Digital Image Processing

Rama Chellappa

Digital Image Processing

Rama Chellappa

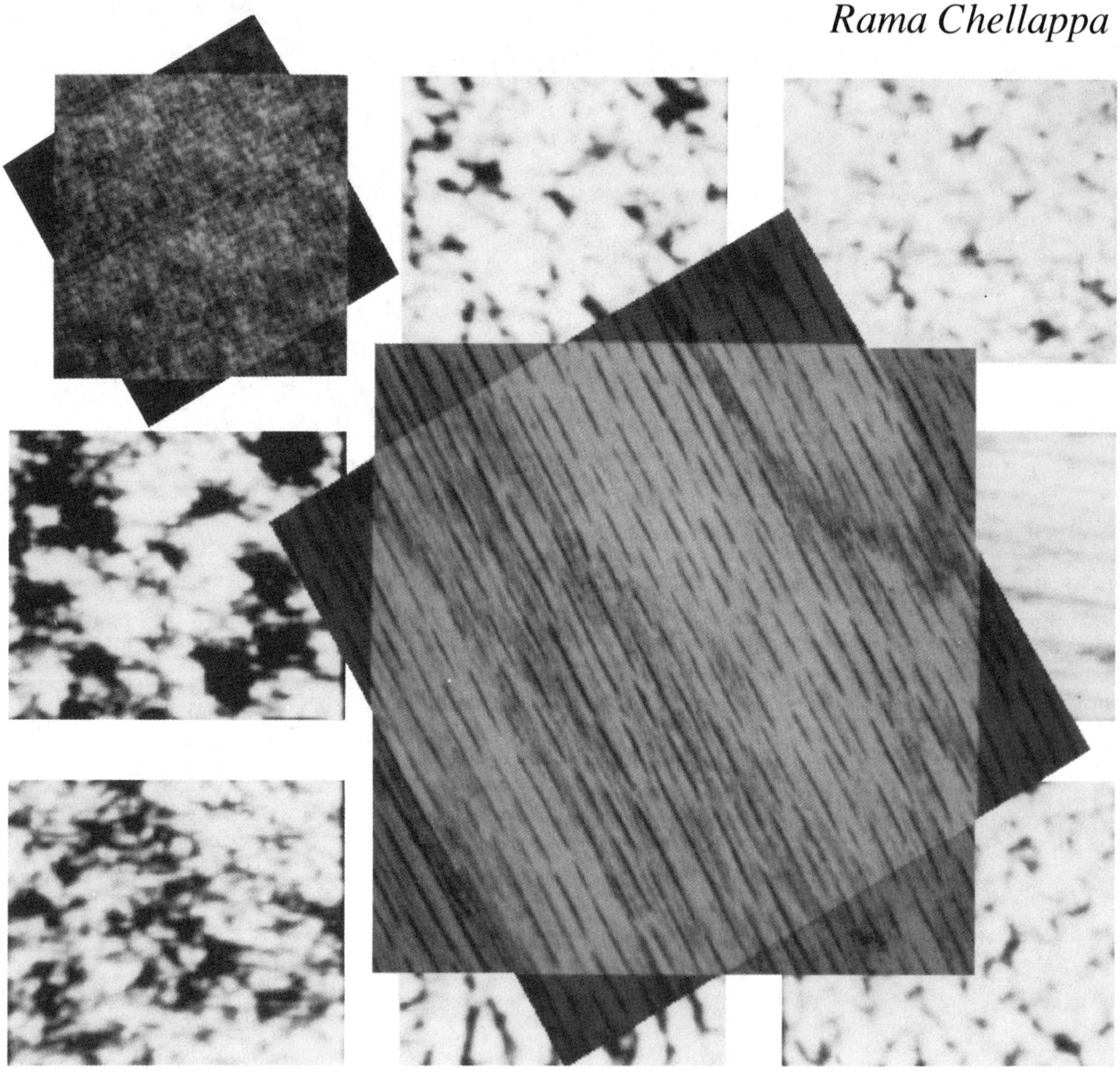

 IEEE Computer Society Press   ◆ The Institute of Electrical and Electronics Engineers, Inc.

Digital Image Processing

Rama Chellappa

IEEE Computer Society Press
Los Alamitos, California

Washington • Brussels • Tokyo

IEEE Computer Society Press Tutorial

Library of Congress Cataloging-in-Publication Data

Digital image processing / [collected by] Rama Chellappa.
    p. cm. — (IEEE Computer Society Press tutorial)
Includes bibliographical references.
ISBN 0-8186-2361-6 (microfiche). — ISBN 0-8186-2362-4 (casebound)
  1. Image processing — Digital techniques. I. Chellappa, Rama. II. Series.
TA1632.D49248 1992   91-33360
621.36'7 — dc20   CIP

Published by the
IEEE Computer Society Press
10662 Los Vaqueros Circle
PO Box 3014
Los Alamitos, CA 90720-1264

© 1992 by the Institute of Electrical and Electronics Engineers, Inc. All rights reserved.

Copyright and Reprint Permissions: Abstracting is permitted with credit to the source. Libraries are permitted to photocopy beyond the limit of US copyright law, for private use of patrons, those articles in this volume that carry a code at the bottom of the first page, provided that the per-copy fee indicated in the code is paid through the Copyright Clearance Center, 27 Congress Street, Salem, MA 01970. Instructors are permitted to photocopy isolated articles, without fee, for non-commercial classroom use. For other copying, reprint, or republication permission, write to IEEE Copyrights Manager, IEEE Service Center, 445 Hoes Lane, PO Box 1331, Piscataway, NJ 08855-1331.

IEEE Computer Society Press Order Number 2362
Library of Congress Number 91-33360
IEEE Catalog Number EH0351-7
ISBN 0-8186-2362-4 (case)
ISBN 0-8186-2361-6 (microfiche)

Additional copies can be ordered from

IEEE Computer Society Press	IEEE Service Center	IEEE Computer Society	IEEE Computer Society
Customer Service Center	445 Hoes Lane	13, avenue de l'Aquilon	Ooshima Building
10662 Los Vaqueros Circle	PO Box 1331	B-1200 Brussels	2-19-1 Minami-Aoyama
PO Box 3014	Piscataway, NJ 08855-1331	BELGIUM	Minato-ku, Tokyo 107
Los Alamitos, CA 90720-1264			JAPAN

Technical Editor: Fred Petry
Production Editor: Lisa O'Conner
Copy Editor: Phyllis Walker
Cover layout by Joe Daigle
Cover art: Texture images developed by Qinsen Zhang and Rama Chellapa.
Printed in the United States of America by Braun-Brumfield, Inc.

 THE INSTITUTE OF ELECTRICAL AND ELECTRONICS ENGINEERS, INC.

Acknowledgments

(This work was completed while the author was a faculty member in the Department of Electrical Engineering-Systems, University of Southern California, Los Angeles, California.)

I would like to express my thanks to several of my former colleagues at the University of Southern California, who gave their invaluable encouragement in the preparation of this tutorial. First of all, I wish to thank Dr. L.M. Silverman, Dean of the School of Engineering at USC, for the support he gave me from the very start of this project. I would also like to thank Dr. L.J. Griffiths, Associate Dean for Research at USC, and Dr. J.M. Mendel, Chairman of the Department of Electrical Engineering-Systems at USC, for their continued interest and encouragement. I would particularly like to thank Professors A. Rosenfeld, R.L. Kashyap, T.S. Huang, and J.W. Woods and Mr. T. Ebrahimi for their valuable suggestions during the various stages of the work. A sincere word of appreciation is due Professor A.A. Sawchuk for his significant contribution to the introduction to the chapter on image restoration. My special thanks to Ms. Delsa Tan for her perseverance and word processing skills in generating several versions of the introductory material for each chapter and of the chapter on additional literature. To Ms. Mayitta Penoliar is my sincere appreciation for the tedious photocopying of the collected papers. I would also like to thank Ms. Lisa O'Conner of the IEEE Computer Society Press, Los Alamitos, California, and Ms. Phyllis Walker, the copy editor, for their tireless efforts in producing this volume.

Most of all, I am grateful to my wife, Vishnu Priya, and son, Vivek, for their patience and understanding during the numerous weekends and late evenings when I was busy at work.

Rama Chellappa
February 14, 1992

Preface

This tutorial on digital image processing is a revised and updated version of an earlier work that I coedited entitled *Digital Image Processing and Analysis: Volume 1: Digital Image Processing* (R. Chellappa and A.A. Sawchuk, IEEE Computer Society Press, 1985). Since the publication of this earlier work, the field of digital image processing (DIP) has matured in some areas, while a number of new results and insights are now being obtained in some other areas. Several new collected works have appeared that are on topics included both in this tutorial and in the earlier work. Keeping this in mind, I extensively revised the earlier work to produce this tutorial. For example, the papers in the earlier work on image transforms were dropped. Image transforms represents one of the most matured topics in DIP, as evidenced by the publication of numerous recent books.

I begin with Chapter 1 on image models — with an emphasis on original work on image models. It is not an exaggeration to say that the topic of image models has been one of the most active topics in the 1980s, with more recent efforts being directed toward specific applications, such as image restoration. Chapter 2 — on image enhancement — emphasizes median and related nonlinear filtering of images. Chapter 3 is on image restoration. Over the last six years, the emphasis in image restoration has been on preserving discontinuities while smoothing or restoring degraded images. A good number of the papers included in Chapter 3 address this important issue. Also included in this chapter are papers on smoothing of speckle images and on some theoretical concepts related to restoration. Chapter 4 — on image data compression — emphasizes recent developments such as second-generation techniques, subband coding, vector quantization, and motion-compensated coding methods. Finally, a new chapter, Chapter 5 — on emerging topics — was added. Six papers representing five emerging topics — wavelets, morphology, neural networks, robust image processing, and high-definition television (HDTV) — are included in this chapter. Chapter 6 is a bibliography that lists selected additional literature.

In an endeavor such as this, the most difficult task is the discriminate selection of papers to be included. Digital image processing has become such an active area of research that one could conceivably compile a collection of papers on each one of the topics discussed herein and still leave out many outstanding papers. I spent much time revising the list of papers to be included. Due to limited space, I could include only 46 papers. My choice of which papers to include was motivated by both subjective preference and a desire to reduce — as much as possible — overlapping with similar published works. I have tried to refer to as many other papers as possible in the introductory material for each chapter and have listed many additional papers in the bibliography (Chapter 6).

Credit for the technical merits of this tutorial must go to the respective authors of the papers included here. This text is appropriate for someone who has had a senior-level or a first-year graduate-level course on image processing. The numerous papers on image models, restoration, and compression would be best appreciated by readers with a background in random processes, such as that normally attained in the first year of graduate curriculum in electrical engineering.

Table of Contents

Acknowledgments v

Preface vi

Chapter 1: Image Models 1

Two-Dimensional Discrete Markovian Fields 8
   J.W. Woods (*IEEE Trans. Information Theory*, March 1972, pp. 232-240)
Advances in Mathematical Models for Image Processing 17
   A.K. Jain (*Proc. IEEE*, May 1981, pp. 502-528)
Markov Random Field Texture Models 44
   G.R. Cross and A.K. Jain (*IEEE Trans. Pattern Analysis and Machine Intelligence*,
   January 1983, pp. 25-39)
Estimation and Choice of Neighbors in Spatial-Interaction Models of Images 59
   R.L. Kashyap and R. Chellappa (*IEEE Trans. Information Theory*, January 1983, pp. 60-72)
Characterization and Estimation of Two-Dimensional ARMA Models 72
   R.L. Kashyap (*IEEE Trans. Information Theory*, September 1984, pp. 736-745)
Stochastic Image Models Generated by Random Tessellations of the Plane 82
   J.W. Modestino, R.W. Fries, and A.L. Vickers (*Computer Graphics and Image Processing*,
   January 1980, pp. 74-98)
Mosaic Models for Textures 107
   N. Ahuja and A. Rosenfeld (*IEEE Trans. Pattern Analysis and Machine Intelligence*,
   January 1981, pp. 1-11)
A Facet Model for Image Data 118
   R.M. Haralick and L. Watson (*Computer Graphics and Image Processing*,
   February 1981, pp. 113-129)
Fractal-Based Description of Natural Scenes 135
   A.P. Pentland (*IEEE Trans. Pattern Analysis and Machine Intelligence*, November 1984,
   pp. 661-674)
Image Segmentation and Image Models 149
   A. Rosenfeld and L.S. Davis (*Proc. IEEE*, May 1979, pp. 764-772)

Chapter 2: Nonlinear Filters for Image Enhancement 158

Nonlinear Mean Filters in Image Processing 163
   I. Pitas and A.N. Venetsanopoulos (*IEEE Trans. Acoustics, Speech, and Signal Processing*,
   June 1986, pp. 573-584)
A Generalization of Median Filtering Using Linear Combination of Order Statistics 175
   A.C. Bovik, T.S. Huang, and D.C. Munson, Jr. (*IEEE Trans. Acoustics, Speech,
   and Signal Processing*, December 1983, pp. 1342-1350)
Theory of Order Statistic Filters and Their Relationship to Linear FIR Filters 184
   H.G. Longbotham and A.C. Bovik (*IEEE Trans. Acoustics, Speech, and Signal Processing*
   February 1989, pp. 275-287)
**Adaptive Nonlinear Filters for Simultaneous Removal of
Different Kinds of Noise in Images** 197
   R. Bernstein (*IEEE Trans. Circuits and Systems*, November 1987, pp. 1275-1291)
Detail Preserving Ranked-Order Based Filters for Image Processing 214
   G.R. Arce and R.E. Foster (*IEEE Trans. Acoustics, Speech, and Signal Processing*,
   January 1989, pp. 83-98)

**Optimal Stack Filtering and the Estimation and
Structural Approaches to Image Processing** 230
   E.J. Coyle, J.-H. Lin, and M. Gabbouj (*IEEE Trans. Acoustics, Speech,
   and Signal Processing*, December 1989, pp. 2037-2057)

Chapter 3: Image Restoration 260

Kalman Filtering in Two Dimensions 265
   J.W. Woods and C.H. Radewan (*IEEE Trans. Information Theory*, July 1977, pp. 473-482)
Correction to "Kalman Filtering in Two Dimensions" 275
   J.W. Woods (*IEEE Trans. Information Theory*, September 1979, p. 567)
Edge-Adaptive Kalman Filtering for Image Restoration with Ringing Suppression 276
   A.M. Tekalp, H. Kaufman, and J.W. Woods (*IEEE Trans. Acoustics, Speech,
   and Signal Processing*, June 1989, pp. 892-899)
Digital Image Restoration Using Spatial Interaction Models 284
   R. Chellappa and R.L. Kashyap (*IEEE Trans. Acoustics, Speech, and Signal Processing*,
   June 1982, pp. 461-472)
Stochastic Relaxation, Gibbs Distributions, and the Bayesian Restoration of Images 296
   S. Geman and D. Geman (*IEEE Trans. Pattern Analysis and Machine Intelligence*,
   November 1984, pp. 721-741)
Simulated Annealing in Compound Gaussian Random Fields 317
   F.-C. Jeng and J.W. Woods (*IEEE Trans. Information Theory*, January 1990, pp. 94-107)
**Pyramid Implementation of Optimal-Step Conjugate-Search Algorithms
for Some Low-Level Vision Problems** 331
   T. Simchony, R. Chellappa, and Z. Lichtenstein (*IEEE Trans. Systems, Man, and Cybernetics*,
   November/December 1989, pp. 1408-1425)
Maximum Likelihood Image and Blur Identification: A Unifying Approach 349
   R.L. Lagendijk, A.M. Tekalp, and J. Biemond (*Optical Engineering*, May 1990, pp. 422-435)
Adaptive Restoration of Images with Speckle 363
   D.T. Kuan, A.A. Sawchuk, T.C. Strand, and P. Chavel (*IEEE Trans. Acoustics, Speech,
   and Signal Processing*, March 1987, pp. 373-383)
A Class of Iterative Signal Restoration Algorithms 374
   A.K. Katsaggelos and S.N. Efstratiadis (*IEEE Trans. Acoustics, Speech,
   and Signal Processing*, May 1990, pp. 778-786)
Digital Signal Restoration Using Fuzzy Sets 383
   M.R. Civanlar and H.J. Trussell (*IEEE Trans. Acoustics, Speech, and Signal Processing*,
   August 1986, pp. 919-936)

Chapter 4: Image Data Compression 401

Image Data Compression: A Review 411
   A.K. Jain (*Proc. IEEE*, March 1981, pp. 349-389)
Second-Generation Image-Coding Techniques 452
   M. Kunt, A. Ikonomopoulos, and M. Kocher (*Proc. IEEE*, April 1985, pp. 549-574)
Recent Results in High-Compression Image Coding 478
   M. Kunt, M. Bénard, and R. Leonardi (*IEEE Trans. Circuits and Systems*, November 1987,
   pp. 1306-1336)
Vector Quantization 509
   R.M. Gray (*IEEE ASSP Magazine*, April 1984, pp. 4-29)
Image Coding Using Vector Quantization: A Review 535
   N.M. Nasrabadi and R.A. King (*IEEE Trans. Communications*, August 1988, pp. 957-971)
Subband Coding of Images 550
   J.W. Woods and S.D. O'Neil (*IEEE Trans. Acoustics, Speech, and Signal Processing*,
   October 1986, pp. 1278-1288)

**Progressive Image Transmission Using Vector Quantization on Images
in Pyramid Form** 561
    L. Wang and M. Goldberg (*IEEE Trans. Communications*, December 1989, pp. 1339-1349)

Advances in Picture Coding 572
    H.G. Musmann, P. Pirsch, and H.-J. Grallert (*Proc. IEEE*, April 1985, pp. 523-548)

**Image Sequence Compression Using a Pel-Recursive
Motion-Compensated Technique** 598
    R.J. Moorhead II, S.A. Rajala, and L.W. Cook (*IEEE J. Selected Areas in Communications*,
    August 1987, pp. 1100-1114)

**Coding of Arbitrarily Shaped Image Segments Based on a Generalized
Orthogonal Transform** 613
    M. Gilge, T. Engelhardt, and R. Mehlan (*Signal Processing: Image Communication*,
    October 1989, pp. 153-180)

Object-Oriented Analysis-Synthesis Coding of Moving Images 641
    H.G. Musmann, M. Hötter, and J. Ostermann (*Signal Processing: Image Communication*,
    October 1989, pp. 117-138)

Tree-Structured Scene Adaptive Coder 663
    P. Strobach (*IEEE Trans. Communications*, April 1990, pp. 477-486)

Combined Source-Channel Coding of Images Using the Block Cosine Transform 673
    J.W. Modestino, D.G. Daut, and A.L. Vickers (*IEEE Trans. Communications*, September 1981,
    pp. 1261-1274)

Optimal Block Cosine Transform Image Coding for Noisy Channels 687
    V.A. Vaishampayan and N. Farvardin (*IEEE Trans. Communications*, March 1990, pp. 327-336)

Chapter 5: Emerging Topics 697

Multifrequency Channel Decompositions of Images and Wavelet Models 699
    S.G. Mallat (*IEEE Trans. Acoustics, Speech, and Signal Processing*, December 1989,
    pp. 2091-2110)

Morphological Systems for Multidimensional Signal Processing 719
    P.A. Maragos and R.W. Schafer (*Proc. IEEE*, April 1990, pp. 690-710)

Image Restoration Using a Neural Network 740
    Y.-T. Zhou, R. Chellappa, A. Vaid, and B.K. Jenkins (*IEEE Trans. Acoustics, Speech,
    and Signal Processing*, July 1988, pp. 1141-1151)

**Complete Discrete 2-D Gabor Transforms by Neural Networks for Image Analysis
and Compression** 751
    J.G. Daugman (*IEEE Trans. Acoustics, Speech, and Signal Processing*, July 1988, pp. 1169-1179)

Robust Image Modeling Techniques with an Image Restoration Application 762
    R.L. Kashyap and K.-B. Eom (*IEEE Trans. Acoustics, Speech, and Signal Processing*,
    August 1988, pp. 1313-1325)

Image Processing for Higher Definition Television 775
    G.J. Tonge (*IEEE Trans. Circuits and Systems*, November 1987, pp. 1385-1398)

Chapter 6: Bibliography of Selected Additional Literature 789

About the Author 801

Chapter 1: Image Models

In the analysis and processing of images, one encounters a large amount of data. In a typical image-processing problem, working with images defined on arrays of dimensions up to as large as 1024 by 1024 or 2048 by 2048 is not uncommon. The intensity values at each one of the grid locations may be quantized up to 16 levels. To enable efficient processing of this data, having an underlying model that explains the dominant statistical characteristics of the given data would be preferable to direct empirical processing of image data. The analysis and processing of the image data could then be done efficiently by using the models fitted to images. Although identifying the underlying mechanisms that could have possibly generated the observed image data is very difficult, any analytical expression that explains the nature and extent of dependency of a pixel intensity on intensities of its neighbors can be said to be a "model."

A typical image is represented by a two-dimensional array of numbers, the gray-level variations defined over a rectangular or square lattice. One of the important characteristics of such data is the special nature of the statistical dependence of the gray level at a lattice point on some of its neighbors. The classification of image models into the different groups suggested in the literature attempts to characterize this dependence among neighboring pixels. Let $\{y(s), s \in \Omega\}$, $\Omega = \{s : s = (i,j), 0 \leq i, j \leq M-1\}$, be the gray levels from an M by M image. One way of characterizing the statistical dependence among neighboring pixels is to represent $y(s)$ as a linear-weighted combination of $\{y(s + r), r \in N\}$, where N is the neighbor set not containing $(0,0)$, and additive noise. Specific restrictions on the members of the neighbor set N yield representations familiar in the image-processing literature. For instance, the popular "causal" models are obtained when N has quarter-plane support.[1] One of the features of using the causal model is that the image-processing algorithms developed by using causal models are recursive. One can generalize causal models to so-called "unilateral" models by including more neighbors, but still preserving the recursive structure of the image-processing algorithms. Unilateral models result when N is a subset of the nonsymmetric half plane S^+, defined recursively as[1]

$$s \in S^+, \ r \in S^+ \rightarrow s + r \in S^+$$

$$s \in S^+ \rightarrow -s \notin S^+$$

$$(0,0) \notin S^+$$

Unlike in one-dimensional discrete time series, where the existence of a preferred direction is inherently assumed, no such preferred ordering is appropriate for a two-dimensional discrete lattice. Thus, the class of unilateral models is possibly a restrictive form of representation for images, compared to noncausal models where an observation $y(s)$ can be dependent on neighboring observations in all directions. The simplest noncausal model is obtained when $y(s)$ is dependent on its east, west, north, and south neighbors. One can consider more general representations by including the diagonal neighbors, and so on.

Whittle[2] authored a pioneering paper on using noncausal models for representing spatial data. He was the first to point out the consequences of introducing noncausality into autoregressive models and to develop approximate Gaussian maximum-likelihood (ML)-estimation methods and hypothesis-testing procedures for noncausal autoregressive (NCAR) models. These models represent $y(s)$ as a linear combination of $\{y(s + r), r \in N\}$, where N is a noncausal neighbor set, and an additive white noise.

Independent of Whittle, Rosanov[3] introduced two-dimensional discrete Gaussian Markovian random fields (MRFs) possessing a two-dimensional noncausal Markov property. The two-dimensional array $\{y(s)\}$ is said to possess a noncausal or bilateral Markov property with respect to a symmetric neighbor set N if

$$p\big[y(s)\big|\text{all } y(r), r \neq s\big] = p\big[y(s)\big|\text{all } y(s+r), r \in N\big] \qquad 1$$

The Markov property defined in Equation 1 is called "locally Markov." Rosanov introduced two-dimensional Gaussian discrete MRF models by using a global Markov property,[4,5] of which Equation 1 is a special case. It turns out that if $\{y(s)\}$ is Gaussian and possesses the two-dimensional Markov property (local or global), then $y(s)$ can be written as a linear-weighted sum of $\{y(s + r), r \in N\}$ and an additive correlated noise. Using Hilbert space arguments, Rosanov developed spectral characterizations of MRF models. In the first reprinted paper in this chapter, Woods — independent of Rosanov — develops basic results regarding the representation of Gaussian MRF models. Woods then describes procedures for generating $\{y(s)\}$, obeying known MRF models, and gives an application of MRF models for two-dimensional spectral estimation.

A seminal work regarding the theory of Gaussian and non-Gaussian MRF models is by Besag.[6] Given a specific noncausal neighbor set, the MRF models can be specified by defining the basic probability structures

$$p[\, y(s) \mid \text{all } y(s+r), r \varepsilon N \,]$$

A natural question is what the constraints are on

$$p[\, y(s) \mid y(s+r), r \varepsilon N \,]$$

such that the resulting Markov field $\{y(s)\}$ has a valid probability structure. Besag gives a simple proof for the structure of allowable conditional densities. Some estimation methods and hypothesis-testing procedures, which are not as efficient as the likelihood-based methods, are also discussed by Besag. Related discussions concerning representation of MRF models may be found in the literature.[7-10]

Thus far, we have discussed two classes of noncausal models: the Gaussian NCAR models and the Gaussian MRF models. Models in these two classes are related in the sense that, given an NCAR model, one can always construct an MRF model whose second-order properties are identical to those of the original NCAR model. For instance, an NCAR model with

$$N = \{(0,1), (0,-1), (-1,0), (1,0)\}$$

has the equivalent (in second-order properties) MRF model with neighbor set

$$N = \{(0,1), (0,-1), (-1,0), (1,0), (-1,1), (1,1), (-1,-1), (1,-1), (0,2), (2,0), (0,-2), (-2,0)\}$$

Thus, an NCAR model with neighbor set N is not Markov with respect to N in the sense of Equation 1, but is Markov with respect to a higher-order neighbor set N', which includes members of N and some extra neighbors. However, the converse is not always true (that is, given an MRF model, an equivalent finite NCAR model does not always exist). For instance, an MRF model with $N = \{(0,1), (0,-1), (-1,0), (1,0)\}$ does not possess an equivalent finite-parameter NCAR model.

The given finite image can be analyzed either as a slice of an infinite image defined over an infinite lattice or as an image defined only on a finite lattice. In general, synthesis and estimation methods are complicated when infinite-lattice models are used. As an alternative, by assuming some boundary conditions, one can develop computationally efficient procedures for estimation, image synthesis, and restoration. Several types of boundary conditions have been analyzed in the literature on image processing.

A useful set of boundary conditions used by several researchers[10,11,12,13,14] is the doubly periodic boundary conditions that lead to toroidal lattice representation. A consequence of this representation is that the covariance matrix of the image is block circulant, which is diagonalizable by fast Fourier transforms (FFTs). Thus, computationally efficient procedures can be developed for image synthesis and restoration. Although — at first sight — the toroidal lattice assumption seems to be restrictive, reported[13,14] theoretical and numerical investigations seem to suggest that toroidal lattice models are excellent approximations for the infinite lattice models. Note that the toroidal lattice assumption has been used in the study of crystal statistics by Onsager[15] and by Besag and Moran[16] for developing estimation methods in Gaussian MRF models.

In the next reprinted paper, by Jain, boundary conditions used are such that the resulting covariance matrix has a symmetric tridiagonal structure, diagonalizable by fast sine transforms. This representation leads to fast algorithms for image restoration. This paper also contains an excellent summary of two-dimensional causal models for image representation and of the usefulness of models in image-processing applications.

The following reprinted paper, by Cross and Jain, illustrates one application of MRF models: synthesis of textures. Specifically, two-level and eight-level textures (obtained after preprocessing of textures scanned from the Brodatz album) are represented by binary and binomial MRF models on a toroidal lattice. The parameters are estimated by using the coding method discussed in the paper by Besag.[6] An iterative algorithm developed by Metropolis et al.[17] is used for the synthesis of textures by using the estimated parameters. Good synthesis results are reported for cork, grass, paper, and sand, while "regular" textures — like brick and tile — are not adequately synthesized.

The coding estimate yields consistent estimates of parameters; however, this estimate is not efficient[16] because of partial use of the data. For Gaussian MRF models, one can improve on the coding estimate by using the least-squares (LS) estimate or the ML estimate. The LS estimate is analyzed in the paper by Kashyap and Chellappa that appears next in this chapter. Specifically, it is shown that the LS estimate is consistent and that its efficiency is between coding and ML estimates for an isotropic nearest-neighbor Gaussian MRF model. Besag and Moran[16] and Künsche[18] discuss the ML-estimation problem in Gaussian MRF models. Owing to noncausal representation, the likelihood is a complicated function that requires the use of numerical optimization procedures. Kashyap and Chellappa also discuss an approximate ML estimation scheme for Gaussian NCAR models. Other papers[19-22] deal with the estimation of parameters in noncausal models.

The LS estimate — often referred to as the pseudolikelihood estimate — was originally proposed by Besag.[23] Subsequently, its efficiency was compared to that of coding and ML estimates[24] for a first-order isotropic Gaussian MRF model. Asymptotic consistency of the pseudolikelihood estimate has also been established.[25,26]

Prior to noncausal models being used for image processing and analysis, the problem of the estimation of the particular neighbor set N to be used must be tackled. Choosing the appropriate N is a multidecision problem involving composite hypotheses. For this problem, Kashyap and Chellappa suggest decision rules with good asymptotic properties. Simulation results are also included in the paper by Kashyap and Chellappa to illustrate the usefulness of these rules.

In the next reprinted paper, Kashyap introduces a general class of finite-order, two-dimensional, autoregressive, moving average (ARMA) models that can represent any process with rational spectral density. Two methods are suggested for parameter estimation in the proposed models. The first method uses empirical correlations and involves the solution of linear equations. The second method is based on a likelihood function derived using toroidal representation.

Most of the algorithms using the image models discussed above use the underlying assumption that the image is wide-sense stationary. Two conditions for wide-sense stationarity are that the mean is constant over the entire image and the autocorrelation function is translation invariant. In real-life images, very often either one or both of the above two conditions are violated; then, it is necessary to develop standard image-processing algorithms for restoration and coding by using nonstationary models.

Several researchers have considered to some extent the problem of developing such image-processing algorithms for nonstationary images. Hunt[27] discusses three cases of increasing complexity, as follows:

- Nonstationary mean, stationary autocorrelation;
- Stationary mean, nonstationary autocorrelation; and
- Nonstationary mean, nonstationary autocorrelation.

The basic idea in developing algorithms is to remove the nonstationarities in the mean and autocorrelation by suitable transformations and then to process the resulting images by using stationary assumptions. Then, the transformations used to create the stationary images are inversely applied to obtain the processed images corresponding to the original nonstationary images. Similar procedures can be developed by using causal two-dimensional autoregressive models. For instance,[13] in analogy with one-dimensional time series observations, one can generate a new image

$$x(s_1, s_2) = y(s_1, s_2) - y(s_1, s_2 - 1)$$

If $\{x(s)\}$ is represented by a stationary two-dimensional autoregressive model, then the original image $\{y(s)\}$ is not stationary. One can process the "difference" image $\{x(s)\}$ and then construct the result corresponding to the original image $\{y(s)\}$.

The handling of nonstationary images poses difficult theoretical, as well as computational, problems. An *ad hoc* technique used very often in image-compression and image-restoration studies is to break the image into supposedly stationary blocks and then process the entire image block by block.

A better approach is to regard the given image as being composed of several stationary patches, each of which is represented by an appropriate causal or noncausal model. The mechanism for choosing a particular model for a given region (which may even be a pixel) may then be described by a stochastic process. These doubly stochastic fields have been very successfully used for image-restoration applications.[28,29] A significant contribution to modeling nonstationary images is in a paper by Geman and Geman;[30] in this work and in subsequent extensions thereof,[31] the intensity array is modeled as either a multilevel or a Gaussian MRF model. The discontinuities are modeled as line processes that are defined at the dual lattice sites interposed between the regular pixel sites. These line processes take values of zero or one, depending on whether an edge is absent or present, respectively. Whenever the line process is on (that is, when it has a value of one), the interaction between pixels on either side is broken. Line processes themselves are modeled as multilevel MRFs. Using these multimodel representations, researchers have developed several stochastic and deterministic algorithms for image restoration[30-34] and texture segmentation.[35-38] (Some of their papers on image restoration are reprinted in Chapter 3 in this tutorial.)

The image models we have discussed so far assume that the spatial dependence is among the neighboring pixels. Very often, images have a distinctly patchy or cellular structure, as in the case of a plastic-bubble or a brick-wall texture. It seems preferable to represent such images by models that characterize statistical dependency among cells or regions that consist of several pixels. One possible approach is to extend the NCAR or MRF model representations to include the analysis of regions by the methods used in geographical analysis.[20] Another approach is to construct cellular stochastic models; this approach is discussed in the next two papers reprinted in this chapter, which are authored by Modestino, Fries, and Vickers and by Ahuja and Rosenfeld. In cellular or tessellation models, it is assumed that the images are composed of cells of nearly constant gray level. These models are characterized by a random mechanism to generate the cells and another random mechanism to account for the coloring of the individual cells. The cells can be generated in a number of ways. For instance, in the Poisson line model,[39] the plane is divided into convex cells by a set of straight lines that have random positions and orientations. Such lines can be generated by dropping points (θ, p) in the strip

$$[0 \leq \theta \leq \pi], -\infty < \rho < \infty$$

according to a Poisson process of intensity τ / π. Each of these points (θ, p) defines a line

$$x\cos\theta + y\sin\theta = p$$

The resulting cells are colored independently or with a specified correlation and distribution. The cells can be generated in several other ways, including using the occupancy model[40] or the Johnson-Mehl model.[41]

Schachter, Rosenfeld, and Davis[42] illustrate an application of cellular stochastic models (referred to as "mosaic models") for textures. Variograms (a measure of second-order properties) are used to assess the appropriateness of particular mosaic models fitted to a given image.

In the next paper reprinted in this chapter, by Modestino, Fries, and Vickers, rectangular, parallel, and polygonal tessellations are modeled by appropriate Poisson processes, and the adjacent cells are colored to possess specified correlation values. The authors derive second-order properties of the resulting realizations and indicate applications to edge detection, image enhancement, and texture discrimination.

The paper by Ahuja and Rosenfeld, also reprinted in this chapter, is the final reprinted paper on cellular models. This paper discusses geometric and correlation properties of the following two classes of mosaic models:

• Cell-structured models (for example, checkerboard, hexagonal, Poisson line, occupancy, and Delanuay models) and
• Coverage (or "bombing") models.

Specifically, the authors give expressions for the expected number of components, as well as for the expected area and width of a component, in the mosaic. Related papers deal with mosaic models for textures.[43-45]

The paper by Haralick and Watson is reprinted next in this chapter. It introduces a different type of model, known as the "facet model." In this model, the given image is partitioned into connected regions, called "facets," each of which satisfies specific gray-tone and shape constraints. The gray tones in each facet are a polynomial function of either zero, one, or two degrees of the row-column coordinates of the pixel in the facet. The usefulness of a special class of facet model for edge and region analysis is discussed in two papers by Haralick.[46,47]

The next paper reprinted in this chapter, by Pentland, suggests using fractal models for the representation of natural scenes such as those containing mountains, trees, and clouds. Mandelbrot[48] first used fractals to represent the surfaces of such natural objects. The essential characteristic of a fractal is what is known as the "fractional dimension (FD)," which roughly corresponds to our intuitive notion of roughness; the higher the FD is, the rougher the surface looks. From an image analysis point of view, the interesting result in Pentland's paper is the development of four propositions regarding transformations between fractal surfaces and image intensity surfaces. Thus, the adequacy of fractal models for a given scene can be verified from the raw image itself. The paper discusses examples drawn from natural scenes and Brodatz textures in order to illustrate the concept of fitting a fractal model to the given image. By using the histogram of fractal dimension computed over eight-by-eight blocks of an aerial image, it is shown that the fractal models can be successfully used for image segmentation. The attractive feature of this segmentation technique is that the results are reasonably stable across wide variations in the scale of the scene. Further discussions regarding the estimation — using fractals — of the slope of a surface, the relationship to existing two-dimensional texture models, and human texture perception are also given in this paper.

We have so far considered what may be called "explicit" image models. Very often, when a particular image-processing algorithm is analyzed, one can identify certain assumptions that the image should satisfy in order for a particular technique to be applicable. The final paper reprinted in this chapter, by Rosenfeld and Davis, discusses the "implicit" models used when images are segmented. The authors discuss image-segmentation techniques from the standpoint of the assumptions that an image should satisfy for a particular technique to be applicable. The paper emphasizes statistical models that describe the pixel population in an image or region and structural models that describe the decomposition of an image into regions.

Some images can be represented as a composition of primitives. For example, in most textures one can identify a basic structure that repeats itself (according to some rules) to form the observed texture. By using the analogy between the structure of images in terms of primitives and relations among primitives and the syntax of a language in terms of grammar rules, formal (syntactic) models for images have been suggested.[49] An excellent summary of image representation using a particular type of grammar, called the "tree grammar," for representing images is given by Fu.[50] By associating probabilities with the production rules of the tree grammar, Fu develops a stochastic tree grammar to handle uncertainties in the images; Fu's paper illustrates the usefulness of the tree grammar in representing textures.

In conclusion, research in image modeling has matured. Several classes of image models have been developed in the literature; these models are not "universal," in the sense that no single model can explain the dominant characteristics of all images. For instance, the NCAR and MRF models may represent random textures, like sand and cork, very well, but they are not adequate for modeling regular patterns, like brick walls. More importantly, the models discussed in the papers reprinted in this chapter do not take into account some of the basic characteristics of image formation; for instance, they do not take into account knowledge about sensors or illumination.[51,52] A realistic image model should integrate the known deterministic characteristics of the imaging system and use statistical models to explain the uncertainties due to noise.

Chapter 1 References

1. A.K. Jain, *Fundamentals of Digital Image Processing*, Prentice-Hall, Englewood Cliffs, N.J., 1988.
2. P. Whittle, "On Stationary Processes in the Plane," *Biometrika*, Vol. 41, 1954, pp. 434-449.
3. Y.A. Rosanov, "On Gaussian Fields with Given Conditional Distributions," *Theory of Probability and Its Applications*, Vol. XII, 1967, pp. 381-391.
4. P. Levy, *Processes References Stochastiques et Mouvement Brownien*, Gautheir-Villars, Paris, France, 1948.
5. P. Levy, "A Special Problem of Brownian Motion, and a General Theory of Gaussian Random Functions," *Proc. Third Berkeley Symp. Math. Statistics and Probability*, Vol. 2, Univ. of Calif. Press, Berkeley, Calif., 1956.
6. J.E. Besag, "Spatial Interaction and the Statistical Analysis of Lattice Systems," *J. Royal Statistical Soc.*, Ser-B, 1974, pp. 192-236.
7. K. Abend, T.J. Harley, and L.N. Kanal, "Classification of Binary Random Patterns," *IEEE Trans. Information Theory*, Vol. IT-11, Oct. 1965, pp. 538-544.
8. E. Wong, "Two-Dimensional Random Fields and Representation of Image," *SIAM J. Applied Math.*, Vol. 16, 1968, pp. 756-770.
9. P.A.P. Moran, "A Gaussian Markovian Process on a Square Lattice," *J. Applied Probability*, Vol. 10, Mar. 1973, pp. 54-62.
10. P.A.P. Moran, "Necessary Conditions for Markovian Processes on a Lattice," *J. Applied Probability*, Vol. 10, Sept. 1973, pp. 605-612.
11. R.L. Kashyap, "Univariate and Multivariate Random Field Models for Images," *Computer Graphics and Image Processing*, Vol. 12, 1980, pp. 257-270.
12. H. Derin and P.A. Kelly, "Discrete-Index Markov-Type Random Processes," *Proc. IEEE*, Vol. 77, Oct. 1989, pp. 1485-1510.
13. R.L. Kashyap, "Analysis and Synthesis of Image Patterns by Spatial Interaction Models," in *Progress in Pattern Recognition*, L.N. Kanal and A. Rosenfeld, eds., Vol. 1, 1981, pp. 149-186, North-Holland, Amsterdam, 1981, pp. 149-186.
14. R. Chellappa, *Stochastic Models for Image Analysis and Processing*, doctoral thesis, School of Electrical Engineering, Purdue Univ., W. Lafayette, Ind., Aug. 1981.
15. L. Onsager, "Crystal Statistics, I: A 2-D Model with an Order-Disorder Transition," *Physics Rev.*, Vol. 65, 1944, pp. 117-149.
16. J.E. Besag and P.A.P. Moran, "On the Estimation and Testing of Spatial Interaction in Gaussian Lattice," *Biometrika*, Vol. 62, Dec. 1975, pp. 555-562.
17. N. Metropolis et al., "Equations of State Calculations by Fast Computing Machines," *J. Chemical Physics*, Vol. 21, June 1953, pp. 1087-1092.
18. H. Künsch, "Thermodynamics and Statistical Analysis of Gaussian Random Fields," *Z. Wahrschienlickeitstheorie verw. Gebiete*, Vol. 58, Nov. 1981, pp. 407-421.
19. G.S. Sharma and R. Chellappa, "A Model Based Approach for the Estimation of 2-D Maximum Entropy Power Spectra," *IEEE Trans. Information Theory*, Vol. IT-31, Jan. 1985, pp. 90-99.
20. K. Ord, "Estimation Methods for Models of Spatial Interaction," *J. Am. Statistical Assoc.*, Vol. 70, Mar. 1975, pp. 120-126.
21. W.E. Larimore, "Statistical Inference on Stationary Random Fields," *Proc. IEEE*, Vol. 65, June 1977, pp. 961-970.
22. J.E. Besag, "Errors-in-Variable Estimation for Gaussian Lattice Scheme," *J. Royal Statistical Soc.*, Series B, Vol. 39, 1977, pp. 73-78.
23. J.E. Besag, "Statistical Analysis of Non-Lattice Data," *The Statistician*, Vol. 24, 1975, pp. 179-195.
24. J.E. Besag, "Efficiency of Pseudo-Likelihood Estimation for Simple Gaussian Fields," *Biometrika*, Vol. 64, 1977, pp. 616-618.
25. S. Geman and C. Graffigne, "Markov Random Field Image Models and Their Applications to Computer Vision," *Proc. Int'l Congress Math.*, A.M. Gleason, ed., Am. Math. Soc., 1987.
26. B. Gidas, "Consistency of Maximum Likelihood and Pseudo-Likelihood Estimators for Gibbs Distributions," *Proc. Workshop on Stochastic Differential Systems in Applications in Electrical Computer Engineering, Control Theory and Operations Research*, IMA, Univ. of Minnesota, Minneapolis, Minn., 1986.
27. B.R. Hunt, "Nonstationary Statistical Image Models (and Their Applications to Image Data Compression)," *Computer Graphics and Image Processing*, Vol. 12, 1980, pp. 173-180.
28. J.W. Woods, "Two-Dimensional Kalman Filtering," in *Two-Dimensional Signal Processing*, T.S. Huang, ed., Topics in Applied Physics, Vol. 43, Springer-Verlag, New York, N.Y., 1981, pp. 155-205.
29. J.W. Woods, S. Dravida, and R. Mediavilla, "Image Estimation Using Doubly Stochastic Gaussian Random Field Models," *IEEE Trans. Pattern Analysis and Machine Intelligence*, Vol. PAMI-9, Mar. 1987, pp. 245-253.
30. S. Geman and D. Geman, "Stochastic Relaxation, Gibbs Distributions and the Bayesian Restoration of Images," *IEEE Trans. Pattern Analysis and Machine Intelligence*, Vol. PAMI-6, Nov. 1984, pp. 721-741.
31. F.C. Jeng and J.W. Woods, "Simulated Annealing in Compound Gaussian Random Fields," *IEEE Trans. Information Theory*, Vol. IT-36, Jan. 1990, pp. 94-107.

32. T. Simchony, R. Chellappa, and Z. Lichtenstein, "Pyramid Implementation of Optimal-Step Conjugate-Search Algorithms for Some Low-Level Computer Vision Problems," *IEEE Trans. Systems, Man, and Cybernetics*, Vol. SMC-19, Nov./Dec. 1989, pp. 1408-1425.
33. T. Simchony, R. Chellappa, and Z. Lichtenstein, "Relaxation Algorithms for MAP Estimation of Gray-Level Images with Multiplicative Noise," *IEEE Trans. Information Theory*, Vol. IT-36, May 1990, pp. 608-613.
34. H. Derin and H. Elliott, "Modeling and Segmentation of Noisy and Textured Images Using Gibbs Random Fields," *IEEE Trans. Pattern Analysis and Machine Intelligence*, Vol. PAMI-9, Jan. 1987, pp. 39-55.
35. F.S. Cohen and D.B. Cooper, "Simple, Parallel, Hierarchical, and Relaxation Algorithms for Segmenting Noncausal Markovian Fields," *IEEE Trans. Pattern Analysis and Machine Intelligence*, Vol. PAMI-9, Mar. 1987, pp. 195-219.
36. B.S. Manjunath, T. Simchony, and R. Chellappa, "Stochastic and Deterministic Networks for Texture Segmentation," *IEEE Trans. Acoustics, Speech, and Signal Processing*, Vol. ASSP-38, June 1990, pp. 1035-1049.
37. D. Geman et al., "Boundary Detection by Constrained Optimization," *IEEE Trans. Pattern Analysis and Machine Intelligence*, Vol. PAMI-12, July 1990, pp. 609-628.
38. J.L. Marroquin, *Probabilistic Solution of Inverse Problems*, doctoral dissertation, Artificial Intelligence Laboratory, MIT, Cambridge, Mass., Sept. 1985.
39. R.E. Miles, "On the Homogeneous Planar Poisson Point Processes," *Math. BioSciences*, Vol. 6, 1970, pp. 85-127.
40. R.E. Miles, "Random Polygons Determined by Random Lines in a Plane," *Proc. US Nat'l Academy Sciences*, Vol. 52, 1964, pp. 901-907.
41. B.J. Schachter and N. Ahuja, "Random Pattern Generation Process," *Computer Graphics and Image Processing*, Vol. 10, June 1979, pp. 95-114.
42. B.J. Schachter, A. Rosenfeld, and L.S. Davis, "Random Mosaic Models for Textures," *IEEE Trans. Systems, Man, and Cybernetics*, Vol. SMC-8, Sept. 1978, pp. 694-702.
43. B.J. Schachter, "Model Based Texture Measures," *IEEE Trans. Pattern Analysis and Machine Intelligence*, Vol. PAMI-2, Mar. 1980, pp. 169-171.
44. J.W. Modestino, R.W. Fries, and A.L. Vickers, "Texture Discrimination Based Upon An Assumed Stochastic Texture Model," *IEEE Trans. Pattern Analysis and Machine Intelligence*, Vol. PAMI-3, Sept. 1981, pp. 557-580.
45. A.L. Vickers and J.W. Modestino, "A Maximum Likelihood Approach to Texture Classification," *IEEE Trans. Pattern Analysis and Machine Intelligence*, Vol. PAMI-4, Jan. 1982, pp. 61-68.
46. R.M. Haralick, "Edge and Region Analysis for Digital Image Data," *Computer Graphics and Image Processing*, Vol. 12, 1980, pp. 60-73.
47. R.M. Haralick, "Digital Steps Edges from Zero-Crossing of Second Directional Derivatives," *IEEE Trans. Pattern Analysis and Machine Intelligence*, Vol. PAMI-6, Jan. 1984 pp. 58-68.
48. B.B. Mandelbrot, *Fractals: Form, Chance, and Dimension*, W.H. Freeman and Company, San Francisco, Calif., 1977.
49. K.S. Fu, *Syntactic Pattern Recognition*, Prentice-Hall, Englewood Cliffs, N.J., 1982.
50. K.S. Fu, "Syntactic Image Modeling Using Stochastic Tree Grammars," *Computer Graphics and Image Processing*, Vol. 12, 1980, pp. 136-152.
51. B.K.P. Horn, "Understanding Image Intensities," *Artificial Intelligence J.*, Vol. 8, Apr. 1977, pp. 201-231.
52. B.K.P. Horn and M.J. Brooks, *Shape from Shading*, MIT Press, Cambridge, Mass., 1989.

Two-Dimensional Discrete Markovian Fields

JOHN W. WOODS, MEMBER, IEEE

Abstract—A definition of discrete Markovian random fields is formulated analogously to a definition for the continuous case given by Lévy. This definition in the homogeneous Gaussian case leads to a difference equation that sets forth the state of the field in terms of its values on a band of minimum width P, where P is the order of the process. The state of the field at position (i,j) is given by the set of values of the nearest neighbors within distance P of the point (i,j). Conversely, given a difference equation satisfying certain conditions relating to stability, there corresponds a homogeneous discrete Markov random field.

This theory is applied to the problem of obtaining spectral estimates of a two-dimensional field, given observation over a limited aperture.

I. INTRODUCTION

IN THE theory of random processes, a very fruitful idea is the concept of a Markov process. In 1956 Lévy [1] proposed a definition of a Markovian random field. In analogy with Lévy's definition, this paper presents a definition of a Markov random field on a discrete space and shows that in the homogeneous Gaussian case this field can be represented by a two-dimensional difference equation driven by a homogeneous nonwhite noise source. The noise source is equivalent to the error in a best linear mean-square-error (MSE) estimate of the field at a point in terms of its nearest neighbors. A P-order homogeneous Gauss–Markov random field is characterized by the correlations among the elements out to distance P.

II. STATIONARY GAUSS–MARKOVIAN SEQUENCES

In one dimension a Markov sequence can be represented by a difference equation.

Theorem 1: For a stationary Gaussian Markov process [2] of order N in discrete time $\{x_n\}$ we can write

$$x_n = \sum_{m=1}^{N} h_m x_{n-m} + w_n, \qquad -\infty < n < +\infty, \quad (1)$$

where i) the h_m are the coefficients of the minimum-mean-square-error (MMSE) estimate of x_n given $\{x_k; \forall k < n\}$, and ii) $E[w_n w_m^*] = c\delta_{mn}$, c being the error in the MMSE estimate mentioned in i).

Proof: The MMSE estimate of x_n given $\{x_k; \forall k < n\}$ is the same as the MMSE estimate of x_n given $\{x_k; n - N < k < n\}$ because the conditional distributions are the same (the Markov assumption). Since the process is stationary Gaussian, the MMSE estimate is linear time invariant. Thus $x_n = \sum_{m=1}^{N} h_m x_{n-m}$ or $x_n = \sum_{m=1}^{N} h_m x_{n-m} + w_n$, where w_n denotes the error in the estimate of x_n. Clearly w_n is stationary Gaussian, and also we recall [2] that w_n is uncorrelated with $x_{n-1}, \cdots, x_{n-N}$ and thus uncorrelated with all the x_i for $i < n$. Now let $l > n$ and consider $E[w_l x_n] = \sum h_m E \cdot [w_l x_{n-m}] + E[w_l w_n]$. Since $E[w_l w_k] = 0$ for all $k < l$ and hence for all $k \leq n$, we have $E[w_l w_n] = 0$, $\forall l > n$. Therefore, by stationarity, $E[w_m w_n] = c\delta_{mn}$. Q.E.D.

Another Markovian assumption would be that the conditional probability of x_n given all other values only depends upon the N nearest neighbors on each side. This would yield the representation

$$x_n = \sum_{\substack{m=-N \\ m \neq 0}}^{+N} h_m x_{n-m} + u_n, \qquad -\infty < n < +\infty, \quad (2)$$

where i) $E[x_n u_m^*] = c'\delta_{mn}$, $c' \geq 0$, and ii)

$$E[u_n u_m^*] = \begin{cases} c', & n - m = 0 \\ -h_{n-m} c', & |n - m| \leq N \\ 0, & \text{elsewhere.} \end{cases}$$

Here the h_i are chosen as the best linear estimator coefficients, hence the error term (drive term) is uncorrelated with all the x_i used in the estimate. Note that, unlike the one-sided process (1), the two-sided process (2) is not driven by a white-noise source.

A second difference concerns its use as a model for a non-Markovian process. In the one-sided case, if an N point estimate is made, the resulting process as defined by (1) always exists, but in the case of the two-sided estimate (2)

Manuscript received June 8, 1970; revised April 27, 1971.
The author is with the VELA Seismological Center, Alexandria, Va. 22314.

the representation may not exist. In the stationary Gaussian case we have to restrict the h_m in (2) to values such that $E[u_n u_0^*]$ is nonnegative definite. The following example shows that a restriction on the h_m in (2) is necessary.

Example 1: Let $\{x_n\}$ be a stationary Gaussian zero-mean sequence with correlation $R_x(n) = \cos(n\pi/6)$. The MMSE predictor coefficient equation for x_0 given x_{-1} and x_{+1} is

$$\begin{bmatrix} 1 & R_2 \\ R_2 & 1 \end{bmatrix} \begin{bmatrix} h_1 \\ h_{-1} \end{bmatrix} = \begin{bmatrix} R_1 \\ R_1 \end{bmatrix},$$

which has solution $h_1 = h_{-1} = R_1(R_2 + 1)^{-1} = 3^{-1/2}$. Now, for $N = 1$, $R_u(n) = E[u_n u_0^*]$ is not nonnegative definite, hence the MMSE estimate does not lead to a two-sided difference equation model in this case.

If we further restrict the h_m so that $R_u(n)$ is positive definite, then it will be shown later (for two dimensions, hence also for one dimension) that (2) always has a unique solution. The larger question concerning the kind of non-Markov processes $\{x_n\}$ that correspond to the positive-definite $R_u(n)$ for given N remains unsolved. (This question is of interest when one is trying to use a Markov process to model a possibly non-Markov process.) However, it is clear that if the process can be represented by (2) for a given N, if then the spectral factorization theorem applies, it can also be represented by (1) for the same N.[1] The advantage of the two-sided representation is that in two dimensions and higher, it turns out that there is no spectral factorization theorem[2] so that (2) as generalized hereafter does not imply a "one-sided" representation.

III. Two-Dimensional Markovian Assumptions

In the two-dimensional case there is no physically meaningful notion of order for the points in the space. As a result, the realizable representation seems to have little meaning, i.e., what points will come before other points. On the other hand, the second symmetric representation (if extended to two dimensions) in terms of the nearest neighbors is intuitively pleasing as an approximation to a two-dimensional field. We next show that Lévy's definition of a Pth-order Markov random field [1] leads to an analogous discrete definition that in the homogeneous [3] Gaussian case has the representation

$$x_{nm} = \sum_{\not{D}_P} h_{kl} x_{n-k,m-l} + u_{nm}$$

where

1) $E[x_{nm} u_{kl}^*] = c \delta_{nk} \delta_{ml}$
2) $D_P = D_P - \{\vec{0}\}$
3) $D_P = \{(k,l) \text{ such that } k^2 + l^2 \leq P^2\}$
4) $E[u_{nm} u_{00}^*] = \begin{cases} c, & m = n = 0 \\ -h_{mn} c, & (m,n) \in \not{D}_P \\ 0, & \text{elsewhere} \end{cases}$

and where the h_{kl} are found as the coefficients of the linear MMSE estimator of x_{nm} given its neighbors out to distance P.

Definition [1],[9]: Let ξ_z be a random field on the metric space $\aleph$. Let $\tilde{\xi}_z$ be an approximation to ξ_z in the neighborhood of a curve ∂G separating the space $\aleph$ into two regions G^+ and G^- where $E|\tilde{\xi}_z - \xi_z| = 0(\delta^P)$, δ being the distance $(z,\partial G)$. Then if given $\tilde{\xi}_z$ we have $\xi_z \in G^+$ independent of $\xi_z \in G^-$ for all ∂G. Then ξ_z is a Markovian random field of order P.

In the case of smooth differentiable sample functions, this condition is equivalent to knowing the partial derivatives of ξ_z on ∂G out to order P. The discrete version would thus concern the partial differences out to order P, thereby enlarging ∂G to a band of minimum width P.

Definition: A band of minimum width P is a set of contiguous lattice points with a well-defined inside and outside G^+ and G^-, such that all points in G^+ are at least distance P from every point in G^-.

Definition of a Discrete Markovian Random Field of Order P: Let a band of minimum width P (∂G the "present") separate discrete space $\aleph$ into two regions G^+ and G^- (Fig. 1), the "future" and "past". Then given ξ_z on ∂G, the future and past are independent, i.e., upon defining ξ_{G^+} as the restriction of ξ to G^+ with $\xi_{\partial G}$ and ξ_{G^-} defined analogously, we have $\Pr\{\xi_{G^+} | \xi_{G^-}, \xi_{\partial G}\} = \Pr\{\xi_{G^+} | \xi_{\partial G}\}$ for all such ∂G.

A. Discrete Gauss-Markov Fields

Let $\{x_{ij}\}$ be a homogeneous second-order non-Markov Gaussian random field with nonsingular covariance in a finite region $\mathscr{D}$ of the discrete space I^2. Form the MMSE estimate of x_{00} given x_{ij} on $\not{D}_P$ where $D_P \subset \mathscr{D}$, we can then write

$$x_{ij} = \sum_{\not{D}_P} h_{kl} x_{i-k, j-l} + u_{ij}, \qquad (3)$$

where u_{ij} is the error random field, i.e., (3) defines u_{ij}. It follows that

$$E[x_{ij} u_{kl}^*] = c \delta_{ik} \delta_{jl} \quad \text{in } D_P, c > 0$$

and

$$c^{-1} E[u_{ij} u_{kl}^*] = \begin{cases} -h_{i-k, j-l}, & i \neq k, j \neq l \\ 1, & i = k, j = l \end{cases} \quad \text{in } \not{D}_P.$$

Now if

$$c^{-1} R_u(i,j) = \begin{cases} 1, & i = j = 0 \\ -h_{ij}, & (i,j) \in D_P \\ 0, & \text{elsewhere} \end{cases} \qquad (4)$$

---

[1] Spectral factorization does not always apply. For example, consider the stationary Gaussian zero-mean sequence $\{x_i\}$ with correlation function $\cos w_0 k$. It is easy to show that this sequence is two-sided Markov with $N = 1$, but it is one-sided Markov with $N = 2$, not $N = 1$. Note that this example is degenerate in the sense that the zero-mean sequence $\{u_i\}$ has zero variance, i.e., the sequence $\{x_i\}$ is deterministic.

[2] The fact that spectral factorization does not exist in two dimensions was pointed out in helpful conversations with J. Burg, then of Texas Instruments Incorporated, Dallas.

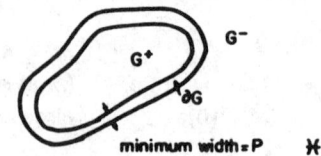

Fig. 1. Regions used in Markov-P field definition.

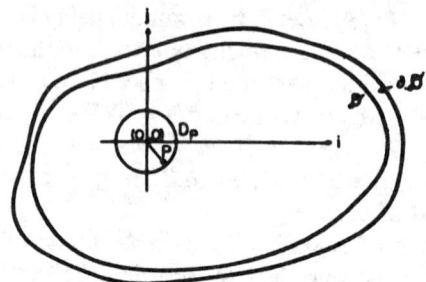

Fig. 2. Solution region for Markov-P field over a finite set.

is positive definite, it can be shown that the solution to (3) driven by $\{u_{ij}\}$ with correlation given by (4) is Markov-P in $\mathcal{D}$ (Fig. 2).

Theorem 2: Let $\{x_{ij}\}$ satisfy (3) in a finite region $\mathcal{D}$ of the discrete space I^2, where the zero-mean homogeneous Gaussian random field $\{u_{ij}\}$ is specified by the positive-definite homogeneous correlation function $R_u(i,j)$ given by (4). Let an arbitrary set of boundary values be specified in P bands immediately surrounding $\mathcal{D}$. Call this boundary region $\partial \mathcal{D}$. Then $\{x_{ij}\}$ is Gauss–Markov-P in $\mathcal{D}$.

Proof: Assume there is a given arbitrary set of boundary values specified in a region $\partial \mathcal{D}$ consisting of P bands immediately surrounding $\mathcal{D}$. Assume that $\{x_{ij}\}$ satisfies (3) where $\{u_{ij}\}$ is given by (4). Then we must show that there exists a unique solution $\{x_{ij}\}$, which is Markov of order P. Let the number of points of $\mathcal{D}$ be $\mathcal{N}$. To facilitate the solution, order the points of $\mathcal{D}$ onto a column vector so that

$$\{x_{ij}\} \leftrightarrow x$$

$$\{u_{ij}\} \leftrightarrow u.$$

Then the difference equation (3) can be written in matrix form $Ax = u - b$ where b is a column vector of linear combinations of boundary conditions. Now by (4) the vector u has a correlation matrix equal to A, the coefficient matrix of the unknown vector x. Thus, since the $\{h_{kl}\}$ are such that $R_u(i,j)$ is positive definite, then the coefficient matrix A is positive definite, and hence its inverse exists so that the solution x exists and is unique. To show that the solution is Markov-P, choose an arbitrary band of minimum width P separating $\mathcal{D}$ into G^+ and G^-. Now by the procedure just used to solve for x_{ij} in $\mathcal{D}$, we can solve for x_{ij} in G^+ given x_{ij} on ∂G. These values will depend on u_{ij} in G^+ and x_{ij} on ∂G. Hence, given x_{ij} on ∂G, these random variables will be independent of x_{ij} in G^- owing to the fact that the u_{ij} in G^+ and the u_{ij} in G^- are independent sets of random variables. Hence $\{x_{ij}\}$ is Markov of order P.

The positive-definite assumption is necessary to guarantee that a solution exists for arbitrary boundary conditions on ∂G and/or values of $\{u_{ij}\}$.

Theorem 3: If $\{x_{ij}\}$ is second-order homogeneous Gauss–Markov-P in a finite region $\mathcal{D}$ of the discrete space I^2, then $\{x_{ij}\}$ satisfies (3) and the estimate error field satisfies (4).

Proof: The proof is immediate. Clearly, we can write (3) where the estimate error u_{00} is uncorrelated with x_{ij} for $(i,j) \in D_P$ since these are the points used in the MMSE estimate. Now since the field is Markov-P, the random variable x_{ij} conditioned on $\{x_{ij}: (i,j) \in \bar{D}_P\}$ is independent of $\{x_{ij}: (i,j) \notin D_P\}$. Therefore this is also the best estimate of x_{00} given all other x_{ij}; $(i,j) \in \mathcal{D}$, so that $E[x_{ij}u_{00}^*] = 0$ for $(i,j) \neq 0$. Homogeneity of $\{x_{ij}\}$ implies that u_{ij} is homogeneous, so $E[x_{ij}u_{kl}^*] = c\delta_{ik}\delta_{jl}$ for all $(i,j), (k,l) \in \mathcal{D}$. Multiplying (3) by u_{kl}^* and taking expected values, we then obtain (4).

Note that $R_u(i,j)$ may be only nonnegative definite.

Since there is no spectral factorization theorem in two dimensions, the field x_{ij} cannot be represented by a "one-sided" difference equation driven by white noise. The following example proves this lack of factorization.

Example 2: Consider a Gaussian random field $\{x_{ij}\}$ with correlation function $R_{ij} = 0$, except at the points shown in Fig. 3. This field exists since its correlation function is nonnegative definite. If we could factor the spectrum, then we could write $x_{ij} = \alpha w_{ij} + \beta w_{i-1,j} + \gamma w_{i-1,j-1}$ for some α, β, γ, where w_{ij} is white Gaussian noise. Now this cannot be done as is easily seen by considering the possible correlation patterns, when this difference equation is autocorrelated. In particular, the zero output at $(i,j) = (0,1) \Rightarrow \beta\gamma = 0$. Let $\beta = 0$, then we cannot satisfy $R_{-1,0} = \frac{1}{4}$. Assume $\gamma = 0$, $R_{1,1} = 0 \neq \frac{1}{4}$. So $\beta\gamma \neq 0$. This is a contradiction.

The reason that spectral factorization fails in two or more dimensions seems to be that the number of constraints exceeds the number of unknowns. One immediately runs into this problem when he tries to factor a general two-dimensional polynomial spectrum.

B. Generation of $\{u_{ij}\}$

If one wanted to generate a Markov-P field by a difference equation in some finite region, he would first have to generate the $\{u_{ij}\}$ as a finite linear combination of white noise. However, this problem can be overcome by going to the discrete Fourier transform (DFT) domain due to the bounded support of $R_u(i,j)$.

Theorem 4: Let $R_u(k,l) = 0$ for $(k,l) \in D_P^c$. Take $N \gg P$. Let $\{w_{kl}\}$ be a unit-variance zero-mean white Gaussian noise sequence defined for $(k,l) \in [-N, +N] \times [-N, +N] = \mathcal{S}_N$. Generate an array of random variables by the equation

$$v_{kl} = w_{kl}\{S_u(k,l)\}^{1/2},$$

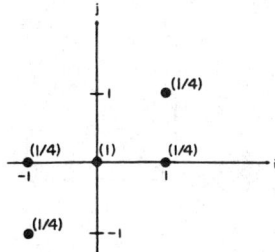

Fig. 3. Correlation diagram for Example 2 of a correlation function whose spectrum cannot be factored.

where

$$S_u(k,l) = \sum_{\mathscr{S}_N} R_u(m,n) \exp\{+j2\pi(km+ln)/(2N+1)\}.$$

Set

$$\mu_{kl} = N^{-1} \sum_{\mathscr{S}_N} v_{mn} \exp\{-j2\pi(km+ln)/(2N+1)\}.$$

Then $\{\mu_{kl}\}$ is Gaussian zero mean with correlation function $R_u(k,l)$ for $(k,l) \in \mathscr{S}\lfloor N/2 \rfloor$ (where $\lfloor \cdot \rfloor$ is the least integer function) and hence is a realization of $\{u_{ij}\}$ in this region.

Proof: Consider $\mu_{kl} = N^{-1} \sum_{mn} v_{mn} \exp\{-j2\pi(km+ln)/(2N+1)\}$. This is a linear combination of zero-mean independent Gaussian random variables; hence the μ_{kl} are jointly Gaussian zero mean. The correlation values are

$$E[\mu_{kl}\mu_{mn}^*] = N^{-2} \sum_{op}\sum_{qr} E[w_{op}w_{qr}^*] S_u^{1/2}(o,p)$$
$$\cdot [S_u^{1/2}(q,r)]^* \exp\{-j2\pi(2N+1)^{-1}$$
$$\cdot [ko + lp - mq - nr]\}$$
$$= N^{-2} \sum_{op} |S_u(o,p)| \exp\{-j2\pi(2N+1)^{-1}$$
$$\cdot [o(k-m) + p(l-n)]\}.$$

Since $S_u(o,p)$ is a spectrum, we have

$$E[\mu_{kl}\mu_{mn}^*] = N^{-2} \sum_{op} S_u(o,p) \exp\{-j2\pi(2N+1)^{-1}$$
$$\cdot [o(k-m) + p(l-n)]\}$$
$$= R_u(k-m, l-n), \quad \text{for } |k-m| \leq N$$
$$\text{and } |l-n| \leq N$$

and hence for $(k,l), (m,n) \in \mathscr{S}N/2$. Thus for the indicated region the field is a realization of $\{u_{ij}\}$.

Note that if R_u were not bounded support, then the DFT of R_u over $\mathscr{S}_N$ would not be the spectrum of R_u; hence the preceding proof would not be valid since we could be sure that $S_u(o,p)$, the DFT of $R_u(k,l)$, was nonnegative.

C. Non-Gaussian Markov Fields

Any field generated by a difference equation of the form of (3) driven by a source $\{u_{ij}\}$ of independent non-Gaussian variables will be a Markov field. In this section we establish that, based upon a stability assumption, these solutions exist and are unique in the mean absolute sense. Let

$$\rho \triangleq \sum_{\mathscr{D}_P} |h_{kl}|.$$

The stability assumption here is that $\rho < 1$. If $h_{kl} = h_{-k,-l}^*$ for all $(k,l) \in \mathscr{D}_P$, then this implies that $1 - H(u,v)$ is positive. However, if h is not Hermitian, then $1 - H(u,v)$ may not even be real.

Theorem 5: Let $\{u_{ij}\}$ be independent random variables with bounded absolute moment defined in a region $\mathscr{D}$. Let $\{x_{ij}^{bc}\}$ be a set of boundary conditions defined on P bands $(\partial \mathscr{D})$ surrounding $\mathscr{D}$. Then the iterative sequence

$$x_{ij}^{(n+1)} = \begin{cases} \sum_{\mathscr{D}_P} h_{kl} x_{i-k,j-l}^{(n)} + u_{ij} & \text{on } \mathscr{D} \\ x_{ij}^{bc} & \text{on } \partial \mathscr{D} \end{cases} \quad (5)$$

with $\rho < 1$ and initial values

$$x_{ij}^{(0)} = \begin{cases} u_{ij} & \text{on } \mathscr{D} \\ x_{ij}^{bc} & \text{on } \partial \mathscr{D} \end{cases}$$

converges to the mean absolute solution to

$$x_{ij} = \sum_{\mathscr{D}_P} h_{kl} x_{i-k,j-l} + u_{ij} \quad \text{on } \mathscr{D} \quad (6)$$

with boundary conditions

$$x_{ij} = x_{ij}^{bc} \quad \text{on } \partial \mathscr{D}. \quad (7)$$

Proof: The proof will consist of three parts:

i) to show that

$$\max_{\mathscr{D}} \sup_n E|x_{ij}^{(n)}| < \infty,$$

ii) to show that

$$\max_{\mathscr{D}} E|x_{ij}^{(m)} - x_{ij}^{(n)}| \to 0 \quad \text{as } m,n \to \infty,$$

iii) to show that the solution is unique.

i) From (5) we have

$$\max_{\mathscr{D}} |x_{ij}^{(n+1)}| \leq \sum_{\mathscr{D}_P} |h_{kl}| \max_{\mathscr{D}} |x_{ij}^{(n)}| + \max_{\mathscr{D}} |u_{ij}|.$$

So taking expectations we have

$$\max_{\mathscr{D}} E|x_{ij}^{(n+1)}| \leq \rho \max_{\mathscr{D}} E|x_{ij}^{(n)}| + M,$$

where

$$M \triangleq \max_{\mathscr{D}} E|u_{ij}| < \infty.$$

Thus

$$\max_{\mathscr{D}} E|x_{ij}^{(n)}| \leq M(1-\rho)^{-1} < \infty$$

independent of n. Thus

$$\max_{\mathscr{D}} \sup_n E|x_{ij}^{(n)}| < \infty.$$

ii) Subtract (5) for nth and mth iterations (where $m \geq n \geq N$) to yield

$$x_{ij}^{(m)} - x_{ij}^{(n)} = \sum h_{kl}(x_{i-k,j-l}^{(m-1)} - x_{i-k,j-l}^{(n-1)}).$$

Thus

$$\max_{\mathscr{D}} |x_{ij}^{(m)} - x_{ij}^{(n)}| \leq (\sum |h_{kl}|) \max_{\mathscr{D}} |x_{ij}^{(m-1)} - x_{ij}^{(n-1)}|.$$

Now take expectations and repeat the process N times to yield

$$\max_{\mathscr{D}} E|x_{ij}^{(m)} - x_{ij}^{(n)}| \leq \rho^N E|x_{ij}^{(m-N)} - x_{ij}^{(n-N)}|$$

$$\leq \rho^N 2M(1-\rho)^{-1} \to 0 \quad \text{as} \quad N \to \infty.$$

So by the Cauchy convergence theorem, $x_{ij}^{(n)} \to x_{ij}$ in mean absolute sense. It is easily verified that x_{ij} is indeed a solution to (6) and (7), and so this step will be omitted.

iii) Say there are two solutions to (6) and (7), x_{ij} and $\tilde{x}_{ij}$. We have

$$x_{ij} - \tilde{x}_{ij} = \sum_{D_P} h_{kl}(x_{i-k,j-l} - \tilde{x}_{i-k,j-l}).$$

Now

$$E \max_{\mathscr{D}} |x_{ij} - \tilde{x}_{ij}| \leq (\sum_{D_P} |h_{kl}|) E \max_{\mathscr{D}} |x_{ij} - \tilde{x}_{ij}|$$

$$< E \max_{\mathscr{D}} |x_{ij} - \tilde{x}_{ij}|$$

so

$$E \max_{\mathscr{D}} |x_{ij} - \tilde{x}_{ij}| = 0.$$

Hence $x_{ij} = \tilde{x}_{ij}$ in the mean absolute sense.

IV. Homogeneous Gauss–Markov Fields Over All Space

In this section we will extend the solution of the Markov difference equation (3) from $\mathscr{D}$, a bounded region, to the whole space. This will be accomplished by solving the equations on a disk D_R of radius R and then finding a limiting solution as $R \to \infty$ for uniformly bounded boundary conditions specified on ∂D_R (Fig. 4). For this section we assume the spectral density of the $\{u_{ij}\}$ field $S_u(\mu,v) > 0$ for all $(\mu,v) \in \mathscr{S}_\pi$, which implies $R_u(i,j)$ is positive definite.

Lemma: If $S_u(\mu,v) > 0$, define $A(\mu,v) \triangleq S_u^{-1}(\mu,v)$. Let

$$\mathscr{A}_{kl} \triangleq \int\int_{\mathscr{S}_\pi} A(\mu,v) \exp[+j(k\mu + lv)] \, d\mu \, dv (2\pi)^{-2}.$$

Then

i) $\sum |\mathscr{A}_{kl}|^2 < \infty,$

ii) $k\mathscr{A}_{kl} \to 0$ as k and/or $l \to \infty,$

iii) $l\mathscr{A}_{kl} \to 0$ as k and/or $l \to \infty.$

Proof: Since the continuous function $S_u(\mu,v) > 0$ in the closed square $\mathscr{S}_\pi$, $A(\mu,v)$ is continuous and positive in this square, hence it is bounded. Applying Parseval's

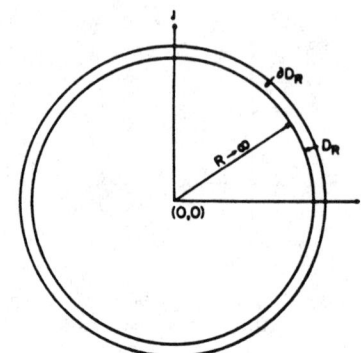

Fig. 4. Solution region for Theorem 6 on all-space extension of Markov difference equation solution.

theorem, we have

$$\sum |\mathscr{A}_{kl}|^2 = \int\int |A(\mu,v)|^2 \, dv \, d\mu (2\pi)^{-2} \leq M < \infty.$$

Also

$$\sum |k\mathscr{A}_{kl}|^2 = \int\int |\partial A/\partial\mu|^2 \, d\mu \, dv (2\pi)^{-2} < \infty$$

since

$$\partial A/\partial \mu = -\sum_{D_P} k h_{kl} \exp[+j(k\mu + lv)]/$$

$$\{1 - \sum_{D_P} h_{kl} \exp[+j(k\mu + lv)]\}^2$$

so that $|\partial A \partial \mu| \leq M' < \infty$. This proves ii).
A similar result holds for $l\mathscr{A}_{kl}$, which proves iii).

We will now solve (3) and (4) using generating functions [8].

Theorem 6: If (3) and (4) are solved in D_R with finite bounded boundary conditions specified on ∂D_R, where $S_u(\mu,v)$, the spectrum of the Gaussian field $\{u_{ij}\}$, is strictly positive, then as R gets large the solution tends to $x_{ij} = \sum_{k,l} \mathscr{A}_{kl} u_{i-k,j-l}$, the "particular" or transform solution, for $(i,j) \in D_{R_1}$ for any fixed R_1.

Proof: Rewrite (3),

$$x_{ij} - \sum_{D_P} h_{kl} x_{i-k,j-l} = u_{ij}.$$

Multiply through by $t^i s^j$ and sum over D_R, taking the terms involving the boundary conditions $\{x_{ij} = x_{ij}^{bc}$ on $\partial D_R\}$ to the right-hand side. We then have

$$[1 - H(t,s)]X(t,s) = W(t,s) + BC(t,s),$$

where

$$X(t,s) \triangleq \sum_{D_R} x_{ij} t^i s^j$$

$$H(t,s) \triangleq \sum_{D_P} h_{kl} t^k s^l$$

$$W(t,s) \triangleq \sum_{D_R} w_{ij} t^i s^j$$

$$BC(t,s) \triangleq \sum_{(i,j) \in \partial D_R} (\sum_{(k,l) \in D_{ij}} h_{k-i,l-j}) x_{ij}^{bc} t^i s^j,$$

where
$$D_{ij} \triangleq \{(k,l) \in D_R \text{ and } (k-i, l-j) \in D_P\}$$

So
$$X(t,s) = W(t,s)[1 - H(t,s)]^{-1} + BC(t,s)[1 - H(t,s)]^{-1}.$$

Thus for $(i,j) \in D_R$
$$x_{ij} = \sum_{D_R} u_{kl} \mathscr{A}_{i-k, j-l} + x_{ij}^h,$$

where x_{ij}^h denotes the homogeneous solution given rise by the boundary conditions. It remains to show that $(i,j) \in D_{R_1}$ with $R_1 \ll R$ implies that $x_{ij}^h \simeq 0$. Toward this end, note that $BC(t,s)$ is a polynomial in t, s, t^{-1}, and s^{-1} of order αR for some finite α, and the boundary conditions are uniformly bounded, say by $M < \infty$, so that

$$|x_{ij}^h| \leq \alpha RM(\sum_{D_P} |h_{kl}|) |\mathscr{A}_{k_0-i, l_0-j}|,$$

where (k_0, l_0) is a point in $D_{R-P}^C \cap D_{R+P}$ that leads to a maximum value for $|\mathscr{A}_{k-i, l-j}|$ for $(i,j) \in D_{R_1}$. Now $R \to \infty$ implies k_0 or $l_0 \to \infty$, so by ii) and iii) of the Lemma, $R|\mathscr{A}_{k_0-i, l_0-j}| \to 0$ as $R \to \infty$. Thus $|x_{ij}^h| \to 0$ as $R \to \infty$.

Since $\sum \mathscr{A}_{kl}^2 < \infty$ [(i) of Lemma], we can write

$$\sum_{D_R} u_{kl} \mathscr{A}_{i-k, j-l} \to \sum_{(k,l)} u_{kl} \mathscr{A}_{i-k, j-l},$$

where $(i,j) \in D_{R_1}$.

Putting these results together yields

$$x_{ij} \to \sum_{k,l} u_{kl} \mathscr{A}_{i-k, j-l} = u_{ij} \otimes \mathscr{A}_{ij},$$

which was to be established.

Based upon Theorem 6, we can say that (3) and (4) determine a solution over the whole space of lattice points. This is analogous to the justification of the "solution for all time" in the case of the one-dimensional differential equation. Therefore, this class ($S_u > 0$) of Markov fields[3] has the spectral representation $S_x(\mu, v) = \{1 - \sum_{D_P} h_{kl} \exp[+j(k\mu + lv)]\}^{-1}$. Furthermore, if one has a difference equation that is stable in the sense that $1 - H(\mu, v) > 0$, then the solution driven by white noise is a discrete Markov random field.

It is easily seen that if $S_u(\mu_0, v_0) = 0$, then adding in varying amounts of $\exp[+j(\mu_0 k + v_0 l)]$ into the boundary conditions will alter the solution well inside of the boundary by the same amounts, thus leading to nonconvergence of the solution as the boundary tends to infinite radius.

Example 3: The case of north-south-east-west direct dependence.

Consider the Gaussian-Markov-1 process generated by

---

[3] There are Gauss-Markov random fields not in this class. Consider $S_x(\mu, v) = \frac{1}{2}\{\delta(\mu - \mu_0) + \delta(\mu + \mu_0)\}$. In this case $\{x_{ij}\}$ is Markov-1 and $S_u(\mu, v) \equiv 0$.

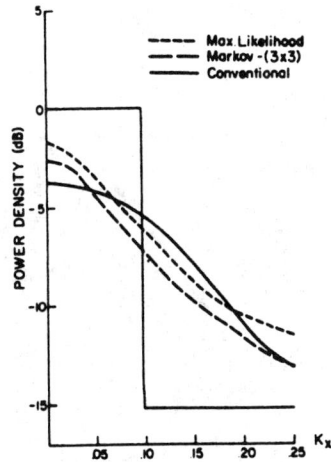

TABLE I

k \	0	1	2	3	4
4	0.10	0.10	0.08	0.05	0.03
3	0.25	0.24	0.16	0.10	0.05
2	0.72	0.53	0.31	0.16	0.08
1	1.90	1.10	0.53	0.24	0.10
0	5.71	1.90	0.72	0.25	0.10

$c = E[x_{00} u_{00}^*] = 4.0$

Fig. 5. $k_y = 0$ slice of spectral estimates for isotropic disk model and 3×3 array.

the difference equation.

$$x_{ij} = \alpha(x_{i,j+1} + x_{i+1,j} + x_{i-1,j} + x_{i,j-1}) + u_{ij},$$

driven by a zero-mean Gaussian source $\{u_{ij}\}$ with correlation

$$c^{-1} R_u(i,j) = \begin{cases} 1, & (i,j) = 0 \\ -\alpha, & i = \pm 1 \text{ and } j = \pm 1 \\ 0, & \text{elsewhere,} \end{cases}$$

where $c = E[x_{00} u_{00}^*] \neq 0$.

We restrict $|\alpha| < \frac{1}{4}$, so that $S_u > 0$. Now $S_x(\mu, v) = c[1 - 2\alpha(\cos 2\pi\mu + \cos 2\pi v)]^{-1}$ so that

$$R_x(k,l) = c \int_{-0.5}^{+0.5} \int_{-0.5}^{+0.5} \exp[+j2\pi(\mu k + vl)]$$
$$\cdot [1 - 2\alpha(\cos 2\pi\mu + \cos 2\pi v)]^{-1} d\mu \, dv.$$

Computer evaluation of this integral for $2\alpha = 0.45$ generates the values shown in Table I. This example shows that the present definition of a discrete Markov field is more general than the definition of Abend *et al.* [5] since it allows north-south-east-west "direct" dependence, which is not obtained in the Markov-Mesh [5] formulation.

V. Application

One application of this idea is in the area of high-resolution wavenumber spectra. Essentially, the problem is

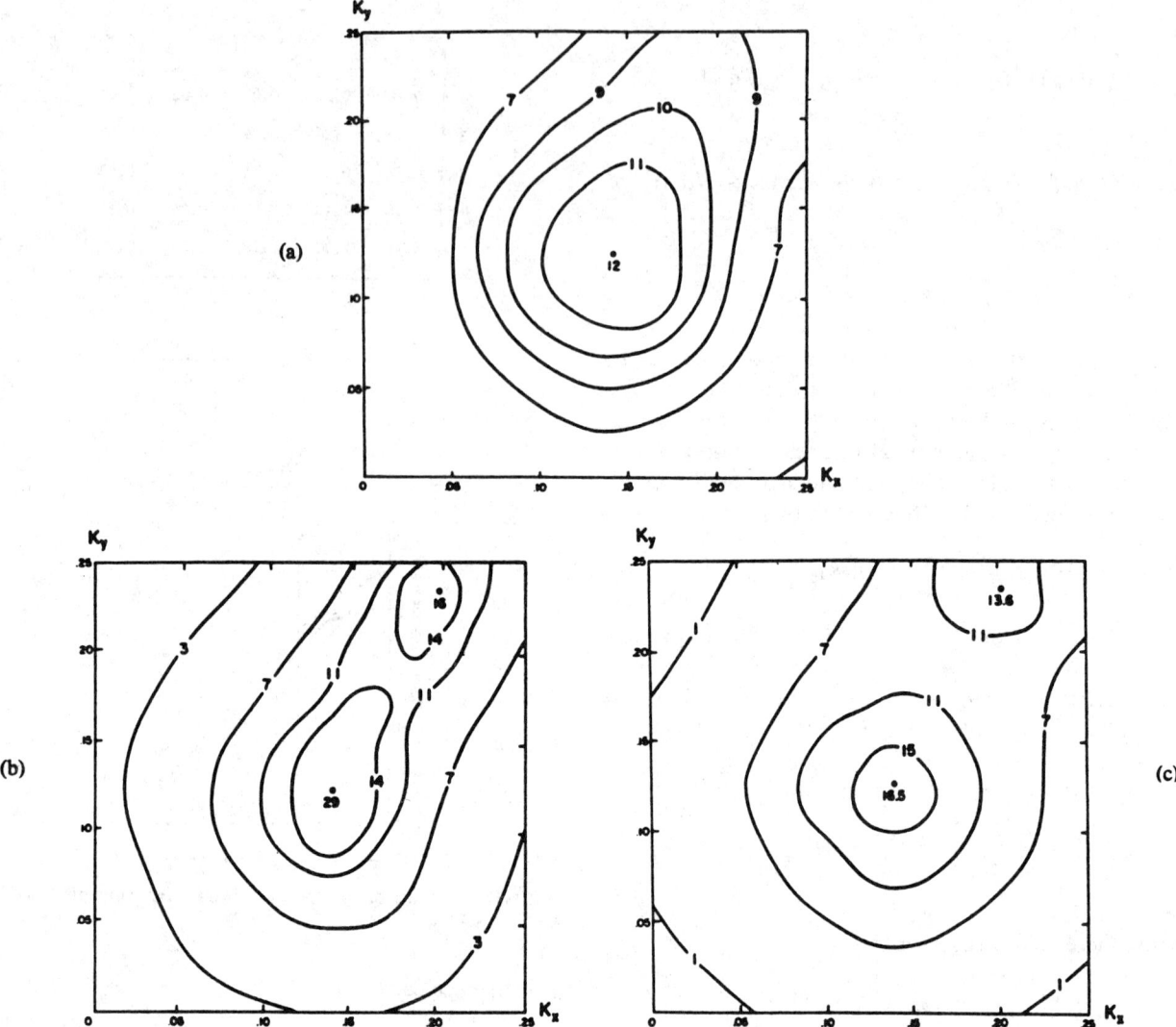

Fig. 6. Portion of spectral estimate for attenuated cosines with $\alpha = 0.2$. (a) Conventional Bartlett estimate. (b) Markov-(4 × 4) estimate. (c) True spectra.

the following. From observing a random function over a limited region of space, say D_R, form an estimate of the spectrum [6],[7]. One method would be to model the data by a Markov-R field, then calculate the spectrum of the model by

$$S_x(\mu,v) = c[1 - H(\mu,v)]^{-1}.$$

Since in the homogeneous Gaussian case the model is equivalent to saying that only those data within R of the origin are useful in the estimate of x_{00}, we can check the appropriateness of the model by seeing if the spectrum changes much when the points at distance R from the origin are added to or deleted from the estimate.

A. Experimental Results

In this section, experimental results are presented on the problem of wavenumber spectral estimation. Covariance data are modeled by Markov spectra in terms of the prediction error covariance function for an estimate of the $x = (0,0)$ value from data in a square of side N centered on the origin. Thus, in this section we speak of Markov-$(N \times N)$ instead of Markov-R.

Two sets of spectra were used in a test of this method of spectral estimation. In the first set the spectrum was an isotropic disk model with corner frequency 0.1 Hz plus white noise at -15 dB. A slice at $k_y = 0$ is shown in Fig. 5. The Markov-(3×3) prediction results are shown along with the maximum-likelihood [6] and conventional estimates (Bartlett or triangular weighting).[4] The Markov results are seen to be comparable to maximum-likelihood results and better than conventional results. For 4 × 4 and larger arrays, the Markov estimate did not exist because the transform of the estimated error matrix went negative around the maximum values of the true spectrum. This behavior is not unexpected since the isotropic band-limited disk has a dependence that drops off only linearly with distance and in fact is singular in the sense that perfect prediction is possible by using all the values not at the origin, hence clearly not Markov.

In the second set of experiments, a covariance function

---

[4] The maximum-likelihood and conventional results are for a 4 × 4 array, hence the comparison is slightly biased against the Markov estimate.

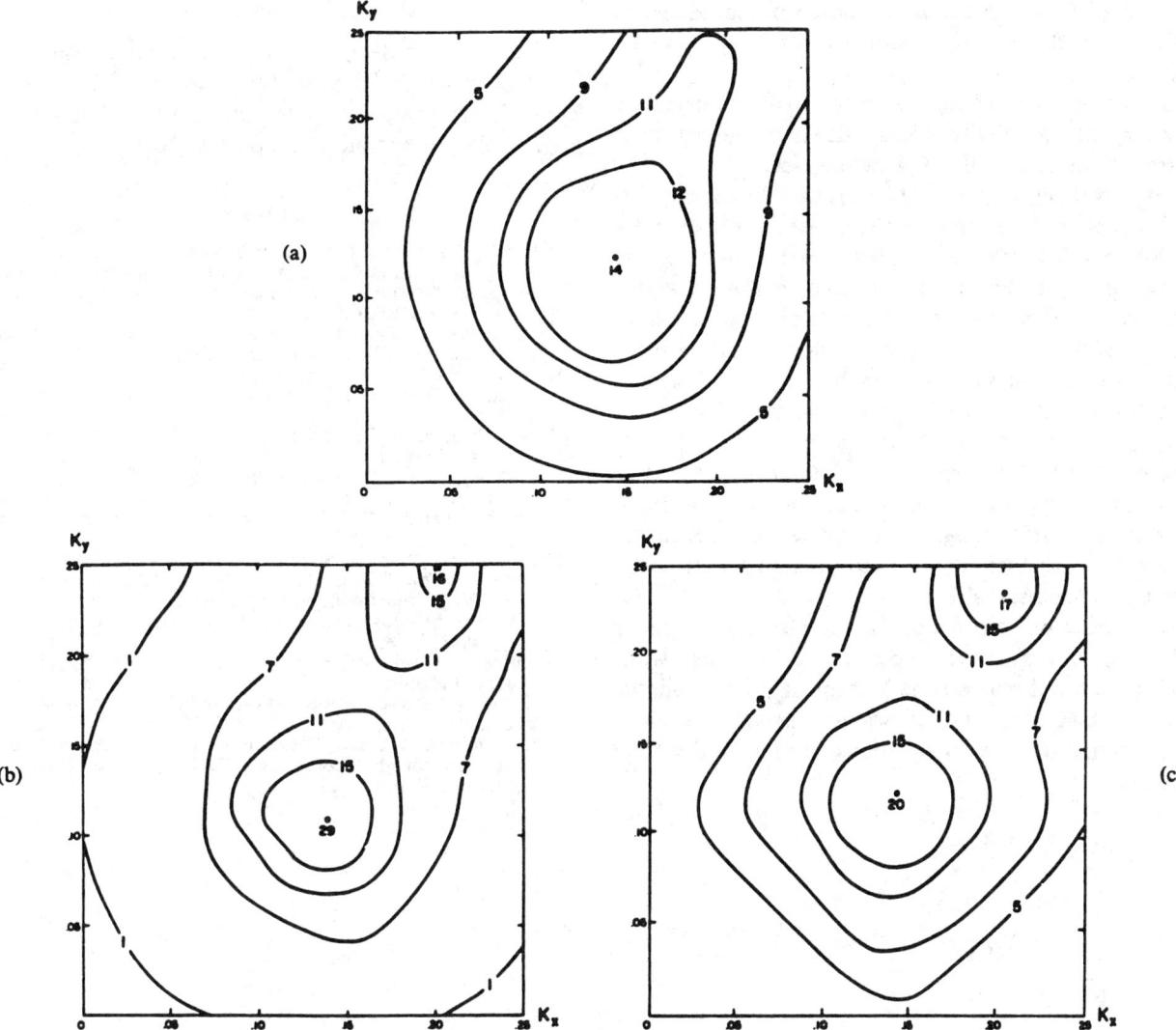

Fig. 7. Portion of spectral estimate for attenuated cosines with $\alpha = 0.1$. (a) Conventional Bartlett estimate. (b) Markov-(4×4) estimate. (c) True spectra.

consisting of two cosine waves at $k_1 = (0.14, 0.12)$ and $k_2 = (0.20, 0.24)$ attenuated by $\exp(-\alpha r)$ was considered. Specifically,

$$R_{kl} = \exp(-\alpha r)[\cos(k_1 \cdot r) + 0.5 \cos(k_2 \cdot r)] + c\delta_{kl}$$

where $r = (k, l)$ and $r = (k^2 + l^2)^{1/2}$.

A portion of the resulting spectrum is shown in Fig. 6 for the case $\alpha = 0.2$ and $c = 0.033$ or -15 dB. Fig. 6(a) shows the conventional estimate for a 4×4 array and Fig. 6(b) shows the Markov-(3×3) estimate. Fig. 6(c) shows the true spectrum computed on a 51×51 correlation array in the conventional manner. It is seen that the conventional[5] estimate (Fig. 6(a)) does not separate the peaks at k_1 and k_2; however, the Markov estimate does. The peak values in the Markov spectrum are exaggerated; the main peak is greatly exaggerated. It is conjectured that this is due to a windowing effect on the prediction error covariance function. Some smoothing of the Markov results could be employed to advantage in this case.

The exponential weighting on the covariance matrix tends to smooth out the spectrum but also tends to keep the estimated Markov error covariance positive definite, thus establishing a tradeoff between resolution and stability. The white-noise level also has this effect; however, as N increases, the value of c must increase to keep the estimate stable in some cases; for example, the isotropic disk model.

Finally, Fig. 7 is the same as Fig. 6, except that $\alpha = 0.1$ and $c = 1$. In this case the Markov peaks are less exaggerated.

VI. Conclusions

This formulation of discrete-space Markov field can be considered a generalization of that presented by Abend et al. [5] in that it allows north-south-east-west "direct" dependence. Also, the present method does not imply any constraints on the directional propagation of the process.

---

[5] Conventional results without the Bartlett or triangular weighting did resolve the peaks in the 4×4 case; however, the resulting spectral estimate was negative for some frequencies. Note also that 4×4 is the data array, thus correlation values are available out to lags of ± 4 in both directions, implying a 9×9 correlation array.

Furthermore, it forms a natural extension of independence in such a way that storage and/or processor size can be controlled.

When the model is valid, it is much easier to calculate high-order joint probability densities and to design optimum processors than would otherwise be the case.

One disadvantage of this technique is that the continuous-space Markov field will not necessarily become a discrete-space Markov field if it is sampled in space on a regular grid. However, if the samples of the continuous-space Markov field are taken closely in comparison to the bandwidths of the field, then the approximation should be good. In the one-dimensional case the result would generally still be Markov essentially because the state variables of the resulting difference equation would be the same state variables as for the differential equation. However, in two dimensions or higher, the state variables of the corresponding partial-differential equations are curves and, hence, are not available as conditional information from finite numbers of spatial samples.

In some cases one can factor the operator $S(\mu,v)$; then a two-dimensional difference equation driven by white Gaussian noise will generate the Markov field. There should be a corresponding theory concerning constant coefficient, "stable" partial-differential equations, and/or ideally band limited field.

Acknowledgment

The maximum-likelihood and conventional results for the isotropic disk model were computed by Dr. C. Ong of Texas Instruments Incorporated, as part of a report on high-resolution wavenumber spectra [10].

References

[1] P. Lévy, "A special problem of Brownian motion, and a general theory of Gaussian random functions," in *Proc. 3rd Berkeley Symp. Mathematical Statistics and Probability*, vol. 2. Berkeley, Calif.: Univ. California Press, 1956.

[2] A. Papoulis, *Probability, Random Variables and Stochastic Processes*. New York: McGraw-Hill, 1965, pp. 528–530.

[3] A. M. Yaglom, *An Introduction to the Theory of Stationary Random Functions*. Englewood Cliffs, N.J.: Prentice-Hall, 1962, pp. 81–84.

[4] ——, "Second-order homogeneous random fields," in *Proc. 4th Berkeley Symp. Mathematical Statistics and Probability*, vol. 2. Berkeley, Calif.: Univ. California Press, 1961.

[5] K. Abend, T. J. Harley, and L. N. Kanal, "Classification of binary random patterns," *IEEE Trans. Inform. Theory*, vol. IT-11, pp. 538–544, Oct. 1965.

[6] J. Capon, "High-resolution frequency-wavenumber spectrum analysis," *Proc. IEEE*, vol. 57, pp. 1408–1418, Aug. 1969.

[7] J. P. Burg, "Maximum entropy spectral analysis," presented at the 37th Meeting Soc. Exploration Geophysicists, Oklahoma City, Okla., 1968.

[8] Jordan, *Calculus of Finite Differences*. New York: Chelsea, 1965, last chapter.

[9] E. Wong, "Two-dimensional random fields and representation of images," *SIAM J. Appl. Math.*, vol. 16, pp. 756–770, 1968.

[10] C. Ong and S. Laster, "High resolution wavenumber spectra," Texas Instruments Incorporated, Dallas, Contract F33657-69-C-1063, Spec. Rep. 1, 1971.

Advances in Mathematical Models for Image Processing

ANIL K. JAIN, MEMBER, IEEE

Invited Paper

Abstract—Several state-of-the-art mathematical models useful in image processing are considered. These models include the traditional fast unitary transforms, autoregressive and state variable models as well as two-dimensional linear prediction models. These models introduced earlier [51], [52] as low-order finite difference approximations of partial differential equations are generalized and extended to higher order in the framework of linear prediction theory. Applications in several image processing problems, including image restoration, smoothing, enhancement, data compression, spectral estimation, and filter design, are discussed and examples given.

I. Introduction

MATHEMATICAL models are becoming increasingly important because of their role in the development of useful algorithms for image processing. Virtually all applications of image processing utilize some sort of mathematical models. The continuing advances in high-speed digital processors, digital memories, and very-large-scale integration (VLSI) have led to successful algorithms for many difficult problems. Table I gives a description of some of the typical problems in image processing and their associated modeling requirements. A typical algorithm requires quantification of the processing criterion and a model such as bandwidth, power spectrum, etc., of the data (input to the algorithm). While most of the problems listed in Table I also occur in one-dimensional signal processing, special care is needed in the development of two- (and higher) dimensional algorithms. The major difference besides the higher dimensionality is that of causality. A large number of one-dimensional signal processing methods are based on the fact that the observed data is the output of a causal system. For two-dimensional images the data coordinates are spatial and any causality associated with an image is purely due to its scanning or acquisition technique. Therefore, it is not surprising that a large number of image processing algorithms for edge extraction, enhancement, restoration, data compression, etc., are noncausal.

The computational efficiency of algorithms is often measured by their memory and operation count requirements. The most efficient algorithms would be such that the required number of operations per pel would be independent of the size of the image. Unfortunately, a large number of algorithms require an operation count which is proportional to log N,

Manuscript received May 28, 1980; revised October 30, 1980. This work was supported by the U.S. Army Research Office, Durham, NC, under Grant DAAG29-78-G-0206.
The author is with the Signal and Image Processing Laboratory, Department of Electrical and Computer Engineering, University of California, Davis, CA 95616.

N, or higher for $N \times N$ images. Table II lists some of the desirable properties of two-dimensional models and algorithms which tend to minimize their computational complexity. In this paper, we will consider mathematical models which are useful for solving image processing problems such as listed in Table I and their tradeoffs with respect to the desirable characteristics of Table II.

We start by series expansion models in Section II, followed by one-dimensional stochastic models in Section III. In Sections IV, V, and VI two-dimensional causal, semicausal, and noncausal models, respectively, are discussed. In Section VII, we consider applications of these models in several image processing problems.

Notation and Definitions

1) We will denote two-dimensional sequences defined on a rectangular grid by $u_{i,j}$, $x_{i,j}$, etc. Upper case letters such as U, X, etc. will denote matrices. For example

$$U \triangleq \{u_{i,j}; 1 \leq i \leq N, 1 \leq j \leq M\}$$

denotes an $N \times M$ matrix whose elements are $u_{i,j}$. Whenever necessary we will also use $[U]_{i,j}$ to denote the (i,j)th element of a matrix U. The jth column of U will be denoted as u_j.

2) If A is a matrix then A^T is its transpose and A^* is its complex conjugate.

3) Let $\{u_{i,j}\}$ be an $N \times M$ sequence. We define an $NM \times 1$ lexicographic ordered vector u_r obtained from this sequence as

$$u_r = \mathcal{O}_r(u_{i,j})$$
$$\triangleq [u_{1,1} u_{1,2} \cdots u_{1,M}, u_{2,1} \cdots u_{2,M} \cdots u_{N,1} \cdots u_{N,M}]^T$$

where $\mathcal{O}_r$ signifies the row by row ordering operation. Similarly we define $\mathcal{O}_c$ as a column by column ordering operator and write

$$u_c = \mathcal{O}_c(u_{i,j}) \triangleq [u_{1,1} u_{2,1} \cdots u_{N,1}, u_{1,2} \cdots u_{N,2},$$
$$\cdots u_{1,M} \cdots u_{N,M}]^T.$$

4) When each $u_{i,j}$ is a random variable, we will call $\{u_{i,j}\}$, a discrete *random field*. A given image could be considered as a sample function of this random field.

5) The mean and covariances of a random field $\{u_{i,j}\}$ are defined as

$$Eu_{i,j} = \mu_{i,j}$$
$$\text{Cov}[u_{i,j}, u_{m,n}] \triangleq E(u_{i,j} - \mu_{i,j})(u_{m,n} - \mu_{m,n}) = r_u(i,j; m,n)$$

$$(1)$$

TABLE I
Typical Problems in Image Processing

	Problem	Description	Models
1.	SMOOTHING:	Given noisy image data filter it to smooth out the noise variations.	Noise & image, Power Spectra
2.	ENHANCEMENT	Bring out or enhance certain features of the image e.g., edge enhancement, contrast stretching, etc.	Features
3.	RESTORATION & FILTERING	Restore an image with known (or unknown) degradation as close to its original form as possible, e.g., image deblurring, image reconstruction, image registration, geometric correction etc.	Degradations, Criterion of "closeness".
4.	DATA COMPRESSION	Minimize the Number of Bits required to store/transmit an image for a given level of Distortion.	Distortion Criterion, Image as an Information source
5.	FEATURE EXTRACTION	Extract certain features from an image, e.g., edges.	Features, detection criterion
6.	DETECTION AND IDENTIFICATION	Detect and identify the presence of an object from a scene e.g., matched filter, pattern recognition and image segmentation, texture analysis etc.	Detection criterion, object and scene
7.	INTERPOLATION/ AND EXTRAPOLATION	Given image data at certain points in a region, estimate the image values of all other points inside this region (interpolation) and also at points outside this region (extrapolation).	Estimation Criterion, and Degree of smoothness of the data
8.	SPECTRAL ESTIMATION	Given image data in a region, estimate its power spectrum.	Criterion of Estimation, A-priori model for data
9.	SPECTRAL FACTORIZATION	Given the magnitude of the frequency response of a filter-design a realizable filter e.g., a stable 'causal' filter.	Criterion of realizability;
10.	SYNTHESIS	Given a description or some features of an image, design a system which reproduces a replica of that image; e.g., texture synthesis.	Features, Criterion of reproduction.

TABLE II
Desirable Properties of Image Processing Algorithms

Property	Description
Linearity	Linear operations on data
Separability	Independent Row and Column operations
Shift Invariance	Operations leading to Toeplitz and Circulant Matrix Manipulations
Markovian or Finite Memory	Only local and/or sparse operation required in each pixel e.g., FIR Filters.

Often we will consider the special case when

$$\mu_{i,j} = \mu = \text{constant}$$

$$r_u(i,j;m,n) = r_u(i-m;j-n). \quad (2)$$

For notational simplicity, whenever there is no confusion, we will drop the subscript u. A random field satisfying (2) is also called *translational (or spatial) invariant, homogeneous, or wide-sense stationary*. For random fields with Gaussian statistics this also implies strict sense stationarity. Unless otherwise mentioned, the term *"stationary"* refers to wide-sense stationarity.

6) A random field $\{x_{i,j}\}$ will be called a *white noise field* whenever the random variables $\{x_{i,j}\}$ are mutually uncorrelated, i.e., its covariance function is of the form

$$r_x(i,j;m,n) = \sigma_x^2(i,j)\,\delta_{i,m}\delta_{j,n}$$

where $\delta_{i,m}$ is the Kronecker delta function and $\sigma_x^2(i,j)$ is the variance of $x_{i,j}$.

II. Series Expansion Models and Image Transforms
A. Unitary Transforms

A classical way of analyzing a function is by its series expansion in terms of a set of complete orthonormal functions. In the context of image processing a general orthogonal series expansion for an $N \times N$ image[1] $\{u_{i,j}\}$ is a pair of *unitary transformations* of the form

$$u_{i,j} = \sum_{k=1}^{N}\sum_{l=1}^{N} v_{k,l}a^*(i,j;k,l) \quad (3)$$

$$v_{k,l} = \sum_{i=1}^{N}\sum_{j=1}^{N} u_{i,j}a(i,j;k,l) \quad (4)$$

where $\{a(i,j,k,l)\}$, usually called the *image transform*, is a

[1] Much of the subsequent analysis is easily generalized to rectangular, $N \times M$ images. But for simplicity we shall only consider square images here.

TABLE III
Typical Fast Unitary Transform Used in Image Processing

Transform	Formula
Discrete Fourier (DFT)	$a_{m,n} = \frac{1}{\sqrt{N}} \exp\left\{-j\frac{2\pi(m-1)(n-1)}{N}\right\}, 1 \leq m,n \leq N$
Discrete Cosine (DCT)	$a_{m,n} = \begin{cases} \frac{1}{\sqrt{N}}, & m=1, 1 \leq n \leq N \\ \sqrt{\frac{2}{N}} \cos\frac{(m-1)(2n-1)\pi}{2N}, & 2 \leq m \leq N, 1 \leq n \leq N \end{cases}$
Discrete Sine (DST)	$a_{m,n} = \sqrt{\frac{2}{N+1}} \sin\frac{mn\pi}{N+1}, 1 \leq m, n \leq N$
Walsh-Hadamard (WHT)	$a_{m,n} = (-1)^{\sum_{i=0}^{p-1} m_i n_i}, 1 \leq m, n \leq N = 2^p$ m_i, n_i = ith binary digit (0 or 1) in the binary expansion of $(m-1)$ and $(n-1)$ respectively.

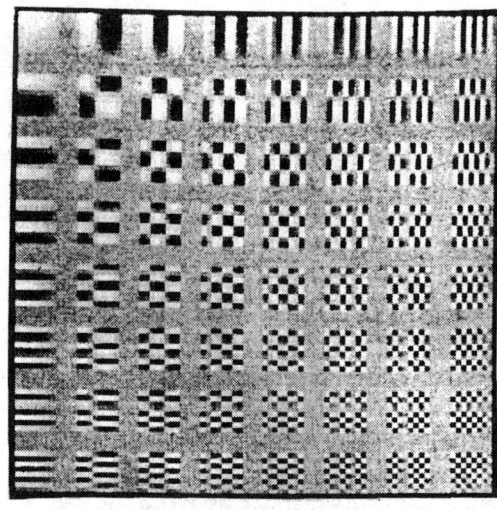

Fig. 1. 8 × 8 basis images of the DCT. Each 8 × 8 basis image if $B_{i,j}$ orthogonal to the rest and represents a spatially varying FIR of a system whose input is an impulse at (i, j).

set of complete orthonormal basis functions satisfying the properties

$$\sum_{k=1}^{N} \sum_{l=1}^{N} a(i,j;k,l) a^*(i',j';k,l) = \delta_{i,i'}\delta_{j,j'} \quad \text{(Orthonormality)}$$

$$\sum_{i=1}^{N} \sum_{j=1}^{N} a(i,j;k,l) a^*(i,j;k',l') = \delta_{k,k'}\delta_{l,l'} \quad \text{(Completeness)}.$$

(5)

The elements $v_{k,l}$ are called the *transform coefficients* and $\{v_{k,l}\}$ the *transformed image*. Equation (3) is a deterministic representation of an image considered as an $N^2 \times 1$ vector. Alternatively, the image $u_{i,j}$ is the output of a linear *spatially variant* (SV) *finite impulse response* (FIR) system whose *impulse response* (IR) or *point spread function* (PSF) is

$$h(i,j;k,l) = a^*(i,j;k,l), \quad 1 \leq i,j,k,l \leq N \quad (6)$$

to a unit impulse $\delta_{i,k}\delta_{j,l}$. For each (i,j) the array $\{a^*(i,j;k,l)\}$ is also called a *basis image*. It is readily seen from (3) and (4) that the general unitary transformation would require $O(N^4)$ operations, one operation being a multiplication and a summation. For typical size ($N = 256$) images this means over a billion operations would be needed to compute the transform coefficients. To reduce dimensionality, the unitary transformations in (3) and (4) are restricted to the *product-separable* class, satisfying the condition

$$a(i,j;k,l) = a_{i,k} b_{j,l} \quad (7)$$

where $A = \{a_{i,j}\}$ and $B = \{b_{i,j}\}$ are unitary matrices (i.e., $A^{-1} = A^{*T}$). Often in image processing one chooses $B = A$ so that (3) and (4) yield

$$V = AUA^T \quad (8)$$
$$U = A^{*T} V A^*. \quad (9)$$

Now the transformations require column operations followed by row operations on the result, reducing the computations to $O(N^3)$ operations. Even this reduction is insufficient and the choice of image transforms is further restricted to *fast transforms*. Typically, these transform matrices have structural properties which lead to fast Fourier transform (FFT) type algorithms. Hence a transformation of the type $y = Ax$, for an $N \times 1$ vector x could be performed in $O(N \log N)$ operations so that for images the operation count is $O(N^2 \log N)$ or $\log N$ per pel. Examples of common fast unitary transforms are the discrete Fourier (DFT), cosine (DCT), sine (DST), Walsh-Hadamard (WHT) transforms [1]-[8] (see Table III), etc. Fig. 1 shows the basis images of the DCT. Other fast transforms include the Haar, Slant [1]-[3], and a family of sinusoidal transforms [9], [10]. A useful property of all unitary transforms is their energy conservation property

$$\sum_{i=1}^{N} \sum_{j=1}^{N} |u_{i,j}|^2 = \sum_{k=1}^{N} \sum_{l=1}^{N} |v_{k,l}|^2 \quad (10)$$

known as Parseval's relation. This follows from the fact that a unitary transformation is simply a rotation of the image viewed as a vector in an N^2 dimensional vector space so that the length of the vector remains unchanged.

B. The Karhunen-Loeve Transform

Of particular significance among unitary transforms is the so-called Karhunen-Loeve transform (KLT) for random fields. Without loss of generality we are assuming zero-mean random fields. More generally, one could consider the autocorrelation function instead. It is the complete orthonormal set of basis images $\phi(i,j;k,l)$ determined from the eigenvalue equation

$$\sum_{m=1}^{N} \sum_{n=1}^{N} r(k,l;m,n) \phi(i,j;m,n) = \lambda_{i,j} \phi(i,j;k,l) \quad (11)$$

where $r(\cdot)$ is the image covariance function. For separable covariance functions, the KLT is also separable. Two significant properties which make the KLT very desirable are as follows [1], [11]-[13].

1) It completely decorrelates the transform coefficients, i.e.,

$$\text{Cov}[v_{k,l}(\mathcal{A}), v_{m,n}(\mathcal{A})] = \sigma_{k,l}^2(\mathcal{A}) \delta_{k,m} \delta_{l,n}, \quad \text{for } \mathcal{A} = \Phi$$

(12)

where $\mathcal{A}$ denotes an arbitrary $N^2 \times N^2$ unitary transform Φ

TABLE IV
TYPICAL COVARIANCE FUNCTION MODELS USED IN IMAGE PROCESSING

Model Description	Covariance Function $r(k,\ell) \triangleq \text{Cov}[u_{i,j}, u_{i+k,j+\ell}]$	Comments
Separable	$\sigma^2 \rho_1^{\|k\|} \rho_2^{\|\ell\|}$	Typically $\rho_1 = \rho_2 = 0.95$. ρ_1, ρ_2 are one step correlation parameters
Nonseparable Exponential or Isotropic	$\sigma^2 \exp\{-\sqrt{\alpha_1 k^2 + \alpha_2 \ell^2}\}$	For $\alpha_1 = \alpha_2$, this is called the Isotropic model. $\rho_1 = \exp(-\alpha_1)$, $\rho_2 = \exp(-\alpha_2)$.

is the KLT and $\sigma_{k,l}^2(\mathcal{A})$ are the variances of the $\mathcal{A}$-transform coefficients $v_{k,l}(\mathcal{A})$.

2) Compared to all other unitary transforms, the KLT packs the maximum expected energy in a given number of samples M, i.e.,

$$\sum\sum_{k,l \in \mathcal{M}(\Phi)} \sigma_{k,l}^2(\Phi) \geq \sum\sum_{k,l \in \mathcal{M}(\mathcal{A})} \sigma_{k,l}^2(\mathcal{A}), \quad \forall 1 \leq M \leq N^2 \tag{13}$$

where $\mathcal{M}(\mathcal{A})$ is the set containing M index pairs (k,l) corresponding to the largest M variances in the $\mathcal{A}$-transform domain. This property serves as a basis for transform data compression techniques.

Table IV shows the two commonly used stationary covariance models used in image processing. For the separable model, the KLT is given by

$$\phi(i,j; k,l) = \psi_1(i,k) \psi_2(j,l) \tag{14}$$

where $\psi_n(i,j)$ is the KLT corresponding to the one dimensional covariance function $\rho_n^{|i-j|}$, $n = 1, 2$. Unfortunately, Ψ_n is not a fast transform. Depending on the value of ρ_n, it has been shown that a suitable fast sinusoidal transform [9], [10] could be found as a good approximation to the KLT. For example for $-0.5 \leq \rho_n \leq 0.5$, the sine transform (see Table III) and for $0.5 \leq \rho_n \leq 1$, the cosine transform [10], [14] are good substitutes for the KLT. For common monochrome images, the correlation parameters ρ_1 and ρ_2 are close to unity so that the DCT is the preferred fast transform. It has also been shown [10], [15] that the sinusoidal transforms have equivalent performance as $N \to \infty$. In image processing N can be quite large, and one often processes smaller blocks (typically 16×16) of an image at a time. The performance differences between the various transforms are significant enough to warrant the use of the KLT or a reasonable substitute of it. Recently it has been shown [16] that the separable DCT is a good substitute for the nonseparable KLT of other stationary random fields also, including those modeled by the nonseparable exponential covariance function shown in Table IV. Fig. 2 shows the data compression efficiency of the various unitary transforms for random fields modeled by the nonseparable exponential covariance function of Table IV. Here we are plotting the residual expected energy (also called the basis restriction error [10])

$$\sigma_e^2(\mathcal{A}, M) = 1 - \left(\sum\sum_{k,l \in \mathcal{M}} \sigma_{k,l}^2(\mathcal{A}) \bigg/ \sum_{k=1}^{N} \sum_{l=1}^{N} \sigma_{k,l}^2(\mathcal{A}) \right) \tag{15}$$

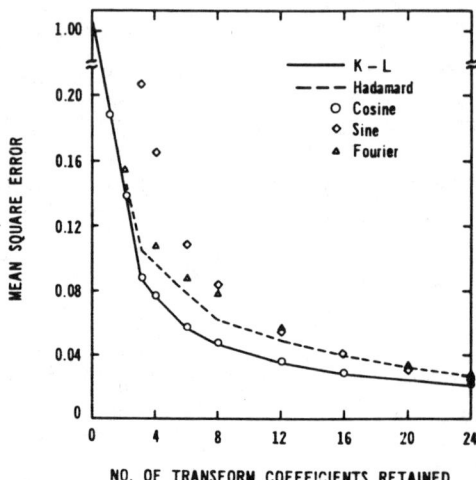

Fig. 2. Data compression efficiency of various transforms for 8×8 random fields with covariance function $r(k,l) = (0.95)^{\sqrt{k^2+l^2}}$.

remaining in the $N^2 - M$ samples of the $\mathcal{A}$-transform. Clearly we see that the DCT has the best performance for the chosen values of ρ_1 and ρ_2. In the later sections we will see that the DCT and DST are useful in other statistical representations of images also. Image transforms have been applied extensively in data compression, noise smoothing, and restoration of images [1]-[3], [7], [17]-[19].

C. The Singular-Value Decomposition (SVD) Representation

Considering an $N \times N$ image as a matrix U of real numbers, it is possible to express it as [20]-[22]

$$U = \sum_{m=1}^{K} \lambda_m^{1/2} \psi_m \phi_m^T \tag{16}$$

where K is the rank of U and ψ_m and ϕ_m are the orthonormal eigenvector solutions of

$$U^T U \phi_m = \lambda_m \phi_m$$
$$UU^T \psi_m = \lambda_m \psi_m. \tag{17}$$

The quantities λ_m, $m = 1, \cdots, K$ are positive and (16) is called the singular value or the outer product expansion of U and can also be written as

$$U = \Psi \Lambda^{1/2} \Phi^T \tag{18}$$

where Ψ and Φ are $N \times K$ matrices whose column vectors are ψ_m and ϕ_m, respectively, and $\Lambda^{1/2}$ is the diagonal matrix of elements $\{\lambda_m^{1/2}\}$. If the singular values λ_m are arranged in decreasing order then the partial sum

$$U_M \triangleq \sum_{m=1}^{M} \lambda_m^{1/2} \psi_m \phi_m^T \quad (19)$$

is the best least squares approximation of U for any $M \geq 0$, i.e., the error

$$e_M = \sum_{i=1}^{N} \sum_{j=1}^{N} (u_{i,j} - u_{i,j}^{\cdot})^2 \quad (20)$$

is minimum for any fixed M. This means the energy packed in the M coefficients $\{\lambda_m, 1 \leq m \leq M\}$ is maximized by the SVD transform. We note that the KLT maximizes the *average energy* packed in M samples for an ensemble of images. Thus, for any given image, the SVD transform would be more efficient in terms of its data compression (and other least squares processing) ability. However, in view of (17) this transform would be different for each different image. Hence, unlike the KLT, a good fast transform substitute, independent of the image, cannot be found for the SVD. Although SVD transform has potential applications in image data compression and restoration problems [23]-[26], the computational burden introduced by it overwhelms its desirable least squares property. Fortunately, some of the iterative least squares algorithms [95] could be employed to achieve practically the same results. The SVD has other applications [27], e.g., in approximation of a two-dimensional power spectrum by a separable product of one-dimensional power spectra (see Section V), in the design of digital filters [22], [28] and also in texture analysis of images [29].

III. IMAGE REPRESENTATION BY ONE-DIMENSIONAL STOCHASTIC PROCESSES

Often it is desired to design image processing algorithms for an ensemble of images. For practical reasons this ensemble is generally characterized by the mean and covariance functions. These functions could be specified by a mathematical formula (e.g., as in Table IV) or via the SDF, or simply as arrays of numerical values. An alternative is to consider the image ensemble as being generated by a linear system forced by white noise or a random sequence of known SDF. The impulse response of this linear system is often specified by a difference equation. Computational complexity as well as performance of various processing algorithms can be studied in terms of this difference equation.

A simple way to characterize an image is to consider it as a collection of one-dimensional signals, e.g., as an output of a raster scanner, or as a sequence of rows (or columns) ignoring the interrow (or column) dependencies. For such cases, one-dimensional representations of stochastic processes are useful. One dimensional stochastic models have been applied in line by line processing of images for DPCM coding, hybrid coding, recursive filtering and restoration, etc. [17], [38]-[42], [46], [52], [58].

A. Autoregressive Representations

If $\{u_k\}$ is a zero-mean stationary Gaussian random sequence, then a causal representation of the type

$$u_k, \forall k = \sum_{n=1}^{p} a_n u_{k-n} + \epsilon_k \quad E\epsilon_k = 0 \quad E\epsilon_k \epsilon_l = \beta^2 \delta_{k,l} \quad (21)$$

is called a (one-sided) autoregressive (AR) representation. The sequence $\{\epsilon_k\}$ is a zero-mean white-noise random process independent of the past outputs. AR models have the following important properties.

1) The quantity

$$\bar{u}_k = \sum_{n=1}^{p} a_n u_{k-n}$$

$$= E[u_k | u_n, \forall n \leq k - 1] \quad (22)$$

is the best mean-square predictor of u_k based on all of its past and depends only on the past p samples. Thus (21) becomes

$$u_k = \bar{u}_k + \epsilon_k \quad (23)$$

which says the sample at k is the sum of its minimum variance causal prediction estimate plus the prediction error. This is also called the *innovations representation*. The sequence $\{u_k\}$ defined by (21) is called a pth-order Markov process.

2) The AR process is stationary and causally stable (in the usual bounded-input-bounded-output (BIBO) sense) if and only if the roots of the polynomial

$$A_p(z) = 1 - \sum_{n=1}^{p} a_n z^{-n} \quad (24)$$

lie inside the unit circle. If stationary, then its spectral density function (SDF) is given by

$$S_u(z) = \beta^2 / [A_p(z) A_p(z^{-1})], \quad z = e^{j\omega}, \quad -\pi < \omega < \pi. \quad (25)$$

From (21), it is seen that the transfer function of an AR representation is $1/A_p(z)$ which is an all pole model.

3) *Theorem 1:* Given an arbitrary set of positive definite real covariances $\{r_k\}$ on a window $W = \{-p \leq k \leq p\}$, there exists a unique AR model (21) whose parameters are identified by solving the linear Toeplitz system of equations

$$r_k - \sum_{n=1}^{p} a_n r_{k-n} = \beta^2 \delta_{k,0}, \quad 0 \leq k \leq p. \quad (26)$$

Moreover, this model is causally stable and stationary.

The significance of this theorem is that the covariances generated by the model (obtained by the Fourier inverse of (25)) would match exactly the given covariances on the window W. The model covariances outside this window provide a positive definite *extrapolation* of the given covariance sequence.

An important consequence of this result is that any given SDF can be approximated arbitrarily closely by a finite-order AR spectrum. In other words, if $\{r_k\}$ is a covariance sequence corresponding to a given positive and analytic SDF $S(z)$, and if $\{a_n^p, n = 1, \cdots, p\}$ and β_p^2 denote the solution of (26), then

$$\lim_{p \to \infty} \beta_p^2 / [A_p(z) A_p(z^{-1})] = S(z), \quad z = \exp(j\omega)$$

where $A_p(z)$ is given by (24) with a_n replaced by a_n^p. This relation states that the solution of (26), as $p \to \infty$, provides the spectral factorization of $S(z)$. If $S(z)$ happens to be a rational all pole spectrum, the a_n^p will be zero when $n > p$, for some $p < \infty$. In general (26) can be used to find a rational, all

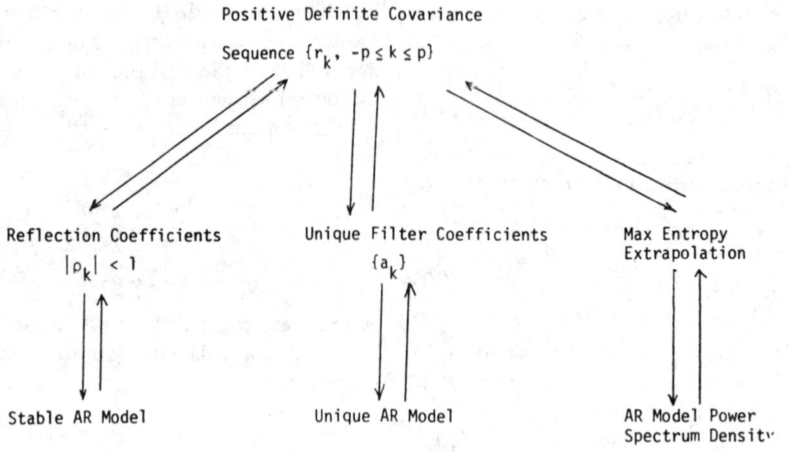

Fig. 3. Properties of the AR models.

pole spectral approximation of an arbitrary positive SDF. For these and other related ideas see Whittle [30] and Astrom [31].

4) *Levinson Algorithm [32], [33]*: The Toeplitz system of equations (26), also called the *normal equations*, can be solved in $O(p^2)$ operations by the recursions

$$a_{n+1,k} = \begin{cases} a_{n,k} - \rho_{n+1} a_{n,n+1-k}, & a_{n,0} = 1, \quad 1 \leq k \leq n \\ \rho_{n+1}, & k = n+1 \end{cases}$$

$$\beta_{n+1}^2 = \beta_n^2 (1 - \rho_{n+1}^2), \qquad \beta_0^2 = r_0$$

$$\rho_{n+1} = \frac{1}{\beta_n^2}\left[r_{n+1} - \sum_{k=1}^{n} a_{n,k} r_{n+1-k}\right], \quad \rho_1 = r_1/r_0 \quad (27)$$

where $\beta^2 = \beta_p^2$, $a_n = a_{p,n}$ are the coefficients required in (26). The elements $\{\rho_n, 1 \leq n \leq p\}$ are called the *reflection coefficients*. If the covariance matrix $\{r_{k-n}, 0 \leq k, n \leq p\}$ is positive definite then it could be shown that $|\rho_n| < 1$. Moreover the sequences $\{r_k\}$, $\{a_k\}$ and $\{\rho_k\}$ are unique.

5) A necessary and sufficient condition for the stability of the AR model is that $|\rho_n| < 1$, $\forall n$, or equivalently that the matrix $\{r_{k-n}, 0 \leq k, n \leq p\}$ be positive definite.

6) *Theorem 2 (Maximum Entropy Extrapolation)*: The given positive definite covariance sequence $\{r_k, -p \leq k \leq p\}$ has a unique maximum entropy extrapolation and is given by the covariances generated by the AR model of (21).

Although the proof of this result is available at various places in the literature [34], [36], the following simple proof is offered. We define as entropy of a covariance sequence $\{r_k, -N \leq k \leq N\}$ the average entropy of $(N+1)$ Gaussian random variables which is given by (within an additive constant)

$$H_N = \frac{1}{N+1} \log |R_N| \quad (28)$$

where $|R_N|$ is the determinant of the Toeplitz covariance matrix associated with the covariance sequence. From the theory of Toeplitz matrices it is easy to show that the determinant of R_N follows the simple recursion [35]

$$|R_N| = |R_{N-1}| \beta_N^2, \qquad \beta_N^2 \leq \beta_{N-1}^2$$

From this, H_N is monotonically nonincreasing function of N. For $N \geq p$, to maximize H_N, we therefore simply need to have $\beta_k^2 = \beta_p^2$ for $N \geq k \geq p$. This means the optimum ρ_k are zero for $k > p$ and one obtains

$$a_{n+p,k} = \begin{cases} a_{p,k}, & \text{for } n \geq 0, \quad 1 \leq k \leq p \\ 0, & k \geq p+1. \end{cases} \quad (29)$$

Thus the pth-order AR model maximizes the entropy. By setting $\rho_{n+p} = 0$ in (27) the extrapolated covariances are obtained as

$$r_{n+p} = \sum_{k=1}^{p} a_k r_{n+p-k}, \quad n \geq 1. \quad (30)$$

The SDF given by (25), determined via the coefficients $\{a_k\}$ is called the *maximum entropy spectrum* of the given covariance sequence. It is interesting to note that (29) provides the necessary conditions for extrapolation of $\{r_k\}$ from $k = p+1$ to $k = N$, for any $N > p$.

7) The reflection coefficients are such that at recursion step n in (27), the sum of the forward and backward predictive errors is minimized, i.e., if we define

$$\sigma_e^2 \triangleq E(\epsilon_{m,k}^+)^2 + E(\epsilon_{n,k}^-)^2 \quad (31)$$

$$\epsilon_{n,k}^+ \triangleq x_k - \sum_{m=1}^{n} a_{n,m} x_{k-m} = \epsilon_{n-1,k}^+ - \rho_n \epsilon_{n-1,k}^- \quad (32)$$

$$\epsilon_{n,k}^- \triangleq x_{k-n} - \sum_{m=1}^{n} a_{n,m} x_{k-n+m} = \epsilon_{n-1,k-1}^- - \rho_n \epsilon_{n-1,k}^+ \quad (33)$$

then ρ_n is such that σ_e^2 is minimized. This relation is useful in finding ρ_n directly when observed samples of the random process rather than their covariances are available [34].

Fig. 3 summarizes the properties of the AR models. In image processing, AR models have been found useful in modeling images line by line, as illustrated by the following examples.

Example 1: Consider zero-mean monochrome images whose covariance function models are listed in Table IV. If the image is processed one column at a time then the covariance function of pels on any column is of the form

$$r_k = E u_{i,j} u_{i+k,j} = \sigma^2 \rho_1^{|k|} \quad (34)$$

for both the models of Table IV. The corresponding AR representation is

$$x_i = \rho_1 x_{i-1} + \epsilon_i \qquad \beta^2 = E \epsilon_i^2 = \sigma^2 (1 - \rho_1^2). \quad (35)$$

Example 2: In certain image processing applications, each column (or row) of an image is first unitarily transformed, i.e., for the jth column

$$v_j = A u_j, \quad j = 1, \cdots, N \qquad (36)$$

and each element $v_j(i)$ is modeled as a first-order AR process, i.e.,

$$v_j(i) = a_1(i) v_{j-1}(i) + e_j(i), \quad i = 1, \cdots, N. \qquad (37)$$

If A is the KLT, i.e., the elements $v_j(i)$ and $v_j(k)$ are uncorrelated (independent under Gaussian assumptions) for $i \neq k$, then (37) represents a set of N decoupled AR models. Such algorithms have been called *hybrid* (i.e., a combination of nonrecursive and recursive procedures) and have been used in image restoration and coding [17], [52], [58]. For a tutorial review of AR models see [37]. Practical examples are discussed in section VI.

Example 3: Common images represent a nonnegative luminance function. In many applications from the physics of image formation it is possible to model the image as a power spectrum. For example, in high-resolution radar imaging a target can be considered as a set of distributed scatterers. The overall radar cross section (RCS) of the target measured as a function of aspect angle has the properties of a power spectrum. Let $S(x)$, $-\frac{1}{2} < x < \frac{1}{2}$ represent a line of the image. Assume $S(x) > 0$ and that the Fourier series of $S(x)$ is uniformly convergent. Then its inverse Fourier transform is a valid covariance sequence. For a sampled image, if s_k, $\{0 \leq k \leq N-1\}$ represents a set of positive and bounded real numbers, it can be shown [38] that its DCT coefficients given by

$$r_{-k} \triangleq r_k = \frac{1}{N} \sum_{m=0}^{N-1} s_m \cos \frac{\pi k}{N} \left(m + \frac{1}{2}\right), \quad 0 \leq k \leq N-1 \qquad (38)$$

is a covariance sequence. Hence it is possible to find a pth-order AR model whose output covariances would match the $\{r_k\}$ over $[-p, p]$. In other words, one could synthesize each line of the image arbitrarily closely by a suitable AR model. Note that the image itself is being modeled by a deterministic function even though the AR model may characterize a random process whose covariances are related to the image. Fig. 4 shows an original and a synthesized image line by line by segments of $N = 32$ pels, generated by an eighth-order AR model. This figure also shows the image obtained by cosine transform coding when the same number of transform coefficients are retained. The higher resolution provided by the AR model approach is the result of the covariance extrapolation performed by that model. For other examples and details see [38].

B. State Variable Models

State variable models have been used to represent two-dimensional images considered as the output of a raster scanner. The scanner output is modeled as a one-dimensional random process and is characterized by a set of state variable equations of the form

$$\frac{dx(t)}{dt} = A(t) x(t) + B(t) \varepsilon(t)$$

$$y(t) = C(t) x(t) \qquad (39)$$

where $y(t)$ is the scanner output at time t, and $x(t)$ is an

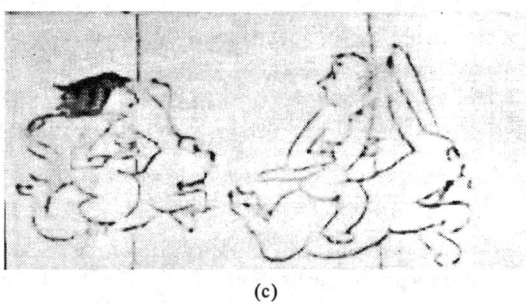

Fig. 4. Line by line synthesis of an image by eighth-order AR models. Each line has been synthesized by line segments of 32 pixels. (a) Original. (b) Synthesis using Cosine transform, 4 to 1 sample reduction. (c) Synthesis using AR model, 4 to 1 sample reduction.

$n \times 1$ vector, $\varepsilon(t)$ is a $p \times 1$ zero-mean white-noise vector such that

$$E \varepsilon(t) \varepsilon^T(t') = K \delta(t - t'). \qquad (40)$$

A, B, C, K are appropriate matrices which are determined such that $y(t)$ satisfies (approximately, if not exactly) the statistics of the scanner output.

The first attempt to model images by state variable techniques was made by Nahi and Asseffi [39], [40]. Although their final model has limitations because of several approximations, their modeling procedure does expose several difficulties in representing two-dimensional random field by one-dimensional models.

Consider an image being raster scanned from left to right and top to bottom with instantaneous repositioning so that the scanner output is continuous. Let $u(i, x)$ denote the brightness at a point x of the ith scanned line of the image, where $i = 0, \pm 1, \pm 2, \cdots, \pm \infty$, and x lies in the continuous interval $[0, M]$. The scanner output at any instant

$$t = jM + x, \quad 0 \leq x \leq M \qquad (41)$$

is $s(t) = u(j, x)$, where the scanner speed is assumed to be unity. Thus the scanner acts like a stacking operator which stacks one row after another. It is easy to show that the scanner output $s(t)$ is a nonstationary process even though $u(i, x)$ is a two-dimensional stationary random field. Defining

$$\tau = iM + y, \quad 0 \leqslant y \leqslant M, \quad i = 0, 1, 2, \cdots \quad (42)$$

the covariance of the scanner output is given by [39]

$$r_s(x, y) = Es(t)s(t+\tau) = \begin{cases} r(i, y), & x + y \leqslant M. \\ r(i+1, M-y), & x + y > M. \end{cases} \quad (43)$$

Since r_s depends on both x and y, it is a nonstationary covariance function. It could be *approximated* as a stationary covariance by averaging it over $[0, M]$ to yield

$$\tilde{r}(\tau) = \frac{M-y}{M} r(i, y) + \frac{y}{M} r(i+1, M-y). \quad (44)$$

Now $\tilde{r}$ depends only in i and y (the parameters of τ). Thus it is a function of τ only and is therefore stationary. Now a rational approximation of $\tilde{r}(\tau)$ is made from which a state variable model can be determined using conventional spectral factorization techniques in one dimension. For an example see [39].

C. State Variable Model for the Nonstationary Scanning Process $s(t)$ [41], [42]

Instead of approximating the covariance function $r_s(x, y)$ by a stationary covariance model, a time varying state variable model can be determined for the scanning process. Suppose the image has N scan lines and its covariance function is separable, i.e.,

$$r(n, \tau) = r_1(n) r_2(\tau) \quad (45)$$

where r_1, r_2 are stationary covariance functions. Suppose $r_2(\tau)$ has a state variable realization (A, B, C, K) and the $N \times N$ covariance matrix $R_1 = \{r_1(i-j), 1 \leqslant i, j \leqslant N\}$ has a lower-upper triangular (LU) factorization $R_1 = HH^T$. Then $r(n, \tau)$ has the realization

$$\dot{x} = Ax + B\epsilon$$

$$x(kM) = x_k$$

$$y = Cx$$

$$E\epsilon(t)\epsilon^T(\tau) = K\delta(t - \tau)$$

$$s(t) = s_k(t) = \sum_{j=0}^{k} h_{k,j} y(t - (k-j)M),$$

$$kM < t \leqslant (k+1)M. \quad (46)$$

These equations give a nonstationary or the so-called *cyclostationary* representation of $s(t)$. This is because (46) is to be reinitialized after every M time units. Also, because of the delays involved, this representation is non-Markovian.

The derivation of (46) is quite simple, especially in comparison to the elaborate procedure of the earlier development. However, it is time varying, and being non-Markovian its usefulness as such is limited.

D. A Vector Scanning Model

Suppose the image considered above is scanned by a column of N raster scanners and define

$$\hat{s}(t) = [s_0(t) s_1(t) \cdots s_{N-1}(t)]^T$$

$$\hat{x}(t) = [x^T(t), \quad x^T(t - (N-2)M), \cdots, x^T(t - (N-1)M)]^T,$$

$$(N-1)M \leqslant t \leqslant NM.$$

Then the vector scanner $s(t)$ has a state variable Markovian representation

$$\frac{d\hat{x}}{dt} = \mathcal{A}\hat{x} + \mathcal{B}\hat{\epsilon}(t)$$

$$E\hat{x}_0^T \hat{x}_0 \triangleq P_0 = R_1$$

$$E\hat{\epsilon}(t)\hat{\epsilon}^T(\tau) = (I \otimes K)\delta(t - \tau), \quad (N-1)M \leqslant t, \tau \leqslant NM$$

$$\hat{s}(t) = (H \otimes C)\hat{x} \quad (47)$$

where $\mathcal{A} = I \otimes A$, $\mathcal{B} = I \otimes B$, and $\otimes$ denotes the Kronecker product. Now we have a Markov model, but its dimensional has increased.

State variable models have been found useful in restoration of images degraded by spatially varying PSF's where Fourier techniques are not applicable and particularly when the PSF can be modeled as a finite impulse response and/or the degradation is a causal process (e.g., motion blur). For details see [45].

E. Noncausal Models [18], [46]

Earlier we saw that a causal AR representation is of the type

$$u_k = \bar{u}_k + \epsilon_k, \quad E\epsilon_k = 0$$

where $\bar{u}_k$ is the best linear mean square predictor of u_k based on the past values $\{u_l, l < k\}$ and $\{\epsilon_k\}$ is a white-noise sequence. Thus $\bar{u}_k$ is a minimum variance causal predictor of u_k. In an analogous fashion, we can define a minimum variance noncausal predictor $\bar{u}_k$ which depends on the past as well as the future values of u_k. Let $\{u_k\}$ be any zero-mean Gaussian random sequence and let $\bar{u}_k$ denote the best linear mean-square estimate of u_k based on all $\{u_l, l \neq k\}$. Writing

$$\bar{u}_k \triangleq \sum_{l \neq k} a_{k,l} u_l \quad (48)$$

we determine coefficients $a_{k,l}$ by minimizing the mean-square error $E[(u_k - \bar{u}_k)^2]$. This minimization gives the result as

$$r_{k,l} - \sum_{j \neq k} a_{k,j} r_{j,l} = \beta_k^2 \delta_{k,l}, \quad \beta_k^2 = \min E(u_k - \bar{u}_k)^2. \quad (49)$$

In matrix form after defining $a_{k,k} = -1$, this becomes

$$-AR = B \quad \text{or} \quad -A = BR^{-1} \quad (50)$$

where B is a diagonal matrix of elements β_k^2 and R is assumed to be positive definite. The noncausal *minimum variance representation* (MVR) of the (scalar) nonstationary random process $\{u_k\}$ is now defined as

$$u_k - \sum_{l \neq k} a_{k,l} u_l = v_k \quad \text{or} \quad -Au = v \quad (51)$$

where u and v are vectors of elements $\{u_k\}$ and $\{v_k\}$ respectively and v is a random process that represents the noncausal prediction error. Using (50) and (51) we get

$$R^{-1} u = B^{-1} v. \quad (52)$$

It is interesting that the minimum variance noncausal representation of (52) does not require any spectral factorization, but only needs the inversion of the covariance matrix R. Note that the random process $\{v_k\}$ is not a white-noise sequence. Instead, it is a "colored"-noise sequence whose covariance is obtained via (52) to give

$$R_\nu \triangleq E\mathbf{v}\mathbf{v}^T = BR^{-1}B. \quad (53)$$

The elements of the diagonal matrix B are determined by noting that $B \equiv \text{diag}[R_\nu]$ and are given by

$$\beta_k^2 = \frac{1}{[R^{-1}]_{k,k}}. \quad (54)$$

Hence, the noncausal representation (51) is complete by specifying R^{-1}. For an infinite stationary process with analytic SDF $S(\omega)$, the noncausal MVR becomes

$$r_0^+ u_k + \sum_{\substack{l=-\infty \\ l \neq 0}}^{\infty} r_l^+ u_{k-l} = \beta^{-2} v_k \quad (55)$$

where

$$r_k^+ = \frac{1}{2\pi} \int_{-\pi}^{\pi} S^{-1}(\omega) \exp(jk\omega) \, d\omega$$

is the covariance sequence corresponding to $1/S(\omega)$ and

$$\beta^2 = 1/r_0^+. \quad (56)$$

Example 4: A special case of interest is to find the noncausal MVR for causal AR processes. From (55), it follows that for the pth-order AR model of (21), the noncausal MVR is given by

$$u_k - \sum_{n=1}^{p} h_n(u_{k-n} + u_{k+n}) = v_k, \quad \forall k$$

$$h_n = \frac{-\sum_{k=0}^{p} a_k a_{n+k}}{\sum_{k=0}^{p} a_k^2}, \quad a_0 \triangleq -1$$

$$r_\nu(k) \triangleq E v_j v_{j+k} = \beta_\nu^2 \left[\delta_{k,0} - \sum_{n=1}^{p} h_n(\delta_{k,n} + \delta_{k,-n}) \right]$$

$$\beta_\nu^2 = \frac{\beta^2}{\sum_{k=1}^{p} a_k^2}. \quad (57)$$

This is a $2p$th-order stochastic difference equation forced by a pth-order moving average process $\{v_k\}$.

If we define $N \times 1$ vectors $u = \{u_k\}$, $\mathbf{v} = \{v_k\}$, etc., (57) can be written as

$$Hu = \mathbf{v} + b \quad E\mathbf{v}b^T = 0$$
$$R_\nu \triangleq E\mathbf{v}\mathbf{v}^T = \beta_\nu^2 H \quad (58)$$

where H is the $N \times N$ symmetric banded Toeplitz matrix whose entries along the mth subdiagonal are $-h_m$, and the $N \times 1$ vector b contains $2p$ nonzero terms involving the boundary variables $\{u_{1-k}, u_{N+k}, 1 \leq k \leq p\}$. Defining

$$u^0 = H^{-1}\mathbf{v} \quad u^b = H^{-1}b \quad (59)$$

we obtain an orthogonal decomposition of u

$$u = u^0 + u^b \quad E[u^0(u^b)^T] = O \quad (60)$$

which is such that the covariance matrix of u^0 is

$$R^0 \triangleq Eu^0 u^{0T} = \beta_\nu^2 H^{-1} \quad (61)$$

and the process u^b is completely determined by the $2p$ boundary variables $\{u_{1-k}, u_{N+k}, 1 \leq k \leq p\}$. This representation provides the following result which is useful in developing the so-called fast KLT algorithms [18].

Theorem 3: Let $\{u_k\}$ be a stationary, pth-order AR sequence. For any $N > 1$ if the $2p$ boundary values $\{u_{1-k}, u_{N+k}, 1 \leq k \leq p\}$ are given then the KLT of the sequence $\{u_k, 1 \leq k \leq N\}$ conditioned on these boundary values is the orthonormal set of eigenvectors of the $N \times N$ banded Toeplitz matrix H.

This theorem could be proven following [18] where the special case $p = 1$ was considered. It has been shown [10] that for a given H, a fast sinusoidal transform could be found as a good approximation to its KLT. For the case $p = 1$, the KLT is the fast sine transform (see Table III). Noncausal representations are useful in data compression and restoration of images using image transforms [46]–[53]. The boundary variables are processed first (e.g., filtered in image estimation problems) and $\tilde{u}^b$, an estimate of u^b is determined. The residual process $\tilde{u}^0 = u - u^b$ is then processed by the KLT of u^0. For example it has been shown for $p = 1$ that the noncausal representation can be used for block by block coding of a sequence in such a way that interblock redundancy could be exploited (via the boundary values) leading to an algorithm more efficient than the conventional block by block KLT coding where one does not consider the interblock effects. For details see [9], [17], [19]. Algorithms in other applications [93] will require manipulation of the banded Toeplitz matrix and certain circulant [54] and other [10], [49] decompositions have been found useful. In the sequel we will find the above theory useful in developing semicausal and noncausal representations for two-dimensional images.

IV. Linear Prediction Models in Two Dimensions

One important property of many one-dimensional systems is that of causality. For two-dimensional images, causality is not inherent in the data. Moreover, the data could be such that a causal realization by a finite-order linear system is not possible, even if the SDF is a rational function. This is because it is generally not possible to factorize a two-dimensional polynomial as a product of lower order polynomials. In general, one can think of causal, semicausal, and noncausal representations for two-dimensional images. These representations are the discrete equivalent of the classical categories, viz., initial-value (or hyperbolic), initial-boundary value (or parabolic) and boundary value (or elliptic), of two-dimensional linear systems characterized by partial differential equations. In this section we define such models in the framework of linear prediction. In the next section we will consider their realization from a given SDF.

Linear prediction models in two dimensions are useful in image data transmission and storage via DPCM coding and hybrid coding, design of recursive, semirecursive and nonrecursive filters for image estimation, restoration and filtering and in image analysis. Examples are considered in Section VI.

Let $\{u_{i,j}\}$ be an arbitrary zero-mean Gaussian random field and let $\bar{u}_{i,j}$ denote a prediction estimate of the random variable $u_{i,j}$.

A. Causal Prediction

Suppose the samples of the random field $\{u_{i,j}\}$ are arranged in any desired, one-dimensional ordered sequence $\{u(k)\}$. Then $\bar{u}_{i,j}$ is defined as a *causal prediction* of $u_{i,j}$ if it depends only

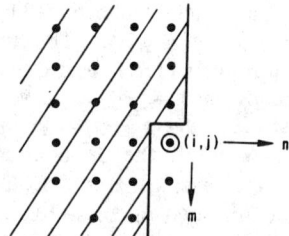

Fig. 5. Prediction region for causal models.

on the elements that occur before the element $u_{i,j}$. A common example occurs when an image is raster scanned, say, column by column, and $\bar{u}_{i,j}$ is a linear estimate based on all the elements scanned before arriving at (i, j), i.e.,

$$\bar{u}_{i,j} = \sum_{m,n \in \mathcal{S}} a(i, j; m, n) u_{m,n},$$

$$\mathcal{S} = \{m, n: n < j, \forall m\} \cup \{m, n: n = j, m < i\}. \quad (62)$$

Fig. 5 shows the set $\mathcal{S}$ for causal prediction at (i, j). This definition of causality includes, as a special case, single quadrant causal predictors of the type

$$\bar{u}_{i,j} = \sum_{\substack{m=0 \\ (m,n) \neq (0,0)}}^{\infty} \sum_{n=0}^{\infty} a(i, j; m, n) u_{i-m, j-n}. \quad (63)$$

If u_j denotes the jth column vector of the image, (62) gives

$$\bar{u}_j = A_{j,j}^0 u_j + \sum_{n < j} A_{j,n} u_n \quad (64)$$

where $A_{j,j}^0$ is a lower triangular matrix whose diagonal entries are zero.

B. Semicausal Prediction[2]

If the estimate $\bar{u}_{i,j}$ is causal in one of the coordinates and noncausal in the other, it is called a *semicausal predictor*. For example, a linear semicausal predictor which is causal in "j" and noncausal in "i" would be of the form

$$\bar{u}_{i,j} = \sum_{m,n \in \mathcal{S}} a(i, j; m, n) u_{m,n},$$

$$\mathcal{S} = \{m, n: n < j, \forall m\} \cup \{m, n: n = j, \forall m \neq i\} \quad (65)$$

where $\mathcal{S}$ is shown in Fig. 6. In vector notation this becomes

$$\bar{u}_j = A_{j,j}^0 u_j + \sum_{n < j} A_{j,n} u_n \quad (66)$$

where $\{A_{j,n}\}$ are matrices of elements $\{a(i, j; m, n) \forall i, m\}$ and $A_{j,j}^0$ has zeros at its diagonal elements.

C. Noncausal Prediction

The quantity $\bar{u}_{i,j}$ is defined as a noncausal prediction of $u_{i,j}$ if it can be written as a linear combination of possibly all the

[2] We note that in the two-dimensional literature the term 'causal' is often used for single quadrant models only and the model of (62) is sometimes called 'semicausal' or nonsymmetric half-plane (NSHP) model. Our definition of semicausality includes all of the half-plane as indicated in (65).

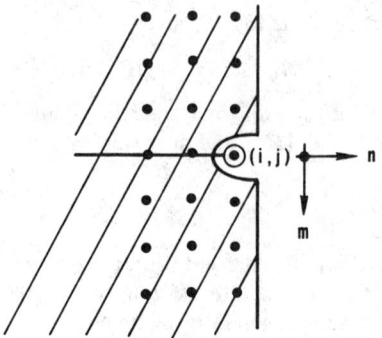

Fig. 6. Prediction region for semicausal models.

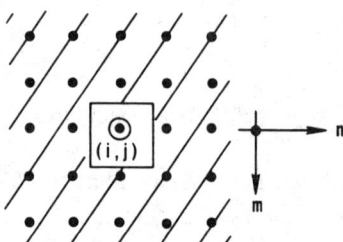

Fig. 7. Prediction region for noncausal models.

variables in the random field, except $u_{i,j}$ itself. For example, a *linear noncausal predictor* would be of the type

$$\bar{u}_{i,j} = \sum_{m,n \in \mathcal{S}} a(i, j; m, n) u_{m,n},$$

$$\mathcal{S} = \{m, n; (m, n) \neq (i, j)\} \quad (67)$$

and is shown in Fig. 7. Note that $\bar{u}_{i,j}$ contains terms from all the four quadrants about the point (i, j).

Example 4: The following are examples of causal, semicausal, and noncausal predictors.

Causal:

$$\bar{u}_{i,j} = a_1(i, j) u_{i-1,j} + a_2(i, j) u_{i,j-1} + a_3(i, j) u_{i-1,j-1}.$$

Semicausal:

$$\bar{u}_{i,j} = a_1(i, j) u_{i-1,j} + a_2(i, j) u_{i+1,j} + a_3(i, j) u_{i,j-1}.$$

Noncausal:

$$\bar{u}_{i,j} = a_1(i, j) u_{i-1,j} + a_2(i, j) u_{i+1,j} + a_3(i, j) u_{i,j-1}$$
$$+ a_4(i, j) u_{i,j+1}.$$

D. Minimum Variance Prediction

A minimum variance prediction estimate is one that minimizes the mean-square error

$$e_{i,j} = E(u_{i,j} - \bar{u}_{i,j})^2 \quad (68)$$

at each i, j. For a Gaussian random field, the minimum variance predictors would be linear, whose coefficients $a(\cdot\cdot;\cdot\cdot)$ could be determined from its covariance function. Minimization of (68) and use of (62), (65), or (67) yields the orthogonality relation

$$E\left[u_{i,j} - \sum_{m,n \in \underline{\mathcal{S}}} a(i, j; m, n) u_{m,n} \right] u_{p,q} = \beta_{i,j}^2 \delta_{i,p} \delta_{j,q},$$

$$p, q \in \mathcal{S}_0 \quad \mathcal{S}_0 \triangleq \mathcal{S} \cup [i, j] \quad (69)$$

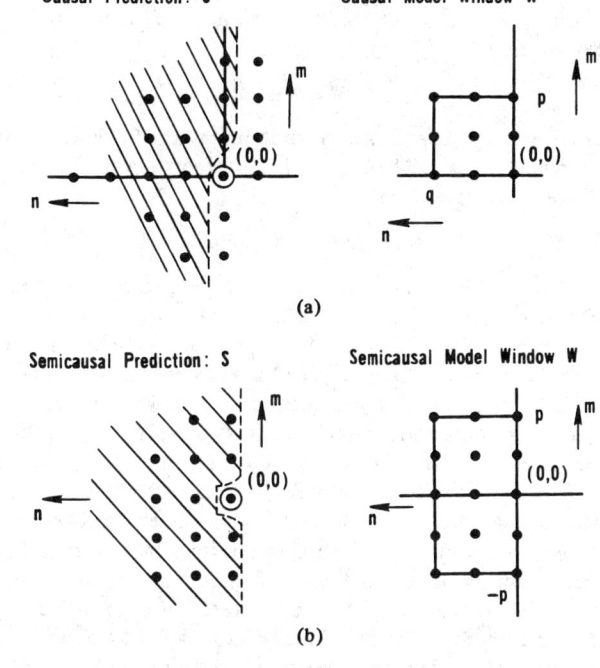

Fig. 8. Prediction regions and windows for stationary models.

Written in terms of covariances, we obtain

$$r(i,p;j,q) - \sum_{m,n \in \mathcal{S}} a(i,m;j,n) r(m,p;n,q)$$
$$= \beta_{i,j}^2 \delta_{i,p} \delta_{j,q}, \quad p,q \in \mathcal{S}_0 \quad (70)$$

where $\mathcal{S}$ depends on whether $\bar{u}_{i,j}$ is causal, semicausal, or noncausal, and $\beta_{i,j}^2$ is the minimized value of $e_{i,j}$. A solution of the simultaneous equations (70) gives the unknowns $a(\cdot\,\cdot\,;\,\cdot\,\cdot)$ and $\beta_{i,j}^2$.

E. Stochastic Representation of Gaussian Fields

Let $\bar{u}_{i,j}$ be an arbitrary prediction of $u_{i,j}$. Then we define a stochastic representation of the random field $\{u_{i,j}\}$ as

$$u_{i,j} = \bar{u}_{i,j} + \epsilon_{i,j} \quad (71)$$

where $\{\epsilon_{i,j}\}$ is another random field such that the given covariance properties of $\{u_{i,j}\}$ are satisfied. There are three types of representations that we would be interested in considering here. These are as follows:

(i) minimum variance representations (MVR)
(ii) white-noise-driven representations (WNDR)
(iii) autoregressive moving average (ARMA) representations.

For minimum variance representations, $\bar{u}_{i,j}$ is chosen to be a minimum variance predictor. These representations could be causal, semicausal, or noncausal in structure. One basic difference among these representations is their spatial structure which leads to different types of processing algorithms. For WNDR $\{\epsilon_{i,j}\}$ is chosen to be a white-noise field resulting in several types of models including the Karhunen–Loeve representations. In ARMA representations, $\{\epsilon_{i,j}\}$ is a colored noise field with a truncated covariance function, i.e.,

$$E\epsilon_{i,j}\epsilon_{m,n} = 0, \quad \forall |i-m| > K, \quad |j-n| > L \quad (72a)$$

for some fixed integers $K > 0, L > 0$. For example the function

$$r_\epsilon(i,j;m,n) = \begin{cases} 1, & i=m, j=n \\ \alpha, & |i-m|=1, |j-n|=1 \\ 0, & \text{otherwise} \end{cases} \quad (72b)$$

represents a stationary moving average field.

F. Stationary Models

For stationary random fields, the covariances become a function of two variables, i.e.,

$$r(i,j;m,n) = r(i-m, j-n)$$

and the various predictors become spatially invariant (or shift invariant) yielding the representation

$$u_{i,j} = \sum_{m,n \in \hat{\mathcal{S}}} a_{m,n} u_{i-m,j-n} + \epsilon_{i,j} \quad (73)$$

where $\hat{\mathcal{S}}$ is a window of index pairs (m,n) which is now independent of i,j and is defined as

$$\hat{\mathcal{S}} = \begin{cases} \{n \geq 1, \forall m\} \cup \{n=0, m \geq 1\}, \\ \qquad \text{for causal models} \\ \{n \geq 1, \forall m\} \cup \{n=0, \forall m \neq 0\}, \\ \qquad \text{for semicausal models} \quad (74) \\ \{\forall (m,n) \neq (0,0)\}, \quad \text{for noncausal models.} \end{cases}$$

Note that $\hat{\mathcal{S}}$ does not contain the origin $(0, 0)$. Fig. 8 shows $\hat{\mathcal{S}}$ for the various cases above. Often one is only interested in representations where $a_{m,n}$ are nonzero only over a finite window W, (see Fig. 8 for examples) called the *prediction window*, which is a subset of $\hat{\mathcal{S}}$, so that

$$u_{i,j} = \sum_{m,n \in W} a_{m,n} u_{i-m,j-n} + \epsilon_{i,j}. \quad (75)$$

In that event (75) becomes a constant coefficient stochastic difference equation with a rational transfer function

$$H(z_1^{-1}, z_2^{-1}) = \frac{1}{A(z_1^{-1}, z_2^{-1})}$$
$$\triangleq \left[1 - \sum_{m,n \in W} a_{m,n} z_1^{-m} z_2^{-n} \right]^{-1} \quad (76)$$

The SDF of random fields represented by these stationary

models becomes

$$S_u(z_1, z_2) = \frac{S_\epsilon(z_1, z_2)}{\left[1 - \sum\sum_{m,n \in W} a_{m,n} z_1^{-m} z_2^{-n}\right]\left[1 - \sum\sum_{m,n \in W} a_{m,n} z_1^{m} z_2^{n}\right]} \quad (77)$$

where $S_\epsilon(z_1, z_2)$ is the SDF of $\{\epsilon_{i,j}\}$. In general, $\{\epsilon_{i,j}\}$ would be a moving average field so that (77) is a rational function expressed as a ratio of two-dimensional polynomials in z_1 and z_2.

Minimum Variance Models: If (75) is a minimum variance representation of a stationary field, then the orthogonality condition (69) becomes

$$r(k,l) - \sum\sum_{m,n \in W} a_{m,n} r(k-m, l-n) = \beta^2 \delta_{k,0} \delta_{l,0},$$
$$k, l \in \hat{S}_0 \quad \hat{S}_0 = \hat{S} \cup (0,0). \quad (78)$$

Defining

$$a_{0,0} \triangleq -1 \quad W_0 = W \cup (0,0) \quad (79)$$

(78) reduces to

$$-\sum\sum_{m,n \in W_0} a_{m,n} r(k-m, l-n) = \beta^2 \delta_{k,0} \delta_{l,0}, \quad (k,l) \in \hat{S}_0. \quad (80)$$

Mapping the arrays $\{a_{m,n}\}$, $\{u_{m,n}\}$, $\{\delta_{k,0}\delta_{l,0}\}$ with support on W_0 into vectors a, u, l, respectively, by column ordering, we obtain

$$\mathcal{R} a = -\beta^2 l \quad (81)$$

where $\mathcal{R}$ is the covariance matrix of the vector u. For example, if W_0 is the noncausal rectangular window $[-p, p] \times [-q, q]$ then a is of size $(2p+1)(2q+1)$ and $\mathcal{R}$ is a $(2p+1) \times (2p+1)$ doubly block Toeplitz matrix with basic dimension $(2p+1) \times (2p+1)$. The unit vector l takes the value 1 at the location i_0, which corresponds to the $(0,0)$ location in the window W_0. Equations (79) and (81) can be solved to give

$$a = -\beta^2 \mathcal{R}^{-1} l$$
$$\triangleq -\beta^2 \mathcal{L}_{i_0}$$
$$\beta^2 = 1/\mathcal{L}_{i_0}(i_0)$$
$$= 1/[\mathcal{R}^{-1}]_{i_0, i_0}. \quad (82)$$

These equations are much easier to solve than (70) because the dimensionality of $\mathcal{R}$ equals the square of the number of points in the window W_0 rather than the square of the number of points in the image. For a given positive definite $\mathcal{R}$, a unique solution of (81) is obtained. However, for a given admissible set of predictor coefficients $a_{m,n}$, there is not a unique $\mathcal{R}$ which will yield these coefficients as the solution of (81). Moreover, for an arbitrary positive definite $\mathcal{R}$, the solution of (81) does not assure prediction coefficients which would yield stable models. In spite of these shortcomings, equation (81) is useful because i) it is a linear (Toeplitz block) system of equations and ii) it could be used in finding approximate causal, semicausal and noncausal MVR's which are stable.

G. White-Noise-Driven Representations (WNDR)

Consider an arbitrary matrix operator $\mathcal{A}$ and the linear representation

$$\mathcal{A} u = \epsilon \quad (83)$$

where u and ϵ are vectors corresponding to the fields $\{u_{i,j}\}$ and $\{\epsilon_{i,j}\}$, respectively. When $\{\epsilon_{i,j}\}$ is required to be a white-noise field, we must have

$$\mathcal{A} \mathcal{R} \mathcal{A}^T = \mathcal{B} = \text{Diagonal} \quad \mathcal{R} = E u u^T, \quad \mathcal{B} = E \epsilon \epsilon^T. \quad (84)$$

Thus, any white noise driven linear representation must satisfy the factorization equation (84). However, it does not have a unique solution $\mathcal{A}$ and therefore many different representations are possible. If $\mathcal{A}$ is a lower triangular matrix, then (83) is a causal representation. As we shall see, the causal MV representations are of this type. When $\mathcal{A}$ is a block lower triangular matrix, then (83) becomes a semicausal WNDR (but not necessarily MVR). Otherwise, it would be a noncausal WNDR. Since $\mathcal{R}$ is a covariance matrix, another solution of (84) is obtained when $\mathcal{A}$ is a unitary matrix containing the eigenvectors of $\mathcal{R}$ and $\mathcal{B}$ is the diagonal matrix of its eigenvalues. This would yield the KL representation of the random field. The choice of the operator $\mathcal{A}$ for WNDR's depends on the algorithmic considerations or on a given physical situation.

V. REALIZATION OF THE TWO-DIMENSIONAL PREDICTION MODELS

Now we consider the problem of identifying the foregoing three types of representations given the covariance function, or equivalently, (for the stationary case) the spectral density function of the image. When the desired representation is required to be causal and stable, the above problem is also called the *spectral factorization problem*. Let $S(z_1, z_2)$ represent the two-dimensional z-transform of a covariance sequence $r(m, n)$. When $z_1 = \exp(j\omega_1)$, $z_2 = \exp(j\omega_2)$, this becomes the SDF and will also be written as $S(\omega_1, \omega_2)$. The main result of this section is that it is possible to find finite order, stable causal, semicausal, and noncausal MVR's which would match a given well behaved SDF arbitrarily closely. Details are given in the Appendix.

A. Separable Models

When the covariance function is separable, e.g., in the stationary case, if $r(k-m, l-n) = r_1(k-m) r_2(l-n)$, the solution of (80) reduces to two independent one-dimensional models. For example, if $r_1(m)$ and $r_2(n)$ have the one-dimensional realizations

$$\sum_{m \in W_1} a_1(m) x(k-m) = e_1(k)$$

$$\sum_{m \in W_2} a_2(n) y(l-n) = e_2(l).$$

Then $r_1(m) r_2(n)$ has the realization

$$\sum_{m \in W_1} \sum_{n \in W_2} a_1(m) a_2(n) u_{k-m, l-n} = \epsilon_{k,l}$$

$$r_\epsilon(m, n) = r_{e_1}(m) r_{e_2}(n). \quad (85)$$

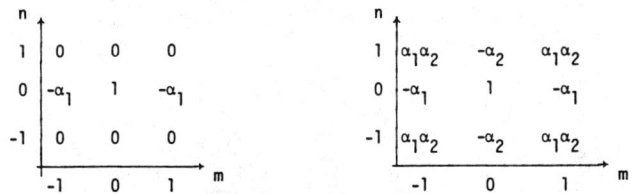

Fig. 9. Correlation arrays $\rho_\epsilon(m, n)$ for semicausal and noncausal model prediction errors.

Example 5: Consider the separable covariance model shown in Table IV. Using the above result the minimum variance causal, semicausal, and noncausal models are obtained as follows [51], [52].

Causal model (C1):

$$u_{i,j} = \rho_1 u_{i-1,j} + \rho_2 u_{i,j-1} - \rho_1 \rho_2 u_{i-1,j-1} + \epsilon_{i,j}$$

$$r_\epsilon(m, n) = \sigma^2 (1 - \rho_1^2)(1 - \rho_2^2) \delta_{m,0} \delta_{n,0}. \tag{86}$$

Semicausal MVR (SC2):

$$u_{i,j} = \alpha_1 (u_{i-1,j} + u_{i+1,j}) + \rho_2 u_{i,j-1}$$
$$- \rho_2 \alpha_1 (u_{i-1,j-1} + u_{i+1,j+1}) + \epsilon_{i,j}$$

$$r_\epsilon(m, n) = \sigma^2 \frac{(1 - \rho_1^2)(1 - \rho_2^2)}{(1 + \rho_2^2)} \rho_\epsilon(m, n)$$

$$\alpha_1 \triangleq \frac{\rho_1}{(1 + \rho_1^2)}. \tag{87}$$

Noncausal MVR (NC3):

$$u_{i,j} = \alpha_1 (u_{i-1,j} + u_{i+1,j}) + \alpha_2 (u_{i,j-1} + u_{i,j+1})$$
$$- \alpha_1 \alpha_2 (u_{i-1,j-1} + u_{i+1,j-1}$$
$$+ u_{i-1,j+1} + u_{i+1,j+1}) + \epsilon_{i,j}$$

$$r_\epsilon(m, n) = \sigma^2 \frac{(1 - \rho_1^2)(1 - \rho_2^2)}{(1 + \rho_1^2)(1 + \rho_2^2)} \cdot \rho_\epsilon(m, n). \tag{88}$$

Fig. 9 shows the correlation arrays $\rho_\epsilon(m, n)$ for the above two models.

Remarks:

1) The prediction window is necessarily rectangular for separable models. Thus causal MVR's are necessarily quarter-plane models for separable covariance functions although the converse is not true.

2) All the three models in the above example represent the same stationary random field. The spatial structural differences yield different types of algorithms. For example, it has been shown [9], [17], that the causal, semicausal and the noncausal models yield naturally the predictive, hybrid and transform coding algorithms for data compression of images. For other applications see [1], [52], [53], [55].

3) While the causal MVR's are white noise driven, the semicausal and noncausal MVR's are not.

4) If the given SDF $S(\omega_1, \omega_2)$ is not separable, then its best least squares separable approximation can be found via its singular value decomposition as

$$S(\omega_1, \omega_2) \simeq \hat{S}(\omega_1, \omega_2) \triangleq \lambda S_1(\omega_1) S_2(\omega_2)$$

where $S_1(\omega_1)$ and $S_2(\omega_2)$ are the solutions corresponding to the largest eigenvalue λ of the following eigenvalue equations

$$\int_{-\pi}^{\pi} K_1(\omega_1, y) S_1(y) dy = \lambda S_1(\omega_1), \quad \int_{-\pi}^{\pi} S_1^2(\omega) d\omega = 1$$

$$\int_{-\pi}^{\pi} K_2(x, \omega_2) S_2(x) dx = \lambda S_2(\omega_2), \quad \int_{-\pi}^{\pi} S_2^2(\omega) d\omega = 1$$

where

$$K_1(x, y) = \int_{-\pi}^{\pi} S(x, y') S(y, y') dy'$$

$$K_2(x, y) = \int_{-\pi}^{\pi} S(x', x) S(x', y) dx'.$$

If $S(\omega_1, \omega_2) > 0$, then it is easy to show that $\lambda > 0$, $S_1(\omega_1) > 0$, $S_2(\omega_2) > 0$ and S_1, S_2 would be valid one-dimensional SDF's if S is a valid two-dimensional SDF. Now $\hat{S}$ is a separable SDF and therefore an appropriate causal, semicausal or noncausal realization of $\hat{S}$ could be found. A similar method of approximating a SDF (or equivalently, the magnitude of the frequency response of a filter) by a positive separable function has been used in [27] for the design of separable two-dimensional filters when the given SDF is discrete. In that case, the above equations reduce to the matrix SVD relations of Section II-C.

B. Causal Minimum Variance Representations

It can be shown that the causal MVR's are also white-noise driven representations. In general identification of a causal MVR requires a two-stage factorization. For example if the SDF is a rational function of the form

$$S(z_1, z_2) = \frac{C_0}{\left[\sum_{n=-q}^{q} \sum_{m=-p_1}^{p_1} \alpha_{m,n} z_1^{-m} z_2^{-n} \right]} \tag{89}$$

where C_0 is a constant, then, the first-stage factorization is achieved by solving a set of normal equations (see (A12) in Appendix) parametric in z_1 and the result is

$$S(z_1, z_2) = \frac{\sum_{n=0}^{q} \hat{a}_n^q(z_1) r_n(z_1)}{\left[1 + \sum_{n=1}^{q} \hat{a}_n^q(z_1) z_2^{-n} \right] \left[1 + \sum_{n=1}^{q} \hat{a}_n^q(z_1^{-1}) z_2^n \right]}. \tag{90}$$

Then a second stage factorization of S (equation (A13)) gives

$$S(z_1, z_2) = \frac{\beta^2}{\left[\sum_{n=0}^{q} a_n^q(z_1) z_2^{-n} \right] \left[\sum_{n=0}^{q} a_n^q(z_1^{-1}) z_2^n \right]}. \tag{91}$$

In general $a_n^q(z_1)$ will be irrational functions expressed by their infinite Laurent series. Under certain conditions of positivity and analyticity of the SDF the causal model so determined would be stable and causally invertible (i.e., "minimum-phase"). However, one is confronted with the problem of solving an infinity of sets of q simultaneous equations ((A12)

```
                              m                          -.0247  -.0503  .0802 | 2
       -.0805  .532 | 1                                  -.0503   .001   .534 | 1
         .532   -1  | 0                                   .0802   .534   -1   | 0
    n ─────────────                                    n ──────────────────────
            1    0                                           2      1     0
```

Fig. 10. Single quadrant causal MVR coefficients.

and (A13)) for the rational SDF of (89). An *approximate* rational factorization of S could be obtained by finding a rational approximation for $a_n^q(z_1)$. For example, let

$$a_n^q(z_1) \simeq \sum_{m=-p}^{p} a_{m,n} z_1^{-m}, \quad n \geq 1$$

$$a_0^q(z_1) \simeq \sum_{m=0}^{p} a_{m,0} z_1^{-m}.$$

Then with the analyticity constraint on S, it is possible to find a suitable integer $p < \infty$, such that $\tilde{S}$, the rational factorized form obtained by replacing $a_n^q(z_1)$ by their approximations above would be of the form given in (77) and would be arbitrarily close to S. The realization of $\tilde{S}$ would now be of the form of (75). Thus it is possible to find finite-order causal MVR's which would come arbitrarily close to the infinite order causal MVR's of a given SDF. It can also be shown that the solution of (82) for a causal window W_0 and for suitably large p and q should yield a causal MVR which would realize the given SDF arbitrarily closely. The proof of this and related considerations such as stability will be considered elsewhere. Another approach of rationalizing (91) and retaining stability is via a reflection coefficient design method proposed by Marzetta [56].

Example 6: Consider the nonseparable exponential covariance model in Table IV with $\alpha_1 = \alpha_2 = 0.05$. Single quadrant causal MVR coefficients $a_{m,n}$ over $[0,1] \times [0,1]$ and $[0,2] \times [0,2]$ regions are obtained as shown in Fig. 10.

Fig. 11 compares the given covariance array with the one generated by the model on the $[4 \times 4]$ grid for the $[2 \times 2]$ model. Although both the models above turn out to be stable, the given and the model covariances do not match exactly. However, as the model order is increased, e.g., from $[1 \times 1]$ to $[2 \times 2]$ the covariance match has been found to improve.

C. Semicausal Minimum Variance Representations

For these models only a single stage factorization of the SDF is required. Unlike causal MVR's, semicausal MVR's are not white-noise-driven models. However, for a given semicausal MVR, a causal MVR can always be found under some mild restrictions [see Appendix]. But the causal realization may have a higher (even infinite) order and/or may become spatially varying as shown by the following example.

Example 7: Consider a spatially invariant, semicausal MVR which is noncausal in the "i" variable and causal in the "j" variable

$$u_{i,j} = a(u_{i-1,j} + u_{i+1,j}) + b u_{i,j-1} + \epsilon_{i,j}.$$

Let $\{u_{i,j}\}$ be a random field with $1 \leq i, j \leq N$, $u_{0,j} = u_{N+1,j} = 0$, $0 < a < \frac{1}{2}$, $|2a + b| < 1$. In vector notation this becomes

$$Q u_j = b u_{j-1} + \epsilon_j \quad (92)$$

$$r(k, \ell) = \exp\left\{-.05 \sqrt{k^2 + \ell^2}\right\}$$

.868	.894	.905	.894	.868
.894	.932	.951	.932	.894
.905	.951	1.000	.951	.905
.894	.932	.951	.932	.894
.868	.894	.905	.894	.868

ACTUAL COVARIANCES ON W_c

.696	.730	.697	.579	.479
.730	.819	.840	.701	.579
.697	.840	1.000	.840	.697
.579	.701	.840	.819	.730
.479	.579	.697	.730	.696

ESTIMATED COVARIANCES BY $p=q=2$ CAUSAL MODEL

.821	.853	.866	.853	.821
.858	.907	.932	.907	.858
.874	.934	1.000	.934	.874
.858	.907	.932	.907	.858
.821	.853	.866	.853	.821

ESTIMATED COVARIANCES BY $p=q=2$ SEMICAUSAL MODEL

Fig. 11. Covariances estimated by the causal and semicausal models.

where Q is a symmetric tridiagonal Toeplitz matrix whose diagonal elements are unity, and the subdiagonal elements equal $-a$. For this to be a minimum variance representation, the orthogonality conditions require (see (A14))

$$E \epsilon_j \epsilon_k^T = \beta^2 Q \delta_{j,k}$$

where β^2, the variance of $\epsilon_{i,j}$ is assumed to be constant. The matrix Q has an lower-upper factorization $Q = L^T \Gamma^{-1} L$, where

$$L = \begin{bmatrix} 1 & & & & \\ -r_2 & 1 & & & \\ & -r_3 & 1 & & \\ & & \ddots & \ddots & \\ & & & & -r_N & 1 \end{bmatrix}$$

$$\Gamma^{-1} = \text{Diag}\left\{\frac{a}{r_1}, \frac{a}{r_2}, \cdots, \frac{a}{r_N}\right\}$$

and $\{r_k\}$ are given by the backward recursion

$$r_k = \frac{a}{1 - a r_{k+1}}, \quad r_{N+1} = 0, \quad 1 \leq k \leq N.$$

Following Appendix A.2, we get a causal MVR as

$$u_{i,j} = r_i u_{i-1,j} + \frac{br_i}{a} \sum_{k=0}^{N-i+1} \alpha_{i,k} u_{i+k,j-1} + v_{i,j}$$

where $\alpha_{i,k}$ is the element in the kth upper diagonal and the ith row of $(L^T)^{-1}$. Now the sparse structure of the semicausal representation has been lost by this causal representation. Also, it is no longer a constant coefficient model. In the steady state, i.e., as i and $N \to \infty$, the asymptotic values of r and $\alpha_{i,k}$ are given by

$$r \triangleq r_\infty = \frac{1 - \sqrt{1 - 4a^2}}{2a}, \quad \alpha_{i,k} = r^k, \quad 0 < r < 1$$

and we obtain a constant coefficient, infinite order, causal MVR

$$u_{i,j} = r u_{i-1,j} + \frac{b}{a} \sum_{k=0}^{\infty} r^{k-1} u_{i+k,j-1} + v_{i,j}$$

$$E v_{i,j}^2 = \beta^2 (1 + r^2).$$

In a practical situation, one would truncate the summation to a finite number of terms to obtain an approximate, finite-order causal model. However, the number of terms that may have to be retained to achieve stability could well be quite large resulting in a high-order model.

For a rational SDF as in (89), one needs to solve (A25) for the given value of q from which a_n^q are determined. This gives the first stage of factorization in the z_2 variable and we obtain

$$S = \frac{-\beta^2 a_0^q(z_1)}{\left[\sum_{n=0}^{q} a_n^q(z_1) z_2^{-n}\right]\left[\sum_{n=0}^{q} a_n^q(z_1^{-1}) z_2^{n}\right]}. \quad (93)$$

No second stage factorization is required for semicausal MVR's. As in the case of causal models $\{a_n^q(z_1)\}$ will be generally irrational but analytic functions in the neighborhood of $|z_1| = 1$. When approximated by suitable rational functions, e.g., letting

$$a_n^q(z_1) \simeq \sum_{m=-p}^{p} a_{m,n} z_1^{-m}, \quad a_{0,0} = -1, \quad n > 0 \quad (94)$$

we obtain a finite-order semicausal MVR

$$u_{i,j} = \sum_{\substack{m=-p \\ m \neq 0}}^{p} a_{m,0} u_{i-m,j} + \sum_{n=1}^{q} \sum_{m=-p}^{p} a_{m,n} u_{i-m,j-n} + \epsilon_{i,j} \quad (95)$$

where $\{\epsilon_{i,j}\}$ is a moving average with SDF

$$S_\epsilon(z_1, z_2) = \beta^2 \left[1 - \sum_{m=-p}^{p} a_{m,0} z_1^{-m}\right]. \quad (96)$$

The SDF of this semicausal MVR is

$$S_u = \frac{S_\epsilon}{\left[\sum_{n=0}^{q}\sum_{m=-p}^{p} a_{m,n} z_1^{-m} z_2^{-n}\right]\left[\sum_{n=0}^{q}\sum_{m=-p}^{p} a_{m,n} z_1^{m} z_2^{n}\right]}. \quad (97)$$

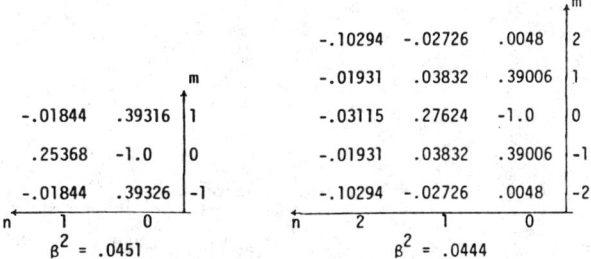

Fig. 12. Semicausal MVR coefficients.

Thus it is possible to find finite-order semicausal MVR's which would realize a given positive and analytic SDF arbitrarily closely. It can also be shown that for a semicausal prediction window with suitably large but finite values of p and q, the finite-order semicausal MVR obtained via the solution of (82) would realize a given positive and analytic SDF arbitrarily closely. Thus, even though the solution of (82) corresponding to a fixed size window W need not ensure an admissible (i.e., stable) representation, solving it successively (or recursively) for increasing size windows should eventually lead to an admissible as well as a reasonably accurate representation. The advantage, of course, is that one would be solving only finite-order equations, whereas the approach via equations (A24), (A25), in general requires solving an infinite set of equations (i.e., for every $|z_1| = 1$). In many examples (see below and in the next section), the acceptable values of p and q have been found not to be very large.

Remarks

1) The finite-order semicausal MVR's realize SDF's which contain both numerator and denominator polynomials (see (97)). However, the numerator polynomial is one dimensional and is in the noncausal dimension.

2) The above remark implies semicausal MVR's are driven by colored noise. In fact $\{\epsilon_{i,j}\}$ is a moving average process in the "i" variable and is white in the "j" variable.

3) Semicausal MVR's were introduced in [9] and have been found useful in developing semirecursive or the so-called hybrid algorithms which are recursive in one direction and are transform based in the other directions. See examples in Section VI and [51], [52], [55], [57]–[59].

4) The semicausal models are recursive (or causal) only in the j variable. A re-indexing in the i-variable to attempt to represent it as a two-dimensional causal model would yield an unstable model. Thus the model in Example 7 written as

$$u_{i,j} = \frac{1}{a} u_{i-1,j} - u_{i-2,j-1} - \frac{b}{a} u_{i-1,j-1} - \frac{1}{a} \epsilon_{i-1,j}$$

would be unstable if solved recursively in i and j.

Example 8: We return to the nonseparable exponential covariance function considered in Example 5. Fig. 12 shows the semicausal MVR coefficients for $p = q = 1$ and $p = q = 2$.

Fig. 11 shows the covariance match achieved by the semicausal MVR model. Compared to single quadrant causal model for $p = q = 2$, we find a better covariance fit is provided by the semicausal model (see Fig. 13).

D. Noncausal Representations

The results for two-dimensional noncausal MVR's are analogous to the one dimensional results discussed in Section III-E. All the relevant equations for the two-dimensional case are given in the Appendix. The following conclusions are made.

	.905 .894 .868		.209 .315 .389		.039 .041 .047
n	.951 .932 .894	n	.111 .231 .315	n	.019 .025 .036
↑	1.00 .951 .905	↑	0. .111 .208	↑	0. .017 .031
	→ m		→ m		→ m

| Actual covariances $r(m,n)$ $r(-m,n) = r(m,-n) = r(-m,-n)$ | Causal Model Covariance Mismatch | Semicausal Model Covariance Mismatch |

Fig. 13. Covariance mismatch of the causal and semicausal models.

1) An arbitrary positive SDF can be realized arbitrarily closely by a stationary finite-order noncausal MVR provided S^{-1} has a uniformly convergent Fourier series. Conversely, if the given SDF S is a rational function with a zeroth-order numerator polynomial, then there exists a unique finite-order noncausal MVR realization of S.

2) As in the case of causal and semicausal models, an admissible finite-order noncausal MVR with a specified spectral mismatch error could be identified via the finite-order block Toeplitz equation (82).

Example 9: Consider the SDF

$$S(z_1, z_2) = [1 - \alpha(z_1 + z_1^{-1} + z_2 + z_2^{-1})]^{-1}, \quad 0 < \alpha < \tfrac{1}{4}. \quad (98)$$

Since S^{-1} is a two-dimensional polynomial, the *noncausal MVR* is

$$u_{i,j} = \alpha(u_{i+1,j} + u_{i-1,j} + u_{i,j+1} + u_{i,j-1}) + \epsilon_{i,j} \quad (99)$$

$$r_\epsilon(k,l) = \begin{cases} 1, & (k,l) = (0,0) \\ -\alpha, & (k,l) = (\pm 1, 0), (0, \pm 1) \\ 0, & \text{otherwise.} \end{cases}$$

Now let us consider finding a semicausal MVR. Comparing S with (89) we see $q = 1$. The equation for $r_n(z)$ is obtained via (A11) and (98) as

$$[1 - \alpha(z_1 + z_1^{-1})] r_n(z_1) - \alpha[r_{n-1}(z_1) + r_{n+1}(z_1)] = \delta_{n,0}$$

which solves to give

$$r_n(z_1) = r_n(z_1^{-1}) = AC^{|n|}$$
$$A = 1/\sqrt{\alpha_0^2 - 4\alpha^2}$$
$$\alpha_0 = 1 - \alpha(z_1 + z_1^{-1})$$
$$C = [\alpha_0 - \sqrt{\alpha_0^2 - 4\alpha^2}]/2\alpha.$$

Using this in (A25) and (A26) for $q = 1$ and simplifying we obtain

$$\hat{a}_1 = \hat{a}_1^1 = -C(z_1^{-1})$$
$$h(z_1) = A^{-1}[1 - C(z_1) C(z_1^{-1})]^{-1} = \tfrac{1}{2}\{\alpha_0 + \sqrt{\alpha_0^2 - 4\alpha^2}\}$$
$$a_0 = a_0^1 = -\beta^2 h(z_1)$$
$$a_1 = \beta^2 h(z_1) C(z_1^{-1}) = \alpha\beta^2.$$

Note $h(z_1)$ is an irrational function of z_1. Assuming $0 < \alpha \ll 1$, we obtain the rational approximation

$$h(z_1) = 1 - \alpha(z_1 + z_1^{-1}) + 0(\alpha^2).$$

Ignoring $0(\alpha^2)$ terms we obtain

$$\beta^2 \simeq 1, \; a_0(z_1) = -1 + \alpha(z_1 + z_1^{-1}), \; a_1(z_1) = \alpha, \; S_\epsilon = -a_0(z_1)$$

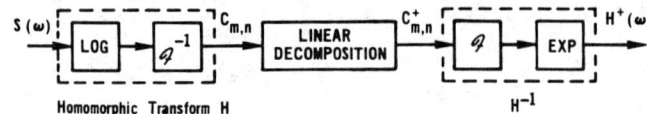

Fig. 14. Homomorphic transform method for two-dimensional spectral factorization.

and the finite-order semicausal MVR

$$u_{i,j} = \alpha(u_{i-1,j} + u_{i+1,j}) + \alpha u_{i,j-1} + \epsilon_{i,j} \quad (100)$$

$$r_\epsilon(k,l) = \delta_{l,0} \begin{cases} 1, & k = 0 \\ -\alpha, & |k| = 1 \\ 0, & \text{otherwise.} \end{cases}$$

For $0 < \alpha < \tfrac{1}{3}$, equation (100) can be shown to be a stable semicausal model. The SDF corresponding to this model is

$$S_u = \frac{[1 - \alpha(z_1 + z_1^{-1})]}{[1 - \alpha(z_1 + z_1^{-1}) - \alpha z_2^{-1}][1 - \alpha(z_1^{-1} + z_1) - \alpha z_2]}.$$

For $a = b = \alpha$ in Example 7, we see (100) and the model considered there are identical. A causal MVR approximation of (100) is obtained as discussed in that example.

E. Causal and Semicausal Model Realizations Via Homomorphic Transformation

The factorization required in the causal and semicausal models could be achieved via the so-called homomorphic transformation[3] shown in Fig. 14. One starts with the Fourier series of $\log S$ (the homomorphic transform of S) as

$$\tilde{S}(z_1, z_2) \triangleq \log S(z_1, z_2) = \sum_{m=-\infty}^{\infty} \sum_{n=-\infty}^{\infty} c_{m,n} z_1^{-m} z_2^{-n},$$

$$|z_1| = 1, |z_2| = 1 \quad (101)$$

where it is assumed the sequence $\{c_{m,n}\}$, also called the *Cepstrum*, is absolutely summable, i.e.,

$$\sum_m \sum_n |c_{m,n}| < \infty. \quad (102)$$

Now, if $\tilde{S}$ is decomposed as a sum of, say, three components as

$$\tilde{S} \triangleq \tilde{S}_\epsilon + \tilde{H}^+ + \tilde{H}^- \quad (103)$$

then

$$S = \frac{e^{\tilde{S}_\epsilon}}{[e^{-\tilde{H}^+} e^{-\tilde{H}^-}]} \triangleq S_\epsilon H^+ H^- \quad (104)$$

is a product of three factors. If the decomposition is such that

---
[3] Also called Wiener-Doob factorization [61], [62] or Hilbert transformation [56].

$H^+(z_1, z_2) = H^-(z_1^{-1}, z_2^{-1})$ and $S_\epsilon(z_1, z_2) = S_\epsilon(z_1^{-1}, z_2^{-1})$ then there exists a stable two-dimensional linear system with transfer function $H^+(z_1, z_2)$ such that the SDF of the output is S if the SDF of the input is S_ϵ.

This algorithm is due to Ekstrom and Woods [64] and is a direct extension in two dimensions of a method by Wiener [61]. The causal and the semicausal models can be realized by finding their respective decompositions in such a way that the impulse response $h^+_{m,n} = \mathcal{F}^{-1}\{H^+(\omega_1, \omega_2)\}$ has causal and semicausal regions of support $\hat{S}_0 = \hat{S} \cup (0, 0)$ where $\hat{S}$ is defined in (74). We give the specific decompositions for causal MVR, semicausal WNDR, and semicausal MVR models.

Causal MVR:

$$\tilde{H}^+ = \sum_{m=1}^{\infty} c_{m,0} z_1^{-m} + \sum_{m=-\infty}^{\infty} \sum_{n=1}^{\infty} c_{m,n} z_1^{-m} z_2^{-n}$$

$$\tilde{H}^- = \sum_{m=-\infty}^{-1} c_{m,0} z_1^{-m} + \sum_{m=-\infty}^{\infty} \sum_{n=-\infty}^{-1} c_{m,n} z_1^{-m} z_2^{-n}$$

$$\tilde{S}_\epsilon = c_{0,0}. \tag{105}$$

In view of (102), $\tilde{H}^+(z_1, z_2)$ is analytic in the region $\{|z_1| = 1, |z_2| \geq 1\} \cup \{|z_1| \geq 1, z_2 = \infty\}$. Hence $H^+(z_1, z_2)$ will be analytic in the same region. Therefore, the impulse response $h^+_{m,n}$ will be zero for $[-\infty \leq m \leq -1, n = 0] \cup [n < 0, \forall m]$, i.e., $\{h^+_{m,n}\}$ is causal.

Semicausal WNDR:

$$\tilde{H}^+ = \frac{1}{2} \sum_{m=-\infty}^{\infty} c_{m,0} z_1^{-m} + \sum_{m=-\infty}^{\infty} \sum_{n=1}^{\infty} c_{m,n} z_1^{-m} z_2^{-n}$$

$$\tilde{H}^- = \frac{1}{2} \sum_{m=-\infty}^{\infty} c_{m,0} z_1^{-m} + \sum_{m=-\infty}^{\infty} \sum_{n=-\infty}^{-1} c_{m,n} z_1^{-m} z_2^{-n}$$

$$\tilde{S}_\epsilon = 0. \tag{106}$$

Now $\tilde{H}^+$ and hence H^+ will be analytic in the region $\{|z_1| = 1, |z_2| \geq 1\}$ and impulse response $h^+_{m,n}$ will be zero for $\{\forall m, n < 0\}$, i.e., $h^+_{m,n}$ is semicausal.

Semicausal MVR: A simple examination of (95)–(97) reveals that semicausal MVR's require that within a constant multiplier S_ϵ should equal $1/H^+(z_1, \infty)$. Using this condition, we obtain

$$\tilde{H}^+ = \sum_{m=-\infty}^{\infty} c_{m,0} z_1^{-m} + \sum_{m=-\infty}^{\infty} \sum_{n=1}^{\infty} c_{m,n} z_1^{-m} z_2^{-n}$$

$$\tilde{H}^- = \sum_{m=-\infty}^{\infty} c_{m,0} z_1^{-m} + \sum_{m=-\infty}^{\infty} \sum_{n=-\infty}^{-1} c_{m,n} z_1^{-m} z_2^{-n}$$

$$\tilde{S}_\epsilon = -\sum_{m=-\infty}^{\infty} c_{m,0} z_1^{-m}. \tag{107}$$

The region of analyticity of $\tilde{H}^+$ and H^+ is $\{|z_1| = 1, |z_2| \geq 1\}$ and that of $\tilde{S}_\epsilon$ and S_ϵ is $\{|z_1| = 1, \forall z_2\}$. Hence $h^+_{m,n}$ is semicausal and S_ϵ is a SDF.

Example 10: Consider the SDF of Example 9. Assuming $0 < \alpha \ll 1$, we obtain

$$\tilde{S} \simeq \alpha(z_1 + z_1^{-1} + z_2 + z_2^{-1}) + 0(\alpha^2).$$

Ignoring $0(\alpha^2)$ terms we obtain

$$H^+ = \begin{cases} \alpha(z_1^{-1} + z_2^{-1}), & \text{causal MVR} \\ \frac{1}{2}\alpha(z_1 + z_1^{-1}) + \alpha z_2^{-1}, & \text{semicausal WNDR} \\ \alpha(z_1 + z_1^{-1}) + \alpha z_2^{-1}, & \text{semicausal MVR} \end{cases}$$

$$\tilde{S}_\epsilon = \begin{cases} 0, & \text{for causal MVR and semicausal WNDR} \\ -\alpha(z_1 + z^{-1}), & \text{for semicausal MVR}. \end{cases}$$

This gives

$$H^+ = 1/e^{-H^+} \simeq \begin{cases} 1/[1 - \alpha z_1^{-1} - \alpha z_2^{-1}], & \text{causal MVR} \\ 1/[1 - \frac{\alpha}{2}(z_1 + z_1^{-1}) - \alpha z_2^{-1}], & \\ & \text{semicausal WNDR} \\ 1/[1 - \alpha(z_1 + z_1^{-1}) - \alpha z_2^{-1}], & \\ & \text{semicausal MVR} \end{cases}$$

$$S_\epsilon \simeq \begin{cases} 1, & \text{causal MVR and semicausal WNDR} \\ 1 - (z_1 + z_1^{-1}), & \text{semicausal MVR}. \end{cases}$$

Remarks

1) We note that for noncausal models, one need not go through the above procedure. A suitable truncation of the Fourier series of S^{-1} yields the desired model.

2) In general, the Fourier series of $\tilde{S}$ and H^+ will contain an infinite number of terms even if S and $\tilde{H}^+$ (or its approximation) respectively were (finite order) polynomials. Therefore, a practical algorithm requires two stages of numerical approximations. First, in the evaluation of $\tilde{S}$ and then in the evaluation of H^+. An algorithm utilizing the DFT to obtain such an approximate spectral factorization and its error analysis has been considered by Rino [63] for one-dimensional problems. Extension of the algorithm in two dimensions is given in [64].

3) From the foregoing discussion the BIBO stability condition for finite-order causal and the semicausal models can be stated quite simply as follows.[4]

Theorem 4: A causal MVR whose transfer function H is given by

$$H(z_1, z_2) = 1/A(z_1, z_2)$$

$$A(z_1, z_2) = 1 - \sum_{m=1}^{p} a_{m,0} z_1^{-m} - \sum_{m=-p}^{p} \sum_{n=1}^{q} a_{m,n} z_1^{-m} z_2^{-n}$$

is stable if and only if i) $A(z_1, z_2) \neq 0$, $|z_1| \geq 1$, $z_2 = \infty$, ii) $A(z_1, z_2) \neq 0$, $|z_1| = 1$, $|z_2| \geq 1$.

Theorem 5: A semicausal WNDR or MVR whose transfer function H is given by

$$H = 1/A$$

$$A(z_1, z_2) = 1 - \sum_{\substack{m=-p \\ m \neq 0}}^{p} a_{m,0} z_1^{-m} - \sum_{m=-p}^{p} \sum_{n=1}^{q} a_{m,n} z_1^{-m} z_2^{-n}$$

---

[4] It is assumed that the causal, semicausal, and the noncausal model equations are solved, respectively, as initial, initial-boundary, and boundary value problems.

is stable if and only if $A(z_1, z_2) \neq 0, |z_1| = 1, |z_2| \geq 1$.

Theorem 6: A noncausal MVR or WNDR whose transfer function is given by

$$H = 1/A, \quad A(z_1, z_2) = 1 - \sum_{m=-p}^{p} \sum_{n=-q}^{q} a_{m,n} z_1^{-m} z_2^{-n}$$

is stable if and only if $A(z_1, z_2) \neq 0, |z_1| = 1, |z_2| = 1$.

The conditions stated in these theorems assure H to be analytic in the appropriate regions in the z_1, z_2 hyperplanes so that its stability conditions are satisfied. Two-dimensional stability has been discussed almost invariably for causal models and occasionally for noncausal models. For details see [65]–[68].

F. Other Methods

Since exact factorization of a two-dimensional SDF $S(\omega_1, \omega_2)$ (rational or not) as the magnitude square of a rational function $H(\omega_1, \omega_2)$ is not possible in general, any number of other methods which could give reasonable rational approximations should be possible. The advantage of model identification via the prediction model orthogonality equations (Sections V-A to V-D) is that the equations to be solved are linear. The advantage of the homomorphic transform approach is that a suitable FFT (even if large in size) could be used to obtain the approximate models. In both procedures, however, situations exist where the model order may get very large in order to be stable.

In image processing applications it is generally desirable that the model order not be very large. This is because the image data is often processed block by block (often 16×16) and if the model order approaches the size of a column (or row), then nonrecursive or transform based methods become more efficient (even computationally). Therefore, identification techniques which give reasonable (low-) order models with assurance of stability would be useful in many applications such as restoration and data compression. High-order models, on the other hand, could be useful in image synthesis, object identification, spectral estimation, and digital filter design applications.

Among the various other methods for identifying image models, perhaps the most direct is the parameter identification method via the maximum-likelihood approach [69]. Sugimoto *et al.* [70], [71] have applied this method for identification of finite order semicausal models. Similar approaches are possible for causal and noncausal models although the algorithmic details would differ considerably.

Another method suggested in [51], [52] is based on the fact that the causal, semicausal, and noncausal models can also be considered as finite difference approximations of hyperbolic, parabolic, and elliptic partial differential equations, respectively. Hence, low-order stable models can be determined by identifying the parameters of the finite difference approximations subject to their stability constraints which are known from the theory of their parent partial differential equations.

Since the semicausal MVR and WNDR require only factorization in only one variable, one-dimensional system identification techniques [72] could potentially be applied for identifying these models. Once the semicausal MVR is known, the causal realization (or an approximation of it), if desired, could be found via the method of Section V-C.

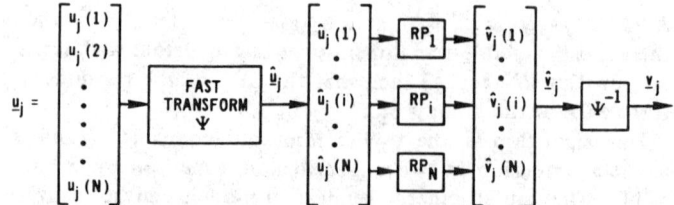

Fig. 15. Parallel structure of semicausal algorithms. RP_i is the ith channel recursive processor such as a recursive filter for image restoration or a DPCM encoder for data compression.

VI. APPLICATIONS IN IMAGE PROCESSING

The three types of models discussed in the foregoing have applications in most of the image processing problems listed in Table I. As mentioned before the choice of a particular model depends not only on the accuracy of the model but also on the associated algorithmic architecture. The three models yield three quite different processing techniques which will be described briefly.

A. Algorithmic Structures

The causal models can be easily viewed to represent images as the output of a line scanner and hence yield, quite naturally, algorithms which are recursive in nature. Causal MVR's have been found most useful in data compression of images [17] for real time transmission where the successive transmitted samples represent the prediction error between the new imagepel and its predicted value based on the past transmission. Causal MVR's have usefulness in the design of recursive filters for noise smoothing and restoration of blurred images (especially when the blurring process is also causal, e.g., in motion blur). It should be mentioned, however, that two-dimensional images generally do not have any causality (or dynamics) associated with them and the usual solutions of smoothing and most restoration problems are boundary valued (or noncausal). The recursive methods therefore have to sweep back and forth between the boundaries. This, together with the algorithmic complexities of two-dimensional recursions, have kept the users favor with more direct Fourier transform based algorithms [6], [7], [73], [75]. However, potential for these algorithms seems to be substantial for space variant restoration problems where Fourier techniques do not apply.

The semicausal models yield hybrid algorithms which are transform based (nonrecursive) in one dimension and recursive in the other. The finite-order semicausal MVR's have a structure where the model coefficients (e.g., matrices in (66)) be represented by banded Toeplitz matrices. It is possible to find a fast unitary sinusoidal transform [10] which would reduce these matrices to their diagonal forms (or nearly so). For example, the semicausal model of (92) reduces to a set of N decoupled first-order Markov processes

$$\lambda_k \hat{u}_j(k) = b \hat{u}_{j-1}(k) + \hat{\epsilon}_j(k), \quad k = 1, \cdots, N \quad (108)$$

under the transformation $\hat{u}_j = \psi u_j$, ψ = DST (see Table III), where λ_k are the eigenvalues of Q. Now, several image processing problems, e.g., noise smoothing, data compression, restoration, system identification etc. can be formulated as N one-dimensional problems, which could be solved in parallel. Fig. 15 shows the parallel structure of semicausal algorithms. Each line u_j of the image is first unitarily transformed and each transformed element $\hat{u}_j(k)$ is processed recursively in the 'j' variable. The output vector $\hat{v}_j$ is inverse transformed to give the processed vector v_j.

Semicausal models have been used in real-time data compression of images for transmission from remotely piloted vehicles (RPV) [17], [58], [74], in restoration and noise smoothing problems [52], [55], [70], [71] spectral estimation [59], etc. The associated algorithms combine the advantages of low memory and hardware complexity of recursive methods and the relatively high performance of transform processing methods.

Noncausal models have been used most widely either as moving average models or via the transform methods. A large number of commonly used image processing operators, e.g., spatial smoothing, gradient and compass edge detectors, bilinear interpolation, unsharp masks, etc., are moving average operators. It has been shown that noncausal MVR's naturally lead to transform domain algorithms and have been found useful in most of the problems listed in Table I.

B. Smoothing, Enhancement, and Restoration of Images

The common smoothing problem is to find the best linear mean-square estimate of the image $u_{i,j}$ given the noisy observations

$$y_{i,j} = u_{i,j} + n_{i,j}$$

where $\{n_{i,j}\}$ is a white-noise field independent of $\{u_{i,j}\}$. Causal models have been used by several authors [52], [76]–[79] to develop recursive filter implementations. Semicausal and vector scanning models have been considered in [52], [55], [70], [71], [80] to develop semirecursive or line to line recursive algorithms. Noncausal models have been shown to yield fast transform based nonrecursive algorithms [52], [73] and have also been found useful in developing moving average FIR filters.

The following two examples show how some of the commonly used operators in image processing are related to the linear prediction models. Use of appropriate prediction models (depending on the images) can lead to similar but better operators.

Example 11: Consider an image represented by the noncausal MVR of (99). The optimum filter transfer function is given by another noncausal MVR as

$$G(z_1, z_2) = \beta^2 / \{\beta^2 + \sigma_n^2 [1 - \alpha(z_1 + z_1^{-1} + z_2 + z_2^{-1})]\}$$

where σ_n^2 is the variance of the noise. At signal-to-noise ratios (SNR) of approximately 5, G can be approximated by the FIR filter [52]

$$G \simeq T(z_1, z_2) = \tfrac{1}{2} [1 + \tfrac{1}{4}(z_1 + z_1^{-1} + z_2 + z_2^{-1})]$$

which is simply a commonly used spatial averaging filter. At a different signal to noise ratios another suitable moving average approximation can be found whose region of support would increase with the reciprocal of SNR. In fact, moving average filters can be adapted (via the noncausal models) to local changes in SNR. Fig. 16 shows that a noisy (SNR = 5) image optimally filtered via an appropriate noncausal model or its approximate spatial averaging filter is better than using the optimal (Wiener) filter based on the usual separable covariance model [52].

Example 12 (Enhancement): The prediction operator (causal, semicausal, or noncausal) denoted by $A(z_1, z_2)$ generally performs some sort of differentiation. When applied to a real-world image, the prediction error generally contains a nonstationary component which generally represents high spatial frequencies, e.g., edges. Thus the operator

$$C(z_1, z_2) = 1 + \lambda A(z_1, z_2)$$

would add to the image a quantity proportional to high spatial frequencies (or gradient). For example, in the case of the noncausal MVR considered above, with $\alpha \simeq \tfrac{1}{4}$

$$C = (1 + \lambda) - \frac{\lambda}{4}(z_1 + z_1^{-1} + z_2 + z_2^{-1}).$$

Now the operator A is simply a discrete Laplacian and C is called the *"Unsharp Mask"* used often for edge enhancement of images.

Image models have also been used in restoration of images blurred due to motion, atmospheric turbulence and other shift invariant PSF. State variable, line recursive as well as frame-recursive models have been used to develop recursive algorithms for deblurring of images [60]. Noncausal models have been used to develop transform-domain deblurring algorithms. Other restoration techniques such as iterative gradient methods, singular value decomposition have mostly been used [7], [73], [75], [95] for solving deterministic (e.g., least squares interpolation) problems although image models could be used (especially to improve their performance in the presence of noise).

C. Image Data Compression

This is one application where image models have probably had the most significant impact. Causal prediction models have been used most widely in the design of intraframe and interframe predictive or the so-called DPCM coders. Semicausal models have been employed in transform/DPCM coding for RPV and teleconferencing applications. Noncausal models give rise to transform coding algorithms which have been found to give high performance. The prediction model parameters determine the coder design details such as quantizer design, bit allocation, optimum transform, etc. These details and other related considerations for image data compression may be found in the recent survey articles [17], [81] and in [16], [57].

Example 13: Consider the semicausal model of (92) when it is white noise driven. It reduces to (108) after sine transformation of the vectors u_j. Fig. 17 shows images encoded via this model at an average rate of 1 bit/pel. This model has also been used effectively to simultaneously filter and encode noisy images. For details see [17], [57], [58].

D. Edge Extraction

Example 14 (Edge Extraction): An image can be considered as being composed of two components, i.e.,

$$u_{i,j} = u_{i,j}^s + u_{i,j}^b$$

where $u_{i,j}^s$ and $u_{i,j}^b$ represent the stationary and nonstationary (boundaries and edges) components respectively. Such two source models for images have been considered by Schreiber, Yan and Sakrison, Jain and Wang, and others [82]–[84], [57]. Using a WNDR for the stationary component, the image can be expressed as

$$\epsilon_{i,j} = \epsilon_{i,j}^s + \epsilon_{i,j}^b$$

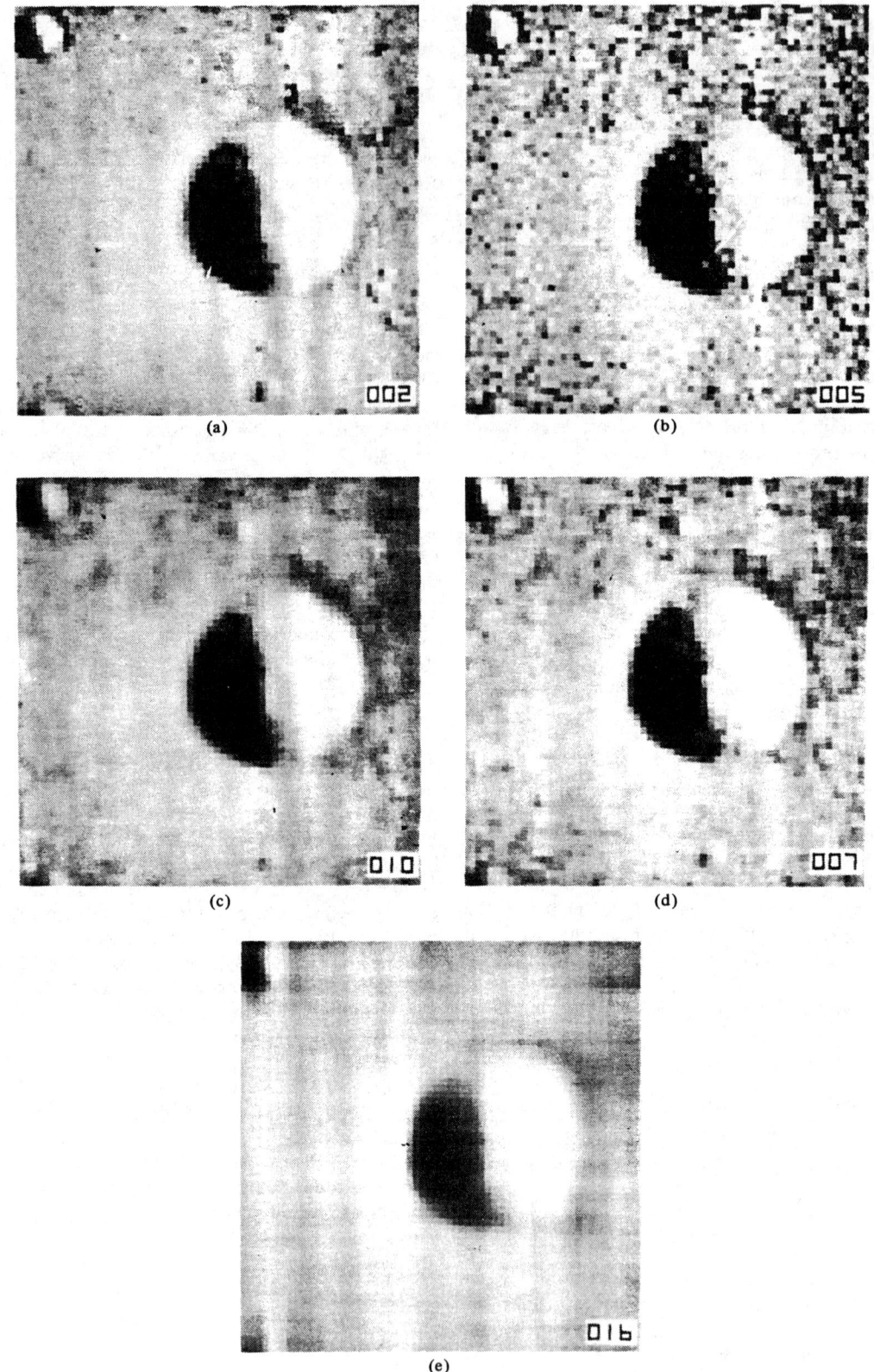

Fig. 16. Smoothing of a noisy image. (a) Original. (b) Noisy. (c) Optimum filtered using a noncausal model. (d) Spatial averaged. (e) Optimum filtered based on the separable covariance model.

where $\epsilon = \mathcal{L}[u]$, and $\mathcal{L}$ is the whitening prediction operator (causal, semicausal or noncausal). Now, $\epsilon_{i,j}$ can be viewed as a sum of signal $\epsilon_{i,j}^b$ (edges) and white noise $\epsilon_{i,j}^s$. The edge detection problem is therefore reduced to the detection of a signal in the presence of noise. Fig. 18 shows the edges detected using a noncausal model. Such two source models are useful in designing "edge preserving" image-processing algorithms.

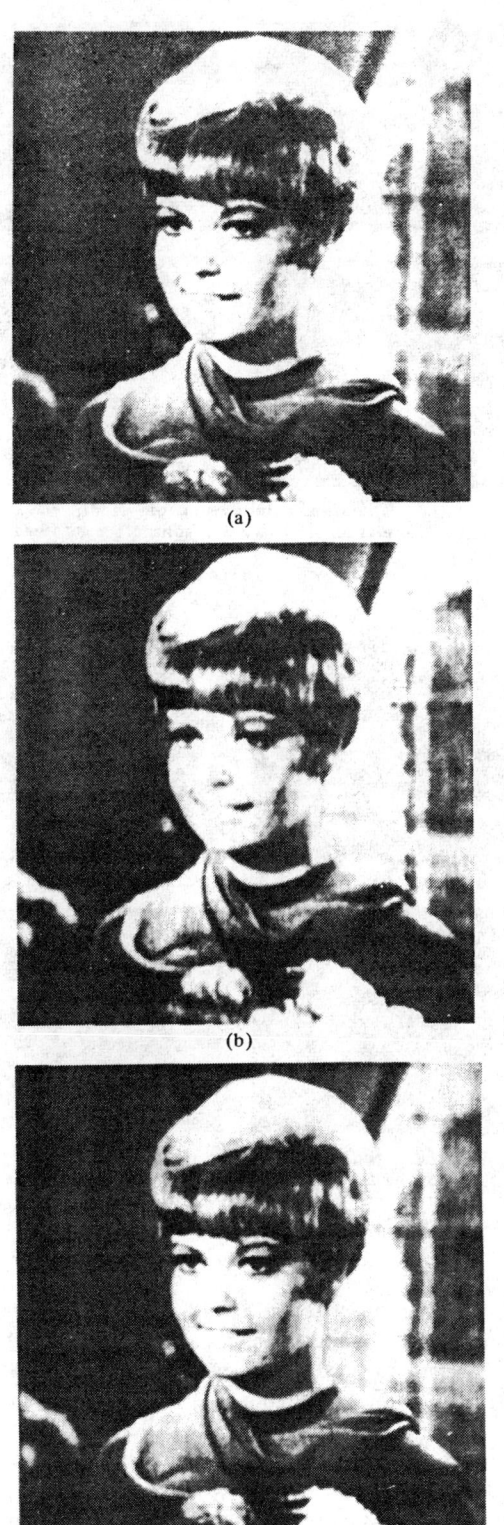

Fig. 17. Data compression of images via a semicausal model. (a) Original. (b) Encoded. 1 bit/pel. (c) Adaptive codings, 1 bit/pel. In the adaptive method, the model parameters are updated after every 16 × 16 block of pels. Mean-square error improvement due to adaptation is in excess of 3 dB.

E. Two-Dimensional Spectral Estimation

Let $r(m, n)$ be a two-dimensional positive definite covariance sequence given on a rectangular window $W_c = [-p_c, p_c] \times [-q_c, q_c]$. The problem is to find an estimate of the SDF

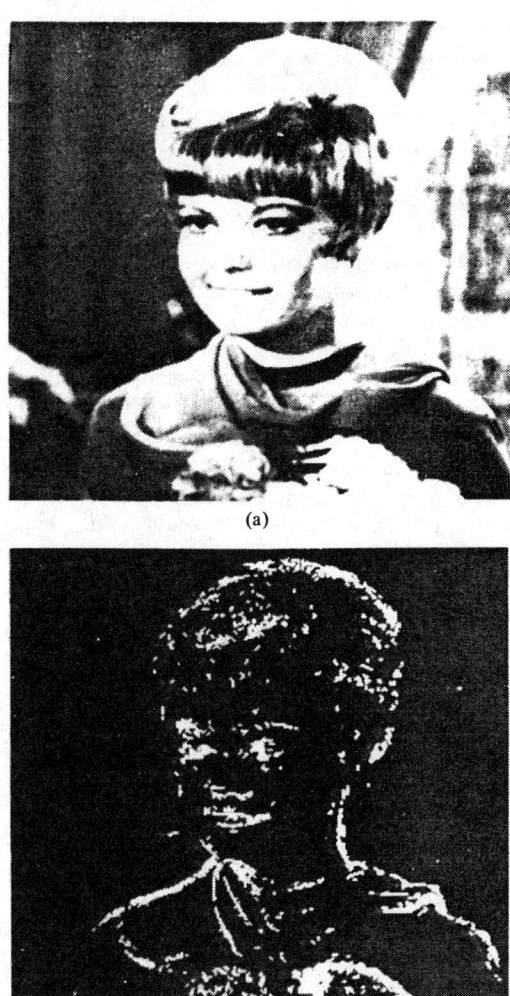

Fig. 18. Edges extracted using a noncausal model.

associated with this covariance sequence. In two dimensions, the maximum entropy spectral estimation problem is to *find a positive definite extension of $r(m, n)$ outside W_c such that the entropy*

$$H = \frac{1}{4\pi^2} \int_{-\pi}^{\pi} \int_{-\pi}^{\pi} \log S(\omega_1, \omega_2) \, d\omega_1 \, d\omega_2$$

is maximized. Note that it is required that the Fourier coefficients of the estimated spectrum S match the given covariances exactly on W_c. The solution, if it exists, requires that the Fourier series of $1/S$ should be truncated outside the window W_c, i.e., S should be the SDF of a noncausal MVR, i.e., of the form

$$S(z_1, z_2) = \beta^2 \left[\sum_{m,n \, \in W_c} \alpha_{m,n} z_1^{-m} z_2^{-n} \right]^{-1},$$

$$|z_1| = 1, \quad |z_2| = 1 \quad (109)$$

where the coefficients $\alpha_{m,n}$, β^2 are determined by matching the given covariances to the Fourier coefficients of S on W_c. Unfortunately, this maximum entropy solution need not exist because, in two (and higher) dimensions, a positive definite sequence on a rectangular window need not have a positive definite extension [85], [86]. However, if $r(m, n)$ has at least one positive definite extension then the maximum entropy solution (109) exists and is unique [94]. When the solution exists, the problem of finding $\alpha_{m,n}$ is nonlinear and cannot be, in general, reduced to a linear problem as in the one-dimensional case. This is because of the spectral factorization difficulty mentioned earlier.

However, it is possible to obtain positive SDF estimates if we relax the condition of exact covariance match on W_c. This is motivated by the fact that often the available covariances are estimated from data and are noisy. The foregoing finite-order causal, semicausal, and noncausal MVR's could be used to estimate the SDF. The algorithm simply requires solving (80) for $(k, l) \in W_0$ or equivalently (81) and (82) where W_0 is a subset of $\hat{S}_0$ and could be a causal, semicausal, or noncausal prediction filter window. Note that the W_0 and W_c are not of equal size. For example, for a causal MVR, if $W_0 = [0, p] \times [0, q]$ then the covariance sequence is needed over $W_c = [-p, p] \times [-q, q]$. After having solved (80), the estimated SDF (if admissible) is given as follows.

Causal MVR:

$$S(z_1, z_2) = \beta^2 \bigg/ \bigg|1 - \sum_{m,n \,\in\, W} a_{m,n} z_1^{-m} z_2^{-n}\bigg|^2,$$

$$|z_1| = 1, \quad |z_2| = 1. \quad (110)$$

Semicausal MVR:

$$W_0 = [-p, p] \times [0, q], \quad W_c = [-2p, 2p] \times [-q, q],$$

$$W = W_0 - (0, 0)$$

$$S(z_1, z_2) = S_\epsilon(z_1, z_2) \bigg/ \bigg|1 - \sum_{m,n \,\in\, W} a_{m,n} z_1^{-m} z_2^{-n}\bigg|^2,$$

$$|z_1| = 1, \quad |z_2| = 1$$

$$S_\epsilon(z_1, z_2) = \beta^2 \left[1 - \sum_{m=1}^{p} a_{m,0}(z_1^{-m} + z_1^{m})\right]. \quad (111)$$

Noncausal MVR:

$$W_0 = [-p, p] \times [-q, q],$$

$$W_c = [-2p, 2p] \times [-2q \times 2q], \quad W = W_0 - (0, 0)$$

$$S(z_1, z_2) = \beta^2 \left[1 - \sum_{m,n \,\in\, W} a_{m,n} z_1^{-m} z_2^{-n}\right]^{-1},$$

$$|z_1| = 1, \quad |z_2| = 1. \quad (112)$$

It should be noted that the solution of (81) and (82), while it guarantees admissible predictor coefficients, the estimated spectrum may not always be positive (i.e., admissible) for any arbitrary positive definite $\mathcal{R}$. This is because the solution yields coefficients which satisfy (80) only partially, i.e., for $k, l \in W_0$ (and not necessarily for all $k, l \in \hat{S}_0$). However, for a large enough W_0 and covariances that come from an analytic SDF, an admissible SDF can be found. In many practical examples, the window size W_0 has been found to be not large and in many cases it is actually quite small for admissible SDF.

Example 15: Consider the covariance sequence

$$r(m, n) = \frac{\cos 2\pi(m + n)}{8} + \frac{\cos 2\pi(m + n)}{12} + 0.05 \delta_{m,0} \delta_{n,0}$$

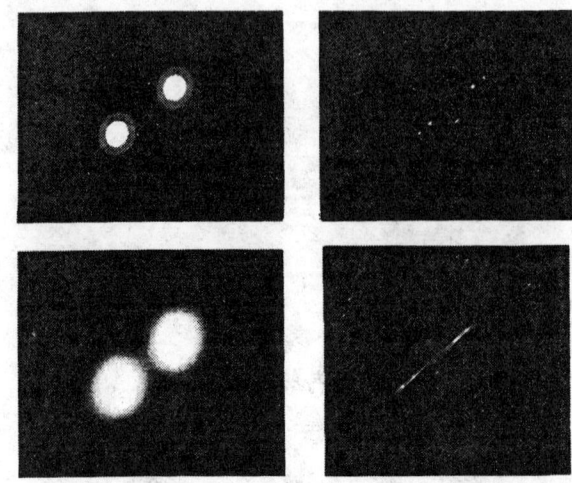

Fig. 19. Spectral estimation comparison of windowed DFT versus semicausal MVR methods. Top row; from left windowed DFT spectrum amplitude versus semicausal MVR spectrum amplitude. Bottom row; same quantities shown on dB scale.

Fig. 20. Spectral estimation comparison of causal versus semicausal models. Top row from left; model spectrum amplitude versus semicausal model spectrum amplitude. Bottom row; same quantities shown on dB scale.

whose SDF has line spectra at $\pm(\frac{1}{8}, \frac{1}{8})$ and $\pm(\frac{1}{12}, \frac{1}{12})$ in the frequency plane. The covariances are available over $[-4, 4] \times [-2, 2]$. Figs. 19 and 20 shows the spectra estimated by a) Bartlett windowing and taking DFT, b) single quadrant causal MVR for $p = q = 5$, c) semicausal MVR, $p = 3, q = 4$. Note that objects not resolved by the DFT method are resolved by the causal and semicausal estimates. Spurious peaks appear in the causal model and the covariance match over the window W_c is not very good. The semicausal estimate is much more accurate both in terms of resolution, peak location and its covariance match. For other examples and more discussion see [59].

Remarks:

1) The causal and noncausal MVR spectra (110) and (112) are of the same form as the maximum entropy spectrum (109). However, they would not be equal in general. If the given covariance sequence is separable, then the maximum entropy and the causal, the semicausal and noncausal spectra would be identical.

2) The semicausal MVR spectra is ARMA type and is therefore not a maximum entropy spectra.

3) All the equations for calculating the prediction model coefficients are linear.

4) As expected from the theory of these two-dimensional prediction models, experimentally, it has been observed that the covariance match on the window W_c improves as p, q are increased.

F. Extension to Adaptive Models and Other Applications

Other applications of image models are in adaptive processing where the model parameters are updated with the changes in image properties—Fig. 17, for example, shows the result of adapting the semicausal model of (108) block by block. In general adaptations could be made continuously and recursively from pel to pel, as is done in many DPCM techniques for image coding. However, it has been observed that models which are adapted at every pel tend to be sensitive to noise and rarely show any significant improvement over more practical block by block adaptive models.

Applications also exist in identification, recognition and synthesis of images of texture. Image models also provide a priori information concerning performance bounds such as achievable signal to noise ratio, compression versus distortion, etc., [16], [52].

VII. Summary and Conclusions

We have presented several mathematical models which have been used and are of potential use in image processing. Included in our discussion were several traditional models (e.g., series expansion, one dimensional AR, state variable etc.) and some new models (viz. the causal, semicausal and noncausal prediction models). Not included in our discussion were considerations of the Markovian property, stability tests, controllability, observability and other such notions. Also, not considered were models for vector random fields which have potential applications in multispectral and color image processing. Theoretical results for these and related topics can be found in [66], [87]-[92]. It was shown however, that the models considered do have a large number of applications in image (and two-dimensional signal) processing. Among the prediction models considered, the semicausal and noncausal models seem to offer several algorithmic and performance tradeoffs against the purely causal (or recursive) methods.

Appendix

A.1 Causal Minimum Variance Representations

First we consider the general nonstationary case for arbitrary random fields. Let us define a block matrix $\mathcal{R}$ whose elements are the matrices $R_{j,k}$ which are the cross covariances $Eu_j u_k^T$. Then $\mathcal{R}$ is the covariance matrix of the column ordered array vector u. Let $\{u(k)\}$, $\{\bar{u}(k)\}$ and $\{e(k)\}$ be the column ordered sequences corresponding to the arrays $\{u_{i,j}\}$, $\{\bar{u}_{i,j}\}$ and $\{\epsilon_{i,j}\}$, respectively. From our definition of causality, we can write

$$u(k) = \bar{u}(k) + e(k).$$

The orthogonality condition (69) requires that $e(k)$ be orthogonal to $u(l)$ for $\forall l < k$. This means $\{e(k)\}$ must be a white-noise sequence because

$$Ee(l)e(k) = E[u(l) - \bar{u}(l)]e(k) = 0, \quad \forall l < k.$$

Since $Ee(l)e(k) = Ee(k)e(l)$, the above is true also for $k < l$. Thus *causal MVR's are also white-noise driven representations*. If $\beta_{i,j}^2$ denotes the variance of $\epsilon_{i,j}$, we have

$$E\epsilon_{i,j}\epsilon_{i+m,j+n} = \beta_{i,j,n}^2 \delta_{m,0} \delta_{n,0}. \quad (A1)$$

In matrix notation, equations (64) and (71) become

$$-A_{j,j}u_j = \sum_{n<j} A_{j,n} u_n + \epsilon_j, \quad \forall j$$

where

$$-A_{j,j} \triangleq I - A_{j,j}^0 \quad (A2)$$

is a unit lower triangular matrix (i.e., the diagonal entries are 1). This equation can also be written in terms of a *block lower triangular* matrix $\mathcal{A}$ whose block elements are the matrices $A_{j,n}$, as

$$-\mathcal{A}u = e \quad \mathcal{A} = \{A_{j,n}\}. \quad (A3)$$

Since the diagonal blocks of $\mathcal{A}$ are $\{A_{j,j}\}$, which are lower triangular matrices themselves, the matrix $\mathcal{A}$ is a strictly lower triangular matrix. Equation (A3) implies

$$\mathcal{A}[Euu^T]\mathcal{A}^T = Eee^T \quad \text{or} \quad \mathcal{R} = \mathcal{A}^{-1} \mathcal{R}_e (\mathcal{A}^{-1})^T$$

$$\text{or} \quad \mathcal{R}^{-1} = \mathcal{A}^T \mathcal{R}_e^{-1} \mathcal{A} \quad (A4)$$

where $\mathcal{R}_e$ is a diagonal matrix of the variances of $e(k)$. This is a *lower-upper* factorization of $\mathcal{R}$. Thus, the causal MVR requires a factorization of the block covariance matrix $\mathcal{R}$ by a strictly lower triangular matrix. For a positive definite $\mathcal{R}$, such a factorization always exists and can be obtained in two stages of factorization. The first stage requires a block-lower triangular factorization of $\mathcal{R}$. The second stage requires lower triangular factorization of a sequence of matrix blocks. For example, for $N \times N$ images, define

$$\hat{A}_{j,n} \triangleq A_{j,j}^{-1} A_{j,n} \quad R_{n,k} \triangleq Eu_n u_k^T. \quad (A5)$$

Then the desired solution of (A4) is obtained by first solving for $\hat{A}_{j,n}$ the so called normal equation

$$\sum_{n=1}^{j-1} \hat{A}_{j,n} R_{n,k} = -R_{j,k}, \quad 1 \leq k \leq j-1, \quad j = 2, \cdots, N$$

$$(A6)$$

which is a set of $(j-1) \times (j-1)$ block matrix equations.

Given $\{\hat{A}_{j,n}, n \leq j\}$, the unit lower triangular matrix $A_{j,j}$ is obtained by the lower-upper factorization

$$\left[\sum_{n=1}^{j} \hat{A}_{j,n} R_{n,j}\right]^{-1} = A_{j,j}^T (R_j^\epsilon)^{-1} A_{j,j} \quad (A7)$$

where R_j^ϵ is the covariance matrix of the prediction error vector ϵ_j and is diagonal. Once $A_{j,j}$ is known, $A_{j,n}$ is obtained via (A5). In practice the above algorithm will be quite tedious because the size of $\mathcal{R}$ is $N^2 \times N^2$ and the number of operations would be $O(N^6)$.

In the case of stationary models defined on the infinite plane if one starts with (73), a parallel result corresponding to (A1), (A5)-(A7), is obtained as

$$-A_0 u_j = \sum_{n=1}^{\infty} A_n u_{j-n} + \epsilon_j \quad E\epsilon_j \epsilon_k^T = \beta^2 I \delta_{j,k} \quad (A8)$$

and

$$-\sum_{n=1}^{q} \hat{A}_n^q R_{n-j} = R_{-j}, \quad 1 \leq j \leq q, \quad q = 1, 2, \cdots$$

$$\left[\sum_{n=1}^{q} \hat{A}_n^q R_n\right]^{-1} = \frac{1}{\beta^2} [A_0^q]^T [A_0^q], \quad R_n \triangleq E u_j u_{j+n}^T \quad \text{(A9)}$$

$$A_n^q \triangleq A_0 \hat{A}_n^q, \quad A_n = \lim_{q \to \infty} A_n^q, \quad \forall n \geq 0 \quad \text{(A10)}$$

where A_0 is a unit lower triangular matrix and $\hat{A}_n^q$, A_n^q, R_n, etc., are all doubly infinite Toeplitz matrices. If the given SDF $S(\omega_1, \omega_2)$ is positive and analytic, then following [56], it could be shown that there exists a unique[5] causal realization such as (A8). Moreover, the coefficients A_n could be obtained by solving the sequence of normal equations of (A9) and taking the limit $q \to \infty$ as in (A10). In terms of Z_1-transforms

$$r_n(z_1) \triangleq \sum_{m=-\infty}^{\infty} r(m,n) z_1^{-m}$$

$$a_n(z_1) \triangleq \sum_{m=-\infty}^{\infty} a_{m,n} z_1^{-m}, \quad n \geq 1$$

$$a_0(z_1) \triangleq \sum_{m=0}^{\infty} a_{m,0} z_1^{-m}, \quad \text{etc.} \quad \text{(A11)}$$

Equations (A9), (A10) reduce to scalar qth-order AR model equations, parametric in z_1

$$-\sum_{n=1}^{q} \hat{a}_n^q(z_1) r_{n-j}(z_1) = r_j(z_1^{-1}), \quad j = 1, \cdots, q \quad \text{(A12)}$$

where

$$-\sum_{n=0}^{q} \hat{a}_n^q(z_1) r_n(z) = \beta^2 / [a_0^q(z_1^{-1}) a_0^q(z_1)]$$

$$a_n^q(z_1) = a_0^q(z_1) \hat{a}_n^q(z_1), \quad \hat{a}_0^q(z_1) = 1, \quad n = 1, \cdots q \quad \text{(A13)}$$

where $a_0^q(z_1)$ is such that all its roots are inside the unit circle $|z_1| = 1$. If the SDF is a rational function of the form of (89), these equations can be used to obtain the causal MVR for the given value of q. In general this representation will be of infinite order. A finite-order approximation may be obtained as explained in Section V-B.

A.2 Semicausal Minimum Variance Representation

For semicausal models the orthogonality conditions require that for $\forall k < j$, the prediction error vector ϵ_j be orthogonal to u_k, and at $k = j$, the elements $\epsilon_j(i)$ be orthogonal to $u_j(m)$, $\forall m \neq i$. These conditions yield the representation equation

$$-A_{j,j} u_j = \sum_{n<j} A_{j,n} u_n + \epsilon_j, \quad A_{j,j} \triangleq -I + A_{j,j}^0, \quad \forall j$$

$$E u_k \epsilon_j^T = B_j \delta_{j,k}, \quad k \leq j$$

$$E \epsilon_k \epsilon_j^T = E \epsilon_j \epsilon_k^T = -A_{j,j} B_j \delta_{j,k}, \quad \forall j, k \quad \text{(A14)}$$

---

[5] This means the infinite predictor coefficients $a_{m,n}$ and the covariance sequence $r(m,n)$ are unique with respect to one another.

where

$$B_j = \text{Diag } \{E \epsilon_{i,j}^2\} \triangleq \text{Diag } \{\beta_{i,j}^2\}.$$

From above $-A_{j,j} B_j$ is a covariance matrix and must therefore be symmetric. Since B_j is diagonal, $A_{j,j}$ could not be lower or upper triangular.[6] Also, $\{\epsilon_j\}$ is a white-noise vector sequence. However, $\{\epsilon_{i,j}\}$ need not be a white-noise field because the elements of ϵ_j could be mutually correlated. Recall that in the case of causal MVR's, $\{\epsilon_{i,j}\}$ was a white-noise field. Now (A14) can be written as a block lower triangular matrix equation

$$-\mathcal{A} u = \epsilon \quad \mathcal{A} = \{A_{j,n}\} \quad \text{(A15)}$$

where $A_{j,j}$ is no longer lower triangular (compare with (A3)). Once again the $\mathcal{A}$ satisfies an equation similar to (A4), the difference being $\mathcal{R}_\epsilon$ would now be block diagonal and $\mathcal{A}$ is block lower triangular (rather than also being lower triangular). Now, the matrices $A_{j,n}$ could be found by a single stage lower-upper factorization by solving

$$-\sum_{n=1}^{j} A_{j,n} R_{n,k} = B_j \delta_{j,k}, \quad k \leq j. \quad \text{(A16)}$$

The solution is given by

$$A_{j,n} = A_{j,j} \hat{A}_{j,n}$$

$$A_{j,j} = -B_j H_j \quad H_j \triangleq \left[\sum_{n=1}^{j} \hat{A}_{j,n} R_{n,j}\right]^{-1}$$

$$B_j(i,i) \triangleq \beta_{i,j}^2 = 1/H_j(i,i) \quad \text{(A17)}$$

where $\hat{A}_{j,n}$ is the solution of (A6).

It is now worth noting that a causal MVR could always be obtained from a semicausal MVR whenever the covariance matrix $R_j^\epsilon = E \epsilon_j \epsilon_j^T = -A_{j,j} B_j$ is positive definite so that it has a factorization

$$R_j^\epsilon = L_j^T \Gamma_j^{-1} L_j \quad \text{(A18)}$$

where $\Gamma_j = \{\gamma_j(k)\}$, is a diagonal matrix and L_j is a unit-lower triangular matrix. Then the first equation in (A14) can be written as

$$-\tilde{A}_{j,j} u_j = \sum_{n<j} \tilde{A}_{j,n} u_n + v_j \quad \text{(A19)}$$

where

$$\tilde{A}_{j,j} \triangleq B_j L_j B_j^{-1} \quad \tilde{A}_{j,n} \triangleq B_j \Gamma_j (L_j^T)^{-1} A_{j,n}$$

$$v_j \triangleq B_j \Gamma_j (L_j^T)^{-1} \epsilon_j. \quad \text{(A20)}$$

From these it follows that $\tilde{A}_{j,j}$ is also a unit-lower triangular matrix and $\{v_{i,j}\}$ is a white-noise random field since

$$R_j^v = E v_j v_j^T = B_j \Gamma_j B_j \quad \text{(A21)}$$

is a diagonal matrix. Comparison of (A19) with (A2) shows that it is now a causal MVR. Given a semicausal MVR, a causal MVR is guaranteed provided the lower-upper factorization of (A18) exists, i.e., if R_j^ϵ is positive definite. However, it may not always be desirable to get to a causal representation because the spatial structure of this representation may be-

---

[6] Except when $A_{j,j}$ is diagonal. In that case however, equation (A14) will reduce to a causal model and would not be admissible here.

come more cumbersome than the semicausal case as shown by Example 7 in Section V-C.

In the case of stationary semicausal MVR's defined on the infinite plane the equations corresponding to (A16) and (A17) become

$$-A_0 u_j = \sum_{n=1}^{\infty} A_n u_{j-n} + \epsilon_j \quad E\epsilon_j \epsilon_k^T = -\beta^2 A_0 \delta_{j,k} \quad (A22)$$

$$-\sum_{n=1}^{q} \hat{A}_n^q R_{n-j} = R_{-j}, \quad 1 \leq j \leq q, \quad q = 1, 2, \cdots$$

$$-A_0^q = \beta^2 \left[R_0 + \sum_{n=1}^{q} \hat{A}_n^q R_n \right]^{-1}$$

$$A_n^q = A_0^q \hat{A}_n^q, \quad \lim_{q \to \infty} A_n^q = A_n \quad (A23)$$

where $-A_0$ now is a symmetric, positive definite Toeplitz matrix. Written in terms of Z_1-transform variables defined in (A11) with

$$a_0(z_1) = \sum_{m=-\infty}^{\infty} a_{m,0} z_1^{-m} \quad (A24)$$

we obtain, again, the scalar qth-order AR model equations

$$-\sum_{n=1}^{q} \hat{a}_n^q(z_1) r_{n-j}(z_1) = r_j(z_1^{-1}), \quad j = 1, \cdots, q \quad (A25)$$

and

$$-a_0^q(z_1) = \beta^2 h(z_1), \quad h(z_1) \triangleq \left[r_0(z_1) + \sum_{n=1}^{q} \hat{a}_n^q(z_1) r_n(z_1) \right]^{-1}$$

$$\beta^2 = 1 \bigg/ \left(\frac{1}{2\pi} \int_{-\pi}^{\pi} h(z_1) \, d\omega \right), \quad z_1 = e^{j\omega},$$

$$S_\epsilon(z_1, z_2) = -\beta^2 a_0^q(z_1), \quad a_n^q(z_1) = a_0^q(z_1) \hat{a}_n^q(z_1),$$

$$a_n(z_1) = \lim_{q \to \infty} a_n^q(z_1). \quad (A26)$$

For a positive and analytic SDF, a unique semicausal MVR such as (A22) can be shown to exist and its coefficients could be identified via (A23) or equivalently via (A25) and (A26).

A.3 Noncausal Representations

For noncausal MVR's, the orthogonality condition gives

$$r(i,j;p,q) - \sum\sum_{(m,n) \neq (i,j)} a(i,j;m,n) r(m,n;p,q)$$

$$= \beta_{i,j}^2 \delta_{i,p} \delta_{j,q}.$$

Define

$a(i,j;i,j) = -1, A_{j,n} = \{a(i,j;m,n), \forall i,m\}, B_j = \text{Diag}\{\beta_{i,j}^2, \forall i\}.$

Using these we obtain the matrix equations similar to (50)

$$-\sum_n A_{j,n} R_{n,q} = B_j \delta_{j,q}, \quad \text{or} \quad -\mathcal{A}\mathcal{R} = \mathcal{B},$$

$$\text{or} \quad -\mathcal{A} = \mathcal{B}\mathcal{R}^{-1} \quad (A27)$$

where $\mathcal{A}$, $\mathcal{R}$, and $\mathcal{B}$ are block matrices defined as

$$\mathcal{A} = \{A_{j,n}, \forall j, n\}, \quad \mathcal{R} = \{R_{j,n}, \forall j, n\}, \quad \mathcal{B} = \text{Diag}\{B_j, \forall j\}.$$

From this, we can obtain, as in (54)

$$\beta_{i,j}^2 = 1/[(\mathcal{R}^{-1})_{i,i}]_{j,j}. \quad (A28)$$

Thus $\beta_{i,j}^2$ is obtained by finding the jth diagonal block of $\mathcal{R}^{-1}$. Then the ith diagonal term of this matrix block equals $\beta_{i,j}^{-2}$. $\mathcal{A}$ is now obtained directly from (A27).

The orthogonality condition also requires

$$Eu_{i,j} \epsilon_{p,q} = \beta_{i,j}^2 \delta_{i,p} \delta_{j,q}, \quad \forall i, j$$

which gives

$$E\epsilon_{i,j}\epsilon_{p,q} = r_\epsilon(i,p;j,q) = \begin{cases} \beta_{i,j}^2, & (i,j) = (p,q) \\ -a(i,j;p,q)\beta_{i,j}^2, & (i,j) \neq (p,q). \end{cases}$$
(A29)

Hence, the noncausal MVR of an arbitrary Gaussian field $\{u_{i,j}\}$ is given by

$$u_{i,j} = \sum\sum_{(m,n) \neq (i,j)} a(i,j;m,n) u_{m,n} + \epsilon_{i,j} \quad (A30)$$

where $\{\epsilon_{i,j}\}$ is a zero-mean *nonwhite* Gaussian random field whose covariances are given by (A29). For stationary random fields defined on the infinite plane, the two-dimensional noncausal MVR is obtained by a direct extension of the one-dimensional result (see (55) and (56)) as

$$r_{0,0}^+ u_{i,j} + \sum_{k=-\infty}^{\infty} \sum_{\substack{l=-\infty \\ (k,l) \neq (0,0)}}^{\infty} r_{k,l}^+ u_{i-k,j-l} = r_{0,0}^+ \epsilon_{i,j} \quad (A31)$$

$$r_{k,l}^+ = \frac{1}{2\pi} \int_{-\pi}^{\pi} S^{-1}(\omega_1, \omega_2) \exp\{j(k\omega_1 + l\omega_2)\} d\omega_1 d\omega_2,$$

$$\forall k, l \quad (A32)$$

$$E\epsilon_{i,j}\epsilon_{i+k,j+l} = r_\epsilon(k,l) = \begin{cases} 1/r_{0,0}^+, & (k,l) = (0,0) \\ r_{k,l}^+/(r_{0,0}^+)^2, & (k,l) \neq (0,0). \end{cases}$$
(A33)

A rational approximation of $S^{-1}(z_1, z_2)$ will yield a finite-order (approximate) realization. Clearly factorization of S is not required in the case of noncausal MVR's. Thus if S^{-1} is a two-dimensional polynomial

$$S^{-1}(z_1, z_2) = \sum_{k=-p}^{p} \sum_{l=-q}^{q} r_{k,l}^+ z_1^{-p} z_2^{-q} \quad (A34)$$

then the noncausal MVR is

$$\sum_{k=-p}^{p} \sum_{l=-q}^{q} r_{k,l}^+ u_{i-k,j-l} = r_{0,0}^+ \epsilon_{i,j} \quad (A35)$$

where $\{\epsilon_{i,j}\}$ is a zero mean moving average field with SDF

$$S_\epsilon(z_1, z_2) = \left(\sum_{k=-p}^{p} \sum_{l=-q}^{q} r_{k,l}^+ z_1^{-p} z_2^{-q} \right) \bigg/ (r_{0,0}^+)^2. \quad (A36)$$

REFERENCES

[1] A. K. Jain, *Multidimensional Techniques in Digital Image Processing*. To be published.

[2] W. K. Pratt, *Digital Image Processing*. New York: Wiley, 1978.

[3] N. Ahmed and K. R. Rao, *Orthogonal Transforms for Digital Signal Processing*. New York: Springer Verlag, 1975.

[4] E. O. Brigham, *The Fast Fourier Transform*. Englewood Cliffs, NJ: Prentice-Hall, 1974.

[5] H. F. Harmuth, *Transmission of Information by Orthogonal Signals*. New York: Springer Verlag, 1970.

[6] H. C. Andrews, *Computer Techniques in Image Processing*. New York: Academic Press, 1970.

[7] H. C. Andrews and B. R. Hunt, *Digital Image Restoration*. Englewood Cliffs, NJ: Prentice-Hall, 1977.

[8] A. Rosenfeld and A. Kak, *Digital Picture Processing*. New York: Academic Press, 1976.

[9] A. K. Jain, "Some new techniques in image processing," in *Proc. Symp. Current Math Problems in Image Science* (Naval Post Graduate School, Monterey, CA). North Hollywood, CA: Western Periodicals Co., Nov. 1976.

[10] A. K. Jain, "A sinusoidal family of unitary transforms," *IEEE Trans. Pattern Anal. Mach. Intelligence*, vol. PAMI-1, pp. 356-365, Oct. 1979.

[11] H. Hotelling, "Analysis of a complex of statistical variables into principal components," *J. Educ. Psychol.*, vol. 24, pp. 417-441, and 498-520, 1933.

[12] S. Watanabe, "Karhunen-Loeve expansion and factor analysis, theoretical remarks and applications," *Trans. 4th Prague Conf. Inform. Theory, Statist. Decision Functions, and Random Processes* (Prague, Czechoslovakia) pp. 635-660, 1965.

[13] H. P. Kramer and M. V. Mathews, "A linear coding for transmitting a set of correlated signals," *IRE Trans. Inform. Theory*, vol. IT-2, pp. 41-46, Sept. 1956.

[14] N. Ahmed, T. Natarajan, and K. R. Rao, "Discrete cosine transform," *IEEE Trans. Computers*, vol. C-23, pp. 90-93, Jan. 1974.

[15] M. Hamidi and J. Pearl, "Comparison of the cosine and Fourier transforms of Markov-1 signals," *IEEE Trans. Acoust. Speech, Signal Processing*, vol. ASSP-24, pp. 428-429, Oct. 1976.

[16] J. R. Jain and A. K. Jain, "Interframe adaptive data compression techniques for images," Tech. Rep. SIPL-79-2, Signal and Image Processing Lab., Dep. Elec., Comput. Eng., Univ. California, Davis, Aug. 1979.

[17] A. K. Jain, "Image data compression—A review," *Proc. IEEE*, vol. 69, pp. 349-389, Mar. 1981.

[18] —, "A fast Karhunen Loeve transform for a class of random processes," *IEEE Trans. Commun*, vol. COM-24, pp. 1023-1029, Sept. 1976.

[19] A. K. Jain, S. H. Wang, and Y. Z. Liao, "Fast Karhunen Loeve transform data compression studies," presented at Nat. Telecommun. Conf., Dallas, TX, Nov.-Dec. 1976.

[20] G. E. Forsythe and P. Henrici, "The cyclic Jacobi method for computing the principal values of a complex matrix," *Proc. Amer. Math. Soc.*, vol. 94, pp. 1-23, 1960.

[21] G. H. Golub and C. Reinsch, "Singular value decomposition and least squares solutions," *Numer. Math.*, vol. 14, pp. 403-420, 1970.

[22] S. Treitel and J. L. Shanks, "The design of multistage separable planar filters," *IEEE Trans. Geosci. Electron.*, vol. GE-9, pp. 10-27, Jan. 1971.

[23] T. S. Huang, W. F. Schreiber, and O. J. Tretiak, "Image processing," *Proc. IEEE*, vol. 59, pp. 1586-1609, Nov. 1971.

[24] M. M. Sondhi, "Image restoration: The removal of spatially invariant degradations," *Proc. IEEE*, vol. 60, pp. 842-853, July 1972.

[25] H. C. Andrews, "Two dimensional transforms," in *Picture Processing and Digital Filtering*, T. S. Huang, Ed. (Topics in Applied Physics Series, vol. 6), Berlin, Germany: Springer-Verlag, 1975.

[26] H. C. Andrews and C. L. Patterson, "Singular value decomposition (SVD) image coding," *IEEE Trans. Commun.*, vol. COM-24, pp. 425-432, Apr. 1976.

[27] R. E. Twoogood and S. K. Mitra, "Computer aided design of separable two-dimensional digital filters," *IEEE Trans. Acoust. Speech Signal Processing*, vol. ASSP-25, pp. 165-169, Apr. 1977.

[28] V. C. Klema and A. J. Laub, "The singular value decomposition: Its computation and some applications," *IEEE Trans. Automat. Contr.*, vol. AC-25, pp. 164-176, Apr. 1980.

[29] B. Ashjari and W. K. Pratt, "Supervised classification with singular value decomposition texture," USCIPI Rep. 860, Image Proc. Inst., USC, Los Angeles, CA. Mar. 1979.

[30] P. Whittle, *Prediction and Regulation by Linear Least-Squares Methods*. London, England: English Univ. Press, 1954.

[31] K. Astrom, *Introduction to Stochastic Control Theory*. New York: Academic Press, 1970.

[32] N. Levinson, "The Wiener RMS error criterion in filter design and prediction," *J. Math. Phys.*, vol. 25, pp. 261-278, Jan. 1947.

[33] J. Durbin, "The filtering of time series models," *Rev. Int. Inst. Stat.*, vol. 28, pp. 233-244, 1960.

[34] J. Burg, "Maximum entropy spectral analysis," Ph.D. dissertation, Dep. Geophysics, Stanford Univ., Stanford, CA, 1975.

[35] S. Zohar, "Toeplitz matrix inversion: The algorithm of W. F. Trench," *J. Assoc. Comput. Mach.*, vol. 16, pp. 592-601, Oct. 1969.

[36] T. J. Ulrych and T. N. Bishop, "Maximum entropy spectral analysis and autoregressive decomposition," *Rev. Geophys. Space Phys.*, vol. 13, pp. 183-200, Feb. 1975.

[37] J. Makhoul, "Linear prediction: A tutorial review," *Proc. IEEE*, vol. 63, pp. 561-580, Apr. 1975.

[38] A. K. Jain and S. Ranganath, "Image coding by autoregressive synthesis," *Proc. IEEE ICASSP '80* (Denver, CO), pp. 770-773, Apr. 1980.

[39] N. E. Nahi and T. Assefi, "Bayesian recursive image estimation," *IEEE Trans. Comput.* (Short Notes), vol. C-21, pp. 734-738, July 1972.

[40] T. Assefi, "Two dimensional signal processing with application to image restoration," Tech. Rep. 32-1596, JPL, Caltech, Pasadena, CA, Sept. 1, 1974.

[41] N. E. Nahi and C. A. Franco, "Application of Kalman filtering to image enhancement," in *Proc. IEEE Conf. Decision and Control* (New Orleans, LA), pp. 63-65, Dec. 1972.

[42] S. R. Powell and L. M. Silverman, "Modeling of two dimensional covariance functions with application to image restoration," *IEEE Trans. Automat. Cont.*, vol. AC-19, pp. 8-12, Feb. 1974.

[43] N. E. Nahi, *Estimation Theory and Applications*. New York: Wiley, 1969.

[44] A. H. Jazwinsky, *Stochastic Processes and Filtering Theory*. New York: Academic Press, pp. 70-92, 1970.

[45] A. O. Aboutalib and L. M. Silverman, "Restoration of motion degraded images," *IEEE Trans. Circuits Syst.*, vol. CAS-22, pp. 278-286, Mar. 1975.

[46] A. K. Jain, "Noncausal representations for finite discrete signals," in *Proc. IEEE Conf. Decision and Control* (Tucson, AZ), 1974.

[47] A. K. Jain and E. Angel, "Image restoration, modeling and reduction of dimensionality," *IEEE Trans. Comput.*, vol. C-23, pp. 470-476, May 1974.

[48] A. K. Jain, "A fast Karhunen-Loeve transform for recursive filtering of images corrupted by white and colored noise," *IEEE Trans. Comput.*, vol. C-26, pp. 560-571, June 1977.

[49] —, "An operator factorization method for restoration of blurred images," *IEEE Trans. Comput.*, vol. C-25, pp. 1061-1071, Nov. 1977.

[50] —, "Image coding via a nearest neighbors image model," *IEEE Trans. Commun.*, vol. COM-23, pp. 318-331, Mar. 1975.

[51] —, "Partial differential equations and finite difference methods in image processing, Part I—Image representation," *J. Optimization Theory Appl.*, vol. 23, no. 1, pp. 65-91, Sept. 1977.

[52] A. K. Jain and J. R. Jain, "Partial differential equations and finite difference methods in image processing, Part II: Image restoration," *IEEE Trans. Automat. Contr.*, vol. AC-23, pp. 817-834, Oct. 1978.

[53] A. Zvi Meiri, "The pinned Karhunen Loeve transform of a two dimensional Gauss-Markov field," in *Proc. 1976 SPIE Meeting* (San Diego, CA), 1976.

[54] A. K. Jain, "Fast inversion of banded Toeplitz matrices circular decompositions," *IEEE Trans. ASSP*, vol. ASSP-26, pp. 121-126, Oct. 1978.

[55] —, "A semicausal model for recursive filtering of two dimensional images," *IEEE Trans. Comput.*, vol. C-26, pp. 343-350, Apr. 1977.

[56] T. L. Marzetta, "A linear prediction approach to two dimensional spectral factorization and spectral estimation," Ph.D. dissertation, Dep. Elec. Eng. Comput. Sci., MIT, Cambridge, MA, Feb. 1978.

[57] S. H. Wang, "Applications of stochastic models for image data compression," Ph.D. dissertation, Dep. Elec. Eng., SUNY Buffalo, NY, Sept. 1979; Also see S. H. Wang and A. K. Jain, Tech. Rep. SIPL-79-6, Signal and Image Processing Lab., Dep. Elec. Comput. Eng., Univ. California Davis, Sept. 1979.

[58] A. K. Jain and S. H. Wang, "Stochastic image models and hybrid coding," Final Rep., NOSC Contract N00953-77-C-003MJE, Dep. Elec. Eng., SUNY Buffalo, NY, Oct. 1977.

[59] A. K. Jain, "Spectral estimation and signal extrapolation in one and two dimensions," in *Proc. RADC Spectrum Estimation Workshop* (Rome, NY), pp. 195-214, Oct. 1979.

[60] E. Angel and A. K. Jain, "Frame to frame restoration of diffusion images," *IEEE Trans. Automat. Contr.*, vol. AC-23, pp. 850-855, Oct. 1978.

[61] N. Wiener, *Extrapolation, Interpolation and Smoothing of Stationary Time Series*. New York: Wiley, 1949.

[62] J. L. Doob, *Stochastic Processes*. New York: Wiley, 1953.

[63] C. L. Rino, "Factorization of spectra by discrete Fourier transforms," *IEEE Trans. Inform. Theory*, vol. IT-16, pp. 484-485, July 1970.

[64] M. P. Ekstrom and J. W. Woods, "Two dimensional spectral factorization with application in recursive digital filtering," *IEEE Trans. Acoust. Speech Signal Processing*, vol. ASSP-24, pp. 115-128, Apr. 1976.

[65] T. S. Huang, "Stability of two dimensional recursive filters," *IEEE Trans. Audio Electroacoust.*, vol. AU-20, pp. 158-163, June 1972.

[66] *Proceedings IEEE*, vol. 65, Special Issue on Multidimensional Systems (Guest Editor N. K. Bose), June 1977.

[67] D. Goodman, "Some stability properties of two dimensional linear shift invariant filters," *IEEE Trans. Circuits Syst.*, vol. CAS-24, pp. 201-208, Apr. 1977.

[68] J. W. Woods, "Two dimensional discrete Markov fields," *IEEE Trans. Inform. Theory*, vol. IT-18, pp. 232-240, Mar. 1972.

[69] W. E. Larimore, "Statistical inference on stationary random fields," *Proc. IEEE*, vol. 65, pp. 961-970, June 1977.

[70] S. Sugimoto, H. Mizutani and T. Mizokawa, "Causality and recursive estimation of two dimensional random image fields," in *Proc. 8th SICE Symp. Control Theory*, pp. 145-150, Hachigi, Tokyo, 1979.

[71] H. Mizutani and S. Sugimoto, "Semicausal models and smoothing for 2-D random image fields," in *Proc. 11th JAACE Symp. Stoch. Syst.* (Tokyo, Japan), pp. 161-164, Nov. 1979.

[72] T. Kailath, D. O. Mayne, and R. K. Mehra, Eds., *IEEE Trans. Aut. Contr.*, Special Issue on System Identification and Time Series Analysis, vol. AC-19, Dec. 1974.

[73] B. R. Hunt, "The application of constrained least squares estimation to image restoration by digital computer," *IEEE Trans. Comput.*, vol. C-22, pp. 805-812, Sept. 1973.

[74] R. W. Means, E. H. Wrench, and H. J. Whitehouse, "Image transmission via spread spectrum techniques," ARPA Quart. Tech. Rep. ARPA-QR6, Nav. Ocean Syst. Cent., San Diego, CA, Jan.-Dec. 1975; Also see ARPA-QR8, Annu. Rep., Jan.-Dec. 1975.

[75] B. R. Hunt, "Digital image processing," *Proc. IEEE*, vol. 63, pp. 693-708, Apr. 1975.

[76] A. Habibi, "Two dimensional Bayesian estimate of images," *Proc. IEEE*, vol. 60, pp. 878-883, July 1972.

[77] M. Strintzis, "Comments on two dimensional Bayesian estimate of images," *Proc. IEEE*, vol. 64, pp. 1255-1257, Aug. 1976.

[78] N. E. Nahi and A. Habibi, "Decision directed recursive image enhancement," *IEEE Trans. Circuits Syst.*, vol. CAS-22, pp. 286-293, Mar. 1975.

[79] J. W. Woods and C. H. Radewan, "Kalman filtering in two dimensions," *IEEE Trans. Inform. Theory*, vol. IT-23, pp. 473-482, July 1977.

[80] M. S. Murphy and L. M. Silverman, "Image model representation and line by line recursive restoration," in *Proc. Conf. Decision Contr.* (Clearwater Beach, FL), pp. 601-606, Dec. 1976.

[81] A. Netravali and J. Limb, "Picture coding: A survey," *Proc. IEEE*, vol. 68, pp. 366-406, Mar. 1980.

[82] W. F. Schreiber, C. F. Knapp, and N. D. Kay, "Synthetic highs: An experimental TV bandwidth reduction system," *J. Soc. Motion Pic. Television Engrs.*, vol. 68, pp. 525-537, Aug. 1959.

[83] D. N. Graham, "Image transmission by two dimensional contour coding," *Proc. IEEE*, vol. 55, pp. 336-346, Mar. 1967.

[84] J. K. Yan and D. J. Sakrison, "Encoding of images based on a two component source model," *IEEE Trans. Commun.*, vol. COM-25, pp. 1315-1322, Nov. 1977.

[85] W. Rudin, "The extension problem for positive definite functions," *Ill. J. Math.*, vol. 7, pp. 532-539, 1963.

[86] B. W. Dickinson, "Two dimensional Markov spectrum estimates need not exist," *IEEE Trans. Inform. Theory*, vol. IT-26, pp. 120-121, Jan. 1980.

[87] R. P. Roesser, "A discrete state space model for linear image processing," *IEEE Trans. Automat. Contr.*, vol. AC-20, pp. 1-10, Feb. 1975.

[88] S. Attasi, "Modelling and recursive estimation for double indexed sequences," IRIA Rep. IA/129, Domaine de Volvceau, Racquencourt, 78150 Le Chesnay, B.P. 5, France, July 1975.

[89] E. Fornasini and G. Marchesini, "State space realization theory of two dimensional filters," *IEEE Trans. Automat. Contr.*, vol. AC-21, pp. 484-492, Aug. 1976.

[90] E. Wong, "Recursive causal linear filtering for two dimensional random fields," *IEEE Trans. Inform. Theory*, vol. IT-24, pp. 50-59, Jan. 1978.

[91] M. Morf, B. Levy, and S. Y. Kung, "New results in 2-D systems theory, Part I: 2-D polynomial matrices, factorization and coprimeness," *Proc. IEEE*, vol. 65, pp. 861-872, June 1977.

[92] S. Y. Kung, B. C. Levy, M. Morf, and T. Kailath, "New results in 2-D systems theory, Part II: Realization and the notions of controllability, observability and minimality," *Proc. IEEE*, vol. 65, pp. 945-960, June 1977.

[93] A. K. Jain and K. W. Au, "On linear estimation via fast Fourier transform," in *Proc. Conf. Decision and Control* (Ft. Lauderdale, FL), Dec. 1979.

[94] J. W. Woods, "Two dimensional Markov spectral estimation," *IEEE Trans. Inform. Theory*, vol. IT-22, pp. 552-559, Sept. 1976; also see vol. IT-26, pp. 129-130, Jan. 1980.

[95] E. S. Angel and A. K. Jain, "Restoration of images degraded by spatially varying point spread functions by a conjugate gradient method," *Appl. Opt.*, vol. 17, pp. 2186-2190, July 1980.

Markov Random Field Texture Models

GEORGE R. CROSS, MEMBER, IEEE, AND ANIL K. JAIN, MEMBER, IEEE

Abstract—We consider a texture to be a stochastic, possibly periodic, two-dimensional image field. A texture model is a mathematical procedure capable of producing and describing a textured image. We explore the use of Markov random fields as texture models. The binomial model, where each point in the texture has a binomial distribution with parameter controlled by its neighbors and "number of tries" equal to the number of gray levels, was taken to be the basic model for the analysis. A method of generating samples from the binomial model is given, followed by a theoretical and practical analysis of the method's convergence. Examples show how the parameters of the Markov random field control the strength and direction of the clustering in the image. The power of the binomial model to produce blurry, sharp, line-like, and blob-like textures is demonstrated. Natural texture samples were digitized and their parameters were estimated under the Markov random field model. A hypothesis test was used for an objective assessment of goodness-of-fit under the Markov random field model. Overall, microtextures fit the model well. The estimated parameters of the natural textures were used as input to the generation procedure. The synthetic microtextures closely resembled their real counterparts, while the regular and inhomogeneous textures did not.

Index Terms—Binomial model, goodness-of-fit, hypothesis test, image modeling, Markov random field, texture.

I. INTRODUCTION

THE subject of image modeling involves the construction of models or procedures for the specification of images. These models serve a dual role in that they can describe images that are observed and also can serve to generate synthetic images from the model parameters. We will be concerned with a specific type of image model, the class of texture models.

There are four important areas of image processing in which texture plays an important role: classification [25], [51], image segmentation [15], [40], [49], realism in computer graphics [5], [6], [9], [10], [13], [17], and image encoding [16], [39]. Besides being an intrinsic feature of realistic objects [32], [42], texture also gives important information on the depth and orientation of an object. Julesz [30], [31] considers the problem of generation of familiar textures an important one from both the theoretical and practical viewpoints. Understanding texture is also an essential part of understanding human vision [36], [37]. These considerations have led to an increased activity in the area of texture analysis and synthesis.

There is no universally accepted definition for texture. Part of the difficulty in giving a definition of texture is the extremely large number of attributes of texture that we would like to subsume under a definition. We consider a texture to be a stochastic, possibly periodic, two-dimensional image field. We mention a study by Tamura *et al.* [48] which attempted to find statistical features corresponding to the usual attributes of texture. The study delimited six attributes: coarseness, contrast, directionality, line-likeness, regularity, and roughness.

Most texture research can be characterized by the underlying assumptions made about the texture formation process. There are two major assumptions, and the choice of the assumption depends primarily on the type of textures to be considered in the study. The first assumption, which is called the placement rule viewpoint [43], [53], considers a texture to be composed of primitives. These primitives may be of varying or deterministic shape, such as circles, hexagons, or even dot patterns. Macrotextures have large primitives, whereas microtextures are composed of small primitives. These terms are relative to the image resolution [14]. The textured image is formed from the primitives by placement rules which specify how the primitives are oriented, both on the image field and with respect to each other. Examples of such textures include tilings of the plane, cellular structures such as tissue samples, and a picture of brick wall.

The second viewpoint regarding texture generation processes involves the stochastic assumption. The placement rule paradigm for textures may include a random aspect; in the stochastic point of view, however, we take a more extreme position and consider that the texture is a sample from a probability distribution on the image space. The image space is usually an $N \times N$ grid and the value at each grid point is a random variable in the range $\{0, 1, \cdots, G-1\}$. Textures such as sand, grass, and water are not appropriately described by a placement model. The key feature of these images is that the primitives are very random in shape and cannot be easily described.

In this paper we will explore the use of a Markov random field model for the generation and analysis of textured images. The goal of the research is to produce a texture analysis and synthesis system which will take as input a texture, analyze its parameters according to the Markov random field model, and then generate a textured image that both resembles the input texture visually and matches it closely from a statistical point of view. This can be considered a kind of Turing test for image generation [50], in that the proof of the viability of the system will be to produce textures that cannot be distinguished by humans from their real counterparts. We will not perform a rigorous psychological study of the correspondence, but will concentrate on the statistical evaluation of the goodness-of-fit of the observed texture and the generated texture.

II. Texture Models

By a model of a texture, we mean a mathematical process which creates or describes the textured image. The primary goal of texture modeling is the description of real textures. A secondary goal of texture modeling is classification of textures. The numerical parameters of the model can be used as features to classify the texture. There is a distinction between model-based studies and attempts to find good features for the classification of textures. In a model-based environment, we have the capability to produce, for example, textures that match observed textures. In a feature-based texture analysis, the textural features are measured without an ideal or representative texture in mind. A substantial portion of texture research has been done at the feature-based level. A survey of the well-known and commonly used texture features appears in a recent paper [26].

Our interest here is in texture models which take the stochastic process approach. Ideally, we would like to find a stochastic process that is physically meaningful and related to the texture which we are modeling. One can use more prior information about the texture in a model-based approach than in the feature-based approach. In the stochastic process approach, brightness levels or pixel gray values are the random variables. The level $X(i,j)$ at some point (i,j) is not independent of the levels at other points in the image. In fact our principal concern is about the correlations between the $\{X(i,j)\}$.

The models which have been used to generate and represent textures include:
1) time series models [34]
2) fractals [35]
3) random mosaic models [2], [39], [44], [45]
4) mathematical morphology [46]
5) syntactic methods [18], [33]
6) linear models [15], [16].

III. Markov Random Fields

The brightness level at a point in an image is highly dependent on the brightness levels of neighboring points unless the image is simply random noise. In this section, we explain a precise model of this dependence, called the Markov random field. The notion of near-neighbor dependence is all-pervasive in image processing. Focusing directly on this property is a promising approach to the overall problem of microtextures.

The study of Markov random fields has had a long history, beginning with Ising's 1925 thesis [29] on ferromagnetism. Although it did not prove to be a realistic model for magnetic domains, it is approximately correct for phase-separated alloys, idealized gases, and some crystals [41]. The model has traditionally been applied to the case of either Gaussian or binary variables on a lattice. Besag [4] allows a natural extension to the case of variables that have integer ranges, either bounded or unbounded. These extensions, coupled with estimation procedures, permit the application of the Markov random field to texture modeling.

The Markov random field model has been briefly investigated by Hassner and Sklansky [27]. Their work was limited to an exposition of the equivalence between the Gibbs field and Markov random field expressions for the conditional probability distributions (see Spitzer [47] for the proof) and generation of a few examples of textures. Moreover, they limited their attention to the binary case.

An alternative to the full two-dimensional Markov random field for images is to traverse the lattice along a scan line and provide a direct analog to the usual Markov chain [1]. Connors and Harlow [11] generated streaky line textures according to a simple Markov chain that ignores the correlations between pixels in neighboring rows. Haralick and Yokoyama [52] generated essentially one-dimensional textures using scans, but provided some correlations between neighboring rows by considering changes in the features computed from the co-occurrence matrices.

A. Definitions

Our exposition follows Besag [4] and Bartlett [3]. Let $X(i,j)$ denote the brightness level at a point (i,j) on the $N \times N$ lattice L. We simplify the labeling of the $X(i,j)$ to be $X(i)$, $i = 1, 2, \cdots, M$ where $M = N^2$.

Definition 1: Let L be a lattice. A *coloring of L* (or a *coloring of L with G levels*) denoted X is a function from the points of L to the set $\{0, 1, \cdots, G - 1\}$. The notation **0** denotes the function that assigns each point of the lattice to 0.

Definition 2: The point j is said to be a neighbor of the point i if

$$p(X(i)|X(1), X(2), \cdots, X(i-1), X(i+2), \cdots, X(M))$$

depends on $X(j)$.

Note that Definition 2 does not imply that the neighbors of a point are necessarily close in terms of distance, although this is the usual case. Now we can give the definition of a Markov random field.

Definition 3: A *Markov random field* is a joint probability density on the set of all possible colorings X of the lattice L subject to the following conditions.
1) *Positivity:* $p(X) > 0$ for all X.
2) *Markovianity:*

$p(X(i)|\text{all point in the lattice except } i)$
$= p(X(i)|\text{neighbors of } i)$

3) *Homogeneity:* $p(X(i)|\text{neighbors of } i)$ depends only on the configuration of neighbors and is translation invariant (with respect to translates with the same neighborhood configuration).

The Hammersley-Clifford theorem [4] delimits the functions admissible as conditional probability distributions at each point of the lattice and provides a connection between the purely graph-theoretic relationships on a lattice with the algebraic form of the density function. The general formulation of distributions satisfying the above three conditions is given by Besag [4]. We limit our attention to the case where the probability of a point $X(i,j)$ having gray level k is binomial, with parameter determined by its neighbors. This is Besag's formulation of the *autobinomial* distribution.

B. Order Dependence and Anisotropy

In most cases, we are interested in the models where the point i is a neighbor of the point j if i is close to j.

The probability $p(X = k|\text{neighbors})$ is binomial with parameter $\theta(T)$ and number of tries $G - 1$ where G is the number of gray levels. The value of T is given in (1)-(5) for models of various orders. The $b(i, k)$ are the parameters of the model and are 0 for all i larger than the order. The value of a indirectly controls the lattice process. We have limited our attention to case of a maximum fourth-order dependence since higher order parameters cannot be estimated from 64×64 images:

$$\theta = \frac{\exp(T)}{1 + \exp(T)} \tag{1}$$

where a first-order model has the form for T:

$$T = a + b(1, 1)(t + t') + b(1, 2)(u + u'). \tag{2}$$

A second-order model has a T of the form

$$T = a + b(1, 1)(t + t') + b(1, 2)(u + u') + b(2, 1)(v + v') + b(2, 2)(z + z'). \tag{3}$$

A third-order model takes the form

$$T = a + b(1, 1)(t + t') + b(1, 2)(u + u') + b(2, 1)(v + v') + b(2, 2)(z + z') + b(3, 1)(m + m') + b(3, 2)(1 + 1'). \tag{4}$$

Finally, a fourth-order model is obtained by adding an additional term of the form

$$b(4, 1)(o1 + o1' + o2 + o2') + b(4, 2)(q1 + q1' + q2 + q2') \tag{5}$$

to the form for the third-order T. Additional high-order terms can be obtained by extending the orders in a similar way beyond those in Fig. 1.

The formal definition of order can now be given.

Definition 4: The *order* of a Markov random field process on a lattice is the largest value of i such that $b(i, 1)$ or $b(i, 2)$ is nonzero.

Definition 5: A Markov random field is *isotropic at order i* if $b(i, 1) = b(i, 2)$. Otherwise, it is said to be *anisotropic at order i*. The notation $b(i, \cdot)$ implies isotropy at order i and signifies the common value of $b(i, 1) = b(i, 2)$.

The notion of anisotropy agrees with our intuitive notion of directionality in textures. For example, positive values of the clustering parameter $b(1, 1)$ cause clustering in the horizontal direction, whereas $b(1, 2)$ controls clustering in the vertical direction. The $b(2, 1)$ and $b(2, 2)$ control clustering in the diagonal directions. Positive values of these parameters cause attraction; negative values result in repulsion, or a checkerboard effect. More complex types of anisotropy and nonlinear terms can be put into (2)-(5). Cross [12] discusses other models.

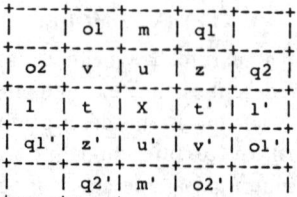

Fig. 1. Neighbors of the point X.

The binary case, where the point variables have range $\{0, 1\}$, is a special case of the binomial model. We obtain the conditional probability of x by

$$p(X = x|T) = \frac{\exp(xT)}{1 + \exp(T)}. \tag{6}$$

When dealing with a finite rectangular lattice and using the definitions of neighbor and order above, points on the edge of the lattice have fewer neighbors than the interior points. We compensate for this by assuming that the lattice has a periodic or torus structure. This means that the left edge is connected to the right edge and the upper edge is connected to the lower edge.

IV. Simulation of Markov Random Fields

In order to generate textures that are the visual representation of Markov random fields, we need a procedure that yields a sample from a Markov random field with given parameters. Fortunately, such procedures exist and have been used extensively in physics to investigate the properties of two- and three-dimensional Ising lattice [7], [22], [20]. Hassner and Sklansky use a procedure that seems to be similar to the classical ones with the addition of a preprocessing step that seems to eliminate some unlikely neighborhood configurations [28]. Simulation is usually needed to estimate many of the properties of Markov random fields since the analytical calculations are, for the most part unsatisfactory [21].

The required theory for the simulation of Markov random fields comes from the theory of discrete, finite-state Markov chains. We want a Markov chain whose states are the set of colorings $\{X\}$ with limiting distribution $\{p(X)\}$. We can sample such a chain and observe colorings $\{X\}$ with frequency given by $\{p(X)\}$. Theorems are available which do the following.

1) Give sufficient conditions for a Markov chain to have a unique limiting distribution [19, p. 393]. These conditions are met in our case.

2) Show how to convert a relatively arbitrary symmetric Markov chain to one with specified limiting distribution $\{q(j)\}$. The key feature of this theorem is the fact that we need only know the ratios $\{q(j)/q(i)\}$ in order to obtain the desired chain [24].

Theorem: Consider a symmetric, aperiodic, irreducible Markov chain with transition matrix P^*. Let $\{q(j)\}$ be a set of positive numbers with sum 1. Then the Markov chain with transition matrix P has limit distribution $\{q(j)\}$, where P is

```
while not STABLE do
    begin
        choose sites X(1),X(2) with X(1) <> X(2);
        r := P(Y)/P(X);
        if r => 1
            then switch X(1),X(2)
            else
                begin
                    u:=uniform random on [0,1];
                    if r > u
                        then switch X(1),X(2)
                        else retain X
                end
    end;
```

Fig. 2. Algorithm for generating Markov random field with joint probability function $p(X)$. The coloring Y is obtained from the coloring X by switching the values of the points $X(1)$ and $X(2)$. Variables with underbars appear boldface in text.

defined by

$$p(i,j) = \begin{cases} p^*(i,j) q(j)/q(i) & \text{if } q(i) > q(j) \\ p^*(i,j) & \text{if } q(j) \geq q(i) \end{cases}$$

$$p(i,i) = p^*(i,i) + \sum_{j}' p^*(i,j)(1 - q(j)/q(i))$$

where the prime on the summation means summation over all indices with j with $q(j)/q(i)$ less than 1.

3) Allow us to calculate the set of ratios $\{q(j) q/(i)\} = \{p(Y)/p(X)\}$ from the conditional distribution of a Markov random field without explicit calculation of the set of $\{p(X)\}$ [4].

Theorem: Let X and Y be two colorings of the Markov random field lattice L. Then

$$\frac{p(Y)}{p(X)} = \prod_{i=1}^{M} \frac{p(X(i) = y(i)|X(1), X(2), \cdots, X(i-1), Y(i+1), \cdots, Y(N))}{p(X(i) = x(i)|X(1), X(2), \cdots, X(i-1), Y(i+1), \cdots, Y(N))}.$$

A. Texture Generation Procedure

In general, we are interested in textures with the same number of pixels at each gray level. This is done by starting with an image that is generated by coloring the point (i,j) with level k, where k is chosen with equal probability from the set $\{0, 1, 2, \cdots, G-1\}$. The convergence to the limit distribution is unaffected by the choice of initial configuration; only the rate at which equilibrium is reached depends on the choice of the initial configuration. Given a state (i.e., coloring) X, we choose the next state Y to be the same as X except that the gray values of two randomly selected points are interchanged. The algorithm is diagrammed in Fig. 2. The algorithm was used by Flinn [21] and was invented by Metropolis et al. [38].

B. Convergence Properties

A theorem of Hammersley [24] guarantees that the application of the algorithm in Fig. 2 will eventually result in a lattice with the desired distribution. The practical question is how long this will take.

We first need to define a time-dimension for the simulation. Suppose that the lattice is $N \times N$ and let $M = N^2$. We consider M attempted exchanges or switches to constitute one *iteration*. Notice that this ignores attempted exchanges between pixels of the same color. It was observed experimentally that in ten iterations or less, either the number of changes drops to 1 percent of M or the measured parameters match the input parameters to within about 5 percent. These guidelines define the variable "STABLE" in Fig. 2. On a PDP-11/34 computer, the time required for one iteration on a 64 × 64 image was 2-3 min depending on the number of gray levels.

We give an example of the convergence for a specific case. The purpose of this example is not to prove convergence, which is a consequence of the mathematical results discussed at the beginning of this section, but rather to give some indication of the convergence rate. We want to simulate a first-order binary Markov random field with parameters

$$a = -2$$
$$b(1, \cdot) = 1$$

on a 128 × 128 lattice. The estimated parameters $b(1, \cdot)$ are shown plotted against number of iterations in Fig. 3. The graph flattens rather quickly and stays rather within 0.05 of the intended value of 1.0 for $b(1, \cdot)$. The parameter estimate which is plotted in Fig. 4 is the average of two estimates, performed on two different codings, as explained in Section V-A. The two estimates agree within about 12 percent. Fig. 4 shows the number of changes observed per 256 attempted exchanges, as the estimates were made every 1/64 iteration. Thus, although in an iteration of M attempted exchanges we are still observing nearly $M/2$ changes, the chain is near equilibrium, as the observed model parameters are within a small tolerance of the intended parameters.

C. Examples of Textures

We present some examples of textures generated according to various settings of Markov random field parameters. These images are representative of the kind of results that can be

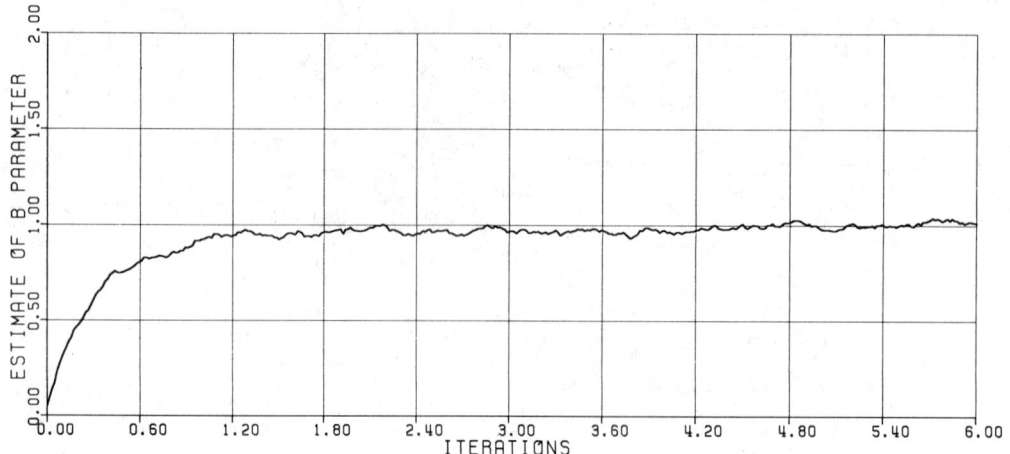

Fig. 3. Convergence of $b(1, \cdot)$.

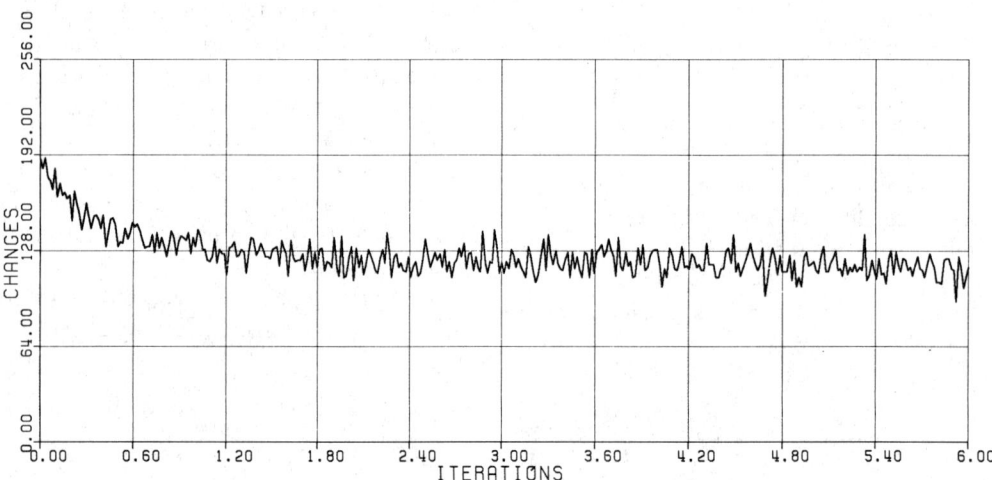

Fig. 4. Behavior of number of exchanges.

achieved but are not necessarily attempts to imitate real textures. They should rather be considered to be an "alphabet" of Markov random field textures. In Section V, we exhibit generated textures matching observed textures.

1) *Clustering Effects:* Fig. 5 shows a series of 64 × 64 binary textures generated according to an isotropic first-order model. Fig. 5(a) represents "noise," i.e., the probability of a pixel being black or white is 0.5, independently of all other pixels. In Markov random field terms,

$a = b(1, \cdot) = 0.$

The value of $b(1, \cdot)$ is increased from 0 to Fig. 5(a) to 3.0 in Fig. 5(h). The increase in clustering is clearly visible.

2) *Anisotropic Effects:* Fig. 6 shows extreme anisotropy in first-order and second-order model on a 64 × 64 lattice. The quantity $b(1, 1)$ controls the horizontal clustering; $b(1, 2)$ causes vertical clustering. In Fig. 6(a), large positive values of $b(1, 2)$ and large negative values of $b(1, 1)$ result in "clean" vertical lines. Contrast this with Fig. 6(b), which has thickened and noisy horizontal lines because of the small positive value of the vertical clustering parameters. The decidedly diagonal effect of Fig. 6(c) results from the use of a second-order structure. The clustering i the NW-SE direction is pronounced since the parameter in this direction is 1.9 and the parameters in all other directions are quite small.

3) *Ordered Patterns:* Many of the applications of the Ising model involve studying the checkerboard-like patterns obtained with negative clustering parameters [41]. This is illustrated by Fig. 7, where the most likely configuration is a black pixel surrounded by four white pixels or vice versa.

4) *Attraction-Repulsion Effects:* An attraction-repulsion process involves having low-order parameters positive, resulting, in clustering but high-order parameters negative in order to inhibit the growth of clusters. If high-order parameters were also positive, large clusters would result, whereas negative high-order parameters yield small clusters. Fig. 8 shows the effect of anisotropic clustering with inhibition. Fig. 8(b) contains longer horizontal and vertical lines than Fig. 8(a) because of the larger values of the first-order clustering parameters $b(1, 1)$ and $b(1, 2)$. Fig. 9 shows two isotropic attraction-repulsion textures. Cluster sizes are small here because of the high-order inhibition.

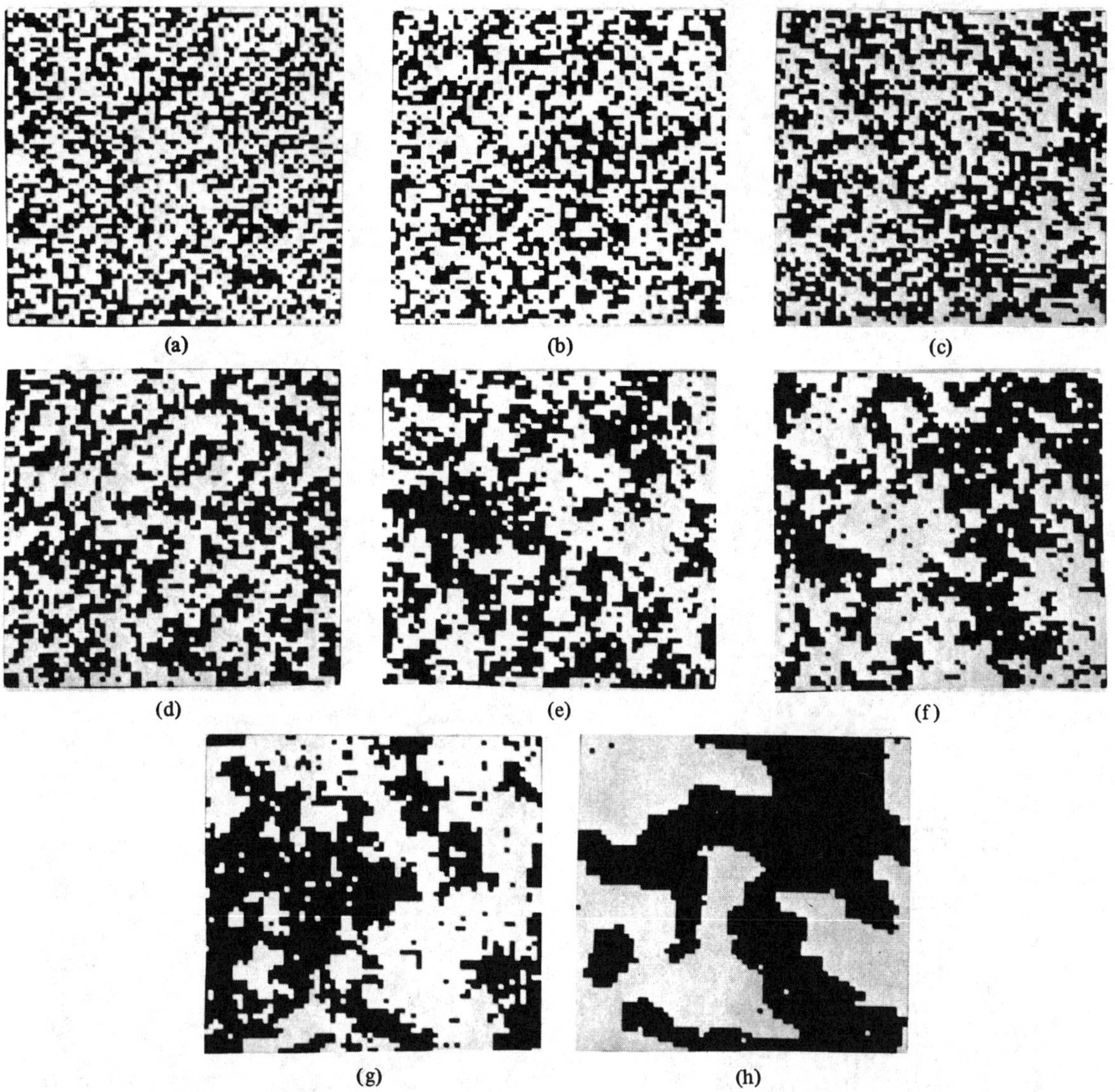

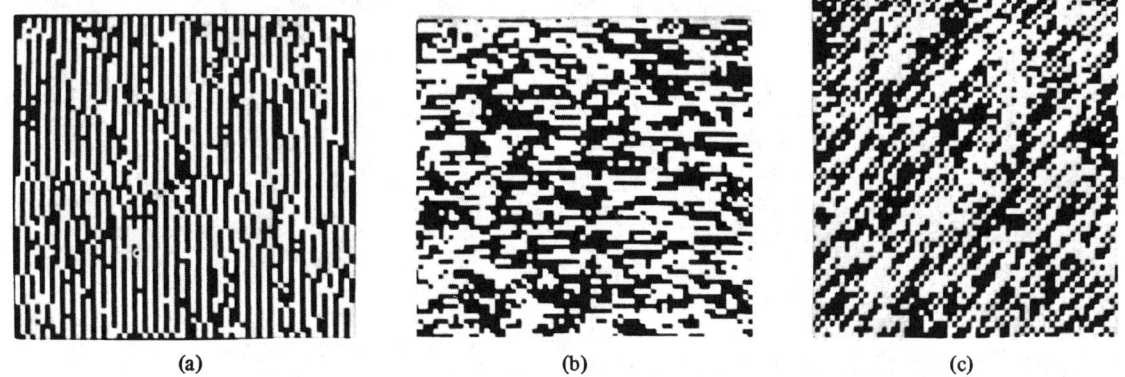

Fig. 5. Isotropic first-order textures. The $b(1, \cdot)$ parameters are: (a) 0.0, (b) 0.50, (c) 0.75, (d) 1.1, (e) 1.26, (f) 1.52, (g) 1.79, (h) 3.0. In all cases, the a parameter is $-2b(1, \cdot)$.

Fig. 6. Anisotopic line textures. The parameters are (a) $a = -0.26$, $b(1, 1) = -2$, $b(1, 2) = 2.1$, $b(2, 1) = 0.13$, $b(2, 2) = 0.015$. (b) $a = -2.04$, $b(1, 1) = 1.93$, $b(1, 2) = 0.16$, $b(2, 1) = 0.07$, $b(2, 2) = 0.02$. (c) $a = -1.9$, $b(1, 1) = -0.1$, $b(1, 2) = 0.1$, $b(2, 1) = 1.9$, $b(2, 2) = -0.075$.

Fig. 7. Ordered pattern. The parameters are $a = 5.09$, $b(1, 1) = -2.25$, $b(1, 2) = -2.16$.

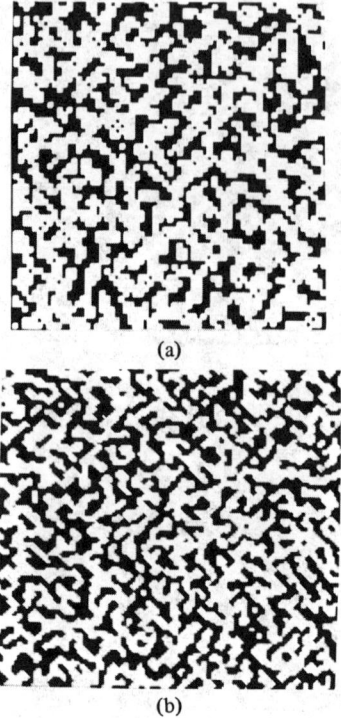

Fig. 9. Isotropic inhibition textures. The parameter values are (a) $a = -0.97$, $b(1, \cdot) = 0.94$, $b(2, \cdot) = 0.94$, $b(3, \cdot) = -0.42$, $b(4, \cdot) = -0.49$. (b) $a = -4.6$, $b(1, \cdot) = 2.62$, $b(2, \cdot) = 2.17$, $b(3, \cdot) = -0.78$, $b(4, \cdot) = -0.85$.

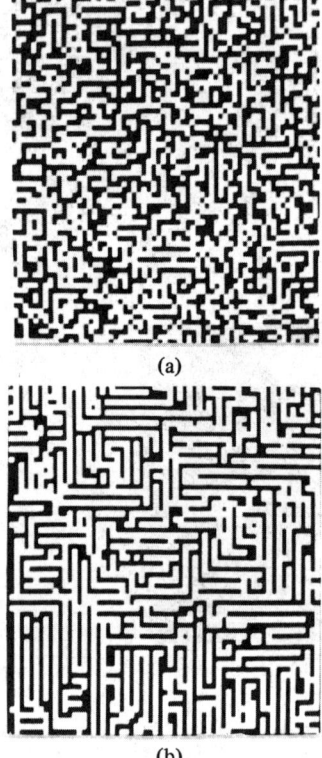

Fig. 8. Diagonal inhibition textures. The parameters are (a) $a = 2.19$, $b(1, 1) = -0.088$, $b(1, 2) = -0.009$, $b(2, 1) = -1$, $b(2, 2) = -1$. (b) $a = 0.16$, $b(1, 1) = 2.06$, $b(1, 2) = 2.05$, $b(1, 2) = -2.03$, $b(2, 2) = -2.10$.

5) Multiple Gray Scale Textures: We now turn our attention to the binomial model. Fig. 10 shows a 4-gray level picture with considerable clustering. Fig. 10(a) is isotropic and first-order, whereas Fig. 10(b) is second-order anisotropic with diagonal clustering. Fig. 11(a) and (b) represents typical multiple gray scale pictures with isotropic clustering.

Fig. 12 shows a pattern similar to Fig. 6, but with 32 gray levels. The resemblance to wood-grain is apparent. Fig. 13(a) and (b) shows the result of attraction–repulsion processes with multiple gray levels. Fig. 13(a) has the appearance of reticulated photographic film due to strong third- and fourth-order inhibition. The diagonality in Fig. 13(b) is a result of strong repulsion in some directions and clustering in others.

It should be noted that many of these images appear blurry

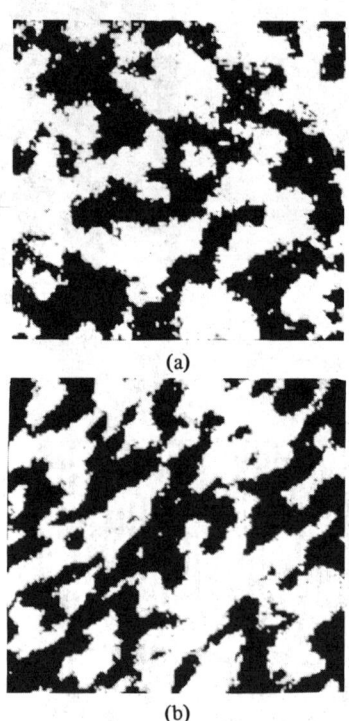

Fig. 10. Clustered textures with 4 gray levels. The parameters are (a) $a = -2$, $b(1, 2) = 1.0$. (b) $a = -2$, $b(1, \cdot) = 1.0$, $b(2, 1) = 1.0$, $b(2, 2) = 0.0$.

and out of focus. This effect is not due to the reproduction process but is intrinsic to the binomial model. If there is no inhibition (via negative high-order parameters), then the bi-

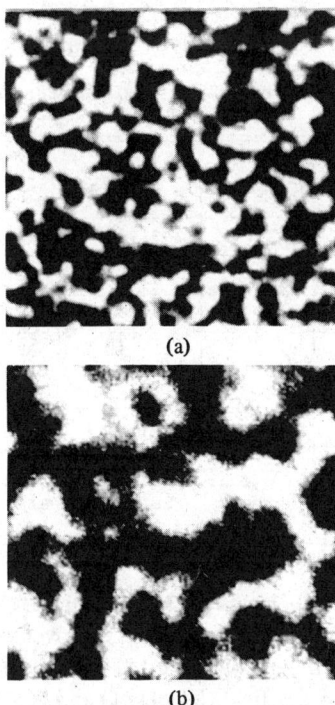

Fig. 11. Clustered textures with 16 and 32 gray levels. The parameters are (a) 16 levels, $a = -2.0$, $b(1, \cdot) = b(2, \cdot) = b(3, \cdot) = b(4, \cdot) = 0.05$. (b) 32 levels, $a = -2.0$, $b(1, \cdot) = b(2, \cdot) = b(3, \cdot) = b(4, \cdot) = 0.05$.

Fig. 12. Horizontal texture with 16 gray levels. The parameters are $a = -2.0$, $b(1, 1) = 0.08$, $b(1, 2) = 1.0$.

nomial model tends to have smooth transitions from black to white. The binomial distribution is unimodal and, as a consequence, values above and below the mean gray value are highly probable also. This results in a tapering of the gray scale around maxima and minima. Such a tapering as one moves away from black or white points has an effect similar to a neighborhood averaging or low-pass filter.

V. Modeling of Natural Textures

In previous sections, we have discussed the probabilistic structure of Markov random fields and have shown how samples from Markov random fields can be generated. We now implement a statistical measure of the correspondence between an observed texture and a texture model. No prior study has performed this kind of evaluation. All prior studies in texture modeling have considered a model adequate if its parameters yielded good classification in pattern recognition experiments or if it was found to be the best-fitting among a number of models tested. For example, Deguchi and Mori-

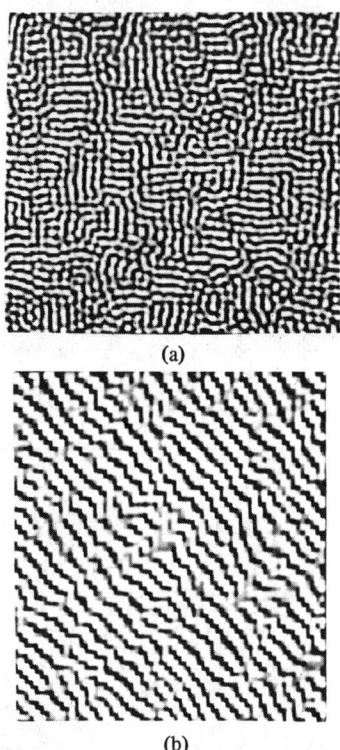

Fig. 13. Attraction–repulsion textures with 16 gray levels. The parameters are (a) $a = -2$, $b(1, \cdot) = b(2, \cdot) = 0.2$, $b(3, \cdot) = b(4, \cdot) = -0.1$. (b) $a = -2$, $b(1, \cdot) = 0.2$, $b(2, 1) = -2.2$, $b(2, 2) = 0.2$, $b(3, 1) = -0.5$, $b(3, 2) = 0.05$, $b(4, 1) = -0.05$, $b(4, 2) = 0.05$.

shita [15] determine the best size for a neighborhood in an autoregressive scheme, but do not give any overall guidelines on when the autoregressive scheme fits the observed texture.

A. Estimation of Parameters

The technique used to estimate the parameters $\{b(j, k)\}$ is maximum likelihood estimation. Let $p(x|\cdot)$ denote the conditional probability $p(X = x|\text{neighbors of } X)$, where X is a point of the lattice L. The usual log likelihood is given by

$$1 = \sum_X \ln(p(X|\cdot)) \qquad (7)$$

where the summation in (7) extends over all points of the lattice.

The summands in (7) are not independent. Instead of forming 1 as a sum over all points of the lattice, the lattice is partitioned into disjoint sets of points called *codings*. Each coding is chosen so that its points are independent. This can be done by adequately spacing the X points so that if $X(i)$ and $X(j)$ are two points in a coding, then $X(i)$ is not a neighbor of $X(j)$ in the Markov random field sense.

A first-order process requires at least two codings for estimation purposes. A second-order process requires spacing so that 3×3 neighborhoods do not interfere. This yields four codings. Nine codings are needed for third- and fourth-order processes. These codings are shown in Figs. 14, 15, and 16.

The actual estimation procedure is straightforward. Let $1(i)$ be the log likelihood for the ith coding obtained by extending the summation only over those points which are in coding i. In (7), $p(X|\cdot)$ depends on the order of the Markov

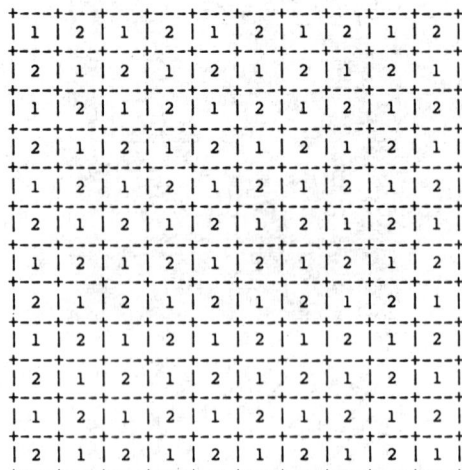

Fig. 14. First-order codings.

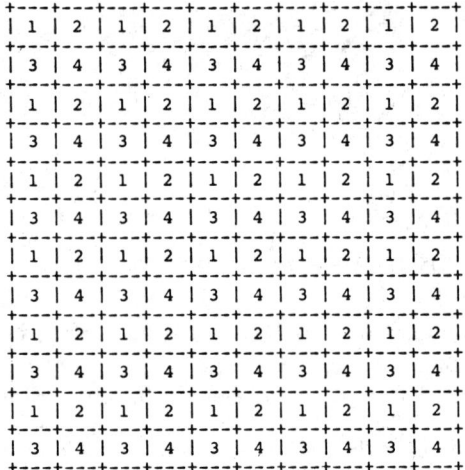

Fig. 15. Second-order codings.

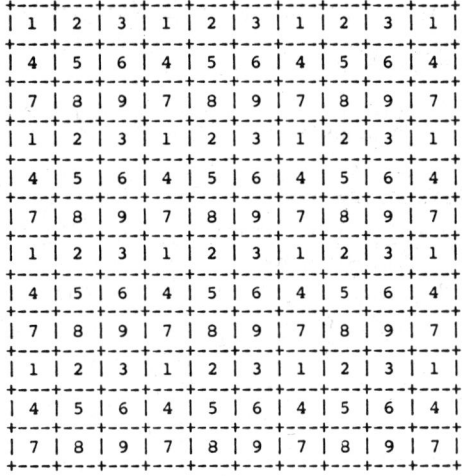

Fig. 16. Third- and fourth-order codings.

random field whose parameters are being estimated. An estimate of the parameter vector for the ith coding is obtained by maximizing $l(i)$. Our final estimate of the parameters is the average value over all the codings. Besag [4] mentions some

TABLE I
EXAMPLE OF A CHI-SQUARE TEST FOR A BINARY 64×64 TEXTURE. A FIRST-ORDER ANISOTROPIC SCHEME WAS FITTED. THE RESULTS OF CODING NUMBER 1 ARE SHOWN ABOVE. THE CHI-SQUARE VALUE IS 12.30957, ON 6 df.

$u + u'$	$v + v'$	$X = 0$	$X = 1$
0	0	625(621.)	5(9.)
0	1	240(244.)	20(16.)
0	2	14(17.)	8(5.)
1	0	79(80.)	19(18.)
1	1	93(91.)	85(87.)
1	2	21(14.)	52(59.)
2	0	4(3.)	8(9.)
2	1	12(17.)	244(239.)
2	2	8(8.)	512(512.)

doubt about the efficiency of this procedure. We have noted little variation in the estimates of textures over various codings. For example, on the 16 binary brick textures estimated as an anisotropic first-order field, let $b(1, 1)$ and $b(1, 1)'$ denote the estimates of the horizontal parameters while $b(1, 2)$ and $b(1, 2)'$ denote the estimates of the vertical parameters on the two codings. Then over the 16 samples we observed that

$$0.24 = \sum |b(1, 1) - b(1, 1)'|$$

and

$$0.09 = \sum |b(1, 2) - b(1, 2)'|.$$

This represents about a 13 percent average difference for the horizontal parameter (1.82) and 3 percent average difference for the vertical parameter (2.75).

B. Hypothesis Testing

Note that we really have only one sample from the unknown distribution $p(X)$ on the set of colorings of the lattice L. From the conditional probability point of view, each observed configuration of neighbors and the value of the center point X is a sample. In this sense, we have $M = N^2/k$ samples of the conditional density $p(X|\cdot)$ for the $N \times N$ lattice 1, where k is the number of codings. We can thus perform a chi-square test of the fit between the expected frequencies for each center pixel and the observed frequency. The expected frequencies are computed using the estimated parameters with an appropriate reduction in degrees of freedom. The null hypothesis is as follows.

H_0: The texture is a sample from a Markov random field with the estimated parameters set $\{a, b(j, k)\}$

while the alternative hypothesis is simply the negation of H_0.

Table I shows an example of a chi-square test for a first-order, anisotropic binary lattice. The entries in the table are of the form "observed (expected)" and the expected entry is computed using the conditional probability distribution with the estimated parameters ($a = -4.26$, $b(1, 1) = 2.70$, and $b(1, 2) = 1.5$). The degrees of freedom are computed by means of the formula

$$df = (G - 1) \cdot N_C - E$$

where G is the number of gray levels, N_C is the number of neighborhood configurations (in Table I, each neighborhood configuration is a row), and E is the number of estimated parameters. In the example of Table I, we have $(2 - 1) \cdot 9 - 3 = 6\, df$. We also use the convention of having at least one expected observation per cell. This results in a reduction in the number of cells and degrees of freedom.

Since we are performing a number of tests on the same data (one on each of k codings), there is a great likelihood of having the hypothesis of a fit to a Markov random field scheme accepted on some codings and rejected on others. The results of the tests are not independent. If they were independent, and we performed k tests at a level α, then the probability of no rejections would be $(1 - \alpha)^k$. A conservative strategy is to take the overall significance level of the test to be kp, where p is the level at which the most significant result was obtained over k codings [4].

The study of natural textures was based on 12 pictures from the Brodatz texture album [8]. The plates used are given in Tables II. Each plate was photographed on 35 mm film to form 24 × 36 mm slides. The slides were digitized in such a way that the small dimension occupied slightly over 256 pixels of the 480 × 640 image of a Spatial Data Eyecom system. The 256 × 256 images were split into 16 nonoverlapping 64 × 64 subimages and also into four 128 × 128 nonoverlapping subimages. The gray scale of each subimage was reduced from 256 gray levels to both two and eight gray levels using equal probability quantizing [25].

C. Evaluation of the Fit

The textures were evaluated for their fit to various models. The purpose of this analysis is twofold. First, we need to validate that the Markov random field model is generally applicable to textured images. The second objective is to formulate some general guidelines on how to choose an appropriate model, in terms of order and the degree of anisotropy and isotropy, to generate specific types of textures.

1) Binary Texture Results: Except for the screen texture, some first- or second-order model was able to give at least ten acceptances, under the previously mentioned conservative decision rule, for each texture sample. Detailed analysis of the screen texture samples showed very few distinct neighborhood configurations. This is a consequence of its regularity. The few neighborhood configurations dominate the computation of the Markov random field parameters. However, the low frequency neighbor probabilities are not properly controlled by these parameters, resulting in large chi-square values. Essentially, the histogram is so skewed toward these configurations that the positivity condition of Section III-A is nearly violated.

A number of models were tried out for testing binary textures. A test against a first-order model results in two hypothesis tests, one for each coding. There are 16 subimages of each texture, and each may be rejected on zero, one, or two codings at the five percent level. The number of conservative

TABLE II
TEXTURES USED IN THE STUDY. THE PLATE NUMBERS REFER TO THE BRODATZ TEXTURE ALBUM [8].

Name	Plate Number
Brick Wall	D94
Ceiling Tile	D86
Pressed Cork	D4
Calf Fur	D93
Grass Lawn	D9
Handmade Paper	D57
Pebbles	D31
Beach Sand	D29
Straw Screening	D49
Water	D38
Wood Grain (1)	D69
Wood Grain (2)	D70

TABLE III
BEST FITTING BINARY TEXTURE MODELS. IN THE TABLE BELOW, THE "*I*" INDICATES THAT THE FEWEST REJECTIONS WERE OBTAINED BY USING ISOTROPIC ESTIMATION, WHILE "*A*" INDICATES THAT THE BEST RESULTS WERE OBTAINED USING ANISOTROPIC PARAMETERS. THE SYMBOL "—" IN THE SECOND-ORDER COLUMN SIGNIFIES THAT THE BEST RESULTS WERE OBTAINED USING A FIRST-ORDER MODEL.

Texture Name	First Order	Second Order	Acceptances at 5%
Bricks	I	---	16
Ceiling Tile	I	---	16
Cork	I	A	14
Fur	I	I	12
Grass	A	---	16
Paper	I	---	15
Pebbles	I	---	14
Sand	A	A	14
Screen	A	A	5
Water	A	A	14
Wood (1)	A	A	14
Wood (2)	A	A	14

acceptances, of which there are a maximum of sixteen possible, is recorded in Table III. Besag [4] makes the point that one cannot compare the fit of a second-order model to the fit of a first-order model unless the same coding scheme is used in both cases. Table III gives the best results on second-order coding for each of the binary textures. The general good fit of the first-order model should be reconciled with the fact that there are only two codings rather than the four for a second-order scheme, which means that fewer rejections are likely.

We have limited our attention to the case of 64 × 64 textures. Although third-order estimates can be made which give good visual results in texture generation experiments explained later, we cannot reliably perform a chi-square test of them on the 64 × 64 lattice. The number of cells with only one member is very large since the number of theoretically possible cells with a fully anisotropic third-order model is 729, yet there is a maximum of 455 distinct configurations in a single third-order coding.

Our preferred choices for the best-fitting model are based on a simple rule: choose the model that gives the largest number of acceptances with a conservative decision rule. The results of this rule are displayed in Table III. We would not consider a fit to be adequate unless the majority of samples from the texture class fit the model.

2) Binomial Texture Results: With the experience gained from the binary fits, we limited our attention to four samples of size 128 × 128 from each of eight gray level pictures. First-

TABLE IV
BEST FITTING EIGHT GRAY LEVEL TEXTURE MODELS. IN THE TABLE BELOW, THE "*I*" INDICATES THAT THE FEWEST REJECTIONS WERE OBTAINED BY USING ISOTROPIC ESTIMATION, WHILE "*A*" INDICATES THAT THE BEST RESULTS WERE OBTAINED USING ANISOTROPIC PARAMETERS. THE SYMBOL "—" INDICATES THAT NEITHER MODEL WAS APPROPRIATE.

Texture Name	First Order	Second Order	Acceptances at 5%
Bricks	A	I	3
Ceiling Tile	A	I	3
Cork	A	A	4
Fur	I	A	4
Grass	A	A	4
Paper	A	A	4
Pebbles	---	---	0
Sand	A	A	4
Screen	---	---	0
Water	---	---	0
Wood (1)	A	A	1
Wood (2)	---	---	0

order models yielded consistently negative results. The binomial model is not suitable for bimodal or uniform conditional probabilities because it always has a peak at exactly one value for any choice of θ. Also, if there are two likely gray values which are not contiguous, then no choice of the parameter θ can yield the correct probabilities.

As in the binary case, third-order analysis cannot be performed on samples of size 64 × 64 for eight gray level textures. Good results were obtained for all but the inhomogeneous textures: water, wood, and pebbles. The binomial model has difficulty in handling large areas of equal brightness. All of the textures which did not fit the model well are either blotchy or regular, like the image of the screen. Fine-grained textures can be handled and, as we shall see, generated by the binomial model easily. The best results of the two sets are shown in Table IV.

In both Tables III and IV, the interpretation of the acceptances column requires some clarification. Each texture is estimated four times (on each of the four codings) for a second-order model. The conservative decision rule at the 5 percent significance level says that if any of the significances of the chi-square values are under $0.05/4 = 0.0125$, then we reject the texture at the 5 percent level as belonging to the texture class.

D. Texture Matching Experiments

This section examines the viability of the Markov random field as a supervised texture generation procedure. The input texture is measured using the maximum likelihood approach described in Section V-C. The results of that evaluation are used as input to the generation procedure in Fig. 2. As mentioned in Section V-A, the third-order model on a 64 × 64 texture cannot be reliably fitted since it causes too many empty or near-empty cells. Limited experimentation showed that if the image size was increased to 128 × 128, a sensible chi-square estimate could be made, although the parameters did not change very much from the estimates made on the 64 × 64 textures.

The steps performed in the texture matching experiments were as follows.

a) The parameters of a digitized natural texture were estimated using a model of some order.

b) If the texture was accepted as a Markov random field using the conservative hypothesis test, then an attempt was made to generate a synthetic texture using the estimated parameters of the natural texture.

c) The parameters of the synthetic texture were estimated in order to assure that the synthetic texture has the same (or very nearly) parameters as the original texture sample.

d) At this point, we have two textures with the same Markov random field parameters. The two textures can then be compared to see if they are visually similar.

1) Binary Texture Matching: The parameters used to generate the synthetic textures were obtained by averaging the parameter estimates from each of the codings of a single subimage. The choice of subimage was arbitrary. A third-order estimate was used in all cases except for the pictures of wood grain (1) and pebbles. In these two cases, a first-order model gave better visual results. First-order models tend to form in blob-like aggregations and cannot correctly characterize fine-structured textures. Moreover, they are inadequate in showing any directionality except vertical and horizontal.

The regularity and neat rectangles are not present in the synthetic texture of brick. The inhomogeneity of fur, wood(1), and wood(2) is missed in the synthetic examples. The remaining eight textures (cork, screen, sand, ceiling tile, grass, water, paper, and pebbles) are reasonably approximated by the simulated textures.

The clustering present in the pebbles image, Fig. 17(a), is shown clearly in the synthetic version, Fig. 17(a1). In the picture of cork, Fig. 17(b), diagonality is the overriding feature and this is correctly modeled. The screen image, Fig. 17(c1), is remarkably similar to the original, Fig. 17(c). The third-order repulsion effect provides the curious checkerboard effects along the lines in both the original and the generated texture.

2) Binomial Texture Matching: A 128 × 128 image size was used for both estimation and matching. The natural textures were quantized to have eight gray levels using histogram equalization. In all cases, a third-order model was estimated and used to generate the synthetic textures. Textures which failed in this matching experiment were: water, wood grain (1), wood grain (2), and pebbles. When considered as an eight-gray level image, these textures take on a distinctly inhomogeneous appearance. At this size, they look like pictures of objects, whereas the generated textures look like a fine-grain field. The Markov random field always results in a homogeneous covering of the image, which cannot be a blotchy image unless the parameters are extreme. As an example, the fur pictures, Fig. 18(a) and (a1), show the result of an inhomogeneity in the image.

The other clear failure is the bricks picture. As in the binary case, the bricks image has a regular structure. The Markov random field can only detect a hint of a vertical structure. Ceiling tile, cork, grass, paper, and sand are handled adequately. Missing are the large black holes in the synthetic tile picture, but there are some dense black patches [Fig. 18(c) and (c1)]. The distinctly three-dimensional appearance of the handmade paper, admittedly a tactile property is not captured either [Fig. 18(b) and (b1)].

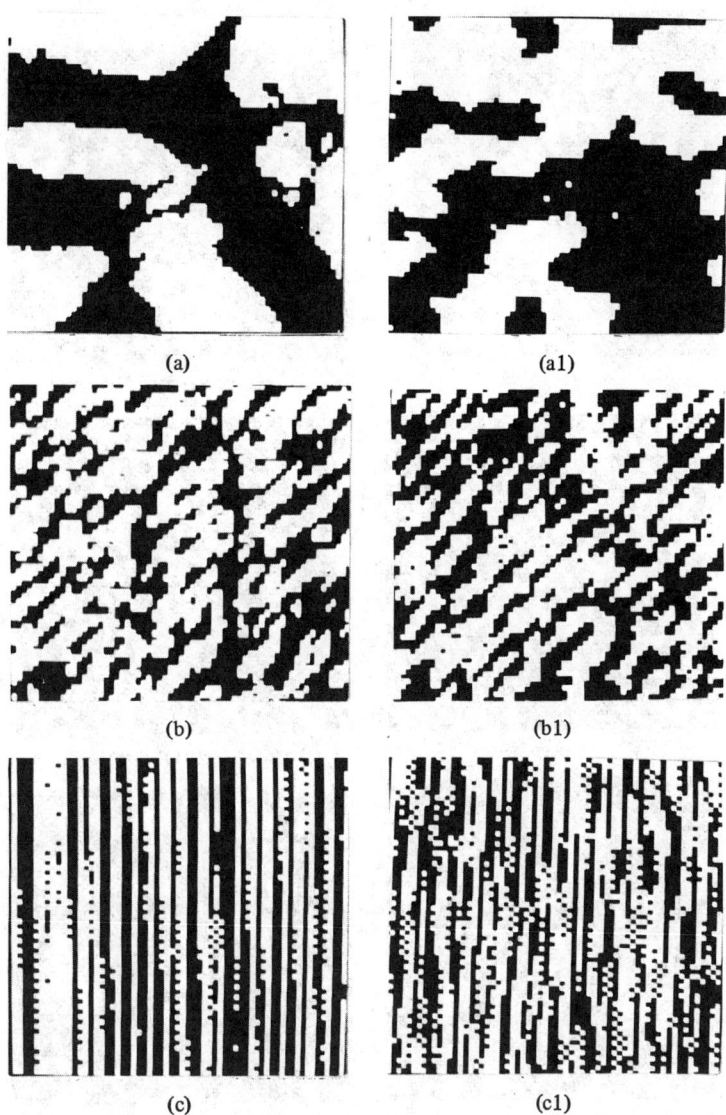

Fig. 17. Real and synthetic binary textures: (a) binary pebbles, (a1) synthetic binary pebbles, (b) binary cork, (b1) synthetic binary cork, (c) binary screen, (c1) synthetic binary screen.

The model seems to be adequate for duplicating the microtextures, but is incapable of handling strong regularity or cloud-like inhomogeneities. These experiments should be taken as an exploration of the limits of a purely statistical approach to texture without any *a priori* knowledge at all. For example, if we knew that the bricks picture was supposed to have rectangles of a certain size and orientation, then we could start with them as an outline and then fill in the rectangles with a Markov random field.

VI. Conclusions and Discussion

A. Summary

The focus of this research was on the application of the binomial model for texture, with special attention to the selection of an appropriate conditional distribution for the points of a lattice. It was demonstrated that the Markov random field parameters control the strength and direction of the clustering of the image. Overall, the microtextures, grass, sand, cork, ceiling tile, and paper, obeyed the Markov random field model well.

Using the estimation procedure for Markov random fields, the parameters of the natural textures were measured. The measured parameters were used as input to the texture generation procedure. This was an attempt to see how far the statistical approach alone could be carried in the absence of any structural information about the texture. Microtextures were successfully generated although the regular and inhomogeneous textures bore little resemblance to their synthetic counterparts.

The positive aspects of the Markov random field model are given as follows.

1) The model is fully two-dimensional and does not assume

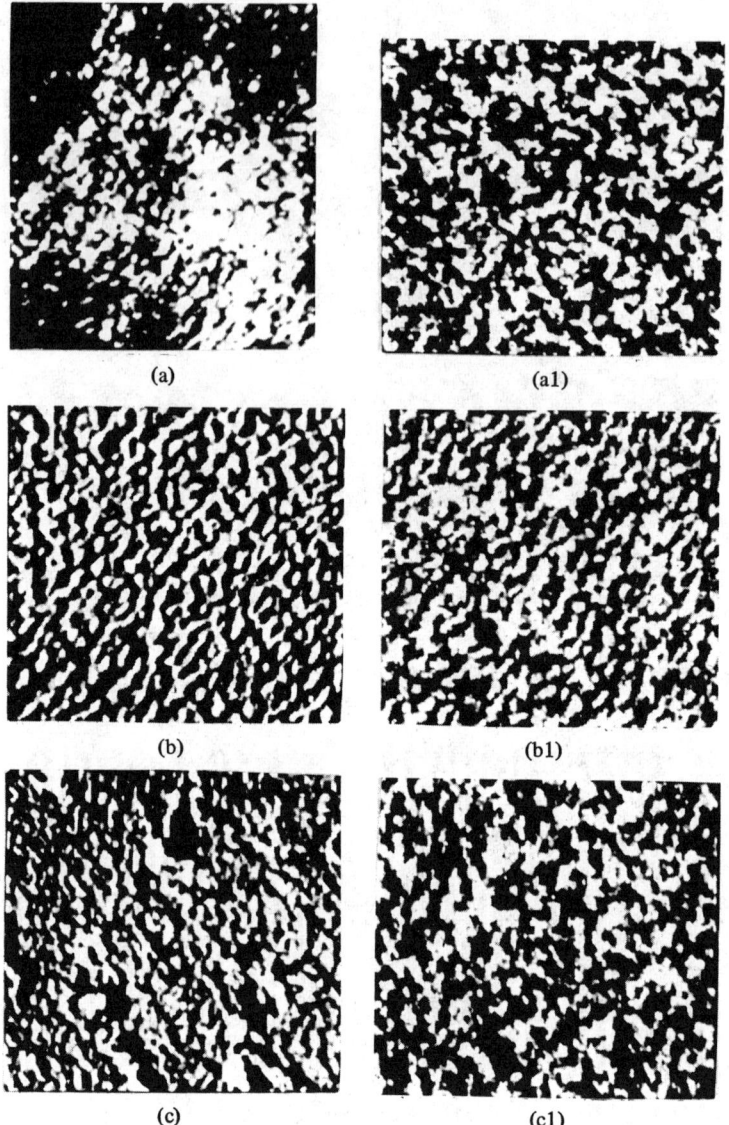

Fig. 18. Real and synthetic eight level textures. (a) fur, (a1) synthetic fur, (b) paper, (b1) synthetic paper, (c) ceiling tile, (c1) synthetic ceiling tile.

a causal (unilateral) dependence [11], [34]. This means that the Markov property is not relative to a particular direction. The Markov random field model allows us to consider neighbors in all directions.

2) The texture parameters are measurable from samples and the appropriateness of the model can be assessed objectively by a hypothesis test. Moreover, the Markov random field model allows the fitting of the sample texture directly to the model parameters. The current state of most models requires indirect fits by using variograms and correlation matches [15], [45].

3) The model parameters themselves are sufficient to generate images. In a purely feature-based approach, we do not have the capability to generate images from features because the features do not uniquely define a texture class.

4) The pattern formation process, although specified locally, implies a global pattern. The consistency conditions enforced by the Markov random field cause a pattern over the entire lattice. As Besag explains in the discussion of his lattice model paper, [4]:

Incidentally, the fact that a scheme is formally described as "locally interactive" does not imply that the patterns it produces are local in nature (cf. the extreme case of long-range order in the Ising model).

5) The patterns formed are realistic. The binomial model allows natural smooth peaks and valleys in the gray level height field over the plane.

6) The patterns generated by varying the model parameters can be studied and classified. Directionality, coarseness, gray level distribution, and sharpness can all be controlled by choice of the parameters.

7) The parameter estimation procedure can be implemented in a parallel algorithm. Each parameter estimate is performed on disjoint codings, each of which can be processed separately and then averaged to form the final result. Even the hypothesis tests could be done in parallel.

The Markov random field model has the following disadvantages.

1) Regular textures are not modeled very well.

2) The textural primitives of the Markov random field are nongeometric.

3) Large images are required to get good parameter estimates.

4) The theoretical properties of the model are, in general, difficult to obtain. We are currently computing the co-occurrence matrices as a function of the Markov random field parameters.

Several additional experiments can be done to determine the limitations and power of the Markov random field models. The full second-order model involving nonlinear terms may provide sufficient information about the image without any need to go as far as third-order. The full second-order model has only four codings, which is a distinct computational advantage.

The Brodatz texture samples certainly do not exhaust the possibilities of the model. It may be possible, for example, to use the Markov random field as a method of modeling film grain noise [23]. The binomial model textures have a distinctly biomedical flavor and may be of use in modeling images obtained by microscopy.

The Markov random field model can be used in a hierarchical manner. First, estimate the parameters on the given resolution. Next, consider the lattice of dimension half the original dimension by either averaging nonoverlapping two by two neighborhoods or simply selecting every other point. The reduced lattice parameters are then estimated and the process is repeated to get a sequence of parameter vectors which may describe the structure of the image better than a single set. We are investigating the use of Markov random field parameters for texture discrimination.

A test of homogeneity is needed. The Markov random field model assumes homogeneity in the image. Some verification of this should be made before estimating the parameters and assessing the goodness-of-fit.

References

[1] K. Abend, T. J. Harley, and L. N. Kanal, "Classification of binary random patterns," *IEEE Trans. Inform. Theory*, vol. IT-11, pp. 538-544, 1965.

[2] N. Ahuja, "Mosaic models for image analysis and synthesis," Ph.D. dissertation, Dep. Comput. Sci., Univ. Maryland, College Park, 1979.

[3] M. S. Bartlett, *The Statistical Analysis of Spatial Pattern*. London: Chapman and Hall, 1976.

[4] J. Besag, "Spatial interaction and the statistical analysis of lattice systems (with discussion)," *J. Royal Statist. Soc.*, series B, vol. 36, pp. 192-326, 1974.

[5] J. F. Blinn and M. E. Newell, "Texture and reflection in computer generated images," *Commun. Ass. Comput. Mach.*, vol. 19, p. 542, 1976.

[6] ——, "Simulation of wrinkled surfaces," *Comput. Graphics*, vol. 12, no. 3, p. 286, 1978.

[7] A. B. Bortz, M. H. Kalos, J. L. Lebowitz, and M. A. Zendejas, "Time evolution of a quenched binary alloy: Computer simulation of a two-dimensional model system," *Phys. Rev. B*, vol. 10, pp. 535-541, 1974.

[8] P. Brodatz, *Textures*. New York: Dover, 1966.

[9] E. Catmull, "Computer display of curved surfaces," in *Proc. Conf. Comput. Graphics, Pattern Recognition, Data Structures*, IEEE Pub. 75CH0981-1C, 1975, pp. 11-17.

[10] E. Catmull and A. R. Smith, "3-D transformations of images in scanline order," in *Proc. Siggraph Conf.*, Seattle, WA, July 1980, pp. 279-285.

[11] R. W. Connors and C. A. Harlow, "A theoretical comparison of texture algorithms," *IEEE Trans. Pattern Anal. Machine Intell.*, vol. PAMI-2, pp. 204-222, 1980.

[12] G. R. Cross, "Markov random field texture models," Ph.D. dissertation, Dep. Comput. Sci., Michigan State Univ., East Lansing, 1980.

[13] C. Csuri, R. Hackathorn, R. Parent, W. Carlson, and M. Howard, "Towards an interactive high visual complexity animation system," *Comput. Graphics*, vol. 13, pp. 289-299, 1979.

[14] L. S. Davis, S. Johns, and J. K. Aggarwal, "Texture analysis using generalized co-occurrence matrices," *IEEE Trans. Pattern Anal. Machine Intell.*, vol. PAMI-1, pp. 251-259, 1979.

[15] K. Deguchi and I. Morishita, "Texture characterization and texture-based image partitioning using two-dimensional linear estimation techniques," *IEEE Trans. Inform. Theory*, vol. IT-27, pp. 738-745, 1978.

[16] E. T. Delp, R. L. Kashyap, O. R. Mitchell, and R. B. Abhyankar, "Image modeling with a seasonal autoregressive time series with applications to data compression," in *Proc. IEEE Comput. Soc. Conf. Pattern Recognition and Image Processing*, Chicago, IL, 1978, pp. 100-104.

[17] W. Dungan, "A terrain and cloud computer generation model," *Comput. Graphics*, vol. 13, no. 2, pp. 143-150, 1979.

[18] R. W. Ehrich and J. P. Foith, "A view of texture topology and texture description," *Comput. Graphics Image Processing*, vol. 8, pp. 174-202, 1978.

[19] W. Feller, *An Introduction to Probability Theory and Its Applications*, vol. 1, 3rd ed. New York: Wiley, 1968.

[20] P. A. Flinn and G. M. McManus, "Monte Carlo calculation of the order-disorder transformation in the body-centered cubic lattice," *Physical Rev.*, vol. 124, pp. 54-59, 1961.

[21] P. A. Flinn, "Monte Carlo calculation of phase separation in a 2-dimensional Ising system," *J. Statist. Phys.*, vol. 10, pp. 89-97, 1974.

[22] L. D. Fosdick, "Calculation of order parameters in a binary alloy by the Monte Carlo method," *Physical Rev.*, vol. 116, pp. 565-573, 1959.

[23] G. K. Froehlich, J. F. Walkup, and R. B. Asher, "Optimal estimation in signal-dependent film-grain noise," in *Proc. ICO-11 Conf.*, Madrid, 1978, pp. 367-369.

[24] J. M. Hammersley and D. C. Handscomb, *Monte Carlo Methods*. London: Methuen and Company, 1964.

[25] R. M. Haralick, K. Shanmugam, and I. Dinstein, "Textural features for image classification," *IEEE Trans. Syst., Man, Cybern.*, vol. SMC-3, pp. 610-621, 1973.

[26] R. M. Haralick, "Statistical and structural approaches to texture," in *Proc. 4th Int. Joint Conf. Pattern Recognition*, Kyoto, Japan, Nov. 1978, pp. 45-69.

[27] M. Hassner and J. Sklansky, "The use of Markov random fields as models of texture," *Comput. Graphics Image Processing*, vol. 12, pp. 357-370, 1980.

[28] ——, "Markov random field models of digitized image texture," in *Proc. Int. Joint Conf. Pattern Recognition*, Kyoto, Japan, Nov. 1978, pp. 522-540.

[29] E. Ising, *Zeitschrift Physik*, vol. 31, p. 253, 1925.

[30] B. Julesz, "Visual pattern discrimination," *IRE Trans. Inform. Theory*, vol. IT-8, pp. 84-97, 1962.

[31] ——, *Foundations of Cyclopean Perception*. Chicago, IL: Univ. Chicago Press, 1971.

[32] A. L. Kraft and W. A. Winnick, "The effect of pattern and texture gradient on slant and shape judgments," *Perception and Psychophys.*, vol. 2, pp. 141-147, 1967.

[33] S. Y. Lu and K. S. Fu, "A syntactic approach to texture analysis," *Comput. Graphics Image Processing*, vol. 7, pp. 303-330, 1978.

[34] B. H. McCormick and S. N. Jayaramamurthy, "Time series model for texture synthesis," *Int. J. Comput. Inform. Sci.*, vol. 3, pp. 329-343, 1974.

[35] B. B. Mandelbrot, *Fractals–Form, Chance, Dimension*. San Francisco, CA: W. H. Freeman, 1977.

[36] D. Marr, "Analyzing natural images: A computational theory of

textures vision," in *Proc. Cold Spring Harbor Symp. Quantative Biol.*, vol. 40, 1976, pp. 647–662.
[37] —, "Early processing of visual information," *Phil. Trans. Royal Soc. London*, series B, vol. 275, pp. 483–519, 1976.
[38] N. Metropolis, A. W. Rosenbluth, M. N. Rosenbluth, A. H. Teller, and E. Teller, "Equations of state calculations by fast computing machines," *J. Chem. Phys.*, vol. 21, pp. 1087–1091, 1953.
[39] J. W. Modestino and R. W. Fries, "Stochastic models for images and applications," in *Pattern Recognition and Signal Processing*, C. H. Chen, Ed. Alphen aan den Rijn, The Netherlands: Sitjhoff and Noordhoff.
[40] R. Nevatia, "Locating object boundaries in textured environments," *IEEE Trans. Comput.*, vol. C-25, pp. 1170–1175, 1976.
[41] G. F. Newell and E. W. Montroll, "On the theory of the Ising model of ferromagnetism," *Rev. Modern Phys.*, vol. 25, pp. 353–389, 1953.
[42] W. M. Newman and R. F. Sproull, *Principles of Interactive Computer Graphics*. New York: McGraw-Hill, 1979.
[43] A. Rosenfeld and A. Troy, "Visual texture analysis," Univ. Maryland, Rep. TR 70-116, June 1970.
[44] B. Schacter, A. Rosenfeld, and L. S. Davis, "Random mosaic models for textures," *IEEE Trans. Syst., Man, Cybern.*, vol. SMC-8, pp. 694–702, 1978.
[45] B. Schacter and N. Ahuja, "Random pattern generation processes," *Comput. Graphics Image Processing*, vol. 10, pp. 95–114, 1979.
[46] J. Serra, "Boolean model and random sets," *Comput. Graphics Image Processing*, vol. 12, pp. 99–126, 1980.
[47] F. Spitzer, "Markov random fields and Gibbs ensembles," *Amer. Math. Monthly*, vol. 78, pp. 142–154, 1971.
[48] H. Tamura, S. Mori, and T. Yamawaki, "Textural features corresponding to visual perception," *IEEE Trans. Syst., Man, Cybern.*, vol. SMC-8, pp. 460–473, 1978.
[49] W. B. Thompson, "Textural boundary analysis," *IEEE Trans. Comput.*, vol. C-24, pp. 272–276, 1977.
[50] A. M. Turing, "Computing machinery and intelligence," *Mind*, vol. 59, pp. 433–460, 1950.
[51] J. Weszka, C. Dyer, and A. Rosenfeld, "A comparative study of texture measures for terrain classification," *IEEE Trans. Syst., Man, Cybern.*, vol. SMC-6, pp. 269–285, 1976.
[52] R. Yokoyama and R. M. Haralick, "Texture pattern image generation by regular Markov chain," *Pattern Recognition*, vol. 11, pp. 225–234, 1979.
[53] S. W. Zucker, "On the foundations of texture: A transformation approach," Univ. Maryland, Rep. TR-331, Sept. 1974.

George R. Cross (S'79–M'80) was born in New York, NY, on December 22, 1946. He received the B.A. degree in mathematics from the University of Rochester in 1969, the M.A. degree in mathematics from the State University of New York, New Paltz, in 1973, and the M.S. and Ph.D. degrees in computer science from Michigan State University in 1979 and 1980, respectively.

From 1969 to 1973, he was a Senior Associate Programmer with International Business Machines, Kingston, NY. In 1981 he joined the Department of Computer Science, Louisiana State University, Baton Rouge, where he is currently an Assistant Professor. His research interests include pattern recognition and image processing.

Dr. Cross is a member of the Association for Computing Machinery, the Pattern Recognition Society, the AAAI, and the AAAS.

Anil K. Jain (S'70–M'72) was born in Basti, India, on August 5, 1948. He received the B.Tech. degree with distinction from the Indian Institute of Technology, Kanpur, India, in 1969, and the M.S. and Ph.D. degrees in electrical engineering from Ohio State University in 1970 and 1973, respectively.

From 1971 to 1972, he was a Research Associate in the Communications and Control Systems Laboratory, Ohio State University. Then from 1972 to 1974, he was an Assistant Professor in the Department of Computer Science, Wayne State University, Detroit, MI. In 1974, he joined the Department of Computer Science, Michigan State University, where he is currently a Professor. He served as the Program Director of the Intelligent Systems Program at the National Science Foundation from September 1980 to August 1981. His research interests are in the areas of pattern recognition and image processing.

Dr. Jain is a member of the Association for Computing Machinery, the Pattern Recognition Society, and Sigma Xi. He is also an Advisory Editor of *Pattern Recognition Letters*.

Estimation and Choice of Neighbors in Spatial-Interaction Models of Images

RANGASAMI L. KASHYAP, FELLOW, IEEE, AND RAMALINGAM CHELLAPPA, MEMBER, IEEE

Abstract—Some aspects of statistical inference for a class of spatial-interaction models for finite images are presented: primarily the simultaneous autoregressive (SAR) models and conditional Markov (CM) models. Each of these models is characterized by a set of neighbors, a set of coefficients, and a noise sequence of specified characteristics. We are concerned with two problems: the estimation of the unknown parameters in both SAR and CM models and the choice of an appropriate model from a class of such competing models. Assuming Gaussian-distributed variables, we discuss maximum likelihood (ML) estimation methods. In general, the ML scheme leads to nonlinear optimization problems. To avoid excessive computation, an iterative scheme is given for SAR models, which gives approximate ML estimates in the Gaussian case and reasonably good estimates in some non-Gaussian situations as well. Likewise, for CM models, an easily computable consistent estimate is given. The asymptotic mean-squared error (mse) of this estimate for a four-neighbor CM model is shown to be substantially less than the mse of the popular coding estimate. Asymptotically consistent decision rules are given for choosing an appropriate SAR or CM model. The usefulness of the estimation scheme and the decision rule for the choice of neighbors is illustrated by using synthetic patterns. Synthetic patterns obeying known SAR and CM models are generated, and the models corresponding to true and several competing neighbor sets are fitted. The estimation scheme yields estimates close to the parameters of the true models, and the decision rule for the choice of neighbors picks up the true model from the class of competing models.

I. INTRODUCTION

SPATIAL-interaction models (often known as random field models) have many applications in image processing and analysis. For instance, they can be used for the design of image restoration algorithms [1]–[3], for image coding [4], and for texture analysis [5]–[8]. Typically, an image is represented by two-dimensional scalar data, the gray level variations defined over a rectangular or square lattice. One of the important characteristics of such data is the special nature of the statistical dependence of the gray level at a lattice point on those of its neighbors.

The spatial-interaction models characterize this statistical dependency by representing $y(s)$, the gray level at location s, as a linear combination of the gray levels $\{y(s + s'), s' \in N\}$ and an additive noise, where N is called the neighbor set which does not include $(0, 0)$.

Specific restrictions on the members of neighbor set N yield representations familiar in the image processing literature. For instance, the familiar *causal* models [4]-[6] are obtained when N is defined as $N = \{(i, j): i \leq 0, j \leq 0, (i, j) \neq (0, 0)\}$. Likewise, the unilateral neighbor set used in [3] result when N is a finite subset of a half plane defined in [9]. Neighbor sets more general than the causal or the unilateral have been of much interest in image processing [1], [2], [7], [8], [10] in the analysis of wheat data on fields [11], [12], in navigational problems [13], and in the analysis of geographic data [14].

There are two nonequivalent ways [12] of specifying the underlying interaction among the given observations leading to two classes of models, the simultaneous models [12], [15], [16] and the conditional Markov models [7], [8], [10], [12], [16]. Within the class of simultaneous models there are simultaneous autoregressive (SAR) models [11]-[16], simultaneous moving average (SMA) models [17], and simultaneous autoregressive and moving average (SARMA) [17] models, as in one-dimensional time series models. The class of SAR models is a subset of the class of CM models, i.e., for every SAR model there exists a unique conditional Markov (CM) model with equivalent spectral density function, but the converse is not always true. Still the class of SAR models deserves detailed study for the following reasons. SAR models are parsimonious, i.e., the CM model in general is characterized by more parameters than the equivalent SAR model (if one exists). Secondly, the study of SAR models can be extended to include SMA and SARMA models which are not subsets of CM models. Hence the study of elementary SAR models considered in this paper will be of considerable use.

Given a finite image we are interested in fitting an appropriate model from the class of SAR or CM models. Given a SAR or CM model the finite image can be analyzed either as a finite block of an infinite image defined over an infinite lattice, or as an image defined only on a finite lattice. In general, the estimation methods are complicated when infinite lattice representations are used for SAR and CM models. To overcome this problem we will consider some finite lattice representations. The finite lattice models can be justified in their own right or as approximations to infinite lattice models. After choosing a finite lattice representation, two problems have to be tackled in fitting an appropriate model, namely, a method of estimating the parameters of the model given the structure of the model, and a criterion to choose between different possible structures.

The classical least square (LS) estimates are asymptotically consistent and efficient for SAR models characterized by *unilateral* neighbor sets, but they are not even consistent [11], [14] for bilateral neighbor sets. Asymptotically consistent and efficient estimates can be obtained via the maximum likelihood (ML) estimation method with an appropriate distribution assumption for $\{y(s)\}$. In general due to the fact that the Jacobian of the transformation matrix for bilateral SAR or CM models is not unity, the log-likelihood function is a complicated function even for Gaussian variables. An asymptotic approximation developed in [11] for infinite lattice SAR models will be of use for very simple models only.

However, by using a finite lattice representation [14]-[17] for SAR models an explicit expression can be written for the log-likelihood function for any arbitrary distribution. Specifically, a toroidal lattice representation given in Section II-B yields a transformation matrix that is block-circulant whose eigenvalues, and hence the log-likelihood function can be written down explicitly. Unfortunately, the resulting function is nonquadratic in the parameters, requiring the use of nonlinear numerical optimization algorithms. To avoid excessive computations, we give an iterative scheme that yields approximate ML estimates for Gaussian distributions. These estimates are reasonably good in some non-Gaussian situations as well.

For CM models we use the consistent estimation scheme suggested in [10] which involves inverting an $m \times m$ symmetric matrix, where m is the number of independent parameters to be estimated. However, this estimate is not efficient. Actual comparison of efficiencies for a simple isotropic CM model with $N = \{(0, 1), (0, -1), (-1, 0), (1, 0)\}$ indicates that the efficiency of this estimate is superior to that of the popular coding estimate [8], [12].

The second problem considered is the choice of appropriate neighbors in SAR and CM models. As illustrated in [18], [19], different neighbor sets in SAR or CM models account for different image patterns and the quality of regeneration is dependent upon the particular underlying model. From one-dimensional time series analysis, it is known that the use of an appropriate model leads to good results in forecasting and similar applications. We give asymptotically consistent decision rules for the appropriate choice of neighbors in conditional or simultaneous models. The derivation of this decision rule for SAR models may be found in [20]. The decision rule for choosing between different neighbor sets in CM models is similar in structure to that in simultaneous models. The usefulness of the estimation scheme and the decision rule for the choice of neighbors can be demonstrated by applying them to synthetic patterns for which the underlying true model of the synthetic pattern is known.

The organization of the paper is as follows. In Section II, we consider the estimation problem in SAR models and give an iterative estimation scheme. The results of applying this estimation scheme to synthetic data generated by known models are also given. A consistent estimation scheme for CM models is presented in Section III along with the results for synthetic data. An expression for the MSE of this estimate is also derived. The need for using an appropriate SAR or CM model is discussed, and decision rules for the choice of neighbors in SAR or CM models are given in Section IV.

II. Estimation Schemes in SAR Models

A. Model Representation and Estimation in Infinite Lattice SAR Models

Assume that the stationary image $\{y(s)\}$ obeys the infinite lattice SAR model in (2.1), with associated neighbor set N

$$y(s) = \sum_{r \in N} \theta_r y(s+r) + \sqrt{\rho}\, \omega(s). \quad (2.1)$$

In (2.1), $(\theta_r, r \in N)$ and ρ are unknown parameters, and $\omega(\cdot)$ is an independent and identically distributed (i.i.d.) noise sequence with zero mean and unit variance. By stationarity $E(y(s)) = 0$. A sufficient condition on $\theta^T = \{\theta_r, r \in N\}$ to ensure stationarity of $y(\cdot)$ is

$$\left\{1 - \sum_{(i,j) \in N} \theta_{i,j} z_1^i z_2^j \neq 0\right\},$$

for all z_1, z_2 such that $|z_1| = 1, |z_2| = 1;$ (2.2)

N need not be symmetric. If N is symmetric we have to assume that the coefficients of the symmetrically opposite neighbors are equal, i.e., $\theta_{k,l} = \theta_{-k,-l}$. Otherwise, the parameters may not be identifiable [12]. Note that $y(\cdot)$ is not Markov with respect to any arbitrary bilateral neighbor set N, i.e.,

$$p(y(s)|\text{all } y(r), s \neq r) \neq p(y(s)|\text{all } y(s+r), r \in N). \quad (2.3)$$

Given a finite image defined on a square $M \times M$ grid Ω, we are interested in estimating the parameters of the model characterizing the image. A popular method of estimation is that of least squares (LS), which yields the estimate in (2.4)

$$\hat{\theta} = \left[\sum_s z(s) z^T(s)\right]^{-1} \left(\sum_s z(s) y(s)\right), \quad (2.4)$$

$$\hat{\rho} = \frac{1}{M^2} \sum_s (y(s) - \hat{\theta}^T z(s))^2, \quad (2.5)$$

$$z(s) = \text{col}[y(s+r), r \in N]. \quad (2.6)$$

One of the drawbacks of the LS is that in general $\hat{\theta}$ is not consistent for nonunilateral neighbor sets [14]. A qualitative explanation for the inconsistency of $\hat{\theta}$ can be given as follows. Substitute (2.1) into (2.4) to obtain after simplification,

$$S(\hat{\theta} - \theta) = \sum_s z(s) \omega(s), \quad (2.7)$$

where $S = \sum_s z(s) z^T(s)$. Multiplying the left-hand side (LHS) of (2.7) by its transpose and taking expectations, we get

$$E(S(\hat{\theta} - \theta)(\hat{\theta} - \theta)^T S) = E\left[\sum_r \sum_s z(s) \omega(s) \omega(r) z^T(r)\right]. \quad (2.8)$$

Since

$$E(z(s)\omega(s)) \neq 0 \quad (2.9)$$

with nonunilateral neighbor sets, the right-hand side (RHS) of (2.8) does not go to zero even as M tends to infinity leading to the inconsistency of $\hat{\theta}$. Another popular method is the ML method, which yields asymptotically consistent and efficient estimates. As mentioned earlier, the derivation of the log-likelihood function is extremely difficult, even in the Gaussian case, for SAR models with nonunilateral neighbor sets since the Jacobian of the transformation matrix is a complicated function of the model parameters. It has been shown [11] that for large values of M, an approximate expression can be obtained for the determinant of the transformation matrix. Typically, for a SAR model with spectrum inversely proportional to

$$\|1 - \sum_{r \in N} \theta_r \exp(\sqrt{-1}\, w^T r)\|^2$$

the log of the determinant is approximately equivalent to the absolute term in the expansion of

$$-2\log\left(1 - \sum_{r \in N} \theta_r \exp(\sqrt{-1}\, w^T r)\right).$$

This approximation is useful only for very simple SAR models. These considerations motivate us to use another class of representations, known as finite lattice SAR models. The finite lattice models considered here can be analyzed either as approximations to infinite lattice models or as an independent class of models.

B. SAR Model Representation on Finite Lattices: [15], [16]

Suppose we partition the finite lattice Ω into mutually exclusive and totally inclusive subsets Ω_I, the interior set, and Ω_B, the boundary set, such that

$$\Omega_B = \{s = (i,j): s \in \Omega \text{ and } (s+r) \notin \Omega$$

$$\text{for at least one } r \in N\},$$

and

$$\Omega_I = \Omega - \Omega_B.$$

For every $s \in \Omega_B$, there exists a $r \in N$ so that $(s+r) \notin \Omega$ and consequently $y(s+r)$ is not defined by (2.1). Hence (2.1) needs modification.

The toroidal lattice SAR model for a *finite* image $\{y(s), s \in \Omega\}$ is defined by two equations for s in Ω_I and Ω_B as in (2.10) and (2.11).

$$y(s) = \sum_{r \in N} \theta_r y(s+r) + \sqrt{\rho}\,\omega(s), \quad s \in \Omega_I, \quad (2.10)$$

$$y(s) = \sum_{r \in N} \theta_r y_1(s+r) + \sqrt{\rho}\,\omega(s), \quad s \in \Omega_B, \quad (2.11)$$

$y_1(s+(k,l))$ with $s = (i,j)$,
$= y(s+(k,l)), \quad \text{if } (s+(k,l)) \in \Omega$
$= y[(k+i-1) \bmod M + 1, (l+j-1) \bmod M + 1],$
$\quad \text{if } (s+(k,l)) \notin \Omega. \quad (2.12)$

In the RHS of (2.11), y_1 takes the role of y in (2.10). $y_1(s)$ in (2.12) is a function of $y(r)$, $r \in \Omega$ even when $s \notin \Omega$. If the image $y(\cdot)$ were folded into a torus, $y_1(s) = y(s)$.

Equations (2.10) and (2.11) give M^2 equations relating the image variables $\{y(s)\}$ and i.i.d. random variables $\{\omega(s)\}$. Denoting y and ω as $M^2 \times 1$ vectors of lexicographic ordered arrays $\{y(\cdot)\}$ and $\{\omega(\cdot)\}$, (2.10)–(2.11) can be rewritten as $B(\boldsymbol{\theta})y = \sqrt{\rho}\,\omega$, where $B(\boldsymbol{\theta})$ is a block-circulant matrix:

$$B(\boldsymbol{\theta}) = \begin{bmatrix} B_{1,1} & B_{1,2} & \cdots & B_{1,M} \\ B_{1,M} & B_{1,1} & \cdots & B_{1,M-1} \\ \cdots & \cdots & & \cdots \\ B_{1,2} & \cdots & & B_{1,1} \end{bmatrix}.$$

For instance when the neighbor set of dependence N is $\{(-1,0),(0,1),(1,0),(0,-1)\}$ we have

$$B_{1,1} = \text{circulant}(1, -\theta_{0,1}, 0, \cdots, -\theta_{0,-1}),$$
$$B_{1,2} = \text{circulant}(-\theta_{1,0}, 0, \cdots, 0),$$
$$B_{1,M} = \text{circulant}(-\theta_{-1,0}, 0, \cdots, 0),$$

and

$$B_{1,j} = 0 \quad j \neq 1, 2, M.$$

To ensure stationarity, the coefficients $\{\theta_r, r \in N\}$ must obey [17]:

$$\mu_s(\boldsymbol{\theta}) \triangleq (1 - \boldsymbol{\theta}^T \psi_s) \neq 0, \quad s \in \Omega, \quad (2.13)$$

where

$$\psi_s = \text{col}\left[\exp\left[\sqrt{-1}\,\frac{2\pi}{M}(s-\mathbf{1})^T r, r \in N\right]\right], \quad \mathbf{1} = (1,1).$$

The finite lattice representation on a toroidal lattice is only one of several possible finite lattice representations [17].

C. Estimation in Toroidal Lattice SAR Models

1) Least Squares and ML Estimates: The LS estimate in (2.4) is not consistent for toroidal lattice SAR model. The ML estimation method yields asymptotically consistent and efficient estimates. To obtain an expression for the log-likelihood function, we impose a Gaussian structure on the noise sequence $\omega(\cdot)$. Then the likelihood of the observations can be written as

$$\ln p(y|\boldsymbol{\theta}, \rho) = \ln \det B(\boldsymbol{\theta}) - (M^2/2)\ln 2\pi\rho$$
$$- \frac{1}{2\rho}\sum_\Omega (y(s) - \boldsymbol{\theta}^T z(s))^2, \quad (2.14)$$

Since $\det B(\boldsymbol{\theta}) = \prod_\Omega (1 - \boldsymbol{\theta}^T \psi_s)$,

$$\ln p(y|\boldsymbol{\theta}, \rho) = \sum_\Omega \ln(1 - \boldsymbol{\theta}^T \psi_s) - (M^2/2)\ln 2\pi\rho$$
$$- \frac{1}{2\rho}\sum_\Omega (y(s) - \boldsymbol{\theta}^T z(s))^2, \quad (2.15)$$

The ML estimates are obtained by maximizing (2.15) with respect to $\boldsymbol{\theta}$ and ρ. Since the log-likelihood function is nonquadratic in $\boldsymbol{\theta}$, the estimation involves the use of numerical optimization methods, such as Newton–Raphson approach, which are computationally expensive.

We give an iterative method which yields estimates close to the ML estimates with a faster convergence rate.

2) An Iterative Estimation Scheme: This method is derived by replacing the term $\ln(1 - \boldsymbol{\theta}^T \psi_s)$ in (2.15) with the approximation $\ln(1 + a) = a - a^2/2$. The corresponding approximation of $\ln p(y|\boldsymbol{\theta}, \rho)$ denoted as $J(\boldsymbol{\theta}, \rho)$ can be written as

$$J(\boldsymbol{\theta}, \rho) = -V^T\boldsymbol{\theta} + 0.5\boldsymbol{\theta}^T R \boldsymbol{\theta} - (M^2/2)\ln 2\pi\rho$$
$$- \frac{1}{2\rho}\sum_{s \in \Omega}(y(s) - \boldsymbol{\theta}^T z(s))^2, \quad (2.16)$$

where

$$V = \sum_\Omega C_s, \quad m \times 1 \text{ vector}, \quad (2.17)$$

$$R = \sum_\Omega (S_s S_s^T - C_s C_s^T), \quad m \times m \text{ matrix}, \quad (2.18)$$

$$C_s = \text{col}\left[\cos\frac{2\pi}{M}((s-\mathbf{1})^T r), r \in N\right], \quad (2.19)$$

$$S_s = \text{col}\left[\sin\frac{2\pi}{M}((s-\mathbf{1})^T r), r \in N\right]. \quad (2.20)$$

Theorem 1: The estimates $\bar{\boldsymbol{\theta}}, \bar{\rho}$ maximizing $J(\boldsymbol{\theta}, \rho)$ are obtained as the limits of $\boldsymbol{\theta}_t, \rho_t$ defined by

$$\boldsymbol{\theta}_{t+1} = \left(R - \frac{1}{\rho_t}S\right)^{-1}\left(V - \frac{1}{\rho_t}U\right), \quad t = 0, 1, 2, \cdots \quad (2.21)$$

and

$$\rho_t = \frac{1}{M^2}\sum_\Omega (y(s) - \boldsymbol{\theta}_t^T z(s))^2, \quad t = 0, 1, 2, 3, \cdots, \quad (2.22)$$

where

$$S = \sum_\Omega z(s)z^T(s), \quad m \times m \text{ matrix}, \quad (2.23)$$

and

$$U = \sum_\Omega z(s)y(s), \quad m \times 1 \text{ vector}. \quad (2.24)$$

The initial value $\boldsymbol{\theta}_0$ is chosen as $\boldsymbol{\theta}_0 = S^{-1}U$. All the summations in (2.22)–(2.24) are over $s \in \Omega$ and m is the dimension of $\boldsymbol{\theta}$.

$\boldsymbol{\theta}_{t+1}$ in (2.21) is the value of $\boldsymbol{\theta}$ maximizing $J(\boldsymbol{\theta}, \rho_t)$. ρ_t in (2.22) is the value of ρ maximizing $J(\boldsymbol{\theta}_t, \rho)$. These facts allow us to establish Theorem 1.

Comments

1) Usually, the numerical optimization methods require the evaluation of the first and possibly the second derivatives of the likelihood function with respect to the unknown parameters at each step of the iteration. In our scheme we approximate the second derivative by a function of matrices R and S which are indepen-

dent of iterations and can be evaluated once the neighbor set N, and the image data are known.

2) It is difficult to analyze the asymptotic distribution properties of the estimate $\bar{\theta}$ because of the approximations involved. Numerical experiments indicate that these estimates are close to the ML estimates.

3) The iterative estimation method has been obtained by using the toroidal lattice representation. It is a natural question to ask if the toroidal lattice assumption is reasonable. Simulation results reported elsewhere [18] indicate that the toroidal lattice models are good approximations to the infinite lattice models. Specifically, second-order properties, like the correlation function, of the infinite lattice model and the toroidal lattice model are numerically very close to each other.

D. Experimental Results

We give the results of applying the estimation scheme in Section II-B to some synthetic data generated from known SAR models. The estimates of the model should be very close to the true parameters. The scheme used to generate the synthetic data is in [16].

Experiment I: (Gaussian data and a SAR model with $N = \{(-1,0), (1,0), (-1,1), (1,-1), (1,1), (-1,-1)\}$.)

The parameters of that true model are $\alpha = 30.00$, $\rho = 1.1111$, and $\theta_{-1,0} = \theta_{1,0} = 0.12$, $\theta_{1,1} = \theta_{-1,-1} = -0.14$, and $\theta_{-1,1} = \theta_{1,-1} = 0.28$. The parameter α is the expected value of $\{y(s)\}$. For simplicity we assumed $\alpha = 0$ in Section II-A. To facilitate easy display of the data generated by a SAR model as an image with gray level variations in (0-63) range, we have used $\alpha = 30.0$. α can be estimated from the given image as the sample mean. Using this model the synthetic data is generated using a Gaussian pseudo-random number generator. For estimation of the parameters the sample mean of the window was subtracted and the iterative scheme in (2.21)–(2.22) is used. The numerical values of the estimates corresponding to the model with neighbor set N are $\bar{\theta}_{-1,0} = \bar{\theta}_{1,0} = 0.1262$, $\bar{\theta}_{1,1} = \bar{\theta}_{-1,-1} = -0.1613$, $\bar{\theta}_{-1,1} = \bar{\theta}_{1,-1} = 0.3116$ and $\bar{\rho} = 1.0520$. On the other hand the LS estimates obtained from (2.4) and (2.5) are

$$\hat{\theta}_{-1,0} = \hat{\theta}_{1,0} = 0.1470, \quad \hat{\theta}_{1,1} = \hat{\theta}_{-1,-1} = -0.1526,$$

$$\hat{\theta}_{-1,-1} = \hat{\theta}_{1,1} = 0.3680, \quad \hat{\rho} = 1.0126.$$

Note the approximate ML estimates $(\bar{\theta}, \bar{\rho})$ are much closer to the true parameters than the LS estimates $(\hat{\theta}, \hat{\rho})$.

Experiment II: (Synthetic data generated by using uniform random numbers and SAR model with $N = \{(-1,0), (1,0), (-1,1), (1,-1), (1,1), (-1,-1)\}$.)

The approximate ML estimation scheme has been developed by using Gaussian assumption for the variables. It should be of interest to see how good the estimation scheme is for non-Gaussian variables, as it would be unreasonable to assume that all images are generated by Gaussian random fields. Synthetic data obeying the same SAR model as in Experiment I but with $\omega(\cdot)$ obeying a uniform distribution was generated and the estimation scheme in Theorem 1 was used to estimate the parameters. The numerical values of the estimates are

$$\bar{\theta}_{-1,0} = \bar{\theta}_{1,0} = 0.1343, \quad \bar{\theta}_{-1,-1} = \bar{\theta}_{1,1} = -0.1562,$$

$$\bar{\theta}_{-1,1} = \bar{\theta}_{1,-1} = 0.3187, \quad \bar{\rho} = 1.0113.$$

The LS estimates are

$$\hat{\theta}_{-1,0} = \hat{\theta}_{1,0} = 0.1541, \quad \hat{\theta}_{-1,-1} = \hat{\theta}_{1,1} = -0.1530,$$

$$\hat{\theta}_{-1,1} = \hat{\theta}_{1,-1} = 0.3711, \quad \hat{\rho} = 0.9732.$$

Compared to the case of Gaussian data, the estimates $(\bar{\theta}, \bar{\rho})$ obtained for uniform data are inferior, understandably so. Nevertheless, the estimates are not too far from the true parameter values. Further the iterative estimate $\bar{\theta}$ is superior to the LS estimate.

III. ESTIMATION SCHEMES IN CM MODELS

A. Model Representation

Infinite Lattice Models [10]: Assume that the observations $\{y(s), s \in \Omega\}$ have zero mean and obey the CM model on an infinite lattice,

$$y(s) = \sum_{r \in N} \theta_r y(s+r) + e(s). \quad (3.1)$$

The neighbor set N is symmetric:

$$\theta_r = \theta_{-r}, \quad \text{for all } r \in N.$$

The stationary Gaussian noise sequence $\{e(s)\}$ is defined by

$$E(e(s) | \text{all } y(r), r \neq s) = 0,$$
$$E[e(s)] = 0,$$
$$E[e^2(s)] = \nu, \quad (3.2)$$

Using (3.1) and (3.2) one can prove that the noise sequence $\{e(s)\}$ has the correlation structure given below:

$$E(e(s)e(r)) = \begin{cases} \nu, & s = r, \\ -\theta_{s-r}\nu, & (s-r) \in N, \\ 0, & \text{otherwise.} \end{cases} \quad (3.3)$$

It can be shown [10] that the observation $y(s)$ obeying (3.1) satisfies the Markov condition,

$$p(y(s) | y(r), \text{all } r, r \neq s) = p(y(s) | y(s+r), \forall r \in N).$$

2) *Finite Lattice Models* [7], [16], [17], [21]: The finite lattice models used in this paper assume a toroidal lattice representation. The representation is characterized by (3.1) defined over $s \in \Omega_I$ together with

$$y(s) = \sum_{r \in N} \theta_r y_1(s+r) + e(s), \quad s \in \Omega_\beta, \quad (3.4)$$

where $y_1(\cdot)$ is defined in Section II-B. Equations (3.1) and (3.4) yield M^2 equations relating $\{e(s)\}$ and $\{y(s)\}$ through

$$H(\theta)y = e, \quad (3.5)$$

where $H(\theta)$ is a block-circulant symmetric matrix. To

ensure stationarity, we need

$$\mu'_s \triangleq (1 - 2\boldsymbol{\theta}^T \boldsymbol{\phi}_s) > 0, \quad \text{for all } s \in \Omega$$

$$\boldsymbol{\theta} = \text{col}[\theta_r, r \in N_s],$$

and

$$\boldsymbol{\phi}_s = \text{col}\left[\cos\frac{2\pi}{M}((s-1)^T r, r \in N_S\right]$$

where N_S is the asymmetrical half of N, i.e.,

$$N = N_S \cup \overline{N}_S,$$
$$\overline{N}_S = \{r: -r \in N_S\},$$
$$N_S \cap \overline{N}_S = \emptyset$$

B. Estimation in CM Models

1) Coding and ML Methods: Given an image and the infinite lattice conditional Markov model (3.1), we are interested in estimating the model's parameters. This problem has received some attention in the image processing literature [7]–[8]. The coding method [12] developed in statistical literature has been used for modeling the textures in [7], for the case of binary and binomial variables. Consider the case of a Gaussian CM model with $N = \{(0, 1), (1, 0), (0, -1), (-1, 0)\}$, characterized by $\boldsymbol{\theta} = \text{col}(\theta_{0,1}, \theta_{1,0})$. The conditional probability density of $y(\cdot)$ is

$$p(y(s)|y(s+r), r \in N)$$
$$= \frac{1}{(2\pi\nu)^{1/2}} \exp\left\{-\frac{1}{2\nu}\left[y(s) - \sum_{r \in N} \theta_r y(s+r)\right]^2\right\}.$$

The coding estimate $\boldsymbol{\theta}'_C$ of $\boldsymbol{\theta}$ is given by

$$\boldsymbol{\theta}'_C = \left[\sum_{\Omega_0} q(s) q^T(s)\right]^{-1} \sum_{\Omega_0} q(s) y(s), \quad (3.6)$$

where

$$q(s) = \text{col}[y(s+r) + y(s-r); r = (0, 1), (1, 0)],$$

and Ω_0 is a subset of Ω with every other site of Ω skipped. One of the main disadvantages of this method is that the estimates thus obtained are not efficient [21] due to a partial utilization (50 percent) of the data. The coding estimate is not unique. The coding scheme yields another estimate, say $\boldsymbol{\theta}''_C$, obtained from (3.6), where s is summed over $\Omega - \Omega_0$. The different coding estimates for the same parameter can differ considerably. For instance, in the Mercer–Hall wheat data and a CM model with $N = \{(0, 1), (0, -1), (1, 0), (-1, 0), (1, 1), (-1, -1), (-1, 1), (1, -1)\}$ the estimates of $\theta_{0,1}$ obtained by four possible coding schemes are 0.043, 0.085, 0.243, 0.236 [12]. These estimates are dependent and hence a simple averaging of these highly dependent estimates is not satisfactory.

An estimate with good asymptotic properties like consistency and efficiency can be obtained by the ML procedure. This method involves assuming an appropriate distribution for $\{e(s)\}$. But it is difficult to derive an explicit expression for the log-likelihood function even in Gaussian case due to the problem of evaluating the Jacobian of the transformation matrix. The ML estimate for general CM models can be obtained by assuming the toroidal lattice representation for $\{y(s)\}$ and Gaussian structure for $\{e(s)\}$ and maximizing the log-likelihood function. For the toroidal representation corresponding to (3.5) the log-likelihood function $\ln p(y|\boldsymbol{\theta}, \nu)$ can be written as [21]

$$\ln p(y|\boldsymbol{\theta}, \nu) = \sum (1/2) \ln(1 - 2\boldsymbol{\theta}^T \boldsymbol{\phi}_s)$$
$$- (M^2/2) \ln 2\pi\nu - \frac{1}{2\nu} y^T H(\boldsymbol{\theta}) y. \quad (3.7)$$

Note that the contribution of the exponential term of the probability density function is linear in $\boldsymbol{\theta}$ unlike the SAR models. Numerical optimization procedures like the Newton–Raphson approach can be applied to obtain the ML estimates. The ML estimates are consistent and efficient, but computationally unattractive. We give below an estimate which is consistent and computationally efficient.

2) A Consistent Estimation Scheme: Consider the estimate

$$\boldsymbol{\theta}^* = \left[\sum_{\Omega_I} q(s) q^T(s)\right]^{-1}\left(\sum_{\Omega_I} q(s) y(s)\right) \quad (3.8)$$

and

$$\nu^* = \frac{1}{M^2} \sum_{\Omega_I} (y(s) - \boldsymbol{\theta}^{*T} q(s))^2, \quad (3.9)$$

where Ω_I is as in Section II-B. The estimate $\boldsymbol{\theta}^*$ is an improvement over the coding estimates like $\boldsymbol{\theta}'_C$, $\boldsymbol{\theta}''_C$, etc. We will state a theorem regarding the consistency of the estimate $\boldsymbol{\theta}^*$ and give an expression for the asymptotic variance of the estimate $\boldsymbol{\theta}^*$. Although this estimate was suggested in [10], no results are known regarding its statistical behavior. An expression for the asymptotic variance of $\boldsymbol{\theta}^*$ for an isotropic conditional model with $N = \{(0, 1), (1, 0), (0, -1), (-1, 0)\}$ is given.

Theorem 2: Let $y(s)$, $s \in \Omega$ be the set of observations obeying the CM model (3.1). Then

a) the estimate $\boldsymbol{\theta}^*$ is asymptotically consistent;
b) the asymptotic covariance matrix of $\boldsymbol{\theta}^*$ is

$$E(\boldsymbol{\theta} - \boldsymbol{\theta}^*)(\boldsymbol{\theta} - \boldsymbol{\theta}^*)^T$$
$$= \frac{1}{M^2}\left[\nu Q^{-1} + 2\nu^2 Q^{-2} - \frac{\nu}{M^2} Q^{-1} \sum_s \sum_{\substack{r \\ (s-r) \in N}} \theta_{(s-r)} T_{r,s} Q^{-1}\right], \quad (3.10)$$

where $Q = E[q(s) q^T(s)]$, and $T_{r,s} = E[q(r) q^T(s)]$;
c) for the isotropic conditional model with $N = \{(0, 1), (1, 0), (0, -1), (-1, 0)\}$ and $\theta_r = \theta$, for all $r \in N$ the asymptotic expected mean square error is

$$E(\theta - \theta^*)^2 = \frac{2\theta^2(1 - 4\theta\alpha_{1,0})^2}{4M^2\alpha_{1,0}^2}, \quad (3.11)$$

TABLE I
COMPUTATION OF ASYMPTOTIC VARIANCES AND EFFICIENCIES OF DIFFERENT ESTIMATES IN ISOTROPIC CONDITIONAL MODEL WITH $N = \{(0, 1), (0, -1), (-1, 0), (1, 0)\}$; COLUMN 5 IS FROM [21]

4θ	$M^2 \text{var}(\hat{\theta}_{ML})$	$M^2 \text{var}(\theta_C')$	$M^2 \text{var}(\theta^*)$	$\text{eff}(\theta_C')$	$\text{eff}(\theta^*)$
.1	.4928	.497	.494	.991	.9975
.2	.472	.489	.478	.965	.987
.3	.437	.474	.450	.921	.971
.4	.390	.454	.412	.859	.946
.5	.333	.427	.365	.779	.912
.6	.267	.393	.309	.681	.864
.7	.197	.349	.244	.564	.807
.8	.1243	.296	.1753	.419	.709
.9	.0556	.224	.1004	.248	.553

where

$$\alpha_{k,l} = \frac{\text{cov}(y(s), y(s + (k, l)))}{\text{cov}(y^2(s))}. \quad (3.12)$$

The elements of matrices Q and $T_{r,s}$ are functions of normalized autocorrelation coefficients $\alpha_{k,l}$. The proof is given in Appendix II.

Equation (3.8) can also be used for estimation in toroidal lattice representations by summing over Ω instead of Ω_I. The resulting difference in the numerical values is negligible for sufficiently large M.

C. Comparison of Estimates

We compare the asymptotic variance of the estimate (3.8), with the asymptotic variances of the coding estimate and the ML estimate for the isotropic conditional model in part c) of Theorem 2. From [21], the asymptotic variance of the coding estimate is

$$M^2 \text{var}(\theta_C^*) = \frac{\theta(1 - 4\theta\alpha_{1,0})}{2\alpha_{1,0}}. \quad (3.13)$$

Also from [21], the variance of the ML estimate $\hat{\theta}_{ML}$ is

$$\text{var}(\hat{\theta}_{ML}) = \frac{0.5}{M^2(I(\theta) - 4V_{10}^2(\theta))}, \quad (3.14)$$

where

$$I(\theta) = \frac{1}{4\pi^2} \int\int_0^{2\pi} \frac{(\cos x + \cos y)^2 \, dx \, dy}{(1 - 2\theta(\cos x + \cos y))^2}$$

and

$$V_{st}(\theta) = \frac{1}{4\pi^2} \int\int_0^{2\pi} \frac{\cos(sx + ty) \, dx \, dy}{(1 - 2\theta(\cos x + \cos y))}.$$

Tabulated values of $V_{10}(\theta)$, $\alpha_{1,0}$, and $I(\theta)$ are available in [21] for different values of θ. Using these values, (3.11), (3.15), and (3.16), the columns 2–4 of Table I are computed. The asymptotic efficiencies, in columns 5 and 6 are defined by

$$\text{eff}(\theta_C') = \frac{\text{var}(\theta_{ML})}{\text{var}(\theta_C')}$$

and

$$\text{eff}(\theta^*) = \frac{\text{var}(\theta_{ML})}{\text{var}(\theta^*)}.$$

It is evident that the estimate θ^* computed using (3.8) is more efficient than the coding estimate for all θ. For small values of θ, the efficiencies of both θ_C' and θ^* are nearly one. But as θ approaches 0.25, the efficiency of θ_C falls compared to that of θ^*. For $\theta = 0.9/4$, the efficiency of θ^* is more than twice that of θ_C'. Note that column 5 is available in [21].

D. Experimental Results

We give the results of applying the estimation scheme (3.8)–(3.9) to some synthetic data generated from known CM models. The synthetic generation scheme is given in Appendix I and the results of the estimation scheme are given below.

Experiment III: (Gaussian Data and a CM model with $N = \{(-1, 1), (1, 1), (1, -1), (-1, -1)\}$.)

In the true model the values of α and ν are 30.0 and 1.1111 respectively, $\theta_{-1,1} = -0.14$, and $\theta_{1,1} = 0.28$. Using this model, synthetic data was generated. For estimation of the parameters, the sample mean was subtracted and (3.13)–(3.14) were used. The actual values of the estimates of the estimates are $\theta_{-1,1}^* = -0.1410$, $\theta_{1,1}^* = 0.2787$, and $\nu^* = 1.1033$ which are quite close to the true parameters.

Experiment IV: (Synthetic data generated by uniform distribution and the neighbor set in experiment III.)

The estimate θ^* was not derived using any specific assumption regarding the underlying distribution of y and consequently it should be fairly robust. To test this hypothesis $y(\cdot)$ was synthesized for the model in experiment III, the sequence $\eta(\cdot)$ being obtained from a uniform random number generator with zero mean and unit variance. The values of estimates are $\theta^*_{-1,1} = -0.14282$, $\theta^*_{1,1} = 0.27572$, and $\nu^* = 1.146$ which are not much different from the true θ compared to the estimates for Gaussian data.

IV. Choice of Neighbors in Simultaneous and Conditional Models

A. Motivation and Possible Approaches

We briefly discuss the need for choosing appropriate SAR or CM models, consider possible approaches and suggest decision rules. From one-dimensional time series analysis, it is known that a model of appropriate order should be fitted to obtain good results in applications like forecasting and control. A similar situation is true in the case of two-dimensional models. The problem becomes more difficult due to the rich variety of model structures. In the two-dimensional case, within the same class of (say) SAR models, different neighbor sets account for different patterns as shown in [18], [19]. Thus the quality of the reconstructed image varies considerably depending on how similar the underlying model is to the true model, and so the use of appropriate neighbor set is important.

Suppose we have an original image, (say) a 64×64 window from one of the Brodatz textures, and fit different SAR of CM models to the texture. It may be argued that by visual inspection of the reconstructed patterns corresponding to the different fitted models, a decision can be made regarding the appropriate model. There are several criticisms of this procedure. First the decision rule is subjective and no quantitative measure of possible error in the decision is given. More significantly, the reconstructed patterns corresponding to an original model and another model which includes the original model and some extra neighbors look very similar. Hence, a decision based on visual inspection is unreliable. Given an arbitrary image it should be possible to choose on a quantitative basis without visual inspection an appropriate model from a family of such models. In the context of this paper, different models should be interpreted as representing different neighbor sets N. We discuss the possible statistical procedures for both SAR and CM models and suggest decision rules separately.

The possible approaches are using pairwise hypothesis testing [8], [11], [12], Akaike's information criterion (AIC) [13], and the Bayes approach [20]. The pairwise hypothesis method has been used for SAR models in [11], [12] for wheat and orange data, for conditional models in field data [12] and texture modeling [8]. The main criticisms of this approach are that the resulting decision rules are not transitive, i.e., if a model C_1 is preferred to C_2 and C_2 is preferred to C_3, then it does not follow that C_1 is preferred to C_3 [22]. Also the decision rules are not consistent, i.e., the probability of choosing an incorrect model does not go to zero even as the number of observations goes to infinity. In the literature on the choice of an appropriate CM model [8], [12] the test statistics are computed using the estimate derived by coding methods. As discussed in Section III, the coding estimates are not efficient and in general more than one estimate results for a given CM model. The use of coding estimates in the choice of neighbor sets leads to several problems [8] and some *ad hoc* decision rules are used.

The model selection problem comes under the category of a multiple decision problem. A method that is well-suited to this problem is to compute a test statistic for different models and choose the one corresponding to the minimum. The AIC criterion and the Bayes method are two such procedures. The AIC method has been used for the choice of SAR models in the literature [13]. The AIC method, in general, gives transitive decision rules but is not consistent even for one-dimensional autoregressive models [23].

B. Bayes Decision Rules for Choice of the SAR Model

We formulate the problem and give the test statistic. The actual derivation of the test statistic can be done by using standard Bayes decision theory as in [20] for SAR models.

Suppose we have three sets N_1, N_2, and N_3 of neighbors containing m_1, m_2, and m_3 neighbors respectively. Corresponding to each N_i, we have a toroidal SAR model C_i

$$y(s) = \sum_{r \in N_k} \theta_{kr} y(s+r) + \sqrt{\rho_k}\, \omega(s), \quad s \in \Omega_I, \quad (4.1)$$

$$y(s) = \sum_{r \in N_k} \theta_{kr} y_1(s+r) + \sqrt{\rho_k}\, \omega(s), \quad s \in \Omega_B, \quad (4.2)$$

where $y_1(\cdot)$ is as in Section II-B, $\theta_{k,r} \neq 0$, $r \in N_k$, and $\rho_k > 0$, $k = 1, 2, 3$ and the noise sequence $\{\omega(s)\}$ is Gaussian.

The models C_i, $i = 1, 2, \cdots$ are mutually exclusive. According to Bayesian theory, the optimal decision rule for minimizing the average probability of decision error chooses the model C_i which maximizes the posterior probability $P(C_i/y)$, where y is the vector of all the observations. The quantity $P(C_i/y)$ is computed from the Bayes rule, $P(C_i/y) = p(y/C_i) P(C_i)/P(y)$. We will set $P(C_i)$ same for all i in the absence of any contrary information, so that

$$p(y/C_k) = \int p(y/\theta, \rho) p(\theta, \rho/C_k) |d\theta|\, d\rho.$$

The representation (4.1)–(4.2) together with the Gaussian assumption yields an expression for $p(y/\theta, \rho)$ similar to (2.14) in Section II-C. By assuming that $p(\theta, \rho/C_i)$ is a regular prior density and using asymptotic integration results [24] for large values of M, it can be shown that [20]

$$p(y/C_k) \approx -(M^2/2) \ln \bar{\rho}_k$$
$$+ (1/2) \sum_{s \in \Omega} \ln(1 - \bar{\theta}_k^T C_{ks} + \bar{\theta}_k^T Q_{ks} \bar{\theta}_k)$$
$$- (m_k/2) \ln(M^2) + \ln p(\bar{\theta}_k, \bar{\rho}_k/C_k).$$

If the prior densities $p(\theta, \rho/C_k)$ are known they can be substituted in $p(y/C_k)$ given above. In general, for the model selection problem the prior densities are hard to

TABLE II
Details of SAR Models Fitted to Gaussian Data Generated by $N = \{(-1,0), (1,0), (-1,1), (1,-1), (-1,-1), (1,1)\}$, $\alpha = 30.0$, $\rho = 1.1111$, $\theta_{-1,0} = \theta_{1,0} = 0.12$, $\theta_{-1,1} = \theta_{1,-1} = 0.28$, $\theta_{-1,-1} = \theta_{1,1} = -0.14$[1]

Number	Neighbor Set N	$\hat{\rho}$	Estimate of Coefficients	Test Statistic C_k
1	$(-1,0), (1,0),$ $(-1,1), (1,-1),$ $(-1,-1), (1,1)$	1.0520	$\theta_{-1,0} = \theta_{1,0} = .1262$ $\theta_{-1,1} = \theta_{1,-1} = .3116$ $\theta_{-1,-1} = \theta_{1,1} = -.1613$	2088.3 *
2	$(0,-1), (0,1),$ $(-1,1), (1,-1),$ $(-1,-1), (1,1)$	1.1540	$\theta_{0,-1} = \theta_{0,1} = .0396$ $\theta_{-1,1} = \theta_{1,-1} = .3254$ $\theta_{-1,-1} = \theta_{1,1} = -.1691$	2480.
3	$(-1,0), (0,-1),$ $(-1,-1)$	2.5713	$\theta_{0,-1} = .0504$ $\theta_{-1,0} = .2826$ $\theta_{-1,-1} = -.5625$	3863.3
4	$(0,-1) (0,1),$ $(-1,0), (1,0)$	3.4651	$\theta_{0,-1} = \theta_{0,1} = .0524$ $\theta_{-1,0} = \theta_{1,0} = .1705$	5381.7
5	$(-1,1), (1,-1),$ $(-1,-1), (1,1)$	1.1595	$\theta_{-1,1} = \theta_{1,-1} = .3332$ $\theta_{-1,-1} = \theta_{1,1} = -.1638$	2523.5
6	$(0,-1), (0,1),$ $(-1,0), (1,0),$ $(-1,1), (1,-1),$ $(-1,-1), (1,1)$	1.0535	$\theta_{0,-1} = \theta_{0,1} = .0169$ $\theta_{-1,0} = \theta_{1,0} = .1233$ $\theta_{-1,1} = \theta_{1,-1} = .3086$ $\theta_{-1,-1} = \theta_{1,1} = -.1638$	2103.1
7	$(-1,0), (1,0),$ $(-1,1), (1,-1),$ $(-1,-1), (1,1),$ $(-2,0), (2,0)$	1.0558	$\theta_{-1,0} = \theta_{1,0} = .1276$ $\theta_{-1,1} = \theta_{1,-1} = .3095$ $\theta_{-1,-1} = \theta_{1,1} = -.1578$ $\theta_{-2,0} = \theta_{2,0} = .0079$	2114.7

[1] The estimate of $\alpha = 30.034$.

specify. Hence we derive an approximate test statistic by dropping the terms due to prior densities. Then the decision rule for the choice of appropriate neighbor set is the following.

Choose the neighbor set N_{k*} if

$$k^* = \arg\min_k \{C_k\}, \quad (4.3)$$

where

$$C_k = \left\{-\sum_{s \in \Omega} \ln(1 - 2\bar{\theta}^T C_{ks} + \bar{\theta}_k^T Q_{ks} \bar{Q}) + M^2 \ln \bar{\rho}_k + m_k \ln(M^2)\right\},$$

$$Q_{ks} = S_{ks} S_{ks}^T + C_{ks} C_{ks}^T,$$

$$C_{ks} = \text{col}\left[\cos \frac{2\pi}{M}((s-1)^T r), r \in N_k\right], \quad (4.4)$$

and

$$S_{ks} = \text{col}\left[\sin \frac{2\pi}{M}((s-1)^T r), r \in N_k\right].$$

Note that if the kth CM model has a unilateral SAR representation, then the decision statistics reduce to

$$C_k = M^2 \ln \bar{\rho}_k + m_k \ln M^2. \quad (4.5)$$

This expression follows from the fact that the Jacobian of the transformation matrix $B(\theta)$ from the noise variates to the observations is approximately unity. The model selection procedure consists of computing C_k for different models, which may be causal or noncausal, and choosing the one corresponding to the lowest C_k. The difference between the Akaike rule and the rule in (4.5) is that the coefficient of m_k in (4.5) is $\ln M^2$ whereas it is 2 (independent of M) in the Akaike rule.

C. Experimental Results

To illustrate the usefulness of the decision rule in (4.2), we consider the synthetic Gaussian data generated by the SAR model $N = N_0 = \{(-1,0), (1,0), (-1,1), (1,-1), (-1,-1), (1,1)\}$. The test statistics C_k for each of the fitted models are given in Table II together with the model description and estimates of parameters. The decision rule correctly picks up the true model. Note that the numerical values corresponding to closely competing models are quite close.

It would be interesting to see if the conclusion reached by the decision rule (4.4) derived using Gaussian assumption for $\{\omega(\cdot)\}$ agrees with visual inspection. To answer

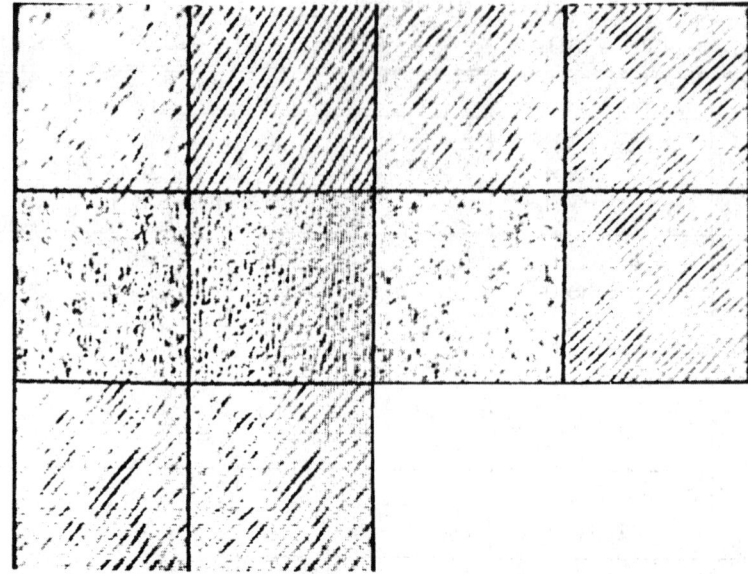

Fig. 1. Synthetic images generated by different SAR models fitted to data generated by the SAR model with true $N = \{(-1,0), (1,0), (-1,1), (1,-1), (-1,-1), (1,1)\}$ in Table II. Windows $(1,1)$, $(1,2)$, and $(1,3)$ are generated by true N, with true parameters, LS estimates and approximate ML estimates respectively. Windows $(2,2)$ through $(3,2)$ are generated by models 3 through 7 in Table II and Window $(1,4)$ from model 2 in Table II. Window $(2,1)$ is generated by a SAR model with $N = \{(-1,0), (1,0), (0,-1)\}$.

this query, synthetic patterns corresponding to some of the fitted models in Table II are given in Fig. 1. We shall use matrix notation in referring to the windows in Fig. 1. The image $(1,1)$ corresponds to the true model in Table II and $(1,2)$ is generated by the true neighbor set N, with the LS estimates replacing the true parameters. Note that the quality of the image in $(1,2)$ is poor, due to the inconsistency of the LS estimate. The window $(1,3)$ corresponds to the true neighbor set with the parameters estimated by the approximate ML scheme and is similar to the original pattern. The windows $(2,2)$ through $(3,2)$ are generated by models 3 through 7 in Table II. Approximate ML estimation method is used for parameter estimation in these windows. The image $(2,1)$ is generated by the model with $N = \{(-1,0), (0,-1), (-1,-0)\}$ and is not at all good. The window $(2,3)$ is generated by $N = \{(0,1), (0,-1), (-1,0), (1,0)\}$ and does not possess the diagonal patterns present in the original image in $(1,1)$. The window $(2,4)$ is generated by a SAR model with $N = \{(-1,1), (1,-1), (-1,-1), (1,1)\}$, a subset of the neighbor set of the true model and is not as good as the image $(1,3)$. Lastly, the image $(3,1)$ depends on the eight nearest neighbors and looks very similar to image $(1,3)$.

In general, the patterns corresponding to two SAR models with neighbor sets N_1 and N_0, such that $N_0 \subseteq N_1$, the common coefficients being same, others being negligible, are visually very similar to one another but the decision rule picks up the true model. Similar results are noted for the case, when the underlying distribution of $\omega(\cdot)$ is uniform. The quality of synthesized pictures is inferior compared to the Gaussian case, due to the violation of the distribution assumption.

D. Bayes Decision Rule for the Choice of CM Models

Suppose we have three sets N_1, N_2, N_3 of neighbors containing $2m_1$, $2m_2$, $2m_3$ members respectively. Corresponding to each N_k, we write the CM model as

$$y(s) = \sum_{r \in N_k} \theta_{kr} y(s+r) + e(s), \quad s \in \Omega_I, \quad (4.6)$$

$$y(s) = \sum_{r \in N_k} \theta_{kr} y_1(s+r) + e(s), \quad s \in \Omega_B, \quad (4.7)$$

where $y_1(\cdot)$ is defined in Section II-B, $\theta_{kr} \neq 0$, $r \in N_k$, $\nu_k > 0$, $k = 1, 2, 3$, and $\{e(s)\}$ is Gaussian. Then the decision rule for the choice of appropriate neighbors is: choose the neighbor set N_{k*} if,

$$k^* = \arg\min_k \{C_k\}, \quad (4.8)$$

where

$$C_k = -\sum_{s \in \Omega} \ln(1 - 2\theta_k^{*T}\phi_{ks}) + M^2 \ln \nu_k + m_k \ln(M^2), \quad (4.9)$$

$$\theta_k^* = \text{col}[\theta_r^*, r \in N_{Sk}],$$

and

$$\phi_{k,s} = \text{col}\left[\cos \frac{2\pi}{M}((s-1)^T r, r \in N_{Sk}\right]$$

where N_{Sk} is the asymmetrical half of N_k, i.e.,

$$N_k = N_{Sk} \cup \overline{N}_{Sk},$$
$$\overline{N}_{Sk} = \{r: -r \in N_{Sk}\}, N_{Sk} \cap \overline{N}_{Sk} = \emptyset.$$

The model selection procedure consists of computing C_k

TABLE III
DETAILS OF CM MODELS FITTED TO THE GAUSSIAN DATA GENERATED BY $N = \{(-1,1), (1,1), (1,-1),$
$(-1,-1)\}, \alpha = 30.0, \nu = 1.1111, \theta_{-1,1} = \theta_{1,-1} = -0.14,$ AND $\theta_{1,1} = \theta_{-1,-1} = 0.28$[2]

	Number	Neighbor Set N_1	$\hat{\nu}$	Estimate of Coefficients	Test Statistics C_k
	1	(1,1)	1.1638	$\theta_{1,1} = .3116$	1575.3
	2	(-1,1)	1.3520	$\theta_{-1,1} = .2093$	1628.9
True Model	3	(-1,1), (1,1)	1.1033	$\theta_{-1,1} = -.1410$ $\theta_{1,1} = .27875$	1464.30*
	4	(0,1), (1,0)	1.4934	$\theta_{0,1} = -.0052$ $\theta_{1,0} = -.0020$	1659.7
	5	(-1,1), (1,1) (1,0)	1.1033	$\theta_{-1,1} = -.14101,$ $\theta_{1,1} = .27877,$ $\theta_{1,0} = -.0051$	1472.7
	6	(-1,1), (1,1), (0,1)	1.1033	$\theta_{-1,1} = -.1410,$ $\theta_{1,1} = .27873,$ $\theta_{0,1} = -.001717$	1472.2
	7	(-1,1), (1,1) (0,1), (1,0)	1.1033	$\theta_{-1,1} = -.14101,$ $\theta_{1,1} = .27876$ $\theta_{1,0} = .0049,$ $\theta_{0,1} = -.0009$	1481.0

[2] The estimate of $\hat{\alpha} = 30.00$.

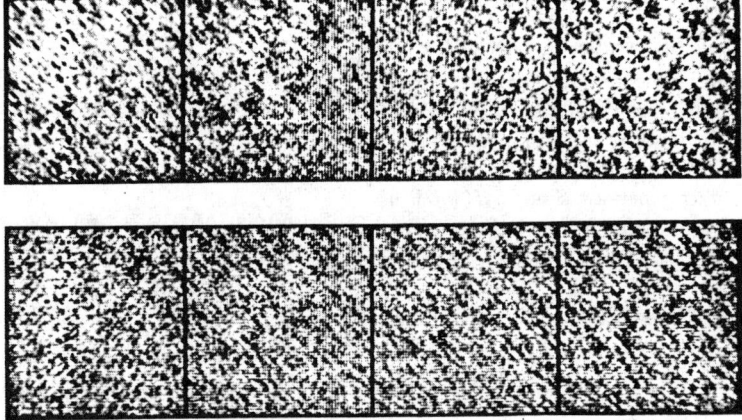

Fig. 2. Synthetic images generated by different CM models fitted to data generated by the CM model with true $N = \{(-1,1), (1,-1), (-1,-1), (1,1)\}$ in Table III. Window (1, 1) is generated by the true model in Table III. The images (1, 2) through (2, 4) are generated by models 1 through 7 in Table III. Windows (2, 2), (2, 3), and (2, 4) corresponding to models which include true N and some extra neighbors look visually similar to the window (1, 4) corresponding to true N but the decision rule (4.9) correctly eliminates the former models.

for different models and choosing the one corresponding to the lowest C_k.

E. Experimental Results

To illustrate the usefulness of the decision rule in (4.8), we consider the synthetic data generated by the CM model with $N = \{(-1,1), (1,1), (1,-1), (-1,-1)\}$ considered in experiment III. The test statistics C_k in (4.9) was computed for each of the fitted models in Table III. The decision rule correctly picks up the true model.

The synthetic patterns corresponding to some of the fitted models in Table III are given in Fig. 2. The window (1, 1) corresponds to the pattern generated by the neighbor set N mentioned above and parameters $\theta_{-1,1} = -0.14$ and $\theta_{1,1} = 0.28$. The images (1, 2) through (2, 4) are generated by models 1 through 7 in Table III. The parameters are estimated by least squares method. Image (1, 4) is generated with the true neighbor set and estimated parameters and is very similar to the image (1, 1). The window (2, 1) corresponds to the inappropriate model with $N = \{(0, 1), (1, 0), (0, -1), (-1, 0)\}$ and is comparatively of poor quality. Image (2, 4) is generated by a CM model with $N = \{(1,0), (0,1), (-1,1), (1,1), (-1,0), (0,-1), (1,-1), (-1,-1)\}$ and is very similar to the original. However, the decision rule correctly eliminates this model in preference to correct model.

V. Conclusion

We have considered some aspects of statistical inference in spatial interaction models. Specifically, we have considered some estimation schemes in both SAR and CM models. We have also given decision rules for the choice of neighbors in these models. We have not suggested any preference of simultaneous AR models over conditional models or vice versa. The appropriateness of one class of models over the other for the given data should be inferred from the data itself.

Acknowledgment

The authors would like to thank the reviewers for their comments which have improved the readability of the paper. The second author would like to sincerely thank Professor Azriel Rosenfeld for his continued interest and encouragement.

Appendix I

Synthetic Generation of Data Obeying Known CM Models

Equation (3.5) can be equivalently written as [17] $\sqrt{H(\theta)}\, y = \sqrt{\nu}\, \eta$, where η is an i.i.d. noise sequence with zero mean and unit variance, and is of known distribution, not necessarily Gaussian. The synthetic generation is done by assigning some arbitrary values in the stationary region to θ and the noise sequence is generated from a random number generator. Since $\sqrt{H(\theta)}$ is a block-circulant matrix Fourier computations can be used. The synthetic generation scheme is as follows [17]:

$$y = \sum_{\Omega} \left(f_s x_s / \sqrt{\mu'_s(\theta)} \right) + \alpha(\mathbf{1}), \quad \text{(A1)}$$

where $x_s = (\sqrt{\nu}/M^2) f_s^{*T} \eta$, $\mathbf{1} = (1,1,\cdots,1)$, M^2-vector, and $\mu'_s(\theta)$, and $s \in \Omega$ are defined in Section III-A2).

We generate the vector η from pseudorandom numbers, generate its Fourier transform $\{x_s\}$, and finally use (A1).

Appendix II

Proof of Theorem 2: a) We have from (3.8)

$$\theta^* = \left[\sum_\Omega q(s) q^T(s) \right]^{-1} \left(\sum_\Omega q(s) y(s) \right). \quad \text{(A2)}$$

Substituting for $y(s)$ from (3.1) and simplifying, we have

$$\left[\sum_\Omega q(s) q^T(s) \right] (\theta^* - \theta) = \sum_\Omega q(s) e(s). \quad \text{(A3)}$$

Since $E(q(s)e(s)) = 0$ by (3.2) and $[\sum_\Omega q(s) q^T(s)]$ is a positive definite matrix, the consistency of the estimate θ follows.

b) To make our calculations easy we assume from now on that $e(s)$ is normally distributed. Multiplying (A3) by its transpose and taking expectations, we have

$$E\left[\sum_s q(s) q^T(s) (\theta^* - \theta)(\theta^* - \theta^T) \left(\sum_s q(s) q^T(s) \right) \right]$$

$$= E\left[\sum_s q(s) e(s) \sum_r (q(r) e(r))^T \right]. \quad \text{(A4)}$$

The RHS of (A4)

$$= \sum_s \sum_r E(q(s) e(s)) E(q^T(r) e(r))$$
$$+ \sum_s \sum_r E(q(s) e(r)) E(q^T(r) e(s))$$
$$+ \sum_s \sum_r E(e(s) e(r)) E(q(r) q^T(s))$$
$$= I + II + III, \quad \text{(A5)}$$

where

$$I = 0, \quad \text{by using (3.2)}, \quad \text{(A6)}$$

$$II = 2M^2 \nu^2 I_{m \times m}, \quad \text{by using (3.2) and } E(e(s) y(s)) = \nu, \quad \text{(A7)}$$

$$III = \nu \sum_s E(q(s) q^T(s))$$
$$\quad - \nu \sum_{\substack{r \ s \\ (s-r) \in N}} \theta(s-r) E(q(r) q^T(s)), \quad \text{using (3.3)}. \quad \text{(A8)}$$

Defining

$$E(q(s) q^T(s)) = Q, \quad m \times m \text{ matrix},$$
$$E(q(r) q^T(s)) = T_{r,s}, \quad m \times m \text{ matrix},$$
$$III = M^2 \nu Q - \nu \sum_{\substack{s \ r \\ (s-r) \in N}} \theta(s-r) T_{r,s}. \quad \text{(A9)}$$

Substituting (A6), (A7), and (A9) the RHS of (A4)

$$= M^2 \left[\nu Q + 2\nu^2 I_{m \times m} - \nu \sum_{\substack{s \ r \\ (s-r) \in N}} \theta_{(s-r)} T_{r,s} \right]. \quad \text{(A10)}$$

For large values of M,

$$\frac{1}{M^2} \sum_s q(s) q^T(s) = Q + \xi(M), \quad \text{(A11)}$$

where $\xi(M)$ is such that

$$E(\xi^2(M)) = O(1/M^2). \quad \text{(A12)}$$

Using (A11)

$$(\text{LHS of (A4)})/M^4$$
$$= E\left[(Q + \xi(M))(\theta^* - \theta)(\theta^* - \theta)^T (\theta + \xi(M))^T \right] \quad \text{(A13)}$$

$$\simeq Q E\left[(\theta^* - \theta)(\theta^* - \theta)^T \right] Q + O(1/M^2), \quad \text{by (A12)}. \quad \text{(A14)}$$

Substitution of (A10) and (A13) into (A4) yields (3.10). Q.E.D.

c) Consider the isotropic conditional model with $N = \{(0,1), (1,0), (0,-1), (-1,0)\}$, we have

$$y(s) = \theta q(s) + e(s), \quad (A15)$$

where $q(s) = y(s + (0,1)) + y(s + (0,-1)) + y(s + (1,0)) + y(s + (-1,0))$.

The part b) of Theorem 2 yields

$$E(\theta^* - \theta)^2 = \frac{1}{M^2} \frac{1}{(E(q^2(s)))^2}$$

$$\cdot \left[4\nu^2 + \nu E(q^2(s)) - \theta \nu \sum_s \sum_{\substack{r \\ (s-r) \in N}} E(q(s)q(r)) \right]. \quad (A16)$$

Let

$$\gamma_{k,l} = E[y(s)y(s + (k,l))] \quad (A17)$$

and

$$\gamma_{k,l} = \gamma_{|k|,|l|} = \gamma_{l,k}. \quad (A18)$$

Express the higher order correlations $\gamma_{2,1}$, $\gamma_{2,0}$, and $\gamma_{3,0}$ in terms of $\gamma_{0,0}$, $\gamma_{1,0}$, and $\gamma_{1,1}$ by the following formulas

$$\gamma_{0,0} = \nu / (1 - 4\theta \alpha_{1,0}), \quad (A19)$$

$$\gamma_{2,1} = \frac{1}{2\theta} \gamma_{1,1} - \gamma_{1,0}, \quad (A20)$$

$$\gamma_{3,0} = \gamma_{1,0}\left(1 + \frac{1}{\theta^2}\right) - \frac{\gamma_{0,0}}{\theta} - \frac{3\gamma_{1,1}}{\theta}, \quad (A21)$$

$$\gamma_{2,0} = \frac{1}{\theta} \gamma_{1,0} - \gamma_{0,0} - 2\gamma_{1,1}. \quad (A22)$$

Equations (A19)–(A22) can be obtained by multiplying $y(s)$ by appropriately chosen $y(s + (k,l))$ and taking expectations on both sides of the equation.

Consider the various terms in (A16).

$$E(q^2(s)) = \frac{1}{\theta} 4\gamma_{1,0}, \quad \text{using (A22), (A23)}$$

$$\sum_s \sum_{\substack{r \\ (s-r) \in N}} E(q(s)q(r)) = 4[9\gamma_{1,0} + \gamma_{3,0} + 6\gamma_{2,1}]$$

$$= 4\left[4\gamma_{1,0} + \frac{1}{\theta^2}\gamma_{1,0} - \frac{1}{\theta}\gamma_{0,0}\right],$$

$$\times \text{ by (A20)-(A21)}, \quad (A24)$$

Substitution of (A23) and (A24) in (A16) yields

$$E(\theta^* - \theta)^2 = \frac{1}{M^2} \frac{\theta^2}{16\gamma_{1,0}^2} \left[4\nu^2 + 4\nu\gamma_{0,0} - 16\theta\gamma_{1,0}\nu\right],$$

which on using (A19) and $\alpha_{1,0} = \gamma_{1,0}\gamma_{0,0}$ yields

$$E(\theta^* - \theta)^2 = \frac{2\theta^2(1 - 4\theta\alpha_{1,0})^2}{4M^2\alpha_{1,0}^2}.$$

References

[1] A. K. Jain and J. R. Jain, "Partial difference equations and finite difference methods in image processing—Part 2: image restoration," *IEEE Trans. Automat. Contr.*, vol. AC-23, pp. 817–833, Oct. 1978.

[2] R. L. Kashyap and R. Chellappa, "Image restoration using random fields," in *Proc. Eighteenth Ann. Allerton Conf. Commn., Contr., Comput.*, University of Illinois, Urbana, IL, pp. 956–965, Oct. 1980.

[3] J. W. Woods, "Markov image modeling," *IEEE Trans. Automat. Contr.*, vol. AC-23, pp. 846–850, Oct. 1978.

[4] E. J. Delp, R. L. Kashyap, and O. R. Mitchell, "Image data compression using autoregressive time series models," *Pattern Recog.*, vol. 11, pp. 313–323, Dec. 1979.

[5] B. H. McCormick and S. N. Jayaramamurthy, "Time series models for texture synthesis," *Int. J. Comput. Inform. Sci.*, vol. 3, no. 4, pp. 329–343, 1974.

[6] J. T. Tou, "Pictorial feature extraction and recognition via image modeling," *Comput. Graphics Image Proc.*, vol. 12, pp. 376–406, Apr. 1980.

[7] M. Hassner and J. Sklansky, "The use of Markov random fields as models of textures," *Comput. Graphics Image Proc.*, vol. 12, pp. 357–370, Apr. 1980.

[8] G. R. Cross and A. K. Jain, "Markov random field texture models," in *Proc. IEEE Comput. Soc. Conf. Pattern Recog. Image Proc.*, Dallas, TX, pp. 597–601, Aug. 1981.

[9] D. M. Goodman and M. P. Ekstrom, "Multi-dimensional spectral factorization and unilateral AR models," *IEEE Trans. Automat. Contr.*, vol. AC-25, pp. 258–262, Apr. 1980.

[10] J. W. Woods, "Two-dimensional discrete Markov random fields," *IEEE Trans. Inform. Theory*, vol. 18, pp. 232–240, Mar. 1972.

[11] P. Whittle, "On stationary processes in the plane," *Biometrika*, vol. 41, pp. 434–449, 1954.

[12] J. E. Besag, "Spatial interaction and statistical analysis of lattice systems," *J. Royal Stat. Soc., Ser. B*, vol. B-36, pp. 192–236, 1974.

[13] W. E. Larimore, "Statistical inference on stationary random fields," in *Proc. IEEE*, vol. 65, pp. 961–960, June 1977.

[14] K. Ord, "Estimation methods for models of spatial interaction," *J. Amer. Stat. Ass.*, vol. 70, pp. 120–126, Mar. 1975.

[15] R. L. Kashyap, "Univariate and multivariate random field models for images," *Comput. Graphics Image Proc.*, vol. 12, pp. 257–270, Mar. 1980.

[16] —, "Random field models on finite lattices for finite images," in *Proc. 5th Int. Conf. Pattern Recog.*, Miami, FL, Dec. 1980.

[17] —, "Finite lattice random field models for finite images," presented at the Conf. Inform. Sci. Syst., Baltimore, MD, Mar. 1981.

[18] R. Chellappa, "Stochastic models for image analysis and processing," Ph.D. dissertation, Purdue University, W. Lafayette, IN, Aug. 1981.

[19] R. Chellappa and R. L. Kashyap, "Synthetic generation and estimation in random field models of images," in *Proc. IEEE Comput. Soc. Conf. Pattern Recog. Image Proc.*, Dallas, TX, pp. 577–582, Aug. 1981.

[20] R. L. Kashyap, R. Chellappa, and N. Ahuja, "Decision rules for the choice of neighbors in random field models of images," *Comput. Graphics Image Proc.*, vol. 15, pp. 301–318, Apr. 1981.

[21] P. A. P. Moran and J. E. Besag, "On the estimation and testing of spatial interaction in Gaussian Lattices," *Biometrika*, vol. 62, no. 3, pp. 555–562, 1975.

[22] R. L. Kashyap, "A Bayesian comparison of different classes of models using empirical data," *IEEE Trans. Automat. Contr.*, vol. AC-22, pp. 715–727, Oct. 1977.

[23] —, "Inconsistency of the AIC rule for estimating the order of autoregressive models," *IEEE Trans. Automat. Contr.*, vol. AC-25, pp. 996–998, Oct. 1980.

[24] D. V. Lindley, "The use of prior probability distributions in statistical inference and decisions," in *Proc. Fourth Berkeley Symp. Math. Statist. Prob.*, vol. 1, pp. 453–468, 1961.

[25] R. Chellappa and R. L. Kashyap, "Digital image restoration using spatial interaction models," *IEEE Trans. Acous., Speech, Signal Processing*, pp. 461–472 June 1982.

[26] A. K. Jain, "Advances in mathematical models for image processing," in *Proc. IEEE*, vol. 69, no. 5, pp. 512–528, May 1981.

[27] N. K. Bose, *Applied Multidimensional Systems Theory*. New York: Van Nostrand Reinhold, 1982.

Characterization and Estimation of Two-Dimensional ARMA Models

RANGASAMI L. KASHYAP, FELLOW, IEEE

Abstract — A class of finite-order two-dimensional autoregressive moving average (ARMA) is introduced that can represent any process with rational spectral density. In this model the driving noise is correlated and need not be Gaussian. Currently known classes of ARMA models or AR models are shown to be subsets of the above class. The three definitions of Markov property are discussed, and the class of ARMA models are precisely stated which have the noncausal and semicausal Markov property without imposing any specific boundary conditions. Next two approaches are considered to estimate the parameters of a model to fit a given image. The first method uses only the empirical correlations and involves the solution of linear equations. The second method is the likelihood approach. Since the exact likelihood function is difficult to compute, we resort to approximations suggested by the toroidal models. Numerical experiments compare the quality of the two estimation schemes. Finally the problem of synthesizing a texture obeying an ARMA model is considered.

I. INTRODUCTION

PARAMETRIC representations for two-dimensional random fields are useful in many applications such as image synthesis, classification, spectral estimation, etc. This paper develops a finite stochastic difference equation model for regular two-dimensional random fields having rational spectral densities and discusses related topics such as the various definitions of weak Markov processes, parameter estimation, and synthesis of textures resembling a given non-Gaussian texture.

We will first give the background information regarding the structural representations. Rosanov [1], Woods [2], and Besag [3] have shown that any Gaussian Markov field having an all-pole spectral density (i.e., a reciprocal of a linear sinusoidal function) possesses a finite difference equation representation, the so-called conditional autoregressive (CAR) model in which the driving input noise is correlated but does not have, in general, a moving average representation. The set of models suggested earlier, such as the simultaneous AR models [3], [4], and causal recursive models [5], [6] is a proper subset of the set of CAR models.

As discussed later, the various types of two-dimensional autoregressive moving average (ARMA) models discussed in [7]–[9], [11] have the restriction that the denominator of the corresponding spectral density, say $A(z)$, is factorable, i.e., $A(z) = D_1(z_1, z_2) D_1(z_1^{-1}, z_2^{-1})$. Thus no general *finite* difference equation model is available for representing a discrete random field having a rational spectral density in which both the numerator and the denominator are not factorable. We emphasize the use of the word "finite" since a simple spectral density such as $[1 + \phi(\cos\lambda_1 + \cos\lambda_2)]/[1 - \theta(\cos\lambda_1 + \cos\lambda_2)]$, $|\phi|, |\theta| < 0.5$, $\phi \neq \theta$, cannot be represented by any of the ARMA models in [7]–[9], [11] using a *finite* number of parameters, but can always be represented by these models using an *infinite* number of parameters. But the principle of parsimony precludes the use of a model having a large number of parameters especially in tasks such as fitting models to the given data. In contrast, the class of recursive finite ARMA models in one dimension can represent any process with a rational spectral density of finite order.

The two-dimensional case differs significantly from the one-dimensional case in relation to the Markov property. There are three types of weak Markov property, namely, causal [10], semicausal [8], [9] and noncausal [1]–[3]. In contrast to the one-dimensional case, where a process obeying an ARMA model is a projection of a vector Markov process, the general ARMA model in the two-dimensional case is neither Markovian according to any of the three definitions, nor a projection of another Markov process. However, a particular subset of ARMA models is shown to possess the semicausal Markov property that was introduced in [8], [9]. We will clarify the precise structure of the ARMA models having the requisite semicausal Markov property without imposing any special boundary conditions.

The next topic to be covered is the estimation of parameters in a model to fit a given finite image. We present two approaches. In the first approach the parameter estimates are computed from the empirical correlations by solving linear equations. There are no iterations in contrast to the one-dimensional ARMA model parameter estimation problems. The second approach utilizes the likelihood. The exact expression for the likelihood of the given observations in terms of the parameters is very complicated. We consider an approximation that is easy to handle. The approximation happens to be the exact likelihood when the observations obey a variant of the ARMA model, the so-called toroidal ARMA model. Finally we discuss a procedure for synthesizing a texture obeying a given ARMA model.

Section II deals with the general ARMA representation and the relation to existing two-dimensional difference

---

Manuscript received August 16, 1982; revised February 14, 1984. This work was partially supported by the National Science Foundation under Grant ECS-80-09041 and a grant by the Office of Naval Research, under Grant N00014-82-K-0360.

The author is with the School of Electrical Engineering, Purdue University, West Lafayette, IN 47907.

equation models. Section III deals with the Markovian properties of the ARMA models. Section IV contains the parameter estimation using the estimated correlations. Section V deals with the likelihood approach, which includes the results of numerical experiments on the quality of estimates. Section VI deals with the problems of synthesizing a texture to resemble a real texture.

II. THE ARMA MODEL

Note that j, k, p, and q stand for integers and r and s stand for integer pairs. $z = (z_1, z_2)$. Let $y(s), s \in L$ be a two-dimensional random field $L = \{(j, k): j, k \text{ are integers}\}$. Let $y(\cdot)$ be stationary and have the correlation function $R(s)$ and spectral density $S(z)$,

$$S(z) = \sum_{j=-\infty}^{\infty} \sum_{k=-\infty}^{\infty} R(j,k) z_1^j z_2^k \quad (1)$$

$$= \nu B(z)/A(z), \quad z = [\exp 2\pi i \lambda], i = \sqrt{-1}, \quad (2)$$

$$A(z) = 1 - \sum_{r \in N_1} \theta_r z^r,$$

$$B(z) = 1 + \sum_{r \in N_2} \phi_r z^r, \theta_r = \theta_{-r}, \phi_r = \phi_{-r}. \quad (3)$$

Hereafter the notation $z = (\exp 2\pi i \lambda)$ stands for the vector $z = (\exp i 2\pi \lambda_1, \exp i 2\pi \lambda_2)$. N_i are *finite* subsets of $(L - (0,0))$ and are symmetric, i.e., if $(j, k) \in N_i$, then $(-j, -k) \in N_i$, $i = 1, 2$. A and B are finite-order polynomials. $A(z_1, z_2) = A(z_1^{-1}, z_2^{-1})$. The same applies for B.

$$A(z) \neq 0 \text{ and } B(z) \neq 0 \text{ for all } z \text{ such that } |z_i| = 1,$$
$$i = 1, 2. \quad (4)$$

$$A(z) \text{ and } B(z) \text{ have no common zero.} \quad (5)$$

Conditions (3) and (4) assure that $S(z)$ is finite, and positive for all real $\lambda = (\lambda_1, \lambda_2)$. The correlations $R(\cdot)$ of $y(\cdot)$ can be obtained from $S(\cdot)$ by the usual inversion formula

$$R(r) = \int_0^1 \int_0^1 S(z = \exp i 2\pi \lambda) \exp[2\pi i \lambda \cdot r] d\lambda_1 d\lambda_2. \quad (6)$$

In the two-dimensional case, $R(r = (j, k))$ is not necessarily a linear combination of exponentially decaying functions of j and k or exponentially decaying sinusoids, as in the one-dimensional case.

We will show the existence of a sequence obeying a spectral density in (2) by a constructive procedure. Let $\{w(s), s \in \Omega_M\}$ be a finite $M \times M$ sequence of i.i.d. (independent identically distributed) $(0, 1)$ variables with any appropriate density, and let $\{W_r, r \in \Omega_M\}$ be its corresponding DFT where

$$\Omega_M = \{(j, k), 0 \leq j, k \leq M - 1\}.$$

Let $\{y_M(s), s \in \Omega_M\}$ be the inverse DFT of the sequence $\{Y_{Ms}, s \in \Omega_M\}$ defined

$$Y_{Ms} = \left(\sqrt{\nu} \sqrt{B_s}/\sqrt{A_s}\right) W_s, s \in \Omega_M, \quad (7)$$

where $A_s = A(z = \exp i 2\pi s/M)$ and B_s can be defined similarly.

Theorem 1: As M tends to infinity, the correlations $R_M(s)$ of the sequence $\{y_M(s)\}$ tend to the corresponding correlations $R(s)$ in (6) that are associated with the spectral density (2).

Proof: The discrete spectral density of the sequence $y_M(\cdot)$ is $\{S_{Mr}, r \in \Omega_M\}$

$$S_{Ms} = E[Y_{Ms} Y_{Ms}^*]$$
$$= \nu B_s/A_s. \quad (8)$$

Thus the spectral density S_{Mr} is numerically equal to the spectral density (2) at all the grid points. The correlations $\{R_M(\cdot)\}$ can be obtained from $\{S_{Mr}\}$ by inverse DFT

$$R_M(p, q) = (1/M^2) \sum_{j=0}^{M-1} \sum_{k=0}^{M-1} (\nu B_{j,k}/A_{j,k})$$
$$\cdot \exp[i(2\pi/M)(pj + qk)]. \quad (9)$$

The summand in (9) and the integrand in (6) are identical at all the grid points of Ω_M and finite for all M. Hence as M tends to infinity, the summation $R_M(s)$ in (9) tends to the corresponding integral $R(s)$ in (6) by the definition of integral. □

A two-dimensional ARMA model is defined by the following difference equation (10), in which the driving input $e(\cdot)$ is correlated

$$y(s) = \sum_{r \in N_1} \theta_r y(s + r) + \sqrt{\nu} e(s), \quad (10)$$

or

$$A(z) y(s) = \sqrt{\nu} e(s), \quad (11)$$

where $e(\cdot)$ is a zero-mean correlated sequence with spectral density

$$S_e(z) = A(z) B(z), \quad (12)$$

A and B are defined in (3).

It is easy to verify that the spectral density of $y(\cdot)$ obeying (10) is $\nu B(z)/A(z)$. Unlike the one-dimensional case, $e(\cdot)$ cannot be replaced by a finite moving average representation excited by an i.i.d. sequence, since $\sqrt{A(z) B(z)}$ is not, in general, a finite-order polynomial in z.

The model in (10) is useful for analysis only; it is not useful for synthesis. To synthesize a sequence $y(\cdot)$ obeying (10), we have to proceed as in the proof of Theorem 1.

In view of (12) the sequence $e(s)$ has nonzero autocorrelation only over a finite number of lags, as displayed in (13)

$$E[e(t) e(t + s)] = \begin{cases} -\sum_{r \in N_1} \phi_r \cdot \theta_{s-r}, & \text{if } s \in N'', \\ 0, & \text{otherwise,} \end{cases} \quad (13)$$

where

$$N_i' = N_i \cup \{0,0\} \quad N'' = \{r + s : r \in N_1', s \in N_2'\},$$
$$\phi_{0,0} = 1 \quad \theta_{0,0} = -1,$$
$$\phi_s = 0, \quad \text{if } s \notin N_2', \quad \theta_r = 0, \quad \text{if } r \notin N_1'.$$

The sequence $e(s)$ has nonzerocorrelation with $y(s + r)$ only for a *finite* number of values of r. To prove this statement, let us find the cross-spectral density $S_{ey}(\cdot)$ from (10).

$$S_{ey}(z) = (\sqrt{\nu}/A(z))S_e(z)$$
$$= \sqrt{\nu} B(z). \tag{14}$$

Equating the coefficients of z^r on either side, we get

$$E[e(s)y(s+r)] = \begin{cases} \sqrt{\nu}\,\phi_r, & \text{if } r \in N_2', \\ 0, & \text{otherwise} \end{cases} \tag{15}$$

Relation to Currently Known ARMA Models

Case 1: The conditions autoregressive model [1]–[3] is a special case of (10), with $B(z) = 1$. The CAR models are called as minimum variance representations (MVR) in [9].

Case 2: The simultaneous AR model [3], [9], [10], also called a white noise driven representation (WNDR) in [9], is a special case of (10), where $B(z) = 1$ and $A(z)$ has a factorization as in (16).

$$A(z) = KD(z)D(z^{-1}), \quad D(z) = 1 - \sum_N \theta_r z^r, \tag{16}$$

N need not be symmetric. A simultaneous ARMA model [9], [11], [24] is a special case of (10), in which both A and B have a factorization as in (16).

Case 3: Consider the two-dimensional ARMA models introduced in [7] in which $\Phi(z)$, a special two-dimensional transform of the correlation function defined in (17), is a rational function as in (18).

$$\Phi(z_1, z_2) = \sum_{i=0}^{\infty} \sum_{j=-\infty}^{\infty} R(i_1, j_2) z_1^i z_2^j, \tag{17}$$

$$= C(z)/D(z), \tag{18}$$

where

$$C(z) = \sum_{i=0}^{M_1} \sum_{j=0}^{M_2} c_{ij} z_1^i z_2^j \quad D(z) = \sum_{i=0}^{M_1} \sum_{j=0}^{M_2} d_{ij} z_1^i z_2^j.$$

We emphasize that $\Phi(\cdot)$ is distinct from the spectral density S defined in (1) even though Φ is also called a spectral density in [7]. The ARMA models that possess a Φ function as in (18) are a *proper subset* of the processes having spectral density S as in (2) and hence are a proper subset of the ARMA models defined in (10). This result is stated as Theorem 2.

Theorem 2: If there exists a stationary process $y(\cdot)$ with its Φ function as in (18), its spectral density S has the structure as in (19)

$$S = \nu B(z)/D_1(z)D_1(z^{-1}) \quad D_1(z) = \sum_{i=0}^{M_1} \sum_{j=0}^{M_2'} d_{ij}' z_1^i z_2^j, \tag{19}$$

$M_2' \geq M_2$, B need not be factorable.

Proof:

$$\sum_{i=-\infty}^{0} \sum_{j=-\infty}^{\infty} R(i,j) z_1^i z_2^j = \sum_{i=0}^{\infty} \sum_{j=-\infty}^{\infty} R(-i,j) z_1^{-i} z_2^j,$$

and by replacing j by $-j$ it becomes

$$\sum_{i=0}^{\infty} \sum_{j=-\infty}^{\infty} R(-i,-j) z_1^{-i} z_2^{-j},$$

but $R(i, j) = R(-i, -j)$, so that

$$\sum_{i=0}^{\infty} \sum_{j=-\infty}^{\infty} R(i,j) z_1^{-i} z_2^{-j} = \Phi(z_1^{-1}, z_2^{-1}),$$

in view of (17).

$$\sum_{j=-\infty}^{\infty} R(0, j) z_2^j = \frac{G_1(z_2)G_1(z_2^{-1})}{G_2(z_2)G_2(z_2^{-1})},$$

where

$$G_i(z_2) = \sum_{k=0}^{M_{3i}} g_{ik} z_2^k,$$

in view of the factorability of one-dimensional polynomials.

From (1)

$$S(z_1, z_2) = \left(\sum_{i=0}^{\infty} \sum_{j=-\infty}^{\infty} + \sum_{i=-\infty}^{0} \sum_{j=-\infty}^{\infty} \right) R(i,j) z_1^i z_2^j$$
$$- \sum_{j=-\infty}^{\infty} R(0,j) z_2^j$$
$$= \Phi(z_1, z_2) + \Phi(z_1^{-1}, z_2^{-1})$$
$$- G_1(z_2)G_1(z_2^{-1})/G_2(z_2)G_2(z_2^{-1})$$
$$= \frac{C(z)}{D(z)} + \frac{C(z^{-1})}{D(z^{-1})} - \frac{|G_1(z_2)|^2}{|G_2(z_2)|^2}$$
$$= \frac{\nu B(z)}{[D(z)G_2(z_2)][D(z^{-1})G_2(z_2^{-1})]}$$
$$= \nu B(z)/D_1(z)D_1(z^{-1}),$$

where $B(z)$ is the numerator normalized so that its constant term is one and

$$D_1(z) = D(z)G_2(z_2)$$
$$= \left(\sum_{i=0}^{M_1} \sum_{j=0}^{M_2} d_{ij} z_1^i z_2^j \right) \left(\sum_{j=0}^{M_{32}} g_{2j} z_2^j \right)$$
$$= \sum_{i=0}^{M_1} \sum_{j=0}^{M_2'} d_{ij}' z_1^i z_2^j, \quad M_2' > M_2.$$

□

Comment: A simple consequence of Theorem 2 is that a process $y(\cdot)$ with spectral density as in (2) with a nonfactorable denominator A cannot have a Φ function as in (19) and thus cannot have the corresponding ARMA representation given in [7].

Case 4: Consider the spectral density in (2), in which both A and B have the following factorization:

$$A(z) = K_1 D_1(z) D_1(z^{-1}) \quad B(z) = K_2 D_2(z) D_2(z^{-1}),$$

$$D_1(z) = 1 - \sum_{r \in N_4} d_r z^r, \quad D_2(z) = 1 - \sum_{r \in N_5} d'_r z^r.$$

$N_4, N_5 \subset L^-, (0,0) \not\subset N_4, (0,0) \not\subset N_5$. Both N_4 and N_5 are subsets of the nonsymmetrical half-plane (NSHP) L^- indicated in Fig. 1. Then the corresponding ARMA difference equation can be written as

$$y(s) = \sum_{r \in N_4} d_r y(s + r) + \sqrt{v''}\left(w(s) + \sum_{r \in N_5} d'_r w(s+r)\right),$$

where $w(\cdot)$ is i.i.d. $(0,1)$ sequence. The above equation is the analog of the traditional ARMA model in time series.

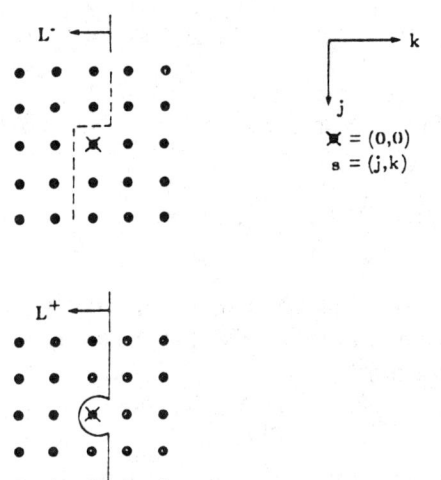

Fig. 1. Nonsymmetrical half plane L^- and half plane L^+.

In the above equation, if $B(z) = 1$ or, equivalently, $d'_r = 0$, then the corresponding process $y(\cdot)$ possesses the weak linear *causal* Markov property, i.e.,

$$E[y(s)| \text{all } y(s+r), r \in L^-]$$
$$= \sum_{r \in N_4} d_r y(s+r), N_4 \subset L^-. \quad (20)$$

The corresponding difference equation is called as a causal AR representation [9]. In this case it is possible to divide the image at any point s into three parts, namely, s is the present, the set $\{s + r : r \in L^-\}$ is the past, and $\{s + r, r \neq (0,0), r \notin L^-\}$ is the future.

Case 5: Theorem 5, to be proved later, shows that semicausal models [9] are a subclass of the general ARMA class.

Toroidal ARMA Model

A toroidal variant of the ARMA model in (10), defined only over a finite $M \times M$ lattice Ω_M, is defined as

$$y_M(s) = \sum_{r \in N_1} \theta_r y_M(s \oplus r) + \sqrt{v}\, e_M(s), s \in \Omega_M, \quad (21)$$

where $\oplus$ stands for summation modulo M and

$$\{e_M(s), s \in \Omega_M\} = \text{inverse DFT of } \{E_M(r), r \in \Omega_M\}$$
$$E_M(r) = \sqrt{A_r B_r}\, W_r$$
$$\{W_r, r \in \Omega_M\} = \text{DFT of } \{w(s), s \in \Omega_M;$$
$$w(\cdot) \text{ is i.i.d. } (0,1)\}.$$

Equivalently, the toroidal ARMA model equation can be written as

$$\sqrt{A_r}\, Y_r = \sqrt{B_r}\, W_r \sqrt{v}, \quad (22)$$

where $\{Y_r, r \in \Omega_M\}$ is the D.F.T. of $\{y(s), s \in \Omega_M\}$.

The spectral density of $y_M(\cdot)$ exists only for the frequencies corresponding to the grid points of Ω_M, and in such cases, it equals the corresponding spectral density of the process $y(\cdot)$ obeying the ARMA model in (10).

The toroidal model is useful not only for synthesis, as indicated in the proof of Theorem 1, but also in parameter estimation as well.

III. Markov Properties

The Markov property can be defined in a number of ways in the two-dimensional case. A process $y(\cdot)$ obeying an ARMA model (10) does not have any type of Markov property. However, we will show that special subsets of the model in (10) do possess a variety of Markov properties.

Let us evaluate the conditional expectation of $y(s)$, given all other values for the general model in (10).

Theorem 3: The sequence $y(\cdot)$ obeying (10) and having a Gaussian density has the following conditional expectation and variance

$$y_1(s) \triangleq E[y(s)| \text{all } y(s+r), r \neq (0,0)]$$
$$= \sum_{r \neq (0,0)} g_r y(s+r), \quad (23)$$

$$E\left[(y(s) - y_1(s))^2\right] = v/K, \quad (24)$$

where K and g_r are defined as

$$K\left(1 - \sum_{r \in L'} g_r z^r\right) = A(z)/B(z), \quad (25)$$

$$L' = L - (0,0), g_r = g_{-r}.$$

Proof: Let $G(z) = \sum_{r \in L} g_r z^r$.

$$u(s) \triangleq y(s) - y_1(s) = (1 - G(z)) y(s). \quad (26)$$

The cross spectral density between v and y is

$$S_{vy}(z) = (1 - G(z)) S_{yy}(z),$$
$$= v/K, \text{ from (2)}.$$

Hence
$$E[u(s)y(s+r)] = 0, \quad \text{for all } r \neq (0,0).$$

Thus (23) is true since $y(\cdot)$ is Gaussian. To prove (24), we have from (26) that
$$S_{vv}(z) = (1 - G(z))^2 S_{yy}(z),$$
and by (2) and (25) this becomes
$$= (\nu/K)\left(1 - \sum g_r z^r\right).$$

Hence $E[v^2(s)] = \nu/K$. □

The conditional expectation in (23) has, in general, an infinite number of terms. Next we must determine the conditions under which the conditional expectation in (23) has a finite number of terms. The answer is given in Theorem 4.

Definition: A sequence $y(\cdot)$ is weak *noncausal* Markov if the following is true: $E[y(s)|$ all $y(s+r), r \neq 0, 0] = E[y(s)|$ all $y(s+r), r \in N, N$ is finite, symmetric, $(0,0) \notin N]$.

Theorem 4: A stationary sequence is weak noncausal Markov and possesses a finite linear conditional expectation indicated in (27) if and only if the process $y(\cdot)$ has an all-pole spectral density, i.e., $B(z)$ in (2) is a constant,
$$E[y(s)|\text{all } y(s+r), r \neq (0,0)] = \sum_{r \in N_1} g_r y(s+r), \quad (27)$$
where $(0,0) \notin N_1$, N_1 is symmetric and finite, $g_r = g_{-r}$.

Proof—"If" Part: Let the spectral density of y be $\nu/A(z)$. By Theorem 3, the conditional expectation is defined in terms of g_r in (25),
$$g_r = \theta_r, \text{ if } r \in N_1,$$
$$= 0, \quad r \neq (0,0), r \notin N_1.$$

Hence the conditional expectation has a finite number of terms.

"Only if" Part: Let
$$u(s) = y(s) - y_1(s)$$
$$= y(s) - \left(\sum_{r \in N_1} g_r z^r\right) y(s). \quad (28)$$

Since $y_1(\cdot)$ is the conditional expectation,
$$E[u(s)y(s+t)] = 0, \quad \text{for all } t \neq (0,0). \quad (29)$$

Let $E[u(s)y(s)] = K_1$. Multiply (28) on both sides by $y(s+t)$ and take expectation. Let $R(t) = E[y(s)y(s+t)]$
$$R(t) - \sum_{r \in N} g_r R(t-r) = 0, \quad \text{if } t \neq (0,0),$$
$$= K_1, \quad \text{if } t = (0,0),$$
by (29). Take Fourier transform on both sides of the above equation.
$$\left(1 - \sum_{r \in N_1} g_r\right) S_y(z) = K_1$$

i.e., $S_y(z)$ has an all-pole spectral density. □

Comment 1: Parts of Theorem 4 have been known in the literature [1]–[3]. The theorem is given to show the equivalence of the following three statements.

a) $y(\cdot)$ has the conditional expectation in (27).
b) $y(\cdot)$ has an all pole spectral density $\nu/A(z)$.
c) $y(\cdot)$ obeys the *conditional AR* model in (10) where the driving input $e(\cdot)$ has the spectral density $A(z)$.

This equivalence is never explicitly stated in the literature. For instance, in [2] both a) and b) are used together in defining the CAR model.

Comment 2: Every sequence $y(\cdot)$ that is causal Markov and has the linear expectation in (20) defined by a neighbor set N_4 also possesses the noncausal Markov property in (27) with neighbor set N_1, $N_1 \supset N_4$. The reverse is not true [3].

We mentioned earlier that $y(\cdot)$ obeying a general ARMA model in (10) does not possess the noncausal Markov property. However a small subset of ARMA models possesses another Markov property called semicausal or half-plane Markov.

Definition: (semicausal or half-plane Markov): $y(\cdot)$ is said to be linear *half-plane* Markov with respect to the neighbor set N if
$$E[y(s)/\text{all } y(s+r), r \in L^+] = \sum_{r \in N} \theta_r y(s+r), \quad (30)$$
where $L^+ = \{(j,k): k \leq 0, (j,k) \neq (0,0)\}$. L^+ is displayed in Fig. 1. N is any subset of L^+ defined below
$$N = N_1 \cup N_2, \quad (31)$$
$$N_1 = \{(i,0), (-i,0); i = 1, \cdots, m_1\}$$
$$N_2 = \{(i,j), j = -1, \cdots, -m_2, i = \pm 1, \pm 2, \cdots, \pm m\}.$$

We will presently display a subset of ARMA models, the so-called semicausal models that have the semicausal Markov property
$$A(z)y(s) = \sqrt{\nu}\, e(s), \quad (32)$$
where
$$A(z) = 1 - \sum_{r \in N} \theta_r z^r, \quad N \text{ in } (31)$$
$$= 1 - \sum_{k=1}^{m_1} \theta_{k,0}(z_1^k + z_1^{-k})$$
$$- \sum_{k=-m_1}^{m_1} \sum_{l=1}^{m_2} \theta_{k,l} z_1^k z_2^{-l}.$$

The correlated sequence $e(\cdot)$ has zero-mean, Gaussian probability density and spectral density as in (33) or correlation function as in (34),
$$S_e(z) \triangleq B(z) \triangleq 1 - \sum_{p=0}^{m_1} \theta_{p,0}(z_1^p + z_1^{-p}), \quad (33)$$

$R_{ee}(k,l) = 0, \quad \text{if } l \neq 0$

$$R_{ee}(k,0) = \begin{cases} \theta_{k,0}, & \text{if } k = \pm 1, \cdots, \pm m_1, \theta_{k,0} = \theta_{-k,0} \\ 1, & \text{if } k = 0 \\ 0, & \text{otherwise.} \end{cases}$$
(34)

Equation (32) can be written as the difference equation in (35),

$$y(i,j) = \sum_{k=1}^{m_1} \theta_{k,0}[y(i+k,j) + y(i-k,j)]$$
$$+ \sum_{k=-m_1}^{m_1} \sum_{l=1}^{m_2} \theta_{k,l} y(i+k, j-l) + \sqrt{\nu} e(i,j). \quad (35)$$

A necessary and sufficient condition for the stability of (35) [9, Theorem 5] is

$$A(z_1, z_2) \neq 0 \text{ for } |z_1| = 1, \quad |z_2| \geq 1. \quad (36)$$

The model in (31) is called semicausal because it is causal in the index j, i.e., in the right-hand side of (35), $j+l, l > 1$ does not appear.

Theorem 5:

The stationary sequence $y(\cdot)$ defined in (31) and (32) possesses the weak half-plane Markov property in (29) if and only if the input sequence $e(\cdot)$ in it has the correlation function in (34) or, equivalently, $y(\cdot)$ has the spectral density $\nu B(z)/\|A(z)\|^2$.

Proof—"If" part:

$S_{ey}(z)$ = cross-spectral density of $e(\cdot)$ and $y(\cdot)$,

$$= \frac{\nu S_{ee}(z)}{A(z^{-1})} = \nu B(z)/A(z^{-1}).$$

Expanding $S_{ey}(z)$ in power series, we see that the coefficient of any term involving z_2^{-l}, $l \geq 1$ is zero. Hence

$$R_{ey}(k,l) \triangleq E[e(i,j) y(i-k, j-l)] = 0, \quad \text{if } l > 0. \quad (37)$$

Let
$$R(k) \triangleq R_{ey}(k,0). \quad (38)$$

Multiply (35) by $e(i+k, j)$, take expectation on both sides, and use (37) and (38).

$$R(k) - \sum_{p=1}^{m_1} \theta_{p,0}[R(k+p) - R(k-p)] = R_{ee}(k,0). \quad (39)$$

Let $S(z_1)$ be the one-dimensional discrete Fourier transform of $R(k)$. Multiply (39) by z^{-k}, sum from $k = -\infty$ to ∞, and use $R_{ee}(k,0)$ in (34).

$$B(z_1)S(z_1) = \nu B(z_1).$$

Hence $S(z_1) = \nu$ or
$$R_{ey}(k,0) = 0, \quad \text{if } k \neq 0. \quad (40)$$

Hence (37) and (40) yield

$$E[e(s)y(s+r)] = 0, \quad \text{for all } r \in L^+. \quad (41)$$

Since $e(\cdot)$ and $y(\cdot)$ are Gaussian, the above equation yields

$$E[e(s)|\text{all } y(s+r), r \in L^+] = 0. \quad (42)$$

Taking conditional expectation of $y(s)$ given all $y(s+r), r \in L^+$, on both sides of (32) and using (42) yields (30).

"Only if" part:

Since (30) is true, (41) is true. Multiplying (35) by $e(k,l), l \neq j$, and taking expectations on both sides by using (41), we get

$$E[e(i,j)e(k,l)] = 0, \quad \text{for all } j \neq l. \quad (43)$$

Multiplying (35) by $e(i,j)$ and taking expectation on both sides using (41), we get

$$E[e(i,j)y(i,j)] = E[e^2(i,j)] = \nu. \quad (44)$$

Multiplying (35) by $e(i+k, j)$ and taking expectations on both sides we have

$$R_{ey}(k,0) = \sum_{p=1}^{m_1} \theta_{p,0}[R_{ey}(k+p,0) + R_{ey}(k-p,0)]$$
$$+ R_{ee}(k,0) \quad (45)$$

and by (41)

$$R_{ey}(k,0) = 0, \quad \text{if } k \neq 0. \quad (46)$$

Substituting for $R_{ey}(k,0)$ in (45) from (46) and (44), we get the desired expression for $R_{ee}(k,0)$ in (34). □

Comment 1: For images with *specific boundary* conditions Jain [8], [9] has shown that the models in (26) have the weak semicausal property. In theorem 5, we have established the converse also without imposing any specific boundary conditions.

Comment 2: A semicausal Markov sequence is also causal Markov *only* in the degenerate case $B(z) = 1$, i.e., $\theta_{k,0} = 0$ if $k \neq 0$. In this degenerate case, it also possesses the noncausal Markov property with respect to a suitable symmetric set N_4. Apart from this case, a semicausal Markov sequence is never noncausal Markov or vice versa.

Comment 3: In this entire section we have discussed only the weak Markov property. In the Gaussian case the weak Markov property is the same as the strong Markov property involving the factorization of probability density. Some additional results connected with the strong (noncausal) Markov property can be found in [3], [13].

IV. Parameter Estimation from Correlations

Given a finite image over the $M \times M$ grid Ω, we want to develop a procedure for fitting an ARMA model (10) to it, i.e., estimating the unknown parameters in it after fixing the neighbor sets N_1 and N_2. We will give two procedures. In this section the parameters are estimated using the estimated correlations, and the procedure is independent of the density of the image. The method is computationally easy and does not involve any iteration. This is in contrast to the parameter estimation of ARMA models in the time series case. We will point out the reason for the difference. Note that here $\theta_r = \theta(r)$ and $R_r = R(r)$. N_i, $i = 1, 2, \cdots$, are finite symmetric subsets of $\{L - (0,0)\}$. N_{Si} and $\overline{N}_{Si}$ are mutually exclusive *antisymmetric* subsets defined by

the following relations:
$$N_i = N_{Si} \cup \bar{N}_{Si}, \quad N_{Si} \cap \bar{N}_{Si} = 0$$
$$(i, j) \in N_{Sk} \Rightarrow (-i, -j) \notin N_{Sk}.$$

Without loss of generality we can make N_{Si} a subset of $(L - L^- - (0,0))$, where L^- is defined in Fig. 1. Let the polynomials A and B in the spectral density of the process $y(\cdot)$ in (2) be

$$A(z) = 1 - \sum_{r \in N_{S1}} \theta_r(z^r + z^{-r}), \quad \#N_{S1} = m_1,$$

$$B(z) = 1 + \sum_{r \in N_{S2}} \phi_r(z^r + z^{-r}), \quad \#N_{S2} = m_2,$$

where the symbol $\#$ means "size of".

Let $N_{S1} = \{r_1, \cdots, r_{m_1}\}$, $N_{S2} = \{s_1, \cdots, s_{m_2}\}$. The corresponding ARMA model equation is

$$y(s) = \sum_{j=1}^{m_1} \theta(r_j)(y(s + r_j) + y(s - r_j)) + \sqrt{\nu} e(s), \tag{47}$$

where $e(\cdot)$ has the following cross-spectral density
$$S_{ey}(z) = \sqrt{\nu} B(z),$$

i.e.,

$$E[e(s)y(s+r)] = \begin{cases} \sqrt{\nu}, & \text{if } r = 0, \quad \text{(48a)} \\ \sqrt{\nu} \phi_r, & \text{if } r \in N_2, \quad \text{(48b)} \\ 0, & \text{otherwise.} \quad \text{(48c)} \end{cases}$$

Choose a symmetric set N_3 having $2m_1$ nearest neighbors of $(0, 0)$ so that $N_3 \cap N_2 = 0$. Note that N_3 is not unique.

$$N_{S3} = \{t_1, t_2, \cdots, t_{m2}, t_{m2+1}, \cdots, t_{m1}\}$$

We will obtain an explicit expression for the coefficients θ_r, ϕ_r, ν in terms of the correlations $R(s)$.

Multiplying (47) by $y(0)$ and taking expectation on both sides, using (48a), we have

$$R(0) = 2 \sum_{j=1}^{m_1} \theta(r_j) R(r_j) + \nu. \tag{49}$$

Multiplying (47) by $y(s + s_i), s_i \in N_{S2}$, on both sides and taking expectation using (48b), we obtain

$$R(s_i) = \sum_{j=1}^{m_1} \theta(r_j)[R(r_i + s_j) + R(s_i - r_j)] + \nu\phi(s_i),$$
$$i = 1, \cdots, m_2. \tag{50}$$

Multiplying (47) by $y(s + t_i), t_i \in N_{S3}$ on both sides and taking expectation, using (48c), we get

$$R(t_i) = \sum_{j=1}^{m_1} \theta(r_j)\{R(t_i + r_j) + R(t_i - r_j)\},$$
$$i = 1, \cdots, m_1. \tag{51}$$

In (49), (50) and (51), the true correlations $R(\cdot)$ can be replaced by their estimates, and the resulting equations can be solved for $\theta(\cdot), \phi(\cdot)$, and $\nu(\cdot)$ as indicated below. The steps are as follows.

a) Choose the set N_{S3}.
b) Estimate the various correlation needed in (49) through (51),
$$\hat{R}(r) = \frac{1}{M_1 - 1} \sum_s y(s) y(s + r),$$
where the summation extends over all valid s in Ω, and M_1 is the number of admissible values of s.
c) Solve the m_1 linear equations in (51) for $\theta(r_1), \cdots, \theta(r_{m_1})$ to yield the corresponding estimates $\hat{\theta}$.
d) Solve the linear equation (49) for ν after replacing $\theta(\cdot)$ by $\hat{\theta}$, yielding the estimate $\hat{\nu}$.
e) Solve the linear equation (50) for $\phi(\cdot)$ after replacing θ by $\hat{\theta}$ and ν by $\hat{\nu}$.

It is important to note that the computation does not involve any iteration. One can show that the estimates are consistent, i.e., as the size of the image M goes to infinity, the estimates tend to their true values provided $A(z)$ and $B(z)$ do not have any common factors.

Comment 1: The procedure needs the choice of the set N_3. The set could be arbitrary as long as it is exclusive of N_2. Empirical evidence indicates that the one suggested here, namely having $2m_1$ *nearest* neighbors, leads to the estimate with higher accuracy than other choices.

Comment 2: As noted earlier, no iteration is needed in the computation. In contrast, the estimation of parameters by the covariance method in the one-dimensional ARMA model is much more complicated and involves iteration. The reason for the different behavior is the difference in the model equations. This section directly estimates the coefficients occurring in the spectral density, whereas in the traditional one-dimensional ARMA case, we estimate the coefficients of $C(z_1)$ and $D(z_1)$ where $S(z_1) = \|C(z_1)\|^2/\|D(z_1)\|^2$. If we convert the one-dimensional ARMA equation into a form similar to (4.1), then the computation procedure indicated in this section can be used for the one-dimensional case as well.

The sequence of computation is illustrated by an example.

Example 1: Let the ARMA model be as in (52) and (53)
$$y(s) = \theta \sum_{r \in N_1} y(s + r) + \sqrt{\nu} e(s), \tag{52}$$

$$N_1 = \{(0, 1), (0 - 1), (1, 0), (-1, 0)\}$$

$$A(z) = 1 - \theta \sum_{r \in N_1} z^r \quad B(z) = 1 + \phi \sum_{r \in N_2} Z^r, N_2 = N_1.$$
$$\tag{53}$$

The required choice of $N_{S3} = (1, 1)$. Note that $R_{i,j} = R_{i,-j}$

$= R_{j,i}$. From (50) we get

$$R_{0,0} = 4\theta R_{1,0} + \nu. \quad (54)$$

From (51) we get

$$R_{1,0} = \theta[R_{0,0} + R_{2,0} + 2R_{1,1}] + \nu\phi. \quad (55)$$

From (52) we get

$$R_{1,1} = 2\theta[R_{1,0} + R_{1,2}]. \quad (56)$$

Solving (54) through (56) for θ, ϕ and ν is straightforward. The numerical results are given in the next section.

V. Likelihood

When the number of parameters to be estimated is not very small compared to the image size M^2, then the estimates given earlier may not be accurate. Hence, we introduce the more accurate method of estimation, the so-called likelihood method. As before, let the given set of observations by y

$$y = \text{Col}[y(s), s \in \Omega]$$
$$\Omega = \{(i,j), 0 \leq i, j \leq M - 1\}.$$

Let the spectral density of y be $\nu B(z)/A(z)$. Let us assume that y is Gaussian. Then we can find the correlation function $R(s)$ of $y(\cdot)$ as a function of θ_i, ϕ_i and ν from the spectral density. This gives the covariance of the vector y, say C. Thus y is Gaussian $[0, C(\theta, \phi, \nu)]$. But the matrix C is of dimension $M^2 \times M^2$ and $R(s)$ is not a simple function of s, θ, ν and ϕ. Hence the above density expression for y is not useful for tasks such as its maximization to find the parameter estimates. We have to be content with an approximation to the probability density function of y so that it is amenable to optimization.

Let $\{Y_r, r \in \Omega\}$ be the discrete Fourier transform of the finite sequence $\{y(s), s \in \Omega\}$. Then as M tends to infinity, the sequence $\{Y_r\}$ is independent and Gaussian with mean zero and variance $M^2 S_r(\theta, \phi, \nu)$ [14] where

$$S_r(\theta, \phi, \nu) = \frac{\nu B(z = \exp(i(2\pi/M)r))}{A(z = \exp(i(2\pi/M)r))}, \quad i = \sqrt{-1},$$
$$= \frac{\nu(1 + \phi^T \psi_r)}{1 - \theta^T \alpha_r}, \quad (57)$$

$$\psi_r = \text{Col}(2\cos(2\pi/M)r^T s, s \in N_{S2}),$$
$$\alpha_r = \text{Col}(2\cos(2\pi/M)r^T s, s \in N_{S1}),$$
$$\phi = \text{Col}(\phi_r, r \in N_{S2}), \theta = \text{Col}(\theta_r, r \in N_{S1}).$$

Asymptotically, the probability density of $\{Y_r\}$ is given by

$$p(Y_r, r \in \Omega; \theta, \phi, \nu)$$
$$\simeq \left[\prod_{r \in \Omega} 1/(2\pi S_r(\theta, \phi, \nu))\right]^{1/2}$$
$$\cdot \exp\left[-(1/2)\sum_{r \in \Omega} \|Y_r\|^2 / M^2 S_r(\theta, \phi, \nu)\right]. \quad (58)$$

We can show [12] that, the RHS of (58) is the *exact* probability density of $\{Y_r\}$ obeying the toroidal variant of the ARMA model described in (21) or (22).

The expression on the RHS of (58) has to be maximized with respect to θ, ϕ, and ν. It is more convenient to work with the log likelihood

$$J_1(\theta, \phi, \nu)$$
$$= -(M^2/2)\ln(2\pi\nu)$$
$$-1/2\sum_r \log[1 + \phi^T \psi_r)/1 - \theta^T \alpha_r)]$$
$$-(1/2)\sum_{r \in \Omega} \|Y_r\|^2(1 - \theta^T\alpha_r)/\nu(1 + \phi^T\psi_r)M^2.$$
(59)

Maximizing J_1 with respect to ν yields

$$\nu = \left(\sum_r \|Y_r\|^2(1 - \theta^T\alpha_r)/(1 + \phi^T\psi_r)\right)/M^4. \quad (60)$$

Substituting it back and simplifying, we see that the maximum likelihood (ML) estimates of θ and ϕ are obtained by minimizing $J(\theta, \phi)$ with respect to θ and ϕ, where

$$J(\theta, \phi) = \sum_{r \in \Omega} \log\left[(1 + \phi^T\psi_r)/(1 - \theta^T\alpha_r)\right]$$
$$+ M^2 \log \sum_{r \in \Omega} \|Y_r\|^2 \frac{(1 - \theta^T\alpha_r)}{1 + \phi^T\psi_r}.$$

Since the minimum value of (θ, ϕ) has to yield a finite value for $J(\cdot)$, the ML estimates of θ and ϕ automatically satisfy the conditions $1 + \phi^T\psi_r \neq 0$, $1 - \theta^T\alpha_r \neq 0$ for all r in Ω.

We cannot make such a claim for the estimates obtained by the correlation methods, especially for small M. The numerical aspects of maximization have been discussed in [4], [5] for the case of AR models.

The likelihood approach can be adapted to the particular situation on hand. If we know that the observation is the sum of a signal obeying a CAR model and an additive noise, then we can directly write the likelihood and estimate the parameters of the CAR model and the corresponding spectrum. If the signal plus noise assumption is true, any spectral estimation method that ignores the noise will not give good results. This feature has been documented in [16].

Numerical Experiments

The correlation and maximum likelihood estimates are compared via numerical experiments. The image model in Example 1 of Section IV is considered, with numerical values $\theta = 0.22$, $\phi = 0.2$, and $\nu = 1$. Ten different images of size 64×64 obeying this model were synthesized using different random sequences, as discussed in Section VI. In each case the parameter estimates were computed by both the methods. For ϕ, θ, and ν, the mean of the ten estimates, the standard duration (SD) of the ten estimates and

TABLE I

Grid Size		θ			φ			ν		
		Mean	S.D.	RMSE	Mean	S.D.	RMSE	Mean	S.D.	RMSE
64*64	Corr.	.2216	.0050	.0053	.1988	.0110	.0110	.8987	.0206	.1033
	ML.	.2240	.0044	.0060	.1973	.0044	.0051	.9542	.1092	.1142
32*32	Corr.	.2019	.0146	.0182	.2125	.0300	.0325	.8060	.0618	.2036
	ML.	.2238	.0119	.0124	.1930	.0130	.0148	.8930	.1257	.1651
16*16	Corr.	.2148	.0379	.0383	.1974	.0528	.0529	.5845	.0971	.4269
	ML.	.2447	.0070	.0257	.1759	.0179	.0300	1.0861	.3535	.3639

The summary of the parameter estimates of ten runs by the correlation method and ML (maximum likelihood) method in the model of Example 1 of Section IV. "Mean" is the mean of the 10 estimate values of the 10 images and S.D. is the corresponding standard duration. RMSE is the square root of the mean of the squared error between the estimates and the true value. The true values of the parameters are $\theta = 0.22$, $\phi = 0.2$ and $\nu = 1.0$.

the root mean square value of the deviation of the estimate from the true value root mean square error (RMSE) are given in Table I for both correlation and ML estimates. Similar experiments were performed with images of size 32×32 and 16×16 and the results are also given in Table I.

For 64×64 images the SD and the RMSE are close to one another. Further, the correlation estimates and the ML estimates of ϕ and θ have similar accuracy. The correlation estimate of ν appears to be slightly biased. But as the size of the image decreases, the RMSE values of the ML estimates are less than the corresponding values of the correlation estimate. This feature is to be expected. But the quality of correlation estimate is not unduly low. For instance, for 32×32 image the RMSE values for ML and correlation estimates of θ are 0.0124 and 0.0182, not a very drastic difference. In many image processing problems the correlation estimates appear to be adequate, especially in view of their low computational demand.

VI. Synthesis

An interesting problem in image processing is the synthesis of an image that resembles a real texture. There are many methods of synthesizing images, each one based on a different type of model. Synthesis has been done using various types of two-dimensional AR models [5], [13], [17]–[20], and mosaic models [21], [22]. Our aim is to explore the use of ARMA model.

The synthesis of a finite $M \times M$ image to obey *exactly* the difference equation in (10) is very difficult. It involves the factorization of a $M^2 \times M^2$ matrix whose elements are the correlation of various lags. It is still more difficult to ensure that the density of the synthesized $y(\cdot)$ has the prespecified form. Instead it is easy to generate a finite $M \times M$ image $y_M(\cdot)$ obeying the toroidal variant of the ARMA model in (22):

$$\sqrt{A_r}\, Y_r = \sqrt{\nu}\, \sqrt{B_r}\, W_r, \tag{61}$$

with zero mean, unit variance and the histogram P mentioned later on. By Theorem 1, as M tends to infinity, the second-order properties of the sequence $y_M(\cdot)$ obeying the toroidal ARMA model in (61) tend to that of the general ARMA model in (10).

The parameters θ_r and ϕ_r can be estimated from the given image by parameter estimation techniques. The sets N_{S1} and N_{S2} needed in the definition of A_r and B_r can be chosen as in [12], [23]. To determine the histogram P of $w(\cdot)$, we proceed as follows. Using the *given image*, say $\{y'(s), s \in \Omega\}$, and the (estimated) parameters θ, ϕ, ν, etc., generate W_r' by

$$W_r' = Y_r' \sqrt{A_r / B_r \nu},$$

where $\{Y_r', r \in \Omega\}$ is the DFT of $\{y'(s), s \in \Omega\}$. The inverse DFT of $\{W_r', r \in \Omega\}$ yields $\{w'(s), s \in \Omega\}$. The histogram of w' is the required histogram P.

The synthesis procedure is as follows.

a) Generate a sequence $\{w(s), s \in \Omega\}$ drawn from an i.i.d. population with zero mean, unit variance, and histogram P. Compute its DFT $\{W_r, r \in \Omega\}$.
b) Compute $\{Y_r, r \in \Omega\}$ from (61), and its inverse DFT yields $\{y(s), s \in \Omega\}$.

VII. Conclusion

We have introduced a general class of two-dimensional ARMA models that can represent any discrete rational spectral density and have shown that the various classes of two-dimensional difference equation models, discussed in the literature, are subclasses of this general class. We have also given various definitions of weak Markov processes and have precisely characterized subclasses of ARMA models having the various types of Markov properties. Two methods are given for estimating the parameters in the model. Finally, a technique is given for synthesizing an image obeying a given ARMA model.

Acknowledgment

The author would like to thank Mr. G. Boray for carrying out the numerical experiments of Section V.

REFERENCES

[1] Y. A. Rosanov, "On Gaussian fields with given conditional distributions," *Theory Probab. Appl.*, vol. 12, no. 3, pp. 381–391, 1967.

[2] J. W. Woods, "Two-dimensional discrete Markov random fields," *IEEE Trans. Inform. Theory*, vol. IT-18, no. 2, pp. 232–249, March 1972.

[3] J. E. Besag, "Spatial interaction and statistical analysis of lattice systems," *J. Roy. Statist. Soc.*, ser. B., vol. B-36, pp. 192–236, 1974.

[4] R. Chellappa and R. L. Kashyap, "Digital image restoration using spatial interaction models," *IEEE Trans. Acoust., Speech and Signal Proc.*, vol. ASSP-30, no. 3, pp. 461–472, June 1982.

[5] B. H. McCormick and S. N. Jayaramurthy, "Time series models for texture synthesis," *Int. J. Comput. Inform. Sci.*, vol. 4, pp. 329–343, Dec. 1974.

[6] E. J. Delp, R. L. Kashyap, and O. R. Mitchell, "Image data compression using autoregressive time series models," *Patt. Recognition*, vol. 11, pp. 313–323, 1979.

[7] M. G. Strintzis, "Dynamic representation and recursive estimation of cyclic and two-dimensional processes," *IEEE Trans. Automat. Contr.*, vol. AC-23, no. 5, pp. 801–808, 1978.

[8] A. K. Jain and J. R. Jain, "Partial difference equations and finite difference methods in image processing, Part 2: Image restoration," *IEEE Trans. Automat. Contr.*, vol. AC-23, pp. 817–833, Oct. 1978.

[9] A. K. Jain, "Advances in mathematical models for image processing," *Proc. IEEE*, vol. 69, pp. 512–528, May 1981.

[10] P. Whittle, "On the stationary processes in the plane," *Biometrika*, vol. 41, pp. 434–449, 1954.

[11] R. L. Kashyap, "Random field models on finite lattices for finite images," in *Proc. Conf. Inform. Sci.*, Johns Hopkins University, March 1981.

[12] R. L. Kashyap and R. Chellappa, "Estimation and choice of neighbors in spatial interaction models of images," *IEEE Trans. Inform. Theory*, vol. IT-29, no. 1, pp. 60–72, Jan. 1983.

[13] G. R. Cross and A. K. Jain, "Markov random field texture models," in *Proc. IEEE Comput. Soc. Conf. Patt. Recognition and Image Processing*, Dallas, TX, pp. 597–602, Aug. 1981.

[14] D. R. Brillinger, *Time Series: Data Analysis and Theory*. New York: Holt, Rinehart and Winston, 1975.

[15] R. Chellappa and S. Y. Kung, "On two-dimensional Markov spectral estimation," in *Proc. 1982 CISS*, Princeton, March 1982.

[16] T. Ulrych and C. J. Walker, "High resolution two-dimensional power spectral estimation," in *Applied Time Series Analysis II*, D. Findley, Ed. San Diego, CA: Academic, pp. 71–99, 1981.

[17] D. D. Garber and A. A. Sawchuk, "Computational models for texture analysis and synthesis," in *Proc. Image Understanding Workshop*, pp. 69–88, April 1981.

[18] M. Hassner and J. Sklansky, "The use of Markov random fields as models of textures," *Comput. Graph. and Image Processing*, vol. 12, pp. 376–406, April 1980.

[19] R. Chellappa and R. L. Kashyap, "Synthetic generation and estimation in random field models of images," in *Proc. IEEE Comput. Soc. Conf. Patt. Recognition and Image Processing*, Dallas, TX, pp. 577–582, Aug. 1981.

[20] R. Chellappa, "Stochastic models in image analysis and processing," Ph.D. dissertation, Purdue University, Aug. 1981.

[21] B. J. Schacter *et al.*, "Random mosaic models for textures," *IEEE Trans. Syst. Man, Cyber.*, vol. SMC-8, pp. 694–702, Sept. 1978.

[22] J. W. Modestino, R. W. Fries, and A. L. Vickers, "Texture discrimination based upon an assumed stochastic texture model," *IEEE Trans. Patt. Anal. and Mach. Intel.*, vol. PAMI-3, pp. 557–580, Sept. 1981.

[23] R. L. Kashyap, R. Chellappa, and N. Ahuja, "Decision rules for the choice of neighbors in random field models of images," *Comput. Graph. Image Processing*, vol. 15, pp. 301–318, April 1981.

[24] R. L. Kashyap, "Analysis and synthesis of image patterns by spatial interaction models," in *Progress in Pattern Recognition*, Vol. I. Ed. L. Kanal and A. Rosenfeld. New York: North Holland, 1981.

[25] R. L. Kashyap, and A. R. Rao, Stochastic dynamic models from empirical data. San Diego, CA: Academic Press, 1976.

"Stochastic Image Models Generated by Random Tessellations of the Plane" by J.W. Modestino, R.W. Fries, and A.L. Vickers from *Computer Graphics and Image Processing*, January 1980, pages 74-98. Copyright © 1980 by Academic Press, Inc., reprinted with permission.

Stochastic Image Models Generated by Random Tessellations of the Plane*

J. W. Modestino, R. W. Fries,† and A. L. Vickers

Electrical and Systems Engineering Department, Rensselaer Polytechnic Institute Troy, New York 12181

A useful class of two-dimensional (2-D) random fields is described which can be generated by random tessellations of the plane. The random tessellations are in turn generated by marked point processes evolving according to a spatial parameter. Gray levels are assigned within elementary disjoint regions generated by the tessellations to have specified correlation properties with gray levels in contiguous regions. A complete second-order statistical description of the resulting class of random fields is provided. This includes not only autocorrelation functions and power spectral densities but joint probability density functions. Several applications are discussed including the modeling of real-world imagery possessing inherent edge structure.

1. INTRODUCTION

In a number of image processing applications it is important to have available a realistic and conveniently parameterized stochastic model for the class of images of interest. Examples include image enhancement, image coding, texture discrimination, and edge detection in noisy digitized images. This latter application provided the initial motivation for the work described here. It is clearly important in this case to have available a stochastic model for edge structure in two-dimensional (2-D) imagery data. This is also the case in several other applications to be described.

The ubiquitous 2-D Gaussian random field [1–4] has often been proposed as an appropriate model for real-world imagery. This has been particularly the case in image coding applications (cf. [5, 6]). Unfortunately, the 2-D Gaussian random field, except under pathological assumptions on the covariance, cannot account for the predominant and pronounced edge structure present in real-world imagery. It is of some interest then to develop alternative and more appropriate 2-D stochastic models for image data exhibiting inherent edge structure.

In this paper a useful class of 2-D random fields appropriate for this purpose are described and several of their more important properties discussed. This

---

* This work was supported in part by ONR under Contract N00014-75-C-0281 and in part by USAF RADC under Contract AF30602-78-C-0083.

† R. W. Fries is now with Pattern Analysis and Recognition Corp., Rome, N.Y.

class of random fields is modeled as a marked point process [7] evolving according to a spatial parameter. According to this model the plane is randomly partitioned or tessellated into a number of disjoint geometric regions by an appropriately defined field of random lines which form the boundaries of these regions. The density of these random lines, or edges, is defined in terms of a rate parameter λ. Gray levels are then assigned within elementary regions to possess a specified correlation coefficient ρ with gray levels in contiguous regions. We describe several schemes for tessellating the plane into elementary geometrical regions where the line process generating the tessellation is modeled in terms of a stationary renewal point process possessing a gamma distributed interarrival distribution with characteristic parameter ν.

Given a particular tessellation scheme, the random fields are then completely defined in terms of the three parameters λ, ρ, and ν. The parameter λ represents the "edge busyness" associated with an image while ρ is indicative, at least on an ensemble basis, of the "edge contrast." For ρ large (in magnitude) and negative there is an abrupt almost black-to-white or white-to-black transition across an edge boundary. If $\rho > 0$, on the other hand, the transition across an edge boundary is much more gradual. Finally, the parameter ν provides a measure of the degree of randomness or "homogeneity" of the resulting mosaic appearance. These properties are closely related to real-world image properties.

This class of random fields has proved a useful and conveniently parameterized stochastic image model in a number of important applications. These include: the development of a class of edge detectors based upon 2-D least mean-square filtering concepts, image enhancement based upon 2-D stochastic homomorphic filtering, a stochastic texture model in the development of statistically optimum texture discriminators, and a stochastic source model for image coding applications. Several of these applications will be discussed.

2. PRELIMINARIES

We consider an image as a family of random variables $\{f_\mathbf{x}(\omega), \mathbf{x} \in R^2\}$, or a random field, defined on some fixed but unspecified probability space $(\Omega, \mathcal{A}, P)$. For convenience we suppress the functional dependence upon the underlying probability space and consistently write $f(\mathbf{x})$ for $f_\mathbf{x}(\omega)$. The covariance function of the random field then becomes[1]

$$R_{ff}(\mathbf{x}, \mathbf{y}) = E\{f(\mathbf{x})f(\mathbf{y})\}; \qquad \mathbf{x}, \mathbf{y} \in R^2, \tag{1}$$

where $E\{\cdot\}$ represents the expectation operator. If a random field $\{f(\mathbf{x}), \mathbf{x} \in R^2\}$ possesses a covariance function invariant under all Euclidean motions it will be called *homogeneous and isotropic* (cf. [2] for definitions). In this case the covariance function of the field evaluated at two points can depend only upon the Euclidean distance between these two points so that

$$E\{f(\mathbf{x} + \mathbf{u})f(\mathbf{x})\} = R_{ff}(\|\mathbf{u}\|), \tag{2}$$

where $\mathbf{u}^T = (u_1, u_2)$ is an element of R^2 and $\|\mathbf{u}\|$ represents the ordinary Euclidean

[1] We assume the field is of second order (i.e., variances exist) and possesses zero mean.

norm defined in terms of an inner product $\langle \cdot, \cdot \rangle$ according to

$$\|\mathbf{u}\|^2 = \langle \mathbf{u}, \mathbf{u} \rangle = u_1^2 + u_2^2. \tag{3}$$

By construction, the 2-D random fields to be described here are of this category. Furthermore, they have been explicitly constructed so that the joint probability density function (p.d.f.) of the field evaluated at two points likewise depends only upon the Euclidean distance between these points. More specifically, define the random variables $f_1 = f(\mathbf{x})$ and $f_2 = f(\mathbf{x} + \mathbf{u})$. The joint p.d.f. associated with these two random variables, parameterized by the spatial coordinates, then satisfies

$$p\{f_1, f_2; \mathbf{x}, \mathbf{x} + \mathbf{u}\} = p\{f_1, f_2; \|\mathbf{u}\|\}, \tag{4}$$

which is the 2-D concept of stationarity [8] or invariance which will be most useful for our purposes.

The corresponding power spectral density function is given by

$$S_{ff}(\boldsymbol{\omega}) = \int_{R^2} R_{ff}(\|\mathbf{u}\|) \exp\{-j\langle \boldsymbol{\omega}, \mathbf{u} \rangle\} d\mathbf{u}, \tag{5}$$

where $\boldsymbol{\omega}^T = (\omega_1, \omega_2)$ represents a 2-D spatial frequency vector and $d\mathbf{u}$ is the differential volume element in R^2. This expression can be evaluated up to functional form with the aid of a theorem of Bochner [9] with the result

$$S_{ff}(\boldsymbol{\omega}) = S(\Omega) = 2\pi \int_0^\infty \lambda R_{ff}(\lambda) J_0(\lambda \Omega) d\lambda, \tag{6}$$

where $\Omega \triangleq \|\boldsymbol{\omega}\| = (\omega_1^2 + \omega_2^2)^{\frac{1}{2}}$ represents radial frequency. Here $J_0(\cdot)$ denotes the ordinary Bessel function of the first kind of order zero. The quantities $S_{ff}(\cdot)$ and $R_{ff}(\cdot)$ are then related through a Hankel transform [10, 11].

3. CONSTRUCTION PROCEDURE

In the present section we describe several construction procedures for homogeneous and isotropic random fields generated by random tessellations of the plane. Relevant second-order properties are discussed in the next section. We begin with the case where the plane is tessellated into random *rectangular* regions.

Rectangular tessellations. A fundamental role in the construction of this class of processes will be played by the integer-valued random field[2] $\{N(\mathbf{x}), \mathbf{x} \geq 0\}$ which provides a 2-D generalization of a counting process [12]. In particular, suppose the vector $\tilde{\mathbf{x}}$ is obtained from $\mathbf{x}$ according to $\tilde{\mathbf{x}} = \mathbf{A}\mathbf{x}$, where $\mathbf{A}$ is the unitary matrix

$$\mathbf{A} = \begin{bmatrix} \cos\theta & \sin\theta \\ -\sin\theta & \cos\theta \end{bmatrix}, \tag{7}$$

defined for some $\theta \epsilon [-\pi, \pi]$. This transformation results in a rotation of the Cartesian coordinate axes (x_1, x_2) by θ radians as illustrated in Fig. 1.

[2] By the notation $\mathbf{x} \geq 0$ we mean that $\mathbf{x}^T = (x_1, x_2)$ is such that $x_i \geq 0$, $i = 1, 2$.

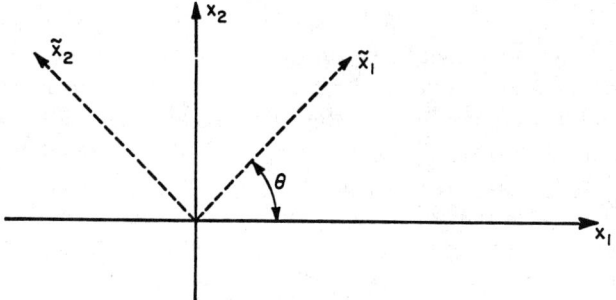

Fig. 1. Rotation of Cartesian coordinate axes.

Consider now the integer-valued random field defined by

$$N(\mathbf{x}) = N_1(\tilde{x}_1) + N_2(\tilde{x}_2); \quad \mathbf{x} \geq 0, \tag{8}$$

where $\theta \epsilon [-\pi, \pi]$ is chosen according to some p.d.f. $p(\theta)$ and $\{N_i(l), l \geq 0\}$, $i = 1, 2$, are mutually independent 1-D counting processes. That is, $N_i(l)$ represents the number of events which have occurred in the interval $[0, l]$. We will be particularly concerned with the case where $\{N_i(l), l \geq 0\}$, $i = 1, 2$, are renewal point processes defined in terms of their interarrival distribution.

The random field $\{N(\mathbf{x}), \mathbf{x} \geq 0\}$ in (8) then assumes constant integer values on nonoverlapping rectangles whose sides are parallel to the transformed coordinate axes $(\tilde{x}_1, \tilde{x}_2)$ and whose locations are determined by the event times of the corresponding point processes $\{N_i(l), l \geq 0\}$, $i = 1, 2$. Consider now the random field $\{f(\mathbf{x}), \mathbf{x} \geq 0\}$ which undergoes transitions at the boundaries of these elementary rectangles. The gray level assumed throughout any elementary rectangle is zero-mean Gaussian[3] with variance σ^2 and correlation coefficient ρ with the gray levels in contiguous rectangles. More specifically, let $X_{i,j}$ represent the amplitude or gray level assumed by the random field after i transitions in the $\tilde{x}_1$ direction and j transitions in the $\tilde{x}_2$ direction. The sequence $\{X_{i,j}\}$ is assumed generated recursively according to

$$X_{i,j} = \rho X_{i-1,j} + \rho X_{i,j-1} - \rho^2 X_{i-1,j-1} + W_{i,j}; \quad i, j \geq 1, \tag{9}$$

where $|\rho| \leq 1$, and $\{W_{i,j}\}$ is a 2-D sequence of independent and identically distributed (i.i.d.) zero-mean Gaussian variates with common variance $\sigma_w^2 = \sigma^2(1 - \rho^2)^2$. The initial values $X_{k,0}$, $X_{0,l}$, $k, l \geq 0$ are jointly distributed zero-mean Gaussian variates with common variance σ^2 and covariance properties chosen to result in stationary conditions. An alternative interpretation of the sequence $\{X_{i,j}\}$ is as the output of a separable 2-D recursive filter excited by a white noise field. It is easily seen that

$$E\{X_{i,j} X_{i+k_1,j+k_2}\} = \sigma^2 \rho^{k_1+k_2}; \quad k_1, k_2 \geq 0. \tag{10}$$

Typical computer-generated realizations of the resulting random field are

[3] For definiteness we assume Gaussian statistics. This assumption is not critical to the development which follows and is easily removed.

illustrated in Fig. 2 for selected values of ρ when $p(\theta)$ is uniform over $[-\pi, \pi]$ and $\{N_i(l), l \geq 0\}$, $i = 1, 2$, are Poisson with intensities $\lambda_1 = \lambda_2 = \lambda$. The displayed images here and throughout this paper are square arrays consisting of 256 elements or samples on a side. In Fig. 2, λ is measured in normalized units of events per sample distance so that there are on average 256λ transitions along each of the orthogonal axes. Similarly, in Fig. 3 we illustrate realizations of the resulting random field when the point processes $\{N_i(l), l \geq 0\}$, $i = 1, 2$, undergo jumps of unit height at equally spaced intervals $l = 1/\lambda$. The starting positions ϵ_i, $i = 1, 2$, will be assumed uniformly distributed over the interval $[0, l]$.

The preceding two examples are special cases of the situation where the point processes $\{N_i(l), l \geq 0\}$, $i = 1, 2$, are stationary renewal processes [13, 14] with gamma distributed interarrival times. This class of random fields represents a 2-D generalization of the class of 1-D processes described in [15]. In particular, we assume the common interarrival distribution of the two mutually independent

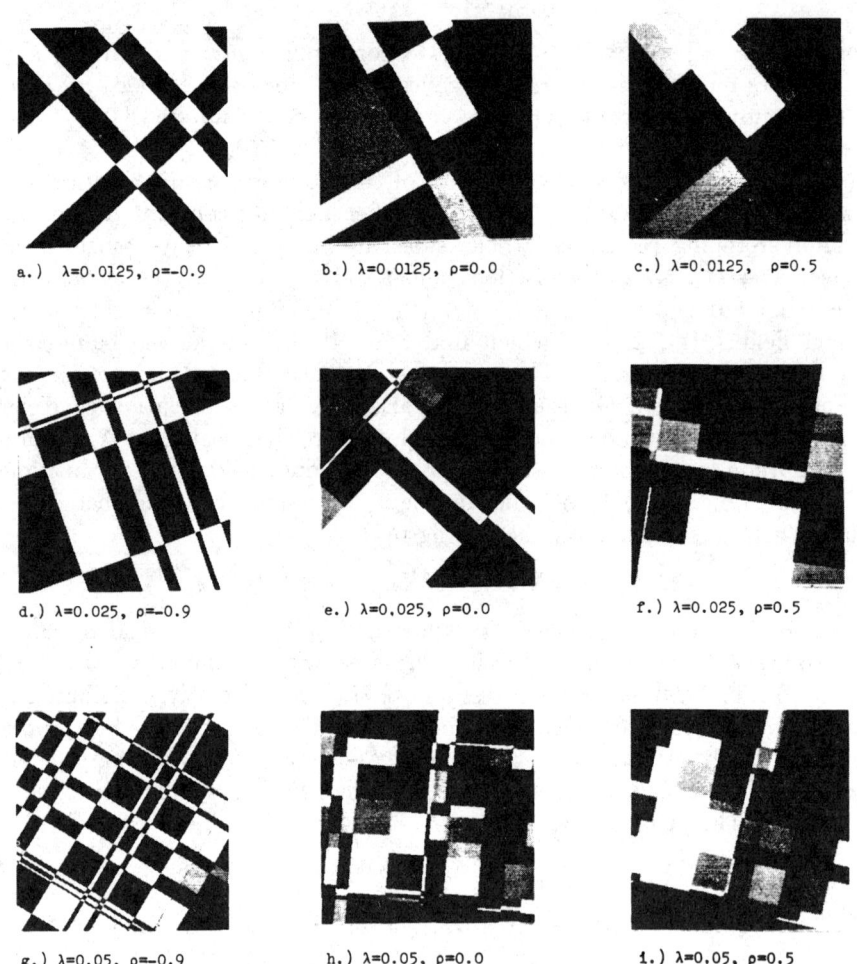

FIG. 2. Selected realizations of random field generated by Poisson partitions.

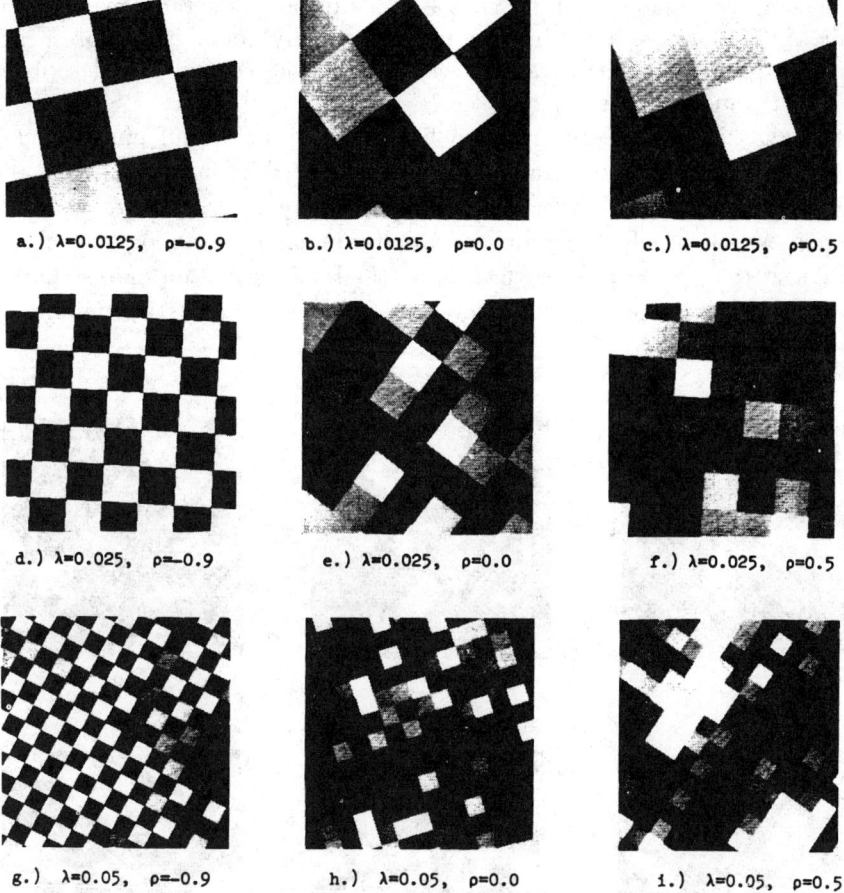

Fig. 3. Selected realizations of random field generated by periodic partitions.

point processes $\{N_i(l), l \geq 0\}$, $i = 1, 2$, possesses p.d.f.

$$f(x) = \frac{x^{\nu-1}}{\Gamma(\nu)\beta^\nu} \exp\{-x/\beta\}, \qquad (11)$$

where $\nu = 1, 2, \ldots,$ and $\beta = 1/\lambda\nu$ for fixed $\lambda > 0$. For example, if $\nu = 1$ we have the exponential distribution

$$f(x) = \lambda e^{-\lambda x}; \qquad x \geq 0, \qquad (12)$$

associated with the Poisson process, while in the limit $\nu \to \infty$ we have

$$f(x) = \delta(x - 1/\lambda); \qquad x \geq 0, \qquad (13)$$

corresponding to the case of periodic partitions as illustrated in Fig. 3.

In Fig. 4 we illustrate selected realizations of the resulting random field for several values of ν all with $\lambda = 0.05$ and $\rho = 0.0$. Clearly the parameter ν provides a measure of the degree of randomness or "homogeneity" of the structure. For small ν the random field $\{f(\mathbf{x}), \mathbf{x} \in R^2\}$ appears as a random rectangular mosaic. As ν increases, individual realizations rapidly approach a more periodic mosaic in appearance. The parameters λ, ρ, and ν then completely describe this class of 2-D random fields.

Although this class of 2-D random fields provides a useful image model in selected applications, the rectangular mosaic exhibited by individual realizations is not entirely consistent with edge structure in real-world imagery. That is, we would expect the edge structure to exhibit a much more random edge orientation. An alternative approach then is to randomly partition or tessellate the plane into more complex geometric regions. In what follows we describe two possible alternatives.

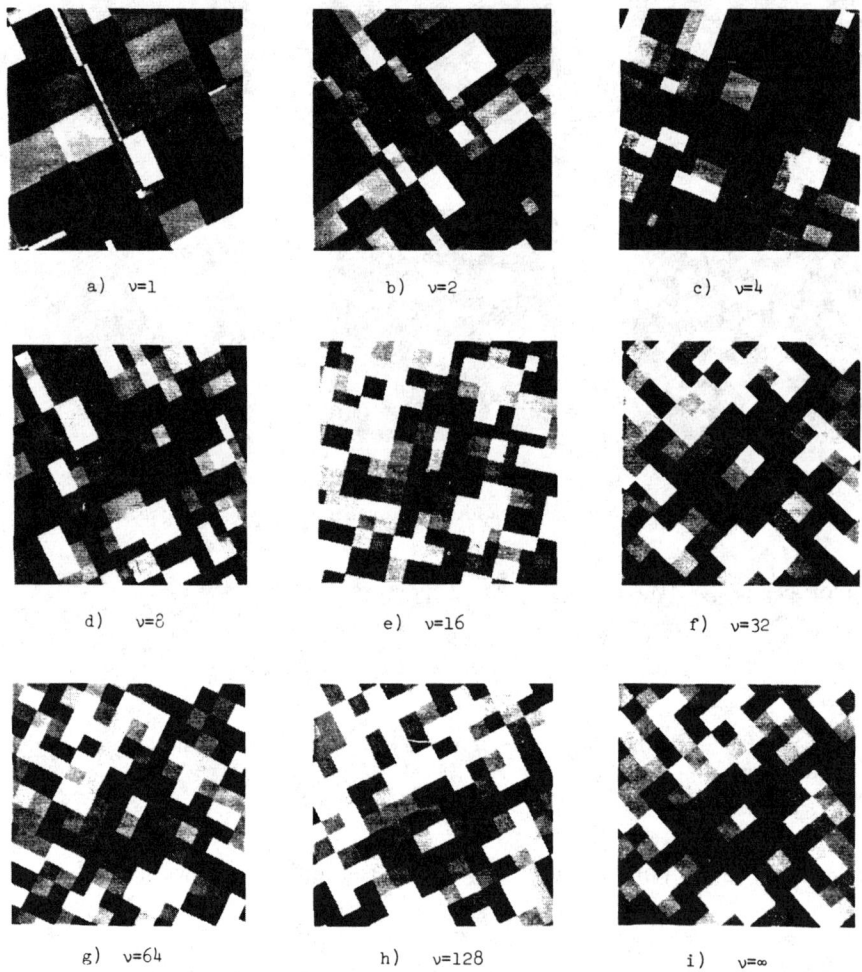

FIG. 4. Selected realizations of random field generated by stationary renewal point processes possessing gamma distributed interarrival distribution and with $\lambda = 0.05$ and $\rho = 0.0$.

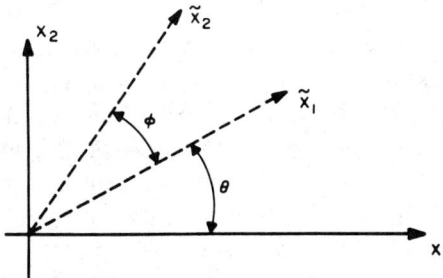

Fig. 5. Nonisometric transformation of Cartesian coordinate frame.

Parallelogram tessellations. Again the plane is partitioned by two mutually independent renewal point processes evolving along appropriately defined coordinate axes. In this case, however, these coordinate axes are determined by a nonunitary or nonisometric transformation of the Cartesian coordinate frame. More specifically, we suppose the vector $\tilde{\mathbf{x}}$ is obtained from $\mathbf{x}$ according to the linear transformation $\tilde{\mathbf{x}} = \mathbf{A}\mathbf{x}$ where now $\mathbf{A}$ is the 2×2 matrix defined for ϕ, $\theta \in [-\pi, \pi]$ according to

$$\mathbf{A} = \frac{1}{\sin \phi} \begin{bmatrix} \sin (\theta + \phi) & -\cos (\theta + \phi) \\ -\sin \theta & \cos \theta \end{bmatrix}. \qquad (14)$$

This transformation has an interpretation as a distance-preserving rotation of the Cartesian coordinate frame by θ radians followed by a non-distance-preserving scaling. The new coordinate axes $(\tilde{x}_1, \tilde{x}_2)$ are illustrated in Fig. 5. In what follows we assume that the angle ϕ is fixed while θ is chosen uniformly on $[-\pi, \pi]$. The point processes $\{N_i(l), l \geq 0\}$ now evolving along the respective coordinate axes $\tilde{x}_i$, $i = 1, 2$, result in a tessellation of the plane into elementary regions comprised of disjoint parallelograms whose sides are parallel to the new coordinate axes. Gray levels are then assigned within these elementary regions as described previously.

In Fig. 6 we illustrate typical realizations of the resulting 2-D random field for selected values of ϕ all with $\lambda = 0.025$ and $\rho = 0.0$. The point processes generating the random field in this case are Poisson corresponding to gamma distributed interarrival times with parameter $\nu = 1$. Typical realizations for the case $\nu = \infty$, corresponding to periodic partitions, are illustrated in Fig. 7. This class of random fields results in a distinctive herringbone or tweed mosaic.

Polygonal tessellations. Consider the tessellation of the plane R^2 by a field of random sensed lines. More specifically, an arbitrary sensed line can be described in terms of the 3-tuple (r, θ, ζ). Here r represents the perpendicular or radial distance to the line in question, $\theta \in [-\pi, \pi]$ represents the orientation of this radial vector, and finally ζ is a binary random variable assuming values ± 1 which specifies the sense or direction imparted to this line segment. The pertinent geometry is illustrated in Fig. 8 for the case $\zeta = 1$. By virtue of the direction imposed on this line segment the plane is partitioned into two disjoint regions, R (right of line) and L (left of line) such that $R \cup L = R^2$.

Now consider the field of lines generated by the sequence $\{r_i, \theta_i, \zeta_i\}$. Here the sequence $\{r_i\}$ represents the "event times" associated with a homogeneous Poisson process $\{N(r), r \geq 0\}$ with intensity λ events/unit distance evolving according to the radial parameter r. The sequence $\{\theta_i\}$ is i.i.d. and uniform on $[-\pi, \pi]$ while $\{\zeta_i\}$ is also i.i.d. assuming the value ± 1 with equal probability.

The field of random lines so generated results in a partition of the plane into disjoint polygonal regions. Gray levels are assigned as described in [16] to result in correlation coefficient ρ with gray levels in contiguous regions. Typical realizations of the resulting random field are illustrated in Fig. 9 for selected values of

FIG. 6. Selected realizations of nonrectangular random field generated by Poisson point processes with $\lambda = 0.025$ and $\rho = 0.0$.

FIG. 7. Selected realizations of nonrectangular random field generated by periodic point processes with $\lambda = 0.025$ and $\rho = 0.0$.

$\lambda_e = \lambda/\pi$ and ρ. The quantity λ_e represents the average edge density along any randomly chosen line segment.[4] This random field is again described in terms of the two parameters λ_e, or equivalently λ, and ρ. This class of 2-D random fields can be extended to include more general point processes $\{N(r), r \geq 0\}$ controlling the radial evolution; for example, stationary renewal processes with gamma

[4] Similarly, in the case of rectangular tessellations it is easily shown that the average edge density along any randomly chosen line segment is $\lambda_e = 4\lambda/\pi$.

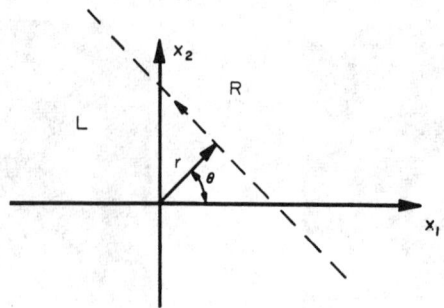

Fig. 8. Parameterization of directed line segment.

distributed interarrival times. Unfortunately, the analysis of the resulting processes becomes quite complicated and as a result we will not pursue this generalization here.

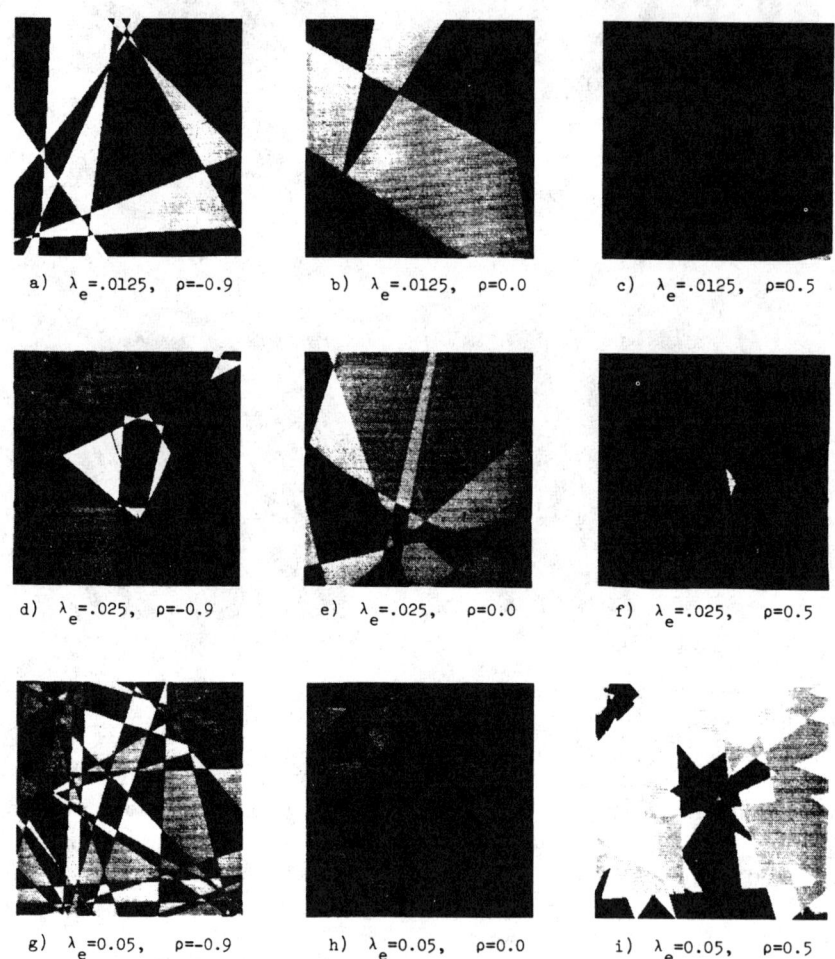

a) $\lambda_e = .0125$, $\rho = -0.9$
b) $\lambda_e = .0125$, $\rho = 0.0$
c) $\lambda_e = .0125$, $\rho = 0.5$

d) $\lambda_e = .025$, $\rho = -0.9$
e) $\lambda_e = .025$, $\rho = 0.0$
f) $\lambda_e = .025$, $\rho = 0.5$

g) $\lambda_e = 0.05$, $\rho = -0.9$
h) $\lambda_e = 0.05$, $\rho = 0.0$
i) $\lambda_e = 0.05$, $\rho = 0.5$

Fig. 9. Selected realizations of random field generated by polygonal partitions.

4. SECOND-ORDER PROPERTIES

We turn now to the second-order properties of the class of 2-D random fields described in the preceding section. In the interests of brevity the treatment will be condensed and will make extensive use of results reported elsewhere.

Rectangular tessellations. As a first step in the development of the covariance function, assume that the random orientation $\theta \in [-\pi, \pi]$ has been chosen and that k transitions have occurred[5] between the two points $\mathbf{x}$ and $\mathbf{x} + \mathbf{u}$ where we assume for the moment $\mathbf{u} \geq 0$. It follows from (10) that

$$E\{f(\mathbf{x} + \mathbf{u})f(\mathbf{x})|\theta, k\} = \sigma^2 \rho^k; \qquad k = 0, 1, 2, \ldots. \tag{14}$$

The conditioning upon k is easily removed according to

$$E\{f(\mathbf{x} + \mathbf{u})f(\mathbf{x})|\theta\} = \sum_{k=0}^{\infty} E\{f(\mathbf{x} + \mathbf{u})f(\mathbf{x})|\theta, k\} p_{k|\theta}(\mathbf{u}), \tag{15}$$

where $p_{k|\theta}(\mathbf{u})$ is the probability of k transitions between $\mathbf{x}$ and $\mathbf{x} + \mathbf{u}$ given that θ is acting. We exploit the stationary renewal properties of the point processes $\{N_i(l), l \geq 0\}$, $i = 1, 2$, in writing this probability as a function only of the displacement $\mathbf{u}$. In particular, $p_{k|\theta}(\mathbf{u})$ can be evaluated according to

$$p_{k|\theta}(\mathbf{u}) = \sum_{j=0}^{k} q_{k-j|\theta}^{(1)}(\tilde{u}_1) q_{j|\theta}^{(2)}(\tilde{u}_2); \qquad k = 0, 1, \ldots, \tag{16}$$

where $q_{j|\theta}^{(i)}(\tilde{u}_i)$ is the probability that $\{N_i(l), l \geq 0\}$ has undergone j transitions in the interval $\tilde{u}_i$, $i = 1, 2$, which depends upon $\mathbf{u}^T = (u_1, u_2)$ and θ according to

$$\tilde{u}_1 = u_1 \cos \theta + u_2 \sin \theta, \tag{17a}$$

and

$$\tilde{u}_2 = u_2 \cos \theta - u_1 \sin \theta. \tag{17b}$$

Substituting (14) and (16) into (15) we obtain

$$E\{f(\mathbf{x} + \mathbf{u})f(\mathbf{x})|\theta\} = \sigma^2 \sum_{k=0}^{\infty} \rho^k \sum_{j=0}^{k} q_{k-j|\theta}^{(1)}(\tilde{u}_1) q_{j|\theta}^{(2)}(\tilde{u}_2), \tag{18}$$

and by simple rearrangement of the double summation in this last expression we find

$$E\{f(\mathbf{x} + \mathbf{u})f(\mathbf{x})|\theta\} = \sigma^2 \sum_{j=0}^{\infty} \sum_{k=j}^{\infty} \rho^{k-j} q_{k-j|\theta}^{(1)}(\tilde{u}_1) \rho^j q_{j|\theta}^{(2)}(\tilde{u}_2)$$

$$= \sigma^2 \Big[\sum_{m=0}^{\infty} \rho^m q_{m|\theta}^{(1)}(\tilde{u}_1)\Big] \cdot \Big[\sum_{n=0}^{\infty} \rho^n q_{n|\theta}^{(2)}(\tilde{u}_2)\Big]. \tag{19}$$

---

[5] By this we mean that $k = k_1 + k_2$, where k_i, $i = 1, 2$, represents the number of transitions along each of the orthogonal axes which have now been rotated by θ radians.

Assuming a uniform distribution for θ, it follows that the covariance function becomes

$$R_{ff}(\mathbf{x} + \mathbf{u}, \mathbf{x}) = \frac{1}{2\pi} \int_{-\pi}^{\pi} E\{f(\mathbf{x} + \mathbf{u})f(\mathbf{x}) | \theta\} d\theta, \qquad (20)$$

with the integrand given by (19). While not immediately apparent, it is easily shown that this last expression depends only upon $\|\mathbf{u}\|$ so that the resulting random field is indeed homogeneous and isotropic.

While explicit evaluation of (20) is in general quite cumbersome, it can be evaluated in special cases. For example, in the Poisson case $\nu = 1$ it can be shown [18] that

$$R_{ff}(\|\mathbf{u}\|) = \frac{2\sigma^2}{\pi} \int_0^{\pi/2} \exp\{-2^{\frac{1}{2}}(1-\rho)\lambda\|\mathbf{u}\| \cos(\theta - \pi/4)\} d\theta, \qquad (21)$$

while the corresponding power spectral density computed according to (6) becomes

$$S_{ff}(\Omega) = \frac{8(1-\rho)\lambda\sigma^2}{\Omega^2 + 2(1-\rho)^2\lambda^2} \left[\frac{1}{\Omega^2 + (1-\rho)^2\lambda^2}\right]^{\frac{1}{2}}. \qquad (22)$$

Typical covariance surfaces together with intensity plots of the corresponding power spectral density in the case of periodic partitions (i.e., $\nu = \infty$) are illustrated in Fig. 10. The autocorrelation functions are plotted as a function of the normalized spatial variable[6] $\|\mathbf{u}\|/l$ over the range $0 \leq \|\mathbf{u}\|/l \leq 3$, while the power spectral density is plotted as a function of the normalized spatial frequency variable $\Omega/2\pi\lambda$ over the range $0 \leq \Omega/2\pi\lambda \leq 5$. Additional details can be found in [18]. Explicit evaluation of these quantities for the general case of gamma distributed interarrival times is provided in [19].

Similarly, the conditional joint probability of $f_1 = f(\mathbf{x})$ and $f_2 = f(\mathbf{x} + \mathbf{u})$ given both the random angle θ and the number of transitions k between $\mathbf{x}$ and $\mathbf{x} + \mathbf{u}$ is easily shown to be given by[7]

$$p\{f_1, f_2; \mathbf{x}, \mathbf{x} + \mathbf{u} | \theta, k\} = \frac{1}{2\pi\sigma^2(1-\rho^{2k})^{\frac{1}{2}}} \exp\left\{-\frac{f_1^2 - 2\rho^k f_1 f_2 + f_2^2}{2\sigma^2(1-\rho^{2k})}\right\}; \quad k > 0$$

$$= \frac{1}{(2\pi)^{\frac{1}{2}}\sigma} \exp\left\{-\frac{f_1^2}{2\sigma^2}\right\} \delta(f_1 - f_2); \quad k = 0. \qquad (23)$$

Note that this quantity is independent of $\mathbf{x}$, $\mathbf{x} + \mathbf{u}$, and θ; we will make use of this observation later.

---

[6] Here $l = 1/\lambda$ with λ the common rate parameter of the two mutually independent point processes which provide a rectangular partition of the plane.

[7] It is at this point that the Gaussian assumption is crucial.

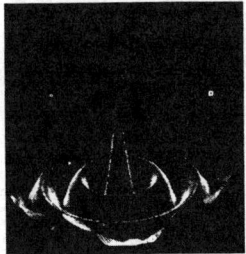
a) Autocorrelation Function
$\rho = -0.9$

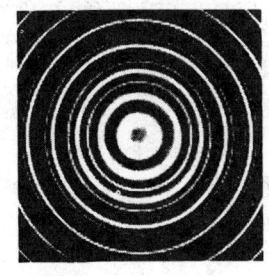
b) Power Spectral Density
$\rho = -0.9$

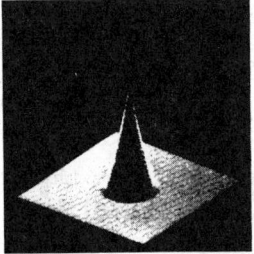
c) Autocorrelation Function
$\rho = 0.0$

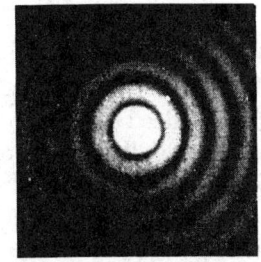
d) Power Spectral Density
$\rho = 0.0$

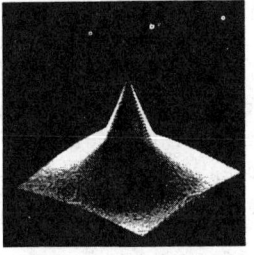
e) Autocorrelation Function
$\rho = 0.5$

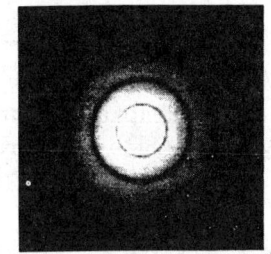
f) Power Spectral Density
$\rho = 0.5$

FIG. 10. Autocorrelation function and power spectral density of 2-D random checkerboard process generated by periodic partitions.

The conditioning upon k in this case is easily removed according to

$$p\{f_1, f_2; \mathbf{x}, \mathbf{x} + \mathbf{u} | \theta\} = \sum_{k=0}^{\infty} p\{f_1, f_2; \mathbf{x}, \mathbf{x} + \mathbf{u} | \theta, k\} p_{k|\theta}(\mathbf{u})$$

$$= \sum_{k=0}^{\infty} h_k(f_1, f_2) p_{k|\theta}(\mathbf{u}), \qquad (24)$$

where $p_{k|\theta}(\mathbf{u})$ has been defined previously as the probability of k transitions between $\mathbf{x}$ and $\mathbf{x} + \mathbf{u}$ given that θ is acting. We have used $h_k(f_1, f_2)$ in the second expression of (24) in order to emphasize the functional independence of the spatial parameters $\mathbf{x}$ and $\mathbf{x} + \mathbf{u}$ and the rotation angle θ.

Again under the assumption of uniform distribution for θ, the joint p.d.f. can be evaluated as

$$p\{f_1, f_2; \mathbf{x}, \mathbf{x} + \mathbf{u}\} = \frac{1}{2\pi} \int_{-\pi}^{\pi} p\{f_1, f_2; \mathbf{x}, \mathbf{x} + \mathbf{u} | \theta\} d\theta$$

$$= \sum_{k=0}^{\infty} h_k(f_1, f_2) p_k(\|\mathbf{u}\|), \quad (25)$$

where

$$p_k(\|\mathbf{u}\|) \triangleq \frac{1}{2\pi} \int_{-\pi}^{\pi} p_{k|\theta}(\mathbf{u}) d\theta, \quad (26)$$

and we have made explicit use of the fact that the integral on the right-hand side of this last expression depends only upon the Euclidean distance $\|\mathbf{u}\|$. It follows that (4) is indeed satisfied and hence the 2-D random field is homogeneous and isotropic through all second-order statistics.

To complete the evaluation of the joint p.d.f. $p\{f_1, f_2; \|\mathbf{u}\|\}$ it remains to provide explicit evaluation of $p_k(\|\mathbf{u}\|)$ in (26). This has proved rather cumbersome in general, although quite tractable in several important special cases. For example, again in the case $\nu = 1$ corresponding to Poisson partitions, it can be shown [19] that

$$p_k(\|\mathbf{u}\|) = \frac{4[2^{\frac{1}{2}}\lambda\|\mathbf{u}\|]^k}{\pi k!} \int_0^{\pi/4} \cos^k \theta \exp\{-2^{\frac{1}{2}}\lambda\|\mathbf{u}\| \cos \theta\} d\theta;$$

$$k = 0, 1, \ldots, \quad (27)$$

which does not seem capable of further simplification. At any rate, this expression is easily evaluated by numerical integration. Substitution into (25) then yields explicit evaluation of $p\{f_1, f_2; \|\mathbf{u}\|\}$. Actually, for evaluation and display purposes, it proves convenient to consider a normalized version of this joint p.d.f. defined according to[8]

$$p_0\{f_1, f_2; \|\mathbf{u}\|\} = \sigma^2 p\{\sigma f_1, \sigma f_2; \|\mathbf{u}\|\}, \quad (28)$$

which is plotted in Fig. 11 as a function of f_1, f_2 for selected values of ρ and the *normalized displacement* $d' \triangleq \lambda_c \|\mathbf{u}\|$. Here the point $f_1 = f_1 = 0$ appears in the center and the plots cover the range $-3 \leq f_i \leq 3$, $i = 1, 2$. Note the high concentration of discrete probability mass along the diagonal $f_1 = f_2$ for small values of d'. This is a direct result of the high probability of $\mathbf{x}$ and $\mathbf{x} + \mathbf{u}$ falling in the same rectangular regions and thus resulting in identical values for $f_1 = f(\mathbf{x})$ and $f_2 = f(\mathbf{x} + \mathbf{u})$. This probability diminishes for increasing d'. Indeed, as indicated in Fig. 11, this "ridge line" along the diagonal has virtually disappeared for $d' = 8$. The off-diagonal probability mass visible for $\rho = -0.9$ is a direct

---

[8] The net effect of this normalization is that the f_1, f_2 axes can be considered normalized to the standard deviation σ.

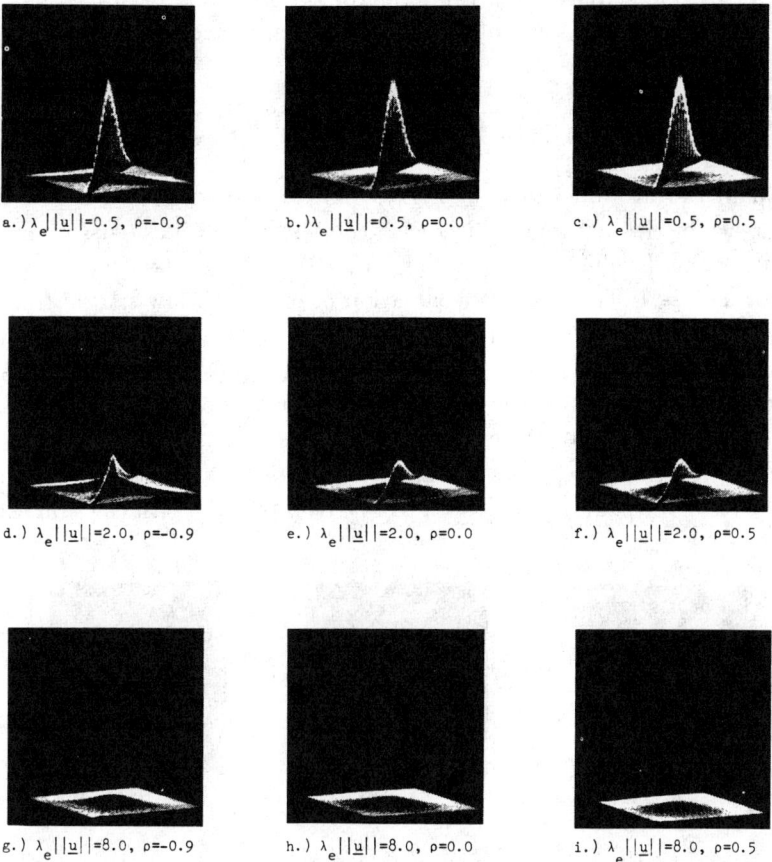

Fig. 11. Selected joint probability density functions for rectangular partition process, $\nu = 1$.

result of the negative correlation while for $\rho = 0.5$, as expected, there is visible probability mass distributed along the main diagonal. For $\rho = 0$, of course, this distribution is circularly symmetric about the origin. These observations are more apparent in Fig. 12 which illustrates intensity plots of the logarithms of the corresponding p.d.f.'s in Fig. 11. Note, in particular, the almost identical circularly symmetric distributions which result for large d' independent of the value of ρ.

Nonrectangular tessellations. Corresponding second-order properties of 2-D random fields generated by nonrectangular tessellations, although somewhat more complicated than in the rectangular case, have been determined as reported in [16, 19], to which the reader is referred to for details. For example, in the case of polygonal tessellations it is shown in [16] that, under the assumption of a Poisson line process generating the partitions, the autocorrelation function is given by

$$R_{ff}(\|\mathbf{u}\|) = \sigma^2 e^{-\lambda_e \|\mathbf{u}\|}\{I_0(\lambda_e\|\mathbf{u}\|) + 2\sum_{k=1}^{\infty}\rho^k I_k(\lambda_e\|\mathbf{u}\|)\}, \qquad (29)$$

where $I_k(\cdot)$ is the modified Bessel function of the first kind of order k. Similarly, the corresponding power spectral density is evaluated according to

$$S_{ff}(\Omega) = \frac{2\sigma^2(1-\rho^2)}{\lambda_e^2} \int_0^\pi \left[\frac{1-\cos\phi}{1-2\rho\cos\phi+\rho^2}\right] \frac{d\phi}{[(\Omega/\lambda_e)^2 + (1-\cos\phi)^2]^{\frac{3}{2}}}. \quad (30)$$

These quantities are illustrated in Fig. 13 for various values of ρ. One notable characteristic of this random field is that the power spectral density behaves as $(\Omega/\lambda_e)^{-\frac{1}{2}}$ for small values of (Ω/λ_e), i.e., $S_{ff}(\Omega)$ has a singularity at the origin except for $\rho = -1$. This high concentration of energy at low spatial frequencies is a direct result of the construction procedure which allows relatively large correlations between gray levels in regions relatively far apart. We feel that this characteristic is typical of selected image processing applications and as a result it was purposely built into the construction procedure.

Similarly, for the case of polygonal tessellations generated by Poisson point processes, the joint p.d.f. is easily seen to be given by (25) with the sum extended

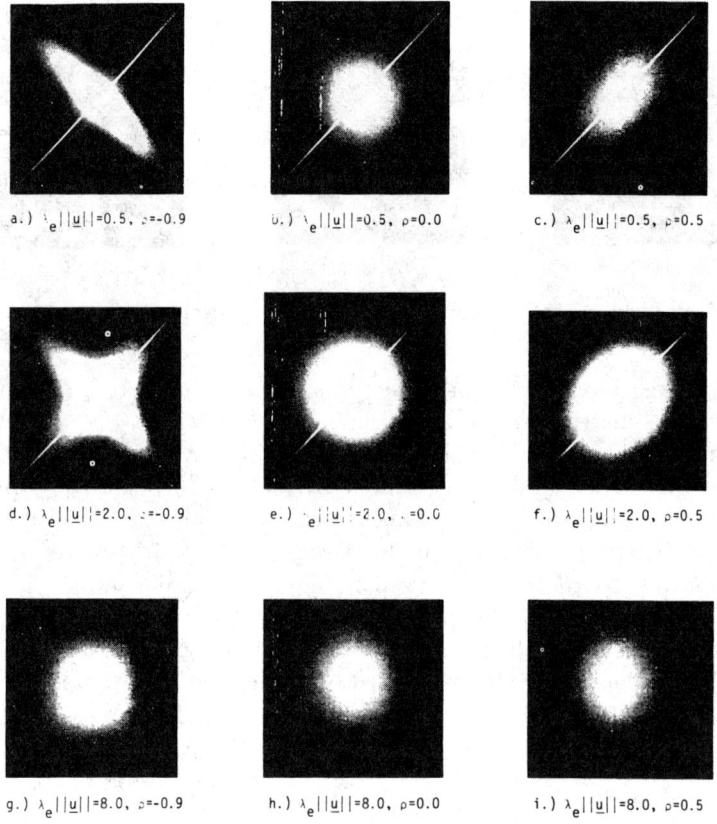

Fig. 12. Intensity plots of logarithm of selected joint probability density functions for rectangular partition process, $\nu = 1$.

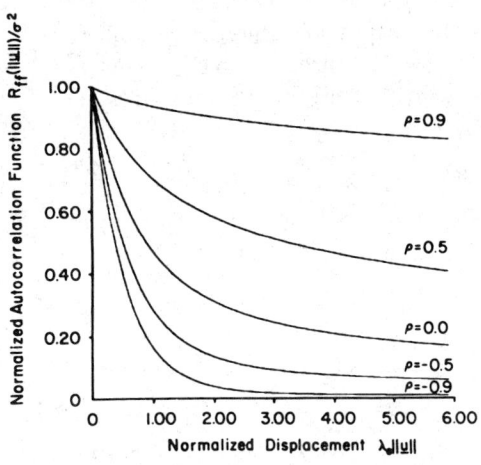 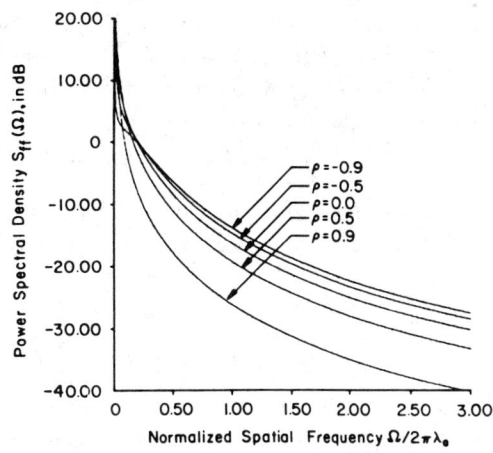

a.) NORMALIZED AUTOCORRELATION FUNCTION   b.) POWER SPECTRAL DENSITY

Fig. 13. Autocorrelation function and power spectral density of 2-D random field generated by polygonal partitions.

over both positive and negative values of k and now

$$p_k(\|\mathbf{u}\|) = [\lambda_e\|\mathbf{u}\|/2]^{|k|} \exp\{-\lambda_e\|\mathbf{u}\|\} \sum_{l=0}^{\infty} \frac{[\lambda_e\|\mathbf{u}\|/2]^{2l}}{(l+|k|)!l!};$$

$$k = 0, \pm 1, \pm 2, \ldots. \quad (31)$$

In Fig. 14 we provide intensity plots of the logarithm of $p_0\{f_1, f_2; \|\mathbf{u}\|\}$ as a function of f_1 and f_2 for selected values of ρ and $d' = \lambda_e\|\mathbf{u}\|$. An interesting observation to be drawn here is the persistence of the diagonal "ridge line" with increasing values of d'. This is, of course, a direct result of the construction procedure which allows return to the same gray level at distant spatial locations with relatively high probability.

5. APPLICATIONS

We consider now some selected applications of the 2-D random fields described in the preceding.

Edge detection. This problem is treated in some detail in [17]. We assume that the true edge structure in an image is described by the random field $f(\mathbf{x})$ modeled as one of the previously developed 2-D random fields. In many applications, the observed image is a noise-corrupted version of $f(\mathbf{x})$ described by

$$g(\mathbf{x}) = f(\mathbf{x}) + n(\mathbf{x}), \quad (32)$$

where $n(\mathbf{x})$ is a zero-mean homogeneous and isotropic noise field possessing noise spectral density $S_{nn}(r) = \sigma_n^2$, i.e., a white noise field. Here one assumes that the noise field $n(\mathbf{x})$ represents any additive noise or spurious detail not considered part of the essential contours or edges represented by the random field $f(\mathbf{x})$.

In [17] the problem on edge detection was posed as a 2-D Wiener filtering problem. More specifically, if $l(\mathbf{x})$ represents the output of some desired operation on $f(\mathbf{x})$ then design the imaging system with optical transfer function (OTF) $H_0(\boldsymbol{\omega})$ whose output $\hat{l}(\mathbf{x})$ in response to $g(\mathbf{x})$ at its input minimizes the mean-square error

$$I_e = E\{[l(\mathbf{x}) - \hat{l}(\mathbf{x})]^2\}. \tag{33}$$

Assuming the desired operation possesses OTF $H_d(\boldsymbol{\omega}) = \|\boldsymbol{\omega}\|^2 \exp\{-\tfrac{1}{2}\|\boldsymbol{\omega}\|^2\}$ (cf. [17] for justification) the optimum Wiener filter is isotropic with OTF

$$H_0(\Omega) = \frac{\Omega^2 e^{-\Omega^2/2} S_{ff}(\Omega)}{S_{ff}(\Omega) + \sigma_n^2}; \qquad \Omega \geq 0. \tag{34}$$

For example, if $\{f(\mathbf{x}), \mathbf{x} \in R^2\}$ is the rectangular 2-D random field with Poisson partitions then the power spectral density $S_{ff}(\Omega)$ is given by (22). The resulting Wiener filter is then completely defined in terms of the three parameters λ, ρ, and $\zeta \triangleq \sigma^2/\sigma_n^2$ which represents the signal-to-noise ratio (SNR). Typical results

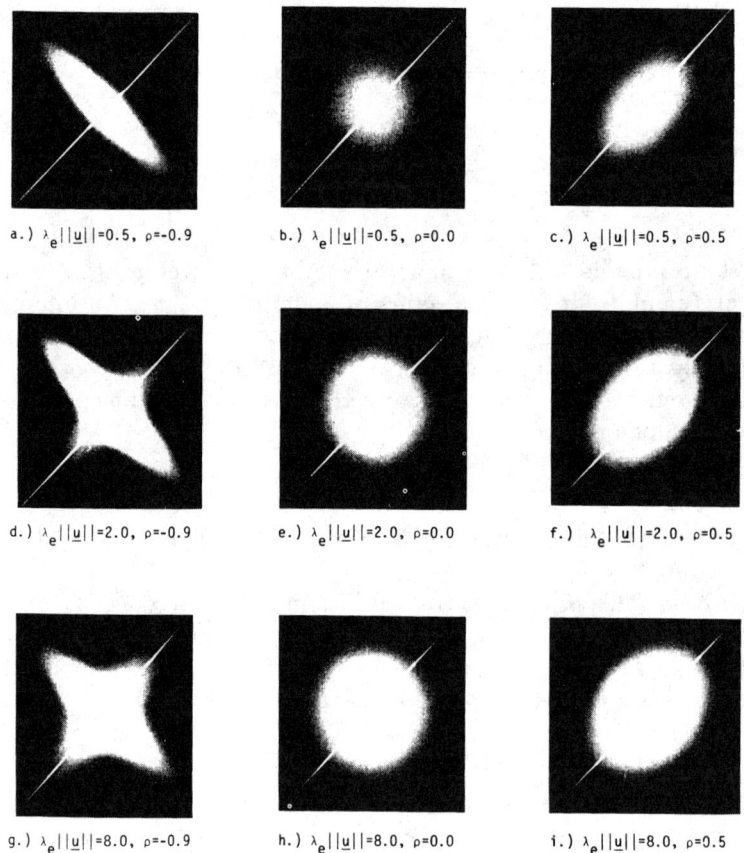

FIG. 14. Selected joint probability density functions for polygonal partition process.

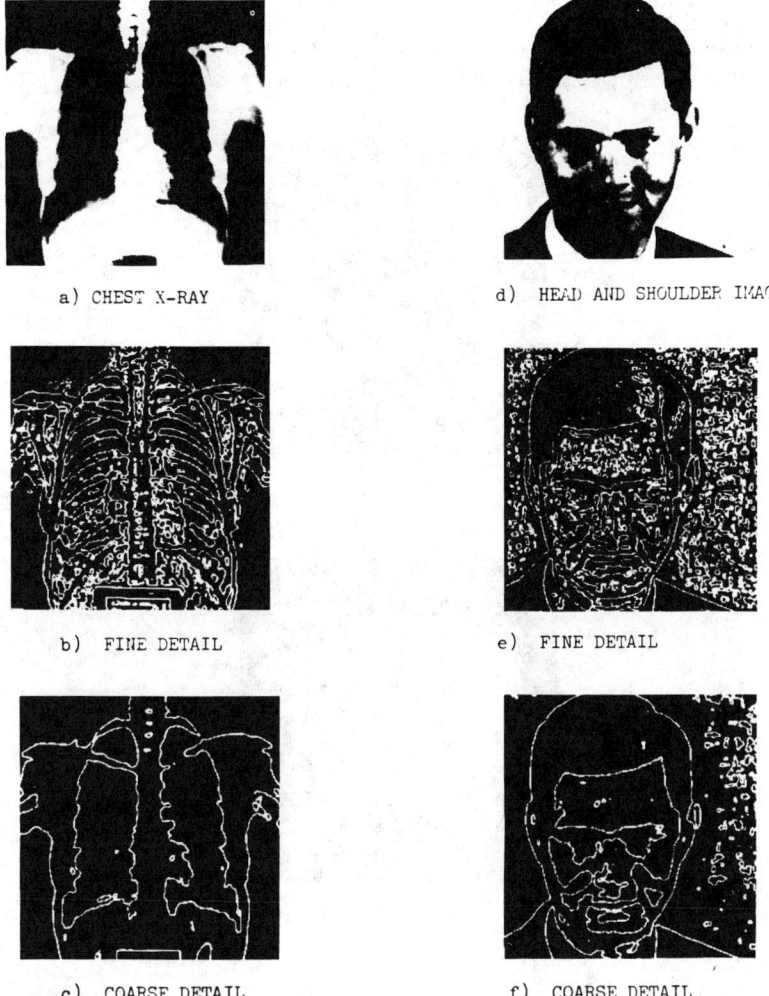

Fig. 15. Typical results of Wiener edge detector applied to real-world images.

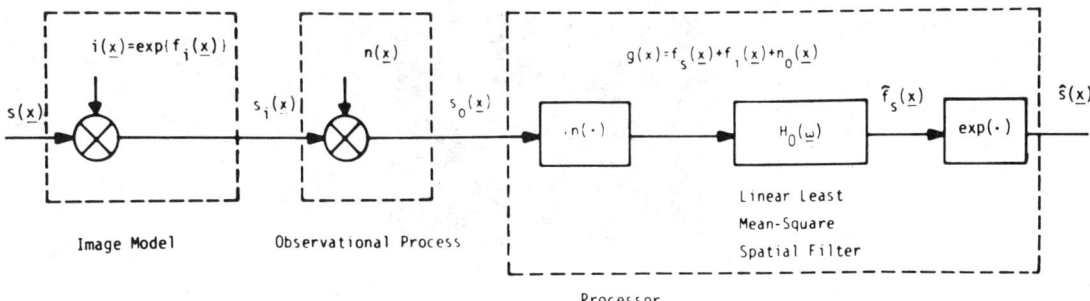

Fig. 16. Homomorphic filtering of degraded images.

are illustrated in Fig. 15 employing a digital implementation of the optimum Weiner filter. Additional results appear in [20].

Image enhancement. This class of 2-D random fields has found application as a stochastic model for spatially varying illumination in homomorphic filtering of

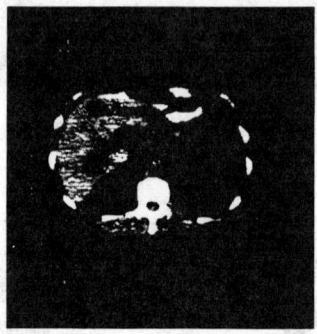

a) ORIGINAL

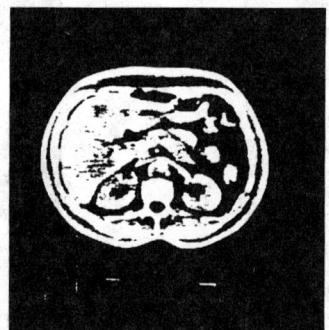

b) PROCESSED VERSION 1

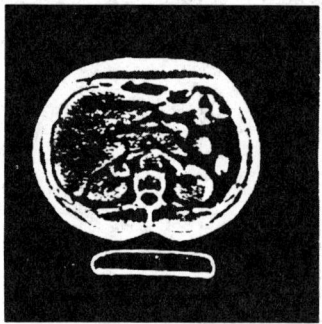

c) PROCESSED VERSION 2

FIG. 17. Typical results of homomorphic filtering of transaxial tomography image.

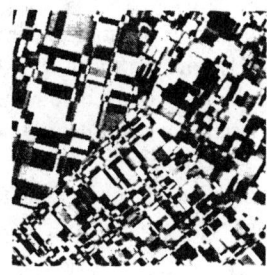
a.) Original; NW, $\rho=0.0$, $\lambda=0.16$; NE, $\rho=0.5$, $\lambda=0.32$; S, $\rho=0.0$, $\lambda=0.32$

b.) Log – Likelihood Discriminator

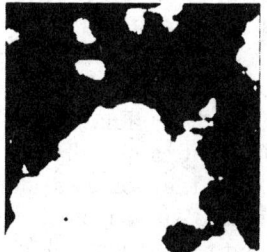
c.) Correlation Discriminator

d.) Correlation / Edge Discriminator

Fig. 18. Illustration of texture discrimination results.

images. More specifically, consider the formation of an image as indicated in Fig. 16. Here the observed image $s_i(\mathbf{x})$ is the product of the true image $s(\mathbf{x})$ and the illumination function $i(\mathbf{x}) = \exp\{f_i(\mathbf{x})\}$, where $f_i(\mathbf{x})$ is a 2-D random field with polygonal partitions as described in the preceding section. The true image $s(\mathbf{x})$ will be similarly modeled although the edge density will be assumed much higher than that of the illumination process. Finally, we assume that the observational or recording process introduces the multiplicative white noise field $n(\mathbf{x})$. The image available for processing is then

$$s_0(\mathbf{x}) = s(\mathbf{x}) \cdot i(\mathbf{x}) \cdot n(\mathbf{x}). \qquad (34)$$

As indicated in Fig. 16, by a simple application of homomorphic filtering concepts [21, 22] it is possible to design a linear least mean-square spatial filter to provide an estimate $\hat{s}(\mathbf{x})$ of the true image field. This approach attempts to minimize the effects of both the nonconstant illumination and the multiplicative noise. Typical results are indicated in Fig. 17 for a transaxial tomography image. Additional results can be found in [23].

Texture discrimination. This class of 2-D random fields has also been used as a stochastic texture model leading to a class of texture discrimination algorithms which approximate the statistically optimum maximum likelihood classifier. The details are provided in [24]. Typical performance of this texture discrimination scheme is illustrated in Fig. 18. Here Fig. 18a illustrates a source image which consists of realizations of three distinct rectangular Poisson tessellation processes for various parameter choices. The NW and NE corners have $\lambda = 0.16$, $\rho = 0.0$, and $\lambda = 0.32$, $\rho = 0.5$, respectively. These values were chosen to result in identical second-moment properties. As a result these two fields cannot be discriminated on the basis of autocorrelation functions and/or power spectral densities alone. The field in the S side has $\lambda = 0.32$ while $\rho = 0.0$. Since it possesses the same edge density as the field in the NE corner, these two textures cannot be discriminated on the basis of edge density alone.

As indicated in Fig. 18b, the log-likelihood discriminator does an excellent job of discriminating the three texture regions except in the vicinity of either texture or image boundaries. Included in Fig. 18 for comparison purposes is the performance of alternative more conventional texture discrimination schemes. In Fig. 18c we demonstrate the performance of a conventional correlation discriminator. This algorithm implements a threshold test on a least-squares estimate of the correlation of pixels separated by distance d which has been optimized in this case. The optimum threshold has been chosen empirically on the basis of histogram techniques. While this approach is useful in discriminating the texture in the S side from that in either the NW or NE corner, it cannot discriminate between the NW and NE regions due to the fact that they possess identical second-moment properties. As a partial remedy to this situation we have devised a discriminant that employs both correlation and edge density information. Using this correlation/edge density discriminator some degree of success has been

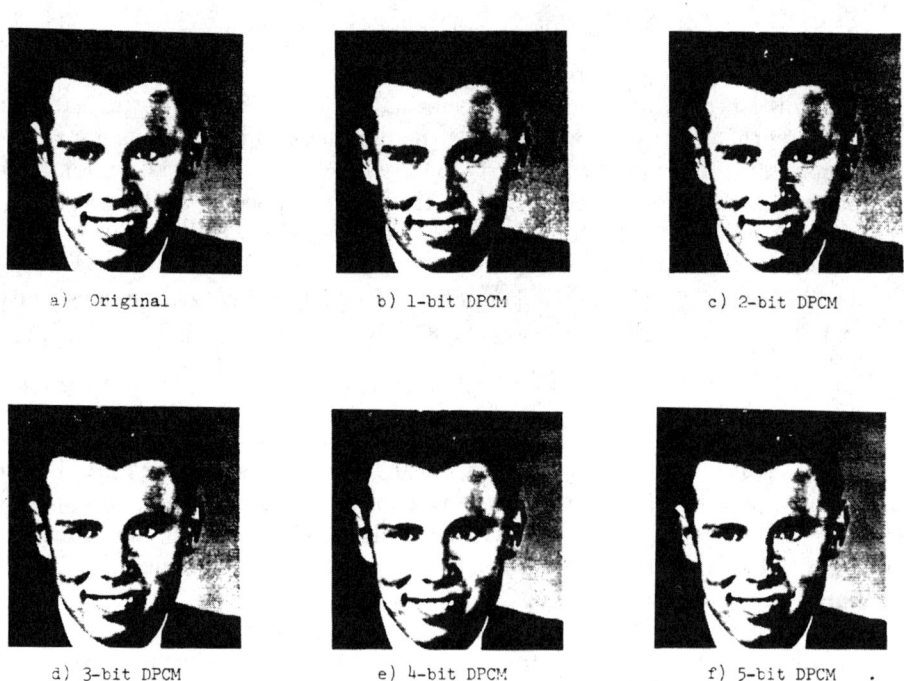

FIG. 19. 2-D DPCM encoding of face image using recursive predictor for $\lambda = 0.05$ and $\rho = -0.9$.

achieved in discriminating between the NW and NE regions as illustrated by the results in Fig. 18d. The results are, however, generally inferior to the performance of the log-likelihood discriminator.

Image coding. A 2-D differential pulse code modulation (DPCM) encoder for images has been developed using the rectangular Poisson tessellation process as an image model as an alternative to the conventional autoregressive (AR) modeling assumptions. This encoder performs better at 1 bit/pixel quantization than previous designs [25] based upon the AR model. The details are provided in [19]. In Fig. 19 we illustrate typical performance of this encoder on a head-and-shoulders image. Even at 1 bit/pixel it has achieved accurate reproduction of edges without excessive granular noise in regions of constant intensity.

6. SUMMARY AND CONCLUSIONS

A class of 2-D homogeneous and isotropic random fields has been described which we feel provides a useful model for real-world imagery possessing pronounced edge structure. This model is conveniently parameterized by several physically meaningful quantities. Several of the more important properties of this class of 2-D random fields have been discussed and some applications described.

REFERENCES

1. E. Wong, Homogeneous Gauss–Markov random fields, *Ann. Math. Statist.* **40**, 1969, 1625–1634.
2. E. Wong, Two-dimensional random fields and the representation of images, *SIAM J. Appl. Math.* **16**, 1968, 756–770.
3. E. Wong, *Stochastic Processes in Information and Dynamical Systems*, Chap. 7, McGraw-Hill, New York, 1971.
4. A. M. Yaglom, Second-order homogeneous random fields, In *Proc. 4th Berkeley Symp. Math. Stat. and Prob.*, Vol. 2, pp. 593–620, 1961.
5. D. J. Sakrison and V. R. Algazi, Comparison of line-by-line and two-dimensional encoding of random images, *IEEE Trans. Inform. Theory* **IT-17**, July 1971, 386–398.
6. J. B. O'Neal, Jr., and T. Raj Natarajan, Coding isotropic images, *IEEE Trans. Inform. Theory* **IT-23**, Nov. 1977, 697–707.
7. D. L. Synder, *Random Point Processes*, Wiley, New York, 1975.
8. A. Papoulis, *Probability, Random Variables and Stochastic Processes*, Chap. 11, McGraw-Hill, New York, 1965.
9. S. Bochner, *Lectures on Fourier Integrals*, Annals, of Math. Studies, No. 42, pp. 235–238, Princeton Univ. Press, Princeton, N.J., 1959.
10. A. Papoulis, Optical systems, singularity functions, complex Hankel transforms, *J. Opt. Soc. Soc. Amer.* **57**, 1967, 207–213.
11. A. Papoulis, *Systems and Transforms with Applications in Optics*, McGraw-Hill, New York, 1968.
12. E. Parzen, *Stochastic Processes*, Holden-Day, San Francisco, 1962.
13. E. Cinlar, *Introduction to Stochastic Processes*, Prentice-Hall, Englewood Cliffs, N.J., 1975.
14. W. Feller, *An Introduction to Probability and Its Applications*, Vol. 2, Wiley, New York, 1971.
15. J. W. Modestino and R. W. Fries, A generalization of the random telegraph wave, submitted.
16. J. W. Modestino and R. W. Fries, Construction and properties of a useful two-dimensional random field, *IEEE Trans. Inform. Theory*, in press.
17. J. W. Modestino and R. W. Fries, Edge detection in noisy images using recursive digital filtering, *Computer Graphics Image Processing* **6**, 1977, 409–433.
18. J. W. Modestino, R. W. Fries, and D. G. Daut, A generalization of the two-dimensional random checkerboard process, *J. Opt. Soc. Amer.* **69**, 1979, 897–906.

19. R. W. Fries, *Theory and Applications of a Class of Two-Dimensional Random Fields*, Ph.D. thesis, Electrical and Systems Engineering Dept., RPI, Troy, N.Y., in preparation.
20. R. W. Fries and J. W. Modestino, An empirical study of selected approaches to the detection of edges in noisy digitized images, submitted.
21. A. V. Oppenheim, R. W. Schafer, and T. G. Stockham, Jr., Nonlinear filtering of multiplied and convolved signals, *Proc. IEEE* **56**, Aug. 1968, 1264–1291.
22. A. V. Oppenheim and R. W. Schafer, *Digital Signal Processing*, Chap. 10, Prentice–Hall Englewood Cliffs, N.J., 1975.
23. R. W. Fries and J. W. Modestino, Image enhancement by stochastic homomorphic filtering, *IEEE Trans. Acoust., Speech, Signal Processing*, in press.
24. J. W. Modestino, R. W. Fries, and A. L. Vickers, Texture discrimination based upon an assumed stochastic texture model, submitted.
25. J. W. Modestino and D. G. Daut, Combined source-channel coding of images, *IEEE Trans. Commun.* **COM-27**, 1644–1659.

Mosaic Models for Textures

NARENDRA AHUJA AND AZRIEL ROSENFELD, FELLOW, IEEE

Abstract — This paper deals with a class of image models based on random geometric processes. Theoretical and empirical results on properties of patterns generated using these models are summarized. These properties can be used as aids in fitting the models to images.

Index Terms — Image models, mosaics, random geometry, texture.

I. INTRODUCTION

TEXTURE perception is an important part of human vision [1]. Objects may often be distinguished by their characteristic textures in spite of similar colors or shapes. Textural cues are important in the perception of orientations and relative distances of surfaces [1]. The texture of a surface is characterized by properties such as fine, coarse, smooth, granulated, rippled, mottled, irregular, random, lineated, etc. [2].

Despite its ubiquity in scene analysis a precise definition of texture does not exist. Clearly, any such definition must be relatively simple and incorporate all important features of the texture that determine its various perceptual attributes. Pickett [1] views texture as consisting of a large number of elements, each in some degree visible, and, on the whole, densely and evenly (possibly randomly) arranged over the field of view such that there is a distinct characteristic spatial repetitiveness in the pattern.

All treatments of texture so far have taken one of the following two approaches.

The *statistical* approach [1], [3] attempts a global characterization of texture. Statistical properties of the spatial distribution of gray levels are used as texture descriptors. The key feature of this approach is the sole dependence of the description on point properties, with no explicit use of elements or subregions.

The *structural* approach conceives of texture as an arrangement of a set of spatial subpatterns according to certain placement rules [4]. The subpatterns themselves are, in general, made up of smaller subpatterns, positioned according to some placement rules. This recursive nature of the approach captures the hierarchical structure of natural scenes. Both the subpatterns and their placement may be characterized statistically.

Most existing texture models are based upon the first approach. While statistical models may be successfully used in discriminating sets of textures, and in other such limited tasks, it is our contention that they are inherently less powerful than the structural models that use probabilistic subpattern selection and placement. For the case of images on grids this is not hard to see. Consider a subpattern that consists of a single pixel. It is obvious that its characteristics and placement rules can be designed so as to make the resulting model identical to any given statistical model, since both have control over the same set of image primitives and can incorporate the same types of primitive interactions. This shows that the structural models are at least as powerful as the statistical models. On the other hand, it is obvious that images that are piecewise uniform with respect to some property, and are known to have been generated by a structural approach, must be better modeled using the structural approach. Similar arguments apply to Euclidean plane textures. However, it is not clear if the lower power of the statistical approaches really makes them less useful for image modeling, since limitations of human visual perception may make the additional power of the structural approach unexploitable, and hence, insignificant.

Natural phenomena involve objects of variable physical extent. At any resolution, therefore, natural textures are likely to consist of more than one pixel. However, it is not obvious what the structure should be. At times, a good guess about the physical processes that may have given rise to a given pattern may provide clues as to the appropriate structure a model must incorporate. Pattern generation processes in nature are certainly very complex, and usually impossible to simulate exactly. However, it may be useful to single out some important features of these processes. If a model can incorporate such features, the patterns it describes may be similar to real textures in significant ways.

As we will see in Section II, little effort has been devoted to the structural approach. Even for the few structural models that have been considered, there has not been a reasonable amalgamation of the various properties we have discussed above. These methods either are not generative or involve training based upon some arbitrarily selected features, or are not well analyzed as regards their properties.

In this paper we describe a class of generative models called mosaic models that use random pattern generation processes in the plane to provide image structure.

In Section II we review the models of texture that have been proposed earlier, including both statistical and structural models.

Section III describes two classes of mosaic models, called cell structure and coverage ("bombing") models, and gives several examples of each. The general treatment of mosaic models in the rest of the paper uses these examples as illustrations. As we will note in Section VII, a variety of models could be added to the small set used here. We also discuss some aspects of the grid version of the mosaics originally defined in the Euclidean plane. We conclude the section by outlining a methodology for obtaining a model for a given image.

Some of the geometrical features proposed in Section III are obtained for the cell structure models in Section IV. We derive expressions for the expected area of a connected component, expected width of a component, expected number of components, and expected total perimeter in the image, for the three regular and three random cell structure models that constitute our repertoire of such models. We also obtain the same set of geometrical properties for the square and circular coverage models, for both the binary and multicolored cases.

In Section V we discuss properties of the mosaic models that represent the correlation between the pixels in terms of their relative positions. We derive the joint gray level probability density of pixels at a given distance and orientation for the two classes of models. These density functions are then used to obtain the autocorrelation function, the edge density, and the variogram for the models. The relationship between the responses of some digital edge operators and the Euclidean plane perimeter is also discussed.

Section VI briefly discusses the problem of fitting mosaic models to real textures, and presents some preliminary results. Section VII summarizes the work presented in this paper. It critically reviews the mosaic model approach in comparison with the other methods. Some projects that could be undertaken to further investigate the application of mosaic models are suggested.

II. TEXTURE MODELS

This section reviews texture models under the statistical and structural classes. See [14] for an alternate classification.

A. Statistical Models

The models based upon the statistical approach can be divided into two major classes: time series models and random field models.

1) Time Series Models: Time series analysis [5] has been extensively used to study visual textures. In the simplest form, the image is TV scanned to provide a one-dimensional series of gray level fluctuations, which is treated as a one-dimensional stochastic process evolving in "time." Alternatively, a point is assumed to depend upon a certain part of its neighborhood and on Gaussian noise. The coefficients of dependence are extracted from the images by using time series analysis techniques. Various forms of the dependence provide different models.

By studying the statistical properties of a given texture, e.g., its autocorrelation function, etc., McCormick and Jayaramamurthy [6] have made a choice of a best fitting time series model for a given texture. They also use the same information to estimate the required set of parameter values, and generate synthetic textures using the model.

In an earlier paper Whittle [7] pointed out the difficulty of using time series for two-dimensional processes. The problem is that in a two-dimensional process, the dependence of a point extends in all directions, and there is no direct way to map the two-dimensional grid points onto a series such that the original dependence is preserved, although it is unilateral (depends only on the past values). In view of this, one would like to try to capture as much of the two-dimensional dependence as possible without getting into the analytical problems due to bilateral dependence. Tou *et al.* [8] have done this by making a point depend on its upper and left neighbors. They consider fitting a model to a given texture. The choice among the various models, as well as the choice of the order of the process, is made by comparing the behavior of some observed statistical properties, e.g., the autocorrelation function, with that predicted by each of the different models. For each of the possibly many choices of models, the values of the parameters are determined so as to minimize, say, the least-square error in fit. In a subsequent paper, Tou and Chang [9] use the maximum likelihood principle to optimize the values of the parameters, in order to obtain a refinement of the preliminary model as suggested by the autocorrelation function.

2) Random Field Models: The second class of models treats the image as a two-dimensional random field (for a definition of random field, see Wong [10]).

One way to describe a random field would be in terms of the joint probability density of the properties (say, gray level) of the pixels, although this may be an overspecification, i.e., the modeling may not represent enough abstraction. It also implies estimation of the spatial probability density functions of gray levels, which means inference on the joint probability density of a large number of random variables corresponding to the pixels in the entire image. One immediate simplification that could be introduced is to assume that not all points in an image are simultaneously constrained by a high-dimensional probability density function, but that this is only true of small neighborhoods of pixels. However, even for a neighborhood of size 3×3 (or 5×5) and nonparametric representation one has to deal with densities in a 9- (or 25-) dimensional space, along with the associated sample size and storage problems. This makes the approach unwieldy.

Read and Jayaramamurthy [11] and McCormick and Jayaramamurthy [12] make use of switching theory techniques to identify textures by describing their local gray level patterns using minimal functions. If each pixel can take one out of N_g gray levels, then a given neighborhood of n pixels from an image can be represented by a point in an $(n \times N_g)$-dimensional space. If many such neighborhoods from a given texture are considered then they are likely to provide a cluster of points in the above space. The differences in the local characteristics of different textures are expected to result in different clusters. The set covering theory of Michalski and McCormick [13], which is a generalization of the minimization machinery of switching theory already available, is used [12] to describe the sets of points in each cluster. These maximal descriptions also allow coverage of empty spaces within and around clusters, and thus the samples do not have to be exhaustive but only have to be large enough to provide a good representation of the underlying texture.

Haralick *et al.* [14] confine the local descriptions to 2×1 neighborhoods. They identify a texture by the gray level cooccurrence frequencies at neighboring pixels, which are the first estimates of the corresponding probabilities. They use several different features, all derived from the cooccurrence matrix, for texture classification.

Deguchi and Morishita [15] use a noncausal model for the dependence of a pixel on its neighborhood centered at the pixel. The weights are determined by minimizing the mean-square estimation error. The optimal two-dimensional estimator characterizes the texture. They use such a characterization for classification and for segmentation of images consisting of more than one textural region.

In view of the seemingly difficult task of describing or extracting the joint probability densities, attempts have been made to use parametric models where the form of the probability density is assumed, or to model the field density by specifying some "important" properties of the field that may correspond to more than one probability density function.

Among parametric models of the joint density of pixels in a window, the multivariate normal has been the one most commonly used because of its tractability. However, it has been found to have limited applicability [16]. Hunt [17], [18] points out that stationary, Gaussian modeling of images is an oversimplification. He proposes a nonstationary Gaussian model which differs from the stationary model only in that the mean vector has unequal components. He shows the appropriateness of this model by subtracting, from each point on the image, its local ensemble average, and showing that the resulting picture fits a stationary Gaussian model.

Trussel and Kruger [19] show that the Laplacian density function constitutes a more valid model for high-pass filtered imagery than the Gaussian model. They show that this discrepancy neither seriously weakens the applicability of this class of models to a major restoration method nor challenges any other conclusions of the work based on the Gaussian model.

Longuet-Higgins [20]-[22] treats the ocean surface as a random field satisfying the following assumptions:

a) the wave spectrum contains a single, narrow band of frequencies; and

b) the wave energy is being received from a large number of different sources whose phases are random.

Some of the results that he derives are:

1) the probability distribution of the surface elevation, and that of the magnitude and orientation of the gradient;

2) the average number of zero crossings per unit distance along a line in an arbitrary direction;

3) the average length of contour per unit area;

4) the average density of maxima and minima per unit area; and

5) for a narrow spectrum, the probability distribution of the heights of maxima and minima.

All the results are expressed in terms of the two-dimensional energy spectrum up to a finite order only. The converse of the problem is also studied and solved, i.e., given certain statistical properties of the surface, to find a convergent sequence of approximations to the energy spectrum.

The analogy between this work and image processing, and the significance of the results obtained therein, is obvious. Fortunately, the assumptions made are also acceptable for images.

Panda [23] uses an analogous approach to analyze background regions selected from forward-looking infrared (FLIR) imagery. He derives expressions for 1) density of border points and 2) average number of connected components in a row of the thresholded picture. There is good agreement between the observed and the predicted values in most cases, for most of the pictures considered. Panda [24] also uses the same model to predict the properties of the pictures obtained by running several edge operators (based on differences of average gray levels) on some synthetic pictures with normally distributed gray levels, and having different correlation coefficients. The images are assumed to be continuous-valued stationary Gaussian random fields with continuous parameters.

Matheron [25] uses the change in pixel properties as a function of distance to model a random field. He uses the term regionalized variables to emphasize the particular features of the pixels whose complex mutual correlation reflects the structure of the underlying phenomenon. He assumes weak stationarity of the increments in the gray levels between pixels. The second moment of the increments for pixels at an arbitrary distance, called the variogram, is used to reflect the structure of the field. Knowledge of the variogram is useful for the estimates of many global and local properties of the field. Huijbregts [26] discusses several properties of the variogram and relates them to the structural features of the regionalized variables. For nonhomogeneous fields having spatially varying mean, the variogram of the residuals with respect to the local means is used.

A characterization similar to the variogram is given by the autocorrelation function. In work on image restoration, images have often been modeled by a two-dimensional random field with a given mean and autocorrelation. An autocorrelation function that has been found to be reasonably good for a variety of pictorial data is

$$R(\tau_1, \tau_2) = \sigma^2 \exp\left[-\alpha_1 |\tau_1| - \alpha_2 |\tau_2|\right],$$

which is stationary and separable.

Nahi and Jahanshahi [27] suggest modeling the image as a background statistical process combined with a set of foreground statistical processes, each replacing the background in the regions occupied by the objects of the category which it is assumed to characterize.

In a subsequent paper Nahi and Lopez-Mora [28] use a more complex γ function. For each row, γ either indicates the absence of the object or provides a vector estimate of the object width and its geometric center in that row. The two-dimensional vector possesses information about the object size and skewness, and is assumed to be a first-order Markov process.

Abend *et al.* [16] introduce Markov Meshes to model dependence of a pixel on a certain immediate neighborhood. The joint probability density for the entire image, then, is the product of local conditional probability densities at each pixel. Using Markov chain methods on the sequences of pixels from various causal dependency neighborhoods of a pixel they show that in many cases such a causal dependence translates into a noncausal dependence. For example, the dependence of a pixel on its west, northwest and north neighbors translates into its dependence upon all its eight neighbors. Interestingly, the causal neighborhood that results in a 4-neighbor noncausal dependence is not known.

Hassner and Sklansky [29] also discuss a Markov random field model for images. They present an algorithm that generates a texture from an initial random configuration and a set of independent parameters that specify a consistent collection of nearest neighbor conditional probabilities which characterize the Markov random field.

Pratt and Faugeras [30] and Gagalowicz [31] view texture as the output of a homogeneous spatial filter excited by white noise, not necessarily Gaussian. The image is then characterized by its mean, the histogram of the input white noise, and the transfer function of the filter. For a given texture, the model parameters are obtained as follows.

- The mean is readily estimated from the image.
- Computing the autocorrelation function (second-order moments) determines the magnitude of the transfer function.
- Computing higher order moments determines the phase of the transfer function.

Inverse filtering gives the white noise image and hence its histogram and probability density. For a Markov field of order 1 it may be sufficient to replace the decorrelation operator by a Laplacian, or by gradient operators. However, the whitened field estimate of the independent identically distributed noise process obtained above will only identify the spatial operator in terms of the autocorrelation function, which is not unique. Thus, the white noise probability density and the spatial filter do not, in general, make up a complete set of descriptors [32]. But it may be possible that they are sufficient descriptors from the standpoint of visual texture discrimination.

Mandelbrot also takes a similar approach although he views the pixel gray levels as defining a Brownian surface [33].

B. Structural Models

The next three models use the notion of a structural primitive, although both the shapes of the primitives and the rules to generate the textures from the primitives may be specified statistically. This statistical-structural nature of these models brings them closer to the models discussed in the following sections than any of the models described so far.

Matheron [34] and Serra [35] propose a model that views a binary texture as produced by a set of translations of a structural element. All locations of the structural elements such that the entire element lies within the foreground of the texture are identified. Note that there may be (narrow) regions which cannot be covered by any placement of the structural element, as all possible arrangements of the element that cover a given region may not lie completely within the foreground. Thus, only an "eroded" version of the image can be spanned by the structural element which is used as the representation of the original image. Textural properties can be obtained by appropriately parameterizing the structure element. It is interesting to note that for a structural element consisting of two pixels at distance d, the area of the eroded image is the value of the autocovariance, at distance d, of the original image. More complicated structural elements would provide a generalized autocovariance function which has more structural information. Matheron and Serra show how the generalized covariance function can be used to obtain various texture features.

Zucker [36] conceives of a real texture as being a distortion of an ideal texture which is a spatial layout of primitives as cells in a regular or semiregular tessellation. Certain transformations are applied to the primitives to distort them to provide a realistic texture. The statistical nature of the texture can be provided through these transformation rules.

Yokoyama and Haralick [37] describe a growth process to synthesize textures. Their method consists of the following steps.
1) Mark some of the pixels in a clean image as seeds.
2) The seeds grow into curves called skeletons.
3) The skeletons thicken to become regions.
4) The pixels in the regions thus obtained are transformed into gray levels in the desired range.
5) A probabilistic transformation is applied, if desired, to modify the gray level cooccurrence probability in the final image.

The distribution processes in step 1) and the growth processes in steps 2) and 3) can be deterministic or random. The dependence of the properties of the images generated on the nature of the underlying operations is not obtained. This makes the approach unsuitable for texture description or classification.

There are a number of other studies of texture that are more technique oriented, and describe some ad hoc texture feature selection and classification schemes which are not based upon any specific model of the texture. We are concerned here with models of texture and hence will not discuss these studies; see [2] for a good survey.

III. Mosaic Models

This section briefly reviews some planar geometrical processes that define the proposed class of models. A more detailed treatment of this material can be found in [38].

A. Cell Structure Models

Cell structure mosaics are constructed in two steps.
1) Tessellate a planar region into cells. We will only consider tessellations composed of bounded convex polygons.

2) Independently assign one of m colors to each cell according to a fixed set of probabilities

$$p_1, \cdots, p_m; \quad \sum_{i=1}^{m} p_i = 1.$$

The set of colors may correspond to a set of values of any property, not necessarily gray level.

Cell structure models form a family whose members differ in the manner in which the plane is tessellated. We will describe some important members of this family, starting from the three regular tessellations and progressing towards random ones.

1) Checkerboard Model: In this model, the origin and orientation of the axes are chosen randomly, and the plane is tessellated into squares.

2) Hexagonal Model: This is analogous to the checkerboard model, except that the plane is tessellated into regular hexagons.

3) Triangular Model: This is analogous to the first two models, but based on a tessellation into equilateral triangles.

4) Poisson Line Model: In this model, a Poisson process chooses points in the strip $0 \leq \theta < \pi$, $-\infty < \rho < \infty$. Each of these points defines a line of the form $x \cos \theta + y \sin \theta = \rho$, and these lines define a tessellation of the plane.

5) Occupancy Model: In this model, a Poisson process chooses points (called "nuclei") in the plane. Each nucleus defines a "Dirichlet cell" consisting of all the points in the plane that are nearer to it than to any other nucleus.

6) Delaunay Model: The Delaunay tessellation is obtained by joining all pairs of nuclei whose Dirichlet cells are adjacent.

B. Coverage Models

Coverage or "bombing" models constitute the second class of mosaic models that we consider. A coverage mosaic is obtained by a random arrangement of a set of geometric figures ("bombs") in the plane.

We will first describe the process defining the class of binary models. Consider the geometric figure in the plane and identify it by 1) the location of some distinguished point in the figure, e.g., its center of gravity, hereafter called the center of the figure; and 2) the orientation of some distinguished line in the figure, e.g., its principal axis of inertia. Let a point process drop points on the plane and let each point represent the center of a figure. Let each figure have an orientation θ according to some distribution function $F(\theta)$. By this process any fixed region A is randomly partitioned into A_0 and $A_1 = A - A_0$, where A_1 consists of that part of A that is covered by the figures. By assigning two different colors to A_0 and A_1, we get a binary coverage mosaic.

A multicolored coverage mosaic is obtained by considering figures of more than one color. The color of a given figure is randomly chosen from a known vector of colors $\bar{c} = (c_1, c_2, \cdots, c_m)$ according to a predetermined probability vector $\bar{p} = (p_1, p_2, \cdots, p_m)$. Let c_0 denote the background color. Since the figures, in general, overlap, we must have a rule to determine the colors of the regions that are covered by figures of more than one color. We will give one example of such a rule.

Let us view the point process as dropping the centers sequentially in time. Each time a new point falls, the area covered by the associated figure is colored with the color of that figure irrespective of whether any part of the area has already been included in any of the previously fallen figures. The color of a point in the final pattern is thus determined by the color of the latest figure that covered it. (Note that we could just as well have allowed a figure to cover only an area not included in any of the previous figures.)

More generally, we can have more than one type of geometric figure, with the sizes of each class of figures governed by a certain probability distribution. These along with the nature of the point process and the choices of the probability distributions for color and orientation selection provide different ways of controlling the characteristics of the resulting patterns.

The coverage models discussed in this paper use a Poisson point process for dropping centers, and figures of a fixed shape and size. Some examples of the figures that can be considered are line segments, ellipses, circles, rectangles, and squares.

C. Digital Mosaics

All the models described above use processes that are defined in the Euclidean plane. On a grid these processes can at best be simulated only coarsely. Often, many of the concepts of the Euclidean plane must be almost completely redefined in order to be adaptable to a grid. Moreover, even with the modified definitions, the digital plane patterns are not as well behaved as the Euclidean plane patterns. Many measures become meaningless for extreme values of the quantities they describe. As a general rule, digital versions of Euclidean plane phenomena become better and better behaved with increasing resolution, i.e., with a finer and finer grid. Therefore, we can expect digital mosaics to behave only approximately as they would in the Euclidean plane, and we should preferably work at high resolution.

During the course of the work described in this paper we have faced several problems originating from the discrete nature of the grid. We have had to modify several Euclidean plane definitions to suit the grid patterns. To illustrate this, we briefly discuss the Poisson process on the grid.

In the Euclidean plane, a point process is said to be a homogeneous Poisson point process of intensity λ if:

1) the number of points in any region of area A has a Poisson distribution with parameter λA; and

2) the numbers of points in disjoint regions are independent random variables.

Any finite region in the Euclidean plane is mapped onto a finite number of points on the grid, so that whereas the actual Poisson process can drop an unlimited number of points with positive probability in such a region, the digital Poisson process can drop at most as many points as there are grid points in the region. Since each grid point represents a square of unit area centered at that point in the plane, it will be selected by the digital Poisson process whenever even a single point is dropped by the Euclidean Poisson process in the square. From property 1) above, we have

$p \equiv$ Pr {a given point on the grid is occupied by the digital Poisson process of intensity λ}

= Pr {a square of unit area in the Euclidean plane contains at least one point due to a Poisson process of intensity λ}

$= 1 - e^{-\lambda}$.

A digital Poisson point process is thus a binomial process with parameter $p = 1 - e^{-\lambda}$, and

Pr {n points fall in a region consisting of N grid points}

$= \binom{N}{n} p^n (1-p)^{N-n}$.

To simulate a Poisson process on the grid thus amounts to making a binary decision at each of its points.

D. Analysis of Models

In applying models such as those discussed above to images, we should use properties of the models that can be directly measured for a given image, so that we can determine the degree of the fit of the model to the image. Some examples of such properties are as follows.

1) What is the probability that a pair of points distance d apart will fall in regions of colors c_i and c_j? In other words, for each d, what is the color cooccurrence matrix?

2) What is the expected number of connected components of color c_i?

3) What is the expected area of a connected component of color c_i? Or, what is the total area having color c_i? Note that in the case of cell structure models this information is implicit in the answer to question 2) above, since from the model we already know the stationary probability vector of the colors. This is because the cells are nonoverlapping. However, in the case of coverage models this question involves a different property.

4) What is the nature of the autocorrelation function?

5) What is the expected perimeter density? Alternatively, what is the edge density?

6) What is the expected squared color difference (variogram) for point pairs?

In the following sections we present results regarding these properties for the models discussed above.

IV. Geometric Properties of Components

A connected component of uniformly colored points in a mosaic will be called a component of the mosaic. These components are unions of identically colored, adjacent units (cells or figures). Geometrical properties of components are important because, in analyzing an image, we cannot isolate single units.

In this section we discuss geometrical properties of components in both cell structure and coverage mosaics, including the expected area and width of a component, the expected number of components, and the expected total component perimeter in the mosaic. Only a brief summary of the results is given here; the details can be found in two papers [39], [40].

A. Cell Structure Mosaics

Let us first consider an $M \times N$ checkerboard mosaic in which the squares have two possible colors, black and white, with the probability of a black square being p, and that of a white square being $q = 1 - p$. Let $E(r)$ be the expected number of runs (of black squares) of length r in a row; readily we have $E(N) = p^N$, while $E(r) = (N - r - 1) p^r q^2 + 2p^r q$ for $0 < r < N$. Moreover, the total expected number of runs in a row is $(N - 1) qp + p$. Let $T(r)$ be the expected number of distinct components reaching a given row whose runs in that row are overlapped by a run of length r in the next row; we have estimated $T(r)$ empirically. Then the increment in the number of components when a row is added is given by

$$\sum_{r=1}^{N} E(r)[q^r + (1 - q^r)(1 - T(r))].$$

The expected number of components in the mosaic is then

$$C = C_0 + (M - 1) \Delta = \frac{\sum_{r=1}^{N} E(r) + (M - 1) \Delta}{M} + (M - 1) \Delta$$

where C_0 is the expected number of components in the first row.

The expected number of black squares in the mosaic is $B = pMN$; hence the expected number of squares in a component is $A = B/C$. It is not hard to show that the expected perimeter in a component (i.e., the expected number of pairs of adjacent black and white squares such that the black square belongs to the component) is $P = 4Aq$, since $4q$ is the expected number of white neighbors of a black square.

We can carry out an analogous analysis for a hexagonal mosaic, by treating it as a checkerboard in which alternate rows have been shifted by half the square size. Here we use increments Δ_o and Δ_e corresponding to the addition of odd- and even-numbered rows, respectively. We then have

$$C = C_0 + \left\lceil \frac{M-1}{2} \right\rceil \Delta_e + \left\lfloor \frac{M-1}{2} \right\rfloor \Delta_o.$$

The expected number of black cells is $B = p(\lceil M/2 \rceil \lceil N/2 \rceil + \lfloor M/2 \rfloor \lfloor N/2 \rfloor)$, and the expected number of hexagons in a component is thus $A = B/C$. Similarly, the expected number of white neighbors of a black cell is $6q$, and P is thus $6Aq$.

The analysis for a triangular mosaic is also analogous, except that here we have $B = pMN$ (as in the checkerboard case), and the expected number of white neighbors of a black cell is $3q$.

Let us now consider any regular tessellation in which each cell has K neighbors (sharing an edge with it), and V cells meet at each vertex. Evidently, for the square, hexagonal, and triangular tessellations we have $K = 4, 6, 3$, and $V = 4, 3, 6$, respectively. It is easily seen that the results obtained above apply to any mosaics having the same K and V values.

Finally, consider a random tessellation in which the expected number of neighbors of each cell is K, and the expected number of cells meeting at a vertex is V. We conjecture that in the random mosaic defined by any such tessellation, the expected values for the number, area, and perimeter of

TABLE I
PREDICTED AND OBSERVED NUMBERS OF BLACK COMPONENTS IN A
100-CELL RANDOM MOSAIC

Black cell probability (p)	Poisson line mosaic		Occupancy mosaic		Delaunay mosaic	
	Predicted	Observed	Predicted	Observed	Predicted	Observed
.1	8.0	8.0	8.6	7.0	8.2	10.7
.2	14.2	14.7	11.8	10.7	14.4	15.7
.3	14.5	13.7	11.7	9.3	17.1	17.3
.4	12.1	10.0	10.2	10.0	19.3	15.3
.5	8.9	9.0	7.2	5.0	16.4	17.3
.6	6.2	4.7	4.1	3.7	11.9	9.0
.7	3.1	2.3	2.7	2.3	9.7	6.0
.8	1.6	2.3	2.0	1.7	4.3	3.3
.9	1.0	1.3	2.0	1.0	1.7	1.0

black components are the same as those for a regular mosaic with the same K and V values. Now it is known [38] that the expected K and V values for the Poisson line, occupancy, and Delaunay tessellations are the same as the K and V values for the regular square, hexagonal, and triangular tessellations, respectively. Also the area and perimeter properties of the individual cells of these tessellations are known [38]. Hence our conjecture enables us to predict the expected number, area, and perimeter of black components in the cell structure models.

The predictions and observed values for the expected numbers C of components in random mosaics having 100 cells are summarized in Table I as functions of the black cell probability p. We see that the agreement is generally good, especially when p is small. This analysis readily extends to mosaics with more than two colors, since we can group all but one of the colors together to obtain the two-color case.

Finally, we consider the expected width W of a component, i.e., the expected run length of points of a given color along a line drawn across the mosaic. Let p_i be the probability that a cell has the given color. For a checkerboard mosaic of square side b, we can show that

$$W = \frac{\sqrt{2}b}{\pi(1-p_i)} \ln \frac{\sqrt{2}+1}{\sqrt{2}-1}.$$

Similarly, for a triangular mosaic we have

$$W = \frac{3\sqrt{3}b}{4\pi(1-p_i)} \ln 3.$$

The expression for the hexagonal mosaic is more complicated and will not be given here.

For the random mosaics, we can use the fact that the mean chord length of a convex region of area A and perimeter P is $\pi A/P$. Applying this to the cells of the mosaics, we have

$$W = \frac{\pi}{1-p_i} E(A/P)$$

where $E(\ )$ means "the expected value of." For a Poisson line model in which the Poisson process has intensity τ/π, we have $E(A) = \pi/\tau^2$ and $E(P) = 2\pi/\tau$. For an occupancy or Delaunay model in which the process has intensity λ, we similarly have $E(A) = 1/\lambda$, $E(P) = 4/\sqrt{\lambda}$ and $E(A) = 1/2\lambda$, $E(P) = 32/3\pi\sqrt{\lambda}$, respectively. We can use these values, together with the approximation $E(A/P) = E(A)/E(P)$ [39], to estimate W for these mosaics.

B. Coverage Mosaics

Our approach to estimating the expected number of connected components in a coverage mosaic is also based on analysis of runs of overlapping components; for an $M \times N$ digital image it has the form

$$C = C_0 + (M-1)\Delta$$

just as in Section IV-A. Now the expected image area occupied by the figures is

$$A_c = MN(1 - e^{-\lambda\alpha})$$

where λ is the intensity of the Poisson process and α is the area of each figure. Thus the expected area of a component is A_c/C. Explicit expressions for C_0 and Δ can be given in the cases of square and circular figures.

The estimation of expected perimeter for coverage mosaics depends on determining, for each figure, the total length of its border segments that are not intersected by any other figure. An exact formula can be given for the expected perimeter in Euclidean plane mosaics. However, for the grid case we have obtained only an approximate expression.

For square figures, Table II shows expected and predicted number of components, covered area, and perimeter for a 200×200 image. These quantities are tabulated as functions of the expected number n of square centers per square area. (This parameter n takes into account both the intensity λ of the Poisson process and the area a of the squares.) The agreement appears to be quite good.

We can also consider the expected component width W in coverage mosaics; the details will not be given here. These results all assume a two-color mosaic (figures and background); the generalization to multicolor mosaics is quite complicated (except for the expected perimeter and covered area), and has not been attempted.

V. CORRELATION PROPERTIES OF MOSAICS

This section discusses properties involving the gray levels of pairs of points in an image generated by a mosaic model. We discuss the joint gray level probability density for pairs of

TABLE II
PREDICTED AND OBSERVED NUMBERS OF COMPONENTS, COVERED AREAS,
AND PERIMETERS FOR A SQUARE COVERAGE MOSAIC

Square centers per square area	Number of components		Covered area		Perimeter	
	Predicted	Observed	Predicted	Observed	Predicted	Observed
.1	125.6	129.2	3806.5	3939.4	3183.8	3421.6
.5	200.7	205.6	15738.8	15408.0	8189.2	9108.6
1.0	38.8	38.0	25284.8	25286.0	7858.0	9150.6
1.5	4.3	3.0	31074.8	31065.8	5986.6	6798.8
2.0			34586.6	34688.8	4206.3	4569.4
2.5			36716.6	36630.4	2843.0	3052.0
3.0			38008.5	37934.0	1880.1	1942.0
4.0			39267.4	34276.2	792.9	702.8

points at given separations, and also derive from it the autocorrelation, edge density, and variogram (expected squared gray level difference) for the mosaics. Only a brief summary of results is given here; the details can be found in [41].

A. Joint Gray Level Probability

For the cell structure models, let $W(d)$ be the probability that two points distance d apart lie in the same cell. Explicit expressions for $W(d)$ can be given for the square, hexagonal, and triangular tessellations; for example, for squares of side b we have

$$W(d) = \begin{cases} 1 - (4d/\pi b) + (d^2/\pi b^2) & d \leq b \\ 1 - (2/\pi) - (4/\pi) \cos^{-1}(b/d) - (d^2/\pi b^2) \\ \quad + (4/\pi)\sqrt{(d^2/b^2) - 1} & b < d \leq \sqrt{2}b \\ 0 & d > \sqrt{2}b. \end{cases}$$

For the Poisson line model with intensity τ/π we have $W(d) = e^{-2\tau d/\pi}$. Explicit expressions for $W(d)$ for the occupancy and Delaunay models are not known, but we have empirically estimated these functions.

In terms of $W(d)$, the probability density $P_{ij}(d)$ for one of a randomly selected pair of points at distance d having color c_i, given that the other point has color c_j, is given by

$$P_{ij}(d) \equiv p_i p_j (1 - W(d)) + \delta_{ij} W(d)$$

where δ_{ij} is the Kronecker delta.

For the coverage models, the analysis depends on the probabilities that figure centers do or do not occur in specified areas centered at the two points. For any area A, no centers occur in A with probability $e^{-\lambda A}$, and at least one center occurs with probability $1 - e^{-\lambda A}$, where λ is the intensity of the Poisson process. For a two-color model the probabilities are of the form

$$P_{\text{white, white}}(d, \theta) = e^{-\lambda(2A_1 - A_2(d,\theta))}/p_{\text{white}}$$
$$P_{\text{white, black}}(d, \theta) = 2e^{-\lambda A_1}[1 - e^{-\lambda(A_1 - A_2(d,\theta))}]/p_{\text{black}}$$
$$P_{\text{black, white}}(d, \theta) = -2e^{\lambda A_1}[1 - e^{-\lambda(A_1 - A_2(d,\theta))}]/p_{\text{white}}$$
$$P_{\text{black, black}}(d, \theta) = \{1 - e^{-\lambda A_1}[2 - e^{-\lambda(A_1 - A_2(d,\theta))}]\}/p_{\text{black}}.$$

The areas themselves have relatively complicated expressions determined by the geometry of the figures. For example, for upright black squares of side length $2a + 1$ on a white background, we have

$$A_1 = 4a^2$$

and

$$A_2(d, \theta) = 4a^2 - 2ad(\sin\theta + \cos\theta) + (d^2/2)\sin 2\theta$$
$$\text{for } 0 \leq d \leq 2a$$
$$\text{or } \cos^{-1}(2a/d) \leq \theta \leq \pi/4$$
$$= 0 \quad \text{otherwise.}$$

The expressions for multicolored models are more complicated.

B. Autocorrelation

For a cell structure model the covariance $\text{cov}(d)$ of two points distance d apart having gray levels x and y is $E(xy) - E(x)E(y)$, where $E(xy) = W(d)E(x^2) + (1 - W(d))E^2(x)$, so that $\text{cov}(d) = W(d)[E(x^2) - E^2(x)]$. Hence, the autocorrelation coefficient $\rho(d)$ is $\text{cov}(d)/\text{cov}(0) = W(d)$. It is interesting to note that for the Poisson line model $W(d)$ is negative exponential, a commonly assumed form for the autocorrelation of an image; but for the other cell structure models, this is not the case.

For a two-color coverage model it can be shown that

$$\rho(d, \theta) = \frac{e^{-\lambda A_1}}{1 - e^{-\lambda A_1}} [e^{\lambda A_2(d,\theta)} - 1]$$

where A_1 and A_2 are as in Section V-A. Expressions for autocorrelation for the multicolored models can also be obtained.

C. Edge Density

Let P be the expected border length per unit area in a continuous mosaic as discussed earlier. Since in all our models the border consists of randomly oriented straight line segments, it is not very hard to see that the expected number of horizontal and vertical steps in the chain code of the digital border is $4P/\pi$, and the expected number of diagonal steps is

$$4P(\sqrt{2} - 1)/\pi.$$

Let δ denote the expected absolute difference between two different colors; then the expected (e.g., horizontal) edge value per unit area is $2P\delta/\pi$. Analogous expressions can be obtained for other edge operators.

D. Variogram

The variogram of an image is the expected squared difference between the gray levels of two randomly selected points at a given separation. For the cell structure models we have

$$\gamma(d) = (1 - W(d)) \sum_{i,j=1}^{m} (c_i - c_j)^2 p_i p_j.$$

For two-color coverage models we have

$$\gamma(d, \theta) = 2e^{-\lambda A_1} [1 - e^{-\lambda(A_1 - A_2(d,\theta))}] (B - W)^2$$

where B and W are the two colors, and A_1, A_2 are as in Section V-A. The corresponding expression for multicolored coverage models can also be obtained.

VI. Fitting Mosaic Models to Textures

In [42] some preliminary experiments on fitting mosaic models to real textures were described. Predicted variograms were computed for two models, checkerboard and Poisson line, and were fitted to the actual variograms of ten texture samples from Brodatz' album. These textures were also thresholded, and average component widths were computed for them. This width agreed very closely with the width predicted by the better fitting model in each case.

Some further experiments on mosaic model fitting are reported in [43]. Samples of four Brodatz textures and three terrain textures were segmented, and average component area and perimeter and total number of components were computed. Values predicted by six cell structure models (checkerboard, hexagonal, triangular, Poisson line, occupancy, and Delaunay) were also computed. (Predictions were also made for the square bombing model, but they were very poor in all cases.) For each texture, the model parameters were adjusted to make the area predictions match the observed values, and the resulting errors in predicted perimeter were tabulated; and vice versa. The minimum area error and minimum perimeter error models for each texture were the same in nearly all cases, and were consistent from sample to sample for nearly all the textures.

VII. Concluding Remarks

The following are some specific points of comparison between mosaic models and conventional statistical texture models, such as time series and random field models.

1) Mosaic models describe images by specifying geometrical processes that may have generated the visual pattern under consideration. Such a constructive description, therefore, inherently encompasses the specification of all the information about the pattern. One may extract from the model as much information as desired, e.g., autocorrelation properties, which may not be unique to the image. For example, characterization of a pattern in terms of its autocorrelation properties ignores any phase information.

It may be interesting to note that certain features of some of the mosaic models are the same as have been commonly used to model images. At the same time, other mosaic models take different values for the same features, thus implying that mosaic models should prove to be a more general class of models. As an example, the Poisson line model has an exponential autocorrelation function, a model that has been extensively used in the literature; while other mosaic models exhibit different forms of autocorrelations.

2) Time series models allow the current value of an image point to depend on a finite number of previous values. There is, thus, an inherent assumption in the definition of the model about the Markovianity of the data. While it is a different issue how useful the model could still be in practice, such an assumption places a definite theoretical restriction on the generality of the model. Both the random field and mosaic models are free of such a restriction.

3) Images are inherently two-dimensional and hence should be treated as such. Time series models clearly fail to meet this requirement. They allow a point to depend on, at best, only a part of its neighborhood. A time series model also cannot make use of the rich class of two-dimensional features, e.g., shape and orientation of subpatterns, edge density, connectedness of components, etc., which seem to play an important role in human perception of images. Some of these features have one-dimensional counterparts which could, in principle, be used. But they are much less useful because of their lesser semantic relevance. The random field and mosaic models, on the other hand, are two-dimensional models.

4) In time series modeling the choice of the model is based upon a qualitative assessment of the autocorrelation function. The order of the underlying process is guessed, to begin with, and then iteratively improved until a set of parameter values is found that, along with the chosen order of the model, predicts an autocorrelation function sufficiently close to the observed one. Thus, the process of model specification involves some amount of trial and error.

For random field models there is a much larger gap between the variety of models proposed and the attempts at fitting them to images. Except for some simple parametric models, however, the model fitting does appear to be a complex process.

Furthermore, the model arrived at in order to obtain a good fit of properties such as autocorrelation may, in fact, turn out to be worse than expected, due to the fact that the characterization of the image in terms of correlation properties ignores phase information, as pointed out in 1) above.

It may be observed that in both the time series and random field models the complexity of modeling is very unevenly shared by the two levels of a) model selection and b) parameter evaluation. There is only a limited choice about the type of model to be selected, and the parameterization of the chosen model is the major part of the modeling process. The variety of natural images must, therefore, be represented only by the assignment of distinct values to the parameter set of the model.

Mosaic models, on the other hand, are much richer in variety, and each of these models is simpler to specify, as compared to the time series and random field models. The complete process of modeling thus gets more evenly split into the two steps. This should have the effect of reducing the size of the search space when fitting models to a given image.

5) Natural visual patterns can often be characterized by a repetitive arrangement of certain subpatterns, according to a set of rules. The subpatterns, recursively, may be patterns of smaller extent, but of independent complexity (busyness, entropy, fineness). A small set of relatively less busy subpatterns with sharp borders may give the image a patchy appearance, whereas a large set of busy patterns may give rise to a finer, textured pattern.

One reason why mosaic models may be more appropriate for complex natural images is that they provide a hierarchical character to the problem of image modeling. The arrangement of the components, possibly of more than one type, in the mosaic is often specified statistically.

For the nonpatchy class of patterns, both the time series and random field models may not turn out to be very complex. Although one could also attempt to apply these models to images with regularly shaped patches having relatively sharp borders, such an approach is likely to defy an easy analysis, and is likely to provide a complex model. For example, the order of the resultant time series model may be very high in order to incorporate enough information about the gray level jumps across the patch borders. Clearly, although the interior patch-points do not contain much information, they do increase the order of the model, making it more complex and computationally more expensive.

Not surprisingly, in view of the above observations, the time series models have been used only for those images that are relatively well suited for such an approach, as pointed out above. The images used for most of the random field models that have been tried also are relatively nonpatchy.

It may be seen that an image from the patchy category can be transformed into a picture of the nonpatchy category by sampling it sufficiently coarsely. Since this transformation should not change the structure of the image, the model should still be valid with a different set of parameter values. The validity of the choice of a mosaic model thus appears to be insensitive to scale changes, and mimics the underlying generating process of the image so as to incorporate as much of the detail as is captured in the image to be modeled.

Under certain conditions the mosaic models and the random field models may produce similar patterns. For example, a random field model may fit certain coarsely sampled (dense) mosaics.

6) Mosaic models are likely to be intuitively more meaningful. A pattern corresponding to a specified model, and the implications for it of the variations in parameter values, may be easier to visualize in case of the mosaic models than the others.

In conclusion, mosaic models provide a powerful set of tools for texture analysis and synthesis. The large number of possible models provides a means of controlling or matching many different texture features. It is planned to undertake a series of studies in which these models are applied to the analysis of real textures.

ACKNOWLEDGMENT

The authors express their thanks to E. Slud for many helpful discussions and to K. Riley for her help in preparing this paper.

REFERENCES

[1] R. M. Pickett, "Visual analysis of texture in the detection and recognition of objects," in *Picture Processing and Psychopictorics*, B. S. Lipkin and A. Rosenfeld, Eds. New York: Academic, 1970, pp. 289-308.
[2] R. M. Haralick, "Statistical and structural approaches to texture," in *Proc. 4th Int. Joint Conf. Pattern Recognition*, Nov. 1978, pp. 45-69.
[3] J. K. Hawkins, "Textural properties for pattern recognition," in *Picture Processing and Psychopictorics*, B. S. Lipkin and A. Rosenfeld, Eds. New York: Academic, 1970, pp. 347-370.
[4] A. Rosenfeld and B. S. Lipkin, "Texture synthesis," in *Picture Processing and Psychopictorics*, B. S. Lipkin and A. Rosenfeld, Eds. New York: Academic, 1970, pp. 309-322.
[5] J. E. P. Box and G. M. Jenkins, *Time Series Analysis*. San Francisco, CA: Holden-Day, 1976.
[6] B. H. McCormick and S. N. Jayaramamurthy, "Time series model for texture synthesis," *Int. J. Comput. Inform. Sci.*, vol. 3, pp. 329-343, 1974.
[7] P. Whittle, "On stationary processes in the plane," *Biometrika*, vol. 41, pp. 434-449, 1954.
[8] J. T. Tou and Y. S. Chang, "An approach to texture pattern analysis and recognition," in *Proc. 1976 IEEE Conf. Decision Contr.*, Dec. 1976, pp. 398-403.
[9] J. T. Tou, D. B. Kao, and Y. S. Chang, "Pictorial texture analysis and synthesis," in *Proc. 3rd Int. Joint Conf. Pattern Recognition*, Nov. 1976.
[10] E. Wong, "Two-dimensional random fields and representations of images," *SIAM J. Appl. Math.*, vol. 16, pp. 756-770, 1968.
[11] J. S. Read and S. N. Jayaramamurthy, "Automatic generation of texture feature detectors," *IEEE Trans. Comput.*, vol. C-21, pp. 803-812, 1972.
[12] B. H. McCormick and S. N. Jayaramamurthy, "A decision theory method for the analysis of texture," *Int. J. Comput. Inform. Sci.*, vol. 4, pp. 1-38, 1975.
[13] R. S. Michalski and B. H. McCormick, "Interval generalization of switching theory," in *Proc. 3rd Annu. Houston Conf. Comput. Syst. Sci.*, Houston, TX, Apr. 1971, pp. 213-226.
[14] R. M. Haralick, K. Shanmugam, and I. Dinstein, "Textural features for image classification," *IEEE Trans. Syst., Man, Cybern.*, vol. SMC-3, pp. 610-621, 1973.
[15] K. Deguchi and I. Morishita, "Texture characterization and texture-based image partitioning using two-dimensional linear estimation techniques," *IEEE Trans. Comput.*, vol. C-27, pp. 846-850, 1978.
[16] K. Abend, T. J. Harley, and L. N. Kanal, "Classification of binary random patterns," *IEEE Trans. Inform. Theory*, vol. IT-11, pp. 538-544, 1965.
[17] B. R. Hunt, "Bayesian methods in nonlinear digital image restoration," *IEEE Trans. Comput.*, vol. C-26, pp. 219-229, 1977.
[18] B. R. Hunt and T. M. Cannon, "Nonstationary assumptions for Gaussian models of images," *IEEE Trans. Syst., Man, Cybern.*, vol. SMC-6, pp. 876-882, 1976.
[19] H. J. Trussel and R. P. Kruger, "Comments on nonstationary assumptions for Gaussian models in images," *IEEE Trans. Syst., Man, Cybern.*, vol. SMC-8, pp. 579-582, 1978.
[20] M. S. Longuet-Higgins, "The statistical analysis of a random moving surface," *Phil. Trans. Roy. Soc. London*, vol. A249, pp. 321-387, Feb. 1957.
[21] —, "Statistical properties of an isotropic random surface," *Phil. Trans. Roy. Soc. London*, vol. A250, pp. 151-171, Oct. 1957.
[22] —, "On the statistical distribution of the heights of sea waves," *J. Marine Res.*, vol. 11, pp. 245-266, 1952.
[23] D. P. Panda, "Statistical properties of thesholded images," *Comput. Graphics Image Processing*, vol. 18, pp. 334-354, 1978.
[24] D. P. Panda and T. Dubitzki, "Statistical analysis of some edge operators," *Comput. Graphics Image Processing*, vol. 11, pp. 313-348, 1979.
[25] G. Matheron, "The theory of regionalized variables and its applications," *Les Cahiers du Centre de Morphologie Math. de Fontainbleau*, vol. 5, 1971.

[26] C. Huijbregts, "Regionalized variables and quantitative analysis of spatial data," in *Display and Analysis of Spatial Data*, J. Davis and M. McCullagh, Eds. New York: Wiley, 1975, pp. 38-51.
[27] N. E. Nahi and M. H. Jahanshahi, "Image boundary estimation," *IEEE Trans. Comput.*, vol. C-26, pp. 772-781, 1977.
[28] N. E. Nahi and S. Lopez-Mora, "Estimation detection of object boundaries in noisy images," *IEEE Trans. Automat. Contr.*, vol. AC-23, pp. 834-845, 1978.
[29] M. Hassner and J. Sklansky, "Markov random field models of digitized image texture," in *Proc. 4th Int. Joint Conf. Pattern Recognition*, Nov. 1978, pp. 538-540.
[30] W. K. Pratt and O. D. Faugeras, "Development and evaluation of stochastic-based visual texture features," in *Proc. 4th Int. Joint Conf. Pattern Recognition*, Nov. 1978, pp. 545-548.
[31] A. Gagalowicz, "Analysis of texture using a stochastic model," in *Proc. 4th Int. Joint Conf. Pattern Recognition*, Nov. 1978, pp. 541-544.
[32] W. K. Pratt, O. D. Faugeras, and A. Gagalowicz, "Visual discrimination of stochastic texture fields," *IEEE Trans. Syst., Man, Cybern.*, vol. SMC-8, pp. 796-804, 1978.
[33] B. Mandelbrot, *Fractals—Form, Chance, and Dimension*. San Francisco, CA: Freeman, 1977.
[34] G. Matheron, *Elements pour une Theorie des Milieux Poreux*. Paris: Masson, 1967.
[35] J. Serra and G. Verchery, "Mathematical morphology applied to fibre composite materials," *Film Sci. Technol.*, vol. 6, pp. 141-158, 1973.
[36] S. Zucker, "Toward a model of texture," *Comput. Graphics Image Processing*, vol. 5, pp. 190-202, 1976.
[37] R. Yokoyama and R. M. Haralick, "Texture synthesis using a growth model," *Comput. Graphics Image Processing*, vol. 8, pp. 369-381, 1978.
[38] B. Schachter and N. Ahuja, "Random pattern generation processes," *Comput. Graphics Image Processing*, vol. 10, pp. 95-114, 1979.
[39] N. Ahuja, "Mosaic models for images, 1: Geometric properties of components in cell structure mosaics," *Inform. Sci.* to be published.
[40] —, "Mosaic models for images, 2: Geometric properties of components in coverage mosaics," *Inform. Sci.* to be published.
[41] —, "Mosaic models for images, 3: Spatial correlation in mosaics," *Inform. Sci.* to be published.
[42] B. J. Schachter, A. Rosenfeld, and L. S. Davis, "Random mosaic models for textures," *IEEE Trans. Syst., Man, Cybern.*, vol. SMC-8, pp. 694-702, 1978.
[43] N. Ahuja and A. Rosenfeld, "Fitting mosaic models to textures," in *Image Texture Analysis*, R. M. Haralick, Ed. New York: Plenum, 1981.
[44] —, "Image models," in *Handbook of Statistics*, P. R. Krishnarah and L. N. Kanal, Eds., to be published.

Narendra Ahuja was born in Achnera, India, on December 8, 1950. He received the B.E. degree with honors in electronics engineering from the Birla Institute of Technology and Science, Pilani, India, in 1972, the M.E. degree with distinction in electrical communication engineering from the Indian Institute of Science, Bangalore, India, in 1974, and the Ph.D. degree in computer science from the University of Maryland, College Park, in 1979.

From 1974 to 1975 he was Scientific Officer in the Department of Electronics, Government of India, New Delhi. From 1975 to 1979 he was at the Computer Vision Laboratory, University of Maryland, College Park, as a Graduate Research Assistant (1975-1978), as a Faculty Research Assistant (1978-1979), and as a Research Associate (1979). In 1979 he joined the University of Illinois, Urbana-Champaign, where he is currently a Research Assistant Professor in the Coordinated Science Laboratory and an Assistant Professor in the Department of Electrical Engineering. His research interests are in computer vision and pattern recognition.

Dr. Ahuja is included in *Who's Who in Technology Today*, and is a member of the Association for Computing Machinery, the IEEE Computer Society, and Sigma Xi.

Azriel Rosenfeld (M'60-F'72) was born in New York, NY, on February 19, 1931. He received the B.A. degree in physics from Yeshiva University, New York, NY, and the Ph.D. degree in mathematics from Columbia University, New York, NY, in 1950 and 1957, respectively.

From 1954 to 1956, he was a Physicist with the Fairchild Controls Corporation, New York, NY; from 1956 to 1959, he was an Engineer with the Ford Instrument Company, Long Island City, NY; and from 1959 to 1964, he was Manager of Research with the Budd Company Electronics Division, Long Island City, NY, and Information Sciences Center, McLean, VA. Since 1964, he has been a Professor of Computer Science at the University of Maryland, College Park. He has published ten books and nearly 250 papers, most of them dealing with the computer analysis of pictorial information. He edits the journal *Computer Graphics and Image Processing* and was Chairman of the Third International Joint Conference on Pattern Recognition.

A Facet Model for Image Data*

ROBERT M. HARALICK AND LAYNE WATSON

Virginia Polytechnic Institute and State University, Blacksburg, Virginia 24061

Received February 25, 1980

Image processing algorithms implicitly or explicitly assume an idealized form for the image data on which they operate. The degree to which the observed data meets the assumed idealized form is typically not examined or accounted for. This causes processing errors often attributed to noise. In this paper we discuss a facet model for image data which has the potential for fitting the form of the real idealized image, and for describing how the observed image differs from the idealized form. It is also an appropriate form for a variety of image processing algorithms. We give a relaxation procedure, and prove its convergence, for determining an estimate of the ideal image from observed image data.

1. INTRODUCTION

Operations on image data are designed to determine or estimate properties about the scene being imaged. A typical problem, for example, might be to determine homogeneous object parts or object edges. Such properties often cannot be determined without error. Sometimes it is because the algorithm works best for image data meeting certain assumptions actually not met by the observed image data.

The statistical uncertainty due to noise is unavoidable. However, the error due to using an algorithm on data that does not meet an assumed form is avoidable by first preprocessing the observed data and generating from it an estimate of its ideal form.

This decomposition of the problem into the two parts of getting an estimate of the ideal image underlying the observed image and then processing the estimate to determine the image properties is suggestive of the way this kind of problem is handled in stochastic control: get the best estimate of system state and then use a deterministic control assuming the best estimate of the actual system state. For the classical linear system with additive Gaussian noise this approach is the optimal one. For nonlinear systems it is not the best approach. But even here it gives good enough answers that it is frequently used nevertheless.

The advantage of the decomposition is its simplicity: it handles the noise when it estimates the ideal image, a process which we can call noise cleaning. Its disadvantage is that errors between the assumed form of the ideal image and the actual form of the ideal image will be exaggerated and propagated by any processing algorithm using the restored image.

In this paper we suggest a facet model for image data. The model specifies how the order and regularity in the world manifests itself in the ideal image and how the real image differs from the ideal image. The model is our working hypothesis. Our exploration here will use the facet model in its simplest form.

*© 1979 IEEE. Reprinted, with permission, from *Proceedings, IEEE Computer Society Conference on Pattern Recognition and Image Processing* (August 6–8, 1979, Chicago, Illinois) (79CH1428-2C).

The facet model for ideal image data assumes that the image is everywhere simple. This means that the spatial domain of the image can be partitioned into connected regions called facets each of which satisfies certain gray tone and shape constraints. The gray tones in each facet must be a polynomial function of the row–column coordinates of the pixels in the facet. In this paper we assume that the polynomial function is of degree zero, one, or two. Hence if we consider the gray tones as composing a surface above the resolution cells of the facet, then for the ideal image having a degree-one polynomial function, the surface is a sloped plane. Thus, "sloped facet model" would be an appropriate description of this specialized facet model.

The shape constraint is also simple: Each facet must be sufficiently smooth in shape. We assume that each region in the image can be exactly represented as the union of $K \times K$ blocks of pixels. The value of K associated with an image means that the narrowest part of each of its facets is at least as large as a $K \times K$ block of pixels. Hence, images which can have large values of K have very smoothly shaped regions. In this paper, we will take K less than or equal to 3.

To make these ideas precise, let Z_r and Z_c be the row and column index set for the spatial domain of an image. For any $(r, c) \in Z_r \times Z_c$, let $I(r, c)$ be the gray value of resolution cell (r, c) and let $B(r, c)$ be the $K \times K$ block of resolution cells centered around resolution cell (r, c). Let $\pi = \{\pi_1, \ldots, \pi_N\}$ be a partition of the spatial domain of $Z_r \times Z_c$ into its facets.

In the sloped facet model, for every resolution cell $(r, c) \in \pi_n$, there exists a resolution cell $(i, j) \in Z_r \times Z_c$ such that:

(1) Shape region constraint: $(r, c) \in B(i, j) \subseteq \pi_n$;
(2) Region gray tone constraint: $I(r, c) = \alpha_n r + \beta_n c + \gamma_n$.

An observed image J differs from its corresponding ideal image I by the addition of random stationary noise having zero mean and covariance matrix proportional to a specified one.

$$J(r, c) = I(R, c) + \eta(r, c),$$

where

$$E[\eta(r, c)] = 0,$$

$$E[\eta(r, c)\eta(r', c')] = k\sigma(r - r', c - c').$$

The flat facet model of Tomita and Tsuji [2] and Nagao and Matsuyama [1] differs from the sloped facet model only in that the coefficients α_n and β_n are assumed to be zero and Nagao uses a more generalized shape constraint which is also suitable here.

In Section 2 we describe a relaxation procedure which generates images satisfying the facet form. The relaxation procedure is proved to converge in Section 3 and has the important properties suggested by Rosenfeld [3]: in a coordinated and parallel manner, the strong influence the weak in their neighborhoods causing the weak to become consistent with the strong. In Section 4 we show some results.

2. NOISE CLEANING UNDER THE FACET MODEL

Noise cleaning is a procedure by which a noisy image is operated on in a manner which produces an image which has less noise and has the form of an ideal image. The facet model suggests the following simple nonlinear relaxation procedure to iteratively operate on the image until the image of ideal form is produced. Each resolution cell is contained in K^2 different $K \times K$ blocks. The gray tone distribution in each of these blocks can be fit by either a flat horizontal plane or a sloped plane. One of the K^2 blocks has smallest error of fit. Set the output gray value to be that gray value fitted by the block having smallest error. For the flat facet model this amounts to computing the variance for each $K \times K$ block a pixel participates in. The output gray value is then the mean value of the block having smallest variance (Tomita and Tsuji [2], Nagao and Matsuyama [1]).

For the sloped facet model, the procedure amounts to fitting a sloped plane to each of the blocks a given resolution participates in and outputting the fitted gray value of the given resolution cell from the block having the lowest fitting error.

The relaxation process associated with the facet model is similar in some respects to Diday's dynamic clusters method [4]. The main differences are: (1) the dynamic clusters method is a *finite* process (since there are only finitely many possible partitions and samples), while the sloped facet filtering process produces (in general) an *infinite* sequence of distinct points; (2) the residuals in each partition strictly decrease with the dynamic clusters method, whereas the sloped facet filter residuals (or sum of residuals) are not necessarily monotone; (3) the dynamic clusters method changes assignments of data points but not the points themselves, whereas the facet model relaxation repeatedly changes the data themselves.

Since the relaxation procedure for the sloped facet model is more complicated, we give a derivation here of the required equations. We assume that the block lengths are odd so that one of the block's pixels is its center. Let the block be $(2L + 1) \times (2L + 1)$ with the upper left-hand corner pixel having relative row-column coordinates $(-L, -L)$ and the lower right-hand corner pixel having relative row-column coordinates (L, L). Let $J(r, c)$ be the gray value at row r, column c. According to the sloped facet model, for any block entirely contained in a facet

$$J(r, c) = \alpha r + \beta c + \gamma + \eta(r, c),$$

where $\eta(r, c)$ is the noise.

A least-squares procedure may be used to determine the estimates for α, β, and γ. Let

$$f(\alpha, \beta, \gamma) = \sum_{r=-L}^{L} \sum_{c=-L}^{L} (\alpha r + \beta c + \gamma - J(r, c))^2.$$

The least-squares estimates for α, β, and γ are those which minimize f. To determine these values, we take the partial derivatives of f with respect to α, β, and

γ, set these to zero and solve the resulting equations for α, β, and γ.

$$\frac{df}{d\alpha} = 2 \sum_{r=-L}^{L} \sum_{c=-L}^{L} (\alpha r + \beta c + \gamma - J(r,c))r,$$

$$\frac{df}{d\beta} = 2 \sum_{r=-L}^{L} \sum_{c=-L}^{L} (\alpha r + \beta c + \gamma - J(r,c))c,$$

$$\frac{df}{d\gamma} = 2 \sum_{r=-L}^{L} \sum_{c=-L}^{L} (\alpha r + \beta c + \gamma - J(r,c)).$$

Setting the partial derivatives to zero results in

$$\sum_{r=-L}^{L} \sum_{c=-L}^{L} (\alpha r^2 + \beta rc + \gamma r - J(r,c)r) = 0,$$

$$\sum_{r=-L}^{L} \sum_{c=-L}^{L} (\alpha rc + \beta c^2 + \gamma c - J(r,c)c) = 0,$$

$$\sum_{r=-L}^{L} \sum_{c=-L}^{L} (\alpha r + \beta c + \gamma - J(r,c)) = 0.$$

Using the facts that $\sum_{i=-K}^{K} i = 0$ and $\sum_{i=-K}^{K} i^2 = \frac{1}{3} K(K+1)(2K+1)$ we obtain

$$\tfrac{1}{3} L(L+1)(2L+1)^2 \alpha - \sum_{r=-L}^{L} r \sum_{c=-L}^{L} J(r,c) = 0,$$

$$\tfrac{1}{3} L(L+1)(2L+1)^2 \beta - \sum_{c=-L}^{L} c \sum_{r=-L}^{L} J(r,c) = 0,$$

$$(2L+1)^2 \gamma - \sum_{r=-L}^{L} \sum_{c=-L}^{L} J(r,c) = 0.$$

Therefore,

$$\alpha = \frac{3}{L(L+1)(2L+1)^2} \sum_{r=-L}^{L} r \sum_{c=-L}^{L} J(r,c),$$

$$\beta = \frac{3}{L(L+1)(2L+1)^2} \sum_{c=-L}^{L} c \sum_{r=-L}^{L} J(r,c),$$

$$\gamma = \frac{1}{(2L+1)^2} \sum_{r=-L}^{L} \sum_{c=-L}^{L} J(r,c).$$

The meaning of this result can be readily understood for the case when the block size is 3 × 3. Here $L = 1$ and

$$\alpha = \tfrac{1}{6}[J(+1, \cdot) - J(-1, \cdot)],$$
$$\beta = \tfrac{1}{6}[J(\cdot, 1) - J(\cdot, -1)],$$
$$\gamma = \tfrac{1}{9}J(\cdot, \cdot),$$

where an argument of J taking the value dot means that J is summed from $-L$ to L in that argument position. Hence, α is proportional to the slope down the row dimension, β is proportional to the slope across the column dimension, and γ is the simple gray value average over the block. See Beaudet [5] for least-squares estimates of higher-order derivatives.

The fitted gray tone for any resolution cell (r, c) in the block is given by

$$\hat{J}(r, c) = \alpha r + \beta c + \gamma.$$

For the case where $L = 1$, the 3 × 3 block,

$$\hat{J}(r, c) = \tfrac{1}{6}[J(1, \cdot) - J(-1, \cdot)]r$$
$$+ \tfrac{1}{6}[J(\cdot, 1) - J(\cdot, -1)]c$$
$$+ \tfrac{1}{9}J(\cdot, \cdot).$$

Writing this expression out in full:

$$\hat{J}(r, c) = \tfrac{1}{18}\{J(-1, -1)(-3r - 3c + 2)$$
$$+ J(-1, 0)(-3r + 2)$$
$$+ J(-1, 1)(-3r + 3c + 2)$$
$$+ J(0, -1)(-3c + 2)$$
$$+ J(0, 0)(2)$$
$$+ J(0, 1)(3c + 2)$$
$$+ J(1, -1)(3r - 3c + 2)$$
$$+ J(1, 0)(3r + 2)$$
$$+ J(1, 1)(3r + 3c + 2)\}.$$

This leads to the set of linear filter masks shown in Fig. 1 for fitting each pixel position in the 3 × 3 block.

The sloped facet model relaxation procedure examines each of the K^2 $K \times K$ blocks a pixel (r, c) belongs to. For each block, a block error can be computed by

$$\epsilon^2 = \sum_{r=-L}^{L} \sum_{c=-L}^{L} (\hat{J}(r, c) - J(r, c))^2.$$

$\hat{J}(-,1)$

8	5	2
5	2	-1
2	-1	-4

$\hat{J}(-1,0)$

5	5	5
2	2	2
-1	-1	-1

$\hat{J}(-1,1)$

2	5	8
-1	2	5
-4	-1	2

$\hat{J}(0,-1)$

5	2	-1
5	2	-1
5	2	-1

$\hat{J}(0,0)$

2	2	2
2	2	2
2	2	2

$\hat{J}(0,1)$

-1	2	5
-1	2	5
-1	2	5

$\hat{J}(1,-1)$

2	-1	-4
5	2	-1
8	5	2

$\hat{J}(1,0)$

-1	-1	-1
2	2	2
5	5	5

$\hat{J}(1,1)$

-4	-1	2
-1	2	5
2	5	8

FIG. 1. 3×3 linear estimators of a pixel's grey tone for the nine different 3×3 neighborhoods the pixel participates in. If the pixel's position is (i,j) in the neighborhood, the estimate is $\hat{J}(i,j)$. Each mask must be normalized by dividing by 18.

One of the $K \times K$ blocks will have lowest error. Let (r^*, c^*) be the coordinates of the pixel (r, c) in terms of the coordinate system of the block having smallest error. The output gray value at pixel (r, c) is then given by $\hat{J}(r^*, c^*)$, where $\hat{J}$ is the linear estimate of gray values for the block having smallest error of fit.

3. CONVERGENCE

We now prove that the sequence of images produced by relaxation using either the flat facet or sloped facet model converges. Only the one-dimensional simplest versions of the facet models are considered because these proofs capture the essence of the more general cases where technical details obscure the proof. The proofs are readily generalized to two dimensions and larger neighborhoods.

We think of the gray tones at the mth iteration as a finite sequence of numbers

$$X_1^{(m)}, \ldots, X_N^{(m)}$$

which becomes the sequence

$$X_1^{(m+1)}, \ldots, X_N^{(m+1)}$$

after one application of the relaxation procedure for the flat facet or sloped facet model.

3.1. The Flat Facet Model

We discuss the convergence of the flat facet model using a one-dimensional sequence of gray tones and a neighborhood size of 2. The flat facet relaxation has the interesting property that the algebraic order of a pair of gray tones in a block is unchanged by the relaxation. Hence if $X_k^{(m)} \geq X_{k+1}^{(m)}$, then $X_k^{(m+1)} \geq X_{k+1}^{(m+1)}$. It is this property which drives the convergence monotonically.

PROPOSITION 1. *Let a, b, c be numbers and*

$$b' = \frac{a+b}{2} \quad \text{if } |a - b| \leq |b - c|$$
$$= \frac{b+c}{2} \quad \text{if } |a - b| > |b - c|.$$

Then (1) $b \geq c$ *implies* $(b + c)/2 \leq b' \leq b + (b - c)/2$,

(2) $b \leq c$ *implies* $b + (b - c)/2 \leq b' \leq (b + c)/2$.

Proof. From the definition of b', $|b' - b| \leq |(b - c)/2|$.

(1) Suppose $b \geq c$. Then $|b' - b| \leq (b - c)/2$. Hence, $-(b - c)/2 \leq b' - b \leq (b - c)/2$ so that $b - (b - c)/2 \leq b' \leq b + (b - c)/2$.

(2) Suppose $b \leq c$. Then $|b' - b| \leq (c - b)/2$. Hence, $-(c - b)/2 \leq b' - b \leq (c - b)/2$ so that $b - (c - b)/2 \leq b' \leq b + (c - b)/2$.

PROPOSITION 2. *Let $a, b, c, d,$ and e be numbers. Define*

$$f(x, y, x) = (x + y)/2 \quad \text{if } |y - x| \leq |y - z|$$
$$= (y + z)/2 \quad \text{if } |y - x| > |y - z|.$$

Let $b' = f(a, b, c)$, $c' = f(b, c, d)$, $d' = f(c, d, e)$, and $c'' = f(b', c', d')$. Suppose $b < c < d$. Then

(1) $c \leq c'$ *implies* $c' \leq c''$,

(2) $c \geq c'$ *implies* $c' \geq c''$.

Proof. By Proposition 1, $b < c < d$ implies $b + (b - c)/2 \leq b' \leq (b + c)/2 \leq c' \leq (c + d)/2 \leq d' \leq d + (d - c)/2$.

(1) Suppose $c \leq c'$. Then since $b < c < d$ it follows from the definition of f that $c' = (c + d)/2$ and $d - c \leq c - b$. Now note that

$$d' - c' \leq [d + (d - c)/2] - (c + d)/2 = d - c$$

and

$$c' - b' \geq (c + d)/2 - (b + c)/2 = (d - c)/2 + (c - b)/2$$
$$\geq (d - c)/2 + (d - c)/2.$$

Hence, $d' - c' \leq d - c \leq c' - b'$. Since $b' \leq c' \leq d'$ we must have by definition of f, $c'' = (c' + d')/2 \geq (c' + e')/2 = c'$.

(2) Suppose $c \geq c'$. Then since $b < c < d$ it follows from the definition of f that $c' = (b + c)/2$ and $c - b \leq d - c$. Now note that

$$d' - c' \geq (c + d)/2 - (b + d)/2 = (c - b)/2 + (d - c)/2$$
$$\geq (c - b)/2 + (c - b)/2$$

and

$$c' - b' \leq (b + c)/2 - [b + (b - c)/2] = c - b.$$

Hence, $c' - b' \leq c - b \leq d'c'$. Since $b' \leq c' \leq d'$ we must have by definition of f, $c'' = (b' + c')/2 \leq (c' + c')/2 = c'$.

THEOREM 1. *Let $X_1^{(0)}, \ldots, X_N^{(0)}$ be a given sequence of numbers, and define sequences $X_1^{(m)}, \ldots, X_N^{(m)}$, $m = 1, 2 \ldots$, by best adjacent least-squares averaging:*

$$X_k^{(m+)} = \frac{X_{k-1}^{(m)} + X_k^{(m)}}{2}, |X_{k-1}^{(m)} - X_k^{(m)}| \leq |X_k^{(m)} - X_{k+1}^{(m)}| \quad \text{or} \quad k = N$$
$$= \frac{X_k^{(m)} + X_{k+1}^{(m)}}{2}, \quad \text{otherwise.}$$

Then (1) the algebraic order of $X_1^{(0)}, \ldots, X_N^{(0)}$ is preserved by each sequence $X_1^{(m)}, \ldots, X_N^{(m)}$;

(2) If $X_i^{(0)}$ is a local min(max), then so is $X_i^{(m)}$;

(3) For all k and m, $\min_i X_i^{(0)} \leq X_k^{(m)} \leq \max_i X_i^{(0)}$;

(4) For fixed k, $X_k^{(m)}$ is either monotone increasing or decreasing;

(5) $\lim_{m \to \infty} [X_1^{(m)}, \ldots, X_N^{(m)}] = [X_1^\infty, \ldots, X_N^\infty]$ exists, and each X_k^∞ is a local nonstrict extremum.

Proof. (1) The proof is by induction on m. Suppose $X_k^m \leq X_{k+1}^m$. Then by Proposition 1, part (1), $X_{k+1}^{m+1} \geq (X_k^m + X_{k+1}^m)/2$ and by Proposition 1, part (2), $X_k^{m+1} \leq (X_k^m + X_{k+1}^m)/2$. Hence, $X_k^{m+1} \leq X_{k+1}^{m+1}$. Similarly, if $X_k^m \geq X_{k+1}^m$ then by Proposition 1, part (1), $X_k^{m+1} \geq (X_k^m + X_{k+1}^m)/2$ and by Proposition 1, part (2), $X_{k+1}^{m+1} \leq (X_k^m + X_{k+1}^m)/2$. Hence $X_{k+1}^{m+1} \leq X_k^{m+1}$.

(2) Since order relationships between neighboring points are preserved, as proved in (1), local extrema must remain extrema.

(3) If X_k^0 is a local minimum, then by (2) X_k^m remains the local minimum for all m. The averaging process can do nothing but increase X_k^m. Hence, X_k^m must be monotonically increasing. It now follows from (1) that $\min_i X_i^0 \leq X_j^m$ for all j and m. Similarly, every local maximum is preserved and if X_k^0 is a local maximum, then X_k^m is monotonically decreasing. Also, because of (1), $\max_i X_i^0 \geq X_j^m$ for all j and m.

(4) The proof is by induction on m. If X_k^m is a local extremum, the result follows from (2) and the observation made in the proof of (3). If X_k^m is not a local extremum then we have two cases depending on whether $X_{k-1}^{m-1} < X_k^{m-1} < X_{k+1}^{m-1}$ or $X_{k-1}^{m-1} > X_k^{m-1} > X_{k+1}^{m-1}$. But these cases are really identical since reordering the

indices in one case will produce the other. Thus without loss of generality we suppose $X_{k-1}^{m-1} < X_k^{m-1} < X_{k+1}^{m-1}$. Now by Proposition 2, $X_k^{m-1} \leq X_k^m$ implies $X_k^m \leq X_k^{m+1}$ and $X_k^{m-1} \geq X_k^m$ implies $X_k^m \geq X_k^{m+1}$.

(5) By (3) and (4), for each fixed k, X_k^m is a bounded monotone sequence. Therefore, by the Bolzano–Weierstrass theorem, the sequence converges

$$\lim_{m \to \infty} X_k^m = X_k^\infty.$$

Taking limits in the definition of X_k^m yields that X_k^∞ equals either $(X_k^\infty + X_{k+1}^\infty)/2$ or $(X_k^\infty + X_{k-1}^\infty)/2$, which implies X_k^∞ equals either X_{k-1}^∞ or X_{k+1}^∞. Hence X_k is a nonstrict local extremum for every k, $1 \leq k \leq N$.

3.2. The Slope Facet Model

We discuss the convergence of the slope facet model using a one-dimensional sequence and a neighborhood size of 3. The slope facet relaxation has the interesting convergence property that those neighborhoods of points most collinear converge first. Hence, the strongly consistent neighborhoods do not change much and force the weakly consistent neighborhoods to be consistent with the strongly consistent neighborhoods which have already converged. What happens is very similar to the property of relaxation procedures desired by Rosenfeld [3].

LEMMA 1. *Let $y = ax + b$ be the best polynomial least-squares approximation of degree ≤ 1 to the data points (x_1, y_1), (x_2, y_2), (x_3, y_3), where $x_1 < x_2 < x_3$ are equally spaced. Then a residual $y_i - ax_i - b = 0$ for some i if and only if the three points are collinear.*

Proof. By scaling and translating the points if necessary, it may be assumed without loss of generality that $x_1 = -1$, $x_2 = 0$, $x_3 = 1$. Solving the normal equations gives the least-squares fit

$$y = \frac{-y_1 + y_3}{2} x + \frac{y_1 + y_2 + y_3}{3}.$$

For each i, $ax_i + b - y_i = 0$ implies $(y_1 + y_3)/2 = y_2$, which implies (x_2, y_2) is the midpoint of the line segment between (x_1, y_1) and (x_3, y_3). Hence the points are collinear. The converse is trivial.

LEMMA 2. *Let $x_1 < x_2 < x_3$ be equally spaced points and $P(x)$ the best polynomial discrete least-squares approximation of degree ≤ 1 to the points (x_1, y_1), (x_2, y_2), (x_3, y_3). Then*

$$p(x_1) = \frac{5y_1 + 2y_2 - y_3}{6}, \qquad y_1 - p(x_1) = \frac{y_1 + y_3 - 2y_2}{6} = s,$$

$$p(x_2) = \frac{y_1 + y_2 + y_3}{3}, \qquad y_2 - p(x_2) = -2s,$$

$$p(x_3) = \frac{5y_3 + 2y_2 - y_1}{6}, \qquad y_3 - p(x_3) = s.$$

Proof. As in the proof of Lemma 1 it may be assumed that $x_1 = -1$, $x_2 = 0$, $x_3 = 1$. The results then follow from the explicit formula for $p(x)$ given in the proof of Lemma 1.

THEOREM 2. *Let $y_1^0, \ldots, y_N^0$ be a given sequence of numbers, and define sequences $y_1^m, \ldots, y_N^m$, $m = 1, 2, \ldots$, by*

$$y_i^{m+1} = p(i),$$

where $p(x)$ is the polynomial of degree of ≤ 1 producing the best least-squares approximation among all polynomials of degrees ≤ 1 of best discrete least-squares approximation to any three consecutive points from

$$(i-2, y_{i-2}^m), (i-1, y_{i-1}^m), (i, y_i^m), (i+1, y_{i+1}^m), (i+2, y_{i+2}^m).$$

Then $\lim_m y_i^m$ exists for all i, $1 \leq i \leq N$.

Proof. The proof is by induction on the number K of consecutive points which are converging. Let $(k-1, y_{k-1}^0), (k, y_k^0), (k+1, y_{k+1}^0)$ be the three points which have the best least-squares fit $p(x)$ over all the points (i, y_i^0). Then by definition, $y_j^1 = p(j)$, $j = k-1, k, k+1$, and these three new points are collinear. By the definition of the sequences, collinear points remain collinear, and therefore these three points converge. Hence, $K \geq 3$. Applying this same argument to the remaining points produces, after a finite number of iterations, blocks of three or more consecutive points which remain fixed.

For the inductive step, suppose that $y_k, y_{k+1}, \ldots, y_l$ are converging and the next block of converging points starts with y_r. (The following argument also applies if there is no y_r.) Take m large enough that $y_k^m, \ldots, y_l^m, y_r^m, y_{r+1}^m, \ldots$, may be considered fixed. Consider the minimum least-squares error at the points $y_{l+1}^m, y_{l+2}^m, \ldots, y_{r-1}^m$. There are some three points, say

$$y_{t-1}^m, y_t^m, y_{t+1}^m,$$

whose least-squares error is the smallest. If $l < t-1 < t+1 < r$, then $y_{t-1}^{m+1}, y_t^{m+1}, y_{t+1}^{m+1}$ are collinear, hence converging, and the induction is complete. Otherwise the minimum residual occurs at one of the ends. There are two cases:

Case 1. $l = t$ (the case $r = t$ is similar). By Lemma 2, $y_{l+1}^{m+1} = \frac{1}{6}(5y_{l+1}^m + 2y_l^m - y_{l-1}^m)$, $y_l^{m+1} = y_l^m$, $y_{l-1}^{m+1} = y_{l-1}^m$, and a short calculation shows that the residual at $y_{l-1}^{m+1}, y_l^{m+1}, y_{l+1}^{m+1} \leq \frac{5}{6}$ (residual at $y_{l-1}^m, y_l^m, y_{l+1}^m$).

Case 2. $l = t - 1$ (the case $r = t + 1$ is similar). Using Lemma 2 again, a short calculation shows that the residual at $y_l^{m+1}, y_{l+1}^{m+1}, y_{l+2}^{m+2} \leq \frac{1}{6}$ (residual at $y_l^m, y_{l+1}^m, y_{l+2}^m$).

As $m \to \infty$, either the minimum residual occurs in the middle, in which case the induction is complete, or at one of the ends, in which case the minimum residual decreases by a factor of $\frac{5}{6}$ or $\frac{1}{6}$ at each iteration. Therefore, the minimum residual converges to zero, and either y_{l+1}^m or y_{r-1}^m converges, completing the induction step.

3.3. Remarks

Theorems 1 and 2 are true in a number of extensions:

(1) The neighborhood size can be increased to an arbitrary K points.

(2) The domain of the points can be extended from one dimension to two dimensions, thereby making the results true for image data.

(3) The neighborhood shape does not have to be square or even rectangular in the case of the two-dimensional data. This takes care of the variety of neighborhood shapes employed by Nagao and Matsuyama [1] in their flat facet iterations.

(4) The theorems are true even if norms other than the L_2 norm are used to determine the best approximation. For example, they are true for the L_1 norm and L_∞ norm.

The theorems were stated and proved in their present form only in order to provide as much insight as possible. The proofs of the extensions just mentioned are conceptually the same as the proofs given here, but they present considerably more technical and notational difficulties.

Although the relaxation has been proved to converge, the meaning of the limit in relation to the starting point has not been established. In other words, this relaxation procedure suffers the same fault of many of the probabilistic relaxation labeling procedures used in image processing: the results are interesting and

FIG. 2. Original 256 × 256 test image.

FIG. 3. Result of processing the original image of Fig. 2 with five iterations of the slope facet procedure.

perhaps useful, but the problem being solved has not been stated or understood. We are actively working to try to remedy this weakness.

4. RESULTS

Figure 2 illustrates a 256 × 256 outdoor scene which the VISIONS group at the University of Massachusetts is working with and has supplied to us. Figure 3 illustrates the image after five iterations using the slope facet relaxation technique with a 3 × 3 window. Contrast between different regions has improved. Any region depicting features smaller or thinner than the 3 × 3 window is degraded. Most noticeable is the light above the garage door, the linear gutter feature, and the leaves on the trees. In general, textured areas become smoother and coarser textured. Edge boundaries become sharper and homogeneous areas have less noise.

To help discover what changed between the original image of Fig. 2 and the slope facet image, the absolute value of the difference between the original and the first slope facet iteration is shown in Fig. 4. Most of the changes have occurred along edges and in textured regions. This suggests that the slope facet model is a good model for the interior of any region in the image. But at the edges of region or for regions which are smaller than the $K \times K$ window size used, the model does not fit well.

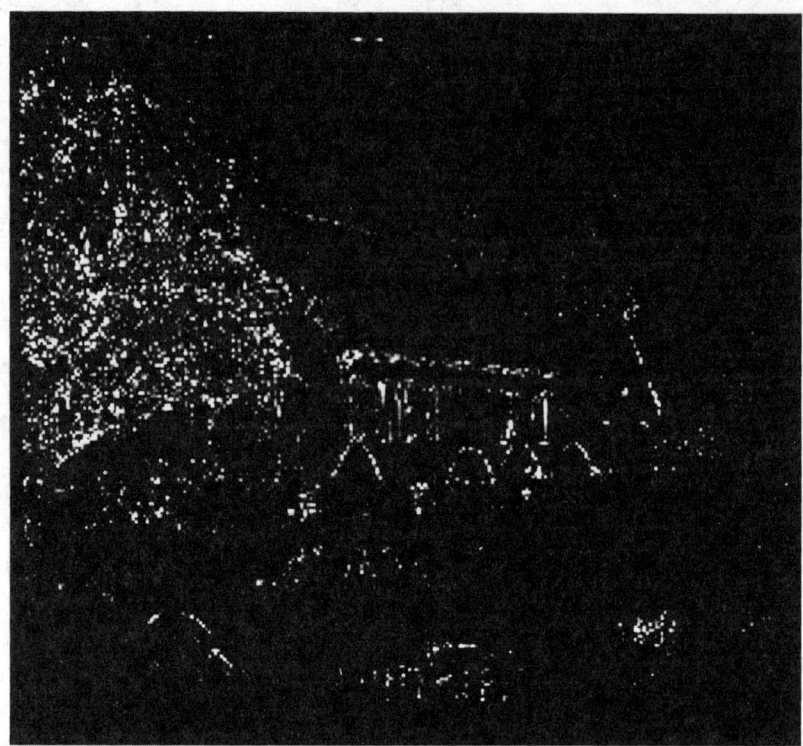

Fig. 4. The absolute value of the difference between the original and the result of the first iteration of the slope facet procedure.

Just for the sake of comparison, Fig. 5 illustrates the fifth iteration of the flat facet procedure. Note the blocky, flat appearance the image has. This image clearly cannot be the ideal underlying image for the original of Fig. 2. Figure 6 shows the absolute value of the difference between the original and the first iteration of the flat facet procedure. The changes certainly occur everywhere they did with the slope facet procedure except that they are larger in magnitude and larger in area.

The quadratic facet model allows a much better fit to occur near the edges. Figure 7 shows a blow-up of rows 80 to 143 and columns 60 to 123 of the left-hand corner of the house. Figure 8 shows the corresponding blow-up of the fifth iteration quadratic facet. Aside from the difference due to the photographic developing process, the images look the same at the pixel level. Confirming this, Fig. 9 illustrates the absolute value of the differences between the original in Fig. 7 and the quadratic facet result of Fig. 8. There is relatively little spatial structure in the difference image.

For the sake of comparison, Fig. 10 shows the same section after processing with five iterations of the slope facet procedure and Fig. 11 the same for five iterations of the flat facet procedure. These images confirm our earlier comments about the flat facet model being really incorrect and the slope facet model being correct in region interiors but not at edges.

FIG. 5. The result of processing the original image of Fig. 2 with five iterations of the flat facet procedure.

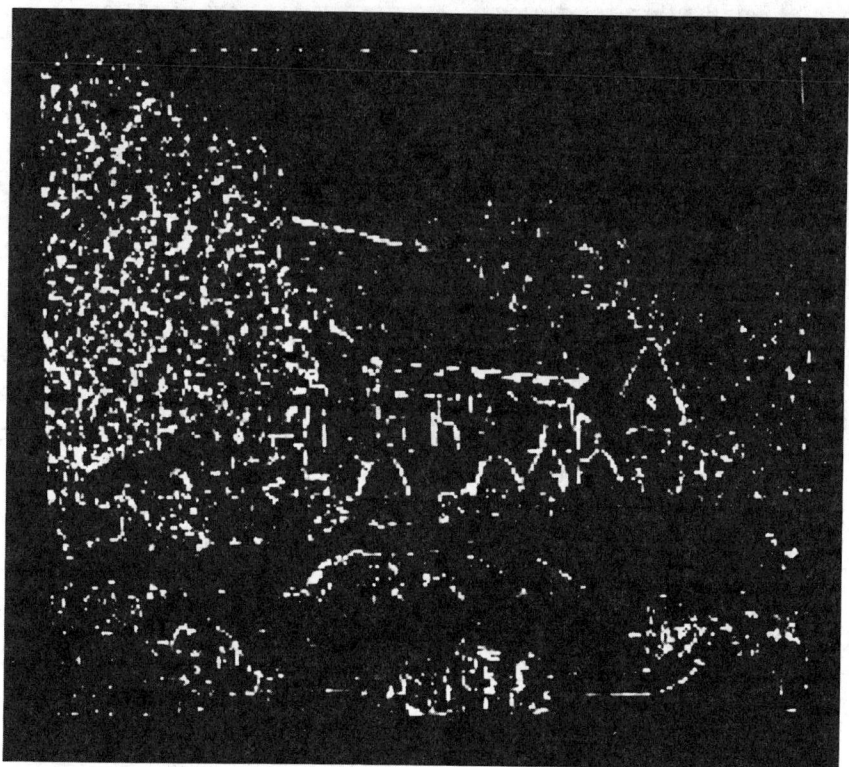

FIG. 6. The absolute value of the difference between the original and the first iteration of the flat facet procedure.

FIG. 7. Blow-up of the left corner of the house of the image of Fig. 2.

FIG. 8. The result of processing the image of Fig. 7 with the quadratic facet model procedure.

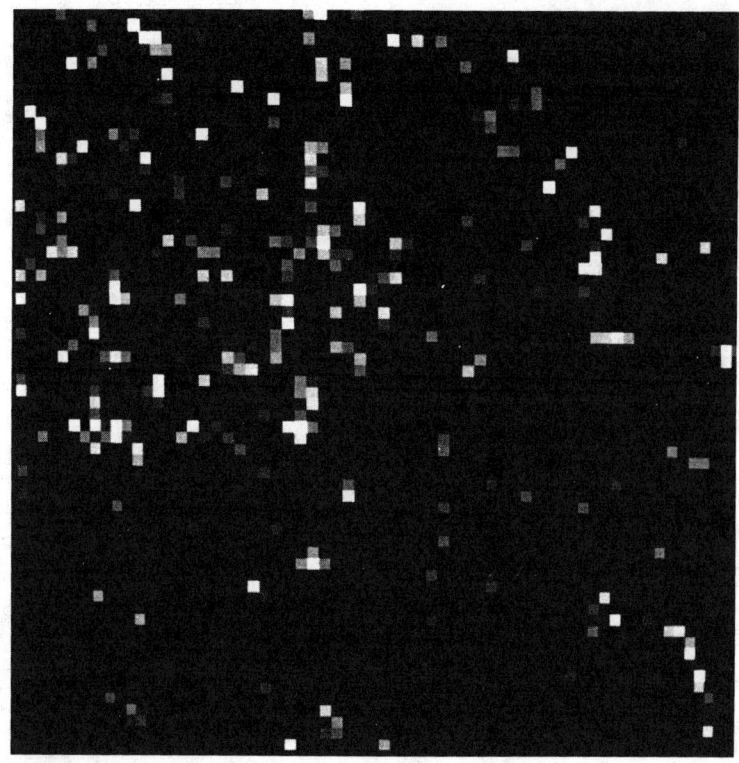

FIG. 9. The absolute value of the difference between the original of Fig. 7 and the quadratic facet image of Fig. 8.

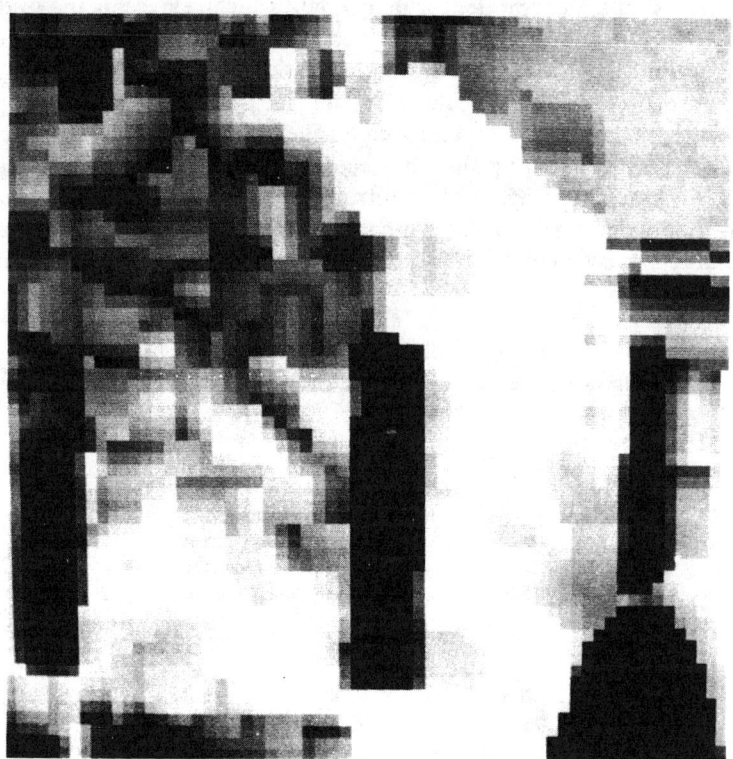

FIG. 10. The result of processing the blow-up of Fig. 7 with five iterations of the slope facet procedure.

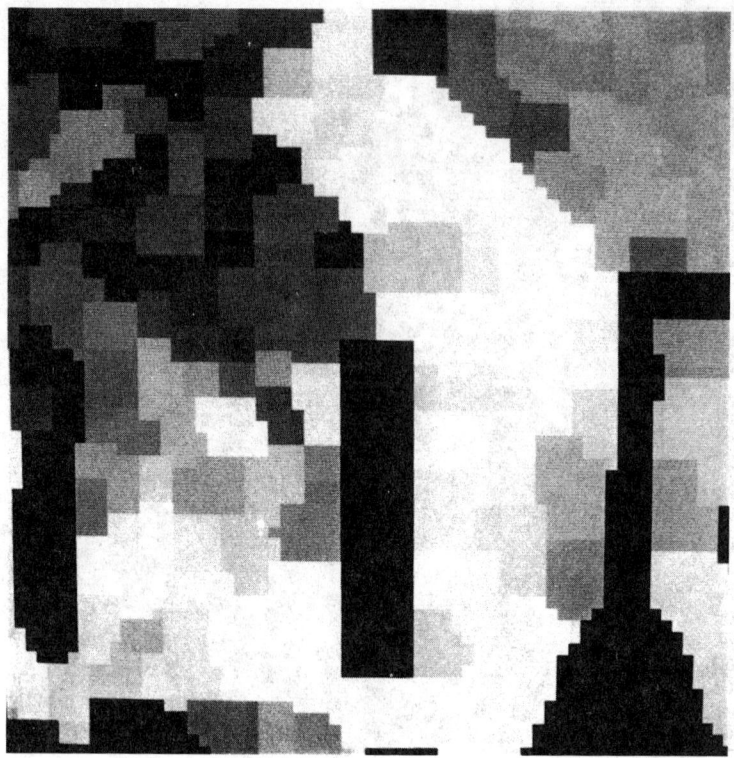

FIG. 11. The result of processing the blow-up of Fig. 7 with five iterations of the flat facet procedure.

5. CONCLUSION

We have discussed a facet model for image data which represents the underlying ideal image as a piecewise polynomial function, each piece being called a facet. We have suggested that those image processing operations that require an image to be in idealized form first restore the image to that ideal form by the facet iteration algorithm which we described and proved convergent. There is much work that remains to be done concerning the choice of the slope facet or quadratic facet model for any particular image and the size of window that is most appropriate. Experiments using the resulting facet image as the input image to various edge operators and region segmentation operators need to be tried and we will report on them in future papers.

REFERENCES

1. M. Nagao and T. Matsuyama, Edge preserving smoothing, in *Proceedings, Fourth International Joint Conference on pattern Recognition, Kyoto, Japan, November 1978.*
2. F. Tomita and S. Tsuji, Extraction of multiple regions by smoothing in selected neighborhoods, *IEEE Trans. Syst. Man Cybernet.* **SMC-7**, No. 2, 1977, 107–109.
3. A. Rosenfeld, Iterative methods in image analysis, *Pattern Recognition* **10**, 1978, 181–187.
4. E. Diday, The dynamic clusters method in non-hierarchial clustering, *Int. J. Comput. Inform. Sci.* **2**, No. 1, 1973, 61–88.
5. P. R. Beaudet, Rotationally invariant image operators, in *Proceedings, Fourth International Joint Conference on Pattern Recognition, Kyoto, Japan, November 1978,* pp. 579–583.

Fractal-Based Description of Natural Scenes

ALEX P. PENTLAND

Abstract—This paper addresses the problems of 1) representing natural shapes such as mountains, trees, and clouds, and 2) computing their description from image data. To solve these problems, we must be able to relate natural surfaces to their images; this requires a good model of natural surface shapes. Fractal functions are a good choice for modeling 3-D natural surfaces because 1) many physical processes produce a fractal surface shape, 2) fractals are widely used as a graphics tool for generating natural-looking shapes, and 3) a survey of natural imagery has shown that the 3-D fractal surface model, transformed by the image formation process, furnishes an accurate description of both textured and shaded image regions.

The 3-D fractal model provides a characterization of 3-D surfaces and their images for which the appropriateness of the model is verifiable. Furthermore, this characterization is stable over transformations of scale and linear transforms of intensity.

The 3-D fractal model has been successfully applied to the problems of 1) texture segmentation and classification, 2) estimation of 3-D shape information, and 3) distinguishing between perceptually "smooth" and perceptually "textured" surfaces in the scene.

Index Terms—Fractals, image segmentation, shading, texture models, texture perception, 3-D shape estimation, 3-D shape models.

Fig. 1. Fractal-based models of natural shapes (by Mandelbrot and Voss [10]).

I. INTRODUCTION

THE world that surrounds us, except for man-made environments, is typically formed of complex, rough, and jumbled surfaces (e.g., Fig. 1). If we are to develop machines competent to deal with the natural world, therefore, we need a representational framework that is able to describe such shapes succinctly. The problem, then, is how shall we describe the shape of a crumpled newspaper? A clump of leaves? A jagged mountain?

Current representational schemes employ Plato's notion of ideal forms—e.g., spheres, cylinders, and cubes—to describe three-dimensional shapes. Such shape-primitive representations function well in man-made carpentered environments. When we attempt to describe the crenulated, crumpled surfaces typical of natural objects, however, the result is usually implausibly complex. Such awkwardness makes these shape-primitive representations difficult to envisage as the basis for human-performance-level capabilities.

Furthermore, how can we expect to extract 3-D information from the image of a rough or cumpled surface when all of our models refer to smooth surfaces only? We have no models that describe either the shape of such complex surfaces or how they evidence themselves in an image. The lack of a 3-D model for such naturally occurring surfaces has generally restricted image-understanding efforts to a world populated exclusively by smooth objects, a sort of "Play-Doh" world [1] that is not much more general than the blocks world.

Shape-from-shading [2], [3] and surface interpolation methods [4], for instance, all employ the heuristic of "smoothness" to relate neighboring points on a surface. Such heuristics are applicable to many man-made surfaces, of course, but are demonstrably untrue of most natural surfaces. Texture descriptors, similarly, have dealt only with patterns assumed to lie on a smooth surface [5], [6], or have discarded 3-D notions entirely and worked only with ad hoc statistical measures of the image intensity surface. Before we can employ such techniques in the *natural* world, we must be able to determine which surfaces are smooth and which are not—or else generalize our techniques to include the rough, crumpled surfaces typically found in nature.

In either case, we must have recourse to a 3-D model competent to describe naturally occurring surfaces. A good model of natural surfaces, together with the physics of image formation, would provide the analytical tools necessary for relating natural surfaces to their images. A formulation able to relate image to surface can provide the necessary leverage for usefully representing natural surfaces, as well as the computation of such descriptions from the image data.[1]

Manuscript received October 17, 1983; revised February 13, 1984. This work was supported by the Defense Advanced Research Projects Agency under Contract MDA 903-83-C-0027 (monitored by the U.S. Army Engineer Topographic Laboratory) and by National Science Foundation Grant DCR-83-12766.

The author is with the Artificial Intelligence Center, SRI International, Menlo Park, CA 94025.

[1] The word representation will be used to refer to the formal language in which *descriptions* of particular objects are couched.

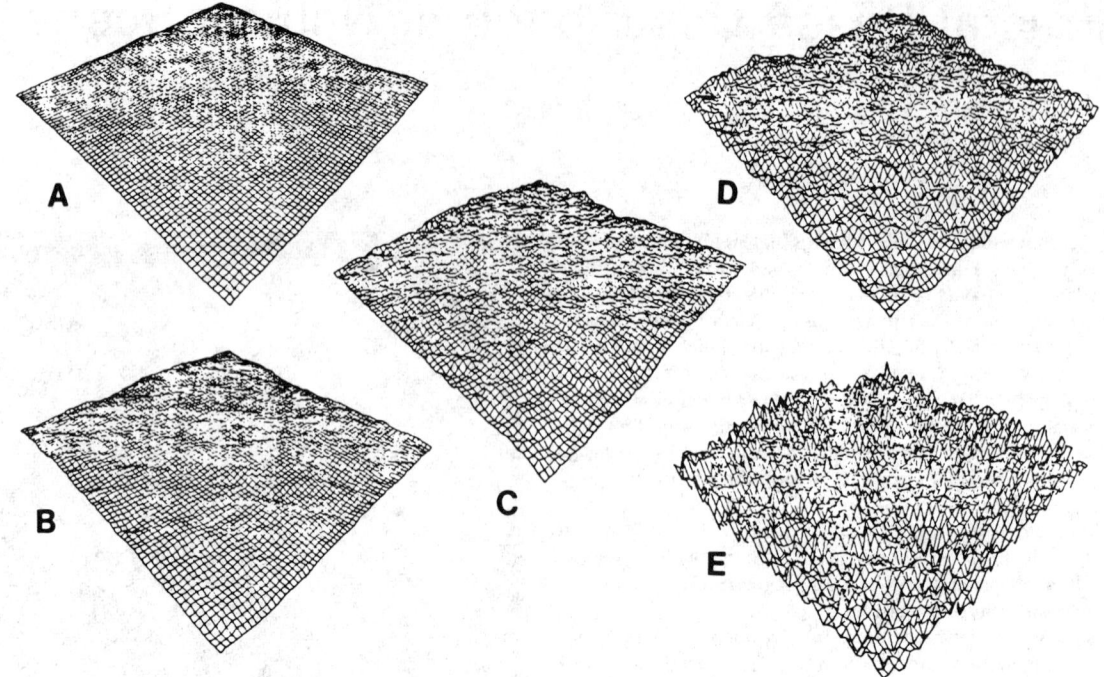

Fig. 2. Surfaces of increasing fractal dimension. The fractal dimension corresponds closely to our intuitive notion of roughness.

This paper, therefore, addresses two related problems: 1) finding a representation of shape capable of describing succinctly the surfaces of such natural objects as mountains, trees, and clouds, and 2) determining how such a description might be computed, given only raw image data. The first step towards solving these problems, of course, is to obtain a model of natural surface shapes.

Fractal functions appear to provide such a model, in part, because many basic physical processes produce fractal surfaces (and thus fractals are quite common in nature), but perhaps even more importantly because fractals *look* like natural surfaces. This natural appearance has spurred recent computer graphics research to focus on using fractal processes[2] for simulating natural shapes and textures (as in Fig. 1). Mountains, clouds, water, plants, trees, and even primitive animals [7]–[13] are all among the objects that have been realistically portrayed by use of fractal functions. This is important information for workers in computer vision because the natural appearance of fractals is strong evidence that they capture all of the perceptually relevant shape structure of natural surfaces.

Additional support for the fractal model comes from a recently conducted survey of natural imagery [14]. This survey found that the fractal model of imaged 3-D surfaces furnishes an accurate description of most textured and shaded image regions, thereby further validating this physics-derived model for both image texture and shading.

II. Fractals and the Fractal Model

During the last 20 years, B. B. Mandelbrot has developed and popularized a relatively novel class of mathematical functions known as *fractals* [7], [10]. Fractals are found extensively in

[2]Most computer graphics techniques actually employ a stochastic approximation of true fractal functions [9]; however, this distinction is not important for our purposes.

nature [7], [8], [10]. Mandelbrot, for instance, shows that fractal surfaces are produced by a number of basic physical processes, ranging from the aggregation of galaxies to the curdling of cheese.

The defining characteristic of a fractal is that it has a *fractional dimension*, from which we get the word "fractal." Technically, a fractal is defined as a set for which the Hausdorff-Besicovich dimension is strictly larger than the topological dimension, i.e., a set for which the only consistent description of its metric properties requires a "dimension" value larger than our standard, intuitive definition of the set's "dimension."

The fractal dimension of a surface corresponds quite closely to our intuitive notion or roughness. Thus, if we were to generate a series of scenes with the same 3-D relief but with increasing fractal dimension D, we would obtain a sequence of surfaces with linearly increasing perceptual roughness, as is shown in Fig. 2: (a) shows a flat plane ($D \approx 2.0$), (b) rolling countryside ($D \approx 2.1$), (c) an old, worn mountain range 2.3), (d) a young, rugged mountain range ($D \approx 2.5$) and, finally (e), a stalagmite-covered plane ($D \approx 2.8$).

One general characterization of fractals is that they are the end result of physical processes that modify shape through local action. Such processes will, after innumerable repetitions, typically produce a fractal surface shape. Examples are erosion, aggregation (e.g., galaxy formation, meteorite accretion, and snowflake growth), and turbulent flow (e.g., of rivers or lava).

Experimental Note:

Ten naive subjects (natural-language researchers) were shown sets of fifteen 1-D curves and 2-D surfaces with varying fractal dimension but constant range (e.g., see Fig. 2), and asked to estimate roughness on a scale of one (smoothest) to ten (roughest). The mean of the subject's estimates of roughness had a nearly perfect

0.98 correlation ($p < 0.001$) with the curve's fractal dimension, i.e., fractal dimension accounted for 96 percent of the variance in the roughness estimates. The fractal measure of perceptual roughness is therefore almost twice as accurate as any other reported to date, e.g., [29].

An Illustration of Fractal Dimension: One familiar example of naturally occurring fractal curves is coastlines. When we examine a coastline (as in Fig. 1), we see a familiar scalloped curve formed by innumerable bays and peninsulas. If we then examine a finer-scale map of the same region, we shall again see the same type of curve. It turns out that this characteristic scalloping is present at almost all scales of examination [8], i.e., the statistics of the curve are invariant with respect to transformations of scale.

To illustrate the importance of fractal dimension, let us suppose that we wish to measure the area of an island or the length of its coastline. Metric properties are, in general, estimated by taking a measuring instrument of size λ, determining that n such instruments will "cover" the curve or area to be measured, and applying the formula

$$M = n\lambda^D$$

where M is the metric property to be measured (e.g., length, area), and D the topological dimension of the measuring instrument.

The fact that the coastline is scalloped at all scales causes a problem when we attempt to measure it because all of the curve's features that are smaller than the size of the measuring tool will be missed, whatever the size of the measuring tool selected. When we attempt to estimate the length of such a curve, therefore, the measurement we obtain depends not only on the coastline but also on the length of the measurement tool itself [8]!

Mandelbrot pointed out that, in order to obtain a consistent measurement of the coastline's length, we must generalize the notion of dimension to include fractional dimensions. The use of a fractional power in our mensuration formula compensates, in effect, for the length or area lost because of details smaller than λ. The unique fractional power that yields consistent estimates of a set's metric properties in called that set's *fractal dimension*. Because it provides the correct adjustment factor for all those details smaller than λ, it may also be viewed as a measurement of the shape's roughness.

One of the more important lessons such examples teach us is the following: standard notions of length and area do NOT produce consistent measurements for many natural shapes. The basic metric properties of these shapes vary as a function of their fractal dimension. Fractal dimension, therefore, is a necessary part of any consistent description of the metric properties of such shapes, for any description that lacks it will not be correct at more than one scale of examination.

Fractal Brownian Functions: Virtually all fractals encountered in physical models have two additional properties: 1) each segment is statistically similar to all others; 2) they are statistically invariant over wide transformations of scale. The path of a particle exhibiting Brownian motion is the canonical example of this type of fractal; the discussion that follows, therefore, will be devoted exclusively to fractal Brownian functions, a mathematical generalization of Brownian motion.

A random function $I(x)$ is a fractal Brownian function if for all x and Δx

$$\Pr\left(\frac{I(x + \Delta x) - I(x)}{\|\Delta x\|^H} < y\right) = F(y) \quad (1)$$

where $F(y)$ is a cumulative distribution function [7]. Note that x and $I(x)$ can be interpreted as vector quantities, thus providing extension to two or more topological dimensions. If $I(x)$ is scalar, then the fractal dimension D of the graph described by $I(x)$ is

$$D = 2 - H. \quad (2)$$

If $H = 1/2$ and $F(y)$ comes from a zero-mean Gaussian with unit variance, then $I(x)$ is the classical Brownian function.

The fractal dimension of these functions can be measured either directly from $I(x)$ by use[3] of (1), or from $I(x)$'s Fourier power spectrum $P(f)$, as the spectral density of a fractal Brownian function is proportional[4] to f^{-2H-1}.

A. Fractals and the Imaging Process

Before we can use a fractal model of natural surfaces to help us understand images we must determine how the imaging process maps a fractal surface shape into an image intensity surface.

The first step is to define our terms carefully. Real images and surfaces can not, of course, be true mathematical fractals, because the latter are defined to exist at all scales. Physical surfaces, in contrast, have an overall size that places an upper limit on the range of applicable scales. A lower limit is set by the size of the surfaces' constituent particles. Fractals, in common with all mathematical abstractions, can only approximate physical objects over a range of physical parameters.

Because it is unreasonable to expect a physical surface to be fractal over all scales, the only physically reasonable definition of a "fractal surface" is a surface that may be accurately approximated by a single fractal function over a range of scales. We shall say, therefore, that a surface is *fractal* if the fractal dimension is stable over a wide range of scales, the implication being that it can be accurately approximated over that range of scales by a single fractal function.

These considerations prompt the following two definitions, the first applicable to a two-dimensional function such as the image intensity surface, the second applicable to a topologically two-dimensional surface embedded in three dimensions, such as the surface of a mountain.

Definition: A *fractal Brownian surface* is a continuous function that obeys the statistical description given by (1) with x as a two-dimensional vector at all scales (i.e., values of Δx) between some smallest ($\Delta x_{\min}$) and largest ($\Delta x_{\max}$) scales.

Definition: A *spatially isotropic fractal Brownian surface* is a surface in which the components of the surface normal $N = (N_x, N_y, N_z)$ are themselves fractal Brownian surfaces of identical fractal dimension.

---

[3] See the beginning portions of Section III and Section IV-A.
[4] Discussion of the rather technical proof of this proportionality may be found in [1].

In the next section, I will present evidence showing that many natural surfaces are spatially isotropic fractals, with Δx_{min} and Δx_{max} being the size of the projected pixel and the size of the examined surface patch, respectively. Further, it is interesting to note that practical fractal-generation techniques, such as those used in computer graphics, have had to constrain the fractal generating function to produce spatially isotropic fractal Brownian surfaces in order to obtain realistic imagery [9]. Thus, it appears that many real 3-D surfaces are spatially isotropic fractals, at least over a wide range of scales.

With these definitions in hand, we can now address the problem of how 3-D fractal surfaces appear in the 2-D image.

Proposition 1: A 3-D surface with a spatially isotropic fractal Brownian shape produces an image whose intensity surface is fractal Brownian and whose fractal dimension is identical to that of the components of the surface normal, given a Lambertian surface reflectance function and constant illumination and albedo.

Proof: Under the Lambertian and constancy assumptions, the image intensity I at a point P is a function of the surface normal N at the surface point that projects to P:

$$I = \rho \lambda N \cdot L \quad (3)$$

where ρ is the albedo of the surface, λ is the illuminant intensity, and $L = (l_x, l_y, l_z)$ is the illuminant direction. Variations in I, therefore, are dependent only upon variations in N.

The proposition claims that the image intensity I will obey the rule

$$\Pr\left(\frac{I(x, y) - I(x + \Delta x, y)}{\|\Delta x\|^H} < y\right) = F(y).$$

To show this, we let N_1 be the normal at point (x, y) and N_2 be the normal at point $(x + \Delta x, y)$. Then we expand using (3), yielding

$$\Pr\left(\frac{\rho\lambda(N_1 \cdot L) - \rho\lambda(N_2 \cdot L)}{\|\Delta x\|^H} < y\right) = F(y).$$

Expanding the dot products, we obtain

$$\Pr\left(\frac{\rho\lambda(N_{1x}l_x + N_{1y}l_y + N_{1z}l_z) - \rho\lambda(N_{2x}l_x + N_{2y}l_y + N_{2z}l_z)}{\|\Delta x\|^H}\right.$$
$$\left. < y\right) = F(y).$$

As N_x, N_y, and N_z are all fractal Brownian functions, by virtue of the surface being assumed a spatially isotropic fractal Brownian function and, as ρ, λ, and L are constant, then $\rho\lambda N_x l_x$, $\rho\lambda N_y l_y$, and $\rho\lambda N_z l_z$ are also fractal Brownian (see Proposition 2 in the following section); thus

$$I = \rho\lambda(N \cdot L) = \rho\lambda(N_x L_x + N_y L_y + N_z l_z)$$

must also be. Note that this proof may be generalized to include all cases in which the reflectance function is an affine transformation of N. The dimension of I is the same as that of the components of N since multiplication does not affect fractal dimension (see Proposition 2). ∎

This proposition demonstrates that the fractal dimension of the surface normal dictates the fractal dimension of the image intensity surface and, of course, the dimension of the physical surface.[5] Simulation of the imaging process with a variety of imaging geometries and reflectance functions indicates that this proposition will hold quite generally; the "roughness" of the surface seems to dictate the "roughness" of the image. If we know that the surface is homogeneous,[6] therefore, we can estimate the fractal dimension of the surface by measuring the fractal dimension of the image data.

What we have developed, then, is a method for inferring a basic property of the 3-D surface—its fractal dimension—from the image data. That fractal dimension is required to obtain a scale-invariant description of a surface's metric properties is an indication of its usefulness. That fractal dimension has also been shown to correspond closely to our intuitive notion of roughness shows the fundamental importance of the measurement: we can now discover from the image data whether the 3-D surface is rough or smooth, isotropic or anisotropic. We can know, in effect, what kind of cloth the surface was cut from.

Experimental Note:

15 naive subjects (mostly language researchers) were shown digitized images of eight natural textured surfaces drawn from Brodatz [15]. These are shown in Fig. 8. They were asked "if you were to draw your finger horizontally along the surface pictured here, how rough or smooth would the surface feel?," i.e., they were asked to estimate the 3-D roughness/smoothness of the viewed surfaces. This procedure was then repeated for the vertical direction, yielding a total of 16 roughness estimates for each subject. A scale of one (smoothest) to ten (roughest) was used to indicate 3-D roughness/smoothness. The fractal dimension of the 2-D image was then computed along the horizontal and vertical directions by the use of (5), as described in the following section, and the viewed surface's 3-D fractal dimension was estimated by the use of Proposition 1. The mean of the subject's estimates of 3-D roughness had an excellent 0.91 correlation ($p < 0.001$) with roughnesses predicted by use of the image's 2-D fractal dimension and Proposition 1, i.e., the 3-D fractal dimension predicted by use of the measured 2-D image's fractal dimension accounted for 83 percent of the variance in the subject's estimates of 3-D roughness. This result, therefore, supports the general validity of Proposition 1.

Properties of Fractal Brownian Functions: Fractal functions must be stable over common transformations if they are to be useful as a descriptive tool. The following propositions prove that the fractal dimension of a surface is invariant with respect to linear transformations of the data and to transformation of scale. Estimates of fractal dimension, therefore, may be expected to remain stable over smooth monotonic transformations of the image data and over changes of scale.

---

[5] The surface normal is a function of the first derivative of depth; thus, we can construct an integration procedure that converts surface normals into surface shape (as a depth map).

[6] Rubin and Richards [28] describe a scheme whereby the homogeneity of a surface may be determined from its imaged color.

Proposition 2: A linear transformation of a fractal Brownian function is a fractal Brownian function with the same fractal dimension.

Proof: The proposition claims that if $I(x)$ is a fractal Brownian function, i.e., obeys (1) then

$$\Pr\left(\frac{(AI(x)+B)-(AI(x+\Delta x)+B)}{\|\Delta x\|^H}<y\right)=F(y)$$

will be true of $AI(x)+B$. This second expression may be rewritten as

$$\Pr\left(\frac{I(x)-I(x+\Delta x)}{\|\Delta x\|^H}<\frac{y}{A}\right)=F(y)$$

or

$$\Pr\left(\frac{I(x)-I(x+\Delta x)}{\|\Delta x\|^H}<y\right)=F(yA)$$

thus proving the proposition; linear transforms merely scale the distribution $F(y)$. ∎

Proposition 3: The fractal dimension of a fractal Brownian function is invariant over transformations of scale.

Proof: The proposition claims that, if $I(x)$ is a fractal Brownian function, i.e., it obeys (1), then

$$\Pr\left(\frac{I(x)-I(x+k\Delta x)}{\|k\Delta x\|^H}<y\right)=F(y)$$

will be true of $I(x)$. This is trivially true; we need only set $\Delta x^* = k\Delta x$, and then the second expression may be rewritten as

$$\Pr\left(\frac{I(x)-I(x+\Delta x^*)}{\|\Delta x^*\|^H}<y\right)=F(y)$$

thus proving the proposition. ∎

B. Contours and the Imaging Process

We have described a method whereby the fractal dimension of the surface can be inferred for homogeneous uniformly lit surfaces. Even if the surface is not homogeneous or uniformly illuminated, however, we can still hope to infer the fractal dimension of the surface from imaged surface contours and bounding contours.

Contour shape is often primarily a function of surface shape; this is especially true for contours that lie mostly within a plane intersecting the surface. Common examples of such approximately-planar contours are bounding contours and contours that are "drawn" on the surface, e.g., cast shadows. The imaged projection of such planar contours is simply a linear transform of the 3-D contour; recalling that linear transforms do not alter the fractal dimension of a function, we see that the fractal dimension of these imaged contours is the same as that of the 3-D contour.

Thus, we may use the fractal dimension of imaged contours to directly infer that of the 3-D surface (the surface's dimension is simply one plus the contours' dimension). Consequently, the estimate of fractal dimension obtained from contours can be used to corroborate the one derived from image intensities.

III. APPLICABILITY OF THE FRACTAL MODEL

Proposition 1 proved that a fractal surface implies that the image intensity surface is itself fractal. The reverse is also true, as is proved in the following proposition. This proposition, therefore, gives us a method of evaluating the usefulness of the fractal surface model for particular image data: to determine whether or not a 3-D surface is fractal, all we need to do is to determine whether its image is fractal (given that we have first determined that the surface is homogeneous, perhaps by use of color information [28]).

Proposition 4: If an image intensity surface is a two-dimensional fractal Brownian then the imaged 3-D surface must be spatially-isotropic fractal Brownian, given that the surface is Lambertian and the illumination and albedo are constant.

Proof: For a Lambertian surface, the image intensity I is a linear function of the components of the surface normal N_x, N_y, and N_z, e.g.,

$$I = \rho\lambda(N\cdot L) = \rho\lambda(N_x l_x + N_y l_y + N_z l_z). \tag{4}$$

To prove that a fractal Brownian image intensity surface necessarily entails a 3-D surface that is spatially-isotropic fractal Brownian, it suffices (by definition) to prove that a fractal image implies that the components of the surface normal are fractal.

We first note that Proposition 2 proves that linear transforms do not affect the fractal nature of a function nor its dimension. Thus, (4) shows that the fractal nature (and dimension) of the image intensity surface is determined by the sum of N_x, N_y, and N_z. As the finite sum of nonfractal functions is nonfractal, we see that if the image intensity surface is fractal Brownian then so must be at least one of the components of the surface normal. If the image is two-dimensionally fractal (e.g., fractal in both the x and y image directions), then at least two independent components of the surface normal must be fractal. Thus, as the surface normal has only two degrees of freedom (by virtue of being constrained to have unit magnitude), a two-dimensionally fractal Brownian image intensity surface implies that all of the surface normals' components must be fractal Brownian and the surface is therefore spatially-isotropic fractal Brownian. ∎

To evaluate the applicability of the fractal model for a particular surface and its image data, then, we need only verify the homogeneity of the surface and the fractal nature of the image intensity surface. It appears that verification of surface homogeneity can be done by use of color information [28]; in order to verify the fractalness of the image we first rewrite (1) to obtain the following description of the manner in which the second-order statistics of the image change with scale:

$$E(|\Delta I_{\Delta x}|)\|\Delta x\|^{-H} = E(|\Delta I_{\Delta x=1}|) \tag{5}$$

where $E(|\Delta I_{\Delta x}|)$ is the expected value of the change in intensity over distance Δx. Equation (5) is a hypothesized relation among the image intensities; a hypothesis that we may test statistically. If we find that (5) is true of the image intensity surface within a homogeneous image region,[7] then

---

[7] i.e., we calculate the quantities $E(|\Delta I_{\Delta x}|)$ for various Δx, use a least squares regression [using the log of (5)] to estimate H, and examine the residuals.

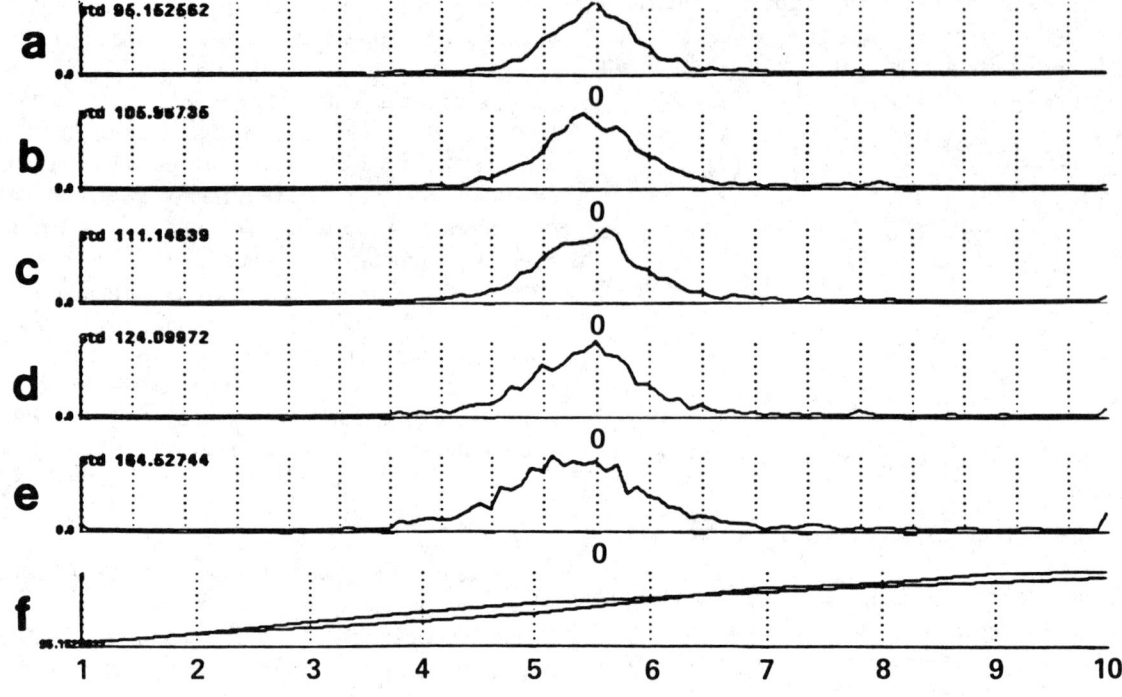

Fig. 3. Results for a typical textured patch.

Proposition 4 tells us that the viewed surface must be a 3-D fractal Brownian surface, and thus the fractal model is appropriateness for particular image data because it means that we can know when (and when not) to use the model.

To evaluate the suitability of the fractal model for natural surfaces, the homogeneous regions from each of six images of natural scenes were densely sampled. In addition, detailed images of 12 textured surfaces (see Brodatz [15]) were digitized and examined. The intensity values within each of these regions were then approximated by a fractal Brownian function and the approximation error observed.

Fig. 3 shows the results for a typical textured patch. The graphs (a)-(e) show the distribution of intensity differences (i.e., the second-order difference statistics) at one, two, three, five, and ten pixel distances; the distributions are approximately Gaussian. Fig. 3(f) shows a plot of the standard deviation of these distributions as a function of scale (i.e., $E(|\Delta I_{\Delta x}|)$ as a function of Δx in pixels). Overlaid on this graph is a least-squares fit of a fractal rule. As can be seen, the fit is quite good—implying that the intensity surface in this region is actually a fractal Brownian function, at least over the 10:1 range of scales measured.

For the majority of the textures examined (77 percent), the fit was as good or better than the example shown. In 15 percent of the cases the region was constant except for random, zero-mean perturbations; consequently, the fractal function correctly approximates the image data, although the estimated fractal dimension is equal to the topological dimension.[8] The fit was poor in only 8 percent of the regions examined. In some of these cases it appeared that the image digitization

[8] In these cases the data's dimensionality is technically not "fractional," but this distinction need not concern us here

had become saturated, and thus the poor fit may have been artifactual.

The fact that the vast majority of the regions examined were quite well approximated by a fractal Brownian function indicates that the fractal model will often provide a useful description of natural surfaces and their images. In those cases for which the fractal description is appropriate, the only statistical structure that remains unaccounted for by the fractal Brownian function is zero-mean unit-variance Gaussian noise—indicating that the fractal description effectively exhausts all of the second-order difference information within the image.

Following initial report of this work [14] a similar investigation was conducted by Peleg et al. [27]. In their work high-resolution images drawn from Brodatz [15] were examined over much larger ranges of scale, and their data show that the images' fractal dimension was not constant over all scales but rather only over ranges of scale. These data might be naively interpreted as indicating that these textures are not fractal, however, such an interpretation is incorrect.

As observed earlier, physical processes do not typically act at all possible scales but rather only over a *range* of scales. Thus, we should expect that a physical surface (and thus its image) will change its fractal characteristics when we pass from a range of scales dominated by one formative process to a range of scales that was shaped in a different manner. It is this realization that real surfaces will be fractal over ranges of scale, rather than fractal over all scales, that prompted the careful inclusion of *limited* ranges of scale in this papers' definition of 2-D and 3-D fractal surfaces. The ranges of constant fractal dimension observed in the Peleg et al. data, therefore, are consistent with (and provide independent confirmation of) the fractal surface model.

A. The Relationship Between Fractals and Regular Patterns

Fractal Brownian functions do not, of course, describe regular or large-scale spatial structures such as are seen in the image of a brick wall or a tiled floor. Such structures must be accounted for by other means. It is important to realize, however, that while fractal Brownian surfaces are required to have particular second-order statistics, this does not mean that they cannot be regularly patterned.

To understand this, consider that the probability of a random number generator producing the string "1010..." is exactly the same as the probability of any other particular string with half 1's, half 0's. Both strings have the same statistics, and thus the same probability of occurrence, although one is regularly patterned and the other is not. Similarly, a surface such as a brick wall can be a perfectly good Brownian fractal: the overall distribution of second-order statistics is correct; it simply contains position-dependent patterns.

The fact that fractal Brownian functions can exhibit regularities allows us to smoothly pass from random chaotic surfaces to regular patterned ones within the same conceptual framework [16]. Regular surfaces, for instance, can be generated by adding constraints (patterning) to the random-number generator used in conjunction with computer graphics techniques for recursively generating fractal Brownian functions [9].

B. Detection of Edge Points

It is an important characteristic of the fractal model that we can determine its appropriateness for particular image data because this allows us to know when, and when not, to use the model. If we discover an image region that does not fit the fractal model, Proposition 4 allows us to infer that we are not viewing a homogeneous fractal surface.

Boundaries between homogeneous regions are one example of a physical configuration that does not fit well into the fractal model. Thus, when we examine points that lie on the boundary between two image regions we find that the fit between the fractal model and the image data is normally poor. The fact that boundaries seem to be the most common event giving rise to a nonfractal intensity surface provides a method of detecting image points that are likely to be edges.

One simple way to find such points is examination of the computed fractal dimension. It turns out that when we compute the fractal dimension of a region covering a boundary between two homogeneous areas, by using the regions's Fourier power spectrum,[9] we normally calculate a fractal dimension that is less than the topological dimension. As this is a physical impossibility, the implication is that the assumptions of the fractal model are inappropriate for that specific image data. When we observe a measured fractal dimension that is less than the topological dimension, therefore, we can reasonably expect that we have found a texture edge. Examples of this will be shown in the following sections.

IV. INFERRING SURFACE PROPERTIES

Fractal functions appear to provide a good description of natural surface textures and their images; thus, it is natural to use the fractal model for image segmentation, texture classification, shape-from-texture, and the estimation of 3-D roughness from image data. It is also natural to inquire into the relationship between the fractal surface model and the various other models of shape and texture that have previously been reported. This section, consequently, describes the research performed in these areas.

A. Examples of Image Segmentation

Proposition 1 tells us that, within a homogeneous region, the fractal dimension in the image is dependent upon that of the 3-D surface, thus giving us a technique for inferring a 3-D property of the viewed surface that closely corresponds to people's concept of roughness/smoothness. This suggests that measurement of the fractal dimension in the image will be useful in segmenting natural imagery.

Fig. 4(a) shows an aerial view of San Francisco Bay. This image was digitized and the fractal dimension computed for each 8 × 8 block of pixels by means of the Fourier technique, i.e., the parameter H was estimated by a least-squares regression of the Fourier-domain fractal definition onto the power spectrum of the block of pixels.[9] Orientational information was not incorporated into measurement of the local fractal dimension, i.e., differences in dimension among various image directions at a point were collapsed into one average measurement. Fig. 4(b) shows a histogram of the fractal dimensions computed over the whole image.[10]

This histogram of fractal dimension was then broken at the "valleys" between the modes of the histogram, and the image segmented into pixel neighborhoods belonging to one mode or another. Fig. 4(c) shows the segmentation obtained by thresholding at the breakpoint indicated by the arrow under (b); each pixel in (c) corresponds to an 8 × 8 block of pixels in the original image. As can be seen, a good segmentation into water and land was achieved—one that cannot be obtained by thresholding on image intensity.

Proposition 3 indicates that this segmentation should be stable over transformations of scale. To test this prediction, the image was averaged down, from 512 × 512 pixels to 256 × 256 and 128 × 128 pixel images, and the fractal dimension recomputed for each of the reduced images. Fig. 4(d) and (e) illustrate the segmentations produced by using the same breakpoint as had been employed in the original full-resolution segmentation. These results, therefore, demonstrate the stability of the fractal dimension measure across wide (4:1) variations in scale, as predicted by Proposition 3.

---

[9]That is, since the power spectrum $P(f)$ is proportional to f^{-2H-1}, we may use a linear regression on the log of the observed power spectrum as a function of f(e.g., a regression using $\log(P(f)) = -(2H+1)\log(f) + k$ for various values of f) to determine the power H and thus the fractal dimension.

[10]The values to the left of the large spike in (b) have a computed fractal dimension that is less than the topological dimension; thus, these points are likely caused by patches that cross distinct regional boundaries; in fact, they all occur along the water-land boundary and delineate that boundary.

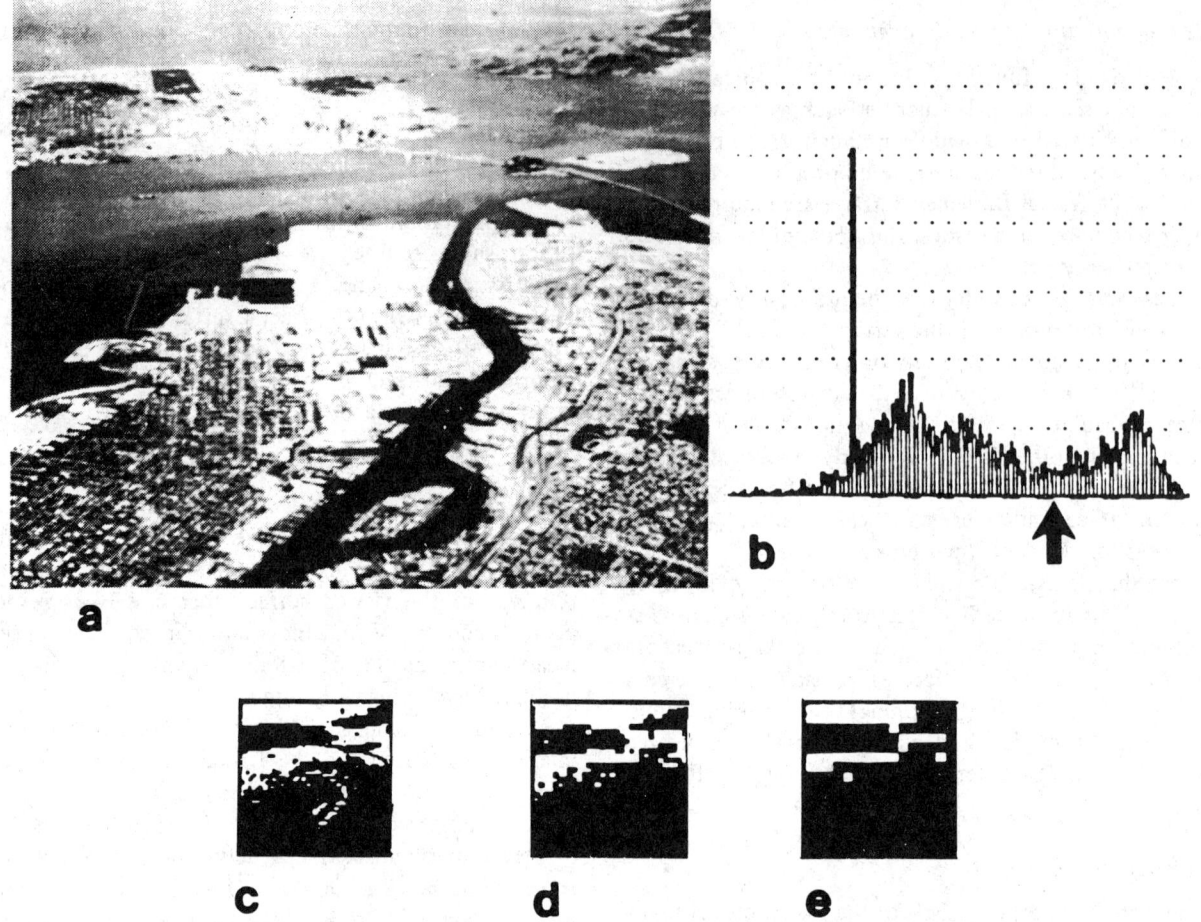

Fig. 4. San Francisco Bay.

Fig. 5(a) shows a view of Mount Dawn. This image was digitized into 512 × 512 pixels and the fractal dimension computed as before; (b) shows a histogram of the computed fractal dimension. Arrows at the bottom of (b) show where the distribution of fractal dimension was broken to produce a segmentation of the image. Fig. 5(c) shows the image segmented into two classes (land; snow-and-sky) at the first histogram breakpoint. Fig. 5(d) shows the sky separated from the land and snow by the second histogram breakpoint. Taken together, (c) and (d) demonstrate a good segmentation into mountain, snow, and sky. Note that the distinction between snow and sky is very subtle; it is impressive that this fine of a separation can be made by use of a simple image-wide histogram of roughnesses.

This image was also averaged down to 256 × 256, 128 × 128, and 64 × 64 pixel images, and the fractal dimension recomputed for each of the reduced images. Fig. 5(e)–6(j) illustrate the segmentations that result from using the same cut points as were employed in the original, full-resolution segmentation; it can be seen that the segmentations in these figures are quite similar, again demonstrating the stability of the fractal description across wide (8:1) variations in scale.

Images of smooth, man-made surfaces can also be usefully segmented, as shown in Fig. 6. Fog. 6(a) shows a picture of a mug and, just behind it, a chairback. This image was digitized into 256 × 256 pixels and the fractal dimension computed; (b) is a histogram of the computed fractal dimensions with the breakpoint indicated by an arrow. Fig. 6(c) shows the image segmented into two classes at the point indicated by arrow 1. A good partial segmentation results.[11] Fig. 6(d) illustrates the points whose computed fractal dimension is less than the topological dimension [the points to the left of arrow 2 in (b)], as expected, these are edge points.

One final example is the desert scene shown in Fig. 7(a). This scene was segmented into three classes based on the histogram shown in (b); the segmentations are shown in (c) (road and sky versus desert) and (d) (road and desert versus sky). As can be seen, there is a good segmentation into desert, road, and sky.

Several other images have been segmented in this manner and, in each case, a good segmentation was achieved. The computed fractal dimension (and thus the segmentation) was always stable over at least 4:1 variations in scale; most segmentations were stable over a range of 8:1.

Stability of the fractal description is to be expected because the fractal dimension of the image is directly related to the fractal dimension of the viewed surface, which is a property of 3-D natural surfaces that is typically stable with respect to transformations of scale [8]. The fact that the fractal descrip-

[11] Nor can this segmentation be achieved by thresholding on intensity values.

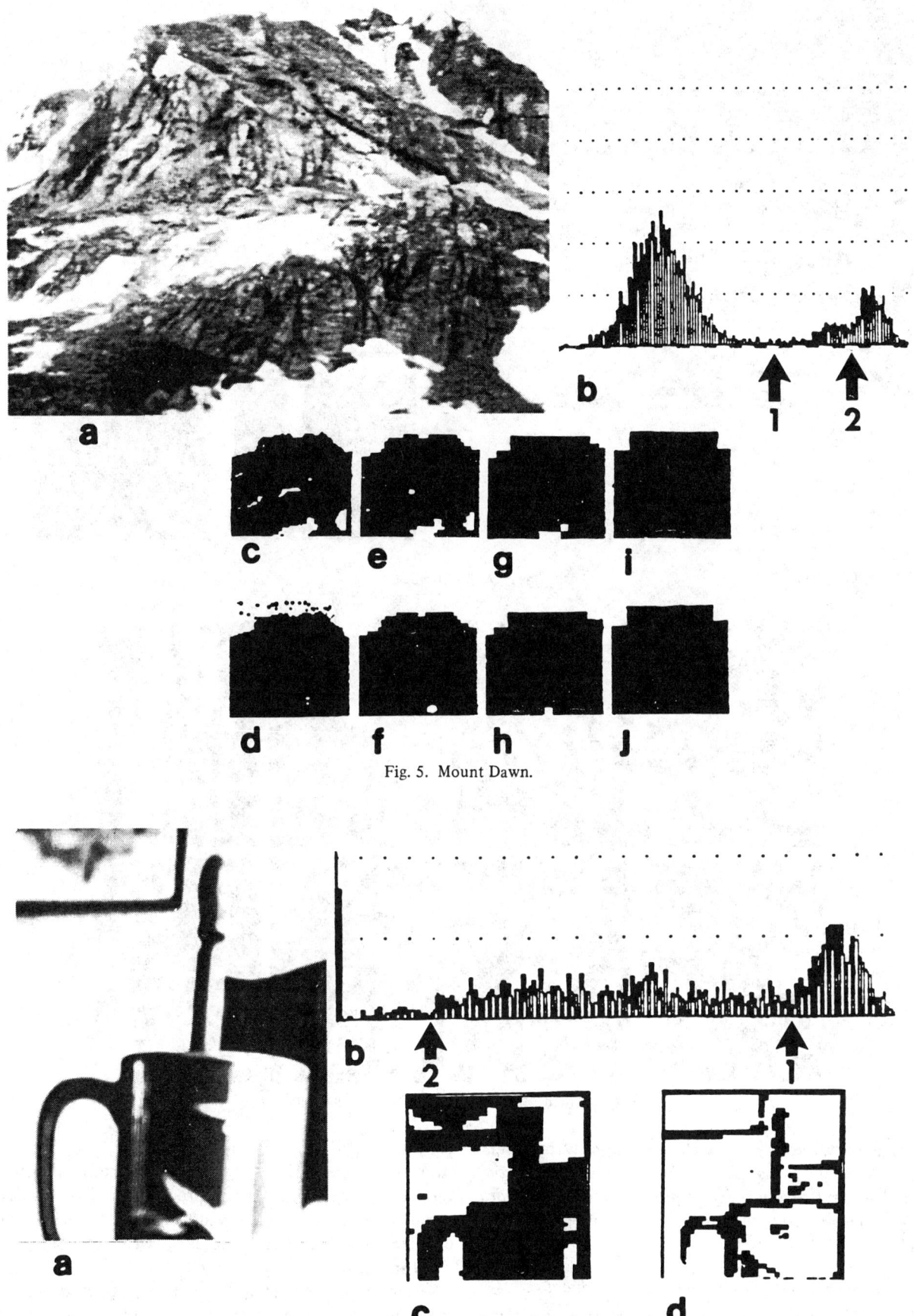

Fig. 5. Mount Dawn.

Fig. 6. A picture of a mug.

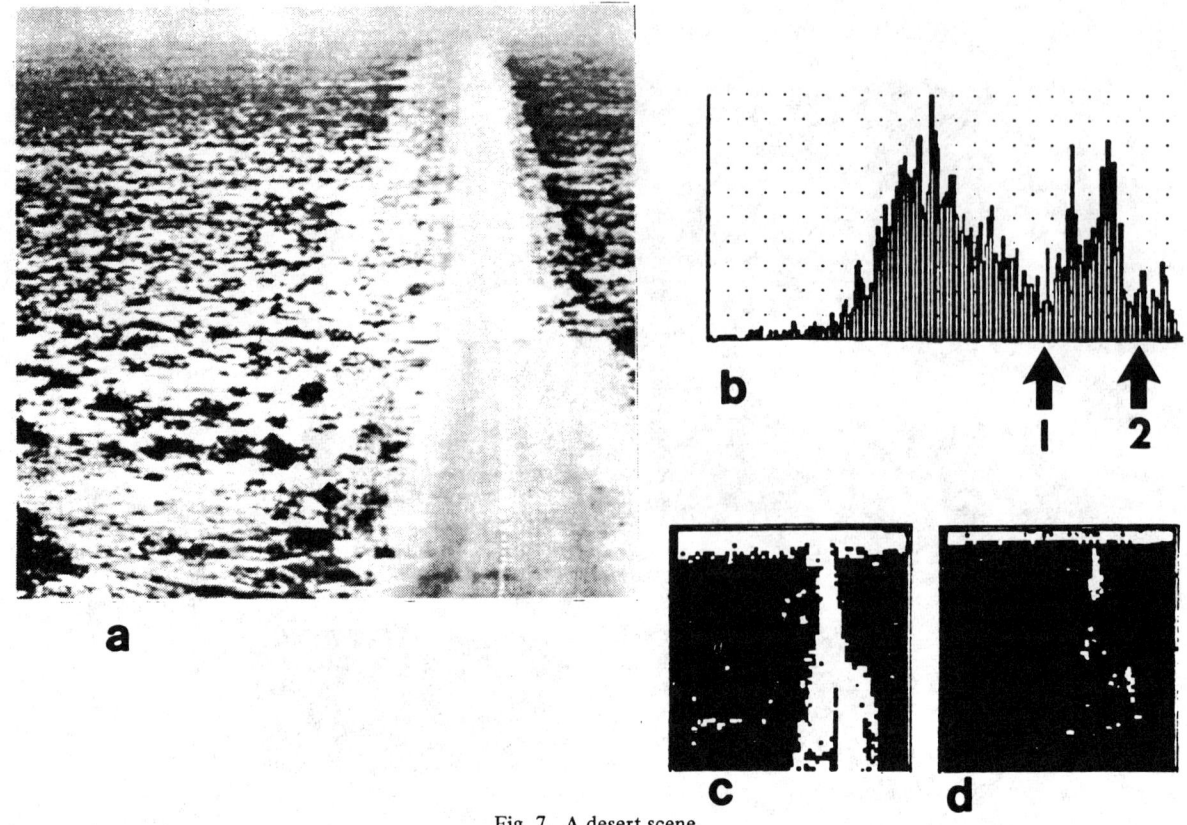

Fig. 7. A desert scene.

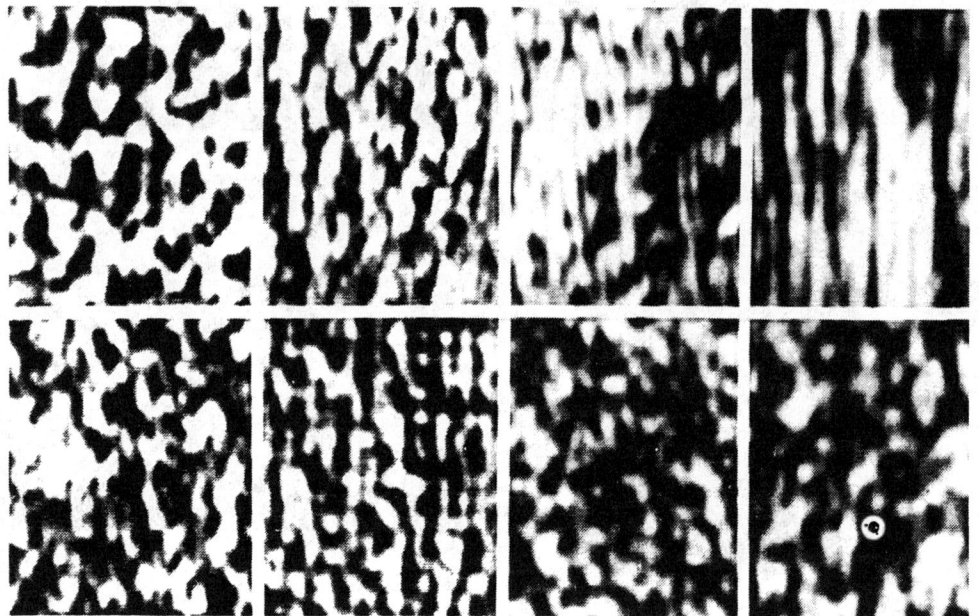

Fig. 8. The Brodatz textures used for comparison.

tion is stable with respect to scale is a critically important property. After all, let us consider: *how can we hope to compute a stable, viewer-independent representation of the world if our information about the world is not stable with respect to scale?*

B. Comparison to Established Segmentation Techniques

To obtain an objective comparison to established segmentation techniques, a mosaic of eight images of natural surfaces [15] was digitized. The mosaic, shown in Fig. 8, was constructed by Laws [17], [18] for the purpose of comparing various texture segmentation procedures. The images that comprise this data set were chosen to be as visually similar as possible; gross statistical differences were removed by mean-value and histogram-equalization.

Segmentation performance on these data exists for several techniques and, although differences in digitization complicate any comparisons we might wish to make, Laws' performance figures nevertheless serve as a useful yardstick for assessing performance on these data.

For this comparison, simple orientational information was incorporated into the fractal description; the fractal dimension was calculated separately along the x and y image directions. Fractal dimension was estimated, by using (5), within five 16 × 16 pixel nonoverlapping subregions extracted from each of the eight regions. These data were next used to estimate the mean and variance of fractal dimension in the x and y directions, and theoretical classification probabilities were then computed.

The two-parameter fractal segmenter yielded a classification accuracy of 84.4 percent. This performance compares quite favorably to other segmentation techniques—despite the much larger number of texture features employed by these alternative methods. For example, Laws [17] reports accuracies of 65 percent for correlation statistics [19], [20], 72 percent for cooccurrence statistics [21], [22], and a theoretical accuracy of 87.4 percent for texture energy statistics.[12] The results of this comparison, therefore, indicate that fractal-based segmentation will likely prove a general and powerful technique.[13]

C. Shape Estimates

There are two ways surface shape is reflected in image patterning: 1) projection foreshortening, a function of the angle between the viewer and the surface normal, and 2) perspective gradients, which are due to increasing distance between the viewer and the surface. These two phenomena are independent in that they have separate causes. Thus, they can serve to confirm each other, i.e., if projection foreshortening is used to estimate surface tilt, that estimate is *independently confirmed* if there is a perspective gradient of the proper magnitude and same direction [6], [25]. We may be confident our estimate is correct when such independent confirmation is found.

The fractal dimension found in the image, by virtue of its independence with respect to scale, appears to be nearly independent of the orientation of the surface. Fractal dimension, therefore, cannot be used to measure projection foreshortening. Projection foreshortening does, however, affect the variance of the distribution $F(y)$ associated with the fractal dimension (see Proposition 2) in the same manner in which it affects the distribution of tangent direction. Thus, to estimate surface orientation, we might assume that the surface's structure is isotropic and estimate surface orientation on the basis of previously derived shape-from-contour and shape-from-texture results [5], [6].

This estimation technique often works; for instance, a vertical tilt and 45° slant was estimated for the image in Fig. 4, and a vertical tilt and 47° slant was estimated for the upper portion of the image in Fig. 7. The necessity of assuming isotropy, however, is a serious shortcoming of this technique—for, when the assumption is wrong, the estimate may be very much in error.

An important new result, therefore, is that we may partially cure this problem by observing the fractal dimensions in the x and y directions. If they are unequal we have *prima facie* evidence of anisotropy in the surface, because fractal dimension is largely unaffected by projection.

Regardless of how a foreshortening-derived estimate of surface orientation is produced, we may still seek confirmation of it by measuring the perspective gradient; if confirmation is found, we may be confident of our estimate. Such a gradient appears in Fig. 4: the houses dwindle in size with increasing distance from the viewer.

Fig. 9(a) and (b) shows relief plots of the fractal dimension computed from Fig. 4(a) and 7(a), respectively. In Fig. 9(a) and (b) the x and y axes correspond to the horizontal and vertical directions in Fig. 4(a) and 7(a); i.e., they are viewed as if from the left-hand side of the original images. The z axis shows the computed fractal dimension for each 8 × 8 block of pixels.

In both of these examples there is a gradual rise in the estimated fractal dimension with increasing distance. We can track this effect of perspective foreshortening and thus observe the perspective gradient.

It is at first somewhat puzzling to observe the fractal dimension changing with increasing distance, for fractal dimension is stable with respect to changes in scale. What we are in fact observing in these examples in interaction between our sampling rate and the range of scales over which the fractal approximation is valid (see Section II-A).

Real surfaces are not fractal at all scales; there are smallest and largest components to their shape (e.g., grain size and region size). These largest and smallest components define the limits between which the surface can be described with a single fractal function. When the projected size of a pixel becomes comparable to either of these limits, the fractal approximation can break down. If the pixel size is large with respect to the largest shape components, we observe the familiar Nyquist sampling behavior: the surface appears to become smoother as the pixel size is increased. When the pixel size is less than the smallest shape components, we observe "texture" edges, i.e., inhomogeneities in the shape structure.

By observing the limits within which the fractal approximation holds,[14] we measure a property intrinsic to the surface: the range of scales over which the surface obeys the fractal rule. Because such measurement is in terms of pixel size, it relates the size of the projected pixel relative to the (presumably invariant) size distribution of the surface's shape components. Measuring the largest scale at which a single fractal rule holds, therefore, gives us the ratio between pixel size and an aspect of the surfaces' intrinsic structure and thus allows us to observe the perspective gradient.

---

[12] See [17, p. 148].

[13] On a data set of 12 Brodatz textures, in which the textures were somewhat less similar, the classification accuracy was 87.6 percent. Following initial report of this work [14], Peleg *et al.* [27] investigated other techniques for calculating fractal dimension and have reported essentially 100 percent accuracy on similar Brodatz textures, by using separate estimates of fractal dimension at many different scales. This allowed them to incorporate information about Δx_{min} and Δx_{max}, the limits at which the textures behave as a single fractal, and thus to improve their classification accuracy.

[14] By use of (5). Also see Peleg *et al.* [27], which describes an alternate fractal-dimension technique for discovery of these scale limits.

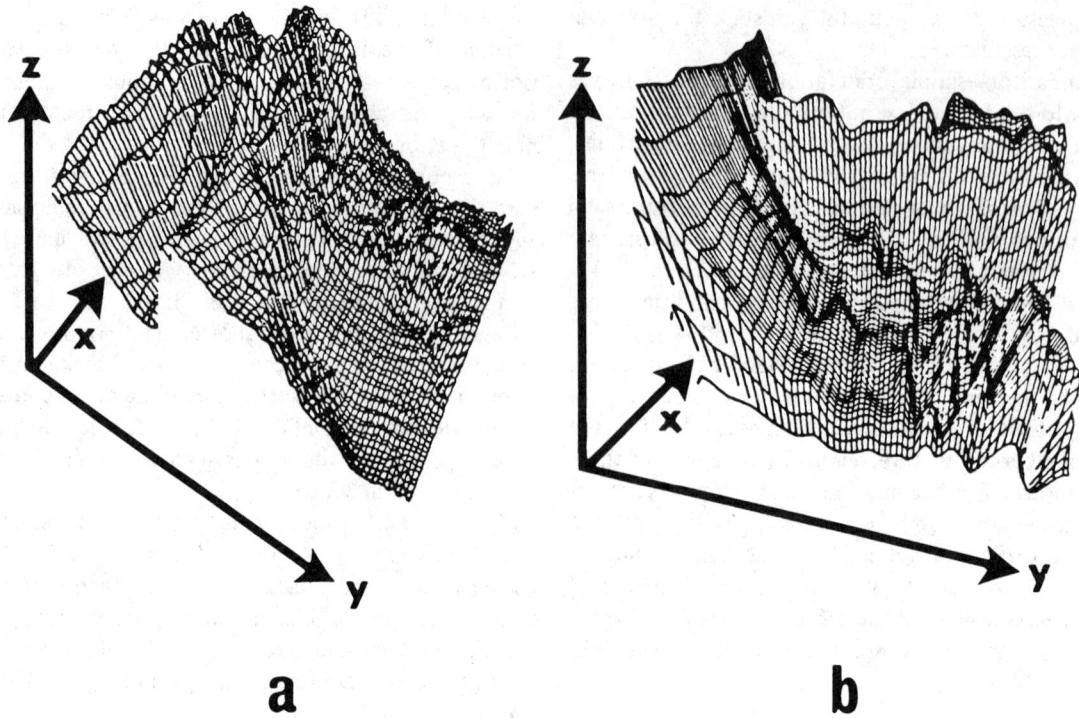

Fig. 9. Relief plots of the computed fractal dimension for Figs. 4(a) and 7(a).

In Fig. 9 we are measuring the size of the surface's largest shape components by using the fact that the apparent smoothness of the viewed surface increases with increasing size of the projected pixel, given that the pixels' projected size is comparable to that of the surface's largest shape components. Measurements of fractal dimension may thus be used to measure the perspective gradient, thereby providing independent confirmation of the foreshortening-derived estimates of surface orientation. In imagery of large planar regions it may also be possible to use the magnitude of the perspective gradient to estimate the surface's orientation.

Note, however, that in Fig. 9(b) the portion of the image closest to the viewer does not exhibit a smooth gradient because the size of the region used to compute the fractal dimension was small relative to the size of the rocks and bushes. In this near area the image data used to compute fractal dimension are often *boundaries* between homogeneous areas, and therefore do not fit the fractal model. As described previously, the appropriateness of the fractal model may be determined for the specific image data under consideration. In the case of the image in Fig. 7(a), the fractal model is inappropriate for much of the data in the near portion of the image. Thus, most of the apparent "perspective gradients" in the near portion of Fig. 9(b) can be identified as artifacts.

These two new results—the ability to obtain evidence of surface anisotropy and the measurement of the perspective gradient—represent significant advances in shape estimation because they offer a way to substantially improve the reliability of shape-from-foreshortening [5], [6] techniques.

D. Shading into Texture

Fractal functions with $H \approx 0$ do not change their statistics as a function of scale. Such surfaces are planar except for random variations described by the function $F(y)$ in (1); e.g., they are stationary. Because these surfaces are judged by people to be "smooth"[15] the fractal model with small values of H is appropriate for modeling smooth, shaded regions of the image. In contrast, fractals with $H > 0$ are not perceived as smooth, but rather as rough or textured.

The fractal model can therefore encompass both image shading and texture, with shading as a limiting case in the spectrum of texture granularity.[16] The fractal model thus allows us to make a reasonable, rigorous, and perceptually plausible definition of the categories "texture" and "shading" in terms that can be measured by using the image data.

The ability to differentiate between "smooth" and "rough" surfaces is critical to the performance of such techniques as shape-from-shading [3], [4], [26], surface interpolation [4], and shape-from-texture [5], [6]—to mention only the obvious cases. Thus, use of the fractal model to infer qualitative 3-D shape, i.e., smoothness/roughness, has the potential to significantly improve the utility of many other machine vision methods.

E. Relationship to 2-D Texture Models

One of the more interesting aspects of the fractal surface model is that it relates 2-D texture measures based on co-

---

[15] The surface may, however, have significant local fluctuations: these are usually seen as "dust" or some other extraneous effect modifying the smooth surface. It may also be that beyond some limiting value of the variance of $F(y)$ the surface is no longer perceived as smooth.

[16] If we assume that incident light is reflected at the angle of incidence and we make the variance of $F(y)$ small relative to the pixel size, the surface will be mirrorlike. If, on the other hand, the variance of $F(y)$ is large relative to the pixel size, the surface will become more isotropically reflecting. Thus, we can use the fractal model to capture the intuitive notion that reflectance functions are due to the structure of the microtexture.

occurrence statistics [21], [22], Fourier spectra [23]–[25], Markov processes [13], or autocorrelation [19], [20] to each other and to 3-D surface structure.

We have seen that fractal Brownian functions may be defined in terms of either the way interpixel differences (second-order statistics) change with distance, or the rate at which the Fourier power spectrum falls off with increasing frequency. Similarly, fractal functions may be characterized by the way the autocorrelation function falls off [7], [10], or by Markov processes [10], [13]. Because the fractal image of a 3-D fractal surface may be described in any of these terms, it follows that for fractal images we may relate each of these texture measures to the other and to the 3-D fractal surface model. The fractal surface model, therefore, offers the potential of unifying and simplifying these various 2-D texture descriptions, as well as the possibility of interpreting them in terms of the 3-D structure of the world.

To say that the fractal model can be described in these other terms in not to say that the fractal model is equivalent to these other models: the fractal model is clearly a 3-D model, whereas the texture models are only 2-D. Further, although it is true that a fractal function can be characterized in terms of Fourier spectra, co-occurrence matrices, etc., it is not true that any characterization of an image in these terms captures the 3-D properties of the viewed surface, as is the case with the fractal description. Characterization of an image in terms of radial slices of the Fourier domain (for instance) is completely orthogonal to the fractal description and, as a result, constrains the shape of the 3-D surface hardly at all.[17] As a consequence, we cannot expect the image segmentation performance of these texture techniques to be generally indicative of the performance of the fractal surface model.

One may still ask, since we can "translate" the fractal surface model into these various texture descriptions, why should one employ the fractal model rather than some other? The principal advantage of describing textures in terms of fractal surfaces, rather than in any of these other vocabularies, is that it allows us to capture a simple physical relationship that underlies the texture structure; a relationship that allows us to interpret the 2-D texture measurements in terms of the 3-D world. The fact that this physical interpretation can be lost with the 2-D characterizations of texture makes it seem advantageous to characterize texture problems in terms of the 3-D fractal surface model.

F. Relationship to Human Texture Perception

In light of the fact that the fractal surface model has been shown to predict peoples' perception of 3-D roughness (see Section II), it is worth examining the relationship between the fractal surface model and models of human texture perception.

The most widely-known model of human texture perception is due to Julesz [30] who suggested that preattentive texture perception is dependent upon the global second-order statistics of the texture. Although this suggestion is now known to be wrong, Gagalowicz [31] has presented evidence that the problems with Julesz's conjecture are obviated by making texture discrimination dependent upon only the *local* second-order statistics. Others, such as Richards and Polit [32], have presented evidence that texture perception is mediated by spatial-frequency tuned channels.

It turns out that both the second-order statistics and the Fourier models fit well with the notion that people use the fractal dimension of the image (and thus of the 3-D surface) in preattentive discrimination of unpatterned textures. That the fractal surface model and these perceptual models complement each other is not so surprising, for we have already described how to measure the images' fractal dimension either by use of the local second-order statistics[7] or the Fourier power spectrum.[9]

Let us look first at Gagalowicz's model of texture perception, and for the sake of argument let us assume that discrimination between unpatterned texture is based on the perceived roughness of the corresponding 3-D surface. In this case the fractal surface model agrees with Gagalowicz's claim that texture discrimination will be dependent the local second-order statistics—as these determine the images' roughness (i.e., its fractal dimension) and thus the roughness of the 3-D surface.

Similarly, because the images' fractal dimension can also be measured from its Fourier power spectrum, the image and surface roughness (fractal dimension) can be determined by use of spatial frequency channels. Thus, the suggestion that spatial frequency channels mediate human texture perception also agrees with the fractal surface model and the assumption that preattentive texture discrimination depends on perceived roughness.

V. SUMMARY

Fractal functions seem to provide a good model for describing the rough, crenulated, and crumpled 3-D surfaces typical of natural scenes. The evidence in support of this assertion is the following:

1) Many basic physical processes produce fractal surfaces.
2) Fractal surfaces *look* like natural surfaces, and thus appear to capture all of the shape structure relevant to human perception.
3) We have conducted a survey of natural imagery and found that a fractal model of imaged 3-D surfaces, when transformed by the image formation process, furnishes an accurate description of both textured and shaded regions in most natural imagery.

Fractal functions, therefore, are useful for describing the complex 3-D surfaces typical of natural objects. By transforming this 3-D model through the image formation process we can obtain a useful model of how such surfaces appear in the image data. One important aspect of this model is that it is easy to test its appropriateness for particular image data.

Characterization of image texture by means of a 3-D fractal surface model has shed considerable light on the physical basis for several of the 2-D texture techniques currently in use, and made it possible to describe image texture in a manner that is stable over transformations of scale and linear transforms of intensity. These properties of the fractal surface model allow

---

[17]Illumination effects can account for most variation in such a description. In general, a description in these other terms will constrain the 3-D interpretation only to the extent that the description allows recovery of the image's fractal parameters.

it to serve as the basis for an accurate image segmentation procedure that is similarly stable over a wide range of scales.

Because fractal dimension is not affected by projection distortion, its measurement can significantly enhance our ability to estimate shape from foreshortening. Specifically, measurement of fractal dimension can provide 1) evidence of surface anisotropy, and 2) an estimate of the perspective gradient. Both capabilities are extremely important because they provide a way to obtain independent confirmation of the assumptions on which previously reported techniques are based.

One further important result is that measurement of the 2-D image fractal dimension enables estimation of the 3-D fractal dimension. Knowledge of the 3-D fractal dimension has been shown to be a nearly perfect predictor of people's perception of roughness. Thus, the 3-D fractal model allows us to determine which imaged regions are perceived as smooth, and which ones appear textured. This discrimination is of special importance to shape-from-shading, shape-from-texture, and surface interpolation methods as their performance relies on assumptions about the smoothness or roughness of the viewed surface.

The encouraging progress that has already been achieved in research on these problems augers well for the fractal-based approach. It appears that the 3-D fractal model of surface shape will constitute a significant aid in efforts to proceed from the image of a natural scene to its description.

Acknowledgment

The author would like to thank K. Laws for his expertise and advice, M. Fischler and A. Witkin for their feedback, and A. Hanson for getting me interested in fractals in the first place.

References

[1] H. G. Barrow and J. M. Tenenbaum, "Recovering intrinsic scene characteristics from images," in *Computer Vision Systems*, A. Hanson and E. Riseman, Eds. New York: Academic, 1978.

[2] B. K. P. H. Horn, "Shape from shading: A method for obtaining the shape of a smooth opaque object from one view," Project MAC, A. I. Tech. Rep. 79, 1970.

[3] B. K. P. H. Horn and K. Ikeuchi, "Numerical shape from shading and occluding boundaries," *Artifical Intelligence*, Special Issue on Computer Vision, vol. 15, pp. 141-184, 1981.

[4] W. E. L. Grimson, "Computing shape using a theory of human stereo vision," Ph.D. dissertation, Dep. Mathematics, Massachussetts Inst. Technol., Cambridge, MA, 1980.

[5] J. R. Kender, "Shape from texture: An aggregation transform that maps a class of textures into surface orientation," *Proc. Sixth Int. Joint Conf. Artificial Intell.*, Tokyo, Japan, 1979.

[6] A. P. Witkin, "Recovering surface shape and orientation from texture," *Artificial Intelligence*, vol. 17, pp. 17-47, 1981.

[7] B. B. Mandelbrot, *Fractals: Form, Chance and Dimension*. San Francisco, CA: Freeman, 1977.

[8] L. F. Richardson, "The problem of contiguity: An appendix of statistics of deadly quarrels," *General Systems Yearbook*, vol. 6, pp. 139-187, 1961.

[9] A. Fournier, D. Fussel, and L. Carpenter, "Computer rendering of stochastic models," *Commun. ACM*, vol. 25, no. 6, pp. 371-384, 1982.

[10] B. B. Mandelbrot, *The Fractal Geometry of Nature*. San Francisco, CA: Freeman, 1982.

[11] A. Norton, "Generation and display of geometric fractals in 3-D," *Comput. Graphics*, vol. 16, no. 3, pp. 61-67, 1982.

[12] Y. Kawaguchi, "A morphological study of the form of nature," *Comput. Graphics*, vol. 16, no. 3 pp. 223-232, 1982.

[13] L. C. Carpenter, "Vol libre," computer-generated movie, 1980.

[14] A. Pentland, "Fractal-based description of natural scenes," in *Proc. IEEE Conf. Comput. Vision and Pattern Recognition '83*, Arlington, VA, July 1983. See also, A. Pentland, "Fractal-based description," in *Proc. Int. Joint Conf. Artificial Intel. '83*, Karlsruhe, Germany, Aug. 1983.

[15] P. Brodatz, *Textures: A Photographic Album for Artistis and Designers*. New York: Dover, 1966.

[16] T. Pavlidis, personal communication.

[17] K. Laws, "Textured image segmentation," USC Image Processing Institute, Los Angeles, CA, Rep. 940, 1980.

[18] D. H. Ballard and C. M. Brown, *Computer Vision*. Englewood Cliffs, NJ: Prentice-Hall, 1982.

[19] W. K. Pratt, O. D. Faugeras, and A. Gagalowicz, "Visual discrimination of stochastic texture," *IEEE Trans. Syst., Man, Cybern.*, vol SMC-8, pp. 460-473, 1978.

[20] K. Deguchi and I. Morishita, "Texture characterization and texture-based image partitioning using two-dimensional linear estimation techniques," *IEEE Trans Comput.*, vol C-27, pp. 739-745, 1978.

[21] A. Rosenfeld and E. B. Troy, "Visual texture analysis," in *IEEE Conf. Feature Extraction and Analysis*, Argonne, IL, pp. 115-124, Oct 1970.

[22] R. M. Haralick, K. Shanmugam, and J. Dinstein, "Textural features for image classification," *IEEE Trans. Syst., Man, Cybern.*, vol. SMC-3, pp. 610-621, 1973.

[23] R. Bajacsy and L. Lieberman, "Computer description of real outdoor scenes," in *Proc. 2nd Int. Joint Conf. Pattern Recognition*, Copenhagen, Denmark, Aug 1974, pp. 174-179.

[24] H. Maurer, "Texture analysis with Fourier series," in *Proc. 9th Int. Sympo. Remote Sensing of the Environment*, Ann Arbor, MI, Apr. 1974, pp 1411-1420.

[25] R. Bajacsy and L. Lieberman, "Texture gradient as a depth cue," *Comput. Graphics Image Processing*, vol. 5, no. 1, pp 52-67, 1976.

[26] A. P. Pentland, "Local Computation Of Shape," in *Proc. Nat. Conf. Artifical Intell.*, Pittsburgh, PA 1982.

[27] S. Peleg et al., Univ. Maryland, College Park, MD, Dep. Comput. Sci., TR-1306. July, 1983.

[28] J. M. Rubin and W. A. Richards, "Color vision and image intensities: When Are changes material?," *Biol. Cyber.*, vol, 45, pp. 215-226, 1982.

[29] H. Tamura, S. Mori, and T. Yamawaki, "Textural features corresponding to visual perception," *IEEE Trans. Syst., Man, Cybern*, vol. SMC-8, pp. 460-473, June 1978.

[30] B. Julesz, "Texture and visual perception," *Sci. Am.*, vol. 212, pp. 38-48, 1965.

[31] A. Gagalowicz, "A new method for texture fields synthesis: Some applications to the study of human vision," *IEEE Trans. Pattern Anal. Machine Intell.*, vol. PAMI-3, pp. 520-533, Sept. 1981.

[32] W. Richards and A. Polit, "Texture matching," *Kybernetik*, vol. 16, pp. 155-162, 1974.

Alex P. Pentland, for a photograph and biography, see p. 187 of the March 1984 issue of this Transactions.

Image Segmentation and Image Models

AZRIEL ROSENFELD AND LARRY S. DAVIS

Abstract—This paper discusses image segmentation techniques from the standpoint of the assumptions that an image should satisfy in order for a particular technique to be applicable to it. These assumptions, which are often not stated explicitly, can be regarded as (perhaps informal) "models" for classes of images. The paper emphasizes two basic classes of models: *statistical* models that describe the pixel population in an image or region, and *spatial* models that describe the decomposition of an image into regions.

I. INTRODUCTION

THIS SEMITUTORIAL paper discusses image segmentation techniques from the standpoint of the assumptions that an image should satisfy in order for a particular technique to be applicable to it. These assumptions, which are often not stated explicitly, can be regarded as "models" for classes of images. The paper emphasizes two basic classes of such models: *statistical* models that describe the pixel population in an image or region, and *spatial* models that describe the decomposition of an image into regions.

Most image analysis systems deal with specific classes of images, e.g., photomicrographs of blood cells or satellite TV images of cloud cover. Ideally, the design of techniques for segmenting such images should make use of specialized knowledge about the given class of scenes, e.g., knowledge based on hematology, meteorology, etc., as well as about the image acquisition system that was used—microscope, TV camera, etc. In practice, however, most image segmentation techniques are designed to be relatively general purpose, i.e., applicable to a wide class of images. Examples of such techniques include thresholding and spectral signature classification, region growing, edge detection, border following, template matching, etc. A review of these and other segmentation techniques can be found in [1, ch. 8].

Although these standard segmentation techniques are fairly widely applicable, it is not always obvious, given a class of images, which of them are applicable to that class. In fact, the applicability of a given technique depends on the image satisfying a particular set of assumptions; but these assumptions are often not explicitly stated. Our goal in this paper is to discuss the assumptions that underlie various basic segmentation techniques, and the resultant constraints on the types of images to which these techniques are applicable.

We will consider in this paper only relatively low-level segmentation techniques, such as those listed earlier, that make decisions about image points or small sets of points on the basis of properties of the points themselves, or of their neighborhoods, or of their spatial arrangement. We will not consider hierarchical (e.g., syntactic) segmentation schemes here. We will also restrict ourselves to images of essentially two-dimensional scenes—e.g., terrain seen from satellites, radiographs, photomicrographs, etc.; this will allow us to treat two-dimensional image models without having to consider three-dimensional scene models or be concerned with the process of projecting three dimensions onto two.

Image models have many uses in image processing and analysis; for example, they can be used for image synthesis, for the design of optimal enhancement or restoration algorithms, for shape or texture description, etc. In this paper we will consider only their relationship to image segmentation.

Most of the image models that have been investigated are relatively simple, and do not provide adequate descriptions of real images. We will attempt to indicate, at various points, directions in which further work is needed in developing more realistic classes of models. We will also cite a number of papers in which image models are used, either implicitly or explicitly; but these references are not intended to be complete.

Section II deals with models that describe an image's gray-level population, while Section III treats models that describe an image in terms of regions.[1] For any given image model we may consider the following questions:
 a) how does one use the model to predict the performance of a given segmentation technique?
 b) how should one design a segmentation technique to take the greatest possible advantage of the information that the model gives about the images?
We will address these questions primarily on an informal level.

II. STATISTICAL MODELS

The models considered in this section are basically statistical in nature; they describe the pixel population and its spatial distribution. We assume here, for the most part, that the image is black-and-white, so that each pixel has a single gray-level value. The generalization to color or multispectral images will also be briefly discussed.

Image texture is often described using statistical methods. First-order gray-level statistics describe properties such as lightness and contrast, while higher order statistics of gray levels, or first-order statistics of local properties, can be used to describe properties such as coarseness/busyness or directionality. Textures can thus be modeled in terms of first-order and higher order gray-level probability densities, or of probability densities of local property values. They can also be modeled in terms of two-dimensional random fields

---

Manuscript received May 8, 1978; revised November 17, 1978. This work was supported by the Mathematical and Computer Sciences Division of the National Science Foundation under Grant MCS-76-23763.
 A. Rosenfeld is with the Computer Science Center, University of Maryland, College Park, MD 20742.
 L. S. Davis is with the Computer Science Department, University of Texas, Austin, TX 78712.

[1] The models of Section II may also assume that the image is made up of regions, but they say nothing about the shapes of the regions; at most, the models imply that the regions are big enough to have large interiors, which will give rise to large clusters of, e.g., local property values.

or time series. Models of all of these types will be discussed in this section. Other approaches to texture description, e.g., in terms of the Fourier power spectrum, also deserve mention here, but will not be discussed in detail. For a comprehensive review of texture analysis see the paper by Haralick in this issue.

A. First-Order Models

First-order statistical models describe the pixel population in a class of images without regard to its spatial distribution. The simplest description of this type is provided by the images' gray-level probability density (GLPD). For digital images this is a discrete density; it is a probability vector of the form $\bar{p} = (p_1, \cdots, p_k)$, where k is the number of possible gray levels. Given an image, we can estimate its class GLPD by computing its *gray-level histogram*, which specifies how often each gray level occurs in the image. If the histogram is $\bar{h} = (h_1, \cdots, h_k)$, then $\sum_{i=1}^{k} h_i = A$ is the image area (= total number of pixels), and h_i/A is an estimate of p_i, $1 \leq i \leq k$.

Prior to digitization, the gray level $g(x, y)$ at point (x, y) of an image is proportional to the product of

$i(x, y)$—the illumination incident on point (x, y) in the scene
$r(x, y)$—the reflectivity of that point.

The digitization process samples g, usually by taking a weighted integral over a neighborhood of (x, y), and quantizes the resulting value. A realistic model for the digital image's gray-level population would have to be based on a probabilistic description of illumination and reflectivity and the effects of digitization. In practice, this is not done. (See, however, the work of Horn [2] on the relationship between illumination, surface orientation, and gray level.) Instead, one assumes that the GLPD $\bar{p}$ is a discrete truncated approximation to some standard probability density function, e.g., Gaussian, or to a mixture of such densities. This type of assumption is commonly used in image segmentation by thresholding (see below). A more realistic class of models for $\bar{p}$ would be highly desirable.

Given a model for the GLPD of an image, e.g., a mixture of Gaussians, the only basis that we have for segmenting the image is to classify the pixels using gray level as a feature. If we know the means and standard deviations of the Gaussians, it is straightforward to determine the minimum-error threshold(s) for this classification (see, e.g., [1, sect. 8.1.3]). If we do not know them, but we know how many of them there are supposed to be, say k, we can find a linear combination of k Gaussians that best fits the image's histogram (e.g., [3]) and then find the minimum-error thresholds for these Gaussians. Analogous methods can be used for other simple types of probability densities (PD's).

A number of standard threshold selection techniques have been developed that determine thresholds by analyzing the image's histogram. Perhaps the best known of these is the approach of identifying peaks and valleys on the histogram, and picking thresholds at the bottoms of the valleys. In certain special cases, this is equivalent to minimum-error thresholding, but under more general assumptions, where the components of the mixture have unequal standard deviations or unequal weights, it is not, as discussed in [1, sect. 8.1.2-3]. Given a model for the GLPD, it is straightforward to predict the expected numbers of errors that will be made if the valley-bottom approach is used.

If we know that an image is composed of two types of regions having different GLPD's, we can attempt to detect edges between the regions by comparing the histograms in pairs of adjacent subimages. Here the subimages must be small enough to fit inside the regions, yet large enough to contain adequate numbers of pixels to make the comparison of histograms meaningful. For example, one could use a χ^2 or Kolmogorov-Smirnov test to determine whether the two histograms come from a single population or from different populations; or, if the forms of the GLPD's are known, one could design an appropriate optimal test. Some early examples of this idea can be found in [4]-[6]. Edge detection will be discussed further in Section II-C.

The segmentation techniques discussed in this section can, in principle, be generalized to color or multispectral images. Here the pixels are vector-valued, and we must deal with multivariate PD's, or with sets of univariate PD's. In the case of color, a variety of coordinate systems can be used—e.g., (red, green, blue), (intensity, hue, saturation), etc. It is often assumed that these PD's are of some standard form, such as Gaussian. The use of a set of univariate PD's to segment a color image by recursive thresholding is described in [7]; multivariate decision surfaces can also be used, as indicated in [8]. Pixel classification in the spectral signature feature space is the standard method of segmenting multispectral images in remote sensing; for a review of this subject see, e.g., [9].

B. Higher Order Models

First-order models are quite useful for segmenting many types of images, but they contain very little information about the image. One usually expects an image to be composed of coherent pieces of some sort (texture elements, objects, etc.), but first-order models ignore this completely; the GLPD $\bar{p}$ remains unchanged under arbitrary spatial rearrangement of the pixels. In this subsection we discuss higher order models for the pixel population that take into account spatial relationships among the pixels.

The *nth order GLPD* of a class of images specifies the probability with which every possible n-tuple of gray levels occurs in a given set of relative positions or "displacements." Each such set of displacements is defined by an $(n-1)$-tuple of coordinate pairs $((x_2, y_2), \cdots, (x_n, y_n))$ which specify the coordinates of the last $n-1$ points relative to the first. For each set of displacements, the nth order discrete density is a k^n-tuple of probabilities, one for each of the k^n possible n-tuples of gray levels.

For example, the second order GLPD is a function of a single relative position (x, y), and specifies the probability that each of the k^2 possible pairs of gray levels occurs in that relative position. For a given (x, y), this GLPD is an n-by-n matrix of probabilities p_{ij}, where p_{ij} is the probability that the pair of gray levels (i, j) occurs at the given displacement. Given an image and a displacement, we can estimate the corresponding GLPD by computing a *gray-level cooccurrence matrix*, which specifies how often each pair of gray levels occurs in the image at the given displacement. Let the matrix be

$$C = \begin{pmatrix} C_{11} & \cdots & C_{1k} \\ \vdots & & \vdots \\ C_{k1} & \cdots & C_{kk} \end{pmatrix}$$

then
$$\hat{C} = \sum_{i,j=1}^{k} C_{ij}$$

is the number of point pairs in the image at the given displacement. Note that this is less than the area of the image, since for positions sufficiently near the image border, one of the points in the pair will fall outside the image. Thus $C_{ij}/\hat{C}$ is an estimate of the probability p_{ij}.

In practice, the second and higher order GLPD's are of interest only for relatively small displacements. In fact, as the displacement becomes large, the image gray levels at that displacement become independent of one another, so that in the second-order case the probability p_{ij} reduces to the product $p_i p_j$—or equivalently, the matrix of p_{ij}'s becomes the product of the column vector $\bar{p}$ and row vector $\bar{p}^t$. Thus it is not too cumbersome to specify an estimated second order GLPD by constructing cooccurrence matrices for a small set of displacements.[2] Such matrices are sometimes used to describe textures; see [1, sect. 10.2.1].

Little or no consideration has been given to formulating plausible models for the second or higher order GLPD's of images. A heuristic discussion of the expected form of a gray level cooccurrence matrix, for images composed of dark objects on a light background or vice versa, separated by blurred edges, can be found in [10]. Intuitively, for such images, the cooccurrence matrix for a small displacement should consist of two clusters of high values located near the main diagonal, corresponding to pairs of points interior to the objects and to the background, respectively; these are near the diagonal since two gray levels in the objects or in the background will be close to one another. There should also be higher valued elements representing pairs of intermediate gray levels, corresponding to pairs of points on or near the object/background edges. The form of the clusters, however, is not easy to specify. Realistic models for the cooccurrence matrices of various classes of images would be highly desirable.

If we are given a model for some higher order GLPD, say second order, we can consider classifying the pixels using a set of gray levels, at a pixel and at various neighbors of it, as features. For example, suppose that the second-order GLPD for a given displacement is a mixture of bivariate Gaussians. If we know the means and covariance matrices of these Gaussians, it is straightforward to determine the minimum-error decision surface for classifying a pixel based on the feature vector (z, z'), where z is the gray level of the pixel and z' is that of its neighbor at the given displacement, as belonging to one of the Gaussians. If we do not know the parameters of the Gaussians, but we know how many of them there are supposed to be, we can find a linear combination of Gaussians that best fits the image's cooccurrence matrix for the given displacement, and then determine the decision surfaces for the best-fitting Gaussians.

In [11], n-tuples of gray levels were employed as features for pixel classification, using both a trainable linear classifier and an unsupervised clustering procedure. Local average gray levels were also used as features in some experiments;

[2] Note also that many types of images are isotropic, so that their second order GLPD's depend only on the magnitude of the displacement, not on its direction.

compare Section II-C. The results obtained were reasonable, but little can be said about their optimality in the absence of a good model for the n-dimensional feature space.

In [12], cooccurrence matrices were used to obtain sharpened "gray-level histograms" for images composed of objects on a background by projecting various parts of the matrix onto its main diagonal, thus mapping each feature vector (z, z') into the average gray level $(z + z')/2$. These histograms can then be used to segment the image by thresholding. An alternative might have been to project the matrix onto its principal eigenvector, i.e., to find a linear combination of z and z' that maximizes the discriminability of the clusters. It would be desirable to investigate this approach for various models of the cooccurrence feature space.

Higher order PD's can also be used, in principle, to analyze color or multispectral images; but up to now they have been used primarily for gray-scale images.

C. Models for Local Property Values

An alternative method of describing the spatial relationships that exist among the pixels in a class of images is to use the PD's of the values of various local image properties. For example, suppose that the images have a bimodal GLPD; this means that the images contain a mixture of light and dark pixels, but we cannot tell whether these are randomly mixed together or whether they form large light and dark clumps. If we know the PD of *average gray levels*, for averages taken over neighborhoods of various sizes, we can get some insight into the spatial arrangement of the light and dark pixels; if they are randomly mixed, the average even over a relatively small neighborhood will have a unimodal PD, whereas if they are clumped, a larger degree of averaging will be required before the PD becomes unimodal. Alternatively, suppose that we know the PD of *gray-level differences* for pairs of points having various displacements; if the light and dark points are randomly mixed, this PD will show the presence of high absolute differences even for small displacements, whereas if they are clumped, a small displacement will yield primarily small absolute differences.

Let π be a local property whose value at (x, y) depends on the gray levels of n pixels in the vicinity of (x, y). Then the PD of π can be derived from the images' nth-order GLPD for the set of displacements of these n pixels relative to (x, y). For example, the PD of gray level differences for pairs of pixels having a given displacement can be derived from the images' second-order GLPD for that displacement.

To estimate the PD of a local property, we can compute the histogram of its values—i.e., count how often each value occurs in the image. For a property whose value depends only on a pair of points, this histogram can be derived from the corresponding gray level cooccurrence matrix. For example, given the cooccurrence matrix C for a specified displacement, if we sum its entries along lines parallel to its main diagonal, we obtain the gray-level difference histogram for the given displacement. Gray-level difference histograms, like cooccurrence matrices, provide useful descriptions of textures, as discussed in [1, sect. 10.2.1].

An advantage of using local property PD's, rather than the higher order GLPD's themselves, is that one can choose local properties that are relatively uncorrelated with one another. In the joint PD of a set of such properties, it may be possible to detect relatively compact clusters corresponding to differently textured image regions. Unfortunately, little is known about the expected nature of such distributions, except for the simplest types of local properties.

Specifying second-order GLPD's, or even gray-level difference PD's, for a set of displacements involves a large amount of information, even if the image is assumed to be isotropic. As a simplification, one can compute the value of some statistic of the PD for each displacement d, and use the value of this statistic as a function of d as a descriptor of the image. For example, the expected (= mean) squared gray-level difference, as a function of d, is sometimes employed as an image descriptor; it is known as the *variogram* of the image [13].

Local properties that respond to the presence of edges, e.g., the values of various difference operators that measure digital versions of the gray level "gradient," are especially useful for image segmentation. Edge detection in an image is usually done by thresholding the values of some such property, but little or no work has been done on the selection of optimal thresholds for this purpose. In fact, the form of the edge value PD has been investigated only for the simplest classes of images and the simplest difference operators. In order to predict this PD we must know something about the relative frequencies of occurrence of region interior and border points in the image, as well as about the GLPD's in the interiors of the various types of regions, and about the blurredness of the interregion edges.

If we know the edge value PD for given types of homogeneous regions, we can use it to predict the edge detection false alarm rate in an image composed of these types of regions. This idea was investigated in [14] for a particular class of regions and for various edge-detecting operators.

In an image containing two types of regions, the joint PD of gray level and edge value should consist of two clusters near zero edge value, representing the interiors of the regions, joined by a band that arches into higher edge values, representing the interregion borders [15]. This model suggests that if we want to discriminate between the regions, we should design a gray-level classifier for the subpopulation of pixels having low edge values, since in this subpopulation the clusters will be more cleanly separated. Alternatively, we might examine the subpopulation of pixels having high edge values, and use, e.g., its mean as a threshold, since this is the mean gray level of the border points. These methods, and several variations on them, are discussed in [16].

Other sets of local properties, including local averages of the gray level and various local "busyness" measures, have been employed to classify pixels using clustering procedures [8], [17]. If models for the joint PD's of such properties could be derived, optimal classification techniques could be used. Local property statistics can also be used to analyze color or multispectral images, but little or nothing has been done along these lines as yet.

D. Random Field Models

The nth-order GLPD of a class of images depends only on the relative positions of the n points, not on their absolute positions. In particular, the first-order GLPD is independent of position. For many types of images, e.g., cloud patterns or blood smears, this is a reasonable assumption, since objects can occur anywhere in the scene. For other types of images, however, e.g., chest X-rays or portrait photographs, it is not reasonable to assume position independence. In this section we discuss random field models for classes of images, which provide, in general, for the possibility that the image gray levels are space-variant.

A two-dimensional discrete *random field* is a family of random variables $\tilde{z}(x, y)$ corresponding to the points of a digital image. It is described by specifying the joint PD's of n-tuples of these random variables, for various values of n and for all possible (absolute) positions of the n pixels. An elementary discussion of random fields can be found in [1, sect. 2.4]. Note that since the PD of a given pixel depends on the position of that pixel, it cannot be estimated by computing a gray level histogram for a single image; rather, one must compute a histogram of the gray levels at that pixel in an ensemble of images, all of which are presumed to belong to the given random field, i.e., to be "outcomes" of the given array of random variables.

A random field is call *homogeneous* if
a) the random variables all have the same mean value $(E(\tilde{z}(x, y)) = \mu$ for all $x, y)$; note that their densities need not be the same;
b) the autocorrelation of any two of the random variables, i.e., the expected value $E(\tilde{z}(x, y) \tilde{z}(u, v))$ of their product, depends only on their relative position, i.e., on $(x - u, y - v)$; note that their joint density may still depend on absolute position.

Images are often modeled as samples generated by a homogeneous random field. This is less restrictive than modeling them by nth-order GLPD's, but it still assumes a high degree of space invariance.

As a further simplification, the random fields used to model images are often assumed to have the following properties:
a) the random variables all have Gaussian PD's, say with mean μ and variance σ^2;
b) the autocorrelation of two random variables at relative position $(\Delta x, \Delta y)$ is of the form

$$\sigma^2 \exp(-\alpha|\Delta x| - \beta|\Delta y|).$$

These assumptions have been empirically validated for a variety of image ensembles.

Rather than modeling an image directly as a discrete random field, one can model the original scene as a random field (which may be continuous—i.e., a random variable is defined for every position (x, y) in the plane), and then consider the effects of the processes of imaging and digitization on this random field. In general, imaging will introduce both blur and noise, while digitization discretely samples and quantizes the resulting field.

Random field models have not been extensively used as a basis for designing image segmentation techniques; further work in this area would be very desirable. As a simple example of how they might be used, if we threshold an image that was generated by a homogeneous random field, it is possible to predict the expected values of various geometrical properties (area, perimeter, etc.) of the above-threshold regions [18]. This analysis is useful in defining criteria, based on geometrical properties, for discriminating between "noise regions," resulting when the image background is thresholded, and objects that are extracted from the background by thresholding. It would be of interest to study the application of general random field models to the design of optimal space-variant thresholding and edge detection procedures.

Textures can be modeled as homogeneous random fields that are obtained by applying local filtering operations to an initial uncorrelated random field [19]. This implies that the following should be good texture descriptors:

1) the autocorrelation of the image;
2) the PD of the random variable at any position, after a whitening transformation such as a Laplacian-like operator has been applied to the image to decorrelate it.

E. Time Series Models

Another approach to modeling the spatial dependence of gray levels in an image is to regard the image as a sequence of random variables, each of which is dependent on some of the preceding ones. The sequence might, for example, correspond to a row-by-row scan of the image, as in a TV raster.

Let $\tilde{z}_i$ be the ith random variable in the sequence. One usually assumes that the mean μ of the $\tilde{z}_i$'s has been subtracted from each of them. Let $\tilde{\nu}$ be a Gaussian random variable with mean 0 and variance σ^2. We say that the sequence of $\tilde{z}$'s is *autoregressive* if

$$\tilde{z}_i = \sum_{j=1}^{n} \alpha_j \tilde{z}_{i-j} + \tilde{\nu}(i)$$

so that each $\tilde{z}_i$ is a linear combination of the n preceding $\tilde{z}$'s, and also depends on the current "noise" term $\tilde{\nu}$.

In the autoregressive model, each $\tilde{z}_i$ depends on the current $\tilde{\nu}$ and on the preceding $\tilde{z}$'s, which in turn depend on the preceding $\tilde{\nu}$'s and on still earlier $\tilde{z}$'s. In the *moving average* model, we assume that $\tilde{z}_i$ depends only on the current and preceding $\tilde{\nu}$'s, i.e.,

$$\tilde{z}_i = \sum_{j=0}^{n} \beta_j \tilde{\nu}(i-j)$$

so that the sequence of $\tilde{z}$'s can be regarded as observations on linearly filtered noise. One can also assume a *mixed* model which includes both the preceding $\tilde{z}$'s and the preceding $\tilde{\nu}$'s.

If μ remains constant, the models described above are called *stationary*. Other models can be formulated which display nonstationary or periodic ("seasonal") behavior. Such models have been used for texture analysis and synthesis by fitting them to a given image or ensemble of images [20]–[23].

A serious objection to time series models for images is the fact that they are unilateral, i.e., the random variables depend only on "preceding" ones, rather than on their neighbors on all sides. Note that the "preceding" pixels need not be on the same row as the given pixel; one can allow dependence on neighbors both to the left of and above the pixel. However, this is still asymmetrical. Unfortunately, symmetrical dependence is mathematically much less tractable than the models defined above. Little work has been done on the use of time series models in defining segmentation schemes; see, however, the work of Nahi described at the end of Section III-D. No work seems to have been done on the modeling of color or multispectral images by vector-valued random fields or time series.

III. Spatial Models

The models considered in Section II assumed, typically, that an image is composed of regions, each of which is statistically homogeneous. Still more generally, one could consider hierarchical models in which the regions are in turn composed of subregions, etc.; but we shall not do so here. No consideration has yet been given to questions of region definition and description. In this section we discuss such questions.

Region description has at least three different aspects; they are as follows.

a) *Interregion Interaction:* The regions may consist of sparsely separated blobs, or scattered points, on a background; or they may touch or interpenetrate to various extents. At another extreme, the image may be partitioned into a set of regions, so that every region is bordered by others on all sides. This aspect of region modeling will be discussed in Sections III-A and III-B.

b) *Interregion Transitions:* The region/region or region/background boundaries may be sharp, or blurred, or gradual. This aspect will be treated in Section III-C.

c) *Region Size and Shape:* The regions may be small or large, compact or elongated or jagged, etc. Region shapes can be described in two ways, one based on boundary curvature, the other on "local size." These approaches to shape description will be discussed in Sections III-D and III-E, respectively. The former approach must be used when dealing with regions that are themselves thin curves.

On the general problem of modeling classes of shapes and patterns see [24].

Models that specify how an image is broken up into regions generally give more information about the image than models that specify gray level statistics. Given a statistical description of the regions, one can often derive the GLPD's, but the reverse is usually not true.

As already pointed out, some assumptions about region size and between-region edges, as well as how many different region types are present, are needed in order to formulate reasonable statistical image models that involve higher order GLPD's or PD's of local properties. On the other hand, such models do not require information as to whether the image consists of objects on a background or is partitioned into regions, or detailed information about region shapes.

A. Objects on a Background

Images may be composed of "objects" on a background, where the objects may be of one or several types. The simplest such situation is that in which the objects are relatively widely spaced, so that they rarely or never touch. As an extreme case of this, the image may be composed of isolated points scattered over the background. The placement of the objects can range from regular to random. Note that if there are many objects, it may be possible to regard the object/background mixture as a homogeneous image that has biased higher order GLPD's; but modeling the image as scattered objects on a background should provide more insight into the structure of the image. On such models see also [25].

Decompositions of an image into scattered objects can be characterized statistically by describing

a) statistics of object sizes and shapes; see Sections III-D5;
b) statistics of object positions and orientations.

These position statistics can be first-order or higher order. If we think of an object's position as being specified by the coordinates of (say) its centroid, we can describe the spatial distribution of objects by a binomial random field, i.e., an array of binomially distributed random variables $\tilde{z}(x, y)$; this is equivalent to specifying an array of probabilities $p(x, y)$, each of which is the probability that an object centroid is located at (x, y). If the objects are equally likely to appear anywhere, we need only specify a single probability p. Constraints on the relative positions of objects are defined by the higher order statistics of the random field; for example, the autocorrelation $E(\tilde{z}(x, y)\tilde{z}(u, v))$ gives the joint probability that a pair of objects will exist at positions (x, y) and (u, v). If the objects' positions are uncorrelated, this reduces to $p(x, y)p(u, v)$, the product of the individual object probabilities. As in Section II-D, we may sometimes want to assume that the random field is homogeneous, i.e., that $E(\tilde{z}(x, y)) = p(x, y) = p$ is independent of (x, y), and that $E(\tilde{z}(x, y)\tilde{z}(u, v))$ depends only on the relative positions of (x, y) and (u, v). We can use relative position constraints to ensure, for example, that objects are always at least a certain minimum distance apart.

It often suffices to describe spatial distributions of object positions in terms of statistics of the distances from an object to its nearest neighbors. It can be shown [26] that for a Poisson object probability that is independent of position and uncorrelated with the probabilities at other positions, the distance to the kth nearest neighbor has a χ^2 distribution. One can use nth-order PD's of various object properties as image descriptors, where the n-tuples of objects are chosen on the basis of neighbor relationships; this idea is discussed further at the end of this section.

A special class of object position models which have been studied extensively are the so-called "bombing" models of random geometry, in which regions of a given shape are dropped at random positions, so that the random field of object occurrences is homogeneous and uncorrelated. For various types of region shapes (circular, rectangular, etc.), it is possible to compute the first and second order GLPD's of the images produced in this way, given the first and second order GLPD's of the objects and the background. A summary of the properties of images generated by bombing models can be found in [27, sect. 4]. It would be desirable to extend these results to other types of object position models.

The distribution of object orientations can be characterized by associating a distinguished axis with each object, e.g., its principal axis of inertia, and specifying the PD of orientations for each position as a random field in which the random variables have values in the range $(0, 2\pi)$. Analogous remarks apply, of course, to the PD's of other object properties, whether geometrical (Sections III-D and III-E) or statistical (as in Section II).

As the objects become relatively large or relatively closely spaced, it becomes increasingly important to consider situations in which objects touch or overlap. When overlap occurs, one object may "occlude" the other, i.e., we use the statistical description of the occluding object in the region of overlap; or the two objects may "mix"—e.g., we use an average statistical description. Note that if the objects all have the same statistical description, it makes no difference whether we regard them as occluding or mixing.

Description of object positions need not be statistical. They can sometimes be template like, i.e., they can specify particular relative positions in which the objects must occur. More generally, they can allow deviations from these ideal positions ("rubber templates"). On models for pattern deformation see [24].

Still another way to describe relative object positions is in terms of fuzzy spatial relations such as above/below, to the left/right of, near/far, etc. On quantitative definitions of these relations see [28]; on the difficulty of defining them for extended objects see [29].

Given a spatial distribution of objects on a background, it still remains to choose statistical models for the pixel populations in the objects. Even for a regular distribution of objects, these choices can be random. We can describe the choices using a random field whose variables have outcomes in the space of statistical models; e.g., the choice of model for an object is determined by the outcome of the random variable at the position of that object's centroid. This allows us to make the choices dependent on the absolute or relative positions of the objects. Another way to introduce dependencies among the choices is in terms of the nearest neighbor relations between pairs of objects. The first-order statistics of object properties, and second-order statistics of pairs of neighboring objects, provide more insight into the image structure than do the statistics of pixel gray levels, and in particular provide an important class of texture descriptors [30]. In particular, the "objects" can be defined by local extrema of some local property; on the use of local extrema in texture description see [31].

B. Image Decompositions

Rather than regarding an image as consisting of objects on a background, we can regard it as *partitioned* into regions. In this section we discuss "mosaic models" for such image partitions. Incidentally, another class of models, which will not be discussed here, involves *packed* objects on a background, where the objects are pushed together until they touch and no further pushing is possible without overlap. On random packings of objects see [32].

Image partitions can be generated by various types of geometrical processes. There is a wide variety of regular partitions, such as checkerboards, hexagonal grids, and other tessellations of the plane. If these paritions are periodic, they are specified by defining a single period, which is then repeated. (Two-dimensional periodicity is defined in general by a "period parallelogram" whose repetitions cover the plane.) Some regular partitions can be generated by starting with a regular array of points and allowing them to grow (into regions) until they collide; others can be generated by cutting up the plane with a regular family of lines or curves. First- and second-order GLPD's for regular checkerboard models are given in [27, sect. 3.3].

Growth processes can also be used to generate a variety of random image partitions, by starting with an arbitrary spatial distribution of points, generated by a random field as in Section III-A, and allowing them to grow into regions. This method of generating an image partition is called an *occupancy model* ([27, sect. 3.2b]). It is easy to show that the resulting regions must all be convex polygons; they are called *Thiessen polygons* (or sometimes *Voronoi polygons*). If the points do not all start to grow simultaneously, the regions can be concave and can have circular-arc boundaries; this method of generating an image partition is called the *Johnson-Mehl model* [27]. Various properties of the regions generated by occupancy models, e.g., statistics of area, perimeter, etc., are summarized in [27], for the case where the initial spatial distribution of points is homogeneous and uncorrelated.

Dissections of the plane by random families of curves can also be used to define random image partitions. A random family of curves is defined by parameterizing the set of possible curves, e.g., a straight line is defined by its slope and its distance from the origin, and creating an arbitrary distribution of points, defined by a random field, in the resulting parameter space. An extensively studied model of this type is the *Poisson line model*, where the curves are straight lines defined by a homogeneous, uncorrelated set of points in (slope, distance) space. Many properties of the regions defined by this model (first- and second-order gray-level statistics, as well as statistics of area, etc.) are summarized in [27, sect. 3.2a]. Another approach to dissecting the plane using curves is to start with a spatial distribution of points and allow them to execute *random walks* until they collide; this approach is discussed in [33, appendix B]. An example of the use of such models in texture analysis can be found in [34].

Given an image partition, it still remains to choose statistical models for the pixel populations in the individual regions. As at the end of Section III-A, these choices can be defined using a random field, or in terms of the neighbor (=adjacency) relations between pairs of regions. The first-order statistics of region properties, and the second-order statistics of properties of pairs of neighboring regions, provide important descriptors of the image [35].

When an image has been generated by partitioning it into regions and choosing statistical models for the regions, it may be difficult or impossible to determine what the original partition was, since neighboring regions may have overlapping or even identical statistics. In principle it should be possible, from a knowledge of the classes of models that were used, to derive optimal estimates of the partition and the region models; but in practice this can only be done in relatively simple cases. An extensive discussion of this subject can be found in [36].

It should be pointed out that only a few simple image decomposition models have been described in this section. A wide variety of physical processes may give rise to decompositions of natural scenes into regions. Further work on mathematically defining such models would be desirable.

C. Interregion Transitions

The boundaries between objects and background, or between adjacent pairs of regions, in a scene may be sharp or gradual. In addition, the processes of imaging the scene and digitizing the image will introduce blur and noise, as well as sampling and quantization effects.

In [37], qualitative models for interregion transitions of various types are discussed. For example, in scenes containing polyhedra, convex edges may have highlights, concave edges may be shadowed, and occluding edges may be relatively step-like, while shadow edges may be more gradual. Under some circumstances, edges may give rise to changes in the rate of change of gray level, rather than to gray-level steps. Some recent work on image segmentation [38] is based on the assumption that objects are connected regions having above-threshold gray levels and are surrounded by steep edges.

Quantitative models for the region edges in digital images have not been formulated to any great extent. Such models would be very useful in designing optimal edge detection operators, as well as in predicting the expected form of second- or higher order GLPD's (cooccurrence matrices) or of first-order PD's of local properties, since for small neighborhoods or displacements, such PD's are quite sensitive to the transitions that occur at edges.

D. Region Shape: Interiors

Region shape is difficult to model statistically, since it has very many degrees of freedom. We shall discuss two approaches to shape modeling, one based on boundary curvature (in Section III-E), the other based on "local size" (in this section). Shape modeling becomes especially complicated if the shape is allowed to have holes, so that it has multiple borders, i.e., an outer border and a set of nonintersecting inner borders that are surrounded by the outer border. In this and the next section we will deal primarily with shapes that do not have holes.

At each point P of a region R, there is a largest neighborhood N_p that is contained in R. Some of these N_p's may be contained in neighborhoods of other points; those that are not will be called *maximal*. It is easily seen that R is the union of the maximal neighborhoods. The set of centers and radii of the maximal neighborhoods is called the *skeleton* or *medial axis* of R [1, sect. 9.2.3].

These observations suggest that a shape can be defined by specifying a set of arcs or curves, i.e., the loci of skeleton points, and their associated radii. An arc can be defined, e.g., by specifying its coordinates as functions of a given parameter, as in Section III-E; the radius can also be specified as a function of the parameter. On this approach to defining various types of shapes see [39].[3] There is no need to use only the maximal neighborhoods; any set of centers and radii specifies a shape, perhaps redundantly.

To model a class of shapes using skeletons, we must specify a class of position functions, possibly for a set of arcs, and a class of associated radius functions. However, not all the properties that we might want our shapes to have are equally easy to control in this way. For example, we can make our shapes generally elongated by keeping the radii small relative to the length(s) of the arc(s), and we can make them generally compact by keeping the arc lengths short and the radii large; but it is much harder to control such properties as convexity when we use a skeleton representation.

For some purposes, it may be sufficient to give a simplified characterization of a class of shapes in terms of the set of radii of the neighborhoods N_p. For example, suppose that we specify only the first- and second-order statistics of the radius function, where second order statistics are defined in terms of relative position. The first order statistics, which we might call the "size spectrum," correspond to a bombing model with a given PD of bomb radii, while the second-order statistics constrain the relative positions of the bombs. For an image consisting of the given shape on a background, such a model should suffice to determine the probability of a given image point lying in the shape, or of a given pair of points both lying in the shape or one lying inside and the other outside, even though the shape itself is quite underdetermined. Given the statistical descriptions of the object and background, this in turn determines the first- and second-order GLPD's of the image. A size spectrum model can also be used to determine optimal smoothing radii for various image segmentation techniques.

If a region shape model is available, the design of pixel classification techniques based on local properties can be refined to reflect the available shape information. For exam-

---

[3] Analogous methods of describing three-dimensional shapes in terms of the radius functions of "generalized cylinders" are treated in [40].

ple, if we have statistical information about local size of the regions, we should be able to predict more accurately the expected numbers of points for which the local property neighborhoods will fit inside a region—or, more generally, to predict the PD of degree of overlap between these neighborhoods and the regions. This in turn allows us to more accurately predict PD's of local property values.

Shape models are also potentially useful in segmentation techniques such as region growing. Given a region fragment, we examine blocks of pixels adjacent to it and decide whether or not to merge them into the fragment. This decision should be based not only on a comparison of statistical properties of the block and fragment, but also on the desired region shape. For example, if the region is a strip of known width, pixel blocks that would cause this width to be exceeded are inadmissible. Analogous remarks apply to region splitting criteria, and to schemes for constructing piecewise approximations of images.

One can also characterize the shape of a region in terms of the lengths and positions of the runs of points in which the rows of the image meet the region. These runs can be regarded as the one-dimensional analogs of the neighborhoods N_p; thus this approach can be thought of as based on a row-by-row "skeleton" description. The shape is defined by specifying a set of pairs of functions of y (the row number), one specifying the x-coordinate of the run center and the other specifying the "radius" (=[half] run length). Region descriptions of this type, using only a single pair of functions, are used in [41], [42].

E. Region Shape: Borders

A region without holes is determined by specifying its border, which is a closed curve. Thus we can model classes of region shapes by defining classes of curves. The same methods can be used to model the shapes of skeleton arcs, as mentioned in Section III-D. If a region is itself a thin arc or curve, its skeleton radii are all zero, so that arc or curve shape is the only basis on which to model it. On digital arcs and curves, and their representation, segmentation, and description, see [1, sect. 9.3].

An arc or curve can be defined in various ways by specifying a function of one variable. For example, one can use *parametric equations* of the form

$$x = f(t) \quad y = g(t)$$

or one can combine them into a single complex-valued function: $x + iy = f(t) + ig(t)$, where the parameter t varies over some interval. This representation depends on the position and orientation, as well as the size, of the curve. A position-independent representation is obtained by using the *slope intrinsic equation* $y' = F(s)$, where s is arc length from an arbitrary starting point; while a representation independent of both position and orientation is obtained by using the *curvature intrinsic equation* $y'' = G(s)$.[4]

To model a class of shapes in terms of their equations, we must impose constraints on the functions to insure that the curves they define are closed and do not cross themselves; this is much easier to do for parametric equations than for intrinsic equations. We can insure that the shapes are, e.g., convex by constraining the boundary curvature never to change sign, and we can make them smooth by constraining the rate of change of curvature; but it is much harder to control such properties as compactness and elongatedness in terms of boundaries.

Curve modeling can also be done using transforms of the functions that define the curve, rather than the functions themselves. In particular, it is sometimes useful to work with Fourier transforms, since this makes it easy to specify curve properties such as symmetry and periodicity, as well as rate of change of slope or curvature ("wiggliness"). A comparison of various transform techniques for curve description can be found in [43].

For some purposes, it may be sufficient to characterize a class of curves in terms of their sets of slopes or curvatures, rather than completely specifying their equations. For example, if we specify only the PD of slopes, we can detect the general orientation of the curve; and if we specify the second-order slope PD for pairs of points that are close together along the curve, or the first-order curvature PD, we can determine the curve's "wiggliness." The slope histogram of a curve is sometimes called its "directionality spectrum." Such a model should be adequate for determining the first- and second-order GLPD's of an image consisting of the given region on a background, where the region and background have given statistical descriptions (compare the analogous remarks in Section III-D), even though the region shape itself is quite underdetermined.

Models for border curvature are very important in designing criteria for accepting successive points in border following algorithms. They are also useful in designing methods of segmenting region borders, e.g., by angle detection, "spur" detection, lobe detection, piecewise approximation, etc.; see [1, sect. 9.3.2]. However, little explicit use of such models has been made in designing such segmentation techniques.

IV. Concluding Remarks

This paper has reviewed some basic ideas about image models and indicated how they can be used in the design and evaluation of segmentation techniques. We have discussed only a relatively elementary class of segmentation methods. Many other approaches to segmentation are also subject to analysis in terms of the image models to which they are applicable. Some of these will now be briefly mentioned.

Local template matching operations, as used, e.g., for line or curve detection, are subject to analysis in terms of statistical models for the background, which determine false alarm rates, and of shape models for the curves to be detected. Similar remarks apply to more global matching operations, e.g., to the detection of straight lines or of curves of a given shape using the Hough transform. For a discussion of the false alarm statistics of template matching see [44]–[45]. On the performance of Hough transforms in noisy or textured environments see [46].

Iterative "relaxation" techniques, e.g., for curve enhancement, can be analyzed in terms of joint detection probabilities at neighboring points, but little has yet been done to characterize the expected behavior of such processes. A review of various applications of these techniques can be found in [47].

---

[4] An often proposed method of representing a curve by a function is to use a *polar equation* $r = h(\theta)$, where r is the distance of the curve from the origin; this can be made position-independent by taking the origin to be at some standard point such as the centroid of the curve. However, if the curve is nonconvex, this may not be a single-valued function—i.e., the curve may not be "star-shaped" from its centroid.

On the use of image statistics to determine coefficients for relaxation processes see [48].

Image segmentation is a key initial step in syntactic image analysis, since it provides the primitives on which this analysis is based. Conversely, a syntactic model for a class of images can be used, in principle, as a guide in segmenting the images. For example, given a stochastic image grammar one should be able to find a maximum-likelihood parse of the image, and in particular, to find the most likely primitives in it. On the general subject of syntactic image models see [49]. Some examples of hierarchical and syntactic models for texture are [50]-[52].

It is hoped that this paper will serve to stimulate further work on model-based image segmentation, with the eventual goal of putting the topic of segmentation on a firm mathematical footing.

References

[1] A. Rosenfeld and A. C. Kak, *Digital Picture Processing*, New York: Academic Press, 1976.

[2] B. Horn, Obtaining shape from shading information, in P. H. Winston, Ed., *The Psychology of Computer Vision*. New York: McGraw-Hill, 1975.

[3] J. H. Wolfe, "Pattern clustering by multivariate mixture analysis," *Behavioral Research*, vol. 5, pp. 329-350, 1970.

[4] W. S. Holmes, H. R. Leland, and G. E. Richmond, "Design of a photo interpretation automaton," in *Proc. Eastern Joint Computer Conf.*, pp. 27-35, 1962.

[5] J. L. Muerle and D. C. Allen, "Experimental evaluation of techniques for automatic segmentation of objects in a complex scene," in G. C. Cheng *et al.*, Eds., *Pictorial Pattern Recognition*, Washington, DC, Thompson, 1968, pp. 3-13.

[6] J. L. Muerle, "Some thoughts on texture discrimination by computer," in B. S. Lipkin and A. Rosenfeld, Eds., *Picture Processing and Psychopictorics*. New York: Academic Press, 1970, pp. 371-379.

[7] R. Ohlander, K. Price, and D. R. Reddy, "Picture segmentation using a recursive region splitting method," *Computer Graphics Image Processing*, vol. 8, pp. 313-333, 1978.

[8] B. J. Schachter, L. S. Davis, and A. Rosenfeld, "Some experiments in image segmentation by clustering of local feature values," *Pattern Recognition*, in press.

[9] R. M. Haralick, "Automatic remote sensor image processing," in A. Rosenfeld, Ed., *Digital Picture Analysis*. Berlin, Germany: Springer, 1976, pp. 5-63.

[10] J. S. Weszka and A. Rosenfeld, "Threshold evaluation techniques," *IEEE Trans. Systems, Man, Cybern.*, vol. SMC-8, pp. 622-629, 1978.

[11] N. Ahuja, L. S. Davis, R. M. Haralick, and D. P. Panda, "Image segmentation based on local gray level patterns," Computer Science Center, Univ. Maryland, College Park, TR-551, June 1977.

[12] N. Ahuja and A. Rosenfeld, "A note on the use of second-order gray level statistics for threshold selection," *IEEE Trans. Systems, Man, Cybern.*, in press.

[13] C. J. Huijbregts, "Regionalized variables and quantitative analysis of spatial data," in J. C. Davis and M. J. McCullagh, Eds., *Display and Analysis of Spatial Data*. New York: Wiley, 1975, pp. 38-53.

[14] D. P. Panda, "Statistical analysis of some edge operators," Computer Science Center, Univ. Maryland, College Park, TR-558, July 1977.

[15] D. P. Panda and A. Rosenfeld, "Image segmentation by pixel classification in (gray level, edge value) space," *IEEE Trans. Comput.*, vol. C-27, pp. 875-879, 1978.

[16] J. S. Weszka and A. Rosenfeld, "Histogram modification for threshold selection," *IEEE Trans. Systems, Man, Cybern.*, in press.

[17] G. Coleman and H. C. Andrews, "A bottom up image segmentor," in *Proc. Image Understanding Workshop*, pp. 44-54, Apr. 1977. H. C. Andrews, "Analytic results of the Coleman segmentor," *ibid.*, pp. 96-103, Oct. 1977.

[18] D. P. Panda, "Statistical properties of thresholded images," *Comput. Graphics Image Processing*, vol. 8, pp. 334-354, 1978.

[19] W. K. Pratt, "Quantitative design and evaluation methods for edge and texture feature extraction," in *Proc. Image Understanding Workshop*, pp. 103-109, Nov. 1978.

[20] B. H. McCormick and S. N. Jayaramamurthy, "Time series model for texture synthesis," *J. Comput. Inform. Sci.*, vol. 3, pp. 329-343, 1974; "A decision theory method for the analysis of texture," *ibid.*, vol. 4, pp. 1-38, 1975.

[21] J. T. Tou, D. B. Kao, and Y. S. Chang, "Pictorial texture analysis and synthesis," in *Proc. Third Int. Joint Conf. Pattern Recognition*, pp. 590-590p, Nov. 1976.

[22] J. T. Tou and Y. S. Chang, "Picture understanding by machine via textural feature extraction," in *Proc. IEEE Conf. Pattern Recognition and Image Processing*, pp. 392-399, June 1977.

[23] M. Hassner and J. Sklansky, "Markov random fields as models of digitized image texture," *ibid.*, pp. 346-351, May 1978.

[24] U. Grenander, *Pattern Synthesis*. New York: Springer, 1976.

[25] A. Rosenfeld and B. S. Lipkin, "Texture synthesis," in *Picture Processing and Psychopictorics*, B. S. Lipkin and A. Rosenfeld, Eds. New York: Academic Press, 1970, pp. 309-346.

[26] M. G. Kendall and P. A. P. Moran, *Geometrical Probability*. New York: Hafner, 1963.

[27] B. Schachter and N. Ahuja, Random pattern generation processes, *Computer Graphics Image Processing*, in press.

[28] R. Haar, "Solving layout problems using relaxation labeling," *IEEE Trans. Systems, Man, Cybernetics*, vol. SMC-7, pp. 557-559, 1977.

[29] P. H. Winston, "Learning structural descriptions from examples," M.I.T. Artificial Intelligence Laboratory, Cambridge, MA, TR-231, 1970.

[30] L. S. Davis, S. Johns, and J. K. Aggarwal, "Texture analysis using generalized cooccurrence matrices," in *Proc. IEEE Conf. Pattern Recognition and Image Processing*, pp. 313-318, May 1978.

[31] O. R. Mitchell, C. R. Myers, and W. Boyne, "A max-min measure for image texture analysis," *IEEE Trans. Comput.*, vol. C-26, pp. 408-414, 1977.

[32] C. A. Rogers, *Packing and Covering*. Cambridge, England: Cambridge Univ. Press, 1964.

[33] N. Ahuja, "Mosaic models for image analysis and synthesis," Computer Science Center, Univ. Maryland, College Park, MD, TR-607, Nov. 1977.

[34] B. J. Schachter, A. Rosenfeld, and L. S. Davis, "Random mosaic models for textures," *IEEE Trans. Systems, Man, Cybern.*, vol. SMC-8, pp. 694-702, 1978.

[35] J. T. Maleson, C. M. Brown, and J. A. Feldman, "Understanding natural texture," in *Proc. Image Understanding Workshop*, pp. 19-27, Oct. 1977.

[36] U. Grenander, *Pattern Analysis*. New York: Springer, 1978.

[37] A. Herskovits and T. Binford, "On boundary detection," M.I.T. Artificial Intelligence Laboratory, Cambridge, MA, AIM-183, 1970.

[38] D. L. Milgram, "Region extraction using convergent evidence," in *Proc. Image Understanding Workshop*, pp. 58-64, Apr. 1977; "Progress report on segmentation using convergent evidence," *ibid.*, pp. 104-108, Oct. 1977.

[39] H. Blum and R. N. Nagel, "Shape description using weighted symmetric axis features," in *Proc. IEEE Conf. Pattern Recognition and Image Processing*, pp. 203-215, June 1977.

[40] R. Nevatia and T. O. Binford, "Description and recognition of curved objects," *Artificial Intelligence*, vol. 8, pp. 77-98, 1977.

[41] N. E. Nahi, "Image modeling by replacement processes," in *Image Science Mathematics*, C. O. Wilde and E. Barrett, Eds. North Hollywood, CA: Western Periodicals Co., 1977, pp. 99-106.

[42] N. E. Nahi and M. H. Jahanshahi, "Image boundary estimation," *IEEE Trans. Comput.*, vol. C-26, pp. 772-781, 1977.

[43] B. Shapiro, "The use of orthogonal expansions for biological shape description," Computer Science Center, Univ. Maryland, College Park, MD, TR-472, Aug. 1976.

[44] G. J. VanderBrug and A. Rosenfeld, "Two-stage template matching," *IEEE Trans. Comput.*, vol. C-26, pp. 384-393, 1977.

[45] A. Rosenfeld and G. J. VanderBrug, "Coarse-fine template matching," *IEEE Trans. Systems, Man, Cybernetics*, vol. SMC-7, pp. 104-107, 1977.

[46] A. Iannino and S. D. Shapiro, "A survey of the Hough transform and its extension for curve detection," in *Proc. IEEE Conf. on Pattern Recognition and Image Processing*, pp. 32-38, May 1978.

[47] A. Rosenfeld, "Iterative methods in image analysis," *ibid.*, pp. 14-18, June 1977; *Pattern Recognition*, vol. 10, pp. 181-187, 1978.

[48] A. Rosenfeld and S. Peleg, "Determining compatibility coefficients for curve enhancement relaxation processes," *IEEE Trans. Systems, Man, Cybern.*, vol. SMC-8, pp. 548-555, 1978.

[49] K. S. Fu, *Syntactic Methods in Pattern Recognition*, Academic Press, New York, 1974.

[50] R. W. Ehrich and P. F. Lai, "Elements of a structural model of texture," in *Proc. IEEE Conf. Pattern Recognition and Image Processing*, pp. 319-326, May 1978.

[51] S. Y. Lu and K. S. Fu, "Stochastic tree grammar inference for texture synthesis and discrimination," *ibid.*, pp. 340-343.

[52] ——, "A syntactic approach to texture analysis," *Computer Graphics Image Processing*, vol. 7, pp. 303-330, 1978.

Chapter 2: Nonlinear Filters for Image Enhancement

Image enhancement consists of a collection of techniques that seek to improve the visual appearance of an image or to convert the image into a form that is more amenable to human and machine analyses. Because it is difficult to define a criterion characterizing a "good-quality" image, no unified theory of image enhancement exists at the present time. The enhancement problem is made more difficult because image quality is decided by the not-so-well-understood human visual system. Image enhancement is today a collection of techniques that improve the quality of the given image.

Images can be of less-than-good quality because of such things as an imperfect photographic process, imperfect display devices, poor contrast, unequal distribution of gray level, channel noise, salt-and-pepper noise, quantization noise, and artifacts introduced by some processing algorithm. As the nature of these imperfections are varied, so are the various enhancement techniques. A technique that works well for a particular degradation may not be well suited for other types of degradations.

Andrews[1] identified the following three types of enhancement techniques:

- Pointwise techniques,
- Spatial techniques, and
- Artifacts techniques.

Pointwise techniques vary from the simplest gray-scale reversal to more complicated histogram-modification algorithms. These techniques operate on individual pixels, with the operator usually being space invariant, memoryless, and nonlinear. Typical algorithms are film gamma correction, gray-scale reversal, stretching of gray levels, and modification of the histogram to the desired function. Some of these techniques — for instance, gray-scale stretching or reversal — are deterministic, while others — for instance, histogram modification — use statistical distribution of the pixels.

Spatial techniques deal with modifying the gray level of the pixel by using the gray levels of the pixels in a neighborhood surrounding the pixel that is being modified. These techniques are useful in reducing additive or multiplicative noise. If precise locations of the noisy pixels are known, one can selectively replace the noisy pixels by a weighted average of gray levels of their neighbors. In practice, the precise locations of the noisy pixels are not available, and so the averaging operation is done by using a window over the entire image. This operation may be thought as convolving the averaging window with the image, and one can implement this operation in either the spatial or the transform domain.

It is easy to see why the averaging operation — performed by a mean filter — should achieve noise reduction. Suppose the image noise array consists of independent pixels, each with variance σ^2. If each pixel is replaced by its sample mean taken over n pixels, then the variance of the pixels in the smoothed image is σ^2/n. Note that the amount of reduction in variance using a mean filter is independent of the distribution of the underlying noise pixels (that is, the amount of reduction is independent of the distribution of the corrupting noise). This independence is not satisfactory, since the noise due to a heavy-tailed distribution — such as double exponential or lognormal noise — is more disturbing to the eye than Gaussian noise, because the former can produce pixels whose intensities vary significantly from those of their neighbors. It is desirable to have a filter that is adaptive to the underlying noise structure. This problem with the mean filter is also illustrated by the fact that the averaging operation is not robust against outliers. (That is, when pixels of intensities that are significantly different from those of their neighbors are present, the averaging operation simply includes the outliers in computing the mean.) Another related problem with the mean filter is that it tends to blur edges present in the images; hence, it may not be useful as a front end in image feature-extraction tasks.

A filter or noise-cleaning technique that does not possess the drawbacks just described is the popular median filter.[1] Median filtering is a nonlinear technique in which the given pixel in the image is replaced by the sample median of the pixels in a window surrounding the pixel to be corrected. For a constant-signal model, the reduction in variance achieved when median filtering is done over a window with n pixels, n odd, is approximately[2]

$$\frac{1}{4nf^2(m)}$$

where m is the theoretical median and $f(m)$ is the probability density of the underlying pixels in the given image. It is assumed that the pixels are independent and identically distributed. Thus, the median filter is adaptive to the distribution of the corrupting noise.

One can compare the smoothing performances of the mean and median filters operating on the window of same size by using

$$\eta = \frac{1}{4\sigma^2 f^2(m)}$$

where σ^2 is the variance of the noisy image pixel and η is simply the ratio of variance of a median to that of the mean. By simple calculations,[3] one can show that $\eta = 3$ for uniform noise, 1.57 for Gaussian noise, and 0.5 for double-exponential noise. Thus, if blurring of edges is not of serious concern, it does not pay to use the median filter for light-tailed noise such as Gaussian noise. However, the median filter outperforms the mean filter in heavy-tailed noisy cases like double-exponential noise. One can also infer that the median filter will perform better for impulse noise.

A qualitative explanation for robustness of the median filter against outliers can be provided as follows: If $x(1), x(2), \ldots, x(n)$, n odd, denotes a one-dimensional sequence, then the median is nothing but the middle number in size (that is, if $x(n)$'s are arranged in ascending order), as

$$x_{(1)} < x_{(2)} < \ldots < x_{(n)}$$

where $x_{(1)}$ is the smallest of $x(.)$'s, $x_{(2)}$ is the second smallest of $x(.)$'s, and $x_{(n)}$ is the largest of $x(.)$'s. Then the median is $x_{(n+1)/2}$. Thus, when outliers are present, they make up the tail end of the ordered sequence; provided there are not too many of them, the median is relatively unaltered. (A comprehensive discussion on median filters may be found in an excellent chapter in a book by Justusson.[3] This chapter, which includes a discussion of median filtering of correlated noise and impulse noise, as well as a discussion of frequency response of median filters, is highly recommended because this material is not available elsewhere.) Another important property of the median filter is that it does not blur the edges present in the given image.

Artifacts techniques — the third of Andrews' enhancement techniques — deal with removing artifacts that arise in processed images as a result of some algorithms. The artifacts may be due to such things as contouring, spatial filtering, psychovisual phenomena, and the scanner. There is no general technique available for removing artifacts, since they arise because of various reasons. The techniques of artifacts removal are cumbersome. Andrews[1] provides a brief discussion of this often-overlooked part of image-processing literature.

Thus far, we have elaborated on basic methods of image enhancement. We have not covered techniques such as edge crispening, histogram modification, and geometric correction, because discussion of these techniques may be found in standard textbooks.[4,5]

A paper by Lee[6] and one by Narayanan and Rosenfeld[7] are examples of papers that deal with using local and global information to smooth the given images. In the paper by Lee,[6] estimates of the local mean and variance obtained from the given image are used for contrast enhancement and filtering of additive and multiplicative noise. The main features of algorithms in Lee's paper are simplicity and amenability to parallel implementation. One of the decisions to be made in smoothing using neighbors is the choice of particular neighbors to be used. In their paper, Narayanan and Rosenfeld[7] describe two methods to use when choosing the appropriate neighbors prior to smoothing. The first method uses those neighbors whose probabilities, as estimated from the histogram, are higher than that of the given pixel. The second method uses a neighbor only if there is no significant concavity in the histogram between the pixel and the neighbor. Each of these methods gives better results than simply using local neighbors in cases where the noise in a region belongs to the same histogram peak as that of the region's average.

Earlier work on median filtering concentrated on computational aspects. For instance, Narendra[8] introduced a separable two-dimensional median filter, which is computationally more efficient than the regular two-dimensional median filter. The regular two-dimensional median filter operates like a one-dimensional median filter in that the median is now taken over the pixels in a two-dimensional window. Justusson[3] gives different types of windows that may be used. The separable two-dimensional median filter first computes the median of the pixels along each row in the window; then, the median of the row medians is computed and used as the median of the window. Although both of the methods — that is, using the separable and the regular two-dimensional median filters — use all of the pixels in the window, their outputs generally differ. However, if the pixels within the window are monotonic, both filters give the same outputs. The idea of a separable two-dimensional median filter is an extension of Tukey's work.[9] The advantages of the separable median filter are computational savings and easy hardware implementation. However, its variance is higher than that of a regular two-dimensional median filter; hence, it is not statistically as efficient as the regular two-dimensional median filter.

Huang, Yang, and Tang[10] describe a fast algorithm for two-dimensional median filtering. Because the median of $\{x_{(1)}, x_{(2)}, \ldots, x_{(n)}\}$ is the middle number $x_{(n+1)/2}$ in the ordered sequence $x_{(1)} < x_{(2)} < \ldots x_{(n)}$, conventional sorting techniques like quicksort can be used to compute the median. In the computation of the median of m by n numbers, the average number of comparisons is typically proportional to m times n, assuming that the original ordering is random. The algorithm due to Huang, Yang, and Tang computes the median of m by n numbers with computer time that is proportional to n. The fast median-filtering algorithm is developed by storing the gray-level histogram of m times n pixels in the running window and updating this histogram as the window moves. Other authors have written papers on efficient computation of median filters.[11-13]

One of the first papers to analyze the behavior of median filters is one by Gallagher and Wise.[14] Their paper is concerned with the invariance of certain sequences to median filtering and the effects of repeatedly median filtering a given sequence. Gallagher and Wise refer to sequences that are invariant to median filtering as "root signals" of the median filter; Tyan, in his work, refers to such sequences as "fixed points."[15,16] All three of the above-mentioned papers[14-16] derive the structure of sequences that are invariant to a median filter of finite length. Since the edges in images satisfy the local monotonicity condition required of sequences in order to be termed "fixed points," edges are not perturbed by median filters. Gallagher and Wise[14] show that if a given sequence is not a root signal of the median filter, the nonroot signal — upon repeated median filtering — becomes a root-signal or fixed-point sequence (that is, it becomes invariant to the median filter). The number of repetitions of median filtering required to attain a root-signal or fixed-point sequence is $(n-2)/2$, where n is the length of the sequence. Tyan[16] discusses fixed points of two-dimensional median filtering.

Over the last 10 years, activity in median filters has been explosive. Generalizations of median filters are referred to as rank order filters, order statistic filters, and stack filters. In this chapter, six papers on nonlinear filters for image enhancement are reprinted. One of these six papers deals with generalizations of mean filters, while the other five concentrate on generalizations of median filters. Owing to space limitations, we concentrate only on the theoretical aspects of these filters. Specific implementations of some of these filters may be found elsewhere in the literature.[13,17-19]

The first paper reprinted in this chapter, by Pitas and Venetsanopoulos, presents a smoothing filter defined as a general nonlinear function of the weighted average of the neighboring gray values. Conventional smoothers — such as arithmetic, harmonic, and geometric means — are special cases of the smoother presented by Pitas and Venetsanopoulos. A Taylor's series expansion[20] is used to write the mean and variance of the output in terms of the first- and second-order statistics of the inputs, very much as in the analyses presented by Gibbons[2] and Papoulis.[21] Pitas and Venetsanopoulos show that — like mean filters — nonlinear mean filters are better than median filters in smoothing additive, white, uniform, or Gaussian noise. Nonlinear mean filters are also better than mean filters in suppressing impulsive noise. However, while median filters are capable of removing positive and negative spikes, the nonlinear mean filter presented by Pitas and Venetsanopoulos can remove impulses of either the positive or negative type, but not both at the same time. Also, nonlinear mean filters preserve edges better than arithmetic or geometric mean filters, with or without noise. The authors give experimental results to support the usefulness of the nonlinear mean filter.

As mentioned before, the standard median filter is a specific-order statistic. For a number of years, there has been interest in generalizing median filters by using combinations of different-order statistics.[3] The next reprinted paper, by Bovik, Huang, and Munson, presents a generalization of median filtering using a weighted linear combination of order statistics of the input sequence. The weights are chosen so as to minimize the output mean-square error when the input is a constant signal and white noise of different distributions. As the noise becomes more and more impulsive, the optimal-order statistics filter (OOSF) tends toward the median filter and combines properties of both the averaging and median filters. The paper also gives extensions to nonconstant signal models.

In the next reprinted paper, by Longbotham and Bovik, a firm theoretical foundation for order statistic (OS) filters is given by using the relationships of OS filters to linear filters. Note that OS filters are modifications of nonrecursive or finite-impulse, discrete linear filters through a nonlinear ordering. The paper derives necessary and/or sufficient conditions on both the filter coefficients and the signal process in order that nonrecursive OS and linear filtering become equivalent operations.

The next reprinted paper, by Bernstein, presents the signal adaptive median (SAM) filter, which — in a single pass — enables the simultaneous removal of a combination of signal-dependent, additive, random noise. The SAM filter could be recursive or nonrecursive and has an adjustable window size; the adjustment is decided by the nature of the image region being processed — that is, by whether it has edges or is a flat region.

In the next reprinted paper, Arce and Foster give an extensive analysis of a class of filters known as "multistage median filters." Multistage filtering[22] is accomplished by combining the outputs of basic subfilters, which are designed to preserve a specific feature — such as edges or lines. The particular multistage filters considered in this paper are designed using a median of subfilter outputs, which themselves are medians taken along specific directions. Statistical threshold-decomposition theory[23] is then used to derive the noise-reduction and detail-preserving characteristics of the multistage median filters. Using mean-square, mean-absolute, and subjective visual criteria, Arce and Foster give performance comparisons of the multistage median filter with a square median, multistage median, finite-impulse response (FIR)-median hybrid and with morphological filters. The effectiveness of each filter is dependent on the type of image, the error criterion used, and the nature and amount of contaminating noise. Useful observations regarding the best filters for various combinations of signal-to-noise ratio and the nature of contaminating noise are made in the paper.

In the final paper reprinted in this chapter, Coyle, Lin, and Gabbouj discuss in detail a class of nonlinear filters for image enhancement known as "stack filters." Stack filters — introduced in a paper by Wendt, Coyle, and Gallagher[24] — constitute a large class of nonlinear filters, which includes rank-order filters as well as morphological filters; filters in this class are easily implemented using very large scale integration (VLSI) technology. The reprinted paper — by Coyle, Lin, and Gabbouj — presents an excellent summary of multilevel and multistage median filters, morphological filters, order statistic filters, and stack filters. Stack filters are analyzed in some detail.

Chapter 2 References

1. H.C. Andrews, "Monochrome Digital Image Enhancement," *Applied Optics*, Vol. 15, Feb. 1976, pp. 495-503.
2. J.D. Gibbons, *Nonparametric Statistical Inference*, McGraw-Hill, New York, N.Y., 1971.
3. B.I. Justusson, "Median Filtering: Statistical Properties," in *Two-Dimensional Digital Signal Processing, II: Transforms and Median Filters*, Topics in Applied Physics, Vol. 43, Springer-Verlag, New York, N.Y., 1981.
4. A. Rosenfeld and A.C. Kak, *Digital Picture Processing*, Vol. 1, Academic Press, Inc., New York, N.Y., 1982.
5. W.K. Pratt, *Digital Image Processing*, John Wiley Interscience, New York, N.Y., 1991.
6. J.S. Lee, "Digital Image Enhancement and Noise Filtering by Use of Local Statistics," *IEEE Trans. Pattern Analysis and Machine Intelligence*, Vol. PAMI-2, Mar. 1980, pp. 165-168.
7. K.A. Narayanan and A. Rosenfeld, "Image Smoothing by Local Use of Global Information," *IEEE Trans. Systems, Man, and Cybernetics* Vol. SMC-11, Dec. 1981, pp. 826-831.
8. P.M. Narendra, "A Separable Median Filter for Image Noise Smoothing," *IEEE Trans. Pattern Analysis and Machine Intelligence*, Vol. PAMI-3, Jan. 1980, pp. 20-29.
9. J.W. Tukey, "The Ninther: A Robust Estimate of Location," in *Contributions to Surrey's Sampling and Applied Statistics*, H.A. David, ed., Academic Press, Inc., New York, N.Y., 1978.
10. T.S. Huang, G.J. Yang, and G.Y. Tang, "A Fast Two-Dimensional Median Filtering Algorithm," *IEEE Trans. Acoustics, Speech, and Signal Processing*, Vol. ASSP-27, Feb. 1979, pp. 13-18.
11. E. Ataman, V.K. Aatre, and K.M. Wong, "A Fast Method for Real-Time Median Filtering," *IEEE Trans. Acoustics, Speech, and Signal Processing*, Vol. ASSP-28, Aug. 1980, pp. 415-421.
12. V. B. Rao and K. S. Rao, "A New Algorithm for Two-Dimensional Median Filtering," *IEEE Trans. Acoustics, Speech, and Signal Processing*, Vol. ASSP-34, Dec. 1986, pp. 1674-1675.
13. M.V. Ahmad and D. Sundararajan, "A New Algorithm for Real-Time Median Filtering," *IEEE Trans. Circuits and Systems*, Vol. CAS-34, Nov. 1987, pp. 1364-1374.
14. N.C. Gallagher and G.L. Wise, "A Theoretical Analysis of the Properties of Median Filters," *IEEE Trans. Acoustics, Speech, and Signal Processing*, Vol. ASSP-29, Dec. 1981, pp. 1136-1141.
15. S.G. Tyan, "Fixed Points of Running Medians," *Tech. Report*, Polytechnic Inst. of New York, Brooklyn, N.Y., 1977.
16. S.G. Tyan, "Median Filtering: Deterministic Properties," in *Two-Dimensional Digital Signal Processing*, T.S. Huang, ed., Topics in Applied Physics, Vol. 43, Springer-Verlag, New York, N.Y., 1981.
17. K. Oflazer, "Design and Implementation of a Single Chip 1-D Median Filter," *IEEE Trans. Acoustics, Speech, and Signal Processing*, Vol. ASSP-31, Oct. 1983, pp. 1164-1168.
18. C.G. Boncelet, Jr., "Recursive Algorithms and VLSI Implementations for Median Filtering," *Proc. IEEE Int'l Symp. Circuits and Systems*, 1988, pp. 1745-1747.
19. G.R. Arce, P.J. Warter, and R.E. Foster, "Theory and VLSI Implementations of Multilevel Median Filters," *Proc. IEEE Int'l Symp. Circuits and Systems*, 1988, pp. 2795-2798.
20. S.M. Selby, *Standard Math. Tables*, CRC Press, Inc., Boca Raton, Fla., 1973.
21. A. Papoulis, *Probability Random Variables and Stochastic Processes*, McGraw-Hill, New York, N.Y., 1965.
22. A. Nieminen, P. Heinonen, and Y. Neuvo, "A New Class of Detail-Preserving Filters for Image Processing," *IEEE Trans. Pattern Analysis and Machine Intelligence*, Vol. PAMI-9, Jan. 1987, pp. 74-90.
23. G.R. Arce, "Statistical Threshold Decomposition for Recursive and Nonrecursive Median Filters," *IEEE Trans. Information Theory*, Vol. IT-32, Mar. 1986, pp. 243-253.
24. P.D. Wendt, E.J. Coyle, and N.C. Gallagher, Jr., "Stack Filters," *IEEE Trans. Acoustics, Speech, and Signal Processing*, Vol. ASSP-34, Aug. 1986, pp. 898-911.

Nonlinear Mean Filters in Image Processing

IOANNIS PITAS, STUDENT MEMBER, IEEE, AND
ANASTASIOS N. VENETSANOPOULOS, SENIOR MEMBER, IEEE

Abstract—The use of nonlinear means in image processing is introduced. The properties of these means in the presence of different types of noise are investigated. It is shown that nonlinear filters based on these means behave well for both additive and impulse noise. Their performance in the presence of signal dependent noise is satisfactory. They preserve the edges better than linear filters, and they reject the noise better than median filters.

I. INTRODUCTION

ONE of the most important tasks in image processing is noise filtering [1], [2]. Noise removal in images is a particularly difficult task due to the following various reasons.

1) Images are nonstationary two-dimensional processes [1].
2) They are often corrupted by additive, impulse, and signal dependent noise [1].
3) The exact characteristics of our visual system are not well understood [1]. However, experimental results indicate that the first processing levels of our visual system possess nonlinear characteristics [3].
4) Our visual perception is heavily based on edge information [1]. Thus, noise filtering must preserve edges.

The first techniques used for noise removal were linear [1], [2]. Linear techniques possess mathematical simplicity but have the disadvantage that they blur the edges. They also do not perform well in the presence of signal dependent noise. Powerful linear techniques, such as Wiener filtering, are meaningful only when additive noise is present [1], [2]. These disadvantages led to the use of nonlinear filtering in image processing [1]. Initially, logarithmic homomorphic filtering was applied for multiplicative noise removal [4]. Later median filtering was shown to be computationally efficient and to preserve edge information [5], [6]. These two characteristics made it attractive for image processing. Recently, a new class of generalized mean filters was proposed [7]. Also, some homomorphic filters were used for the removal of signal dependent noise [8].

The purpose of this paper is to investigate some general nonlinear means for image processing, which include those of [4], [7], and [8] as special cases, and to evaluate their performance in the presence of edges, additive noise, impulse noise, and signal dependent noise. The analysis of the performance of homomorphic filters is a special case of our analysis. The outline of this paper is the following. Section II includes the definition of nonlinear means. Section III evaluates their performance in the presence of additive noise. Section IV describes their performance in the presence of impulse noise. Their effect on edges is considered in Section V. Their performance in the reduction of signal dependent noise is described in Section VI. Section VII contains some results of image processing and a discussion.

II. NONLINEAR MEAN FILTERS

Consider the numbers x_i, $i = 1, \cdots, N$. We define as nonlinear mean the following function:

$$y = g^{-1}\left(\frac{\sum_{i=1}^{N} a_i g(x_i)}{\sum_{i=1}^{N} a_i}\right) \quad (1)$$

where $g(x)$ is a single valued, analytic nonlinear function, and a_i are weights.

If the weights a_i are constants then the nonlinear mean filters reduce to the well-known homomorphic filters [4], [8] shown in Fig. 1. This is the case for the following nonlinear means [9] of interest in signal processing:

$$g(x) = \begin{cases} x & \text{arithmetic mean } \bar{x} \\ 1/x & \text{harmonic mean } y_H \\ \log x & \text{geometric mean } y_G \\ x^p\, p \epsilon Q - \{-1, 0, 1\} & L_p \text{ mean } y_{L_p} \end{cases}$$

Other functions $g(x)$ can be also considered.

If the weights a_i are not constants, other classes of nonlinear means can be obtained by appropriate choice of the parameters a_i. Such a useful class is generated by choosing $g(x)$ in a similar way and a_i

$$a_i = x_i^p. \quad (2)$$

A useful nonlinear mean of this class is the contraharmonic mean

$$y_{CH_p} = \frac{\sum_{i=1}^{N} x_i^{p+1}}{\sum_{i=1}^{N} x_i^p} \quad (3)$$

Manuscript received May 15, 1984; revised January 28, 1985 and August 8, 1985. This work was supported by the Natural Sciences and Engineering Research Council of Canada under Strategic Grant G-1236.
I. Pitas is with the Department of Electrical Engineering, University of Thessaloniki, Thessaloniki, Greece, 54006.
A. N. Venetsanopoulos is with the Department of Electrical Engineering, University of Toronto, Toronto, Ont., Canada.
IEEE Log Number 8607567.

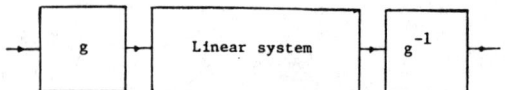

Fig. 1. Structure of a homomorphic filter.

which can be interpreted as an arithmetic mean having weights a_i given by (2).

The nonlinear means previously described have the following well-known property [9], which will be used in their analysis:

$$\min\{x_i\} \le y_{CH-p} \le y_{L-p} \le y_H \le y_G \le \bar{x}$$
$$\le y_{L_p} \le y_{CH_p} \le \max\{x_i\}. \quad (4)$$

Having defined the nonlinear statistical means, we shall try to evaluate their performance in noise filtering. The analysis is general and it encompasses all filters described by (1). Sometimes it is focused on specific nonlinear means which are of interest for the type of noise examined.

III. STATISTICAL PROPERTIES OF NONLINEAR MEAN FILTERS

From (1) it is apparent that y is a function of N variables:

$$y = f(x_1, \cdots, x_N). \quad (5)$$

Let m_i, $\sigma_{x_i}^2$ be the mean and the variance of a variable x_i ($1 \le i \le N$):

$$m_i = \int x_i p(x_i) \, dx_i \quad (6)$$

$$\sigma_{x_i}^2 = \int (x_i - m_i)^2 p(x_i) \, dx_i \quad (7)$$

and define the function $R_{i_1, i_2, \cdots, i_k}(j_1, j_2, \cdots, j_k)$ as follows:

$$R_{i_1, i_2, \cdots, i_k}(j_1, j_2, \cdots, j_k)$$
$$= \int \int \cdots \int (x_{j_1} - m_{j_1})^{i_1}$$
$$\cdot (x_{j_2} - m_{j_2})^{i_2} \cdots (x_{j_k} - m_{j_k})^{i_k}$$
$$\cdot p(x_1, \cdots, x_k) \, dx_1, \cdots, dx_k \quad (8)$$

where $p(x_1, \cdots, x_k)$ is the joint density function of the random variables $x_1, \cdots, x_k$.

We attempt to determine the mean m_y and the variance σ_y^2 of the output y of (5), when the first- and second-order statistics m_i, $\sigma_{x_i}^2$ $R_{11}(i, j)$, $i, j = 1, \cdots, N$ are known. The higher order statistics of the inputs x_i are usually not known and are difficult to evaluate. On the other hand, the accurate analysis of the performance of nonlinear filters usually requires the knowledge of all statistics of the input [10], [11]. Here we shall perform an approximate analysis of the performance of the nonliner filters (5), based on the multidimensional Taylor series expansion [12]. Such an approximate analysis has already been used for the evaluation of the performance of nonlinear one-dimensional functions [10].

The Taylor series expansion of a function $f(x_1, \cdots x_N)$ around the point $(m_1, \cdots, m_N)$ has the following form:

$$y = f(m_1, \cdots, m_N) + \left[\sum_{i=1}^{N} (x_i - m_i) \frac{\partial}{\partial x_i}\right]$$
$$\cdot f + \cdots + \frac{1}{n!}\left[\sum_{i=1}^{N} (x_i - m_i) \frac{\partial}{\partial x_i}\right]^n f + \cdots \quad (9)$$

where all the partial derivatives are calculated on the point $(m_1, \cdots, m_N)$. A truncated version of the Taylor series expansion, which includes up to second-order terms is the following:

$$y \cong f(m_1, \cdots, m_N) + \sum_{i=1}^{N} f_i'(x_i - m_i)$$
$$+ \frac{1}{2} \sum_{i=1}^{N} f_i''(x_i - m_i)^2 + \sum_{\substack{i=1 \\ i>j}}^{N} \sum_{j=1}^{N} f_{ij}''(x_i - m_i)(x_j - m_j) \quad (10)$$

where the symbols f_i', f_i'', f_{ij}'' denote

$$f_i' = \left.\frac{\partial f}{\partial x_i}\right|_{(m_1, \cdots, m_N)} \quad (11)$$

$$f_i'' = \left.\frac{\partial^2 f}{\partial x_i^2}\right|_{(m_1, \cdots, m_N)} \quad (12)$$

$$f_{ij}'' = \left.\frac{\partial^2 f}{\partial x_i \partial x_j}\right|_{(m_1, \cdots, m_N)} \quad (13)$$

The truncated Taylor series is valid if the values x_i are close to m_i.

The mean value m_y of y is given by

$$m_y = \int \int \cdots \int f(x_1, \cdots, x_N)$$
$$\cdot p(x_1, \cdots, x_N) \, dx_1, \cdots, x_N \quad (14)$$

and it can be calculated accurately by using the Taylor series expansion (9) in place of $f(x_1, \cdots, x_N)$ in (14). If only up to second-order statistics are available, then its truncated version (10) can be used in (14) to obtain

$$m_y \cong f(m_1, \cdots, m_N) + \frac{1}{2} \sum_{i=1}^{N} f_i'' \sigma_{x_i}^2$$
$$+ \sum_{\substack{i=1 \\ i>j}}^{N} \sum_{j=1}^{N} f_{ij}'' R_{11}(i, j). \quad (15)$$

The variance σ_y^2 of the output y is given by

$$\sigma_y^2 = \int \int \cdots \int [f(x_1, \cdots, x_N) - m_y]^2$$
$$\cdot p(x_1, \cdots, x_N) \, dx_1, \cdots, dx_N$$
$$= \int \int \cdots \int f^2(x_1, \cdots, x_N) p(x_1, \cdots, x_N)$$
$$\cdot dx_1, \cdots, dx_N - m_y^2. \quad (16)$$

TABLE I
PARTIAL DERIVATIVES OF VARIOUS NONLINEAR MEANS

	Geometric $(a_i=1, i=1,N)$	L_p $(a_i=1, p_i=1,N)$	Contraharmonic
$\dfrac{\partial f}{\partial x_i}$	$\dfrac{1}{N}\left(\prod\limits_{k=1}^{N} x_k\right)^{\frac{1}{N}} x_i^{-1}$	$\dfrac{x_i^{p-1}}{N\left(\sum\limits_{k=1}^{N} x_k^p/N\right)^{\frac{p-1}{p}}}$	$\dfrac{(p+1)x_i^p \sum\limits_{k=1}^{N} x_k^p - p x_i^{p-1} \sum\limits_{k=1}^{N} x_k^{p+1}}{\left(\sum\limits_{k=1}^{N} x_k^p\right)^2}$
$\dfrac{\partial^2 f}{\partial x_i^2}$	$-\dfrac{N-1}{N}\left(\prod\limits_{k=1}^{N} x_k\right)^{\frac{1}{N}} x_i^{-2}$	$\dfrac{p-1}{N^2} x_i^{p-2} \dfrac{\sum\limits_{k=1}^{N} x_k^p - x_i^p}{\left(\sum\limits_{k=1}^{N} x_k^p/N\right)^{\frac{2p-1}{p}}}$	$\dfrac{\left[p(p+1)x_i^{p-1}\sum\limits_{k=1}^{N} x_k^p - p(p-1)x_i^{p-2}\sum\limits_{k=1}^{N} x_k^{p+1}\right]\left(\sum\limits_{k=1}^{N} x_k^p\right) - 2px_i^{p-1}\left[(p+1)x_i^p\sum\limits_{k=1}^{N} x_k^p - px_i^{p-1}\sum\limits_{k=1}^{N} x_k^{p+1}\right]}{\left(\sum\limits_{k=1}^{N} x_k^p\right)^3}$
$\dfrac{\partial^2 f}{\partial x_i \partial x_j}$	$\dfrac{1}{N^2}\left(\prod\limits_{k=1}^{N} x_k\right)^{\frac{1}{N}} x_i^{-1} x_j^{-1}$	$-\dfrac{x_i^{p-1} x_j^{p-1}}{N^2} \dfrac{p-1}{\left(\sum\limits_{k=1}^{N} x_k^p/N\right)^{\frac{2p-1}{p}}}$	$\dfrac{\left[p(p+1)x_i^p x_j^{p-1} - p(p+1)x_i^{p-1} x_j^p\right]\left(\sum\limits_{k=1}^{N} x_k^p\right) - 2px_j^{p-1}\left[(p+1)x_i^p\sum\limits_{k=1}^{N} x_k^p - px_i^{p-1}\sum\limits_{k=1}^{N} x_k^{p+1}\right]}{\left(\sum\limits_{k=1}^{N} x_k^p\right)^3}$

An approximation of the variance σ_y^2 can be found by substituting (10) and (15) in (16)

$$\sigma_y^2 \cong \int \int \cdots \int [f(m_1, \cdots, m_N) + \sum_{i=1}^{N} f_i'(x_i - m_i) + \frac{1}{2} \sum_{i=1}^{N} f_i''(x_i - m_i)^2 + \sum_{i=1}^{N}\sum_{\substack{j=1 \\ i>j}}^{N} f_{ij}''(x_i - m_i)(x_j - m_j)]^2 p(x_1, \cdots, x_N) \cdot dx_1, \cdots, dx_N - m_y^2. \quad (17)$$

By evaluating (17) and dropping the terms which require statistics of an order higher than two, we obtain

$$\sigma_y^2 \cong \sum_{i=1}^{N} f_i'^2 \sigma_{x_i}^2 + 2\sum_{i=1}^{N}\sum_{\substack{j=1 \\ i>j}}^{N} f_i' f_j' R_{11}(i,j) - \left[\frac{1}{2}\sum_{i=1}^{N} f_i'' \sigma_{x_i}^2 + \sum_{i=1}^{N}\sum_{\substack{j=1 \\ i>j}}^{N} f_{ij}'' R_{11}(i,j)\right]^2. \quad (18)$$

The partial derivatives f_i', f_i'', f_{ij}'' for the geometric $L_p(a_i = 1, i = 1, N)$ and contraharmonic means are tabulated in Table I.

Comments

1) The results (15), (18) are valid for any joint probability distribution $p(x_1, \cdots, x_N)$, under the constraint that the function $f(x_1, \cdots, x_N)$ is adequately approximated by a second-order Taylor series expansion around the point $(m_1, \cdots, m_N)$. This constraint is satisfied if the differences $x_i - m_i$, $i = 1, N$ are sufficiently small. This is true when the variances $\sigma_{x_i}^2$, $i = 1, N$ are small and the probability distributions $p(x_i)$ are short tailed (e.g., uniform). This is also approximately true (in a probabilistic sense) when the variances $\sigma_{x_i}^2$, $i = 1, N$ are small and the probability distributions $p(x_i)$ are medium-tailed ones (e.g., Gaussian), because in this case there is a low probability of occurrence of large differences $x_i - m_i$, $i = 1, N$. The above-mentioned constraints are already known from the analysis of the statistical properties of the nonlinear functions of one random variable [10].

2) The variance $\sigma_{\bar{x}}^2$ of the arithmetic mean $\bar{x}$ is given by the following formula:

$$\sigma_{\bar{x}}^2 = \frac{1}{N^2}\left[\sum_{i=1}^{N} \sigma_{x_i}^2 + 2\sum_{i=1}^{N}\sum_{\substack{j=1 \\ i>j}}^{N} R_{11}(i,j)\right]. \quad (19)$$

We cannot draw any direct conclusion by comparing (18) to (19) because of the existence of f_i', f_i'', f_{ij}'' in (18). However, if we consider the case where $m_1 = m_2 = \cdots = m_N = m$, and if we take into account the values of the derivatives given in Table II, (18) becomes

$$\sigma_y^2 \cong \frac{1}{N^2}\left[\sum_{i=1}^{N} \sigma_{x_i}^2 + 2\sum_{i=1}^{N}\sum_{\substack{j=1 \\ i>j}}^{N} R_{11}(i,j)\right] - \left[\frac{1}{2}\sum_{i=1}^{N} f_i'' \sigma_{x_i}^2 + \sum_{i=1}^{N}\sum_{\substack{j=1 \\ i>j}}^{N} f_{ij}'' R_{11}(i,j)\right]^2. \quad (20)$$

Specific expressions are tabulated in Tables II and III for geometric, L_p, and contraharmonic means. Comparing

TABLE II
Partial Derivatives of Various Nonlinear Means for $x_i = m$

	$\frac{\partial f}{\partial x_i}$	$\frac{\partial^2 f}{\partial x_i^2}$	$\frac{\partial^2 f}{\partial x_i \partial x_j}$
Geometric mean ($a_i=1, i=1,N$)	$\frac{1}{N}$	$-\frac{N-1}{N^2 m}$	$\frac{1}{N^2 m}$
L_p mean ($a_i=1, i=1,N$)	$\frac{1}{N}$	$\frac{(p-1)(N-1)}{N^2 m}$	$-\frac{p-1}{N^2 m}$
Contraharmonic mean	$\frac{1}{N}$	$\frac{2p(N-1)}{N^2 m}$	$-\frac{2p}{N^2 m}$

TABLE III
Performance of Various Filters in the Presence of Additive White Noise, Expressed as σ_y^2/σ_x^2 for $m_i = m$, $\sigma_{x_i}^2 = \sigma_x^2$

Noise Probability distribution	Arithmetic mean	Geometric mean	L_p mean	Contraharmonic mean	Median
Uniform ($a_i=1, i=1,N$)	$\frac{1}{N}$	$\frac{1}{N} - \frac{(N-1)^2}{4N^2 m^2}\sigma_x^2$	$\frac{1}{N} - \frac{(p-1)^2(N-1)^2}{4N^2 m^2}\sigma_x^2$	$\frac{1}{N} - \frac{p^2(N-1)^2}{N^2 m^2}\sigma_x^2$	$\frac{3}{N+2}$
Gaussian ($a_i=1, i=1,N$)	$\frac{1}{N}$	$\frac{1}{N} - \frac{(N-1)^2}{4N^2 m^2}\sigma_x^2$	$\frac{1}{N} - \frac{(p-1)^2(N-1)^2}{4N^2 m^2}\sigma_x^2$	$\frac{1}{N} - \frac{p^2(N-1)^2}{N^2 m^2}\sigma_x^2$	$\frac{\pi}{2(N+\pi/2-1)}$
Double Exponential	$\frac{1}{N}$	*	*	*	$\frac{1}{2N-1}$

(19) to (20), we realize that the nonlinear mean filters have smaller output variance than the arithmetic mean over homogeneous image regions. This implies that they suppress the noise better than arithmetic mean filters.

3) It is very well known that median filters have larger output variance than the arithmetic mean $\bar{x}$, for additive white, uniform, or Gaussian noise [6]. Thus, nonlinear mean filters also have smaller output variance than median filters, as can also be seen in Table III. The comparison of the performance of nonlinear mean filters and median filters in the case of the white noise having long-tailed probability distribution is not easy for the following two reasons.

1) The variance of the output of the nonlinear statistical filters depends on the mean value m, on the variance σ_x^2, and on p.

2) In this case, (20) is approximately valid only for very small variances $\sigma_{x_i}^2$, $i = 1, N$. In extremely long-tailed distributions (e.g., impulse noise), (20) is not valid. This case will be considered in more detail in Section IV.

The analysis we have done in this section is general and it can be applied both to one-dimensional and two-dimensional filtering. In the second case, the inputs $x_1, \cdots, x_N$ are values of the pixels s_{ij} of an image corrupted by noise n_{ij}

$$x_{ij} = s_{ij} + n_{ij}.$$

The noise n_{ij} is assumed to be additive, zero mean, white, or colored. The analysis shows that the nonlinear mean filters examined reduce the noise variance more than the linear arithmetic mean filters for homogeneous image regions. It is also shown that they perform better than median filters in the homogeneous image regions, for short-tailed and medium-tailed noise probability distributions.

Another kind of noise encountered in images is impulse noise. We shall try to evaluate the performance of nonlinear mean filters in the presence of impulse noise.

IV. Impulse Noise Filtering

Impulse noise consists of very large positive or negative spikes of short duration. Positive spikes have values much larger than those of the background signal and appear like bright spots on the image. Negative spikes have values much smaller than those of the background signal and appear like dark spots on the image. Both are easily detected by the eye and degrade the image quality. Their removal is an important task in image processing.

Image processing by a linear arithmetic mean filter tends to reduce impulse noise and to distribute it to its surrounding pixels. Thus, linear filtering is not a useful tool in impulse noise removal. Filtering by the nonlinear means y_G, y_H, y_{L-p}, y_{CH-p} tends to reduce the average signal level, as can be seen by inequality (4). Thus, it can be used for positive spike suppression. On the other hand, the nonlinear means y_{L_p}, y_{CH_p} tend to increase the signal level and thus they can be used for negative spike suppression.

We shall try to find quantitative criteria to determine if the nonlinear mean filters suppress successfully positive spikes. Let the background signal have a mean m and the spikes a mean $M = bm (b \gg 1)$. Let

$$x_{ij} = \begin{cases} bm & \text{with probability } q \\ m & \text{with probability } 1 - q. \end{cases} \quad (20)$$

Our analysis will be based on the local mean image statistics as it is seen in (20). This makes only a negligible difference in the case of true impulse noise, since

$$\frac{x_{ij} - m}{b} \ll m. \quad (21)$$

For the purpose of statistical analysis, we define successful spike suppression as occurring when the following inequality for the expected value of the output of the nonlinear mean filter holds:

$$E(|y|) \leq am \quad a = 1 + \epsilon \quad \epsilon \geq 0 \quad (22)$$

for a positive spike.

Let N be the length of our filter and k the number of spikes found in the filter window. Then statistically q may be approximated by

$$q \simeq \frac{k}{N}. \quad (23)$$

We now estimate the maximum probability of occurrence of spikes, under which the spike suppression can be considered successful by criterion (22).

If the L_{-p} mean is used, then

$$\left(\frac{(N-k)m^{-p} + kM^{-p}}{N}\right)^{-1/p} \leq am,$$

hence,

$$q \leq \frac{a^{-p} - 1}{b^{-p} - 1}. \quad (24)$$

Equation (24) shows that by choosing p high enough, we can successfully suppress spikes, even when there is a large probability of occurrence. If the geometric mean is used, then

$$\sqrt[N]{m^{N-k}(bm)^k} \leq am, \quad \text{hence,} \quad q \leq \frac{\log a}{\log b}. \quad (25)$$

Since $\log a$ is only slightly larger than zero according to (22) and (25), it is clear that the geometric mean can remove only quite sparse spikes. If the contraharmonic mean y_{CH-p} is used

$$\frac{(N-k)m^{-p+1} + k(bm)^{-p+1}}{(N-k)m^{-p} + k(bm)^{-p}} \leq am,$$

hence,

$$q \leq \frac{a - 1}{a - 1 + b^{-p}(b - a)}. \quad (26)$$

Equation (26) also shows that we can suppress positive spikes with high probability, if we choose an appropriate power of p.

A similar analysis can be done for the suppression of negative spikes.

Let the background signal have a mean m and the spikes a mean $M = bm$ ($0 < b \ll 1$). Let the spike occurrence be described by (20) and a successful spike suppression be described by

$$y \geq am \quad a = 1 - \epsilon \quad \epsilon > 0. \quad (27)$$

If we use the y_{L_p} mean for negative spike suppression, we have

$$\left(\frac{(N-k)m^p + kM^p}{N}\right)^{1/p} \geq am,$$

hence,

$$q \leq \frac{1 - a^p}{1 - b^p}. \quad (28)$$

If we use the y_{CH_p} mean for negative spike suppression, we have

$$\frac{(N-k)m^{p+1} + kM^{p+1}}{(N-k)m^p + kM^p} \geq am,$$

hence,

$$q \leq \frac{1 - a}{1 - a + b^p(a - b)}. \quad (29)$$

It can be seen from (28) and (29) that even negative spikes with a high probability of occurrence can be suppressed by a choice of a sufficiently high power of p.

The major drawback in the use of nonlinear mean filters for impulse noise removal is that they cannot remove simultaneously positive and negative spikes. The nonlinear means y_{CH_p}, y_{L_p} tend to distribute positive spikes to their surrounding pixels. The nonlinear means y_H, y_{L-p}, y_{CH-p} tend to distribute negative spikes to their surrounding pixels.

Median filters have been extensively used for impulse noise removal [6]. Their performance is very satisfactory, but it deteriorates rapidly by increasing the probability of spike occurrence, or by decreasing their window extent [6]. One of their advantages lies in their suitability for fast computation and their ability to remove combined positive negative spikes. In the case of impulse noise removal, we conclude that nonlinear mean filters are better than median filters, only when we have one kind of impulse noise, with high probability of occurrence (≥ 0.4). Some simulation results of the previous analysis are described in Section VII.

In the next section, we shall examine some properties of nonlinear mean filters in the presence of signal dependent noise.

V. Signal Dependent Noise Filtering by Nonlinear Means

Signal dependent noise is a special kind of noise described by the formula

$$x = s + h(s)n \quad (30)$$

where n is white noise, s is the signal, x is the noise corrupted signal, and $h(s)$ is a function which governs the dependence of the noise term $h(s)n$ on the signal s. Two usual kinds of signal dependent noise are the multiplicative noise [1], [3], [4], [8]:

$$x = s + csn \quad c = \text{constant}, \quad (31)$$

and the film-grain noise [1], [8]:

$$x = s + cs^m n \quad (32)$$

where c, m are parameters describing the noise.

$$g(x) = g(s) + g^{(1)}(s) cs^m n + \frac{1}{2} g^{(2)}(s) c^2 s^{2m} n^2 + \cdots + \frac{1}{k!} g^{(k)}(s) c^k s^{mk} n^k + \cdots \underbrace{\qquad\qquad\qquad\qquad\qquad\qquad\qquad\qquad\qquad\qquad\qquad}_{N(n,\,s)}. \quad (38)$$

Signal dependent noise cannot be removed by conventional linear techniques, as it is done with additive noise. Nonlinear techniques have been used for its filtering. Homomorphic filtering has been used for the removal of multiplicative [4] and film-grain noise [8]. Such techniques attempt to decouple the noise from the signal and to transform signal dependent noise to additive noise. Then conventional linear techniques, e.g., Wiener filter-

$$g(x) = g(s) + cn - \frac{1}{2} mc^2 \left(\frac{s^m n}{s}\right)^2 s^{-m+1} + \cdots + \frac{c^k}{k!(1-m)} \prod_{i=1}^{k} (-m + 2 - i) \left(\frac{s^m n}{s}\right)^k s^{-m+1} + \cdots \underbrace{\qquad\qquad\qquad\qquad\qquad\qquad\qquad\qquad\qquad\qquad\qquad}_{N(s,\,n)}. \quad (41)$$

ing [1], can be used to remove the additive noise. Homomorphic filters have the form of Fig. 1. As we have mentioned in Section II, homomorphic filters can be considered a special case of (1).

The following theorem is proven in the Appendix.

Theorem: The only kind of signal dependent noise (30) which is completely reduced to additive noise by homomorphic filtering by an analytical function g

$$g[s + h(s)n] = g(s) + N(n) \quad (33)$$

is multiplicative noise. In this case, the analytic function g is the natural logarithm.

$$g(x) = \ln x. \quad (34)$$

In all other kinds of signal dependent noise, the function g produces a noise $N(n, s)$

$$g[s + h(s)n] = g(s) + N(n, s) \quad (35)$$

which consists of several terms, given by the Taylor series expansion

$$N(n, s) = \sum_{k=1}^{\infty} \frac{g^{(k)}(s)}{k!} h^k(s) n^k \quad (36)$$

where $g^{(k)}(s)$ is the kth derivative of $g(s)$.

If we choose $g(s)$ such that

$$g^{(1)}(s) h(s) = 1, \quad (37)$$

the most significant term of $N(n, s)$ is signal independent. Thus, the noise is partially decoupled from the signal. This noise is removed by any conventional linear technique. After the removal of $N(s, n)$, the nonlinear function $g^{-1}(x)$ is applied on $g(s)$ of (35) to recover the signal s.

We shall try to apply homorphic filtering to the film-grain noise described by (32).

In this case, the Taylor series expansion becomes

If we choose

$$g^{(1)}(s) = s^{-m} \quad (39)$$

this is satisfied by

$$g(s) = \frac{1}{1-m} s^{-m+1} \quad (40)$$

and the series expansion becomes

We see that $N(s, n)$ is still signal dependent, although it includes the term n which is additive noise. Its dependence on s is significantly reduced, since the higher order terms of $N(s, n)$ progressively vanish when the noise levels are below the signal level.

$$|cs^m n| \leq |s|. \quad (42)$$

The term n of $N(s, n)$, which is the most significant one, can be efficiently reduced by the use of linear techniques. The corresponding nonlinear mean is an L_{-p} mean with $p = 1 - m$.

The previous analysis shows that the use of nonlinear

means in the presence of signal dependent noise of the form (30) leads at least to the partial decoupling of signal and noise.

So far we have tried to determine the behavior of nonlinear mean filters in the presence of different kinds of noise. We shall now consider the properties of nonlinear mean filters in the presence of edges.

VI. Performance of Nonlinear Means in the Presence of Edges

Edge information is very important in image processing [1], [3]. Good quality images have sharp, clear edges. Any degradation of edge sharpness causes a deterioration of the subjective quality of the image. It is generally known [6] that linear filtering blurs the edges. This is one of the major drawbacks of linear filtering. Median filtering tends to preserve the edges. This fact and its computational simplicity have made it popular in image processing. We shall try to evaluate the performance of nonlinear mean filters in the presence of edges.

The edge which will be examined is shown in Fig. 2. It is a step edge having values b and $b + h$ on each side. Ramp edges will not be examined in this work. The filtered edge by various nonlinear means is shown in Fig. 2. The blurring effects of the arithmetic and geometric mean filters are clearly shown. Regions of increased values (plateaus) are decreased in area under the y_{L-p} and y_{CH-p} means, and regions of decreased values are decreased in area under the y_{L_p} and y_{CH_p} means. The nonlinear means y_{L_p}, y_{CH_p}, y_{L-p}, y_{CH-p} tend to preserve edges better than the arithmetic or geometric means, although they shift them a little. This shift is not significant, if the length of the filter is small and, above all, not observed by the human eye. The higher the value of p, the better the edge preservation is.

We also consider the performance of the nonlinear mean filters in the presence of noise edges. The model which will be used is the following:

$$x = s + n \quad (43)$$

where s is a deterministic step edge having values b and $b + h$, on each side, and n is a white uniform noise of mean value zero and variance σ_n^2. The output mean m_y and the variance σ_y^2 are given by relations (15) and (18), respectively. Since white noise is assumed, (15) and (18) are specialized to this case:

$$m_y \simeq f(m_1, \cdots, m_N) + \frac{1}{2} \sum_{i=1}^{N} f_i'' \sigma_n^2 \quad (44)$$

$$\sigma_y^2 = \sum_{i=1}^{N} f_i'^2 \sigma_n^2 - \left(\frac{1}{2} \sum_{i=1}^{N} f_i'' \sigma_n^2 \right)^2 \quad (45)$$

where $m_1, \cdots, m_N$ are equal to b or $b + h$ according to the actual position of the filter window.

Equation (44) shows that the nonlinear mean response in the presence of noisy edges follows approximately the filter response for the same edge without noise, when the

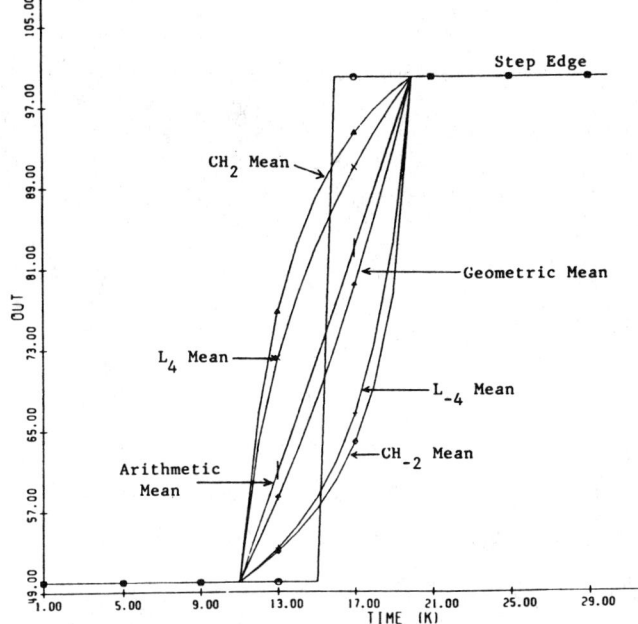

Fig. 2. The response of nonlinear statistical means in the presence of an ideal step edge. (○ step edge, △ CH_2 mean, × L_4 mean, | arithmetic mean, ↑ geometric mean, + L_{-4} mean, ◇ CH_{-2} mean).

noise levels are small enough. Thus, nonlinear means y_{L_p}, y_{CH_p}, y_{L-p}, y_{CH-p} tend to preserve edges, even if they are noisy. Figs. 4 and 8 show the mean values m_y of the L_3 and CH_{-2} nonlinear filters in the presence of noise. Equation (45) is only a crude approximation of the output variance of nonlinear means. The variances σ_y^2 of the L_3 and CH_{-2} nonlinear mean filters are shown in Figs. 6 and 10.

We now consider some simulations to check the theoretical results.

VII. Simulation and Conclusions

We have performed three kinds of experiments to check our analysis. The first set of experiments are one-dimensional simulations for the verification of our theoretical results presented in Sections III and VI. These results are valid for noise having any medium-tailed or short-tailed probability density function of sufficiently small variance. The test signal is a step edge with $b = 50$, $h = 50$ corrupted with additive uniformly distributed white noise. The performance of various nonlinear mean filters in such an edge is shown in Fig. 3. The theoretical mean and variance of the output of the nonlinear mean filters are given by (44) and (45). The theoretical and the experimental results for the y_{L_3} mean are described in Figs. 4–7. The experimental results have been obtained by applying the nonlinear statistical means to 100 different test signals. These test signals have been generated by adding noise produced by a random number generator to the step edge. The formulas used to find the estimates $\hat{m}_y$ and $\hat{\sigma}_y^2$ of the output mean and variance were the following:

$$\hat{m}_y = \frac{1}{M} \sum_{i=1}^{M} f(x_{li}, \cdots, x_{Ni}), \quad (46)$$

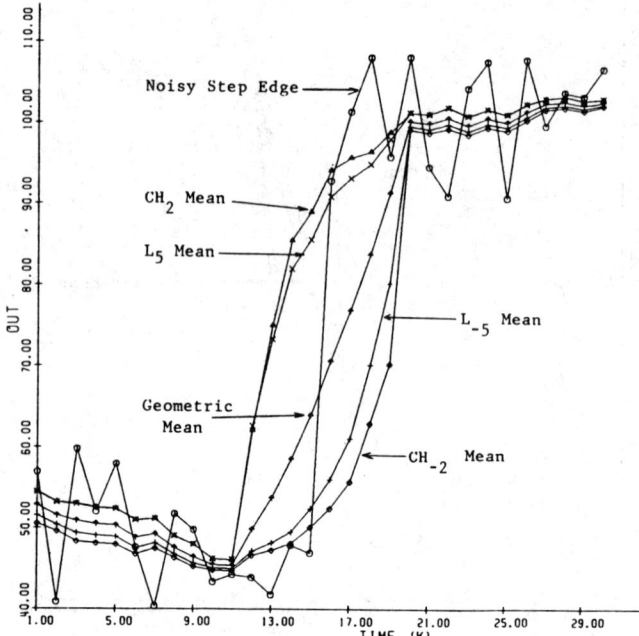

Fig. 3. The response of nonlinear statistcal means in the presence of a noisy step edge (○ step edge, △ CH_2 mean, × L_5 mean, ↑ geometric mean, + L_5 mean, ◊ CH_{-2} mean).

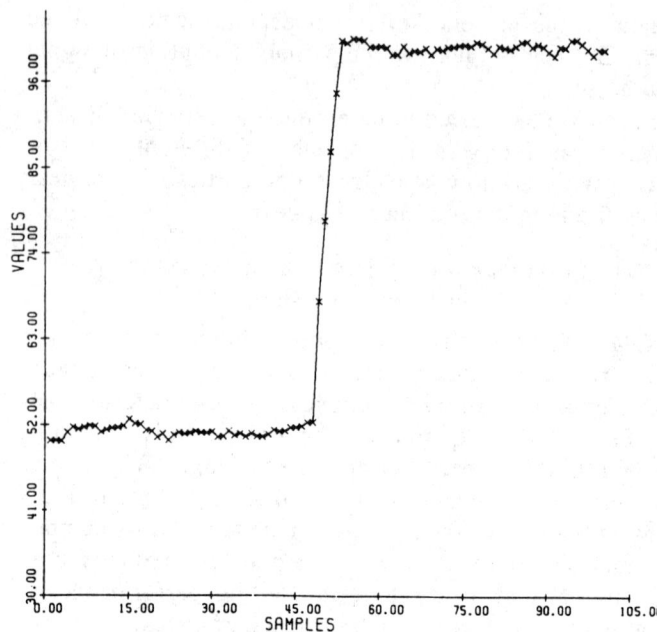

Fig. 5. Experimental mean of the output of an L_3 mean filter in the presence of a step edge corrupted by additive, uniformly distributed noise of variance 75.

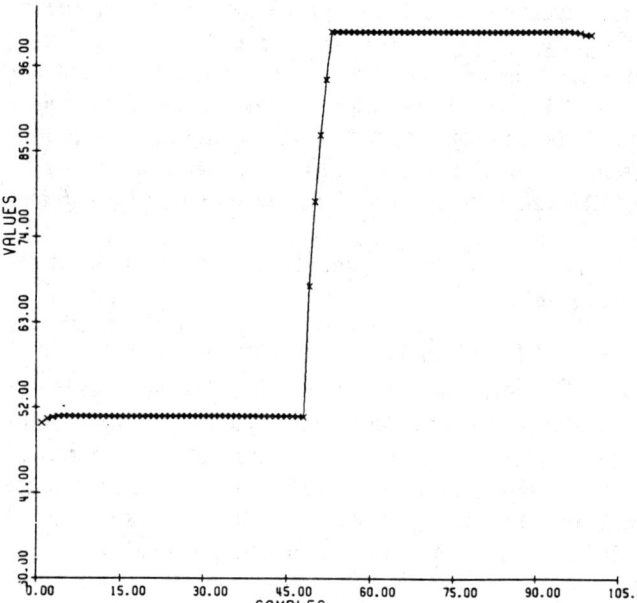

Fig. 4. Theoretical mean of the output of an L_3 mean filter in the presence of a step edge corrupted by additive, uniformly distributed noise of variance 75.

$$\hat{\sigma}_y^2 = \frac{1}{M} \sum_{i=1}^{M} [f(x_{li}, \cdots, x_{Ni}) - \hat{m}_y]^2 \quad (M = 100).$$

(47)

The theoretical results approximate very well the experimental ones. The theoretical and experimental results for the $y_{CH_{-2}}$ mean are presented in Figs. 8–11. The only discrepancy between the theoretical and the experimental results is in the variance of the output points near the lower part of the edge. This is explained by the fact that the

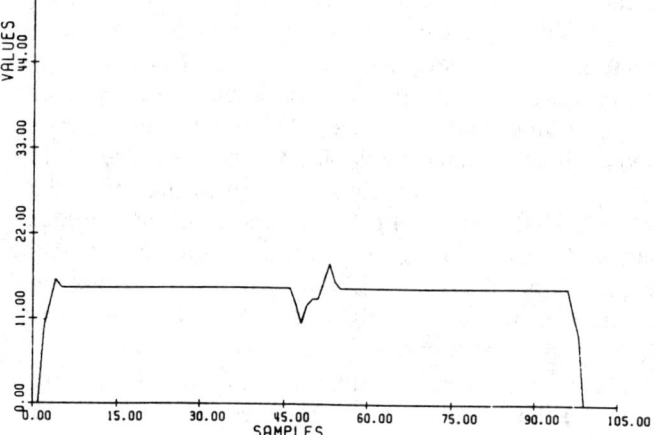

Fig. 6. Theoretical variance of the output of an L_3 mean filter in the presence of a step edge corrupted by additive, uniformly distributed noise of variance 75.

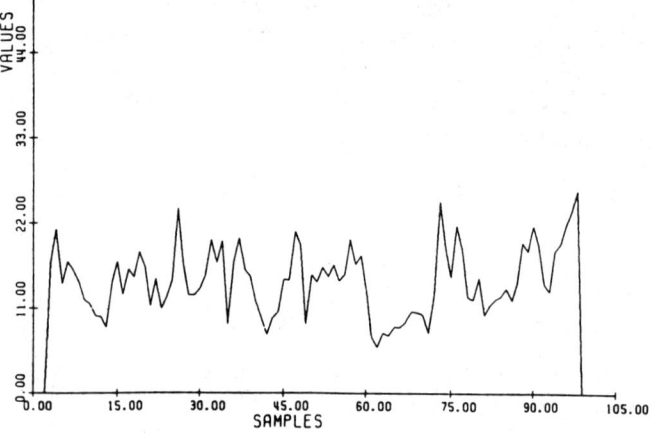

Fig. 7. Experimental variance of the output of an L_3 mean filter in the presence of a step edge corrupted by additive, uniformly distributed noise of variance 75.

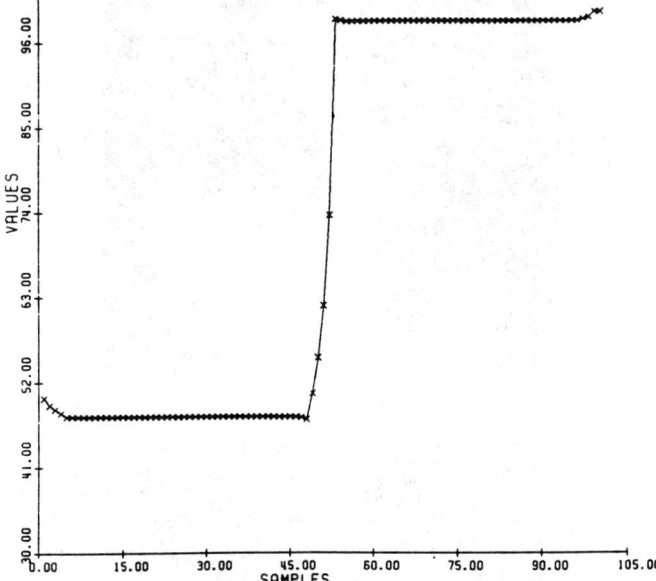

Fig. 8. Theoretical mean of the output of a CH_{-2} mean filter in the presence of a step edge corrupted by additive, uniformly distributed noise of variance 75.

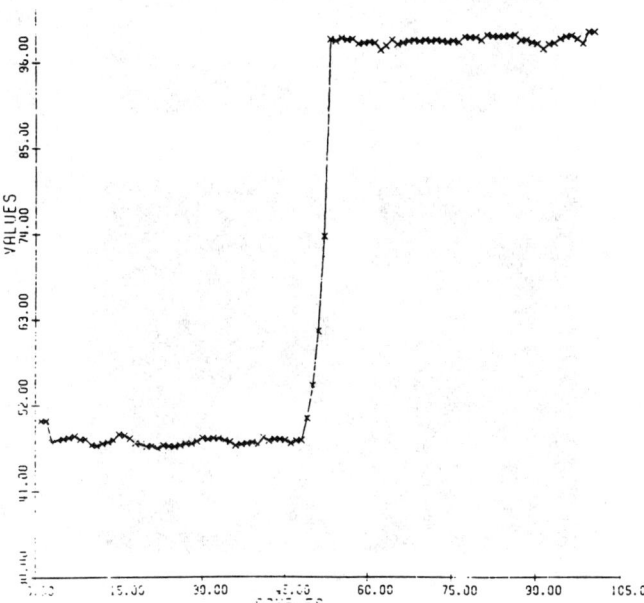

Fig. 9. Experimental mean of the output of a CH_{-2} mean filter in the presence of a step corrupted by additive, uniformly distributed noise variance 75.

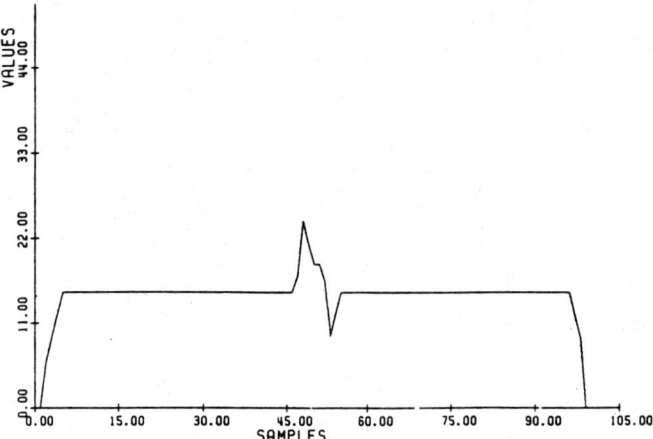

Fig. 10. Theoretical variance of the output of a CH_{-2} mean filter in the presence of a step edge corrupted by additive, uniformly distributed noise of variance 75.

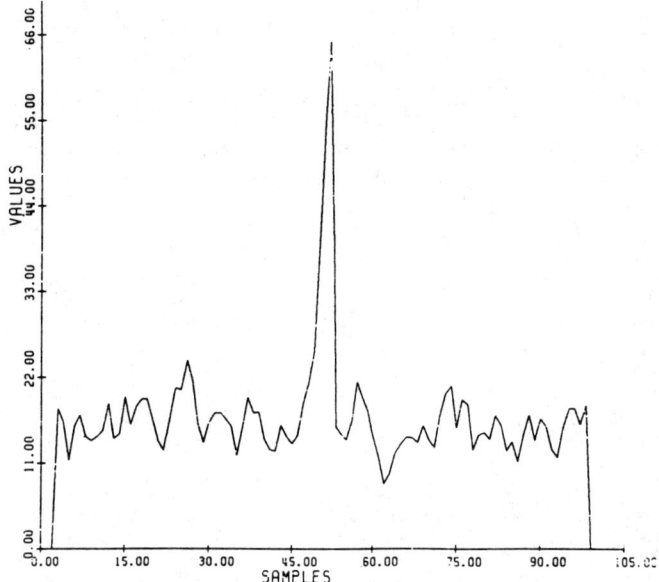

Fig. 11. Experimental variance of the output of a CH_{-2} mean filter in the presence of a step edge corrupted by additive, uniformly distributed noise of variance 75.

nonlinearity of the $y_{CH_{-2}}$ mean is high and it is not always well approximated by a second-order approximation of the form (45).

A test signal consisting of uniformly distributed white noise was used for positive spike removal by nonlinear means is shown in Fig. 12. The performance of the $y_{L_{-3}}$ mean and the $y_{CH_{-2}}$ mean are shown in Figs. 13 and 14, respectively. The spike suppression is very good.

The second set of experiments is performed on the test image of Fig. 15(a). The same image corrupted by positive impulse noise with probability of occurrence 0.30 is shown in Fig. 15(b). The result of a 3 × 3 median filter is shown in Fig. 15(c). The median filter fails to remove all the spikes. The result of a 3 × 3 $y_{CH_{-2}}$ nonlinear mean filter is shown in Fig. 15(d). It removes perfectly all the spikes.

The third set of experiments has been performed on the test image shown in Fig. 16(a). This image was corrupted by additive uniformly distributed white noise of variance $\sigma_n^2 = 200$ and is shown in Fig. 16(b). This image is filtered by an arithmetic mean filter, a median filter, and a y_H nonlinear mean filter of a 5 × 5 extent. The results are shown in Fig. 16(c)-(e), respectively. It is clearly seen that a median filter preserves the edges but it does not reduce significantly the background noise. The contrary is valid for an arithmetic mean filter. The filter y_H reduces the background noise better than the median filter and preserves the edges better than the arithmetic mean filter. The conclusions drawn from the previous analysis are outlined

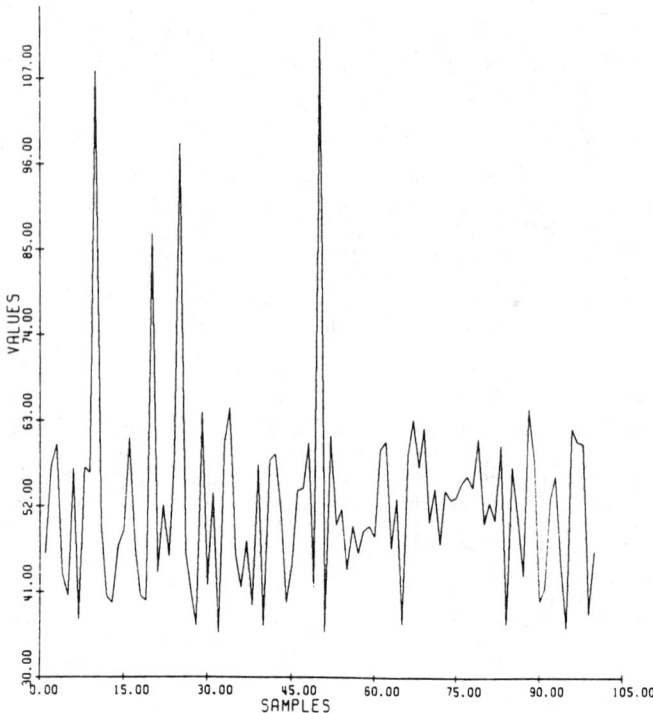

Fig. 12. Positive spikes superimposed to a uniform white noise of mean 50 and variance 75.

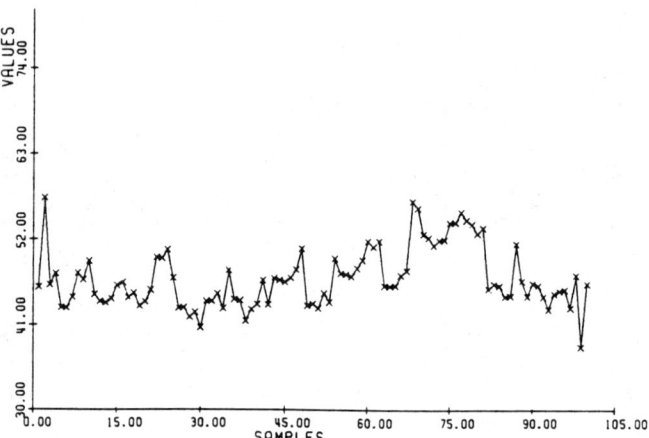

Fig. 13. Filtering of signal of Fig. 12 by an L_{-3} mean. Positive spikes are removed.

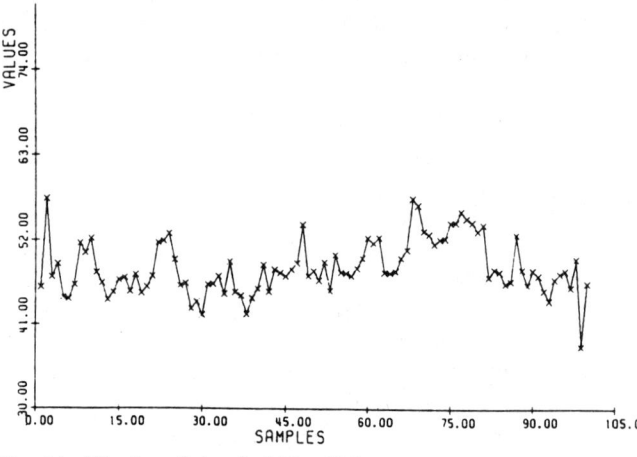

Fig. 14. Filtering of signal of Fig. 13 by a CH_{-2} mean. Positive spikes are removed.

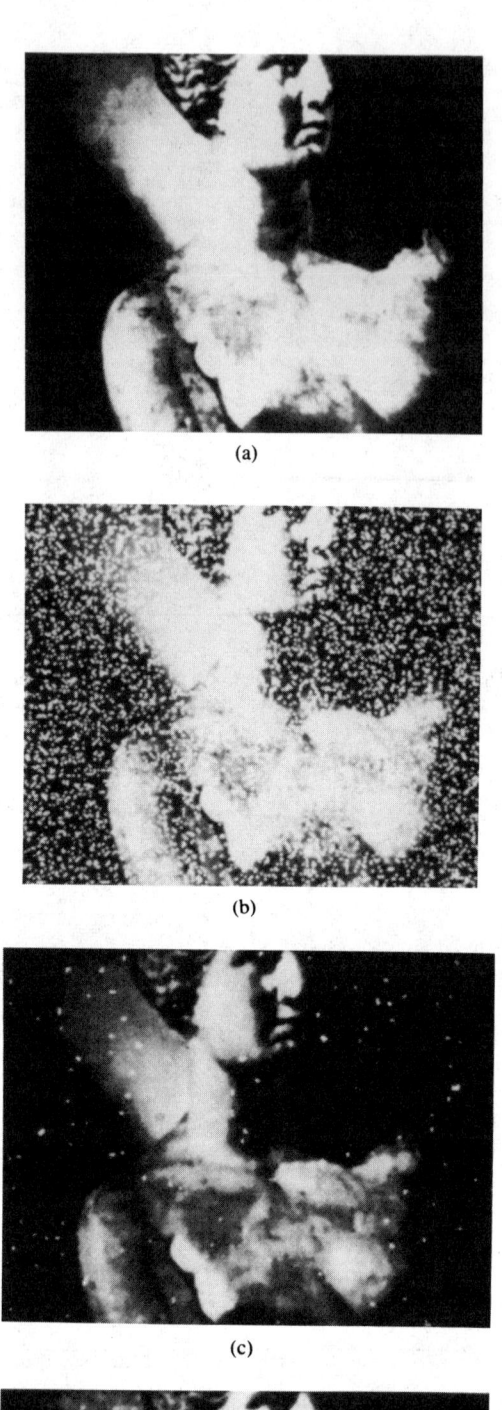
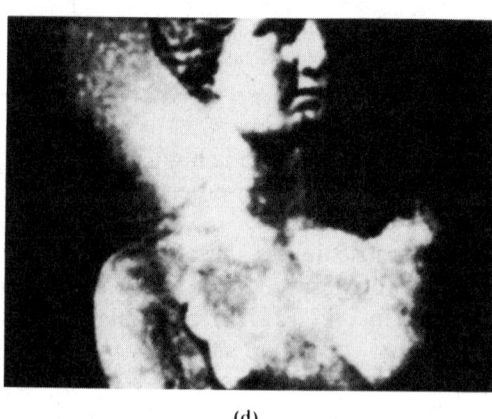

Fig. 15. (a) Test image. (b) Test image corrupted by impulse noise. (c) Image 15(b) filtered by a 3 × 3 medium filter. (d) Image 15(b) filtered by a 3 × 3 CH_{-2} mean.

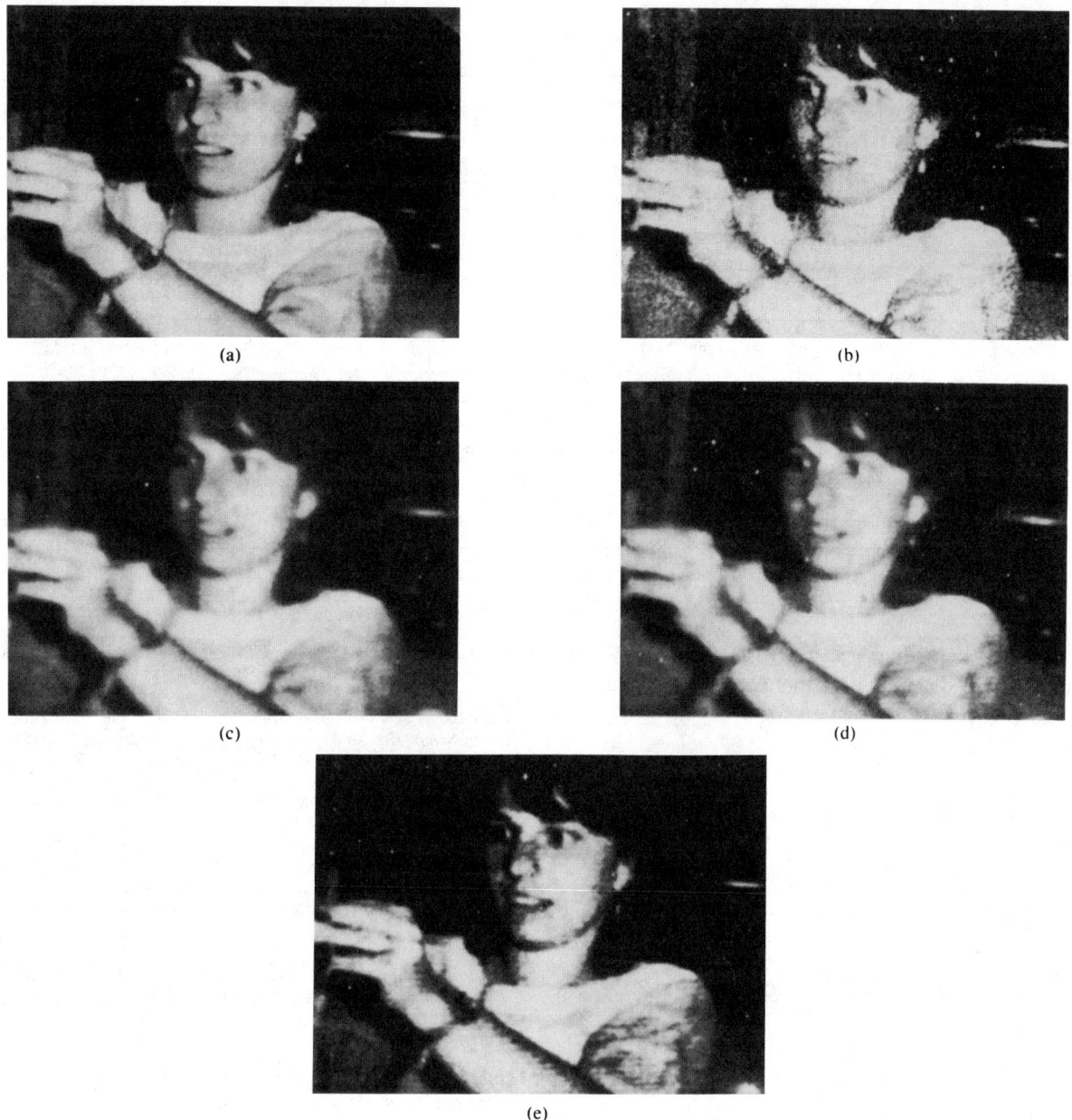

Fig. 16. (a) Test image. (b) Test image corrupted by uniformly distributed white noise of variance $\sigma_n^2 = 200$. (c) Image 16(b) filtered by an arithmetic mean filter. (d) Image 16(b) filtered by a median filter. (e) Image 16(b) filtered by a harmonic mean filter.

in Table IV. This table summarizes the properties of various filters used in image processing for noise removal. It cannot of course encompass all the qualitative quantitative results describing the performance of the various filters, but gives an overview of their characteristics.

APPENDIX

Proof of the Theorem of Section V: The signal dependent noise is described by

$$x = s + h(s)\, n. \tag{A1}$$

We shall try to find the form of $h(s)$, which allows a decoupling of noise and signal by a function $g(x)$

$$g[s + h(s)\, n] = g(s) + N(n) \tag{A2}$$

where $N(n)$ is a function of noise n only.

By using a Taylor series expansion of $g(x)$, we have

$$g[s + h(s)\, n] = g(s) + g^{(1)}(s)\, h(s)\, n$$
$$+ \frac{1}{2} g^{(2)}(s)\, h^2(s)\, n^2 + \cdots$$
$$+ \frac{g^{(k)}(s)}{K!} h^k(s)\, n^k + \cdots$$

$$N(n, s) = \sum_{k=1}^{\infty} \frac{g^{(k)}(s)}{k!} h^k(s)\, n^k \tag{A3}$$

where (k) denotes the kth derivative of a function.

TABLE IV
OVERVIEW OF THE PERFORMANCE OF VARIOUS FILTERS IN THE PRESENCE OF DIFFERENT KINDS OF NOISE

	Arithmetic mean	Geometric mean	L_p mean	Contraharmonic mean	Median
Short-tailed additive noise	Good	Good	Good	Good	Poor
Heavy-tailed additive noise	Poor	Poor	Poor	Poor	Good
Positive spikes	Poor	Poor	Good	Good	Good
Negative spikes	Poor	Poor	Good	Good	Good
Mixed spikes	Poor	Poor	Poor	Poor	Good
Multiplicative noise	Poor	Good	Poor	Poor	Poor
Film-grain noise	Poor	Poor	Good	Poor	Poor
Edge preservation	Poor	Poor	Good	Good	Good

The Taylor series expansion (36) is unique [13]. The noise part $N(n, s)$ of (19) is independent of s, iff the following set of equation is satisfied for every k:

$$\frac{g^{(k)}(s)}{k!} h^k(s) = a \quad (A4)$$

$$\frac{g^{(k+1)}(s)}{(k+1)!} h^{(k+1)}(s) = b \quad (A5)$$

where a, b are constants. Equations (A4) and (A5) are valid iff

$$h^{(1)}(s) = \frac{b}{a} \frac{(k+1)}{k} \quad (A6)$$

which implies

$$h(s) = cs. \quad (A7)$$

This function corresponds to multiplicative noise.
Q.E.D.

The function $g(x)$ used in this case is the logarithmic function. The additive noise $N(n, s)$ can be removed by a linear technique. Finally, the application g^{-1} on the remaining part $g(s)$ of (36) gives an estimate of the original signal n. The logarithmic homorphic filter corresponds to the geometric mean filter.

References

[1] W. K. Pratt, *Digital Image Processing*. New York: Wiley, 1978.
[2] B. R. Hunt and H. C. Andrews, *Digital Image Restoration*. Englewood Cliffs, NJ: Prentice-Hall, 1976.
[3] A. V. Oppenheim, *Applications of Digital Signal Processing*. Englewood Cliffs, NJ: Prentice-Hall, 1978.
[4] A. V. Oppenheim, R. W. Schafer, and T. G. Stockham, "Nonlinear filtering of multiplied and convolved signals," *Proc. IEEE*, vol. 56, pp. 1264-1294, Aug. 1963.
[5] S. G. Tyan, "Median filtering: Deterministic properties," in *Two-Dimensional Digital Signal Processing*, vol. II, T. S. Huang, Ed. New York: Springer-Verlag, 1981.
[6] B. J. Justusson, "Median filtering: Statistical properties," in *Two-Dimensional Digital Signal Processing*, vol. II, T. S. Huang, Ed. New York: Springer-Verlag, 1981.
[7] A. Kundu, S. K. Mitra, and P. P. Vaidyanathan, "Generalized mean filters: A new class of nonlinear filters for image processing, in *Proc. 6th Symp. Circuit Theory Design*, Sept. 1983, pp. 185-187.
[8] H. H. Arsenault and M. Denis, "Image processing in signal-dependent noise," *Canadian J. Phys.*, vol. 61, pp. 309-317, 1983.
[9] B. G. Kendall, *The Advanced Theory of Statistics*, vol. 1. London, England: Griffin, 1973.
[10] A. Papoulis, *Probability, Random Variables and Stochastic Processes*. New York: McGraw-Hill, 1965.
[11] W. B. Davenport and W. L. Root, *Random Signals and Noise*. New York: McGraw-Hill, 1958.
[12] S. M. Selby, *Standard Mathematical Tables*. Boca Raton, FL: CRC, 1973.
[13] R. V. Churchill, W. Brown, and R. F. Verhey, *Complex Variable and Applications*. New York: McGraw-Hill, 1974.

Ioannis Pitas (S'80), for a photograph and biography, see p. 572 of this issue.

Anastasios N. Venetsanopoulos (S'66-M'69-SM'79) received the Mechanical and Electrical Engineering degree from the National Technical University of Athens, Greece, in 1965. He received the M.S., M.Phil., and Ph.D. degrees from the Department of Engineering and Applied Science, Yale University, New Haven, CT, in 1966, 1968, and 1969, respectively.

He joined the University of Toronto, Ont., Canada, in September 1968, where he is now a Professor and the Chairman of the Communications Group, Department of Electrical Engineering. His research interests span the fields of digital signal/image processing and digital communications. He has conducted research, taught, and consulted extensively in Europe and North and South America. He was Program Chairman of the International Communications Conference (ICC-78) and will be again for ICC-86; he was Editor of the *Canadian Electrical Engineering Journal*; and he was the President of the Canadian Society of Electrical Engineering.

Dr. Venetsanopoulos is a member of the Association of Professional Engineers of Ontario, the New York Academy of Sciences, Sigma Xi, and the Technical Chamber of Greece. He has served as Chairman of the Central Canada Council of IEEE. He is presently a Fellow of the Engineering Institute of Canada and Associate Editor for Digital Signal Processing of the IEEE TRANSACTIONS ON CIRCUITS AND SYSTEMS.

A Generalization of Median Filtering Using Linear Combinations of Order Statistics

ALAN C. BOVIK, STUDENT MEMBER, IEEE, THOMAS S. HUANG, FELLOW, IEEE, AND
DAVID C. MUNSON, JR., MEMBER, IEEE

Abstract—We consider a class of nonlinear filters whose output is given by a linear combination of the order statistics of the input sequence. Assuming a constant signal in white noise, the coefficients in the linear combination are chosen to minimize the output MSE for several noise distributions. It is shown that the optimal order statistic filter (OSF) tends toward the median filter as the noise becomes more impulsive. The optimal OSF is applied to an actual noisy image and is shown to perform well, combining properties of both the averaging and median filters. A more general design scheme for applications involving nonconstant signals is also given.

I. INTRODUCTION

MEDIAN filtering has recently been recognized as an effective alternative to the linear smoother for some applications [1]–[4]. In particular, the moving median of a time or spatial series has been shown to preserve edges or monotonic changes in trend, while eliminating impulses of short duration. In these respects, the median smoother is superior to the linear filter.

The median is a particular case of the ith order statistic (or rank statistic) of a finite set of real numbers. The ith order statistic of N real numbers $x_1, \cdots, x_N$ where N is usually odd for digital filtering applications, is defined as the ith largest number in algebraic value. Here we shall denote the ith order statistic by $x_{(i)}$ in keeping with the mathematical literature. The minimum is then $x_{(1)}$, the maximum $x_{(N)}$, and the median $x_{((N+1)/2)}$.

Little work has been done in digital filtering applications using order statistics other than the median. It is the object of this paper to present an order statistic filter design scheme, where the output of the filter is a linear combination of the order statistics of several input samples considered simultaneously. The order statistic filter (OSF) is nonlinear due to the ordering process, which considerably complicates the analysis.

Before introducing the OSF, a short review of previous work in median filtering follows.

Manuscript received November 22, 1982; revised April 27, 1983. This work was supported by the Joint Services Electronics Program under Contract N00014-79-C-0424. Portions of this manuscript were presented at the IEEE International Conference on Acoustics, Speech, and Signal Processing, Paris, France, May 3-5, 1982.
The authors are with the Coordinated Science Laboratory and the Department of Electrical Engineering, University of Illinois, Urbana, IL 61801.

A. Median Filtering

The median filter was introduced in 1974 by Tukey [1], who used the moving median as a smoothing technique in time series analysis. Rabiner *et al.* [2] used the median filter and series combinations of linear filters and median filters to smooth speech waveforms in a qualitative study, and reported favorable results. They found that the median filter was generally superior to a Hamming window of similar length for smoothing several waveforms such as log input energy of a speech signal, zero-crossing rate, and pitch period. The median smoother was noted to preserve discontinuities of sufficient duration while eliminating local roughness in the signal, whereas the linear smoother was seen to be inadequate in that much information was lost due to smearing. They deemed the median-linear series combination to be yet more effective for their application, but there is no evidence to support this for the general application.

Jayant [3] performed a similar study involving the suppression of impulse noise due to bit errors in the transmission of digital speech signals. He compared moving average and moving median-based filters in computer simulations and informal listening tests for various filter lengths. He concluded that for independently occurring errors the two techniques performed similarly. However, he noted that for dependent error occurrences, which were interpreted as clusterings of the errors, the averager was generally superior.

Median filtering has also come into recent use for enhancing images. Pratt [4] made a rather qualitative study of two-dimensional median filters of various sizes and shapes, and examined application of one-dimensional medians to a picture corrupted by impulsive noise. He concluded that although the median filter is extremely useful for suppressing impulsive and "salt-and-pepper" noise, it should be considered an ad hoc method dependent upon the particular application.

There has been some more recent work in actual implementation of median filtering. Huang *et al.* [5] have devised a fast algorithm to implement two-dimensional median filters. Their algorithm is based upon the fact that as the filter window is moved from column to column across the image, most of the pixels are retained within the filter window. The algorithm updates the histogram corresponding to the new pixel values entering the window. A considerable reduction in computer time is attainable when compared with conventional sorting algorithms. In particular, for an $n \times n$ filter window the number of comparisons required for computation of each pixel is about $(2n + 10)$; using ordinary sorting methods the number of comparisons is significantly higher.

An algorithm for real-time median filtering has been developed by Ataman, Aatre, and Wong [6].[1] This algorithm allows on-line computation of the running median.

It is possible that some of these methods, or variations, could be used for general order statistic filtering; however, that is beyond the scope of this paper, and will not be discussed here.

B. The Order Statistic Filter

The output of an order statistic filter of length N operating on a sequence $\{x_j\}$ for N odd is given by

$$y_k = \text{OSF}(\{x_j\}_{j=k-M}^{k+M}) = \sum_{i=1}^{N} \alpha_i x_{(i)}^k \qquad (1)$$

where $M = (N-1)/2$ and $x_{(i)}^k$ are the order statistics of $x_{k-M}, \cdots, x_k, \cdots, x_{k+M}$. The α_i are constants that may be chosen for a particular application. We can generalize this to two dimensions by considering the points within the window as the values to be ranked and linearly combined, regardless of the shape and size of the window. Generally the window is symmetric about its center and we replace the center pixel value with the output value.

The median filter is a particular case of (1), with coefficients

$$\alpha_i = \begin{cases} 1; & i = (N+1)/2 \\ 0; & \text{otherwise.} \end{cases}$$

We can also define a maximum filter, for example, by taking

$$\alpha_i = \begin{cases} 0; & i = 1, \cdots, N-1 \\ 1; & i = N. \end{cases}$$

As a generalization, we may constrain all of the coefficients of the order statistics to be zero except for the ith, which we set to unity. The result is called an ith ranked-order operation. Nodes and Gallagher [7] have found that an $(N-1)$th ranked-order operation is effective for digital AM detection both with and without corruption by impulse noise. Similarly, an Nth ranked-order operation (the maximum filter) can be used for peak detection.

In this paper we consider the design of a general OSF. In Section II we assume a constant signal in additive white noise and derive an explicit expression for the coefficients in the OSF minimizing the output MSE. The optimal coefficients are given for different filter lengths for several common noise distributions.

In Section III we compute the optimal OSF coefficients for a number of generalized exponential noise distributions. It is shown that as the noise becomes more impulsive (i.e., the tails of the noise density become heavier), the optimal OSF tends toward the median filter.

In Section IV, the optimal OSF for a constant signal is applied to an actual noisy image. The OSF performs well and is found to share properties of both the averaging and median filters.

Finally, Section V provides a more general design scheme for applications involving nonconstant signals.

II. Optimal OSF Coefficients for a Constant Signal in White Noise

We consider a constant signal s corrupted by zero-mean additive white noise; thus, the OSF input samples are of the form

$$x_j = s + n_j$$

where the n_j are independent, identically distributed random variables satisfying $E\{n_j\} = 0$. In addition, it will be assumed that the noise distribution is symmetric.

In the following, we will use the MSE as an optimality criterion, but we will also insist that the order statistic estimator be unbiased, i.e.,[2]

$$s = E\{y_k\} = E\left\{\sum_{i=1}^{N} \alpha_i x_{(i)}\right\} = s \sum_{i=1}^{N} \alpha_i + \sum_{i=1}^{N} \alpha_i E\{n_{(i)}\}. \qquad (2)$$

The noise distribution is symmetric so that the optimal α_i are symmetric and

$$E\{n_{(i)}\} = -E\{n_{(N-i+1)}\}.$$

Therefore, the unbiasedness condition (2) reduces to

$$\sum_{i=1}^{N} \alpha_i = 1. \qquad (3)$$

A. Minimization of the Mean Squared Error

The MSE is given by

$$\text{MSE} = E\{(y_k - s)^2\} = E\left\{\left(\sum_{i=1}^{N} \alpha_i x_{(i)} - s\right)^2\right\}$$

which can be simplified to

$$\text{MSE} = E\left\{\left(\sum_{i=1}^{N} \alpha_i n_{(i)}\right)^2\right\} \qquad (4)$$

by substituting $x_{(i)} = s + n_{(i)}$ and using (3). Expanding (4) gives the form

$$\text{MSE} = \sum_{i=1}^{N} \sum_{j=1}^{N} \alpha_i \alpha_j H_{ij} \qquad (5)$$

where

$$H_{ij} = E\{n_{(i)} n_{(j)}\}. \qquad (6)$$

Equation (5) is a quadratic form that can be expressed as

$$\text{MSE} = \alpha^T H \alpha \qquad (7)$$

where H is the $N \times N$ correlation matrix of the random vector $(n_{(1)}, n_{(2)}, \cdots, n_{(N)})^T$ and α is the constant vector $(\alpha_1, \alpha_2, \cdots, \alpha_N)^T$.

---

[1] Also, see [6] for a more complete list of references on median filtering.

[2] To simplify notation we will write $x_{(i)}$ instead of $x_{(i)}^k$, and $n_{(i)}$ instead of $n_{(i)}^k$.

The minimization of (7) subject to (3) is a straightforward quadratic optimization problem that can be solved using Lagrange multipliers. The Lagrangian function is given by (where e denotes a column of ones)

$$F(\alpha, \lambda) = \alpha^T H \alpha + \lambda(1 - e^T \alpha).$$

Setting the derivative with respect to α equal to zero yields

$$2H\alpha - \lambda e = 0. \tag{8}$$

The correlation matrix H is generally positive definite (it must be at least nonnegative definite). In this case (7) is strictly convex and a unique solution can be obtained by multiplying (8) by $e^T H^{-1}$ and using (3) in the form $e^T \alpha = 1$ to give

$$\lambda = 2/[e^T H^{-1} e].$$

Substituting into (8) yields the optimal coefficients

$$\alpha = H^{-1} e / [e^T H^{-1} e]. \tag{9}$$

A more general expression for α has been derived by Lloyd [8], using the Gauss-Markov least-squares theorem. This expression does not require that the parent distribution be symmetric as we assumed in deriving (9), but does require computation of the expected values of the ordered noise variates.

In order to compute the optimal coefficients using (9), it is first necessary to compute the elements of H, given by (6). We now consider this problem.

B. Computation of the Correlation Matrix

Evaluation of the H_{ij} in (6) requires expressions for the marginal and bivariate densities of the $n_{(i)}$. For this, we refer to the monograph on order statistics by David [9]. Denoting the parent distribution and density of the noise as $F_n(\cdot)$ and $f_n(\cdot)$, respectively, the density of $n_{(i)}$ for $i = 1, \cdots, N$ is given by

$$g_{n_{(i)}}(x) = K_i F_n^{i-1}(x) [1 - F_n(x)]^{N-i} f_n(x) \tag{10}$$

where $K_i = N!/[(i-1)!(N-i)!]$.

The joint density of $n_{(i)}$ and $n_{(j)}$ for $i, j = 1, \cdots, N$ ($i < j$) is

$$g_{n_{(i)} n_{(j)}}(x, y) = K_{i,j} F_n^{i-1}(x) [F_n(y) - F_n(x)]^{j-i-1}$$
$$\cdot [1 - F_n(y)]^{N-j} f_n(x) f_n(y) \tag{11}$$

where $K_{i,j} = [N!/[(i-1)!(j-i-1)!(N-j)!]]$.

Using the above notation, the H_{ij} are given by

$$H_{ij} = \iint_{-\infty}^{\infty} xy\, g_{n_{(i)} n_{(j)}}(x, y) \, dx\, dy \quad (i < j) \tag{12}$$

$$H_{ii} = \int_{-\infty}^{\infty} x^2 g_{n_{(i)}}(x) \, dx. \tag{13}$$

Due to the complexity of (10) and (11), numerical integration is generally required for evaluation of the H_{ij}, even for simple parent distributions of the original noise. The number of required integrations can be approximately quartered, however, by making use of the following symmetry relations:
a) $H_{ij} = H_{ji}$
b) $H_{ij} = H_{N-i+1, N-j+1}$

where b) assumes a symmetric parent density f_n.

Equations (12) and (13) were used to compute H for six different noise distributions and all odd values of N ranging from 3 to 25. The results are quite voluminous and hence are tabulated in [10], rather than here. The noise distributions chosen were the U-shaped, uniform, parabolic, triangular, normal, and Laplacian. These have been considered by Sarhan [11]-[13] for some small values of N (both odd and even) in estimating population means and variances in the mid-1950's. The U-shaped and parabolic densities are given by

$$f_U(x) = \sqrt{27/125}\, (3x^2/2\sigma^2); \quad |x| < \sqrt{5/3}\, \sigma$$

and

$$f_P(x) = 3(\sqrt{5}\, \sigma + x)(\sqrt{5}\, \sigma - x)/20\sqrt{5}\, \sigma^3; \quad |x| < \sqrt{5}\, \sigma$$

where σ is the standard deviation. We have taken $\sigma = 1$ for all distributions. This is without loss of generality, since Sarhan has shown that the optimal OSF coefficients are independent of σ.

C. Optimal Coefficients and Comparison of MSE

The resulting optimal values of the coefficients $\{\alpha_i\}_{i=1}^N$ were computed for each of the six noise distributions and for all odd values of N ranging from 3 to 25, and are available in [10]. Tables I-III list the optimal coefficients for $N = 3, 9,$ and 25.

The results obtained for the uniform and normal distributions are expected, since the midpoint ($\alpha_1 = \alpha_N = 1/2$) and the average ($\alpha_i = 1/N; i = 1, \cdots, N$) are the respective maximum likelihood estimators for these distributions. The resulting α_i for the Laplacian case are not surprising either, as we see that most of the weight is located in the center α_i. In fact, we note that the weight in the central coefficient becomes more pronounced as the noise distribution grows heavier tailed.

Table IV compares the MSE of the optimal OSF with that of both the median filter and the averaging filter for $N = 3$. It can be shown that the averaging filter is the best linear unbiased estimator (BLUE) for the problem under consideration. Note that the optimal OSF performs at least as well as either the median or BLUE for any noise distribution. This occurs because both the median and BLUE are OSF filters.

We next consider a family of generalized exponential noise distributions to further explore the relationship between the tail behavior of the noise and the properties of the OSF.

III. A FAMILY OF GENERALIZED EXPONENTIAL NOISE DISTRIBUTIONS

Consider the noise density

$$f_n(x) = k e^{-\gamma |x|^\beta}; \quad |x| < \infty \tag{14}$$

where γ and β are positive, and where k is chosen such that

$$\int_{-\infty}^{+\infty} f_n(x) \, dx = 1.$$

Integration yields

$$k = (\beta \gamma^{1/\beta})/2\Gamma(1/\beta)$$

TABLE I
OPTIMAL OSF COEFFICIENTS FOR $N = 3$

DISTRIBUTION	α_1	α_2
U-shaped	0.54000	-0.08000
Uniform	0.50000	0.00000
Parabolic	0.44048	0.11905
Triangular	0.39456	0.21088
Normal	0.33333	0.33333
Laplacian	0.15168	0.69663
	α_3	α_2

TABLE II
OPTIMAL OSF COEFFICIENTS FOR $N = 9$

DISTRIBUTION	α_1	α_2	α_3	α_4	α_5
U-shaped	0.55478	-0.02627	-0.01460	-0.00988	-0.00806
Uniform	0.50000	0.00000	0.00000	0.00000	0.00000
Parabolic	0.34031	0.06134	0.04428	0.03623	0.03568
Triangular	0.25913	0.04914	0.05734	0.08392	0.10094
Normal	0.11111	0.11111	0.11111	0.11111	0.11111
Laplacian	-0.01899	0.02904	0.06965	0.23795	0.36469
	α_9	α_8	α_7	α_6	α_5

TABLE III
OPTIMAL OSF COEFFICIENTS FOR $N = 25$

DISTRIBUTION	α_1	α_2	α_3	α_4	α_5
U-shaped	0.49732	0.00177	0.00320	0.00387	0.00394
Uniform	0.50000	0.00000	0.00000	0.00000	0.00000
Parabolic	0.28292	0.04758	0.03169	0.02393	0.01936
Triangular	0.21685	0.03614	0.02411	0.01811	0.01457
Normal	0.04000	0.04000	0.04000	0.04000	0.04000
Laplacian	0.00550	0.00335	-0.00427	-0.00101	-0.00008
	α_{25}	α_{24}	α_{23}	α_{22}	α_{21}

DISTRIBUTION	α_6	α_7	α_8	α_9	α_{10}
U-shaped	0.00081	-0.00122	-0.00197	-0.00206	-0.00180
Uniform	0.00000	0.00000	0.00000	0.00000	0.00000
Parabolic	0.01641	0.01447	0.01316	0.01204	0.01147
Triangular	0.01248	0.01190	0.01341	0.01786	0.02610
Normal	0.04000	0.04000	0.04000	0.04000	0.04000
Laplacian	0.00065	0.00314	0.01064	0.02907	0.06499
	α_{20}	α_{19}	α_{18}	α_{17}	α_{16}

DISTRIBUTION	α_{11}	α_{12}	α_{13}
U-shaped	-0.00162	-0.00150	-0.00146
Uniform	0.00000	0.00000	0.00000
Parabolic	0.01096	0.01068	0.01066
Triangular	0.03684	0.04643	0.05039
Normal	0.04000	0.04000	0.04000
Laplacian	0.11835	0.17195	0.19541
	α_{15}	α_{14}	α_{13}

TABLE IV
COMPARISON BETWEEN MSE OF THE OPTIMAL OSF FILTER, THE MEDIAN FILTER, AND THE BLUE

DISTRIBUTION	$\frac{\text{MSE(OPTIMAL)}}{\text{MSE(MEDIAN)}}$	$\frac{\text{MSE(OPTIMAL)}}{\text{MSE(BLUE)}}$
U-shaped	0.306	0.749
Uniform	0.500	0.900
Parabolic	0.603	0.963
Triangular	0.667	0.988
Normal	0.742	1.000
Laplacian	0.900	0.862

with

$$\gamma = [\Gamma(3/\beta)/\Gamma(1/\beta)]^{\beta/2} \sigma^{-\beta}$$

where Γ is the ordinary gamma function and σ, the standard deviation, will be taken to be 1. Obviously, if β is small, the above density will have heavy tails and the resulting noise will be impulsive in nature. Conversely, if β is large, the tails will be shallow and the noise will be comparatively smooth.

The techniques used in Section II can be applied to obtain the optimal coefficients for various β. As β decreases, the time required for computation of the correlation matrix, H, increases dramatically since very small intervals are required in the numerical integration routine. This limitation is not particularly disturbing, however, since the optimal OSF will be seen to approach the median for such extremely impulsive noise.

The Laplacian case with $\beta = 1$ and the normal case with $\beta = 2$ have already been considered. In this section we also consider $\beta = 1/2, 3/4, 3/2$, and 3. The correlation matrices were computed for $N = 3$ and are available in [10]. Filter lengths larger than $N = 3$ would have entailed prohibitive computational time for the cases with $\beta < 1$. The resulting optimal OSF coefficients were computed from (9) and are listed in Table V.

Note that as β grows smaller, there is a dramatic tendency towards the median; the value of α_2 approaches one very rapidly, and the value of $\alpha_1 = \alpha_3$ approaches zero. This strengthens the notion that median and almost-median type filters are very effective for suppressing additive noise which is more impulsive than the Laplacian case, at least for a nearly constant background signal.

Fig. 1 shows a plot of MSE(optimal)/MSE(median) and MSE(optimal)/MSE(BLUE) versus β for the above values of β. It is clear that the optimal OSF performs significantly better than the BLUE for $\beta < 1$, corresponding to impulse noise, and that the OSF performs better than the median filter for $\beta > 1$, corresponding to shallow-tailed noise.

In a related study, Gastwirth and Cohen [14] considered the behavior of several robust estimators, most of which are OSF's. In particular, they found the optimal coefficients α given by (9) for the contaminated normal densities $CN(\epsilon, D)$ given by

TABLE V
OPTIMAL OSF COEFFICIENTS FOR GENERALIZED EXPONENTIAL NOISE AND $N = 3$

β	α_1	α_2
3.0	0.4054	0.1891
2.0	0.3333	0.3333
1.5	0.2626	0.4748
1.0	0.1517	0.6966
0.75	0.0773	0.8453
0.5	0.0052	0.9897
	α_3	α_2

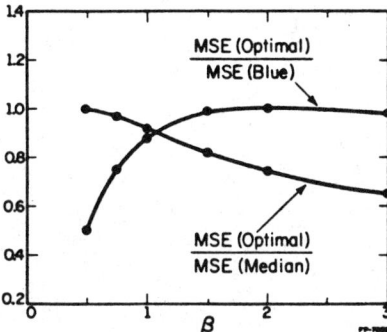

Fig. 1. Comparison between the MSE of the optimal OSF filter, the median filter, and the BLUE for generalized exponential noise.

$$f_{\epsilon,D}(x) = \frac{1}{\sqrt{2\pi}} \left\{ (1-\epsilon) e^{-x^2/2} + \frac{\epsilon}{D} e^{-x^2/2D^2} \right\}$$

for $\epsilon = 0.01, 0.05, 0.10$ and $D = 3$. This corresponds to an assumed standard normal noise contaminated by a fraction ϵ of $\eta(0, 3)$ noise. They found that for reasonably small samples the optimal α were very similar to the coefficients associated with the δ-trimmed mean. The δ-trimmed mean corresponds to an OSF with coefficients

$$\alpha_i = \begin{cases} 1/(N - 2[\delta N]); & [\delta N] + 1 \leq i \leq N - [\delta N] \\ 0; & \text{otherwise} \end{cases}$$

where N is the sample size, δ is the fraction trimmed from each end of the ordered sample, and $[\mu]$ denotes the integer part of μ.

The densities $CN(\epsilon, D)$ do not represent a class of increasingly heavy-tailed densities like those in (14), but rather represent a degree of contamination suitable for robustness studies. Gastwirth and Cohen found that in small samples ($N < 20$) both the OSF's for the contaminated normal densities and suitably trimmed means were very robust over densities ranging from the normal to the Laplacian, where robustness was defined in terms of the efficiency relative to the optimal OSF for each density. They concluded that for simplicity and reliability a moderately trimmed mean ($\delta \sim 0.20$) is very effective for small to moderate sample sizes.

IV. APPLICATION OF A DESIGNED FILTER TO A NOISY IMAGE

In this section an optimal OSF for a constant signal is applied to an image corrupted by pseudorandom computer-generated noise. The image under consideration consists of 240 × 240 pixel values with eight bits of resolution per pixel. The original, uncorrupted image is shown in Fig. 2(a). Zero-mean Laplacian noise ($\sigma^2 = 100$) was added to the image, as shown in Fig. 2(b). The optimal 3 × 3 (9 point) Laplacian OSF, with coefficients given in Table II, was then applied with the result shown in Fig. 2(c).

A 3 × 3 averaging filter and a 3 × 3 median filter were also applied for comparison. The averaging filter was noted to produce a slightly blurrier image than either the OSF or the median filter, whereas the median filter produced sharp edges in the image but also introduced some blotches in areas of fairly constant value. The Laplacian OSF combined qualities of both the other filters, yielding sharp edges but with a slight smoothing effect reminiscent of the averager. The differences in the filtered versions were rather slight, however, and were deemed to be too small to show in reproduction; hence the filtered versions corresponding to the averager and the median are not shown.

In order to better preserve discernible differences after reproduction, Fig. 3(a)–(e) compares a single line of the original image with the filtered versions.[3] The averaging filter smoothed out some information-carrying features that are present in the original, particularly edge-type structures. The median filter preserved edges well, but flattened narrow peaks that were present in the original image. The Laplacian OSF yielded a compromise between the other two filters.

A useful quantitative comparison of the performances of the three filters is the empirical mean squared error given by

$$e = \frac{1}{K^2} \sum_{i=1}^{K} \sum_{j=1}^{K} (f_{ij} - o_{ij})^2$$

where K is the number of pixels per line (240), o_{ij} are the pixel values in the original image, and f_{ij} are the pixel values in the filtered image. Table VI lists the empirical MSE for the Laplacian OSF, the median filter, and the averaging filter. The Laplacian OSF performed better than the median filter and significantly better than the averaging filter.

V. GENERALIZATION FOR NONCONSTANT SIGNALS

Most practical applications deal with unknown signals, but unfortunately, given a statistical description of such a signal, the design of an optimal OSF is generally intractable. There are cases though, such as in detection, where the signal may be nonconstant, but known. In this section we extend the results of Section II to the case of a nonconstant known signal.

Consider a known signal s_j corrupted by white noise n_j, resulting in the sequence

---
[3] Note that for a 3 × 3 window, the filtered versions also depend on the two lines adjacent to that shown in Fig. 3(b).

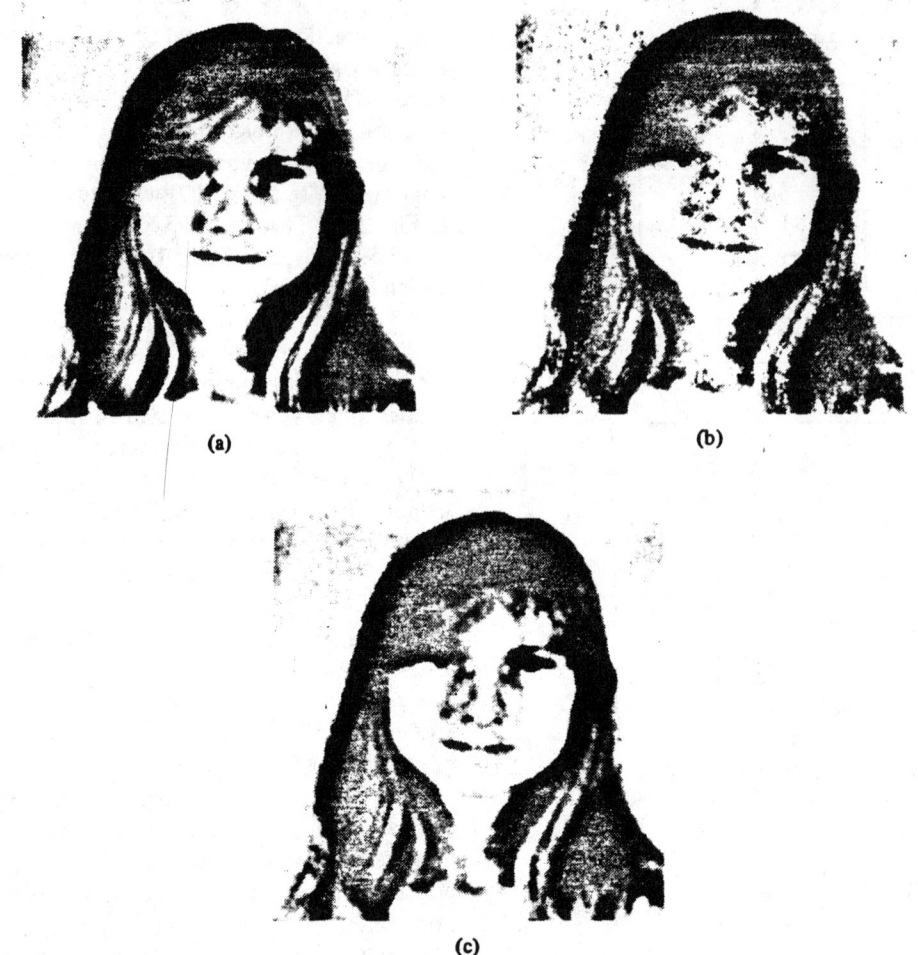

Fig. 2. (a) Original image. (b) Image corrupted by zero-mean Laplacian noise ($\sigma^2 = 100$). (c) Noisy image filtered by Laplacian OSF.

$$x_j = s_j + n_j.$$

In this case the optimal OSF is time or spatially varying with coefficients $\alpha_k = (\alpha_1^k, \alpha_2^k, \cdots, \alpha_N^k)^T$. The filter output is

$$y_k = \sum_{i=1}^{N} \alpha_i^k x_{(i)}^k$$

so that the MSE for the kth output is

$$\text{MSE}_k = E\{(y_k - s_k)^2\} = E\left\{\left(\sum_{i=1}^{N} \alpha_i^k x_{(i)}^k - s_k\right)^2\right\}.$$

As before, this can be rewritten using a quadratic form. Let H_k be the correlation matrix with elements $h_{ij}^k = E\{x_{(i)}^k x_{(j)}^k\}$ and let μ_k be the mean vector with elements $\mu_i^k = E\{x_{(i)}^k\}$ for $i, j = 1, \cdots, N$. The MSE can then be expressed as

$$\text{MSE}_k = \alpha_k^T H_k \alpha_k - 2 s_k \alpha_k^T \mu_k + s_k^2. \tag{15}$$

Again, we will insist that the estimate be unbiased, i.e.,

$$s_k = E\{y_k\} = \sum_{i=1}^{N} \alpha_i^k E\{x_{(i)}^k\} = \alpha_k^T \mu_k. \tag{16}$$

Substitution of the unbiasedness condition into (15) yields

$$\text{MSE}_k = \alpha_k^T H_k \alpha_k - s_k^2. \tag{17}$$

The minimization of (17) subject to (16) can be solved as before using the Lagrange multiplier method. The Lagrangian function is

$$F(\alpha_k, \lambda) = \alpha_k^T H \alpha_k - s_k^2 + \lambda(s_k - \alpha_k^T \mu_k).$$

Setting the derivative with respect to α_k equal to zero yields

$$2 H_k \alpha_k - \lambda \mu_k = 0$$

which, combined with the unbiasedness constraint (16), gives the optimal coefficients

$$\alpha_k = s_k H_k^{-1} \mu_k / \mu_k^T H_k^{-1} \mu_k.$$

Notice that unlike the constant signal case, the optimal coefficients now depend on the signal.

Computation of μ_k and H_k requires both the marginal and bivariate densities of the $x_{(i)}^k$. The densities given by (10) and (11) cannot be used, since the N independent observations $x_{k-M}, \cdots, x_k, \cdots, x_{k+M}$ are no longer identically distributed

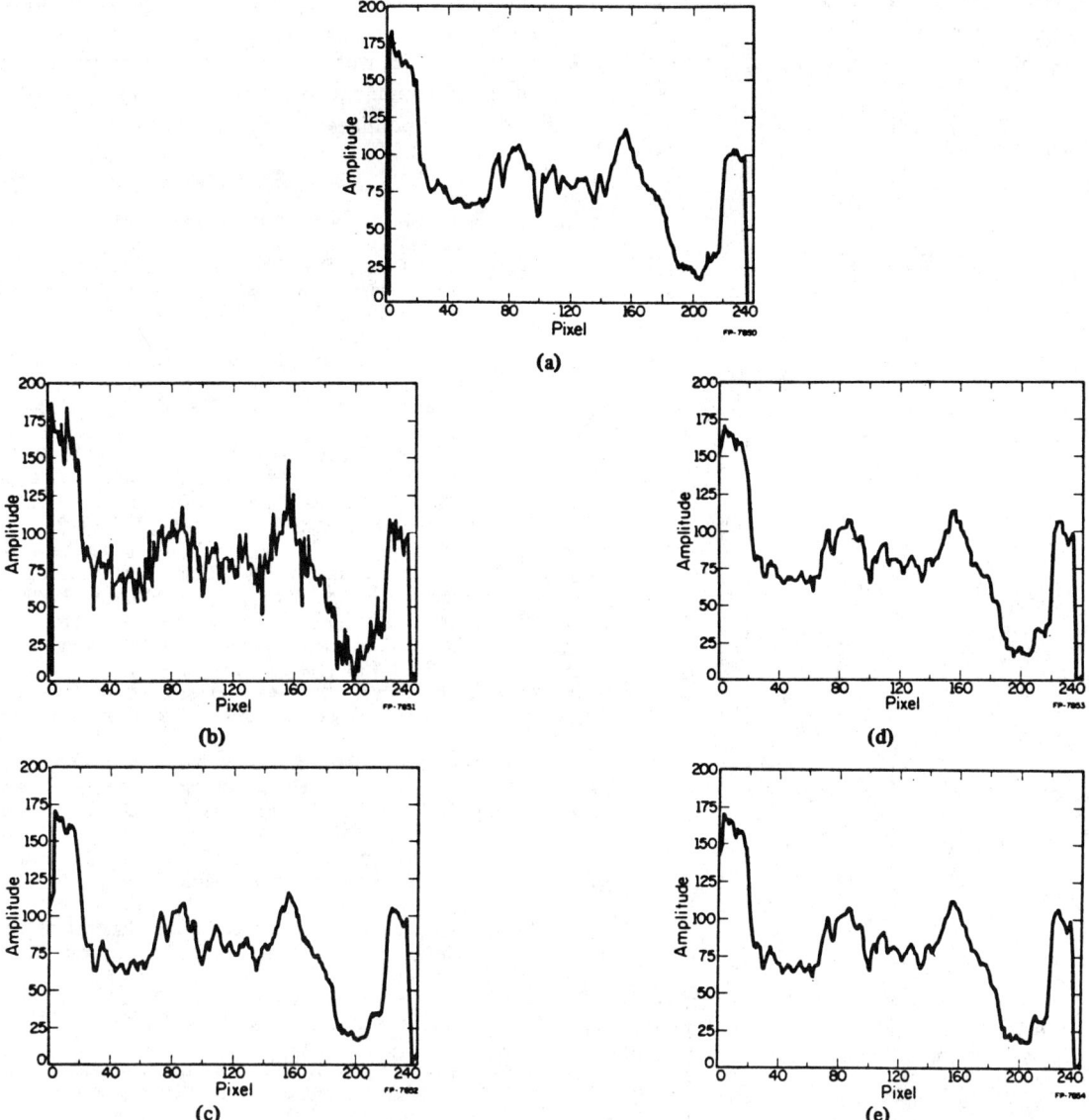

Fig. 3. (a) Horizontal line through mouth region in Fig. 2(a) (uncorrupted original). (b) Line from Fig. 3(a) with Laplacian noise ($\sigma^2 = 100$) added. (c) Noisy image filtered by averaging filter (horizontal line through mouth region). (d) Noisy image filtered by median filter (horizontal line through mouth region). (e) Noisy image filtered by Laplacian OSF (horizontal line through mouth region).

TABLE VI
COMPUTED EMPIRICAL MSE FOR FILTERED VERSIONS OF IMAGE CORRUPTED BY LAPLACIAN NOISE
($\sigma^2 = 100$)

Filter	MSE
Laplacian OSF	60.4
Median Filter	66.0
Averaging Filter	74.1

(the means are different). Denoting the densities of the unordered observations by $f_j^k(x)$ and the distributions by $F_j^k(x)$ for $j = 1, \cdots, N$, the marginal density of $x_{(i)}^k$ for $i = 1, \cdots, N$ is given by

$$g_i^k(x) = L_i \, {}^+|A_i^k(x)|^+$$

where

$$L_i = \frac{1}{(N-i)!(i-1)!}$$

and

$$A_i^k(x) = \begin{bmatrix} F_1^k(x) & \cdots & F_N^k(x) \\ \vdots & & \vdots \\ F_1^k(x) & \cdots & F_N^k(x) \\ f_1^k(x) & \cdots & f_N^k(x) \\ 1 - F_1^k(x) & \cdots & 1 - F_N^k(x) \\ \vdots & & \vdots \\ 1 - F_1^k(x) & \cdots & 1 - F_N^k(x) \end{bmatrix} \begin{matrix} \} \, i-1 \text{ rows} \\ \\ \} \, 1 \text{ row} \\ \\ \} \, N-i \text{ rows} \end{matrix}$$

where $^+|\cdot|^+$ denotes the *permanent* of the matrix, which is simply the determinant with all of the signs in the expansion positive rather than alternating [15].

Similarly, the joint density of $x_{(i)}^k$ and $x_{(j)}^k$ where $i < j$ is given by

$$g_{ij}^k(x,y) = L_{ij}{}^+ \left| A_{ij}^k(x,y) \right|^+$$

where

$$L_{ij} = \frac{1}{(i-1)!(j-i-1)!(N-j)!}$$

and

$$A_{ij}^k(x,y) =$$

$$\begin{bmatrix} F_1^k(x) & \cdots & F_N^k(x) \\ \vdots & & \vdots \\ F_1^k(x) & \cdots & F_N^k(x) \\ f_1^k(x) & \cdots & f_N^k(x) \\ F_1^k(y) - F_1^k(x) & \cdots & F_N^k(y) - F_N^k(x) \\ \vdots & & \vdots \\ F_1^k(y) - F_1^k(x) & \cdots & F_N^k(y) - F_N^k(x) \\ f_1^k(y) & \cdots & f_N^k(y) \\ 1 - F_1^k(y) & \cdots & 1 - F_N^k(y) \\ \vdots & & \vdots \\ 1 - F_1^k(y) & \cdots & 1 - F_N^k(y) \end{bmatrix} \begin{matrix} \left.\begin{matrix}\\ \\ \\ \end{matrix}\right\} i-1 \text{ rows} \\ \left.\begin{matrix}\\ \end{matrix}\right\} 1 \text{ row} \\ \left.\begin{matrix}\\ \\ \\ \end{matrix}\right\} j-i-1 \text{ rows} \\ \left.\begin{matrix}\\ \end{matrix}\right\} 1 \text{ row} \\ \left.\begin{matrix}\\ \\ \\ \end{matrix}\right\} N-j \text{ rows.} \end{matrix}$$

It should be noted that these expressions are valid for the order statistics of any set of N independent nonidentically distributed random variables.

VI. CONCLUSION

We have studied a new class of nonlinear filters whose output is given by a linear combination of the order statistics of the input sequence. Both the median and averaging filters are members of this class. Assuming a constant signal in additive white noise, an explicit expression was derived for the optimal OSF coefficients. Both qualitative and quantitative comparisons suggested that OSF's (designed for a constant signal) can probably perform better than the median and averaging filters in some applications.

Computation of the optimal OSF coefficients requires the correlation matrices of the order statistics. A number of these matrices are available in a separate report [10] and may also be of use in other endeavors.

The dependence of the OSF coefficients on the impulsivity of the additive noise was investigated using a family of generalized exponential distributions. For noise more impulsive than the Laplacian case, the optimal OSF quickly tends toward the median.

A generalization of the OSF design scheme was given for known nonconstant signals. This could prove useful for applications such as signal detection.

Finally, more work needs to be done in this area, particularly on the development of performance measures for comparison of different nonlinear filtering schemes.

REFERENCES

[1] J. W. Tukey, "Nonlinear (nonsuperposable) methods for smoothing data," in *Conf. Rec., 1974 EASCON*, p. 673.
[2] L. R. Rabiner, M. R. Sambur, and C. E. Schmidt, "Applications of a nonlinear smoothing algorithm to speech processing," *IEEE Trans. Acoust., Speech, Signal Processing*, vol. ASSP-23, pp. 552-557, Dec. 1975.
[3] N. S. Jayant, "Average and median-based smoothing techniques for improving digital speech quality in the presence of transmission errors," *IEEE Trans. Commun.*, vol. COM-24, pp. 1043-1045, Sept. 1976.
[4] W. K. Pratt, *Digital Image Processing*. New York: Wiley, 1978.
[5] T. S. Huang, G. J. Yang, and G. Y. Tang, "A fast two-dimensional median filtering algorithm," *IEEE Trans. Acoust., Speech, Signal Processing*, vol. ASSP-27, pp. 13-18, Jan. 1979.
[6] E. Ataman, V. K. Aatre, and K. M. Wong, "A fast method for real-time median filtering," *IEEE Trans. Acoust., Speech, Signal Processing*, vol. ASSP-28, pp. 415-420, Aug. 1980.
[7] T. M. Nodes and N. C. Gallagher, Jr., "Median filtering," in *Proc. 18th Allerton Conf. Commun., Contr., Comput.*, Monticello, IL, Oct. 8-10, 1980, pp. 926-934.
[8] E. H. Lloyd, "Least-squares estimation of location and scale parameters using order statistics," *Biometrika*, vol. 39, pp. 88-95, 1952.
[9] H. A. David, *Order Statistics*. New York: Wiley, 1981.
[10] A. C. Bovik, "Nonlinear filtering using linear combinations of order statistics," Coordinated Sci. Lab., Univ. Illinois, Urbana, Rep. R-935, 1982.
[11] A. E. Sarhan, "Estimation of the mean and standard deviation by order statistics," *Ann. Math. Statist.*, vol. 25, pp. 317-328, 1954.
[12] —, "Estimation of the mean and standard deviation by order statistics, part II," *Ann. Math. Statist.*, vol. 26, pp. 505-511, 1955.
[13] —, "Estimation of the mean and standard deviation by order statistics, part III," *Ann. Math. Statist.*, vol. 26, pp. 576-592, 1955.
[14] J. L. Gastwirth and M. L. Cohen, "Small sample behavior of some robust linear estimators of location," *J. Amer. Statist. Ass.*, vol. 65, pp. 946-973, 1970.
[15] R. J. Vaughan and W. N. Venables, "Permanent expressions for order statistic densities," *J. Roy. Statist. Soc.*, vol. 34, pp. 308-310, 1972.

Alan C. Bovik (S'80) was born in Kirkwood, MO, on June 25, 1958. He received the B.S. degree in computer engineering and the M.S. degree in electrical engineering from the University of Illinois, Urbana-Champaign, in 1980 and 1982, respectively. He is currently completing the Ph.D. degree in electrical engineering at the same university.

He has served as both Research Assistant in the Coordinated Science Laboratory and as Teaching Assistant in the Department of Electrical Engineering at the University of Illinois. His current research interests are in the areas of statistical signal and image processing, computer vision, and computational aspects of human vision.

Mr. Bovik is a member of Phi Kappa Phi.

Thomas S. Huang (S'61-M'63-SM'76-F'79), for a photograph and biography, see p. 649 of the June 1983 issue of this TRANSACTIONS.

 David C. Munson, Jr. (S'75–M'79) was born in Red Oak, IA, on October 19, 1952. He received the B.S. degree in electrical engineering from the University of Delaware, Newark, in 1975, and the M.S., M.A., and Ph.D. degrees in electrical engineering from Princeton University, Princeton, NJ, in 1977, 1977, and 1979, respectively.

Since August 1979, he has been with the University of Illinois, Urbana-Champaign, IL, where he is currently an Associate Professor in the Department of Electrical Engineering and an Associate Research Professor in the Coordinated Science Laboratory.

His research interests include the effects of finite register length in digital signal processing, signal processing architectures, multidimensional and time-varying signal processing, and image reconstruction in sensor array processing systems such as synthetic aperture radar.

Dr. Munson is a member of Eta Kappa Nu and Tau Beta Pi.

Theory of Order Statistic Filters and Their Relationship to Linear FIR Filters

HAROLD GENE LONGBOTHAM, MEMBER, IEEE, AND ALAN CONRAD BOVIK, MEMBER, IEEE

Abstract—Order statistic (OS) filters are a class of nonlinear digital filters which have proved useful in applications where robust signal smoothing is required. OS filters can be viewed either as a modification to linear FIR filters (the samples are algebraically ordered prior to linear weighting), or as a generalization of the median filter (all of the ordered samples are utilized instead of a single one). While there exist signal processing domains where OS filters afford advantages over linear filters, there are many more situations where the converse holds, or where the filters produce similar results. Before a design methodology for OS filters can be developed, these application domains must be delineated. A first approach to solving this problem involves finding those signals for which OS and linear filtering produces identical results, when the filters are defined with identical coefficients.

In this paper, necessary and/or sufficient conditions on both the filter coefficients and the signal process are derived in order that nonrecursive OS and linear filtering are equivalent operations. The results indicate that an understanding of OS filters hinges on a better understanding of the properties of signals containing locally monotonic components. The results obtained extend a number of previous theories characterizing the well-known median and ranked-order filters, and extend them to a broader class of filters and input signals.

I. INTRODUCTION

A. Historical Perspective

THE median filter was proposed by Tukey in 1971 [1] as a smoothing device for discrete signals. In particular, he noted the filter to be particularly effective for suppressing impulse noise while simultaneously preserving locally monotonic signal structures often containing significant information. These properties made the median filter a natural choice for noise reduction purposes in many problems of practical interest; over the next ten years, many papers appeared demonstrating the efficacy of the filter for applications such as speech [2] and image processing [3], and fast algorithms [4], [5], and dedicated architectures [6] were developed to accelerate its computation. Despite these advances and the apparent value of the technique, the median filter was widely regarded as a curiosity with no solid foundation in signal processing theory. This changed in 1981 when Gallagher and Wise [7] and Tyan [8] developed certain deterministic properties of the filter; in particular, they showed that certain signals (labeled *root signals* in [7]) are invariant to median filtering if they possess a minimum degree of smoothness (local monotonicity), and that repeated application of the filter to any finite-length signal converges to a root in a finite number of passes.

These results gave the median filter a theoretical groundwork, and spurred the development of a number of extensions and generalizations, including *ranked-order filters* (RO filters), where a single order statistic (generally other than the median) from the windowed data set is reproduced at each signal coordinate [9], and the more general *order stastic filters* (OS filters or *L-filters*) [10], [11], where a linear combination of the order statistics is taken as the filter output at each coordinate. OS filters are interesting because a) they offer a compromise in performance between linear filters and median filters, and b) it is possible to design an optimal (among OS filters) MSE filter for estimating a constant signal level immersed in any iid noise, whose performance will be superior to linear filtering. Moreover, there exists a vast body of literature on the use of order statistics for parameter estimation (see, e.g., the extensive bibliography in [12]) which lends strong justification for using moving functions of OS for recovering smoothly varying signals immersed in iid noise; unfortunately, the statistical design for general signals or correlated noise has proved more difficult. However, means have been found for computing the optimal MSE OS filter coefficients for estimating nonconstant signals in iid noise [13] and for restoration of Markov sequences [14]. Efficient VLSI implementations for OS-type filters have also been suggested, and a chip is available which can perform any RO operation of window width nine or less [15]. The chip design is based on the so-called threshold decomposition property of RO filters [16]: RO filtering of a quantized sequence is equivalent to separately filtering and recombining a set of binary signals composing the input. Recently, OS and RO filters have been shown to be a subset of a broader class of operations known as mathematical morphology [17]; in this approach, the filtering operation can be interpreted as a (geometric) signal-shaping process. An approach for combining the outputs of OS and linear filters into a single response has also been proposed [18]; this promising technique allows the definition of a nonlinear filter possessing certain linear attributes (frequency selectivity) as well as robustness against iid additive noise. Thus, the concept of median filtering as an *ad hoc* signal processing tool is metamorphosing into a rich theory for signal esti-

---

Manuscript received February 19, 1987; revised June 16, 1988.

The authors are with the Department of Electrical and Computer Engineering, The University of Texas at Austin, Austin, TX 78712-1084.

IEEE Log Number 8825137.

mation/restoration which provides significant advantages over linear filtering methodologies, both in performance and in implementation.

B. Motivation and Overview

Despite the promising developments outlined above, many questions regarding the applicability of OS filters for more general signal processing applications remain unanswered. The most generic goal of a digital filter is to enhance or preserve some component of an input signal, while suppressing some other component. The Fourier interpretation of frequency selection has made linear filtering an irreplaceable tool for manipulating signals, e.g., there is no clearly defined theory for designing a "highpass" nonlinear filter of any type. While there clearly exist applications where OS filters afford an advantage over linear filtering strategies, it must also be realized that there are many more situations where the converse holds, or where the filters produce identical or similar results. Before a concrete methodology can be advanced for designing OS filters as an alternative to linear filtering, these application domains must be delineated from both a deterministic and a statistical point of view.

In this paper, we address the deterministic analysis of OS filters based on their relationship with linear filters. As indicated in Fig. 1, OS filters may be regarded as modifications of nonrecursive or finite impulse response (FIR) discrete linear filters (windowing followed by linear weighting) via the inclusion of a nonlinear ordering operation between windowing and weighting. The problem may be restated as: for what signal processing application does the inclusion of an ordering element produce a benefit? Unfortunately, the answer to this question requires specific knowledge of the application being considered. More generally it may be asked: how do the outputs resulting from OS and linear filtering of a signal relate? A first approach to this question involves finding those signals for which OS and linear filtering produce identical results, when the filters are defined with identical coefficients, viz., identifying those signals for which inclusion of the ordering element produces no difference at the output. Early papers on median and RO filters [7]-[9] provide a clue to determining what these signals are; it turns out that the signal must either be monotonic or locally monotonic, depending on the form of the filter coefficient set, unless the signal is bivalued.

Some of the significant results obtained in the paper are summarized below.

- The relationship between OS and nonrecursive linear filters having the same coefficient sets can be characterized completely for signals which possess a certain degree of smoothness measured in terms of local monotonicity. The results obtained indicate that over sufficiently smooth regions, OS and linear filters are equivalent operations. Depending on the filter coefficients, the operation of the filters may be low-pass (smoothness-preserving) or otherwise.

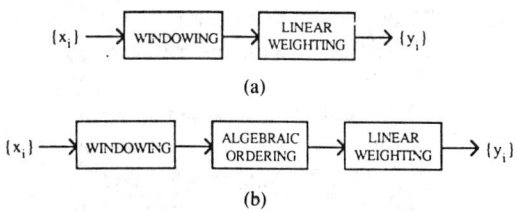

Fig. 1. Diagram illustrating the difference between (a) nonrecursive linear FIR filtering and (b) nonrecursive OS filtering.

- For signals which are not sufficiently smooth, OS and linear filters must result in different outputs. Although the relationship between the outputs is difficult to characterize in this case, OS filters can be defined which supply similar signal-shaping performance to the linear filter, with increased robustness against noise.

- The results obtained encapsulate most of the single-pass deterministic properties of the median filter and the more general RO filters [7]-[9], and extend them to a broader class of filters and input signals.

Previous studies of OS and related nonlinear filters have clearly demonstrated their utility for smoothing noise in discrete signals [1]-[3], [7]-[11], [13]-[23]. The results obtained here strengthen the notion of OS filters as smoothing devices, and quantify their behavior relative to a better-understood class of filters (linear filters). This increased understanding also provides motivation for using combined OS/linear filtering structures for smoothing noise while maintaining certain frequency attributes [18] since, by proper selection of the OS coefficients, the output can be made to conform to certain smoothing specifications, while specification of the linear filter coefficients allows retention of the desired frequencies. By combining the outputs, a smoother signal possessing the desired frequency response can be obtained.

Although many of the results obtained here are limited to "smoothing" OS filters, a number of other filters are characterized as well. While the results provided do not supply a specific design methodology for OS filters, it is hoped that a number of tools for their understanding have been provided which will lead to a framework for design.

II. ORDER STATISTIC FILTERS

The notation used throughout the paper is summarized first.

A. Notation

$\{x_i\}$ Two-sided infinite real- and finite-valued data sequence to be filtered.

$\{\mathbf{x}_i\}$ Sequence of windowed data vectors $\mathbf{x}_i = (x_{1:i}, x_{2:i}, \cdots, x_{2N+1:i})^T$, where $x_{j:i} = x_{i+j-N-1}$, so that at each coordinate i, the filter is centered at i. Unless otherwise stated, the window span is taken to be $2N + 1$, where $N > 0$.

$\{\mathbf{x}_{(i)}\}$ Sequence of ordered data vectors $\mathbf{x}_{(i)} = $ order $\{\mathbf{x}_i\} = (x_{(1):i}, \cdots, x_{(2N+1):i})^T$, so that $x_{(j):i} \leq x_{(k):i}$ whenever $j \leq k$.

a	Coefficient vector $(a_1, \cdots, a_{2N+1})^T$ associated with an arbitrary OS or linear filter.
$\bar{a}$	The vector $(a_{2N+1}, a_{2N}, \cdots, a_1)^T$, i.e., a with elements in reversed order.
b	Coefficient vector $(b_1, b_2, \cdots, b_{N+1}, \cdots, b_2, b_1)^T$ associated with an arbitrary *symmetric* OS or linear filter, i.e., $b = \bar{b}$.
1	Constant-valued vector $(1, 1, \cdots, 1)^T$ of length $2N + 1$.
$\{\omega_a(x_i)\}$	OS-filtered sequence with elements $\omega_a(x_i) = a^T x_{(i)}$.
$\{\lambda_a(x_i)\}$	Linear-filtered sequence with elements $\lambda_a(x_i) = a^T x_i$.

A separate notation is used for filters defined with symmetric coefficients, since they are treated as a special case in Section IV; the results derived for symmetric filters do not extend to the general case. While it will generally be assumed that the input sequence $\{x_i\}$ and filter coefficients a can take any finite real values, the results presented also hold for integer-valued or quantized input data and filter coefficients, although the output and input ranges may not coincide. As in Tyan [8], the input sequence is assumed to be two-sided infinite; similar conditions to those used there will be required in establishing many of the results. However, the results given here can also be proven using the input signal model in [7], viz., that the input is a finite length sequence which has been padded at either end.

B. Basic Properties of OS Filters

The sequence resulting from a (nonrecursive) OS filtering of an arbitrary data sequence $\{x_i\}$ is denoted $\{\omega_a(x_i)\}$ with elements $\omega_a(x_i) = a^T x_{(i)}$, where $a = (a_1, \cdots, a_{2N+1})^T$ is an arbitrary real finite-valued vector of length $2N + 1$. Although OS filters differ from linear FIR filters only via the inclusion of an ordering element, this provides a very nonlinear characteristic which may greatly effect the response of the filter. However, OS filters do enjoy a limited number of "linear" properties, e.g., they are translation-invariant, preserve linear trends [11], and the following also hold.

Properties: Suppose that $c = c1$ where c is any constant. Then, for any vectors x_i and a of length $2N + 1$,

1) $\omega_a(x_i + c) = \omega_a(x_i) + \omega_a(c)$
2) $\omega_a(cx_i) = c\omega_a(x_i)$ if $c \geq 0$, and $\omega_a(cx_i) = c\omega_{\bar{a}}(x_i)$ if $c < 0$
3) $\omega_{a+c}(x_i) = \omega_a(x_i) + \omega_c(x_i)$
4) $\omega_{ca}(x_i) = c\omega_a(x_i)$
5) $\omega_a(x_i) = \lambda_a(x_i)$ $[\omega_a(x_i) = \lambda_{\bar{a}}(x_i)]$ if x_i is nondecreasing [nonincreasing]. If $a = \bar{a}$, then $\omega_a(x_i) = \lambda_a(x_i)$ if x_i is either nonincreasing or nondecreasing.

Proof: Since $\omega_a(x_i) = a \cdot x_{(i)}$ and $\lambda_a(x_i) = a \cdot x_i$, where $\cdot$ is the usual vector inner product, 1)-5) are simple consequences of the vector interpretation of nonrecursive OS and linear filters. Simple proofs are available in [19]. ◊

Properties 1-4 are important reasons why OS filters are particularly useful for signal and image smoothing applications, particularly if the filter coefficients sum to unity. The reason for this is that scaling or translating the signal or filter coefficients results in an identically scaled or translated filter output.

An erroneous property often attributed to OS filters is their tendency to "preserve edges" and "suppress impulses." This idea has largely come about as a byproduct of the interpretation of OS filters as "generalized median filters" [10], [11]. Actually, no OS filter preserves edges better than a linear FIR filter with identical coefficients; in fact, the only OS filters which preserve ideal (step) edges up to a shift are the RO filters. An RO filter is an OS filter with all zero coefficients except one, which is set to unity: $a_j = 0$; $j = 1, \cdots, 2N + 1, j \neq k$, and $a_k = 1$ for some $k \in \{1, \cdots, 2N + 1\}$.

Fact: The only OS filters which preserve ideal (step) edges up to a shift are the RO filters.

Proof: An ideal step edge is either nondecreasing or nonincreasing. By Property 5, OS filtering of a positive-going (negative-going) step edge is identical to linear FIR filtering of the step edge using the same coefficients (in reverse order). However, the only FIR filters which preserve edges up to a shift are delay elements, which have the same coefficients as the RO filters. ◊

In particular, the only OS filter which exactly preserves edges is the median filter. However, OS filters do a better job of *simultaneously* preserving edges and smoothing noise, at least for additive white noise of arbitrary distribution [20]. Moreover, if the span of an OS filter is extended by padding the coefficient set with zeros on either side, a further improvement in noise reduction with no loss of edge preservation can be obtained. Such a process is known as *censoring* in the statistical parlance; good examples of this are the median filter where, by increasing the span of the filter, additional noise suppression is effected, and the *trimmed mean filters*, which are discussed later. However, edge preservation and noise suppression are not the only important goals in signal filtering. In the following, some fundamental properties are given that relate OS filters and linear FIR filters which are defined with identical coefficients.

C. Basic Relationships Between OS and Linear FIR Filters

In this section, Property 5 is extended for arbitrary OS filters. Finding necessary and sufficient conditions on the input $\{x_i\}$ and the filter coefficient vector a, such that $\omega_a(x_i) = \lambda_a(x_i)$ everywhere, is, in general, a very difficult problem. The problem is complicated by the fact that in taking a linear combination of the ordered data samples at any signal coordinate i, the output may be the same as that obtained by a linear weighting of the unordered samples, even if the order statistics and the unordered data samples do not coincide at any point: $x_{(k):i} \neq x_{k:i}$ for $k = 1, \cdots, 2N + 1$. However, when $\omega_a(x_i) = \lambda_a(x_i)$ everywhere for *any* coefficient vector a, or for *any* input sequence $\{x_i\}$, certain conditions are induced on the sequence and filter coefficients, respectively.

Lemma 1: Suppose that $c = c\mathbf{1}$ where c is any constant. Then $\omega_a(x_i) = \lambda_a(x_i) \ \forall \ i \Leftrightarrow$ each of the following hold $\forall \ i$:

a) $\omega_{a+c}(x_i) = \lambda_{a+c}(x_i)$
b) $\omega_{ca}(x_i) = \lambda_{ca}(x_i)$
c) $\omega_a(x_i + c) = \lambda_a(x_i + c)$.

Furthermore, if $a = \bar{a}$, then $\omega_a(x_i) = \lambda_a(x_i) \ \forall \ i \Leftrightarrow$ the following holds $\forall \ i$:

d) $\omega_a(cx_i) = \lambda_a(cx_i)$.

Proof: Again, a)-c) follow from simple vector algebra. Item d) follows for $c \geq 0$ for the same reason. For $c < 0$, note that $\omega_a(cx_i) = -\omega_a(-cx_i) = -\lambda_a(-cx_i) = \lambda_a(cx_i)$. ◊

The above properties indicate that if an OS and linear FIR filter yield the same output when operating on a particular sequence, then performing linear operations on either the input sequence or filter coefficients does not change the fact that the outputs are equal. These properties greatly simplify the development of many of the results stated later.

In order to determine the circumstances under which the outputs of OS and linear filters can be related, restrictions must be imposed on either the filter coefficients or the input sequence, or both. In fact, there is only one type of filter coefficient set for which OS and linear FIR filtering yields identical results for *any* input sequence; not surprisingly, these filters are both OS and linear.

Theorem 1: The following two statements are equivalent:

a) $\omega_a(x_i) = \lambda_a(x_i) \ \forall \ i$ for any and every sequence $\{x_i\}$
b) $a = c\mathbf{1}$ for some real scalar c.

Proof: That b) ⇒ a) follows since the data values are weighted equally regardless of their ordering. To show that a) ⇒ b), consider the sequence $\{x_i\}$ taking value 0 everywhere except $x_0 = -1$. Although for $i \notin \{-N, \cdots, N-1\}$ $\omega_a(x_i) = \lambda_a(x_i)$ for any a, for $i \in \{-N, \cdots, N-1\}$, $\omega_a(x_i) = \lambda_a(x_i) \Rightarrow a_1 = a_{N+1-i}$; hence, $\omega_a(x_i) = \lambda_a(x_i) \ \forall \ i \Rightarrow a$ is constant-valued. ◊

Thus, scalar multiples of the averaging filter are the only linear filters which yield the same output as OS filters defined with the same coefficients for *any* input. A similar question arises regarding the filter input: for what sequences does OS and linear filtering produce identical results for *any* set of filter coefficients? The following Corollaries to Lemma 2 in Section III address this.

Corollary 1: The following two statements are equivalent.

a) The elements of the vector x_i are nondecreasing.
b) $\omega_a(x_i) = \lambda_a(x_i)$ for any and every a.

Proof: That a) ⇒ b) follows from Property 5. That b) ⇒ a) follows by considering $a = (1, 0, 0, \cdots, 0)$, and by using Lemma 2. ◊

Corollary 1 states that ω_a and λ_a filter an input sequence $\{x_i\}$ identically for any $a \Leftrightarrow$ if $\{x_i\}$ is everywhere nondecreasing. A similar result also holds for $\{x_i\}$ everywhere non*in*creasing:

Corollary 2: The following two statements are equivalent.

a) The elements of the vector x_i are nonincreasing.
b) $\omega_a(x_i) = \lambda_{\bar{a}}(x_i)$ for any and every a.

Proof: Identical to that for Corollary 1, but using Corollary 3 instead of Lemma 2. ◊

These results suggest that any relationship between OS filters and linear filters must be developed from an understanding of their action on monotonic signal structures. The preceding properties relating OS and linear filters will be of utility in developing some of the more powerful theorems that will be considered shortly for the more specific cases of RO filters and symmetric filters. Most of the preceding results are highly intuitive; however, many of the results presented in later sections are not, and many are quite surprising.

III. Ranked-Order Filters

A. Ranked-Order Filters as Linear Delay Elements on Monotonic Signals

Hereafter an RO filter with all coefficients zero except for the kth will be referred to as a *kth ranked-order (RO) filter*. The output of a kth RO filter is $\omega_a(x_i) = x_{(k):i}$, and the *median filter* is defined by $\omega_a(x_i) = x_{(N+1):i}$. Nodes and Gallagher [9] discussed many properties of RO filters. In particular, they found that an ideal (step) edge is shifted $(k - N - 1)$ units when filtered with a kth RO filter, where the edge is advanced if the edge is positive-going, and delayed if the edge is negative-going. This is precisely the result obtained by the linear filter $\lambda_a(x_i) = x_{k:i}$ if the edge is positive-going, and by $\lambda_a(x_i) = x_{2N+2-k:i}$ if the edge is negative-going. Noting that ideal step edges are either monotonic nondecreasing or monotonic nonincreasing, it could be hypothesized that kth RO filters and linear delay elements yield identical results *only* when operating on monotonic signals, with special provision made for the median filter. It turns out that this is the case, provided that the signal is *somewhere* monotonic, as will be shown in Theorem 2. There are two exceptions to this which must be treated separately.

Lemma 2: The following three statements are equivalent.

a) The sequence $\{x_i\}$ is everywhere nondecreasing.
b) $x_{(1):i} = x_{1:i} \ \forall \ i$.
c) $x_{(2N+1):i} = x_{2N+1:i} \ \forall \ i$.

Proof: That a) ⇒ b) and c) follows from Property 5. To show that b) ⇒ a), note that $x_{(1):i} = x_{1:i} \forall i \Rightarrow x_{1:i} \leq x_{2:i} = x_{1:i+1} \forall i \Rightarrow \{x_i\}$ is everywhere nondecreasing. Similarly, c) ⇒ a) since $x_{(2N+1):i} = x_{2N+1:i} \forall i \Rightarrow x_{2N+1:i} \geq x_{2N:i} = x_{2N+1:i-1} \forall i \Rightarrow \{x_i\}$ is everywhere nondecreasing. ◊

Thus, filtering with a min (max) filter is equivalent to filtering with a linear delay element ⇔ the input is everywhere nondecreasing, where the shift is N units to the left (right). For nonincreasing sequences, the direction of shift is reversed.

Corollary 3: The following three statements are equivalent.

  a) The sequence $\{x_i\}$ is everywhere nonincreasing.
  b) $x_{(1):i} = x_{2N+1:i} \forall i$.
  c) $x_{(2N+1):i} = x_{1:i} \forall i$.

Proof: The sequence $\{y_i\} = \{-x_i\}$ is nondecreasing ⇔ $\{x_i\}$ is nonincreasing. Furthermore, $y_{(k):i} = y_{k:i} \forall i \Leftrightarrow x_{(2N+2-k):i} = x_{2N+2-k:i} \forall i$, for any $k \in \{1, 2, \cdots, 2N+1\}$. Applying Lemma 2 to $\{y_i\}$ and using the above yields the desired results. ◊

Similar results for RO filters other than the min/max filters require the input to be sufficiently smooth in at least one local region, in the sense that it must contain at least one monotonic segment; moreover, the length of the segment depends on the filter used.

Theorem 2: The following two statements are equivalent.

  a) $\{x_i\}$ is everywhere nondecreasing.
  b) $x_{(k):i} = x_{k:i} \forall i$, and $\{x_i\}$ contains at least one nondecreasing segment of length $R = \min\{k, 2N+2-k\}$, where $k \in \{2, \cdots, 2N\}, k \neq N+1$.

Proof: Appendix. ◊

The direction of shift is reversed for nonincreasing sequences, although the magnitude of the shift remains unchanged.

Corollary 4: The following two statements are equivalent.

  a) $\{x_i\}$ is everywhere nonincreasing.
  b) $x_{(k):i} = x_{2N+2-k:i} \forall i$, and $\{x_i\}$ contains at least one nonincreasing segment of length $R = \min\{k, 2N+2-k\}$, where $k \in \{2, \cdots, 2N\}, k \neq N+1$.

Proof: By applying Theorem 2 to the sequence $\{y_i\}$ defined in the proof of Corollary 3. ◊

The assumption that $\{x_i\}$ contains a monotonic region of length R is necessary in Theorem 2 and Corollary 4 (unless the input sequence is assumed to be of finite length with padding at either end, as in [7] and [9]). In this case, the statements of Theorem 2 and Corollary 4 resemble those of Lemma 2 and Corollary 3 (since padding introduces a constant region of length $N + 1 > R$ at each end of the input sequence). For example, if $\{x_i\}$ is composed of the pattern (0, 1, 1, 1) repeated indefinitely in either direction, then $x_{(5):i} = x_{5:i}$ for every i for $N = 8$. However, the only sequences of this type are bivalued, as discussed in Section III-B. For any sequence that is not restricted to be bivalued, Theorem 2 and Corollary 4 indicate that (nonmedian) RO filtering will produce a change in the shape of the sequence (aside from a shift), unless the sequence is globally monotonic. If the sequence is monotonic, then it will be shifted but not changed in shape. Theorem 2 and its Corollary do not include the median filter for the simple reason that they do not hold for $k = N + 1$ (as detailed in the Appendix). However, under different monotonicity conditions (local monotonicity), median filtering is equivalent to linear identity filtering (i.e., not filtering), provided that there is at least one monotonic region present in the input, as given in the following restatement of a theorem due to Tyan [8].

Definition: A sequence $\{x_i\}$ is *locally monotonic of order n*, or LOMO(n), if $(x_j, \cdots, x_{j+n-1})$ is monotonic (either nonincreasing or nondecreasing) for every j.

Theorem 3: Suppose that $\{x_i\}$ contains at least one monotonic segment $(x_p, \cdots, x_{p+N})$ of length $N + 1$. Then the following two statements are equivalent:

  a) $\{x_i\}$ is LOMO($N + 2$)
  b) $x_{(N+1):i} = x_{N+1:i} \forall i$.

Proof: See [8]. ◊

Tyan also showed that the only sequences not containing at least one such locally monotonic region for which b) holds are oscillating bivalued sequences. In subsection B of this section, it is shown that this is also the case for RO filters.

The preceding has established that the subclass of OS filters known as RO filters are equivalent to linear delay elements when operating on sequences which are sufficiently smooth in the sense that they are monotonic, and that they yield different results otherwise. The exception to this is the median filter, which is the only RO filter having symmetric coefficients. The idea that symmetric OS filters may have a different relationship to linear FIR filters is particularly interesting, since symmetric OS filters are most widely used for signal smoothing purposes. Noting that linear FIR digital filters are linearly combined delay elements, and that OS filters are linear combinations of RO filters, one may wonder whether similar conditions exist under which FIR and OS filtering are equivalent operations for more general symmetric coefficient sets. This question is addressed in Section IV.

B. Ranked-Order Filters as Linear Delay Elements on Bivalued Signals

It has been noted that certain bivalued sequences exist for which RO filters and linear delay elements produce identical results, but which are nowhere monotonic in the senses of Theorems 2 and 3. As it turns out, all sequences of this type are necessarily bivalued, suggesting that they may not be of particular interest in most applications. For the case of the median filter, Tyan [8] noted that if a sequence does contain highly oscillating bivalued regions, filtering may be of little use if it is desirable to smooth the oscillation; with this in mind, he proposed several modifications to the filter to overcome this problem. However, it is not clear whether these sequences present a particular problem for RO filters in general; in any case, the emphasis here is in finding those sequences for which OS and linear filters produce identical results. In the following theorem, the extreme value filters ($k = 1$ or $k = 2N + 1$) are not considered, as a consequence of Lemma 2; also, the median filter ($k = N + 1$) is not included, since the input sequence is only restricted to nowhere contain a *nondecreasing* segment of specific length. For $k = N + 1$, the theorem is modified by replacing *nondecreasing* with *monotonic*.

Theorem 4: If $x_{(k):i} = x_{k:i} \ \forall \ i$ for some $k \in \{2, \cdots, 2N\}$, $k \neq N + 1$, and if $\{x_i\}$ nowhere contains a nondecreasing segment of length $R = \min(k, 2N + 2 - k)$, then $\{x_i\}$ is bivalued.

Proof: The proof is very similar to that given in [8] for the median filter. Since little additional insight can be obtained from it, the reader is referred to [19]. ◊

As with the median filter [8], it is difficult to completely classify the bivalued sequences satisfying Theorem 4; however, it is clear that such sequences must vary rapidly. It is also possible that they must be periodic, although we have not been able to show this to be true. However, there is a certain class of periodic sequences for which filtering by RO filters and linear delay filters produces identical results for an infinite number of filter spans $2N + 1$ and rank orders k.

Definition: The bivalued sequence $\{x_i\} = \{(a - b)y_i + b\}$ ($a \neq b$) is (p, q)-periodic for integers $p \geq 2$, $q \geq 1$, if $\{y_i\}$ is a binary sequence of period pq, where each period contains q values 0 and $(p - 1)q$ values 1. Specifically, if $a < b$ ($a > b$), then $\{x_i\}$ is *negative* (*positive*) (p, q)-periodic.

It is not required that pq be the smallest period characterizing the sequence $\{x_i\}$: $\{x_i\}$ may also be (p', q')-periodic, where $p'q' < pq$. Note here that a (p, q)-periodic sequence nowhere contains a nondecreasing segment of length $jpq + 1$, and $jpq + 1 \leq jp^2q + 1 - jpq$ for any integer $j \geq 1$.

Theorem 5: If $\{x_i\}$ is a negative (positive) (p, q)-periodic sequence, then $x_{(jpq+1):i} = x_{jpq+1:i}$ ($x_{(2N+1-jpq):i} = x_{2N+1-jpq:i}$) $\forall \ i$, if $2N + 1 = jp^2q + 1$ for some integer $j \geq 1$.

Proof: Suppose that $\{x_i\}$ is a negative (p, q)-periodic sequence taking values $c_1 < c_2$, and that $j = 1$. Then for $2N + 1 = p^2q + 1$, the following hold.

For any i such that $x_{1:i} = c_1$, then $x_{pq+1:i} = c_1$ also. Furthermore, $x_{2N+1:i} = x_{p^2q+1:i} = c_1$, so exactly $pq + 1$ elements of x_i take value c_1. Hence, $x_{(pq+1):i} = c_1$ as well.

For any i such that $x_{1:i} = c_2$, then $x_{pq+1:i} = c_2$ and $x_{2N+1:i} = c_2$ also. Then there are only pq elements of x_i that are equal to c_1, so that $x_{(pq+1):i} = c_2$ as well.

For any integer $j > 1$, $\{x_i\}$ is also negative (p, jq)-periodic. Applying the above argument establishes that $x_{(jpq+1):i} = x_{jpq+1:i} \ \forall \ i$ as well, where $2N + 1 = jp^2q + 1$.

The proof for positive (p, q)-periodic sequences is entirely analogous. ◊

The preceding theorem states that any (p, q)-periodic sequence $\{x_i\}$ is filtered identically by an infinite set of RO filters and their linear counterparts (those satisfying Theorem 5). Specifically, if p is even, then for every N which is a positive multiple of $p^2/2$, there is an RO/linear delay filter pair of length $2N + 1$ for which filtering produces identical results. For example, the alternating sequence $(\cdots, c_1, c_2, c_1, c_2, \cdots)$, where $p = 2$, $q = j = 1$, satisfies this for every even N. If p is odd, then the result holds for every N which is a positive multiple of p^2. However, the converse does not hold: for a given N, there is no guarantee that there will exist such a (p, q)-periodic sequence, e.g., for $N = 11$, there is no such sequence since $2N \neq jp^2q$ for all integers j, p, q.

IV. Symmetric Order Statistic Filters

Symmetric OS filters are of particular interest since they have found many applications in signal smoothing, noise removal, and image restoration. For constant signals embedded in noise characterized by a symmetric distribution, the optimal (MSE) OS filter will always be symmetric. Moreover, it has been noted [11] that if a nonrecursive OS filter and a nonrecursive linear filter are defined with identical, symmetric coefficient sets, then they will yield identical outputs if applied to a monotonic (nonincreasing or nondecreasing) sequence. In the following, it is shown that these conditions may be relaxed considerably by imposing various conditions on the filter coefficients.

A. Equivalence of Symmetric OS and Linear FIR Filtering of LOMO Signals

Corollary 1 is extended for the case of filters defined with symmetric coefficients in the following.

Theorem 6: The following two statements are equivalent.

a) The sequence $\{x_i\}$ is LOMO($2N + 1$).
b) $\omega_b(x_i) = \lambda_b(x_i) \ \forall \ i$, for any and every symmetric b.

Proof: The proof is given in the Appendix since it involves several steps and some additional lemmas. The reason for this is that it is not assumed that $\{x_i\}$ contains any smooth (monotonic) region; moreover, Theorem 6 is not true for a single segment x_i. ◊

While the class of inputs for which ω_b and λ_b produce identical outputs for all symmetric vectors b includes only LOMO($2N + 1$) sequences, more specific results may be achieved by applying certain restrictions to the filter coefficients. For length three filters, a very simple result is obtained using Lemma 1 and Theorems 3 and 6.

Lemma 3: Suppose that $\boldsymbol{b} = (b_1, b_2, b_1)^T$ is an arbitrary length three symmetric vector such that $b_1 \neq b_2$. Then the following two statements are equivalent:

a) $\{x_i\}$ is LOMO(3)
b) $\omega_b(x_i) = \lambda_b(x_i) \; \forall \; i$.

Proof: That a) $\Rightarrow$ b) follows from Theorem 6. To show that b) $\Rightarrow$ a), assume that $\boldsymbol{b}$ is as given, and that $\omega_b(x_i) = \lambda_b(x_i) \; \forall \; i$. From Lemma 1a, $\omega_{b'}(x_i) = \lambda_{b'}(x_i)$ where $\boldsymbol{b'} = (0, b_2 - b_1, 0)^T$. From Lemma 1d, $\omega_{b''}(x_i) = \lambda_{b''}(x_i)$ where $\boldsymbol{b''} = (0, 1, 0)^T$, which is the median/identity filter. Since any sequence contains a monotonic segment of length 2 ($= N + 1$), $\{x_i\}$ is LOMO(3) from Theorem 3. ◇

Lemma 3 is also a consequence of Theorem 7 which will be detailed later. It is important to note that this result cannot be generalized for symmetric nonconstant coefficient vectors of arbitrary length without some restriction on the input sequence and, as it turns out, on the coefficients. For example, suppose $\boldsymbol{b} = (1, 1, 0, 0, 0, 1, 1)^T$. If $\{x_i\} = \{\cdots, c, d, c, d, \cdots\}$ ($c \neq d$) where the pattern alternates indefinitely in both directions, $\{x_i\}$ is not LOMO(7) and yet $\omega_b(x_i) = \lambda_b(x_i) \; \forall \; i$; thus, it is possible that OS and linear filtering produces identical results even if the input sequence is not LOMO($2N + 1$) [it is only LOMO(2) in the example]. However, $\omega_b(x_i) = \lambda_b(x_i)$ everywhere for the $\boldsymbol{b}$ given above $\Leftrightarrow$ if the input is LOMO(6), if the input sequence is required to contain at least one smooth (monotonic) segment of length five. The following lemmas will be used to prove this more powerful result for arbitrary filter lengths; Lemmas 4 and 5, respectively, supply characterizations of LOMO sequences in terms of the local structure of such sequences near changes in monotonicity, and in the relative behavior of pairs of RO filters whose ranks are symmetric about the median rank $N + 1$. Lemma 5 is interesting in itself, since it indicates that filters defined as sums of symmetrically placed RO filters yield outputs identical to those of symmetrically placed linear delay elements, provided that the input is only LOMO rather than monotonic.

Lemma 4: The sequence $\{x_i\}$ is LOMO(k) $\Leftrightarrow$ for any $j \in \{2, \cdots, k\}$ $\exists \; i$ such that either $x_{1:i} \leq \cdots \leq x_{j-1:i} > x_{j:i}$ or $x_{1:i} \geq \cdots \geq x_{j-1:i} < x_{j:i}$, then $x_{1:i} = \cdots = x_{j-1:i}$.

Proof: A simple proof is given in [8]. ◇

Lemma 5: The following three statements are equivalent for $N + 1 \leq k \leq 2N$:

a) $\{x_i\}$ is LOMO($k + 1$)
b) $\{x_i\}$ is LOMO(k) and $\{x_{k:i}, x_{2N+2-k:i}\} = \{x_{(k):i}, x_{(2N+2-k):i}\} \; \forall \; i$
c) $\{x_i\}$ contains at least one monotonic segment of length $N + 1$, and $\{x_{j:i}, x_{2N+2-j:i}\} = \{x_{(j):i}, x_{(2N+2-j):i}\} \; \forall \; i$ for $N + 1 \leq j \leq k$.

Proof: First it is shown that a) $\Rightarrow$ b). If $\{x_i\}$ is LOMO($k + 1$), then it is also LOMO(k). For any i, if x_i is nondecreasing, then $\{x_{k:i}, x_{2N+2-k:i}\} = \{x_{(k):i}, x_{(2N+2-k):i}\}$. Thus, assume instead that ($x_{1:i}, \cdots, x_{k+1:i}$) is nondecreasing and let $p = \min \{r: k + 2 \leq r \leq 2N + 1, x_{r-1:i} > x_{r:i}\}$. From a) $x_{p-k:i} = \cdots = x_{p-1:i}$ and $x_{p-1:i} = \max \{x_{k:i}: x_{k:i} \in \boldsymbol{x}_i\}$. Since $2 \leq p - k \leq 2N + 1 - k$, then $x_{k:i}, x_{2N+2-k:i} \in \{x_{p-k:i}, \cdots, x_{p-1:i}\}$. But at least $2N + 2 - k$ elements of $\boldsymbol{x}_i$ are $\leq x_{(2N+2-k):i}$, and at most $2N + 1 - k$ elements of $\boldsymbol{x}_i$ are $< x_{p-k:i}$, hence, $x_{(k):i}, x_{(2N+2-k):i} \in \{x_{p-k:i}, \cdots, x_{p-1:i}\} \Rightarrow x_{(k):i} = x_{(2N+2-k):i}$. The same result is obtained by identical reasoning if it is instead assumed that $\boldsymbol{x}_i$ is nonincreasing.

To show that b) $\Rightarrow$ a), assume that $\{x_i\}$ is LOMO(k) but is not monotonic, since otherwise a) holds trivially. By Lemma 4, $\exists \; i$ such that $x_{1:i} \leq x_{2:i} = x_{3:i} = \cdots = x_{k:i} > x_{k+1:i}$. It is only necessary to show that b) $\Rightarrow x_{1:i} = x_{2:i}$ for any such i. Since $N + 1 \leq k \leq 2N$, also $2 \leq 2N + 2 - k \leq N + 1$, so that $x_{k:i}, x_{2N+2-k:i} \in \{x_{2:i}, \cdots, x_{k:i}\}$. If $x_{1:i} < x_{2:i}$, exactly $2N + 2 - k$ elements of $\boldsymbol{x}_i$ are $< x_{k:i}$, so that $x_{k:i} \neq x_{(2N+2-k):i}$ which contradicts b); hence, $x_{1:i} = x_{2:i}$. By identical reasoning it can be shown that for every i such that $x_{1:i} \geq x_{2:i} = x_{3:i} = \cdots = x_{k:i} < x_{k+1:i}$, b) $\Rightarrow x_{1:i} = x_{2:i}$. Hence, $\{x_i\}$ is LOMO($k + 1$).

To show that c) $\Rightarrow$ a), assume that $\{x_i\}$ contains a monotonic segment of length $N + 1$ and that $x_{N+1:i} = x_{(N+1):i} \; \forall \; i$; then Theorem 3 $\Rightarrow \{x_i\}$ is LOMO($N + 2$). If $\{x_{N:i}, x_{N+2:i}\} = \{x_{(N):i}, x_{(N+2):i}\} \; \forall \; i$, then $\{x_i\}$ is LOMO($N + 3$) since b) $\Rightarrow$ a) for $k = N + 2$. Similarly, if $\forall \; (p, j)$ satisfying $N + 1 \leq p \leq j \leq k$, it is true that $\{x_{p:i}, x_{2N+2-p:i}\} = \{x_{(p):i}, x_{(2N+2-p):i}\} \; \forall \; i$. then $\{x_i\}$ is LOMO($j + 1$) $\Rightarrow \{x_i\}$ is LOMO($k + 1$). Hence, c) $\Rightarrow$ a) and c) $\Rightarrow$ b).

The proof is completed by showing that a) and b) taken together $\Rightarrow$ c). Either a) or b) $\Rightarrow \{x_i\}$ contains a monotonic segment of length $N + 1$. Suppose that

i) $\{x_{j:i}, x_{2N+2-j:i}\} = \{x_{(j):i}, x_{(2N+2-j):i}\} \; \forall \; i$ for some $j \in \{N + 2, \cdots, k\}$.

Since a) $\Rightarrow \{x_i\}$ is LOMO($k + 1$) $\Rightarrow \{x_i\}$ is LOMO(j), then b) and i) $\Rightarrow$

ii) $\{x_{j-1:i}, x_{2N+3-j:i}\} = \{x_{(j-1):i}, x_{(2N+3-j):i}\} \; \forall \; i$.

Finally, since a) and b) $\Rightarrow$ i) for $j = k$, then i) and ii) $\Rightarrow \{x_{j:i}, x_{2N+2-j:i}\} = \{x_{(j):i}, x_{(2N+2-j):i}\} \; \forall \; i$ for $j \in \{N + 1, \cdots, k\}$, proving c). ◇

The following theorem is a principal result of this paper, since it gives the weakest conditions under which OS and linear FIR filtering produce identical results. The OS filters characterized by the theorem include many practical filters of both the OS and FIR variety. While the input sequence is required to be LOMO in order for the conditions of the theorem to hold, the necessary degree of local monotonicity is found to depend upon the filter coefficients in an interesting way.

Theorem 7 (Equivalence Theorem): Suppose that the elements of the length $2N + 1$ symmetric vector $\boldsymbol{b}$ satisfy

$b_1 = b_2 = \cdots = b_{2N+1-k}$ ($N + 1 \leq k \leq 2N$) and one of the following:

a) $b_1 < \min \{b_{2N+2-k}, \cdots, b_{N+1}\}$,
b) $b_1 > \max \{b_{2N+2-k}, \cdots, b_{N+1}\}$.

Then the following two statements are equivalent:

c) $\{x_i\}$ contains at least one monotonic segment of length k and $\lambda_b(x_i) = \omega_b(x_i) \; \forall \; i$
d) $\{x_i\}$ is LOMO($k + 1$).

Proof: Lemma 1a and Lemma 1b $\Rightarrow$ it suffices to consider $b_1 = 0$ and case a). To show that c) $\Rightarrow$ d), note that $\lambda_b(x_i) = \omega_b(x_i) \; \forall \; i \Rightarrow$

$$\sum_{n=2N+2-k}^{N+1} b_n \gamma_{n:i} = 0 \quad \forall \; i \quad (1)$$

where $\gamma_{n:i} = [x_{n:i} - x_{(n):i} + x_{2N+2-n:i} - x_{(2N+2-n):i}]$; $2N + 2 - k \leq n \leq N$ and $\gamma_{N+1:i} = [x_{N+1:i} - x_{(N+1):i}]$. Now assume $\exists \; j$ such that $(x_{1:j}, \cdots, x_{k:j})$ is monotonic $\Rightarrow$ either $x_{n:j} \geq x_{(n):j}$ for $1 \leq n \leq k$ or $x_{n:j} \leq x_{(2N+2-n):j}$ for $1 \leq n \leq k$. Then $b_n > 0 \; \forall \; n \in N = \{2N + 2 - k, \cdots, N + 1\} \Rightarrow$ either $b_n \gamma_{n:j} \geq 0 \; \forall \; n \in N$ or $b_n \gamma_{n:j} \leq 0 \; \forall \; n \in N$. Hence, 1) $\Rightarrow \gamma_{n:j} = 0 \; \forall \; n \in N$.

Now suppose $(x_{1:j}, \cdots, x_{k:j})$ is nondecreasing $\Rightarrow$ $x_{n:j} = x_{(n):j} \; \forall \; n \in M = \{2N + 2 - k, \cdots, k\} \Rightarrow$ $x_{n-1:j+1} - x_{(n-1):j+1} = x_{(n):j} - x_{(n-1):j+1} \geq 0 \; \forall \; n \in M$. There are only two possibilities.

i) If $x_{k:j+1} \geq x_{k:j}$, then $y_j = (x_{1:j}, \cdots, x_{k+1:j})$ is nondecreasing.

ii) If $x_{k:j+1} < x_{k:j}$, then $x_{n-1:j+1} = x_{k:j} \; \forall \; n \in M$, since otherwise $\exists \; n \in M$ such that n elements of x_j are $< x_{n:j} \Rightarrow x_{n:j} \neq x_{(n):j}$ (contradiction). Note that 1) $\Rightarrow x_{2N+1:j+1} \leq x_{k:j}$, since $x_{2N+1:j+1} > x_{k:j} \Rightarrow x_{(n-1):j+1} = x_{n:j} \; \forall \; n \in M$; in this case 1) $\Rightarrow x_{k:j+1} = x_{(k):j+1} \geq x_{(k-1):j+1} = x_{k:j}$ (contradiction). Hence, $x_{2N+1:j+1} \leq x_{k:j} \Rightarrow x_{(n):j+1} = x_{n:j} \; \forall \; n \in M, n \neq 2N + 2 - k$, which combined with 1) $\Rightarrow x_{k:j+1} = x_{(2N+2-k):j+1}$. Finally, $x_{1:j} = x_{k:j}$, since $x_{1:j} < x_{k:j} \Rightarrow x_{k:j} = x_{(2N+2-k):j+1}$ (contradiction). Hence, y_j is nonincreasing.

Thus, i) and ii) $\Rightarrow y_j$ is monotonic; the same result is attained if $(x_{1:j}, \cdots, x_{k:j})$ is instead assumed nonincreasing. Since this conclusion only required 1) and the assumption that $(x_{1:j}, \cdots, x_{k:j})$ is monotonic, 1) $\Rightarrow y_i$ is monotonic $\forall \; i \geq j$. By identical reasoning, it can be shown that y_{j-1} is monotonic, hence, 1) $\Rightarrow y_i$ is monotonic $\forall \; i \leq j \Rightarrow \{x_i\}$ is LOMO($k + 1$).

That d) $\Rightarrow$ c) follows since if $\{x_i\}$ is LOMO($k + 1$), Lemma 5 $\Rightarrow \{x_i\}$ contains a monotonic segment of length k, and $\gamma_{n:j} = 0$ for $n \in N \; \forall \; i \Rightarrow \lambda_b(x_i) = \omega_b(x_i) \; \forall \; i$. Note that this implication does not require either a) or b) to hold. ◇

In the preceding, it is necessary that $N + 1 \leq k \leq 2N$, since $k < N + 1 \Rightarrow N$ is empty and $k = 2N + 1 \Rightarrow$ neither a) nor b) is true. The assumption that $\{x_i\}$ contains a monotonic segment of *minimum* length k is necessary, since otherwise it is not true that 1) $\Rightarrow \gamma_{k:j} = 0$. For finite-length sequences with padding as in [7], the existence of a monotonic segment is required when $k > N + 2$; however, the padding process could be modified by further extending the length of the sequence by $k - (N + 2)$ elements at each end, thus ensuring the presence of a monotonic segment of length k.

A natural question that arises is whether there are any filter coefficient vectors b other than those characterized in Theorem 7 for which $\omega_b(x_i) = \lambda_b(x_i) \; \forall \; i \Leftrightarrow \{x_i\}$ is LOMO. We believe that there are not. While we have not been able to show this for arbitrary N, we have been able to prove it to be so for $2N + 1 \leq 11$ (by exhausting all possibilities of relative weightings of the OS).

In the following, we describe several properties of filters satisfying Theorem 7, and discuss a number of well-known filters falling in this class.

Definition: If an OS filter ω_b and linear filter λ_b satisfy the conditions of Theorem 7, then they are *LOMO($k + 1$)-equivalent*.

The following corollaries mainly derive from Theorem 7. In each it is assumed, as usual, that b is symmetric and of length $2N + 1$.

Corollary 5: Suppose that ω_b and λ_b are LOMO($k + 1$)-equivalent. Then if the symmetric vector b' is of length $2M + 1$ ($M > N$), where $b'_j = b_1$ for $j = 1, \cdots, M - N$ and $b'_j = b_{j+N-M}$ for $j = M - N + 1, \cdots, M + 1$, then $\omega_{b'}$ and $\lambda_{b'}$ are LOMO($k + 1$)-equivalent.

Proof: If b satisfies the condition of Theorem 7, then b' does also. Hence, $\omega_{b'}$ and $\lambda_{b'}$ are LOMO($k + 1$)-equivalent. ◇

Corollary 5 is of particular interest for the following reason. Consider a symmetric ($2N + 1$)-vector b associated with a linear FIR filter, where all of the elements of b are either positive or negative. Defining an OS filter of length $2M + 1$ ($M > N$) as having coefficients $b' = (0, \cdots, 0, b_1, \cdots, b_{N+1}, \cdots, b_1, 0, \cdots, 0)$, $\omega_{b'}$ and λ_b will yield similar or identical outputs if the input sequence is sufficiently smooth (locally monotonic); however, since filters of this type are invariably smoothing filters, the OS filter will impart a much greater degree of noise suppression than the linear filter. This is one of the strongest reasons for using OS filters for signal smoothing purposes.

Corollary 6: Suppose that $\{x_i\}$ is LOMO(M) but not LOMO($M + 1$), and that $\{x_i\}$ contains at least one segment of length k which is monotonic. If ω_b and λ_b are LOMO($k + 1$)-equivalent, then $\omega_b(x_i) = \lambda_b(x_i) \; \forall \; i \Leftrightarrow M \geq k + 1$.

Proof: Clearly, $\omega_b(x_i) = \lambda_b(x_i) \; \forall \; i$ if $M \geq k + 1$, since x_i is monotonic $\forall \; i$. It is equally clear that $\omega_b(x_i) \neq \lambda_b(x) \; \forall \; i$ if $M < k + 1$, as a consequence of Theorem 7. ◇

Theorem 7 is an extension of the well-known result (Theorem 3) for median filters, viz., median filters of length $2N + 1$ are LOMO($N + 2$)-equivalent to linear identity filters. However, there are several other well-known filters which are characterized by Theorem 7.

Definitions: A symmetric OS filter with coefficients $b_j = 0$; $j = 1, \cdots, N - k$ and $b_j = 1/(2k + 1)$; $j = N - k + 1, \cdots, N + 1$ is a *k-inner median filter*. A symmetric OS filter with coefficients $b_j = 1/2k$; $j = 1, \cdots, k$ and $b_j = 0$; $j = k + 1, \cdots, N + 1$ is a *k-outer mean filter*.

Inner and outer mean filters (also known as trimmed mean filters) have been noted to possess properties similar to those of both the linear averaging filter and the highly nonlinear median filter. Bednar and Watt [21] conjectured that repeated filterings of a given input sequence with a *k*-inner mean filter will eventually converge to the same result as obtained by repeatedly filtering the signal with a linear averaging filter of length $2k + 1$. The following corollary shows this to be true for LOMO signals; here of course convergence is obtained in a single pass. It should be noted that any linear filter remains unchanged by "padding" with zeros at either end of the coefficient vector.

The following corollaries are simple consequences of Theorem 7 and Corollary 5 and are stated without proof.

Corollary 7: Linear averaging filters of length $2k + 1$ and *k*-inner mean filters are LOMO($k + 1$)-equivalent for $N \geq k + 1$.

Corollary 8: A *k*-outer mean filter of length $2N + 1$ and a linear filter defined with the same coefficients are LOMO($N - k + 1$)-equivalent for $N \geq k + 1$.

The class of filters characterized by Theorem 7 includes many other linear filters of practical significance, including triangle-shaped filters, Hamming windows, Gaussian-shaped filters of finite extent, and filters defined by differencing averaging filters of different spans. This last type of filter is of particular interest, since the linear variety is a bandpass filter which is useful for detecting edges in signals or images. Since the corresponding OS filter (a difference of inner mean filters) is LOMO-equivalent, and since edge structures are ideally locally monotonic, the OS version can also be applied to this task. If there is noise present in the signal, then the OS version may supply more robust detection of edges and suppression of false edges [22].

In the following, it is shown that filters characterized by Theorem 7, and having outer coefficient(s) equal to zero, enjoy certain smoothing properties (the linear versions are always low-pass, and both the linear and OS versions always preserve local monotonicity).

B. Smoothing LOMO-Equivalent Filters

In the preceding, several linear filters were discussed which are LOMO-equivalent to their OS counterparts (OS filters of the same length and having the same coefficients). Those filters mentioned for which the outer coefficient(s) are zero were all of the low-pass variety. If a length-($2N + 1$) linear filter λ_b is LOMO($k + 1$)-equivalent to the OS filter ω_b, and if $b_1 = 0$, then λ_b is a length-$2k + 1$ linear filter with all positive or negative coefficients. Such a filter is never of the "high-pass" type; moreover, ω_b enjoys certain smoothing properties as well.

Definition: If ω_b and λ_b are LOMO($k + 1$)-equivalent, and if $b_1 = 0$, then ω_b and λ_b are *($k + 1$)-smoothing*.

In the following, $B(e^{j\nu})$ = frequency response of the linear filter with coefficient vector b.

Lemma 6: Suppose that b is the length $2k + 1$ coefficient vector ($k > 0$) of a symmetric linear filter, where $b_i b_j > 0$ for $i \neq j$. Then $|B(e^{j0})| > |B(e^{j\nu})|$ for $\nu \in (0, \pi)$.

Proof: For simplicity, assume that the impulse response $\{b_i\}$ of b is zero for $|i| > k$, and $b_i > 0$ for $|i| \leq k$. Then $|B(e^{j\nu})| = |b_0 + 2\{b_1 \cos(\nu) + b_2 \cos(2\nu) + \cdots + b_k \cos(k\nu)\}| \leq b_0 + 2\{b_1|\cos(\nu)| + b_2|\cos(2\nu)| + \cdots + b_k|\cos(k\nu)|\} < b_0 + 2\{b_1 + b_2 + \cdots + b_k\} = |B(e^{j0})|$, since $|\cos(c\nu)| < 1$ for $\nu \in (0, \pi)$, $c \neq 0$. ◇

Thus, any ($k + 1$)-smoothing OS filter acts low-pass when applied to an LOMO($k + 1$) sequence. In a related study [23], it was found that OS filtering of iid random sequences leads to sequences having maximum power at zero frequency, regardless of the filter coefficients. This suggests that OS filters have a smoothing tendency which is invariant to the coefficient vector, viz., that ordering the windowed data values imparts a high degree of correlation at the output. This is not the case for arbitrary linear filters, suggesting that OS-filtered sequences are smoother in some sense than their LOMO-equivalent linear-filtered counterparts, unless the input is LOMO.

Lemma 7 (Monotonicity Preserving Property): Suppose that ω_b and λ_b are ($k + 1$)-smoothing. Then if $\{x_i\}$ is LOMO(M), where $M \geq k + 1$, then both $\{\omega_b(x_i)\}$ and $\{\lambda_b(x_i)\}$ either everywhere preserve (if $b_{N+1} > 0$) or everywhere reverse (if $b_{N+1} < 0$) monotonicity.

Proof: For any i,

$$\lambda_b(x_{i+1}) - \lambda_b(x_i) = \sum_{n=2N+2-k}^{N+1} b_n \Delta_{n:i}, \quad (2)$$

where $\Delta_{n:i+1} = [x_{n:i+1} - x_{n:i} + x_{2N+2-n:i+1} - x_{2N+2-n:i}]$: $2N + 2 - k \leq n \leq N$, $\Delta_{N+1:i} = [x_{N+1:i+1} - x_{N+1:i}]$. If $\{x_i\}$ is LOMO(M), where $M \geq k + 1$, then for $N + 1 \leq k \leq 2N$, either $x_{n:i+1} \geq x_{n:i}$ $\forall n \in M = \{2N + 2 - k, \cdots, k\}$ (when $x_{i+1} \geq x_i$) or $x_{n:i+1} \leq x_{n:i}$ $\forall n \in M$ (when $x_{i+1} \leq x_i$). Since ω_b and λ_b are ($k + 1$)-smoothing, either a) $b_n > 0$ $\forall n \in N = \{2N + 2 - k, \cdots, N + 1\}$ or b) $b_n < 0$ $\forall n \in N$. In case a), if $x_{i+1} \geq x_i$, then $\Delta_{n:i} \geq 0$ $\forall n \in N$, and hence, (2) ⇒ $\lambda_b(x_{i+1}) \geq \lambda_b(x_i)$. If $x_{i+1} \leq x_i$ then (2) ⇒ $\lambda_b(x_{i+1}) \leq \lambda_b(x_i)$. Hence, λ_b everywhere preserves monotonicity. Similarly, in case b), $x_{i+1} \leq x_i$ ⇒ $\lambda_b(x_{i+1}) \geq \lambda_b(x_i)$ and $x_{i+1} \geq x_i$ ⇒ $\lambda_b(x_{i+1}) \leq \lambda_b(x_i)$. Hence, λ_b everywhere reverses monotonicity. Finally, by Theorem 7, $\omega_b(x_i) = \lambda_b(x_i)$ $\forall i$ ⇒ $\omega_b(x_i)$ either everywhere preserves or everywhere reverses monotonicity. ◇

Lemma 7 does not imply that ($k + 1$)-smoothing filters are LOMO-preserving, since there is no guarantee that $x_{i+1} = x_i$ ⇒ $\lambda_b(x_{i+1}) = \lambda_b(x_i)$, even if $\{x_i\}$ is LOMO(M), $M \geq k + 1$. Thus, constant segments that separate monotonic regions of opposite polarity in the input sequence may be reduced in size, thus reducing the degree of local monotonicity. For example, if the 4-smoothing OS filter $b = (0, 1, 1, 1, 0)^T$ is applied to $\{x_i\} = \{\cdots, 0, 0, 0, 1, 1, 1, 1, 0, 0, 0, \cdots\}$, ($x_i = 0$ everywhere else), the output $\{\omega_b(x_i)\} = \{\cdots, 0, 0, 1, 2, 3, 3, 2, 1, 0, 0, \cdots\}$ results, which is LOMO(3) even though $\{x_i\}$ is LOMO(5).

Finally, we show that the level (intuitively, the limiting average value) of a signal is preserved under linear FIR filtering if the filter coefficients sum to unity. However, such a condition is not sufficient for OS filters, unless the conditions of the Equivalence Theorem are satisfied.

Definition: The sequence $\{x_i\}$ has *level* L_x if for any i

$$\lim_{m \to \infty} \sum_{n=i-m}^{i+m} x_n/(2m+1) = L_x.$$

Theorem 8: If the elements of the arbitrary vector a satisfy $a^T 1 = 1$ and if $\{y_i\} = \{\lambda_a(x_i)\}$, then $L_y = L_x$.

Proof: Assume $a^T 1 = 1$ and define

$$S_m = \sum_{i=-m}^{m} \sum_{n=1}^{2N+1} a_n x_{n:i}/(2m+1)$$

$$= [a_1 x_{-m-N} + (a_1 + a_2) x_{-m-N+1} + \cdots$$

$$+ (a_1 + a_2 + \cdots + a_{2N}) x_{-m+N-1}]/(2m+1)$$

$$+ [x_{-m+N} + x_{-m+N+1} + \cdots + x_{m-N}]/$$

$$(2m+1) + [(a_{2N+1} + a_{2N} + \cdots + a_2)$$

$$\cdot x_{m-N+1} + \cdots + (a_{2N+1} + a_{2N}) x_{m+N-1}$$

$$+ a_{2N+1} x_{m+N}]/(2m+1).$$

Hence, the output level is

$$L_y = \lim_{m \to \infty} S_m = \lim_{m \to \infty} [x_{-m+N} + \cdots + x_{m-N}]/$$

$$(2m+1) = L_x. \quad \diamond$$

Now consider the sequence $\{x_i\}$ with elements $x_i = (-1)^i$, and let $\{y_i\} = \{\omega_a(x_i)\}$, where $\omega_a(x_i) = x_{(2N+1):i}$, i.e., $a = (0, 0, \cdots, 1)$. Then $L_x = 0$ and $L_y = 1$ although $a^T 1 = 1$. Hence, it is not sufficient for the filter coefficients to sum to unity in order that ω_a be level-preserving; some other restrictions must be added. Clearly, the conditions on both the input sequence and the filter set given in the Equivalence Theorem apply.

Theorem 9: Suppose that λ_b and ω_b are LOMO($k+1$)-equivalent, where the elements of the symmetric vector b satisfy $b^T 1 = 1$, and let $\{y_i\} = \{\omega_a(x_i)\}$. Then if $\{x_i\}$ is LOMO(M), where $M \geq k + 1$, then $L_y = L_x$.

Proof: By Theorems 7 and 8. $\quad \diamond$

V. Concluding Remarks

In this paper, several (necessary and/or sufficient) conditions were derived on both the input sequence and on the filter coefficient set for OS and linear FIR filters defined with identical coefficients to yield identical outputs. The results extend highly popularized theorems for the median filter, and have shown that the notion of a "root signal" can be appropriately interpreted in terms of the relationship between OS and linear filters. In particular, for filters which preserve smoothness (those characterized by Lemma 7), OS and linear filters operate identically on signals which are sufficiently smooth, even if they contain "edges."

Several significant results were obtained for filters defined with symmetric coefficients sets; it was found that if the filter is of the "smoothness-preserving" type, then the OS and linear filters yield identical results if and only if the input is sufficiently smooth (LOMO), provided it is smooth *somewhere*. Thus, the idea of local monotonicity becomes important in the study of the class of OS filters, rather than being confined to median filter theories. Extensions of these results could give rise to a more complete theory of OS filtering, perhaps involving the decomposition of input signals into monotonic or locally monotonic components. One can offer several conjectures at this point. It is possible that a $(k+1)$-smoothing OS filter always produces a result which is more nearly LOMO (in some sense) than its LOMO-equivalent linear filter, except when operating on LOMO inputs. For coefficient sets which are not $(k+1)$-smoothing, it may be that for certain filters/signals the OS filter may give a result which is "more LOMO" than the linear counterpart, while for others the reverse may be true. Hopefully, some means can be developed for determining the conditions on the filter coefficients and on the input data for each to hold. With this in mind, we are currently investigating the notion of "LOMOtonic regression," similar to the concept of isotonic regression: associated with any sequence $\{x_i\}$ there exists a unique sequence among the class of monotonic sequences which is closest to $\{x_i\}$ in the mean-square sense [24]. It is also possible that for a given $\{x_i\}$, there exists a unique member $\{y_i\}$ of the class L_k of real-valued LOMO(k) sequences which is closest to $\{x_i\}$, viz., $\{y_i\} = \arg\{\min_{\{z_i\} \in L_k} \|\{x_i\} - \{z_i\}\|\}$ where $\|\cdot\|$ is a suitable distance norm.

Appendix

The proofs of Theorems 2 and 6 are given here, along with several additional lemmas required in the proofs.

Lemma A.1: Suppose that $2 \leq k \leq 2N$. Let $n < m$ be integers and let $x_{k:n} > x_{k:i} > x_{k:m} \; \forall \; i$ satisfying $n < i < m$. If $x_{(k):n} = x_{k:n}$ and $x_{(k):m} = x_{k:m}$, then

 a) $m - n \leq \min(k - 1, 2N + 1 - k)$, unless $k = N + 1$.
 b) either $x_{k:j} \geq x_{k:n}$ or $x_{k:j} \leq x_{k:m}$ for $j \in \{n + 1 - k, \cdots, n\} \cup \{m, \cdots, 2N + 1 + m - k\}$
 c) $x_{k:j} \geq x_{k:n}$ for $n + 1 - k \leq j \leq \min\{m - k, n\}$, and $x_{k:j} \leq x_{k:m}$ for $\max\{m, 2N + 2 + n - k\} \leq j \leq 2n + 1 + m - k$.

Proof:

a) Consider the four separate possible cases of overlap between x_n and x_m.

 i) If $x_{k:n} \in x_m$, viz., if $x_{k:n} = x_{j:m}$ for some $j \in \{1, \cdots, k - 1\}$, then $m - n = k - j \leq k - 1$ and

$x_{j:m} > x_{j+1:m}, \cdots, x_{k-1:m} > x_{k:m}$, i.e., $k - j$ elements of x_m are $>x_{k:m}$. But at most $2N + 1 - k$ elements of x_m are $>x_{k:m}$, so $m - n \leq 2N + 1 - k$. Thus, if $m - n \leq k - 1$, then $m - n \leq 2N + 1 - k$.

ii) If $x_{k:n} \notin x_m$, then $m - n \geq k$, and $x_{1:m}, \cdots, x_{k-1:m} > x_{k:m}$, i.e., $k - 1$ elements of x_m are $>x_{k:m}$. But at most $2N + 1 - k$ elements of x_m are $>x_{k:m}$, so $k - 1 \leq 2N + 1 - k$. Thus, if $m - n \geq k$, then $k \leq N + 1$.

iii) If $x_{k:m} \in x_n$, conclude analogous to i) that if $m - n \leq 2N + 1 - k$, then $m - n \leq k - 1$.

iv) If $x_{k:m} \notin x_n$, it follows as in ii) that if $m - n \geq 2N + 2 - k$, then $k \geq N + 1$.

Finally, i)–iv) yield a).

b) Assume the conditions in a) are satisfied. Then if $x_{(k):n} = x_{k:n}$, then x_n contains at least $2N + 2 - k$ elements which are $\geq x_{k:n}$, and similarly, if $x_{(k):m} = x_{k:m}$, then x_m contains at least k elements which are $\leq x_{k:m}$. Since $x_{k:n} > x_{k:i} > x_{k:m}$ $\forall n < i < m$, there are at least $2N + 2 - k$ elements $\geq x_{k:n}$ and at least k elements $\leq x_{k:m}$ contained in $(x_{k:n+1-k}, \cdots, x_{k:n}) \cup (x_{k:m}, \cdots, x_{k:2N+1+m-k})$, which contains exactly $2N + 2$ elements.

c) Assume the conditions in a) are satisfied. If $\exists j$ satisfying $n + 1 - k \leq j \leq \min\{m - k, n\}$ such that $x_{k:j} \leq x_{k:m}$, then x_m contains at most $k - 1$ elements which are $\leq x_{k:m}$, contradicting the assumption that $x_{(k):m} = x_{k:m}$. Thus, $x_{k:j} \geq x_{k:n}$ for $n + 1 - k \leq j \leq \min\{m - k, n\}$. Similarly, if $\exists j$ satisfying $\max\{m, 2N + 2 + n - k\} \leq j \leq 2n + 1 + m - k$ such that $x_{k:j} \geq x_{k:n}$, then x_n contains at most $2N + 1 - k$ elements which are $\geq x_{k:n}$, contradicting the assumption that $x_{(k):n} = x_{k:n}$. Thus, $x_{k:j} \leq x_{k:m}$ for $\max\{m, 2N + 2 + n - k\} \leq j \leq 2n + 1 + m - k$. ◇

Proof of Theorem 2: That a) $\Rightarrow$ b) follows from Property 5.

To show that b) $\Rightarrow$ a) for $2 \leq k \leq N$, suppose that $\exists p$ such that $(x_p, \cdots, x_{p+R-1})$ is nondecreasing; without loss of generality, suppose $p = k - R + 1$. Since $k \leq N$, also $R = k$, so $(x_1, \cdots, x_k)$ is nondecreasing. By contradiction assume that monotonicity is violated to the right of x_k. Let $j = \min\{i: i \geq 0, x_{k:i+N+1} > x_{k:i+N+2}\}$. We may take $j = 0$, since otherwise we could take $p = k + j - R + 1$. Then

i) $x_1 \leq \cdots \leq x_k > x_{k+1}$.

Moreover, since by hypothesis $x_k = x_{k:N+1} = x_{(k):N+1}$ and $x_{k+1} = x_{k:N+2} = x_{(k):N+2}$, by Lemma A.1 it follows that

ii) either $x_{k+j-N-1} \geq x_k$ or $x_{k+j-N-1} \leq x_{k+1}$ for $j \in \{N + 2 - k, \cdots, N\} \cup \{N + 3, \cdots, 3N + 3 - k\}$,

and

iii) $x_1 \geq x_k$ and $x_{2N+2} \leq x_{k+1}$.

But i) and iii) $\Rightarrow x_1 = \cdots = x_k > x_{k+1}$. Since $x_{k+1} = x_{k:N+2} = x_{(k):N+2}$, at least k elements of $S = \{x_{k+1}, \cdots, x_{2N+2}\}$ are $\leq x_{k+1}$. However, at most k elements of S are $<x_k$, and one of these is x_{2N+2}, from iii). Furthermore, ii) $\Rightarrow$ every element of S is either $\geq x_k$ or $\leq x_{k+1}$, so exactly k elements of S are $\leq x_{k+1}$, and exactly $2N + 2 - 2k$ elements of S are $\geq x_k$. Let $n = \min\{i: x_i \in S, x_i \geq x_k\}$. Then $k + 2 \leq n \leq 2k$ since $x_n \notin \{x_{k+1}, x_{2N+2}\}$. Since $x_n = x_{k:n-k+N+1}$ and $x_{n-k+N+1} = (x_{n-k+1}, \cdots, x_{n-k+2N+1})$, the k elements of S that are $\leq x_{k+1} < x_k$ all lie in $x_{n-k+N+1}$. Since these elements are also $<x_n$, $x_n \neq x_{(k):n-k+N+1}$, which is a contradiction. Thus, $\{x_i: 1 \leq i < \infty\}$ is everywhere nondecreasing.

Now assume by contradiction that monotonicity is violated to the left of x_1. Reasoning as before, take $x_0 > x_1$, or $x_{k:N+1-k} > x_{k:N+2-k}$. Since $x_{k:N+1-k} = x_{(k):N+1-k}$ and $x_{k:N+2-k} = x_{(k):N+2-k}$, Lemma A.1 $\Rightarrow x_{2N+2-k} \leq x_1$; thus, $x_0 > x_1 = \cdots = x_{2N+2-k}$. Thus, the $2N + 1 - k$ elements $x_1, \cdots, x_{2N+1-k} \in x_{N+1-k}$ are all $<x_0$; since $2N + 1 - k > k$ (for $2 \leq k \leq N$), then $x_0 \neq x_{(k):N+1-k}$, which is a contradiction. Thus, $\{x_i\}$ is everywhere nondecreasing.

The proof that b) $\Rightarrow$ a) for $N + 2 \leq k \leq 2N$ is accomplished in an identical manner by first showing that $\{x_i\}$ is everywhere nondecreasing to the *left* of the monotonic segment. ◇

In the preceding proof, a contradiction is not reached if $k = N + 1$ (the median filter) were allowed, since in order to have $x_{N+1:N+1} = x_{(N+1):N+1}$, we would require that $x_1 = \cdots = x_{N+1} > x_{N+2}$, and that exactly $N + 1$ elements of $S = \{x_{N+2}, \cdots, x_{2N+2}\}$ be $\leq x_{N+2}$. Therefore, no element of S is $>x_{N+2}$ and no similar contradiction can be reached.

The remainder of the Appendix is devoted to proving Theorem 6. A number of definitions and lemmas will be required to accomplish the proof.

Definitions: Consider the segment $x_i = (x_{i-N}, \cdots, x_{i+N})$, $N \geq 1$. If x_i is not monotonic, then x_i can take one of four other forms.

i) x_i is of *Type I* if it is not monotonic and $\exists$ at least one $j \in \{1, \cdots, N\}$ such that $x_{j:i} \neq x_{(j):i}$ and $x_{j:i} \neq x_{(2N+2-j):i}$, but $x_{k:i} + x_{2N+2-k:i} = x_{(k):i} + x_{(2N+2-k):i}$ $\forall k \in \{1, \cdots, N + 1\}$.

ii) x_i is of *Type II* if it is not monotonic, $x_{N+1:i} = x_{(N+1):i}$, and x_i contains p values $j \in \{1, \cdots, N\}$ such that $x_{j:i} = x_{(j):i}$ and $x_{2N+2-j:i} = x_{(2N+2-j):i}$, and $N - p$ values $k \in \{1, \cdots, N\}$ such that $x_{k:i} = x_{(2N+2-k):i}$ and $x_{2N+2-k:i} = x_{(k):i}$, for some $p \in \{1, \cdots, N - 1\}$.

iii) x_i is of *Type III* if it is not monotonic and if $x_{1:i} = x_{(2N+1):i}$ ($x_{1:i} = x_{(1):i}$), $x_{2N+1:i} = x_{(1):i}$ ($x_{2N+1:i} = x_{(2N+1):i}$), and $x_{j:i} = x_{(j):i}$ ($x_{j:i} = x_{(2N+2-j):i}$) for $j = 2, \cdots, N + 1$.

iv) x_i is of *Type IV* if $\exists j \in \{1, \cdots, N\}$ such that $x_{j:i} + x_{2N+2-j:i} \neq x_{(j):i} + x_{(2N+2-j):i}$.

If x_i is not monotonic, then it must be of Type I, II, III, or IV. If x_i is of Type III, then it is also of Type II. If x_i is of Type I, then it cannot be of Type II or III. If x_i is of Type IV, then it cannot be of Types I, II, or III. Finally, if $N = 1$, then x_i cannot be of Types I, II, or III.

Lemma A.2: If $\{x_i\}$ contains a Type I segment of length $2N + 1$, then it contains a Type IV segment of length $2N + 1$.

Proof: Assume that $\boldsymbol{x}_i = (x_{i-N}, \cdots, x_{i+N})$ is of Type I. Let $n = \max \{j; 1 \leq j \leq N, x_{j:i} \neq x_{(j):i}, x_{j:i} \neq x_{(2N+2-j):i}\} \Rightarrow$ either $x_{j:i} = x_{(j):i}$ or $x_{j:i} = x_{(2N+2-j):i}$ $\forall j \in \{1, \cdots, N + 1\}$. Since $\boldsymbol{x}_i$ and $\boldsymbol{x}_{(i)}$ are $1-1$, $x_{n:i} \notin \{x_{(n):i}, \cdots, x_{(2N+2-n):i}\}$. However, since $\boldsymbol{x}_i$ and $\boldsymbol{x}_{n+i-N-1}$ differ in exactly $N + 1 - n$ elements, $x_{(N+1):n+i-N-1} \in \{x_{(n):i}, \cdots, x_{(2N+2-n):i}\}$. Hence, $x_{n:i} = x_{N+1:n+i-N-1} \neq x_{(N+1):n+i-N-1} \Rightarrow x_{n+i-N-1}$ is of Type IV. ◊

Lemma A.3: If $\{x_i\}$ contains a Type III segment of length $2N + 1$, then it contains a Type IV segment of length $2N + 1$.

Proof: Assume that $\boldsymbol{x}_i = (x_{i-N}, \cdots, x_{i+N})$ is of Type III. Specifically, suppose that $x_{1:i} = x_{(2N+1):i}$, $x_{2N+1:i} = x_{(1):i}$, and that $x_{j:i} = x_{(j):i}$ for $j = 2, \cdots, N + 1$. Then $\exists n = \min \{j: 2 \leq j \leq 2N - 1, x_{2N+1:i} \leq x_{j:i} < x_{j+1:i} \leq x_{1:i}\}$ since otherwise $\boldsymbol{x}_i$ is monotonic and not of Type III. Then $\boldsymbol{x}_{i+1}$ is not monotonic, hence it is of Type I, II, or IV. By Lemma A.2 it must be assumed that $\boldsymbol{x}_{i+1}$ is of Type II. Then $n = 2$ and $x_{2:i} \leq x_{2N+1:i} \Rightarrow x_{2N:i+1} = x_{1:i+1} < x_{2:i+1} = x_{3:i+1} = \cdots = x_{2N-1:i+1} \leq x_{2N+1:i+1}$. Then $\boldsymbol{x}_{i+2}$ is also not monotonic, and $x_{2N-1:i+2} < x_{1:i+2} = x_{2:i+2} = \cdots = x_{2N-2:i+2} \leq x_{2N:i+2}$. Hence, $x_{2N-1:i+2} \neq x_{(2N-1):i+2}$ and $x_{2N-1:i+2} \neq x_{(3):i+2} \Rightarrow \boldsymbol{x}_{i+2}$ is not of Type II $\Rightarrow \boldsymbol{x}_{i+2}$ is of Type I or IV $\Rightarrow \{x_i\}$ contains a Type IV segment of length $2N + 1$. ◊

Lemma A.4: If $\boldsymbol{x}_i = (x_{i-N}, \cdots, x_{i+N})$ is of Type II, then for $1 \leq M \leq N$, $(x_{i-M}, \cdots, x_{i+M})$ is either monotonic or of Type II.

Proof: By definition of Type II segments. Clearly, if $M = 1$, then $(x_{i-M}, \cdots, x_{i+M})$ is monotonic. ◊

Lemma A.5: If $\{x_i\}$ contains a Type II segment of length $2N + 1$, then it contains a Type IV segment of length $2N + 1$.

Proof: Assume that $\boldsymbol{x}_i = (x_{i-N}, \cdots, x_{i+N})$ is of Type II for some $p \in \{1, \cdots, N - 1\}$. Let $M' = \min \{M: 2 \leq M \leq N, (x_{i-M}, \cdots, x_{i+M}) \text{ is of Type II}\}$. Then $(x_{i-M'}, \cdots, x_{i+M'})$ is of Type III, hence, by Lemma A.3, $\{x_i\}$ contains a length $2M' + 1$ segment $(x_{j-M'}, \cdots, x_{j+M'})$ of Type IV for some $j \neq i$. Then $\boldsymbol{x}_j = (x_{j-N}, \cdots, x_{j+N})$ is not monotonic, and by Lemma A.4 it is not of Type II, hence, it is of Types I or IV $\Rightarrow \{x_i\}$ contains a Type IV segment of length $2N + 1$ by Lemma A.2. ◊

Proof of Theorem 6: That a) $\Rightarrow$ b) follows from Property 5. To show that b) $\Rightarrow$ a), assume that $\forall i$.

$$\lambda_b(\boldsymbol{x}_i) - \omega_b(\boldsymbol{x}_i) = \sum_{j=1}^{N+1} b_j \gamma_{j:i} = 0 \quad (3)$$

for every symmetric $\boldsymbol{b}$, where $\gamma_{j:i} = (x_{j:i} + x_{2N+2-j:i} - x_{(j):i} - x_{(2N+2-j):i})$ for $j = 1, \cdots, N$ and $\gamma_{N+1:i} = (x_{N+1:i} - x_{(N+1):i})$. Since (3) holds for *any* $\boldsymbol{b}$, then $\gamma_{j:i} = 0$ for $j = 1, \cdots, N + 1$ $\forall i \Rightarrow \{x_i\}$ nowhere contains

a Type IV segment of length $2N + 1$. By contradiction assume that $\{x_i\}$ is not LOMO($2N + 1$). Then $\{x_i\}$ contains a segment of length $2N + 1$ which is of Types I, II, or III. But by Lemmas A.2, A.3, and A.5, then $\{x_i\}$ must also contain a segment of length $2N + 1$ which is of Type IV, which is a contradiction. Hence, $\{x_i\}$ must be LOMO($2N + 1$). ◊

References

[1] J. W. Tukey, *Exploratory Data Analysis.* Reading, MA: Addison-Wesley, 1971.

[2] L. R. Rabiner, M. R. Sambur, and C. E. Schmidt, "Applications of a nonlinear smoothing algorithm to speech processing," *IEEE Trans. Acoust., Speech, Signal Processing*, vol. ASSP-23, pp. 552–557, Dec. 1975.

[3] B. R. Frieden, "A new restoring algorithm for the preferential enhancement of edge gradients," *J. Opt. Soc. Amer.*, vol. 66, pp. 280–283, Mar. 1976.

[4] T. S. Huang, G. J. Yang, and G. Y. Tang, "A fast two-dimensional median filtering algorithm," *IEEE Trans Acoust., Speech, Signal Processing*, vol. ASSP-27, pp. 13–18, Jan. 1979.

[5] E. Ataman, V. K. Aatre, and K. M. Wong, "A fast method for real-time median filtering," *IEEE Trans. Acoust., Speech, Signal Processing*, vol. ASSP-28, pp. 415–420, Aug. 1980.

[6] K. Oflazer, "Design and implementation of a single-chip median filter," *IEEE Trans. Acoust., Speech, Signal Processing*, vol. ASSP-31, Oct. 1983.

[7] N. C. Gallagher and G. L. Wise, "A theoretical analysis of the properties of median filters," *IEEE Trans. Acoust., Speech, Signal Processing*, vol. ASSP-29, pp. 1136–1141, Dec. 1981.

[8] S. G. Tyan, "Median filtering: Deterministic properties," in *Two-Dimensional Signal Processing: Transforms and Median Filters*, T.S. Huang, Ed. New York: Springer-Verlag, 1981.

[9] T. A. Nodes and N. C. Gallagher, Jr., "Median filters: Some modifications and their properties," *IEEE Trans. Acoust., Speech, Signal Processing*, vol. ASSP-30, pp. 739–746, Oct. 1982.

[10] A. C. Bovik, T. S. Huang, and D. C. Munson, Jr., "A generalization of median filtering using linear combinations of order statistics," *IEEE Trans. Acoust., Speech, Signal Processing*, vol. ASSP-31, pp. 1342–1350, Dec. 1983.

[11] Y. H. Lee and S. A. Kassam, "Generalized median filtering and related nonlinear filtering techniques," *IEEE Trans. Acoust., Speech, Signal Processing*, vol. ASSP-33, pp. 672–683, June 1985.

[12] H. A. David, *Order Statistics.* New York: Wiley, 1982.

[13] A. C. Bovik and L. Naaman, "Least-squares signal estimation using order statistic filters," in *Proc. 20th Annu. Conf. Info. Sci. Syst.*, Princeton, NJ, Mar. 1986, pp. 735–739.

[14] F. Palmieri and C. G. Boncelet, Jr., "Optimal mse linear combination of order statistics for restoration of Markov processes," in *Proc. 20th Annu. Conf. Info. Sci. Syst.*, Princeton, NJ, Mar. 1986, pp. 729–734.

[15] P. D. Wendt, E. J. Coyle, and N. C. Gallagher, "Stack filters," *IEEE Trans. Acoust., Speech, Signal Processing*, vol. ASSP-34, pp. 898–911, Aug. 1986.

[16] J. P. Fitch, E. J. Coyle, and N. C. Gallagher, Jr., "Median filtering by threshold decomposition," *IEEE Trans. Acoust., Speech, Signal Processing*, vol. ASSP-32, Dec. 1984.

[17] P. Maragos and R. W. Schafer, "A unification of linear, median, order statistic, and morphological filters under mathematical morphology," in *Proc. IEEE Int. Conf. Acoust., Speech, Signal Processing*, Tampa, FL, Mar. 1985.

[18] F. Palmieri and C. G. Boncelet, "Design of order statistic filters with a given spectral behavior," in *Proc. 21st Annu. Conf. Info. Sci. Syst.*, Baltimore, MD, Mar. 1987.

[19] H. G. Longbotham and A. C. Bovik, "Theory of order statistic filters and their relationship to linear FIR filters," Comput. Vis. Res. Center, Tech. Rep. TR-87-2-34, Univ. Texas, Austin, Mar. 1987.

[20] L. Naaman and A. C. Bovik, "Optimal order statistic filters with coefficient censoring," in *Proc. IEEE Int. Conf. Acoust., Speech, Signal Processing*, New York, Apr. 11–14, 1988.

[21] J. B. Bednar and T. L. Watt, "Alpha-trimmed means and their relationship to median filters," *IEEE Trans. Acoust., Speech, Signal Processing*, vol. ASSP-32, pp. 145–153, Feb. 1984.

[22] A. C. Bovik and A. Restrepo, "Adaptive L-filters," in *Proc. 23rd Annu. Allerton Conf. Commun., Contr., Comput.*, Monticello, IL, Oct. 2-4, 1985.
[23] A. Restrepo and A. C. Bovik, "Spectral analysis of order statistic filters," in *Proc. IEEE Int. Conf. Acoust., Speech, Signal Processing*, Tokyo, Japan, Apr. 7-11, 1986.
[24] A. C. Bovik, T. S. Huang, and D. C. Munson, Jr., "Edge sensitive image restoration using order-constrained least-squares methods," *IEEE Trans. Acoust., Speech, Signal Processing*, vol. ASSP-33, pp. 1253-1263, Oct. 1985.

Harold Gene Longbotham (S'85-M'87) was born in Baytown, TX, on September 4, 1946. He received the B.S. degree in mathematics and physics from Stephen F. Austin University, Nacadoches, TX, in 1968, the M.S. degree in physics from the University of New Mexico in 1971, the M.S. degree in statistics from the University of Texas at San Antonio in 1983, and the M.S. and Ph.D. degrees in electrical engineering from the University of Texas at Austin in 1984 and 1987.

From 1968 to 1970 he was at the Houston Manned Spacecraft Center working for Lockheed Electronics Company in the area of Fourier transform holography. During the period from 1971 to 1983 he taught at several institutions, including the Pine Ridge Indian Reservation, the University of New Mexico, Texas Lutheran College, and the University of Texas at San Antonio. Since 1983 he has been a full-time graduate student at the University of Texas at Austin. He is currently an Assistant Professor at the University of Texas at San Antonio. His current research interests include digital signal processing, digital filter design with emphasis on nonlinear filters, and digital control theory.

Mr. Longbotham was elected to *Who's Who in American Colleges and Universities*, and is a member of Alpha Chi and Sigma Phi Sigma.

Alan Conrad Bovik (S'80-M'84) was born in Kirkwood, MO, on June 25, 1958. He received the B.S. degree in computer engineering in 1980, and the M.S. and Ph.D. degrees in electrical and computer engineering in 1982 and 1984, respectively, all from the University of Illinois, Urbana-Champaign.

He is currently an Associate Professor in the Departments of Electrical and Computer Engineering and Biomedical Engineering at the University of Texas at Austin, where he is the Director of the Laboratory for Vision Systems in the Computer and Vision Research Center. His current research interests include the application of nonlinear statistical methods to problems in digital signal and image processing, biomedical image processing, and computer vision, and computational aspects of biological visual perception.

Dr. Bovik currently holds the Stark Centennial Endowed Fellowship in Engineering. He is a member of the Pattern Recognition Society, the International Neural Network Society, and the Honor Society of Phi Kappa Phi. He is an Honorable Mention winner of the Annual Pattern Recognition Society Award, and is Associate Editor of the international journal *Pattern Recognition*.

Adaptive Nonlinear Filters for Simultaneous Removal of Different Kinds of Noise in Images

REINHARD BERNSTEIN

Abstract —A novel adaptive median filter is proposed. It allows the simultaneous removal of a combination of signal-dependent and additive random noise in addition to mixed impulse noise in images, processed in a single filtering pass. The adaptation algorithm is based on the local signal-to-noise ratio. An extension of the class of nonlinear mean filters to adaptive filters is considered. The performance of the adaptive median filter is compared to the commonly used median filter and the nonlinear mean filter.

Keywords: Signal-adaptive median filter, adaptive nonlinear mean filter, noise removal, digital image processing.

I. INTRODUCTION

MOST IMAGE-PROCESSING algorithms and applications deal with special tasks. One of the most important tasks is noise filtering. Some of the first techniques for noise removal used linear, signal, and space invariant two-dimensional filters as extensions of filters applied in one-dimensional signal processing (e.g., [1], [6], [7]). However, their use is not appropriate for different reasons.

In images, edges very often contain essential information. Furthermore, our visual perception is heavily based on edge information. Therefore, any filtering should preserve the edges. But a linear space invariant noise filter tends to blur the edges [8].

For a typical image, each part differs sufficiently from other parts such that a description by a nonstationary two-dimensional process might be appropriate [5]. As a consequence, the noise filtering should be done by nonstationary or signal-adaptive methods [10], [11].

In general, images can be corrupted by signal-dependent (multiplicative) noise, signal-independent (additive) noise, and impulse noise. The impulse noise might be caused in a camera by a faulty sensor and, in the transmission of coded images, by a faulty communication in noisy channels. In the presence of impulse noise, a reasonable noise suppression can be achieved by nonlinear filters only. Thus, the use of nonlinear filters in image processing increases permanently.

One of the most popular nonlinear filters for noise removal is the median filter. Initially, it was suggested by Tukey [2] as a tool in time series analysis. Its application to image processing was first published by Pratt [3] and Frieden [4]. It is computationally efficient [13], suppresses impulse noise, and preserves edge information. In recent years, the generalization of the median filter to a linear combination of order statistic filters was performed by Bovik, Huang, and Munson [14]. Lee and Kassam [15] proposed an extension of the median filter to the linear and nonlinear order statistic filters (L. M. and MTM filters), which stem from robust estimation theory [15].

A new class of generalized mean filters designed especially for impulse noise suppression was introduced by Kundu and Mitra [16], while a class of general nonlinear mean filters was defined by Venetsanopoulos and Pitas [17]. Recently, a further extension to nonlinear order statistic filters for image processing was published by the same authors [18]. Although the defined class is large enough to include, in principle, all known nonrecursive linear and nonlinear filters applied for pointwise image processing, the explicitly treated filters have some unsatisfying properties. In these filters, the input signal is mapped by a nonlinearity. For noise removal, this nonlinearity is adjusted to a particular noise, without referring to the actual signal. Therefore, these filters offer a reasonably good suppression of one special kind of noise only, e.g., negative *or* positive impulse noise or signal-dependent or additive noise. Moreover, the result of filtering depends strongly on the nature of the image and the number representation of the image data. This disadvantage is avoided by the median filter.

The purpose of this paper is to introduce a new signal-adaptive median filter (SAM filter) with variable windows. A comparison with the conventional median filter and the generalized nonlinear mean filter shows its favorable performance. It is suitable to remove a mixture of different noise in one processing step. We consider a combination of multiplicative, additive, and impulse noise with positive and/or negative impulses. An extension to signal-dependent noise, which is not purely multiplicative, in combination with signal-independent noise will be performed. The SAM filter to be proposed is a conceptionally simple and robust point estimator suitable for parallel processing as well.

The outline of the paper is as follows. At first, Section II describes the signal-adaptive averaging (SAA) since the proposed adaptation on the local features of the noisy signal, applied to all kinds of filters under investigation,

Manuscript received January 6, 1987; revised June 4, 1987.
The author is with the Lehrstuhl für Nachrichtentechnik, University of Erlangen-Nürnberg, D-8520 Erlangen, Cauerstrasse 7, West Germany.
IEEE Log Number 8716562.

can be derived from them. Apart from some useful supplements, it is related basically to our proposal, published in [10]. Section III describes the structure of our SAM filter. In Section IV, a short description of the generalized nonlinear mean filters and the extension to a signal-adaptive version follows. On the basis of several test pictures of various types which are corrupted by different noise, a comparison with the SAM filter will be performed in Section IV. Conclusions are drawn in Section VI.

II. Adaptive Noise Suppression

The general system for signal-adaptive digital image processing (enhancement, noise removal, etc.) is shown in Fig. 1. It can be divided into three blocks.

The first block models the image formation or, specifically for noise filtering, the formation of the available noise image $x(k,l)$ as a function of the (commonly unknown) noise-free image $u(k,l)$ and the shared noise processes. In general, the image $u(k,l)$ does not necessarily agree with the original or source image $v(k,l)$ itself. Often it is a linear or nonlinear function of $v(k,l)$. (Here and in the following, k and l are the discrete space variables.)

The second block consists of a linear or nonlinear filter, which is adjusted to the actual input signal $x(k,l)$. The adjustment is controlled by a third block, denoted "control system." The task of the control system is to perform the filter adaptation by an appropriate criterion derived from the local signal features of the noisy signal $x(k,l)$, taking into account the available *a priori* knowledge about the noise-free signal $u(k,l)$ and the noise, based on the model of noisy image formation (first block).

The particular blocks will be specified first, assuming that impulse noise does not occur.

A. Model for the Noise-Corrupted Signal (Block 1)

In order to model the noisy digital image $x(k,l)$, we introduce the following equation in accordance with Fig. 2:

$$x(k,l) = u_1(k,l) + u_2(k,l)q(k,l) + r(k,l). \quad (1)$$

Here, $q(k,l)$ and $r(k,l)$ are random variables with zero mean, belonging to independent ergodic random processes being stationary over the entire image. The image components $u_1(k,l)$ and $u_2(k,l)$ are linear or nonlinear functions f_1 and f_2 of the noise-free input signal $u(k,l)$, respectively. Therefore, they are correlated with each other, but assumed to be statistically independent of the noise $q(k,l)$ and $r(k,l)$. For some important special cases, we get the functions listed below.

1) Signal-Dependent Purely Multiplicative Noise with an "Additive Mean" p: In this case, we have

$$x(k,l) = u(k,l) \cdot \tilde{p}(k,l)$$

with

$$\tilde{p}(k,l) = p + q(k,l).$$

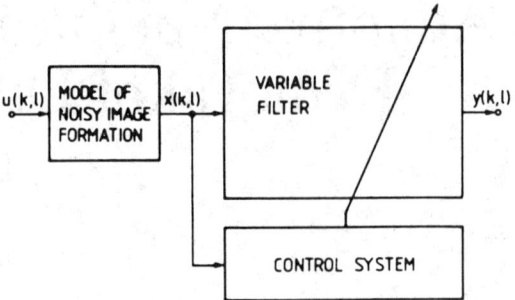

Fig. 1. General adaptive image enhancement system.

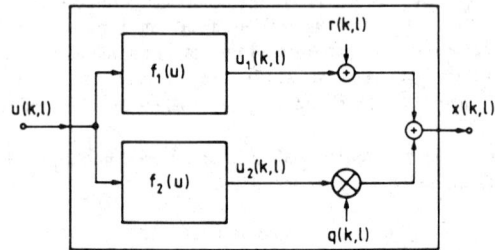

Fig. 2. Model of the noisy image formation.

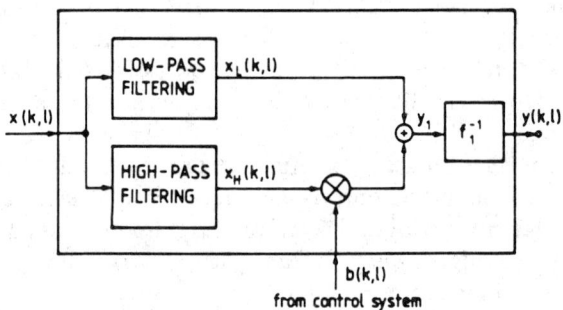

Fig. 3. Implementation of the variable filter as a two-channel filter.

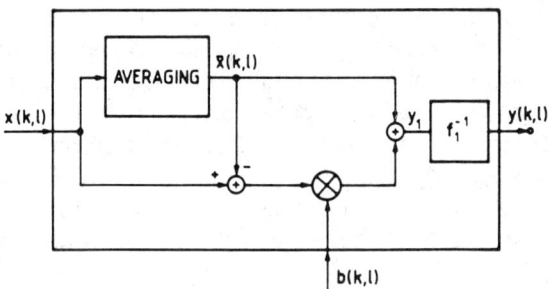

Fig. 4. The adaptive averaging filter.

In (1), this means the identification of

$$u_1(k,l) = pu(k,l) \rightarrow f_1(u) = p \cdot u \quad (2)$$

$$u_2(k,l) = u(k,l) \rightarrow f_2(u) = u. \quad (3)$$

2) Film Grain Noise [19]: This is a special case of 1) with $p=1$

$$u_1(k,l) = u_2(k,l) = u(k,l). \quad (4)$$

The noise-free input image $u(k,l)$ depends on the original image $v(k,l)$ according to the nonlinear function

$$u(k,l) = c_1[v(k,l)]^{\gamma_1}, \quad \gamma_1, c_1 = \text{const.} \quad (5)$$

3) Photo-Electronic Systems for Image Detection and Recording (e.g., TV cameras or tubes) [19]: In this case,

$$u_1(k,l) = u(k,l) = c_2[v(k,l)]^{\gamma_2},$$
$$\gamma_2, c_2 = \text{const.} \quad (6)$$

$$u_2(k,l) = [u_1(k,l)]^{1/2} \to f_2(u) = [u]^{1/2}. \quad (7)$$

B. The Adaptive Filter (Block 2)

For the variable filter, we use a two-channel filter as shown in Fig. 3. The filter input signal $x(k,l)$ is split up into a low-frequency signal $x_L(k,l)$ and a high-frequency signal $x_H(k,l)$ by appropriate filters. The high-frequency part is weighted with a signal-dependent weighting factor $b(k,l)$. For simplification, we substitute the high-frequency signal by the difference signal $x_H(k,l) = x(k,l) - x_L(k,l)$, provided that the applied low-pass filter has zero phase response, which implies a nonrecursive system. A two-component model like this is suitable not only for noise suppression, but also for many other enhancement operations, e.g., statistical differencing [20], and contrast enhancement [12], [21], shadow correction, cloud cover removal [21], and enhancement of X-ray images in medical radiography [22].

All these algorithms are distinguished by a different signal-dependent weighting factor $b(k,l)$, beside some task-dependent additional nonlinearities in each channel. For our application of noise removal, it is possible to derive $b(k,l)$ analytically, if we substitute the low-pass filter by a simple average filter, which leads to the system of Fig. 4. The output signal

$$y_1(k,l) = \bar{x}(k,l) + b(k,l)[x(k,l) - \bar{x}(k,l)] \quad (8)$$

should be an estimate of the noise-free signal $u_1(k,l)$. To get an estimation of the input signal $u(k,l)$, we have to map $y_1(k,l)$ point by point by the inverse function f_1^{-1}

$$y(k,l) = \hat{u}(k,l) = f_1^{-1}(y_1(k,l)) \quad (9)$$

if

$$u_1(k,l) = f_1(u(k,l)). \quad (10)$$

C. Derivation of the Signal-Dependent Weighting Factor

We determine the weighting factor $b(k,l)$ of (8) minimizing the mean-square error of the difference between the noise-free signal $u_1(k,l)$ and its estimate according to (8) over some random ensemble at (k,l). This leads to the criterion

$$\text{minimize } E\{[u_1(k,l) - y_1(k,l)]^2\} \quad (11)$$

where E denotes expectation. Substitution of $y_1(k,l)$ by (8) gives

$$E\{[u_1(k,l) - y_1(k,l)]^2\}$$
$$= E\{[u_1(k,l) - \bar{x}(k,l)]^2\} + b^2(k,l) \cdot \sigma_x^2(k,l)$$
$$- 2b(k,l) \cdot E\{u_1(k,l)[x(k,l) - \bar{x}(k,l)]\}. \quad (12)$$

With (1), it is easy to verify that the last term can be expressed as

$$E\{u_1(k,l)[x(k,l) - \bar{x}(k,l)]\} = \sigma_{u_1}^2(k,l) \quad (13)$$

if we assume, that the noise variables $q(k,l)$ and $r(k,l)$ are signal-independent random variables with zero mean. Therefore, setting the derivative of (12) with respect to $b(k,l)$ to zero yields

$$b(k,l) = \frac{\sigma_{u_1}^2(k,l)}{\sigma_x^2(k,l)} \quad (14)$$

as the quotient of the variances of u_1 and x at (k,l). The basic assumption used up to now is according to [9] that the ensemble mean at the point (k,l) is equal, or at least sufficiently close, to the local mean derived by averaging over the pixels of a small area surrounding the point (k,l). This implies that we assume the image to be divided into small subimages, each of which was generated by an at least wide-sense stationary ergodic process. The validity of this assumption is debatable especially from the theoretical point of view, but it is justified by experimental results. As mentioned above, we assume that the noise components $q(k,l)$ and $r(k,l)$ in (1) are generated by independent stationary random processes with zero mean. With (1), the local variance of u_1 can be expressed as

$$\sigma_{u_1}^2(k,l) = \sigma_x^2(k,l) - \left[\overline{u_2^2}(k,l) \cdot \sigma_q^2 + \sigma_r^2\right] \quad (15)$$

with

$$E\{u_2^2(k,l)\} = \overline{u_2^2}(k,l). \quad (16)$$

Substituting (15) into (14) yields the equation

$$b(k,l) = 1 - \frac{\overline{u_2^2}(k,l) \cdot \sigma_q^2 + \sigma_r^2}{\sigma_x^2(k,l)}. \quad (17)$$

The mean $\overline{u_2^2}(k,l)$ is usually not available because $u_2(k,l)$ is unknown. Nevertheless, for the cases discussed previously, it is possible to replace it by variables related to the known filter input signal $x(k,l)$. This is discussed in the sequel.

1) Purely Multiplicative Signal-Dependent Noise with Mean p According to 1) and 2) of Section II-A: Substitution of (2) and (3) in (1) results in

$$x(k,l) = u(k,l)[p + q(k,l)] + r(k,l) \quad (18)$$

and therefore

$$\bar{x}(k,l) = \bar{u}_1(k,l) = \bar{u}(k,l). \quad (19)$$

Taking this into account, we can write

$$\overline{u_2^2}(k,l) = \frac{1}{p^2}\left[\sigma_{u_1}^2(k,l) + \bar{x}^2(k,l)\right] \quad (20)$$

and, with (14), we replace $\sigma_{u_1}^2(k,l) = b(k,l) \cdot \sigma_x^2(k,l)$, which leads to

$$\overline{u_2^2}(k,l) = \frac{1}{p^2}\left[b(k,l) \cdot \sigma_x^2(k,l) + \bar{x}^2(k,l)\right]. \quad (21)$$

Substitution of this expression into (17) yields

$$b(k,l) = \frac{1}{1+\tilde{\sigma}_q^2}\left[1 - \frac{\bar{x}^2(k,l)\cdot\tilde{\sigma}_q^2 + \sigma_r^2}{\sigma_x^2(k,l)}\right] \quad (22)$$

with

$$\tilde{\sigma}_q^2 = \sigma_q^2/p^2. \quad (23)$$

For most applications, we have $\tilde{\sigma}_q^2 \ll 1$. Therefore, we obtain from (22)

$$b(k,l) \approx 1 - \frac{\bar{x}^2(k,l)\cdot\tilde{\sigma}_q^2 + \sigma_r^2}{\sigma_x^2(k,l)}. \quad (24)$$

2) Signal-Dependent Noise not Purely Multiplicative According to 3) of Section II-A: If we substitute $u_2(k,l)$ given by (7) into (1), we obtain

$$x(k,l) = u_1(k,l) + \sqrt{u_1(k,l)}\, q(k,l) + r(k,l) \quad (25)$$

and, with (6)

$$\bar{x}(k,l) = \bar{u}_1(k,l) = \overline{c_2[v(k,l)]^{\gamma_2}}. \quad (26)$$

From (7), we get

$$u_2^2(k,l) = u_1(k,l) \quad (27)$$

and therefore

$$\overline{u_2^2(k,l)} = \bar{u}_1(k,l) = \bar{x}(k,l). \quad (28)$$

With this equation, we rewrite (17) finally as

$$b(k,l) = 1 - \frac{\bar{x}(k,l)\cdot\sigma_q^2 + \sigma_r^2}{\sigma_x^2(k,l)}. \quad (29)$$

3) Generalization: A further generalization is evident. If it is possible to describe, or at least to approximate, the mean $\overline{u_2^2(k,l)}$ by a function $g\{\bar{u}_1(k,l)\}$ (analytically or numerically by a look-up table), we obtain from (17) with $\bar{x}(k,l) = \bar{u}_1(k,l)$

$$b(k,l) = 1 - \frac{g\{\bar{x}(k,l)\}\cdot\sigma_q^2 + \sigma_r^2}{\sigma_x^2(k,l)}. \quad (30)$$

As mentioned already, we assume that the ensemble mean and variance of x at the point (k,l) can be sufficiently well estimated by the local values, derived from the pixels of a small range surrounding (k,l) with

$$m_x(k,l) = \hat{\bar{x}}(k,l) = \frac{1}{w}\sum_\kappa \sum_\lambda x(k+\kappa, l+\lambda) \quad (31)$$

and

$$\hat{\sigma}_x^2(k,l) = \frac{1}{w}\sum_\kappa \sum_\lambda \left[x(k+\kappa, l+\lambda) - m_x(k,l)\right]^2. \quad (32)$$

The range, including w pixels, must not necessarily be rectangular. But for convenience, we use in the following a square window including $w = N \times N$, $N = (2n+1)$ pixels centered at (k,l). This allows us to calculate the local values of the running mean and variance recursively by partial sums from the previous ones [23]. It is worth noting that this can be accomplished by a fixed number of additions and multiplications independent of the mask size. Unfortunately, this is only an approximation, but the applied algorithm is rather insensitive to small deviations of the mean and variance. Therefore, this is not a real problem in practice. Nevertheless, we must be aware that $b(k,l)$ is positive per definition. This can be achieved easily by slightly modifying (30):

$$b(k,l) = \begin{cases} 1 - \dfrac{\sigma_n^2(k,l)}{\hat{\sigma}_x^2(k,l)}, & \text{if } \sigma_n^2(k,l) < \hat{\sigma}_x^2(k,l) \\ 0, & \text{else} \end{cases} \quad (33)$$

with

$$\sigma_n^2(k,l) = g\{m_x(k,l)\}\cdot\sigma_q^2 + \sigma_r^2. \quad (34)$$

Therefore, the weighting factor $b(k,l)$ is computable for each pixel of the noisy image $x(k,l)$, if the global variances σ_q^2, σ_r^2 of the random noise components $q(k,l)$ and $r(k,l)$ are known. These constants can be estimated from the noisy image, too, according to our proposal in [10].

Let us discuss now the physical significance of $b(k,l)$. From (33), we recognize that $0 \le b(k,l) \le 1$ holds. Furthermore, $b(k,l)$ is a measure of the local signal activity. In flat regions of the image, it becomes rather small or zero. Close to or on edges, $b(k,l)$ approaches one. Therefore, $b(k,l)$ can be regarded as a noise-insensitive edge detector. Beside this qualitative description, there exists an equivalent to the well-known Wiener filter applied in the case of additive noise only. Equation (34) describes the effective mean local noise power at (k,l). According to (15), we have

$$\sigma_x^2(k,l) = \sigma_{u_1}^2(k,l) + \sigma_n^2(k,l) \quad (35)$$

and we can rearrange (33) as

$$b(k,l) = 1 - \frac{1}{1 + \dfrac{\sigma_{u_1}^2(k,l)}{\sigma_n^2(k,l)}}, \quad \text{if } \sigma_n^2(k,l) \ne 0 \quad (36)$$

which can be identified with

$$b(k,l) = 1 - \frac{1}{1 + (S/N)_{(k,l)}} \quad (37)$$

where

$$(S/N)_{(k,l)} = \frac{\sigma_{u_1}^2(k,l)}{\sigma_n^2(k,l)} \quad (38)$$

describes the local signal-to-noise ratio at (k,l) of the difference signal $u_1(k,l) - \bar{u}_1(k,l)$ and the effective local noise. In the case of additive noisy only, we find a similar expression for the Wiener filter in the frequency domain

$$H_w(\omega_1, \omega_2) = 1 - \frac{1}{1 + (S/N)_{(\omega_1, \omega_2)}}. \quad (39)$$

Equation (39) may be extended, using a "signal equivalent

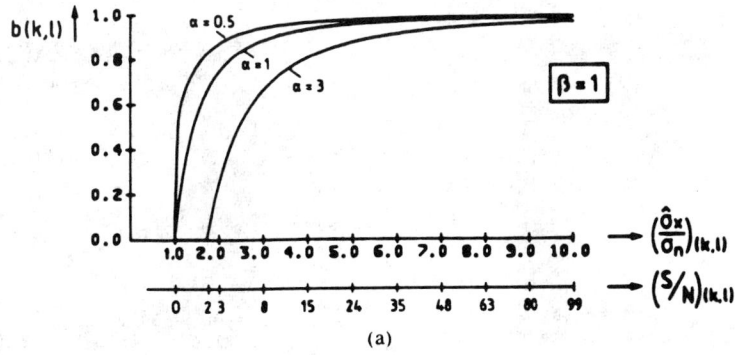

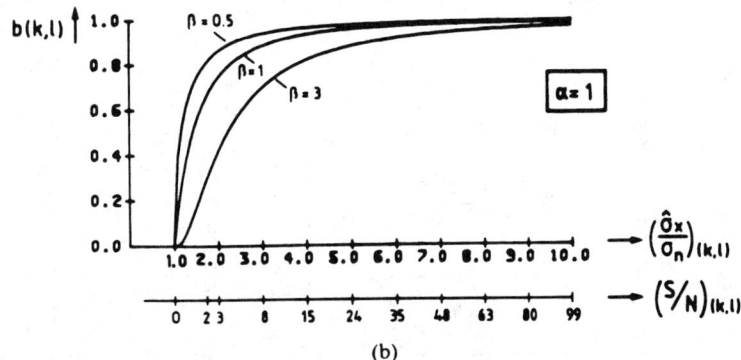

Fig. 5. Generalized weighting factor as a function of the local signal-to-noise ratio and the parameters α and β. (a) Dependence on parameter α, if $\beta = 1$. (b) Dependence on parameter β, if $\alpha = 1$.

approach" as in [24], according to

$$H_e(\omega_1, \omega_2) = \left[1 - \frac{\alpha}{1 + (S/N)_{(\omega_1,\omega_2)}}\right]^\beta \quad (40)$$

where α and β are properly choosen real constants. This includes the following cases (if $\alpha > 0$):

Wiener filtering, if $\alpha = \beta = 1$,
parametric Wiener filtering, if $\alpha \neq 1$, $\beta = 1$ [19],
power spectrum filtering, if $\alpha = 1$, $\beta = 0.5$,
short space spectral subtraction, if $\alpha > 1$, $\beta = 0.5$ [25],
generalized spectral subtraction, if $\alpha \neq 1$, $\beta \neq 1$ [26],
anisotropic filtering, if α and/or β depend on the spatial directions [11], [26].

Similar to (40), we extend (33) to

$$b(k,l) = \begin{cases} \left[1 - \alpha \dfrac{\sigma_n^2(k,l)}{\hat{\sigma}_x^2(k,l)}\right]^\beta, & \text{if } \alpha \cdot \sigma_n^2(k,l) < \hat{\sigma}_x^2(k,l) \\ 0, & \text{else.} \end{cases}$$

(41)

Fig. 5 shows this function for different values of α and β. If $\alpha \geq 1$, the parameter α controls essentially the threshold of the local signal-to-noise ratio (38) up to which the high-frequency components are suppressed entirely. For $\alpha = \alpha_0 < 1$, and $\beta = 1$, we get essentially an approximation of the function derived for $\alpha = 1$, $\beta = \alpha_0 < 1$ as is shown by a comparison of Fig. 5(a) with Fig. 5(b) for $\alpha_0 = 1/2$.

The parameter β controls the suppression of noise especially close to edges. A large local signal-to-noise ratio indicates high-frequency image components (i.e., edges). If this occurs, edge preservation is more important than noise reduction according to the masking effect by human vision. The masking effect stems from the fact that noise is perceived by a human eye differently, depending upon whether it occurs close to or far from an edge. The eye is quite sensitive to a small amount of noise in a flat field, but it is able to tolerate a large amount of noise in the neighborhood of an edge. Nevertheless, in order to avoid abrupt changes of noise suppression and to achieve a better signal adaptation, we adjust the window size of the averaging filter pointwise according to $b(k,l)$. This is accomplished by a simple strategy. Starting with the window size used for the previous point or an initial window size at the beginning (e.g., 5×5 or 7×7), we increase the size (e.g., from 5×5 to 7×7). If $b(k,l)$ becomes greater than an appropriately choosen threshold b_t, we decrease the window size until the weighting factor $b(k,l)$ becomes less than the threshold b_t or it reaches the minimum window size of 3×3. Otherwise, we increase the size of the window up to a maximum size. The first increase of the size leads to a better noise reduction in the neighborhood of edges, since the deviation of the local noise variances from the expected values becomes smaller for larger masks. The applied threshold b_t depends slightly on the image signal and the noise. To illustrate the performance of a signal-adaptive weighting factor and the proposed mask size adaptation, we give an example.

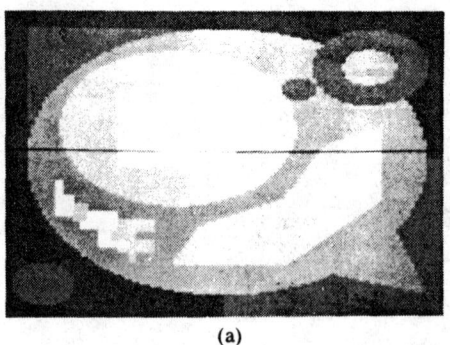
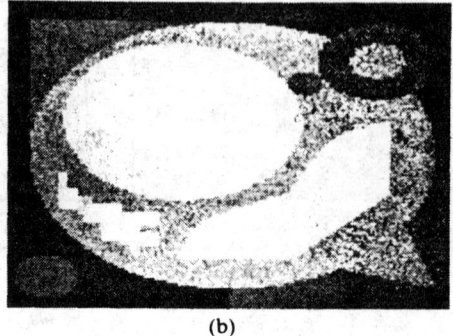

Fig. 6. Test-image "graphic" (256×256 pixels, 8 bit/pixel). (a) Original image $u(k,l)$ (the row $k = k_0 = 120$ is marked dark). (b) Noisy image $x(k,l)$ corrupted by multiplicative gaussian distributed noise ($\sigma_q^2 = 0.01$, unity mean) and uniformly distributed additive noise ($\sigma_r^2 = 100$, zero mean).

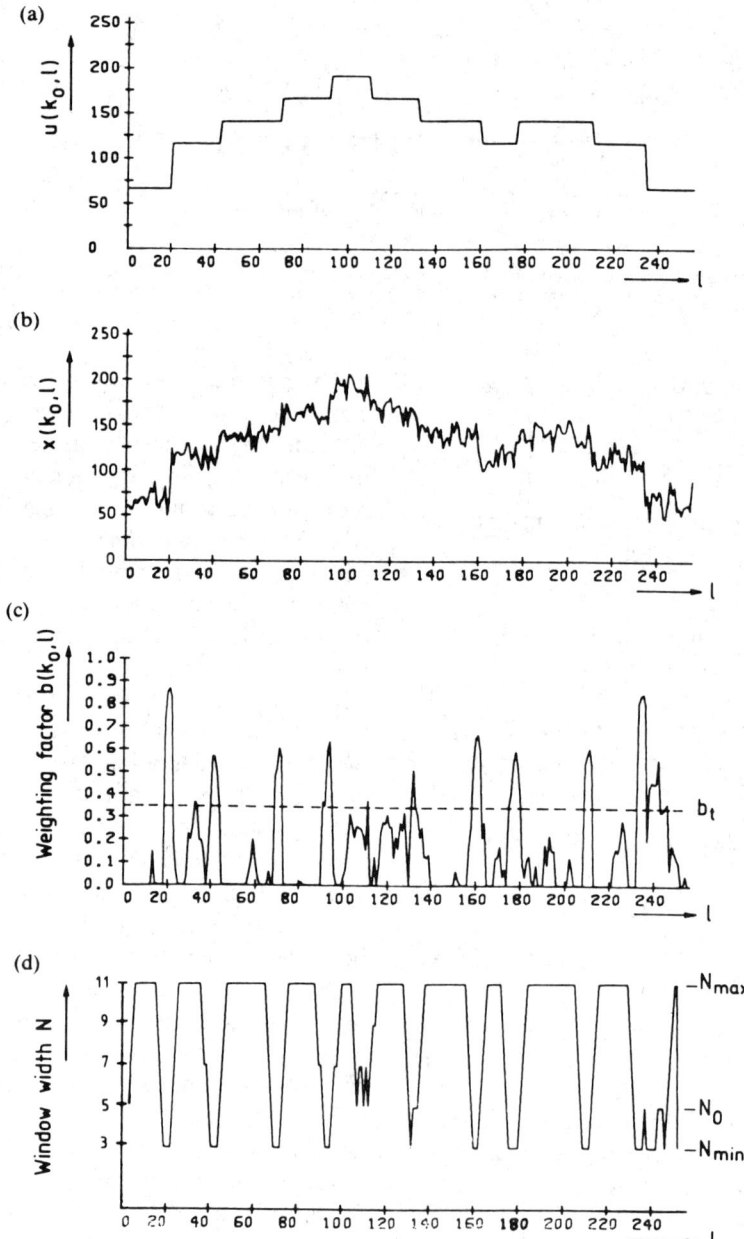

Fig. 7. (a) Plot of the noise-free image of Fig. 6(a) along line 120. (b) The same line of the noisy image of Fig. 6(b). (c) Signal-dependent weighting factor along the line 120 and threshold b_t for the window size adaptation. (d) Width of the adaptive window, adjusted between 3×3 and 11×11.

The image under consideration is a computer-generated test picture and therefore absolutely noise-free. It consists of 256·256 pixel values with an 8-bit resolution per pixel. The noise-free image $u(k, l)$ is shown in Fig. 6(a). The row $k_0 = 120$ is marked as a dark horizontal line. The image was corrupted by multiplicative gaussian noise ($\sigma_q^2 = 0.01$) with unity mean ($p = 1$) and additive zero-mean, uniformly distributed noise ($\sigma_r^2 = 100$), as shown in Fig. 6(b). For the row indicated in Fig. 6(a), the noiseless signal $u(k_0, l) = u_1(k_0, l)$ is shown in Fig. 7(a) and the corresponding noisy signal $x(k_0, l)$ in Fig. 7(b). The signal-dependent weighting factor $b(k_0, l)$ determined by (24) for a fixed mask size of 5·5 is depicted in Fig. 7(c). Based on this line plot, we choose the threshold for the mask size adaptation to $b_t = 0.35$. For all test images considered in this paper, we found that the appropriate value of b_t lies between 0.2 and 0.35. This corresponds to a minimum mean local signal-to-noise ratio between 0.25 and 0.54 according to Fig. 5 with $\alpha, \beta = 1$. We use a square window including $w = N \times N$ pixels, with variable window width N. It is adjusted according to $b(k, l)$ between $N_{\min} = 3$ and $N_{\max} = 11$, starting with an initial window width $N_0 = 5$, as shown in Fig. 7(d).

The moving average filter as considered up to now (or any other linear low-pass filter used to get the low-frequency component of the image) can be applied successfully only to images without impulse noise. If, in addition, impulse noise is present, our algorithm has to be changed as follows. First, we replace the linear low-pass filter by an appropriate nonlinear filter. Second, we complete the signal-adaptive weighting factor by an additional criterion for the impulse noise detection. If we choose the median filter, we get a signal-adaptive median filter (SAM filter).

III. SIGNAL-ADAPTIVE MEDIAN FILTERING

It is well known that the median filter removes impulse noise and reduces random noise (especially when the noise probability density has large tails), but preserves the edges and monotonic trends of the signal. Therefore, it is often applied in image processing. The commonly used median filter is nonrecursive. The two-dimensional median filtering (nonrecursive or recursive) can be effectively implemented by an algorithm introduced by Huang *et al.* [13]. An algorithm for on-line computation of the running median for real-time applications has been published already [27]. For a single filter pass, the recursive median filter reduces the noise better than a nonrecursive median filter with the same window size. In contrast to a recursive linear filter, the recursive median filter is inherently stable since the value of the median is per definition equal to one of the input samples. Therefore, the median value is bounded if the input signal is bounded.

With respect to an appropriate window size w, two effects must be taken into account. The noise suppression increases with increasing window size w; conversely, the space resolution decreases with increasing window size. In particular, a median filter removes all objects on a flat background which contain less than $(w+1)/2$ pixels. To solve this problem, commonly a small window (e.g., 3×3) is used, and the median filtering is repeated, until the resulting output is sufficiently smooth or until no further changes occur. Recently, it has been shown [28] that, under repeated median filtering, any sequence is converted to a sequence which is invariant to further median filtering. This sequence is denoted "root signal" and depends on the form of the used window. Though the convergence property of repeated median filtering is useful in the analysis of median filters [28] and in image coding [29], the repeated median filtering does not necessarily lead to a sufficient noise reduction [28].

Therefore, we propose a median filter (recursive or nonrecursive) with a variable window size, adjusted automatically depending on the nature of the processed part of the signal, i.e., whether it is an edge or a flat region. To achieve this, algorithms for histogram windowing and impulse detection must be introduced.

A. Histogram Windowing

In a monochromatic digitized image, the value of each pixel is represented by an integer number in the range between $S_{\min}$ and $S_{\max}$. In a black and white image, the minimum grey-level $S_{\min}$ appears black and the maximum grey-level $S_{\max}$ appears white. The actual values of $S_{\min}$ and $S_{\max}$ depend on the chosen numerical representation.

For a linear system, the result is independent of the internal numerical representation, apart from an additive constant. This is true also for order statistic filters, e.g., the median filter. For other nonlinear filters treated in this paper, this does not hold. Hence, we have to take into account that the numerical values of the pixels are usually physically associated with intensities, which are always positive.

To define the model for an impulse-noise corrupted image $x_i(k, l)$, we assume that positive impulses appear as white dots ($S_{\max}$) with probability p_p, and negative impulses appear as black dots ($S_{\min}$) with probability p_n. This yields

$$x_i(k, l) = \begin{cases} S_{\min}, & \text{with probability } p_n \\ S_{\max}, & \text{with probability } p_p \\ x(k, l), & \text{with probability } 1 - (p_p + p_n) \end{cases} \quad (42)$$

where $x(k, l)$ describes the image signal already corrupted by signal-dependent and signal-independent noise according to the model shown in Fig. 2.

As mentioned previously, we use the histogram-updating algorithm of Huang *et al.* [13] to evaluate the running median. Based on this algorithm, we perform some necessary modifications.

From the histogram of all pixels within a window with size w, centered at point (k, l), we derive the frequency of occurrence of the pixels with the value $S_{\min}$, denoted by $h_{\min}(k, l)$, and the one of the pixels, which has a value equal to $S_{\max}$, denoted by $h_{\max}(k, l)$. The *a priori* frequency

h_n of negative and h_p of positive impulses inside the window can be described according to (42), by

$$h_n = \text{NINT}[w \cdot p_n] \quad (43a)$$

and

$$h_p = \text{NINT}[w \cdot p_p] \quad (43b)$$

where $\text{NINT}[x]$ denotes rounding x to the next integer.

In the modified histogram, the frequencies of occurrence $h_{\min}(k,l)$, $h_{\max}(k,l)$ are changed according to

$$\tilde{h}_{\min}(k,l) = h_{\min}(k,l) - \Delta h_{\min}(k,l)$$
$$= \begin{cases} 0, & \text{if } h_{\min}(k,l) - h_n < \delta \\ h_{\min}(k,l) - h_n, & \text{else} \end{cases} \quad (44a)$$

and

$$\tilde{h}_{\max}(k,l) = h_{\max}(k,l) - \Delta h_{\max}(k,l)$$
$$= \begin{cases} 0, & \text{if } h_{\max}(k,l) - h_p < \delta \\ h_{\max}(k,l) - h_p, & \text{else} \end{cases} \quad (44b)$$

with an appropriate choosen threshold δ, taking into account that the local impulse frequencies commonly differ from the assumed a priori frequencies of (43a,b). For a square window including $w = (2n+1) \cdot (2n+1)$ pixels, we choose $\delta = n$. This causes only objects with at least n pixels of grey-level $S_{\min}$ or $S_{\max}$ to become relevant for filtering.

This algorithm can be regarded as a kind of adaptive "histogram windowing." It is evident that this procedure can be performed analogously if only one type of impulse occurs. Moreover, it can be applied in a similar way for recursive median filtering as well, taking into account that $(w/2) - 1$ elements in the window are already processed. Therefore, the applied a priori impulse frequencies according to (43a,b) must be reduced approximately by one half. The windowed histogram is used now to evaluate the modified median $\tilde{x}_M(k,l)$, similar to the original procedure.

To determine the actual weighting factor $b(k,l)$ according to Section II-A, we use the modified local mean

$$\tilde{m}_x(k,l) = \frac{1}{\tilde{w}(k,l)} \left\{ \left[\sum_\kappa \sum_\lambda x_i(k+\kappa, l+\lambda) \right] \right.$$
$$- [\Delta h_{\min}(k,l) \cdot S_{\min}$$
$$\left. + \Delta h_{\max}(k,l) \cdot S_{\max}] \right\} \quad (45)$$

and the modified local variance

$$\tilde{\sigma}_x^2(k,l) = \frac{1}{\tilde{w}(k,l)} \left\{ \left[\sum_\kappa \sum_\lambda x_i^2(k+\kappa, l+\lambda) \right] \right.$$
$$\left. - [\Delta h_{\min}(k,l) \cdot S_{\min}^2 + \Delta h_{\max}(k,l) \cdot S_{\max}^2] \right\}$$
$$- \tilde{m}_x^2(k,l) \quad (46)$$

for the reduced window size

$$\tilde{w}(k,l) = w - [\Delta h_{\min}(k,l) + \Delta h_{\max}(k,l)]. \quad (47)$$

As mentioned already, we obtain these values very efficiently by updating the corresponding values of the point processed previously. Obviously, it can be derived directly from the windowed histogram as well, but this would require a considerably higher computational effort.

In the presence of impulse noise, it is necessary to apply the modified values of the local mean and variance, otherwise the local statistical properties are changed significantly due to the impulses, as demonstrated by the example in Fig. 8. The noisy image of Fig. 6(b) was corrupted, in addition, by positive impulse noise with a probability of occurrence $p_p = 0.1$. Fig. 8(a) shows the noise-free image signal $u_1(k,l)$ in addition to the noisy signal $x_i(k,l)$ for the row at $k = k_0 = 120$, indicated in Fig. 6(a). The signal-dependent weighting factor $b(k,l)$ along this row, derived with the unchanged local mean (31) and variance (32) shows Fig. 8(b). It is not suitable to control smoothing and window size adaptation of the median filter. In contrast to that, the modification of the local mean and variance according to (45) and (46) yields a weighting factor as shown in Fig. 8(c). It is comparable to the one derived in absence of impulse noise, as a comparison with Fig. 7(c) shows. Therefore, the median filter window size adaptation can be performed now according to the procedure described in Section II-C. Nevertheless, we have to take care that the weighting factor becomes zero if the processed pixel is an impulse. Due to this reason, an additional criterion for impulse detection is necessary.

B. Impulse Detection

To detect whether a pixel $x_i(k,l)$ is affected by an impulse or not, we apply the criterion

$$x_i(k,l)$$
$$= \begin{cases} \text{negative impulse,} & \text{if } x_i(k,l) - \tilde{x}_M(k,l) < \tau_n \\ \text{positive impulse,} & \text{if } x_i(k,l) - \tilde{x}_M(k,l) > \tau_p \\ x(k,l), & \text{else} \end{cases}$$
$$(48)$$

where $\tilde{x}_M(k,l)$ describes the modified median, and τ_n and τ_p are appropriately choosen thresholds. Recently, Mitra and Kundu [16] introduced signal-dependent thresholds, which offer a more sensitive impulse detection than constants. For the regarded application of signal-adaptive median filtering, we introduce the more convenient thresholds

$$\tau_p(k,l) = c \cdot [S_{\max} - \tilde{x}_M(k,l)] \geq 0 \quad (49a)$$

and

$$\tau_n(k,l) = c \cdot [S_{\min} - \tilde{x}_M(k,l)]$$
$$= \tau_p(k,l) - c \cdot (S_{\max} - S_{\min}) \leq 0 \quad (49b)$$

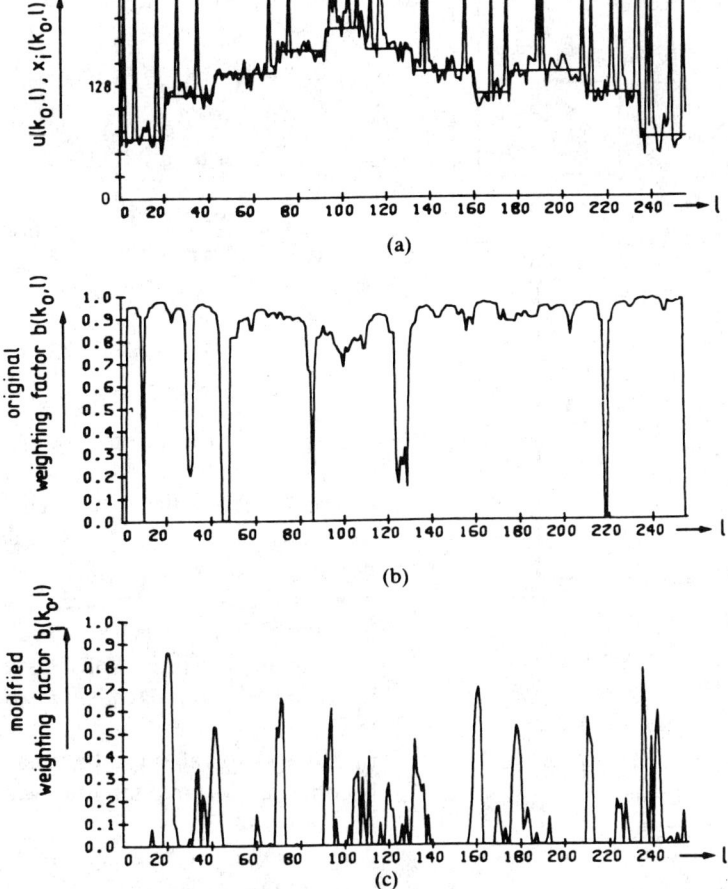

Fig. 8. Image of Fig. 6(b), additionally corrupted by 10-percent positive impulses. (a) Original signal $u(k,l)$ and noisy signal $x_i(k,l)$ at line $k = k_0 = 120$. (b) Weighting factor without modification. (c) Modified weighting factor (after histogram windowing).

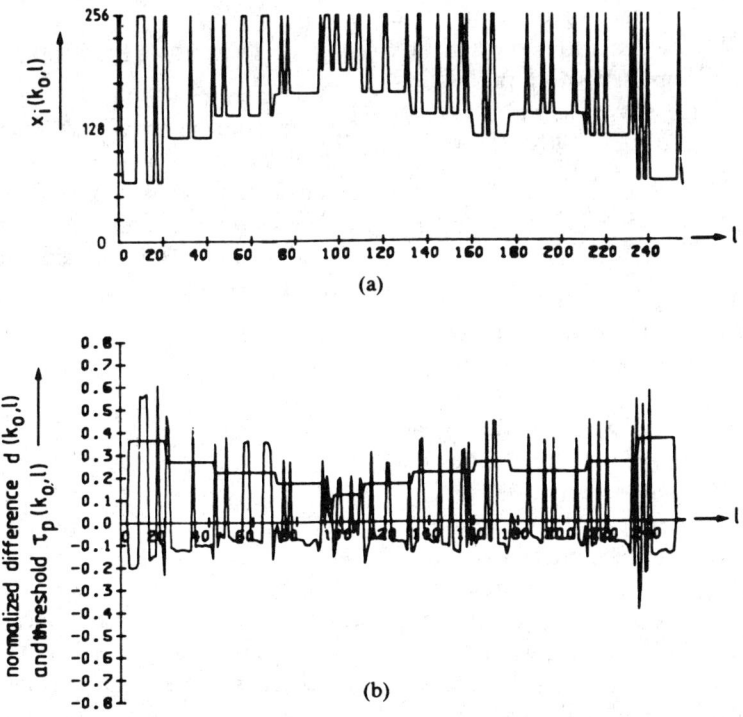

Fig. 9. Impulse detection with adaptive thresholds (line $k_0 = 120$). (a) Image signal of Fig. 6(a), corrupted by 20-percent positive impulses. (b) Difference d between signal and modified median (normalized by 256) and signal-adaptive threshold τ_p.

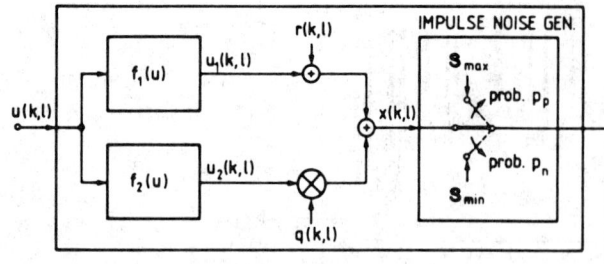
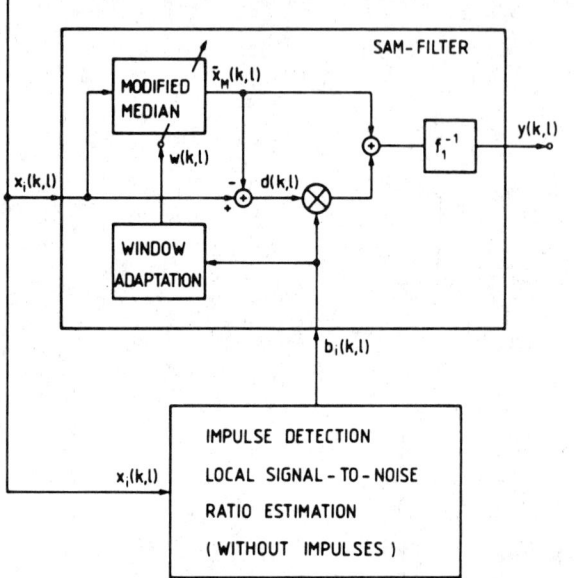

Fig. 10. SAM filtering algorithm for different kinds of noise.

where c is a constant. We found $c = 1/2, \cdots, 5/6$ appropriate.

Fig. 9 demonstrates the performance of these adaptive thresholds for an example. We use again the image of Fig. 6(a) and corrupt it by positive impulses with a probability of occurrence $p_p = 0.2$. Fig. 9(a) shows this noisy signal $x_i(k, l)$ for the row $k = k_0 = 120$. Fig. 9(b) shows the difference

$$d(k, l) = x_i(k, l) - \tilde{x}_M(k, l) \qquad (50)$$

of (48) and the threshold $\tau_p(k, l)$ for the same row k_0. It is easy to recognize that all impulses are detected by this threshold (the pixels on the left and right borders are not taken into account for filtering).

To smooth the nonimpulsive noise, we apply the signal-dependent weighting factor $b(k, l)$ of (41) for the median filter as well. It is able to do that without any disadvantage as long as the median is equal to or at least comparable to the local mean, i.e., in flat homogeneous image partitions. Close to or on edges, the weighting factor approaches one and the input signal remains unfiltered, independent of the type of filter. Applying a filter with adaptive window size, most of the pixels are members of one of these two classes. Therefore, the weighting factor of (41) derived for the averaging filter is still suitable for the SAM filter. In addition, we complete it by the impulse detection criterion discussed here. This yields

$$b_i(k,l) = \begin{cases} 0, & \text{if } x_i(k,l) - \tilde{x}_M(k,l) < c \cdot [S_{\min} - \tilde{x}_M(k,l)] \\ & \text{or } x_i(k,l) - \tilde{x}_M(k,l) > c \cdot [S_{\max} - \tilde{x}_M(k,l)] \\ & \text{or } \alpha \cdot \tilde{\sigma}_n^2(k,l) \geq \tilde{\sigma}_x^2(k,l) \\ \left[1 - \alpha \cdot \dfrac{\tilde{\sigma}_n^2(k,l)}{\tilde{\sigma}_x^2(k,l)}\right]^{\beta}, & \text{else} \end{cases} \qquad (51)$$

with $c = 5/6$. The expression

$$\tilde{\sigma}_n^2(k,l) = g\{\tilde{m}_x(k,l)\} \cdot \sigma_q^2 + \sigma_r^2 \qquad (52)$$

is an estimate of the effective local power of the nonimpulsive noise similar to (34). The modified median $\tilde{x}_M(k, l)$ is computed from the windowed histogram. The modified local mean $\tilde{m}_x(k, l)$ can be calculated by (45), and the modified local variance $\tilde{\sigma}_x^2(k, l)$ by (46).

Applying the procedure described in Section II-C, $b_i(k, l)$ of (51) can be used to adjust the window size of the running median filter. For the special case of impulse-noise removal only, we set $\tilde{\sigma}_n^2(k, l)$ to an appropriate constant (e.g., $1, \cdots, 4$). This has the effect that the local variance of the image signal must be greater than this constant to become important for the window-size adaptation algorithm.

Our SAM filtering algorithm, as shown in Fig. 10, is complete now. The performance of this algorithm in comparison with related, recently published nonlinear filters will be shown in Section V. To clarify the subject, we give a short description of these techniques, and some useful additions.

IV. Some Related Nonlinear Filters

The nonlinear filters described in this section are the generalized nonlinear mean filters, introduced by Venetsanopoulos and Pitas [17], [18], and the nonlinear mean filtering algorithm of Kundu and Mitra [16].

The *nonlinear mean* of all pixels of an image signal $x(k, l)$ included by a square window of size $w = (2n+1) \cdot (2n+1)$ is defined by

$$y(k, l) = g^{-1}\left(\dfrac{\sum_{\kappa=-n}^{n}\sum_{\lambda=-n}^{n} a(k+\kappa, l+\lambda) \cdot g[x(k+\kappa, l+\lambda)]}{\sum_{\kappa=-n}^{n}\sum_{\lambda=-n}^{n} a(k+\kappa, l+\lambda)}\right). \qquad (53)$$

Here, $g(x)$ denotes a nonlinear function and $g^{-1}(x)$ the inverse function. The weights $a(k + \kappa, l + \lambda)$ are not necessarily constants. They can be a nonlinear function of x as well. With respect to our application, we consider only the case that $g(x) = x^p$, with p being a rational number excluding $(-1, 0)$.

If the weights equal one, we derive from (53) the L_p-mean

$$y_{L_p}(k,l) = \left(\frac{1}{w} \sum_{\kappa=-n}^{n} \sum_{\lambda=-n}^{n} x^p(k+\kappa, l+\lambda) \right)^{1/p} \quad (54)$$

If $g(x) = x$ and the weights are a function of the input signal according to

$$a(k+\kappa, l+\lambda) = x^p(k+\kappa, l+\lambda) \quad (55)$$

(53) yields the contraharmonic mean or CH_p-mean

$$y_{CH_p}(k,l) = \frac{\sum_{\kappa=-n}^{n} \sum_{\lambda=-n}^{n} x^{p+1}(k+\kappa, l+\lambda)}{\sum_{\kappa=-n}^{n} \sum_{\lambda=-n}^{n} x^p(k+\kappa, l+\lambda)}. \quad (56)$$

The L_p- and the CH_p-mean filters offer a good suppression of positive impulses for $p<1$ and of negative impulses for $p>1$. According to our experience, the result derived by the CH_{-2}-mean and the L_{-3}-mean filter differ only slightly in most cases.

The filtering algorithm, introduced by Kundu and Mitra [16], also uses an L_p-mean, but only for those pixels that are detected as impulses. Otherwise, the signal remains unchanged. The impulse detection is performed by the criterion

$$x_i(k,l)$$
$$= \begin{cases} \text{negative impulse}, & \text{if } m_x(k,l) - x_i(k,l) > \tau_1(k,l) \\ \text{positive impulse}, & \text{if } m_x(k,l) - x_i(k,l) < \tau_2(k,l) \\ x(k,l), & \text{else} \end{cases}$$
(57)

where $m_x(k,l)$ describes the local mean of all pixels within a $3 \cdot 3$ window. The signal-dependent thresholds are derived to be

$$\tau_1(k,l) = (S_h(k,l) - S_{\min})/3 \quad (58a)$$

and

$$\tau_2(k,l) = (S_l(k,l) - S_{\max})/3 \quad (58b)$$

where $S_h(k,l)$ denotes the highest and S_l the lowest value of all pixels within the window.

A slightly better performance can be achieved if the mean $m_x(k,l)$ is replaced by the mean of all pixels, except of the pixel being processed. This yields the thresholds

$$\tau_1'(k,l) = \tfrac{9}{8}\tau_1(k,l) \quad (59a)$$

and

$$\tau_2'(k,l) = \tfrac{9}{8}\tau_2(k,l). \quad (59b)$$

Due to the fact that the input signal $x_i(k,l)$ is filtered only if it is detected as an impulse, this algorithm is restricted to impulse-noise removal exclusively.

The L_p- and CH_p-mean filter performance depends strongly on the dynamic range of the signal and its numerical representation. To avoid numerical problems with x^p for p negative and x zero, we choose $S_{\min} = 1$.

Compared with the median filter or the SAM filter, the L_p-mean filter and the CH_p-mean filter have the main disadvantage that only one kind of impulse may be suppressed: positive impulses for $p<1$ and negative impulses for $p>1$. If an image is corrupted by both types, the filtering leads to poor results: A single pixel within the window with a value comparable to that of a negative impulse (generated by the signal itself or by the noise) results in an output signal with w negative pixels, according to the window size w, if the filter is designed for suppression of positive impulses ($p<1$).

Furthermore, we observed that the L_p-mean filter does not preserve the edges as well as the median filter. The moving nonlinear mean filters allow the suppression of impulse noise with higher probability of spike occurrence than the median filter, even for a window size 3×3. This advantage is at the expense of less space resolution, since the filter algorithm does not distinguish between several singular impulses and an object, represented by a few pixels of similar value. To reduce this effect, commonly the smallest window of 3×3 pixels is used; however, in this case, the smoothing of nonimpulsive noise deteriorates. To avoid this problem, we propose to make the nonlinear mean filters signal-adaptive, similar to the technique described in Section III. To achieve this, we adjust the window size and the smoothing properties by a signal-dependent weighting factor, according to the technique described previously. In particular, we choose

$$b_i(k,l) = \begin{cases} 0, & \text{if } \tilde{m}_x(k,l) - x_i(k,l) > \tau_1'(k,l) \\ & \text{or } \tilde{m}_x(k,l) - x_i(k,l) < \tau_2'(k,l) \\ & \text{or } \tilde{\sigma}_n^2(k,l) \geq \tilde{\sigma}_x^2(k,l) \\ 1 - \dfrac{\tilde{\sigma}_n^2(k,l)}{\tilde{\sigma}_x^2(k,l)}, & \text{else} \end{cases}$$
(60)

with $\tilde{\sigma}_n^2(k,l)$ according to (52). There are two differences in comparison with the weighting factor of (51) for the SAM filter. Since the modified median is not available now, we replace it with the modified mean $\tilde{m}_x(k,l)$ of (45). The thresholds $\tau_1'(k,l)$ and $\tau_2'(k,l)$ are choosen according to (59a,b). As a comparison between the nonadaptive and the adaptive version of the L_p-mean and the CH_p-mean shows, the performance becomes much better. This will be demonstrated now.

V. Comparison of the Filter Performances

Based on a set of test images, we performed a comparison between the conventional median filter, the nonlinear (adaptive and nonadaptive) CH_p-mean and L_p-mean filters, and our SAM filter [30]. For the special case of pure impulse noise, we also include the algorithm of Kundu and Mitra. A quantitative comparison is performed on the basis of an objective quality measure, denoted *enhancement factor* F_e, which is defined by the ratio of the mean-square error before and after filtering of all processed

TABLE I
IMPULSE NOISE CORRUPTED IMAGES AND THE ENHANCEMENT
FACTOR OBTAINED BY FILTERING

Test image no.	Original image	Noise		Enhancement factor F_e					
		positive impulses	negative impulses	L_p-mean filtering $p = \div 3$ (3 × 3)	median filtering (3 × 3)	algorith. of Kundu/ Mitra (3 × 3)	adapt. CH_p-mean $p = \div 2$	adapt. L_p-mean $p = \div 3$	SAM filtering
1	Graphic	20%	-	35.26	9.38	23.02	126.60	112.47	221.64
2	Playboy	15%	-	5.00	6.64	4.93	18.49	19.16	45.58
3	Lady	3%	-	2.67	5.87	13.53	19.49	19.89	73.83
4	Lady	-	3%	4.79	7.82	13.73	61.45	69.76	159.89
5	Lady	10%	-	8.38	13.40	15.25	45.55	45.23	94.95
6	Lady	-	10%	12.25	18.43	11.94	87.47	75.19	158.70
7	Lady	2.5%	2.5%	0.09	11.02	18.47	6.73	2.68	101.66
8	Lady	7.5%	7.5%	0.26	24.55	13.89	3.30	0.98	100.00

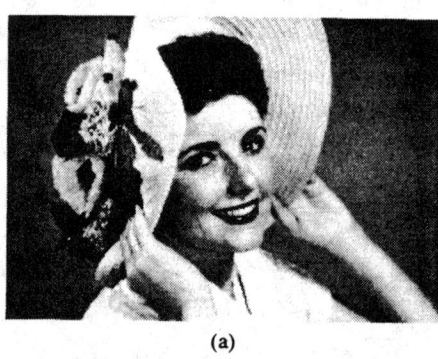

Fig. 11. Original images (256 × 256 pixels, 8 bit/pixel). (a) Test image "lady." (b) Test image "playboy."

pixels of the entire image (we exclude the nonprocessed pixels near the borders). This yields

$$F_e = \frac{\sum_k \sum_l [u(k,l) - x_i(k,l)]^2}{\sum_k \sum_l [u(k,l) - y(k,l)]^2} \quad (61)$$

with the noise-free image signal $u(k,l)$, the noise-corrupted filter input signal $x_i(k,l)$, and the "enhanced" filter output signal $y(k,l)$.

Obviously, the measure can be applied to test images only, since for "real-world" images the noise-free image is unknown. To generate a set of test images, we start with three images (256 × 256 pixels, 8 bit/pixel) of different types. The first one, called "graphic," is shown in Fig. 6(a). It consists essentially of some constant regions with different grey levels and sharp edges. The second one (Fig. 11(a)) shows the portrait of a lady with a straw hat. The third image, a boy playing with toys (abbreviated as "playboy") is shown in Fig. 11(b). This image is interesting due to the sharp edges and fine details. Corrupting these three images by positive and negative impulse noise with different probabilities of spike occurrence, as listed in Table I, we get the noisy test images numbered from 1 to 8. The test images 9 to 16 are generated as follows.

First, we corrupt the original image (according to the model in Fig. 2) by multiplicative gaussian noise of unity mean, and additive noise of zero mean and uniform distribution. In addition, we corrupt it by positive impulse noise with various probabilities of occurrence, as listed in Table 2. We use only positive impulses due to the fact that the nonlinear mean filters cannot remove positive and negative impulses simultaneously, in contrast to the median and the SAM filter. The achieved enhancement factors F_e after one filtering pass are listed in Table I for the images corrupted by impulse noise only and in Table II for a mixture of noise. Fig. 12 shows these results summarized in a diagram. We can recognize that the degree of enhancement depends strongly on the kind of image and the kind of noise. For the test images 7, 8, 11, and 12, the nonadaptive nonlinear mean filtering leads to an enhancement factor less than one, which indicates that the mean-square error after filtering increases. Furthermore, it can be clearly recognized that the adaptive filters perform significantly better than the nonadaptive ones. The best overall perfor-

TABLE II
TABLE OF TEST IMAGES, CORRUPTED BY MULTIPLICATIVE AND ADDITIVE RANDOM NOISE IN ADDITION TO POSITIVE IMPULSE NOISE AND THE ENHANCEMENT FACTOR, OBTAINED BY FILTERING.

Test image no.	Original image	Noise random add.	Noise random mult.	positive impulses	Enhancement factor F_e CH_{-2}-mean filtering (3 x 3)	L_{-3}-mean filtering (3 x 3)	median filtering (3 x 3)	adapt. CH_{-2}-mean filtering	adapt. L_{-3}-mean filtering	SAM filtering
9	Graphic	$\sigma_r=10$	-	-	3.21	3.21	2.74	7.40	7.40	7.40
10	Graphic	$\sigma_r=10$	$\sigma_q=.1$	-	3.00	3.00	3.11	6.00	6.00	7.58
11	Playboy	$\sigma_r=13$	-	-	0.20	0.21	0.68	1.89	1.89	2.35
12	Playboy	$\sigma_r=13$	$\sigma_q=.2$	-	0.25	0.26	1.05	1.19	1.22	2.66
13	Graphic	$\sigma_r=10$	-	20%	47.70	41.14	9.65	96.79	80.27	158.92
14	Graphic	$\sigma_r=10$	$\sigma_q=.1$	10%	45.51	42.10	31.77	112.27	105.25	126.41
15	Playboy	$\sigma_r=13$	-	15%	4.09	4.30	6.65	12.65	13.13	24.52
16	Playboy	$\sigma_r=13$	$\sigma_q=.2$	10%	2.24	2.34	6.40	5.51	5.72	16.02

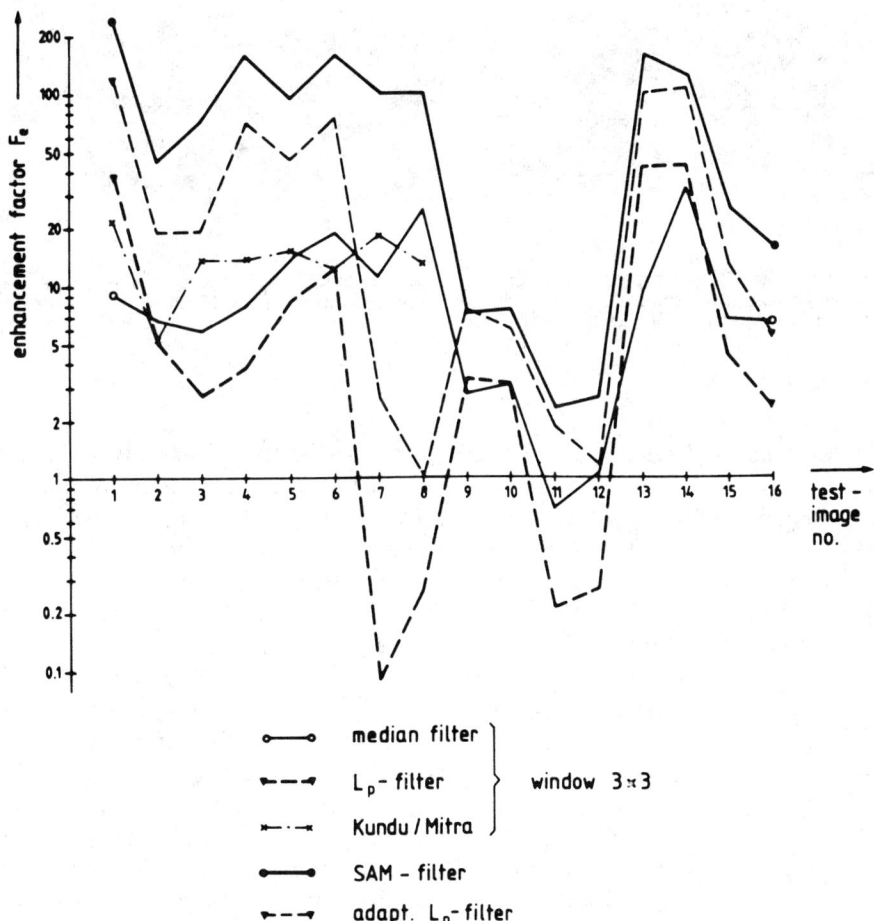

Fig. 12. Comparison of the enhancement factor between some nonlinear filtering algorithms and the SAM filter, using the 16 test images listed in Tables I and II.

Fig. 13. (a) Image of Fig. 11(b) corrupted with 15-percent positive impulses (according to test image 2 of Table I). (b) Median filtered version (3×3 window). (c) Nonadaptive L_{-3}-mean filtered. (d) Filtered with the algorithm of Kundu and Mitra. (e) Adaptive L_{-3}-mean filtered. (f) SAM filtered.

mance has been achieved with the SAM filter, as described in this paper.

Besides this objective criterion, finally, the filter performance should be examined by a more important subjective criterion: the human visual perception. Some examples are addressed, according to Tables I and II.

First, we regard the test image 2 of Table I, shown in Fig. 13(a). It is corrupted by positive impulse noise, with probability of occurrence $p_p = 0.15$. Noise filtering yields the image of Fig. 13(b) for the (3×3) median filter and the image of Fig. 13(c), applying the (3×3) nonlinear L_{-3}-mean filter. The disadvantage of poor space resolution can be easily recognized looking for fine details (e.g., the stripes of the boy's shirt). This effect can be reduced by an adaptive nonlinear mean filter (Fig. 13(e)), as described in the previous section. Applying the algorithm of Kundu and Mitra leads to the image of Fig. 13(d). With the SAM filter, the best noise reduction is achievable (Fig. 13(f)).

The performance for noise with negative impulses is demonstrated by the example of test image 6 of Table I, as shown in Fig. 14(a). Fig. 14(b) shows the result achieved by the algorithm of Kundu and Mitra. With the adaptive L_3-mean filter, we get the image shown in Fig. 14(c). The SAM filter has the best performance, as Fig. 14(d) shows.

The performance in the case of mixed impulse noise is demonstrated with the example of test image 8 of Table I. Fig. 15(a) shows the noisy image ($p_n = p_p = 0.075$). Both the filtering algorithm of Kundu and Mitra (Fig. 15(b)), and the adaptive L_{-3}-mean filter (Fig. 15(c)) yield an insufficient noise reduction. Furthermore, from Fig. 15(c), we recognize the already mentioned effect that the L_{-3}-mean filter cannot reduce the positive spikes if at least one negative spike (generated by the signal or the noise) within the window occurs. If this happens, the impulse is replaced by a dark square, according to the actual window. To upgrade the performance of the L_p-mean, we change $p =$

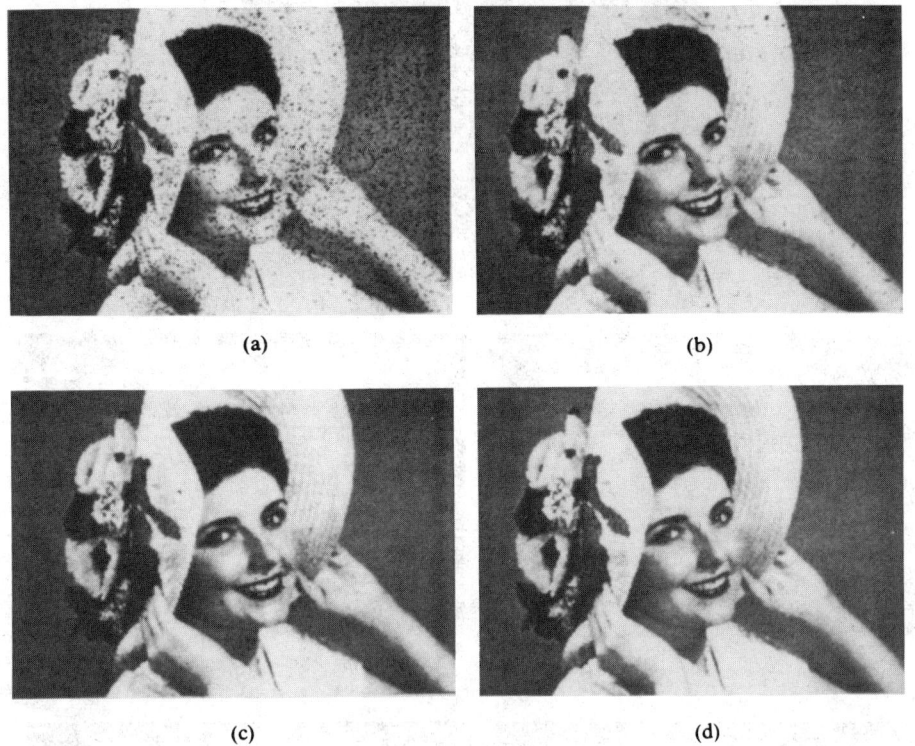

Fig. 14. (a) Image of Fig. 11(a) corrupted with 10-percent negative impulses (according to test image 6 of Table I). (b) Filtered with the algorithm of Kundu and Mitra. (c) Adaptive L_{+3}-mean filtered. (d) SAM filtered.

Fig. 15. (a) Image of Fig. 11(a) corrupted by mixed impulse noise with 7.5-percent positive and negative impulses (according to test image 8 of Table I). (b) Filtered with the algorithm of Kundu and Mitra. (c) Adaptive L_{-3}-mean filtered. (d) SAM filtered.

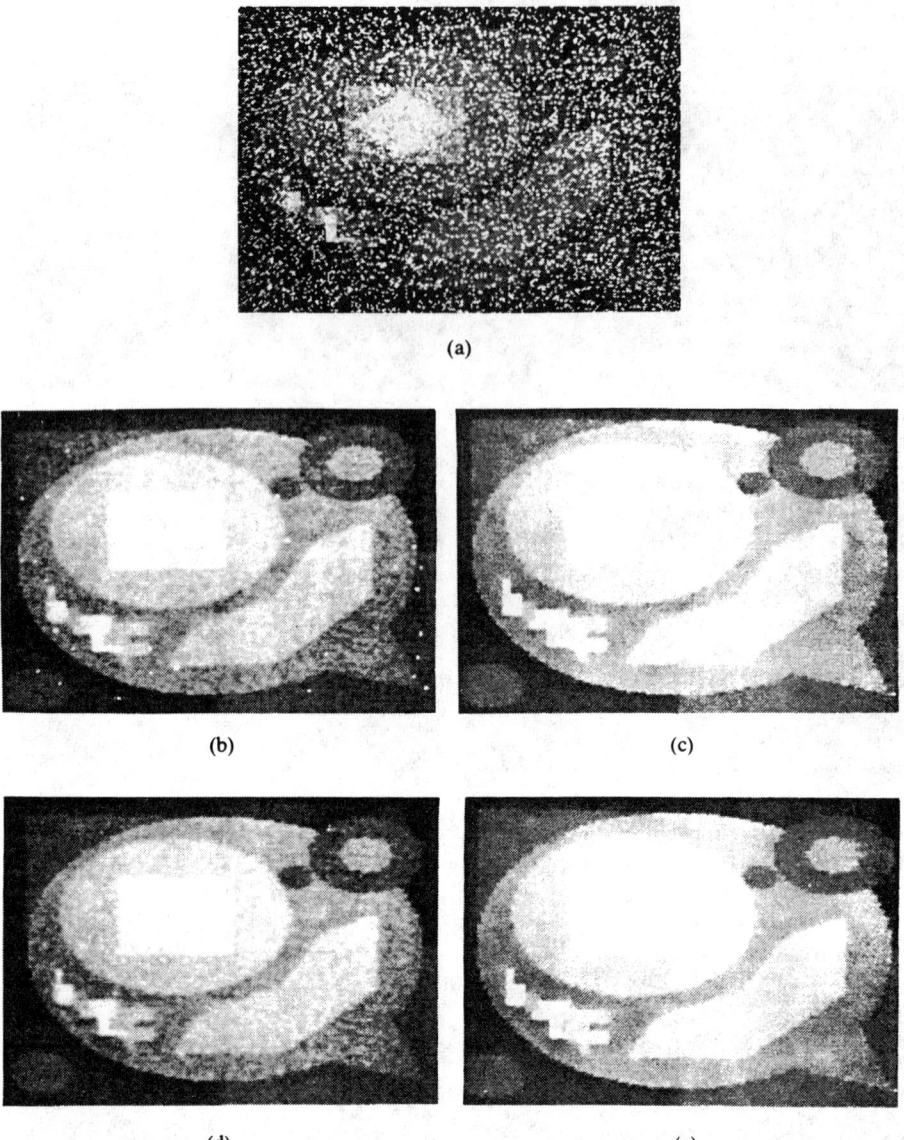

Fig. 16. (a) Image of Fig. 6(b) additional corrupted with 10-percent positive impulses (according to test image 14 of Table II). (b) Nonadaptive median filtered (3×3 window). (c) SAM filtered. (d) Nonadaptive L_{-3}-mean filtered. (e) Filtered with the adaptive L_{-3}-mean filter.

−3 to $p = 3$ if a negative spike is encountered. Though the enhancement factor increases from 0.55 to 0.98, a remarkable subjective quality improvement cannot be achieved. Another undesired effect occurs: Since the impulse probability is high, there can be some additional positive or negative impulses enclosed by the filter window. If this happens, the negation of p replaces the negative spike by a positive one and vice versa. Our SAM filter avoids this problem, as Fig. 15(d) shows.

Finally, with the last example, we treat the case of mixed random and positive impulse noise. Fig. 16(a) shows test image 14 of Table II. The conventional median filter (mask size: 3×3) results in the image of Fig. 16(b). The L_{-3}-mean filter allows a better impulse-noise suppression (Fig. 16(d)), but the smoothing is rather bad, in contrast to the corresponding adaptive versions. This is shown in Fig. 16(c) for the SAM filter and in Fig. 16(e) for the adaptive L_{-3}-mean filter.

VI. Conclusions

The objective of this paper is the description of a new signal-adaptive version of the median filter (SAM filter). Thereby, the performance of smoothing and space resolution is controlled by an appropriate weighting factor as a function of the local signal-to-noise ratio, estimated from the noisy image. The derived adaptation algorithm is not restricted to the median filter; it can be applied in a similar way to other kinds filters, as well. An adaptive version of the nonlinear mean filters was introduced. Our goal (noise removal of images corrupted by a combination of impulse noise, signal-dependent, and additive random noise, performed in a single filtering pass) can be achieved sufficiently well only by the described SAM filter, as various examples demonstrate.

ACKNOWLEDGMENT

Prof. Dr.-Ing. H. W. Schüßler constantly encouraged the author to carry out this work. He, as well as the colleages at the Lehrstuhl für Nachrichtentechnik, provided both stimulating discussions and valuable help in preparing this paper. The author wishes to express his sincere gratitude to all of them.

REFERENCES

[1] H. W. Schüßler, *Digitale Systeme zur Signalverarbeitung.* Berlin, Heidelberg, New York: Springer-Verlag, 1973.
[2] J. W. Tukey, *Exploratory Data Analysis.* Reading, MA: Addison-Wesley, preliminary ed. 1971, final ed. 1977.
[3] W. K. Pratt, "Median filtering," in *Semianual Report*, Image Proc. Institute, Univ. of Southern California, pp. 116–123, Sept. 1975.
[4] B. R. Frieden, "A new restoring algorithm for the preferential enhancement of edge gradients," *J. Opt. Soc. Amer.*, vol. 66, pp. 280–283, 1976.
[5] W. K. Pratt, *Digital Image Processing.* New York: Wiley, 1978.
[6] R. Bernstein, "Contributions to the processing of two-dimensional signals" (in German), in *Ausgewählte Arbeiten über Nachrichtensysteme*, H. W. Schüßler, Ed., no. 46, Univ. Erlangen, FRG, 1981.
[7] H. G. Zimmer, H. Kronberg, R. Bernstein, and V. Neuhoff, "Improvements in microphotometry by digital signal processing," *Pattern Recognition*, vol. 13, pp. 79–82, 1982.
[8] R. Bernstein, "A comparison of signal independent and signal dependent two-dimensional filtering," in *Proc. Sixth Summer Symp. on Circuit Theory* (Prague), July 1982, pp. 21–25.
[9] J. S. Lee, "Digital image enhancement and noise filtering by use of local statistics," *IEEE Trans. Pattern Anal. Machine Intell.*, vol. PAMI-2, pp. 165–168, Mar. 1980.
[10] R. Bernstein, "Signal adaptive two-dimensional noise filtering using local signal features," in *Signal Proc. II: Theories and Applications*, H. W. Schüßler, Ed. North Holland Pub., EUSIPCO, pp. 239–242, Sept. 1983.
[11] H. E. Knutsson, R. Wilson, and G. H. Granlund, "Anisotropic nonstationary image estimation and its applications: Part I—Restoration of noisy images," *IEEE Trans. Commun.*, vol. COM-31, no. 3, pp. 388–406, Mar. 1983.
[12] R. Bernstein, "Contrast enhancement of noisy images by signal adaptive two-dimensional filtering," in *Proc. Conf. Digital Signal Processing*, (Florence), Sept. 1984, pp. 519–523.
[13] T. S. Huang, G. J. Yang, and G. Y. Tang, "Fast two-dimensional median filtering algorithm," *IEEE Trans. Acoust., Speech, Signal Process.*, vol. ASSP-27, pp. 13–18, Feb. 1979.
[14] A. C. Bovik, T. S. Huang, and D. C. Munson, Jr., "A generalization of median filtering using linear combinations of order statistics," *IEEE Trans. Acoust., Speech, Signal Process.*, vol. ASSP-31, pp. 1342–1349, Dec. 1983.
[15] Y. H. Lee and S. A. Kassam, "Generalized median filtering and related nonlinear filtering techniques," *IEEE Trans. Acoust., Speech, Signal Process.*, vol. ASSP-33, no. 3, pp. 672–683, June 1985.
[16] A. Kundu, S. K. Mitra, and P. P. Vaidyanathan, "Application of two-dimensional generalized mean filtering for removal of impulse noises from images," *IEEE Trans. Acoust., Speech, Signal Process.*, vol. ASSP-32, no. 3, pp. 600–609, June 1984.
[17] A. N. Venetsanopoulos and I. Pitas, "A class of nonlinear mean filters for image processing," in *Proc. ECCTD*, (Prague), Sept. 1985, pp. 594–597.
[18] I. Pitas and A. N. Venetsanopoulos, "Nonlinear order statistic filters for image filtering and edge detection," *Signal Processing*, vol. 10, pp. 395–412, June 1986.
[19] H. C. Andrews and B. R. Hunt, *Digital Image Restoration.* Englewood Cliffs, NJ: Prentice Hall, 1977.
[20] R. W. Wallis, "An approach to the space variant restoration and enhancement of images," in *Proc. Symp. Current Math. Problems in Image Science* (Monterey, CA) Nov. 1976.
[21] T. Peli and J. S. Lim, "Adaptive filtering for image enhancement," *Optical Eng.*, vol. 21, no. 1, pp. 108–112, Feb. 1982.
[22] G. Garibotto, "Adaptive and interactive X-ray enhancement techniques: Comparison of performances," in *Proc. Conf. Digital Signal Processing*, (Florence), Sept. 1984, pp. 706–709.
[23] M. Kiesel, "Adaptive zweidimensionale Filterung von Bildsignalen mit signalabhängiger Veränderung der Maskengröße," Diploma thesis, Lehrstuhl für Nachrichtentechnik, Univ. Erlangen-Nürnberg, FRG, May 1983.
[24] J. F. Abramatic and L. M. Silverman, "Nonlinear restoration of noisy images," *IEEE Trans. Pattern Analysis and Machine Intelligence*, vol. PAMI-4, pp. 141–148, Mar. 1982.
[25] J. S. Lim, "Image restoration by short space spectral substraction," *IEEE Trans. Acoustics, Speech, Signal Process.*, vol. ASSP-28, pp. 191–197, Apr. 1980.
[26] H.-J. Seyfried, "Vergleich zweier Verfahren zur adaptiven Rauschunterdrückung," Diploma thesis, Lehrstuhl für Nachrichtentechnik, Univ. Erlangen-Nürnberg, FRG, Dec. 1985.
[27] E. Ataman, V. K. Aatre, and K. M. Wong, "A fast method for real-time median filtering," *IEEE Trans. Acoustics, Speech, Signal Process.*, vol. ASSP-28, pp. 415–420, Aug. 1980.
[28] N. C. Gallagher, Jr., and G. L. Wise, "A theoretical analysis of the properties of median filters," *IEEE Trans. Acoustics, Speech, Signal Process.*, vol. ASSP-29, pp. 1136–1141, Dec. 1981.
[29] G. R. Arce and N. C. Gallagher, Jr., "BTC image coding using median filter roots," *IEEE Trans. Commun.*, vol. COM-31, pp. 784–793, June 1983.
[30] L. Dittrich, "Nichtlineare Filter zur Unterdrückung von Impulsstörungen und Rauschen in Bildsignalen," Diploma thesis, Lehrstuhl für Nachrichtentechnik, Univ. Erlangen-Nürnberg, FRG, Oct. 1986.

✱

Reinhard Bernstein received the Dipl.-Ing. and Dr.-Ing. degrees in electrical engineering from the University of Erlangen-Nürnberg, West Germany, in 1974 and 1981, respectively.

From 1974 to 1975, he worked for Siemens AG, Erlangen, in the field of signal processing for medical applications. Since 1975, he has been working as a Research Assistant at the Lehrstuhl für Nachrichtentechnik, University Erlangen. His current research interests include digital signal processing and its application to multidimensional signal and image processing.

Detail-Preserving Ranked-Order Based Filters for Image Processing

GONZALO R. ARCE, MEMBER, IEEE, AND RUSSELL E. FOSTER

Abstract—Multistage (multilevel) median and FIR-median hybrid filters have been shown to be effective in preserving image detail as well as in attenuating noise. The analysis of multistage FIR-median hybrid filters has been reported in [1]. In this paper, the theoretical analysis of multistage median filters is developed. It is shown that multistage median filters are a combination of max/median and min/median filters. Since multistage median filters belong to the class of two-dimensional stack filters, they have threshold decomposition attributes making their theoretical analysis simple. Statistical threshold decomposition is applied to derive the statistical characteristics of these filters, and the results are used to evaluate the performance of these two types of multistage filters. Finally, a quantitative and qualitative comparison of the multistage filters and of other efficient detail-preserving filters is presented. The comparisons are made using the mean squared error (MSE) and the mean absolute error criteria (MAE). This comparison should help researchers in evaluating the performance of new, nonadaptive, detail-preserving filter algorithms.

I. INTRODUCTION

MEDIAN filtering is a simple and efficient point estimator frequently used in signal and image processing applications. In a one-dimensional domain, running medians track local monotonic signal trends (including edges) [10]. Although some questions remain unanswered, one-dimensional median filters are rather well understood and their performance is, if not optimal, satisfactory in most cases.

Two-dimensional median filters have been used with some success in image processing applications. Here a $(2N + 1) \times (2N + 1)$ running window is scanned across the entire image, where the output associated with the center of the window is the median of the samples inside the square window. Although noise suppression is obtained, too much signal distortion is introduced, and features such as thin lines and other fine details are distorted or lost. These undesirable effects are not acceptable in many applications where the preservation of structure is important.

Recently, several new detail-preserving, median, and ranked-order-based filter structures have been proposed in the literature [1]-[12]. These filters fall, roughly, into one of two categories. The first class is the set of adaptive ranked-order filters [4], [5], [8], [9], [11], [12]. This class of filters is generally preferred in low signal-to-noise environments. The second class encompasses structure-preserving ranked-order filters with fixed (nonadaptive) windows [1]-[3], [6], [7], [18]. Local statistics are used extensively to specify the samples to be considered by adaptive ranked-order filters. The principal advantage of nonadaptive filters is that neither *a priori* information of the image is required such as minimum edge height, nor do local statistics need to be computed inside the filter's window. As expected, the filters in the second class have less computational complexity, and should be easier to implement than their adaptive counterparts.

In this paper, we will only consider nonadaptive, structure-preserving filters. In particular, we will analyze the class of multistage median filters, and we will compare the efficiency of these filters with other detail-preserving filters classes including *Multistage FIR-Median Hybrid*, *Morphological*, and *Multistage Max/median* filters. We have selected these because of their effectiveness, and also because they are a good representation of the different approaches taken in the design of detail-preserving filters. Other nonadaptive structures are not included because of space limitations. For completeness, we have also included results for the square median filter.

The objective of this paper is twofold. First, multistage median filters are analyzed thoroughly. Second, using these results, along with the results derived for the other filters defined in [1], [2], and [7], we compare their performance in a deterministic and a statistical approach. It is hoped that the comparison of these efficient structure-preserving filters will not only indicate the relative efficiency of each of the filters considered here, but should also help researchers in evaluating the performance of new algorithms.

The definitions of the filter structures are given in Section II. In Section III, we derive several properties for the multistage median filter proposed in [1], and for the multistage max/median filter introduced in Section II. The statistical description of these two filters is developed in Section IV. A comparison of the nonadaptive, detail-preserving filters defined in this section is done in Section V.

II. MULTISTAGE FILTERING SCHEMES

Multistage filtering[1] was introduced in [1] as a method to combine the output of basic subfilters, so as to match

---

Manuscript received August 17, 1987; revised June 17, 1988.
G. R. Arce is with the Department of Electrical Engineering, University of Delaware, Newark, DE 19716.
R. E. Foster was with the Department of Electrical Engineering, University of Delaware, Newark, DE. He is now with AT&T Bell Laboratories, Allentown, PA 18103.
IEEE Log Number 8824489.

[1]Multistage filtering was originally introduced in [1] as multilevel filtering.

the structure spanned by the filters window. Each subfilter is designed to preserve a feature in one direction. By including enough subfilters, a basic feature oriented in any direction is preserved by the filter. The type of feature to be preserved determines the subclass of the multistage filter. If the feature spans a one-dimensional line segment, the multistage filter subclass is defined as *Unidirectional Multistage Filters*. If the feature spans two line segments, each in orthogonal directions, the subclass is defined as *Bidirectional Multistage Filters*. In principle, we can extend this idea to define subclasses of filters that will preserve more complex features. However, it can be experimentally observed that such extensions will diminish the detail-preserving characteristics of these multistage filters. Thus, following the definitions in [1], we define two subclasses of multistage filters.

A. Unidirectional Multistage Filters

Let $\{a(\cdot, \cdot)\}$ be a discrete 2-dimensional sequence $\{a(n_1, n_2); n_1, n_2 \in Z\}$ where the index Z is the set of all integers, $Z = \{\cdots, -1, 0, 1, \cdots\}$, and consider the set of samples inside a $(2N+1) \times (2N+1)$ window centered at the (n_1, n_2) location $\{a(n_1 + l_1, n_2 + l_2): -N \leq l_1, l_2 \leq N\}$. For notational simplicity, we will use the vector notation $(n_1, n_2) = n$, where $n \in Z^2$. Define the subsets, W_1, W_2, W_3, W_4, of the square window as

$$W_1[a; (n)] = \{a(n_1 + l_1, n_2): -N \leq l_1 \leq N\},$$
$$W_2[a; (n)] = \{a(n_1 + l_1, n_2 + l_1): -N \leq l_1 \leq N\},$$
$$W_3[a; (n)] = \{a(n_1, n_2 + l_1): -N \leq l_1 \leq N\},$$
$$W_4[a; (n)] = \{a(n_1 + l_1, n_2 - l_1): -N \leq l_1 \leq N\} \quad (1)$$

These sets specify the samples inside the masks shown in Fig. 1(a). Moreover, let

$$z_l(n) = median[a(\cdot, \cdot) \in W_l[a; (n)]] \quad 1 \leq l \leq 4. \quad (2)$$

Filters using the windows in (1) are unidirectional because the subwindows W_l span one direction only. Using (2), the following unidirectional filters are defined.

Definition 1: The *Max/median* and *Min/median* filter outputs are defined by the operations

$$y_{max}(n) = max_{1 \leq l \leq 4} [z_l(n)],$$
$$y_{min}(n) = min_{1 \leq l \leq 4} [z_l(n)], \quad (3)$$

respectively [2]. □

The unidirectional max/median (min/median) filter was shown to preserve positive (negative) image features, as well as to attenuate noise effectively [2]. In applications where both positive and negative features exist, the max/median or min/median filter, alone, are not adequate. A combination of these two filters can be used to overcome the shortcomings of each. This combination filter is de-

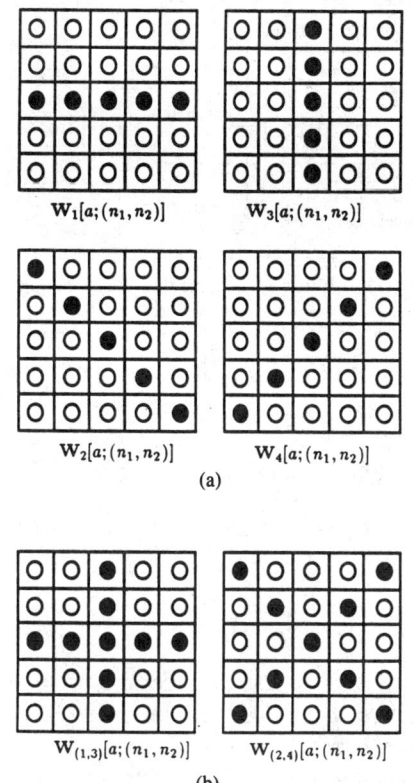

Fig. 1. Subwindows used by multilevel filters: (a) unidirectional; (b) bidirectional.

fined as the *multistage max/median* filter, and it uses a combination scheme used by Nieminen *et al.* [1].

Definition 2: The output of the *Multistage max/median* filter is defined by

$$y_{m/max}(n) = med[y_{max}(n), y_{min}(n), a(n)]. \quad (4)$$

□

The multistage nature of this last class of filters is depicted in Fig. 2. Another filter structure that uses combinations of medians was proposed in [1] and is defined next.

Definition 3: The *Multistage Median* filter output is described by

$$y_{m/med}(n) = med[y_{w_1, w_3}(n), y_{w_2, w_4}(n), a(n)], \quad (5)$$

where

$$y_{w_1, w_3}(n) = median[z_1(n), z_3(n), a(n)],$$
$$y_{w_2, w_4}(n) = median[z_2(n), z_4(n), a(n)]. \quad (6)$$

□

In Sections III and IV, we will examine the properties of this last filter.

By replacing the median within the z_l structures, by an averaging operation we form the class of *FIR-median Hybrid* filters [1].

Definition 4: The *FIR-median Hybrid* filter output is described by

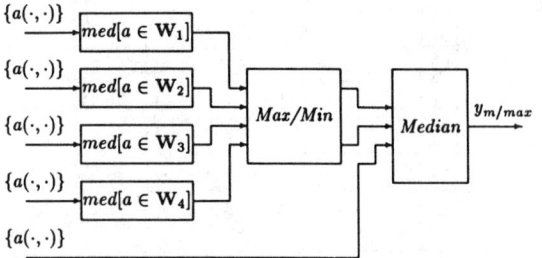

Fig. 2. Multistage max/median filter structure.

$$y_{fir}(n) = med[\bar{y}_{w_1,w_3}(n), \bar{y}_{w_2,w_4}(n), a(n)], \quad (7)$$

where

$$\bar{y}_{w_1,w_3}(n) = median[\hat{z}_1(n), \hat{z}_3(n), a(n)],$$
$$\bar{y}_{w_2,w_4}(n) = median[\hat{z}_2(n), \hat{z}_4(n), a(n)], \quad (8)$$

where

$$\hat{z}_l = med[z_{la}(n), z_{lb}(n), a(n)], \quad 1 \le l \le 4, \quad (9)$$

and where z_{la} and z_{lb} are the average of the samples in each of the two halves of the window W_l, excluding the center sample $a(n)$. □

In [1], the unidirectional multistage median and FIR-median hybrid filters are referred to as the 3-level median (3LM−) and the 3-level unidirectional FIR-median hybrid filters (3LH−), respectively. These filters are denoted as "3-level" due to the three sequential operations used by these two multistage filters. It should be mentioned that, for all filters considered here, we have limited the number of unidirectional window subsets W_l to four. The number of window subsets can be increased as the span of the filter's window grows. Roughly, each substructure will preserve detail along its longitudinal direction. Hence, if we are interested in preserving details along the horizontal, vertical, and diagonal directions, we should use the four substructures defined above. As discussed in Section V, by including additional substructures, the filters will preserve details in other directions as well.

B. Bidirectional Multistage Filters

If the basic subwindows are of bidirectional type, we form another class of multistage detail-preserving filters [1]. Define the subsets $W_{(1,3)}$, $W_{(2,4)}$, of the $(2N + 1) \times (2N + 1)$ square window, as

$$W_{(1,3)}[a; (n)] = W_1[a; (n)] \cup W_3[a; (n)],$$
$$W_{(2,4)}[a; (n)] = W_2[a; (n)] \cup W_4[a; (n)]. \quad (10)$$

These sets specify the samples inside the masks shown in Fig. 1(b). Let

$$z_{1,3}(n) = median[a(\cdot) \in W_{(1,3)}[a; (n)]],$$
$$z_{2,4}(n) = median[a(\cdot) \in W_{(2,4)}[a; (n)]], \quad (11)$$

then, the bidirectional multistage filters are defined as follows.

Definition 5: The output of the *Bidirectional Multistage Max/median* filter is defined by

$$y^+_{m/max}(n) = med[y^+_{max}(n), y^+_{min}(n), a(n)], \quad (12)$$

where

$$y^+_{max}(n) = max[z_{1,3}(n), z_{2,4}(n)],$$
$$y^+_{min}(n) = min[z_{1,3}(n), z_{2,4}(n)]. \quad (13)$$
□

Similarly, we have Definition 6.

Definition 6: The *Bidirectional Multistage median* (2LM+) filter output is described by [1]

$$y^+_{m/med}(n) = median[z_{1,3}(n), z_{2,4}(n), a(n)]. \quad (14)$$
□

Again, by replacing the median within the z structures, by an averaging operation we form the class of *Bidirectional FIR-median Hybrid* filters [1].

Definition 7: The *Bidirectional FIR-median Hybrid* (2LH+) filter output is described by [1]

$$y^+_{fir}(n) = med[\bar{y}_{w_{1,3}}(n), \bar{y}_{w_{2,4}}(n), a(n)], \quad (15)$$

where $\bar{y}_{w_{1,3}}$ is the median of: the center sample and the averages of each of the four quarters [excluding the center sample $a(n)$] of the window $W_{(1,3)}$. Similarly, $\bar{y}_{w_{2,4}}$ is the median of: the center sample and the averages of each of the four quarters [excluding the center sample $a(n)$] of the window $W_{2,4}$. □

In [1], the bidirectional multistage median and FIR-median hybrid filters are denoted as the two-level median (2LM+) and the 2-level FIR-median hybrid (2LH+) filters, respectively. They are referred to as "2-level" because of the two sequential operations of the filters. Moreover, the superscript (+) used to denote the bidirectional multistage filters resembles the shape of the basic subwindows. For notational simplicity, we have not added a superscript when referring to the unidirectional multistage filters.

In Section V, we compare the performance of each type of multistage filter. Also, we compare multistage filters to detail-preserving *Morphological Filters*. This comparison is included since morphological filters have been shown to be very efficient and are also nonadaptive in nature. Moreover, they are closely related to ranked-order based filters [14]. Mathematical Morphology has been shown to be effective in quantitatively describing image geometric structures. Referring to (1), if we partition each window $W_l[a; (n)]$ into $(N + 1)$ overlapping subsets, $S_{l,m}$, of $(N + 1)$ consecutive elements, then the *Morphological* filter is defined as [6], [7], [14].

Definition 8: The *2-dimensional Close-Open* filter (2DCO) output is defined as

$$y_{2DCO}(n) = \max_{\substack{1 \le l \le 4 \\ 1 \le m \le N+1}} \left(min[a(\cdot) \in S_{l,m}[C; (n)]] \right),$$
$$(16)$$

where
$$C(n) = \min_{\substack{1 \leq l \leq 4 \\ 1 \leq m \leq N+1}} \left(\max [a(\cdot) \in S_{l,m}[a; (n)]] \right). \tag{17}$$

□

III. Multistage Median and Max/Median Filters

The use of multistage filtering operations was introduced by Nieminen et al. [1] for the preservation of fine-structure in image processing. In [1], the multistage *FIR-Median Hybrid* filter was analyzed and shown to give promising results. The *multistage median* filter was also introduced in [1], however, no analytical results were presented. In this section, we will derive some deterministic properties of this filter. In particular, we show that both the multistage median and multistage max/median filters have the *Threshold Decomposition* property [16]; furthermore, we show that these two filters are identical. Finally, based on results obtained for the max/median and min/median, we describe root signal structures for these filters.

Let the input to the multistage filters be $\{a(n)\}$. The thresholded signal $\{t^i(n)\}$ associated with the input is defined by

$$t^i(n) = \begin{cases} 1 & \text{if } a(n) \geq i; \\ 0 & \text{if } a(n) < i, \end{cases} \tag{18}$$

where $1 \leq i \leq k - 1$ is the level of thresholding. Since the multistage median and multistage max/median operations embody positive Boolean functions only, it follows from the theory of stack filters that these multistage filters have the threshold decomposition attribute [13]. Hence, if we denote either of the multistage median operators (unidirectional or bidirectional) on the input signal by $m/med[a(\cdot)]$, and either of the multistage max/median operator by $m/max[a(\cdot)]$, then

$$y_{m/max}(n) = m/max[a(n)]$$
$$= \sum_{i=1}^{k-1} x_{m/max}^i(n), \tag{19}$$

and
$$y_{m/med}(n) = m/med[a(n)]$$
$$= \sum_{i=1}^{k-1} x_{m/med}^i(n), \tag{20}$$

where
$$x_{m/max}^i(n) = m/max[t^i(n)],$$
$$x_{m/med}^i(n) = m/med[t^i(n)]. \tag{21}$$

In summary, this property states that we can threshold the k-level input signal into $k - 1$ binary signals, filter each of these binary signals with the multistage median (multistage max/median) filter, and combine the $k - 1$ binary filtered signals, as in (20) and (21), to obtain the k-level output. As will be seen throughout this and the next sections, the threshold decomposition property greatly simplifies the analysis of these nonlinear operators.

A. Unidirectional Multistage Filters

Here, we assume that the subwindows used in the multistage filter structures are of a unidirectional type. Before we state the first property, we specify some notation for the sake of simplicity. Let the ith-level thresholded sequence, filtered by a max/median, min/median, multistage max/median, and multistage median, be denoted as $x_{max}^i(\cdot)$, $x_{min}^i(\cdot)$, $x_{m/max}^i(\cdot)$, and $x_{m/med}^i(\cdot)$, respectively. Moreover, let $z_l^i(n)$ be the medians of each substructure in (2) when the input signal is $\{t^i(\cdot)\}$.

Property 1: The outputs of the multistage median, $y_{m/med}$, and multistage max/median filters, $y_{m/max}$, are identical.

Proof: Using the threshold decomposition property, it is sufficient to show that each of the $k - 1$ binary filtered signals in (21) is identical.

Case 1: Assume $t^i(n) = 0$. With this condition, the output of the max/median can be expressed as

$$x_{m/max}^i(n) = med[x_{max}^i(n), x_{min}^i(n), 0]. \tag{22}$$

Since $x_{min}^i \leq x_{max}^i$, then (22) reduces to

$$x_{m/max}^i(n) = 1 - I(x_{min}^i(n) = 0),$$
$$= 1 - I(\text{at least one subfilter}$$
$$\text{median } z_l^i \text{ is zero}), \tag{23}$$

where $I(A)$ is the indicator function

$$I(A) = \begin{cases} 1, & \text{if } A \text{ is true}; \\ 0, & \text{if } A \text{ is false}. \end{cases} \tag{24}$$

Referring to (6), the output of the multistage median is

$$x_{m/med}^i(n) = med[x_{w_1w_3}^i(n), x_{w_2w_4}^i(n), 0]. \tag{25}$$

If any of the subfilter medians z_l^i is zero, then at least one term inside the median operator in (25) is also zero, consequently,

$$x_{m/med}^i(n) = 1 - I(\text{at least one subfilter}$$
$$\text{median } z_l^i \text{ is zero}). \tag{26}$$

Since (23) and (26) are identical, so are the outputs of these filters.

Case 2: Assume $t^i(n) = 1$. With this condition, the output of the max/median can be expressed as

$$x_{m/max}^i(n) = med[x_{max}^i(n), x_{min}^i(n), 1]. \tag{27}$$

Since $x_{min}^i \leq x_{max}^i$, then (27) reduces to

$$x_{m/max}^i(n) = 1 - I(x_{max}^i(n) = 0)$$
$$= 1 - I(\text{all of the subfilter}$$
$$\text{medians } z_l^i \text{ are zero}). \tag{28}$$

Similarly, the output of the multistage median is

$$x^i_{m/med}(n) = med[x^i_{w_1w_3}(n), x^i_{w_2w_4}(n), 1]. \quad (29)$$

If any of the subfilter medians z^i_l is one, then at least one of the two terms inside the median operator in (29) is one; thus,

$$x^i_{m/med}(n) = I(\text{at least one subfilter median } z^i_l \text{ is one}),$$
$$= 1 - I(\text{all of the subfilter medians } z^i_l \text{ are zero}). \quad (30)$$

Since (30) is identical to (28), property 1 is proved. □

Thus, since multistage max/median and multistage median filters are identical, we will refer to them as multistage median filters only. From the definition of these filters, it is interesting to note that the multistage median filter chooses its output as the maximum substructure median value if the input sample is greater than this value. If the input falls below the value of the minimum substructure median, then the output is set to the value of the minimum median. Finally, if the sample is between the maximum and minimum of these substructure medians, the filter does not modify the input sample. Fig. 3 illustrates the output characteristics of this filter for a constant value input signal embedded in Laplacian noise. The dashed curve is the input, and the solid curves are the *max/median* (y_{max}) and *min/median* (y_{min}) outputs, respectively. The output signal is bounded below and above by the two solid curves. The smoothing efficacy is obvious from this graph.

An important property of the multistage median filter is that it has a *Root* signal set. A root signal is invariant to the multistage median filter operation. The existence of such signals for the multistage median filter can be proven by a simple example [an $(N + 1) \times (N + 1)$ square object of value one, with a background of value zero]. Although a complete root signal analysis is not included here, it is simple to show that a sample belonging to either $N + 1$ consecutive zeros, or $N + 1$ consecutive ones in any subset direction, is a fixed point to the multistage filter [2]. The root signal characteristics of the multistage median filter will be further illustrated in Section V.

B. Bidirectional Multistage Filters

In this section, all the filters considered are of a bidirectional type; therefore, we omit the (+) superscript in (12)–(15) for the sake of notational simplicity. Let the $z^i_{1,3}(n)$ and $z^i_{2,4}(n)$ be the medians of each substructure in (10) when the input signal is $\{t^i(\cdot)\}$. The *i*th-level thresholded sequences, filtered by a max/median, min/median, multistage max/median, and multistage median, are denoted as $x^i_{max}(\cdot)$, $x^i_{min}(\cdot)$, $x^i_{m/max}(\cdot)$, and $x^i_{m/med}(\cdot)$, respectively. In particular,

$$x^i_{max}(n) = max[z^i_{1,3}(n), z^i_{2,4}(n)],$$
$$x^i_{min}(n) = min[z^i_{1,3}(n), z^i_{2,4}(n)],$$
$$x^i_{m/max}(n) = med[x^i_{min}(n), x^i_{max}(n), t^i(n)],$$
$$x^i_{m/med}(n) = med[z^i_{1,3}(n), z^i_{2,4}(n), t^i(n)]. \quad (31)$$

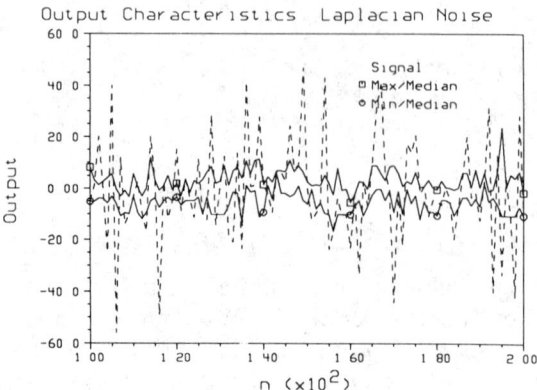

Fig. 3. Output of multistage median filter bounded above and below by the maximum and minimum median substructure, respectively; $N = 5$.

Since the samples in the two bidirectional subwindows, $\{W_{(1,3)}\}$ and $\{W_{(2,4)}\}$, are mutually exclusive except for the center sample, the proof of the next property is omitted since it follows closely the proof of property 1.

Property 2: The output of the bidirectional multistage median, $y_{m/med}$, and multistage max/median filters, $y_{m/max}$, are identical. □

The root signal set of bidirectional, multistage median filters is different than that of their unidirectional counterparts. For a window of parameter N, the subwindow of the bidirectional multistage filter spans $4N + 1$ samples as opposed to $2N + 1$ samples included in the unidirectional filter subwindow. At the binary level [i.e., $t^i(\cdot)$], a sample is invariant to bidirectional multistage median filtering if there are $2N$ other samples, inside either subwindow, with the same value. The root signal characteristics of the bidirectional multistage median filter will be further illustrated in Section V.

IV. STATISTICAL THRESHOLD DECOMPOSITION FOR MULTISTAGE MEDIAN FILTERS

The smoothing performance of the multistage median filter can be described by the multivariate output distribution. In general, this is not possible since accurate statistical descriptions of input images are difficult to obtain. It is possible, however, to describe the noise attenuation characteristics of multistage-median filters by the probability measure function (pmf) of the filtered signals in homogeneous regions. In this model, the problem is reduced to the estimation of a constant parameter in additive white noise. In nonstationary regions (edges), the deterministic properties of the filter can be used to evaluate how well the multistage filter preserves fine detail.

Although several of the results in this section could be derived without the use of threshold decomposition, we chose this approach since it follows from the approach of the previous sections. Furthermore, threshold decomposition allows the analysis of recursive systems [18]; thus, this decomposition provides a unified framework for the analysis of these filtering structures. *Statistical Threshold Decomposition* was introduced as a method to describe marginal probability measure functions of median filtered sequences, using probability measure functions of binary median filtered sequences [15]. Here we extend those concepts to the multistage-median filtering of two-dimensional sequences.

Let $\{a(n): n_1, n_2 \in Z\}$ be an independent, identically distributed (i.i.d.), discrete alphabet random sequence, with a probability space (Ω, F, P), where the sample space is $\Omega = Z_k = \{0, 1, \cdots, k-1\}$. The event space F is the power set, and P is the probability measure described by the discrete distribution function $F(i)$, $i \in Z_k$. The thresholded binary sequence $\{t^i(n)\}$ is also i.i.d., with a probability space (Ω_b, F_b, P_b), where the sample space is $\Omega_b = \{0, 1\}$, F_b is the binary power set, and P_b is induced by the probability measure function (pmf)

$$\Pr(t^i(n) = 0) = F(i-1),$$
$$\Pr(t^i(n) = 1) = 1 - F(i-1). \quad (32)$$

A. Unidirectional Windows

Refer to the substructure medians at the ith threshold level as

$$z_l^i(n) = \text{median}[t^i(\cdot) \in W_l[t^i; (n)]],$$
$$l = 1, \cdots, 4. \quad (33)$$

The max/median and min/median at the binary level are denoted as $x_{max}^i(n)$ and $x_{min}^i(n)$, respectively. The multistage median filter at the ith level is denoted as $x_{m/med}^i(n) = x_{m/max}^i(n)$. It was shown in [13] and [15] that the probability measure function describing the sequence $\{y_{m/med}(\cdot)\}$ in the Z_k sample space can be derived from the $k-1$ probability measure functions describing the thresholded filtered sequences $\{x_{m/med}^i(n); 1 \leq k - 1\}$ in the binary sample space. These results are summarized in the next property.

Property 3: If $\{y_{m/med}(n); y \in Z_k\}$ and $\{x_{m/med}^i(n); x^i \in (0, 1); 1 \leq i \leq k-1\}$ are the k-level, and thresholded multistage median filtered signals, then

$$F_y(j) = P_r[y_{m/med}(n) \leq j] = P_r[x_{m/med}^{j+1}(n) = 0]$$
$$= F(j)\left[1 - \left(\sum_{q=N+1}^{2N}\binom{2N}{q}\right.\right.$$
$$\left.\left.\cdot (1 - F(j))^q F(j)^{2N-q}\right)^4\right]$$
$$+ (1 - F(j))\left[\sum_{q=N+1}^{2N}\binom{2N}{q}\right.$$
$$\left.\cdot (1 - F(j))^{2N-q} F(j)^q\right]^4, \quad (34)$$

where $F(j)$ is the probability measure function of the i.i.d. input sequence $\{a(\cdot)\}$.

Proof: Using the total law of probability, we can write (34) as

$$P_r[x_{m/med}^{j+1}(n) = 0]$$
$$= P_r[x_{m/med}^{j+1}(n) = 0/t^{j+1}(n) = 0] P_r[t^{j+1}(n) = 0]$$
$$+ P_r[x_{m/med}^{j+1}(n) = 0/t^{j+1}(n) = 1]$$
$$\cdot P_r[t^{j+1}(n) = 1]. \quad (35)$$

Applying the definition of multistage median filters on the first term of (35), we obtain

$$P_r[x_{m/med}^{j+1}(n) = 0/t^{j+1}(n) = 0]$$
$$= P_r[\text{med}[x_{max}^{j+1}(n), x_{min}^{j+1}(n), 0] = 0]. \quad (36)$$

Since $x_{min}^{j+1} \leq x_{max}^{j+1}$, the above equation reduces to

$$P_r[x_{m/med}^{j+1}(n) = 0/t^{j+1}(n) = 0]$$
$$= P_r[x_{min}^{j+1}(n) = 0/t^{j+1}(n) = 0]$$
$$= P_r[\min_{1 \leq l \leq 4}(z_l^{j+1}(n)) = 0/t^{j+1}(n) = 0]$$
$$= P_r[\text{at least one } z_l^{j+1}(n) = 0/t^{j+1}(n) = 0]$$
$$= 1 - P_r[\text{all } z_l^{j+1}(n) = 1/t^{j+1}(n) = 0]. \quad (37)$$

Since

$$P_r[z_l^{j+1}(n) = 1/t^{j+1}(n) = 0]$$
$$= P_r[\text{at least } N+1 \text{ samples are one}/t^{j+1}(n) = 0]$$
$$= \sum_{q=N+1}^{2N}\binom{2N}{q}(1 - F(j))^q F(j)^{2N-q}, \quad (38)$$

equation (37) reduces to

$$P_r[x_{m/med}^{j+1}(n) = 0/t^{j+1}(n) = 0]$$
$$= \left[1 - \left(\sum_{q=N+1}^{2N}\binom{2N}{q}(1 - F(j))^q F(j)^{2N-q}\right)^4\right]. \quad (39)$$

Similarly, applying the definition of multistage median filters on the second term in (35), we obtain

$$P_r[x_{m/med}^{j+1}(n) = 0/t^{j+1}(n) = 1]$$
$$= P_r[\text{med}[x_{max}^{j+1}(n), x_{min}^{j+1}(n), 1] = 0]. \quad (40)$$

Hence,

$$P_r[x_{m/med}^{j+1}(n) = 0/t^{j+1}(n) = 1]$$
$$= P_r[x_{min}^{j+1}(n) = 0, x_{max}^{j+1}(n) = 0/t^{j+1}(n) = 1]$$
$$= P_r[\text{all } z_l^{j+1}(n) = 0/t^{j+1}(n) = 1]. \quad (41)$$

Since

$$P_r[z_l^{j+1}(n) = 0/t^{j+1}(n) = 1]$$
$$= P_r[\text{at least } N+1 \text{ samples are zero}/t^{j+1}(n) = 1]$$
$$= \sum_{q=N+1}^{2N}\binom{2N}{q}F(j)^q(1 - F(j))^{2N-q}, \quad (42)$$

equation (40) reduces to

$$P_r[x^{j+1}_{m/med}(n) = 0/t^{j+1}(n) = 1]$$
$$= \left[1 - \left(\sum_{q=N+1}^{2N}\binom{2N}{q}(1-F(j))^{2N-q}F(j)^q\right)^4\right]. \tag{43}$$

Property 3 follows directly from (35), (39), and (43). □

As expected, it is simple to show, using property 3, that the multistage median filter is a median unbiased estimator.

B. Bidirectional Windows

Each bidirectional subwindow spans $4N + 1$ samples, as opposed to $2N + 1$ samples spanned by the unidirectional subwindow. Thus, for the same $(2N + 1) \times (2N + 1)$ window span, the bidirectional filter will have better noise removal, and worse detail-preserving characteristics, than the unidirectional multistage median filter. The output distributions quantify the noise attenuation improvement.

Property 4: If $\{y_{m/med}(n); y \in Z_k\}$ and $\{x^i_{m/med}(n); x^i \in (0, 1); 1 \le i \le k - 1\}$ are the k-level, and thresholded bidirectional, multistage median filtered signals, then

$$F_y(j) = P_r[y_{m/med}(n) \le j] = P_r[x^{j+1}_{m/med}(n) = 0]$$
$$= F(j)\left[1 - \left(\sum_{q=2N+1}^{4N}\binom{4N}{q}(1-F(j))^q F(j)^{4N-q}\right)^2\right]$$
$$+ (1-F(j))\left[\sum_{q=2N+1}^{4N}\binom{4N}{q}(1-F(j))^{4N-q}F(j)^q\right]^2, \tag{44}$$

where $F(j)$ is the probability measure function of the i.i.d. input sequence $\{a(\cdot)\}$.

Proof: Using the total law of probability, we can write (44) as

$$P_r[x^{j+1}_{m/med}(n) = 0]$$
$$= P_r[x^{j+1}_{m/med}(n) = 0/t^{j+1}(n) = 0] P_r[t^{j+1}(n) = 0]$$
$$+ P_r[x^{j+1}_{m/med}(n) = 0/t^{j+1}(n) = 1]$$
$$\cdot P_r[t^{j+1}(n) = 1]. \tag{45}$$

Applying the definition of multistage median filters on the first term of (45), we obtain

$$P_r[x^{j+1}_{m/med}(n) = 0/t^{j+1}(n) = 0]$$
$$= P_r[med[z^{j+1}_{1,3}(n), z^{j+1}_{2,4}(n), 0] = 0]$$
$$= 1 - P_r[\text{both subwindows are one}/t^{j+1}(n) = 0]. \tag{46}$$

Since both subwindows, conditioned on the center sample, are mutually exclusive, and since

$$P_r[z^{j+1}_{1,3}(n) = 1/t^{j+1}(n) = 0]$$
$$= P_r[\text{at least } 2N + 1 \text{ samples are one}/t^{j+1}(n) = 0]$$
$$= \sum_{q=2N+1}^{4N}\binom{4N}{q}(1-F(j))^q F(j)^{4N-q}, \tag{47}$$

then, (46) reduces to

$$P_r[x^{j+1}_{m/med}(n) = 0/t^{j+1}(n) = 0]$$
$$= \left[1 - \left(\sum_{q=2N+1}^{4N}\binom{4N}{q}(1-F(j))^q F(j)^{4N-q}\right)^2\right]. \tag{48}$$

Similarly, the second term in (45) reduces to

$$P_r[x^{j+1}_{m/med}(n) = 0/t^{j+1}(n) = 1]$$
$$= \left[1 - \left(\sum_{q=2N+1}^{4N}\binom{4N}{q}(1-F(j))^{4N-q}F(j)^q\right)^2\right]. \tag{49}$$

Property 4 follows directly from (45), (48), and (49). □

Empirically, the bidirectional multistage median filter chooses its output as the maximum substructure, $4N + 1$ long, median value if the input sample is greater than this value. If the input falls below the value of the minimum substructure median, then the output is set to the value of the minimum median. Finally, if the sample is between the maximum and minimum of these substructure medians, then the filter does not modify the input sample.

In impulsive noise environments, if there are several noisy samples clustered together, impulses may not be removed from the image. It is very helpful to quantify the probability of such an event. Define the *Breakdown Probability* as the probability of an impulse occurring at the output of the multistage median filter, and let p be the occurrence probability of an impulse at the input of the filter (the impulse is equally likely to be positive or negative). The breakdown probabilities, in homogeneous image regions, follow from properties 3 and 4.

Property 5: Let p be the probability of an impulse occurring at the input, then the breakdown probabilities for the unidirectional filter $P_r[B-]$, and the breakdown probability of the bidirectional multistage median filter $P_r[B+]$, are

$$P_r[B-] = p\left[1 - \left(\sum_{q=N+1}^{2N}\binom{2N}{q}(1-p)^q p^{2N-q}\right)^4\right]$$
$$+ (1-p)\left[\sum_{q=N+1}^{2N}\binom{2N}{q}(1-p)^{2N-q}p^q\right]^4, \tag{50}$$

TABLE I
Breakdown Probabilities for 3-Level Multistage Median Filter

Breakdown Probability For *3Level-Median Filter*						
Probability, p	$N=1$	$N=2$	$N=3$	$N=4$	$N=5$	$N=6$
0.0620	0.0252	0.0052	0.0010	0.0002	4×10^{-5}	1×10^{-5}
0.125	0.0820	0.0350	0.0139	0.0055	0.0022	0.0008
0.25	0.2249	0.1757	0.1310	0.0958	0.0694	0.0501
0.375	0.3665	0.3481	0.3279	0.3077	0.2880	0.2691
0.50	0.50	0.50	0.50	0.50	0.50	0.50

TABLE II
Breakdown Probabilities for 2-Level Bidirectional Multistage Median Filter

Breakdown Probability For *2Level Bidirectional Median Filter*						
Probability, p	$N=1$	$N=2$	$N=3$	$N=4$	$N=5$	$N=6$
0.0625	0.0026	0.0001	5×10^{-6}	2×10^{-7}	1×10^{-7}	6×10^{-10}
0.125	0.0189	0.0028	0.0004	7.5×10^{-5}	1.3×10^{-5}	2×10^{-6}
0.25	0.1156	0.0542	0.0266	0.0134	0.0068	0.0036
0.375	0.2884	0.2276	0.1843	0.1514	0.1255	0.1048
0.50	0.50	0.50	0.50	0.50	0.50	0.50

TABLE III
Breakdown Probabilities for Median Filter

Probability, p	$N=1$	$N=2$	$N=3$	$N=4$	$N=5$	$N=6$
0.0625	0.011	0.002	5×10^{-4}	9×10^{-5}	2×10^{-5}	4×10^{-6}
0.125	0.043	0.016	0.006	0.002	0.001	4×10^{-4}
0.250	0.156	0.103	0.070	0.048	0.034	0.024
0.375	0.316	0.275	0.243	0.216	0.194	0.175
0.500	0.500	0.500	0.500	0.500	0.500	0.500

and

$$P_r[B+] = p\left[1 - \left(\sum_{q=2N+1}^{4N}\binom{4N}{q}(1-p)^q p^{4N-q}\right)^2\right] + (1-p)\left[\sum_{q=2N+1}^{4N}\binom{4N}{q}(1-p)^{4N-q}p^q\right]^2, \quad (51)$$

respectively. □

Tables I and II show the breakdown probabilities for different values of p and N; hence, for a given performance, we can easily select the size of the filter. Clearly, bidirectional multistage median filters have better noise attenuation characteristics at the expense (as will be shown in Section V) of having less detail-preserving properties. Since the unidirectional (bidirectional) multistage median filter chooses the output to be a $2N + 1$ $(4N + 1)$ median estimate, if the input sample is greater than the maxima or smaller than the minima of these medians, the smoothing performance of the multistage is bounded by the performance of a median estimator of size $2N + 1$ $(4N + 1)$. This bound can be observed in Table III which shows the breakdown probabilities of a simple median filter.

V. Performance Comparison

In an effort to quantify the performance of the filters described in Section II, a number of simulations were done. The question we are interested in answering is: How well, relative to the other filters, does each perform in terms of *noise removal* and *structural preservation*? It is difficult, however, to define an error criteria to accurately quantify image distortion. This issue has been an important area of research for some time and, to date, there is still not a universally accepted error criteria. In this paper, we will base our comparisons on the mean square error (MSE), the mean absolute error (MAE), and a subjective visual criteria. The empirical *normalized mean square error* is given by

$$MSE = \frac{\sum_{n_1=0}^{M-1}\sum_{n_2=0}^{M-1}(f(n) - \hat{f}(n))^2}{\sum_{n_1=0}^{M-1}\sum_{n_2=0}^{M-1}(f(n))^2}, \quad (52)$$

where $\{f(\cdot)\}$ and $\{\hat{f}(\cdot)\}$ are the original image and its estimate (filtered image), respectively. In our simulations, $M = 512$ (512×512 image resolution), and each sample has 8 bits/pixel gray-scale quantization. The empirical *mean absolute error* is defined as:

$$MAE = \frac{\sum_{n_1=0}^{M-1}\sum_{n_2=0}^{M-1}|f(n) - \hat{f}(n)|}{\sum_{n_1=0}^{M-1}\sum_{n_2=0}^{M-1}f(n)}. \quad (53)$$

Finally, we use an absolute difference visual display to quantify the error in a human visual error criteria. If there is no error between the original image and the filtered image, at a sample location, this sample is displayed as white. For a maximum error, the sample is displayed black. This difference image provides us with information about the edge jitter characteristics introduced by a filter, as well as the noise suppression capabilities of the algorithm. The use of all these error measures will allow us to objectively compare the performance of each filter. How much we weight each error criteria depends on the particular application where these filters are used.

In Sections V-A and B, the performance of all the mentioned filters will be evaluated in a deterministic and a statistical approach, respectively.

A. Response of Filters to Test Images

The response of filters to test images is very often used to describe the deterministic properties of the filter. The more subtle details a filter can preserve, the better the filter is considered from a deterministic viewpoint. The root structure of each filter quantifies their structure-preserving characteristics. For all of the filters under consideration, their root signal analysis is, if not complete, adequate in that it gives an accurate understanding of the types of structures which are preserved by the filter [1], [6], [7]. For a window spanning a set of $\{2N + 1 \times 2N + 1\}$ elements, the multistage FIR-median hybrid filter preserves structures of width N. Due to the averaging operator, the end of the structures are distorted [1]. All the other detail-preserving filters considered here preserve structures of width $N + 1$, without distorting the ending of these structures.

The test image is a sampled, linearly swept, frequency modulated signal. In polar coordinates, the continuous signal is given by

$$a(r) = \begin{cases} A \cos(2\pi f_0 r^2/R) & \text{for } r \leq R/2 \\ A \cos(2\pi f_0 r^2/R - f_0(r - R)^2/R)) & \\ & \text{for } R/2 \leq 3R/2 \end{cases} \quad (54)$$

where r is the radius from the center, A is the amplitude of the signal, R is the period of the FM signal, and f_0 is the highest instantaneous frequency [17]. As discussed in [17], the two-dimensional frequency characteristics of the filtering process can be easily observed in this test pattern. For instance, since one of the filter's substructures is positioned horizontally, we can expect our output to preserve detail of the image along the vertical axis (zero horizontal frequency). The moiré patterns observed in this test image are due to the undersampling of certain regions of the image.

Fig. 4(a) shows the original test image which will be filtered by each filter under consideration. To best illustrate the artifacts introduced by the filtering operations, the absolute difference of the original image with the filtered image is displayed in ($N = 2$): (b) the square median filter, (c) the multistage median filter (3LM−), (d) the multistage FIR-median hybrid filter (3LH−), and (e)

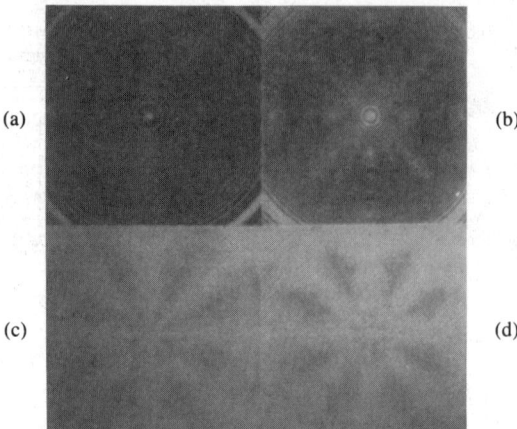

Fig. 4. (a) Original test image; absolute difference between original image, and (b) median filter, (c) multistage median filter (3LM−), (d) multistage FIR-median hybrid (3LH−), (e) 2DCO, and (f) (3LM−) with 8 subwindows, and (g) bidirectional multistage median (2LM+) (top to bottom, left to right).

the morphological (2DCO). The number of subwindows used will determine the number of orientations at which the filter will be able to preserve structure. By selecting four subwindows, we are able to preserve features on the horizontal, vertical, and diagonal directions. The structural-preserving properties of the filter depend not only on the type of ranking operation used in the estimate, but also on the number of orientations of the subwindows. As the span of the window increases, more orientations of the subwindows can be included in the filtering operation. As these additional data are included in the estimate of the pixel, structures oriented along the direction of the subwindow will be preserved. Fig. 4(f) illustrates the effect of adding more window substructures to the multistage median filter. Similar results are expected by adding more subwindows to the other types of filters [1]. To illustrate the effect of the type of subwindows used in multistage filtering, Fig. 4(g) shows the difference image when the estimate used is a bidirectional multistage median filter.

This image is the basis of our subjective error criterion. As mentioned before, a zero difference is shown as a white sample, and a difference of 255 is shown as a black sample. Roughly speaking, the smaller the error, the whiter the image. From these images, it is clear that these filters best preserve features along the directions of their subwindows. It can also be observed that the morphological filter introduces more distortion in the off-axis areas of the image than the multistage filters. As expected, Fig. 4(b) shows the extensive blur introduced by the square median filter. Based on Fig. 4, it can be seen that under a human visual criteria, the multistage FIR-median hybrid filter preserves signal structures best.

Table IV shows the error introduced to the original image by each filtering operation, under a mean squared error and a mean absolute error criteria. We have not tabulated the results of the multistage filter with 8 subwindows, since this filter cannot be compared to those using 4 subwindows. The asterisks in the tables indicate the two lowest distortions achieved under a given criteria. The multistage FIR-median hybrid filter yields the smallest error under the two error criteria. The multistage median filter ranks second followed by the morphological filter. The bidirectional multistage median does not perform well, and, as expected, the square median filter performs very poorly.

B. Response to Noisy Images

As indicated in Section IV, it is difficult to accurately model an image statistically. Even if adequate statistical image models were available, the nonlinear characteristics of all ranked-order-based filters make it difficult to obtain multivariate output distributions. Thus, in this analysis, we will consider the noise attenuation of these filters for two important classes of input signals. First, we analytically compare the noise attenuation characteristics of the filters in constant signals with additive white noise. Second, to compare the filters detail-preserving characteristics, we will apply each filtering operation to real images.

Using the results of Section IV and the statistical results derived for the other filters, the noise attenuation of each filter is plotted versus the window parameter N. Fig. 5(a) shows the results for the constant signal embedded in white, additive, impulsive noise, where each impulse occurs with probability 0.125 and it has an absolute magnitude of 200. Fig. 5(b) shows equivalent results when the noise is white, Gaussian, with a variance of 625. The morphological filter best attenuates the noise under both error criteria. In impulsive noise, however, the performance of the multistage median filter is very close to that of the morphological filter. As can be seen in Fig. 5, the multistage median filter performs better than its FIR-median hybrid counterpart. This follows from the fact that each subwindow estimate in the (3LM−) is taken over $2N + 1$ points. On the other hand, the (3LH−) filter structure makes estimates in subwindows of size N. Although not included here, the results for bidirectional multistage filters are similar. The results in Fig. 5, for a constant signal in noise, give a rough measure of the statistical efficiency of each filter in different types of noise. The efficiency of each filter in nonconstant signals is illustrated next.

Fig. 6(a) and (b) shows an original image and the image corrupted with impulsive noise. The probability of an impulse occurring is 0.125, and if it occurs it can be positive or negative with equal probability. In these simulations, the impulse was set to a height of 200. Fig. 6 also shows the noisy image filtered with: (c) a square median filter,

TABLE IV
RESULTS OF TEST PATTERN SIMULATION

Measured Error	Image: Test Pattern
Type of Filter	MSE
Sq. Median	0.2528
3LM-	0.0124 *
3LH-	0.0095 *
2DCO	0.0203
2LM+	0.0735
2LH+	0.0657
Mean Absolute Error	
Sq. Median	0.4732
3LM-	0.0496 *
3LH-	0.0362 *
2DCO	0.0683
2LM+	0.2020
2LH+	0.1987

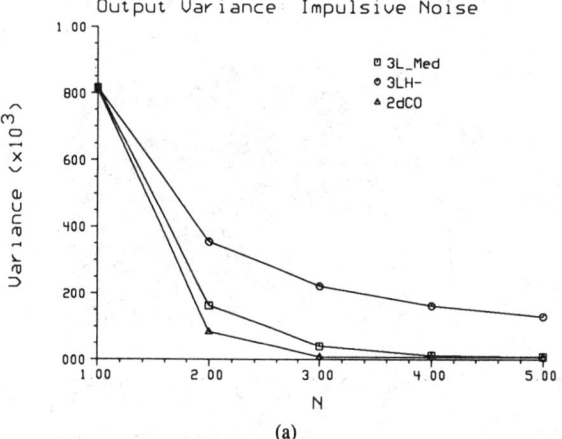

(a)

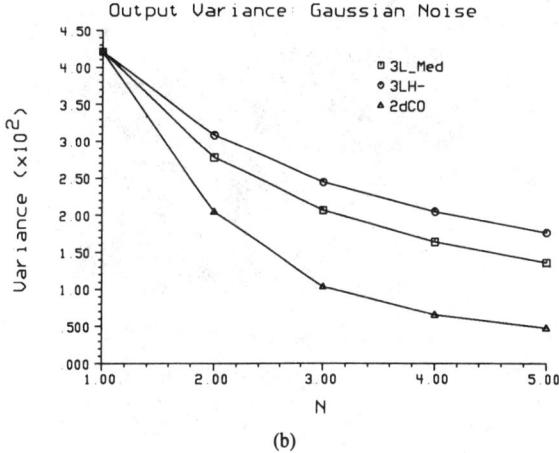

(b)

Fig. 5. Output variance for different window sizes for (a) impulsive noise, (b) Gaussian noise.

Fig. 6. (a) Original image, (b) noisy image (impulsive noise), (c) median filter, (d) (3LM−), (e) (3LH−), (f) 2DCO, (g) (2LM+), and (h) (2LH+). All estimates use $N = 2$.

Fig. 7. Difference image between original and estimate in impulsive noise using (a) noisy image, (b) median filter, (c) (3LM−), (d) (3LM−), (e) 2DCO, (f) (2LM+), and (g) (2LH+).

TABLE V
RESULTS OF IMPULSIVE NOISE SIMULATION ($N = 2$)

Measured Error	Image: Noisy Stream-Bridge	
	Mean Squared Error	
Type of Filter:	Noise type: Impulsive	
2nd Order	$Prob. = .125\ Size = 200$	$Prob. = .25\ Size = 200$
Sq. Median	0.0274	0.8494
3LM-	0.0207	0.0769
3LH-	0.0293	0.0823
2DCO	0.0163 *	0.0516
2LM+	0.0259	0.0149 *
2LH+	0.0186 *	0.0379 *
	Mean Absolute Error	
Sq. Median	0.1134	0.9236
3LM-	0.0439 *	0.1128
3LH-	0.0547	0.1333
2DCO	0.0431 *	0.0920 *
2LM+	0.0627	0.0822 *
2LH+	0.0619	0.1010

(d) the multistage median filter (3LM−), (e) the FIR-median hybrid filter (3LH−), (f) the morphological filter, (g) the bidirectional multistage median filter, and (h) the bidirectional FIR-median hybrid (2LH+) (all with $N = 2$). Fig. 7 shows the difference of the original image with: (a) the noisy image, (b) the median filtered signal, (c) the multistage median filtered image, (d) the FIR-median hybrid filtered image, (e) the morphological filtered image, (f) the bidirectional median filtered signal, and (g) the 2LH+ filtered signal. Table V shows the error introduced by each of the filters under the MSE and MAE error criteria. As indicated by the asterisks, the morphological filter (2DCO) and the (3LM−) outperform the other filters for a low probability of impulses at the input. For higher impulse probabilities, the bidirectional median filter performs best.

Fig. 8 shows the same sequence as Fig. 6, when the additive noise is Gaussian with a standard deviation of 25. Fig. 9 shows the same sequence of difference images as Fig. 7, corresponding to the filtering sequence of Fig. 8. Table VI summarizes the results. For both error criteria, the morphological filter and the bidirectional median filter perform best for small noise standard deviation. For a higher standard deviation, the square median yields the best results. This is not surprising since the square median attenuates more noise at the expense of blurring.

As illustrated in Figs. 10 and 11, we can further attenuate the noise by increasing the window size. The effect of increasing the window size of a multistage median filter is to reduce the breakdown probability as can be seen in Figs. 6(d) and (g) and 10(b) and (e). Using the results of Section III, an impulse can occur in Fig. 6(d) with probability 0.035. By increasing the window parameter, from $N = 2$ to $N = 3$, the breakdown probability in Fig. 10(d) is only 0.013 (in the homogeneous regions of the image). For the bidirectional multistage median filter, the breakdown probability of 0.0028 in Fig. 6(g) is reduced to 0.0004 in Fig. 10(e).

By increasing the window size of a morphological filter, the probability of an impulse occurring at the output of the filter is also reduced. The effect of increasing the window size of the FIR-median hybrid filters is to reduce the height of some of the impulse at the output of the filter; nevertheless, more blurring is introduced in the output image. Table VII summarizes the error introduced by the third-order ($N = 3$) filters. The multistage median filter and the morphological filter perform the best with this larger window.

VI. CONCLUSIONS

Although conventional square median filters are effective in many image processing applications, they have not proven to be adequate for both detail preserving and noise suppression. To overcome these limitations, many filter combinations and structures have been proposed in the literature. In this paper, we only considered nonadaptive, structure-preserving filters. After defining several detail-preserving filter structures, we analyzed the properties of multistage median filters. It was shown that multistage median and the multistage max/median filters are identical. Using the concepts of threshold decomposition and statistical threshold decomposition, we found closed-form

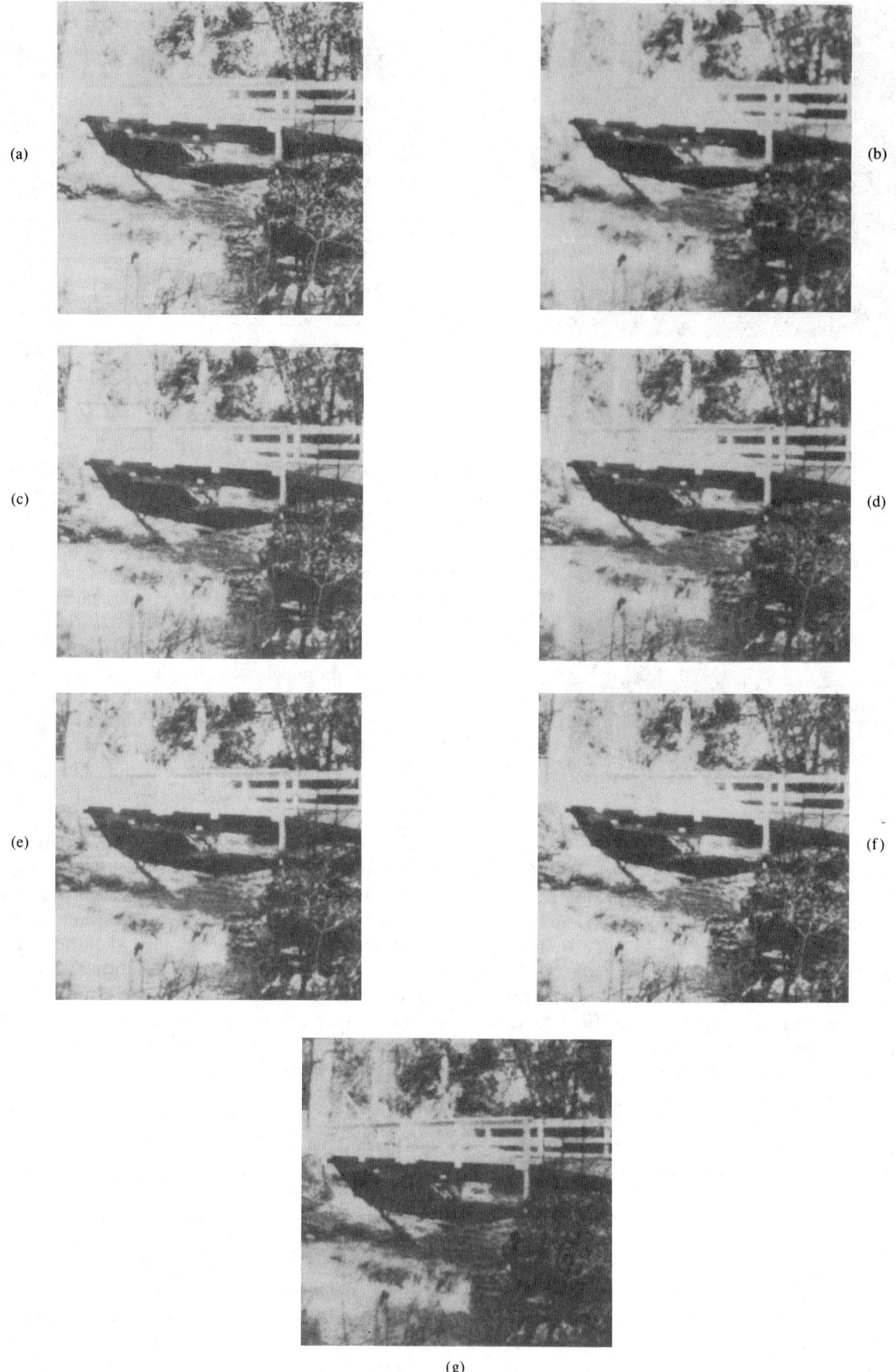

Fig. 8. (a) Noisy image (Gaussian noise), (b) median filter, (c) (3LM−),
(d) (3LH−), (e) 2DCO, (f) (2LM+), and (g) (2LH+)

Fig. 9. Difference image between original and estimate in Gaussian noise using (a) no estimate (noisy), (b) median filter, (c) (3LM−), (d) (3LH−), (e) (2DCO), (f) (2LM+), and (g) (2LH+).

TABLE VI
RESULTS OF GAUSSIAN NOISE SIMULATION ($N = 2$)

Measured Error	Image: Noisy Stream-Bridge	
Mean Squared Error		
Type of Filter:	Noise type: Gaussian	
2nd Order	$\mu = 0.0\ \sigma = 25.0$	$\mu = 0.0\ \sigma = 60.0$
Sq. Median	0.0272	0.0376 *
3LM-	0.0171	0.0714
3LH-	0.0181	0.0753
2DCO	0.0160 *	0.0592
2LM+	0.0168 *	0.0417 *
2LH+	0.0174	0.0433
Mean Absolute Error		
Sq. Median	0.1304	0.1651 *
3LM-	0.1158	0.2429
3LH-	0.1194	0.1845
2DCO	0.1104	0.2179
2LM+	0.1079 *	0.1806 *
2LH+	0.1081 *	0.1847

expression for output distribution functions. Since the class of multistage median filters have the threshold decomposition attribute, they are simpler to analyze than their FIR-median hybrid counterparts.

TABLE VII
RESULTS OF IMPULSIVE NOISE SIMULATION ($N = 3$)

Measured Error	Image: Noisy Stream-Bridge
Mean Squared Error	
Type of Filter:	Impulsive
3rd Order	$Prob. = .125\ Size = 200$
Sq. Median	0.0342
3LM-	0.0162 *
3LH-	0.0244
2DCO	0.0150 *
2LM+	0.0252
2LH+	0.0190
Mean Absolute Error	
Sq. Median	0.4737
3LM-	0.0496 *
3LH-	0.0529 *
2DCO	0.0684
2LM+	0.0887
2LH+	0.0712

Finally, using these results as well as the properties of the other filters under consideration, we compared their efficiency in noise suppression and detail-preserving characteristics. The comparison used the following error criteria: a) a mean squared error, b) an absolute error, and c) a subjective visual error criteria. As expected, the performance of each filter relative to that of the others depends on the type of error criterion used and also in the type of noisy environments. The reader is invited to relate the errors tabulated in Tables IV–VII with their own subjective evaluation of the images. Thus, perhaps, a better interpretation of the (MSE) and (MAE) error criteria can be gained.

For very high signal-to-noise ratio, the multistage FIR-median hybrid filter performs best under all three error criteria. For higher noise power and in heavy-tailed noise environments, the morphological filter and the multistage median filter performed best using all error measures. For Gaussian noise, the morphological filter performed well in higher signal-to-noise ratios. For low signal-to-noise ratio, the square median filter gave the best results under the MSE and MAE error criteria. In all cases (as expected), the square median filter performed very poorly in preserving image structure. The weight used for each error measure depends on the particular application. The comparison of these efficient structure-preserving filters should help researchers in evaluating the performance of new algorithms.

Thus, two-dimensional multistage median filters have been shown to have the same attributes as those of the median filter in a one-dimensional domain. Among the characteristics of multistage median filters are: a) they preserve two-dimensional structures, b) they are good smoothers in heavy-tailed noise environments, c) they allow for simple implementations, and finally, d) they are relatively efficient in different types of noise. The properties of Multistage Median Filters will prove this filtering scheme most useful in detail-preserving image processing applications.

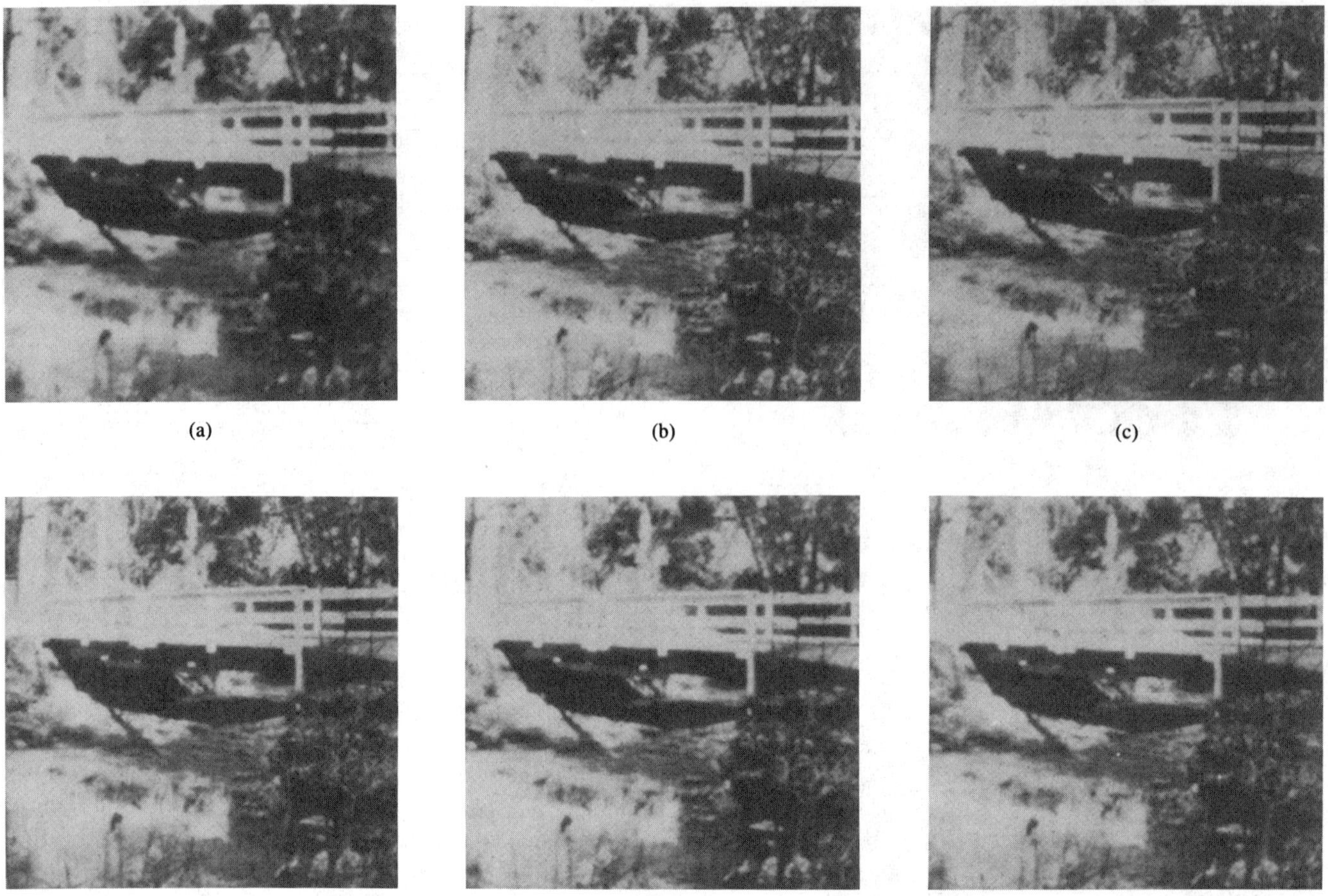

Fig. 10. (a) Median filter, (b) (3LM−), (c) (3LH−), (d) (2DCO), (e) (2LM+), and (f) (2LH+). All filters using $N = 3$.

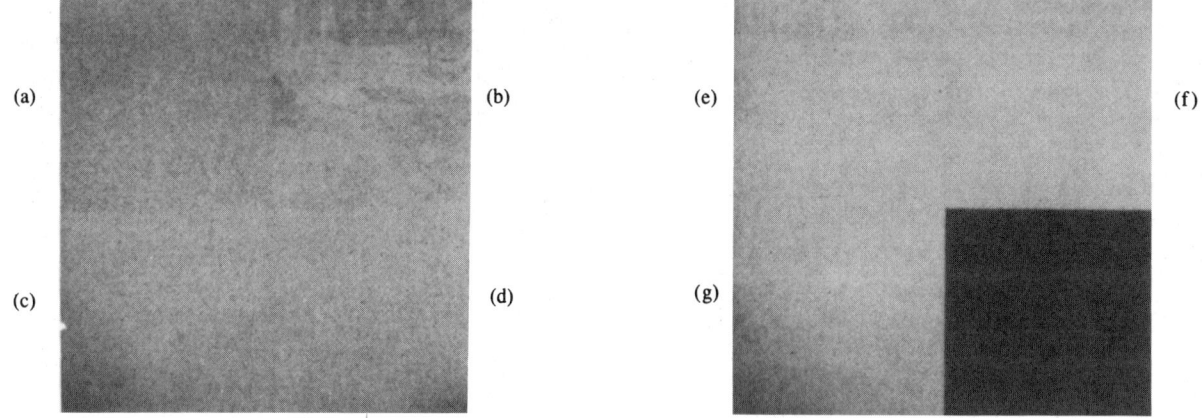

Fig. 11. Difference image between original and estimate in impulsive noise using ($N = 3$). (a) No estimate (noisy), (b) median filter, (c) (3LM−), (d) (3LH−), (e) 2DCO, (f) (2LM+), and (g) (2LH+).

REFERENCES

[1] A. Nieminen, P. Heinonen, and Y. Neuvo, "A new class of detail-preserving filters for image processing," *IEEE Trans. Pattern Anal. Machine Intell.*, vol. PAMI-9, Jan. 1987.

[2] G. R. Arce and M. P. McLoughlin, "Theoretical analysis of max/median filters," *IEEE Trans. Acoust., Speech, Signal Processing*, vol. ASSP-35, Jan. 1987.

[3] I. Pitas and A. N. Venetsanopoulos, "Nonlinear mean filters in image processing," *IEEE Trans. Acoust., Speech, Signal Processing*, vol. ASSP-34, June 1986.

[4] Y. H. Lee and A. T. Fam, "An edge gradient enhancing adaptive order statistic filter," *IEEE Trans. Acoust., Speech, Signal Processing*, vol. ASSP-35, May 1987.

[5] L. S. Davis and A. Rosenfeld, "Noise cleaning by iterated local averaging," *IEEE Trans. Syst., Man, Cybern.*, vol. SMC-8, Sept. 1978.

[6] R. L. Stevenson and G. R. Arce, "Theoretical analysis of morphological filters," in *Proc. 24th Annu. Allerton Conf. Commun., Contr., Comput.*, Monticello, IL, Oct. 1986.

[7] ——, "Morphological filters: Statistics and further syntactical properties," *IEEE Trans. Circuits Syst.*, vol. CAS-34, Nov. 1987.

[8] I. Song and S. A. Kassam, "A class of rank filters based on the Wilcoxon signed rank statistic," in *Proc. 24th Annu. Allerton Conf. Commun., Contr., Comput.*, Monticello, IL, Oct. 1986.

[9] Y. H. Lee and S. A. Kassam, "Generalized median filtering and related nonlinear filtering techniques," *IEEE Trans. Acoust., Speech, Signal Processing*, vol. ASSP-33, June 1985.

[10] G. R. Arce, N. C. Gallagher, and T. A. Nodes, "Median filter: Theory and applications," in *Advances in Computer Vision and Image Processing*, Vol. 2, T. S. Huang, Ed. Greenwich, CT: JAI, 1986.

[11] A. C. Bovik, T. S. Huang, and D. C. Munson, "Edge-sensitive image restoration using order-constrained least squares methods," *IEEE Trans. Acoust., Speech, Signal Processing*, vol. ASSP-33, Oct. 1985.

[12] A. Kundu, S. K. Mitra, and P. P. Vaidyanathan, "Application of two-dimensional generalized mean filtering for removal of impulsive noises from images," *IEEE Trans. Acoust., Speech, Signal Processing*, vol. ASSP-32, June 1984.

[13] P. D. Wendt, E. J. Coyle, and N. C. Gallagher, Jr., "Stack filters," *IEEE Trans. Acoust., Speech, Signal Processing*, vol. ASSP-34, Aug. 1986.

[14] P. A. Maragos and R. W. Schafer, "Morphological filters—Part II," *IEEE Trans. Acoust., Speech, Signal Processing*, vol. ASSP-35, Aug. 1987.

[15] G. R. Arce, "Statistical threshold decomposition for recursive and nonrecursive median filters," *IEEE Trans. Inform. Theory*, vol. IT-32, Mar. 1986.

[16] P. Fitch, E. J. Coyle, and N. C. Gallagher, Jr., "Median filtering by threshold decomposition," *IEEE Trans. Acoust., Speech, Signal Processing*, vol. ASSP-32, Dec. 1984.

[17] T. Thong, "Digital image processing test patterns," *IEEE Trans. Acoust., Speech, Signal Processing*, vol. ASSP-31, June 1983.

[18] G. R. Arce, P. J. Warter, and R. E. Foster, "Recursive multistage median filters," in *Proc. 22nd Annu. Conf. Inform. Sci. Syst.*, Princeton Univ., Princeton, NJ, Mar. 18, 1988.

Gonzalo R. Arce (S'82-M'82) was born in La Paz, Bolivia, on September 20, 1957. He received the B.S. degree in electrical engineering with high honors from the University of Arkansas, Fayetteville, in 1979. In 1980 and 1982, respectively, he received the M.S. and Ph.D. degrees in electrical engineering from Purdue University, West Lafayette, IN.

In September 1982 he joined the Faculty of the Electrical Engineering Department at the University of Delaware, Newark, where he is currently Associate Professor. His research interests include statistical and multidimensional digital signal processing, computer vision, and communication theory. He is author or coauthor of over 40 technical papers in these areas, and is a frequent consultant to industry.

Dr. Arce is a member of Eta Kappa Nu.

Russell E. Foster was born in Bridgeton, NJ, on May 5, 1960. He received the B.S. degree in electronic engineering from Monmouth College, West Long Branch, NJ, in 1986, and the Master degree in electrical engineering from the University of Delaware, Newark, in 1988.

While attending the University of Delaware he was a Research Assistant working on ranked-order filter architectures for VLSI implementation. Currently he is employed by AT&T Bell Laboratories where he is a member of Technical Staff in the Advanced Integrated Circuit Design Department, Allentown, PA. His research interests include multidimensional signal processing algorithms and high-speed circuit design techniques applicable to signal processing and communications IC's.

Mr. Foster is a member of Eta Kappa Nu and Sigma Pi Sigma.

Optimal Stack Filtering and the Estimation and Structural Approaches to Image Processing

EDWARD J. COYLE, MEMBER, IEEE, JEAN-HSANG LIN, STUDENT MEMBER, IEEE, AND MONCEF GABBOUJ, STUDENT MEMBER, IEEE

Abstract—Rank-order based filters such as stack filters, multilevel and multistage median filters, morphological filters, and order statistic filters have all proven to be very effective at enhancing and restoring images. Perhaps the primary reason for their success is that they can suppress noise without destroying important image details such as edges and lines.

Two approaches have been used in the past to design rank-order based nonlinear filters to enhance or restore images. They may be called the *structural approach* and the *estimation approach*. The first approach requires structural descriptions of the image and the process which has altered it, while the second requires statistical descriptions. The many different classes of rank-order based filters that have been developed over the last few decades are reviewed in the context of these two approaches.

One of these filter classes, stack filters, then becomes the focus of the rest of the paper. These filters, which are defined by a weak superposition property and an ordering property, contain all compositions of 2-D rank-order operations.

The recently developed theory of minimum mean absolute error (MMAE) stack filtering is reviewed and extended to two dimensions. Then, a theory of optimal stack filtering under structural constraints and goals is developed for the structural approach to image processing.

These two optimal stack filtering theories are then combined into a single design theory for rank-order based filters.

I. INTRODUCTION

WHENEVER an image is recorded by an electronic system or transmitted over a communication channel, it is altered in some fashion. This alteration may take on many forms. It may be unintentional or unavoidable, such as when white Gaussian noise is added to the observed image by the electronics in the imaging system, or when speckle noise is introduced because a coherent imaging system has been used. Or it may be intentional, which is the case when the image is compressed or used to modulate some signal in preparation for its transmission over some communication channel. No matter what the form of the alteration, though, the goal of the first stage of an image processing system is often the recovery[1] of the original image from the altered version that has been recorded or transmitted.

Nonlinear filters that incorporate rank-order operations have proven to be particularly effective at this task of image recovery. This is because the median filter [1]–[3], stack filters [4], multilevel and multistage median filters [5], [6], morphological filters [7]–[10], order statistic filters [11], and other rank-order based filters can preserve or reconstruct edges, lines, and other image details while also removing the noise or other processes which have altered the image. To perform similarly, other classes of filters, such as linear filters, must use some type of data-dependent scheme.

There has thus been a tremendous amount of activity in the area of filter design for rank-order based filters. As will be seen in the next section, at least 20 different classes of these filters have been defined in the last few decades. They include, to name only a few: the "pure" rank-order operators such as the median filter; compositions of rank-order operators such as stack filters, morphological filters, and multistage median filters [5], [6]; and compositions of linear filters and rank-order operators such as order statistic (L filters) and C filters (Ll filters) [11]–[15].

This activity in the generation of new classes of rank-order based filters is not a sign of chaos. It is a sign that something fundamental is happening. From this primordial soup of different rank-order based filters, several sophisticated new theories of filter design have emerged or are emerging. They are all reviewed in Section II of this paper before one of them, the theory of optimal stack filtering [21]–[24], is developed in detail.

The review proceeds by identifying two different approaches to the design of rank-order based filters. One might be called the *structural* approach, while the other might be called the *estimation* approach. The first approach relies on structural descriptions of the image and the process which has altered it, while the second relies on statistical descriptions. The many different classes of rank-order based filters are reviewed in the context of their contribution to one or the other of these approaches.

The primary goal of this paper, though, is to summarize and extend a new theory [21]–[24] which combines these two filter design approaches into a single formal methodology for the design of *optimal* rank-order based nonlinear filters. This is not to imply that the two approaches have not been used together in the past. It is just that previous efforts to combine them have tended to be either

---

Manuscript received March 17, 1989. This work was supported by the National Science Foundation under Grant EET 87-21333, and by a grant from the AT&T Foundation.

E. J. Coyle and M. Gabbouj are with the School of Electrical Engineering, Purdue University, West Lafayette, IN 47907.

J.-H. Lin was with the School of Electrical Engineering, Purdue University, West Lafayette, IN 47907. He is now with the Department of Electrical Engineering, University of Delaware, Newark, DE.

IEEE Log Number 8931344.

[1]The word recovery is used to denote both *enhancement*, which is often ad hoc, and *restoration*, which implies that some knowledge of the joint statistics of the image and the process which altered it is used to design a filter.

heuristic in nature or have developed design methods over rather limited classes of nonlinear filters. In this paper, the structural and estimation approaches are combined into a methodology capable of determining a best filter from the very large classes of nonlinear filters called stack filters [4] and generalized stack filters [22].

Stack filters contain all combinations and compositions of rank-order operators within a finite window [4]. They thus include median filters [1]–[3], multistage median filters [5], [6], and the opening and closing operations in morphological filtering [7]–[9], all of which have been very successful in image processing. With the proper generalization [22], stack filters include all digital morphological operators, even the gray-scale operators [25].

It is the definition [4] of stack filters which distinguishes them from these other filter classes. It emphasizes two properties originally discovered for the median and other rank-order operators. They are the weak superposition property known as the threshold decomposition [26], [27] and the ordering property known as the stacking property [26]–[28]. These properties are the primary tools of new theories for optimal stack filtering under both structural and estimation error criteria.

This paper is organized as follows. The next section provides a review of previous work on both the structural and estimation approaches for the design of rank-order based filters. Section III reviews the definition of the filters, called stack filters [4] and generalized stack filters [22], which are considered in the rest of the paper.

Section IV reviews already finished work on the estimation approach to the design of these filters [21]–[23], including the development of a theory of optimal adaptive stack filtering under the mean absolute error criterion [23]. Section V provides the nontrivial extension to two dimensions of recent results [24] on the structural approach to the design of optimal stack filters. This involves the definition of local and global structures in images and the development of a method for designing a stack filter that will either meet or come as close as possible to meeting any desired set of structural constraints or goals. This new theory is called optimal stack filtering under structural error criteria.

In Section VI, the theories of optimal filtering under the mean absolute error criterion and optimal filtering under structural error criteria are unified into a single optimal filtering theory.

II. Rank-Order Based Nonlinear Filtering in Image Processing

The history of rank-order based nonlinear filtering in image processing is difficult to condense into a single section in a paper or even into a single book. The reason is that so many different classes of these nonlinear filters have been defined in the last few decades. Since each one derives its own raison d'être from the set of applications in which it has been used successfully, it is difficult to dismiss any one of them from consideration.

Any effort to review all of them, however, very quickly results in chaos or degenerates into a long list of definitions and applications. For instance, a partial list of the classes of nonadaptive filters which incorporate rank-order operations in one way or another would include median filters [1]–[3], weighted median filters [16], [17], [29], rank-order filters [30], [31], recursive median filters [30], multistage recursive median filters [32], alpha-trimmed means [33], stack filters [4], generalized stack filters [22], cellular logic operations [34]–[36], generalized rank-order filters [37], Ξ filters [38], cascaded median filters [19], C filters (Ll filters) [13]–[15], order statistic filters [11], modified trimmed mean filters [39], double window modified trimmed mean filters [39], separable median filters [40], max/median filters [41], morphological filters [7]–[10], [25], [55], [105]–[107], multistage median filters [5], [6], and FIR-median hybrid filters [42].

Stating the definitions of all of these filter classes would by itself require many pages. Even the definitions of some of the most recently developed filters requires a significant amount of space in the Appendix.

One possible solution to this problem is to determine whether some philosophically different approaches to image processing tasks can be identified, and to then discuss the different filters in the context of these approaches. The filters which figure most prominently in the discussion of these approaches are the ones that could then be discussed in some detail.

As already stated in the Introduction, the solution just outlined is the one chosen for this paper. The discussion will be divided along the lines of the structural and the estimation approaches to image recovery.

A. The Structural Approach to Image Recovery with Rank-Order Based Filters

In the structural approach, there is one list of local and/or global gray-scale variations, which will be called structures, which are known to be present in the original image, and another list of structures which are created by whatever process alters the image. The goal is to find or create a rank-order based filter which preserves or modifies in a desired way the structures of the original image, while eliminating those created when the image was altered. Meeting this goal has, until recently, meant either searching through a catalog of filters and their structural behavior to find one with the desired behavior or synthesizing a filter from "simpler" filters with known behavior.

For example, suppose we wish to find a rank-order based filter which preserves structures corresponding to horizontal and vertical edges in images, while removing those structures which correspond to impulses which are less than N points across in the horizontal and vertical directions. A search through the catalog would reveal many 2-D rank-order based filters with this type of structural behavior [5], [6]. It is instructive, though, to try to synthesize a simple filter with this behavior in order to see the difficulties encountered in this approach.

Since the goal is to remove structures shaped like impulses of width N or less while preserving the structure of any edges, the one-dimensional median filter of window width $2N + 1$ immediately comes to mind. It preserves any signal which is a sequence of constant-valued regions, each of length $N + 1$ or greater, which are separated by monotonic regions [2], [3], and it deletes impulses of width N or less [2]. Running this filter along every horizontal line in the image and then along every vertical line in the image should thus produce the desired behavior.

The filter just described is known as the $(2N + 1) \times (2N + 1)$ separable median filter [40]. To find the 2-D representation of this filter, suppose, for simplicity, that $N = 1$ so that each 1-D median filter has a window of width three. Then, defining $X_{i,j}$ to be the i, jth pixel around a reference point of $(0, 0)$, the output at $(0, 0)$ of the 3×3 separable median filter $y_3(\cdot, \cdot)$ is

$$y_3(0, 0) = \text{median} \begin{pmatrix} \text{median}(X_{-1,-1}, X_{0,-1}, X_{1,-1}) \\ \text{median}(X_{-1,0}, X_{0,0}, X_{1,0}) \\ \text{median}(X_{-1,1}, X_{0,1}, X_{1,1}) \end{pmatrix}.$$

(2.1)

From its definition, it would appear that the structural properties of the separable median filter can be determined completely from the structural properties of the 1-D median filters used on each vertical and horizontal line of the image.

This is essentially, but not exactly, the case. Specifically, if every horizontal and vertical line in an image is a fixed point or root signal for the 1-D median filter of window width $2N + 1$, then the image is a 2-D root signal of the $(2N + 1) \times (2N + 1)$ separable median filter. Structurally, this says that every line in the image consists of constant-valued regions of minimum width $N + 1$ separated by monotonic regions called edges. Impulsive structures of width N or less are not allowed.

Unfortunately, not all the roots of the separable median filter can be generated this way. In [43] and [44], it is shown that the 2-D binary images shown in Fig. 1 are roots for the separable median filter. Note that many of the vertical and horizontal lines in these images contain impulsive structures and therefore are *not* root signals of the window width $2N + 1$ 1-D median filter. Thus, the separable median filter preserves some 2-D structures which contain oscillations or impulses.

This is a problem if the noise or other process which altered the image can create structures like that shown in Fig. 1. Such behavior is unlikely, though, since if just one point in this oscillatory structure were different, the structure would no longer be a root signal of the filter [43], [44]. The entire oscillatory structure would be eliminated after a few passes of the separable median filter. The separable median would then be behaving more like the 1-D median; it would preserve edge-like structures, while removing impulsive structures. In this case, the synthesis procedure has worked rather well since the 2-D filter has the desirable characteristics of its 1-D building blocks.

```
110000            1110000000111
110000            1110000000111
110111            1110000000111
110111            0010101010100
000111            0011111111100
000111            0011111111100
                  0011111111100
```

Fig. 1. (From [43].) The two binary images shown above are both roots of the 5×5 separable median filter. Note the presence of impulsive and oscillatory structures in these 2-D roots.

The above discussion points out some of the difficulties encountered in the structural approach. First, it often requires very significant effort to characterize the root signals of 2-D rank-order based filters. Second, the approach has, until recently [16], [24], relied on building a catalog of the structural behavior of many different 2-D filters. In other words, the design process under the structural approach is one of selection or synthesis from a relatively small class of well-understood operations like the 1-D median filter.

One of the goals of this paper is to change this situation by providing an algorithm to find rank-order based filters with any specified structural behavior. Before doing so, though, some other work that has recently taken place on the structural approach is reviewed.

In the separable median filtering example considered above, the properties of the 1-D median filter figured very prominently. Particularly significant was its ability to preserve edges and constant-valued regions, while removing impulsive structures.

The median filter is not, of course, a perfect filtering operation. It may cause edge jitter [45] and streaking [46] or may remove important details from the image [5], [6].

When the median is properly generalized, though, many filters with much better performance can be found or synthesized. This was the original motivation behind the definitions of stack filters, max/median filters, multilevel and multistage median filters, order statistic filters, FIR-median hybrid filters, and generalized stack filters.

The performance of these filters is significantly better than the separable median filter defined above. While the separable median only has two stages of processing, a multistage median filter may have three or more. Furthermore, the median operations used in these different stages are used in many different orientations within the filter's window, not just the horizontal and vertical orientations.

Specifically, in a multistage median filter, there is a median filter oriented in any direction in the image in which there are details to be preserved. These different orientations and the multiple levels of processing allow these other filters to preserve many more structures than the separable median filter. They can, for example, preserve lines in addition to edges [5], [6]. They also have superior noise reduction properties when compared to the separable median [5], [6].

Since these multistage median filters are among the best filters produced so far by the structural approach to the design of rank-order based operations, we now provide an example of a multistage median filter.

In the first level of operation, the median filter of appropriate window width (or, alternatively, an FIR filter

[42]) is applied in all directions along which lines, edges, or other details in the images are to be preserved. This stage can be thought of as producing several intermediate images, one from each filtering direction. The second level of operation is then a pointwise maximum, minimum, or median over all of the outputs produced in the first level of operation.

Suppose, for example, the window is a 5×5 square window consisting of points $X_{i,j}$ where the indexing is relative to the center of the window. The point $X_{0,0}$ is thus the pixel in the middle of the window. One possible version of the multistage or multilevel median [5], [6], called the unidirectional multistage median in [6], would be

$$\text{median} \begin{pmatrix} \text{median}(X_{0,-2}, X_{0,-1}, X_{0,0}, X_{0,1}, X_{0,2}) \\ \text{median}(X_{2,-2}, X_{1,-1}, X_{0,0}, X_{-1,1}, X_{-2,2}) \\ \text{median}(X_{2,0}, X_{1,0}, X_{0,0}, X_{-1,0}, X_{-2,0}) \\ \text{median}(X_{2,2}, X_{1,1}, X_{0,0}, X_{-1,-1}, X_{-2,-2}) \\ X_{0,0} \end{pmatrix}. \quad (2.2)$$

This improved synthesis approach to the design of rank-order based filters has been quite successful. As can be seen in the examples provided in [5] and [6], some of which are repeated in Section IV-D, these filters do a good job of preserving details, while also suppressing noise.

In addition to visual checks to determine whether the appropriate details are being preserved, statistical checks must be performed to determine the filter's effect upon noise. One possible check is to directly compute the empirical absolute error and empirical squared error in the same applications used for the visual evaluation. Such computations were carried out, for instance, for all of the examples in [6].

Another method of comparing these filters statistically is to analytically determine their output distribution. This approach has been used in a large number of papers [5], [6], [19], [39], [41], [47]-[52]. The task of finding the distribution is made much simpler by the algorithm in [53] and by the existence of the technique called statistical threshold decomposition [54].

Morphology[2] and the Structural Approach: It is important to mention here that morphology [7]-[10], [25], [55], [105]-[107], which also uses a synthesis approach to the design of rank-order based filters, has been quite effective in quantitatively describing and manipulating geometric structures in images. There is also a great deal of intuition that has been built up in the area as to how and when to apply a particular rank-order based operation to achieve some desired effect. An example in which this intuition proves to work very nicely is the rolling ball algorithm, which can be used to reduce impulsive noise [25].

As is made clear in [9] (from the morphological point of view), there is a great deal of common ground between morphology and rank-order based signal processing. In fact, much of digital morphology is based on rank-order operations. To see this requires translating morphological language into the language used in this paper.

The structuring elements [7]-[9] used in morphology are equivalent to the windows used in this paper; the set which defines a structuring element specifies the shape of the window over which the morphological operation will be applied. The morphological operations of erosion and dilation by a given structuring element are then min and max operations, respectively, performed in the window defined by the structuring element as this window is moved over the image in the usual fashion. The close-open and open-close operations are compositions of erosions and dilations and are therefore also based on rank-order operations. An example of a morphological filter which has been translated into the language in this paper can be found in the Appendix.

Thus, the area of rank-order based and morphological filtering consider many of the same operations—compositions and linear combinations of rank-order operations—but approach them from different points of view. This close relationship between morphology and rank-order based filtering implies that all of the analytical results developed later in this paper can be applied, after suitable translation, to the field of digital morphology.

Summary: One fact that must be pointed out concerning the work reviewed above is that it concerns the synthesis of filters with desired structural behavior from a few filters with well-studied behavior. The approach thus rests on the often strenuous efforts that must be made to determine the structural behavior of any given filtering operation. Since analyzing every filter for its specific structural behavior and/or output distribution is not feasible, the field of rank-order based filters will not advance far beyond the above efforts in a very timely fashion.

What is needed is a way of searching through the class of all 2-D stack filters, which are all possible compositions of 2-D rank-order filters, to find a filter which either has exactly the properties desired or comes the closest of all of the available filters.

The 1-D foundation of this work can be found in [16] for weighted median filters and in [24] for stack filters. Both of these efforts build on techniques developed in [56], [57] for the median filter. In this paper, the results in [24] are extended to two dimensions, resulting in a theory called optimal stack filtering under structural goals and error criteria.

B. The Estimation Approach to Image Recovery

In the structural approach to image processing summarized above, rank-order based filters are chosen, even for noise-reduction applications, according to their structural behavior. In other words, goals such as edge preservation or specific root signal behavior come first; the statistical effects are then determined once the filter has already been chosen.

---

[2] For a full accounting of morphology, please consult [7]-[9], [25], [55], [105]-[107], and another paper [10] in this issue.

In the estimation approach, the rank-order based filter is chosen for reasons which are statistical rather than structural in nature, and then it may be checked to determine if its structural behavior is desirable.

Three different forms of the estimation approach can be said to exist: the enhancement form, the optimization form, and the data-dependent form. Each of these forms and the filters they have produced are reviewed in the subsections which follow.

The Enhancement Form of the Estimation Approach: In this form of the estimation approach to image processing, a nonlinear filter or filter class is proposed because it has been shown, in the statistics literature [58], [59] or elsewhere, to have precise statistical properties such as robustness or optimality under some error criterion. These properties lead to the application of the filter to tasks in image processing where that particular property is desired. Since the filter design is not based on an explicit model for the image degradation, we refer to this as the enhancement approach.

Perhaps the most well-known example of this form of the estimation approach is the median filter [1]. One of the reasons it has been used in image processing is because of the many optimality properties it is known to possess, even if they do not translate directly into optimality properties for the running median in image processing.

1) The median is the least absolute error estimate of the center of a distribution [29]. This says that the median of i.i.d. samples $x_1, x_2, \cdots, x_n$ of a random variable X achieves the minimum in

$$\min_a \sum_{i=1}^{n} |x_i - a|. \quad (2.3)$$

2) The median of i.i.d. samples of a doubly exponential random variable is the maximum likelihood estimator of the mean of that random variable [29].

3) The conditional median at each time instant t is the minimum mean absolute error estimator of the signal value at time t where the conditioning is on the past history up to time t of the noise corrupted observations of the signal; see, for instance, [60].

4) As shown in [44], the running median is, with high probability, a maximum *a posteriori* estimator of a constant signal in symmetric impulse noise.

In addition to all of these properties, and the results in [83], the median in both one and two dimensions is relatively easy to implement in software and hardware [37], [61]–[77], and as mentioned in Section II-A, it has desirable structural properties. Thus, both the enhancement form of the estimation approach and the structural approach lead to the median filter.

Other examples of rank-order based filters resulting from the enhancement approach include *STM* filters [39], order statistic or *L* filters [11], alpha-trimmed mean filters [33], modified trimmed mean filters [39], and double window modified trimmed mean filters [39]. These filters are usually compared to each other by computing output statistics such as the output variance or by subjectively comparing their outputs to see which one gives the best results.

The Restoration Form of the Estimation Approach:[3] In this form of the estimation approach, a nonlinear filter class is defined as a generalization of some particular filter which is already known to have nice statistical or structural properties. The filter which is the germ of the new class is usually one that was discovered via the enhancement approach described previously. However the class of nonlinear filters arises, the goal is to develop an optimization procedure to find the filter within this class which minimizes some statistical error criterion.

The first class of rank-order based nonlinear filters to succeed in this way was the order statistic or *L* filters [11]. They were defined as a generalization of the median and other rank-order filters. The generalization was to consider linear combinations of the ranked values of the samples in the filter window.

For example, in a 1-D window of length n, let $x_{(1)}, x_{(2)}, \cdots, x_{(n)}$ denote the samples in the window after they have been ordered according to their rank, that is, $x_{(1)} \leq x_{(2)} \leq \cdots \leq x_{(n)}$. The output of the filter is then defined to be

$$\sum_{i=1}^{n} a_i x_{(i)}, \quad (2.4)$$

which is a linear combination of *order* statistics.

Under trivial assignments to some of the a_i's in (2.4), one can derive the median filter, rank-order filters, alpha-trimmed mean filters, etc. Order statistic filters thus provide a reasonably large class of filters over which to optimize.

The goal in [11] was then to pick the a_i's in (2.4) which minimize the mean-squared error between the actual output of the filter and some desired output, given noise-corrupted observations of the desired signal as the input to the filter. The key problem was the computation of the correlation matrix of the order statistics. In general, this prohibited a closed-form solution for the problem, but special cases are known in which closed-form results are possible [11]. Examples showing the application of order statistic filters to a problem in noise reduction in image processing can also be found in [11].

Some recent work on order statistic filters and their generalizations, the *C* filters (*Ll* filters) [12]–[15] has concerned the development of optimal adaptive filtering algorithms. The result is an algorithm to train an order statistic, *C* filter or *Ll* filter to minimize the mean-squared error criterion. This problem reduces to training the linear section of the filter, which then allows the well-developed theory of adaptive linear filtering [78]–[80] to be brought to bear. These adaptive filters should prove useful in image processing.

Analog order statistic filters [81] have recently been de-

---

[3]This approach requires some knowledge of the joint statistics of the image and the process which altered it.

fined, and the relationship between order statistic filters and linear filters has been studied [82].

After the theory for optimal order statistic filters was developed, the next successful nonlinear optimization theory was developed for stack filters [21], [22]. This theory is an extension of the theory in [20] for rank-order filters, which may be regarded as a new interpretation of the results in [83]. A theory of optimal adaptive stack filtering has also been developed [23].

Stack filters are defined in Section III of this paper, and the optimization theory developed for them is reviewed in Section IV.

The Data-Dependent Form: The first step in this form of the estimation approach is the selection of a *set* of filters. They may all be different, or they may all be specific modifications of a particular filter, or some combination of these two extremes. Each filter in the set has a specific desirable property or purpose, such as edge preservation or noise smoothing in a constant-valued region corrupted by noise. Which filter is used at each point in the image is then determined by estimation of local statistics around that point.

It should be noted that this approach is often called the *adaptive approach* in the literature. This can cause confusion with adaptive filtering theories, such as [15], [23], which emphasize the *training* of filters to minimize some specific error criterion.

To avoid confusion, perhaps the name "adaptive approach" should only be used in situations in which the filter is trained by some algorithm, and the name "data-dependent approach" should be used for the "set of filters" approach being discussed in this subsection. This is appropriate since these data-dependent filters perform the same operation whenever a given array of pixel values appears in the filter's window; in other words, the overall operation performed by a data-dependent filter does not change over *time*. In contrast, in the training approach, the filter will change with time.

Terminology aside, some important work has been carried out under the data-dependent approach. Unfortunately, it is hard to describe it all here since each paper considers a different set of filters and/or a different method of determining which filter to use in each location.

Some examples of data-dependent rank-order based filters include gradient median filters [84], the adaptive minimum mean-squared error point estimators considered in [85], signal adaptive median (SAM) filters [86], adaptive length median filters [87], [88], edge gradient enhancing order statistic filters [89], and adaptive order statistic and trimmed mean filters [90], [91].

In essentially all of the papers listed in the previous paragraph, the nonlinear operation performed at each location in the image is determined by the local statistics at that location. Very good results have been obtained in many of these efforts. They are particularly good at preserving edges and other image structures, while reducing a broad range of noise types.

One important point must now be made. For any given data-dependent processing scheme, there is some filtering operation which does not first compute local statistics to determine which of a set of operations to apply. This is possible because each of the data-dependent filters above can still be considered a nondata-dependent function from the space defined by the points in the window to the real line. Developing a general optimization approach over a large enough class of filters would therefore remove the need for the data-dependent filters. It is not clear, though, that such an effort is feasible, although the generalized stack filters discussed later might provide an appropriate context in which to investigate the possibility.

C. Summary

What is needed in this area is an optimality theory for rank-order based nonlinear filters that is as analytically tractable as the theory of optimal linear filtering, yet at the same time includes as many nonlinear operations as possible, especially all the rank-order based operations. The error criterion used in this theory should then incorporate both statistical goals and structural goals and/or constraints in order to allow a filter designer to tailor the error criterion to produce whatever type of result is desired. Such a theory is developed in this paper.

III. THE MEDIAN FILTER, STACK FILTERS, AND GENERALIZED STACK FILTERS

The median filter, rank-order filters, and other filters which can be represented as stack filters [4] or generalized stack filters [22] figured prominently in the preceding discussions of both the structural *and* statistical approaches to image recovery. This indicates that stack filters may provide the appropriate context in which to unify these two approaches to image processing.

To define stack filters, it is best to start with the simplest one first, the median filter. It is a sliding window nonlinear filter whose output at each window position is the middle value of all of the sample values appearing in its window [1]–[3]. In two dimensions, there is a great deal of freedom in selecting the filter's window. It may, for example, be a square, an ×, or a cross.

Fig. 2 shows the motion of a square window median filter over an array of samples, with the resulting output array shown below it. The output point is assigned the same position as the center point in the window, although other assignments are certainly allowed.

Two of the fundamental properties of median filters are the weak superposition property known as the *threshold decomposition* [26], [27], and the ordering property [28] called the *stacking property* in [4], [26], [27].

The threshold decomposition is a superposition property for the median filter. It states that median filtering a gray-level image is the same as first decomposing it into a set of binary images by thresholding, then filtering each binary image with a median filter, and finally, adding up the results of these operations. This is, however, a *weak* superposition property since it works only if the input is decomposed by thresholding. Even though it is a weak su-

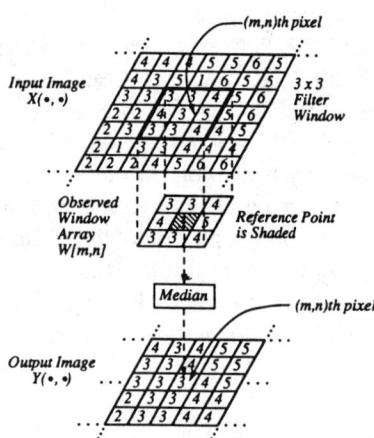

Fig. 2. Filtering with 3 × 3 square window median filter. The output of the filter is placed at the position corresponding to the location in the input image of the reference point of the window.

perposition property, the fact that the median obeys any superposition property is significant since, as can be seen with linear filters, such properties are essential for simplifying the study of filtering operations.

The stacking property is an *ordering* property. It states that the results of applying the median filter to each of the binary images obtained by thresholding the original image will have a specific structure to them. As will be seen later, this structure is what makes the theory of minimum mean absolute error stack filtering possible.

These two properties dramatically simplify the study of the median filter. For this reason, it became logical to ask what other filters possess these two properties. This is how stack filters and generalized stack filters got their start and their names.

Since these properties will form the foundation for all that follows, they are defined, in the context of the median filter, in the next section.

A. The Superposition Property of the Median Filter

Assume that the image X is a 2-D array of points, and denote the m, nth point in the image by $X(m, n)$. At each point, the image takes on some value in the set $Q = \{0, 1, \cdots, M\}$, so that $X(m, n) \in Q$ for all m, n. This implies that the image has been quantized to $M + 1$ levels.

Let W be the window of the filter. Pick some point in the window to be its reference point and give the window a specific orientation about this reference point, relative to the coordinates of the image array. The window's position is then specified by the coordinate of the image point immediately under the reference point of the window.

For simplicity, assume the window W is a $p \times q$ rectangle. Define $W[m, n]$ to be the array of sample points of the image that appears in the window W when its reference point is at position (m, n) in the image coordinates. The (i, j)th entry in $W[m, n]$ is denoted $W[m, n](i, j)$ and is the same as image sample $X(m + i, n + j)$. Note that i and j may take on negative as well as positive values.

We now define the threshold decomposition of the image. The binary image X_l is defined to be the image obtained by thresholding the image X at level l. This thresholding operator is called $T_l(\cdot)$, so that $X_l = T_l(X)$ where $X_l(i, j)$, which is the i, jth point in the binary plane X_l, is specified as follows:

$$X_l(i, j) = \begin{cases} 1, & \text{if } X(i, j) \geq l \\ 0, & \text{else.} \end{cases}$$

One fact that is obvious, yet important, is that X is the sum of its binary threshold images:

$$X = \sum_{l=1}^{M} X_l = \sum_{l=1}^{M} T_l(X). \quad (3.1)$$

The section of the image appearing in the window W can be similarly thresholded, so that

$$W[m, n] = \sum_{l=1}^{M} T_l(W[m, n]) = \sum_{l=1}^{M} w_l[m, n] \quad (3.2)$$

where $w_l[m, n] = T_l(W[m, n])$ is the binary array obtained by thresholding the pixels in the window $W[m, n]$ at level l. Note that the thresholding operator is defined in such a way that its output always has the same dimension, the same number of pixels, as its input.

The median operator is denoted as $S_{\text{med}}(\cdot)$ for reasons that will be clear later. The output image Y is obtained by taking the median of all the points inside the window W at each possible position of the window. The (m, n)th position in the output image Y is thus

$$Y(m, n) = S_{\text{med}}(W[m, n]). \quad (3.3)$$

The threshold decomposition property of the median filter [26], [27] can now be stated:

$$Y(m, n) = S_{\text{med}}(W[m, n]) = S_{\text{med}}\left(\sum_{l=1}^{M} w_l[m, n]\right)$$

$$= \sum_{l=1}^{M} S_{\text{med}}(w_l[m, n]). \quad (3.4)$$

These equalities are illustrated in Fig. 3 with a 3 × 3 square window median filter.

The property expressed in the last equality in (3.4) is clearly a superposition property, but it is a weak one. It holds only if the input to the median filter is decomposed by thresholding. Several other important points should be made regarding this superposition property.

1) The threshold decomposition holds for all rank-order operators of any dimension [27].

2) It also holds for any composition of rank-order operators [4], [27].

3) Since the input to the median filter on any threshold level is binary, the output on that level will also be binary. This is because the output of the median or any other rank-order operation is always one of the values appearing in the window of the filter. The median and other rank-order operators are thus logical operators when the input is binary.

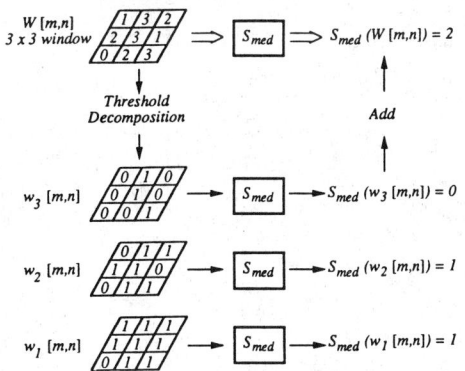

Fig. 3. Weak superposition. The broad arrows show the overall median filtering operation. The slender arrows show the same operation in its threshold decomposition architecture.

For an example illustrating item 3), suppose the bits appearing in a window with three points are x_1, x_2, and x_3. Then the median over this window is given by

$$S_{\text{med}}(x_1, x_2, x_3) = x_1 x_2 + x_2 x_3 + x_3 x_1$$

where multiplication denotes the logical AND, which is the binary version of the minimum operator [28], and addition denotes the logical OR, which is the binary version of the maximum operator [28].

The threshold decomposition reduces much of the study of rank-order operators to the study of their effects on binary signals and images. The effect on multilevel signals and images can then be determined by seeing how the results of the binary studies relate to each other on different levels, as discussed in [57].

The results in [92] illustrate how useful this last observation can be. There it is first shown that the 1-D median filter of window width $2N + 1$ will drive any binary input signal of length L to a root signal after at most

$$p(N, L) = 3 \left\lceil \frac{L - 2}{2(N + 2)} \right\rceil$$

passes of the filter. By observing the decomposition architecture shown in Fig. 3, it is then clear that making k passes of the multilevel median is equivalent to thresholding the input into binary signals, filtering each of these binary signals k times, and then adding up the output. If $k \geq p(N, L)$, then the binary signals on the different levels at the output of the kth pass are all binary root signals. The multilevel signal to which they add must then be a multilevel root signal. Thus, the window width $2N + 1$ median filter will drive any 1-D signal of length L to a root signal after no more than $p(N, L)$ passes.

B. The Stacking Property of the Median Filter

The second fundamental property of the median filter is the stacking property. Stated in its simplest form, it says that if the output of the filter on level k of the threshold decomposition architecture is a 1 at a given window position, then the outputs of all the filters on the levels below k must also be 1 at that window position [26]–[28].

To state this property, we first need the notion of stacking for arrays. The array B_1 is said to stack on (top of) the array B_2, which is assumed to have the same dimension as array B_1, if each entry of B_1 is less than or equal to the corresponding entry of B_2; in other words,

$$B_1(i, j) \leq B_2(i, j), \quad \forall i, j. \quad (3.5)$$

The notation used for this relation between arrays is

$$B_1 \leq B_2. \quad (3.6)$$

Note that any two arrays are not necessarily comparable in this fashion. This relation defines only a partial order on the set of arrays.

A set of arrays in which every pair is comparable in this fashion is the set of binary arrays obtained by thresholding any integer-valued array, or any real-valued array for that matter, at a variety of different levels. In particular, for the binary arrays w_l obtained in (3.2) by thresholding the integer-valued input W at each integer value $1-M$, we have

$$w_l[m, n] \geq w_{l+1}[m, n], \quad l = 1, 2, \cdots, M - 1. \quad (3.7)$$

This thresholding operation and its stacking property can be seen on the left side of Fig. 3.

While this stacking property of the input arrays is simply fundamental to the notion of a well-defined 2-D signal, the fact that is not so obvious, and is of tremendous interest to us, is that the median filter and all other rank-order operators, when in the threshold decomposition architecture shown in Fig. 3, carry the stacking property of the input arrays through to their output:

$$S_{\text{med}}(w_l[m, n]) \geq S_{\text{med}}(w_{l+1}[m, n]),$$
$$l = 1, 2, \cdots, M - 1. \quad (3.8)$$

Thus, the ordering from lowest to highest threshold level of the binary threshold arrays on the left side of Fig. 3 causes the binary digits on the right side of Fig. 3 to always look like a "stack" of ones (1's) with a "stack" of zeros (0's) on top. This fact has several consequences and interpretations.

1) It makes possible the direct VLSI implementation of the threshold decomposition architecture for all rank-order operators [68]. This architecture has since been improved upon; see, for instance, [71].

2) The stacking property can be interpreted as a consistency condition in the context of estimation [21]–[23]. Suppose that the goal of the filter on level k of the threshold decomposition architecture is to make the best decision, 0 or 1, at time t as to whether the signal it is estimating is less than k or not. Because of the stacking property, the level-crossing decisions made by the filters on different levels are constrained to be consistent with each other. The filter on level 3 will not decide the signal is less than 3 by putting out a 0, while the filter on level 5 decides the signal is greater than or equal to 5 by putting out a 1.

3) Any operation from $Q^{p \times q} \to Q$ has a representation in a threshold decomposition architecture with the operators on all the threshold levels satisfying the stacking property relative to each other [22].

The stacking property for a binary function $f(\cdot)$ is called the increasing property in morphology [7]–[9]. What is of interest when comparing the two approaches to nonlinear filtering is that the stacking property is not *required* of morphological operators [7]–[9] when they are implemented in the threshold decomposition architecture, even though each such filter has a representation in this architecture in which this property is obeyed [22]. Instead, morphologists would begin with a binary operator, say $f(\cdot)$, and then define the following multilevel operation for integer-valued input:

$$Y(m, n) = \max_{l} \{l : f(w_l[m, n]) = 1)\}. \quad (3.9)$$

Although (3.4) and (3.9) are equivalent when the logical operator $f(\cdot)$ is a positive Boolean function, the difference in emphasis on the stacking property is one of the primary differences between these two approaches to image processing.

C. Stack Filters and Generalized Stack Filters [4], [22]

The importance of the threshold decomposition to the analysis of the median and other rank-order filters, the importance of the threshold decomposition architecture to the VLSI implementation of these filters, and the nice consequences and interpretations of this architecture in light of the stacking property all indicate that these are fundamental properties which could be used to define a general class of filters. This is the reasoning which led to the definition of stack filters and generalized stack filters.

The first requirement of stack filters is that they have the threshold decomposition architecture, which means they must appear as shown in Fig. 4. The variability that is left in this architecture is in the choice of the function $f(\cdot)$ used on each threshold level.

The operator $f(\cdot)$ is required to be a Boolean operator. The motivation in this case is a practical one; we want the output of the filter to have the same number of quantization levels as the input. This frees the designer from worry about an expansion in number of bits for the computations at successive stages in a cascade of stack filters.

Finally, we require that the filter, which we call $S_f(\cdot)$ to indicate that it consists of a stack of logical operators, to have the following two fundamental properties.

The Threshold Decomposition Property:

$$S_f\left(\sum_{l=1}^{M} W_l\right) = \sum_{l=1}^{M} S_f(W_l) = \sum_{l=1}^{M} f(W_l). \quad (3.10)$$

The Stacking Property:

$$S_f(B_1) \geq S_f(B_2) \quad \text{whenever } B_1 \geq B_2. \quad (3.11)$$

The stacking property is sufficient to ensure that $S_f(\cdot)$ has the threshold decomposition property. The reason is

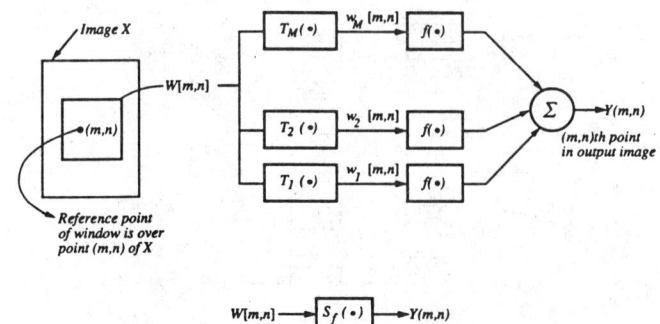

Fig. 4. The threshold decomposition architecture of the stack filter $S_f(\cdot)$. The filter $S_f(\cdot)$ is shown in its gray-level notation and in its threshold decomposition architecture. Note that if $S_f(\cdot)$ has binary input $w_i[m, n]$, then $S_f(w_i[m, n]) = f(w_i[m, n])$.

that, for (3.11) to be met, we must have

$$f(B_1) \geq f(B_2) \quad \text{whenever } B_1 \geq B_2 \quad (3.12)$$

and B_1 and B_2 are binary arrays. Gilbert [93] showed that a necessary and sufficient condition for a Boolean function to satisfy this property is that the operator be a positive Boolean function. These are all logical operators whose *minimum sum of products (MSP) expression* does not have any complements, only AND and OR operations. Also, if the Boolean function is positive, it has a *unique* MSP expression.

For example, the 2-D Boolean operator

$$f\left(\begin{bmatrix} x_{11} & x_{12} \\ x_{21} & x_{22} \end{bmatrix}\right) = x_{11}x_{21} + x_{22}x_{11}x_{12}, \quad (3.13)$$

which is in its MSP form, is positive since it uses only AND operations, which are denoted by multiplication, and OR operations, which are denoted by addition. If complementation is denoted by an overbar, then a Boolean function which is not positive might be

$$f\left(\begin{bmatrix} x_{11} & x_{12} \\ x_{21} & x_{22} \end{bmatrix}\right) = \bar{x}_{11}x_{21} + x_{22}\overline{x_{11}x_{12}}.$$

Since there are no complements, any positive Boolean function has a representation as an OR (MAX) of AND (MIN) terms [4], [9], [28], [37]. If the positive Boolean function is used on each threshold level, then the overall multilevel operation obeys the threshold decomposition since it is simply a composition of rank-order operators and they all obey the threshold decomposition. For instance, the gray-level version of the Boolean operation $f(\cdot)$ in (3.13) is

$$S_f\left(\begin{bmatrix} X_{11} & X_{12} \\ X_{21} & X_{22} \end{bmatrix}\right)$$

$$= \text{MAX}(\text{MIN}(X_{11}, X_{21}), \text{MIN}(X_{22}, X_{11}, X_{12})).$$

Thus, the preservation of the stacking property leads naturally to a definition of a filter class that is exactly the set of all compositions of rank-order filters within a finite window.

One more generalization must be made—to the class of generalized stack filters [22]. In this class of filters, there is still a single logical operator associated with each level in the threshold decomposition architecture, but the number of threshold arrays fed into each filter is allowed to vary. Furthermore, in generalized stack filters, the filters on different levels of the threshold decomposition architecture are allowed to be different. These filters must, however, still obey the stacking property.

When different filters are used on different levels, the stacking property becomes an ordering for operators on neighboring levels. For instance, the logical operators f_l and f_{l+1} on levels l and $l + 1$, respectively, must satisfy

$$f_l(B_1) \geq f_{l+1}(B_2) \quad \text{whenever } B_1 \geq B_2.$$

If $f_l \neq f_{l+1}$, then f_l and f_{l+1} need not be positive to preserve the stacking property.

A generalized stack filter $S_F(\cdot)$ with M levels in its threshold decomposition architecture is defined by an ordered set F of logical operators $F = \{f_1, f_2, \cdots, f_M\}$. If each of these logical operators observes the $2I + 1$ threshold levels nearest to its level where I is any non-negative integer, then the filter's operation is defined as follows:

$$S_F(W) = \sum_{l=1}^{M} f_l(w_{l-I} | w_{l-I+1} | \cdots | w_{l+I}) \quad (3.14)$$

in which the notation "|" implies concatenation of the binary threshold arrays on the indicated levels. In addition, we require the following stacking property:

$$f_l(w_{l-I} | w_{l-I+1} | \cdots | w_{l+I})$$
$$\geq f_{l+1}(w_{l-I+1} | w_{l-I+2} | \cdots | w_{l+I+1}). \quad (3.15)$$

Fig. 5 shows the architecture of a specific generalized stack filter. Both logical operators in this architecture are fed three binary threshold arrays. To keep everything well defined, it is thus necessary to add the binary threshold arrays for levels 3 and 0 to the threshold decomposition of the input. These "dummy levels" allow one to consider each filter in the architecture to have $2I + 1$ binary arrays fed into it without having to worry about the boundaries.

The intuition behind generalized stack filters is quite simple.

1) Suppose that each binary filter's input is the $2I + 1$ threshold arrays nearest to its level: the arrays on its level and the I levels above and below the filter. The output of the multilevel filter implemented this way can change by no more than $2I + 1$ for a change of size 1 in any pixel in the gray-level input array. Through I, the designer controls the degree of smoothing performed by the filter.

2) Since each filter observes more threshold levels as the index I is increased, each one has more information on which to base its output decision. It theoretically can then do a better job of estimating some desired signal in

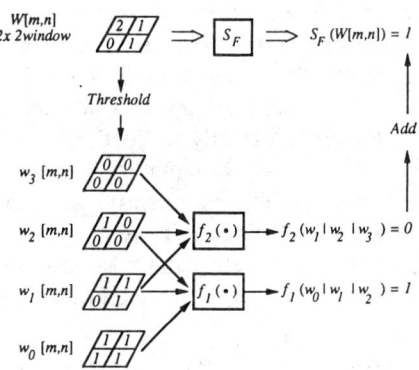

Fig. 5. A simple generalized stack filter $S_F(\cdot)$. The set $F = \{f_1, f_2\}$ of operators is given by $f_1(w_0 | w_1 | w_2) = R_5(w_0 | w_1 | w_2)$, $f_2(w_1 | w_2 | w_3) = R_4(w_1 | w_2 | w_3)$ where $R_n(\cdot)$ is the rank-order operator which puts out the nth largest point in its window.

noise, or of preserving, deleting, or modifying certain structures.

3) The interpretation of the function of the filter on level l as making decisions as to whether the desired image is less than l or not still holds as in stack filters. Consistency between decisions made on different levels is enforced by (3.15).

Even with the requirement that the filters on different levels of a generalized stack filter have the stacking property relative to each other, the class of filtering operations has not been restricted by very much. In fact, if every pixel of the input array takes on values in the set $Q = \{0, 1, \cdots, M\}$, then every function $F: Q^k \rightarrow Q$ where k is the number of pixels in the filter's window has a representation as a generalized stack filter with M threshold levels.

IV. MEAN ABSOLUTE ERROR ESTIMATION AND STACK FILTERS [21]

The stack filters and generalized stack filters defined in the previous section are a very large class of filters. The number of stack filters grows faster than $2^{2^{n/2}}$ where n is the number of pixels in the window of the filter.

This doubly exponential increase in n immediately prohibits simple exhaustive searches for a stack filter which is best for a given application. One possible alternative is to consider only subclasses of stack filters and to develop heuristics for how and when to apply filters from these subclasses. Before settling for this suboptimal alternative, though, it is important to see if an efficient analytical technique can be developed to find a best stack filter.

The search for this efficient analytical approach is set, in this section, in the context of the estimation approach to image processing. The structural approach is considered in Section V.

Within the estimation approach, the first step in the development of a filter design algorithm is the choice of an error criterion. In Section IV-A, the absolute error criterion is chosen since it simplifies in a very nice way in the presence of the stacking property and since it shows some interesting signs of being appropriate for image processing. In Section IV-B, the nonadaptive estimation approach is considered. It leads to a linear program for finding a stack filter which is optimal under the mean absolute error criterion. The theory of optimal adaptive stack filtering [23] is mentioned briefly in Section IV-C.

Finally, some examples showing how this optimization theory may be used in both its adaptive and nonadaptive forms are provided. Of particular interest is how the optimization procedure can select the best window size and shape within the window for which the procedure was run.

A. Selecting an Error Criterion: The Mean Absolute Error

Since stack filters are a generalization of the median filter, it is natural to look to that filter for the choice of an error criterion for estimation with stack filters. The criterion that immediately presents itself is the mean absolute error criterion. The reason is that the conditional median minimizes the mean absolute error criterion.

Before using this error criterion, though, it is important to determine if it is appropriate for image processing. A review of previous work in the area would not seem to indicate that the MAE is appropriate. In fact, previous efforts with both the MAE criterion and its neighbor, the MSE criterion, have not been very successful—see, for instance, the comments and references in [94] with regard to these error criteria and efforts to find an analytic error criterion that agrees with early visual processes. It thus appears that neither of the traditional analytical criteria may be appropriate, so what is to be done?

The first thing to be done is to determine the true source of failure in these previous efforts. It is possible that they failed not because of the error criterion, but because of the class of filters over which the criterion was applied. For instance, a linear filter which is optimal in the mean-squared sense is still a linear filter. It will thus blur any sharp edges in the image. This says a lot about linear filters, but not much about the MSE criterion.

Thus, when considering a new class of filters under a particular error criterion, all pronouncements on the effectiveness of that error criterion that are based on experiences with some other class of filters must be carefully examined.

The above line of argument resurrects both the MSE and MAE criteria, so we are back to asking the question, "Why the MAE criterion?"

One significant reason for using the MAE criterion is robustness. As discussed in the first chapter of [95], the MAE is superior to the MSE from the point of view of distributional robustness. There are, of course, error measures that are even more robust than the MAE, as explicitly pointed out in [96]. In this paper, though, we are only interested in the comparison between the MAE and MSE criteria. For a thorough discussion of the robust estimation approach to image processing, see [96], which discusses robust image models and the class of filters known as M filters.

Another reason for choosing the MAE criterion is some experimental evidence that human beings use the MAE criterion when solving certain estimation problems, and that they actually prefer it to the MSE criterion.[4] This evidence can be found in the results of a psychology experiment reported in [97]. The subjects in the experiment were asked to produce location estimates from i.i.d. observations of a random variable with a J-shaped probability density function. The J shape guaranteed that the median and the mean of the distribution were significantly different. The subjects were rewarded for picking estimates which maximized certain reward functions. The optimal estimate for one reward function was the mean; for the other, it was the median. The interesting result is that under *both* reward functions, the subjects tended to compute the median. This was true even if they had been trained for and would have been more heavily rewarded for computing the mean.

Thus, human beings, at least in this experiment, were able to compute the conditional median, but not the conditional mean. This suggests that the MAE criterion might prove useful in image processing since it leads to the conditional median as the optimal estimator. The examples in Section IV-D provide more evidence in this direction.

B. Superposition, Stacking, and Simplification of the MAE Criterion [21]–[23]

The optimal filtering problem over the class of stack filters is illustrated in Fig. 6. The process $W[m, n]$ appearing in the window of a 2-D stack filter is assumed to be a windowed version of an altered version of some desired image X. The corruption may be caused either by a noise process $N(m, n)$ or by some intentional operation, such as modulation.

At each window position (m, n), the stack filter output is an estimate, called $\hat{X}(m, n)$, of $X(m, n)$, the gray-level value of the desired image at the point (m, n). This estimate is based on $W[m, n]$, the gray-level values observed in the window of the stack filter; thus,

$$\hat{X}(m, n) = S_f(W[m, n]). \quad (4.1)$$

The goal is to pick a stack filter from the class of stack filters with $p \times q$ rectangular windows such that at each window position, the average mean absolute error between the filter's output and the desired signal is minimized. If $W[m, n]$ and $X(m, n)$ are jointly stationary (relative to m and n) random processes, then the cost to be minimized by proper choice of $f(\cdot)$ is

$$\text{MAE}_f = E\big[\big|X(m, n) - S_f(W[m, n])\big|\big]. \quad (4.2)$$

The key to the theory of MMAE stack filtering is that in the context of stack filters, the MAE criterion can be reduced to the sum of the level-crossing decision errors

---

[4]Or at least the estimates humans form, for whatever reason, are the same as those that would be formed if the MAE were being minimized.

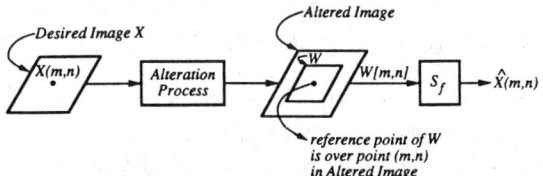

Fig. 6. The optimal stack filtering problem is to find the stack filter $S_f(\cdot)$ or, equivalently, the positive Boolean function $f(\cdot)$ which minimizes $E[|X(m, n) - \hat{X}(m, n)|]$.

incurred by the Boolean filters on each level of the threshold decomposition architecture. The threshold decomposition and stacking properties are what make this reduction possible.

To demonstrate this fact, consider the mean absolute error incurred when the stack filter $S_f(\cdot)$ is used. Let $x_k(m, n) = T_k(X(m, n))$ and $w_k[m, n] = T_k(W[m, n])$ where $T_k(\cdot)$ is again the threshold operation at level k. For each k, $x_k(m, n)$ is a binary digit, while $w_k[m, n]$ is a binary array. Then

$$\text{MAE}_f = E\left[|X(m, n) - S_f(W[m, n])|\right] \quad (4.3)$$

$$= E\left[\left|\sum_{k=1}^{M} \left(x_k(m, n) - S_f(T_k(W[m, n]))\right)\right|\right] \quad (4.4)$$

$$= E\left[\left|\sum_{k=1}^{M} \left(x_k(m, n) - f(w_k[m, n])\right)\right|\right]. \quad (4.5)$$

The second and third equalities are a consequence of the threshold decomposition property of stack filters and (3.1) and (3.2).

Now examine the sum inside (4.5). Note that every term in this sum which is not zero will have the same sign. This follows from the stacking property of thresholding [see (3.7)] and from the stacking property of the positive Boolean function $f(\cdot)$. In more detail, if we look at the row vectors

$$\vec{x} = [x_1(m, n) \, x_2(m, n) \, \cdots \, x_M(m, n)]$$
$$\vec{y} = [f(w_1[m, n]) f(w_2[m, n]) \, \cdots \, f(w_M[m, n])], \quad (4.6)$$

each one must be a string of ones followed by a string of zeros. For $\vec{x}$, this fact is obvious from the definition of thresholding. For $\vec{y}$, it follows since $f(\cdot)$ is a logical operator, so its output is binary since $w_i[m, n] \geq w_{i+1}[m, n]$ for all i, and since $f(\cdot)$ is positive so that it has the stacking property

$$f(w_i[m, n]) \geq f(w_{i+1}[m, n]), \quad \forall \, i. \quad (4.7)$$

Thus, entry-wise subtraction of these vectors always results in another vector whose entries are all nonpositive or all nonnegative. For instance, [11111000] − [11000000] = [00111000].

The consequence of these arguments is that (4.5) becomes

$$\text{MAE}_f = \sum_{k=1}^{M} E\left[|x_k(m, n) - f(w_k[m, n])|\right]. \quad (4.8)$$

Thus, for stack filters, the multilevel mean absolute error is reduced to the sum of the mean absolute errors on each of the levels of the threshold decomposition architecture.

Note, though, that the error on each threshold level is simply the error that results from a level-crossing detection problem. This problem is to find the Boolean function $f(\cdot)$ which makes the best decision at each location (m, n) as to whether the desired image value at (m, n) is less than k or not, subject to the stacking constraint. The stacking constraint simply forces the decisions on different levels to be consistent with each other. As mentioned before, this means the filter on level 3 cannot say the desired image value is less than 3 by putting out a zero if the filter on level 5 has decided the desired image value is greater than or equal to 5.

In summary, for stack filters, the mean absolute error criterion reduces to massively parallel optimal level-crossing decision making when the decisions are all coordinated with each other [21]-[23].

The analytical significance of this tie to detection is that it allows the cost function to be written as a linear function of the decisions the filter makes for each possible binary array observed in the window of the filter. Without going into complete detail, if $p_f(w_j)$ is defined to be the (0 or 1) decision the Boolean function $f(\cdot)$ makes when w_j, the jth of the 2^{pq} possible binary arrays, is in the filter's window, then there are constants C_j such that

$$\text{MAE}_f = \sum_{j=1}^{2^{pq}} C_j p_f(w_j). \quad (4.9)$$

The coefficients C_j depend on the joint statistics of the corrupted and the desired processes. A complete description of the joint statistics is not necessary, only the joint level-crossing behavior of the corrupted and the desired process must be known. Details on the meaning and computation of the C_j's can be found in [21]-[23].

It is important to remember that (4.8) and (4.9) are valid only when $f(\cdot)$ is a positive Boolean function, i.e., when $S_f(\cdot)$ is a stack filter. This must be considered when trying to find the $f(\cdot)$ which minimizes (4.8) and (4.9). Thus, finding the optimal filter requires minimizing the linear function of the $p_f(\cdot)$'s in (4.9) subject to the constraint that these quantities obey the stacking property, i.e., that they define a *positive* Boolean function.

This stacking constraint can be expressed as a set of inequalities in terms of these decision variables:

$$p_f(w_i) \leq p_f(w_j) \quad \text{if } w_i \leq w_j \quad (4.10)$$

where w_i and w_j are the ith and jth possible binary arrays of dimension $p \times q$. Recall that two $p \times q$ binary arrays s and t satisfy $s \leq t$ if and only if each entry of s is less than or equal to the corresponding entry in t. The optimal filtering problem over the class of stack filters under the mean absolute error criterion can therefore be formulated as the following zero-one integer linear program:

$$\text{minimize} \sum_{j=1}^{2^{pq}} C_j p_f(w_j) \qquad (4.11)$$

subject to the constraints

$$p_f(w_i) \leq p_f(w_j) \quad \text{if } w_i \leq w_j \qquad (4.12)$$

$$p_f(w_j) = 0 \text{ or } 1 \quad \text{for all } j. \qquad (4.13)$$

Integer linear programming is, of course, NP complete unless it has special structure. In this case, the structure required is present. When the constraints in (4.12) are rewritten as a matrix, the resulting matrix is TUM (totally unimodular [98]). This implies that the zero-one integer linear program can be formulated as the following linear program [21]-[23]:

$$\text{minimize} \sum_{j=1}^{2^{pq}} C_j p_f(w_j) \qquad (4.14)$$

subject to the constraints

$$p_f(w_i) \leq p_f(w_j) \quad \text{if } w_i \leq w_j \qquad (4.15)$$

$$0 \leq p_f(w_j) \leq 1 \quad \text{for all } j. \qquad (4.16)$$

The linear programming formulation of the optimization problem has a very nice interpretation in terms of the behavior of the Boolean operator $f(\cdot)$. The constraint in (4.16) implies that the filter is allowed to randomize its decisions. The quantity $p_f(w_j)$ is thus the probability the filter puts out a 1 when the binary array w_j is observed. The filter is thus allowed to make soft decisions.

The stacking constraints in (4.15) are still required in this soft decision case, although it should be noted that the binary filters' outputs then stack only in the average sense; at particular time instants, the deterministic stacking constraint may be violated. Even with this extension to soft decisions, *there is always an optimal filter which makes hard decisions* [21]-[23]. This follows from the total unimodularity of the constraint matrix consisting of (4.15) and (4.16). The output of the linear program in (4.14)-(4.16) is always an optimal filter which makes hard decisions.

The constraints in (4.15) and (4.16) have many redundant equations. This redundancy can be easily removed, as shown in [21]. The number of constraints can be reduced to $b2^{b-1}$ where b is the number of pixels in the window. Thus, the number of constraints in the linear program is exponential in the window size. Although this is undesirable, it is much better than the exhaustive search through the more than $2^{2^{b}/2}$ possible stack filters for a b pixel window. Also, the constraint matrix in (4.14) is very sparse—there are only two nonzero entries in each row—so some specialized linear programming algorithm whose complexity is less than exponential in the size of the window might exist.

As an example of an application of this optimization theory, we summarize an example from [99]. There, the input to the filter is a scan line of a binary image that has been corrupted by noise. The uncorrupted version of the scan line was assumed to be a binary root signal for a window width five median filter and the noise was assumed to set the signal to zero or one or leave it uncorrupted, according to which state a particular Markov chain was in. The error criterion used was a weighted mean absolute error criterion—certain errors were assigned higher costs than others. In particular, when $C(\overline{W}, 1, 0) = 1$ in the table below, the error criterion is the (unweighted) mean absolute error criterion.

The goal in this example was to find the best window width five stack filter. The optimal filters which were produced for different weightings of the cost $C(\overline{W}, 1, 0)$ of an incorrect positive-going level-crossing decision can be seen in the table below. When $C(\overline{W}, 1, 0) = 1$, the error criterion is the (unweighted) mean absolute error criterion. Note that none of these optimal filters is the median filter, even though the desired signal is a root of the window width five median filter.

$C(\overline{W}, 1, 0)$	$f(x_1, x_2, x_3, x_4, x_5)$	W.MAE
0.1	$x_2 x_3 x_4$	0.0389
0.2	$x_1 x_3 x_4 + x_2 x_3 x_4 + x_2 x_3 x_5$	0.0694
1.0	$x_2 x_3 + x_3 x_4 + x_1 x_2 x_4 x_5$	0.1662
2.0	$x_3 + x_2 x_4$	0.2164
5.0	$x_2 + x_4$	0.3325
10.0	$x_2 + x_3 + x_4$	0.3614

These results are interesting since the filter was allowed to have a window width of five, *yet in one case, the optimal filter ended up having a split window with only two points in it*. The optimization program thus selected a smaller window within the optimization window as being the best window. The linear program can thus be used to select the best size and shape of a window in addition to selecting the filter to be used within that window.

C. Optimal Adaptive Stack Filtering [23]

The preceding section reviewed a nonadaptive methodology for finding a stack filter which minimizes the mean absolute error between its output and a desired image. There are, at this time, several problems with this methodology.

First, it requires either knowledge or estimation of the coefficients in the cost function which is to be minimized in the linear programming procedure.

Second, the number of variables and constraints in the linear program grows exponentially in the window width of the filter. The largest window size that can be run using standard linear programs, such as the ones available in IMSL, is a 3 × 3 window. This limitation can probably be corrected by exploiting the sparseness of the constraint matrix in (4.15)—it has only two nonzero entries in each row—or by using some interior point algorithm.

Finally, the corrupted process and the desired process were required to be jointly stationary, which is almost certainly never the case in image processing.

With these problems as motivation, a theory of optimal adaptive stack filtering has been developed. This approach eliminates the stationarity assumption, it is computationally efficient, and it does not require direct computation of the statistics of the corrupted and desired images. It does, however, require the existence of a training sequence.

There is not enough space to review this adaptive approach here (see [23] for a full exposition); instead, some examples we have run using this approach are provided.

D. An Example Using Adaptive Stack Filters

The image processing example which will be used to illustrate the performance of the adaptive stack filtering algorithm is the same as the examples used in [6]. This allows direct comparison of the optimal filtering results with the heuristically determined rank-order based filters that are discussed and compared in [6].

Fig. 7(a) repeats the image from [6, Fig. 6(a)]. Fig. 7(b) shows the image in (a) after it has been corrupted with impulsive noise. This is the same noisy image as in [6, Fig. 6(b)].

One-quarter of each of the images in Fig. 7(a) and (b) were fed into the adaptive stack filtering algorithm to train a stack filter with a 4×4 window and a generalized stack filter with a 3×3 window with three binary threshold arrays fed into the filter on each level of the threshold decomposition architecture.

The optimal filters determined by the training algorithm were then used to filter the noisy image. The resulting images are shown in Fig. 7(c) and (d). As can be seen by comparing these two images, the 4×4 stack filter did a better job of removing the noise. This is not surprising since its window was larger, there was less chance of the noise clustering together to form impulses comparable in size to the window. Both of these optimal filters did a very good job of preserving details in the image. The edges of the bridge are sharp, the grass in the foreground has been preserved, and even the foliage in the background is well preserved.

It is instructive to compare the outputs of these optimal filters to the outputs obtained with the various filters used in [6] (see [6, Fig. 6(c)-(h)]. To facilitate this comparison, Fig. 7(e) and (f) repeat the two images in [6] that were obtained with a 5×5 window multistage median filter and a 5×5 morphological filter.

Two conclusions can be drawn from these comparisons. The first is that the structural approach which resulted in the synthesis of the multistage median filter and the morphological filter used in these examples was quite successful. It achieved approximately the same MAE as the optimal stack filter discussed above. The filters it yielded are not as efficient as the optimal stack filter, though, since they require a 25 pixel window instead of a 16 pixel window to achieve the same MAE.

The second conclusion to be drawn is that the MMAE stack filtering approach presented in this paper yields structural results which are at least as good as those obtained with the synthesis-based structural approach. This is significant since the program we used to find the optimal stack filter required approximately 20 h to run, which compares very favorably to the years of design and filtering experience required before the synthesis-based structural approach yielded the multistage median filter and morphological filter which worked so well in the above examples. It is thus clear that if the characteristics of the noise or the image were to change significantly from those in the above examples, the optimal filtering approach should be used to solve the new problem—if only to save time.

The program we used to train the optimal filters described above did not exploit any of the inherent parallelism in the adaptation algorithm nor did it efficiently manipulate the image data—we were more interested in getting the results than in getting them efficiently. Because of this and a very crude method of determining when the training was complete, it took many hours of CPU time to find the optimal filter. Much work is needed to speed up this program; it should take at most a few hours to run.

V. Optimal Stack Filtering Under Structural Constraints [24]

In Section IV, a theory of minimum mean absolute error stack filtering was developed. This, however, is only half of the picture. It shows how to find a filter which is best for removing "noise" from an image, but it does not really allow the designer to incorporate into the filter design procedure any *a priori* knowledge of the structure of the desired image and the structures introduced when the image is altered. In other words, it cannot account for the structural approach to filter design. This is a serious defect since a great deal of success has been achieved with the structural approach to image processing.

This could possibly be corrected if there were an analytical procedure for the design of filters satisfying various structural constraints that could be appended to the estimation procedure. Unfortunately, such a procedure is not currently available, or at least not one that is useful over a class of filters as large as stack filters.

Most previous procedures developed for this problem have, with the exception of the new results reported in [16], largely involved detailed studies of the deterministic behavior of specific filters, and then the use of these studies as guides to which filters to use to achieve the desired structural effect. While this approach has worked fine for problems in which there are not many different structural constraints, it will break down when the number of con-

(a)

Fig. 7. (a) Original image of bridge over stream. Same as [6, Fig. 6(a)]. (b) Noise corrupted image of bridge over stream. Same as [6, Fig. 6(b)]. (c) Output of optimal stack filter with a 4 × 4 rectangular window with image in (b) as input. The filter was trained using one-quarter of (a) and (b). (d) Output of an optimal generalized stack filter with a 3 × 3 rectangular window and three threshold levels fed into each filter. The input image to this filter was (b). The filter was trained using the upper left corners of (a) and (b). (e) Output of 5 × 5 multistage median filter with (b) as input. This is the same as [6, Fig. 6(d)]. The filter is specified in (3) in the Appendix. (f) Output of a morphological filter with (b) as input. This is the same as [6, Fig. 6(f)]. The filter is specified in (6) in the Appendix.

(b)

Fig. 7. (Continued.)

straints becomes large or if the different constraints begin to overlap.

Thus, before the structural approach can be combined with the MMAE approach to stack filtering, a theory of optimal stack filtering under structural constraints must be developed. This is the subject of this section.

A logical place to begin this development is with the study of local and global structures which are invariant to stack filtering operations. By analogy with the median filter, these signals will be called root signals [2].

A general-purpose method is presented in Section V-A for first determining whether a given stack filter has any

(c)

Fig. 7. (Continued.)

root signals and then characterizing the structural behavior of these roots. These results allow characterization of the effects of any stack filter on the global structure of an image. The results in this section are the beginning of the generalization to 2-D of the 1-D results proven in [24]. The results in [24] are themselves a generalization of the approach developed in [56], [57] for the 1-D median filter.

Section V-B presents a technique for determining whether there is any stack filter in the specified window which has the desired structural behavior. This test is important since it determines if one should seek a different

(d)

Fig. 7. (Continued.)

(larger) window for the filter or if one should settle for finding a filter which comes closest to providing the desired behavior. The section ends with an algorithm which will find a stack filter in a given window which, if it does not actually satisfy the structural constraints exactly, will come as close as possible among all filters over that window.

These results should be of great interest to workers in morphology since they provide the first approach to the design of optimal compositions of morphological filters with a desired structural behavior.

A. Existence and Characterization of Root Signals

To determine the root signal behavior of a given stack filter, it is sufficient to determine the root signal behavior of the filter on a binary image. The results for gray-valued

(e)

Fig. 7. (*Continued.*)

images can then be obtained by reversing the threshold decomposition or, more precisely, by determining which binary root signals can be stacked on top of each other in the sense of (3.7). Examples showing how this can be done for the recursive separable median filter can be seen in [100], and a graph-theoretic approach extending the results in [56] to multivalued root signals of the median filter can be found in [57].

This can be most easily illustrated with the 1-D median filter. The finite-length binary root signals of a window width $2N + 1$, 1-D median filter consist of alternating sequences of zeros and ones where each sequence of one of the values is at least $N + 1$ samples long. The multivalued roots for the 1-D median filter can then be determined by seeing which binary root signals can be stacked on top of one another.

(f)

Fig. 7. (*Continued*.)

Thus, we restrict our attention to binary images. The problem of stacking the resulting 2-D binary root signals that are found is not considered here.

Any stack filter has a particular window W through which it observes the binary image. The motion of this window over the binary array is described by the motion of the reference point in the window. We will assume that this reference point touches each point in the image once; that is, none is skipped.

Create a graph, called the *window process graph* [24], which has one node for each of the possible binary arrays that can be seen in the filter's window. There are two sets of directed edges in this graph; the up edges and the right edges. The up edges determine the sequence of binary arrays that can be observed in the window as its reference point is advanced one point at a time in the vertical direction. The right edges determine the sequence of binary arrays that can be observed in the window as its reference point is advanced one point at a time to the right.

As an example, consider the reverse-L shaped window shown in Fig. 8, which has its reference point in the lower right corner. The median operator is performed on the pixel values in this window.

The window process graph for the reverse-L window is shown in Fig. 9 with its right edges shown in part (a) of the figure and its up edges shown in part (b). The full window process graph is obtained by adding the edges from one of the graphs to the other. It is very important, though, to keep the edges labeled as either up or right edges separate since this will be very important later.

Once the window process graph has been specified, it can be used to determine the root signal behavior of any stack filter $S_f(\cdot)$. First, recall that for each possible binary array w_j in the window, we have $f(w_j) = S_f(w_j)$ when the binary array w_j is in the filter's window.

Create a new directed graph, which is called the *stack filter digraph for $S_f(\cdot)$* [24], by thinning the window process graph as follows.

1) Delete any node in the window process graph which corresponds to a binary array w_j for which $f(w_j)$ is different from the value at the reference point in the array. Also, delete any edges ending or originating in the nodes which must be deleted.

2) Delete any nodes which have either no outgoing or no incoming edges.

3) If there is no difference between the output graph from Step 2) and the input graph for Step 2), then stop; otherwise, repeat Step 2).

A particular stack filter digraph is shown in two pieces in Fig. 10. It is for the filter $S_{\text{med}}(\cdot)$ with the window shown in Fig. 8. This filter puts out the middle value appearing in the L-shaped window. The right edges for this graph are shown in (a), the up edges in (b); the entire graph is obtained by adding the edges from one of the graphs to the other.

Once a stack filter's digraph has been determined, it is possible to determine whether the stack filter has any 2-D root signals. A necessary condition for the existence of at least one nontrivial, infinite extent 2-D root is that there be at least one *elementary cycle*[5] of all up edges or one elementary cycle of all right edges in the stack filter's directed graph. This is rather obvious since if there are no cycles, then there is no infinite length sequence of binary arrays for which the filter's output for each of the binary arrays is the same as the reference point in each array.

This test is very simple to apply since there are already many different algorithms, the most reliable of which seems to be [101], for searching directed graphs for

[5]A *cycle* is a subset of nodes interconnected by edges, such that there is a path, which may traverse many nodes, from any one node to any other node in the subset. The cycle is *elementary* if each node appears only once.

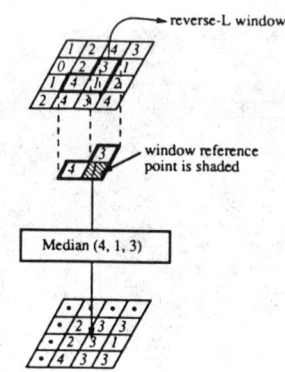

Fig. 8. A reverse-L shaped window which feeds a median filter. The coordinates of the points in the window are measured relative to the reference point.

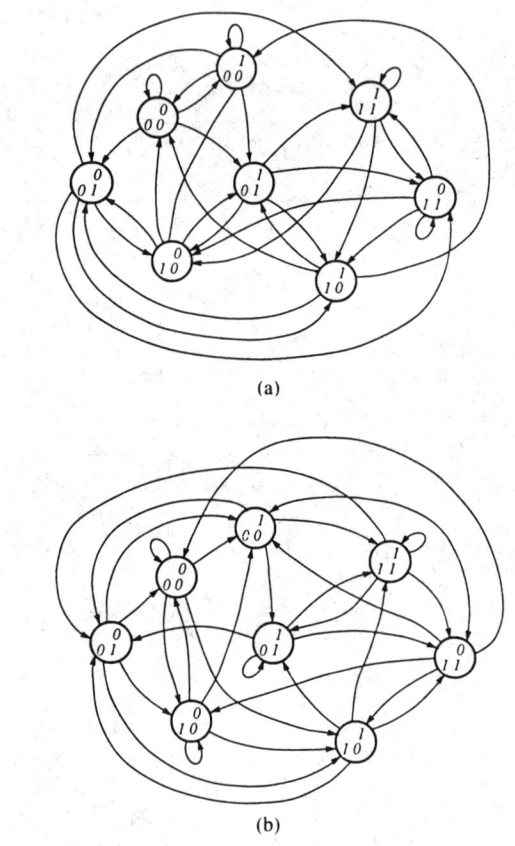

Fig. 9. The window process graph for the reverse-L shaped window shown in Fig. 8. The right edges for this graph are shown in (a), the up edges in (b).

cycles. It should be noted, though, that finding cycles in a graph is an NP-complete problem. There are, however, algorithms of polynomial complexity which can tell, with high probability of being correct, whether there is a Hamiltonian cycle or not [102].

A stronger necessary condition for the existence of a 2-D root signal is that there exists at least one set of nodes in which each node is a member of a cycle of up edges *and* a cycle of right edges. This test, unfortunately, requires enumerating all elementary cycles of up edges and of right edges.

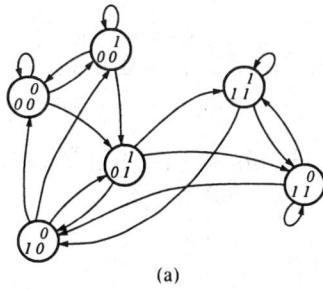

(a)

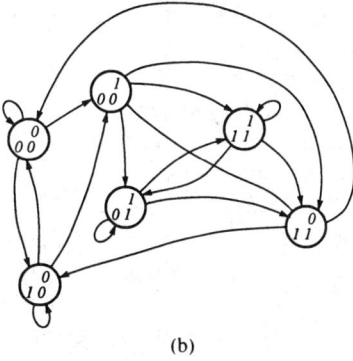

(b)

Fig. 10. The stack filter digraph for the filter $S_{\text{med}}(\cdot)$ with the window shown in Fig. 8. The right edges are shown in (a), the up edges in (b).

A nontrivial, infinite-extent, 2-D root signal exists for a stack filter with a finite window if its stack filter digraph contains at least one nontrivial toroidal network. In this toroidal network, the canonical form of which is shown in Fig. 11, all the vertical cycles are made of up edges from the stack filter digraph, while the horizontal cycles are made of right edges. There are many possible variations from the canonical toroid which are allowed. For instance, not all of the up cycles need have the same number of nodes since a node may be repeated in a cycle.

Fig. 12 shows one of the toroidal networks from the stack filter digraph in Fig. 10. A portion of a 2-D infinite extent periodic root signal that can be generated from this toroid is shown in Fig. 13. More complex behavior can be obtained when toroids intersect with each other. The resulting roots need not be periodic in this case.

The number of different types of root signal behavior exhibited by a given stack filter is determined by the number of distinct *elementary* toroids that its stack filter digraph contains. Toroids which intersect each other can be considered to be in the same equivalence class. Whether a stack filter digraph has more than one equivalence class is an indication of the discrimination ability of the filter.

The above discussion is significant because it shows that the investigation of the root signal behavior of stack filters is very closely related to the study of the topology of directed graphs.

In summary, the concepts of stack filter digraphs and toroids in these graphs provide a means of characterizing the 2-D signals which are preserved by a given stack filter. This is one aspect of significant importance for the structural approach to filter design since one frequent goal of this approach is to pick a filter for which the desired

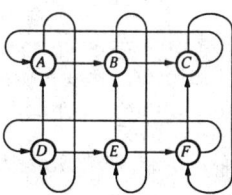

Fig. 11. The canonical form of a vertical period 2, horizontal period 3 toroid. The toroid is elementary if no vertical cycle is repeated, and no horizontal cycle is repeated, i.e., if $C = B$ and $E = F$, then a vertical cycle is repeated and the toroid is no longer elementary.

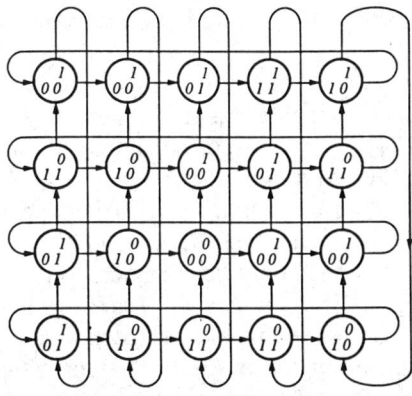

Fig. 12. A toroid constructed from the stack filter digraph in Fig. 10. The vertical edges shown above are up edges in the graph in Fig. 10; the horizontal edges are right edges from Fig. 10. This toroid has a vertical period of 4 and a horizontal period of 5. It generates some of the 2-D periodic roots of the filter $S_{\text{med}}(\cdot)$ with the window shown in Fig. 8.

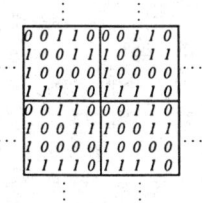

Fig. 13. A periodic 2-D root signal of $S_{\text{med}}(\cdot)$ when it has the reverse-L window shown in Fig. 8. This root was generated from the toroid in Fig. 12 by picking off the reference point in the lower right corner of each node.

image contains structures which are 2-D root signals of this filter.

Of course, the converse of the above problem of characterizing root signals must be considered as well. This is the problem of determining what a given filter does to signals which are not root signals. Does it drive them to a root signal after some number of passes of the filter or do successive passes produce oscillatory or other unstable behavior? This problem appears to be at least several orders of magnitude harder than the problem of finding and characterizing root signals, but it is a very important problem. Results on the convergence question can be found in [2], [4], [43], [44], [92], [103], [104], and [108].

It should be mentioned at this point that much work has also been done in morphology with regard to designing filters which preserve specific signals or structures. The work on morphological filters with multiple structuring elements [105], [106] is a very good example of the work in this area.

The results in the following section indicate how a stack filter which does the best job of providing a specified structural behavior can be determined.

B. Design of Stack Filters with Specific 2-D Behavior

Does there exist a stack filter (or generalized stack filter) which will preserve, delete, or otherwise modify each local or global structure on a list of structures that might appear in some image?

If there is a stack filter with the desired behavior, how can it be found; and if there is not one, how can one that comes the "closest" to doing what is desired be found?

These two questions are really at the heart of the structural approach to the design of nonlinear filters for image processing. They may also be considered the fundamental questions asked in morphology.

Since the class of stack filters is being considered, and since all these filters obey the threshold decomposition, these questions need only be considered in the context of binary images. This follows since any results for the binary case can be extrapolated to the gray-level case through appropriate use of (3.10). In most situations, this is easy since the same structural behavior is usually desired on all the levels of the threshold decomposition architecture for the sake of scale invariant operation of the filter.

If the structural behavior the designer wants from the filter varies from level to level of the image, then some problems may arise with the use of a stack filter. Since the stack filter has the same Boolean operation on each level, it cannot satisfy requirements on different levels which conflict with each other. If, for instance, the goals are to remove all 4×4 square structures appearing in the binary array on level 6 but preserve them on level 3, a stack filter will not work. In such cases, a generalized stack filter, which can have different filters on different levels, must be used.

At any rate, in the remainder of this section, we consider only binary images as the inputs to the stack filter $S_f(\cdot)$. For binary input, the operation of the filter $S_f(\cdot)$ is the same as the operation of the positive Boolean function $f(\cdot)$.

The first step in answering the questions posed above is the development of a measure of how closely a filter's operation comes to providing the desired structural behavior. This measure must be a function of the desired output of the filter and the decisions made by the positive Boolean function $f(\cdot)$.

We will also need some new notation. Again, letting w_j be the jth of all the possible binary arrays seen in the window of the filter, define $r(w_j)$ to be the value of the pixel at the reference point in the window. For instance, if the filter has a reverse-L shaped window as in Fig. 8, with the reference point in the lower right corner of the L, then

$$r\begin{pmatrix} 0 \\ 0 \ 0 \end{pmatrix} = 0, \quad r\begin{pmatrix} 0 \\ 1 \ 1 \end{pmatrix} = 1, \quad r\begin{pmatrix} 1 \\ 1 \ 0 \end{pmatrix} = 0. \tag{5.1}$$

The output of $f(\cdot)$ is specified, as before, by $p_f(w_j)$, which is the filter decision probability for the jth of the possible binary arrays that can appear in the filter's window.

The quantity we are interested in for each binary array w_j is the absolute deviation

$$d(w_j) = |p_f(w_j) - r(w_j)| \tag{5.2}$$

between the filter's output and the value at the reference point.

With this measure of error, we can formulate the preservation, elimination, or modification of certain structures as constraints on the filter decision probabilities $p_f(\cdot)$'s. The different types of constraints will now be broken down into a catalog according to whether the constraint is local or global in nature.

Constraints for Global Structures: The global behavior that can be observed by a filter is completely specified by its window process graph, which depends only upon the window W of the filter. Each toroid in this graph is a complete specification of what can be thought of as 2-D periodic behavior which can exist throughout the extent of the image. It is logical then to specify the global behavior of a filter by specifying its action on the toroids in the window process graph.

Recall that if a toroid is in the stack filter graph of a particular filter $f(\cdot)$, then the global behavior it specifies is a set of 2-D root signals of the filter. In this case, the filter output agrees with the value at the reference point in any binary array that is associated with at least one of the nodes in the toroid.

Thus, we use the set of all possible toroids in the window process graph of the window W to specify the global behavior that can be seen by any filter with that window.

Under this approach, designing a filter with the global behavior associated with a particular toroid amounts to finding a filter which either does or does not have that toroid in its stack filter graph.

To this end, let $T_W(i)$ be the ith toroid in the window process graph for W, and define

$$T(i) = \{w_j : \text{some node of } T_W(i) \text{ is labeled with } w_j\} \tag{5.3}$$

to be the set of all binary arrays that can appear in the window W and which are associated with at least one node in $T_W(i)$. If the filter $f(\cdot)$ is to preserve this toroid, it must satisfy

$$R_f(i) = \sum_{\substack{w_j \in T(i) \\ r(w_j) = 1}} (1 - p_f(w_j)) + \sum_{\substack{w_j \in T(i) \\ r(w_j) = 0}} p_f(w_j) = 0 \tag{5.4}$$

where the notation $R_f(i)$ means $f(\cdot)$ preserves the root images associated with the ith toroid.

Because $p_f(\cdot)$ is always between zero and one for any input array, the quantity $R_f(i)$ is always nonnegative. It is also easy to see that it is exactly zero if and only if the filter's outputs for the w_j's of interest agree exactly with the value of the reference points of the w_j's. Thus, (5.4) is a proper expression of the constraint that the filter preserves the structures associated with the ith toroid.

The fact that $R_f(i)$ is always nonnegative is significant. It says that another way to state that we desire a function $f(\cdot)$ such that $R_f(i) = 0$ is to say that we want to find an $f(\cdot)$ which minimizes $R_f(i)$. The larger the value of $R_f(i)$, the larger the number of nodes of $T_W(i)$ at which the filter's output is not what was desired. In particular, if the filter's decisions are required to be hard (0 or 1) decisions, then the value of $R_f(i)$ is exactly the number of nodes at which the filter output disagrees with the value of the reference point.

If structures associated with the ith toroid are not to be preserved, the designer must determine the extent to which it should be modified. In the simplest case, the designer specifies that the toroid is not to be in the stack filter's digraph. This corresponds to specifying that certain structures are not to be root signals of the filter. The goal is simply to keep the toroid from being in the stack filter's digraph.

This is certainly accomplished if the filter's output disagrees with the reference point value for every possible binary array in $T(i)$. It is also accomplished, though, if the filter's output disagrees with the reference point value for any one of the arrays in $T(i)$. There is thus a great deal of freedom to specify how the structures associated with that toroid are to be modified. If the ith toroid has $t(i)$ nodes, then we can disagree at anywhere between 1 and $t(i)$ of them, and in any combination of nodes, and the toroid will be broken.

This freedom can be summed up in the following equation:

$$k \geq \overline{R}_f(i) = t(i) - \left(\sum_{\substack{w_j \in T_W(i) \\ r(w_j) = 1}} p_f(w_j) + \sum_{\substack{w_j \in T_W(i) \\ r(w_j) = 0}} (1 - p_f(w_j)) \right) \geq l \quad (5.5)$$

where the notation $\overline{R}_f(i)$ means that the ith toroid is not to be in the stack filter digraph of $f(\cdot)$; that is, there are to be no roots of $f(\cdot)$ corresponding to the ith toroid.

If all of the filter decision probabilities are zero or one, the inequalities in (5.5) force the filter decisions to be different from the reference point for at least k, but no more than l, of the binary arrays in $T(i)$. Note that it does not specify at which points the disagreement should occur. Such freedom may be necessary to meet other constraints, and in Section VI, this freedom is used to minimize noise.

By analogy with the case of preserving the ith toroid, we could also say that we wish to find the filter $f(\cdot)$ which does the most complete job of eliminating the ith toroid, in which case our goal is to find the filter $f(\cdot)$ which minimizes $\overline{R}_f(i)$ since then it will have broken the toroid at the maximum number of nodes.

Constraints for Local Structures: Essentially any structural constraint which is meant to be local, even though it may have unforeseen global effects, is lumped into this category. Specifically ruled out of this category, though, are those constraints phrased directly in terms of structures associated with toroids and 2-D roots.

It may be desirable to preset some of the filter's decision probabilities to get a desired structural effect, whether it is preservation, deletion, or modification. A typical constraint in this category would be of the form

$$L_f(i) = \begin{cases} p_f(w_i) & \text{if } r(w_i) = 0 \\ 1 - p_f(w_i) & \text{if } r(w_i) = 1 \end{cases} = 0 \quad (5.6)$$

which sets a particular filter decision probability equal to the value of the reference point in the window and would therefore not alter this particular point of the structure w_i. Alternatively,

$$\overline{L}_f(i) = \begin{cases} 1 - p_f(w_i) & \text{if } r(w_i) = 0 \\ p_f(w_i) & \text{if } r(w_i) = 1 \end{cases} = 0 \quad (5.7)$$

which sets the filter decision probability for binary array w_i equal to the logical complement of the value at the reference point in the binary array w_i. This specifies that the reference point in the structure w_i is to be altered wherever w_i is observed in the input image. Of course, we could as well say we are trying to find the filter $f(\cdot)$ which minimizes $L_f(i)$ or $\overline{L}_f(i)$ and we would be accomplishing the same purposes.

The notation L_f and $\overline{L}_f$ indicates that it is a (very) local constraint, and that the output is to agree with or be the opposite of the point at the reference point in the array of interest.

As mentioned in the previous subsection, cycles play an important role in both local and global behavior. The correct relationship between the local behavior of a filter on a *number* of different cycles is what creates global behavior. Thus, it may be that particular cycles should be preserved, deleted, or otherwise modified. To this end, let $C_W(i)$ be the ith cycle in the window process graph associated with the window W, and define

$$C(i) = \{w_j : \text{a node of } C_W(i) \text{ is labeled with } w_j\} \quad (5.8)$$

which consists of all binary arrays associated with the window W which are themselves associated with the nodes in the ith cycle. If we want a filter $f(\cdot)$ to preserve this cycle, then, as in the case of toroids, we want

$$C_f(i) = \sum_{\substack{w_j \in C(i) \\ r(w_j) = 1}} (1 - p_f(w_j)) + \sum_{\substack{w_j \in C(i) \\ r(w_j) = 0}} p_f(w_j) = 0 \quad (5.9)$$

or, alternatively, to minimize $C_f(i)$.

If we do not want the filter to preserve the cycle, we have to decide how much of it should be modified or deleted. By analogy with the treatment for toroids, we have the constraint, assuming there are $c(i)$ nodes in cycle i,

$$k \geq \overline{C}_f(i) = c(i) - \left(\sum_{\substack{w_j \in Cw(i) \\ r(w_j)=1}} p_f(w_j) + \sum_{\substack{w_j \in Cw(i) \\ r(w_j)=0}} (1 - p_f(w_j)) \right) \geq l \quad (5.10)$$

or, alternatively, we can minimize $\overline{C}_f(i)$.

There are certain other local structural constraints, but the two types above are likely to be the dominant ones.

Design of Filters Satisfying Structural Constraints: Now that there is a method for analytically expressing structural constraints and goals, it is possible to consider the design of a filter which satisfies these constraints or meets these goals.

The list of constraints is assumed to have the following form:

Structural Constraints
Preserve toroids $1-M$; modify toroids $(M+1)-N$
Preserve cycles $1-P$; modify cycles $(P+1)-Q$
Preserve local behavior $1-R$;
modify local behavior $(R+1)-S$.
(5.11)

The most important feature in the above constraints is that each one can be formulated as a linear function of the filter decision probabilities by using (5.4)-(5.10). This is noteworthy since the stacking constraints in (4.12) and the probability constraints in (4.13) are also linear, and they are what guarantees that the filter $f(\cdot)$ is positive in the linear program developed in Section IV-B.

Concatenate all of the constraints listed above—the structural constraints, the stacking constraints, and the probability constraints—into a single set of constraints. If there are any binary solutions to the resulting set of linear equations, then any one of these solutions is a filter $f(\cdot)$ with the desired behavior. Whether there is a solution or not can be determined by running a linear program to check if the constraints are feasible or not.

If the constraints are feasible, then they can be solved via standard techniques to find a filter with the desired behavior. If they cannot be satisfied, then two possibilities present themselves: change the shape and/or size of the window W or find a filter within the original window which comes the "closest" to providing the desired behavior.

There are very few guides at this point as to how to change the window shape and size to accomplish the desired goal. This is an area requiring a great deal of research. It is also one of the reasons that it is best to start the above procedure with the largest possible window.

The second alternative is actually surprisingly easy to implement. It is accomplished via a linear program in which some or all of the structural constraints are incorporated in the cost function instead of as constraints. For simplicity, assume that all of them have been moved to the cost function, which is stated as follows:

$$\text{STRUCT}_f = \sum_{i=1}^{M} \beta_R(i) R_f(i) + \sum_{j=M+1}^{N} \beta_{\overline{R}}(j) \overline{R}_f(j)$$
$$+ \sum_{k=1}^{P} \beta_C(k) C_f(k)$$
$$+ \sum_{l=P+1}^{Q} \beta_{\overline{C}}(l) \overline{C}_f(l) + \sum_{m=1}^{R} \beta_L(m) L_f(m)$$
$$+ \sum_{n=R+1}^{S} \beta_{\overline{L}}(n) \overline{L}_f(n). \quad (5.12)$$

The variables $\beta_x(i)$ are simply weights which either the designer or some high-level system can vary to specify a hierarchy in importance among the structural goals.

Any function $f(\cdot)$ which minimizes STRUCT_f will do the best possible job of satisfying the constraints, although it will probably violate some of them. If the resulting filter does not do what is desired, the weights in (5.12) can be adjusted and the program can be repeated.

The linear program to design a stack filter with window W which does the best job of meeting the structural constraints or goals is thus

Find f which minimizes STRUCT_f

subject to

stacking constraints in (4.15).

The two linear programming approaches outlined above may be combined. Some of the structural constraints may be expressed as constraints in the linear program above instead of including them in the cost function.

An example showing how the above results may be used in the design of stack filters can be found in the following section.

VI. Unification of the Structural and Estimation Approaches

Both the structural and the estimation approaches to the design of optimal filters resulted in linear programs to find an optimal filter. These linear programs are restated here in an abstract fashion.

For Finding a Stack Filter $S_f(\cdot)$ with Optimal Structural Behavior

Find an $f(\cdot)$ which minimizes STRUCT_f
subject to

stacking constraints on $f(\cdot)$ and (possibly) structural constraints.

For Finding a Stack Filter $S_f(\cdot)$ which Minimizes the MAE

Find an $f(\cdot)$ which minimizes MAE_f
subject to
stacking constraints on $f(\cdot)$.

If one wishes to both minimize noise and at the same time have specific structural behavior, then one need only combine the above two linear programs. The new objective function is just a weighted sum of the two objective functions stated above. In other words, add them after multiplying one by β and the other by $(1 - \beta)$ where $\beta \in [0, 1]$. The quantity β determines whether noise reduction or structural behavior is considered more important. The constraints on the new objective function are just the concatenation of those for the individual objective functions.

This linear program can be solved either directly, in which case detailed statistical descriptions are needed of the image and the process which alters it, or the adaptive approach in [23] may be used to train a filter to do the job.

We now illustrate how the above unified approach to stack filter design can be used in a one-dimensional binary filtering problem. We have chosen a one-dimensional filtering example for simplicity of presentation and because, at this time, our programs can find elementary cycles, but not elementary toroids, in directed graphs.

The following is the Boolean expression of a binary stack filter of window width five which is the MMAE filter for a particular one-dimensional binary filtering problem:

$$f(x_1, x_2, x_3, x_4, x_5)$$
$$= x_1 x_3 x_5 + x_1 x_4 + x_2 x_3 + x_2 x_5 + x_3 x_4.$$

The stack filter digraph for this filter has 13 elementary cycles. One of the elementary cycles is Cycle 1:

$$01010 \to 10101 \to 01010.$$

One of the many possible root signals that can be generated by this cycle is the binary oscillation

$$\cdots 0101010101010 \cdots.$$

Other root signals which contain segments which are binary oscillations are also possible since this elementary cycle shares nodes with other elementary cycles.

Another elementary cycle in the digraph of $f(\cdot)$ is given by Cycle 2:

$$01100 \to 11000 \to 10001 \to 00011 \to 00110 \to 01100$$

which can generate the following root signal:

$$\cdots 0110001100011 \cdots.$$

Suppose that we are told that the structures corresponding to the binary oscillations listed above should not appear at the output of the filter. If they appear in the input, though, they will appear at the output since they will be preserved by the stack filter $f(\cdot)$. We would thus like to rerun the MAE optimization program with the additional constraints that Cycles 1 and/or 2 listed above should be broken in at least one position.

We will first try to break Cycle 1, then Cycle 2, and finally, both Cycle 1 and Cycle 2.

Since Cycle 1 consists of binary oscillations, it will be eliminated by adding the constraint

$$p_f(01010) + (1 - p_f(10101)) \geq 1 \quad (6.1)$$

to the linear program to find the MMAE filter. Once this is done, the new optimal filter has the following Boolean expression:

$$f_1(x_1, x_2, x_3, x_4, x_5) = x_1 x_4 + x_2 x_3 + x_2 x_5 + x_3 x_4.$$

The stack filter digraph for $f_1(\cdot)$ contains 12 cycles, only Cycle 1 has been removed. It has been removed because this new optimal filter $f_1(\cdot)$ has $p_{f_1}(10101) = 0$ and $p_{f_1}(01010) = 0$. This causes any binary oscillation to be set to all 0's after one pass of the filter.

To break Cycle 2 in at least one position, the following must hold:

$$p_f(00011) + (1 - p_f(00110)) + (1 - p_f(01100))$$
$$+ p_f(10001) + p_f(11000) \geq 1. \quad (6.2)$$

The new optimal filter has the following Boolean expression:

$$f_2(x_1, x_2, x_3, x_4, x_5) = x_1 x_3 + x_1 x_4 + x_2 x_5 + x_3 x_4.$$

The stack filter digraph for $f_2(\cdot)$ contains ten cycles. Two extra cycles were destroyed in addition to Cycle 2.

Finally, to break both Cycle 1 and Cycle 2, both (6.1) and (6.2) are used as constraints. The new optimal filter has the following expression:

$$f_3(x_1, x_2, x_3, x_4, x_5)$$
$$= x_1 x_3 + x_1 x_4 + x_2 x_4 + x_2 x_5 + x_3 x_4.$$

The stack filter digraph for $f_3(\cdot)$ contains only nine cycles instead of the original 13.

This example shows that it is not always possible to eliminate a particular type of structural behavior without eliminating other types of behavior. In other words, when you delete one specific cycle, it may take others with it.

Much work remains to be done on this new combined MAE and structural approach to stack filtering. It shows great promise of being able to design filters for many different purposes—not just noise reduction.

VII. CONCLUSIONS

The simplicity, in Section VI, of the unification of the estimation and structural approaches to stack filter design belies its significance. It provides the designer with an analytical tool to accomplish essentially whatever is desired in the way of image recovery. Only the goals need to be specified, and then the crank can be turned to find the filter which meets those goals.

This is not to imply that all is finished in this area since it certainly is not. The complexity problem is one that must be examined for this approach.

For instance, although the linear programming problems grow exponentially in the window size of the filter, the constraint matrix is very, very sparse. Exploitation of this fact should drastically reduce the complexity of the linear program and allow very large window size optimization procedures to be executed. Interior point algorithms should also be examined, especially since the constraint matrix for a given window width stays the same from one estimation problem to the next.

APPENDIX
DEFINITIONS OF SOME FILTERS DISCUSSED IN SECTION II

Section II provided a list of the rank-order based filtering operations that have been defined over the years. Some of the most recently defined filters are defined below for reference purposes. These definitions come directly from [6].

Let $\{a(\cdot, \cdot)\}$ be a discrete two-dimensional sequence $\{a(n_1, n_2); n_1, n_2 \in Z\}$ where the index set Z is the set of all integers, and consider the set of samples inside a $2N + 1 \times 2N + 1$ square window W centered at the (n_1, n_2). The points in the window are thus $\{a(n_1 + l_1, n_2 + l_2): -N \leq l_1, l_2 \leq N\}$. For notational simplicity, we will use the vector notation $(n_1, n_2) = n$, where $n \in Z^2$. Define the following subsets of the window W:

$$W_1[a; (n)] = \{a(n_1 + l_1, n_2): -N \leq l_1 \leq N\}$$

$$W_2[a; (n)] = \{a(n_1 + l_1, n_2 + l_1): -N \leq l_1 \leq N\}$$

$$W_3[a; (n)] = \{a(n_1, n_2 + l_1): -N \leq l_1 \leq N\}$$

$$W_4[a; (n)] = \{a(n_1 + l_1, n_2 - l_1): -N \leq l_1 \leq N\}$$

$$W_{(1,3)}[a; (n)] = W_1 \cup W_3$$

$$W_{(2,4)}[a; (n)] = W_2 \cup W_4. \quad (A.1)$$

Also define the following median operations inside the specified window:

$$z_l(n) = \text{median}[a(\cdot, \cdot) \in W_l[a; (n)]] \quad 1 \leq l \leq 4.$$

$$z_{1,3}(n) = \text{median}[a(\cdot, \cdot) \in W_{(1,3)}[a; (n)]]$$

$$z_{2,4}(n) = \text{median}[a(\cdot, \cdot) \in W_{(2,4)}[a; (n)]]. \quad (A.2)$$

In what follows, the variable y, with different subscripts, will denote the outputs of the various filters.

1) Max/median $y_{\max}$ and min/median $y_{\min}$ filters:

$$y_{\max}(n) = \max_{1 \leq l \leq 4}[z_l(n)] \quad y_{\min}(n) = \min_{1 \leq l \leq 4}[z_l(n)]. \quad (A.3)$$

2) Multistage max/median filter $y_{m/\max}$:

$$y_{m/\max}(n) = \text{med}[y_{\max}(n), y_{\min}(n), a(n)] \quad (A.4)$$

where the operations $y_{\max}$ and $y_{\min}$ were defined above.

3) Multistage median filter $y_{m/\text{med}}$:

$$y_{m/\text{med}}(n) = \text{med}[y_{w_1,w_3}(n), y_{w_2,w_4}(n), a(n)] \quad (A.5)$$

where

$$y_{w_1,w_3}(n) = \text{median}[z_1(n), z_3(n), a(n)]$$

$$y_{w_2,w_4}(n) = \text{median}[z_2(n), z_4(n), a(n)]. \quad (A.6)$$

4) FIR-median hybrid $y_{\text{fir}}(n)$:

$$y_{\text{fir}}(n) = \text{median}[\bar{y}_{w_1,w_3}(n), \bar{y}_{w_2,w_4}(n), a(n)] \quad (A.7)$$

where

$$\bar{y}_{w_1,w_3} = \text{median}[\hat{z}_1(n), \hat{z}_3(n), a(n)]$$

$$\bar{y}_{w_2,w_4} = \text{median}[\hat{z}_2(n), \hat{z}_4(n), a(n)] \quad (A.8)$$

where

$$\hat{z}_l = \text{median}[z_{la}(n), z_{lb}(n), a(n)],$$
$$1 \leq l \leq 4 \quad (A.9)$$

in which z_{la} and z_{lb} are the average of the samples in each of the two halves of the window W_l, excluding the center sample $a(n)$.

5) Bidirectional multistage median $y_{m/\text{med}}^+$:

$$y_{m/\text{med}}^+(n) = \text{median}[z_{1,3}(n), z_{2,4}(n), a(n)]. \quad (A.10)$$

6) The two-dimensional close–open morphological filter y_{2DCO}: Referring to (A.1), partition each window $W_l[a; (n)]$ into $(N + 1)$ overlapping subsets $S_{l,m}$ of $(N + 1)$ consecutive points. Then

$$y_{\text{2DCO}}(n) = \max_{\substack{1 \leq l \leq 4 \\ 1 \leq m \leq N+1}} \left(\min[a(\cdot) \in S_{l,m}[C; (n)]]\right)$$

(A.11)

where

$$C(n) = \min_{\substack{1 \leq l \leq 4 \\ 1 \leq m \leq N+1}} \left(\max[a(\cdot) \in S_{l,m}[a; (n)]]\right).$$

(A.12)

ACKNOWLEDGMENT

We would like to thank G. R. Arce and R. E. Foster of the University of Delaware for providing the computer files containing the images in Fig. 7(a) and (b). We would also like to thank the reviewers, J. P. Allebach, A. C. Kak, and R. L. Kashyap, for their help in improving this paper.

REFERENCES

[1] J. W. Tukey, "Nonseparable (nonsuperposable) methods for smoothing data," in *Conf. Rec., EASCON*, 1974, p. 673, and *Exploratory Data Analysis*. Reading, MA: Addison-Wesley, 1977.

[2] N. C. Gallagher, Jr. and G. L. Wise, "A theoretical analysis of the properties of median filters," *IEEE Trans. Acoust., Speech, Signal Processing*, vol. ASSP-29, pp. 1136–1141, Dec. 1981.

[3] S. G. Tyan, "Median-filtering: Deterministic properties," in *Two-Dimensional Digital Signal Processing. II: Transforms and Median Filters*, ch. 5, vol. 42, pp. 197–217, *Topics in Applied Physics*. T. S. Huang, Ed. New York: Springer-Verlag, 1981.

[4] P. D. Wendt, E. J. Coyle, and N. C. Gallagher, Jr., "Stack filters," *IEEE Trans. Acoust. Speech, Signal Processing*, vol. ASSP-34, pp. 898–911, Aug. 1986.

[5] A. Nieminen, P. Heinonen, and Y. Neuvo, "A new class of detail-preserving filters for image processing," *IEEE Trans. Pattern Anal. Machine Intell.*, vol. PAMI-9, pp. 74–90, Jan. 1987.

[6] G. R. Arce and R. E. Foster, "Detail preserving ranked-order based filters for image processing," *IEEE Trans. Acoust., Speech, Signal Processing*, vol. 37, pp. 83–98, Jan. 1989.

[7] J. Serra, *Image Analysis and Mathematical Morphology*. New York: Academic, 1982.

[8] R. M. Haralick, S. R. Sternberg, and X. Zhuang, "Image analysis using mathematical morphology," *IEEE Trans. Pattern Anal. Machine Intell.*, vol. PAMI-9, pp. 532–550, July 1987.

[9] P. A. Maragos and R. W. Schafer, "Morphological filters—Part I: Their set theoretic analysis and relations to linear shift invariant filters," and "Morphological filters—Part II: Their relations to median, order statistic and stack filters," *IEEE Trans. Acoust., Speech, Signal Processing*, vol. ASSP-35, pp. 1153–1184, Aug. 1987.

[10] R. M. Haralick, X. Zhuang, C. Lin, and J. S. J. Lee, "The digital morphological sampling theorem," this issue, pp. 2067–2090.

[11] A. C. Bovik, T. S. Huang, and D. C. Munson, Jr., "A generalization of median filtering using linear combinations of order statistics," *IEEE Trans. Acoust., Speech, Signal Processing*, vol. ASSP-31, pp. 1342–1350, Dec. 1983.

[12] P. P. Ghandi, S. R. Peterson, and S. A. Kassam, "Frequency/selective signal restoration using nonlinear combination filters," in *Proc. 1988 Int. Conf. Acoust., Speech, Signal Processing*, New York, NY, Apr. 1988, pp. 1522–1525.

[13] S. R. Peterson and S. A. Kassam, "General order statistic-based structures for nonlinear signal processing," in *Proc. 1986 Conf. Inform. Sci. Syst.*, Princeton, NJ, Mar. 1986, pp. 723–728.

[14] S. A. Kassam and S. R. Peterson, "Nonlinear finite moving window filters for signal restoration," presented at the IEEE Pacific RIM Conf. Commun., Comput., Signal Processing, Canada, June 1987.

[15] F. Palmieri and C. G. Boncelet, Jr., "A class of nonlinear adaptive filters," in *Proc. 1988 Int. Conf. Acoust., Speech, Signal Processing*, New York, NY, Apr. 1988, pp. 1483–1486.

[16] O. Yli-Harja, J. Astola, and Y. Neuvo, "A response-based design method for weighted median filters," Dep. Inform. Technol., Lappeenranta Univ. Technol., Lappeenranta, Finland, Res. Rep. 9/1988, 1988.

[17] ——, "Analysis of the properties of median and weighted median filters using threshold logic and stack filter representations," Dep. Inform. Technol., Lappeenranta Univ. Technol., Lappeenranta, Finland, Res. Rep. 10/1988, 1988.

[18] A. Nieminen, P. Heinonen, and Y. Neuvo, "Median-type filters with adaptive substructures," *IEEE Trans. Circuits Syst.*, vol. CAS-34, pp. 842–847, July 1987.

[19] G. R. Arce and R. L. Stevenson, "On the synthesis of median filter systems," *IEEE Trans. Circuits and Syst.*, vol. CAS-34, pp. 420–429, Apr. 1987.

[20] E. J. Coyle, "Rank order operators and the mean absolute error criterion," *IEEE Trans. Acoust., Speech, Signal Processing*, vol. 36, pp. 63–76, Jan. 1988.

[21] E. J. Coyle and J.-H. Lin, "Stack filters and the mean absolute error criterion," *IEEE Trans. Acoust., Speech, Signal Processing*, vol. 36, pp. 1244–1254, Aug. 1988.

[22] J.-H. Lin and E. J. Coyle, "Minimum mean absolute error nonlinear filtering," in *Proc. 1988 Int. Conf. Acoust., Speech, Signal Processing*, New York, NY, Apr. 1988 pp. 1439–1442; and "Minimum mean absolute error estimation over the class of generalized stack filters," *IEEE Trans. Acoust., Speech, Signal Processing*, to appear, Apr. 1990.

[23] J.-H. Lin, T. M. Sellke, and E. J. Coyle, "Adaptive stack filtering under the mean absolute error criterion," in *Proc. 1988 Conf. Adv. Commun. Contr. Syst.*, Baton Rouge, LA, Oct. 1988; pp. 392–405; and *IEEE Trans. Acoust., Speech, Signal Processing*, to appear, June 1990.

[24] M. Gabbouj and E. J. Coyle, "Minimum mean absolute error stack filtering with structural constraints," *IEEE Trans. Acoust., Speech, Signal Processing*, to appear, June 1990.

[25] S. R. Sternberg, "Grayscale morphology," *Comput. Vision, Graphics, Image Processing*, vol. 35, pp. 333–355, 1986.

[26] J. P. Fitch, E. J. Coyle, and N. C. Gallagher, Jr., "Median filtering by threshold decomposition," *IEEE Trans. Acoust., Speech, Signal Processing*, vol. ASSP-32, pp. 1183–1188, Dec. 1984.

[27] ——, "Threshold decomposition of multidimensional rank order operators," *IEEE Trans. Circuits Syst.*, vol. CAS-32, pp. 445–450, May 1985.

[28] Y. Nakagawa and A. Rosenfeld, "A note on the use of local min and max operations in digital picture processing," *IEEE Trans. Syst., Man, Cybern.*, vol. SMC-8, pp. 632–635, Aug. 1978.

[29] B. I. Justusson, "Median filtering: Statistical properties," in *Two-Dimensional Digital Signal Processing, II: Transforms and Median Filters*, ch. 4, vol. 42, pp. 161–196, *Topics in Applied Physics*, T. S. Huang, Ed. New York: Springer-Verlag, 1981.

[30] T. A. Nodes and N. C. Gallagher, Jr., "Median filters: Some modifications and their properties," *IEEE Trans. Acoust., Speech, Signal Processing*, vol. ASSP-29, pp. 739–746, Oct. 1982.

[31] V. Kim and L. Yaroslavskii, "Rank algorithms for picture processing," *Comput. Vision, Graphics, Image Processing*, vol. 35, pp. 234–258, 1986.

[32] G. R. Arce, P. J. Warter, and R. E. Foster, "Recursive multistage median filters," in *Proc. 22nd Annu. Conf. Inform. Sci. Syst.*, Princeton, NJ, Mar. 1988.

[33] J. B. Bednar and T. L. Watt, "Alpha-trimmed means and their relationship to median filters," *IEEE Trans. Acoust., Speech, Signal Processing*, vol. ASSP-32, pp. 145–153, Feb. 1984.

[34] M. J. B. Duff and T. J. Fountain, *Cellular Logic Image Processing*. London: Academic, 1986.

[35] K. Preston, Jr., M. J. B. Duff, S. Levialdi, P. E. Norgren, and J.-I. Toriwaki, "Basics of cellular logic with some application in medical image processing," *Proc. IEEE*, vol. 67, pp. 826–856, May 1979.

[36] K. Preston, Jr., "Multidimensional logical transforms," *IEEE Trans. Pattern Anal. Machine Intell.*, vol. PAMI-5, Sept. 1983.

[37] J. P. Fitch, "Software and VLSI algorithms for generalized ranked order filtering," *IEEE Trans. Circuits Syst.*, vol. CAS-34, pp. 553–559, May 1987.

[38] K. Preston, Jr., "Ξ-filters," *IEEE Trans. Acoust., Speech, Signal Processing*, vol. ASSP-31, pp. 861–876, Aug. 1983.

[39] Y. H. Lee and S. A. Kassam, "Generalized median filtering and related nonlinear filtering techniques," *IEEE Trans. Acoust., Speech, Signal Processing*, vol. ASSP-33, pp. 672–683, June 1985.

[40] P. M. Narendra, "A separable median filter for image noise smoothing," *IEEE Trans. Pattern Anal. Machine Intell.*, vol. PAMI-3, pp. 20–29, Jan. 1981.

[41] G. R. Arce and M. P. McLoughlin, "Theoretical analysis of the max/median filter," *IEEE Trans. Acoust., Speech, Signal Processing*, vol. ASSP-35, pp. 60–69, Jan. 1987.

[42] P. Heinonen and Y. Neuvo, "FIR-median hybrid filters," *IEEE Trans. Acoust., Speech, Signal Processing*, vol. ASSP-35, pp. 832–838, June 1987.

[43] T. A. Nodes and N. C. Gallagher, Jr., "Two-dimensional root structures and convergence properties of the separable median filter," *IEEE Trans. Acoust., Speech, Signal Processing*, vol. ASSP-31, pp. 1350–1365, Dec. 1983.

[44] T. A. Nodes, "Theoretical results on the properties of median type operations," Ph.D. dissertation, School Elec. Eng., Purdue Univ., West Lafayette, IN, Dec. 1982.

[45] A. C. Bovik, T. S. Huang, and D. C. Munson, Jr., "The effect of median filtering on edge estimation and detection," *IEEE Trans. Pattern Anal. Machine Intell.*, vol. PAMI-9, pp. 181–194, Mar. 1987.

[46] A. C. Bovik, "Streaking in median filtered images," *IEEE Trans. Acoust., Speech, Signal Processing*, vol. ASSP-35, pp. 493–503, Apr. 1987.

[47] F. Kuhlmann and G. L. Wise, "On second moment properties of median filtered sequences of independent data," *IEEE Trans. Commun.*, vol. COM-29, pp. 1374–1379, Sept. 1981.

[48] E. Ataman, V. K. Aatre, and K. M. Wong, "Some statistical properties of median filters," *IEEE Trans. Acoust., Speech, Signal Processing*, vol. ASSP-29, pp. 1073–1075, Oct. 1981.

[49] T. A. Nodes and N. C. Gallagher, Jr., "The output distribution of median type filters," *IEEE Trans. Commun.*, vol. COM-32, pp. 532–541, May 1984.

[50] G.-Y. Liao, T. A. Nodes, and N. C. Gallagher, Jr., "Output distributions of two-dimensional median filters," *IEEE Trans. Acoust., Speech, Signal Processing*, vol. ASSP-33, pp. 1280–1295, Oct. 1985.

[51] S. R. Peterson, Y. H. Lee, and S. A. Kassam, "Some statistical properties of alpha-trimmed mean and standard type M filters," *IEEE Trans. Acoust., Speech, Signal Processing*, vol. 36, pp. 707–713, May 1988.

[52] G. R. Arce, N. C. Gallagher, Jr., and T. A. Nodes, "Median filters: Theory for one and two dimensional filters," in *Image Enhancement and Restoration*, ch. 3, pp. 90–166, *Advances in Computer Vision and Image Processing*, vol. 2, T. S. Huang, Ed. Greenwich, CT: JAI Press, 1986.

[53] C. G. Boncelet, Jr., "Algorithms to compute order statistic distributions," *SIAM J. Sci. Stat. Comput.*, vol. 8, Sept. 1987.

[54] G. R. Arce, "Statistical threshold decomposition for recursive and nonrecursive median filters," *IEEE Trans. Inform. Theory*, vol. IT-32, pp. 243–253, Mar. 1986.

[55] R. L. Stevenson and G. R. Arce, "Morphological filters: Statistics and further syntactic properties," *IEEE Trans. Circuits Syst.*, vol. CAS-34, pp. 1292–1305, Nov. 1987.

[56] G. R. Arce and N. C. Gallagher, Jr., "State descriptions of the root signal set of median filters," *IEEE Trans. Acoust., Speech, Signal Processing*, vol. ASSP-30, pp. 894–902, Dec. 1982.

[57] D. H. Yom and S. Ann, "Directed graph representation for the root signal set of median filters," *Proc. IEEE*, vol. 75, pp. 1542–1544, Nov. 1987.

[58] P. J. Huber, *Robust Statistics*. New York: Wiley, 1981.

[59] D. F. Andrews *et al.*, *Robust Estimation of Location*. Princeton, NJ: Princeton University Press, 1972.

[60] D. L. Snyder, *Random Point Processes*. New York: Wiley, 1975.

[61] M. I. Shamos, "Robust picture processing operators and their implementation as circuits," in *Proc. Image Understanding Workshop*, Pittsburgh, PA, Nov. 1978.

[62] W. L. Eversole, D. J. Mayer, F. B. Frazee, and T. F. Cheek, Jr., "Investigation of VLSI technologies for image processing," in *Proc. Image Understanding Workshop*, Pittsburgh, PA, Nov. 1978.

[63] T. S. Huang, G. J. Yang, and G. Y. Tang, "A fast two-dimensional median filtering algorithm," *IEEE Trans. Acoust., Speech, Signal Processing*, vol. ASSP-27, pp. 13–18, Feb. 1979.

[64] E. Ataman, V. K. Aatre, and K. M. Wong, "A fast method for real-time median filtering," *IEEE Trans. Acoust., Speech, Signal Processing*, vol. ASSP-28, pp. 415–421, Aug. 1980.

[65] P. E. Danielsson, "Getting the median faster," *Comput. Vision Graphics, Image Processing*, vol. 17, pp. 71–78, 1981.

[66] D. R. Morgan, "Analog sorting network ranks inputs by amplitude and allows selection," *Electron. Design*, pp. 72–74, Jan. 18, 1973.

[67] K. Oflazer, "Design and implementation of a single-chip 1-D median filter," *IEEE Trans. Acoust., Speech, Signal Processing*, vol. ASSP-31, pp. 1164–1168, Oct. 1983.

[68] R. G. Harber, S. C. Bass, and G. W. Neudeck, "VLSI implementation of a fast rank order filtering algorithm," in *Proc. 1985 IEEE Int. Conf. Acoust., Speech, Signal Processing*, Tampa, FL, Mar. 1985.

[69] J. A. Roskind, "A fast sort-selection filter chip with effectively linear hardware complexity," in *Proc. 1988 IEEE Int. Conf. Acoust., Speech, Signal Processing*, Mar. 1985.

[70] K. Chen, P. Heinonen, Q. Ye, and Y. Neuvo, "Analog/digital hybrid median filter realizations," in *Proc. 1987 Int. Conf. Digital Signal Processing*, Florence, Italy, 1987, pp. 349–352.

[71] K. Chen, "Realizations of a class of nonlinear filters using a bit-serial approach," in *Proc. 1988 IEEE Int. Symp. Circuits Syst.*, Helsinki, Finland, June 1988, pp. 1749–1752.

[72] C. G. Boncelet, Jr., "Recursive algorithms and VLSI implementations for median filtering," in *Proc. 1988 IEEE Int. Symp. Circuits Syst.*, Helsinki, Finland, June 1988, pp. 1745–1747.

[73] G. R. Arce, P. J. Warter, and R. E. Foster, "Theory and VLSI implementation of multilevel median filters," in *Proc. 1988 IEEE Int. Symp. Circuits Syst.*, Helsinki, Finland, June 1988, pp. 2795–2798.

[74] V. Bapeswara Rao and K. Sankara Rao, "A new algorithm for real-time median filtering," *IEEE Trans. Acoust., Speech, Signal Processing*, vol. ASSP-34, pp. 1674–1675, Dec. 1986.

[75] M. O. Ahmad and D. Sundararajan, "A fast algorithm for two-dimensional median filtering," *IEEE Trans. Circuits Syst.*, vol. CAS-34, pp. 1364–1374, Nov. 1987.

[76] R. T. Hoctor and S. A. Kassam, "An efficient structure for nonlinear L- and C-filters," in *Proc. 1988 IEEE Int. Symp. Circuits Syst.*, Helsinki, Finland, June 1988, pp. 1507–1510; and *IEEE Trans. Circuits Syst.*, to be published.

[77] E. Ochoa, J. P. Allebach, and D. W. Sweeney, "Optical median filtering using threshold decomposition," *Appl. Opt.*, vol. 25, Jan. 1987.

[78] S. T. Alexander, *Adaptive Signal Processing: Theory and Applications*. New York: Springer-Verlag, 1986.

[79] M. L. Honig and D. G. Messerschmitt, *Adaptive Filters: Structures, Algorithms and Applications*. Boston, MA: Kluwer Academic, 1984.

[80] S. Haykin, *Adaptive Filter Theory*. Englewood Cliffs, NJ: Prentice-Hall, 1986.

[81] H. G. Longbotham and A. C. Bovik, "Relating analog and digital order statistic filters," in *Proc. 1988 IEEE Int. Conf. Acoust., Speech, Signal Processing*, New York, NY, Apr. 1988, pp. 1526–1529.

[82] ——, "Theory of order statistic filter and their relationship to linear FIR filters," *IEEE Trans. Acoust., Speech, Signal Processing*, vol. 37, pp. 275–287, Feb. 1989.

[83] P. Bloomfield and W. L. Steiger, *Least Absolute Deviations*. Boston, MA: Birkhauser, 1983.

[84] J. Astola, O. Yli-Harja, P. Heinonen, and Y. Neuvo, "Gradient median filter," in *Proc. 1987 IEEE Int. Symp. Circuits Syst.*, Philadelphia, PA, May 1987, pp. 246–251.

[85] R. Kasturi, J. Walkup, and T. Krile, "Adaptive point estimation in signal-dependent noise," *IEEE Trans. Syst., Man, Cybern.*, vol. SMC-15, pp. 352–359, May–June 1985.

[86] R. Bernstein, "Adaptive nonlinear filters for simultaneous removal of different kinds of noise in images," *IEEE Trans. Cirucits Syst.*, vol. CAS-34, pp. 1275–1291, Nov. 1987.

[87] H.-M. Lin and A. N. Willson, Jr., "Median filters with adaptive length," *IEEE Trans. Circuits Syst.*, vol. 35, pp. 675–690, June 1988.

[88] C. Pomalaza-Raez and C. D. McGillem, "An adaptive, nonlinear edge-preserving filter," *IEEE Trans. Acoust., Speech, Signal Processing*, vol. ASSP-32, pp. 571–576, June 1984.

[89] Y. H. Lee and A. T. Fam, "An edge-gradient enhancing adaptive order statistic filter," *IEEE Trans. Acoust., Speech, Signal Processing*, vol. ASSP-35, pp. 680–695, May 1987.

[90] R. Ding and A. N. Venetsanopoulos, "Generalized homomorphic and adaptive order statistic filters for the removal of impulsive and signal-dependent noise," *IEEE Trans. Circuits Syst.*, vol. CAS-34, pp. 948–955, Aug. 1987.

[91] A. Restrepo and A. C. Bovik, "Adaptive trimmed mean filters for image restoration," *IEEE Trans. Acoust., Speech, Signal Processing*, vol. 36, pp. 1326–1337, Aug. 1988.

[92] P. D. Wendt, E. J. Coyle, and N. C. Gallagher, Jr., "Some convergence properties of median filters," *IEEE Trans. Circuits Syst.*, vol. CAS-33, pp. 276–286, Mar. 1986.

[93] E. N. Gilbert, "Lattice-theoretic properties of frontal switching functions," *J. Math. Phys.*, vol. 33, pp. 57–67, Apr. 1954.

[94] R. Kasturi and J. F. Walkup, "Nonlinear image restoration in signal dependent noise," in *Image Enhancement and Restoration*, ch. 4, pp. 167–212, *Advances in Computer Vision and Image Processing*, vol. 2, T. S. Huang, Ed. Greenwich: CT: JAI Press, 1986.

[95] P. J. Huber, *Robust Statistical Procedures*. Philadelphia, PA: SIAM, 1977.

[96] R. L. Kashyap and K. B. Eom, "Robust image models and their applications," *Adv. Electron. Electron. Phys.*, vol. 70, pp. 79–157, 1988.

[97] C. Peterson and A. Miller, "Mode, median and mean as optimal estimators," *J. Exp. Psychol.*, vol. 68, no. 4, pp. 363–367, 1964.

[98] C. Papadimitriou and K. Steiglitz, *Combinatorial Optimization: Algorithms and Complexity*. Englewood Cliffs, NJ: Prentice-Hall, 1982.

[99] M. Gabbouj, "Optimal stack filter examples and positive Boolean functions," M.S. thesis, School Elec. Eng., Purdue Univ., West Lafayette, IN, Dec. 1986.

[100] M. P. McLoughlin and G. R. Arce, "Deterministic properties of the separable recursive median filter," *IEEE Trans. Acoust., Speech, Signal Processing*, vol. ASSP-35, pp. 98–106, Jan. 1987.

[101] A. T. Berztiss, "A K-tree algorithm for simple cycles of a directed graph," Dep. Comput. Sci., Univ. Pittsburgh, Pittsburgh, PA, Tech. Rep. 73-6, May 14, 1973.

[102] D. Auglin and L. G. Valiant, "Fast probabilistic algorithms for Hamiltonian circuits and matchings," *J. Comput. Syst. Sci.*, vol. 18, pp. 155–193, 1979.

[103] P. D. Wendt, "Nonrecursive and recursive stack filters and their filtering behavior," submitted to *IEEE Trans. Acoust., Speech, Signal Processing*.

[104] P.-T. Yu and E. J. Coyle, "Convergence behavior and N-roots of stack filters," submitted to *IEEE Trans. Acoust., Speech, Signal Processing*.

[105] J. Song and E. J. Delp, "The analysis of morphological filters with multiple structuring elements," *Comput. Vision, Graphics, Image Processing*, to appear.

[106] ——, "A generalization of morphological filters using multiple structuring elements," in *Proc. 1989 IEEE Symp. Circuits Syst.*, Portland, OR, May 1989.

[107] C.-H. H. Chu and E. J. Delp, "Impulsive noise suppression and background normalization of electrocardiogram signals using morphological operators," *IEEE Trans. Biomed. Eng.*, vol. 36, pp. 262–273, Feb. 1989.

[108] J. P. Fitch, E. J. Coyle, and N. C. Gallagher, Jr., "Root properties and convergence rates of median filters," *IEEE Trans. Acoust., Speech, Signal Processing*, vol. ASSP-33, pp. 230–240, Feb. 1985.

Edward J. Coyle (S'79–M'82) was born in Philadelphia, PA, on April 22, 1956. He received the Bachelor of Electrical Engineering degree from the University of Delaware, Newark, in 1978, and the Master's and Ph.D. degrees in electrical engineering and computer science from Princeton University, Princeton, NJ, in 1980 and 1982, respectively.

Since 1982 he has been with the School of Electrical Engineering, Purdue University, West Lafayette, IN, where he is currently an Associate Professor. His research interests lie in the areas of nonlinear signal and image processing and performance analysis of computer communication networks.

Dr. Coyle is a member of the Operations Research Society of America, the Association for Computing Machinery, Phi Kappa Phi, Tau Beta Pi, and Eta Kappa Nu. He is co-recipient with Dr. J. P. Fitch of the 1986 Best Paper Award for authors under the age of 30 from the IEEE Acoustics, Speech, and Signal Processing Society.

Jean-Hsang Lin (S'84) received the B.S.E.E. degree from Chung-Yuan University, Taiwan, in 1977, the M.S.E.E. degree from the University of Texas, Arlington, in 1984, and the Ph.D. degree in electrical engineering from Purdue University, West Lafayette, IN, in 1988.

He is currently an Assistant Professor in the Department of Electrical Engineering, University of Delaware, Newark. His research interests include nonlinear signal processing, image processing, adaptive filtering, and computer vision.

Moncef Gabbouj (S'85) was born in Monastir, Tunisia, in 1962. He received the B.S. degree in electrical engineering in 1985 from Oklahoma State University, Stillwater, and the M.S. degree in electrical engineering from Purdue University, West Lafayette, IN, in 1986.

Currently he is with the School of Electrical Engineering, Purdue University, where he is working toward the Ph.D. degree. His research interests include nonlinear signal and image processing, mathematical morphology, neural networks, and artificial intelligence.

Chapter 3: Image Restoration

Image restoration is an estimation process that attempts to recover an ideal, high-quality image from a degraded recording. Restoration is applied to remove

- Systematic degradations (such as blurring due to optical-system aberrations, atmospheric turbulence, motion, and diffraction) and
- Statistical degradations (such as noise and measurement errors).

These two types of degradations lead to conflicting requirements on the restoration filter. It is difficult to improve image quality by emphasizing high spatial frequencies while — at the same time — suppressing noise. The overall quality of image-restoration algorithms benefits greatly from

- Better models for the image-formation process, including better models for both systematic and statistical degradations;
- Better modeling of objects to be restored by using nonstationary or local statistical models; and
- Better modeling of image quality criteria and properties of the human observer and visual system.

The papers reprinted in this chapter provide an overview of recent work that makes use of the facts presented above. In addition, they review new methods of implementation, such as recursive techniques, parallel algorithms, and spatial-domain (non-Fourier) processing.

This chapter begins with a reprinted paper by Woods and Radewan that presents several techniques for extending Kalman filtering to two dimensions. The authors define an exact two-dimensional Kalman scalar filter (one that observes and updates one image point at a time) and an exact two-dimensional Kalman vector filter (one that observes and updates one line at a time); they show each filter to have both an excessive computational load and memory requirements for any image of practical size. In general, the computations per point and the memory requirements are each proportional to M^2, where M is the image width in pixels. Woods and Radewan then present two processing techniques that reduce computational load by two to three orders of magnitude. Both techniques take advantage of the fact that image pixels outside the local neighborhood of the pixel to be estimated generally have low correlation with that pixel to be estimated.

Woods and Radewan also describe a Kalman strip processor as a suboptimal implementation of the Kalman vector processor. The image is sectioned onto vertical overlapping strips; the vector processor operates locally only within each strip. By extracting and recombining pixels from the center of each strip, computations are greatly reduced — with some loss of estimation accuracy. They also describe a reduced update Kalman filter (RUKF) that updates only those state elements in a certain local neighborhood of the pixel being estimated. This and the Kalman strip processor considerably reduce the computational and memory requirements — again, with minimal loss of estimation accuracy.

A related paper is one by Woods and Ingle.[1] This paper extends the RUKF described in the previous paper to image-restoration problems that combine noisy observations with blurring of the original object data. Further, Woods and Ingle provide details on implementing the RUKF, considering the effects of boundary conditions at the edges of the image. Additional work that compares theoretical and experimental performances is described.

In the next reprinted paper, by Tekalp, Kaufman, and Woods, the original work of Woods and Radewan in developing Kalman filters for image restoration is extended to the space-varying case to preserve edges and suppress ringing while restoring. The basis for such a generalization is the multiple-model approach originally suggested by Woods.[2] In this multiple-model approach, a bank of five linear, space-invariant reduced update Kalman filters is designed such that the five filters correspond to the five models used to represent images. Based on a conditional maximum a posteriori probability decision logic, a decision is made at each pixel to use one of the five filters.

The application of Wiener filters to the image-restoration problem has received considerable attention.[3,4] A paper by Ekstrom[5] provides a detailed extension of one-dimensional classical Wiener mean-square estimation theory to two-dimensional problems. Ekstrom's paper concentrates on causal — that is, realizable and unilateral — estimators that use only past and present observations. The results are applicable to prediction (estimation of future values), filtering (estimation of present values), and smoothing (estimation of past values), given past and present observations. In analogy with the one-dimensional solution, Ekstrom derives an optimal realizable filter as the solution of a two-dimensional discrete Wiener-Hopf equation. This equation is solved by using a spectral-factorization procedure. Ekstrom obtains various error expressions, and he provides extensions to multicategory Wiener filters that could better account for the nonnegativity of image values and the nonstationary nature of image statistics.

The application of partial differential equation (PDE) models for image statistics in the restoration of noisy images is discussed by Jain and Jain.[6] Using PDE models for the stochastic representation of the image avoids the classically difficult problem of two-dimensional spectral factorization that has been inherent in most previous filtering algorithms. Jain and Jain show that hyperbolic, parabolic, and elliptic classes of PDEs produce recursive, semirecursive, and nonrecursive classes of filtering algorithms, respectively. The authors give practical details concerning applying these filters and make a detailed experimental evaluation in comparing their results with Fourier-Wiener and spatial-averaging methods. In addition, the paper explores trade-offs and performance bounds.

The next reprinted paper, by Chellappa and Kashyap, presents several methods of nonrecursive minimum mean-square error (MMSE) restoration of images in which the image statistics are represented by more general types of models than those used by Jain and Jain.[6] The blurring function is assumed to be generally nonseparable and space invariant. In MMSE restoration, a covariance matrix C_f for the original object function f is needed. Most previous algorithms assume that accurate a priori information about C_f is given or that a prototype image is available so that the parameters of C_f can be estimated. This paper presents restoration algorithms that do not require a prototype. Two classes of parametric image models are used, as follows:

- NCAR models and
- Gaussian MRF models.

Chellappa and Kashyap present procedures for estimating the model parameters from the observed blurred and noisy data. The resulting models are then used directly for MMSE restoration. The authors generalize previous restrictions (found in earlier papers, including the one by Jain and Jain[6]) to isotropic and/or causal models, and their intent is to reduce the errors in restoration due to inappropriate models and inaccurate techniques of model parameter estimation. Chellappa and Kashyap give experimental results using several different classes of models and different signal-to-noise ratios.

Abramatic and Silverman[7] present a unified approach to nonstationary-image restoration in which the form or parameters of a linear estimation filter change with spatial position. Because of their basically low pass characteristics, traditional stationary Wiener filters often smooth noise at the expense of image details being blurred. In the original object, edges generally carry the most visually useful information; edges can be considered as boundaries between regions of stationary statistics. The general philosophy is to estimate the location and visual significance of the edges from a noisy recorded image and to use this information to implement a linear nonstationary filter. The human eye and visual system are much more sensitive to errors in spatially broad, flat, low-frequency regions than they are at edges; thus, the nonstationary filter smooths over large regions in low-frequency areas and smooths over very small regions near edges. Because the edge information comes from the recorded image and is used to modify the restoration filter, the overall procedure is really a nonlinear filter. Abramatic and Silverman carefully explore the trade-offs between noise reduction and resolution and define several categories of "spatial-masking functions" containing estimated edge information. They present several generalizations of Wiener filtering and simplified models, and they give experimental results for various types of filters and masking functions.

As discussed in the chapter on image models (Chapter 1), a significant amount of work is being done in the field of modeling nonstationary images and developing algorithms for image restoration and other applications. The work of Geman and Geman, reported on in the next reprinted paper, is in this field. By noting the equivalence of MRFs and Gibbs distributions, the authors begin by representing the binary or multilevel gray-level image (a maximum of three levels was considered in this paper) with a Gibbs distribution.[8] More importantly, discontinuities in the image are represented using binary MRF or Ising models whose lattice sites are located in between the pixel sites. Note that these characterizations involve several parameters that need to be estimated from the degraded image or prototype of the original image (if available). Using the probability density of noise corrupting the image, they formulate image restoration as a maximum a posteriori (MAP) estimation problem.

Because the particular criterion function that needs to be maximized is nonconvex, the authors give a simulated annealing algorithm[9,10] that asymptotically converges to the global MAP estimate. An important contribution of this paper is in establishing the constraints on the annealing schedule to ensure convergence to the global estimate. One of the drawbacks of simulated annealing is an enormous computational load. Murray, Kashko, and Buxton[11] discuss special-purpose hardware for implementing the Geman and Geman algorithm.

The next reprinted paper, by Jeng and Woods, extends the work of Geman and Geman to the case in which the stationary regions of the image are represented using Gauss MRF models. Through the use of Lyapunov functions,[12] convergence results for the simulated annealing algorithm are established. Owing to the computational intensity of the simulated annealing algorithm, several researchers have looked at developing deterministic algorithms that do not usually converge to the global MAP estimate, but nevertheless yield acceptable results in a reasonable number of iterations. One result of such efforts is the iterated conditional mode method developed by Besag.[13] Another is the graduated nonconvexity (GNC) algorithm developed by Blake and Zisserman.[14] The GNC algorithm starts with a convex approximation F^* to the nonconvex function F to be minimized. Then, a whole sequence of cost functions $F^{(p)}$ — where $0 \leq p \leq 1$ — is constructed such that $F^{(0)} = F$ (the original nonconvex function) and $F^{(1)} = F^*$. In between $F^{(0)}$ and $F^{(1)}$, $F^{(p)}$ changes continuously. The GNC algorithm optimizes a whole sequence of $F^{(p)}$ — for example, $\{F^{(1)}, F^{(1/2)}, F^{(1/4)}, F^{(1/8)}, F^{(1/16)}\}$ — one after another, using the optimum solution of the previous optimization step as the starting point for the next step. In the original work reported on by Blake and Zisserman,[14] the optimization step was performed using the sequential-over-relaxation (SOR) method.

In the next reprinted paper, by Simchony, Chellappa, and Lichtenstein, the GNC algorithm is applied to MAP estimation of gray-scale images corrupted by Gaussian noise. The noise-free images are represented using the compound Gauss MRF models presented in the previous paper (by Jeng and Woods). Instead of the SOR method, the line-search method of Polak and Ribiere (discussed by Luenberger[15]) is used for the optimization step in the GNC algorithm. Simchony, Chellappa, and Lichtenstein utilize the special structure of Gibbs energy functions that arise due to MRF representation of the underlying images to map the algorithm to a highly parallel implementation. After the completion of the iterations, one obtains not only a smoothed estimate, but also an indication of where the edges are present in the image. The authors use examples to illustrate applications to edge detection and shape from shading.

In developing image-restoration algorithms, one usually needs information concerning such things as blur function and noise variance. For a number of years, researchers simply assumed that such information was available. Recently, several methods were developed for the estimation of blur and image.[16-18] In the next reprinted paper, by Lagendijk, Tekalp, and Biemond, an overview of existing methods for image and blur identification is given using an ML framework. The authors show that several of the recently published image- and blur-identification algorithms are different implementations of the same ML estimator, but they result from different modeling assumptions. They give examples of ML-estimation techniques for real-image and blur identification.

Most of the papers on image restoration assume that the corrupting noise is additive and signal independent. In radar or in other images formed with coherent illumination, the noise appears as speckles that are multiplicative or signal dependent. Although the paper by Kondo, Ichioka, and Suzuki[4] discusses Wiener filtering of images corrupted by multiplicative and signal-dependent noise, this paper assumes a lot of a priori information.

Frost et al.[19] consider the application of locally adaptive smoothing filters to the restoration of radar images degraded by multiplicative noise. They present a model for the coherent formation of synthetic aperture radar images in which the noise is multiplicative. Estimates of local image statistics — such as mean and variance — are made from the degraded image and used in an adaptive-smoothing filter implemented in the spatial domain. The authors provide experimental results that compare the filter with standard stationary filters and with an *ad hoc* median filter. The motivation for and implementation of the restoration method are similar to those described by Lee[20] for image enhancement.

Kuan et al.[21] design filters for the restoration of images with signal-dependent noise. Restoration filters adapt to local changes in image statistics based on a nonstationary-mean, nonstationary-variance image model. The degradations in the image are assumed to be due to uncorrelated, signal-dependent noise, which includes multiplicative, film-grain, and Poisson noise. The important assumption in the paper by Kuan et al.[21] is that the original image, adjusted for its local mean, is a nonstationary, uncorrelated, random process. For the case of uncorrelated, signal-dependent noise and no blur, this assumption results in a filter that becomes a point processor similar to Lee's filter.[20] However, for multiplicative noise, the smoothing filter is an extension of Lee's algorithm that allows for various types of signal-dependent noise. All of the nonstationary-image statistical parameters needed for the filter are estimated from the noisy image.

The next reprinted paper, by Kuan, Sawchuk, Strand, and Chavel, describes the application of nonstationary, two-dimensional recursive filtering to the restoration of images with signal-dependent speckle noise. Speckle noise exists in all imaging systems with coherent illumination, including synthetic aperture radar, coherent acoustic imaging, sonar, and laser-illuminated scenes. In this paper, the speckle is modeled as a signal-dependent noise, and an adaptive linear minimum mean-square estimation filter is defined for restoration of degraded images. The nonstationary-image mean, variance, and physical parameters of the speckle are estimated from the degraded image. Also, the authors discuss another technique for speckle reduction. This technique, which employs MAP restoration, is applicable to complex-amplitude speckle images in which both the amplitude and the phase of the degraded data are preserved. Experimental results are given in the paper.

The next reprinted paper, by Katsaggelos and Efstratiadis, presents a class of iterative signal-restoration algorithms that use a representation theorem for the generalized inverse of a matrix. Also, the authors propose methods for incorporating a priori knowledge about the solution into the form constraints.

The final paper reprinted in this chapter, by Civanlar and Trussell, also presents an elegant framework for incorporating a priori knowledge into image-restoration algorithms using the notion of fuzzy sets. Applications to image restoration, image coding, and tomography are highlighted in the paper.

Restoration of degraded images is a reasonably matured research topic with several practical applications. Research is still carried out on the following topics: restoration of image sequences, multichannel restoration, nonstationary images, synthetic aperture, infrared, and range images. Also, attempts are being made to develop algorithms that make as few assumptions as possible.

Chapter 3 References

1. J.W. Woods and V.K. Ingle, "Kalman Filtering in Two Dimensions: Further Results," *IEEE Trans. Acoustics, Speech, and Signal Processing*, Vol. ASSP-29, Apr. 1981, pp. 188-197.
2. J.W. Woods, "Two Dimensional Kalman Filtering," in *Two-Dimensional Digital Signal Processing I: Linear Filters*, T.S. Huang, ed., Topics in Applied Physics, Vol. 42, Springer-Verlag, New York, N.Y., 1981.
3. H.C. Andrews and B.R. Hunt, *Digital Image Restoration*, Prentice-Hall, Inc., Englewood Cliffs, N.J., 1977.
4. K. Kondo, Y. Ichioka, and T. Suzuki, "Image Restoration by Weiner Filtering in the Presence of Signal-Dependent Noise," *Applied Optics*, Vol. 16, Sept. 1977, pp. 2554-2558.
5. M.P. Ekstrom, "Realizable Wiener Filtering in Two Dimensions," *IEEE Trans. Acoustics, Speech, and Signal Processing*, Vol. ASSP-30, Feb. 1982, pp. 31-40.
6. A.K. Jain and J.R. Jain, "Partial Differential Equations and Finite Difference Methods in Image Processing " Part II: Image Restoration," *IEEE Trans. Automatic Control*, Vol. AC-23, Oct. 1978, pp. 817-834.
7. J.F. Abramatic and L.M. Silverman, "Nonlinear Restoration of Noisy Images," *IEEE Trans. Pattern Analysis and Machine Intelligence*, Vol. PAMI-4, Mar. 1982, pp. 141-149.
8. R. Kinderman and J.L. Snell, *Markov Random Fields and Their Application*, Am. Math. Soc., Providence, R.I., 1980.
9. S. Kirkpatrick, C.D. Gellatt, Jr., and M.P. Vecchi, "Optimization by Simulated Annealing," *Science*, Vol. 220, May 1983, pp. 671-680.
10. N. Metropolis et al., "Equations of State Calculations by Fast Computing Machines," *J. Chemical Physics*, Vol. 21, 1953, pp. 1087-1091.
11. D.W. Murray, A. Kashko, and H. Buxton, "A Parallel Approach to the Picture Restoration Algorithm of Geman and Geman on an SIMD Machine," *Image Vision Computing*, Vol. 4, Aug. 1986, pp. 133-142.
12. A. Lasota and M.C. Mackey, *Probabilistic Properties on Deterministic Systems*, Cambridge Univ. Press, New York, N.Y., 1985.
13. J.E. Besag, "On the Statistical Analysis of Dirty Pictures," *J. Royal Statistical Soc.*, Ser-B, Vol. 48, 1986, pp. 259-302.
14. A. Blake and A. Zisserman, *Visual Reconstruction*, MIT Press, Cambridge, Mass., 1987.
15. D. Luenberger, *Linear and Nonlinear Programming*, Addison-Wesley, Reading, Mass., 1984.
16. A.M. Tekalp, H. Kaufman, and J.W. Woods, "Identification of Image and Blur Parameters for the Restoration of Noncausal Blurs," *IEEE Trans. Acoustics, Speech, and Signal Processing*, Vol. ASSP-34, 1986, pp. 963-972.
17. A.M. Tekalp, H. Kaufman, and J.W. Woods, "On Statistical Identification of a Class of Linear Space Invariant Blurs Using Non-Minimum Phase ARMA Models," *IEEE Trans. Acoustics, Speech, and Signal Processing*, Vol. ASSP-36, 1988, pp. 1360-1363.
18. J. Biemond, F.G. Van der Putten, and J.W. Woods, "Identification and Restoration of Images with Symmetric Noncausal Blurs," *IEEE Trans. Circuits and Systems*, Vol. 23, 1988, pp. 385-394.
19. V.S. Frost et al., "A Model for Radar Images and Its Application to Adaptive Digital Filtering of Multiplicative Noise," *IEEE Trans. Pattern Analysis and Machine Intelligence*, Vol. PAMI-4, Mar. 1982, pp. 157-166.
20. J.S. Lee, "Digital Image Enhancement and Noise Filtering by Use of Local Statistics," *IEEE Trans. Pattern Analysis and Machine Intelligence*, Vol. PAMI-2, Mar. 1980, pp. 165-168.
21. D.T. Kuan et al., "Adaptive Noise Smoothing Filter for Images with Signal-Dependent Noise," *IEEE Trans. Pattern Analysis and Machine Intelligence*, Vol. PAMI-7, Mar. 1985, pp. 165-177.

Kalman Filtering in Two Dimensions

JOHN W. WOODS, MEMBER, IEEE, AND CLARK H. RADEWAN, MEMBER, IEEE

Reprinted from *IEEE Transactions on Information Theory*, Volume IT-23, Number 4, July 1977, pages 473-482. Copyright © 1977 by The Institute of Electrical and Electronics Engineers, Inc.

Abstract—The Kalman filtering method is extended to two dimensions. The resulting computational load is found to be excessive. Two new approximations are then introduced. One, called the strip processor, updates a line segment at a time; the other, called the reduced update Kalman filter, is a scalar processor. The reduced update Kalman filter is shown to be optimum in that it minimizes the post update mean-square error (mse) under the constraint of updating only the nearby previously processed neighbors. The resulting filter is a general two-dimensional recursive filter.

I. INTRODUCTION

IN RECENT YEARS there have been many attempts to extend Kalman filtering to two dimensions [1]–[3]. This is a direct result of the method's great success in one dimension. In the two-dimensional (2-D) case, the enormity of the data calls particularly for an efficient recursive processor. Unfortunately, the previous efforts to achieve a truly recursive 2-D Kalman filter were of only limited success because of both the difficulty in establishing a suitable 2-D recursive model and also the high dimension of the resulting state vector. In fact, a straightforward extension of one-dimensional (1-D) Kalman filter techniques would result in a number of state variables proportional to N for the filtering of an $N \times N$ digital image.

In this paper, we propose two schemes which to a large extent overcome the computational problems that have precluded the use of 2-D Kalman-like processors. We develop two new approximations: one to the 2-D Kalman vector processor (updates a line at a time), called the Kalman strip filter; and another to the 2-D Kalman scalar processor, (updates a point at a time) called the reduced update filter. Both of these processors offer computationally effective solutions to the problem of 2-D Kalman filtering. These results have application to a wide range of problems involving estimation on 2-D data fields, including the image processing problem where the utility of linear filtering is well-established. The theory includes the case of space-variant models, allowing a better match to local source statistics, in turn permitting a greater noise reduction. Further, it should be possible to treat nonlinear space-variant models via techniques similar to those of the 1-D extended Kalman filtering [5].

We start with a brief review of the concept of state and its role in 1-D Kalman filtering. Then we define the 2-D Kalman scalar and vector filters, and we point out their undesirable computational properties in that the state vector grows with the image size. Next, we present the Kalman strip filter and the reduced update Kalman filter. Finally, we present examples of application of the filters in a simulated data environment.

The Concept of State

The concept of state is central to linear system theory in one dimension. The state is defined as the minimum information about the past and present needed to determine all future responses given the future input [4]. For systems governed by differential or difference equations, the state is simply a sufficient set of initial conditions for the one-point boundary value problem. The state concept carries over to the case of stochastic differential and difference equations in Kalman filtering. In fact, the state vector of the dynamical system signal model determines the order of the Kalman calculations. In this random case, the state can be defined as the minimum amount of information about past and present estimates needed to determine an optimal causal estimate of future response given future noisy observations. The dynamical model for this case is given by [5]

$$s(m) = Fs(m-1) + Gu(m) \quad (1)$$

$$r(m) = Hs(m) + v(m), \quad (2)$$

where s is the signal state vector, r is the observation or received signal, v is the observation noise, and u is the random process which generates the signal. The matrices F, G, and H are, respectively, the system, drive, and observation matrices.

In (1) and (2), u and v are uncorrelated white Gaussian zero mean noise sources with correlation

$$E[u(m)u^T(k)] = Q_u \delta_{mk}$$

and

$$E[v(m)v^T(k)] = Q_v \delta_{mk},$$

where Q_u and Q_v are correlation matrices and δ_{mk} is the Kronecker delta. The Kalman filtering equations for this model are [5]

$$\hat{s}_b(m) = F\hat{s}_a(m-1) \quad (3)$$

$$P_b(m) = FP_a(m-1)F^T + GQ_uG^T \quad (4)$$

$$K(m) = P_b(m)H^T(HP_b(m)H^T + Q_v)^{-1} \quad (5)$$

$$\hat{s}_a(m) = \hat{s}_b(m) + K(m)[r(m) - H\hat{s}_b(m)] \quad (6)$$

Manuscript received May 3, 1976; revised October 25, 1976. This work was supported in part by the U.S. Energy Research and Development Administration under contract number W-7504-ENG-48 and in part by the Defense Advanced Research Projects Agency of the Department of Defense under ARPA Order No. 2436.

J. W. Woods was with Lawrence Livermore Laboratory, Livermore, CA. He is now with the Electrical and Systems Engineering Department, Rensselaer Polytechnic Institute, Troy, NY 12181.

C. H. Radewan is with the Lawrence Livermore Laboratory, Livermore, CA 94550.

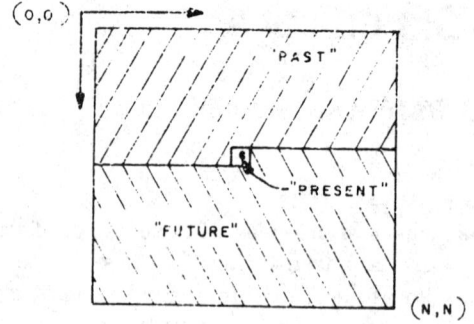

Fig. 1. Scalar scanning rectangular region using raster scan.

$$P_a(m) = [I - K(m)H]P_b(m), \quad (7)$$

where

$$P_i(m) \triangleq E[(s - \hat{s})_i(s - \hat{s})_i^T], \quad i = a,b$$

is the error covariance matrix. The subscripts a and b indicate "after" and "before" updating, respectively.

These equations have the following simple interpretation. First, in (3), we project the last estimate forward using the dynamics of the system model. Then in (6) we update this estimate using the new observation $r(m)$. Equation (5) is the gain matrix for the updating in (6). The remaining equations (4) and (7) are the error covariances necessary to calculate the new gain matrix.

II. KALMAN FILTERING IN TWO DIMENSIONS

A) A Scalar 2-D Kalman Filter

When we try to extend the above formalism to two dimensions, we encounter a problem concerning the 1-D definition of state as we will now show. First, we consider a particular scanning of a discrete 2-D square region consisting of an $N \times N$ regularly spaced lattice. Since the scanning does not qualitatively affect the results, we will assume the raster scan, i.e., left to right, advance one line, then repeat. Continuing with this procedure for the next $N-2$ lines we complete the scan. Thus at any point in the picture, some points will be the "past," one point will be the "present," and the remaining points will be the "future." These words will thus have their conventional meaning with respect to the order in which the points are processed (see Fig. 1). Next, we generalize our dynamical model (1). We obtain, by application of a recently developed 2-D spectral factorization routine [6], the $(M \times M)$th order (see Appendix) scalar equation,[1]

$$s(m,n) = \sum_{R_{\oplus +}} c_{kl} s(m-k, n-l) + u(m,n), \quad (8)$$

where $R_{\oplus +} = \{m \geq 0, n \geq 0\} \cup \{m < 0, n > 0\}$, which is to be compared to the scalar version of (1),

$$s(m) = \sum_{k=1}^{M} c_k s(m-k) + u(m). \quad (9)$$

[1] Inclusion of zeroes in the model leads to additional complications. To simplify the discussion, we consider only all-pole dynamical systems.

The model of (8) is called a nonsymmetric half-plane (NSHP) model [7].

Now we are in a position to appreciate the difficulty with state in two dimensions. For while (8) only uses $O(M^2)$ points for each computation of a new output point, so that the amount of computation is related to the order of the filter as in (9), when (8) moves across the image, values of s will be needed from the previous M lines. Thus the memory requirements of (8) are not of order related to the order of the filter as in (9). Because of this large memory requirement, the state vector for (8) must contain the M previous lines and hence has $O(MN)$ components.

It is convenient to take the part of the state vector on the support of the filter and give it a special name. Thus we define a new term *pseudo-state* as the minimum part of the state vector needed to compute the present output given the present input. This pseudo-state has a number of elements related to the order of the filter and hence its size determines the order of computation of the filter. However, the storage requirements are related to the size of the state vector. In the ordinary 1-D case, the pseudo-state vector is the state vector.

Next we will consider the Kalman filtering equations for this model. We will find that both the per point computation and the memory grow with N^2, the square of the width of the image field. Because of this unsatisfactory situation, we then turn to some approximate filters which greatly reduce the computation while only slightly affecting the accuracy of the estimate.

To obtain the Kalman filtering equations for the signal model of (8) and the observation equation

$$r(m,n) = s(m,n) + v(m,n), \quad (10)$$

where u and v are independent white Gaussian sources, we note that the scanning operation transforms the 2-D problem into an equivalent 1-D problem. Thus (8) can be put into the form (1) by defining the state vector of $M(N+1)$ components

$$s(m,n) = [s(m,n), s(m-1,n),$$
$$\cdots, s(1,n); s(N, n-1), \cdots, s(1, n-1);$$
$$\cdots; s(N, n-M), \cdots, s(m-M, n-M)]^T.$$

With this transformation, we obtain

$$s(m,n) = Fs(m-1, n) + Gu(m,n) \quad (11)$$

with corresponding observational model

$$r(m,n) = Hs(m,n) + v(m,n) \quad (12)$$

which is identical in form to (1) and (2) with line by line scanning understood. Thus we could immediately write down the Kalman equations. They would be (3) to (7) with the above interpretation of the s vector. The difficulty with these equations is the amount of computation and memory requirements associated with them. For example, consider an $(M \times M)$th order system model as in (8) and an observation region consisting of an $N \times N$ square with $N \gg M$. Then the dimension of the matrix equations (3) to (8) is approximately MN. This means that in general the order of the computation is $O(M^3N^3)$. However, taking advantage of the spatial invariant structure of the signal model, this can be reduced to $O(M^2N^2)$ as will be shown below. For $M = 4$ and $N = 100$, we require on the order of 160 000 multiplies and adds per output point. The overall total computation for the 10 000 element picture would be $O(10^9)$. At 1 μs/operation, the computer time for such a calculation would be 10^3 s or approximately 20 min. In addition, the data storage problems are immense. To store $P_{b,a}$ at each stage we need $O(MN)^2$ storage locations. For the above M and N, this is 160 000 words of storage to be accessed at each picture point! These numbers tell us that the exact 2-D Kalman scalar filter is computationally unmanageable, given today's state of the computer art. However, not only that, it is also wasteful of computation as will be pointed out below.

Next we consider the 2-D Kalman vector filter [8]. This is also an exact processor as is the scalar one mentioned above; however, the vector processor observes a line at a time instead of a point at a time.

B) A Kalman Vector Filter

In this formulation, we consider a vector scanning [8] consisting of a (horizontal) line at a time, as is necessary to do optimal Kalman vector filtering. We can write a recursive signal model

$$s(n) = Fs(n-1) + Gu(n) \quad (13)$$

with vector observations

$$r(n) = Hs(n) + v(n). \quad (14)$$

Here

$$s(n) \triangleq [s(1,n), \cdots, s(N,n); s(1,n-1), \cdots, s(N,n-1); \cdots; s(1,n-M+1), \cdots, s(N,n-M+1)]^T$$

and

$$r(n) = [r(1,n), \cdots, r(N,n)]^T.$$

Since (13) and (14) are of the form of (1) and (2), the Kalman equations are (3) thru (7) with the above interpretations for the s and r vectors. We note that these matrix equations are of order $O(MN)$ as in the 2-D Kalman scalar filter. However, each iteration of the vector filter yields N estimates (a whole line), so for the example given for the scalar filter, the vector filter computation times are reduced by a factor of N yielding an $O(M^3N^2)$ computation. The storage requirements are the same and hence this is again a computationally unmanageable solution.[2]

We will see below how splitting the picture up into partially overlapping strips can greatly reduce the computation of this vector filter. Further reductions in the order of the computation can be realized by using the special block form of the matrices F, G, and H in (13) and (14). These reductions in computation permit the practical implementation of the Kalman vector filter. As in the 2-D scalar case, we can construct the recursive dynamical model (13) by using a 2-D spectral factorization procedure [6].

III. NEW DEVELOPMENTS

In this section, we will summarize new approximate methods for realizing the 2-D Kalman scalar and vector filters [10], [11]. While both these techniques provide 2 to 3 orders of magnitude reduction in computation and storage, it can be anticipated that the reduction in the optimality of the estimate will be only slight. The reason for this surprising result is that the cause of the excessive computations is "purely theoretical," that is, the very uncommon but possible occurrence of high correlation at great distances. We will first develop an approximate Kalman vector filter called the strip processor. Then we will present a scalar filter called the reduced update Kalman filter.

A) A Kalman Strip Processor

The Kalman strip filter arises from the following considerations. First, although the vector filter has a state vector whose dimension is the width of the picture as is required for theoretical optimality, experience suggests that very few images will have the large correlation at great distances to justify such computation. Rather, most images show significant correlation only over rather compact neighborhoods of a given point. Thus we consider processing strips of the picture independently. The strips are overlapped with only the middle points being used as the final estimate. If the strip width is greater than the correlation distance of the signal and noise field, then close to optimum performance can result for points near the center. Processing the picture in these strips can greatly reduce the order of the computation and storage.

Second, we observe that if the data are stationary in the horizontal direction, we can save computation and storage by the following scheme: take the strips in the vertical direction and note that the filters for the different strips will all be the same. Thus the Kalman covariance equations (4) and (7) and the gain equation (5) need be calculated only for the first strip. Then the corresponding line in each of the remaining strips may be updated via (6) using the same gain matrix. In this way, storage need be provided for the covariance and gain matrices only in the first strip. Thus these two simplifications allow us to construct a good approximation to the Kalman vector filter which is computationally manageable. We will now elaborate on the details of constructing such a Kalman strip filter. This will consist of two parts: first, a discussion of the model, second, a discussion of the filter for that model.

1) The Strip Dynamical Model: The recursive signal model is the same as given in (13) with vector observations given in (14) with the exception that the vectors now are

---

[2] Note that the term vector processor was used in [8] to refer to a processor less than a line wide. However, we will reserve this term for the full width processor.

of dimension MW, where W is the strip width ($W \ll N$). We start the model development from a general NSHP recursive model (see Appendix), and develop from it a vector recursive model,

$$s(n) = Fs(n-1) + Gu(n) \quad (15)$$
$$r(n) = Hs(n) + v(n), \quad (16)$$

where

$$s(n) \triangleq [s(1,n), \cdots, s(W,n); s(1,n-1), \cdots, s(W,n-1); \cdots; s(1,n-M+1), \cdots, s(W,n-M+1)]^T$$

and

$$r(n) \triangleq [r(1,n), \cdots, r(W,n)]^T.$$

To obtain $r = s + v$, choose

$$H = [I:0:\cdots:0]^T.$$

Now F, G, and Q_u must be chosen so that s approximately satisfies (8). The conversion from (8) to (15) is most easily seen in the Z-transform domain. Taking the Z-transform of (8), we see that the system function transforming s into u is

$$\frac{U(z_1,z_2)}{S(z_1,z_2)} = 1 - C(z_1,z_2), \quad (17)$$

where

$$C(z_1,z_2) = \sum_{\mathcal{R}_{\oplus+}} c_{pq} z_1^{-p} z_2^{-q}. \quad (18)$$

Equation (17) can be factored as

$$1 - C(z_1,z_2) = (1 - C(z_1,\infty))(1 - C^{(1)}(z_1,z_2)), \quad (19)$$

where

$$C(z_1,\infty) = \sum_{p>0} c_{p0} z_1^{-p},$$

and where $C^{(1)}(z_1,z_2)$ contains only $q > 0$ terms and is generally of infinite order in z_1^{-1}.

Now $C^{(1)}$ can be approximately represented by F since it represents an operation on the previous rows. The first factor on the right side of (19) can be inverted and represented by G. In this way we arrive at the following form for F:

$$F = \begin{bmatrix} A_1 & A_2 & \cdots & A_M \\ I & O & \cdots & O \\ O & I & O & O \\ O & & \ddots & \ddots \\ O & & \cdots & O I O \end{bmatrix}, \quad (20)$$

which is $MW \times MW$ with $W \times W$ blocks I and A_m; $m = 1, \cdots, M$. Here

$$A_m = [I - C_0]^{-1} C_m \quad (21)$$

where the C_m are given by

$$(C_m)_{ij} = c_{m,i-j}. \quad (22)$$

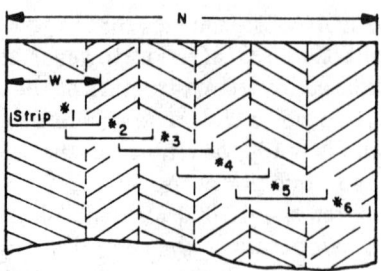

Fig. 2. Kalman strip processing example (dotted lines indicate estimate boundaries).

In like manner, we could set

$$G = [(I - C_0)^{-1} : O : O : O : \cdots : O]^T.$$

However, the edge effects due to the small strip width W would be expected to cause significant errors. To lessen this problem, we choose G to make the correlations of models (15) and (8) agree exactly in the current row. This procedure leaves uncorrected slight errors in the correlations with the $(M-1)$ previous rows in the model. Since the errors are both small and concentrated near the strip edges, they are expected to be insignificant in effect on the "saved" estimates in the middle section of the strip.

2) The Kalman Strip Filter: The Kalman equations for this model are

$$\hat{s}_b^i(n) = F \hat{s}_a^i(n-1) \quad (23)$$
$$\hat{s}_a^i(n) = \hat{s}_b^i(n) + K^1(n)[r^i(n) - H \hat{s}_b^i(n)], \quad (24)$$

where i is the number of the strip. In addition, to calculate the gain matrix for the nth line we must compute

$$P_b^1(n) = F P_a^1(n-1) F^T + G Q_u G^T \quad (25)$$
$$K^1(n) = P_b^1(n) H^T [H P_b^1(n) H^T + Q_v]^{-1} \quad (26)$$
$$P_a^1(n) = [I - K^1(n) H] P_b^1(n). \quad (27)$$

We note that for the horizontally stationary case, (25) through (27) need only be computed once for each line, while the estimates (23) and (24) are computed for all the strips at the nth line before proceeding to line $(n+1)$. Initial conditions are needed for (23) and (25) at the first line. They are given by

$$s_b^i(1) = E[s^i(1)] = o \quad (28)$$

and

$$P_b^1(1) = E[s^i(1) s^{iT}(1)] = R_s, \quad (29)$$

where R_s is the $MW \times MW$ correlation matrix of the model.

Fig. 2 shows a diagram for strip processing where the middle third of the elements are retained for the final estimate of s. The overlap would require a factor of three in computation. In the scheme used in the example of Section IV, a width of $W = 25$ is used with retention of the middle 15 elements. In this case, the "extra" computation due to the overlap is reduced to a factor of two. The amount of "extra" computation can be traded off for uniformity in the estimation error.

3) Optimization of Strip Width: To minimize the amount of computation for the completely nonstationary case, we can choose the number of retained elements N_R and the strip width W consistent with obtaining near optimum performance. To keep the saved points at least D from the strip edge, where D is the "correlation distance" of the signal s, we get

$$W = 2D + N_R.$$

The number of computations per point is proportional to

$$\frac{(2D + N_R)^3}{N_R}, \quad \text{for } N \gg 2D.$$

The minimum occurs at

$$N_R^o = D \tag{30}$$

which yields

$$W^o = 3D \tag{31}$$

to minimize computation.

When the data are stationary horizontally, then the number of computations is asymptotically

$$\frac{(2D + N_R)^2}{N_R}, \quad \text{for } N \gg 2D.$$

The minimum turns out to be

$$N_R^o = 2D$$

which yields

$$W^o = 4D. \tag{32}$$

B) Reduced Update Kalman Filtering

In this section, we will treat an approximation to the 2-D Kalman scalar processor presented in Section II-A. This involves the dynamical model (8) and the scalar observation (10). As indicated earlier, the state vector for this filter is $O(MN)$ dimensional, where M is the order of the recursive model and N is the width of the picture. Thus all these points must be updated in an equation equivalent to (6). The main concept of the reduced update filter is that the Kalman equations are composed of two steps: a prediction part and an update part. Now the prediction part, as set forth in (3), is a computationally straightforward projection of $O(M^2)$ previous estimates. However, the update part involves calculations involving each of the $O(MN)$ random variables in the state vector. Since $N \gg M$, we can reduce the bulk of the computation by reducing the update process. Thus we choose to update only those elements of the state vector within a certain distance of the point currently being processed, (m,n). We can expect this procedure to result in a good approximation because significant updates will be confined to a region around the observation at (m,n). Therefore, omitting the update of points far away should only minimally impact performance. For convenience of notation, we take this region to be the support of the NSHP recursive signal model in

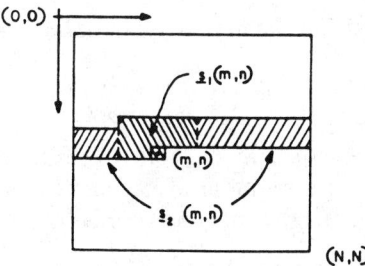

Fig. 3. Assignment of points to partitioned state vector.

(8). Hence, there are only $O(M^2)$ points to update, i.e., we only update the pseudo-state vector for each observation. In the remainder of this section, we will derive the equations for the optimal updating of the pseudo-state vector. We will see that these equations can point the way to further simplifications which are expected again to result in only slightly suboptimum performance.

Let the signal model be generated by

$$s(m,n) = \sum_{\mathcal{R}_{\oplus +}} c_{kl} s(m-k, n-l) + w(m,n), \tag{33}$$

where $\{w(m,n)\}$ is a zero mean homogeneous white Gaussian source with variance σ_w^2. The received signal is

$$r(m,n) = s(m,n) + v(m,n), \tag{34}$$

where $\{v(m,n)\}$ is zero mean homogeneous white Gaussian noise, independent of $\{w(m,n)\}$, with variance σ_v^2.

Let the field $\{r(m,n)\}$ be observed over an $N \times N$ rectangular region. Next, introduce a vector notation for the pseudo-state vector corresponding to a scalar line by line scan, viz.,

$$s_1(m,n) \triangleq [s(m,n), \cdots, s(m-M, n); s(m+M, n-1),$$
$$\cdots, s(m-M, n-1);$$
$$\cdots; s(m+M, n-M), \cdots, s(m-M, n-M)]^T. \tag{35}$$

Order the remaining points of the state vector onto $s_2(m,n)$. Thus the resulting assignment of points is as shown in Fig. 3. With this convention the state vector can be written

$$s(m,n) = (s_1^T(m,n), s_2^T(m,n))^T. \tag{36}$$

The state dynamical model can then be written

$$s(m,n) = Cs(m-1, n) + w(m,n), \tag{37}$$

where C is the system propagation matrix determined by $\{c_{kl}\}$ and by the ordering of the state vector $s(m,n)$. Note that (37) holds for all the points (m,n), except near the boundaries where boundary conditions must be incorporated. The drive vector is given as

$$w(m,n) \triangleq (w(m,n), 0, \cdots, 0)^T. \tag{38}$$

The scalar observation equation is

$$r(m,n) = Hs(m,n) + v(m,n), \tag{39}$$

where

$$H = (1, 0, \cdots, 0). \tag{40}$$

We can partition the matrix C similarly to s as

$$C = \begin{pmatrix} C_{11} & C_{12} \\ C_{21} & C_{22} \end{pmatrix}. \quad (41)$$

It then turns out that C_{11} and C_{12} contain all the $\{c_{kl}\}$ terms, and the remainder of C constitutes a shift transformation. Thus (37) may be rewritten as

$$s_1(m,n) = C_{11}s_1(m-1,n) + w_1(m,n) + C_{12}s_2(m-1,n), \quad (42)$$

where w has been partitioned similarly to s. Equation (42) focuses on the computation to be performed at (m,n). That is, s_2 requires only the shifting of previously computed values. We can similarly partition $H = (H_1, H_2)$ with $H_2 = O$ to get a new observation equation

$$r(m,n) = H_1 s_1(m,n) + v(m,n). \quad (43)$$

1) Derivation of Reduced Update Filter: Assume that the received array $\{r(m,n)\}$ is scanned in line by line fashion. Then the Kalman filtering equations can be written immediately from (3) through (7) as discussed in Section I.

  a) Extrapolation:
$$m \to m+1$$
$$P_b(m,n) = CP_a(m-1,n)C^T + GQ_w G^T \quad (44)$$
$$\hat{s}_b(m,n) = C\hat{s}_a(m-1,n) \quad (45)$$

  b) Update:
$$K(m,n) = P_b(m,n)H^T[HP_b(m,n)H^T + \sigma_v^2]^{-1} \quad (46)$$
$$\hat{s}_a(m,n) = \hat{s}_b(m,n) + K(m,n)[r(m,n) - H\hat{s}_b(m,n)] \quad (47)$$
$$P_a(m) = [I - K(m,n)H]P_b(m,n). \quad (48)$$

If an arbitrary gain matrix is used instead of the one prescribed in (46), the covariance P_a given in (48) changes to [5]

$$P_a(m,n) = (I - K(m,n)H)P_b(m,n)(I - K(m,n)H)^T + K(m,n)\sigma_v^2 K^T(m,n). \quad (49)$$

Let $K(m,n)$ have the form

$$K(m,n) = \begin{bmatrix} K_1(m,n) \\ \hline O \end{bmatrix}, \quad (50)$$

where the partitioning corresponds to that of $s(m,n)$. We now choose $K_1(m,n)$ to minimize the trace of $P_a(m,n)$ as given in (49) for $K(m,n)$ as given in (50). The result is the reduced update Kalman filter.

  c) Extrapolation:
$$m \to m+1$$
$$P_b(m,n) = CP_a(m-1,n)C^T + GQ_w G^t \quad (51)$$
$$\hat{s}_{1b}(m,n) = C_{11}\hat{s}_{1a}(m-1,n) + C_{12}\hat{s}_{2a}(m-1,n). \quad (52)$$

  d) Update:
$$K_1(m,n) = P_{11,b}(m,n)H_1^T(H_1 P_{11,b}(m,n)H_1^T + \sigma_v^2)^{-1} \quad (53)$$

$$\hat{s}_{1a}(m,n) = \hat{s}_{1b}(m,n) + K_1(m,n)[r(m,n) - H_1\hat{s}_{1b}(m,n)] \quad (54)$$

$$P_{11,a}(m,n) = [I - K_1(m,n)H_1]P_{11,b}(m,n) \quad (55a)$$
$$P_{12,a}(m,n) = [I - K_1(m,n)H_1]P_{12,b}(m,n) \quad (55b)$$

where P_a and P_b have been partitioned similarly to s.

Equations (51)–(55) can provide great computational savings over the standard Kalman filtering equations. To understand these equations better, it is helpful to convert them back to scalar notation. First, we note that (52) will become, in scalar notation,

$$\hat{s}_b^{(m,n)}(m,n) = \sum_{\mathcal{R}_{\oplus+}} c_{kl}\hat{s}_a^{(m-1,n)}(m-k,n-l), \quad (56)$$

since it represents propagation of the previous estimates through the dynamics of the system. In these scalar equations, the superscript indicates the step in the filtering, while the argument represents the position of the data. Equation (51) represents the error in this predicted estimate; thus it becomes

$$R_b^{(m,n)}(m,n;k,l)$$
$$= \sum_{op} c_{op} R_a^{(m-1,n)}(m-o, n-p; k,l), \quad (k,l) \in \mathcal{S}_{\oplus+}^{(m,n)} \quad (57)$$

$$R_b^{(m,n)}(m,n;m,n)$$
$$= \sum_{kl} c_{kl} R_b^{(m,n)}(m,n; m-k, n-l) + \sigma_w^2, \quad (58)$$

where $\mathcal{S}_{\oplus+}^{(m,n)}$ is the support of the state vector $s(m,n)$.

Equation (53) computes a $K_1(m,n)$ which has the same support as $s_1(m,n)$, namely, $\mathcal{R}_{\oplus+}^{(m,n)}$, the support of the pseudo-state vector. The scalar equation identical to (53) is

$$K^{(m,n)}(i,j) = \frac{R_b^{(m,n)}(m,n;i,j)}{R_b^{(m,n)}(m,n;m,n) + \sigma_v^2},$$
$$(i,j) \in \mathcal{R}_{\oplus+}^{(m,n)}. \quad (59)$$

Similarly, (54) becomes

$$\hat{s}_a^{(m,n)}(i,j) = \hat{s}_b^{(m,n)}(i,j) + K^{(m,n)}(m-i, n-j)[r(m,n) - \hat{s}_b^{(m,n)}(m,n)], \quad (i,j) \in \mathcal{R}_{\oplus+}^{(m,n)}. \quad (60)$$

Finally, (55a) and (55b) both are expressible as the set of scalar equations

$$R_a^{(m,n)}(i,j;k,l) = R_b^{(m,n)}(i,j;k,l) - K^{(m,n)}(m-i, n-j)R_b^{(m,n)}(m,n;k,l),$$
$$\text{for } (i,j) \in \mathcal{R}_{\oplus+}^{(m,n)}; (k,l) \in \mathcal{S}_{\oplus+}^{(m,n)}. \quad (61)$$

The reduced update Kalman filter comprising (56) to (61) has been derived as an optimal approximation to the 2-D Kalman scalar filter. The prediction part of the Kalman filter is left unchanged, and the update is optimized under the constraint of updating only the nearest previously processed neighbors. It is thus perhaps not clear that the resulting reduced update filter is overall optimal in the class of 2-D recursive filters of the same order as itself because the prediction part of the Kalman filter was

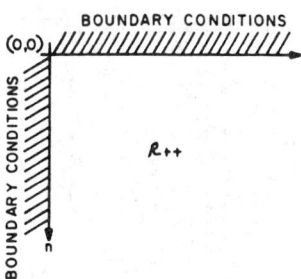

Fig. 4. Data region to be filtered by reduced update equations.

held fixed in the above derivation. However, it turns out that this procedure is indeed overall optimal as will now be seen.

Theorem: The reduced update Kalman filter is optimal under its constraint, i.e., it minimizes the mse over the class of spatially varying, linear, 2-D recursive filters of similar order.

Proof: Consider filtering the region $\mathcal{R}_{\oplus+}$ with boundary conditions (bc) on the upper and left edges as shown in Fig. 4. The method of proof will be induction. The signal model is given by (33) with observations given by (34). For the first point $(m,n) = 0$, obviously the best prediction will be

$$\hat{s}_b^{(0,0)}(0,0) = \sum_{\mathcal{R}_{\oplus+}} c_{kl} s^{(bc)}(-k,-l). \quad (62)$$

If this is followed by the optimal constrained update, we obtain

$$\hat{s}_a^{(0,0)}(0,0) = \hat{s}_{\text{mmse}}(0,0),$$

the best mse estimate subject to constraint. Now assume we have the best constrained mse estimate at (m,n). Then the best prediction based on the pseudo-state is

$$\hat{s}_b^{(m+1,n)}(m+1,n) = \sum c_{kl} \hat{s}_a^{(m,n)}(m+1-k, n-l), \quad (63)$$

as can be seen by applying to (33) the conditional expectation operator $E[\cdot \mid \hat{s}_1(m,n)]$. Finally, the optimal constrained update generates the optimal constrained mse estimate at $(m+1,n)$. This completes the proof.

From this theorem follows the very important fact that for homogeneous data the Kalman reduced update filter will converge to an optimal 2-D NSHP recursive filter for estimating the data. Now, in one dimension, such a filter could be obtained via Wiener's spectral design procedure [9]. However, the same procedure in the 2-D case leads to an infinite-order filter, thus the optimal finite-order filter is not obtained. Hence, the reduced update Kalman filter is also particularly attractive from the standpoint of design of spatially invariant filters for homogeneous random fields.

2) Order of Computation: Next we investigate the order of computation of the reduced update Kalman filter. We will consider each of (56) thru (61) separately. First, (56) will be $O(M^2)$ for an Mth order NSHP model. Equation (56) will thus be $O(M^2)$ for each (k,l). Since there are $O(MN)$ points in $\mathcal{S}_{\oplus+}^{(m,n)}$, we obtain $O(M^3N)$ for (57). Equation (58) is $O(M^2)$, as are (58) and (60). Equation (61) is simple, but has to be computed for each pair (i,j) and (k,l) with $(k,l) \in \mathcal{S}_{\oplus+}^{(m,n)}$, thus giving a computational total of $O(M^3N)$ as in (57). Summing up, we get the overall total computation per point as $O(M^3N)$. This is to be compared with $O(M^3N^3)$ for the general Kalman scalar filter and $O(M^2N^2)$ for the $(M \times M)$th order half-plane filter model.

The overall savings of a factor N^2 results from two simplifications. First, the reduced update has reduced the orders of the matrices from $MN \times MN$ to $M^2 \times MN$. Second, for the $(M \times M)$th order filter model, the scalar equations (56) to (61) write only the newly computed values at point (m,n). Equation (51), for example, contains many more error covariance values than (57) and (58). However, only the first row (and column) of $P_b(m,n)$ actually changes. The other elements simply get shifted. The scalar equations were written with respect to a fixed reference, the origin in the data plane. Thus no shifting appears in that notation. Another way of looking at this is as follows. The C matrix is composed of zeroes and ones except for the first row. These zeroes and ones simply serve to shift the data in the state vector, one place down as each new element is put in. This computation can be avoided by using indirect addressing and simply writing the new element over the oldest element in storage. Then a pointer or indirect address can be used to keep track of the "head" of the vector. This is essentially the reason for not counting the shifting operations, as they can be avoided with minimal computational effort on many machines.

For the reasons outlined in the previous paragraph, (56) thru (61) not only provide a convenient way to perceive the two-dimensional nature of the reduced update filter, but also present its essential computational aspects. The main computation was observed to be in (57) and (61). Equation (56) computes the error covariance between the "predicted point" (m,n) and the previous estimates in the filters state vector. Experience suggests this will be peaked at the point (m,n) with rapid decay with distance from (m,n). Thus it is a reasonable approximation to compute (57) only in a fixed size region including $\mathcal{R}_{\oplus+}^{(m,n)}$. This reasoning can also be applied to (61), where (k,l) would be restricted to a region significantly smaller than $\mathcal{S}_{\oplus+}^{(m,n)}$ and of fixed size for increasing N. Calling such a region $\mathcal{T}_{\oplus+}^{(m,n)}$ we can rewrite (57) and (61) as

$$R_b^{(m,n)}(m,n;k,l) = \sum c_{op} R_a^{(m-1,n)}(m-o, n-p; k,l), \quad (k,l) \in \mathcal{T}_{\oplus+}^{(m,n)} \quad (64)$$

$$R_a^{(m,n)}(i,j;k,l) = R_b^{(m,n)}(i,j;k,l) - K^{(m,n)}(m-i, n-j) R_b^{(m,n)}(m,n;k,l),$$
$$\text{for } (i,j) \in \mathcal{R}_{\oplus+}^{(m,n)}; (k,l) \in \mathcal{T}_{\oplus+}^{(m,n)}. \quad (65)$$

These approximate reduced update equations reduce the order of the computation to $O(M^4)$, a constant with respect to N. Fig. 5 sets forth the envisioned region assignment. As mentioned above, the adverse effects of substituting $\mathcal{T}$

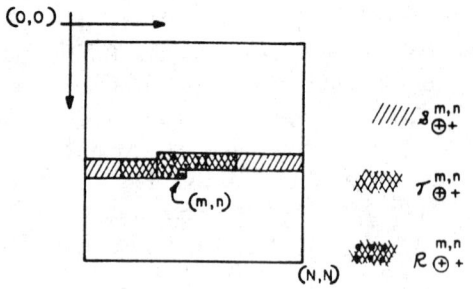
Fig. 5. Region assignment for $T_{\oplus+}^{(m,n)}$, covariance update region.

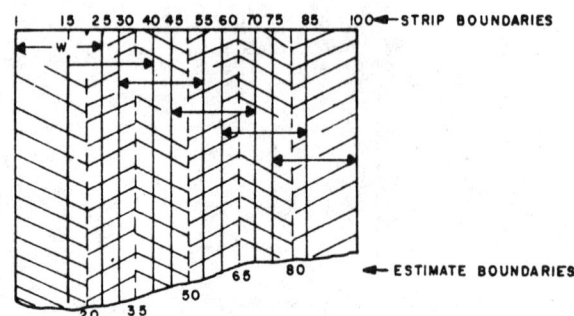
Fig. 6. Strip arrangement detail.

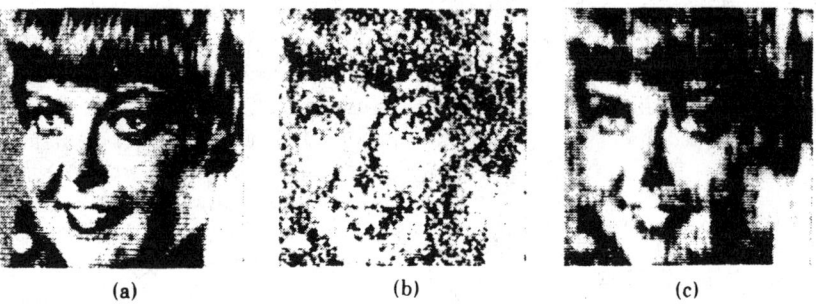
Fig. 7. Strip processing example. (a) Original. (b) Noisy (SNR = 1). (c) Estimate.

for $\mathcal{S}$ are expected to be minimal for most pictures. This is so both for the reasons mentioned previously and also because (59), the Kalman gain calculation does not directly make use of points outside $\mathcal{R}_{\oplus+}^{(m,n)}$. Thus the effect of this "truncation" would seem to be at worst second-order.

If we look at memory requirements, we find that they are dominated by the need to store the $\boldsymbol{R}_a$ error covariances. For the 2-D Kalman scalar filter, this storage will be $(M^2 N^2)$. For the reduced update filter we get the same amount of storage, only a portion of which is accessed at every point. For the approximate reduced update filter, we obtain $O(M^3 N)$. A little thought reveals that this is the minimal possible dependence on N, i.e., linear, for a spatially varying processor.[3] Thus we cannot hope for further improvements here. However, for homogeneous regions, these storage requirements can be greatly relaxed. Then one only has to run the processor over a much smaller region to obtain near convergence to the steady-state filter. Subsequently, only (56) and (60) need be computed at a substantially lower amount of computational effort.

IV. Experimental Results

A noisy picture was processed with the Kalman strip filter. The signal was a 100 × 100 element center segment from a standard SMPTE test picture. The 8-bit original had an estimate of its mean removed prior to processing. The picture was then scaled so that its variance equaled one. White Gaussian noise was added at unit variance to

[3] To see this, note that the processor must minimally have access to the error variances for the entire previous line.

produce a SNR of unity. The original with mean removed was also used to generate a (10 × 4)th order $+\oplus$ NHSP model [6], [7]. (See Appendix). This turns out to be a model for the transposed pictures. Thus the noisy image was transposed and inserted into the Kalman strip filter program with the above NSHP model. The strip arrangement is shown in detail in Fig. 6. There are six strips, each 25-points wide, with five-element overlap on each side for the interior strips. The middle 15 elements of the strips cover the picture and provide a fairly uniform error covariance. The mean value was added back and the estimate images transposed for presentation.

Fig. 7(a) shows the original image. Fig. 7(b) shows the noisy image. Fig. 7(c) shows the strip filter estimate. The measured SNR improvement was 7.7 dB. This compares favorably with previous results. As the model and noise were stationary, convergence was obtained; in this case, in 10 lines. The computer time was under 15 s on a CDC 7600 computer. The error covariance values were within 3 percent of their minimum value over the 15-element middle region of the strip. On the strip edge, it was as much as 60 percent above the minimum error variance value which was near the center.

The noisy picture of Fig. 7(b) was also modeled with a (3 × 3)th order $\oplus+$ NSHP factor and processed by the approximate reduced update Kalman filter for various sizes of $T_{\oplus+}$. In particular, region half-widths of 3, 5, 7, and 9 were tried. The results were approximately the same in all cases, indicating both that the error decorrelates fast for our model and that the filter is fairly robust with respect to this type of error. The measured SNR improvement was 8.3 dB with output shown as Fig. 8. Convergence

Fig. 8. Reduced update estimate.

was obtained in 10 lines or less with a run time of 40 s. This run time could be greatly shortened if the filter were updated only for the first 10 columns in the first 10 lines instead of the entire first 10 lines. The error covariance values of a sampling of the columns indicate that such a change in the algorithm would have negligible effect on the final result. This is because the chosen covariance model, as is typical of images, does not show substantial correlation over distances on the order of ten or more pixels.

V. Conclusions

The Kalman strip filter was introduced as a new approximation to the Kalman vector filter which processes a line at a time. The new filter is not limited to separable correlation functions and provides nearly uniform estimation error over the image by incorporating strip overlap. An optimum strip width was chosen to minimize computation. The reduced update Kalman filter was introduced and shown to be optimum in that it minimizes the post update mse under the constraint of updating only the nearby previously processed neighbors. It was shown that for all-pole data models, the Kalman reduced update filter coverges to an optimum 2-D recursive filter in the homogeneous case.

Appendix

Spectral Factorization in Two Dimensions [6]

In this Appendix, we review some of the properties of two-dimensional (2-D) spectral factorization that are pertinent to the development of 2-D recursive models. Since our recursive model consists of a recursive filtering of spatially white Gaussian noise, the problem can be thought of as a filter design problem.

In [7] it is shown that under mild conditions, one may factor a 2-D spectrum into nonsymmetric half-plane (NSHP) factors. The support of the filter numerator a and denominator b is restricted to a nonsymmetric half-plane, that is, a half-plane with the negative axis removed, as shown in Fig. 9. This removal allows the filter to be recursible. Fig. 10 shows how the NSHP support of b permits the 2-D recursion from left to right and top to bottom. This recursion can be accomplished precisely, because only previously computed points are used in the computation of the present output.

By the order of an NSHP filter, we mean the following: let the support of b and a be given by the union of an $(M_1 + 1) \times (M_2 + 1)$ square and an $M_1 \times M_2$ square situated as shown in Fig. 11. We will agree to call such a filter an $(M_1 \times M_2)$th-order NSHP

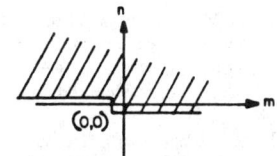

Fig. 9. Nonsymmetric half-plane.

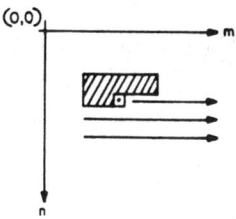

Fig. 10. Recursion of filter with NSHP support.

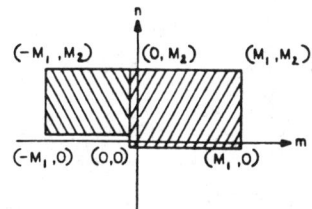

Fig. 11. Diagram illustrating concept of order of NSHP filter.

filter. This notation is then indicative of the highest powers of z_1, z_2, z_1^{-1}, and z_2^{-1} in the filter's 2-D Z-transform

$$B(z_1,z_2) = \sum_{m=0}^{M_1} \sum_{n=0}^{M_2} b_{mn} z_1^{-m} z_2^{-n} + \sum_{m=-1}^{-M_1} \sum_{n=-1}^{-M_2} b_{mn} z_1^{-m} z_2^{-n}. \quad (A1)$$

As mentioned above, these recursive factors arise from a spectral factorization, in this case, that of the signal spectrum S_s. In general, the exact factors of S_s will be infinite-order, however, finite-order approximations can result in a specified small error. We can obtain such an approximation, in the simplest case, by simply truncating the factors to finite support. Thus we can solve the following rational approximation problem.

Given $\epsilon > 0$, choose the NSHP filter order $M_1 \times M_2$ high enough so that

$$\left|\left| S_s(u,v) - \left|\frac{A(e^{ju},e^{jv})}{B(e^{ju},e^{jv})}\right|^2 \right|\right| < \epsilon, \quad (A2)$$

where A and B are the 2-D Z-transforms of the filter numerator a and denominator b, respectively, and where $||\cdot||$ is a suitable functional norm, e.g., L^1, L^2, L^∞, etc., and most importantly where the resulting 2-D recursive filter is *stable*. In [6], a window method is advanced as a simple way to design these filters. This method was used to obtain the models in this paper. More elaborate and efficient design methods are presently under investigation.

References

[1] A. Habibi, "Two-dimensional Bayesian estimate of images," *Proc. IEEE*, vol. 60, p. 878–883, July 1972.

[2] N. E. Nahi, "Role of the recursive estimation in statistical image enhancement," *Proc. IEEE*, vol. 60, p. 872–877, July 1972.

[3] S. R. Powell and L. M. Silverman, "Modeling of two-dimensional covariance functions with application to image restoration," *IEEE Trans. Auto. Control*, vol. AC-19, p. 8–13, Feb. 1974.
[4] P. Padulo and M. A. Arbib, *System Theory*. Philadelphia, PA: W. B. Saunders, 1974, p. 21.
[5] A. P. Sage and J. L. Melsa, *Estimation Theory with Applications to Communications and Control*. New York: McGraw-Hill, 1971, p. 89–90.
[6] M. P. Ekstrom and J. W. Woods, "Two-dimensional spectral factorization with applications in recursive digital filtering," *IEEE Trans. Acoust., Speech and Signal Proc.*, vol. ASSP-24, pp. 115–128, Apr. 1976.
[7] J. W. Woods and M. P. Ekstrom, "Nonsymmetric half-plane recursive filters—characterization, stability theory and test," in *Proceedings 1975 Int'l Sympos. on Circuits and Systems*, Newton, MA, Apr. 1975, p. 447–450.
[8] N. E. Nahi and C. A. Franco, "Recursive image enhancement by vector scanning," *IEEE Trans. Commun.*, vol. C-21, pp. 305–311, April 1973.
[9] N. Wiener, *The Extrapolation, Interpolation, and Smoothing of Stationary Time Series*. New York: Wiley, 1949.
[10] J. W. Woods and C. H. Radewan, "The Kalman strip filter—a two-dimensional recursive vector processor," in *Proc. 9th Asilomar Conference Circuits, Sys. & Comp.*, Pacific Grove, CA, Nov. 1975.
[11] J. W. Woods and C. H. Radewan, "Reduced update Kalman filter—a two-dimensional recursive processor," presented at *Johns Hopkins Conf. on Inform. Sci. & Sys.*, Baltimore, MD, Apr. 1976.

Correction to "Kalman Filtering in Two Dimensions"

JOHN W. WOODS, MEMBER, IEEE

Reprinted from *IEEE Transactions on Information Theory*, Volume IT-25, Number 5, September 1979, page 628. Copyright © 1979 by The Institute of Electrical and Electronics Engineers, Inc.

In the above paper,[1] the two-dimensional (2-D) reduced update Kalman filter was introduced as an optimal approximation to the 2-D Kalman filter for scalar observations obtained from a raster scan. The reduced update filter consists of two parts: a prediction part and a reduced update part, i.e., an update of

TABLE I
MEAN-SQUARE PREDICTION ERROR SUMMARY (SNR = 3 DB, $\sigma_v^2 = 1440$)

Update Region	Example 1		Example 2		Example 3	
	$\sigma^2(\underline{c})$	$\sigma^2(\underline{b})$	$\sigma^2(\underline{c})$	$\sigma^2(\underline{b})$	$\sigma^2(\underline{c})$	$\sigma^2(\underline{b})$
Fig. 1 (a)	727	725	363	359	515	512
Fig. 1 (b)	740	727	367	360	526	516

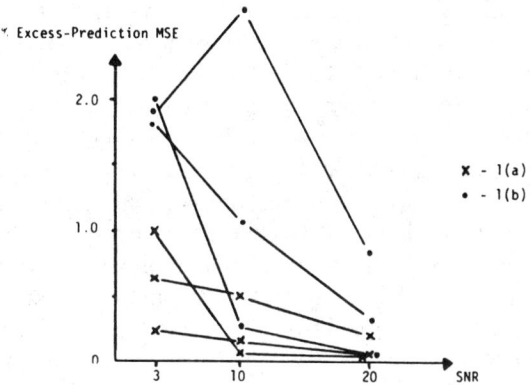

Fig. 1. Two updated regions. (·) indicates current data location.

Fig. 2. Percent excess prediction mean-square error versus SNR in dB.

points near the scalar observation. The algorithm was derived to be *weakly optimal*, in that at each point the reduced updating is performed optimally with respect to mean square error in the Gaussian case. The prediction is performed using the 2-D dynamical model, and it was claimed that this prediction part was also optimal in the sense of being an optimal estimate conditioned on the current estimate of the pseudo-state vector, the filters active memory. When both the prediction and update are optimal, the filter will be called *strongly optimal*.

Unfortunately the 2-D reduced update filter is not strongly optimal. In particular (63) of the paper was based on

Manuscript received July 24, 1978. This work was supported by the Air Force Office of Scientific Research, Air Force Systems Command, USAF, under Grant 77-3361.

The author is with the Electrical and Systems Engineering Department, Rensselaer Polytechnic Institute, Troy, NY 12181.

[1] J. W. Woods and C. H. Radewan, *IEEE Trans. Inform. Theory*, vol. IT-23, pp. 473–482, July 1977.

$$E[s_1(m,n)|\hat{s}_1(m,n)] = \hat{s}_1(m,n), \quad (1)$$

which can be shown to be necessary and sufficient for the optimality of dynamical prediction. However (1) is not generally true for the reduced update filter. This is because as the pseudo-state vector $\hat{s}_1(m,n)$, the data on which the dynamical prediction is based, moves across the picture, old elements move from the inactive memory into the active or updated memory. Therefore the elements of $\hat{s}_1(m,n)$ may not be jointly optimal in the sense of (1). Having observed this, one may construct a counterexample to show the nonoptimality of the dynamical model for 2-D prediction. Thus the 2-D reduced update filter is not strongly optimal. Two questions arise: how does one modify the reduced update filter to be strongly optimal, and is the reduced update filter approximately strongly optimal? These questions are answered below.

MODIFICATIONS FOR STRONG OPTIMALITY

The most straightforward modification for strong optimality is to calculate an optimal prediction vector

$$\boldsymbol{b}(m,n) \triangleq E\big[\hat{s}_1(m,n)\hat{s}_1^T(m,n)\big]^{-1} E[s(m+1,n)\hat{s}_1(m,n)]. \quad (2)$$

Then the resulting optimal prediction is

$$\hat{s}(m+1,n) = \boldsymbol{b}^T(m,n)\hat{s}_1(m,n) = \sum_{\mathcal{R}_{\oplus+}} b_{k,l}^{(m,n)} \hat{s}^{(m,n)}(m-k, n-l), \quad (3)$$

where the $b_{k,l}^{(m,n)}$ are the properly ordered elements of $\boldsymbol{b}(m,n)$. The reduced update part of the algorithm is unchanged. However, in order to calculate (2), one must additionally compute and update the estimate covariances and cross-covariances between the estimate and the signal. While this represents a significantly increased design burden, the computational complexity of the steady-state filter is not adversely affected.

APPROXIMATE STRONG OPTIMALITY

To demonstrate the approximate strong optimality of the unmodified reduced update Kalman filter, several examples were run using homogeneous data whose statistics exactly match those of several (2×2)th order models. Steady-state reduced update filters were generated and used to filter the data. Running average estimates of the covariance matrix and cross-covariance vector of (2) were calculated over the 128×128 images (leaving out a ten-pixel border on all sides). An optimal steady-state prediction vector $\boldsymbol{b}$ was thus determined. In a second filter run, this optimal $\boldsymbol{b}$ was used to predict s_1 as a side calculation, and the mean-square prediction error was tabulated. The mean-square prediction error using the dynamical model c vector was also calculated. The dynamical and optimal prediction error variances are shown in Table I for two slightly different updated regions, a 13-pixel one shown in Fig. 1(a) and a 12-element one shown in Fig. 1(b). The prediction error values in Table I show that the dynamical prediction is nearly optimal for these examples, especially using the update region of Fig. 1(a). Fig. 2 shows the percent excess prediction mean-square error versus signal-to-noise ratio (SNR) for the three examples of Table I.

Edge-Adaptive Kalman Filtering for Image Restoration with Ringing Suppression

A. MURAT TEKALP, MEMBER, IEEE, HOWARD KAUFMAN, SENIOR MEMBER, IEEE, AND JOHN W. WOODS, FELLOW, IEEE

Abstract—We extend the two-dimensional (2-D) linear space-invariant (LSI) reduced update Kalman Filter (RUKF) to edge-adaptive space-variant restoration of noisy and blurred images using a decision-directed approach. The edge-adaptive RUKF was motivated by the need to suppress the ringing artifacts caused by LSI processing. We show that ringing artifacts can be suppressed to a great extent by using multiple image models that provide a better match to local edge orientation. The maximum *a posteriori* probability decision procedure developed in this paper, for model selection at each pixel, can be used with other 2-D Kalman filtering algorithms as well.

I. INTRODUCTION

IMAGE restoration may be defined as the process of undoing imaging degradations based on mathematical model of these degradations. The aim of image restoration is to remove blur and noise incurred in recording the image. Blur removal is a deconvolution-type problem [1], which is often ill posed[1] owing to the presence of observation noise as well as any singularity of the inverse system. Hence, direct-inversion (i.e., pseudoinverse filtering) may cause large oscillations in the solution due to noise amplification.

It is possible, however, to formulate a well-posed stochastic extension of the ill-posed restoration problem [2]. Hence, many researchers [3]-[5] have attempted to solve the image restoration problem using Kalman filtering techniques, where a statistical model of the image can be utilized to effectively regularize the ill-posed deconvolution problem. The better the model fits the image, the better the regularization that can be achieved.

A straightforward extension of the well-known 1-D Kalman filter into two dimensions creates dimensionality and computational problems. To this effect, Woods and Radewan [6] derived a suboptimal but efficient approximation to the 2-D Kalman filter defined as the reduced-update Kalman filter (RUKF). In [6], the development was presented for the estimation-in-noise problem. In a subsequent paper, Woods and Ingle [5] extended RUKF to deconvolution-type problems.

Kalman filtering for the restoration of degraded images has some advantages when compared to other stochastic filtering techniques. First, since it is recursive in the spatial domain, it does not require too much storage. Therefore, it is suitable for implementation on microcomputers. Second, it can be easily extended to optimal adaptive filtering of images through the use of space-variant image and blur models to improve its performance.

Many researchers [7], [8] have found that much better results, in terms of both mean-square error and visual quality, could be obtained through the use of adaptive, space-variant filters for the estimation of images in the presence of noise. This follows from the fact that linear space-invariant (LSI) filters smooth out the edges and reduce the contrast, which invariably results in poor visual quality. Space-variant image models [9] provide a better match to local image statistics, thus helping to preserve edges with greater noise reduction in nonedge regions. Woods *et al.* [8] addressed the optimal space-variant estimation of images in the presence of noise with a given number of *a priori* selected image models in a switching environment, where at each pixel one of the steady-state LSI filters designed for these models is chosen. The method of the current paper can be considered as an extension of the decision-directed method of [8] to deconvolution-type problems.

In the image restoration problem, the shortcomings of the LSI filter are quite different from the ones mentioned for the estimation problem. Image deblurring is a high-frequency emphasis operation. Therefore, the LSI filter does not cause excessive smoothing of edges. However, any sharp edges may cause ringing when LSI filters are utilized for image restoration [10]. The edge-adaptive RUKF is motivated by the need to suppress the ringing artifacts caused by LSI processing. In another adaptive nonlinear Kalman filtering approach for the image restoration problem, Rajala and DeFigueiredo [11] partitioned the image based on local spatial image activity in accordance with the masking effect [7]. The partitioning was implemented by a thresholding operation on the measure of spatial activity, where the thresholds were chosen sub-

---

Manuscript received August 19, 1987; revised September 24, 1988. This work was based in part upon research performed under a grant from Eastman Kodak Company, and by the NSF under Grant ECS-8313889 to Rensselaer Polytechnic Institute. The revised version of this paper was performed under NSF Grant MIP-8809291 to the University of Rochester.

A. M. Tekalp was with Photographic Research Laboratories–Photographic Products Group, Eastman Kodak Company, Rochester, NY. He is now with the Electrical Engineering Department, University of Rochester, Rochester, NY 14627.

H. Kaufman and J. W. Woods are with the Electrical, Computer, and Systems Engineering Department, Rensselaer Polytechnic Institute, Troy, NY 12180.

IEEE Log Number 8927466.

[1]According to Hadamard's definition [2].

jectively. One might argue that if the observed image is significantly smeared, then the masking function, or any other FIR edge detection operator computed from the noisy and blurred image, may not lead to a meaningful segmentation. This is unlike the situation in the proposed method where the computation of the decision statistic includes the RUKF which takes the blur model into account.

In Section II we elaborate on the causes of ringing in image restoration, and introduce an edge-adaptive image modeling approach. In Section III we develop a new decision-directed edge-adaptive RUKF for image restoration to suppress the ringing artifacts caused by the LSI filters. In Section IV we demonstrate the ability of the edge-adaptive RUKF to suppress the ringing artifacts by providing experimental results.

II. Ringing Artifacts and Edge-Adaptive Image Modeling

A. Degradation Models

The degradations that occur during the image formation and recording process can be divided into two categories: i) deterministic (but possibly unknown) degradations, i.e., the blur, and ii) stochastic degradations, i.e., the noise.

1) The Blur: In this paper, we consider space-invariant, finite impulse response blurs. The model for the blurred image is then given by the following convolution summation:

$$b(m, n) = \sum_{(k,l) \in \mathcal{B}} h_{k,l} s(m - k, n - l), \quad (1)$$

where $\{h_{k,l}\}$ denote the point spread function (PSF) of the blur, $\mathcal{B}$ is the support of the PSF as depicted in Fig. 1, and $\{s(m, n)\}$ denote the undistorted original image. The support of the PSF need not be causal, and in general most real-life blurs are modeled with noncausal PSF's. The blurring PSF modeled in this manner is a $K \times K$th-order finite impulse response (FIR) filter.

2) The Noise: Images are subject to statistical degradations that are commonly called noise. For instance, the images recorded on a photographic film are affected by film-grain noise, whereas electronic images suffer from photoelectric noise. For practical purposes, both types of noise can be modeled to some degree of accuracy by an additive white Gaussian field, $v(m, n)$, with zero-mean and appropriate variance σ_v^2. Hence, the combined degradation model becomes

$$r(m, n) = \sum_{(k,l) \in \mathcal{B}} h_{k,l} s(m - k, n - l) + v(m,n), \quad (2)$$

where $r(m, n)$ represents the observed noisy version of the blurred image.

B. On Ringing Artifacts in Image Restoration

We define the ringing artifacts as periodic overshoots and undershoots, about an edge, that decay in spatial coordinates as we move further from the edge. The image restoration problem is ill posed because the magnitude of

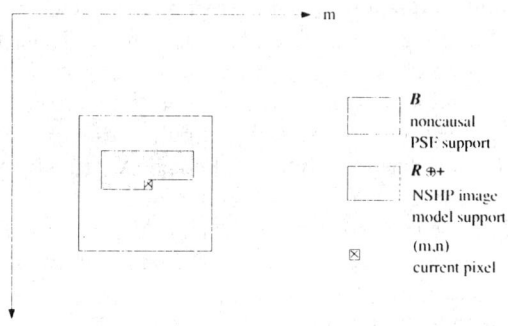

Fig. 1. Model supports.

the direct inverse of the blur transfer function would be infinite at those frequencies where the blur transfer function has zeros, and typically large at some neighborhood of these zeros and also at high frequencies. This results in excessive amplification of any sensor noise at these frequencies. Ringing arises in an effort to regularize the ill-posed image restoration problem through the use of an LSI filter when the transfer function of the blur has periodic zeros.

Some well-known LSI regularized inversion techniques include the constrained least squares filter [1], the Wiener filter, and the Kalman filter. Inevitably, the regularized filter deviates from the exact inverse at the frequencies where the exact inverse tends to large values. It is this deviation of the regularized filter from the exact inverse that causes the ringing artifacts [12]. To elaborate on this fact, let us denote the discrete Fourier transform (DFT) of an image, that is restored using an LSI filter, by $\hat{S}(k, l)$. Then,

$$\hat{S}(k, l) = \tilde{H}(k, l) R(k, l) \quad (3)$$

where $\tilde{H}(k, l)$ denotes the frequency response of an LSI regularized restoration filter, and $R(k, l)$ denotes the DFT of the degraded image. Writing (2) in the DFT domain and substituting into (3),

$$\hat{S}(k, l) = \tilde{H}(k, l) H(k, l) S(k, l) + \tilde{H}(k, l) V(k, l) \quad (4)$$

where $H(k, l)$, $S(k, l)$, and $V(k, l)$ denote the DFT of the blur transfer function, the original image, and the noise sequences, respectively. Adding and subtracting $S(k, l)$ to the right-hand side of (2), we have

$$\hat{S}(k, l) = S(k, l) + [\tilde{H}(k, l) H(k, l) - 1] S(k, l)$$
$$+ \tilde{H}(k, l) V(k, l)$$
$$= S(k, l) + E_S(k, l) + E_N(k, l) \quad (5)$$

where $E_S(k, l) \doteq [\tilde{H}(k, l) H(k, l) - 1] S(k, l)$ is the signal dependent error term, and $E_N(k, l) \doteq \tilde{H}(k, l) V(k, l)$ is the noise dependent error term. In the case where $H(k, l)$ has periodic zeros, $E_S(k, l)$ manifests itself as ringing artifacts. Let us define $\epsilon(k, l) \doteq [\tilde{H}(k, l) H(k, l) - 1]$. It can easily be seen that $\epsilon(k, l) = -1$ at the zeros of the blur transfer function. Hence, the presence of certain frequencies, that correspond to the zeros of the blur transfer function, in $S(k, l)$ excites $\epsilon(k, l)$ to produce ringing artifacts which are periodic with the period of these zeros. It was shown in [12] that in the case of uniform linear motion blur, the ringing artifacts occur with the period of zero crossings in the transfer function of the blur.

In the case of LSI Kalman filtering, the better the image model fits the image, the better the noise suppression that can be achieved. But, noise suppression can be achieved at the expense of ringing artifacts as can be seen from (5). The fact that LSI RUKF produces ringing artifacts in exchange for noise amplification can be observed in Figs. 5(b), 6(b), and 7(b) for the case 7×1 uniform motion blur. One of the important observations to note from Figs. 5(b), 6(b), and 7(b) is that ringing artifacts initiate at the sharp edges in an image. This can also be seen from the above mathematical discussion, since sharp edges are likely to contain the frequencies that excite $\epsilon(k, l)$ to produce the ringing artifacts. Indeed, this is the rationale behind the edge-adaptive restoration of images for ringing suppression. It is the piecewise (switching) structure of the model (which enables one to avoid filtering across the edges) that suppresses the ringing artifacts. Otherwise, we can state that no single image model, no matter how good, would be able to prevent ringing artifacts.

C. Edge-Adaptive Multiple Image Modeling

We define a digital image to be an $N \times N$ array of pixels. A conventional raster-type scan from left to right and from top to bottom will be followed. A causality is introduced in the representation of images by the scanning process. This causality is related only to the scanning process, and not to the properties of the image. For our representations, nonsymmetric half plane (NSHP) causality [13] has been chosen.

The LSI RUKF [5] is based on a space-invariant autoregressive (AR) model of an image which is assumed to be a realization of a homogeneous random field. Woods [13] shows that homogeneous Gauss–Markov random fields can be represented by the following NSHP causal autoregressive (AR) difference equation model:

$$s(m, n) = \sum_{(k,l) \in \mathcal{R}_{\oplus+}} c_{k,l} s(m - k, n - l) + w(m, n)$$

(6)

where $\{c_{k,l}\}$ are the NSHP model coefficients, and $w(m, n)$ is a zero-mean, white Gaussian field with variance σ_w^2, to account for uncertainty in the model. The region $\mathcal{R}_{\oplus+}$ denotes the NSHP model support, shown in Fig. 1, and is defined by:

$$\mathcal{R}_{\oplus+} = \{(k, l) | (1 \leq k \leq M, 0 \leq l \leq M)$$
$$\cdot U(-M \leq k \leq 0, 1 \leq l \leq M)\}. \quad (7)$$

In the following, the image model (6) will be referred to as an $M \times M$th-order AR model. The above model can be made edge adaptive if we quantize all possible edge orientations into $L - 1$ levels, and represent each edge orientation with a different $M \times M$th-order AR model. An Lth model is used to represent more uniform image areas. This representation is referred to as edge-adaptive image modeling.

The image model is then given by

$$s(m, n) = \sum_{(k,l) \in \mathcal{R}_{\oplus+}} c_{k,l}(\theta(m, n)) s(m - k, n - l)$$
$$+ w(m, n) \quad (8)$$

where $\{\theta(m, n)\}$ are random variables representing the model selected at (m, n), and $\{c_{k,l}(\theta(m, n))\}$ are the corresponding model coefficients. The pixel locations at which the model transitions take place are *a priori* unknown, and have to be detected from the noisy and blurred observations during the filtering procedure. The image model (8) then constitutes a space-variant system in a randomly switching environment, especially suited to represent images that have abrupt changes of gray levels (i.e., sharp edges).

In Section III, we develop a decision-directed multiple-model image restoration algorithm based on image model (8), with on-line model detection capability. We set L equal to five, to represent edges of 0, 45, 90, and 135 degrees plus a nonedge or textural model. This corresponds to smoothing along the edges or the major correlation directions.

III. Decision-Directed Edge-Adaptive RUKF

In this section, we present a decision-directed edge-adaptive image restoration technique based on multiple-model Kalman filtering. We set the number of models L equal to five. Four edge models, corresponding to major correlation directions of 0, 45, 90, and 135 degrees, plus a nonedge model are used to represent the image. We then design 5 steady-state, LSI RUKF's, one for each model, prior to filtering. As will be seen below, in the filtering a decision is made at each pixel, based on a conditional maximum *a posteriori* probability (CMAP) decision logic, to estimate the edge orientation. This, in turn, defines the best deconvolution model from the given set of multiple models. The overall effect of the algorithm is space-variant deconvolution efficiently implemented with the aid of a bank of five steady-state LSI RUKF's.

A. On-Line Decision Procedure

The pixel locations at which the model transitions take place are *a priori* unknown, and have to be detected from the noisy and blurred observations during the filtering procedure. In this section, we develop a decision algorithm, based on a local decision window, which classifies each pixel as belonging to one of these five categories.

1) The Decision Window: The decision window, denoted by $X(m, n)$, consists of $I \times J$ pixels centered around the current pixel (m, n). For each decision window, there is also an associated boundary region, denoted by $Y(m, n)$. The support of the boundary region, $Y(m, n)$, is defined as the union of the image and blur model supports for every pixel that lies on the boundary of the decision window, as shown in Fig. 2. In Fig. 2 the decision window was depicted for the case of a 1×1 image model and a 7×1 motion blur. Obviously, the boundary region, $Y(m, n)$, will change as the supports for the image and blur models change. The pixel values within the boundary region that are in the past of (m, n) are set equal to their best available estimates at (m, n), while those that are in the future of (m, n) are set equal to the blurred and noisy observations. This boundary region is needed for the estimation of the parameters as described below.

On labeling the observations in the decision window, $X(m, n)$, by $x_1, x_2, \cdots, x_{N_X}$, where $N_X = I \cdot J$ is the number of pixels in the window, and assuming that the undistorted signal $s(m, n)$ is Gaussian distributed, we can easily show that x_q, $q = 1, \cdots, N_X$ are conditionally Gaussian distributed as

$$p[x_q | \theta(m, n) = j, x_1, \cdots, x_{q-1}, Y(m, n)]$$
$$= N[\hat{r}_j(m, n), \sigma_j(m, n)]. \quad (9)$$

2) Estimation of the Parameters: The parameters of the class-conditional distribution (9), the conditional mean $r_j(m, n)$, and the variance $\sigma_j^2(m, n)$, can be estimated from an RUKF running on the decision window with fixed boundaries $Y(m, n)$ and the model $\theta(m, n) = j$. This must be repeated at each decision window location.

The conditional mean is given for a generic point (m, n), using (2) as

$$\hat{r}_j(m, n) = \sum_{(k,l) \in \mathcal{B}} h_{kl} \hat{s}_{b,j}^{(m,n)}(m - k, n - l) \quad (10)$$

where $\hat{s}_{b,j}^{(m,n)}(m - k, n - l)$ denotes the predicted estimates obtained from the RUKF for model $\theta(m, n) = j$ running on the decision window with fixed boundaries $Y(m, n)$.

The conditional variance is the 2-D innovation variance given as

$$\sigma_j^2(m, n) = E\{[r(m, n) - \hat{r}_j(m, n)]^2\}. \quad (11)$$

Substituting (2) and (10) into (11) gives

$$\sigma_j^2(m, n) = E\left\{\left[\sum_{k,l} h_{k,l} e_{b,j}^{(m,n)}(m - k, n - l)\right]^2\right\}$$
$$+ E\{v^2(m, n)\}, \quad (12)$$

where

$$e_{b,j}^{(m,n)}(m - k, n - l)$$
$$\doteq s(m - k, n - l) - \hat{s}_{b,j}^{(m,n)}(m - k, n - l),$$
$$(k, l) \in \mathcal{B}$$

denotes the prediction error for model j. Hence,

$$\sigma_j^2(m, n) = \sum_{k,l} \sum_{o,p} h_{k,l} h_{o,p} R_{b,j}^{(m,n)}(m - k, n - l;$$
$$m - o, n - p) + \sigma_v^2, \quad (13)$$

where $R_{b,j}^{(m,n)}(m, n; k, l)$ is the *a priori* error covariance for constant model j. In the experiments that follow, the

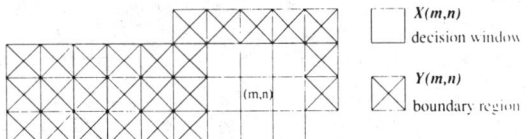

Fig. 2. The decision window and the associated boundary region for the case of a 7×1 PSF and a 1×1 image model.

estimates (13) are approximated by steady-state filter outputs corresponding to L fixed models, with corresponding steady-state innovation variance, σ_j^2, $j = 1, \cdots, L$.

3) Derivation of the Decision Statistic: The CMAP estimate for $\theta(m, n)$ at each decision window maximizes the conditional probability $P[\theta(m, n) = j | X, Y]$, where the argument (m, n) of both X and Y is omitted for notational convenience. By recursively using the Bayes' rule in the decision window, we obtain

$$P[\theta(m, n)$$
$$= j | X, Y] = k \cdot P[\theta(m, n) = j | Y]$$
$$\cdot P[x_1 | \theta(m, n) = j, Y]$$
$$\cdot \prod_{q=2}^{N_X} P[x_q | \theta(m, n) = j, x_1, \cdots, x_{q-1}, Y]$$
$$(14)$$

where k is a normalization constant indicating the terms not depending on $\theta(m, n)$.

Substituting (9) into (14) and taking natural logarithms, we obtain the equivalent CMAP statistic

$$S_j = N_X \ln \sigma_j + \ln P[\theta(m, n) = j | Y]$$
$$- \frac{1}{2} \sum_{(k,l) \in X} \left\{\frac{[r(k, l) - \hat{r}_j(k, l)]}{\sigma_j}\right\}^2. \quad (15)$$

Finally, the $P[\theta(m, n) = j | Y]$ are approximated with *a priori* probabilities $P[\theta(m, n) = j]$ to get the final decision statistic. The estimate of the model acting at (m, n), $\hat{\theta}(m, n)$, is then chosen to maximize the decision statistic (15).

The only *ad hoc* parameters in the proposed algorithm are these *a priori* probabilities. At worst, if there is not enough information about how to choose these probabilities, one can set them all equal, in which case the method reduces to conditional maximum likelihood model detection.

B. Filtering Procedure

Having determined the image model at (m, n) by the above procedure, the prediction and update at this pixel is then performed by one of the L steady-state deconvolution-type RUKF's.

The bank of steady-state Kalman filters, shown in Fig. 3, should be designed off-line, prior to filtering. The L image models are identified on a prototype test image having well-defined edges of 0, 45, 90, and 135 degrees. One such test image is the "geometric image" shown in Fig.

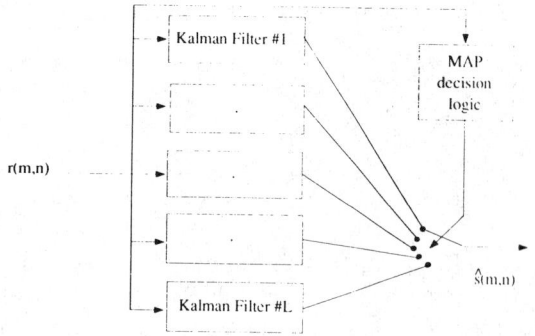

Fig. 3. Block diagram for multiple-model filtering procedure.

Fig. 4. Original images: (a) geometric image, (b) cameraman image, (c) face image.

4(a). In particular, each model should be identified separately only over a neighborhood of those pixels corresponding to approximately that edge orientation. The PSF of the blur is either assumed to be known or obtained from the observed image itself using the techniques given in [14]–[16]. Then, to obtain the steady-state Kalman gains for each filter, we would iterate the error-covariance equations of [5] until an approximate steady state is reached, once for each model. The convergence can generally be achieved by processing 10 lines.

Then, the filtering equations for the multiple-model restoration algorithm are given as follows:

$$\hat{s}_b^{(m,n)}(m, n) = \sum_{(k,l) \in \Re_+} c_{k,l}(\hat{\theta}(m, n)) \hat{s}_a^{(m-1,n)}(m-k, n-l), \quad (16)$$

and

$$\hat{s}_a^{(m,n)}(i, j) = \hat{s}_b^{(m,n)}(i, j) + k_{m-i, n-j}(\hat{\theta}(m, n))$$
$$\cdot \left| r(m, n) - \sum_{(k,l) \in \Re} h_{k,l} \hat{s}_b^{(m,n)}(m-k; n-l) \right|,$$
$$(i, j) \in \mathcal{U}_{\oplus +}. \quad (17)$$

where $\hat{\theta}(m, n)$ denotes the model chosen at (m, n), and $c_{k,l}(\hat{\theta}(m, n))$ and $k_{m-i, n-j}(\hat{\theta}(m, n))$ denote, respectively, the corresponding image parameters and the steady-state Kalman gains for the model chosen. The local state support $\mathcal{U}_{\oplus +}$ remains as in [5].

Most of the computation of the decision-directed algorithm is thus in the model detection, which can be computed in parallel for the L models. Experimental results are provided in the next section to illustrate the improvement obtained over LSI filtering, especially in ringing suppression.

IV. EXPERIMENTAL RESULTS

We first demonstrate the ability of this technique to suppress ringing artifacts on a test image where every pixel falls exactly into one of the five categories. This image, shown in Fig. 4(a), called the geometric image, is 128 × 128 pixels in size.

The geometric image, blurred with a 7 × 1 linear uniform motion blur, is immersed in white noise at 40 dB blurred signal-to-noise ratio (BSNR). The BSNR is defined as follows:

$$BSNR(\text{dB}) = 10 \log \left\{ \frac{\text{Variance of blurred image}}{\text{Variance of noise}} \right\}. \quad (18)$$

The resulting image is shown in Fig. 5(a).

The restored image using the LSI RUKF with the image model coefficients obtained over the original image via a least-squares prediction method is shown in Fig. 5(b). The image displays ringing artifacts, which initiate from the edges of objects and extend in the direction of the blurring. Fig. 5(c) shows a restoration obtained by using the multiple-model algorithm. In this case, five a priori image models were identified over the original image within the respective regions. The image model coefficients for these five models are given in Table I. The edge mask, indicating the pixel locations where an edge is detected, obtained by the on-line decision procedure using the noisy and blurred image, is shown in Fig. 5(d). For the results reported in this paper, the decision window consisted of only the current pixel and the associated boundary region. The result shows that ringing can be suppressed by properly adapting the Kalman filter to the approximate local edge orientation.

Next, we present results on two real images: the cameraman image shown in Fig. 4(b) and the face image shown in Fig. 4(c). Both of these images are 256 × 256 pixels in size. The set of simulation results for the case of 7 × 1 uniform motion blur at 40 dB BSNR is shown in Figs. 6(a)–(d) and 7(a)–(d), respectively, for these images. The visual improvement due to edge-adaptive restoration is significant in both images; however, it is more dramatic in the cameraman image. This is because the cameraman image has a larger variance, i.e., more contrast, than the face image. We note that in processing these images, the edge models and the uniform region model

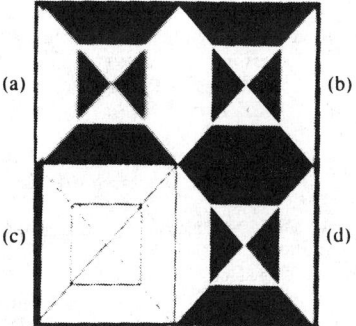

Fig. 5. Restoration results for the geometric image: (a) 7 × 1 uniform motion blur at 40 dB BSNR, (b) LSI RUKF, (c) edge-adaptive RUKF, (d) edge mask.

TABLE I
IMAGE MODEL COEFFICIENTS USED IN EDGE-ADAPTIVE RUKF

MODEL ORIENTATION	COEFFICIENTS				
	$C_{1,1}$	$C_{0,1}$	$C_{-1,1}$	$C_{1,0}$	σ_ω^2
0° edge	0.02461	-0.00180	0.00643	0.96977	32.2181
45° edge	0.00088	0.01183	0.96874	0.01819	32.1013
90° edge	0.03989	0.92556	0.03650	-0.00263	31.8146
135° edge	0.93956	0.02923	0.00085	0.03029	31.2738
non-edge	0.26247	0.24658	0.24430	0.24573	32.2035

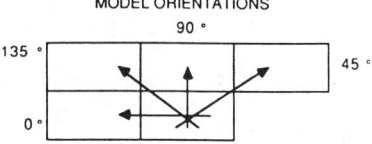

Fig. 6. Restoration results for the cameraman image: (a) 7 × 1 uniform motion blur at 40 dB BSNR, (b) LSI RUKF, (c) edge-adaptive RUKF, (d) edge mask.

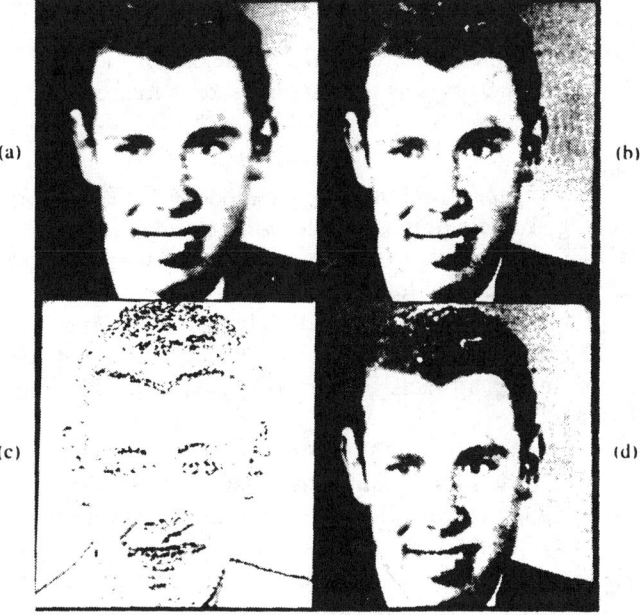

Fig. 7. Restoration results for the face image: (a) 7 × 1 uniform motion blur at 40 dB BSNR, (b) LSI RUKF, (c) edge-adaptive RUKF, (d) edge mask.

were obtained from the geometric image. Therefore, the edge-adaptive RUKF is robust with respect to image-model parameters.

The *a priori* probabilities, $P[\theta(m, n) = j]$, $j = 1, \cdots, 5$, can be computed as an estimate of the ratio of pixels belonging to class, j, to the total number of pixels in the image. Obviously, these probabilities are image dependent. In our experiments, we computed them globally using the entire geometric image. The resulting *a priori* probabilities were 0.10 for each of the edge models, and 0.60 for the nonedge model. In the cameraman and face images, we also tried 0.15 for each of the edge models and 0.40 for the nonedge model, the resulting differences in the detected edges (i.e., the edge-mask) and the mean square restoration error (an increase of about 1 percent) was not noticeable. For the cameraman and face images, when the *a priori* probabilities were all set equal to 0.2 for each model (i.e., the conditional maximum likelihood detection), the number of false edges detected increased noticeably. This also led to about a 16 percent increase in the mean square restoration error compared with the reported results. Ideally, the *a priori* probabilities should be updated based on local properties to reduce the number of detection errors. We are currently working for such an algorithm.

The MSE improvements for the experiments mentioned above are tabulated in Table II. The decibel improve-

TABLE II
MSE Improvements in Decibels, for the Case of 7 × 1 Linear Motion Blur at 40 dB BSNR

IMAGE	LSI RUKF (in dB)	EDGE-ADAPTIVE RUKF (in dB)
Geometric	11.33	20.72
Cameraman	10.49	12.57
Face	11.86	12.45

ments are computed as follows:

$$\text{MSE Improvement (dB)} = 10 \log \left\{ \frac{\text{MSE of the degraded image}}{\text{MSE of the restored image}} \right\} \quad (19)$$

where MSE stands for the mean square error.

The computation required for the multiple-model filter with a 1 × 1 decision window is approximately 6 times that of the LSI filter. For example, for a 256 × 256 image, the edge-adaptive RUKF requires 2.5 min CPU time on a VAX 11/785. At lower BSNR's, to eliminate the effects of observation noise on the model detection, one may consider increasing the size of the decision window. Obviously, the computational complexity of the decision algorithm increases as the window size increases.

V. Conclusions

In this paper, we showed a method to overcome the ringing artifacts in image restoration by adapting the LSI RUKF to local edge orientations. The decision-directed edge-adaptive multiple-model RUKF shows significant improvement over the LSI RUKF both visually and in the MSE sense. We experimentally verified that it can suppress ringing artifacts that are a byproduct of LSI regularization.

This ringing suppression is due to the fact that the decision-directed RUKF smooths along edges in images by choosing the best prediction model, at each pixel, among a set of *a priori* designed multiple edge models. In other words, the prediction is performed as a linear combination of pixels that are always on the same side of an edge by virtue of these edge models. Therefore, the filter avoids predicting across an edge in the direction of the recursion.

Finally, we note that the proposed edge-adaptive filtering method can be used with other 2-D Kalman filtering algorithms as well.

References

[1] H. C. Andrews and B. R. Hunt, *Digital Image Restoration*. Englewood Cliffs, NJ: Prentice-Hall, 1977.
[2] J. N. Franklin, "Well-posed stochastic extension of ill-posed linear problems," *J. Math. Anal. Appl.*, vol. 31, pp. 682–716, 1970.
[3] M. S. Murphy and L. M. Silverman, "Image model representation and line by line recursive restoration," *IEEE Trans. Automat. Contr.*, vol. AC-23, pp. 809–816, Oct. 1978.
[4] J. Biemond, J. Rieske, and J. Gerbrands, "A fast Kalman filter for images degraded by both blur and noise," *IEEE Trans. Acoust., Speech, Signal Processing*, vol. ASSP-31, pp. 1248–1256, Oct. 1983.
[5] J. W. Woods and V. K. Ingle, "Kalman filtering in two dimensions—Further results," *IEEE Trans. Acoust., Speech, Signal Processing*, vol. ASSP-29, pp. 188–197, Apr. 1981.
[6] J. W. Woods and C. W. Radewan, "Kalman filtering in two dimensions," *IEEE Trans. Inform. Theory*, vol. IT-23, pp. 473–482, July 1977.
[7] G. L. Anderson and A. N. Netravali, "Image restoration based on a subjective criterion," *IEEE Trans. Syst., Man, Cybern.*, vol. SMC-6, pp. 845–853, Dec. 1976.
[8] J. W. Woods, S. Dravida, and R. Mediavilla, "Image estimation using doubly stochastic Gaussian random field models," *IEEE Trans. Pattern Anal. Machine Intell.*, vol. PAMI-9, pp. 245–253, Mar. 1987.
[9] A. M. Tekalp, H. Kaufman, and J. W. Woods, "Fast recursive estimation of the parameters of a space-varying autoregressive image model," *IEEE Trans. Acoust., Speech, Signal Processing*, vol. ASSP-33, pp. 469–472, Apr. 1985.
[10] A. M. Tekalp, "Identification and restoration of noisy and blurred images," Ph.D. dissertation, Rensselaer Polytechnic Inst., Troy, NY, 1984.
[11] S. Rajala and R. J. P. DeFigueiredo, "Adaptive nonlinear image restoration by a modified Kalman filtering approach," *IEEE Trans. Acoust., Speech, Signal Processing*, vol. ASSP-29, pp. 1033–1042, Oct. 1981.
[12] R. L. Lagendijk, J. Biemond, and D. E. Boekee, "Iterative image restoration with ringing reduction," in *Signal Processing III: Theories and Applications*. New York: Elsevier Science, EURASIP, 1986.
[13] J. W. Woods, "Markov image modeling," *IEEE Trans. Automat. Contr.*, vol. AC-23, pp. 846–850, Oct. 1978.
[14] A. M. Tekalp, H. Kaufman, and J. W. Woods, "Identification of image and blur parameters for the restoration of noncausal blurs," *IEEE Trans. Acoust., Speech, Signal Processing*, vol. ASSP-34, pp. 963–972, Aug. 1986.
[15] A. M. Tekalp and H. Kaufman, "On statistical identification of a class of linear space-invariant image blurs using nonminimum-phase ARMA models," *IEEE Trans. Acoust., Speech, Signal Processing*, vol. 36, pp. 1360–1363, Aug. 1988.
[16] M. Cannon, "Blind deconvolution of spatially invariant image blurs with phase," *IEEE Trans. Acoust., Speech, Signal Processing*, vol. ASSP-24, pp. 58–63, Feb. 1976.

A. Murat Tekalp (S'80–M'85) was born in 1958. He received the B.S. degree in electrical engineering, and the B.S. degree in mathematics from Boğaziçi University, Istanbul, Turkey, in 1980, with the highest honors, and the M.S. and Ph.D. degrees in electrical, computer and systems engineering from Rensselaer Polytechnic Institute (RPI), Troy, NY, in 1982 and 1984.

He began his career as a Teaching Assistant at Boğaziçi University, Istanbul, Turkey, as an undergraduate student in 1978. From January 1981 to December 1984 he was a Research Assistant at RPI working in the areas of image estimation/restoration, and system identification. From December 1984 to August 1987 he was a Research Scientist, and then a Senior Research Scientist at Eastman Kodak Company, Rochester, NY. He is currently an Assistant Professor of Electrical Engineering at the University of Rochester, Rochester, NY, where he is teaching graduate and undergraduate courses in signal and image processing. He has been an Adjunct Faculty at the University of Rochester from September 1986 to December 1986, and a Visiting Assistant Professor at Rensselaer Polytechnic Institute from January 1987 to June 1987. His current research interests include multidimensional digital signal processing, adaptive image restoration, blur identification, higher-order spectrum analysis, medical image processing, and pattern recognition.

Dr. Tekalp was a scholar of the Turkish Scientific and Technical Research Association. He is a member of Sigma Xi and the IEEE ASSP Society. He is the organizer and first Chairman of the Rochester Chapter of the ASSP Society. He has been a technical reviewer for several IEEE TRANSACTIONS, *Signal Processing*, and the *Journal of the Optical Society of America*.

Howard Kaufman (S'64-M'66-SM'75) received the B.E.E., M.E.E., and Ph.D. degrees from the Department of Electrical Engineering, Rensselaer Polytechnic Institute, Troy, NY, in 1962, 1963, and 1965, respectively.

He joined the Computer Research Department of Cornell Aeronautical Laboratory, Buffalo, NY, in 1965, where he was engaged in the development of procedures for applying digital computers to process estimation, identification, and control.

In 1968 he joined the General Electric Research and Development Center as a System Engineer and developed computer simulations of large scale industrial processes. Since 1969 he has been a member of the Electrical, Computer, and Systems Engineering Department of Rensselaer Polytechnic Institute, Troy, NY, where he is a Professor teaching courses in systems analysis, optimal and adaptive control theory, and digital systems. His research interests are in the areas of digital adaptive control, and estimation theory, optimal control, and digital signal processing. He has written many papers in these areas and has served as a consultant to General Electric Corporation Research and Development in related projects. During the summer of 1972 he was awarded a NASA Summer Faculty Fellowship at NASA-Langley Research Center where he conducted research in the development of digital adaptive flight control systems, and during the summer of 1982, he was an NSF Industrial Research Participant at General Electric Corporate Research and Development where he was involved in computer aided control systems design.

Dr. Kaufman is a member of Sigma Xi, Eta Kappa Nu, and Tau Beta Pi honor societies.

John W. Woods (S'67-M'70-SM'83-F'88) was born in Washington, DC, on December 5, 1943. He received the B.S., M.S., E.E., and Ph.D. degrees in electrical engineering from the Massachusetts Institute of Technology, Cambridge, in 1965, 1967, and 1970, respectively.

From 1970 to 1973 he was at the VELA Seismological Center, Alexandria, VA, working on array processing of digital seismic data. From 1973 to 1976 he was at the Lawrence Livermore Laboratory, University of California, working on two-dimensional digital signal processing. Since 1976 he has been with the ECSE Department at Rensselaer Polytechnic Institute, Troy, NY, where he is currently a Professor. He has taught courses in digital signal processing, probability and stochastic processes, information theory, and communication systems. His research interests include estimation/restoration, detection, recursive digital filtering, and data compression of images and other multidimensional data. He has authored or coauthored over 50 papers in these fields. He has coauthored one text in the area of probability, random processes, and estimation. During the academic year 1985/1986, he was Visiting Professor in the Information Theory Group at Delft University of Technology, The Netherlands. He is presently directing the Circuits and Signal Processing program at the National Science Foundation, Washington, DC.

Dr. Woods was co-recipient of the 1976 and 1987 Senior Paper Awards of the IEEE Acoustics, Speech, and Signal Processing (ASSP) Society. He is a former member of their Digital Signal Processing Committee. He was Chairman of the Schenectady joint ASSP/Communications Society Chapter in 1977-1978. He was an Associate Editor for Signal Processing of the IEEE TRANSACTIONS ON ACOUSTICS, SPEECH, AND SIGNAL PROCESSING. He was Co-chairman of the Third ASSP Workshop on Multidimensional Signal Processing held at Lake Tahoe, CA, October 1983. He is a former Chairman of the ASSP Technical Committee on Multidimensional Signal Processing. He is currently an elected member of the Administrative Committee of the ASSP Society and serves as the Society's Educational Chairman. He is a member of Sigma Xi, Tau Beta Pi, Eta Kappa Nu, and the AAAS.

Digital Image Restoration Using Spatial Interaction Models

R. CHELLAPPA, MEMBER, IEEE, AND R. L. KASHYAP, FELLOW, IEEE

Abstract—This paper is concerned with developing fast nonrecursive algorithms for the minimum mean-squared error restoration of degraded images. The degradation is assumed to be due to a space invariant, periodic, nonseparable known point-spread function, and additive white noise. Our basic approach is to represent the images by a class of spatial interaction models, namely the simultaneous autoregressive models and the conditional Markov models defined on toroidal lattices, and develop minimum mean-squared error restoration algorithms using these models. The restoration algorithms are optimal, if the parameters characterizing the interaction models are exactly known. However, in practice, the parameters are estimated from the images. By using spatial interaction models, we develop restoration algorithms that do not require the availability of the original image or its prototype. The specific structure of the underlying lattice enables the implementation of the filters using fast Fourier transform (FFT) computations. Several restoration examples are given.

I. Introduction

THE restoration of degraded images has many fields of application, including space and biomedical imagery [1], [2]. The literature on image restoration is too enormous to be listed in detail and there are many different methodologies like minimum mean-square error (MMSE) restoration, maximum *a posteriori* probability restoration, and maximum entropy restoration [3]. In this paper, we are concerned with MMSE methods of restoration.

Suppose y and x represent lexicographic ordered arrays of the original and degraded image, related as in (1.1).

$$x = Hy + \eta. \tag{1.1}$$

In (1.1), H is the block-circulant matrix corresponding to the blur caused by a nonseparable, space-invariant point-spread function (PSF) and η is a signal independent additive white noise of variance γ. Then, it is well known [1] that $\hat{y}$, the MMSE estimate of y, can be written as

$$\hat{y} = Q_y H^T (H Q_y H^T + \gamma I)^{-1} x \tag{1.2}$$

where Q_y is the covariance matrix of y. There are two problems to be considered in the evaluation of $\hat{y}$, namely, the determination of the covariance matrix Q_y and the inversion of the matrix in (1.2). We discuss the second problem first. For an image of size $M \times M$, Q_y is of dimension $M^2 \times M^2$, and it is not uncommon to have $M = 128$ in typical restoration applications. Thus, some assumptions have to be made to reduce the computational load. In [1, ch. 7], the block-Toeplitz covariance matrix Q_y is approximated by a block-circulant matrix. Since block-circulant matrices possess an eigenfunction expansion in terms of Fourier vectors, fast Fourier transform (FFT) computations are used for the implementation of (1.2). In the stochastic representation of images by finite difference approximations of partial differential equations [4], appropriate assumptions are made regarding the model representation for y so that Q_y has a symmetric, tridiagonal Toeplitz form. Since symmetric tridiagonal matrices are diagonalized by sine transforms, fast algorithms for the implementation of (1.2) have been developed. Another approach [5]-[7] is to assume an underlying causal model for the image y displayed as a state space model. Then $\hat{y}$ could be computed by recursive algorithms of the Kalman type.

The other problem in evaluating (1.2) is the determination of Q_y. Most of the MMSE algorithms assume the availability of a prototype of the original image. Then the covariance matrix Q_y is evaluated from the prototype by making appropriate assumptions about the correlation structure of the prototype image. For instance, considerable attention has been paid [2] to the exponential separable autocorrelation function, whose parameters are estimated from the prototype. In [1, ch. 7], $\hat{y}$ of (1.2) is written in terms of spectral density function (SDF) of the prototype image, which is often estimated from the periodogram of the prototype. In [8], the correlation function is assumed to be separable, corresponding to an underlying causal separable model. The method of estimating Q_y or equivalently, the parameters of the corresponding model, is arbitrary.

The actual mean-square error (MSE) between the original y and its estimate $\hat{y}$ will be larger than the theoretical minimum value since the covariance matrix Q_y is not known in practice, and an estimate of Q_y obtained from either y or x is used in place of Q_y. The error in the covariance estimation is caused either by the use of inappropriate assumptions like causality or separability for the underlying models or by the use of inconsistent spectral estimates such as periodograms. By using more general classes of models and consistent spectral estimates, one can hope to reduce the errors due to inappropriate modeling, and this is precisely what we attempt in this paper.

Manuscript received May 21, 1981; revised December 15, 1981 and January 25, 1982. This work was supported in part by the National Science Foundation under Grant ECS-80-09041 and in part by the U.S. Air Force Office of Scientific Research under Grant AFOSR-77-3271.

R. Chellappa was with the School of Electrical Engineering, Purdue University, West Lafayette, IN 47907, and the Computer Vision Laboratory, University of Maryland, College Park, MD 20742. He is now with the Department of Electrical Engineering, Systems and Image Processing Institute, University of Southern California, Los Angeles, CA 90007.

R. L. Kashyap is with the School of Electrical Engineering, Purdue University, West Lafayette, IN 47907.

We assume that the images are represented by a class of models known as spatial interaction models. One of the important characteristics of an image is the statistical dependence of the gray level at a lattice point on those of its neighbors. We characterize the dependency using a neighbor set N which is a finite set of pairs of integers excluding $(0, 0)$ such that $y(s)$, the gray level at location s, is a linear combination of the set of gray levels $\{y(s+r), r \in N\}$, and an additive noise. Among the spatial interaction models, we are primarily interested in the class of simultaneous autoregressive (SAR) models [9]-[12] and conditional Markov (CM) models [10]-[14] defined on finite toroidal lattices. These two classes of models are nonequivalent in that, given a SAR model, an equivalent CM model with the same spectral density function can always be found; however, the converse is not always true. For instance, there is no equivalent SAR model for the CM model with dependence on the east, west, north, and south neighbors. More elaborate comparisons of CM and SAR models are given in Section II.

We are interested in the use of SAR and CM models in developing nonrecursive restoration schemes. We represent either the given degraded image, x in (1), or the original y by appropriate SAR or CM models and formulate the MMSE restoration problem. The representation on a toroidal lattice leads to covariance matrices having a block-circulant structure leading to fast implementation of filters using FFT algorithms. All the relevant quantities like Q_y and γ are estimated from the given degraded image.

The contributions of this paper can be summarized as follows. First, the SAR and CM models used in this paper are more general than the models used in [4], [8], [15]. We do not make any isotropy assumption present in almost all the models used in [4]. The use of CM models in nonrecursive image restoration thus far has been limited to simple separable models. In general, the SDF corresponding to CM models do not factorize, and for these models, recursive Kalman-type algorithms [7] are approximations to the nonrecursive algorithms developed here. The Kalman-type recursive algorithms use unilateral models for images whose SDF is only an approximation to the SDF of the true CM model. More importantly, the methods developed here do not require that a prototype of the original image be available.

The organization of the paper is as follows. In Section II, we give a brief description of the representations of images using SAR or CM models. The different restoration algorithms using SAR models are given in Section III together with examples. The application of CM models is considered in Section IV with some examples of restoration. Finally, a brief discussion is given in Section V.

II. Representation of Finite Images Using Spatial Interaction Models

We discuss the two different representations used for the images, namely, the SAR models and the CM models. The image is described by a finite set of gray levels $\{y(s), s = (i, j) \in \Omega\}$, $\Omega = \{s = (i, j), 1 \leq i, j \leq M\}$ where $y(s)$ is the gray level of the cell s. Let N be a neighbor set, a set of points (i, j) where i and j are integers and $(0, 0) \notin N$. Geometrically, $(0, 1)$ is to the right of $(0, 0)$ and $(1, 0)$ is at the bottom of $(0, 0)$.

A. SAR Model Representation [9]-[12]

Suppose we partition the finite lattice Ω into mutually exclusive and totally inclusive subsets Ω_B, the boundary set, and Ω_I, the interior set:

$$\Omega_B = \{s = (i, j): s \in \Omega \text{ and } (s + r) \notin \Omega) \text{ for at least one } r \in N\}.$$

$$\Omega_I = \Omega - \Omega_B$$

We are interested in fitting a SAR model characterized by the neighbor set N so that $y(s)$ is the sum of a linear combination of gray levels $[y(s+r), r \in N]$ and an additive white noise $w(s)$ as in (2.1) below. For every $s \in \Omega_B$, there exists an $r \in N$ so that $(s + r) \notin \Omega$, and consequently, $y(s+r)$ is not defined. Then we define a proxy $y_1(\cdot)$ to take its place and define a new equation (2.2).

The SAR model for a *finite* image $[y(s), s \in \Omega]$ is in (2.1)-(2.3)

$$y(s) = \sum_{r \in N} \theta_r y(s+r) + \sqrt{\rho} \, w(s), \quad s \in \Omega_I \quad (2.1)$$

$$y(s) = \sum_{r \in N} \theta_r y_1(s+r) + \sqrt{\rho} \, w(s), \quad s \in \Omega_B \quad (2.2)$$

$$y_1[(k, l) + (i, j)] = y[(k, l) + (i, j)] \quad \text{if } (k, l) + (i, j) \in \Omega,$$
$$= y[(k + i - 1) \bmod M + 1,$$
$$\cdot (l + j - 1) \bmod M + 1],$$
$$\text{if } (k, l) + (i, j) \notin \Omega. \quad (2.3)$$

We need a separate equation (2.2) for $y(s)$, $s \in \Omega_B$ for reasons mentioned above. In the RHS of (2.2), y_1 takes the role of y in (2.1). y_1 in (2.3) is a function of $y(s')$, $s' \in \Omega$ even when $s \notin \Omega$. If the image $y(\cdot)$ were folded into a torus, $y_1(s) = y(s)$. By defining y_1 in (2.3), we do not have to assume that the image is toroidal. In (2.1) and (2.2), $\{w(s)\}$ is a sequence of independent and identically distributed (IID) random variables of zero mean and unit variance, and N denotes the associated neighbor set. Equation (2.1) is characterized by a set of parameters $[(\theta_r, r \in N), \rho]$. Denoting y and w as $M^2 \times 1$ vectors of lexicographically ordered arrays $[y(\cdot)]$ and $[w(\cdot)]$ and $\theta = \text{col}\,[\theta_r, r \in N]$, (2.1)-(2.2) can be written as

$$B(\theta) y = \sqrt{\rho} \, w \quad (2.4)$$

where $B(\theta)$ is an $M^2 \times M^2$ block circulant matrix given below:

$$B(\theta) = \begin{bmatrix} B_{1,1} & B_{1,2} & \cdots & B_{1,M} \\ B_{1,M} & B_{1,1} & \cdots & B_{1,M-1} \\ B_{1,M-1} & \cdots & B_{1,1} & B_{1,M-2} \\ \vdots & \vdots & \vdots & \vdots \\ B_{1,2} & \cdots & \cdots & B_{1,1} \end{bmatrix}$$

where each of the component matrices is circulant. For the case $N = [(0, 1), (1, 1), (0, -1), (-1, 0)]$

$B_{1,1}$ = circulant $(1, \theta_{0,1}, 0, \cdots, \theta_{0,-1})$

$B_{1,2}$ = circulant $(0, \theta_{1,1}, 0, \cdots)$

$B_{1,M}$ = circulant $(\theta_{-1,0}, 0, \cdots, 0)$

$B_{1,j} = 0, \quad j \neq 1, 2, M.$

See the Appendix for the definition of circulant.

In general, the component matrices $B_{i,j}$ can be constructed from θ_r as shown below

$(B_{1,i})_{1j}$ = jth element of first row of $B_{1,i}$

$\quad = 1 \quad$ if $i = 1, j = 1$

$\quad = \theta_{i_1, j_1} \quad$ if $(i_1, j_1) \in N$, $i_1 \mod M = i - 1$

$\quad$ and $j_1 \mod M = j - 1$, $i = 1, \cdots, M$, $j = 2, \cdots, M.$

$\quad = 0 \quad$ otherwise. $\hfill(2.5)$

One of the requirements of the representation in (2.4) is that an input w with bounded variance yields an output with a bounded variance. A necessary and sufficient condition to ensure a bounded output for a bounded input is that all the eigenvalues of the block-circulant transformation matrix $B(\theta)$, namely μ_s, $s \in \Omega$, be not zero, i.e.,

$\mu_s \triangleq (1 - \theta^T \psi_s) \neq 0$

$\psi_s = \text{col } [\exp \sqrt{-1} \, (2\pi/M)(s^T - (1,1))r, r \in N]. \hfill(2.6)$

The derivation of μ_s in (2.6) is given in the Appendix. Since $B(\theta)^{-1}$ exists by virtue of (2.6), (2.4) yields

$$y = \sqrt{\rho} \, B(\theta)^{-1} w. \hfill(2.7)$$

The image covariance matrix

$$Q_y = \text{cov}(y) = \rho [B^T(\theta) B(\theta)]^{-1} \hfill(2.8)$$

is also block-circulant with eigenvalues $\rho/\|\mu_s\|^2$, $s \in \Omega$. The spectral density of y is

$S_y(\lambda_1, \lambda_2) = \rho/\|\mu_{i,j}\|^2 \quad$ if $\lambda_1 = 2\pi i/M$, $\lambda_2 = 2\pi j/M.$

Another possible representation for the image $y(s)$, $s \in \Omega$ is by using the so-called infinite lattice models [11], [13], [14], where $[y(s)]$ obeys (2.1) for all s, i.e., the pixels $y(s)$, $s \in \Omega_B$ do not obey a separate equation like (2.2). One of the disadvantages of the infinite lattice representation is that the corresponding covariance matrix Q_y does not possess an orthogonal representation in terms of fast transforms like Fourier, sine, etc. Consequently, the inversion of $M^2 \times M^2$ matrix Q_y required to compute $\hat{y}$ is computationally expensive. As will be discussed in Section V, the finite lattice representation in (2.1) and (2.2) is a good approximation to the infinite lattice model, with the advantages of computational simplicity, since Q_y in (2.8) resulting from the finite lattice representation has an orthogonal representation in terms of Fourier vectors.

B. CM Model Representation [10]-[14]

We consider two classes of two-dimensional (2-D) Markov models, known as unilateral Markov models and bilateral Markov models.

An image obeying a unilateral Markov model can be divided into two parts, the "past" and "future," so that the definition of Markovianity is similar to the definition in the one-dimensional time series case. However, an arbitrary image cannot be divided into the two parts mentioned above. For such images, we need the class of bilateral Markov models which involve a new definition of Markovianity different from that in the 1-D case.

1) Unilateral Markov Models: The unilateral models obey

$$y(s) = \sum_{r \in N} \theta_r y(s+r) + \sqrt{\rho} \, w(s). \hfill(2.9)$$

$w(\cdot)$ is IID with zero mean, unit variance, and Gaussian. The neighbor set N is a subset of the nonsymmetric half plane S^+ [16] defined below:

$s_1 \in S^+$, $s_2 \in S^+ \to s_1 + s_2 \in S^+$

$s \in S^+ \to -s \notin S^+$, $(0,0) \notin S^+.$

The definition of S^+ is not unique. We can make it unique without any loss of any generality by assuming

$(0,1) \notin S^+$, $(1,1) \notin S^+$, $(-1,1) \in S^+.$

S^+ is given in Fig. 1(a). For any given s, we can divide an arbitrary infinite image into two parts, namely $\Omega_{s,N}$ (defined below) and its complement using the neighbor set N [17]

$s \notin \Omega_{s,N}$, $(s+r) \in \Omega_{s,N}$

$\quad$ for all $r \in N.$

$r \in \Omega_{s,N} \to (r+t) \in \Omega_{s,N}$

$\quad$ for all $t \in N$ provided $r + t \neq s.$

Some possible structures of $\Omega_{s,N}$ are shown in Fig. 1(b) and (c). With respect to s, the set $\Omega_{s,N}$ can be interpreted as the "past" and the remaining part excluding s as the "future." The unilateral Markov model possesses the one-dimensional Markov property defined below:

$$p(y(s)|\text{all } y(r), r \in \Omega_{s,N}) = p(y(s)|\text{all } y(s+r), r \in N).$$
$$\hfill(2.10)$$

The popular class of causal models which includes the familiar three neighbor model with $N = [(0,-1), (-1,0), (-1,-1)]$ is a special class of unilateral models so that N is a subset of the top left quadrant centered around the origin, and $\Omega_{s,N}$ is also a quadrant centered around s. This is illustrated in Fig. 1(b). In view of the definition of N, an image obeying the unilateral model can be synthesized recursively using appropriate initial conditions. In the causal model, with $N = [(0,-1), (-1,0), (-1,-1)]$ the required initial conditions are the topmost row and leftmost column.

2) Bilateral Markov Models: As mentioned earlier, there are many images which do not possess the unilateral Markov property. In this group, there are some images which possess another type of Markov property labeled as bilateral Markov property.

Definition: An image $\{y(\cdot)\}$ is said to possess the bilateral Markov property with respect to the symmetric neighbor set N if the following is true:

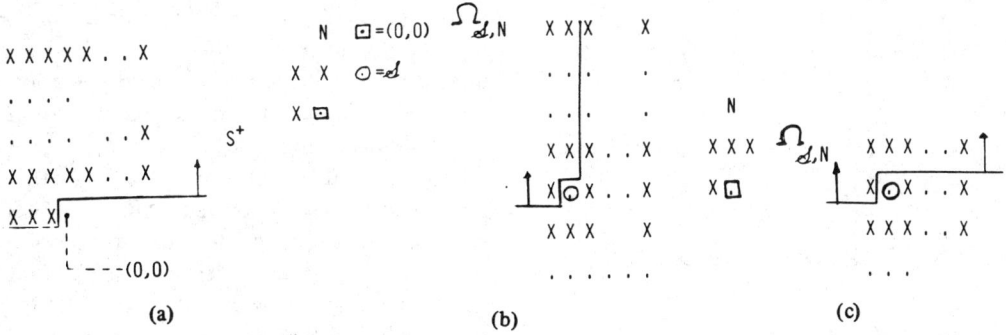

Fig. 1. (a) Structure of nonsymmetric half plane. (b) Causal unilateral model. (c) Noncausal unilateral model.

$$p(y(s)|\text{all } y(r), \text{ except } r \neq s) = p(y(s)|\text{all } y(s+r), r \in N). \quad (2.11)$$

We will presently give a difference equation representation for an image so that it has the bilateral Markovian property. It is more convenient to work with the subset N_S of N defined below:

$$s \in N_S \rightarrow -s \notin N_S; \quad N = [s: s \in N_S \text{ or } -s \in N_S].$$

Let the infinite image $y(\cdot)$ obey the difference equation (2.12)

$$y(s) = \sum_{r \in N_S} \theta_r(y(s+r) + y(s-r)) + \sqrt{\nu}\, e(s) \quad (2.12)$$

where the correlated noise sequence $e(\cdot)$ has the following properties:

$$\left.\begin{array}{l} e(\cdot) \text{ is stationary and Gaussian} \\ E[e(s)] = 0 \\ E[e(s)e(r)] = -\theta_{s-r}, \quad (s-r) \in N \\ \qquad\qquad\quad = 1 \qquad \text{if } s = r \\ \qquad\qquad\quad = 0 \qquad \text{otherwise.} \end{array}\right\} \quad (2.13)$$

If we are interested only in second-order properties, we do not need the Gaussian assumption on e. By taking the Fourier transform of (2.12) and using (2.13), one can show that the cross-spectral density between $e(\cdot)$ and $y(\cdot)$ is a constant $\sqrt{\nu}$ so that

$$\begin{array}{rl} E[y(s)e(r)] = \sqrt{\nu} & \text{if } s = r \\ = 0 & \text{if } s \neq r. \end{array} \quad (2.14)$$

Since $y(\cdot)$ and $e(\cdot)$ are Gaussian, (2.14) implies

$$E[e(s)|\text{all } y(r), r \neq s] = 0.$$

Taking expectation of (2.12) and utilizing the above equation, we find that $y(\cdot)$ possesses the bilateral Markov property in (2.11) with respect to the neighbor set N.

Given a sequence $y(\cdot)$ which possesses a strict bilateral Markov property with respect to the symmetric neighbor set N_1, there may not exist any neighbor set N such that $y(\cdot)$ is unilateral Markov with respect to the neighbor set N. This feature is due to the lack of spectral factorization in two dimensions. However, the converse is true, i.e., given a sequence $y(\cdot)$ which obeys a unilateral Markov model with neighbor set N, we can construct a neighbor set N_1 so that $y(\cdot)$ is bilateral Markov with the neighbor set N_1. An example is in Fig. 2.

As before, the infinite lattice model is computationally cumbersome for handling finite images. Hence, we will introduce the toroidal lattice models. As before, Ω is divided into 2 subsets Ω_B and Ω_I

$$y(s) = \sum_{r \in N_S} \theta_r(y(s+r) + y(s-r)) + \sqrt{\nu}\, e(s), \quad s \in \Omega_I,$$

$$y(s) = \sum_{r \in N_S} \theta_r(y_1(s+r) + y_1(s-r)) + \sqrt{\nu}\, e(s), \quad s \in \Omega_B$$

$$(2.15)$$

where $y_1(\cdot)$ is related to $y(\cdot)$ as in (2.3). The noise sequence $e(\cdot)$ obeys (2.13). Using the vector matrix notation, (2.15) can be written as

$$A(\theta) y = \sqrt{\nu}\, e \quad (2.16)$$

where $A(\theta)$ is a block-circulant and a symmetric matrix. As in SAR models, to ensure bounded output for a bounded input a necessary and sufficient condition is that the eigenvalues of $A(\theta)$ be positive, i.e.,

$$\mu_s' \triangleq (1 - 2\theta^T \phi_s) > 0 \quad \text{for all } s \in \Omega$$

$$\theta = \text{col}\, (\theta_r, r \in N_S)$$

$$\phi_s = \text{col}\left[\cos \frac{2\pi}{M}[(s-1)^T r], r \in N_S\right]. \quad (2.17)$$

The M^2 eigenvalues of $A(\theta)$, viz. μ_s', $s \in \Omega$, can be derived using the method in the Appendix and the fact that $A(\theta)$ is symmetric.

In view of (2.17), (2.16) can be inverted

$$y = \sqrt{\nu}\, A^{-1}(\theta) e \quad (2.18)$$

$$E[ey^T] = \sqrt{\nu}\, I, \quad \text{from (2.14).} \quad (2.19)$$

Consequently, multiplying both sides of (2.18) by y^T, taking expectation and using (2.19), we obtain the following expression for the covariance matrix Q_y

$$Q_y = \nu A^{-1}(\theta). \quad (2.20)$$

Note that Q_y is block circulant with eigenvalues ν/μ_s', $s \in \Omega$. The spectral density of $y(\cdot)$ is

```
            X    X X
        X . N X . X            N₁
            X X
```

Fig. 2. Neighbor sets in two equivalent unilateral (N) and bilateral (N_1) models.

$$S_y(\lambda_1, \lambda_2) = \nu/\mu'_{ij} \quad \text{if} \quad \lambda_1 = 2\pi i/M, \quad \lambda_2 = 2\pi j/M.$$

C. Comparison of SAR and CM Models

An SAR model with a neighbor set N does not possess, in general, a bilateral Markov property with respect to N. However, when $y(\cdot)$ is Gaussian, it is possible to construct a set N_1 which is a superset of N such that $y(\cdot)$ obeying a Gaussian SAR model with neighbor set N is bilateral Markov with neighbor set N_1. For instance, if $N = [(0, 1), (0, -1), (1, 0), (-1, 0)]$ then $N_1 = [s: s \in N_S \text{ or } -s \in N_S]$ where $N_S = [(1, 0), (0, 1), (1, 1), (-1, 1), (0, 2), (2, 0)]$. Consequently, even when $y(\cdot)$ is not Gaussian, we can construct a CM model which has the same spectral density as an SAR model. However, the higher order properties of these two models may be different.

The converse is not true. Given a CM model with neighbor set N, there may not exist any SAR model with the same second-order properties. A simple example is the CM model with N having the four nearest neighbors. The discussion of [18] is also relevant here.

However, CM models have their own disadvantages. For an image $y(\cdot)$ obeying a CM model, we can write an explicit expression for the joint density of the entire image only when y or $e(\cdot)$ is Gaussian, and in a few other special cases [13]. Consequently, it is not possible to use good parameter estimation methods like maximum likelihood except when $y(\cdot)$ is Gaussian or $y(\cdot)$ belongs to other special cases. In contrast, in SAR models, we can write an expression for the joint density of the entire image, given the common density of the input noise w. In addition, SAR models can be generalized into simultaneous autoregressive moving average (SARMA) models. These models are not a subset of CM models.

III. Restoration Schemes Using SAR Models

In developing restoration algorithms, three different cases might arise.

Case i): An SAR model with parameters θ and ρ is assumed for the *original* undegraded image y. The parameters (θ, ρ) are unknown. A prototype of the original image is available, from which θ and ρ can be estimated.

Case ii): An SAR model characterized by parameters θ' and ρ' is assumed for the given *degraded* image, x. A prototype of the original image is not available. The parameters θ' and ρ' can be estimated from the degraded image.

Case iii): Assume an SAR model with unknown parameters (θ, ρ) for the original image y, and that a prototype original is *not* available. Estimate (θ, ρ) using the degraded image.

Of the three cases considered above, Case i) is not realistic since a prototype is rarely available. Cases ii) and iii) are realistic as they do not require any prototype of the original.

Although Case i) does not correspond to a realistic situation, it is briefly mentioned here to serve as a benchmark. For instance, the goodness of the approximation used in Case iii) may be evaluated by comparing the mean square error in restored images under Cases i) and iii).

Case iii) is different from Case ii) in that the undegraded image y is represented by an SAR or CM model in the former, while in the latter, the degraded image x itself is represented by an SAR or CM model. The motivation for considering these two cases is as follows. The MMSE restoration algorithms require the estimation of power spectrum S_y of the undegraded image y, related to S_x, the power spectrum of the degraded image as

$$S_x = S_y \|H(\lambda)\|^2 + S_\eta \tag{2.21}$$

where $\|H(\lambda)\|^2$ is the scale factor due to PSF matrix H, and S_η is the noise power spectrum. Under Case ii), we directly estimate S_x and try to infer S_y using (2.21). This method works well (as shown later), when the degradation is due to noise alone ($\|H(\lambda)\|^2 \equiv 1$); due to the ill-conditioned nature of PSF matrix, a poor estimate of S_y results when the degradation due to PSF matrix is also included. Hence, Case iii) is a practical compromise, where the required estimate of S_y is the estimate of S_x obtained from the degraded image.

A. Restoration Using SAR Model for x (Case ii)

Assume that we are given a degraded image x related to y as in (1.1), and represent x by the SAR model in (3.1) and (3.2):

$$x(s) = \sum_{r \in N} \theta'_r x(s+r) + \sqrt{\rho'} \, w(s), \quad s \in \Omega_I \tag{3.1}$$

$$x(s) = \sum_{r \in N} \theta'_r x_1(s+r) + \sqrt{\rho'} \, w(s), \quad s \in \Omega_B \tag{3.2}$$

where $x_1(\cdot)$ obeys an equation similar to $y_1(\cdot)$ in (2.3). The covariance matrix Q_x of x, under the transformation in (1.1) is

$$Q_x = H Q_y H^T + \gamma I \tag{3.3}$$

$$Q_y = H^{-1}(Q_x - \gamma I)(H^T)^{-1}. \tag{3.4}$$

Very often, due to the ill-conditioned nature of the PSF matrix, H^{-1} does not exist. Under these situations, a suitable generalized inverse may be substituted for H^{-1}. With this assumption, the substitution of (3.4) into (1.2) yields the MMSE estimate $\hat{y}$

$$\hat{y} = H^{-1}(Q_x - \gamma I)(Q_x)^{-1} x. \tag{3.5}$$

Since Q_x is a block-circulant matrix with eigenvalues $\rho'/\|\mu'_s\|^2$, $s \in \Omega$, and H is block circulant with eigenvalues $\bar{h}_s$, $s \in \Omega$, $\hat{y}$ can be computed as

$$\hat{y} = 1/M^2 \sum_s f_s [(\rho' - \gamma \|\mu_s\|^2)/\rho' \bar{h}_s] f_s^{*T} x. \tag{3.6}$$

In (3.6) f_s, $s \in \Omega$ are the M^2 Fourier vectors defined below:

$$f_{i,j} = \text{col } [t_j, \lambda_i t_j, \cdots, \lambda_i^{M-1} t_j], \quad M^2 \text{ vector}$$

$$t_j = \text{col } [1, \lambda_j, \lambda_j^2, \cdots, \lambda_j^{M-1}], \quad M \text{ vector}$$

$$\lambda_i = \exp [\sqrt{-1} \, 2\pi(i-1)/M].$$

Equation (3.6) yields an optimal $\hat{y}$ if the parameters $\boldsymbol{\theta}'$, ρ', and γ are known exactly. In practice, they are not known and are estimated from the degraded image. One can use the steady state component of the spectral density of the degraded image as an estimate of γ [1]. The reasoning behind this method is as follows. Since the additive noise is white, S_x, the power spectrum of noisy image is a sum of a constant (corresponding to γ) and the term involving S_y. For relatively large frequencies, S_y becomes relatively small and the corresponding value of S_x is the required estimate of γ. The expression for this estimate of γ is given below for a 64 × 64 image.

$$\hat{\gamma} = (1/(4)^2) \sum_{s \in \Omega_S} \rho'/\|\mu_s\|^2,$$

$$\Omega_S = [s = (i, j), 29 \leq i, j \leq 32]. \quad (3.7)$$

The estimates of $\boldsymbol{\theta}'$ and ρ' are computed from the given degraded image. The popular methods of estimation are the least squares (LS) and the maximum likelihood (ML) methods. The LS method yields consistent estimates for unilateral neighbor sets, but, in general, the estimates are inconsistent for SAR models with nonunilateral neighbor sets. For Gaussian SAR models with nonunilateral neighbor sets, the log-likelihood function is a nonquadratic function of parameters. Consequently, the ML method requires the use of computationally expensive gradient methods. An approximate iterative estimation scheme suggested in [19] yields, with less computation, estimates close to ML estimates for Gaussian variables and performs reasonably well in non-Gaussian situations as well.

The approximate ML estimates $\bar{\boldsymbol{\theta}}$, $\bar{\rho}$ are obtained as limits of $\boldsymbol{\theta}_{t+1}$, ρ_t given below:

$$\boldsymbol{\theta}_{t+1} = (\boldsymbol{R} - [1/\rho_t] \boldsymbol{S})^{-1} (\boldsymbol{V} - (1/\rho_t) \boldsymbol{U}], \quad t = 0, 1, 2, \cdots \quad (3.8)$$

$$\rho_t = (1/M^2) \sum [x(s) - \boldsymbol{\theta}_t^T z(s)]^2, \quad t = 1, 2, 3, \cdots \quad (3.9)$$

$$z(s) = \text{col } [x(s + r), r \in N], \quad m \text{ vector}$$

$$\boldsymbol{S} = \sum z(s) z^T(s), \quad \boldsymbol{U} = \sum z(s) x(s) \quad (3.10)$$

$$\boldsymbol{V} = \sum \boldsymbol{C}_s, \quad \boldsymbol{R} = \sum (\boldsymbol{S}_s \boldsymbol{S}_s^T - \boldsymbol{C}_s \boldsymbol{C}_s^T) \quad (3.11)$$

$$\boldsymbol{C}_s = \text{col } [\cos (2\pi/M) \{s^T - (1, 1)\} r, r \in N]$$

$$\boldsymbol{S}_s = \text{col } [\sin (2\pi/M) \{s^T - (1, 1)\} r, r \in N].$$

The initial value $\boldsymbol{\theta}_0$ is $\boldsymbol{\theta}_0 = \boldsymbol{S}^{-1} \boldsymbol{U}$.

All the summations in (3.9)-(3.11) are over $s \in \Omega$ and m is the dimension of $\boldsymbol{\theta}$. The details of the derivation of the estimation method may be found in [19], [20]. For unilateral models, $\boldsymbol{R}$ and $\boldsymbol{V}$ given by (3.10) and (3.11) are equal to the null matrix and vector, respectively, so that $\boldsymbol{\theta}_{t+1}$ is the (LS) estimate. This estimation scheme has been used in texture synthesis [20] and the image restoration applications reported here, and usually converges within four or five iterations. The computational load is in the inversion of $m \times m$ matrix in (3.8). The matrix $\boldsymbol{R}$ and vector $\boldsymbol{V}$ remain unaltered during all the iterations.

Fig. 3. Original image.

The practical implementation of (3.6), when there is no blur ($H = I$), is straightforward and gives good results, reported in the next section. When $H \neq I$, there may be computational problems due to some eigenvalues $\bar{h}_s$ being small. These problems can be avoided to some extent by using some approximate methods [1, ch. 7], [2, ch. 7].

Consider the case $H = I$, i.e., degradation is due to noise alone. The estimate $\hat{y}$ in (3.6) is reduced to

$$\hat{y} = (1/M^2) \sum_\Omega f_s(\rho' - \gamma \|\mu_s\|^2) f_s^{*T} x/\rho'.$$

The parameters γ, ρ' and $\boldsymbol{\theta}$ are estimated from the noisy image. The application of this restoration scheme is illustrated by the following experiments.

B. Experimental Results (Case ii)

A 64 × 64 window of the original girl's face [15] in Fig. 3 was corrupted by an additive white noise sequence such that the signal-to-noise ratio (SNR), defined as the ratio of signal variance to noise variance, equals a specified value.

It is assumed that only the noisy image is available. SAR models of different neighbor sets N were fitted to the noisy image. The filtered images using these models are in Fig. 4 where SNR = 7 dB, and in Fig. 5 where SNR = 0 dB. The details of models used are given in Table I. In Fig. 4, the filtered images using models with neighbor sets N_4, N_5, and N_6 are good. Interestingly, for this image, the filtered image corresponding to a simple causal model performs well compared to the models with neighbor sets N_2 and N_3. For the noisy image of SNR = 0 dB, the filtered image using the neighbor set N_4 is the best. Some of the features of the image, such as the upper lip of the girl's mouth which is barely visible in the noisy image, are well defined in the filtered images.

We now give some numerical measures for the evaluation of the quality of the restoration. For the model with neighbor set N_5 the best estimate of γ for the 7 dB image was 386.61, the true value being 393.01. For the 0 dB noisy image, the estimate of γ was 1804.1 (the true value of γ being 1965.05), using the model with neighbor set N_4. An indication of the quality of the filtered estimate $\hat{y}$ may be obtained by computing the mean square error (MSE)

$$(1/(64)^2) \sum_{s \in \Omega} [y(s) - \hat{y}(s)]^2.$$

The MSE's between the original and the noisy images are 378.53 and 1728.5 corresponding to the 7 dB and 0 dB noisy images, respectively. The best filtered image y, obtained using

Fig. 4. Filtering of noisy image using SAR models when prototype of the original is not available. *Top*—noisy image of SNR = 5. *Second row*—(left to right) filtered images using models N_1, N_2, and N_3. *Third row*—(left to right) filtered images using models N_4, N_5, and N_6.

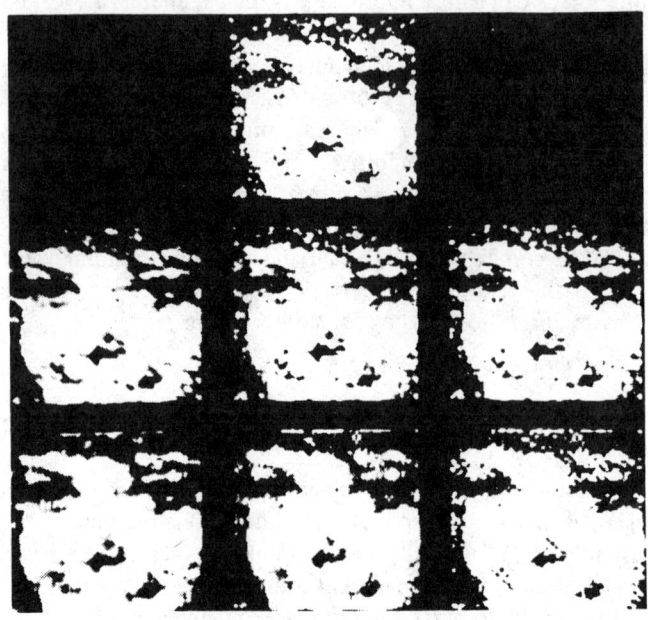

Fig. 5. Filtering of noisy image using SAR models when prototype of the original is not available. *Top*—noisy image of SNR = 1. *Second row*—filtered images using models N_1, N_2, and N_3. *Third row*—filtered images using models N_4, N_5, and N_6.

TABLE I
DETAILS OF SAR MODELS CORRESPONDING TO THE RESTORED IMAGES IN FIGS. 4–6

Number	Neighborset N
N_1	{(-1,0), (0,-1), (-1,-1)}
N_2	{(-1,0), (1,0), (0,-1)}
N_3	{(-1,0), (1,0), (0,-1), (0,1)}
N_4	{(-1,0), (-1,1), (0,1), (1,1), (1,0), (1,-1), (0,-1), (-1,-1)}
N_5	{(-1,0), (-1,1), (0,1), (1,1), (1,0), (1,-1), (0,-1), (-1,-1), (-2,0), (2,0)}
N_6	{(-1,0), (-1,1), (0,1), (1,1), (1,0), (1,-1), (0,-1), (-1,-1), (-2,0), (2,0), (0,-2), (0,2)}

TABLE II
MEAN SQUARE ERROR BETWEEN y AND $\hat{y}$ OBTAINED USING SAR MODELS

Model Number	MSE 7 db	MSE 0 db
N_1	137.59	394.62
N_2	181.61	689.20
N_3	198.44	731.96
N_4	112.40	347.40
N_5	113.87	566.88
N_6	160.04	1204.9
No Model	1728.5	378.53

the neighbor set N_4, has MSE of 112.40. The same filter gave the best results for the SNR = 0 dB image, with the MSE being 347.40. The numerical values of MSE between y and $\hat{y}$ for all the models N_1–N_6 are listed in Table II.

C. SAR Model for y (Case iii)

Assume that the undegraded image y is represented by an SAR model with neighbor set N in (2.1) and (2.2) and parameters (θ, ρ). A prototype of the original image is not available. An SAR model with neighbor set N is fitted to the given degraded image, and the resulting estimates are used in place of the unknown parameters (θ, ρ). The MMSE estimate $\hat{y}$ can be computed as

$$\hat{y} = (1/M^2) \sum f_s [\rho \bar{h}_s^* / (\rho \|\bar{h}_s\|^2 + \gamma \|\mu_s\|^2)] f_s^{*T} x \quad (3.12)$$

where ρ and θ are replaced by estimates computed using the degraded image. Some experimental results using this method are given below.

D. Experimental Results

The original image in Fig. 3 was blurred by using the PSF

$$h(k, l) = (0.4/\pi) \exp\{-0.4(k^2 + l^2)\}, \quad 0 \leq k, l \leq 2. \quad (3.13)$$

The additive Gaussian noise has SNR = 5. The SAR models in Table I were fitted to the degraded image and (3.12) was used. The degraded as well as restored images are shown in Fig. 6. The improvement is noticeable with the filters corresponding to models with neighbor sets N_4, N_5 and N_6. We give the following numerical figures to evaluate the quality of restoration. The MSE between the original and the noisy and blurred images is 511.43. The MSE between the original and restored images using the neighbor set N_4 is 160.06 when

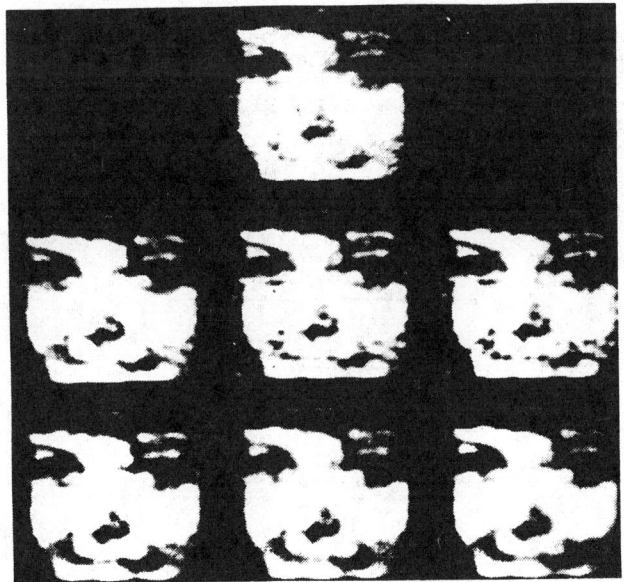

Fig. 6. Restoration of noisy and blurred image using SAR models when the prototype of the original is not available. Restoration is done using (3.12) and parameters estimated from the degraded image. Top—noisy and blurred image of Fig. 3, the degradation being due to Gaussian blur (3.13) and additive white noise of SNR = 5. Second row—restored images using models N_1, N_2, and N_3. Third row—restored images using models N_4, N_5, and N_6.

Fig. 7. Filtering of noisy images using CM models when the prototype of the original is not available. Top—noisy image of SNR = 5. Second row—filtered images using models N_{S1} and N_{S2}. Third row—filtered images using models N_{S3} and N_{S4}.

the estimates obtained from the degraded image are used, and is 151.90 when the estimates obtained from the original prototype are used. This indicates that the additional MSE caused by the replacement of the unknown parameters by their estimates obtained from the degraded image is within 2 percent.

IV. Restoration Using CM Models

The development in this section will parallel Section III and, hence, the discussion is kept to a bare minimum.

A. CM Model for x

Algorithms using CM models for the restoration of images degraded by a finite PSF and additive noise can be derived similar to SAR models discussed in Section III-A. For the sake of brevity, we will consider the case of degradation due to additive noise only, i.e.,

$$x = y + \eta. \quad (4.1)$$

Assume that x obeys a CM model in (4.2) and (4.3):

$$x(s) = \sum_{r \in N_S} \theta'_r [x(s+r) + x(s-r)] + \sqrt{\nu'}\, e(s), \quad s \in \Omega_I \quad (4.2)$$

$$x(s) = \sum_{r \in N_S} \theta'_r [x_1(s+r) + x_1(s-r)] + \sqrt{\nu'}\, e(s), \quad s \in \Omega_B \quad (4.3)$$

where $[x_1(\cdot)]$ obeys an equation similar to (2.3). The covariance matrix Q_x of $[x(\cdot)]$ is

$$Q_x = Q_y + \gamma I. \quad (4.4)$$

Substitution of Q_y from (4.4) into (1.2) with $H = I$ yields $\hat{y}$, an estimate of the original image

$$\hat{y} = (Q_x - \gamma I)\, Q_x^{-1} x. \quad (4.5)$$

$\hat{y}$ in (4.5) can be computed using the Fourier computations as in (4.6).

$$\hat{y} = \sum_\Omega f_s\, [(\nu' - \gamma\mu'_s)\, f_s^{*T} x/\nu'] \quad (4.6)$$

where μ'_s are defined in (2.17). The parameters θ', ν', and γ can be estimated from the noisy image. There are several methods to estimate (θ', ν') for CM models. The coding method in [13] is very simple in principle and yields consistent but very inefficient estimates. The ML method in [23] yields consistent and efficient estimates but the procedure is computationally unattractive except for simple isotropic models. A simple consistent estimate whose efficiency lies between the coding and ML methods, given in [19] is used to estimate ν' and θ'. The estimates $\hat{\theta}'$ and $\hat{\nu}'$ are given by

$$\hat{\theta}' = \left[\sum_{s \in \Omega} q(s)\, q^T(s)\right]^{-1} \left[\sum_{s \in \Omega} x(s)\, q(s)\right], \quad (4.7)$$

$$\hat{\nu}' = (1/M^2) \sum_{s \in \Omega} [x(s) - \hat{\theta}'^T q(s)]^2, \quad (4.8)$$

$$q(s) = \text{col}\, [\{x(s+r) + x(s-r)\}, r \in N_S] \quad (4.9)$$

B. Experimental Results

The original girl's image in Fig. 3 is corrupted by additive white noise of SNR = 7 dB. CM models of different neighbor sets N_S were fitted to the noisy image and (4.6) was used. The noisy image together with the filtered images are given in Fig. 7 for SNR = 7 dB, and in Fig. 8 for SNR = 0 dB. The filtered images of the 7 dB noisy image corresponding to neighbor sets N_{S3} and N_{S4} are good. Most of the filtered images with CM models appear smoother than the filtered images obtained by SAR models. The improvement is noticeable in the filtered images of 0 dB noisy image corresponding

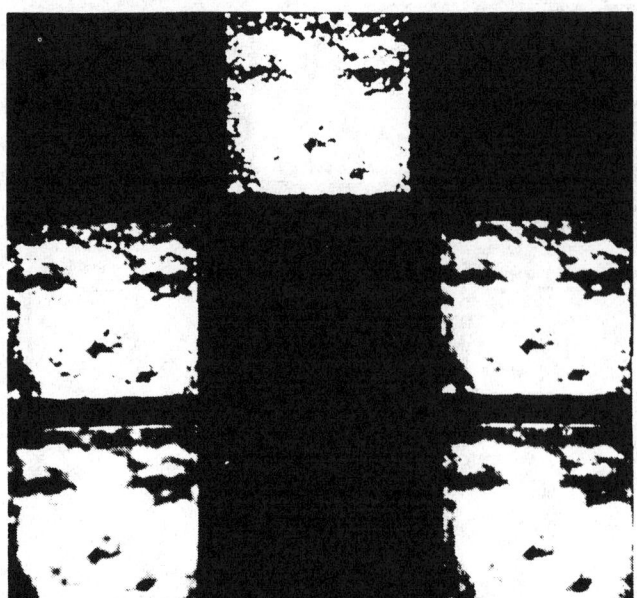

Fig. 8. Filtering of noisy images using CM models when the prototype of the original is not available. *Top*—noisy image of SNR = 1. *Second row*—filtered images using models N_{S1} and N_{S2}. *Third row*—filtered images using models N_{S3} and N_{S4}.

TABLE III
DETAILS OF CM MODELS CORRESPONDING TO THE RESTORED IMAGES IN FIGS. 7–9

Number	Neighborset N_s
N_{S1}	{(0,1), (1,0)}
N_{S2}	{(0,1), (1,0), (1,1)}
N_{S3}	{(1,0), (1,-1), (0,1), (1,1)}
N_{S4}	{(1,0), (0,1), (1,1), (1,-1), (0,2), (2,0)}

TABLE IV
MEAN SQUARE ERROR BETWEEN y AND $\hat{y}$ OBTAINED USING CM MODELS

Model Number	7 db	0 db
N_{S1}	129.35	499.90
N_{S2}	103.81	332.21
N_{S3}	93.28	321.79
N_{S4}	91.06	339.58
No Model	378.53	1728.5

to a model with neighbor set N_{S4}. Table III gives the details of the CM models filtered to the noisy image. Using the model with the neighbor set N_{S4}, the best estimate of γ for 7 dB noisy image was obtained as 378.74 (true value being 393.01). For 0 dB noisy image, the estimate of γ was 1917.9 (true value being 1965.05) using the model with neighbor set N_{S3}. The MSE corresponding to the best filter in Fig. 7 was 91.08 using the neighbor set N_{S4} with the error between the original and noisy being 378.53, roughly a reduction in the MSE by a factor of 4. The corresponding numerical values for 0 dB SNR image are 321.79 and 1728.5 using N_{S3}. Note that the MSE's reported above are less than the errors corresponding to the best SAR filters, confirming our visual judgment. The numerical values of the MSE between y and $\hat{y}$ for the models in Table III are given in Table IV.

C. CM Models for "y" (Case iii)

Assume that the undegraded image y is represented by a CM model in (2.11)-(2.12). The MMSE estimate y can be computed as

$$\hat{y} = (1/M^2) \sum f_s (\nu \bar{h}_s^* / (\nu \|\bar{h}_s\|^2 + \gamma \mu_s') f_s^{*T} x. \quad (4.10)$$

The parameters (θ, ν, γ) of the CM model are estimated using the given *degraded* image and (4.7)-(4.9). The estimate of γ is obtained from the degraded image using

$$\hat{\gamma} = (\tfrac{1}{16}) \sum_{s \in \Omega_S} \nu/\mu_s', \quad \Omega_S = \{s = (i,j), 29 \leq i, j \leq 32\}.$$

$$(4.11)$$

In our experiment, a degraded image is obtained by using the PSF in (3.13) and an additive white noise of SNR = 5. The CM models used are listed in Table III. Equation (4.10) was used to compute $\hat{y}$ with θ, ν, and γ replaced by their estimates obtained from the degraded image. The restored images are in Fig. 9 and the improvement is evident. To get some idea regarding the performance of this method we give some numerical figures below. The MSE between the original and degraded image is 511.43. The MSE between the original and the best restored image obtained using the neighbor set N_{S4} is 169.29, when estimates obtained from the degraded image are used; on the other hand, the MSE is 146.99 when the estimates obtained from the original prototype image are used, indicating that the increase in MSE due to using the estimates from the degraded image when no prototype of original is available is within 5 percent.

V. Discussion

We have developed a class of MMSE restoration algorithms for the restoration of degraded images, without requiring that the prototype of the original image be available. The underlying model representations are more general than the models considered in [4]-[8]. Consequently, the structures of the correlation functions of the models are more varied than the correlation functions corresponding to the models in [4]-[8]. We have used estimates of parameters obtained from asymptotically consistent methods. The representation on toroidal lattices leads to fast computations using FFT algorithms. Fast restoration filters have been considered in the literature [4], [8] for a much smaller class of neighbor sets N motivated by discrete approximations of second-order continuous partial differential equations. Since fast sine transforms diagonalize symmetric, *tridiagonal* Toeplitz matrices, the fast algorithms in [4], [8] are valid only for a restricted class of models like [4], [8] nearest neighbor models. For instance, for neighbor sets like N_5 and N_6 (Table I) and N_{S4} (Table III), exact fast implementation of filters using sine transforms is not possible since these neighbor sets lead to banded Toeplitz covariance matrices. Almost all the models in [4], [8] are isotropic, which is not usually true in real images.

For the girl's image used in this paper, it was found that the

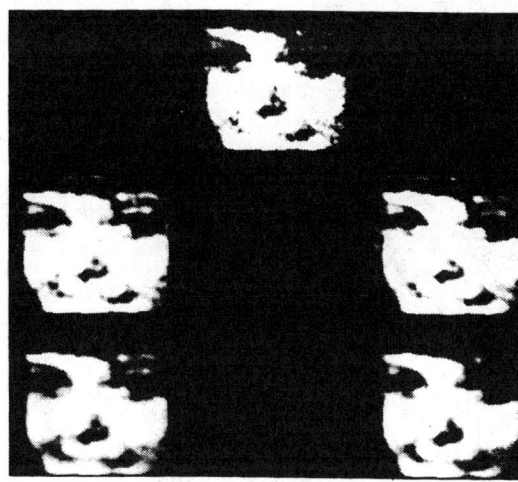

Fig. 9. Restoration of noisy and blurred image using CM models when the prototype of the original is not available. Restoration is done using (4.10) and parameters estimated from the degraded image. *Top*—noisy and blurred image same as in Fig. 6. *Second row*—restored images using models N_{S1} and N_{S2}. *Third row*—restored images using models N_{S3} and N_{S4}.

filtering of noisy images was better with CM models than with SAR models, judging from the actual MSE computed and visual inspection. A quantitative decision can be made regarding the appropriateness of a particular filter structure by using the decision rules in [20], [26]. The increase in MSE that results due to the use of estimates of parameters obtained from the degraded image instead of the original image is within 2 percent for SAR models and about 5 percent for CM models. In our experiments, we have used images of size 64 × 64. Due to the Fourier computations involved, much larger images can be restored with reasonable computational load. Since large images cannot be adequately represented by one stationary model, it is preferable to restore the large image using several different models fitted to overlapping or nonoverlapping blocks of the image. One can also consider different values of PSF matrix H in the different image blocks.

Note that the bilateral SAR and CM models used here naturally lead to nonrecursive restoration algorithms. Compared to several recursive formulations known in the literature [7], the nonrecursive algorithms require more memory since the images are transformed as a block. Since the algorithms use FFT routines, the main computational load is in obtaining the estimates of the parameters characterizing the model. For CM and SAR models, the estimation method involves inverting an $m \times m$ matrix. A similar matrix inversion is also required in unilateral models, except in the case of the simplest causal separable model, with $N = \{(0, 1), (-1, 0), (-1, -1)\}$, where the required estimates can be obtained by measuring the row and column correlations. Thus, the computational load in the estimation is of the same order in bilateral CM models and recursive models, but in general, the estimation in bilateral SAR models does involve extra computations. It should be pointed out that recursive structures are obtained from a subset of all possible neighbor sets. If the underlying model is characterized by a neighbor set N whose spectral density function does not factorize (which is often true in two dimensions), any recursive algorithm will only be an approximation [7] to the nonrecursive algorithms. Furthermore, obtaining recursive filter structures involves some computations.

In Sections III and IV, finite lattice models were used for developing computationally elegant restoration schemes. The finite lattice models involve assumptions regarding the distribution of boundary pixels. An alternative representation without any such assumptions is the infinite lattice models mentioned in Section II-A. One of the great impediments of infinite lattice models is the enormous computations involved in the inversion of the matrix in (2). Typically, for a 64 × 64 image, Q_y is of dimension 4096 × 4096 and the storage and inversion of the matrix in (2) is very expensive. On the other hand, the toroidal lattice models lead to a manageable computational load with relatively high quality of restoration. Restrictive as it may appear, the toroidal structure has been widely used in several investigations. Onsager [21] showed in a pioneering work that in two dimensions using periodic boundary, one can solve problems relating to finite lattices analytically and then obtain limiting results corresponding to infinite lattice models. Moran [22] assumed a CM model on a toroidal lattice, and constructed a CM model on an infinite lattice as a limiting case of the periodic lattice structure. Periodic boundary assumptions have been made to obtain maximum likelihood estimates in [23]. One of the important conclusions of these investigations is that the final results obtained by using models with periodic boundary conditions and infinite lattice models are not significantly different from each other. Specifically numerical quantities of spectral density function, correlation function, etc., are very close to each other.

Suppose $S_I(\eta_1, \eta_2)$ denotes the spectral density function of the infinite lattice model and $S_F(\lambda_i, \lambda_j)$, $i, j = 0, 1, \cdots, M-1$, $\lambda_i = 2\pi i/M$ denote the SDF of the toroidal lattice model; then it can be shown that

$$S_I(\eta_1 = \lambda_i, \eta_2 = \lambda_j) = S_F(\lambda_i, \lambda_j), \quad i, j = 0, 1, \cdots, M-1.$$

As a consequence, the normalized autocorrelation function (ACF) of infinite and toroidal lattice models are numerically close. To illustrate the numerical proximity, the normalized ACF of isotropic CM model with $\theta = 0.24$ and $N_S = \{(0, 1), (1, 0)\}$ was evaluated at lower lags using the toroidal lattice assumption, and was compared with the corresponding quantities for the infinite lattice model available in [24, Table I]. We have for the normalized ACF computed with infinite lattice model, $\rho_{1,0} = 0.434$, $\rho_{1,1} = 0.295$, $\rho_{0,2} = 0.220$, $\rho_{2,1} = 0.180$. The corresponding quantities computed using toroidal lattice assumption are $\rho_{1,0} = 0.4329$, $\rho_{1,1} = 0.2935$, $\rho_{0,2} = 0.2181$, and $\rho_{2,1} = 0.1785$, which are very close to one another. Since the $\rho_{k,l}$'s can be expressed in terms of $\rho_{1,0}$ and $\rho_{1,1}$, any $\rho_{k,l}$ in the infinite lattice model will be very close to the corresponding $\rho_{k,l}$ of the toroidal model, for $|k| \leq [M/2]$ and $|l| \leq [M/2]$. In addition, the estimates of the corresponding parameters of the finite and infinite lattice models will also be numerically close. Hence, we can regard the finite toroidal lattice models as excellent approximations to the infinite lattice models.

VI. Conclusions

We have developed several algorithms using a class of spatial interaction models, for the restoration of images degraded by blur and additive noise. These algorithms are fast and nonrecursive and do not involve any restrictive assumptions like isotropy or causality. We do not require the availability of a prototype of the original image, an assumption present in almost all of the MMSE restoration methods.

Appendix
Evaluation of Eigenvalues of a Block-Circulant Matrix [11]

Definition: An $M \times M$ matrix $A = \{a_{ij}\}$ is said to be circulant if

$$a_{i,j} = a_{i \bmod M + 1, j \bmod M + 1} \quad \text{for all } i, j = 1, \cdots, M.$$

Such a matrix can be specified by its first row since other rows can be generated from the first row by shifting operation. For instance

$$A = \text{circulant } (\theta_1, \cdots, \theta_M)$$

$$= \begin{bmatrix} \theta_1 & \theta_2 & \cdots & \theta_M \\ \theta_M & \theta_1 & \cdots & \theta_{M-1} \\ \theta_{M-1} & \theta_M & \cdots & \theta_{M-2} \\ \theta_2 & \theta_3 & \cdots & \theta_1 \end{bmatrix}.$$

Lemma 1: The eigenvalues of the circulant matrix given above are

$$\mu_i = \sum_{k=1}^{M} \theta_k \lambda_i^k, \quad \lambda_i = \exp\left[\sqrt{-1}\,(i-1)\,2\pi/M\right], \, i = 1, \cdots, M.$$

The eigenvector corresponding to the eigenvalue μ_i is the Fourier vector t_i

$$t_i^T = (1, \lambda_i, \lambda_i^2, \cdots, \lambda_i^{M-1}).$$

The proof of Lemma 1 can be found in [25].

Derivation of μ_s in (2.6): Define a set of coefficients $\theta_{i,j}$, $(i,j) \notin N$ as follows:

$$\theta_{0,0} = 1$$

$$\theta_{i_1, j_1} = \theta_{i_1 \bmod M, j_1 \bmod M} \quad \text{if } (i_1, j_1) \in N. \tag{A1}$$

All other $\theta_{i,j}$ are zero. By (2.5) and (A1)

$$B_{1,i} = \text{circulant } (\theta_{i-1,0}, \theta_{i-1,1}, \cdots, \theta_{i-1,M-1}),$$

$$i = 1, \cdots, M. \tag{A2}$$

Let h_{ij} be the eigenvalue of the circulant matrix $B_{1,i}$ corresponding to the eigenvector t_j.

$$h_{1,j} = (\text{first row of } B_{1,1})^T t_j$$

$$= 1 + \sum_{k:\,(0,k) \in N} \theta_{0,k} \lambda_j^k, \quad \text{using (A1)}, \cdots \tag{A3}$$

$$h_{i,j} = (\text{first row of } B_{1,i})^T t_j$$

$$= \sum_{(l,k) \in N} \theta_{l,k} \lambda_j^k, \quad \text{where } l \bmod M = i - 1. \tag{A4}$$

Let

$$B(\theta) f_{ij} = \text{column } [a_{i1}, a_{i1}, \cdots, a_{iM}] \tag{A5}$$

where $a_{i,j}, j = 1, \cdots, M$ are all M vectors

$$a_{i1} = \sum_{k=1}^{M} B_{1,k} t_j \lambda_i^{k-1}, \quad \text{by (A5)}$$

$$= \sum_{k=1}^{M} h_{kj} t_j \lambda_i^{k-1},$$

since h_{kj} is eigenvalue of $B_{1,k}$ for eigenvector t_j

$$= t_j \left[\left(1 + \sum_{\substack{k \\ (0,k) \in N}} \theta_{0,k} \lambda_j^k \right) + \sum_{\substack{l,k \\ (l,k) \in N, l \neq 0}} \theta_{l,k} \lambda_j^k \lambda_i^l \right],$$

by (A2), (A3) and definition of λ_j

$$= \left(1 + \sum_{(l,k) \in N} \theta_{l,k} \lambda_i^l \lambda_j^k \right) t_j$$

$$= \mu_{ij} t_j, \quad \text{by definition of } \mu_{ij}.$$

We can prove similarly that

$$a_{ik} = \mu_{ij} t_j \lambda_i^{k-1}, \quad k = 2, \cdots, M.$$

Hence

$$B(\theta) f_{ij} = \mu_{ij} f_{ij}, \quad i, j = 1, \cdots, M.$$

Hence, $\{f_{ij}, \mu_{ij}, i, j = 1, \cdots, M\}$ are the eigenvectors and eigenvalues of $B(\theta)$.

Acknowledgment

The authors would like to thank the referees for their suggestions, which have substantially increased the readability of the paper, and Prof. E. J. Delp for providing the image data. The first author would also like to acknowledge the encouragement and support of Prof. A. Rosenfeld.

References

[1] H. C. Andrews and B. R. Hunt, *Digital Image Restoration*. Englewood Cliffs, NJ: Prentice-Hall, 1977.

[2] A. Rosenfeld and A. C. Kak, *Digital Picture Processing*. New York: Academic, 1976.

[3] B. R. Freiden, "Image enhancement and restoration," in *Picture Processing and Digital Filtering*, T. S. Huang, Ed. New York: Springer-Verlag, 1979.

[4] A. K. Jain and J. R. Jain, "Partial difference equations and finite differences in image processing—Part II: Image restoration," *IEEE Trans. Automat. Contr.*, vol. AC-23, pp. 817-833, Oct. 1978.

[5] S. R. Powell and L. M. Silverman, "Modeling of two-dimensional covariance functions with applications to image restoration," *IEEE Trans. Automat. Contr.*, vol. AC-19, pp. 8-13, Feb. 1976.

[6] M. S. Murphy and L. M. Silverman, "Image model representation and line by line recursive restoration," *IEEE Trans. Automat. Contr.*, vol. AC-23, pp. 808-816, Oct. 1978.

[7] J. W. Woods and C. H. Radewan, "Kalman filtering in two dimensions," *IEEE Trans. Inform. Theory*, vol. IT-23, pp. 473-482, July 1977.

[8] A. K. Jain, "A fast Karhunen-Loeve transform for digital restoration of images degraded by white and colored noise," *IEEE Trans. Comput.*, vol. C-26, pp. 560-571, June 1977.

[9] R. L. Kashyap, "Univariate and multivariate random field models

for images," *Comput. Graphics and Image Processing*, vol. 12, pp. 257–270, Mar. 1980.
[10] —, "Random field models on torus lattices for finite images," in *Proc. 5th Int. Conf. Pattern Recognition*, Miami, FL, Dec. 1980.
[11] —, "Random field models on finite lattices for finite images," presented at the Symp. Inform. Sci., Baltimore, MD, Mar. 1981.
[12] R. L. Kashyap and R. Chellappa, "Image restoration using random field models," *Proc. 18th Annu. Allerton Conf. Commun., Contr., and Computing*, Univ. Illinois, Urbana, pp. 956–965, Oct. 1980.
[13] J. Besag, "Spatial interaction and statistical analysis of lattice systems," *J. Roy. Stat. Soc., Ser. B.*, vol. B-36, pp. 199–236, 1974.
[14] J. W. Woods, "Two-dimensional discrete Markovian fields," *IEEE Trans. Inform. Theory*, vol. IT-18, pp. 232–240, Mar. 1972.
[15] W. K. Pratt and F. Davarian, "Fast computational techniques for pseudo inverse and Wiener image restoration," *IEEE Trans. Comput.*, vol. C-26, pp. 571–580, June 1977.
[16] D. M. Goodman and M. P. Ekstrom, "Multidimensional spectral factorization and unilateral AR models," *IEEE Trans. Automat. Contr.*, vol. AC-25, pp. 258–262, Apr. 1980.
[17] R. L. Kashyap, "Analysis and synthesis of image patterns by spatial interaction models," in *Progress in Pattern Recognition*, vol. 1, L. N. Kanal and A. Rosenfeld, Eds. Amsterdam, The Netherlands: North-Holland, 1981.
[18] D. Brook, "On the distinction between the conditional probability and the joint probability approaches in the specification of nearest-neighbor systems," *Biometrika*, vol. 51, pp. 481–483, 1964.
[19] R. Chellappa and R. L. Kashyap, "Synthetic generation and estimation in random field models of images," in *Proc. IEEE Comput. Soc. Conf. Pattern Recognition, Image Processing*, Dallas, TX, Aug. 1981, pp. 577–582.
[20] R. Chellappa, "Stochastic models in image analysis and processing," Ph.D. dissertation, Purdue Univ., West Lafayette, IN, Aug. 1981.
[21] L. Onsager, "Crystal statistics, I: A two-dimensional model with an order–disorder transition," *Phys. Rev.*, vol. 65, pp. 117–149, 1944.
[22] P. A. P. Moran, "A Gaussian Markovian process on a square lattice," *J. Appl. Prob.*, vol. 10, pp. 605–612, 1973.
[23] P. A. P. Moran and J. E. Besag, "On the estimation and testing of spatial interaction in Gaussian lattices," *Biometrika*, vol. 62, pp. 555–562, 1975.
[24] J. E. Besag, "On the correlation structure of some two-dimensional stationary processes," *Biometrika*, vol. 59, pp. 43–48.
[25] R. Bellman, *Introduction to Matrix Analysis*. New York: McGraw-Hill, 1960.
[26] R. L. Kashyap, R. Chellappa, and N. Ahuja, "Decision rules for choice of neighbors in random field models of images," *Comput. Graphics and Image Processing*, vol. 15, pp. 301–318, 1981.

R. Chellappa (S'78–M'81) received the B.E. (Hons.) degree in electronics and communication engineering from the University of Madras, Madras, India, in 1975, the M.E. degree with distinction in electrical communication engineering from the Indian Institute of Science, Bangalore, India, in 1977, and the M.S.E.E. and Ph.D. degrees from Purdue University, West Lafayette, IN, in 1978 and 1981, respectively.

He was a recipient of a National Scholarship from the Government of India from 1969 to 1975. From 1979 to 1981, he was also associated with the Computer Vision Laboratory, University of Maryland, College Park, as a Graduate Research Assistant and Faculty Research Assistant.

Since September 1981, he has been an Assistant Professor in the Department of Electrical Engineering, Systems and Image Processing Institute, University of Southern California, Los Angeles. His research interests include image processing, pattern recogn' ̀ multidimensional signal processing, and statistical inference.

Dr. Chellappa is a member of Eta Kappa Nu and Ta   a Pi.

R. L. Kashyap (M'70–SM'77–F'79) received the D.I.I.Sc. and M.E. degrees from the Indian Institute of Science, Bangalore, India, in 1960 and 1962, respectively, and the Ph.D. degree in engineering from Harvard University, Cambridge, MA, in 1965.

During 1965 and 1966 he was a Postdoctoral Fellow in applied mathematics at Harvard University, where he conducted research in stochastic automata. In 1966 he joined the faculty of Purdue University, West Lafayette, IN, where he currently holds the rank of Professor of Electrical Engineering. During spring semester of 1974, he was a Visiting Research Associate at the University of California, Berkeley, in the Department of Electrical Engineering and Computer Science, engaged in research in data management systems and time series analysis. In the fall semester of 1974, he was a Visiting Professor at the Division of Engineering and Applied Physics, Harvard University. He was an Associate Editor of the IEEE TRANSACTIONS ON AUTOMATIC CONTROL. He is the coauthor of the book *Stochastic Dynamic Models from Empirical Data* (New York: Academic, 1976).

Dr. Kashyap is a member of Sigma Xi and the Association for Computing Machinery. In 1966 he won the National Electronics Conference Annual Best Research Paper Award for his paper "Optimization of stochastic finite-state machines." He was the Coprogram Chairman of the 1978 IEEE Computer Society Conference on Pattern Recognition and Image Processing.

Stochastic Relaxation, Gibbs Distributions, and the Bayesian Restoration of Images

STUART GEMAN AND DONALD GEMAN

Abstract—We make an analogy between images and statistical mechanics systems. Pixel gray levels and the presence and orientation of edges are viewed as states of atoms or molecules in a lattice-like physical system. The assignment of an energy function in the physical system determines its Gibbs distribution. Because of the Gibbs distribution, Markov random field (MRF) equivalence, this assignment also determines an MRF image model. The energy function is a more convenient and natural mechanism for embodying picture attributes than are the local characteristics of the MRF. For a range of degradation mechanisms, including blurring, nonlinear deformations, and multiplicative or additive noise, the posterior distribution is an MRF with a structure akin to the image model. By the analogy, the posterior distribution defines another (imaginary) physical system. Gradual temperature reduction in the physical system isolates low energy states ("annealing"), or what is the same thing, the most probable states under the Gibbs distribution. The analogous operation under the posterior distribution yields the maximum *a posteriori* (MAP) estimate of the image given the degraded observations. The result is a highly parallel "relaxation" algorithm for MAP estimation. We establish convergence properties of the algorithm and we experiment with some simple pictures, for which good restorations are obtained at low signal-to-noise ratios.

Index Terms—Annealing, Gibbs distribution, image restoration, line process, MAP estimate, Markov random field, relaxation, scene modeling, spatial degradation.

I. INTRODUCTION

THE restoration of degraded images is a branch of digital picture processing, closely related to image segmentation and boundary finding, and extensively studied for its evident practical importance as well as theoretical interest. An analysis of the major applications and procedures (model-based and otherwise) through approximately 1980 may be found in [47]. There are numerous existing models (see [34]) and algorithms and the field is currently very active. Here we adopt a Bayesian approach, and introduce a "hierarchical," stochastic model for the original image, based on the *Gibbs distribution*, and a new restoration algorithm, based on stochastic relaxation and *annealing*, for computing the maximum *a posteriori* (MAP) estimate of the original image given the degraded image. This algorithm is highly parallel and exploits the equivalence between Gibbs distributions and *Markov random fields* (MRF).

The essence of our approach to restoration is a stochastic relaxation algorithm which generates a sequence of images that converges in an appropriate sense to the MAP estimate. This sequence evolves by *local* (and potentially *parallel*) changes in pixel gray levels and in locations and orientations of boundary elements. Deterministic, iterative-improvement methods generate a sequence of images that monotonically increase the posterior distribution (our "objective function"). In contrast, stochastic relaxation permits changes that *decrease* the posterior distribution as well. These are made on a *random* basis, the effect of which is to avoid convergence to *local maxima*. This should not be confused with "probabilistic relaxation" ("relaxation labeling"), which is deterministic; see Section X.

The stochastic relaxation algorithm can be informally described as follows.

1) A local change is made in the image based upon the current values of pixels and boundary elements in the immediate "neighborhood." This change is *random*, and is generated by sampling from a local conditional probability distribution.

2) The local conditional distributions are dependent on a global control parameter T called "temperature." At *low* temperatures the local conditional distributions concentrate on states that *increase* the objective function, whereas at high temperatures the distribution is essentially uniform. The limiting cases, $T = 0$ and $T = \infty$, correspond respectively to greedy algorithms (such as gradient ascent) and undirected (i.e., "purely random") changes. (High temperatures induce a loose coupling between neighboring pixels and a chaotic appearance to the image. At low temperatures the coupling is tighter and the images appear more regular.)

3) Our image restorations avoid local maxima by beginning at high temperatures where many of the stochastic changes will actually decrease the objective function. As the relaxation proceeds, temperature is gradually lowered and the process behaves increasingly like iterative improvement. (This gradual reduction of temperature simulates "annealing," a procedure by which certain chemical systems can be driven to their low energy, highly regular, states.)

Our "annealing theorem" prescribes a schedule for lowering temperature which guarantees convergence to the global maxima of the posterior distribution. In practice, this schedule may be too slow for application, and we use it only as a guide in choosing the functional form of the temperature-time dependence. Readers familiar with Monte Carlo methods in statistical physics will recognize our stochastic relaxation algorithm as a "heat bath" version of the *Metropolis algorithm* [42]. The idea of introducing temperature and simulating annealing is due to Černý [8] and Kirkpatrick et al. [40], both of whom used it for combinatorial optimization, including the traveling salesman problem. Kirkpatrick also applied it to computer design.

Since our approach is Bayesian it is model-based, with the "model" captured by the prior distribution. Our models are "hierarchical," by which we mean layered processes reflecting the type and degree of *a priori* knowledge about the class of images under study. In this paper, we regard the original image as a pair X = (F, L) where F is the matrix of observable pixel intensities and L denotes a (dual) matrix of unobservable edge elements. Thus the usual gray levels are considered a marginal process. We refer to F as the *intensity process* and L as the *line process*. In future work we shall expand this model by adjoining other, mainly geometric, attribute processes.

The degradation model allows for noise, blurring, and some nonlinearities, and hence is characteristic of most photochemical and photoelectric systems. More specifically, the degraded image G is of the form $\phi(H(F)) \odot N$, where H is the blurring matrix, ϕ is a possibly nonlinear (memoryless) transformation, N is an independent noise field, and $\odot$ denotes any suitably invertible operation, such as addition or multiplication. Surprisingly, these nonlinearities do not affect the computational burden.

To pin things down, let us briefly discuss the Markovian nature of the intensity process; similar remarks apply to the line process, the pair (F, L), and the distribution of (F, L) conditional on the "data" G. Of course, all of this will be discussed in detail in the main body of the paper.

Let $Z_m = \{(i, j) : 1 \leq i, j \leq m\}$ denote the $m \times m$ integer lattice; then $F = \{F_{i,j}\}$, $(i, j) \in Z_m$, denotes the gray levels of the original, digitized image. Lowercase letters will denote the values assumed by these (random) variables; thus, for example, $\{F = f\}$ stands for $\{F_{i,j} = f_{i,j}, (i, j) \in Z_m\}$. We regard F as a sample realization of a random field, usually isotropic and homogeneous, and with significant correlations well beyond nearest neighbors. Specifically, we model F as an MRF, or, what is the same (see Section IV), we assume that the probability law of F is a Gibbs *distribution*. Given a *neighborhood system* $\mathcal{F} = \{\mathcal{F}_{i,j}, (i, j) \in Z_m\}$, where $\mathcal{F}_{i,j} \subseteq Z_m$ denotes the neighbors of (i, j), an MRF over $(Z_m, \mathcal{F})$ is a stochastic process indexed by Z_m for which, for every (i, j) and every f,

$$P(F_{i,j} = f_{i,j} | F_{k,l} = f_{k,l}, (k, l) \neq (i, j))$$
$$= P(F_{i,j} = f_{i,j} | F_{k,l} = f_{k,l}, (k, l) \in \mathcal{F}_{i,j}). \quad (1.1)$$

The MRF–Gibbs equivalence provides an explicit formula for the *joint* probability distribution $P(F = f)$ in terms of an *energy function*, the choice of which, together with $\mathcal{F}$, supplies a powerful mechanism for modeling spatial continuity and other scene features.

The relaxation algorithm is designed to maximize the conditional probability distribution of (F, L) given the data G = g, i.e., find the mode of the *posterior distribution* $P(X = x | G = g)$. This form of Bayesian estimation is known as *maximum a posteriori* or MAP estimation, or sometimes as *penalized maximum likelihood* because one seeks to maximize log $P(G = g | X = x) + \log P(X = x)$ as a function of x; the second term is the "penalty term." MAP estimation has been successfully employed in special settings (see, e.g., Hunt [31] and Hansen and Elliott [25]) and we share the opinion of many that the MAP formulation (and a Bayesian approach in general; see also [24], [43], [45]) is well-suited to restoration, particularly for handling general forms of spatial degradation. Moreover, the distribution of G itself need not be known, which is fortunate due to its usual complexity. On the other hand, MAP estimation clearly presents a formidable computational problem. The number of possible intensity images is L^{m^2}, where L denotes the number of allowable gray levels, which rules out any direct search, even for small ($m = 64$), binary ($L = 2$) scenes. Consequently, one is usually obliged to make simplifying assumptions about the image and degradation models as well as compromises at the computational stage. Here, the computational problem is overcome by exploiting the pivotal observation that the posterior distribution is again Gibbsian with approximately the same neighborhood system as the original image, together with a sampling method which we call the *Gibbs Sampler*. Indeed, our principal theoretical contribution is a general, practical, and mathematically coherent approach for investigating MRF's by sampling (Theorem A), and by computing modes (Theorem B) and expectations (Theorem C).

The Gibbs Sampler generates realizations from a given MRF by a "relaxation" technique akin to site-replacement algorithms in statistical physics, such as "spin-flip" and "exchange" systems. The prototype is due to Metropolis et al. [42]; see also [7], [18], and Section X. Cross and Jain [12] use one of these algorithms invented for studying binary alloys. ("Relaxation labeling" in the sense of [13], [30], [46], [47] is different; see Section X.) The Markov property (1.1) permits parallel updating of the line and pixel sites, each of which is "refreshed" according to a simple recipe determined by the governing distribution. Thus, both parts of the MRF–Gibbs equivalence are exploited, for computing and modeling, respectively. Moreover, minimum mean-square error (MMSE) estimation is also feasible by using the (temporal) ergodicity of the relaxation chain to compute *means* w.r.t. the posterior distribution. However, we shall not pursue this approach.

We have used a comparatively slow, raster scan-serial version of the Gibbs Sampler to generate images and restorations (see Section XIII). But the algorithm is parallel; it could be executed in essentially one-half the time with two processors running simultaneously, or in one-third the time with three, and so on. The full parallel potential is realized by assigning one (simple) processor to each site of the intensity process and to each site of the line process. Whatever the number of processors, parallel implementation is made feasible by a small communications requirement among processors. The communications burden is related to the neighborhood size of the graph associated with the image model, and herein lies much of the power of the hierarchical structure: although the field model X = (F, L) has a local graph structure, the *marginal* distribution on the observable intensity process F has a *completely connected graph*. The introduction of a hierarchy dramatically expands the richness of the model of the observed process while only moderately adding to the computational burden. We shall return to these points in Sections IV and XI.

The MAP algorithm depends on an *annealing schedule*, which refers to the (sufficiently) slow decrease of a ("control") parameter T that corresponds to *temperature* in a physical system. As T decreases, samples from the posterior distribution are forced towards the minimal energy configurations; these correspond to the mode(s) of the distribution. Theorem B makes this precise, and is, to our knowledge, the first theoretical result of this nature. Roughly speaking, it says that if the temperature $T(k)$ employed in executing the kth site replacement (i.e., the kth image in the iteration scheme) satisfies the bound

$$T(k) \geq \frac{c}{\log(1+k)}$$

for every k, where c is a constant independent of k, then with probability converging to one (as $k \to \infty$), the configurations generated by the algorithm will be those of minimal energy. Put another way, the algorithm generates a Markov chain which converges *in distribution* to the uniform measure over the minimal energy configurations. (It should be emphasized that *pointwise* convergence, i.e., convergence *with probability one*, is in general not possible.) These issues are discussed in Section XII, and the algorithm is demonstrated in Section XIII on a variety of degraded images. We also discuss the nature of the constant c in regard to practical convergence rates. Basically, we believe that the logarithmic rate is best possible. However, the best (i.e., smallest) value of c that we have obtained to date (see the Appendix) is far too large for computational value and our restorations are actually performed with small values of c. As yet, we do not know how to bring the theory in line with experimental results in this regard.

The role of the Gibbs (or Boltzmann) distribution, and other notions from statistical physics, in the construction of "expert systems" is expanding. To begin with, we refer the reader to [21] for the original formulation of our computational method and of a general approach to expert systems based on maximum entropy extensions. As previously mentioned, Černý [8] and Kirkpatrick *et al.* [40] introduced annealing into combinatorial optimization. Other examples include the work of Cheeseman [9] on maximum entropy and diagnosis and of Hinton and Sejnowski [29] on neural modeling of inference and learning.

This paper is organized as follows. The degradation model is described in the next section, and the undegraded image models are presented in Section IV after preliminary material on graphs and neighborhood systems in Section III. In particular, Section IV contains the definitions of MRF's, Gibbs distributions, and the equivalence theorem. Due to the plethora of Markovian models in the literature, we pause in Section V to compare ours to others, and in Section VI to explain some connections with maximum entropy methods. In Section VII we raise the issues of parameter estimation and model selection, and indicate why we are avoiding the former for the time being. The posterior distribution is computed in Section VIII and the corresponding optimization problem is addressed in Section IX. The concept of stochastic relaxation is reviewed in Section X, including its origins in physics. Sections XI and XII are devoted to the Gibbs Sampler, dealing, respectively, with its mechanical and mathematical workings. Our experimental results appear in Section XIII, followed by concluding remarks.

II. Degraded Image Model

We follow the standard modeling of the (intensity) image formation and recording processes, and refer the reader to [31] or [47] for better accounts of the physical mechanisms.

Let H denote the "blurring matrix" corresponding to a shift-invariant point-spread function. The formation of F gives rise to a blurred image $H(\text{F})$ which is recorded by a sensor. The latter often involves a nonlinear transformation of $H(\text{F})$, denoted here by ϕ, in addition to random sensor noise $\text{N} = \{\eta_{i,j}\}$, which we assume to consist of independent, and for definiteness, Gaussian variables with mean μ and standard deviation σ.

Our methods apply to essentially arbitrary noise processes $\text{N} = \{\eta_{i,j}\}$, discrete or continuous. However, computational feasibility requires that the description of N as an MRF (this can always be done; see Section IV) has an associated graph structure that is approximately "local"; the same requirement is applied to the image process $\text{X} = (\text{F}, \text{L})$. For clarity, we forgo full generality and focus on the traditional Gaussian white noise case. Extension to a general noise process is mostly a matter of notation.

The degraded image is then a function of $\phi(H(\text{F}))$ and N, say $\psi(\phi(H(\text{F})), \text{N})$, for example, addition or multiplication. (To compute the posterior distribution, we only need to assume that $b \to \psi(a, b)$ is invertible for each a.) For notational ease, we will write

$$\text{G} = \phi(H(\text{F})) \odot \text{N}. \tag{2.1}$$

At the pixel level, for each $(i, j) \in Z_m$,

$$G_{i,j} = \phi\left(\sum_{(k,l)} H(i-k, j-l) F_{k,l}\right) \odot \eta_{i,j}. \tag{2.2}$$

The mathematical results require an additional assumption, namely, that F and N be independent as stochastic processes (and likewise for L and N) and we assume this henceforth. This is customary, although we recognize the limitation in certain contexts, e.g., for nuclear scan pictures.

For computational purposes, the degree of locality of F should be approximately preserved by (2.1), so that the neighborhood systems for the prior and posterior distributions on (F, L) are comparable. This is achieved when H is a simple convolution over a small window. For instance, take

$$H(k, l) = \begin{cases} \frac{1}{2}, & k = 0, l = 0 \\ \frac{1}{16}, & |k|, |l| \leq 1, (k, l) \neq (0, 0) \end{cases} \tag{2.3}$$

so that the intensity at (i, j) is weighted equally with the average of the eight nearest neighbors. The function ϕ is unrestricted, bearing in mind that the true noise level depends on ϕ, $\odot$, and σ. Typically, ϕ is logarithmic (film) or algebraic (TV).

An important special case, which occurs in two-dimensional (2-D) signal theory, is the segmentation of noisy images into coherent regions. The usual model is

$$G = F + N \qquad (2.4)$$

where N is white noise and the number of intensity levels is small. This is the model entertained by Hansen and Elliott [25] for simple, binary MRF's F, and by many other workers with varying assumptions about F; see [14], [16], [17]. In this case, namely (2.4), we can extract simple images under extremely low signal-to-noise ratios.

The full degraded image is (G, L); that is, the "line process" is not transformed.

III. Graphs and Neighborhoods

Here and in Section IV we present the general theory of MRF's on graphs, focusing on the aspects and examples which figure in the experimental restorations. The level of abstraction is warranted by the variety of MRF's, graphs, and probability distributions simultaneously under discussion.

Let $S = \{s_1, s_2, \cdots, s_N\}$ be a set of *sites* and let $\mathcal{G} = \{\mathcal{G}_s, s \in S\}$ be a *neighborhood system* for S, meaning any collection of subsets of S for which 1) $s \notin \mathcal{G}_s$ and 2) $s \in \mathcal{G}_r \Leftrightarrow r \in \mathcal{G}_s$. Obviously, $\mathcal{G}_s$ is the set of *neighbors* of s and the pair $\{S, \mathcal{G}\}$ is a graph in the usual way. A subset $C \subseteq S$ is a *clique* if every pair of distinct sites in C are neighbors; $\mathcal{C}$ denotes the set of cliques.

The special cases below are especially relevant.

Case 1: $S = Z_m$. This is the set of pixel sites for the intensity process F; $\{s_1, s_2, \cdots, s_N\}$, $N = m^2$, is any ordering of the lattice points. We are interested in homogeneous neighborhood systems of the form

$$\mathcal{G} = \mathcal{F}_c = \{\mathcal{F}_{i,j}, (i,j) \in Z_m\}; \mathcal{F}_{i,j}$$
$$= \{(k,l) \in Z_m : 0 < (k-i)^2 + (l-j)^2 \leq c\}.$$

Notice that sites at or near the boundary have fewer neighbors than interior ones; this is the so-called "free boundary" and is more natural for picture processing than torodial lattices and other periodic boundaries. Fig. 1(a), (b), (c) shows the (interior) neighborhood configurations for $c = 1, 2, 8$; $c = 1$ is the first-order or nearest-neighbor system common in physics, in which $\mathcal{F}_{i,j} = \{(i, j - 1), (i, j + 1), (i - 1, j), (i + 1, j)\}$, with adjustments at the boundaries. In each case, (i, j) is at the center, and the symbol $\circ$ stands for a neighboring pixel. The cliques for $c = 1$ are all subsets of Z_m of the form $\{(i, j)\}$, $\{(i, j), (i, j + 1)\}$ or $\{(i, j), (i + 1, j)\}$, shown in Fig. 1(d). For $c = 2$, we have the cliques in Fig. 1(d) as well as those in Fig. 1(e). Obviously, the number of clique types grows rapidly with c. However, only small cliques appear in the model for F actually employed in this paper; indeed, the degree of progress with only *pair* interactions is somewhat surprising. Nonetheless, more complex images will likely necessitate more complex energies. Our experiments (see Section XIII) suggest that much of this additional complexity can be accommodated while maintaining modest neighborhood sizes by further developing the hierarchy.

Case 2: $S = D_m$, the "dual" $m \times m$ lattice. Think of these sites as placed midway between each vertical or horizontal pair of pixels, and as representing the possible locations of "edge

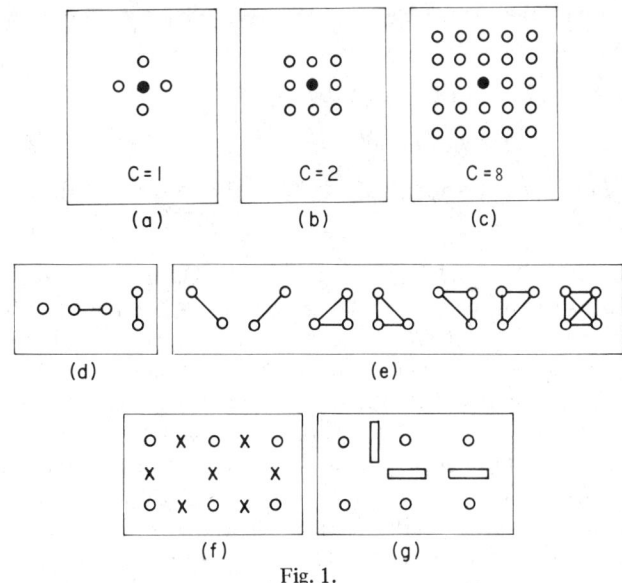

Fig. 1.

elements." Shown in Fig. 1(f) are six pixel sites together with seven line sites denoted by an $\times$. The six surrounding $\times$'s are the neighbors of the middle $\times$ for the neighborhood system we denote by $\mathcal{L} = \{\mathcal{L}_d, d \in D_m\}$. Fig. 1(g) is a segment of a realization of a binary line process for which, at each line site, there may or may not be an edge element. We also consider line processes with more than two levels, corresponding to edge elements with varying orientations.

Case 3: $S = Z_m \cup D_m$. This is the setup for the field (F, L). Z_m has neighborhood system $\mathcal{F}_1$ (nearest-neighbor lattice) and D_m has the above-described system. The pixel neighbors of sites in D_m are the two pixels on each side, and hence each (interior) pixel has four line site neighbors.

IV. Markov Random Fields and Gibbs Distributions

We now describe a class of stochastic processes that includes both the prior and posterior distribution on the original image. In general, this class of processes (namely, MRF's) is neither homogeneous nor isotropic, assuming the index set S has enough geometric structure to even *define* a suitable family of translations and rotations. However, the *particular* models we choose for prior distributions on the original image are in fact both homogeneous and isotropic in an appropriate sense. (This is not the case for the *posterior* distribution.) We refer the reader to Section XIII for a precise description of the prior models employed in our experiments, and in particular for specific examples of the role of the line elements.

As in Section III, $\{S, G\}$ denotes an arbitrary graph. Let $X = \{X_s, s \in S\}$ denote *any* family of random variables indexed by S. For simplicity, we can assume a common state space, say $\Lambda \triangleq \{0, 1, 2, \cdots, L - 1\}$, so that $X_s \in \Lambda$ for all s; the extension to site-dependent state spaces, appropriate when S consists of both line and pixel sites, is entirely straightforward (although not merely a notational matter due to the "positivity condition" below). Let Ω be the set of all possible *configurations*:

$$\Omega = \{\omega = (x_{s_1}, \cdots, x_{s_N}) : x_{s_i} \in \Lambda, 1 \leq i \leq N\}.$$

As usual, the event $\{X_{s_1} = x_{s_1}, \cdots, X_{s_N} = x_{s_N}\}$ is abbreviated $\{X = \omega\}$.

X is an MRF with respect to $\mathcal{G}$ if

$$P(X = \omega) > 0 \quad \text{for all} \quad \omega \in \Omega; \tag{4.1}$$

$$P(X_s = x_s | X_r = x_r, r \neq s) = P(X_s = x_s | X_r = x_r, r \in \mathcal{G}_s) \tag{4.2}$$

for every $s \in S$ and $(x_{s_1}, \cdots, x_{s_N}) \in \Omega$. Technically, what is meant here is that the pair $\{X, P\}$ satisfies (4.1) and (4.2) relative to some probability measure on Ω. The collection of functions on the left-hand side of (4.2) is called the *local characteristics* of the MRF and it turns out that the (joint) probability distribution $P(X = \omega)$ of *any* process satisfying (4.1) is *uniquely* determined by these conditional probabilities; see, e.g., [6, p. 195].

The concept of an MRF is essentially due to Dobrushin [15] and is one way of extending Markovian dependence from 1-D to a general setting; there are, of course, many others, some of which will be reviewed in Section V.

Notice that *any* X satisfying (4.1) is an MRF if the neighborhoods are large enough to encompass the dependencies. The utility of the concept, at least in regard to image modeling, is that priors are available with neighborhoods that are small enough to ensure feasible computational loads and yet still rich enough to model and restore interesting classes of images (and textures: [12]).

Ordinary 1-D Markov chains are MRF's relative to the nearest-neighbor system on $S = \{1, 2, \cdots, N\}$ (i.e., $\mathcal{G}_1 = \{2\}$, $\mathcal{G}_i = \{i - 1, i + 1\}$ $2 \leq i \leq N - 1$, $\mathcal{G}_N = \{N - 1\}$) if we assume all positive transitions and the chain is started in equilibrium. In other words, the "one-sided" Markov property

$$P(X_k = x_k | X_j = x_j, j \leq k - 1) = P(X_k = x_k | X_{k-1} = x_{k-1})$$

and the "two-sided" Markov property

$$P(X_k = x_k | X_j = x_j, j \neq k) = P(X_k = x_k | X_j = x_j, j \in \mathcal{G}_k)$$

are equivalent. Similarly for an rth order Markov process on the line with respect to the r nearest neighbors on one side and on both sides. (This appears to be doubted in [1] but follows, eventually, from straightforward calculations or immediately from the Gibbs connection.)

Gibbs models were introduced into image modeling by Hassner and Sklansky [28], although the treatment there is mostly expository and limited to the binary case.

A *Gibbs distribution* relative to $\{S, \mathcal{G}\}$ is a probability measure π on Ω with the following representation:

$$\pi(\omega) = \frac{1}{Z} e^{-U(\omega)/T} \tag{4.3}$$

where Z and T are constants and U, called the *energy function*, is of the form

$$U(\omega) = \sum_{C \in \mathcal{C}} V_C(\omega). \tag{4.4}$$

Recall that $\mathcal{C}$ denotes the set of cliques for $\mathcal{G}$. Each V_C is a function on Ω with the property that $V_C(\omega)$ depends only on those coordinates x_s of ω for which $s \in C$. Such a family $\{V_C, C \in \mathcal{C}\}$ is called a *potential*. Z is the normalizing constant:

$$Z \doteq \sum_\omega e^{-U(\omega)/T} \tag{4.5}$$

and is called the *partition function*. Finally, T stands for "temperature"; for our purposes, T controls the degree of "peaking" in the "density" π. Choosing T "small" exaggerates the mode(s), making them easier to find by sampling; this is the principle of annealing, and will be applied to the posterior distribution $\pi(f, l) = P(F = f, L = l | G = g)$ in order to find the MAP estimate. Of course, we will show that $\pi(f, l)$ is Gibbsian and identify the energy and neighborhood system in terms of those for the priors. The *choice* of the prior distributions, i.e., of the particular functions V_C for the image model $\pi(\omega) = P(X = \omega)$, will be discussed later on; see Section VII for some general remarks and Section XIII for the particular models employed in our experiments.

The terminology obviously comes from statistical physics, wherein such measures are "equilibrium states" for physical systems, such as ferromagnets, ideal gases, and binary alloys. The V_C functions represent contributions to the total energy from external fields (singleton cliques), pair interactions (doubletons), and so forth. Most of the interest there, and in the mathematical literature, centers on the case in which S is an *infinite*, 2-D or 3-D lattice; singularities in Z may then occur at certain ("critical") temperatures and are associated with "phase transitions."

Typically, several free parameters are involved in the specification of U, and Z is then a function of those parameters—notoriously intractable. For more information see [3], [5], [6], [23], [32], and [39].

The best-known of these lattice systems is the Ising model, invented in 1925 by E. Ising [33] to help explain ferromagnetism. Here, $S = Z_m$ and $\mathcal{G} = \mathcal{F}_1$, the nearest-neighbor system. The most general form of U is then

$$U(\omega) = \sum V_{\{i,j\}}(x_{i,j}) + \sum V_{\{(i,j), (i+1,j)\}}(x_{i,j}, x_{i+1,j})$$
$$+ \sum V_{\{(i,j), (i,j+1)\}}(x_{i,j}, x_{i,j+1}) \tag{4.6}$$

where the sums extend over all $(i, j) \in Z_m$ for which the indicated cliques make sense. The Ising model is the special case of (4.6) in which X is binary ($L = 2$), homogeneous (= strictly stationary), and isotropic (= rotationally invarient):

$$U(\omega) = \alpha \sum x_{i,j} + \beta \left(\sum x_{i,j} x_{i+1,j} + \sum x_{i,j} x_{i,j+1} \right) \tag{4.7}$$

for some parameters α and β, which measure, respectively, the external field and bonding strengths.

Returning to the general formulation, recall that the local characteristics

$$\pi(x_s | x_r, r \neq s) = \frac{\pi(\omega)}{\sum_{x_s \in \Lambda} \pi(\omega)} \quad s \in S, \omega \in \Omega$$

uniquely determine π for any probability measure π on Ω, $\pi(\omega) > 0$ for all ω. The difficulty with the MRF formulation *by itself* is that

i) the *joint* distribution of the X_s is not apparent;

ii) it is extremely difficult to spot local characteristics, i.e., to determine when a given set of functions $\psi(x_s | x_r, r \neq s)$, $s \in S$, $(x_{s_1}, \cdots, x_{s_N}) \in \Omega$, are conditional probabilities for some (necessarily unique) distribution on Ω.

For example, Chellappa and Kashyap [10] allude to i) as a disadvantage of the "conditional Markov" models. See also the discussion in [6]. In fact, these apparent limitations to the MRF formulation have been noted by a number of authors, many of whom were obviously not aware of the following theorem.

Theorem: Let $\mathcal{G}$ *be a neighborhood system. Then* X *is an MRF with respect to* $\mathcal{G}$ *if and only if* $\pi(\omega) = P(X = \omega)$ *is a Gibbs distribution with respect to* $\mathcal{G}$.

Among other benefits, this equivalence provides us with a simple, practical way of specifying MRF's, namely by specifying potentials, which is easy, instead of local characteristics, which is nearly impossible. In fact, with some experience, one can choose U's in accordance with the desired *local* behavior, at least at the intensity level. In short, the modeling and consistency problems of i) and ii) are eliminated.

Proofs may be found in many places now; see, e.g., [39] and the references therein, or the approach via the Hammersley-Clifford expansion in [6]. An influential discussion of this correspondence appears in Spitzer's work, e.g., [48]. Explicit formulas exist for obtaining U from the local characteristics. Conversely, the local characteristics of π are obtained in a straightforward way from the potentials: use the defining ratios and make the allowable cancellations. Fix $s \in S$, $\omega = (x_{s_1}, \cdots, x_{s_N}) \in \Omega$, and let ω^x denote the configuration which is x at site s and agrees with ω everywhere else. Then if $\pi(\omega) = P(X = \omega)$ is Gibbsian,

$$P(X_s = x_s | X_r = x_r, r \neq s) = Z_s^{-1} \exp - \frac{1}{T} \sum_{C: s \in C} V_C(\omega) \quad (4.8)$$

$$Z_s \doteq \sum_{x \in \Lambda} \exp - \frac{1}{T} \sum_{C: s \in C} V_C(\omega^x). \quad (4.9)$$

Notice that the right-hand side of (4.8) only depends on x_s and on x_r, $r \in \mathcal{G}_s$, since any site in a clique containing s must be a neighbor of s. These formulas will be used repeatedly to program the Gibbs Sampler for local site replacements.

For the Ising model, the conditional probability that $X_{i,j} = x_{i,j}$, given the states at $S \setminus \{i, j\}$, or equivalently, just the four nearest neighbors, reduces to

$$\frac{e^{-x_{ij}(\alpha + \beta v_{i,j})}}{1 + e^{-(\alpha + \beta v_{i,j})}}$$

where $v_{i,j} = x_{i,j-1} + x_{i-1,j} + x_{i,j+1} + x_{i+1,j}$. This is also known as the autologistic model and has been used for texture modeling in [12]. More generally, if the local characteristics are given by an exponential family and if $V_C(\omega) \equiv 0$ for $|C| > 2$, then the pair potentials always "factor" into a product of two like terms; see [6].

We conclude with some further discussion of a remark made in Section I: that the hierarchical structure introduced with the line process L expands the graph structure of the *marginal* distribution of the intensity process F. Consider first an arbitrary MRF X with respect to a graph $\{S, \mathcal{G}\}$. Fix $r \in S$ and let $\hat{X} = \{X_s, s \in S, s \neq r\}$. The marginal distribution $\hat{P}$ of $\hat{X}$ is derived from the distribution P of X by summing over the range of X_r. Use the Gibbs representation for P and perform this summation: the resulting expression for $\hat{P}$ can be put in the Gibbs form, and from this the neighborhood system on $\hat{S} \doteq S \setminus \{r\}$ can be inferred. The conclusion of this exercise is that $s_1, s_2 \in \hat{S}$ are, in general, neighbors if either i) they were neighbors in S under $\mathcal{G}$ or ii) each is a neighbor of $r \in S$ under $\mathcal{G}$. Now let $X = (F, L)$, with neighborhood system defined at the end of Section III. Successive summations of the distribution of X over the ranges of the elements of L yields the marginal distribution of the observable intensity process F. Each summation leaves a graph structure associated with the marginal distribution of the remaining variables, and this can be related to the original neighborhood system by following the preceding discussion of the general case. It is easily seen that when all of the summations are performed, the remaining graph is completely connected; under the marginal distribution of F, all sites are neighbors. This calculation suggests that significant long-range interactions can be introduced through the development of hierarchical structures without sacrificing the computational advantages of local neighborhood systems.

V. Related Markov Image Models

The use of neighborhoods is, of course, pervasive in the literature: they offer a geometric framework for the clustering of pixel intensities and for many types of statistical models. In particular, the Markov property is a natural way to formalize these notions. The result is a somewhat bewildering array of Markov-type image models and it seems worthwhile to puase to relate these to MRF's. The process under consideration is $F = \{F_{i,j}, (i, j) \in Z_m\}$, the gray levels, or really any pixel attribute.

An early work in this direction is Abend, Harley and Kanal [1] about pattern classification. Among many novel ideas, there is the notion of a *Markov mesh* (MM) process, in which the Markovian dependence is *causal:* generally, one assumes that, for all (i, j) and f,

$$P(F_{i,j} = f_{i,j} | F_{k,l} = f_{k,l}, (k, l) \in A_{i,j})$$
$$= P(F_{i,j} = f_{i,j} | F_{k,l} = f_{k,l}, (k, l) \in B_{i,j}) \quad (5.1)$$

where $B_{i,j} \subseteq A_{i,j} \subseteq \{(k, l): k < i \text{ or } l < j\}$. A common example is $B_{i,j} = \{(i - 1, j), (i - 1, j - 1), (i, j - 1)\}$. Besag [6], Kanal [37], and Pickard [44] also discuss such "unilateral" processes, which are usually a subclass of MRF's, although the resulting (bilateral) neighborhoods can be irregular. Anyway, for MM models the emphasis is on the causal, iterative aspects, including a recursive representation for the joint probabilities. Incidentally, a Gibbs type description of rth order Markov chains is given in [1]; of course, the full Gibbs-MRF equivalence is not perceived and was not for about five years. Derin *et al.* [14] model F as an MM process and use recursive Bayes smoothing to recover F from a noisy version $F + N$; the algorithms exploit the causality to maximize the univariate posterior distribution at each pixel based on the data over a strip containing it, and are very effective at low S/N ratios for some simple images.

Motivated by a paper of Lévy [41], Woods [51] defined "P-Markov" processes for the resolution of wavenumber spectra. The definition involves two spatial regions separated by a "boundary" of width P, and correspond to the past, future, and present in 1-D. Woods also considers a family of "wide-sense" Markov fields of the form

$$F_{i,j} = \sum_{(k,l) \in W_p} \theta_{k,l} F_{i-k, j-l} + U_{i,j} \quad (5.2)$$

where $W_p = \{(k, l): 0 < k^2 + l^2 \leq P\}$, $\theta_{k,l}$ are the MMSE coefficients for projecting $F_{i,j}$ on $\{F_{k,l}, (k, l) \in (i, j) + W_p\}$, and $\{U_{i,j}\}$ is the error, generally nonwhite. The main theoretical result is that if $\{U_{i,j}\}$ is homogeneous, Gaussian, and satisfies a few other assumptions, then F is Gaussian, P-Markov and vice-versa. In general, there are consistency problems and the P-Markov property is hard to verify. In the nearest-neighbor case, one gets a Gaussian MRF.

Other "wide-sense" Markov processes appear in Jain and Angel [35] and Stuller and Kurz [49]. The assumptions in [35] are a nearest-neighbor system, white noise, and no blur; restoration is achieved by recursively filtering the rows $\{F_{i,j}\}_{j=1}^{m}$, which form a vector-valued, second-order Markov chain, to find the optimal interpolator of each row. In [49], causality is introduced and earlier work is generalized by considering an arbitrary "scanning pattern."

The "spatial interaction models" in Chellappa and Kashyap [10], [38] satisfy (5.2) for general coefficients and W's. The model is causal if W lies in the third quadrant. The authors consider "simultaneous autoregressive" (SAR) models, wherein the noise is white, and "conditional Markov" (CM) models, wherein the "bilateral" Markov property holds (i.e., (1.1) with $\mathcal{F}_{i,j} = (i, j) + W$) in addition to (5.2), and the noise is nonwhite. Thus, the CM models are MRF's, although in [10], [38] the boundary of Z_m is periodic, and hence boundary conditions must be adjoined to (5.2). Given any (homogeneous) SAR process there exists a unique CM process with the same spectral density, although different neighborhood structure. The converse holds in the Gaussian case but is generally false (see the discussion in Besag [6]). MMSE restoration of blurred images with additive Gaussian noise is discussed in [10]; the original image is SAR or CM, usually Gaussian.

Finally, Hansen and Elliott [25] and Elliott et al. [17] design MAP algorithms for the segmentation of remotely sensed data with high levels of additive noise. The image model is a nearest-neighbor, binary MRF. However, the autologistic form of the joint distribution is not recognized due to the lack of the Gibbs formulation. The conditional probabilities are approximated by the product of four 1-D transitions, and segmentation is performed by dynamic programming, first for each row and then for the entire images. More recent work in Elliott et al. [16] is along the same lines, namely MAP estimation, via dynamic programming, of very noisy but simple images; the major differences are the use of the Gibbs formulation and improvements in the algorithms. Similar work, applied to boundary finding, can be found in Cooper and Sung [11], who use a Markov boundary model and a deterministic relaxation scheme.

VI. MAXIMUM ENTROPY RESTORATION

There are several contact points. The Gibbs distribution can be derived (directly from physical principles in statistical mechanics) by maximizing entropy: basically, it has maximal entropy among all probability measures (equilibrium states) on Ω with the same *average* energy. Thus it is no accident that, like maximum entropy (ME) methods, ours are well-suited to nonlinear problems; see [50]. Moreover, based on the success of ME restoration (along the lines suggested by Jaynes [36]) for recovering randomly pulsed objects (cf. Frieden [19]), we intend in the future to analyze such data (e.g., starfield photographs) by our methods.

We should also like to mention the interesting observation of Trussell [50] that conventional ME restoration is a special case of MAP estimation in which the prior distribution on F is

$$P(\mathrm{F} = f) = \exp\left(-\beta \sum f_{i,j} \log f_{i,j}\right) \Big/ (\text{normalizing constant}).$$

By "conventional ME," we refer to maximizing the entropy $\sum f_{i,j} \log f_{i,j}$ subject to $\sum \eta_{i,j}^2 = $ constant ($\eta_{i,j}$ is here again the noise process); see [2]. Other ME methods (e.g., [19]) do not appear to be MAP-related.

VII. MODEL SELECTION AND PARAMETER ESTIMATION

The quality of the restoration will clearly depend on choices made at the modeling stage, in our case about specific energy types, attribute processes, and parameters. Cross and Jain [12] use maximum likelihood estimation in the context of Besag's [6] "coding scheme," as well as standard goodness-of-fit tests, for matching realizations of autobinomial MRF's to real textures. Kashyap and Chellappa [38] introduce some new methods for parameter estimation and the choice of neighborhoods for the SAR and CM models, mostly in the Gaussian case. These are but two examples.

For uncorrupted, simple MRF's, the coding methods do finesse the problem of the partition function. However, for more complex models and for corrupted data, we feel that the coding methods are ultimately inadequate due to the complexity of the distribution of G. This view seems to be shared by other authors, although in different contexts. Of course, for MRF's, the obstacles facing conventional statistical inference due to Z have often been noted. Even for the Ising model, analytical results are rare; a famous exception is Onsager's work on the correlational structure.

At any rate, we have developed a new method [20] for estimating clique parameters from the "noisy" data, and this will be implemented in a forthcoming paper. For now, we are obliged to choose the parameters on an ad hoc basis (which is common), but hasten to add that the quality of restoration does not seem to have been adversely affected, probably due to the relative simplicity of the MRF's we actually use for the line and intensity processes; see Section XIII.

One should also address the *general* choice of π and $\mathcal{G}$. This is really quite different than parameter estimation and somewhat related to "image understanding": how does one incorporate "real-world knowledge" into the modeling process? In image interpretation systems, various semantical and hierarchical models have been proposed (see, e.g., [26]). We have begun our study of hierarchical Gibbs models in this paper. A *general theory* of interactive, self-adjusting models that is practical and mathematically coherent may lie far ahead.

VIII. Posterior Distribution

We now turn to the posterior distribution $P(F = f, L = l | G = g)$ of the original image given the "data" g. In this section we take $S = Z_m \cup D_m$, the collection of pixel and line sites, with some neighborhood system $\mathcal{G} = \{\mathcal{G}_s, s \in S\}$; an example of such a "mixed" graph was given in Section III. The configuration space is the set of all pairs $\omega = (f, l)$ where the components of f assume values among the allowable gray levels and those of l among the (coded) line states.

We assume that X is an MRF relative to $\{S, \mathcal{G}\}$ with corresponding energy function U and potentials $\{V_C\}$:

$$P(F = f, L = l) = e^{-U(f,l)/T}/Z$$

$$U(f, l) = \sum_C V_C(f, l).$$

For convenience, take $T = 1$.

Recall that $G = \phi(H(F)) \odot N$, where N is white Gaussian noise with mean μ and variance σ^2 and is independent of X.

We emphasize that what follows is easily extended to processes N that are more general MRF's, although we still require that N be independent of X. The operation $\odot$ is assumed invertible and we will write $N = \Phi(G, \phi(H(F))) = \{\Phi_s, s \in Z_m\}$ to indicate this inverse.

Let $\mathcal{H}_s$, $s \in Z_m$, denote the pixels which affect the blurred image $H(F)$ at s. For instance, for the H in (2.3), $\mathcal{H}_s$ is the 3×3 square centered at s. Observe that Φ_s, $s \in Z_m$, depends only on g_s and $\{f_t, t \in \mathcal{H}_s\}$. By the shift-invariance of H, $\mathcal{H}_{r+s} = s + \mathcal{H}_r$ where $\mathcal{H}_r \subseteq Z_m$, $s + r \in Z_m$, and $s + \mathcal{H}_r$ is understood to be intersected with Z_m, if necessary. In addition, we will assume that $\{\mathcal{H}_s\}$ is "symmetric" in that $r \in \mathcal{H}_0 \Rightarrow -r \in \mathcal{H}_0$. Then the collection $\{\mathcal{H}_s \setminus \{s\}, s \in Z_m\}$ is a neighborhood system over Z_m. Let $\mathcal{H}^2$ denote the second-order system, i.e.,

$$\mathcal{H}_s^2 = \bigcup_{r \in \mathcal{H}_s} \mathcal{H}_r, \quad s \in Z_m.$$

Then it is not hard to see that $\{\mathcal{H}_s^2 \setminus \{s\}, s \in Z_m\}$ is also a neighborhood system. Finally, set $\mathcal{G}^P = \{\mathcal{G}_s^P, s \in S\}$ where

$$\mathcal{G}_s^P = \begin{cases} \mathcal{G}_s, & s \in D_m \\ \mathcal{G}_s \cup \mathcal{H}_s^2 \setminus \{s\}, & s \in Z_m. \end{cases} \quad (8.1)$$

The "P" stands for "posterior"; some thought shows that $\mathcal{G}^P$ is a neighborhood system on S.

Let $\mu \in \mathbb{R}^M (M = N^2)$ have all components $= \mu$ and let $\|\cdot\|$ denote the usual norm in $\mathbb{R}^M$: $\|V\|^2 = \sum_1^M V_i^2$.

Theorem: For each g fixed, $P(X = \omega | G = g)$ is a Gibbs distribution over $\{S, \mathcal{G}^P\}$ with energy function

$$U^P(f, l) = U(f, l) + \|\mu - \Phi(g, \phi(H(f)))\|^2/2\sigma^2. \quad (8.2)$$

Proof: Using standard results about "regular conditional expectations," we can and do assume that

$$P(X = \omega | G = g) = \frac{P(G = g | X = \omega) P(X = \omega)}{P(G = g)} \quad (8.3)$$

for all $\omega = (f, l)$, for each g.

Since $P(G = g)$ is a constant and $P(X = \omega) = e^{-U(\omega)}/Z$, the key term is

$$P(G = g | X = \omega) = P(\phi(H(F)) \odot N = g | F = f, L = l)$$
$$= P(N = \Phi(g, \phi(H(f))) | F = f, L = l)$$
$$= P(N = \Phi(g, \phi(H(f))))$$

(since N is independent of F and L)

$$= (2\pi\sigma^2)^{-M/2} \exp -\left(\frac{1}{2\sigma^2}\right) \|\mu - \Phi\|^2.$$

We will write Φ for $\Phi(g, \phi(H(f)))$. Collecting constants we have, from (8.3),

$$P(X = \omega | G = g) = e^{-U^P(\omega)}/Z^P$$

for U^P as in (8.2); Z^P is the usual normalizing constant (which will depend on g). It remains to determine the neighborhood structure.

Intuitively, the line sites should have the *same* neighbors whereas the neighbors $\mathcal{G}_s$ of a pixel site $s \in Z_m$ should be augmented in accordance with the blurring mechanism.

Take $s \in D_m$. The local characteristics at s for the posterior distribution are, by (8.2),

$$P(L_s = l_s | L_r = l_r, r \neq s, r \in D_m, F = f, G = g)$$
$$= \frac{e^{-U^P(f,l)}}{\sum_{l_s} e^{-U^P(f,l)}} = \frac{e^{-U(f,l)}}{\sum_{l_s} e^{-U(f,l)}}$$

where the sum extends over all possible values of L_s. Hence $\mathcal{G}_s^P = \mathcal{G}_s$.

For $s \in Z_m$, the term in (8.2) involving Φ does not cancel out. Now $\Phi(g, \phi(H(f))) = \{\Phi_s, s \in Z_m\}$ and let us denote the dependencies in Φ_s by writing $\Phi_s = \Phi_s(g_s; f_t, t \in \mathcal{H}_s)$. Then

$$P(F_s = f_s | F_r = f_r, r \neq s, r \in Z_m, L = l, G = g)$$
$$= \frac{e^{-U^P(f,l)}}{\sum_{f_s} e^{-U^P(f,l)}}; U^P(f,l)$$
$$= U(f,l) + \sum_{r \in Z_m} (\Phi_r - \mu)^2/2\sigma^2. \quad (8.4)$$

Decompose U^P as follows:

$$U^P(f,l) = \sum_{C: s \in C} V_C(f,l)$$
$$+ (2\sigma^2)^{-1} \sum_{r: s \in \mathcal{H}_r} (\Phi_r(g_r; f_t, t \in \mathcal{H}_r) - \mu)^2$$
$$+ \sum_{C: s \notin C} V_C(f,l)$$
$$+ (2\sigma^2)^{-1} \sum_{r: s \notin \mathcal{H}_r} (\Phi_r(g_r; f_t, t \in \mathcal{H}_r) - \mu)^2.$$

Since the last two terms do not involve f_s (remember that V_C only depends on the sites in C), the ratio in (8.4) depends only on the first two terms above. The first term depends only on coordinates of (f, l) for sites in $\mathcal{G}_s (s \in C \Rightarrow C \subseteq \mathcal{G}_s)$ and the second term only on sites in

$$\bigcup_{r:s \in \mathcal{H}_r} \mathcal{H}_r = \bigcup_{r \in \mathcal{H}_s} \mathcal{H}_r \doteq \mathcal{H}_s^2.$$

Hence, $\mathcal{G}_s^P = \mathcal{G}_s \cup \mathcal{H}_s^2 \setminus \{s\}$, as asserted in the theorem. □

IX. THE COMPUTATIONAL PROBLEM

The posterior distribution $P(X = \omega|g)$ is a powerful tool for image analysis; in principle, we can construct the optimal (Bayesian) estimator for the original image, examine images sampled from $P(X = \omega|g)$, estimate parameters, design near-optimal statistical tests for the presence or absence of special objects, and so forth. But a conventional approach to any of these involves prohibitive computations. Specifically, our job here is to find the value(s) of ω which maximize the posterior distribution for a fixed g, i.e., *minimize*

$$U(f, l) + \|\mu - \Phi(g, \phi(H(f)))\|^2 / 2\sigma^2, (f, l) \in \Omega \quad (9.1)$$

where (see Section VIII) Φ is defined by $\phi(H(f)) \odot \Phi = g$. Even without L, the size of Ω is at least 2^{4000}, corresponding to a binary image on a small (64×64) lattice. Hence, the identification of even near-optimal solutions is extremely difficult for such a relatively complex function.

In Sections XI and XII we will describe our stochastic relaxation method for this kind of optimization. The same method works for sampling and for computing expectations (and hence forming likelihood ratios), as will be explained in Section XI. The algorithm is highly parallel, but our current implementation is serial: it uses a single processor. The restoration of more complex images than those in Section XIII, probably involving more levels in the hierarchy, may necessitate *some* parallel processing.

X. STOCHASTIC RELAXATION

There are many types of "relaxation," two of them being the type used in statistical physics and the type developed in image processing called "relaxation labeling" (RL), or sometimes "probabilistic relaxation." Basically, ours is of the former class, referred to here as SR, although there are some common features with RL.

The "Metropolis algorithm" (Metropolis *et al.* [42]) and others like it [7], [18] were invented to study the equilibrium properties, especially ensemble averages, time-evolution, and low-temperature behavior, of very large systems of essentially identical, interacting components, such as molecules in a gas or atoms in binary alloys.

Let Ω denote the possible configurations of the system; for example, $\omega \in \Omega$ might be the molecular positions or site configuration. If the system is in thermal equilibrium with its surroundings, then the probability (or "Boltzmann factor") of ω is given by

$$\pi(\omega) = e^{-\beta \mathcal{E}(\omega)} / \sum_\omega e^{-\beta \mathcal{E}(\omega)}, \quad \omega \in \Omega$$

where $\mathcal{E}(\omega)$ is the potential energy of ω and $\beta = 1/KT$ where K is Boltzmann's constant and T is absolute temperature. We have already seen an example in the Ising model (4.7). Usually, one needs to compute ensemble averages of the form

$$\langle Y \rangle = \int_\Omega Y(\omega) \, d\pi(\omega) = \frac{\sum_\omega Y(\omega) e^{-\beta \mathcal{E}(\omega)}}{\sum_\omega e^{-\beta \mathcal{E}(\omega)}}$$

where Y is some variable of interest. This cannot be done analytically. In the usual Monte Carlo method, one restricts the sums above to a *sample* of ω's drawn uniformly from Ω. This, however, breaks down in the situation above: the exponential factor puts most of the mass of π over a very small part of Ω, and hence one tends to choose samples of very low probability. The idea in [42] is to choose the samples from π instead of uniformly and then weight the samples evenly instead of by $d\pi$. In other words, one obtains $\omega_1, \omega_2, \cdots, \omega_R$ from π and $\langle Y \rangle$ is approximated by the usual ergodic averages:

$$\langle Y \rangle \approx \frac{1}{R} \sum_{r=1}^R Y(\omega_r). \quad (10.1)$$

Briefly, the sampling algorithm in [42] is as follows. Given the state of the system at "time" t, say $X(t)$, one randomly chooses another configuration η and computes the energy change $\Delta \mathcal{E} = \mathcal{E}(\eta) - \mathcal{E}(X(t))$ and the quantity

$$q = \frac{\pi(\eta)}{\pi(X(t))} = e^{-\beta \Delta \mathcal{E}}. \quad (10.2)$$

If $q > 1$, the move to η is allowed and $X(t+1) = \eta$, whereas if $q \leq 1$, the transition is made *with probability* q. Thus we choose $0 \leq \xi \leq 1$ uniformly and set $X(t+1) = \eta$ if $\xi \leq q$ and $X(t+1) = X(t)$ if $\xi > q$. (A "parallel processing variant" of this for simulating certain binary MRF's is given by Berger and Bonomi [4].)

In binary, "single-flip" studies, $\eta = X(t)$ except at one site, whereas in "spin-exchange" [18] systems, a pair of neighboring sites is selected. In either case, the "flip" or "exchange" is made with probability $q/(1 + q)$, where q is given in (10.2). In special cases, the single-flip system is equivalent to our Gibbs Sampler. The exchange algorithm in Cross and Jain [12] is motivated by work on the evolution of binary alloys. The samples generated are used for visual inspection and statistical testing, comparing the real and simulated textures. The model is an autobinomial MRF; see [6] or [12]. The algorithm is not suitable (nor intended) for restoration: for one thing, the intensity histogram is constant throughout the iteration process. This is necessarily the case with exchange systems which depend heavily on the initial configuration.

The algorithm in Hassner and Sklansky [28] is apparently a modification of one in Bortz *et al.* [7]. Another application of these ideas outside statistical mechanics appears in Hinton and Sejnowski [29], a paper about neural modeling but a spiritual cousin of ours. In particular, the parallel nature of these algorithms is emphasized.

The essence of every SR scheme is that changes $(\omega \rightarrow \eta)$ which *increase* energy, i.e., *lower* probability, are permitted.

By contrast, deterministic algorithms only allow jumps to states of lower energy and invariably get "stuck" in *local* minima. To get to samples from π, we must occasionally "backtrack."

All of these algorithms can be cast in a general theory involving Markov chains with state space Ω. See Hammersley and Handscomb [27] for a readable treatment. The goal is an irreducible, aperiodic chain with equilibrium measure π. If $\omega_1, \omega_2, \cdots, \omega_R$ is a realization of such a chain, then standard results yield (10.1), in fact at a rate $O(R^{-1/2})$ as $R \to \infty$. In this setup an auxiliary transition matrix is used to go from ω to η, and the general replacement recipe involves the same ratio $\pi(\eta)/\pi(\omega)$. The Markovian properties of the Gibbs Sampler will be described in the following sections.

Chemical annealing is a method for determining the low energy states of a material by a gradual lowering of temperature. The process is delicate: if T is lowered too rapidly and insufficient time is spent at temperatures near the freezing point, then the process may bog down in nonequilibrium states, corresponding to flaws in the material, etc. In *simulated* annealing, Kirkpatrick *et al.* [40] identify the solution of an optimal (computer) design problem with the ground state of an imaginary physical system, and then employ the Metropolis algorithm to reach "steady-state" at each of a decreasing sequence of temperatures $\{T_n\}$. This sequence, and the time spent at each temperature, is called an "annealing schedule." In [40], this is done on an ad hoc basis using guidelines developed for chemical annealing. Here, we prove the existence of annealing schedules which guarantee convergence to minimum energy states (see Section XII for formal definitions), and we identify the *rate* of decrease relative to the number of full sweeps.

Turning to RL, there are many similarities with SR, both in purpose and, at least abstractly, in method. RL was designed for the assignment of numeric or symbolic labels to objects in a visual system, such as intensity levels to pixels or geometric labels to cube edges, in order to achieve a "global interpretation" that is consistent with the context and certain "local constraints." Ideally, the process evolves by a series of *local* changes, which are intended to be simple, homogeneous, and performed in parallel. The local constraints are usually so-called "compatibility functions," which are much like statistical correlations, and often defined in reference to a graph. We refer the reader to Davis and Rosenfeld [13] for an expository treatment, to Rosenfeld *et al.* [46] for the origins, to Hummel and Zucker [30] for recent work on the logical and mathematical foundations, and to Rosenfeld and Kak [47] for applications to iterative segmentation.

But there are also fundamental differences. First, most variants of RL are rather ad hoc and heuristic. Second, and more importantly, RL is essentially a *nonstochastic* process, both in the interaction model and in the updating algorithms. (Indeed, various probabilistic analogies are often avoided as misleading; see [30], for example.) There is nothing in RL corresponding to an equilibrium measure or even a joint probability law over configurations, whereas there is no analogue in SR of the all-important, iterative updating *formulas* and corresponding sequence of "probability estimates" for various hypotheses involving pixel or object classification.

In summary, there are shared goals and shared features (locality, parallelism, etc.) but SR and RL are quite distinct, at least as practiced in the references made here.

XI. Gibbs Sampler: General Description

We return to the general notation of Section IV: $X = \{X_s, s \in S\}$ is an MRF over a graph $\{\mathcal{G}_s, s \in S\}$ with state spaces Λ_s, configuration space $\Omega = \Pi_s \Lambda_s$, and Gibbs distribution $\pi(\omega) = e^{-U(\omega)/T}/Z, \omega \in \Omega$.

The general computational problems are

A) sample from the distribution π;
B) minimize U over Ω;
C) compute expected values.

Of course, we are most concerned with B), which corresponds to MAP estimation when π is the posterior distribution. The most basic problem is A), however, because A) together with annealing yields B) and A) together with the ergodic theorem yields C). We will state three theorems corresponding to A), B), and C) above. Theorem C is not used here and will be proven elsewhere; we state it because of its potential importance to other methods of restoration and to hypothesis testing.

Let us imagine a simple processor placed at each site s of the graph. The connectivity relation among the processors is determined by the bonds: the processor at s is connected to each processor for the sites in $\mathcal{G}_s$. In the cases of interest here (and elsewhere) the number of sites N is very large. However, the size of the neighborhoods, and thus the number of connections to a given processor, is modest, only eight in our experiments, including line, pixel and mixed bonds.

The state of the machine evolves by discrete changes and it is therefore convenient to discretize time, say $t = 1, 2, 3, \cdots$. At time t, the state of the processor at site s is a random variable $X_s(t)$ with values in Λ_s. The total configuration is $X(t) \doteq (X_{s_1}(t), X_{s_2}(t), \cdots, X_{s_N}(t))$, which evolves due to state changes of the individual processors. The starting configuration, $X(0)$, is arbitrary. At each epoch, only *one* site undergoes a (possible) change, so that $X(t-1)$ and $X(t)$ can differ in at most one coordinate. Let $n_1, n_2, \cdots$ be the sequence in which the sites are "visited" for replacement; thus, $n_t \in S$ and $X_{s_i}(t) = X_{s_i}(t-1), i \neq n_t$. Each processor is programmed to follow the same algorithm: at time t, a sample is drawn *from the local characteristics* of π for $s = n_t$ and $\omega = X(t-1)$. In other words, we choose a state $x \in \Lambda_{n_t}$ from the conditional distribution of X_{n_t} given the observed states of the neighboring sites $X_r(t-1)$, $r \in \mathcal{G}_{n_t}$. The new configuration $X(t)$ has $X_{n_t}(t) = x$ and $X_s(t) = X_s(t-1), s \neq n_t$.

These are *local* computations, and *identical* in nature when π is homogeneous. Moreover, the actual calculation is *trivial* since the local characteristics are generally very simple. These conditional probabilities were discussed in Section IV and we refer the reader again to formulas (4.8) and (4.9). Notice that Z does not appear.

Given an initial configuration $X(0)$, we thus obtain a sequence $X(1), X(2), X(3), \cdots$ of configurations whose convergence properties will be described in Section XII. The limits obtained do not depend on $X(0)$. The sequence (n_t) we actually use is simply the one corresponding to a raster scan, i.e., repeatedly visiting all the sites in some "natural" fixed order. Of course, in this case one does not actually need a processor at each site. But the theorems are valid for very general (not necessarily periodic) sequences (n_t) allowing for *asynchronous* schemes in which each processor could be driven *by its own clock*. Let us briefly discuss such a parallel implementation of the Gibbs Sampler and its advantage over the serial version.

Computation is parallel in the sense that it is realized by simple and alike units operating largely independently. Units are dependent only to the extent that each must transmit its current state to its neighbors. Most importantly, the amount of time required for one complete update of the entire system is *independent of the number of sites*. In the raster version, we simply "move" a processor from site to site. Upon arriving at a site, this processor must first load the local neighborhood relations and state values, perform the replacement, and move on. The time required to refresh S grows linearly with $N = |S|$. Thus, for example, for the purposes at hand, the parallel procedure is potentially at least 10^4 times faster than the raster version we used, and which required considerable CPU time on a VAX 780. Of course, we recognize that the fully parallel version will require extremely sophisticated new hardware, although we understand that small prototypes of similar machines are underway at several places.

A more modest degree of parallelism can be simply implemented. Since the convergence theorems are independent of the details of the site replacement scheme $n_1, n_2, \cdots$ the graph associated with the MRF $\mathbb{X}$ can be divided into collections of sites with each collection assigned to an independently running (asynchronous) processor. Each such processor would execute a raster scan updating of its assigned sites. Communication requirements will be small if the division of the graph respects the natural topology of the scene, provided, of course, that the neighborhood systems are reasonably local. Such an implementation, with five or ten micro- or minicomputers, represents a straightforward application of available technology.

XII. GIBBS SAMPLER: MATHEMATICAL FOUNDATIONS

As in Section XI, (n_t), $t = 1, 2, \cdots$, is the sequence in which the sites are visited for updating, and $X_s(t)$ denotes the state of site s after t replacement opportunities, of which only those for which $n_\tau = s$, $1 \leq \tau \leq t$, involve site s. For simplicity, we will assume a common state space $\Lambda_s \equiv \Lambda = \{0, 1, \cdots, L-1\}$, and as usual that $0 < \pi(\omega) < 1$ for all $\omega \in \Omega$ or, what is the same, that $\sup_\omega |U(\omega)| < \infty$. The initial configuration is $X(0)$.

We now investigate the statistical properties of the random process $\{X(t), t = 0, 1, 2, \cdots\}$. The evolution $X(t-1) \to X(t)$ of the system was explained in Section XI. In mathematical terms,

$$P(X_s(t) = x_s, s \in S)$$
$$= \pi(X_{n_t} = x_{n_t} | X_s = x_s, s \neq n_t) P(X_s(t-1)$$
$$= x_s, s \neq n_t) \qquad (12.1)$$

where, of course, $\pi = e^{-U/T}/Z$ is the Gibbs measure which drives the process. Our first result states that the distribution of $X(t)$ converges to π as $t \to \infty$ regardless of $X(0)$. The only assumption is that we continue to visit every site, obviously a necessary condition for convergence.

Theorem A (Relaxation): Assume that for each $s \in S$, the sequence $\{n_t, t \geq 1\}$ contains s infinitely often. Then for every starting configuration $\eta \in \Omega$ and every $\omega \in \Omega$,

$$\lim_{t \to \infty} P(X(t) = \omega | X(0) = \eta) = \pi(\omega). \qquad (12.2)$$

The proof appears in the Appendix, along with that of Theorem B. Like the Metropolis algorithm, the Gibbs Sampler produces a Markov chain $\{X(t), t = 0, 1, 2, \cdots\}$ with π as equilibrium distribution. The only complication is that the transition probabilities associated with the Gibbs Sampler are nonstationary, and their matrix representations do not commute. This precludes the usual algebraic treatment. These issues are discussed in more detail at the beginning of the Appendix.

We now turn to annealing. Hitherto the temperature has been fixed. Theorem B is an "annealing schedule" or rate of temperature decrease which forces the system into the lowest energy states. The necessary programming modification in the relaxation process is trivial, and the *local* nature of the calculations is preserved.

Let us indicate the dependence of π on T by writing π_T, and let $T(t)$ denote the temperature at stage t. The annealing procedure generates a different process $\{X(t), t = 1, 2, \cdots\}$ such that

$$P(X_s(t) = x_s, s \in S)$$
$$= \pi_{T(t)}(X_{n_t} = x_{n_t} | X_s = x_s, s \neq n_t)$$
$$\cdot P(X_s(t-1) = x_s, s \neq n_t). \qquad (12.3)$$

Let

$$\Omega_0 = \{\omega \in \Omega : U(\omega) = \min_\eta U(\eta)\}, \qquad (12.4)$$

and let π_0 be the uniform distribution on Ω_0. Finally, define

$$U^* = \max_\omega U(\omega),$$
$$U_* = \min_\omega U(\omega),$$
$$\Delta = U^* - U_*. \qquad (12.5)$$

Theorem B (Annealing): Assume that there exists an integer $\tau \geq N$ such that for every $t = 0, 1, 2, \cdots$ we have

$$S \subseteq \{n_{t+1}, n_{t+2}, \cdots, n_{t+\tau}\}.$$

Let $T(t)$ be any decreasing sequence of temperatures for which

a) $T(t) \to 0$ as $t \to \infty$;
b) $T(t) \geq N\Delta/\log t$
    for all $t \geq t_0$ for some integer $t_0 \geq 2$.

Then for any starting configuration $\eta \in \Omega$ and for every $\omega \in \Omega$,

$$\lim_{t \to \infty} P(X(t) = \omega | X(0) = \eta) = \pi_0(\omega). \qquad (12.6)$$

The first condition is that the individual "clocks" do not slow to an arbitrarily low frequency as the system evolves, and imposes no limitations in practice. For raster replacement,

$\tau = N$. The major practical weakness is b); we cannot truly follow the "schedule" $N\Delta/\log t$. For example, with $N = 20{,}000$ and $\Delta = 1$, it would take $e^{40{,}000}$ site visits to reach $T = 0.5$. We single out this temperature because we have obtained good results by making T decrease from approximately $T = 4$ to $T = 0.5$ over 300–1000 sweeps ($= 300N - 1000N$ replacements), using a schedule of the form $C/\log(1+k)$, where k is the number of full sweeps. (Notice that the condition in b) is then satisfied provided C is sufficiently large.) Apparently, the bound in b) is far from optimal, at least as concerns the constant $N\Delta$. (In fact, the proof of Theorem B does establish something stronger, namely that Δ can be taken as the largest absolute difference in energies associated with pairs ω and ω^* which differ at only one coordinate. But this improvement still leaves $N\Delta$ too large for actual practice.) On the other hand, the logarithmic rate is not too surprising in view of the widespread experience of chemists that T must be lowered very slowly, particularly near the freezing point. Otherwise one encounters undesirable physical embodiments of *local* energy minima.

Concerning ergodicity, in statistical physics one attempts to predict the observable quantities of a system in equilibrium; these are the "time averages" of functions on Ω. Under the "ergodic hypothesis," one assuumes that (10.1) is in force, so that time averages approach the corresponding "phase averages" or expected values. The analog for our system is the assertion that, in some suitable sense,

$$\lim_{n \to \infty} \frac{1}{n} \sum_{t=1}^{n} Y(X(t)) = \int_{\Omega} Y(\omega)\, d\pi(\omega). \quad (12.7)$$

(Here again T is fixed.) As we have already stated, a direct calculation of the righthand side of (12.7), namely,

$$\sum_{\omega} Y(\omega) e^{-U(\omega)/T} \Big/ \sum_{\omega} e^{-U(\omega)/T}$$

is impossible in general. The left-hand side of (12.7) suggests that we use the Gibbs Sampler and compute a time average of the function Y. For most physical systems, the ergodic hypothesis is just that—a *hypothesis*—which can rarely be verified in practice. Fortunately, for our system it is not too difficult to directly establish ergodicity.

Theorem C (Ergodicity): Assume that there exists a τ such that $S \subseteq \{n_{t+1}, \cdots, n_{t+\tau}\}$ for all t. Then for every function Y on Ω and for every starting configuration $\eta \in \Omega$, (12.7) holds with probability one.

XIII. Experimental Results

There are three groups of pictures. Each contains an original image, several degraded versions, and the corresponding restorations, usually at two stages of the annealing process to illustrate its evolution. The degradations are formed from combinations of

i) ϕ absent or $\phi(x) = \sqrt{x}$;
ii) multiplicative or additive noise;
iii) signal-to-noise levels.

The signal-to-noise ratios are all very low. For blurring, we always took the convolution H in (2.3). The restorations are all MAP estimates generated by the serial Gibbs Sampler with annealing schedule

$$T(k) = \frac{C}{\log(1+k)}, \quad 1 \leq k \leq K$$

where $T(k)$ is the temperature during the kth *iteration* (= full sweep of S), so that K is the total number of iterations. In each case, $C = 3.0$ or $C = 4.0$. No pre- or postfiltering, nor anything else was done. The models for the intensity and line processes were kept as simple as possible; indeed, only cliques of size two appear in the intensity model.

Group 1: The original image [Fig. 2(a)] is a sample of an MRF on Z_{128} with $L = 5$ intensities and the eight-neighbor system (Fig. 1, $c = 2$). The potentials $V_C = 0$ unless $C = \{r, s\}$, in which case

$$V_C(f) = \begin{cases} \frac{1}{3}, & f_s = f_r \\ -\frac{1}{3}, & f_s \neq f_r. \end{cases}$$

Two hundred iterations (at $T \equiv 1$) were made to generate Fig. 2(a).

The first degraded version is Fig. 2(b), which is simply Fig. 2(a) plus Gaussian noise with $\sigma = 1.5$ *relative to* gray levels f, $1 \leq f \leq 5$. Fig. 2(c) is the restoration of Fig. 2(b) with $K = 25$ iterations only, i.e., early in the annealing process. In Fig. 2(d), $K = 300$.

The second degraded image [Fig. 3(b)] uses the model

$$G = H(F)^{1/2} \cdot N \quad (13.1)$$

where $\mu = 1$ and $\sigma = 0.1$, again relative to intensities $1 \leq f \leq 5$. Fig. 3(c) and 3(d) shows the restorations of Fig. 3(b) with $K = 25$ and $K = 300$, respectively.

Group 2: Fig. 4(a) is "hand-drawn." The lattice size is 64×64 and there are three gray levels. Gaussian noise ($\mu = 0$, $\sigma = 0.7$) was added to produce Fig. 4(b). We tried two types of restoration on Fig. 4(b). First, we used the "blob process" which generated Fig. 2(a) for the F-model. There was no line process and $K = 1000$. Obviously these are flaws; see Fig. 4(c).

A line process L was then adjoined to F for the original image model, and the corresponding restoration after 1000 iterations is shown in Fig. 4(d). L itself was described in Case 2 of Section III and the neighborhood system for (F, L) on $Z_{64} \cup D_{64}$ was discussed in Case 3 of Section III. The (prior) distribution on $X = (F, L)$ was as follows. The range of F is $\{0, 1, 2\}$ ($L = 3$ intensities). The energy $U(f, l)$ consists of two terms, say $U(f|l) + U(l)$. To understand the interaction term $U(f|l)$, let d denote a line site, say between pixels r and s. If $L_d = 1$, i.e., an edge element is "present" at d, then the bond between s and r is "broken" and we set $V_{\{r,s\}}(f_r, f_s) = 0$ regardless of f_r, f_s; otherwise ($L_d = 0$) $V_{\{r,s\}}$ is as before except that $\pm \frac{1}{3}$ are replaced by ± 1. As for $U(l)$, only cliques of size four are nonzero, of which there are six distinct types up to rotations. These are shown in Fig. 5(a) with their associated energy values.

Then we corrupted the hand-drawn figure using (13.1) with the same noise parameters as Fig. 3(b), obtaining Fig. 6(b), which is restored in Fig. 6(c) using the same prior on (F, L) as above and with $K = 1000$ iterations.

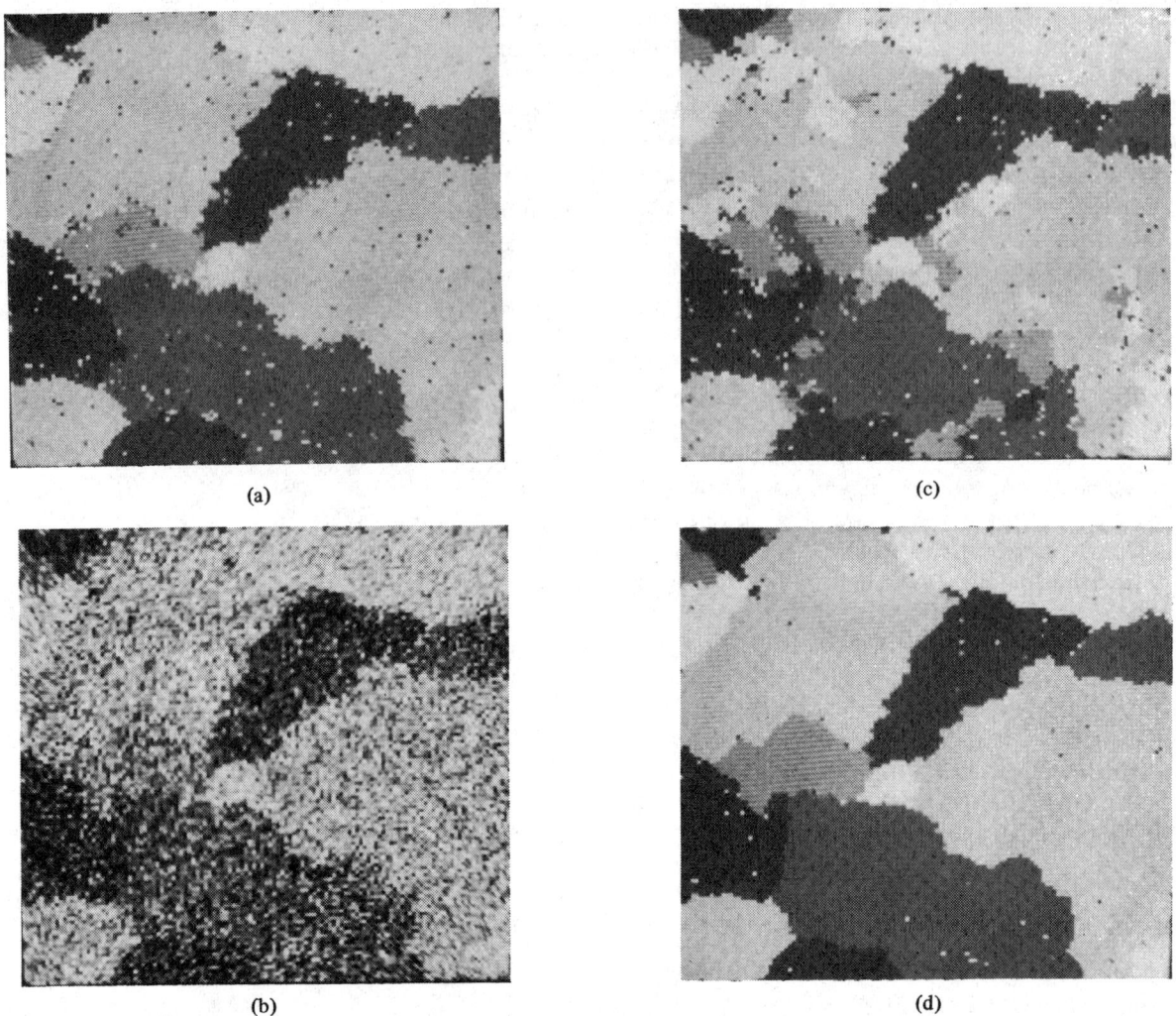

Fig. 2. (a) Original image: Sample from MRF. (b) Degraded image: Additive noise. (c) Restoration: 25 iterations. (d) Restoration: 300 iterations.

Group 3: The results in Group 2 suggest a boundary-finding algorithm for general shapes: allow the line process more directional freedom. Group 3 is an exercise in boundary finding at essentially 0 dB. Fig. 7(a) is a 64 × 64 segment of a roadside photograph that we obtained from the Visions Research Group at the University of Massachusetts. The levels are scaled so that the (existing) two peaks in the histogram occur at $f = 0$ and $f = 1$. We regard Fig. 7(a) as the *blurred image* $H(F)$. Noise is added in Fig. 7(b); the standard error is $\sigma = 0.5$ *relative to the two main gray levels* $f = 0, 1$.

Figs. 7(c) and 7(d) are "restorations" of Fig. 7(b) for $K = 100$ and $K = 1000$ iterations, respectively. The outcome of the line process is indicated by painting black any pixels to the left of or above a "broken bond." The two main regions, comprising the sign and the arrow, are perfectly circumscribed by a continuous sequence of line elements.

The model for X is more complex than the one in Group 2. There are now four possible states for each line site corresponding to "off" ($l = 0$) and three directions, shown in Fig. 5(b). The $U(f|l)$ term is the same as before in that the pixel bond between r and s is broken whenever $l_d \neq 0$. The range of F is $\{0, 1\}$ ($L = 2$).

Only cliques of size four are nonzero in $U(l)$, as before. However, there are now many combinations for $(l_{d_1}, l_{d_2}, l_{d_3}, l_{d_4})$ given such a clique $C = \{d_1, d_2, d_3, d_4\}$ of line sites, although the number is substantially reduced by assuming rotational invariance, which we do. Fig. 5(c) shows the convention we will use for the ordering and an example of the notation. The energies for the possible configurations (l_{d_i}, $1 \leq i \leq 4$) range from 0 to 2.70. (Remember that high energies correspond to low probability, and that the exponential exaggerates differences.) We took $V(0, 0, 0, 0) = 0$ and $V(l_{d_i}, 1 \leq i \leq 4) = 2.70$ otherwise, except when exactly two of the l_{d_i} are nonzero. Parallel segments [e.g., (1, 0, 1, 0)] receive energy 2.70; sharp turns [e.g., (0, 2, 1, 0)] and other "corner" types get 1.80; mild turns [e.g., (0, 2, 3, 0)] are 1.35; and continuations [e.g., (2, 0, 2, 0) or (0, 1, 3, 0)] are 0.90.

XIV. Concluding Remarks

We have introduced some new theoretical and processing methods for image restoration. The models and estimates are noncausal and nonlinear, and do not represent extensions into two dimensions of one-dimensional filtering and smoothing

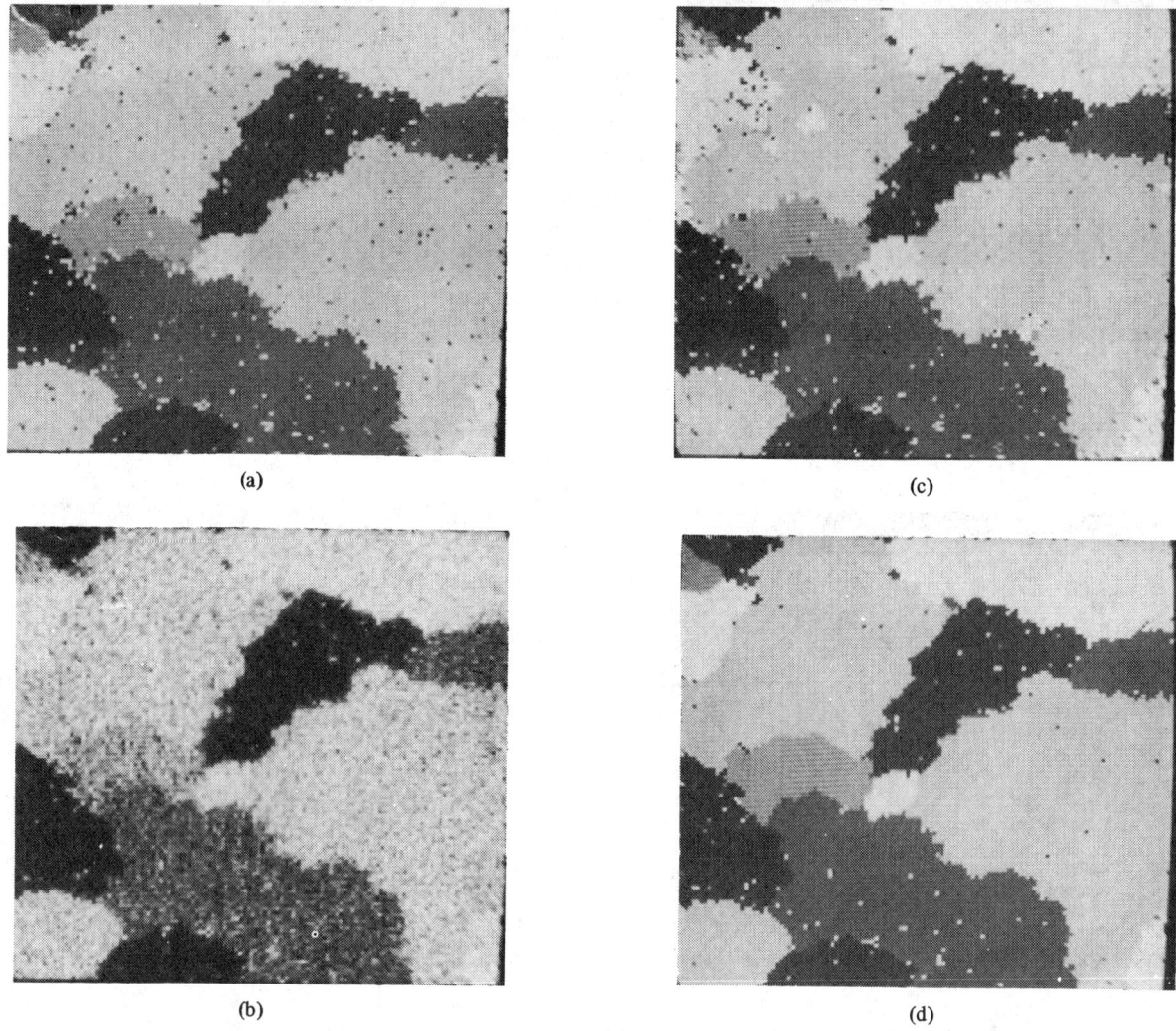

Fig. 3. (a) Original image: Sample from MRF. (b) Degraded image: Blur, nonlinear transformation, multiplicative noise. (c) Restoration: 25 iterations. (d) Restoration: 300 iterations.

algorithms. Rather, our work is largely inspired by the methods of statistical physics for investigating the time-evolution and equilibrium behavior of large, lattice-based systems.

There are, of course, *many* well-known and remarkable features of these massive, homogeneous physical systems. Among these is the evolution to minimal energy states, regardless of initial conditions. In our work posterior (Gibbs) distribution represents an *imaginary* physical system whose lowest energy states are exactly the MAP estimates of the original image given the degraded "data."

The approach is very flexible. The MRF-Gibbs class of models is tailor-made for representing the dependencies among the intensity levels of nearby pixels as well as for augmenting the usual, pixel-based process by other, unobservable attribute processes, such as our "line process," in order to bring exogenous information into the model. Moreover, the degradation model is almost unrestricted; in particular, we allow for deformations due to the image formation and recording processes. All that is required is that the posterior distribution have a "reasonable" neighborhood structure as a MRF, for in that case the computational load can be accommodated by appropriate variants (such as the Gibbs Sampler) of relaxation algorithms for dynamical systems.

APPENDIX
PROOFS OF THEOREMS

Background and Notation

Recall that $\Lambda = \{0, 1, 2, \cdots, L-1\}$ is the common state space, that η, η', ω, etc. denote elements of the configuration space $\Omega = \Lambda^N$, and that the sites $S = \{s_1, s_2, \cdots, s_N\}$ are visited for updating in the order $\{n_1, n_2, \cdots\} \subset S$. The resulting stochastic process is $\{X(t), t = 0, 1, 2, \cdots\}$, where $X(0)$ is the initial configuration.

For Theorem A, the transitions are governed by the Gibbs distribution $\pi(\omega) = e^{-U(\omega)/T}/Z$ in accordance with (12.1), whereas, for Theorem B (annealing), we use $\pi_{T(t)}$ (see Section XII) for the transition $X(t-1) \to X(t)$ [see (12.3)].

Let us briefly discuss the process $\{X(t), t \geq 0\}$, restricting attention to constant temperature; the annealing case is essentially the same. To begin with, $\{X(t), t \geq 0\}$ is indeed a Markov chain; this is apparent from its construction. Fix t and

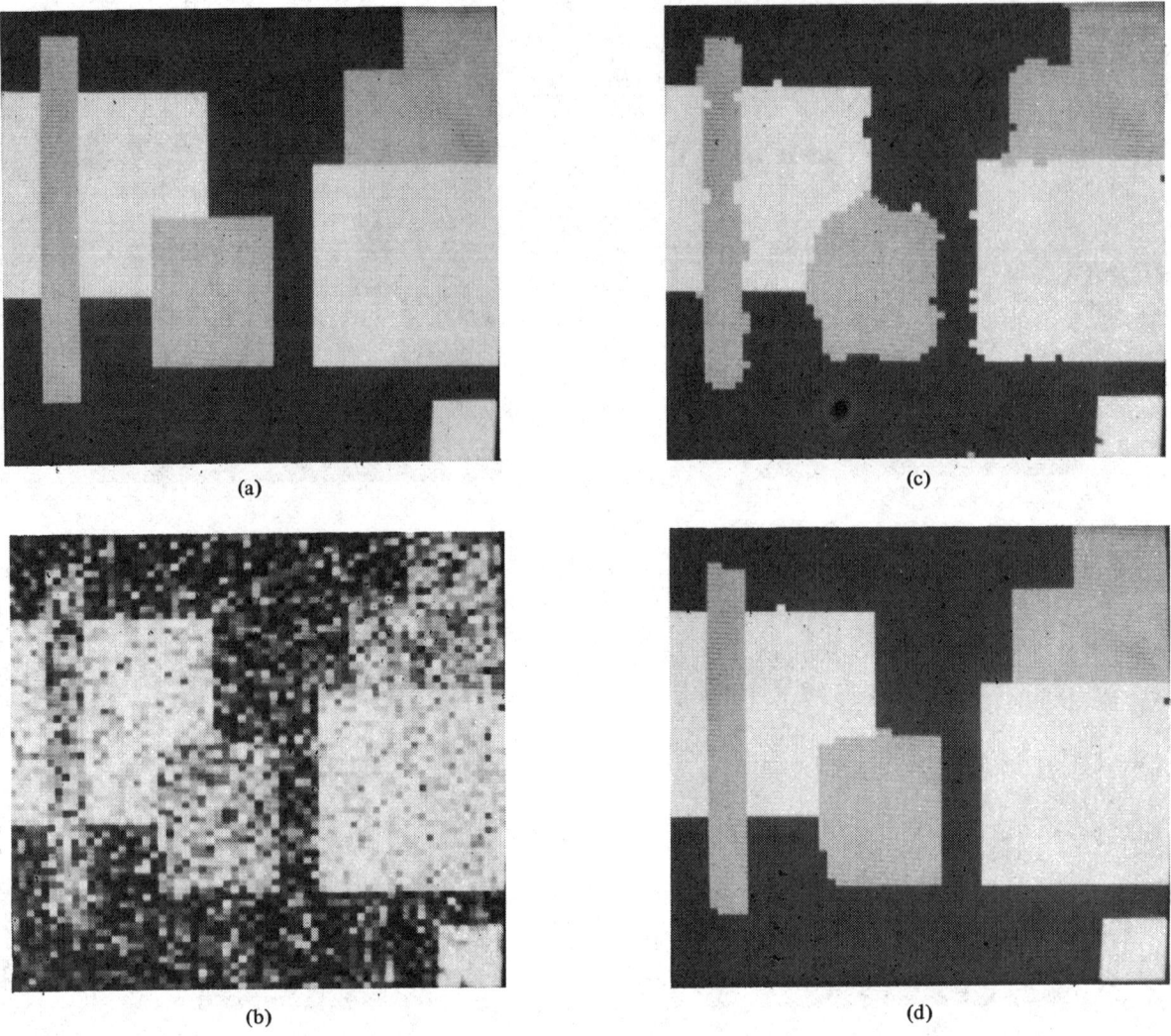

Fig. 4. (a) Original image: "Hand-drawn." (b) Degraded image: Additive noise. (c) Restoration: Without line process; 1000 iterations. (d) Restoration: Including line process; 1000 iterations.

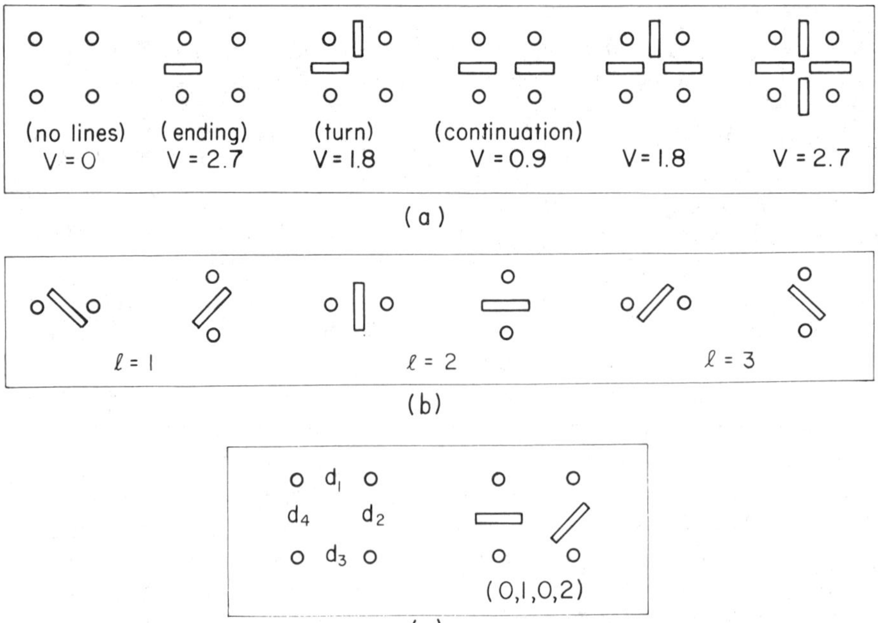

Fig. 5.

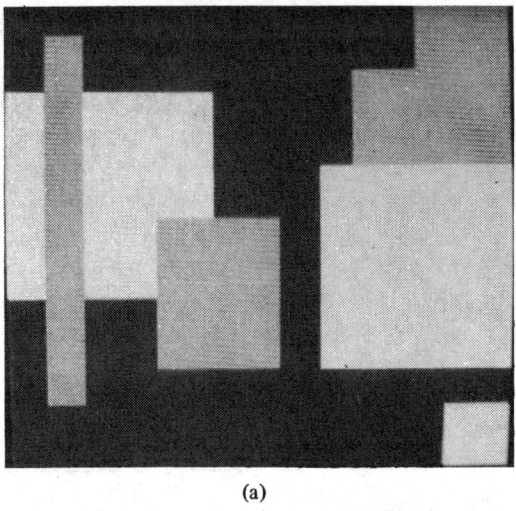
(a)

(b)

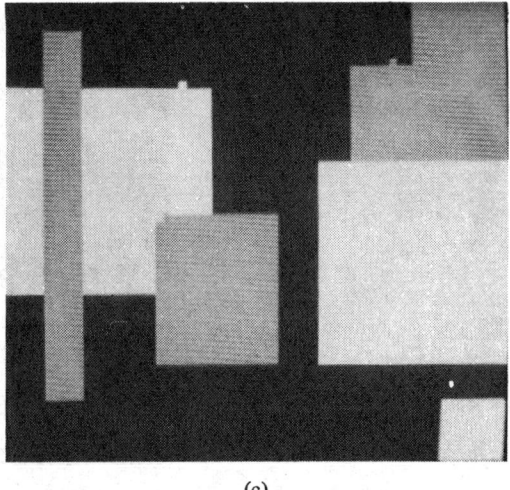
(c)

Fig. 6. (a) Original image: "Hand-drawn." (b) Degraded image: Blur, nonlinear transformation, multiplicative noise. (c) Restoration: including line process; 1000 iterations.

$\omega \in \Omega$. For any $x \in \Lambda$, let ω^x denote the configuration which is x at site n_t and agrees with ω elsewhere. The transition matrix *at time t* is

$$(M_t)_{\eta, \omega} = \begin{cases} \pi(X_{n_t} = x_{n_t} | X_s = x_s, s \neq n_t), \\ \quad \text{if } \eta = \omega^x \text{ for some } x \in \Lambda \\ 0, \quad \text{otherwise} \end{cases}$$

where $(M_t)_{\eta, \omega}$ denotes the row η, column ω entry of M_t, and $\omega = (x_{s_1}, x_{s_2}, \cdots, x_{s_N})$. In particular, the chain is *nonstationary*, although clearly *aperiodic* and *irreducible* (since $\pi(\omega) > 0 \; \forall \omega$). Moreover, given any starting vector (distribution) μ_0, the distribution of $X(t)$ is given by the vector $\mu_0 \prod_{j=1}^{t} M_j$, i.e.,

$$P_{\mu_0}(X(t) = \omega) = \left(\mu_0 \times \prod_{j=1}^{t} M_j \right)_\omega$$

$$= \sum_\eta P(X(t) = \omega | X(0) = \eta) \mu_0(\eta).$$

Notice that π is the (necessarily) unique invariant vector, i.e., for every $t = 1, 2, \cdots,$

$$\pi(\omega) = (\pi M_t)_\omega = \sum_\eta P(X(t) = \omega | X(0) = \eta) \pi(\eta). \quad (A.1)$$

To see this, fix t and $\omega = \{x_s\}$, and write

$$(\pi M_t)_\omega = \sum_\eta \pi(\eta) (M_t)_{\eta, \omega}$$

$$= \sum_{x \in \Lambda} \pi(\omega^x) (M_t)_{\omega^x, \omega}$$

$$= (M_t)_{\omega^{x'}, \omega} \sum_{x \in \Lambda} \pi(\omega^x) \quad (\text{for any } x' \in \Lambda)$$

$$= \pi(X_{n_t} = x_{n_t} | X_s = x_s, s \neq n_t) \pi(X_s = x_s, s \neq n_t)$$

$$= \pi(\omega).$$

It will be convenient to use the following, semistandard notation for transitions. For nonnegative integers $r < t$ and $\omega, \eta \in \Omega$, set

$$P(t, \omega | r, \eta) = P(X(t) = \omega | X(r) = \eta)$$

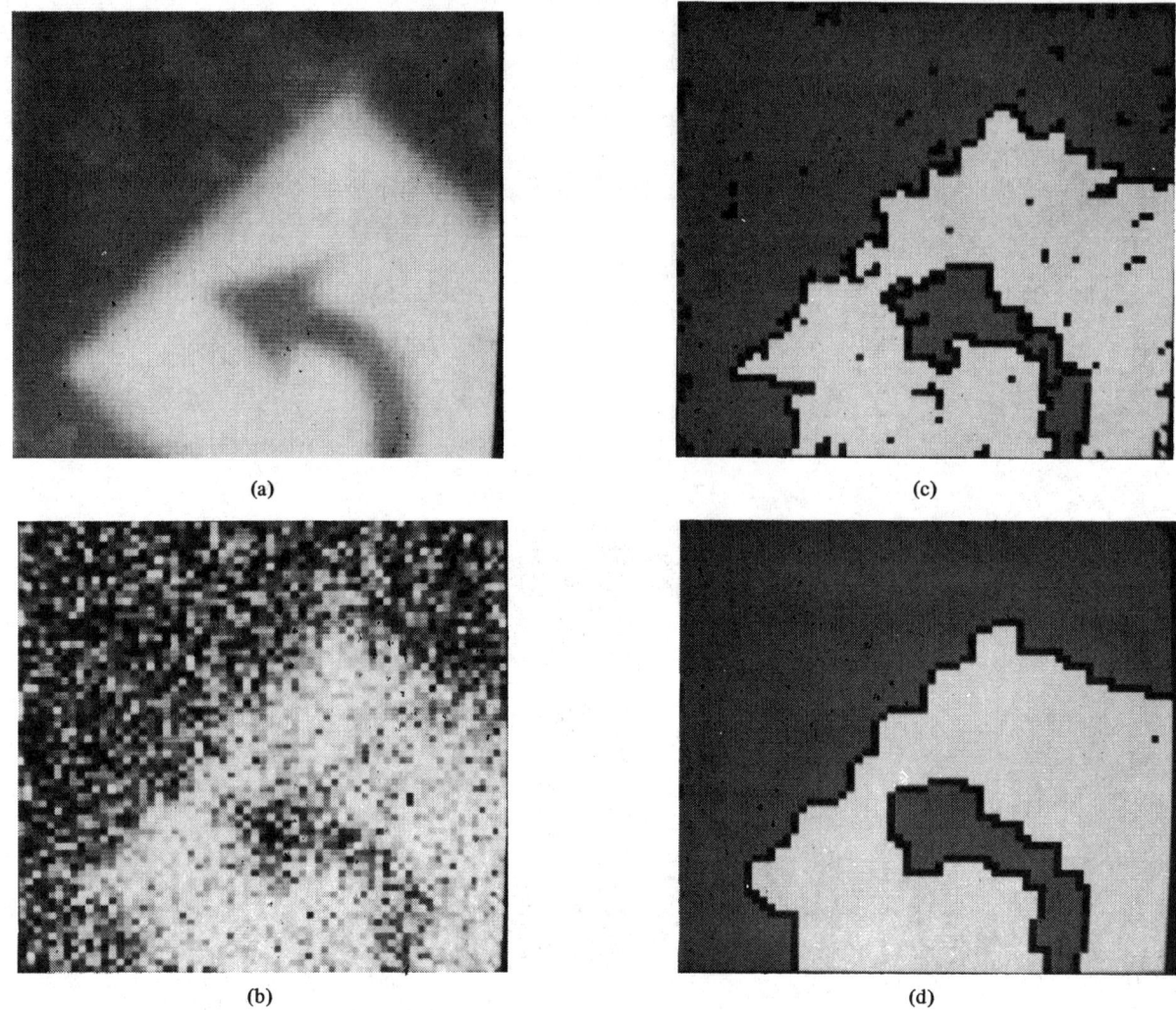

Fig. 7. (a) Blurred image (roadside scene). (b) Degraded image: Additive noise. (c) Restoration including line process; 100 iterations. (d) Restoration including line process; 1000 iterations.

and, for any *distribution* μ on Ω, set

$$P(t, \omega | r, \mu) = \sum_\eta P(t, \omega | r, \eta) \mu(\eta).$$

Finally, $\|\mu - \nu\|$ denotes the L^1 distance between two distributions on Ω:

$$\|\mu - \nu\| = \sum_\omega |\mu(\omega) - \nu(\omega)|.$$

Obviously, $\mu_n \to \mu (n \to \infty)$ in distribution (i.e., $\mu_n(\omega) \to \mu(\omega)$ $\forall \omega$) if and only if $\|\mu_n - \mu\| \to 0$, $n \to \infty$. (Remember that Ω is finite.)

Proof of Theorem A: Set $T_0 = 0$ and define $T_1 < T_2 < \cdots$ such that

$$S \subseteq \{n_{T_{k-1}+1}, n_{T_{k-1}+2}, \cdots, n_{T_k}\}, \quad k = 1, 2, \cdots.$$

This is possible since every site is visited infinitely often. Clearly (at least) k iterations or full sweeps have been completed by "time" T_k. In particular, $kN \leq T_k < \infty \, \forall k$. Let

$$K(t) = \sup \{k : T_k < t\}.$$

Obviously $K(t) \to \infty$ at $t \to \infty$. The proof of Theorem A is based on the following lemma, which also figures in the proof of the annealing theorem.

Lemma 1: There exists a constant r, $0 \leq r < 1$, such that for every $t = 1, 2, \cdots$,

$$\sup_{\omega, \eta', \eta''} |P(X(t) = \omega | X(0) = \eta') - P(X(t)$$

$$= \omega | X(0) = \eta'')| \leq r^{K(t)}.$$

Assume for now that the lemma is true. Since π is an invariant vector for the chain:

$$\overline{\lim_{t \to \infty}} \sup_{\omega, \eta} |P(X(t)$$

$$= \omega | X(0) = \eta) - \pi(\omega)|$$

$$= \overline{\lim_{t \to \infty}} \sup_{\omega, \eta} \left| \sum_{\eta'} \pi(\eta') \{P(X(t)$$

$$= \omega | X(0) = \eta) - P(X(t) = \omega | X(0) = \eta')\} \right|$$

[by (A.1)]
$$\leq \varlimsup_{t \to \infty} \sup_{\omega, \eta', \eta''} |P(X(t) = \omega | X(0) = \eta')$$
$$- P(X(t) = \omega | X(0) = \eta'')|$$
$$= 0, \text{ by Lemma 1.}$$

So it suffices to prove Lemma 1.

Proof of Lemma 1: For each $k = 1, 2, \cdots$ and $1 \leq i \leq N$, let m_i be the time of the last replacement of site s_i before $T_k + 1$, i.e.,

$$m_i = \sup \{t : t \leq T_k, n_t = s_i\}.$$

We can assume, without loss of generality, that $m_1 > m_2 > \cdots > m_N$; otherwise, relabel the sites. For any $\omega = (x_{s_1}, \cdots, x_{s_N})$ and ω',

$$P(X(T_k) = \omega | X(T_{k-1}) = \omega')$$
$$= P(X_{s_1}(m_1) = x_{s_1}, \cdots, X_{s_N}(m_N)$$
$$= x_{s_N} | X(T_{k-1}) = \omega')$$
$$= \prod_{j=1}^{N} P(X_{s_j}(m_j) = x_{s_j} | X_{s_{j+1}}(m_{j+1})$$
$$= x_{s_{j+1}}, \cdots, X_{s_N}(m_N) = x_{s_N}, X(T_{k-1}) = \omega').$$

Let δ be the smallest probability among the local characteristics:

$$\delta = \inf_{\substack{(x_{s_1}, \cdots, x_{s_N}) \in \Omega \\ 1 \leq i \leq N}} \pi(X_{s_i} = x_{s_i} | X_{s_j} = x_{s_j}, j \neq i).$$

Then $0 < \delta < 1$ and a little reflection shows that every term in the product above is at least δ. Hence,

$$\inf_{\substack{k=1,2,\cdots \\ \omega, \omega'}} P(X(T_k) = \omega | X(T_{k-1}) = \omega') \geq \delta^N. \quad (A.2)$$

Consider now the inequality asserted in Lemma 1. It is trivial for $t \leq T_1$ since in this case $K(t) = 0$. For $t > T_1$,

$$\sup_{\omega, \eta', \eta''} |P(X(t) = \omega | X(0) = \eta') - P(X(t) = \omega | X(0) = \eta'')|$$
$$= \sup_{\omega} \{\sup_{\eta} P(X(t) = \omega | X(0) = \eta)$$
$$- \inf_{\eta} P(X(t) = \omega | X(0) = \eta)\}$$
$$= \sup_{\omega} \{\sup_{\eta} \sum_{\omega'} P(X(t) = \omega | X(T_1)$$
$$= \omega') P(X(T_1) = \omega' | X(0) = \eta)$$
$$- \inf_{\eta} \sum_{\omega'} P(X(t) = \omega | X(T_1)$$
$$= \omega') P(X(T_1) = \omega' | X(0) = \eta)\}$$
$$\doteq \sup_{\omega} Q(t, \omega).$$

Certainly, for each $\omega \in \Omega$,

$$\sup_{\eta} \sum_{\omega'} P(X(t) = \omega | X(T_1) = \omega') P(X(T_1) = \omega' | X(0) = \eta)$$
$$\leq \sup_{\mu} \sum_{\omega'} P(X(t) = \omega | X(T_1) = \omega') \mu(\omega')$$

where the supremum is over all probability measures μ on Ω which, by (A.2), are subject to $\mu(\omega') \geq \delta^N \, \forall \omega'$. Suppose $\omega' \to P(X(t) = \omega | X(T_1) = \omega')$ is maximized at $\omega' = \omega^*$ (which depends on ω). Then the last supremum is attained by placing mass δ^N on each ω' and the remaining mass, namely, $1 - |\Omega| \delta^N = 1 - L^N \delta^N$, on ω^*. The value so obtained is

$$(1 - (L^N - 1) \delta^N) P(X(t)$$
$$= \omega | X(T_1) = \omega^*)$$
$$+ \delta^N \sum_{\omega' \neq \omega^*} P(X(t) = \omega | X(T_1) = \omega').$$

Similarly,

$$\inf_{\eta} \sum_{\omega'} P(X(t) = \omega | X(T_1) = \omega') P(X(T_1) = \omega' | X(0) = \eta)$$
$$\geq (1 - (L^N - 1) \delta^N) P(X(t)$$
$$= \omega | X(T_1) = \omega_*)$$
$$+ \delta^N \sum_{\omega' \neq \omega_*} P(X(t) = \omega | X(T_1) = \omega_*)$$

where $\omega' \to P(X(t) = \omega | X(T_1) = \omega')$ is *minimized* at ω_*. It follows immediately that

$$Q(t, \omega) \leq (1 - L^N \delta^N) \{P(X(t)$$
$$= \omega | X(T_1) = \omega^*) - P(X(t) = \omega | X(T_1) = \omega_*)\},$$

and hence,

$$\sup_{\omega, \eta', \eta''} |P(X(t) = \omega | X(0) = \eta') - P(X(t) = \omega | X(0) = \eta'')|$$
$$\leq (1 - L^N \delta^N) \sup_{\omega, \eta', \eta''} |P(X(t)$$
$$= \omega | X(T_1) = \eta') - P(X(t)$$
$$= \omega | X(T_1) = \eta'')|.$$

Proceeding in this way, we obtain the bound

$$(1 - L^N \delta^N)^{K(t)} \sup_{\omega, \eta', \eta''} |P(X(t)$$
$$= \omega | X(T_{K(t)}) = \eta') - P(X(t) = \omega | X(T_{K(t)}) = \eta'')|$$

and the lemma now follows with $r = 1 - L^N \delta^N$. Notice that $r = 0$ corresponds to the (degenerate) case in which $\delta = L^{-1}$, i.e., all the local characteristics are uniform on Λ. Q.E.D.

Proof of Theorem B: We first state two lemmas.

Lemma 2: For every $t_0 = 0, 1, 2, \cdots$,

$$\lim_{t \to \infty} \sup_{\omega, \eta', \eta''} |P(X(t)$$
$$= \omega | X(t_0) = \eta') - P(X(t) = \omega | X(t_0) = \eta'')| = 0.$$

Lemma 3:
$$\varlimsup_{t_0 \to \infty} \sup_{t \geq t_0} \|P(t, \cdot \mid t_0, \pi_0) - \pi_0\| = 0.$$

Recall that π_0 is the uniform probability measure over the minimal energy states $\Omega_0 = \{\omega : U(\omega) = \min_\eta U(\eta)\}$.

First we show how these lemmas imply Theorem B, which states that $P(X(t) = \cdot \mid X(0) = \eta)$ converges to π_0 as $t \to \infty$. For any $\eta \in \Omega$,

$$\varlimsup_{t \to \infty} \|P(X(t) = \cdot \mid X(0) = \eta) - \pi_0\|$$

$$= \varlimsup_{t_0 \to \infty} \varlimsup_{\substack{t \to \infty \\ t \geq t_0}} \left\| \sum_{\eta'} P(t, \cdot \mid t_0, \eta') \cdot P(t_0, \eta' \mid 0, \eta) - \pi_0 \right\|$$

$$\leq \varlimsup_{t_0 \to \infty} \varlimsup_{\substack{t \to \infty \\ t \geq t_0}} \left\| \sum_{\eta'} P(t, \cdot \mid t_0, \eta') \cdot P(t_0, \eta' \mid 0, \eta) - P(t, \cdot \mid t_0, \pi_0) \right\|$$

$$+ \varlimsup_{t_0 \to \infty} \varlimsup_{\substack{t \to \infty \\ t \geq t_0}} \|P(t, \cdot \mid t_0, \pi_0) - \pi_0\|.$$

The last term is zero by Lemma 3. Furthermore, since $P(t_0, \cdot \mid 0, \eta)$ and π_0 have total mass 1, we have

$$\left\| \sum_{\eta'} P(t, \cdot \mid t_0, \eta') P(t_0, \eta' \mid 0, \eta) - P(t, \cdot \mid t_0, \pi_0) \right\|$$

$$= \sum_\omega \sup_{\eta''} \left| \sum_{\eta'} (P(t, \omega \mid t_0, \eta') - P(t, \omega \mid t_0, \eta''))\right.$$
$$\left. \times (P(t_0, \eta' \mid 0, \eta) - \pi_0(\eta')) \right|$$

$$\leq 2 \sum_\omega \sup_{\eta', \eta''} |P(t, \omega \mid t_0, \eta') - P(t, \omega \mid t_0, \eta'')|.$$

Finally, then,

$$\varlimsup_{t \to \infty} \|P(X(t) = \cdot \mid X(0) = \eta) - \pi_0\|$$

$$\leq 2 \sum_\omega \varlimsup_{t_0 \to \infty} \varlimsup_{\substack{t \to \infty \\ t \geq t_0}} \sup_{\eta', \eta''} |P(t, \omega \mid t_0, \eta') - P(t, \omega \mid t_0, \eta'')|$$

$$= 0 \quad \text{by Lemma 2.} \qquad \text{Q.E.D.}$$

Proof of Lemma 2: We follow the proof of Lemma 1. Fix $t_0 = 0, 1, \cdots$ and define $T_k = t_0 + k\tau$, $k = 0, 1, 2, \cdots$. Recall that $S \subseteq \{n_{t+1}, \cdots, n_{t+\tau}\}$ for all t by hypothesis, that $\pi_{T(t)}(\omega) = e^{-U(\omega)/T(t)}/Z$ and that U^*, U_* are the maximum and minimum of $U(\omega)$, respectively, the range being $\Delta = U^* - U_*$. Let

$$\delta(t) = \inf_{\substack{1 \leq i \leq N \\ (x_{s_1}, \cdots, x_{s_N}) \in \Omega}} \pi_{T(t)}(X_{s_i} = x_{s_i} \mid X_{s_j} = x_{s_j}, j \neq i).$$

Observe that

$$\delta(t) \geq \frac{e^{-U^*/T(t)}}{Le^{-U_*/T(t)}} = \frac{1}{L} e^{-\Delta/T(t)}.$$

Now fix k for the moment and define the m_i as before:

$$m_i = \sup\{t : t \leq T_k, n_t = s_i\}, \quad 1 \leq i \leq N.$$

We again assume that $m_1 > m_2 > \cdots > m_N$. Then

$$P(X(T_k) = \omega \mid X(T_{k-1}) = \omega')$$
$$= P(X_{s_1}(m_1) = x_{s_1}, \cdots, X_{s_N}(m_N)$$
$$= x_{s_N} \mid X(T_{k-1}) = \omega')$$
$$= \prod_{j=1}^N P(X_{s_j}(m_j) = x_{s_j} \mid X_{s_{j+1}}(m_{j+1})$$
$$= x_{s_{j+1}}, \cdots, X_{s_N}(m_N) = x_{s_N}, X(T_{k-1}) = \omega')$$
$$\geq \prod_{j=1}^N \delta(m_j) \quad \text{(using (12.3) and the definition of } \delta\text{)}$$
$$\geq L^{-N} \prod_{j=1}^N e^{-\Delta/T(m_j)}$$
$$\geq L^{-N} \exp-\left\{\frac{\Delta N}{T(t_0 + k\tau)}\right\} \quad \text{(since } m_j \leq T_k$$
$$= t_0 + k\tau, j = 1, 2, \cdots, N, \text{ and } T(\cdot) \text{ is decreasing)}$$
$$\geq L^{-N}(t_0 + k\tau)^{-1}$$

wherever $t_0 + k\tau$ is sufficiently large. In fact, for a sufficiently small constant C, we can and do assume that

$$\inf_{\omega, \omega'} P(X(T_k) = \omega \mid X(T_{k-1}) = \omega') \geq \frac{CL^{-N}}{t_0 + k\tau} \tag{A.3}$$

for every $t_0 = 0, 1, 2, \cdots$ and $k = 1, 2, \cdots$, bearing in mind that T_k depends on t_0.

For each $t > t_0$, define $K(t) = \sup\{k : T_k < t\}$ so that $K(t) \to \infty$ as $t \to \infty$. Fix $t > T_1$ and continue to follow the argument in Lemma 1, but using (A.3) in place of (A.2), obtaining

$$\sup_{\omega, \eta', \eta''} |P(X(t) = \omega \mid X(t_0) = \eta') - P(X(t) = \omega \mid X(t_0) = \eta'')|$$

$$\leq \prod_{k=1}^{K(t)} \left(1 - \frac{C}{t_0 + k\tau}\right).$$

Hence it will be sufficient to show that

$$\lim_{m \to \infty} \prod_{k=1}^m \left(1 - \frac{C}{t_0 + k\tau}\right) = 0 \tag{A.4}$$

for every t_0. However, (A.4) is a well-known consequence of the divergence of the series $\sum_k (t_0 + k\tau)^{-1}$ for all t_0, τ. This completes the proof of Lemma 2.

Proof of Lemma 3: The probability measures $P(t, \cdot \mid t_0, \pi_0)$ figure prominently in the proof, and for notational ease we prefer to write $P_{t_0, t}(\cdot)$, so that for any $t \geq t_0 > 0$ we have

$$P_{t_0, t}(\omega) = \sum_\eta P(X(t) = \omega \mid X(t_0) = \eta) \pi_0(\eta).$$

To begin with, we claim that for any $t > t_0 \geq 0$,

$$\|P_{t_0, t} - \pi_{T(t)}\| \leq \|P_{t_0, t-1} - \pi_{T(t)}\|. \tag{A.5}$$

Assume for convenience that $n_t = s_1$. Then

$$\|P_{t_0, t} - \pi_{T(t)}\|$$
$$= \sum_{(x_{s_1}, \cdots, x_{s_N})} |\pi_{T(t)}(X_{s_1} = x_{s_1} | X_s = x_s, s \neq s_1)$$
$$\cdot P_{t_0, t-1}(X_s = x_s, s \neq s_1)$$
$$- \pi_{T(t)}(X_s = x_s, s \in S)|$$
$$= \sum_{x_{s_2}, \cdots, x_{s_N}} \left\{ \sum_{x_{s_1} \in \Lambda} \pi_{T(t)}(X_{s_1} = x_{s_1} | X_s = x_s, s \neq s_1) \right.$$
$$\times |P_{t_0, t-1}(X_s = x_s, s \neq s_1)$$
$$\left. - \pi_{T(t)}(X_s = x_s, s \neq s_1)| \right\}$$
$$= \sum_{x_{s_2}, \cdots, x_{s_N}} |P_{t_0, t-1}(X_s = x_s, s \neq s_1)$$
$$- \pi_{T(t)}(X_s = x_s, s \neq s_1)|$$
$$= \sum_{x_{s_2}, \cdots, x_{s_N}} \left| \sum_{x_{s_1}} \{P_{t_0, t-1}(X_s = x_s, s \in S) \right.$$
$$\left. - \pi_{T(t)}(X_s = x_s, s \in S)\} \right|$$
$$\leq \sum_{(x_{s_1}, \cdots, x_{s_N}) \in \Omega} |P_{t_0, t-1}(X_s = x_s, s \in S)$$
$$- \pi_{T(t)}(X_s = x_s, s \in S)|$$
$$= \|P_{t_0, t-1} - \pi_{T(t)}\|.$$

Observe that $\|\pi_0 - \pi_{T(t)}\| \to 0$ as $t \to \infty$. To see this, let $|\Omega_0|$ be the size of Ω_0. Then

$$\pi_{T(t)}(\omega) = \frac{e^{-U(\omega)/T(t)}}{\sum_{\omega' \in \Omega_0} e^{-U(\omega')/T(t)} + \sum_{\omega' \in \Omega \setminus \Omega_0} e^{-U(\omega')/T(t)}}$$
$$= \frac{e^{-(U(\omega) - U_*)/T(t)}}{|\Omega_0| + \sum_{\omega' \in \Omega \setminus \Omega_0} e^{-(U(\omega') - U_*)/T(t)}}$$
$$\xrightarrow{t \to \infty} \begin{cases} 0, & \omega \notin \Omega_0 \\ \frac{1}{|\Omega_0|}, & \omega \in \Omega_0. \end{cases} \quad (A.6)$$

Next, we claim that

$$\sum_{t=1}^{\infty} \|\pi_{T(t)} - \pi_{T(t+1)}\| < \infty. \quad (A.7)$$

Since

$$\sum_{t=1}^{\infty} \|\pi_{T(t)} - \pi_{T(t+1)}\| = \sum_{\omega} \sum_{t=1}^{\infty} |\pi_{T(t)}(\omega) - \pi_{T(t+1)}(\omega)|$$

and since $\pi_{T(t)}(\omega) \to \pi_0(\omega)$ for every ω, it will be enough to show that, for every ω, $\pi_T(\omega)$ is monotone (increasing or decreasing) in T for all T sufficiently small. But this is clear from (A.6): if $\omega \notin \Omega_0$, then a little calculus shows that $\pi_T(\omega)$ is strictly increasing for $T \in (0, \epsilon)$ for some ϵ, whereas if $\omega \in \Omega_0$, then $\pi_T(\omega)$ is strictly decreasing for all $T > 0$.

Lemma 3 can now be obtained from (A.5) and (A.7) in the following way. Fix $t > t_0 \geq 0$:

$$\|P_{t_0, t} - \pi_0\|$$
$$\leq \|P_{t_0, t} - \pi_{T(t)}\| + \|\pi_{T(t)} - \pi_0\|$$
$$\leq \|P_{t_0, t-1} - \pi_{T(t)}\| + \|\pi_{T(t)} - \pi_0\|, \quad \text{by (A.5)}$$
$$\leq \|P_{t_0, t-1} - \pi_{T(t-1)}\| + \|\pi_{T(t-1)} - \pi_{T(t)}\| + \|\pi_{T(t)} - \pi_0\|$$
$$\leq \|P_{t_0, t-2} - \pi_{T(t-1)}\| + \|\pi_{T(t-1)} - \pi_{T(t)}\| + \|\pi_{T(t)} - \pi_0\|$$
$$\leq \|P_{t_0, t-2} - \pi_{T(t-2)}\| + \|\pi_{T(t-2)} - \pi_{T(t-1)}\| + \|\pi_{T(t-1)} - \pi_{T(t)}\|$$
$$+ \|\pi_{T(t)} - \pi_0\|.$$

Proceeding in this way,

$$\|P_{t_0, t} - \pi_0\| \leq \|P_{t_0, t_0} - \pi_{T(t_0)}\| + \sum_{k=t_0}^{t-1} \|\pi_{T(k)} - \pi_{T(k+1)}\| + \|\pi_{T(t)} - \pi_0\|.$$

Since $P_{t_0, t_0} = \pi_0$ and $\|\pi_{T(t)} - \pi_0\| \to 0$ as $t \to \infty$, we have,

$$\varlimsup_{t_0 \to \infty} \sup_{t \geq t_0} \|P_{t_0, t} - \pi_0\|$$
$$\leq \varlimsup_{t_0 \to \infty} \sup_{t > t_0} \sum_{k=t_0}^{t-1} \|\pi_{T(k)} - \pi_{T(k+1)}\|$$
$$= \varlimsup_{t_0 \to \infty} \sum_{k=t_0}^{\infty} \|\pi_{T(k)} - \pi_{T(k+1)}\|$$
$$= 0 \quad \text{due to (A.7).} \qquad \text{Q.E.D.}$$

Acknowledgment

The authors would like to acknowledge their debt to U. Grenander for a flow of ideas; his work on pattern theory [23] prefigures much of what is here. They also thank D. E. McClure and S. Epstein for their sound advice and technical assistance, and V. Mirelli for introducing them to the practical side of image processing as well as arguing for MRF scene models.

References

[1] K. Abend, T. J. Harley, and L. N. Kanal, "Classification of binary random patterns," IEEE Trans. Inform. Theory, vol. IT-11, pp. 538-544, 1965.
[2] H. C. Andrews and B. R. Hunt, Digital Image Restoration. Englewood Cliffs, NJ, Prentice-Hall, 1977.
[3] M. S. Bartlett, The Statistical Analysis of Spatial Pattern. London: Chapman and Hall, 1976.
[4] T. Berger and F. Bonomi, "Parallel updating of certain Markov random fields," preprint.
[5] J. Besag, "Nearest-neighbor systems and the auto-logistic model for binary data," J. Royal Statist. Soc., series B, vol. 34, pp. 75-83, 1972.
[6] —, "Spatial interaction and the statistical analysis of lattice systems (with discussion)," J. Royal Statist. Soc., series B, vol. 36, pp. 192-326, 1974.
[7] A. B. Bortz, M. H. Kalos, and J. L. Lebowitz, "A new algorithm

for Monte Carlo simulation of Ising spin systems," *J. Comp. Phys.*, vol. 17, pp. 10-18, 1975.
[8] V. Cerný, "A thermodynamical approach to the travelling salesman problem: an efficient simulation algorithm," preprint, Inst. Phys. & Biophys., Comenius Univ., Bratislava, 1982.
[9] P. Cheeseman, "A method of computing maximum entropy probability values for expert systems," preprint.
[10] R. Chellappa and R. L. Kashyap, "Digital image restoration using spatial interaction models," *IEEE Trans. Acoust., Speech, Signal Processing*, vol. ASSP-30, pp. 461-472, 1982.
[11] D. B. Cooper and F. P. Sung, "Multiple-window parallel adaptive boundary finding in computer vision," *IEEE Trans. Pattern Anal. Machine Intell.*, vol. PAMI-5, pp. 299-316, 1983.
[12] G. C. Cross and A. K. Jain, "Markov random field texture models," *IEEE Trans. Pattern Anal. Machine Intell.*, vol. PAMI-5, pp. 25-39, 1983.
[13] L. S. Davis and A. Rosenfeld, "Cooperating processes for low-level vision: A survey," 1980.
[14] H. Derin, H. Elliott, R. Christi, and D. Geman, "Bayes smoothing algorithms for segmentation of images modelled by Markov random fields," Univ. Massachusetts Tech. Rep., Aug. 1983.
[15] R. L. Dobrushin, "The description of a random field by means of conditional probabilities and conditions of its regularity," *Theory Prob. Appl.*, vol. 13, pp. 197-224, 1968.
[16] H. Elliott, H. Derin, R. Christi, and D. Geman, "Application of the Gibbs distribution to image segmentation," Univ. Massachusetts Tech. Rep., Aug. 1983.
[17] H. Elliott, F. R. Hansen, L. Srinivasan, and M. F. Tenorio, "Application of MAP estimation techniques to image segmentation," Univ. Massachusetts Tech. Rep., 1982.
[18] P. A. Flinn, "Monte Carlo calculation of phase separation in a 2-dimensional Ising system," *J. Statist. Phys.*, vol. 10, pp. 89-97, 1974.
[19] B. R. Frieden, "Restoring with maximum likelihood and maximum entropy," *J. Opt. Soc. Amer.*, vol. 62, pp. 511-518, 1972.
[20] D. Geman and S. Geman, "Parameter estimation for some Markov random fields," Brown Univ. Tech. Rep., Aug. 1983.
[21] S. Geman, "Stochastic relaxation methods for image restoration and expert systems," in *Proc. ARO Workshop: Unsupervised Image Analysis*, Brown Univ., 1983; to appear in *Automated Image Analysis: Theory and Experiments*, D. B. Cooper, R. L. Launer, and D. E. McClure, Eds. New York: Academic, 1984.
[22] U. Grenander, *Lectures in Pattern Theory*, Vols. I-III. New York: Springer-Verlag, 1981.
[23] D. Griffeath, "Introduction to random fields," in *Denumerable Markov Chains*, Kemeny, Knapp and Snell, Eds. New York: Springer-Verlag, 1976.
[24] A. Habibi, "Two-dimensional Bayesian estimate of images," *Proc. IEEE*, vol. 60, pp. 878-883, 1972.
[25] F. R. Hansen and H. Elliott, "Image segmentation using simple Markov field models," *Comput. Graphics Image Processing*, vol. 20, pp. 101-132, 1982.
[26] A. R. Hanson and E. M. Riseman, "Segmentation of natural scenes," in *Computer Visions Systems*. New York: Academic, 1978.
[27] J. M. Hammersley and D. C. Handscomb, *Monte Carlo Methods*. London: Methuen, 1964.
[28] M. Hassner and J. Sklansky, "The use of Markov random fields as models of texture," *Comput. Graphics Image Processing*, vol. 12, pp. 357-370, 1980.
[29] G. E. Hinton and T. J. Sejnowski, "Optimal perceptual inference," in *Proc. IEEE Conf. Comput. Vision Pattern Recognition*, 1983.
[30] R. A. Hummel and S. W. Zucker, "On the foundations of relaxation labeling processes," *IEEE Trans. Pattern Anal. Machine Intell.*, vol. PAMI-5, pp. 267-287, 1983.
[31] B. R. Hunt, "Bayesian methods in nonlinear digital image restoration," *IEEE Trans. Comput.*, vol. C-23, pp. 219-229, 1977.
[32] V. Isham, "An introduction to spatial point processes and Markov random fields," *Int. Statist. Rev.*, vol. 49, pp. 21-43, 1981.
[33] E. Ising, *Zeitschrift Physik*, vol. 31, p. 253, 1925.
[34] A. K. Jain, "Advances in mathematical models for image processing," *Proc. IEEE*, vol. 69, pp. 502-528, 1981.
[35] A. K. Jain and E. Angel, "Image restoration, modeling and reduction of dimensionality," *IEEE Trans. Comput.*, vol. C-23, pp. 470-476, 1974.
[36] E. T. Jaynes, "Prior probabilities," *IEEE Trans. Syst. Sci. Cybern.*, vol. SSC-4, pp. 227-241, 1968.
[37] L. N. Kanal, "Markov mesh models," in *Image Modeling*. New York: Academic, 1980.
[38] R. L. Kashyap and R. Chellappa, "Estimation and choice of neighbors in spatial interaction models of images," *IEEE Trans. Inform. Theory*, vol. IT-29, pp. 60-72, 1983.
[39] R. Kinderman and J. L. Snell, *Markov Random Fields and Their Applications*. Providence, RI: Amer. Math. Soc., 1980.
[40] S. Kirkpatrick, C. D. Gellatt, Jr., and M. P. Vecchi, "Optimization by simulated annealing," IBM Thomas J. Watson Research Center, Yorktown Heights, NY, 1982.
[41] P. A. Levy, "A special problem of Brownian motion and a general theory of Gaussian random functions," in *Proc. 3rd Berkeley Symp. Math. Statist. and Prob.*, vol. 2, 1956.
[42] N. Metropolis, A. W. Rosenbluth, M. N. Rosenbluth, A. H. Teller, and E. Teller, "Equations of state calculations by fast computing machines," *J. Chem. Phys.*, vol. 21, pp. 1087-1091, 1953.
[43] N. E. Nahi and T. Assefi, "Bayesian recursive image estimation," *IEEE Trans. Comput.*, vol. C-21, pp. 734-738, 1972.
[44] D. K. Pickard, "A curious binary lattice process," *J. Appl. Prob.*, vol. 14, pp. 717-731, 1977.
[45] W. H. Richardson, "Bayesian-based iterative method of image restoration," *J. Opt. Soc. Amer.*, vol. 62, pp. 55-59, 1972.
[46] A. Rosenfeld, R. A. Hummel, and S. W. Zucker, "Scene labeling by relaxation operations," *IEEE Trans. Syst., Man, Cybern.*, vol. SMC-6, pp. 420-433, 197.
[47] A. Rosenfeld and A. C. Kak, *Digital Picture Processing*, vols. 1, 2, 2nd ed. New York: Academic, 1982.
[48] F. Spitzer, "Markov random fields and Gibbs ensembles," *Amer. Math. Mon.*, vol. 78, pp. 142-154, 1971.
[49] J. A. Stuller and B. Kruz, "Two-dimensional Markov representations of sampled images," *IEEE Trans. Commun.*, vol. COM-24, pp. 1148-1152, 1976.
[50] H. J. Trussell, "The relationship between image restoration by the maximum a posteriori method and a maximum entropy method," *IEEE Trans. Acoust., Speech, Signal Processing*, vol. ASSP-28, pp. 114-117, 1980.
[51] J. W. Woods, "Two-dimensional discrete Markovian fields," *IEEE Trans. Inform. Theory*, vol. IT-18, pp. 232-240, 1972.

Stuart Geman received the B.A. degree in physics from the University of Michigan in 1971, the M.S. degree in physiology from Dartmouth College in 1973, and the Ph.D. degree in applied mathematics from the Massachusetts Institute of Technology in 1977.

Since 1977 he has been a member of the Division of Applied Mathematics at Brown University, Providence, RI, where he is currently an Associate Professor. His research interests include statistical inference, parallel computing, image processing, and stochastic processes.

Dr. Geman is an Associate Editor of *The Annals of Statistics* and is a recipient of the Presidential Young Investigator Award.

Donald Geman, for a photograph and biography, see this issue, p. 720.

Simulated Annealing in Compound Gaussian Random Fields

FURE-CHING JENG, MEMBER, IEEE, AND JOHN W. WOODS, FELLOW, IEEE

Abstract — It is well-known that searching for globally optimal solutions is very difficult. In most cases only locally optimal solutions are found, usually by deterministic searches. Recently, a stochastic relaxation technique called simulated annealing has been developed to search for a globally optimal solution in image estimation and restoration problems. The convergence of simulated annealing has been proved only for random fields with a compact range space. Because of this, images were modeled as random fields with bounded discrete or continuous values. However, in most image processing problems, it is more natural to model the image as a random field with values in a noncompact space, e.g., conditional Gaussian models. The proof of convergence of the stochastic relaxation method is extended to a class of compound Gauss–Markov random fields. Simulation results are provided to show the power of these methods.

I. INTRODUCTION

IN IMAGE PROCESSING, the state of the art for image estimation has been advanced by modeling images as compound Markov random fields [3], [17]. Estimation results for these compound Markov models are visually better than those of an LSI model [16]. That is, the resulting estimates retain the edges, which are very important to human vision. Generally speaking, a compound Markov model consists of several simple image models having different characteristics, along with a structure model, a two-dimensional random field with a finite number of discrete values which governs transitions between the different submodels. Although compound models can produce better results, optimal solutions to estimation problems with these models are far more computationally demanding.

Recently, a powerful optimization method called simulated annealing (stochastic relaxation) has been introduced to solve a variety of optimization problems [3], [8], [13]. A nice feature of simulated annealing is that the algorithm itself is easy to implement and this simplicity is independent of problem size. On the other hand, this algorithm takes quite a long time to find the optimal solution. One application of simulated annealing is to image estimation and segmentation. The first paper published on simulated annealing for image processing was written by Geman and Geman [3]. They modeled images as Markov random fields with a finite number of levels, i.e., two-dimensional (2-D) Markov chains. Regarding the whole image as a random vector, they showed that the sequence of random vectors generated by the simulated annealing algorithm is a one-dimensional (1-D) vector-valued Markov chain and that this 1-D Markov chain converges to the optimal MAP solution. The results they obtained were visually quite impressive.

A limitation of their theoretical work was that images were modeled in a finite range space which is generally not appropriate for our problem of image estimation. Often, it is more natural to model the image as a Gauss–Markov random field, which has a noncompact range space. When applying simulated annealing in this case, a proof for the convergence of simulated annealing to an optimal estimate in this noncompact range space has been lacking. Although previous convergence results can be straightforwardly extended from a finite number of levels to a compact (discrete or continuous) range space, these methods do not extend to a noncompact range space. In particular, both the Gemans' approach [3] and the ergodic coefficient approach [13] fail in the case of a continuous noncompact range space. In this paper, we use a different method called the Liapunov function approach [10] which had been used for obtaining the convergence of stochastic approximation [15]. Here this method is used in a proof of the convergence of simulated annealing for a broad class of compound Gauss–Markov random fields appropriate to image estimation.

As pointed out in [13], the convergence of simulated annealing is related to the asymptotic properties of the probability density function of an inhomogeneous Markov chain. The asymptotic properties of probability mass or density functions of inhomogeneous Markov chains with a compact range space have been well established [4], [11], and [13]. However, for a Markov chain with a noncompact range space, the asymptotic properties of probability density functions are more difficult, and the available results are not very general. In this paper, we first study the asymptotic properties of inhomogeneous Markov chains. Then we review some known solution approaches. We also point out their limitations by applying them to a homogeneous Markov sequence with a noncompact range space.

Manuscript received February 5, 1988; revised November 8, 1988. Portions of this paper were presented at the MDSP Workshop, Noordwijkerhoot, The Netherlands, October 1987. This work was supported in part by the National Science Foundation under Grant ECS-8313880.

F. C. Jeng was a Rensselar graduate student visiting at the Center for Automation Research, University of Maryland. He is now with Bell Communications Research, Morristown, NJ.

J. W. Woods is with the Electrical, Computer, and Systems Engineering Department, Rensselaer Polytechnic Institute, Troy, NY 12180-3590.

IEEE Log Number 8933120.

Using Liapunov functions, a solution approach used by Lasota and Mackey [10] can deal with the case of a noncompact range space. By extending the results of homogeneous Markov chains in [10] to inhomogeneous Markov chains, we are able to prove convergence for inhomogeneous Markov vector sequences generated by the iterations of simulated annealing for a broad class of compound Gauss–Markov random fields. Finally, we present results of applying the simulated annealing method to compound Gauss–Markov (CGM) random fields (a generalization of the Gemans' models). We also compute the conventional LSI estimate for comparison.

II. Problem Statement

We shall pose a classical probability problem that concerns the asymptotic properties of the probability density function of a Markov chain. The reason for studying this problem is that the convergence of the Gibbs sampler or the simulated annealing algorithm can be formulated in this way, and hence the solution to this problem is the same as solving the convergence problem of the Gibbs sampler or the simulated annealing algorithm. The Gibbs sampler is a special case of simulated annealing with a fixed temperature. It leads to a random sequence which is a homogeneous Markov chain. Its main application is to realize a Markov random field using a Monte Carlo simulation, for example to approximate the mean or conditional mean. Before stating the problem, we will define some notation for the sake of clarity.

We assume a measure space (Ω, Σ, μ) and a conditional density function $p_n(s_n|s_{n-1})$ which defines a Markov chain $s_1, s_2, \cdots, s_n, \cdots$. In our case the s_i are vector-valued, with a number of elements equal to the number of pixels in the image. For simplicity, we assume Ω is R^d, and μ is a Lebesgue measure on R^d. Define a Markov operator P_n: $L^1 \to L^1$ as follows:

$$P_n f(s_n) \triangleq \int_\Omega p_n(s_n|s_{n-1}) f(s_{n-1}) \, ds_{n-1}. \quad (1)$$

By P_n^m we mean composite operations of the operators $P_{n+m} P_{n+m-1} \cdots P_{n+2} P_{n+1}$.

As mentioned before, the convergence problem of the simulated annealing algorithm is the same as the convergence of P_0^m as $m \to \infty$. Hence we are interested in finding when P_0^m will converge as $m \to \infty$.

III. Solution Approaches

There are two known methods, the Gemans' [3] and ergodic approaches [13], for solving this problem in the case where the state space Ω is compact. Neither of these two methods can be extended to a noncompact range space. We have used the method suggested in [10] for the noncompact case. In this section we present these three approaches and give an example of a homogeneous Markov chain that occurs in the Gibbs sampler to illustrate our point. First, we present this simple, but often occurring, Markov sequence [2] which will be used throughout this section.

Let the autoregressive (AR) random sequence s_n satisfy the following equation:

$$s_n = \rho s_{n-1} + w_n, \qquad 0 < \rho < 1 \quad (2)$$

where w_n is a zero-mean white Gaussian sequence with variance $1 - \rho^2$. Clearly, s_n is a Gauss-Markov sequence. The conditional probability density function $p_n(s_n|s_{n-1})$ is

$$p_n(s_n|s_{n-1}) = p(s_n|s_{n-1})$$
$$= \frac{1}{\sqrt{2\pi(1-\rho^2)}} e^{-(s_n - \rho s_{n-1})^2 / 2(1 - \rho^2)}. \quad (3)$$

and

$$P_0^m f(s_m) = \int_R \frac{1}{\sqrt{2\pi(1-\rho^{2m})}} e^{-(s_m - \rho^m s_0)^2 / 2(1 - \rho^{2m})} f(s_0) \, ds_0. \quad (4)$$

One can easily show that $P_0^m f(s_m)$ converges to a probability density function that does not depend on f [2], i.e.,

$$\lim_{m \to \infty} P_0^m f(s_m) = \frac{1}{\sqrt{2\pi}} e^{-s^2/2}. \quad (5)$$

A. The Gemans' Approach

In [3], Geman and Geman first defined a coefficient $r(P_n)$ of the operator P_n and used this coefficient to obtain the convergence of P_0^m. The coefficient $r(P_n)$ is defined as follows:

$$r(P_n) \triangleq \inf_{s_n, s_{n-1}} p_n(s_n|s_{n-1}). \quad (6)$$

They obtained the following theorem for the convergence of P_0^m.

Theorem 1: If there exists an $m' > 0$ such that $\sum_{i=1}^\infty r(P_{(i-1)m'}^{m'}) = \infty$, then $P_0^m f(s_m)$ converges to a probability density function that does not depend on f.

This theorem works in a compact range space, however as one can easily check, for $m, n > 0$ we have that $r(P_n^m) = 0$ in the previous example. Hence this approach fails to apply to this example. In fact, it will not work for the case of the noncompact range space in general. This is because, when we take the infimum of a transition density function in a noncompact range space, we always get zero, hence this theorem fails to apply.

B. Ergodic Coefficient Approach

In [1], Dobrushin introduced the ergodic coefficient to study the behavior of an inhomogeneous Markov chain with a finite number of levels. He obtained a sufficient condition on the convergence of P_0^m in terms of ergodic coefficients. Madsen [11] then generalized this to the case of a compact range space in a straightforward way. The ergodic coefficient $\gamma(P_n)$ of the Markov operator is defined as follows:

$$\gamma(P_n) \triangleq 1 - \frac{1}{2} \int_\Omega \sup_{s'_{n-1}, s''_{n-1}} |p_n(s_n|s'_{n-1}) - p_n(s_n|s''_{n-1})| \, ds_n \quad (7)$$

Using the ergodic coefficient, we have the following theorem due to Madsen [11], which uses the ergodic coefficient.

Theorem 2: If there exists an $m' > 0$ such that $\sum_{i=1}^\infty \gamma(P_{(i-1)m'}^{m'}) = \infty$, then $P_0^m f(s_m)$ converges to a probability density function that does not depend on f.

Although the sufficient condition in Theorem 2 is easy to verify, it is not useful in noncompact range space, e.g., a Gauss–Markov process. We now show that Theorem 2 fails to apply to the previous example. The ergodic coefficient $\gamma(P_n^m)$ of this AR random sequence introduced previously is 0 for all $m, n > 0$, which can be checked as follows:

$$\gamma(P_n^m) = 1 - \frac{1}{2} \int_\Omega \sup_{s'_n, s''_n} \frac{1}{\sqrt{2\pi(1-\rho^{2m})}}$$
$$\cdot \left| e^{-(s_{n+m} - \rho^m s'_n)^2/2(1-\rho^{2m})} - e^{-(s_{n+m} - \rho^m s''_n)^2/2(1-\rho^{2m})} \right| ds_{n+m}$$
$$= 0.$$

Hence Theorem 2 also fails to apply in this simple case.

C. Liapunov Function Approach

An alternative approach [10], reminiscent of the stability methods developed by Liapunov, offers a way to examine the asymptotic properties of iterates of probability density functions by Markov operators. Although the approach in [10] applies only to a homogeneous Markov chain, it is not difficult to extend their results to the inhomogeneous case. Before stating the theorem of convergence, we need some lemmas and definitions.

Definition: A continuous nonnegative function $V: \Omega \to R$ is a *Liapunov function* if

$$\lim_{\|s\| \to \infty} V(s) = \infty \quad (8)$$

where $\|\cdot\|$ is a norm.

Let D be the set of all probability density functions with respect to Lebesgue measure and the L_1 norm is defined as follows:

$$\|f\|_1 \triangleq \int_\Omega |f(s)| \, ds, \quad \forall f \in L^1.$$

Definition: Let $P_n: L^1 \to L^1$ be a Markov operator. Then $\{P_n\}$ is said to be *asymptotically stable* if for any $f_1, f_2 \in D$

$$\lim_{m \to \infty} \|P_0^m(f_1 - f_2)\|_1 = 0. \quad (9)$$

The following theorem, which is an extension of [10, theorem 5.7.1], gives for sufficient conditions on the convergence of P_0^m in terms of transition density functions.

Theorem 3: Let (Ω, Σ, μ) be a measure space and μ be a Lebesgue measure in R^d. If there exists a Liapunov function $V: \Omega \to R$ and a positive integer $\tilde{m} > 0$ such that

$$\int_\Omega V(s_n) p_n(s_n|s_{n-1}) \, ds_n \leq \alpha V(s_{n-1}) + \beta,$$
$$\text{for } 0 \leq \alpha < 1 \text{ and } \beta \geq 0, \quad \forall n \quad (10)$$

and

$$\sum_{i=1}^\infty \|g_{m_i}\|_1 = \infty, \quad m_i = i\tilde{m} \quad (11)$$

where

$$g_{m_i}(s_{m_i}) \triangleq \inf_{\|s_{m_i-1}\| \leq r} p_{m_i}(s_{m_i}|s_{m_i-1}) \quad (12)$$

and r is a positive number satisfying the following inequality:

$$V(s) > 1 + \frac{\beta}{(1-\alpha)}, \quad \forall \|s\| > r,$$

then, for the Markov operator $P_n: L^1(\Omega) \to L^1(\Omega)$ defined by (1), we have that P_0^m is asymptotically stable.

Proof: The proof can be obtained by minor modifications to the proofs of [10, theorems 5.7.1 and 5.6.2] and is presented in the Appendix.

In the following we will apply Theorem 3 to the AR random sequence s_n. Since s_n is a homogeneous Markov sequence, it is easier to check the sufficient conditions of Theorem 3 in this example. The transition density function for s_n is

$$p(s_n|s_{n-1}) = \frac{1}{\sqrt{2\pi(1-\rho^2)}} e^{-(s_n - \rho s_{n-1})^2/2(1-\rho^2)}.$$

Choose a Liapunov function $V(s)$ as follows:

$$V(s) = |s|^2. \quad (13)$$

By simple calculations, we have

$$\int_R |s_n|^2 \frac{1}{\sqrt{2\pi(1-\rho^2)}} e^{-(s_n - \rho s_{n-1})^2/2(1-\rho^2)} \, ds_n$$
$$\leq (1 - \rho^2) + \rho^2 |s_{n-1}|^2 \quad (14)$$

where $\rho < 1$. Also the following condition is satisfied:

$$\int_R \inf_{\|s_{n-1}\| \leq r} \frac{1}{\sqrt{2\pi(1-\rho^2)}} e^{-(s_n - \rho s_{n-1})^2/2(1-\rho^2)} \, ds_n = \gamma > 0,$$
$$\forall r > 0. \quad (15)$$

Hence, from Theorem 3, we know that P_0^m is asymptotically stable. Theorem 3 will be used to prove the convergence of the simulated annealing algorithm for a broad class of compound Gauss–Markov (CGM) random fields.

IV. Simulated Annealing for Compound Gauss–Markov Random Fields

As described in the Introduction, a linear-shift invariant AR model is insufficient to describe images for image estimation and restoration. Recently, a class of models called compound models [3], [16] has been proposed for better modeling. As mentioned before, compound models can be significantly better, but the optimal image estimate based on these models is difficult to calculate. The simulated annealing method is just the right tool for solving this dilemma. In this section we will introduce a new class of compound models called compound Gauss–Markov (CGM) random fields to model images for image estimation. By applying the convergence result of Theorem 3, we can show that the simulated annealing algorithm works for a broad class of such models.

A. Compound Gauss–Markov Random Fields

A compound Gauss–Markov (CGM) model is a Gauss–Markov (GM) model [7], [17] plus a line process (field) as introduced by Geman and Geman [3]. In the following, we will give mathematical descriptions for GM and CGM models.

A Gauss–Markov model can be described as follows:

$$s(m,n) = \sum_{kl \in \mathcal{R}} c_{kl} s(m-k, n-l) + w(m,n) \quad (16)$$

where $w(m,n)$ is a Gaussian random field satisfying the following covariance constraint:

$$E[w(m,n)w(k,l)]$$
$$= \begin{cases} \sigma_w^2, & \text{if } (m,n) = (k,l) \\ -c_{m-k, n-l}\sigma_w^2, & \text{if } (m-k, n-l) \in \mathcal{R} \\ 0, & \text{otherwise,} \end{cases} \quad (17)$$

and a first-order support of $\mathcal{R}$ is shown in Fig. 1. A random field described by (17) is a Markov random field with a neighborhood support $\mathcal{R}$ [7], [17]. By the equivalence of Markov random fields and Gibbs distributions, we can write down the probability density function $p(S)$ in terms of the Gibbs distribution as follows:

$$p(S) = \frac{1}{Z_1} e^{-U_s(S)}$$

and

$$U_s(S) \triangleq \sum_{c_s \in C_s} V_{c_s}(S) \quad (18)$$

where c_s is a clique, C_s denotes the set of cliques for the Markov neighborhood system, Z_1 is a normalizing constant that is functionally independent of S, and

$$S \triangleq \begin{pmatrix} s_{11} \\ s_{12} \\ \vdots \\ s_{1N} \\ s_{21} \\ \vdots \\ s_{NN} \end{pmatrix}.$$

Each $V_{c_s}(S)$ is a function on the sample space with the property $V_{c_s}(S)$ depends only on those $s(m,n)$ of S for which $(m,n) \in c_s$. In the above GM model, we have

$$V_{c_s}(S) = \frac{s^2(m,n)}{2\sigma_w^2} \quad \text{or} \quad -\frac{c_{m-k, n-l} s(m,n) s(k,l)}{\sigma_w^2}.$$

A CGM model can be described as follows:

$$s(m,n) = \sum_{kl \in \mathcal{R}} c_{kl}^{l(m,n)} s(m-k, n-l) + w^{l(m,n)}(m,n) \quad (19)$$

where $w^{l(m,n)}(m,n)$ is a Gaussian random field with the variance controlled by the $l(m,n)$ and $l(m,n)$ is a vector that consists of four nearest neighbors of the line field surrounding the pixel $s(m,n)$ and $l(m,n)$ is the line field[1] which is defined on the interpixel grid system [3]. This line field has two values indicating whether a *bond* is broken or not. If a bond is broken between adjacent pixels, then there is little correlation between these two pixels, otherwise, a strong correlation exists.

The joint mixed probability density function of (S, L) is Gibbsian and distribution that can be described in terms of potential functions. That is,

$$p(S, L) = \frac{1}{Z_2} e^{-[U_s(S|L) + U_l(L)]/T} \quad (20)$$

where Z_2 is a normalizing constant which is independent of (S, L), and T is a temperature parameter, U_s is defined in (18), and U_l is of the form

$$U_l(L) = \sum_{c_l \in C_l} V_{c_l}(L)$$

where

$$L \triangleq \begin{pmatrix} l_{11} \\ l_{12} \\ \vdots \\ l_{1N'} \\ l_{21} \\ \vdots \\ l_{N'N'} \end{pmatrix}$$

and N'^2 is the total number of points in the line field.

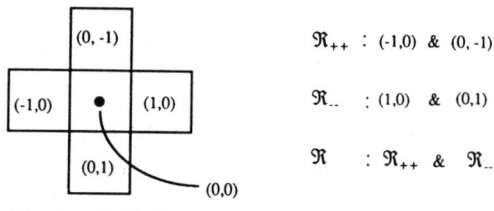

Fig. 1. Coefficient support regions $\mathcal{R}$, $\mathcal{R}_{++}$, and $\mathcal{R}_{--}$.

---
[1]In the Gemans' paper [3], $l(m,n)$ is called the line process. We will call it the line field because it is a two-dimensional (2-D) field.

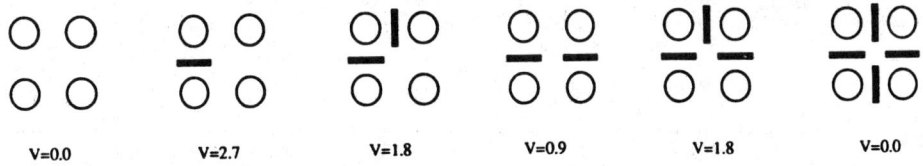

Fig. 2. Clique system c_l.

The clique system c_l we will use in this paper is the system used in [3] as shown in Fig. 2. For a CGM model to be a valid conditional Markov random field for any given line field L, such as Gauss-Markov models in (17), we have covariance constraints on $w^{l(m,n)}(m,n)$:

$$E\left[w^{l(m,n)}(m,n)w^{l(k,l)}(k,l)\right]$$

$$= \begin{cases} \sigma^2_{w_{l(m,n)}(m,n)}, & \text{if } (m,n) = (k,l) \\ -c^{l(k,l)}_{m-k,n-l}\sigma^2_{w_{l(m,n)}(m,n)}, & \text{if } (m-k,n-l) \in \mathcal{R} \\ 0, & \text{otherwise.} \end{cases}$$

By commutativity of correlation of two random variables, we have the following constraint on the model coefficients:

$$c^{l(k,l)}_{m-k,n-l}\sigma^2_{w_{l(m,n)}(m,n)} = c^{l(m,n)}_{k-m,l-n}\sigma^2_{w_{l(k,l)}(k,l)},$$

$$\text{if } (m-k,n-l) \in \mathcal{R}. \quad (21)$$

This constraint reduces the total number of free parameters that can be used in the models. Consequently, they should be enforced in parameter identification.

Since the CGM model is Gibbsian, it is a Markov random field. Depending on the functional $U_s(S|L)$ however, the random field L itself may or may not be a Markov random field. This can be seen from the following expression for the probability mass function $P(L)$,

$$P(L) = \frac{1}{Z_2}\int_S e^{-[U_s(S|L) + U_l(L)]/T}\,dS$$

$$= \frac{e^{-U_l(L)/T}}{Z_2}\int_S e^{-[U_s(S|L)]/T}\,dS.$$

If $\int_S e^{-U_s(S|L)/T}\,dS$ has the form of a Gibbs mass function for L, then L is a Markov random field, otherwise it is not. In general, $\int_S e^{-U_s(S|L)/T}\,dS$ may not be a Gibbs mass function for L.

B. Simulated Annealing Algorithm

We will discuss the simulated annealing procedure for CGM random fields. The main purpose of simulated annealing is to find the maximum *a posteriori* probability estimate from noisy observations. We thus assume that the observations $r(m,n)$ are corrupted by an independent white Gaussian noise $v(m,n)$ i.e.,

$$r(m,n) = s(m,n) + v(m,n).$$

Denoting

$$R \triangleq \begin{pmatrix} r_{11} \\ r_{12} \\ \vdots \\ r_{1N} \\ r_{21} \\ \vdots \\ r_{NN} \end{pmatrix},$$

the joint mixed probability density function of S, L, R is then

$$p(S,L,R) = (R|S,L)p(S,L) = p(R|S)p(S,L). \quad (22)$$

Simulated annealing proceeds by scanning through the pixels in some fashion and replacing the current values of $s(m,n)$ and $l(m,n)$ by randomly selected quantities that depend on the current state of the system. We now present the two conditional probabilities for $s(m,n)$ and $l(m,n)$ which are used in this Monte Carlo type procedure. The conditional a posteriori density function $\pi^s(m,n)$ for $s(m,n)$ is

$$\pi^s(m,n) \triangleq p(s(m,n)|S_{(m,n)}, L, R)$$

$$= \frac{p(S,L,R)}{\int p(S,L,R)\,ds(m,n)}.$$

From (22) and (20), we can obtain by completing the square

$$\pi^s(m,n) = \frac{1}{Z_3}\exp\left[-\frac{\left(s(m,n) - \sum_{kl}c^{l(m,n)}_{kl}s(m-k,n-l)\right)^2}{2T\sigma^2_{w_{l(m,n)}}} - \frac{(s(m,n) - r(m,n))^2}{2T\sigma^2_v}\right]$$

$$= \left(1\bigg/\sqrt{2\pi T\frac{\sigma^2_v \sigma^2_{w_{l(m,n)}}}{\sigma^2_v + \sigma^2_{w_{l(m,n)}}}}\right)e^{\Psi(s(m,n))} \quad (23)$$

where Z_3 is a normalizing constant and

$$\Psi(s(m,n)) \triangleq -\frac{\left(s(m,n) - \sum_{kl} \frac{\sigma_v^2}{\sigma_v^2 + \sigma_{w_{l(m,n)}}^2} c_{kl}^{l(m,n)} s(m-k, n-l) - \frac{\sigma_{w_{l(m,n)}}^2}{\sigma_v^2 + \sigma_{w_{l(m,n)}}^2} r(m,n)\right)^2}{2T \frac{\sigma_v^2 \sigma_{w_{l(m,n)}}^2}{\sigma_v^2 + \sigma_{w_{l(m,n)}}^2}}$$

with

$$S_{(m,n)} \triangleq \{s(k,l): (k,l) \neq (m,n)\}.$$

The conditional *a posteriori* probability mass function $\pi^l(m,n)$ for $l(m,n)$ is

$$\pi^l(m,n) \triangleq \frac{p(S,L,R)}{\sum_{l(m,n)} p(S,L,R)}.$$

From (22) and (20), we can obtain

$$\pi^l(m,n) = \frac{1}{Z_4} e^{\Phi(l(m,n))} \qquad (24)$$

where Z_4 is a normalizing constant and

$$\Phi(l(m,n)) = -\frac{\frac{s^2(i,j)}{2\sigma_{w_{l(i,j)}}^2} - \frac{c_{i-i', j-j'} s(i,j) s(i',j')}{\sigma_{w_{l(i,j)}}^2} + \frac{s^2(i',j')}{2\sigma_{w_{l(i',j')}}^2} + \sum_{(m,n) \in c_l} V_{c_l}(L)}{T}$$

and $l(m,n)$ is located between two neighboring pixels $s(i,j)$, $s(i',j')$.

The simulated annealing method can be implemented in a sequential or parallel way. We first describe sequential simulated annealing, e.g., raster scanning. Due to the sequential visiting of each pixel, we establish a linear ordering on the whole image. Thus, if a pixel at (m,n) is processed before the other pixel at (k,l) within a sweep of the image, we will denote the ordering relation as $(m,n) < (k,l)$ or $(k,l) > (m,n)$. For ease of the convergence proof, we keep the temperature constant within a sweep of the image and reduce the temperature only after each complete sweep (iteration) of the whole image. Since $\pi(S,L)$, $\pi^s(m,n)$ and $\pi^l(m,n)$ all depend on T, then $\pi(S,L)$, $\pi^s(m,n)$ and $\pi^l(m,n)$ also vary with t, which we denote by $\pi_t(m,n)$, $\pi_t^s(m,n)$, and $\pi_t^l(m,n)$, respectively.

1) Sequential Simulated Annealing Procedure: The sequential simulated annealing algorithm can be described in the following procedure. Let (m_t, n_t), $t=1,2,\cdots$, be the sequence in which the sites are visited for updating.

1) Set $t=0$ and assign an initial configuration denoted as S_{-1} and an initial temperature $T(0) = 1$.
2) The evolution $L_{t-1} \to L_t$ of the state of the line field can be obtained by sampling the next point of the line field from the raster-scanning scheme based on the conditional probability function $\pi_t^l(m_t, n_t)$ and keeping the rest unchanged.
3) Set $t = t+1$. Repeatedly go back to Step 2 until the whole line field is sampled.
4) The evolution $S_{t-1} \to S_t$ of the state of the observed field can be obtained by sampling the new value of the intensity field $s(m_t, n_t)$ based on the conditional density function $\pi_t^s(m_t, n_t)$ and keeping the rest unchanged.
5) Set $t = t+1$. Repeatedly go back to Step 4 until the whole intensity field is sampled.
6) Decrease T and go to Step 2 until $t > t_f$, where t_f is a specified integer.

Before going on to state the main theorem, we would first like to obtain some useful expressions that will be used in the implementation of the algorithm and the proof of the main theorem. Denote by t_k the number of iterations for k iteration sweeps of the whole image. From the simulated annealing procedure, we then have

$$p(S_{t_k}, L_{t_k} | S_{t_{k-1}}, L_{t_{k-1}}, R)$$
$$= p(S_{t_k} | S_{t_{k-1}}, L_{t_k}, L_{t_{k-1}}, R) P(L_{t_k} | S_{t_{k-1}}, L_{t_{k-1}}, R)$$
(by Bayes' rule)
$$= p(S_{t_k} | S_{t_{k-1}}, L_{t_k}, R) P(L_{t_k} | S_{t_{k-1}}, L_{t_{k-1}})$$
(by simulated annealing). (25)

Furthermore, we have the conditional pdf factorization
$$p(S_{t_k} | S_{t_{k-1}}, L_{t_k}, R)$$
$$= \prod_{mn} p\left[s_{t_k}(m,n) | S_{t_{k-1}}, \{s_{t_k}(i,j), (i,j) < (m,n)\}, L_{t_k}, R\right]$$
(by the chain rule)
$$= \prod_{mn} p\left[s_{t_k}(m,n) | \{s_{t_{k-1}}(i,j), (i,j) > (m,n)\}, \{s_{t_k}(i,j), (i,j) < (m,n)\}, L_{t_k}, R\right]$$
(by simulated annealing)[2]
$$= \prod_{mn} \pi_{t_k}^s(m,n) \qquad (26)$$

where

$$\pi_{t_k}^s(m,n) = \left(1 \bigg/ \sqrt{2\pi T(t_k) \frac{\sigma_v^2 \sigma_{w_{l_{t_k}(m,n)}}^2}{\sigma_v^2 + \sigma_{w_{l_{t_k}(m,n)}}^2}}\right) e^{\Psi_{t_k}(s(m,n))}$$

[2] Note that in simulated annealing the conditional density function is only a function of the current state of the system.

from (23),

$$\Psi_{t_k}(s(m,n)) \triangleq - \frac{\left[s_{t_k}(m,n) - C_+^{l_{t_k}(m,n)} * s_{t_k}(m,n) - C_-^{l_{t_k}(m,n)} * s_{t_{k-1}}(m,n) - \frac{\sigma_{w_{l_{t_k}(m,n)}}^2}{\sigma_v^2 + \sigma_{w_{l_{t_k}(m,n)}}^2} r(m,n)\right]^2}{2T(t_k) \frac{\sigma_v^2 \sigma_{w_{l_{t_k}(m,n)}}^2}{\sigma_v^2 + \sigma_{w_{l_{t_k}(m,n)}}^2}}$$

and

$$C_+^{l_{t_k}(m,n)} * s_{t_k}(m,n)$$
$$\triangleq \sum_{kl \in \mathcal{R}_{++}} \frac{\sigma_v^2}{\sigma_v^2 + \sigma_{w_{l_{t_k}(m,n)}}^2} c_{kl}^{l_{t_k}(m,n)} s_{t_k}(m-k, n-l)$$

$$C_-^{l_{t_k}(m,n)} * s_{t_{k-1}}(m,n)$$
$$\triangleq \sum_{kl \in \mathcal{R}_{--}} \frac{\sigma_v^2}{\sigma_v^2 + \sigma_{w_{l_{t_k}(m,n)}}^2} c_{kl}^{l_{t_k-1}(m,n)} s_{t_{k-1}}(m-k, n-l),$$

with $\mathcal{R}_{++}$ and $\mathcal{R}_{--}$ as illustrated in Fig. 1. Rewriting (26) into vector-matrix form, we have

$$p(S_{t_k}|S_{t_{k-1}}, L_{t_k}, R)$$
$$= \frac{1}{Z_6} \exp\left[-\frac{1}{2T(t_k)}[S_{t_k} - AS_{t_{k-1}} - Q_1 R]^T \cdot Q^{-1}(t_k)[S_{t_k} - AS_{t_{k-1}} - Q_1 R]\right] \quad (27)$$

where $C_+^{l_{t_k}}$ and $C_-^{l_{t_k}}$ are matrices corresponding to the operators $C_+^{l_{t_k}}$, $C_-^{l_{t_k}}$, Z_6 is a normalizing constant and

$$A \triangleq (I - C_+^{l_{t_k}})^{-1} C_-^{l_{t_k}},$$

$$Q_1 \triangleq \frac{1}{\sigma_v^2}(I - C_+^{l_{t_k}})^{-1} Q_0,$$

$$Q \triangleq (I - C_+^{l_{t_k}})^{-1} Q_0 (I - C_+^{l_{t_k}})^{-T}.$$

By the structure of the operators $C_+^{L_{t_k}}$ and $C_-^{L_{t_k}}$, the matrices $C_+^{l_{t_k}}$ and $C_-^{l_{t_k}}$ are, respectively, upper and lower triangular matrices with zeros on the diagonal. The matrix Q_0 is diagonal with elements $\sigma_v^2 \sigma_{w_{l_{t_k}}(m,n)}^2 / (\sigma_v^2 + \sigma_{w_{l_{t_k}}(m,n)}^2)$. Analogously, we have the following useful expressions for the line field:

$$P(L_{t_k}|S_{t_{k-1}}, L_{t_{k-1}}) = \prod_{mn} \pi_{t_k}^l(m,n) \quad (28)$$

and

$$\pi_{t_k}^l(m,n) = \frac{1}{Z_5(t_k)} e^{\Phi_{t_k}(l(m,n))} \quad (29)$$

where the normalizing constant $Z_5(t_k)$ is

$$Z_5(t_k) = \sum_{l(m,n)} e^{\Phi_{t_k}(l(m,n))}$$

and $\Phi_{t_k}(l(m,n))$ is

$$\Phi_{t_k}(l(m,n)) \triangleq -\frac{\frac{s_{t_{k-1}}^2(i,j)}{2\sigma_{w_{l(i,j)}}^2} - \frac{c_{i-i',j-j'} s_{t_{k-1}}(i,j) s_{t_{k-1}}(i',j')}{\sigma_{w_{l(i,j)}}^2} + \frac{s_{t_{k-1}}^2(i',j')}{2\sigma_{w_{l(i',j')}}^2} + \sum_{(m,n) \in c_l} \tilde{V}_{c_l}^{(m,n)}(L_{t_k}, L_{t_{k-1}})}{T(t_k)}$$

and

$$\tilde{V}_{c_l}^{(m,n)}(L_{t_k}, L_{t_{k-1}})$$
$$= V_{c_l}(l(m,n), \{l_{t_k}(p,q): (p,q) > (m,n)\}, \{l_{t_{k-1}}(p,q): (p,q) < (m,n)\}).$$

Now we present the main theorem.

Theorem 4: If the following conditions are satisfied:

a) $\sum_{kl} |c_{kl}^l| = \rho < 1, \forall l$;
b) let $T(t) \to 0$ as $t \to \infty$; and
c) $T(t) \geq C/\log(1 + k(t))$ where C is a sufficiently large positive constant that is specified in the Appendix;

then for any starting configuration S_{-1}, L_{-1}, we have

$$p(S_t, L_t | S_{-1}, L_{-1}, R) \to \pi_0(S, L), \quad \text{as } t \to \infty$$

where $\pi_0(\cdot, \cdot)$ is the uniform distribution over the MAP solutions and $k(t)$ is the iteration number of sweeps up to time t.

Proof: See the Appendix.

2) Parallel Simulated Annealing Procedure: As pointed out in [3], [13], stochastic relaxation converges very slowly to the optimal solution because of the logarithmic temperature cooling schedule. In [3], it was suggested that simulated annealing can be implemented in an asynchronous parallel machine, a so-called multiple-instruction multiple-data (MIMD) machine, to speed up the processing. However, an MIMD machine is rather difficult to implement

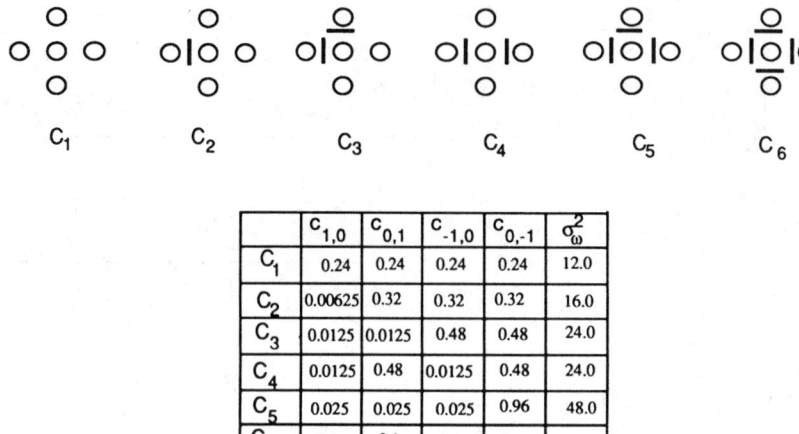

	$c_{1,0}$	$c_{0,1}$	$c_{-1,0}$	$c_{0,-1}$	σ_ω^2
C_1	0.24	0.24	0.24	0.24	12.0
C_2	0.00625	0.32	0.32	0.32	16.0
C_3	0.0125	0.0125	0.48	0.48	24.0
C_4	0.0125	0.48	0.0125	0.48	24.0
C_5	0.025	0.025	0.025	0.96	48.0
C_6	0.1	0.1	0.1	0.1	192.0

Fig. 3. Model coefficients c_{kl} of upper level random fields.

and use compared with a single-instruction multiple-data (SIMD) machine. To guarantee the convergence of simulated annealing in an SIMD machine, a coding scheme has been employed by Murray, *et al.* in [14]. The total speedup depends on the size k of the neighborhood of the Markov random field. In theory, we can have $2N^2/k$ speedup if we have enough processors where N^2 is the total number of pixels.

Naturally, the following question will be raised: "Could stochastic relaxation be implemented in a fully parallel way?" Here, the fully parallel processing of the stochastic relaxation method means that one could update the whole image simultaneously based on the previous iteration results. Unfortunately, the answer to the question is negative. Basically, this procedure does not work because the random field thus created at each iteration does not obey the *a posteriori* density function of the original Markov random field. Hence we expect that the whole procedure may still converge but not to a MAP estimate. A good example is given in [6] showing that fully parallel processing of the Gibbs sampler (which is the special case of simulated annealing with the temperature held constant) for Gauss–Markov random fields does not work, and hence it must also fail in the case of simulated annealing.

V. Simulation Results

Now we present image estimate results based on compound Gauss–Markov (CGM) random fields by using simulated annealing. The image size is 256×256. A Wiener filter estimate based on a conventional LSI Gauss–Markov random field is also computed for comparison. As mentioned in the previous section, CGM models have constrained model coefficients as described in (21), and consequently, difficulties will arise in parameter identification. Often, parameters obtained from a real image by using least-squares methods do not satisfy constraints. Although a consistent set of solutions for model coefficients may be obtained by brute force, i.e., using an update nonlinear programming technique, it will be computationally involved. One way to get around this problem is to modify identification results from the least squares method to make these solutions consistent. Another way is to assign a set of consistent model coefficients that seems reasonable, as was done in [3]. Here we use the latter approach to obtain a consistent set of model coefficients for our simulations. The values of our model coefficients for the upper level fields (up to rotational symmetry) are shown in Fig. 3. The potential functions V_c of our line field are shown in Fig. 2 and are the same as [3].

We consider the unblurred image estimation problem in white Gaussian noise at SNR = 10 dB. An original lady's face image is shown in Fig. 4(a). Fig. 4(b) shows the 10-dB noisy image. Fig. 4(c) shows a Wiener filter result

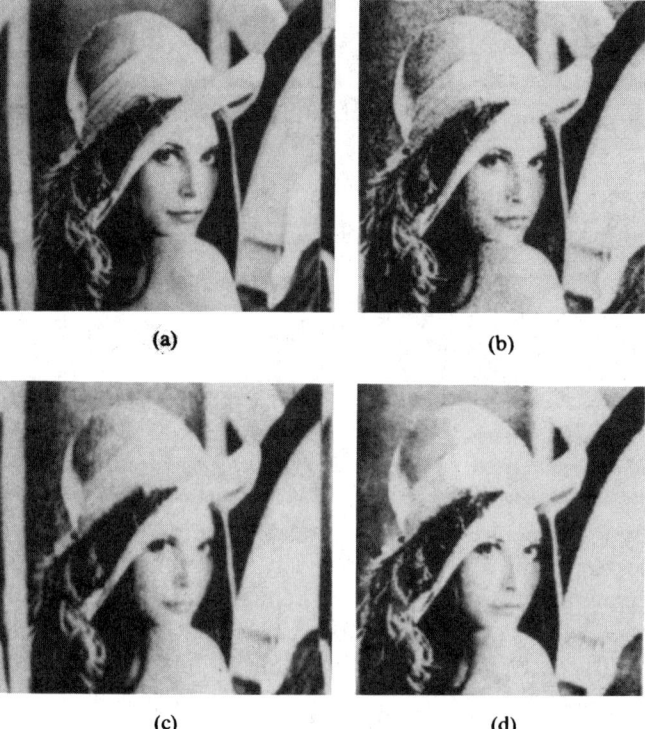

Fig. 4. (a) Original lady's face image. (b) Noisy image with SNR = 10 dB. (c) Wiener filter result for LSI Gauss–Markov model. (d) Simulated annealing result for CGM model at 200 iterations.

obtained using a first-order Gauss–Markov model. Fig. 4(d) shows a filtering result from simulated annealing using a first-order CGM model and 200 iterations. It is clearly seen that CGM models can produce better visual quality compared with LSI Gauss–Markov models.

VI. CONCLUSION

Compound random field models are more appropriate than simple Gauss–Markov models for image estimation. Although compound models are better, it is in general difficult to find an analytic solution. Simulated annealing is a very good tool for finding optimal estimates for these compound models. The work reported in this paper provides theoretical support for the convergence of simulated annealing on CGM models.

Future work is needed to extend our convergence proof to CGM models without a constraint on the sum of absolute values of the model coefficients. Also, parameter identification for valid CGM model coefficient sets is an important issue to be solved.

ACKNOWLEDGMENT

The authors wish to thank Prof. Azriel Rosenfeld for providing access to the computer facilities while F.-C. Jeng was visiting at the Center for Automation Research, University of Maryland.

APPENDIX

We now present the proof of Theorems 3 and 4. Before presenting these proofs, we give norm definitions and lemmas which will be useful later.

Definition [9]: Let x be a vector with components x_i and Q be a matrix with components q_{ij}. We define $\|x\|_\infty$ and $\|Q\|_\infty$ as follows:

$$\|x\|_\infty \triangleq \max_i |x_i|$$

$$\|Q\|_\infty \triangleq \sup_x \frac{\|Qx\|_\infty}{\|x\|_\infty} = \max_i \sum_j |q_{ij}|.$$

Definition [9]: Let x be a vector with components x_i and Q be a matrix with components q_{ij}. We define $\|x\|_2$ and $\|Q\|_2$ as follows:

$$\|x\|_2 \triangleq \left(\sum_i |x_i|^2 \right)^{1/2}$$

$$\|Q\|_2 \triangleq \sup_x \frac{\|Qx\|_2}{\|x\|_2} = \max_i (\lambda_i)^{1/2}$$

where the λ_i are the eigenvalues of matrix QQ^T.

Lemma 1: If $\sum_{k,l} |c^l_{k,l}| < 1$, $\forall l$, then

$$\left\| (I - C^l_+)^{-1} C^l_- \right\|_\infty < 1$$

where C^l_+, C^l_- are previously defined (just after (27)).

Proof: For purposes of our proof, we assume that the value of the image boundary is zero. First, define the matrix A as

$$A \triangleq (I - C^l_+)^{-1} C^l_-.$$

From the definition of matrix norm, we only need to prove that

$$\max_i \sum_j |a_{i,j}| < 1.$$

We will prove this by induction. Since we use raster scanning, i can be represented as $i = (m'-1)N + n'$ for $1 \le m' \le N$ and $1 \le n' \le N$.

1) For $(m', n') = (1,1)$, i.e., $i = 1$, we have

$$\sum_{(p,q)} |a_{1,(p-1)N+q}| = \sum_{k,l \in \mathcal{R}} |c^{l(1,1)}_{k,l}| < 1$$

(from the given conditions).

2) For all $(m', n') < (m, n)$ (i.e., $\{m' < m$ or $m' = m, n' < n\}$), i.e., $i = (m'-1)N + n'$, we assume that the following inequality holds:

$$\sum_{(p,q)} |a_{(m'-1)N+n',(p-1)N+q}| < 1.$$

3) Next we show that, for $i = (m-1)N + n$, we have

$$\sum_{(p,q)} |a_{i,(p-1)N+q}| < 1.$$

First note that

$$\sum_{(p,q)} a_{(m-1)N+n,(p-1)N+q} s_{t_k-1}(p,q)$$

$$= \frac{\sigma_r^2}{\sigma_r^2 + \sigma_{w_{t_k}(m,n)}^2} \left(\sum_{(k,l) \in \mathcal{R}_{--}} c^{l_{t_k}(m-k,n-l)}_{k,l} s_{t_k-1}(m-k, n-l) \right.$$

$$\left. + \sum_{(k,l) \in \mathcal{R}_{++}} c^{l_{t_k}(m-k,n-l)}_{k,l} s_{t_k}(m-k, n-l) \right) \text{ (by definition)}$$

$$= \frac{\sigma_r^2}{\sigma_r^2 + \sigma_{w_{t_k}(m,n)}^2} \left(\sum_{(k,l) \in \mathcal{R}_{--}} c^{l_{t_k}(m,n)}_{k,l} s_{t_k-1}(m-k, n-l) \right.$$

$$\left. + \sum_{(k,l) \in \mathcal{R}_{++}} c^{l_{t_k}(m,n)}_{k,l} \left(\sum_{(c,d)} a_{(m-k-1)N+n-l,(c-1)N+d} s_{t_k-1}(c,d) \right) \right)$$

·(substituting for s_{t_k})

where the previous relations come from the simulated annealing procedure. Hence

$$\sum_{(p,q)} |a_{(m-1)N+n,(p-1)N+q}| \leq \frac{\sigma_r^2}{\sigma_r^2 + \sigma_{w_{l_k(m,n)}}^2} \left(\sum_{(k,l) \in \mathcal{R}} |c_{k,l}^{l_k}{}^{(m,n)}| \right.$$

$$\left. + \sum_{(k,l) \in \mathcal{R}_{++}} |c_{k,l}^{l_k}{}^{(m,n)}| \left(\sum_{(c,d)} |a_{(m+k-1)N+n-l,(c-1)N+d}| \right) \right)$$

(by the triangle inequality)

$$\leq \sum_{(k,l) \in \mathcal{R}} |c_{k,l}^{l_k}{}^{(m,n)}| + \sum_{(k,l) \in \mathcal{R}_{++}} |c_{k,l}^{l_k}{}^{(m,n)}|$$

$$\cdot \left(\sum_{(c,d)} |a_{(m+k-1)N+n-l,(c-1)N+d}| \right)$$

$$\cdot \left(\text{since } \frac{\sigma_r^2}{\sigma_r^2 + \sigma_{w_{l_k(m,n)}}^2} \leq 1 \right)$$

$$\leq \sum_{(k,l) \in \mathcal{R}} |c_{k,l}^{l_k}{}^{(m,n)}| + \sum_{(k,l) \in \mathcal{R}_{++}} |c_{k,l}^{l_k}{}^{(m,n)}|$$

$$\cdot \left(\text{since } \sum_{(c,d)} |a_{(m+k-1)N+n-l,(c-1)N+d}| \leq 1 \ \forall (k,l) \in \mathcal{R}_{++} \right)$$

$$< 1$$

from the given conditions. □

Lemma 2: Assume $\boldsymbol{B}$ is a d-dimensional positive definite matrix with eigenvalues $\lambda_1 \geq \lambda_2 \geq \cdots \geq \lambda_d > 0$ and $\boldsymbol{B} = \boldsymbol{J}^T \Lambda \boldsymbol{J}$ where Λ is a diagonal matrix that carries of the eigenvalues. Then

$$\frac{1}{\sqrt{(2\pi)^d |\boldsymbol{B}|}} \int_{\|x\|_2 > b} e^{-(x^T \boldsymbol{B}^{-1} x)/2} \, d\boldsymbol{x} \geq q \left(\frac{b}{\sqrt{\lambda_d}} \right)^{d-2} e^{-b^2/2\lambda_d}$$

where the constant q does not depend on b.

Proof:

$$\frac{1}{\sqrt{(2\pi)^d |\boldsymbol{B}|}} \int_{\|x\|_2 > b} e^{-(x^T \boldsymbol{B}^{-1} x)/2} \, d\boldsymbol{x}$$

$$= \frac{1}{\sqrt{(2\pi)^d \lambda_1 \lambda_2 \cdots \lambda_d}} \int_{\|x'\|_2 > b} e^{-(x'^T \Lambda^{-1} x')/2} \, d\boldsymbol{x}'$$

$$\cdot (x' = \boldsymbol{J}\boldsymbol{x}, \boldsymbol{J} \text{ is unitary})$$

$$= \frac{1}{\sqrt{(2\pi)^d \lambda_1 \lambda_2 \cdots \lambda_d}} \int_{\|x'\|_2 > b} \exp\left(-\sum_{i=1}^d \frac{x_i'^2}{2\lambda_i} \right) d\boldsymbol{x}'$$

$$= \frac{1}{\sqrt{(2\pi)^d}} \int_{\sum_i \lambda_i x_i''^2 > b^2} \exp\left(-\sum_{i=1}^d \frac{x_i''^2}{2} \right) d\boldsymbol{x}''$$

$$\cdot \left(x'' = x'/\sqrt{\lambda_i} \right)$$

$$\geq \frac{1}{\sqrt{(2\pi)^d}} \int_{\lambda_d \sum_i x_i''^2 > b^2} \exp\left(-\sum_{i=1}^d \frac{x_i''^2}{2} \right) d\boldsymbol{x}''$$

$$= q \int_{r > b/\sqrt{\lambda_d}} r^{d-1} e^{-r^2/2} \, dr$$

(using a d-dimensional polar coordinate transformation)

$$\geq q \left(\frac{b}{\sqrt{\lambda_d}} \right)^{d-2} e^{-b^2/2\lambda_d}$$

(Q function approximation [18]). □

A. Proof of Theorem 3

The proof can be divided into two parts. The first part shows that there exists an integer $\tilde{m}$ which depends on f such that

$$P_n^m f(s) \geq \epsilon g_{n+m}(s), \qquad \forall m \geq \tilde{m}.$$

The second part shows that

$$\|P_0^{i\tilde{m}}(f_1 - f_2)\|_1 \leq \prod_{j=1}^i \left(1 - \|h_{m_j}\|_1 \right)$$

where $h_{m_j} \triangleq \epsilon g_{m_j}$ and $m_j = j\tilde{m}$ and $0 < \epsilon < 1$ will be determined later. Hence, by the given condition, i.e., $\sum_{j=1}^\infty \|g_{m_j}\|_1 = \infty$, we can reach the conclusion.

Part 1: This part of proof is a modification of the proof of [10, theorem 5.7.1]. First define the function

$$E_n^m(V|f) \triangleq \int_\Omega V(s) P_n^m f(s) \, ds,$$

which can be thought of as the expected value of $V(s)$ with respect to the density $P_n^m f(s)$. By the definition of $P_n^m f$, we have directly

$$E_n^m(V|f) = \int_\Omega V(s) \, ds \int_\Omega p_{n+m}(s|t) P_n^{m-1} f(t) \, dt \quad (30)$$

$$= \int_\Omega P_n^{m-1} f(t) \, dt \int_\Omega p_{n+m}(s|t) V(s) \, ds. \quad (31)$$

Substituting (10) into (31) then yields

$$E_n^m(V|f) \leq \int_\Omega P_n^{m-1} f(t)[\beta + \alpha V(t)]\, dt$$
$$= \beta + \alpha \int_\Omega P_n^{m-1} f(t) V(t)\, dt$$
$$= \beta + \alpha E_n^{m-1}(V|f).$$

By an induction argument, it is easy to show that from this equation, we obtain

$$E_n^m(V|f) \leq \frac{\beta}{1-\alpha} + \alpha^m E_n^0(V|f).$$

Even though $E_n^0(V|f)$ is clearly dependent on our initial choice of f, it is equally clear that, for every f such that

$$E_n^0(V|f) < \infty,$$

there is some integer $\tilde{m} = \tilde{m}(f)$ such that

$$E_n^m(V|f) \leq [\beta/(1-\alpha)] + 1, \quad \text{for all } m \geq \tilde{m} - 1.$$

Now let

$$\Omega_a \triangleq \{ s \in \Omega : V(s) < a \},$$

so that from the Chebyshev inequality, we have

$$\int_{\Omega_a} P_n^m f(s)\, ds \geq 1 - \frac{E_n^m(V|f)}{a}. \tag{32}$$

Further, choose

$$a > 1 + [\beta/(1-\alpha)];$$

then

$$\frac{E_n^m(V|f)}{a} \leq \frac{1}{a}\left(1 + \frac{\beta}{1-\alpha}\right) < 1, \quad \text{for } m \geq \tilde{m} - 1,$$

and thus (32) becomes

$$\int_{\Omega_a} P_n^m f(s)\, ds \geq 1 - \frac{1}{a}\left(1 + \frac{\beta}{1-\alpha}\right) \triangleq \epsilon > 0, \quad \text{for } m \geq \tilde{m} - 1.$$

Since $V(s) \to \infty$ as $\|s\| \to \infty$, there is an $r > 0$ such that $V(s) > a$ for $\|s\| > r$. Thus the set Ω_a is entirely contained in the ball $\|s\| \leq r$, and we may write

$$P_n^{m+1} f(s) = \int_\Omega p_{n+m+1}(s|t) P_n^m f(t)\, dt$$
$$\geq \int_{\Omega_a} p_{n+m+1}(s|t) P_n^m f(t)\, dt$$
$$\geq \inf_{t \in \Omega_a} p_{n+m+1}(s|t) \int_{\Omega_a} P_n^m f(t)\, dt$$
$$= \inf_{\|t\| \leq r} p_{n+m+1}(s|t) \int_{\Omega_a} P_n^m f(t)\, dt$$
$$\geq \epsilon \inf_{\|t\| \leq r} p_{n+m+1}(s|t), \quad \text{for all } m \geq \tilde{m} - 1. \tag{33}$$

By setting

$$g_m(s) = \inf_{\|t\| \leq r} p_m(s|t),$$

we have

$$P_n^m f(s) \geq \epsilon g_{n+m}(s), \quad \forall m \geq \tilde{m}.$$

Part 2: This part of proof is a modification of the proof of [10, Theorem 5.6.2]. The goal is to show that

$$\|P_0^{i\tilde{m}}(f_1 - f_2)\|_1 \leq \prod_{j=1}^{i}\left(1 - \|h_{m_j}\|_1\right).$$

First we show that for every pair of densities $f_1, f_2 \in D$, the $\|P_n^m(f_1 - f_2)\|_1$ is a decreasing function of m for any fixed n. To see this, note that, every Markov operator is contractive, i.e.,

$$\|P_n f\|_1 \leq \|f\|_1,$$

and, as a consequence,

$$\|P_n^{l+m} f\|_1 \leq \|P_n^m f\|_1.$$

Now set $g \triangleq f_1 - f_2$ and note that, since $f_1, f_2 \in D$,

$$c \triangleq \|g^+\|_1 = \|g^-\|_1 = \|g\|_1/2.$$

Assume $c > 0$. We have $g = g^+ - g^-$ and

$$\|P_n^m g\|_1 = c\|(P_n^m(g^+/c) - h_{n+m}) - (P_n^m(g^-/c) - h_{n+m})\|_1 \tag{34}$$

where $g^+ \triangleq \max(0, g)$ and $(g)^- \triangleq -\min(0, g)$. Since g^+/c and g^-/c belong to D, there must exist an integer $\tilde{m}$ such that for all $m \geq \tilde{m}$

$$P_n^m(g^+/c)(s) \geq h_{n+m}(s) \quad \text{and} \quad P_n^m(g^-/c)(s) \geq h_{n+m}(s). \tag{35}$$

Hence $\|(P_n^m(g^+/c) - h_{n+m})\|_1$ and $\|(P_n^m(g^-/c) - h_{n+m})\|_1$ can be expressed as follows:

$$\|(P_n^m(g^+/c) - h_{n+m})\|_1$$
$$\triangleq \int_\Omega |P_n^m(g^+/c)(s) - h_{n+m}(s)|\, ds$$
$$= \int_\Omega (P_n^m(g^+/c)(s) - h_{n+m}(s))\, ds \quad \text{(from (35))}$$
$$= \int_\Omega P_n^m(g^+/c)(s)\, ds - \int_\Omega h_{n+m}(s)\, ds$$
$$= \|P_n^m(g^+/c)\|_1 - \|h_{n+m}\|_1$$
$$= 1 - \|h_{n+m}\|_1, \quad \text{for } m \geq \tilde{m}.$$

Analogously,

$$\|(P_n^m(g^-/c) - h_{n+m})\|_1 = 1 - \|h_{n+m}\|_1, \quad \text{for } m \geq \tilde{m}.$$

Thus (34) gives

$$\|P_n^m g\|_1 \leq c\|(P_n^m(g^+/c) - h_{n+m})\|_1 + c\|(P_n^m(g^-/c) - h_{n+m})\|_1$$
$$= 2c(1 - \|h_{n+m}\|_1)$$
$$= \|g\|_1(1 - \|h_{n+m}\|_1), \quad \text{for } m \geq \tilde{m}. \tag{36}$$

From (36), for any $f_1, f_2 \in D$, we can find an integer $\tilde{m}$ such that

$$\|P_n^{\tilde{m}}(f_1 - f_2)\|_1 \leq \|f_1 - f_2\|_1(1 - \|h_{n+\tilde{m}}\|_1).$$

By applying the same argument, we have

$$\|P_0^{i\tilde{m}}(f_1 - f_2)\|_1 \leq \|P_0^{(i-1)\tilde{m}}(f_1 - f_2)\|_1 (1 - \|h_{m_i}\|_1)$$
$$\leq \|f_1 - f_2\|_1 \prod_{j=1}^{i}\left(1 - \|h_{m_j}\|_1\right)$$

where $m_j = j\tilde{m}$. Since we have

$$\sum_{j=1}^{\infty} \|h_{m_j}\|_1 = \infty,$$

this implies
$$\lim_{m \to \infty} \| P_0^{m}(f_1 - f_2) \|_1 = 0. \qquad \square$$

B. Proof of Theorem 4

We prove that the simulated annealing algorithm converges for a broad class of CGM models. The proof of this theorem essentially has two parts. The first part is to prove the convergence of the simulated annealing algorithm using Theorem 3. The second part proves that it actually converges to the MAP estimate. This part is the same as the Gemans' proof [3]. Here, we will not present the proof of this latter part. As described in [3], the sequence generated by simulated annealing is an inhomogeneous Markov sequence and hence showing convergence of simulated annealing is the same as showing that this Markov sequence is asymptotically stable. Therefore, to prove this theorem, we need only check that this Markov sequence satisfies the sufficient conditions of Theorem 3. The proof of this part consists of two steps. Step 1 shows that (10) holds, and Step 2 shows that (11) holds. Then convergence follows from Theorem 3.

Step 1: Show that

$$\sum_{L_{t_k}} \int_{S_{t_k}} V(S_{t_k}, L_{t_k}) p(S_{t_k}, L_{t_k} | S_{t_{k-1}}, L_{t_{k-1}}, R) \, dS_{t_k}$$
$$\leq \beta + \alpha V(S_{t_{k-1}}, L_{t_{k-1}}) \qquad (37)$$

where $V(S, L)$ is the Liapunov function

$$V(S, L) \triangleq V_1(S) + V_2(L)$$

$$V_1(S) \triangleq \|S\|_\infty \triangleq \max_{(m,n)} |s(m,n)|$$

$$V_2(L) \triangleq \|L\|_\infty \triangleq \max_{(m,n)} |l(m,n)|.$$

We first establish (37) for $V_1(S)$ in Step 1.1, then for $V_2(L)$ in Step 1.2, and then combine both these results to get (37).

Step 1.1: Show that

$$\int_R V_1(S_{t_k}) p(S_{t_k} | S_{t_{k-1}}, L_{t_k}, R) \, dS_{t_k} \leq \beta_1 + \alpha V_1(S_{t_{k-1}}), \qquad \forall L_{t_k}$$

where $0 \leq \beta_1 < \infty$, and $0 < \alpha < 1$.

Proof: From (27), we have

$$\int_\Omega V_1(S_{t_k}) p(S_{t_k} | S_{t_{k-1}}, L_{t_k}, R) \, dS_{t_k}$$
$$= \int_\Omega \|S_{t_k}\|_\infty p(S_{t_k} | S_{t_{k-1}}, L_{t_k}, R) \, dS_{t_k}$$
$$= \int_\Omega \|S'_{t_k} + A S_{t_{k-1}} + QR\|_\infty \frac{1}{Z_6}$$
$$\cdot \exp\left\{-\frac{1}{2T(t_k)} [S'_{t_k}]^T Q^{-1}(t_k) [S'_{t_k}]\right\} dS'_{t_k}$$

(by change of variables)

$$\leq \int_\Omega (\|S'_{t_k}\|_\infty + \|A S_{t_{k-1}}\|_\infty + \|QR\|_\infty) \frac{1}{Z_6}$$
$$\cdot \exp\left\{-\frac{1}{2T(t_k)} [S'_{t_k}]^T Q^{-1}(t_k) [S'_{t_k}]\right\} dS'_{t_k}$$

(by triangle inequality)

$$\leq \int_\Omega (\|S'_{t_k}\|_2 + \|A S_{t_{k-1}}\|_\infty + \|QR\|_\infty) \frac{1}{Z_6}$$
$$\cdot \exp\left\{-\frac{1}{2T(t_k)} [S'_{t_k}]^T Q^{-1}(t_k) [S'_{t_k}]\right\} dS'_{t_k}$$

(because $\|S\|_2 \geq \|S\|_\infty$)

$$\leq [T(t_k)]^{1/2} [Tr(Q)]^{1/2} + \|QR\|_\infty + \|A\|_\infty \|S_{t_{k-1}}\|_\infty$$
$$\leq \beta_1 + \|A\|_\infty V_1(S_{t_{k-1}})$$
$$= \beta_1 + \alpha V_1(S_{t_{k-1}})$$

where

$$Tr(Q) \triangleq \sum_i^{N^2} q_{ii}$$

$$\alpha \triangleq \max_L \|A\|_\infty$$

and

$$\beta_1 \triangleq \sup_{T(t_k)} \max_L \left[[T(t_k)]^{1/2} [Tr(Q)]^{1/2} + \|QR\|_\infty\right].$$

From Lemma 1, we have

$$0 < \alpha < 1.$$

Since the temperature $T(t_k)$ decreases to zero as $k \to \infty$, we also have

$$0 \leq \beta_1 < \infty. \qquad \square$$

Step 1.2: Show that

$$\sum_{L_{t_k}} P(L_{t_k} | L_{t_{k-1}}, S_{t_{k-1}}) V_2(L_{t_k}) \leq \beta_1 + \alpha V_2(L_{t_{k-1}})$$

Proof: Since L_{t_k} has only a finite number of levels, choosing β_1 big enough, the above inequality obviously holds.

Proof of Step 1: Set $\beta = \beta_1 + \beta_2$ and $\alpha < 1$. Then

$$\sum_{L_{t_k}} \int_{S_{t_k}} V(S_{t_k}, L_{t_k}) p(S_{t_k}, L_{t_k} | S_{t_{k-1}}, L_{t_{k-1}}, R) \, dS_{t_k}$$

$$= \sum_{L_{t_k}} \int_{S_{t_k}} (V_1(S_{t_k}) + V_2(L_{t_k})) p(S_{t_k} | S_{t_{k-1}}, L_{t_k}, R) P(L_{t_k} | S_{t_{k-1}}, L_{t_{k-1}}) \, dS_{t_k}$$

$$= \sum_{L_{t_k}} \int_{S_{t_k}} V_1(S_{t_k}) p(S_{t_k} | S_{t_{k-1}}, L_{t_k}, R) P(L_{t_k} | S_{t_{k-1}}, L_{t_{k-1}}) \, dS_{t_k} + \sum_{L_{t_k}} \int_{S_{t_k}} V_2(L_{t_k}) p(S_{t_k} | S_{t_{k-1}}, L_{t_k}, R) P(L_{t_k} | S_{t_{k-1}}, L_{t_{k-1}}) \, dS_{t_k}$$

$$\leq \beta_1 + \alpha V_1(S_{t_{k-1}}) + \beta_2 + \alpha V_2(L_{t_{k-1}}) \qquad \text{(from Steps 1.1 and 1.2)}$$

$$= \beta + \alpha V(S_{t_{k-1}}, L_{t_{k-1}}). \qquad \square$$

Step 2: Show that if temperature $T(t)$ decreases as $C_T/\log(1+k(t))$, then for any $n_0 > 0$, we have

$$\sum_{m=1}^{\infty} \|h_{mt_{n_0}}\|_1 = \infty$$

where C_T is a constant and $k(t)$ is the iteration number of sweeps up to time t.

Proof: This result can be obtained by establishing the lower bound for $\|h_{t_k}\|_1$. First recall that

$$h_{t_k} = \inf_{(S_{t_{k-1}}, L_{t_{k-1}}) \in R_a} p(S_{t_k}, L_{t_k} | S_{t_{k-1}}, L_{t_{k-1}}, R)$$

where R_a is defined as

$$R_a \triangleq \{(S, L): V(S, L) \leq a\}.$$

By definition of L_1 norm, we have

$$\|h_{t_k}\|_1 = \sum_{l_{t_k}} \int \inf_{(S_{t_{k-1}}, L_{t_{k-1}}) \in R_a} p(S_{t_k}, L_{t_k} | S_{t_{k-1}}, L_{t_{k-1}}, R) \, dS_{t_k}.$$

From (25), we have

$$\|h_{t_k}\|_1 = \sum_{l_{t_k}} \int \inf_{(S_{t_{k-1}}, L_{t_{k-1}}) \in R_a} p(S_{t_k} | S_{t_{k-1}}, R) \, dS_{t_k}$$

$$= \sum_{l_{t_k}} \int \inf_{(S_{t_{k-1}}, L_{t_{k-1}}) \in R_a} p(S_{t_k} | S_{t_{k-1}}, L_{t_{k-1}}, R)$$

$$\cdot P(L_{t_k} | S_{t_{k-1}}, L_{t_{k-1}}) \, dS_{t_k}$$

$$\geq \inf_{l_{t_k}} \left[\inf_{(S_{t_{k-1}}, L_{t_{k-1}}) \in R_a} P(L_{t_k} | S_{t_{k-1}}, L_{t_{k-1}}) \right.$$

$$\left. \cdot \int \inf_{(S_{t_{k-1}}, L_{t_{k-1}}) \in R_a} p(S_{t_k} | S_{t_{k-1}}, L_{t_k}, R) \, dS_{t_k} \right]$$

$$\geq \inf_{(L_{t_k}, L_{t_{k-1}})} \inf_{\|S_{t_{k-1}}\|_\infty \leq a} \left[P(L_{t_k} | S_{t_{k-1}}, L_{t_{k-1}}) \right]$$

$$\cdot \inf_{l_{t_k}} \left[\int \inf_{\|S_{t_{k-1}}\|_\infty \leq a} p(S_{t_k} | S_{t_{k-1}}, L_{t_k}, R) \, dS_{t_k} \right]. \quad (38)$$

Since

$$P(L_{t_k} | S_{t_{k-1}}, L_{t_{k-1}}) = \prod \pi_{t_k}^l(m, n)$$

(from (28)), we need to have a lower bound for $\pi_{t_k}^l(m, n)$ to obtain a lower bound for $P(L_{t_k} | S_{t_{k-1}}, L_{t_{k-1}})$. Denoting

$$\delta_{\min} \triangleq \inf_{\|S\|_\infty \leq a, l} \left(\frac{s^2(i,j)}{2\sigma^2_{w_{R(i,j)}}} - \frac{c_{i-i',j-j'}(i,j)s(i',j')}{\sigma^2_{w_{R(i,j)}}} \right.$$

$$\left. + \frac{s^2(i',j')}{2\sigma^2_{w_{R(i',j')}}} + \sum_{(m,n) \in c_l} V_{c_l}(L) \right)$$

$$\delta_{\max} \triangleq \sup_{\|S\|_\infty \leq a, l} \left(\frac{s^2(i,j)}{2\sigma^2_{w_{R(i,j)}}} - \frac{c_{i-i',j-j'}s(i,j)s(i',j')}{\sigma^2_{w_{R(i,j)}}} \right.$$

$$\left. + \frac{s_2(i',j')}{2\sigma^2_{R(i',j')}} + \sum_{(m,n) \in c_l} V_{c_l}(L) \right),$$

and from (29), we have

$$\pi_{t_k}^l(m, n) = \frac{e^{\Phi_{t_k}(l(m,n))}}{\sum_{l(m,n)} e^{\Phi_{t_k}(l(m,n))}}$$

$$\geq \frac{e^{\delta_{\max}/T(t_k)}}{\sum_{l(m,n)} e^{\delta_{\min}/T(t_k)}}$$

$$= \frac{1}{M} e^{\Delta/T(t_k)}, \quad \forall \|S_{t_{k-1}}\|_\infty \leq a$$

where M is the number of levels for the line field l and

$$\Delta \triangleq \delta_{\max} - \delta_{\min}.$$

Therefore,

$$\inf_{(L_{t_k}, L_{t_{k-1}})} \inf_{\|S_{t_{k-1}}\|_\infty \leq a} P(L_{t_k} | S_{t_{k-1}}, L_{t_{k-1}})$$

$$= \inf_{(L_{t_k}, L_{t_{k-1}})} \inf_{\|S_{t_{k-1}}\|_\infty \leq a} \prod \pi_{t_k, l}^l(m, n)$$

$$\geq \left(\frac{1}{M} e^{\Delta/T(t_k)}\right)^{N^2}$$

$$= C_2 e^{C_1/T(t_k)}$$

where

$$C_1 \triangleq N'^2 \Delta \qquad C_2 \triangleq \left(\frac{1}{M}\right)^{N^2}.$$

Hence, from (38), we have

$$\|h_{t_k}\|_1 \geq C_2 e^{C_1/T(t_k)} \inf_{l_{t_k}} \left[\int \inf_{\|S_{t_{k-1}}\|_\infty \leq a} p(S_{t_k} | S_{t_{k-1}}, L_{t_k}, R) \, dS_{t_k} \right]. \quad (39)$$

Now from (27),

$$p(S_{t_k} | S_{t_{k-1}}, L_{t_k}, R) = \frac{1}{Z_0} \exp\left\{ -\frac{1}{2T(t_k)} [S_{t_{k-1}} - AS_{t_{k-1}} - Q_1 R]^T \right.$$

$$\left. \cdot Q^{-1}(t_k)[S_{t_{k-1}} - AS_{t_{k-1}} - Q_1 R] \right\}$$

it can be shown that there exists a finite number b with $b \gg a$ such that

$$\int \inf_{\|S_{t_{k-1}}\|_\infty \leq a} p(S_{t_k} | S_{t_{k-1}}, L_{t_k}, R) \, dS_{t_k}$$

$$\geq \frac{1}{\left[(2\pi)^d T(t_k) |Q(t_k)|\right]^{1/2}}$$

$$\cdot \int_{\|S_{t_k}\|_2 > b} \exp\left[-\frac{1}{2T(t_k)} S_{t_k}^T Q^{-1}(t_k) S_{t_k} \right] dS_{t_k}.$$

From Lemma 2, we can establish the following inequality.

$$\frac{1}{\left[(2\pi)^d T(t_k) |Q(t_k)|\right]^{1/2}}$$

$$\cdot \int_{\|S_{t_k}\|_2 > b} \exp\left[-\frac{1}{2T(t_k)} S_{t_k}^T Q^{-1}(t_k) S_{t_k} \right] dS_{t_k}$$

$$\geq q \left(\frac{b}{\sqrt{T(t_k)\lambda_d}}\right)^{d-2} e^{-b^2/2T(t_k)\lambda_d}$$

where λ_d is the smallest eigenvalue of $Q(t_k)$ and q is a positive constant.[3] Obviously λ_d and b depend on L_{t_k}. Denoting λ_d^* and b^* such that

$$\left(\frac{b^*}{\sqrt{T(t_k)\lambda_d^*}}\right)^{d-2} e^{-b^{*2}/2T(t_k)\lambda_d^*}$$

$$= \inf_{L_{t_k}} \left(\frac{b}{\sqrt{T(t_k)\lambda_d}}\right)^{d-2} e^{-b^2/2T(t_k)\lambda_d},$$

we have

$$\|h_{t_k}\|_1 \geq C_2 e^{-c_1/T(t_k)} q \left(\frac{b^*}{\sqrt{T(t_k)\lambda_d^*}}\right)^{d-2} e^{-b^{*2}/2T(t_k)\lambda_d^*}.$$

Finally, we obtain the lower bound for $\|h_{t_k}\|_1$ for temperature $T(t_k) = C_T/\log(1+k)$ as follows:

$$\|h_{t_k}\|_1 \geq \frac{C^*(\log(1+k))^{(d-2)/2}}{1+k}$$

where

$$C^* \triangleq C_2 q \left(\frac{b^*}{\sqrt{C_T \lambda_d^*}}\right)^{d-2} \qquad C_T \triangleq C_1 + \frac{b^{*2}}{2\lambda_d^*}.$$

Therefore,

$$\sum_{m=1}^{\infty} \|h_{mt_{n_0}}\|_1 \geq \sum_{m=1}^{\infty} \left(\frac{C^*(\log(1+mn_0))^{(d-2)/2}}{1+mn_0}\right) = \infty$$

since

$$\sum_{i=1}^{\infty} \frac{C^*(\log(in_0))^{(d-2)/2}}{in_0} \geq \sum_{i=1}^{\infty} \frac{C^*}{in_0} = \infty.$$

---

[3] Note that there are only a finite number of possible different $Q(t_k)$ due to the fact of the line field L_{t_k} has a finite number of different realizations.

REFERENCES

[1] R. L. Dobrushin, "Central limit theorems for nonstationary Markov chains II," *Theory Probab. Appl.*, vol. 1, pp. 329–383, 1954 (English translation).
[2] J. L. Doob, *Stochastic Processes*. New York: Wiley, 1953, pp. 170–291.
[3] S. Geman and D. Geman, "Stochastic relaxation, Gibbs distributions, and the Bayesian restoration of images," *IEEE Trans. Pattern Anal. Machine Intell.*, vol. PAMI-6, pp. 721–741, Nov. 1984.
[4] B. Gidas, "Nonstationary Markov chains and convergence of the annealing algorithm," *J. Statist. Phys.*, vol. 39, pp. 73–131, 1985.
[5] J. M. Hammersley and D. C. Handscomb, *Monte Carlo Methods*. London: Methuen, 1965, pp. 113–126.
[6] F. C. Jeng, "Compound Gauss–Markov random fields for image estimation and restoration," Ph. D. dissertation, Rensselaer Polytech. Inst., Troy, NY, June, 1988.
[7] R. Kashyap and R. Chellappa, "Estimation and choice of neighbors in spatial-interaction models of images," *IEEE Trans. Inform. Theory*, vol. IT-29, pp. 60–72, Jan. 1983.
[8] S. Kirkpatrick, C. D. Gelatt, and M. P. Vecchi, "Optimization by simulated annealing," *Science*, vol. 220, pp. 671–680, May 1983.
[9] E. Kreyszig, *Introductory Functional Analysis with Applications*. New York: Wiley, 1978, pp. 102–103.
[10] A. Lasota and M. C. Mackey, *Probabilistic Properties on Deterministic Systems*. New York: Cambridge Univ. Press, 1985.
[11] R. W. Madsen and D. L. Isaacson, "Strongly ergodic behavior for nonstationary Markov processes," *Ann. Probab.*, vol. 1, No. 2, pp. 329–335, 1973.
[12] N. Metropolis, A. W. Rosenbluth, M. N. Rosenbluth, A. H. Teller, and E. Teller, "Equations of state calculations by fast computing machines," *J. Chem. Phys.*, vol. 21, pp. 1087–1092, 1953.
[13] D. Mitra, F. Romeo, and A. Sangiovanni-Vincentelli, "Convergence and finite-time behavior of simulated annealing," *Adv. Appl. Probab.*, vol. 18, pp. 747–771, 1986.
[14] D. W. Murray, A. Kashko, and H. Buxton, "A parallel approach to the picture restoration algorithm of Geman and Geman on an SIMD machine," *Image Vision Comput.*, vol. 4, pp. 133–142, Aug. 1986.
[15] M. B. Nevelson and R. Z. Hasminskii, *Stochastic Approximation and Recursive Estimation* (translations of Mathematical Monographs, vol. 47) Providence, RI: Amer. Math. Soc., 1973.
[16] J. W. Woods, S. Dravida, and R. Mediavilla, "Image estimation using doubly stochastic Gaussian random field models," *IEEE Trans. Pattern Anal. Machine Intell.*, vol. PAMI-9, pp. 245–253, Mar. 1987.
[17] J. W. Woods, "Two dimensional discrete Markovian fields," *IEEE Trans. Inform. Theory*, vol. IT-18, pp. 232–240, Mar. 1972.
[18] J. M. Wozencraft and I. M. Jacobs, *Principles of Communication Engineering*. New York: Wiley, 1965, pp. 82.

Pyramid Implementation of Optimal-Step Conjugate-Search Algorithms for Some Low-Level Vision Problems

TAL SIMCHONY, MEMBER, IEEE, RAMALINGAM CHELLAPPA, SENIOR MEMBER, IEEE, AND ZE'EV LICHTENSTEIN

Abstract —Optimization of a cost function arises in several low-level vision problems. The cost functions in these problems are usually derived from discretization of functionals obtained from regularization principles or stochastic estimation techniques using Markov random field models. A parallel pyramid implementation of the line search conjugate gradient algorithm for minimizing the cost functions is presented. By viewing the global cost function as a Gibbs energy function, we efficiently compute the gradients, inner products and the optimal-step size using the pyramid. The global Gibbs energy of a given configuration is broken into its basic energy terms associated with different cliques. The authors let each low-level processor sum the energies associated with its cliques. The local energy terms are added by the intermediate levels of the pyramid to the top, where the step size is determined by an efficient univariate search. Such implementation allows us to calculate the global energy in $O(\log n)$ operations, where n is the number of grid points in each direction. Implementation of this algorithm to shape from shading results in a multiresolution conjugate gradient algorithm. Robustness and efficiency of the algorithm are demonstrated for edge detection using the graduated nonconvexity (GNC) algorithm. The authors also present the usefulness of this formulation to image estimation based on Markov models. A compound model for the original image is defined consisting of a two-dimensional (2-D) noncausal Gauss-Markov random field (GMRF) to represent the homogeneous regions, and a line process to represent the discontinuities. A new deterministic algorithm based on the GNC formulation is derived to obtain a near optimal Maximum aposteriori probability (MAP) estimate of images corrupted by additive Gaussian noise. Since the algorithm depends on the model parameters, a new estimation technique for obtaining the compound GMRF model parameters is derived based on the expectation maximization (EM) algorithm. Experimental results are provided to illustrate the usefulness of this method.

I. INTRODUCTION

MANY physical phenomena that govern the processes that are of interest to researchers in computer vision, can be described by their local characteristics. They are formulated mathematically using differential or integral equations in the deterministic approach, or Markov fields in the stochastic formulation. Examples for the deterministic formulation are the image irradiance equation, the optical flow equation [1], etc. An example for the stochastic formulation is image restoration using Markov random fields models [2]. Computer vision research is usually focused on the inverse problem [3], i.e., given an observation (usually an image, or a sequence of images), find a dense depth map, the velocity field, etc. These problems are in many cases ill posed in the sense of Hadamard [4]. In order to overcome the ill posedness, regularization methods have been suggested [3]. In this approach the original problems are reformulated as optimization problems. Instead of solving the original differential equation exactly, an integral consisting of two elements is constructed. The first element minimizes the mean square error between the observation and the corresponding calculated quantity (from the differential equation). The second term is a penalty term that favors smooth solutions. The desired solution is the minimum of this functional (integral).

There are several ways to obtain the minimum of the functional. One can use calculus of variations to convert the optimization problem into a set of differential equations [5]. This variational approach was extensively explored for the shape from shading (SFS) problem [6], which deals with the reconstruction of the orientation map of a surface from a single image using the irradiance equation. This formulation leads to nonlinear differential equations, which are not easy to solve unless the penalty term in the functional is sufficiently large (the solution is far from the original problem). Alternatively one can use direct optimization [5]. Direct methods discretize the integral in the functional and replace the partial derivatives by finite difference approximations to obtain cost functions of the different attributes' values at all grid points (which we call configurations). In the SFS problem one obtains a cost function on the orientation of the surface at all the grid points. The minimum of this cost function is the desired solution to the SFS problem [7]. Using standard calculus [7], the configuration that sets the gradient of the cost function with respect to the orientation at each grid point to zero is searched for. The same methodology is

Manuscript received September 16, 1988; revised March 30, 1989. This work was partially supported by the NSF Grant No. MIP-84-51010 and matching funds from IBM and AT&T and Hughes Aircraft Company. T. Simchony was supported by ECI Telecom. This work was partially presented at the Second International Conference on Computer Vision, Tampa, FL, December 1988.

The authors are with the University of Southern California, Signal and Image Processing Institute, Dept. of EE-Systems, University Park/MC-0272, Los Angeles, CA 90089.

IEEE Log Number 8930348.

used in [8], leading to a system of sparse nonlinear equations. The solution is obtained via a relaxation method in [7] or a direct method in [8]. The algorithms converge only when the penalty term is large, which yields an oversmoothed solution.

Cost functions also yield a suitable formulation for problems involving discontinuities in the observation or in the reconstructed attribute. An example for this is the weak membrane formulation [9] for the surface interpolation problem. A weak membrane (weak membrane is a membrane that satisfies weak continuity constraints) is fitted to noisy data, and used for edge detection by marking the points where discontinuities in the membrane height occur. The cost function derived using this model is not convex. To find the global minimum of the cost function F, it is suggested that the graduated nonconvexity algorithm (GNC) may be used. The GNC algorithm starts with a convex approximation F^* to the cost function F. Then a whole sequence of cost functions $F^{(P)}$, $0 \le P \le 1$ is constructed, so that $F^{(0)} = F$, the original nonconvex function, and $F^{(1)} = F^*$. In between, $F^{(P)}$ changes continuously, between $F^{(1)}$ and $F^{(0)}$. The GNC algorithm optimizes a whole sequence of $F^{(P)}$, for example $\{F^{(1)}, F^{(1/2)}, F^{(1/4)}, F^{(1/8)}, F^{(1/16)}\}$, one after the other, using the optimal solution of previous optimization step as the starting point for the next. The optimization step is then performed using the sequential over relaxation (SOR) method. The authors report a big degradation in the convergence rate of the SOR method when the processed image is corrupted with excessive noise.

The third cost function formulation is derived from stochastic modeling. When one models a process by a Markov field, and exploits the Gibbs–Markov equivalence theorem, a Gibbs energy function is obtained for the different configurations. As an example consider the problem of image estimation. We assume that the original image is represented by a compound model consisting of a two-dimensional (2-D) noncausal Gauss–Markov random field (GMRF) to represent the homogeneous regions and a line process model to represent the discontinuities (note that GMRF models can be viewed as extended regularization models). This model can also be used for modeling piecewise continuous functions required for surface interpolation and edge detection. The noise is assumed to be additive Gaussian and spatially independent. The objective is the maximum *aposteriori* distribution (MAP) solution, or the configuration that corresponds to the minimum of the Gibbs energy function. This problem illustrates the equivalence between a Gibbs energy function, and the cost functions obtained by direct optimization. Since the Gibbs energy function corresponding to the posterior distribution is not convex it can be minimized using simulated annealing [2], a computationally extensive proposition.

In this paper we propose a unified and practical method for minimizing the cost functions resulting from the deterministic and stochastic formulations described previously. The method exploits the equivalence between direct optimization of a deterministic problem, and the MAP solution using the Markov random fields, through the use of Gibbs energy function, and treats the two problems with the same algorithm. We chose an optimization algorithm [10] that is amenable to parallel computation to cope up with the computational complexity induced by the high-dimensional cost functions. The special structure of Gibbs energy functions is utilized to map the algorithm to a highly parallel implementation. Since in general the cost function is not quadratic, we use an extended version of the original conjugate gradient method—the line search extension proposed by Polak and Ribiere [10]. The algorithm is very efficient in solving high-dimensional unconstrained optimization problems. The complete algorithm is as follows.

- Step 1) Given X_0 compute $G_0 = \nabla f(X_0)$ and set $D_0 = -G_0$.
- Step 2) For $k = 0, 1, \cdots, n-1$:
  a) Set $X_{k+1} = X_k + \alpha_k D_k$ where α_k minimizes $f(X_k + \alpha D_k)$;
  b) Compute $G_{k+1} = \nabla f(X_{k+1})$;
  c) Unless $k = n-1$, set $D_{k+1} = -G_{k+1} + \beta_k D_k$ where
  $$\beta_k = \frac{(G_{k+1} - G_k)^T G_{k+1}}{G_k^T G_k};$$
  d) Check termination criteria.
- Step 3) Replace X_0 by X_n and go back to Step 1).

The use of the algorithm requires computations of inner products in Step 2c), and finding the optimal step in Step 2a). The value of the optimal step depends on the global cost function. We use a pyramid to efficiently calculate the global cost function and the inner products required for computing β_k. We view the global cost function as a Gibbs energy function corresponding to a given configuration. We break the energy function to its basic energy terms associated with different cliques. We let each low-level processor sum the energies associated with its cliques, making sure that each clique's energy is summed only once. The local energy terms are added by the intermediate levels of the pyramid to the top, where the step size is determined by an efficient univariate search. Such an implementation allows us to calculate the global energy in $O(\log n)$ operations, where n is the number of grid points in each direction. This search is bound to converge to a maximal point of the cost function. The additional component of the algorithm is the computation of the gradient in Step 2b). This computation can be implemented in parallel at the bottom of the pyramid, because the gradients of the cost functions (for this class of problems) depend only on the values of the function in a small neighborhood of the pixel.

An additional improvement can be obtained for the SFS problem if one searches for the minimum of the discrete cost function using a multigrid conjugate gradient algorithm. The rate of convergence of the multigrid search is an order of magnitude faster than the single resolution version. This improvement is due to better propagation of low frequency information on the coarse grid. Determination of the higher frequency modes occurs as the grid gets finer and finer. This multigrid search utilizes the same properties that make multigrid relaxation method so successful [11]. In our work we experimented with V-shape multigrid schedules, and we believe that other schedules such as W-shape will perform equally well.

We have also studied the use of the extended conjugate gradient search to replace the SOR step in Blake and Zisserman's [9] graduated nonconvexity (GNC) algorithm. Once again we use the Gibbs formulation in order to obtain an efficient and parallel implementation. The results we obtain using the conjugate gradient algorithm require a smaller number of iterations than the SOR method [9]. The convergence rate of the algorithm is much less sensitive to noise. This example demonstrates the robustness of the algorithm in comparison to other methods.

A deterministic relaxation algorithm is presented for obtaining the MAP estimate of gray-level images modeled by a compound GMRF, and degraded by additive Gaussian noise. This algorithm, which is an extension of the GNC algorithm, is able to find the near optimal MAP estimate corresponding to the nonconvex posterior Gibbs energy function. As a by-product, the line process configuration determined by the MAP estimate produces an accurate edge map without any additional cost. Unlike the simulated annealing method, the deterministic algorithm converges in a small number of iterations. Each of the optimization steps required by the GNC algorithm is performed using the extended conjugate gradient search implemented on a pyramid.

Due to the modeling assumption the restoration algorithm depends on the compound GMRF model parameters. We obtain estimates of the compound GMRF model parameters from the original image using a new expectation maximization (EM) estimation technique. The EM algorithm enables estimation of the GMRF model parameters without being affected by the edges present in the image.

Hierarchical pyramid based algorithms have been proposed for many computer vision tasks. High-level applications include multiresolution and top-down/bottom-up image analysis tasks, such as feature extraction for object recognition [12]. The pyramid structure is very efficient for a variety of low-level processes, e.g., averaging, histograming, edge detection, median filtering, and image segmentation [13]–[19]. Algorithms implemented on the pyramid exploit the pyramid's massively parallel and shallowly serial hierarchical computing ability. In this paper we use the pyramid structure to obtain a fast parallel implementation of the line search conjugate gradient algorithm, which we implement in both single-resolution, and multigrid fashion.

The organization of the paper is as follows. In Section II, the SFS problem is briefly discussed, and the multiresolution conjugate gradient algorithm for reconstructing the orientation of a surface is presented. A synthetic sphere image is experimented with both single- and multiresolution versions of the algorithm to show the reduction in computation time obtained with the multiresolution implementation. In Section III, we present the GNC algorithm with a modified optimization step, based on the conjugate gradient search. Experimental results for edge detection are presented. The experiments indicate that the algorithm is more robust than SOR. Section IV discusses estimation of gray-level images corrupted by additive noise. We present the compound GMRF model, and derive an extended GNC algorithm for obtaining the MAP estimate. A new parameter estimation technique for obtaining the compound model parameters is derived. We present experiments to show the performance of the new algorithm on real images, and obtain both image estimates and edge maps.

II. Shape From Shading

A. Discrete Cost Function for SFS and Gibbs Representation

The SFS problem is the problem of reconstructing the surface orientation from the observed image intensity. Let $E(x, y)$ be the observed image of intensity related to a surface $Z(x, y)$ as

$$E(x, y) = R(p, q, \beta, l, \rho) \tag{1}$$

where β is the illumination direction vector, l is the vector from the surface to the camera, ρ is the albedo term, $p = Z_x$ and $q = Z_y$ are the surface slopes and R is the reflectance map. In the case of a Lambertian surface, one can further write (1) as

$$E(x, y) = \frac{\rho \beta \cdot (-p, -q, 1)}{(1 + p^2 + q^2)^{1/2}}. \tag{2}$$

The discrete set up for the SFS problem was first suggested by Strat [7], using the following cost function:

$$\epsilon^2 \sum_{i=1}^{n} \sum_{j=1}^{m} \left(E_{ij} - R(p_{ij}, q_{ij}) \right)^2 + \frac{\lambda}{\epsilon^2} \sum_{i=1}^{n} \sum_{j=1}^{m} e_{ij}^2 \tag{3}$$

where the first term corresponds to the irradiance error. The second term e_{ij} is the integrability penalty term that corresponds to an estimate for the integral around an elementary square path in the counter-clockwise direction, with the picture cell (i, j) in the lower left corner, i.e.,

$$e_{ij} = \frac{\epsilon}{2} [p_{i,j} + p_{i+1,j} + q_{i+1,j} + q_{i+1,j+1}$$
$$- p_{i+1,j+1} - p_{i,j+1} - q_{i,j+1} - q_{i,j}]. \tag{4}$$

In our work we use Strat's integrability term. A different discrete cost function was suggested by Lee [8]:

$$\mu = \epsilon^2 \sum_{i=1}^{n} \sum_{j=1}^{m} \left(E_{ij} - R(f_{ij}, g_{ij}) \right)^2 + \kappa \sum_{i=1}^{n} \sum_{j=1}^{m} r_{ij} \tag{5}$$

where f and g are the surface orientation in stereographic coordinates and r_{ij} is a smoothing penalty term

$$r_{ij} = \left[(f_{i+1,j} - f_{i,j})^2 + (f_{i,j+1} - f_{i,j})^2 \right.$$
$$\left. + (g_{i+1,j} - g_{i,j})^2 + (g_{i,j+1} - g_{i,j})^2 \right] \Big/ h^2.$$

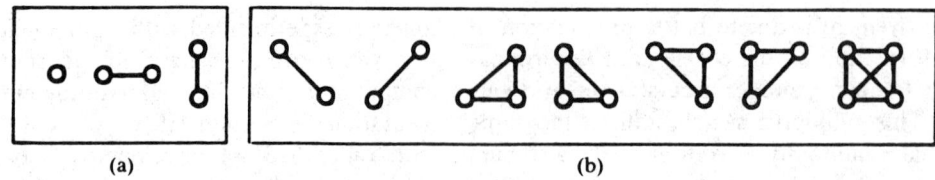

Fig. 1. Gibbs energy cliques. (a) First-order MRF cliques ($c = 1$). (b) Second-order MRF cliques ($c = 2$).

In our formulation we work with p and q and use two different cost functions. The first is a straight forward modification of (5) to p and q coordinates, and the second adds the integrability constraint described in (3) and (4) to obtain:

$$\epsilon^2 \sum_{i=1}^{n} \sum_{j=1}^{m} \left(E_{ij} - R(p_{ij}, q_{ij}) \right)^2$$

$$+ \frac{\lambda}{\epsilon^2} \sum_{i=1}^{n} \sum_{j=1}^{m} e_{ij}^2 + \kappa \sum_{i=1}^{n} \sum_{j=1}^{m} r_{ij}. \quad (6)$$

We now explain the Gibbs formulation for the cost function.

Let $S = \{s_1, s_2, \cdots, s_N\}$ be the set of sites (grid points), $\mathcal{G} = \{\mathcal{G}_s, s \in S\}$ be a neighborhood system for S, meaning any collection of subsets of S for which 1) $s \notin \mathcal{G}_s$ and 2) $s \in \mathcal{G}_r \Leftrightarrow r \in \mathcal{G}_s$. $\mathcal{G}_s$ is the set of neighbors of s and $\{S, \mathcal{G}\}$ is a graph in the usual way. A subset $C \subset S$ is a clique if every pair of distinct sites in C are neighbors. $\mathscr{C}$ denotes the set of cliques [2]. In our problem S is the set of pixel sites (grid points) of the image intensity, $N = n^2$ where n is the number of grid points in each direction. It is easier to view s_m as a two-dimensional vector $s_m = \{(i, j) | i, j \in [1 \cdots n]\}$. One can look into a homogeneous neighborhood system of the form

$$\mathcal{G} = \mathcal{F}_c = \{\mathcal{F}_{i,j}^c, (i, j) \in S\}$$

$$\mathcal{F}_{i,j}^c = \{(k, l) \in S | 0 < (k - i)^2 + (l - j)^2 < c\}.$$

Notice that the sites near the boundary have fewer neighbors than the interior ones. The cliques for $c = 1$ are all of the form $\{(i, j)\}, \{(i, j), (i, j+1)\}, \{(i, j), (i+1, j)\}$ as shown in Fig. 1(a), and for $c = 2$ we have the previously mentioned and the additional cliques described in Fig. 1(b). The cost function:

$$U(p, q) = \sum_{i,j} \epsilon^2 \left(E_{ij} - R(p_{ij}, q_{ij}) \right)^2$$

$$+ \kappa \left[(p_{i,j+1} - p_{i,j})^2 + (p_{i+1,j} - p_{i,j})^2 \right.$$

$$\left. + (q_{i,j+1} - q_{i,j})^2 + (q_{i+1,j} - q_{i,j})^2 \right] \quad (7)$$

can be broken into a sum of energy terms corresponding to a nearest neighbor system. The only cliques we need to consider correspond to $c = 1$. Thus we can write

$$U(p, q) = \sum_{c \in \mathscr{C}} V_C(p, q).$$

Where $\mathscr{C}$ denote the set of cliques for $\mathcal{G} = \mathcal{F}_1$. In general the stencil we use for finite difference approximation to differential operators determines the spatial dependence of the cost function. It is reflected in the type of cliques we have to use when we break the cost function into its primal components. Thus for (6) the cliques consist of one or two elements corresponding to $c = 2$. In (7) the spatial dependence corresponds to $c = 1$ and the additional cliques consist of at most two elements. Note that to each pixel corresponds a two-element vector of unknowns: $(p_{i,j}, q_{i,j})$. The unknowns are coupled together in the Gibbs energy function. This energy function is very similar to energy functions of coupled Markov Processes [2]. Minimizing our cost function is totally equivalent to solving for the configuration with maximum probability. A deterministic algorithm for solving this problem was suggested in [20], in which Besag minimizes the cost function for a grid point (i, j) given the values of its neighbor set. The algorithm uses only local computation, and can be implemented in parallel. The problem with using the algorithm when the unknowns can take values in a continuous set, is that the computations involved in minimizing the energy of the conditional distribution are not trivial. Thus this algorithm is not practical for our problem. All the deterministic algorithms have one limitation in common—they all guarantee convergence only to a local minimum. To avoid the difficulty we assumed that the minimum is unique. This is not always true, as discussed in [21]. We can use our formulation to deal with the multiple minima case. An algorithm for finding the global minimum of a Gibbs energy function was suggested by Geman and Hwang in [22], using an algorithm based on a simulated diffusion process. The algorithm performs a gradient search combined with a Brownian motion component, which is gradually attenuated to zero. This search can be implemented efficiently, on the architecture suggested in this paper. The only modification required, is adding a white noise component to each element of the computed gradient.

B. The Multiresolution Conjugate-Gradient Algorithm Implemented on a Pyramid

We first calculate the gradient corresponding to (5):

$$\frac{\partial \mu}{\partial p_{i,j}} = 2\epsilon^2 \left(E_{i,j} - R_{i,j} \right) \frac{\partial R_{i,j}}{\partial p_{i,j}} + \kappa (4 p_{i,j} - \hat{p}_{i,j}) \quad (8)$$

where

$$\hat{p}_{i,j} = p_{i,j+1} + p_{i,j-1} + p_{i+1,j} + p_{i-1,j}$$

and

$$\frac{\partial \mu}{\partial q_{i,j}} = 2\epsilon^2 (E_{i,j} - R_{i,j}) \frac{\partial R_{i,j}}{\partial q_{i,j}} + \kappa(4q_{i,j} - \hat{q}_{i,j}) \quad (9)$$

where

$$\hat{q}_{i,j} = q_{i,j+1} + q_{i,j-1} + q_{i+1,j} + q_{i-1,j}$$

for the Lambertian reflectance map, and light source located at the camera, (8) and (9) become:

$$\frac{\partial \mu}{\partial p_{i,j}} = 2\epsilon^2 \left(E_{i,j} - \frac{1}{\left(1 + p_{i,j}^2 + q_{i,j}^2\right)^{\frac{1}{2}}} \right) \frac{p_{i,j}}{\left(1 + p_{i,j}^2 + q_{i,j}^2\right)^{\frac{3}{2}}}$$
$$+ \kappa(4p_{i,j} - \hat{p}_{i,j})$$

$$\frac{\partial \mu}{\partial q_{i,j}} = 2\epsilon^2 \left(E_{i,j} - \frac{1}{\left(1 + p_{i,j}^2 + q_{i,j}^2\right)^{\frac{1}{2}}} \right) \frac{q_{i,j}}{\left(1 + p_{i,j}^2 + q_{i,j}^2\right)^{\frac{3}{2}}}$$
$$+ \kappa(4q_{i,j} - \hat{q}_{i,j}). \quad (10)$$

Note that the spatial communication required is only with the nearest neighbors. Next we note that if the boundary and initial conditions are trivial, the gradient is zero—we are at a local maximum of the energy function. We can now use the previous example to illustrate the importance of enforcing integrability in the gradient search. One can see that if we start with an initial condition that satisfies ($p = q$) and the condition holds on the boundary, the search is then limited to the subspace ($p = q$), because the gradient is the same for p and q in every iteration. This problem is solved when the integrability term is added to obtain:

$$\frac{\partial \mu}{\partial p_{i,j}} = 2\epsilon^2 \left[E_{i,j} - \frac{1}{\left(1 + p_{i,j}^2 + q_{i,j}^2\right)^{\frac{1}{2}}} \right] \frac{p_{i,j}}{\left(1 + p_{i,j}^2 + q_{i,j}^2\right)^{\frac{3}{2}}}$$
$$+ \kappa(4p_{i,j} - \hat{p}_{i,j}) + \frac{\lambda}{\epsilon^2}(e_{i,j} + e_{i,j-1}$$
$$- e_{i-1,j-1} - e_{i-1,j})$$

$$\frac{\partial \mu}{\partial q_{i,j}} = 2\epsilon^2 \left[E_{i,j} - \frac{1}{\left(1 + p_{i,j}^2 + q_{i,j}^2\right)^{\frac{1}{2}}} \right] \frac{q_{i,j}}{\left(1 + p_{i,j}^2 + q_{i,j}^2\right)^{\frac{3}{2}}}$$
$$+ \kappa(4q_{i,j} - \hat{q}_{i,j}) + \frac{\lambda}{\epsilon^2}(e_{i,j-1}$$
$$+ e_{i-1,j-1} - e_{i,j} - e_{i-1,j})$$

where $e_{i,j}$ was defined in (4). We now give the algorithm as follows.

1) Set the initial resolution to $l = 2^k$ and choose an initial solution on the coarse grid.
2) Given the initial configuration p^0, q^0 compute
$$G_0 = \nabla \mu(p^0, q^0) \text{ and set } D_0 = -G_0.$$
3) Calculate the optimal step for the given D_k using the global energy function (at the top of the pyramid) as described in the next paragraph.
4) Perform the descent step
$$p^{k+1} = p^k + \alpha_k D_k^p$$
$$q^{k+1} = q^k + \alpha_k D_k^q.$$
5) Calculate the gradient vector G_{k+1} for the given resolution (at the bottom of the pyramid).
6) Calculate a new conjugate direction
$$D_{k+1} = -G_{k+1} + \beta_k D_k$$
where
$$\beta_k = \frac{(G_{k+1} - G_k)^T G_{k+1}}{G_k^T G_k}.$$
7) Repeat Steps 3)–6) until either the reduction in the global energy is below a threshold or a fixed number of iterations have been completed.
8) Stop if you have reached the desired resolution.
9) Refine the resolution ($l = 2^{k+1}$), perform a local coarse to fine extension of the solution to obtain an initial configuration for the finer level.
10) Go back to Step 2).

Step 3) of the algorithm is implemented in the following manner. The top of the pyramid performs univariate minimization using an iterative algorithm, such as golden section search [23], to determine the optimal step. The algorithm uses the values of the cost function corresponding to different step sizes. In each iteration, a new value for the step size is propagated down the pyramid to the bottom layer, so that the processors on the bottom can calculate the updated values of p and q and then sum the energy terms associated with the cliques that correspond to their location. In order to avoid repeated terms in the sum, each energy term is weighted by a reciprocal of the number of elements that construct the corresponding clique. Then, the intermediate levels of the pyramid sum the energy terms corresponding to their "sons," in order to obtain the global energy for the configuration at the top. When the optimal step is determined at the top, it is propagated down to the bottom layer, and Step 4) is performed.

C. Experimental Results

The experiments were performed on a synthetic sphere image illuminated from the previously mentioned. The two gradients corresponding to the cost functions (6), (7) were used to obtain a reconstruction of the surface, assuming a Lambertian reflectance map, and constant albedo. The parameters λ and κ were chosen experimentally. We found that the rate of convergence is highly affected by the choice of λ and κ. Setting the smoothing part to small values slowed down the convergence rate significantly. As expected if smoothing dominated, the results started to differ from the original surface, because we have solved a different problem. The results for (7) were obtained using ten or less iterations at each resolution, starting with a 4×4 grid and finishing at 64×64 and 128×128 grids. The L_2 error is $O(10^{-2})$. When we decreased the smoothing

TABLE I
COMPARISON OF SINGLE AND MULTIRESOLUTION ALGORITHMS
TO SHAPE FROM SHADING

Grid Size	Resolution	Iteration	Energy	L_2 Error $\times 10^{-2}$
64	multi	40	2.960476	2.12969
	single	104	2.888647	2.11380
128	multi	50	2.876788	1.15690
	single	252	2.851924	2.09900

part, better results were obtained and the accuracy improved to $O(10^{-3})$.

We repeated the first experiment with a single-resolution conjugate gradient search. The results are summarized in Table I. The experiment supports the belief that multiple resolutions increase the rate of convergence significantly.

III. EDGE DETECTION USING THE GRADUATED NONCONVEXITY ALGORITHM

Edge detection can be viewed as the problem of fitting a weak membrane (that is, an elastic membrane under weak continuity constraints) to a surface [9]. The location of discontinuities in the weak membrane correspond to discontinuities in the intensity (step edges). The problem has the following mathematical form. Find the configuration that minimizes the following functional corresponding to a weak membrane with a simple line process

$$F = \int \{(u-d)^2 + \lambda^2(\nabla u)^2\} dA + \alpha \int dl \quad (11)$$

where u is the estimated membrane height and d is the noisy data. The first integral is evaluated over the area in which the data d is defined, and the second along the length of all discontinuities. α is a penalty per unit length of discontinuity. λ is a characteristic length for smoothing the continuous portions of the data and is also a characteristic distance for interaction between discontinuity. Since the data is only available on grid points, and the problem does not have a closed form solution, we need to discretize the problem. Blake [9] suggests minimizing the cost function as

$$F = D + \sum_{ij} h_{\alpha,\lambda}(u_{i,j} - u_{i-1,j}, l_{ij})$$
$$+ \sum_{ij} h_{\alpha,\lambda}(u_{i,j} - u_{i,j+1}, m_{ij}) \quad (12)$$

where

$$D = \sum_{ij}(u_{i,j} - d_{i,j})^2 \quad (13)$$

l_{ij} activates the line process in the northernly direction and

$$h_{\alpha,\lambda}(t,l) = \lambda^2(t)^2(1-l) + \alpha l$$

m_{ij} activates the line process in the easternly direction. The problem is thus reduced to the following optimization problem

$$\min_{\{u_{ij}\}} \left(D + \min_{\{l_{ij}\}} \left(\sum_{ij} h_{\alpha,\lambda}(u_{i,j} - u_{i-1,j}, l_{ij}) \right) \right.$$
$$\left. + \min_{\{m_{ij}\}} \left(\sum_{ij} h_{\alpha,\lambda}(u_{i,j} - u_{i,j+1}, m_{ij}) \right) \right).$$

As D does not involve l_{ij}, m_{ij}, minimization over l_{ij}, m_{ij} can be performed and one is then left with minimization with respect to u_{ij}:

$$\min_{\{u_{ij}\}} F = \min_{\{u_{ij}\}} \left(D + \sum_{ij} g_{\alpha,\lambda}(u_{i,j} - u_{i-1,j}) \right.$$
$$\left. + \sum_{ij} g_{\alpha,\lambda}(u_{i,j} - u_{i,j+1}) \right)$$

where

$$g_{\alpha,\lambda}(t) = \min_{l \in \{0,1\}} h_{\alpha,\lambda}(t,l) \doteq \min(\lambda^2(t)^2, \alpha).$$

By applying a convex approximation to F Blake obtains:

$$F^* = D + \sum_{ij} g^*_{\alpha,\lambda}(u_{i,j} - u_{i-1,j}) + \sum_{ij} g^*_{\alpha,\lambda}(u_{i,j} - u_{i,j+1}) \quad (14)$$

where

$$g^*_{\alpha,\lambda}(t) = \begin{cases} \lambda^2(t)^2, & |t| < q \\ \alpha - c^*(|t|-r)^2/2, & q \leq |t| < r \\ \alpha, & |t| \geq r \end{cases}$$

where

$$r^2 = \alpha\left(\frac{2}{c^*} + \frac{1}{\lambda^2}\right), \quad q = \frac{\alpha}{\lambda^2 r}, \quad \text{and } c^* = \frac{1}{4} \text{ for membrane}.$$

A one parameter family of cost functions $F^{(P)}$ is then defined by replacing g^* in (14) by $g^{(P)}$. $g^{(P)}$ is similar to g^* except that c^* is replaced by a variable c^{**}, that varies with P as

$$F^{(P)} = D + \sum_{ij} g^{(P)}_{\alpha,\lambda}(u_{i,j} - u_{i-1,j}) + \sum_{ij} g^{(P)}_{\alpha,\lambda}(u_{i,j} - u_{i,j+1}) \quad (15)$$

with

$$g^{(P)}_{\alpha,\lambda}(t) = \begin{cases} \lambda^2(t)^2, & |t| < q \\ \alpha - c^{**}(|t|-r)^2/2, & q \leq |t| < r \\ \alpha, & |t| \geq r \end{cases}$$

where

$$c = \frac{c^*}{P}, \quad r^2 = \alpha\left(\frac{2}{c^{**}} + \frac{1}{\lambda^2}\right), \quad \text{and} \quad q = \frac{\alpha}{\lambda^2 r}.$$

The GNC algorithm begins by minimizing $F^{(P=1)} = F^*$. Then P is decreased from 1 to 0, which makes $g^{(P)}$ change steadily from g^* to g. For every value of P we minimize $F^{(P)}$ starting with the last configuration corresponding to the previous P (local minimum of $F^{(2P)}$). We suggest that minimization of $F^{(P)}$ can be performed efficiently using the optimal step conjugate gradient algorithm described in Section II. The conjugate gradient algorithm takes fewer number of iterations than SOR, but each iteration requires substeps to determine the optimal step. The conjugate gradient search is less sensitive to the noise present in the image. The number of iterations increases only by 40 percent in the presence of 0 dB noise, while the SOR algorithm requires double the number of iterations. We view $F^{(P)}$ as a Gibbs energy function for the global configuration. The energy function is then broken into terms that correspond to cliques of a nearest neighbor system. The zero order terms are of the form

$$(u_{ij} - d_{ij})^2.$$

The energy terms corresponding to cliques of two elements e.g., $(i, j)(i, j+1)$ is of the form

$$g_{\alpha,\lambda}^{(P)}(t) = \begin{cases} \lambda^2(t)^2, & |t| < q \\ \alpha - c^{**}(|t|-r)^2/2, & q \leq |t| < r \\ \alpha, & |t| \geq r \end{cases}$$

where $t = (u_{i,j} - u_{i-1,j})$ in the x direction and $t = (u_{i,j} - u_{i,j+1})$ in the y direction. Note that the energy term is a nonlinear function of the cliques' elements. We proceed by calculating the gradient of $F^{(P)}$ for points in the interior

$$\frac{\partial F^{(P)}}{\partial u_{ij}} = 2(u_{i,j} - d_{i,j}) + g_{\alpha,\lambda}^{(P)'}(u_{i,j} - u_{i,j-1})$$
$$+ g_{\alpha,\lambda}^{(P)'}(u_{i,j} - u_{i-1,j}) + g_{\alpha,\lambda}^{(P)'}(u_{i,j} - u_{i,j+1})$$
$$+ g_{\alpha,\lambda}^{(P)'}(u_{i,j} - u_{i+1,j}) \qquad (16)$$

where

$$g_{\alpha,\lambda}^{(P)'}(t) = \begin{cases} 2\lambda^2(t), & |t| < q \\ -c^{**}(|t|-r)\sin(t), & q \leq |t| < r. \\ 0, & |t| \geq r \end{cases}$$

On the boundary we need a modification, for the corner $i=0, j=0$:

$$\frac{\partial F^{(P)}}{\partial u_{00}} = 2(u_{0,0} - d_{0,0}) + g_{\alpha,\lambda}^{(P)'}(u_{0,0} - u_{0,1})$$
$$+ g_{\alpha,\lambda}^{(P)'}(u_{0,0} - u_{1,0}) \qquad (17)$$

and similarly at the other corners. For the boundary side $i=0, j=1, \cdots, N-1$:

$$\frac{\partial F^{(P)}}{\partial u_{ij}} = 2(u_{0,j} - d_{0,j}) + g_{\alpha,\lambda}^{(P)'}(u_{0,j} - u_{0,j-1})$$
$$+ g_{\alpha,\lambda}^{(P)'}(u_{0,j} - u_{0,j+1}) + g_{\alpha,\lambda}^{(P)'}(u_{0,j} - u_{1,j}) \qquad (18)$$

and similarly for the other sides.

We now have all the building blocks required for our algorithm, presented next.

1) Choose λ, h_0 (scale and sensitivity).
2) Set $\alpha = h_0^2 \lambda / 2$.
3) Set $P = 1.0$.
4) Given an initial configuration u^0 compute $G_0 = \nabla F^P(u^0)$ and set $D_0 = -G_0$.
5) Calculate (using a univariate search) the optimal step for the given D_k using the global energy function (at the top of the pyramid).
6) Perform the descent step

$$u^{(k+1)} = u^{(k)} + \alpha_k D_k$$

7) Calculate the gradient vector $G_{k+1} = \nabla F^P(u^{(k+1)})$ (at the bottom of the pyramid).
8) Calculate a new conjugate direction

$$D_{k+1} = -G_{k+1} + \beta_k D_k$$

where

$$\beta_k = \frac{(G_{k+1} - G_k)^T G_{k+1}}{G_k^T G_k}.$$

9) Repeat Steps 5)–8) until $\max_{i,j} |u_{i,j}^{(k+1)} - u_{i,j}^{(k)}| < \epsilon$, or the energy reduction is below some level.
10) If $P > c^*/\lambda$ then $P = P/2 u^0 = u^{(k+1)}$ go back to Step 4).
11) Calculate the edge location using the following rules:

$$l_{i,j} = \begin{cases} 1, & \text{if } |u_{i,j} - u_{i-1,j}| > r \\ 0, & \text{if } |u_{i,j} - u_{i-1,j}| < q \\ \text{ambiguous}, & \text{otherwise} \end{cases}$$

$$m_{i,j} = \begin{cases} 1, & \text{if } |u_{i,j} - u_{i,j+1}| > r \\ 0, & \text{if } |u_{i,j} - u_{i,j+1}| < q \\ \text{ambiguous}, & \text{otherwise.} \end{cases}$$

The $l_{i,j}$ and $m_{i,j}$ are the edge indicator functions in the northernly and easternly directions respectively.

A. Experimental Results

1) Edge Detection using Conjugate Gradient: The experiments in this section were performed on a 128×128 airport image. We used the Polak–Ribiere conjugate gradient search. Edge detection was performed on the original image and the original image corrupted by additive Gaussian noise. The conjugate gradient method proved to be robust to noise in the sense that the convergence properties were not affected considerably by the amount of noise in the processed image. In each step of the GNC algorithm the termination criterion used was: stop if $f(x_k) - f(x_{k+1}) \leq 100$. We preferred this test over the one: stop when $\|u_{k+1} - u_k\|_\infty \leq a$ (where a is some constant), because it requires a smaller number of iterations without degradation in the computed edges. The GNC steps were performed till $p = c^*/\lambda$.

Experimental results are summarized in Fig. 2. Figs. 2(a) and 2(b) are the original airport image and the result obtained with $h = 10$, $\lambda = 4$ after 157 iterations. Figs. 2(c) and 2(d) are the image with 5-dB noise ($\sigma_n = 12$), and the result obtained with $h = 16$, $\lambda = 4$, where the number of

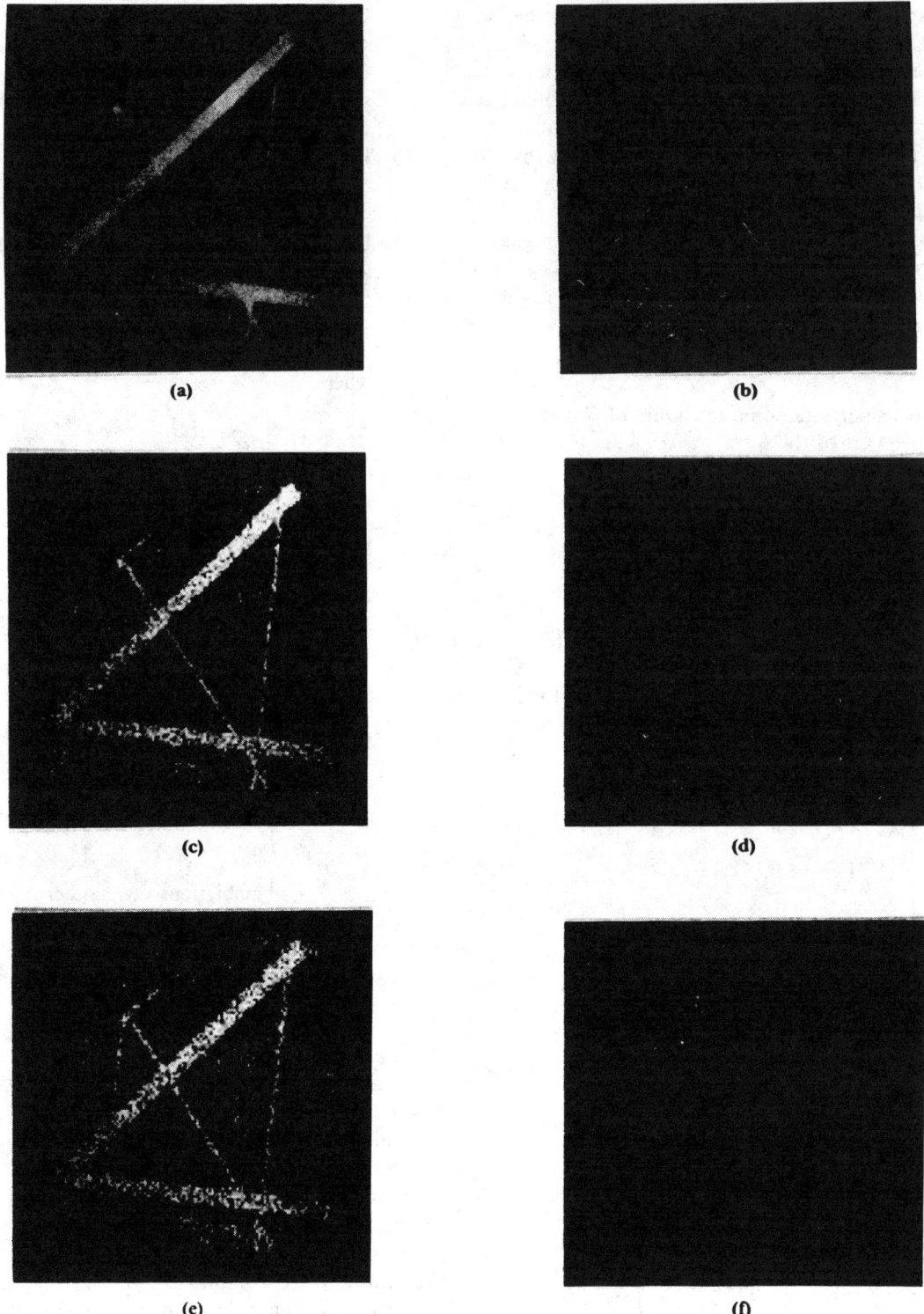

Fig. 2. Edge detection using conjugate gradient-based GNC algorithm. (a) Original airport image. (b) Edge estimate on original airport image. (c) Airport image corrupted by 5-dB additive noise. (d) Edge estimate on 5-dB noisy airport image. (e) Airport image corrupted by 0-dB additive noise. (f) Edge estimate on 0-dB noisy airport image.

iteration increased to 198. Figs. 2(e) and 2(f) are the image with 0-dB noise ($\sigma_n = 22$), and the result obtained with $h = 20$, $\lambda = 4$ with the algorithm terminating after 224 iterations.

2) Comparison between Conjugate Gradient and SOR: We first compared the sequential SOR and the black and red (parallel) SOR. The number of iterations and the final results were the same for these two algorithms. In order to compare the SOR and the conjugate gradient we used several images with different noise levels. The number of iterations in the SOR increases considerably when the noise level is increased, while the number of iterations in the conjugate gradient method is not so sensitive to the noise. The number of iterations in the SOR is greater than

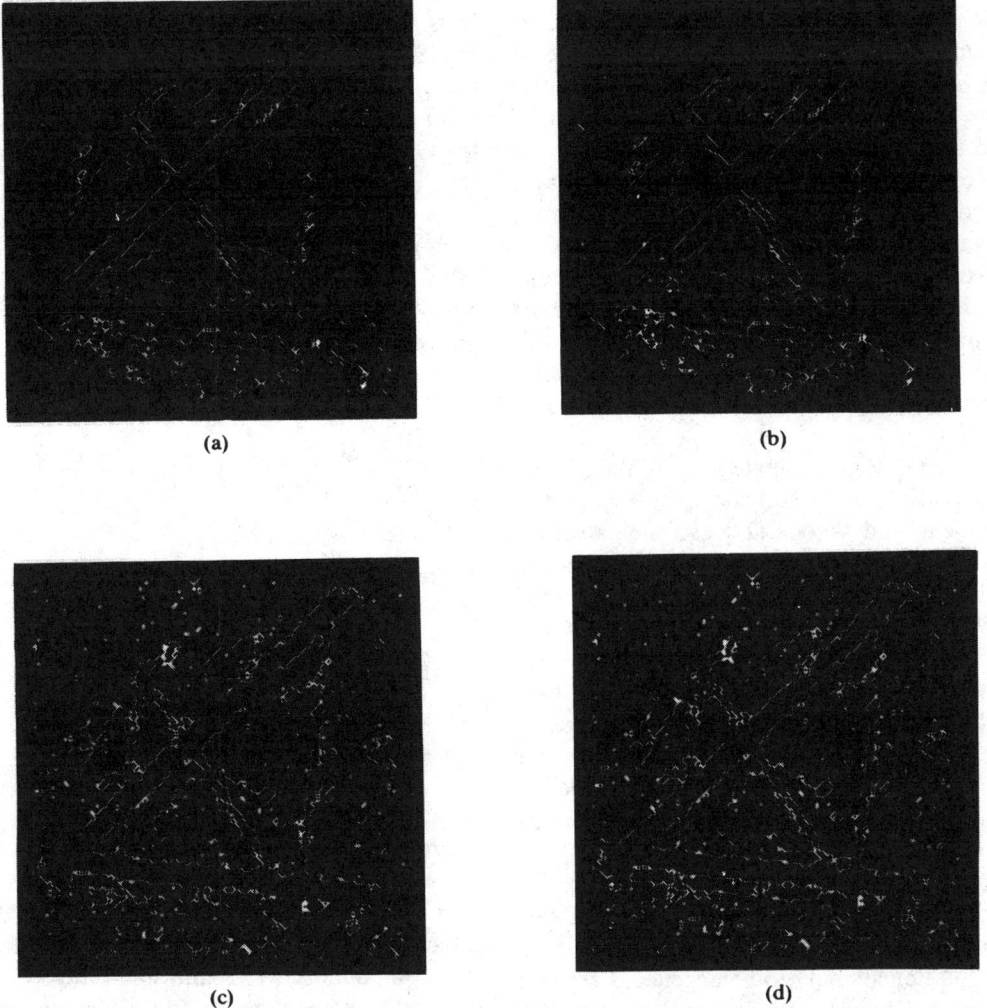

Fig. 3. Comparison between SOR and conjugate-gradient GNC results. (a) SOR edge estimate on 5-dB image in Fig. 2(c). (b) CG edge estimate on 5-dB image in Fig. 2(c). (c) SOR edge estimate on 0-dB image in Fig. 2(e). (d) CG edge estimate on 0-dB image in Fig. 2(e).

that of the conjugate gradient, but in each conjugate gradient step we perform more computations. The final results for these two methods are the same for all the noise levels. In Table II we summarize the results.

In Fig. 3 we present the comparison results for the two algorithms. Figs. 3(a) and 3(c) are the results from the 5-dB and 0-dB images using SOR algorithm, where Figs. 3(b) and 3(d) were obtained by using the conjugate gradient algorithm.

TABLE II
COMPARISON BETWEEN CONJUGATE GRADIENT AND SOR ALGORITHMS

Image	Algorithm	Iterations	Final Energy $\times 10^6$	Undefined $l_{i,j}, m_{i,j}$
Airport	SOR	328	1.3101	336
	CG	157	1.3088	336
Airport with 5-dB noise	SOR	477	4.1830	279
	CG	198	4.1814	253
Airport with 0-dB noise	SOR	617	8.9788	244
	CG	224	8.9722	227

IV. GRADUATED NONCONVEXITY ALGORITHM FOR IMAGE ESTIMATION USING COMPOUND GMRF MODELS

Image estimation of gray-level images requires the ability of the estimate to preserve the sharpness of edges, which play an important role in human interpretation of images. Linear filters [24], [25], as well as MAP estimation using the homogeneous Gauss–Markov random field (GMRF) model [26] for the intensity tend to smear the edges. To avoid this problem a class of models called compound GMRF was suggested in [27]. The model suggested is a GMRF coupled with a line process. In this model the structure of the line process determines the value of the GMRF model coefficients. The GMRF parameters are required to satisfy some symmetry constraint, and the choice of the parameters for a given line configuration remains an open problem. Our simplified compound GMRF model is a member of the class of models proposed in [27]. In our formulation the line process breaks the correlation between neighboring pixels when the gray-level jump is above a threshold. The model can be viewed as an extension of the weak membrane model [9] used for surface interpolation and edge detection. The GMRF breaks when edges occur, which in turn creates homogeneous GMRF patches separated by the line process. Qualitative and quantitative values correspond to all the new model parameters, and they can be estimated from the image. As an example the regularization term in the weak membrane model is replaced by the ratio of the noise variance to the GMRF model variance.

Given the distribution of the corrupting noise we write the conditional density of the degraded image conditioned on the original image. The degradation we consider in this work is additive white Gaussian noise. Thus the posterior density is written in terms of the GMRF model parameter estimates.

To obtain the global MAP estimate for an image obeying a compound GMRF model and corrupted by additive Gaussian noise, Jeng and Woods [27] use simulated annealing. This stochastic algorithm is slow, and can not in practice obey the theoretical requirement on the initial temperature. We use a modified version of the GNC algorithm [9]. The algorithm is deterministic and good results are obtained in less than 100 iterations. We have used the algorithm on a real airport image and obtained good restoration results. The configuration of the line process is determined by the MAP estimate. It provides an accurate estimate of the image edges without any additional cost.

In this section we also address the problem of estimating the GMRF model parameters from a noise-free realization of the original image. In order to avoid the edges one can limit the estimation domain only to homogeneous regions, which will make maximum likelihood (ML) estimation impractical. Instead we have developed the following procedure. We detect the edges on the image using the GNC algorithm [9] and discard the intensity data in a strip of four pixels centered at each edge. We develop an EM algorithm [28] that calculates the conditional expectation of the intensity given the parameters of the model and the neighboring intensity levels that is used to replace the discarded data, and then calculate the new parameters estimate from the smoothed image using least squares (LS) [25] or ML techniques. The process is repeated till it converges. As initial parameters we used the LS estimates of the image including the edges. The current version includes only results based on LS, and we are implementing the ML version. The parameters we obtain have much lower model variance then the parameters estimated from the image with the edges, although the image variance reduced only slightly. In the future we would like to extend this process to estimation from the noisy image itself.

A. Image and Noise Models

The GMRF models have been successfully used for modeling homogeneous intensity regions, such as natural texture (sand, grass, calf) [29], [30]. The GMRF model is not suitable for composite real-world scenes because it is unable to capture sharp transitions (edges). These problems can be partially overcome by introducing composite models [2], [27]. We develop a composite model able to describe homogeneous regions as well as sharp transitions from one region to the other. The model is an extension of the GMRF models. We first review the GMRF model and then extend it to the compound GMRF.

1) GMRF Model: Suppose that the original image $\{y(s)\}$ is defined on a finite lattice $\Omega = \{s = (i, j): 1 \le i, j \le M\}$. Consider a stationary Gauss–Markov model with mean y_m, parameters $\Theta_{s,r} = \Theta_{\{s-r\}}$ and toroidal boundaries for which

$$p(y(s)|y(r), r \in \Omega) = p(y(s)|y(r), r \in N_s)$$
$$= \frac{1}{\sqrt{2\pi\nu}} \exp\left\{-\frac{1}{2\nu}\left[y(s) - y_m - \sum_{r \in N_s} \Theta_{s,r}(y(r) - y_m)\right]^2\right\} \quad (19)$$

where N_s characterizes the neighborhood dependence. This leads to the joint density function [31]:

$$p(y) = \frac{1}{\{(2\pi)^{M^2} \det(\nu B(\Theta)^{-1})\}^{\frac{1}{2}}}$$
$$\cdot \exp\left\{-\frac{1}{2\nu}(y - y_m)'B(\Theta)(y - y_m)\right\} \quad (20)$$

where $B(\Theta)$ is a $M^2 \times M^2$ block-Toeplitz matrix, and y_m is the $M^2 \times 1$ vector of the constant mean y_m.

2) The Compound GMRF Model: In this section we extend the weak membrane (12) and GMRF (19) models to a compound GMRF and line process model. Since the parameters corresponding to the compound GMRF model can be estimated from the noisy image using bias compensated least square (BCLS) techniques [32], this extension enables us to get better reconstruction of weakly continuous surfaces. It also gives a qualitative meaning to λ in the weak membrane algorithm and allows us to estimate its value from the noise and model variances.

We define the following conditional distribution for the compound GMRF model as

$$p(y(s)|y(s+\tau), y(s-\tau), l(s,\tau), l(s-\tau,\tau), \tau \in N^*)$$
$$= \frac{e^{-u(y(s)|y(s+\tau), y(s-\tau), l(s,\tau), l(s-\tau,\tau), \tau \in N^*)}}{Z}$$

where N^* is the set of shift vectors corresponding to the neighborhood of the GMRF model.

The line process notation is illustrated in Fig. 4. For a second order GMRF model $N^* = \{(0,1), (1,0), (1,1), (-1,1)\}$:

$$U(y(s)|y(s+\tau), y(s-\tau), l(s,\tau), l(s-\tau,\tau), \tau \in N^*)$$
$$= \frac{1}{2\nu}\left[\sum_{\tau \in N^*} \Theta_\tau\left[(y(s) - y(s+\tau))^2(1 - l(s,\tau))\right.\right.$$
$$\left.+ (y(s) - y(s-\tau))^2(1 - l(s-\tau,\tau))\right]$$
$$\left.+ \left(1 - \sum_{\tau \in N^*} 2\Theta_\tau\right)y(s)^2\right].$$

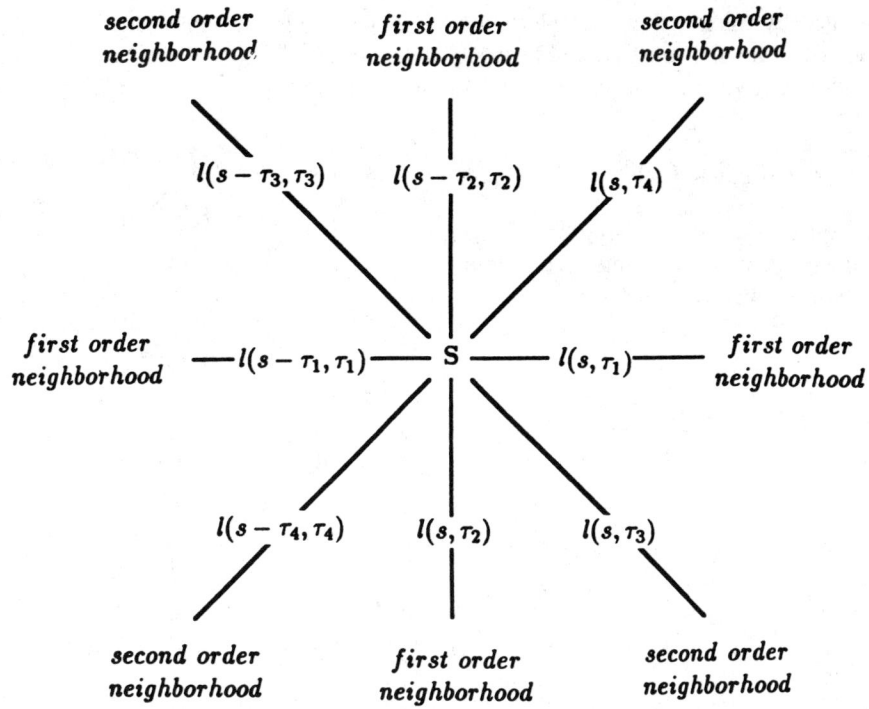

Fig. 4. Line process notation. $\tau_1 = (0,1)$, $\tau_2 = (1,0)$, $\tau_3 = (1,1)$, $\tau_4 = (-1,1)$.

The line process is now defined on the edges that connect the nodes (the grid points) that are neighbors of a given pixel.

The prior probability of the line process is

$$p(l(s,\tau_i)|l(r,\tau), r \in \Omega, \tau \in N^*, (r,\tau) \neq (s,\tau_i))$$

$$= \frac{e^{-U(l(s,\tau_i)|l(r,\tau), r \in \Omega, \tau \in N^*, (r,\tau) \neq (s,\tau_i))}}{Z}$$

where

$$U(l(s,\tau_i)|l(r,\tau), r \in \Omega, \tau \in N^*, (r,\tau) \neq (s,\tau_i))$$
$$= \beta l(s,\tau_i).$$

Recall from (19) that for a zero-mean GMRF model

$$U(y(s)|y(s+\tau), y(s-\tau), \tau \in N^*)$$

$$= \frac{1}{2\nu}\left(y(s) - \sum_{\tau \in N^*} \Theta_\tau [y(s+\tau) + y(s-\tau)]\right)^2.$$

It is obvious that the conditional distribution of the compound GMRF model is equal to the GMRF model when $l(s,\tau) = 0$, $l(s-\tau,\tau) = 0$, for all $\tau \in N^*$. We shall assume that all $\Theta_\tau > 0$, which is almost always the case for the first order neighborhoods.

The corresponding joint distribution of the compound GMRF is

$$p(y,l) = \frac{e^{-U(y,l)}}{Z}$$

where

$$U(y,l)$$
$$= \sum_{s \in \Omega} \left\{ \sum_{\tau \in N^*} \Theta_\tau \left[\frac{1}{2\nu}(y(s) - y(s+\tau))^2 (1 - l(s,\tau)) \right. \right.$$
$$\left. \left. + \beta l(s,\tau) \right] + \frac{1}{2\nu}\left(1 - \sum_{\tau \in N^*} 2\Theta_\tau\right) y(s)^2 \right\}.$$

One can see that if $(y(s) - y(s+\tau))$ is bigger than a threshold, it is cheaper to break the connection and introduce an edge in the same way it is done in the weak membrane formulation.

The Noise Model and the MAP Equation: We consider the following model for image intensity degraded by additive Gaussian noise [33]

$$x(s) = y(s) + n(s). \qquad (21)$$

Since $n(s)$ is a spatially independent Gaussian noise variable, we can express the conditional density function $p(x|y)$ as

$$p(x|y) = \frac{1}{(2\pi\sigma_n^2)^{M^2/2}} \exp\left\{-\frac{1}{2\sigma_n^2} \sum_{s \in \Omega} (x(s) - y(s))^2\right\}. \qquad (22)$$

Knowing the statistical properties of the original image y and the degradations, one can construct the *aposteriori* density function $p(y|x)$ from the observation x. Thus Bayes law leads to the *aposteriori* density

$$p(y|x) = \frac{p(x|y)p(y)}{p(x)} \qquad (23)$$

where y is the original image we wish to estimate. The

MAP estimate is obtained by maximizing the *aposteriori* density function $p(y|x)$ to find the most probable value of y. Since the observation x is given, $p(x)$ can be treated as a constant, and we have

$$p(y|x) = Kp(x|y)p(y) \qquad (24)$$

where constant K is equal to $1/p(x)$. Using the Gibbs formulation the global energy corresponding to the compound GMRF model with additive noise is

$$\begin{aligned}
U(y,l|x) &= \sum_{s \in \Omega} \left\{ \frac{(x(s)-y(s))^2}{2\sigma^2} + \frac{\left(1-\sum_{\tau \in N^*} 2\Theta_\tau\right)y(s)^2}{2\nu} \right. \\
&\quad + \sum_{\tau \in N^*} \Theta_\tau \left[\frac{1}{2\nu}(y(s)-y(s+\tau))^2(1-l(s,\tau)) \right. \\
&\quad \left. \left. + \beta l(s,\tau) \right] \right\} \\
&= \frac{1}{2\sigma^2} \sum_{s \in \Omega} \left\{ (x(s)-y(s))^2 \right. \\
&\quad + \lambda^2 \left(1 - \sum_{\tau \in N^*} 2\Theta_\tau\right) y(s)^2 \\
&\quad + \sum_{\tau \in N^*} \Theta_\tau \left[\lambda^2 (y(s)-y(s+\tau))^2 (1-l(s,\tau)) \right. \\
&\quad \left. \left. + \alpha l(s,\tau) \right] \right\} \qquad (25)
\end{aligned}$$

where $\lambda^2 = \sigma^2/\nu$, $\alpha = 2\beta\sigma^2$. The regularization parameter λ that did not have a quantitative value in the weak membrane model, has both qualitative meaning and quantitative value in the new model. It reflects the confidence we have in the data, as it is the ratio of the measurement noise variance to the GMRF model variance.

B. The GNC-GMRF Algorithm

One can see the similarity between the global energy function corresponding to the posterior density in (25) and the global energy Blake suggested to minimize in the weak membrane formulation (12). The weak membrane model is a special case of the compound GMRF model with a first order neighborhood system and isotropic parameters $\Theta_x = \Theta_y = 0.25$ and with appropriate scaling of λ and α. Blake has developed the GNC algorithm to find the global minimum of (12). We modify the GNC algorithm to obtain an algorithm that is able to find a near optimal MAP solution for the compound GMRF model. For simplicity in the formulation we restrict our attention to a first order compound GMRF model although there are no difficulties in deriving the algorithm for higher order neighborhood systems. For the first order compound GMRF model we can write

$$\begin{aligned}
U(y,l,m|x) &= \sum_{i,j \in \Omega} \frac{1}{2\sigma^2} \left\{ (x_{i,j} - y_{i,j})^2 \right. \\
&\quad + \lambda^2 (1 - 2(\Theta_x + \Theta_y)) y_{i,j}^2 \\
&\quad + \Theta_x \left[\lambda^2 (y_{i,j} - y_{i-1,j})^2 (1 - l_{i,j}) + \alpha l_{i,j} \right] \\
&\quad \left. + \Theta_y \left[\lambda^2 (y_{i,j} - y_{i,j+1})^2 (1 - m_{i,j}) + \alpha m_{i,j} \right] \right\}
\end{aligned}$$

where $l_{i,j}, m_{i,j}$ activate the line process in the x and y directions respectively. We can write the posterior energy function in the form

$$\begin{aligned}
U &= \frac{1}{2\sigma^2} \left\{ D + \sum_{ij} \Theta_x h_{\alpha,\lambda}(y_{i,j} - y_{i-1,j}, l_{ij}) \right. \\
&\quad \left. + \sum_{ij} \Theta_y h_{\alpha,\lambda}(y_{i,j} - y_{i,j+1}, m_{ij}) \right\} \qquad (26)
\end{aligned}$$

where

$$D = \sum_{ij}(y_{i,j} - x_{i,j})^2 + \lambda^2(1 - 2(\Theta_x + \Theta_y))y_{i,j}^2 \qquad (27)$$

where

$$h_{\alpha,\lambda}(t,l) = \lambda^2(t)^2(1-l) + \alpha l.$$

Note that $(1 - 2(\Theta_x + \Theta_y)) > 0$ because of the positivity requirement of the spectral density of the GMRF model. The problem is thus reduced to the following optimization problem:

$$\min_{\{y_{ij}\}} \left(\frac{1}{2\sigma^2} \left[D + \min_{\{l_{ij}\}} \left(\sum_{ij} \Theta_x h_{\alpha,\lambda}(y_{i,j} - y_{i-1,j}, l_{ij}) \right) \right. \right.$$
$$\left. \left. + \min_{\{m_{ij}\}} \left(\sum_{ij} \Theta_y h_{\alpha,\lambda}(y_{i,j} - y_{i,j+1}, m_{ij}) \right) \right] \right).$$

As D does not involve l_{ij}, m_{ij}, minimization over l_{ij}, m_{ij} can be performed and one is then left with minimization with respect to y_{ij}:

$$\min_{\{y_{ij}, l_{ij}, m_{ij}\}} U = \min_{\{y_{ij}\}} \left\{ \frac{1}{2\sigma^2} \left[D + \sum_{ij} \Theta_x g_{\alpha,\lambda}(y_{i,j} - y_{i-1,j}) \right. \right.$$
$$\left. \left. + \sum_{ij} \Theta_y g_{\alpha,\lambda}(y_{i,j} - y_{i,j+1}) \right] \right\}$$

where

$$g_{\alpha,\lambda}(t) = \min_{l \in \{0,1\}} h_{\alpha,\lambda}(t,l) = \min(\lambda^2(t)^2, \alpha).$$

In the following, we assume that y is presented by a one-dimensional (1-D) array with a lexicographic order. Following Blake we look for a convex approximation U^*. The convexity of U^* is guaranteed by requiring that it has a positive definite Hessian matrix $H = \partial^2 U^*/\partial y_{ij} \partial y_{k,l}$. Suppose g^* is designed to satisfy

$$\forall t \; g^{*\prime\prime}(t) \geq -c^*$$

where $c^* > 0$. Then the "worst case" of H occurs when

$$\forall i,j \; g^{*\prime\prime}(y_{i,j} - y_{i,j+1}) = -c^* \text{ and } g^{*\prime\prime}(y_{i,j} - y_{i-1,j})$$
$$= -c^*$$

so that

$$H = [2 + 2\lambda^2(1 - 2(\Theta_x + \Theta_y))]I - c^*R.$$

The matrix R is a symmetric tri-diagonal block Toeplitz matrix:

$$R = \begin{bmatrix} Q & -\Theta_x I & & & \\ -\Theta_x I & Q & -\Theta_x I & & \\ & -\Theta_x I & Q & -\Theta_x I & \\ & & -\Theta_x I & Q \end{bmatrix}$$

$$Q = \begin{bmatrix} 2\Theta_x + 2\Theta_y & -\Theta_y & & & \\ -\Theta_y & 2\Theta_x + 2\Theta_y & -\Theta_y & & \\ & -\Theta_y & 2\Theta_x + 2\Theta_y & -\Theta_y & \\ & & -\Theta_y & 2\Theta_x + 2\Theta_y \end{bmatrix}.$$

To prove that H is positive definite it is sufficient to show that the largest eigenvalue $\mathscr{E}_{max}$ of R satisfies $\mathscr{E}_{max} \leq 2 + 2\lambda^2(1 - 2(\Theta_x + \Theta_y))/c^*$.

The eigenvalues $\mathscr{E}_{i,j}$, $i, j \in (0 \cdots M-1)$ of R can be found using the sine transform [34].

$$\mathscr{E}_{i,j} = \Theta_x \left(2 - 2\cos\frac{2\pi i}{M} \right) + \Theta_y \left(2 - 2\cos\frac{2\pi j}{M} \right)$$

So that max $\mathscr{E}_{i,j} = 4(\Theta_x + \Theta_y)$, thus to guarantee convexity c^* must satisfy

$$c^* \leq \frac{1 + \lambda^2(1 - 2(\Theta_x + \Theta_y))}{2(\Theta_x + \Theta_y)}.$$

Following Blake we construct the best quadratic approximation g^* with a given bound $-c^*$ on its second derivative, satisfying the extra condition: for all t $g^*(t) \leq g(t)$

$$g_{\alpha,\lambda}^*(t) = \begin{cases} \lambda^2(t)^2, & |t| < q \\ \alpha - c^*(|t|-r)^2/2, & q \leq |t| < r \\ \alpha, & |t| \geq r \end{cases}$$

where

$$r^2 = \alpha\left(\frac{2}{c^*} + \frac{1}{\lambda^2}\right), \qquad q = \frac{\alpha}{\lambda^2 r}.$$

Thus we obtain the convex approximation for U:

$$U^* = \frac{1}{2\sigma^2}\left[D + \sum_{ij} \Theta_x g_{\alpha,\lambda}^*(y_{i,j} - y_{i-1,j}) + \sum_{ij} \Theta_y g_{\alpha,\lambda}^*(y_{i,j} - y_{i,j+1})\right]. \quad (28)$$

A one parameter family of cost functions $U^{(P)}$ is then defined by replacing g^* in (28) by $g^{(P)}$. $g^{(P)}$ is similar to g^* except that c^* is replaced by a variable c^{**}, that varies with P

$$U^{(P)} = \frac{1}{2\sigma^2}\left[D + \sum_{ij} \Theta_x g_{\alpha,\lambda}^{(P)}(y_{i,j} - y_{i-1,j}) + \sum_{ij} \Theta_y g_{\alpha,\lambda}^{(P)}(y_{i,j} - y_{i,j+1})\right] \quad (29)$$

with

$$g_{\alpha,\lambda}^{(P)}(t) = \begin{cases} \lambda^2(t)^2, & |t| < q \\ \alpha - c^{**}(|t|-r)^2/2, & q \leq |t| < r \\ \alpha, & |t| \geq r \end{cases}$$

where

$$c^{**} = \frac{c^*}{P}, \qquad r^2 = \alpha\left(\frac{2}{c^{**}} + \frac{1}{\lambda^2}\right), \quad \text{and} \quad q = \frac{\alpha}{\lambda^2 r}.$$

The GNC–GMRF algorithm is derived similar to the GNC algorithm in Section III. In the GNC–GMRF algorithm we no longer choose the value of λ, but compute it from the equation $\lambda = \sqrt{\sigma^2/\nu}$. The GNC–GMRF algorithm begins by minimizing $U^{(P=1)} = U^*$. Then P is decreased from 1 to 0, which makes $g^{(P)}$ change steadily from g^* to g. For every value of P we minimize $U^{(P)}$ starting with the last configuration corresponding to the previous P (local minimum of $U^{(2P)}$). The minimization of $U^{(P)}$ is performed efficiently using the optimal step conjugate gradient algorithm.

C. Parameter Estimation

The compound GMRF model presented in Section IV-A-2 presents a new problem in parameter estimation. We would like to estimate the GMRF parameters only in homogeneous regions that do not include edges. The problem is that even if the location of the edges is known, removing the adjacent pixels from the rectangular domain we started with, leaves a highly irregular domain, which is cumbersome to work with. Furthermore in the case of ML estimation, the irregularity of the domain makes it impossible to write a close form expression for the likelihood function even if toroidal assumption are made. Instead we suggest a new algorithm based on the EM algorithm [28]. For the time being, we present the algorithm for estimating the parameters from the original image. We believe that the method can be extended to estimation techniques such as BCLS [32] that are based on the noisy image.

The idea behind the new algorithm is that we ignore the intensity data in strips centered at the edges and replace this data by the conditional mean of the GMRF model given the model parameters and the neighboring pixels intensity data. The conditional mean is calculated using a relaxation method, i.e., for the first order neighborhood we repeatedly set

$$y^{k+1}(i,j) = \Theta_x(y^k(i+1,j) + y^k(i-1,j)) + \Theta_y(y^k(i,j+1) + y^k(i,j-1)). \quad (30)$$

Note that we modify the intensity only in the strips centered at the edges. The iterations are bound to converge, because the stability requirement of the GMRF model parameters ensure that the eigenvalues of the iteration matrix are smaller than 1. Once we computed the condi-

TABLE III
PARAMETER ESTIMATION RESULTS FOR AIRPORT IMAGE USING THE EM ALGORITHM

Iteration	Θ_x	$\hat{\Theta}_x$	Θ_y	$\hat{\Theta}_y$	ν	$\hat{\nu}$	Image Variance
0	0.282700	0.266150	0.247330	0.232850	25.6184	51.97603	469.4704
1	0.300411	0.291597	0.213673	0.207403	6.55542	16.98208	359.0647
5	0.310806	0.304306	0.198853	0.194694	5.99739	12.96653	336.8897
14	0.312426	0.306504	0.196215	0.192496	5.98000	12.55508	350.1088

tional mean, we perform an estimation step based on LS or ML on the smoothed image. We use the estimated parameters to calculate a new conditional mean for the pixels in the edge vicinity, which in turn are used for a new parameter estimation step. In this paper we present results for the EM algorithm based on LS. We are currently working on the ML version. We use Blakes edge detector [9] to find the location of the edges in the image. In the future we intend to combine the image and parameters estimation. The results we obtain with the new algorithm differ significantly from the results obtained directly from the original image. For example the estimated model variance is much smaller, although the image variance is reduced only slightly. The results show the importance of suppressing the edges effect in the parameter estimation. The new algorithm is summarized as follows.

1) Get an initial estimate for the model parameters, using the LS technique on the original image.
2) Find the image edges location using the GNC algorithm [9].
3) By using the current estimate of the model parameters find the conditional mean of the intensity in a strip four pixels wide centered at the edge using the relaxation equation (30).
4) Calculate a new parameter estimate on the smoothed image calculated in Step 3).
5) Check if the parameters are stable. If not scale them by multiplying the vector Θ by

$$\psi = \frac{0.499}{\max_{s \in \Omega} \sum_{\tau_i \in N^*} \Theta_{\tau_i} \Phi_{s,\tau_i}}$$

where

$$\Phi_{s,\tau_i} = \cos\left(\frac{2\pi s^T \tau_i}{M}\right),$$

and

$$N^* = \{\tau_1, \tau_2\} = \{(0,1),(1,0)\}$$

are the shift vectors corresponding to the first order GMRF model, to ensure that the scaled parameters $\hat{\Theta}_{\tau_i}, \tau_i \in N^*$ satisfy

$$\left(1 - 2\sum_{\tau_i \in N^*} \hat{\Theta}_{\tau_i} \Phi_{s,\tau_i}\right) > 0 \; \forall \; s \in \Omega. \quad (31)$$

6) If the change in the parameters is small enough stop, else go back to step 3).

Steps 4) and 5) of the algorithm can be replaced by constraint maximization of the likelihood function. We are currently working on the ML version of the algorithm. We experimented with the new algorithm on a real airport image and obtained the results summarized in Table III. Note that the parameter values do not change much after ten iterations.

D. Restoration Results

The original airport image corrupted by 5-dB and 10-dB additive white Gaussian noise was reconstructed using the modified GNC algorithm. As an initial condition for the algorithm we used the noisy image. Parameters were estimated from the original image using the new EM algorithm described in Section III. The results were obtained using at most 25 iterations for each value of P. For some values of P the algorithm converged in less than 20 iterations.

In the first experiment we restored an image corrupted by 10-dB additive white Gaussian noise. The edge threshold was chosen to be $h = 20$ and the noise variance was assumed to be known. The results after 100 iterations are presented in Fig. 5. We then repeated the experiment for the 5-dB additive white Gaussian noise case. In this experiment h was set to 25. The results are presented in Fig. 6. The results obtained for 10-dB noise case are very good. The estimates include all the information in the original image and in addition we obtain a precise edge map. We compare the results obtained assuming a GMRF model for the image intensity and show that the image estimates are substantially blurred. In the 5-dB case the results are good also, but a few noisy points were isolated by the line process. This is an inherent problem owing to the simple line process used in this model. It can partially be overcome by increasing λ. One can also modify the line process to include an energy term that will inhibit the formation of such edges as in [2], but the GNC algorithm can no longer be used for the more sophisticated line process.

V. CONCLUSION

In this paper, we used the stochastic formulation for low level vision problems, and demonstrated the equivalence between direct optimization of functionals and MAP estimates obtained from stochastic modeling. We used the Gibbs formulation to present the Markov field model, and the Gibbs energy functions to link the deterministic and stochastic formulations. Using the Gibbs formulation, we derived a pyramid implementation for the line-search con-

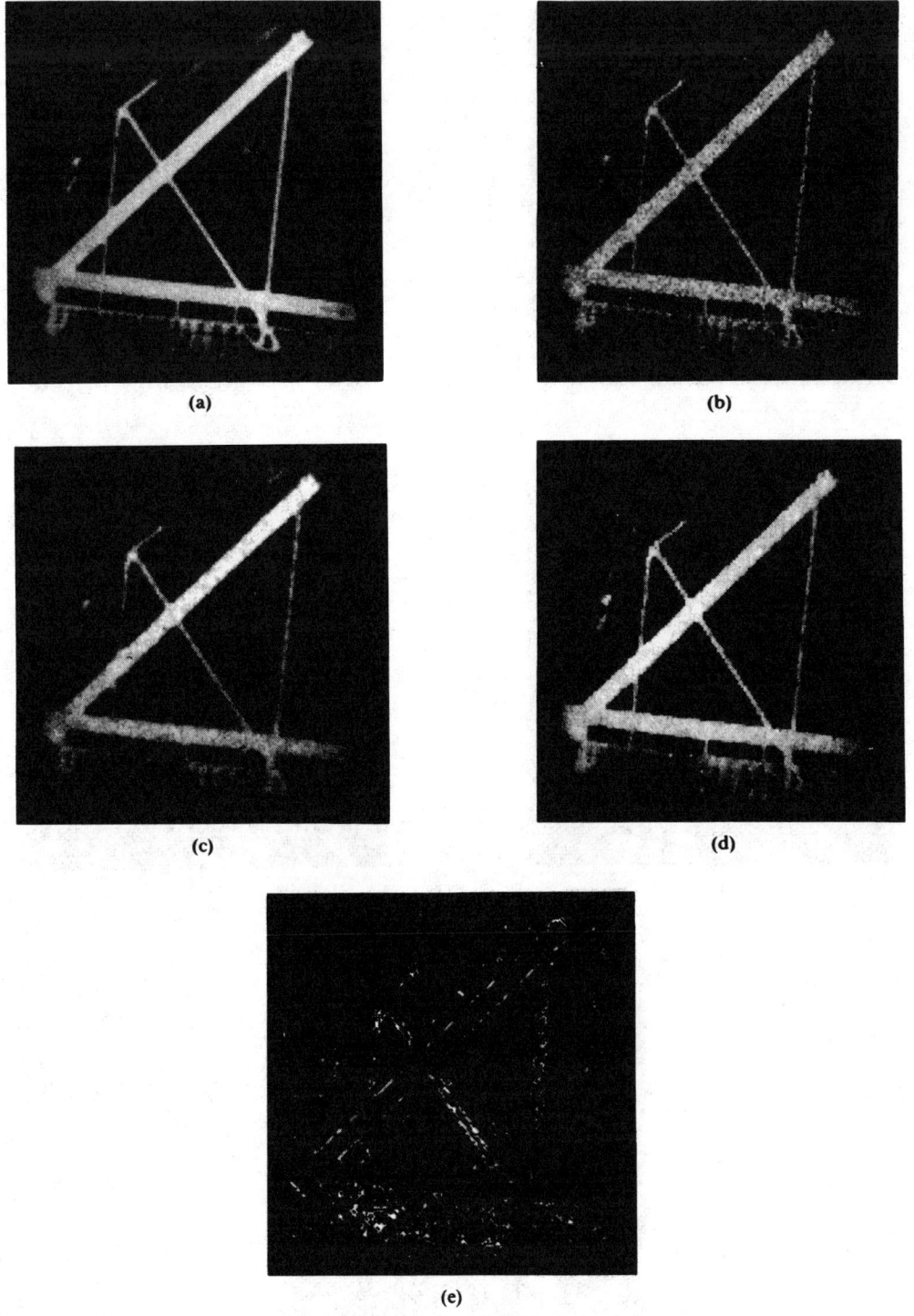

Fig. 5. Restoration and edge detection on airport image with 10-dB noise. (a) Original 128×128 airport image. (b) Image corrupted by 10-dB noise. (c) GMRF estimate after 100 iterations. (d) Compound GMRF estimate using GNC after 100 iterations. (e) Edge map obtained from GNC algorithm.

jugate gradient algorithm for early vision problems. The line-search conjugate algorithm was successfully used for nonlinear optimization problems, arising in SFS, image estimation and edge detection. We have also shown that the multigrid methods can successfully be incorporated in our algorithms to improve their convergence rate.

Coupled Markov fields models (such as compound GMRF) suggest a more realistic description of real life scenes. This observation is supported by the large reduction in the model variance, due to the ability to cope with the edges in the scene by using line processes. The new models require new parameter estimation techniques. An algorithm for obtaining the GMRF model parameters from the original image via an EM algorithm, was derived in this paper. The estimated parameters emphasize the importance of suppressing the influence of edges, when estimat-

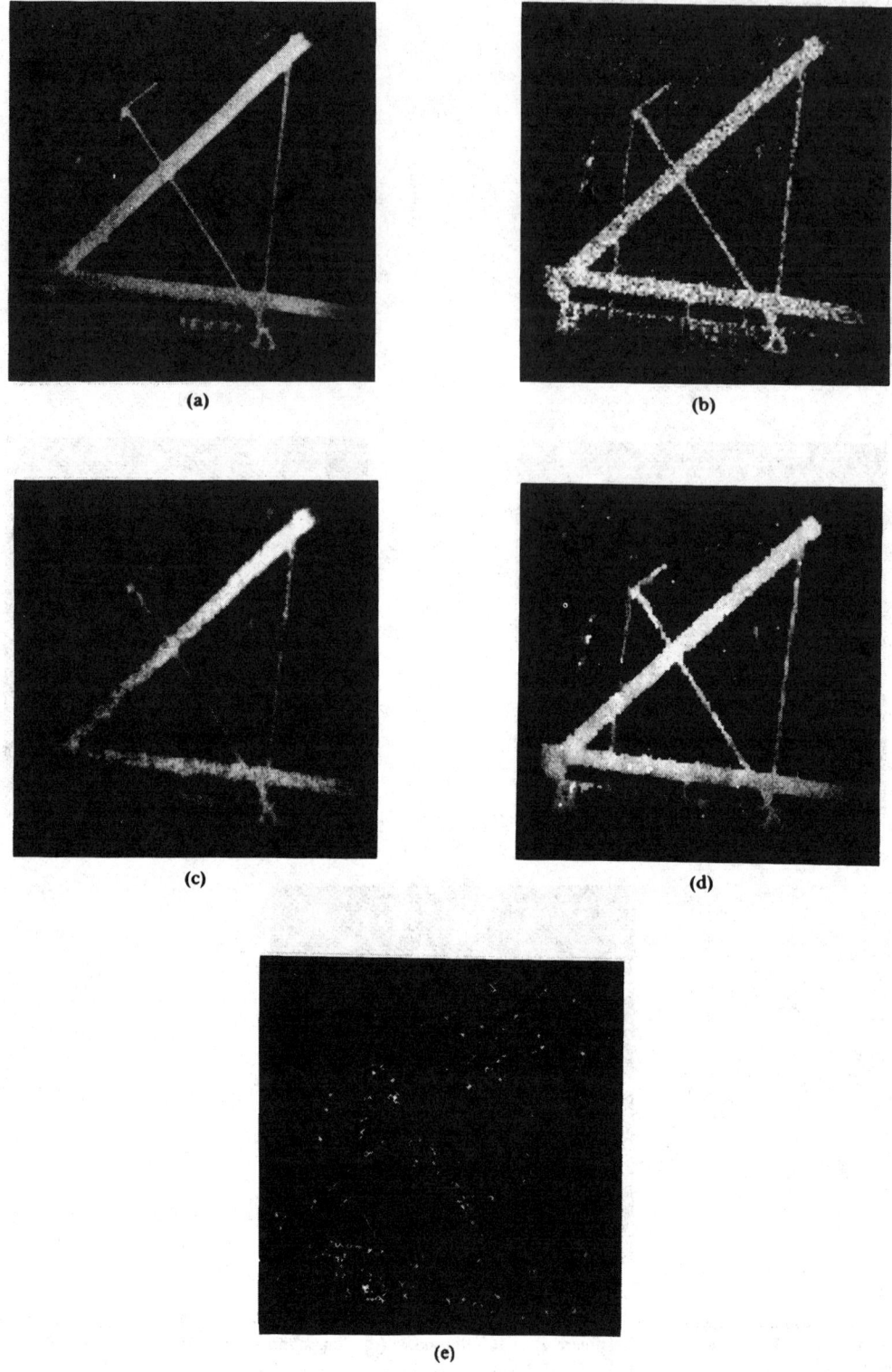

Fig. 6. Restoration and edge detection on airport image with 5-dB noise. (a) Original 128×128 airport image. (b) Image corrupted by 5-dB noise. (c) GMRF estimate after 100 iterations. (d) Compound GMRF estimate using GNC after 100 iterations. (e) Edge map obtained from GNC algorithm.

ing the parameters of the homogeneous regions. The work in the paper needs to be extended to a parameter estimation method from noisy images. We feel that it can be done using an EM algorithm

Existing stochastic relaxation techniques for optimizing the nonconvex cost functions are computationally un-attractive. In some restricted cases one can use the GNC formulation to find the global minimum of these nonconvex cost functions. We have exploited the equivalence between the stochastic and deterministic formulations through the use of Gibbs energy function, to extend the GNC algorithm to image estimation in compound GMRF for the additive noise case. The results are very encouraging, and the GNC–GMRF algorithm is fast and robust. Recently we have developed suboptimal relaxation methods in order to optimize nonconvex cost functions obtained from more sophisticated line processes than the one handled by the GNC formulation [35]. We have used a constrained minimization approach and let the line process variables evolve to the set $\{0,1\}$ gradually. Simulations results are encouraging.

References

[1] B. K. P. Horn, *Robot Vision*. Cambridge, MA: The MIT Press, 1986.
[2] S. Geman and D. Geman, "Stochastic relaxation, Gibbs distributions, and Bayesian restoration of images," *IEEE Trans. Pattern Anal. Machine Intell.*, vol. PAMI-6, pp. 721–741, Nov. 1984.
[3] T. Poggio and V. Torre, "Ill-posed problems and regularization analysis in early vision," Artificial Intelligence Lab., M.I.T., A.I.M 773, Apr. 1984.
[4] J. Hadamard, *Lectures on the Cauchy Problem in Linear Partial Differential Equations*. New Haven, CT: Yale University Press, 1923.
[5] R. Courant and D. Hilbert, *Methods of Mathematical Physics*, vol. 1. New York: Interscience, 1953.
[6] M. J. Brooks and B. K. P. Horn, "Shape and source from shading," in *Proc. Int. Joint Conf. Artificial Intell.*, Los Angeles, CA, Aug. 1985, pp. 932-936.
[7] M. Strat, "A numerical method for shape from shading from a single image," MS Thesis, M.I.T., Dept. of Elect. Engrg. and Comp. Sci., 1979.
[8] D. Lee, "A provably convergent algorithm for shape from shading," in *Proc. DARPA Image Understanding Workshop*, Miami Beach, FL, Dec. 1985, pp. 489-496.
[9] A. Blake and A. Zisserman, *Visual Reconstruction*. Cambridge, MA: MIT Press, 1987.
[10] D. Luenberger, *Linear and Nonlinear Programming*. Reading, MA: Addison-Wesley, 1984.
[11] D. Terzopoulos, "Image analysis using multigrid relaxation methods," *IEEE Trans. Pattern Anal. Machine Intell.*, vol. PAMI-8, pp. 129–139, Mar. 1986.
[12] Z. Li and L. Uhr, "Pyramid vision using key features to integrate image-driven bottom-up and model-driven top-down processes," *IEEE Trans. Syst. Man Cybern.* vol. SMC-17, pp. 250–263, Mar. 1987.
[13] P. J. Burt, T. H. Hong, and A. Rosenfeld, "Segmentation and estimation of image region properties through cooperative hierarchical computation," *IEEE Trans. Syst. Man Cybern.*, vol. SMC-11, pp. 801–809, 1981.
[14] P. J. Burt and G. S. van der Wal, "Iconic image analysis with the pyramid vision machine," *Comput. Architecture Pattern Anal. Machine Intell.*, pp. 137–144, 1987.
[15] R. Miller, "Pyramid computer algorithms," Ph.D. Thesis, Dept. of Math., State Univ. of New York, Binghamton, 1984.
[16] A. Rosenfeld, *Multiresolution Image Processing and Analysis*. New York: Springer-Verlag, 1984.
[17] ——, "A report on the DARPA image understanding architectures workshop," in *Proc. of DARPA Image Understanding Workshop*, Los Angeles, CA, Feb. 1987, pp. 298-302.
[18] S. L. Tanimoto, "Paradigm for pyramid machine algorithms," *Parallel Structures for Comput. Vision*, M. T. B. Duff, Ed. New York: Academic, pp. 173–194, 1987.
[19] M. Shneier, "Using pyramid to define local thresholds for blob detection," *IEEE Trans. Pattern Anal. Machine Intell.*, vol. PAMI-5, pp. 345–349, May 1983.
[20] J. Besag, "On the statistical analysis of dirty pictures," *J. Roy. Statist. Soc. B*, vol. 48, pp. 259–302, 1986.
[21] T. Simchony and R. Chellappa, "Direct analytical methods for solving Poisson equations in computer vision problems," in *IEEE Comput. Society Workshop Comput. Vision Problems*, Miami Beach FL, Nov. 1987.
[22] S. Geman and C. Hwang, "Diffusions for global optimization," *SIAM J. Contr. Optimization*, vol. 24, pp. 1031–1043, Sept. 1986.
[23] L. E. Scales, *Introduction to Non-Linear Optimization*. New York: Spinger-Verlag, 1985.
[24] A. K. Jain and J. R. Jain, "Partial difference equations and finite differences in image processing, part II: Image restoration," *IEEE Trans. Automatic Contr.*, vol. AC-23, pp. 817–833, Oct. 1978.
[25] R. Chellappa and R. L. Kashyap, "Digital image restoration using spatial interaction models," *IEEE Trans. Acoust. Speech Signal Process.*, vol. ASSP-30, pp. 461–472, June 1982.
[26] H. Jinchi, T. Simchony, and R. Chellappa, "Maximum *aposteriori* restoration of images corrupted by multiplicative noise," in *Proc. ICASSP 87, IEEE Conf. Acoust. Speech Signal Process.*, Dallas, TX, Apr. 1987.
[27] F. C. Jeng and J. W. Woods, "Image estimation by stochastic relaxation in the compound Gaussian case," in *Proc. ICASSP 88, IEEE Conf. Acoust. Speech Signal Process.*, New York, N.Y., Apr. 1988.
[28] A. P. Dempster, N. M. Laird, and D. B. Rubin, "Maximum likelihood from incomplete data via the EM algorithm," *Roy. Statis. Soc. B*, no. 39, 1977.
[29] R. Chellappa and R. L. Kashyap, "Texture synthesis using two-dimensional noncausal autoregressive models," *IEEE Trans. Acoust. Speech Signal Process.*, vol. ASSP-33, pp. 194–203, Feb. 1985.
[30] R. Chellappa, S. Chatterjee, and R. Bagdazian, "Texture synthesis and coding using Gaussian Markov random field models," *IEEE Trans. Syst. Man Cybern.*, vol. SMC-15, pp. 298–303, Mar. 1985.
[31] J. Besag, "Spatial interaction and the statistical analysis of lattice systems," *J. Roy. Statist. Soc. B*, vol. 36, pp. 192–236, 1974.
[32] H. Kaufman *et al.*, "Estimation and identification of two-dimensional images," *IEEE Trans. Automatic Contr.*, vol. AC-28, no. 7, pp. 745–755, July 1983.
[33] B. R. Hunt, "Digital image processing," *Proc. IEEE*, vol. 63, Apr. 1975, pp. 693–708.
[34] A. K. Jain, "A sinusoidal family of unitary transforms," *IEEE Trans. Pattern Anal. Machine Intell.*, vol. PAMI-1, pp. 356–365, Oct. 1979.
[35] A. Rangarajan, R. Chellappa, and T. Simchony "Networks for image estimation using penalty mehtod," *Proc. Int. Joint Conf. Neural Networks*, Washington DC, June, 1989.

Tal Simchony (S'86–M'88) received the B.Sc. degree in mathematics and computer science and the M.Sc. degree in applied mathematics from Tel Aviv University in 1982 and 1985, respectively, and the Ph.D. degree in electrical engineering from University of Southern California, Los Angeles, CA in 1988.

In 1982–1985 he worked in the software industry, for ECI Telecom Ltd., Tel Aviv, Israel. He is currently a research associate in the Signal and Image Processing Institute, University of Southern California. His current research interests include image processing, computer vision and neural networks. He joined ECI Telecom in 1989.

Ramalingam Chellappa (S'78–M'79–SM'83) was born in Madras, India. He received the B.S. degree (honors) in electronics and communications engineering from the University of Madras in 1975, and the M.S. degree (with distinction) in electrical communication engineering from the Indian Institute of Science, Bangalore, India, in 1977, and the M.S. and Ph.D. degrees in electrical engineering from Purdue University, West Lafayette, IN, in 1978 and 1981, respectively.

During 1979–1981, he was a Faculty Research Assistant at the Computer Vision Laboratory, University of Maryland, College Park, MD. Since 1986 he has been an Associate Professor in the Electrical Engineering Systems, and as of September 1988, he became the Director of the Signal and Image Institute at the University of Southern California, Los Angeles. His current research interest are in signal and image processing, computer vision, and pattern recognition.

Dr. Chellappa is a member of the Tau Beta Pi and Eta Kappas Nu. He is a coeditor of two volumes of selected papers on image analysis and processing, published in Fall 1985, and an Associate Editor for IEEE TRANSACTIONS ON ACOUSTICS, SPEECH AND SIGNAL PROCESSING. He was a recipient of a National Scholarship from the Government of India during 1969-1975. He received the 1975 Jawaharlal Nehru Memorial Award from the Department of Education, Government of India, the 1985 Presidential Young Investigator Award, and the 1985 IBM Faculty Development Award. He was the General Chairman of the IEEE Computer Society Conference on Computer Vision and Pattern Recognition, San Diego, CA, June, 1989, IEEE Computer Society workshop on Artificial Intelligence for Computer Vision, and Program Co-Chairman of the NSF-sponsored workshop on Markov random fields.

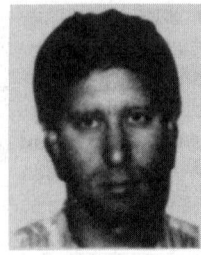

Ze'ev Lichtenstein received the B.S.E.E. degree from Tel-Aviv University, Tel-Aviv, Israel in 1986.

In 1983-1987, he was with Scitex Corp., Israel, where he was involved in a design of a new scanner. Currently he is a research assistant in the Signal and Image Processing Institute at the University of Southern California, Los Angeles. His current research interests include signal processing, and optimization techniques for computer vision.

Maximum likelihood image and blur identification: a unifying approach

Reginald L. Lagendijk
Delft University of Technology
Department of Electrical Engineering
P.O. Box 5031
2600 GA Delft, The Netherlands

A. Murat Tekalp
University of Rochester
Electrical Engineering Department
Rochester, New York 14627

Jan Biemond
Delft University of Technology
Department of Electrical Engineering
P.O. Box 5031
2600 GA Delft, The Netherlands

Abstract. A number of different algorithms have recently been proposed to identify the image and blur model parameters from an image that is degraded by blur and noise. This paper gives an overview of the developments in image and blur identification under a unifying maximum likelihood framework. In fact, we show that various recently published image and blur identification algorithms are different implementations of the same maximum likelihood estimator resulting from different modeling assumptions and/or considerations about the computational complexity. The use of the maximum likelihood estimation in image and blur identification is illustrated by numerical examples.

Subject terms: image restoration; blur identification; maximum likelihood; parameter estimation.

Optical Engineering 29(5), 422-435 (May 1990).

"Maximum Likelihood Image and Blur Identification: A Unifying Approach" by R.L. Lagendijk, A.M. Tekalp, and J. Biemond from *Optical Engineering*, Volume 29, Number 5, May 1990, pages 422-435. Copyright © 1990 Society of Photo-Optical Instrumentation Engineers, reprinted with permission.

CONTENTS

1. Introduction
2. Model development
   2.1. Image model
   2.2. Blur model
   2.3. Some considerations in modeling
3. Maximum likelihood (ML) parameter identification: theory
   3.1. Definition of the likelihood function
   3.2. Uniqueness of the estimates
   3.3. Analytic solution
4. ML parameter identification: implementation
   4.1. Gradient-based optimization
   4.2. EM-algorithm-based implementation
   4.3. Prediction-error-based implementation
   4.4. Least squares implementation
   4.5. Parallel 1-D least squares implementation
5. Experimental results
   5.1. Effect of observation noise
      5.1.1. Motion blur
      5.1.2. Defocusing blur
   5.2. Estimation of the point-spread function support
6. Discussion
7. Acknowledgments
8. References

Invited Paper RR-103 received Dec. 15, 1989; revised manuscript received Dec. 20, 1989; accepted for publication Dec. 20, 1989.
© 1990 Society of Photo-Optical Instrumentation Engineers.

1. INTRODUCTION

In many applications recorded images represent a degraded version of the original scene. The degradations may be due to blurring and observation noise. Two major causes of blurring are (1) relative motion between the imaging system and the original scene and (2) out-of-focus imaging systems. In certain cases, the blurring due to these phenomena may completely mask important information in the image, such as the diagnostic information in medical imaging or the legal evidence in photographs of one-of-a-kind documents. The noise usually originates from the recording medium or from the quantization of the data for digital storage. Although the blur is the most important degradation visually, the noise that is inevitably mixed with the data constitutes an important limitation in restoring blurred images.

The field of image restoration is concerned with the estimation of the original image from a noisy and blurred version. Over the past decades, a variety of image restoration methods have been developed, including Fourier domain,[1] recursive,[2] and iterative[3] procedures. However, in the literature it generally has been assumed that the point-spread function (PSF) of the blurring system and some other parameters of the restoration filter are known a priori. Since this is not usually the case in practice, one of the most challenging current problems in image restoration is how to estimate this information.

Earlier work in blur identification has concentrated on PSFs whose Fourier magnitude contains a regular pattern of zero crossings (such as uniform linear motion blur). Since these zeros usually can also be located in the power spectrum of the blurred image, spectral or cepstral techniques can be used to identify the PSF from the distance between the zeros in the power spectrum of the blurred image.[4,5] Shortcomings of this approach are that the PSFs that do not satisfy these conditions cannot be identified and that the presence of noise in the observed image is not taken into account.

In more recent work, the original scene has been modeled by a two-dimensional autoregressive (AR) process, and the blurring has been modeled by a 2-D linear system with finite impulse response (the PSF). In this paper, we follow the same modeling assumptions. We refer to estimating the PSF of the blurring system as blur identification, whereas by image identification we refer to estimating the parameters of the 2-D AR process modeling the second-order statistics of the image. Various apparently unrelated methods to estimate these unknown parameters have been proposed in the literature.[6-16] This paper aims at reviewing recent developments in image and blur identification under a unifying maximum likelihood (ML) framework. In fact, we show that these methods are different implementations of the same maximum likelihood estimator, resulting from different modeling assumptions and/or considerations about the computational complexity.

In Sec. 2 we start with the basic image and blur model development. Section 3 discusses the formulation of the image and blur identification problem as a ML problem. From this formulation, it follows that except for one specific parameter, an analytic solution that optimizes the likelihood function cannot be obtained. Therefore, in Sec. 4 we develop several numerical implementations of the ML estimator. In many of these methods, iterative optimization procedures play an important role, which are based on either numerical or analytical gradient computations. In discussing the various methods we emphasize their advantages and disadvantages. We show that there are basically two classes of implementations: one based on the assumption of noiseless data and one that incorporates the presence of noise into the algorithm. In Sec. 5 we compare two important representatives of each of these classes and focus, in particular, on their usefulness for identifying various blurs at various signal-to-noise ratios. Although the currently available maximum-likelihood-based image and blur identification algorithms cannot handle blurs that are both nonsymmetric and nonminimum phase, the ML approach will nevertheless be shown to be a powerful tool for image and blur identification in many applications.

2. MODEL DEVELOPMENT

2.1. Image model

In this paper we assume that the original image $f(i,j)$ can be characterized by a 2-D homogeneous Gauss-Markov process that is represented by the following 2-D AR model[17]:

$$f(i,j) = \sum_{k,l \in \mathcal{S}_a} a(k,l) f(i-k, j-l) + v(i,j) , \quad (1)$$

where $a(k,l)$ are the image model coefficients, $\mathcal{S}_a$ is the causal image model support, and i,j represent the vertical and horizontal coordinates, respectively. The modeling error $v(i,j)$ is a zero-mean homogeneous Gaussian distributed white noise process with covariance $Q_v(i,j) = \sigma_v^2 \delta(i,j)$ and is independent of $f(i,j)$. It is assumed that the coefficients $a(k,l)$ are chosen in such a way that Eq. (1) is a stable image model.[17]

A more compact notation for Eq. (1) can be arrived at by stacking the image data into a vector through conventional raster scanning, $f = [f(0,0), f(0,1), \ldots f(N-1, N-1)]'$,[18] yielding

$$f = Af + v , \quad (2)$$

where A is a matrix formed by the image model coefficients and the vector v is obtained from $v(i,j)$ through the raster scanning.

The probability density function (pdf) of f, given the pdf of v and the model (2), is given by

$$p(f;A,Q_v) = \left(\frac{\det|I - A|^2}{2\pi^{N^2} \det|Q_v|} \right)^{1/2} \exp\left[-\frac{1}{2} f'(I-A)' Q_v^{-1} (I-A) f \right] , \quad (3)$$

where $Q_v = \sigma_v^2 I$ is the covariance matrix of the modeling error v.

2.2. Blur model

The observed image $g(i,j)$ is modeled as the output of a 2-D finite impulse response (FIR) linear space-invariant system, which is characterized by its PSF $d(m,n)$. The observation noise $w(i,j)$ is assumed to be an additive zero-mean homogeneous Gaussian distributed process with covariance $Q_w(i,j) = \sigma_w^2 \delta(i,j)$. Then, the noisy blurred image is given by[1]

$$g(i,j) = \sum_{m,n \in \mathcal{S}_d} d(m,n) f(i-m, j-n) + w(i,j) , \quad (4)$$

where $\mathcal{S}_d$ is the support of the PSF $d(m,n)$. Since image formation systems normally do not absorb or generate energy, the PSF should satisfy

$$\sum_{m,n \in \mathcal{S}_d} d(m,n) = 1.0 . \quad (5)$$

Furthermore, since both the original and observed images represent intensity distributions that cannot take negative values, the PSF coefficients are always nonnegative. Again, Eq. (4) can be written in a more compact matrix-vector form:

$$g = Df + w , \quad (6)$$

where the definitions of the matrix D and the vectors g, f, and w follow from the raster scanning.

The probability density of g, given the pdf of the observation noise, the model for the blurring system, and the original image, can be expressed as

$$p(g/f;D,Q_w) = \frac{1}{\sqrt{2\pi^{N^2}\det|Q_w|}} \exp\left[-\frac{1}{2}(g - Df)^t Q_w^{-1}(g - Df)\right] , \quad (7)$$

where $Q_w = \sigma_w^2 I$ is the covariance matrix of the observation noise w. Observe that g is conditioned on both the original image (denoted by g/f) and the deterministic parameters D and Q_w (which we denote by $g;D,Q_w$).

2.3. Some considerations in modeling

One of the considerations in modeling images is that images are always of finite extent. As a result, Eqs. (1) and (4) can never model the data near the boundaries of the image accurately. We therefore have to preprocess the observed blurred image around its boundaries such that Eq. (4) is consistent with either the circular or linear convolution of $d(i,j)$ with $f(i,j)$. Suitable preprocessing operations have been suggested by Woods et al.[2,19] In the following, we assume that Eqs. (1) and (4) indicate circular convolution, when we consider the discrete Fourier transform (DFT) domain implementations, so that the observation matrix D and the image model matrix A can be assumed to be block-circulant.[18] In the recursive implementations, we assume that Eqs. (1) and (4) indicate linear convolution so that the observation matrix D and the image model matrix A can be assumed to be block-Toeplitz.[18]

It is almost always the case that the support of the PSF $\mathcal{S}_d$ is noncausal in the sense that it contains pixels that are both in the past and in the future (with respect to the direction of scanning) of the current pixel. However, given the FIR blur model (4), identification algorithms that are based just on the given blurred observations are insensitive to any shift of the support of the PSF. Hence, we can assume, without any loss of generality, that the support of the PSF can be shifted such that it is first quadrant causal. Then, recursive restoration and identification procedures, which demand a certain definition of causality, can be applied. However, many PSFs, such as symmetric PSFs, correspond to nonminimum phase systems, which cannot be identified recursively. Since shifting the support of the PSF does not address this problem, we have to conclude that for the application of recursive identification methods, both $a(k,l)$ and $d(m,n)$ need to represent causal minimum phase systems. If this assumption is not satisfied, recursive methods will identify the spectrally minimum phase equivalent of the actual nonminimum phase PSF.[6,8,20] For nonrecursive methods there is a related consideration. With hindsight to Sec. III, we observe that the ML approach to image and blur identification uses only second-order statistics of the blurred image, because all probability density functions are assumed to be Gaussian. Then, the Fourier phase of the ML solution is generally undetermined and the solution is nonunique since the second-order statistics of the blurred image do not contain information about the Fourier phase of the blur. Hence, to obtain a unique and/or stable solution to the ML image and blur identification problem, additional constraints on the PSF are required.

3. ML PARAMETER IDENTIFICATION: THEORY

To derive a restoration filter that aims at obtaining an estimate $\hat{f}$ that is "as close as possible" to the original image f, the PSF $d(m,n)$, the variance σ_w^2 of the observation noise, and the model of the original image [$a(k,l)$ and σ_v^2] need to be known. In this section, we derive the maximum likelihood estimator of these parameters. We consider various implementations of this ML estimator in the following section.

3.1. Definition of the likelihood function

For notational convenience, we denote the unknown parameters by the vector θ, i.e.,

$$\theta = (\theta_1, \theta_2, \ldots, \theta_M)^t$$
$$= (d(m,n), a(k,l), \sigma_w^2, \sigma_v^2)^t . \quad (8)$$

The maximum likelihood estimator of the parameter vector θ is defined by[20,21]

$$\hat{\theta}_{ml} = \arg\left\{\max_{\theta \in \Theta} \mathcal{L}^*(\theta)\right\} = \arg\left\{\max_{\theta \in \Theta} \log p(g;\theta)\right\} , \quad (9)$$

where $\mathcal{L}^*(\theta)$ denotes the (log-)likelihood function of θ; $p(g;\theta)$ denotes the a priori probability density function of the observed image, given θ; and Θ specifies the range of the parameters θ. By combining Eqs. (3) and (7), dropping all constant terms and premultiplying the result by -2 [the maximization in Eq. (9) now becomes a minimization], we obtain the equivalent likelihood function $\mathcal{L}(\theta)$:

$$\mathcal{L}(\theta) = \log(\det|P|) + g^t P^{-1} g , \quad (10)$$

where

$$P = \text{cov}(g) = \sigma_v^2 D(I - A)^{-1}(I - A)^{-t} D^t + \sigma_w^2 I . \quad (11)$$

If the matrices D and A are assumed to have a block-circulant structure, P has a block-circulant structure as well. Associated with P is the following 2-D convolution kernel $p(i,j)$:

$$p(i,j) = \sigma_v^2 d(i,j) * [1 - a(i,j)]^{-1}$$
$$* [1 - a(-i,-j)]^{-1} * d(-i,-j) + \sigma_w^2 . \quad (12)$$

We observe that all matrices in Eq. (11) commute because they are related to convolutions. The covariance matrix P is positive definite provided that $\sigma_w^2 > 0$. Since there is always noise present in the blurred image, this condition is satisfied. As a consequence, the inverse of P and the logarithm of $\det|P|$ always exist.

We should note that the dimension of P is $N^2 \times N^2$, where typical values of N are 128, 256, or even larger. Hence, direct evaluation of Eqs. (10) and (11) may not be feasible in practice.

If, however, we assume that the matrices A and D are block-circulant, they can be diagonalized by employing a 2-D discrete Fourier transform.[18] The eigenvalues of A, D, and P are given by the DFT coefficients corresponding to $a(k,l)$, $d(m,n)$, and $p(i,j)$, respectively. For this reason, the likelihood function $\mathcal{L}(\theta)$ can be evaluated very efficiently in the frequency domain:

$$\mathcal{L}(\theta) = \log\left[\prod_{u,v} P(u,v)\right] + \sum_{u,v} \frac{|G(u,v)|^2}{P(u,v)}$$

$$= \sum_{u,v}\left[\log P(u,v) + \frac{|G(u,v)|^2}{P(u,v)}\right] , \quad (13)$$

where

$$P(u,v) = \sigma_v^2 \frac{|D(u,v)|^2}{|1 - A(u,v)|^2} + \sigma_w^2 , \quad (14)$$

and $D(u,v)$, $A(u,v)$, $P(u,v)$, and $G(u,v)$ are the DFTs of $d(m,n)$, $a(k,l)$, $p(i,j)$, and $g(i,j)$, respectively. Alternatively, Eqs. (10) and (11) may be evaluated recursively in the spatial domain by using the concept of prediction error. This approach is discussed in Sec. 4.3.

3.2. Uniqueness of the estimates

From Eqs. (13) and (14) we observe that $\mathcal{L}(\theta)$ is independent of the phases of $1 - A(u,v)$ and $D(u,v)$, which was already mentioned in Sec. 2.3. However, this fact does not constitute a problem for the uniqueness of the estimates of $a(k,l)$ since we have assumed that the model (1) is stable and its support is causal. Then, the zeros of $1 - A(u,v)$ always lie inside the unit bicircle. As a result, $1 - A(u,v)$ always has minimum phase. This eliminates the phase ambiguity for $1 - A(u,v)$ and results in unique estimates for $a(k,l)$.

On the other hand, the estimates of $d(m,n)$ are not unique, in the absence of any additional constraints, mainly because blurs may have any kind of Fourier phase. Hence, the ML procedures are able to correctly identify only the magnitude-squared of $D(u,v)$, i.e., $|D(u,v)|^2$. Nonuniqueness of the estimates of $d(m,n)$ can in general be avoided by enforcing the solution to satisfy a set of constraints. In many papers dealing with blur identification, the PSF is assumed to be symmetric, i.e., $d(m,n) = d(-m,-n)$. In this way, the Fourier phase of the PSF is enforced to be either zero or $\pm \pi$. Unfortunately, even when we exploit the symmetry of the PSF, the Fourier phase of the solution is not defined uniquely because of the presence of $\pm \pi$, which translates into an ambiguity of the sign of $D(u,v)$. In practice, however, the sign ambiguity is not a serious problem because two additional constraints can be imposed on the solution to alleviate this problem. These are (1) the PSF coefficients are nonnegative and (2) the support of the PSF, $\mathcal{S}_d$, is finite.

The above constraints are almost always restrictive enough to obtain a unique estimate for the PSF. In the next section, in developing the algorithms for the optimization of $\mathcal{L}(\theta)$ we assume that the actual PSF is symmetric, positive, and has finite support, thereby restricting the class of PSFs that can be correctly identified. It should be noted that other forms of symmetries, such as $d(m,n) = d(-m,n)$ or $d(m,n) = d(m,-n)$, could also be used as constraints.

3.3. Analytic solution

In a first attempt to optimize $\mathcal{L}(\theta)$, we may consider an explicit analytic solution. Although the partial derivatives of the likelihood function with respect to the elements of θ can be computed (see Sec. 4.1), equating these to zero does not lead to any useful analytic expressions for the parameters to be estimated, mainly because of the nonquadratic behavior of $\log(\det|P|)$.

There is, however, one important exception. Let us introduce a new variable α, defined by

$$\alpha = \frac{\sigma_w^2}{\sigma_v^2} . \quad (15)$$

Substituting α into the likelihood function allows us to derive an analytic expression for either σ_v^2 or σ_w^2. Confining ourselves to the analytic expression for σ_v^2 (the other case is similar), we find for the ML estimator of σ_v^2 the following result:

$$\hat{\sigma}_v^2 = \frac{1}{N^2} g^t \tilde{P}^{-1} g . \quad (16)$$

Here $\tilde{P}$ is a modified covariance function appearing at the resulting ML estimation procedure:

$$\hat{\theta}'_{ml} = \arg\min_{\theta' \in \Theta'}\left\{N^2 \log(\sigma_v^2) + \log(\det|\tilde{P}|) + \frac{1}{\sigma_v^2} g^t \tilde{P}^{-1} g\right\} , \quad (17)$$

where

$$\tilde{P} = D(I - A)^{-1}(I - A)^{-t}D^t + \alpha I \quad (18)$$

and $\theta' = (d(m,n), a(k,l), \alpha)^t$. The interpretation of Eqs. (17) and (18) is that for a given θ', the optimal value of σ_v^2 can be determined analytically. Contrary to this, the minimization in Eq. (17) requires the optimal value of σ_v^2. Therefore, the above procedure does not make the actual optimization of the likelihood function much easier. More important, however, Eq. (15) reflects the well-known fact that in image restoration only the ratio of σ_w^2 to σ_v^2 is relevant and not their actual values. This ratio is typically known as the regularization parameter, which regulates the trade-off between deblurring and noise amplification.[3] In this sense, the elimination of the actual noise variances from the image and blur identification procedure is very natural.

In Sec. 4.4, it is shown that for the hypothetical case $\alpha = 0$ (i.e., the observed blurred image is noiseless), the likelihood function can be optimized independently of σ_v^2. For values of α that are much smaller than the diagonal elements of $D(I - A)^{-1}(I - A)^{-t}D^t$, we may very well assume that the effect of α in Eq. (18) is negligible. This means that we are allowed to apply identification methods that are based on noiseless data[6,8–10] to noisy data and account for the presence of noise later on. We study the effects of this assumption in Sec. 5. On the other hand, for very noisy data, αI dominates $D(I - A)^{-1}(I - A)^{-t}D^t$. In this case $\tilde{P}$ becomes independent of D and A, the entries of which can therefore no longer be identified correctly. The solution to Eq. (17) is then given by

$$\hat{\sigma}_w^2 = \frac{1}{N^2} g^t g , \quad (19)$$

i.e., the observed image is considered to contain noise only.

4. ML PARAMETER IDENTIFICATION: IMPLEMENTATION

Since an analytic solution for $\hat{\theta}$ cannot be found in general, except for σ_v^2 or σ_w^2, we consider numerical solution strategies in order to maximize $\mathcal{L}(\theta)$. An exhaustive search method or any other more intelligent search method could theoretically be applied to find a solution to Eq. (17). The dimension of the solution space is, however, very large due to the total number of unknowns. For example, a moderate blur with an extent of 5×5 pixels and a nonsymmetric half-plane image model support would already lead to a 17-dimensional solution space. Unless extremely tight constraints can be enforced onto the PSF and image model, global search strategies are not feasible for optimizing the likelihood function. In the following sections we consider recursive and nonrecursive algorithms, in which various forms of iterative optimization procedures play a prominent role.

4.1. Gradient-based optimization

To maximize $\mathcal{L}(\theta)$, we first consider a basic iterative optimization algorithm, which has the following structure:

$$\hat{\theta}^{(k+1)} = \hat{\theta}^{(k)} - B^{(k)} \nabla_\theta \mathcal{L}(\hat{\theta}^{(k)}) , \qquad (20)$$

where the gradient of $\mathcal{L}(\theta)$ is defined by

$$\nabla_\theta \mathcal{L}(\theta) = \left[\frac{\partial \mathcal{L}(\theta)}{\partial \theta_1}, \frac{\partial \mathcal{L}(\theta)}{\partial \theta_2}, \ldots, \frac{\partial \mathcal{L}(\theta)}{\partial \theta_M} \right]^t$$

$$= \left[\frac{\partial \mathcal{L}(\theta)}{\partial d(m,n)}, \frac{\partial \mathcal{L}(\theta)}{\partial a(k,l)}, \frac{\partial \mathcal{L}(\theta)}{\partial \sigma_v}, \frac{\partial \mathcal{L}(\theta)}{\partial \sigma_w} \right]^t \qquad (21)$$

and $B^{(k)}$ is the gain matrix that controls the convergence behavior of the iterations. Typical choices for this gain matrix are the identity matrix multiplied by a scalar, or the Hessian.[21]

For the image-blur identification problem, the partial derivative of $\mathcal{L}(\theta)$ with respect to one of the elements of θ (say θ_i) is given by

$$\frac{\partial \mathcal{L}(\theta)}{\partial \theta_i} = \frac{\partial}{\partial \theta_i} [\log(\det|P|)] + \frac{\partial}{\partial \theta_i} [g^t P^{-1} g] \qquad (22)$$

$$= \mathrm{tr}\left\{ \frac{\partial P}{\partial \theta_i} P^{-1} \right\} - \mathrm{tr}\left\{ g P^{-1} \frac{\partial P}{\partial \theta_i} P^{-1} g^t \right\} , \qquad (23)$$

where $\mathrm{tr}\{A\}$ denotes the trace of the matrix A. Thus, the iterative optimization algorithm (20) can be realized if we can evaluate the partial derivatives of P with respect to θ_i.

Since P itself is quadratic in $d(m,n)$, $a(k,l)$, σ_v, and σ_w, the evaluation of $\partial P/\partial \theta_i$ is relatively simple, yielding

$$\frac{\partial P}{\partial d(m,n)} = \sigma_v^2 (I - A)^{-1} (I - A)^{-t} (S_{m,n} D^t + S_{-m,-n} D) , \qquad (24)$$

$$\frac{\partial P}{\partial a(k,l)} = \sigma_v^2 D (I - A)^{-1} (I - A)^{-t} D^t$$
$$\times [S_{k,l}(I - A)^{-1} + S_{-k,-l}(I - A)^{-t}] , \qquad (25)$$

$$\frac{\partial P}{\partial \sigma_v} = 2\sigma_v D(I - A)^{-1}(I - A)^{-t} D^t , \qquad (26)$$

$$\frac{\partial P}{\partial \sigma_w} = 2\sigma_w I . \qquad (27)$$

Here $S_{m,n}$ is a "shift operator," which is a block-circulant matrix defined through the convolution kernel $\delta(i-m, j-n)$, i.e.,

$$S_{m,n} \sim \delta(i-m, j-n) = \begin{cases} 1, & i=m \text{ and } j=n , \\ 0, & \text{elsewhere} . \end{cases} \qquad (28)$$

Alternatively, Eq. (22) can also be evaluated in the DFT domain as

$$\frac{\partial \mathcal{L}(\theta)}{\partial \theta_i} = \sum_{u,v} \left\{ \left[\frac{1}{P(u,v)} - \frac{|G(u,v)|^2}{P(u,v)^2} \right] \frac{\partial P(u,v)}{\partial \theta_i} \right\} . \qquad (29)$$

The counterparts of Eqs. (24) through (27) in the Fourier domain become

$$\frac{\partial P(u,v)}{\partial d(m,n)} = \sigma_v^2 \frac{1}{|1 - A(u,v)|^2} \left\{ D(-u,-v) \exp\left[-\frac{2\pi j}{N}(um + vn) \right] \right.$$
$$\left. + D(u,v) \exp\left[\frac{2\pi j}{N}(um + vn) \right] \right\} , \qquad (30)$$

$$\frac{\partial P(u,v)}{\partial a(k,l)} = \sigma_v^2 \frac{|D(u,v)|^2}{|1 - A(u,v)|^2} \left\{ \frac{1}{1 - A(u,v)} \exp\left[-\frac{2\pi j}{N}(uk + vl) \right] \right.$$
$$\left. + \frac{1}{1 - A(-u,-v)} \exp\left[\frac{2\pi j}{N}(uk + vl) \right] \right\} , \qquad (31)$$

$$\frac{\partial P(u,v)}{\partial \sigma_v} = 2\sigma_v \frac{|D(u,v)|^2}{|1 - A(u,v)|^2} , \qquad (32)$$

$$\frac{\partial P(u,v)}{\partial \sigma_w} = 2\sigma_w . \qquad (33)$$

Lagendijk et al.[10] considered the application of the above iterations when the observed data are noiseless. In addition, they showed that it is possible to explicitly incorporate linear relations among the PSF and image model coefficients [such as the symmetry and Eq. (5)] into the computation of $\partial P/\partial \theta_i$. In this way, the uniqueness of the solution obtained by the above iterations could be guaranteed.

4.2. EM-algorithm-based implementation

From the work of Dempster et al.,[22] it is known that any likelihood function $\mathcal{L}(\theta)$ can be optimized by the following iterative scheme:

$$\mathcal{L}(\theta; \hat{\theta}^{(k)}) = E\{\log p(\mathcal{X}; \theta)/\mathcal{Y}; \hat{\theta}^{(k)}\} , \qquad (34)$$

$$\hat{\theta}^{(k+1)} = \arg\left\{ \max_{\theta \in \Theta} \mathcal{L}(\theta; \hat{\theta}^{(k)}) \right\} , \qquad (35)$$

where $\mathcal{L}(\theta; \hat{\theta}^{(k)})$ is the conditional likelihood function. The above iterations are known as the expectation-maximization (EM) algorithm: Eq. (34) is called the E-step and Eq. (35) the M-step. In Eq. (34) $\mathcal{X}$ denotes an appropriately chosen "complete data" set, which includes the observed "incomplete data" $\mathcal{Y}$ as a subset. The choice of the complete and incomplete data in the image and blur identification problem is discussed in the following. Convergence of the EM algorithm to a stationary point of $\mathcal{L}(\theta)$ was established by Dempster et al.[22] The EM algorithm is a particularly powerful tool to optimize $\mathcal{L}(\theta)$ if the maximization of $\mathcal{L}(\theta;\hat{\theta}^{(k)})$ in Eq. (35) can be performed easily. Furthermore, since the EM-based iterative scheme is not controlled by a gain matrix, such as $B^{(k)}$ in Eq. (20), its convergence is very robust. The convergence speed, on the other hand, may be slower than the maximally achievable one using the gradient-based iterations in Eq. (20).

For the image-blur identification problem, Lagendijk et al.[11,16] chose $\mathcal{X} = \{f,g\}$ and $\mathcal{Y} = \{g\}$. The particular choice of this complete data is motivated by the following: (1) for an entirely known complete data set, the image-blur identification problem can be solved uniquely, illustrating the meaning of "complete" data, and (2) both the E-step and the M-step can be solved relatively easily. The use of other definitions of $\mathcal{X}$ and $\mathcal{Y}$ in the iteration Eqs. (34) and (35) was considered by Lay et al.[14] Substituting the above choice for $\mathcal{X}$ and $\mathcal{Y}$ into the EM algorithm, together with the models of Sec. 2, leads to the following iteration[16]:

- E-step:

$$\hat{f}^{(k)} = E(f/g;\theta^{(k)}) = V^{(k)}D^t Q_w^{-1} g \ , \quad (36)$$

$$V^{(k)} = \text{cov}(f/g;\theta^{(k)})$$
$$= [(I - A)^t Q_v^{-1}(I - A) + D^t Q_w^{-1} D]^{-1} \ . \quad (37)$$

- M-step:

$$\{\hat{a}(k,l), \hat{\sigma}_v^2\} \leftarrow \min_{a(k,l),\sigma_v^2} \left\{ N^2 \log \sigma_v^2 + \frac{1}{\sigma_v^2} \text{tr}\{(I - A)\, \hat{\mathcal{R}}_{ff}^{(k)}\,(I - A)^t\} \right\} \ , \quad (38)$$

$$\{\hat{d}(m,n), \hat{\sigma}_w^2\} \leftarrow \min_{d(m,n),\sigma_w^2} \left\{ N^2 \log \sigma_w^2 + \frac{1}{\sigma_w^2} g^t g \right.$$
$$\left. - \frac{2}{\sigma_w^2} \text{tr}\{D\hat{\mathcal{R}}_{fg}^{(k)}\} + \frac{1}{\sigma_w^2} \text{tr}\{D\hat{\mathcal{R}}_{ff}^{(k)} D^t\} \right\} \ . \quad (39)$$

The conditional autocorrelation matrix $\hat{\mathcal{R}}_{ff}^{(k)}$ and crosscorrelation matrix $\hat{\mathcal{R}}_{fg}^{(k)}$ are given by

$$\hat{\mathcal{R}}_{ff}^{(k)} = E(ff^t/g;\hat{\theta}^{(k)}) = V^{(k)} + \hat{f}^{(k)}\hat{f}^{(k)t} \ , \quad (40)$$

$$\hat{\mathcal{R}}_{fg}^{(k)} = E(fg^t/g;\hat{\theta}^{(k)}) = \hat{f}^{(k)} g^t \ . \quad (41)$$

Since the M-step involves minimizing quadratic expressions only, it can be replaced by the following set of linear equations[16]:

$$\hat{r}_{ff}^{(k)}(p,q) = \sum_{k,l \in \mathcal{S}_a} \hat{a}(k,l) \hat{r}_{ff}^{(k)}(p-k, q-l) \ , \quad \forall (p,q) \in \mathcal{S}_a \ , \quad (42)$$

$$\hat{\sigma}_v^2 = \hat{r}_{ff}^{(k)}(0,0) - \sum_{k,l \in \mathcal{S}_a} \hat{a}(k,l)\, \hat{r}_{ff}^{(k)}(k,l) \ , \quad (43)$$

$$\hat{r}_{fg}^{(k)}(-p,-q) = \sum_{m,n \in \mathcal{S}_d} \hat{d}(m,n) \hat{r}_{ff}^{(k)}(p-m, q-n) \ ,$$
$$\forall (p,q) \in \mathcal{S}_d \ , \quad (44)$$

$$\hat{\sigma}_w^2 = \frac{1}{N^2} \sum_{i,j=1}^{N} g(i,j)^2 - \sum_{m,n \in \mathcal{S}_d} \hat{d}(m,n)\, \hat{r}_{fg}^{(k)}(-m,-n) \ . \quad (45)$$

Here $\hat{r}_{ff}^{(k)}(p,q)$ and $\hat{r}_{fg}^{(k)}(p,q)$ denote the auto- and crosscorrelation sequences associated with the correlation matrices $\hat{\mathcal{R}}_{ff}^{(k)}$ and $\hat{\mathcal{R}}_{fg}^{(k)}$, respectively. Symmetry conditions and the constraint Eq. (5) can be incorporated into the above set of equations in a straightforward way.[16]

The application of the EM algorithm to the image-blur identification problem results in an entirely linear iterative procedure,[11,16] the complexity of which is significantly less than the gradient-based optimization described in the previous section. In the E-step, the conditional mean of the original image is computed based on the current parameter estimates. In the M-step, the estimates of $\{d(m,n),\sigma_w^2\}$ and $\{a(k,l),\sigma_v^2\}$ are updated by solving two independent sets of linear equations. The image model parameters are determined from the conditional mean $\hat{f}$ as computed in the E-step, while the PSF coefficients are computed by identifying the linear system that has $\hat{f}$ as its input and g as the resulting output. These updated parameters are then used in the next E-step.

We conveniently implement the E-step of the algorithm in the DFT domain, making use of the assumed block-circulant nature of the matrices that are involved in these equations. Hence, Eq. (36) in fact corresponds to a Wiener filter defined by the available parameter estimates at the $(k-1)$st iteration. Alternatively, the recursive counterpart of the Wiener filter, i.e., the Kalman filter,[2] may be employed to implement the E-step in the spatial domain.

4.3. Prediction-error-based implementation

Both the gradient-based and the EM-algorithm-based formulations have been implemented in the DFT domain in order to avoid huge matrix operations in the spatial domain. Alternatively, it is possible to efficiently compute the likelihood function in the spatial domain by expressing the likelihood function in a recursive form.

Following Angwin,[15] we first assume that the image is raster scanned and that the elements of the observed noisy blurred image g become available one by one. (Note that in the derivation of the gradient-based and the EM-algorithm-based implementations, we used the matrix-vector notation, which assumes that all data g are available at once.) We can then represent the data at pixel position (i,j) in a recursive prediction error equation form[23]:

$$g(i,j) = \hat{g}(i,j;\theta) + \varepsilon(i,j;\theta) \ , \quad (46)$$

where $\hat{g}(i,j;\theta)$ is the predicted value of $g(i,j)$ using all observed image data up to the pixel (i,j), given the parameter vector θ, and $\varepsilon(i,j;\theta)$ denotes the resulting prediction error.

Next, we consider the linear minimum variance predictor for $\hat{g}(i,j;\theta)$ in Eq. (46) in order for $\varepsilon(i,j;\theta)$ to possess certain desired properties that will be made use of in rewriting $\mathcal{L}(\theta)$ recursively. The minimum variance prediction $\hat{g}(i,j;\theta)$ can be computed recursively[11] by employing a 2-D Kalman filter.[2] By using the usual definition of state vector $x(i,j)$ in two dimensions, the image model (1) and observation Eq. (4) can be expressed in the following state-space form:

$$x(i,j) = \mathcal{C}x(i,j-1) + (1,0,\ldots,0)'v(i,j) , \quad (47)$$
$$g(i,j) = \mathcal{H}x(i,j) + w(i,j) ,$$

where $\mathcal{C}$ and $\mathcal{H}$ denote the state transition matrix and degradation vector, whose definitions follow directly from the image model and the observation equation, respectively. The estimated state vector $\hat{x}_a(i,j)$ is then given by

$$\hat{x}_b(i,j) = \mathcal{C}\hat{x}_a(i,j-1) , \quad (48)$$
$$\hat{x}_a(i,j) = \hat{x}_b(i,j) + \mathcal{K}(i,j)\{g(i,j) - \mathcal{H}\hat{x}_b(i,j)\} ,$$

where $\mathcal{K}(i,j)$ is the Kalman gain, which is computed through the Ricatti equation; $\hat{x}_b(i,j)$ and $\hat{x}_a(i,j)$ denote the state estimation at the pixel (i,j) before and after updating, respectively.

Based on the above Kalman filter, we can write an expression for both the recursive prediction $\hat{g}(i,j;\theta)$ and the variance of the prediction error $\varepsilon(i,j;\theta)$ as

$$\hat{g}(i,j;\theta) = \mathcal{H}\hat{x}_b(i,j) , \quad (49)$$
$$\sigma^2_{\varepsilon(i,j;\theta)} = E[\varepsilon(i,j;\theta)\varepsilon(i,j;\theta)'] = \mathcal{H}P_b(i,j)\mathcal{H}' + \sigma^2_w ,$$

where $P_b(i,j) = E[(x(i,j) - \hat{x}_b(i,j))(x(i,j) - \hat{x}_b(i,j))']$ denotes the state error covariance matrix at the pixel (i,j) and can be obtained from the Kalman filter.

Given that $\hat{g}(i,j;\theta)$ is the minimum variance prediction of $g(i,j)$ and that $g(i,j)$ has a Gaussian distribution, we can conclude that $\varepsilon(i,j;\theta)$ is a white process uncorrelated with $\hat{g}(i,j;\theta)$ and its pdf $q(\varepsilon(i,j);\theta)$ is Gaussian with zero mean and variance $\sigma^2_{\varepsilon(i,j;\theta)}$.

In order to express the likelihood function in a recursive form, we let $g_{(m,n)} = [g(0,0), g(0,1), \ldots, g(m,n)]'$, i.e., the image vector containing all of the observed data up to and including $g(m,n)$, and $\mathcal{L}_{(m,n)}(\theta)$ denote the likelihood function of the observed data up to and including $g(m,n)$. Then we have[23]

$$\begin{aligned}\mathcal{L}_{(m,n)}(\theta) &= \log p(g_{(m,n)}; \theta) \\ &= \log p(g(m,n)/g_{(m,n-1)}; \theta) \cdot p(g_{(m,n-1)}; \theta) \\ &= \log q(g(m,n) - \hat{g}(m,n); \theta) \cdot p(g_{(m,n-1)}; \theta) \\ &= \log \prod_{(i,j)=(0,0)}^{(m,n)} q(g(i,j) - \hat{g}(i,j); \theta) \\ &= \sum_{(i,j)=(0,0)}^{(m,n)} \log q(g(i,j) - \hat{g}(i,j); \theta) \\ &= \sum_{(i,j)=(0,0)}^{(m,n)} \log q(\varepsilon(i,j); \theta) . \end{aligned} \quad (50)$$

Substituting the pdf $q(\varepsilon(i,j); \theta)$ into Eq. (50), dropping all constant terms, and multiplying the result by -2 leads to

$$\mathcal{L}_{(m,n)}(\theta) = \sum_{(i,j)=(0,0)}^{(m,n)}\left\{\log\sigma^2_{\varepsilon(i,j;\theta)} + \frac{[g(i,j) - \hat{g}(i,j)]^2}{\sigma^2_{\varepsilon(i,j;\theta)}}\right\} . \quad (51)$$

Equation (51) shows that the likelihood function can be evaluated as a sum of scalar functions, which is considerably simpler than the direct evaluation of Eqs. (10) and (11). Substituting Eq. (49) into Eq. (51) yields a computable recursive expression for the likelihood function, in which the 2-D Kalman filter is utilized to recursively compute the prediction errors and the prediction error variance. Optimizing $\mathcal{L}(\theta)$ in Eq. (10), which uses all of the available data $g(i,j)$, $i,j \in [0,N-1]$, is now equivalent to optimizing $\mathcal{L}_{(N-1,N-1)}(\theta)$, given by Eq. (51).

It should be noted that the recursive computation of the likelihood function unfortunately does not lead to a recursive parameter identification procedure. For example, suppose that the likelihood function $\mathcal{L}_{(m,n)}(\theta)$ has been optimized with respect to θ. The addition of a single new observed data point $g(m,n+1)$ to Eq. (51) requires a new likelihood function $\mathcal{L}_{(m,n+1)}(\theta)$ to be optimized, the result of which cannot be expressed analytically in terms of the parameter estimates at (m,n). Hence, the proposed solution does not easily extend to an adaptive (finite memory) parameter identification scheme.

Another problem with this formulation is that the partial derivatives of the likelihood function (51) cannot be obtained analytically because of the nonlinearities introduced by the Ricatti equation. Therefore, numerical procedures have to be utilized in order to compute the partial derivatives of the likelihood function with respect to each of the unknown parameters. This, however, involves filtering the blurred image a number of times. Therefore, even if efficient implementations are employed,[2,15] the use of a 2-D Kalman filter usually requires more computation than the frequency domain approach, especially for large PSFs. Note that the technique described in this section is essentially a mixed iterative-recursive identification method, where numerical gradients are used to iteratively optimize the likelihood function, which is computed recursively.

4.4. Least squares implementation

In the following two sections we discuss implementations of the likelihood estimator that are based on the assumption of noiseless observed image data, i.e., $\sigma^2_w = 0$. In the presence of observation noise, the estimates obtained by using these procedures are no longer the maximum likelihood solutions but are the least squares solutions, as will be shown. For small values of σ^2_w, the difference between the least squares and the ML estimates are, however, negligible (see Sec. 5).

In the case $\sigma^2_w = 0$, the covariance matrix P in Eq. (11) becomes

$$P = \sigma^2_v D(I - A)^{-1}(I - A)^{-t}D' . \quad (52)$$

Furthermore, if we assume, without loss of generality, that the PSF of the degrading system is first-quadrant causal and that D and A are associated with linear convolutions, the determinant of the covariance matrix P becomes equal to $[\sigma^2_v d(0,0)^2]^{N^2}$. The likelihood function $\mathcal{L}(\theta)$ in Eq. (10) can then be rewritten as

$$\mathcal{L}(\theta') = N^2\log\{[d(0,0)\sigma_v]^2\}$$
$$+ \frac{1}{[d(0,0)\sigma_v]^2} g'D'^{-t}(I - A)'(I - A)D'^{-1}g . \quad (53)$$

Here

$$D' = \frac{1}{d(0,0)}D , \quad (54)$$

or

$$d'(m,n) = \frac{d(m,n)}{d(0,0)} , \quad (55)$$

indicates a normalization of the PSF in both matrix and scalar notation and θ' is composed of the image model parameters $a(k,l)$ and the normalized PSF coefficients $d'(m,n)$. Equation (53) shows that for a given D' and A, $\mathcal{L}(\theta')$ can be optimized analytically with respect to $\mu = d(0,0)^2\sigma_v^2$, yielding

$$\mu = d(0,0)^2\sigma_v^2 = \frac{1}{N^2}g'D'^{-t}(I - A)^t(I - A)D'^{-1}g . \qquad (56)$$

Taking Eq. (5) and the fact that $d(0,0) \geq 0$ into account, both $d(0,0)$ and σ_v^2 can be obtained from Eq. (56). Hence, under the assumption of noiseless data, analytic expressions for $d(0,0)$ and σ_v^2 can be found. Furthermore, the optimization of Eq. (53) can be done independent of σ_v^2, as was already mentioned in Sec. 3.3.

The normalized PSF coefficients $d'(m,n)$ and image model coefficients $a(k,l)$ can be determined by a gradient-based optimization of $\mathcal{L}(\theta')$ in the DFT domain, similar to the one in Sec. 4.1. Alternatively, a gradient-based optimization of $\mathcal{L}(\theta')$ using recursive spatial domain computations has been proposed by Tekalp et al.[6,8] To this end, we first introduce a new variable ε, called the (prediction) error signal:

$$\varepsilon = (I - A)D'^{-1}g ,$$

or

$$\varepsilon(i,j) = g(i,j) - \sum_{k,l \in \mathcal{S}_a} a(k,l)g(i-k, j-l) - \sum_{m,n \in \mathcal{S}_d \setminus \{(0,0)\}} d'(m,n)\varepsilon(i-m, j-n) . \qquad (57)$$

Minimizing the likelihood function $\mathcal{L}(\theta')$ in Eq. (53) then reduces to minimizing the variance of ε:

$$\mathcal{L}(\theta') = c_1 + \frac{1}{[d(0,0)\sigma_v]^2}\varepsilon^t\varepsilon$$
$$= c_1 + \frac{1}{[d(0,0)\sigma_v]^2}\sum_{i,j}\varepsilon^2(i,j) , \qquad (58)$$

where only $\varepsilon(i,j)$ is a function of $a(k,l)$ and $d'(m,n)$. We observe that for noiseless blurred images, the original ML identification problem can be rewritten as an equivalent 2-D least squares problem.

Recursive equations can be employed[6,8] to compute $\varepsilon(i,j)$ and the gradient of $\mathcal{L}(\theta')$. The gradient of Eq. (58) can be computed analytically with respect to each of the unknowns θ'_k and can be expressed in recursive form as follows:

$$\frac{\partial \mathcal{L}(\theta')}{\partial \theta'_k} = 2\sum_{i,j}\varepsilon(i,j)\frac{\partial \varepsilon(i,j)}{\partial \theta'_k} , \qquad (59)$$

where the partial derivatives of $\varepsilon(i,j)$ are recursively given by

$$\frac{\partial \varepsilon(i,j)}{\partial a(k,l)} = -g(i-k, j-l)$$
$$- \sum_{p,q \in \mathcal{S}_d \setminus \{(0,0)\}} d'(p,q)\frac{\partial \varepsilon(i-p, j-q)}{\partial a(k,l)} , \qquad (60)$$

$$\frac{\partial \varepsilon(i,j)}{\partial d'(m,n)} = -\varepsilon(i-m, j-n)$$
$$- \sum_{p,q \in \mathcal{S}_d \setminus \{(0,0)\}} d'(p,q)\frac{\partial \varepsilon(i-p, j-q)}{\partial d(m,n)} . \qquad (61)$$

To guarantee the stability of these recursive equations, the normalized PSF $d'(i,j)$ must be a minimum phase bisequence. Since this, in general, cannot be assumed to be the case, the following two computational methods were proposed: (1) Decompose the unknown PSF model into four quarter-plane convolutional factors, each of which is stable in its direction of recursion, and next identify one of these factors, using the symmetry of the factors, by the above sketched identification method. The final PSF is formed by cascading the individual convolutional factors.[6] (2) Decompose the magnitude square of the PSF into two nonsymmetric half-plane factors in order to identify the magnitude response of the PSF.[8] Tekalp et al.[6] also suggested solution strategies when there is observation noise based on the spectral factorization of a combined noise process.

It can be shown that the above formulation is equivalent to the maximum likelihood identification of a 2-D causal autoregressive moving-average (ARMA) model in the absence of observation noise. Rearranging Eq. (57), we obtain

$$g = Ag + D'\varepsilon$$

or

$$g(i,j) = \sum_{k,l \in \mathcal{S}_a} a(k,l)g(i-k, j-l) + \sum_{m,n \in \mathcal{S}_d} d'(m,n)\varepsilon(i-m, j-n) . \qquad (62)$$

The input-output relation Eq. (62) constitutes a 2-D ARMA model, which formed the basis of the pioneering work by Tekalp et al.[6] in the area of image-blur identification. In Eq. (62) the AR coefficients represent the image model, and the MA parameters stand for the normalized PSF coefficients. Hence, the image and blur identification problem becomes a 2-D ARMA model identification problem, which states that identifying the PSF coefficients is equivalent to finding the zeros of the MA polynomial in the complex $z_1 - z_2$ plane. Thus, the proposed procedures can be considered as a generalization of the classical blur identification methods, which are based on locating the zeros of the frequency response of the PSF. We note that under the assumption that the observed data are noiseless and the image and blur models are causal, the ML and the least squares solutions are the same.

4.5. Parallel 1-D least squares implementation

Having noticed that the image-blur identification can be interpreted as a 2-D ARMA model identification problem, one wonders whether the well-known 1-D ML ARMA model identification procedures can be used to address the ML ARMA identification problem in two dimensions. It was shown[9,12,13] that under certain conditions, it is possible to decompose the 2-D ARMA model identification problem into a set of parallel 1-D complex ARMA model identification problems. Well-known 1-D least squares identification methods were subsequently applied to each of the parallel channels independently to obtain the least squares estimates of the parameters.

In this section, we consider the ML estimation of the 2-D ARMA model by 1-D ML identification of each of the channels independently. It is shown that such an independent optimization can be done only if the blurred image is noiseless. As a result, the methods described in this section are essentially least squares techniques in the presence of observation noise.

We first rewrite the likelihood function $\mathcal{L}(\theta)$ in Eq. (13) as the sum of N likelihood functions each of which is based on a column of the image. This is done by simply splitting the summation over both the columns and rows in Eq. (13) into a separate summation over the rows (denoted by the summation index u), followed by a separate summation over the columns (denoted by v):

$$\mathcal{L}(\theta) = \sum_{u,v} \left[\log P(u,v) + \frac{|G(u,v)|^2}{P(u,v)} \right]$$

$$= \sum_{v} \left\{ \sum_{u} \left[\log P_v(u) + \frac{|G_v(u)|^2}{P_v(u)} \right] \right\}$$

$$= \sum_{v} \left[\log \prod_{u} P_v(u) + \sum_{u} \frac{|G_v(u)|^2}{P_v(u)} \right]$$

$$= \sum_{v} \left(\log \det|P_v| + g_v^t P_v^{-1} g_v \right) = \sum_{v} \mathcal{L}_v(\theta) , \quad (63)$$

where $G_v(u)$ denotes the vth column of $G(u,v)$ and $g_v = (g_v(0), g_v(1), \ldots, g_v(N-1))^t$ denotes the inverse 1-D DFT of $G_v(u)$. Similarly, $P_v(u)$ denotes the vth column of $P(u,v)$ and P_v is the circulant matrix associated with the convolution kernel $p_v(i)$, which is the inverse 1-D DFT of $P_v(u)$. Referring to Eqs. (11) and (14), we can write

$$P_v = \sigma_v^2 D_v (I - A_v)^{-1} (I - A_v)^{-t} D_v^t + \sigma_w^2 I , \quad (64)$$

or

$$P_v(u) = \sigma_v^2 \frac{|D_v(u)|^2}{|1 - A_v(u)|^2} + \sigma_w^2 , \quad \forall v . \quad (65)$$

Associated with these relations is the following convolution kernel for each of the columns:

$$p_v(i) = \sigma_v^2 d_v(i) * [1 - a_v(i)]^{-1} * [1 - a_v(-i)]^{-1}$$
$$* d_v(-i) + \sigma_w^2 , \quad \forall v . \quad (66)$$

$D_v(u)$ and $A_v(u)$ are the vth column of $D(u,v)$ and $A(u,v)$, respectively, and $d_v(i)$ and $a_v(i)$ are their 1-D column-wise inverse DFTs. Alternatively, we may also regard $d_v(i)$ as the vth DFT coefficient resulting from a 1-D *forward* DFT of the ith row of $d(i,j)$. Similar results hold for $a_v(i)$, $p_v(i)$ and $g_v(i)$.

The interpretation of Eq. (63) is that if we apply a 1-D DFT to each of the rows of $g(i,j)$, as proposed by Biemond et al.,[9] we can compute the value of the likelihood function $\mathcal{L}(\theta)$ as the sum of the individual likelihood functions $\mathcal{L}_v(\theta)$, each of which is related to a column (or "channel") of $g(i,j)$. We would now like to optimize $\mathcal{L}(\theta)$ by optimizing each of the individual likelihood functions $\mathcal{L}_v(\theta)$ independently (possible in parallel). Note that this decoupled optimization cannot be performed directly by equating the gradients of $\mathcal{L}_v(\theta)$ with respect to θ to zero because the channels are not decoupled with respect to the elements of θ. However, it can be observed from Eq. (66) that the channels are decoupled with regard to the coefficients $a_v(i)$ and $d_v(i)$. Therefore, each $\mathcal{L}_v(\theta)$ can be optimized independently with respect to these transformed coefficients.

Unfortunately, such an independent optimization is not possible for σ_w^2 and σ_v^2 because they appear in the expressions for each $\mathcal{L}_v(\theta)$. However, if we (initially) assume that the observation noise is negligible ($\sigma_w^2 \approx 0$), it is then sufficient to optimize $\mathcal{L}(\theta)$ only with respect to the image model and PSF coefficients, as shown in Sec. 3.3. As a result, however, we obtain least squares estimates of the parameters $d_v(i)$ and $a_v(i)$ instead of the ML estimates.

We now define $\theta_v = (d_v(i), a_v(i))^t$ ($\forall v$) and write $\mathcal{L}_v(\theta) = \mathcal{L}_v(\theta_v)$ to stress that the likelihood function of channel v need be optimized only with respect to the parameter vector θ_v. If we assume that $d_v(i)$ and $a_v(i)$ denote linear convolutions, we can rewrite $\mathcal{L}_v(\theta_v)$ as follows:

$$\mathcal{L}_v(\theta_v) = N \log[d_v(0)^2 \sigma_v^2]$$
$$+ \frac{1}{d_v(0)^2 \sigma_v^2} g_v^t D_v'^{-t} (I - A_v)^t (I - A_v) D_v'^{-1} g_v$$

$$= c_1 + \frac{1}{c_2} \varepsilon_v^t \varepsilon_v = c_1 + \frac{1}{c_2} \sum_i \varepsilon_v^2(i) . \quad (67)$$

Here $D_v' = D_v/d_v(0)$ indicates a normalization of the PSF and $\varepsilon_v = (I - A_v) D_v'^{-1} g_v$ is the error signal in the vth channel.

Finally, the optimization of $\mathcal{L}(\theta)$ with respect to θ can be done by solving the following set of equations:

$$\nabla_\theta \mathcal{L}(\theta) = \nabla_\theta \sum_v \mathcal{L}_v(\theta_v) = \sum_v \frac{\partial \theta}{\partial \theta_v} \nabla_{\theta_v} \mathcal{L}_v(\theta_v) = 0 , \quad (68)$$

where $\partial \theta/\partial \theta_v$ denotes the Jacobian matrix of the transform from θ to θ_v (i.e., the 1-D row-wise DFT). Since the parameter vectors θ_v are mutually uncoupled, an obvious solution to Eq. (68) is given by

$$\nabla_{\theta_v} \mathcal{L}_v(\theta_v) = 0 , \quad \forall v , \quad (69)$$

or

$$\frac{\partial}{\partial a_v(k)} \mathcal{L}_v(\theta_v) = \frac{\partial}{\partial a_v(k)} \sum_{i=0}^{N-1} \varepsilon_v^2(i) = 0 , \quad \forall v , \quad (70)$$

$$\frac{\partial}{\partial d_v(m)} \mathcal{L}_v(\theta_v) = \frac{\partial}{\partial d_v(m)} \sum_{i=0}^{N-1} \varepsilon_v^2(i) = 0 , \quad \forall v . \quad (71)$$

After identifying the parameters $d_v(m)$ and $a_v(k)$ in each of the channels, the original parameters $d(m,n)$ and $a(k,l)$ can be found by a 1-D row-wise inverse DFT. Finally, σ_v^2 can be obtained by using Eq. (16).

Using a discussion similar to the one in Sec. 4.4, it is straightforward to show that solving Eqs. (70) and (71) is equivalent to identifying a 1-D (complex) ARMA model using least squares. In this respect, the algorithm resulting from the above reformulation of the 2-D ML problem is identical to the approach suggested by Biemond et al.[9] A variety of "standard" 1-D identification procedures can be applied to solve $a_v(i)$ and $d_v(i)$ from Eqs. (70) and (71), respectively, for each of the parallel channels. One-dimensional recursive identification methods, such

Fig. 1. Original cameraman image.

Fig. 2. Cameraman image blurred by horizontal motion at SNR = 40 dB.

TABLE I. Identified PSF coefficients for horizontal motion blur.

Method	SNR	$d(0,0)$	$d(0,1)$	$d(0,2)$	$d(0,3)$	$d(0,4)$	σ_w^2	η_{SNR}	$\eta_{SNR,\,max}$
RLS	60	0.128	0.126	0.124	0.123	0.061	-	12.25	13.11
EM	60	0.134	0.131	0.128	0.118	0.056	0.007	10.77	
RLS	40	0.124	0.132	0.119	0.129	0.058	-	7.09	7.66
EM	40	0.126	0.125	0.124	0.127	0.060	0.32	7.51	
RLS	30	0.133	0.139	0.122	0.117	0.055	-	3.78	4.89
EM	30	0.122	0.122	0.122	0.142	0.053	2.98	4.75	
RLS	20	0.081	0.150	0.072	0.189	0.048	-	2.24	2.81
EM	20	0.123	0.127	0.111	0.161	0.039	30.2	2.80	
RLS	10	0.031	0.142	0.063	0.278	0.001	-	2.52	3.19
EM	10	0.133	0.124	0.050	0.239	0.020	302.9	3.16	

TABLE II. Identified image model coefficients for horizontal motion blur.

Method	SNR	$a(-1,-1)$	$a(-1,0)$	$a(-1,1)$	$a(0,-1)$	σ_v^2
RLS	60	-0.317	0.552	0.194	0.570	225.2
EM	60	-0.303	0.659	0.152	0.483	261.6
RLS	40	-0.246	0.553	0.325	0.363	238.5
EM	40	-0.391	0.643	0.155	0.595	176.9
RLS	30	-0.123	0.388	0.283	0.448	262.7
EM	30	-0.477	0.636	0.148	0.688	128.3
RLS	20	-0.115	0.430	0.269	0.395	311.1
EM	20	-0.526	0.627	0.154	0.742	105.7
RLS	10	0.056	0.083	0.220	0.635	471.1
EM	10	-0.457	0.514	0.206	0.731	147.8

as the recursive maximum likelihood or recursive extended least squares methods, have been used by Das[7] and Katayama et al.[12]; the nonrecursive Graupe, Moore, and Krause technique was used by Biemond et al.,[9] while Blanc-Féraud et al.[13] considered the use of gradient-based optimization procedures.

5. EXPERIMENTAL RESULTS

5.1. Effect of observation noise

In the preceding section we showed that there are basically two classes of image-blur identification methods. The first class incorporates the fact that there is noise in the observed blurred image. In the second class, the presence of noise is neglected in deriving the identification algorithm. These methods can, however, also be applied to noisy data as long as the signal-to-noise ratio is high enough. The SNR is defined by

$$\text{SNR} = 10 \log_{10}\left(\frac{\text{variance of the blurred image}}{\text{variance of the noise}}\right) \text{ (dB)} . \quad (72)$$

In this first experiment we consider the effects of noise on the identified parameters. Two aspects are studied: (1) At what SNR does the second class of implementations break down, and (2) how good are the estimated parameters, both in numerical respect and in terms of the improvement in SNR for the restored image. The measure of improvement in SNR is defined by

$$\eta_{SNR} = 10 \log_{10} \frac{\sum_{i,j}[g(i,j) - f(i,j)]^2}{\sum_{i,j}[\hat{f}(i,j) - f(i,j)]^2} \text{ (dB)} , \quad (73)$$

where $\hat{f}(i,j)$ denotes the restored image based on the estimated parameters. The results presented in the experimental section involve two implementations, one representing algorithms incorporating the presence of noise (EM-algorithm-based implementation) and the other representing the class of algorithms based on the assumption of noiseless data (2-D recursive least squares implementation). The restoration results are obtained in either case by using a 2-D Wiener filter.

5.1.1. Motion blur

We artificially blurred the original cameraman image of Fig. 1 by horizontal linear motion blur over nine pixels and added noise that corresponds to 60, 40, 30, 20, and 10 dB SNR. Figure 2 shows the blurred image with SNR = 40 dB. The nonsymmetric half-plane image model coefficients identified from the original image using a least squares method are given by

$$\begin{bmatrix} a(-1,-1) & a(-1,0) & a(-1,1) \\ a(0,-1) & & \end{bmatrix} = \begin{bmatrix} -0.498 & 0.594 & 0.139 \\ 0.756 & & \end{bmatrix},$$

and the variance of the modeling error $\sigma_v^2 = 227.5$. The PSF used in blurring the image is given by

$$[d(0,-4), d(0,-3), d(0,-2), d(0,-1), d(0,0), d(0,1), d(0,2), d(0,3), d(0,4)] =$$
$$[0.0625, 0.125, 0.125, 0.125, 0.125, 0.125, 0.125, 0.125, 0.0625] ,$$

and σ_w^2 equals 0.0035, 0.35, 3.5, 35.0, and 350.0 for SNR = 60, 40, 30, 20, and 10 dB, respectively.

In identifying the image model and PSF coefficients, we assumed that the PSF is symmetric and used a 1×9 PSF support. The boundaries of the image were preprocessed to approximately satisfy the assumption of a linear (RLS approach) or circulant (EM algorithm) convolution between $f(i,j)$ and $d(i,j)$. The identification results are listed in Table I (PSF coefficients) and Table II (image model coefficients). Table I also lists the SNR im-

Fig. 3. Wiener filter restoration from Fig. 2 using (a) ideal parameters, (b) estimated parameters by the RLS method, and (c) estimated parameters by the EM algorithm.

provement obtained by restoring the image using the identified parameters (denoted by η_{SNR}) and the one obtained by using the exact parameters (denoted by $\eta_{SNR,max}$). From these tables, it can be seen that at high SNRs the least squares and ML approaches yield comparable results. At 60 dB SNR the least squares results are even better than the true ML estimates, which is mainly due to numerical inaccuracies in the implementation of the EM algorithm. For decreasing SNRs the least squares method appears to break down below 40 dB, while the ML estimation computed through the EM algorithm are acceptable up to a SNR of 20 dB.

To show the effects of the deviations of the estimated parameters from their ideal values, Fig. 3 shows the Wiener filter restoration result of the blurred image in Fig. 2 using (a) the ideal parameters, (b) the parameters estimated by the 2-D RLS method, and (c) the parameters obtained from the EM algorithm. As can be seen from the restoration results, the estimation errors of approximately 5% in the parameters have hardly any effect on the quality of the restoration result.

5.1.2. Defocusing blur

In the next experiment, the cameraman image was blurred by the following 2-D PSF:

$$\begin{bmatrix} d(-2,-2) & d(-2,-1) & d(-2,0) & d(-2,1) & d(-2,2) \\ d(-1,-2) & d(-1,-1) & d(-1,0) & d(-1,1) & d(-1,2) \\ d(0,-2) & d(0,-1) & d(0,0) & d(0,1) & d(0,2) \\ d(1,-2) & d(1,-1) & d(1,0) & d(1,1) & d(1,2) \\ d(2,-2) & d(2,-1) & d(2,0) & d(2,1) & d(2,2) \end{bmatrix} =$$

$$\begin{bmatrix} 0.0175 & 0.031 & 0.031 & 0.031 & 0.0175 \\ 0.031 & 0.062 & 0.062 & 0.062 & 0.031 \\ 0.031 & 0.062 & 0.062 & 0.062 & 0.031 \\ 0.031 & 0.062 & 0.062 & 0.062 & 0.031 \\ 0.0175 & 0.031 & 0.031 & 0.031 & 0.0175 \end{bmatrix}.$$

The blurred image with noise added at 40 dB is shown in Fig. 4. The restored image using the ideal parameters is given in Fig. 5(a) (η_{SNR} = 6.00 dB), while Figs. 5(b) and 5(c) show the restoration results using the identified parameters by the RLS (η_{SNR} = 5.81 dB) and EM methods (η_{SNR} = 5.77 dB), respectively. The identified PSF coefficients associated with these restored images are

Fig. 4. Defocused cameraman image at SNR = 40 dB.

$$\hat{d}_{RLS}(m,n) = \begin{bmatrix} 0.017 & 0.032 & 0.031 & 0.032 & 0.017 \\ 0.031 & 0.063 & 0.061 & 0.063 & 0.031 \\ 0.030 & 0.063 & 0.061 & 0.063 & 0.030 \\ 0.031 & 0.063 & 0.061 & 0.063 & 0.031 \\ 0.017 & 0.032 & 0.031 & 0.032 & 0.017 \end{bmatrix},$$

$$\hat{d}_{EM}(m,n) = \begin{bmatrix} 0.019 & 0.031 & 0.032 & 0.029 & 0.018 \\ 0.033 & 0.060 & 0.059 & 0.061 & 0.031 \\ 0.029 & 0.065 & 0.065 & 0.065 & 0.029 \\ 0.031 & 0.061 & 0.059 & 0.060 & 0.033 \\ 0.018 & 0.029 & 0.032 & 0.031 & 0.019 \end{bmatrix}.$$

The identified image model coefficients are given by

$$\hat{a}_{RLS}(k,l) = \begin{bmatrix} -0.311 & 0.502 & 0.198 \\ 0.610 & & \end{bmatrix},$$

$$\hat{a}_{EM}(k,l) = \begin{bmatrix} -0.410 & 0.599 & 0.167 \\ 0.636 & & \end{bmatrix}.$$

The identified variances are, for the 2-D recursive least squares method, σ_v^2 = 247.3, and for the EM-algorithm-based identification, σ_w^2 = 0.316, σ_v^2 = 201.

If the SNR is decreased, the least squares method does not lead to useful results anymore. Again, the true ML estimator yields acceptable results up to a SNR of 20 dB. At that noise level, the estimated PSF and image model coefficients are given by

Fig. 5. Wiener filter restoration from Fig. 4 using (a) ideal parameters, (b) estimated parameters by the RLS method, and (c) estimated parameters by the EM algorithm.

(a)

(b)

Fig. 6. Wiener filter restoration at SNR = 20 dB using (a) the ideal parameters and (b) the estimated parameters.

$$\hat{d}_{EM}(m,n) = \begin{bmatrix} 0.012 & 0.054 & 0.017 & 0.041 & 0.021 \\ 0.022 & 0.064 & 0.060 & 0.058 & 0.030 \\ 0.024 & 0.064 & 0.068 & 0.064 & 0.024 \\ 0.030 & 0.058 & 0.060 & 0.064 & 0.022 \\ 0.021 & 0.041 & 0.017 & 0.054 & 0.012 \end{bmatrix},$$

$$\hat{a}_{EM}(k,l) = \begin{bmatrix} -0.424 & 0.561 & 0.170 \\ 0.686 & & \end{bmatrix},$$

and $\sigma_w^2 = 31.2$, $\sigma_v^2 = 182.2$. The improvement in SNR of the restored image using these estimated parameters is 1.81 dB, compared with 1.95 dB for the ideal parameters. Both restored images are shown in Fig. 6.

5.2. Estimation of the PSF support

In the above experiments we assumed that the exact size of the support $\mathscr{S}_d$ of the PSF $d(m,n)$ was known a priori. In this section we consider the effects of using an incorrect support size and show that it is possible to choose the correct PSF support among various alternatives by inspecting the values of the likelihood function or by visual inspection of the restoration results.

In identifying the defocusing blur in the image in Fig. 4 (SNR = 40 dB), we used a PSF support size of 3×3, 5×5, and 7×7. The identified PSF coefficients, image models, and variances, together with the associated value of the likelihood function, are given next. The restored images are shown in Figs. 7(a), $\mathscr{S}_d = 3 \times 3$, 7(b), $\mathscr{S}_d = 5 \times 5$, and 7(c), $\mathscr{S}_d = 7 \times 7$.

- $\mathscr{S}_d = 3 \times 3$:

$$\hat{d}(m,n) = \begin{bmatrix} 0.056 & 0.159 & 0.042 \\ 0.136 & 0.214 & 0.136 \\ 0.042 & 0.159 & 0.056 \end{bmatrix},$$

$$\hat{a}(k,l) = \begin{bmatrix} -0.682 & 0.680 & 0.142 \\ 0.861 & & \end{bmatrix},$$

$\hat{\sigma}_w^2 = 0.301$,

$\hat{\sigma}_v^2 = 22.22$,

$\mathscr{L}(\hat{\theta}) = 1.78$ per pixel.

- $\mathscr{S}_d = 5 \times 5$:

$$\hat{d}(m,n) = \begin{bmatrix} 0.019 & 0.031 & 0.032 & 0.029 & 0.018 \\ 0.033 & 0.060 & 0.059 & 0.061 & 0.031 \\ 0.029 & 0.065 & 0.065 & 0.065 & 0.029 \\ 0.031 & 0.061 & 0.059 & 0.060 & 0.033 \\ 0.018 & 0.029 & 0.032 & 0.031 & 0.019 \end{bmatrix},$$

$$\hat{a}(k,l) = \begin{bmatrix} -0.410 & 0.599 & 0.167 \\ 0.636 & & \end{bmatrix},$$

$\hat{\sigma}_w^2 = 0.316$,

$\hat{\sigma}_v^2 = 201.3$,

$\mathscr{L}(\hat{\theta}) = 1.67$ per pixel.

Fig. 7. Wiener filter restoration from Fig. 4 for various PSF support sizes: (a) $\mathcal{S}_d = 3\times 3$, (b) $\mathcal{S}_d = 5\times 5$, and (c) $\mathcal{S}_d = 7\times 7$.

- $\mathcal{S}_d = 7\times 7$:

$\hat{d}(m,n) =$
$$\begin{bmatrix} 0.002 & 0.000 & 0.004 & 0.006 & 0.002 & 0.007 & 0.001 \\ -0.003 & 0.018 & 0.030 & 0.031 & 0.031 & 0.017 & 0.001 \\ -0.002 & 0.029 & 0.058 & 0.059 & 0.059 & 0.030 & 0.000 \\ -0.003 & 0.030 & 0.062 & 0.063 & 0.063 & 0.030 & -0.003 \\ 0.000 & 0.030 & 0.059 & 0.059 & 0.058 & 0.029 & -0.002 \\ 0.001 & 0.017 & 0.031 & 0.031 & 0.030 & 0.018 & -0.003 \\ 0.001 & 0.007 & 0.002 & 0.006 & 0.004 & 0.000 & 0.002 \end{bmatrix},$$

$\hat{a}(k,l) = \begin{bmatrix} -0.450 & 0.574 & 0.141 \\ 0.725 & & \end{bmatrix},$

$\hat{\sigma}_w^2 = 226.2 ,$

$\hat{\sigma}_v^2 = 0.315 ,$

$\mathcal{L}(\hat{\theta}) = 1.66$ per pixel.

By inspection of the value of the likelihood function, it becomes already apparent that the 5×5 PSF support is most likely. The same conclusion can be reached by (visually) evaluating the restored images.

6. DISCUSSION

In this paper, we have considered the identification of image and blur model parameters under a unifying maximum likelihood approach. Five different ways of evaluating the likelihood function are described, each leading to a certain implementation. We have shown both recursive space domain and nonrecursive DFT domain methods for the evaluation of the likelihood function. All of the methods, except the EM algorithm, required a gradient-based iterative optimization procedure. In some implementations the gradient of the likelihood function can be obtained analytically, while in other implementations numerical methods to evaluate the gradient have to be used. The sensitivity of the estimated parameters to observation noise and the assumed model order is shown experimentally.

The efficiency of the various implementations depends strongly on the available computational resources. For instance, if DFTs can be efficiently evaluated, by using parallel or pipelined machines or special-purpose hardware, the methods of Secs. 4.1 and 4.2 are most attractive. On the other hand, the recursive spatial domain methods of Secs. 4.3, 4.4, and 4.5 are more efficient for sequential implementations.

A major problem in all of the methods discussed in this paper is that the likelihood function may contain several local optima. As a result, the identified parameters are relatively sensitive to the initial or boundary conditions, especially when the number of parameters is large. Therefore, many initial guesses or boundary conditions need to be tried in order to find the global optimum of the likelihood function. One way to avoid this problem is to make use of even more a priori knowledge about the solution. For example, if there is available knowledge about the physics of the underlying blurring process, the PSF can often be described by a function with one or two parameters.[16] By reducing the number of unknown parameters, many suboptima will disappear, which simplifies the problem.

Another possibility to avoid local optima is the use of hierarchical identification strategies.[24] Such methods start with identifying the image and blur model from a reduced resolution image and then using those results to initialize the identification process at higher resolution levels. Additional advantages of hierarchical procedures are that they are computationally less expensive and that they allow for easier estimation of the support of the PSF.

Another more recent direction in image and blur identification is the use of higher-order spectra.[25] In these methods, it is possible to estimate the Fourier phase of the PSF as well as its Fourier magnitude square. Hence, a unique solution can be obtained both for the image and blur model parameters without using any additional a priori information or constraints about the PSF. In theory, these methods are capable of estimating any type of PSF. The shortcomings of these techniques are (1) it is not possible to incorporate a criterion, such as ML, into the estimation procedures and (2) the sensitivity of the estimates to observation noise has not yet been considered.

7. ACKNOWLEDGMENTS

This paper is based on research supported in part by NATO under grant 0124/87 to the Delft University of Technology and grant number 88-IJ-CX-0038 from the U.S. Department of Justice and grants MIP-8809291 and CDA-8820693 from the National Science Foundation to the University of Rochester. The authors would like to thank Richard P. Kleihorst, a graduate student from the Delft University of Technology, for his contributions to this paper.

8. REFERENCES

1. H. C. Andrews and B. R. Hunt, *Digital Image Restoration*, Prentice-Hall, Englewood Cliffs, N.J. (1977).
2. J. W. Woods and V. K. Ingle, "Kalman filtering in two-dimensions: further results," IEEE Trans. Acoust. Speech Signal Proc. 29(2), 188–197 (1981).
3. R. L. Lagendijk, J. Biemond, and D. E. Boekee, "Regularized iterative image restoration with ringing reduction," IEEE Trans. Acoust. Speech Signal Proc. 36(12), 1874–1888 (1988).
4. T. G. Stockham, T. M. Cannon, and R. B. Ingebretsen, "Blind deconvolution through digital signal processing," Proc. IEEE 64(4), 678–692 (1975).
5. M. Cannon, "Blind deconvolution of spatially invariant image blurs with phase," IEEE Trans. Acoust. Speech Signal Proc. 24, 58–63 (1976).
6. A. M. Tekalp, H. Kaufman, and J. W. Woods, "Identification of image and blur parameters for the restoration of noncausal blurs," IEEE Trans. Acoust. Speech Signal Proc. 34, 963–972 (1986).
7. B. Das, "Comparative study of stationary and non-stationary techniques for the restoration of images degraded by blur and noise," Tech. Rep., Rensselaer Polytechnic Inst. Dept. ECSE (1986).
8. A. M. Tekalp and H. Kaufman, "On statistical identification of a class of linear space-invariant blurs using non-minimum-phase ARMA models," IEEE Trans. Acoust. Speech Signal Proc. 36(8), 1360–1363 (1988).
9. J. Biemond, F. G. van der Putten, and J. W. Woods, "Identification and restoration of images with symmetric noncausal blurs," IEEE Trans. Circ. Syst. 23(3), 385–394 (1988).
10. R. L. Lagendijk, A. K. Katsaggelos, and J. Biemond, "Iterative identification and restoration of images," in *Proc. 1988 IEEE Int. Conf. on Acoustics, Speech and Signal Processing*, pp. 992–995 (1988).
11. R. L. Lagendijk, D. L. Angwin, H. Kaufman, and J. Biemond, "Recursive and iterative methods for image identification and restoration," in *Proc. Fourth European Signal Processing Conf.*, J. G. Lacoume, ed., pp. 235–238, North Holland, Amsterdam (1988).
12. T. Katayama, T. Hirai, and K. Okamura, "A fast Kalman filter approach to restoration of blurred images," Signal Proc. 14, 165–175 (1988).
13. L. Blanc-Féraud, M. Barlaud, and P. Mathieu, "Image restoration and blur estimation using a constrained maximum likelihood method," in *Proc. 3rd Int. Workshop on Time-Varying Image Processing and Moving Object Recognition* (1989).
14. K. T. Lay and A. K. Katsaggelos, "Blur identification and image restoration based on the EM-algorithm," Opt. Eng. 29(5) (1990).
15. D. L. Angwin, "Adaptive image restoration using reduced order model based Kalman filters," Ph.D. thesis, Rensselaer Polytechnic Inst., Dept. ECSE (1989).
16. R. L. Lagendijk, J. Biemond, and D. E. Boekee, "Identification and restoration of noisy blurred images using the expectation-maximization algorithm," IEEE Trans. Acoust. Speech Signal Proc., to appear (July 1990).
17. A. K. Jain, "Advances in mathematical models for image processing," Proc. IEEE 69(5), 502–528 (1981).
18. W. K. Pratt, "Vector space formulation of two-dimensional signal processing operations," Comput. Graph. Image Proc. 4, 1–24 (1975).
19. J. W. Woods, J. Biemond, and A. M. Tekalp, "Boundary value problem in image restoration," in *Proc. 1985 IEEE Int. Conf. on Acoustics, Speech, and Signal Processing*, pp. 692–695 (1985).
20. L. Ljung and T. Söderström, *Theory and Practice of Recursive Identification*, MIT Press, Cambridge (1983).
21. F. C. Schweppe, *Uncertain Dynamic Systems*, Prentice-Hall, Englewood Cliffs, N.J. (1973).
22. A. P. Dempster, N. M. Laird, and D. B. Rubin, "Maximum likelihood from incomplete data," J. Royal Statist. Soc. B 39, 1–38 (1977).
23. K. J. Åstrom, "Maximum likelihood and prediction error methods," Automatica 16, 551–574 (1980).
24. R. L. Lagendijk, J. Biemond, and D. E. Boekee, "Hierarchical blur identification," in *Proc. 1990 IEEE Int. Conf. on Acoustics, Speech, and Signal Processing* (1990).
25. A. T. Erdem and A. M. Tekalp, "Image-blur identification using higher-order spectra," in *Proc. 1990 IEEE Int. Conf. on Acoustics, Speech, and Signal Processing* (1990).

Reginald L. Lagendijk was born in Leiden, The Netherlands, in 1962. He received the M.Sc. degree in electrical engineering from the Delft University of Technology in 1985. Since 1985, he has been working toward the Ph.D. degree in the Information Theory Group of the university and is currently on the faculty of the Department of Electrical Engineering. His research interests include information theory and multidimensional signal processing, with emphasis on image identification and restoration and data compression of image sequences.

A. Murat Tekalp: Biography and photograph appear with the guest editorial in this issue.

Jan Biemond was born in De Kaag, The Netherlands, in 1947. He received the MS and Ph.D. degrees in 1973 and 1982, respectively, from the Delft University of Technology, where he is currently a professor in the Laboratory for Information Theory of the Department of Electrical Engineering. His research interests include multidimensional signal processing, image enhancement and restoration, data compression of images, and motion estimation, with application in image coding and computer vision. He has authored or coauthored more than 40 papers in these fields. In 1983 he was a visiting researcher at Rensselaer Polytechnic Institute in Troy, N.Y., and at the Georgia Institute of Technology in Atlanta. Dr. Biemond is a member of the IEEE-ASSP Technical Committee on Multidimensional Signal Processing and of the IEEE-CAS Technical Committee on Visual Signal Processing and Communication. He served as the general chairman of the Fifth ASSP/EURASIP Workshop on Multidimensional Signal Processing, held at Noordwijkerhout, The Netherlands, in September 1987.

Adaptive Restoration of Images with Speckle

DARWIN T. KUAN, MEMBER, IEEE, ALEXANDER A. SAWCHUK, SENIOR MEMBER, IEEE, TIMOTHY C. STRAND, MEMBER, IEEE, AND PIERRE CHAVEL

Abstract—Speckle is a granular noise that inherently exists in all types of coherent imaging systems. The presence of speckle in an image reduces the resolution of the image and the detectability of the target. Many speckle reduction algorithms assume speckle noise is multiplicative. We instead model the speckle according to the exact physical process of coherent image formation. Thus, the model includes signal-dependent effects and accurately represents the higher order statistical properties of speckle that are important to the restoration procedure. Various adaptive restoration filters for intensity speckle images are derived based on different model assumptions and a nonstationary image model. These filters respond adaptively to the signal-dependent speckle noise and the nonstationary statistics of the original image.

I. INTRODUCTION

SPECKLE occurs in all types of coherent imagery such as synthetic aperture radar (SAR) imagery, acoustic imagery, and laser illuminated imagery. It is due to the random interference of the wavelets scattered by the microscopic fluctuations of the object surface within one resolution element. Several references provide details about the origin of speckle and its statistical properties [1], [2]. Unlike multiplicative noise or Poisson noise, speckle noise is not only signal-dependent but is also spatially correlated. The signal-to-noise ratio (SNR) of fully developed speckle is equal to one, and the correlation function of speckle noise depends on the coherent point spread function of the imaging system and the original image intensity.

It is useful to distinguish between two situations; in a usual linear imaging system described by the convolution equation between the object function and the system point spread function, either the object or the point spread function may be affected by noise and originate speckle.

The case of a noisy object (case A) corresponds to the fully coherent situation of a scattering object illuminated by a coherent wavefront. This situation occurs with laser or radar illumination if the scattering object reflectance modulus is the only meaningful information and the random phase variations of the reflectance are of no particular concern. Speckle is then created by the random interferences between the various phasors.

Manuscript received March 14, 1985; revised May 21, 1986.
D. T. Kuan is with FMC Corporation, Central Engineering Labs., Artificial Intelligence Center, Santa Clara, CA 95052.
A. A. Sawchuk is with the Image Processing Institute, University of Southern California, Los Angeles, CA 90007.
T. C. Strand is with IBM Corporation, Almaden Research Center, San Jose, CA 95120.
P. Chavel is with the Institut d'Optique, Université de Paris Sud, Orsay, France.
IEEE Log Number 8611739.

The case of a noisy imaging system (case B) corresponds to a randomly variable transmitting medium. This situation occurs, in particular, in astronomy because of the atmospheric turbulence. Speckle is then created by the random phase variation of the wavefront originating from each source point. The noisy point spread functions corresponding to all image points add on an intensity or amplitude basis depending on the coherence of the source.

While in case A, a mere superposition of images of the same object with statistically independent phase terms converges to an incoherent, noise-free image, this is not true in case B where such a superposition leads to a severe blur. Sophisticated methods have been developed and applied in the last 15 years to partly recover the information and resolution from large sets of statistically independent images in case B [12]–[16].

Our work aims at applying the techniques of *a posteriori* signal processing to the problem of speckle reduction. These could be applied to any speckle situation, possibly in conjunction with the above-mentioned techniques using multiple statistically independent images. However, the present paper is solely devoted to case A.

An important property of fully developed speckle is that the ensemble mean of the speckle image is equal to the incoherent image of the original object. This property serves as the basis of frame averaging techniques where multiple frames of uncorrelated speckle images of the same object are generated and averaged on an intensity basis [3], [4]. This averaging process increases the SNR from 1 to $M^{1/2}$ where M is the number of uncorrelated speckle images. While these methods are effective for speckle reduction, they require multiple frames of speckle images and do not consider the image statistics. In recent years, digital methods for processing SAR data and digitally processed SAR images have become available. Interests in applying digital image enhancement and restoration techniques to speckle reduction are high [5]–[7]. However, these approaches have assumed that speckle noise is multiplicative, and have used multiplicative noise filtering algorithms to suppress speckle noise. The multiplicative noise model for speckle noise is only a rough approximation [8], and these techniques ignore the correlation of speckle that is useful for speckle reduction.

In this paper, we model the speckle according to the exact physical process of coherent image formation. Thus, the model includes signal-dependent effects and accurately represents the higher order statistical properties of speckle that are important to the restoration procedure.

We first derive an adaptive noise smoothing filter and a maximum *a posteriori* (MAP) filter for a limiting situation when the discrete speckle samples can be assumed independent of each other. These filters only require the local mean and local variance estimates of the noisy image and fall into the multiplicative noise filtering category. We then use our accurate speckle model and a nonstationary mean, nonstationary variance (NMNV) image model to derive a local minimum mean square error (LLMMSE) filter for speckle reduction. The filter responds adaptively to the signal-dependent speckle noise and the nonstationary content of the image. More importantly, the correlation properties of speckle are taken into account. Extensions of these adaptive speckle reduction techniques to the multiple frames case are developed, and simulation results for synthetic speckle images are presented.

II. Speckle Model and Speckle Statistics

Speckle is due to the random interference of wavelets scattered by the microscopic fluctuations of an optically rough object surface. Consider the coherent imaging system in Fig. 1. A transparency of complex amplitude transmittance $t(x, y)$ is illuminated by a unit-amplitude coherent beam. Here $t(x, y)$ is the product of the object amplitude transmittance $f^{1/2}(x, y)$ and the random phasor $\exp(j\phi(x, y))$ introduced by the roughness of the object surface. A block diagram of the mathematical model of speckle is shown in Fig. 2, where $h(x, y)$ is the coherent point spread function of the system, $b(x, y)$ is the complex amplitude speckle image, and $g(x, y)$ is the speckle intensity image. Due to our lack of knowledge of the detailed structure of the object surface, speckle is best described by its statistical properties. The speckle restoration problem is a signal estimation problem where we extract the signal component $f(x, y)$ from the noisy data $g(x, y)$ or $b(x, y)$. Since the adaptive speckle reduction filter is implemented digitally, we will give a discrete formulation of speckle model and statistics.

A. Single Phase Speckle Model

In many practical applications, the object surface is extremely rough compared to the optical wavelength. This is the so-called "fully developed" speckle. In this case, the phase function $\phi(x, y)$ is an uncorrelated random field uniformly distributed between 0 and 2π. We also assume that $\phi(x, y)$ is statistically independent of the original image intensity $f(x, y)$. Goodman [1] used a discrete model for fully developed speckle and assumed that the object surface can be modeled as a collection of a large number of independent random scatterers. In this case, the discrete complex amplitude speckle image $b(m, n)$ can be written as

$$b(m, n) = \sum_i \sum_k h(m - i, n - k) f^{1/2}(i, k) \cdot \exp(j\phi(i, k)). \quad (1)$$

The speckle intensity $g(m, n)$ is given by $g(m, n) =$

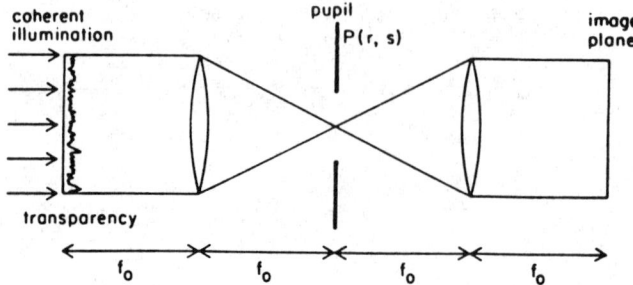

Fig. 1. Coherent imaging system.

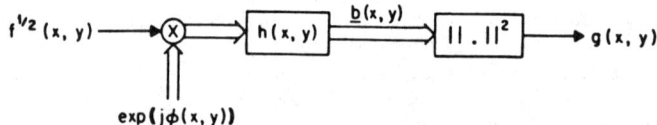

Fig. 2. Block diagram of speckle model.

$|b(m, n)|^2$. In this paper, we only consider fully developed speckle. Based on these assumptions and with the help of the central limit theorem, it is easy to show that the weighted two-dimensional random walk process $b(m, n)$ in (1) can be approximated by a complex circular Gaussian process. Consequently, $g(m, n)$ has a negative exponential probability density function

$$P(g(m, n)|f) = \begin{cases} \dfrac{1}{I(m, n)} \exp\left[-\dfrac{g(m, n)}{I(m, n)}\right] \\ \qquad \text{for } g(m, n) \geq 0 \\ 0 \qquad \text{otherwise} \end{cases} \quad (2)$$

where $I(m, n)$ is the incoherent image of the original image given by

$$I(m, n) = \sum_i \sum_k h^2(m - i, n - k) f(i, k). \quad (3)$$

The assumption of fully developed speckle often applies because many objects are very rough compared to optical and even radar wavelengths. The negative exponential probability density function can be easily verified on real speckle images [17].

It is interesting to see that the conditional mean of speckle intensity image $g(m, n)$ given f is equal to the incoherent image $I(m, n)$ of the original object through the same imaging system. This property serves as the basis of frame averaging techniques [1]. Unlike multiplicative noise or Poisson noise, speckle noise is not only signal dependent but also correlated. This can be observed from the coarseness, texture, or the "speckle size" of a speckle image. The speckle size or the correlation region of a speckle image is approximately the size of the incoherent point spread function of the system and is important for speckle reduction. These second-order statistics will be discussed in detail in Section IV for designing an adaptive speckle reduction filter where correlation properties of the speckle are considered.

B. Multiple Phase Speckle Model

The sampling frequency used in the single phase speckle model is usually several times larger than the bandwidth of the system and signal. Let us assume that the sampling frequency of the single phase speckle model is r times larger than the maximum of the bandwidths of the incoherent imaging system and the signal in both x and y directions. In this case, it is reasonable to have the following approximations:

$$f^{1/2}(ri + s, rk + t) \simeq f^{1/2}(ri, rk) \text{ and}$$
$$h(ri + s, rk + t) \simeq h(ri, rl) \text{ for } 0 \leq s, t < r. \quad (4)$$

With these approximations, we have the multiple phase speckle model

$$b(m, n) = \sum_i \sum_k h(m - i, n - k) f^{1/2}(i, k) a(i, k) \quad (5)$$

where position (m, n) in the multiple phase model is the corresponding point (rm, rn) in the single phase model, and

$$a(i, k) = \sum_{s=0}^{r-1} \sum_{t=0}^{r-1} \exp(j\phi(ri + s, rk + t)). \quad (6)$$

The complex random variable $a(i, k)$ can be approximated by a circular Gaussian random variable since r is usually a large number. This speckle model not only reduces the sampling rate to the minimum value required for accurately representing the statistics of speckle, but also abstracts the dependence of speckle model on the object surface. The introduction of an intermediate phasor $a(i, k)$ also avoids the singular probability density function problem associated with $\exp(j\phi(i, k))$ in the estimation procedure and preserves the same statistical properties as in the single phase speckle model.

III. Adaptive Speckle Reduction Techniques— Independent Speckle Samples

In some situations, the speckle intensity image has been undersampled such that the sampling interval is greater than the correlation length of speckle. Therefore, the correlation information of the speckle is lost and the speckle samples are independent. In this case, speckle reduction becomes a noise smoothing problem. In this section, we consider adaptive speckle reduction techniques for independent speckle samples.

A. Adaptive Noise Smoothing Filter

Consider the linear space-invariant image formation model with additive noise degradation. The lexicographic representation [9] of this model is given by

$$g = Hf + v \quad (7)$$

where g is the noisy observation, f is the original image, H is the blur matrix, and v is the observation noise. The conventional stationary image model assumes that an image is a wide-sense stationary field. The statistical properties of an image are characterized globally rather than locally by its stationary correlation function. This assumption enables the use of FFT-based algorithms in the restoration procedure and consequently reduces the computation time dramatically. However, the restoration filter designed accordingly is insensitive to abrupt changes of the image intensity, and tends to smooth the edges where stationarity is not justified. To overcome these disadvantages and to have improved restoration result, we introduce a nonstationary mean, nonstationary variance (NMNV) image model [9]. In this image model, the nonstationary mean describes the gross structure of a nonstationary image and the nonstationary variance characterizes edge and elementary texture information of the image. If we assume that the original image f can be modeled by its nonstationary mean and nonstationary variance, the linear minimum mean square error filter (LMMSE) has the form

$$\hat{f}_{\text{LMMSE}} = \bar{f} + C_{fg} C_g^{-1} (g - \bar{g}). \quad (8)$$

Here $\bar{f}$ is the nonstationary mean of f; C_{fg} and C_g are the nonstationary covariance matrices. In order to distinguish this filter from the conventional Wiener filter, we shall call it local linear minimum mean square error (LLMMSE) filter to emphasize its locally adaptive properties.

For the independent speckle samples case, the speckle intensity $g(m, n)$ in (2) can be represented as a multiplicative noise model, and we have

$$g(m, n) = u(m, n) I(m, n) \quad (9)$$

where $u(m, n)$ is a signal-independent, white noise process and has a normalized negative exponential distribution with unit mean and unit variance

$$P(u(m, n)) = \begin{cases} \exp(-u(m, n)) & \text{for } u(m, n) \geq 0 \\ 0 & \text{otherwise.} \end{cases} \quad (10)$$

Because $u(m, n)$ is a white noise process and we use the NMNV image model, it is easy to see that the covariance matrices C_{Ig} and C_g are both diagonal matrices. Therefore, the LLMMSE filter for speckle reduction becomes a set of scalar equations

$$\hat{I}_{\text{LLMMSE}}(m, n) = \bar{I}(m, n) + \frac{\sigma_I^2(m, n)}{\sigma_I^2(m, n) + \bar{I}^2(m, n) + \sigma_I^2(m, n)} \cdot (g(m, n) - \bar{I}(m, n)) \quad (11)$$

where $\sigma_I^2(m, n)$ is the nonstationary variance of $I(m, n)$. Usually the nonstationary mean and nonstationary variance of the original image are not known *a priori* and have to be estimated from the degraded image. If we assume that ensemble statistics can be replaced by local spatial statistics estimated from the degraded image, we have the adaptive noise smoothing filter

$$\hat{I}_A(m, n) = \mu_I(m, n) + \frac{v_I(m, n)}{v_I(m, n) + \mu_I^2(m, n) + v_I(m, n)} \cdot (g(m, n) - \mu_I(m, n)) \quad (12)$$

where $\mu_I(m, n)$ is the local mean estimate of $I(m, n)$, and $v_I(m, n)$ is the local variance estimate of $I(m, n)$. The adaptive noise smoothing filter makes a balance between the local mean estimate and the speckle observation according to the local statistics of the image.

The performance of the adaptive noise smoothing filter depends on the method used to calculate the local statistics. One way to obtain the local mean and local variance estimates of $g(m, n)$ is to calculate the sample mean and sample variance over a uniform moving average window centered at (m, n). The local statistics of $I(m, n)$ can be calculated from the local statistics of $g(m, n)$ by assuming the relationship between their ensemble statistics also holds for their local statistics. Therefore, the functional forms of these transformations depend on the particular noise structure. For the multiplicative speckle noise model in (9), it is straightforward to show that [9]

$$\mu_I(m, n) = \mu_g(m, n)$$

$$v_I(m, n) = \frac{v_g(m, n) - \mu_g^2(m, n)\sigma_u^2}{1 + \sigma_u^2}.$$

B. Maximum A Posteriori (MAP) Filter

The adaptive noise smoothing filter only considers the mean and variance of speckle and is the optimal MMSE filter for Gaussian statistics. Since the speckle intensity $g(m, n)$ has a negative exponential distribution which is very different from Gaussian distribution, it is useful to consider the nonlinear MAP filter for better performance. The MAP estimate of I is obtained by maximizing the *a posteriori* probability density function

$$P(I|g) = \frac{P(g|I) P(I)}{P(g)} \quad (13)$$

with respect to I. Because the logarithm function is a monotonically increasing function, we can take the logarithm on both sides of (13) and then differentiate it with respect to I. Thus, we have the MAP equation

$$\left. \frac{\partial \ln P(g|I)}{\partial I} + \frac{\partial \ln P(I)}{\partial I} \right|_{I = \hat{I}_{\text{MAP}}} = 0 \quad (14)$$

where we use the fact that $P(g)$ is a constant with respect to I. The first term in (14) is the maximum likelihood (ML) term, and the second term is the *a priori* term of the incoherent image. Because of the NMNV image model and the independent speckle samples assumption, the MAP equation can be expressed as a set of scalar equations

$$\left. \frac{\partial \ln P(g(m, n)|I(m, n))}{\partial I(m, n)} + \frac{\partial \ln P(I(m, n))}{\partial I(m, n)} \right|_{I(m,n) = \hat{I}_{\text{MAP}}(m,n)} = 0. \quad (15)$$

The first term of (15) can be written as

$$\frac{\partial \ln P(g(m, n)|I(m, n))}{\partial I(m, n)} = -\frac{1}{I(m, n)} + \frac{g(m, n)}{I^2(m, n)}. \quad (16)$$

Setting (16) to zero, we have the ML estimate

$$\left. -\frac{1}{I(m, n)} + \frac{g(m, n)}{I^2(m, n)} \right|_{I(m,n) = \hat{I}_{\text{ML}}(m,n)} = 0$$

or $\quad (17)$

$$\hat{I}_{\text{ML}}(m, n) = g(m, n).$$

It is interesting to see that the ML estimate of the incoherent image is the speckle image itself. For the NMNV image model, we have

$$P(I(m, n)) = \frac{1}{\sqrt{2\pi\sigma_I^2(m, n)}} \cdot \exp\left[-\frac{[I(m, n) - \bar{I}(m, n)]^2}{2\sigma_I^2(m, n)} \right] \quad (18)$$

where $\sigma_I^2(m, n)$ and $\bar{I}(m, n)$ are the nonstationary variance and mean of $I(m, n)$. Thus, the second term of (15) can be written as

$$\frac{\partial \ln P(I(m, n))}{\partial I(m, n)} = -[I(m, n) - \bar{I}(m, n)]/\sigma_I^2(m, n). \quad (19)$$

From (15), (16), and (19), we have the MAP equation

$$\left. \frac{g(m, n)}{I^2(m, n)} - \frac{1}{I(m, n)} - \frac{1}{\sigma_I^2(m, n)} [I(m, n) - \bar{I}(m, n)] \right|_{I(m,n) = \hat{I}_{\text{MAP}}(m,n)} = 0$$

or

$$-\hat{I}_{\text{MAP}}^2(m, n)[\hat{I}_{\text{MAP}}(m, n) - \bar{I}(m, n)] + \sigma_I^2(m, n)[g(m, n) - \hat{I}_{\text{MAP}}(m, n)] = 0. \quad (20)$$

It is easy to see from (20) that $\hat{I}_{\text{MAP}}(m, n)$ is the real root of a cubic equation whose value is between $\bar{I}(m, n)$ and $g(m, n)$. Again, the MAP estimate is a balance between the local mean estimate and the speckle intensity observation. Here, the weights are determined by the first-order probability density function of speckle intensity. The local statistics estimates are calculated the same way as in the adaptive noise smoothing filter.

C. Multiple Frame Speckle Reduction Filters

In some applications, we may have several independent speckle images of the same object. Frame averaging techniques can be applied to increase the SNR. The adaptive speckle reduction techniques that consider the local image statistics can be extended to process multiple frames easily by modifying the speckle noise statistics in the restoration equations.

The average of M independent speckle images ($g^{(i)}(m, n)$, $i = 1, \cdots, M$) can be expressed as

$$g^{(a)}(m, n) = \frac{1}{M} \sum_{i=1}^{M} g^{(i)}(m, n).$$

The random variable $g^{(a)}(m, n)$ has a gamma probability density function because it is the average of M independent negative exponential random variables. The conditional mean and variance of $g^{(a)}(m, n)$ are given by

$$E[g^{(a)}(m, n) | I(m, n)] = I(m, n) \quad \text{and}$$

$$\text{Var}[g^{(a)}(m, n) | I(m, n)] = I^2(m, n)/M.$$

Therefore, the adaptive noise smoothing filter for the multiple frame averaged speckle image is the same as the adaptive noise smoothing filter for multiplicative noise with unit mean and variance equal to $1/M$. Similarly, the MAP equation of the multiple frame speckle case can be derived based on the gamma probability density function and is similar to the one-point MAP equation (20) derived based on a negative exponential probability density function. The difference is that the frame number M puts a weight on the term $[g^{(a)}(m, n) - \hat{I}_{\text{MAP}}(m, n)]$ in (20).

D. Simulation Results

In this section, we show some simulation results of different adaptive speckle reduction filters for the independent speckle samples case. The original aerial photograph is shown in Fig. 3(a). The independent samples speckle image shown in Fig. 3(b) is generated according to the multiplicative noise model with negative exponential distribution. The SNR is equal to one and the speckle samples are independent. The local mean is calculated using a 7 × 7 uniform weight window and is shown in Fig. 3(c). The local variance estimate is similarly calculated [9], and the adaptive noise smoothing estimate and one-point MAP estimate are shown in Fig. 3(d) and (e). These adaptive estimates have much better resolution than the low-pass filtered result. Because of the low SNR in a speckle intensity image, we will not have a good local statistics estimate. This fact explains the noisy appearance in Fig. 3(d) and (e). If we estimate the local mean and variance from the adaptively smoothed image, we have the second iteration adaptive noise smoothing estimate and the MAP estimate that are shown in Fig. 3(f) and (g). It is easy to see that the noise is further smoothed without much loss of image resolution.

For the multiple frame case, the original aerial image is given in Fig. 4(a). The average of 4 independent speckle images is shown in Fig. 4(b). The SNR of this picture increases from 1 to 2 due to the averaging process. This fact will help us to have a more accurate local statistics estimate. The adaptive noise smoothing estimate and the one-point MAP estimate for the multiple frames case are shown in Fig. 4(c) and (d), respectively. The image quality improvement of using our adaptive speckle reduction techniques after the 4 frames averaging process is significant.

IV. Adaptive Speckle Restoration Techniques— Correlated Speckle Samples

The speckle reduction techniques discussed in the last section assume that the discrete samples of a speckle intensity image are statistically independent and only the first-order statistics of speckle are used for speckle reduction. The correlation properties of speckle are ignored and we only have an estimate of the incoherent image rather than the original object intensity. In this section, we derive an LLMMSE estimate of the original image that takes into account the second-order statistics of speckle. This approach is the first time that second-order statistics have been considered in speckle reduction algorithms.

From (8), the LLMMSE filter for correlated speckle samples has the form

$$\hat{f}_{\text{LLMMSE}} = \bar{f} + C_{fg} C_g^{-1} (g - \bar{g}). \quad (21)$$

Note that in this formulation, our objective is to estimate the object intensity using the correlation properties of speckle. From (3), the conditional and unconditional means of g can be expressed as

$$E[g|f] = H_I f \quad \text{and} \quad E[g] = H_I \bar{f} \quad (22)$$

where H_I is the incoherent point spread matrix of the system. The cross-covariance matrix of f and g is given by

$$\begin{aligned} C_{fg} &= E[(f - \bar{f})(g - \bar{g})^T] \\ &= E[(f - \bar{f})(g - H_I f + H_I f - H_I \bar{f})^T] \\ &= E[(f - \bar{f})(g - H_I f)^T] \\ &\quad + E[(f - \bar{f})(f - \bar{f})^T H_I^T] \\ &= C_f H_I^T \end{aligned} \quad (23)$$

where C_f is the covariance matrix of f. The covariance matrix of g is given by

$$\begin{aligned} C_g &= E[(g - \bar{g})(g - \bar{g})^T] \\ &= E[(g - H_I f + H_I f - H_I \bar{f})(g - H_I f \\ &\quad + H_I f - H_I \bar{f})^T] \\ &= E[(g - H_I f)(g - H_I f)^T] + H_I C_f H_I^T. \quad (24) \end{aligned}$$

The first part of (24) is the speckle noise term and the second part is the signal term since $E[g|f] = H_I f$. The (i, j)th element of the first term in (24) is equal to

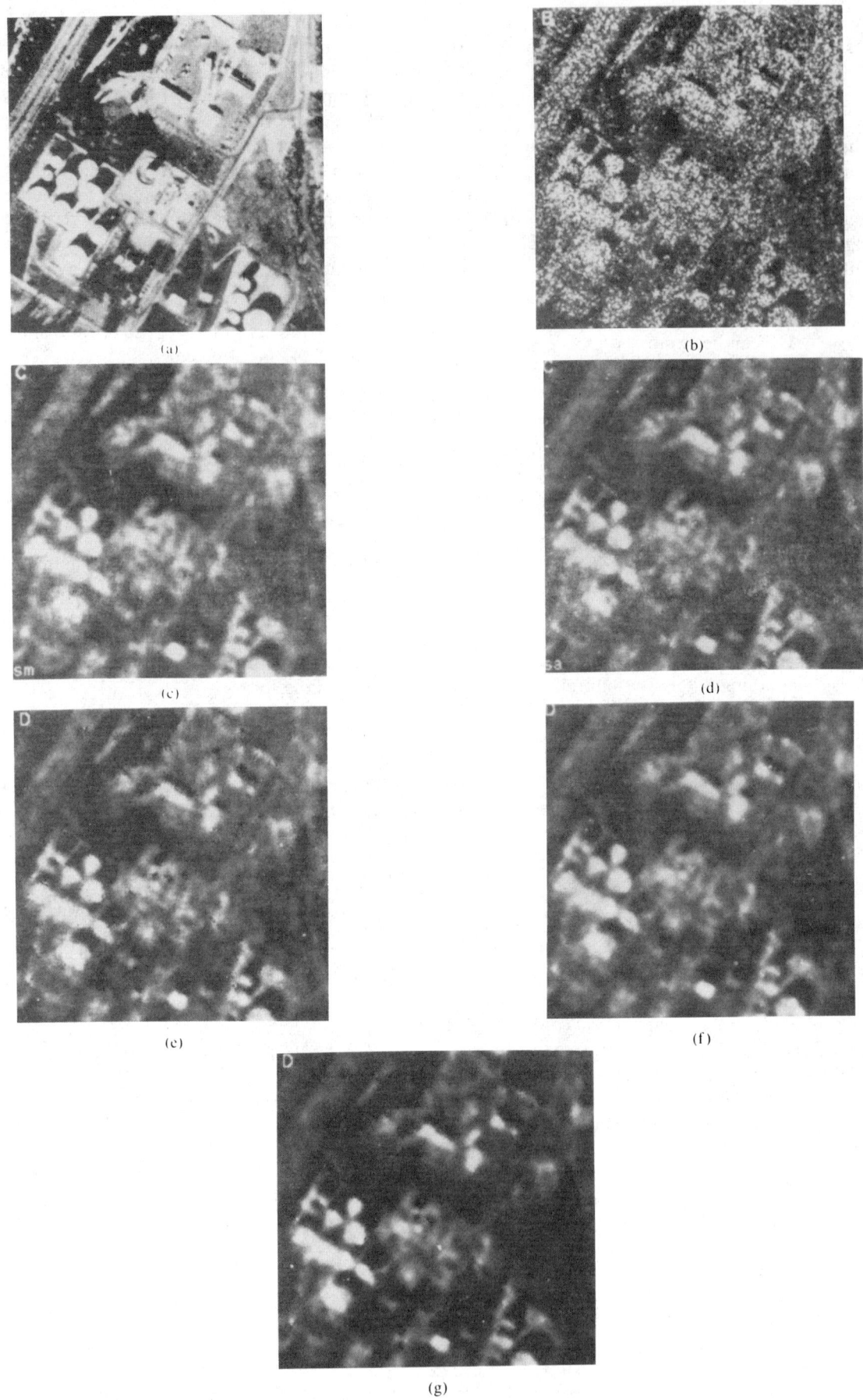

Fig. 3. Adaptive speckle reduction filter simulation—single frame, independent speckle samples. (a) Original image. (b) Speckle image. (c) 7 × 7 local mean of speckle image in (b). (d) Adaptive noise smoothing estimate. (e) One-point MAP estimate. (f) Second iteration adaptive noise smoothing estimate. (g) Second iteration MAP estimate.

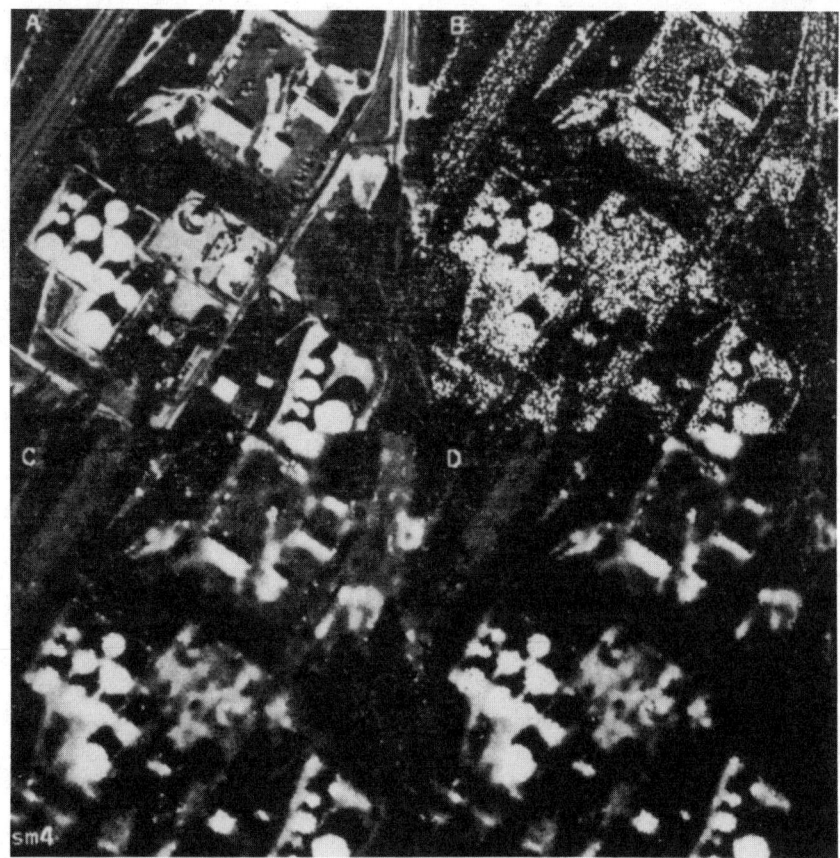

Fig. 4. Adaptive speckle reduction filter simulation—4 frames, independent speckle samples. (a) Original image. (b) Speckle image (4 frames average). (c) Adaptive noise smoothing estimate. (d) One-point MAP estimate.

$E[C_g(m, n; m_1, n_1|f)]$, where (m, n) and (m_1, n_1) are the actual spatial coordinates in the image. The corresponding lexicographic representation indexes are $i = (m - 1)*N + n$ and $j = (m_1 - 1)*N + n_1$, where N is the number of columns in the image. Because $g(m, n) = |b(m, n)|^2$, we have

$$E[C_g(m, n; m_1, n_1|f)]$$
$$= E\big[E[b(m, n) b^*(m, n) b(m_1, n_1) b^*(m_1, n_1)|f]\big]^2$$
$$- E[g(m, n)|f] E[g(m_1, n_1)|f]$$
$$= E\big[|E[b(m, n) b^*(m_1, n_1)|f]|^2\big], \quad (25)$$

where we applied the following complex circular Gaussian moment theorem [1].

Theorem: Let u, v, s, and t be complex circular Gaussian random variables, then

$$E[u^*v^*st] = E[u^*s] E[v^*t] + E[u^*t] E[v^*s].$$

From (1), (25) can be expressed as

$$E[C_g(m, n; m_1, n_1|f)]$$
$$= E\big[|E[b(m, n) b^*(m_1, n_1)|f]|^2\big]$$
$$= E\bigg[\bigg|E\bigg[\sum_i \sum_k \sum_r \sum_s f^{1/2}(i, k) f^{1/2}(r, s) h(m - i,$$

$$n - k) h(m_1 - r, n_1 - s) a(i, k) a^*(r, s)\bigg|f\bigg]\bigg|^2\bigg]$$
$$= E\bigg[\bigg|\sum_i \sum_k h(m - i, n - k)$$
$$h(m_1 - i, n_1 - k) f(i, k)\bigg|^2\bigg]$$
$$= E\bigg[\sum_i \sum_k \sum_r \sum_s h(m - i, n - k) h(m_1 - i, n_1 - k) f(i, k) h(m - r, n - s) h(m_1 - r, n_1 - s) f(r, s)\bigg]$$
$$= \sum_i \sum_k \sum_r \sum_s h(m - i, n - k) h(m_1 - i, n_1 - k) h(m - r, n - s) h(m_1 - r, n_1 - s) E[f(i, k) f(r, s)]. \quad (26)$$

If we assume that the object intensity can be modeled by its nonstationary mean and nonstationary variance, then (26) can be expressed as

$$E[C_g(m, n, m_1, n_1|f)]$$
$$= \sum_i \sum_k \sum_r \sum_s h(m - i, n - k) h(m_1 - i, n_1$$

Fig. 5. Adaptive speckle restoration filter simulation—single frame, correlated speckle samples (5×5 coherent PSF). (a) Original image. (b) Speckle image. (c) 7×7 local mean of (b). (d) Restored image.

$$\cdot [\bar{f}(i,k)\bar{f}(r,s) + \sigma_f^2(i,k)\delta(i-r,k-s)]$$

$$= \sum_i \sum_k \sum_r \sum_s h(m-i, n-k) h(m_1-i, n_1-k) h(m-r, n-s) h(m_1-r, n_1-s) \bar{f}(i,k)\bar{f}(r,s)$$

$$+ \sum_i \sum_k h^2(m-i, n-k) h^2(m_1-i, n_1-k) \sigma_f^2(i,k) \quad (27)$$

$$= \left| \sum_i \sum_k h(m-i, n-k) h(m_1-i, n_1-k) \bar{f}(i,k) \right|^2$$

$$+ \sum_i \sum_k h^2(m-i, n-k) h^2(m_1-i, n_1-k) \sigma_f^2(i,k).$$

From (25) and (27), (24) can be expressed as

$$C_g = [H\bar{F}H^T]^2 + H_lC_fH_l^T + H_lC_fH_l^T \quad (28)$$

where the operator $[A]^2$ takes the magnitude square of each element of matrix A, and $\bar{F}$ matrix is defined as

$$\bar{F} = \begin{bmatrix} \bar{f}(1,1) & & & 0 \\ & \bar{f}(1,2) & & \\ & & \cdots & \\ 0 & & & \bar{f}(N,N) \end{bmatrix}.$$

Substituting these statistics into (21), we have the LLMMSE speckle reduction filter for correlated speckle samples.

The local statistics used in the LLMMSE speckle reduction filter have to be estimated from the degraded image $g(m, n)$. The local mean and local variance of $g(m, n)$ is readily available. However, the speckle reduction filter requires the local mean and local variance of the original image $f(m, n)$. One way to get the local mean of $f(m, n)$ is to apply the inverse system of H_l on the local mean estimate of $g(m, n)$. The quality of this estimate depends on the stability of the inverse system and problems of error accumulation may occur due to the inexact knowledge of the blurring function and the instability of the inverse system.

Another local mean estimate of $f(m, n)$ can be ob-

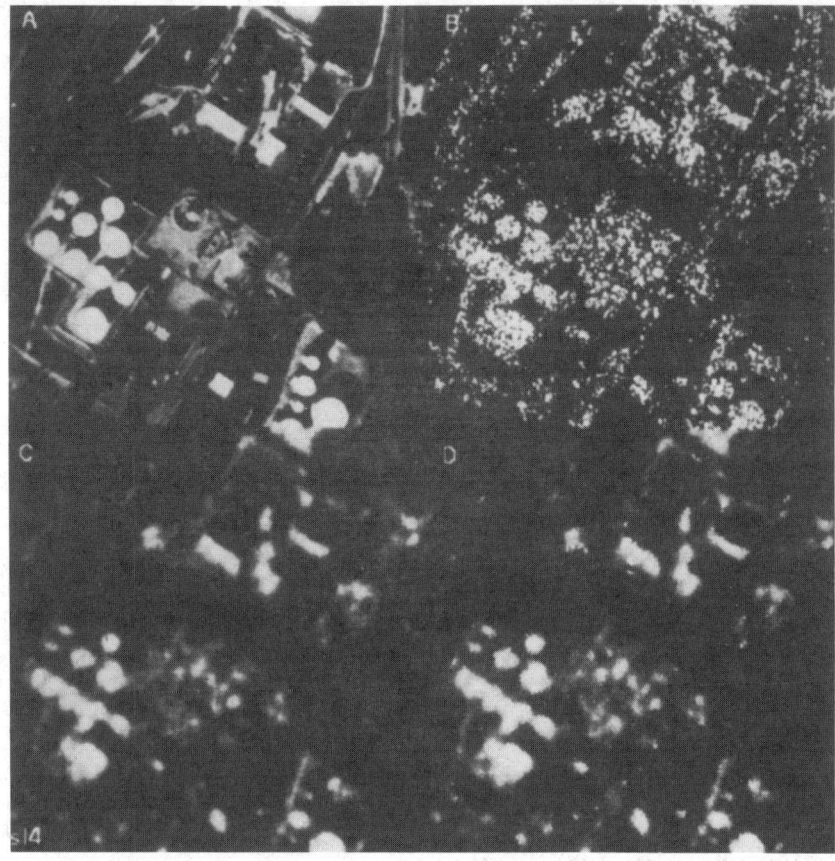

Fig. 6. Adaptive speckle restoration filter simulation—4 frames, correlated speckle samples (5 × 5 coherent PSF). (a) Original image. (b) Speckle image (4 frames average). (c) 7 × 7 local mean of (b). (d) Restored speckle image.

tained by using the blurring function as the weighting function for calculating the local mean of $g(m, n)$ and using the inverse filter to calculate the local mean of $f(m, n)$. It is easy to see the net effect is to set the local mean of $f(m, n)$ equal to $g(m, n)$. Due to the low SNR in speckle images, this is not a good estimate. In here, we estimate the local mean of $f(m, n)$ from $g(m, n)$ by local averaging, then convolve the local mean estimate of $f(m, n)$ with the blurring function H_l to get a consistent local mean estimate of $g(m, n)$. Similarly, the local variance estimate of $f(m, n)$ is calculated from $g(m, n)$ by assuming a multiplicative speckle noise model as in the adaptive noise smoothing filter case.

A. Simulation Results

The LLMMSE speckle reduction filter requires the inverse of C_g which is of dimension $N^2 \times N^2$. For a common image $N = 256$, this task will take a tremendous amount of computation and memory space. Here, we use a sectioning method that divides an image into overlapping sections of size 12 × 12 to reduce the computation load. The reason for using overlapping sections is to avoid section boundary effects. The 2-D recursive implementation of this filter is discussed in [10].

The simulation results for correlated speckle samples are shown in Fig. 5. The speckle image in Fig. 5(b) is generated according to the accurate speckle model in Fig. 2 with a 5 × 5 coherent point spread function. The correlation properties of this speckle image can be visualized by comparing the speckle size in Figs. 3 and 5(b). We use a 7 × 7 uniform weight moving average window to calculate the local mean of Fig. 5(b), and the result is shown in Fig. 5(c). The adaptively restored image is shown in Fig. 5(d). The same filter with modified statistics can be applied to a multiple frames case. The average of 4 independent frames of spatially correlated speckle images is shown in Fig. 6(b). The 7 × 7 local mean estimate is given in Fig. 6(c). The adaptively restored image is shown in Fig. 6(c). The restored image has much better resolution than the result of a low-pass filter.

V. Conclusions

In this paper, we developed several adaptive speckle reduction filters for intensity speckle images where only the speckle intensity is recorded and the phase information is lost in the recording process. For the case of independent speckle samples, speckle reduction becomes a noise smoothing problem and speckle noise can be modeled as a multiplicative noise with negative exponential distribution. In this situation, the one-point maximum *a posteriori* (MAP) filter and the adaptive noise smoothing filter can adapt themselves to the local image statistics and the first-order statistics of speckle noise to suppress speckle noise effectively. In general, however, the second-order statistics of speckle are also important for speckle reduction. The local linear minimum mean square error (LLMMSE) filter developed here takes into account both the local image statistics and the correlation of speckle, a factor which has been previously ignored. These adaptive speckle reduction techniques can be extended directly to process multiple frames of speckle intensity images. Simulation results for various speckle model assumptions and various adaptive restoration filters are presented. The optimal MAP speckle reduction filter for complex amplitude speckle images, where both the amplitude and phase data are available, is discussed in [11].

References

[1] J. W. Goodman, "Some fundamental properties of speckle," *J. Opt. Soc. Amer.*, vol. 66, pp. 1145-1149, Nov. 1976.

[2] S. Lowenthal and H. Arsenault, "Image formation for coherent diffuse objects: Statistical properties," *J. Opt. Soc. Amer.*, vol. 60, pp. 1487-1493, Nov. 1970.

[3] L. J. Porcello, N. G. Massey, R. B. Innes, and J. M. Marks, "Speckle reduction in synthetic aperture radars," *J. Opt. Soc. Amer.*, vol. 66, pp. 1305-1311, Nov. 1976.

[4] J. S. Zelenka, "Comparison of continuous and discrete mixed-integrator processors," *J. Opt. Soc. Amer.*, vol. 66, pp. 1295-1304, Nov. 1976.

[5] J. S. Lim and H. Nawab, "Techniques for speckle noise removal," *Opt. Eng.*, vol. 20, pp. 472-480, May/June 1981.

[6] J. S. Lee, "Speckle analysis and smoothing of synthetic aperture radar images," *Comput. Graph. Image Processing*, vol. 17, pp. 24-32, 1981.

[7] V. S. Frost, J. A. Stiles, K. S. Shanmugan, and J. C. Holtzman, "A model for radar images and its application to adaptive digital filtering for multiplicative noise," *IEEE Trans. Pattern Anal. Machine Intell.*, vol. PAMI-4, pp. 157-166, Mar. 1982.

[8] M. Tur, K. C. Chin, and J. W. Goodman, "When is speckle noise multiplicative," *Appl. Opt.*, vol. 21, pp. 1157-1159, Apr. 1982.

[9] D. T. Kuan, A. A. Sawchuk, T. C. Strand, and P. Chavel, "Adaptive noise smoothing filter for images with signal-dependent noise," *IEEE Trans. Pattern Anal. Machine Intell.*, vol. PAMI-7, pp. 165-177, Mar. 1985.

[10] —, "Nonstationary 2-D recursive filter for speckle reduction," in *Proc. 1982 IEEE Int. Conf. Acoust., Speech, Signal Processing*, Paris, France, May 1982.

[11] —, "MAP speckle reduction filter for complex amplitude speckle images," in *Proc. 1982 IEEE Conf. Pattern Anal. Machine Intell.*, Las Vegas, NV, June 1982.

[12] R. H. T. Bates, "Astronomical speckle imaging," *Physics Rep.*, vol. 90, pp. 203-297, 1982.

[13] R. H. T. Bates and R. A. Minard, "Compensation for multiple reflection," *IEEE Trans. Sonics Ultrason.*, vol. SU-31, pp. 330-336, July 1984.

[14] R. A. Minard, B. S. Robinson, and R. H. T. Bates, "Full-wave computed tomography. Part 3: Coherent shift-and-add imaging," *IEE Proc.*, vol. 132, part A, no. 1, pp. 50-58, Jan. 1985.

[15] G. Weigelt and B. Wirnitzer, "Image reconstruction by the speckle-masking method," *Opt. Lett.*, vol. 8, no. 7, pp. 389-391, July 1983.

[16] B. R. Hunt, W. R. Fright, and R. H. T. Bates, "Analysis of the shift-and-add method for imaging through turbulent media," *J. Opt. Soc. Amer.*, vol. 73, no. 4, pp. 456-465, Apr. 1983.

[17] J. C. Dainty, "Laser speckle and related phenomena," in *Topics in Applied Physics*, vol. 9. Berlin, Germany: Springer-Verlag, 1975.

Darwin T. Kuan (S'81-M'82) received the B.S. degree from the National Taiwan University in 1978 and the M.S. and Ph.D. degrees from the University of Southern California, Los Angeles, in 1979 and 1982, respectively, all in electrical engineering.

From 1979 to 1982 he was a Research Assistant in the Signal and Image Processing Institute at the University of Southern California. He spent three months of 1982 at the Institut d'Optique, Orsay, France, as a Visiting Scientist working on speckle noise reduction techniques. From 1982 to 1983 he was with Advanced Decision Systems, Mountain View, CA. He is currently Principal Computer Scientist at the Artificial Intelligence Center, FMC Corporation, Santa Clara, CA, where he is working on autonomous vehicles and artificial intelligence. His research interests include computer vision, artificial intelligence, and image and signal processing.

Alexander A. Sawchuk (S'65-M'71-SM'79) was born in Washington, DC, in 1945. He received the B.S. degree from the Massachusetts Institute of Technology, Cambridge, in 1966 and the M.S. and Ph.D. degrees from Stanford University, Stanford, CA, in 1968 and 1972, respectively, all in electrical engineering.

He has been employed in instrumentation and communications systems analysis by the National Bureau of Standards, the NASA Goddard Space Flight Center, and the Communications Satellite Corporation. In 1971 he joined the University of Southern California, Los Angeles, where he is presently Director of the Signal and Image Processing Institute, and Professor in the Department of Electrical Engineering. His research interests include optical information processing, digital image processing, multidimensional signal processing, machine vision, and image analysis.

Dr. Sawchuk is a Fellow of the Optical Society of America and Chair of its Technical Council. He is a Fellow of the Society of Photo-Optical Instrumentation Engineers, and is a member of the Optical Society of Southern California, the Society of Information Display, and Sigma Xi. In 1980 he received the Halliburton Award for Exceptional Service from the University of Southern California.

Timothy C. Strand (M'80) received the B.A. degree in physics from the University of Iowa and the M.S. and Ph.D. degrees in applied physics from the University of California at San Diego.

From 1976 until 1983 he was associated with the Image Processing Institute at the University of Southern California where he was involved in teaching and research in the areas of optical information processing, image processing, holography, and optical computing. He is currently Manager of the Machine Vision Sensing Group at the IBM Almaden Research Center.

Pierre Chavel was born in Strasbourg, France, in 1950. He received the Agrégation de Physique from Ecole Normale Supérieure de Saint-Cloud in 1972, and the Doctorat ès Sciences from the Université de Paris-Sud, Orsay, France, in 1979.

Since 1972 he has been a Research Scientist at CNRS (Centre National de la Recherche Scientifique), working at the Institut d'Optique, Orsay. He spent the academic year 1979–1980 as a Visiting Scientist at the Image Processing Institute, University of Southern California, Los Angeles. His research interests include optical-digital image processing, optical coherence, and optical computing.

Dr. Chavel is the Secretary of Société Française d'Optique and a member of the Optical Society of America, SPIE, the European Physical Society, Société Française de Physique, and Union des Physiciens.

A Class of Iterative Signal Restoration Algorithms

AGGELOS K. KATSAGGELOS, MEMBER, IEEE, AND SERAFIM N. EFSTRATIADIS, STUDENT MEMBER, IEEE

Abstract—In this paper, a class of iterative signal restoration algorithms is derived based on a representation theorem for the generalized inverse of a matrix. These algorithms exhibit a first or higher order of convergence, and some of them consist of an on-line and an off-line computational part. The conditions for convergence, the rate of convergence of these algorithms, and the computational load required to achieve the same restoration results are derived. A new iterative algorithm is also presented which exhibits a higher rate of convergence than the standard quadratic algorithm with no extra computational load. These algorithms can be applied to the restoration of signals of any dimensionality. Iterative restoration algorithms that have appeared in the literature represent special cases of the class of algorithms described here. Therefore, the approach presented here unifies a large number of iterative restoration algorithms. Furthermore, based on the convergence properties of these algorithms, combined algorithms are proposed that incorporate *a priori* knowledge about the solution in the form of constraints and converge faster than the previously used algorithms.

I. INTRODUCTION

THE recovery or restoration of a signal that has been distorted is one of the most important problems in signal processing applications [1], [18]. More specifically, the following degradation model is considered:

$$y = Dx, \quad (1)$$

where the vectors y and x represent, respectively, lexicographically ordered blurred and original signals. The matrix D represents a linear deterministic distortion which may be space varying or space invariant. When y and x represent images, then the distortion may be due to motion between the camera and the scene or due to atmospheric turbulence. The signal restoration problem is then to invert (1) or to find a signal as close as possible to the original one, subject to a suitable optimality criterion given y and D. Equation (1) also represents the more general degradation model where an additive noise term is considered. In this case, the restoration problem takes again the form of solving (1) for x, where D is replaced by a square well-conditioned matrix and y by $D^T y$, where ^{T} denotes the transpose of a matrix or vector. This case will be separately studied in Section III, since computationally simpler algorithms can be used.

Iterative algorithms are used in our work in solving the signal restoration problem. Iterative restoration algorithms have a number of advantages over direct or recursive restoration techniques, and they have been used extensively in the literature [18]. Most of these algorithms have a linear or first-order convergence rate. Singh *et al.* [19] derived an iterative restoration algorithm with a quadratic rate of convergence, when the matrix D in (1) is invertible. Morris *et al.* [14]–[16] and Lagendijk *et al.* [13] generalized this algorithm for higher orders of convergence. In their derivation, the matrix D in (1) was invertible. In [14]–[16] it was further assumed that D represents a convolution operator.

In this paper, we extend the results in [13]–[16] and [19] by showing that when D is singular, the higher order algorithms converge to the minimum norm solution of (1), provided that a solution exists. This is a very important result because for a large number of distortions of practical interest (motion, out-of-focus), the matrix D is singular. Furthermore, we derive iterative algorithms with linear and higher order convergence rates for the general case when D in (1) is a rectangular matrix. In this case, the limiting solution of these algorithms is the minimum norm least-squares (MNLS) solution of (1). The derivation of these algorithms is based on a representation theorem for the generalized inverse D^+ of the matrix D. Iterative restoration algorithms benefit a great deal from the use of constraints which incorporate properties of the solution into the restoration process. However, the direct use of constraints with the higher order algorithms may result in divergence or meaningless results. We propose techniques which allow us to effectively use constraints with a combination of linear and higher order iterative algorithms.

The derivation of the linear and higher order algorithms obtaining the MNLS solution of (1) is presented in Section II. Computationally simpler higher order algorithms solving for the minimum norm solution of (1), when D is a square, positive semidefinite matrix, are presented in Section III. Such a situation may result, for example, when a noise term is added to (1). Then, after regularization, the restoration problem is again the solution of a set of linear equations analogous to (1), where D and y are replaced by another matrix A and a vector b, respectively. These algorithms extend the results reported in [13]–[16] and [19]. In Section IV, the algorithms are compared with respect to their computational load. The incorporation of constraints are discussed in Section V, and a number of experimental results are presented in Section VI. Finally, conclusions are presented in Section VII.

Manuscript received August 2, 1988; revised June 16, 1989. This work was supported in part by the National Science Foundation under Grant MIP-8614217.

The authors are with the Department of Electrical Engineering and Computer Science, Northwestern University, The Technological Institute, Evanston, IL 60208-3118.

IEEE Log Number 9034417.

II. Minimum Norm Least-Squares Solution

In this section we assume that the matrix D in (1) is an $m \times n$ matrix, where $m \geq n$. That is, $D \in L(\mathbf{R}^n, \mathbf{R}^m)$, $x \in \mathbf{R}^n$ and $y \in \mathbf{R}^m$, where $L(\mathbf{R}^n, \mathbf{R}^m)$ is the set of matrices that map $\mathbf{R}^n$ into $\mathbf{R}^m$, the n-dimensional and m-dimensional Euclidean spaces, respectively. Let $\mathcal{R}(D)$ and $\mathcal{N}(D)$ denote, respectively, the range and the null space of D and let $\dim(S)$ denote the dimensionality of the subspace S [20]. If $\dim(\mathcal{R}(D)) = r$, then since $\dim(\mathcal{R}(D^T)) = r$, we get that $\dim(\mathcal{N}(D)) = n - r$ and $\dim(\mathcal{N}(D^T)) = m - r$. Equation (1) has at most one solution if and only if $r = n$, and we get no solution if $y \in \mathcal{N}(D^T)$. The degradation model of (1) can be modified so that D is a square matrix ($m = n$), by increasing the size of x, by adding zeros, or by reducing the size of y. Even in this case, however, for a large number of common distortions (motion, out-of-focus), the distortion matrix is singular, that is, $r < n$. Since in both cases (square and rectangular D) it cannot be guaranteed that $y \in \mathcal{R}(D)$, a least-squares (LS) solution is sought (the case when D is square and $y \in \mathcal{R}(D)$ will be studied in Section III). Such a solution minimizes the Euclidean norm $\|Dx - y\|$. The LS solution satisfies the normal equations

$$D^T D x = D^T y. \tag{2}$$

The set of x's that satisfy (2) forms a closed convex set which contains a unique vector of minimum norm [5]. Then the generalized inverse $D^+ \in L(\mathbf{R}^m, \mathbf{R}^n)$ is defined by $D^+ y = x^+$, where x^+ is the minimum norm least-squares (MNLS) solution of (1). A general theorem representing D^+ as the limit of a sequence of matrices, presented in Groetch [5], is presented next without proof, due to its significance.

A. Representation of D^+ and x^+

Theorem 1: Suppose $D \in L(\mathbf{R}^n, \mathbf{R}^m)$ and let $D^* = D^T D / \mathcal{R}(D^T)$. If Ω is an open set with $\sigma(D^*) \subset \Omega \subset (0, \infty)$ and $\{f_k(z)\}$ is a family of continuous real valued functions on Ω with $\lim_k f_k(z) = z^{-1}$ uniformly on $\sigma(D^*)$, then

$$D^+ = \lim_k f_k(D^*) D^T, \tag{3}$$

where the convergence is in the uniform topology for $L(\mathbf{R}^m, \mathbf{R}^n)$. Furthermore,

$$\|f_k(D^*) D^T - D^+\| \leq \sup\{|1 - z f_k(z)|\} \cdot \|D^+\|, \tag{4}$$

where the supremum is taken over all $z \in \sigma(D^*)$. □

Some of the notation used above is as follows. The spectral radius of a square matrix T and the restriction of T to a subspace S of $\mathbf{R}^n$ are, respectively, denoted by $\sigma(T)$ and T/S [20]. Clearly, the matrix D^* is symmetric and positive definite. Therefore, its spectral radius is a subset of the set $(0, \infty)$.

Theorem 1 is very powerful because it provides us with a general expression (3) for representing and iteratively computing the generalized inverse of a matrix. Furthermore, it provides us with a measure of the rate of convergence (4). Therefore, it unifies a large number of iterative restoration techniques. Any family of functions $\{f_k\}$ with the properties stated by Theorem 1 can result in a new representation for D^+. Clearly, some of these families of functions result in more attractive representations, from a computational point of view. It is noted here that Theorem 1 holds not only for matrices but for any linear operator with a closed range [5].

In signal restoration we are primarily interested in solving for x^+. Expressions for x^+ instead of D^+ are derived as follows. The convergence of the sequence $\{f_k(D^*) D^T\}$ to D^T is in the uniform topology for $L(\mathbf{R}^m, \mathbf{R}^n)$, which means that [5]

$$\lim_k \|f_k(D^*) D^T - D^+\| = 0. \tag{5}$$

The uniform convergence of $\{f_k(D^*) D^T\}$ to D^+ implies strong convergence of $\{f_k(D^*) D^T\}$ to D^+, which means that for each $y \in \mathbf{R}^m$

$$\lim_k \|f_k(D^*) D^T y - D^+ y\| = 0. \tag{6}$$

Therefore, (3) and (4) are written, respectively, as [3], [10]

$$x^+ = \lim_k f_k(D^*) D^T \tag{7}$$

and

$$\|f_k(D^*) D^T y - x^+\| \leq \sup\{|1 - z f_k(z)|\} \cdot \|x^+\|, \tag{8}$$

where the supremum is again over all $z \in \sigma(D^*)$. Therefore, Theorem 1 can be restated with (7) and (8) replacing (3) and (4), respectively. In the following section, different iterative restoration algorithms will be derived, corresponding to different choices of $\{f_k(z)\}$, by using (7) and (8).

B. A Linear Algorithm

Consider the sequence of functions $\{f_k(z)\}$ defined by

$$f_0(z) = \beta > 0$$

$$f_k(z) = f_0(z) \sum_{i=0}^{k} (1 - z f_0(z))^i. \tag{9}$$

It is shown [3], [5] that $\lim_{k \to \infty} f_k(z) = z^{-1}$ uniformly on compact subsets of the set

$$\Omega_\beta = \{z : |1 - \beta z| < 1\} = \left\{z : 0 < z < \frac{2}{\beta}\right\}. \tag{10}$$

According to Theorem 1 and (9), by setting $x_k = f_k(D^*) D^T y$, we get the iteration

$$x_0 = \beta D^T y$$

$$x_{k+1} = x_k + \beta D^T (y - D x_k)$$

$$= (I - \beta D^T D) x_k + \beta D^T y, \tag{11}$$

which converges to x^+ for

$$0 < \beta < 2 \cdot \|D\|^{-2}. \tag{12}$$

Iteration (11) also results from a successive approximations approach to the solution of the normal equations (2). It has been studied and used extensively for signal restoration [7], [18]. According to (8), the rate of convergence of iteration (11) is linear and it is characterized by the relation

$$\frac{\|x_k - x^+\|}{\|x^+\|} \leq c^{k+1}, \tag{13}$$

where [5]

$$c = \max\left\{\left|1 - \beta \cdot \|D\|^2\right|, \left|1 - \beta \cdot \|D^+\|^{-2}\right|\right\}. \tag{14}$$

An equivalent way of describing the linear rate of convergence of iteration (11) is with the use of the residual error at step k of iteration (9) [3]. It is defined as

$$r_k = 1 - zf_k(z) \tag{15}$$

and it represents the residual error associated with each eigenvalue of D^*, since $z \in \sigma(D^*)$. Then, according to iteration (9),

$$r_{k+1} = r_0 r_k. \tag{16}$$

Equation (16) represents a straight line on the $r_k r_{k+1}$-plane.

C. Higher Order Algorithms

Consider the sequence of functions $\{f_k(z)\}$ for an integer $p \geq 2$

$$f_0(z) = \beta > 0,$$

$$f_{k+1}(z) = f_k(z) \sum_{i=0}^{p-1} (1 - zf_k(z))^i. \tag{17}$$

The sequence defined by (17) converges uniformly to z^{-1} on compact subsets of Ω_β (10) [3], [5]. Application of Theorem 1 results in the algorithm [3], [5], [8]–[10]

$$D_0 = \beta D^T D, \quad x_0 = \beta D^T y, \tag{18a}$$

$$\Phi_k = \sum_{i=0}^{p-1} (I - D_k)^i, \tag{18b}$$

$$D_{k+1} = \Phi_k D_k, \quad x_{k+1} = \Phi_k x_k. \tag{18c}$$

An advantage of iteration (18) is that the matrix sequence $\{\Phi_k\}$ or $\{D_k\}$ can be computed in advance or *off-line*, although for a general D this may result in excessive storage. The solution sequence $\{x_k\}$ is then computed *on-line* after the distorted data y are available. As observed from (18), the limit of D_k is the projection onto the row space of D. This projection is equal to the identity matrix when D is invertible. That is, the distortion matrix is also updated. This means that if x_k is interpreted as the observed distorted signal at each iteration, then the distortion op-

erator, which maps the original signal into x_k, is approaching the identity operator (if the inverse exists) as the iteration number increases.

Algorithm (18) exhibits pth order of convergence. That is, according to relation (8) [3], [6],

$$\frac{\|x_k - x^+\|}{\|x^+\|} \leq c^{p^k}, \tag{19}$$

where the convergence factor c is given by (14). Equivalently, it is easily shown that [3]

$$r_{k+1} = r_k^p, \tag{20}$$

where r_k is defined by (15). Equation (20) represents a pth-order curve on the $r_k r_{k+1}$-plane. Certain of these curves for $p = 2, 3, 4, 9, 20$ are shown in Fig. 1. The curve representing the rate of convergence of the linear algorithm (16) is also shown. Clearly, as p increases, the residual error for most of its values tends to go to zero in one iteration. Notice that the values -1 and 1 are excluded from the range of values that r_k takes.

D. A New Iterative Algorithm

Let us regard z^{-1} as the root of the function $f(u) = (u^{-1} - z)^\eta$, where $\eta > 0$. If the Newton–Raphson method is used in approximating this root, then the sequence $\{u_k\}$ is generated according to [3]

$$u_{k+1} = u_k\left[1 + \frac{1}{\eta}(1 - zu_k)\right], \tag{21}$$

for a suitable u_0. Suppose that for $\beta > 0$, a sequence of functions $\{f_k(z)\}$ is defined by

$$f_0(z) = \beta$$

$$f_{k+1}(z) = f_k(z)\left[1 + \frac{1}{\eta}(1 - zf_k(z))\right]. \tag{22}$$

The convergence and the rate of convergence of this algorithm can be described by considering r_k defined by (15). That is, it is found in a straightforward way that

$$r_{k+1} = \frac{1}{\eta} r_k(r_k + \eta - 1). \tag{23}$$

Note that for $\eta = 1$, this algorithm becomes the quadratic algorithm ($p = 2$) of (17). The curves described by (23) for different values of η are shown in Fig. 2. The lines $r_{k+1} = r_k$ and $r_{k+1} = -r_k$, also shown in this figure, are dividing the space into the regions I and II, defined, respectively, by $|r_{k+1}| < |r_k|$ and $|r_{k+1}| \geq |r_k|$. Clearly, if part of the curve represented by (23) for a certain η lies in region I, and if $|r_0| < 1$, iteration (22) converges; otherwise, it may not converge. For example, for $\eta > 1$ and $|r_0| < 1$, iteration (22) converges to z^{-1} on compact subsets of Ω_β, although the convergence rate of the algorithm may be slower than that of the quadratic.

On the other hand, for $0.5 < \eta < 1$, the part of the curve (23) for which $r_k \leq -\eta$ lies in the region II. Therefore, we need to restrict the residuals to satisfy $r_k > -\eta$,

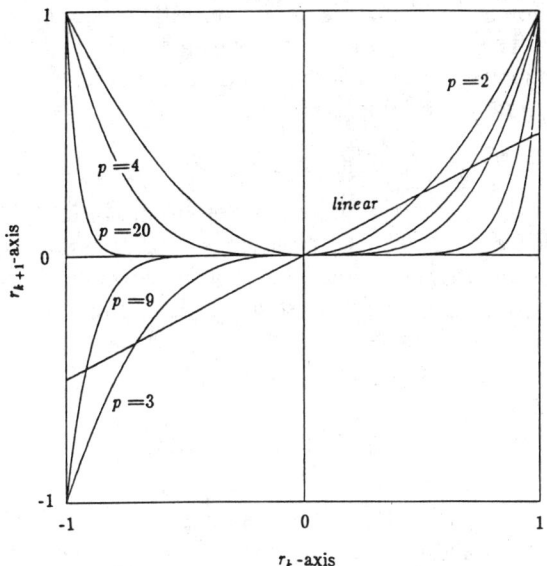

Fig. 1. Representation of the residual error of (16) and (20), respectively, for various values of the order p.

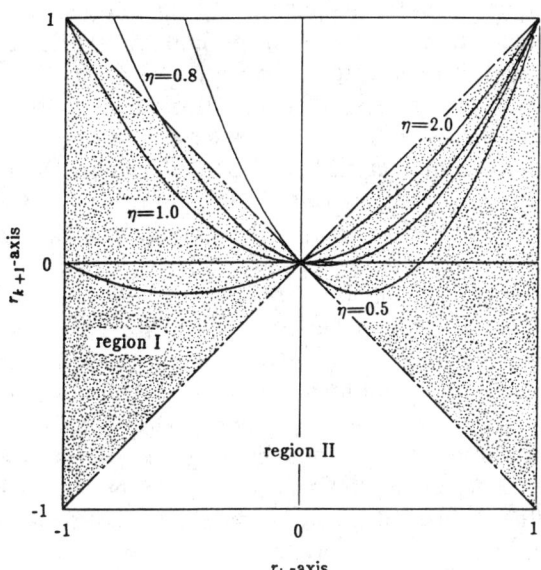

Fig. 2. Representation of the residual error of (23), for various values of η.

or $r_k \geq 0$. One way to accomplish this is by using $\eta = 1$ in evaluating $r_1(k = 0)$ and then changing η to any value such that $0.5 < \eta < 1$. The rate of convergence of iteration (22) is pictorially represented by the slope of the curves shown in Fig. 2. For example, for $r_k \geq 0.2$, iteration (22) converges faster with $\eta = 0.8$ than with $\eta = 1.0$. With the conditions on η imposed according to Fig. 2 in mind, application of Theorem 1 results in the iteration [3]

$$D_0 = \beta D^T D, \quad x_0 = \beta D^T y, \quad (24a)$$

$$\Phi_k = I + \frac{1}{\eta}(I - D_k), \quad (24b)$$

$$D_{k+1} = \Phi_k D_k, \quad x_{k+1} = \Phi_k x_k, \quad (24c)$$

where $\eta = 1$ for $k = 0$ and $0.5 < \eta < 1$ for $k \geq 1$. In general, the rate of convergence of iteration (24) depends on the distribution of the eigenvalues of the matrix D^* defined by Theorem 1.

III. Minimum Norm Solution

In this section we consider the solution of

$$Ax = b, \quad (25)$$

where A is a square positive semidefinite matrix and $b \in \mathcal{R}(A)$. This is a case of special interest. Equation (25) may be the degradation model of (1), when, for example, $D = A$ represents the degradation due to atmospheric turbulence. Equation (25) may also result from the regularization of the ill-posed signal restoration problem. More specifically, the following degradation model is considered.

$$y = Dx + w, \quad (26)$$

where y and x represent, respectively, the lexicographically ordered distorted and original signals, and w denotes the additive noise. According to a regularization approach presented in [7] and [11], the solution of (26) is replaced by the solution of the well-conditioned system of equations

$$(D^T D + \alpha C^T C)x = D^T y. \quad (27)$$

The matrix C represents a high-pass filter and its role is to restrict the energy of the restored signal at high frequencies, due primarily to the amplified noise. The regularization parameter α is a function of the signal-to-noise ratio [7]. Therefore, the presence of additive noise in the degradation model does not alter the form of the iterative algorithms presented in Section II, since (1) is now replaced by (25).

Clearly, (25) can be solved by using any of the algorithms presented in Section II. A key difference, however, between (1) and (25) is that although matrix D is in general a rectangular matrix, matrix A is always square, positive definite, or positive semidefinite. Therefore, (25) might have a solution, which means that $b \in \mathcal{R}(A)$. As a matter of fact, the constraint C can be designed in such a way that $b \in \mathcal{R}(A)$ [7]. In this case, the minimum norm solution can be found with fewer computations than those required by the least-squares approach, as is shown next.

An iteration due to Bialy [2] with linear rate of convergence, suitable for finding the solution of (25), is presented by the following theorem.

Theorem 2: Let $A: \mathbf{R}^n \to \mathbf{R}^n$ be a positive semidefinite matrix. For $b \in \mathbf{R}^n$, $x_0 \in \mathbf{R}^n$ consider the iterative process

$$x_{k+1} = x_k + \beta(b - Ax_k), \quad (28)$$

where $0 < \beta < 2 \cdot \|A\|^{-1}$. Then, the sequence $\{x_k, k \geq 0\}$ converges to $x^* = \hat{x} + P_{\mathcal{N}(A)}\{x_0\}$, where $\hat{x}$ is the minimum norm solution of $Ax = b$ and $P_{\mathcal{N}(A)}\{x_0\}$ is the projection of x_0 onto the null space of A, if and only if $b \in \mathcal{R}(A)$. □

We can think of iterations (11) and (28) as forming a

pair, since they both have a linear rate of convergence. Iteration (11) successively approximates the solution to the normal equations (2), while iteration (28) successively approximates the solution to (25). In extending the above-mentioned correspondence between the linear algorithms (11) and (28) to the higher order algorithms, we present the following theorem [3], [8].

Theorem 3: Let $A: \mathbf{R}^n \to \mathbf{R}^n$ be a positive semidefinite matrix. For a given integer $p \geq 2$ and $\beta > 0$, consider the iterative process

$$A_0 = \beta A^T, \quad x_0 = \beta b, \tag{29a}$$

$$\Phi_k = \sum_{i=0}^{p-1} (I - A_k)^i, \tag{29b}$$

$$A_{k+1} = \Phi_k A_k, \quad x_{k+1} = \Phi_k x_k, \tag{29c}$$

where $0 < \beta < 2 \cdot \|A\|^{-1}$. Then the sequence $\{x_k, k \geq 0\}$ converges to $x^* = \hat{x}$, where $\hat{x}$ is the minimum norm solution of $Ax = b$, if and only if $b \in \mathcal{R}(A)$. □

The proof of Theorem 3 is presented in the Appendix. Algorithm (29) with $p = 2$ was proposed by Singh *et al.* [19] for the case that $\|I - A\| < 1$, and by Morris *et al.* [14] for the case that A is positive definite and represents a linear space invariant system (convolution case). Algorithm (29) for any $p \geq 2$ was proposed by Morris *et al.* [14], [15] and by Lagendijk *et al.* [13] for the case that A is positive definite. Therefore, Theorem 3 extends the previously reported results.

IV. COMPARISON BASED ON THE COMPUTATIONAL LOAD

The question we address in this section is the following. For a specific restoration problem, which of the iterative algorithms presented in Sections II (B, C, and D) and III should one use? We answer this question by considering the amount of computation required by each algorithm in obtaining the same solution point or in satisfying the same error criterion.

Clearly, algorithms (28) and (29), if applicable, should be used, since they require fewer computations than their counterparts, iterations (11) and (18), respectively. Additionally, iteration (24) should be used over iteration (18) for $p = 2$, if η is chosen according to the discussion in Section II-D, since the former requires the same number of computations as the latter, with the exception of an additional multiplication by the scalar $1/\eta$. Therefore, in the following, the algorithms of Section II-B and C will be compared. The same comparison holds true for the algorithms of Section III.

Iterative algorithms give the exact solution as $k \to \infty$, but in practice the iterative process is terminated after a finite number of iterations. Since the distortion operator is known, c in (14) is known, therefore, the number of iterations required by the algorithms to reach an approximate solution can be computed. More specifically, let us denote by k_1 and k_p the iteration steps of the first and pth-order algorithms, respectively. Let us also suppose that m_p iterations of the pth-order algorithm are run, that is, $k_p = 1, \cdots, m_p$. Then, according to (13) and (19), the k_pth iteration step of algorithm (18) is equivalent to $N(k_p)$ iterations of the linear algorithm, where

$$N(k_p) = p^{k_p} - p^{k_p - 1}. \tag{30}$$

That is, had the k_pth iteration step of algorithm (18) been replaced by $N(k_p)$ iteration steps of algorithm (11), the restoration results would have been the same. Now, the total number of iteration steps of algorithm (11) denoted by m_1, which are equivalent to m_p iteration steps of algorithm (18), are given by the expression

$$m_1 = \sum_{k_p=1}^{m_p} N(k_p) = p^{m_p} - 1. \tag{31}$$

According to (31), due to the exponential relation between m_1 and m_p, a tremendous number of iterations may be required by the linear algorithm in obtaining the same result with a higher order algorithm. For example, if $p = 5$ and $m_5 = 10$, then $m_1 = 9\,765\,624$. However, the relation between the computational load required by the linear and pth-order algorithm in running, respectively, m_1 and m_p iterations, is not exponential, as explained below.

In the general case, let us assume that matrix D has dimensions $m \times n$; then D^* is an $n \times n$ square matrix. Thus, the computational load for the linear algorithm after m_1 iterations is $M_1 = mn^2 + (m_1 + 1)mn$ multiplies and $A_1 = n^2(m - 1) + (m_1 + 1)mn$ additions, with a total of $C_1 = n^2(2m - 1) + 2(m_1 + 1)mn$ operations. On the other hand, m_p iterations of the pth-order algorithm require $M_p = nm + m_p[nm + (p - 1)n^2m]$ multiplies and $A_p = n(m - 1) + m_p[n(m - n) + (p - 1)n^2m]$ additions, with a total of $C_p = n(2m - 1) + m_p[n(2m - n) + 2(p - 1)n^2m]$ operations. The efficiency of the higher order algorithms over the linear depends on the order chosen, the dimensions m and n of the matrix D, and the number of iterations required. Table I shows the smallest number of iterations which the quadratic algorithm ($p = 2$) must run in order to be computationally more efficient than the linear algorithm, as a function of the dimensions of the matrix D. In this case, matrix D is considered to be square ($m = n$) and multiplies and additions are assumed to require the same amount of computation. According to Table I, although the required number of computations per iteration is greater for the higher order algorithms, the overall computational load is indeed less than that required by the linear algorithm, after a small number of iterations. The latter is due to the fact that the error for a given p decreases exponentially with a factor p, whereas the number of computations increases linearly with the same factor.

The computational savings with the use of the higher order algorithms increases when the distortion matrix D has a special form. For example, consider the common case when D is circulant. Then the algorithms are implemented using the Discrete Fourier Transform (DFT). For the linear algorithm, the number of computations after m_1

TABLE I
SMALLEST NUMBER OF ITERATIONS (m_2) FOR WHICH THE QUADRATIC ALGORITHM IS COMPUTATIONALLY MORE EFFICIENT THAN THE LINEAR ALGORITHM, AS A FUNCTION OF THE DIMENSION n OF THE SQUARE MATRIX D

n	m_2
2	3
3,4	4
5-7	5
8-11	6
12-20	7
21-35	8
36-63	9
64-113	10
114-204	11
...	...

TABLE II
COMPUTATION OF THE REQUIRED NUMBER OF ITERATIONS AND THE COMPUTATIONAL LOAD OF THE VARIOUS ALGORITHMS, GIVEN c AND ϵ (D CIRCULANT). THE MINIMUM C_p/N_F INDICATES THE OPTIMUM ORDER p_{opt}

$c = 0.9$	p	1	2	3	4	5	6	7	8	9	10
$\epsilon = 10^{-3}$	m_p	65	7	4	4	3	3	3	3	2	2
	C_p/N_F	133	22	21	29	28	34	40	46	35	39
$\epsilon = 10^{-6}$	m_p	131	8	5	4	4	3	3	3	3	3
	C_p/N_F	265	25	26	29	37	34	40	46	52	58

iterations is $M_1 = (m_1 + 2)N_F$ complex multiplies and $A_1 = (m_1 + 1)N_F$ complex additions, with a total of $C_1 = (2m_1 + 3)N_F$ complex operations, where N_F is the extent of the DFT. For the pth-order algorithm, the number of computations after m_p iterations is $M_p = (m_p p + 1)N_F$ complex multiplies and $A_p = m_p(p - 1)N_F$ complex additions, with a total of $C_p = [m_p(2p - 1) + 1]N_F$ complex operations. Clearly, since C_1 and C_p depend linearly on m_1 and m_p, respectively, while the relation between m_1 and m_p is exponential, according to (31), C_p decreases relatively to C_1, as the order p and iteration number m_p increase. For example, consider the case when $p = 2$ and $m_2 = 8$; then $C_2 = 25N_F$. According to (31), the equivalent number of iterations for the linear algorithm is $m_1 = 255$ and $C_1 = 513N_F$. If $p = 3$ and $m_3 = 8$, then $C_3 = 41N_F$. In this case, the linear algorithm requires $m_1 = 6560$ and $C_1 = 13\,123N_F$ complex operations.

The analysis of the required computational load can be carried out from a different point of view, if we assume that an error threshold ϵ is determined in advance in terminating the iteration. Then, we are interested in finding the smallest m_1 or m_p, and of course that choice of the order p which minimizes the total number of computations. By using (13), m_1 is determined by $m_1 = \lceil \log(\epsilon/c)/\log(c) \rceil$, where $\lceil x \rceil$ is the smallest integer which is greater than or equal to x. For the higher order algorithms, m_p is given by

$$m_p = \left\lceil \frac{\log(\log(\epsilon)/\log(c))}{\log(p)} \right\rceil, \quad (32)$$

and the optimum order p_{opt} minimizes C_p/N_F. Two examples with $c = 0.9$, are given in Table II. In the first example, $\epsilon = 10^{-3}$ and $p_{opt} = 3$, $m_3 = 4$, and $C_3 = 21N_F$. In the second example, $\epsilon = 10^{-6}$ and $p_{opt} = 2$, $m_2 = 8$, and $C_2 = 25N_F$. Note that in the last example, the linear algorithm would require $m_1 = 131$ iterations and $C_1 = 265N_F$ complex operations in order to meet the same error criterion.

In conclusion, the computational load required by the pth-order algorithm is indeed smaller when compared to the computational load required by the linear algorithm. This statement is further amplified if the order p is a composite number. Then arithmetic computations are reduced dramatically, due to the decomposition of the pth-order algorithm into lower order algorithms, as was discussed by Morris et al. [16].

V. COMBINED ALGORITHMS

An attractive feature of the linear iterative algorithms of (11) and (28) is the possibility of incorporating prior knowledge about the solution into the restoration process, in the form of constraints [18]. Among the different constraints, the nonlinear positivity constraint has been shown to be very powerful and useful [18]. However, according to our experimental evidence, when the positivity constraint is used with the higher order algorithms, it generally leads to erroneous results or causes divergence. The qualitative explanation we offer at this point is that this behavior is due to the decoupling of the computation of D_k from the computation of x_k in (18), (24), and (29). That is, there is no adjustment mechanism in the higher order algorithm as with the linear algorithm via the error term ($y - Dx_k$) in (11) or the error term ($b - Ax_k$) in (28). Therefore, the development of constrained higher order algorithms is an open research topic. A first step toward this direction is an iterative algorithm which makes use of both the linear and the pth-order algorithms along with the application of constraints, as discussed next for the algorithm in Section II [3], [10].

Let us denote by k_1 and k_p the iteration numbers of the first and pth order algorithms, respectively. According to (30) and (31), a combination of these algorithms can produce the same restoration results as each algorithm alone. More specifically, given a positive number ϵ, the required total number of iterations m_1 and m_p for algorithms (11) and (18), respectively, are determined as discussed in Section IV. If m_p is even (odd), then the pth order algorithm updates the solution only at its odd (even) iteration steps except at the last one, while its even (odd) iteration steps are replaced by $N(k_p)$ equivalent iterations of algorithm (13). (The opposite occurs for m_p odd.) The last iteration of the pth order algorithm is replaced by $K = m_1$

$- p^{m_p - 1}$ iterations of algorithm (13). For example, if m_p is even, then for $k_p = 1, 3, \cdots, m_p - 1$, we have $k_1 = 0$, while for $k_p = 2, 4, \cdots, m_p - 2$, we have $k_1 = 1, 2, \cdots, N(k_p)$, and for $k_p = m_p$, we have $k_1 = 1, 2, \cdots, K$. In general, if we denote by k the iteration number of the combined algorithm, then

$$k = \left\lceil \frac{k_p}{2} \right\rceil - \mathrm{mod}\,(m_p, 2) + \sum_{l=1}^{k_p - 1} N(k_p)$$
$$\cdot \mathrm{mod}\,(l \cdot m_p, 2) + k_1, \quad (33)$$

where mod $(i, 2)$ represents the modulo operation. When the combined algorithm is used, the proper deterministic constraint(s) can be imposed whenever algorithm (11) is applied. Note that, since after the incorporation of constraints (30) does not hold as is, the range of k_1 can be smaller than $N(k_p)$.

Adaptive regularized iterative image restoration algorithms have also appeared in the literature [6], [11], based on iterations (11) and (28). We have proposed a combined adaptive iterative algorithm based on iterations (18), (24), and (29) [4]. The same idea is used as the one described above. That is, one iteration of the pth-order algorithm (18), for example, is combined with $N(k_p)$ iterations (30) of the linear adaptive algorithm, in forming a combined adaptive iteration step.

VI. Experimental Results

Certain experimental results which demonstrate some of the basic ideas of the previous sections are described in this section. A synthetic signal of length 64 samples consisting of two impulses, $x(n) = \delta(n - 30) + \delta(n - 35)$, is used in our experiments. The simulated distortion is due to motion over 11 samples. The impulse response of such a distorting system is a rectangle, resulting in a singular matrix D. The normalized residual error [left-hand side of conditions (13) and (19)] is shown in Fig. 3, resulting respectively from the application of iterations (11) and (18) for different values of p. In our simulations, the value of x^+ was substituted by the available signal x_{or}. The normalized error is shown again in Fig. 4 with the application of the positivity constraint. The combined algorithm described in Section V for m_p even is implemented in this case for the higher order algorithms. It is observed in this case that the smaller the parameter p, the higher the convergence rate. This is due to the fact that the smaller the parameter p, the more often the higher order algorithm is applied. Due to this observation, the linear algorithms combined with the algorithm proposed in Section II-D is not shown in Fig. 4, since its performance is very similar with the performance of the quadratic algorithm.

Finally, the algorithm with quadratic convergence is compared to the algorithm proposed in Section II-D. The distortion is the same as before, while an image line is used as a test signal. The normalized error is shown in Fig. 5. The faster convergence of the new algorithm over the quadratic algorithm is obtained with no extra computational load.

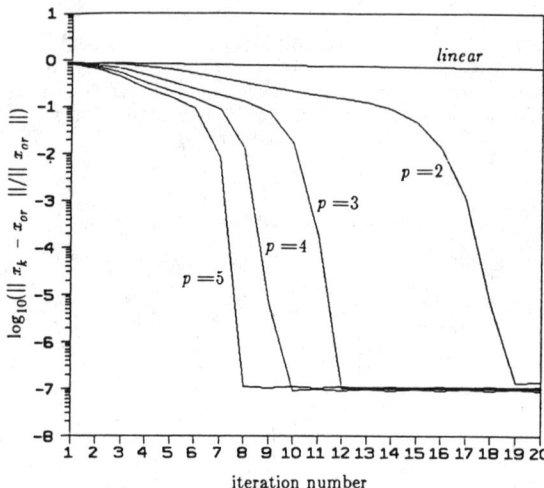

Fig. 3. Normalized residual error versus number of iteration for algorithms (11) and (18), for various values of p.

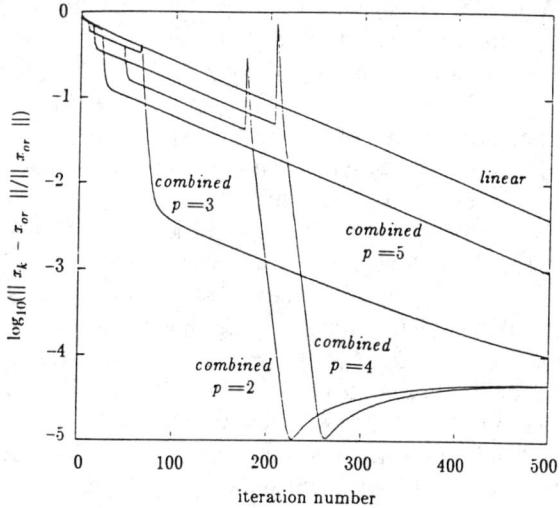

Fig. 4. Normalized residual error versus iteration number for the linear and combined algorithms of Section V, for various values of p, with the incorporation of the positivity constraint.

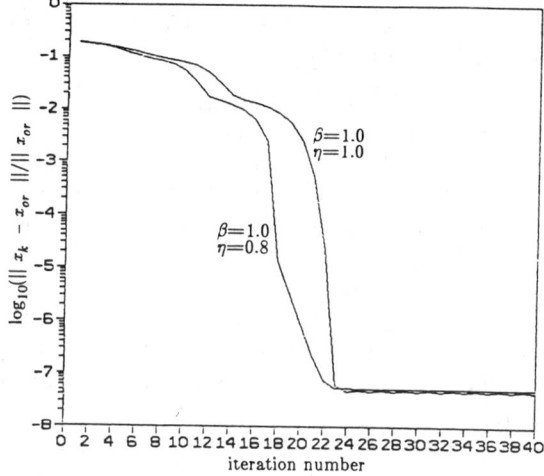

Fig. 5. Normalized residual error versus iteration number for algorithm (24) for various values of η ($\eta = 1.0$ corresponds to the quadratic algorithm).

VII. Discussion and Conclusions

A number of iterative signal restoration algorithms have been derived based on a representation theorem for the generalized inverse of a matrix. Some of these algorithms have appeared in the literature and some are new. An algorithm relating to the method of stochastic approximations can be also derived based on Theorem 1 [3], [5], [12]. Therefore, the approach followed here unifies the derivation of a large number of iterative restoration algorithms. These algorithms are applicable to the general case when additive noise is considered in the distortion model. The restoration approach is the same since the solution of (1) is replaced by the solution of (25). According to the analysis of Section IV, the application of the higher order algorithms is more advantageous due to the computational savings. In addition, due to the fact that they require a smaller number of iterations to converge, truncation or roundoff errors may be less pronounced.

One of the attractive properties of the linear restoration algorithms is the possibility of incorporating constraints in the iteration, which express *a priori* knowledge about the solution. Although the straightforward incorporation of constraints in the higher order algorithms results in undesirable results, we have proposed an algorithm which combines the constrained linear and the pth-order iterations. This combined algorithm converges faster than the constrained linear algorithm and with less overall computational load.

The algorithms presented can be used for the restoration of signals of any dimensionality as well as for the solution of any type of inverse problem which accepts the formulation of (1) or (25). The application of the algorithms to band-limited signal extrapolation is currently under investigation. Since the approach presented here in deriving iterative restoration algorithms is general, the use of other families of functions $f_k(z)$ which satisfy Theorem 1, and may lead to useful iterative restoration algorithms, is also currently under investigation.

Appendix
Proof of Theorem 3

Denote by λ_i, $i = 1, \cdots, n$ the eigenvalues of A. Since A is positive semidefinite, $\lambda_i > 0$ for $i = 1, \cdots, r$ and $\lambda_i = 0$ for $i = r + 1, \cdots, n$, where r is the rank of the matrix. Since A is symmetric, it has a complete set of orthonormal eigenvectors $u_1, \cdots, u_n$, where $(u_i, u_j) = \delta_{ij}$. That is, A can be written as

$$A = U\Lambda U^T = [u_1 \cdots u_n] \begin{bmatrix} \lambda_1 & & \varnothing \\ & \ddots & \\ \varnothing & & \lambda_n \end{bmatrix} \begin{bmatrix} u_1^T \\ \vdots \\ u_n^T \end{bmatrix}. \quad (A-1)$$

If we define

$$T = (I - \beta A) = U(I - \beta \Lambda) U^T, \quad (A-2)$$

and $T_k = I - A_k$, then the iterative algorithm (29) can be written as

$$T_0 = T, \quad x_t = \beta b,$$

$$T_{k+1} = T_k^p, \quad x_{k+1} = \left\{ \sum_{i=0}^{p-1} T_k^i \right\} x_k. \quad (A-3)$$

Solving for x_k, we obtain the following formula:

$$x_k = \left\{ \sum_{i=0}^{p^k - 1} T^i \right\} \beta b, \quad (A-4)$$

or by using (A-2),

$$x_k = \beta \sum_{i=0}^{p^k - 1} U(I - \beta \Lambda)^i U^T b. \quad (A-5)$$

Since A is symmetric, $\mathbf{R}^n = \mathfrak{N}(A) \oplus \mathfrak{R}(A^T) = \mathfrak{N}(A^T) \oplus R(A)$. The $(n - r)$ eigenvectors that correspond to the zero eigenvalues of A span $\mathfrak{N}(A)$ since

$$Au_i = \lambda_i u_i = 0, \quad \text{or} \quad u_i \in N(A)$$

$$\text{for } i = r + 1, \cdots, n$$

and $(u_i, u_j) = \delta_{ij}$

$$\text{for } i, j \in (r + 1, n).$$

Then $\mathfrak{R}(A) = \mathfrak{R}(A^T) = \text{span}\{u_1, \cdots, u_r\}$ and b can be written as

$$b = Uc \quad \text{or } U^T b = c, \quad (A-6)$$

where $c = [c_1, \cdots, c_n]^T$ is the coefficient column vector. From (A-5) and (A-6) we get

$$x_k = \beta \sum_{i=0}^{p^k - 1} U(I - \beta \Lambda)^i c$$

$$= \beta \sum_{j=1}^{n} \left\{ c_j u_j \sum_{i=0}^{p^k - 1} (1 - \beta \lambda_j)^i \right\}. \quad (A-7)$$

Since A is positive semidefinite, $0 < \lambda_{\max} \leq \|A\|$. In fact, $\lambda_{\max} = \|A\|_2$. It is assumed that

$$0 < \beta \cdot \|A\| < 2 \quad \text{or} \quad 0 < \beta \lambda_{\max} < 2$$

$$\text{or} \quad |1 - \beta \lambda_{\max}| < 1. \quad (A-8)$$

Therefore, since $\lambda_i > 0$ for $i = 1, \cdots, r$

$$|1 - \beta \lambda_i| < 1 \quad (A-9)$$

and

$$(1 - \beta \lambda_i)^{\nu(k)} \to 0 \quad \text{for } k \to \infty, \quad (A-10)$$

where ν is a positive, strictly increasing function of k such that $\nu(1) \geq 1$. Now, if $b \in \mathfrak{R}(A)$

$$c_{r+1} = \cdots = c_n = 0. \quad (A-11)$$

Finally, from (A-7) we get

$$x_k = \sum_{j=1}^{r} c_j \lambda_j^{-1} [1 - (1 - \beta \lambda_j)^{p^k}] u_j \quad (A-12)$$

and for $k \to \infty$, due to (A-10),

$$\hat{x} = x_\infty = \sum_{j=1}^{r} c_j \lambda_j^{-1} u_j, \quad (A-13)$$

where $\hat{x}$ is the minimum norm solution, since $A\hat{x} = b$ and the infinite set of solutions is equal to $x = \hat{x} + \bar{x}$, where $\bar{x} \in \mathfrak{N}(A)$. Now if $b \notin \mathfrak{R}(A)$, from (A-7) and (A-10), we get

$$x_k = \beta \sum_{j=1}^{r} \left\{ c_j u_j \sum_{i=0}^{p^k-1} (1 - \beta \lambda_j)^i \right\} + \beta p^k \sum_{j=r+1}^{n} c_j u_j \tag{A-14}$$

and for $k \to \infty$, $x_k \to \infty$ since at least one of the c_i, where $i = r + 1, \cdots, n$, is different from zero. Q.E.D.

References

[1] H. C. Andrews and B. R. Hunt, *Digital Image Restoration*. Englewood Cliffs, NJ: Prentice-Hall, 1977.

[2] H. Bialy, "Iterative Behandlung Linearen Funktionalgleichungen," *Arch. Ration. Mech. Anal. 4*, pp. 166–176, July 1959.

[3] S. N. Efstratiadis, "Fast iterative signal restoration algorithms," M.S. thesis, Northwestern Univ., Dep. Elec. Eng., Comput. Sci., June 1988.

[4] S. N. Efstratiadis and A. K. Katsaggelos, "Fast adaptive iterative image restoration algorithms," in *Proc. SPIE Symp. Visual Commun. Image Processing '88*, Cambridge, MA, Nov. 1988, pp. 10–18.

[5] C. W. Groetch, *Generalized Inverses of Linear Operators*. New York: Marcel Dekker, 1977.

[6] A. K. Katsaggelos, J. Biemond, R. M. Mersereau, and R. W. Schafer, "Nonstationary iterative image restoration," in *Proc. 1985 Int. Conf. Acoust., Speech, Signal Processing*, Tampa, FL, Mar. 1985, pp. 696–699.

[7] —, "A general formulation of constrained iterative restoration algorithms," in *Proc. 1985 Int. Conf. Acoust., Speech, Signal Processing*, Tampa, FL, Mar. 1985, pp. 700–703.

[8] A. K. Katsaggelos, "A unified approach to iterative image restoration," in *Proc. SPIE Symp. Visual Commun. Image Processing '87*, Cambridge, MA, Oct. 1987, pp. 163–167.

[9] A. K. Katsaggelos and S. N. Efstratiadis, "Fast iterative image restoration algorithms," in *Proc. 25th Annu. Allerton Conf. Commun., Contr., Comput.*, Monticello, IL, Sept. 1987, pp. 493–502.

[10] —, "A unified approach to iterative signal restoration," in *Proc. IEEE Int. Conf. Acoust., Speech, Signal Processing*, New York, Apr. 1988, pp. 1028–1031.

[11] A. K. Katsaggelos, "Iterative image restoration algorithms," *Opt. Eng.*, vol. 28, no. 7, pp. 735–748, July 1989.

[12] H. J. Kushner and D. S. Clark, *Stochastic Approximation Methods for Constrained and Unconstrained Systems*. New York: Springer-Verlag, Appl. Math. Sci., vol. 26, 1978.

[13] R. L. Lagendijk, R. M. Mersereau, and J. Biemond, "On increasing the convergence rate of regularized image restoration algorithms," in *Proc. Int. Conf. Acoust., Speech, Signal Processing*, Dallas, TX, Apr. 1987, pp. 28.2.1–4.

[14] C. E. Morris, M. A. Richards, and M. H. Hayes, "Iterative deconvolution algorithm with quadratic convergence," *J. Opt. Soc. Amer. A*, vol. 4, no. 1, pp. 200–207, Jan. 1987.

[15] —, "A generalized fast iterative deconvolution algorithm," in *Proc. 1987 Int. Conf. Acoust., Speech, Signal Processing*, Dallas, TX, Apr. 1987, pp. 36.1.1–36.1.4.

[16] —, "Fast reconstruction of linearly distorted signals," *IEEE Trans. Acoust., Speech, Signal Processing*, vol. 36, pp. 1017–1025, July 1988.

[17] A. W. Naylor and G. R. Sell, *Linear Operator Theory in Engineering and Science*, 2nd ed. New York: Springer-Verlag, 1982.

[18] R. W. Schafer, R. M. Mersereau, and M. A. Richards, "Constrained iterative restoration algorithms," *Proc. IEEE*, vol. 60, pp. 432–450, Apr. 1981.

[19] S. Singh, S. N. Tandon, and H. M. Gupta, "An iterative restoration technique," *Signal Processing 11*, pp. 1–11, 1986.

[20] G. Strang, *Linear Algebra and Its Applications*, 2nd ed. New York: Academic, 1980.

Aggelos K. Katsaggelos (S'80–M'85) was born in Arnea, Greece, on April 17, 1956. He received the Diploma degree in electrical and mechanical engineering from the Aristotelian University of Thessaloniki, Thessaloniki, Greece, in 1979. He received the M.S. and Ph.D. degrees, both in electrical engineering, from the Georgia Institute of Technology, Atlanta, in 1981 and 1985, respectively.

From 1980 to 1985 he was a Research Assistant at the Digital Signal Processing Laboratory of the Electrical Engineering School of Georgia Tech, where he was engaged in research on image restoration. He is currently an Assistant Professor in the Department of Electrical Engineering and Computer Science at Northwestern University, Evanston, IL. During the 1986–1987 academic year he was an Assistant Professor at Polytechnic University, Department of Electrical Engineering and Computer Science, Brooklyn, NY. His current research interests include signal and image processing, processing of moving images, computational vision, and VLSI implementation of signal processing algorithms. He is the Editor of the book *Digital Image Restoration* (New York: Springer-Verlag).

Dr. Katsaggelos is a member of SPIE, the IEEE-CAS Technical Committee on Visual Signal Processing and Communications, the Technical Chamber of Commerce of Greece, and Sigma Xi.

Serafim N. Efstratiadis (S'89) was born in Greece in 1964. He received the Diploma degree in electrical engineering from the Aristotelian University of Thessaloniki, Thessaloniki, Greece, in 1986 and the M.S. degree in electrical engineering from Northwestern University, Evanston, IL, in 1988. He is currently working toward the Ph.D. degree in the area of motion compensated image sequence restoration.

He has been a Research Assistant, and currently he is a Teaching Assistant, in the Department of Electrical Engineering and Computer Science at Northwestern University. His research interests include multidimensional signal processing, image modeling, identification, restoration, and video communications.

Mr. Efstratiadis is a member of the Technical Chamber of Commerce of Greece.

Digital Signal Restoration Using Fuzzy Sets

MEHMET REHA CIVANLAR, MEMBER, IEEE, AND H. JOEL TRUSSELL, MEMBER, IEEE

Abstract—A new signal restoration method with considerable flexibility in incorporating *a priori* information is developed. The method defines a fuzzy set for each piece of information to restrict the set of acceptable solutions. Using fuzzy sets makes it possible to model partially defined information as well as exact knowledge. The intersection of all the fuzzy sets is the feasibility set. The original signal is a member of this set with a high membership value, and any high membership valued element of this set is a nonrejectable solution. Such solutions can be computed by using optimization techniques.

Ideally, the feasibility set contains only the original signal. The chance of recovering the original signal decreases as the feasibility set gets larger. Thus, the size of the feasibility set gives a quality measure for the solution.

The method generated successful results in many restorations for which the conventional techniques have failed, and may be applied in image coding and tomography.

I. INTRODUCTION

THE general signal restoration problem is to estimate the original form of a degraded and noise corrupted signal. A large number of techniques has been developed for the solution of this problem under different degradation models, varying degrees of distortions, and various amounts of *a priori* knowledge [1], [2]. A major problem in signal restoration is using all of the knowledge which is available. This paper presents a new method which extends the range of restorable distortions by the application of fuzzy set theory to model *a priori* information.

The earliest approach to the restoration problem may be the inverse filtering which, in general, causes noise amplification [1], [3]. Better methods are obtained through the use of *a priori* information. Examples include: the Wiener filter [1], which uses the covariance structure of the original signal and the contaminating noise; the constrained least-squares method [4], which assumes a smooth original signal and needs only the noise variance; and the stochastic estimation techniques [1], [5], which require probability density functions (pdf) of the signal and the noise. Obviously, the more information combined in a restoration algorithm, the better the restoration will be. However, to find an operator that generates an estimate consistent with all available information becomes considerably difficult when the amount of *a priori* knowledge increases.

Iterative techniques are flexible in combining *a priori* information in the restoration process, and they have become popular in signal restoration because of this flexibility. In their survey paper, Schafer *et al.* [6] formulate the constrained iterative restoration methods as finding the fixed point of a transformation $O[\cdot]$ defined as

$$O[\cdot] = C[\cdot] + \lambda\{g - T[C[\cdot]]\} \tag{1}$$

where g is the degraded signal and $T[\cdot]$ is the degradation operator. Any *a priori* knowledge about the original signal is expressed through the operator $C[\cdot]$ by constructing it such that the original signal is a fixed point, i.e., $C[f] = f$. The nonzero scalar λ is to be used for controlling the rate of convergence. Several constraint operators for different kinds of *a priori* knowledge are studied in [6].

If the operator $O[\cdot]$ of (1) is a contraction, then it has a unique fixed point and this fixed point is the original signal. For nonexpansive $O[\cdot]$'s, the fixed point is not unique. However, if f is a fixed point of $O[\cdot]$, either the residual signal which is defined by

$$r \triangleq g - T[C[f]] \tag{2}$$

is null or f does not satisfy the constraints. The second is not possible for the unique fixed-point case, and for the nonexpansive case, a fixed point which does not satisfy the constraints can easily be discarded as a wrong solution. Thus, practically, when the iterations converge the residual signal is zero. For unconstrained iterations such as Landweber [7] and Van Cittert [8], the convergence point is a pseudoinverse filter solution and is sensitive to noise. The conditioning of the problem can be improved by using constraints. However, the solution is still sensitive to noise [6].

The sensitivity of the solution to noise contamination can easily be seen by including additive noise in the degradation model. For this case, the degraded signal is

$$g = T[f] + n \tag{3}$$

where n is the noise. A solution, making the residual signal zero, is

$$f' = f + (TC)^{-1}[n]. \tag{4}$$

The additional noise term may dominate this solution. A cure for this may be found in defining a new convergence criterion and stopping the iterations accordingly. In the work of Strand [9], the effects of early truncation on the Landweber iteration are studied in detail. Trussell [10] uses the residual signal's sample variance for deciding on the convergence of the iterations. The iterations are stopped when the sample variance equals the variance of

---

Manuscript received September 24, 1984; revised January 6, 1986.
M. R. Civanlar is with the Center for Communication and Signal Processing, North Carolina State University, Raleigh, NC 27695-7914.
H. J. Trussell is with the Department of Electrical and Computer Engineering, North Carolina State University, Raleigh, NC 27695-7911.
IEEE Log Number 8608141.

the contaminating noise. This method has proven to be successful.

A problem with modeling *a priori* information as fixed points of an operator is that many times the operator will not be simple. It will be very difficult to investigate the properties such as nonexpansivity of complex operators. On the other hand, almost any kind of *a priori* knowledge can easily be modeled as a set in the signal space. Any signal in the intersection of these sets is consistent with all the available *a priori* information and is a nonrejectable solution. In [11] these solutions were called "feasible solutions."

If all of the sets used in the description of the solution are closed and convex, a feasible solution can be found using the method of projections onto the closed convex sets (POCS). This method is presented by Bregman [12], and extended by Gubin *et al.* [13]. The Gerchberg-Papoulis algorithm [14], [15] may be considered as the first application of POCS in signal processing. In [16], POCS is used in tomographic image reconstruction. In the works of Youla and Webb [17] and Sezan and Stark [18], a collection of closed and convex sets to be used in signal restoration applications are discussed.

A collection of sets describing the feasible solutions can be defined using the residual signal. Clearly, if the original signal is exactly recovered, the residual signal will be identical with the noise. The noise sequence is unknown; however, in most of the applications, many statistics of the noise are available. Consequently, the sample statistics of the residual signal should be made to agree with the available noise statistics. The idea of using the residual signal's statistics for defining closed convex sets in signal space can be used in almost all restoration problems.

In order to use a piece of information to define an ordinary set, the information must be well defined. Partially defined information is difficult to use. If the sets constructed using this kind of information are too small, their intersection may be empty; if they are too large, their effect on the solution will be reduced. The convexity requirement is another factor restricting the information that can be used by the POCS technique. Application of a broader class of *a priori* information can be made possible by using fuzzy sets instead of ordinary sets. In fact, among all the available methods for modeling *a priori* information, using fuzzy sets may be considered as the most general one. Almost all of the restoration algorithms can be derived using the fuzzy sets formulation and can be extended to include additional *a priori* knowledge.

II. Signal Restoration by POCS

In this section, a brief outline of the POCS method used in [11] will be given for completeness. In [11] the feasible solutions were defined for the standard linear model which is given by

$$g = Hf + n \qquad (5)$$

where g is the recorded signal of length N; f is the original signal to be estimated of length N; H is the impulse response matrix ($N \times N$), usually representing convolution; and n is signal independent noise of length N. If only the matrix H and some statistics of the noise are known, the feasible solutions can be defined by using the residual signal given in (2). If the original signal is recovered, the residual will be identical with the noise. Hence, a feasible solution should generate a residual signal having statistics consistent with those of the noise.

Many statistics of the contaminating noise can be estimated. Theoretically, all of these should be used in defining feasible solutions. However, in practical applications, computational problems make a selection necessary. The mean value, the variance, the power spectrum, and the maximum deviation from the mean are the statistics used in [11]. In many applications, these statistics of the noise sequence are assumed to be known [1], [4]. The definition of the feasible solutions for a Gaussian, zero mean, white noise sequence with known variance was given in [11]. For other noise sequences with different properties, similar definitions can easily be constructed. There are many other constraints which can reasonably be applied to the restoration problem [17]. These constraints depend upon the characteristics of the specific signal under consideration.

Individually, each of the constraints may be quite easy to satisfy. However, it is usually very difficult to satisfy all of them simultaneously. The POCS method was used for this purpose. The main result of POCS theory which was used in [11] is as follows: let $C_0 = \cap_i C_i$ be nonempty, where C_i is a closed and convex set in R^N. Let P_i be the projection operator which projects a vector onto C_i. The iteration given by

$$f^{k+1} = P_1 P_2 \cdots P_M[f^k] \qquad (6)$$

converges to a point in C_0. According to this result, a feasible solution can be found using the successive projections onto individual sets.

The projection operator onto a convex set C can be found by solving the following minimization problem:

$$\min_{f_p} \|f_p - f\|^2 \quad \text{such that} \quad f_p \in C \qquad (7)$$

where f is the signal to be projected onto C, and f_p is the projection. The projection operators for the sets modeling the residual signal's statistics were given in [11]; projection operators for other sets can be found in [17].

There are many factors which influence the solution obtained. Among the most important are the parameters of the signal formation model (5), the impulse response H, and the noise. The initial estimate f_0 used to start the iterations can be quite influential also. It is possible to relate all of the factors effecting the solution to the size of the intersection set. If the size of the intersection set is large, there are many feasible solutions, and so, the chances of recovering the original signal diminishes.

Mathematically, the largest distance between any two points of a set can be defined as its size. It is very difficult to determine the size of the intersection set in this sense.

However, upper bounds for the sizes of the component sets can be found in terms of the parameters of the model. The size of the intersection set is related to that of the component sets, at least it will always be less than or equal to the smallest one.

The quantitative effect of the extent of the impulse response and noise power on the size of the convex sets defined by residual signal's statistics is studied in [11] and it was shown that

$$\max_{f_1, f_2 \in C_i} \|f_1 - f_2\| \leq 2\delta_i \|H^{-1}\| \quad (8)$$

for the convex sets defined using the variance, the power spectrum, and the maximum deviation from the mean value of the residual signal. The matrix norm is the one derived from the Euclidean norm, and the δ parameters are related to the noise power.

The set defined using the mean value has infinite extent, and in the case of a singular H, the sizes of the sets defined by the residual statistics are unbounded. For this case, other *a priori* knowledge may restrict the set of feasible solutions. It should be noted that a set with unbounded size is not useless. Most of the sets describing *a priori* knowledge about the signal, such as nonnegativity, have infinite extent, however, they may severely limit the size of the intersection set. Finally, the amplitude or the energy of a signal can always be restricted using a reasonable limit.

In the case of a severe degradation without enough *a priori* knowledge, the set of feasible solutions can be very large or unbounded. Using an appropriate initial signal might help in such cases. In POCS, each estimate is projected to the closest element in the next convex set. Intuitively, this means that the solution should be "close" to the initial estimate. In fact, if all of the sets are linear varieties, the solution is the closest point of their intersection to the initial estimate. Although all the sets used in the restoration problem are not linear varieties, in [21], the solution was shown to be affected by the initial estimate. If the estimate starting the iterations is reasonable, the solution to which the method converges is also reasonable.

The method described is a recent formulation in signal restoration. It is capable of generating high-quality restorations through the use of a large class of *a priori* information that can be modeled by convex sets of signals. However, partially defined information cannot be used effectively. Fuzzy sets formulation will solve this problem and significantly extend the range of *a priori* information that can be used in signal restoration.

III. A Review of the Fuzzy Set Theory

Many useful classifications of objects in everyday life are vaguely defined. The set of men over 6 ft in height is well defined. A man is either a member of this set or not. However, it is not the same for the set of tall men. There is no fixed height separating tall men from the others. The transition is gradual. Still the classification of tall is useful. The tall men's stores cater to this vaguely defined set of people. It is the purpose of fuzzy set theory to give us a mathematical tool with which to manipulate this partially defined knowledge.

Imprecise information is common in signal restoration. Consider the following examples. Physical filters have transition regions, thus, bandwidth of a filtered signal is not exact (unless we artificially assume so). For a lossless system, the energy of the output signal, in the sense of mean-squared signal value, is equal to that of the input signal; however, because of noise we cannot estimate it accurately. The covariance structure of similar images are similar; however, they are not equal. If the original signal is known to be "impulsive," we can judge a restoration using this knowledge; however, it is not easy to incorporate this knowledge in the restoration algorithm.

The requirements for the statistics of the residual signal, which are described in Section II, can be formulated better using fuzzy sets instead of ordinary sets. The following example may help in demonstrating this. Let the noise in the linear degradation model (5) be zero mean, white, and normal, and let the sample mean of a residual signal be m. If the noise and the residual are the same, m is a normal random variable with zero mean and known variance σ^2. For the application of the POCS technique, it is necessary to set limits for acceptable m's. Practically, it is obvious that if $|m| = \sigma$, it is acceptable; and if $|m| = 100\sigma$, it is not. However, for $|m| = 2.5\sigma$, the decision is not easy. A limit for the convex set can be set using some level of confidence. Let that limit be 2σ corresponding to approximately 95 percent confidence. Under this limit, a residual signal with $m_1 = 1.9999\sigma$ will be considered acceptable, i.e., a member of the set, while another one with $m_2 = 2.00001\sigma$ will be rejected. However, the belief in the consistency of the data does not change abruptly. That is, there is no natural limit separating the acceptable and unacceptable m's, that transition occurs in a region. Thus, the set defined by the sample mean of the residual signal has a vague boundary and a fuzzy version of it will be more appropriate.

The theory of fuzzy sets was founded by Zadeh [22] in 1964. There has been a large number of studies on this subject, and it has been applied in many areas including automatic control and operations research. In [23] and [24], lists of references covering almost all of these works are included.

A. Definitions

The characteristic (indicator) function $\mu_A: X \to \{0, 1\}$ of an ordinary (nonfuzzy) set A in a universe X is defined as

$$\mu_A(x) = \begin{cases} 1 & \text{iff } x \in A \\ 0 & \text{otherwise} \end{cases} \quad (9)$$

where $\{0, 1\}$ is called a valuation set. If the valuation set is the real interval $[0, 1]$, then A is called a fuzzy set [24]. $\mu_A(x)$ is the grade of membership of x in A, and is called

TABLE I
OPERATIONS ON FUZZY SETS

	Intersection $\mu_{A \cap B}(x)$	Union $\mu_{A \cup B}(x)$	Complement $\mu_{\bar{A}}(x)$
Min-Max	$\min(\mu_A(x), \mu_B(x))$	$\max(\mu_A(x), \mu_B(x))$	$1 - \mu_A(x)$
Probabilistic	$\mu_A(x)\mu_B(x)$	$\mu_A(x) + \mu_B(x) - \mu_A(x)\mu_B(x)$	
Bold	$\max(0, \mu_A(x) + \mu_B(x) - 1)$	$\min(1, \mu_A(x) + \mu_B(x))$	

the membership function of the fuzzy set A. Qualitatively, the membership function describes the strength of our belief that x is a member of A. If $\mu_A(x) = 1$, it is certain that x is in A; and if $\mu_A(x) = 0$, it is certain that x is not in A. Thus, a fuzzy set can be considered as a subset of X with vague boundaries.

Two fuzzy sets A and B are equal iff $\mu_A(x) = \mu_B(x)$ for all x in the universe X, and A is a subset of B iff $\mu_A(x) \leq \mu_B(x)$ for all x in X. The set of x's, for which $\mu_A(x) > 0$, is called the support of the fuzzy set A. The height of a fuzzy set is defined as

$$\text{hgt}(A) = \sup_{x \in X} \mu_A(x), \quad (10)$$

and finally, a fuzzy set is normalized if its height is unity.

The membership function is the key in fuzzy set theory. There are guidelines for the construction of membership functions for special applications [24]. General techniques are not available. A guideline for finding the membership functions for fuzzy sets to be used in the signal restoration problem will be discussed in Section IV.

B. Fuzzy Set Algebra

In the scope of this paper, fuzzy sets are used to enforce several constraints in signal restoration; thus, it is necessary to deal with several fuzzy sets and set operations. The ordinary set theoretic operations, union, intersection, and complement are extended to fuzzy sets. However, there is more than one set of the definitions which are given in Table I.

All of the intersection operators given in Table I are triangular norms [24]. A triangular norm is a function from $[0, 1] \times [0, 1]$ to $[0, 1]$ with the following properties:

1) $T(0, 0) = 0$; $T(a, 1) = T(1, a) = a$;
2) $T(a, b) \leq T(c, d)$ whenever $a \leq c$ and $c \leq d$;
3) $T(a, b) = T(b, a)$; and
4) $T(T(a, b), c) = T(a, T(b, c))$.

These properties may be used for defining other intersection operators.

The best set of operators depends on the problem, and specifically what is meant by the words intersection, union, and complement. The selection of the suitable set of operators for the restoration problem is discussed in Section IV.

C. Measures for Fuzzy Sets

A mathematical way of "defining" an acceptable solution is restricting the set of solutions by using the available *a priori* information. If the definition is perfect, there should be a unique signal satisfying it. If the solution is not well defined, there will be many signals which can be accepted as the solution, and if the definitions are inconsistent, no solutions will be satisfactory. Thus, the "size" and the "height" of the intersection set can be used for measuring the quality of the definition. If the solution is well defined, then clearly its quality will be high.

Two measures, energy and entropy, have been proposed for fuzzy sets [25]. In [26], the energy measure is shown to be better suited for decision theoretic applications. The "size" of a fuzzy set, in the sense used here, is related to the energy measure.

A general definition for the energy measure of a fuzzy set A is [26]

$$e(A) = \int_X \varphi(\mu_A(x)) \, dw(x) \quad (11)$$

where, φ is nondecreasing on $[0, 1]$; $\varphi(x) = 0$ iff $x = 0$; and w is a totally finite positive measure. For the most general case, the measure w must be defined on a σ-algebra of subsets of X. In many cases, the set of all possible subsets of X can be used as the σ-algebra. Most of the measures can be made totally finite by defining X as a finite but large enough subset of the signal space so that it contains every possible solution. The main properties of this energy measure are as follows:

1) $e(A)$ is defined only for measurable fuzzy sets;
2) if $A_1 \subset A_2$ then $e(A_1) \leq e(A_2)$;
3) $e(A) = 0$ iff A is an empty set, or $\mu_A(x)$ vanishes almost everywhere; and
4) if φ is strictly increasing on $[0, 1]$, $e(A)$ is maximized when $A = X$.

While the form of (11) is completely general, we most often use the simple measure $w(x) = x$. Using this measure, two simple forms for the energy measure may be given as

$$e(A) = \frac{1}{\text{hgt}(A)} \int \mu_A(x) \, dx \quad (12)$$

$$e(A) = \frac{1}{\text{hgt}^2(A)} \int \mu_A^2(x) \, dx. \quad (13)$$

Clearly, for a "small" set, the energy measure is close to zero.

IV. FUZZY SETS FORMULATION

The signal restoration problem can be formulated as finding an element of the intersection of various sets describing the original signal. In using partially defined information, if it is necessary to guarantee that the original signal is contained in the intersection, the sets may be forced to be very large. Obviously, larger sets have less effect on the solution. In the fuzzy sets formulation, the partially defined information can be used more effectively because any set assigning a high membership value to the original signal can be included in the collection of sets defining the solution. If all fuzzy sets used are expected to contain the original signal with a high membership value, then so is their intersection. Hence, a reasonable estimate for the original signal is one of the members of the fuzzy intersection set with a high membership value.

The fuzzy sets formulation can be divided into three tasks. The first is finding an objective and methodical way for the construction of membership functions. Choosing the intersection operator is the second task. Finally, a computational technique must be developed to find a solution.

A. Membership Functions

The major problem with using fuzzy sets is to define the membership functions in an objective and systematic way. For signal restoration applications, this can be done by using prototypes or statistical information.

In [27] a guideline for constructing the membership function for a fuzzy set which has a deformable prototype element is discussed. The prototype element is described by a finite number of parameters and it can be deformed by perturbing these parameters. The membership function of an element is based on two considerations: the amount of the perturbation required to approximate the element and the quality of that approximation. In [27], a measure, called the "dissimilarity" between the prototype and the element, is defined as

$$D(x) = \min_{p_1, \cdots, p_n} (m(x; p_1, \cdots, p_n) + w\delta(p_1, \cdots, p_n)) \quad (14)$$

where p_i's are the parameters of the prototype; m is the distance between the element x and the prototype (the approximation error); δ is a function describing the deformation energy (in other words, the degree of perturbation made on the prototype); and w is a weighting factor. An example of a membership function for the fuzzy set described by the prototype may be

$$\mu_p(x) = 1 - (D(x)/\sup D). \quad (15)$$

This method has been used for defining membership functions of fuzzy sets describing handwritten characters and certain classes of ECG signals [27]. In signal restoration, it is possible to use this technique for constructing fuzzy sets around prototype signals. Another important application may be the modeling of a signal which is known to be the output of a system defined by a set of parameters. As an example, consider a speech signal. The coefficients of a linear predictive coder can be used as the parameters of the prototype. The error made by coding the signal with specified number of coefficients is the distance part of the dissimilarity. The deformation energy is related to the difference between the prototype's coefficients and the coefficients used for coding the signal. The fuzzy set constructed this way can be used for incorporating information such as "voiced speech" or "speech of a certain speaker" in a restoration algorithm.

Another possibility in constructing membership functions is to rely on statistics as in the case of finding probabilities. This idea is applied in deriving membership functions for fuzzy sets to be used in linguistic applications [29] and in social sciences [30]. In [24], normalization of a histogram to make the highest ordinate equal to one is proposed for obtaining a membership function. Considering the fuzzy sets defined on the real line, if a histogram or probability density function for the elements of a certain fuzzy set is available, assigning high membership values to those portions of the real line corresponding to high number of occurrences is reasonable. However, this does not justify using a function proportional to the histogram as a membership function.

In constructing a fuzzy set using information in the form of a histogram or a probability density function of a parameter, a set of requirements can be imposed and a function satisfying these can be determined. Let s be a parameter, such as the sample mean of the residual signal, to be used for the construction of a fuzzy constraint set. A reasonable membership function for this fuzzy set may be expected to satisfy the following set of requirements.

1) $E\{\mu(s) | s$ is calculated for the original signal$\} \geq c$, where c should be close to 1. Qualitatively, this requirement forces the average value of the membership of the original signal in this fuzzy set to be larger than c. It should be noted that the original signal is not needed for the calculation of the required expected value. Using the sample mean example, this condition requires

$$\int \mu(m) p(m | \hat{f} = f) \, dm \geq c \quad (16)$$

where m is the sample mean of the residual signal, and the conditional pdf p is the density function of a zero mean normal random variable with variance σ^2 for the case described in Section III. If the proposed solution $\hat{f}$ is not equal to the original signal f, the pdf of the sample mean may not be p because the residual signal will not be equal to the noise unless the difference between the proposed solution and the original signal lies entirely in the null space of H.

2) $0 \leq \mu(x) \leq 1$ because, as far as the specific parameter used in defining the fuzzy set is concerned, there may be signals which are totally unacceptable as a solution ($\mu(x) = 0$), signals which are indistinguishable from the solution ($\mu(x) = 1$), and signals which are in between.

3) $\int \mu^2(x) \, dx$ should be minimized. This condition is required for obtaining a "selective" membership function, that is, the grade for signals which differ from the original signal should be as low as possible. The integral of the squared membership function is related to the size

of a fuzzy set. Thus, by minimizing it, the "smallest" set satisfying the other requirements can be obtained.

The optimal membership function defined by these conditions can be derived using constrained optimization techniques for infinite-dimensional spaces [31]. This derivation is presented in [44] where the optimal membership function is shown to be

$$\mu(x) = \begin{cases} \lambda p(x) & \text{if } \lambda p(x) < 1 \\ 1 & \text{otherwise} \end{cases} \quad (17)$$

where $p(x)$ is the pdf or its estimate derived from the histogram of the parameter used for defining the fuzzy set, and the constant λ is to be solved from

$$\lambda \int_{\lambda p(x) < 1} p^2(\eta) \, d\eta + \int_{\lambda p(x) \geq 1} p(\eta) \, d\eta - c = 0. \quad (18)$$

For standard normal pdf, the relation between the parameter λ and the confidence level is given in Appendix A. For a specific pdf, λ can be solved from (18) using numerical techniques.

It should be noted that the optimal membership function depends on the size measure used in the third requirement. For example, if the integral of the membership function is used as the measure, the optimal solution is an ordinary set which is nothing but a classical confidence interval having the parameter "c" of the first condition as the confidence level. In other words, the same sets used with the POCS method are optimal if the integral of the membership function is minimized [44]. However, as explained in Section III, there is an abrupt change from nonmembership to full membership in these sets which is not realistic for many cases.

If probabilistic knowledge is not available, the membership function should be defined using the available data so that its value for the original signal is close to one and it is as selective as possible. For example, if the original signal is known to be low-pass filtered using a filter with a finite transition region, all signals band-limited to the union of the passband and the transition band of this filter should have high membership in the set describing this information. However, lower membership values should be assigned to the signals which have their significant components only in the transition band.

The membership functions for a collection of fuzzy sets which have potential in signal processing applications are listed below.

1) Sets Derived from Residual Signal's Statistics: As in [11], when defining these sets, the underlying signal degradation model is assumed to be linear with additive zero mean, normal, and white noise with variance σ^2 (5). Nonlinear degradation models with different noise characteristics can be modeled similarly at the cost of increased complexity.

Mean Value: The sample mean of a feasible residual signal is a normal random variable (r.v.) with zero mean and variance σ^2/N. Thus, a fuzzy set can be defined using the parameter

$$p_m = \frac{1}{\sigma \sqrt{N}} \Sigma [r]_i \quad (19)$$

where r is the ith sample of the residual signal, and p_m is a standard normal r.v. The membership function can easily be constructed for any confidence level and is given as

$$\mu_m(p_m) = \begin{cases} 1 & |p_m| \leq a(c) \\ \frac{\lambda(c)}{\sigma \sqrt{2\pi}} e^{-1/2 p_m^2} & \text{otherwise} \end{cases} \quad (20)$$

where c is the confidence level, and $a(c)$ and $\lambda(c)$ are the optimal parameters for normal pdf's, as given in Appendix A.

Variance: The sum of the squares of a feasible residual signal divided by the noise variance has a chi-square distribution with degrees of freedom N. However, for most of the applications, the number of samples is large enough to approximate the chi-square by the normal. The parameter used in defining this set is

$$p_v = \sqrt{2 \frac{\Sigma [r]_i^2}{\sigma^2}} - \sqrt{2N - 1}. \quad (21)$$

The distribution of this parameter is approximately standard normal [32]. Thus, the membership function can be obtained from μ_m by replacing p_m with p_v.

Power Spectrum: For discrete frequencies between 1 and $(N/2 - 1)$, the magnitude squared DFT coefficients of a feasible residual signal have a chi-square distribution with two degrees of freedom [20]. Thus, the pdf of the maximum magnitude square in these frequencies can be obtained as follows. Let

$$p_{pk} = \frac{2|R(k)|^2}{N\sigma^2} \quad (22)$$

where $R(k)$ is the kth discrete frequency component of the residual signal. The parameter p_{pk} has an exponential distribution with parameter 0.5 for $0 < k < N/2$. If p_{pm} denotes the maximum p_{pk}, then its probability distribution function can be calculated as

$$F_{pm}(x) = P\{p_{pm} \leq x\} = P\{p_{pk} \leq x, \forall k\}$$
$$= \left(\int_0^x \tfrac{1}{2} e^{-\eta/2} \, d\eta \right)^{N'} = (1 - e^{-x/2})^{N'} \quad (23)$$

where $N' = N/2 - 1$. The pdf can be obtained by differentiating (23) and is given by

$$f_{pm}(x) = \frac{N'}{2} (1 - e^{-x/2})^{(N'-1)} e^{-x/2}. \quad (24)$$

This is a unimodal pdf, hence, the corresponding membership function has the following form:

$$\mu_{pm}(x) = \begin{cases} 1 & \text{if } a < x < b \\ \lambda f_{pm}(x) & \text{otherwise} \end{cases} \quad (25)$$

where the parameters a, b, and λ depend on the number of samples N and are to be found numerically. In Appendix A, the values for the parameters a and b are tabulated for various confidence levels and numbers of samples.

Maximum Deviation from the Mean: Individual entries of the residual signal have a normal distribution. The derivation of the pdf of the maximum value of the residual signal is similar to the derivation for the power spectrum, and the pdf is given by

$$f_o(x) = N\sqrt{\frac{2}{\pi}} [1 - 2Q(x)]^{(N-1)} e^{-x^2/2} \quad (26)$$

where $Q(x)$ is the probability of having a standard normal random variable larger than x. The function $f_o(x)$ is a unimodal pdf, thus, the form of the corresponding membership function is the same as μ_{pm}. The parameters of the membership function are dependent on N, and must be found numerically. A table of the a and b values is given in Appendix A.

2) Fuzzy Sets Defined Using Signal's Statistics: In many applications, in addition to the noise statistics, various statistics of the original signal can be estimated also. Several restoration techniques are based on the availability of this information. The power spectrum equalization technique [33] assumes the availability of the original signal's power spectrum. In the Wiener filter, the covariance of the signal is used. Maximum *a posteriori* probability technique assumes the availability of a pdf for the original signal [34].

Obviously, fuzzy sets describing this information can be constructed. The membership functions derived for the sets defined by the residual signal's statistics can be used for the sets describing the same statistics of the original signal. Using the technique for deriving membership functions from statistical information, fuzzy sets defined by other statistics of the original signal can be constructed.

3) Fuzzy Sets Defined Using Signal Specifications:

Energy of the Signal: In several applications, it is possible to estimate the energy of the original signal. In photography, the average light intensity can be measured. Even if this measurement is not available, for many applications, a measurement done on a similar view can give a ''close'' value to the original one. Similarly, in speech processing, a knowledge about the average signal energy can be obtained by measuring the energy level of a similar speech signal. Imposing a bound on the maximum energy of the original signal is very useful in restricting the size of the feasibility set but, as can be seen from the examples above, generally, the upper bound of the energy is not known exactly. However, a fuzzy set can be used for introducing a soft upper bound. The membership function for this set may be of the form

$$\mu_{eu}(f) = e^{-\alpha f^t f}. \quad (27)$$

In addition to the upper bound, a soft lower bound can be imposed on the energy of the signal for restricting the size of the feasibility set. A soft lower bound can be obtained by considering the attenuating nature of a general degradation system and the energy of the output signal.

Another use of a lower bound on the energy is in defining impulsiveness which is a rather vague concept. In [19], maximizing the energy of the restored signal is shown to be useful in impulsive signal restoration. The reason for this is the relatively high autocorrelation of these signals at zero lag [45].

A soft lower bound on the energy of a signal can be modeled by a fuzzy set with a parametric membership function of the form

$$\mu_{el}(f) = 1 - e^{-\beta f^t f}. \quad (28)$$

It should be noted that this set cannot be approximated by an ordinary convex set.

Prototype Signals: It is possible to construct a fuzzy set around a signal which is expected to be similar to the original signal. There are two ways of obtaining a prototype signal. The first one is using the result of a prerestoration. In prerestoration, a conventional restoration technique may be used. It is observed that simple and fast techniques, such as thresholding for finite level signals, are capable of generating useful prototypes. The second method for finding a prototype signal is using the available information about a property of the original signal. For example, if the signal is a text image, it is possible to estimate many letters using the meaning of the text.

A parametric membership function for a fuzzy set around a prototype signal can be

$$\mu_{pr}(f) = \exp\left(-\sum_{i=1}^{N} \alpha_i ([f]_i - [f_p]_i)^2\right) \quad (29)$$

where f_p is the prototype signal and α coefficients reflect the confidence in the prototype.

Smoothness: If the original signal is known to be smooth, a fuzzy set can be constructed using the approximate time or space derivative of the signal. In the constrained least-squares method [4], the original signal is assumed to be as smooth as possible. In the fuzzy set formulation, an adjustable weight can be assigned to the smoothness of the signal. A parametric membership function for this set may be

$$\mu_s(f) = e^{-\gamma f^t D^t D f} \quad (30)$$

where D is a difference operator and γ is used for adjusting the required smoothness.

Finite Number of Levels: There are many cases for which the original signal is known to have only a finite number of levels. An example for this can be given from industrial tomography. If the sample to be scanned is known to be made of certain kind of materials, then in the reconstructed image there will be finite number of gray levels.

A membership function for a fuzzy set modeling the finite level signals may be

$$\mu_{fl}(f) = \prod_{i=1}^{N} \sum_{j=1}^{M} \beta_j \exp\left(-\alpha_j([f]_i - [flv]_j)^2\right) \quad (31)$$

where flv is a vector containing m possible finite levels, and α and β parameters can be adjusted using the relative amount of the number of levels.

Time, Amplitude, and Bandlimits: Similar to the ordinary sets case, the knowledge about the time or space extent, the bandwidth, and the amplitude range of the original signal can be used for defining fuzzy sets. However, fuzzy sets have the advantage of being able to model imprecise limits. The best example for this is the bandlimit of a low-pass filtered signal which is outlined above.

B. Selecting the Intersection Operator

After the construction of the fuzzy sets defining the solution, the next step is to find the set of feasible solutions. In the case of ordinary sets, a feasible solution must be a member of all sets used in defining the solution, and any signal which is a member of all these sets must be a feasible solution. Therefore, the feasibility set is the largest common subset or the intersection of the sets defining the solution.

In the case of fuzzy sets, the largest common subset of a class of sets is their intersection defined using the minimum operator. Straightforward extension of the ordinary sets formulation suggests using the minimum as the intersection operator. However, it is not necessary to construct the fuzzy sets formulation as an extension of the ordinary sets case, and there are various operators that can be used for defining the intersection of fuzzy sets.

Essentially, if a feasible solution is defined as one which has a high grade of membership in the intersection set, the selection of a particular triangular norm will not have a major effect on the solution. However, the computation of the solution will be different for different intersection operators. This subject is addressed below. Another aspect of the problem, for which the selection of the intersection operator plays an important role, is the calculation of the size of the feasibility set. The same classes of sets may have different sizes of intersection for different intersection operators, and the meanings of these measures are different. This may be used to obtain a better definition for the shape of the feasibility set by comparing its sizes calculated using different intersection operators.

C. Computing the Solution

The first step in extending the convex ordinary sets formulation is using convex fuzzy sets. A fuzzy set is said to be convex iff its α-level sets are convex for all α values in [0, 1] [22]. An α-level set of a fuzzy set A with a membership function $\mu_A(x)$ is an ordinary set which is defined [22] as

$$A_\alpha = \{x : \mu_A(x) \geq \alpha\}. \quad (32)$$

Hence, if all fuzzy sets used in defining the solution of a signal restoration problem are convex, their α-level sets form a collection of ordinary convex sets. A signal in the intersection of these α-level sets can be found using the POCS technique, and such a signal will have a grade of membership larger than or equal to α in every individual fuzzy set. Obviously, its grade of membership in the fuzzy intersection set depends on the intersection operator. However, if there exist signals with a specified grade of membership in the intersection set defined by a particular operator, it is possible to find one of them by using POCS and adjusting the parameter α according to the intersection operator.

In the most general case, the problem imposed by the fuzzy sets formulation is an unconstrained nonlinear optimization problem in the signal space, and finding a solution is nothing but locating a maximum of a certain combination of nonlinear functions. However, no algorithm is capable of solving every nonlinear optimization problem. For special problems, there are various techniques which are more efficient than more general methods. Thus, in solving a signal restoration problem formulated using fuzzy sets, the first step must be a search for a special technique suitable for the problem. Using POCS may be an example for exploiting a special case of the problem, namely, convexity of the individual sets.

For the general case, iterative algorithms for nonlinear optimization can be used to find a solution. In these algorithms, the membership value of the estimate in the intersection set may be used as a convergence criterion. The iterations may be terminated when the membership value reaches a certain level which may be a constant or a function of the number of completed iterations. Since no assumptions are made about the convexity of the membership functions, the algorithm may converge to a local suboptimal solution determined by the initial estimate. However, since the range of the membership function and an acceptable level for its value is available, this will not cause a serious problem. If a specific algorithm converges to a point with a low membership value, it may be executed again using some other initial estimate.

As indicated in Section IV-B, the straightforward extension of the ordinary POCS formulation requires the use of the minimum operator for the intersection of fuzzy sets. Using this operator, the problem can be stated as

$$\max_{f} \mu_{\min}(f) \quad (33)$$

where $\mu_{\min}(f)$ is the value of the minimum membership function in the set of membership functions defining the solution. This is the classic Chebyshev problem [35]. Clearly, even if all of the membership functions are differentiable, $\mu_{\min}(f)$ is not necessarily differentiable. Thus, conventional unconstrained optimization techniques cannot be applied to this problem. There are various specialized solution techniques for the Chebyshev problem [35]–[38]. The algorithms described in [37] and [38] are based on finding an appropriate direction which gives a local increase to the function to be maximized. These algorithms converge to the global optimum solution if all of the involved functions are pseudoconcave and the functions satisfy some regularity condition. In the case of nonpseudoconcave functions, the algorithm may converge to a local optimum. This method, essentially being a hill-climbing technique, will generate a better estimate than the initial signal, even if it is terminated prematurely.

A differentiable membership function for the intersection set can be obtained by using forms of the intersection operator other than the minimum. There are various iterative algorithms for the solution of nonlinear optimization problems with differentiable cost functions [40].

A differentiable cost function can be obtained by using the p-norm approximation for the minimum intersection. In [41], the following formulation is proposed as a general form for the intersection operator:

$$\mu_{\cap_p}(f) = 1 - \min\left\{1, \left[\sum_{i=1}^{m}(1-\mu_i(f))^p\right]^{1/p}\right\}. \quad (34)$$

$\mu_{\cap_p}$ converges to minimum intersection operator as p approaches infinity. It is a triangular norm, and for $p = 1$, it is the bold intersection operator defined in Section III [41].

In using the p-norm as the intersection operator for finding the solution of the restoration problem, the following simplified equivalent problem can be solved:

$$\min \sum_{i=1}^{m}(1-\mu_i(f))^p. \quad (35)$$

The parameter p is adjusted by considering the desired level of interdependence and the computational feasibility.

Product form of the intersection also gives a differentiable formulation. Since most of the membership functions are exponentials, taking the logarithm of the membership function of the intersection set simplifies this formulation. An important difference is the interdependent nature of the latter. The membership of an element in the intersection set defined by the product operator changes when its membership in any of the component sets change unless one of them is zero. For the minimum operator, any change in the membership value in a intersecting set will not affect the result provided that it is above the minimum membership value. Clearly, the membership value calculated by the product operator is always less than or equal to the one calculated by the minimum operator.

The main difficulty in finding the optimal solution is the high dimensionality of the problem. The large size of the Hessian matrix makes Newton's method impractical even if the membership functions are twice differentiable. For the same reason, quasi-Newton or variable metric methods are not suitable. An ordinary steepest ascent technique involves the smallest number of calculations and storage area per iteration; but its speed of convergence is quite slow. In order to have an algorithm with a faster convergence rate, a version of conjugate feasible directions techniques may be useful. In [39], [40], and [42], the feasible direction algorithm developed by Polak is recommended for nonconvex problems with large dimensions. A detailed description of the method can be found in [39].

An interesting similarity exists among the iterations generated by the four different formulations described above [45]. Consider a restoration problem where m fuzzy sets with pseudoconcave membership functions are used. At each iteration of the four different formulations, estimates are modified using a combination of the gradients of those membership functions with small values.

In order to demonstrate this, let the estimate at the kth iteration be denoted by f^k. In using the POCS technique with a specified α value, the equation for the kth iteration will be

$$f^{k+1} = P_1 P_2 \cdots P_m(f^k) \quad (36)$$

where P_i's are the projectors. The projection of the signal f^{ki}, which is inside the ith set at kth iteration, onto the $i + 1$th set can be found by solving

$$\min \|f^{ki} - f^{k(i+1)}\|^2$$
$$\text{s.t. } \mu_{i+1}(f^{k(i+1)}) \geq \alpha. \quad (37)$$

If f^{ki} is already inside the α-level set of the $i + 1$th fuzzy set, then its projection is itself. Otherwise, the Kuhn-Tucker conditions give the following form for the solution:

$$f^{(i+1)k} = f^{ik} + \lambda_{(i+1)k}\nabla\mu_{i+1}(f^{ik}) \quad (38)$$

where $\lambda_{(i+1)k}$'s are constants. Thus, the equation giving the kth iteration of the POCS algorithm is

$$f^{k+1} = f^k + \sum_{ik \in H_k}\lambda_{ik}\nabla\mu_{ik}(f^{ik}) \quad (39)$$

where H_k is the set of indexes of the fuzzy sets which are projected on in the kth iteration.

If the same problem is solved using the minimum operator as the fuzzy intersection, the kth iteration will have the following form:

$$f^{k+1} = f^k + \tau \sum_{ik \in H(f^k, \delta)}\lambda_i'\nabla\mu_i(f^k) \quad (40)$$

where τ is to be found with one-dimensional optimization, $H(f^k, \delta)$ is the set of indexes of those membership functions which are within δ distance to the minimum, and where λ_i''s are constants.

If the product of membership functions is used for finding the membership function of the intersection set, the kth iteration of a steepest ascent algorithm used for maximizing the logarithm of the cost formation will be

$$f^{k+1} = f^k + \tau'\sum_{i=1}^{m}\frac{1}{\mu_i(f^k)}\nabla\mu_i(f^k) \quad (41)$$

where τ' is to be found by one-dimensional optimization. Similarly, if the p-norm is used with the same algorithm, the equation for the kth iteration is given by

$$f^{k+1} = f^k + \tau'\sum_{i=1}^{m}p(1-\mu_i(f^k))^{p-1}\nabla\mu_i(f^k). \quad (42)$$

In (40), using the gradients of the minimal membership functions is explicitly stated. In (41) and (42), the gradients of the smaller valued membership functions will dominate the summations. Finally, in the POCS technique, those sets assigning high membership values to the estimate will not take part in the projections. The gradients of various quantities used in membership functions are given in Appendix B.

V. A Measure for the Quality of a Restoration

A. Size of the Intersection Set

Ideally, the fuzzy feasibility set must be a singleton containing only the original signal. For this case, the available information uniquely defines the original signal. However, in practice, a complete definition of the original signal is almost never available and the intersection set has many elements with above-threshold membership values. An arbitrary one of these can be the solution obtained by the techniques described in the previous section.

In a consistent formulation, the height of the intersection set is close to one. Hence, the elements with maximal membership in the intersection set are nonrejectable solutions. However, their "closeness" to the original signal depends on the "size" of their intersection set. Heuristically, the size of the intersection set is a measure for the combined information about the original signal. If the size is small, the original signal is well defined; any signal in the intersection set is close to the original signal, and is a high-quality restoration. However, the chance of obtaining a high-quality restoration by selecting an arbitrary element of a large intersection set is small.

The size of the intersection set can be computed before obtaining the solution. If this computation is less complex than finding a solution, the size measure may be found first and, depending on the result, a decision can be made on computing the solution.

In [11], the size of an ordinary set was defined to be

$$\text{size}(C) = \sup_{f_1, f_2 \in C} \|f_1 - f_2\| \tag{43}$$

where the Euclidean norm was used. This definition is certainly in complete agreement with the size concept in this context. In fact, it is an upper bound for the error. An easy extension of this definition to fuzzy sets can be obtained by using the α-level sets of a fuzzy set. The sizes of all α-level sets as a function of α convey considerable information about a fuzzy set. The rate of change of this function is particularly important because it reflects the sensitivity of the results to the membership level.

In addition to the maximum distance between the elements of α-level sets, the energy measures given in Section III-C may be used to measure the size. It is shown that, in the case of a fuzzy set of alternatives, the measure given in (13) is a better indicator for the existence of a dominant alternative [26]. In the restoration problem, the feasibility set may be considered as a set of alternative solutions. Hence, the same conclusion holds. This can be

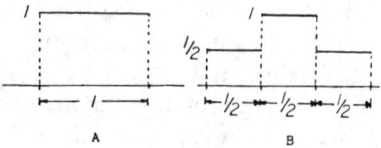

Fig. 1. The area under the membership functions A and B are equal to one unit. The area under the squared membership function A is one; however, the area under the squared membership function B is 0.75.

demonstrated by an example. Among the fuzzy sets A and B, whose membership functions are as depicted in Fig. 1, the definition of the original signal is, clearly, better in set B; but when computed using (12), both sets have the same energy measure. On the other hand, under (13), the energy of the fuzzy set B is smaller.

Following these arguments, it may be concluded that a small intersection set is an indication of a well-defined solution and high-quality restoration. This is valid under the assumption of a consistent formulation. The intersection set may have a very small size but this may be because of a low height, indicating an inconsistency in the incorporated information. In such cases, the formulation of the problem must be checked for the source of an inconsistency. This may be done by removing some of the sets from the formulation and calculating the height of the new intersection set. In the following, a consistent formulation is assumed.

B. Computational Aspects

In many applications, because of the null space of the degradation operator, the upper bounds given in [11] for the sizes of individual sets are undefined. Even when some of the sets in the collection have known bounds, these may be extremely large and of little value. In specific cases, it may be possible to find an analytical expression for the size of the intersection set. However, developing a general, analytical technique does not seem possible. These necessitate the approximate computation of the size measures by Monte Carlo experiments.

The maximum distance between two elements of an α-level set of the fuzzy intersection set can be approximated by the largest distance between the random signals generated over this set. Probabilistic confidence levels on such an approximation can be calculated [43]. Similarly, an estimate for the energy of the intersection set can be computed by

$$e(\cap_\alpha) = \frac{V}{NS} \sum_{i=1}^{NS} \mu^2(f_i) \tag{44}$$

where NS is the total number of random signals used in the experiment, and V is the volume over which the signals are distributed uniformly.

In order to find a limited region over which the random signals are to be generated, some information about the original signal is required. In the worst case, this region can be defined using a large enough energy or amplitude bound on the original signal. However, if a large region is used, the high dimensionality of the signal space necessitates performing an enormous number of experiments. Fortunately, in many cases, the size of this region can be restricted using some of the sets defining the solution. For example, if the original signal is known to be positive, there is no reason for generating test signals with negative components.

If a solution is required regardless of the size of the intersection set, or if the experimentation region is too large for being computationally feasible, a solution is computed. After finding the solution, the size of the intersection set can be used as a quality measure for it. Certainly, to know a solution helps a great deal in designing the experiment. For example, to find the maximum distance between the elements, it is possible to search for the furthest element of the intersection set from the solution in randomly generated directions. If the solution is obtained by the POCS technique, it will be on the boundary of at least one of the intersecting α-level sets. For this case, instead of random directions, the normals of the surfaces of the α-level sets can be used as search directions. In order to compute the energy measure, a sphere centered on the solution can be used as the experimentation region. The size of this sphere can be adjusted during the experiment to contain a reasonable proportion of the generated random signals.

Using randomly generated signals as initial signals, and finding the distances between the obtained restorations, is another technique for size computation. This is based on the results obtained in [21], indicating the profound effect of the initial estimate on the solution. However, solving the problem several times involves a large amount of computation.

Another approach to size computation may be to use a reasonable prototype signal "similar" to the original. As an example, consider a degraded image. Most of the time, the main scene such as buildings, ships, human faces, text, etc., can be identified. After such an identification, it is possible to find a similar picture. Degrading this picture with the same degradation, a new degraded picture can be obtained. Since the original of the new degraded picture is available, experiments can be done as if a solution is available. It is reasonable to assume that the size of the intersection set of this simulation is close to that of the original case. This approach may also be used in classifying the most effective sets for a certain group of signals. The effectiveness of various types of information for restricting the set of solutions can be studied by computing the size reduction obtained by the inclusion of a new set in a collection of sets describing a signal.

C. Results

In order to demonstrate the effects of variations in the parameters of a degradation system and the α-level on the size of the intersection set, Monte Carlo experiments were performed on the linear degradation system described in Section II. The original signal is a simulated X-ray spectrum and is shown in Fig. 2. It is convolved with a Gaussian-shaped impulse response, and zero mean, white noise

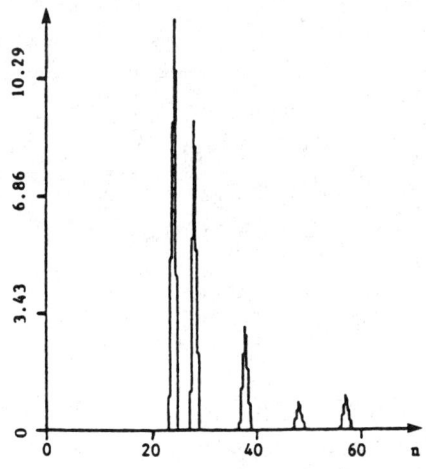

Fig. 2. Original signal.

TABLE II
THE ENERGY OF THE INTERSECTION SET

Noise Variance	Impulse Response's Variance	Side of the 64-Cube	Number of Points with Membership > 0.1	Energy
0.01	4.0	0.5	309	$10.52e - 21$
0.10	4.0	2.0	166	$1.79e + 18$
0.10	8.0	2.0	196	$2.12e + 18$

is added to obtain the degraded signal. The severity of the degradation is varied by changing the spread of the impulse resonance and the noise variance. The sets used in the experiments are those defined by the residual signal's statistics and nonnegativity.

To estimate the energy measure of the intersection set under varying degradation levels, uniform random signals are generated inside an N-dimensional cube around the original signal, and the energy measure defined in (13) is calculated using (44). The results are presented in Table II where 1000 signals, which are uniformly distributed inside a hypercube with noted sidelength, are used for each experiment. The size of the hypercube is adjusted according to the severity of the degradation so that a reasonable number of points have practically nonzero membership values in the intersection set defined by the minimum operator. It should be noted that changing the size of the hypercube while keeping the number of trials constant causes a change in the variance of the estimated energy. It is possible to estimate this variance and improve the experiment; however, in this paper, a detailed experiment design will not be investigated. The results obtained by this simple experiment are consistent with the theoretical expectations.

The maximum distance between the elements of the α-level sets of the intersection set is estimated by generating random signals so that their DFT coefficients are nonzero at the frequencies for which the DFT coefficients of the degrading function are almost zero. The sets defined by the residual signal's statistics are insensitive to the signals in these frequencies. However, when the nonnegativity

TABLE III
MAXIMUM DERIVATION FROM THE ORIGINAL SIGNAL

Noise Variance	Impulse Response's Variance	Conf. Level	Range of Coeff. Magnitude	Number of Points in the Intersection	Maximum Squared Distance
0.01	4.0	0.99	6.0	36	1.05
0.01	4.0	0.10	8.0	21	1.87
0.10	4.0	0.99	23.0	18	11.17
0.10	4.0	0.10	25.0	120	14.10
0.10	8.0	0.99	25.0	15	11.44
0.10	8.0	0.10	25.0	100	15.07

constraint is enforced, the size of the intersection set is reduced significantly. As in the case of estimating energy, a restricted range is used for the frequency coefficients so that a reasonable proportion of 500 generated signals is contained in the intersection set. The results presented in Table III are consistent with the expectations and are encouraging for further studies on the subject.

The estimate for the maximum distance between the elements of the intersection set seems to be more meaningful than the energy measure. However, the latter can be used of a relative comparison of different formulations. The computation of the size measures using Monte Carlo experiments is long and costly but, for the cases in which the collection of the fuzzy sets defining the solution is fixed, this drawback may be easier to overcome by performing experiments with prototype data.

VI. RESULTS

A. Using the POCS Method

The POCS method can be used when all fuzzy sets defining the solution are convex. The fuzzy sets constructed using the residual signal's statistics, with the exception of the one using the mean value, are not convex. However, as in [11], it is reasonable to assume that initially the statistics of the residual signal are more likely to be larger than the upper bounds and stay in the same region during the iterations. Under this assumption, the convex hull of the nonconvex α-level sets can be used. The convex approximations for the α-level sets of the fuzzy sets defined using residual signal's statistics are given in Appendix C.

In order to observe the effect of the α-level on the quality of the restoration and the computation time, consider the degraded signal shown in Fig. 3. This signal is obtained by convolving the signal displayed in Fig. 2 by a Gaussian-shaped impulse response with variance four, and adding zero mean, white, Gaussian noise with variance 0.001. Restorations are computed using three different α-levels. The sets defined by residual signal's statistics and nonnegativity are used in the restoration. The nonnegativity requirement is also made fuzzy using the following membership functions:

$$\mu_{nn}(f_i) = \begin{cases} e^{\alpha_{nn} f_i} & f_i < 0 \\ 1 & \text{otherwise} \end{cases} \quad (45)$$

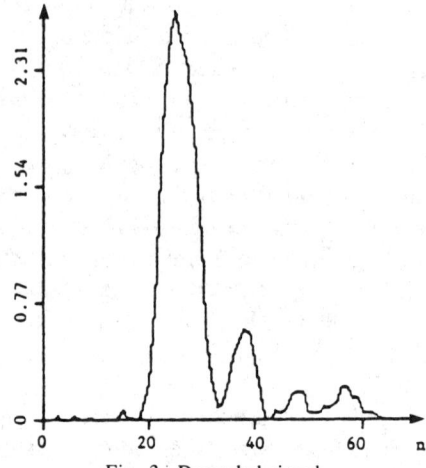

Fig. 3. Degraded signal.

where α_{nn} is adjusted for an acceptable negative value when the membership value of f_i is close to one.

The restoration shown in Fig. 4(a) is obtained using 0.1 level sets in 64 iterations. In Fig. 4(b), the restoration at 0.5 level is displayed. This result is computed in 135 iterations. The result demonstrated in Fig. 4(c) is obtained in 151 iterations and its membership in each set is larger than 0.99. As expected, the quality of the restoration gets higher and the amount of the computations for obtaining it increases as α gets larger.

Because of the logarithmic relation between α and δ values (Appendix C), the relative sensitivity of the results to changing α values decreases as α gets larger. For the example demonstrated in Fig. 4, to obtain the result at 0.89 level, 149 iterations are required. That is, only two iterations are gained by a 0.1 reduction in α. However, finding a solution, when α is 0.2, takes 99 iterations. Thus, the difference between the number of iterations for obtaining solutions at α levels 0.1 and 0.2 is 35.

Many other factors may affect the sensitivity of the results to membership level. Number of samples, noise variance, and severity of the degradation are some of these factors. As can be seen from (C.5) in the Appendix C, the derivatives of the δ bounds of the sets with respect to α are functions of these factors.

It should be noted that, if the sensitivities of the sets used in a restoration problem varies significantly, the order of projections will affect the membership value of a result obtained after a certain number of iterations. Pro-

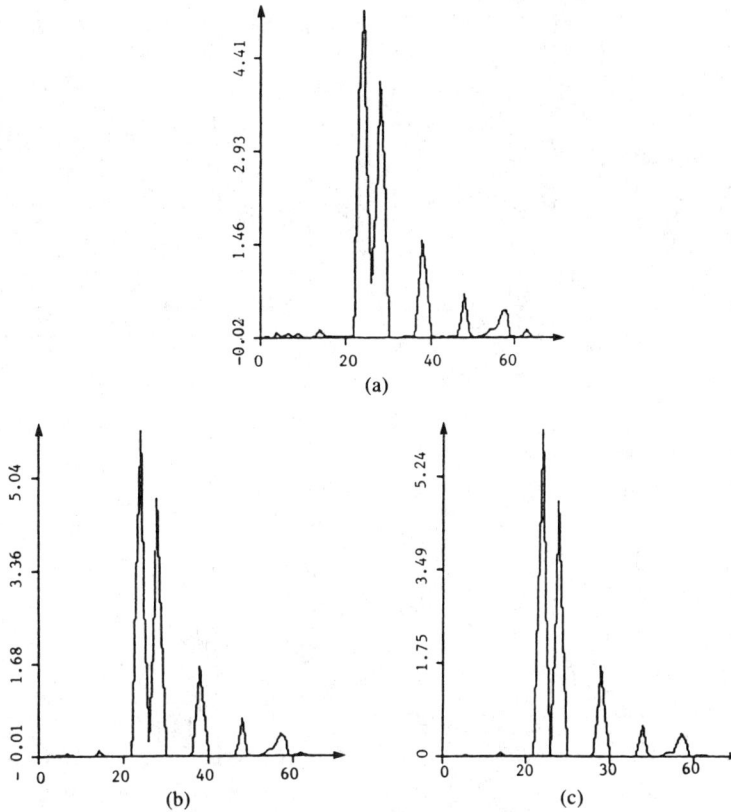

Fig. 4. (a) Restoration when $\alpha = 0.1$. (b) Restoration when $\alpha = 0.5$. (c) Restoration when $\alpha = 0.99$.

jecting onto more sensitive sets last may reduce the number of iterations required for obtaining a solution with a certain membership value.

In cases for which the noise sequence has improbable sample statistics, or a degradation model with an erroneous parameter, the intersection set may be very small for high α values. This causes a large number of iterations. Reducing α to enlarge the sizes of the sets can be a solution for this problem. The membership level may also be reduced if a solution is required in a small number of iterations.

These methods were tested by adding large spurious noise spikes to the degraded signal. A standard restoration was run 285 iterations with $\alpha = 0.99$ which failed to converge. A second restoration was run with 30 iterations with $\alpha = 0.99$, followed by 30 iterations with $\alpha = 0.5$, and finally, 2 iterations with $\alpha = 0.1$. The quality of the two restorations was comparable. For this example, a 78 percent reduction in the computation time is achieved by using the relaxation technique and lowering the required quality. If, instead of relaxing the α-level, it is kept constant at 0.99 and the iterations are terminated at the 62th iteration, the results will not be much different. However, there is no way of finding the sufficient number of iterations before the experiment.

Another way of approaching the outliers problem may be using a successive contraction. For this approach, a solution with a low membership value is computed first. Depending on the number of iterations for obtaining the solution with the low membership value, a decision can be made on running more iterations or terminating the process. For example, for the case described in the successive relaxation application, finding a solution at 0.1 level takes 40 iterations, while for the same signal without the added spike, 24 iterations are enough for obtaining a solution at the same level. Increasing the level to 0.2 takes another 120 iterations for the case with outlier while the second one reaches 0.99 level in 8 additional iterations.

B. Results Obtained by Using Optimization Techniques

There are two main motivations for investigating different optimization techniques. The first one is to find a more efficient algorithm than the POCS method for collecting of convex fuzzy sets, and the second one is to be able to use nonconvex fuzzy sets which cannot be approximated by convex sets.

In order to investigate the performance of various algorithms to compute a solution in the case of convex fuzzy sets, experiments were performed using the three forms of the intersection operator. A conjugate gradient-type algorithm was utilized with the p-norm and the product intersections, and the special algorithm described in [38] is used with the minimum intersection. The results obtained using different intersection operators and algorithms were similar to the ones obtained by using the POCS method. The number of iterations required for obtaining a solution with a given membership value is observed to be smaller for the minimum intersection operator used with the spe-

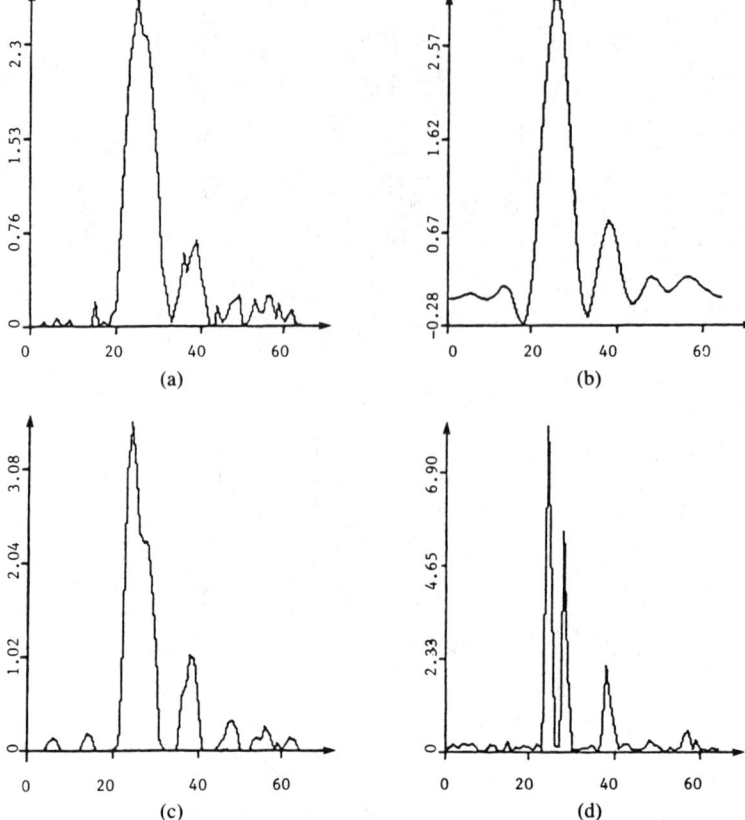

Fig. 5. (a) Degraded signal. (b) Restoration by constrained least-squares method. (c) Restoration by POCS. (d) Restoration by imposing a lower bound on energy of the signal.

cial algorithm. However, this does not result in a significant reduction in the computation time required by the POCS method because of extra computations performed in each iteration, such as calculation of the gradients, determination of the optimal direction, and line search. However, it should be noted that one of the techniques described above, or a completely different technique, might be superior to others for a special collection of sets.

In the formulation of the signal restoration problem using fuzzy sets, *a priori* knowledge which cannot be modeled as a convex set may also be utilized. In the following restoration examples, nonconvex fuzzy sets for imposing a lower bound on the energy and finite levels on the signal are used. The intersection operator used is the product of membership functions. A straightforward hill-climbing algorithm with line search is utilized. The iterations are stopped when the membership values of the estimates in the intersection set are larger than 0.95.

The fuzzy sets imposing upper and lower bounds on the energy of the restored signal were discussed in Section IV. In this example, the effect of the fuzzy set placing a soft lower bound on the energy will be demonstrated. The degraded signal shown in Fig. 5(a) is obtained from the same degradation system and the original signal used in Figs. 2 and 3. However, the noise variance is increased to 0.01. In Fig. 5(b) and (c), the restorations obtained by the constrained least-squares [4] and the POCS methods are displayed, respectively. In the POCS algorithm, the fuzzy sets defined by the residual signal's statistics and nonnegativity are used. Fig. 5(d) displays the restoration obtained when the collection of the fuzzy sets defining the solution includes an additional fuzzy set enforcing a soft lower bound on the energy of the signal. Considering the performance of the other techniques at this noise level, the superiority of the result is obvious. The three large impulses of the original signal are completely recovered, the remaining two impulses are not very clear, however, they are at the correct places.

In determining the membership function of the lower bound set, the energy of the degraded signal is used to locate the lowest value of the membership function. The energy of the degraded signal is less than that of the original signal because of the attenuating nature of the degrading system's impulse response. Determination of the nonrejectable energy level requires *a priori* knowledge about the energy of the original signal. In many applications this kind of information is available. For example, in image restoration a prototype can be used for determining an acceptable energy level. In X-ray spectroscopy, an estimate for the composition of the test material can be made to derive an approximate bound on the expected energy of the resulting signal. It should be noted that the result is not very sensitive to the errors in the acceptable energy levels. In the demonstrated example,

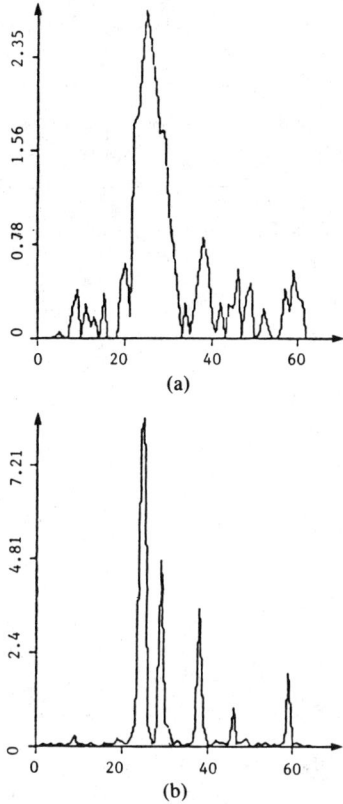

Fig. 6. (a) Degraded signal. (b) Restoration.

any signal with an energy higher than 180 units is assigned a membership value larger than 0.99, while the energy of the original signal is 235.65 units. The quality of the result does not change for a ±10 percent change around this energy level.

In Fig. 6 the degraded and restored signals corresponding to 0.5 noise variance are displayed. The resolution of the impulses are still excellent; however, the locations of some of the impulses are different from the original signal by one sample. This indicates that, for higher noise levels than this one, the result may not be correct and more information about the original signal may be necessary.

Another nonconvex set is the one modeling a finite number of levels. In many applications, such as restoring text pictures or industrial tomography, the original signal is known to have finite levels. In such cases, the classical approach is thresholding a restoration of the signal obtained by a convenient algorithm. Usually, successful results can be obtained by this technique. In order to apply thresholding, the possible levels of the original signal must be known *a priori*. However, in many applications these levels are not known exactly, but their ranges are available. Additionally, the signal may vary around the possible levels. An example for this was discussed in Section IV. In such cases, a fuzzy set modeling this property of the original signal can easily be constructed and included in the collection.

In Fig. 7(a) and (b), a finite-level signal and its degraded form are displayed, respectively. The degrading impulse response is of Gaussian shape with variance 6.

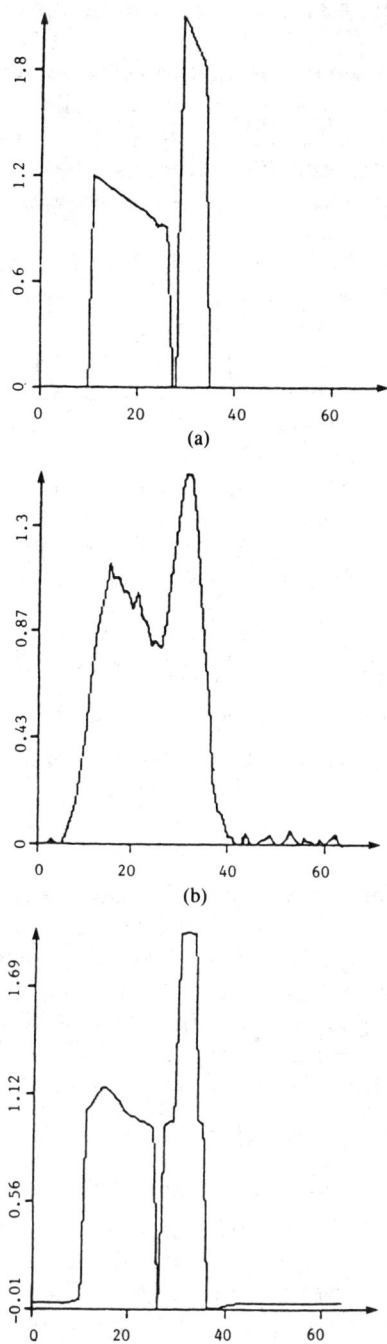

Fig. 7. (a) Original signal. (b) Degraded signal. (c) Restored signal.

Zero mean, white noise with variance 0.001 is added on the degraded signal. To obtain the restoration shown in Fig. 7(c), the fuzzy sets defined by the residual signal's statistics, nonnegativity, and a fuzzy set modeling known ranges for signal values are utilized. The obtained restoration is reasonable at the stated degradation level.

VII. Conclusions and Suggestions

The method presented can be used in multidimensional signal restoration, and it is capable of generating high-quality restorations in cases for which the conventional techniques have failed. It has considerable flexibility in incorporating a large collection of information to define the solution. Using fuzzy sets makes it possible to use partially defined information as well as exact information.

The method is a general and extendible technique. It can easily be adjusted according to the requirements of varying signal restoration problems. The quality of an obtained restoration can be improved by the addition of new sets to the existing collection.

In addition to the basic signal restoration and reconstruction applications, the new technique can be used in image coding. In transmitting or storing images, instead of the actual image, a collection of parameters describing the sets, which in turn define the actual image, may be transmitted or stored. In restoration applications, it has been observed that a few sets may be adequate to approximate a signal well. If these sets can be defined by a small number of parameters, using these parameters instead of the image may reduce the required amount of stored or transmitted information considerably.

APPENDIX A
OPTIMAL MEMBERSHIP FUNCTIONS FOR SPECIFIC PDF'S

A. Gaussian Distribution

If the probability density function $p(x)$ is

$$p(x) = \frac{1}{\sqrt{2\pi}} e^{-(1/2)x^2}, \quad \text{(A.1)}$$

then the optimal membership function is determined by a single scalar "a" which is a function of the confidence level c defined in Section IV. A sample membership function for the standard normal distribution is illustrated in Fig. 8. The plot given in Fig. 9 shows the values of the parameter a versus the confidence level c. The optimal Lagrange multiplier can be calculated using

$$\lambda^*(c) = \sqrt{2\pi}\ e^{a^2/2}. \quad \text{(A.2)}$$

B. PDF's for Power Spectrum and Maximum Deviation

The probability density functions for the power spectrum of the residual and maximum residual value were given in (24) and (26), respectively. These are unimodal densities, and the membership functions derived from them can be specified by two parameters, namely, the starting value "a," and the final value "b" of the region in which the membership function equals to 1. The values of these parameters for various confidence levels and number of samples are given in Table IV.

APPENDIX B
GRADIENTS

In this appendix, the derivatives of some of the residual signal's functions with respect to the estimated signal are given. For the linear signal degradation model, the residual signal is

$$r = g - Hf. \quad \text{(B.1)}$$

If the matrix H represents circular convolution, any row is enough in specifying the whole matrix. The signal

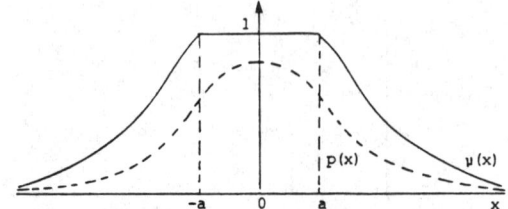

Fig. 8. The membership function corresponding to the standard normal density.

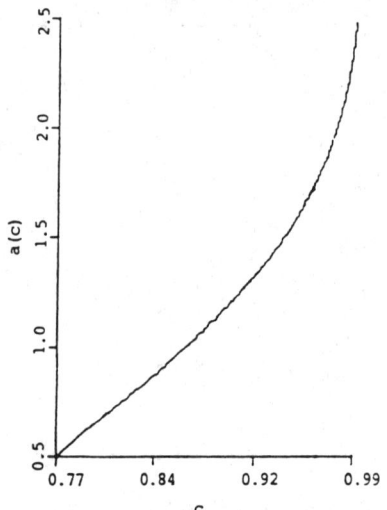

Fig. 9. The parameter "a" of the membership function corresponding to the standard normal density versus confidence level.

TABLE IV
OPTIMAL PARAMETERS FOR THE MEMBERSHIP FUNCTIONS OF THE SETS DESCRIBED BY THE POWER SPECTRUM AND THE MAXIMUM VALUE OF THE RESIDUAL SIGNAL

N	c	Power Spectrum Set			Max. Residual Set		
		lambda	a	b	lambda	a	b
64	0.90	13	4.75	10.25	2.4	2.03	3.05
64	0.95	25	4.23	11.75	5.0	1.90	3.31
64	0.98	48	3.87	13.14	14.0	1.78	3.62
128	0.90	13	6.14	11.67	2.3	2.30	4.26
128	0.95	25	5.61	13.17	4.9	2.18	3.51
128	0.98	47	5.24	14.51	14.0	2.06	3.81
256	0.90	13	7.53	13.06	2.2	2.54	3.45
256	0.95	25	7.00	14.57	4.8	2.43	3.58
256	0.98	46	6.63	15.87	14.0	2.32	3.99
4096	0.90	13	13.08	18.62	1.8	3.38	4.13
4096	0.95	25	12.54	20.13	4.2	3.30	4.35
4096	0.98	45	12.17	21.38	13.5	3.21	4.62
6384	0.90	13	15.85	21.39	1.6	3.75	4.43
6384	0.95	25	15.31	22.90	3.5	3.67	4.62
6384	0.98	44	14.96	24.11	8.5	3.61	4.81
65 576	0.90	13	18.63	24.17	1.2	4.11	4.66
65 576	0.95	25	18.08	25.67	2.3	4.04	4.82
65 576	0.98	40	17.79	26.68	7.0	3.96	5.00

whose samples are the elements of the first row of H will be called the point spread function (psf), and will be denoted by h. A signal, such as r, has three representations, namely, vector form as in (B.1), which is denoted by a small letter, sequence form as $h(n)$, and discrete Fourier transformed (DFT) form, which will be denoted by using a capital letter with explicit frequency dependence, as in $R(k)$. $[\ ]_i$ denotes the ith element of a vector; and the subscripts "$\cdot, i$" and "$i, \cdot$" denote the ith column vector and ith row vector of a matrix, respectively.

A. Sum of Residual Elements

The sum of the residual signal's elements is used in defining the set based on the sample mean statistics. The gradient of this quantity is

$$\nabla_f \sum_{i=1}^{i=N} [r]_i = -\left[\sum_{i=1}^{i=N} [H_{\cdot,1}]_i, \sum_{i=1}^{i=N} [H_{\cdot,2}]_i, \cdots, \sum_{i=1}^{i=N} [H_{\cdot,N}]_i\right]^t. \quad \text{(B.2)}$$

If H represents circular convolution, then

$$\nabla_f \sum_{i=1}^{i=N} [r]_i = -\sum_{i=1}^{i=N} [h]_i [1, 1, \cdots, 1]^t. \quad \text{(B.3)}$$

In many applications, the sum of the elements of the psf is unity. For this case, the gradient is an N-dimensional vector of ones.

B. Sum of Squared Residual Elements

$$\nabla_f \sum_{i=1}^{i=N} [r]_i^2 = -2 H^t r. \quad \text{(B.4)}$$

If H represents circular convolution, then the following form of (B.4) can be computed easily using FFT:

$$\nabla_f \sum_{i=1}^{i=N} [r]_i^2 = -2 \text{ IDFT} \{H(k)^* R(k)\} \quad \text{(B.5)}$$

where IDFT is the inverse DFT.

C. Maximum Deviation from the Mean Value

The absolute value of the maximum deviation is not continuously differentiable. However, an approximation for it can be calculated by using the p-norm approximation for the Chebyshev's norm. Using a sufficiently large p value, an approximate gradient for the maximum deviation can be obtained as follows:

$$\nabla_f |[r]_i|_{\max} = \nabla_f \left(\sum_{i=1}^{i=N} [r]_i^p\right)^{1/p}$$

$$= -\sum_{i=1}^{i=N} \left(\frac{[r]_i}{rx}\right)^{(p-1)} H_{i,\cdot}. \quad \text{(B.6)}$$

where

$$rx = \left(\sum_{i=1}^{i=N} [r]_i^p\right)^{1/p} \quad \text{(B.7)}$$

and p is a large even integer. For the circular convolution case, $H_{i,\cdot}$ is the $(i-1)$ times circularly rotated psf.

D. Maximum Power Spectrum Value

As in the maximum deviation case, only an approximate derivative can be found. If the periodogram is denoted by $P(k)$, then

$$\nabla_f P(k)_{\max} = \nabla_f \left(\sum_{i=2}^{i=N/2} |R(i)|^{2p}\right)^{1/p}$$

$$= -2 \sum_{i=2}^{i=N/2} \left(\frac{|R(i)|^2}{Pmx}\right)^{(p-1)}$$

$$\cdot \text{Re}\{R(i) H^*(i) [w^0, w^i, \cdots, w^{(N-1)i}]^t\} \quad \text{(B.8)}$$

where

$$Pms = \sum_{i=2}^{i=N/2} (|R(i)|^{2p})^{1/p}$$

and $w = \exp[j(2\pi/N)]$.

APPENDIX C
CONVEX APPROXIMATIONS FOR α-LEVEL SETS

In [11], the convex sets constructed using the residual signal's sample mean, sample variance, maximum periodogram value, and maximum deviation from the mean value are denoted as C_m, C_v, C_p, and C_m, respectively. These sets are

$$C_m = \left\{f \mid \left|\sum_{i=1}^{N} ([g]_i - [Hf]_i)\right| \leq \delta_m\right\} \quad \text{(C.1)}$$

$$C_v = \{f \mid \|g - Hf\|^2 \leq \delta_v\} \quad \text{(C.2)}$$

$$C_p = \Big\{f \mid |G(k) - H(k) F(k)|^2 \leq \delta_p,$$

$$k = 1, 2, \cdots, \frac{N}{2} - 1\Big\} \quad \text{(C.3)}$$

$$C_0 = \{f \mid |[g]_i - [Hf]_i| \leq \delta_0\}. \quad \text{(C.4)}$$

The convex approximations for the α-level sets of the fuzzy sets defined using residual signal's statistics have the same form as the sets given above, however, the δ parameters are α dependent. The relations between α and δ parameters are as follows:

$$\delta_m = cl\sigma_n \sqrt{N}$$

$$\delta_v = \sigma_n^2 N \left(1 + \frac{cl^2}{2(N-1)} + \frac{cl\sqrt{2N-1}}{N-1}\right)$$

$$\delta_p = \sigma_n^2 N \left(\frac{b(c)}{2} - \ln \alpha\right)$$

$$\delta_0 = \sigma_n \sqrt{b^2(c) - 2 \ln \alpha} \quad \text{(C.5)}$$

where

$$cl = \sqrt{a^2(c) - 2 \ln \alpha}, \quad \text{(C.6)}$$

and $a(c)$ and $b(c)$ are confidence level dependent parameters as defined in Appendix A.

REFERENCES

[1] W. K. Pratt, *Digital Image Processing*. New York: Wiley, 1978.
[2] H. C. Andrews and B. R. Hunt, *Digital Image Restoration*. Englewood Cliffs, NJ: Prentice-Hall, 1977.
[3] A. Rosenfeld and A. C. Kak, *Digital Picture Processing*. New York: Academic, 1982.
[4] B. R. Hunt, "The application of constrained least squares estimation to image restoration by digital computer," *IEEE Trans. Comput.*, vol. C-2, pp. 805-812, Sept. 1973.
[5] —, "Bayesian methods of nonlinear digital image restoration," *IEEE Trans. Comput.*, vol. C-26, pp. 219-229, Mar. 1977.
[6] R. N. Schafer, R. M. Mersereau, and M. A. Richards, "Constrained iterative restoration algorithms," *Proc. IEEE*, vol. 69, Apr. 1981.
[7] P. H. Van Cittert, "Zum Einfluss der Spaltbreite auf die Intenstatswerteilung in Spektallinien II," *Z. fur Physik*, vol. 69, pp. 298-308, 1931.
[8] L. Landweber, "An iteration formula for Fredholm integral equation of the first kind," *Amer. J. Math.*, vol. 73, pp. 615-624, 1951.
[9] O. N. Strand, "Theory and methods related to the singular function expansion and Landweber's iteration for integral equations of the first kind," *SIAM J. Numer. Anal.*, vol. 14, no. 4, pp. 798-825, 1974.
[10] H. J. Trussell, "Convergence criteria for iterative restoration methods," *IEEE Trans. Acoust., Speech, Signal Processing*, vol. ASSP-31, pp. 129-136, Feb. 1983.
[11] H. J. Trussell and M. R. Civanlar, "Feasible solution in signal restoration," *IEEE Trans. Acoust., Speech, Signal Processing*, vol. ASSP-32, pp. 201-212, Apr. 1984.
[12] L. M. Bregman, "The method of successive projection for finding a common point of convex sets," *Doklady, Akad. Nauk. SSSR*, vol. 162, no. 3, pp. 688-692, 1965.
[13] L. G. Gubin, B. T. Polyak, and E. V. Raik, "The method of projections for finding the common point of convex sets," *USSR Comput. Math. Mathemat. Phys.*, vol. 7, no. 6, pp. 1-24, 1967.
[14] R. W. Gerchberg, "Super resolution through error energy reduction," *Opt. Acta*, vol. 14, no. 9, pp. 709-720, Sept. 1979.
[15] A. Papoulis, "A new algorithm in spectral analysis and band-limited extrapolation," *IEEE Trans. Circuits Syst.*, vol. CAS-22, pp. 735-741, Sept. 1975.
[16] A. Lent and H. Tuy, "An iterative method for the extrapolation of bandlimited functions," *J. Math. Anal. Appl.*, vol. 83, pp. 554-565, 1981.
[17] D. C. Youla and H. Webb, "Image reconstruction by the method of convex projections, Part 1—Theory," *IEEE Trans. Med. Imaging*, vol. MI-1, pp. 81-94, Oct. 1982.
[18] M. I. Sezan and H. Stark, "Image restoration by the method of convex projections: Part 2—Applications and numerical results," *IEEE Trans. Med. Imaging*, vol. MI-1, pp. 95-101, Oct. 1982.
[19] H. J. Trussell, "Maximum power signal restoration," *IEEE Trans. Acoust. Speech, Signal Processing*, vol. ASSP-29, pp. 1059-1061, Oct. 1981.
[20] G. M. Jenkins and D. G. Watts, *Spectral Analysis and Its Applications*. San Francisco, CA: Holden-Day, 1968.
[21] H. J. Trussell and M. R. Civanlar, "The initial estimate in constrained iterative restoration," in *ICASSP Proc.*, vol. 2, Apr. 14-16, 1983.
[22] L. A. Zadeh, "Fuzzy sets," *Inf. Contr.* 8, pp. 338-353, 1965.
[23] A. Kandel and W. J. Byatt, "Fuzzy sets, fuzzy algebra and fuzzy statistics," *Proc. IEEE*, vol. 66, pp. 1619-1639, Dec. 1978.
[24] D. Dubois and H. Prade, *Fuzzy Sets and Systems: Theory and Applications*. New York: Academic, 1980.
[25] A. DeLuca and S. Termini, "Entropy and energy measures of fuzzy sets," in *Advances in Fuzzy Set Theory and Applications*. Amsterdam, The Netherlands: North-Holland, 1979, pp. 321-338.
[26] E. Czogala, S. Gottwald, and W. Pedrycz, "Contribution to application of energy measure of fuzzy sets," *Fuzzy Sets Syst.*, no. 8, pp. 205-214, 1982.
[27] H. Bremermann, "Pattern recognition," in *System Theory in Social Sciences*, H. Bossel, S. Klaszko, and N. Muller, Eds. Basel, Switzerland: Birkhauser, 1976, pp. 116-159.
[28] M. Kochen and A. N. Badre, "On the precision of adjectives which denote fuzzy sets," *J. Cybern.*, vol. 4, no. 1, pp. 49-59, 1976.
[29] H. M. Hersh and A. Caramazza, "A fuzzy set approach to modifiers and vagueness in natural languages," *J. Exp. Psych.*, vol. 105, pp. 254-276, 1976.
[30] M. Nowakowska, "Fuzzy concepts in social sciences," *Behav. Sci.*, vol. 22, pp. 107-115, 1977.
[31] D. G. Luenberger, *Optimization by Vector Space Methods*. New York: Wiley, 1969.
[32] P. G. Hoel, *Introduction to Mathematical Statistics*. New York: Wiley, 1971.
[33] E. R. Cole, "The removal of unknown image blurs by homomorphic filtering," ARPA, Tech. Rep. UTEC-CSc-74-029, 1974.
[34] H. J. Trussell and B. R. Hunt, "Improved methods of maximum *a posteriori* restoration," *IEEE Trans. Comput.*, vol. C-27, pp. 57-62, Jan. 1979.
[35] T. Hald and K. Madsen, "Combined LP and quasi-Newton methods for minimax optimization," *Math. Progr.*, vol. 20, 1981.
[36] S. P. Han, "Variable metric methods for minimizing a class of non-differentiable functions," *Math. Progr.*, vol. 20, pp. 1-13, 1981.
[37] W. J. Zangwill, "An algorithm for the Chebyshev problem with an application to concave programming," *Manag. Sci.*, vol. 14, pp. 58-78, 1967.
[38] C. Charalambous and A. R. Conn, "An efficient method to solve the minimax problem directly," *SIAM J. Numer. Anal.*, vol. 15, no. 1, pp. 162-187, Feb. 1978.
[39] R. Fletcher, *Practical Methods of Optimization*, vol. 1. New York: Wiley, 1980.
[40] G. Zoutendijk, *Mathematical Programming Methods*. Amsterdam, The Netherlands: North-Holland, 1976.
[41] W. Pedrycz, "Some aspects of fuzzy decision making," *Kybernetes*, vol. 11, pp. 297-301, 1982.
[42] E. Polak, *Computational Methods in Optimization: A Unified Approach*. New York: Academic, 1971.
[43] W. Freiberger and U. Grenander, *A Short Course in Computational Probability and Statistics*. New York: Springer-Verlag, 1977.
[44] M. R. Civanlar and H. J. Trussell, "Constructing membership functions using statistical data," *Int. J. Fuzzy Sets Syst.*, vol. 18, pp. 1-13, Jan. 1986.
[45] M. R. Civanlar, "Digital signal restoration using projection and fuzzy set techniques," Ph.D. dissertation, N.C. State Univ., Raleigh, July 1984.

Mehmet Reha Civanlar (S'83-M'85) was born in Ankara, Turkey, on March 7, 1956. He received the B.S. and M.S. degrees from the Middle East Technical University, Turkey, and the Ph.D. degree from North Carolina State University, Raleigh, all in electrical engineering, in 1979, 1981, and 1984, respectively.

He was a Research Assistant in the Process Control Laboratory of the Middle East Technical University during 1979-1981. While working toward the Ph.D. degree he held research and teaching assistantships and instructed in the Department of Electrical and Computer Engineering of the North Carolina State University. Now he is a Research Associate in the Center for Communication and Signal Processing of the same Department. His current research interests include signal restoration with applications in tomography, and speech and image coding techniques.

Dr. Civanlar is a Fulbright Scholar and a member of Sigma Xi, Tau Beta Pi, Phi Kappa Phi, and the IEEE Acoustics, Speech, and Signal Processing Society.

H. Joel Trussell (S'74-M'76) was born in Atlanta, GA, on February 3, 1945. He received the B.S. degree from the Georgia Institute of Technology, Atlanta, in 1967, the M.S. degree from Florida State University, Tallahassee, in 1968, and the Ph.D. degree from the University of New Mexico, Albuquerque, in 1976.

In 1969 he joined the Los Alamos Scientific Laboratory, Los Alamos, NM, where he began work in image and signal processing in 1971. During 1978-1979 he was a Visiting Professor at Heriot-Watt University, Edinburgh, Scotland. In 1980 he joined the Department of Electrical Engineering, North Carolina State University, Raleigh. His current interests include signal restoration/reconstruction and mathematical methods.

Dr. Trussell is a member of Sigma Xi, Tau Beta Pi, Phi Kappa Phi, and the IEEE Acoustics, Speech, and Signal Processing Society.

Chapter 4: Image Data Compression

Image data compression has been, and is still to some extent, one of the major areas of research in image processing. Very often, in practical situations, one encounters images defined over $1K$ by $1K$ or $2K$ by $2K$ lattices. Assuming that each pixel is represented by 16 bits (corresponding to gray-level variations between zero and 255), the image data represent approximately 16 megabytes (or 64 megabytes of memory), which is quite high. It is desirable to represent the information in the image with considerably fewer bits and — at the same time — to be able to reconstruct an image that is close to the original image.

Applications of data compression are primarily in the transmission and storage of information. In transmission applications, compression techniques are constrained by real time and on-line considerations that limit the size and complexity of the hardware. Image-transmission techniques are useful in such areas as broadcast television, remote sensing via satellite, aircraft, radar, sonar, teleconferencing, computer communications, and facsimile transmission. In storage applications, the requirements are less stringent than in transmission applications, because much of the preprocessing can be done off line. Image storage is required most commonly for such things as medical images and educational and business documents.

The basic idea in image-compression techniques is to use an invertible linear transformation to transform the given correlated image array to an array of uncorrelated variables that can be represented by much fewer bits compared to in the original image array. As an example, if we represent each of the pixels in the original M by M image array and in the decorrelated array with eight bits and one bit, respectively, then the compression factor is approximately

$$\frac{8M^2}{m+M^2}$$

where m denotes the number of bits required to code the decorrelating transformation used. Usually, $m << M^2$ and a compression factor of eight is achieved.

Traditionally, two classes of image-compression techniques have been developed, as follows:

- Transform coding techniques and
- Predictive coding techniques.

In the transform coding technique, a linear, invertible two-dimensional discrete transform is applied to the given image; a subset of the transformed coefficients is retained, quantized, and then stored or transmitted. When it is required to generate an image close to the original image from the stored/transmitted information, the quantized transformed coefficients are reconstructed, followed by the application of the inverse transform. In the transform coding scheme, we can identify the following basic problems to be solved: the choice of the discrete decorrelating transform and the choice of the appropriate transform coefficients to be retained.

Similarly, in predictive coding schemes, the basic idea is to generate an array of uncorrelated random variables from the given image by using an invertible transformation. The structure of the transformation is defined by using an appropriate image model (see Chapter 1). By fitting a model to the given image, one generates the so-called "residuals," which are differences between the image gray levels and the gray levels predicted by the model. The residuals are less correlated than the original image pixels and — hence — can be represented by much fewer bits. Given the quantized residuals and parameters of the model, an image close to the original can be generated. Hybrid image compression is also possible by the transform and predictive coding schemes being combined.

Since most of the image-compression techniques are implemented in digital format, the design of quantizers for quantizing the transform coefficients, residuals, and parameters of the transformations forms an integral part of any compression scheme. Several types of quantizers, including Max's optimal quantizer,[1] nonparametric quantizers,[2] visual quantizers,[3] and color quantizers,[4] have been used in image-compression research. Evaluating the performance of the image coder is done through visual judgment of the reconstructed image. Although visual judgment of the reconstructed image is probably the natural criterion for evaluating the quality of reconstruction, such judgment is subjective and difficult to model and represent. Consequently, the mean-square error between the original image and the reconstructed image is usually used as the criterion for measuring the quality of the reconstructed image. Because the mean-square error is not an especially accurate measure of visual fidelity, several other methods for measuring visual fidelity have been suggested.[5,6]

The best invertible transform is the one that produces uncorrelated transform coefficients. Of all of the linear orthonormal transforms — such as the Fourier, Hadamard, cosine, sine, and Karhunen-Loeve transforms — the Karhunen-Loeve transform (KLT) is the only one that always produces exactly uncorrelated transform coefficients for finite images. (Rosenfeld and Kak[7] provide a simple proof to show that the KLT coefficients are uncorrelated.) Furthermore, for a given arbitrary number n of the transform coefficients retained, the KLT minimizes the ensemble mean-square error between the original image and the image reconstructed by using n transform coefficients. This fact follows from the observations given below.

(1) The ensemble mean-square error is the sum of variances of the discarded transform coefficients and
(2) By simply packing maximum variances in the first n transform coefficients (where n is an arbitrary number), the KLT minimizes the ensemble mean-square error.

Giri[8] provides a proof for the second of these observations.

Although the KLT possesses the nice properties mentioned above, its use poses serious computational problems, as it is determined by eigenvectors of the M^2 by M^2 covariance matrix of the M by M image (M is usually 128, 256, or 512). As a computational compromise, the use of several different transforms — such as the Fourier, Hadamard, cosine, and sine transforms — has been considered. In a classic paper by Wintz,[9] an excellent summary of the different transforms compression methods is given, followed by experimental results of image compression by using the Fourier transform, the Hadamard transform, and the KLT. The given image is divided into several small blocks of size 16 by 16, and each block is processed independently. This paper is noted for its historical notes regarding the KLT and a discussion of quantizer design. Fourier transform coding of images appeared in an earlier paper.[10]

Ahmed, Natarajan, and Rao[11] suggest a transform coding scheme using the discrete cosine transform (DCT). The DCT is an approximate substitute for the KLT in that the resulting transform coefficients are not exactly uncorrelated. It turns out that if the given data obey a first-order causal Markov model with normalized correlation coefficient $\rho = 0.9$, then the DCT is a good approximation for KLT. Good results using the discrete sine transform (DST)[12] may be obtained for some other values of ρ.

As mentioned before, the computation of variances of transform coefficients is an important aid in the selection of coefficients to be retained and in the normalization of coefficients to unit variance. Since the variances of Fourier transform coefficients are proportional to the spectral-density function evaluated at corresponding frequencies of the data, one can obtain estimates of variances of Fourier coefficients by using the periodogram method.[13] However, the periodogram method often yields inconsistent estimates of the spectral-density function. An alternative method would be to fit an image model such as the NCAR or MRF model. With the modeling assumption, the spectral-density function becomes an explicit function of parameters of the model and can be easily estimated.

To summarize, the stumbling block to using the optimal KLT is the computational complexity; on the other hand, the computationally efficient Fourier transform, DCT, DST, and Hadamard transform compression schemes are not optimal. A desirable compression scheme would be to combine the optimality of the KLT with the computational efficiency of the fast transforms, like the fast Fourier transform (FFT), the DCT, the DST, and the Hadamard transform. Jain[14] assumes appropriate boundary conditions for the original image such that the resulting covariance matrix is symmetric, tridiagonal, Toeplitz, and diagonalizable by the DST. Thus, the modified image (the original image along with the boundary conditions) is optimally coded by using the DST. With the boundary conditions also coded and transmitted/stored, the synthetic image corresponding to the original is recovered at the receiver. This technique is useful only when images are generated by the specific nearest-neighbor Markov models assumed. Chellappa and Bagdazian[15] present a fast KLT coding of closed image boundaries on a plane by using FFT.

The KLT is optimal in the sense of minimizing the ensemble mean-square error. Suppose we have only one image to be coded. For this case, the singular value decomposition (SVD) is optimal in the sense of minimizing the sample error

$$\frac{1}{M^2} \sum_{s \in \Omega} [y(s) - \hat{y}(s)]^2$$

where $\{\hat{y}(s)\}$ is reconstructed by retaining only a specific number of singular values. Thus, SVD coding is a deterministic technique in that it is optimal in the least-square sense, while the KLT is optimal in a statistical or ensemble mean-square sense. Andrews and Patterson[16] describe an SVD image-coding technique and give experimental results. They point out that a major drawback of SVD coding is its computational complexity.

We have so far discussed several transform coding schemes in which an array of uncorrelated coefficients is produced by using an invertible, unitary transform. A complimentary technique, the so-called "predictive coding technique," uses image models to generate an array of uncorrelated residuals. Suppose that the given image $\{y(s)\}$ can be adequately represented by a unilateral autoregressive model, as in

$$y(s) = \sum_{r \in N} \theta_r y(s+r) + \sqrt{\beta}\, \omega(s) \qquad 2$$

where $\{\omega(s)\}$ is a mutually uncorrelated sequence of noise variables with zero mean and unit variance and N is an arbitrary unilateral neighbor set. Given $\{y(s)\}$, one can obtain LS estimates $\{\theta_r^*\}$, β^* of parameters $\{\theta_r\}$, β, respectively, and can generate estimates of the noise sequence, the so-called "residual set" $\{\omega^*(s)\}$, by using the recursive relation

$$\omega^* = \frac{1}{\sqrt{\beta^*}} \left[y(s) - \sum_{r \in N} \theta_r^* y(s+r) \right]$$

To the extent that the model in Equation 2 is adequate to represent $\{y(s)\}$, the residuals in the set $\{\omega^*(s)\}$ possess statistical characteristics similar to those of $\{\omega(s)\}$. In particular, the residuals are uncorrelated and hence can be represented by fewer bits compared to the original data. An image close to the original is generated from the quantized residuals, parameters, and initial conditions by replacing the true values by their quantized values in Equation 2. Typically, for $N = \{(0, -1), (-1, -1), (-1, 0)\}$, the first row and the column of the image serve as the initial condition set. Since the difference between the original pixel and a predicted pixel is quantized, this method is known as the differential pulse code modulation (DPCM) scheme.

Delp, Kashyap, and Mitchell[17] use a seasonal autoregressive model to represent the image. The basic model is that of Equation 2, with $N = \{(0, -1), (-1, -1), (-1, 0)\}$. By concatenating the rows, the one-dimensional version of Equation 2 is obtained as

$$y(k) = \theta_1 y(k-M) + \theta_2 y(k-M-1) + \theta_3 y(k-1) + \omega(k) \qquad 3$$

where $s = (i,j)$, $k = (i-1)M + j$, and $\theta_1 = \theta_{0,-1}$, $\theta_2 = \theta_{-1,-1}$, and $\theta_3 = \theta_{-1,0}$. The LS method is used to obtain the estimates of parameters $\{\theta_i\}$, and Equation 3 is used to generate the image. Several images are generated using the DPCM scheme and a feedback quantizer. Because the optimal quantizer requires the knowledge of the probability distribution of the residuals (which is rarely available), a nonparametric quantizer[2] — which preserves the first two moments of the residuals — is used. Similar predictive coding schemes that use the two-dimensional causal model[18] and region-based stochastic models (discussed in Chapter 1) may be found in a paper by Daut, Fries, and Modestino.[19]

As remarked in Chapter 1, it is desirable to generalize predictive coding schemes by using noncausal models. As an illustration of how this may be done, assume that in Equation 2, N now represents a noncausal neighbor set. Equation 2 can be written in matrix vector format as

$$B(\underline{\theta})\underline{y} = \sqrt{\beta}\,\underline{\omega}$$

where $\underline{y}$ and $\underline{\omega}$ are M^2 by 1 vectors of $\{y(s)\}$ and $\{\omega(s)\}$, respectively, arranged in lexicographic order; $\underline{\theta} = \mathrm{col.}\,[\theta_r, r \in N]$; and $B(\underline{\theta})$ is the transformation matrix from ω to y. The estimates of parameters $\underline{\theta}$ and β can be obtained by using the ML method developed by Kashyap and Chellappa.[20] (This paper is reprinted in Chapter 1.) Let $\underline{\theta}^*$ and β^* denote these estimates. The residuals $\{\hat{\omega}(s)\}$ corresponding to the noncausal model may be obtained by

$$\underline{\hat{\omega}} = \frac{1}{\sqrt{\beta^*}} B(\underline{\theta}^*)\underline{y}$$

The image can be reconstructed as

$$\underline{y}^* = \sqrt{\beta^*} B^{-1}(\underline{\theta}^*)\underline{\hat{\omega}}$$

In the above two equations, $\underline{\theta}^*$ and β^* are the quantized parameters and $\{\hat{\omega}(s)\}$ is the residual set. Since we are, by assumption, using a noncausal model, the generation of $\underline{y}^*$ involves inverting an M^2 by M^2 matrix $B(\theta)$, which is not computationally attractive. However, by assuming some special boundary conditions, one can generate $\underline{y}^*$ more efficiently; specifically, the toroidal lattice representation enables the generation of $\underline{y}^*$ by using a two-dimensional FFT. Other efficient solutions are possible using other finite lattice representations.[12] Chellappa, Chatterjee, and Bagdazian[21] present some work regarding the use of noncausal MRF models for texture coding. In addition to transform compression, predictive compression, and a combination thereof (often referred as "hybrid compression"[22-25]), several novel image-compression schemes have been considered in the literature. Two examples are given below.

(1) Modestino, Bhaskaran, and Anderson[26] describe a robust tree encoding procedure that uses the class of cellular stochastic models described in a paper by Modestino, Fries, and Vickers.[27] (This paper is reprinted in Chapter 1.) The tree coding scheme is less sensitive to channel errors and produces images of less distortion than classical DPCM schemes.[18]

(2) Delp and Mitchell[28] developed a block truncation coding (BTC) scheme. In this scheme, the given image is divided into 4 by 4 blocks, each of which is coded independently. Each block is represented by its quantized representations of the sample mean, the standard deviation, and a 4 by 4 array of zeros and ones. The array of zeros and ones indicates whether pixels are below or above the threshold of a one-bit, moment-preserving, nonparametric quantizer. Several modifications of this basic BTC scheme — with higher compression factors — are also discussed.

As of now, the basic ideas behind image data compression are well understood. Still, significant work remains to be done in designing compression methods with very high compression factors (compression factor > 30) that also produce high-quality images for video coding and coding of multisource information. In order to cover the mature, as well as the novel, ideas that have evolved in the field of image data compression, I decided to reprint in this chapter a number of survey papers, along with several examples of papers presenting novel ideas. While deciding on the papers to be included, I made a conscious attempt to avoid significant overlapping with the text by Netravali and Prasada on visual communication systems.[29]

The first paper reprinted in this chapter is an excellent survey paper by Jain. In this paper, standard image-compression schemes — such as DPCM, predictive coding, transform coding, hybrid coding, interframe coding, and adaptive coding — are reviewed in detail. Effects of channel errors are discussed. This award-winning paper is noted for its extensive bibliography.

The methods reviewed in Jain's paper are quite good for obtaining a compression factor of about 10. For achieving a higher compression — say in excess of 30 — a different approach is needed. Methods that give very high compression, with tolerable image quality, are discussed in the next reprinted paper, a survey paper by Kunt, Ikonomopoulos, and Kocher. These methods — referred to as "second-generation methods" — can be classified into two groups:

• Methods using local operators and
• Methods using contour-texture operators.

Four methods (two from each of the above groups) are discussed in detail in the paper by Kunt, Ikonomopoulos, and Kocher. First, the authors review briefly the first-generation coding methods described in the reprinted paper by Jain and in another paper, by Netravali and Limb;[30] then, they give an excellent summary of vision mechanisms. Needless to say, the topic of vision mechanisms — often overlooked in image-compression literature — is very important, since it is the human eye that evaluates the quality of the reconstructed image.

Methods using local operators are discussed by Kunt, Ikonomopoulos, and Kocher; these methods include the pyramidal coding scheme and the anisotropic nonstationary predictive coding method of Wilson, Knutsson, and Granlund.[31]

In contrast to local-operator-based methods, methods using contour-texture operators segment the image into textured regions surrounded by contours. Contours and texture information are then coded separately. Region-growing[32] or edge-detection[33] techniques are used to extract the contours. Specific details regarding the methods used for coding contours and textures may be found in the reprinted paper by Kunt, Ikonomopoulos, and Kocher and in the references therein. It is important to note that a compression factor of 70 is achievable using these methods.

In the next reprinted paper, by Kunt, Benard, and Leonardi, several improvements and advances to the second-generation coding methods described in the previous reprinted paper are discussed. Specific advances presented are directional decomposition and adaptive split-and-merge methods.

The next two reprinted papers — one by Gray and the other by Nasrabadi and King — are important survey papers on vector quantization, an active research topic in speech and image compression. Prior to 1980, almost all image-compression systems employed scalar quantization techniques (such as the one reported on by Max[1]) — or variations of these techniques — to code the transform coefficients or residuals that arise in DPCM schemes. In 1980, the idea of scalar quantization was generalized to vector quantization where a sequence of vectors are coded. The vectors could be from consecutive samples of a speech wave form or they could be from consecutive rows or parts of rows in an image-compression system. Results from information theory support the usefulness of vector quantization in achieving better compression factors. The paper by Gray is an authoritative, lucid exposition of basic concepts behind the design of vector quantizers (VQs), with applications to speech and image coding. The paper by Nasrabadi and King is a more specialized review of vector quantization for image coding.

Burt and Adelson[34] describe a novel image-compression scheme that uses images of different resolutions of the given image. Let $\{y_0(s), s \varepsilon \Omega_0\}$ be the given image, represented as the base (or zero level) of a pyramid. Then, the first level of the pyramid contains a low pass filtered version of $\{y_0(s)\}$ — denoted as $\{y_1(s), s\varepsilon\Omega_1\}$ — where Ω_1 is a lattice smaller than Ω_0. Each pixel in Ω_1 is a weighted average of pixels in a 5 by 5 neighborhood of Ω_0. This process is repeated until a pyramid of a certain height is constructed. In this construction, the images at successively higher levels of the pyramid correspond to lower-resolutions copies of the original image $\{y_0(s)\}$. A sequence of difference images is then constructed, using $L_i(y_i(s) - y_{i+1}(s))$, where — before the subtraction is done — the pixel values in Ω_{i+1} are interpolated down to Ω_i. The two important properties of the difference images $\{L_i(s)\}$ are that they are less correlated in comparison with the sequences of images $\{y(s)\}$ and that

$$y_0(s) = \sum_{i=0}^{N} L_i(s)$$

where N denotes the number of levels of the pyramid. The advantages of the Laplacian pyramid code are:

(1) The Laplacian code is very similar to image representation in the human visual system;
(2) The difference images at different levels can be quantized using a different number of bits, which gives more flexibility in the assignment of bits; and
(3) The Laplacian code tends to enhance salient image features.

Laplacian pyramid coding is generalized substantially in the next reprinted paper, by Woods and O'Neil. The authors generalize the technique known as "subband coding" of speech to images.[35] The basic principle behind subband coding is to divide the frequency band of the signal and then to code each subband using compression techniques outlined in the paper by Jain reprinted in this chapter. The advantages of dividing up the frequency into subbands are that coding errors can be confined within subbands and that variable bit assignments for the different subbands are possible.

Woods and O'Neil present a set of quadrature mirror filters (QMFs) for a specific frequency-domain partition. The subbands obtained after quadrature mirror filtering are coded using the DPCM technique. Optimal quantization is achieved using the Laplacian distribution for the residuals. Assignment of bits between subbands is also optimized to obtain the minimum mean-squared error in total reconstruction. Simulation results show that compression factors higher than 10 can be achieved easily, with good reconstruction. An adaptive subcoding scheme in which bits within a subband are assigned depending on whether a given block is in busy, nonbusy, or quiet categories is presented, with supporting simulation results. This paper by Woods and O'Neil is well cited in the image-compression literature.

The next reprinted paper, by Wang and Goldberg, discusses an example of a hybrid method where two or more popular techniques are combined to see if the resulting method captures the best of constituent techniques. In the mid-1970s, several hybrid techniques that effectively combined predictive and transform compression methods were proposed.[22-24] Similarly, Wang and Goldberg combine the pyramidal compression scheme and vector quantization to arrive at a hybrid method for progressive transmission. The pyramid image is first produced by computing the truncated mean over 2 by 2 blocks. Then, a new difference pyramid — created by computing the difference between the pixels in one level and in the level below in the original pyramid — is coded using vector quantization. The scheme is very similar in spirit to the Laplacian pyramid compression scheme presented in the paper by Burt and Adelson.[34]

One restrictive assumption made in most transform and predictive coding techniques is that the image is stationary, which is rarely true. Real images consist of lines and edges that constitute substantive nonstationarities in the image model. A practical solution to the difficult problem of handling nonstationarities in images is to make the coding technique adapt itself to the local variations in the signal statistics. Habibi[36] reviews several such adaptive transform and predictive coding techniques.

The next five reprinted papers deal with a topic of significant interest in image compression: compression of a sequence of images. Schemes using this type of compression are useful in point-to-point transmission of commercial television programs, satellite transmission, and video teleconferencing. One approach to this problem is to directly extend the techniques known for compression of two-dimensional still images. For instance, one can transform code blocks of images including the third dimension along a time axis and proceed as in the case of still images. Or one can predict the pixel in the current frame in terms of previously scanned pixels in the current and previous frames and then implement a DPCM compression technique. Roese, Pratt, and Robinson[37] and O'Neal[38] give examples of such transform and DPCM coding schemes. Since time-varying images usually consist of objects in motion, significant improvements can be obtained if object motion is taken into account, leading to motion-compensated coding schemes. For instance, if the displacement field of the image is known, better prediction of the current frame can be obtained by shifting and interpolating the parts of the previous frame. Thus, a motion-compensated predictive coder involves the estimation of object displacement, the use of these displacement estimates to obtain motion-compensated prediction, and the coding of the prediction error and information regarding displacement estimates. Displacement estimates can be obtained by using one of the several methods discussed by Huang and Tsai.[39]

Some of the pioneering work on image sequence coding is by Netravali and Robbins,[40] who discuss a motion-compensated predictive coding scheme, and by Netravali and Stuller,[41] who describe a motion-compensated transform coding scheme. One of the problems of the transform coding scheme for a sequence of images is the large amount of storage required. The paper by Netravali and Stuller discusses a hybrid transform DPCM to partly overcome the storage problem. Healy and Mitchell extend the BTC technique[28] discussed earlier in this chapter to a sequence of satellite images by using motion detection for optimal bit assignments. An excellent summary of image sequence coding may be found in a paper by Dubois, Prasada, and Sabri.[43]

My main consideration in selecting papers as reprints in this chapter was to avoid significant overlapping with the collected works by Netravali and Prasada[29] — on visual communication systems — and by Chellappa and Sawchuk[44] — on digital image processing and analysis. (The latter is the earlier work that I coedited, which is referred to in the preface of this tutorial.) However, since tutorial papers always add breadth to a collected work, I decided to include in the five reprinted papers on image sequence coding an excellent paper by Musmann, Pirsch, and Grallert that was also reprinted in the text by Netravali and Prasada.[29] This paper gives a review of the advances made during the period from 1981 to 1985 in coding of image sequence. Motion compensation is an important component in achieving high-compression factors. This paper gives a lucid comparison of displacement-estimation algorithms. This comparison is followed by a survey of predictive and transform coding methods as they apply to broadcast-television and video-teleconferencing applications.

One of the standard methods used to reduce the bit rate in compressing an image sequence is skipping frames at the transmitter and interpolating the skipped frames at the receiver. Standard techniques, such as frame repetition and linear interpolation, cause undesirable side effects. In order to avoid these side effects — which include jerkily moving objects in the reconstructed picture and blurring in moving areas — motion-adaptive frame-interpolation techniques are being developed. A typical method would operate on the principle that pixels in the moving area will be reconstructed using a local average, while pixels in the nonmoving area will be replaced by corresponding pixels from the previous reconstructed frame. The reprinted paper by Musmann, Pirsch, and

Grallert concludes with a nice discussion of several motion-adaptive frame-interpolation methods.

The next reprinted paper, by Moorhead, Rajala, and Cook, discusses a pixel-recursive, motion-compensated technique, along with simulation results. First, the authors provide a rigorous analysis of convergence conditions of existing recursive algorithms for displacement estimation; then, they present a new technique known as "projection-along-the-motion-trajectory."

Conventional motion-compensated predictive and transform compression techniques divide the images into nonoverlapping blocks and code them independently. Such techniques will produce undesirable results when parts of a block do not have any portion of a moving object and thus get wrongly compensated. Such undesirable results can be avoided by coding objects rather than blocks.

The next reprinted paper, by Gilge, Engelhardt, and Mehlan, presents an object-oriented orthogonal transform coding method for the compression of still and video images. In this method, the extracted contours of objects are first coded and transmitted. The contents of each object are represented using a generalized orthogonal transform in which orthogonalization is performed by including only pixels inside the object. At first notice, it may appear that one has to code and transmit the shape-specific transform coefficients for each object, resulting in a significant reduction in compression factor. However, because the computation of transform coefficients that define the contents of the object (the interior) can be done at the receiver using the reconstructed contour elements, reasonable compression factors can be achieved. Also discussed in this paper are progressive transmission, segmentation methods for video coding, and details regarding quantization. The coding rate reported in this paper is less than the 64 kilobits per second reported in the next two reprinted papers. The use of several improvements that are suggested at the end of the paper may help this rate to be achieved.

The next reprinted paper, by Musmann, Hötter, and Ostermann, presents an interesting scheme in which the image is also coded using object motion, shape, and color information. Object motion is represented using pure parameters[45] extracted from two frames at a time. The extracted pure parameters are coded by DPCM techniques using stored parameters from the previous image. Object shape is represented using contours, but only the differences in the boundaries are coded. Color information is coded using a hybrid scheme that combines motion-compensation prediction and interframe coding techniques. The authors also present extensions of their techniques to three-dimensional objects. An interesting feature of their work is that no explicit object-recognition tasks are involved. By synthesizing an image from previously coded information, one can obtain the required information about objects. The paper presents experimental investigations by means of simulation at a transmission rate of 64 kilobits per second.

The final reprinted paper on image sequence coding, by Strobach, presents interesting quadtree-based methods. Arguing that the motion-compensated prediction error image has mostly line, boundary-like structures, the author uses a quadtree-based, structured DPCM technique that produces very good results at a rate of 64 kilobits per second. An added attraction of the proposed method is the simplicity of the quadtree-based method.

Most of the image-compression techniques using transform and predictive model-based approaches are concerned with the problem of efficient image representation and coding of transformed information. These techniques work rather well in the absence of channel errors. Global transform-based methods have better performance in the presence of channel errors than random field model-based predictive methods; however, the performance of both of these methods can be drastically affected in the presence of significant channel errors or recording errors. To overcome this drawback, it is better to view image data compression as a joint source/channel coding problem. Because such an approach may increase the required bandwidth, it should be applied carefully. The next two reprinted papers, by Modestino, Daut, and Vickers and by Vaishampayan and Farvardin, discuss methods for combined source/channel coding of images that are applicable to the two-dimensional DCT-based compression technique.

We have thus far considered techniques that are useful for compression of gray-tone images. In applications such as the transmission or storage of geographical maps, weather maps, fingerprint cards, and newspaper pages, the images of interest are normally two tone. Huang[46] reviews relevant concepts and techniques of efficient coding for storage and transmission of two-tone images. Huang discusses the digitization of two-tone images and then discusses in detail heuristic and mathematical schemes for efficient coding.

Although the mean-square error is used as a criterion for measuring the quality of image reconstruction, it is not general enough: This criterion completely ignores the psychovisual properties of the human vision system. Clearly, because images are viewed and evaluated by human observers, a realistic image-coding technique should incorporate characteristics that are peculiar to the human visual system. The main reason for lack of activity in this research area is perhaps the complexity of visual models and the interdisciplinary nature of the field.

Sakrison[47] surveys characteristics of the human visual system and its sensitivity to coding errors for still, monochromatic images. Several ways of determining the response of the human observer are discussed, and a "model" for the human observer is derived by using a set of psychophysical experiments. Sakrison shows how this model can be used to derive a distortion measure that could be the basis for optimal coding schemes. Note that the optimal Max quantizer uses the mean-square error, a performance criterion that does not truly reflect the properties of the human visual systems. Sharma and Netravali[48] designed a quantizer that minimizes a weighted mean-square error in which weights are derived on the basis of subjective tests. The incorporation of complete human visual properties into the design of image-compression techniques should prove to be a challenging research area for the future.

Chapter 4 References

1. J. Max, "Quantizing for Minimum Distortion," *IEEE Trans. Information Theory*, Vol. IT-6, Mar. 1960, pp. 7-12.
2. E.J. Delp, *Moment Preserving Quantization and Its Application in Block Truncation Coding*, doctoral thesis, School of Electrical Engineering, Purdue Univ., W. Lafayette, Ind., Aug. 1979.
3. F. Kretz, "Subjectively Optimal Quantization of Pictures," *IEEE Trans. Communications*, Vol. COM-23, Nov. 1975, pp. 1288-1292.
4. A.K. Jain and W.K. Pratt, "Color Image Quantization," presented at National Telecommunication Conf., Houston, Texas, Dec. 1972.
5. J.L. Mannos and D.J. Sakrison, "The Effects of a Visual Fidelity Criterion on the Encoding of Images," *IEEE Trans. Information Theory*, Vol. IT-20, July 1974, pp. 525-536.
6. V.R. Algazi, "The Psycho-Physics of Vision and Their Relation to Picture Quality and Coding Limitation," *Acta Eletron.*, Vol. 19, 1976, pp. 25-232.
7. A. Rosenfeld and A.C. Kak, *Digital Picture Processing*, Vol. 1, Chapter 5, Academic Press, Inc., Orlando, Fla., 1982.
8. N.C. Giri, *Multivariate Statistical Inference*, Chapter 10, Academic Press, Inc., Orlando, Fla., 1977.
9. P.A. Wintz, "Transform Picture Coding," *Proc. IEEE*, Vol. 60, July 1972, pp. 809-820.
10. H.C. Andrews and W.K. Pratt, "Fourier Transform Coding of Images," *Proc. Hawaii Int'l Conf. System Sciences*, Jan. 1968, pp. 677-679.
11. N. Ahmed, T. Natarajan, and K.R. Rao, "Discrete Cosine Transform," *IEEE Trans. Computers*, Vol. C-23, Jan. 1974, pp. 90-93.
12. A.K. Jain, "A Sinusoidal Family of Unitary Transforms," *IEEE Trans. Pattern Analysis and Machine Intelligence*, Vol. PAMI-1, Oct. 1979, pp. 356-365.
13. L.H. Koopmans, *The Spectral Analysis of Time Ser.*, Academic Press, Inc., Orlando, Fla., 1973.
14. A.K. Jain, "A Fast Karhunen-Loeve Transform for a Class of Random Processes," *IEEE Trans. Communications*, Vol. COM-24, Sept. 1976, pp. 1023-1029.
15. R. Chellappa and R. Bagdazian, "Fourier Coding of Image Boundaries," *IEEE Trans. Pattern Analysis and Machine Intelligence*, Vol. PAMI-6, Jan. 1984, pp. 102-105.
16. H.C. Andrews and C.L. Patterson, "Singular Value Decomposition (SVD) Image Coding," *IEEE Trans. Communications*, Vol. COM-24, Apr. 1976, pp. 425-432.
17. E.J. Delp, R.L. Kashyap, and O.R. Mitchell, "Image Data Compression Using Autoregressive Time Series Models," *Pattern Recognition*, Vol. 11, 1979, pp. 313-323.
18. P.A. Maragos, R.W. Schafer, and R.M. Mersereau, "Two-Dimensional Linear Prediction and Its Application to Adaptive Predictive Coding of Images," *IEEE Trans. Acoustics, Speech, and Signal Processing*, Vol. ASSP-32, Dec. 1984, pp. 1213-1229.
19. D.G. Daut, R.W. Fries, and J.W. Modestino, "Two-Dimensional DPCM Image Coding Based on an Assumed Stochastic Image Model," *IEEE Trans. Communications*, Vol. COM-29, Sept. 1981, pp. 1365-1379.
20. R.L. Kashyap and R. Chellappa, "Estimation and Choice of Neighbors in Spatial-Interaction Models of Images," *IEEE Trans. Information Theory*, Vol. IT-29, Jan. 1983, pp. 60-72.
21. R. Chellappa, S. Chatterjee, and R. Bagdazian, "Texture Synthesis and Coding Using Gaussian Markov Random Field Models," *IEEE Trans. Systems, Man, and Cybernetics*, Vol. SMC-15, Mar./Apr., 1985, pp. 298–303.
22. A. Habibi, "Hybrid Coding of Pictorial Data," *IEEE Trans. Communications*, Vol. COM-22, May 1974, pp. 614-626.
23. A.K. Jain and S.H. Wang, "Stochastic Image Models and Hybrid Coding," Tech. Report #SIPL-79-6, Univ. of California, Davis, Calif., Sept. 1979.
24. J.A. Roese, W.K. Pratt, and G.S. Robinson, "Interframe Cosine Transform Image Coding," *IEEE Trans. Communications*, Vol. COM-25, Nov. 1977, pp. 1329-1338.
25. J.R. Jain and A.K. Jain, "Displacement Measurement and Its Application in Interframe Image Coding," *IEEE Trans. Communications*, Vol. COM-29, Dec. 1981, pp. 1799-1808.
26. J.W. Modestino, V. Bhaskaran, and J.B. Anderson, "Tree Encoding of Images in the Presence of Channel Errors," *IEEE Trans. Information Theory*, Vol. IT-27, Nov. 1981, pp. 677-697.
27. J.W. Modestino, R.W. Fries, and A.L. Vickers, "Stochastic Image Models Generated by Random Tessellations of the Plane," *Computer Graphics and Image Processing*, Jan. 1980, pp. 74-98.
28. E.J. Delp and O.R. Mitchell, "Block Truncation Coding," *IEEE Trans. Communications*, Vol. COM-27, Sept. 1979, pp. 1335-1342.
29. A.N. Netravali and B. Prasada, *Visual Communication Systems*, IEEE Press, New York, N.Y., 1989.
30. A.N. Netravali and J.O. Limb, "Picture Coding: A Review," *Proc. IEEE*, Vol. 68, Mar. 1980, pp. 366-406.
31. R. Wilson, H.E. Knutsson, and G.H. Granlund, "Anisotropic Nonstationary Image Estimation and Its Applications: Part II - Predictive Image Coding," *IEEE Trans. Communications*, Vol. COM-31, Mar. 1983, pp. 398-406.
32. M. Kocher and M. Kunt, "Image Data Compression by Contour-Texture Modelling," *Proc. SPIE Int'l Conf. Applications of Digital Image Processing*, Geneva, 1987, pp. 131-139.
33. A. Ikonomopoulos and M. Kunt, "High Compression Image Coding via Directional Filtering," *Signal Processing*, Vol. 8, Apr. 1981, pp. 179-203.

34. P.J. Burt and E.H. Adelson, "The Laplacian Pyramid as a Compact Image Code," *IEEE Trans. Communications*, Vol. COM-31, Apr. 1983, pp. 532-540.
35. R.E. Crochiere, S.A. Webber, and J.L. Flanagan, "Digital Coding of Speech in Subbands," *Bell Systems Tech. J.*, Vol. 55, Oct. 1976, pp. 1069-1085.
36. A. Habibi, "A Survey of Adaptive Image Coding Techniques," *IEEE Trans. Communications*, Vol. COM-25, Nov. 1977, pp. 1275-1284.
37. J.A. Roese, W.K. Pratt, and G.S. Robinson, "Interframe Cosine Transform Image Coding," *IEEE Trans. Communications*, Vol. COM-25, Nov. 1977, pp. 1329-1339.
38. J.B. O'Neal, "Predictive Quantizing Systems (Differential Pulse Code Modulation) for the Transmission of Television Signals," *Bell Systems Tech. J.*, Vol. 45, May-June 1966, pp. 689-721.
39. T.S. Huang and R.Y. Tsai, "Image Sequences Analysis: Motion Estimation in Image Sequence Analysis," T.S. Huang, ed., Vol. 5, *Springer Ser. Information Sciences*, Springer-Verlag, New York, N.Y. 1981.
40. A.N. Netravali and J.D. Robbins, "Motion-Compensated Television Coding - Part I," *Bell Systems Tech. J.*, Vol. 58, Mar. 1979, pp. 631-670.
41. A.N. Netravali and J.A. Stuller, "Motion-Compensated Transform Coding," *Bell Systems Tech. J.*, Vol. 58, Sept. 1979, pp. 1703-1718.
42. D.J. Healy and O.R. Mitchell, "Digital Video Bandwidth Compression Using Block Truncation Coding," *IEEE Trans. Communications*, Vol. COM-29, Dec. 1981, pp. 1809-1817.
43. E. Dubois, B. Prasada, and M.S. Sabri, "Image Sequence Coding in Image Sequence Analysis," T.S. Huang, ed., *Springer Ser. in Information Sciences*, Springer-Verlag, New York, N.Y., 1981.
44. R. Chellappa and A.A. Sawchuk, *Digital Image Processing and Analysis: Vol. 1: Digital Image Processing,* IEEE CS Press, Los Alamitos, Calif., 1985.
45. R.Y. Tsai and T.S. Huang, "Estimating Three-Dimensional Motion Parameters of a Rigid Planar Patch," *IEEE Trans. Acoustics, Speech, and Signal Processing*, Vol. ASSP-29, Dec. 1981, pp. 1147-1152.
46. T.S. Huang, "Coding of Two-Tone Images," *IEEE Trans. Communications*, Vol. COM-25, Nov. 1977, pp. 1406-1424.
47. D.J. Sakrison, "On the Role of the Observer and a Distortion Measure in Image Transmission," *IEEE Trans. Communications*, Vol. COM-25, Nov. 1977, pp. 1251-1267.
48. D.K. Sharma and A.N. Netravali, "Design of Quantizers for DPCM Coding of Picture Signals," *IEEE Trans. Communications*, Vol. COM-25, Nov. 1977, pp. 1267-1274.

Image Data Compression: A Review

ANIL K. JAIN, MEMBER, IEEE

Invited Paper

Abstract—With the continuing growth of modern communications technology, demand for image transmission and storage is increasing rapidly. Advances in computer technology for mass storage and digital processing have paved the way for implementing advanced data compression techniques to improve the efficiency of transmission and storage of images. In this paper a large variety of algorithms for image data compression are considered. Starting with simple techniques of sampling and pulse code modulation (PCM), state of the art algorithms for two-dimensional data transmission are reviewed. Topics covered include differential PCM (DPCM) and predictive coding, transform coding, hybrid coding, interframe coding, adaptive techniques, and applications. Effects of channel errors and other miscellaneous related topics are also considered. While most of the examples and image models have been specialized for visual images, the techniques discussed here could be easily adapted more generally for multidimensional data compression. Our emphasis here is on fundamentals of the various techniques. A comprehensive bibliography with comments is included for a reader interested in further details of the theoretical and experimental results discussed here.

I. INTRODUCTION

IMAGE DATA compression is concerned with minimization of the number of information carrying units used to represent an image. Perhaps the simplest and most dramatic form of data compression is the sampling of the band-limited images where an infinite number of image points per unit sampling area is reduced to a single image sample without any loss of information (assuming an ideal low-pass filter is available). Consequently, the number of samples per unit area is infinitely reduced! In digital image processing, each image sample, also called a *pel*, is quantized to a fixed but sufficient number of bits, and then the image is stored (or transmitted) digitally. The usefulness of data compression arises in storage and transmission of images, where the aim is to minimize the memory for storage and bandwidth for transmission. Typically, a compressed image when decoded to reconstruct its original form will be accompanied by some distortion. The efficiency of a compression algorithm is measured by its data compressing ability, the resulting distortion and as well by its implementation complexity. The complexity of data compression algorithms is a particularly important consideration in their hardware implementation.

A. Image Raw Data Rates

Typical television images have spatial resolution of approximately 512 × 512 pels per frame. At 8-bit/pel intensity resolution and 30 frames/s this translates into a rate of nearly 60×10^6 bit/s. Depending on the application digital image raw data rates typically vary from 10^5 bit/frame to 10^8 bit/frame or 10^6 bit/s to 10^9 bit/s or higher. The large memory and/or channel capacity requirements for digital image transmission and storage make it mandatory to consider data compression techniques.

B. Data Compression versus Bandwidth Compression

The mere process of converting an analog video signal into a digital signal results in increased bandwidth requirements for transmission. For example, a 4-MHz television signal sampled at Nyquist rate with 8 bit/sample would require a bandwidth of 32 MHz when transmitted using a digital modulation scheme, such as phase-shift keying (PSK) which requires 1 Hz per 2 bits. Thus, while digitized information has advantages over its analog form in terms of processing flexibility, easy or random access in storage, higher signal-to-noise ratio (SNR), possibility of errorless transmission, etc., one has to pay the price in terms of this eight-fold increase in bandwidth. Data compression techniques seek to minimize this cost and on occasion use the processing flexibility to reduce the bandwidth of the digital signal below its analog bandwidth requirements.

Applications of data compression are primarily in transmission and storage of information. For transmission, compression techniques are greatly constrained by real time and on-line considerations which tend to limit severely the size and complexity of the hardware. For storage applications, "compressor" requirements are less stringent because much of the preprocessing can be done off line. However, the decoding or decompression (or retrieval) should be quick and efficient to minimize the turn around or response time. Image transmission applications are in broadcast television, remote sensing via satellite, aircraft, radar, sonar, teleconferencing, computer communications, facsimile transmission, etc. Image storage is required most commonly for educational and business documents, medical images used in patient monitoring systems, etc. Because of their wide application, data compression and coding schemes have been of great importance in digital image processing [1]–[10], [209]. Application of data compression is also possible in the development of fast algorithms where the number of operations required to implement an algorithm is reduced by working with the compressed data.

Image data compression methods can be classified in two basically different categories. In the first category are those methods which exploit *redundancy* in the data. Redundancy is a characteristic which is related to *predictability*, *randomness*, *smoothness*, etc., in the data. For example, an image

---

Manuscript received March 26, 1980; revised October 20, 1980. This work was supported by the Army Research Office, Durham, under Grant DAAG29-78-G-0206.

The author is with the Signal and Image Processing Laboratory, Department of Electrical and Computer Engineering, University of California, Davis, CA 95616.

of constant gray levels is fully predictable once the gray level of the first pel is known. On the other hand, a white-noise random field is totally unpredictable and every pel has to be stored to reproduce the image. Thus many data compression algorithms attempt to represent a given sampled image array $\{u_{i,j}\}$, by another array $\{\epsilon_{i,j}\}$, which has no redundancy, and such that $\{u_{i,j}\}$ can be determined uniquely from $\{\epsilon_{i,j}\}$. The raw data rate of $\{\epsilon_{i,j}\}$ then determines the data rate of $\{u_{i,j}\}$. Often, such a process results in some compression but with an accompanying distortion in the reproduced array $\{u_{i,j}\}$. Efficient compression techniques tend to minimize this distortion. Techniques such as *differential pulse code modulation* (DPCM) and other *predictive coding* methods fall in this category when the field $\{\epsilon_{i,j}\}$ is determined "causally" from $\{u_{i,j}\}$, where causality is imposed by the scanning mechanism of the image.

In the second category, compression is achieved by an energy preserving transformation of the given image into another array such that maximum information is *packed* into a minimum number of samples. Such techniques are labeled "*transform coding*" and are related to noncausal representations [11] of signals. Other image data compression algorithms exist which use a combination of these two methods.

C. Information Rates

Raw image data rates do not necessarily represent information rates. For example, monochrome images, are quantized typically to 8 bits giving the data rate of 8 bit/pel. Whereas, the average information rate is given by the entropy (measured in bits)

$$H(u) = -\sum_{i=1}^{L} p_i \log_2 p_i \qquad (1)$$

where p_i is the probability that a quantized sample u takes the value r_i, say, from a set of $L = 2^n$, ($n = 8$ here) values. This is called the zeroth-order entropy since no consideration is given to the fact that a given sample may have statistical dependence on its neighbors. For monochrome images the zeroth-order entropy is generally around 4-6 bits. The first-order entropy is defined as

$$H(u_k | u_{k-1}) = -\sum_{i_1=1}^{L} \sum_{i_2=1}^{L} P_{i_1, i_2} \log_2 (P_{i_1, i_2} / P_{i_2}) \qquad (2)$$

where $P_{i_1, i_2} = \text{Prob}[u_k = r_{i_1}, u_{k-1} = r_{i_2}]$; u_{k-1} is a pel "previous" to u_k and P_{i_1}, P_{i_2} are the marginal probabilities of u_k and u_{k-1}, respectively. This is considered as the average information content of u_k if the state of u_{k-1} is known. Second and higher order entropies can be defined similarly. For six-bit raw image data, Schreiber [12] has estimated the zeroth-, first- and second-order entropies to be 4.4, 1.9, and 1.5 bit/pel, respectively.

Since according to Shannon's *noiseless coding theorem* [13]-[16], it is possible to code without distortion, a source of entropy H bit/sample using $H + \epsilon$ bit/sample where ϵ is an arbitrarily small positive quantity, the maximum achievable compression C, defined by

$$C = \frac{\text{Average bit rate of the original raw data}}{\text{Average bit rate of the encoded data}} = \frac{n}{n_a}$$

is $n/(H + \epsilon) \simeq n/H$. Computation of such a compression ratio for images is impractical if not impossible. For example an $N \times M$ digital image with n bit/pel is one of $L = 2^{nNM}$ possible image patterns that could occur. Thus, if p_i, the probability of the ith image pattern were known, one could compute the entropy, i.e., the information rate for n bit/pel $N \times M$ images. Then, one could store all the L possible image patterns and encode the image by its address—using an entropy coding scheme. However, even for relatively small N and M, L is prohibitively large; e.g.,[1] for $n = 8$ and $N = M = 16$, $L = 2^{2048} \simeq 10^{614}$. Although it is physically impractical to measure p_i, it is believed that the entropy of such an ensemble of images is likely to be very low since only a few of the L images are likely to occur often.

D. Fidelity Measures

Techniques commonly employed for image data compression result in some degradation of the reconstructed image. A widely used measure of reconstructed image fidelity for an $N \times M$ size image is the average mean-square error defined as

$$e_{ms}^2 = \frac{1}{NM} \sum_{i=1}^{N} \sum_{j=1}^{M} E(u_{i,j} - u_{i,j}^*)^2 \qquad (3a)$$

where $\{u_{i,j}\}$ and $\{u_{i,j}^*\}$ represent the $N \times M$ original and the reproduced images, respectively. Experimentally, the average mean-square error is often estimated by the average sample mean-square error in the given image defined by

$$e_{ms}^2 \simeq \frac{1}{NM} \sum_{i=1}^{N} \sum_{j=1}^{N} (u_{i,j} - u_{i,j}^*)^2. \qquad (3b)$$

There are two definitions of SNR that are used corresponding to the above error. These are defined as

$$\text{SNR} = 10 \log_{10} \frac{(\text{Peak to peak value of the original image data})^2}{e_{ms}^2} \quad (\text{dB}) \qquad (4)$$

$$\text{SNR}' = 10 \log_{10} \frac{\sigma_u^2}{e_{ms}^2} \quad (\text{dB}) \qquad (5)$$

where σ_u^2 is the variance of the original image.

Although SNR' is more widely used as a measure of SNR in the signal processing literature (since it is related to the signal power and noise power), and is perhaps more meaningful because it gives 0 dB for equal signal and noise power, SNR is used more commonly in the image coding field. Often, the original image raw data is given as discrete samples quantized to a relatively large number of gray levels. Typically, the number of levels is 256 (or 8 bits) so that the peak to peak value is 255. Hence (4) becomes

$$\text{SNR} = 10 \log_{10} \frac{(255)^2}{e_{ms}^2}.$$

The mean-square error criterion of (3a) may not always be desirable especially when one is dealing with images which have to be evaluated visually [17]-[21]. This is because the mean-square error is not an especially accurate measure of visual fidelity. Several visual fidelity measures for images

---

[1] The number of molecules in a gallon of water, by comparison, is only 1.3×10^{26}.

have been recently suggested. In [17], [19], these measures evaluate a weighted mean-square error of contrast (rather than intensity, cf. Section II-E1), e.g.,

$$e = \iiiint |\epsilon(x', y') h(x - x', y - y')|^2 \, dx' \, dy' \, dx \, dy$$

$$\epsilon(x, y) = f(u(x, y) - u^*(x, y)) \tag{6}$$

where $u(x, y)$ is the image intensity field, $f(\cdot)$ is a nonlinear function and $h(x, y)$ is a two-dimensional weighting function. In terms of Fourier domain quantities $\mathcal{E}(\omega_1, \omega_2) = \mathcal{F}\{\epsilon(x, y)\}$ and $H(\omega_1, \omega_2) = \mathcal{F}\{h(x, y)\}$, (6) becomes

$$e = \iint |\mathcal{E}(\omega_1, \omega_2) H(\omega_1, \omega_2)|^2 \, d\omega_1 \, d\omega_2. \tag{7}$$

Mannos and Sakrison [17] have found the following definitions of $f(u)$ and H to be useful (at normal viewing distance)

$$f(u) = u^{1/3}$$

$$H(\omega_1, \omega_2) = H(\omega) = A\left[a + \left(\frac{\omega}{\omega_0}\right)^\alpha\right] \exp -\left\{\left(\frac{\omega}{\omega_0}\right)^\beta\right\}$$

$$\omega = (\omega_1^2 + \omega_2^2)^{1/2} \quad A = 2.6 \quad a = 0.0192$$

$$\omega_0 = 1/0.114 \quad \alpha = 1 \quad \beta = 1.1. \tag{8}$$

The criterion (7) suggests that for visual evaluation, the image contrast field ($u^{1/3}$) should be passed through a linear spatial filter whose transfer function is $H(\omega)$ defined in (8). Then the output of this filter represents the visual signal whose quality can be measured by the ordinary mean-square criterion. Measurements of $H(\omega)$ show that the human visual response to spatial frequencies in nonuniform and that the mid-spatial frequencies are emphasized more than the low- and high-spatial frequencies [18], [21], [22]. Other measures [20], [209] based on spatial domain characteristics such as "visibility" will be considered in Section III-F.

E. Subsampling, Coarse Quantization Frame Repetition, and Interlacing [23]-[26]

One obvious method of data compression would be to reduce the sampling rate, the number of quantization levels and the refresh rate (number of frames/s for motion images). While this would reduce the amount of data, the associated phenomena of aliasing, contouring, and flickering, respectively, would occur. The compression achieved for acceptable image fidelity by these methods is relatively small compared to more advanced methods available for data compression. For motion images, successive frames have to be refreshed at a rate above the so-called critical fusion frequency (CFF) to avoid a flickering appearance. For most observers this frequency is 50-60 pictures/s. Typically, to capture motion a refresh rate of 25-30 frames/s is generally sufficient. (This, of course, depends on the type of motion e.g., the speed of motion). Thus a compression of 2 to 1 could be achieved by transmitting (or storing) only 30 frames/s, but refreshing at 60 frames/s by repeating each frame [23], [24]. This, however, requires a frame storage and an image breakup [23] or jump effect (not flicker) is often observable. Note that the frame repetition rate is chosen at 60/s rather than, say 55/s, to avoid any interference with the line frequency of 60 Hz (in the U.S.).

Instead of frame repetition, line interlacing is found to give better visual rendition. Each frame is divided into an "odd field" containing the odd line addresses, and an "even field" containing the even line addresses and are transmitted alternately. However, each field is displayed for a duration of $2/n$ s if n is the refresh rate in frames/s. The storage requirement now is $\frac{1}{2}$ frame. Although the jump or image breakup effect is significantly reduced by line interlacing, spatial frequency resolution is somewhat degraded. An appropriate increase in the scan rate (i.e., lines per frame) with line interlacing gives an actual compression of about 37 percent for the same subjective quality as the 60 frames/s refresh rate without repetition [24]. Other interlacing techniques such as vertical line interlace or dot interlace (for higher compression) seem possible [25], [26] but are more objectionable to the viewer.

II. Image Quantization

Since most digital image data compression algorithms require a quantizer, it is helpful to begin with a review of some of the common quantization methods. Let u be a real scalar random variable with a continuous probability density function $p_u(x)$. For example, u could represent the contrast or brightness of an image pel and $p_u(x)$ could be represented by the image histogram. A quantizer maps the continuous variable u into a discrete variable u^* which belongs to a finite set $\{r_1, \cdots, r_L\}$ of real numbers. This mapping is generally a staircase function (Fig. 1) and the quantization rule is as follows.

Define $\{t_j, j = 1, \cdots, L + 1\}$ as a set of increasing *transition* or *decision levels*. If u lies in the interval $(t_j, t_{j+1}]$, then u is mapped to r_j, $j \in [1, L]$. The quantity r_j, called the reconstruction level, is the quantized value of u and also lies in the interval $(t_j, t_{j+1}]$. The quantizer design problem is to determine the optimum transition and reconstruction levels, given the probability density and an optimization criterion. Since the quantizer mapping is irreversible, the quantizer introduces distortion which any reasonable quantizer design must attempt to minimize. There are several quantizer designs available that offer various tradeoffs between simplicity and performance. Some of these are discussed in the sequel. Quantization of image samples for digital transmission is called pulse code modulation (PCM) (Fig. 2).

A. The Optimum Mean Square or Lloyd-Max Quantizer [27]-[28]

Here the criterion is to minimize the mean-square quantization error for a fixed number of quantization levels. This error is defined as

$$E = \int_{u_1}^{u_{L+1}} [x - u^*(x)]^2 \, p_u(x) \, dx = E[(u - u^*)^2]. \tag{9}$$

Minimization of this error gives the transition levels that lie half way between the reconstruction levels and gives reconstruction levels that lie at the center of mass of the density in the transition intervals. Mathematically, they are given by the solutions of the simultaneous nonlinear equations

$$t_k = (r_k + r_{k-1})/2 \tag{10}$$

$$r_k = \int_{t_k}^{t_{k+1}} x p_u(x) \, dx \bigg/ \int_{t_k}^{t_{k+1}} p_u(x) \, dx = E[u | u \in I_k] \tag{11}$$

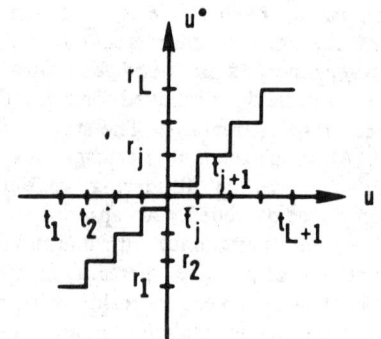

Fig. 1. Typical input-output characteristics of a quantizer.

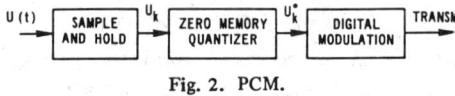

Fig. 2. PCM.

where I_k is the kth transition interval $(t_k, t_{k+1}]$. An estimate for the quantizer distortion is given by

$$E = \frac{1}{12L^2}\left[\int_{t_L}^{t_{L+1}} p^{1/3}(x)\,dx\right]^3. \quad (12)$$

This is a useful expression because it gives an estimate of the quantizer error directly in terms of the probability density and the number of quantization levels.

When u is uniformly distributed, the Lloyd-Max quantizer equations become linear, and yield

$$\left.\begin{array}{l} t_k = t_1 + (k-1)q \\ r_k \triangleq t_k + q/2 \\ q = (t_{L+1} - t_1)/L \end{array}\right\} \quad (13)$$

Thus all the transition as well as reconstruction levels are equally spaced. This quantizer is also called the *"linear quantizer."*

The minimum mean-square quantizer has two interesting properties.

1) The quantizer output is an unbiased estimate of the input, i.e.,

$$Eu^* = Eu. \quad (14)$$

2) The quantization error is orthogonal to the quantizer output, i.e.,

$$E(u - u^*)u^* = 0. \quad (15)$$

This relation[2] gives an interesting model for the quantizer as

$$u = u^* + \eta, \quad Eu\eta = E\eta^2 \quad (16)$$

where η denotes *quantizer noise* which is uncorrelated with the *quantizer output*. In Section VII, we will find this model useful in developing data compression techniques for transmission over noisy channels.

[2] This result is also of theoretical interest because it *does not* follow from the principle of orthogonality since u^* is not constrained to be a linear estimate of u. It does follow, however, from (11) and it implies that regardless of how the transition levels are chosen, the reconstruction level should be the conditional mean of $p_u(x)$ over the corresponding transition interval for the minimization of mean-square error.

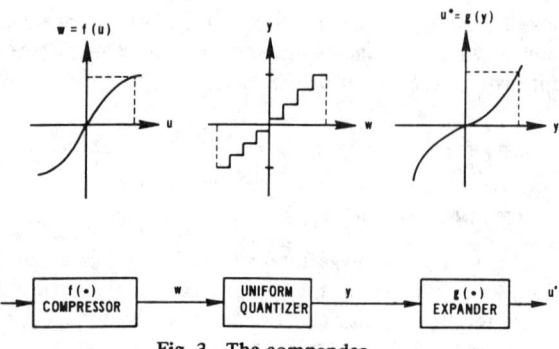

Fig. 3. The compander.

Often a nonuniform random variable is quantized by a uniform quantizer. Then the uniform quantizer which minimizes, with respect to q (the quantization step size), the mean-square error, is called the *optimum uniform quantizer*.

B. A Compander Design [28]-[31]

A compander (compressor-expander) is a uniform quantizer preceded and succeeded by nonlinear transformations as shown in Fig. 3. The random variable u is first passed through a nonlinear memoryless transformation $f(\cdot)$ to yield another random variable w. This random variable is uniformly quantized to give $y \in \{y_i\}$, which is nonlinearly transformed by $g(\cdot)$ to give the output u^*. The overall transformation from u to u^* is a nonuniform quantizer. The functions f and g are determined so that the overall system approximates the Lloyd-Max quantizer. The result is obtained as

$$g(x) = f^{-1}(x)$$

$$f(x) = -a + 2a\left[\int_{t_1}^{x} p_u^{1/3}(z)\,dz \middle/ \int_{t_1}^{t_{L+1}} p_u^{1/3}(z)\,dz\right] \quad (17)$$

for which $[-a, a]$ is the range of w over which the uniform quantizer operates.

As an example, consider the truncated Laplacian density which is used often as a probabilistic model of the prediction error signal in DPCM, i.e.,

$$p_u(x) = c e^{-\alpha|x|}, \quad -a \leq x \leq a \quad (18)$$

where $c = \alpha/2[1 - \exp(-\alpha a)]^{-1}$. Use of (17) gives

$$f(x) = \begin{cases} a\dfrac{[1 - \exp(-\alpha x/3)]}{[1 - \exp(-\alpha a/3)]}, & x \geq 0 \\ -f(-x), & x \leq 0 \end{cases} \quad (19)$$

$$g(x) = \begin{cases} -\dfrac{3}{\alpha}\ln\left[1 - \dfrac{x}{a}(1 - \exp(-\alpha a/3))\right], & 0 \leq x \leq a \\ -g(-x), & -a \leq x < 0. \end{cases} \quad (20)$$

It should be remarked that the transformed random variable $w = f(u)$ is not uniformly distributed in general.[3] Companders for more general criteria have been considered by Algazi [32].

[3] Hence, the uniform quantizer in the compander is (by design) not the Lloyd-Max quantizer for w.

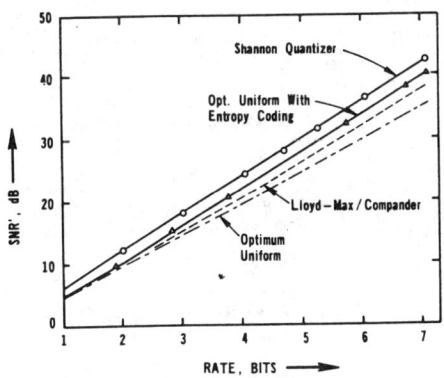

Fig. 4. SNR' versus rate for Gaussian density quantizers.

C. Comparisons

The Gaussian and the Laplacian densities are two commonly used models for quantization in image data compression algorithms. Comparison among various quantizers could be made in at least two different ways. First, suppose the quantizer output is to be coded by a fixed number of levels. This would be the case for a fixed word length analog to digital conversion. Then one would compare the quantizing error variance as a function of number of quantization bits n. Fig. 4 shows SNR' curves for the Lloyd-Max, the compander, and the optimum uniform quantizers for the Gaussian case. As expected, the Lloyd-Max quantizer gives the best performance. The performance difference between the Lloyd-Max (optimum nonuniform) and the optimum uniform quantizers is about 2 dB for $n = 6$. In the case of the Laplacian density this difference is about 4.3 dB. The performances of the compander and the Lloyd-Max quantizer are indistinguishable.

From rate distortion theory it is known [35] that block quantization of independent Gaussian samples of variance σ^2, could be achieved at an average bit rate

$$n = \frac{1}{2} \log_2 \frac{\sigma^2}{D} \quad (21)$$

as the block length approaches infinity (infinite dimensional quantizer), where $D < \sigma^2$, is the average mean-square distortion per sample. This can also be written as

$$D = \sigma^2 2^{-2n}, \quad n \geq 0 \quad (22)$$

and represents a lower bound on the attainable distortion of any finite length block quantizer for Gaussian random variables. This is also called the Shannon lower bound and the associated (hypothetical) optimal block encoder will be called the *Shannon quantizer*. The various quantizers in Fig. 4 are also compared with this quantizer. Equation (22) also gives an upper bound on attainable distortion by optimal block encoders for non-Gaussian random variables. Zero memory quantizers, also called one-dimensional quantizers (block length is one), for the same rate, generally do not attain distortion levels which are less than given by (22). The optimum one-dimensional quantizer for a uniform random variable of variance σ^2 attains this distortion, however. Thus, for any fixed distortion D, the rate of the Shannon quantizer may be considered to give the minimum achievable by a zero memory quantizer for most probability distributions of interest in coding of images. From Fig. 4 it can be seen that for the Gaussian distributions the zero memory optimum mean-square quantizer performs within about $\frac{1}{2}$ bit of its Shannon quantizer.

The second comparison is based on the entropy of the quantizer output versus its distortion. If the quantized variables are entropy coded by a variable length coding scheme such as Huffman coding, then the average number of bits needed to code them could be less than $\log_2 L$. An optimum quantizer under this criterion would be the one that minimizes the distortion for a specified output entropy [35]-[38]. Entropy coding would undoubtedly increase the complexity of the encoding-decoding algorithm and would require extra buffer storage at the transmitter and receiver to maintain a constant bit rate over the communication channel. From Fig. 4 it is seen that the uniform quantizer with entropy coding has a better performance than the Lloyd-Max quantizer (without entropy coding). It has been found that the uniform quantizer is quite a good approximation of the "optimum quantizer" based on entropy versus mean-square distortion criterion [33], [34], if the quantization step size is optimized with respect to this criterion. In fact, for uniform distributions the one-dimensional optimum mean-square quantizer performs within $\frac{1}{4}$ bit of its Shannon quantizer.

D. Quantization of Complex Gaussian Random Variables [39], [40]

In many situations (e.g., in radar and coherent imaging) one has to quantize complex random variables. Let $z = x + jy$ be a complex random variable, where x and y are independent Gaussian random variables each with zero mean and variance σ^2. One obvious way of quantization of x and y is via their Lloyd-Max quantizers. Now suppose it is desired to quantize the amplitude and phase variables, A and θ defined by

$$z = A \exp(j\theta), \quad A = \sqrt{x^2 + y^2}, \quad \theta = \tan^{-1}(y/x).$$

$$(23)$$

It is easy to show that when x and y are independent Gaussian random variables, A and θ are also independent where A has a Rayleigh density and θ is uniformly distributed. Let L_1 and L_2 be the number of quantization levels for A and θ, respectively, such that $L_1 L_2 = L$ = constant. Let $\{v_n\}$ and $\{w_n\}$ be, respectively, the decision and reconstruction levels of A, if it were quantized by its own Lloyd-Max quantizer (i.e., without regard to θ or z). Also, let $\{t_n\}$ and $\{r_n\}$ be the corresponding quantities for quantization of A such that the mean-square error of z is minimized (where θ is quantized uniformly). It has been shown [39], [40] that the transition and reconstruction levels of the optimum quantizer of z are related to the Lloyd-Max quantizer of A as follows:

$$\left. \begin{array}{l} t_n = v_n \\ r_n = w_n \dfrac{\sin \pi/L_2}{\pi/L_2} \end{array} \right\} \quad (24)$$

If L_2 is large, then $\sin \pi/L_2 / \pi/L_2 \to 1$ and the phase and amplitude can be quantized independently. For a given number of bits, the optimum allocation of L_1 and L_2 requires that for rates ≥ 4.6 bits, the phase should be allocated 1.37 bits more than the amplitude.

The performance of the amplitude-phase quantizer is found to be only marginally better than the independent quantization of x and y by their Lloyd-Max quantizers. However, the above results could be useful when one is required to quantize

A and θ, e.g., in radar and coherent imaging applications where amplitude and glint (or phase) measurements are made.

E. Visual Quantization [41]–[51]

The foregoing methods can be applied for gray scale quantization of monochrome images. The number of quantization levels or gray levels should be sufficient to suppress any contouring effects. Uniform quantization of typical images, where the pels represent the luminance function, requires about 64 gray levels or 6 bits. Contouring effects start becoming visible at or below 5 bit/pel. Mean-square quantizers matched to the histogram of a given image may need only 5 bit/pel to suppress the contouring effects.

In quantizing images which have to be visually processed (or examined) the eye seems to be quite sensitive to contours and errors which affect the local structure [41]. However, the contours do not contribute very much to the mean-square error. Thus a visual quantization scheme should attempt to hold the quantization contours below the level of visibility over the range of luminances to be displayed. We consider two methods for achieving this (other than allocating the full 6 bit/pel).

1) Contrast Quantization

The human visual system does not perceive equal changes in luminances equally. However, visual sensitivity is nearly uniform with respect to normalized, just noticeable, changes in luminance. That is, if L and $L + \Delta L$ are just noticeably different luminance, then

$$\frac{\Delta L}{L} \simeq \text{constant.} \quad (25)$$

This is called Weber's law [42]. Define

$$C = \log L \quad (26)$$

then $\Delta C \simeq \Delta L / L$ is nearly constant. This means visual sensitivity is nearly uniform to changes in C, which is called *contrast*. Several different nonlinear transformations have been suggested in the literature to represent contrast accurately. The common functions are

$$C = \begin{cases} \alpha \log(1 + \beta L), & L \in [0, 1] \quad (27) \\ \alpha L^\beta \quad (28) \end{cases}$$

where α and β are constants. For example, in (28) the values $\alpha = 1$, $\beta = \frac{1}{3}$ (see [17]), and in (27) the values $\alpha = \beta/\log(1 + \beta)$ and α lying between 6 and 18 have been suggested (Kretz [43]).

Once the contrast representation $f(\cdot)$ is known, one simply performs the optimum mean-square quantization of the contrast field (see Fig. 5). To display (or reconstruct) the image, the quantized contrast is transformed back to the luminance value by the inverse transformation $f^{-1}(\cdot)$. Experimental studies indicate that with four-bit quantization of contrast, the contouring effects can be greatly minimized [43].

2) Pseudorandom Noise Quantization

Another method for suppressing contouring effects is due to Roberts [44]. First we add a small amount of pseudorandom uniformly distributed noise to the luminance samples before quantization. This pseudorandom noise is also called *dither*. To display the image, the same (or another) pseudorandom sequence is subtracted from the quantizer output. The input noise causes some pels to go above the original

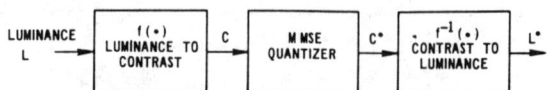

Fig. 5. Visual contrast quantizer.

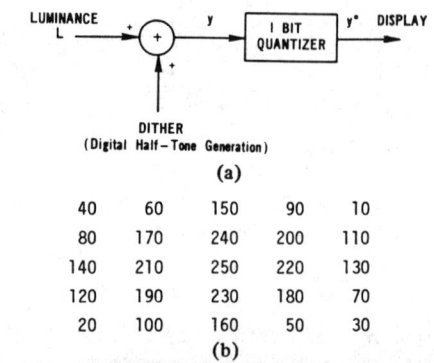

Fig. 6. Halftone image quantization. (a) Digital halftone generation. (b) A 5 × 5 halftone dither matrix. Repeat periodically over the image. (c) Clockwise, original 256 × 256 8 bit/pel image; 1 bit/pel quantization; 1 bit/pel halftone with dither; halftone negative 1/bit pel.

decision level and others below the decision level. Thus the average value of the quantized pels is about the same with and without the additive noise. During display, the noise tends to fill-in the regions of contours in such a way that the spatial average is unchanged. The amount of dither added should be kept small enough to maintain the spatial resolution but large enough to allow the luminance values to vary randomly about the quantizer decision levels. Usually, the noise should affect the least significant bit of the quantizer. Reasonable image quality is achievable by a 4- or 5-bit quantizer. For details and examples, see [44]–[49].

3) Halftone Image Quantization

The above method is closely related to the method of generating halftone images from gray level images. Halftone images are binary images which give a gray scale rendition. Examples are the common printed images (e.g., all the images printed in this paper are halftones). To each pel of the given image (often oversampled e.g., a 256 × 256 image may be printed on a 1024 × 1024 grid of black and white dots) is added a random number (dither sample) and the resulting signal is quantized by a one bit quantizer. The output (0 or 1) represents a black or white dot. In practice the dither signal is a finite two-dimensional pseudorandom pattern of thresholds (e.g., a 5 × 5 dither matrix) [50], [51] which is repeated periodically over the image (Figs. 6(a) and 6(b)). The halftone image may exhibit moire patterns if the image and the dither matrix have similar periodicities. Good halftoning algorithms are designed to minimize the Moire effect. Fig. 6(c) shows a 256 × 256 one-bit halftone generated digitally from the original 256 × 256 × 8-bit image. Compared to a one-bit quantized image, the one-bit halftone has a much better visual rendition. The gray level rendition in halftones is due to local spatial averaging performed by the eye.

4) Color Quantization [52]

Perceptual considerations become even more important in quantization of color signals. A pel of a color image could be considered as a three-dimensional vector C, its elements C_1, C_2, C_3 representing the three color primaries. The color gamut (i.e., the set of all perceived colors) is a highly irregular solid in the three-dimensional space. Quantization of a color image requires allocating quantization cells to colors in the color gamut. Moreover, the quantization cells will be unequal in size because equal changes in color coordinates do not, in general, result in equal changes in color perception. In the NTSC (national television systems committee, which has specified U.S. television standards) color coordinate system, the reproducible color gamut is the cube $[0, 1] \times [0, 1] \times [0, 1]$. It has been shown that uniform quantization of each color coordinate in this system provides the best results (based on a color perception measure) as compared to uniform quantization in several other coordinate systems. For more on color image coding see Limb *et al.* [53].

III. PREDICTIVE TECHNIQUES FOR IMAGE DATA COMPRESSION

A. Predictive Quantization

In the previous section we considered zero memory quantization of scalar random variables, i.e., the successive inputs to a quantizer were treated independently. Often, the available data sequence has statistical dependency or redundancy from one sample to the next. Consider a random sequence $\{u_n\}$ and suppose information in the samples up to $n = k - 1$ has been transmitted somehow. Let u_n^* denote the reproduced value of u_n. When u_k is to be transmitted, advantage is taken of the fact that the previously transmitted elements might contain some information about it. Accordingly, a quantity $\overline{u}_k^*$, an estimate of u_k is predicted from the previously transmitted samples and a prediction error sequence defined as

$$e_k \triangleq u_k - \overline{u}_k^* \qquad (29)$$

is formed. Now it is sufficient to quantize e_k instead of u_k for transmission. If e_k^* is the quantized value of e_k, u_k^* the reproduced value of u_k is given by

$$u_k^* = \overline{u}_k^* + e_k^*. \qquad (30)$$

A common data transmission method utilizing predictive quantization is called DPCM. The overall system concept is shown in Fig. 7. The principal components of a DPCM sys-

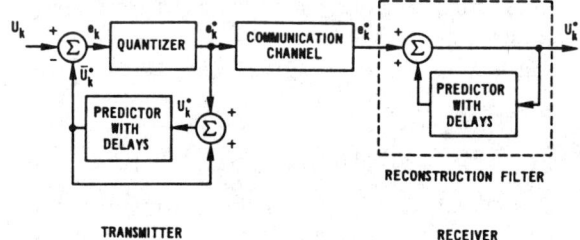

Fig. 7. DPCM.

tem are its predictor and quantizer. From (29) and (30) it is easy to deduce that the error in reproduction of u_k, given by

$$\delta u_k \triangleq u_k - u_k^* = e_k - e_k^* = q_k \qquad (31)$$

is equal to the error in quantization of e_k. Hence, to minimize $\sigma_e^2(k)$, the variance of the prediction error, $\overline{u}_k^*$ should be the best mean-square estimate of u_k and is given by its conditional mean, i.e.,

$$\overline{u}_k^* = E[u_k | \dot{U}_k^-] \qquad (32)$$

where $\dot{U}_k^-$ is the set of past reproduced values, i.e.,

$$\dot{U}_k^- = \{u_l^*, l < k\}. \qquad (33)$$

From (31), the mean-square distortion of u_k is given by

$$E[\delta u_k^2] = \sigma_q^2(k) \qquad (34)$$

and the minimum achievable rate (using a zero memory quantizer) is[4] (see (21))

$$n_{\text{DPCM}} = \tfrac{1}{2} \log_2 \, (\sigma_e^2(k)/\sigma_q^2(k)). \qquad (35)$$

If the original sequence were quantized by a zero memory quantizer (PCM), the minimum achievable rate for u_k would be

$$n_{\text{PCM}} = \tfrac{1}{2} \log_2 \, (\sigma_u^2(k)/\sigma_q^2(k)) \qquad (36)$$

for the same quantizing distortion $\sigma_q^2(k) \leqslant \sigma_e^2(k)$. Since $\sigma_e^2(k) \leqslant \sigma_u^2(k)$, the reduction in achievable rate of predictive quantization over PCM is

$$n_{\text{PCM}} - n_{\text{DPCM}} = \tfrac{1}{2} \log_2 \, (\sigma_u^2(k)/\sigma_e^2(k)). \qquad (37)$$

From (37), the data compression ability depends on the variance reduction by prediction i.e., the ability to predict u_k and therefore on intersample dependence of the sequence $\{u_n\}$. If all the samples are mutually independent then $\overline{u}_k^* = E[u_k]$ and $\sigma_u^2(k) = \sigma_e^2(k)$, resulting in no advantage over PCM. Hence, the underlying philosophy of predictive quantization is to remove mutual redundancy between successive samples and quantize only the new information, i.e., the residuals. An important aspect of this scheme is emphasized by (32) which says that prediction is based on the output rather than the input samples from the past. This results in the predictor being in the feedback loop around the quantizer (see Fig. 7) so that quantizer noise at a given step is fed back to the quantizer input at the next step. This has a stabilizing effect that prevents accumulation of errors in the reconstructed signal u_k^*. At the receiver the feedback loop of the quantizer reconstructs the signal.

[4] Recall from Section II-C our comment that common zero memory quantizers do not achieve a rate lower than the Shannon quantizer for Gaussian distributions.

It is interesting to note that if we consider the error sequence called "innovations"

$$\epsilon_k = u_k - \overline{u}_k \qquad (38)$$

where

$$\overline{u}_k = E[u_k|U_k^-], \quad U_k^- = \{u_l; l < k\} \qquad (39)$$

i.e., the predictor $\overline{u}_k$ is based on the past *input* values, then the variance of this sequence is smaller than that of e_k. Defining[5]

$$E\epsilon_k\epsilon_l \triangleq \beta_k^2 \delta_{k,l} \qquad (40)$$

we must have

$$\beta_k^2 < \sigma_e^2(k). \qquad (41)$$

This is true because $\overline{u}_k^*$ is based on the samples $\{u_l^*, l < k\}$ which contain quantization noise and could never be quite as good as $\overline{u}_k$. As the number of quantization levels goes to infinity $\sigma_e^2(k)$ will approach β_k^2. Hence, a lower bound on the rate is

$$n_{\min} = \frac{1}{2} \log_2 \frac{\beta_k^2}{\sigma_q^2(k)} < n_{\text{DPCM}}. \qquad (42)$$

When the quantization error is small, n_{DPCM} approaches $n_{\min}$. This expression is useful because often it is much easier to evaluate β_k^2 than $\sigma_e^2(k)$ and could be used to estimate the achievable compression. The SNR' corresponding to $\sigma_q^2(k)$ is given by

$$\text{SNR}' = 10 \log_{10} \frac{\sigma_u^2(k)}{\sigma_q^2(k)}$$

$$= 10 \log_{10} \frac{\sigma_u^2(k)}{\sigma_e^2(k) f(n)} < 10 \log_{10} \frac{\sigma_u^2(k)}{\beta_k^2 f(n)} \qquad (43)$$

where $f(n)$ is the quantizer mean-square distortion function for a unit variance input, and n quantization bits. For equal distortion, the gain in SNR of predictive quantization over PCM is

$$\text{SNR}' - (\text{SNR}')_{\text{PCM}} = \Delta \text{SNR}$$

$$= 10 \log_{10} \frac{\sigma_u^2(k)}{\sigma_e^2(k)} < 10 \log_{10} (\sigma_u^2(k)/\beta_k^2) \qquad (44)$$

which is proportional to the variance reduction ratio.

B. Delta Modulation [57]-[69]

The simplest form of predictive coding is one where the predictor is simply a one-step delay function and a one-bit quantizer is used to achieve a one-bit representation of the signal. Thus we have

$$\overline{u}_k^* = u_{k-1}^* \qquad e_k = u_k - u_{k-1}^*. \qquad (45)$$

This is called "linear modulation" or "delta modulation" (DM) and is shown in Fig. 8(a). An important aspect of this scheme is that it does not require sampling of the input signal. The predictor simply performs integration of the quantizer output signal, which is a sequence of binary pulses. The receiver is also a simple integrator. Fig. 8(b) shows typical input-output signals of a delta modulator. The primary limitations of DM

---
[5] It is worth noting that while the innovations sequence $\{\epsilon_k\}$ is uncorrelated, the prediction error sequence $\{e_k\}$ is not and therefore still contains some redundancy.

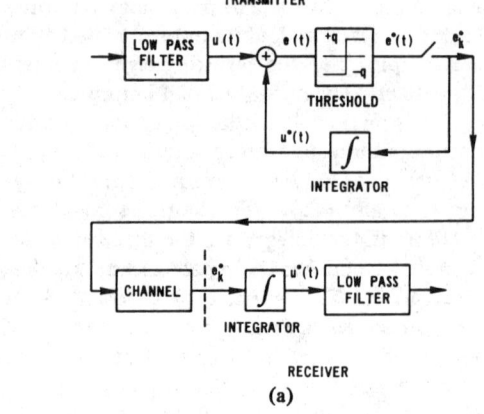

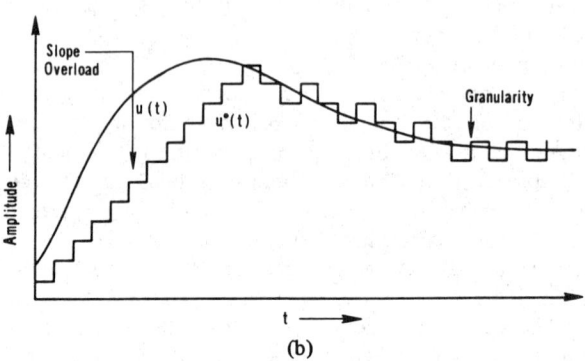

Fig. 8. (a) DM. (b) Input-output signals of DM.

are 1) slope overload 2) granularity noise and 3) instability to channel errors. Slope overload occurs whenever there is a large jump or discontinuity in the signal to which the quantizer can respond only in several delta steps. Granularity noise is the steplike nature of the output when the input signal is almost constant. Both of these errors could be compensated to a certain extent by low-pass filtering the input and output signals. Slope overload can also be reduced by increasing the sampling rate which will reduce the achievable compression. An alternative for reducing granularity, while retaining simplicity, is to go to a *Tristate DM* scheme. Here, the quantizer has three levels and the quantizer output could be coded either by 1) a simple two-bit binary code, or 2) a variable length Huffman code, or 3) a run-length code. The advantage of this method in picture coding is that a large number (65-85 percent) of the pels are found to be in the "level" or "0" state and only the remaining pels are in the "rise" or +1 and "fall" or -1 state. When the output is Huffman coded (which in this case is very simple, e.g., use a code, 0 for 0 states, 10 for +1 states and 11 for -1 states), average rates of around 1.2 bit/pel have been achieved. Alternatively, use of run-length code for 0 states and a two-bit code for the other states have been shown to yield rates around 1 bit/pel for different images [63]. The reconstruction filter of the delta modulator which is a simple integrator is unstable. In the presence of channel errors, the receiver output can accumulate large levels of error. The prediction filter can be stabilized by attenuating the predicted value by a constant $0 < \rho < 1$ (called "leak").

Other variations of DM, such as adaptive DM could further improve its performance (see, e.g., [69]). However, the increase in complexity has to be measured against the more general case of DPCM coding and other techniques for data compression. In application of DM to image coding, the signal is generally presented line by line and no advantage is taken of the two-dimensional correlation in the data. The performance of the system will depend largely on how good the previous element prediction rule is. A simple model for many images is to represent each line of the image as a first order Gauss-Markov process

$$u_k = \rho u_{k-1} + \epsilon_k \quad E\epsilon_k^2 = (1 - \rho^2)\sigma_u^2 = \beta^2 \quad Eu^2 \triangleq \sigma_u^2 \quad (46)$$

where ρ, the one-step correlation is approximately 0.95. The mean-square distortion of the delta modulated signal is given approximately by [8]

$$D = E[\delta u^2] = \left[\frac{2(1-\rho)f(1)}{1-(2\rho-1)f(1)}\right]\sigma_u^2. \quad (47)$$

The corresponding SNR' is

$$\text{SNR}' = 10\log_{10}(\sigma_u^2/D). \quad (48)$$

Assuming the prediction error to be Gaussian and quantized by its Lloyd-Max quantizer, and $\rho = 0.95$, the SNR' is 12.8 dB, which is an 8.4-dB improvement over PCM at 1 bit/pel. This amounts to a compression of 2.5 or a savings of about 1.5 bit/pel. From (47) and (48), the SNR of DM can be improved by increasing ρ which can be done by increasing the sampling rate of the quantizer output. For example, by doubling the sampling rate in this example, ρ will be increased to 0.975 and the SNR' will increase by 3 dB. At the same time the data rate is doubled. Better performance is obtained by increasing the quantizer bits which is done in DPCM. In fact, a large number of ills of DM can be cured by DPCM thereby making it more attractive than DM for data compression.

C. Differential Pulse-Code Modulation of Markov Processes

Many times a signal is modeled by a pth-order Gauss-Markov process

$$u_k - \sum_{j=1}^{p} a_j u_{k-j} = \epsilon_k. \quad (49)$$

For such processes, the best mean-square predictor of u_k given U_k^- is

$$\overline{u}_k = \sum_{j=1}^{p} a_j u_{k-j}. \quad (50)$$

For DPCM of such signals, the predictor $\overline{u}_k^*$ is taken to be the right side of (50) with u_{k-j} replaced by u_{k-j}^* giving

$$\overline{u}_k^* = \sum_{j=1}^{p} a_j u_{k-j}^*. \quad (51)$$

While this is not the optimal estimate of u_k given $\dot{U}_k^-$, it is a good linear approximation if the quantization errors are small. From (40) and (41), assuming u_k is a stationary process (i.e., in steady state), we have

$$\sigma_e^2(k) < \beta^2 = \sigma_u^2 \left(1 - \sum_{j=1}^{p} a_j \rho_j\right) \quad (52)$$

where $\rho_j = E[u_k u_{k+j}]/\sigma_u^2$, is the correlation between u_k and u_{k+j}. For a first-order Markov process, the SNR of the DPCM signal is estimated by

$$\text{SNR}' = -10\log_{10}((1-\rho^2)f(n)/(1-\rho^2 f(n))). \quad (53)$$

If an image is transmitted line by line then the foregoing Markov model is appropriate. For many images, the probability density of the differential signal e_k, is modeled by the Laplacian density function and roughly 8-10 dB improvement in SNR over PCM is obtained at rates of 1-3 bit/pel.

D. Differential Pulse-Code Modulation of Linear State Variable Systems

Sometimes an image may be modeled by a state variable system [111], [112], e.g., when a scanned image contains additive noise and/or is degraded due to interaction between the sensing elements (e.g., in a charge-coupled device (CCD) camera) or is degraded by other phenomena. It is possible to filter (for restoration and noise smoothing) and compress the digitized scanner output simultaneously. Consider a state variable linear system

$$\left.\begin{array}{l} u_{k+1} = A_k u_k + B_k \epsilon_k \\ y_k = C_k u_k + n_k \end{array}\right\}. \quad (54)$$

The output is y_k but the image pel information is contained in u_k and $C_k u_k$. DPCM of the output can be performed via the associated Kalman filter and the necessary equations are as follows.

Quantizer Input:

$$e_k = y_k - C_k s_k^*$$

where

$$\left.\begin{array}{l} s_k^* = A_{k-1} s_{k-1}^* + G_{k-1} e_{k-1}^*, \\ G_k = A_k R_k C_k^T Q_k^{-1} \\ Q_k = N_k + C_k R_k C_k^T \\ R_{k+1} = A_k R_k A_k^T + B_k K_k B_k^T - G_k Q_k G_k^T, R_0 = P_0 \end{array}\right\}. \quad (55)$$

The quantity s_k^* is the one step predictor that arises in Kalman filtering and e_k^* is the quantizer output. The gain G_k is the Kalman filter gain which is computed by solving the Riccati equation for R_k. The matrices K_k, N_k, and P_o represent the covariances of ϵ_k, η_k, and u_0, respectively. At the receiver, the reproduced estimates of u_k and y_k are given by s_k^* and y_k^*, respectively, as

$$\left.\begin{array}{l} s_{k+1}^* = A_k s_k + G_k e_k^* \\ y_k^* = C_k s_k^* + e_k^* \end{array}\right\} \quad (56)$$

Note that this method tends to preserve the output y_k as well as $\hat{y}_k = Cs_k$, which is the best linear estimate of Cu_k. In other words, there is no need to first filter the observations and then perform DPCM; the Kalman filter in the prediction loop suffices. Thus filtering as well as DPCM quantization are performed simultaneously. If there is no additive noise, this method is valid if $C_k R_k C_k^T$ is positive definite. The filter gains are obtained by simply setting $N_k = 0$.

E. Two-Dimensional DPCM [73]-[77]

The foregoing DPCM methods are easily extended to two dimensions whenever a reasonable causal predictor for every pel in the two-dimensional image is available. As an example consider the often used causal model for images

$$u_{i,j} = a_1 u_{i-1,j} + a_2 u_{i,j-1} - a_3 u_{i-1,j-1} + \epsilon_{i,j}. \quad (57)$$

If $a_3 = a_1 a_2$ and $\epsilon_{i,j}$ is a white-noise field then this would rep-

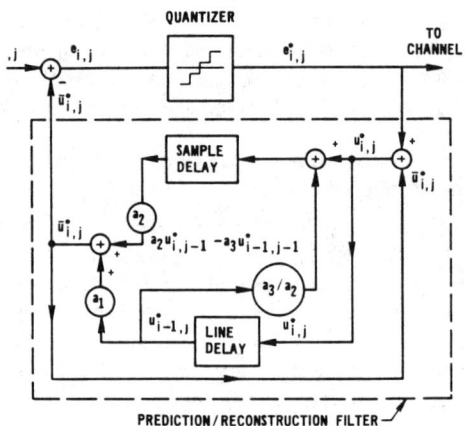

Fig. 9. Two-dimensional DPCM for images represented by the causal model of (57).

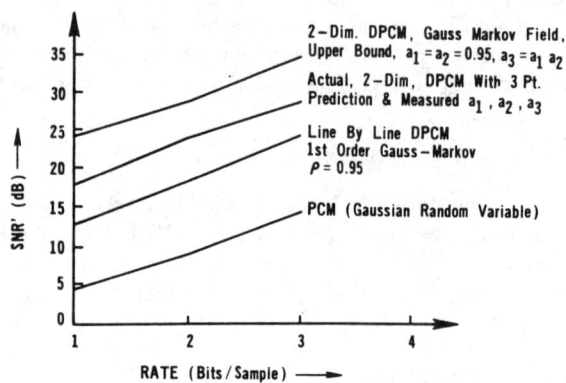

Fig. 10. SNR versus Rate of DPCM of two-dimensional, separable covariance causal model images and its comparison with line-by-line DPCM and with PCM.

resent a random field whose autocorrelation is

$$r(m, n) = E u_{i,j} u_{i+m, j+n} = \sigma_u^2 a_1^{|m|} a_2^{|n|}. \quad (58)$$

The quantities a_1, a_2 are the one-step correlations of the random field along the "i" and "j" axes respectively and the prediction error variance is

$$\beta^2 \triangleq E \epsilon_{i,j}^2 = \sigma_u^2 (1 - a_1^2)(1 - a_2^2). \quad (59)$$

The DPCM equations for images represented by (57) would be as follows (Fig. 9)

$$\begin{aligned} \text{Predictor:} & \quad \overline{u}_{i,j}^* = a_1 u_{i-1,j}^* + a_2 u_{i,j-1}^* - a_3 u_{i-1,j-1}^* \\ \text{Quantizer Input:} & \quad e_{i,j} = u_{i,j} - \overline{u}_{i,j}^* \\ \text{Reconstructor:} & \quad u_{i,j}^* = \overline{u}_{i,j}^* + e_{i,j}^* \end{aligned}$$

(60)

For monochrome images generally $a_1 \simeq a_2 \simeq 0.95$ from which it is deduced that at small distortion levels two-dimensional DPCM should perform better than PCM by about 20 dB or equivalently by about 3.25 bit/pel (see (37) and (44)). In practice two-dimensional DPCM does not achieve quite as much as 20 dB improvement over PCM. This is because the separable covariance model of (58) is "overly optimistic" about the variance of the prediction error. It has also been found [73] that increasing the order of the predictor substantially does not give any appreciable improvement in performance and a three or four point prediction is satisfactory for DPCM coding of images. The predictor coefficients are found by minimizing the mean-square prediction error (of the input data $u_{i,j}$). This leads to a set of linear equations which can be solved from knowledge of the image autocorrelations. Unlike in one dimension, this method of designing a two-dimensional linear predictor could give rise to an unstable causal model [210], [211]. This means while the prediction error will be minimized (ignoring the quantization effects) the reconstruction filter could be unstable causing any transmission error to be amplified greatly at the receiver. Therefore, the predictor rule has to be stabilized (at the cost of either increasing the prediction error variance or increasing the predictor order) before it is used in the DPCM algorithm.

Fig. 10 shows the performance characteristics of various DPCM methods and PCM. Since the entropy of the quantizer output is generally less than the number of quantizing bits, a variable length Huffman code is employed to reduce the average bit rate. Experimental results on images have shown that for a Laplacian density based three-bit Max quantizer, the entropy of the quantized output is roughly 2.3 bits. Thus the compression achieved by two-dimensional DPCM techniques for typical 8 bit/pel raw image data is about 3–3.5.

Overall, DPCM is a simple and easy to implement on-line technique which yields favorable compression results. The major drawbacks are 1) its sensitivity to variations in image statistics, 2) its high sensitivity to channel errors, and 3) its increase in complexity for other types of data such as represented by two dimensional *autoregressive moving average* (ARMA) models (rather than *autoregressive* (AR) models only), and other stochastic models such as semicausal and noncausal models [211]. DPCM techniques can be adapted to local variations in image statistics by adjusting the number of quantization levels according to the local activity (measured by local gradients or variance etc.) in the image and/or modifying the prediction rule whenever a nonstationarity such as slope overload or edge etc., is encountered. Examples of such adaptations are considered in Section VI-C. For ARMA and semicausal fields, vector-DPCM models can yield effective results as we shall see in Section VI. For noncausal random fields DPCM is still possible [8] although other techniques such as transform coding are more suitable (see Section V-C).

F. Differential Pulse-Code Modulation Under a Visual Criterion

Visually, the effect of quantization errors in DPCM is to cause local degradations in areas of large slopes or edges in the picture. Improvement in visual appearance could be made by designing the quantizer which attaches weight to quantization errors according to "visibility" rather than the probability of a given prediction error. Such studies have been made by Candy and Bosworth [78] and Netravali [79].

The visibility of the prediction error e, depends on a combination of factors such as its probability, perceptibility etc. A visibility function is defined as one which relates the subjective visibility of noise added to an image pel to the magnitude of prediction error at the pel. In the case of the previous pel prediction rule, as in DM, e is called the slope of illuminance function. In a more general setting one measures what is called a *masking function* which is a weighted linear combination of the magnitude of the slopes over a window, and the visibility function is related to the value of the masking function.

For prediction errors in a DPCM coder, their visibility function (for a given image) can be measured as follows. For some fixed interval $[x, x + \Delta x]$ (for suitability small Δx), add white noise to all those pels in the original image where the prediction error magnitude $|e|$ (or the masking function) lies in this interval. Let P_m be the power of the noise. Then obtain another image by adding white noise of power P_w to all the pels such that the two images are subjectively equivalent. Then the visibility function $v(x)$ is defined as [20]

$$v(x) = \frac{-dV(x)}{dx} \quad (61)$$

where $V(x) = P_w/P_m$. The visibility function, therefore, represents the subjective visibility in a scene of unit prediction (or masking) noise. This function varies with the scene. Experimental results have shown that for predictors, such as the one used in (57), the visibility function decays faster than the probability density function of the prediction error. On the other hand, for single element predictors (line-by-line, one-dimensional DPCM), the visibility function of prediction errors decays more slowly than the probability density function.

Given the visibility function of the prediction error, the quantizer in the DPCM loop can be designed to minimize the *mean-square subjective (quantization) error* (MSSE) defined by [8], [79]

$$\text{MSSE} = \sum_{i=1}^{L} \int_{t_i}^{t_{i+1}} v(x) \, (e(x) - r_i(x))^2 \, dx. \quad (62)$$

With this design, it has been found that a 27-level quantizer ($L = 27$) gives almost no perceptible errors (i.e., all quantization errors are below their visibility threshold). The entropy of the quantizer output is found to be around 3.4 to 3.8 bit/pel (for head and shoulder type images). Equivalent quality is achieved by a 35-level Lloyd–Max quantizer (entropy $\simeq 4.0$). For large but acceptable levels of visual distortions, e.g., corresponding to the output entropy of 2.6 bit/pel of the Lloyd–Max quantizer in DPCM, a quantizer design based on the above criterion could save about 1 bit/pel. Therefore by considering a visual fidelity criterion, DPCM techniques could achieve compressions of about 4 to 5 for acceptable levels of visual distortion (e.g., corresponding to about 30-dB SNR based on peak to peak to rms error ratio) [79].

G. Predictive Coding of Interframe Images

Predictive coding ideas considered above can also be extended to a sequence of motion and other images which have significant frame to frame redundancy. Much of the research on interframe image coding has been done recently and is based on predictive techniques [81]–[97]. This is primarily due to relatively simpler hardware implementation and low storage requirements of these techniques.

Common situations where interframe images occur are broadcast television, teleconferencing, etc. Typically, the pel values from one frame to the next (at a fixed x, y location) differ substantially only in the areas of relative motion. In what follows we will assume that the object being viewed is always within the camera view (i.e., in the image frame), but it may be displaced by translation, rotation, or any other form of motion.

1) Conditional Replenishment

This technique developed by Mounts [81] and subsequently refined by Candy, Haskell, Limb, Pease *et al.* [82]–[85] is based on a simple method of detection and coding of the moving areas which are replenished from frame to frame. If $u_{i,j,k}$ denotes the pel at location (i, j) in frame k, then the interframe difference signal is

$$e_{i,j,k} = u_{i,j,k} - u^*_{i,j,k-1} \quad (63)$$

where $u^*_{i,j,k-1}$ is the reproduced value of $u_{i,j,k-1}$ at the $(k-1)$th frame. If the magnitude of $e_{i,j,k}$ is greater than a predetermined threshold then it is quantized and coded for transmission. At the receiver, a pel is reconstructed either by repeating the value of that pel location from the previous frame if it came from a stationary area or is replenished by the decoded difference signal if it came from a moving area, i.e.,

$$u^*_{i,j,k} = \begin{cases} u^*_{i,j,k-1} + e^*_{i,j,k}, & \text{if } |e_{i,j,k}| > \eta \\ u^*_{i,j,k-1}, & \text{otherwise.} \end{cases} \quad (64)$$

For transmission, code words representing the quantized values and their addresses are generated. Evidently the average rate achieved will depend on the extent and duration of moving areas so that a reasonably sized buffer with appropriate buffer control strategy is necessary to achieve a steady bit rate and a small chance of buffer overflow. A common scheme of buffer control is to raise the threshold whenever overflow is imminent.

2) Spatial and Temporal Resolution Exchange by Subsampling

It has been noted by Pease and Limb [82] that the spatial resolution in the moving areas and the temporal resolution in the stationary areas could be reduced without noticeable degradation of the perceived scene. This property of exchange of spatial and temporal resolution could be utilized in obtaining further compression. In the areas of rapid or violent motion, temporal prediction is poor and spatial prediction could be utilized to reduce the prediction error. Experiments based on these ideas have achieved data rates of 0.25 to 1 bit/pel (or 0.25 to 1 Mbit/s) for 1-MHz signal.

3) Conditional Replenishment with Cluster Coding

A typical interframe predictive coding algorithm requires the following sequence of steps:

1) segmentation of moving and stationary areas;
2) prediction of a pel in a given area from pels in the previous frame(s) and from pels in the given frame;
3) spatial and temporal resolution exchange used in bit allocation;
4) temporal filtering to reduce jerkiness of motion in the reconstructed image;
5) buffer control.

Now we consider in some detail an example which utilizes most of the above steps. This method [84]–[86] mainly requires transmitting the addresses and quantized amplitudes of significant interframe differences of consecutive frames. The significant interframe differences tends to occur in clusters along a frame line. Hence their addresses are efficiently coded by transmitting the beginning address of a cluster and a cluster terminator code. Isolated points or very small clusters are ignored to keep the address coding scheme efficient.

Fig. 11 shows a typical buffer control scheme with different control levels. In the beginning the first three lines of the first

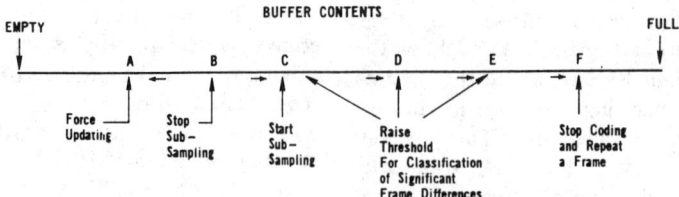

Fig. 11. Buffer control for conditional replenishment interframe coding.

frame are force updated, i.e., transmitted at 8 bit/pel. In subsequent frames the next group of 3 lines is force updated except when the coder is in a buffer overflow state. At this rate, a complete frame is refreshed every 85th frame (for a 256 line image frame) or approximately every 3 s for 30 frame/s. If the contents of the buffer fall below state A, force update is continued. Beyond the state C, the frame differences in a cluster are subsampled by transmitting every other frame difference. At the receiver the missing samples are linearly interpolated. This continues until the buffer contents fall below B. Beyond C, D, and E the threshold is increased to lower the number of significant changes. Beyond the point F, coding is stopped for one frame period and subsampling is continued for the next frame period.

Since the buffer control plays a leading role, the above method is sensitive to available buffer capacity. Often the buffer length is taken to be the average number of bits per frame. Simulation studies [97] have shown that a 1 bit/pel rate could be achieved conveniently with an average SNR of about 33 dB. The SNR in stationary areas is higher (39 dB) and in moving areas it is lower (30 dB). The buffer overflow occurs about 7 percent of the time. Lowering the rate to $\frac{1}{2}$ bit/pel degrades the performance substantially to 59 percent buffer overflow rate and 28-dB SNR. Figs. 12(a) and (b) show encoded images and the encoding error magnitudes[6] for a typical frame at $\frac{1}{2}$ bit/pel and 1 bit/pel rates. A high rate of buffer overflow results in jerky reproduction of motion as evidenced by Fig. 12(a). It should be noted that most distortion is in the temporal direction (because the previous frame is repeated whenever the prediction signal does not replenish) and is evident from the error image. At a 1 bit/pel rate, buffer overflow is significantly reduced leading to a considerable improvement in performance.

H. Adaptive-Predictive Coding and Motion Compensation

Predictive techniques are local in structure and are therefore quite sensitive to changes in the data. Nonstationarities in interframe statistics are introduced by motion in the successive frames. Reasonable adaptations of the predictor and encoder to compensate for the changes due to motion could be made to achieve considerable gains in performance. Several motion compensation schemes [90], [94]-[97] have been proposed to improve the performance of interframe predictive coding methods. We consider one such adaptive scheme which is based on a motion classifier. Fig. 13 shows the overall scheme (for a sequence of frames without interlace). A pel at location (i, j, k) is first classified as belonging to an area of stationary (C_s), moderate/slow (C_M), or rapid (C_R) motion. Classification is based on an activity index $\alpha_{i,j,k}$ which is measured as a weighted average of the interframe difference signal e.g.,

$$\alpha_{i,j,k} = \sum_{(x,y) \in \mathcal{H}} w_{x,y} |u^{\bullet}_{i+x, j+y, k} - u^{\bullet}_{i+x, j+y, k-1}| \quad (65)$$

where $w_{x,y} \geq 0$ are some predetermined weights (typically $w_{x,y} = 1$) and $\mathcal{H}$ is a suitable spatial neighborhood of $(0, 0)$. A large value of $\alpha_{i,j,k}$ indicates a large amount of motion in the neighborhood of the pel. The current pel, $u_{i,j,k}$ is classified by specifying suitable thresholds for the three classes. Its prediction is chosen as

$$\overline{u}^{\bullet}_{i,j,k} = \begin{cases} u^{\bullet}_{i,j,k-1}, & \text{if } u_{i,j,k} \in C_S \\ u^{\bullet}_{i-q, j-r, k-1}, & \text{if } u_{i,j,k} \in C_M \\ \rho_r^p u^{\bullet}_{i,j-p,k} + \rho_h u^{\bullet}_{i-1,j,k} - \rho_h \rho_v u^{\bullet}_{i-1,j-p,k}, & \text{if } u_{i,j,k} \in C_R \end{cases} \quad (66)$$

where $p = 2$ in the 2 to 1 subsampling mode and $p = 1$, otherwise. Also, ρ_h and ρ_v are the one step correlation coefficients along i and j, respectively, and q and r are chosen so that $\overline{u}^{\bullet}_{i,j,k}$ is the intensity value at the nearest neighbor of $u_{i,j,k}$. This is done by estimating the average displacement of the neighborhood $\mathcal{H}$ which gives the minimum activity. Observe that for the case of rapid motion, the two-dimensional causal model in (60) has been used. This is, because due to rapid motion, temporal prediction would be difficult. In the case of moderate motion, we are simply searching the nearest neighbor of $u_{i,j,k}$ in the previous frame. For each class a different quantizer is used, the number of quantization levels of which depends on the variance of the prediction error. Generally, this criterion allocates more bits to areas of high activity and fewer bits to stationary areas. Fig. 12(c) shows the result of this method at 0.5 bit/pel utilizing the same buffer length as in the case of Fig. 12(a). Comparison of error images shows a significant improvement. In terms of the SNR, the improvement is about 7 dB and the buffer overflow rate is 7 percent.

I. Predictive Coding with Motion Compensation and Interpolation

In principle, for compression of interframe motion images, if the motion trajectory of each pel could be measured, then only the initial or reference frame and the trajectory information need to be coded for transmission/storage. To reproduce the images one could simply propagate each pel along its trajectory. In practice, one could only measure the motion trajectory of a group of pels. For example, the interframe motion could be modeled by piecewise linear translations of the moving objects followed by a measurement of the magnitude and direction of this translation. Rocca, Cufforio et al. [94]-[96] have considered techniques for segmentation and measurement of displacement of moving objects in a stationary

---

[6] The error magnitudes have been amplified ten times to enhance their display.

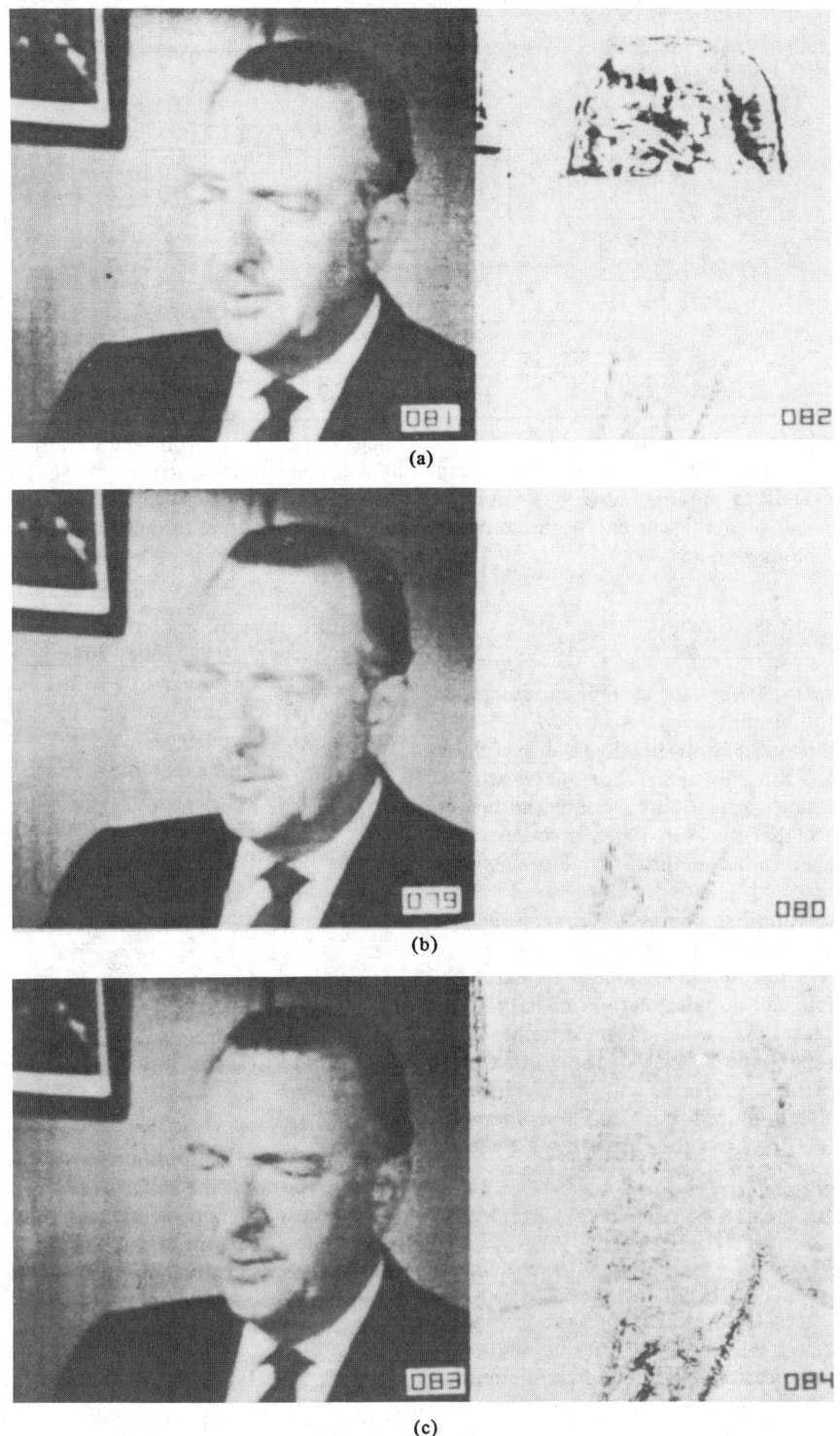

Fig. 12. Encoded images (left) and error images (right) obtained by the interframe conditional replenishment and adaptive predictive coding methods. (a) Encoded images by conditional replenishment, 0.5 bit/pel, SNR = 27.9 dB. (b) Encoded images by conditional replenishment, 1.0 bit/pel, SNR = 33 dB. (c) Adaptive classification prediction coding, 0.5 bit/pel, SNR = 34.8 dB.

background. Another method [97] which does not require coding the moving object boundaries is to divide the image frame into fixed size small rectangular blocks. Each block is assumed to undergo a linear translation and the displacement vector of each block is coded. Image registration techniques such as area correlation, affine transformation and others often employed in geometric correction and interpolation [113]–[114] could be employed. Performance of area correlation techniques has been found to be rather poor for small block sizes, in areas of low spatial activity, and for blocks not under-

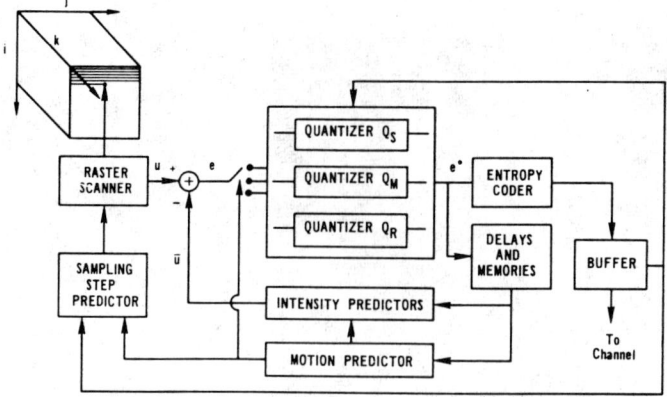

Fig. 13. Adaptive classification predictive coding scheme.

going pure translation. An effective algorithm which searches for the *direction of minimum distortion* (DMD) has been proposed in [97]. The DMD is obtained at a location (i,j) such that the distortion between the current frame and the reference frame block is minimized, i.e.,

$$D(i,j) \triangleq \sum_{m=1}^{M} \sum_{n=1}^{N} \{u(m,n) - u_0(m+i, n+j)\}^2$$

where $\{u(m,n)\}$ and $\{u_0(m,n)\}$ are the current and reference frames respectively, is minimized.

For interframe motion estimation usually the search is limited to a window of 5×5 pels or so. For images with a monotonically nonincreasing correlation function, the search could be speeded up such that the search area is successively reduced to a half or less. For other methods of motion estimation see [212], [213].

Having estimated the motion compression is achieved by skipping the image frames until the next reference frame. For simplicity suppose only the alternate frames are skipped. Frame skipping is a simple and popular method of data compression of interframe images even when no measurements of motion are available. Let U_{2k} be a block of the $2k$th frame which has been skipped for $k = 1, 2, \cdots$. In the absence of motion compensation the reproduced frame could be obtained as follows:

Frame Repetition: $\quad u_{2k}^*(m,n) = u_{2k-1}^*(m,n) \quad (67)$

Frame Interpolation: $u_{2k}^*(m,n) = \frac{1}{2}[u_{2k-1}^*(m,n)$
$\qquad\qquad\qquad\qquad + u_{2k+1}^*(m,n)]. \quad (68)$

Frame interpolation reduces the jerkiness present in frame repetition methods but requires an additional frame memory. The motion trajectory information can be used in prediction as well as interpolation. Thus with motion compensation one would have

Frame Repetition: $\quad u_{2k}^*(m,n) = u_{2k-1}^*(m+q, n+l) \quad (69)$

Frame Interpolation: $u_{2k}^*(m,n) = \frac{1}{2}[u_{2k-1}^*(m+q, n+l)$
$\qquad\qquad\qquad\qquad + u_{2k+1}^*(m+q', n+l')] \quad (70)$

where (q,l) and (q',l') are the displacement vectors of U_{2k} relative to the preceding and following frames, respectively. Fig. 14 shows the effect of motion compensation in interframe image data compression. Here we show the reproduced images in a skipped frame obtained via (67)-(70) and the corresponding error. The improvement due to motion compensation, roughly 10 dB, is quite significant.

J. Predictive Coding of Facsimile Images [98]-[110]

The principles of predictive coding could be easily applied to binary images. The main difference is that the prediction error is also a binary variable so that no quantizer is needed. If the original data has redundancy, then the prediction error sequence will have large runs of "0"s (or "1"s).

Let $\{u_{i,j}\}$ denote a binary image and $\overline{u}_{i,j}$ denote its predicted value based on the values of pels in its prediction window S^- which contains some of the pels that have already been scanned and encoded. The prediction error e is defined as

$$e_{i,j} = \begin{cases} 0, & \text{if } \overline{u}_{i,j} = u_{i,j} \\ 1, & \text{if } \overline{u}_{i,j} \neq u_{i,j} \end{cases} \quad (71)$$

$$= u_{i,j} \oplus \overline{u}_{i,j} \quad (72)$$

where $\oplus$ denotes the EXCLUSIVE-OR operation. Given the error sequence, the reconstruction is simply

$$u_{i,j} = \overline{u}_{i,j} \oplus e_{i,j}. \quad (73)$$

Since $\overline{u}_{i,j}$ is a causal predictor, it can be determined from $u_{i,j}$ contained in S^-. The binary prediction error sequence can be coded by a run-length or entropy coding scheme [104]-[110] by assuming the variables $e_{i,j}$ to be independent with probability p_i. As an example consider a binary image scanned from top to bottom and left to right. At any (i,j), let the prediction window be

$$S^- = \{(i-1, j-1), (i, j-1), (i+1, j-1), (i-1, j)\}. \quad (74)$$

Then $u_{i,j}$ is decided to be "0" or "1", the state in majority among the pels in S^-. This defines a prediction rule.

1) Choice of Predictors [98]-[103]

A reasonable criterion is to choose a predictor so that the prediction error probability is minimized. If n is the number of pels in the prediction window S^-, then at each pel the elements of S^- can take 2^n different states. Let $k = 1, 2, \cdots, 2^n$ denote the kth state of S^- and define

$$p_k = \text{Probability } S^- \text{ is in state } k$$
$$q_k = \text{Prob } [u_{i,j} = 1|k]. \quad (75)$$

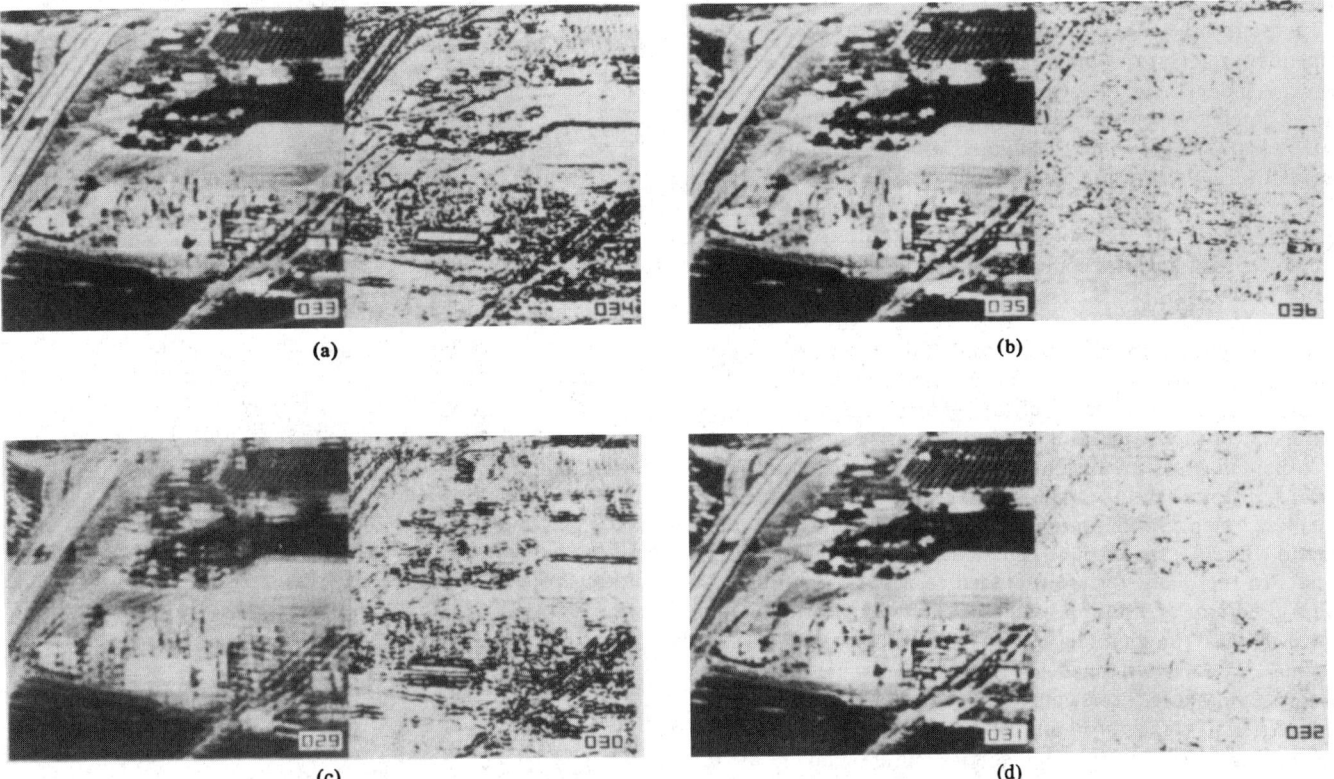

Fig. 14. Effects of motion compensation on interframe prediction and interpolation. (a) Frame repetition from the preceding frame (i) along temporal axis, SNR = 16.9 dB, equation (67), (ii) along motion trajectory, SNR = 26.69 dB, equation (69). (b) Frame interpolation from the preceding and the following frames (temporal filtering) (i) along temporal axis, SNR = 19.34 dB, equation (68) (ii) along motion trajectory, SNR = 29.56, equation (70).

The optimum prediction rule for minimum probability of prediction error is

$$\bar{u}_{i,j} = \begin{cases} 1, & \text{if } q_k \geq 0.5 \\ 0, & \text{if } q_k < 0.5. \end{cases} \quad (76)$$

If the random process $\{u_{i,j}\}$ is assumed to be strict sense stationary, then the various probabilities are the same at every (i, j) and therefore the prediction rule stays the same. In practice a suitable choice of n has to be made to achieve a tradeoff between prediction error probability and the complexity of the predictor due to large values of n. Experimentally 4-7 pel predictors have been found to be adequate. Corresponding to the prediction rule of (76), the minimized prediction error is

$$p_e = \sum_{k=1}^{2^n} p_k \min(q_k, 1 - q_k). \quad (77)$$

2) Adaptive Predictors

Such predictors are useful in practice because the image data is generally nonstationary. In general, any pattern classifier or a discriminant function could be used as a predictor. A simple classifier is a *linear learning machine* or *adaptive threshold logic unit* (TLU) [99], [100] which calculates the threshold q_k as a linear functional of the states of the pels in the prediction window. Another type of pattern classifier is a network of TLU's called layered machines and includes piecewise linear discriminant functions and the so-called "α-perceptron" [99], [100].

A practical adaptive predictor for facsimile images has been proposed by Kobayashi and Bahl [98] where a counter C_k of L bits is associated with each of the $k \in [1, 2^n]$ states. The counter runs from 0 to $2^L - 1$. The adaptive prediction rule is

$$\bar{u}_{i,j} = \begin{cases} 1, & \text{if } C_k \geq 2^{L-1} \\ 0, & \text{if } C_k < 2^{L-1}. \end{cases}$$

After prediction of a pel has been performed, the counter is updated as

$$C_k = \begin{cases} \min(C_k + 1, 2^L - 1), & \text{if } u_{i,j} = 1 \\ \max(C_k - 1, 0), & \text{if } u_{i,j} = 0. \end{cases}$$

The value $L = 3$ has been found to yield minimum prediction error for a typical printed page.

3) Performance of Predictive Coders

Experimental results reported in [98] show that a 4-pel adaptive predictor and a 7-pel fixed predictor yield the best tradeoff between the prediction error probability and the predictor complexity. For a typical journal printed page (with no line drawings) the value of p_e is about 0.05, giving the entropy to be 0.286 bit/pel. The maximum achievable compression would be 3.5 if the prediction error sequence was independent. For other printed documents which have line drawings or are less dense, higher compressions have been achieved.

There are other predictive coding algorithms which consider dependency of run lengths by considering one-dimensional Markov models of run lengths (see e.g., Arps [103]) or two-dimensional Markov models of prediction errors (Preuss [101]-[102]). Another technique which makes use of the correlation between scan lines is called the predictive differential quantizing (PDQ) technique. Instead of coding run lengths, the differences between corresponding run lengths of successive scan lines are coded.

IV. ONE-DIMENSIONAL TRANSFORM CODING

An alternative to predictive coding is *transform coding*, which is sometimes also called *block quantization*. Here a long sequence of data samples is divided into blocks of N samples, and each block treated as a vector is quantized independently of other blocks. An optimum block quantizer could be defined as the one that minimizes the average distortion of the quantized elements of the vector for a given number of quantization levels. In optimum predictive coding, the successive inputs to the quantizer are whitened recursively and the optimum predictor is a nonlinear causal filter. In practice, a suboptimal linear predictor is used. In transform coding all the samples are first whitened jointly and then quantized. The optimal whitening filter which minimizes the distortion in the reconstructed signal turns out to be a noncausal, linear filter (as opposed to the causal-predictive filter) known as the Karhunen–Loeve (KL) transform. In practice, the KL transform is substituted by a suboptimal but fast unitary transform.

A. The Karhunen-Loeve Transform and Block Quantization [115]-[118]

Consider a vector u which comes from a (real) Gaussian random process of zero mean and covariance R (see Fig. 15). This vector is linearly transformed by an $N \times N$ (complex) matrix A to produce a (complex) vector v whose components $\{v_k\}$ are mutually uncorrelated. Each component v_k is quantized independently. The output vector v^* is linearly transformed by a matrix B to yield a vector u^*. The problem is to find the optimal decorrelating matrix A, the reconstruction matrix B, and the optimum quantizers such that the overall average mean-square distortion

$$D = \frac{1}{N} E \sum_{k=1}^{N} (u_k - u_k^*)^2 \qquad (78)$$

is minimized. The solution of this problem is obtained as follows (Segall [116]).

1) The optimal reconstruction matrix B is given by

$$B = A^{-1}\Gamma \qquad (79)$$

where Γ is a diagonal matrix of elements

$$\gamma_k = (E[v_k v_k^{*\ast}])/(E[v_k^\ast v_k^{*\ast}]) \qquad (80)$$

where the * indicates the complex conjugate.

2) The optimal decorrelating matrix A is the KL transform of u, i.e., the rows of A are the orthonormalized eigenvectors of the covariance matrix R.

3) For any quantizing scheme, the quantizer minimizing the overall mean-square error is the Lloyd–Max quantizer. Thus the quantizer that minimizes the quantization error between each v_k and v_k^* also minimizes the overall mean-square error. With Lloyd–Max quantizers we get $B = A^{*T}$.

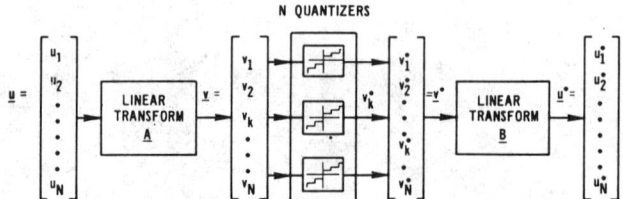

Fig. 15. One-dimensional transform coding.

The KL transform has the property that for any $M \leq N$ it packs the maximum average energy into some M samples of v. Although the KL transform is optimal, it is often difficult to compute and has no fast algorithm associated with it. For stationary random sequences there are many fast unitary transforms which approach the energy packing efficiency of the KL transforms. Examples are the cosine, Fourier, and sine transforms. These transforms have been shown to be members of a larger family of sinusoidal transforms [136] all of which have a performance equivalent to the KL transform as the size N of the data vector goes to infinity. For first-order stationary Markov processes [see (46)] the cosine transform matrix defined as [131]

$$C_{i,j} = \begin{cases} \dfrac{1}{\sqrt{N}}, & i = 1, \ 1 \leq j \leq N \\ \sqrt{\dfrac{2}{N}} \cos \dfrac{(2j-1)(i-1)\pi}{2N}, \\ & 2 \leq i \leq N, \ 1 \leq j \leq N \end{cases} \qquad (81)$$

has been shown to perform very closely to the KL transform when the correlation parameter ρ lies in the interval $(0.5, 1)$, even when N is small [136]. The transformation $y = Cx$ can be computed via the fast Fourier transform (FFT) in $O(N \log N)$ operations. These properties have made the cosine transform a useful substitute for the KL transform in image processing since many images can be modeled by low-order Markov processes with high interpel correlation.

Nonsinusoidal unitary transforms such as the Hadamard, Haar, Slant transforms (which are square-wave transforms) are also used since they are computationally faster than the FFT-based fast sinusoidal transform. Therefore, in transform coding practice, the KL transform is substituted by a suitable fast unitary transform. The Lloyd-Max quantizer may also be substituted by another quantizer.

B. Distortion-Rate Characteristics and Bit Allocation

Regardless of the choice of the unitary transform and the quantizer, the distortion D defined by (78) becomes

$$D = \frac{1}{N} \sum_{k=1}^{N} \sigma_k^2 f(n_k) \qquad (82)$$

where σ_k^2 is the variance of the transform coefficient v_k and $f(n)$, as mentioned before [see (43)], is the distortion function of the quantizer for a unity variance input. To complete the design of the transform coder, one has to determine the bit allocation $\{n_k\}$ among the various samples $\{v_k\}$. Let the average desired bit rate per sample be p. Then

$$\frac{1}{N} \sum_{k=1}^{N} n_k = p. \qquad (83)$$

For a fixed value of p, it is required to find the allocation of $n_k \geq 0$ bits to v_k such that the distortion D is minimized. In the case of the Shannon quantizer

$$f(n) = 2^{-2n} \qquad (84)$$

the optimum bit allocation is given by

$$n_k = n_k(\theta) = \max\left[0, \frac{1}{2}\log_2\left(\frac{\sigma_k^2}{\theta}\right)\right] \qquad (85)$$

where θ is determined such that

$$\frac{1}{N}\sum_{k=1}^{N} n_k(\theta) = p. \qquad (86)$$

The minimized distortion at the rate p is given by

$$D_{\min} = \frac{1}{N}\sum_{k=1}^{N} \min(\theta, \sigma_k^2). \qquad (87)$$

Equations (85)–(87) also give the distortion versus rate characteristics of any unitary transform A used in transform coding. We note that the performance of a transform is completely determined by the variances σ_k^2 which are given by

$$\sigma_k^2 = \sigma_k^2(A) = [ARA^{*T}]_{k,k} \qquad (88)$$

Since A is unitary, $\sum_{k=1}^{N}\sigma_k^2(A) = N\sigma^2$ is constant for all A's. Hence the distortion versus rate characteristic depends on how the *total energy* $N\sigma^2$ is distributed by A among the various coefficients $\{v_k\}$. The KL transform distributes it in the most efficient way [119]–[129]. The distortion versus rate characteristics when other quantizers are used can also be determined (see e.g., [116], [118]). In practice, the bit allocation requires minimizing (82) subject to (83) and the constraint that the n_k be nonnegative integers. The solution of this problem is found via a theory of marginal analysis due to Fox [117], by the following simple algorithm [118].

Step 1: Start with the allocation $n_k = 0, 1 \leq k \leq N$ and set $j = 1$.

Step 2: Let $n_k^j = n_k^{j-1} + \delta_{k,i}$, where $\delta_{k,i}$ is the Kronecker delta function and i is any index for which $\Delta_k = \sigma_k^2[f(n_k^{j-1}) - f(n_k^{j-1} + 1)]$ is maximum.

Step 3: If $\Sigma n_k^j > Np$, stop; otherwise set $j \to j+1$ and go to step 2. If ties occur for the maximizing index, the procedure is successively initiated with the allocation $n_k^j = n_k^{j-1} + \delta_{i,k}$ for each one. Note that this algorithm simply means that the marginal returns defined by $\Delta_{k,j} = \sigma_k^2[f(j) - f(j+1)]$; $k = 1, \cdots, N$; $j = 0, 1, \cdots, N$, are arranged in a decreasing order and bits are distributed one by one according to this order. For an average bit rate of p, the total number of marginal returns to be sorted is N^2p for an $N \times 1$ vector.

C. Fast Karhunen–Loeve Transform Coding

Sometimes it is possible to approach the data compression efficiency of the KL transform by decomposing a random process into two mutually orthogonal processes with fast KL transforms. Consider, for example, the elements u_k, $0 \leq k \leq N+1$ of a stationary, first-order Gauss–Markov sequence with zero mean and covariance

$$r_m \triangleq Eu_k u_{k+m} = \rho^{|m|}. \qquad (89)$$

Let u represent the $N \times 1$ vector of elements $\{u_k, 1 \leq k \leq N\}$. It has been shown that this vector has a decomposition[7] [137]

$$u = u^0 + u^b \qquad (90)$$

where

$$u^b = \alpha Q^{-1}b, \; b = [u_0, \underbrace{0 \cdots\cdots\cdots 0}_{N-2 \text{ zeros}}, u_{N+1}]^T$$

such that u^0 and u^b are zero mean, mutually orthogonal random vectors, i.e., $E[u^0(u^b)^T] = 0$. The matrix Q is a symmetric, tridiagonal, Toeplitz matrix with unity along the main diagonal and $-\alpha$ along the other two diagonals and $\alpha = \rho/(1+\rho^2)$. The KL transform of the sequence $\{u_k^0\}$ is the fast sine transform defined as

$$\psi_{i,j} = \sqrt{\frac{2}{N+1}}\sin\frac{ij\pi}{N+1}, \quad 1 \leq i, j \leq N \qquad (91)$$

and the KL transform of the 2×1 vector $[u_0, u_{N+1}]^T$ is the 2×2 sine transform

$$\Phi = \frac{1}{\sqrt{2}}\begin{bmatrix} 1 & 1 \\ 1 & -1 \end{bmatrix}. \qquad (92)$$

Given the original $(N+2) \times 1$ sequence $\{u_k, 0 \leq k \leq N+1\}$, the $N \times 1$ sequences $\{u_k^0\}$ and $\{u_k^b\}$ are realized as follows. First the boundary variables (u_0, u_{N+1}) are passed through a time varying finite impulse response (FIR) filter whose impulse response $h_{m,n}$ equals $\alpha[Q^{-1}]_{m,n}$ and its duration is N to give u_k^b and $u_k^0 = u_k - u_k^b$. (See Fig. 16.)

Now instead of transform coding the original $(N+2) \times 1$ sequence by its KL transform we code u^0 and u_b separately by one of the following three methods.

Method I: (see Fig. 17) The boundary variables (u_0, u_{N+1}) and the residual process $\{u_k^0\}$ are transform coded independently by their respective KL transforms and are combined at the receiver according to (90). Fig. 20 shows the performance of this is below the KL transform by only about 0.5 dB at SNR$' = 20$ dB.

Method II: The performance of the above method is improved when the boundary values are quantized before the residual is coded (Fig. 18). Fig. 20 shows the result. Clearly, at small distortion levels ($D \leq 3$ percent) the performance is indistinguishable from the KL transform. It is interesting to note that in this method, if the boundary variables are not allocated any bits then $u^0 = u$, the method reduces to sine transform coding of u. Thus the sine transform coder provides a lower bound of the performance of the fast KL transform coder.

Method III: Recursive Block Coding. In all of the foregoing transform coding methods, it is assumed that successive blocks of data are independent. In practice, however, when a long sequence of data is divided into blocks of M samples, the successive blocks are correlated. If the block length is large, the interblock correlation could be ignored. But if the block size is chosen to be small (e.g., when the data statistics are slowly changing or the transform size is kept small to reduce hardware cost) it may be desirable to exploit the interblock redundancy. The noncausal decomposition of (90) could be

---

[7] This decomposition expresses the finite segment of a stationary process as a two source model. The first source has a fast KL transform and the second source is determined by a few (two in this example) boundary variables.

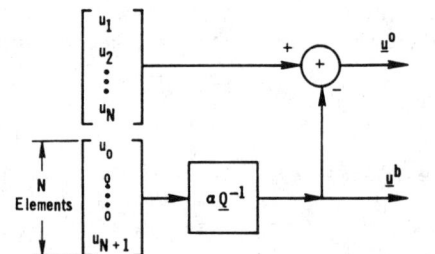

Fig. 16. Realization of fast KL transform decomposition.

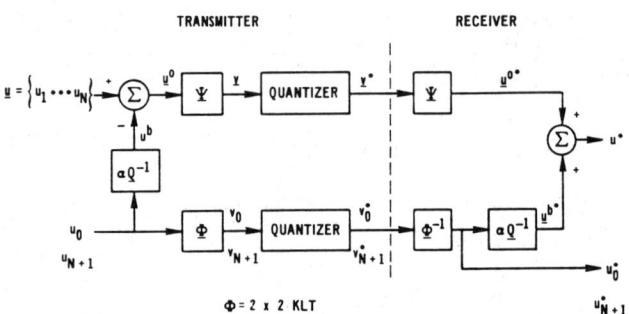

Fig. 17. Fast KL transform coding: Method I.

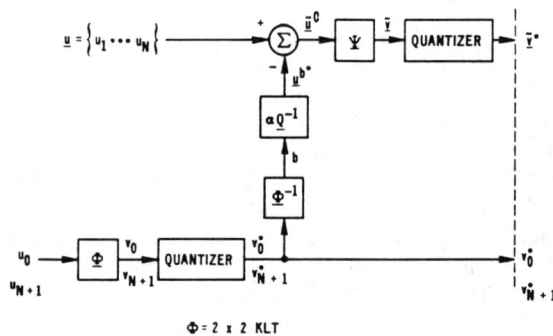

Fig. 18. Fast KL transform coding: Method II.

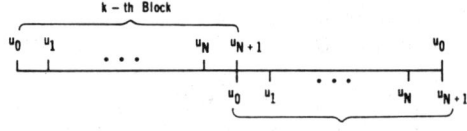

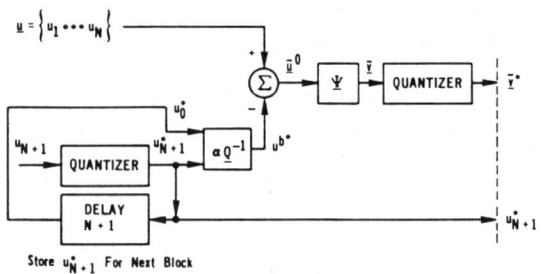

Fig. 19. Recursive block coding: Method III.

exploited to design a *recursive block coding scheme* which does this (Fig. 19). Now in coding of the $(k+1)$th block of $M = N + 2$ samples, the first sample u_0 comes from the $(N+1)$th sample of the previous block which has already been coded. Hence for each successive block one only needs to quantize u_{N+1} and the residual process $\tilde{u}_k^0$. Now, the rate distortion function [214] yields a performance which is better than even the conventional KL transform coding (see Fig. 20). This result can be used in designing small size transform coders which achieve the efficiency of large size coders. For example, it has been shown in [135] that a block recursive coder of size 8 can achieve the efficiency of a KL transform coder of block length 16.

D. Transform Coding versus Differential Pulse-Code Modulation [8], [130]

It is interesting to compare the performances of the KL transform coding and DPCM methods. For first-order stationary Gauss–Markov sequences of N samples, and for a small fixed average mean-square distortion $D < (1 - \rho)/(1 + \rho)$, the rate R_{DPCM} achievable via DPCM could be shown to satisfy the bounds

$$\frac{1}{2N} \log_2 \frac{\sigma_u^2}{D} + \frac{(N-1)}{2N} \log_2 \left(1 + \frac{\rho^2 D}{(1-\rho^2)\sigma_u^2}\right) \leq R_{\text{DPCM}}$$
$$\leq \frac{1}{2N} \log_2 \frac{\sigma_u^2}{D} + \frac{(N-1)}{2N} \log_2 \left(\rho^2 + \frac{(1-\rho^2)\sigma_u^2}{D} + \frac{\sigma_u^2}{(N-1)D}\right). \tag{93}$$

The KL transform coding method could achieve a rate

$$R_{\text{KL}} = \frac{1}{2N} \log_2 \frac{\sigma_u^2}{D} + \frac{(N-1)}{2N} \log_2 \frac{(1-\rho^2)\sigma_u^2}{D},$$
$$0 < D < (1-\rho)/(1+\rho). \tag{94}$$

Comparing (97) and (98), we find $\Delta R = R_{\text{DPCM}} - R_{\text{KL}}$ satisfies

$$\frac{(N-1)}{2N} \log_2 \left(1 + \frac{\rho^2 D}{(1-\rho^2)\sigma_u^2}\right) \leq \Delta R \leq \left(\frac{N-1}{2N}\right)$$
$$\cdot \log_2 \left(1 + \frac{\rho^2 D}{(1-\rho^2)\sigma_u^2} + \frac{1}{(N-1)(1-\rho^2)}\right). \tag{95}$$

As $N \to \infty$, this gives

$$\Delta R = R_{\text{DPCM}} - R_{\text{KL}} = \frac{1}{2} \log_2 \left(1 + \frac{\rho^2 D}{(1-\rho^2)\sigma_u^2}\right). \tag{96}$$

For $D = 0.01\,\sigma^2$, $\text{SNR}' = 20$ dB, and $\rho = 0.95$, one obtains $R_{\text{DPCM}} - R_{\text{KL}} = 0.062$ bit/sample and $R_{\text{KL}} = 1.16$ bit/sample. Thus DPCM performs quite close to KL transform coding at low distortion levels as the block size $N \to \infty$. For $N = 16$ one obtains $0.058 \leq \Delta R \leq 0.381$ so that the performance of DPCM could get worse if it were reinitialized after short intervals. DPCM is quite sensitive to changes in the data statistics e.g., via (96), it could be shown for small distortions, that

$$\frac{d(\Delta R)}{\Delta R} \simeq \frac{2}{(1-\rho^2)} \Delta \rho, \quad \text{for } |\rho| \lesssim 1 \tag{97}$$

which shows that a 2.5 percent change in ρ would change the incremental rate of DPCM over KL transform coding by 50 percent at $\rho = 0.95$. This together with the fact that generally the available data is not stationary, leads to a performance of DPCM which is much worse than estimated via (96), especially when the distortion is higher (i.e., for larger compression). At very low distortions, however, $(D \simeq 0.001\,\sigma_u^2)$ DPCM and KL transform methods are found to perform quite closely on actual images. Finally, we should note that the above analysis

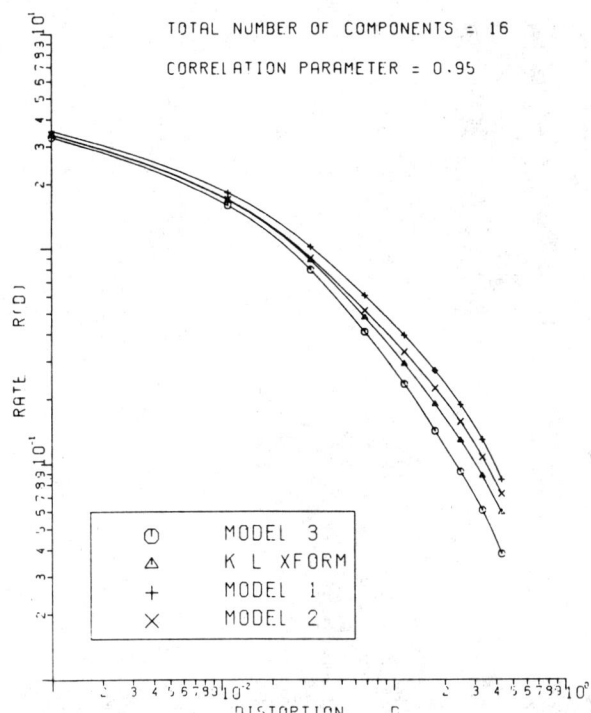

Fig. 20. Distortion versus rate characteristics of fast KL transform coding.

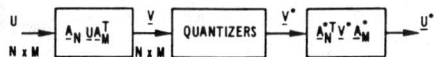

Fig. 21. Two-dimensional transform coding.

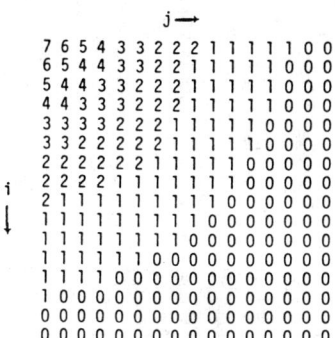

Fig. 22. Typical bit allocation for 16 × 16 block cosine transform coding at approximately 1 bit/pel for images modeled by the exponential covariance function of (103).

is only valid for Markov processes. For general ARMA models, state variable models, or two-dimensional models, ΔR is likely to be more significant.

V. Multidimensional Transform Coding

A. Two-Dimensional Transform Coding [145]–[165]

The transform coding results of Section IV-A are easily extended to two-dimensional images by considering an $N \times M$ image $\{u_{i,j}\}$ as a one-dimensional $NM \times 1$ vector u obtained by stacking up the rows of the image. The optimal unitary transform should then be the KL transform of the vector u. Often the image can be characterized such that the KL transform of u is separable, i.e.,

$$\mathcal{Q} = A_M \otimes B_N \qquad (98)$$

where A_M and B_M are $M \times M$ and $N \times N$, respectively, unitary matrices and $\otimes$ denotes the Kronecker product. Then the transformation

$$\mathcal{V} = \mathcal{Q} u \qquad (99)$$

can be written in matrix form as

$$V = A_M U B_N^T. \qquad (100)$$

Often A and B are the same transforms of appropriate sizes so that

$$V = A_N U A_M^T. \qquad (101)$$

If the KL transform is not fast, it is substituted by a fast transform. Fig. 21 shows the overall two-dimensional transform coding algorithm. The bit allocation algorithm for the quantizer design requires the knowledge of the variances (or second moments) of the random variables $\{v_{k,l}\}$. Defining

$$\sigma_{k,l}^2 = E|v_{k,l}|^2 \qquad (102)$$

the bit allocation $\{n_{k,l}\}$ can be found as before, by simply mapping $\{\sigma_{k,l}^2\}$ to a one-dimensional sequence of variances and using the algorithms described in Section IV-B. In practice, to make transform coding computationally efficient in terms of storage and speed, a given image is divided into small rectangular blocks, and each block is transform coded independently. For example, if a 256 × 256 image divided into 16 × 16 blocks, the storage requirement is reduced by a factor of 256 and the speed is improved by a factor of 2 for a transform which requires $O(N \log_2 N)$ operations to transform an $N \times 1$ vector.

The variances $\sigma_{k,l}^2$ are calculated either directly from transformed blocks of test images or from the knowledge of the power spectral density, or equivalently, the autocorrelation function of the image. The separable covariance function of (58) is often used to estimate the transform domain variances. Another function which generally provides a better fit of covariances is given as

$$r(k,l) = \sigma^2 \exp\{-\sqrt{\alpha_1 k^2 + \alpha_2 l^2}\}. \qquad (103)$$

Fig. 22 shows the bit allocation for cosine transform coding of a 16 × 16 block of an image to achieve an average rate of 1 bit/pel when the image covariance function is modeled by (103). Figs. 23(a) and (b) show the cosine transform coded images (and the error images) at average rates of 0.5 bit/pel and 1 bit/pel, respectively.

B. Zonal Versus Threshold Coding

Examination of the bit allocation pattern of Fig. 22 reveals that a substantial number of transformed samples are allocated zero bits (except at very high average rates). Thus only a small *zone* of transformed image is transmitted. Denoting by I_t, the address set of transmitted samples

$$I_t = \{k, l; n_{k,l} \geq 1\} \qquad (104)$$

and letting n_t be the number of transmitted samples, we can define a *zonal mask*

$$m(k,l) = \begin{cases} 1, & k, l \in I_t \\ 0, & \text{otherwise} \end{cases} \qquad (105)$$

which takes values of unity in the zone of largest n_t variances

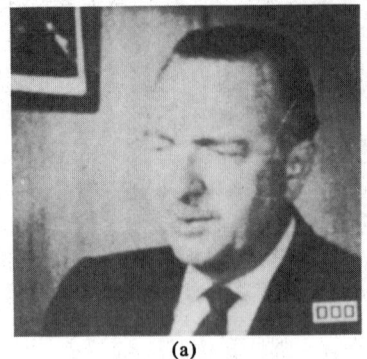
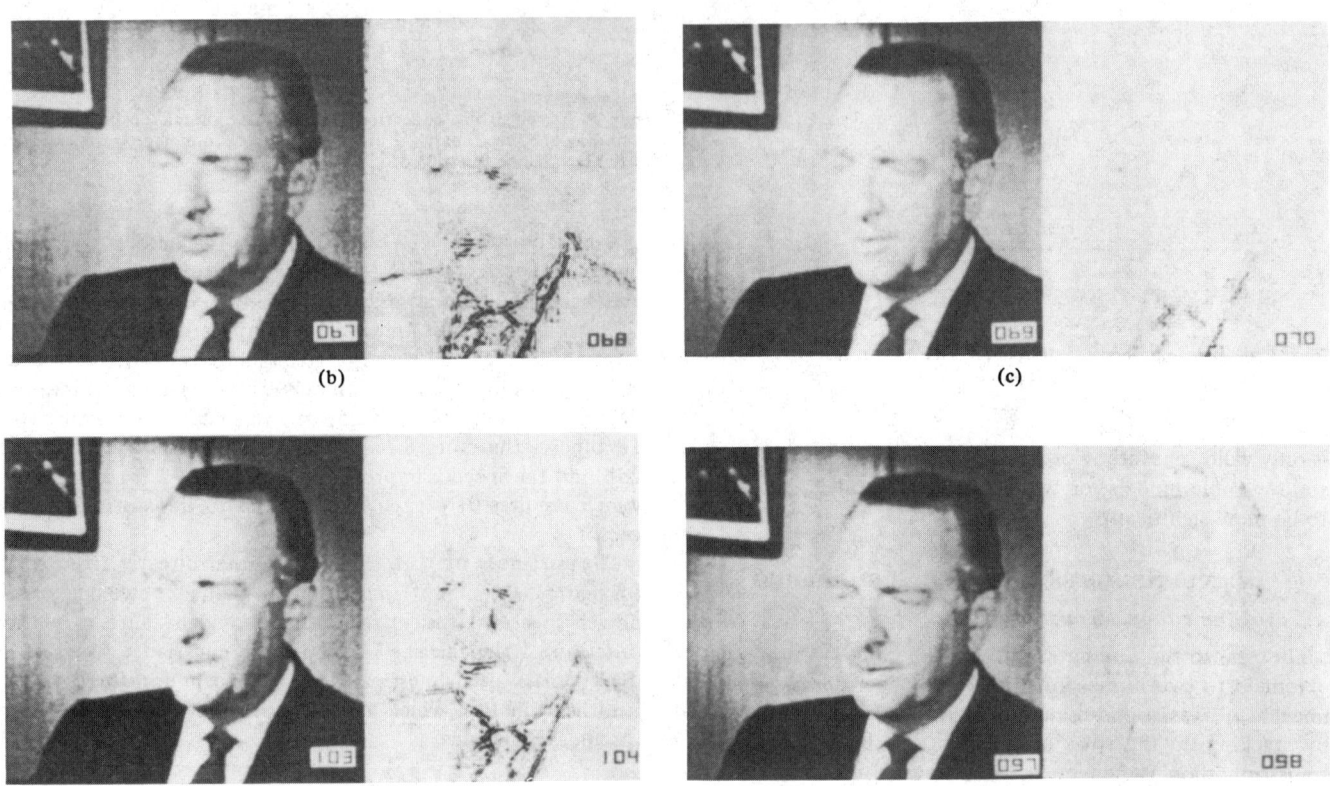

Fig. 23. Cosine transform coded images and error images. (a) Original. (b) Intraframe 16 × 16 block coded, 0.5 bit/pel, SNR = 34.4 dB. (c) Intraframe 16 × 16 block coded, 1 bit/pel, SNR = 40.3 dB. (d) Interframe transform, 16 × 16 × 16 block coded, 0.5 bit/pel, SNR = 36.8 dB. (e) Adaptive transform coded, 16 × 16 × 16 block coded, SNR = 41.2 dB.

of the transformed samples. Thus in transform coding one applies a zonal mask on the transformed image and quantizes only the nonzero elements for transmission or storage. This method is also called *zonal coding*.

If instead of transmitting/storing the n_t elements of maximum variance, one considers n_t samples of maximum amplitude (for the given image) in the transform domain, we get what is called *threshold coding*. The address set of transmitted samples is now

$$I'_t = \{(k, l): |v_{k,l}| > \eta\} \quad (106)$$

where η is a suitably chosen threshold which controls the achievable average bit rate. For a given class of images, since the variances of the transform samples are fixed, the zonal mask remains unchanged from one image to the next (or one block to the next) for a fixed bit rate. However, the *threshold mask* m_η defined as

$$m_\eta(k, l) = \begin{cases} 1, & (k, l) \in I'_t \\ 0, & \text{otherwise} \end{cases} \quad (107)$$

could change from block to block because the I'_t of largest amplitude samples need not be the same for different blocks. The samples retained after thresholding are typically quantized by a constant word length quantizer followed by a variable word length entropy coder.

Although for the same number of transmitted samples (or the number of quantizing bits) a threshold mask would give a better choice of transmission samples (i.e., lower distortion) it would also result in an increased bit rate because the addresses of the transmitted samples (i.e., the boundary of the threshold mask) have to be coded for every image block. Typically, a sample line by line run-length coding scheme is implemented to code the transition boundaries in the threshold mask. Usually this results in a somewhat more complex scheme than zonal transform coding. However, threshold coding has merits since it is adaptive in nature and is particularly useful when the image statistics might change rapidly so that a fixed zonal mask is inefficient.

C. Transform Coding of Random Fields via Noncausal Models

The fast KL transform decomposition described in Section IV-C arises quite naturally when two-dimensional images or random fields are represented by certain noncausal models [186]. For example, consider a two-dimensional Markov-1 random field image represented by the stochastic difference equation[8]

$$u_{i,j} - \alpha(u_{i-1,j} + u_{i+1,j} + u_{i,j-1} + u_{i,j+1}) = \epsilon_{i,j} \quad (108)$$

where $\alpha < \frac{1}{4}$ and $\epsilon_{i,j}$ is a two-dimensional zero mean random sequence whose covariance function is given by

$$r_\epsilon(k,l) = E\epsilon_{i,j}\epsilon_{i+k,j+l} = \beta^2 \begin{cases} 1, & (k,l) = (0,0) \\ -\alpha_1, & (k,l) = (\pm 1, 0) \text{ or } (0, \pm 1) \\ 0, & \text{otherwise.} \end{cases} \quad (109)$$

Let U be an $N \times N$ image block. In matrix form (108) becomes

$$QU + UQ = \epsilon + B_1 + B_2 \quad (110)$$

$$B_1 = \alpha \begin{bmatrix} b_1^T \\ 0 \\ b_3^T \end{bmatrix}, \quad B_2 = \alpha [b_2 \vdots 0 \vdots b_4] \quad (111)$$

where b_1, b_2, b_3 and b_4 are $N \times 1$ vectors which contain the boundary elements of the image (see Fig. 24) and the elements of Q are defined by

$$q_{i,j} = \begin{cases} \frac{1}{2}, & i = j \\ -\alpha, & i - j = 1 \\ 0, & \text{otherwise.} \end{cases} \quad (112)$$

It could be shown that such a random field has a decomposition

$$U = U^0 + U^b$$

where U^b is determined from the boundary values and the KL transform of U^0 is the fast Sine transform. Specifically,

$$\left. \begin{array}{l} u^b = \mathcal{Q}^{-1}(b_1 + b_2), \quad \mathcal{Q} \triangleq (I \otimes Q + Q \otimes I) \\ u^0 = u - u^b \end{array} \right\} \quad (113)$$

where u, u^0, u^b, b_1 and b_2 are $N^2 \times 1$ vectors obtained by lexicographic ordering of the $N \times N$ matrices U, U^0, U^b, B_1, and B_2, respectively. Two-dimensional fast KL transform coding algorithms similar to those discussed in Section IV-C could now be designed. Fig. 25 shows, for example, an appli-

---

[8] It is called a noncausal model because a pel is related directly via this model to neighbors in all the four quadrants.

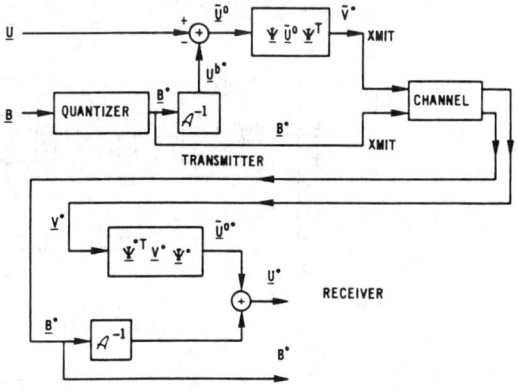

Fig. 24. Boundary variables of the noncausal model.

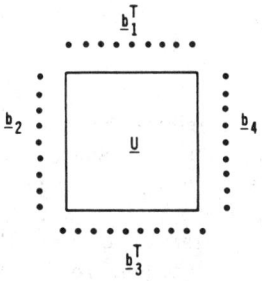

Fig. 25. Fast KL transform coding of images; ψ is the KL transform of U^0.

cation of the method II of Section IV-C. Recursive block coding algorithms which use small image blocks (e.g., for adaptive coding methods) and exploit interblock redundancy could also be designed following Section IV-C.

D. Transform Coding of Two Source Models

It is noteworthy that the foregoing algorithm is based on a two source model of a stationary random field, viz.

$$U = U^0 + U^b \quad (114)$$

where the two source outputs U^0 and U^b are realizable from the given image block U and its boundary variables B. One could extend this idea to represent an image as a nonstationary field

$$U = U_s + U_b \quad (115)$$

where U_s is a stationary component and U_b is a nonstationary component. The two components are coded separately to preserve the different features in the image. Suppose the stationary component has a representation

$$\mathcal{L}[U_s] = \epsilon_s \quad (116)$$

where ϵ_s is a zero mean unity variance white noise field. Applying L on U we get

$$\begin{aligned} \epsilon &\triangleq \mathcal{L}[U] = \mathcal{L}[U_s] + \mathcal{L}[U_b] \\ &\triangleq \epsilon_s + \epsilon_b \end{aligned} \quad (117)$$

The operator $\mathcal{L}$ could be realized in various ways. For example, a common method is to let $\mathcal{L}$ be such that U_s is a low-pass filtered version of U and U_b contains the high spatial frequencies such as edges.

A two source coding scheme similar to the above method

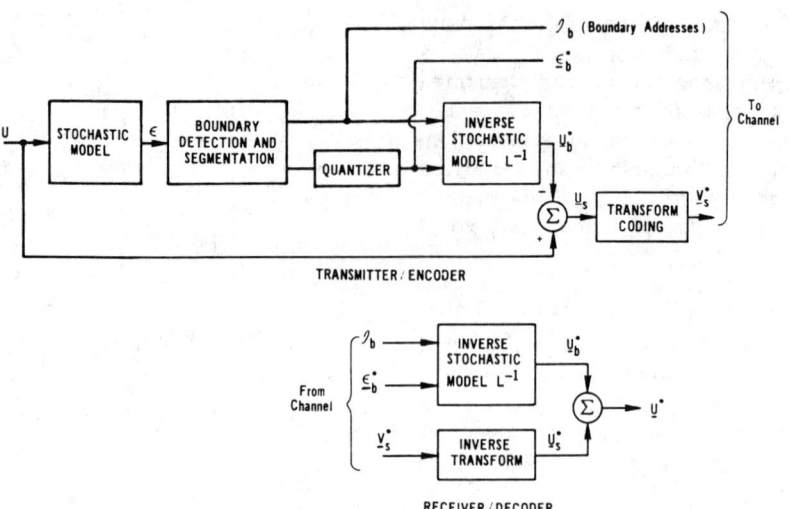

Fig. 26. Two source transform coding.

was first proposed by Schreiber *et al.* [174]–[175]. The given image is segmented into its low and high spatial frequency components. The low-frequency component and the addresses (I_b) of the boundary points are encoded. At the receiver the original image is synthesized by adding to the low-frequency component a quantity proportional to the Laplacian of a step function called *synthetic highs* at the locations of the boundary points. Another two source coding scheme has been studied by Yan and Sakrison [164], where the image decomposition in two sources is performed by subtracting the sharp changes in the local mean of the image from the image. The corner points and the values of changes are coded separately, and the residual image, which is a much better candidate for a stationary random field, is transform coded. Jain and Wang [184] have considered certain stochastic image models to achieve the two source decomposition. For an appropriate $\mathcal{L}$ in (117), $\epsilon_{i,j}$ is a sum of $\epsilon_b(i,j)$ (signal) and $\epsilon_s(i,j)$ (white noise). If the original image data contains only a small amount of additive noise, then ϵ_b and ϵ_s could be segmented by a simple threshold scheme e.g., as follows:

$$\left. \begin{array}{l} \epsilon_b(i,j) = \begin{cases} 0, & |\epsilon_{i,j}| < t \\ t \operatorname{sgn} \epsilon_{i,j}, & |\epsilon_{i,j}| > t \end{cases} \\ \epsilon_s(i,j) = \epsilon_{i,j} - \epsilon_b(i,j) \end{array} \right\} \quad (118)$$

where t is a suitable threshold. A simple connectivity algorithm (e.g., check to see if each feature $\epsilon_b(i,j)$ has at least one neighbor which is also a feature sample) is used to minimize the effects of noise. I_b is the set of addresses where $\epsilon_b(i,j) \neq 0$, and the quantized values $\epsilon_b^*(i,j)$ are coded for transmission. The residual field

$$U_s = U - \mathcal{L}^{-1}[\boldsymbol{\epsilon}_b] \quad (119)$$

is transform coded. The overall average rate depends on the choice of threshold which has to be found experimentally. For $t = \infty$, this method reduces to the usual transform coding method. Fig. 26 shows the block diagram of this method.

Fig. 27 shows the results of this method for a 256×256 image coded in 64×64 blocks. Figs. 27(a) and (b) show the stochastically segmented components U_s and U_b for the threshold $t = \sigma_\epsilon$ where σ_ϵ is the standard deviation of $\epsilon_{i,j}$. Fig. 27(c) and (d) show the reconstructed components U_s^* and U_b^*. Fig. 27(e) shows the final encoded image at 1 bit/pel average rate.

Fig. 27(f) shows the edge map I_b–which is preserved by this coding method.

Compared to ordinary transform coding, for the same mean-square error this method offers several choices in terms of the subjective quality of the receiver image. However, the complexity of the algorithm is increased substantially compared to other adaptive transform coding methods.

E. Transform Coding Under Visual Criteria

In Section I-D it was mentioned that the ordinary mean-square criterion was of limited use for the visual evaluation of images. A weighted mean-square criterion proposed by Mannos and Sakrison [17] has been found to be useful. Fig. 28 shows a transform coding scheme that takes into account the visual criterion. The image luminance field is first converted to a contrast field via a memoryless nonlinear transformation. This image field is then Fourier transformed. The transform domain elements are multiplied by a frequency weighting function $H(\omega_1, \omega_2)$ (see Section I-D) and the resulting samples are quantized using the usual mean-square criterion. Inverse weighting followed by inverse Fourier transformation gives the reconstructed contrast field.

For large image block sizes, the frequency weighting function $H(\omega_1, \omega_2)$ can be applied in the DFT domain. To apply this method for coding images block by block via an arbitrary transform the image constrast field should first be convolved with $h(x, y)$, the Fourier inverse of $H(\omega_1, \omega_2)$. For practical implementation, it would then be desirable to seek discrete finite support approximations of h and h^{-1}. The resulting field $z_{i,j}$ could then be coded by any desired method. At the receiver, the encoded field $z_{i,j}$ must now be convolved with the inverse function $h^{-1}(i,j)$. The reader should note that the transform domain quantizer design and bit allocation now depends on the statistics of the field $\{z_{i,j}\}$.

F. Three-Dimensional Transform Coding

In many applications, (for example, in multispectral imaging interframe video imaging, biomedical cineangiography and computer-aided tomographic (CAT) scanning, etc.), one has to work with three-dimensional (or higher) data. Transform coding schemes are possible for compression of such data. The basic ideas of the foregoing sections are extended in this development.

Fig. 27. Images coded by two source transform coding. (a) Original. (b) U_b, nonstationary component. (c) U_s, stationary component. (d) 1.5 bit/pel coded image. (e) Edges preserved by the coder.

A three-dimensional (separable) transform of an $L \times M \times N$ sequence $\{u_{i,j,k}\}$ is defined as

$$v_{l,m,n} = \sum_{i=1}^{L} \sum_{j=1}^{M} \sum_{k=1}^{N} u_{i,j,k} a_L(l,i) a_M(m,j) a_N(n,k) \quad (120)$$

where $1 \leq l \leq L$, $1 \leq m \leq M$, $1 \leq n \leq N$ and $\{a_L(i,j)\}$ are the elements of an $L \times L$ unitary matrix A_L. In higher dimensions, one simply takes the A-transform with respect to each index.

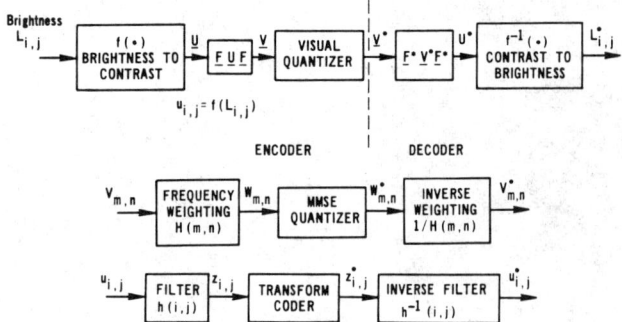

Fig. 28. Transform coding under visual criterion.

For an arbitrary A, the number of operations is $LMN(L + M + N)$. If A is a fast transform, such as the DFT, sine, cosine, etc., then the operation count is generally $LMN(\log_2 LMN)$. The storage requirement for the data is LMN. To reduce the online storage and computation requirements, often one partitions the available data into smaller blocks (e.g., $16 \times 16 \times 16$) and each block is processed independently. The coding algorithm after transformation is the same as before except that one is working with triple indexed variables. Fig. 23(c) shows a frame of a sequence of cosine transform coded images at 0.5 bit/pel. The improvement over intraframe coding is seen by comparing it with Fig. 23(b).

G. Adaptive Transform Coding

Performance of transform coding schemes could be improved substantially by adapting them to changes in image statistics. For three-dimensional data, this could be quite useful because the statistical properties along the temporal dimension could vary quite a lot depending on motion or other temporal changes. There are essentially three types of adaptation that could be made, viz.

1) adaptation of transform
2) adaptation of bit allocation
3) adaptation of quantizer levels.

Theoretically, a change in statistics of the data could require all of these adaptations. Adaptation of the transform basis vectors is the most difficult and expensive, because ideally one should find a new set of KL basis vectors for any change in the statistical parameters. A method of this type was considered by Tasto and Wintz [158]. From a practical standpoint, if one knows the range and type of statistical variations, one may choose a single transform which would be least sensitive to such changes.

A more practical and perhaps more effective method is to adapt the bit assignment to changes in statistics. For example, one could classify an image block into one of several categories and allocate a larger number of bits to blocks that have larger activity and fewer bits to ones having lower activity. This results in a variable average rate from block to block, but gives a better utilization of the total bits over the entire ensemble of image blocks. Adaptations of this type have been considered by Chen [163] for two-dimensional transform coding, by Jain and Wang [118, sec. 6] for hybrid coding and by Jain and Jain [97] for a three-dimensional transform coding. Fig. 23(d) shows a frame of interframe-cosine transform adaptively coded images. The significant improvement over intraframe (Fig. 23(b)) or nonadaptive interframe (Fig. 23(c)) is evident.

Another adaptive scheme is to allocate bits to image blocks so that each block has the same distortion [215]. This results in a uniform degradation of the image and appears less objectionable to the eye. In adaptive quantization schemes, the bit allocation is kept the same but the quantizer levels are adjusted according to changes in the variances of the transform domain samples. Transform domain variances may be estimated by either updating the statistical parameters of the covariance model or may be estimated in real time by local averaging (or prediction) of the squared magnitude of the transform domain samples. One such approach has been considered by Tescher [159].

H. Transform Coding of Tomographic (Computer-Aided Tomographic Scanned) X-Ray Images

In many applications where one has a sequence U_k, of two-dimensional images, where the temporal axis (k) need not be time (as in the case of motion images). Examples are the tomographic X-ray images where a three dimensional object is imaged by illuminating it by an X-ray source on a two-dimensional plane. By rotating the object relatively to the source, several views or projections $\{U_k\}$ of the object are obtained. If $f(x, y, z)$ is the transmissivity of the object, then $U_k(i,j) \triangleq u_{i,j,k}$ is given by

$$u_{i,j,k} = \int_{S_{i,j,k}} f(x, y, z)\, dS \qquad (121)$$

where $S_{i,j,k}$ is the path of the X-ray from the source to the (i,j)th pel on the image in the kth projected view. It is known that if one has several such projection images, one could "reconstruct" a reasonable estimate of $f(x, y, z)$. Once $f(x, y, z)$ or its estimate is known, one could obtain other views (e.g., cross sections) which may otherwise be impractical to obtain. The number of projection views and the associated data rates with such images often achieves unmanageable proportions [169]. Hence compression of projection images for storage of this data for subsequent reconstruction and analysis becomes very desirable.

Fig. 29(a) shows an 8 bit/pel projection image (128×128) of a dog's thorax. Figs. 29(b) and (c) show results of three-dimensional transform coded projections at 0.5 bit/pel and 0.04 bit/pel giving compressions of 16 and 200, respectively. The size of each image block for three-dimensional transform coding was chosen to be $32 \times 16 \times 8$. Note that high SNR values are achieved even at large values of compression. The high values of compression are achieved because imaging a projection is equivalent to low-pass filtering so that the data has large interpel correlation. Also, there is substantial redundancy from one projection to the next.

From a clinical standpoint, one is more interested in the reconstructed images than the projection images. Fig. 30(a) shows a cross section of the object reconstructed from the original (uncompressed) and the transform coded projections. Hence the fidelity criterion is to minimize the error in the reconstructed object for a given bit rate of the projection data. Fig. 30(b) shows the error images of the reconstructed cross section. These results show compression ratios of 16 and above may be achieved for projection images while preserving medically useful information. Higher compression is achievable for X-ray cineangiographic images where the third dimension represents time [97], [169].

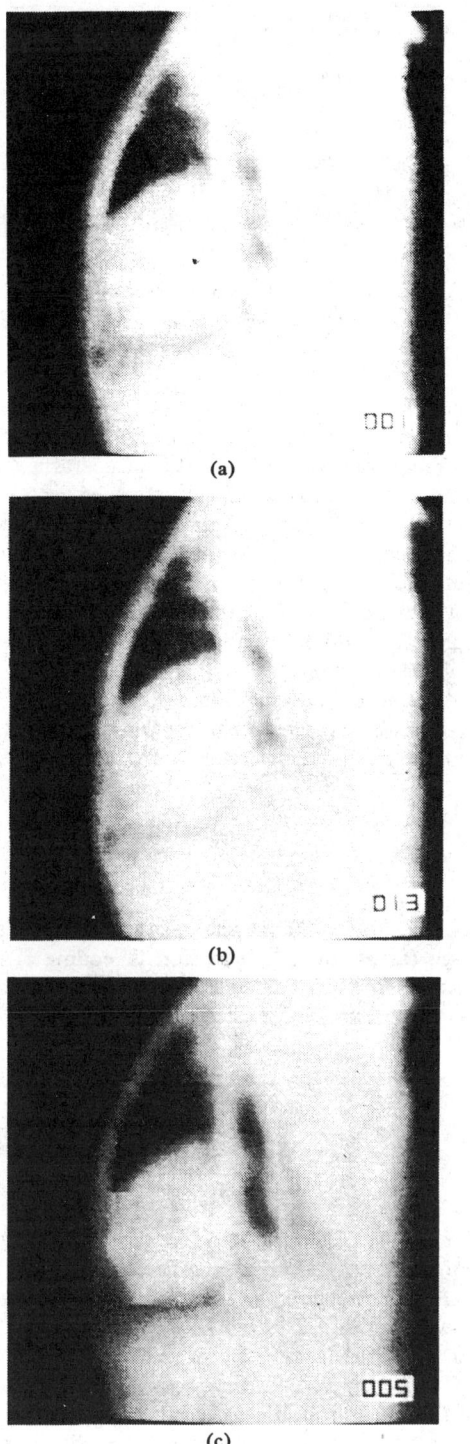

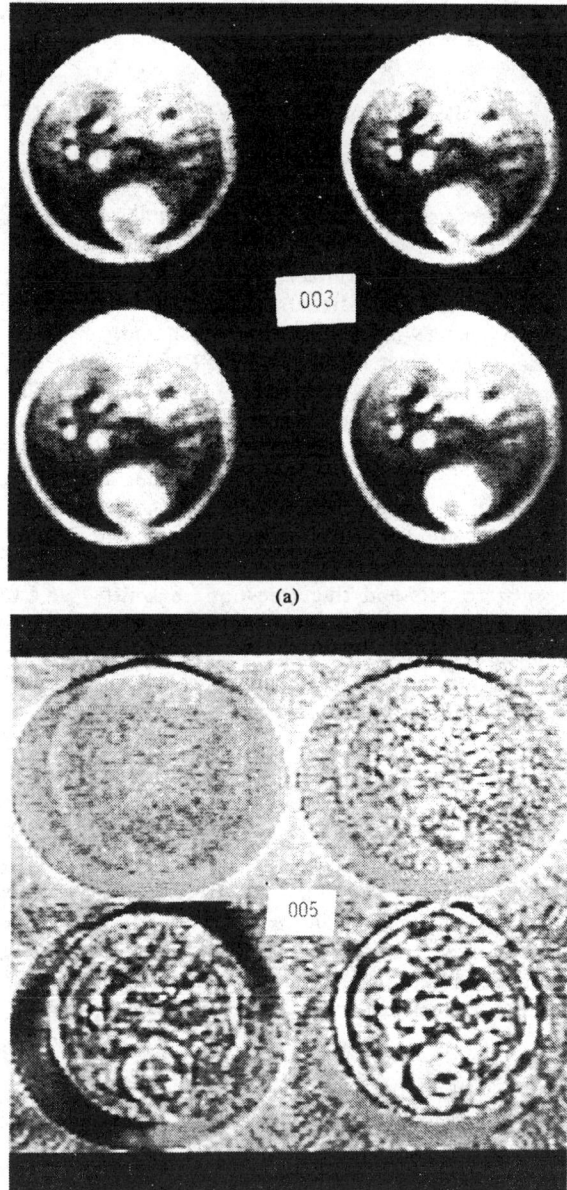

Fig. 29. Transform coding of CAT scanned images, CR = compression ratio. (a) original 8 bit/pel. (b) 0.5 bit/pel, CR = 16, SNR = 49.3 dB. (c) 0.04 bit/pel, CR = 200, SNR = 40.7 dB.

I. Summary of Transform Coding

In summary, transform coding achieves relatively larger compression compared to predictive methods. Generally, any distortion due to quantization and channel errors gets distributed, over the entire image, during the inverse transformation. Visually, this is less objectionable than the errors in predictive coding where it is distributed locally at the source. Although for one-dimensional autoregressive processes, transform and

Fig. 30. Reconstructed cross section from compressed projection images. (a) Reconstructed images clockwise from top left, original, CR = 4, CR = 16, CR = 8. (b) Error in reconstructed images due to data compression, clockwise from top left, CR = 4, CR = 16, CR = 200, CR = 64.

predictive coding schemes are theoretically close in performance, their differences on real world data are substantial. This is because of two reasons. First, often the real world data is not stationary. Predictive coding compared to transform coding, is quite sensitive to changes in the statistics of the data. Hence, in practice, only adaptive predictive coding algorithms achieve the efficiency of (nonadaptive) transform coding methods. Second, in two dimensions finite order causal predictors may never achieve a compression ability close to transform coding because a finite order autoregressive representation of a two-dimensional random field may not exist [211]. From an implementation point of view, predictive coding has much lower complexity both in terms of memory requirements and number of operations to be performed. However, with rapidly decreasing cost of digital hardware and computer memory, the hardware complexity of transform coders may not remain a disadvantage for very long.

VI. Hybrid Image Coding and Vector Differential Pulse-Code Modulation

A. Hybrid Coding

The term refers to techniques which combine transform and predictive coding techniques. Typically, first a two-dimensional image is unitarily transformed in one of its dimensions to obtain a sequence of one dimensional, independent, sequences. Each of these sequences is then coded independently by a one dimensional predictive technique such as DPCM. This technique combines the advantages of hardware simplicity of DPCM and the robust performance of transform coding. Fig. 31 shows the overall scheme. The hardware complexity of this method is that of a one-dimensional transform coder and at most N DPCM channels, where N is the size of the transform basis vectors. The number of DPCM channels is significantly less than N because many elements of the transformed vector are allocated zero bits and therefore not transmitted at all. In practice, the transformed samples are multiplexed into a single DPCM channel which adjusts its quantizer and predictor according to the statistics of the input samples. Consider an $N \times M$ image and let u_j denote its jth column, i.e.,

$$u_j = [u_{1,j} u_{2,j} \cdots u_{N,j}]^T. \tag{122}$$

A unitary transformation

$$v_j = \Psi u_j, \quad 1 \leq j \leq M. \tag{123}$$

is performed on each vector u_j such that the elements of v_j are mutually uncorrelated. Further, for each i, the sequence $\{v_j(i)\}$, is modeled by a suitable autoregressive process. It has been shown [118], [184] that several random field models for images lead to a first-order Markov model

$$v_j(i) = \rho_i v_{j-1}(i) + e_j(i), \quad 1 \leq i \leq N \tag{124}$$

for the transformed vector v_j. For example, consider a random field represented by the semicausal stochastic finite difference equation

$$\left. \begin{array}{l} u_{i,j} = \alpha(u_{i-1,j} + u_{i+1,j}) + \gamma u_{i,j-1} + \epsilon_{i,j} \\ E\epsilon_{i,j} = 0, E\epsilon_{i,j}\epsilon_{k,l} = \beta^2 \delta_{i,k} \delta_{j,l} \quad \alpha < \tfrac{1}{2}, |2\alpha + \gamma| < 1 \end{array} \right\}. \tag{125}$$

This is called a semicausal model (because a pel at (i, j) is related to pels that occur both before and after it in the "i" direction and to pels that occur only before it in the "j" direction). If we assume that at the boundaries of the image $u_{i,j} \simeq u_{i-1,j}$ (highly correlated) then the cosine transform plays the role of Ψ and (125) reduces to (124) with

$$\rho_i = \gamma \lambda_c(i), E[e_j^2(i)] = \beta^2/\lambda_c^2(i)$$

$$\lambda_c(i) = 1 - 2\alpha \cos \frac{(i-1)\pi}{N}, \quad 1 \leq i \leq N. \tag{126}$$

The DPCM equations for the ith channel now follow from Section III-C as

Predictor: $\bar{v}_j(i) = \rho_i v_{j-1}(i)$ \hfill (127a)
Quantizer Input: $\tilde{e}_j(i) = v_j(i) - \bar{v}_j(i)$ \hfill (127b)
Reconstruction Filter: $v_j(i) = \bar{v}_j(i) + \tilde{e}_j(i)$. \hfill (127c)

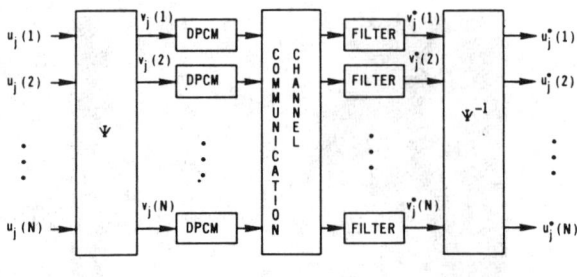

Fig. 31. Hybrid coding of two-dimensional images.

The encoding scheme requires, first, taking the transform of each column vector u_j. This is followed by the DPCM channels for predictive coding of successive transform vectors. The receiver simply reconstructs the transformed vectors according to (127a) and (127c) and performs the inverse transformation Ψ^{-1}. It has been shown [118] that in practice a fast sinusoidal transform such as the sine or cosine (depending how the boundary values are handled) is useful for monochrome images. To complete the design we now need to specify the quantizer in each DPCM channel.

Letting p denote the average desired bit rate in bit/pel, n_i the number of bits allocated to the ith DPCM channel and $\sigma_e^2(i)$ the quantizer mean-square error in the ith channel we could write

$$p = \frac{1}{N} \sum_{i=1}^{N} n_i, \quad n_i \geq 0. \tag{128}$$

Assuming that all the DPCM channels are in their steady state, the average (mean-square) distortion in coding of any vector (for noiseless channels) can be shown to be simply the average distortions in various DPCM channels, viz.

$$D = \frac{1}{N} \sum_{i=1}^{N} g_i(n_i) \sigma_e^2(i) \tag{129}$$

$$g_i(x) = \frac{f(x)}{1 - \rho_i^2 f(x)}$$

where $f(x)$ is the distortion-rate function of the quantizer and $g_i(x)$ represents the mean square distortion of the ith DPCM channel if the corresponding Markov process prediction error variance were unity. The bit allocation problem for hybrid coding is to minimize (129), subject to the constraints of (128). This is now in the framework of the problem defined in Section IV-B and the solution could be obtained as indicated there. In a typical hybrid coding scheme with $N = 16$ (block size) the bit allocations are (3, 3, 3, 2, 2, 1, 1, 1, 0, 0, 0, 0, 0, 0, 0, 0) for an average rate of 1 bit/pel. Fig. 32 shows a 256 $\times$ 256 image hybrid coded in blocks of 16 $\times$ 256 using the cosine transform and the semicausal model of (125).

B. Hybrid Coding of Noisy Images

In many situations the observed image may be noisy (and/or blurred). Then, it is desirable to design a coder which does not waste bits in coding the noise. As explained in Section III-D, a Kalman filter could be employed for prediction, in each DPCM channel of the hybrid coder. This is particularly useful when the image data is represented by a suitable semi-

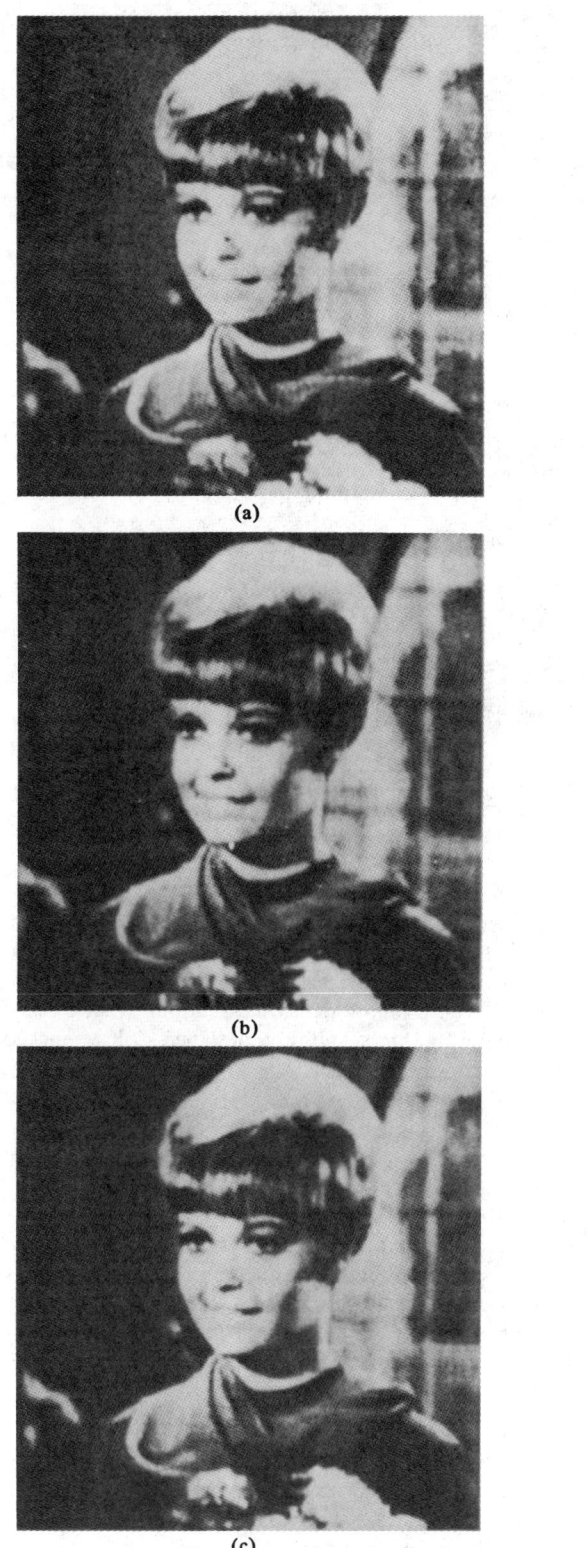

Fig. 32. Hybrid encoded images via semicausal model of (125) at 1 bit/pel. (a) Nonadaptive, SNR = 31 dB. (b) Adaptive variance estimation, SNR = 31.5 dB. (c) Adaptive classification, SNR = 33 dB.

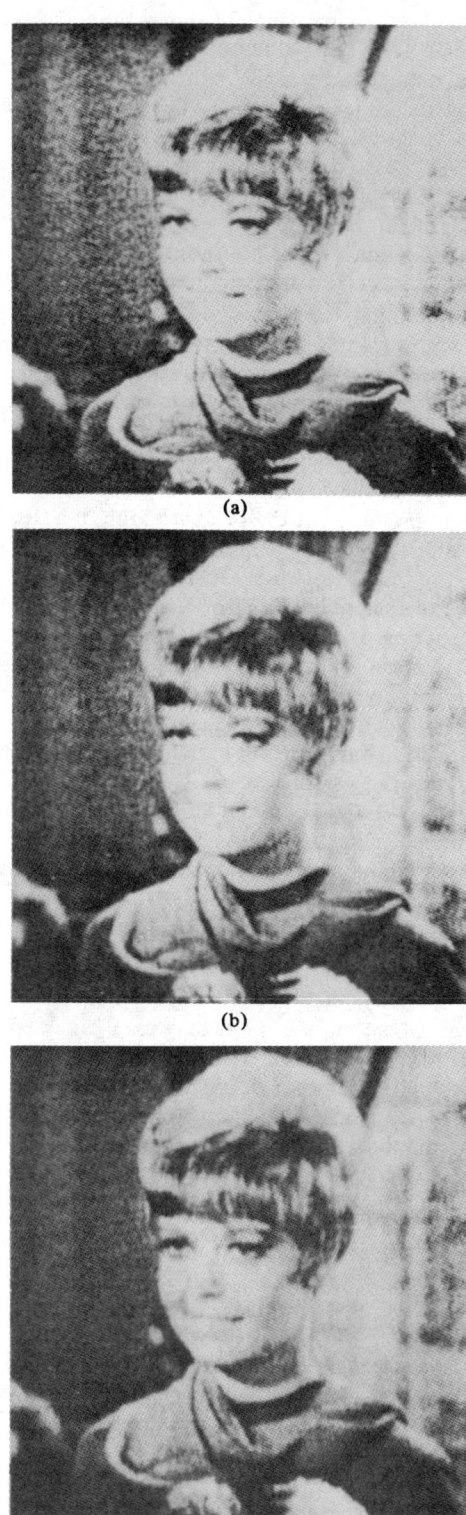

Fig. 33. Hybrid coding of noisy images via semicausal model. (a) Noisy image. (b) Restored image 8 bit/pel. (c) Encoded image 1 bit/pel.

causal model [184], since the Kalman predictor equations for the noisy image would correspond to the simple one-dimensional state variable model

$$v_j(i) = \rho_i v_{j-1}(i) + e_j(i) \qquad (130)$$

$$z_j(i) = v_j(i) + \eta_j(i). \qquad (131)$$

Fig. 33 shows the result of hybrid coding of a noisy image. The following observations have been made.

1) Because of presence of noise, the encoded data could have higher fidelity than the observed data due to filtering

combined with encoding. Fig. 33 shows this. Except at low rates and small noise (e.g., at rate = 0.5 bit/pel and $\sigma_n = 0.2 \sigma_u$), the encoded data has a better SNR then the observed data.

2) The overall coder performance depends on additive noise in observed image versus quantizer noise (or bit rate). At large noise levels ($\sigma_n > 0.5 \sigma_u$), the additive noise dominates so that quantization noise due to compression results in only a marginal degradation in performance. At small noise levels ($\sigma_n \lesssim 0.2\sigma_u$), quantization effects are more visible (as in the noise free case) since this effect starts to dominate.

C. Extensions of Hybrid Coding

The coding scheme of the previous section could be adapted to images whose spatial statistics vary slowly by updating the parameters of the model. It is important to consider adaptive schemes which offer reasonable tradeoffs between performance and complexity of the coder.

For a fixed predictor in the feedback loop of a DPCM channel, the variance of the prediction error will fluctuate with changes in the image statistics. A simple method is to update the variance of the prediction error at each step j, and use it to adjust the spacing of the quantizer levels in each DPCM channel. For a mean-square error criterion, this adaptation is achieved by simply normalizing the prediction error using its updated standard deviation. Then the quantizer levels are designed for a unit variance input random variable.

Let $\tilde{\sigma}_j^2(i)$ be the variance of $\tilde{e}_j(i)$, the prediction error at step j of the ith DPCM loop, and let $\dot{\sigma}_j^2(i)$ denote the variance of the quantized values. Since the quantized variables $\tilde{e}_j(i)$ are available both at the receiver and the transmitter, it is easy to estimate $\dot{\sigma}_j^2(i)$. A simple estimate of $\dot{\sigma}_j^2(i)$, called an exponential average variance estimator, is of the form [189]

$$\dot{\sigma}_{j+1}^2(i) = (1 - \gamma) e_j^2(i) + \gamma \dot{\sigma}_j^2(i), \quad j = 1, 2, \cdots. \quad (132)$$

For small quantization errors one may use $\dot{\sigma}_j$ as an estimate of $\tilde{\sigma}_j$. For the Lloyd–Max quantizers (or approximations thereof) a more accurate estimate of $\tilde{\sigma}_j$ is possible. Since the variance of a Lloyd–Max quantizer input equals the sum of the variances of the quantizer output and the quantization error (Section II-C), one could obtain the recursion [118]

$$\tilde{\sigma}_{j+1}^2(i) = \frac{1-\gamma}{1-f(n_i)} e_j^2(i) + \gamma \tilde{\sigma}_j^2(i), n_i > 1, \quad 0 < \gamma < 1. \quad (133)$$

The above estimates become poor for DPCM channels which are assigned a small number of bits ($n_i \simeq 1$). For these channels $\tilde{\sigma}_j(i)$ could be estimated by an extrapolation procedure [118].

Another adaptation is based on the classification method discussed earlier in Section V-G. Here each image column is classified as belonging to one of K predetermined classes that are fixed according to the activity in that image column, which is measured by its variance. Quantization bits are allocated according to their dynamic activity. The classification information is communicated by sending an extra $\log_2 K$ bits per column. Fig. 32 shows results of adaptive hybrid coding and compares them with the nonadaptive algorithm. Experimentally, it is found that the compression increases by a factor of 2 for the adaptive techniques [118].

Hybrid coding is particularly useful in interframe image data

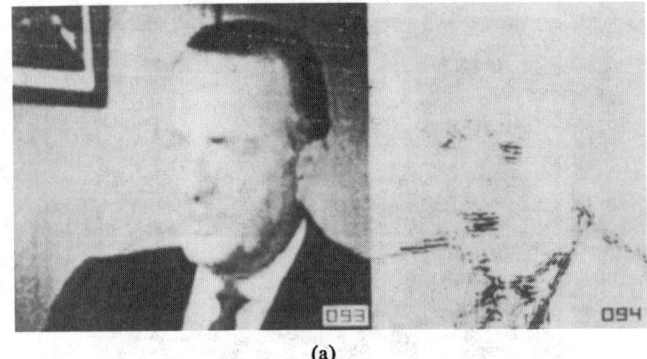

(a)

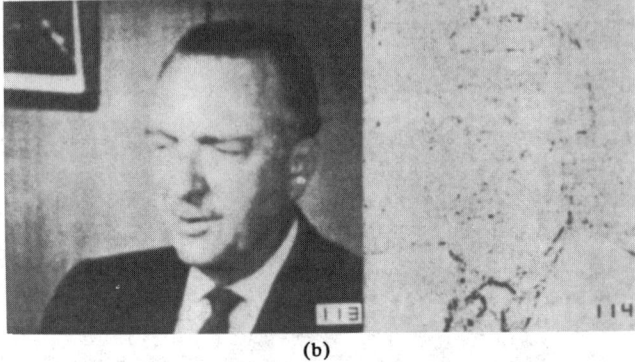

(b)

Fig. 34. Interframe adaptive hybrid coding. (a) Nonadaptive without motion compensation, 0.5 bit/pel, SNR = 34 dB. (b) Adaptive with motion compensation, 0.125 bit/pel, SNR = 36.7 dB.

compression of motion images. A two-dimensional $M \times N$ block of the kth frame, denoted U_k, is first transformed to give V_k. For each (m, n) the sequence $\{v_k(m, n), k = 1, 2, \cdots\}$ is considered a one-dimensional random process, and is coded independently by a suitably designed DPCM method. The receiver simply performs the two-dimensional inverse transform of the sequence $\{v_k(m, n)\}$. Since motion is characterized by deterministic variations along the temporal axis, the various motion compensation schemes discussed in Section III-I on predictive coding can be applied. Fig. 34 shows an interframe, 0.125 bit/pel via an adaptive hybrid coding method with motion compensation based on trajectory estimation and frame skipping. Such adaptations are not feasible in three-dimensional transform coding. Thus with motion compensation the adaptive hybrid coding method performs better than adaptive predictive coding as well as adaptive three-dimensional transform coding [97].

D. Hybrid Coding–Conclusions

In practice, hybrid coders combine the advantages of simple hardware complexity of DPCM coders and the high performance of transform coders, particularly at moderate bit rates (e.g., 1 bit/pel for two-dimensional images). In general, hybrid coding performance lies between transform coding and DPCM. It is easily adaptable to coding and filtering of noisy images and to changes in data statistics. It is less sensitive to channel errors than DPCM, but is not as robust as transform coding. Hybrid coders have been implemented for real-time data compression of images acquired by remotely piloted vehicles (RPV) [188].

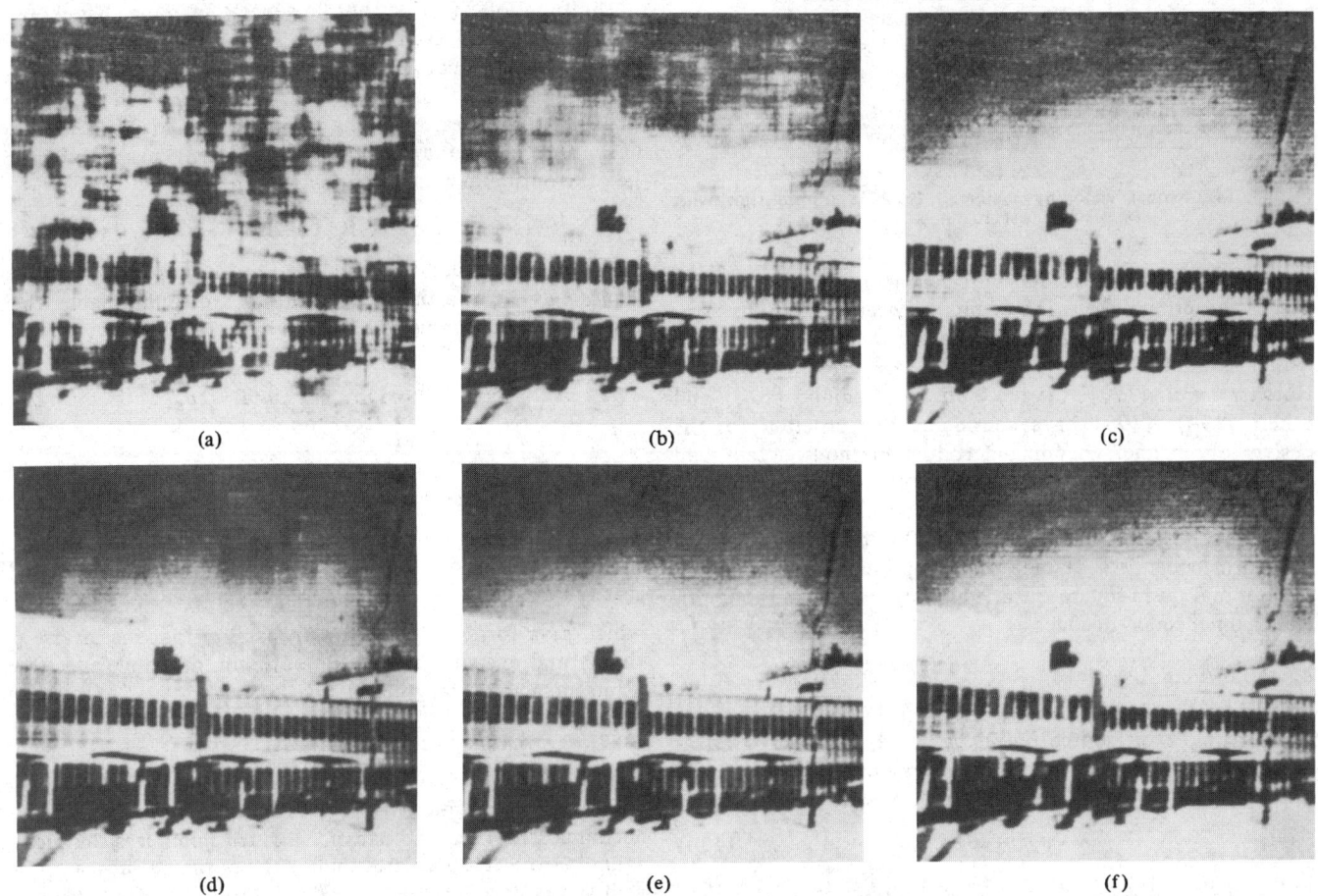

Fig. 35. Effect of channel errors in DPCM coding of images at 3 bit/pel; n = bit/pel assigned to the quantizer, k = length constraint on the channel code word, R = code rate for the convolutional codes used, SNR_i = signal to noise ratio at the channel input. From Modestino and Daut [216].

VII. Image Coding in the Presence of Channel Errors

In the data compression designs considered in the foregoing sections we ignored the channel effects by assuming noiseless channels (for transmission or storage). In practice, error correcting bits are appended to quantized samples before encoding to compensate for channel errors. Often, the error correcting codes used are designed to reduce the probability of bit errors, and for simplicity, equal protection is provided to all the samples. To account for channel errors, one has to add redundancy to the input. On the other hand, the data compression techniques tend to remove the redundancy in the source data. Thus a proper tradeoff between source coding (redundancy removal) and channel coding (redundancy injection) has to be achieved in the design of data compression systems.

In predictive coding, it is essential that the reconstruction filter be stable. Otherwise the channel errors could accumulate to arbitrarily large values. For example, as mentioned in Section III-B, the predictor of the delta modulator has to be stabilized by providing a "leak" factor. For multidimensional predictive coding, special care has to be taken to ensure the stability of the predictor model. Even when the predictor models are stable, the channel error is usually amplified by the reconstruction filter. For example, in DPCM coding of a first-order Markov process with intersample correlation ρ, the distortion that appears in the output signal in steady state due to channel noise (assumed white) is amplified by a factor of $(1 - \rho^2)^{-1}$. For $\rho = 0.95$, this amplification factor is 10. At the same time the achievable compression is also proportional to this factor. Therefore, while high compression is achievable for large value of ρ, the channel distortion is also large. Visually, channel noise in DPCM tends to create streaks that originate at the time the first channel error occurs and terminate when the coder is reinitialized. When isolated erroneous scan lines appear, post processing such as its replacement by the previous line or an average of the neighbors can be done [218]. A median filter operating orthogonally to the scanning direction could also be effective. Other techniques involve using error correcting codes at the source or modifying the reconstruction filter. These and related considerations have been studied in [76], [216]-[220].

Modestino and Daut have considered a combined source-channel coding approach for DPCM transmission of images. Error control protection is provided to bits which contribute most significantly to the reconstruction error. Fig. 35 shows that a proper bit allocation between the quantizer and the channel coder for error protection can improve the performance of DPCM schemes designed for unaided channels.

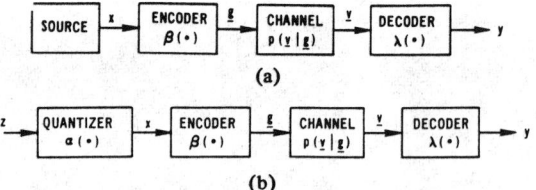

Fig. 36. (a) Channel encoding system. (b) PCM transmission with channel encoding.

In this section we consider source channel encoding methods based on optimal allocation of bits between the various error sources as well as the use of "optimal channel coder-decoder" which minimize the overall mean-square error. Crimmins, Horwitz et al. [190], [191], Wolf and Redinbo [192] and others [194], [195] have considered this criterion for the design of channel encoding-decoding methods. Jain and Jain [97], [193] have used this criterion for optimization of PCM and transform image coding algorithms to compensate for channel errors. The key result is that the overall optimal transform coder is a cascade of the optimal transform (KL), the optimal mean-square quantizer (Lloyd-Max) and the optimal channel coder-decoder.

A. Definitions

Consider Fig. 36(a). Let S be the set of $K = 2^k$ data symbols representing k bit source output words x_i. Let V be an n-dimensional binary vector space and let C be a k-dimensional subspace of V, $k \leq n$. If v_1 and v_2 are elements of V, then

$$v = v_1 \oplus v_2 \qquad (134)$$

is also an element of V. Here "$\oplus$" sign implies the EXCLUSIVE-OR operation. C contains n-bit binary words of order K such that if $g_1, g_2 \in C$, then $g = g_1 \oplus g_2 \in C$. Since C is a k-dimensional subspace of V, it could be described by a set of k basis vectors, each being an n-tuple. Moreover, every k-dimensional binary vector can be mapped onto C.

Let the channel be a memoryless, binary symmetric channel with bit-error probability p_e. We will assume the channel error does not depend on the channel input. Let $\beta(\cdot)$ denote the mapping which maps the k-bit source output $x_i \in S$ into the n-bit code words $g_i \in C$ by a one-to-one encoding rule. The channel maps the elements of C into the elements of V. At the receiver, $\lambda(\cdot)$ denotes the mapping of elements of V into elements on the real line R, i.e.,

$$\lambda: V \xrightarrow{\text{into}} R. \qquad (135)$$

B. The Optimum Mean-Square Decoder [192]

The mean-square error between the decoder output and the encoder input is given by

$$\sigma_c^2 = \sigma_c^2(\beta, \lambda) \triangleq E(y - x)^2 \qquad (136)$$

and depends on the mappings β and λ. It has been shown that for a fixed encoding rule β, the decoder that minimizes this error is given by the conditional mean of x, i.e.,

$$y = \lambda(v) = \sum_{x \in S} x p(x|v) = E(x|v) \qquad (137)$$

where $p(x|v)$ is the conditional probability of x given the channel output v [192].

The function $\lambda(v)$ does not, in general, map the channel output into the set S even if $n = k$. Sometimes it may be desired to map the decoder output into a predefined set of levels y^* which contain 2^n or less levels. Then it could be shown [192] that the best decoding rule is to find $\lambda(v)$ according to (137) and then round off each value to $[y]$; the nearest $y^* \in y^*$, i.e., the optimum mapping λ^* is now given by

$$\lambda^*(v) = [\lambda(v)]^*. \qquad (138)$$

If β is the natural encoding of the integers into binary k-tuples ($n = k$), and the source outputs are equiprobable, then the optimum decoding rule is given by

$$\lambda(v) = (2^k - 1)p_e + \sum_{i=1}^{k} v_i(1 - 2p_e)2^{k-i} \qquad (139)$$

where $v_i = 0, 1$ are the elements of the channel output vector v. For $p_e \ll 1$, this yields $\lambda = \beta^{-1}$, i.e.,

$$\lambda(v) \simeq \sum_{i=1}^{k} v_i 2^{k-i} \qquad (140)$$

which says for small bit-error probability that the inverse of the natural encoding rule is the optimum decoding rule. (See Yamaguchi and Huang [195].)

C. The Optimum Encoding Rule

In the foregoing we considered the optimum decoding rule for any given encoding rule β. It is desirable to find as well the encoding rule (i.e., the pair β, λ) which minimizes the mean-square error. This requires finding the optimum subspace C as well as the encoding rule β. For uniformly distributed source output, Wolf and Redinbo [192] have given a procedure for obtaining the optimal mapping β. In general, an exhaustive minimization procedure which searches over all subspaces of V is required. In practice suboptimal solutions are found by restricting the search to a particular set of subspaces. Table I shows a set of suboptimal basis vectors calculated by Jain and Jain [97] for various combinations of pairs (n, k), from which β is obtained as follows. Let $b = [b(1), b(2), \cdots, b(k)]$, be the binary representation of an element of S, then

$$g = \beta(b) = \sum_{j=1}^{k} \oplus b(j) \cdot \phi_j \qquad (141)$$

where $\Sigma \oplus$ denotes EXCLUSIVE-OR summation, "·" denotes the binary product and $\{\phi_j\}$ are the basis vectors of C as listed in Table I. The codes generated by this method are called (n, k) Group Codes. These codes for other combinations of n and k have been tabulated in [97].

Example: Let $n = 4$, $k = 2$. Then $\phi_1 = [1\ 0\ 1\ 1]$, $\phi_2 = [0\ 1\ 0\ 1]$ and β is given as follows:

x	b	$g = \beta(b)$
0	0 0	0 0 0 0 = $0 \cdot \phi_1 \oplus 0 \cdot \phi_2$
1	0 1	0 1 0 1 = $0 \cdot \phi_1 \oplus 1 \cdot \phi_2$
2	1 0	1 0 1 1 = $1 \cdot \phi_1 \oplus 0 \cdot \phi_2$
3	1 1	1 1 1 0 = $\phi_1 \oplus \phi_2$.

In general the basis vectors ϕ_i depend on the bit error probability p_e. In the special cases of Table I and those tabulated in [97], these vectors have been found to be almost independent of p_e [97], [192]. For most image coding applications, the

TABLE I
Basis Vectors $\{\phi_i, i = 1, \cdots, k\}$ of Group G for (n, k) Group Codes

i	k	n-k=0	1	2	3	4
1	4	1000	10001	100011	1000110	10001110
2		0100	01000	010001	0100101	01001010
3		0010	00100	001000	0010011	00100101
4		0001	00010	000100	0001111	00010011
1	3	100	1001	10011	100110	1001110
2		010	0100	01001	010101	0101010
3		001	0010	00100	001011	0010101
1	2	10	101	1011	10110	010111
2		01	010	0101	01101	101110
1	1	1	11	111	1111	11111

group codes given in [97] are sufficient. Although these codes are for equiprobable source outputs, we shall use these codes for other distributions as well. This will degrade the performance of the channel encoder somewhat, but it is a second-order effect compared to the overall improvement in performance.

D. Optimization of PCM Transmission

In PCM the source is a memoryless quantizer whose outputs are independently coded for transmission. Let k be the number of quantizer bits for each sample, $\{x_i\}$ the output levels arranged in the ascending order of their values, and $\{p(x_i)\}$ their probabilities. If b_i is the binary vector representation of the index i, we use (141) to define the mapping β for any given pair (n, k). The decoder equation (137) gives the reproduced values. Consider the PCM scheme in Fig. 36(b) where a continuous random variable z is quantized for transmission. The mean square distortion between the quantizer input z and the decoder output is given by

$$\sigma_t^2 = E(z - y)^2. \tag{142}$$

It has been shown [97] that for a fixed n-bit channel encoder $\beta(\cdot)$, the k-bit quantizer $\alpha(\cdot)$ and the channel decoder $\lambda(\cdot)$ that minimize the mean-square error σ_t^2 are given by

$$\lambda(v) = E(x|v) \tag{143}$$

$$x = \alpha(z) = E(z|z \in I_j) \tag{144}$$

where $I_j, j = 1, \cdots, 2^k$ denotes the jth quantization interval of the quantizer.

This means that the optimum decoder is independent of the optimum quantizer, which is the Lloyd-Max quantizer. Thus the optimal design can be accomplished by designing the quantizer and the decoder individually.

Let $f(k)$ and $c(n, k)$ denote the mean-square distortions due to the k-bit Lloyd-Max quantizer and the channel respectively when the quantizer input is a unit variance random variable. Then we could write the total mean-square error for the input z of variance σ_z^2,

$$\left. \begin{array}{l} \sigma_t^2 = \sigma_z^2 \hat{\sigma}_t^2 \\ \hat{\sigma}_t^2 \triangleq [f(k) + c(n, k)] \\ \sigma_q^2 \triangleq \sigma_z^2 f(k), \sigma_e^2 \triangleq \sigma_z^2 c(n, k). \end{array} \right\} \tag{145}$$

where σ_q^2 and σ_e^2 represent the quantizer and channel distortions, respectively. The channel distortion depends on the

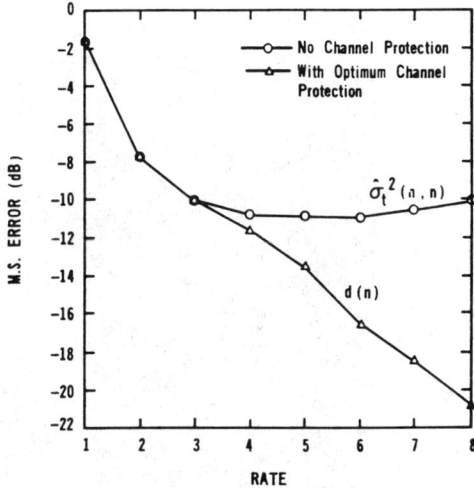

Fig. 37. Distortion versus rate characteristics of PCM transmission over a binary symmetric channel.

(n, k) group code as well as the bit error probability p_e. For a fixed n and $k \leq n$, $f(k)$ is a monotonically decreasing function of k, whereas $c(n, k)$ is a monotonically increasing function of k. Hence for every n there is an optimum value of $k = k(n)$ for which $\hat{\sigma}_t^2$ is minimized. Let $d(n)$ denote the minimum value of $\hat{\sigma}_t^2$ with respect of k. Fig. 37 shows the plot of the distortions $\hat{\sigma}_t^2(n, n)$ and $d(n)$ versus the rate for n-bit PCM transmission of a Gaussian random variable when $p_e = 0.01$. It shows, for example, the optimum combination of error protection and quantization could improve the system performance by about 11 dB for an 8-bit transmission. The quantity $\hat{\sigma}_t^2(n, n)$ represents the distortion of the PCM system if no channel error protection is provided and all the bits are used for quantization. With k optimized, we write

$$k = k(n)$$

$$d(n) = \min_k \{\hat{\sigma}_t^2(n, k)\} = \hat{\sigma}_t^2(n, k(n)). \tag{146}$$

Thus $d(n)$ represents the optimized distortion function.

E. Optimization of Transform Coding

The results above could be exploited in designing transform coders which are protected against channel errors. A transform coder contains several PCM channels, each operating on one transformed sample. If we represent z_j as the jth trans-

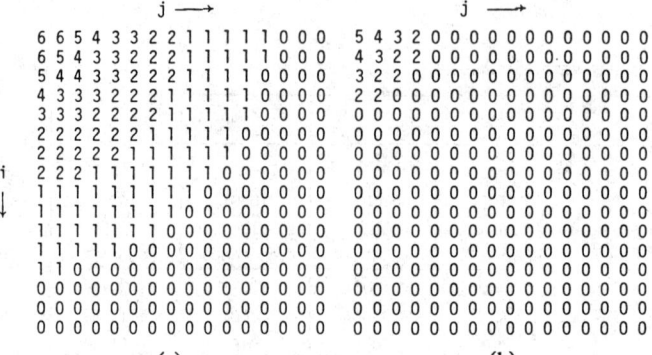

Fig. 38. Bit allocations for quantization and error protection in 16 × 16 block cosine transform coding of images. Images modeled by the exponential covariance function of (103). Average bit rate is 1 bit/pel and channel error rate is 1 percent. (a) $k_{i,j}$, bits allocated to quantizers (b) $n_{i,j} - k_{i,j}$, channel protection bits allocated to quantizer outputs.

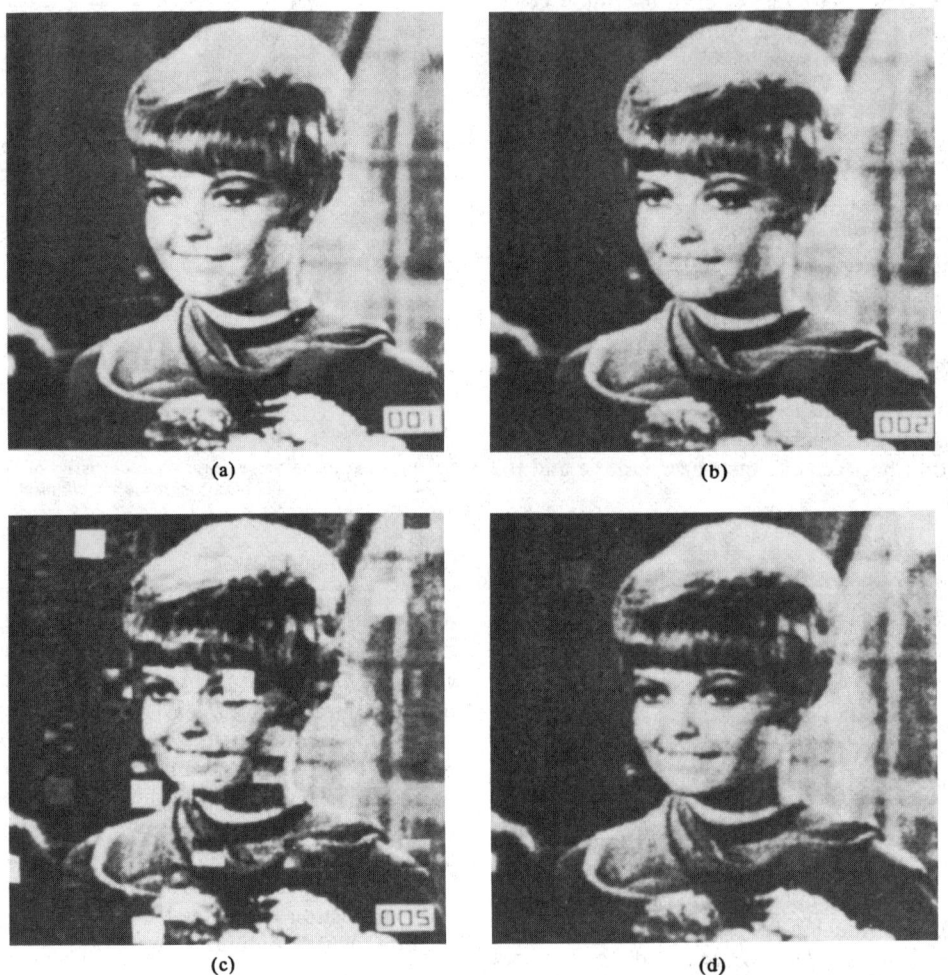

Fig. 39. Transform coding of images with channel error protection. (a) original (b) 1 bit/pel with no channel errors (c) 1 bit/pel, $p_e = 0.01$, without channel error protection (d) 1 bit/pel, $p_e = 0.01$ with error protection.

form domain sample and let $\sigma_j^2 = \text{var}(z_j)$, then the average mean-square distortion of a transform coding scheme in the presence of channel errors becomes

$$D = \sum_j \sigma_j^2 \, d(n_j) \qquad (147)$$

where n_j is the total number of bits allocated to the jth PCM channel.

The index j takes values over the set of integers $\{1, 2, \cdots, J\}$, where J is the number of PCM channels. Since we could evaluate the function $d(n)$ via (146), any transform coding scheme could be designed by finding the bit allocation n_j for

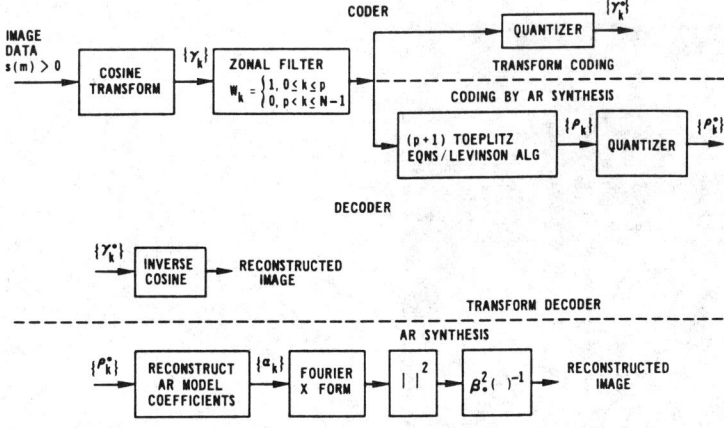

Fig. 40. Transform coding versus coding by AR synthesis.

a desired average rate by following the integer bit allocation algorithm of Section IV-C. Knowing n_j, we can find $k_j = k(n_j)$, the optimum number of quantizer bits corresponding to n_j.

Fig. 38 shows the bit allocation (k_j) pattern for the quantizers and the allocation of channel protection bits ($n_j - k_j$) at an overall average bit rate of 1 bit/pel for 16 × 16 block coding of an isotropic random field. Clearly, more protection is provided to samples which have larger variances (and hence are more important for transmission). The overhead due to channel protection, even for the high value of $p_e = 0.01$, is only 15 percent. For $p_e = 0.001$, the overhead is about 4 percent.

Fig. 39 shows the results of applying the foregoing techniques to transform coding of an image in the presence of channel errors. The improvement in SNR is 10 dB at $p = 0.01$ and is also significant visually. This scheme is quite robust with respect to fluctuations in the channel error rates (p_e).

VIII. Other Methods

Several specialized methods not described so far include variable velocity scanning, pseudorandom scanning, image coding by splines, interpolative coding, countour coding, cluster and feature coding, singular value decomposition (SVD) coding, autoregressive coding, etc. We briefly discuss them now.

In variable velocity scanning [203], the image is sampled at a rate proportional to the slope of the scanned intensity. This provides a higher number of samples in areas of edges and large activity and fewer samples in smooth areas. Pseudo random scanning proposed by Huang and Tretiak [205] for binary facsimile images, is a multiplexing scheme where pseudorandom scans of 1's and 0's from several images are passed sequentially through a logical OR gate. At the receiver the transmitter pseudorandom scanning sequence is repeated by each channel. A "1" will be displayed correctly in some of the channels but will appear as random noise in others. Up to four channels have been found to be easily multiplexed giving a 4 to 1 compression.

Since image activity is not regularly spaced in common images, non-uniform sampling could be performed via the use of variable knot splines [208]. Basically the image is sampled at locations (called knots) where its Laplacian (for cubic splines) exceeds a threshold. Cubic splines in two dimensions are then fitted through the knots. This method becomes quite similar to the stochastic decomposition method of Section V-D, if we identify $\mathcal{L}$ to be the Laplacian operator and allocate all the quantization bits to the deterministic part ϵ_b. The reconstructed image is obtained by finding a least squares smoothing solution of the problem $\mathcal{L}[u] = \epsilon_b$. A somewhat different approach to this problem is via splines [208]. For other interpolative coding schemes, see [206], [207].

Contour coding is useful for boundaries and curves and has applications in transmission of weather maps as well as in two source coding discussed in Section V-C. These algorithms have been studied by Wintz, Wilkins *et al.*, Freeman, Graham, Schreiber, and others [171]-[181]. An important class of algorithms useful for multispectral images is called cluster or feature coding. In multispectral images, at each (x, y) location a vector of multispectral intensities is represented. Each vector is mapped into a feature vector. Areas of the images which have similar features "cluster" together in the feature space. First, a set of cluster centroids is determined. Then, for each pel, its membership to this set is found. Only the information pertaining to its membership and the set of feature vectors are coded. Hilbert, Wintz, and others [222], [223] have developed algorithms for cluster coding. Usually, the fidelity criterion for these algorithms is the classification (rather than mean square) accuracy of the encoded data.

Since an image is most easily represented by a matrix, its SVD can be used for data compression. Consider an $N \times M$ image U of rank r. Its SVD could be written as

$$U = \sum_{i=1}^{r} \lambda_i \phi_i \psi_i^T \tag{148}$$

where ϕ_i and ψ_i are, respectively, $N \times 1$ and $M \times 1$ vectors, and $\lambda_1 \geqslant \lambda_2 \geqslant \lambda_3 \cdots \geqslant \lambda_r > 0$ are called the singular value of U. The first term $\lambda_1 \phi_1 \psi_1^T$ represents the best least squares, rank one matrix approximation of U. To achieve data compression, define

$$U_1 = U - \lambda_1^* \phi_1^* (\psi_1^*)^T$$
$$U_{k+1} = U_k - \lambda_{1,k}^* \phi_{1,k}^* (\psi_{1,k}^*)^T, \quad k = 1, 2, \cdots, k_m \tag{149}$$

where $\lambda_{1,k} \phi_{1,k} \psi_{1,k}^T$ is the best least squares rank one approximation of U_k and $\lambda_{1,k}^*, \phi_{1,k}^*, \psi_{1,k}^*$ are the quantized values of $\lambda_{1,k}, \phi_{1,k}$ and $\psi_{1,k}$, respectively. Generally, one chooses $k_m \ll r$. At the receiver, the reproduced image is given by

$$U^* = \sum_{k=1}^{k_m} \lambda_{1,k}^* \phi_{1,k}^* (\psi_{1,k}^*)^T. \tag{150}$$

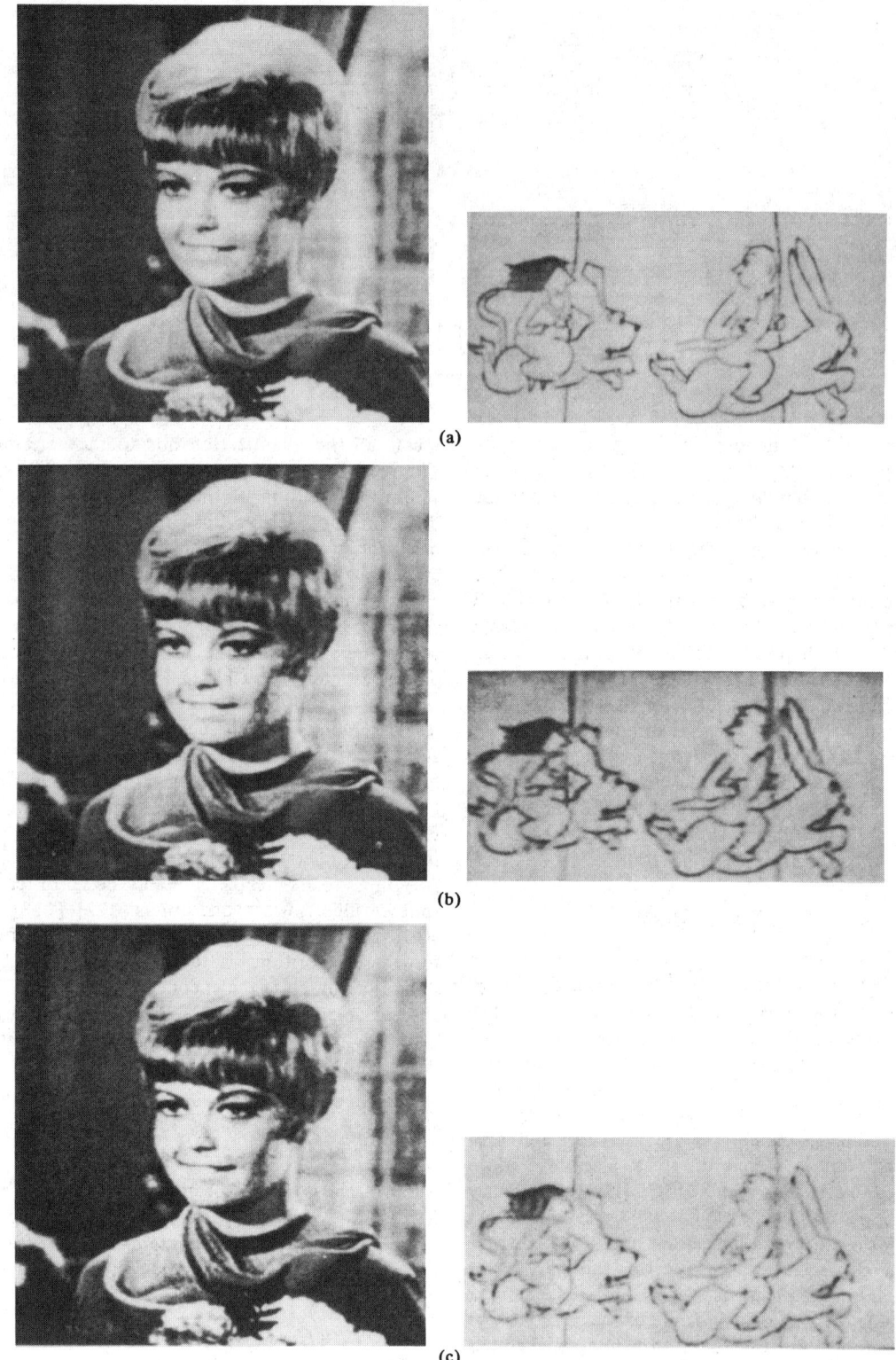

Fig. 41. Line-by-line compression of images by AR synthesis with 4 to 1 sample reduction. (a) Original. (b) Cosine transform coded. (c) Coding by AR synthesis.

For small quantization errors, one would have $\lambda_{1,k}^* \simeq \lambda_k$, $\phi_{1,k}^* \simeq \phi_{1,k}$ and $\psi_{1,k}^* \simeq \psi_k$. Andrews and Patterson [173] have used the expansion of (148) although differently for coding of images. All the quantities λ_k, ϕ_k and ψ_k are calculated first, then quantized and coded. The received image is simply calculated as

$$U^* = \sum_{k=1}^{k_m} \lambda_k^* \phi_k^* (\psi_k^*)^T. \qquad (151)$$

TABLE II
Summary of Image Data Compression Methods

Method	Typical Average Rates Bits/Pixel	Comments
Zero Memory Methods		Simple to implement
PCM	6-8	
Contrast Quantization	4-5	
Pseudorandom Noise - Quantization	4-5	
Line Interlace	4	
Dot Interlace	2-4	
Predictive Coding		
Delta Modulation	1	Performance poorer than DPCM over sample data for improvement.
Intraframe DPCM	2-3	Predictive methods are generally simple to implement, are sensitive to data statistics. Adaptive techniques improve performance substantially. Channel error effects are commulative and severely degrade image quality.
Intraframe Adaptive DPCM	1-2	
Interframe Conditional - Replenishment	1-2	
Interframe DPCM	1-1.5	
Interframe Adaptive DPCM	0.5-1	
Transform Coding		Achieve high performance, small sensitivity to fluctuation in data statistics, channel and quantization errors distributed over the image block. Easy to provide channel protection. Hardware complexity is high.
Intraframe	1-1.5	
Intraframe Adaptive	0.5-1	
Interframe	0.5-1	
Interframe Adaptive	0.1-0.5	
Hybrid Coding		Achieve performance close to transform coding at moderate rates (.5 to 1 bit/pixel). Complexity lies midway between transform coding and DPCM.
Intraframe	1-2	
Intraframe Adaptive	0.5-1.5	
Interframe	0.5-1	
Interframe Adaptive	0.25-0.5	

Bit rates of 2 bit/pel have been achieved at acceptable distortion levels. The method according to (149) and (150) should perform better, since the quantization error at any step is fed to the next step for correction. Compared to usual transform coding, SVD coding is not very attractive because the vectors ϕ_i, ψ_i have to be computed for each image.

In recent years AR models have been found to have extensive applications [198]. Their success has been notable in high resolution spectral estimation and in the theory of linear prediction. Recently, it has been shown [197] that the AR models can be useful in image data compression also.

From the theory of image formation, since the intensity distribution of an image is nonnegative, it can be considered as a power spectrum. Therefore its Fourier transform is an autocorrelation function. In AR modeling an underlying AR random process is realized such that the Fourier transform of the image is the autocorrelation of that random process. For simplicity we consider the one-dimensional case. It has been shown [197] that the discrete cosine transform of a positive sequence $\{u_m\}$

$$\gamma_k = \gamma_{-k} = \frac{1}{N} \sum_{m=0}^{N-1} u_m \cos \frac{\pi k}{N} \left(m + \frac{1}{2}\right), \quad 0 \leq k \leq N-1 \quad (152)$$

is an autocorrelation sequence. Hence, there exists a pth-order AR model, viz.

$$a(k) = \sum_{m=1}^{p} \alpha_m a(k-m) + \epsilon(k) \quad (153)$$

where $\epsilon(k)$ is a stationary zero-mean white noise process, such that its first $(p+1)$ autocorrelations are the same as $\{\gamma_k, 0 \leq k \leq p\}$. The corresponding power spectrum of the sequence $\{a(k)\}$ is given by

$$s(x) = \beta^2 / |1 - \sum_{m=1}^{p} \alpha_m \exp\{-j2\pi mx\}|^2, \quad -\frac{1}{2} \leq x \leq \frac{1}{2} \quad (154)$$

$$\beta^2 \triangleq E[\epsilon^2(k)] = \gamma_0 - \sum_{m=1}^{p} \alpha_m \gamma(m). \quad (155)$$

The information in the image line $\{u_m\}$ is thus coded into the $(p+1)$ coefficients α_m and β^2. The quantity $s(x)$ gives an interpolated estimate of the samples image sequence $\{u_m\}$. The α_m and β^2 may be obtained by solving a system of linear Toeplitz equations whose solution can be obtained via Levinson's algorithm [197]-[200], which gives the quantities ρ_m, known as reflection coefficients. These are less than 1 in magnitude and have been shown in speech synthesis [201], [202] to be more desirable for quantization. Fig. 40 shows the AR coding algorithm and compares it with transform coding.

For highly correlated gray-level images, this method has only a marginal advantage over the cosine transform coding. However for binary and high contrast images (with few gray levels) this method performs much better than transform coding (Fig. 41). Hence it could be considered as a universal transform coding algorithm which could be used for transform coding of composite images. Further development is required to extend this method to two-dimensional block coding (rather than line by line).

IX. SUMMARY AND CONCLUSIONS

We have discussed the fundamentals as well as details of several basic and state of the art techniques in image data compression. Many of these techniques, e.g., predictive, transform and hybrid coding have been hardware implemented for image transmission/storage applications (see [9], [188]). Table II provides a summary of performance of the three classes of algorithms considered in detail here. Excluded from our specific discussion here is color image coding. The principles outlined here are valid for color images. However, the details differ substantially because of perceptual considerations in color. A recent survey article [53] addresses these issues.

Much of our discussion in this paper has been devoted to pel by pel reproduction of an image. In many applications such as image understanding systems, one desires to code only the description of the image. For example, if the various objects of the scene could be recognized by a machine, then it may suffice to synthesize a similar scene at the receiver from the description of the objects. Such a technique is called coding by synthesis. One method of coding by synthesis is to code the unrecognized objects pel by pel and synthesize the image background or other areas which may contain some easily identifiable texture such as grass, ivy, brick, or a nearly uniform background. Such an approach requires a marriage of image analysis and segmentation techniques with the pel by pel coding techniques discussed here. Future image coding advances seem to point in this direction.

BIBLIOGRAPHY AND COMMENTS

Section 1

Data compression has been a topic of immense interest in digital image processing. Several special issues and review papers have been devoted to this. For details, see

[1] Special Issue on Redundancy Reduction, *Proc. IEEE*, vol. 55, Mar. 1967.
[2] Special Issue of Digital Communications, *IEEE Commun. Tech.*, vol. COM-19, part I, Dec. 1971.
[3] T. S. Huang and O. J. Tretiak, Eds., *Picture Bandwidth Compression*. New York: Gordon and Breach, 1972.
[4] Special Issue of Image Bandwidth Compression, *IEEE Trans. Commun.*, vol. COM-25, Nov. 1977.
[5] L. D. Davisson and R. M. Gray, Eds., *Data Compression* (Benchmark Papers in Electrical Engineering and Computer Science). Stroudsberg, PA: Dowden Hutchinson & Ross, 1976.
[6] T. S. Huang, "PCM picture transmission," *IEEE Spectrum*, vol. 12, pp. 57-60, Dec. 1965.
[7] W. K. Pratt, *Digital Image Processing*. New York: Wiley, 1978, pp. 591-710.
[8] A. K. Jain, *Multidimensional Techniques in Digital Image Processing*. To be published.
[9] P. Camana, "Video bandwidth compression: A study in tradeoffs," *IEEE Spectrum*, pp. 24-29, June 1979.
[10] W. K. Pratt, Ed., *Image Transmission Techniques*. New York: Academic Press, 1979.
[11] A. K. Jain, "Some new techniques in Image Processing," in *Image Science Mathematics*, C. O. Wilde and E. Barrett, Eds. North Hollywood, CA: West Periodical Co., 1977, pp. 201-223.

For entropy and probability measures of image data, see [10] and

[12] W. F. Schreiber, "The measurement of third order probability distributions of television signals," *IRE Trans. Inform. Theory*, vol. IT-2, pp. 94-105, Sept. 1956.

For Shannon's original work, see

[13] C. E. Shannon, "The mathematical theory of communication," Parts I and II, *Bell Syst. Tech. J.*, vol. 27, pp. 379 and 623, 1948. Also see, C. F. Shannon and W. Weaver, *The Mathematical Theory of Communication*. Urbana, IL: The University of Illinois Press, 1949.

Shannon's theory and the fundamentals of source coding and different encoding schemes can be found in textbooks on Information theory, e.g.,

[14] F. M. Reza, *An Introduction to Information Theory*. New York: McGraw-Hill, 1961.
[15] N. Abramson, *Information Theory and Coding*. New York: McGraw-Hill, 1963.
[16] R. G. Gallagher, *Information Theory and Reliable Communication*. New York: Wiley, 1968.

For visual fidelity criteria based on spatial frequency response, see Sakrison in [4, p. 1251] and

[17] J. L. Mannos and D. J. Sakrison, "The effects of a visual fidelity criterion on the encoding of images," *IEEE Trans. Inform. Theory*, vol. IT-20, pp. 525-236, July 1974.

For other related results on visual fidelity criterion and visual perception,

[18] D. H. Kelly, "Effects of sharp edges on the visibility of sinusoidal gratings," *J. Opt. Soc. Amer.*, vol. 60, pp. 98-103, Jan. 1970.
[19] V. R. Algazi, "The psycho-physics of vision and their relation to picture quality and coding limitations," *Acta Electron.*, vol. 19, no. 3, pp. 225-232, 1976.
[20] A. Netravali and B. Prasada, "Adaptive quantization of picture signals using spatial masking," *Proc. IEEE*, vol. 65, pp. 536-548, April 1977.
[21] Z. L. Budrikis, "Visual fidelity criterion and modeling," *Proc. IEEE*, vol. 60, pp. 771-779, July 1972.
[22] T. N. Cornsweet, *Visual Perception*. New York: Academic Press, 1970.

For effects of frame rate reduction, interlacing and related methods of compression, see

[23] M. W. Baldwin, "Demonstration of some visual effects of using frame storage in television transmission," in *IRE Conv. Rec.*, p. 107, 1958.
[24] R. C. Brainard, F. W. Mounts, and B. Prasada, "Low resolution TV: Subjective effects of frame repetition and picture replenishment," *Bell Syst. Tech. J.*, vol. 56, no. 1, pp. 261-271, Jan. 1967.
[25] S. Deutsch, "Pseudo-random dot scan television systems," *IEEE Trans. Broadcasting*, vol. BC-11, pp. 11-21, July 1965.
[26] G. G. Gouriet, "Dot Interlaced Television," *Electron. Eng.*, vol. 24, no. 290, pp. 166-171, Apr. 1952.

Section II

[27] S. P. Lloyd, "Least squares quantization in PCM," unpublished memorandum, Bell Laboratories, 1957 (Copy available by writing the author).
[28] J. Max, "Quantizing for minimum distortion," *IRE Trans. Inform. Theory*, vol. IT-6, pp. 7-12, 1960.
[29] P. F. Panter and W. Dite, "Quantizing distortion in pulse-code modulation with nonuniform spacing levels," *Proc. IRE*, vol. 39, pp. 44-48, 1951.

[30] B. Smith, "Instantaneous companding of quantizing signals," *Bell Syst. Tech. J.*, vol. 27, pp. 446–472, 1948.
[31] G. M. Roe, "Quantizing for minimum distortion," *IEEE Trans. Inform. Theory*, vol. IT-10, pp. 384–385, 1964.
[32] V. R. Algazi, "Useful approximations to optimum quantization," *IEEE Trans. Commun.*, vol. COM-14, pp. 297–301, 1966.
[33] T. J. Goblick and J. L. Holsinger, "Analog source digitization: A comparison of theory and practice," *IEEE Trans. Inform. Theory*, vol. IT-13, pp. 323–326, Apr. 1967.
[34] H. Gish and J. N. Pierce, "Asymptotically efficient quantization," *IEEE Trans. Inform. Theory*, vol. IT-14, pp. 676–681, 1968.
[35] T. Berger, *Rate Distortion Theory*. Englewood Cliffs, NJ: Prentice-Hall, 1971.
[36] —, "Optimum quantizers and permutation codes," *IEEE Trans. Inform. Theory*, vol. IT-16, pp. 759–765, Nov. 1972.
[37] A. N. Netravali and R. Saigal, "An algorithm for the design of optimum quantizers," *Bell Syst. Tech. J.*, vol. 55, pp. 1423–1435, Nov. 1976.
[38] D. K. Sharma, "Design of absolutely optimal quantizers for a wide class of distortion measures," *IEEE Trans. Inform Theory*, vol. IT-24, pp. 693–702, Nov. 1978.
[39] N. C. Gallagher, Jr., "Quantizing schemes for the discrete fourier transform of a random time-series," *IEEE Trans. Inform. Theory*, vol. IT-24, pp. 156–163, Mar. 1978.
[40] W. A. Pearlman, "Quantizing error bounds for computer generated holograms," Stanford University Information Systems Laboratory, Stanford, CA, Tech. Rep. 6 503-1, Aug. 1974. Also see Pearlman and Gray, *IEEE Trans. Inform. Theory*, vol. IT-24, pp. 683–692, Nov. 1978.
[41] F. W. Scoville and T. S. Huang, "The subjective effect of spatial and brightness quantization in PCM picture transmission," *NEREM Rec.*, pp. 234–235, 1965.
[42] S. Hecht, "The visual discrimination of intensity and the Weber-Fechner law," *J. Gen. Physiol.*, vol. 7, p. 241, 1924.
[43] F. Kretz, "Subjectively optimal quantization of pictures," *IEEE Trans. Commun.*, vol. COM-23, pp. 1288–1292, Nov. 1975.
[44] L. G. Roberts, "Picture coding using pseudo-random noise," *IRE Trans. Inf. Theory*, vol. IT-8, pp. 145–154, Feb. 1962.
[45] J. E. Thompson and J. J. Sparkes, "A pseudo-random quantizer for television signals," *Proc. IEEE*, vol. 55, pp. 353–355, Mar. 1967.
[46] J. O. Limb, "Design of dither waveforms for quantized visual signals," *Bell Syst. Tech J.*, vol. 48, pp. 2555–2583, Sept. 1969.
[47] B. Lippel, M. Kurland, and A. H. March, "Ordered dither patterns for coarse quantization of pictures," *Proc. IEEE*, vol. 59, pp. 429–431, Mar. 1971.
[48] B. Lippel and M. Kurland, "The effects of dither on luminance quantization of pictures," *IEEE Trans. Commun. Tech.*, vol. COM-19, pp. 879–889, Dec. 1971.
[49] J. E. Thompson, "A 36-MBIT/S television coder employing pseudorandom quantization," *IEEE Trans. Commun. Tech.*, vol. COM-19, pp. 872–879, Dec. 1971.
[50] C. N. Judice, "Digital video: A buffer-controlled dither processor for animated images," *IEEE Trans. Commun.*, vol. COM-25, pp. 1433–1440, Nov. 1977.
[51] P. G. Roetling, "Halftone method with edge enhancement and moiré suppression," *J. Opt. Soc. Amer.*, vol. 66, pp. 985–989, 1976.
[52] A. K. Jain and W. K. Pratt, "Color image quantization," in *Nat. Telecommunication Conf. 1972 Rec.* (Houston, TX), Dec. 1972 (IEEE Publication No. 72CH0601-S-NTC).
[53] J. O. Limb, C. B. Rubinstein, and J. E. Thompson, "Digital coding of color video signals," *IEEE Trans. Commun.*, vol. COM-25, pp. 1329–1385, Nov. 1977.

Section III

For some initial work on predictive coding, see

[54] B. N. Oliver, "Efficient coding," *Bell Syst. Tech. J.*, vol. 31, pp. 724–750, July 1952.
[55] C. W. Harrison, "Experiments with linear prediction in television," *Bell Syst. Tech. J.*, pp. 764–768, July 1952.
[56] P. Elias, "Predictive Coding—Part I and Part II," *IRE Trans. Inform. Theory*, vol. IT-1, pp. 16–33, Mar. 1955.

For delta modulation analysis of Markov and Wiener processes, see

[57] D. Slepian, "On delta modulation," *Bell Syst. Tech. J.*, vol. 51, pp. 2101–2137, Dec. 1972.
[58] T. L. Fine, "The response of a particular nonlinear system with feedback to each of two random processes," *IEEE Trans. Inform. Theory*, vol. 14, pp. 255–264, Mar. 1968.

For applications of delta modulation in transmission of signals and video images, see

[59] R. Steele, *Delta Modulation Systems*. New York: Wiley, 1975.
[60] J. B. O'Neal, Jr., "Delta modulation quantizing noise—Analytic and computer simulation results for gaussian and television inputs signals," *Bell Syst. Tech. J.*, vol. 45, pp. 117–141, Jan. 1966.
[61] R. S. Bosworth and J. C. Candy, "A companded one-bit coder for PICTUREPHONE transmission," *Bell Syst. Tech. J.*, vol. 58, no. 5, pp. 1459–1479, May 1969.
[62] H. R. Schindler, "Delta modulation," *IEEE Spectrum*, vol. 7, pp. 69–78, Oct. 1970.
[63] I. M. Paz, G. C. Collins, and B. H. Batson, "A tri-state delta modulator for run-length encoding of video," *Proc. Nat. Telecomm. Conf.* (Dallas, TX), vol. I, pp. 6.3-1–6.3-6, Nov. 1976.

For adaptive delta modulation algorithms and applications to image transmission, see

[64] J. E. Abate, "Linear and adaptive delta modulation," *Proc. IEEE*, vol. 55, pp. 298–308, Mar. 1967.
[65] C. L. Song, J. Garodnick, and D. L. Schilling, "A variable step-size robust delta modulator," *IEEE Trans. Commun.*, vol. COM-19, pp. 1033–1044, Dec. 1971.
[66] N. S. Jayant, "Adaptive delta modulation with one bit memory," *Bell Syst. Tech. J.*, vol. 49, pp. 321–342, Mar. 1970.
[67] D. Mitra, "Mathematical analysis of an adaptive quantizer," *Bell Syst. Tech. J.*, vol. 53, no. 5, pp. 867–896, May 1974.
[68] C. C. Cutler, "Delayed encoding: Stabilizer for adaptive coders," *IEEE Trans. Commun.*, vol. COM-19, pp. 898–906, Dec. 1971.
[69] T. R. Lei, N. Scheinberg, and D. L. Schilling, "Adaptive delta modulation systems for video encoding," *IEEE Trans. Commun.*, vol. COM-25, Nov. 1977.

The original design of DPCM systems was developed in

[70] C. C. Culter, "Differential quantization of communication systems," U. S. Patent 2 605 361, July 29, 1952.

For other early work in DPCM and its applications in image data compression see [54], [55] and

[71] R. E. Graham, "Predictive quantization of television signals," in *IRE Wescon Conv. Rec.*, Part 4, pp. 147–156, Aug. 1958.
[72] J. B. O'Neal, Jr., "Predictive quantizing systems (differential pulse code modulation) for the transmission of television signals," *Bell Syst. Tech. J.*, vol. 45, pp. 689–721, May–June 1966.

For more recent work on DPCM of two-dimensional images, see

[73] A. Habibi, "Comparison of the nth-order DPCM encoder with linear transformations and block quantization techniques," *IEEE Trans. Commun. Tech.*, vol. COM-19, pp. 948–956, Dec. 1971.
[74] S. K. Goyal and J. B. O'Neal, Jr., "Entropy coded differential pulse code modulation for television," *IEEE Trans. Commun.*, vol. COM-23, pp. 660–666, June 1975.
[75] J. B. O'Neal, Jr., "Differential pulse-code modulation (DPCM) with entropy coding," *IEEE Trans. Inform. Theory*, vol. IT-21, pp. 169–174, Mar. 1976.
[76] R. Lippmann, "Influence of channel errors on DPCM picture coding," *Acta Electron.*, vol. 19, no. 4, pp. 289–294, 1976.
[77] J. B. O'Neal, Jr., and T. R. Natarajan, "Coding isotropic images," *IEEE Trans. Inform. Theory*, vol. IT-23, pp. 697–707, Nov. 1977.

For DPCM techniques based on visual fidelity, see [20] and

[78] J. C. Candy and R. H. Bosworth, "Methods for designing differential quantizers based on subjective evaluations of edge busyness," *Bell Syst. Tech. J.*, vol. 51, no. 7, pp. 1495–1516, 1972.
[79] A. N. Netravali, "On quantizers for DPCM coding of picture signals," *IEEE Trans. Inform. Theory*, vol. IT-23, pp. 360–370, May 1977.

[80] D. K. Sharma and A. N. Netravali, "Design of quantizers for DPCM coding of picture signals," *IEEE Trans. Commun.*, vol. COM-25, pp. 1267-1274, Nov. 1977.

Predictive coding techniques have been studied extensively for interframe image data compression. Greater details of the techniques described in the text may be found in

[81] F. W. Mounts, "A video encoding system with conditional picture-element replenishment," *Bell Syst. Tech. J.*, vol. 48, pp. 2545-2554, Sept. 1969.
[82] R.F.W. Pease and J. O. Limb, "Exchange of spatial and temporal resolution in television coding," *Bell Syst. Tech. J.*, vol. 50, pp. 191-200, Jan. 1971.
[83] J. O. Limb and R.F.W. Pease, "A simple interframe coder for video telephony," *Bell Syst. Tech. J.*, vol. 50, pp. 1877-1888, Aug. 1971.
[84] J. C. Candy et al., "Transmitting television as clusters of frame-to-frame differences," *Bell Syst. Tech. J.*, vol. 50, pp. 1889-1917, Aug. 1971.
[85] B. G. Haskell et al., "Interframe coding of video-telephone pictures," *Proc. IEEE*, vol. 60, pp. 792-800, July 1972.
[86] J. O. Limb et al., "Combining intraframe and frame-to-frame coding for television," *Bell Syst. Tech. J.*, vol. 53, pp. 1137-1173, Aug. 1974.
[87] D. J. Connor and J. O. Limb, "Properties of frame-difference signals generated by moving images," *IEEE Trans. Commun.*, vol. COM-22, p. 1564, Oct. 1974.
[88] B. G. Haskell, "Entropy measurements for nonadaptive and adaptive frame-to-frame, linear predictive coding of videotelephone signals," *Bell Syst. Tech. J.*, vol. 54, pp. 1155-1175, Aug. 1975.
[89] B. G. Haskell and R. L. Schmidt, "A low bit-rate interframe coder for video-telephone," *Bell Syst. Tech. J.*, vol. 54, pp. 1475-1495, Oct. 1975.
[90] B. G. Haskell et al., "Interframe coding of 525-line, monochrome television at 1.5 Mbits/s," *IEEE Trans. Commun.*, vol. COM-25, pp. 1339-1348, Nov. 1977.

For other designs and considerations of interframe DPCM, see

[91] H. Yasuda et al., "Transmitting 4-MHz TV signals by combinational difference coding," *IEEE Trans. Commun.*, vol. COM-25, pp. 508-516, May 1977.
[92] T. Ishiguro et al., "Composite interframe coding of NTSC color television signals," *Nat. Telecommunications Conf.* (Dallas, TX), pp. 6.4-1-6.4-5, 1976.
[93] J. O. Limb et al., "Digital coding of color video signals—A review," *IEEE Trans. Commun.*, vol. COM-25, pp. 1349-1385, Nov. 1977.

For adaptive interframe predictive coding methods, see [84], [86] and

[94] F. Rocca and S. Zanoletti, "Bandwidth reduction via movement compensation on a model of the random video process," *IEEE Trans. Commun.*, vol. COM-20, pp. 960-965, Oct. 1972.
[95] C. Cafforio and F. Rocca, "Methods for measuring small displacements of television images," *IEEE Trans. Inform. Theory*, vol. IT-22, pp. 573-579, Sept. 1976.
[96] S. Broferrio and F. Rocca, "Interframe redundancy reduction of video signals generated by translating objects," *IEEE Trans. Commun.*, pp. 448-455, Apr. 1977.
[97] J. R. Jain and A. K. Jain, "Interframe adaptive data compression techniques for images," Sig. & Image Proc. Lab., Dep. Elec. and Comput. Eng., Univ. CA, Davis, Aug. 1979.
Also see, J. R. Jain, Ph.D. dissertation, Dep. Elec. Eng., SUNY, Buffalo, Sept. 1979.

For predictive coding of facsimile images, different prediction rules and data compression results, see

[98] H. Kobayashi and L. R. Bahl, "Image data compression by predictive coding I: Prediction algorithms" and "II: Encoding algorithms," *IBM J. Res. Dev.*, vol. 18, no. 2, pp. 164-179, Mar. 1974.
[99] N. J. Nilsson, *Learning Machines*. New York: McGraw-Hill, 1965.
[100] K. S. Fu, "Learning control systems—Review and outlook," *IEEE Trans. Automat. Contr.*, vol. AC-15, p. 210, 1970.

[101] T. S. Huang, "Coding of two tone images," *IEEE Trans. Commun.*, vol. COM-25, pp. 1406-1424, Nov. 1977.
[102] D. Preuss, "Two-dimensional facsimile source coding based on Markov Model," *Nachrichtentech. Z.*, vol. 28, pp. 358-363, Oct. 1975.
Also see, H. G. Musmann and D. Preuss, "Comparison of redundancy rendering codes for facsimile transmission of documents," *IEEE Trans. Commun.*, vol. COM-25, no. 11, pp. 1425-1433, Nov. 1977.
[103] R. B. Arps, "Entropy of printed matter at the threshold of legibility for efficient coding in digital image processing," Stanford Electronics Lab., Stanford, CA, Rep. No. 31, 1969.

For other encoding schemes with applications to facsimile image data, see Huang [3, p. 221] and

[104] J. Capon, "A probabilistic model for run-length coding of pictures," *IRE Trans. Inform. Theory*, vol. IT-5, pp. 157-163, Dec. 1959.
[105] S. W. Golomb, "Run length encodings," *IEEE Trans. Inform. Theory*, vol. IT-12, pp. 399-401, July, 1966.
[106] J. O. Limb, "Efficiency of variable length binary encoding," in *Proc. UMR Mervin J. Kelly Communications Conf.* (Rolla MO), pp. 13.3-1-13.3-9, Oct. 1970.
[107] T. S. Huang, "An upper bound on entropy of runlength coding," *IEEE Trans. Inform. Theory*, vol. IT-21, pp. 00-00, Sept. 1975.
[108] H. Meyr, H. G. Rosdolski and T. S. Huang, "Optimum runlength codes," *IEEE Trans. Commun.*, vol. COM-22, pp. 00-00, June 1974.
[109] D. A. Huffman, "A method for the construction of minimum redundancy codes," *Proc. IRE*, vol. 40, pp. 1098-1101, Sept. 1952.
[110] A. E. Laemmel, "Coding processes for bandwidth reduction in picture transmission," Microwave Res. Inst., Poly. Inst. Brooklyn, NY, Rep. R-246-51, PIB-187, Aug. 30, 1951.

Other references for Section III

[111] N. E. Nahi and T. Asseffi, "Bayesian recursive estimation," *IEEE Trans. Comput.*, vol. C-21, pp. 734-738, July 1972.
[112] S. R. Powell and L. M. Silverman, "Modelling of two-dimensional random fields with application to image restoration," *IEEE Trans. Automat. Contr.*, vol. AC-19, pp. 8-13, Feb. 1974.
[113] R. Bernstein, Ed., *Digital Image Processing for Remote Sensing*. New York: IEEE Press, 1978.
[114] G. L. Turin, "An introduction to matched filters," *IRE Trans. Inform. Theory*, vol. IT-6; pp. 311-329, June 1960.

Section IV

For the optimality of the KL transform in one-dimensional transform coding, bit allocations, and related results see

[115] J.J.Y. Huang and P. M. Schultheiss, "Block quantization of correlated Gaussian random variables," *IEEE Trans. Commun. Syst.*, pp. 280-296, Sept. 1963.
[116] A. Segall, "Bit allocation and encoding for vector sources," *IEEE Trans. Inform. Theory*, vol. IT-22, pp. 162-169, Mar. 1976.
[117] B. Fox, "Discrete optimization via marginal analysis," *Management Sci.*, vol. 13, pp. 201-216, Nov. 1966.
[118] A. K. Jain and S. H. Wang, "Stochastic image models and hybrid coding," Dep. Elec. Eng., SUNY, Buffalo, Final Rep., NOSC Contract N00953-77-C-003MJE, Oct. 1977.

The KL transform is often also called the method of *Principal Components* or the *Hotelling Transform* due to original work of Hotelling reported in

[119] H. Hotelling, "Analysis of a complex of statistical variables into principal components," *J. Educ. Psychology*, vol. 24, pp. 417-441, and 498-520, 1933.

For theory of KL transform and its further historic development see

[120] H. Karhunen, "Ueber Lineare Methoden in der Wahrscheinlichkeitsrechnung," *Ann. Acad. Science Fenn*, Ser. A.I. 37,

Helsinki, 1947. (see translation by I. Selin, The Rand Corp., Doc. T-131, Aug. 11, 1960.)

[121] M. Loeve, "Fonctions aleatoires de seconde ordre," in P. Levy, *Processus Stochastiques et Mouvement Brownien*. Paris, France: Hermann, 1948.
Also see, M. Loeve, *Probability Theory*. New York: Van Nostrand, pp. 478-479, 1960.

[122] A. Koschman, "On the filtering of nonstationary time series," in *Proc. Nat. Electron Conf.*, p. 126, 1954.

[123] J. L. Brown, Jr., "Mean square truncation error in series expansion of random functions," *J. SIAM*, vol. 8, pp. 18-32, Mar. 1960.

[124] I. Selin, *Detection Theory*. Princeton, NJ: Princeton University Press, 1965.

[125] R. E. Totty and J. C. Hancock, "On optimum-finite dimensional signal representation," in *Proc. 1st Annu. Allerton Conf. on Circuits and System Theory*, 1963.

[126] S. Wantanabe, "Karhunen-Loeve expansion and factor analysis, theoretical remarks and applications," *Prague Conf. Inform. Theory, Statistics, Decision Functions, and Random Processes* (Prague, Czechoslovakia), pp. 635-660, 1965.

[127] W. D. Ray and R. M. Driver, "Further decomposition of the Karhunen Loeve series representation of a stationary random process," *IEEE Trans. Inform. Theory*, vol. IT-11, pp. 663-668, Nov. 1970.

For results on energy compaction properties see Wantanabe [126] and

[128] H. P. Kramer and M. V. Mathews, "A linear coding for transmitting a set of correlated signals," *IRE Trans. Inform. Theory*, vol. IT-2, pp. 41-46, Sept. 1956.

[129] V. R. Algazi and D. J. Sakrison, "On the Optimality of Karhunen-Loeve Expansion," *IEEE Trans. Inform. Theory*, pp. 319-321, Mar. 1969.

For rate distortion aspects of KL transform coding see [35] and

[130] L. D. Davisson, "Rate distortion theory and application," *Proc. IEEE*, vol. 60, pp. 800-808, July 1972.

For Cosine, Sine, and other sinusoidal transforms, their relationship to the KL transforms and asymptotic properties see

[131] N. Ahmed, T. Natarajan, and K. R. Rao, "Discrete cosine transform," *IEEE Trans. Comput.*, vol. C-23, pp. 90-93, Jan. 1974.

[132] Y. Yemini and J. Pearl, "Asymptotic properties of discrete unitary transforms," School Eng. Appl. Sci., UCLA, Los Angeles, UCLA-ENG-REPORT-7566, Nov. 1975.

[133] M. Hamidi and J. Pearl, "Comparison of the cosine and Fourier transforms of Markov-1 signals," *IEEE Trans. Acoust., Speech, Signal Processing*, vol. ASSP-24, pp. 428-429, Oct. 1976.

[134] R. M. Gray, "Toeplitz and circulant matrices: A review," Stanford Univ. Stanford, CA, Tech. Rep. SV-SEL-71-032, June 1971.
Also see, "On the asymptotic eigenvalue distribution of Toeplitz matrices," *IEEE Trans. Inform. Theory*, vol. IT-18, pp. 725-730, Nov. 1972.

[135] A. K. Jain, "Some new techniques in image processing," in *Proc. Symp. on Current Mathematical Problems in Image Science* (Naval Post Graduate School, Monterey, CA) Nov. 1976.

[136] A. K. Jain, "A sinusoidal family of unitary transforms," *IEEE Trans. Pattern Anal. Machine Intell.*, vol. PAMI-1, pp. 356-365, Oct. 1979.

For details of the Fast KL transform and related results see [135] and

[137] A. K. Jain, "A fast Karhunen-Loeve transform for a class of stochastic processes," *IEEE Trans. Commun.*, vol. COM-24, pp. 1023-1029, Sept. 1976.

[138] A. K. Jain, S. H. Wang, and Y. Z. Liao, "Fast KL transform data compression studies," *National Telecomm. Conf.*, Dallas, Texas, Nov-Dec. 1976.

[139] A. Z. Meiri, "The pinned Karhunen-Loeve transform of a two-dimensional Gauss-Markov field," in *Proc. 1976 SPIE Advances in Image Transmission Techniques* (San Diego, CA), vol. 87, pp. 155-164, Aug. 1976.

For fast transforms and the general theory of transforms see

[140] N. Ahmed and K. R. Rao, *Orthogonal Transforms for Digital Signal Processing*. New York: Springer Verlag, 1975.

[141] E. O. Brigham, *The Fast Fourier Transform*. Englewood Cliffs, NJ: Prentice-Hall, 1974.

[142] H. F. Harmuth, *Transmission of Information by Orthogonal Signals*. New York: Springer Verlag, 1970.

[143] B. S. Nagy, *Introduction to Real Functions and Orthogonal Expansions*. New York: Oxford Univ. Press, 1965.

[144] *Proc. Symp. Applications of Walsh Functions* (University of Maryland, IEEE-EMC), 1970-1973, and Catholic Univ. America, 1974.

Section V

Transform coding of two-dimensional images was introduced by Andrews and Pratt. The original work is reported in

[145] H. C. Andrews and W. K. Pratt, "Fourier transform coding of images," in *Proc. Hawaii Int. Conf. System Science*, pp. 677-679, Jan. 1968.

[146] H. C. Andrews, J. Kane, and W. K. Pratt, "Hadamard transform image coding," *Proc. IEEE*, vol. 57, pp. 58-68, Jan. 1969.

[147] W. K. Pratt and H. C. Andrews, "Application of Fourier-Hadamard transformation to bandwidth compression," in *Picture Bandwidth Compression*, T. S. Huang and O. J. Tretiak, Eds. New York: Gordon and Breach, 1972, pp. 515-554.

[148] H. C. Andrews and W. K. Pratt, "Transform image coding," in *Proceedings Computer Processing Communications*. New York: Polytechnic Press, 1969, pp. 63-84.

[149] H. C. Andrews, *Computer Techniques in Image Processing*. New York: Academic Press, 1970.

For subsequent developments and refinements, see

[150] A. Habibi and P. A. Wintz, "Image coding by linear transformation and block quantization," *IEEE Trans. Commun. Tech.*, vol. COM-19, pp. 50-63, Feb. 1971.

[151] H. Enomoto and K. Shibata, "Orthogonal transform coding system for television signals," *IEEE Trans. Electromagn. Compat.*, Special Issue on Walsh Functions, vol. EMC-13, pp. 11-17, Aug. 1971.

[152] J. W. Woods and T. S. Huang, "Picture bandwidth compression by linear transformation and block quantization," in *Picture Bandwidth Compression*, T. S. Huang and O. J. Tretiak, Eds. New York: Gordon and Breach, 1972, pp. 555-573.

[153] P. A. Wintz, "Transform picture coding," *Proc. IEEE*, vol. 60, pp. 809-823, July 1972.

[154] G. B. Anderson and T. S. Huang, "Piecewise Fourier transformation for picture bandwidth compression," *IEEE Trans. Commun.*, vol. COM-20, pp. 388-491, June 1972.

[155] W. K. Pratt, W. H. Chen, and L. R. Welch, "Slant transform image coding," *IEEE Trans. Commun.*, vol. COM-22, pp. 1075-1093, Aug. 1974.

[156] A. K. Jain, "A fast Karhunen-Loeve transform for finite discrete images," in *Proc. Nat. Electronics Conf.* (Chicago, IL), pp. 322-328, Oct. 1974.

[157] K. R. Rao, M. A. Narasimhan, and Revuluri, "Image Data Processing by Hadamard-Haar Transform," *IEEE Trans. Comput.*, vol. C-23, pp. 888-896, Sept. 1975.

[158] M. Tasto and P. A. Wintz, "Image coding by adaptive block quantization," *IEEE Trans. Commun. Tech.*, vol. COM-19, pp. 956-972, Dec. 1971.

[159] H. C. Andrews and A. G. Tescher, "The role of adaptive phase coding in two and three dimensional Fourier and Walsh image compression," in *Proc. Walsh Function Symp.* (Washington, DC), Mar. 1974.
Also see, A. G. Tescher, "The role of phase in adaptive image coding," Ph.D. dissertation, Univ. Southern California, Los Angeles, Jan. 1974.

[160] J. I. Gimlett, "Use of activity classes in adaptive transform image coding," *IEEE Trans. Commun.*, vol. COM-23, pp. 785-786, July 1975.

[161] R. V. Cox and A. G. Tescher, "Channel rate equalization techniques for adaptive transform coder," *Proc. SPIE Conf. Advances in Image Transmission Techniques* (San Diego, CA), Aug. 1976.

[162] C. Reader, "Intraframe and interframe adaptive transform coding," *Proc. SPIE*, vol. 66, pp. 108-118, Aug. 1975.

[163] W. H. Chen and C. H. Smith, "Adaptive coding of monochrome and color images," *IEEE Trans. Commun.*, vol. COM-25, pp. 1285-1292, Nov. 1977.

[164] J. K. Yan and D. J. Sakrison, "Encoding of images based on a two component source model," *IEEE Trans. Commun.*, vol. COM-25, pp. 1315–1322, Nov. 1977.
[165] A. Habibi, "Survey of adaptive image coding techniques," *IEEE Trans. Commun.*, vol. COM-25, pp. 1275–1284, Nov. 1977.

For three-dimensional transform coding with applications in data compression of color images, medical X-ray images, etc., see

[166] W. K. Pratt, "Spatial transform coding of color images," *IEEE Trans. Commun. Tech.*, vol. COM-19, pp. 980–982, Dec. 1971.
[167] J. A. Rose and W. K. Pratt, "Theoretical performance models for interframe transform and hybrid transform/DPCM coders," in *Proc. SPIE Conf. Advances in Image Transmission Techniques* (San Diego, CA), Aug. 1976.
[168] J. A. Roese, W. K. Pratt, and G. S. Robinson, "Interframe cosine transform image coding," *IEEE Trans. Commun.*, vol. COM-25, pp. 1329–1338, Nov. 1977.
[169] J. R. Jain, A. K. Jain, and R. A. Robb, "Data compression of multidimensional X-ray Images," to be published.
[170] T. R. Natrajan and N. Ahmed, "On interframe transform coding," *IEEE Trans. Commun.*, vol. COM-25, pp. 1323–1329, Nov. 1977.

For other topics related to transform image coding, see

[171] W. K. Pratt, "Transform image coding spectrum extrapolation," in *Proc. Hawaii Systems Science Conf.*, Jan. 1974.
[172] M. N. Huhns, "Optimum restoration of quantized correlated signals," University of Southern California, Los Angeles, Image Processing Institute, USCIPI 600, Aug. 1975.
[173] H. C. Andrews and C. L. Patterson, "Singular value decomposition (SVD) image coding," *IEEE Trans. Commun.*, vol. COM-24, pp. 425–432, Apr. 1976.

For contour and boundary coding algorithms, see

[174] W. F. Schreiber and C. F. Knapp, "TV bandwidth reduction by digital coding," *IRE Nat. Conv. Rec.*, vol. 6, part 4, pp. 88–89, 1958.
[175] W. F. Schreiber, C. F. Knapp, and N. D. Kay, "Synthetic highs: An experimental TV bandwidth reduction system," *J. Soc. Motion Pict. Telev. Eng.*, vol. 68, pp. 525–537, Aug. 1959.
[176] H. Freeman, "On the encoding of arbitrary geometric configurations," *IRE Trans. Electron. Comput.*, vol. EC-10, pp. 260–268, June 1961.
[177] D. N. Graham, "Image transmission by two-dimensional contour coding," *Proc. IEEE*, vol. 55, pp. 336–346, Mar. 1967.
[178] H. Freeman, "Boundary encoding and processing," in *Picture Processing and Psychopictorics*, B. S. Lipkin and A. Rosenfeld, Eds. New York: Academic Press, pp. 241–266.
[179] P. A. Wintz and L. C. Wilkins, "Studies on data compression, Part I: Picture coding by contours, Part II: Error analysis of run-length codes," Purdue University, Lafayette, IN, School of Engineering, Rep. TR-EE-70-17, Sept. 1970.
[180] L. C. Wilkins and P. A. Wintz, "Image coding by coding contours," *Proc. Int. Conf. Communications* (San Francisco, CA), vol. 1, 1970.
[181] W. F. Schreiber, T. S. Huang, and O. J. Tretiak, "Contour coding of images," in *Picture Bandwidth Compression*, T. S. Huang and O. J. Tretiak, Eds. New York: Gordon and Breach, pp. 443–448, 1972.

Section VI

[182] A. Habibi, "Hybrid coding of pictorial data," *IEEE Trans. Commun.*, vol. COM-22, pp. 614–624, May 1974.
[183] R. A. Jones, "Adaptive hybrid picture coding," *Proc. SPIE*, vol. 87, pp. 247–255, Aug. 1976.

For detailed analysis of hybrid coding via stochastic models and simulation results, see Jain and Wang [118] and

[184] S. H. Wang, "Applications of stochastic models for image data compression," Ph.D. dissertation, Dep. Elec. Eng., State Univ. New York, Buffalo, Sept. 1979.

For interframe hybrid coding and its applications, see Roese *et al.* [168], Jain *et al.* [97]. For other hybrid processing applications, see

[185] A. K. Jain, "A semicausal model for recursive filtering of two-dimensional images," *IEEE Trans. Comput.*, vol. C-26, pp. 343–350, Apr. 1977.
[186] A. K. Jain, "Partial differential equations and finite difference methods in image processing, Part I: Image representation," *J. Optimiz. Theory Appl.*, vol. 23, pp. 65–91, Sept. 1977.
[187] A. K. Jain and J. R. Jain, "Partial differential equations and finite difference methods in image processing, Part II: Image restoration," *IEEE Trans. Automat. Contr.*, vol. AC-23, pp. 817–834, Oct. 1978.
[188] R. W. Means, E. H. Wrench, and H. J. Whitehouse, "Image transmission via spread spectrum techniques," Naval Ocean Systems Center, San Diego, CA, ARPA Quarterly Tech. Rep. ARPA-QR6, Jan.–Dec. 1975.
Also see, ARPA-QR8, Annu. Rep., Jan–Dec. 1975.

For variance estimation in DPCM, see

[189] P. Castellino, G. Madena, L. Nebbia, and C. Sengliala, "Bit rate reduction by automatic adaptation of quantizer step-size in DPCM systems," in *Proc. 1974 Int. Zurich Sem. Digital Communications*, pp. B6(1)–B6(6), 1974.

Section VII

Use of Fourier transform theory on finite Abelian groups, to find the optimal mean-square encoding rule β for nonredundant codes ($n = k$) is reported in

[190] T. R. Crimmins, H. M. Horwitz, C. J. Palermo, and R. V. Palermo, "Minimization of mean square error for data transmitted via group codes," *IEEE Trans. Inform. Theory*, vol. IT-15, pp. 72–78, Jan. 1969.
[191] T. R. Crimmins and H. M. Horwitz, "Mean square error optimum coset leaders for group codes," *IEEE Trans. Inform. Theory*, vol. IT-16, pp. 429–432, July 1970.

Extension to include redundant codes ($n \geq k$) and the optimal mean-square decoding rule was proposed in

[192] G. A. Wolf, "The optimum mean square estimate for decoding binary block codes," Ph.D. dissertation, Dep. Elec. Eng., Univ. Wisconsin, Madison, 1973.
Also see, G. A. Wolf and R. Redinbo, *IEEE Trans. Inform. Theory*, vol. IT-20, pp. 344–351, May 1974.

Extension of these results to optimize PCM and image transform coding methods are discussed in [97] and

[193] J. R. Jain and A. K. Jain, "Optimization of image data compression algorithms for transmission over noisy channels," Presented at Int. Picture Coding Symp., Ipswich, U.K., July 1979. (To be published.)

Other designs of mean-square quantizers cascaded to noisy channels (with a fixed encoding rule) have been considered for PCM transmission, e.g., see

[194] A. J. Kurtenbach and P. A. Wintz, "Quantizing for noisy channels," *IEEE Trans. Commun. Tech.*, vol. COM-17, pp. 291–302, Apr. 1969.

For other related results, see

[195] Y. Yamaguchi and T. S. Huang, "Optimum binary fixed length block codes," Research Lab of Electronics, Massachusetts Institute of Technology, Cambridge, MA, Quarterly Report, vol. 78, July 1965.
[196] W. Rudin, *Fourier Analysis on Groups*. New York: Interscience, 1967.

Section VIII

[197] A. K. Jain and S. Ranganath, "Image coding by autoregressive synthesis," in *Proc. IEEE ICASSP* (Denver, CO), Apr. 1980.
[198] J. Makhoul, "Linear prediction: A tutorial review," *Proc. IEEE*, vol. 63, pp. 561–580, Apr. 1975.
[199] J. P. Burg, "Maximum entropy spectral analysis," Ph.D. disserta-

[200] T. J. Ulrych and T. N. Bishop, "Maximum entropy spectral analysis and autoregressive decomposition," *Rev. Geophysics Space Phys.*, vol. 13, pp. 183-200, Feb. 1975.
[201] J. D. Markel and A. H. Gray, "On autocorrelation equations as applied to speech analysis," *IEEE Trans. Audio and Electroacoustics*, vol. AU-21, #2, pp. 69-77, April 1973.
[202] R. Viswanathan and J. Makhoul, "Quantization properties of transmission parameters in linear prediction systems," *IEEE Trans. Acoust., Speech, Signal Processing*, vol. ASSP-23, pp. 309-321, June 1975.

Section IX

For variable velocity scanning, pseudorandom scanning, interpolative coding, variable knot splines, SVD, and other methods, see

[203] E. E. Wright, "Velocity modulation in television," *Proc. Phys. Soc. (London)* vol. 46, p. 512-514, July 1934.
[204] M. P. Beddoes, "Experiments with slope feedback coder for TV compression," *IRE Trans. Broadcasting*, vol. BC-7, pp. 12-28, Mar. 1961.
[205] T. S. Huang and O. J. Tretiak, "A pseudorandom multiplex system for facsimile transmission," *IEEE Trans. Commun. Tech.*, vol. COM-16, pp. 436-438, June 1968.
[206] C. M. Kortman, "Redundancy reduction: A practical method of data compression," *Proc. IEEE*, vol. 55, pp. 253-263, Mar. 1967. (See this issue for other data compression schemes also.)
[207] L. D. Davisson, "Data compression using straight line interpolation," *IEEE Trans. Inform. Theory*, vol. IT-14, pp. 390-394, May 1968.
[208] D. McCaughey, "The degrees of freedom of sampled images," Ph.D. dissertation, USCIPI Rep. No. 730, University of Southern California, Los Angeles, June 1977.

ADDITIONAL BIBLIOGRAPHY

[209] A. N. Netravali and J. O. Limb, "Picture coding: a review," *Proc. IEEE*, vol. 68, pp. 366-406, Mar. 1980.
[210] J. Woods, "Stability of DPCM coders for television," *IEEE Trans. Commun.*, vol. COM-23, pp. 845-846, Aug. 1975.
[211] A. K. Jain, "Advances in mathematical models for image processing," *Proc. IEEE*, to be published.
[212] A. N. Netravali and J. D. Robbins, "Motion compensated television coding—Part I," *Bell Syst. Tech. J.*, pp. 631-670, Mar. 1979.
[213] J. A. Stuller and A. N. Netravali, "Transform domain motion estimation," *Bell Syst. Tech J.*, pp. 1673-1702, Sept. 1979. (Also see pp. 1703-1718 of the same issue for application to coding.)
[214] A. K. Jain, "The rate vs distortion characteristics of some fast Karhuenen Loeve transform coding algorithms," Tech. Rep. Signal and Image Processing Lab., Dep. Elec. and Comput. Eng., Univ. California, Davis, Sept. 1980.
[215] V. R. Algazi and D. J. Sakrison "Computer processing in communications," pp. 85-100, Polytechnic Institute of Brooklyn, Brooklyn, NY, 1969.
[216] J. W. Modestino and D. G. Daut, "Combined source channel coding of images," *IEEE Trans. Commun.*, vol. COM-27, pp. 1644-1659, Nov. 1979.
[217] H. G. Musmann, "Predictive image coding," in *Image Transmission Techniques*. New York: Academic Press, 1979.
[218] E. G. Bowen and J. O. Limb, "Subjective effects of substituting lines in a video telephone signal," *IEEE Trans. Commun.*, pp. 1208-1211, Oct. 1976.
[219] N. F. Maxemchuk and J. A. Stuller, "Reduction of transmission error in adaptively predicted DPCM encoded picture," *Bell Syst. Tech. J.*, vol. 58, pp. 1413-1425, July-Aug. 1979.
[220] W. Zschunek, "DPCM picture coding with adaptive prediction," *IEEE Trans. Commun.*, vol. COM-25, pp. 1295-1302, Nov. 1977.
[221] I. Dukhovich and J. B. O'Neal, "A three dimensional spatial nonlinear predictor for television," *IEEE Trans. Commun.*, vol. COM-26, pp. 578-583, May 1978.
[222] F. E. Hilbert, "Cluster compression algorithm, a joint clustering/data compression concept," Jet Propulsion Laboratory, Pasadena, CA, JPL Publication 77-43, Dec. 1, 1977.
[223] J. N. Gupta and P. A. Wintz, "A boundary finding algorithm and its applications," *IEEE Trans. Circuits Syst.*, vol. CAS-22, pp. 351-362, Apr. 1975.

Second-Generation Image-Coding Techniques

MURAT KUNT, SENIOR MEMBER, IEEE, ATHANASSIOS IKONOMOPOULOS, AND MICHEL KOCHER

Invited Paper

The digital representation of an image requires a very large number of bits. The goal of image coding is to reduce this number, as much as possible, and reconstruct a faithful duplicate of the original picture. Early efforts in image coding, solely guided by information theory, led to a plethora of methods. The compression ratio, starting at 1 with the first digital picture in the early 1960s, reached a saturation level around 10:1 a couple of years ago. This certainly does not mean that the upper bound given by the entropy of the source has also been reached. First, this entropy is not known and depends heavily on the model used for the source, i.e., the digital image. Second, the information theory does not take into account what the human eye sees and how it sees.

Recent progress in the study of the brain mechanism of vision has opened new vistas in picture coding. Directional sensitivity of the neurones in the visual pathway combined with the separate processing of contours and textures has led to a new class of coding methods capable of achieving compression ratios as high as 70:1. Image quality, of course, remains as an important problem to be investigated. This class of methods, that we call second generation, is the subject of this paper. Two groups can be formed in this class: methods using local operators and combining their output in a suitable way and methods using contour–texture descriptions. Four methods, two in each class, are described in detail. They are applied to the same set of original pictures to allow a fair comparison of the quality in the decoded pictures. If more effort is devoted to this subject, a compression ratio of 100:1 is within reach.

I. INTRODUCTION

Every image acquisition system, be it high-resolution microdensitometer or TV camera, produces pictorial data by sampling in space and quantizing in brightness analog scenes. The sampling step size is usually chosen small enough to avoid interpolation before display and relies on the integration ability of the human visual system. A digital image is thus an N by N array of integer numbers or picture elements (pels) requiring N^2B bits for its representation where B is the number of bits per pel. This array is commonly referred to as the canonical form of a digitized

Manuscript received July 29, 1984; revised November 2, 1984.
M. Kunt and A. Ikonomopoulos are with the Signal Processing Laboratory, Swiss Federal Institute of Technology, Lausanne, CH-1007 Lausanne, Switzerland.
M. Kocher was with AT&T Bell Laboratories, Holmdel, NJ 07733, USA. He is now with CERAC Institute, Ecublens, Switzerland.

picture, because it is assumed that the two-dimensional sampling theorem is respected. Generally, the canonical form requires a very large number of bits for its representation. For example, with a 512 by 512 raster and 8 bits per pel, 2×10^6 bits are needed, a rather large number! This paper is confined to grey-level still pictures.

A. The Problem

The goal of image coding is to reduce (to compress), as much as possible, the number of bits necessary to represent and reconstruct a faithful duplicate of the original picture. This is a very reasonable goal for two related reasons.

First, any data originated from what is called an image, are not random. Adjacent samples have similar grey values, exhibiting thus an important spatial correlation. If this correlation is exploited in an appropriate way, there is no doubt that the number of N^2B bits can be reduced. We call "first generation" the set of techniques based on this classical view of the image coding problem, although at least one of them (see Section II) was in advance for its time.

The second reason extends the first one and is as follows. Consider the canonical form of a natural image such as a portrait, a scene with trees and houses, or a building, etc., and let us ask the following question: Can we find a representation for such an image worse than its canonical form? (worse in the sense of not efficient or economical). Probably the answer is no. Following the famous sentence by Descartes stating that a picture is worth a thousand words, about 20 bits should be enough to represent it. Unfortunately, like Shannon, he did not tell us how to do it! The summary of this is that data compression is not only possible but has to be done by several orders of magnitude. How this can be achieved when the limits of compression have been reached within the framework of information theory and coding theory (see Fig. 1)? By simply going out of this framework. The reason for this is that often forgotten assumptions of ergodicity and stationarity are not satisfied for image data. The entropy of the image data source is not known and depends heavily on the model used. We call "second generation" the ensemble of techniques capable

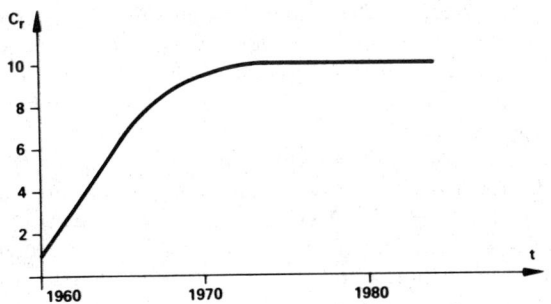

Fig. 1. Average compression ratio (sketch) of the first-generation image coding techniques.

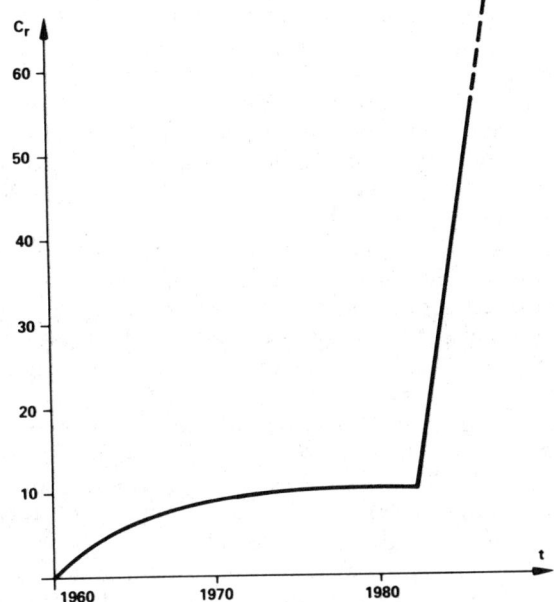

Fig. 2. Average compression ratio (sketch) of both generations.

of achieving high compressions beyond this saturation level (Fig. 2). The purpose of this paper is to report on the recent attempts made in this direction.

Another view of the difference between the techniques of the first and the second generation is as follows. Image coding is basically carried out in two steps: first, image data are converted into a sequence of messages and, second, code words are assigned to the messages. Methods of the first generation put the emphasis on the second step, whereas methods of the second generation put it on the first step and use available results for the second step.

B. A Way to a Possible Solution

The very end of almost every image-processing system is the human eye. Although our visual system is by far the best image-processing system one can think of, it is also far from being perfect. So, if the coding scheme is matched to the human visual system and attempts to imitate its functions, at least for the known part of it, high compressions can be expected. A few methods designed with these aims give encouraging compressions as high as 70:1 as shown in Fig. 2. Therefore, it does not seem unreasonable to preprocess the canonical form in this way before applying the classical coding theory to achieve high compression.

What are needed now are guidelines for preprocessing. An image can be described in terms of several possible entities such as pels of the canonical form, a group of pels in small blocks, Fourier or other transform coefficients, linearly predicted values, or derivatives. With the continuous progress in visual pattern recognition and scene analysis, another possibility is to describe an image in terms of contour and texture [1].

Contours are commonly referred to as abrupt changes in grey level [1], [2]. According to the abruptness, refinements such as strong or weak contours can be used. Texture, on the other hand, became a great center of interest in Pattern Recognition [3]–[6]. Although a large number of studies have been done on purely textured images [7], a clear-cut definition of texture does not exist. This is mainly because, in this context, texture is related to human visual perception and has a subjective component as well. The most suitable definition [8] relies on the shift invariance and shows the small amount of semantic information contained in it. In the context of coding, texture will be defined as anything else in images, beside contours.

The suggested way to a possible solution for high-compression image coding is therefore to represent an image in terms of textured regions surrounded by contours in such a way that the regions correspond, as faithfully as possible, to the objects of the scene. Efficient codes exist for contour coding. Because of the low information content, textured areas can also be coded efficiently.

C. Organization of the Paper

In Section II a brief overview of first-generation coding techniques is given. Its purpose is not to replace excellent well-known reviews by Netravali and Limb [9], by Jain [10], or the most recent by Musmann contained in this issue, but to summarize the tremendous amount of effort devoted to this particular problem over the last two decades. One particular technique that we consider as advanced for its time is described in some detail because of the insight it gave for the development of the second-generation techniques, providing thus a basis for their introduction.

Section III is devoted to the mechanism of vision and to the translation, into engineering language, of recent results from neurophysiology. Properties of the human visual system which can be used in image processing and coding are described. Successful applications, other than coding, are indicated.

Sections IV and V describe four techniques which can be considered as second generation. The first two are based on local operators whereas the last two use contour–texture models. Results showing decoded pictures are discussed in Section VI. Unless otherwise stated, all the pictures used in this paper are digitized with a 256 by 256 raster and quantized to 256 levels, thereby permitting an 8-bit representation. Output pictures are reproduced on a laser-receiver using dry silver paper with an optical density of 1.6.

II. Brief Review of First-Generation Coding Techniques

A. Preliminary Remarks

A digitized picture can be characterized by a sequence of messages. There are many ways of selecting the messages. The only requirement is to be able to reconstruct a faithful duplicate of the original picture from a sequence of messages. A source-coding technique is then applied to this sequence of messages to reduce its redundancy. The particular way of selecting the messages and assigning code words to them becomes a specific image-coding method. For example, the messages can be the brightness level of each pel (canonical form), or a group of pels, or values of a function computed from a group of pels. In this section, major image-coding techniques that we classed as "first generation" will be listed. For more detail, the reader may refer to [9], [10] or to the companion paper by Musmann in this issue.

A first classification of the coding methods can be made as information-lossless or information-lossy techniques. The former are able to reconstruct the original picture exactly, whereas the latter introduce some distortions which should be kept as unnoticeable as possible.

A second classification can be based on the space where the method is applied. For example a method combining the values of pels in an appropriate way is labeled as spatial method. In contrast, a method which uses a set of transform coefficients is called transform method. Finally, methods which are applied in both the spatial and the transform domain are referred to as hybrid methods.

Another classification is often made as fixed or adaptive methods in the sense that the parameters used are fixed or change as a function of the local data in the image.

B. Major Techniques of the First Generation

Spatial methods:

1) Pulse-Code Modulation (PCM): Acceptable quality pictures are obtained with 3 bits per pel. The compression ratio is then $C = 2.6$ to 1. Dithering, as introduced by Roberts [11], may be used to improve the quality. The properties of the human visual system are not used at all.

2) Predictive Coding: Predictive methods do not normally make use of the properties of the human visual system. With respect to the 8-bit canonical form, the compression ratio obtained by two-dimensional prediction is around 4 to 1. They can be made adaptive if the prediction parameters are adapted to the data in an appropriate way. For example, a local activity measure can be defined and prediction parameters can be updated at each noticeable change of activity. In this way compression ratio may be increased by about 10 to 20 percent.

Of interest are the particular cases of the prediction.

3) Differential Pulse-Code Modulation (DPCM): This technique allows compression ratios around $2.5:1$. Adaptive DPCM schemes exist leading to compression ratios as high as $3.5:1$.

4) Delta Modulation: Average compression ratio obtained with delta modulation is also not very high but the technique is rather simple.

5) Interpolative Coding: Most commonly used interpolators are zero-order and first-order interpolators, giving compression ratios around $4:1$. Higher order polynomials or splines can also be used, but their computational complexities do not justify the results. Again, properties of the human visual system are not used.

6) Bit-Plane Coding [12]: With bit-plane coding an average compression around $4:1$ can be obtained without making any use of the properties of the human visual system.

Transform methods: The basic motivation behind transform coding is to transform a set of data (pels) into another set of "less correlated" or "more independent" coefficients, before coding. The inverse transform recovers the original picture. Most commonly used transformations are linear transformations implemented with fast algorithms for computational efficiency.

1) Karhunen–Loéve transform: The Karhunen–Loéve transform is the best linear transformation in the sense that it leads to uncorrelated coefficients. It is, however, not often used in practice because of its computational load. It gives an indication about the upper bound of what other transformations, computationally more efficient, should attempt to reach in decorrelating data samples.

2) Fast transformations: There are several linear transforms which can be computed with $N \log_2 N$ operations as compared to $N**2$. The most important ones are labeled as Fourier, Hadamard, Haar, sine, cosine, and slant. One important difference between these transformations and the Karhunen–Loéve transformation is that these transformations do not depend on the statistics of the input image.

3) Coding strategies: There are several coding strategies in transform coding. First the dimensionality of the transformation must be determined. A still picture can either be transformed by a two-dimensional transform or by a one-dimensional transform to be coded on a line-by-line basis. The next parameter to be fixed is the size of the transform. A commonly used strategy is to subdivide the image into subpictures of size M by M with M much smaller than the size N of the image (for example, $M = 32$ and $N = 512$) and to transform each subpicture separately. The important characteristic of these transformations is that all the "important" coefficients are packed into a specific area of the transform domain. Important compressions (up to $10:1$) can be obtained depending on the number of coefficients retained in a given area. Another possibility is to put a threshold on the transform coefficient magnitude and set to zero all those below the threshold. Higher compression ratios (around $15:1$) can be obtained with good-quality decoded pictures. Although there is some evidence that the human visual system is not a linear transformer, its basic properties may be included in the design of a transform coder.

Transform coding may also be adaptive by matching the parameters of the coder to the statistics of the subpicture being coded. Adaptation can be made at the level of the transform, of bit assignment, or of quantizer level assignment. Coding efficiency can be increased by about 25–30 percent compared to the nonadaptive case.

Hybrid methods [13]: In its common use, hybrid coding refers to methods combining predictive coding and transform coding. Both DPCM and transform coding techniques have some attractive characteristics and some limitations. Combining these two techniques leads to hybrid coding methods capable of achieving compressions around $8:1$, having the advantages of hardware simplicity (DPCM) and robust performances (transform coding).

C. Synthetic High System [14]–[20]

Although presented in this section mainly for chronological reasons, it is our belief that this technique is the only one which was in advance for its time. It is surprising to see that it is even not referred to in general surveys. This technique has been known for more than two decades! In the early days of image coding it was considered a heavy

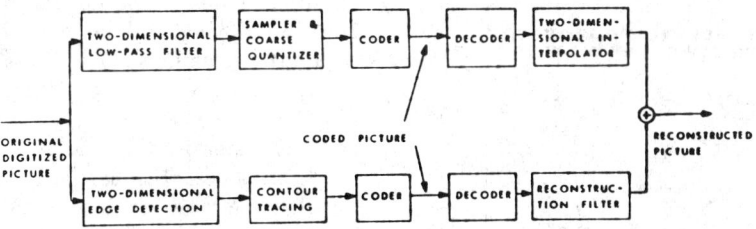

Fig. 3. Block diagram of the synthetic high system.

method because of its computational complexity, but today, it is as easy to implement as anything else with present technology. Compared to its contemporary methods, it gives very high compression ratios. Also, it gave a lot of insight to develop "second-generation" techniques. A number of studies [21]–[24] using the decomposition of a picture into low-frequency and high-frequency components are, directly or indirectly, based on the synthetic high system.

The sequence of messages for the synthetic high system is selected in the following manner. The original picture is split into two parts: the low-pass picture giving the general area brightness without sharp contours, and the high-pass picture containing sharp edge information. In its analog form, it is an information-lossless technique. According to the two-dimensional sampling theorem, the low-pass picture can be represented with very few samples. These samples are the messages characterizing the canonical form of the low-pass picture. The edge detection is performed either by a gradient or a Laplacian operator. A nonlinear operation, thresholding, is performed on the high-pass picture to determine whether an edge point is important. Then the method becomes information-lossy. Finally, the location and the magnitude of each selected edge point are coded. These variables are the messages characterizing the high-pass picture.

A two-dimensional reconstruction filter, whose properties are determined uniquely by the low-pass filter used for the low-pass picture is used to synthesize the high-frequency part from edge information. This "synthetic high" signal is then added to the low-pass picture to give the final output. A block diagram of this system is shown in Fig. 3. The reader may refer to [15]–[20] for more detail.

The synthetic high system exploits elegantly the properties of the visual system at its early processing levels by making use of the lateral inhibition phenomenon (see Section III-C). Thereby, it permits a considerable amount of redundancy reduction. Fig. 4 shows an original X-ray picture

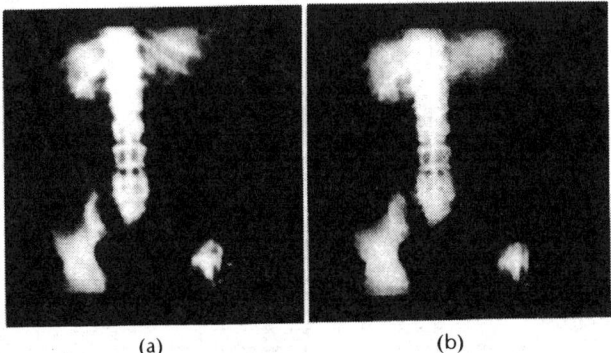

Fig. 4. An original X-ray picture (a) and its reconstructed version obtained with the synthetic high system (b). Compression ratio: $C = 8.37$.

and its reconstructed version obtained with the synthetic high system with a compression of 8.3:1. The values of the thresholds used in this system are of primary importance for the compression ratios and for the quality of the reconstructed pictures. A high compression ratio is obtained but a large amount of texture and detail are lost if these thresholds are kept too high. On the other hand, a good picture quality but a poor compression ratio are obtained if they are kept too low. With a lack of theoretical method, the compromise between compression ratio and image quality can best be found with an empirical cut-and-try procedure. The directional decomposition based method, discussed in Section V-B, can be viewed as a refinement of the synthetic high system, where the ability to extract and code edges is improved with directional filters.

III. Mechanism of Vision

As discussed earlier, the very end of almost every image processing system is the human eye. Therefore, it is useful to know how and what the eye sees. The answers to these questions lie far outside from our usual engineering context. That is why, a summary of the brain mechanism of vision is given here from [25] and [26] along with our engineering interpretations.

A. General Description

The human visual system is a part of the nervous system. The latter is doubtlessly the most complicated communication network. It is managed by the most powerful computer: the brain. The communication in this network is carried out through nerve cells called neurons. The brain contains about 10^{11} neurons, roughly the same number as that of stars in our galaxy.

A neuron has a body of size varying between 5 and 100 μm. A main fiber called the axon and a number of fiber branches called dendrites are attached to this body. Fig. 5 depicts some typical neurons.

The information transfer from one neuron to another is made electrochemically. The junction between two neurons is called the synapse. The transmitting and the receiving neurons are called presynaptic and postsynaptic, respectively. The information generated in a presynaptic neuron travels its axon like an electrical signal in a cable. Terminal branches of the axon transmit this signal to the dendrites of the postsynaptic neuron. During this transmission, the electrical signal generates chemicals at the end of the axon which are deposited on the postsynaptic neuron. In turn, these chemicals generate a new electrical signal in the postsynaptic neuron. A neuron can receive signals from thousands of presynaptic neurons and can transmit to thousands of postsynaptic neurons. A given neuron can handle up to 200 000 synapses. This shows how capable a

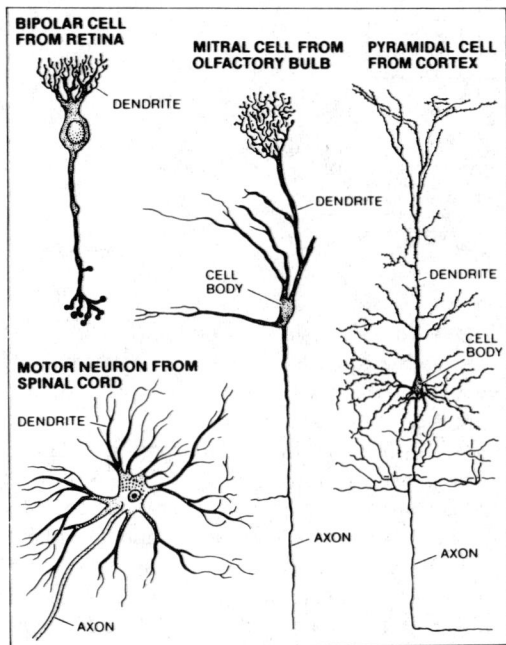

Fig. 5. Typical neurons (after [26]).

neuron is compared to an integrated circuit whose fanouts cannot exceed a few dozen. The action of a neuron can be of two types: excitatory or inhibitory. The first one generates pulses in the postsynaptic neuron whereas the second inhibits the existing pulses. This basic behavior is at the origin of a variety of phenomena such as Mach bands, band-pass characteristic of the visual frequency response, and the edge and line detection mechanism of the eye. Moreover, it provides the justification for the existing so-called local operators for edge detection.

To have an idea on the complexity of the nervous system, just imagine a network of 10^{12} neurons connected in cascade, in parallel, and with feedback! A schematic view of this organization is depicted in Fig. 6. A successful application of this structure is the architecture used in the WISARD system developed by Aleksander and his team [27] to recognize faces. The analysis of such a complex network of neurons seems, *a priori*, quite difficult if not impossible. There are however a number of features which simplify the study. These features make it possible, nowadays, to analyze the nervous system on a cell-by-cell basis. The first characteristic is that there are only two types of signals in the nervous system: one for long distances and the other for short distances. The second characteristics is that these signals are almost identical in all neurons regardless of the information they carry: visual, tactile, audible, etc. Moreover, their shape does not vary from species to species. A signal recorded from a cat is similar to that recorded from a human being. The signals received and processed by the brain are thus symbols representing external events. The nervous system is analyzed with three basic tools of the neurobiologist: the microscope, the selective stain, and the microelectrode. The signal recorded at a given neuron is a pulse train. Each pulse has a magnitude of about 100 mV and a duration of about 1 ms. The repetition rate (frequency) of these pulses is proportional to the intensity of the stimulus. The nervous system communicates through frequency modulation. What allows the brain to distinguish between two identical signals is the pathway used by each of the signals, in other words the wiring. There is thus a specific ensemble of neurons corresponding to each type of excitation. From a mathematical point of view, there is a one-to-one mapping between different parts of the body and the brain.

B. The Eye

The eye is the sensor of visual signals. It focuses them to form the image on the retina. The latter analyzes the image and sends the message to the brain through the optical nerve and optical paths in the head. Very roughly stated, the eye can be viewed as a photo camera (see Fig. 7). The light passes through the cornea and aqueous humor and enters the inner eye through the pupil. The amount of light allowed to enter is regulated by the pupil as a diaphragm. The lens focuses the light on the photoreceptive cells of the retina. The volume of the eye is not large (6.5 cm^3). Its diameter is about 24 mm and it weighs 7 g. The lens of the eye is not perfect even for persons with no weakness of

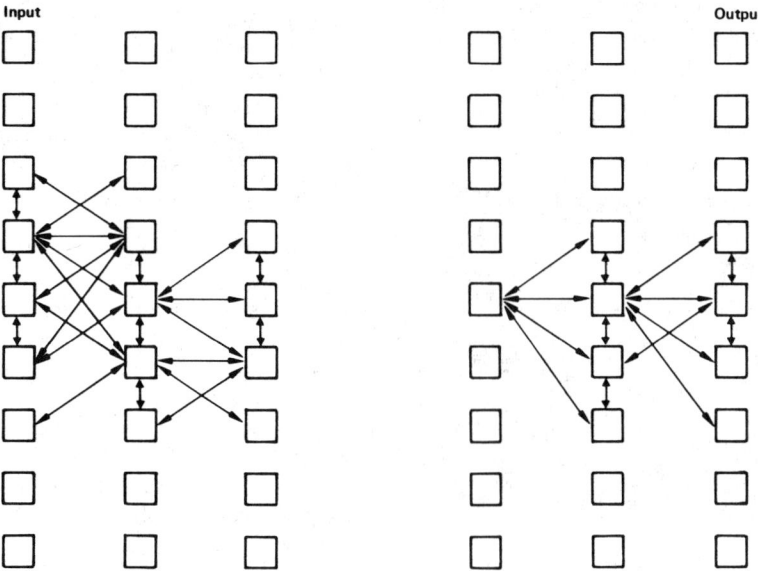

Fig. 6. Block diagram of the nervous system.

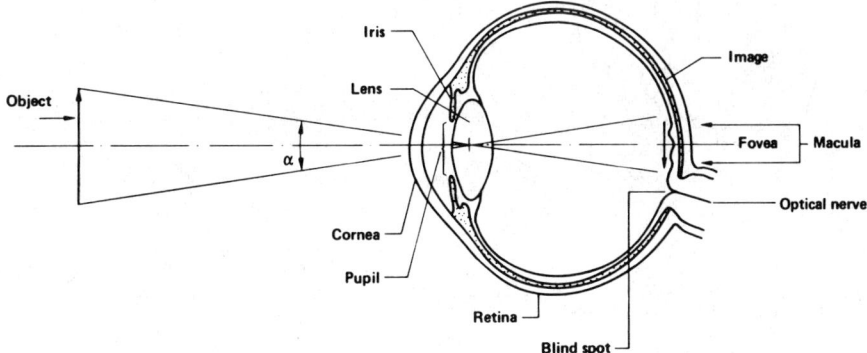

Fig. 7. Schematic view of the eye.

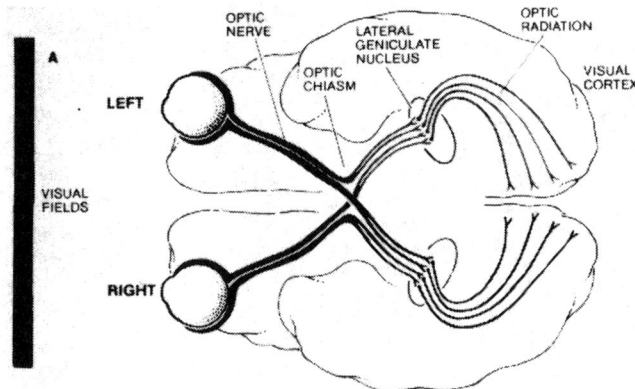

Fig. 8. Pathways in the human visual system.

vision. This imperfection is the source of the spherical aberration which appears as a blur in the focal plane. Such a blur can be modeled as a two-dimensional low-pass filter. The pupil's diameter varies between 2 and 9 mm. This aperture can also be modeled as a low-pass filter. The highest cutoff frequency corresponds to 2 mm. Continuous enlargement of the pupil's diameter decreases the cutoff frequency.

C. The Retina

The retina is the neurosensorial layer of the eye and its area is about 12.5 cm^2. It transforms the incoming light into electrical signals that are transmitted to the visual cortex through the optic nerve. Optical pathways in the visual system are depicted in Fig. 8. It should be noticed that at the optic chiasm, the output of each eye is divided into two. Consequently, the information content of the left half of the visual field is processed by the right side of the brain and the information content of the right half of the visual field is processed by the left side of the brain.

The anatomy of the retina shows five types of cells organized in layers as schematized in Fig. 9. Notice here an illustration of the general wiring principles of Fig. 6. The furthest layer from the incoming light is that of photocells. There are two types of photocells: rods and cones. A normal eye contains about 130 million rods and 6.5 million cones. Rods and cones are different enough to be examined separately. Rods are sensitive to shapes and need low luminance (scotopic vision). In contrast, cones need daylight (photopic vision). They detect color and distinguish details.

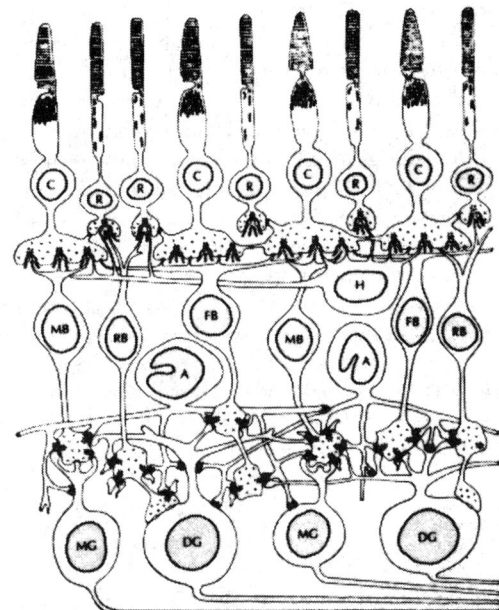

Fig. 9. Cells of the retina (after [29]).

Their distribution in the retina is highest in the vicinity of the optical axis of the eye. That is why a precise detail vision is obtained only when the eye "fix" them, in other words, when their image is formed at the fovea. In this region there are about 120 cones per degree which fix the visual resolution to 1 min of arc.

Photoreceptors are responsible for transforming the in-

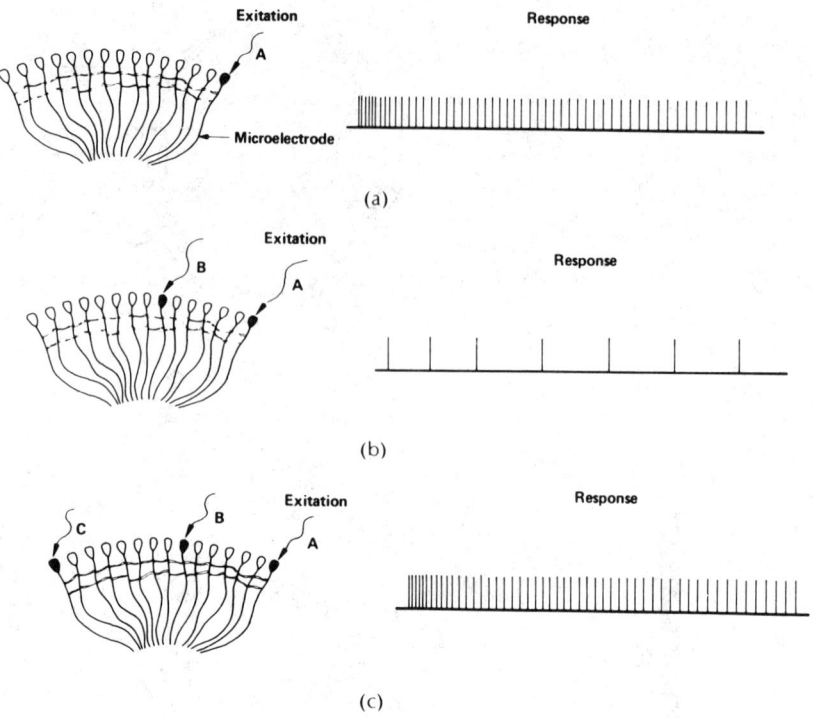

Fig. 10. Illustration of the lateral inhibition. An active cell A (a). Activation of B cells inhibit cell A (b). Disinhibition of A (c).

coming light into electric signals, while compressing its dynamic range. This compression is made according to a nonlinear law whose classical interpretation leads to a logarithmic curve (Weber–Fechner law). It is obtained by the following experiment. If a visual field of luminance L is divided into two parts along a straight line and the luminance of one part is increased by ΔL until a difference is noticed, the ratio $\Delta L/L$ remains constant for very large variations of L. If this result is interpreted as a small increase ΔB in brightness, $\Delta B = \alpha \Delta L/L$ and by integration we obtain $B = \alpha \log L + \beta$. More recent experiments, done with complex scenes, led to power laws $B = aL^\gamma$, with $\gamma = 1/2$ or $1/3$ depending on bright or dark surrounding, respectively, as nicely reported in [28].

In serial connections of the retina (Fig. 9), photoreceptors are connected to bipolar cells which, in turn, are connected to ganglion cells, whose axons make up the optical nerve. In parallel connections, horizontal cells receive synapses from photocells and may act on bipolar cells and photocells. Amacrin cells receive synapses from bipolar cells and may act on ganglion cells and bipolar cells. Some of these actions indicate feedback loops in parallel connections.

These parallel and feedback connections are responsible for the so-called lateral inhibition [29]. This phenomenon can be summarized as follows (Fig. 10). When a given cell A is excited, it produces a pulse train whose frequency is proportional to the intensity of light (Fig. 10(a)). If other neighboring cells B are excited as well, they inhibit the pulse train generated by A (Fig. 10(b)). A disinhibition of cell A may occur when the inhibition exerted on it by B cells is partially released by exciting other cells C, in the close neighborhood of B, that inhibit the action of B but are too far away from the cell A to act on it (Fig. 10(c)). If the responses of these cells are recorded spatially, a point-spread function or a spatial impulse response is obtained as depicted in Fig. 11. Clearly, this corresponds to a high-pass filter. It is interesting to note that the same effect, due to totally different mechanisms, occurs in xerographic copying which does not reproduce faithfully large black areas, un-

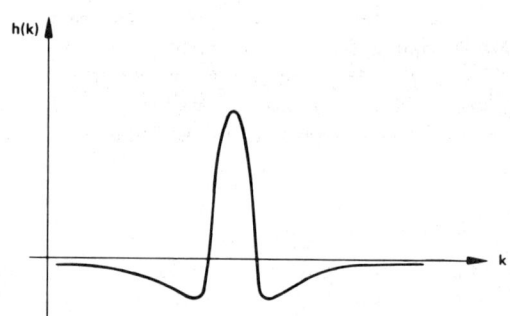

Fig. 11. Spatial impulse response of the retinal cells.

less a halftone screen is used to brake up the original black pattern into small dots. Also noticeable is the fact that the synthetic high system is the first image-coding method which makes an elegant use of this property.

As one may suspect, the high-pass behavior of the lateral inhibition does not extend infinitely. Beyond a radial spatial frequency of about 10 cycles per degree of solid angle, an integration takes place due to previously described low-pass filters and to the limited number of cells per unit retina length. If two excitations are closer than 1 min of arc to each other, their projections on the retina fall on the same cell and, therefore, are not distinguishable. As a summary, at this level of the visual system, a linear model with a bandpass frequency response can be assumed, as shown in Fig. 12.

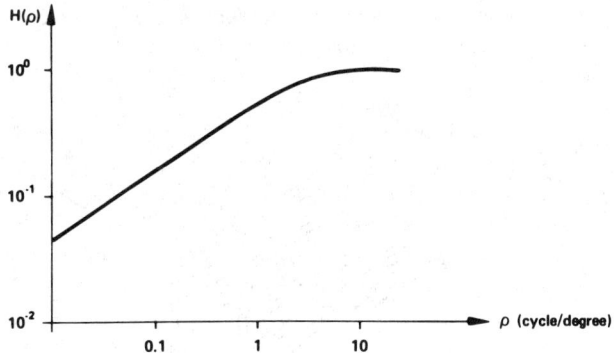

Fig. 12. Frequency response (radial) of the retinal cells.

D. Ganglion Cells and the Lateral Geniculate Nucleus

To study specialized cells, such as ganglion cells or the other cells in the visual cortex, two concepts need to be introduced. The first one is that of the receptive field of a cell. It is simply the area of the retina which can influence the behavior of that cell. The second is that of the most effective excitation. It is the stimulus which produces a pulse train of highest frequency. Because of parallel and feedback connections, a receptive field is divided into regions. Some of them are excitatory whereas some others are inhibitory. They are often called "on areas" and "off areas," respectively. The effective excitation of a ganglion cell is a circular spot whose diameter is around 0.2 mm. The receptive fields are also circular and there are two types: those which are "on" in the center and "off" at the border and those which are "off" in the center and "on" on the border (Fig. 13). At this level in the visual system, the information is processed independently from spatial orientation. Notice also that the absolute light intensity is ignored by ganglion cells which measure only differences in their receptive fields. A systematic analysis shows that even a very small spot (0.1 mm in diameter) can cover several overlapping receptive fields, some of the ganglions cells being excited and some inhibited. These cells are spatially grouped. More generally, cells in the visual system processing information coming from a given area of the retina are grouped. This is thus an economical arrangement of the wiring. The receptive fields in the vicinity of the fovea are smaller than the others (high visual resolution). Their area increases progressively as we go away from the fovea. With this last observation, the previous high-pass filter can be said to be shift-variant because of nonconstant spatial resolution. Simultaneous contrast effect and edge detection are mainly due to ganglion cells. Their effect can be modeled as a two-dimensional high-pass filter. Lateral excitations and inhibitions are also the source of the so-called Mach phenomenon which is the subjective enhancement of sharp luminance changes between relatively uniform regions.

The information processed by the retina reaches the lateral geniculate nucleus after division at the optic chiasma. The cellular analysis of this nucleus shows also a layered organization of cells. Cells on each layer receive information only from one eye. This is called ocular dominance. Moreover, here also, neurons receiving information from a given area of the retina are grouped, independently from the specific layer. Even if the exciting eye is changed, the position in the visual field remains stable. The cells in the lateral geniculate nucleus function in a way very similar to that of ganglion cells. Independence of orientation is maintained.

E. The Visual Cortex

Located at the back of the brain, the visual cortex is a folded layer of neurons of about 2 mm in thickness. The information transmitted from the lateral geniculate nucleus is received at the "area 17" of the cortex which is connected to areas 18 and 19. Cellular analysis of the cortex indicates also that 10^{10} neurons contained in it are hierachically organized in layers with only a few types of neurons. They are classified as simple cells, complex cells, hypercomplex cells, and higher order hypercomplex cells.

The receptive field of a simple cell is elliptical. The center is bar shaped and surrounded by two opposed areas (on and off). The effective excitation is not a circular spot but a slit oriented in the same direction as that of the central bar of the receptive field. If the slit is rotated, other simple cells start reacting depending on the angle. It is at this level of the visual system that specific processing for a given orientation is introduced. For a fixed orientation, if the excitation is slid in the receptive field, the pulse train vanishes progressively. Fig. 14 shows the receptive field of a simple cell. The receptive field of some simple cells may have only two antagonistic areas. In this case the most effective excitation is a border between the zones. It is interesting to note here the similarity between this receptive field (also the one in Fig. 13) and various masks used for edge and line detection by local operators such as Roberts, Sobel, Kirsch, Hueckel, and Mero-Vasy [2]. One may wonder if these operators were designed on this basis!

Complex cells are also sensitive to the orientation of the

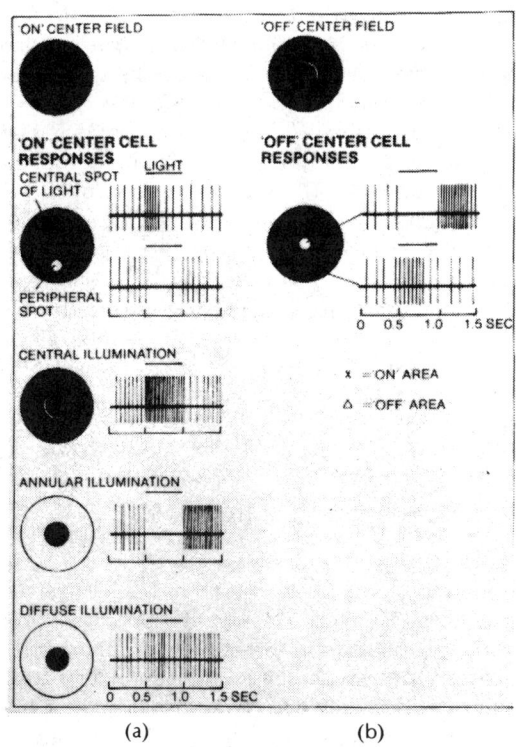

Fig. 13. Receptive fields of ganglion cells. Center on surround off (a) and center off surround on (b) (after [26]).

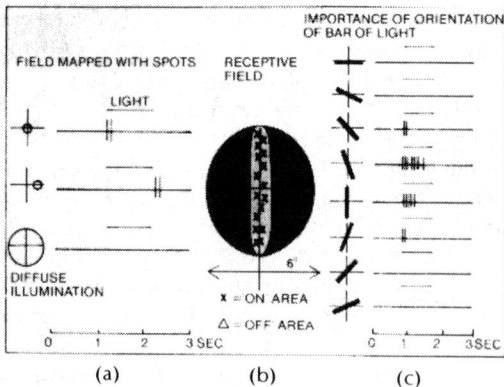

Fig. 14. Receptive field of a simple cell (after [26]).

excitation. In contrast with simple cells, however, they are not sensitive to the position of the excitation in the receptive field. Complex cells indicate orientation independently from the position.

The effective excitation for hypercomplex cells also requires a specific orientation, but in addition, it needs a discontinuity such as a corner or the end of a line. Fig. 15 summarizes the functions of these various cells in the perception of a white rectangle on a dark background.

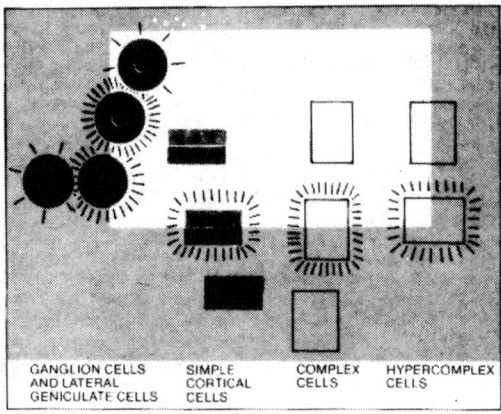

Fig. 15. Perception of a white rectangle on a dark background by cortical cells (after [26]).

F. Visual System Model

A systematic, cell-by-cell analysis of the cortex indicates a columnar organization in both ocular dominance and direction dominance. If a microelectrode penetrates perpendicularly to the cortex, all the cells it encounters respond to excitation coming from one eye only. A neighboring penetration shows cells responding to the other eye. Finally, if the penetration is slanted from one layer to the next, the ocular dominance alternates from one eye to the other.

It is interesting to note that if the same experiment is repeated by looking, not for the ocular dominance, but the response to a given orientation, the same columnar organization can be observed. A perpendicular penetration shows that all the cells encountered respond to the same orientation. In the neighboring column, the orientation is slightly different. There are roughly thirty quantized directions.

Combining the results of these two experiments, a columnar model of the cortex is obtained, as shown in Fig. 16, where the bars in the columns indicate the preferred direction.

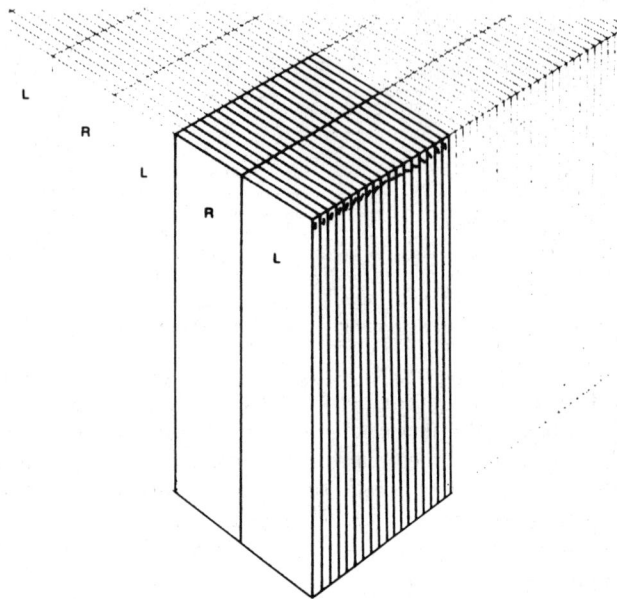

Fig. 16. Hubel and Wiesel's columnar model.

All the properties described in this section can be summarized in a block diagram (see Fig. 17) where parts related to the lens, the retina, and the cortex are indicated. Bars in the boxes indicate the directional filters followed by another filter bank for detecting the intensity of the stimulus. The first block is a spatial, isotropic, low-pass filter. It represents the spherical aberration of the lens, the effect of the pupil, and the frequency limitation by the finite number of photoreceptors. It is followed by the nonlinear characteristic of the photoreceptors. Here, a logarithmic curve for simplicity or a law of the type L^γ for more accuracy, can be used. At the level of the retina, this nonlinear and very likely memoryless transformation is followed by an isotropic high-pass filter corresponding to the lateral inhibition phenomenon of the ganglion cells. The processing done by the cells in the lateral geniculate nucleus can be included in this high-pass filter.

Finally, there is a directional filter bank that represents the processing performed by the cortex' cells. It should be noted that the whole system is shift-variant because of the decrease in resolution away from the fovea. This block diagram is the basis of the GOP system which will be described in Section IV.

IV. Local Operator Based Techniques

A. Pyramidal Coding [30]

1) General Remarks: Because it combines features of predictive and transform coding methods and because the compressions obtained are not too high (around 10:1), this pyramidal coding technique could have been described as a hybrid method of the first generation. It is included in this section, however, since its hierarchical structure is similar to that of the nervous system, and it uses functions close to

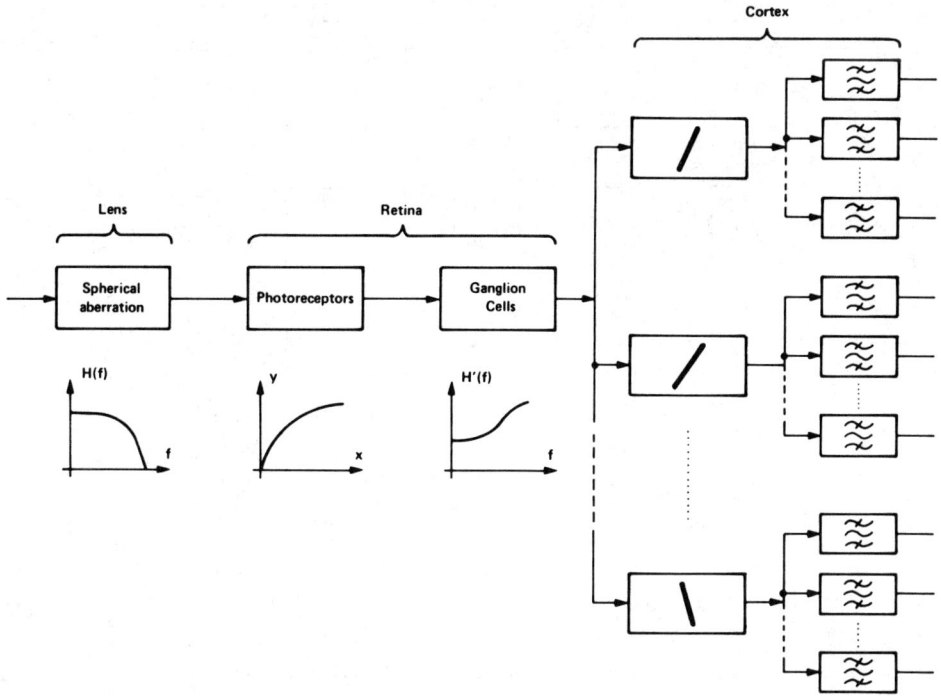

Fig. 17. Block diagram of the human visual system.

those of the human visual system. It has also elegant capabilities for progressive transmission or reconstruction. The reader may notice the role played by the synthetic high system in the design of this method.

2) Basic Method: Starting from the original picture $x(k, \ell)$ to be coded, a low-pass version $x_1(k, \ell)$ of it is computed using local averaging with a unimodal Gaussian-like two-dimensional impulse response. The low-pass image, with a cutoff frequency of f_1, can be viewed as a prediction of $x(k, \ell)$. The prediction error is then

$$e_1(k, \ell) = x(k, \ell) - x_1(k, \ell). \quad (1)$$

Clearly, coding $e_1(k, \ell)$ and $x_1(k, \ell)$ is equivalent to directly coding the picture itself. The compression that can be expected is due to two facts. a) $e_1(k, \ell)$, by its nature, is a high-pass image. Because of the low sensitivity of the eye at these frequencies, fewer bits per sample than those used for the original picture could be sufficient. b) $x_1(k, \ell)$ is a low-pass image. It can be represented by fewer samples than those necessary to represent the original image, because of the two-dimensional sampling theorem.

At this level, beside particular interpretations and specific functions used, this method is conceptually identical to the synthetic high system. The refinement is that the basic operations described above are iterated. More specifically, $x_1(k, \ell)$ is again low-pass filtered, say at a cutoff frequency f_2, and the result, $x_2(k, \ell)$ is used as a prediction of $x_1(k, \ell)$. The error for this prediction is then

$$e_2(k, \ell) = x_1(k, \ell) - x_2(k, \ell). \quad (2)$$

Note that this second error image is smaller than $e_1(k, \ell)$ by a factor which is the ratio of the two cutoff frequencies f_1/f_2. After n iterations, a series of prediction error images $e_1(k, \ell), e_2(k, \ell), \cdots, e_n(k, \ell)$ are obtained. At each iteration, the dimensions of these images are reduced by a factor $f_i/f_{(i+1)}$. For a simple implementation, a factor of two can be used at each iteration. If these images are viewed as stacked one above another, the result is a pyramidal data structure. The image at a given level of this structure is the difference of two Gaussian-like functions convolved with the original image. The difference of two Gaussian-like two-dimensional functions is a good approximation of the impulse response representing the lateral inhibition phenomenon of the human visual system. These functions are extensively used to detect intensity changes [31], [32].

A fast algorithm is proposed in [30] to obtain a series of prediction error images. A 5 by 5 separable Gaussian kernel is used to determine equivalent two-dimensional impulse responses $h_i(k, \ell)$ for each level i of the pyramid. Convolving the original image with these impulse responses leads directly to the error images. These images are then quantized and coded. To reconstruct the decoded image, interpolation filters are designed and used to compensate the decimation performed at each level. When all the error images are decoded and interpolated to reach the original resolution, their pel-by-pel sum gives the decoded image. Fig. 18 shows a block diagram of this system. A nice feature of this system is that the quality of the decoded picture can be improved as desired at the expense of a lower compression ratio. Good-quality pictures with an average compression ratio around 10:1 are obtained as shown in [30] and in Section VI.

B. Anisotropic Nonstationary Predictive Coding [33]

1) General Remarks: Like the pyramidal coding procedure described previously, this method can also be classified as a hybrid method for combining prediction and transform coding. We consider it as a "second-generation" method because of the extensive use of the properties of the human visual system and because of the high compressions achieved. It is a good example showing the emphasis put on the selection of messages before coding, an im-

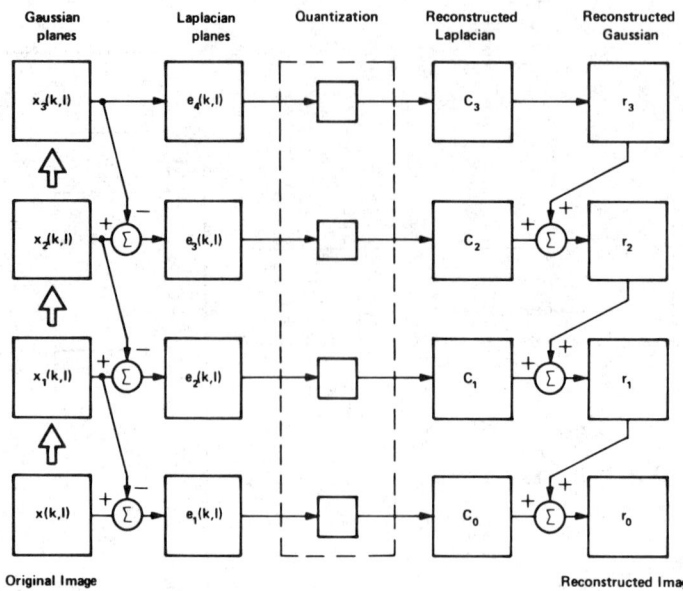

Fig. 18. Block diagram of the pyramid coding method (after [30]).

portant feature of the second-generation methods. Impacts of the synthetic high system in the design of this method are also quite visible.

2) Principles of the Method: The principles of the anisotropic, nonstationary predictive coding can be viewed as a by-product of a scheme for image restoration [34]. Starting with the classical estimation problem of recovering the estimate $\hat{x}(k,\ell)$ of an image $x(k,\ell)$ corrupted with additive, stationary, and independent white noise, refinements for the well-known Wiener filter are derived. The resulting restoration filter has three components.

The first component is the classical isotropic Wiener filter expressed as

$$H_1(\rho) = \frac{\Phi_x(\rho)}{\Phi_x(\rho) + \sigma_n^2} \quad (3)$$

where ρ is the radial frequency in the Fourier domain, $\Phi_x(\rho)$ the power spectrum of the original image, and σ_n^2 the noise power. This filter has a low-pass characteristic since the image has more low-frequency energy than the noise.

The second component is also an isotropic filter given by

$$H_2(\rho) = \frac{\sigma_n^2}{\Phi_x(\rho) + \sigma_n^2}. \quad (4)$$

In contrast with the first component, it has a high-pass characteristic. The combination of these two components leads to a bandpass behavior such as that of the early stages of the human visual system (see Fig. 12).

The third component is an anisotropic filter given by

$$H_3[\rho,\theta,\varphi(k,\ell)] = \frac{\cos^2[\varphi(k,\ell) - \theta]\sigma_n^2}{\Phi_x(\rho) + \sigma_n^2} \quad (5)$$

where θ is the polar angular frequency in the Fourier domain. This filter is used to weight local noise according to its direction with respect to that of a local anisotropy indicated by $\varphi(k,\ell)$. Local noise components aligned with $\varphi(k,\ell)$ are enhanced, whereas those which are orthogonal to $\varphi(k,\ell)$ are attenuated for better restoration.

The final restoration filter is a weighted sum of these three components

$$H(\rho,\theta,k,\ell) = H_1(\rho) + \beta(k,\ell)\tau(k,\ell)H_2(\rho)$$
$$+ \beta(k,\ell)[1 - \tau(k,\ell)]H_3[\rho,\theta,\varphi(k,\ell)]. \quad (6)$$

Weight function $\beta(k,\ell)$ is related to the magnitude of locally rectilinear features (edges and lines) in the vicinity of the point (k,ℓ) whereas $\tau(k,\ell)$ represents the variability in angle of the same feature. The weight $\beta(k,\ell)$ can be viewed as direction-insensitive estimation of a local nonstationarity. Thus together with the directional information $\varphi(k,\ell)$, it forms a vector image which indicates the magnitude and the direction of locally rectilinear features of the image. All the unknown functions in (6), such as $\beta(k,\ell)$, $\varphi(k,\ell)$, $\tau(k,\ell)$, and the frequency responses of the filters must be estimated from the available data. To alleviate the computational burden on these estimations, spatially limited filters (local operators) are suggested in [34] as arrays of at most 15 elements. Furthermore, the restoration can be performed iteratively by several passes over the data. Good restoration results are obtained by using a high-speed, parallel GOP processor [36].

3) Application to Coding: The logical way to use the restoration filter for picture coding is to transform it into a prediction filter and to use the prediction error as the messages to be coded. In this scheme, the discrete cosine transform is first applied to the prediction error before quantization and coding. Weighting functions $\beta(k,\ell)$, $\varphi(k,\ell)$, and $\tau(k,\ell)$, estimated from the original picture, must be coded and transmitted (or stored) as well.

In general, the restoration filter need not be recursive. The prediction filter, however, must be recursive. This requires the truncation of the corresponding impulse responses involved in (6) to obtain a recursive two-dimensional differential equation to implement the prediction. When the prediction and its error are computed, a one-dimensional discrete cosine transform is applied to each line of the prediction error image. The transform coefficients are then quantized in a two-level process: adaptive coding of the stationary part and threshold coding of the nonstationary part.

Weighting functions are coded in a rather simple way.

These functions have low bandwidth. Accordingly, they are coded with 1:6 undersampling in both directions. Magnitudes, angles, and the variations in angle are coded with 2, 4, and 1 bits, respectively. This leads to a very high compression, higher than 70:1, for representing the weighting functions. Taking into account the number of bits used to code the prediction error, global compressions as high as 35:1 are obtained with good-quality decoded pictures.

V. Contour–Texture Oriented Techniques

In contrast with local operator based methods, contour–texture oriented techniques attempt to segment the image into textured regions surrounded by contours such that the contours correspond, as much as possible, to those of the objects in the image. Contour and texture informations are then coded separately. Contours may be extracted in two ways: by region growing or by using the by now well-known contour extraction—or edge detection—techniques [1], [2]. In the first case, closed contours are obtained which makes it simple to list regions and their properties. The segmented image looks like a puzzle image. In the second case, contours that are obtained are not necessarily closed. Combination of this information with texture information becomes thus more problematical. Two techniques using these approaches are described below, leading to compressions as high as 70:1.

A. Region Growing Based Coding [37]–[40]

1) Segmentation: In the first stage of this method, the image is segmented to classify its pels into contour pels and texture pels. This procedure partitions the image into a set of adjacent regions under the constraint that the variation of the grey level within the region does not contain any sharp discontinuities, i.e., contours. A similar idea was suggested in [20]. Segmentation is carried out in three steps: preprocessing, region growing, and elimination of artifacts.

The preprocessing is intended to reduce the local granularity of the original image without affecting its contours, so that not too many small regions are obtained after region growing. Furthermore, these small regions do not correspond, in general, to real objects of the original image and thus become false contours. The key problem in this preprocessing is the reconciliation of apparently two contradictory goals; namely, granularity removal and edge preservation. Most of the granularity removal filters have low-pass characteristics and therefore smooth the edges as well. The inverse gradient filter [41] is chosen because of its ability to adapt its coefficients according to local contrast. Accordingly, this filter behaves like a low-pass filter in areas free of contours and like an all-pass filter in highly contrasted areas. Since its frequency characteristics are not perfectly low-pass or all-pass, it is not very efficient in removing granularity, at least in one pass. That is why it has to be applied iteratively until the granularity has been sufficiently removed. The result of applying this filter to a one-dimensional signal is shown in Fig. 19.

The mechanism of region growing is the following. Regions to be extracted must be characterized with some property in the first step. The property might be, for example, the grey level of a pel, the variation of the grey level, or the energy within a given frequency band. The selection of this property plays a very important role in the complexity

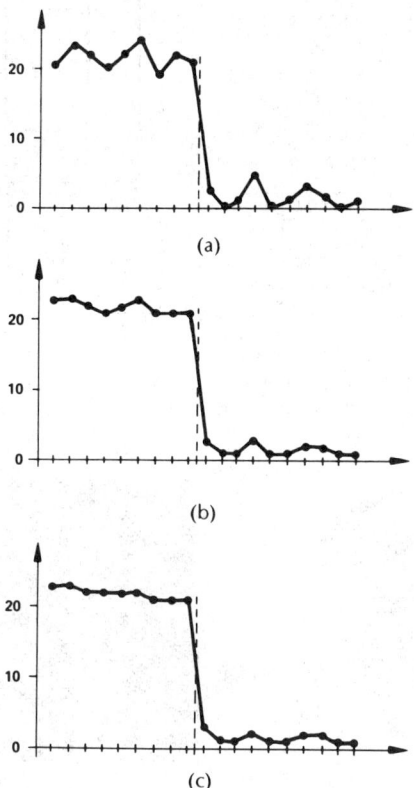

Fig. 19. Inverse gradient filtering of a one-dimensional signal. The original signal (a), result after one iteration (b), result after two iterations (c).

of the method and in the exactness of the contours obtained after segmentation. Then, starting with a given pel in the picture, its neighboring pels are examined to see whether they share the same property. If this is the case, that pel is included in the region, and in turn, its neighboring pels are examined, and so on. When there are no more pels left, connected to the region and sharing the same property, the procedure stops and restarts at any other pel which is not included in the first region. The segmentation is complete when all the pels of the picture are assigned to some region. The property used in the example below is very simple: it is a fixed grey-level interval. Although it has a constant width, this interval is made adaptive by moving it up and down on the grey-level scale in order to intercept the maximum number of pels. This displacement is constrained, however, so that previously intercepted pels always remain in the region. After this region growing, two types of artifacts are obtained: Contours which do not completely separate two regions and contours that are two pels wide. Fig. 20 shows these artifacts. They are easily eliminated with an appropriate procedure [38]. Two original pictures and the results of the region growing are shown in Fig. 21. The number of regions are 1001 and 1111 for the cameraman picture and the building picture, respectively.

At this level, the resulting image can be viewed as that of a puzzle with one-point thick closed contours. Unfortunately, because of the simple property used, the number of these contours is much higher than that of the objects in the original image. Two procedures are available to overcome this problem: introduction of some distortions by eliminating insignificant regions and their contours, or the use of a more refined property. The first alternative is

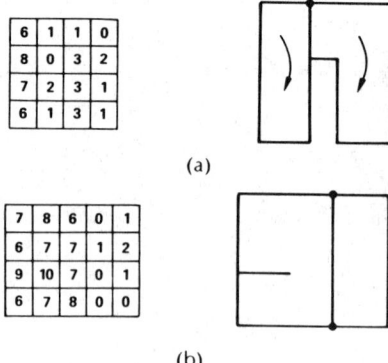

Fig. 20. Artifacts resulting from region growing. Two-point thick contours (a) and incompletely separated regions (b).

Fig. 21. Two original images and the result of region growing with a grey-level interval of 10 in both cases.

described below whereas the second is under investigation at present.

There are two heuristics to decrease the number of regions obtained by region growing: elimination of the small regions and merging weakly contrasted adjacent regions.

Fig. 22 shows the histogram and the cumulative histogram of the number of regions as a function of their size expressed in terms of the number of inner points resulting from the image of the building in Fig. 21. These curves indicate that roughly 70 percent of the regions have less than 15 pels. There are two reasons for this result. First, the granularity is not completely eliminated during preprocessing, and second, small areas of high gradient in the original image are segmented into several small regions because of the property used. If it is assumed that regions containing a number of pels less than a threshold are not significant, their elimination decreases drastically the number of regions. To avoid the creation of holes in the image, these regions are included in one of their adjacent regions. To minimize the corresponding distortion, the enclosing region is chosen as the adjacent region whose mean grey level is closest to that of the small region to be included.

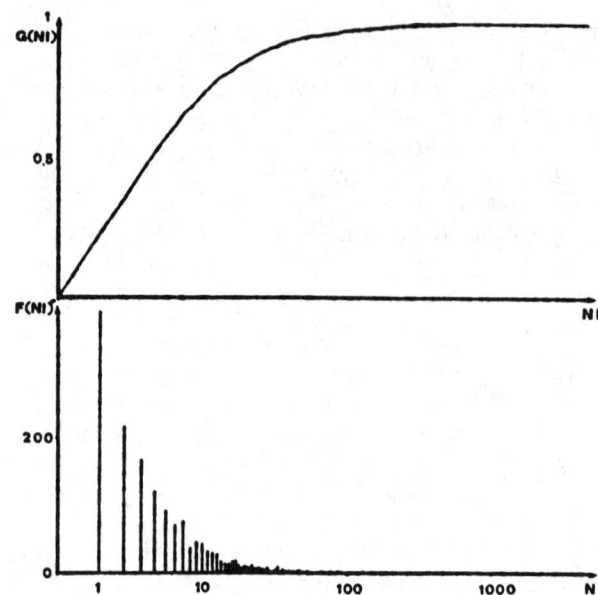

Fig. 22. Histogram and the cumulative histogram of the number of regions in the picture of the building from Fig. 25 as a function of their size.

By observing areas of constant luminance gradient in the pictures of Fig. 21 (the sky for example), it can be noticed that they are subdivided into regions even though there is no real contour. This is due to the property used in region growing which divides the image into regions of fixed grey-level dynamic range. The second possibility to decrease the number of regions is thus to merge adjacent regions whose contrast is below a certain level. The contrast between adjacent regions is defined as the mean grey level difference calculated along their common border. Notice that this procedure does not introduce any distortion. Fig. 23 shows the histogram and the cumulative histogram of the number of adjacent regions in the image of the building as a function of their common contrast. These

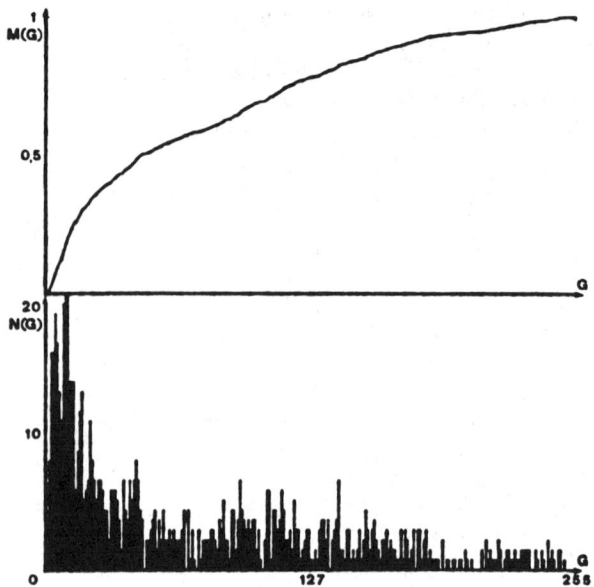

Fig. 23. Histogram and the cumulative histogram of the number of adjacent regions in the picture of the building from Fig. 25 as a function of their common contrast.

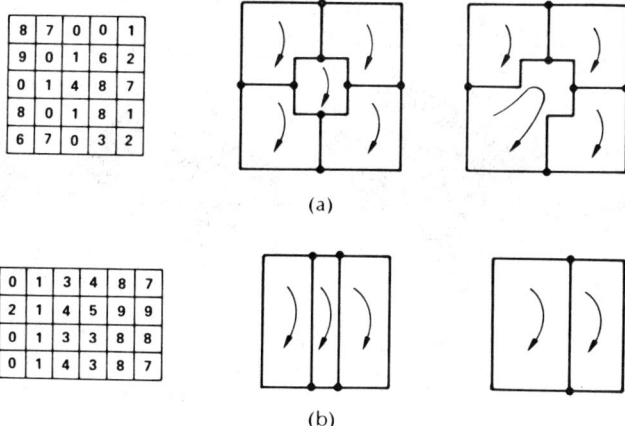

Fig. 24. Procedure for the elimination of small regions (a) and for merging adjacent regions whose local contrast is small (b).

curves indicate that roughly 35 percent of the region borders in the building image have a local contrast of less than 15 grey levels. If it is assumed that adjacent regions whose local contrast is lower than a threshold can be merged without introducing discontinuities, the number of regions is reduced further. The schematic views of these two elimination procedures are depicted in Fig. 24. The result of their application to segmented images of Fig. 21 is shown in Fig. 25. The number of regions are now 195 and 164 for the cameraman picture and the building picture, respectively.

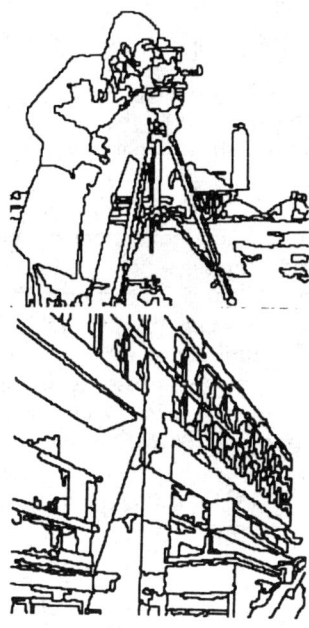

Fig. 25. Final results of the segmentation procedure.

The entire segmentation procedure has two interesting features: it is parametric in the sense that the number of regions can be fixed *a priori*, and there is no discontinuity in grey level within the regions which allows the use of global analytic functions (splines or polynomials) for their description. We are now investigating a region growing procedure using polynomial approximations over larger regions with better fidelity.

2) Contour Coding: Efficient description of the contours obtained after segmentation is a part of the messages to be coded. As discussed in Section III, a precise description of contours is essential for the human visual system. In this technique contour coding is carried out in two steps.

Since regions are closed, contour points along the border of two adjacent regions are described twice, once for each region. In the first step, these points are removed from one of the regions to be described and coded only once.

In the second step, remaining contour segments are described in a three-mode procedure [42]: 1) approximation by line segments, 2) approximation by circle segments, and 3) without approximation. Starting from the first contour point, the longest straight-line segment and circle segment are drawn under the constraint that the maximum error between the original data and their approximation does not exceed a given bound. The cost, associated with each mode, in terms of number of bits for coding, is evaluated. The "cheapest" mode is chosen. This procedure leads to an average of 1.6 bits per contour point for natural pictures if the error bound is 1.1 pels. Recently, a more refined code [43] without approximation has been proposed, using about 1.2 bits per contour point.

3) Texture Coding: The missing part of the messages after contour coding is texture coding. Note that within each region there is no longer any sharp discontinuity and hence the variation of the grey level within a region can be described with smooth two-dimensional polynomial functions. Texture coding is also carried out in two steps.

In the first step, the general shape of the grey level in each region is approximated by a two-dimensional polynomial function. The order of the polynomial is determined as a function of the approximation error and of the cost involved in coding polynomial coefficients. The approximation criterion used is the mean-square error which is minimized over each region for polynomials of order 0, 1, and 2. A three-dimensional view of these approximations is shown in Fig. 26. In this particular case, the best ("cheapest") approximation is obtained with a first-order polynomial function.

In the second step, the granularity removed with preprocessing is added back in the form of a pseudo-random noise to render the image more natural and less "painted by numbers." The mean-square error between the original image and the image reconstructed with polynomial functions is computed in each region. This error is used to control the variance of zero-mean Gaussian pseudo-random signal added as microtexture or "salt-and-pepper." Fig. 27

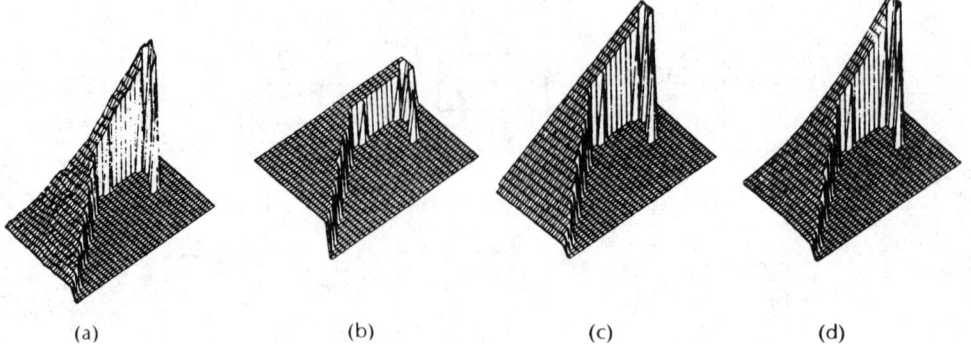

Fig. 26. Approximation of the grey level of a region with two-dimensional polynomial functions. Original data (a), zero-order approximation (b), first-order approximation (c), and second-order approximation (d).

Fig. 27. Decoded pictures with compression ratio 50:1.

shows the final state of the decoded pictures with compressions around 50:1. Additional results of this method are discussed in the next section.

4) Remarks: The region growing based technique seems to be a powerful approach for high-compression image coding. Its weak aspect is the property used in region growing which leads to a rather large number of regions whose borders are not necessarily the contours of the objects in the image. We are currently investigating another property for region growing; namely, two-dimensional polynomial approximation, for obtaining a smaller number of larger regions with better quality. A number of special procedures were designed to combat unnecessary artifacts resulting from region growing. Also under investigation are better ways to analyze and synthesize texture.

B. Directional Decomposition Based Coding

1) General Remarks: In this method, heavy emphasis is placed on edge detection to preserve edge information in the best possible way. According to the properties of the human visual system discussed in Section III with reference to coding, features required for an edge detector are precision of the edge position, economy in the sense that the smallest possible set of representative edge points are detected, and the ability to reconstruct the original edge. It is not obvious that most of these edge detection operators are simultaneously optimal with respect to all these features. The commonly used point-based definition of edge elements leads to the detection of redundant information. The weakness of this kind of operator is visible in the enormous amount of work that has been done (edge thinning, edge tracking, etc.) to improve these results. That is why it is preferable to define an edge element (EE) to be a two-dimensional step function of a given width and given direction. For notational ease it will be represented by a vector $\vec{e}$ with:

$$|\vec{e}| = \ell \quad \text{and} \quad a_1 < \arg(\vec{e}) < a_2. \tag{7}$$

The goal is to obtain a representation of the edges of an image by means of such edge elements. The set of edge elements that provides this representation constitute the edge element set (ES). An edge detection scheme which uses this representation and produces the necessary information for reconstructing the edges, satisfies all the requirements mentioned previously. An edge element subset (EES) is defined to be a subset of the edge element set containing edge elements confined to limited directions, bounded by two angles a_1 and a_2

$$S_k = \{\vec{e}_k | \|\vec{e}_k\| = \ell, \ \arg(\vec{e}_k) \in (a_1, a_2)\}. \tag{8}$$

With each EES we associate a principal direction corresponding to the bisector of the angle (a_1, a_2) and an orthogonal direction which is perpendicular to the principal direction.

Using these definitions, a directional image is defined to be an image containing edge elements belonging to only one edge element subset.

2) Directional Filtering: Directional filtering is based on the relationship between the presence of an edge in an image and its contribution to the image spectrum. It is largely motivated by the existence of direction-sensitive neurones in the human visual system. The discrete Fourier transform of an image $x(k, \ell)$ is given by

$$X(m,n) = \sum_{k=0}^{N-1} \sum_{\ell=0}^{N-1} x(k,\ell) \exp[-j2\pi(mk + n\ell)/N]. \tag{9}$$

If the content of the spectrum along a line passing through the origin of the Fourier domain is examined, choosing (for computational ease) the line $X(0, n)$ we have

$$X(0,n) = \sum_{k=0}^{N-1} \sum_{\ell=0}^{N-1} x(k,\ell) \exp[-j2\pi n\ell/N]$$

$$= \sum_{\ell=0}^{N-1} \exp[-j2\pi n\ell/N] \sum_{k=0}^{N-1} x(k,\ell). \tag{10}$$

This equation can be viewed as the Fourier transform of a one-dimensional signal which represents the mean values of the image $x(k,\ell)$ along the k axis (see Fig. 28(a)). If there is an edge parallel to this axis (Fig. 28(b)), the signal corresponding to the second part of (10) is a step-like

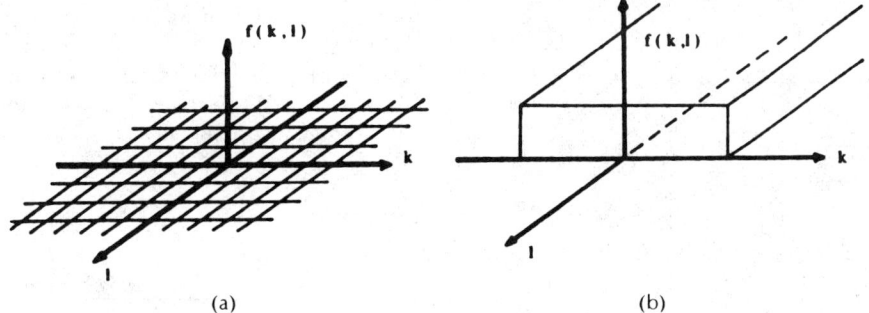

Fig. 28. Coordinate system to project an image along the k axis (a) and an ideal edge parallel to it (b).

function. Therefore, the contribution of the edge along the m axis of the Fourier domain may be deduced from the Fourier transform of this signal. In a similar way, the result for other directions can be found by turning the k axis to the left and to the right up to 90° and computing the projection of the image on the ℓ axis. The series of signals that is obtained is shown in Fig. 29. A theoretical aspect of

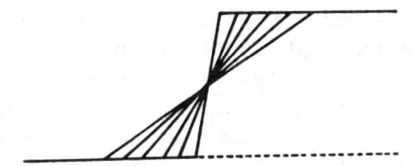

Fig. 29. Projections of an ideal edge for various directions.

the Fourier transforms of these signals may be obtained by approximating them by means of the following series of error functions:

$$g_n(z) = \frac{2\pi}{\sigma_n} A \int_{-z}^{z} \exp\left(-x^2/2\sigma_n^2\right) dx. \quad (11)$$

They are shown in Fig. 30. The Fourier transforms of these

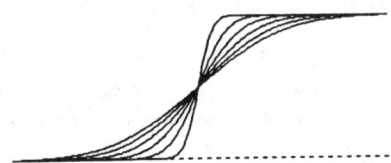

Fig. 30. Approximation for the signals of Fig. 33.

functions are given by

$$G_n(f) = \frac{A}{j2\pi f} \exp\left(-\sigma_n^2 f^2\right). \quad (12)$$

It can be deduced from this equation that as σ_n^2 decreases, getting closer to the step function, the high-frequency content of the Fourier transform increases. The contribution of an edge is distributed all over the spectrum; the highest frequency component lies in the direction orthogonal to that of the edge, and as we turn away from this direction, the frequency of the contributions decreases, to vanish at 90°. Therefore, to detect an edge element subset, the sector of the spectrum that corresponds to the interval of directions of the EES should be retained. A filter whose frequency response covers a sector or a part of a sector in

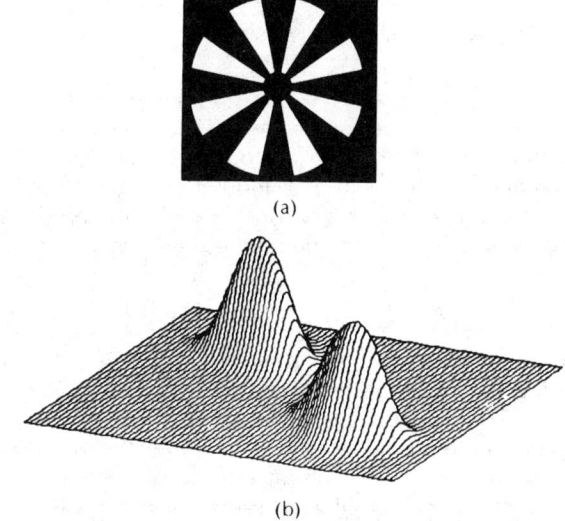

Fig. 31. Sectors covered by directional filters (a) and a low-pass filter in the Fourier domain designed with a Gaussian window of large variance (b).

the frequency domain is called a directional filter. To make edge detection with these filters easier, high-pass filtering along the principal direction is introduced. Areas of the Fourier domain corresponding to these filters are shown in Fig. 31. The entire frequency plane is thus covered with n directional filters and one low-pass filter. The ideal frequency response of the ith directional filter is given by

$$H_i(f,g) = \begin{cases} 1, & \text{if } \left[\theta(i) < \tan^{-1}(g/f) < \theta(i+1)\right. \\ & \left. \text{and if } \left(f^2 + g^2\right) > \rho_c \right\} \\ 0, & \text{otherwise} \end{cases}$$

with $\quad (13)$

$$\theta(i) = (i-1)\pi/2n$$
$$\theta(i+1) = (i+1)\pi/2n$$

and

$$|f|, |g| < 0.5$$

where f and g are spatial frequencies, ρ_c is the cutoff frequency of the low-pass filter, and where a unity sampling step size is assumed.

Accordingly, a directional filter is a high-pass filter along its principal direction and a low-pass filter along the orthogonal direction. The bandwidth along this direction is

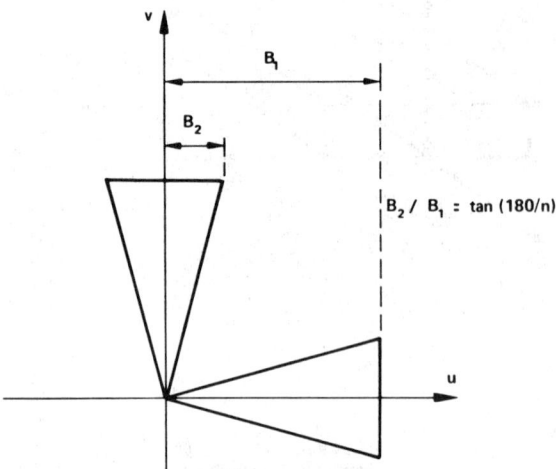

Fig. 32. Bandwidth of a directional filter.

$g \tan(\pi/2n)$ (see Fig. 32). Because of the Gibbs phenomenon, the ideal frequency response of the directional filters should be modified by an appropriate window function. The purpose is to avoid oscillation around zero crossings corresponding to real edges. One of the most appropriate window functions for this purpose is the Gaussian window given by

$$w(k, \ell) = \exp\left[-(k^2 + \ell^2)/s^2\right]. \quad (14)$$

It can be shown [45] that, after windowing the filters and filtering, the superposition of all the directional images and the low-pass image leads to the original image. Thus the directional filtering, as defined, is an information preserving transformation. An example of directional decomposition with eight directional filters is shown in Fig. 33. There is,

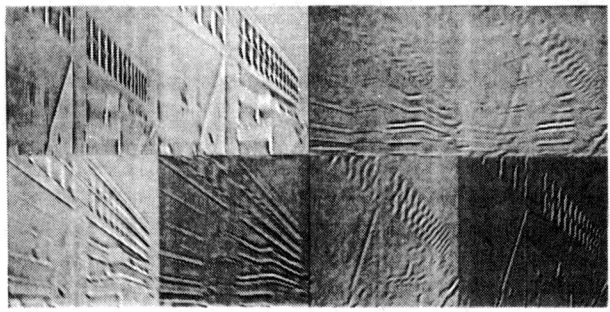

Fig. 33. Directional decomposition in eight components and the resulting sum.

however, a compromise to be made. If the variance s^2 of the window function is too large, directional filters are more selective in their sector but quite poor as low-pass filters along the orthogonal direction. This introduces undesirable oscillations. In contrast, if this parameter is too small, these oscillations are considerably attenuated to the detriment of the directional selectivity. The same edge may appear in several directional images. A solution to this compromise may be found by using the following nonlinear transformation. It consists of first computing the sum of the values of the image points lying on the same position in all the directional images and retaining the point of the maximum value. Then, all the other points are set to 0 except the point of maximum value, which now takes the value of the sum. An illustration of this transformation is given in Fig. 34. This transformation considerably improves the directional selectivity and keeps the undesirable oscillations at an acceptable level.

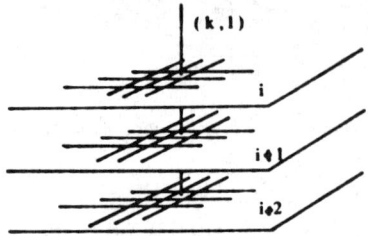

Fig. 34. Illustrating the nonlinear transformation to improve the directional selectivity.

There are two other parameters involved in the directional filters: their number and the cutoff frequency of the low-pass filter. The number of filters is directly related to the minimum width of edge elements that is accepted *a priori* in the image. Therefore, a direct way to define the number of filters (directions) is obtained by fixing the minimum length of accepted edge elements. The segmentation of curved edges (curvature quantization) resulting from the definition of edge elements is another fact that must also be taken into account. From a physiological point of view [25], it seems that the quantization of the directions is made by 20 to 30 different groups of cells, each one specialized to a limited interval of directions. However, to better define the range of acceptable quantization, experimental work is required. Since the choice of the cutoff frequency influences only the compression ratio and the quality of the decoded image, it will be discussed in the next section.

3) Coding: The messages to be coded are the directional images and the low-pass image. Note that the following scheme is not information lossless and that a certain quality degradation is assumed when coding. The main objective is to achieve the highest compression for a given degradation. The low-frequency component is, by its nature, adapted to transform coding. Criticism of transform coding was based on its weakness in coding edges. Since there are no edges in the low-frequency component, transform coding is the preeminently adequate method. As it will be shown, there is no degradation resulting from low-frequency component coding.

High-frequency images will be used for detecting and coding edges. A loss of information and hence a quality degradation is associated with this coding procedure. The loss of information comes from the inevitable choice between weak and strong edges. If the compression ratio is set to high rates, very weak edges must be eliminated. On the other hand, the indirect approximation of the edges by line segments, as assumed by the definition of the edge elements, introduces some degradations at the locations of high curvature. Edge detection in the directional images is based on the high-pass character of the directional filters along their principal direction. Filtering a signal with a high-pass filter gives zero crossings at the locations of abrupt changes (edges). Accordingly, edge detection in the directional images is performed by searching the zero crossings along the principal direction of each image.

For ease of implementation, a normalization of all the principal directions on the horizontal direction is introduced. It is based on interpolation, rotation, and resampling. The details of this algorithm can be found in [48]. Edge detection in the normalized images is done by searching the zero crossings along the columns. The following parameters are used:

$$p_1 = x_i(k,\ell) \cdot x_i(k+1,\ell)$$
$$p_2 = x_i(k,\ell) \cdot x_i(k+2,\ell) \qquad (15)$$

where $x_i(k,\ell)$ represents the ith directional image.

The existence of a zero crossing is established by the condition $p_1 < 0$ or $p_1 = 0$ and $p_2 < 0$. Another variable which must be used after this stage is the magnitude of the zero crossings, defined as

$$p_3 = |x_i(k,\ell) - x_i(k+k',\ell)| \qquad (16)$$

where k' equals 1 or 2 if $p_1 < 0$ or $p_1 = 0$ and $p_2 < 0$, respectively. By setting a threshold on this variable, it is possible to control the strength of the edges to be retained.

Because of the bandwidth reduction along the lines (orthogonal direction) and the subsampling, edge detection is applied to smaller directional images. Accordingly, each zero crossing detected corresponds to an edge element as defined by (7). Its direction belongs to the sector determined by the directional filter ($180/2n$) and its length in pels is equal to the subsampling rate. An example of zero crossing edge detection is given in Fig. 35. The first directional image of the set given in Fig. 33 is shown again in Fig. 35(a) whereas the zero crossings detected from this image

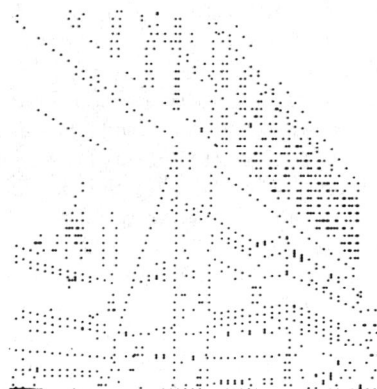

Fig. 36. Global result of zero crossing edge detection in eight directional images.

Fig. 37. Edges obtained after interpolation.

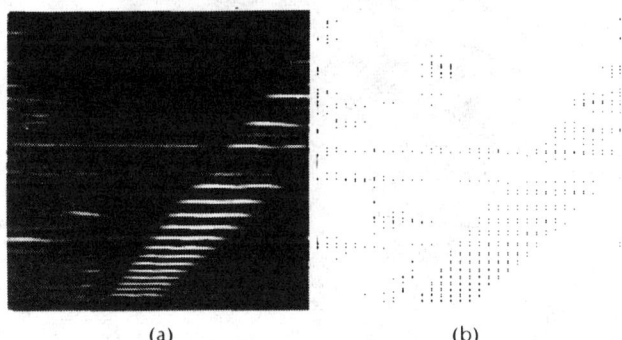

Fig. 35. Zero crossing edge detection (b) in one directional image (a).

by applying the detection algorithm to every fifth column (subsampling rate 5:1), are plotted in Fig. 35(b). When edges in all the directional images are detected, the global result is as shown in Fig. 36. This image was obtained by rotating and superposing each directional image after edge detection. Fig. 37 shows the edge image obtained by interpolation between the zero crossings of each directional image before rotation and superposition. Notice that the representation of Fig. 36, which contains 1107 points, permits the reconstruction of the image of Fig. 37 which contains 5381 points. This result shows that the requirements of precise and economical detection are largely satisfied.

Each directional image is represented by the positions and the magnitudes of the zero crossings. The positions are coded with run-length coding using the Huffman code, requiring an average of 4.5 bits per position. The magnitudes of zero crossings are coded by trying different number of quantization levels. Exploiting the low sensitivity to contrast at high frequencies, a 3-bit code word was finally retained for coding the magnitudes of the zero crossings. The improvements obtained by using larger code words are not enough to justify the price payed. Smaller code words lead to objectionable distortions.

The low-frequency image can be coded in two equivalent ways. Since the maximum frequency of this component is much lower, it can be resampled using the two-dimensional sampling theorem and the resulting pixels can be coded by a standard procedure. The alternative is transform coding. The choice of the transform technique is directly dictated by the filtering that was used. The locations of the Fourier coefficients are known from the characteristics of the filter, and the importance of all these coefficients excludes any elimination by thresholding. This falls, therefore, in the category of zonal coding. After experimenting with several possibilities such as logarithmic quantization, bit-allocation plane, etc., the coefficients are quantized linearly. Fixed-length words are used to code the phase and variable-length words, as attributed by the Huffman code, are used to code the magnitudes.

4) Decoding: In order to reconstruct the original image, all the components have to be decoded and added. The low-frequency component is obtained by inversely transforming the coded coefficients. The high-frequency component is obtained by synthesizing the directional images from the zero crossings. The synthesis of edge profiles from the zero crossing information and the interpolation between the columns of the normalized directional images, are the most critical procedures for the quality of the decoded image. The edge model, that was introduced in Section V-B1, offers the theoretical basis for the synthesis of the one-dimensional signals along the columns. Equation (11) requires two parameters: the magnitude A of zero crossings representing the contrast of the edge and the standard deviation related to the steepness of the slope of the edge. As the magnitude of zero crossings is coded, the only unknown parameter is the standard deviation. Two possible solutions were studied. The first consists of assuming a constant value for the standard deviation. This solution gives a standard, more-or-less step-like edge. The second consists of assuming a dependence of the standard deviation on the contrast. Experimental results indicate that a linear variation of the standard deviation with the contrast gives more realistic edges. The prototype wavelet which was adopted for approximating the profiles of zero crossings is the following:

$$g(u) = (u/Ak) \exp[-u^2/Ak] \qquad (17)$$

where u is the distance from the zero crossing at $u = 0$, A the magnitude, and k a constant. The family of these functions for different values of A is illustrated in Fig. 38.

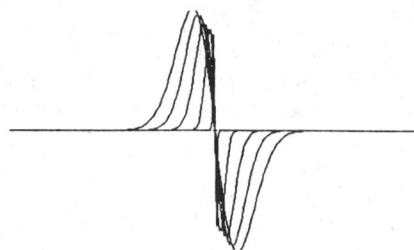

Fig. 38. Synthetic zero crossing profiles.

Note that the prototype wavelet of (17) is closely related to the derivative of (11).

Once the synthesis of zero crossing profiles is carried out at coded locations, the whole directional image is reconstructed by interpolation between the columns of the subsampled images. For a perfect interpolation between the columns of these images, the fact that the edge elements assumed by the presence of each zero crossing may have any direction within this interval must be taken into account. The interpolation algorithm looks for a neighboring point not only on the same line but also on the two preceding or following lines.

An example of coding the low- and high-frequency components is given in Fig. 39. Low- and high-frequency images

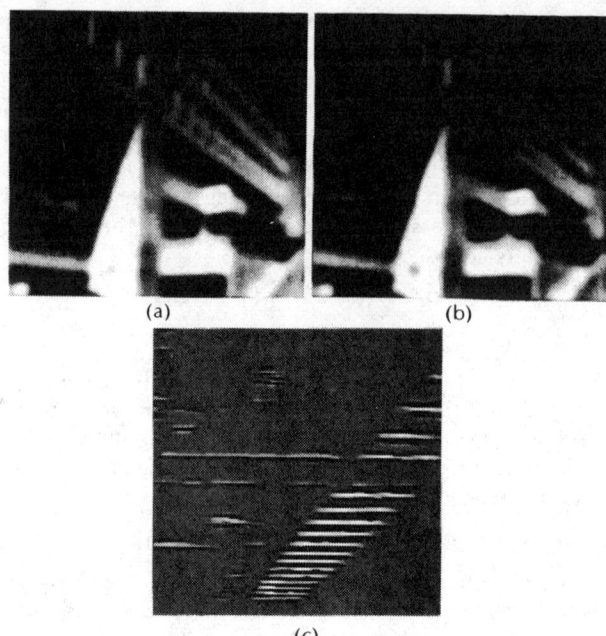

Fig. 39. The low-pass image before coding (a) and after coding (b). Decoded one directional image (c).

before coding are shown in Figs. 39(a) and 35(a), respectively. Their reconstructed versions after coding and decoding are shown in Fig. 39(b) and (c). The final result of decoding is given in Fig. 40 with a compression ratio of 41:1.

IMAGE CODING BASED ON A DIRECTIONAL DECOMPOSITION
number of directions (filters) : 8
cutoff frequency : 0.12
subsampling rate : 5
zero-cros. detection threshold : 25
total number of zero cros. : 1107
phase mean coding length : 4
compression ratio : 41.27

Fig. 40. An example of coded and decoded image with a compression ratio of 41:1.

VI. SIMULATION RESULTS

All the decoded pictures which will be shown and discussed in this section are obtained with information-lossy methods. It would have been useful to derive a criterion to evaluate the distortions. As is well known, commonly used mean-square error criterion does not correspond to the subjective judgement of human observers. Although several attempts have been made to combine objective and subjective components into one mathematically tractable criterion, the results are not convincing, at least for the authors. For this reason, quality evaluation of the decoded pictures are left to the judgement of the reader. Coding methods have been applied to three original images shown in Fig. 41.

Fig. 41. Three original digitized pictures.

As mentioned earlier, these images are digitized with a 256 by 256 raster and each pel is quantized to 256 levels. Accordingly, their canonical form requires 524 288 bits for each of them. Compression ratios given in this section are the ratios of this number to the number of bits required for the coded versions. Results presented and discussed in this section are related to two first-generation methods and four second-generation methods described in Sections IV and V. Last but not least, errorless channel or storage is assumed for all the results.

A. First-Generation Methods

The purpose for giving here indicative results obtained with the first-generation techniques is not to provide comparison grounds and to disgrace these techniques, but to show, as a reminder, the type of results obtained in the early 1970s. Two examples of such results are given: one with DPCM coding and the other with transform coding. These two methods have been applied in the simplest possible way and all the refinements to improve the quality or the compression ratio by a few percent are omitted. These little improvements do not play an important role in this context.

Fig. 42 shows the image of the building after transform coding and decoding. Fourier transform and threshold coding are used to retain 2521 Fourier coefficients out of 32 768. The magnitude and the phase of each of them are coded with code words of average length of 5.44 and 5 bits, respectively. Addresses of the retained coefficients are coded with run-length coding requiring 3.08 bits per address. The compression ratio is therefore 15.4:1. Although

Fig. 42. An example of transform coded and decoded picture with a compression ratio of 15.4:1.

Fig. 43. An example of DPCM coded and decoded picture with a compression ratio of 3.7:1.

distortions are visible, the quality of this picture can be considered as very good.

An example of simple DPCM coded and decoded picture is shown in Fig. 43, for which the difference signal is quantized to 32 levels and coded with Huffman code. The compression ratio is 3.7:1. The price paid for the excellent quality of the result is the low compression ratio. Further increase of the compression leads to rapid deterioration of the image quality.

B. Pyramidal Coding

To generate the series of images $x_i(k, \ell)$ and $e_i(k, \ell)$, the low-pass filters and their cutoff frequencies must be fixed. A 5 by 5 separable weighting function is used for low-pass filtering. In one dimension, these weights are $w(0) = 0.7$, $w(-1) = w(1) = 0.25$, and $w(-2) = w(2) = 0.1$. The pyramid generated with these weights is shown in Fig. 44. The ratio of two cutoff frequencies $f(i)/f(i + 1)$ in each level of the pyramid is fixed at 2. In this structure, each picture has four times fewer pels than its predecessor. Fig. 45 shows the results obtained with this technique with a compression ratio of about 6:1. A good quality is observed in all the results when compared to the original images (Fig. 41). If the compression is set at a higher ratio (16:1 or 32:1) degradations become visible due to successive decimations and interpolations, as shown in Figs. 46 and 47. These degradations may be eliminated at the expense of a higher computational cost.

C. Anisotropic Nonstationary Predictive Coding

This method, as described in Section IV-B, was also applied to our original images. Fig. 48 shows the results. The average compression ratio is around 20:1 with good-

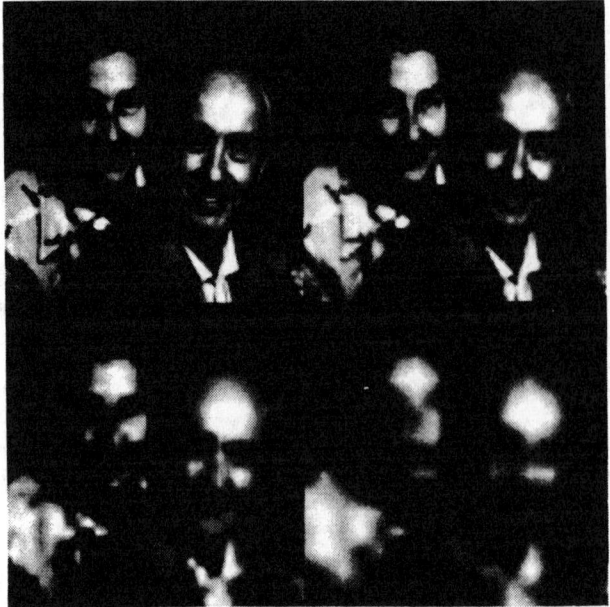

Fig. 44. First four levels of the Gaussian pyramid.

Fig. 46. Pyramidal coding results. The compression ratio is 16:1.

Fig. 45. Pyramidal coding results. The compression ratio is 6:1.

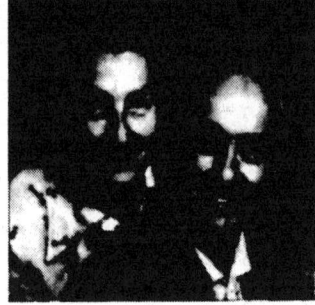

Fig. 47. Pyramidal coding results. The compression ratio is 32:1.

quality decoded images. Other examples with higher compression ratios but on larger images (512 by 512) can be found in [33].

D. Region Growing Based Coding

This method is a succession of parametric procedure as described in Section V-A. As in any parametric method, the ideal value of each parameter is data and goal dependent. The first step of this method is inverse gradient filtering to attenuate local granularity in the image. Its parameters are the size of the mask used in the convolution and the number of iterations. Experiments indicate that a 3 by 3 mask and 10 iterations are appropriate for most of the natural images. The second step is that of region growing, requiring a grey-level interval as the unique parameter. If its value is too small, a large number of regions is obtained decreasing the compression ratio. In contrast, if it is too large, the number of regions is small, leading to a high compression ratio. The price paid for this is the unacceptable distortions in the decoded image. In the third step, small regions are eliminated and strongly connected regions are merged using two threshold parameters. These parameters are the most important parameters of the method. The value of the first threshold on the region size depends on

Fig. 48. Anisotropic nonstationary predictive coding results.

the distortions accepted or tolerated. Experimental results show that regions containing more than 20 inner points should not be eliminated. The second threshold is on the gradient along the common border of two adjacent regions. These regions are merged if the average gradient is less than 15–20 grey levels compared to the full dynamic range of 256 levels. For high compression, the number of regions after segmentation should not exceed 100 or 110. The contours of these regions are coded using the new procedure described in [43], using 1.173 bits per contour point. Finally, texture components, deterministic as well as random, are coded depending on the order of the two-dimensional polynomial function used. The compression ratio for this method is given by

$$C = \frac{524\,288}{0.634P + 10N0 + 30N1 + 60N2} \qquad (18)$$

where P is the number of contour points, $N0$ the number of regions approximated with a zero-order polynomial, $N1$ the number of regions approximated with a first-order polynomial, and $N2$ the number of regions approximated with a second-order polynomial function. Three series of coded and decoded images are shown in Figs. 49–51 along with the corresponding compression ratios. For high compression, several defects appear. Many of them are due to the elimination of the small regions (lips of the cameraman, an ash tray on the wall of the building, etc.). Accordingly, this method is suitable for images which can be described by a small number of large regions. This is not the case of the couple image as reflected by the low compression ratios and poor quality of the results. There is no doubt that the quality of the decoded pictures can be improved if the property used for region growing is replaced by a more powerful one.

E. Directional Decomposition Based Coding

The compression ratio and the quality of an image coded with this scheme depend on the following parameters: the cutoff frequency of the filters, the subsampling rate, the zero crossing detection threshold, and the quantization of the low-frequency components. The value of the cutoff frequency determines the amount of detail preserved in the low-frequency component: the larger the cutoff frequency,

Fig. 49. Region growing based coding results. The parameters used are: (a) $P = 21\,210$, $N0 = 182$, $N1 = 59$, $N2 = 21$, and $C = 29:1$; (b) $P = 16\,448$, $N0 = 160$, $N1 = 38$, $N2 = 8$, and $C = 38:1$; (c) $P = 25\,352$, $N0 = 249$, $N1 = 91$, $N2 = 41$, and $C = 22:1$.

Fig. 50. Region growing based coding results. The parameters used are: (a) $P = 18\,046$, $N0 = 129$, $N1 = 40$, $N2 = 10$, and $C = 38:1$; (b) $P = 14\,590$, $N0 = 122$, $N1 = 35$, $N2 = 5$, and $C = 44:1$; (c) $P = 22\,350$, $N0 = 179$, $N1 = 72$, $N2 = 31$, and $C = 26:1$.

Fig. 51. Region growing based coding results. The parameters used are: (a) $P = 15\,188$, $N0 = 96$, $N1 = 25$, $N2 = 5$, and $C = 45:1$; (b) $P = 11\,952$, $N0 = 98$, $N1 = 31$, $N2 = 3$, and $C = 60:1$; (c) $P = 19\,140$, $N0 = 131$, $N1 = 50$, $N2 = 24$, and $C = 32:1$.

the richer in detail the low-frequency component, the better the quality of the decoded image, but lower the compression ratio. The subsampling rate is directly related to the number of directional filters and to the length of the assumed edge elements. For the results presented here, the number of directional images is fixed at eight. The subsampling rate may vary from three to five resulting in more or less visible distortions in edge reconstruction. For a larger number of directional filters, the directional selectivity is improved at the level of zero crossing profile synthesis but the short edge elements are eliminated causing objectionable distortions.

The zero crossing detection threshold controls the importance of edges to be detected and reconstructed. Fig. 52 is a

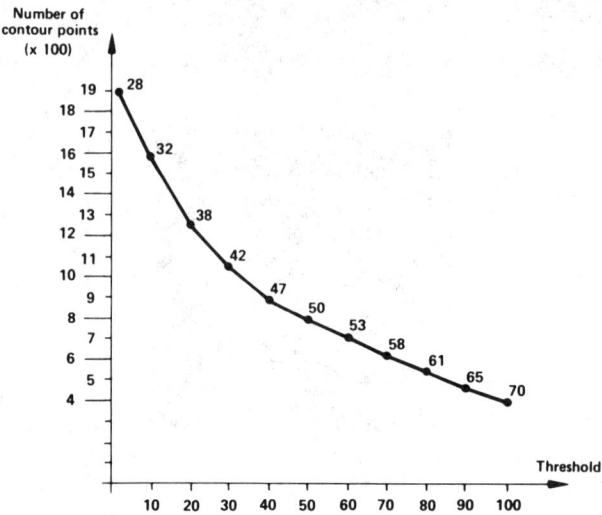

Fig. 52. The number of zero crossings as a function of the threshold.

plot of the number of zero crossings as a function of the threshold, as computed in the picture of the building. The compression ratio for a given set of parameters is indicated for each point of this curve. For a threshold value larger than 30, important contours are eliminated causing visible distortions.

The quality of the low-frequency component depends on the quantization of the magnitude and the phase of the coefficients to be coded. In Fig. 53, the root mean-square error between a low-pass image and its coded version is

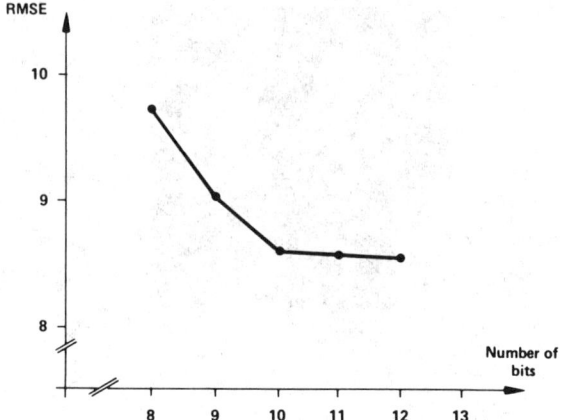

Fig. 53. Root mean-square error as a function of the number of bits used for coding the magnitudes of the Fourier coefficients.

plotted as a function of the number of bits used to code the magnitude. As this plot indicates, in contrast with regular images, the subjective differences between the corresponding images are not as important. The low-pass image coded with 10 bits has no visible distortion and the one coded with 8 bits is acceptable. If the number of bits for the magnitude is kept constant (10 bits), and that for the phase is varied, a similar result is obtained, as depicted in Fig. 54.

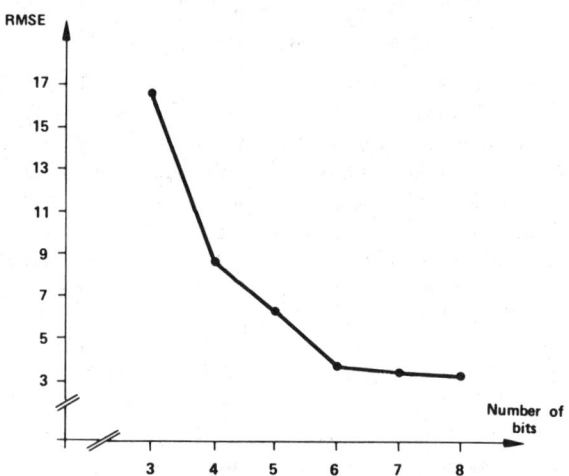

Fig. 54. Root mean-square error as a function of the number of bits used for coding the phase of the Fourier coefficients.

Using 5 bits for the phase, a perfect low-pass image is obtained. The result obtained with 4 bits is acceptable. A lower number of bits introduces important distortions.

The first series of results of decoded images obtained with a low compression ratio is shown in Fig. 55. The average compression ratio is around 20:1 and the quality of the picture is quite high. Comparing these results to those of Fig. 49, one can notice the difference of quality especially in the image of the couple. By decreasing the cutoff frequency and increasing the zero crossing detection threshold, a second series of results is obtained with higher compression ratios, as shown in Fig. 56. They illustrate a typical performance of this method. In this case, the compression ratio varies from 33:1 for the image of the building to 51:1 for the image of the couple.

One may wonder what an image looks like after compression with a very high compresssion ratio close to 100:1. By setting the important parameters beyond their acceptable limits, very high compression ratios can be obtained with rather poor quality results, as shown in Fig. 57. The elimination of important edges and distortions in the edge and low-frequency component reconstruction are quite visible. These results can be improved by the introduction of post-processing procedure after decoding, especially by better matching low- and high-frequency components.

VII. Conclusions

In this paper a brief overview is first given of image-coding techniques using only (or mainly) statistical properties of the information source. The compression ratio achievable with these techniques has reached a saturation limit which does not correspond to the entropy of the source. This entropy, so far, is model dependent. Furthermore, information theory and coding theory do not take into

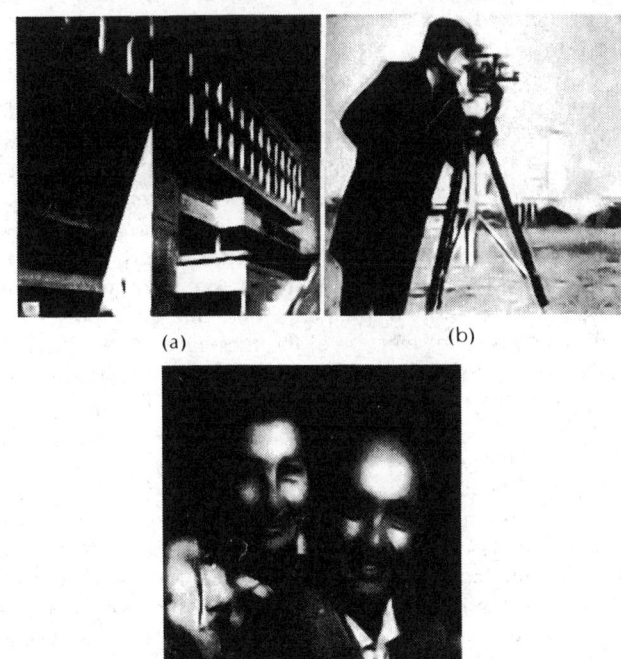

Fig. 56. Directional decomposition based coding results. The parameters used are: $\rho_c = 0.12$, subsampling rate = 4, zero crossing detection threshold = 25, magnitude and phase quantized to 1024 and 32 levels, respectively. The compression ratios are 33:1 (a), 40:1 (b), and 51:1 (c).

Fig. 57. Directional decomposition based coding results. The parameters used are: $\rho_c = 0.12$, subsampling rate = 5, zero crossing detection threshold = 50, magnitude and phase quantized to 256 and 16 levels, respectively. The compression ratios are 56:1 (a), 65:1 (b), and 92:1 (c).

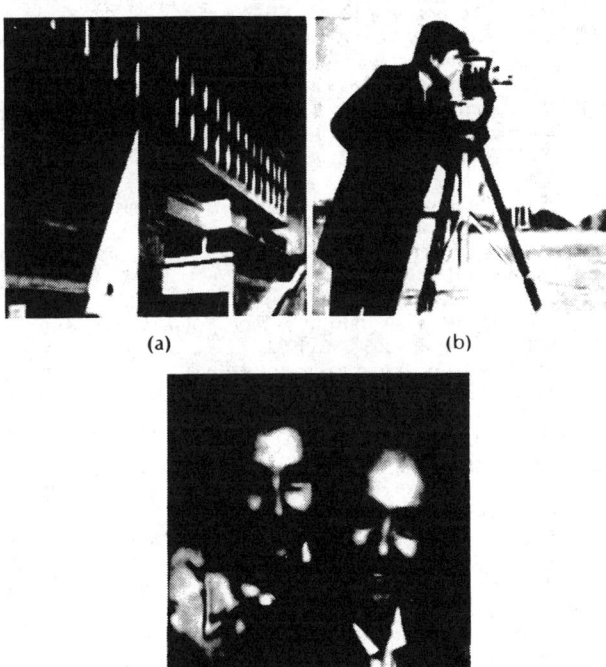

Fig. 55. Directional decomposition based coding results. The parameters used are: $\rho_c = 0.19$, subsampling rate = 3, zero crossing detection threshold = 15, magnitude and phase quantized to 1024 and 32 levels, respectively. The compression ratios are 17:1 (a), 20:1 (b), 24:1 (c).

account the properties of the receiver, i.e., the human visual system. These techniques are classified as first-generation techniques. They are characterized by the use of a signal processing approach in the selection of the messages to be coded and the application of the coding theory to code them.

Given the importance of the human visual system, recent neurophysiological results are discussed and a block diagram of this system is presented. These results suggest strongly the use of a general contour–texture model for image processing and coding. Techniques attempting to use this model are classified as second-generation techniques. It is interesting to note that the synthetic high system, designed 25 years ago, is the starting point for many of the second-generation techniques. These methods put heavy emphasis on the selection of the messages to be coded. In this context, signal processing approaches are not as successful as pattern recognition or artificial intelligence approaches. The coding is done in the classical way.

Four methods were described as second-generation techniques. The first two, namely pyramidal coding and anisotropic nonstationary predictive coding, as based on local operators designed in agreement with the processing done in the human visual system. They produce good-quality results at high compression ratios. The other two methods are based on contour–texture models. They need several improvements to produce better quality images at the same compression ratio or to reach higher compression ratios for the same quality. The goal to be reached is to segment the image into regions corresponding to the real objects of the scene, without missing small ones and without introducing false objects and hence false contours. Powerful representations should be designed to describe the grey level evolution within each region. Recent efforts in texture analysis and synthesis will be of great value to image coding to render the natural look when added to the representation of regions. It is hoped that image coding will remain a center of interest for researchers and that, one day, Descartes' limit will be reached.

ACKNOWLEDGMENT

Several individuals have contributed to our experience in picture coding and hence to this paper through various kinds of interactions. We would like to acknowledge contributions particularly from Prof. F. de Coulon, Prof. W. K. Schreiber, Prof. M. Eden, Prof. I. T. Young, Prof. G. H. Granlund, Prof. W. Frei, and Dr. A. N. Netravali, Dr. C. Rubinstein, Dr. R. Forcheimer, and Dr. P. Stucki.

Special thanks are due to Dr. P. J. Burt, Dr. E. H. Adelson, Dr. R. Wilson, Dr. H. Knutson, and Prof. G. H. Granlund for making their technique available to us to code our images.

REFERENCES

[1] M. Kunt, "Edge detection: A tutorial review," in *Proc. ICASSP 82* (Paris, France, May 2–5, 1982), pp. 1172–1176.
[2] S. Levialdi, "Edge extraction techniques," in *Fundamentals in Computer Vision*, O. D. Feugeras, Ed. Cambridge, England: Cambridge Univ. Press, 1983, pp. 117–144.
[3] R. M. Haralick, "Statistical and structural approaches to textures," *Proc. IEEE*, vol. 67, pp. 786–804, May 1979.
[4] A. Rosenfeld, "Survey, picture processing 1982," *Comput. Vis. Graph. Image Process.*, vol. 22, pp. 339–387, June 1983.
[5] ———, "Survey, picture processing 1981," *Comput. Vis. Graph. Image Process.*, vol. 19, pp. 35–76, May 1982.
[6] H. Wechler, "Texture analysis—A survey," *Signal Process.*, vol. 3, pp. 271–282, July 1980.
[7] P. Brodatz, *Textures—A Photographic Album for Artists and Designers*. New York: Dover, 1966.
[8] M. Unser, "Caractérisation statistique de texture: application à l'inspection automatique," Ph.D. dissertation, Dep. Elec. Eng., Swiss Federal Inst. Technol., Lausanne, Switzerland, June 1984.
[9] A. N. Netravali and J. O. Limb, "Picture coding: A review," *Proc. IEEE*, vol. 63, pp. 366–406, Mar. 1980.
[10] A. K. Jain, "Image data compression: A review," *Proc. IEEE*, vol. 69, pp. 349–389, Mar. 1981.
[11] L. G. Roberts, "Picture coding using pseudo-random noise," *IRE Trans. Informat. Theory*, vol. IT-8, pp. 145–154, Jan. 1962.
[12] *Proc. IEEE* (Special Issue on Digital Encoding of Graphics), A. N. Netravali, Guest Ed., vol. 68, pp. 757–944, July 1980.
[13] A. Habibi, "Hybrid coding of pictorial data," *IEEE Trans. Commun.*, vol. COM-22, pp. 614–624, May 1974.
[14] W. F. Schreiber, C. F. Knapp, and N. D. Kay, "Synthetic highs, an experimental TV bandwidth reduction system," *J. SMPTE*, vol. 68, pp. 525–537, Aug. 1959.
[15] W. F. Schreiber, "The mathematical foundation of the synthetic highs system," *MIT, RLE Quart. Progr. Rep.*, no. 68, p. 140, Jan. 1963.
[16] J. W. Pan, "Reduction of information redundancy in pictures," Sc.D. dissertation, MIT, Dep. Elec. Eng., 1966.
[17] D. N. Graham, "Image transmission by two-dimensional contour coding," Ph.D. dissertation, MIT, Dep. Elec. Eng., 1966.
[18] G. Walpert, "Image bandwidth compression by detection and coding of contours," Ph.D. dissertation, MIT, Dep. Elec. Eng., 1970.
[19] W. F. Schreiber, "Picture coding," *Proc. IEEE*, vol. 55, pp. 320–330, Mar. 1967.
[20] W. F. Schreiber, T. S. Huang, and O. J. Tretiak, "Contour coding of images," in *Picture Bandwidth Compression*, T. S. Huang and O. J. Tretiak, Eds. New York: Gordon and Breach, 1972.
[21] J. K. Tan and D. J. Sakrison, "Encoding of images based on a two-component source model," *IEEE Trans. Commun.*, vol. COM-25, pp. 1315–1322, Nov. 1977.
[22] B. R. Hunt, "Nonstationary statistical image models (and their application to image data compression)," *Comput. Graph. Image Process.*, vol. 12, pp. 173–186, Feb. 1980.
[23] D. E. Troxel *et al.*, "A two-channel picture coding system: I—Real-time implementation," *IEEE Trans. Commun.*, vol. COM-29, pp. 1841–1849, Dec. 1981.
[24] W. F. Schreiber and R. R. Buckley, "A two-channel picture coding system: II—Adaptive companding and color coding," *IEEE Trans. Commun.*, vol. COM-29, pp. 1849–1858, Dec. 1981.
[25] D. H. Hubel and T. N. Wiesel, "Brain mechanisms of vision," *Sci. Amer.*, vol. 241, pp. 150–162, Sept. 1979.
[26] S. W. Kuffler and J. G. Nicholls, *From Neuron to Brain*. Sunderland, MA: Sinauer Assoc., 1976.
[27] I. Aleksander, T. J. Stonham, and R. A. Wilkie, "Computer vision systems for industry," *Digital Syst. Indust. Automat.*, vol. 1, no. 4, pp. 305–320, 1982.
[28] D. E. Pearson, *Transmission and Display of Pictorial Information*. New York: Wiley, 1975, pp. 38–42.
[29] T. N. Cornsweet, *Visual Perception*. New York, Academic Press, 1970, pp. 270–310.
[30] P. J. Burt and E. H. Adelson, "The Laplacian pyramid as a compact image code," *IEEE Trans. Commun.*, vol. COM-31, pp. 532–540, Apr. 1983.
[31] D. Marr and E. Hildreth, "Theory of edge detection," *Proc. Roy. Soc. London*, B 207, pp. 187–217, Mar. 1980.
[32] D. Marr, *Vision*. San Fransisco, CA: H. Freeman and Co., 1982.
[33] R. Wilson, H. E. Knutsson, and G. H. Granlund, "Anisotropic nonstationary image estimation and its applications: Part II—Predictive image coding," *IEEE Trans. Commun.*, vol. COM-31, pp. 398–406, Mar. 1983.
[34] H. E. Knutsson, R. Wilson, and G. H. Granlund, "Anisotropic nonstationary image estimation and its applications: Part I—Restoration of noisy images," *IEEE Trans. Commun.*, vol.

COM-31, pp. 388–397, Mar. 1983.
[35] G. H. Granlund, "In search of a general picture processing operator," *Comput. Graph. Image Process.*, vol. 8, pp. 155–173, Oct. 1978.
[36] ——, "GOP—A fast flexible processor for image analysis," in *Proc. IEEE Conf. Pattern Recognition* (Miami, FL, 1980), pp. 489–492.
[37] M. Kocher and M. Kunt," A contour-texture approach to picture coding," in *Proc. ICASSP-82* (Paris, France, May 1982), pp. 436–440.
[38] M. Kocher, "Codage d'images à haute Compression basé sur un modèle Contour-texture," Ph.D. dissertation, no. 476, Dep. Elec. Eng., Swiss Federal Inst. Technol., Lausanne, Switzerland, Mar. 1983.
[39] M. Kocher and M. Kunt, "Image data compression by contour-texture modelling," in *SPIE Int. Conf. on the Applications of Digital Image Processing* (Geneva, Switzerland, Apr. 1983), pp. 131–139.
[40] ——, "A contour-texture approach to picture coding," in *Proc. Melecon-83* (Athens, Greece, May 24–26), 1983, paper C2.03.
[41] D. C. C. Wang and A. H. Wagnucci, "Gradient inverse filtering weighted smoothing scheme and the evaluation of its performance," *Comput. Graph. Image Process.*, vol. 15, pp. 167–181, Feb. 1981.
[42] P. Faeh and M. Kunt, "Efficient coding of high resolution typographic characters," in *Proc. ICASSP-82* (Paris, France, May 1982), pp. 440–443.
[43] M. Eden and M. Kocher, "On the performance of a contour coding algorithm in the context of image coding. Part II: Coding and contour graphs," *Signal Process.*, vol. 8, May 1985, to be published.
[44] A. Ikonomopoulos and M. Kunt, "Image coding based on a directional decomposition," in *Proc. Int. Picture Coding Symp.* (Davis, CA, Mar. 28–30, 1983), pp. 13–15.
[45] ——, "Directional filtering, zero crossing, edge detection and image coding," in *Proc. EUSIPCO-83* (Erlangen, RFA, Sept. 1983), pp. 203–206.
[46] A. Ikonomopoulos, M. Kocher, and M. Kunt, "Image coding based on human visual system properties for optimal reduction of redundancy," in *Proc. 3rd Scandinavian Conf. on Image Analysis* (Copenhagen, Denmark, July 12–14, 1983), pp. 216–222.
[47] M. Kunt, A. Ikonomopoulos, and M. Kocher, presented at the "Compression d'images: Méthodes de la deuxième génération" (invited lecture), Premièr Colloque GRETSI–CESTA, Biarritz, France, May 21–25, 1983.
[48] A. Ikonomopoulos and M. Kunt, "High compression image coding via directional filtering," *Signal Process.*, vol. 8, no. 3, May 1985, to be published.

Recent Results in High-Compression Image Coding

MURAT KUNT, FELLOW, IEEE, MICHEL BÉNARD, MEMBER, IEEE, AND RICCARDO LEONARDI, STUDENT MEMBER, IEEE

(Invited Paper)

Abstract—The digital representation of an image requires a very large number of bits. The goal of image coding is to reduce this number as much as possible, and to reconstruct a faithful duplicate of the original picture. Early efforts in image coding, solely guided by information theory, led to a plethora of methods. The compression ratio reached a plateau of about 10:1 several years ago. Recent progress in the study of the brain mechanism of vision and of scene analysis has opened new vistas in picture coding. The concept of directional sensitivity of neurones in the visual cortex combined with the separate processing of contours and textures has led to a new class of coding methods, called second generation, capable of achieving compression ratios as high as 100:1. In this paper, recent results on object-based coding methods are reported, exhibiting improvements in the previous second-generation methods.

Key words: Image coding, high compression, contour-texture modeling, 2-D approximation, directional decomposition, region growing, split and merge.

I. INTRODUCTION

SINCE THE VERY beginning of digital image processing in the late fifties, image coding has been recognized as an important problem. The reason for this is the large amounts of data which need to be handled for transmission or storage of digital images. The data are obtained by sampling in space and quantizing analog scenes into brightness levels. For example, for the rather common size of a 512×512 scanning raster and 8 bits per picture element (pixel), 2×10^6 bits are needed, a rather large number. It is mandatory that this number be reduced in order to use available channels or to store them in a reasonably efficient manner. The first attempts toward this goal have led to a plethora of methods [1]-[3] over the last two decades, reducing the number of bits by an order of magnitude. Although very elegant alternatives guided by information theory were proposed, a plateau in the compression ratio was reached at about 10 to 1. This certainly does not mean that the upper bound given by the entropy of the source has also been reached. First, the entropy of an image is unknown and depends heavily on the model used, and second, information theory is not customarily used to take into account what the human eye sees and how it sees.

Fig. 1 is the general block diagram of a communication system, be it for images or speech or any other information source. It is also the first figure of any book on communication theory. Our attention is confined to the first block labeled source coding. There are two main components in this operation: extraction of messages and assignment of code words to messages (Fig. 2). The above-mentioned methods, referred to as the first-generation methods, use very simple messages such as two adjacent pixels, or a combination of a small group of neighboring pixels. However, they place a very heavy emphasis on the code word assignment.

This was accomplished according to information theoretic procedures (for example, Huffman coding). Within this framework, the saturation in compression is achieved by code word assignment for poorly representative messages.

With the continuous progress in technology, wider and more reliable channels and cheaper memories have become available. Accordingly, one might have been satisfied with a 10 to 1 compression. Unfortunately, for some people (and fortunately for some others), the same technological progress opened the way for much wider application to digital images where higher definition (hence, a larger number of bits) was still required to represent the image satisfactorily. Image coding is thus still an important present day problem and it is likely to stay as such for years to come.

How can we compress a digital image more than 10 to 1? As a first step, let us consider another question: Is there any natural scene (for example, a portrait, a scene with trees and houses, a building, etc.) in which a pixel corresponds to a real entity? The answer is obviously no. Pixels are consequences of technical constraints in transforming an analog scene into digital data. Any effort to describe images in terms of more nearly physical entities such as contours or regions should lead to more compact representations and hence to higher compressions. To do this, much heavier emphasis must be put on the first block of Fig. 2, i.e., on the extraction of messages. Efforts in this direction were developed extensively within the last decade and progress in compression still continues. These new

---

Manuscript received April 20, 1987. This work was supported in part by the Swiss National Funds for Scientific Research under Grants 2.670-082 and 2.357-084, and in part by the Swiss Federal Institute of Technology.

The authors are with the Signal Processing Laboratory, Swiss Federal Institute of Technology, 16 Ch. de Bellerive, CH-1007 Lausanne, Switzerland.

IEEE Log Number 8716556.

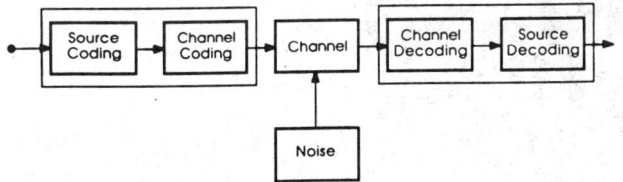

Fig. 1. General block diagram of a communication system.

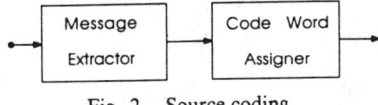

Fig. 2. Source coding.

methods, referred to as second-generation methods, were introduced in [4]. This paper reports recent results in two of the main avenues of research.

Section II gives a brief summary of the new techniques and discusses their weak and strong points. In Section III, advances made in directional decomposition-based coding are described. An alternative to region growing for segmentation is described in Section IV as adaptive split-and-merge-based coding. Results showing decoded pictures are discussed in Section V. Unless otherwise stated, all the grey-level pictures used in this paper are digitized with a 256×256 raster and quantized to 256 levels, thereby permitting an 8-bit representation. Compression ratios are thus referred to $256 \cdot 256 \cdot 8 = 524\,288$ bits of the original data. Output pictures are reproduced on a laser receiver using dry silver paper with an optical density range of 1.6.

II. Brief Review of the Second-Generation Coding Techniques

A. Preliminary Remarks

Two groups can be formed in the class of second-generation coding techniques, depending on the approach used. One group is characterized by the use of local operators. These are two-dimensional (2-D) impulse responses of certain filters or filter banks convolving the image data in the conventional sense. Each impulse response, or mask (as it is often referred to), is designed so as to extract a context-dependent feature. Outputs of these filters are then combined appropriately to obtain the messages to be coded. Pyramidal coding [5] and anisotropic nonstationary predictive coding [6], [7] are the main examples of this group of methods.

Methods of the second group use a different approach. They attempt to describe an image in terms of contour and texture. These entities seem to be more natural in that they coincide with psychological concepts of vision. Each object in a natural scene is characterized by its borders (contours) surrounding its surfaces (texture). This may imply that contour extraction is of primary importance and that the plethora of edge detectors [8] using local operators may be used to locate contours, eliminating the need to consider the two approaches as being different. Contour extraction is indeed of primary importance, but local operator-based edge detection or contour extraction suffers from an important weakness: since contextual information is considered only in a very limited region, there is no way to distinguish between contours corresponding to object borders from those which do not. In addition, a rather heavy processing burden is necessary to achieve this goal. Even with this high overhead cost, the final result contains a nonnegligible number of irrelevant contours, often not connected to each other and costly (in bits) to represent in the coding.

In spite of these drawbacks, a rather elegant technique [9] produces grey-level images from the contour information alone and leads to high compression ratios. The idea is to detect the perceptually relevant contours first, using a smoothed Laplacian mask. Grey-level information on both sides of each contour is coded along with the contour locations. The grey-level image is recovered from these messages by using constrained overrelaxation. The constraint is that of maximal smoothness. The difference between the original image and the reconstructed image, called residual, is coded using the previously mentioned pyramidal coding. For further details and the application of these ideas to image sequences, the reader may refer to [10].

Contours resulting from a segmentation procedure seem to be more suitable for compact representations. The segmentation of a digital image consists in dividing it into a set of contiguous regions of any shape, so that the final result looks like a jig-saw puzzle. Segmentation techniques should produce regions whose frontiers correspond to the borders of the objects. Directional decomposition-based coding [11] and segmentation-based coding [12] are two major examples of this second group of methods. We summarize them below before presenting in detail recent progress achieved in improving them.

B. Directional Decomposition-Based Coding [4], [11]

Using as a concept for image-processing implementation the neurophysiological evidence of direction sensitive cells in the human visual system, a reversible transformation is introduced as a directional decomposition. It is implemented with a 2-D filter bank producing one low-pass component image and N directional images containing high-frequency components in a given direction. All the possible directions between 0 and 180° are quantized to a rather small number N (8 or 16) so that each directional filter covers a sector in the Fourier domain as shown in Fig. 3. It should be noted here that each directional image is high pass in the direction assigned to it, but low pass in the perpendicular direction. Fig. 4 shows an original image and its sixteen directional components.

The coding strategy is rather simple. The low-pass component is coded by undersampling and quantization or by transform coding using classical first-generation techniques. High-pass components are used to detect edges. An information loss is introduced here: strong edges are selected and weak ones are neglected. Edges in these components are located on the zero crossings which are

Fig. 3. Sectors covered by directional filters in the Fourier domain. The origin is at the center of the picture.

Fig. 4. An original image and its directional components.

Fig. 5. Original digital images used in this study.

Fig. 6. Directional decomposition-based coding results. The compression ratios are (a) 43 to 1 and (b) 62 to 1, and (c) 50 to 1.

easy to detect. Their strength is measured by the magnitude of the waveform around the zero crossing. These positions and magnitudes are the messages to be coded. Run-length coding is used for the position, whereas magnitudes are coded with fixed-length code words. In the early version of this technique, a rotation was introduced to establish a fixed zero-crossing search algorithm [11]. It was implemented with interpolation and resampling. The reconstructed directional image was then rotated back to its original direction using the same procedure.

The decoding is carried out as follows. The low-pass component is retrieved by interpolation between decoded and subsampled values. Directional images are reconstructed by using synthetic zero crossing profiles whose parameters are matched to the decoded position and magnitude information. Reconstructed images are then added together to give the final result. Fig. 5 shows three original images. The result of their coding by this technique is shown in Fig. 6. Parameters are selected to give a high compression with noticeable degradation.

This scheme has a number of weak points.

First, if ideally sharp transition frequency filters are used, directional images are subject to the well-known Gibbs phenomenon. In order to avoid it, windows must be introduced. Because of its relation to neurophysiological properties, Gaussian windows are introduced. If isotropy is assumed, the standard deviation is the unique parameter. As will be shown in the next section, for better control of the directional selectivity and high-pass/low-pass separation, anisotropic windows seem to be preferable.

Second, codes more efficient than run-length coding can be used to code zero-crossing locations. Since the directional images are band limited in the perpendicular direction assigned to them, an undersampling along the zero-crossing locations is a better choice.

Third, more variability in the synthetic zero-crossing profiles, using polynomials for example, is necessary to improve the quality.

Fourth, although error-free in theory, some degradations are introduced in rotating back-and-forth directional images for the zero-crossing scans. A rotating scan procedure needs to be introduced to avoid these degradations.

Finally, the correlation between two adjacent directional images is also a source of redundancy that can be exploited. Improvements obtained along these lines are presented in Section III.

C. Segmentation-Based Coding [12]

There are a number of ways to perform the segmentation. Region growing and split-and-merge are the main ones which will be discussed here. Split-and-merge is used in our work to overcome some of the difficulties of region growing and is described in Section IV. In this paragraph, a brief overview of region growing is given. To perform region growing, a particular property must first be defined. Starting from a particular pixel, its neighboring pixels are examined to select those sharing the same property. The procedure stops when all the connected pixels sharing the same property are labeled, producing a single region. Another region is grown, next to the previous one, beginning with the first pixel that does not share the property. One of the simplest properties is membership in a given grey-level interval. This can be viewed as the zero-order 2-D approximation of the image data. To avoid, insofar as is possible, regions not corresponding to visual surfaces of real objects, preprocessing must first be applied to reduce the local granularity of the original image without affecting its contours. An inverse gradient filter can be used for this purpose. Fig. 7 shows the result of region growing

Fig. 7. Two original images and the result of region growing with a grey-level interval of 10 in both cases.

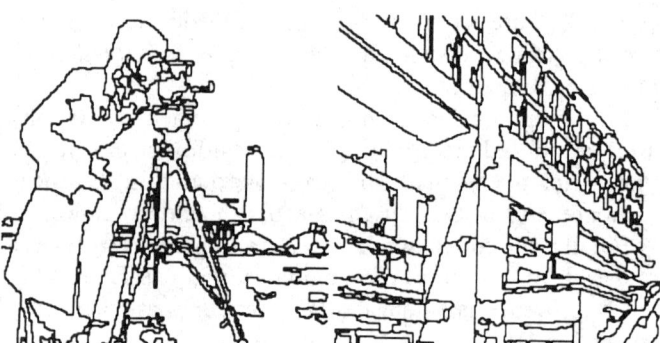

Fig. 8. Final results of the segmentation procedure.

on two images. The number of regions are 1001 and 1111 for the cameraman picture and the building picture, respectively. Unfortunately, because the chosen property is too simple, the number of regions is too large and many of them do not correspond to any real object surface. Two procedures can be used to avoid this problem: introduction of some distortion by eliminating "insignificant" regions and their contours, or the use of a more refined property that is likely to introduce unwanted complexity. This led us to consider a recursive procedure that depends in the first instance on a simple property and which we shall discuss as the split-and-merge technique (Section IV). Small regions can be eliminated easily. False contours can be eliminated by merging adjacent regions whose contrast along this contour is below a chosen, arbitrary level. Fig. 8 displays the final result of segmentation.

To this point, each region has been characterized by a mean gray level and the location of its contour points. The entire image looks like those "painted by numbers." In the next step, the difference between the original image and this intermediate result is approximated over each region

Fig. 9. Region-growing-based coding results. The compression ratios are (a) $C = 38$ to 1, (b) $C = 44$ to 1.

by a 2-D polynomial least-square fit to introduce more realism. The final "touch" is given by a salt and pepper noise equivalent to the granularity removed during preprocessing. Final results obtained with this technique are shown in Fig. 9. Objectionable distortions can be expected when a relatively high compression is attained.

The weak link in this technique is the property employed for region growing. It is so simple that a series of post processings is necessary to overcome its drawbacks, while the results are still highly distorted. The introduction of a more refined property generally leads to dramatic increases in complexity of simulation on general-purpose computers. For example, region growing with a 2-D polynomial whose coefficients are updated for each new pixel included in the region requires several hours of CPU time for a few regions. Since contour-texture representation of an image is a very compact one, for higher compression and quality, the segmentation has been carried out by a split-and-merge procedure as described in Section IV.

III. Improvements of the Directional Decomposition-Based Coding

A. Introductory Comments

The directional decomposition of an image $x(k,l)$ is performed with the following filter bank [4] shown in Fig. 3:

$$G_{lf}(f,g) = \begin{cases} 1, & \text{for } (f^2 + g^2) < \rho_c^2 \\ 0, & \text{otherwise} \end{cases} \quad (1)$$

is the frequency response of the low-pass filter and

$$G_i(f,g) = \begin{cases} 1, & \text{for } (f^2 + g^2) \geq \rho_c^2 \\ & \text{and } (i-1)\pi/N < tg^{-1}(g/f) \leq i\pi/N \\ 0, & \text{otherwise} \end{cases}$$

(2)

(with $i = 1, \cdots, N$) are the frequency responses of the N directional filters. In these equations, f and g are the continuous spatial frequency variables and the parameter ρ_c is the cutoff frequency of the low-pass filter.

In the Fourier domain, low-frequency and directional components are obtained by multiplying the Fourier transform $X(f,g)$ of the image $x(k,l)$ with these filter responses. They are then transformed into the image domain by the inverse Fourier transform. The main property of a directional filter $G_i(f, g)$ is that its output contains only edges whose directions are within the interval $[(i-1)\pi/N + \pi/2, i\pi/N + \pi/2]$. The directional selectivity is thus directly determined by the number N of filters. Neurophysiological references suggest about 20 to 30 neural filters, and, in our work, 16 filters are used for computational ease.

If the above-defined filters are established with sharp transitions, a Gibbs phenomenon in the directional components will result. This phenomenon has two visual effects: dispersion in the direction of the edge and ripples in the perpendicular direction.

An isotropic Gaussian window can be convolved with the frequency responses of the filters [4] to attenuate these undesired drawbacks. To reduce them to an acceptable level, however, large windows must be used to weaken the directional selectivity and the low-pass/high-pass separation. A compromise we have previously used [4], [11], [16] performs a nonlinear transformation. It consists of assigning a given edge point to the most likely direction. Unfortunately, this solution introduces discontinuities along edge grey-level profiles, unless the nonlinear transformation is made properly context-dependent. These drawbacks can be avoided by using separate attenuation functions for the principal direction and the perpendicular direction of each filter. A new filter bank is thus obtained in the frequency domain

$$G_{lf}(f, g) = H(\rho, \rho_c, \sigma_\rho) \qquad (3)$$

$$G_i(f, g) = [1 - H(\rho, \rho_c, \sigma_\rho)][1 - H(0, i\pi/N, \sigma_\theta)] \qquad (4)$$

where

$$H(x, m, s) = \int_{-\infty}^{x} \frac{1}{\sqrt{2\pi} s} \exp\left[-\frac{(t-m)^2}{2s^2}\right] dt \qquad (5)$$

$$\rho = (f^2 + g^2)^{1/2} \text{ and } \theta = \text{Arctg}(g/f).$$

The two parameters σ_ρ and σ_θ are the standard deviations of the Gaussian window along the main direction and the perpendicular direction, respectively. They are introduced to monitor the attenuation of the two Gibbs phenomena independently: σ_ρ acts on the ripples perpendicular to the edge direction, whereas σ_θ reduces the dispersion in the edge direction. These new filters are shown in Fig. 10. The effects of their parameters can be seen in Fig. 11, comparing the same directional image with and without a Gaussian window. The most important properties of this improved definition will be exhibited during different stages of the edge coding process.

B. Coding Strategy

After the directional decomposition, each component is coded independently. The method for coding the low-frequency component is rather conventional and will be summarized here.

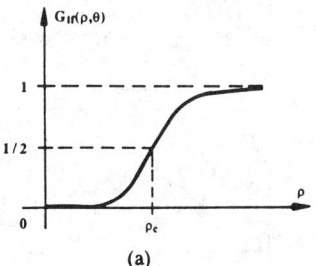

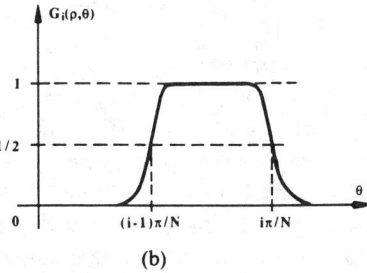

Fig. 10. Frequency response of the smoothed filters in polar coordinates.

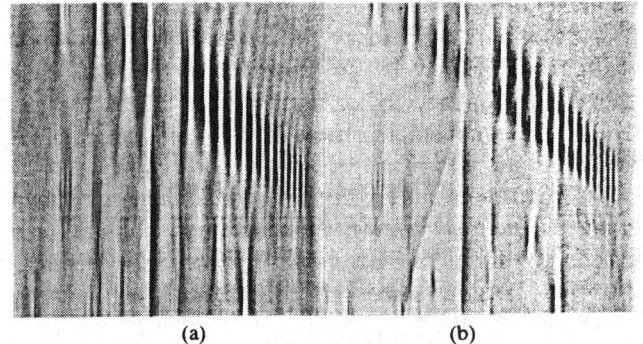

Fig. 11. First directional component obtained with ideally sharp filters. (a) $\sigma_\rho = \sigma_\theta = 0$ and with smoothed filters (b) $\sigma_\rho = 2\rho_c/3$ and $\sigma_\theta = 0.1$). Notice the information content of the edges.

By definition, the low-frequency image is a band-limited signal, limited to ρ_c cycles per degree in both directions (see (3)). Two equivalent methods can be used to code this signal: transform coding or subsampling in the image domain. A quality criterion is necessary to select a method and to determine its parameters. Unfortunately, objective measures based on signal-to-noise ratio are not valid for every kind of image [17]. On the other hand, a direct subjective comparison is inadequate because it is very difficult for the human eye to compare two low-frequency pictures. For these reasons, our quality criterion is based on the comparison of the original image with the sum of the decoded low-frequency image and the original high-frequency component [16]. Quantization artifacts, as well as aliasing errors, may thus be observed easily.

Our experiments shows that the subsampling method is slightly better than transform coding; that is, given the same bound for the number of bits used for coding the low-frequency component, the quality of the reconstructed picture derived by subsampling seems to be higher. However, compression ratios higher than 5 to 1 for these

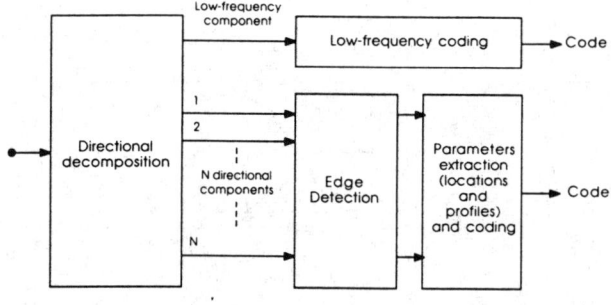

Fig. 12. Coding strategy.

low-pass images cannot be reached with these techniques if degradations are to be kept to an acceptable level. Higher rates lead to considerable distortion due to aliasing and quantization errors. Two conflicting requirements are placed on the filter. To avoid these distortions in the decoded low-frequency image, the cutoff frequency of the low-pass filter must be set as low as possible. On the other hand, to assign relevant information to the zero crossings of the directional images, their dc components should be suppressed as far as possible, requiring a rather high cutoff frequency for the same filter. Given the lack of a theoretical method, this frequency is set to 5 percent of the maximum frequency by an empirical cut-and-try procedure. Low-frequency coding must thus be considered as a necessary but nonefficient stage toward high compression via directional filtering.

The situation is quite different for the directional images for which the most relevant information must be defined, detected, and coded. Early work on directional decomposition [4], [11] showed that this information is concentrated in edges, as illustrated in Fig. 11. The coding strategy must then be centered on edge detection, representation, and coding as schematized in Fig. 12. A set of parameters describing the edge locations and profiles is therefore computed for each directional image as described in the following sections.

C. Edge Detection

The first task of the coding strategy shown in Fig. 12 is edge detection. Two different approaches may be used. The first is to detect edges within each directional image. In the second, edges are detected in the isotropic, global high-frequency component, and their directions are classified using the directional images. Since the detection principle is the same for both approaches, it is described first. Then the selection of the most reliable approach is discussed for edge location and profile coding.

1) Zero-Crossing Detection: As a first step in edge detection, let us examine the response of high-frequency filters to an ideal edge as shown in Fig. 13(a). One-dimensional signals and systems are used here for simplicity, without loss of generality. If the filter is ideal with a sharp transition at its cutoff frequency, as shown in Fig. 13(b), its response to the ideal edge has a zero-crossing at the location of the edge and side lobes as well. Side lobes are particularly disturbing in the location of zero-crossings

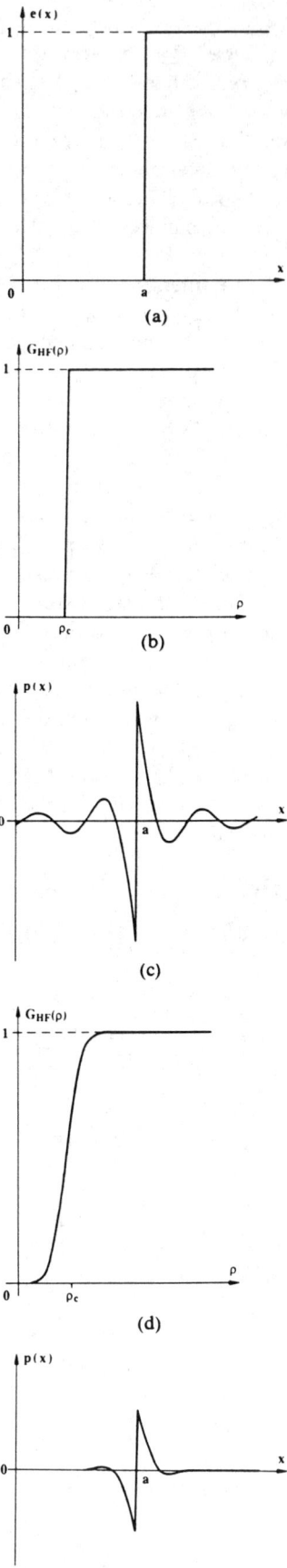

Fig. 13. Response of high-frequency filters to an ideal edge. (a) The ideal edge. (b) Frequency response of the ideally sharp filter and (c) its response to the ideal edge. (d) Frequency response of the smoothed filter and (e) its response to the ideal edge.

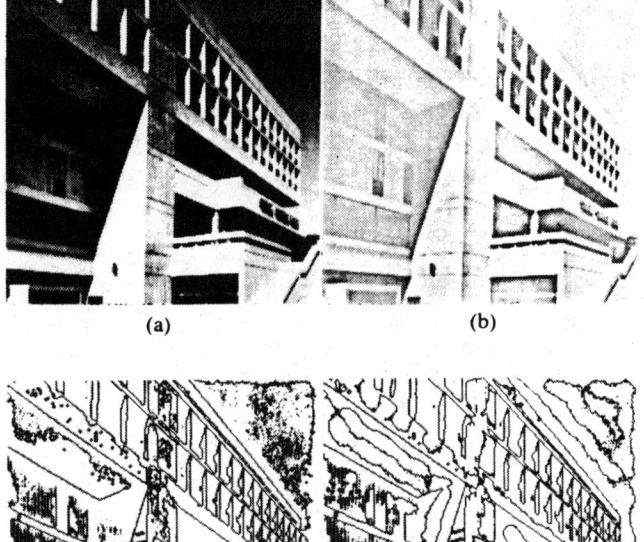

Fig. 14. Zero-crossing detection. (a) An original image, (b) The high-frequency image obtained as the sum of directional components, and detected zero-crossings with (c) $\sigma_\rho/3$ and (d) with $\sigma_\rho = \rho_c/20$.

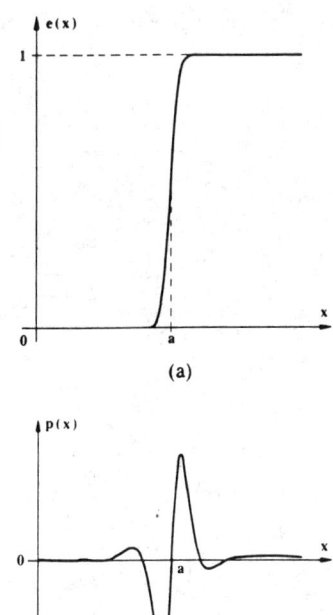

Fig. 15. Response of the (b) high-frequency filter to (a) a nonideal edge (a).

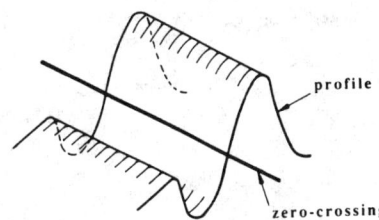

Fig. 16. Profile around an edge point candidate (i.e., a zero-crossing).

because they introduce ambiguities. These lobes, shown in Fig. 13(c), are consequences of a well-known problem in filter design. To eliminate them, the infinite-length impulse response corresponding to the filter of Fig. 13(b) needs to be truncated by a window function. The Fourier transform of this function convolves the ideal response and leads to the frequency response of the smoothed filter shown in Fig. 13(d). The response of this filter to the same ideal edge is that of Fig. 13(e), where only the central zero-crossing is present. Unambiguous detection of this zero-crossing is then performed easily by separating the positive and negative parts of the signal.

This result may be extended to two-dimensional signals. Figs. 14(a) and (b) show an original image and its isotropic high-frequency component, respectively. The latter is obtained by summing all the directional images obtained with a given σ_ρ. Zero-crossings are detected on this high-frequency image by again separating the positive and negative pixels. For a given cutoff frequency ρ_c, the result depends on the value of σ_ρ. For low values of σ_ρ (below $\rho_c/2$), false zero-crossings are present due to the side lobes as shown in Fig. 14(c). These undesired zero-crossings disappear when the value of σ_ρ is increased to $2\rho_c/3$ as depicted in Fig. 14(d). Larger values of σ_ρ should not be used, otherwise some primary zero-crossings may be lost when there is a nonnegligible dc-component in the high-frequency image.

2) Magnitude Determination, Thresholding, and Edge Tracking: The method we have just described locates all the edge point candidates and may thus be favorably compared with the equivalent scheme used in [4]. In our case, errors induced by the rotation of directional images are avoided.

As described earlier [11], magnitudes in the neighborhood of zero-crossings are measured and thresholded to select the edge points among all candidates. The magnitude measure used in [11] and [19] is not robust enough because it is limited to the magnitude of the difference of only two samples on each side of the zero-crossing. In the case of a nonideal edge, as shown in Fig. 15, the sign of the zero-crossing slope may even be false. To improve performance, a new measure based on the energy of the local profile is introduced (Fig. 16). In a directional image, a profile is extracted on a line perpendicular to the edge direction and its energy is computed as the sum of the squares of the samples along this line. The extent of the profile is determined by that of the first side lobe. If the isotropic high-frequency component is used (the sum of directional images), the energy is computed along all the possible profile directions and then averaged. The importance of the zero-crossing is considered to be proportional to the measured energy.

Then a decision, degenerating often to a simple threshold measurement, must be made to obtain a binary image of

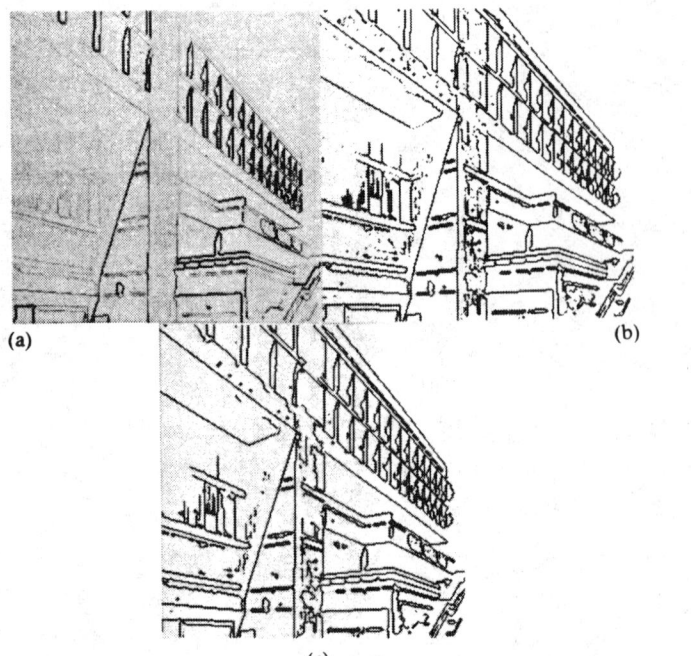
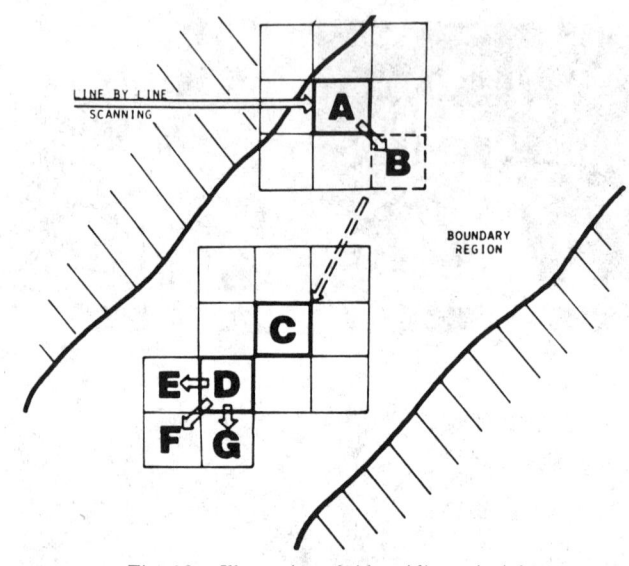

Fig. 17. Edge detection by magnitude thresholding. (a) Magnitudes of zero-crossings to be thresholded. (b) Result of a noncontextual thresholding. (c) Result of ridge riding.

Fig. 18. Illustration of ridge-riding principle.

Fig. 19. Results of edge detection on three original images.

edge points. A fixed threshold for the entire image, or any trivial variations around it, often destroy the continuity in detected edges. Fig. 17(a) displays the energy associated with the zero-crossings, that is, gray-level proportional to energy. The result of simple thresholding appears in Fig. 17(b) and shows several discontinuities. A more refined technique, known as ridge riding or edge tracking as suggested in [13] and [14], gives better results (Fig. 17(c)). In edge tracking, a first threshold, called contour start threshold (CST), is used to detect edge points corre-sponding to large magnitudes. Then, starting from these points, edge points are traced within a 3×3 window in the direction of the largest magnitude. The tracing continues until a second (lower) threshold, called edge point threshold (EPT), is reached. This procedure is depicted in Fig. 18. Since this is a sequential algorithm, irrelevant edge pieces may also be eliminated using a test on the length of the connected edge chain. Three original images and detected edge locations are shown in Fig. 19. Notice that if this edge detection technique is used for a purpose other than

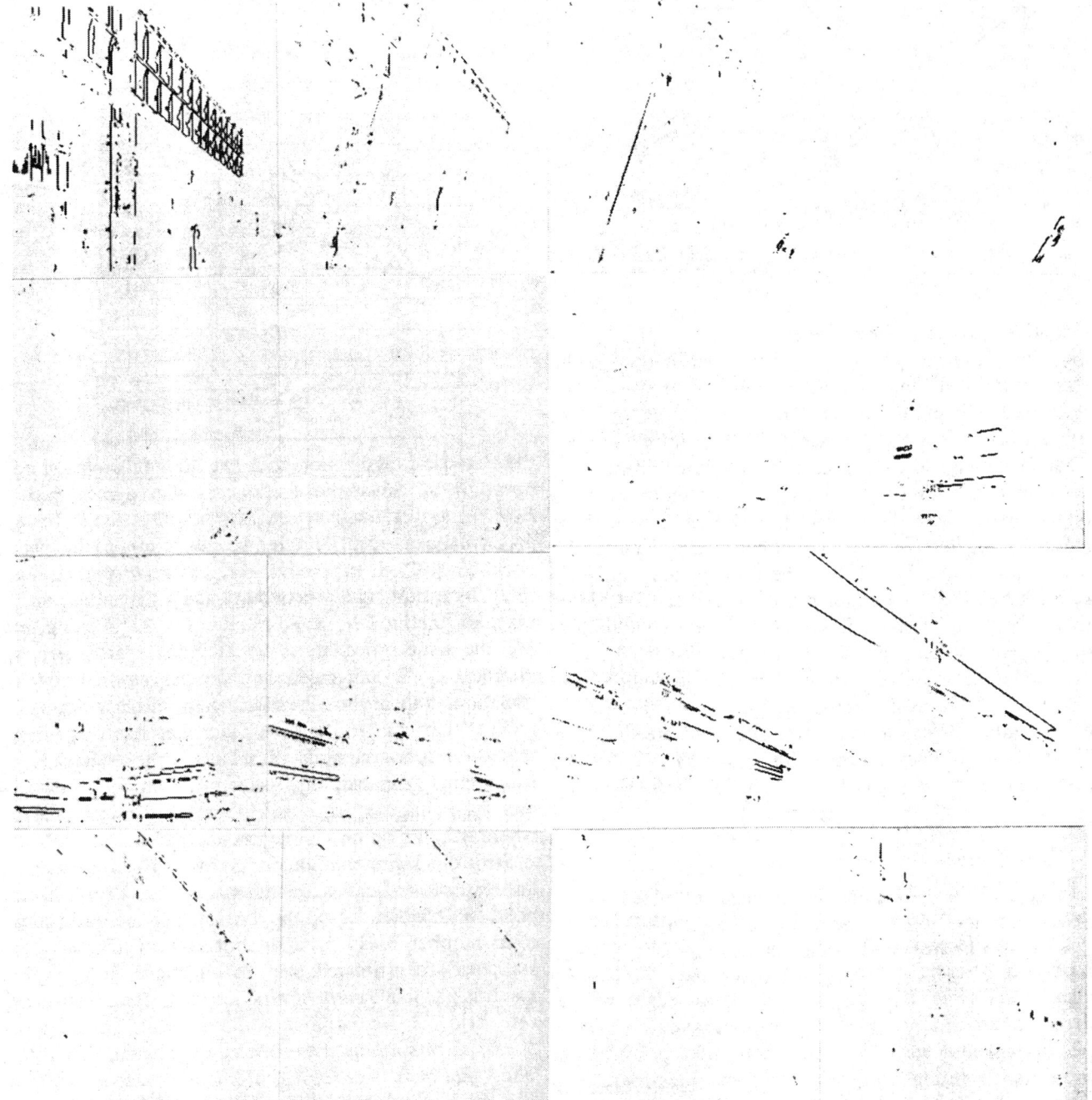

Fig. 20. Results of edge direction determination. Each detected edge point is in the directional edge image corresponding to the local edge direction numbered from 1 to 16.

high compression coding, a different set of parameters may be needed. In some applications, it may be necessary to keep weaker and shorter edges.

3) Remarks: As mentioned earlier, the edge detection scheme we have described may be used on directional images as well as on the isotropic global high-frequency image.

In the first case, due to leakage from one directional filter to its neighbors (windowing with σ_θ), the same edge may be detected in two or more directional images at slightly different locations. This may happen for edges whose directions are along the border of adjacent directional filters. To avoid this redundancy, the overlap of adjacent directional filters in the frequency domain must be decreased as much as possible by decreasing the parameter σ_θ of the directional filters. Unfortunately, the price paid is the appearance of the Gibbs phenomenon, i.e., dispersion terms in the edge direction. As a result, spurious edge continuations corresponding to these dispersion terms are detected. As mentioned before, the nonlinear transformation used in [11] may assign an edge to only one direction, but may affect the edge's continuity (for example, whenever an edge direction changes too rapidly).

In the second case, edge detection is performed in the isotropic high-frequency component and false edges due to

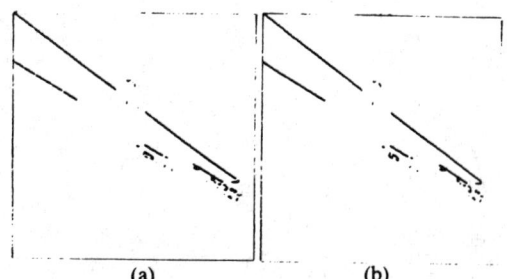

Fig. 21. Preprocessing edges in directional edge images (a) before and (b) after preprocessing.

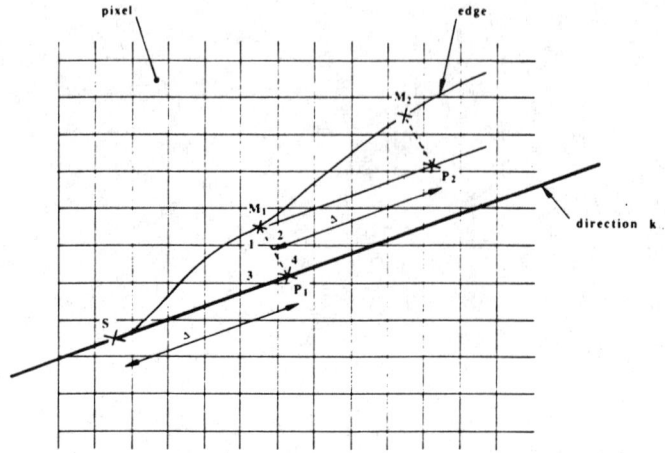

Fig. 22. Edge location coding strategy.

secondary zero-crossings are easily avoided by an appropriate value of σ_ρ as shown earlier. The price paid is the loss of local directional information that needs to be recovered. Directional images are used for this purpose. For each edge point detected in the isotropic high-frequency image, the local energy is computed at the same location and within a small (say 5×5) window in each directional image. The local edge direction is defined as identical to that of the directional image having the maximum energy. In this case, the value of the parameter σ_θ must be small enough to ensure good directional selectivity. On the other hand, if it is too small, the computation of the energy may be altered by the dispersion. Our experience shows that $\sigma_\theta = \pi/2N$ is a good compromise and leads to the result shown in Fig. 20. In this figure, edge points assigned to local edge directions are shown in 16 directional images. Using this last result, it is now possible to perform edge location coding for each direction.

D. Edge Position Coding

Edge position coding has been studied extensively and a plethora of methods can be found in the literature. None of them can be used here as they do not take into account important information available to us: each directional edge image (Fig. 20) contains only those edges whose directions are in a given interval. Furthermore, this fact is the fundamental basis for high compression and justifies directional filtering instead of isotropic high-frequency image coding as suggested in [13] and [14].

1) Directional Edge Preprocessing: Edge preprocessing is necessary to prepare the directional edge images for directional edge position coding. The preprocessing consists mainly in imposing topological properties on the edge structures. They should be 8-connected, not have forks nor crosses, and gaps must be filled. The result of this operation (we may call it "edge cleaning") is shown in Fig. 21.

2) Edge Subsampling and Coding: Edge coding is based on subsampling due to the low-pass characteristic of a directional image in the direction of the edge.

Let S be the starting point of an edge in the directional image number k as shown in Fig. 22 and Δ the subsampling rate. We denote P_1 the point such that $SP_1 = \Delta$ along the main direction $k\pi/N$. Notice that P_1 is located at a point whose coordinates take real, rather then integer values only. It is unlikely that this point will fall exactly on the Cartesian digitization grid. Let M_1 be the closest edge point to P_1. Since the direction of the edge is close to $k\pi/N$, the distance between M_1 and P_1 is small. In fact, M_1 will be a pixels (in the discrete grid) in the neighborhood of P_1. It is possible to represent M_1 with respect to P_1 by a number d_1 between 1 and 4 depending on the pixel assigned to M_1, as indicated in Fig. 22. Starting from M_1, the same procedure is repeated and a new deviation number d_2 is obtained. The process stops when the remaining part of the edge has a length smaller than $\Delta/2$.

Note that edges of length smaller than Δ are not represented and are eliminated because their coding is bit consuming. A coded edge segment is thus represented by the following sequence of messages: $[S, n, d_1, \cdots, d_n]$, where n is the number of edge samples.

With this representation and using Huffman coding, for an edge of n samples, 13 bits are required for the start point S, 2.5 bits for n, and 2.6 for each d_i leading to a total number of $15 \cdot 5 + 2 \cdot 6n$ bits. The Huffman coding statistics are estimated over 16 directional images. This result is particularly interesting for long edges, for which a rate below 1 bit/contour point is easily obtained (for $\Delta = 5$, 36 bits are used to code an edge having 40 points). The value of Δ is chosen according to the target compression ratio and to the smallest edge length that may not be eliminated.

3) Reconstruction of Edge Locations: The previous coding strategy is uniquely decodable. The reconstructed (decoded) directional edge images exhibit only minor differences from the originals as shown in Fig. 23. Edge lengths shorter than Δ (except possibly for the terminal lengths) are not coded, and hence not reconstructed. Reconstructed edge segments can be slightly shorter or longer than the original ones. The visual effect of these changes depends on the value of the parameter Δ, which in turn is determined largely by the desired compression ratio. If set too high, distortions may be objectionable. In conclusion, edge-position coding described here is more economical than the run-length coding first used [11]. Table I gives the number of bits necessary to code edge positions as a function of Δ for various original images.

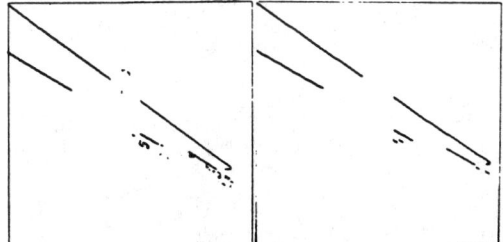

Fig. 23. Result of edge location coding and decoding with $\Delta = 3$. Directional edge image (a) before and (b) after coding, decoding, and reconstruction.

TABLE I
NUMBER OF BITS FOR EDGE LOCATION CODING WITH RESPECT TO Δ

	$\Delta = 3$	$\Delta = 5$	$\Delta = 7$
Fig. 5 : building	9977	6881	4631
Fig. 19 : test image	5944	4590	3275
Fig. 19 : cameraman	8520	4807	3165
Fig. 19 : portrait	10023	5511	3452

E. Edge Profile Extraction and Coding

The second component of an edge to be coded is its grey-level profile perpendicular to the edge direction. This section presents its extraction, representation, and coding.

1) Properties of the Edge Profile and its Extraction: For the optimal profile extraction, it is necessary to take into account its properties. Without loss of generality, one-dimensional signals and systems will be used again for simplicity. The edge profile of a directional image will be created by filtering a simple edge with the corresponding high-pass filter. Let us consider, in the image domain, an edge $e(x, \sigma)$ given by

$$e(x, \sigma) = \frac{1}{\sqrt{2\pi}\,\sigma} \int_{-\infty}^{x} \exp\left(-\frac{t^2}{2\sigma^2}\right) dt. \quad (6)$$

The shape of $e(x, \sigma)$ is controlled by σ. It may vary from the ideal step edge ($\sigma = 0$) to any smoothed edge ($\sigma > 0$) as shown in Figs. 24(a) and (b). If such an edge is filtered with the high-pass filter previously discussed (see Section III-C and Fig. 13(d)), the result depends, in theory, on the cutoff frequency ρ_c of the filter and on the attenuation parameters σ_ρ of the filter, σ of the edge given by (6):

$$p(x, \rho_c, \sigma_\rho, \sigma) = e(x, \sigma) * g(x, \rho_c, \sigma_\rho) \quad (7)$$

where $g(x, \rho_c, \sigma_\rho)$ is the impulse response of the high-pass filter and $*$ represents convolution.

Notice that the response $p(x, \rho_c, \sigma_\rho, \sigma)$ is the edge profile in which we are interested. One of its important features is the distance d between the central zero-crossing at the edge location and the first secondary zero-crossing (Figs. 24(c) and (d), and 25). A first property that can be established on the basis of numerical simulations, is that d

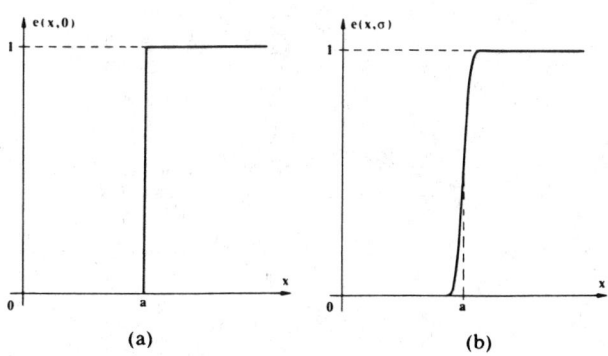

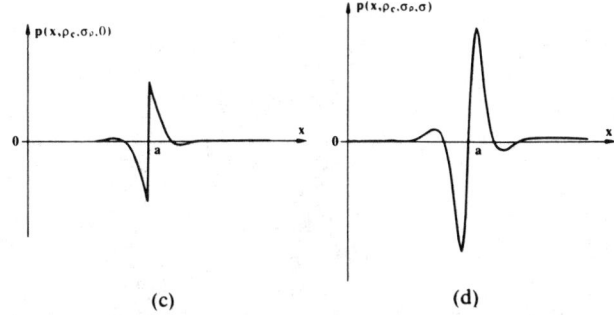

Fig. 24. Response of smoothed high-frequency filters to different edges. An ideally sharp edge with (a) $\sigma = 0$ and a smooth edge (b) with $\sigma > 1$. Response of the filter to (c) the sharp edge and to the (d) smoothed edge.

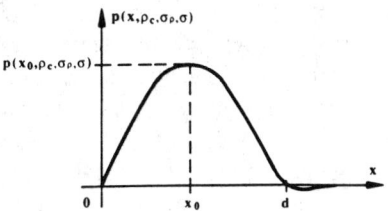

Fig. 25. Parameters of a half profile $p(x, \rho_c, \sigma_\rho, \sigma)$.

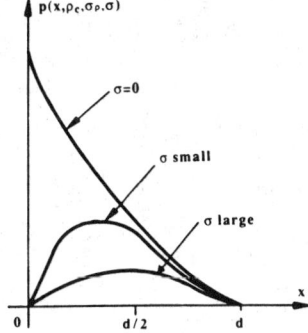

Fig. 26. Variation of the profile $p(x, \rho_c, \sigma_\rho, \sigma)$ as a function of the edge slope parameter.

depends mainly on the cutoff frequency ρ_c as it is roughly proportional to ρ_c^{-1}. The second property is related to the abcissa x_0 of the first maximum in the profile $p(x, \rho_c, \sigma_\rho, \sigma)$; x_0 varies from 0 for the ideal edge ($\sigma = 0$) and tends to $d/2$ for increasing values of σ, that is, for highly smoothed edges. The positive portion of the profile for a zero-centered edge, for various values of σ, is depicted in Fig. 26. These two properties will play an important role in profile modeling.

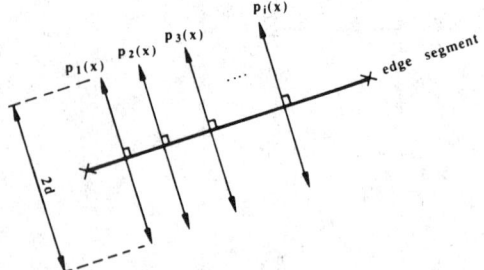

Fig. 27. Edge profile extraction.

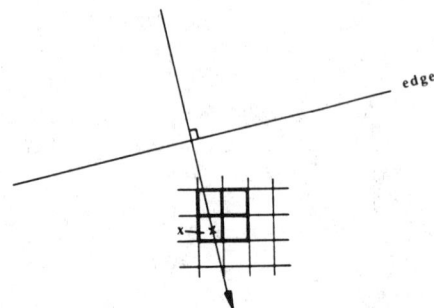

Fig. 28. Resampling the edge profile.

The problem now is to extract numerical data for the profile and estimate parameters for its modeling. The extraction is of course done in the high-frequency images. To be precise, one grey-level profile needs to be determined for each edge point, perpendicular to the edge direction. It would be a bit-consuming operation were all the information to be coded; but profiles extracted from neighboring edge points are very similar and exhibit a high correlation. It is therefore more economical to extract one profile per edge segment of length Δ, or even per entire edge segment if a very high compression ratio is desired. In any case, the extracted profile $p(x)$ must represent the average grey-level variation, perpendicular to both sides of the edge segment or entire edge:

$$p(x) = \frac{1}{n} \sum_{i=1}^{n} p_i(x) \tag{8}$$

where $p_i(x)$ is the profile extracted at the ith point of the edge segment as shown in Fig. 27.

To extract a particular profile $p_i(x)$, it is necessary to interpolate and resample the data since the space variable x is continuous and will rarely follow the discrete Cartesian sampling grid. This is done by linear interpolation of the grey-levels found in the high-frequency image at the four nearest neighboring pixels of x (Fig. 28). Finally, the extent of x must be limited. Since the maximum length between first and second zero-crossings is d (see previous paragraph), the profile $p_i(x)$ is extracted at regularly spaced discrete values of x within the interval $[-d, +d]$ with respect to an edge point. As shown in Fig. 25, the profile must not exhibit any sign change for x within $[0, d]$ or $[-d, 0]$. It may, of course, happen in practice that this sign will change because profiles originated by one or several neighboring edges are superimposed. In these cases, values after (or before) a sign change are discarded.

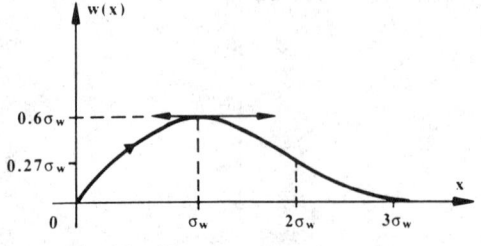

Fig. 29. Wavelet as used in [4] and [19].

2) Profile Representation: The shapes of a half profile for various slopes of the input edge were shown in Fig. 26. Unfortunately, the analytical function representing these curves with respect to σ does not have a simple form and cannot be easily computed and tabulated. Therefore, the theoretical form of the profile must be approximated on the basis of a model.

A first possibility is to consider only the response to an ideal unit step edge ($\sigma = 0$, in (6)) and use it to approximate the response to all other edges as suggested in [14]. This approximation is motivated by the Mach phenomenon, which explains the subjective enhancement of sharp brightness changes in our visual system. In practice, the profile or the so-called "synthetic high" is the response of the system whose frequency response is $[1 - G_{lf}(f, g)]$ to a unit impulse input [14], where $G_{lf}(f, g)$ is given by (3). This model is quite convenient for unit step-like edges and increases synthetically the contrast of softer edges. The price paid is the introduction of occasional false sharp edges at the location of soft ones that have been overenhanced by the Mach phenomenon.

The second possibility is the approximation of real profiles by exponential functions [11], [19] such as

$$w(x) = Ax \exp(-x^2/2\sigma_w^2) \tag{9}$$

where only two parameters are involved, A and σ_w. The first one, A, is simply the magnitude of the synthetic wavelet $w(x)$, while the second, σ_w, is a measure of its extent. These two parameters are computed via cross-correlation between $w(x)$ and the profile to be approximated. A typical wavelet is shown in Fig. 29 and can be compared to those shown in Fig. 26. It can be noticed that the wavelet (9) is well suited for edges of intermediate slope (moderate or large values for σ in (6)), but inappropriate for sharp edges ($\sigma = 0$). As a consequence, the global contrast of sharp edges will be decreased by this model.

Considering the disadvantages of these two models, it seems necessary to consider the approximation problem more generally, i.e., for every kind of profile, be it ideally sharp or very smooth, as shown in Fig. 26. For this reason, an attempt has been made to use polynomials to approximate edge profiles. The limited number of points of the profiles to be approximated suggests polynomials of order 1 or 2. Coefficients of the polynomials are computed via cross-correlation as before. As illustrated in Fig. 30, this third model gives better graphical results for various edge profiles than the two previous ones, especially when

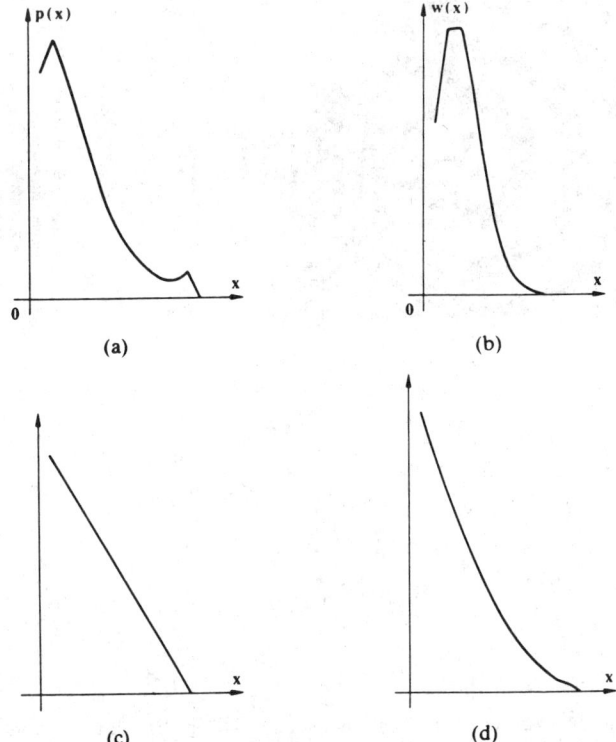

Fig. 30. (a) Approximation of a profile with (b) a wavelet ($A = 64$ and $\sigma_w = 4$), with (c) a first-order polynomial $33 - 3x$ and with (d) a second-order polynomial $42 - 5x + 0.2x$

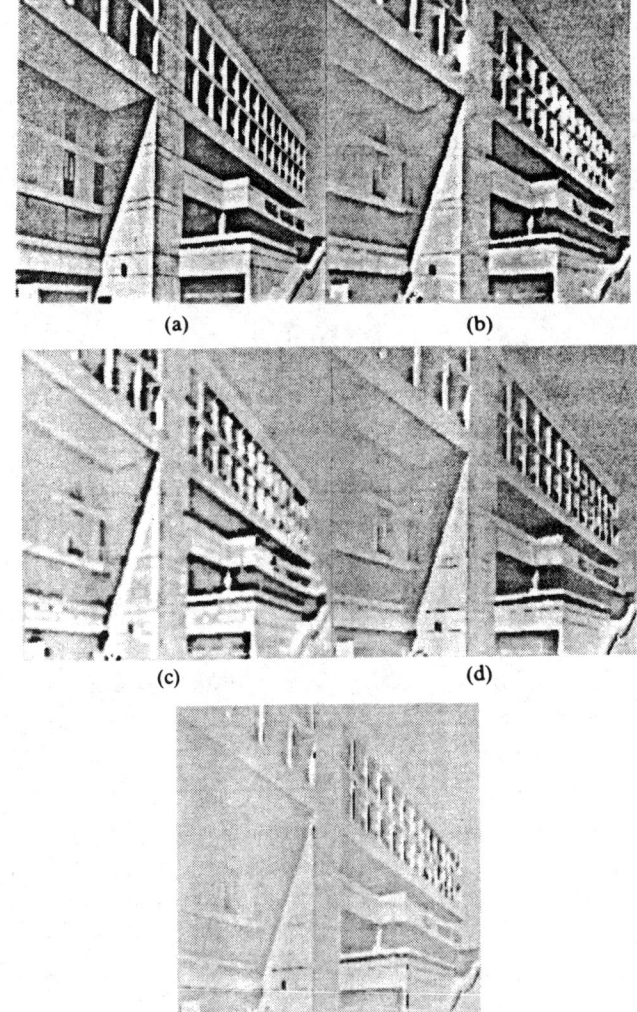

Fig. 31. Effect of the edge-profile approximation on the high-frequency image reconstruction. (a) A high-frequency image approximated respectively with (b) synthetic highs, (c) wavelets, (d) first-order polynomials, and (e) second-order polynomials.

second-order polynomials are chosen. Visual comparison between these models is presented in Fig. 31.

Three models are thus available for profile representation, each requiring different approximations and consequently exhibiting different reconstruction qualities. To compare them in terms of compression ratios, it is now necessary to estimate the numbers of bits required per profile for each.

3) Coding: The problem is to quantize and code the coefficients associated with the analytical expression. For "synthetic highs," one magnitude parameter must be coded, while one magnitude and one dispersion parameter are necessary for the wavelets. Two coefficients are involved in first-order and three in second-order polynomials. Equivalently, two and three points, respectively, on the first- and second-order polynomials can be coded instead. Coding profiles with "synthetic highs" is thus less bit-consuming than coding with wavelets. Also, coding profiles with wavelets is more bit-saving than coding them by polynomials. Since the histograms of the different coefficients exhibit no particular shape (see Fig. 32) a uniform quantization with zero-overload is used in our study. The number of bits per coefficient also influences the quality of the decoded image.

F. Linear Prediction

A new step can be made to decrease the redundancy by relating neighboring directional edges through a predictive model [20].

1) Predictive Model for Directional Images: Fig. 33 shows the first three neighboring directional components of a synthetic image, used here for clarity. The correlation between edges in neighboring components suggests the design of a predictive model to estimate an edge in one directional image given its spatial neighbors in the other directional images.

A typical situation is shown in Fig. 34 giving the first four directional images after edge detection. Edges corresponding to the first directional component (direction number 1) are shown in Fig. 34(a). These edges are detected as strong edges above a given high threshold and as weak edges above a lower threshold. They are represented in Fig. 34 by dark and light grey, respectively. Edges in the neighboring directions, which are also above the same thresholds, are detected as strong edges in their direction but they become weak edges in neighboring directions. In Fig. 34(b), strong edges are detected in component number 2, while the same ones are detected in components number 1 and 3 as weak edges. The same convention applies for Figs. 34(c) and (d). Starting from a strong edge of Fig. 34(a), which has a neighboring weak edge, and following

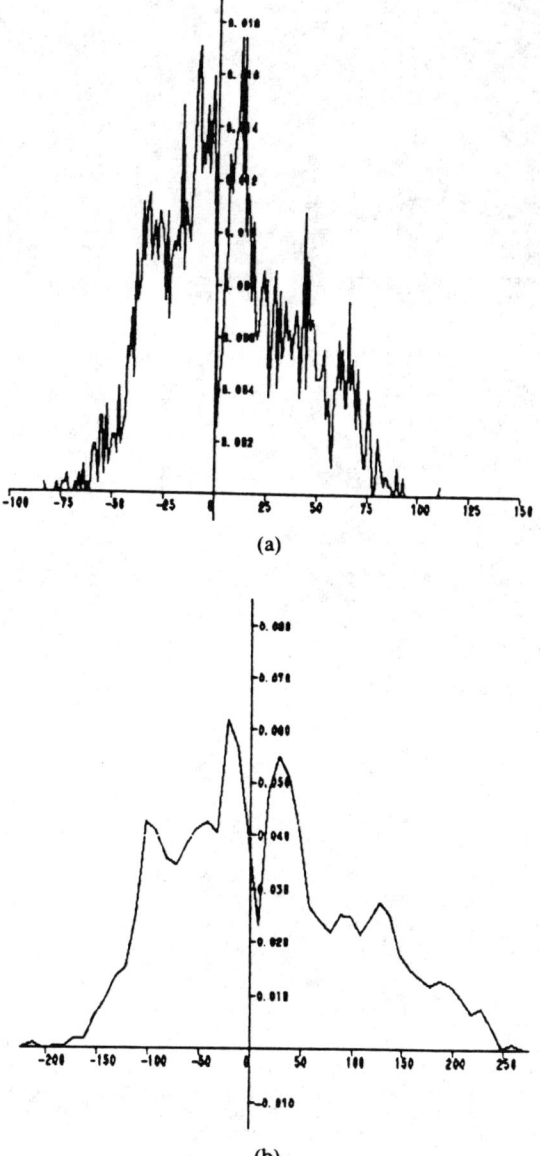

Fig. 32. Histograms of the approximation coefficients. (a) Synthetic highs magnitudes and (b) wavelet magnitudes.

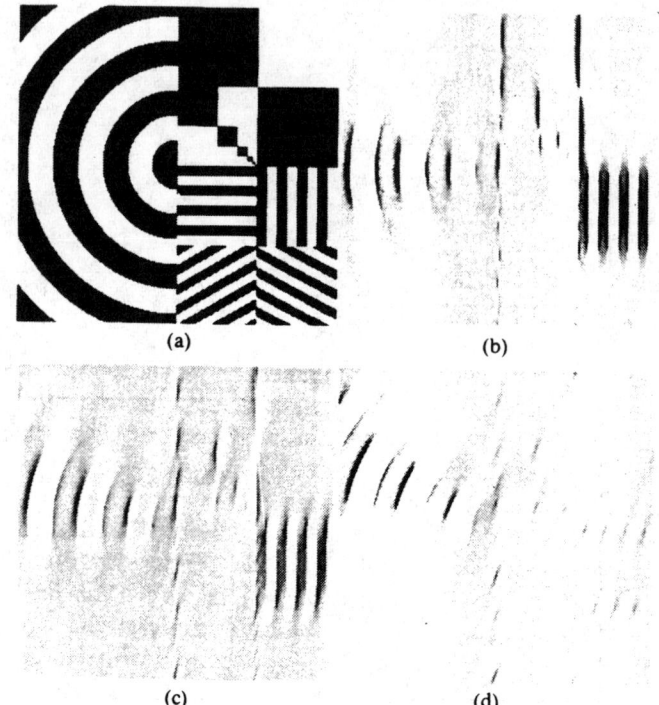

Fig. 33. (a) An original test image and (b)–(d) its first three directional components.

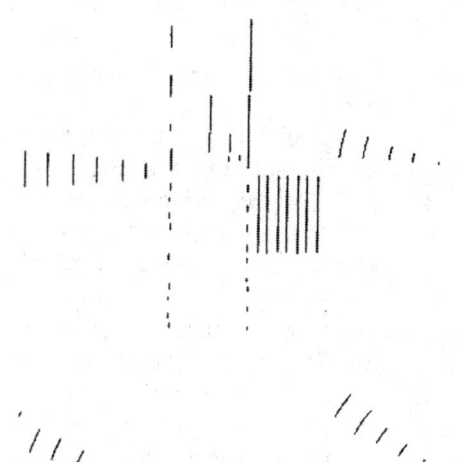

Fig. 34. Strong (dark) and weak (grey) edges in the first four directional images.

the corresponding curve in Figs. 34(b), (c) and (d), the strong edge of Fig. 34(c) can be predicted from the strong edges of Figs. 34(a) and (b) using a second-order predictive model. Then the strong edge of Fig. 34(d) can be predicted from the strong edge of Fig. 34(b) and the predicted edge in Fig. 34(c). Since this property is limited to particular regular curves (circles, spirals), a necessary extension consists in defining a more general prediction structure.

The prediction structure may be defined by considering the edge image in Fig. 35(a). In this image, it is possible to follow curves formed by adjacent segments issued from different directional images. Such curves are called prediction structures. One of them is shown in Fig. 35(b).

A prediction structure is thus a set of N neighboring edges $E(n)$, $n = 0, 1, \cdots, N-1$, each edge $E(n)$ being in a particular directional edge image and having a direction denoted by $D(n)$. The prediction model is defined over these structures. Let $x(n)$ be a K-dimensional vector characterizing the edge $E(n)$. The 2-D linear prediction consists of defining the predicted value $x_p(n)$ of $x(n)$ as follows:

$$x_p(n) = \sum_{i=1}^{M} a(i) \cdot x(n-i) \quad (10)$$

where M is the order of the prediction and $a(i)$ are K by K matrices. The prediction error is

$$e(n) = x(n) - x_p(n). \quad (11)$$

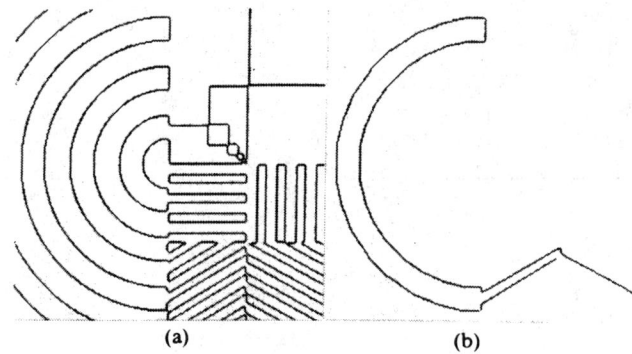

Fig. 35. (a) An edge image and (b) an extracted prediction structure.

First data set
$S(0)$, $x(0)..x(M-1)$, $a(1)..a(M)$
Second data set
$e(M)..e(M+N1)$, end of the first structure.
$S(M+N1+1)$, $e(M+N1+1)..e(M+N1+N2)$, end of the second structure.
etc.

The prediction parameters $a(i)$ are obtained by solving the following well-known equations:

$$\sum_{i=1}^{M} a(i) \cdot c(i,j) = -c(0,j),$$

$$\text{for } j = 1, \cdots, M \qquad (12)$$

where

$$c(i,j) = \sum_{n=n_0}^{n_1} x(n-i) \cdot x(n-j).$$

Since there are MK^2 equations with MK^2 unknowns, $x(n)$ should contain as few parameters as possible to avoid computation induced by large K. The following synthetic description of the edge $E(n)$ by $x(n)$ was chosen. The first two components of $x(n)$ are its length $L(n)$ and its direction $D(n)$. With the coordinates of the start point $S(n)$, they allow an exact reconstruction of the position of the edge $E(n)$. But the coordinates of $S(n)$ are equal to these of the end point of $E(n-1)$, and so it is not necessary to include them in $x(n)$. The other components are related to the description of the edge grey-level profile. There is one magnitude component if the synthetic highs model is chosen. There are one magnitude and one dispersion component for the wavelet model. Finally, two (or three) parameters are necessary if a first- (or second-) order polynomial is used.

2) Implementation: Two data sets are involved in the implementation of the Mth-order predictive model on a structure of N edges. The first includes the coordinates of the start point $S(0)$ of the first edge $E(0)$, the vectors $x(0)..x(M-1)$ needed to begin the prediction and prediction matrix $a(1)..a(M)$. The second contains the sequence of the prediction errors $e(M)..e(N-1)$. Using (10) and (11), it is easy to reconstruct exactly the N edges of the prediction structure from these two data sets. However, it is not necessary to assign a prediction model for each structure. First, some structures may have a number N of edges smaller than the order M of the prediction. Second, it is a waste of bits in the coding context to require the first data set for each structure, in cases where the prediction errors are very small. Therefore, the implementation of the same model is extended to several structures by adding to the second data set the coordinates of the start point of the first edge for every structure change. This leads to the following implementation scheme:

This scheme is extendable to any number of prediction structures and of edges per structure.

Another point to consider is the order M of the predictive model. Large orders require coding several K matrices $a(i)$. A compromise has to be found between maximum efficiency obtained for large values and coding requirements for small values of M. Finally, the coefficients of the matrices $a(i)$ must be computed using an edge sequence representing a typical curve of the considered image, such as a part of the circle in our example of Fig. 35(b). The result associated with this example is the following. The total number of edges found in Fig. 35(a) is 266. Among them, 21 are isolated in a single directional image and cannot be included in a prediction structure. The 245 remaining edges are contained in 19 prediction structures. A wavelet model is used to code the edge profiles. To code the two data sets defined above, the following bit distributions were obtained after optimal Huffmann coding with a prediction model of order 2: 12 bits per position S, 10 bits for the first two vectors $x(0)$ and $x(1)$, 8 bits per coefficient of $a(1)$ and $a(2)$, and 8 bits per prediction error vector $e(i)$.

Note that the use of prediction structures spares many bits devoted to edge position and profile coding. Therefore, this technique can be used efficiently for images with edge structures such as curves or circles as in a portrait picture. For images such as a building, however, the prediction strategy is inefficient since these pictures largely contain edges isolated to one directional image.

G. Reconstruction and Post-Filtering

1) Edge Reconstruction and Superposition: Position and profile parameters are coded for each edge segment. Reconstructing the locations of edge segments is straightforward, starting from the description that includes the start point, number of samples, and deviations (see Section III-D). Then the grey-level variation around this location must be computed from the parameters of the grey-level

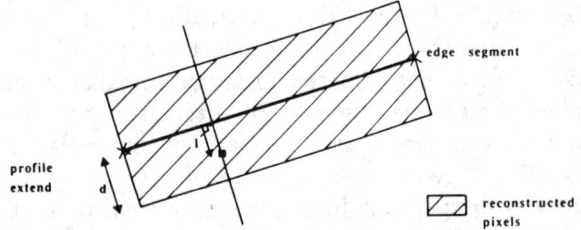

Fig. 36. Reconstruction area around an edge segment. Pixels are computed over the shaded area.

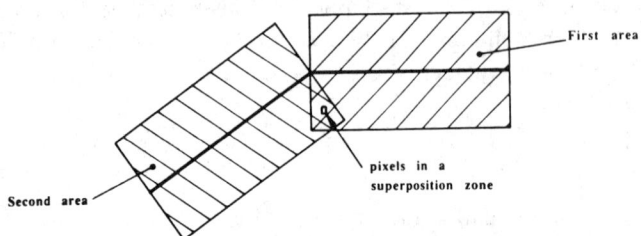

Fig. 37. Superposition of two reconstruction areas.

Fig. 38. Reconstructed high-frequency image.

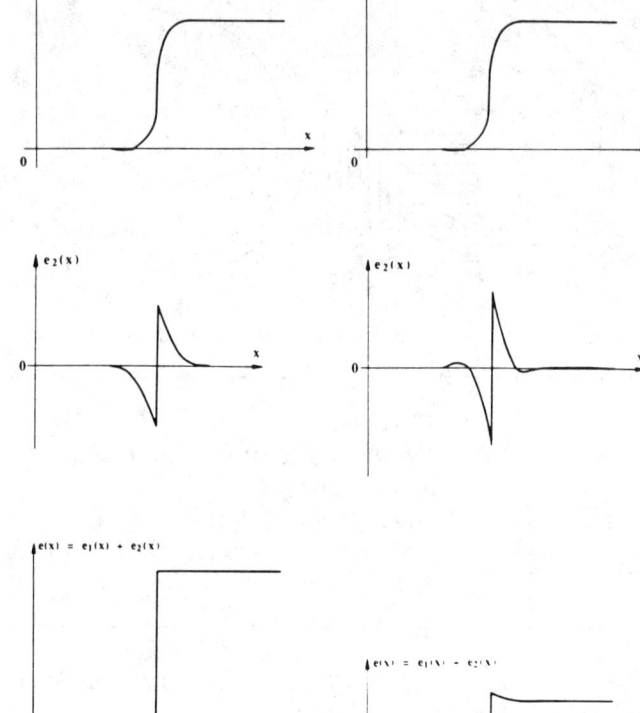

Fig. 39. Adding low-frequency and high-frequency components (a) in theory and (b) in practice.

profile. Fig. 36 displays the area whose pixels are associated with a given edge segment in the reconstructed high-frequency directional image. These pixels belong to a rectangular area whose length is equal to the length of the edge segment and whose width is twice the extent of the one-sided profile. The value of the grey-level at a particular pixel of this area situated at a distance x of the edge segment is given by the value $p(x)$ of the profile.

This process reconstructs the high-frequency image with all its edge segments. However, a pixel located at the vicinity of crossing edges may be affected by several edge segments (Fig. 37) due to the superposition of reconstruction areas. In this case, there is an ambiguity as to profile value. Experimental work suggests that the maximum absolute value should be chosen. Alternatives (interpolation, relaxation) introduce visual artifacts such as false edges.

An example of reconstruction of high-frequency images from edge descriptions based on this principle is shown in Fig. 38.

2) Post-Filtering: Once the high-frequency image is reconstructed, the last task performed by the decoder is to add this image to the reconstructed low-frequency image. As mentioned in [13], in theory this summation should recreate the original image, as shown for one dimension in Fig. 39(a). In practice, however, since the high-frequency signal is not perfectly reconstructed due to errors introduced by the synthetic description, the final signal has ripples or noise terms located mostly near but not at the edge position. The sum of the two images in actual practice is illustrated in one dimension in Fig. 39(b).

Post-filtering is therefore necessary to recover from these undesired artifacts. A median filter is used to perform this task, except that the vicinities of edge positions are not filtered. This avoids distortions of edge slopes and their location. Again, the particular filter used by us was chosen on the basis of experiment and visual inspection. A result of this filtering process is shown in Fig. 40.

IV. Adaptive Split-and-Merge

In this section, we address the problem of representing an image once it has been segmented into a set of regions. The directional decomposition described in Section III has provided further evidence of the importance of contour information. Contour locations and high-frequency profiles are essential to preserve the semantic information. Similarly, when segmentation is the basis for an image representation, contours must be preserved. Furthermore, region boundaries should fit contours. The region bound-

Fig. 40. A reconstructed image (a) before and (b) after post-filtering.

aries will be modified recursively so as to optimize the fit between the original image data and the synthetic description of grey-level variations, that is, pels or subregions will be adjoined to a test region in a way that minimizes a matching criterion. It is thus possible to obtain a symbolic representation of the segmented image. Coding will then be applied to symbols, which will guarantee high compression.

The principles of a segmentation approach will now be outlined for image modeling and coding. To guide the segmentation process, a control image of the contours will be defined. Then, it is shown how to approximate the characteristics of any homogeneous region of the image using a set of 2-D functions. Finally, error measures used to estimate the quality of the segmentation are described.

A. Adaptive Segmentation

1) Introductory Comments: To obtain a segmentation, one tries to find a mathematical or statistical model of the spatial variations of grey-level intensity [21]. For any region obtained by segmentation, the grey-level information will be represented by a set of two-dimensional functions. The method will define optimal partition and represent it by adaptively modifying the approximation parameters and the region shapes.

To prevent the segmentation process from creating significant distortion, contour information must be preserved. This can be done by preserving insofar as possible the visually real contours and avoiding the creation of arbitrary boundaries.

The overall coding procedure is based on the following steps: 1) reproduce faithfully the contours of the objects in the scene, i.e., region boundaries that are put into correspondence with them; 2) minimize the number of regions to avoid artificial boundaries (boundaries that do not correspond to contours) and the number of parameters to specify the approximation for each region; 3) allow a certain degradation in representing the signal within each region; 4) add a random component to the decoded image to render its natural aspect.

To reach the corresponding segmentation, an adaptive approach is necessary given the nonstationary nature of images. A local, then global, analysis of the image will be made by successively modifying the segmentation shape.

2) Control Images and their Extraction: Ideally, a region's borders should match the contours of the objects

Fig. 41. Edge extraction using the Marr-Hildreth operator (upper row) and the high-pass filter obtained as the sum of directional filters given by (4).

in the scene. The decision to resegment a region may be taken only if a region is crossed by a contour. In our experience, a contour image is thus required to control the segmentation.

As mentioned earlier, there is a plethora of contour extraction algorithms ranging from simple masks such as Sobel's or Robert's to sophisticated edge detectors derived with the variational formulation [26] via over-emphasized Marr-Hildreth's Gaussian smoothed Laplacian [24], [25]. The theory of the GOP operators, mentioned previously [6], [7], has included such filters since 1978. Nonlinear edge preserving smoothing filters, such as median or Nagao filters, are also popular.

After several unsuccessful experiments with these operators, losing precision at the location of sharp contour crossings, we used an isotropic high-pass filter obtained by merging the directional filters given by (4). In other words, it is an ideal filter smoothed by a Gaussian function. Edge detection capabilities of this filter have been extensively discussed in Section III. Fig. 41 shows the edge detection obtained for the building and the portrait pictures using the Marr-Hildreth operator and by the high-pass filter obtained as the sum of directional filters given by (4).

To guide the segmentation operation, a second control image is created that classifies pixels in the neighborhood of contour locations; pixels having the same sign (positive or negative), after high-pass filtering, belong to the same region on one side of a contour. This sign image is shown in Fig. 42 for the building and the portrait pictures.

3) Data Approximation: The data approximation procedure not only serves to approximate the signal within each region but also enables the segmentation to be performed. The approximation problem has been extensively covered in the literature [27], [28]. It should, however, be

Fig. 42. Sign images for building and portrait.

reconsidered in the context of segmentation. Let G be a space spanned by a set of 2-D analytical functions $\psi_i(x, y)$ $(i = 1, \cdots, r)$. Any function belonging to G can be written as

$$\hat{g}(x, y) = \sum_{i=1}^{r} u_i \psi_i(x, y) \tag{13}$$

or using a vector notation

$$\hat{g}(x, y) = \psi^T(x, y) \cdot u. \tag{14}$$

In our case, the function $\hat{g}(x, y)$ will be represented by a set of N samples taken over a domain D of any shape, along the traditional Cartesian grid. If k and l represent the discrete coordinates in the image plane, the data set is denoted by $g(k_j, l_j)$ with $j = 1, \cdots, N$, where j is the discrete set variable. The approximation problem is then that of choosing the optimal set of coefficients u_i. As a criterion, a distance measure is introduced. For example, $\hat{g}_1(x, y)$ is better than $\hat{g}_2(x, y)$ in approximating $g(x, y)$, if and only if

$$d(g, \hat{g}_1) < d(g, \hat{g}_2) \tag{15}$$

where $d(g, \hat{g}_i)$ is the distance between $g(x, y)$ and $\hat{g}_i(x, y)$.

For a variety of considerations outlined in [29], the approximation criterion we have used is the least-square error between the original and approximated data. In essence, this criterion has the advantage of being insensitive to local distortions. If contours are preserved by the segmentation, the signal within each region will fit the original pixels harmoniously. Finding the optimal set of parameters u_i is equivalent to solving the system of r linear equations:

$$\partial d(g, \hat{g}) / \partial u_i = 0 \quad \text{for } i = 1, \cdots, r \tag{16}$$

where $d(.,.)$ represents the usual Euclidean distance

$$d(g, \hat{g}) = \sum_{j=1}^{N} e_j^2 = (g - \hat{g})^T (g - \hat{g}). \tag{17}$$

Vectors g and $\hat{g}$ contain the original and approximated values, respectively, over the domain D, and e_j defines the error at each pixel location (k_j, l_j) $(j = 1, \cdots, N)$. If we denote by Z^T the $N \times r$ matrix represented by column vectors $[\psi(k_1, l_1) \psi(k_2, l_2) \cdots \psi(k_N, l_N)]$, the solution to (16) is then given by

$$u = (Z^T Z)^{-1} Z^T g \tag{18}$$

or, defining the $r \times r$ matrix $S = Z^T Z$

$$u = S^{-1} Z^T g \tag{19}$$

where the superscript T indicates the transpose. Equation (19) can be solved as long as S is nonsingular, which is ensured for square domains if r is smaller or equal to N [30]. Its computation requires the evaluation of the vectors $\psi(k_j, l_j)$, for $j = 1, \cdots, N$. It is possible to reduce the computational load by taking advantage of various properties of the least-square approximation, as will be outlined in the split and merge steps of the algorithm.

The next task is that of choosing the set of approximation functions $\psi_i(x, y)$, for $i = 1, \cdots, r$. Their number r should be kept relatively small as a large number of pixels should be mapped into a reduced number of "transformed" coefficients u_i for high compression. Assuming that a segmentation is available that fits region borders to the contours of objects in the scene, it is most common to observe that the image data is a slowly varying luminance function over any region. Such variations are very well represented by 2-D polynomials. Moreover, the oscillatory behavior of commonly used orthogonal functions, difficult to define over nonrectangular regions, do not exist for polynomials.

The last point to be considered is the quantization of the approximated signal. The real-valued approximation $g(x, y)$ may take values outside the range of the original image luminance. Linear rescaling is not appropriate as the contrast will be seriously affected, as shown in Fig. 43. To avoid this, the values outside the dynamic range are set either to the maximum or the minimum value of the luminance. All other pixels are rounded to the nearest integer.

4) Error Measures: After approximating a particular region by minimizing the least-square error (LSE), its value is checked for acceptability. If the LSE is too large, the region shape needs to be modified.

Note that the LSE given by (17) is a global evaluation of the approximation quality for the region of interest. No contextual measure is made with respect to the type of information present in the region. In order not to lose contour information, the tolerable LSE must be kept very small. Under this constraint, the segmentation is likely to create a large number of small regions, inefficient for coding.

If the mean-square (MSE) error, obtained by weighting the least-square error by the number of region points, is used, the goodness of approximation can be measured independent of region size, but the cost is likely to be a loss of significant contours.

It seems necessary to introduce a context-sensitive error criterion to take into account the existence of contours traversing the region under consideration. Unless there is no contour within the region, by using the control image of the contours, the quality of the approximation is measured in the contour neighborhoods assuring their preservation. This criterion is called contour error (CE).

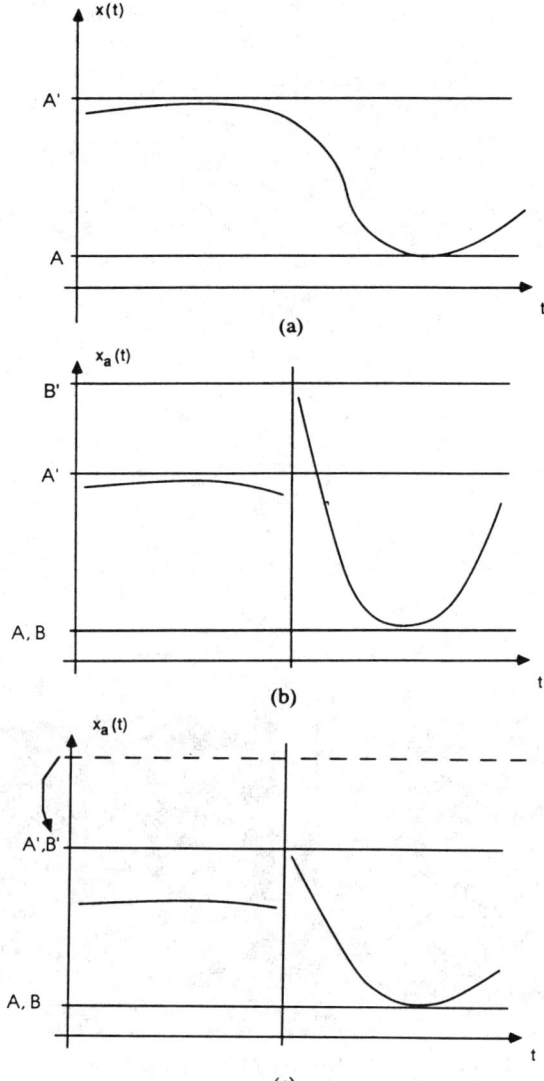

Fig. 43. Illustration of the contrast loss due to linear rescaling in one dimension. (a) An original one-dimensional signal and its dynamic range AA'. (b) Approximation of this signal over two regions within the dynamic range BB' of the approximation and contrast loss after rescaling linearly BB' to AA'.

While the LSE and MSE estimate the fidelity of approximation within a certain region, the CE determines whether real contours have been lost or not. It should be noted that these measures give no indication of the overall approximated image quality; rather, they are used to choose the appropriate segmentation.

B. Split Process

The split process will define homogeneous regions in the image that can be used as "seeds" on which the rest of the segmentation will be build. To find the seeds, the analysis starts from a global look at the data, then goes to a more detailed observation, essentially where important semantic information is present, i.e., at contour locations.

1) Algorithm: To partition the image into an initial set of regions, by an iterative subdivision procedure, a split and stop condition is defined. It will indicate when a region should be subdivided and when it should not. The split procedure will continue as long as the approximation

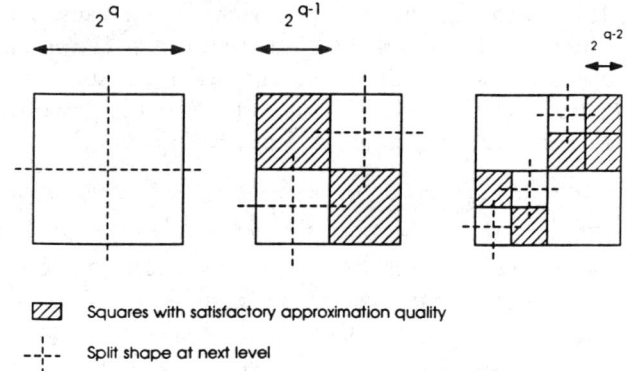

Fig. 44. Illustrating the split process.

error is too large. It should stop, however, when the split induces a region the size of a pixel or when a further subdivision may cause the matrix S to be singular (eq. (19)), that is, whenever the number of points N becomes smaller than the number of approximating functions r.

A region can be split into two or more parts at a time. In our experience, the number of such parts should not be too large in order to guarantee a progressive transition from a global analysis to a local one. For computational ease, a region will be split into subregions of identical shape, say squares, and hence will split into four equal parts. It is assumed that images are of size 2^q in each dimension. Starting with an image of size $2^q \times 2^q$, the best approximation to the entire image in the least-square sense is evaluated with the set 2-D polynomial functions. If the quality of such an approximation is found satisfactory, the process is stopped. If not, the image is divided into four identical squares of size $2^{q-1} \times 2^{q-1}$ and the same process is iterated for each of these squares until the quality measure becomes acceptable. This procedure is shown in Fig. 44. To avoid ill-conditioned solutions for the approximation, the process is stopped whenever $2^{2(q-l-1)}$ becomes smaller than r, defining, then, l as the last level of subdivision. For small values of r, practical experience has shown that the quality of approximation was adequate at this level.

Since, in the final segmentation, the image must be decomposed into a set of regions of any shape and size, it should be possible to split the image down to regions of pixel size. Squares crossed by contours will be processed separately to reach this ultimate split level. The approximation will be said to reproduce faithfully the original data within a given square as long as neither the MSE nor the CE exceed certain thresholds. The threshold values will be kept relatively small so that the approximation error remains negligible before the merging process is begun.

2) Data Structure: The split process may start with squares of size 64×64; it is rare for natural images of size 256×256 or 512×512 to contain homogeneous square regions of larger dimension. The algorithm description has pointed out a quadtree structure that can be implemented in many ways. The number of squares depends on the number of approximating functions r. At the end of the split process, a tree is built with coefficients u_i associated with each leaf, leading to a symbolic description.

It is advantageous to treat regions of the same level (same size squares) together. Indeed, it can be shown that the matrix S has the same expression for squares of identical size if an origin is fixed with respect to the square [31]. Each term of the matrix S can be expressed as

$$s_{mn} = \sum_{j=1}^{N} \psi_m(k_j, l_j) \psi_n(k_j, l_j). \quad (20)$$

Since the domain on which the approximation is evaluated is a square, each coordinate k_j or l_j has $\sqrt{N}$ times the same value if there are N points in the square. Assuming that $\psi_m(x,y) = x^a y^b$ and $\psi_n(x,y) = x^c y^d$, eq. (20) can be rewritten as [29]

$$s_{mn} = \sum_{n=1}^{\sqrt{N}} n^{a+c} \sum_{n=1}^{\sqrt{N}} n^{b+d}. \quad (21)$$

Therefore, each entry of S constitutes a product of two power series of successive integer values that can be evaluated rather simply. Most of the computation will correspond then to the two matrix vector multiplications appearing in (19).

As the region shape is a square, a more simple solution can be found if the approximating function $\hat{g}(x,y)$ is separable, i.e., if

$$\hat{g}(x,y) = \sum_{i=1}^{r_1} \sum_{j=1}^{r_2} u_{ij} x^i y^j \quad (22)$$

which, in a matrix form, becomes for all values (k_j, l_j)

$$G = V_k^T U V_l \quad (23)$$

where V_k and V_l are pseudo-Vandermonde matrices of size $\sqrt{N} \times r_1$ and $\sqrt{N} \times r_2$ along the k and l dimensions, respectively. As shown in [30], the best least-square approximation is given by

$$U = (V_k^T V_k)^{-1} V_k^T G V_l (V_l^T V_l)^{-1}. \quad (24)$$

The number of operations can be substantially reduced since the matrices $V_k^T V_k = H_k$ and $V_l^T V_l = H_l$ are of Hankel type with each element corresponding to a power series from 1 to N. Moreover, the two matrix vector multiplications of size $r_1 r_2 \times N$ appearing in (19) are replaced by five matrix multiplications of respective size $r_1 \times r_1$, $r_1 \times \sqrt{N}$, $\sqrt{N} \times \sqrt{N}$, $\sqrt{N} \times r_2$, and $r_2 \times r_2$. As long as $r_1 r_2$ is larger than 1, the computation is reduced for any value of N [29]. This is shown in Table II for some values of r_1, r_2, and N.

Note that the LSE or MSE can be computed without estimating the approximation for each point of the domain of interest. Indeed, (18) can be rewritten as [29]

$$d(g, \hat{g}) = \text{LSE} = g^T g - u^T S u. \quad (25)$$

It is possible to replace CE by a simple test of the presence of contours within the analyzed square. As a matter of fact, the best approximation in the least-square sense cannot reproduce contours with polynomial functions if the number of points to be approximated is much larger than the number of polynomial coefficients. The split strategy is then simplified as shown in Fig. 45. Each square is divided into four subsquares as long as it contains contour points and N is much greater than r. No least-square approximation is then performed. If no contour points are present, the normal procedure is used without estimating CE.

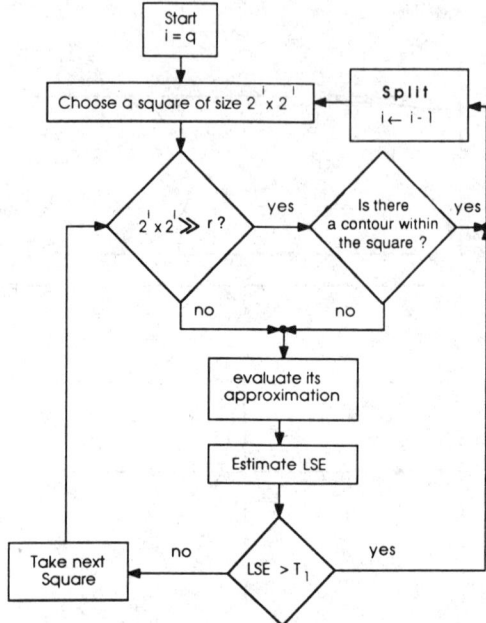

Fig. 45. Simplified split process.

Fig. 46. Result of the split process on the building image. (a) Split regions and (b) the first-order polynomial approximation over these regions. Grey areas in (a) correspond to squares too small to be drawn. Compare Fig. 46(b) to the original image in Fig. 5.

TABLE II
NUMBER OF OPERATIONS REQUIRED TO COMPUTE THE APPROXIMATION COEFFICIENTS

size poly	$N=4^2$	$N=8^2$	$N=16^2$	$N=32^2$	$N=64^2$
$r_1=2$, $r_2=2$	64	176	592	2192	8464
	80	272	1040	4112	16400
$r_1=2$, $r_2=3$	86	206	638	2270	8606
	132	420	1572	6180	24612
$r_1=2$, $r_2=4$	112	240	688	2352	8752
	192	576	2112	8256	32832
$r_1=3$, $r_2=3$	138	318	966	3414	12918
	225	657	2385	9297	36945
$r_1=3$, $r_2=4$	180	372	1044	3540	13140
	336	912	3216	12432	49296

3) Split Results and Information Representation: An example of the split process is presented for the building picture in Fig. 46. The corresponding approximating

Fig. 47. (a) Split result on the portrait picture with 13 903 squares. Zero-order approximation over these squares (b) before and (c) after postprocessing. The compression ratio is 18 to 1.

Fig. 48. (a) Split result on the cameraman picture. Third-order approximation over the squares (b) before and (c) after postprocessing. The compression ratio is 5.6 to 1.

function is a first-order separable polynomial given by

$$\hat{g}(x, y) = u_1 + u_2 x + u_3 y + u_4 xy. \quad (26)$$

The segmented image is composed of 6847 squares of five different sizes (2×2 up to 32×32). A square of size greater than 4×4 is split with no approximation whenever it contains contour points. The tolerated MSE is set to a value of 15^2 if the original picture has a dynamic range of 0 to 255. Very little distortion appears in the approximated image.

The structure of a split graph can be reduced to a quadtree representation [32]. By taking into account geometrical constraints, this graph can be coded with approximatively 0.5 bits per square in the case of natural images. Starting from the initial division of the image into 64×64 squares, a "1" is used to state that a further subdivision is required, a "0" otherwise.

To code the approximation characteristics within each region, an upper limit of eight bits per coefficient can be mathematically justified with virtually no error as long as the original image is represented with an eight-bit dynamic range (see Section IV-D). However, there is still a high correlation between the coefficients of adjacent squares belonging to a homogeneous area of the original signal even after the split process. This suggests merging adjacent squares with the forthcoming strategy.

It may be of interest to see, at this intermediary level of segmentation, the degree of compression and decoded image quality one can obtain with the split process. A simple coding strategy was derived for the zero-order approximation ($\hat{g}(x, y) = u_1$). Instead of representing each square value, the difference between adjacent square values has been coded. For each square, this DPCM-like representation is initiated at the upper-left square. As an example, the portrait picture with a zero-order approximation is shown in Fig. 47. The split leads to 13 903 squares with a compression ratio of 18 to 1. The image of Fig. 47(b) has been postprocessed to eliminate false contours leading to the result of Fig. 47(c).

Using eight bits per coefficient, Fig. 48 shows the cameraman picture coded with cubic functions of the form

$$\hat{g}(x, y) = u_1 + u_2 x + u_3 y + u_4 x^2 + u_5 xy + u_6 y^2. \quad (27)$$

The corresponding compression ratio for this result is 5.6 to 1. Some precision is lost in describing contour information.

C. Merge Process

The merge is the last step in the segmentation process and should lead to the ultimate goal of fitting the region boundaries to contours of the objects in the scene. The final image partition may contain regions of any shape and size. Adjacent squares of the split process are merged if their joint approximation will induce the least degradation of image content with respect to all other possible associations of any two contiguous regions.

1) Algorithm: As a result of the split operation, some squares may contain contours while others define parts of homogeneous areas. The latter will serve as "seeds" for the merge process. On the other hand, pixels in the neighborhood of contours will be associated together to define parts that will be further merged with regions closest to them under the similarity criterion. To guarantee the connectivity of each region, only adjacent regions will be considered for merging.

This part of the segmentation, as was the case for the split operation, involves the definition of merge and stop conditions.

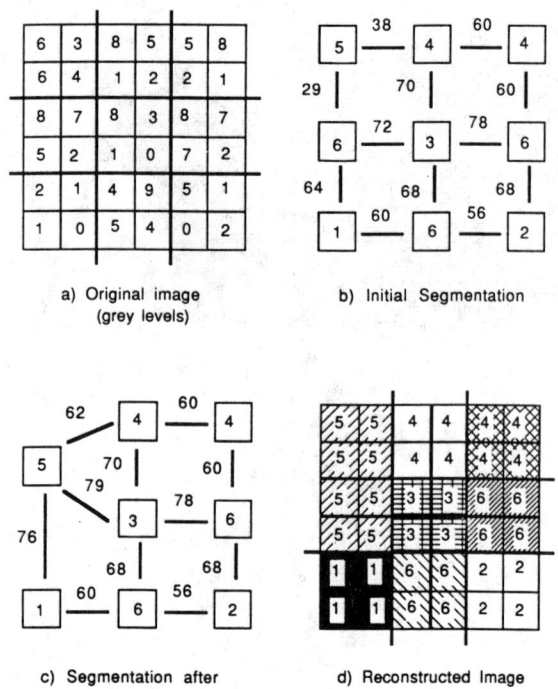

Fig. 49. Illustrating one step merge. (a) An original sample image, (b) its initial segmentation, (c) the result of one step merge, and (d) the reconstructed image.

Two contiguous regions are to be merged whenever they belong to the same homogeneous area of the image. Similarity can be measured with respect to the degree of modification of the approximating function $g(x, y)$ over the two test regions. The smaller the modification, the more likely the homogeneity between them. The key problem is to set the proper threshold. A region-growing technique based on this criterion was proposed by Kocher [33] and later improved [34] to make it adaptive. The latter will be used here. The basic idea is to look for the adjacent region pair that will induce the least degradation. To implement it, a region adjacency graph (RAG) is constructed [35]. Each node in a RAG represents a region and each link defines the adjacency. Then, a cost value is assigned to each link to indicate the degree of dissimilarity between nodes, i.e., two regions. The link with lowest cost identifies the merge of the two most nearly similar regions at each step. The RAG is updated with the evolving segmentation: the node resulting from the association of two regions is linked to the union of all other nodes connected to the two regions. For a given similarity measure or cost function and a set of approximating functions, one is ensured to reach a minimum in the cost function, which will be the optimal image partition except in pathological images. As an example, Fig. 49 presents one step of merging from a certain split image.

Many criteria may be used to establish the stop condition (one, for example, being the number of regions). Indeed, for scene analysis or coding purposes, one can control either the scene complexity or the compression ratio by this means. Another possibility is to limit the degradation of the original signal by measuring the highest error that appears with respect to the two regions that are merged.

2) Approximation and Error Control: The least-square approximation over the union of two regions D_1 and D_2 can be obtained from their individual least-square approximations [29]. The only additional information needed is related to the respective position of the two domains. Let u_1 denote the best set of approximating coefficients, $g_1(k, l)$ the set of N_1 pixels within D_1, S_1 the symmetric matrix defined according to (19) for D_1. Similarly, u_2, $g_2(k, l)$, N_2 and S_2 are defined for the domain D_2. The optimal vector of coefficients u for the area $D = D_1 \cup D_2$ is given by

$$u = (S_1 + S_2)^{-1}(S_1 u_1 + S_2 u_2). \quad (28)$$

Notice that each matrix S_i contains only information related to the approximating functions $\psi_i(k, l)$ defined over the domain D_i and are independent of the data $g_i(k, l)$. The sum of these two matrices denoted by S defines the corresponding information for the domain D. This property is useful since $g_1(k, l)$ and $g_2(k, l)$ need not be used again to obtain the best approximation. To be able to apply (19), the approximations for every region pair must be referenced to a unique origin.

Similarly, it can be shown how most of the error measures used can be obtained from a combination of errors on the merged regions and from a term that does not require the evaluation of the distortion on every pixel [29].

If the LSE is used, it can be expressed over the entire domain D as

$$\text{LSE} = \text{LSE}_1 + \text{LSE}_2 + u_1^T S_1 u_1 + u_2 S_2 u_2 - uSu \quad (29)$$

where LSE_1 and LSE_2 are the least-square errors relative to domains D_1 and D_2, respectively. At each merging step, the LSE increases. Any local, even small, distortion is taken into account. As a homogeneous region becomes larger, the great number of small contributions tend to raise LSE unduly rapidly. In such a case, small regions will tend to be merged even though they are quite different.

Another choice is the MSE measure. Since MSE is the LSE normalized by the number of individual points, after merging a large region with a small one, it will increase only slightly even if the contributions of the small region are relatively large. This criterion will let big regions swallow much smaller ones even if the latter are very different from the large region [29].

The use of a similarity measure independent of region size in the merge is a third possible choice. This is called region ponderated mean-square error (RPMSE). It is obtained by dividing the error contributions of each region by their respective number of points. As with LSE, its expression can be evaluated without estimating the exact approximation for every pixel [29]:

$$\text{RPMSE} = \left(\text{LSE}_1 + u_1^T S_1 u_1 + u^T S u - 2 u^T S_1 u_1\right)/N_1$$
$$+ \left(\text{LSE}_2 + u_2^T S_2 u_2 + u^T S u - 2 u^T S_2 u_2\right)/N_2. \quad (30)$$

With this measure, very small regions that correspond to noisy information may be retained in the final partition. Otherwise, their inclusion in bigger regions could cause a

Fig. 50. Split result of the portrait picture with third-order polynomials which will be merged in Fig. 51.

large increase in RPMSE. The preponderant weight of the large region assures that the noisy region is not merged.

It can be noticed from (29) and (30) that the LSE is used for each merging. This error term increases continuously with each merge and may become very large, dominating the remaining terms in the equations. Equivalent to the LSE, the MSE, and the RPMSE, three other measures may be defined by setting the LSE terms to zero in (29) and (30). This new set of error measures is less sensitive to noise, as they rely only on the approximation coefficients u_i, computed by extensive averaging (see (18)).

A special strategy will govern the use of each of these different measures with respect to the structure of the segmentation, i.e., the physical scene.

3) Overall Merging Strategy: Experimental and mathematical analysis of the effects of each error measure has led us to choose the following strategy. At the start, square regions containing contours are disregarded; the RAG is comprised of homogeneous square regions to be associated, as long as the approximating functions can satisfy their homogeneity characteristics. Two dissimilarity measures are successively applied during this first step: the RPMSE is used initially to allow large regions to appear in the segmentation, then the LSE is used to let localized inhomogeneities, that do not define real contours, disappear. In both cases, the LSE terms are set to zero in (29) and (30) as justified earlier. As an example, this operation was applied to the portrait picture with a 2-D polynomial approximation of order 3 (ten coefficients). Fig. 50(a) and (b) give the split approximation while Fig. 51(a)–(d) show the result of the merge process as described. From the split process, the RPMSE reduces the region number from 1283 to 499, then the LSE diminishes it from 499 to 299. Note that these values do not take into account the regions relative to squares containing contours, shown in white in Fig. 51(a) and (c).

In a second step, the information relative to contours will be inserted. Using the positive and negative sign control image (see Section IV-A2), each square containing a contour is divided into two parts, one for each sign. As long as these parts contain a sufficient number of pixels to allow a unique approximation (N is greater than r), it will define a new node in the RAG, with its individual characteristics. Otherwise, isolated pixels will be considered

Fig. 51. Result of the initial merge with the RPMSE criterion applied to (a) and (b) the split result of Fig. 50, followed by (c) and (d) a merge using LSE. White areas in (a) and (c) indicate squares crossed by contours.

Fig. 52. Final segmentation of the portrait picture with 70 regions.

separately. They will be connected in the RAG to neighboring regions for which an approximation exists. The similarity measure used is based on the LSE. Some artifacts may, however, appear in the final segmentation. Indeed, some parts that have been separated using the second control image may be reassociated whenever the contour that divided them is well represented after approximation. However, a further insertion of the region they define in a neighboring homogeneous zone will change the real contour location, distorting image quality significantly. In Section E, this distortion is reduced by false contour smoothing. As an example, a final segmentation of the portrait picture is presented in Fig. 52 with 70 regions.

D) Information Representation and Coding

The adaptive split-and-merge process has led to a segmented image where each region is represented by a 2-D polynomial function. The approximated image can be reconstructed using the geometric shape and location of the different regions and the approximated data within each region.

1) Region Position and Shape: Since regions are connected, describing the shape of one will define part of its neighbors' borders. To obtain a simple and precise representation, all regions will be described in a single code word. An optimal and easy way of doing it is obtained in tracing each region frontier. This frontier is defined by following a line passing between the pels of one region and its neighbor (or the image boundary).

Given a one-dimensional four-connected graph describing the region frontiers, Eden and Kocher [36] have shown that a code requiring as few as 1.27 its per frontier point can be used. The code contains certain restrictions (in particular, there can be no two successive turns in the same direction). The modifications of the segmentation caused by fulfilling this requirement have no visual effect.

Natural image segmentation by split-and-merge has shown that the average number of frontier points could range from 5000 to 9000, requiring approximately 6500 to 11 500 bits using the above-mentioned code.

2) Data Approximation: Each region is represented by r coefficients. If r pixels are identified in the approximated region, the 2-D polynomials are obtained by using their luminances to compute the coefficients by the inverse polynomials. Assuming that each pixel has an eight-bit precision, at most $8r$ bits are necessary to code the approximating polynomial function. The only possible error appears in the quantization of each pixel. As regions are rather large, this error remains small for r regularly spaced pixels.

A further way to reduce the number of required bits to code the approximation is to use a variable number of coefficients for each region. Given segmentation, diminishing the number of coefficients will necessarily increase the compression ratio. But this may also reduce the reproduction quality. As proposed by Kocher [33], good quality can be preserved by considering polynomials of increasing order. Zero- to third-order polynomials are used in our case. To find the degree of the polynomials to be used within a specific region, the maximum value of each monomial contribution of a certain degree is searched. Starting with the highest possible degree d, if the contribution of the monomial can be neglected for all locations of the region, then the polynomials are of order lower than d. The same procedure is iterated until the right degree is found. Coding a segmented image obtained with a third-order polynomial function will then require two bits per region to state the polynomial order, then 8, 24, 48, or 80 bits per region depending on the order of the polynomials to code the approximating coefficients.

A better way to reduce the cost of approximation is to use a vector quantization scheme to cluster the set of polynomial coefficients for all regions. Among all possible configurations of vectors u, this number is reduced by an appropriate quantization. Indeed, certain regions will be represented by the same vector. This tends to further reduce redundancy for nonconnected regions. Since it is very likely that the distributions of the approximation coefficients are statistically independent, these coefficients are normalized and clustered using the familiar Euclidean distance.

The final strategy for the approximation code first reduces the number of polynomial coefficient configurations using the vector quantization process, then estimates the number of coefficients necessary to represent each of these configurations, and codes them using the above-mentioned technique.

As proposed in [4], a pseudorandom noise can be added to the polynomial approximation of each region to render the image more natural. The LSE between the original and approximated signal within each region is used to control the variance of a zero-mean pseudorandom signal added as "salt-and-pepper" noise.

Natural images can be represented with as few as 25 to 100 regions depending on the desired quality. With an average of 40 bits per region for coding the approximation, this corresponds to a range of 1000 to 4000 bits to the total coding cost. Notice that region location coding is at least three times more expensive than coding the approximated signal within each region. It does not appear possible to disregard the strong requirement of a minimally distorted region frontier shape.

E. Postprocessing

Degradation due to the approximation process is visually detectable mostly at the region's boundaries. The proposed approximation method minimizes the LSE without introducing constraints as to signal continuity between regions. This results in the creation of false contours at the boundaries of some adjacent regions.

An approach to solving this problem is to apply postfiltering to the approximated image. The post-processing filter needs to be low pass and is applied to all boundary points perpendicular to the contour orientation. Its lowpass characteristics depend on the gradient magnitude again calculated perpendicular to the boundary.

An easier and more reliable way to find the regions to be smoothed has been implemented. The smoothing algorithm is as follows. For each boundary point, the control image indicates whether it lies in the neighborhood of a true contour. Typically, it is a true contour if there are other contour points in the control image within a 3×3 window centered at the same location. If so, no postfiltering is performed. Otherwise, a smoothing algorithm that tends to minimize the squared magnitude of the gradient is applied within a specified area around the corresponding false contour point. This area must be large enough to ensure the continuity of the 2-D signal and small enough to avoid smoothing true contours or the destruction of data approximated by the polynomial function. If the false contour is not too critical, both requirements are automatically satisfied in the case that the smoothed region is kept equal to or narrower than the

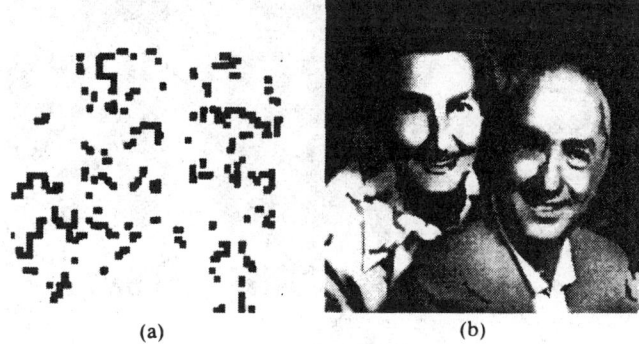

Fig. 53. (a) Postfiltering areas and (b) its result.

analysis window of the true–false state of the boundary point (3×3 in our example).

The smoothing algorithm can be formulated as a constrained optimization problem as described in [9]. It is equivalent to solving the Laplacian equation

$$\nabla^2 \hat{g}(x, y) = 0 \qquad (31)$$

subject to the limit conditions given about $g(x, y)$ along the borders of the regions to be smoothed. This equation can be solved iteratively by using the method of successive overrelaxation [9].

Results of this smoothing procedure are shown in the case of the portrait picture in Fig. 53. To perform it at the decoding end only the portions of region frontiers that do not match real contours of the scene need to be known.

V. Results

This section presents the results of directional decomposition-based coding and adaptive split-and-merge-based coding as described in Sections III and IV, respectively. Unspecified parameters of each method are those indicated in the corresponding section. All the decoded pictures shown in this section are obtained with information-lossy techniques. It would have been useful to derive a criterion to evaluate the distortions. Unfortunately, we do not have an objective quality measure following the subjective judgment of human observers. For this reason, quality evaluation of the decoded pictures is left to the reader, who may compare them to the original ones given in Fig. 5.

A. Directional Decomposition-Based Coding Results

One of the most important components of this method is the model used to approximate edge profiles. Three groups of results will be presented depending on the model used, i.e., synthetic highs, wavelet, and polynomial approximations.

Fig 54 shows reconstructed images assuming an ideal edge model (synthetic highs, Section III-E-2) with average compressions ranging from 50 to 1 to 60 to 1. For example, in the portrait picture (Fig. 54(a)), 563 contour segments are detected in the directional images, requiring 7489 bits to describe their position. A total of 1126 bits are used to represent the associated profiles. Finally, the low-pass

Fig. 54. Directional decomposition-based coding results using the synthetic highs model. The compression ratios are (a) 57 to 1, (b) 59 to 1, and (c) 49 to 1.

Fig. 55. Directional decomposition-based coding results using the synthetic highs model. The compression ratios are (a) 118 to 1, (b) 86 to 1, and (c) 84 to 1.

image is coded with 511 bits. Thus, the decoded image is represented with 9126 bits corresponding to a compression ratio of 57 to 1. Although one may recognize the persons, small details are often lost. The number of bits used for the two other images are roughly the same. By raising the thresholds and increasing the value of other parameters, even more compressed pictures may be obtained. Fig. 55 shows the same pictures with compressions ranging from 90 to 1 to 120 to 1, still using the synthetic highs model.

Fig. 56. Directional decomposition-based coding results using the wavelet model. The compression ratios are (a) 57 to 1, (b) 59 to 1, and (c) 49 to 1.

Fig. 57. Directional decomposition-based coding results using the wavelet model. The compression ratios are (a) 118 to 1, (b) 87 to 1, and (c) 84 to 1.

The compression ratio of the same portrait picture is now twice as high. In this result, 236 contour segments are detected. Their locations are specified with 3452 bits. Profiles are coded with only 472 bits, leading to a total of 4435 bits for the entire picture. The comparison of Figs. 54 and 55 shows that even if the compression is doubled, the quality of the reconstructed pictures is not reduced noticeably.

Figs. 56 and 57 show reconstructed images using the wavelet model for edge profiles. This model requires one more parameter (σ, the extent of the wavelet) than the previous model. For roughly the same compression ratio (60 to 1 for results of Fig. 56 and 120 to 1 for those of Fig. 57), the quality appears to be slightly higher. It may, however, not be visually significant in the signal because of losses in the printing process. As before, for a compression twice as high, the quality does not decrease by the same proportion. It is obvious that very much detail is lost at high compressions.

The results obtained with the third profile model (i.e., polynomial approximations) are shown in Fig. 58. To maintain a relatively high compression averaging around 32 to 1, only first-order polynomials (line segments) are used. Higher order polynojmials require more parameters to be coded. Slightly better quality (more details) may be observed but this may well be due to a lower compression ratio.

In directional decomposition, the decoded picture is the sum of a low-pass picture and the directional images. Before computing this sum, high-frequency components may be weighted to produce more or less sharp pictures. Fig. 59 shows the result of three weights on the building image. The compression ratio is the same for all the cases (60 to 1), but the weighting factor of the high-frequency

Fig. 58. Directional decomposition-based coding results using the first-order polynomial approximation for the profiles. The compression ratios are (a) 27 to 1, (b) 23 to 1, and (c) 28 to 1.

images varies from 0.1 (Fig. 59(a)) to 0.5 (Fig. 59(c)). The best result appears to be obtained with a weight of approximately 0.5.

The last results of directional decomposition-based coding are obtained with linear prediction on directional images. Previously mentioned profile models can again be used in this context. Fig. 60 shows the results using the first-order polynomials (Fig. 60(a)) and the wavelet model (Fig. 60(b)) for the same compression ratio 60 to 1. In this

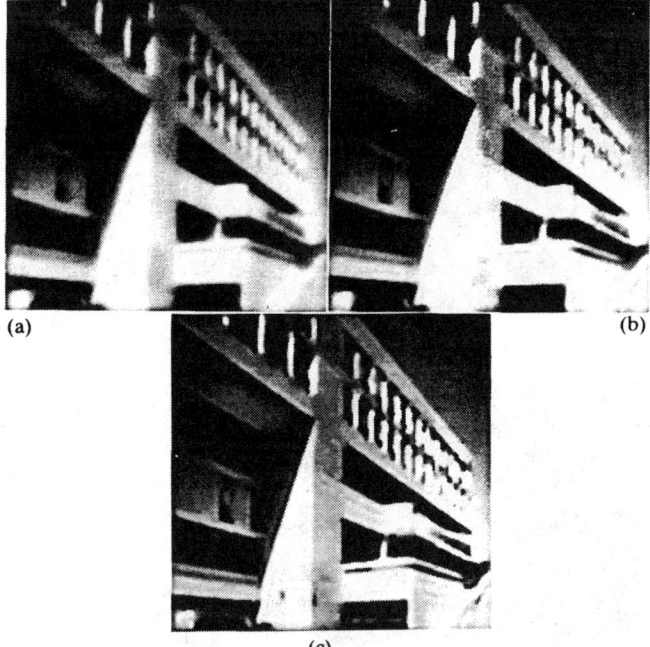

Fig. 59. Directional decomposition-based coding results with different weighting of the high-frequency component. (a) Low weight, (b) moderate weight, and (c) high weight.

Fig. 60. Linear prediction in directional images. Reconstruction using the first-order polynomial approximation of the profiles, compression ratio (a) 50 to 1 and (b) reconstruction using the wavelet model, compression ratio 70 to 1.

case, there is almost no difference between these two profile models.

B. Adaptive Split-and-Merge-Based Coding Results

For the adaptive split-and-merge-based coding method, the order of the polynomials used during the merge process is chosen *a priori* for a given type of image. For example, the building image exhibits linearly varying grey levels (first-order 2-D polynomials), whereas third-order polynomials are more appropriate for the portrait picture. The cameraman picture is reconstructed with zero-order 2-D polynomials. Segmentation result is shown next to each decoded image.

The first series of results are obtained with low compression ratios and are thus of high quality (Fig. 61). For example, the building picture in this figure is segmented into 99 regions whose borders are described by 8968 contour points. The data over each region is approximated by a first-order 2-D polynomial, leading to a compression

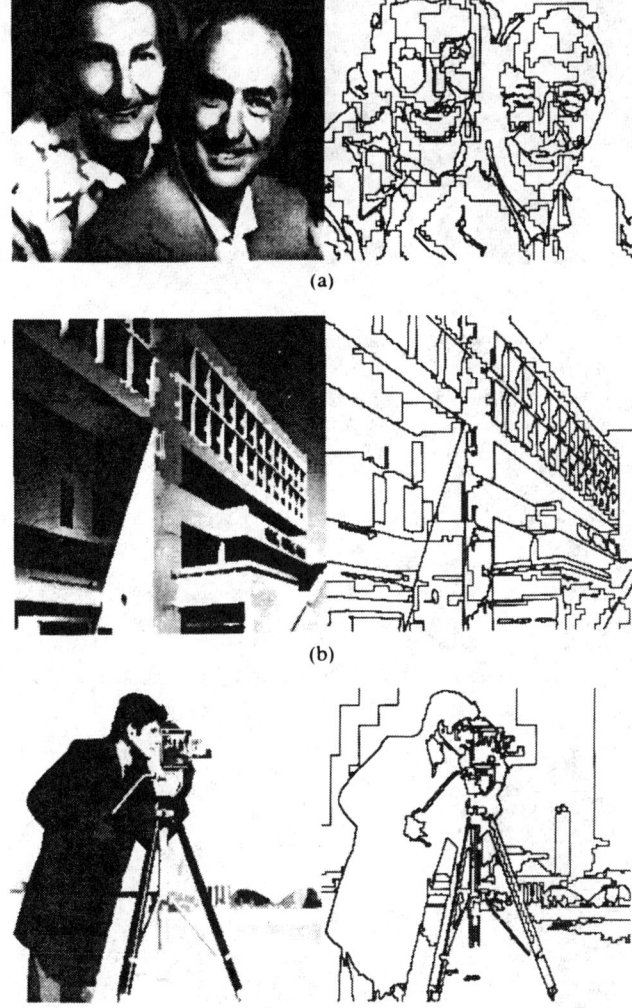

Fig. 61. Adaptive split-and-merge-based coding results. Each image is segmented into 99 regions. The compression ratios are (a) 28 to 1 with third-order polynomials, (b) 38 to 1 with first-order polynomials and (c) 54 to 1 with zero-order polynomials.

ratio of 38 to 1. For the same number of regions, third-order 2-D polynomials yield a compression of 28 to 1 for the portrait picture.

In this method, the key factor controlling compression is the number of regions after segmentation. For the same building picture, if this number is reduced from 99 to 49, the compression ratio increases to 53 to 1 with a corresponding quality shown in Fig. 62. The cameraman picture in this figure is also segmented into 49 regions, but its compression ratio is 68 to 1 using zero-order polynomials. The average compression ratio of this second series of results is 55 to 1.

Fig. 63 shows the third series of results with an average compression ratio of 84 to 1 and 24 regions. These results have not been post-processed to attenuate the visibility of artifacts.

As one would suspect, for equal numbers of regions, higher compression ratios are obtained with lower order polynomials because the number of coefficients is reduced. Currently, we are investigating the possibility of using

Fig. 62. Adaptive split-and-merge-based coding results. Each image is segmented into 49 regions. The compression ratios are (a) 42 to 1 with third-order polynomials, (b) 53 to 1 with first-order polynomials and (c) 68 to 1 with zero-order polynomials.

Fig. 63. Adaptive split-and-merge-based coding results. Each image is segmented into 24 regions except the cameraman picture segmented into 15 regions. The compression ratios are (a) 58 to 1 with third-order polynomials, (b) 76 to 1 with first-order polynomials and (c) 118 to 1 with zero-order polynomials.

variable-order polynomials within the same image, choosing the best approximation over each region.

Comparison of these results with those of directional decomposition-based coding shows that even if the loss of detail is considerable, adaptive split-and-merge-based coding leads to very sharp images, perhaps because region borders also separate different polynomial descriptions of the regions.

As a last series of results, the role of the polynomial's order on the quality of the reconstructed images (for all the other parameters fixed) is shown. These results are displayed in Fig. 64 for the portrait picture, for an average compression ratio of 55 to 1 and without post-processing. As the image contains many curves, the quality obtained with zero-order polynomials is the lowest (Fig. 64(a)). Disturbing false contours appear at the junction of planes in the first-order approximation case (Fig. 64(b)). They may be attenuated by post-filtering at the price of other undesirable outcomes. The best results are obtained with second- and third-order polynomials. To maintain the same compression ratio, the number of regions was reduced for the third-order polynomial computation because more coefficients need to be coded. There still are several false contours but they are less disturbing. Notice, for example, that the chin of the lady is reconstructed within one region with a third-order polynomial (Fig. 64(d)). In some other areas of the picture, lower order polynomials give better results (such as planes on the clothing). For this reason, we are currently investigating an improvement of the technique for selecting the best polynomial for a given region.

VI. Conclusions

In this paper, a brief overview is first given of the "second generation" image coding techniques developed in the early eighties, namely directional decomposition-based coding and segmentation-based coding. These methods attempt to reach high compression using a general

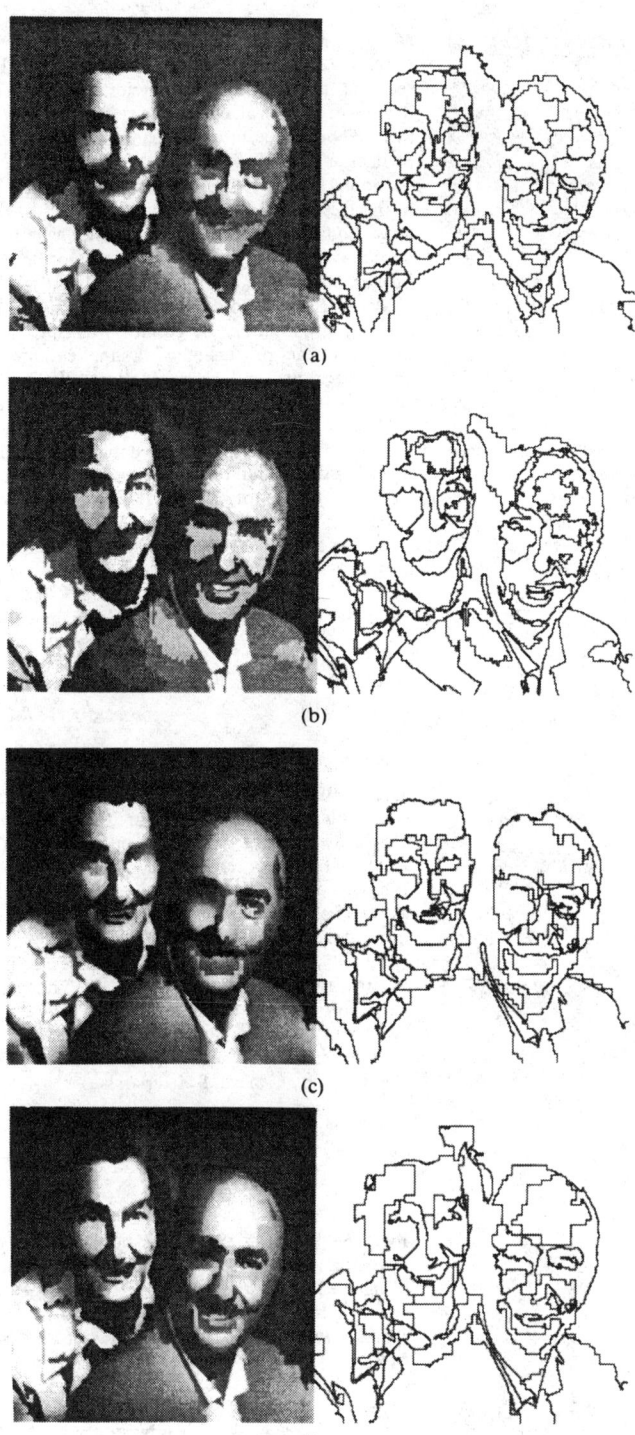

Fig. 64. Adaptive split-and-merge-based coding results. Effect of the polynomial's order on the quality of the reconstructed image. (a) Zero-order polynomials over 39 regions with 7145 contour points and with a compression ratio of 56 to 1. (b) First-order polynomials over 59 regions with 5956 contour points and with a compression ratio of 59 to 1. (c) Second-order polynomials over 39 regions with 5962 contour points and with a compression ratio of 55 to 1. (d) Third-order polynomials over 29 regions with 5563 contour points and with a compression ratio of 56 to 1.

contour-texture model for still pictures. The first technique aims at the contours and at their location directly, whereas the second obtains the contours indirectly, as a result of segmentation. The weak points of the earlier versions of these methods are discussed.

Improvements in these methods are then presented in detail. Directional filters have been improved by introducing two separate attenuations, one for the directional selectivity and another for the low-pass/high-pass selection. Zero-crossing search is simplified by discarding forward-backward rotations which were implemented with interpolation and resampling. Computational errors involved in these procedures were thus eliminated. Precision in zero-crossing location and extraction of edge-point candidates were improved. The importance of edge profiles was measured with a more robust technique using the energy of the profile rather than the slope of a badly defined transition. Three models were used and compared to approximate edge profiles. The efficiency of high-frequency component coding is thus considerably improved. A new avenue is investigated in predicting directional images, exploiting the correlation between two adjacent directional images. For slowly varying data, prediction-based coding seems to provide rather high compressions. As used in our work, prediction elements are those of the directional decomposition-based coding. Other, perhaps more appropriate, elements may also be found and used.

Segmentation-based coding using region growing was the first attempt for high compression. It is, however, limited due to a very simple property used in region growing: the constant grey-level interval. When region growing uses a more refined property, its implementation tends to become too cumbersome. For this reason, still keeping the idea of segmentation, we replaced region growing by the adaptive split-and-merge procedure. It allows us to use polynomials of any order to approximate image data over large regions of any shape, thus decreasing the number of regions and of messages to be coded. This segmentation procedure comes close to the ultimate goal, i.e., to obtain regions corresponding to the real objects of the scene. The quality of reconstructed pictures also appears to be much higher. As a by-product, adaptive split-and-merge produces compact symbols for scene analysis as well.

ACKNOWLEDGMENT

The authors are grateful to Prof. M. Eden for the numerous suggestions he made to improve this paper.

REFERENCES

[1] A. N. Netravali and J. O. Limb, "Picture coding: A review," *Proc. IEEE*, vol. 63, pp. 366–406, Mar. 1980.
[2] A. K. Jain, "Image data compression: A review," *Proc. IEEE*, vol. 69, pp. 349–389, Mar. 1981.
[3] M. Kunt, "Image coding" in *Fundamentals of Computer Vision*, O. D. Faugeras, Ed. London: Cambridge University Press, 1983.
[4] M. Kunt, A. Ikonomopoulos, and M. Kocher, "Second generation image coding techniques," *Proc. IEEE*, vol. 73, pp. 549–574, Apr. 1985.
[5] P. J. Burt and E. H. Adelson, "The Laplacian pyramid as a compact image code," *IEEE Trans. Commun.*, vol. COM-31, pp. 532–540, Apr. 1983.
[6] R. Wilson, H. E. Knutsson, and G. H. Granlund, "Anisotropic nonstationary image estimation and its applications: Part II—Predictive image coding," *IEEE Trans. Commun.*, vol. COM-31, pp. 398–406, Mar. 1983.
[7] H. E. Knutsson, R. Wilson, and G. H. Granlund, "Anisotropic nonstationary image estimation and its applications: Part

I—Restoration of noisy images," *IEEE Trans. Commun.*, vol. COM-31, pp. 388–397, Mar. 1983.
[8] M. Kunt, "Edge detection: A tutorial review," in *Proc. ICASSP'82* (Paris), May 3–5, 1982, pp. 1172–1175.
[9] S. Carlsson, "Image reconstruction from coded edge data," in *Proc. Premier Colloque Image* (Biarritz, France), June 1984, pp. 71–77.
[10] S. Carlsson, "Sketch based representations in image coding," Ph.D. thesis, Dept. Elec. Eng., Royal Institute of Technology, Stockholm, Sweden, Dec. 1986.
[11] A. Ikonomopoulos and M. Kunt, "High compression image coding via directional filtering," *Signal Processing*, vol. 8, no. 2, pp. 179–203, Apr. 1985.
[12] M. Kocher and M. Kunt, "Image data compression by contour-texture modelling," in *Proc. SPIE Int. Conf. on the Applications of Digital Image Processing* (Geneva), Apr. 1983, pp. 131–139.
[13] W. F. Schreiber, C. F. Knapp, and D. Kay, "Synthetic highs: An experimental TV bandwidth reduction system," *J. SMPTE*, vol. 68, pp. 525–537, Aug. 1959.
[14] D. N. Graham, "Image transmission by two-dimensional contour coding," *Proc. IEEE*, vol. 55, pp. 336–346, Mar. 1967.
[15] S. Kuffler and J. Nicholls, *From Neuron to Brain*. Sunderland MA: Sinauer Associates, 1976.
[16] M. Benard and M. Kunt, "Directional decomposition image transformation," presented at IASTED Int. Symp. on Applied Signal Processing and Digital Filtering, Paris, France, June 19–21, 1985.
[17] H. Marmolin, "Subjective MSE measures," *IEEE Trans. Systems, Man Cyber.*, vol,. SMC-16, no. 3, pp. 486–489, May/June 1986.
[18] M. Benard and M. Kunt, "Improvements of directional decomposition based image coding," in *Image Coding*, M. Kunt and T. S. Huang, Eds. *SPIE*, vol. 594, pp. 142–150.
[19] R. Cusani, "New results in directional decomposition based image coding," in *Image Coding*, M. Kunt and T. S. Huang, Eds. *SPIE*, vol. 594, pp. 130–138.
[20] M. Benard and M. Kunt, "Linear prediction in directional images," in *Proc. EUSIPCO-86*, pp. 805–808.
[21] E. M. Riseman and M. A. Arbib, "Survey: Computational techniques in the visual segmentation of static scenes," *Computer Graphics and Image Processing*, vol. 6, pp. 221–276, 1977.
[22] M. Hueckel "An operator which locates edges in digital pictures," *J. ACM*, vol. 18, no. 1, pp. 113–125, Jan. 1971.
[23] R. M. Haralick, "Digital step edges from zero crossing of second directional derivatives," *IEEE Trans. Pattern Anal. Machine Intell.*, vol. 6, pp. 58–68, Jan. 1984.
[24] D. C. Marr and E. C. Hildreth, "Theory of edge detection," *Proc. Roy. Soc. London B*, vol. 207, pp. 187–217, 1980.
[25] V. Torre and T. A. Poggio, "On edge detection," *IEEE Trans. Pattern Anal. Machine Intell.*, vol. PAMI-8, no. 2, pp. 147–163, Mar. 1986.
[26] J. F. Canny, "Finding edges and lines in images," M.I.T. Artificial Intelligence Laboratory, Rep. AI-TR-720, 1983.
[27] P. J. Davis, *Interpolation and Approximation*. Blaisdell Publishing Company, 1963.
[28] M. J. D. Powell, *Approximation Theory and Methods*. London: Cambridge University Press, 1981.
[29] R. Leonardi, "Segmentation adaptative pour analyse et codage d'images à haute performance," Ph.D. thesis, Dept. Elec. Eng., Swiss Federal Institute of Technology, Lausanne, Switzerland, 1987.
[30] M. Eden, M. Unser, and R. Leonardi, "Polynomial representation of pictures," *Signal Processing*, vol. 10, no. 4, pp. 385–393, 1986.
[31] R. Leonardi and M. Kunt, "Adaptive split for image coding," in *Proc. IASTED Int. Symp. on Applied Signal Processing and Digital Filtering* (Paris), June 19–21, 1985.
[32] Y. Cohen, M. S. Landy, and M. Pavel, "Hierarchical coding of binary images,". *IEEE Trans. Pattern Anal. Machine Intell.*, vol. PAMI-7, no. 3, pp. 283–298, May 1985.
[33] M. Kocher, "Codage d'images à haute compression basé sur un modèle contour-texture," Ph.D. thesis No. 476, Dept. Elec. Eng., Swiss Federal Institute of Technology, Lausanne, Switzerland, 1983.
[34] M. Kocher and R. Leonardi, "Adaptive region growing technique using polynomial functions for image approximation," *Signal Processing*, vol. 11, no. 1, pp. 47–60, July 1986.
[35] T. Pavlidis, *Structural Pattern Recognition*. Berlin: Springer, 1977.
[36] M. Eden and M. Kocher, "On the performance of a contour coding algorithm in the context of image coding-Part II: Coding a contour graph," *Signal Processing*, to be published.

Murat Kunt (S'69–M'74–SM'78–F'86) was born in Ankara, Turkey, on January 16, 1945. He received the M.S. degree in physics and the Ph.D. degree in electrical engineering, both from the Swiss Federal Institute of Technology, Lausanne, Switzerland, in 1969 and 1974, respectively.

From 1974 to 1976 he was a visiting scientist at the Research Laboratory of Electronics of the Massachusetts Institute of Technology, where he developed compression techniques for X-ray images and electronic image files. In 1976, he returned to the Swiss Federal Institute of Technology where he is presently Professor of Electrical Engineering. He conducts teaching and research in digital signal and image processing with applications to modeling, coding, pattern recognition, and scene analysis. He is the author or the co-author of more than sixty research papers and eleven books. He is the Editor-in-Chief of the journal *Signal Processing* and is a founding member of EURASIP, the European Association for Signal Processing. He serves on the scientific committees of several international conferences and on the editorial boards of *Pattern Recognition Letters* and *Traitement du Signal*. He was the Cochairman of the first European Signal Processing Conference, which was held in Lausanne in September 1980. He is the President of the Swiss Association for Pattern Recognition.

In 1983, Dr. Kunt received the gold medal of EURASIP for meritorious services.

✠

Michel Bénard (M'84) graduated in 1980 from the Ecole Nationale Supérieure des Télécommunications, Paris, France, and received the Docteur-Ingénieur degree in signal processing in 1983 from the same school. For his thesis, he worked in the Remote Sensing Laboratory of the Ecole des Mines.

In 1984, he worked as a development engineer at IBM, La Gaude. From 1985 to 1987, he was a research engineer in the Signal Processing Laboratory of the Swiss Federal Institute of Technology, Lausanne, where his interest was image coding. He is presently with Apollo Computer Inc., Geneva, Switzerland.

✠

Riccardo Leonardi (S'87) was born in Geneva, Switzerland, in 1962. He received the "Diplôme d'Ingénieur Electricien EPF" from the Swiss Federal Institute of Technology at Lausanne (EPFL), in 1984. He spent one year at Carnegie Mellon University, Pittsburgh, PA, as an exchange student in Electrical Engineering between 1981 and 1982.

In 1985, he made a feasibility study on the visual authentification of signatures for the Swiss industry. He is presently employed at the Signal Processing Laboratory of the EPFL as a teaching and research assistant, where he obtained the Ph.D. degree in June 1987 on image segmentation. His research interests include digital image processing (image coding and scene analysis), pattern recognition, and artificial intelligence.

He is author and coauthor of three scientific publications. He is a member of EURASIP.

Vector Quantization

Robert M. Gray

A vector quantizer is a system for mapping a sequence of continuous or discrete vectors into a digital sequence suitable for communication over or storage in a digital channel. The goal of such a system is data compression: to reduce the bit rate so as to minimize communication channel capacity or digital storage memory requirements while maintaining the necessary fidelity of the data. The mapping for each vector may or may not have memory in the sense of depending on past actions of the coder, just as in well established scalar techniques such as PCM, which has no memory, and predictive quantization, which does. Even though information theory implies that one can always obtain better performance by coding vectors instead of scalars, scalar quantizers have remained by far the most common data compression system because of their simplicity and good performance when the communication rate is sufficiently large. In addition, relatively few design techniques have existed for vector quantizers.

During the past few years several design algorithms have been developed for a variety of vector quantizers and the performance of these codes has been studied for speech waveforms, speech linear predictive parameter vectors, images, and several simulated random processes. It is the purpose of this article to survey some of these design techniques and their applications.

DATA compression is the conversion of a stream of analog or very high rate discrete data into a stream of relatively low rate data for communication over a digital communication link or storage in a digital memory. As digital communication and secure communication have become increasingly important, the theory and practice of data compression have received increased attention. While it is true that in many systems bandwidth is relatively inexpensive, e.g., fiber optic and cable TV links, in most systems the growing amount of information that users wish to communicate or store necessitates some form of compression for efficient, secure, and reliable use of the communication or storage medium.

A prime example arises with image data, where simple schemes require bit rates too large for many communication links or storage devices. Another example where compression is required results from the fact that if speech is digitized using a simple PCM system consisting of a sampler followed by scalar quantization, the resulting signal will no longer have a small enough bandwidth to fit on ordinary telephone channels. That is, digitization (which may be desirable for security or reliability) causes bandwidth expansion. Hence data compression will be required if the original communication channel is to be used.

The two examples of image compression and speech compression or, as they are often called, image coding and speech coding, are probably the currently most important applications of data compression. They are also among the most interesting for study because experience has shown that both types of data exhibit sufficient structure to permit considerable compression with sufficiently sophisticated codes.

Such conversion of relatively high rate data to lower rate data virtually always entails a loss of fidelity or an increase in distortion. Hence a fundamental goal of data compression is to obtain the best possible fidelity for the given rate or, equivalently, to minimize the rate required for a given fidelity. If a system has a sufficiently high rate constraint, then good fidelity is relatively easy to achieve and techniques such as PCM, transform coding, predictive coding, and adaptive versions of these techniques have become quite popular because of their simplicity and good performance [1, 2, 3]. All of these techniques share a fundamental property: The actual quantization or coding or conversion of continuous quantities into discrete quantities is done on scalars, e.g., on individual real-valued samples of waveforms or pixels of images. PCM does this in a memoryless fashion; that is, each successive input is encoded using a rule that does not depend on any past inputs or outputs of the encoder. Transform coding does it by first taking block transforms of a vector and then scalar coding the coordinates of the transformed vector. Predictive coding does it by quantizing an error term formed as the difference between the new sample and a prediction of the new sample based on past coded outputs.

A fundamental result of Shannon's rate-distortion theory, the branch of information theory devoted to data compression, is that better performance can always be achieved by coding vectors instead of scalars, even if the data source is memoryless, e.g., consists of a sequence of independent random variables, or if the data compression system can have memory, i.e., the action of an encoder at each time is permitted to depend on past encoder inputs or outputs [4, 5, 6, 7, 8]. While some traditional compression schemes such as transform coding operate on vectors and achieve significant improvement over PCM, the quantization is still accomplished on scalars and hence these systems are, in a Shannon sense, inherently suboptimal: better performance is always achievable *in theory* by coding vectors instead of scalars, even if the scalars have been produced by preprocessing the original input data so as to make them uncorrelated or independent!

This theory had a limited impact on actual system design because 1) the Shannon theory does not provide constructive design techniques for vector coders, and 2) traditional scalar coders often yield satisfactory performance with enough adaptation and fine tuning. As a result, few design techniques for vector quantizers were considered in the literature prior to the late 1970's when it was found that a simple algorithm of Lloyd [9] for the iterative design of scalar quantization or PCM systems extended in a straightforward way to the design of memoryless vector quantizers, that is, of vector quantizers which encode successive input vectors in a manner not depending on previous encoder input vectors or their coded outputs. Variations of the basic algorithm have since proved useful for the design of vector quantizers with and without memory for a variety of data sources including speech waveforms, speech parameter vectors, images, and several random process models, the latter being useful for gauging the performance of the resulting codes with the optimal performance bounds of information theory.

This paper is intended as a survey of the basic design algorithm and many of its variations and applications. We begin with the simplest example of a memoryless vector quantizer, a vector generalization of PCM. For convenience we use the shorthand VQ for both vector quantization and vector quantizer. Necessary properties of optimal quantizers are described and an algorithm given which uses these properties to iteratively improve a code. For concreteness, we focus on two examples of distortion measures: the ubiquitous mean-squared error and the Itakura-Saito distortion. The first example, which is popular in waveform coding applications, provides a geometric flavor to the development; the second example, which is useful in voice coding applications, helps to demonstrate the generality and power of the technique.

Next, various techniques are described for designing the initial codes required by the algorithm. These techniques also indicate some useful structure that can be imposed on vector quantizers to make them more implementable. Several variations of the basic VQ are described which permit reduced complexity or memory or both at the expense of a hopefully tolerable loss of performance. These include tree-searched codes, product codes, and multistep codes.

We then turn from memoryless vector quantizers to those with memory: feedback vector quantizers such as vector predictive quantizers and finite-state vector quantizers. These codes are not yet well understood, but they possess a structure highly suited to VLSI implementation and initial studies suggest that they offer significant performance gains.

For comparison, we also briefly describe trellis encoding systems or "lookahead" or "delayed decision" or "multipath search" codes which use the same decoder as a feedback vector quantizer but which permit the encoder to base its decision on a longer input data sequence.

A final general code structure is described which uses vector quantization to adapt a waveform coder, which may be another VQ.

We next present a variety of simulation results describing the performance of various VQ systems on various data sources. Examples of all of the above VQ varieties are tested for waveform coding applications on two common data sources: a Gauss Markov source and real sampled speech. One bit per sample coders for these sources are compared on the basis of performance, memory requirements, and computational complexity. Both memoryless and simple feedback vector quantizers are studied for voice coding applications at a rate of 0.062 bits/sample and less and for image coding at a rate of 0.5 bit per sample. One example is given of a simple adaptive predictive vector quantizer for speech waveform coding.

By studying a variety of coding systems on common data sources, the results yield some general comparisons and trends among the various vector quantization techniques. The reader should, however, keep two caveats in mind when interpreting such quantitative results: First, the emphasis here is on low bit rate systems, e.g., speech coders using 1 bit per sample or less and image coders ½ bit per pixel. Comparisons favoring certain systems at such low rates may not be valid for the same systems at higher rates. Second, the numbers reported here are intended to provide comparisons for different systems used on common data sources; they can be compared with other numbers reported in the literature only with great care: the input data and the system design parameters such as sampling rate and pre- or post-filtering may be quite different.

Applications of vector quantization to real data sources such as sampled speech waveforms and images are still young and the algorithms do not yet incorporate the sophisticated "bells and whistles" of many well-established scalar quantization schemes. The preliminary experiments described here, using fairly simple vector quantizers with and without memory, demonstrate that the general approach holds considerable promise for some applications. For example, good quality vocoding systems using VQ and the Itakura-Saito distortion have been developed at 800 bits per second, a significant reduction in the bit rate previously required for comparable quality [10]. While the compression achieved so far in waveform coding and image coding applications using the squared-error distortion has not yet been as significant, we believe that it has yielded comparable or better performance at low rates than traditional scalar schemes of greater complexity. The quality of the ½ bit per pixel images shown here is promising given the simplicity of the coding scheme used.

We attempt to use the minimum of mathematics and a maximum of English in the presentation so as to focus on the intuitive ideas underlying the design and operation of vector quantizers. The detailed descriptions of the various algorithms can be found in the cited references. The reader is also referred to a recent tutorial by Gersho and Cuperman [11] which presents a brief overview of VQ applied to speech waveform coding.

MEMORYLESS VECTOR QUANTIZERS

In this section we introduce the basic definition of memoryless vector quantizers, their properties, and an algorithm for their design.

Quantization

Mathematically, a k-dimensional memoryless vector quantizer or, simply, a VQ (without modifying adjectives) consists of two mappings: an encoder γ which assigns to each input vector $\mathbf{x} = (x_0, x_1, \cdots, x_{k-1})$ a channel symbol $\gamma(\mathbf{x})$ in some channel symbol set $\mathbf{M}$, and a decoder β assigning to each channel symbol v in $\mathbf{M}$ a value in a reproduction alphabet $\hat{\mathbf{A}}$. The channel symbol set is often assumed to be a space of binary vectors for convenience, e.g., $\mathbf{M}$ may be the set of all 2^R binary R-dimensional vectors. The reproduction alphabet may or may not be the same as the input vector space; in particular, it may consist of real vectors of a different dimension.

If $\mathbf{M}$ has M elements, then the quantity $R = \log_2 M$ is called the *rate* of the quantizer in bits per vector and $r = R/k$ is the rate in bits per symbol or, when the input is a sampled waveform, bits per sample.

The application of a quantizer to data compression is depicted in the standard Fig. 1. The input data vectors might be consecutive samples of a waveform, consecutive parameter vectors in a voice coding system, or consecutive rasters or subrasters in an image coding system. For integer values of R it is useful to think of the channel symbols, the encoded input vectors, as binary R-dimensional vectors. As is commonly done in information and communication theory, we assume that the channel is noiseless, that is, that $U_n = \hat{U}_n$. While real channels are rarely noiseless, the joint source and channel coding theorem of information theory implies that a good data compression system designed for a noiseless channel can be combined with a good error correction coding system for a noisy channel in order to produce a complete system. In other words, the assumption of a noiseless channel is made simply to focus on the problem of data compression system design and not to reflect any practical model.

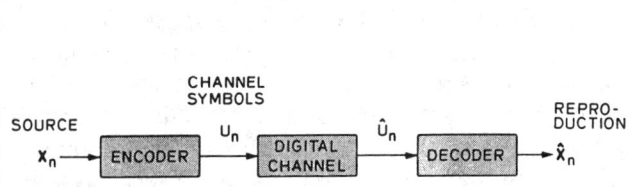

Figure 1. Data Compression System. The data or information source $\{X_n; n = 0, 1, \ldots\}$ is a sequence of random vectors. The encoder produces a sequence of channel symbols $\{U_n; n = 0, 1, 2, \ldots\}$. The sequence $\{\hat{U}_n; n = 0, 1, 2, \ldots\}$ is delivered to the receiver by the digital channel. The decoder then maps this sequence into the final reproduction sequence of vectors $\{\hat{X}_n; n = 0, 1, 2, \ldots\}$.

Observe that unlike scalar quantization, general VQ permits fractional rates in bits per sample. For example, scalar PCM must have a bit rate of at least 1 bit per sample while a k dimensional VQ can have a bit rate of only $1/k$ bits per sample by having only a single binary channel symbol for k-dimensional input vectors.

The goal of such a quantization system is to produce the "best" possible reproduction sequence for a given rate R. To quantify this idea, to define the performance of a quantizer, and to complete the definition of a quantizer, we require the idea of a distortion measure.

Distortion

A distortion measure d is an assignment of a cost $d(\mathbf{x}, \hat{\mathbf{x}})$ of reproducing any input vector $\mathbf{x}$ as a reproduction vector $\hat{\mathbf{x}}$. Given such a distortion measure, we can quantify the performance of a system by an average distortion $Ed(\mathbf{X}, \hat{\mathbf{X}})$ between the input and the final reproduction: A system will be good if it yields a small average distortion. In practice, the important average is the long term sample average or time average

$$\lim_{n \to \infty} \frac{1}{n} \sum_{i=0}^{n-1} d(\mathbf{X}_i, \hat{\mathbf{X}}_i) \tag{1}$$

provided, of course, that the limit makes sense. If the vector process is stationary and ergodic, then, with probability one, the limit exists and equals an expectation $E(d(\mathbf{X}, \hat{\mathbf{X}}))$. For the moment we will assume that such conditions are met and that such long term sample averages are given by expectations. Later remarks will focus on the general assumptions required and their implications for practice.

Ideally a distortion measure should be tractable to permit analysis, computable so that it can be evaluated in real time and used in minimum distortion systems, and subjectively meaningful so that large or small quantitative distortion measures correlate with bad and good subjective quality. Here we do not consider the difficult and controversial issues of selecting a distortion measure; we assume that one has been selected and consider means of designing systems which yield small average distortion. For simplicity and to ease exposition, we focus on two important specific examples:

(1) *The squared error distortion measure:* Here the input and reproduction spaces are k-dimensional Euclidean space

$$d(\mathbf{x}, \hat{\mathbf{x}}) = \|\mathbf{x} - \hat{\mathbf{x}}\|^2 = \sum_{i=0}^{k-1} (x_i - \hat{x}_i)^2,$$

the square of the Euclidean distance between the vectors. This is the simplest distortion measure and the most common for waveform coding. While not subjectively meaningful in many cases, generalizations permitting input-dependent weightings have proved useful and only slightly more complicated. For the squared-error distortion it is common practice to measure the performance of a system by the signal-to-noise ratio (or signal-to-quantization-noise ratio)

$$SNR = 10 \log_{10} \frac{E(\|X\|^2)}{E[d(X, \hat{X})]}.$$

This corresponds to normalizing the average distortion by the average energy and plotting it on a logarithmic scale: Large (small) SNR corresponds to small (large) average distortion.

(2) *The (modified) Itakura-Saito distortion:* This distortion measure is useful in voice coding applications where the receiver is sent a linear model of the underlying voice production process. The distortion measure is based on the "error matching measure" developed in the pioneering work of Itakura and Saito on the PARCOR or LPC approach to voice coding [12]. More generally, this distortion measure is a special case of a minimum relative entropy or discrimination measure; VQ using such distortion measures can be viewed as an application of the minimum relative entropy pattern classification technique introduced by Kullback [13] as an application of information theory to statistical pattern classification. (See also [14, 15].)

We here introduce a minimum of notation to present a definition of the Itakura-Saito distortion measure. Details and generalizations may be found in [16, 17, 14, 15]. Here the input vector can again be considered as a collection of consecutive waveform samples. Now, however, the output vectors have the form $\hat{x} = (\alpha, a_1, a_2, \cdots, a_p)$, where α is a positive gain or residual energy term and where the a_i with $a_0 = 1$ are inverse filter coefficients in the sense that if

$$A(z) = \sum_{i=0}^{p} a_i z^{-i}$$

then the all-pole filter with z-transform $1/A(z)$ is a stable filter. Here the reproduction vectors may be thought of as all-pole models for synthesizing the reproduction at the receiver using a locally generated noise or periodic source, in other words, as the filter portion of a linear predictive coding (LPC) model in a vocoding (voice coding) system. The Itakura-Saito distortion between the input vector and the model can be defined in the time domain as

$$d(\mathbf{x}, \hat{\mathbf{x}}) = \frac{\mathbf{a}^t R(\mathbf{x}) \mathbf{a}}{\alpha} - \ln \frac{\alpha_p(\mathbf{x})}{\alpha} - 1,$$

where $\mathbf{a}^t = (1, a_1, \cdots, a_p)$, $R(\mathbf{x})$ is the $(p + 1) \times (p + 1)$ sample autocorrelation matrix of the input vector $\mathbf{x}$, and where $\alpha_p(\mathbf{x})$ is an input gain (residual energy) term defined as the minimum value of $\mathbf{b}^t R(\mathbf{x}) \mathbf{b}$, where the minimum is taken over all vectors $\mathbf{b}$ with first component equal to 1. There are many equivalent forms of the distortion measure, some useful for theory and some for computation. Frequency domain forms show that minimizing the above distortion can be interpreted as trying to match the sample spectrum of the input vector to the power spectral density of the linear all-pole model formed by driving the filter with z-transform $1/A(z)$ by white noise with constant power spectral density $\sqrt{\alpha}$.

The above formula for the distortion is one of the simplest, yet it demonstrates that the distortion measure is indeed complicated—it is not a simple function of an error vector, it is not symmetric in its input and output arguments, and it is not a metric or distance. Because of the intimate connection of this distortion measure with LPC vocoding techniques, we will refer to VQ's designed using this distortion measure as LPC VQ's.

Average distortion

As the average distortion quantifies the performance of a system and since we will be trying to minimize this quantity using good codes, we pause to consider what the average means in theory and in practice.

As previously noted, in practice it is the long term sample average of (1) that we actually measure and which we would like to be small. If the process is stationary and ergodic, then this limiting time average is the same as the mathematical expectation. The mathematical expectation is useful for developing information theoretic performance bounds, but it is often impossible to calculate in practice because the required probability distributions are not known, e.g., there are no noncontroversial generally accepted accurate probability distributions for real speech and image data. Hence a pragmatic approach to system design is to take long sequences of training data, estimate the "true" but unknown expected distortion by the sample average, and attempt to design a code that minimizes the sample average distortion for the training sequence. If the input source is indeed stationary and ergodic, the resulting sample average should be nearly the expected value and the same code used on future data should yield approximately the same averages [18].

The above motivates a training sequence based design for stationary and ergodic data sources. In fact, even if the "true" probability distributions are known as in the case of a Gauss Markov source, the training sequence approach reduces to a standard Monte Carlo approach.

An immediate objection to the above approach, however, is whether or not it makes sense for real sources which may be neither stationary nor ergodic. The answer is an emphatic "yes" in the following sense: The desired property is that if we design a code based on a *sufficiently long* training sequence and then use the code on future data produced by the same source, then the performance of the code on the new data should be roughly that achieved on the training data. The theoretical issue is to provide conditions under which this statement can be made rigorous. For reasonable distortion measures, a sufficient condition for this to be true for memoryless VQ design is that the source be asymptotically mean stationary, it need not be either stationary nor ergodic [19, 20, 21, 22, 23]. Asymptotically mean stationary sources include all stationary sources, block (or cyclo) stationary sources, and asymptotically stationary sources. Processes such as speech which exhibit distinct short term and long term stationarity properties are well modeled by asymptotically mean stationary sources [21].

The key point here is that the general design approach using long training sequences does not require either ergodicity nor stationarity to have a solid mathematical foundation. In fact, the mathematics suggest the following pragmatic approach: Try to design a code which minimizes the sample average distortion for a very long training sequence. Then use the code on test sequences produced by the same source, but not in the training sequence. If the performance is reasonably close to the design values, then one can have a certain amount of confidence that the code will continue to yield roughly the same performance in the future. If the training and test performance are significantly different, then probably the training sequence is not sufficiently long. In other words, do not try to prove mathematically that a source is asymptotically mean stationary, instead try to design codes for it and then see if they work on new data.

Henceforth for brevity we will write expectations with the assumption that they are to be interpreted as shorthand for long term sample averages. (A sample average $L^{-1} \sum_{i=0}^{L-1} d(\mathbf{X}_i, \hat{\mathbf{X}}_i)$ is, in fact, an expectation with respect to the sample distribution which assigns a probability of $1/L$ to each vector in the training sequence.)

Properties of optimal quantizers

A VQ is optimal if it minimizes an average distortion $Ed\{\mathbf{X}, \beta[\gamma(\mathbf{X})]\}$. Two necessary conditions for a VQ to be optimal follow easily using the same logic as in Lloyd's [9]

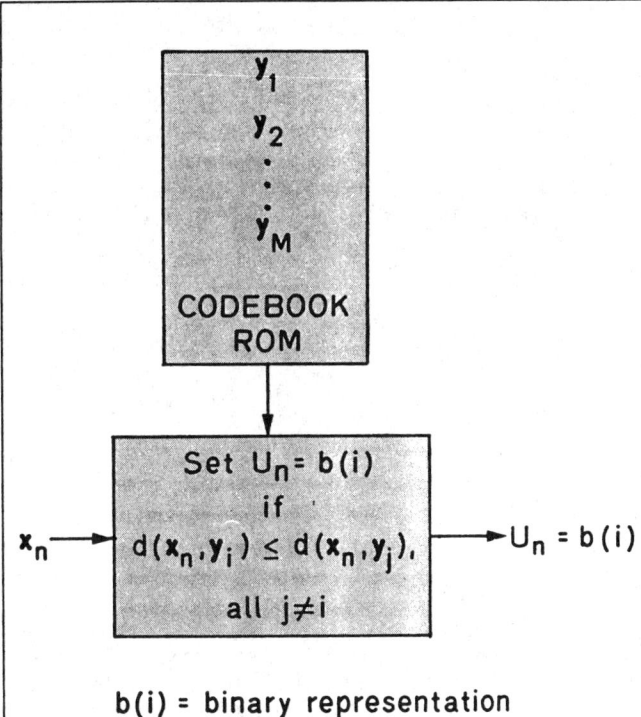

Figure 2. VQ Encoder. The distortion between the input vector and each stored codeword is computed. The encoded output is then the binary representation of the index of the minimum distortion codeword.

classical development for optimal PCM with a mean-squared error distortion measure. The following definition is useful for stating these properties: The collection of possible reproduction vectors $C = \{\text{all } \mathbf{y} : \mathbf{y} = \beta(v)$, some v in $\mathbf{M}\}$ is called the *reproduction codebook* or, simply, *codebook* of the quantizer and its members called *codewords* (or templates). The encoder knows the structure of the decoder and hence all of the possible final output codewords.

Property 1: Given the goal of minimizing the average distortion and given a specific decoder β, no memoryless quantizer encoder can do better than select the codeword v in $\mathbf{M}$ that will yield the minimum possible distortion at the output, that is, to select the channel symbol v yielding the minimum

$$d\{\mathbf{x}, \beta[\gamma(\mathbf{x})]\} = \min_{v \in M} d[\mathbf{x}, \beta(v)] = \min_{y \in C} d(\mathbf{x}, \mathbf{y}). \quad (2)$$

That is, for a given decoder in a memoryless vector quantizer the best encoder is a minimum distortion or nearest neighbor mapping

$$\gamma(\mathbf{x}) = \min_{v \in M}{}^{-1} d[\mathbf{x}, \beta(v)], \quad (3)$$

where the inverse minimum notation means that we select the v giving the minimum of (2).

Gersho [24] calls a quantizer with a minimum distortion encoder a Voronoi quantizer since the Voronoi regions about a set of points in a space correspond to a partition of that space according to the nearest-neighbor rule. The word quantizer, however, is practically always associated with such a minimum distortion mapping. We observe that such a vector quantizer with such a minimum distortion encoder is exactly the Shannon model for a block source code subject to a fidelity criterion which is used in information theory to develop optimal performance bounds for data compression systems.

An encoder γ can be thought of as a partition of the input space into cells where all input vectors yielding a common reproduction are grouped together. Such a partition according to a minimum distortion rule is called a Voronoi or Dirichlet partition. A general minimum distance VQ encoder is depicted in Fig. 2.

A simple example of such a partition and hence of an encoder is depicted in Fig. 3 (a more interesting example follows shortly). Observe that this vector quantizer is just two uses of a scalar quantizer in disguise.

As the minimum distortion rule optimizes the encoder of a memoryless VQ for a decoder, we can also optimize the decoder for a given encoder.

Property 2: Given an encoder γ, then no decoder can do better than that which assigns to each channel symbol v the generalized centroid (or center of gravity or barycenter) of all source vectors encoded into v, that is,

$$\beta(v) = cent(v) = \min_{\hat{x} \in \hat{A}}{}^{-1} E(d(\mathbf{X}, \hat{\mathbf{x}}) | \gamma(\mathbf{X}) = v), \quad (4)$$

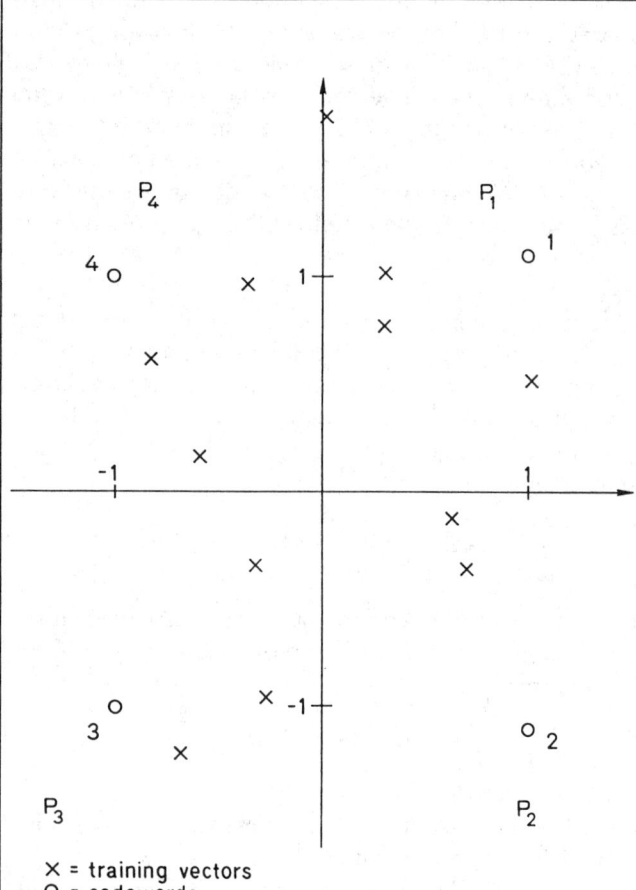

X = training vectors
O = codewords
P_i = region encoded into codeword i

Figure 3. Two-Dimensional Minimum Distortion Partition. The four circles are the codewords of a two-dimensional codebook. The Voronoi regions are the quadrants containing the circles. The x's were produced by a training sequence of twelve two-dimensional Gaussian vectors. Each input vector is mapped into the nearest-neighbor codeword, that is, the circle in the same quadrant.

that is, $\beta(v)$ is the vector yielding the minimum conditional average distortion given that the input vector was mapped into v.

While minimizing such a conditional average may be quite difficult for an arbitrary random process and distortion measure, it is often easy to find for a sample distribution and a nice distortion measure. For example, the centroid in the case of a sample distribution and a squared-error distortion measure is simply the ordinary Euclidean centroid or the vector sum of all input vectors encoded into the given channel symbol, that is, given the sample distribution defined by a training sequence $\{x_i; i = 0, 1, \ldots, L - 1\}$, then

$$\text{cent}(v) = \frac{1}{i(v)} \sum_{x_i : \gamma(x_i) = v} x_i,$$

where $i(v)$ is the number of indices i for which $\gamma(x_i) = v$.

The Euclidean centroids of the example of Fig. 3 are depicted in Fig. 4. (The numerical values may be found in [25].) The new codewords better represent the training vectors mapping into the old codewords, but they yield a different minimum distortion partition of the input alphabet, as indicated by the broken line in Fig. 3. This is the key of the algorithm: iteratively optimize the codebook for the old encoder and then use a minimum distortion encoder for the new codebook.

The Itakura-Saito distortion example is somewhat more complicated, but still easily computable. As with the squared error distortion, one groups all input vectors yielding a common channel symbol. Instead of averaging the vectors, however, the sample autocorrelation matrices for all of the vectors are averaged. The centroid is then given by the standard LPC all-pole model for this average autocorrelation, that is, the centroid is found by a standard Levinson's recursion run on the average autocorrelation.

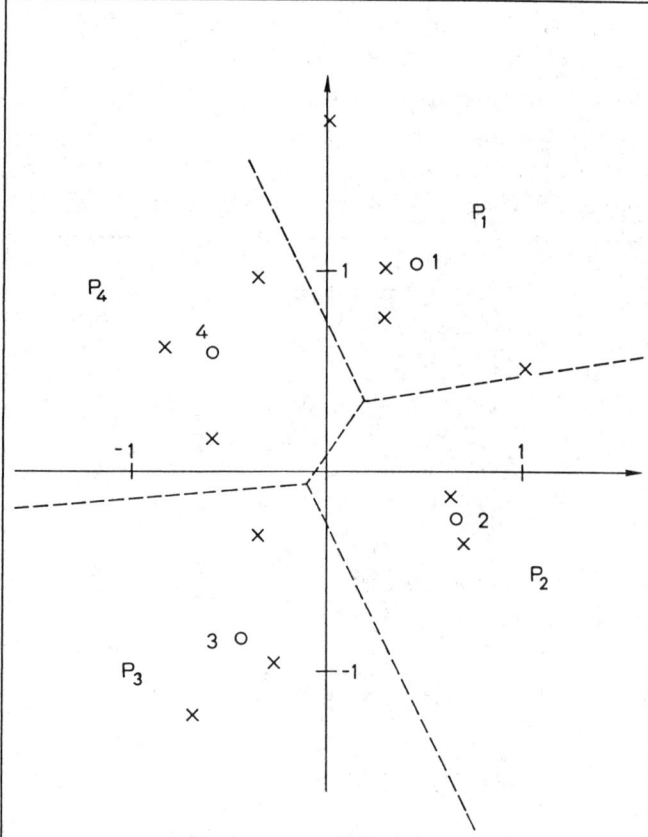

Figure 4. Centroids of Figure 3. The new centroids of the old Voronoi regions of Fig. 3 are drawn as circles. Note that the centroid computation has moved the codewords to better represent the input vectors which yielded those codewords, that is, if one used the same encoder (as in Fig. 3), but replaced the reproduction codewords produced at the decoder by these new centroids, the average distortion would decrease. The broken line delineates the new Voronoi regions for these codewords.

The generalized Lloyd algorithm

The fact that the encoder can be optimized for the decoder and vice versa formed the basis of Lloyd's original optimal PCM design algorithm for a scalar random variable with a known probability density function and a squared error distortion. The general VQ design algorithms considered here are based on the simple observation that Lloyd's basic development is valid for vectors, for sample distributions, and for a variety of distortion measures. The only requirement on the distortion measure is that one can compute the centroids. The basic algorithm is the following:

Step 0. Given: A training sequence and an initial decoder.

Step 1. Encode the training sequence into a sequence of channel symbols using the given decoder minimum distortion rule. If the average distortion is small enough, quit.

Step 2. Replace the old reproduction codeword of the decoder for each channel symbol v by the centroid of all training vectors which mapped into v in Step 1. Go to Step 1.

Means of generating initial decoders will be considered in the next section. Each step of the algorithm must either reduce average distortion or leave it unchanged. The algorithm is usually stopped when the relative distortion decrease falls below some small threshold. The algorithm was developed for vector quantizers, training sequences, and general distortion measures by Linde, Buzo, and Gray [25] and it is sometimes referred to as the LBG algorithm. Previously Lloyd's algorithm had been considered for vectors and difference distortion measures in cluster analysis and pattern recognition problems (e.g., MacQueen [26] and Diday and Simon [27]) and in two-dimensional quantization (e.g., Chen [28] and Adoul et al. [29]). Only recently, however, has it been extensively studied for vector quantization applications using several different distortion measures.

Before continuing, it should be emphasized that such iterative improvement algorithms need not in general yield truly optimum codes. It is known that subject to some mathematical conditions the algorithm will yield locally optimum quantizers, but in general there may be numerous such codes and many may yield poor performance. (See, e.g., [30].) It is often useful, therefore, to enhance the algorithm's potential by providing it with good initial codebooks and perhaps by trying it on several different initial codebooks.

INITIAL CODEBOOKS

The basic design algorithm of the previous section is an iterative improvement algorithm and requires an initial code to improve. Two basic approaches have been developed: One can start with some simple codebook of the correct size or one can start with a simple small codebook and recursively construct larger ones.

"Random" codes

Perhaps the simplest example of the first technique is that used in the k-means variation of the algorithm [26]: Use the first 2^R vectors in the training sequence as the initial codebook. An obvious modification more natural for highly correlated data is to select several widely spaced words from the training sequence. This approach is sometimes called random code generation, but we avoid this nomenclature because of its confusion with the random code techniques of information theory which are used to prove the performance bounds.

Product codes

Another example of the first approach is to use a scalar code such as a uniform quantizer k times in succession and then prune the resulting vector codebook down to the correct size. The mathematical model for such a code is a product code, which we pause to define for current and later use: Say we have a collection of codebooks C_i, $i = 0, 1, \ldots, m - 1$, each consisting of M_i vectors of dimension k_i and having rate $R_i = \log_2 M_i$ bits per vector. Then the product codebook C is defined as the collection of all $M = \Pi_i M_i$ possible concatenations of m words drawn successively from the m codebooks C_i. The dimension of the product codebook is $k = \sum_{i=0}^{m-1} k_i$, the sum of the dimensions of the component codebooks. The product code is denoted mathematically as a Cartesian product:

$$C = \underset{i=0}{\overset{m-1}{\times}} C_i = \{\text{all vectors of the form } (\hat{x}_0, \hat{x}_1, \cdots, \hat{x}_{m-1}); \hat{x}_i \text{ in } C_i; i = 0, 1, \ldots, m - 1\}$$

Thus, for example, using a scalar quantizer with rate R/k k times in succession yields a product k-dimensional vector quantizer of rate R bits per vector. This product code can be used as an initial code for the design algorithm. The scalar quantizers may be identical uniform quantizers with a range selected to match the source, or they may be different, e.g., a positive codebook for a gain and uniform quantizers for $[-1,1]$ for reflection coefficients in an LPC VQ system.

In waveform coding applications where the reproduction and input alphabets are the same—k-dimensional Euclidean space—an alternative product code provides a means of growing better initial guesses from smaller dimensional codes [31]. Begin with a scalar quantizer C_0 and use a two-dimensional product code $C_0 \times C_0$ as an initial guess for designing a two-dimensional VQ. On completion of the design we have a two-dimensional code, say C^2. Form an initial guess for a three dimensional code as all possible pairs from C^2 and scalars from C_0, that is, use the product code $C^2 \times C_0$ as an initial guess. Continuing in this way, given a good $k - 1$ dimensional VQ described by a codebook C^{k-1}, an initial guess for a k-dimensional code design is the product code $C^{k-1} \times C_0$. One can also use such product code constructions with a different initial scalar code C_0, such as those produced by the scalar version of the next algorithm.

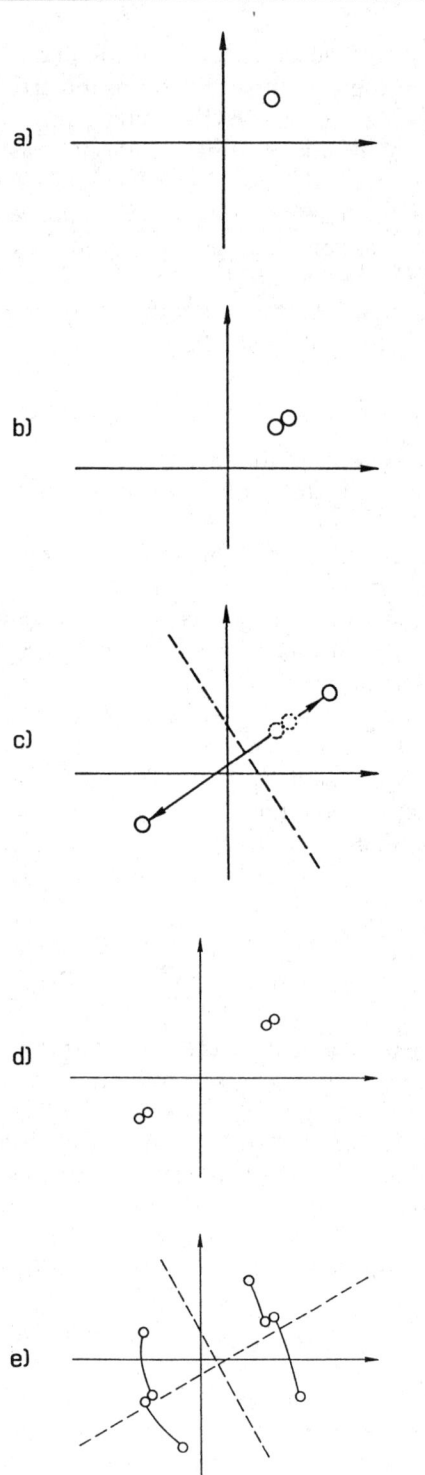

Figure 5. Splitting. A large code is defined in stages: at each stage each codeword of a small code is split into two new codewords, giving an initial codebook of twice the size. The algorithm is run to get a new better codebook. (a) Rate 0: The centroid of the entire training sequence. (b) Initial Rate 1: The one codeword is split to form an initial guess for a two word code. (c) Final Rate 1: The algorithm produces a good code with two words. The dotted line indicates the Voronoi regions. (d) Initial Rate 2: The two words are split to form an initial guess for a four word code. (e) Final Rate 2: The algorithm is run to produce a final four word code.

Splitting

Instead of constructing long codes from smaller dimensional codes, we can construct a sequence of bigger codes having a fixed dimension using a "splitting" technique [25, 16]. This method can be used for any fixed dimension, including scalar codes. Here one first finds the optimum 0 rate code—the centroid of the entire training sequence, as depicted in Fig. 5a for a two-dimensional input alphabet. This single codeword is then split to form two codewords (Fig. 5b). For example, the energy can be perturbed slightly to form a second distinct word or one might purposefully find a word distant from the first. It is convenient to have the original codeword a member of the new pair to ensure that the distortion will not increase. The algorithm is then run to get a good rate 1 bit per vector code as indicated in Fig. 5c. The design continues in this way in stages as shown: the final code of one stage is split to form an initial code for the next.

VARIATIONS OF MEMORYLESS VECTOR QUANTIZERS

In this section we consider some of the variations of memoryless vector quantization aimed at reducing the computation or memory requirements of a full search memoryless VQ.

Tree-searched VQ

Tree-searched vector quantizers were first proposed by Buzo et al. [16] and are a natural byproduct of the splitting algorithm for generating initial code guesses. We focus on the case of a binary tree for simplicity, but more general trees will provide better performance while retaining a significant reduction in complexity.

Say that we have a good rate 1 code as in Fig. 5c and we form a new rate two code by splitting the two codewords as in Fig. 5d. Instead of running a full search VQ design on the resulting 4-word codebook, however, we divide the training sequence into two pieces, collecting together all those vectors encoded into a common word in the 1 bit codebook, that is, all of the training sequence vectors in a common cell of the Voronoi partition. For each of these subsequences of training vectors, we then find a good 1-bit code using the algorithm. The final codebook (so far) consists of the four codewords in the two 1-bit codebooks designed for the two subsequences. A tree-searched encoder selects one of the words not by an ordinary full search of this codebook, but instead it uses the first one bit codebook designed on the whole sequence to select a second code and it then picks the best word in the second code. This encoder can then be used to further subdivide the training sequence and construct even better codebooks for the subsequences. The encoder operation can be depicted as a tree in Fig. 6.

The tree is designed one layer at a time; each new layer being designed so that the new codebook available from each node is good for the vectors encoded into the node. Observe that there are 2^R possible reproduction vectors as in the full search VQ, but now R binary searches are made instead of a single 2^R-ary search. In addition, the encoder

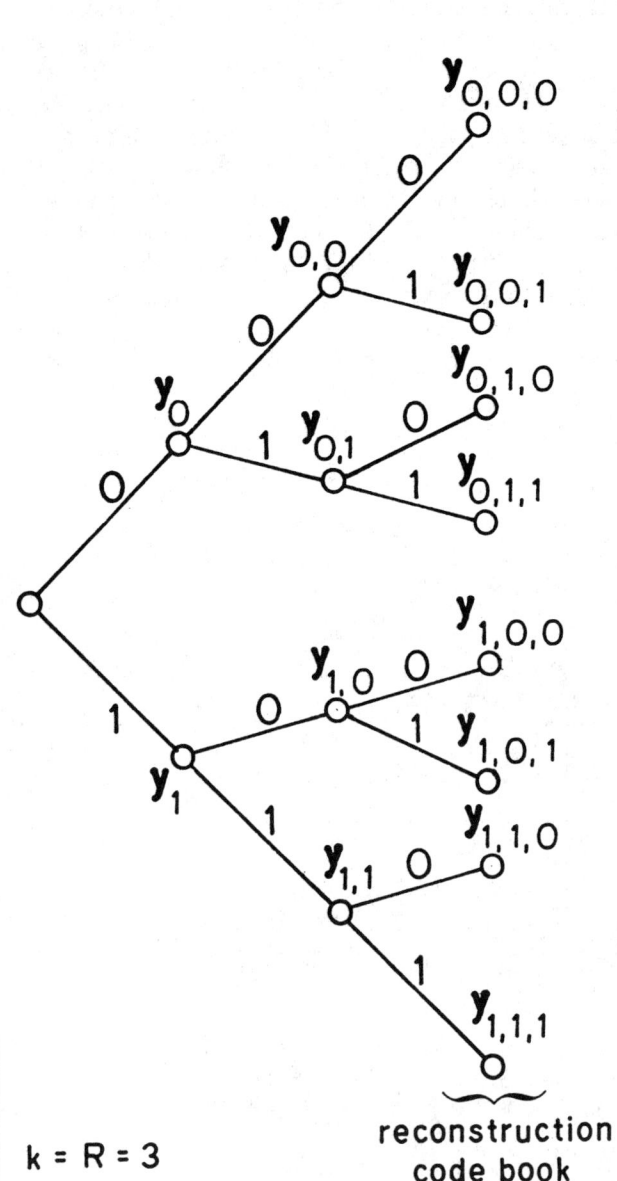

Figure 6. Tree-Searched VQ. A binary encoder tree is shown for a three-dimensional one bit per sample VQ. The encoder makes a succession of R minimum distortion choices from binary codebooks, where the available codebook at each level consists of labels of the nodes in the next level. The labels of the nodes of the final layer are the actual reproduction codewords. At each node the encoder chooses the minimum distortion available label and, if the new index is a 0 (1), sends a channel symbol of 0 (1) and advances up (down) to the next node. After R binary selections the complete channel codeword has been sent and the reproduction codeword specified to the decoder.

storage requirements have doubled. The encoder is no longer optimal for the decoder in the sense of Property 1 since it no longer can perform an exhaustive search of the codebook. The search, however, is much more efficient if done sequentially than is a full search. Thus one may trade performance for efficiency of implementation.

Nonbinary trees can also be used where at the ith layer codebooks of rate R_i are used and the overall rate is then $\Sigma_i R_i$. For example, a depth three tree for VQ of LPC parameter vectors using successive rates of 4, 4, and 2 bits per vector yields performance nearly as good as a full search VQ of the same total rate of 10 bits per vector, yet for the tree search one need only compute $2^4 + 2^4 + 2^2 = 36$ distortions instead of $2^{10} = 1028$ distortions [10].

Other techniques can be used to design tree-searched codes. For example, Adoul et al. [32] use a separating hyperplane approach. Another approach is to begin with a full search codebook and to design a tree-search into the codebook. One technique for accomplishing this is to first group the codewords into close disjoint pairs and then form the centroids of the pairs as the node label of the immediate ancestor of the pair. One then works backwards through the tree, always grouping close pairs. Ideally, one would like a general design technique for obtaining a tree search into an arbitrary VQ codebook with only a small loss of average distortion. Gersho and Cheng [33] have reported preliminary results for designing a variable-length tree search for an arbitrary codebook and have demonstrated its implementability for several small dimensional examples.

Multistep VQ

A multistep VQ is a tree-searched VQ where only a single small codebook is stored for each layer of the tree instead of a different codebook for each node of each layer. Such codes provide the computation reduction of tree-searched codes while reducing the storage requirements below that of even ordinary VQ's. The first example of such a code was the multistage codebook [34]. For simplicity we again confine interest to codes which make a sequence of binary decisions. The first layer binary code is designed as in the tree-searched case. This codebook is used to encode the training sequence and then a training sequence of error or residual vectors is formed. For waveform coding applications the error vectors are simply the difference of the input vectors and their codewords. For vocoding applications, the error vectors are residuals formed by passing the input waveform through the inverse filter $A(z)/\alpha$. The algorithm is then run to design a binary VQ for this vector training sequence of coding errors. The reconstruction for these two bits is then formed by combining the two codewords: For waveform coding this is accomplished by adding the first codeword to the error codeword. For voice coding this is accomplished by using the cascade of two all-pole filters for synthesis. This reproduction can then be used to form a "finer" error vector and a code designed for it. Thus an input vector is encoded in stages as with the tree-searched code, but now only R binary codebooks and hence $2R$ total codewords need to be stored. Observe that there are still 2^R possible final codewords, but we have not needed this much storage because the code can be constructed by adding different combinations of a smaller set of words. A multistage VQ is depicted in Fig. 7.

Product codes

Another useful structure for a memoryless VQ is a prod-

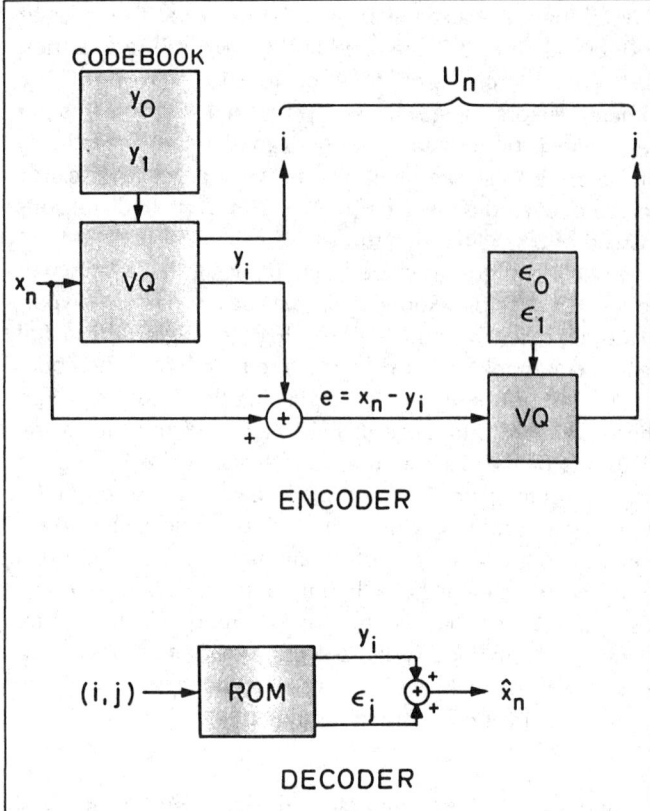

Figure 7. Multistage VQ with 2 Stages. The input vector is first encoded by one VQ and an error vector is formed. The second VQ then encodes the error vector. The two channel symbols from the two VQ's together form the complete channel symbol for the entire encoder. The decoder adds together the corresponding reproduction vectors.

Figure 8 sketches the surprising fact that for the squared error case considered, the two-step selection of the product codeword is an optimal encoding for the given product codebook. We emphasize that here the encoder is optimal for the given product codebook or decoder, but the codebook itself is in general suboptimal because of the constrained product form. A similar property holds for the Itakura-Saito distortion gain/shape VQ. Thus in this case if one devotes R_s bits to the shape and R_g bits to the gain, where $R_s + R_g = R$, then one need only compute 2^{R_s} vector distortions and an easy scalar quantization. The full search encoder would require 2^R vector distortions, yet both encoders yield the same minimum distortion codeword!

uct code. In one extreme, multiple use of scalar quantizers is equivalent to product VQ's and are obviously simple to implement. More general product VQ's, however, may permit one to take advantage of the performance achievable by VQ's while still being able to achieve the higher rates required for good fidelity. In addition, such codes may yield a smaller computational complexity than an ordinary VQ of the same rate and performance (but different dimension). The basic technique is useful when there are differing aspects of the input vector that one might wish to code separately because of different effects, e.g., on dynamic range or finite word length implementation.

Gain/shape VQ

One example of a product code is a gain/shape VQ where separate, but interdependent, codes are used to code the "shape" and "gain" of the waveform, where the "shape" is defined as the original input vector normalized by removal of a "gain" term such as energy in a waveform coder or LPC residual energy in a vocoder. Gain/shape encoders were introduced by Buzo et al. [16] and were subsequently extended and optimized by Sabin and Gray [35, 36]. A gain/shape VQ for waveform coding with a squared-error distortion is illustrated in Fig. 8.

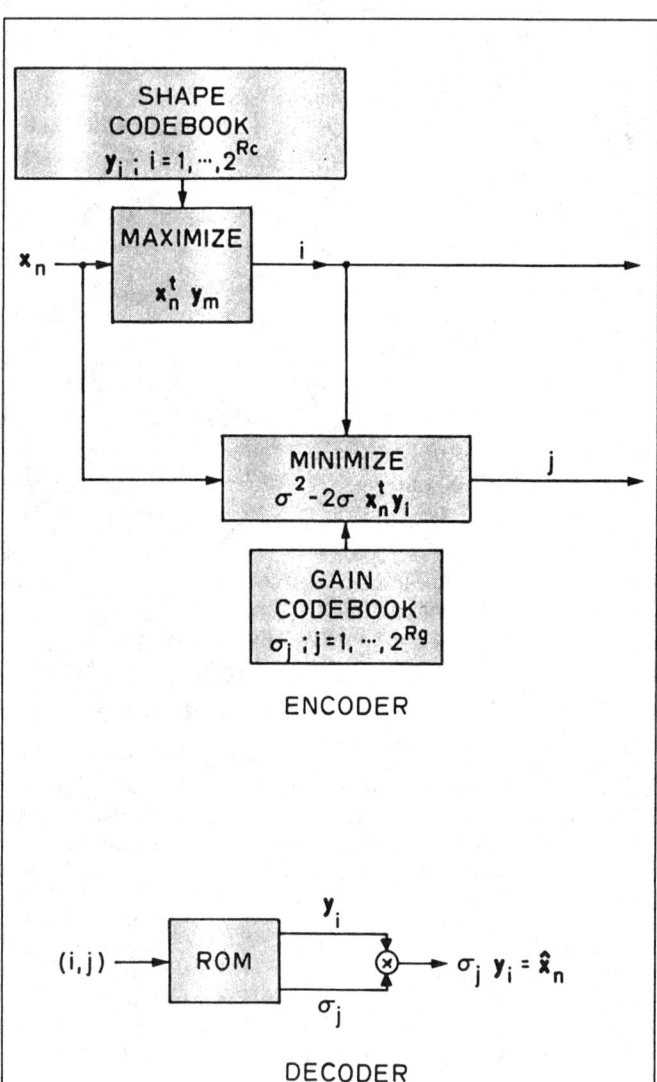

Figure 8. Gain/Shape VQ. First a unit energy shape vector is chosen to match the input vector by maximizing the inner product over the codewords. Given the resulting shape vector, a scalar gain codeword is selected so as to minimize the indicated quantity. The encoder yields the product codeword $\sigma_j y_i$ with the minimum possible squared error distortion from the input vector. Thus this multistep encoder is optimum for the product codebook.

Variations of the basic VQ algorithm can be used to iteratively improve a gain shape code by alternately optimizing the shape for the gain and vice versa. The resulting conditional centroids are easy to compute. The centroid updates can be made either simultaneously or alternately after each iteration [36].

One can experimentally determine the optimal bit allocation between the gain and the shape codebooks.

Separating mean VQ

Another example of a multistep product code is the separating mean VQ where a sample mean instead of an energy term is removed [37]. Define the sample mean $\langle x \rangle$ of a k-dimensional vector by $k^{-1} \sum_{i=0}^{k-1} x_i$. In a separated mean VQ one first uses a scalar quantizer to code the sample mean of a vector, then the coded sample mean is subtracted from all of the components of the input vector to form a new vector with approximately zero sample mean. This new vector is then vector quantized. Such a system is depicted in Fig. 9. The basic motivation here is that in image coding the sample mean of pixel intensities in a small rectangular block represents a relatively slowly varying average background value of pixel intensity around which there are variations.

To design such a VQ, first use the algorithm to design a scalar quantizer for the sample mean sequence $\langle x_j \rangle$, $j = 0, 1, \ldots, L - 1$. Let $q(\langle x \rangle)$ denote the reproduction for $\langle x \rangle$ using the quantizer. Then use the vector training sequence $x_j - q(\langle x_j \rangle)\mathbf{1}$, where $\mathbf{1} = (1, 1, \ldots, 1)$, to design a VQ for the difference. Like the gain/shape VQ, a product codebook and a multistep encoder are used, but unlike the gain/shape VQ it can be shown that the multistep encoder here does not select the best possible mean, shape pair, that is, the multistep encoder is not equivalent to a full search encoder.

Lattice VQ

A final VQ structure capable of efficient searches and memory usage is the lattice quantizer, a k-dimensional generalization of the scalar uniform quantizer. A lattice in k-dimensional space is a collection of all vectors of the form $\mathbf{y} = \sum_{i=0}^{n-1} a_i \mathbf{e}_i$, where $n \leq k$, where $\mathbf{e}_0, \ldots, \mathbf{e}_{n-1}$ are a set of linearly independent vectors in $\mathbf{R}^k$, and where the a_i are arbitrary integers. A lattice quantizer is a quantizer whose codewords form a subset of a lattice. Lattice quantizers were introduced by Gersho [38] and the performance and efficient coding algorithms were developed for many particular lattices by Conway and Sloane [39, 40, 41] and Barnes and Sloane [42]. The disadvantage of lattice quantizers is that they cannot be improved by a variation of the Lloyd algorithm without losing their structure and good quantizers produced by the Lloyd algorithm cannot generally be well approximated by lattices. Lattice codes can work well on source distributions that are approximately uniform over a bounded region of space. In fact, lattices that are asymptotically optimal in the limit of large rate are known for this case in two and three dimensions and good lattices are known for dimensions up to 16.

Ideally, one would like to take a full search, unconstrained VQ and find some fast means of encoding having complexity more like the above techniques than that of the full search. For example, some form of multidimensional companding followed by a lattice quantizer as suggested by Gersho [24] would provide both good performance and efficient implementation. Unfortunately, however, no design methods accomplishing this goal have yet been found.

FEEDBACK VECTOR QUANTIZERS

Memory can be incorporated into a vector quantizer in a simple manner by using different codebooks for each input vector, where the codebooks are chosen based on past input vectors. The decoder must know which codebook is being used by the encoder in order to decode the channel symbols. This can be accomplished in two ways: 1) The encoder can use a codebook selection procedure that depends only on past encoder outputs and hence the codebook sequence can be tracked by the decoder. 2) The decoder is informed of the selected codebook via a special low-rate side channel. The first approach is called feedback vector quantization and is the

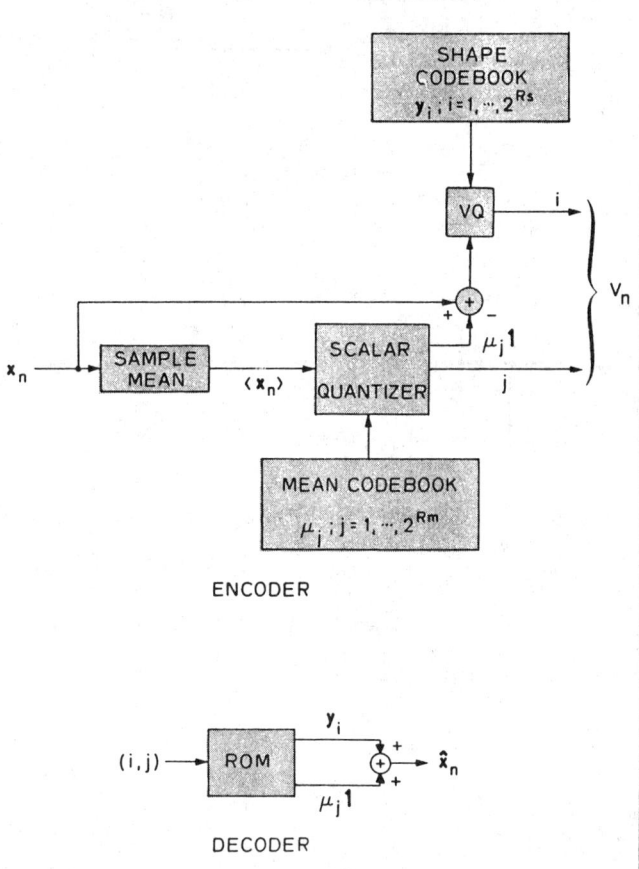

Figure 9. Separating Mean VQ. The sample mean of the input vector is computed, scalar quantized, and then subtracted from each component of the input vector. The resulting vector with approximately zero sample mean is then vector quantized. The decoder adds the coded sample mean to all components of the coded shape vector.

topic of this section. The name follows because the encoder output is "fed back" for use in selecting the new codebook. A feedback vector quantizer can be viewed as the vector extension of a scalar adaptive quantizer with backward estimation (AQB) [3]. The second approach is the vector extension of a scalar adaptive quantizer with forward estimation (AQF) and is called simply adaptive vector quantization. Adaptive VQ will be considered in a later section. Observe that systems can combine the two techniques and use both feedback and side information. We also point out that unlike most scalar AQB and AQF systems, the vector analogs considered here involve no explicit estimation of the underlying densities.

It should be emphasized that the results of information theory imply that VQ's with memory can do no better than memoryless VQ's in the sense of minimizing average distortion for a given rate constraint. In fact, the basic mathematical model for a data compression system in information theory is exactly a memoryless VQ and such codes can perform arbitrarily close to the optimal performance achievable using any data compression system. The exponential growth of computation and memory with rate, however, may result in nonimplementable VQ's. A VQ with memory may yield the desired distortion with practicable complexity.

A general feedback VQ can be described as follows [22]: Suppose now that we have a space **S** whose members we shall call states and that for each state s in **S** we have a separate quantizer: an encoder γ_s, decoder β_s, and codebook C_s. The channel codeword space **M** is assumed to be the same for all of the VQ's. Consider a data compression system consisting of a sequential machine such that if the machine is in state s, then it uses the quantizer with encoder γ_s and decoder β_s. It then selects its next state by a mapping called a next-state function or state-transition function f such that given a state s and a channel symbol v, then $f(v,s)$ is the new state of the machine. More precisely, given a sequence of input vectors $\{x_n; n = 0, 1, 2, \ldots\}$ and an initial state s_0, then the subsequent state sequence s_n, channel symbol sequence v_n, and reproduction sequence $\hat{x}_n$ are defined recursively for $n = 0, 1, 2, \ldots$ as

$$v_n = \gamma_{s_n}(x_n), \qquad \hat{x}_n = \beta_{s_n}(v_n), \qquad s_{n+1} = f(v_n, s_n). \quad (5)$$

Since the next state depends only on the current state and the channel codeword, the decoder can track the state if it knows the initial state and the channel sequence. A general feedback vector quantizer is depicted in Fig. 10. The freedom to use different quantizers based on the past without increasing the rate should permit the code to perform better than a memoryless quantizer of the same dimension and rate.

An important drawback of all feedback quantizers is that channel errors can accumulate and cause disastrous reconstruction errors. As with scalar feedback quantizer systems, this must be handled by periodic resetting or by error control or by a combination of the two.

If the state space is finite, then we shall call the resulting system a finite-state vector quantizer or FSVQ. For an FSVQ, all of the codebooks and the next-state transition table can all be stored in ROM, making the general FSVQ structure amenable to LSI or VLSI implementation [43].

Observe that a memoryless vector quantizer is simply a feedback vector quantizer or finite-state vector quantizer with only a single state. The general FSVQ is a special case

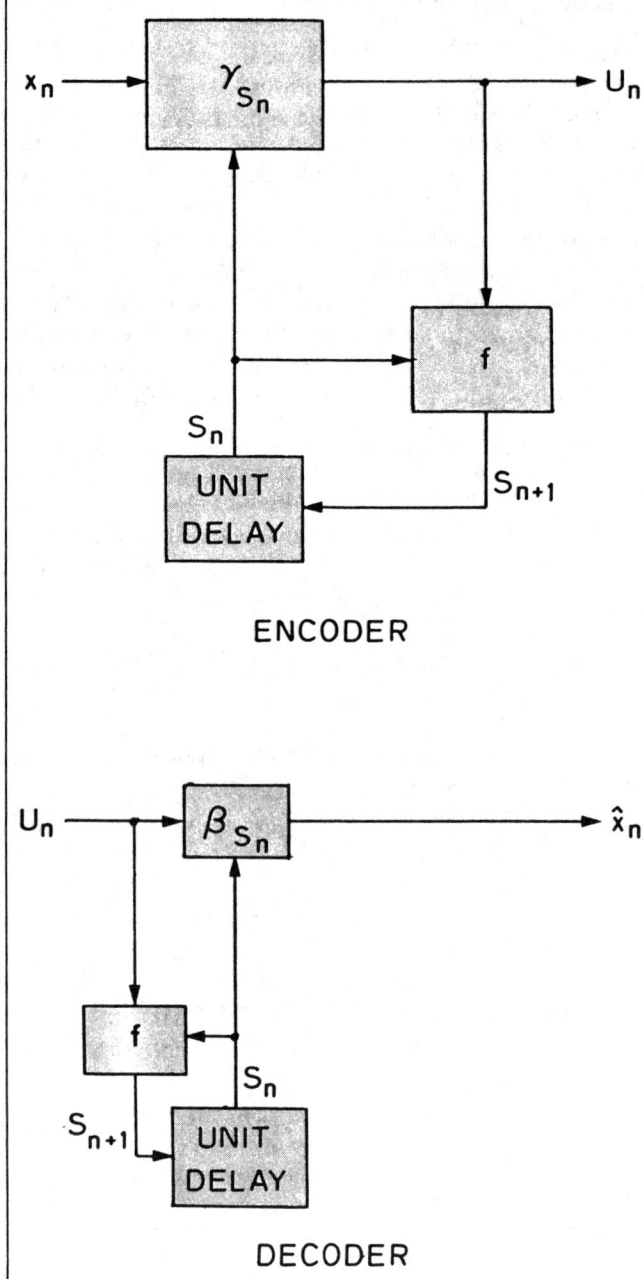

Figure 10. Feedback VQ. At time n both encoder and decoder are in a common state S_n. The encoder uses a state VQ γ_{S_n} to encode the input vector and then selects a new state for the next input vector. Knowing the VQ used and the resulting channel symbol, the decoder can produce the correct reproduction. Note that the state VQ's may be computed at each time from some rule or, if they are small in number, simply stored separately.

of a tracking finite state source coding system [44] where the encoder is a minimum distortion mapping.

Three design algorithms for feedback vector quantizers using variations on the generalized Lloyd algorithm have been recently developed. The remainder of this section is devoted to brief descriptions of these techniques.

Vector predictive quantization

Cuperman and Gersho [45, 46] proposed a vector predictive coder or vector predictive quantizer (VPQ) which is a vector generalization of DPCM or predictive quantization. A VPQ is sketched in Fig. 11. For a fixed predictor, the VQ design algorithm is used to design a VQ for the prediction error sequence. Cuperman and Gersho considered several variations on the basic algorithm, some of which will be later mentioned.

Chang [47] developed an extension to Cuperman and Gersho's algorithm which begins with their system and then uses a stochastic gradient algorithm to iteratively improve the vector linear predictor coefficients, that is, to better match the predictor to the quantizer. The stochastic gradient algorithm is used only in the design of the system, not as an on line adaptation mechanism as in the adaptive gradient algorithms of, e.g., Gibson et al. [48] and Dunn [49]. A scalar version of this algorithm for improving the predictor for the quantizer was developed in unpublished work of Y. Linde.

Product/multistep FVQ

A second basic approach for designing feedback vector quantizers which is quite simple and works quite well is to use a product multistep VQ such as the gain/shape VQ or the separating mean VQ and use a simple feedback quantizer on the scalar portion and an ordinary memoryless VQ on the remaining vector. This approach was developed in [10] for gain/shape VQ of LPC parameters and in [37] for separating mean VQ of images. Both efforts used simple scalar predictive quantization for the feedback quantization of the scalar terms.

FSVQ

The first general design technique for finite-state vector quantizers was reported by Foster and Gray [50, 51]. There are two principal design components: 1. Design an initial set of state codebooks and a next-state function using an *ad hoc* algorithm. 2. Given the next-state function, use a variation of the basic algorithm to attempt to improve the state codebooks. The second component is accomplished by a slight extension of the basic algorithm that is similar to the extension of [52] for the design of trellis encoders: Encode the data using the FSVQ and then replace all of the reproduction vectors by the centroids of the training vectors which map into those vectors; now, however, the centroids are conditioned on both the channel symbol and the state. While such conditional averages are likely impossible to compute analytically, they are easily computed for a training sequence. For example, in the case of a squared error distance one simply forms the Euclidean centroid of all input vectors which correspond to the state s and channel symbol v in an encoding of the training sequence.

As with ordinary VQ, replacing the old decoder or codebook by centroids cannot yield a code with larger distortion. Unlike memoryless VQ, however, replacing the old encoder by a minimum distortion rule for the new decoder can in principle cause an increase in distortion and hence now the iteration is somewhat different: Replace the old encoder (which is a minimum distortion rule for the old decoder) by a minimum distortion rule for the new decoder. If the distortion goes down, then continue the iteration and find the new centroids: If the distortion goes up, then quit with the encoder being a quantizer for the previous codebook and the decoder being the centroids for the encoder. By construction this algorithm can only improve performance. It turns out, however, that in

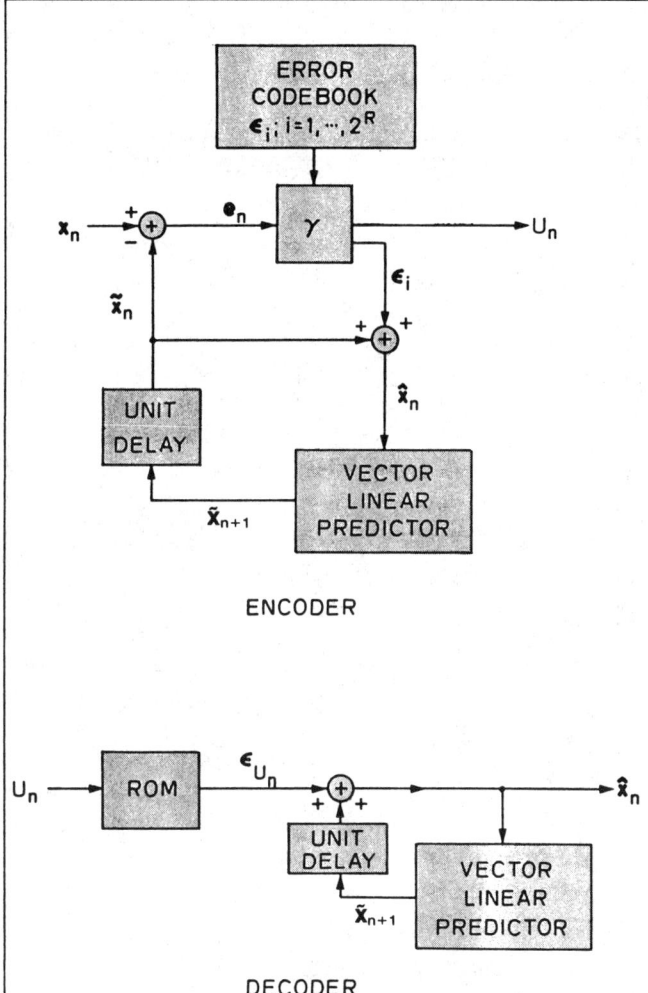

Figure 11. Vector Predictive Quantization. A linear vector predictor for the next input vector of a process given the previous input vector is applied to the previous reproduction of the input vector. The resulting prediction is subtracted from the current input vector to form an error vector which is vector quantized. The decoder uses a copy of the encoder and the received encoded error vectors to construct the reproduction.

practice it is a good idea to not stop the algorithm if the distortion increases slightly, but to let it continue: it will almost always eventually drop back down in distortion and converge to something better.

The first design component is more complicated. We here describe one of the more promising approaches of [51] called the omniscient design approach. Say that we wish to design an FSVQ with K states and rate R bits per vector. For simplicity we label the states as 0 through $K-1$. First use the training sequence to design a memoryless VQ with K codewords, one for each state. We shall call these codewords state labels and this VQ the state quantizer. We call the output of the state VQ the "ideal next state" instead of a channel symbol. Next break up the training sequence into subsequences as follows: Encode the training sequence using the state VQ and for each state s collect all of training vectors which *follow* the occurrence of this state label. Thus for s the corresponding training subsequence consists of all input vectors that occur when the *current* ideal state is s. Use the basic algorithm to design a rate R codebook C_s for the corresponding training sequence for each s.

The resulting state VQ and the collection of codebooks for each state have been designed to yield good performance in the following communication system: The encoder is in an ideal state s chosen by using the state VQ on the last input vector. The encoder uses the corresponding VQ encoder γ_s described by the codebook C_s. The output of γ_s is the channel symbol. In order to decode the channel symbol, the decoder must also know the ideal state. Unfortunately, however, this ideal state cannot be determined from knowledge of the initial state and all of the received channel symbols. Thus the decoder must be omniscient in the sense of knowing this additional side information in order to be able to decode. In particular, this system is not an FSVQ by our definition. We can use the state quantizer and the various codebooks, however, to construct an FSVQ by approximating the omniscient system: Instead of forming the ideal next state by using the state VQ on the actual input vector (as we did in the design procedure), use the state VQ on the current reproduction vector in order to choose the next state. This will yield a state sequence depending only on encoder outputs and the original state and hence will be trackable by the decoder. This is analogous to the scalar practice of building a predictive coder and choosing the predictor as if it knew the past inputs, but in fact applying it to past reproductions.

Combining the previously described steps of (1) initial (state label) codebook design, (2) state codebooks and next-state function design, and (3) iterative improvement of code for given next-state function, provides a complete design algorithm.

In addition to the above design approach, techniques have been developed for iterating on (2) and (3) above in the sense of optimizing the next-state function for a given collection of codebooks. These algorithms, however, are more complicated and require ideas from the theory of adaptive stochastic automata. The reader is referred to [53] for a discussion of these improvement algorithms.

VECTOR TREE AND TRELLIS ENCODERS

As with scalar feedback quantizers, the actions of the decoder of a feedback VQ can be depicted as a directed graph or tree. A simple example is depicted in Fig. 12, where a merged tree or trellis can be drawn since the feedback VQ has only a finite number of states.

Instead of using the ordinary VQ encoder which is only permitted to look at the current input vector in order to decide on a channel symbol, one could use algorithms such as the Viterbi algorithm, M-algorithm or M,L-algorithm, Fano algorithm, or stack algorithm for a minimum cost search through a directed graph and search several levels ahead into the tree or trellis before choosing a channel symbol. This introduces an additional delay into the encoding of several vectors, but it ensures better long run average distortion behavior. This technique is called tree or trellis encoding and is also referred to as look-ahead coding, delayed decision coding, and multipath search coding. (See, e.g., [54, 52] for surveys.) We point out that a tree encoding system uses a tree to denote the

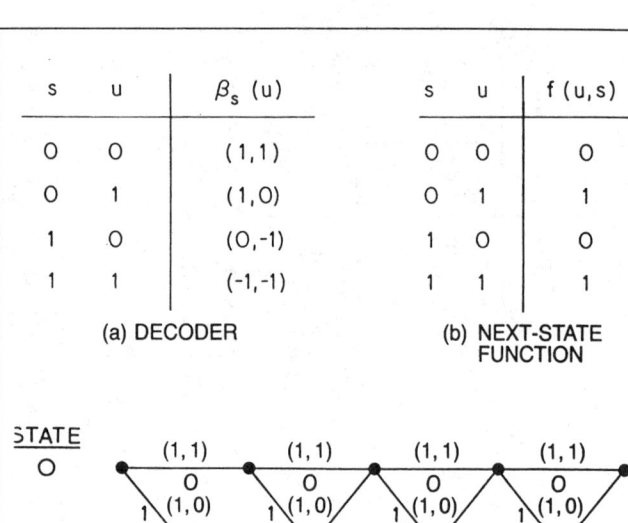

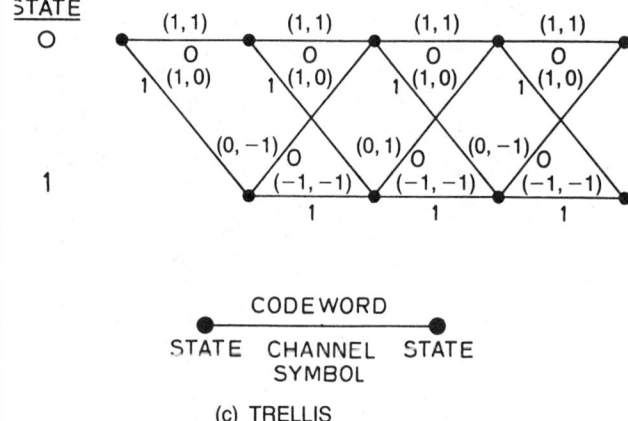

Figure 12. Decoder trellis for a two state 1 bit per vector two dimensional waveform coder. The trellis depicts the possible state transitions for the given next-state function. The transitions are labeled by the corresponding decoder output (in parentheses) and channel symbol produced by the encoder.

operation on successive vectors by the decoder at successive times while a tree-searched VQ uses a tree to construct a fast search for a single vector at a single time.

A natural variation of the basic algorithm for designing FSVQ's can be used to design trellis encoding systems: Simply replace the FSVQ encoder which finds the minimum distortion reproduction for a single input vector by a Viterbi or other search algorithm which searches the decoder trellis to some fixed depth to find a good long term minimum distortion path. The centroid computation is accomplished exactly as with an FSVQ: each branch or transition label is replaced by the centroid of all training vectors causing that transition, that is, the centroid conditioned on the decoder state and channel symbol. Scalar and simple two dimensional vector trellis encoding systems were designed in [52] using this approach.

Trellis encoding systems are not really vector quantization systems as we have defined them since the encoder is permitted to search ahead to determine the effect on the decoder output of several input vectors while a vector quantizer is restricted to search only a single vector ahead. The two systems are intimately related, however, and a trellis encoder can always be used to improve the performance of a feedback vector quantizer. Very little work has yet been done on vector trellis encoding systems.

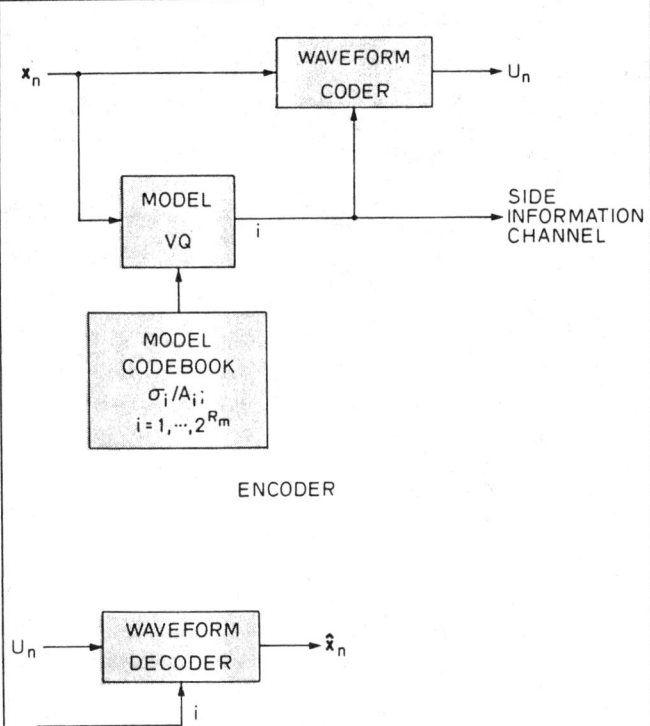

Figure 13. Adaptive VQ. The model VQ uses the Itakura-Saito distortion to select an LPC model to fit the input frame of many sample vectors. This selection in turn determines the waveform coder used to digitize the sample vectors. A side channel then informs the receiver which decoder to use on the channel symbols produced by the waveform coder.

ADAPTIVE VQ

As a final class of VQ we consider systems that use one VQ to adapt a waveform coder, which might be another VQ. The adaptation information is communicated to the receiver via a low rate side information channel.

The various forms of vector quantization using the Itakura-Saito family of distortion measures can be considered as model classifiers, that is, they fit an all-pole model to an observed sequence of sampled speech. When used alone in an LPC VQ system, the model is used to synthesize the speech at the receiver. Alternatively, one could use the model selected to choose a waveform coder designed to be good for sampled waveforms that produce that model. For example, analogous to the omniscient design of FSVQ one could design separate VQ's for the subsequences of the training sequence encoding into common models. Both the model index and the waveform coding index are then sent to the receiver. Thus LPC VQ can be used to adapt a waveform coder, possibly also a VQ or related system. This will yield a system typically of much higher rate, but potentially of much better quality since the codebooks can be matched to local behavior of the data. The general structure is shown in Fig. 13. The model VQ typically operates on a much larger vector of samples and at a much lower rate in bits per sample than does the waveform coder and hence the bits spent on specifying the model through the side channel are typically much fewer than those devoted to the waveform coder.

There are a variety of such possible systems since both the model quantizer and the waveform quantizer can take on many of the structures so far considered. In addition, as in speech recognition applications [55] the gain-independent variations of the Itakura-Saito distortion measure which either normalize or optimize gain may be better suited for the model quantization than the usual form. Few such systems have yet been studied in detail. We here briefly describe some systems of this type that have appeared in the literature to exemplify some typical combinations. All of them use some form of memoryless VQ for the model quantization, but a variety of waveform coders are used.

The first application of VQ to adaptive coding was by Adoul, Debray, and Dalle [32] who used an LPC VQ to choose a predictor for use in a scalar predictive waveform coder. Vector quantization was used only for the adaptation and not for the waveform coding. An adaptive VQ generalization of this system was later developed by Cuperman and Gersho [45,46] who used an alternative classification technique to pick one of three vector predictors and then used those predictors in a predictive vector quantizer. The predictive vector quantizer design algorithm previously described was used, except now the training sequence was broken up into subsequences corresponding to the selected predictor and a quantizer was designed for each resulting error sequence. Chang [47] used a similar scheme with an ordinary LPC VQ as the classifier and with a stochastic gradient algorithm run on each of the vector predictive quantizers in order to im-

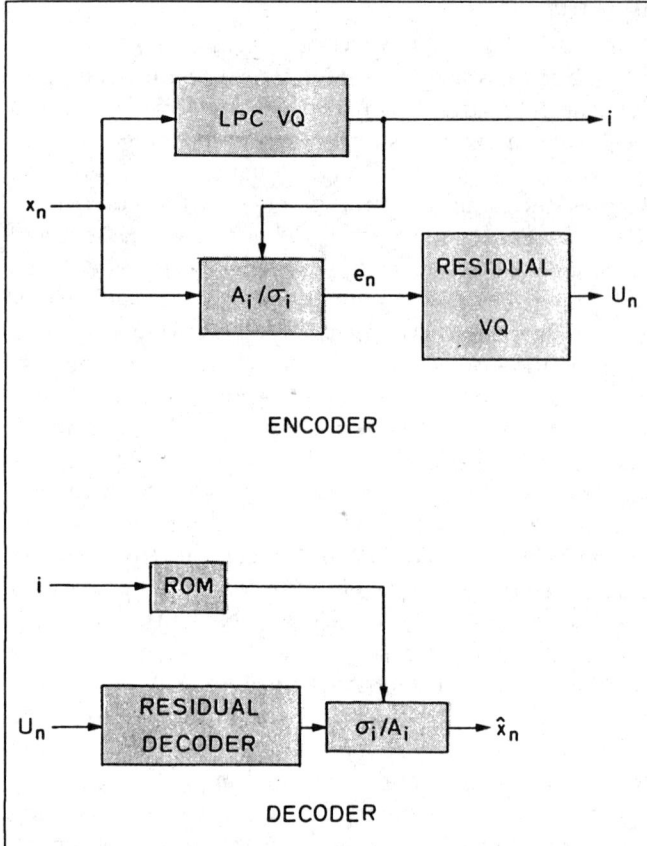

Figure 14. RELP VQ. An LPC VQ is used for model selection and a single VQ to waveform encode the residuals formed by passing the original waveform through the inverse filter $A/\sqrt{\alpha}$. The side information specifies to the decoder which of the model filters $\sqrt{\alpha}/A$ should be used for synthesis.

prove the prediction coefficients for the corresponding codebooks.

Rebolledo et al. [56] and Adoul and Mabilleau [57] developed vector residual excited linear predictive (RELP) systems. (See Fig. 14.) A similar system employing either a scalar or a simple vector trellis encoder for the waveform coder was developed by Stewart et al. [52]. Both of these systems used the basic algorithm to design both the model VQ and the waveform coders.

The RELP VQ systems yielded disappointingly poor performance at low bit rates. Significantly better performance was achieved by using the residual codebooks produced in the RELP design to construct codebooks for the original waveform, that is, instead of coding the model and the residual, code the model and use the selected model to construct a waveform coder for the original waveform as depicted in Fig. 15 [52]. For lack of a better name, this system might be called an inverted RELP because it uses residual codebooks to drive an inverse model filter in order to get a codebook for the original waveform.

Yet another use of LPC VQ to adapt a waveform coder was reported by Heron, Crochiere, and Cox [58] who used a subband/transform coder for the waveform coding and used the side information to adapt the bit allocation for the scalar parameter quantizers.

Many other variations on the general theme are possible and the structure is a promising one for processes such as speech that exhibit local stationarity, that is, slowly varying short term statistical behavior. The use of one VQ to partition a training sequence in order to design good codes for the resulting distinct subsequences is an intuitive approach to the computer-aided design of adaptive data compression systems.

EXAMPLES

We next consider the performance of various forms of vector quantizers on three popular guinea pigs: Gauss Markov sources, speech waveforms, and images. For the speech coding example we consider both waveform coders using the squared error distortion measure and vocoders using the Itakura-Saito distortion. The caveats of the introduction should be kept in mind when interpreting the results.

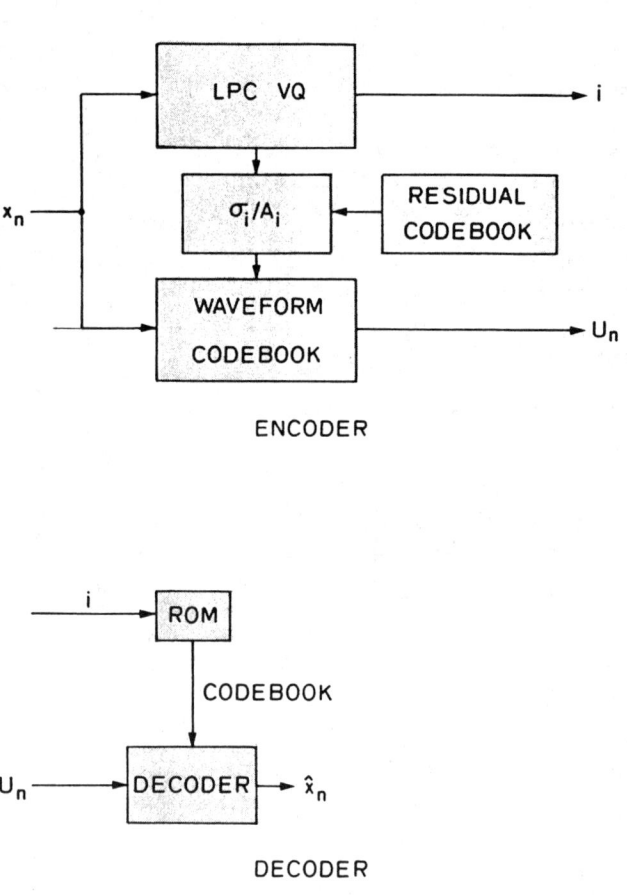

Figure 15. Inverted RELP. An LPC VQ is used to select a model filter σ/A. A waveform codebook is then formed by driving the model filter with all possible residual codewords from a RELP VQ design. Thus, unlike a RELP system, the original waveform (and not a residual) is matched by possible reproduction codewords.

The performance of the systems are given by SNR's for squared error and by an analogous quantity for the Itakura-Saito distortion: In both cases we measure normalized average distortion on a logarithmic scale, where the normalization is by the average distortion of the optimum zero rate code — the average distortion between the input sequence and the centroid of the entire input sequence. This quantity reduces to an SNR in the squared error case and provides a useful dimensionless normalized average distortion in general. We call this quantity the SNR in both cases. The SNR is given in tables instead of graphs in order to facilitate quantitative comparisons among the coding schemes.

Gauss Markov sources

We first consider the popular guinea pig of a Gauss Markov source. This source is useful as a mathematical model for some real data sources and its information theoretic optimal performance bounds as described by the distortion-rate function are known. For this example we consider only the squared error distortion. A Gauss Markov source or a first order Gauss autoregressive source $\{X_n\}$ is defined by the difference equation $X_{n+1} = aX_n + W_n$, where $\{W_n\}$ is a zero mean, unit variance, independent and identically distributed Gaussian source. We here consider the highly correlated case of $a = 0.9$ and vector quantizers of 1 bit/sample. The maximum achievable SNR as given by Shannon's distortion-rate function for this source and rate is 13.2 dB [7].

Various design algorithms were used to design vector quantizers for several dimensions for this source. Table I describes the results of designing several memoryless vector quantizers for a training sequence of 60,000 samples. Given are the design SNR (code performance on the training sequence), the number of multiplications per sample required by the encoder, and the number of real scalars that must be stored for the encoder codebook. The number of multiplications is used as a measure of encoder complexity because it is usually the dominant computation and because the number of additions required is usually comparable. It is given by n = (the number of codewords searched) × (dimension)/(dimension) = the number of codewords searched. The actual storage required depends on the number of bytes used to store each floating point number. Many (but not all) of the final codes were subsequently tested on different test sequences of 60,000 samples. In all cases the open test SNR's were within .25 dB of the design distortion. The systems considered are full search VQ's [25], binary tree-searched VQ's [59], binary multistage VQ's [47], and gain/shape VQ's [36]. The gain and codebook sizes for the gain/shape codes were experimentally optimized.

As expected, the full search VQ yields the best performance for each dimension, but the tree-searched VQ is not much worse and has a much lower complexity. The multistage VQ is noticeably inferior, losing more than 1 dB at the higher dimensions, but its memory requirements are small. The gain/shape VQ compares poorly on the basis of performance vs. rate for a fixed dimension, but it is the best code in the sense of providing the minimum distortion for a fixed complexity and rate.

For larger rates and lower distortion the relative merits may be quite different. For example, the multistage VQ is then capable of better performance relative to the ordinary VQ since the quantization errors in the various stages do not accumulate so rapidly. (See, e.g., [34].) Thus in this

TABLE I
MEMORYLESS VQ FOR A GAUSS MARKOV SOURCE.

	VQ			TSVQ			MVQ			G/SVQ		
k	SNR	n	M	SNR	n	M	SNR	n	M	SNR	n	M
1	4.4	2	2	4.4	2	2	4.4	2	2			
2	7.9	4	8	7.9	4	12	7.6	4	8	7.9	1	3
3	9.2	8	24	9.2	6	42	8.6	6	18	9.3	1	5
4	10.2	16	64	10.2	8	120	8.4	8	32	9.4	2	10
5	10.6	32	160	10.4	10	310	9.3	10	50	9.8	3	17
6	10.9	64	384	10.7	12	756	9.1	12	72	9.9	4	26
7	11.2	128	896	11.0	14	1778	9.4	14	98	10.2	4	31
8							9.9	16	128	10.6	5	43
9										10.9	6	57

Signal to Noise Ratios (SNR), number of multiplications per sample (n), and storage requirements of memoryless vector quantizers: full search memoryless VQ (VQ), binary tree-searched (TSVQ), binary multistage VQ (MVQ), and gain/shape VQ (G/SVQ). Rate = 1 bit/sample. k = vector dimension. Training Sequence = 60000 samples from a Gauss Markov Source with correlation coefficient 0.9.

TABLE II
FEEDBACK VQ OF A GAUSS MARKOV SOURCE.

	FSVQ1				FSVQ2				VPQ		
k	SNR	K	n	M	SNR	K	n	M	SNR	n	M
1	10.0	64	2	64	9.5	16	2	16	10.0	2	2
2	10.8	256	4	512	10.8	32	4	64	11.2	4	8
3	11.4	512	8	1536	11.1	64	8	192	11.6	8	24
4	12.1	512	16	2048	11.3	128	16	512	11.6	16	64

Signal to Noise Ratios (SNR), number of states (K), number of multiplications per sample (n), and storage (M) for feedback quantizers: FSVQ with number of states increased until negligible change (FSVQ1), FSVQ with fewer states (FSVQ2), VPQ. Rate = 1 bit/sample. k = vector dimension. Training Sequence = 60000 samples from a Gauss Markov Source with correlation coefficient 0.9.

TABLE III
MEMORYLESS VQ OF SAMPLED SPEECH.

	VQ				TSVQ			
k	SNRin	SNRout	n	M	SNRin	SNRout	n	M
1	2.0	2.1	2	2	2.0	2.1	2	2
2	5.2	5.3	4	8	5.1	5.1	4	12
3	6.1	6.0	8	24	5.5	5.5	6	42
4	7.1	7.0	16	64	6.4	6.4	8	120
5	7.9	7.6	32	160	7.1	6.9	10	310
6	8.5	8.1	64	384	7.9	7.5	12	756
7	9.1	8.4	128	896	8.3	7.8	14	1778
8	9.7	8.8	256	2048	8.9	8.0	16	4080

	MVQ				G/SVQ			
k	SNRin	SNRout	n	M	SNRin	SNRout	n	M
1	2.0	2.1	2	2				
2	4.3	4.4	4	8				
3	4.3	4.4	6	18	4.5	4.6	4	14
4	4.4	4.5	8	32	6.0	6.1	4	20
5	5.0	5.0	10	50	7.2	6.9	8	44
6	5.0	4.9	12	72	7.7	7.4	16	100
7	5.3	5.1	14	98	8.2	7.7	16	120
8	5.6	5.5	16	128	8.8	8.1	32	264
9					9.3	8.5	64	584
10					9.8	8.9	128	1288
11					10.4	9.3	256	2824

Signal to Noise Ratios inside training sequence (SNRin) of 640000 speech samples, Signal to Noise Ratios outside training sequence (SNRout) of 76800 speech samples, number of multiplications per sample (n), and storage requirements of memoryless vector quantizers: full search memoryless VQ (VQ), binary tree-searched (TSVQ), binary multistage VQ (MVQ), and gain/shape VQ (G/SVQ). Rate = 1 bit/sample. k = vector dimension.

case multistage VQ may be far better because if its much smaller computational requirements.

Table II presents results for three feedback VQ's for the same source. In addition to the parameters of Table I, the number of states for the FSVQ's are given. The first FSVQ and the VPQ were designed for the same training sequence of 60,000 samples. Because of the extensive computation required and the shortness of the training sequence for a feedback quantizer, only dimensions 1 through 4 were considered. The first FSVQ was designed using the omniscient design approach for 1 bit per sample, dimensions 1 through 4, and a variety of numbers of states. For the first example, the number of states was chosen by designing FSVQ's for more and more states until firther increases yielded negligible improvements [51]. It was found, however, that the performance outside of the training sequence for these codes was significantly inferior, by 1 to 2 dB for the larger dimensions. From the discussion of average distortion, this suggests that the training sequence was too short. Hence the second FSVQ design (FSVQ2) was run with a larger training sequence of 128,000 samples and fewer states. The test sequence for these codes always yielded performance within .3 dB of the design value. The VPQ test performance with within .1 dB of the design performance. The scalar predictive quantizer performance and the codebook for the prediction error quantizer are the same as the analytically optimized predictive quantization system of Arnstein [60] run on the same data.

Observe that the scalar FSVQ in the first experiment with 64 states yielded performance quite close to that of the scalar VPQ, which does not have a finite number of states. Intuitively the FSVQ is trying to approximate the infinite state machine by using a large number of states. The VPQ, however, is less complex and requires less memory and hence for this application is superior.

For comparison, the best 1 bit/sample scalar trellis encoding system for this source yields 11.25 dB for this source [52]. The trellis encoding system uses a block Viterbi algorithm with a search depth of 1000 samples for the encoder. It is perhaps surprising that in this example the VPQ and the FSVQ with the short delay of only 4 samples can outperform a Viterbi algorithm with a delay of 1000 samples. It points out, however, two advantages of feedback VQ over scalar trellis encoding systems: 1. The decoder is permitted to be a more general form of finite-state machine than the shift-register based nonlinear filter usually used in trellis encoding systems; and 2. the encoder performs a single full search of a small vector codebook instead of a Viterbi algorithm consisting of a tree search of a sequence of scalar codebooks. In other words, single short vector searches may yield better performance than a "look ahead" sequence of searches of scalar codebooks.

Speech waveform coding

The second set of results considers a training sequence of 640,000 samples of ordinary speech from four different male speakers sampled at 6.5 kHz. The reader is reminded that squared error is not generally a subjectively good distortion measure for speech. Better subjective quality may be obtained by using more complicated distortion measures such as the general quadratic distortion measures with input dependent weightings such as the arithmetic segmented distortions. The VQ design techniques extend to such distortion measures, but the centroid computations are more complicated. (See [30] for the theory and [45, 46] for the application of input-weighted quadratic distortion measures.)

Tables III and IV are the counterparts of Tables I and II for this source. Now, however, the SNR's of the codes on test sequences of samples outside of the training sequence (and by a different speaker) are presented for comparison. In addition, some larger dimensions are con-

TABLE IV
FEEDBACK VQ OF SAMPLED SPEECH.

	FSVQ					VPQ			
k	SNRin	SNRout	K	n	M	SNRin	SNRout	n	M
1	2.0	2.0	2	2	2	2.1	2.6	2	2
2	7.8	7.5	32	4	64	6.4	6.2	4	8
3	9.0	8.3	64	10	192	7.3	6.8	8	24
4	10.9	9.4	512	16	2048	8.0	7.6	16	64
5	12.2	10.8	512	32	2560				

Signal to Noise Ratios inside training sequence (SNRin) of 640000 speech samples, Signal to Noise Ratios outside training sequence (SNRout) of 76800 speech samples, number of states (K), number of multiplications per sample (n), and storage (M) for feedback quantizers: Rate = 1 bit/sample. k = vector dimension.

sidered because the longer training sequence made them more trustworthy. Again for comparison, the best known (nonadaptive) scalar trellis encoding system for this source yields a performance of 9 dB [52]. Here the trellis encoder uses the M-algorithm with a search depth of 31 samples. The general comparisons are similar to those of the previous source, but there are several differences. The tree-searched VQ is now more degraded in comparison to the full search VQ and the multistage VQ is even worse, about 3 dB below the full search at the largest dimension in comparison to about 1 dB for the Gauss Markov case. The complexity and storage requirements are the same except for the shape/gain VQ where different optimum selections of gain and shape codebook size yield different complexity and storage requirements. The VPQ of dimension 4 is inferior to the trellis encoder and the FSVQ of the same dimension. The four dimensional FSVQ, however, still outperforms the scalar trellis encoder.

Observe that an FSVQ of dimension 4 provides better performance inside and outside the training sequence than does a full search memoryless vector quantizer of dimension 8, achieving better performance with 16 4-dimensional distortion evaluations than with 512 8-dimensional distortion computations. The cost, of course, is a large increase in memory. This, however, is a basic point of FSVQ design—to use more memory but less computation.

LPC VQ (vocoding)

Table V presents a comparison of VQ and FSVQ for vector quantization of speech using the Itakura-Saito distortion measure or, equivalently, vector quantization of LPC speech models [16, 14, 53]. The training sequence and test sequence are as above, but now the input dimension is 128 samples and the output vectors are 10th order all-pole models. The training sequence is now effectively shorter since it contains only 5000 input vectors of this dimension. As a result the test results are noticeably different than the design results. Because of the shortness of the training sequence, only FSVQ's of small dimension and few states were considered.

The table summarizes memoryless VQ and two FSVQ designs: the first FSVQ design used was a straightforward application of the design technique outlined previously and the second used the stochastic iteration next-state improvement algorithm of [53]. Observe that the next-state function improvement yields codes that perform better outside of the training sequence then do the ordinary FSVQ codes.

TABLE V
LPC VQ AND FSVQ WITH AND WITHOUT NEXT STATE FUNCTION IMPROVEMENT.

		VQ		FSVQ1		FSVQ2		
R	r	SNRin	SNRout	SNRin	SNRout	SNRin	SNRout	K
1	.008	3.7	2.9					
2	.016	6.1	5.2	7.2	4.3	7.5	6.1	16
3	.023	7.3	6.2	8.4	5.9	9.0	7.5	16
4	.031	8.8	7.9	9.5	7.8	9.6	8.7	4
5	.039	9.7	8.8	10.6	8.9	10.7	9.3	4
6	.047	10.5	9.5					
7	.055	11.6	10.1					
8	.062	12.6	10.7					

Signal to Noise Ratios inside training sequence (SNRin) of 5000 vectors of 128 samples each, Signal to Noise Ratios outside training sequence (SNRout) of 600 vectors of 128 samples each: memoryless VQ, omniscient FSVQ design (FSVQ1), and for omnisicient FSVQ design with next-state function improvement (FSVQ2). K = number of states in FSVQ, R = rate in bits/vector, r = rate in bits/sample. Itakura-Saito distortion measure.

TABLE VI
ADAPTIVE VPQ.

	VPQ	
k	SNRin	SNRout
1	4.12	4.34
2	7.47	7.17
3	8.10	7.67
4	8.87	8.30

Signal to Noise Ratios inside training sequence (SNRin) of 5000 vectors, and Signal to Noise Ratios in test sequence (SNRout) of 600 vectors, rate = 1.023 bits/sample.

Figure 16. Image Training Sequence. The training sequence consisted of the sequence of 3 × 4 subblocks of the five 256 × 256 images shown.

Gain/shape VQ's for this application are developed in [16] and [36]. Tree-searched LPC VQ is considered for binary and nonbinary trees in combination with gain/shape codes in [16] and [10].

Adaptive coding

Table VI presents the results of a simple example of an adaptive VQ, here consisting of an LPC VQ with 8 codewords every 128 samples combined with VPQs of dimensions 1–4. Each of the 8 VPQs is designed for the subsequence of training vectors mapping into the corresponding LPC VQ model [47]. The rate of this system is $1 + 3/128 = 1.023$ bits/sample. The performance is significantly worse than the 10 dB achieved by a hybrid scalar trellis encoder of the same rate [52], but it improves on the nonadaptive VPQ by about ¾ dB. Adaptive vector quantizers are still quite new, however, and relatively little work on the wide variety of possible systems has yet been done.

Image coding

In 1980–1982 four separate groups developed successful applications of VQ techniques to image coding [61, 62, 63, 64, 65, 66, 67, 37]. The only real difference from waveform coding is that now the VQ operates on small rectangular blocks of from 9 to 16 pixels, that is, the vectors are really 2-dimensional subblocks of images, typically squares with 3 or 4 pixels on a side or 3 by 4 rectangles. We here consider both the basic technique and one variation. We consider only small codebooks of 6 bits per 4 × 3 block of 12 pixels for purposes of demonstration. Better quality pictures could be obtained at the same rate of ½ bit per pixel by using larger block sizes and hence larger rates of, say, 8 to 10 bits per block. Better quality could also likely be achieved with more complicated distortion measures than the simple squared error used.

Fig. 16 gives the training sequence of five images. Fig. 17a shows a small portion of the fifth image, an eye, magnified. Fig. 17b is a picture of the $2^6 = 64$ codewords. Fig. 17c shows the decoded eye. Fig. 18 shows the original, decoded image, and error image for the complete picture. The error image is useful for highlighting the problems encountered with the ordinary memoryless VQ. In particular, edges are poorly reproduced and the codeword edges make the picture appear "blocky." This problem was attacked by Ramamurthi and Gersho [62, 67] by constructing segmented (or union or composite) codes — separate codebooks for the edge information and the texture information where a simple classifier was used to distinguish the two in design. In [37] a feedback vector quantizer was developed by using a separating mean VQ with a predictive scalar quantizer to track the mean. Fig. 19 shows the original eye, ordinary VQ, and the feedback VQ. The improved ability to track edges is clearly discernible. Fig. 20 shows the full decoded image for feedback VQ together with the error pattern.

Although image coding using VQ is still in its infancy,

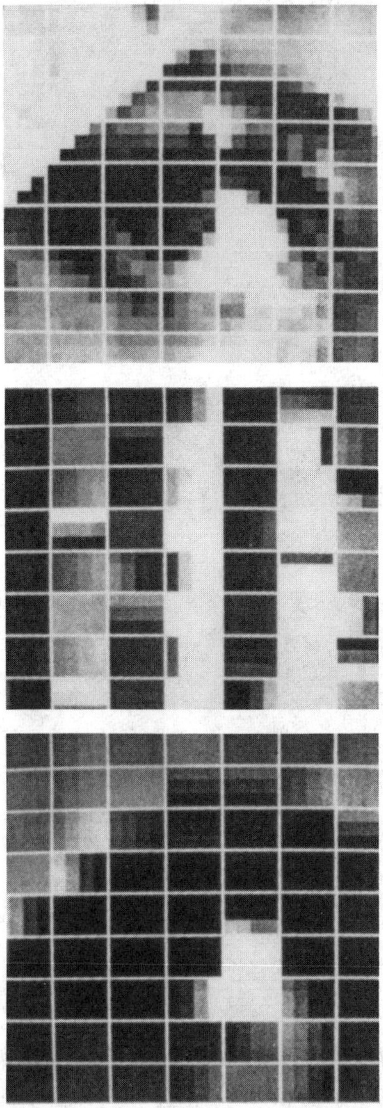

Figure 17. Basic Image VQ Example at ½ bit per pixel. (a) Original Eye Magnified (b) 6 bit codebook VQ codebook for 4 × 3 blocks (c) Decoded Image.

the tradeoffs among performance, rate, complexity, and storage for these codes.

The basic structure of all of the VQ systems is well suited to VLSI implementation: a minimum distortion search algorithm on a chip communicating with off-board storage for codebooks and next-state transition functions. As new and better design algorithms are developed, the chips can be updated by simply reburning the codebook and transition ROM's.

The basic approach can also be incorporated into the design of some traditional scalar data compression schemes, an approach which Gersho calls "imbedded

Figure 18. Full Image for Basic Example (a) Original (b) Decoded Image (c) Error Image.

these preliminary experiments using only fairly simple memoryless and feedback VQ techniques with small codebooks demonstrate that the general approach holds considerable promise for such applications.

COMMENTS

We have described Lloyd's basic iterative algorithm and how it can be used to improve the performance of a variety of vector quantization systems, ranging from the fundamental memoryless full search VQ that serves as the basic model for data compression in information theory to a variety of feedback and adaptive systems that can be viewed as vector extensions of popular scalar compression systems. By a variety of examples of systems and code design simulations we have tried to illustrate some of

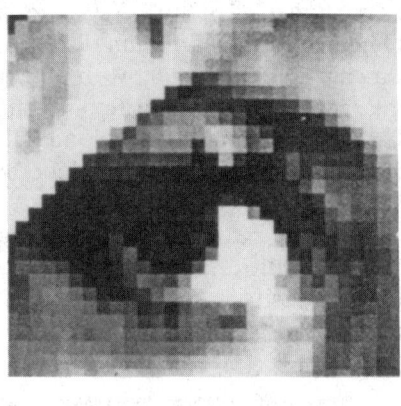

a)

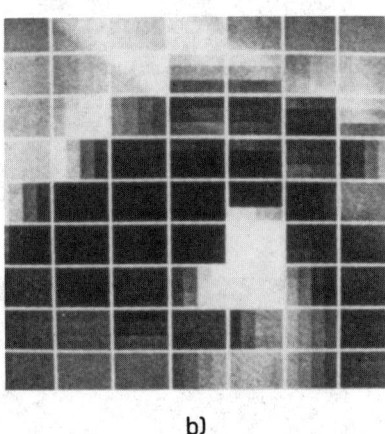

b)

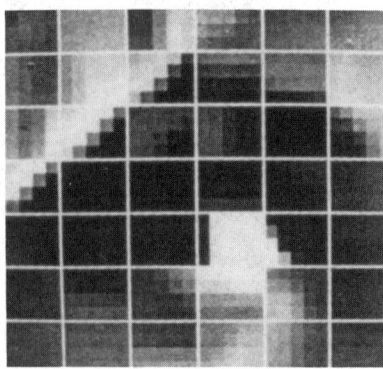

c)

Figure 19. VQ vs. Separating Mean VQ at Rate ½ bit per pixel (a) Original Eye Magnified (b) VQ Decoded Image (c) Separating Mean VQ with DPCM Mean Coding Decoded Image.

a)

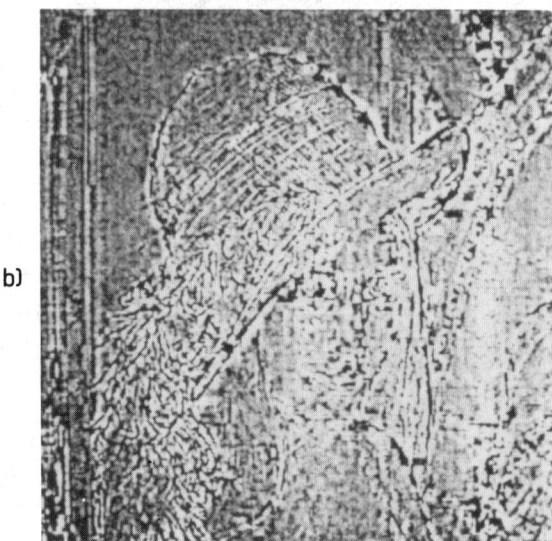

b)

Figure 20. Full Image for Separating Mean Example (a) Decoded Image using Separating Mean VQ with DPCM Mean Coding (b) Error Image.

VQ" [11]. Such schemes typically enforce additional structure on the code such as preprocessing, transforming, splitting into subbands, and scalar quantization, however, and hence the algorithms may not have the freedom to do as well as the more unconstrained structures considered here. Even if the traditional schemes prove more useful because of existing DSP chips or intuitive variations well matched to particular data sources, the vector quantization systems can prove a useful benchmark for comparison.

Recently VQ has also been successfully used in isolated word recognition systems without dynamic time warping by using either separate codebooks for each utterance or by mapping trajectories through one or more codebooks [68, 69, 70, 71, 55, 72]. Vector quantization has also been used as a front end acoustic processor to isolated utterance and continuous speech recognition systems which then do approximately maximum likelihood linguistic decoding based on probabilities estimated using "hidden Markov" models for the VQ output data. [73, 74, 75].

Variations of the basic VQ design algorithm have been tried for several distortion measures, including the squared error, weighted squared error, the Itakura-Saito distortion, and an (arithmetic) segmented signal to noise ratio. (See, e.g., [30, 45, 46]). Other distortion measures are currently under study.

The algorithm has not yet been extended to some of the more complicated distortion measures implicit in noise masking techniques for enhancing the subjective performance of scalar quantization speech coding systems. Whether scalar systems designed by sophisticated techniques matched to subjective distortion measures will sound or look better than vector systems designed for mathematically tractable distortion measures remains to be seen. Whenever the subjective distortion measures can be quantified and a means found to compute centroids, however, the vector systems will yield better quantitative performance. Since the centroid computation is only done in design and not in implementation, it can be quite complicated and still yield useful results.

The generalized Lloyd algorithm is essentially a clustering algorithm and we have attempted to demonstrate its applicability to the design of a variety of data compression systems. Other clustering algorithms may yield better codes in some applications. For example, Freeman [76] proposed a design algorithm for scalar trellis encoding systems using the squared error distortion measure which replaced the Lloyd procedure by a conjugate gradient procedure for minimizing the average distortion for a long training sequence. He found that for a memoryless Gaussian source the resulting codes were superior to those obtained by the Lloyd procedure. It would be interesting to characterize the reasons for this superiority, e.g., the procedure may find a better local minimum or it may simply be numerically better suited for finding a continuous local minimum on a digital computer. It would also be interesting to consider variations of this approach for the design of some of the other systems considered here.

A survey article with many topics cannot provide complete descriptions or exhaustive studies of any of systems sketched. It is hoped, however, that these examples impart the flavor of vector quantizer design algorithms and that they may interest some readers to further delve into the recent and current work in the area.

ACKNOWLEDGMENT

The author gratefully acknowledges the many helpful comments from students and colleagues that aided the preparation of this paper.

Portions of the research described here were supported by the Army Research Office, the Air Force Office of Scientific Research, the National Science Foundation, the John Simon Guggenheim Memorial Foundation, and the Joint Services Electronics Program at Stanford University.

REFERENCES

[1] Davisson, L. D. and Gray, R. M., *Data Compression,* Dowden, Hutchinson, & Ross, Inc., Stroudsbug, PA (1976). Benchmark Papers in Electrical Engineering and Computer Science, Volume 14.

[2] Jayant, N. S., Editor, *Waveform coding quantization and Coding,* IEEE Press, NY (1976).

[3] Jayant, N. S. and Noll, P., *Digital Coding of Waveforms,* Prentice–Hall, Englewood Cliffs, NJ (1984).

[4] Shannon, C. E., "A mathematical theory of communication," *Bell Systems Technical Journal* 27 pp. 379–423, 623–656 (1948).

[5] Shannon, C. E., "Coding theorems for a discrete source with a fidelity criterion," *IRE National Convention Record, Part 4,* pp. 142–163 (1959).

[6] Gallager, R. G., *Information theory and reliable communication,* John Wiley & Sons, NY (1968).

[7] Berger, T., *Rate Distortion Theory,* Prentice-Hall Inc., Englewood Cliffs, NJ (1971).

[8] Viterbi, A. J. and Omura, J. K., *Principles of Digital Communication and Coding,* McGraw-Hill Book Company, New York (1979).

[9] Lloyd, S. P., *Least squares quantization in PCM,* Bell Laboratories Technical Note (1957). (Published in the March 1982 special issue on quantization).

[10] Wong, D., Juang, B.-H., and Gray, A. H., Jr., "An 800 bit/s vector quantization LPC vocoder," *IEEE Transactions on Acoustics Speech and Signal Processing* ASSP-30 pp. 770–779 (October 1982).

[11] Gersho, A. and Cuperman, V., "Vector Quantization: A pattern-matching technique for speech coding," *IEEE Communications Magazine,* (December 1983).

[12] Itakura, F. and Saito, S., "Analysis synthesis telephony based on the maximum liklihood method," *Proceedings of the 6th International Congress of Acoustics,* pp. C-17–C-20 (August 1968).

[13] Kullback, S., *Information Theory and Statistics,* Dover, New York (1969).

[14] Gray, R. M., Gray, A. H., Jr., Rebolledo, G., and Shore, J. E., "Rate distortion speech coding with a minimum discrimination information distortion measure," *IEEE Transactions on Information Theory* IT-27 (6) pp. 708–721 (Nov. 1981).

[15] Shore, J. E. and Gray, R. M., "Minimum-cross-entropy pattern classification and cluster analysis," *IEEE Transactions on Pattern Analysis and Machine Intelligence* PAMI-4 pp. 11–17 (Jan. 1982).

[16] Buzo, A., Gray, A. H., Jr., and Gray, R. M., and Markel, J. D., "Speech coding based upon vector quantization," *IEEE Transactions on Acoustics Speech and Signal Processing* ASSP-28 pp. 562–574. (October 1980).

[17] Gray, R. M., Buzo, A., Gray, A. H., Jr., and Matsuyama, Y., "Distortion measures for speech processing," *IEEE Transactions on Acoustics, Speech, and Signal Processing,* ASSP-28 pp. 367–376 (August 1980).

[18] Gray, R. M., Kieffer, J. C., and Linde, Y., "Locally opti-

mal block quantizer design," *Information and Control* 45 pp. 178–198 (May 1980).

[19] Gray, R. M. and Kieffer, J. C., "Asymptotically mean stationary measures," *Annals of Probability* 8 pp. 962–973 (Oct. 1980).

[20] Kieffer, J. C. and Rahe, M., "Markov channels are asymptotically mean stationary," *Siam Journal of Mathematical Analysis* 12 pp. 293–305 (1980).

[21] Fontana, R. J., Gray, R. M., and Kieffer, J. C., "Asymptotically mean stationary channels," *IEEE Transactions on Information Theory* IT-27 pp. 308–316 (May 1981).

[22] Kieffer, J. C., "Stochastic stability for feedback quantization schemes," *IEEE Transactions on Information Theory* IT-28 pp. 248–254 (March 1982).

[23] Sabin, M. J. and Gray, R. M., *Asymptotic properties of the generalized Lloyd algorithm*, Submitted for publication 1983.

[24] Gersho, A., "On the structure of vector quantizers," *IEEE Transactions on Information Theory* IT-28 pp. 157–166 (March 1982).

[25] Linde, Y., Buzo, A., and Gray, R. M., "An algorithm for vector quantizer design," *IEEE Transactions on Communications* COM-28 pp. 84–95 (January 1980).

[26] MacQueen, J., "Some methods for classification and analysis of multivariate observations," *Proc. of the Fifth Berkeley Symposium on Math. Stat. and Prob.* 1 pp. 281–296 (1967).

[27] Diday, E. and Simon, J. C., "Clustering analysis," in *Digital Pattern Recognition*, ed. K. S. Fu, Springer-Verlag, NY (1976).

[28] Chen, D. T. S., "On two or more dimensional optimum quantizers," *Proceedings, 1977 International Conference on Acoustics, Speech, and Signal Processing*, pp. 640–643 (1977).

[29] Adoul, J.-P., Morissette, S., and Rudko, M., "Bit-rate-halving algorithm for PCM-encoded speech using a new bidimensional data compression scheme," *Record of the 1979 IEEE International Conference on Acoustics Speech and Signal Processing*, pp. 432–435 (April 1979).

[30] Gray, R. M. and Karnin, E., "Multiple local optima in vector quantizers," *IEEE Transactions on Information Theory* IT-28 pp. 256–261 (March 1982).

[31] Abut, H., Gray, R. M., and Rebolledo, G., "Vector quantization of speech and speech-like waveforms," *IEEE Transactions on Acoustics Speech and Signal Processing* ASSP-30 pp. 423–435 (June 1982).

[32] Adoul, J.-P., Debray, J.-L., and Dalle, D., "Spectral distance measure applied to the optimum design of DPCM coders with L predictors," *Proceedings of the 1980 IEEE International Conference on Acoustics Speech and Signal Processing*, pp. 512–515 (April 1980).

[33] Gersho, A. and Cheng, D., "Fast nearest neighbor search for nonstructured Euclidean codes," *Abstracts of the 1983 IEEE International Symposium on Information Theory*, p. 88 (September 1983).

[34] Juang, B.-H. and Gray, A. H., Jr., "Multiple stage vector quantization for speech coding," *Proceedings of the IEEE International Conference on Acoustics Speech and Signal Processing* 1 pp. 597–600 (April 1982).

[35] Sabin, M. J. and Gray, R. M., "Product code vector quantizers for speech waveform coding," *Conference Record Globecom '82*, pp. 1087–1091 (December 1982).

[36] Sabin, M. J. and Gray, R. M., *Product code vector quantizers for waveform and voice coding, IEEE Trans. ASSP*, to appear, (April 1984).

[37] Baker, R. L. and Gray, R. M., "Differential vector quantization of achromatic imagery," *Proceedings of the International Picture Coding Symposium*, (March 1983).

[38] Gersho, A., "Asymptotically optimal block quantization," *IEEE Transactions on Information Theory* IT-25 pp. 373–380 (July 1979).

[39] Conway, J. H. and Sloane, N. J. A., "Voronoi regions of lattices, second moments of polytopes, and quantization," *IEEE Transactions on Information Theory* IT-28 pp. 211–226 (March 1982).

[40] Conway, J. H. and Sloane, N. J. A., "Fast quantizing and decoding algorithms for lattice quantizers and codes," *IEEE Transactions on Information Theory* IT-28 pp. 227–232 (March 1982).

[41] Conway, J. H. and Sloane, N. J. A., "On the Voronoi regions of certain lattices," *SIAM Journal of Alg. Disc. Math.*, (1983). in press

[42] Barnes, E. S. and Sloane, N. J. A., "The optimal lattice quantizer in three dimensions," *SIAM Journal of Alg. Disc. Math.* 4 pp. 30–41 (1983).

[43] Foster, J., Newkirk, J., and Gray, R. M., *VLSI implementation of a finite-state vector quantization waveform encoder*, submitted for publication 1983.

[44] Gaarder, N. T. and Slepian, D., "On optimal finite-state digital transmission systems," *IEEE Transactions on Information Theory* IT-28 pp. 167–186 (March 1982).

[45] Cuperman, V. and Gersho, A., "Adaptive differential vector coding of speech," *Conference Record, GlobeCom 82*, pp. 1092–1096 (December 1982).

[46] Cuperman, V. and Gersho, A., *Vector predictive coding of speech at 16 Kb/s*, Submitted for possible publication 1983.

[47] Chang, P. C., Ph.D. Research, Stanford University 1983.

[48] Gibson, J. D., Jones, S. K., and Melsa, J. L., "Sequentially adaptive prediction and coding of speech signals," *IEEE Transactions on Communications* COM-22 pp. 1789–1797 (November 1974).

[49] Dunn, J. G., "An experimental 9600-bit/s voice digitizer employing adaptive prediction," *IEEE Transactions on Communication Technology* COM-19 pp. 1021–1032 (December 1971).

[50] Foster, J. and Gray, R. M., "Finite-state vector quantization," *Abstracts of the 1982 International Sym-*

posium on Information Theory, (June 1982).

[51] Foster, J., Gray, R. M., and Ostendouf, M., *Finite-state vector quantization for waveform coding,* IEEE Trans. Info. Theory, to appear.

[52] Stewart, L. C., Gray, R. M., and Linde, Y., "The design of trellis waveform coders," *IEEE Transactions on Communications* COM-30 pp. 702–710 (April 1982).

[53] Ostendorf, M. and Gray, R. M., *An algorithm for the design of labeled-transition finite-state vector quantizers,* submitted for publication 1983.

[54] Fehn, H. G. and Noll, P., "Multipath search coding of stationary signals with applications to speech," *IEEE Transactions on Communications* COM-30 pp. 687–701 (April 1982).

[55] Shore, J. E. and Burton, D. K., "Discrete utterance speech recognition without time alignment," *IEEE Transactions on Information Theory* IT-29 pp. 473–491 (July 1983).

[56] Rebolledo, G., Gray, R. M., and Burg, J. P., "A multi-rate voice digitizer based upon vector quantization," *IEEE Transactions on Communications* COM-30 pp. 721–727 (April 1982).

[57] Adoul, J.-P. and Mabilleau, P., "4800 bps RELP vocoder using vector quantization for both filter and residual representation," *Proceedings of the IEEE International Conference on Acoustics Speech and Signal Processing* 1 p. 601 (April 1982).

[58] Heron, C. D., Crochiere, R. E., and Cox, R. V., "A 32-band subband/transform coder incorporating vector quantization for dynamic bit allocation," *Proceedings ICASSP,* pp. 1276–1279 (April 1983).

[59] Gray, R. M. and Linde, Y., "Vector quantizers and predictive quantizers for Gauss-Markov sources," *IEEE Transactions on Communications* COM-30 pp. 381–389 (Feb. 1982).

[60] Arnstein, D. S., "Quantization error in predictive coders," *IEEE Transactions on Communications* COM-23 pp. 423–429 (April 1975).

[61] Yamada, Y., Fujita, K., and Tazaki, S., "Vector quantization of video signals," *Proceedings of Annual Conference of IECE,* p. 1031 (1980).

[62] Gersho, A. and Ramamurthi, B., "Image coding using vector quantization," *Proceedings of the IEEE International Conference on Acoustics Speech and Signal Processing* 1 pp. 428–431 (April 1982).

[63] Baker, R. L. and Gray, R. M., "Image compression using non-adaptive spatial vector quantization," *Conference Record of the Sixteenth Asilomar Conference on Circuits Systems and Computers,* (October 1982).

[64] Murakami, T., Asai, K., and Yamazaki, E., "Vector quantizer of video signals," *Electronic Letters* 7 pp. 1005–1006 (Nov. 1982).

[65] Yamada, Y. and Tazaki, S., "Vector quantizer design for video signals," *IECE Transactions* J66-B pp. 965–972 (1983). (in Japanese)

[66] Yamada, Y. and Tazaki, S., "A method for constructing successive approximation vector quantizers for video signals," *Proceedings of the Annual Conference of the Institute of Television Engineers of Japan,* pp. 6–2 (1983).

[67] Ramamurthi, B. and Gersho, A., "Image coding using segmented codebooks," *Proceedings International Picture Coding Symposium,* (Mar. 1983).

[68] Hamabe, R., Yamada, Y., Murata, M., and Namekawa, T., "A speech recognition system using inverse filter matching technique," *Proceedings of the Ann. Conf. Inst. of Television Engineers,* (June 1981). (in Japanese)

[69] Shore, J. E. and Burton, D. K., "Discrete utterance speech recognition without time alignment," *Proceedings 1982 IEEE International Conference on Acoustics Speech and Signal Processing,* p. 907 (May 1982).

[70] Martinez, H. G., Riviera, C., and Buzo, A., "Discrete utterance recognition based upon source coding techniques," *Proceedings IEEE International Conference on Acoustics Speech and Signal Processing,* pp. 539–542 (May 1982).

[71] Rabiner, L., Levinson, S. E., and Sondhi, M. M., "On the application of vector quantization and hidden Markov models to speaker-independent isolated word recognition," *Bell System Technical Journal* 62 pp. 1075–1106 (April 1983).

[72] Shore, J. E., Burton, D., and Buck, J., "A generalization of isolated word recognition using vector quantization," *Proceedings 1983 International Conference on Acoustics Speech and Signal Processing,* pp. 1021–1024 (April 1983).

[73] Jelinek, F., Mercer, R. L., and Bahl, L. R., "Continuous speech recognition: statistical methods," in *Handbook of Statistics,* Vol. 2, P. R. Khrishaieh and L. N. Kanal, eds., North-Holland, pp. 549–573. (1982).

[74] Billi, R., "Vector quantization and Markov models applied to speech recognition," *Proc. ICASSP 82,* pp. 574–577, Paris (May 1982).

[75] Rabiner, L. R., Levinson, S. E., and Sondhi, M. M., "On the application of vector quantization and hidden Markov models to speaker-independent isolated word recognition," *BSTJ,* Vol. 62, pp. 1075–1105, (April 1983).

[76] Freeman, G. H., "The design of time-invariant trellis source codes," *Abstracts of the 1983 IEEE International Symposium on Information Theory,* pp. 42–43 (September 1983).

[77] Haoui, A. and Messerschmidt, D., "Predictive Vector Quantization," *Proceedings of the IEEE International Conference on Acoustics, Speech, and Signal Processing* (1984).

Robert M. Gray was born in San Diego, CA, on November 1, 1943. He received the B.S. and M.S. degrees from M.I.T. in 1966 and the Ph.D. degree from U.S.C. in 1969, all in Electrical Engineering. Since 1969 he has been with the Information Systems Laboratory and the Electrical Engineering Department of Stanford University, CA, where he is currently a Professor engaged in teaching and research in communication and information theory with an emphasis on data compression. He was Associate Editor (1977–1980) and Editor (1980–1983) of the *IEEE Transactions on Information Theory* and was a member of the IEEE Information Theory Group Board of Governors (1974–1980). He was corecipient with Lee D. Davisson of the 1976 IEEE Information Theory Group Paper Award. He has been a fellow of the Japan Society for the Promotion of Science (1981) and the John Simon Guggenheim Memorial Foundation (1981–1982). He is a fellow of the IEEE and a member of Sigma Xi, Eta Kappa Nu, SIAM, IMS, AAAS, and the Societé des Ingenieurs et Scientifiques de France. He holds an Advanced Class Amateur Radio License (KB6XQ).

Notes added in proof: A similar design technique for FSVQ was independently developed by Haoui and Messerschmidt [77]. It should be pointed out that the FSVQ design algorithm described here is incomplete in that it does not describe the methods used to avoid noncommunicating collection of states and wasted states. These issues are discussed in [51].

Image Coding Using Vector Quantization: A Review

NASSER M. NASRABADI, MEMBER, IEEE, AND ROBERT A. KING

Abstract—This paper presents a review of vector quantization techniques used for encoding digital images. First the concept of vector quantization is introduced, then its application to digital images is explained. Spatial, predictive, transform, hybrid, binary, and subband vector quantizers are reviewed. The emphasis here is on the usefulness of the vector quantization when it is combined with conventional image coding techniques or when it is used in different domains.

I. INTRODUCTION

IMAGE compression is essential for applications such as TV transmission, video conferencing, facsimile transmission of printed material, graphics images, or transmission of remote sensing images obtained from satellites and reconnaissance aircraft. Another area for the application of efficient coding is where pictures are stored in a database, such as archiving medical images, multispectral images, finger prints, and drawings [1] and [2].

The vector quantization algorithms for reducing the transmission bit rate or the storage have recently been extensively investigated for speech and image signals [8] and [11]. In this paper, only the applications of vector quantization to image coding are discussed; the contents are thus restricted to coding techniques that employ vector quantizers (VQ's). Recently, there have been several review articles on general technique of image compression [3]-[6]. In particular, vector quantization has been applied to speech coding for a number of years [7]-[10], and Gray has recently published an excellent review paper on this subject [11].

A fundamental goal of data compression is to reduce the bit rate for transmission or data storage while maintaining an acceptable fidelity or image quality. Numerous bandwidth compression techniques have been developed, such as differential pulse code modulation, transform coding, hybrid coding, and adaptive versions of these techniques in response to the growth of image-processing methods. These techniques usually exploit the psychovisual as well as statistical redundancies in the image data to reduce the bit rate [12]. One deficiency with all of the conventional coding techniques is that quantization is performed on individual real-valued samples of waveforms or pixels of images. For example, transform coding does this by first taking block transforms of a vector and then scalar quantizing the transformed samples within the vector. Predictive coding does it by coding an error term formed as the difference between the current sample and its prediction. These techniques are not optimal since the processed samples are still somehow correlated or dependent.

Paper approved by the Editor for Signal Processing and Communication Electronics of the IEEE Communications Society. Manuscript received October 12, 1984; revised June 16, 1987. This paper was presented at the IEEE Acoustics, Speech, and Signal Processing Conference 1985, Tampa, FL, March 26-29, 1985.
N. M. Nasrabadi is with the Department of Electrical Engineering, Atwater Kent Laboratories, Worcester Polytechnic Institute, MA 01609.
R. A. King is with the Department of Electrical Engineering, Imperial College of Science and Technology, London, SW7, England.
IEEE Log Number 8822470.

According to Shannon's rate-distortion theory, a better performance is always achievable in theory by coding vectors instead of scalars, even though the data source is memoryless.

This paper is not intended as a survey of the basic vector quantization design algorithms or the searching techniques, but rather as a demonstration of the application of vector quantizers to image coding. A definition of the vector quantizer is given followed by its applications to images in the spatial domain, the predictive domain, the transform domain, and combinations of these known as hybrid domains.

II. DEFINITION OF VECTOR QUANTIZATION

Extensive studies of vector quantizers or multidimensional quantizers has recently been performed by many researchers [13]-[17]. The design of optimal vector quantizers from empirical data were proposed and extensively studied by Linde, Buzo, and Gray [9] using a clustering approach which is discussed in Section II-A. This algorithm is now commonly referred to as the LBG algorithm. A vector quantizer can be defined as a mapping Q of K-dimensional Euclidean space R^k into a finite subset Y of R^K. Thus,

$$Q : R^K \to Y \tag{1}$$

where $Y = (\hat{x}_i; i = 1, 2, \cdots, N)$ is the set of reproduction vectors and N the number of vectors in Y. It can also be seen as a combination of two functions: an encoder, which views the input vector x and generates the address of the reproduction vector specified by $Q(x)$, and a decoder, which uses this address to generate the reproduction vector $\hat{x}$. If a distortion measure $d(x, \hat{x})$ which represents the penalty or cost associated with reproducing vectors x by $\hat{x}$ is defined, then the best mapping Q is the one which minimizes $d(x, \hat{x})$ [13]. The LBG algorithm and other variations of this algorithm are based upon this minimization, using a training set as the signal.

One simple distortion measure for waveform coding is the square error distortion given by

$$d(x, \hat{x}) = \|x - \hat{x}\|^2 = \sum_{j=0}^{K-1} (x_j - \hat{x}_j^2). \tag{2}$$

A weighted mean square error (WMSE) distortion can also be used [37]. Other error distortion measures have also been suggested, but they are too expensive computationally [18] for practical implementation. One problem with vector quantization is that a large effort is required by the encoder to search the whole codebook in order to identify the nearest matching vector template to an input vector. Recently, Buzo *et al.* [7] have proposed a tree searched (TSVQ) encoder in order to reduce the search effort of a vector quantizer. A TSVQ encoder can be explained as an encoder that searches a sequence of small codebooks instead of one large codebook. The encoder structure can be depicted as a tree and each search and decision corresponds to advancing one level or stage in the tree, starting from the root of the tree. A detailed description of TSVQ's and TSVQ design algorithms may be found in [19] and [20]. The disadvantages of TSVQ encoders are that their codebook storage requirement is greater than full-search VQ's, and the codewords they select are not, in general, optimum in the sense of minimizing $d(x, \hat{x})$. Other vector quantization techniques that reduce memory as well as encoding complexity can be found in [21]-[22] and [109]-[110] where Fischer designed a quantizer (Pyramid Vector Quantizer) based on the implicit geometry of an independent and identically distributed Laplacian source.

A. Vector Quantizer Design

The goal in designing an optimal vector quantizer is to obtain a quantizer consisting of N reproduction vectors, such that it minimizes the expected distortion. Optimality is said to be achieved if there is no other quantizer that can achieve the minimum expected distortion. Lloyd [17] proposed an iterative nonvariational technique known as his "Method I" for the design of scalar quantizers. Recently, Linde *et al.* [9] extended Lloyds' basic approach to the general case of vector quantizers.

Let the expected distortion be approximated by the time-averaged square error distortion given by the expression

$$D(x, q(x)) = \frac{1}{N} \sum_{i=0}^{N-1} d(x_i, \hat{x}_i). \quad (3)$$

The algorithm for an unknown distribution training sequence is given in [9].

1) Let N = number of levels; distortion threshold $\epsilon \geq 0$. Assume an initial N level reproduction alphabet $\hat{A}_0$, and a training sequence $(x_j; j = 0, 1, \cdots, n - 1)$, and m = number of iterations, set to zero.

2) Given $\hat{A}_m = (y_i; i = 1, \cdots, N)$, find the minimum distortion partition $P(\hat{A}_m) = (S_i; i = 1, \cdots, N)$ of the training sequence: $x_j \in S_i$ if $d(x_j, y_i) \leq d(x_j, y_l)$, for all l. Compute the average distortion

$$D_m = D[(\hat{A}_m, P(\hat{A}_m))] = n-1 \sum_{j=0}^{n-1} \min_{y \in A_m} d(x_j, y). \quad (4)$$

3) If $(D_{m-1} - D_m)/D_m \leq \epsilon$, stop the iteration with $\hat{A}_m$ as the final reproduction alphabet; otherwise continue.

4) Find the optimal reproduction alphabet $\hat{x}(P(\hat{A}_m)) = (\hat{x}(S_i); i = 1, \cdots, N)$ for $P(\hat{A}_m)$ where

$$\hat{x}(S_i) = \frac{1}{\|S_i\|} \sum_{j: x_j \in S_i}^{m} x_j. \quad (5)$$

5) Set $\hat{A}_{m+1} = \hat{x}(S_i)$, increment m to $m + 1$, and go to (2).

In the above iterative algorithm an initial reproduction alphabet $\hat{A}_0$ was assumed in order to start the algorithm. There are a number of techniques to obtain the initial codebook. The simplest technique is to use the first widely spaced words from the training sequence. Linde *et al.* [9] used a splitting technique where the centroid for the training sequence was calculated and split into two close vectors. The centroids or the reproduction vectors for the two partitions were then calculated. Each resulting vector was then split into two vectors and the above procedure was repeated until an N level initial reproduction vector was created. Splitting was performed by adding a fixed perturbation vector ϵ to each vector y_i producing two vectors $y_i + \epsilon$, $y_i - \epsilon$. Another approach for designing initial codebooks is to employ product code techniques [22]. In this approach, a scalar quantizer is used K times successively to yield a K-dimensional vector quantizer.

There are a number of other techniques for designing codebooks, such as Kohonen self-organization feature maps [111]-[112] and simulated annealing (Boltzmann Machine)

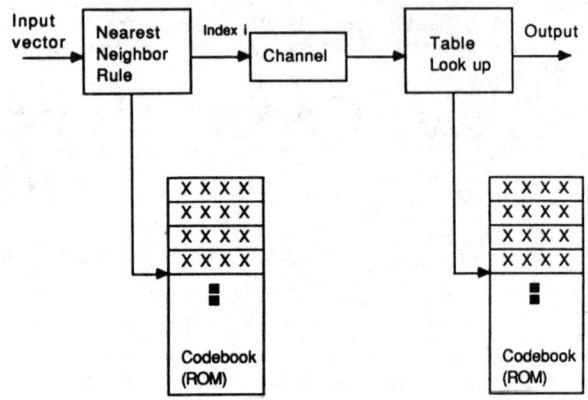

Fig. 1. Block diagram of a simple vector quantizer [37].

[113]-[114]. Kohonen introduced a neural network clustering technique where weights (synaptic strength) between neurons are adaptively sensitized to the prevailing input patterns. The asymptotic values of the weights define the codebook entries. Simulated annealing is an stochastic optimization technique that can be used to find the optimal codebook patterns with respect to the training sequence. It will avoid local minimums by introducing noise in to the system.

III. SPATIAL VECTOR QUANTIZERS (SVQ)

Recently, the performance of vector quantizers on digital images has been investigated in the spatial domain [23]-[45]. Adaptive and nonadaptive vector quantizers have been designed to code single frame images. The basic concept involves partitioning an image into two-dimensional vectors. Each vector is then compared to a set of standard vector templates stored in a ROM, and a codeword identifying the best match is then transmitted. The receiver reconstructs the image using the corresponding templates in place of the original vectors. Fig. 1 shows the block diagram of a simple vector quantization coding system. Murakami *et al.* [30] designed a vector quantizer system by converting each vector (block) of the video signal into a vector with zero mean and unit standard deviation as shown below for a vector of input video samples $S = [s_1, s_2, \cdots, s_k]_l$ of dimension K,

$$m_l = \frac{1}{K} \sum_{i=1}^{K} s_i \quad (6)$$

$$\sigma_l = \left[\frac{1}{K} \sum_{i=1}^{K} (s_i - m_l)^2 \right]^{1/2} \quad (7)$$

$$x_i = \frac{(s_i - m_l)}{\sigma_l} \quad (8)$$

$$X_l = [x_1, x_2, \cdots, x_k]_l \quad (9)$$

where m_l, and σ_l are mean and standard deviations of block l. By the above normalization the probability function $P(X)$ of input vectors X is approximately similar for video signals from different scenes. Each vector X_l is then coded by a codebook designed by the LBG algorithms using a mini-max distortion criterion. The mean and the variance are quantized by a scalar quantizer and then transmitted. A two-dimensional quantizer can also be employed to code these statistical measures.

A. Mean/Shape VQ

Baker and Gray [23]-[26] also designed a similar technique called mean/shape vector quantizer (M/SVQ) this is shown in Fig. 2. The sample mean was scalar quantized and the resulting error vector, obtained by subtracting the sample

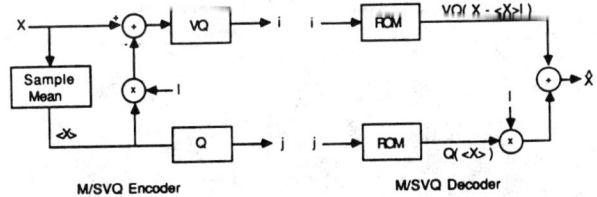

Fig. 2. Mean/shape vector quantizer system [26].

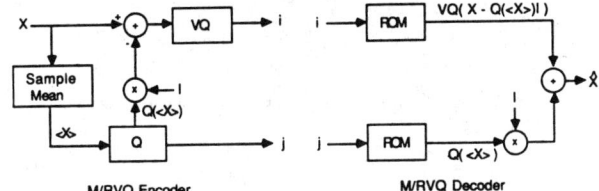

Fig. 3. Mean/residual vector quantizer system [26].

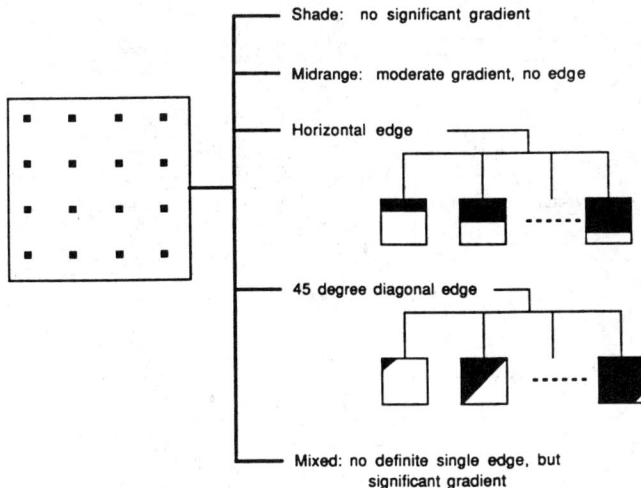

Fig. 5. Each vector is categorized into several classes such as shade and edge blocks [37].

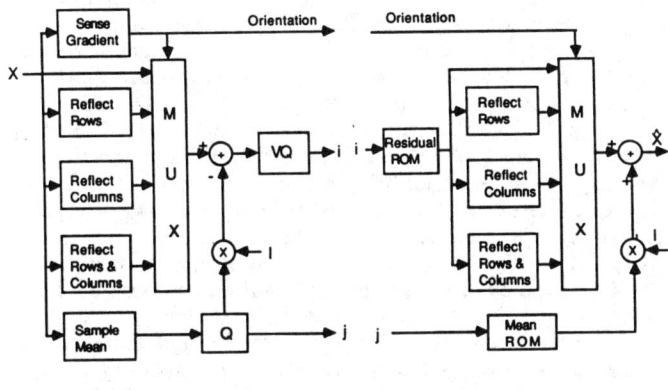

Fig. 4. Mean/reflected residual vector quantizer system [26].

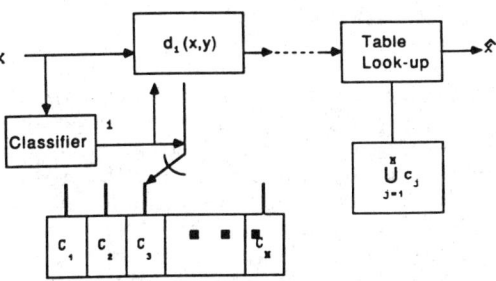

Fig. 6. Classified vector quantizer coding system [37].

mean from the input vector, is vector quantized. A variation of M/SVQ was also introduced, and is called mean/residual vector quantizer (M/RVQ) as shown in Fig. 3. In this coding system, the sample mean is first scalar quantized and then subtracted from the vector so that any error in quantization of the mean is incorporated into the error vector. The M/RVQ system reduces the blocking distortion that is caused by coarse quantization of the sample mean in the M/SVQ system [25]. To exploit the interblock correlation, Baker suggested the use a scalar quantizer with memory. A differential pulse code modulation (DPCM) was used in his system.

Baker also extended his coding system M/RVQ to include the symmetrical properties of the square vectors [26]. Since some square vectors differ only be reflections about their horizontal or vertical axes, it is possible to transmit this orientation as well as the corresponding codebook vector as shown in Fig. 4 this is called mean/reflected residual VQ. The advantage of this approach is that by sending the corresponding reflection information, we do not have to store all the possible code-vectors. An increase in bit rate is expected because information about the symmetry of the vector block has to be sent. If the block size is small 3×3, this increase in side information is significant.

B. Classified VQ

The vector coded images at very low bit rates usually suffer from edge distortion since edges cannot be reproduced perfectly by a small sized codebook. Gersho and Ramamurthi tackled this problem by classifying each vector of the image into several categories [33] and [36]. A simple classification of the training vectors into edge and shade types, followed by a separate codebook design for each class was proposed. They called this approach a classified vector quantizer (CVQ). Each vector was then coded by the appropriate vector quantizer. The computational complexity was also reduced since only one appropriate subclass of the codebook is checked for each input vector. However, since it is of great perceptual importance to preserve the fidelity of edges in location and angular orientation, the authors extended their earlier classification idea to include a larger number of classes [37]. Each edge block was then subdivided into more classes depending upon the orientation and location of the edge. Fig. 5 shows the classification that they used. Subcodebooks were designed separately for each class by using the LBG algorithm. For example, let C represent the overall codebook and C_i represent the codebook for each class i so $C = \bigcup_{i=1}^{M} C_i$ assuming there are M classes. Codebooks were designed by using the LBG algorithm for each class, allowing the training sequence $[x_j; j = 1, \cdots, n]$ to be classified into the appropriate class, $[x_j^i; j = 1, \cdots, d, i = 1, \cdots, M]$; each codebook C_i was designed by using the training sequence that belonged to that class x_j^i. The LBG algorithm was used to minimize the class distortion $d_i(X, Y)$ where x and y were restricted to the corresponding training sequence x^i and the codebook C_i. Fig. 6 shows the coding procedure. Gradient edge operators were employed on the edge enhanced images for classification of each vector image. By increasing the size of the edge codebook, they noticed the quality of the images was seen to be greatly improved.

Finally, Ramamurthi and Gersho extended the above CVQ technique to include different codebooks and appropriate coding processes for each class. For example, the blocks that fall within the midrange class, which represents moderate intensity variation but excluding any definite edges, are two-dimensional transformed by using a discrete cosine transform

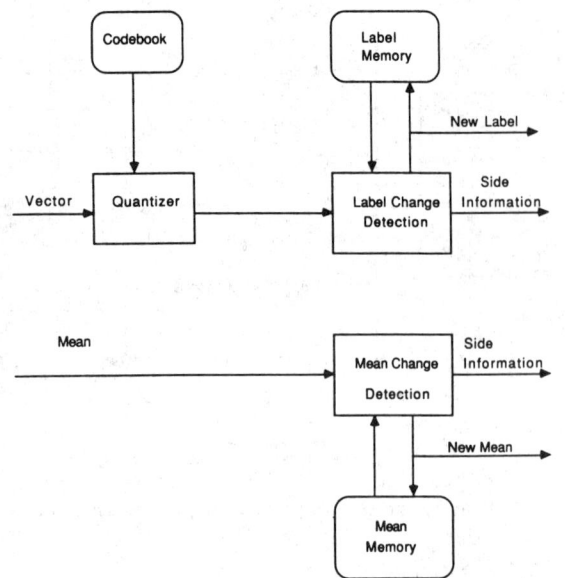

Fig. 7. The block diagram of a codebook replenishment system [40].

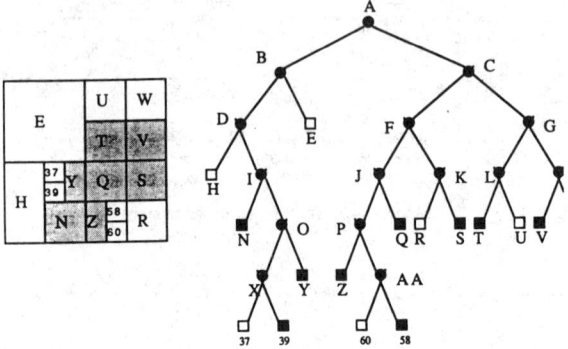

Fig. 8. A typical quad-tree representation of an image [43].

(DCT). A number of high-frequency coefficients are discarded (zonal sampling) [38] thereby reducing the VQ computational complexity in exchange for a small increase in distortion. The distortion is negligible because most of the energy is carried by the low frequency coefficients, especially for the blocks that belong to the midrange class. For the blocks belonging to the edge class, the separate-mean VQ coder of Baker and Gray [23] is employed because the edge blocks are similar in edge orientation and location and differ only in the average intensity level; these can be represented by codebook vectors that are normalized by the mean. These vector quantization techniques can be extended to multidimensional vector quantizers for coding moving images, but the storage for the codebooks as well as the computational complexity will be exponentially increased.

C. Codebook Replenishment VQ

Goldberg *et al.* [39]–[40] introduced an adaptive vector quantizer for the coding of monochromatic and color pictures. In their system, adaptivity was based upon computing and transmitting a small codebook that matched the local statistics of the image to be coded. Fig. 7 shows the block diagram of the proposed adaptive vector quantization system. The image is subdivided into nonoverlapping subimages, and for each subimage, a separate codebook consisting of about 16–64 representative vectors is formed. For each subimage, the locally generated representative vectors of the codebook are transmitted, followed by the codewords or labels for the vectors of the image. Images coded by this technique produce visually acceptable pictures falling between 1–1.5 bit-pixel. The block size of 2×2 was employed in their algorithm. One problem with this method is that the redundancy between different codebooks used in the different subimages is not removed as indicated by the authors [40]. The extension of this technique to color images is discussed in Section VIII. The major problem with this technique is that the new codebooks must be sent to the receiver involving the transformation of a large amount of side information and also needing a large computational effort for designing the new codebooks. Gersho and Yano [41] developed a similar algorithm in which adaptation was applied to change only a small part of the codebook rather than the entire codebook. The algorithm monitors the distortion for each input vector and if it is larger than a predetermined threshold, that input vector is added to the codebook as a new vector.

D. Hierarchical VQ

An important point that has been ignored in adaptive SVQ is that the block size is constant throughout the encoding process. A better technique which could lower the bit rate significantly is to use variable block length. One such technique was introduced by Nasrabadi [42] called adaptive hierarchical VC (AHVQ). In this coding technique, a quad-tree algorithm [43] is first used to partition the image into blocks of size 2×2, 4×4, 8×8, and 16×16. This information about partitioning the image is represented by a quad-tree and is counted as the side information to be transmitted. Fig. 8 shows a typical quad-tree representation. In the coding process, the small blocks, 2×2 and 4×4, are coded by using a typical SVQ. The larger blocks representing constant patterns are encoded by applying VQ in the transform domain. Many of the high-frequency coefficients can be discarded and thus the effective dimension of the blocks is reduced for computational purposes. A similar but one-dimensional algorithm was also proposed for speech [44].

Recently, Vaisey and Gersho [45] implemented such a variable block-size vector quantizer by using a standard split-merging segmentation technique to partition the image into subblocks. Two approaches were studied for vector quantization of images. In the first approach, vector quantizer was used as well as a transform VQ, and in the second approach an adaptive vector quantizer was used where the adaptivity was based upon updating or replenishing the codebook by vector patterns that represent the statistics of the current image more efficiently.

E. Interframe VQ

In an image sequence, successive frames are usually very highly correlated. A simple interframe coding system that only transmits the intensity of the pixels that change between successive frames is known as a frame replenishment coding system. Recently, Goldberg and Sun [39]–[40] introduced several interframe coding systems where the ideas of label replenishment and codebook replenishment were incorporated in their coding system. Fig. 9 shows the schematic diagram for a label replenishment VQ system. In this system, each frame is first divided into two-dimensional blocks, and vectors are then extracted from the resulting blocks either directly in the spatial domain or indirectly through the transform domain. The vectors corresponding to the first frame are taken as the training set for generating the first codebook. The first frame is quantized, and the labels are stored in the label memory and transmitted as indicated by dashed line 2. Each subsequent frame is subdivided into two-dimensional blocks and each vector is quantized. The label is then compared to the one in the label memory, and if it differs, the memory is replenished.

In an image sequence, usually some areas within the image sequence get occluded or are uncovered by the movement of

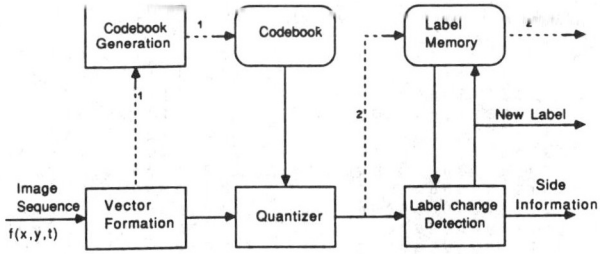

Fig. 9. A schematic diagram for a label replenishment vector quantization system [40].

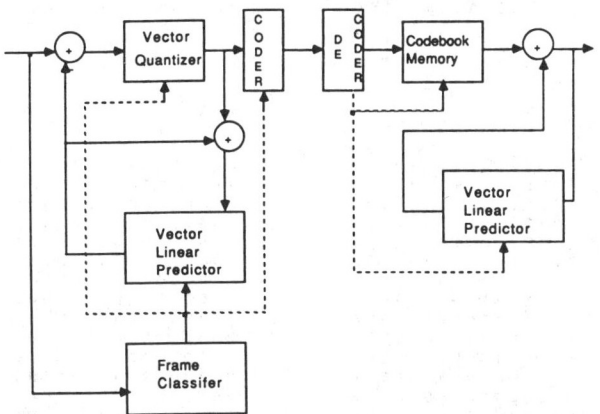

Fig. 10. Adaptive differential vector quantizer [51].

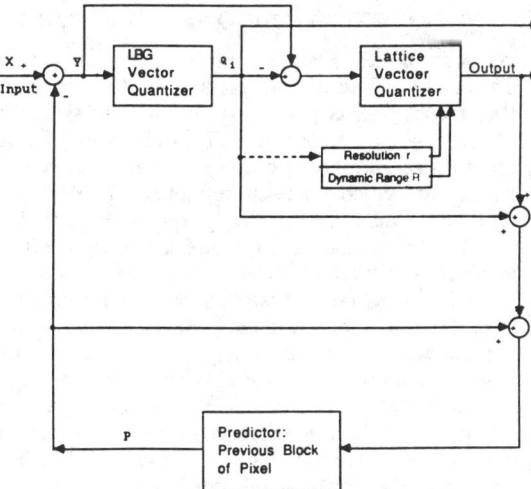

Fig. 11. A two stage hybrid vector quantizer [65].

objects. In order for the codebook to follow the statistics of the image, a codebook replenishment VQ system was suggested in [40]. For each vector from the jth frame, the best representative vector pattern is found from the codebook that was generated using the $j - 1$th frame. If the distance between these vectors is above a threshold, that vector is added to the codebook at the transmitter and the receiver, thereby replenishing the codebooks. If the scene changes drastically, then a large number of new vector patterns has to be transmitted. A better approach would be to use the new frame and form a totally a new codebook as suggested in [40].

IV. PREDICTIVE VECTOR QUANTIZER (PVQ)

In the previous section, we considered zero memory vector quantization of scalar random variables. However, since the consecutive vectors are statistically dependent, better performance can be achieved if intervector correlation is incorporated in the encoder. A memory vector quantizer can be represented by a finite state machine [46]–[48] where each state s represents a separate quantizer with its own codebook C_s. At each state s_i, the encoder uses the codebook C_{s_i} to produce the channel symbols. It selects its next state by a mapping called the state transition function F such that, given a state s_i and a channel symbol v_i then $F(v_i, s_i)$ is the new state of the machine. Feedback vector quantizers are known as finite state vector quantizers (FSVQ) [47]–[50] or predictive vector quantizers [46]. The application of FSVQ to speech and image coding is still not fully developed. A design procedure was developed by Foster et al. [48]. In FSVQ, the codebooks as well as the state transition table are stored in ROM. Recently, Aravind and Gersho [49] and [108] applied a FSVQ coding system to encode digital images. A state transition function F was developed based upon a classifier where intensity and geometric correlations between neighboring blocks were used. The application of FSVQ to image sequences was reported in [50].

A coding system has been introduced by Cuperman and Gersho [51] involving a vector generalization of DPCM and is shown in Fig. 10. The coder consists of a vector predictor and an error vector quantizer. An error vector signal e is formed by subtracting the predicted vector $\hat{x}$ estimated from previous vectors from the actual present sample vector x. This error vector is then coded by using an error codebook. To improve performance, the system is made adaptive by classifying input frames of speech into categories, and using an appropriate predictor and quantizer for each class.

Hang and Woods developed a predictive vector quantizer in [52]–[53]. In their coding system, the input consists of a vector having the current pixel as the first element and the previous inputs as the remaining elements in the vector. The system is like a mapping or a recursive filter predicting the next sample. The mapping is implemented by a VQ lookup table which produces the error signal directly.

The idea of predictive vector quantization can easily be extended to interframe DPCM coders. In conventional interframe coders, usually two frames of an image sequence are stored, and an interframe difference signal is obtained where the moving areas are detected and their resulting difference signal is scalar quantized [54]–[57]. Murakami et al. [58] recently introduced a coding system where vector quantization was used to code the interframe difference signal obtained from the moving areas.

Adaptive predictors, such as motion compensated predictors, have recently been studied extensively [59]–[63]. These adaptive predictors can be incorporated into the interframe predictive vector quantizer. Finally, it should be noted that vector quantization schemes can be employed to code the error signal obtained from conventional hybrid coders [64]; we call these coders hybrid vector quantizers (HVQ).

An interframe predictive vector quantizer was designed by Bage [65]. In his first coding system, the prediction vector P consists of the same spatial block of pixels in the previous frame. An error vector Y is formed by subtracting from an input vector X a prediction vector P. This error vector is then vector quantized by the symbols Q in the codebook. A two-stage hybrid VQ was also proposed as shown in Fig. 11. In this coding system, the first stage is an LBG VQ, in which the difference between the input vector Y and the ith output vector Q of the first stage is Lattice-quantized [65]. This hybrid vector quantization system successively approximates the input vectors by the error vectors in each stage. It uses initially the LBG VQ for coarse quantization in the region where the training set respectively is highest. Then it follows with a Lattice VQ in the region where LBG VQ is less representative. At the decoder, each output vector is formed by component wise addition of the representative vector Q at the output of the first stage and the vector L at the output of the second stage.

V. Transform Vector Quantizer (TVQ)

The purpose of transform coding is to convert statistically dependent or correlated picture elements into independent or uncorrelated coefficients [67]–[73]. Because of the computational complexity an image is usually divided into subimages of reasonable size and then a one- or two-dimensional unitary transform is performed on each subimage. The transformed coefficients are then nonuniformly quantized by a scalar quantizer. The quantization levels are given by a bit assignment matrix in which some of the high-frequency coefficients are discarded. The same bit assignment matrix is stored at the receiver or is transmitted for each image [70]. In adaptive transform coders, several bit assignment matrices are employed where each image block is classified into one of several categories and coded by the corresponding bit assignment matrix [70]. In the following subsections, we introduce the application of the vector quantizer instead of the scalar quantizer to code the transformed coefficients. Transformation has the effect of compressing most of the energy within the vector (block) into some low-frequency coefficients. Thus, if a vector quantizer for an image is designed by the LBG algorithm, using the low-frequency coefficients as the training set, a very low bit rate can be achieved. The codebook designed in the transform domain is believed to be more nearly optimal than the one designed in the space domain because the transformed coefficients have better defined distributions than the image pixels. Also some of the high-frequency coefficients are discarded, and the computational cost is therefore reduced. The correlation between the transformed samples is exploited by the vector quantizer which makes the technique more nearly optimal compared to scalar quantizers.

A. Adaptive Transform Coding Using Vector Quantization

In adaptive transform coders several bit assignment matrices are designed. Each subblock of the image is then classified into one of several classes according to the activity content of the block and coded by the appropriate bit assignment matrix. Typical bit assignment matrices for an adaptive coder with four different classes are shown in Fig. 12. A large number of the high-frequency coefficients are usually discarded. However, these high-frequency coefficients can be transmitted by a vector quantization scheme with a small increase in the bit rate [82]. In this coding system, the bit assignment matrix, as shown in Fig. 13 is now in two parts where the low-frequency coefficients are coded by a scalar quantizer, and the high-frequency coefficients by a vector quantizer. It is shown in [74] that with a small increase in bit rate the high-frequency coefficients are transmitted, and the reconstructed image has a better quality around the edges especially at very low bit rate.

Saito et al. [75] designed a TVQ where images were divided into blocks of 16 × 16 pixels. Each block was transformed by a two-dimensional discrete cosine transform (DCT). The dc coefficient was scalar quantized by an uniform scalar quantizer of 256 levels. The ac coefficients were grouped into several different zones by grouping the coefficients in a zig-zig manner. Each zone was then vector quantized by the appropriate codebook. Vector quantization of transform coefficients has recently received some attention by a number of researchers [76]–[80]. In most of these techniques, a conventional adaptive transform coder is combined with vector quantization. An image is usually divided into blocks of 4 × 4 and then categorized into several classes; each class is then vector quantized by the appropriate codebook. There are several problems with this approach: small blocks (4 × 4) are only feasible with the current computational power so in turn the high-frequency coefficients cannot be discarded. Performing VQ in the transform domain in the above manner where each sub-block is considered as a vector has only one advantage,

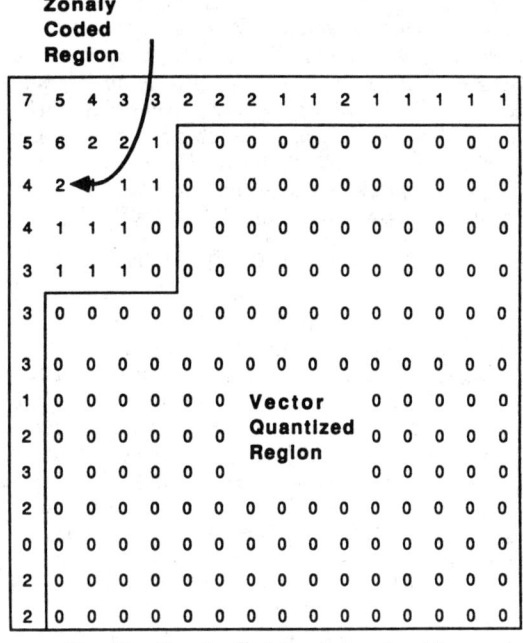

Fig. 12. Typical bit assignment matrices for several different classes.

Fig. 13. An adaptive bit assignment matrix.

that is, that ac coefficients have a well-behaved Laplacian distribution which could be exploited in the designed of the codebook. However, in the following subsections, several TVQ techniques are reviewed. These techniques use VQ to exploit the intra- and interframe correlation between the blocks.

B. One-Dimensional Transform Vector Quantizer

In one-dimensional transform coders, the image lines are transformed by a one-dimensional unitary transform and a bit

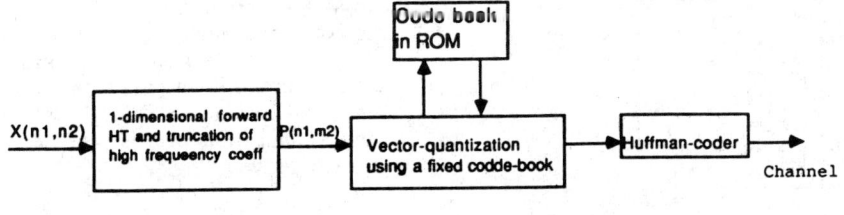

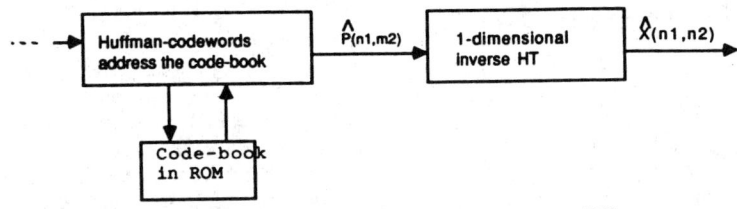

Fig. 14. One-dimensional transform VQ system [81].

assignment matrix is then used to code the normalized coefficients in each transformed line. The quantizer is a scalar where the correlation between the coefficients in each line or previous lines are not incorporated into the quantizer. The correlation within the transformed coefficients in each image line is not very significant since the linear transform is believed to decorrelate the samples within each line. However, the interline correlation is very significant and this can be exploited by a vector quantization scheme. One such technique was proposed by King and Nasrabadi [81], as shown in Fig. 14. A one-dimensional unitary transform is taken along each image line of $N_1 \times N_2$ image data $x(n_1, n_2)$ yielding a sequence of transform coefficients.

$$P(n_1, m_2) = \sum_{n_2=0}^{N_2-1} x(n_1, n_2) A_F(n_2, m_2) \qquad (10)$$

for $m_2 = 0, 1, \cdots, N_2 - 1$ where $A_F(n_2, m_2)$ is the one-dimensional forward transform kernel and m_2 is the transform-domain row coordinate. Each transformed coefficient $P(n_1, m_2)$ is then normalized by its respective standard deviation $\sigma(m_2)$ given by

$$[\sigma(m_2)]^2 = \frac{1}{N_1} \sum_{n_1=0}^{N_1-1} [P(n_1, m_2)]^2 - [\mu(m_2)]^2 \qquad (11)$$

where the mean $\mu(m_2)$ is given by

$$\mu(m_2) = \frac{1}{N_1} \sum_{n_1=0}^{N_1-1} P(n_1, m_2) \qquad (12)$$

for $m_2 = 0, 1, \cdots, N_2 - 1$.

Since most of the energy is contained in the low-frequency coefficients a number of high-frequency coefficients are discarded by a zonal sampling selection process [71] and [72]. The neighboring rows of the transformed image are highly correlated, and this interrow correlation can be exploited by constructed a set of K-dimensional vectors where each vector of the K vector is subsequently compared to an optimized codebook of standard vector templates and is represented by its nearest matching vector template, with the mean square error (MSE) used as a matching criterion. A binary codeword (Huffman codeword) is assigned to each permissible vector template which is then transmitted. At the receiver, these

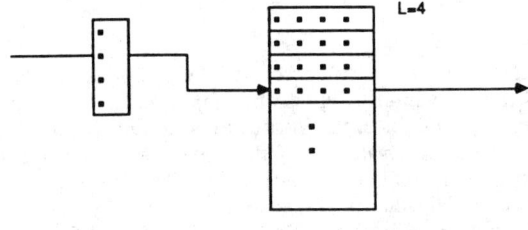

Fig. 15. A codeword addressing a read only ROM.

codewords will address a similar codebook to that of the transmitter to reconstruct the normalized transformed samples. In practice, this reconstruction can be done very rapidly by using the codewords to address a read only memory (ROM) in which the standard vector templates are stored as shown in Fig. 15. The reconstructed samples are then multiplied by the corresponding variances which are either transmitted or estimated at the receiver [73]. A number of the high-frequency coefficients are discarded at the transmitter and each line is padded with zeros at the receiver. Then an inverse unitary transform is performed on each line given by

$$x(n_1, n_2) = \sum_{m_2=0}^{N_2-1} P(n_1, m_2) B_I(n_2, m_2) \qquad (13)$$

where $B_I(n_2, m_2)$ is the one-dimensional inverse transform kernal. The bit rate R achieved is given by

$$R = C \frac{\log_2 M}{K} \qquad (14)$$

where M is the size of the codebook of vectors of dimension, K and C are the ratio of the number of samples retained over the total number of samples in each line (block).

In the above system, some of the high-frequency coefficients are discarded. However, it is possible to design two codebooks, one to code the low-frequency coefficients and one for the high-frequency coefficients. In this system, the low-frequency coefficients with variances above a given threshold are coded by the first codebook and the high-frequency coefficients by the second codebook. The overhead information representing the codebook is also transmitted.

The codebooks are designed by using the LBG algorithm in

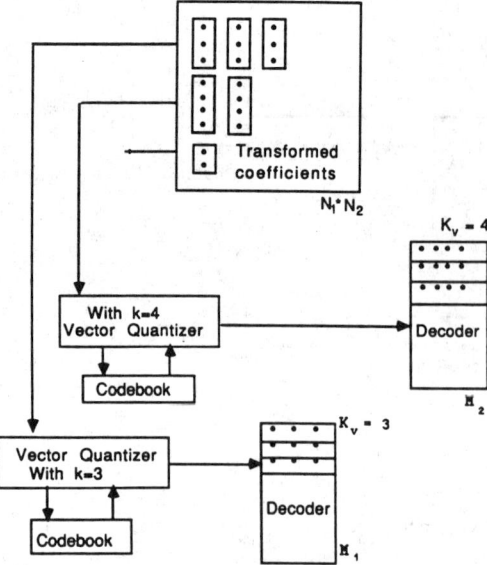

Fig. 16. Adaptive transform vector quantizer where M represents the number of vector patterns in the codebook and K the vector dimension.

the transform domain for vectors of dimension K. A decision on the value K is highly dependent on the spatial resolution and the correlation factor of the images to be coded. One technique would be to find a value of K that gives the distortion error between the original image and the coded image by a fixed optimized codebook of dimension K. However, since the activities within an image could be significantly different from one another, K cannot remain fixed.

An adaptive system was proposed by Nasrabadi et al. [83] where several codebooks of different vector lengths K were employed in the vector quantization scheme as shown in Fig. 16. The adaptivity was accomplished by varying the vector mapping window ($K_v \times 1$) in accordance with the statistical variation in the vertical direction of the row-transformed picture. The statistical variation is described by the Euclidean distance between transformed rows. Thus, the adaptive mapping is such that if there is sufficient intercorrelation between $K_v = b$ neighboring rows, then the rows are encoded with a codebook of vector lengths $K_v = b$. Previously developed codebooks for different template lengths are switched to and addressed in accordance with precomputed thresholds of row interseparation. The system is now a variable bit rate coder. The average bit rate is given by

$$R = A_1 C_1 \frac{\log_2 M}{K_1} + A_2 C_2 \frac{\log_2 M_2}{K_2} + \cdots + A_i C_i \frac{\log_2 M_i}{K_i} \tag{15}$$

where A_i is the number of times the codebook i has been used, M_i is the size of the codebook, and C_i is the percentage of the retained coefficients. Some extra bits are also required to identify each codebook as well as the used adaptivities, such as the zonal discarding of the high-frequency coefficients.

C. Two-Dimensional Transform Vector Quantization

As a consequence of the computational complexity involved in two-dimensional transform coders, an image array $x(n_1, n_2)$ is usually divided into small blocks of $f_i(n_1, n_2)$ for $i = 1, 2, \cdots, Q$ where Q is the number of blocks. Each block is then coded as a unit independent of all other blocks; unfortunately, this reduces the efficiency of the coder since the elements of the various blocks remain correlated in the transform domain. In order to exploit this interblock correlation, Habibi [64] introduced a two-dimensional hybrid coder where the in-

terblock correlation is used by employing a DPCM coder on the corresponding coefficients of the transformed blocks.

A new two-dimensional hybrid coder was introduced by Nasrabadi and King [81] where a vector quantization scheme was used instead of DPCM. In this coding system, a two-dimensional transform is performed on each subblock of the image as given by

$$F_i(m_1, m_2) = \sum_{n_1=0}^{N_1-1} \sum_{n_2=0}^{N_2-1} f_i(n_1, n_2) A_F(n_1, n_2) \tag{16}$$

for $m_1 = 0, 1, \cdots, N_1 - 1, m_2 = 0, 1, \cdots, N_2 - 1$ and $i = 1, 2, \cdots, Q$ where $A_F(n_1, n_2)$ is the forward transform kernel. Since most of the energy is compacted within the low-frequency coefficients, a large number of the high-frequency coefficients are discarded as in the one-dimensional transform coders. However, since the elements of various neighboring blocks are still correlated, this interblock correlation can be exploited by clustering the corresponding retained and normalized transformed samples at m_1 and m_2 of each K neighboring blocks into vectors of dimension K. The vector quantization scheme illustrated in the Section (V-B) is then applied on the vectors, and the corresponding codewords transmitted. At the receiver, these codewords will address the codebook stored in the ROM to reconstruct the transformed blocks by substituting the corresponding vector templates in place of the original vectors. A two-dimensional inverse transform is then applied on each block as given by

$$f_i(n_1, n_2) = \sum_{m_1=0}^{N_1-1} \sum_{m_2=0}^{N_2-1} F_i(m_1, m_2) B_I(m_1, m_2) \tag{17}$$

for $n_1 = 0, 1, \cdots, N_1 - 1, n_2 = 0, 1, \cdots, N_2 - 1$ where $B_I(m_1, m_2)$ is the inverse transform kernel. The vector quantizer employed in this system can be made adaptive as was illustrated for the one-dimensional transform vector quantizer in Section (V-B).

D. Interframe Transform Vector Quantization (ITVQ)

In transform coders, as discussed in Section V, a transformation is performed on a subblock of an image and then coded using a bit assignment matrix. In three-dimensional coders a transformation is applied in each spatial direction as well as in the temporal direction. The resulting coefficients are usually normalized and coded by a three-dimensional bit assignment matrix. However, it is possible to vector quantize these transform coefficients to reduce the bit rate even further. The computational complexity of such a three-dimensional transform coder is very large. Nasrabadi and King [84] introduced a coding system in which a transformation was performed in each spatial direction and a vector quantizer was used along the temporal direction. In the coding system shown in Fig. 17, a two-dimensional unitary transform is performed on each $j \times k$ pixel subblock of L frames. The two-dimensional transform is given by

$$F_i(u, v, l) = \sum_{j=0}^{J-1} \sum_{k=0}^{K-1} f_i(j, k, l) A_F(j, k; u, v) \tag{18}$$

for $u = 0, 1, \cdots, J - 1, v = 0, 1, \cdots, K - 1, l = 0, 1, \cdots, L, i = 1, 2, \cdots, Q^2$ where $f_i(j, k, l)$ denotes the i three-dimensional block amplitude values for a digital image sequence of L frames; $A_F(j, k; u, v)$ represents the forward two-dimensional transform kernel and Q the number of subblocks in each direction. The transformed coefficients are

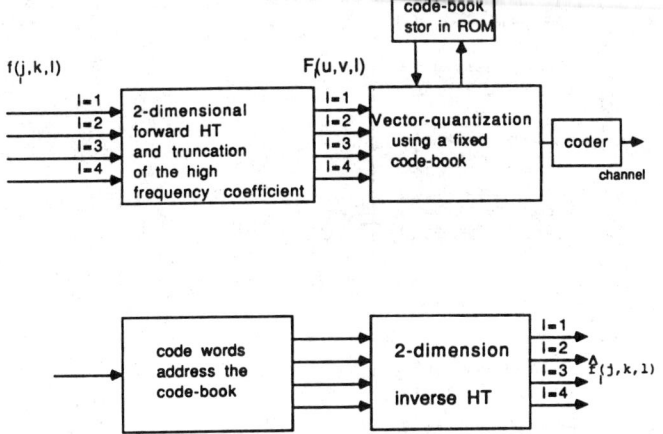

Fig. 17. A block diagram of an interframe transform vector quantizer [81].

then normalized by their corresponding mean and standard deviations given by the following expressions, respectively:

$$\mu(u, v) = \frac{1}{Q^2} \sum_{m=0}^{Q-1} \sum_{n=0}^{Q-1} F_{m,n}(u, v) \quad (19)$$

and

$$\sigma^2(u, v) = \frac{1}{Q^2} \sum_{m=0}^{Q-1} \sum_{n=0}^{Q-1} \{[F_{m,n}(u, v)]^2 - [\mu(u, v)]^2\} \quad (20)$$

for $u = 0, 1, \cdots, J - 1, v = 0, 1, \cdots, K - 1$.

A number of the high-frequency coefficients are zonally discarded. Each spatial frequency (u, v) of L temporally adjacent blocks are clustered into vectors of dimension L. Each vector is then compared to a codebook of standard vector templates and is represented by its nearest (in a mean square error sense) matching vector template as shown in Fig. 18. A binary codeword is then assigned to each permissible vector template and transmitted. At the receiver the transmitted codewords will address the same lookup table codebook where L temporarily adjacent, transformed blocks are reconstructed. The coefficients are rescaled by their corresponding standard deviation and a two-dimensional inverse transform is applied on each block of the frames, as given by expression

$$f_i(j, k, l) = \sum_{u=0}^{J-1} \sum_{v=0}^{K-1} F_i(u, v, l) B_l(u, v; j, k) \quad (21)$$

for $j = 0, 1, \cdots, J - 1, k = 0, 1, \cdots, K - 1, l = 0, 1, \cdots, L, i = 1, 2, \cdots, Q^2$ where $B_l(u, v, j, k)$ is the two-dimensional inverse transform kernel. The bit rate R is obtained from the relation

$$R = C \frac{\log_2 M}{L} \quad (22)$$

where M is the number of patterns (vector templates) in the codebook, L the dimension of the vector (or the number of frames clustered), and C is the number of the retained coefficients divided by the total number of samples in the block.

So far the dimension of the vector templates in the codebook

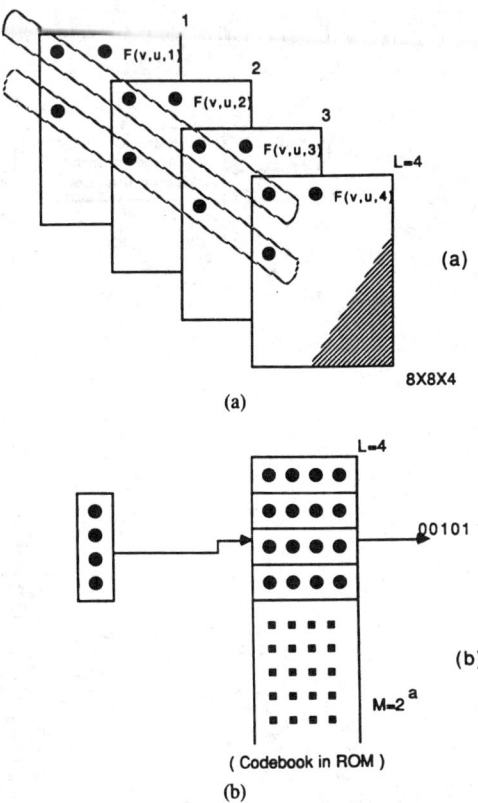

Fig. 18. (a) Shows the clustering of four frames where shaded area represents the high-frequency coefficients that are discarded. (b) Lookup table at the receiver.

has been kept fixed. However, the number of frames that can be clustered depends on the temporal variation within the image sequence. Thus, L should be made variable, changing to exploit the temporal correlation between the frames. Thus, the vector quantizer has to be made adaptive with respect to the movement of the objects within the image sequence, such that in a sequence of frames with little movement a large number of frames are clustered; this is a consequence of the high temporal correlation of frames. However, with a high density of moving objects within the image sequence, a smaller number of frames have to be clustered since the scene changes considerably from one frame to another. Thus, to adapt to the motion of the moving objects within the image sequence several codebooks of different dimensions are employed. The image sequence is then classified, and coded by switching to the appropriate codebook as shown in Fig. 19.

Fig. 20 shows a coding system with only two codebooks of dimension L and $L/2$ which has been simulated on the computer. After performing the two-dimensional transformation, the adaptive quantization scheme first classifies each three-dimensional block as belonging to a stationary area or an area of rapid motion. The classification is based upon a temporal activity index which is a measure given by the difference between the sum of the square of the ac coefficients of each subblock sequence. The three-dimensional block, after being classified, is coded by the appropriate vector quantizer by specifying a suitable threshold indexed for the two classes. The overhead information (identifying the codebook) is minimized by coding each block as a packet where each packet will have a header which specifies the vector quantizer that has been used, any adaptivities, and including any error correcting redundancies.

The above algorithm has been performed on a typical image sequence of frame size (136, 200) quantized to 8 bits/pixel and

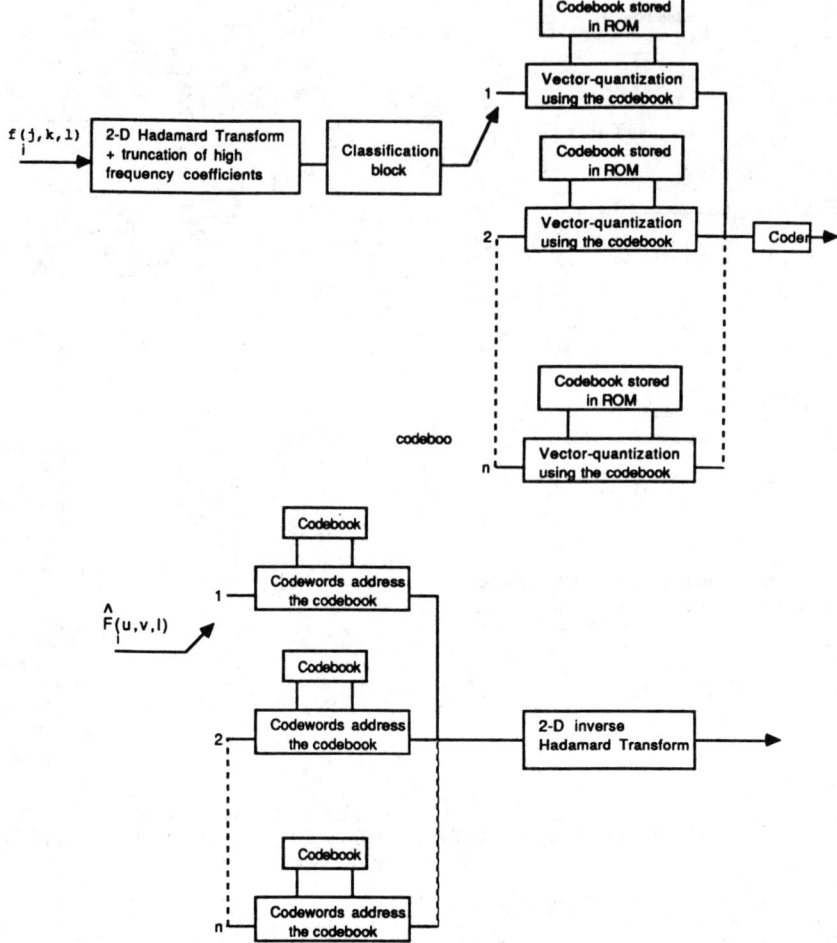

Fig. 19. Adaptive interframe transform vector quantizer system [84].

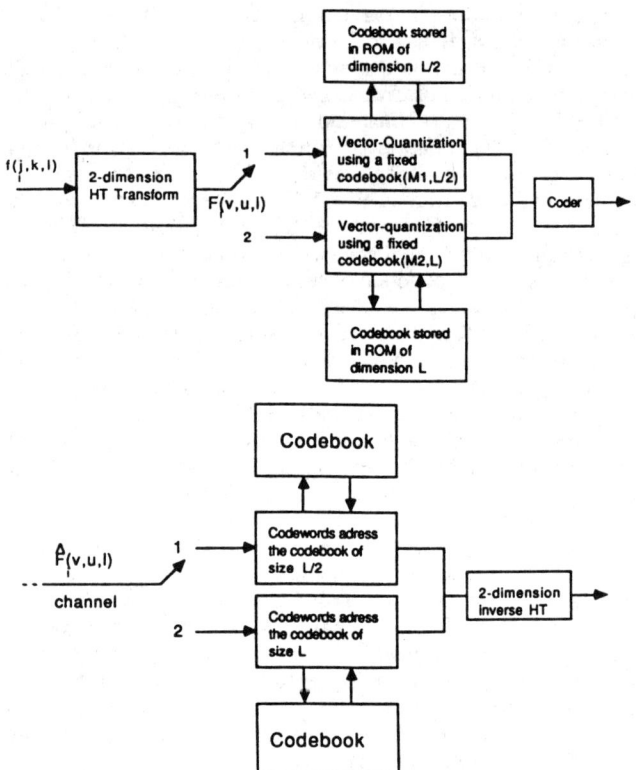

Fig. 20. The simulated adaptive interframe transform VQ coder with only two codebooks [84].

scaled to 5 bits for display as shown in Fig. 21. The codebook was designed using the LBG algorithm. The initial codebook was taken from the training sequence by retaining the most probable patterns with a given distance between them. Processes images are shown in Figs. 22 and 23.

The system shown in Fig. 20 is only adaptive with respect to variation of correlation in the temporal direction. However, other adaptivities such as the use of adaptive zonal discarding of the high-frequency coefficients as well as using specially optimized codebooks to code the high-frequency coefficients are still to be incorporated to provide a fully adaptive system. The bit rates achieved for the processing were obtained by using only two codebooks. A significantly greater reduction is possible if several codebooks or multidimensional vectors are employed. Using a number of codebooks will result in optimized vector quantizers for each particular class as well as the reduction of complexity of searching procedure [11].

VI. Binary Vector Quantizer (BVQ)

A. Facsimile Coding Using BVQ

Digital images such as business letters and documents, weather maps, engineering drawings, geographical maps, and newspaper pages are nominally two-tone (black and white). Efficient coding for the digital transmission or storage of two-tone images has been accomplished by a number of techniques such as run length coding techniques and entropy coding of the original data [1], [2].

One such technique employs entropy coding of vectors obtained by dividing the original image into blocks of N pixels, transmitting short codewords for more frequent vectors and long ones for less frequent vectors. An efficient way to

Fig. 21. Original input image sequence of resolution (136, 200) with amplitude resolution of 8 bits [82].

Fig. 22. Processed image sequence at bit rate of $R = 1.6$ bits/pixel/frame with codebooks of size $CB1 = (285, 3)$ and $CB2 = (111, 6)$ with NMSE $= 9.2 - 9.5 \times 10^{-3}$ [82].

construct such codes is to use Huffman codes which are based upon the joint probability of the pel patterns of the vectors. The bit rate per vector R will satisfy the inequality

$$H_N \leq R \leq H_N + 1 \qquad (23)$$

and the bit rate per pixel r is given by

$$\frac{H_N}{N} \leq r \leq \frac{H_N}{N} + \frac{1}{N} \qquad (24)$$

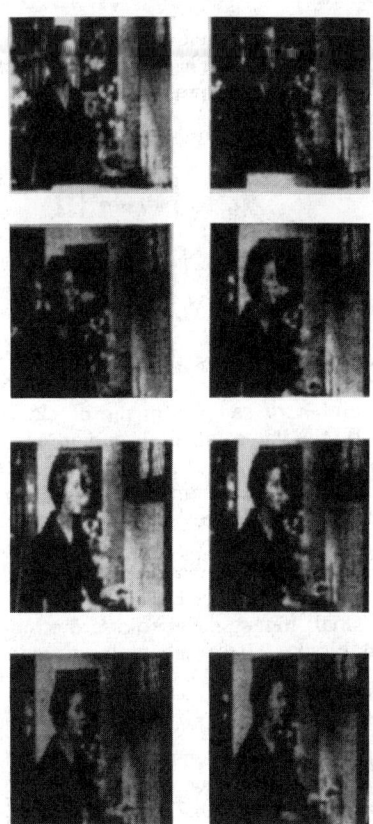

Fig. 23. Processed image sequence at bit rate of $R = 0.6$ bits/pixel/frame with codebooks of size $CB1 = (313, 4)$ and $CB2 = (203, 8)$ with NMSE $= 1.8 - 2.0 \times 10^{-3}$ [82].

where H_N is the entropy of the vectors of length N pixels. It is thus obvious that we can reduce r by making N larger. However, for large N the implementation of the encoder and decoder becomes complicated. A lower bit rate can obviously be achieved by using the conditional entropy [1], but the design and implementation of the Huffman codes will now be very complicated since they require the evaluation of the joint and conditional probabilities and a large lookup table for the storage of the codewords.

One possible way to increase the compression factor is to allow some image degradation in the coding process. One such approximate coding scheme was studied by Knudson [85]. For a given vector size, only a small subset of all possible pixel patterns of the block is allowed. Any pattern which is not allowed is replaced by the pattern in the allowed subset that matches it most closely. This is known as a binary vector quantizer and the codebook could be designed by using the LBG algorithm on a set of training sequences, but there is a high possibility of getting trapped into a local minima. Knudson carried out some experiments using newspaper texts and graphics using blocks of 8×8. It was found that a subset of 62 patterns (out of a possible 2^{64}) was sufficient to obtain satisfactory image quality. It is also possible to use several binary vector quantizers to adapt to the information variations within each block. Huffman codes generated from the statistical distribution measures can be used to represent the permissible block patterns in each codebook.

B. Block Truncation Coding Using Binary Vector Quantization

Recently, a new technique called block truncation coding (BTC) has been developed [86], [87]. This technique uses a one-bit nonparametric quantizer, adaptive over local regions of the image. In general, the picture is divided into $N \times N$

blocks which are coded individually, each into a two-level signal. The levels, a and b, for each block are chosen such that the first two sample moments are preserved. These are given by

$$a = \bar{X} - \bar{\sigma}\sqrt{\left[\frac{q}{m-q}\right]} \quad (25)$$

$$b = \bar{X} - \bar{\sigma}\sqrt{\left[\frac{m-q}{q}\right]} \quad (26)$$

where $\bar{X}$ and $\bar{\sigma}$ are mean and standard deviations of the block, respectively, q is the number of samples greater than $\bar{X}$, and $m = N^2$ is the number of samples in the block. Each block is then described by the values of $\bar{X}$, $\bar{\sigma}$, and an $M \times N$ bit plane consisting of 1's or 0's indicating whether the pixels have values above or below $\bar{X}$. Assuming $\bar{X}$ and $\bar{\sigma}$ are quantized to 8 bits, a data rate of 2 bits/pixel is achieved for blocks of 4 × 4 pixels. In order to decrease this bit rate, an efficient way to code the bit planes must be devised. One approach is to use an entropy coder on the patterns discussed in Section VI-A) above where several small binary codebooks are employed to code each classified block. These suggestions were recently reported in [88].

VII. Subband Vector Quantizers (Subband VQ)

One feature of the human visual system is that the early stages of visual information processing carried out by the brain consist of analyzing the retinal information over multiple, independent channels each of which responds selectively to a narrow-band of spatial frequencies [89].

Subband coding of speech signals was first proposed by Crochiere et al. [90] for medium-to-low rate speech coding systems. In conventional subband coding systems a bank of quadrature mirror filters [91] is employed to produce several replicas of the original signal at different frequency bands; a varying bit assignment strategy for each of these bands is used. Traditionally, fewer numbers of bits are assigned to high-frequency bands than are assigned to low-frequency bands. Recently, vector quantization has been applied to subband speech signals by constructing vectors of dimension K where one sample from successive K subbands was taken [92]-[93]. Recently, Woods [106] designed a subband image coding system. In his system, each band was DPCM coded. In [107], vector quantization was applied to Woods' subband coder in order to exploit the correlation or the redundancies between the spectral bands.

The above techniques can obviously be extended to natural multiband images such as multispectral images [94]-[97] or components of color TV images [98]-[105]. Boucher and Goldberg have recently studied the application of vector quantization to color TV images [98]. They extended their codebook replenishment technique discussed in Section III to color images. The three color signals R, G, and B are first transformed to the *NTSC YIQ* coordinate system by using the standard transformation. The reason for this mapping is that the transformation tends to decorrelate the information and to compact most of the energy in the luminance component Y. Both chrominance components I and Q are severely band limited and there is little correlation between the *NTSC* components Y, I, and Q. In their color coding system, each spectral band, the luminance component Y, and the chrominance components I and Q which were subsampled by a factor of 2 were vector quantized by the codebook replenishment technique.

Yamaguchi [101] designed a coding system where highly correlated R, G, and B, components of color images were vector quantized with bit rates of about 2-3 bits/pixel for each color component. The R, G, and B predictor errors denoted by e_R, e_G, e_B, were then calculated. For the G component signals (intracomponent prediction) the prediction error is $e_G = G - \hat{G}$. For the R and B components the predictor is an intercomponent prediction, for example, $e_R = R - \hat{R}(G')$ where the prediction signal is based on the R component and the decoded G' component. The prediction errors e_R, e_G, e_B are then vector quantized because there exist some correlation between the error components.

Murakami et al. extended his algorithm [103] to code color images. In their technique, a multistage VQ was applied to Y, I, Q components of the color images. A combined component VQ was also designed where a multidimensional vector was used. Budge and Baker used a mean/residual vector quantizer to encode each color component [102] individually where the I and Q components were subsampled by a factor of 4.

VIII. Conclusion

We have presented a survey of vector quantization techniques for image coding. The basic concept of vector quantization was given in Section II. Spatial vector quantizers were discussed in Section III. As digital images are made of nonstationary signals, a variety of SVQ's have been developed such as subtracting the mean and the variance of each vector before using the VQ, or using several codebooks to match the statistics of the image blocks. One major problem with VQ's is that they do not reconstruct the edge vectors efficiently, and this is because the codebook cannot reproduce all possible patterns. A simple way to solve this is to use a codebook replenishment VQ (dynamic VQ). The effect that channel noise has on a spatial VQ coding system has not yet been investigated. Obviously, in a simply VQ system if an error occurs during transmission of a codeword, the vector represented by that codeword is corrupted, therefore, the whole block of 4 × 4 is not correctly reconstructed. A comparison of spatial VQ systems is a difficult task because computational complexity, codebook storage, and overhead information must be considered for each system, as well as the fact that more computational power and large memory storage are becoming more feasible. Since each spatial VQ has its own merit perhaps a combination of them would be the best idea. One major advantage of spatial VQ systems over, for example, transform VQ systems is that the decoder is very simple as it is just a lookup table.

The combination of VQ with conventional coders will result in a more efficient coder than when a conventional coder is used with a scalar quantizer. For example, in an interframe VQ the error signal obtained from two consecutive frmaes are correlated and dependent, but the VQ will exploit this redundancy. Predictive VQ's continue to be developed because designing the codebook and the effect that the channel noise will have on the feedback VQ systems are still major problems.

Several transform VQ systems were also discussed in this paper. The TVQ is computationally complex because of the one- or two-dimensional transformation that has to be performed at the encoder and decoder. TVQ's have several advantages over SVQ's and PVQ's. For example, some of the high-frequency coefficients can be discarded which will reduce the vector size or the bit rate depending on the TVQ system reported in Section V. It can also exploit the intra- and interframe correlation between the vectors to reduce the bit rate. A TVQ will perform better than the conventional hybrid transform/DPCM coders because DPCM coders perform significantly less well in the presence of noise, and the correlation and the dependency between error signal is not fully exploited by scalar quantization. The effect of the channel noise on TVQ will not be so severe because the error is distributed over the whole transform region (block size).

The TVQ should always perform better than conventional transform coders because scalar quantizers are forced to allocate integral numbers of bits to each transform coefficient. However, VQ permits a more distributed allocation.

ACKNOWLEDGMENT

The authors would like to thank Mr. Y. Feng for drawing the block diagrams.

REFERENCES

[1] T. S. Huang, "Coding of two-tone images," *IEEE Trans. Commun.*, vol. COM-25, pp. 1406–1428, Nov. 1977.
[2] A. N. Netravali and F. W. Mounts, "Ordering techniques for facsimile coding: A review," *Proc. IEEE*, vol. 68, pp. 796–807, July 1980.
[3] A. N. Netravali and J. O. Limb, "Picture Coding: A review," *Proc. IEEE*, vol. 68, pp. 366–406, Mar. 1980.
[4] A. K. Jain, "Image data compression: A review," *Proc. IEEE*, vol. 69, pp. 349–389, Mar. 1981.
[5] A. Habibi, "Survey of adaptive image coding techniques," *IEEE Trans. Commun.*, vol. COM-25, pp. 1275–1284, Nov. 1977.
[6] M. Kunt, A. Ikonomopoulos, and M. Kocher, "Second-generation image-coding techniques," *Proc. IEEE*, vol. 73, pp. 549–574, Apr. 1985.
[7] A. Buzo, A. H. Gray, R. M. Gray, and J. D. Markel, "Speech coding based upon vector quantization," *IEEE Trans. Acoust. Speech, Signal Processing*, vol. ASSP-28, pp. 562–574, Oct. 1980.
[8] A. Gersho and V. Cuperman, "Vector quantization: A pattern-matching technique for speech coding," *IEEE Commun. Mag.*, pp. 15–21, Dec. 1983.
[9] Y. Linde, A. Buzo, and R. M. Gray, "An algorithm for vector quantizer design," *IEEE Trans. Commun.*, vol. COM-28, pp. 84–95, Jan. 1980.
[10] H. Abut, R. M. Gray, and G. Rebolledo, "Vector quantization of speech and speech-like waveforms," *IEEE Trans. Acoust., Speech, Signal Processing.*, vol. ASSP-30, pp. 423–435, June 1982.
[11] R. M. Gray, "Vector quantization," *IEEE ASSP Mag.*, pp. 4–29, Apr. 1984.
[12] W. K. Pratt, *Image Transmission Techniques*. New York: Academic, 1979.
[13] A. Gersho, "On the structure of vector quantizers," *IEEE Trans. Inform. Theory*, vol. IT-28, pp. 157–166, Mar. 1982.
[14] J. P. Adoul, C. Collin, and D. Dalle, "Block encoding and its application to data compression of PCM speech," in *Proc. Canadian Commun. EHV Conf.*, Montreal, P.Q., Canada, 1978, pp. 145–148.
[15] D. T. S. Chen, "On two- or more dimensional optimum quantizers," in *Proc. IEEE Int. Conf. Acoust., Speech, Signal Processing*, 1977, pp. 640–643.
[16] A. Gersho, "Asymptotically optimal block quantization," *IEEE Trans. Inform. Theory*, vol. IT-25, pp. 373–380, July 1979.
[17] S. P. Lloyd, "Least-squares quantization in PCM," *IEEE Trans. Inform. Theory*, vol. IT-28, pp. 129–137, Mar. 1982.
[18] R. M. Gray, A. Buzo, A. H. Gray, and Y. Matsuyama, "Distortion measures for speech processing," *IEEE Trans. Acoust., Speech, Signal Processing*, vol. ASSP-28, pp. 367–376, Aug. 1980.
[19] R. M. Gray and H. Abut, "Full search and tree searched vector quantization of speech waveforms," in *Proc. IEEE Int. Conf. Acoust., Speech, Signal Processing*, May 1982, pp. 593–596.
[20] R. M. Gray and Y. Linde, "Vector quantization and predictive quantizers for Gauss Markov source," *IEEE Trans. Commun.*, vol. COM-30, pp. 381–389, Feb. 1982.
[21] B. H. Juang, Jr., and A. H. Gray, "Multiple stage vector quantization for speech coding," in *Proc. IEEE Int. Conf. Acoust., Speech, Signal Processing*, Apr. 1982, pp. 597–600.
[22] M. J. Sabin and R. M. Gray, "Product code vector quantizers for waveform and voice coding," *IEEE Trans. Acoust., Speech, Signal Processing*, vol. ASSP-32, pp. 474–488, June 1984.
[23] R. L. Baker and R. M. Gray, "Differential vector quantization of achromatic imagery," presented at Proc. Int. Picture Coding Symp., Mar. 1983.
[24] S. E. Budge and R. L. Baker, "Compression of color digital images using vector quantization in product codes," in *Proc. IEEE Int. Conf. Acoust., Speech, Signal Procesing*, Apr. 1985, pp. 129–132.
[25] R. L. Baker and R. M. Gray, "Image compression using non-adaptive spatial vector quantization," in *Proc. Conf. Rec. Sixteenth Asilomar Conf. Circuits, Syst., Comput.*, Oct. 1982, pp. 55–61.
[26] R. L. Baker, "Vector quantization of digital images," Ph.D. dissertation, Stanford Univ., Stanford, CA, June 1984.
[27] Y. Yamada, K. Fujita, and S. Tazaki, "Vector quantization of video signals," in *Proc. Ann. Conf. IECE*, 1980, p. 1031.
[28] Y. Yamada and S. Tazaki, "Vector quantizer design for video signals," *IECE Trans. J66-B*, pp. 965–972, 1983 (in Japanese).
[29] ——, "A method for constructing successive approximation vector quantizers for video signals," in *Proc. Ann. Conf. Inst. Television Eng. Japan*, 1983, pp. 6-2.
[30] T. Murakami, K. Asai, and E. Yamazaki, "Vector quantizer of video signals," *Electron. Lett.*, vol. 7, pp. 1005–1006, Nov. 1982.
[31] T. Saito, H. Takeo, H. Harashima, and H. Miyakawa, "A scheme of diminishing performance deterioration due to mismatch in vector quantization of picture signals," presented at Proc. Int. Picture Coding Symp., July 1984.
[32] H. Van Helden, F. Booman, and J. Biemond, "A generalized tree structured algorithm for vector quantization of images," presented at Proc. Int. Picture Coding Symp., July 1984.
[33] A. Gersho and B. Ramamurthi, "Image coding using vector quantization," in *Proc. IEEE Int. Conf. Acoust., Speech, Signal Processing*, Apr. 1982, pp. 428–431.
[34] B. Ramamurthi and A. Gersho, "Image coding using segmented codebooks," presented at Proc. Int. Picture Coding Symp., Mar. 1983.
[35] B. Ramamurthi, A. Gersho, and A. Sekey, "Low-rate image coding using vector quantization," in *Proc. IEEE Global Commum. Conf. Rec.*, Nov. 1983, pp. 184–187.
[36] B. Ramamurthi and A. Gersho, "Image vector quantization with a perceptually-based cell classifier," presented at IEEE Proc. Int. Conf. Acoust., Speech, Signal Processing, Mar. 1984.
[37] ——, "Classified vector quantization of images," *IEEE Trans. Commun.*, vol. COM-34, pp. 1105–1115, Nov. 1986.
[38] B. Ramamurthi, "Vector quantizer of images based on a composite source model," Ph.D. dissertation, Univ. California, Santa Barbara, CA, Apr. 1985.
[39] H. F. Sun and M. Goldberg, "Adaptive vector quantization for image sequence coding," in *Proc. IEEE Int. Conf. Acoust., Speech, Signal Processing*, Mar. 1985, pp. 339–342.
[40] M. Goldberg and H. F. Sun, "Image sequence coding using vector quantization," *IEEE Trans. Commun.*, vol. COM-34, pp. 703–710, July 1986.
[41] A. Gersho and M. Yano, "Adaptive vector quantization by progressive code-vector replacement," in *Proc. IEEE Int. Conf. Acoust., Speech, Signal Processing*, 1985, pp. 133–136.
[42] N. M. Nasrabadi, "Use of vector quantizers in image coding," in *Proc. IEEE Int. Conf. Acoust., Speech, Signal Processing*, Mar. 1985, pp. 125–128.
[43] H. Samet, "The quad-tree and related hierarchical data structures," *ACM Comput. Surveys*, vol. 16, no. 2, pp. 188–260, June 1984.
[44] A. Gersho and Y. Shoham, "Hierarchical vector quantization of speech with dynamic codebook allocation," in *Proc. IEEE Int. Conf. Acoust., Speech, Signal Processing*, 1984, pp. 10.9.1–10.9.4.
[45] D. J. Vaisey and A. Gersho, "Variable block-size image coding," in *Proc. IEEE Int. Conf. Acoust., Speech, Signal Processing*, Apr. 1987, pp. 1051–1054.
[46] A. Haoui and D. Messerschmitt, "Predictive vector quantization," in *Proc. IEEE Int. Conf. Acoust., Speech, Signal Processing*, Mar. 1984, pp. 10.10.1–10.10.4.
[47] M. Dunham and R. Gray, "An algorithm for the design of labelled-transition finite-state vector quantizers," *IEEE Trans. Commun.*, vol. COM-33, pp. 83–89, Jan. 1985.
[48] J. Foster, R. M. Gray, and M. Dunham, "Finite-state vector quantization of waveform coding," *IEEE Trans. Inform. Theory*, vol. IT-31, pp. 348–355, May 1985.
[49] A. Aravind and A. Gersho, "Low-rate image coding with finite-state vector quantization," in *Proc. IEEE Int. Conf. Acoust., Speech, Signal Processing*, Mar. 1986, pp. 137–140.
[50] R. L. Baker and H. H. Shen, "A finite-state vector quantizer for low-rate image sequence coding," in *Proc. IEEE Int. Conf. Acoust., Speech, Signal Processing*, Apr. 1987, pp. 760–763.
[51] V. Cuperman and A. Gersho, "Adaptive differential vector coding of speech," in *Proc. Conf. Rec., GLOBECOM '82*, Dec. 1982, pp. 1092–1096.

[52] H. M. Hang, "Predictive coding of images," Ph.D. dissertation, Elect., Comput., Syst. Dep., Rensselaer Poly. Inst., Troy, NY, Aug. 1984.

[53] H. M. Hang and J. W. Woods, "Predictive vector quantization of images," *IEEE Trans. Commun.*, vol. COM-33, pp. 1208–1219, Nov. 1985.

[54] J. O. Limb and R. F. W. Pease, "A simple interframe coder for video telephony," *Bell Syst. Tech. J.*, vol. 50, pp. 1877–1888, Aug. 1971.

[55] B. G. Haskell et al., "Interframe coding of video-telephone pictures," *Proc. IEEE*, vol. 60, pp. 792–800, July 1972.

[56] B. G. Haskell et al., "Interframe coding of 525-line, monochrome television at 1.5 M bit/s," *IEEE Trans. Commun.*, vol. COM-25, pp. 1339–1348, Nov. 1977.

[57] H. Yasuda et al., "Transmitting 4-MHz TV signals by combinational difference coding," *IEEE Trans. Commun.*, vol. COM-25, pp. 508–516, May 1977.

[58] T. Murakami, K. Asai, A. Itoh, and E. Yamazaki, "Interframe vector coding of color video signals," presented at Proc. Int. Picture Coding Symp., July 1984, also 1983.

[59] C. Cafforio and F. Rocca, "Methods for measuring small displacements of television images," *IEEE Trans. Inform. Theory*, vol. IT-22, pp. 573–579, Sept. 1976.

[60] A. N. Netravali and J. A. Stuller, "Motion compensation transform coding," *Bell Syst. Tech. J.*, pp. 1703–1718, Sept. 1974.

[61] J. R. Jain and A. K. Jain, "Displacement measurement and its application in interframe image coding," *IEEE Trans. Commun.*, vol. COM-29, pp. 1799–1808, Dec. 1981.

[62] E. Dubois, B. Prasada, and S. Sabri, "Image sequence coding," in *Image Sequence Analysis*, T. S. Huang, Ed. New York: Springer-Verlag, 1981, ch. 3.

[63] A. N. Netravali and J. D. Robbins, "Motion-compensated television coding: Part I," *Bell Syst. Tech. J.*, vol. 58, pp. 631–670, Mar. 1979.

[64] A. Habibi, "Hybrid coding of pictorial data," *IEEE Trans. Commun.*, vol. COM-22, pp. 614–624, May 1974.

[65] M. J. Bage, "Interframe predictive coding of images using hybrid vector quantization," *IEEE Trans. Commun.*, vol. COM-34, pp. 411–415, Apr. 1986.

[66] J. A. Roese, W. K. Pratt, and G. S. Robinson, "Interframe cosine transform image coding," *IEEE Trans. Commun.*, vol. COM-25, pp. 1329–1338, Nov. 1977.

[67] H. C. Andrews, J. Kane, and W. K. Pratt, "Hadamard transform image coding," *Proc. IEEE*, vol. 57, pp. 58–68, Jan. 1969.

[68] P. A. Wintz, "Transform picture coding," *Proc. IEEE*, vol. 60, pp. 809–823, July 1972.

[69] W. K. Pratt, W. H. Chen, and L. R. Welch, "Slant transform image coding," *IEEE Trans. Commun.*, vol. COM-22, pp. 1075–1093, Aug. 1974.

[70] W. H. Chen and C. H. Smith, "Adaptive coding of monochrome and color images," *IEEE Trans. Commun.*, vol. COM-25, pp. 1285–1292, Nov. 1977.

[71] G. B. Anderson and T. S. Huang, "Piecewise Fourier transformation for picture bandwidth compression," *IEEE Trans. Commun.*, vol. COM-20, pp. 388–491, June 1972.

[72] M. Tasto and P. A. Wintz, "Image coding by adaptive block quantization," *IEEE Trans. Commun. Technol.*, vol. COM-19, pp. 956–972, Dec. 1971.

[73] K. N. Nagan, "Adaptive transform coding of video signals," *Proc. IEE*, vol. 129, Pt.F, Feb. 1982.

[74] N. M. Nasrabadi and R. A. King, "Computationally efficient adaptive block-transform coding," presented at Proc. EUSIPCO-83, 2nd European Conf. Sig., Sept. 1983.

[75] T. Saito, H. Takeo, K. Aizawa, H. Harashima, and H. Miyakawa, "Adaptive discrete cosine transform image coding using gain/shape vector quantization," in *Proc. IEEE Int. Conf. Acoust., Speech, Signal Processing*, Apr. 1986, pp. 129–132.

[76] J. P. Mareseq and C. Labit, "Vector quantization in transformed image coding," in *Proc. IEEE Int. Conf. Acoust., Speech, Signal Processing*, Apr. 1986, pp. 145–147.

[77] A. A. Abdelwahab and S. C. Kwatra, "Image data compression with vector quantization in the transform domain," in *Proc. IEEE Int. Conf. Commun.*, 1986, pp. 1285–1288.

[78] B. Hammer and M. Schielein, "Image coding by vector quantization of M-Hadamard transform coefficients," *SPIE*, vol. 594, Image Coding, pp. 72–78, 1985.

[79] M. Haqhiri and C. Renius, "An adaptive block-quantizer approach to transform coding of pictures," *SPIE*, vol. 594, Image Coding, pp. 66–71, 1985.

[80] K. S. Thyagarajan, H. Abut, and H. Bheda, "A matrix quantizer for image processing," in *Proc. IEEE Int. Conf. Acoust., Speech, Signal Processing*, Mar. 1984, pp. 48.2.1–48.2.3.

[81] N. M. Nasrabadi and R. A. King, "Image coding using vector quantization in the transform domain," *Pat. Recog. Lett.*, pp. 323–329, 1983.

[82] N. M. Nasrabadi, "Orthogonal transforms and their applications to image coding," Ph.D. dissertation, Imperial College, Univ. London, England, 1984.

[83] N. M. Nasrabadi, J. O. Ibikunle, and R. A. King, "Design of a new codec system for video conferencing," presented at Int. Conf. Digital Signal Proc., Florence, Italy, Sept. 1984.

[84] N. M. Nasrabadi and R. A. King, "A new image coding technique using transform vector quantization," presented at 1984 IEEE Int. Conf. Acoust., Speech, Signal Processing, Mar. 1984.

[85] D. R. Knudson, "Digital encoding of newspaper graphics," Electron. Syst. Lab., Mass. Inst. Technol., Rep. ESL-616, Aug. 1975.

[86] E. J. Delp and D. R. Mitchell, "Image compression using block truncation coding," *IEEE Trans. Commun.*, vol. COM-27, Sept. 1979.

[87] D. J. Healy and D. R. Mitchell, "Digital video bandwidth compression using block truncation coding," *IEEE Trans. Commun.*, vol. COM-29, pp. 1809–1817, Dec. 1981.

[88] V. R. Udpikar and J. P. Raina, "BTC image coding using vector quantization," *IEEE Trans. Commun.*, vol. COM-35, pp. 352–356, Mar. 1987.

[89] G. Westheimer and F. W. Campbell, "Light distribution in the image formed by the living human eye," *J. Opt. Soc. Amer.*, vol. 67, no. 2, pp. 207–212, Feb. 1977.

[90] R. E. Crochiere, S. A. Webber, and J. L. Flanagan, "Digital coding of speech in sub-bands," *Bell Syst. Tech. J.*, vol. 55, Oct. 1986.

[91] J. D. Johnston, "A filter family designed for use in quadrature mirror filter banks," presented at Proc. IEEE Int. Conf. Acoust., Speech, Signal Processing, 1980.

[92] H. Abut and S. A. Luse, "Vector quantization for sub-band coded waveforms," presented at Proc. IEEE Int. Conf. Acoust., Speech, Signal Processing, 1984.

[93] A. Gersho, T. Ramstad, and I. Versvik, "Fully vector-quantized sub-band coding with adaptive codebook allocation," presented at Proc. IEEE Int. Conf. Acoust., Speech, Signal Processing, 1980.

[94] E. E. Hilbert, "Cluster compression algorithm: A joint clustering/data compression concept," *Jet Prop. Lab.*, Pub. 77-43, Dec. 1977.

[95] A. Habibi and A. S. Samulon, "Bandwidth compression of multi-spectral data," *SPIE*, vol. 66, pp. 23–35, 1975.

[96] A. Habibi, "A review of image bandwidth compressed techniques," *SPIE*, vol. 528, Digital Image Processing, pp. 138–144, 1985.

[97] G. E. Lowitz, "Image data reduction," in *Proc. Int. Conf. Spacecraft On-Board Data Manage.*, Nice 24-27, Oct. 1978, pp. 291–294.

[98] P. Boucher, "Adaptive vector quantization of pictorial data," Masters thesis, Univ. Ottawa, Appl. Sci. Elec. Eng., 1984.

[99] P. Boucher and M. Goldberg, "Color image compression by adaptive vector quantization," presented at Proc. IEEE Int. Conf. Acoust., Speech, Signal Processing, 1984.

[100] M. Goldberg, P. R. Boucher, and S. Shlien, "Image compression using adaptive vector quantization," *IEEE Trans. Commun.*, vol. COM-34, Feb. 1986.

[101] H. Yamaguchi, "Efficient encoding of colored pictures in R, G, B components," *IEEE Trans. Commun.*, vol. COM-32, pp. 1201–1209, Nov. 1984.

[102] S. E. Budge and R. L. Baker, "Compression of color digital image using vector quantization in product codes," in *Proc. IEEE Int. Conf. Acoust., Speech, Signal Processing*, Mar. 1985, pp. 129–132.

[103] T. Murakami, K. Asai, and A. Itoh, "Vector quantization of color images," in *Proc. IEEE Int. Conf. Acoust., Speech, Signal Processing*, 1986, pp. 133–135.

[104] J. Barrilleaux, R. Hinkle, and S. Wells, "Efficient vector quantization for color image coding," in *Proc. IEEE Int. Conf. Acoust., Speech, Signal Processing*, 1987, pp. 740–743.

[105] C. L. Yeh, "Color image-sequence compression using adaptive binary-tree vector quantization with codebook replenishment," in *Proc. IEEE Int. Conf. Acoust., Speech, Signal Processing*, Apr. 1987, pp. 1059–1062.

[106] J. W. Woods and S. D. O'Neil, "Sub-band coding of images," *IEEE Trans. Acoust., Speech, Signal Procesing*, vol. ASSP-34, pp. 1278–1289, Oct. 1986.

[107] P. H. Westerink, J. Biemond and D. E. Boekee, "Sub-band coding of images using predictive vector quantizer," in *Proc. IEEE Int. Conf. Acoust., Speech, Signal Processing*, Apr. 1987, pp. 1378–1381.

[108] A. Aravind and A. Gersho, "Image compression based on vector quantization with finite memory," *Opt. Eng.*, vol. 26, no. 7, pp. 570–580, July 1987.

[109] T. R. Fischer, "A pyramid vector quantizer," *IEEE Trans. Inform. Theory*, vol. IT-32, pp. 568–583, July 1986.

[110] H. Tseng and T. R. Fischer, "Transform and hybrid transform/DPCM coding of images using pyramid vector quantization," *IEEE Trans. Commun.*, vol. COM-35, pp. 79–86, Jan. 1987.

[111] T. Kohonen, *Self-Organization and Associative Memory*. New York: Springer-Verlag, 1984.

[112] ——, "The neural phonetic typewriter," *IEEE Comput.*, vol. 21, pp. 11–21, Mar. 1988.

[113] N. Metropolis, A. Rosenbluth, M. Rosenbluth, A. Teller, and E. Teller, "Equation of state calculations by fast computing machines," *J. Chem. Phys.*, vol. 21, no. 6, pp. 1087–1092, June 1953.

[114] S. Kirkpartrick, C. D. Gelatt, Jr., and M. P. Vecchi, "Optimization by simulated annealing," *Science*, vol. 220, no. 4598, pp. 671–680, May 1983.

Nasser M. Nasrabadi (M'84) was born in April 1960. He received the B.Sc. (Eng.) and Ph.D. degrees in electrical engineering from Imperial College, London, England, in 1980 and 1984, respectively.

He is currently an Assistant Professor in the Department of Electrical Engineering at Worcester Polytechnic Institute, Worcester, MA. His primary research interests are in image processing and computer vision.

Robert A. King was born in London, England, in 1923. He obtained the M.A. degree in mechancial sciences from Cambridge University in 1950. He obtained the Ph.D. degree at Imperial College in 1978, and was awarded the D.Sc. (Eng.) degree in 1985.

He is at present a Reader in the Department of Electrical Engineering at the Imperial College of Science and Technology, University of London, London, England. He has been supervising research in the theory, design and application of multidimensional digital filters, and in their application to image processing.

Dr. King is a Fellow of the Institution of Electrical Engineers.

Subband Coding of Images

JOHN W. WOODS, SENIOR MEMBER, IEEE, AND SEAN D. O'NEIL

Abstract—Subband coding has become quite popular for the source encoding of speech. This paper presents a simple yet efficient extension of this concept to the source coding of images. We specify the constraints for a set of two-dimensional quadrature mirror filters (QMF's) for a particular frequency-domain partition, and show that these constraints are satisfied by a separable combination of one-dimensional QMF's. Bits are then optimally allocated among the subbands to minimize the mean-squared error for DPCM coding of the subbands. Also, an adaptive technique is developed to allocate the bits within each subband by means of a local variance mask. Optimum quantization is employed with quantizers matched to the Laplacian distribution. Subband coded images are presented along with their signal-to-noise ratios (SNR's). The SNR performance of the subband coder is compared to that of the adaptive discrete cosine transform (DCT), vector quantization, and differential vector quantization for bit rates of 0.67, 1.0, and 2.0 bits per pixel for 256 × 256 monochrome images. The adaptive subband coder has the best SNR performance.

I. INTRODUCTION

SUBBAND coding of speech was introduced by Crochiere *et al.* [1] in 1976. Since that time, this technique has become quite popular for the medium bandwidth waveform coding of speech. The basic idea of subband coding (SBC) is to split up the frequency band of the signal and then to code each subband with either PCM or DPCM using a coder and bit rate accurately matched to the statistics of that band. In addition to the obvious advantages of such an approach, two other advantages have been found important in speech coding [2]. First, the error in coding a subband is confined to that subband, thus exploiting the masking effect of speech. Second, by varying the bit assignment among the subbands, the noise spectrum can be shaped according to the subjective noise perception of the human ear.

Related previous work in multiband source encoding of images traces back to the splitband quantization method of Kretzmer [3] in 1956. This was a high-frequency–low-frequency PCM-type approach. Another two-band system was the synthetic highs system introduced by Schreiber *et al.* [4] in 1959. More directly related to our method is the recent pyramid coding method of Burt and Adelson [5]. Their approach used a Laplacian pyramid to produce an approximate frequency decomposition but did not explicitly use any subband coding concepts or QMF filters. Independent of the present work [6], the QMF filter was extended to the multidimensional (m-D) case earlier by Vetterli [7] who claimed that separable filters are necessary and sufficient for the most natural four-band extension of the standard two-band QMF filters introduced by Esteban and Galand [8]. Actually, separability is not necessary, and a weaker condition is derived in Section II. It should be noted that no results on image coding are contained in [7].

This paper is organized as follows. Section II summarizes our extension of subband filters of the QMF variety to two dimensions. Section III introduces the concept of subband coding of images. Section IV considers an adaptive extension motivated by previous work in adaptive transform image coding [9]. Section V presents simulation results including a signal-to-noise ratio (SNR) comparison with several other popular encoding methods extending the comparison reported earlier by Baker and Gray [10]. Section VI presents conclusions and suggestions for further work.

II. SUBBAND FILTERS IN TWO DIMENSIONS

This section will summarize our extension of the subband filtering concept to the 2-D case including the method of QMF filter design to eliminate possible aliasing error due to nonideal subband filters. An independent extension of QMF's to the multidimensional case has been published by Vetterli [7]. A key difference is that our derivation substitutes a weaker symmetry constraint for separability of the QMF's, thus allowing the possibility of more general frequency-domain decompositions.

Ideal Filters

Fig. 1 shows the initial 4-band partitioning stage that is the basis for the 16-band filter system to be used in the coding of Section III. After each subband has been split off, it is demodulated to baseband (i.e., zero frequency) by a (2, 2) subsampling [Fig. 2(a)], that is, a decimation by the factor 2 in each dimension. This decimation then makes each subband image fullband at the lower sample rate. For a 16-band system, this process is repeated to further split each subband into four more subbands. It can be seen that the region of support of the resulting subband images would then be reduced by a factor of 4 in each dimension, giving an overall factor of 16 reduction in sample rate for each of the 16 subband images.

After encoding, transmission, and decoding, the filtering process is carried out in reverse [Fig. 2(b)]. Each subband is upsampled by (2, 2) and suitably bandpass filtered

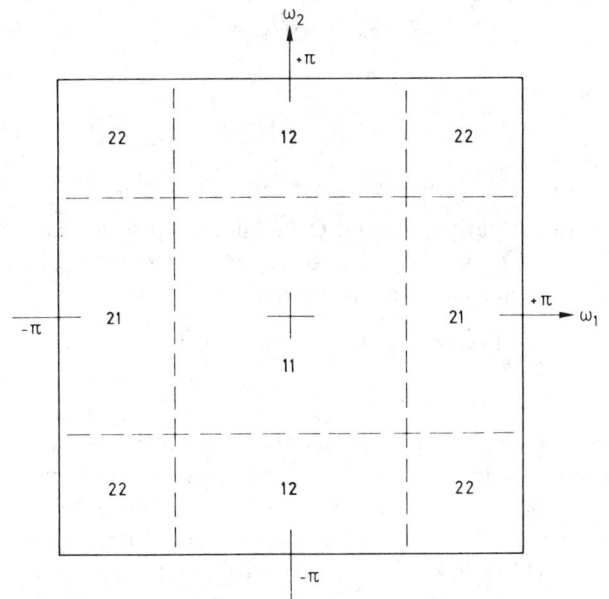

Fig. 1. Initial 4-band partition of frequency domain.

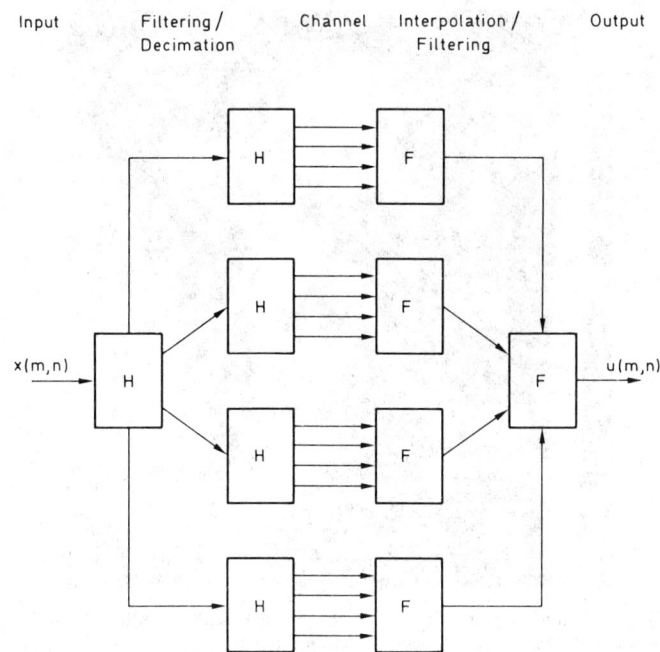

Fig. 3. System diagram of full 16-band system.

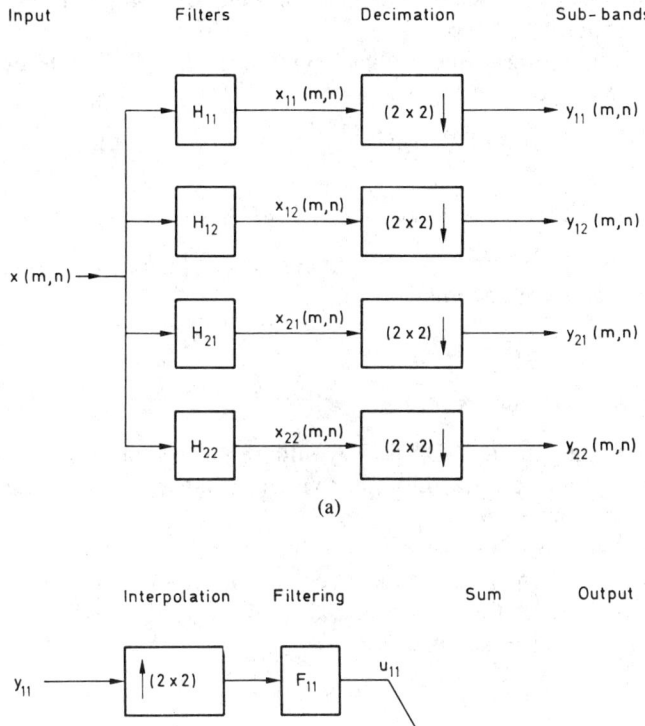

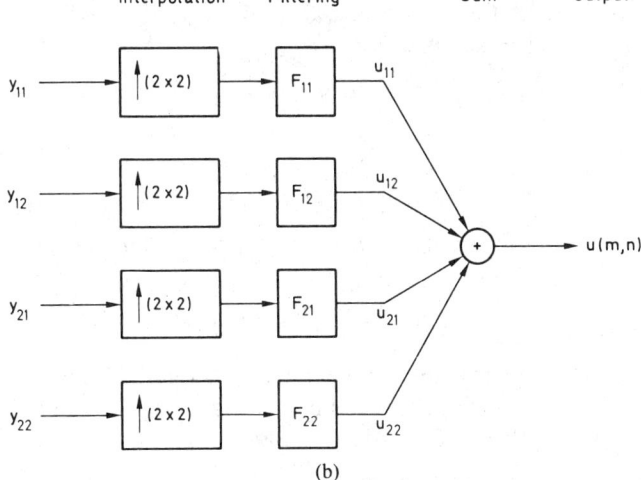

Fig. 2. (a) System diagram of 4-band splitting (done twice for 16 bands). (b) System diagram of 4-band recombination (done twice for 16 bands).

to eliminate aliased copies of the signal produced by the upsampling. The appropriate sets of subbands are then summed to reconstruct the original signal. Again, for 16 bands, this process must be repeated once. A schematic of the full system can be seen in Fig. 3.

FIR Filters

When FIR filters are used to approximate the ideal subband filter characteristics of Fig. 1, either gaps or aliasing error will occur due to the effect of decimation in the transition band of the filter. This effect is well known in the 1-D subband filtering literature [2] where the audio effect of either degradation is deemed unacceptable. We have found these distortions to be similarly unacceptable for subband filtering of images as seen in Fig. 4. Here linear taper filters (i.e., a straight line transition band) are used to partition the subbands and ideal filters are used to recombine them. In the 1-D case, the QMF approach was introduced to cancel out the aliasing effect of the filter transition band in the desirable case where no frequency gaps are allowed between the bands. The extension of the QMF concept to two dimensions is relatively straightforward and proceeds as follows.

Referring to Fig. 2(a) and the initial four-band splitting, we require that the four subband filters H_{11} through H_{22} have mirror-image conjugate symmetry about their mutual boundaries, which for real h_{ij} is equivalent to

$$H_{12}(\omega_1, \omega_2) = H_{11}(\omega_1, \omega_2 + \pi) \quad (1a)$$

$$H_{21}(\omega_1, \omega_2) = H_{11}(\omega_1 + \pi, \omega_2) \quad (1b)$$

$$H_{22}(\omega_1, \omega_2) = H_{11}(\omega_1 + \pi, \omega_2 + \pi). \quad (1c)$$

Denoting the outputs of the filters in Fig. 2(a) as x_{11} through x_{22}, we have the outputs Y_{ij} after (2, 2) downsampling,

Fig. 4. Reconstruction of "Lady" image using linear taper filters for splitting and ideal filters for reconstruction (convolution performed in DFT frequency domain).

$$Y_{ij}(\omega_1, \omega_2) = \frac{1}{4} \sum_{k=0}^{1} \sum_{l=0}^{1} H_{ij}\left(\frac{\omega_1 + k\pi}{2}, \frac{\omega_2 + l\pi}{2}\right)$$
$$\cdot X\left(\frac{\omega_1 + k\pi}{2}, \frac{\omega_2 + l\pi}{2}\right). \quad (2)$$

Ignoring the effects of encoding/decoding and transmission, we find that the outputs U_{ij} of the interpolation filters [Fig. 2(b)] can be expressed as

$$U_{ij}(\omega_1, \omega_2) = Y_{ij}(2\omega_1, 2\omega_2) F_{ij}(\omega_1, \omega_2),$$

and that the final output U can be written as

$$U(\omega_1, \omega_2) = \frac{1}{4} \sum_{k,l} X(\omega_1 + k\pi, \omega_2 + l\pi)$$
$$\cdot \left[\sum_{i,j} H_{ij}(\omega_1 + k\pi, \omega_2 + l\pi) F_{ij}(\omega_1, \omega_2)\right], \quad (3)$$

which is essentially the same as (3.2) in [7]. Splitting U into a desired signal component U_o and an undesired aliasing component U_a such that $U = U_o + U_a$, we get the aliased component

$$U_a(\omega_1, \omega_2) = \frac{1}{4} \sum_{(k,l) \neq (0,0)} X(\omega_1 + k\pi, \omega_2 + l\pi)$$
$$\cdot \left[\sum_{i,j} H_{ij}(\omega_1 + k\pi, \omega_2 + l\pi) F_{ij}(\omega_1, \omega_2)\right],$$

which will vanish if and only if (iff)

$$\sum_{i,j} H_{ij}(\omega_1 + k\pi, \omega_2 + l\pi) F_{ij}(\omega_1, \omega_2) = 0$$
$$\text{for } (k, l) \neq (0, 0). \quad (4)$$

We chose the same reconstruction filters F_{ij} as Vetterli [7],

$$F_{11}(\omega_1, \omega_2) = 4H_{11}(\omega_1, \omega_2) \quad (5a)$$
$$F_{12}(\omega_1, \omega_2) = -4H_{12}(\omega_1, \omega_2) \quad (5b)$$
$$F_{21}(\omega_1, \omega_2) = -4H_{21}(\omega_1, \omega_2) \quad (5c)$$
$$F_{22}(\omega_1, \omega_2) = 4H_{22}(\omega_1, \omega_2), \quad (5d)$$

and found that the aliased terms automatically vanish for $(k, l) = (0, 1)$ or $(1, 0)$. However, in the case $(k, l) = (1, 1)$ the aliased term will vanish iff

$$H_{11}(\omega_1, \omega_2) H_{11}(\omega_1 + \pi, \omega_2 + \pi)$$
$$= H_{11}(\omega_1, \omega_2 + \pi) H_{11}(\omega_1 + \pi, \omega_2). \quad (6)$$

Since the four factors in (6) are evaluations of H_{11} on a square of side π, it follows that both sides of (6) will be zero if the support of H_{11} is contained within $(-\frac{1}{2}\pi, +\frac{1}{2}\pi) \times (-\frac{1}{2}\pi, +\frac{1}{2}\pi)$ whether H_{11} is separable or not, thus contradicting the claim for the necessity of separability in [7]. Note, however, that any separable H_{11} would clearly satisfy (6). An advantage of nonseparable filters would be a directional capability in the subband decomposition. The advantage of separability is, of course, computational simplicity.

Employing a linear phase symmetric $L \times L$ FIR filter for h_{11} with L even, we have

$$h_{11}(m, n) = h_{11}(L - 1 - m, L - 1 - n),$$
$$1 \leq m, n \leq \tfrac{1}{2}L - 1,$$

so that, on removing the linear phase factor, the non-aliased term becomes

$$|H_{11}^2(\omega_1, \omega_2)| + |H_{11}^2(\omega_1, \omega_2 + \pi)| + |H_{11}^2(\omega_1 + \pi, \omega_2)|$$
$$+ |H_{11}^2(\omega_1 + \pi, \omega_2 + \pi)| = 1. \quad (7)$$

Thus, a general 2-D QMF would be generated by a low-pass filter optimized to approximately satisfy (7) with the constraint of (6).

Avoiding this potentially difficult design problem, we proceed here in this first investigation of subband image coding, with the easier separable case. A 1-D QMF filter pair h_1 and h_2 satisfies [8]

$$h_1(n) = h_1(L - 1 - n) \quad 0 \leq n \leq L/2 - 1 \quad (8a)$$
$$h_2(n) = (-1)^n h_1(n) \quad (8b)$$
$$|H_1^2(\omega)| + |H_2^2(\omega)| = 1. \quad (8c)$$

If we define the 2-D baseband filter h_{11} as the separable product

$$h_{11}(m, n) \triangleq h_1(m) h_1(n), \quad (9)$$

take the Fourier transform, and substitute into (6), we see that the 2-D QMF filters can be taken as a separable product of identical 1-D QMF filters [7]

$$H_{ij}(\omega_1, \omega_2) = H_i(\omega_1) H_j(\omega_2), \quad 1 \leq i, j \leq 2. \quad (10)$$

In our coding simulations, we used the 32-point QMF

Fig. 5. Reconstruction of "Lady" image using 16-band 2-D QMF filter (convolution performed in DFT frequency domain).

Fig. 6. Some subband signals of "Lady" image: (a) subband 11-11, (b) subband 11-21, (c) subband 11-12, (d) subband 11-22 (zoomed by 2×2).

designated as $32D$ in [11]. It has a transition bandwidth of 0.043 rad and an overall passband ripple of 0.025 dB. The stopband rejection varies from 38 to 48 dB. Fig. 5 shows a 16-band reconstruction obtained using the separable 2-D QMF based on this 1-D filter. The filtering was performed in the DFT frequency domain with $N = 256$, the image size. Comparison to the original shows it to be virtually identical. Fig. 6 shows four of the subband im-

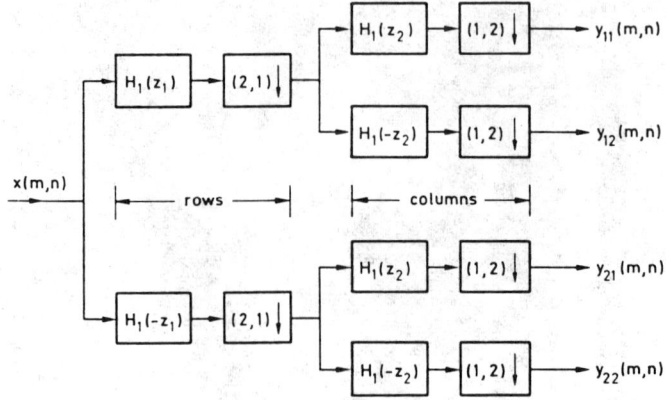

Fig. 7. Separable 4-subband filter.

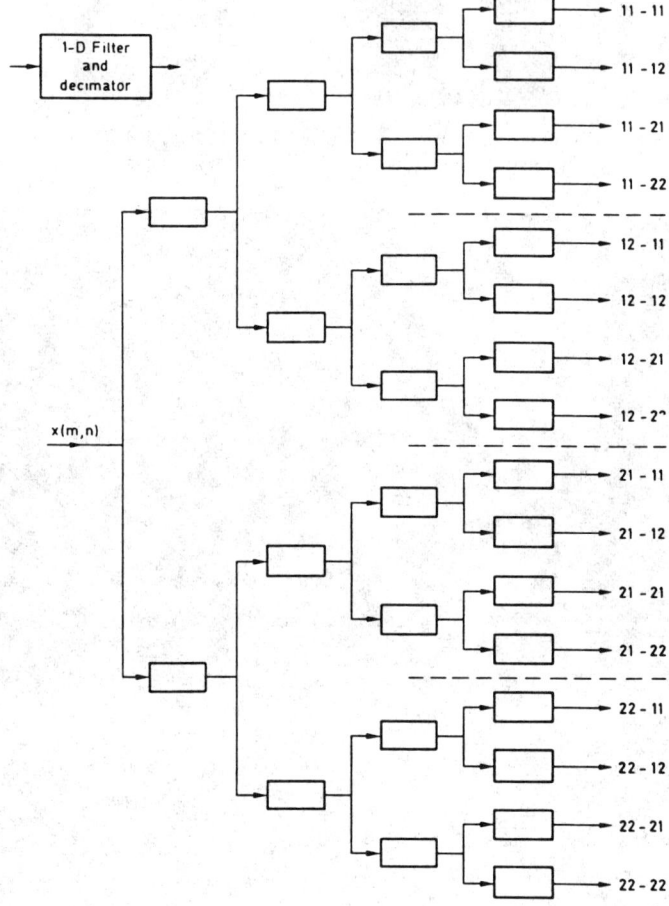

Fig. 8. Tree structure for 16-band separable subband filter.

ages in this decomposition. Fig. 6(a) shows the baseband image 11-11. Fig. 6(b) and (c) shows subband images 11-12, -21, and -22 which have been scaled up for presentation. The rapid black-white transitions in these subband images result from the demodulation by decimation. The frequency axis is effectively folded about the lower band edge, thus interchanging the high and low frequencies. For these subbands, this is equivalent to multiplying by $(-1)^m$, $(-1)^n$, and $(-1)^{m+n}$, respectively. This effect, although visually annoying, would cause no problem for a DPCM predictor.

Filter Tree

Using the 1-D QMF filters, we can perform the 4-band decomposition by the row-column approach shown in Fig. 7. This can be regarded as the first two levels in a filter tree structure with the understanding that the first stage represents row filtering and the second stage represents column filtering. To get a 16-band decomposition, as mentioned above, we iterate the four-band decomposition once to get the filter tree shown in Fig. 8. Here each box represents a 1-D filtering with $h_1(n)$ or $(-1)^n h_1(n)$ followed by a 2↓ subsampling. Also in this diagram, we have the convention that the odd stages represent row filtering while the even stages represent column filtering.

To calculate the computational requirements of this filter tree, we note that stage 1 will require $\frac{1}{2}LN^2$ multiplies where $N \times N$ is the image size and L is the filter length which is assumed to be even. At the second stage, we have one-half as many columns which must be filtered in the same way, but there are two branches, thus, we again require $\frac{1}{2}LN^2$ multiplies. Proceeding to the last two stages we obtain the same results. Thus, the total multiplication requirement becomes $2LN^2$ where we have assumed that the multiplications for filtering with $h_1(n)$ and $(-1)^n h_1(n)$ are performed just once and then added or subtracted as appropriate into the relevant partial product. For $L = 32$, this is 64 multiplies/pixel. These filter trees were also considered by Vetterli [7], who using the concept of pseudo-QMF has reported 10 multiplies/pixel for this four stage filter with $L = 25$. For comparison, a 16×16 DCT using the method of [9] requires about $5\frac{1}{2}$ multiplies/pixel.

III. Subband Coding of Images

This section treats the encoding of the subbands created by the QMF filter tree of the last section. We will be mainly concerned with DPCM as the method to encode the subbands rather than PCM which is often used in subband speech encoders. Our use of DPCM is motivated by the increased efficiency of a predictive encoder for a nonwhite power spectral density. The overall subband coding system is shown in Fig. 9.

In the case of M subbands of equal bandwidth, each subband has been subsampled by sqrt(M) in each dimension. Thus, if we assign B_k bits to subband k, we have the following average bit rate:

$$B = \frac{1}{M} \sum_{k=1}^{M} B_k. \quad (11)$$

Here k represents the subbands ij of the previous section indexed in some convenient order.

To design the DPCM coder for each subband, we need a linear predictive or AR model in the form

$$y_k(m, n) = \sum_{o,p} c_{op}^k y_k(m - o, n - p) + w_k(m, n)$$

with prediction error variance $\sigma_{p,k}^2$. Referring to Fig. 10, we see that for DPCM the reconstruction mean-square error (MSE) is equal to the quantizer MSE

$$E[(y_k(m, n) - \tilde{y}_k(m, n))^2] = E[(e_k(m, n) - q_k(m, n))^2]$$
$$= \text{Var}[r_k(m, n)] \triangleq \sigma_{r,k}^2$$

where $r_k \triangleq y_k - \tilde{y}_k$ is the reconstruction error.

From [2] this is given by

$$\sigma_{r,k}^2 = g(B_k) \text{Var}[e_k(m, n)] 2^{-2B_k} \quad (12)$$
$$\simeq g(B_k) \sigma_{p,k}^2 2^{-2B_k},$$

where $g(B_k)$ is a slowly varying function of the number of bits assigned to subband k. The histogram of prediction errors in subband coding (SBC) of images matches the

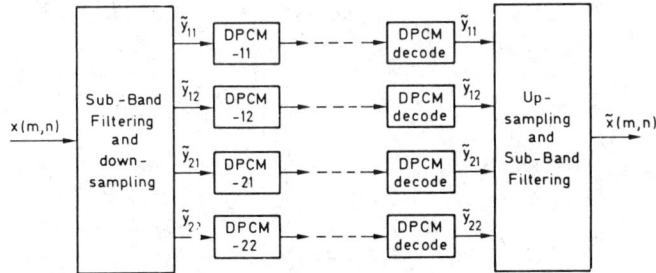

Fig. 9. A subband coding system with four bands.

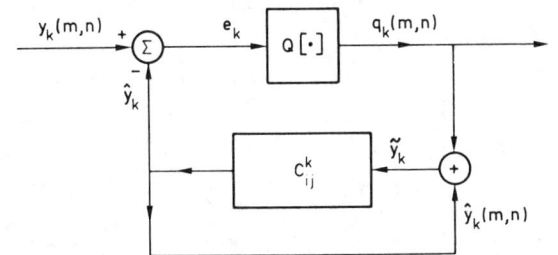

Fig. 10. DPCM for subband k.

Laplacian probability density function (pdf) quite well (see Fig. 11), a property that it no-doubt inherits from fullband DPCM. The optimal pdf optimized quantizer for the Laplacian density was derived by Nitadori [12], and we employ his results in this paper. The value $g(B_k) \simeq g = 4.5$ is valid for this pdf. We can thus write the sum of the error variances of the M subbands as

$$\sum_{k=1}^{M} \text{Var}[r_k(m, n)] = \sum_{k=1}^{M} g \sigma_{p,k}^2 2^{-2B_k}. \quad (13)$$

This MSE is related to the total reconstruction MSE as

$$\text{Var}(r) = E[(y(m, n) - \tilde{y}(m, n))^2]$$
$$= \sum_{k=1}^{M} \text{Var}(r_k). \quad (14)$$

Thus, we must minimize (13) subject to the constraint of (11). This is a standard problem in the optimization of transform encoders [9] whose solution is obtained using Lagrange multipliers. The MSE optimal bit assignment then is

$$B_k = B + \frac{1}{2} \log_2 \left[\frac{\sigma_{p,k}^2}{\sigma_{gm}^2} \right], \quad 1 \leq k \leq M \quad (15)$$

where $\sigma_{gm}^2 \triangleq (\Pi_{k=1}^{M} \sigma_{p,k}^2)^{1/M}$ is the geometric mean of the $\sigma_{p,k}^2$. The minimum overall MSE, then becomes

$$\text{Var}_o(r) = M \sigma_{g,m}^2 2^{-2B}.$$

Calculation of Coding Gain

The coding gain of fullband DPCM with respect to PCM is defined as the ratio of the PCM reconstruction MSE to that of DPCM [2]. Denoting this quantity by $G_{\text{DPCM/PCM}}$, we can express it as

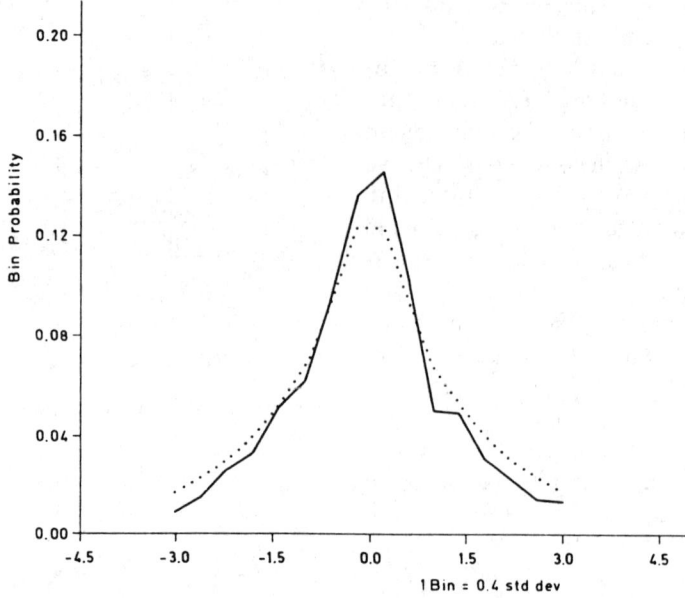

Fig. 11. Histogram of prediction error compared to Laplacian pdf.

$$G_{\text{DPCM/PCM}} = \frac{g \, \sigma_y^2 \, 2^{-2B}}{g \, \sigma_p^2 \, 2^{-2B}}$$

$$= \frac{\sigma_y^2}{\sigma_p^2} \quad \text{(for Gaussian case only)},$$

$$= \gamma_y^{-2},$$

where γ_y^2 is the spectral flatness measure [2] given by

$$\gamma_y^2 \triangleq \frac{\exp \frac{1}{2\pi} \left(\int_{-\pi}^{+\pi} \ln S_y(\omega) \, d\omega \right)}{\sigma_y^2},$$

and where σ_p^2 is the fullband DPCM prediction error. The 2-D version of this result follows from the analogous result that the 2-D prediction error can be expressed as

$$\sigma_p^2 = \exp \left(\frac{1}{(2\pi)^2} \int_{-\pi}^{+\pi} \int_{-\pi}^{+\pi} \ln S_y(\omega_1, \omega_2) \, d\omega_1 \, d\omega_2 \right). \quad (16)$$

If we consider the coding gain of SBC using DPCM to encode the subbands versus fullband DPCM, we have

$$G_{\text{SBC/DPCM}} = \frac{g \, \sigma_p^2 \, 2^{-2B}}{g \sum_{k=1}^{M} \sigma_{p,k}^2 \, 2^{-2B}} \cdot {}^{1}$$

Evaluating at the optimal bit assignment (15) we get

$$G_{\text{SBC/DPCM}} = \frac{\sigma_p^2}{M \sigma_{g,m}^2} \quad (17)$$

where $\sigma_{g,m}^2$ was defined above. Surprisingly, this quantity is exactly equal to one when MSE optimal linear predictors are used for all bands. This can be seen by applying

[1] Note: We can cancel the g's here because SBC and fullband DPCM both have the Laplacian pdf at their quantizers.

(16) to each of the M individual subbands and then multiplying the results together. To do this, we need an expression for the power spectral density of $y_k(m, n)$, the decimated subband signal. It is relatively easy to show that, for ideal filters, we have

$$S_{y_k}(\omega_1, \omega_2) = \frac{1}{M} S_{x_k} \left(\frac{\omega_1}{M}, \frac{\omega_2}{M} \right). \quad (18)$$

The factor $1/M$ is necessary to maintain equal variance between x_k and y_k. Inserting (18) in (16) and carrying out the previously indicated multiplication, we obtain

$$\left(\prod_{k=1}^{M} \sigma_{p,k}^2 \right) = \frac{1}{M^M} \exp \left[\frac{M}{(2\pi)^2} \int_{-\pi}^{+\pi} \int_{-\pi}^{+\pi} \ln S_x(\omega_1, \omega_2) \, d\omega_1 \, d\omega_2 \right]$$

$$= \frac{1}{M^M} \sigma_p^{2M}.$$

Thus,

$$M \sigma_{gm}^2 = \sigma_p^2,$$

so that we have

$$G_{\text{SBC/DPCM}} = 1. \quad (19)$$

The coding gain of SBC relative to PCM is thus the same as that of DPCM relative to PCM

$$G_{\text{SBC/PCM}} = \gamma_y^{-2}. \quad (20)$$

Note that coding gains (17), (19), and (20) are for the case where the bit rate is not too small so that asymptotic formulas such as (12) can be used for the quantizer MSE. Also, the coding gains with respect to PCM assume Gaussian data (in cancelling out the quantizer efficiency factor $g(B)$ which is pdf dependent). Further, these formulas assume optimal linear prediction. In a practical case, we would expect SBC to perform better than DPCM because: 1) restricted to a subband our low-order predictors will be more nearly optimal, and 2) although B is small, the B_k corresponding to bands with significant energy may be large, thus making (13) and (14) more realistic in the subband coding case.

Comments

1) If we took M large enough, we could efficiently use PCM to encode the subbands since their power spectral density would be nearly white. For more modest choices of M, several of the subbands will benefit from DPCM coding.

2) The gain for transform coding with the DFT or DCT is also given by the inverse of the spectral flatness measure in the high rate case [2]. Thus, the SBC coder can theoretically perform equally to the DCT coder at high bit rates for Gaussian images.

3) As M increases from one, the subband coder employing DPCM moves continuously from fullband DPCM towards full-image DFT encoding retaining asymptotic optimality in the sense of (20) at each step.

IV. Adaptive Subband Coding

In addition to bit allocation between the subbands, bits can also be allocated within the subbands, i.e., in the spatial domain. It is clear that within any image there are areas of large change such as edges, and areas of smaller change, as well as regions which are relatively flat. If we divide the image up into 16×16 blocks, corresponding to 4×4 blocks in each of the subband images, we can use the local variance to separate the blocks into busy, nonbusy, and quiet categories. We can then assign more bits to the busy blocks and fewer bits to the other blocks, tacitly accepting an overhead requirement of less than 0.01 bits/pixel. Choosing local variance thresholds to provide equal numbers of blocks in each category, we can see that the reconstruction error variance in subband k will be the average of the subband k error variances in each of the three categories. Denoting the error variance in category j as $\sigma_{k,j}^2$, we have

$$\sigma_r^2 = \frac{1}{3} \sum_{j=1}^{3} \sum_{k=1}^{M} \sigma_{k,j}^2.$$

Then substituting in (12) for each of the three busyness categories, we get

$$\sigma_r^2 = \frac{1}{3} g \sum_{k,j} \sigma_{p,k,j}^2 2^{-2B_{k,j}}.$$

This MSE is optimized using the same method as used on (13) to obtain the bit assignment

$$B_{k,j} = B + \frac{1}{2} \log_2 \left(\frac{\sigma_{p,k,j}^2}{\sigma_{gm,a}^2} \right),$$

$$1 \leq k \leq M, \quad 1 \leq j \leq 3, \quad (21)$$

where

$$\sigma_{gm,a}^2 \triangleq \left(\prod_{k,j} \sigma_{p,k,j}^2 \right)^{1/3M}$$

A problem with (21) as well as (15) earlier is that the B_{kj} may not be integers, and they may (even worse) be negative! Actually, we only need $2^{2B_{kj}}$ to be an integer, and this can often be handled by approximation. The negative values are more of a problem, but it is a standard one in the area of transform coding. Quickly converging iterative algorithms have been developed to deal with negative B_{kj} by truncating the negative values and then evenly subtracting off the excess average bit rate thus created [2]. Generally no more than two iterations of this process are necessary.

Within each category and each subband, we solve the least-squares prediction problem to find the appropriate AR model. The error variance within each category $\sigma_{p,k,j}^2$ then permits the selection of a Laplacian optimized quantizer [12] for the assigned bit rate and, hence, the number of levels.

V. Coding Simulation Results

A coding simulation for SBC was carried out at the Image Processing Laboratory at R.P.I. We considered two monochrome images of size 256×256 with 8-bit gray scales. The encoding was done in the density or log-intensity domain. The images are referred to as "Lady" and "Building" and are seen in Figs. 12(a) and 15, respectively. Both images were encoded at $B = 2.0$ and 1.0 bits per pixel (bpp). The "Lady" image was also encoded at $B = 0.67$ bpp, while the "Building" image was encoded at $B = 0.57$ bpp. The "Lady" image was encoded both adaptively and nonadaptively, however, the "Building" image was only coded adaptively. Convolution was performed circularly with $N = 256$.

For $B = 1.0$ and the "Lady" image, adaptive bit allocation gave the results shown in Table I. These numbers reflect the iterative adjustment to remove negative values. Using normalized Laplacian quantizers with numbers of levels 2, 3, 4, 5, 8, 16, and 32, these values were then modified to the bit assignments shown in Table II. Here the numbers in parentheses indicate 3 and 5 level "midtread" quantizers (i.e., representation levels at zero) which were coded by short length Huffman codes as seen in Table III with the resulting average wordlength as seen in Table II.

Fig. 12 shows the coding results for the "Lady" image using a nonadaptive SBC approach with 16 subbands and 1×1-order quarter-plane predictors. Fig. 12(b) was coded at 0.67 bpp, Fig. 12(c) was coded at 1.0 bpp, and Fig. 12(d) was coded at 2.0 bpp. Fig. 13 shows the corresponding result for adaptive SBC. Fig. 14 shows closeups of the center portion of the adaptive SBC images of Fig. 13. Viewing the original images we discern a slight impairment at 2.0 bpp and a quite noticeable impairment of 0.67 bpp, with the 1.0 bpp result being in between. Fig.

TABLE I
ADAPTIVE BIT ALLOCATIONS FOR THE SUBBANDS OF "LADY" USING (21) AND $B = 1$ bpp
(ALL VALUES HAVE BEEN ADJUSTED TO ELIMINATE NEGATIVE BIT ASSIGNMENTS)[a]

	Sub. 11-11	Sub. 11-12	Sub. 11-21	Sub. 11-22
Quiet	3.68	1.61	0.89	0.76
Nonbusy	4.54	2.65	1.79	1.79
Busy	4.71	3.57	2.58	2.61
	Sub. 12-11	Sub. 12-12	Sub. 12-21	Sub. 12-22
Quiet	0.00	0.86	0.00	0.00
Nonbusy	1.05	1.91	0.43	0.61
Busy	1.75	2.21	1.31	1.96
	Sub. 21-11	Sub. 21-12	Sub. 21-21	Sub. 21-22
Quiet	0.00	0.00	0.00	0.00
Nonbusy	0.00	0.00	0.00	0.10
Busy	0.31	0.21	1.05	1.08
	Sub. 22-11	Sub. 22-12	Sub. 22-21	Sub. 22-22
Quiet	0.00	0.00	0.00	0.00
Nonbusy	0.00	0.00	0.00	0.22
Busy	0.30	0.39	0.48	1.17

[a]Sub. ij-kl refers to the subband resulting from filtering the image by H_{ij} and then by H_{kl}.

TABLE II
ACTUAL BIT ASSIGNMENTS FOR $B = 1$ bpp ON "LADY." ASSIGNMENTS
WERE CALCULATED BY ROUNDING THE VALUES IN TABLE I TO
THE CLOSEST POSSIBLE BIT ASSIGNMENTS. ALLOCATIONS OF 1 AND
2 BITS WERE REPLACED BY 3-LEVEL AND 5-LEVEL QUANTIZERS
FOR SUBBANDS OTHER THAN 11-xx

Sub. 11-11	Sub. 11-12	Sub. 11-21	Sub. 11-22
4	2	1	1
5	3	2	2
5	4	3	3
Sub. 12-11	Sub. 12-12	Sub. 12-21	Sub. 12-22
0	1.36 (3)	0	0
1.17 (3)	1.86 (5)	0	0
1.28 (3)	1.85 (5)	0	1.76 (5)
Sub. 21-11	Sub. 21-12	Sub. 21-21	Sub. 21-22
0	0	0	0
0	0	0	0
0	0	1.10 (3)	1.20 (3)
Sub. 22-11	Sub. 22-12	Sub. 22-21	Sub. 22-22
0	0	0	0
0	0	0	0
0	0	0	1.17 (3)

Total = 47.75/48 = 1.00 bit

TABLE III
VARIABLE LENGTH CODE FOR 3 AND 5 RECONSTRUCTION LEVELS

Reconstruction Level	Code	Code Length
−1.422	10	2
0.0	0	1
1.422	11	2
−2.254	100	3
−0.840	101	3
0.0	0	1
0.840	110	3
2.254	111	3

Reconstructioan levels are normalized.

Fig. 12. Nonadaptive SBC results for "Lady" image: (a) original, (b) 0.67 bpp, (c) 1.0 bpp, (d) 2.0 bpp.

15 shows the corresponding adaptive SBC coding results for the "Building" image. Here the lowest rate is 0.57 bpp. Visual impairments are not evident in the 1.0 and 2.0 bpp "Building" images, however, the 0.57 bpp image seems to have a slightly "muddy" quality. Fig. 16 shows an SNR comparison for adaptive and nonadaptive SBC to three other existing techniques extending the comparison presented in [10]. The other curves plotted are taken from [10] and are the SNR performance of the adaptive DCT of Chen and Smith [9] and two vector quantization approaches. We see that the adaptive SBC gives the best SNR performance at all bit rates in the range 0.67–2.0. Also, the nonadaptive SBC is very competitive

Fig. 13. Adaptive SBC results for "Lady" image: (a) original, (b) 1.0 bpp, (c) 0.67 bpp, (d) 2.0 bpp.

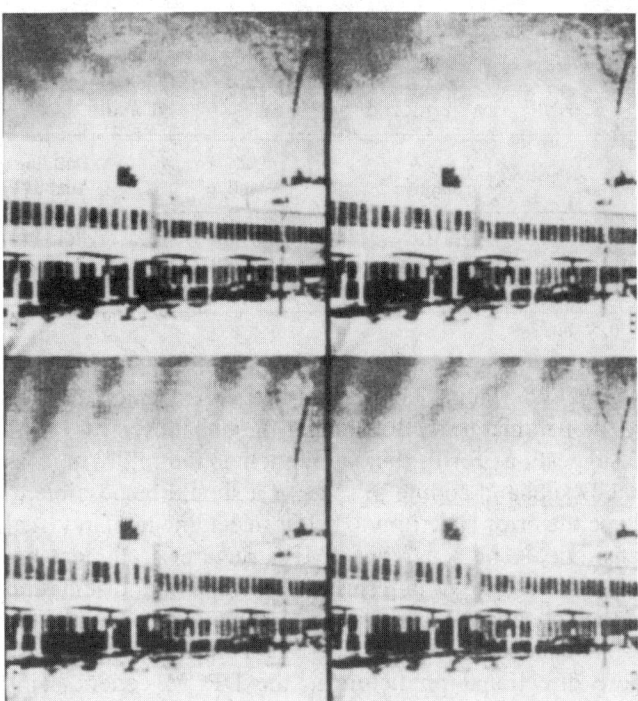

Fig. 15. Adaptive SBC results for "Building" image: (a) original, (b) 0.57 bpp, (c) 1.0 bpp, (d) 2.0 bpp.

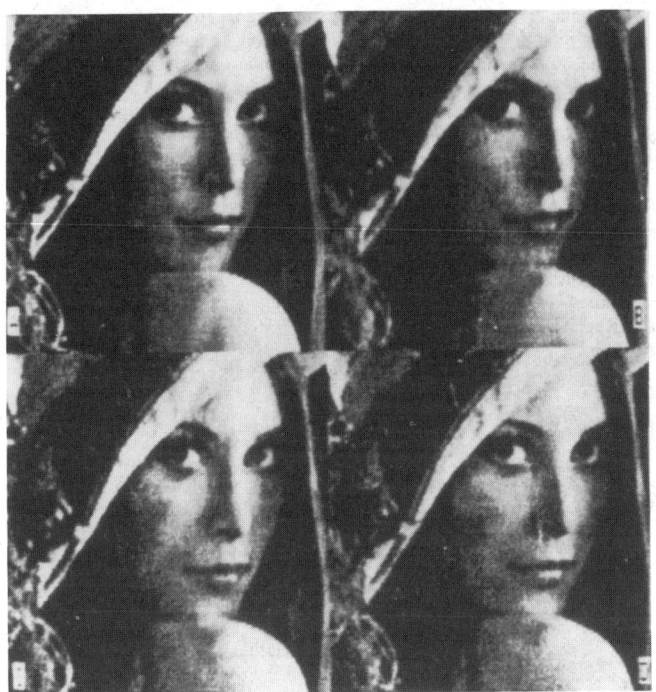

Fig. 14. Closeups of adaptive SBC results of Fig. 13: (a) original, (b) 0.67 bpp, (c) 1.0 bpp, (d) 2.0 bpp.

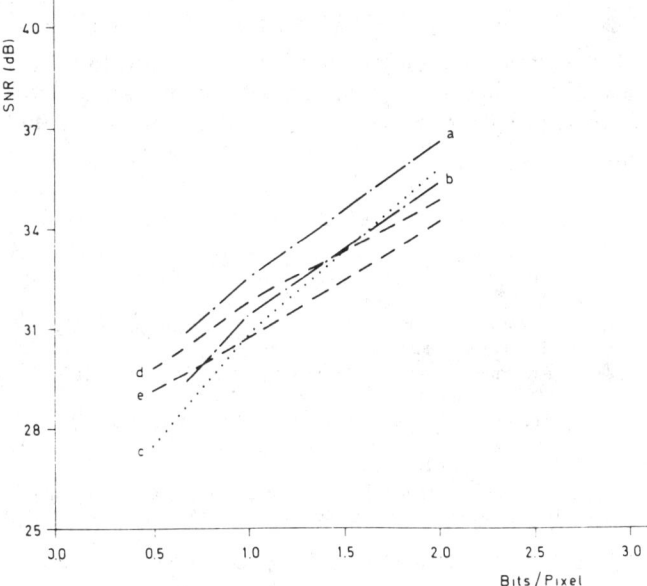

Fig. 16. SNR versus bit rate for "Lady" image using: (a) adaptive SBC, (b) nonadaptive SBC, (c) adaptive DCT, (d) differential VQ, and (e) VQ. (Plots of (c), (d), and (e) are taken from [10].)

with the other techniques over this range. Table IV lists our SNR results for SBC image coding.

VI. Conclusions

In this paper we have analyzed a new method of image coding called subband coding. This method has several advantages. First, it has the best SNR performances of the methods tested. Second, subband coding has good subjective error properties. Third, complexity comparable to transform coders is achievable using pseudo-QMF's. Subband image coding facilitates the progressive transmission approach, whereby lower resolution data are sent first and the detail appears gradually when the image does not change. The SBC technique is compatible with respect to high- and low-definition systems, in that the low-definition receivers can just ignore the higher resolution subbands. The new coding technique seems to have the performance of transform coding at low rates without the attendant blocky structure. Finally, one can see that subband coding unifies transform coding and DPCM by pro-

TABLE IV
SNR VERSUS BIT RATES FOR "LADY" AND "BUILDING"

Bits	"Lady" Nonadaptive	"Lady" Adaptive	"Building" Adaptive
0.67	29.4 dB	30.9 dB	30.6 dB[a]
1.0	31.4 dB	32.5 dB	33.8 dB
2.0	35.4 dB	36.6 dB	38.0 dB

[a] 0.57 bits.

viding a continuum between these two extremes indexed by the parameter M, the number of subbands.

Suggestions for further study include the following. As in 1-D subband coding of speech, it should be possible to shape the error spectrum to better match the human visual sensitivity. The separable QMF structure is efficient but it is also restrictive in terms of the directional orientation of the subbands. For example, one may want to split the 22 subband into 45° and 135° subbands in order to use more directional predictors in the DPCM coders. This cannot be done with separable filters. However, a nonseparable pseudo-QMF structure might exist to solve this problem.

ACKNOWLEDGMENT

The authors would like to thank an anonymous reviewer for pointing out a mistake relating to cancellation of the aliasing terms in (3) in an earlier version of this paper.

REFERENCES

[1] R. E. Crochiere, S. A. Webber, and J. L. Flanagan, "Digital coding of speech in subbands," *Bell. Syst. Tech. J.*, vol. 55, pp. 1069–1085, Oct. 1976.
[2] N. S. Jayant and P. Noll, *Digital Coding of Waveforms*. Englewood Cliffs, NJ: Prentice-Hall, 1984.
[3] E. R. Kretzmer, "Reduced-alphabet representation of television signals," *IRE Convention Rec.*, vol. 4, pp. 140–147, 1956.
[4] W. F. Schreiber, C. F. Knapp, and N. D. Kay, "Synthetic highs, An experimental TV bandwidth reduction systems," *J. SMPTE*, vol. 68, pp. 525–537, Aug. 1959.
[5] P. J. Burt and E. H. Adelson, "The Laplacian pyramid as a compact image code," *IEEE Trans. Commun.*, vol. COM-31, pp. 532–540, Apr. 1983.
[6] S. D. O'Neil, "Sub-band coding of images with adaptive bit allocation," M.S. thesis, ECSE Dep., R.P.I., Troy, NY, Apr. 1985.
[7] M. Vetterli, "Multi-dimensional sub-band coding: Some theory and algorithms," *Signal Processing*, vol. 6, pp. 97–112, Apr. 1984.
[8] D. Esteban and C. Galand, "Application of quadrature mirror filters to split band voice coding schemes," in *Proc. ICASSP*, May 1977, pp. 191–195.
[9] W. H. Chen and C. H. Smith, "Adaptive coding of monochrome and color images," *IEEE Trans. Commun.*, vol. COM-25, pp. 1285–1292, Nov. 1977.
[10] R. L. Baker and R. M. Gray, "Image compression using non-adaptive spatial vector quantization," in *Proc. 16th Asilomar Conf.*, Nov. 1982.
[11] J. D. Johnston, "A filter family designed for use in quadrature mirror filter banks," in *Proc. ICASSP*, Apr. 1980, pp. 291–294.
[12] K. Nitadori, "Statistical analysis of DPCM," *Electron. Commun. Japan*, vol. 48, pp. 17–26, Feb. 1965.

John W. Woods (S'67–M'70–SM'83) was born in Washington, DC, on December 5, 1943. He received the B.S., M.S., E.E., and Ph.D. degrees in electrical engineering from the Massachusetts Institute of Technology, Cambridge, in 1965, 1967, and 1970, respectively.

From 1970 to 1973 he was at the VELA Seismological Center, Alexandria, VA, working on array processing of digital seismic data. From 1973 to 1976 he was at the Lawrence Livermore Laboratory, University of California, Berkeley, working on two-dimensional digital signal processing. Since 1976 he has been with the Department of ECSE at Rensselaer Polytechnic Institute, Troy, NY, where he is currently a Professor. He has taught courses in digital signal processing, probability and stochastic processes, information theory, and communication systems. His research interests include estimation/restoration, detection, recursive digital filtering, and data compression of images and other multidimensional data. He has authored or co-authored over 40 papers in these fields. During the academic year 1985–1986, he was Visiting Professor in the Information Theory Group at Delft University of Technology, Delft, The Netherlands.

Dr. Woods was co-recipient of the 1976 Senior Award of the ASSP Society. He is a former member of the Digital Signal Processing Committee. He was Chairman of the Schenectady joint ASSP/Communications Society Chapter in 1977–1978. He is a former Associate Editor for Signal Processing of the IEEE TRANSACTIONS ON ACOUSTICS, SPEECH, AND SIGNAL PROCESSING. He was Co-chairman of the Third ASSP Workshop on Multidimensional Signal Processing held at Lake Tahoe, CA, in October 1983. He is a former Chairman of the ASSP Technical Committee on Multidimensional Signal Processing. He is a member of Sigma Xi, Tau Beta Pi, Eta Kappa Nu, and the AAAS. He is currently a member of the ASSP AdCom.

Sean D. O'Neil was born in Chicago, IL, on August 30, 1961. He received the B.S. degree in electrical engineering from the Massachusetts Institute of Technology, Cambridge, in 1983, and the M.S. degree from the Rensselaer Polytechnic Institute, Troy, NY, in 1985.

Since 1985 he has been working at the MITRE Corporation, Bedford, MA, on number theoretic signal processing and its implementation in VLSI. His interests include image compression, statistical pattern recognition, machine vision, and their applications.

Progressive Image Transmission Using Vector Quantization on Images in Pyramid Form

LIMIN WANG AND MORRIS GOLDBERG, SENIOR MEMBER, IEEE

Abstract—In this paper, we propose a progressive image transmission scheme in which vector quantization is applied to images represented by pyramids. A mean pyramid representation of an image is first built up by forming a sequence of reduced-size images by averaging over blocks of 2 × 2 pixels. A difference pyramid is then built up by taking the differences between successive levels in the mean pyramid. Progressive transmission is achieved by sending all the nodes in the difference pyramid starting from the top level and ending at the bottom level. The kth approximation image can be formed by adding the information of level k to the previously reproduced $(k - 1)$st approximation. To gain efficiency, vector quantization is applied to the difference pyramid of the image on a level-by-level basis. If the errors due to quantization at level k are properly delivered and included in the next level, $k + 1$, then it is demonstrated that the original image can be reconstructed. It should be emphasized that the error delivery procedure is the key for lossless reproduction of the original image, which makes it possible to reprocess at the lower levels the information lost at the higher levels. Finally, an entropy coder is used to losslessly encode the final residual error image, thus ensuring perfect reproduction of the original image. The experiments demonstrate that it is possible to achieve, simultaneously, lossless, progressive transmission, with compression. It is shown that, at the intermediate levels, the use of vector quantization results in a coding gain over using only a Huffman coder. Furthermore, as a lossy coding scheme, excellent reproduction is achieved at a bit rate of only 0.6 bits/pixel.

I. INTRODUCTION

THE transmission of still images is an important field in interactive image communications, with possible applications in teleconferencing, remote surveillance and browsing of large image databases. With standard raster transmission techniques, a digital image is transmitted as a sequence of rows or lines, implying that to be able to appreciate the image, the viewer must wait for the complete transmission. For example, transmitting an image of size 256 by 256 with 8 bits/pixel over a 1200 baud line would require about 7.28 min. Progressive image transmission [1]–[11] can alleviate this problem by first transmitting a low-resolution approximation image; upon the viewer's request, the low-resolution image can then be progressively improved with further transmission. Eventually, an exact replica of the original image is reconstructed. In other words, in progressive image transmission, successive approximations images are refinements of the earlier images and converge to the final, full resolution image. The primary advantage of progressive image transmission is that the gross structural information of the image appears immediately at the beginning of transmission, so that it may be possible for the viewer to make a decision whether further transmission is necessary, or not.

Paper approved by the Editor for Quantization, Speech/Image Coding of the IEEE Communications Society. Manuscript received February 17, 1987; revised September 16, 1988. This work was supported in part by NSERC under grants. This paper was presented in part at the 30th Midwest Symposium on Circuits abd Systems, Syracuse, NY, August 1987.

The authors are with the Department of Electrical Engineering, University of Ottawa, Ottawa, K1N 6N5 Canada.

IEEE Log Number 8931586.

A variety of approaches to progressive image transmission have been proposed [1]–[11], which generally fall into three categories: pyramidal, transform-based, and iterative encoding. In the pyramidal approach, the different levels in the pyramid correspond to successive approximations of the original image, which can be reconstructed by transmitting the pyramidal data structure from the top to bottom. The contents of the pyramid vary and can include the mean values [1]–[2], the pairs of the mean and difference values [3], and quasibandpass filtered versions of the image [4]. In the transform-based approach, the image first undergoes a block transform and the transformed coefficients are transmitted progressively in some order, usually from low to high order [5]–[6]. In this manner, successive approximations with progressively high resolution are obtained by inverse transforming the coefficients. A third approach is to iteratively encode the residual or difference image, either in the spatial domain or in the transform domain [7]–[11]. At each stage, an error or difference image is formed and then encoded at the next stage.

Vector quantization is a relatively new coding technique which has been successfully applied to speech and image compresssion [12]–[17]. In image vector quantization, the image data to be coded is first decomposed into a set of vectors, e.g., the spatially contiguous blocks. Then, a codebook of representative vectors (codewords) is generated by using an iterative procedure such as the generalized Lloyd clustering algorithm [12]. Quantization involves finding the closest representative vector for a given vector and compression is achieved by transmitting the corresponding label.

In this paper, we propose a progressive image transmission scheme in which vector quantization is applied to images represented by pyramids. The pyramid representation of image is built as follows. A sequence of reduced-size images from the original image is first formed by finding the truncated means over blocks of 2 × 2 pixels. This sequence of reduced-size image is referred to as the "mean" pyramid of the image. Then, the "difference" pyramid of the image is obtained by taking as the node values the differences between successive levels in the mean pyramid, i.e., between the parents and their siblings. The difference pyramid contains all the necessary information to reproduce successive reduced-size approximations of the image. As shown below, there are two important features of the pyramid representation. The first is that as the difference pyramid is composed of a set of differences, the corresponding first order entropy is likely to be much less than the first order entropy of the original image. The second is that if errors introduced at the high levels can be properly delivered to the levels below, the original image can still be reconstructed. To achieve lossless progressive transmission of the original image, all the nodes on the difference pyramid are sent starting from the top level and ending at the bottom level. The kth approximation image can be formed by adding the information of level k to the previously reproduced $(k - 1)$st approximation. Note that since the first order entropy of the difference pyramid is much less than that of the mean pyramid, a significant amount of savings can be expected by transmitting the differences, instead of the means [1], on a pixel-by-pixel basis. To gain efficiency, vector quantization is applied to the difference pyramid of the image on a level-by-level basis where vectors are formed by partitioning the levels into spatially contiguous, nonoverlapping, blocks of $m \times m$ nodes ($m = 2$ and 4 in our simulations). The errors due to quantization at level k are delivered to the next level, $k + 1$; in other words, the information to be transmitted at level $k + 1$ includes all the residual error components. It should be emphasized that the error delivery procedure is the key for lossless reproduction of the original image; this makes it possible to reprocess at the lower levels the information lost at the higher levels. Finally, an entropy coder is used to losslessly encode the final residual error image, thus ensuring perfect reproduction of the original image. The experiments demonstrate that it is possible to achieve, simultaneously, lossless, progressive transmission, with compression. Furthermore, at the intermediate levels, it is shown that the use of vector quantization results in a coding gain over using only a Huffman coder [18].

The rest of this paper is organized as follows. In Section II, an algorithm which reorganizes the image data into a pyramid form suitable for progressive image transmission is first presented. This follows in Section III with the description of the progressive image coding technique, in particular, the application of vector quantization and the method of reprocessing the residual errors due to quantization is discussed. Finally, some simulation results on two images are reported in pictorial form and in terms of rate distortion curves.

II. Pyramid Decomposition of Images

Pyramids are a class of hierarchical representations of images based on the principle of regular decomposition. Such structures have found an important role in the fields of image processing, computer graphics, and geographic information systems [19]–[20]. There are the numerous variants of pyramids differentiated on the basis of the type of data represented and on the decomposition process.

A pyramid data structure (Fig. 1), which is suited for progressive image transmission by vector quantization, is now presented. An image X_n of size $2^n \times 2^n$ is first decomposed into spatially contiguous, nonoverlapping, blocks of 2×2 pixels. Then, a new image at one half the resolution is formed by finding the mean for each block of 2×2 pixels, and truncating the mean to a fixed number of bits. The same process is repeated on the reduced-resolution image to yield a new image at one quarter the resolution. If this process is repeated n times, an image of size 1×1 is eventually produced. The sequence of reduced-resolution images is referred to as the mean pyramid of the image. The corresponding difference pyramid is then formed by taking the differences between successive levels, i.e., between the parents and their siblings, in the mean pyramid. In algorithm form, the mean pyramid is first formed as follows.

A. Formation of the Mean Pyramid

0) Initialization: Let $k = n$ and level k be the original image, i.e., $X_k = X_n$.

1) Formation of level $k - 1$: For each spatially contiguous, nonoverlapping, block of 2×2 nodes at level k, find the truncated mean by (Fig. 2),

$$X_{k-1,[i+1/2],[j+1/2]} = \left[\frac{X_{k,i,j} + X_{k,i,j+1} + X_{k,i+1,j} + X_{k,i+1,j+1}}{4} \right]$$

$$i, j = 1, 3, \cdots 2^k - 1 \quad (2.1)$$

where $[\alpha]$ is the truncation of $\alpha + 0.5$.

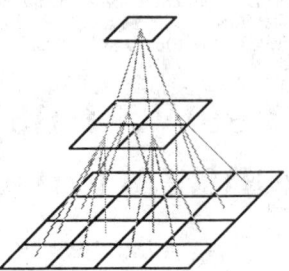

Fig. 1. An example of a pyramid representation of an image of size 4×4 pixels.

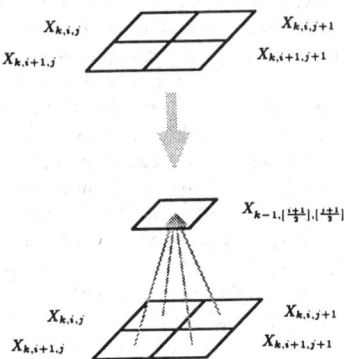

Fig. 2. Formation of mean pyramid. The pixel values at level $k - 1$ of the mean pyramid are obtained by calculating the truncated mean for spatial contiguous, nonoverlapping, block of size 2×2 at level k.

2) Termination: Let $k = k - 1$ and if $k \neq 0$, return to step 1; otherwise, stop.

In other words, the mean pyramid is formed by successively averaging over blocks of 2×2 starting from level $k = n$.

B. Formation of the Difference Pyramid

Once the mean pyramid is built up, the difference pyramid is then formed by taking the differences between the parents and their siblings in the mean pyramid (Fig. 3),

$$\begin{cases} D_{k,i,j} = X_{k-1,[i+1/2],[j+1/2]} - X_{k,i,j} \\ D_{k,i,j+1} = X_{k-1,[i+1/2],[j+1/2]} - X_{k,i,j+1} \\ D_{k,i+1,j} = X_{k-1,[i+1/2],[j+1/2]} - X_{k,i+1,j} \\ D_{k,i+1,j+1} = X_{k-1,[i+1/2],[j+1/2]} - X_{k,i+1,j+1} \end{cases} \quad (2.2)$$

$$k = n, n-1, \cdots 1$$
$$i, j = 1, 3, \cdots 2^k - 1.$$

A detailed example of the mean pyramid and difference pyramid formation for the case $n = 2$ is shown in Fig. 4.

To achieve lossless reproduction of the original image, all that need be transmitted are the top most value of the mean pyramid $X_{0,1,1}$ and the difference sets $\{D_{k,i,j}\}$. At the receiving end, the mean pyramid, corresponding to a sequence of reduced-size approximations of the original image, is built up starting from the top level $k = 1$ and continuing to the bottom level $k = n$ as follows.

C. Reconstruction of the Mean Pyramid

0) Initialization: Let the top level of the mean pyramid X_0 be level 0 and $k = 1$.

1) Reconstruction of level k: The node values of level k

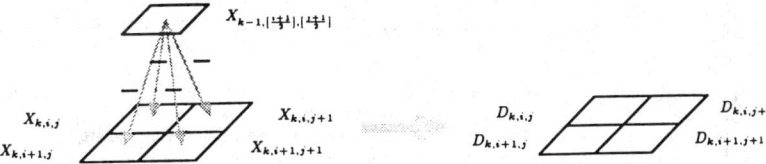

Fig. 3. Formation of difference pyramid. The node values at level k of the difference pyramid are formed by taking differences between successive levels in the mean pyramid, i.e., between the parents and their siblings.

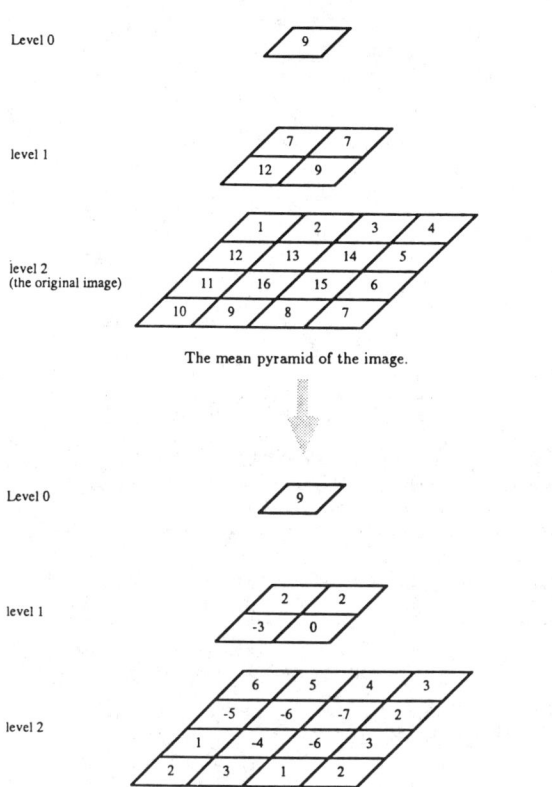

Fig. 4. An example of a mean pyramid followed by the corresponding difference pyramid for image of size 4×4. The mean pyramid of the image. The corresponding difference pyramid.

are obtained by

$$\begin{cases} X_{k,i,j} = X_{k-1,[i+1/2],[j+1/2]} - D_{k,i,j} \\ X_{k,i,j+1} = X_{k-1,[i+1/2],[j+1/2]} - D_{k,i,j+1} \\ X_{k,i+1,j} = X_{k-1,[i+1/2],[j+1/2]} - D_{k,i+1,j} \\ X_{k,i+1,j+1} = X_{k-1,[i+1/2],[j+1/2]} - D_{k,i+1,j+1} \\ \quad i,j = 1, 3, \cdots 2^k - 1 \end{cases} \quad (2.3)$$

which is just the inverse operation of formation of difference pyramid (2.2).

2) *Termination:* Let $k = k + 1$ and if $k \neq n$, return to step 1, otherwise, stop.

Two observations on the difference pyramid are in order. First of all, as the neighboring pixels in most natural images tend to be highly correlated, the values of the differences $\{D_{k,i,j}\}$ will tend to concentrate around zero. Therefore, the first order entropy of the difference pyramid R_q is likely to be much less than the first order entropy of the original image R_o i.e.

$$R_q < R_o. \quad (2.4)$$

Here, R_q and R_o are defined, respectively, as follows:

$$R_q = -\sum_i P_q(i) \log_2 P_q(i), \quad \text{(bits/node)} \quad (2.5)$$

$$R_o = -\sum_i P_o(i) \log_2 P_o(i), \quad \text{(bits/pixel)} \quad (2.6)$$

where $P_q(i)$ and $P_o(i)$ are, respectively, the frequency of occurrence of value i in the difference pyramid and in the original image. Note that the first order entropy defined above is measured on a pixel-by-pixel basis. The second observation regards the number of nodes in the difference pyramid. Since the number of nodes at level k is

$$\frac{2^n \times 2^n}{2^{n-k} \times 2^{n-k}} = 2^k \times 2^k, \quad k = 0, 1, \cdots n, \quad (2.7)$$

the total number of nodes on the pyramid data structure is equal to

$$\sum_{k=0}^{n} \frac{2^n \times 2^n}{2^{n-k} \times 2^{n-k}} = \sum_{k=0}^{n} 2^k \times 2^k$$

$$= \frac{1 - 2^{n+1} \times 2^{n+1}}{1 - 2 \times 2}$$

$$= \frac{4}{3}(2^n \times 2^n) - \frac{1}{3}$$

$$\approx \frac{4}{3}(2^n \times 2^n). \quad (2.8)$$

This implies that the number of nodes on the pyramid is about one third more than the number of pixels on the original image. For comparative purposes, we therefore define an equivalent entropy, R_q^p, measured on a pixel basis.

$$R_q^p = \frac{\frac{4}{3}(2^n \times 2^n) - \frac{1}{3}}{(2^n \times 2^n)} R_q \approx \frac{4}{3} R_q \quad \text{(bits/pixel)}. \quad (2.9)$$

The entropies defined above are measured from two test images, a face image (Fig. 11) and a boat image (Fig. 12). The histograms of the face and boat images shown in, respectively, Figs. 5 and 6, are seen to be more uniformly distributed; whereas the histograms of the corresponding difference pyramids tend to lie around zero. The entropies estimated from the histograms are, respectively, as follows: $R_o = 7.5178$ bits/pixel, $R_q = 4.3861$ bits/node, and $R_q^p = 5.8481$ bits/pixel for the face image; and $R_o = 7.5395$ bits/pixel, $R_q = 5.1582$ bits/node, and $R_q^p = 6.8775$ bits/pixel for the boat image. Note that, for both images, the equivalent entropy of the difference pyramid R_q^p is less than the entropy of the original R_o, i.e.,

$$R_q^p < R_o. \quad (2.10)$$

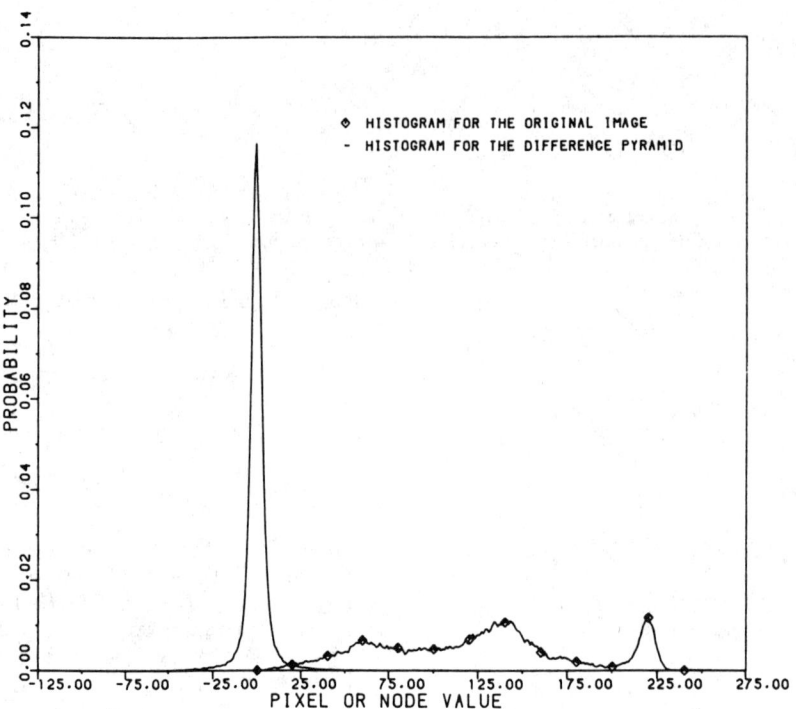

Fig. 5. Histograms for the original face image and the corresponding difference pyramid representation. The former is more uniformly distributed and the latter tends to lie around zero. The entropies estimated from the histograms are, respectively, as follows, $R_o = 7.5178$ bits/pixel; $R_q = 4.3861$ bits/node and $R_q^p = 5.8481$ bits/pixel.

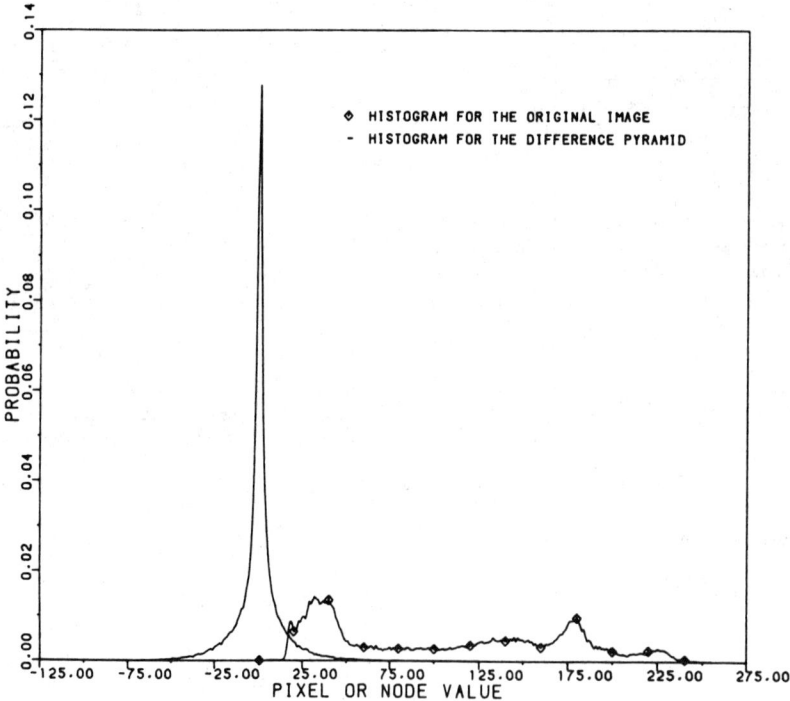

Fig. 6. Histograms for the original boat image and the corresponding difference pyramid representation. The former is more uniformly distributed and the latter tends to lie around zero. The entropies estimated from the histograms are, respectively, as follows, $R_o = 7.5395$ bits/pixel; $R_q = 5.1582$ bits/node and $R_q^p = 6.8775$ bits/pixel.

Consequently, it should be possible to save a certain amount of bits by encoding the images in pyramid form, rather than the original image directly.

A second property of the particular pyramid representation chosen is that of error recovery. In other words, if the errors introduced at the higher levels are properly delivered to the lower levels, the original image can still be reproduced. The principle of error recovery is illustrated in Fig. 7 where an error Δ is introduced at node $(k - 1, [i + 1/2], [j + 1/2])$. The error Δ is delivered to the next level, k, and added to the

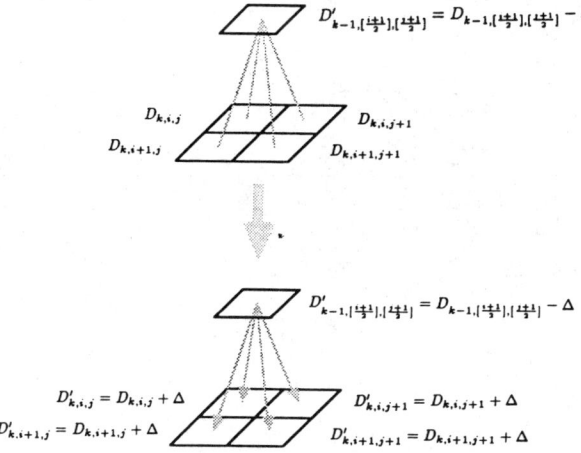

Fig. 7. Error Delivery: An error Δ occurring at node $(k-1, [i+1/2], [j+1/2])$ is delivered to the next level k and added to the four siblings. In other words, the siblings are modified by the error introduced at their parent value.

four siblings $\{D_{k,i+ii,j+jj}, ii, jj = 0, 1\}$ to yield $\{D'_{k,i+ii,j+jj}, ii, jj = 0, 1\}$ (Fig. 7). The corresponding pixel values $\{X'_{k,i+ii,j+jj}, ii, jj = 0, 1\}$ on the kth level of the mean pyramid are then evaluated from (2.3),

$$\begin{aligned}
X'_{k,i+ii,j+jj} &= X_{k-1,[i+1/2],[j+1/2]} - D'_{k,i+ii,j+jj} \\
&= X_{k-2,[[i+1/2]+1/2],[[j+1/2]+1/2]} \\
&\quad - D'_{k-1,[i+1/2],[j+1/2]} - D'_{k,i+ii,j+jj} \\
&= X_{k-2,[[i+1/2]+1/2],[[j+1/2]+1/2]} \\
&\quad - D_{k-1,[i+1/2],[j+1/2]} + \Delta - D_{k,i+ii,j+jj} - \Delta \\
&= X_{k-2,[[i+1/2]+1/2],[[j+1/2]+1/2]} \\
&\quad - D_{k-1,[i+1/2],[j+1/2]} - D_{k,i+ii,j+jj} \\
&= X_{k,i+ii,j+jj} \quad ii, jj = 0, 1. \quad (2.11)
\end{aligned}$$

In other words, the proposed method of error recovery ensures that the original mean pyramid values are reconstructed. The error-recovery technique provides the possibility of lossless encoding of the image even when a lossy coder is employed on the upper levels of the difference pyramid.

Fig. 8 shows an example of error recovery. An error, "e," is introduced at node $(1, 1, 1)$ of the difference pyramid of Fig. 4. The error "e" is delivered to the next level, 2, and added to the four siblings [Fig. 8(a)]. The 1st reduced-size approximation, corresponding to level 1 of the mean pyramid, is formed from level 0 and level 1 of the difference pyramid using (2.3). The 2nd reduced-size approximation, corresponding to level 2 of the mean pyramid, is formed from the previous approximation and level 2 of the difference pyramid with a modified top left quadrant [Fig. 8(c)]. Note that the original image is correctly recovered.

III. Vector Quantization on Pyramid Data Structure of Images

Rate distortion theory [21] indicates that better performance can be always achieved by coding vectors instead of scalars, even in the case of a memoryless source. Furthermore, a well-defined source can be compressed arbitrarily close to the rate distortion function as the coding block size approaches infinity. In vector quantization coding, the input vector set $\{V\}$ drawn from a M-dimensional Euclidean space is mapped into a finite set (codebook) of representative vectors (codewords), $\{\hat{V}_i, i = 1, 2, \cdots N_c\}$, contained in the space, i.e.,

$$q: V \to \hat{V} \quad (3.1)$$

where q is an M-dimensional vector quantization operator. The mapping is completely characterized by the partition $P = \{P_i, i = 1, 2, \cdots N\}$ in the input space, which assigns an input vector $V \in P_i$ to the representative vector $\hat{V}_i$, i.e.,

$$P_i = \{V: q(V) = \hat{V}_i\}. \quad (3.2)$$

A block diagram of the basic steps involved in vector quantization is depicted in Fig. 9. The first step is the decomposition of the input source into a set of vectors. A subset of vectors is chosen as a training sequence and a codebook is generated from the training sequence, by using an iterative clustering algorithm [12]. Finally, in quantizing an input vector, the closest codeword in the codebook is determined and the corresponding label of this codeword transmitted.

To efficiently transmit the image in pyramid form, vector quantization can be applied to the difference pyramid on a level-by-level basis as follows. Level K of the difference pyramid is first vector quantized where $0 < K \leq n$. Then, the errors due to quantization at level K are delivered to the next level $K + 1$ and added to the respective sibling nodes. The process is repeated from high level to low level. Finally, an entropy coder is used to losslessly encode the final residual error image at the bottom most level, thus ensuring perfect reproduction of the original image.

The basic steps involved in vector quantization of the pyramid data structure are as follows (Fig. 10):

0) Let $k = K$ where $0 < K \leq n$.

1) *Vector Formation:* Level k of the difference pyramid is decomposed into a set of vectors corresponding to spatially contiguous, nonoverlapping, square block of $m \times m$ nodes, $\{D_{k,i+ii,j+jj}, ii, jj = 0, 1, \cdots m - 1\}$ where $i, j = 1, m + 1, \cdots 2^k - m + 1$.

2) *Training Sequence Selection:* All the vector formed in step 1 are chosen as the training sequence.

3) *Codebook Generation:* The codebook is generated by applying the generalized Lloyd clustering algorithm [12] where the normalized mean square error (NMSE) is used as the criterion for distortion.

4) *Codebook Encoding:* The codebook obtained is quantized to the same resolution as the difference pyramid and then encoded by a variable length coder based on the frequencies of occurrence of the values in the codebook.

5) *Vector Quantization:* For each vector at level k, the closest codeword in the codebook is determined and the corresponding label of this codeword transmitted.

6) If $k = n$, go to step 9 and otherwise, continue.

7) *Quantization Error Delivery:* In order to losslessly recover the original image, the residual errors $\{e_{k,[i+1/2],[j+1/2]}\}$, due to quantization at level k, are delivered to the next level $k + 1$ and added to the respective sibling nodes (Fig. 7) as follows:

$$\begin{cases}
D'_{k+1,i,j} = e_{k,[i+1/2],[j+1/2]} + D_{k+1,i,j} \\
D'_{k+1,i,j+1} = e_{k,[i+1/2],[j+1/2]} + D_{k+1,i,j+1} \\
D'_{k+1,i+1,j} = e_{k,[i+1/2],[j+1/2]} + D_{k+1,i+1,j} \\
D'_{k+1,i+1,j+1} = e_{k,[i+1/2],[j+1/2]} + D_{k+1,i+1,j+1} \\
\quad i, j = 1, 3, \cdots 2^{k+1} - 1.
\end{cases} \quad (3.3)$$

In other words, the information to be transmitted at level $k + 1$ is modified by the residual error $\{e_{k,[i+1/2],[i+1/2]}\}$ at level k.

8) Set $k = k + 1$ and return to step 1.

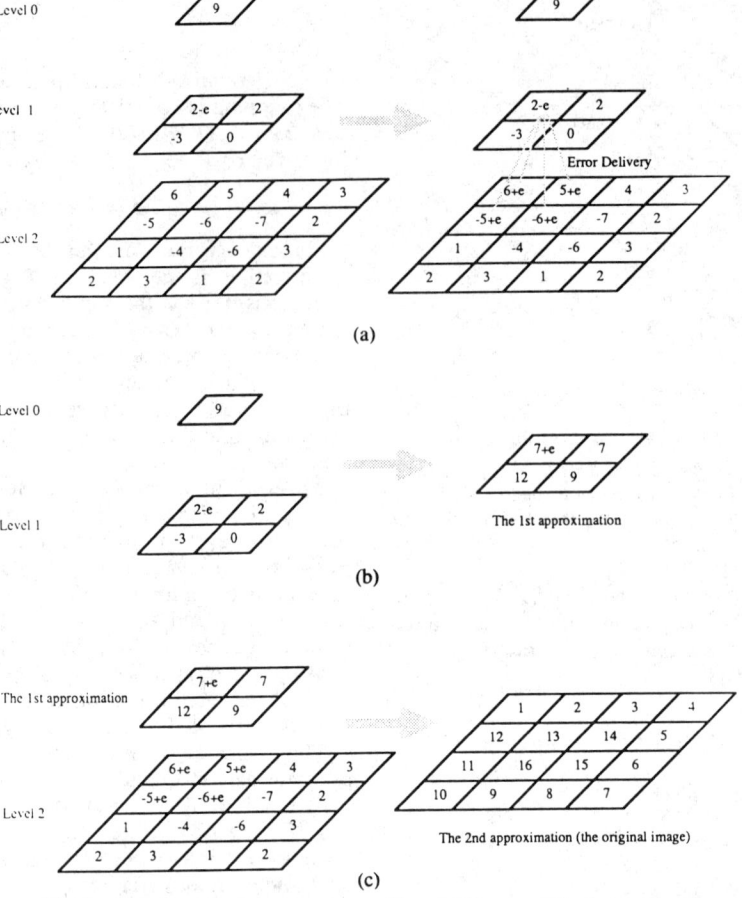

Fig. 8. An example of error recovery effect. (a) For the difference pyramid from Fig. 4, an error "e" introduced at node (1, 1, 1) is delivered to the next level, 2, and added to the four siblings. (b) The first reduced-size approximation is formed from level 0 and level 1 of the difference pyramid. Note the presence of an error "e" in (1, 1, 1) of the mean pyramid. (c) The second reduced-size approximation corresponding to level 2 of the mean pyramid (the original image) is now formed from the 1th reduce-size approximation (1, 1) and level 2 of the difference pyramid with a modified top left quadrant. Note that even though an error "e" is introduced at level 1 of the 1st reduced-size approximation, the second approximation (the original image) is exactly recovered (Fig. 4).

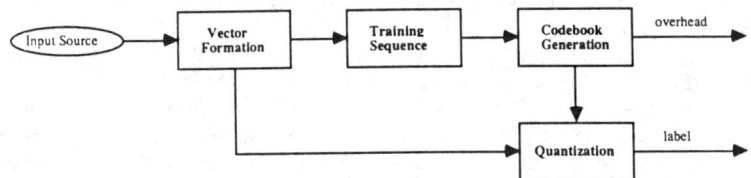

Fig. 9. Vector quantization. The input source is first decomposed into a set of vectors. A subset of vectors in the set is then chosen as a training sequence. The codebook of representative vector (codewords) is generated by using an iterative clustering algorithm. Quantization involves searching, for a given vector, the closest representative vector in the codebook. The label corresponding to the closest codeword is transmitted.

9) Finally, an entropy coder, such as a Huffman coder operating on a pixel-by-pixel basis, is used to losslessly encode the residual error image at level $k = n$, thus ensuring perfect reproduction of the original image.

At the receiver, a sequence of reduced-size approximations of the original image can be obtained by using the reconstruction procedure presented in Section II (2.3) on the quantized difference pyramid. Note that the error delivery in step 7 is the key to achieving lossless reproduction of the original image. This makes it possible to reprocess at the lower levels the residual quantization errors introduced at the higher levels. In this way, all the residual errors due to quantization are passed down, from high level to low level, so that the information to be transmitted at level $k + 1$ actually contains all the residual error components.

IV. SIMULATIONS

Computer simulations using the proposed progressive image transmission scheme on two test images are presented. Both test images are of size 256 × 256 and quantized to 256

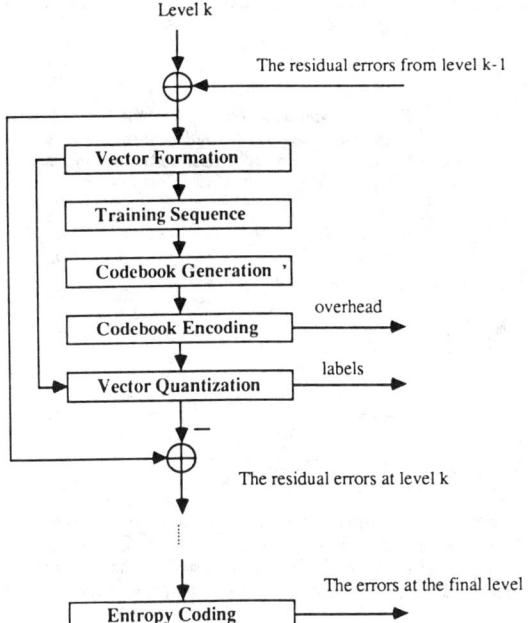

Fig. 10. The steps involved in applying vector quantization to the difference pyramid.

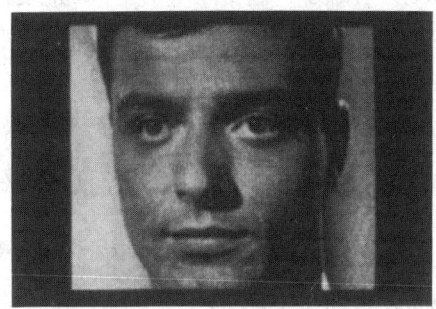

Fig. 11. A face image with relatively low overall detail, but high detail in some areas, such as the eyes.

Fig. 12. A boat image characterized by fine detail, notably many sharp edges.

TABLE I
(a) SIMULATION RESULTS FOR THE FACE IMAGE USING A HUFFMAN CODER ON THE DIFFERENCE PYRAMID. (b) SIMULATION RESULTS FOR THE FACE IMAGE USING VECTOR QUANTIZATION (2 × 2) ON THE DIFFERENCE PYRAMID. (c) SIMULATION RESULTS FOR THE FACE IMAGE USING VECTOR QUANTIZATION (4 × 4) ON THE DIFFERENCE PYRAMID

Level k	Rh(k) (bits/pixel)	Rp(k) (bits/pixel)	NMSE(%)
0	0.0000669	0.0000669	16.2379
1	0.0002677	0.0003346	11.8840
2	0.0010708	0.0014054	8.7855
3	0.0042833	0.0056888	4.4424
4	0.0171334	0.0228223	2.5904
5	0.0685338	0.0913561	1.2322
6	0.2741353	0.3654915	0.5334
7	1.0965415	1.4620330	0.1706
8	4.3861660	5.8481990	0.0000

(a)

Level k	Rh(k) (bits/pixel)	Bit Rate Distribution at Level k			Rp(k) (bits/pixel)	NMSE(%)
		Vector Quantization (2*2)				
		Nc(k)	Rl(k) (bits/pixel)	Rc(k) (bits/pixel)		
0	0.0000669				0.0000669	16.2379
1	0.0002677				0.0003346	11.8840
2	0.0010708				0.0014054	8.7855
3		2	0.0002330	0.0003356	0.0019741	6.0095
4		4	0.0018607	0.0008544	0.0046894	4.0289
5		4	0.0074427	0.0009460	0.0130781	2.6188
6		8	0.0372137	0.0022583	0.0525502	1.1339
7		8	0.1408433	0.0021247	0.1955183	0.4913
8		8	0.5875044	0.0020751	0.7850980	0.1763
9	4.3086748				5.0937728	0.0000

(b)

Level k	Rh(k) (bits/pixel)	Bit Rate Distribution at Level k			Rp(k) (bits/pixel)	NMSE(%)
		Vector Quantization (4*4)				
		Nc(k)	Rl(k) (bits/pixel)	Rc(k) (bits/pixel)		
0	0.0000669				0.0000669	16.2379
1	0.0002677				0.0003346	11.8840
2	0.0010708				0.0014054	8.7855
3		2	0.0000610	0.0023498	0.0038163	6.1119
4		4	0.0004827	0.0052565	0.0095555	3.9734
5		8	0.0027452	0.0110206	0.0233215	2.6082
6		16	0.0136678	0.0240743	0.0610637	1.3580
7		32	0.0645644	0.0502336	0.1758618	0.5424
8		64	0.3180145	0.0931685	0.5870449	0.1671
9	4.3810010				4.9680459	0.0000

(c)

levels. The first, shown in Fig. 11, is a face image with relatively low overall detail, but high detail in some areas, such as the eyes. The second, shown in Fig. 12, is a boat image, characterized by fine detail, notably many sharp edges. The histograms of the original images and the corresponding difference pyramids are reproduced in Fig. 5 and 6, respectively. The entropies estimated from the histograms are, respectively, as follows: $R_o = 7.5178$ bits/pixel, $R_q = 4.3861$ bits/node, and $R_q^p = 5.8481$ bits/pixel for the face image; and $R_o = 7.5395$ bits/pixel, $R_q = 5.1582$ bits/node, and $R_q^p = 6.8775$ bits/pixel for the boat image.

The mean and difference pyramids are formed using (2.1) and (2.2). The pyramid representations contain nine levels; the number of nodes on each level is equal to $2^k \times 2^k$, $k = 0, 1, \cdots 8$. For comparative purposes, a Huffman coder is used to code the images represented by the difference pyramids and the results are reported in Tables I(a) and II(a).

The results obtained by using vector quantization are tabulated in Tables I(b), (c), II(a), and (b). In the implementation, it was found more efficient to code the first three levels of the difference pyramid with a Huffman coder. Vector quantization is applied only to levels 3 to 8 and the vectors are formed by partitioning the levels into spatially contiguous, nonoverlapping, blocks of 2 × 2 or 4 × 4 nodes. At each level $k (\geq 3)$, the codebook is first generated by the generalized Lloyd algorithm [12] and then quantized to the same resolution as the difference pyramid. The errors due to quantization are delivered and added to the next level (3.3). A

TABLE II
(a) SIMULATION RESULTS FOR THE BOAT IMAGE USING A HUFFMAN CODER ON THE DIFFERENCE PYRAMID. (b) SIMULATION RESULTS FOR THE BOAT IMAGE USING VECTOR QUANTIZATION (2 × 2) ON THE DIFFERENCE PYRAMID. (c) SIMULATION RESULTS FOR THE BOAT IMAGE USING VECTOR QUANTIZATION (4 × 4) ON THE DIFFERENCE PYRAMID

Level k	$R_h(k)$ (bits/pixel)	$R_p(k)$ (bits/pixel)	NMSE(%)
0	0.0000787	0.0000787	27.8332
1	0.0003148	0.0003935	19.5735
2	0.0012593	0.0016528	13.8307
3	0.0050373	0.0066901	10.0295
4	0.0201492	0.0268393	7.3884
5	0.0805968	0.1074362	4.3708
6	0.3223875	0.4298238	2.2436
7	1.2895503	1.7193742	0.7282
8	5.1582012	6.8775754	0.0000

(a)

Level k	$R_h(k)$ (bits/pixel)	Vector Quantization (2*2) $N_c(k)$	Vector Quantization (2*2) $R_l(k)$ (bits/pixel)	Vector Quantization (2*2) $R_c(k)$ (bits/pixel)	$R_p(k)$ (bits/pixel)	NMSE(%)
0	0.0000787				0.0000787	27.8332
1	0.0003148				0.0003935	19.5735
2	0.0012593				0.0016528	13.8307
3		2	0.0002187	0.0003356	0.0022073	11.8961
4		4	0.0018109	0.0009460	0.0049643	9.1906
5		4	0.0074661	0.0009765	0.0134070	6.9191
6		8	0.0405449	0.0021972	0.0561492	3.8679
7		8	0.1504987	0.0022277	0.2088757	1.9493
8		8	0.5897188	0.0021667	0.8007613	0.6716
9	5.1581440				5.9589053	0.0000

(b)

Level k	$R_h(k)$ (bits/pixel)	Vector Quantization (4*4) $N_c(k)$	Vector Quantization (4*4) $R_l(k)$ (bits/pixel)	Vector Quantization (4*4) $R_c(k)$ (bits/pixel)	$R_p(k)$ (bits/pixel)	NMSE(%)
0	0.0000787				0.0000787	27.8332
1	0.0003148				0.0003935	19.5735
2	0.0012593				0.0016528	13.8307
3		2	0.0000495	0.0023193	0.0040217	11.8331
4		4	0.0004347	0.0052014	0.0096578	9.8389
5		8	0.0027468	0.0115774	0.0239822	6.9992
6		16	0.0143341	0.0243896	0.0627060	4.6032
7		32	0.0692045	0.0508756	0.1827862	2.2973
8		64	0.3161984	0.1030025	0.6019872	0.7270
9	5.2602968				5.8622840	0.0000

(c)

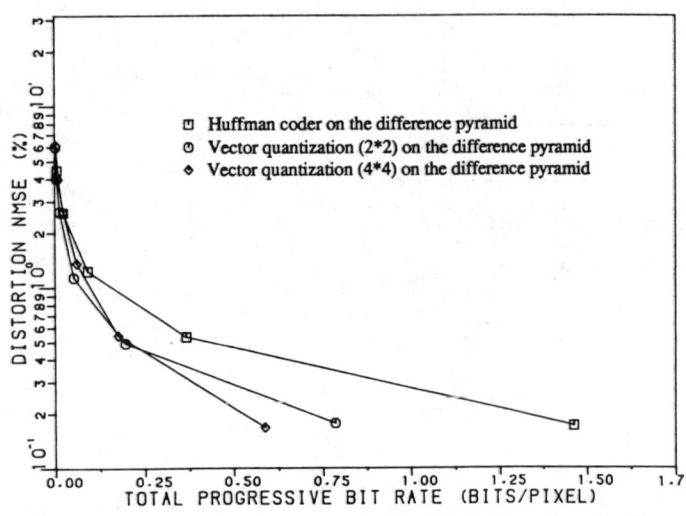

Fig. 13. The rate distortion curves for the face image using a Huffman coder, and vector dimension of block size 2 × 2 and 4 × 4 on the difference pyramid (Table I). It is demonstrated that the use of vector quantization results in a coding gain over a Huffman coder.

set of reduced-size approximations is formed from the quantized difference pyramid by using the reconstruction procedure of the mean pyramid (Section II). The corresponding successive approximations are obtained from the reduced-size approximations as follows:

$$\hat{X}_{k,ii+2^{n-k}(i-1), jj+2^{n-k}(j-1)} = X_{k,i,j} \quad (4.1)$$

where $i, j = 1, 2, \cdots 2^k$ and $ii, jj = 1, 2, \cdots 2^{n-k}$; in other words, the pixels are just repeated.

The results of the computer simulations are listed in Tables I and II where the components shown are defined as follows.

$R_h(k)$—the bit rate required for Huffman coding of the difference pyramid at level k;

$R_l(k)$—the bit rate for transmitting the labels at level k where a variable length coder is employed;

$R_c(k)$—the bit rate for transmitting the codebook at level k where a variable length coder is also used;

$N_c(k)$—the number of codewords in the codebook at level k;

$R_p(k) = \Sigma_{i=0}^{k}(R_h(i) + R_l(i) + R_c(i))$—the total progressive bit rate up to level k.

In evaluation of system performance, the normalized mean square error (NMSE) between the original image X and the kth approximation $\hat{X}_k$ is used,

$$\text{NMSE} = \frac{\Sigma_{i,j=1}^{256}(X_{ij} - \hat{X}_{k,ij})^2}{\Sigma_{ij=1}^{256} X_{ij}^2}, \quad k = 0, 1, \cdots 8 \quad (4.2)$$

where X_{ij} and $\hat{X}_{k,ij}$ represent the (i, j)th element of the original image and its kth approximation, respectively.

Figs. 13 and 14 show the rate distortion curves based on the values in Tables I and II. It is clear that, for both test images, the performance achieved by the proposed scheme is much better than that obtained by simply using an entropy coder, such as a Huffman coder, on the difference pyramid. At an NMSE = 0.17 percent, the saving in bit rate is 0.882 bits/pixel for the face image. At an NMSE = 0.727 percent, the corresponding saving is 1.118 bits/pixel for the boat image. In terms of lossless coding, the original face image can be recovered at a bit rate of about 4.9680 bits/pixel and the original boat image at a bit rate of about 5.8622 bits/pixel. This implies that, as a lossless coder, the proposed scheme is superior to the entropy coder operating on a pixel-by-pixel basis, by about 2.5498 (7.5178–4.9680) bits/pixel for the face image and 1.6773 (7.5395–5.8622) bits/pixel for the boat image, respectively.

Figs. 15 and 16 present the pictorial results for the case when the vectors are formed from 4 × 4 blocks. We note that excellent quality reproduction is obtained at the 8th level at a bit rate of only about 0.6 bits/pixel.

VI. CONCLUSIONS

In this paper, a new progressive image transmission scheme which utilizes the features of pyramid data structure of images and vector quantization has been presented. The experimental results demonstrate that the proposed scheme indeed achieves the goal of lossless, progresssive transmission with compression. The pyramid data structure proposed makes it possible to transmit the images progressively. Compression is obtained by using vector quantization on each level. Lossless reproduction is guaranteed by delivering the residual quantization errors

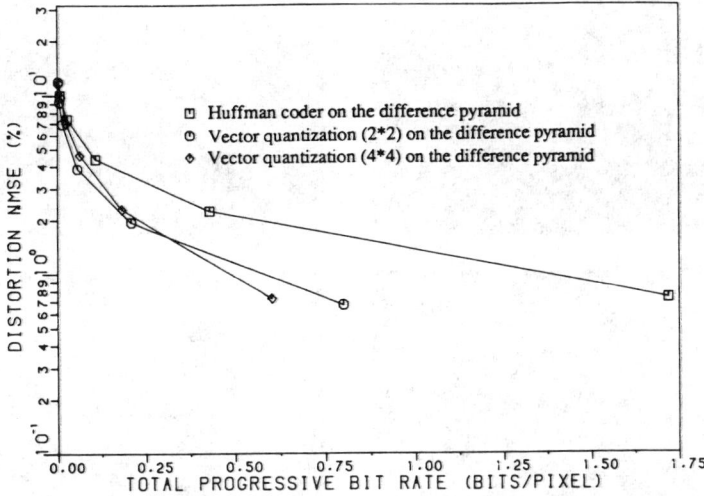

Fig. 14. The rate distortion curves for the boat image using a Huffman coder, and vector dimension of block size 2 × 2 and 4 × 4 on the difference pyramid (Table II). It is demonstrated that the use of vector quantization results in a coding gain over a Huffman coder.

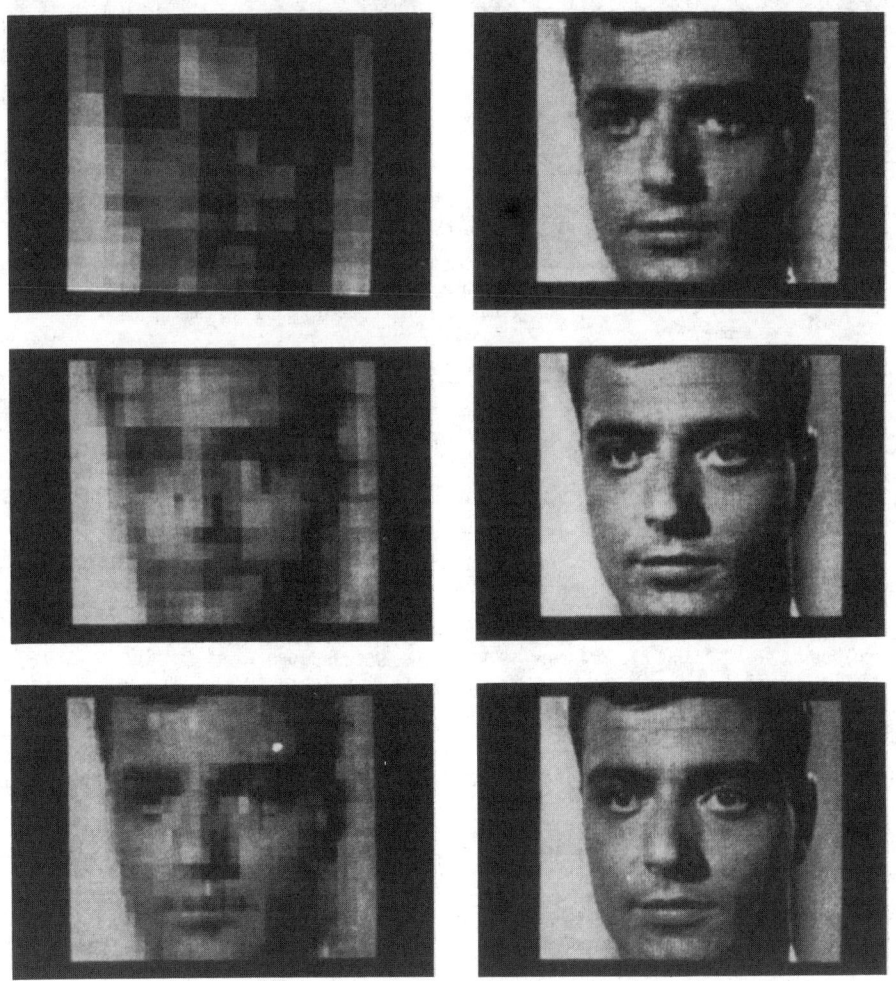

Fig. 15. The sequence of successive approximations (levels 4 through 9 of Table Ic) of the original face image (Fig. 11) with a vector dimension of 4 × 4. The original image has been reproduced as the last one in the sequence.

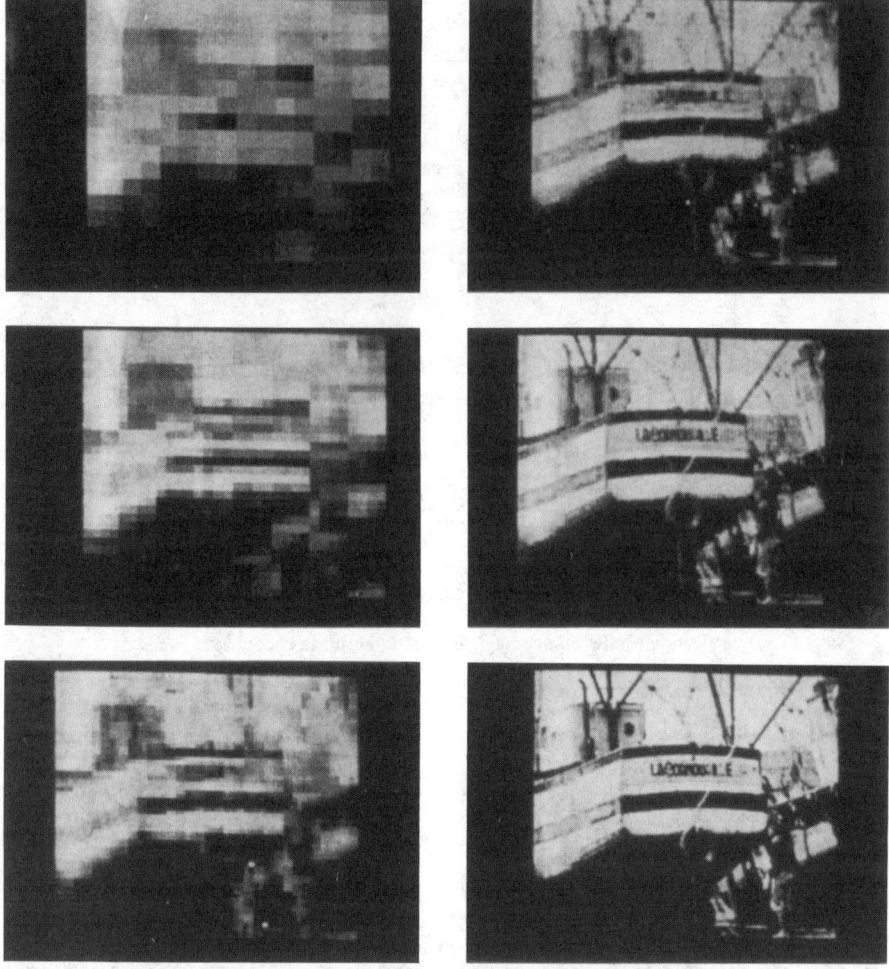

Fig. 16. The sequence of successive approximations [levels 4 though 9 of Table II(c)] of the original boat image (Fig. 12) with a vector dimension of 4 × 4. The original image has been reproduced as the last one in the sequence.

introduced at the higher levels to the lower levels and using an entropy coder on the final residual error image.

ACKNOWLEDGMENT

We wish to acknowledge the diligence of the reviewers which has led to a number of improvements in the paper.

REFERENCES

[1] S. L. Tanimoto, "Image transmission with gross information first," *Comput. Graph. Image Processing*, vol. 9, pp. 72–76, Jan. 1979.
[2] K. Sloan and S. L. Tanimoto, "Progressive refinement of raster images," *IEEE Trans. Comput.*, vol. C-28, pp. 871–874, Nov. 1979.
[3] K. Knowlton, "Progressive transmission of grey scale and binary pictures by simple, efficient, and lossless encoding scheme," *Proc. IEEE*, vol. 68, pp. 885–896, July 1980.
[4] P. J. Burt and E. H. Adelson, "The Laplacian pyramid as a compact image code," *IEEE Trans. Commun.*, vol. COM-31, pp. 532–540, Apr. 1983.
[5] K. N. Ngan, "Image display techniques using the Cosine transform," *IEEE Trans Acoust., Speech, Signal Processing*, vol. ASSP-32, pp. 173–177, Feb. 1984.
[6] E. Dubois and J. L. Moncet, "Encoding and progressive transmission of still pictures in NTSC composite format using transform domain methods," *IEEE Trans. Commun.*, vol. COM-?, pp. 310–319, Mar. 1986.
[7] L. Wang and M. Goldberg, "Progressive image transmission by multistage transform coefficient quantization," *IEEE Int. Conf Commun.*, Toronto, Ont., pp. 419–423, June 1986.
[8] W. D. Hofmann and D. E. Troxel, "Making progressive transmission adaptive," *IEEE Trans. Commun.*, vol. COM-34, pp. 806–813, Aug. 1986.
[9] L. Wang and M. Goldberg, "Lossless progressive image transmission by residual error vector quantization," *Int. Montech'86 IEEE Conf. Antennas Commun.*, Montreal, P.Q., Sept. 1986.
[10] L. Wang and M. Goldberg, "Progressive image transmission by residual error vector quantization in transform domain," *Proc. IEEE Int. Phoenix Conf. Comput. Commun.*, Scottdale, AZ, Feb. 1987, pp. 178–182.
[11] ——, "Progressive image transmission by transform coefficient residual error quantization," *IEEE Trans. Commun.*, vol. 36, pp. 75–87, Jan. 1988.
[12] Y. Linde, A. Buzo, and R. M. Gray, "An algorithm for vector quantization design," *IEEE Trans. Commun.*, vol. COM-28, pp. 84–95, Jan. 1980.
[13] R. M. Gray, "Vector quantization," *IEEE ASSP Mag.*, pp. 4–29, Apr. 1984.
[14] J. Makhoul, S. Roucos, and H. Gish, "Vector quantization in speech coding," *Proc. IEEE*, vol. 73, pp. 1551–1588, Nov. 1985.
[15] A. Gersho and B. Ramamurthi, "Image coding using vector quantization," in *Proc. IEEE Int. Conf. Acoust., Speech, Signal Processing*, May 1982, pp. 428–431.
[16] M. Goldberg, P. R. Boucher, and S. Shlien, "Image compression using adaptive vector quantization," *IEEE Trans. Commun.*, vol. COM-34, pp. 180–187, Feb. 1986.
[17] M. Goldberg and H. Sun, "Image sequence coding using vector quantization," *IEEE Trans Commun.*, vol. COM-34, pp. 703–710, July 1986.
[18] D. A. Huffman, "A method for the construction of minimum-redundancy codes," *Proc. IRE*, pp. 1098–1101, Sept. 1952.
[19] H. Samet, "Data structure for quadtree approximation and compression," *Commun. ACM*, vol. 28, pp. 973–993, 1985.
[20] H. Samet, "Using quadtree to represent spatial data," *NATO ASI Series*, vol. F18, pp. 229–247, 1985.

[21] T. Berger, *Rate Distortion Theory*. Englewood Cliffs, NJ: Prentice-Hall, 1971.

Limin Wang received the M.Sc. degree from Shandong University, China, in 1981, and the Ph.D. degree in electrical engineering from University of Ottawa, Canada, in 1988.

From 1981 to 1984, he was with the Electronics Department of Shandong University. He is presently involved in research on video and image compression using vector quantization, and progressive lossless transmission of medical imagery at the University of Ottawa's Medical Communications Research Centre. His current research interests include digital signal and image processing, data compression, and digital communication.

Morris Goldberg (S'68-M'70-SM'88) received the undergraduate training at the University of McGill and the Ph.D. degree in electrical engineering from Imperial College in 1972.

Since 1974 he has been working in the area of image processing, first for the Canada Centre for Remote Sensing and since 1976 at the University of Ottawa, where he is at present a Professor in the Department of Electrical Engineering. In 1982-1983 he was a Visiting Professor at the ENST in Paris, and in 1986-1987 he spent a sabatical year at Bell Northern Research. He is a Treasurer of the Canadian Image Processing and Pattern Recognition Society, and a reviewer for many journals. His current research interests are the areas of multimedia medical communications, image coding, and knowledge-based user interfaces for image workstations. He leads a large research team of research engineers, graduate students, and postdoctoral fellows funded by the Telecommunications Research Institute of Ontario, by Bell Canada and Bell Northern Research.

Advances in Picture Coding

HANS GEORG MUSMANN, PETER PIRSCH, MEMBER, IEEE, AND HANS-JOACHIM GRALLERT

Invited Paper

This paper presents a review of the advances in digital coding of video signals during the last four years. Displacement estimation algorithms for coding applications are compared first and the relationship between the algorithms is pointed out. The developments in predictive and transform coding are described and discussed with view to broadcast television and video-conferencing applications. One chapter summarizes the first promising results of motion adaptive frame interpolation. Some problems to be solved in the future are pointed out in the conclusions.

I. INTRODUCTION

In this paper advances in image coding are reported starting from the state of image coding as presented in [1]–[3]. In the book edited by Pratt [1], a comprehensive overview is given of the state of image coding in 1979, while [2] and [3] are two reviews on picture coding by Netravali and Limb in 1981 and Jain in 1982. The focus in this paper is oriented to advances in digital coding of television and video-conference signals. Facsimile coding is not included, no hardware systems or codec realizations are described. The emphasis is on new coding algorithms.

One of the main recent developments in image coding is the application of mathematical models describing the motion of objects. Motion considerations have become more and more important, specially for low bit-rate coding. It allows one to improve predictive, transform, and interpolative coding. Because of computation complexity and the required real-time processing mainly motion models describing only the translational component of a motion have been investigated for coding so far. A translational movement generates a frame-to-frame displacement of the moving object. Several methods have been developed to estimate the displacement vector of a moving object from two successive frames. Knowing the displacement vector, we can use it to realize motion-compensated predictive coding, motion-compensated transform coding, and motion-adaptive frame interpolation.

In view of the central role of the displacement estimation techniques for the various coding concepts the whole Section II is devoted to the problems of displacement estimation. Essentially, two groups of estimation algorithms are explained, which are known as recursive algorithms and block-matching algorithms. These displacement estimation techniques are compared with respect to estimation accuracy, convergence rate, and computation complexity.

In Section III advances in predictive coding are discussed. First, the design of differential pulse-code modulation (DPCM) techniques for digital coding of broadcast color television signals is considered, where no visible coding distortions are allowed. Such design methods are based on masking functions which represent visibility thresholds for the quantization error. The design takes care that the DCPM system does not exceed the visibility thresholds. By refinements of this technique improved predictors, as well as fixed and adaptive quantizers have been found. Also new algorithms to adapt the predictor to the nonstationary statistics of an image signal have been developed. This applies to contour prediction as well as to adaptive intra-inter-frame prediction. A considerable research activity can be observed in the field of motion-compensated prediction. Predictors with forward motion estimation generally apply block-matching techniques to estimate the displacement of objects and transmit the displacement vector in addition to the prediction error, whereas predictors with backward motion estimation use recursive estimation techniques and need not transmit the displacement vector.

Advances in transform coding are presented in Section IV. To optimize the quantization of the spectral coefficients the mean-square quantization error has been used as an optimization criterion in the past. New approaches try to control the quantization by the local picture content and to adapt the quantization to the characteristics of the human visual perception. Another attempt to exploit the properties of the human observer for transform coding is the M-transform. This transform uses basis functions of a noise-like structure and generates quantizing error patterns which are

Manuscript received August 27, 1984; revised December 3, 1984.
H. G. Musmann is with the Universität Hannover, Institut für Theoretische Nachrichtentechnik und Informationsverarbeitung, 3000 Hannover, West Germany.
P. Pirsch is with the Standard Elektrik Lorenz Forschungszentrum, 7000 Stuttgart 40, West Germany.
H.-J. Grallert is with Siemens AG, Unternehmensbereich Nachrichten-und Sicherungstechnik Zentrallaboratorium, 8000 München 70, West Germany.

less visible than those of known transforms. In connection with hybrid coding also motion-adaptive techniques have been investigated.

At present, there are only a few publications on motion-adaptive frame interpolation techniques which are described in Section V. A considerable reduction of the data rate can be obtained when frames are skipped at the transmitter and then interpolated at the receiver. However, these techniques run into difficulties if there is motion in the scene. Moving objects become blurred by normal linear interpolation. First promising results show that the blur can be reduced by motion-adaptive frame interpolation. The investigations have also revealed many problems to be solved in the future.

II. Displacement Estimation for Image Sequence Coding

In a sequence of television pictures a moving object generates frame-to-frame luminance changes. These luminance changes can be used to estimate the parameters of a mathematical model that describes the movement of the object. Huang [4] has investigated a motion model that describes translation and rotation of a three-dimensional rigid object. Several methods [5]–[8] have been proposed for estimating the parameters of such motion models from a sequence of television pictures for applications in dynamic scene analysis.

Motion models can also be used to improve the efficiency of predictive and interpolative television coding techniques. Because of the real-time computing requirements, only relatively simple models considering the translational component of motion have been investigated for television coding so far. A translational movement generates a displacement of the moving object from frame to frame. Displacement estimation algorithms for television coding have been proposed for the first time by Limb and Murphy [9] in 1975 and by Cafforio and Rocca [10] in 1976.

The algorithm of Limb and Murphy can be explained by considering a simple moving edge as shown in Fig. 1. The displacement D is estimated by

$$\hat{D} = \hat{dx} = \sum_M |FD| \bigg/ \sum_M |ED| \qquad (1)$$

where $|FD|$ denotes the magnitude of the frame difference signal and $|ED|$ that of the element difference signal. The summation is carried out over the area M which is defined by frame differences greater than a given threshold. The numerator

$$\sum_M |FD|$$

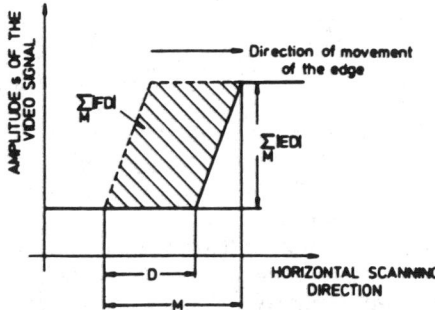

Fig. 1. Illustration of the displacement estimation scheme proposed by Limb and Murphy [9]. The dashed line indicates the position of the edge in the previous frame.

corresponds to the hatched area and the denominator

$$\sum_M |ED|$$

to the height of the parallelogram. Equation (1) does not indicate the direction of the displacement. Cafforio and Rocca start with a different approach and show that their algorithm for displacement estimation includes that of Limb and Murphy as a special simplified solution, whereby the latter one is easier to implement.

Let $s_k(x, y)$ be the luminance value at point x, y of a moving object in frame k. The moving object is assumed not to change its luminances from frame to frame. Then, in case of a pure translational movement that generates a displacement vector D with components dx, dy, the frame differences FD are

$$\begin{aligned} FD(x,y) &= s_k(x,y) - s_{k-1}(x,y) \\ &= s_k(x,y) - s_k(x+dx, y+dy) \\ &= -\frac{\delta s_k(x,y)}{\delta x} \cdot dx - \frac{\delta s_k(x,y)}{\delta y} \cdot dy - n(x,y) \\ &= -D^T \nabla s_k(x,y) - n(x,y) \end{aligned} \qquad (2)$$

where $n(x, y)$ represents the higher order terms of the Taylor series expansion which will be neglected. The gradient ∇s is a vector whose components are element differences ED and line differences LD.

To explain (2), a one-dimensional displacement in the x-direction is considered in Fig. 2. In this special case, the

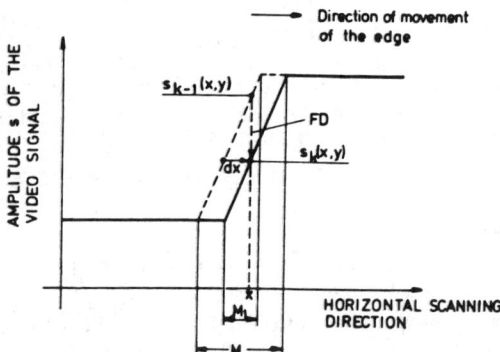

Fig. 2. Illustration of the displacement estimation algorithm proposed by Cafforio and Rocca [10]. The dashed line indicates the position of the edge in the previous frame.

estimate of the displacement vector D reduces to

$$\hat{D} = \hat{dx} = -\frac{FD(x,y)}{\partial s(x,y)/\partial x}. \qquad (3)$$

If the boundary of the moving object is known, (2) can be evaluated for all picture elements of the moving object. Then, using linear regression and neglecting the x, y cross terms, the displacement vector D is approximated by

$$\hat{dx} = -\frac{E[FD(x,y) \cdot \partial s(x,y)/\partial x]}{E[(\partial s(x,y)/\partial x)^2]} = -\frac{\Sigma(FD \cdot ED)}{\Sigma(ED)^2}$$

$$\hat{dy} = -\frac{E[FD(x,y) \cdot \partial s(x,y)/\partial y]}{E[(\partial s(x,y)/\partial y)^2]} = -\frac{\Sigma(FD \cdot LD)}{\Sigma(LD)^2}$$

(4)

where the statistical averages are calculated by summing over the entire area M of the moving object.

The described displacement estimation algorithm of Cafforio and Rocca assumes a linear luminance function at point x, y. For the example in Fig. 2 this assumption is only valid within the area M_1. This area decreases with increasing displacement. Therefore, this estimation algorithm can only be used for measuring small displacements D.

To overcome this problem new estimation algorithms have been developed recently. The algorithms can roughly be classified into two groups, which are denoted as recursive algorithms [11]–[17] and block-matching algorithms [18]–[23]. However, this terminology has not been uniform till now.

A. Recursive Displacement Estimation Algorithms

In 1978, Netravali and Robbins [11] published a first recursive estimation algorithm to improve the estimation accuracy and to increase the measuring range of D. In recursive estimation algorithms it is assumed that an initial estimate $\hat{D}_i$ is used to produce a new improved estimate $\hat{D}_{i+1}$ according to

$$\hat{D}_{i+1} = \hat{D}_i + U_i \quad (5)$$

where U_i is the so-called update term of iteration i. The iterations can be executed either for a single picture element at consecutive picture elements along a scanning line, from line to line, or from frame to frame. Correspondingly, these techniques may be denoted as pel-recursive estimation algorithms with horizontal, vertical, or temporal recursion. Knowing $\hat{D}_i$, a function of the displaced frame difference DFD

$$\text{DFD}(x, y, \hat{D}_i) = s_k(x, y) - s_{k-1}(x - \hat{d}x_i, y - \hat{d}y_i) \quad (6)$$

can be used as a criterion for calculating the estimate $\hat{D}_{i+1}$. Netravali and Robbins propose an estimation algorithm that attempts to minimize the squared value of the displaced frame difference recursively with i using the gradient method

$$\hat{D}_{i+1} = \hat{D}_i - \frac{1}{2}\epsilon \nabla_{\hat{D}_i}[\text{DFD}(x, y, \hat{D}_i)]^2 \quad (7)$$

where $\nabla_{\hat{D}_i}$ is the gradient operator with respect to $\hat{D}_i$ and ϵ is a positive constant. Fig. 3 illustrates how this algorithm approaches the actual displacement D after several iterations. The choice of ϵ requires a compromise. A high value of ϵ yields a quick convergence but a noisy estimate, whereas a small ϵ leads to more accurate displacement estimates. In [11] the ϵ is chosen to be $1/1024$ for motion-compensated predictive coding. Evaluating (7) gives

$$\hat{D}_{i+1} = \hat{D}_i - \epsilon \text{DFD}(x, y, \hat{D}_i) \cdot \nabla_{\hat{D}_i}[\text{DFD}(x, y, \hat{D}_i)] \quad (8)$$

and with the definition (6)

$$\hat{D}_{i+1} = \hat{D}_i - \epsilon \text{DFD}(x, y, \hat{D}_i) \cdot \nabla s_{k-1}(x - \hat{d}x_i, y - \hat{d}y_i) \quad (9)$$

where ∇ is a gradient operator with respect to the horizontal and vertical coordinates x, y.

$$\nabla s_{k-1}(x - \hat{d}x_i, y - \hat{d}y_i) = \begin{bmatrix} \dfrac{\partial}{\partial x} \\ \dfrac{\partial}{\partial y} \end{bmatrix} \cdot s_{k-1}(x - \hat{d}x_i, y - \hat{d}y_i). \quad (10)$$

The algorithm (7) can be extended by calculating the update term from several picture elements, e.g., of an area M, in order to smooth out the effect of quantization noise [11]. Then the update term is given by

$$U_i = -\frac{1}{2}\epsilon \nabla_{\hat{D}_i} \sum_{j \in M} W_j [\text{DFD}(x, y, \hat{D}_i)]^2 \quad (11)$$

where $W_j \geq 0$ and

$$\sum_{j \in M} W_j = 1.$$

The evaluation of DFD and ∇s_{k-1} in (9) requires an interpolation of the luminance $s_{k-1}(x - \hat{d}x_i, y - \hat{d}y_i)$ for nonintegral displacements $\hat{d}x_i, \hat{d}y_i$. Four neighboring picture elements s_A, s_B, s_C, s_D are considered for this interpolation as demonstrated in Fig. 4. First, the integral parts of $\hat{d}x_i$ and

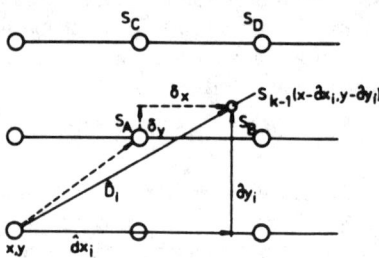

Fig. 4. Position of picture elements in frame s_{k-1} used for interpolation of $s_{k-1}(x - \hat{d}x_i, y - \hat{d}y_i)$.

$\hat{d}y_i$ determine the position of s_A. Then, the fractional parts $\delta x, \delta y$ of $\hat{d}x_i, \hat{d}y_i$ are used for linear two-dimensional interpolation according to

$$s_{k-1}(x - \hat{d}x_i, y - \hat{d}y_i) = (1 - \delta y)[(1 - \delta x)s_A + \delta x s_B] + \delta y[(1 - \delta x)s_C + \delta x s_D]. \quad (12)$$

In order to reduce the implementation complexity Netravali and Robbins also propose simplified versions for the interpolation (12) and displacement estimation algorithm (9) in [11] and [12].

Stimulated by the work of Netravali and Robbins, several new recursive displacement estimation algorithms have been developed. Compared to the algorithm (7) the constant ϵ is substituted by variables in the following displacement estimation techniques to achieve a better adaptation to the local image statistics. The main aim is to improve the

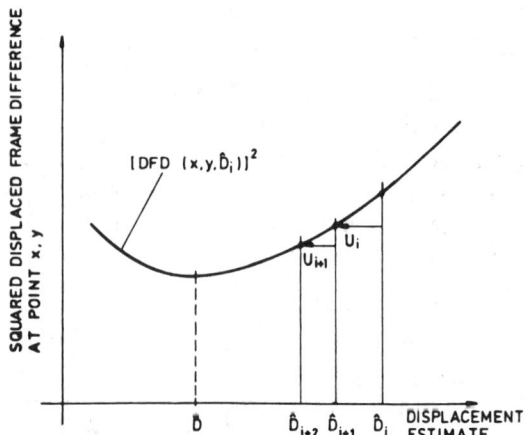

Fig. 3. Illustration of the displacement estimation scheme proposed by Netravali and Robbins [11]. The update term U_i at each iteration is proportional to the gradient $\nabla_{\hat{D}_i}[\text{DFD}(x, y, \hat{D}_i)]^2$ and to the constant ϵ according to (7).

rate of convergence and thus also the accuracy of the displacement algorithms if the number of iterations is limited. To simplify the description of these algorithms only the dx-component of the displacement vector is considered.

Applying the Newton–Raphson algorithm [13] to search for the minimum of DFD^2 results in an update term as

$$U_i = -\frac{\sum_M \frac{\partial}{\partial dx}[DFD(x,y,\hat{D}_i)]^2}{\sum_M \frac{\partial^2}{\partial dx^2}[DFD(x,y,\hat{D}_i)]^2}. \quad (13)$$

Instead of ϵ, a denominator term corresponding to the second-order derivative of DFD^2 is introduced.

In 1982 Cafforio and Rocca [14] published an extended recursive version of their former algorithm (4) which is considered here in a somewhat simplified form

$$U_i = -\frac{\frac{1}{2}\sum_M \frac{\partial}{\partial dx}[DFD(x,y,\hat{D}_i)]^2}{\sum_M \left[\frac{\partial}{\partial x}s_{k-1}(x-\hat{dx}_i,y-\hat{dy}_i)\right]^2 + \eta^2} \quad (14)$$

with $\eta^2 = 100$.

In (14), a correction term η^2 is introduced to avoid problems which would occur in areas of nearly constant luminance where $\partial s_{k-1}/\partial x$ is small.

Bergmann [15] starts from a proposal of Burkhard and Moll [16] and develops a displacement estimation algorithm where the average of two second-order derivatives are used as a denominator

$$U_i = -\frac{\frac{1}{2}\sum_M \frac{\partial}{\partial dx}[DFD(x,y,\hat{D}_i)]^2}{\frac{1}{2}\sum_M \left[\frac{\partial}{\partial x}s_{k-1}(x-\hat{dx}_i,y-\hat{dy}_i) + \frac{\partial}{\partial x}s_k(x,y)\right]\frac{\partial}{\partial x}s_k(x,y)}. \quad (15)$$

The summations in (11), (13), (14), and (15) are taken over the picture elements of an area M. Of course, M can be reduced to contain only one picture element.

To demonstrate the close relationship between the displacement estimation algorithms (11), (13), (14), and (15) we use

$$E[DFD^2] = E\left[\{s_k(x,y) - s_{k-1}(x-dx,y-dy)\}^2\right]$$
$$= E[s_k^2(x,y)] - 2E[s_k(x,y) \cdot s_{k-1}(x-dx,y-dy)]$$
$$+ E[s_{k-1}^2(x-dx,y-dy)]. \quad (16)$$

In the case of

$$E[s_k^2(x,y)] = E[s_{k-1}^2(x-dx,y-dy)] = \text{constant} \quad (17)$$

(16) proves that minimizing $E[DFD^2]$ corresponds to maximizing the cross correlation

$$R_{s_k s_{k-1}}(x,y,D) = E[s_k(x,y) \cdot s_{k-1}(x-dx,y-dy)]. \quad (18)$$

Using (16), (18), and approximating the expectations E by summations over an area M, the described estimation algorithms can be simplified to the expressions in Table 1.

A comparison of the displacement estimation algorithms in Table 1 shows that these algorithms only differ in the denominator of the update term. Fig. 5 illustrates the updating for the Newton–Raphson and Bergmann algorithms. The slope of line ⓐ corresponds to the denominator term of the Newton–Raphson algorithm, while Bergmann's algorithm takes the average of the slopes of line ⓐ and line ⓑ. From Fig. 5 it becomes evident that in this example the Bergmann algorithm converges quicker to the actual displacement dx than the Newton–Raphson algorithm. Since the exact slope of line ⓑ is unknown, the second-order derivative of the cross-correlation function at the actual displacement is approximated by the second-order deriva-

Table 1 Pel-Recursive Displacement Estimation Algorithms, Simplified for Comparison by Assuming (17)

Algorithm	x-Component of the Displacement Estimate $\hat{D}_{i+1}$
Netravali and Robbins [11]	$\hat{dx}_{i+1} = \hat{dx}_i + \epsilon \frac{\partial}{\partial x} R_{s_k s_{k-1}}(x,y,\hat{D}_i), \quad \epsilon = 1/1024$
Newton–Raphson [13]	$\hat{dx}_{i+1} = \hat{dx}_i - \dfrac{\frac{\partial}{\partial x} R_{s_k s_{k-1}}(x,y,\hat{D}_i)}{\frac{\partial^2}{\partial x^2} R_{s_k s_{k-1}}(x,y,\hat{D}_i)}$
Cafferio and Rocca [14]	$\hat{dx}_{i+1} = \hat{dx}_i + \dfrac{\frac{\partial}{\partial x} R_{s_k s_{k-1}}(x,y,\hat{D}_i)}{\left|\frac{\partial^2}{\partial x^2} R_{s_{k-1} s_{k-1}}(x,y,0)\right| + \eta^2}, \quad \eta^2 = 100$
Bergmann [15]	$\hat{dx}_{i+1} = \hat{dx}_i - \dfrac{\frac{\partial}{\partial x} R_{s_k s_{k-1}}(x,y,\hat{D}_i)}{\frac{1}{2}\left[\frac{\partial^2}{\partial x^2} R_{s_k s_{k-1}}(x,y,\hat{D}_i) + \frac{\partial^2}{\partial x^2} R_{s_k s_k}(x,y,0)\right]}$

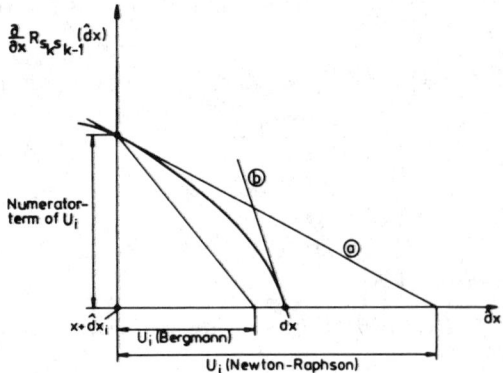

Fig. 5. Illustration of the Newton–Raphson algorithm and a displacement estimation scheme proposed by Bergmann according to Table 1. U_i are the update terms at one iteration. The actual displacement is dx corresponding to maximum cross correlation or minimum of the squared displaced frame differences.

tive of the autocorrelation function at point x, y to calculate the estimate.

Bergmann [15] has investigated the convergence rate of the algorithms in Table 1 in computer simulations using a test sequence showing vertical black bars that move horizontally. The test sequence has been recorded with a camera, sampled with 10 MHz, quantized, and coded with 8 bits per sample. Fig. 6 shows the displacement estimates at consecutive steps of iterations for the different algorithms.

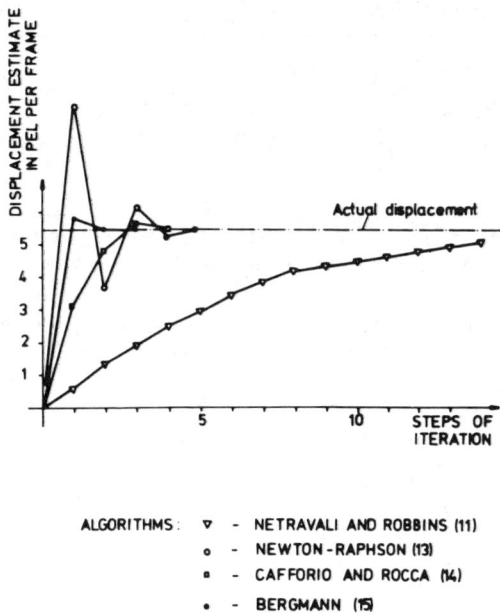

Fig. 6. Displacement estimates at consecutive steps of iterations for various recursive estimation algorithms.

A quicker updating of Netravali and Robbins algorithm can be achieved by increasing the constant ϵ. However, this also implies a decrease of the achievable estimation accuracy which is limited to ϵ. Comparing the Newton–Raphson algorithm with that of Cafforio and Rocca, the results indicate that the correction term η^2 prevents the overshoots. In the case of this special test sequence Bergmann's algorithm proves most favorable. He found that for a good initial estimate the extent of the area M should be chosen about twice as large as the maximum displacement, i.e., $M = 11 \times 11$ pels if $D = dm$ is 5.5 pels. However, it must be pointed out here that the convergence behavior of the recursive estimation algorithms depends also very strongly on the local image details. To illustrate the convergence behavior in the case of a natural test sequence, in Fig. 7 the displaced frame differences of two successive frames are shown after

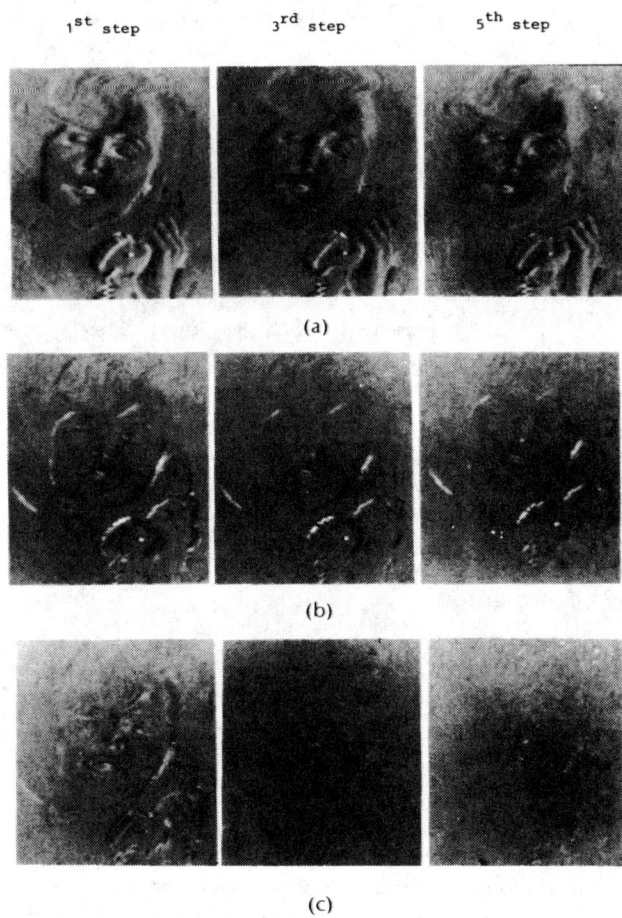

Fig. 7. Illustration of the displaced frame differences of two successive frames at the 1st, 3rd, and 5th step of iteration for various recursive estimation algorithms. $M = 7 \times 5$ pels. (a) Algorithm of Netravali and Robbins [11]. (b) Algorithm of Cafforio and Rocca [14]. (c) Algorithm of Bergmann [15].

consecutive steps of iterations. Positive and negative differences are represented by white and black picture elements, while a zero difference is gray. Also this test confirms the favorable behavior of Bergmann's algorithm. It also indicates some places with residual large differences where the estimation algorithm cannot compensate the displacement.

A second important feature of an estimation algorithm is its range of stability in which the algorithm converges to the correct correlation peak or actual displacement. The stability constraint is given by

$$|D - \hat{D}_{i+1}| < |D - \hat{D}_i|. \quad (19)$$

It requires that the update vector is always directed towards and not opposite to the actual displacement. From this requirement, bounds for the stability ranges of the discussed estimation algorithms can easily be found by considering only the sign of the update terms. In Fig. 8, these bounds are shown for a typical example of a cross-correlation function. The Newton–Raphson algorithm has a smaller stability range compared to that of algorithms (11), (14), and (15). It diverges at the point where the second-order derivative of the cross-correlation function changes its sign.

When displacement estimation algorithms are applied to improve predictive or interpolative coding, the behavior of an estimation algorithm can be affected by quantizing noise superimposed to the image signal. The influence of noise on the accuracy of recursive displacement estimation techniques has been investigated by Sabri [17].

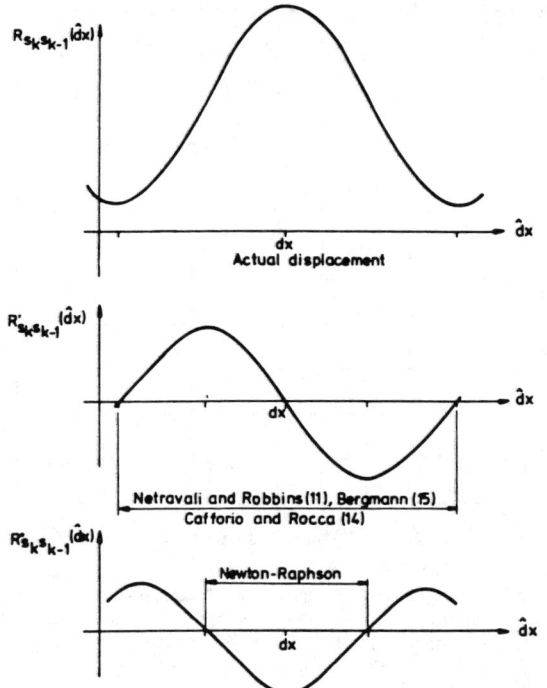

Fig. 8. Stability ranges for various recursive estimation algorithms.

B. Displacement Estimation by Block Matching

Instead of estimating a displacement recursively, a normalized two-dimensional cross-correlation function NCCF

$$\text{NCCF}(D) = \frac{R_{s_k s_{k-1}}(D)}{\sqrt{R_{s_k s_k}(0) \cdot R_{s_{k-1} s_{k-1}}(0)}} \quad (20)$$

can be measured and a displacement estimate be obtained from the position of the correlation peak. To find the displacement for a point x, y, a block of $M \times N$ picture elements centered at point x, y is taken from frame k and correlated with the picture elements in a search area SR of frame $k - 1$ to find the best match. Assuming a maximum horizontal or vertical displacement of dm picture elements the search area SR is given by

$$SR = (M + 2dm) \times (N + 2dm) \quad (21)$$

as shown in Fig. 9. In case of a block size 7×7 and a maximum displacement $dm = 10$ the search area is $SR = 27 \times 27$.

The search for the correlation peak requires an evaluation of NCCF at

$$Q = (2dm + 1)^2 \quad (22)$$

different horizontal and vertical shifts resulting in an excessive number of computations.

On the other hand, investigations by Beyer [24] have shown that a special correlation technique which takes into account the nonstationary behavior of the second moments can reach a very high accuracy of the displacement estimate which is close to the theoretical bounds as given in Fig. 10. These results indicate that an estimation accuracy of 1/10 pel can be obtained with correlation techniques using a practical block size of 7×7 pels.

A first and simple way to reduce the computation complexity is to segment an image into a fixed number of rectangular blocks and to assume that all picture elements of one block have the same displacement. Thus only one displacement vector has to be calculated per block. This technique is called block matching.

A second possibility to reduce the computation complexity is to simplify the matching criterion $D(i, j)$. Instead of evaluating the normalized cross-correlation function NCCF as a matching criterion according to

$$\text{NCCF}(i,j) = \frac{\sum_{m=1}^{M} \sum_{n=1}^{N} s_k(m,n) \cdot s_{k-1}(m+i, n+j)}{\left[\sum_{m=1}^{M} \sum_{n=1}^{N} s_k^2(m,n)\right]^{1/2} \left[\sum_{m=1}^{M} \sum_{n=1}^{N} s_{k-1}^2(m+i, n+j)\right]^{1/2}} \quad (23)$$

where $-dm \leq i, j \leq dm$, J. R. Jain and A. K. Jain [18] apply the mean-square error MSE

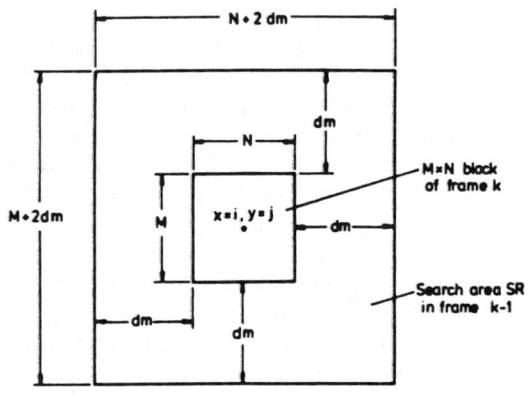

Fig. 9. Geometry of block $M \times N$ and search area SR.

$$\text{MSE}(i,j) = \frac{1}{MN} \sum_{m=1}^{M} \sum_{n=1}^{M} [s_k(m,n) - s_{k-1}(m+i, n+j)]^2 \qquad (24)$$

and Koga et al. [19] propose to use the mean of the absolute frame difference MAD

$$\text{MAD}(i,j) = \frac{1}{MN} \sum_{m=1}^{M} \sum_{n=1}^{N} |s_k(m,n) - s_{k-1}(m+i, n+j)| \qquad (25)$$

with $-dm \leq i,j \leq +dm$. The MAD criterion has the advantage that no multiplications and no divisions are required.

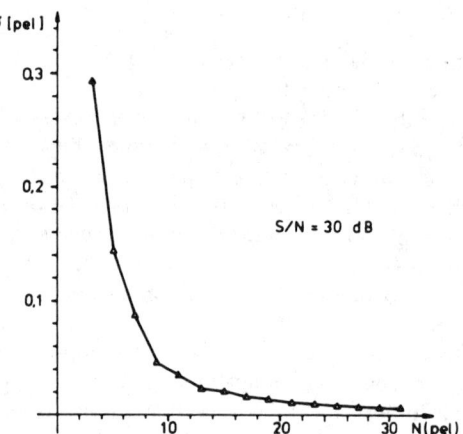

Fig. 10. Lower bound for the standard derivation σ of the displacement estimation error versus block size $N \times N$ according to [24].

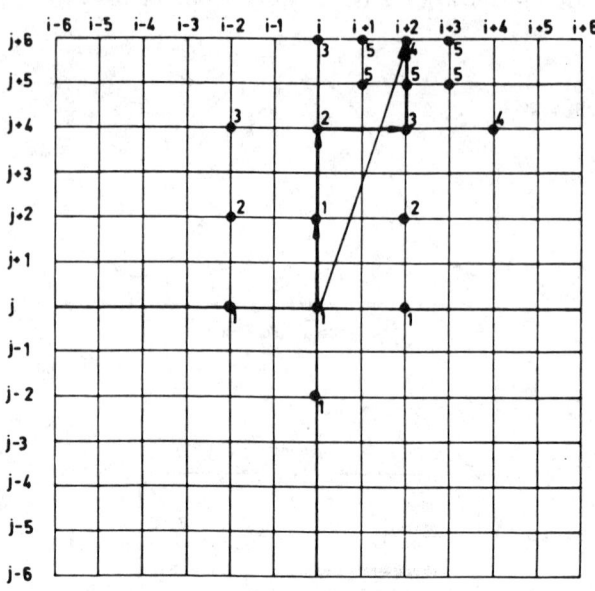

Fig. 11. 2D-logarithmic search procedure [18]. The search points in the search area of frame $k-1$ are shown with respect to a picture element $(x = i, y = j)$ in frame k. In this example, the approximated displacement vectors $(i, j+2)$, $(i, j+4)$, $(i+2, j+4)$, $(i+2, j+6)$, $(i+2, j+6)$ are found in step 1, 2, 3, 4, and 5.

In addition to the matching criterion, J. R. Jain and A. K. Jain in 1981 also suggested a method to reduce the number Q of required shifts to find the best match. The importance of such search procedures can be recognized by considering the extreme situation when an object moves across the television scene of 512 × 512 picture elements within 1 s. This corresponds to a frame-to-frame displacement of about $dm = 20$ and $Q = 1681$ required shifts. For each shift, the criterion (23), (24), or (25) has to be evaluated. To overcome this difficulty, several methods for simplifying the search procedure have been recently investigated [19]–[23]. Three of these techniques, the 2D-logarithmic search [18], the three-step search [19], and the modified conjugate direction search [21] are discussed briefly in the following.

The 2D-logarithmic search procedure, published by J. R. Jain and A. K. Jain, is based on the assumption that the matching criterion $D(i,j) = \text{MSE}(i,j)$ increases monotonically as the search moves away from the direction of minimum distortion. The direction of minimum distortion is defined by (i,j), such that $D(i,j)$ is minimum. The 2D-logarithmic search procedure tracks the direction of minimum distortion. In each step, five search points are checked, as shown in Fig. 11. The distance between the search points is reduced if the minimum is in the center of the search locations or at the boundary of the search area. In this example, five steps are required to find the displacement vector at point $(i+2, j+6)$.

At almost the same time, Koga et al. [19] have published a three-step search procedure which is closely related to the 2D-logarithmic search. Excepting the starting point (i,j), eight search points are tested in the first step. These points are relatively coarsely spaced around the center $x = i, y = j$ as demonstrated in Fig. 12. In this example, point $(i+3,$

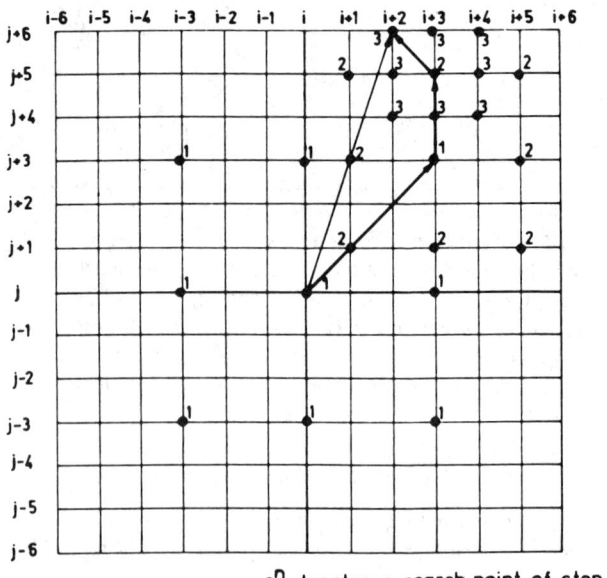

Fig. 12. Three-step search procedure [19]. In this example the points $(i+3, j+3)$, $(i+3, j+5)$, and $(i+2, j+6)$ are the approximated displacement vectors found in step 1, 2, and 3.

$j + 3$) is found as a first approximation of the displacement vector using the MAD criterion (25). In a second step, eight search points are spaced less coarsely around the first approximation and point ($i + 3, j + 5$) is found. The second step is repeated until the required accuracy is achieved. In the case of a search area with $dm \leq 6$ the third step gives the final displacement vector which is at point ($i + 2, j + 6$) in this example.

Recently, Srinivasan and Rao [21] presented an efficient new search procedure, called conjugate direction search. A simplified version of this procedure will be described using the example in Fig. 13. The algorithm searches for the

Table 2 Required Number of Search Points and Sequential Steps for Various Search Procedures and a Search Area Corresponding to a Maximum Displacement of $dm = 6$ Pels per Frame. Total Number of Search Points is $Q = 169$

Search Procedure	Required Number of Search Points		Required Number of Sequential Steps	
	a	b	a	b
2D-logarithmic	18	21	5	7
Three step	25	25	3	3
Conjugate direction (simplified)	12	15	9	12

a) For a special displacement vector ($i + 2, j + 6$).
b) For a worst case situation.

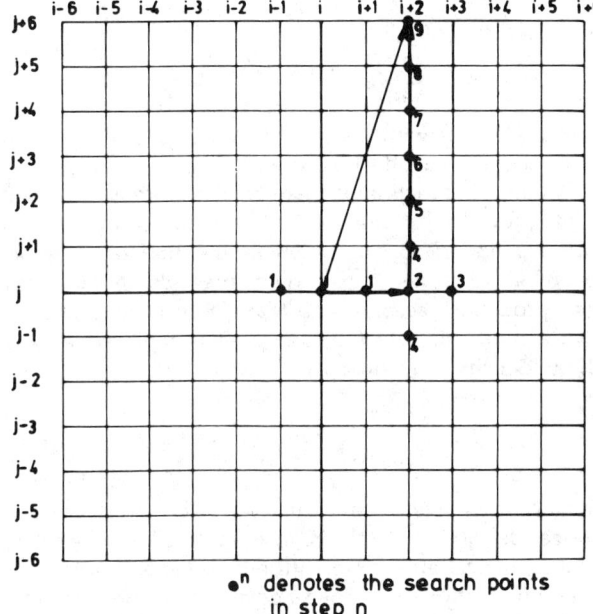

Fig. 13. Conjugate direction search in simplified version [21]. In this example, point ($i + 2, j + 6$) is the displacement vector found in step 9.

direction of minimum distortion $D(i, j)$ which is defined by the MAD (i, j) criterion (25). In a first search, the minimum in the i-direction is determined by computing $D(i - 1, j)$, $D(i, j), D(i + 1, j)$. If $D(i + 1, j)$ proves to be the smallest, $D(i + 2, j)$ also is computed and the smallest value of $D(i, j), D(i + 1, j), D(i + 2, j)$ is found. Proceeding in this fashion, the minimum in the i-direction is detected when the smallest value is situated between two higher values. In a second search, the minimum in the j-direction is determined by the same procedure starting at the minimum of the first search. In case of the example shown in Fig. 13, the first search results in the point ($i + 2, j$) and the second search in ($i + 2, j + 6$).

The computing complexity of a search procedure can be measured by the number of required points. In the above examples, a maximum displacement of $dm = 6$ is assumed. For this case the brute force method requires $Q = 169$ search points. Table 2 presents a comparison of the number of search points and sequential steps required by the explained search procedures. For a real-time hardware realization, the number of the required sequential steps can be a more important feature than the number of search points,

since some of these can be evaluated by parallel computations. If displacement estimates are available from preceding measurements also a tracking method [23] can be used to reduce the search area.

In experiments it has been found that the matching criterion $D(i, j)$ has no significant influence on the search [21]. Therefore, the MAD criterion (25) is recommended since it is relatively simple to implement.

Comparing block matching and recursive estimation algorithms we recognize that the estimation accuracy of the described block-matching algorithms is limited to ± 0.5 picture element. Recursive algorithms allow a more accurate estimate for the cost of more complex computations. However, it should be mentioned that the accuracy of the block-matching techniques could also be improved by additional interpolation.

C. Feature-Based Displacement Estimation Algorithms

These techniques originate from research in the field of dynamic scene analysis where special features of an object are extracted to track and describe its movement. Especially features with high luminance gradients allow a good displacement estimate. The feature-based displacement estimation algorithms which are going to be developed for predictive image coding extract edges in a first step and then use one of the described basic algorithms to estimate the displacement of the edge [25]–[27]. These techniques are still in an early stage requiring very complex computations.

III. Predictive Coding

One of the promising methods for transmission bit-rate reduction of digital video signals is predictive coding. Differential pulse-code modulation (DPCM) is a predictive coding scheme which has been studied extensively since its invention. A block diagram of the basic DPCM system is shown in Fig. 14. In such a system, a prediction $\hat{s}$ of the present sample s is made based upon previously transmitted and decoded information. The difference between the predicted and the present value of the sample is then quantized, coded, and transmitted. After decoding of the transmitted code words, the receiver reconstructs the sample by adding the prediction value to the quantized prediction error. To have the same prediction value at both the transmitter and the receiver, also at the transmitter side the prediction is based on reconstructed samples.

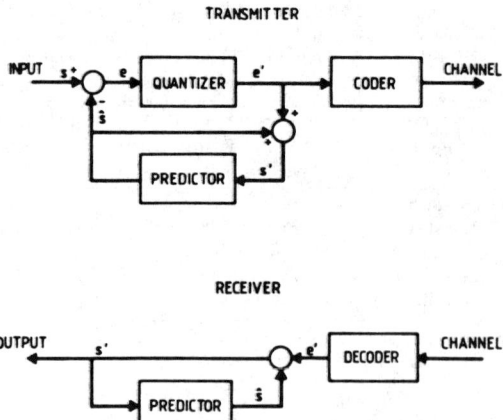

Fig. 14. Block diagram of basic DPCM system.

Methods for designing predictors, quantizers, and coders have been investigated to achieve the smallest transmission rate for a desired picture quality. Several extensions of the basic DPCM system have been made and used for both intraframe and interframe coding of video signals. Besides various adaptive DPCM systems, combinations of different source coding schemes, e.g., DPCM and transform coding, have also been proposed.

The complexity of coding schemes applied to video transmission depends on the kind of service and the tradeoff between hardware expense and transmission costs. Essential for broadcast television is high picture quality. Furthermore, digital cable TV calls for simple hardware realization, because the additional expense for the terminal equipment should be kept small. For video-conference and videophone services, reduction of transmission rate is important. For this reason, more sophisticated coding techniques can be applied. This discussion shows that for an economical coding scheme with reasonable hardware size and cost, there is no general solution. Various factors have impact on the economical solution for a given application. Even if the recent progress in VLSI and digital technology have made complicated signal processing feasible, in addition to new sophisticated predictive coding schemes also improvements in simple DPCM systems are of interest.

A. Subjectively Optimized Quantizers

The transmission bit-rate reduction of DPCM is achieved, to a large extent, by the quantization of the prediction error. An optimum quantizer design for a DPCM system with fixed-length code words should yield a minimum number of quantization levels, and impairments which should be as close as possible to the visibility threshold. Because of the difficulty of incorporating the observer's perception in the quantizer design, simple error measures like "minimum mean-squared error" (MMSE) have frequently been used. Using this distortion measure

$$D_{MMSE} = \sum_{i=0}^{k-1} \int_{d_i}^{d_{i+1}} (e - r_i)^2 p(e) \, de \quad (26)$$

has to be minimized, where $d_0 < d_1 < \cdots < d_K$ and $r_0 < r_1 < \cdots < r_{K-1}$ are decision and representative levels, respectively, and $p(e)$ is the probability density function of the prediction error e. For a given number of levels K, Max [28] has developed a set of equations for optimum decision and reconstruction levels. Subjective tests have shown that the statistically optimized quantizers have too many levels for small prediction errors and *vice versa* too few for large prediction errors. For a small number of levels, these quantizers generate visible edge business and slope overload effects. For this reason several modifications of the MMSE distortion measure have been proposed. A better match to the visibility of distortions is given by a distortion measure with a power of 4 or 6 [29]. Another method of psychovisual quantizer design replaces the probability density function $p(e)$ by a visual weighting function. Limb [30] used the product $p(e)w(e)$, where $w(e)$ is a measure of the local signal change

$$D_{WMSE} = \sum_{i=0}^{k-1} \int_{d_i}^{d_{i+1}} (e - r_i)^2 w(e) p(e) \, de. \quad (27)$$

Candy and Bosworth [31] and Netravali [32] considered the visual masking effect by introducing a visibility function. A visibility function of a particular picture is measured by determination of the visual sensitivity of the eye to distortions added to points where the horizontal signal slope of a video signal exceeds a threshold. A quantizer design procedure according to Max [28] can be applied if the probability density function $p(e)$ is replaced by the visibility density function $v(e)$.

$$D_{SV} = \sum_{i=0}^{k-1} \int_{d_i}^{d_{i+1}} (e - r_i)^2 v(e) \, de. \quad (28)$$

The optimum choice of visual weighting functions for quantizer design is not known. In all cases, physiological as well as statistical effects are considered. A disadvantage of the design methods described above is that the quantization error feedback of the DPCM is not taken into account since the visual weighting functions are determined by added noise [33] instead of real quantization error pattern of DPCM. In addition, an optimal quantizer design, particularly for broadcast television should consider visibility thresholds and should provide the smallest number of levels with no visible impairments.

The first attempt in this direction was made by Kretz [34] who investigated visibility thresholds of specific patterns which imitate the quantization errors of one-dimensional DPCM systems. Real quantization error patterns of various test pictures were generated by non-real-time DPCM simulations on a computer and have been used for threshold measurements by Erdmann [35] and Pirsch [36]. The visibility thresholds were determined by subjective comparison tests of a PCM-encoded picture with a picture which is impaired by DPCM. By selecting specific quantization characteristics and test pictures, thresholds were measured in subjective tests for the various types of impairments such as granular noise, edge busyness, and slope overload [36].

With respect to the masking effect, the measured visibility threshold function is called a masking function. In most investigations on masking, the visibility thresholds were determined for several edge slopes and signal differences on either side of the edge. For signal patterns other than simple one-dimensional edges, a measure for signal change had to be defined, which was denoted as activity function.

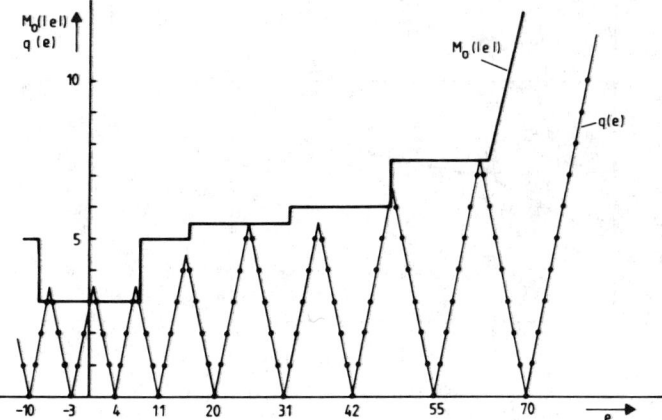

Fig. 15. Masking function and quantization error characteristic versus prediction error of luminance signals sampled at 10 MHz from [38].

In the case of fixed quantizers the maximum quantization error q is dependent on the prediction error e. Hence, the prediction error can be considered as an activity function.

A measured masking function is shown in Fig. 15. The staircase structure of the masking function in Fig. 15 results from the test method and has no subjective evidence. For a given masking function, it is relatively easy to determine a quantizer with a minimum number of levels which always produce quantization errors below threshold [37]. The masking function depends on the predictor used for the subjective tests. Linear predictors with only positive coefficients are advantageous for quantizers with a minimum number of levels [38]. For two-dimensional prediction the algorithm

$$\hat{s}_0 = \frac{1}{2} s'_1 + \frac{1}{8} s'_2 + \frac{1}{4} s'_3 + \frac{1}{8} s'_4 \qquad (29)$$

is recommended [38]. The subscripting of the pels is shown in Fig. 16.

There are several publications on nonadaptive quantizer design based on subjectively measured thresholds. The results can be summarized as follows. For the luminance component sampled at 10 MHz, 13 levels are required for natural test pictures and 21 levels for resolution charts [38].

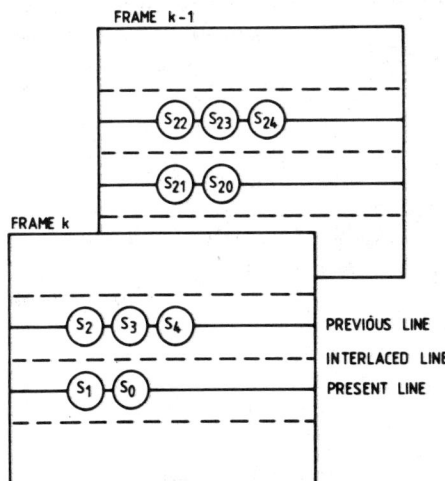

Fig. 16. Sampling raster and subscripting of pels for schemes other than contour predictions.

It has been recognized that the chrominance component B−Y can be quantized more coarsely than R−Y [39], [40]. The number of quantization levels for natural test pictures sampled at 4.4 MHz is 9 for R−Y and 5 for B−Y [40].

The measured threshold functions are picture dependent, but the variation for a class of pictures is not significant. Viewing distance and sampling frequency strongly influence the threshold values. The results reported so far are valid for fixed intraframe prediction. Recent investigations of masking functions for interframe prediction support the known effect that interframe predictors are better than intraframe predictors only for scenes of very slowly moving objects (velocity smaller than 1 pel per frame) [41]. Hence, intraframe predictors are to be prefered for nonadaptive DPCM systems. In the case of interframe prediction, critical test material generates new distortion effects which are described as "temporal overload" and "busy areas" [41]. Measurements of masking functions adapted to these distortions are required for interframe coding.

Subjectively measured masking functions can also be used for the design of adaptive quantizers. By means of more complex activity functions, a picture can be divided into several segments which are quantized differently. There are some proposals for activity functions used for quantizer control in the literature [42], [43], [33], [36]. A typical example of an activity function A is

$$A_{MD} = \max_{i,j \in DN} |d_{i,j}| \qquad (30)$$

where

$$d_{i,j} = s'_i - s'_j \qquad (31)$$

is the difference between neighboring pels and DN describes the index set of pels used for calculation of A_{MD}. To avoid the transmission of additional control information, a causal neighborhood as $DN = \{1,2,3,4\}$ is used in most cases. A heuristic approach leads to a combined masking function which is the maximum of two parts.

$$M = \max \{ M_0(e_0), M_n(A_{MD}) \}. \qquad (32)$$

Here M_0 describes the masking by the present prediction error and M_n describes the masking by surrounding pels. If we assume no interactions between M_0 and M_n than they can be measured independently by subjective threshold tests [36]. An adaptive quantizer can be realized by a set of

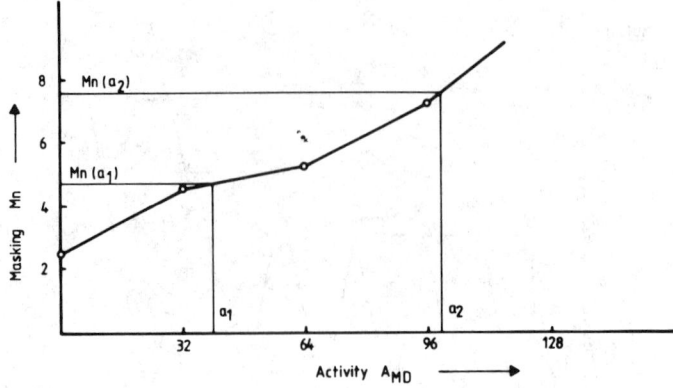

Fig. 17. Masking function $M_n(A_{MD})$ of luminance signals sampled at 10 MHz [36]. The a_1 indicate activity values used for quantizer control.

L separate quantizers which are switched on by the activity value A_{MD} according to

$$Q(e) = \begin{cases} Q_1(e) & A_{MD} < a_2 \\ Q_2(e) & a_2 \leq A_{MD} < a_3 \\ \vdots & \vdots \quad \vdots \\ Q_L(e) & a_L \leq A_{MD} \end{cases} \quad (33)$$

To each of the specific activity values a_1, a masking value $M_n(a_1)$ can be assigned (Fig. 17). Corresponding to (32), each quantization characteristic Q_1 has a uniform quantization with $M_n(a_1)$ as maximum quantization error as long as $M_0(e_0) < M_n(a_1)$. For $M_0(e_0) > M_n(a_1)$, a nonuniform quantization characteristic similar to that of Fig. 15 can be designed. Because of the masking characteristic, the number of levels becomes smaller as the activity becomes greater. Investigations on the statistics of switched quantizers have shown that for smaller activity values, large prediction errors are very rare, particularly for natural pictures. For this reason, a constant word length coding is possible, if for small activity values, the representative levels for large prediction errors are omitted in such a way that for all L characteristics, the same number of levels is used. In this case the largest threshold $M_n(a_L)$ fixes the number of levels.

The described technique has shown some limitations for very detailed pictures [36]. Recent investigations [44] improve adaptive quantizers by extension of the activity function. The term $M_n(A_{MD})$ is replaced by $M_n(A_{MWD})$ where

$$A_{MWD} = \max\{A_{MD}, A_{WD}\} \quad (34)$$

and the activity

$$A_{WD} = \max_{i \in DN}\left\{|\delta_i| + \frac{1}{4}(\delta_i + |\delta_i|)(1 - \text{sign}(e_0))\right\} \quad (35)$$

is based on weighted differences $\delta_i = s'_i - s_0$. The sign function is defined as

$$\text{sign}(x) = \begin{cases} 1, & x > T \\ 0, & |x| \leq T \\ -1, & x < -T \end{cases}$$

$$T = 1. \quad (36)$$

The function A_{WD} considers that transitions to bright values are more strongly masked than transitions to dark values. Application of the extended activity function (34) results in a switched quantizer with four different characteristics each having 11 levels corresponding to 3.5 bits per pel [44]. The representative levels of the four characteristics are listed in Table 3.

Table 3 Positive Representative Levels of Adaptive Quantization with Four Symmetrical Characteristics Each Having 11 Levels [44]

Positive Representative Levels	Activity Range	Masking Value
0, 3, 8, 15, 24, 35	$A_{MWD} < 15$	
0, 7, 14, 23, 34, 47	$15 \leq A_{MWD} < 35$	$M_n(15) = 3$
0, 11, 22, 35, 48, 65	$35 \leq A_{MWD} < 100$	$M_n(35) = 5$
0, 15, 30, 45, 64, 85	$100 \leq A_{MWD}$	$M_n(100) = 7$

Even with very sophisticated control techniques, adaptive quantizers allow only a relatively small reduction of the bit rate in case of constant word length coding. Significantly lower bit rates can be achieved by combining adaptive quantization with variable word length coding. In addition to quantizer control, the activity function is used to assign different codes of variable length to the quantized prediction error. The activity function divides a picture in segments of different statistics. Statistic measurements shows that by variable length coding of the prediction errors, the mean transmission rate could be further reduced by about 0.5 to 1 bit per pel.

Entropy coding with mean transmission rates of less than 2.5 bits per pel for the luminance signal can be reached only if adaptive quantization is combined with subsampling of picture segments at the transmitter side and interpolation of skipped samples at the receiver side [45]. Another well-known approach for low bit-rate coding is conditional replenishment where only pels with significant change from frame to frame are coded and transmitted. Up to now, quantizers for sophisticated, low bit-rate systems have been designed by trial and error and not by psychovisual criteria. The problem of visibility tests for such coding systems starts by selection of scenes with adequate spatial as well as temporal variations.

B. Adaptive Prediction

The picture signal is highly nonstationary and therefore the prediction error can be reduced by adapting the prediction to the local properties of the picture signal. Adaptive prediction reduces the range of possible prediction errors. Hence, picture quality will be improved for a given quantizer.

Contour Prediction: Let the picture be segmented into different areas where to each segment a predictor function h_i is assigned. Differences between proposed adaptive predictors are given by the chosen features of the segments and the control strategy. In case of adaptive intraframe prediction, four different kinds of segments as given below could be used

$$\hat{s}_0 = \begin{cases} h_1 & \text{flat area} \\ h_2 & \text{horizontal contour} \\ h_3 & \text{straight-line contour other than horizontal} \\ h_4 & \text{texture.} \end{cases} \quad (37)$$

Selection of predictor functions is controlled by the state of the neighboring pels. To avoid the transmission of additional information, most predictor selection schemes are based on previously transmitted pels. Frequently signal differences $d_{i,j}$ (31) are used to select the predictor at the present position.

Examples of this approach are adaptive predictors by Graham [46] and Zschunke [47]. Graham used horizontal and vertical prediction only.

$$\hat{s}_0 = \begin{cases} s'_7, & |d_{1,6}| < |d_{6,7}| \\ s'_1, & \text{otherwise.} \end{cases} \quad (38)$$

Because contour prediction requires a larger surrounding of pels for predictor control, a special subscripting according to Fig. 18 is used. Zschunke improved Graham's scheme by

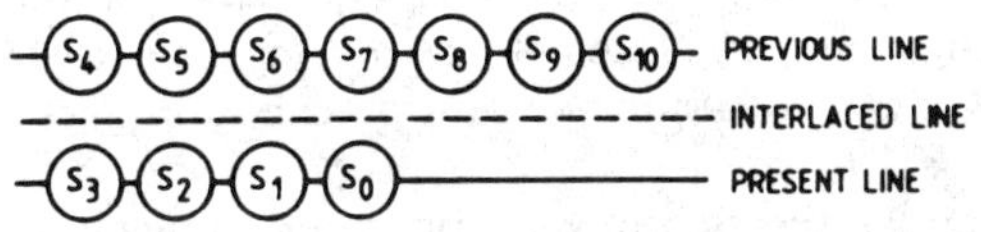

Fig. 18. Subscripting of pels for contour prediction.

separating contour pels from non-contour pels and considering the orientation of straight-line contours.

$$\hat{s}_0 = \begin{cases} s'_k, & \text{straight-line contour} \\ & k \in \{6,7,8\} \\ s'_1, & \text{otherwise.} \end{cases} \quad (39)$$

Contour points from the previous line are determined with reference to the previous pel s_1 by searching for the minimum of $\{|d_{1,5}|, |d_{1,6}|, |d_{1,7}|\}$. In addition, at a detected contour, the sign of the signal change (rising or falling) must be the same at both the previous line and the present line.

Selection control of most adaptive predictors is such that relations of signal differences with reference to the previous pel are used to predict corresponding relations of signal differences at the present pel. This sometimes results in bad prediction for high-detailed picture areas. To reduce the effects of wrong predictor selection, improved selection schemes and predictor functions, with coefficients smaller than one, are proposed. Recent investigations by Zhang [48] recommend the following predictor functions:

$$h_1 = \frac{5}{8}s'_1 + \frac{1}{8}(s'_6 + s'_7 + s'_8)$$

$$h_2 = \frac{3}{4}s'_1 + \frac{1}{4}s'_7$$

$$h_3 = \frac{1}{4}s'_{k-1} + \frac{1}{2}s'_k + \frac{1}{4}s'_{k+1}, \quad k \in \{6,7,8,9\}$$

$$h_4 = \frac{1}{5}(s'_5 + s'_6 + s'_7 + s'_8 + s'_9). \quad (40)$$

The main steps of Zhang's selection scheme can be summarized as follows:

Predictor h_1 for flat areas is used if

$$\min\{|d_{1,2}|, |d_{1,5}|, |d_{1,6}|, |d_{1,7}|\} < 20 \text{ out of } 256.$$

A horizontal edge is assumed for

$$\max\{|d_{1,2}|, |d_{2,3}|\} < \min\{|d_{1,5}|, |d_{1,6}|, |d_{1,7}|, |d_{1,8}|\}.$$

The direction of a contour other than horizontal is identified by

$$\min\{|d_{1,k-1}|\}, \quad k = 6,7,8,9$$

as long as the minimum is smaller than 51 out of 256. In addition, the sign of the signal change at a detected contour has to be identical for neighboring lines. This is checked by

$$\text{sign}(d_{1,2}) \times \text{sign}(d_{k-1,k-2}) = 1.$$

In order to avoid the influence of noise in the contour estimate, the result of the sign function is set to zero for arguments smaller than 7.

Texture is identified by rapid signal changes which will be recognized by

$$\text{sign}(d_{1,2}) \times \text{sign}(d_{k,k-1}) = -1, \quad k = 6,7$$

and

$$\text{sign}(d_{k-1,k-2}) \neq \text{sign}(d_{k,k-1}) = \text{sign}(d_{k+1,k}).$$

Another approach to contour prediction by an edge orientation extrapolation process has been presented by Kretz [26]. An advantage of this recent proposal is the reduced sensitivity to transmission errors.

Adaptive Intra/Interframe Prediction: Contour prediction improves picture quality of scenes with high activity and many high contrast edges. However, for a large class of natural scenes, transmission bit rate reduction is more successful with adaptive intra/interframe predictors. A frame of a scene can be segmented into unchanged and changed areas. The unchanged areas consist of a stationary background with very small frame-to-frame differences whereas changed areas are caused by moving objects. It is obvious, that the best predictor function for unchanged areas is the previous frame predictor. Intraframe predictor is very efficient for changed areas. Hence, several adaptive predictors are proposed. Here either a previous frame or an intraframe predictor is selected, depending on surrounding signal changes. Variations of the coding schemes are basically given by the switching control.

Two approaches will be discussed here. According to the subscripting in Fig. 16 let

$$h_1 = \frac{1}{2}s'_1 + \frac{1}{8}s'_2 + \frac{1}{4}s'_3 + \frac{1}{8}s'_4 \quad (41)$$

be the intraframe predictor and let

$$h_2 = s'_{20} \quad (42)$$

be the previous frame predictor. In the first method [49], switching between both predictors is controlled by a special activity function A_{sj} which is the sum of the magnitudes of the prediction errors for each pel in a small window of neighboring pels. The predictor function, which gives the smallest activity value, is chosen for prediction. The basic selection rule is as follows:

$$\hat{s}_0 = \begin{cases} h_1, & \text{if } A_{s1} < A_{s2} \\ h_2, & \text{otherwise} \end{cases} \quad (43)$$

where

$$A_{sj} = \sum_{i \in DN} |s'_i - h_j(s'_i)|. \quad (44)$$

The notation $h_j(s'_i)$ means the value of predictor function h_j calculated at pel position s_i relative to the present pel s_0.

It has been recognized that the selection schemes described above are sensitive to quantization noise because of recursive control. Better performance for the case of coarse quantization can be provided by activity functions similar to (30) [50]. Here

$$A_{MD1} = \max_{i,j, \in DN} |d_{i,j}| \quad (45)$$

is used as a measure of intraframe activity, and

$$A_{MD2} = \max_{i \in DN} |d_{i, i+20}| \quad (46)$$

as a measure of activity between successive frames. The switching control has been further improved by introducing a weighting factor b and a transitional state. In the transitional state, a three-dimensional predictor

$$h_3 = \frac{1}{4} s'_1 + \frac{1}{8} s'_3 + \frac{5}{8} s'_{20} \quad (47)$$

is used. The adaptation process of this scheme can be described by a state diagram as shown in Fig. 19. A further improvement of picture quality for highly detailed moving areas is possible if the intraframe predictor is combined with contour prediction. An adaptive predictor similar to

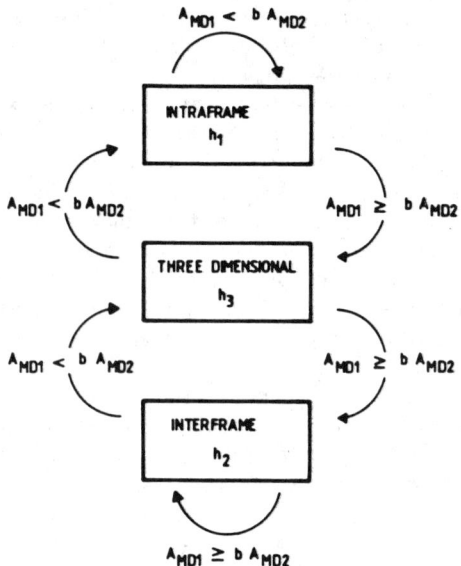

Fig. 19. State diagram of an adaptive intra/interframe predictor [50].

the one described above has been also proposed by Grallert and Starck [51]. Subjective investigations have shown that an eight-level quantizer is sufficient for most television scenes [50].

The application of variable-length coding does not require the restriction to a very small number of quantization levels and allows much lower bit rates than constant word length coding. Using a quantization level zero, optimized prediction provides this level very frequently. Very efficient for such a case is the application of a run-length code for the zero–nonzero pattern of quantization levels within a frame [49], [52].

Other coding schemes cluster a picture in predictable (prediction error level zero) and unpredictable pels and code clusters of predictable pels by run-length [53]. It has been recognized that in case of adaptive prediction, segmentation control by the prediction error is more efficient than a forward segmentor based on frame-to-frame differences as in standard conditional replenishment.

Inter and intraframe prediction are the best for scenes with small and very large motion, respectively. For scenes with moderate motion, interfield predictors are better. This is due to the fact that spatial and interframe correlation is effected differently by motion. For this reason, adaptive inter/intrafield has been proposed [51], [54].

Most of the adaptive schemes are controlled by signal changes of previously transmitted pels to avoid the transmission of overhead information. It has been also shown that systems with overhead information can be as efficient as those without [54]. To keep the transmission costs for overhead information small, switching is performed by clusters of pels.

Motion-Compensated Prediction: Adaptive prediction can be further significantly improved by taking into account the frame-to-frame displacement of moving objects. The success of these schemes obviously depends on the ability to estimate the displacement of moving objects. Methods for displacement estimation are described in Section II of this paper.

In Fig. 20, the transmission bit rate of moving objects is shown as a function of the velocity for the three kinds of predictors. The transmission bit rates have been calculated by assuming a simple signal model [55]. For objects or segments of a scene with small velocity, interframe prediction is obviously the best. For segments with higher velocity, above 1 pel per frame, intraframe prediction does better than interframe prediction. Hence, the transmission rate of adaptive intra/interframe predictors depends on the percentage of pels with slow motion. By application of motion-compensated prediction, transmission rate of moving areas with a velocity above 0.5 pel per frame can be further reduced. It should be recognized, that even with an ideal displacement estimation, there still remains a significant transmission bit rate for highly detailed moving objects in case of noninteger displacements. For this kind of displacement, prediction by the nearest neighbor performs poorer than an interpolation of the four neighboring pels [11].

The methods of motion-compensated prediction can be roughly split into two groups. One set of techniques uses a forward motion estimation on a block-by-block basis (Fig. 21(a)). Block matching is performed by searching for the maximum of the correlation between a block in the present frame and a displaced block in the previous frame [18]–[20].

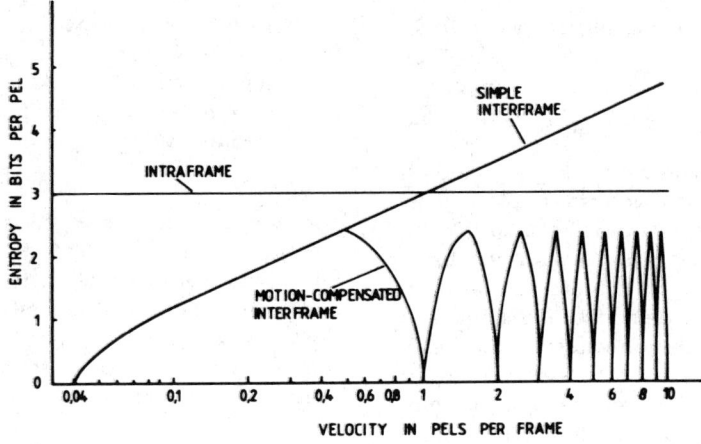

Fig. 20. Transmission rate of moving areas versus velocity for three basic predictors [55].

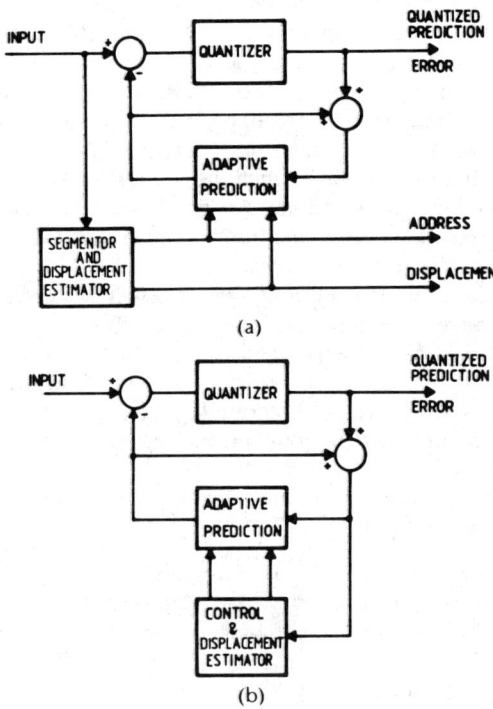

Fig. 21. Block diagram of motion-compensated DPCM codecs. (a) Forward segmentor and motion estimator. (b) Recursive control and motion estimator.

Block size for these correlation techniques is on the order of 7 × 7. To reduce realization expense, the searching of displacement is restricted to a total certain number of possible positions (25) [20]. One of the problems of block-based motion estimation is the segmentation method for moving objects. It is obvious that boundary lines of moving objects within a block influence the estimate.

Instead of block matching, significant spatial luminance gradients within a block can be used for displacement measurement [26]. The results of a two-stage system based on gradients are very promising [56]. Such a system allows separation of objects with different motion within one block.

A disadvantage of the block-wise forward displacement estimator is that the displacement vector needs to be transmitted. To restrict the amount of overhead information, most of the coding schemes with forward estimators use only integer displacements. Overhead information is not necessary with pel recursive displacement estimation based on transmitted pels (Fig. 22(b)). The pel recursive algorithm of Netravali and Robbins [11], [12] has been applied to component and composite color video signals [57], [58]. For stability reasons, the update of the displacement from pel to pel in recursive systems is restricted. Hence, it is advantageous to do predictor selection between motion-compensated prediction and other frame-to-frame and intraframe predictors [53]. Computer simulations on several test sequences have shown the efficiency of motion-compensated prediction with pel recursive displacement estimate. This

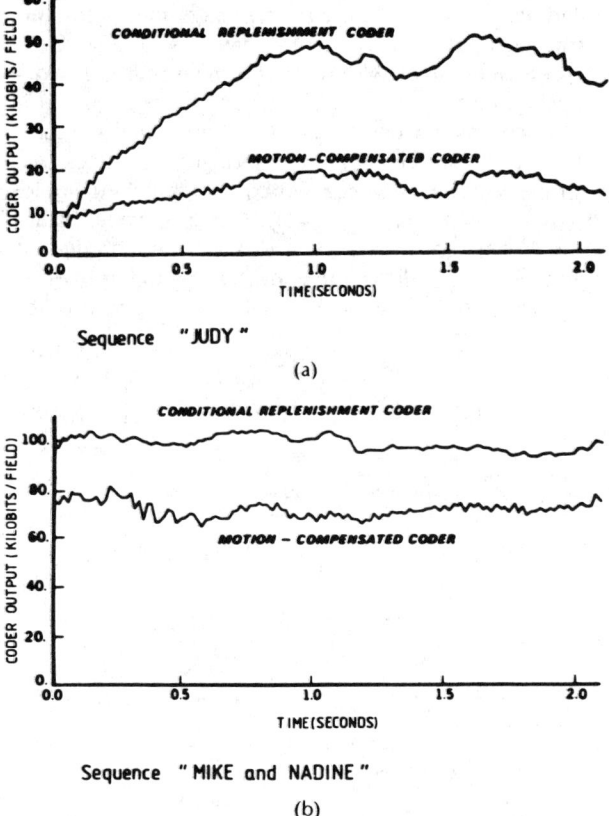

Fig. 22. Performance of conditional replenishment and motion-compensated prediction for two scenes with different activity [12].

kind of prediction reduces the coder bit rate by 30 to 70 percent compared to conditional replenishment (Fig. 22). Using a 35-level quantizer, the maximum bit rates of the scenes are on the order of 0.5 to 2.8 bits per pel depending on the kind of scene [12].

In most cases, motion-compensated prediction based on a forward estimator provides more accurate displacements of large moving objects than recursive systems. But a comparison of prediction techniques with forward and backward estimation using the same bit rate has not yet been reported. Here it has to be considered that the amount of overhead information for a prediction with a forward estimator can be used in addition for prediction error coding in case of recursive estimators. Although the optimal compromise between coding efficiency and hardware costs is not yet known, for low bit-rate systems such as video conferencing with 1.5 Mbits/s and below, a motion compensated predictor performs much better in terms of picture quality than conventional interframe coders. Recent investigations are directed to computationally simpler as well as more robust and effective methods to reduce hardware size and implementation costs [23], [59]. Supported by the progress of VLSI, complex systems such as motion compensation are going from theoretical investigations to actual implementation [60].

IV. Transform Coding

Transform coding denotes a procedure in which the PCM-coded video signal s_n is subjected prior to transmission to an invertible transform with subsequent quantizing and coding. The aim of the transform algorithm is to convert statistically dependent picture elements into independent coefficients. Probably the best known method is the discrete Fourier transform. Fig. 23 shows a block diagram for transform coding of video signals. The input signal s_n representing the picture elements of a sequence of successive television frames is first segmented into blocks (subpictures) of size $M \times N \times K$ (Fig. 24). Typical block sizes are $4 \times 4 \times 4$, $8 \times 8 \times 1$, and $16 \times 16 \times 1$. The coordinates within a block are indicated by i, j, k. Owing to line-by-line and frame-by-frame sampling of television signals, block segmentation calls for M line stores for two-dimensional and K-field or frame stores for three-dimensional transforms. Block-segmentation networks precede the transform circuit at the transmitter and follow it on the receiver side.

A one-dimensional transform

$$S = \bar{T} \cdot s \qquad (48)$$

converts the vector s of the sampling values of a block $(1, N, 1)$ into the vector S of the transform coefficients, which, in order to achieve data compression, are quantized and then subjected to redundancy and irrelevancy reduction. Irrelevancy reduction introduces an irreversible distortion to the video signal whereas elimination of redundancy is a reversible coding operation. At the receiver, the inverse transform

$$s = \bar{T}^{-1} \cdot S = \bar{T}^{-1} \cdot \bar{T} \cdot S = s \qquad (49)$$

restores the picture signal which is affected by the errors produced by irrelevancy reduction. The tolerable distortion is determined by the human observer exclusively. In this paper we distinguish between broadcast picture quality and video telephone quality. The lines of the transform matrix $\bar{T}$ correspond to the samples of the basis functions, e.g., Walsh functions, cosine functions, which determine the characteristics of a transform. For natural pictures, Discrete Cosine Transform (DCT), Karhunen–Loève transform (KLT), Walsh transform (WT), and Slant transform (SLT) lead to an energy concentration in only a few coefficients containing the main part of the picture information. The M transform uses orthogonal pn-sequences as basis functions allowing particularly effective irrelevancy reduction. Various basis function systems are presented in [2], [3]. Fig. 25 shows the basis functions of a one-dimensional M transform for $1 \times 15 \times 1$ blocks [89].

In the past three years investigations have concentrated on the following problems:

- adaptive coding, i.e., quantizing and coding of spectral coefficients controlled by the picture content;
- hybrid coding, i.e., combination of transform coding and DPCM;
- investigation of new basis function systems.

In addition to these investigations, which will be explained in detail, also techniques for reducing the visibility of the block boundaries have been developed.

Transform coding takes advantage of the statistical dependencies of picture elements for redundancy reduction. Because of block segmentation, statistical dependencies beyond block boundaries are not considered. Furthermore, due to irrelevancy reduction at data rates below 1 bit per pel these boundaries may become visible. Schlichte [61], [62], Pearson [63], and Chen [64] are attempting to overcome this deficiency by transform coding with overlapping blocks. This increases the number of blocks per frame or the block size. It is still unknown whether this technique will result in greater reduction factors. This method, however, does make the block boundaries less visible. As the locations of the block boundaries are known, also digital low-pass filtering can be applied to reduce the visibility of the block edges. Reeve and Lim [65] propose two-dimensional filtering for this use. They report that filtering or block overlap coding give almost the same results.

Investigations covered both component and composite

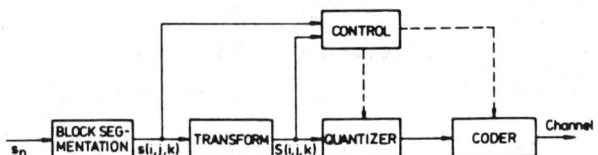

Fig. 23. Block diagram of a transform coder with adaptive control.

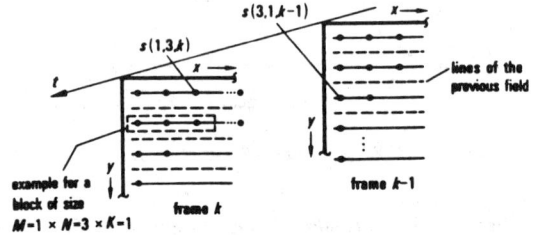

Fig. 24. Sampling structure. The indices x, y, k denote the positions of picture elements in a sequence of frames.

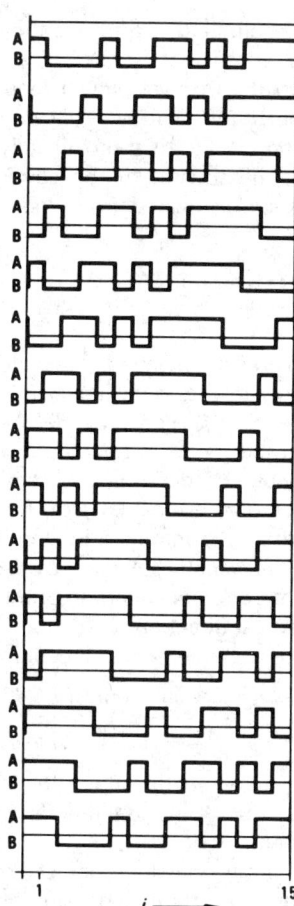

Fig. 25. A one-dimensional m function system with $N = 15$.

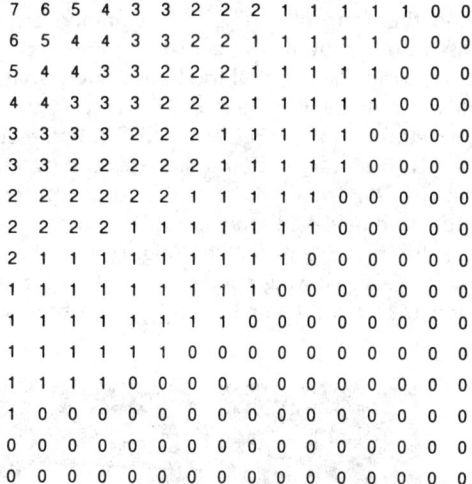

Fig. 26. Typical bit allocation table for $16 \times 16 \times 1$ block cosine transform coding at approximately 1 bit per pel according to Jain [3].

coding of PAL and NTSC signals. The following statements refer to component coding. Composite coding will be described briefly in Section IV-D.

A. Adaptive Coding

The aim of adaptive transform coding is to control the quantizing and coding of the individual coefficients as a function of the picture content or its spectral energy distribution within a block in such a way that the distortions as a result of irrelevancy reduction are kept below a visibility threshold, which is fixed by the human observer. The problems that have to be overcome here are the unique classification of the picture content and the design of suitable quantizers and coders.

From the knowledge of the variances of the spectral coefficients determined from an evaluation of many transform blocks, the so-called bit-allocation or bit-assignment tables can be drawn up which contain the necessary number of quantizing steps for each coefficient. The results of comprehensive investigations on the design of quantizers have been carried out by Mauersberger [66]. Jain [3] gives a typical example in Fig. 26. $S(1,1,1)$ is coded with 7 bits. With increasing indices (i,j) the coefficients $S(i,j,1)$ are quantized more and more coarsely according to the frequency weighting function of the human eye until eventually high-order coefficients are completely suppressed. Once established, the bit-allocation table applies to all the blocks. With such methods it is possible to achieve a reduction to approximately 1 bit per pel for video telephone pictures. This does not, however, apply to highly structured picture contents as it leads to mismatching of the quantizer. Therefore, adaptive coding has to be used for broadcast TV signals or reduction factors greater than 8.

In der Smitten and Hildebrandt [67] have investigated adaptive coding of the Slant coefficients for the transmission of broadcast color TV signals on 34-Mbit/s channels. Classification is based on an analysis of the magnitude spectrum of two-dimensional blocks. If there are predominantly horizontal (H), vertical (V), diagonal (D), or no (0) structures in the picture the investigated block of size $4 \times 4 \times 1$ is assigned to one of the four activity categories H, V, D, or 0. For each category there is a special bit-allocation table. Activity category 0 applies if none of the coefficients achieves 8 percent of its maximum amplitude. Decision for activity category H, V, or D is taken by the activity functions h, v, and d, which are the weighted sums of the absolute values of the coefficients. The following matrix shows the arrangement of the two-dimensional Slant coefficients of one block:

$$S(1,1) \quad S(1,2) \quad S(1,3) \quad S(1,4)$$
$$S(2,1) \quad S(2,2) \quad S(2,3) \quad S(2,4)$$
$$S(3,1) \quad S(3,2) \quad S(3,3) \quad S(3,4)$$
$$S(4,1) \quad S(4,2) \quad S(4,3) \quad S(4,4).$$

Activity functions h, v, and d are calculated by

$$h = 2 \cdot |S(2,1)| + 2 \cdot |S(3,1)| + 2 \cdot |S(4,1)|$$
$$\quad + |S(3,2)| + |S(4,2)|$$
$$v = 2 \cdot |S(1,2)| + 2 \cdot |S(1,3)| + \quad |S(1,4)|$$
$$\quad + |S(2,3)| + |S(2,4)|$$
$$d = 4 \cdot |S(2,2)| + 8 \cdot |S(3,3)|$$
$$\quad + 2 \cdot |S(3,4)| + 2 \cdot |S(4,3)|. \quad (50)$$

If the relevant information is concentrated in one of the categories 0, H, or V, quantizing is controlled by a corresponding bit-allocation table. In case of activity category D the coefficients are subjected to structure coding. The basic idea behind this form of coding is to combine groups of coefficients into a pattern. The actual pattern is compared with a set of basic patterns and the basic pattern that bears the greatest similarity is selected. All the possible basic patterns are stored at the receiver, so that only the storage address needs to be transmitted. Using this coding method and a set of 752 basic patterns, In der Smitten and Hildebrandt have achieved a picture quality that shows no discernible difference between the original and the coded picture under CCIR viewing conditions: [98]. In Fig. 27 the original and the coded luminance signals are represented.

Fig. 27. Luminance component of the test picture. (a) PCM, sampling rates: 10 MHz for luminance, 2.5 MHz for chrominance, line-alternating transmission. (b) Adaptive Slant transform, bit rate 34 Mbits/s, according to [67].

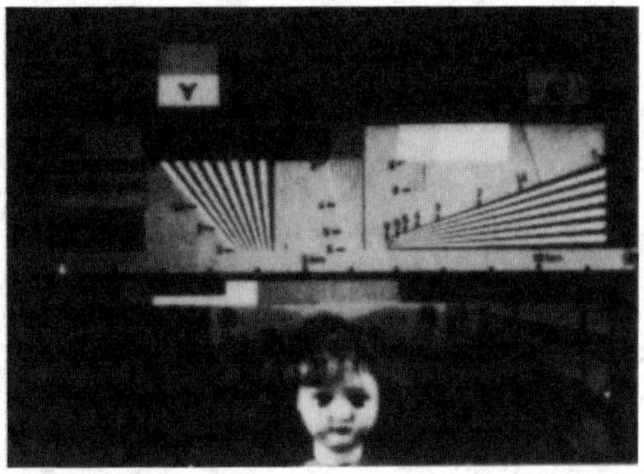

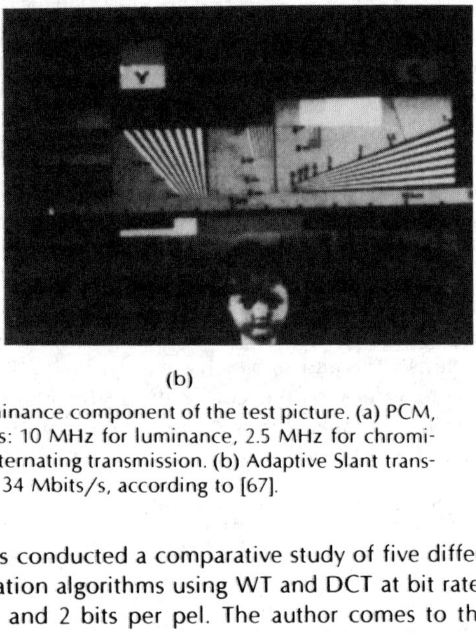

Ngan [68] has conducted a comparative study of five different bit-allocation algorithms using WT and DCT at bit rates between 0.5 and 2 bits per pel. The author comes to the conclusion that bit allocation and type of basis function system are not independent of each other. In general, DCT is clearly superior to WT in terms of data compression achieving a lower bit rate for the same picture quality for all schemes.

Wong and Steele [69], [70] have achieved a data rate of 0.55 bit per pel for monochrome video telephone signals using bit allocation and adaptive selection of the DCT coefficients. For a block size of 16 × 16 × 1, bit allocation takes place in accordance with the following formula:

$$b(i,j) = \text{INTEGER}\left[1/2 \log_2\left(\frac{E[S^2(i,j)]}{E_{mean}} \cdot C\right)\right] \quad (51)$$

where $b(i,j)$ corresponds to the number of bits made available for coding $S(i,j,1)$. E_{mean} is defined as $E[s^2(x,y)]$ for all x, y of the whole field. C is a weighting factor for the individual spectral coefficients. $E[S^2(i,j)]$ as well as E_{mean} must be known to the receiver, which requires the transmission of overhead information. This transform coding scheme reduces the bit rate to approximately 1 bit per pel. In a second step, the squares of the current coefficients $S^2(i,j)$ in a block are estimated from coefficients already coded according to

$$\hat{S}^2(i,j) = 1/3\left[S^2(i,j-1) + S^2(i-1,j) + S^2(i-1,j-1)\right]. \quad (52)$$

If $\hat{S}^2(i,j_0)$ falls below a specified threshold none of the residual coefficients in the same line $S(i,j = j_0,\cdots,16)$ is transmitted. Since $S^2(i,j)$ generally decreases at higher orders i,j this method seems justifiable.

Götze and Ocylok [71] describe a system with adaptive coding of the three-dimensional DCT coefficients for 8 × 8 × 4 blocks. Coding is controlled by the activity vector $\Delta = (\Delta h, \Delta v, \Delta t)$. The variables Δh and Δv denote the maximum absolute difference between adjacent pels s in the horizontal and vertical direction. Δt denotes the maximum absolute difference in the temporal direction within a block

$$\Delta t = \max\left\{(\max s(i,j,k+1) - \min s(i,j,k))k = 1,\cdots,3, \quad i,j = 1,\cdots,8\right\}. \quad (53)$$

If Δt is less than a certain threshold, the block does not contain any visible change in the temporal direction. In this case only coefficients $S(i,j,1)$ $(i,j = 1,\cdots,8)$ are encoded and transmitted. If the classifier detects changes in the temporal direction, the coefficients are divided into 14 activity categories as a function of Δh and Δv. A bit-allocation table is available for each activity category. The authors have achieved a signal-to-noise ratio of about 24 dB for video telephone signals at 0.4 bit per pel.

Attention is drawn to further work on adaptive transform coding, some of it in conjunction with a study of channel coding [72]–[78]; there is no room within this paper for discussing this work in detail.

Lohscheller [79], [80] studies the transmission of still pictures on digital telephone channels. His intention is to overcome the long transmission time by making a coarse structure of the image visible at the receiver after only a few seconds. After two-dimensional DCT with block size 8 × 8 × 1 and quantization according to Mauersberger [66] the coefficients are transmitted in an order according to the size of their spectral variance. After transmission of the first three coefficients of a block, a coarse picture is already visible.

A similiar method allows the inclusion of high-quality photographic images within Videotex data [81]–[83]. Further investigations of the progressive transmission of still pictures in conjunction with transform coding are published by Takikawa [84] and Ngan [85].

B. Hybrid Coding

Hybrid coding denotes the combination of transform coding and DPCM. Owing to the line structure of the television signal, M line stores are used for two-dimensional block segmentation and K frame stores for three-dimensional block segmentation. In order to save memory, it may be suitable to combine a one-dimensional transform in the line direction with DPCM in the column direction or a two-dimensional transform with DPCM in the temporal direction. The block diagram of a hybrid coder based on one-dimensional transform is shown in Fig. 28.

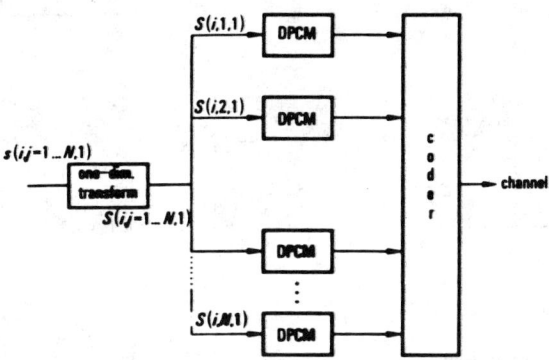

Fig. 28. Block diagram of a hybrid encoder using a one-dimensional transform and DPCM encoders in the second dimension. The block consists of N pels $s(i,j = 1, \ldots, N, 1)$ along a line.

Habibi [86] proposes a system with one-dimensional DCT of block size $1 \times 16 \times 1$. The DPCM is simplified to a previous coefficient predictor that encodes the differences between successive spectral coefficients in the column direction. Then the differences are arranged in blocks of size 64×16. A cutout of such a block is given in Fig. 29.

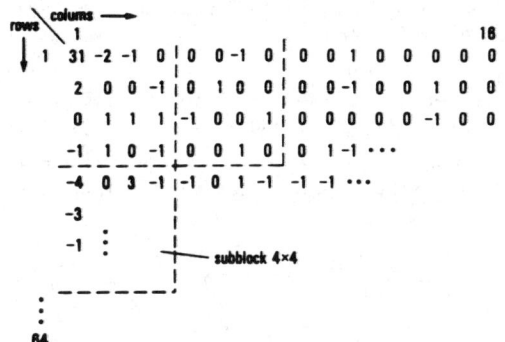

Fig. 29. Typical values of the differences between successive coefficients in column direction [86].

Investigations have shown that a great many of these differences within a block are equal to zero. Habibi divides a block of 64×16 into subblocks of 4×4 differences and applies a special code with variable word length. If a block consists only of zeros, one short code word (01) is transmitted. Otherwise, individual samples of the subblock are encoded corresponding to Table 4.

A buffer is provided to smooth the variable data rate. In order to avoid buffer overflow the resolution of the A/D converter at the system input is controlled by the level to which the buffer is filled. A coarser quantization of the samples results in an increase of the number of zeros in the subblocks. With this adaptive coding scheme, Habibi achieves a signal-to-noise ratio of approximately 36 dB at 1.2 bits per pel with aerial photographs. The quality of these test pictures can be compared with video telephone pictures.

Table 4 Coding with Variable Word Length of Individual Samples of One Subblock According to Habibi [86]

Difference	Code Word
0	1
1	001
−1	0001
2	00001
−2	000001
other	0000001 + PCM

Kamangar and Rao [87] as well as Pearlman and Jakatdar [88] have focused their attention on a two-dimensional transform combined with DPCM in the temporal direction. Pearlman has carried out a full-frame DFT. The differences between temporally successive spectral values are quantized by separate Max quantizers for the real and the imaginary components. Proof that this procedure can be used for videotelephony was furnished with the aid of the test sequence "Walter Cronkite." The signal-to-noise ratio is given as 30 dB for 1 bit per pel per frame and 21.6 dB for 0.2 bit per pel per frame.

By means of two-dimensional DCT, Kamangar and Rao [87] transform blocks of $8 \times 8 \times 1$ picture elements in the field with subsequent one-dimensional DPCM in the temporal direction. Since DPCM fails if there is fast motion in the picture it makes sense to control the coding adaptively. Each block representing the prediction error of DCT coefficients is divided into four subblocks according to Fig. 30.

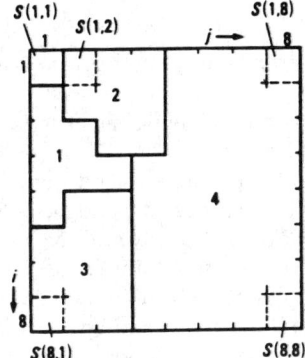

Fig. 30. Structure of subblocks in an 8×8 block of prediction errors in the two-dimensional DCT domain according to Kamangar and Rao [87].

The spatial activity of each subblock is determined by the variance of the coefficients. If the activity exceeds a threshold, more bits are assigned to the prediction errors in that subblock. This method results in a variable output bit rate which requires a buffer to smooth the data stream. The magnitude of the prediction error of the dc coefficient $S(1,1)$ indicates temporal activity. If a block is recognized as temporally active no extra bits will be assigned to subblocks 3 and 4. Coding is thereby adapted to the reduced capacity of the eye to resolve detail in rapid movement. The system supplies a variable data flow. The authors have achieved a signal-to-noise ratio of about 30 dB at 1 bit per pel with the test sequence "Wheel of Fortune." Compared to the test sequence "Walter Cronkite" this sequence shows finer structured details.

Jain and Jain [18] as well as Hein [96] improve the prediction in temporal direction by motion-compensation methods which are carried out in the spatial domain and not in the spectral domain. Jain and Jain calculate the displacement vector for one block of size $16 \times 16 \times 1$ by using the samples $s(i,j,1)$. Then they shift the corresponding block of DCT coefficients $S(i,j,1)$ according to that displacement vector and improve a DPCM in temporal direction in the spectral domain. With 0.253 bit per pel they obtain a signal-to-noise ratio of 38.74 dB in the test sequence "Walter Cronkite."

C. M Transform

M transform is derived from the basis function system of m functions which is presented in [89], [90]. An m-function system arises from the cyclic shifting of one m sequence of binary symbols and subsequent orthonormalization. An m sequence is the maximum-length sequence generated by a feedback shift register [97]. Fig. 25 shows a system of one-dimensional m functions with $N = 15$. The condition for the orthonormalization of this function system reads

$$\frac{1}{15} \sum_{j=1}^{15} m_u(j) \cdot m_v(j) = \begin{cases} 1, & u = v, \\ 0, & u \neq v, \end{cases} \quad u,v = 1,\cdots,15 \tag{54}$$

with

$$\frac{8}{15} A^2 + \frac{7}{15} B^2 = 1, \quad \text{for } u = v$$

and

$$\frac{4}{15} A^2 + \frac{3}{15} B^2 + \frac{8}{15} AB = 0, \quad \text{for } u \neq v \tag{55}$$

the amplitudes A and B can be calculated.

The M transform does not lead to an energy concentration to only a few coefficients and does not reduce redundancy due to statistical dependencies of the picture elements, but allows particularly effective reduction of irrelevancy in the M spectrum. The basis functions have a noise-like structure as shown in Fig. 25. Therefore, the quantizing errors are superimposed on the video signal after the inverse transform as noise-like patterns. The human eye is less sensitive to these patterns than to structures as produced by WT, for example. Measurements have shown that the visibility threshold for the patterns of the m functions are higher than those of Walsh functions.

Using the m functions presented in [89] as a basis, Keesen developed a two-dimensional basis function system, which is shown in Fig. 31. The spectrum produced by this modified M transform is free of dc components [91], [92]. In addition, the mean value of the input function has no effect on the form of the spectrum. Measurements have shown that the variances of all spectral values are nearly the same. Therefore, the same quantizer can be used for all the coefficients.

Fig. 32 shows the block diagram of a coder which has been optimized for the transmission of broadcast color TV signals in 34-Mbit/s channels. The sampling values $s(i,j,1)$ are segmented into blocks of $3 \times 3 \times 1$ prior to transformation. Coding is carried out in three parallel channels. First, the coefficients (S), the activity (a), and the mean value $E(s)$ of a block are computed. Activity is defined as the difference between the maximum and the minimum sample value in a block. The activity controls bit allocation for the quantizing of the mean value and the coefficients. In a block with low activity the mean value is quantized very

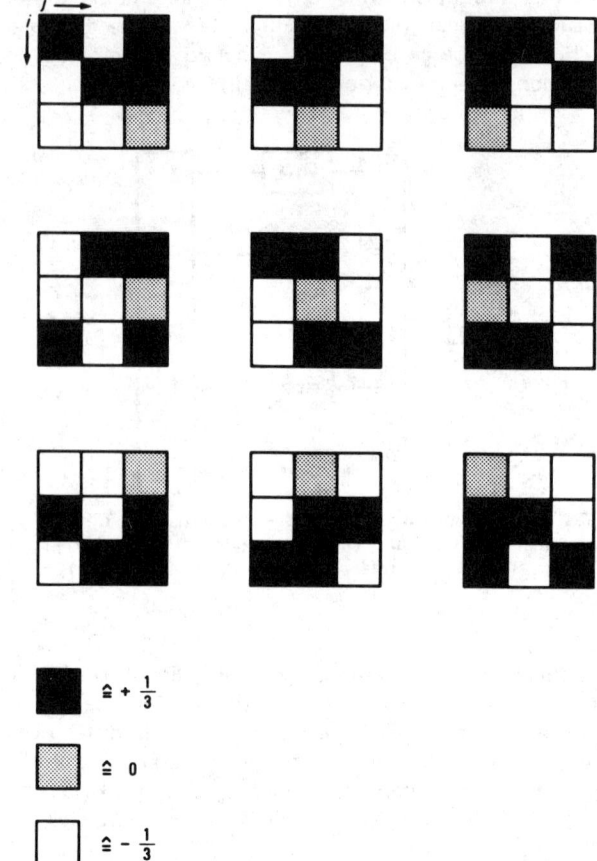

Fig. 31. Basis functions of a modified two-dimensional M transform with block size $3 \times 3 \times 1$.

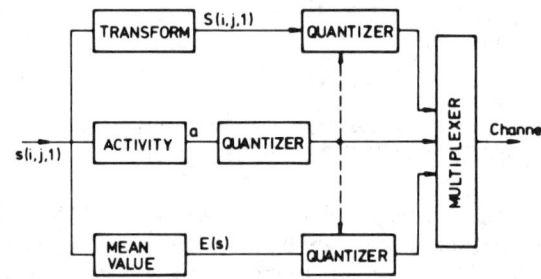

Fig. 32. Block diagram of an adaptive transform coder using modified m functions.

finely and up to 8 bits are spent for its transmission. For high activities about 6 bits are sufficient. Investigations with a realized coder for the luminance signal have shown that for natural pictures there are no visible differences compared with a PCM picture, when 32 bits are used on the average for encoding the information of one block.

D. Composite Coding of NTSC and PAL Signals

In principle, similiar procedures to those used for the adaptive coding of component signals are applied to the adaptive coding of NTSC and PAL signals. The difficulty lies in finding block boundaries in which there is maximum correlation between sampling values.

Playsongsang and Rao [95] describe two different hybrid DCT/DPCM coding schemes for NTSC composite video signals. The first scheme is based on one-dimensional DCT with block size $1 \times 32 \times 1$ with subsequent DPCM in the vertical direction. The authors report, that at 3.5 bits per pel the overall quality for video telephone pictures was good, but there appeared isolated color streaks in areas of sharp changes in color and luminance. The second scheme involves a special form of DCT with block size of $4 \times 4 \times 1$ followed by DPCM between the blocks. The NTSC signal is sampled at three times color subcarrier frequency $3f_{sc}$ and quantized with 8 bits per sample. The samples are arranged in a block consisting of 4 lines of a field and 12 pels per line as shown in Fig. 33. Each block is divided into three subblocks of 4×4 samples having the same subcarrier phase as that in Fig. 34. The data in the subblocks are then

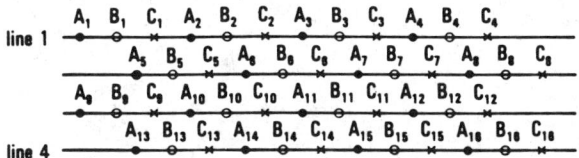

Fig. 33. Samples of one block $4 \times 12 \times 1$. Picture elements indicated with the same symbols have the same subcarrier phase according to Playsongsang and Rao [95].

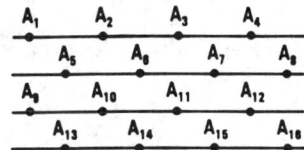

Fig. 34. One subblock with size $4 \times 4 \times 1$ of the block in Fig. 11.

rearranged to be one-dimensional and the DCT of those samples is performed. The first coefficient of each subblock corresponding to the mean value is compared with those of already transmitted adjacent subblocks of the subcarrier phase, as indicated in Fig. 35. The neighboring subblock

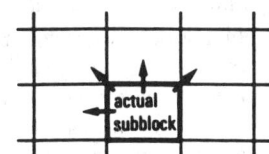

Fig. 35. Intersubblock DPCM according to Playsongsang and Rao [95].

whose mean value is closest to that of the actual block is assumed to have maximum correlation. DPCM is applied between the coefficients of these two subblocks. Two additional bits per subblock indicate the nearest neighbor that has been chosen for DPCM. The signal-to-noise ratio obtained with this method is about 37 dB at a bit rate of 3.5 bits per pel.

Ekambaram and Kwatra [93], [94] describe another adaptive method using two-dimensional DCT with which they achieve a data rate of approximately 2 bits per pel at a "good" picture quality. Unfortunately, the authors do not describe their test sequences.

V. MOTION-ADAPTIVE FRAME INTERPOLATION

Skipping frames at the transmitter and interpolating the skipped frames at the receiver appears as a very attractive method of television coding since it can be combined with known coding techniques to further reduce the bit rate. However, it has been proven that simple frame reconstruction techniques as, e.g., frame repetition, generates jerkily moving objects in the displayed picture [99] or linear interpolation by temporal filtering exhibits blurring in moving areas [100]. The visibility of these degradations is in proportion to the speed of movement. Therefore, linear frame interpolation techniques can only be applied for television sequences with slow movement.

A certain improvement can be achieved if field interpolation is applied instead of frame interpolation [101], since there is less displacement of a moving object between fields than between frames. However, transmitting every second field also reduces the vertical resolution in stationary areas of the displayed picture.

A first step into the direction of motion-adaptive frame interpolation is an adaptive interpolator which is controlled by a movement detector [102]. This technique attempts to improve the picture quality by switching between two different interpolation algorithms in stationary and moving areas. If one of the picture elements F or Z in a present field according to Fig. 36 belongs to a moving area then the picture element in the field to be interpolated is replaced

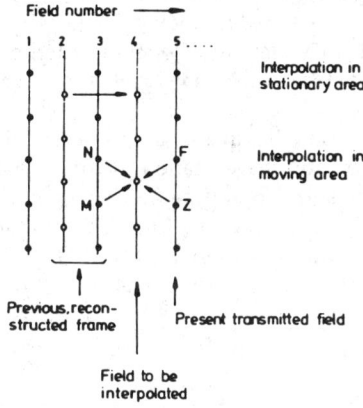

Fig. 36. Position of lines in subsequent fields. The arrows indicate which picture elements are used for interpolation in stationary and moving areas.

by an average of four picture elements Z, F, M, and N. Otherwise it is substituted by the corresponding picture element from the previous reconstructed frame. Compared to linear field interpolation, this nonlinear technique preserves the vertical resolution when combined with coding techniques where no permanent field skipping is applied as, e.g., in conditional replenishment coding.

To avoid blurring in the case of both moderate and rapid movement, the interpolation algorithm must "compensate" the motion of objects. Fig. 37 illustrates that a linear inter-

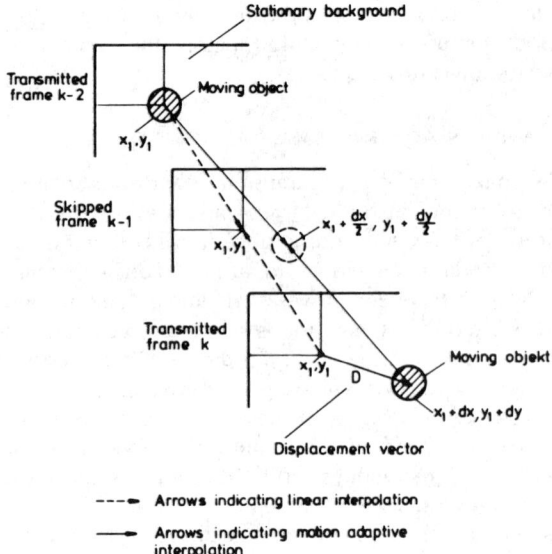

Fig. 37. Illustration of linear and motion-adaptive frame interpolation.

polator reconstructs a picture element with coordinates x_1, y_1 in a skipped frame $k - 1$ from corresponding picture elements x_1, y_1 of the transmitted frames k and $k - 2$. Blurring will be introduced, since picture element amplitudes from a moving object and static background are mixed in the interpolation. For a correct reconstruction of the moving object, its displacement vector $D(dx, dy)$ has to be considered. Thus a picture element at position $x_1 + (dx/2)$, $y_1 + (dy/2)$ in the skipped frame $k - 1$ has to be interpolated from picture elements x_1, y_1 in frame $k - 2$ and $x_1 + dx, y_1 + dy$ in frame k as indicated by arrows. Of course, if there are several moving objects with different displacements in a television scene, the interpolation has to be locally adapted to the individual displacements of the objects.

For this reason, the investigations on motion-adaptive frame interpolation have started with special television scenes which show only one uniformly moving object. Lippmann [103], [104] proposed in 1980 a motion-adaptive frame interpolation scheme for reducing the bit rate of an airborn television camera which scans the ground as demonstrated in Fig. 38. Let A_0, B_0 be two locations on the

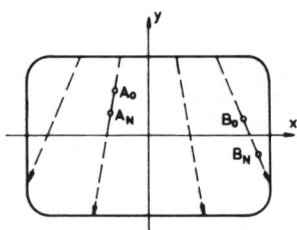

Fig. 38. Geometric imaging configurations of an oblique air-to-ground view. The dashed lines represent the motion paths of fixed ground locations in the television image sequence due to a moving camera.

ground in frame k_0 and A_N, B_N be the corresponding measured, displaced locations in frame k_N. Then all locations C_n in the skipped frames $k_1, \cdots, k_{N-1}$ of Fig. 39 can be calculated from the two measured displacement vectors by use of a simple linear motion model which approximates

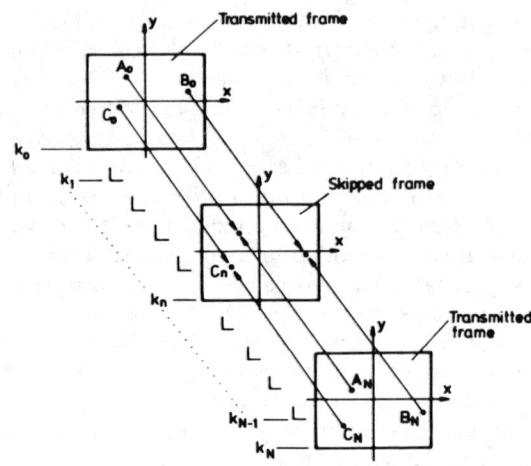

Fig. 39. Interpolation of skipped frames $k_1, \ldots, k_{N-1}$ for a television scene with uniformly moving background according to Lippmann [104].

the motion paths in the image plane by linear trajectories according to

$$y_{C0} = h_1 y_{Cn} + h_2$$
$$x_{C0} = g_1 x_{Cn} + g_2$$

and

$$y_{CN} = h_3 y_{Cn} + h_4$$
$$x_{CN} = g_3 x_{Cn} + g_4 \qquad (56)$$

where the coefficients $g_1, \cdots, g_4$ and $h_1, \cdots, h_4$ are defined by the measured locations A_0, A_N and B_0, B_N. Once the locations C_0 and C_N with amplitudes S_{C0} and S_{CN} have been determined, an amplitude S_{Cn} at location C_n in frame n is interpolated as

$$S_{Cn} = \frac{1}{N}[(N - n)S_{C0} + nS_{CN}]. \qquad (57)$$

This interpolation scheme requires that two point correspondences are measured in two transmitted frames k_0 and k_N. For a more accurate interpolation, the motion has to be described by a model that also considers the rotational components of motion. Assuming that the ground is flat, then five point correspondences have to be measured [4].

Using the explained interpolation scheme for these special aerial television scenes, Lippmann [104] reduces the frame rate at the coder from 25 frames per second to 1 frame per second achieving a bit rate reduction factor of 25.

First research results about motion-adaptive frame interpolation of television signals considering several randomly moving objects have been presented at the 1981 Picture Coding Symposium by Netravali and Robbins [105] and Bergmann [106]. Bergmann points out three major problems which are associated with motion-adaptive frame interpolation and which have to be solved.

i) Moving objects, areas decovered in the present frame and areas going to be covered in the next frame have to be detected and segmented.

ii) Displacement estimation algorithms must be improved to give more accurate estimates for single picture elements. Otherwise, the interpolation will introduce errors, e.g., at the boundaries of moving objects.

iii) An appropriate interpolation filter and algorithm for adapting the coefficients has to be developed.

In 1982 Lenz and Gerhard [107] presented some proposals

for solving the segmentation problem. Sabri, Cuffing, and Prasada reported experiments with 4:1 motion-adaptive field interpolation in noise-free conditions and in low bit-rate coding environment [108], [111]. The first more detailed description of a complete motion-adaptive frame interpolator was published by Bergmann [109] in 1984.

Fig. 40 shows a block diagram of the motion-adaptive frame interpolator. Bergmann uses a displacement estimator

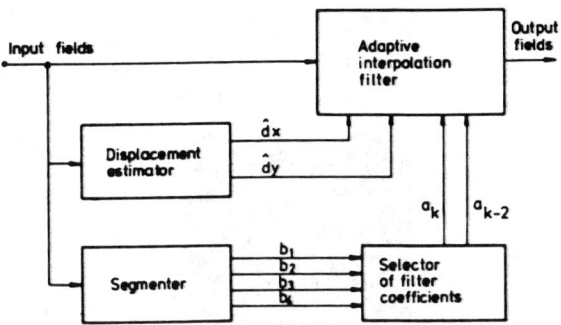

Fig. 40. Block diagram of a motion-adaptive frame or field interpolator.

based on the algorithm (15) as described in Section II. The segmenter according to Fig. 41 indicates for the transmitted field k:

b_1: moving areas
b_2: areas decovered in the present field
b_3: areas going to be covered in the next field
b_4: stationary background.

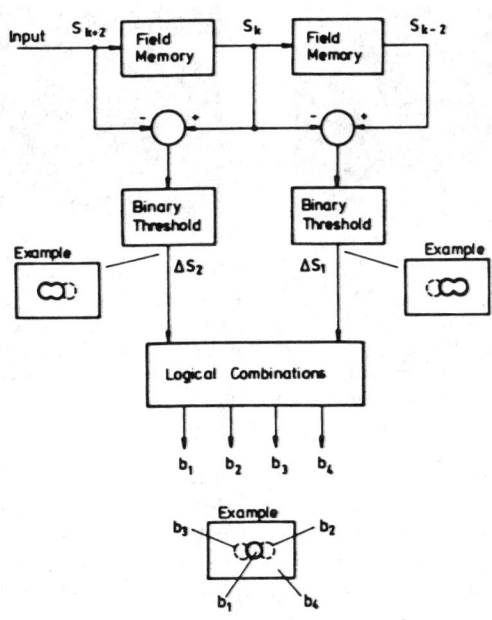

Fig. 41. Block diagram of the segmenter. The examples show the segmentation of a ball moving from right to left.

The segmentation is required for a correct reconstruction of skipped fields. Fig. 42 illustrates how the individual segments have to be reconstructed using image information from field k and $k - 2$, respectively. It also explains that the segments b_2, b_3 cannot be interpolated but must be

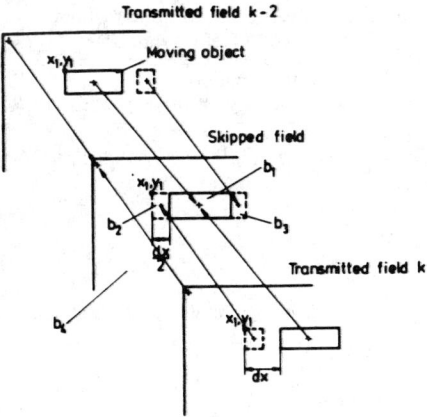

Fig. 42. Ideal segmentation and interpolation of a skipped field. The moving object is assumed to have a horizontal displacement of dx between the transmitted fields k and $k - 2$. Arrows indicate the image information used to reconstruct the skipped field.

extrapolated, since the required image information is available only in the subsequent field for b_2 and in the preceding field for b_3. The stationary background b_4 can be interpolated linearly. To interpolate the moving object b_1, a uniform displacement between field $k - 2$ and field k is assumed.

Unfortunately, the described segmenter only gives a segmentation for transmitted fields. Therefore, Bergmann [109] extrapolates from a segmentation in field k to that in the skipped field. For simplification he assumes that at a picture element position x, y in a skipped field $k - 1$ the same displacement vector is true, as measured for the picture element x, y in field k. Only the size of the displacement vector is divided by a factor of two.

Depending on the segmenter information $b_1, \cdots, b_4$, for a FIR interpolation filter, coefficients a_k, a_{k-2} are selected according to Table 5. Table 5 also shows the resulting interpolation algorithms for the amplitude $s_{k-1}(x, y)$ of the picture element at position x, y. These algorithms correspond to the arrows in Fig. 42.

In case of nonintegral displacements the amplitudes $s_k[x + (dx/2), y + (dy/2)]$ and $s_{k-2}[x - (dx/2), y - (dy/2)]$ have to be evaluated by bilinear interpolation using the four adjacent picture elements according to (12) in Section II. Therefore, the block diagram of the motion-adaptive interpolation filter includes two bilinear spatial interpolators as shown in Fig. 43.

If only every Nth field is transmitted, where $N = 2, 3, 4, \cdots$, then for interpolating the nth field, where $n = 1, 2, 3, \cdots, N - 1$, the filter coefficients have to be chosen according to

$$a_{k-2} = \frac{N - n}{N} \quad a_k = \frac{n}{N} \quad (58)$$

for areas b_1 and b_4.

In order to investigate the performance of the proposed motion-adaptive interpolation technique, simulation with the television test sequence "Ellen" has been carried out. The maximum displacement in this sequence is 16.5 pels per frame. No degradations have been observed in the case that every second field has been skipped ($N = 2$). When skipping two fields ($N = 3$) interpolation errors become visible due to erroneous displacement estimates.

Table 5 Selection of Filter Coefficients and Interpolation Output in Case that Every Second Field is Interpolated ($N = 2$)

Information from Segmenter	Coefficients	Interpolator Output $s_{k-1}(x, y)$
b_1	$a_k = a_{k-2} = \frac{1}{2}$	$\frac{1}{2} \cdot s_{k-2}\left(x - \frac{dx}{2}, y - \frac{dy}{2}\right) + \frac{1}{2} \cdot s_k\left(x + \frac{dx}{2}, y + \frac{dy}{2}\right)$
b_2	$a_k = 1 \quad a_{k-2} = 0$	$1 \cdot s_k(x, y)$
b_3	$a_k = 0 \quad a_{k-2} = 1$	$1 \cdot s_{k-2}(x, y)$
b_4	$a_k = a_{k-2} = \frac{1}{2}$	$\frac{1}{2} \cdot s_{k-2}(x, y) + \frac{1}{2} \cdot s_k(x, y)$

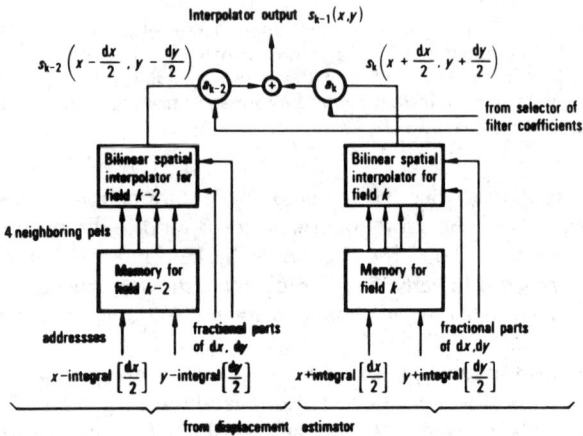

Fig. 43. Block diagram of the motion-adaptive interpolation filter.

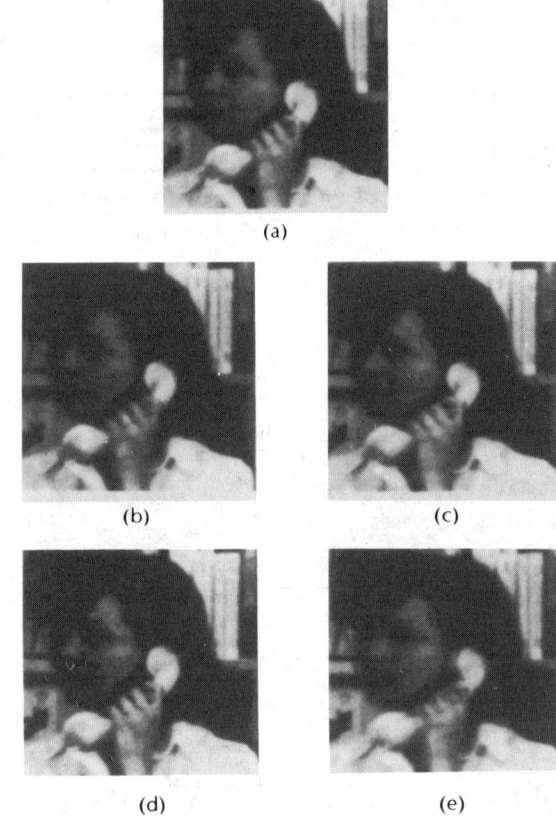

Fig. 44. Interpolated sequence of fields from the test sequence "Ellen." Every third field is transmitted ($N = 3$). (a) Transmitted field k_0. (b), (c) Motion adaptively interpolated fields k_1 and k_2. (d) Transmitted field $k_{N=3}$. (e) Field, reconstructed by linear interpolation.

The photos in Fig. 44 demonstrate the picture quality of the transmitted and motion adaptively interpolated fields in comparison to a field which is reconstructed by pure linear interpolation.

In a recent publication by Furukawa, Koga, and Iinuma [110] the problem of erroneous displacement estimates in motion-adaptive interpolation is discussed. The authors propose a preprocessing of the measured vectors based on a rigid moving object assumption to provide more reliable displacement vectors for the interpolation.

VI. Discussion and Conclusion

The main advances in digital coding of video signals during the last five years are outlined including the areas of predictive coding, transform coding, and motion-adaptive frame interpolation.

In a special section on displacement estimation, the fundamentals and the relationship of two important classes of displacement estimation, known as recursive and block-matching algorithms, are elaborated. It is shown that both classes are iterative estimation techniques which only differ in the search procedure. In the first class, the search procedure is based on measured derivatives of the optimization criterion, in the second the search procedure is based on matching results which are nothing else but checks of the local optimization criterion. Also, it is shown that the algorithms within the first class are closely related although there are essential differences in the performance. In the beginning, only displacements of up to 2 pels per frame could be estimated with an acceptable accuracy in one or two steps of iteration. Now, block-matching techniques allow to measure displacements of up to 6 pels per frame within three steps of iteration while those techniques which are based on derivatives require one to two steps of iteration to reach an accuracy of about ± 0.5 pel per frame.

In the future, especially for application in motion-adaptive frame interpolation, we will need displacement estimation techniques with a measuring range of up to 20 pels per frame. Furthermore, methods will have to be developed which will assure a correct convergence of the estimation algorithms.

Predictive coding is discussed with a view to two areas of application. For coding of broadcast television signals there is the demand that digital encoding should not degrade the picture quality. For such a quality requirement, quantizer design methods based on subjectively measured visibility thresholds are described. Definition and application of activity and masking functions are the main part of this section. More work is needed in order for the activity functions to be better matched to the visual system and for the quantizer control to consider the dynamic feedback of DPCM systems.

Better coder performance in terms of picture quality as a function of bit rate can be reached by adaptive prediction. For high detailed picture areas the use of contour prediction is proposed. Up to now there is a big distinction between adaptive prediction for intraframe and interframe coding because of the hardware expense for the frame store.

Due to the stringent requirements of bit rate reduction for video conferencing, sophisticated adaptive intra/interframe prediction schemes can be applied. Furthermore, in video conferencing, we are allowed to restrict the variety of television scenes to be considered for coding to scenes with slow and moderate movement. Certain distortions may be introduced in coding of rapid movement. A few examples of adaptive prediction schemes are outlined within the paper. Also, two basic approaches of motion-compensated prediction are explained. Better models for describing a scene by an extended set of motion parameters and the development of more robust and accurate motion adaptive prediction schemes are required to improve coder performance.

Transform coding denotes a procedure in which the PCM-coded video signal is subjected prior to transmission to an invertible transform with subsequent quantizing and coding. So far the aim of the transform algorithm has been to convert statistically dependent picture elements into independent coefficients.

In recent years, investigations have focussed on an improvement of adaptive transform coding. Several techniques are discussed where quantizing and coding is controlled by the local picture content and adapted to the perception of the human eye. In addition, a new transform is introduced which does not reduce the statistical redundancy but exploits masking effects of the eye. Three bit per picture element seems to be a lower bound which is attainable in coding of broadcast television signals. In video conferencing the data rate can be reduced to about 0.5 bit per picture element because of the special picture content, e.g., head and shoulder scenes.

It is expected that the combination of transform coding with other pre- and postprocessing methods as motion-compensated three-dimensional transformation or motion-adaptive interpolation will decrease the data rate furthermore in the future. Compared to motion-compensated prediction, motion-adaptive frame interpolation is still in a very early stage. The presented interpolation techniques indicate that at least for video-conferencing scenes a reduction of the field rate by a factor of 2 can be achieved without introducing image degradation. Skipping more than every second field leads to an increase of the displacements and requires more reliable displacement estimation algorithms as well as a development of refined techniques for segmenting the frame to be interpolated. In spite of these problems to be solved, motion-adaptive frame interpolation appears very promising.

REFERENCES

[1] W. K. Pratt, *Image Transmission Techniques*. New York: Academic Press, 1979.

[2] A. N. Netravali and J. O. Limb, "Picture coding: A review," *Proc. IEEE*, vol. 68, pp. 366–406, Mar. 1980.

[3] A. K. Jain, "Image data compression: A review," *Proc. IEEE*, vol. 69, pp. 349–384, Mar. 1981.

[4] T. S. Huang and R. Y. Tsai, "Image sequence analysis: Motion Estimation," in *Image Sequence Analysis*. Berlin, Germany: Springer-Verlag, 1981, pp. 1–18.

[5] J. W. Roach and J. K. Aggarwal, "Determining the movement of objects from a sequence of images," *IEEE Trans. Pattern Anal. Machine Intell.*, vol. PAMI-2, no. 6, pp. 554–562, 1980.

[6] R. Y. Tsai and T. S. Huang, "Estimating three-dimensional motion parameters of a rigid planar patch," *IEEE Trans. Acoust., Speech, Signal Process.*, vol. ASSP-29, no. 6, pp. 1147–1152, Dec. 1981.

[7] R. J. Schalkoff and E. S McVey, "A model and tracking algorithm for a class of video targets," *IEEE Trans. Pattern Anal. Machine Intell.*, vol. PAMI-4, no. 1, pp. 2–10, Jan. 1982.

[8] H. H. Nagel, "Overview on image sequence analysis," in *Image Sequence Processing and Dynamic Scene Analysis*, T. S. Huang, Ed., Berlin, Germany: Springer-Verlag, 1983, pp. 2–39.

[9] J. O. Limb and J. A. Murphy, "Measuring the speed of moving objects from television signals," *IEEE Trans. Commun.*, vol. COM-23, no. 4, pp. 474–478, Apr. 1975.

[10] C. Cafforio and F. Rocca, "Methods for measuring small displacements of television images," *IEEE Trans. Inform. Theory*, vol. IT-22, no. 5, pp. 573–579, Sept. 1976.

[11] A. N. Netravali and J. D. Robbins, "Motion compensated television coding—Part I," *Bell Syst. Tech. J.*, vol. 58, pp. 631–670, Mar. 1979.

[12] J. D. Robbins and A. N. Netravali, "Recursive motion compensation: A review," in *Image Sequence Processing and Dynamic Scene Analysis*, T. S. Huang, Ed. Berlin, Germany: Springer-Verlag, 1983, pp. 76–103.

[13] H. C. Bergmann, "Displacement estimation based on the correlation of image segments," in *IEEE Proc. Int. Conf. on Electronic Image Processing* (York; England), pp. 215–219, July 1982.

[14] C. Cafforio and F. Rocca, "The differential method for image motion estimation," in *Image Sequence Processing and Dynamic Scene Analysis*, T. S. Huang, Ed. Berlin, Germany: Springer-Verlag, 1983, pp. 104–124.

[15] H. C. Bergmann, "Ein schnell konvergierendes Displacement-Schätzverfahren für die Interpolation von Fernsehbildsequenzen," Ph.D. dissertation, Tech. Univ. of Hannover, Hannover, Germany, Feb. 1984.

[16] H. Burkhard and H. Moll, "A modified Newton-Raphson search for the model-adaptive identification of delays," in *Identification and System Parameter Identification*, R. Isermann, Ed. Oxford, England, and New York: Pergamon Press, 1979, pp. 1279–1286.

[17] S. Sabri, "Movement-compensated interframe prediction for NTSC colour TV signals," in *Image Sequence Processing and Dynamic Scene Analysis*, T. S. Huang, Ed. Berlin, Germany: Springer-Verlag, 1983, pp. 156–199.

[18] J. R. Jain and A. K. Jain, "Displacement measurement and its application in interframe image coding," *IEEE Trans. Commun.*, vol. COM-29, pp. 1799–1806, Dec. 1981.

[19] T. Koga, K. Iinuma, A. Hirano, Y. Iijima, and T. Ishiguro, "Motion-compensated interframe coding for video conferencing," in *NTC 81, Proc.*, pp. G5.3.1–G5.3.5 (New Orleans, LA, Dec. 1981).

[20] Y. Ninomiya and Y. Ohtsuka, "A motion-compensated interframe coding scheme for television pictures," *IEEE Trans. Commun.*, vol. COM-30, pp. 201–211, Jan. 1982.

[21] R. Srinivasan and K. R. Rao, "Predictive coding based on efficient motion estimation," in *ICC 1984, Proc.*, pp. 521–526, May 1984.

[22] C. M. Lin and S. C. Kwatra, "Motion compensated interframe color image coding," in *ICC 1984, Proc.*, pp. 516–520, May 1984.

[23] K. Matsuda, T. Tsuda, T. Ito, and S. Make, "A new motion compensation coding scheme for video conference," in *ICC*

1984, Proc., pp. 234–237, May 1984.
[24] S. Beyer, "Displacementschätzverfahren für Fernsehbildsignale mit minimaler Schätzfehlervarianz," pending dissertation at the Tech. Univ. of Hannover, Hannover, Germany.
[25] F. May and W. Wolf, "Picture coding with motion analysis for low bit rate transmission," in ICC 82, Proc., pp. 2G.7.1–2G.7.5, June 1982.
[26] F. Kretz, "Edges in visual scenes and sequences: Applications to filtering, sampling and adaptive DPCM coding," in Image Sequence Processing and Dynamic Scene Analysis, T. S. Huang, Ed., Berlin, Germany: Springer-Verlag, 1983, pp. 125–155.
[27] C. Labit and A. Benveniste, "Motion estimation in a sequence of television pictures," in Image Sequence Processing and Dynamic Scene Analysis, T. S. Huang, Ed. Berlin, Germany: Springer-Verlag, 1983, pp. 292–306.
[28] J. Max, "Quantizing for minimum distortion," IEEE Trans. Inform. Theory, vol. IT-6, pp. 7–12, Mar. 1960.
[29] P. Pirsch and L. Stenger, "Statistical analysis and coding of color video signals," Acta Electronica, vol. 19, no. 4, pp. 277–287, 1976.
[30] J. O. Limb, "Source-receiver encoding of television signals," Proc. IEEE, vol. 55, pp. 364–379, Mar. 1967.
[31] J. C. Candy and R. H. Bosworth, "Methods for designing differential quantizers based on subjective evaluations of edge busyness," Bell Syst. Tech. J., vol. 51, pp. 1495–1516, Sept. 1972.
[32] A. N. Netravali, "On quantizers for DPCM coding of picture signals," IEEE Trans. Inform. Theory, vol. IT-23, no. 3, pp. 360–370, May 1977.
[33] J. O. Limb and C. B. Rubinstein, "On the design of quantizers for DPCM coders: A functional relationship between visibility, probability, and masking," IEEE Trans. Commun., vol. COM-26, pp. 573–578, May 1978.
[34] F. Kretz et al., "Optimization of DPCM video coding scheme using subjective quality criterions," presented at the Conf. on Digital Processing of Signals in Communications, Loughborough, (also in Proc. IERE Conf., no. 37), Sept. 1977.
[35] W. D. Erdmann, "Ein an die Wahrnehmbarkeitseigenschaften des menschlichen Auges angepaßter, gesteuerter Quantisierer für Bildsignale," Ph.D. dissertation, Tech. Univ. of Hannover, Hannover, Germany, 1978.
[36] P. Pirsch, "Design of DPCM quantizers for video signals using subjective tests," IEEE Trans. Commun., vol. COM-29, no. 7, pp. 990–1000, July 1981.
[37] D. K. Sharma, "Design of absolutely optimal quantizers for a wide class of distortion measures," IEEE Trans. Inform. Theory, vol. IT-24, pp. 693–702, Nov. 1978.
[38] P. Pirsch, "A new predictor design for DPCM coding of TV signals," in ICC Conf. Rec., pp. 31.2.1–31.2.5, (Seattle, WA), 1980.
[39] F. Lukas and F. Kretz, "DPCM quantization of color television signals," IEEE Trans. Commun., vol. COM-31, no. 7, pp. 927–932, July 1983.
[40] R. Schäfer, "DPCM coding of the chrominance signals for the transmission of color TV signals at 24 Mbit/s," to appear in Signal Processing.
[41] D. Westerkamp, "The influence of motion on the masking of quantization errors in 3-dimensional DPCM coding," Signal Processing, vol. 7, no. 3, pp. 283–292, Dec. 1984.
[42] A. N. Netravali and B. Prasada, "Adaptive quantization of picture signals using spatial masking," Proc. IEEE, vol. 65, pp. 536–548, Apr. 1977.
[43] H. G. Musmann, "Predictive image coding," in Image Transmission Techniques, W. K. Pratt, Ed. New York: Academic Press, 1979.
[44] R. Schäfer, "Design of adaptive and nonadaptive quantizers using subjective criteria," Signal Processing, vol. 5, no. 4, pp. 333–345, July 1983.
[45] D. Anastassiou et al., "Series/1 based video conferencing system," IBM Syst. J., vol. 22, nos. 1, 2, pp. 97–110, 1983.
[46] R. E. Graham, "Predictive quantizing of television signals," in IRE WESCON Conv. Rec., vol. 2, pt. 4, pp. 147–157, 1958.
[47] W. Zschunke, "DPCM picture coding with adaptive prediction," IEEE Trans. Commun., vol COM-25, no. 11, pp. 1295–1302, Nov. 1977.
[48] C. Zhang, "Ein neuer adaptiver Prädiktor für die DPCM-Codierung von Fernsehsignalen," Frequenz, vol. 36, pp. 161–184, June 1982.
[49] P. Pirsch, "Adaptive intra-interframe DPCM coder," Bell Syst. Tech. J., vol. 61, no. 5, pp. 747–764, May 1982.
[50] D. Westerkamp, "Adaptive intra-interframe DPCM coding for transmission of TV signals with 34 Mbit/s," in Conf. Rec. Int. Zurich Seminar on Digital Communications, Mar. 1984.
[51] H. J. Grallert and A. Starck, "Component encoding of color television signals for transmission in 34, 70 and 140 Mbit/s channels," in Conf. Rec. Int. Zurich Seminar on Digital Communications, Mar. 1984.
[52] T. Koga et al., "A 1.5 Mb/s interframe codec with motion compensation," in ICC Conf. Rec., pp. 1161–1165, June 1983.
[53] J. A. Stuller et al., "Interframe television coding using gain and displacement compensation," Bell Syst. Tech. J., vol. 59, no. 7, pp. 1227–1240, Sept. 1980.
[54] H. Yamamoto, Y. Hatori, and H. Murakami, "30 Mbit/s codec for NTSC color TV signal using an interfield-intrafield adaptive prediction," IEEE Trans. Commun., vol. COM-29, no. 12, pp. 1859–1867, Dec. 1981.
[55] T. Ishiguro and K. Iinuma, "Television bandwidth compression transmission by motion compensated interframe coding," IEEE Commun. Mag., pp. 24–30, Nov. 1982.
[56] F. May, "Codierung von Bildfolgen mit objektbezogener Bewegungskompensation und Signifikanzklassifikation," Ph.D. dissertation, University of Karlsruhe, Karlsruhe, Germany, Feb. 1984.
[57] K. A. Prabhu and A. N. Netravali, "Motion compensated component color coding," IEEE Trans. Commun., vol. COM-30, no. 12, pp. 2519–2527, Dec. 1982.
[58] K. A. Prabhu and A. N. Netravali, "Motion compensated composite color coding," IEEE Trans. Commun., vol. COM-31, no. 2, pp. 216–223, Feb. 1983.
[59] R. Srinivasan and K. R. Rao, "Predictive coding based on efficient motion estimation," in ICC'84 Conf. Rec., pp. 521–526, May 1984.
[60] K. Iinuma et al., "A 1.5 Mb/s full motion videoconference system," in Conf. Rec. 6th Int. Conf. on Digital Satellite Communications (Phoenix, AZ, Sept. 1983).
[61] M. Schlichte, "Block-overlap transform coding of image signals," Siemens Forsch.-u. Entwickl.-Ber., vol. 13, no. 3, 1984.
[62] E. Marschall, M. Schlichte, W. Tengler, and E. Hundt, "Blockübergreifende Transformationscodierung: Theorie und numerische Simulation an Hand von Bildsignalen," in NTG-Fachberichte 84, ISBN 3-8007-1302-0, pp. 249–257.
[63] D. E. Pearson and M. W. Whybray, "Transformcoding with interleaving blocks," in Proc. Conf. on Transform Techniques in Image Processing (London, England), pp. 511–513, May 1983.
[64] T. C. Chen and J. P. de Figueiredo, "An image coding scheme based on spatial domain considerations," IEEE Trans. Pattern Anal. Machine Intell., vol. PAMI-5, pp. 332–337, May 1983.
[65] H. C. Reeve and J. S. Lim, "Reduction of blocking effect in image coding," in Proc. ICASSP 83 (Boston, MA), pp. 1212–1215.
[66] W. Mauersberger, "Adaptive Transformationskodierung von digitalisierten Bildvorlagen," Ph.D. dissertation, Tech. Univ. of Aachen, Aachen, Germany, 1980.
[67] H. G. Hildebrandt, "Untersuchungen zur Optimierung einer adaptiven Transformationscodierung von Farbfernsehsignalen in Echtzeit bei einer Bitflußrate von 34 Mbit/s," Ph.D. dissertation, Univ. of Wuppertal, Wuppertal, Germany, 1983.
[68] K. N. Ngan, "Adaptive transform coding of video signals," Proc. Inst. Elec. Eng., vol. 129, pp. 28–40, Feb. 1982.
[69] W. C. Wong and R. Steele, "Adaptive discrete cosine transformation of pictures using an energy distribution logarithmic model," Radio and Electron. Eng. (GB), vol. 51, pp. 571–578, Nov.–Dec. 1981.
[70] ———, "Adaptive coding of discrete cosine transform video telephone pictures," presented at PCS Ipswich, England, 1979, paper 12.3.
[71] M. Götze and G. Ocylok, "An adaptive interframe transform coding system for images, in Proc. IEEE ICASSP 82, pp. 448–451.
[72] L. Stenger, Th. Kremes, and R. Govaerts, "Optimization of coding algorithms by computer simulation," in Proc. IEEE Globecom 82 (Miami, FL), pp. 305–309, Dec. 1982.
[73] M. Guglielmo, R. Marion, and A. Sciarappa, "Subjective

quality evaluation of different intraframe adaptive transform coding schemes," *CSELT Rapporti Tecnici*, vol. X, pp. 177–181, June 1982.
[74] A. G. Tescher, "Adaptive transform coding of color images at low rate," in *Proc. IEEE NTC 80* (Houston, TX), pp. 36.3/1–4, Dec. 1980.
[75] M. Götze, "Kombinierte Quellen- und Kanalcodierung in adaptiven Transformationscodierungen," in *NTG-Fachberichte 84*, ISBN 3-8007-1302-0, pp. 259–275.
[76] J. W. Modestino, D. G. Daut, and A. L. Vickers, "Combined source-channel coding of images using the block cosine transform," *IEEE Trans. Commun.*, vol. COM-29, pp. 1261–1274, Sept. 1981.
[77] R. Zelinski, "An adaptive transform coding system based on cepstral control and entropy coding," *Frequenz*, vol. 36, pp. 193–198, 1982.
[78] M. Götze, "Combined source channel-coding in adaptive transform coding systems for images," in *Proc. ICC 1984* (Amsterdam, The Netherlands).
[79] H. Lohscheller, "Video-Einzelbildübertragung über Schmalbandkanäle mit zeitlich zunehmender Auflösung," *NTG-Fachberichte*, vol. 74, pp. 335–342, 1980.
[80] ____, "Adaptive transform coding for still picture communication," in *Proc. IEEE Zurich Sem. on Digital Communication, 1984*, pp. 25–31, Mar. 1984.
[81] J. A. Robinson and F. P. Coakley, "Picture coding for photovideotex," *Comput. Commun.*, vol. 6, pp. 3–13, Feb. 1983.
[82] F. Coakley and E. Bisheruwa, "Transform coding techniques for photovideotex," in *Proc. Colloquium on Transform Techniques in Image Processing*, pp. 9/1–9/7 (London, England, May 1983).
[83] "Picture prestel," *Funkschau*, vol. 26, p. 28, 1982.
[84] K. Takikawa, "Fast progressive reconstruction of a transformed image," *IEEE Trans. Informat. Theory*, vol. IT-30, no. 1, pp. 111–117, 1984.
[85] K. N. Ngan, "Image display techniques using cosine transform, *IEEE Trans. Acoust. Speech, Signal Process.*, vol. ASSP-32, no. 1, pp. 173–177, 1984.
[86] A. Habibi, "An adaptive strategy for hybrid image coding," *IEEE Trans. Commun.*, vol COM-29, pp. 1736–1740, Dec. 1981.
[87] F. A. Kamangar and K. R. Rao, "Interfield hybrid coding of component color television signals," *IEEE Trans. Commun.*, vol. COM-29, pp. 1740–1753, Dec. 1981.
[88] W. A. Pearlman and P. Jakatdar, "Hybrid DFT/DPCM interframe image," in *Proc. ICASSP'81* (Atlanta, GA), pp. 1121–1124, Mar. 1981.
[89] H.-J. Grallert, "Application of orthonormalized m-sequences for data reduced and error protected transmission of pictures," in *Proc. IEEE Int. Symp. on Electromagnetic Compatibility, 1980* (Baltimore, MD), pp. 282–287.
[90] ____, "Source encoding and error protected transmission of pictures with help of orthonormalized m-sequences," in *Proc. 12th Int. Television Symp.* (Montreux, Switzerland, 1981), pp. 441–454.
[91] W. G. Keesen, U. Reimann, and H.-J. Grallert, "Codierung von Farbfernsehsignalen mittels modifizierter M-Transformation für die Übertragung über 34-Mbit/s-Kanäle," *Frequenz*, vol. 38, no. 10, pp. 238–243, Oct. 1984.
[92] W. Keesen, U. Reimann, and H.-J. Grallert, "Component encoding using a modified M-transform for transmission over 34-Mbit/s-channels," presented at PCS 84, Rennes, France, July 1984.
[93] C. Ekambaram and S. C. Kwatra, "A new architecture for adaptive transform compression of NTSC composite video signals," in *Proc. IEEE NTC 81* (New Orleans, LA), pp. C9.6/1–5, Dec. 1981.
[94] S. C. Kwatra and H. Fatmi, "NTSC composite video at 1.6 bits/pel," in *Proc. IEEE ICC 83* (Boston, MA), pp. 458–462, June 1983.
[95] A. Playsongsang and K. R. Rao, "DCT/DPCM processing of NTSC composite video signal," *IEEE Trans. Commun.*, vol. COM-30, pp. 541–549, Mar. 1982.
[96] D. N. Hein, "Video data compression using motion compensation," in *MIDCON 82 Conf. Rec.*, pp. 3/4,1–9 (Dallas, TX, Nov. 1982).
[97] S. W. Golomb, *Digital Communications*. Englewood Cliffs, NJ: Prentice-Hall, 1974.
[98] CCIR, Rep. 405-4, in *Recommendations and Reports of the CCIR*. Geneva, Switzerland: CCIR, 1982.
[99] B. G. Haskell and R. L. Schmidt, "A low bit-rate interframe coder for videotelephone," *Bell Syst. Techn. J.*, vol. 54, no. 8, pp. 1475–1495, Oct. 1975.
[100] J. Klie, "Codierung von Fernsehsignalen für niedrige Übertragungsbitraten," Ph.D. dissertation, Tech. Univ. of Hannover, Hannover, Germany, 1978.
[101] H. C. Bergmann, "Übertragung von Bewegtbildern mit niedrigen Übertragungsbitraten," *NTG-Fachberichte*, vol. 74, pp. 370–378, 1980.
[102] B. G. Haskell, P. L. Gordon, R. L. Schmidt, and J. V. Scattaglia, "Interframe coding of 525-line monochrome television at 1.5 Mbit/s," *IEEE Trans. Commun.*, vol. COM-25, no. 11, pp. 1339–1348, Nov. 1977.
[103] R. Lippmann, "Video transmission of aerial scenes at reduced frame rates using motion compensation," presented at the ICC, Seattle, WA, June 1980.
[104] ____, "Continuous movement regeneration in low-frame-rate aerial images," in *Proc. IEEE Int. Conf. on Electronic Image Processing*, Conf. Publ. No. 214, pp. 194–198, July 1982.
[105] A. N. Netravali and J. D. Robbins, "Motion-adaptive interpolation of television frames," presented at the Picture Coding Symp., Montreal, Canada, 1981.
[106] H. C. Bergmann, "Motion-adaptive interpolation of eliminated TV-fields," presented at the Picture Coding Symp., Montreal, Canada, 1981.
[107] R. Lenz and A. Gerhard, "Image sequence coding using scene analysis and spatio-temporal interpolation," in *Image Sequence Processing and Dynamic Scene Analysis*, T. S. Huang, Ed. Berlin, Germany: Springer-Verlag, 1983, pp. 264–274.
[108] S. Sabri, K. Cuffing, and B. Prasada, "Coding of video signals at 50 kbit/s using motion compensation techniques," in *Proc. IEEE Military Communications Conf.*, pp. 809–816, Nov. 1983.
[109] H. C. Bergmann, "Motion adaptive frame interpolation," in *Proc. Int. Zurich Seminar on Digital Communications*, pp. D2.1–D2.5, Mar. 1984.
[110] A. Furukawa, T. Koga, and K. Iinuma, "Motion-adaptive interpolation for videoconference pictures," in *Proc. ICC 1984*, vol. 2, pp. 707–710, May 1984.
[111] B. Prasada, E. Gulko, and S. Sabri, "Evaluation of spatio-temporal interpolation techniques," presented at the Picture Coding Symp., Rennes, France, 1984.

Image Sequence Compression Using a Pel-Recursive Motion-Compensated Technique

ROBERT J. MOORHEAD II, MEMBER, IEEE, SARAH A. RAJALA, SENIOR MEMBER, IEEE, AND LAWRENCE W. COOK, MEMBER, IEEE

Abstract—This paper presents and analyzes a pel-recursive, motion-compensated, image sequence compression algorithm [1]. The analysis retains all the terms of the Taylor's series expansion and yields a set of equations for which the convergence criteria and the convergence rate of the motion estimate are more easily seen. The existing motion prediction schemes are also reviewed and a new motion prediction scheme is presented which is shown to be superior to the existing schemes.

Simulations run on actual image sequences to verify the analytical results indicate that implementing the analytical model as opposed to the generally used heuristic technique does yield a decrease in the information rate and the computational requirements. Simulation results also are included which use the "projection-along-the-motion-trajectory" or PAMT prediction scheme. Third, zeroth-order entropy encoding is shown to reduce the bit rate on the order of 12 percent, and to reduce the mean square error in the reconstructed images on the order of 60 percent when compared to first-order entropy encoding. Fourth, field-to-field motion prediction is compared to frame-to-frame motion prediction.

I. INTRODUCTION

WHEN transmitting or storing image sequences, one would like to send or store the minimum amount of information necessary to reconstruct the sequence to a given level of picture quality. Linear predictive coding has been shown to be very useful in this endeavor [2]. Originally, intensity values were predicted directly from previous intensity values using fixed delays. Later work [1], [3], [4] indicated that a greater compression ratio (with the same picture quality) could be obtained by predicting from displaced locations in the previous frame (or field). The implication is that on the average a better prediction of the intensity values is obtained by using a motion-compensated technique than by using a spatially invariant interframe prediction scheme. Both recursive [1], [3], [4] and nonrecursive [5]–[7] motion estimation techniques exist. This paper will be concerned with one of the most common recursive techniques [1]. Extensive reviews and the advantage of the various techniques can be found in [6], [8], [9].

Since motion-compensated interframe coding was introduced in the 1970's, relatively little analytical work has been done to prove convergence of the motion estimate or to develop rates of convergence. As a result, many of the proposed algorithms and their real-time implementations are ad hoc. By analyzing the convergence requirements and the convergence rates of the motion-compensation technique, a more rigorous (and less computationally intensive) approach is developed and simulated herein.

In Section II the basic pel-recursive gradient technique is reviewed to establish the notation. In Section III the convergence analysis is performed. In Section IV the existing motion prediction schemes are summarized. In Section V a new motion prediction scheme, projection-along-the-motion-trajectory (PAMT), is presented. This new scheme has four advantages over the existing schemes and requires only a minimal increase in computation over the temporal prediction scheme. In particular, this new prediction scheme has been shown to have the potential for much greater information compression than any previously presented scheme. In Section VI simulation results are presented. The first group of results shows that implementing the analytical model, as opposed to the generally used heuristic technique, yields a small, but significant, decrease in the information rate and the computational requirements. The second set of results shows that the PAMT motion prediction scheme offers the potential for increased information compression. Simulation results are also presented which indicate the relative improvements of zeroth-order entropy encoding [10] over first-order entropy encoding and of field-to-field motion estimation over frame-to-frame motion estimation. The results are summarized and a potential circuit diagram is given in Section VII.

II. THE BASIC ALGORITHM

Netravali and Robbins [1] developed a pel-recursive technique for motion-compensated coding. The intensity values within a frame are represented by $I(z, t)$, where z is a two-dimensional spatial vector and t is the frame at time t. If an object moves with purely translational motion, then for some d, where d is the two-dimensional spatial translation displacement vector of the object point

---

Manuscript received September 11, 1986; revised January 29, 1987. This work was supported by the NCSU University/Industry Center of Communications and Signal Processing and the IBM Corporation. This paper was presented in part in a poster session at the Picture Coding Symposium, April 2–4, 1986, Tokyo, Japan.

R. J. Moorhead II was with the Center for Communications and Signal Processing. He is now at the IBM Thomas J. Watson Research Center, Yorktown Heights, NY 10598.

S. A. Rajala is with the Center for Communications and Signal Processing, North Carolina State University, Raleigh, NC 27695.

L. W. Cook was with the Center for Communications and Signal Processing. He is now with Harris Corporation, Melbourne, FL 32902.

IEEE Log Number 8715677.

during the time interval $[t - 1, t]$,
$$I(z, t) = I(z - d, t - 1). \tag{1}$$

Define a function called the displaced frame difference:
$$\text{DFD}(z, \hat{d}^i) = I(z, t) - I(z - \hat{d}^i, t - 1), \tag{2}$$

where $\hat{d}^i$ is an ith estimate of the translation vector. The DFD converges to zero as $\hat{d}^i$ converges to the actual displacement d, of the object point. An iterative equation to find d using the DFD function can be developed using the gradient method [11].

$$\hat{d}^{i+1} = \hat{d}^i - \frac{\epsilon}{2} \nabla_{\hat{d}} [\text{DFD}(z_a, \hat{d})]^2 \big|_{\hat{d} = \hat{d}^i}, \tag{3}$$

where $\nabla_{\hat{d}}$ is the two-dimensional gradient operator with respect to displacement $\hat{d}$, ϵ is the convergence coefficient (a positive scalar), and z_a is the location of the pel under consideration. After algebraic manipulations, the resulting iterative equation for correcting the displacement estimation is [1]

$$\hat{d}^{i+1} = \hat{d}^i - \epsilon \, \text{DFD}(z_a, \hat{d}^i) \, \nabla_z I(z - \hat{d}^i, t - 1) \big|_{z = z_a}. \tag{4}$$

where $\nabla_z I$ is the two-dimensional spatial gradient of the intensity function.

III. Convergence Analysis

Two of the important issues of an iterative algorithm such as the one presented in Section II are to guarantee convergence and to determine the rate of convergence. Almost all previously presented pel-recursive techniques have used only one iteration per pel and assumed convergence over time [1], [3], [12], [13]. This is the approach that is used in this paper, i.e., the displacement vector converges in the mean as the moving area is scanned once for information compression.

Fig. 1 is a one-dimensional example of how the $|\text{DFD}|$ might vary with $\hat{d}^i$, where $\hat{d}^i$ is an estimate of the true one-dimensional displacement d. x_c is the spatial position at which the $|\text{DFD}|$ is minimized, $(x - d)$. If x_b or x_d is the initial spatial location estimate $(x - \hat{d}^0)$, then the displacement estimation equation should converge to d. However, if $(x - \hat{d}^0)$ is at x_a or x_e, problems occur. With an initial spatial location estimation of x_a, the displacement estimate equation would probably converge to the location of the local minimum x_f. With x_e as the initial spatial location estimate, no correction would occur since the spatial gradient at x_e, $(\nabla_x I|_{x_e})$, is zero.

Proof of Convergence of the Displacement Vector Estimate

In this section, it will be proved that the displacement estimation algorithm defined by (4) converges under certain conditions to the true displacement as a moving object is scanned. The proof is similar to one used in [1]. The assumptions are that the motion is purely translational and that the uncovered background is neglected.

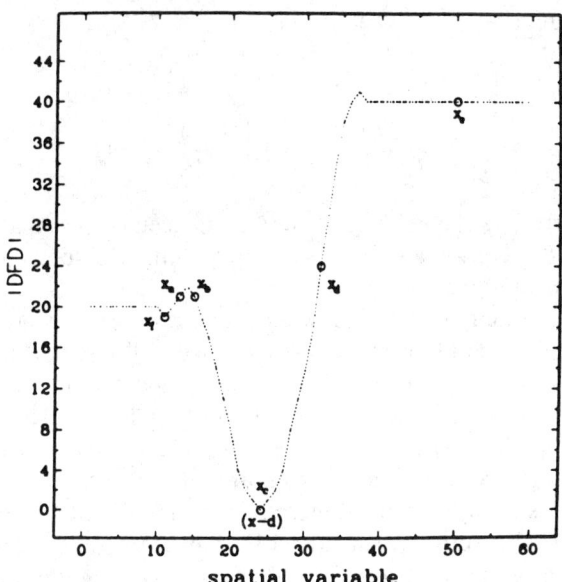

Fig. 1. A sample plot of $|\text{DFD}|$.

Start by substituting (2) into (4) to obtain
$$\hat{d}^{i+1} = \hat{d}^i - \epsilon \{I(z_a, t) - I(z_a - \hat{d}^i, t - 1)\} \nabla_z I(z - \hat{d}^i, t - 1) \big|_{z = z_a}. \tag{5}$$

Substituting from (1) for $I(z_a, t)$,
$$\hat{d}^{i+1} = \hat{d}^i - \epsilon \{I(z_a - d, t - 1) - I(z_a - \hat{d}^i, t - 1)\} \nabla_z I(z - \hat{d}^i, t - 1) \big|_{z = z_a}. \tag{6}$$

The term in braces can be expanded using a Taylor series expansion, i.e.,
$$I(z_a - d, t - 1) - I(z_a - \hat{d}^i, t - 1)$$
$$= (\hat{d}^i - d)^T \nabla_z I(z - \hat{d}^i, t - 1) \big|_{z = z_a}$$
$$+ \tfrac{1}{2} (\hat{d}^i - d)^T \nabla_z^2 I(z - \hat{d}^i, t - 1) (\hat{d}^i - d) \big|_{z = z_a}$$
$$+ O(\hat{d}^i - d)^3, \tag{7}$$

where $\nabla_z^2 I(\ )$ is the 2×2 matrix of second partial derivatives of $I(\ )$ and $O(\hat{d}^i - d)^3$ represents the higher order terms in $(\hat{d}^i - d)$.

The $O(\hat{d}^i - d)^3$ terms cannot be expressed in matrix notation; an open form must be used. Let
$$(\hat{d}^i - d) = \begin{bmatrix} \Delta d_x^i \\ \Delta d_y^i \end{bmatrix} \tag{8a}$$

and
$$\nabla_z I(i) \big|_{z = z_a} = \begin{Bmatrix} \dfrac{\partial}{\partial x} \\ \dfrac{\partial}{\partial y} \end{Bmatrix} I(i) \big|_{\substack{x = x_a \\ y = y_a}}, \tag{8b}$$

where $(i) = (z - \hat{d}^i, t - 1)$. The Taylor series expansion of the difference in the two intensity values can now be rewritten in open form as

$$I(z_a - d, t - 1) - I(z_a - \hat{d}^i, t - 1)$$
$$= \sum_{j=1}^{\infty} \frac{1}{j!} \left\{ \Delta d_x^i \left[\frac{\partial}{\partial x} \right] + \Delta d_y^i \left[\frac{\partial}{\partial y} \right] \right\}^j I(i) \Big|_{\substack{x=x_a \\ y=y_a}}, \quad (9)$$

where Δd_x^i is the error in the x displacement estimate at the ith iteration and Δd_y^i is the error in the y displacement estimate at the ith iteration.

The number of terms in the Taylor series that are required to obtain a good estimate of the difference in the two intensity values is dependent on two factors: 1) the error in the displacement estimation, and 2) the magnitude of the higher order derivatives of the intensity function. There is no reason to assume that a sufficient estimate is always obtained by retaining only the first term of the Taylor series expansion [14]. Therefore, this analysis retains all terms of the Taylor series expansion unlike the analysis in [1].

Substituting (9) into (6),

$$\hat{d}^{i+1} = \hat{d}^i - \epsilon \sum_{j=1}^{\infty} \frac{1}{j!} \left\{ \Delta d_x^i \left[\frac{\partial}{\partial x} \right] \right.$$
$$\left. + \Delta d_y^i \left[\frac{\partial}{\partial y} \right] \right\}^j \begin{pmatrix} \frac{\partial}{\partial x} \\ \frac{\partial}{\partial y} \end{pmatrix} I(i) \Big|_{\substack{x=x_a \\ y=y_a}}. \quad (10)$$

After some intermediate algebra and regrouping of factors,

$$\hat{d}^{i+1} = \hat{d}^i - \epsilon \{\nabla_z I(i) f(i)\} (\hat{d}^i - d) \Big|_{z=z_a}, \quad (11)$$

where $f(i)$ is a 1×2 matrix defined as

$$f(i) = \sum_{j=1}^{\infty} \frac{1}{j!} \left\{ \Delta d_x^i \left[\frac{\partial}{\partial x} \right] \right.$$
$$\left. + \Delta d_y^i \left[\frac{\partial}{\partial y} \right] \right\}^{j-1} \left\{ \frac{\partial}{\partial x} \quad \frac{\partial}{\partial y} \right\} I(i) \Big|_{\substack{x=x_a \\ y=y_a}}. \quad (12)$$

The first two terms of $f(i)$ are indicated in Fig. 2.

Equation (11) can be written as

$$\hat{d}^{i+1} = [J - \epsilon \{\nabla_z I(i) f(i)\}] \hat{d}^i \Big|_{z=z_a}$$
$$+ \epsilon \{\nabla_z I(i) f(i)\} d \Big|_{z=z_a}. \quad (13)$$

where J is the identity matrix. Taking the expected values of both sides over the moving area and assuming the product $\nabla_z I(i) f(i)$ and the displacement are uncorrelated [1], [15], [16],

$$E\{\hat{d}^{i+1}\} = [J - \epsilon E\{\nabla_z I(i) f(i)\}] E\{\hat{d}^i\}$$
$$+ \epsilon E\{\nabla_z I(i) f(i)\} d. \quad (14)$$

Although $E\{\nabla_z I(i) f(i)\}$ may be spatially varying, it is real and symmetric. Therefore, it may be decomposed by a similarity transform into the form

$$E\{\nabla_z I(i) f(i)\} = U(i) S(i) U^T(i), \quad (15)$$

where $U(i)$ is the orthonormal matrix whose columns are the normalized eigenvectors of $E\{\nabla_z I(i) f(i)\}$, and $S(i)$ is the diagonal matrix of eigenvalues of $E\{\nabla_z I(i) f(i)\}$. Furthermore,

$$U^T(i) U(i) = J. \quad (16)$$

Note that $E\{\nabla_z I(i) f(i)\}$ is full rank if there are multiple edge orientations within the random field over which the expected value is taken. The purpose of the similarity transform is to "rotate" the expected displacement vector into a coordinate system in which the expected displacement components are uncoupled. If one were to expand (13), it would be seen that the behavior of $E\{d_x^{i+1}\}$ (and $E\{d_y^{i+1}\}$) is dependent upon both $E\{d_x^i\}$ and $E\{d_y^i\}$. The transformation in (15) provides a set of uncoupled displacements, $v(i)$, for which the convergence properties of the gradient algorithm are more easily displayed. Therefore, let $v(i)$ be the set of uncoupled displacements and be defined by the pair of transformations

$$E\{\hat{d}^i\} = U(i) v(i) \quad (17)$$

and

$$v(i) = U^T(i) E\{\hat{d}^i\}. \quad (18)$$

Substituting (15) and (17) into (14) yields

$$v(i+1) = U^T(i+1) U(i) [J - \epsilon S(i)] v(i)$$
$$+ \epsilon U^T(i+1) U(i) S(i) U^T(i) d. \quad (19)$$

This can be rewritten as

$$v(i+1) = G(i+1) \{[J - \epsilon S(i)] v(i)$$
$$+ \epsilon S(i) U^T(i) d\}, \quad (20)$$

where

$$G(i+1) = U^T(i+1) U(i). \quad (21)$$

Analytically, the product $U^T(i+1) U(i)$ is not easily defined. Since $U^T(i) U(i)$ is the identity matrix and $\hat{d}^{i+1} \approx \hat{d}^i$ within a moving area, as a first approximation assume $G(i+1)$ is approximately equal to J, the identity matrix [16].

As the moving area is scanned, a point is reached at which $E\{\nabla_z I(i) f(i)\}$ remains constant as i increments. At this point, (20) reduces to

$$v(i+1) = [J - \epsilon S] v(i) + \epsilon S U^T d, \quad (22)$$

where the i dependence has been dropped for U and S. To obtain the closed-form solution for the expected displacement vector $E\{\hat{d}^{i+1}\}$, it is necessary to solve (22) for uncoupled displacement vector $v(i+1)$ and utilize (17) for the transformation back to the $E\{\hat{d}^{i+1}\}$.

To solve (22), it is instructive to expand a few terms in

the $v(i)$ sequence:

$i = 0$: $v(1) = [J - \epsilon S] v(0) + \epsilon SU^T d$

$i = 1$: $v(2) = [J - \epsilon S] v(1) + \epsilon SU^T d$

$\quad = [J - \epsilon S]^2 v(0) + [J - \epsilon S] \epsilon SU^T d$

$\quad + \epsilon SU^T d.$ (23)

Following this procedure, the expression for $v(i)$ becomes

$$v(i) = [J - \epsilon S]^i v(0) + \sum_{n=0}^{i-1} \epsilon [J - \epsilon S]^n SU^T d,$$

$i > 0.$ (24)

Since $[J - \epsilon S]$ is a diagonal matrix, the $v_j(i)$ in (24) are uncoupled. Thus, (24) written in terms of a single $v_j(i)$ becomes

$$v_j(i) = (1 - \epsilon \lambda_j)^i v_j(0) + \epsilon c_j \sum_{n=0}^{i-1} (1 - \epsilon \lambda_j)^n \quad (25)$$

where

$$c_j = \lambda_j d_1 u_{j1} + \lambda_j d_2 u_{j2} \quad j = 1, 2 \quad (26)$$

and λ_j is the jth eigenvalue of $E\{\nabla_z I(i) f(i)\}$, d_k is the kth component of the true displacement vector, and u_{jk} is the jkth element of the U matrix.

Performing the summation in (25) produces

$$v_j(i) = (1 - \epsilon \lambda_j)^i v_j(0) + \epsilon c_j \left[\frac{1 - (1 - \epsilon \lambda_j)^i}{1 - (1 - \epsilon \lambda_j)} \right]. \quad (27)$$

Simplifying and using the substitution

$$\gamma_j = 1 - \epsilon \lambda_j, \quad (28)$$

(27) becomes

$$v_j(i) = \gamma_j^i v_j(0) + \frac{c_j}{\lambda_j} (1 - \gamma_j^i), \quad i \geq 0. \quad (29)$$

Several facts are noteworthy:

a) Note $c_j / \lambda_j = d_1 u_{j1} + d_2 u_{j2} \quad j = 1, 2$.

b) For convergent $v_j(i)$ solutions, each of the quantities $|\gamma_j|$ must be less than unity. This implies

$$\frac{2}{\lambda_{\max}} > \epsilon > 0, \quad (30)$$

where $\lambda_{\max}$ is the maximum eigenvalue of the positive semidefinite symmetric matrix $E\{\nabla_z I(i) f(i)\}$. Therefore, the following condition is sufficient for the iterative algorithm to converge.

$$\frac{2}{tr E\{\nabla_z I(i) f(i)\}} > \epsilon > 0, \quad (31)$$

where tr indicates the matrix trace.

If $f(i)$ were to be approximated by $f_1(i)$ (see Fig. 2), then (31) reduces to the constraint equation obtained in

$j = 1$: $f_1(i) = \left\{ \frac{\partial}{\partial x} \frac{\partial}{\partial y} \right\} I(i) \Big|_{\substack{x = x_a \\ y = y_a}},$

$\quad = \nabla_z I^T (z - \hat{d}^i, t - 1) \Big|_{z = z_a}$

$j = 2$: $f_2(i) = \frac{1}{2} \left\{ \Delta d_x^i \left| \frac{\partial}{\partial x} \right| + \Delta d_y^i \left| \frac{\partial}{\partial y} \right| \right\} \left\{ \frac{\partial}{\partial x} \frac{\partial}{\partial y} \right\} I(i) \Big|_{\substack{x = x_a \\ y = y_a}},$

$\quad = \frac{1}{2} \left\{ \Delta d_x^i \left| \frac{\partial^2 I}{\partial x^2} \right| + \Delta d_y^i \left| \frac{\partial^2 I}{\partial x \partial y} \right| \Delta d_x^i \left| \frac{\partial^2 I}{\partial y \partial x} \right| + \Delta d_y^i \left| \frac{\partial^2 I}{\partial y^2} \right| \right\} \Big|_{(z_a - \hat{d}^i, t - 1)}$

$\quad = \frac{1}{2} (\hat{d}^i - d)^T \nabla_z^2 I(z - \hat{d}^i, t - 1) \Big|_{z = z_a}.$

Fig. 2. Expansion of the first two terms of $f(i)$.

the appendix of [1]:

$$\frac{2M}{\sum_{i=1}^{M} \left[\{\nabla_x I(i)\}^2 + \{\nabla_y I(i)\}^2 \right]} > \epsilon > 0, \quad (32)$$

where M iterations are performed in obtaining the displacement estimate and $\nabla_x I(i)$, $\nabla_y I(i)$ are the orthogonal components of $\nabla_z I(i)$, i.e., the gradient vector elements. The $\{\nabla I(i)\}^2$ notation indicates the square of the real-valued gradient component. Note the difference between $\{\nabla I(i)\}^2$ in (32) and $\nabla^2 I(i)$ in (7) and in Fig. 2.

In Section VI, it will be shown that for a typical sequence, (32) constrains ϵ to be less than 0.0020 for low interframe motion and less than 0.0100 for high interframe motion. Many previous implementations of the displacement estimate algorithm [see (4)] have constrained the update term to some arbitrary limit [1], [3], [4], [7], [12], [13]. This is called clipping the update term. The analysis does not require this and the simulations in Section VI will show that it gains nothing.

Musmann et al. [7] have shown that there exist at least three other displacement estimation/correction algorithms which do not clip the update term and converge faster than the one used in [1]; unfortunately all three of them require more computation than (4).

c) There are j modes of convergence.

Each uncoupled displacement $v_j(i)$ convergences in the mean toward its final value c_j / λ_j at a rate controlled by the product $\epsilon \lambda_j$. One may define a convergence constant τ_j for each of the j modes as the number of iterations needed for $v_j(i)$ in (22) to be within e^{-1} of its final value $v_j(\infty)$ [16]. This produces the following equation.

$$v_j(\tau_j) = v_j(\infty) + e^{-1} [v_j(0) - v_j(\infty)]$$

$$= v_j(0) + (1 - e^{-1}) [v_j(\infty) - v_j(0)] \quad (33)$$

which, with the use of (29), may be solved for τ_j

$$\gamma_j^{\tau_j} v_j(0) + \frac{c_j}{\lambda_j} (1 - \gamma_j^{\tau_j}) = v_j(0) + (1 - e^{-1}) \left[\frac{c_j}{\lambda_j} v_j(0) \right]$$

$$= e^{-1} v_j(0) + \frac{c_j}{\lambda_j} (1 - e^{-1}).$$

(34)

This implies that

$$\gamma_j^{\tau_j} = e^{-1}$$

$$(1 - \epsilon\lambda_j)^{\tau_j} = e^{-1}$$

$$\tau_j \ln(1 - \epsilon\lambda_j) = -1$$

$$\tau_j = \frac{-1}{\ln(1 - \epsilon\lambda_j)}. \tag{35}$$

Since each of the λ_j may be quite different, the convergence constants τ_j may vary considerably, resulting in diverse convergence rates for each mode. The largest eigenvalue corresponds to the dominant mode which produces the shortest convergence time. See Example 1 in the Appendix.

Although Example 1 indicates that the larger ϵ, the faster the rate of convergence, Musmann et al. [7] have already noted the tradeoff between rapid convergence and low variance at convergence. While it has been shown that the expected value of the displacement vector converges to the correct value, no consideration has been given to the variance of the displacement vector estimation about the correct value. From (30) it can be seen that if $\epsilon < 2/\lambda_{\max}$, convergence of the displacement vector in the mean sense is assured. However, the variance of the displacement vector about the correct value is proportional to ϵ [11], resulting in conflicting requirements: large ϵ for rapid convergence and small ϵ for small displacement estimate variance. The simulations in Section VI will show that choosing the maximum ϵ is not always prudent. In the next section, the existing motion prediction schemes are reviewed with the intent of introducing a new prediction technique in Section V.

IV. Existing Motion Prediction Schemes

Previously there have been two predominant methods of displacement estimation: spatial and temporal. Most researchers have used a spatially adjacent displacement vector as an initial estimate [1]. Other researchers, mostly from Bell Northern Research, have proposed predicting the displacement along the temporal axis [5]. A third approach is proposed in Section V: project the motion estimation forward along the motion trajectory (PAMT). This would have four advantages and require a minimal increase in computation and no increase in memory over the temporal projection procedure. The problems with the existing schemes are discussed below.

1) Spatial Prediction: By always using a spatially adjacent displacement vector as an initial estimate for the displacement vector under consideration, an implicit assumption is being made that the displacement vectors always have a high spatial correlation. This is not what the original image model implies. The original model assumed that an object is moving over a fixed stationary background. Although the displacement vectors are highly correlated within moving objects and in the stationary background, at the edges of moving objects the displacement vectors are highly uncorrelated. In Section III it was indicated that the number of terms in the Taylor series expansion that are required to obtain a good estimate of the DFD is dependent on two factors, one of which is the error in the displacement estimation. It is questionable whether a spatially adjacent displacement vector is a sufficiently accurate initial estimate to assume convergence of the displacement estimate equation. Consider a one-dimensional example.

In Fig. 3 an edge has moved three units to the left between frames $t - 1$ and t. Scanning from left to right in frame t, a nonzero DFD is first encountered at point x_a (assume $\hat{d}^0 = 0$). This incorrect displacement estimate of 0 will not be corrected since $\nabla_x I|_{t-1} = 0$. No matter how many times the correction equation iterates at x_a, the correct displacement value cannot be found for $I(x_a, t)$. It is not until point x_b is reached that the motion estimation can be corrected (i.e., when $\nabla_x I|_{t-1}$ becomes nonzero). If the correct d has not been determined by the time x_d is reached in the scan line, $\hat{d}$ cannot be corrected further until the spatial gradient in frame $t - 1$ becomes nonzero again, which may not occur until much later in the scan line.

2) Temporal Prediction: Dubois et al. [5] suggested using the temporally adjacent displacement vector as an initial estimate. By projecting the displacement vector estimates over time rather than space, the displacement estimates at the edges can exhibit a sharp discontinuity and this discontinuity can be sharpened over time. However, this approach does not fully solve the problem. It assumes that the spatial location of the moving objects remains the same frame-to-frame.

As one example of the problem with temporal prediction, look again at Fig. 3. The same problem exists here as with spatially adjacent estimation: $\hat{d}^0 = 0$ at x_a. There is no way to converge to d at x_a. The improvement of temporal prediction occurs at x_b where $\hat{d}^0$ is not necessarily zero.

As a second example, consider the object moving to the left in the plane of view with a constant translational velocity in Fig. 4. If the displacement vectors are projected forward parallel to the temporal axis, then there will be errors associated with both the leading and the trailing edge. The intensities along the leading edge (area L in Fig. 4) will not be predicted correctly since in the previous frame (at time $t - 1$), nothing was moving in those pixel locations into which the leading edge has now moved. The trailing edge (area T in Fig. 4) on the other hand has left some pixel locations between time $t - 1$ and t. The intensities at these pixel locations in frame t constitute newly uncovered background. The algorithm will try to predict the intensities for these pixels from displaced intensities in the previous frame. The accuracy of this prediction will depend on the correlation between the intensity values in the displaced region in the previous frame (frame $t - 1$) and the intensity values in the newly

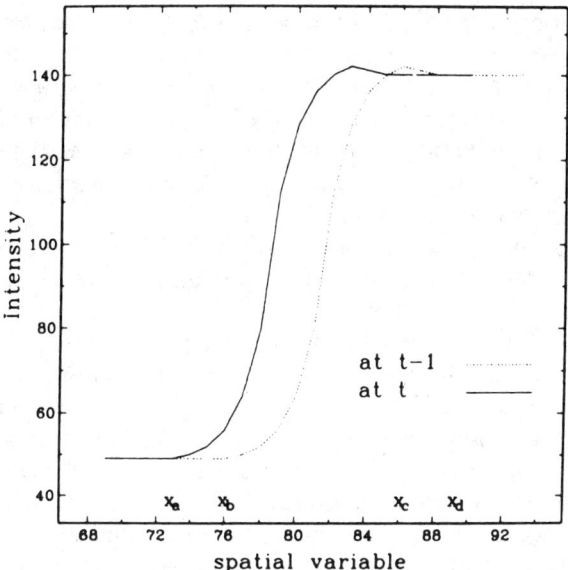

Fig. 3. A moving edge in one dimension.

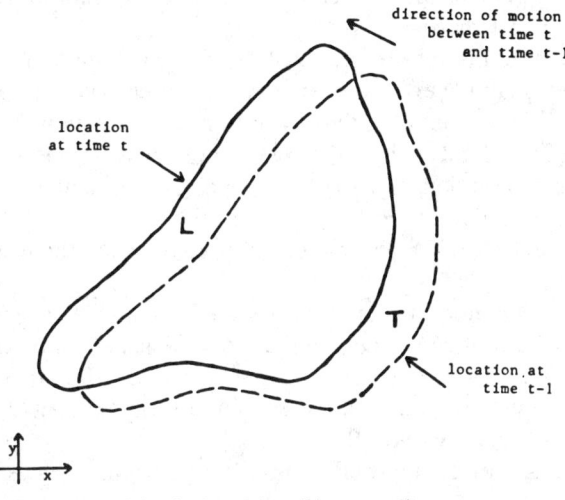

Fig. 4. A moving object, top view.

uncovered background region in the present frame (frame t).

A better prediction scheme would be to assume the motion velocity, not the object location, remains constant. Instead of projecting the motion estimations forward parallel to the temporal axis, project them forward along the motion trajectory. This is the improved motion prediction technique.

V. Proposed Technique: Projection-Along-The-Motion-Trajectory

If the object has a constant velocity frame-to-frame, projecting the displacement vectors forward in the direction of motion can correctly predict the leading edge values. Also, those areas of the image which contain newly uncovered background can be correctly detected.

By projecting the motion vectors forward in the direction of motion, a problem that has existed in the implementation of the algorithm is solved. In proving convergence the uncovered background was neglected [1]. Yet most algorithms [1], [3]–[5], [7], [12], [13], [17]–[19] attempt to determine the intensity values for the newly uncovered background at time t using intensities in the frame at time $t - 1$. The structure of the algorithm is at fault. By obtaining the initial estimates for the displacement vector from spatially or temporally adjacent pels there is no way to detect what regions are newly uncovered background. By predicting the motion vectors forward in the direction of motion, the uncovered background will have no displacement values predicted for it. The uncovered background is then easily detected, allowing a better predictor to be used for it and allowing the implementation to be a true implementation of the algorithm which was proved to converge. The computation requirements for PAMT prediction are only slightly greater than those for temporal prediction. Although it would require another framestore and more computation, a constant acceleration model could be used instead of a constant velocity model with the PAMT technique.

To reiterate and summarize, by projecting the displacement estimates forward along the motion trajectory four improvements are obtained.

1) With respect to spatial prediction, sharp discontinuities can exist at the boundaries between moving objects and the background.

2) With respect to temporal prediction, the actual displacement of the object point can be found more often since the motion, not the location, of the moving area is assumed constant.

3) The number of iterations required for convergence will be decreased due to better initial estimates. Also a smaller displacement prediction error allows a larger ϵ which increases the convergence rate.

4) A substantial portion of the uncovered background is detectable and can be segmented out.

A quantitative comparison of the three displacement prediction schemes (spatial, temporal, and PAMT) is difficult. To say anything substantive, two assumptions must be made: 1) the correct displacement was found for all pels along the leading edge of the moving area in the previous frame, and 2) that the interframe motion is constant. Although these assumptions are somewhat stringent, they allow the improvements of the PAMT technique to be seen. One improvement is the number of pels whose displacement is correctly predicted with the PAMT technique but not with spatial or temporal prediction. These pels are all the pels in the leading edge of the moving area whose $|DFD| > T$ and whose $\nabla_z I(z - \hat{d}^i, t - 1)|_{z=z_a} = [\begin{smallmatrix} 0 \\ 0 \end{smallmatrix}]$. The size of this area is approximately the product of d and the "length" of the leading edge. (See area L in Fig. 4.) The increase in the number of pels whose intensity is "correctly" predicted with PAMT prediction, but not with spatial or temporal prediction, can be determined likewise.

The relative improvement in being able to identify the

uncovered background portion of a frame is much more difficult to ascertain. It is probably most dependent on the similarity between the newly uncovered background and the nearby background which was visible in the previous frame.

As for the validity of the two assumptions, note that even if the interfame motion is not exactly constant, constant motion is a better estimate of the true motion than zero motion, since by the law of entropy, bodies in motion tend to remain in motion. Thus, the PAMT motion prediction technique is intuitively better than temporal prediction, since temporal prediction in effect assumes the moving body has not moved in the time interval $[t-1, t]$. The improvement over spatial prediction is equally obvious.

The validity of the second assumption (that the "correct" displacement was found in the previous frame for all pels along the leading edge of the moving area in the previous frame) is most dependent on whether the leading edge is one of the last edges scanned or one of the first. If the leading edge is one of the last, $\hat{d}^i$ will probably have converged to d; if it is one of the first, $\hat{d}^i$ will probably not have converged to d.

Some simulations run on a synthetic sequence confirmed the dependence of the displacement error on the direction of motion [8]. A hemisphere of radius 16 was translated at various velocities across the image plane. The mean-square error (MSE) in the average displacement estimate was lower for rightward and downward motion than for leftward and upward motion. The entropy and intensity MSE were likewise lower for motion away from the raster scan origin. This result is expected since the gradients are evaluated in the previous frame when $\hat{d}$ must be corrected. For rightward and downward motion, the spatial location of the first moving edge encountered in frame t is "above" the moving object in frame $t-1$. Thus, the spatial gradient is probably nonzero and the value of $\hat{d}$ can start to be "corrected" when an incorrect $\hat{d}$ is first encountered. This is probably not the case for leftward or upward motion.

VI. SIMULATIONS

In this section simulation results are presented which show the increased compression obtained by using the convergence analysis results (and not clipping the update term) and by using the PAMT prediction technique. Simulation results are also included which indicate the relative improvement of using zeroth-order entropy encoding [10] over first-order entropy encoding and of predicting the motion on a field-to-field basis as opposed to a frame-to-frame basis [1]. Information compression is the primary goal herein; motion prediction is a means to that end. The total entropy bit rate is the sum of the information bits and addressing bits. The addressing bits in all the simulation results herein are calculated using run-length encoding. The information bits are based on taking the difference of consecutive nonzero error values (first-order entropy) in most of the runs; the few runs in which it is not will be dutifully noted.

Three algorithms are used in the simulation runs:

1) A motion-compensated (MC) algorithm in which spatial prediction of the motion vectors is used. The motion vector for the pel one line and one pel previous to the pel under consideration is used.

2) An MC algorithm in which the motion vectors are predicted using PAMT. A gap bridging technique is used on the predicted motion-vector field.

3) An MC algorithm in which the predicted motion vector ($\hat{d}^0$) is the average of the motion vectors obtained using spatial and PAMT prediction. Although this prediction technique may increase the prediction error at the edges of moving objects, it will smooth the $\hat{d}^0$ values as a moving object is traversed. The smaller the variance of the motion vector as it converges, the smaller the variance of the intensity error sequence [8]. A small intensity-error variance element-to-element can be exploited to further decrease the information rate by transmitting the difference in consecutive intensity errors rather than the intensity errors directly [1].

The temporal prediction scheme was not simulated herein. However, it appears that it is inferior to the spatial prediction scheme (either in performance or implementation complexity) since the researchers who proposed temporal prediction [3], [5] have since started using a variation of spatial prediction [17]–[19].

The following parameters are used in all three algorithms:

1) The motion vector is corrected if the DFD is greater than 3 out of 255. The percent motion has been previously defined as the percentage of pels which differ in value between two frames by greater than 1.5 percent of the peak-to-peak value [9].

2) A noise-suppression prefilter is used. It does two thresholding operations. In the first section it zeros any frame differences less than four in magnitude. In the second section the frame difference is forced to zero for all pels whose four nearest neighbors have a thresholded frame difference of zero. This prefilter has been used in previous investigations of video teleconferencing by other researchers [1], [12], [13], [20], [21]. The images are *not* low-pass filtered to improve the spatial predictability of the motion. The sequences are of very high quality images with clean, sharp object edges.

3) The intensity-predictor switches between straight interframe prediction and motion-compensated interframe prediction. Motion-compensated prediction is used when the sum of the DFD at the three closest pels on the previous line is less than the frame difference at those same pels. This is the technique proposed in [12].

4) The intensity difference-of-errors sequence is quantized with a 33-level symmetric quantizer whose positive representative values are: 0, 4, 7, 11, 16, 21, 28, 35, 44, 53, 64, 77, 92, 109, 128, 149, 178.

5) As is usually done, the simulation starts with a previous frame at the receiver.

6) The displacement correction algorithm iterates at most once at each pel. This limits the contribution of any one pel in the motion estimation so that the $\hat{d}$ is not unduly influenced by the first few sample points of a moving object [7].

The intent of parameters 1, 2, and 3 is to reduce the bit rate and to apply the displacement estimation algorithm only where appropriate. A more complicated scheme could be used, but the goal was to simulate a codec that could be reasonably expected to function in real-time at low bit rates (e.g., 384 kbits/s).

The algorithms are simulated on three real-time (30 frames/s) image sequences that are typical of ones that might occur in a video teleconferencing environment. These sequences were chosen because they are typical; they exhibit less motion than the sequences used in many other simulations [1], [3], [4], [7], [12], [13]. The sequences have a spatial resolution of 282 lines/frame by 448 pels/line and an intensity resolution of 8 bits/pel for an uncompressed bit rate of 1.01 Mbits/frame. The frames are interlaced. Two frames from each sequence are shown in Fig. 5. All three sequences are 60 frames (2 s), but sometimes only the first 30 frames are used. The percent of interframe motion for each is plotted in Fig. 6.

The improvements in the intensity prediction and the motion prediction are shown by measuring the image compression, the image quality, and the motion predictability. The following tables summarize the simulation results. The first column indicates the ϵ and clip value (if applicable). The second column indicates the maximum entropy bits per frame and the average entropy bits per frame. This measures the image (intensity information) compression. The third column indicates the maximum MSE for any predicted frame and the average MSE for the whole 60-frame sequence of predicted frames. This is one measure of the image quality. The fourth column indicates the maximum and average number of unpredicted pels per frame (or the number of times the displacement estimate is updated). This measures the motion predictability and is a strong measure of the ability to implement the algorithm in real-time, since the motion-correction equation (4) is the most computationally demanding part. The fifth column contains the maximum and minimum value of the average gradient per frame ($E\{\nabla_z I\}$) squared. This determines the upper limit on ϵ. The sixth column indicates the maximum and minimum framewise MSE for the corrected frames, that is the picture quality which is actually viewed at the receiver.

Instead of developing a single cost function involving the bit rate, the picture quality, and the implementation complexity, the ϵ value was varied and the optimum value for the various measures was determined.

A. Convergence Analysis Simulations

The first MC algorithm, which uses spatial prediction, was applied to all three sequences using various ϵ values and various clip values to determine 1) the relative improvement of not clipping the update term in the motion

(a)

(b)

(c)

(d)

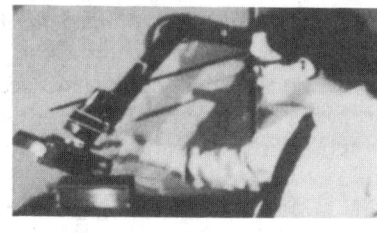
(e)

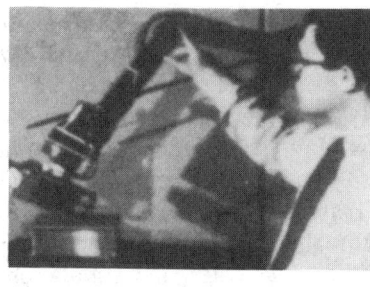
(f)

Fig. 5. (a) Bobsjob, frame 0. (b) Bobsjob, frame 60. (c) Map, frame 0. (d) Map, frame 60. (e) Robot, frame 0. (f) Robot, frame 60.

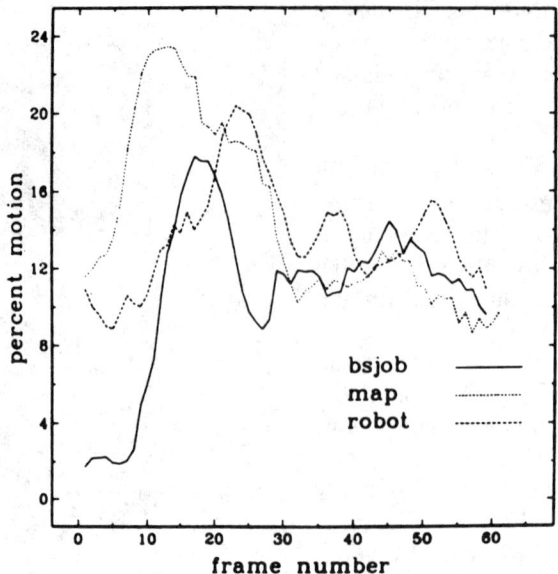

Fig. 6. Percent interframe motion.

TABLE I
SPATIAL PREDICTION OF BOBSJOB SEQUENCE

ε/Clip	Entropy Bits max/aver	Predicted MSE max/aver	Number of Unpredicted Pels max/aver	Average Value of Gradient Squared min/max	Corrected MSE min/max
0.06250/0.0625	121081/ 90910	97.43/25.75	25242/16960	227.5/ 840.0	0.33/1.35
0.00200/1.0000	133962/100474	85.94/22.83	26918/19674	233.9/ 829.1	0.35/1.46
0.00100/ n.c.	130328/ 97571	88.24/23.43	26486/18545	221.8/1004.1	0.37/1.43
0.00050/ n.c.	123381/ 92351	87.33/22.98	25751/17309	219.3/ 724.9	0.38/1.38
0.00025/ n.c.	120663/ 89508	89.68/24.93	25182/16922	218.6/ 699.9	0.33/1.36
0.00010/ n.c.	118330/ 87888	100.71/28.13	24383/16298	227.7/ 602.1	0.26/1.28
0.00001/ n.c.	123801/ 90393	107.41/33.20	24650/15978	209.4/ 552.8	0.26/1.26

n.c.-no clip

correction equation, and 2) the optimum ε and its variance between sequences. The simulation results are tabulated in Tables I–III. The results for the bobsjob sequence are based on 60 frames, while the map and robot sequence results in this section are based on the first 30 frames of each sequence.

An ε value of 0.0010 with a clip value of 0.0625 was used in earlier pel-recursive research [1]. Other ε/clip values that have been used in reported simulations are 0.0078/0.2 and 0.5/0.08 [13]. There is, however, no analytical derivation of these values; they were determined to be the best for a particular sequence by trial and error. The analysis in Section III indicated that $\hat{d}$ should converge to d within the moving area without clipping the update term [see (4)] if the assumptions are valid and the constraints on ε are met. Although one might think that by using a large value of ε and clipping the update term $\hat{d}$ would converge to d faster, the simulation results in Table I do not verify this fact. Granted, all possible pairs of ε and clip values were not tried (that is what is trying to be avoided by doing the analysis), but the heuristic technique does not seem to offer any performance advantages over implementing the analytical technique, i.e., relatively small ε values and no clip. Also note that implementing the analytical model reduces the computational requirements (no clipping or hardlimiting).

For spatial prediction with the ε values tried, the minimum total bit rate was obtained with ε = 0.00010 or 0.00025. The ε which yielded the minimum number of unpredicted pels varied from 0.00001 to 0.00025.

The framewise average of $\{(\nabla_x I)^2 + (\nabla_y I)^2\}$ varied from 209.4 (high motion) to 1004.1 (low motion) for the ε's used in the bobsjob simulations. The average value of $\{(\nabla_x I)^2 + (\nabla_y I)^2\}$ over the whole sequence was about 300. For $\hat{d}$ to converge to d in every frame with a fixed ε value, the largest value of $E\{(\nabla_x I)^2 + (\nabla_y I)^2\}$ should be used to determine ε. For example, if $E\{(\nabla_x I)^2 + (\nabla_y I)^2\} = 1000$, ε is constrained to be less than 0.002 by (32). However, a smaller value of ε may be the optimum value. The simulations indicate such to be the case. For the map and robot sequences, $E\{(\nabla_x I)^2 + (\nabla_y I)^2\}$ was lower, which supports the larger value of ε at which

TABLE II
SPATIAL PREDICTION OF MAP SEQUENCE

ϵ/Clip	Entropy Bits max/aver	Predicted MSE max/aver	Number of Unpredicted Pels max/aver	Average Value of Gradient Squared min/max	Corrected MSE min/max
0.062500/0.0625	157973/134428	72.88/33.55	28387/21668	96.1/228.0	1.24/1.62
0.001000/0.0625	159212/134332	73.20/34.08	28552/21929	95.9/234.5	1.27/1.60
0.500000/0.0800	159758/135176	73.07/32.58	28264/21686	94.2/226.9	1.27/1.59
0.007800/0.2000	162879/138431	67.89/28.44	28359/21954	93.4/223.6	1.34/1.59
0.001000/ n.c.	161891/137889	66.04/28.63	29744/22793	95.8/216.5	1.31/1.65
0.000500/ n.c.	159744/135389	70.71/32.24	28953/22374	94.4/216.7	1.27/2.09
0.000250/ n.c.	157605/134017	72.95/34.40	28424/21994	99.2/235.5	1.22/1.57
0.000100/ n.c.	159646/134798	75.65/36.06	28242/21980	103.3/244.6	1.15/1.61
0.000010/ n.c.	166075/138363	76.53/37.90	29275/22510	103.6/251.2	1.15/1.50
0.000001/ n.c.	166454/138431	76.72/38.03	29175/22509	103.4/250.4	1.15/1.50

n.c.—no clip

TABLE III
SPATIAL PREDICTION OF ROBOT SEQUENCE

ϵ/Clip	Entropy Bits max/aver	Predicted MSE max/aver	Number of Unpredicted Pels max/aver	Average Value of Gradient Squared min/max	Corrected MSE min/max
0.062500/0.062500	141695/109691	47.55/20.99	25644/18441	196.0/422.3	0.98/1.58
0.001000/0.062500	139501/107893	43.96/20.92	25484/18247	197.6/421.8	0.94/1.45
0.500000/0.080000	141503/111154	40.66/20.12	25579/18601	199.5/422.6	1.07/1.47
0.007800/0.200000	147026/119541	31.85/18.07	26197/19985	214.3/394.5	1.16/1.56
0.001000/ n.c.	146919/116616	35.87/19.57	27770/21190	188.2/376.5	1.06/1.48
0.000500/ n.c.	141907/109791	36.73/19.33	26436/18933	189.1/414.7	0.92/1.41
0.000250/ n.c.	137253/107382	42.53/20.73	25389/18334	185.1/428.5	0.93/1.45
0.000100/ n.c.	139149/108227	49.02/22.90	25758/18782	196.0/453.2	0.85/1.33
0.000010/ n.c.	148405/114200	60.98/27.36	27463/19850	191.9/446.0	0.78/1.33
0.000001/ n.c.	149345/114738	62.51/27.83	27421/19881	191.5/447.5	0.78/1.35

n.c.—no clip

the minimum bit rate was obtained for these two sequences. Note that as a general rule the smaller ϵ values yielded a smaller maximum average gradient value.

With respect to the received picture quality, the smaller the value of ϵ, the smaller average MSE in the frames as actually viewed at the receiver. However, the maximum MSE in the corrected frames for all runs was very low. Thus, there was little visual degradations in any of the frames in any of the simulation runs.

Note that the optimum ϵ value was not determined analytically, only an upper limit. Thus, the optimum ϵ must be found by trial and error. However, only one variable needs to be found, not two, and using a relatively small value of ϵ (10^{-3} to 10^{-4}) and no clip appears to yield results which are better than the results obtained by using a relatively large value of ϵ (0.001–0.500) and clipping the update term in the motion correction equation. In effect, better results can be obtained by doing less computation.

B. Comparison of Prediction Techniques

In this section, the performance of the three different prediction schemes is indicated. All three prediction schemes (spatial, PAMT, and mixed) were applied to all three sequences (bobsjob, map, and robot). Since the bobsjob sequence (talking newscaster type) is the most typical sequence, it was chosen to be the primary sequence for further simulation runs. The results of simulating the last two algorithms on the bobsjob sequence are summarized in Table IV.

For the bobsjob sequence, the minimum bit rate for all three prediction schemes was found. These minimum bit rates occur when $\epsilon \approx 0.0001$ and differ by about 2 percent. The minimum number of unpredicted pels for each prediction scheme is also tabulated. These minimum values once again vary by about 2 percent between prediction schemes, but occur at different ϵ values than the entropy minimums. The results are similar for average value of the gradient and the corrected MSE: the minimum values for each prediction scheme vary only slightly and occur at slightly different ϵ values.

In an attempt to see if the same value of ϵ is optimum (or near optimum) for the other two sequences and to see if the PAMT technique offers any relative advantages over the spatial prediction technique in the other sequences, a few sets of parameters were simulated on the map and

TABLE IV
PAMT AND MIXED PREDICTION OF BOBSJOB SEQUENCE

ϵ/clip	Entropy Bits max/aver	Predicted MSE max/aver	Number of Unpredicted Pels max/aver	Average Value of Gradient Squared min/max	Corrected MSE min/max
PAMT					
0.06250/0.0625	121345/ 90064	103.94/31.48	23983/15823	219.4/ 840.0	0.27/1.37
0.00200/0.0625	120259/ 90208	104.26/31.59	23840/15845	214.9/ 787.3	0.27/1.37
0.00200/1.0000	124979/ 93785	93.53/26.12	23698/16522	241.4/ 829.1	0.34/1.44
0.01000/1.0000	133985/ 99482	93.82/26.69	24358/18054	273.4/ 597.9	0.28/1.39
0.00200/ n.c.	130769/ 98208	105.77/33.50	24655/17703	275.1/ 549.0	0.32/1.49
0.00100/ n.c.	122626/ 92470	92.15/27.97	23594/15995	227.3/1004.1	0.28/1.41
0.00050/ n.c.	119588/ 90233	95.52/28.63	23489/15751	194.7/ 724.9	0.28/1.38
0.00025/ n.c.	121470/ 89640	101.77/30.85	24010/15794	210.3/ 699.9	0.26/1.33
0.00010/ n.c.	123703/ 90182	106.57/32.79	24428/15894	208.9/ 602.1	0.26/1.28
mixed					
0.00100/ n.c.	118537/ 88916	86.87/22.81	23350/15835	220.2/1004.1	0.32/1.42
0.00050/ n.c.	117120/ 87990	91.43/24.73	23743/15791	206.0/ 724.9	0.31/1.38
0.00025/ n.c.	116263/ 87423	98.08/27.15	23773/15880	214.1/ 699.9	0.26/1.20

n.c.—no clip

TABLE V
MAP SEQUENCE SIMULATION RESULTS, 60 FRAMES

ϵ	Entropy Bits max/aver	Predicted MSE max/aver	Number of Unpredicted Pels max/aver	Average Value of Gradient Squared min/max	Corrected MSE min/max
spatial					
0.00100	162282/121997	67.95/17.41	29469/18726	91.2/210.2	1.14/1.70
0.00050	160078/119766	72.58/18.95	28898/18296	89.1/214.8	1.09/1.65
PAMT					
0.00100	160085/121466	72.64/19.71	27930/18649	78.7/210.2	1.16/1.70
0.00050	159632/120288	72.74/20.07	28298/18420	79.7/214.8	1.11/1.65
0.00025	161713/120307	74.01/20.55	28616/18422	86.5/230.5	1.09/1.55
mixed					
0.00100	155707/120494	73.03/19.74	27572/19156	80.7/210.3	1.17/1.70
0.00050	155304/119037	72.78/19.95	28006/18486	84.5/214.8	1.09/1.65

robot sequence. The results are summarized in Tables V and VI. These runs were made using all 60 frames of each sequence. Spatial results are included in Tables V and VI, since the runs in Tables II and III were made with only the first 30 frames of each sequence. Most of the average and minimum values for the map sequence drop from Table II to Table V because there is more motion in the first 30 frames of the sequence than in the last 30 frames.

As with the bobsjob sequence all three prediction schemes yield similar results for the map sequence. The largest difference is in the average value of the gradient within a frame. Using the values obtained with spatial prediction as a benchmark, the average gradient is 11–14 percent less using PAMT prediction and 6–12 percent less using mixed prediction. For the simulation runs on the robot sequence only one ϵ value was used; no significant differences occurred in the results for the three prediction schemes.

The failure of the PAMT (and mixed) prediction scheme to show much improvement over spatial prediction is probably most attributable to the crude motion correction scheme and to a high variance in the motion estimates pel-to-pel. In the present motion correction scheme, $\hat{d}$ may not converge to d until most of the moving object has been processed. The $\hat{d}^0$ values in the first part of the moving object may be greatly in error. Since the improvement of the PAMT scheme occurs by utilizing the $\hat{d}$ information in the previous frame, if the $\hat{d}^N$ values in the previous frame are erroneous, little (if any) advantage is gained by using them. In other words, with a better motion-correction scheme, better performance should be obtainable with the PAMT technique. Also in tests done on the synthetic image sequences [8], in which the location of the moving object and the value of d is known, the PAMT scheme had a smaller error in the average displacement estimate than either the spatial or mixed scheme. Unfortunately a smaller average displacement error does not necessarily produce a smaller average intensity prediction error,

TABLE VI
ROBOT SEQUENCE SIMULATION RESULTS, 60 FRAMES

ϵ	Entropy Bits max/aver	Predicted MSE max/aver	Number of Unpredicted Pels max/aver	Average value of Gradient Squared min/max	Corrected MSE min/max
spatial 0.0001	139470/110565	49.27/21.58	25953/19061	189.4/439.3	0.84/1.31
PAMT 0.0001	143474/111397	53.20/23.00	27063/19358	187.1/439.3	0.85/1.33
mixed 0.0001	141994/110772	51.90/22.49	26807/19211	190.4/439.3	0.86/1.34

which is the goal herein. A technique that should reduce the variance of the $\hat{d}$'s pel-to-pel is a postprocessing filter to smooth the displacement estimate within the moving areas and within the background. Another way to improve the performance of the PAMT scheme would be to develop a better gap bridging scheme; further results from the simulation runs on the synthetic sequences showed the $\hat{d}$'s from the PAMT scheme to still have a large pel-to-pel variance due to gaps in the predicted motion field caused by rounding. The $\hat{d}$'s are stored as nonintegers, but are projected forward using integer projections.

C. Zeroth-Order Entropy Information Transmission

In all the simulation runs reported so far the difference of consecutive intensity prediction errors was transmitted (first-order entropy encoding [10]). This had been shown to reduce the bit rate in pel-recursive motion-compensated coders by 5–15 percent [1] over transmitting the intensity prediction errors directly. The only perceptual picture quality degradation in any of the previous simulation runs herein was some slight horizontal streaking. In an attempt to remove these degradations, all 60 frames of the bobsjob sequence were compressed by transmitting the intensity prediction errors directly (zeroth-order entropy encoding [10]). The results are in Table VII. They were surprising. The bit rate was 12–14 percent lower and was minimized at a larger ϵ value. The number of unpredicted pels dropped by 17 percent and the average MSE in the reconstructed frames dropped by 60 percent! All this with less computation.

It should be noted that the intensity MSE in the reconstructed sequences is rather small and may not really be noise, but rather the absence of the noise which was in the original frame. Recall that a noise prefilter was used in the simulations and that the corrected MSE is the error between the original picture and the picture viewed at the receiver. Subjectively no degradations were readily noticeable.

D. Field-to-Field Prediction of Motion

In all the previous simulation runs the motion has been predicted on a frame-to-frame basis. Most researchers who have simulated a switched predictor have used field-to-field intensity prediction in the motion-compensated (MC) section and frame-to-frame intensity prediction in the conditional replenishment (CR) section [1], [3], [12], [13]. This tactic results in a precise prediction of the non-moving background by using frame-to-frame prediction, but smaller displacement vectors by using field-to-field prediction.

In an attempt to confirm this, the first two algorithms were run on the bobsjob sequence using field-to-field motion prediction with the best ϵ determined from the previous runs, namely an ϵ of 0.0001. Both zeroth-order and first-order entropy encoding was used. The results are tabulated in Table VIII. This set of runs was made with only the first 30 frames of the sequence. Once again zeroth-order entropy encoding was better than first-order and the PAMT motion prediction scheme failed to show any improvement over the spatial prediction scheme.

VII. CONCLUSIONS

Four accomplishments are reported in this paper.

1) The pel-recursive motion-compensated algorithm has been more thoroughly analyzed and the analytical model is shown by simulation to yield better results than the heuristic technique of large ϵ values and clipping the update term in (4).

2) A new motion prediction scheme, "projection-along-the-motion-trajectory" or PAMT, is introduced. Although experimentally it failed to show any improvement over the spatial prediction technique, that can be explained, at least in part, by the poor motion correction scheme and the noisy $\hat{d}$ field.

3) The simulation results also indicated that the previously shown fact of greater information compression by coding the difference of consecutive intensity errors [1] was false for at least one typical sequence. A 12–14 percent decrease was obtained by coding the intensity errors directly.

4) Field-to-field motion prediction was reconfirmed to be superior to frame-to-frame motion prediction [1].

Some facts should be emphasized about these image sequences and the simulation parameters when comparing

TABLE VII
ZEROTH-ORDER ENTROPY TRANSMISSION OF BOBSJOB SEQUENCE

ϵ	Entropy Bits max/aver	Predicted MSE max/aver	Number of Unpredicted Pels max/aver	Average Value of Gradient Squared min/max	Corrected MSE min/max
spatial					
0.00100	117476/77269	88.37/21.81	21507/14612	263.0/1043.7	0.00/0.58
0.00050	117819/76855	86.25/21.51	21197/13746	257.4/1158.6	0.00/0.59
0.00025	120287/78184	89.17/23.53	21448/13741	255.2/1053.1	0.00/0.57
PAMT					
0.00200	124247/80926	104.69/32.00	21877/14600	309.4/ 836.1	0.00/0.57
0.00100	123015/80119	90.72/27.06	21028/13162	250.1/1268.5	0.00/0.52
0.00050	124700/81267	95.14/27.83	21362/13156	214.3/1124.5	0.00/0.50

TABLE VIII
FIELD-TO-FIELD MOTION PREDICTION, BOBSJOB SEQUENCE

ϵ	Entropy Bits max/aver	Predicted MSE max/aver	Number of Unpredicted Pels max/aver	Average Value of Gradient Squared min/max	Corrected MSE min/max
spatial/0 0.0001	112794/63171	51.6/14.6	19342/10182	72.5/623.1	0.01/1.21
spatial/1 0.0001	112294/72260	54.9/17.2	21864/13860	61.6/533.0	0.46/1.92
PAMT/0 0.0001	120732/65682	83.7/19.8	20534/10592	76.4/439.5	0.01/1.19
PAMT/1 0.0001	119544/74254	85.9/22.6	23020/14135	67.6/398.7	0.46/2.36

these simulation results and the simulation results of other researchers:

1) As has been noted, the motion in the sequence used for the simulations herein is lower than the motion in the sequences used in most other motion-compensated codec simulations [1], [4], [7], [12], [13]; these sequences are intended to be realistic, as opposed to unusual or exceptional.

2) The frames were not low-pass filtered to blur the edges. The sequences are very high quality sequences with sharp edges. This may explain why zeroth-order entropy encoding was superior, since sharp edges have small transition regions.

3) The results are affected by the endpoints of the quantizer bins and the threshold values in the codec. The values used for the simulations reported herein are noted at the beginning of Section VI.

A potential solution to the inability to correct the displacement vector could be averaging the spatial gradients in the two frames with a 2:1 weighting. (Less weight being given to the gradient values obtained from the present frame since backward differences must be used.) At least this would yield a nonzero spatial gradient in the correct direction without putting too much weight on a noisy estimate. Alternatively one could first see if the $\nabla_z I |_{t-1} = 0$ when $|DFD| > T$ and then (and only then) use $\nabla_z I |_t$. This is similar to the technique attributed to Bergmann in [7].

A potential circuit diagram using the PAMT prediction scheme is shown in Fig. 7. The codec diagrammed transmits zeroth-order entropy information. A few terms need to be defined:

1) $I(z, t)$ is the actual intensity captured by the camera.
2) $\hat{I}(z, t)$ is the predicted intensity, which contains prediction error.
3) $\tilde{I}(z, t)$ is the reconstructed intensity, which contains quantization error.
4) R/W is read/write. One line state indicates read; the other write.

The interpolation portion of the algorithm is not indicated. The condition queue is used to indicate whether the $\hat{d}$ value needs to be corrected or not.

In the correction circuit there are two framestore pairs; one pair is labeled "frame-store" (intensity framestore) and the other pair is labeled "displacement estimate" (displacement-estimate framestore). The addressing and clocking to each pair is alternated each frame (frame-to-frame motion prediction is used for simplicity). During

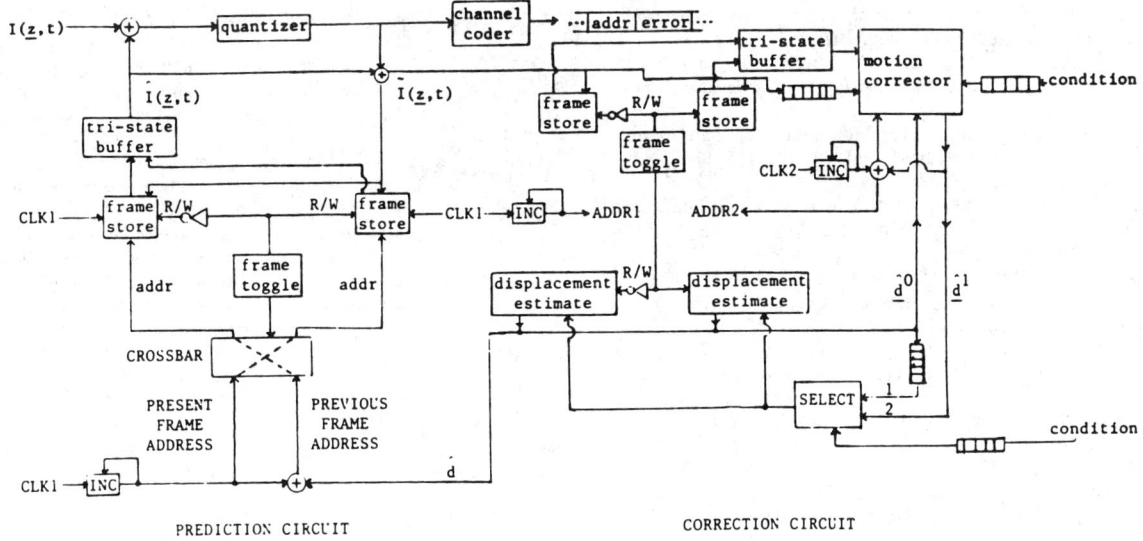

Fig. 7. A potential PAMT circuit diagram.

one frame-processing time, one pair (one intensity framestore and one displacement-estimate framestore) are clocked by CLK1, the same clock that is used in the prediction circuit. Intensity data are stored and displacement estimates are output. This pair is addressed by an incrementer. The second intensity framestore and the second displacement-estimate framestore are clocked by CLK2, an asynchronous clock, and are addressed by the motion corrector using $\hat{d}^1$ and an incrementer. For this pair, intensity data are output and displacement estimates are stored. CLK2 must toggle the same number of times in one frame interval as CLK1 does. Most of the time CLK2 can be faster than CLK1 since in the correction circuit $\hat{d}^0$ is simply copied from one displacement estimate memory into the other with no intervening computation. When motion correction is being done, CLK2 cannot toggle as fast as CLK1 since more computation is being done in the correction circuit loop than in the prediction circuit loop.

APPENDIX
EXAMPLE 1: CONVERGENCE RATE FOR DISPLACEMENT ESTIMATES

Consider an object which moves leftward 2 pels between frames, i.e.,

$$d = \begin{bmatrix} 2 \\ 0 \end{bmatrix}$$

and has the following "gradient" characteristics:

$$E\{\nabla_z I(i) f(i)\} = \begin{bmatrix} 400 & 100 \\ 100 & 200 \end{bmatrix}.$$

The eigenvalues and eigenvectors of $E\{\nabla_z I(i) f(i)\}$ are

$$[\lambda_1 \quad \lambda_2] = [441.4214 \quad 158.5786]$$

$$U = \begin{bmatrix} -0.3827 & 0.9239 \\ 0.9239 & 0.3827 \end{bmatrix}.$$

Using (31), the convergence coefficient ϵ is constrained to be less than 0.0033. If ϵ is chosen to be 0.00100, then the convergence constants are

$$\tau_1 = \frac{-1}{\ln(1 - 0.4414214)} = 1.7172$$

$$\tau_2 = \frac{-1}{\ln(1 - 0.1585786)} = 5.7916.$$

Thus, the analysis indicates both uncoupled displacement estimates should be within e^{-1} of their final value within six iterations if ϵ is 0.00100. However, if ϵ is 0.00010, then the convergence constants are $\{22, 63\}$ and if ϵ is 0.00001, then the convergence constants are $\{226, 630\}$, which are appreciably larger convergence coefficients.

REFERENCES

[1] A. N. Netravali and J. D. Robbins, "Motion compensated television coding, Part I," *Bell Syst. Tech. J.*, vol. 58, pp. 631–670, Mar. 1979.
[2] J. B. O'Neal, Jr., "Predictive quantizing systems (differential pulse code modulation) for the transmission of television signals," *Bell Syst. Tech. J.*, vol. 45, pp. 689–722, May–June 1966.
[3] R. Paquin and E. Dubois, "A spatio-temporal gradient method for estimating the displacement field in time-varying imagery," *Comput. Vision, Graphics, Image Processing*, vol. 21, pp. 205–221, 1983.
[4] D. R. Walker and K. R. Rao, "Improved pel recursive motion compensation," *IEEE Trans. Commun.*, vol. COM-32, pp. 1128–1134, Oct. 1984.
[5] E. Dubois, B. Prasada, and M. S. Sabri, "Image sequence coding," in *Image Sequence Analysis*, T. S. Huang, Ed. Berlin, Germany: Springer-Verlag, 1981, pp. 229–287.
[6] W. B. Thompson and S. T. Barnard, "Lower-level estimation and interpretation of visual motion," *Computer*, vol. 14, pp. 20–28, Aug. 1981.
[7] H. G. Musmann, P. Pirsch, and H.-J. Grallert, "Advances in picture coding," *Proc. IEEE*, vol. 73, pp. 523–548, Apr. 1985.
[8] R. J. Moorhead, "Image sequence compression using a motion-compensated technique," Ph.D. dissertation, North Carolina State Univ., June 1985.
[9] A. N. Netravali and J. O. Limb, "Picture coding: A review," *Proc. IEEE*, vol. 68, pp. 366–406, Mar. 1980.
[10] A. K. Jain, "Advances in mathematical models for image processing," *Proc. IEEE*, vol. 69, pp. 502–528, May 1981.

[11] D. G. Luenberger, *Introduction to Linear and Nonlinear Programming*. Reading, MA: Addison-Wesley, 1973.
[12] J. D. Robbins and A. N. Netravali, "Interframe television coding using movement compensation," in *Proc. Int. Conf. Commun.*, 1979, pp. 23.4.1-23.4.5.
[13] A. N. Netravali and J. D. Robbins, "Motion-compensated coding: Some new results," *Bell Syst. Tech. J.*, vol. 59, pp. 1735-1745, Nov. 1980.
[14] R. J. Moorhead and S. A. Rajala, "Motion-compensated interframe coding," in *Proc. ICASSP '85*, Tampa, FL, Mar. 1985, pp. 347-350.
[15] B. Widrow and J. M. McCool, "A comparison of adaptive algorithms based on the methods of steepest descent and random search," *IEEE Trans. Antennas Propagat.*, vol. AP-24, pp. 615-637, Sept. 1976.
[16] S. T. Alexander, "Adaptive image compression using the least mean square (LMS) algorithm," Ph.D. dissertation, North Carolina State Univ., 1982.
[17] S. Sabri and B. Prasada, "Coding of broadcast TV signals for transmission over satellite channels," *IEEE Trans. Commun.*, vol. COM-32, pp. 1323-1330, Dec. 1984.
[18] S. Sabri, "Movement compensated interframe prediction for NTSC color TV signals," *IEEE Trans. Commun.*, vol. COM-32, pp. 954-968, Aug. 1984.
[19] E. Dubois and S. Sabri, "Noise reduction in image sequences using motion-compensated temporal filtering," *IEEE Trans. Commun.*, vol. COM-32, pp. 826-831, July 1984.
[20] B. G. Haskell, P. L. Gordon, R. L. Schmidt, and J. V. Scattaglia, "Interframe coding of 525 line, monochrome television at 1.5 Mbits/s," *IEEE Trans. Commun.*, vol. COM-25, pp. 1339-1348, Nov. 1977.
[21] H. Kuroda, N. Mukawa, T. Matsuoka, and S. Okudo, "1.5 Mbit/s interframe codec for video teleconferencing signals," in *Proc. 1982 IEEE GLOBECOM*, Nov. 1982, pp. E2.5.1-E2.5.5.

Sarah A. Rajala (S'73-M'79-SM'84) received the B.S.E.E. degree from Michigan Technological University, Houghton, in 1974, and the M.S. and Ph.D degrees in electrical engineering from Rice University, Houston, TX, in 1977 and 1979, respectively.

Since 1979, she has been a member of the Department of Electrical and Computer Engineering, North Carolina State University, Raleigh, where she is currently an Associate Professor. In 1985, she was appointed an adjunct Associate Professor of the Radiology Department at the Bowman Gray School of Medicine, Wakeforest University, Winston-Salem, NC. She has been an active researcher in the areas of time-varying image analysis with application to image coding, target acquistion and tracking, image restoration, and medical image processing. She is the author of over 30 publications and has served as a consultant to many industrial organizations.

Dr. Rajala is a member of SWE, Sigma Xi, Eta Kappa Nu, and Tau Beta Pi.

Robert J. Moorhead II (S'81-M'85) was born in Atlanta, GA, on February 12, 1958. He received the B.S.E.E. degree from Geneva College, Beaver Falls, PA, in 1980 and the M.S. and Ph.D. degrees in electrical and computer engineering from North Carolina State University, Raleigh, in 1982 and 1985, respectively.

Since 1985 he has been a Research Staff Member at the IBM Thomas J. Watson Research Center, Yorktown Heights, NY, in the Image Technologies Department. His current professional interests include image sequence processing algorithms and architectures.

Lawrence W. Cook (S'81-M'86) was born in Arlington, VA, in 1961. He received the B.S. degree in electrical engineering in 1984 from North Carolina State University, Raleigh.

He is currently conducting M.S. degree studies at North Carolina State University in the area of communications and signal processing. In September 1986 he joined Government Systems of Harris Corporation where he is involved with the design of video and signal processing communications systems.

Mr. Cook is a member of Tau Beta Pi and Eta Kappa Nu.

Signal Processing: *Image Communication* 1 (1989) 153-180
Elsevier Science Publishers B.V.

CODING OF ARBITRARILY SHAPED IMAGE SEGMENTS BASED ON A GENERALIZED ORTHOGONAL TRANSFORM

Michael GILGE, Thomas ENGELHARDT and Ralf MEHLAN

Institute for Communication Engineering, RWTH Aachen Melatener Str. 23, 5100 Aachen, Fed. Rep. Germany

Received 8 February 1989
Revised 17 April 1989

Abstract. Region oriented image representation offers several advantages over block-oriented schemes, e.g. adaptation to the local image characteristics, or object motion compensation as opposed to block-wise motion compensation. For the task of image data compression, i.e. image coding, new algorithms are needed which work on arbitrarily shaped image regions, called segments, instead of rectangular image blocks. Based on a generalized moment approach, the luminance function inside the segment is approximated by a weighted sum of basis functions, for example polynomials. A set of basis functions which is orthogonal with respect to the shape of the segment to be coded can be obtained using orthogonalization schemes. This results in the derivation of a generalized shape-adapted transform coder. Suitable coder and decoder structures are introduced which do *not* necessitate the transmission of the basis functions for each segment. Finally an application of the derived algorithms to image sequence coding at low data rates is shown, which is based on a segmentation of the motion compensated prediction error image.

Zusammenfassung. Eine regionenorientierte Bildbeschreibung bietet gegenüber blockorientierten Verfahren einige Vorteile, so wird zum Beispiel eine bessere Adaption an den lokalen Bildinhalt oder eine objektbezogene Bewegungskompensation ermöglicht. Zur Bilddatenreduktion, d.h. Bildcodierung, werden neue Algorithmen benötigt, die beliebig geformte Bildregionen anstatt der bisherigen rechteckigen Bildbereiche verarbeiten können. Ausgehend von einem Ansatz mit verallgemeinerten Momenten wird eine Approximation des Helligkeitsverlaufes innerhalb der Segmentgrenzen mit Hilfe von Polynomen erzielt. Durch den Einsatz von Orthogonalisierungsverfahren kann ein Satz von Basisfunktionen erzeugt werden, der bezüglich der Form des zu codierenden Segmentes orthogonal ist. Dies führt zu einer allgemeinen, formangepaßten Transformationscodierung. Geeignete Strukturen für den Bildcoder und -decoder, welche *ohne* die Übertragung des Basisfunktionensatzes für jedes Segment auskommen, werden eingeführt. Schließlich werden die vorgestellten Algorithmen zur Bewegtbildcodierung mit niedriger Datenrate eingesetzt. Das gezeigte Verfahren beruht auf einer Segmentierung des bewegungskompensierten Prädiktionsfehlerbildes.

Résumé. Les représentations d'images basées sur des régions offrent plusieurs avantages par rapport aux méthodes basées sur des blocs, tels que l'adaptation aux caractéristiques locales de l'image ou la compensation de mouvement d'objet par opposition à la compensation de mouvement par bloc. Pour la compression des données images, c'est-à-dire pour le codage d'images, de nouveaux algorithmes sont nécessaires qui peuvent travailler sur des régions de forme quelconque, appelées segments au lieu des blocs d'image rectangulaire. En utilisant une approche des moments généralisés, la fonction de luminance à l'intérieur du segment est approchée par une somme pondérée de fonctions de base, par exemple des polynômes. Un ensemble de fonctions de base qui est orthogonal par rapport à la forme du segment à coder peut être obtenu en utilisant des méthodes d'orthogonalisation. Ceci conduit à l'établissement d'un codeur transformé adapté à la forme. Des structures appropriées de codeurs et de décodeurs qui ne nécessitent pas la transmission des fonctions de base pour chaque segment sont introduites. Finalement, une application de l'algorithme obtenu au codage de séquence d'images à faible débit est montrée, basée sur la segmentation de l'image d'erreur de prédiction de mouvement.

Keywords. Coding of image segments, moment theory, orthogonalization, orthogonal polynomials, generalized transform coding, prediction error segmentation.

0923-5965/89/$3.50 © 1989, Elsevier Science Publishers B.V.

1. Introduction

Image coding is a key-technique for a wide variety of applications ranging from medical imagery, remote sensing, image communication (e.g. video conference, picture phone), commercial products (e.g. digital VCRs) up to the printing industry. Today's products mostly use DPCM algorithms for image data reduction due to the simplicity of implementation. With the progress in the development of powerful microcomputers and signal processors, now products employing transform coding are at the edge of becoming available products. The data compression reached using transform coding, e.g. for still pictures, is somewhere about 1:15. Although the number of published transform coding algorithms suggests further improvements, a saturation point with respect to compression ratio seems to be reached for transform coding [21].

The exploitation of new degrees of freedom not yet used is necessary to leave the mentioned level of saturation. Consider the block-segmentation shown in Fig. 1: Partitioning the image into rectangular blocks and coding each block separately yields several advantages (e.g. no transmission of shape information due to fixed block-size and low computational complexity). On the other hand the independent treatment of each block often results in a visibility of the block boundaries in the reconstructed image called blocking-effect, especially at low data rates, due to discontinuities in the gray values between adjacent blocks. Another disadvantage is that most algorithms do not exploit inter-block correlation. Several schemes, known from literature, attempt to increase the degrees of freedom using variable block size [30], overlapping blocks [9, 24] or a combination of blockwise DPCM with transform coding [32] and thereby attempt to overcome one or more of the above stated problems.

The next generation of image coders will no longer use a block-oriented image segmentation but a region-oriented segmentation as indicated in Fig. 2. This approach is often called "*contour/texture model*" in the literature. The now quasi-stationary image regions should enable a higher data compression, while the instationarities in the image are represented by segment borders and are separately coded. Because of the additional

Fig. 1. Example of block-oriented image coding, "Alexis".

Fig. 2. Example of region-oriented image coding, "Alexis".

overhead needed for the transmission of the segment borders, a region-oriented coder is not necessarily more efficient than a traditional block-oriented one. Only if powerful representation schemes for both, segment contours and the segment content are available, further compression and better image quality will be achieved.

Up to now, not too many papers in the literature have considered the problem of coding image regions of arbitrary shape: Eden et al. [6] have investigated a polynomial representation, but restrict themselves for the sake of fast implementation and mathematical stability to rectangular regions. Kocher and Leonardi [20] tackle the problem of arbitrary shape using the Gauss–Jordan algorithm to solve the equations, but they only consider polynomials up to the second order. In the comparison between block-wise DCT and segmented image coding by Biggar et al. [2], only zero and first order polynomials are used for region representation. Other authors report about spline-functions for image approximation [4, 33] or polynomials, but again used on small rectangular blocks [13].

This contribution aims at the introduction of a generalized transform coding scheme which works on arbitrarily shaped image segments, instead of just rectangular image regions. The approach contains the conventional block-wise transform coding as a special case. In Section 2 generalized moments are introduced as image properties which include all transforms as special cases, e.g. Fourier. The reconstruction from the moment representation leads to a least mean squares (LMS) approximation of the luminance function. It will be shown that transform coding and LMS approximation are equivalent. Usually the normal equations for LMS approximation are solved by using the Gauss–Jordan algorithm. An orthogonalization of the basis-functions with respect to the segment shape yields a mathematically well posed set of equations. Especially the Gauss–Jordan algorithm is no longer needed because the orthogonalization delivers a set of *uncoupled* equations. In Section 3 a suitable coder and decoder structure is derived which does *not* necessitate the transmission of the basis functions used for the approximation. The scheme also allows user interaction and/or progressive image built-up. A quantization of the approximation coefficients enables further data-reduction. Section 4 shows experimental results using the algorithm for the coding of moving video.

Fig. 3. Segmented image with region-of-interest marked.

Therefore the error image after motion compensated prediction is segmented into regions where motion compensation succeeded—no further transmission is necessary—and regions where motion compensation (partly) failed—transmission of update (i.e. intraframe) information is necessary. Section 5 summarizes the most significant results and discusses possible extensions and further work.

2. Approximation theory in the discrete case

Assume an image patch with the gray-values given by the function $f(x, y)$. The region is a result of a previous segmentation procedure. To give an example, Fig. 4 shows a 3-dimensional plot of a region obtained by a segmentation of the image as shown in Fig. 3.

We are in search of a representation for $f(x, y)$, say $g(x, y)$, which approximates the given gray values and describes them in a compact form because we want to reach data compression. The compression ratio is defined as follows: The number of bits needed to represent the given original gray values $f(x, y)$ (usually 8 bits/pixel) divided by the number of bits needed to describe the approximation $g(x, y)$. For the case of arbitrarily shaped image segments which is considered here, the number of bits to code the segment shape has to be added to the bit count for the representation of $g(x, y)$. As we are only concerned with the

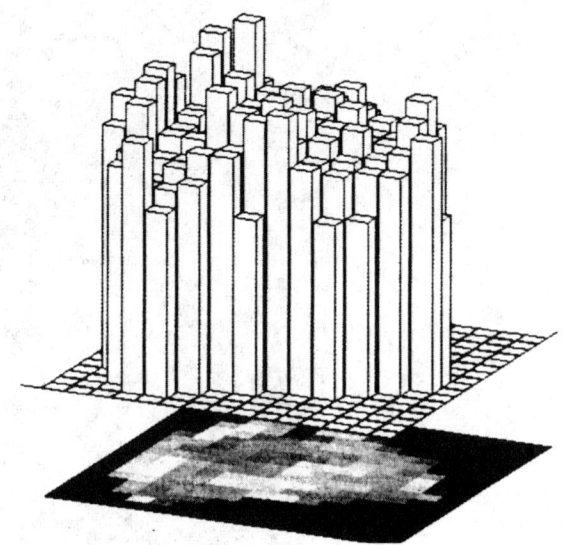

Fig. 4. 3-D plot of the gray values, extracted region from Fig. 3.

description of the luminance inside the segment in this contribution, the contour information will not be considered in the following.

2.1. Generalized moments

A 2-dimensional probability density function of a 2-dimensional random variable is considered. Without loss of generalization any image function $f(x, y)$ restricted to a finite area can be considered a density due to the non-negativity constraint. The function $f(x, y)$ has non-zero values only in a finite part of the x–y plane, namely the region D corresponding to the shape of the segment. We can derive linear properties from the given function using the following operation

$$m_{ij} = \int_{-\infty}^{\infty} \int_{-\infty}^{\infty} h_{ij}(x, y) f(x, y) \, dx \, dy$$
$$= \int_D \int h_{ij}(x, y) f(x, y) \, dx \, dy. \quad (1)$$

The measurements or properties m_{ij} are called generalized moments. A uniqueness theorem [16] states that the sequence of moments $\{m_{ij}\} = \{m_{00}, m_{01}, \ldots, m_{kl}\}$ is uniquely defined by the density $f(x, y)$, and conversely $f(x, y)$ is uniquely defined by its associated sequence of moments $\{m_{ij}\}$.

The specification of the measurement kernel $h_{ij}(x, y)$ depends on the application. The approach is general enough to show that different, commonly used measures all involve the same mathematics. For example, consider the kernel

$$h_{ij} = \exp[-j2\pi(u_i x + v_j y)]. \qquad (2)$$

We then obtain m_{ij} as samples of the 2-dimensional Fourier-transform of the image at the spatial frequency (u_i, v_j). With the choice

$$h_{ij} = h(x_i - x, y_j - y), \qquad (3)$$

the measurements become samples of the convolution of the image with the point spread function h. Finally we take

$$h_{ij} = x^i y^j \qquad (4)$$

and obtain m_{ij} as the geometric moments with the order of the moments denoted by $i+j$. The above definition has the form of a projection of the function $f(x, y)$ onto the monomial $x^i y^j$. This basis functional set $\{x^i y^j\}$ is complete, which is expressed by the Weierstrass approximation theorem [3], but not orthogonal. Orthogonal basis functional sets will be considered in Section 2.3.

Before we can employ the above derivations, we have to solve two main problems:

(1) Given a sequence of generalized moments, we need to find an inverse transform to retrieve $f(x, y)$ or at least an approximation of $f(x, y)$. In the case of Fourier transform we know an inverse exists but does an inverse from the geometric moment representation exist?

(2) Assuming we found an inverse operation for example using the geometric moments the sequence of possible moments is infinite. How many and which of the moments do we need for an approximation satisfying a given error constraint?

It has been shown in [10] that no direct inverse exists for the case of a finite number of geometrical moments and a continuous function $f(x, y)$. Of course, for the discrete case, i.e. sampled image function, (1) can be written in a form with the integrals replaced by summations over the defined area of the given segment

$$m_{ij} = \sum_x \sum_y x^i y^j f(x, y), \qquad (5)$$

or in matrix form

$$\begin{bmatrix} m_{00} \\ m_{10} \\ \vdots \\ m_{ij} \end{bmatrix} = \begin{bmatrix} 1 & 1 & \cdots & 1 \\ x_1 & x_2 & \cdots & x_M \\ \vdots & \vdots & & \vdots \\ x_1^i y_1^j & x_2^i y_2^j & \cdots & x_M^i y_M^j \end{bmatrix}$$
$$\times \begin{bmatrix} f(x_1, y_1) \\ f(x_2, y_2) \\ \vdots \\ f(x_M, y_M) \end{bmatrix}, \qquad (6)$$

$$\mathbf{m} = \mathbf{\Phi} \mathbf{f}. \qquad (7)$$

If we additionally assume to calculate exactly K moments for $K = M$ given image samples, the above equation has the form of a one to one transformation. We know that the inverse is given rightaway by

$$\mathbf{f} = \mathbf{\Phi}^{-1} \mathbf{m}, \qquad (8)$$

with $\mathbf{\Phi}^{-1}$ as the inverse matrix of $\mathbf{\Phi}$. Unfortunately, inverting the matrix $\mathbf{\Phi}$ is a mathematically ill-posed problem. Besides we want less moments than the given number of pixels to suffice as a description of $f(x, y)$. As a solution out of this situation we will introduce the method of "moment matching" in the following. This nicely turns out to be equivalent to the method of least squares approximation, discussed in Section 2.2.

A finite set of K known moments m_{ij} is given and we use a model function $g(x, y)$ which may be expressed in parametrical form with N unknown parameters a_n, by

$$g(x, y) = a_1 \varphi_1(x, y) + a_2 \varphi_2(x, y)$$
$$+ \cdots + a_N \varphi_N(x, y). \qquad (9)$$

The functions $\varphi_n(x, y)$ are called the basis functional set. For the task of approximation the set must be complete (Weierstrass approximation theorem). If we now require the moments M_{ij} of

$g(x, y)$ to be identical to the given moments m_{ij}

$$m_{ij} \stackrel{!}{=} M_{ij}$$

$$\Rightarrow \sum_x \sum_y h_{ij} f(x, y) \stackrel{!}{=} \sum_x \sum_y h_{ij} g(x, y)$$

$$= \sum_x \sum_y h_{ij} \sum_{n=1}^{N} a_n \varphi_n(x, y), \quad (10)$$

we get a coupled set of K equations. If the number of parameters N is equal to the number of moments K, the set of equations has exactly one solution and we can solve for the vector $\boldsymbol{a}^N$ (the superscript N denotes a vector consisting of N components). Please note that the closeness of the approximation is determined by the number of moments used. The sequence of given moments approximates $f(x, y)$ by the estimate $g(x, y)$ which follows from the uniqueness theorem:

$$f(x, y) \approx g(x, y) = \boldsymbol{\Phi} \boldsymbol{a}^N. \quad (11)$$

The equality holds in the discrete case for $K = N \rightarrow M$ or in the continuous case for $K = N \rightarrow \infty$.

Before we can attempt an application we have to make three decisions first:
(1) Select a measurement kernel h_{ij}.
(2) Select approximation functions $\varphi_i(x, y)$.
(3) Determine the number of moments.

We decide to use a geometrical moment generating measurement kernel $h_{ij} = x^i y^j$. For the approximation function $g(x, y)$ we use a polynomial with the simple basis functions

$$\varphi_i(x, y) = x^{k(i)} y^{l(i)}, \quad k + l \leq N. \quad (12)$$

Using geometrical moments, and especially polynomial basis functions for $g(x, y)$, is interesting with regard to image representation for several reasons:
• Under certain constraints all functions can be developed as polynomials, e.g. Taylor-series. We therefore have a kind of a generalized tool.
• Images predominantly consist of slowly varying surfaces which are well represented by polynomials. The subjective quality of the reconstructed images is pleasant to the human eye.
• Polynomials have mathematically very simple expressions.

To give an example we consider only the moments m_{ij} up to first order, making it a total of three moments ($K = 3$), namely $\boldsymbol{m} = \{M_{00}, M_{01}, M_{10}\}$:

$$m_{ij} = \sum_x \sum_y h_{ij} g(x, y), \quad (13)$$

$$m_{ij} = \sum_x \sum_y h_{ij} \sum_{n=1}^{N} a_n \varphi(x, y). \quad (14)$$

Using $\varphi_1 = 1$, $\varphi_2 = y$, and $\varphi_3 = x$ we can write

$$m_{ij} = \sum_x \sum_y x^i y^j (a_1 + a_2 y + a_3 x), \quad (15)$$

$$m_{00} = \sum_x \sum_y (a_1 + a_2 y + a_3 x),$$

$$m_{01} = \sum_x \sum_y (a_1 y + a_2 y^2 + a_3 xy),$$

$$m_{10} = \sum_x \sum_y (a_1 x + a_2 xy + a_3 x^2). \quad (16)$$

The summation is over the area of the given segment (including M pixels). In the following chapter it will be shown that the above approach is identical to the least mean square approximation if the basis functions $\varphi_n(x, y)$ agree with the measurement kernel h_{ij}.

2.2. Least squares approximation and normal equations

Two kinds of errors are connected with an approximation of the original image region:
(1) *Measurement errors.* Taking the samples (pixels) from the original continuous luminance function can be thought of as a measuring process. The obtained values differ from the true brightness values by the measurement error, e.g. due to camera noise. Denoting the true but unknown gray values by $s(x, y)$ and the error term by $e(x, y)$, the following equation holds:

$$f(x, y) = s(x, y) + e(x, y). \quad (17)$$

(2) *Modelling errors.* The approximation tries to fit the measurements to a selected model. Depending on the physical data generating process, the selected model is more or less suited for the description. Only in rare cases do we know the physics behind the data generating process which dictates the choice of the model. In the case of modelling the image intensities, little can be assumed about the nature of $s(x, y)$: the function is positive and bounded. When we are considering the human observer, we can also assume that $s(x, y)$ is bandlimited, otherwise it would contain information a human observer cannot perceive anyway. Summarizing it can be said that the approximation error is dependent on the used model.

In order to find the "best" approximation for a given set of data we have to select not only a suited model but we also have to express "best" in a defined way. For an approximation $g(x, y)$ for $f(x, y)$ in the least mean square sense we have to use the Euclidean distance also called sum of the squared errors:

$$d(f, g) = \sum_x \sum_y (g(x, y) - f(x, y))^2. \quad (18)$$

The least squares approximation was introduced by Gauss as far back as 1795 [27]. This method enjoys the following advantages [26]:
- Easy to implement.
- Does not require an iterative solution.
- Filters zero mean, finite variance noise in an unbiased manner.
- If the measurement error $e(x, y)$ has Gaussian distribution and if the measured data are considered to be realizations of a stochastic process, then the obtained estimate $g(x, y)$ using the least squares criterion yields the minimum variance unbiased estimate among all unbiased estimators. Furthermore the estimate $g(x, y)$ is the maximum likelihood estimate.

The approximating function $g(x, y)$ can be written in a generalized form as

$$g(x, y) = a_1 \varphi_1(x, y) + a_2 \varphi(x, y)$$
$$+ \cdots + a_N \varphi_N(x, y), \quad (19)$$

with the basis functions $\varphi_1, \varphi_2, \ldots, \varphi_N$ given through the selected model, e.g. polynomials, and $a_1, a_2, \ldots, a_N$ being the parameters which are to be determined in a way that (18) will be minimum:

$$d(f, g) = \sum_x \sum_y \left(\sum_{n=1}^N a_n \varphi_n(x, y) - f(x, y) \right)^2$$
$$\to \text{MIN}. \quad (20)$$

To find the vector a^N corresponding to a minimum squared error, we differentiate (20) with respect to every component a_q of a^N and require it to be zero for the minimum:

$$\frac{\partial d}{\partial a_q} = 2 \sum_x \sum_y \left(\sum_{n=1}^N a_n \varphi_n(x, y) \right.$$
$$\left. - f(x, y) \right) \varphi_q(x, y)$$
$$\stackrel{!}{=} 0, \quad \text{for } q = 1, \ldots, N \quad (21)$$

$$\Rightarrow \sum_{n=1}^N a_n \sum_x \sum_y \varphi_n(x, y) \varphi_q(x, y)$$
$$\stackrel{!}{=} \sum_x \sum_y f(x, y) \varphi_q(x, y), \quad \text{for } q = 1, \ldots, N \quad (22)$$

Equation (10), with the measurement kernel h_{ij} chosen to be $\varphi_q(x, y)$, is exactly equivalent to the Gaussian method of least squares approximation. Therefore it proves our earlier statement. Equation (22) are called the normal equations because in an N-dimensional Euclidean space the smallest error vector $e(x, y) = g(x, y) - f(x, y)$ is perpendicular (normal) to the hyperplane spanned by the basis functions $\varphi_q(x, y)$, see Fig. 5. The maximum dimension of the Euclidean space is given by the number of pixels in the current segment, M in our case.

The N equations can be solved for the N values of a^N minimizing the approximation error. With regard to the number of unknowns N and the number of given pixels M we can distinguish between three cases:

(1) $M < N$: We have less data points than

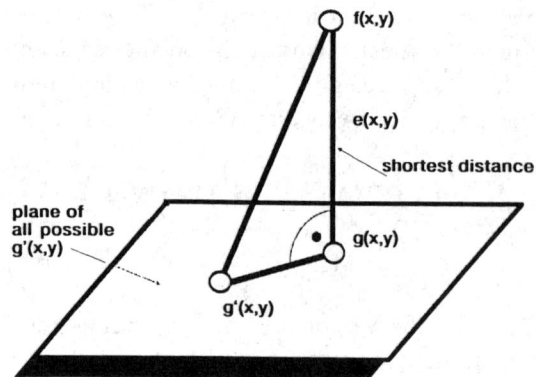

Fig. 5. Relationship between given function f, approximation g, error e.

unknowns which we cannot solve for. The system is said to be underdetermined.

(2) $M = N$: We have as many data points (pixels) as parameters and the system is guaranteed to have exactly one solution if the columns of Φ are linearly independent. The solution can be viewed two ways:

(i) We are mapping the data values onto the basis functional set given by the matrix Φ. Obtaining a is a *transformation* into another coordinate system and the values of a are often called coefficients.

(ii) Another interpretation is that we now have an analytical function $g(x, y)$ which agrees with $f(x, y)$ on the nodes of the sampling grid. But unlike $f(x, y)$ we know all values in between sampling positions which is also called an *interpolation*.

(3) $M > N$: Now we have more data points than parameters which is what we want for data compression. But the distance between g and f usually cannot be zero for all M positions. This directly follows when attempting to fit a straight line, determined by two parameters, through more than two points. The system of linear equations is said to be overdetermined. It can be solved by distributing the fitting error in a way that minimizes the squared error.

The third case $M > N$ in connection with image data compression offers the following potential:

• $f(x, y)$ is corrupted by measurement errors as stated above, therefore an exact reproduction of $f(x, y)$ requires not only the information but also the noise to be coded. A least squares approximation on the other hand can reduce stochastic errors.

• Approximating the function by less parameters than given points yields a compact description, which means data compression (unless the representation of the fewer parameters requires more bits than the given pixels, see Section 3.2).

• The function g can be selected to give smooth spatial gray values changes, e.g. polynomials, which represent the predominantly found slowly varying surfaces in images well. This reduces the oscillatory effects found in reconstruction using periodic functions, e.g. Fourier transform.

• The analytic representation simplifies geometrical operation, e.g. affine transformations, and/or mathematical operations as derivation or integration.

The set of equations is coupled and mathematically not necessarily stable. A solution for a^N can be obtained through the Gauss–Jordan algorithm which is computationally expensive. Another drawback makes the pure approach derived above impractical: In an attempt to improve the approximation quality by including more coefficients (this is necessary for example if we think about progressive transmission, see Section 3.1 for details) all equations have to be solved again from the beginning. This is due to the coupled nature of the equations. A solution to this problem can be obtained through orthogonalization of the basis functions. For orthogonal basis functions the following condition holds:

$$\sum_x \sum_y \varphi_n(x, y) \varphi_q(x, y) = 0, \quad \text{for } n \neq q. \quad (23)$$

The notion of orthogonality greatly simplifies the solution of (22). Now the system of equations is decoupled, yielding

$$\sum_{n=1}^{N} a_n \sum_x \sum_y \varphi_n(x, y) \varphi_q(x, y)$$
$$= \sum_x \sum_y f(x, y) \varphi_q(x, y), \quad \text{for } q = 1, \ldots, N,$$
$$(24)$$

$$\Rightarrow a_q \sum_x \sum_y \varphi_q(x,y)\varphi_q(x,y)$$
$$= \sum_x \sum_y f(x,y)\varphi_q(x,y), \quad \text{for } q=1,\ldots,N, \tag{25}$$

$$a_q = \frac{\sum_x \sum_y f(x,y)\varphi_q(x,y)}{\sum_x \sum_y \varphi_q(x,y)\varphi_q(x,y)}, \quad \text{for } q=1,\ldots,N. \tag{26}$$

If the system of basis functions is even orthonormal, i.e.,

$$\sum_x \sum_y \varphi_q(x,y)\varphi_q(x,y) = 1, \tag{27}$$

we can simplify (26) further

$$a_q = \sum_x \sum_y f(x,y)\varphi_q(x,y), \quad \text{for } q=1,\ldots,N. \tag{28}$$

As we see, the system of equations can be solved very easily for each of the approximation coefficients by just mapping the given image onto the respective basis function $\varphi_q(x,y)$. Even including more coefficients does *not* necessitate the recalculation of previously computed coefficients. This is very useful for progressive image build-up. The main advantage however connected with the orthogonal basis functions is the mathematical stability and simplicity of the approach with no matrix inversion or iterative solutions necessary, but instead, we get a well conditioned system of equations.

Summarizing, we have shown that from a generalized moment representation which includes many well known techniques as a special case, for example Fourier analysis, we can obtain a reconstruction of the original function by the method of moment matching. This method nicely turns out to be equivalent to a least squares approximation. The cumbersome mathematics involved in the method can be avoided completely by using orthogonal basis functions. Taking as many approximation coefficients as given segment pixels results in a perfect error-free reconstruction. For a smaller set of coefficients an approximation can be recovered. The data compression ratio depends on the basis functions used. In the following section we will investigate, how to obtain orthogonal basis functions with respect to segments of arbitrary shape.

2.3. Orthogonalization with respect to shape

The notion of orthogonality is closely connected to those of norm and dot product. The method of least squares is based on the Euclidean semi-norm [8], given by

$$\|f\|_2 = \left(\sum_{x_i}\sum_{y_j} f^2(x_i,y_j)\right)^{1/2} \tag{29}$$

and connected with the scalar or dot product

$$(f,f) = \|f\|_2^2. \tag{30}$$

The scalar product of two functions f and g is given by

$$(f,g) = \sum_{x_i}\sum_{y_j} f(x_i,y_j)g(x_i,y_j). \tag{31}$$

If $(f,g)=0$ holds the functions are said to be orthogonal. To obtain the property of orthogonalization with respect to the shape of the segment, the summation in (31) is carried out only for coordinate pairs (x_i,y_j) inside the segment boundaries. Another possibility is given by the introduction of a weight function $w(x_i,y_j)$ which is zero outside the given segment and equal to 1 inside:

$$(f,g) = \sum_x \sum_y w(x,y)f(x,y)g(x,y)$$
$$= 0. \tag{32}$$

Now the summation can be carried out over an circumscribing rectangle with the functions f and g being orthogonal with respect to the weight function $w(x,y)$. A sample image segment, the sampling grid, and the values of the corresponding weight function is sketched in Fig. 6. It is clear that two given functions cannot be orthogonal with respect to several differently shaped segments. Segments do vary in shape and/or the number of pixels they include. Therefore it is necessary to

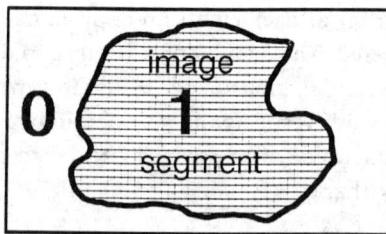

Fig. 6. Example of a window function.

find a specific set of orthogonal functions for each of the different segments given. Please note that a rectangular image block is included in the treatment here as a special shape.

We are guaranteed by the following theorem to find orthogonal basis functions for a given shape:

Theorem. *If the set of functions $u_0, u_1, \ldots, u_n$ is linearly independent in a n-dimensional sub-space A_n then there exists a set of functions $q_0, q_1, \ldots, q_n$ which are orthogonal with respect to the same sub-space and moreover the functions q_n are linear combinations of the functions $u_0, u_1, \ldots, u_n$.*

The proof of the theorem can be found in the literature [31]. In the Appendix, two algorithms are reviewed which generate orthogonal basis functions for a given shape and given independent approximation functions.

Conventional image coding algorithms segment the image into not overlapping rectangular blocks and mostly use transform coding. These algorithms, e.g. DCT or approximation by polynomials, are special cases of the more general method introduced here.

For a rectangular grid and starting with the simple polynomials 1, x, y, x^2, xy, $y^2 \ldots$ we get, after orthogonalization, the well known Gram-Schmidt polynomials. These polynomials are a discrete orthogonal version of the Legendre-

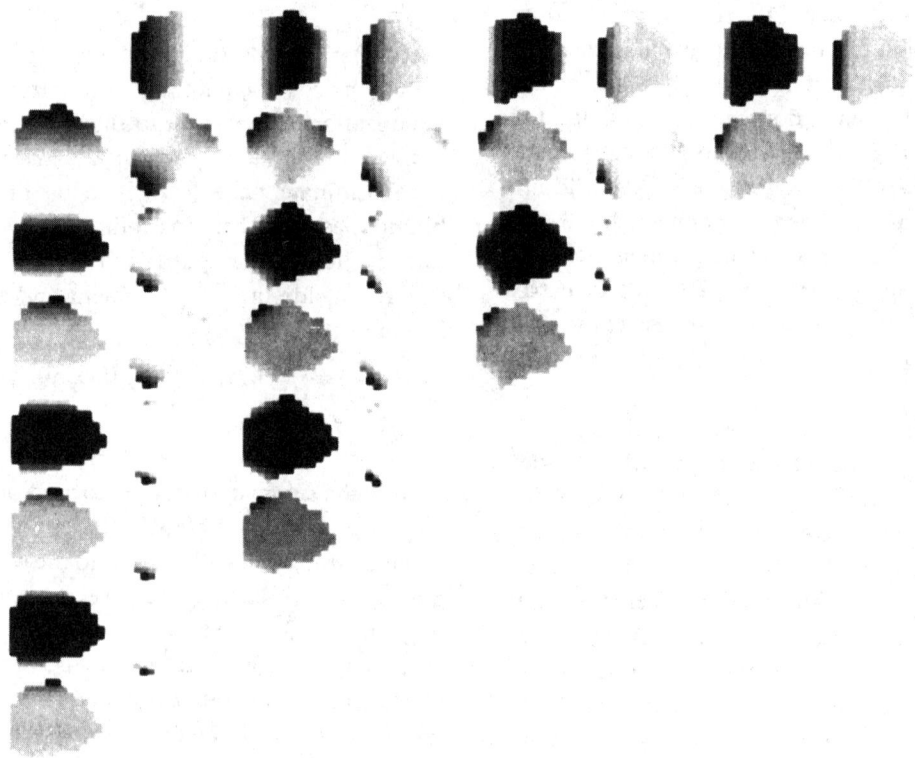

Fig. 7. Basis images for non-orthogonal polynomials.

polynomials which are only orthogonal in the continuous case. Starting with cosine functions (DCT), we do not need to orthogonalize for the case of rectangular regions, as cosine functions are orthogonal not only in the continuous case but also in the discrete case.

For the segment depicted in Fig. 4, the initial basis functions, i.e. the polynomials $x^i y^j$, and the orthogonalized basis functions are shown in Figs. 7 and 8 respectively. A sample reconstruction using the orthogonal basis images of Fig. 8 is shown in Fig. 9. The segment consists of 132 pixels while

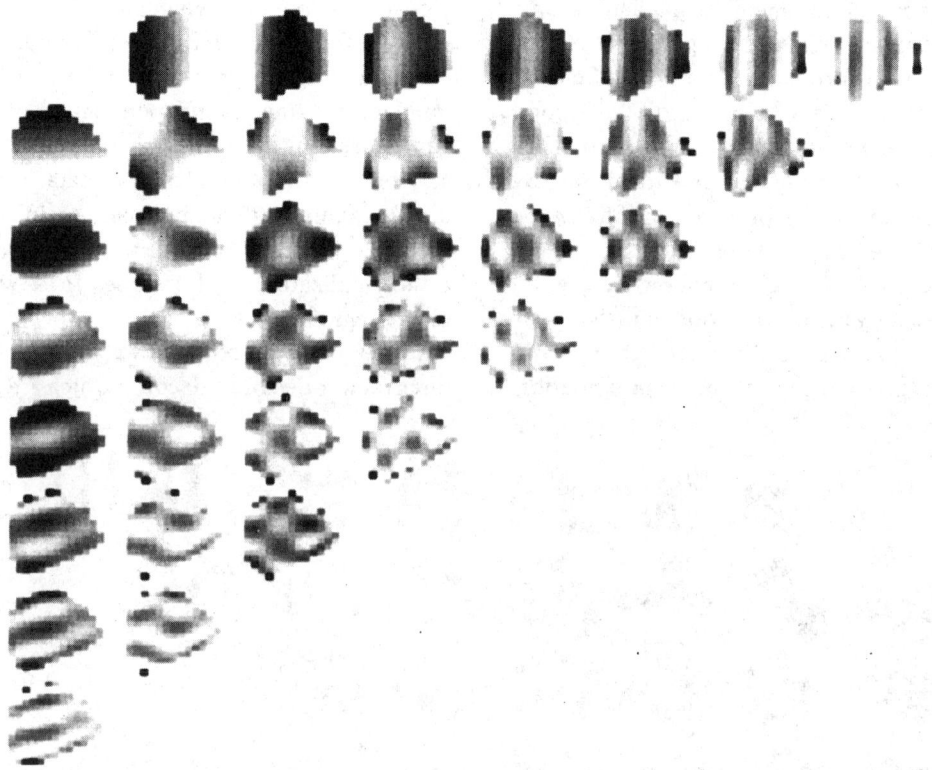

Fig. 8. Basis images after orthogonalization with respect to shape.

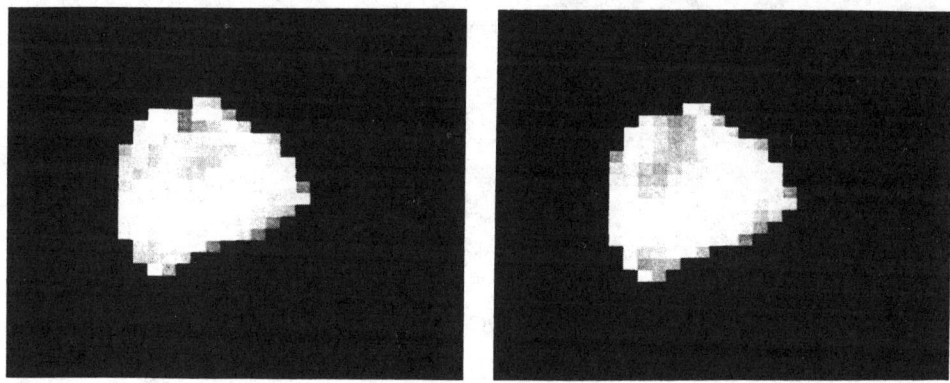

Fig. 9. Sample reconstruction using the orthogonal basis images of Fig. 8. Original segment (left), reconstructed segment (right).

the reconstruction uses up to 9th order polynomials, totalling 45 coefficients. The figure clearly shows the noise reducing effect of the approximation. At the same time the irregular structures inside the segment are far better reproduced than would be possible using only second order polynomials.

In the literature [17] it has been shown that the DCT gives very good energy compaction and approaches the decorrelation properties of a Karhunen–Loève transform (KLT) for a specific class of image functions. We want to exploit these good properties on the one hand and want to use arbitrarily shaped image segments too. By orthogonalization with respect to a specific shape we obtain a shape adapted DCT. The basis images for the segment given in Fig. 4 are shown in Fig. 10.

Summarizing, by the introduction of orthogonal basis functions which are orthogonal to the specific shape of the given segment, the approximation problem for arbitrarily shaped regions can be solved. The approach is characterized by mathematically stable and simple operations, i.e. no iterations and no matrix inversion. The set of approximation coefficients is finite unlike the infinite set of non-orthogonal moments. For a progressive or improved reconstruction, higher order coefficients can be added *without* recalculation of any previously computed coefficients. This property is required for an hierarchical representation. As the orthogonalization process is not limited to polynomials, any linearly independent set of functions can be used for the approximation. Basis functions suitable for the task of image data compression are for example polynomials and cosine functions. These functions have been used for a sample orthogonalization with respect to a real world image segment.

In the following sections we will propose structures for a coder and a decoder which are necessary

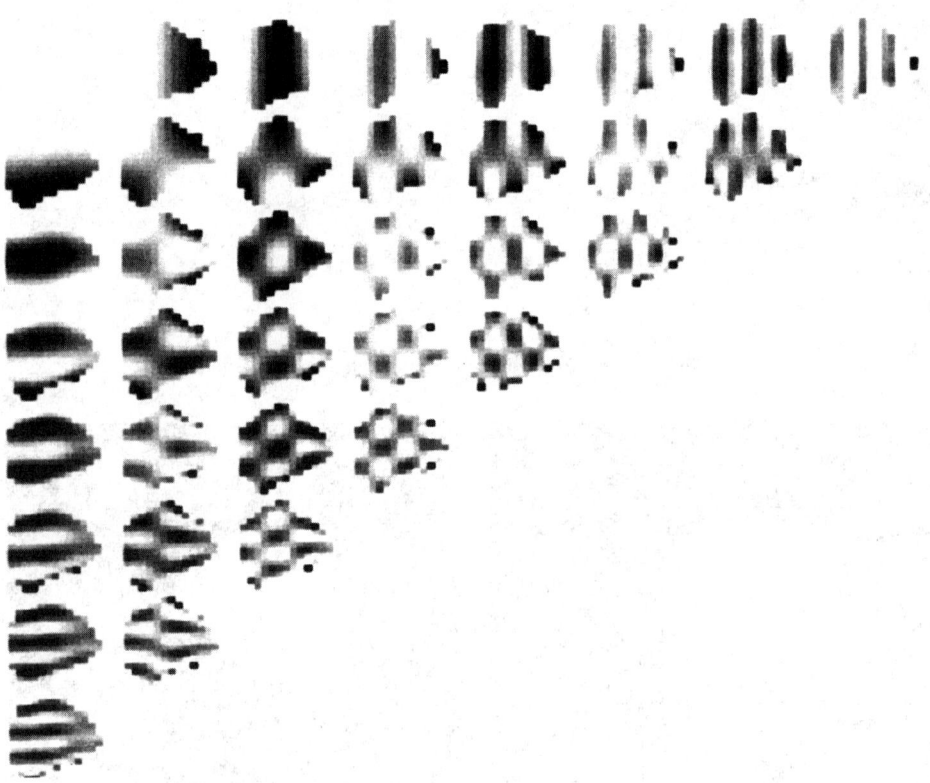

Fig. 10. Shape adapted cosine basis images –> shape adapted DCT.

to make a complete image coder using the introduced transform method.

3. A generalized orthogonal transform

Before we can use the methods introduced in the previous sections, we have to segment the image first. The segmentation has to be connected to the coding and also heavily depends on the application. For example in the case of still image coding a segmentation into quasi-stationary image regions is adequate. One criterion for a good segmentation—keeping maximum data compression as the goal in mind—is the codability of a segment. Therefore the segmentation and coding should be considered as a combined optimization problem [20]. A similar argument holds in the case of the segmentation of image sequences. The performance of a moving video coding system depends to a good degree on the ability to compensate motion in the scene (motion compensated prediction). Therefore the segmentation and the motion compensation have to be considered a mutually dependent problem [14]. To express it even clearer, a segmentation of image sequences without consideration of the motion compensation aspect is likely to be suboptimal.

Image segmentation, especially if carried out as stated above, is computationally very expensive. To concentrate on the coding aspect of the segments themselves we will start our discussion of the coder structure with a given segmentation and assume that this segmentation is the result of the optimization with regard to coding. As far as image sequence coding is concerned we will introduce an alternative solution to the time-consuming segmentation of the images of the sequence by a segmentation of the prediction error which can be obtained straightforward.

3.1. Structure of the coder and decoder

A set of orthogonal basis functions can only be orthogonal with respect to the considered shape and not to several shapes at the same time. This generally means that besides the contour-code and the approximation coefficients for the content, we are required to transmit the used set of basis functions to enable a reconstruction at the receiver. This additional overhead transmission however would most likely cancel the obtained gain due to segment-oriented coding. In the following a scheme is introduced which does not necessitate the transmission of the used basis functional set. Fig. 11 shows a general block diagram of the proposed coding scheme. Starting with a given segmentation the coder can be structured roughly into a contour coder and a content coder.

The *contour* coder has to find an efficient representation for the border or shape of the current segment to be coded. The representation can either be exact, e.g. using run-length codes, or approximative. Error-free encoding of the contour is usually more expensive than coding with respect to a fidelity criterion. The former case needs approximately 1.2 bits/contour-point [5]. But for an approximative contour description we have to implement an algorithm to resolve the overlap and "no-mans-land" situations. Besides we need a reconstruction of the approximated contour inside the transmitter (= coder) to base the orthogonalization on.

The *content* coder operates segment by segment. The current segment under coding for example is labeled A, Fig. 11. Based on a set of basis functions P_{ij} the so-called "basic-knowledge", an orthogonal

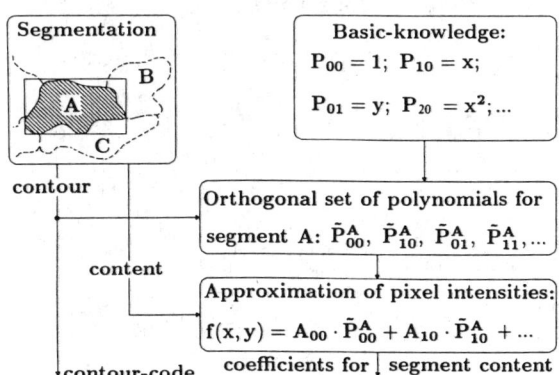

Fig. 11. Structure of region-oriented image coder.

set of basis functions $\tilde{P}_{ij}^A$ with respect to the shape of the segment is generated. The orthogonalization procedure needs the shape information which in case of an approximative contour description needs to be reconstructed at the coder site. Finally the produced orthogonal basis functions are used for the segment content approximation. The approximation coefficients A_{ij} are transmitted to the receiver together with the contour information. The algorithm then proceeds to the next segment.

A block-diagram of the decoder is shown in Fig. 12. After the reception of the contour code, the shape of the current segment, labeled A in our example, is reconstructed. Now it becomes clear why the transmission of the used basis functional set is not necessary using this scheme. If the receiver has the same basic-knowledge, e.g. uses the same starting polynomials, the orthogonal basis functional set can be re-generated at the receiver. The coded and transmitted segment shape contains the information how to derive the basis functions. Finally the approximation coefficients determine the amount of each basis function needed for the content reconstruction, in other words the segment is recovered by a weighted summation of the basis functional set with the approximation coefficients as the weighting factors.

Summarizing, the coding and decoding process is done in three steps:

Coder:
(1) Description of the current segment's contour.
(2) Generation of a set of orthogonal basis functions for the current segment.
(3) Approximation of the current segment's content.

Transmission:
(1) Contour-code.
(2) Approximation coefficients.

Decoder:
(1) Recovering the contour of the current segment.
(2) Generation of a set of orthogonal basis functions for the current segment.
(3) Reconstruction of the current segment's content.

Several parameters of the above introduced coding scheme can be adapted to fit the specific application. Some of these concerning the description of the segment content will be mentioned in the following.

What was called basic-knowledge in the block-diagrams Figs. 11 and 12 is of course not limited to simple polynomials. As already mentioned in Section 2.3 the only constraint limiting the range of possible functional sets is the requirement of linear independence which is not a serious limitation. This gives the possibility to use a wide variety of basis functional sets to start the orthogonalization with. Even more interesting is the thought of adapting the used set to the properties of the current segment under coding: Smooth luminance transition might give favourable results using polynomials, while Walsh-functions might be better suited for areas containing texts. Finally cosine basis functions resembling a shape adapted DCT might be best for the representation of textured segments. A more in depth study about particular properties of different basis functions is currently in progress and will be published soon. For now we will concentrate on the basic concept and its generic potential for coding.

Another possible adaptation parameter is the quality of approximation or synonymous the number of approximation coefficients taken into consideration. All polynomial representation schemes published so far, use a fixed order of approximation, for example Eden et al. [6] use polynomials up to the second order. This is due to the usage of non-orthogonal functions: In Section 2.2 we

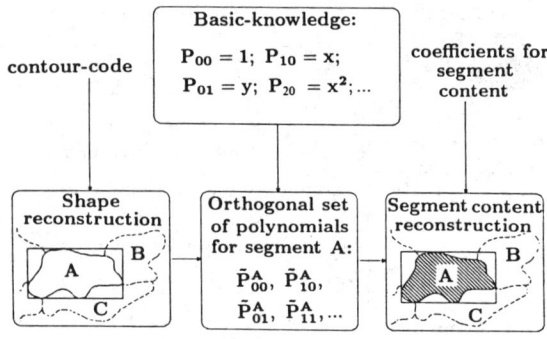

Fig. 12. Structure of decoder.

showed that the recalculation of all previously determined coefficients results if one more approximation coefficient is to be included. The situation changes for an orthogonal function set. The normal equations are now decoupled and further approximation coefficients and the reconstruction itself can be improved by adding more coefficients without recalculation of the previous description/approximation. Therefore hierarchical schemes as for example progressive image built-up or user interaction are investigated in the following.

Progressive image built-up is a technique where coarse picture information is transmitted first. In the beginning the viewer recognizes a kind of low-pass filtered version of the image lacking any detail. In successive steps more detail is added. The advantage of this approach as opposed to line sequential image built-up is that useful information is transmitted to a human observer in a very early stage of the transmission. One example is image retrieval out of data bases. The user can decide very quickly if the image contains the information he needs and prompt the system to add more detail, or, in the other case, stop the transmission and save transmission time (and money). Another example is a system without user interaction but with different reconstruction quality: Segments are classified according to their content and/or their position in the image. Segments at the peripheral of human vision or segments containing parts classified as non-critical will be reconstructed with low priority. Subsequently these segments will be reconstructed using only a few approximation coefficients. High priority segments—e.g. segments in the region of interest or center of vision—on the other hand, are coded with higher fidelity in the beginning. If there is any data-rate left, additional approximation coefficients may be transmitted according to the rank of the segments.

A scheme implementing the above ideas is shown in Fig. 13. Basically the diagram is identical to the coder structure depicted in Fig. 11 insofar as the shape is coded and transmitted: Shape information is used for the generation of orthogonal

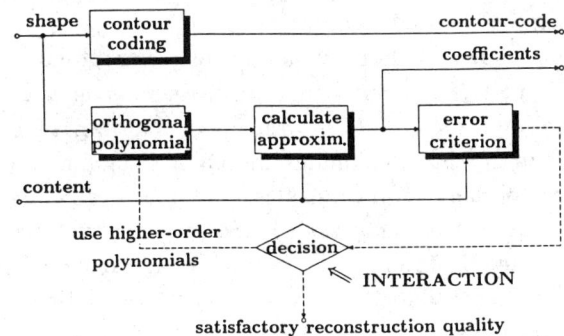

Fig. 13. Variable reconstruction quality—Progressive image built-up.

basis functions and an approximation of the segment content is carried out. Two additional blocks implement the above mentioned capabilities: By reconstructing the approximation inside the coder and comparing the approximated segment to the original image segment, an error measure can be derived. The error criterion can be used for user interaction or adaptation purposes. If the reconstruction quality is not satisfactory an improved approximation can be produced by including higher order basis functions. Please note that the orthogonal basis functions for a specific segment can either be computed all at once by using Householder's algorithm, or can be computed when necessary by Schmidt's algorithm. The already determined orthogonal functions for one segment can be preserved in a memory and recovered later e.g. for further improvements if other segments are to be processed in between.

Even a way to overcome the orthogonalization of the basis functions can be obtained using the following idea: Any 2-dimensional image segment can be sorted into a 1-dimensional vector. For any length which is a multiple of four, 2-dimensional Hadamard matrices can be constructed [23] where the lines are orthogonal with respect to each other. These lines can be used to represent the sorted image vector. To go even further, 3-dimensional orthogonal matrices exist (e.g. Hadamard matrices) with the 2-dimensional planes orthogonal to each other [23]. Each of these planes can be resorted to fit the shape of the segment to be coded without violating the orthogonality property. The planes are now the basis images for the representation. Unfortunately the sorting is not arbitrary but determines the energy compaction performance of the thus designed transform. Only if the basis images resemble image structures commonly found in real world image segments, significant data compression can be obtained. Imagine sorting a set of Hadamard matrices to fit a specific shape but in a way that each basis image only consists of high spatial frequency structures. In this case smooth gray-value transitions in the original segment could only be represented by an excessive number of basis images. Our above introduced method avoids this problem at the cost of the orthogonalization process.

3.2. Quantization of coefficients

A transform is a special kind of approximation where all approximation coefficients are calculated and therefore an exact reconstruction (in the discrete case) is possible. So far a transform alone does not give any data compression. Only in connection with a quantization of the coefficients an irreversible reduction in the amount of data is obtained. Usually not all coefficients are transmitted. State-of-the-art coding schemes for block-oriented transform coding are zonal coders or threshold coders [18]. Our approach differs in so far as not all coefficients are calculated in the beginning.

A region-oriented image data compression algorithm will outperform block-oriented schemes only if the savings in the representation of the content as compared to block-wise coding exceed the data rate necessary for the contour. The number of bits to represent the content of a segment is the product of the number of approximation coefficients used and the number of bits allotted to each coefficient. Originally, the approximation is computed using a floating point format for all values and requiring 32 bits/coefficient. Any quantization of the coefficients leads to an increase in the reconstruction error. The investigation of the dependency between reconstruction error and the accuracy of coefficient quantization is the topic of this section.

Let us consider an example first. Fig. 2 shows an original still image with the overlayed segmentation result into 128 different regions. Using a total

Fig. 14. Reconstructed image: "Alexis" *without* quantization.

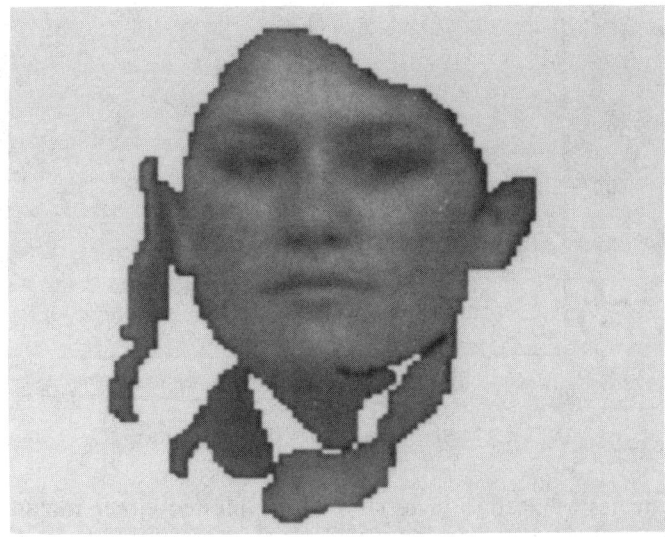

Fig. 15. Original enlarged portion of the face.

of 3209 coefficients for an approximation with orthogonal polynomials which are not quantized but represented in floating point (32 bits), a reconstruction was computed and is given in Fig. 14. The order of the polynomials used depends on the size of the segments: Due to memory constraints the large background segment is approximated using only up to second order polynomials while smaller segments are approximated with polynomials up to an order of 9. A close-up comparison between original and reconstruction using a few important segments from the face is shown in Fig. 15 (original segments) and Fig. 16 (reconstructed segments without quantization). To decide on

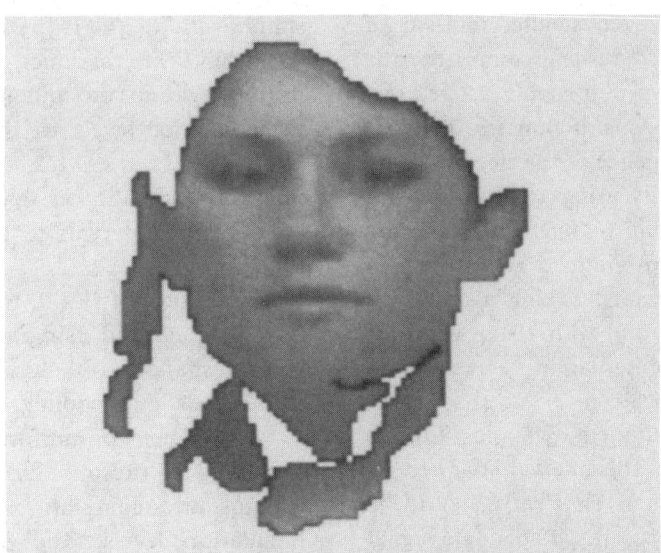

Fig. 16. Reconstructed face segments *without* quantization of coefficients.

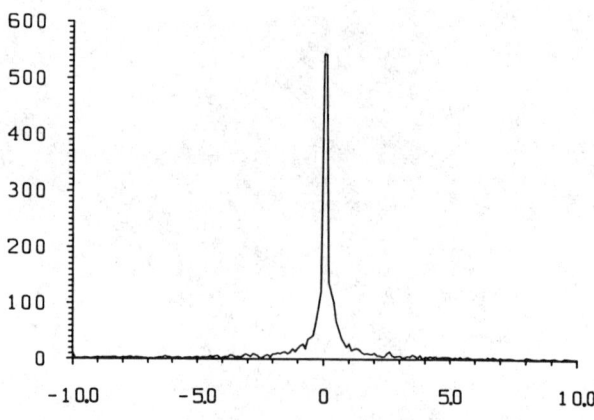

Fig. 17. Histogram of coefficient amplitudes.

possible quantization schemes we need to investigate the amplitude distribution of the coefficients first. The reconstruction quality is a tradeoff between errors caused by quantization of the coefficients and errors caused by the restriction to a finite (as small as possible) number of approximation coefficients.

Fig. 17 shows a histogram of the coefficient's amplitudes, averaged over all approximation coefficients of all orders for the test image "Alexis" shown in Fig. 14. The distribution is highly peaked: about 90% of the coefficients are in the small interval [−10.0, +10.0] and indeed 67% of all coefficients are in the even smaller interval of [−1.0, +1.0]. Quantizer design comprises the optimum tradeoff between dynamic range, resolution and resulting reconstruction errors.

Fig. 18 shows the influence of the step width on the reconstruction quality using a uniform quantizer. The step size should be finer than or equal to 0.01. For bigger step widths a rapid drop in signal to noise ratio results. Taking a quantizer range of [−10.0, +10.0] and with a step width of 0.01, requires 2000 representation values, i.e. 11 bits to represent one coefficient.

The influence of a limited dynamic range is investigated in Fig. 19. The interval spanned by quantizer representation levels clearly should be bigger than [−2.0, +2.0] to reach adequate signal to noise ratios. Fortunately the peaked shape of the coefficient's probability density function can be exploited either for an entropy coding of the representation levels or for the design of a non-uniform quantizer.

Quantization with minimum square error, often called optimum quantization, depends on the probability density functions of the coefficients to be quantized. Because of the changing statistics for different images, the quantizer design has to be based upon an adequate underlying model statistic. Designing optimum quantizers is a computationally expensive method [22, 25] because the decision levels and the representation levels of the quantizer are optimized iteratively. A simplification, [7, 19], can be obtained if the coefficients are assumed to be uniformly distributed within the quantization intervals. The representation levels are then centered inside the intervals at $(v_{i+1} - v_i)/2$, while the second condition for optimality is satisfied by adapting the quantization intervals to the probability density function.

In the range of [−1.0, +1.0] the coefficients are linearly quantized using a step size of 0.01. The peaked shape of the histogram is exploited by variable length coding. Outside the interval [−1.0, +1.0] non-uniform quantization is employed to account for the dynamic range without introducing an excessive number of representation levels. The described quantization scheme is depicted in Fig. 20. The dependency between the reconstruction quality and the number

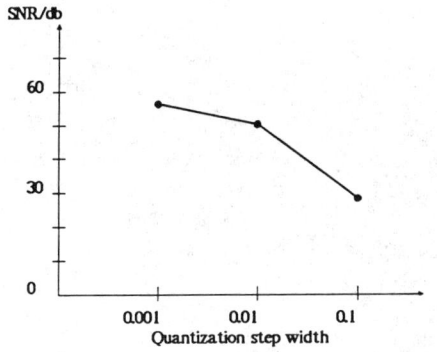

Fig. 18. Influence of quantizer step-size on the reconstruction SNR.

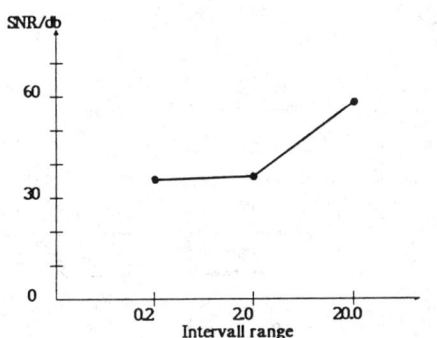

Fig. 19. Influence of quantizer range on the reconstruction SNR.

of bits per coefficient is shown in Fig. 21. Choosing 8 bit/coefficient results in a reconstruction quality mostly degraded by the number of approximation coefficients and not by the coarseness of quantization. The reconstruction of Fig. 16, but now with the coefficients quantized to 8 bit, is depicted in Fig. 22.

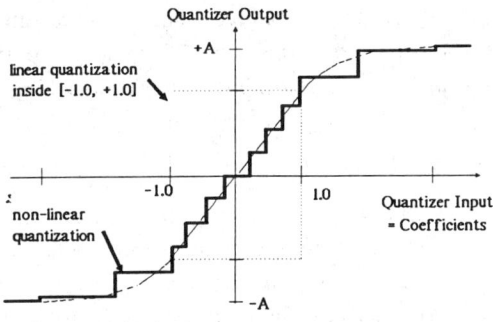

Fig. 20. Quantization scheme.

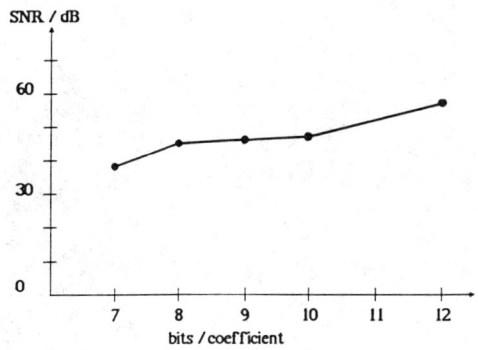

Fig. 21. Bits/coefficients versus SNR in reconstruction.

Conventional schemes, e.g. DCT, use either a predetermined number of bits for each coefficient (zonal coder) or only use coefficients exceeding a certain threshold (threshold coder) [34]. Coder performance can be improved employing a feedback coding scheme: After computing an additional orthogonal basis function φ_q and the corresponding approximation coefficient a_q the reconstruction including the new basis function is compared to the previous reconstruction. Only if the reconstruction quality is improved by a given threshold, the coefficients a_q will be transmitted.

Summarizing, in spite of the wide dynamic range of the coefficients and a necessary fine resolution for small coefficient values, a quantization scheme has been designed, using at most 8 bit/coefficient. A feedback selection technique for the transmitted coefficients results in a further reduction of the total amount of data.

4. Image sequence coding

As already indicated in the leading remarks of Section 3, segmentation is a very time consuming task, especially in combination with the coding of image sequences. Efficient coders for low data rates, for example 64 kbit/s, have to perform a motion compensated prediction. For an accurate motion compensation the boundaries of the objects have to be known, while for a correct segmentation an accurate description of motion is necessary [14].

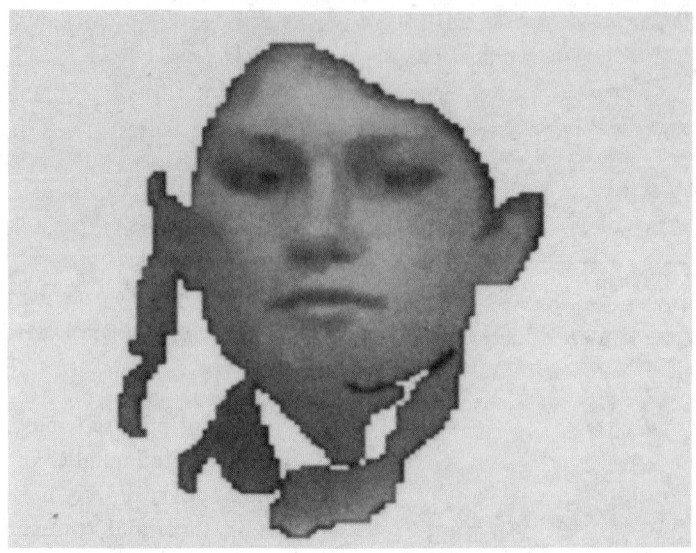

Fig. 22. Reconstructed face segments *with* quantization of coefficients.

Therefore only a joint treatment of both procedures will resolve the mutual influences. An alternative approach which is attractive for implementation due to a low computational complexity will be introduced in the following. The idea especially aims at low bit rate moving video coding but is not restricted by any means to this field of application.

Block-oriented motion compensation, for example by block-matching, has been thoroughly investigated in the past and appeals because of its low computational complexity. In our proposed coding scheme for image sequences which is depicted in Fig. 23 we use block-oriented motion estimation by hierarchical block-matching [11]. The motion compensated prediction image is then subtracted from the actual incoming new image yielding the prediction error image. Fig. 24 illustrates the result of motion compensated prediction: Predicting the current frame, Fig. 24(b), by the previous frame, Fig. 24(a), without any motion compensation yields the prediction error shown in Fig. 24(c). Motion compensated prediction produces the error image depicted in Fig. 24(d) (amplified four times). The statistical properties of the prediction error image have been investigated [11, 12, 29] and have shown a low correlation

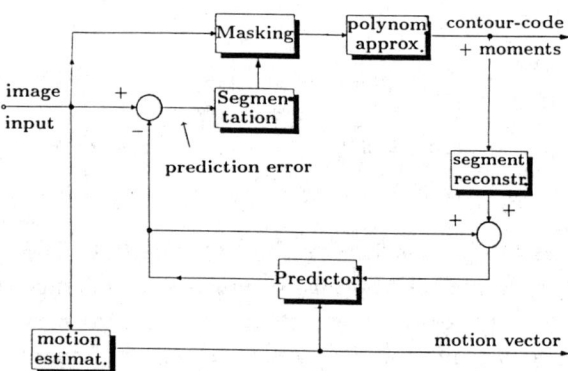

Fig. 23. Image sequence coding—block diagram.

between adjacent pixels. This means that conventional intraframe coding schemes, for example DCT, do not work satisfactorily as they exploit the correlation of the pixels in a block. One possible block-oriented solution has been proposed in [11].

4.1. Segmentation of the prediction error image

The apparent line drawing-like structure of the prediction error image which appears in areas where motion compensation fails partly or completely as shown in Fig. 24(d) makes the prediction error image a candidate for segmentation: Only areas with high prediction error values need to be

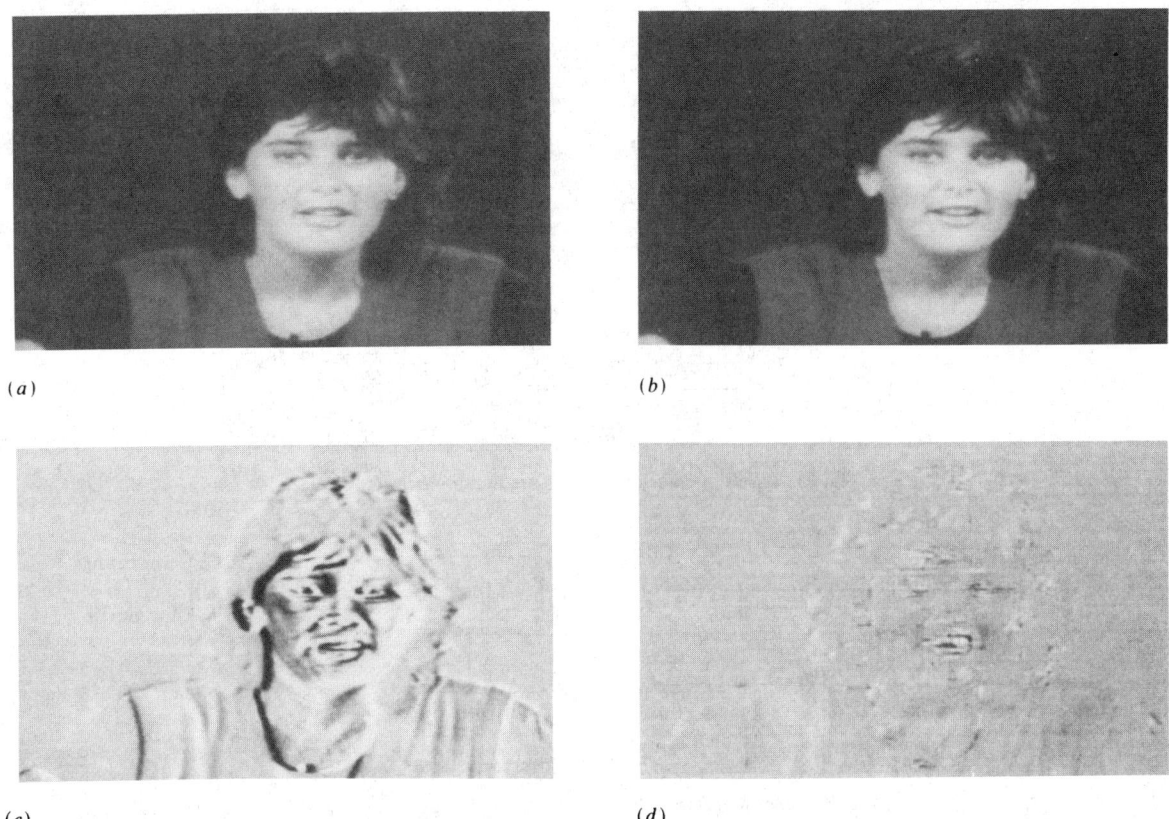

Fig. 24(a) Original frame number 80 from sequence "Miss America". (b) Original frame number 83 from sequence "Miss America". (c) Difference between original frames (amplified four times). (d) Motion compensated prediction error image (amplified four times).

coded. A block-oriented approach is very coarse as the structures are often only a few pixels wide and therefore many additional pixels are unnecessary coded although motion compensation worked for them. A possible segmentation of the prediction error image consists of a simple thresholding operation and a filtering step.

By applying a thresholding operation to the motion compensated prediction error image of Fig. 24(d) all pixels where motion compensated prediction worked well are masked. The result obtained with a threshold value of ±5 is shown in Fig. 25. All pixels shown in black exceed an error value of ±5. Next to regions corresponding to insatisfactory motion compensation many other pixels appear, scattered over the image, which are caused by noise. In a filtering step the super-threshold pixels induced by noise are to be eliminated. A modified median filtering using a neighbourhood of 3 × 3 is employed to keep only those points which have at least 5 super-threshold points in their direct surrounding. Finally all small segments including no more than 8 pixels are discarded. The result is a segmentation yielding only larger areas where motion compensation failed and an update-coding (intraframe) is required. A block-diagram of the thresholding and filtering steps is depicted in Fig. 26, while the simulation result after filtering is shown in Fig. 27. Finally connected regions are identified and labelled, indicated by different gray values for the different segments in Fig. 28. The value of the threshold, the required neighbourhood density for the pixels to be kept, and the number for the smallest allowed segment can be adapted

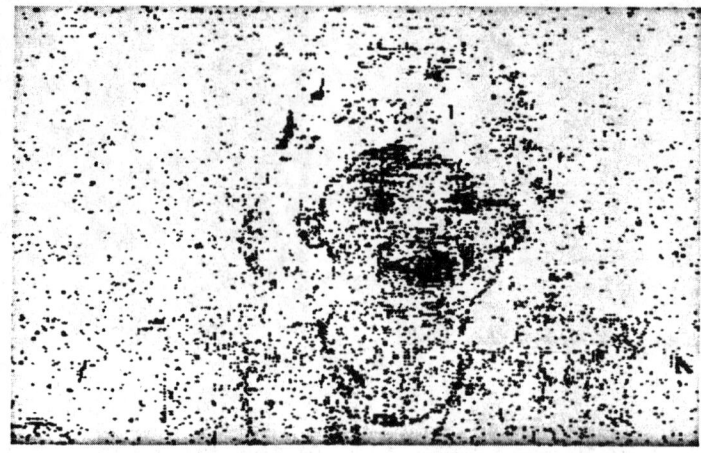

Fig. 25. Result of thresholding the prediction error image.

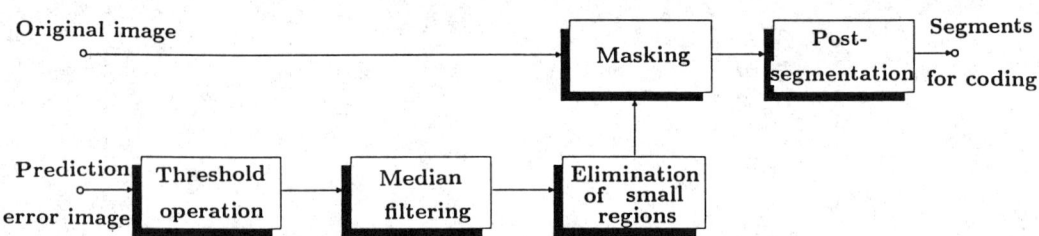

Fig. 26. Block diagram of the prediction error image segmenter.

to the available data-rate. Inside a coder architecture working with a constant channel data-rate the buffer-fullness can be used to control these values.

Statistical investigations of motion-compensated prediction error images reveal a low correlation between adjacent pixels and a high-pass characteristic of the error image [11, 12]. A direct approximation of the prediction error segments especially when using low order polynomials is therefore not very promising. Instead, the prediction error

Fig. 27. Thresholded prediction error image after median filtering.

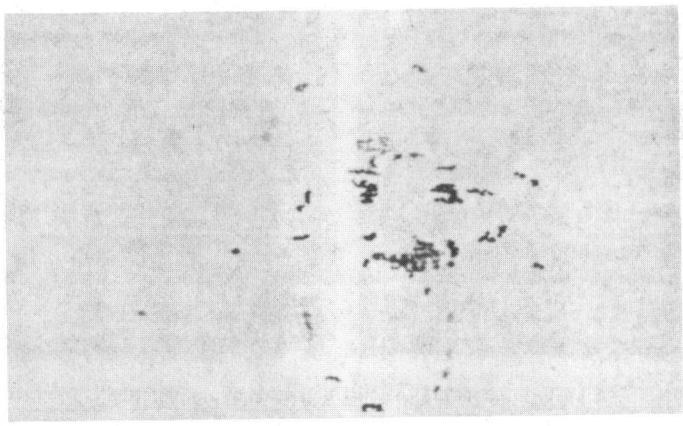

Fig. 28. Labelled segmentation result.

segments are used to mask the corresponding regions in the original image frame. The original image mainly consists of smooth gray value transitions which are well suited for a polynomial approximation. But the segmentation process so far was with disregard of the image to be approximated. Especially larger segments may contain discontinuities, e.g. if the motion compensation failed at a luminance edge, most likely both sides of the edge will appear in the same prediction error segment. To overcome this situation, big segments including more than 40 pixels are subjected to a post-segmentation. This post-segmentation can be a region growing or split and merge technique for example as used for still images in the literature. The segmentation of the prediction error still is computationally efficient because the post-segmentation is only performed on a few small-sized segments. The next section will summarize the results of a computer simulation for image sequence coding employing the above algorithm.

4.2. Experimental results

A complete moving video codec has been simulated for operation at very low data-rates using the structure shown in Fig. 23. The hierarchical motion estimation [11] works on blocks of size 16×16 pixels. The image format is 352×288 pixels at 15 Hz (common intermediate format, every second frame taken). Employing the above introduced segmentation of the prediction error to mask the original frame we get reconstructed frames as shown in Figs. 29 and 30 along with the respective original frames. The accounting information for

Fig. 29. Original and reconstructed frame number 80.

Fig. 30. Original and reconstructed frame number 100.

the frames is given in Tables 1 and 2. Please note that the bit-count includes the contour code: We assumed a rate of 1.2 bit/contour point [5].

So far the data-rate exceeds a rate of 64 kbit/s. We feel however that by an optimization of the algorithm, especially by an approximative contour coding scheme, the rate of 64 kbit/s is within reach.

5. Conclusion

A coding scheme for arbitrarily shaped image segments is introduced. The general case of approximating the gray values inside image segments in a least squares sense is considered. It is shown that the least squares approach can equivalently be described by a generalized moment transformation which includes other transforms, e.g. Fourier, as special cases. The practical problems encountered when implementing the pure algorithm in the field of image data compression
—coupled set of equations,
—mathematically ill posed,
—non-hierarchical description,
—infinite number of descriptors,
could all be overcome by introducing the notion of orthogonal basis functions. Two schemes for the orthogonalization of the basis functions have been described in the Appendix.

Based on the theoretical results, a coder- and decoder-structure is introduced, which implements a shape adapted transform coding without the need

Table 1

Accounting information for frame number 80

Number of segments	186	Motion vectors	1 814 bits
Number of contour pixels	1969	Contour code	2 362 bits
Number of approximation coefficients	1107	Content code	8 856 bits
SNR 35.7 dB		Total bit count	13 032 bits/frame

Table 2

Accounting information for frame number 100

Number of segments	142	Motion vectors	2 140 bits
Number of contour pixels	1 894	Contour code	2 272 bits
Number of approximation coefficients	891	Content code	7 128 bits
SNR 35.6 dB		Total bit count	11 540 bits/frame

to transmit the set of basis functions for each segment. Extensions of the system for user interaction or progressive/adaptive image transmission are discussed. Savings in data-rate by approximating large segments by a small number of coefficients can even be increased by a quantization of the approximation coefficients. A non-linear quantizer gives almost imperceptible reconstruction errors at a rate of 8 bit/coefficient.

An application covering the field of image sequence coding has been derived, combining a conventional, economic block-matching motion estimation with an extremely cost effective segmentation of the prediction error image. Using the segmentation as a mask information, the segments of the original frame are obtained and approximated by orthogonal polynomials. The quality of the reconstruction and the low computational complexity makes the scheme very attractive.

Extension of the proposed algorithms include the investigation of different basis functional sets for the approximation which is currently under study. Another point of consideration is an application of the algorithm to a field called compact disk interactive. Image sequences are stored on CD in a compressed form and the user can select different sequences, level of detail displayed or work on the images. The imbedded hierarchical representation is a necessary prerequisite for this kind of application. Finally more investigations are needed, how the many new degrees of freedom gained by the shaped adapted approach can be optimized together with the many parameters for the best tradeoff between compression ratio and reconstruction quality.

Appendix

Orthogonalization scheme of Schmidt

Before we give the general algorithm, we will consider the problem of finding an appropriate second basis function which is orthogonal to the first. Starting from a linear independent set of functions $u_0, u_1, \ldots, u_n$ we consider the function

$$q_1 = u_1 - r_{01} n_0,$$

with

$$n_0 = \frac{q_0}{\|q_0\|} \quad \text{and} \quad q_0 = u_0. \tag{A.1}$$

By choosing

$$r_{01} = (u_1, n_0) \Rightarrow q_1 = u_1 - (u_1, n_0) n_0, \tag{A.2}$$

we get a q_1 which is orthogonal to q_0. The term $r_{01} q_0$ yields the projection of u_1 onto q_0. The difference of u_1 and its projection has to be normal to q_0 [1]. The orthogonality test yields

$$(q_1, n_0) = ((u_1 - r_{01} n_0), n_0)$$
$$= (u_1, n_0) - r_{01}(n_0, n_0) = 0. \tag{A.3}$$

In general we can write

$$q_k = u_k - r_{0k} q_0 - r_{1k} n_1 - r_{2k} n_2$$
$$- \cdots - r_{k-1\,k} n_{k-1}, \tag{A.4}$$

with

$$r_{lk} = (u_k, n_l) \quad \text{and} \quad n_l = \frac{q_l}{\|q_l\|}. \tag{A.5}$$

Using matrix notation with all the functional values of u_k or q_k standing in the kth column of the following matrices respectively

matrix of given basis functions

$$U = \{u_0, u_1, \ldots, u_n\}, \tag{A.6}$$

matrix of the orthogonal basis functions

$$Q = \{q_0, q_1, \ldots, q_n\}, \tag{A.7}$$

we get

$$U = QR, \tag{A.8}$$

where R is an upper triangular matrix from the orthogonalization coefficients:

$$R = \begin{bmatrix} 1/\|q_0\| & r_{01} & r_{02} & \cdots & r_{0n} \\ 0 & 1/\|q_1\| & r_{12} & \cdots & r_{1n} \\ 0 & 0 & 1/\|q_2\| & \cdots & r_{2n} \\ \vdots & \vdots & \vdots & & \vdots \\ 0 & 0 & 0 & \cdots & 1/\|q_n\| \end{bmatrix}. \tag{A.9}$$

The above algorithm gives orthogonal basis functions step by step which means that we start with two given functions obtaining two orthogonal functions. Successively a third, fourth and so on orthogonal function can be calculated until U and Q are quadratic. This happens when we have as many functions as given data points. Any further function has to be linearly dependent on the others.

Orthogonalization scheme of Householder

With the matrix R as defined above and a $n \times n$-matrix U, consisting of n linear independent basis functions u_k each given at the n nodes of the sampling grid, Householder's scheme uses the following factorization $PU = R$, [15, 28]. The matrix P is the wanted $n \times n$-matrix of the orthogonal basis functions. Please note that in contrast to Schmidt's scheme the orthogonal functions are now along the rows of the matrix P, instead of along the columns. To obtain P we start with a $n \times n$-matrix P_1

$$P_1 = E - 2ww^T, \qquad (A.10)$$

with the identity matrix E and the normalized column vector w: $w^Tw = 1$. P_1 is a symmetrical and orthogonal matrix as can be seen by evaluating the following two equations:

$$P_1^T = E^T - (2ww^T)^T = E - 2(w^T)^Tw^T$$
$$= E - 2ww^T = P_1, \qquad (A.11)$$

$$P_1^T P_1 = P_1 P_1 = (E - 2ww^T)(E - 2ww^T)$$
$$= E - 2ww^T - 2ww^T + 4ww^T$$
$$= E. \qquad (A.12)$$

For a special vector w, which will be derived later, we get a matrix P_1 that maps the first column of the matrix U into a column vector with just one nonzero element in the first position. With the first column of U as the vector x and the first column of the identity matrix as e_1 we can write

$$ke_1 = P_1 x$$
$$\leftrightarrow \begin{bmatrix} k \\ 0 \\ 0 \\ \vdots \\ 0 \end{bmatrix} = P_1 \begin{bmatrix} x_1 \\ x_2 \\ x_3 \\ \vdots \\ x_n \end{bmatrix}. \qquad (A.13)$$

Applying P_1 to $U^{(0)} = U$ we get a new matrix $U^{(1)}$:

$$U^{(1)} = P_1 U^{(0)}. \qquad (A.14)$$

The first line of this matrix $U^{(1)}$ is the first row of the wanted matrix R. The first column contains zeroes below the first element. We now construct a matrix P_2' which is smaller by one row and one column, i.e. the matrix has the size $(n-1) \times (n-1)$. This matrix is used in (A.13) instead of P_1 with the vector x, which now contain the lower $n-1$ elements of the matrix $U^{(1)}$. Finally P_2' is fitted with the identity matrix to yield a $n \times n$-matrix P_2:

$$P_2 = \begin{bmatrix} E & 0 \\ 0 & P_2' \end{bmatrix}. \qquad (A.15)$$

Now the product with $U^{(1)}$ yields a matrix where the first two rows are identical to R:

$$U^{(2)} = P_2 U^{(1)}. \qquad (A.16)$$

After $n-1$ steps, we get the matrix $U^{(n-1)}$ which is identical to the wanted matrix R:

$$P_{n-1} P_{n-2} \cdots P_1 U = R. \qquad (A.17)$$

All matrices P_k are orthogonal, therefore the product matrix P is also orthogonal:

$$P = P_{n-1} P_{n-2} \cdots P_1, \quad \text{with } P^T P = E. \qquad (A.18)$$

Comparing the two algorithms, we see that the matrix P^T is identical to the matrix Q of Schmidt's algorithm: $U = P^T R$.

We still have to select a vector w that satisfies the equation $ke_1 = P_k' x$. This vector w is given by

$$w = \frac{x - ke_1}{\|x - ke_1\|},$$

with

$$k = -\|x\| = -\sqrt{(x, x)}. \quad (A.19)$$

Proof.

$$\begin{aligned}
ke_1 &= P'_k x \\
&= (E - 2ww^T)x \\
&= x - 2ww^T x \\
&= x - 2 \frac{(x - ke_1)(x - ke_1)^T x}{\|x - ke_1\|^2}, \quad (A.20)
\end{aligned}$$

with

$$\begin{aligned}
\|x - ke_1\|^2 &= (x - ke_1)^T (x - ke_1) \\
&= x^T x - kx^T e_1 - ke_1^T x + k^2 \\
&= k^2 - 2kx_1 + k^2 = 2(k^2 - kx_1) \quad (A.21)
\end{aligned}$$

and

$$\begin{aligned}
(x - ke_1)(x - ke_1)^T x &= (x - ke_1)(x^T x - ke_1^T x) \\
&= (x - ke_1)(k^2 - kx_1).
\end{aligned} \quad (A.22)$$

Substituting (A.21) and (A.22) into (A.20) we obtain:

$$ke_1 = x - (x - ke_1) \quad \square$$

Householder's algorithm differs from Schmidt's algorithm in two respects: Householder computes all orthogonal functions at once while Schmidt allows for a successive orthogonalization of single functions. Householder's scheme is mathematically better posed as all computations are done using orthogonal matrices. If almost linearly dependent functions u_k are input to Schmidt's scheme, it may happen that the resulting functions q_k are not orthogonal due to the accumulation of rounding errors. In the same case, Householder's algorithm is more likely to produce functions which are sufficiently orthogonal. Although both algorithms are quite different, they do give the same orthogonal functions if we neglect rounding errors and a scaling factor for now.

References

[1] N.I. Achieser, *Vorlesungen über Approximationstheorie*, Akademie-Verlag, Berlin, 1953.

[2] M.J. Biggar, O.J. Morris and A.G. Constantinides, "Segmented-image coding: Performance comparison with the discrete cosine transform", *IEE Proc.*, Vol. 135, No. 2, April 1988, pp. 121-132.

[3] A. Björck and G. Dahlquist, *Numerische Methoden*, Oldenbourg Verlag, München Wien, 1979.

[4] A.K. Chan, C.K. Chui and K.B. Chan, "Image reconstruction by bivariate quadratic splines", *IEEE Trans. Acoust. Speech, Signal Process.*, Vol. 36, No. 9, September 1988, pp. 1525-1529.

[5] M. Eden and M. Kocher, "On the performance of a contour coding algorithm in the context of image coding—Part I: Contour segment coding", *Signal Process.*, Vol. 8, No. 4, July 1985, pp. 381-386.

[6] M. Eden, M. Unser and R. Leonardi, "Polynomial representation of pictures", *Signal Process.*, Vol. 10, No. 4, June 1986, pp. 385-393.

[7] J.D. Eggerton and M.D. Srinath, "A visually weighted quantization scheme for image bandwidth compression at low data rates", *IEEE Trans. Commun.*, Vol. 34, No. 8, August 1986, pp. 840-847.

[8] G. Engeln-Müllges and F. Reutter, *Numerische Mathematik für Ingenieure*, Bibliographisches Institut, Wein Zürich, 1987.

[9] P.M. Farelle and A.K. Jain, "Recursive block coding—A new approach to transform coding", *IEEE Trans. Commun.*, Vol. 34, No. 2, February 1986, pp. 161-179.

[10] M. Gilge, "Coding of arbitrarily shaped image segments using moment theory", in: J.L. Lacoume et al., eds., *Signal Processing IV, Theories and Applications* (*Proc. 4th Eur. Signal Processing Conf. EUSIPCO '88*), Grenoble, France, September 1988, Elsevier, Amsterdam 1988.

[11] M. Gilge, "A high quality videophone coder using hierarchical motion estimation and structure coding of the prediction error", *Proc. SPIE Conf., Visual Commun. Image Process. '88*, Vol. 1001, Cambridge, USA, November 1988, pp. 864-874.

[12] B. Girod, "The efficiency of motion compensated prediction for hybrid coding of video sequences", *IEEE J. SAC*, Vol. 5, No. 7, August 1987, pp. 1140-1154.

[13] R.M. Haralick and L. Watson, "A facet model for image data", *Signal Process.*, Vol. 15, 1981, pp. 113-129.

[14] M. Hötter and R. Thoma, "Image Segmentation based on object oriented mapping parameter estimation", *Signal Process.*, Vol. 15, No. 3, October 1988, pp. 315-334.

[15] A.S. Householder, *The Theory of Matrices in Numerical Analysis*, Blaisdell Publishing Co., New York, 1964.

[16] M.-K. Hu, "Visual pattern recognition by moment invariants", *IRE Trans. Inf. Theory*, February 1962, pp. 179-187.

[17] A.K. Jain, "A fast Karhunen-Loéve transform for a class of stochastic processes". *IEEE Trans. Commun.*, Vol. 24, No. 9, 1976, pp. 1023-1029.

[18] A.K. Jain, "Image data compression: A review", *Proc. IEEE*, Vol. 69, No. 3, March 1981, pp. 349-389.

[19] N.S. Jayant and P. Noll, *Digital Coding of Waveforms*, Prentice-Hall, Englewood Cliffs, NJ, 1984.

[20] M. Kocher and R. Leonardi, "Adaptive region growing technique using polynomial functions for image approximation", *Signal Process.*, Vol. 11, No. 1, July 1986, pp. 47-60.

[21] M. Kunt, A. Ikonomopoulos and M. Kocher, "Second generation image-coding techniques", *Proc. IEEE*, Vol. 73, No. 4, April 1985, pp. 549-574.

[22] S.P. Lloyd, "Least squares quantization in PCM", *IEEE Trans. Inf. Theory*, Vol. 28, 1982, pp. 129-137.

[23] H.D. Lüke, "Binäre und fast binäre orthogonale Folgen und Matrizen", *Frequenz*, Vol. 41, 1987, pp. 310-314.

[24] E. Marschall, M. Schlichte, W. Tengler and E. Hundt, "Blockübergreifende Transformationscodierung: Theorie und numerische Simulation anhand von Bildsignalen", *NTG-Fachberichte*, Vol. 84, 1983, pp. 249-257.

[25] J. Max, "Quantization for minimum distortion", *IRE Trans. Inf. Theory*, Vol. 6, 1960, pp. 7-12.

[26] M. Schlatter and J. Eichler, "An introduction to the Gaussian least squares approximation and its application in signal processing and system modeling", *Signal Process.*, Vol. 1, No. 3, July 1979, pp. 211-225.

[27] H.W. Sorenson, "Least squares estimation: From Gauss to Kalman". *IEEE Spectrum*, New York, July 1970.

[28] J. Stoer, *Einführung in die Numerische Mathematik*, Springer-Verlag, Berlin, 1983.

[29] P. Strobach, D. Schütt and W. Tengler, "Space-variant regular decomposition quadtrees in adaptive interframe coding", *Proc. Int. Acoust. Speech Signal Process. ICASSP '88*, New York, 1988.

[30] J. Vaisey and A. Gersho, "Variable rate image coding using quad-trees and vector quantization", in: J.L. Lacoume et al., eds., *Signal Processing IV, Theories and Applications* (*Proc. 4th Eur. Signal Processing Conf. EUSIPCO '88*), Grenoble, France, September 1988, Elsevier, Amsterdam 1988.

[31] J.L. Walsh, *Interpolation and Approximation by Rational Functions in the Complex Domain*, American Mathematical Society, Providence, RI, 1965.

[32] L.T. Watson, R.M. Haralick and O.A. Zuniga, "Constrained transform coding and surface fitting", *IEEE Trans. Commun.*, Vol. 31, No. 5, May 1983, pp. 717-726.

[33] L.T. Watson, T.J. Laffey and R.M. Haralick, "Topographic classification of digital image intensity surfaces using generalized splines and the discrete cosine transform", *Comput. Vision, Graphics Image Process.*, Vol. 29, 1985, pp. 143-167.

[34] S. Yuan and K.-B. Yu, "Zonal sampling and bit allocation of HT coefficients in image data compression", *IEEE Trans. Commun.*, Vol. 34, No. 12, December 1986, pp. 1246-1251.

OBJECT-ORIENTED ANALYSIS–SYNTHESIS CODING OF MOVING IMAGES

Hans Georg MUSMANN, Michael HÖTTER and Jörn OSTERMANN

Institut für Theoretische Nachrichtentechnik und Informationsverarbeitung, Universität Hannover, Appelstr. 9a, D-3000 Hannover 1, Fed. Rep. Germany

Received 13 February 1989
Revised 13 May 1989

Abstract. An object-oriented analysis-synthesis coder is presented which encodes objects instead of blocks of $N \times N$ picture elements. The objects are described by three parameter sets defining the motion, shape and colour of an object. The parameter sets are obtained by image analysis based on source models of either moving 2D-objects or moving 3D-objects. Known coding techniques are used to encode the parameter sets. An object-depending parameter coding allows to introduce geometrical distortions instead of quantization errors. Using the transmitted parameter sets an image can be reconstructed by model-based image synthesis.

Experimental results achieved with a first implementation of the coder are given and are discussed.

Zusammenfassung. Es wird ein objektorientierter Analyse-Synthese Coder vorgestellt, der Objekte anstelle von Blöcken der Größe $N \times N$ Bildpunkte codiert. Die Objekte werden durch drei Parametersätze beschrieben, die die Bewegung, die Berandung und die Farbe eines Objektes definieren. Die Parametersätze werden durch eine Bildanalyse gewonnen, die entweder auf dem Quellenmodell bewegter 2D-Objekte oder bewegter 3D-Objekte basiert. Für die Codierung der Parametersätze werden bekannte Codiertechniken benutzt. Eine objektabhängige Parametercodierung gestattet es, geometrische Verzerrungen anstelle von Quantisierungsfehlern einzuführen. Mit Hilfe der übertragenen Parametersätze kann ein Bild durch modellgestützte Bildsynthese rekonstruiert werden.

Experimentelle Ergebnisse, die mit einer ersten Implementierung des Coders erzielt wurden, werden vorgestellt und diskutiert.

Résumé. Ce texte porte sur un codeur d'analyse-synthèse encodant les objets plutôt que les blocs $N \times N$ constituant l'image. Les objets sont décrits par trois ensembles de paramètres décrivant leur trajectoire, leur forme et leur couleur. Ces ensembles sont obtenus par une analyse de l'image basée sur des modèles de source d'objets 2D ou 3D en mouvement. Des techniques de codage connues sont utilisées pour encoder ces ensembles. Ce codage par objets introduit des distorsions géométriques au lieu d'erreurs de quantification. A l'aide des ensembles de paramètres transmis une image peut être reconstruite par synthèse basée sur modèle.

Des résultats expérimentaux obtenus lors d'une première mise en oeuvre du codeur sont présentés et commentés.

Keywords. Model-based image analysis, parameter coding, model-based analysis-synthesis image coding.

1. Introduction

In order to encode moving video signals at low bit rates each image of a sequence is usually subdivided into blocks of $N \times N$ picture elements (pels) and the luminance and chrominance signals of each block are encoded by motion compensated predictive and transform coding algorithms [16, 17]. Thus an image is described by independently moving square blocks which can lead to visible distortions known as blocking and mosquito effects of low bit rate codecs. To avoid these image distortions more appropriate source models for describing the image have to be introduced. This paper presents a coding method called object-oriented analysis-synthesis coding which subdivides each image into moving objects and encodes each object by three sets of parameters defining the motion, shape and colour information of the object.

The objects and their parameters are obtained by an automatic analysis of the actual input image at the coder. Using the encoded and transmitted parameters an image can be reconstructed by image synthesis at the decoder as well as at the coder.

Analysis–synthesis coding techniques have been published in [1, 4, 6, 7, 12, 15, 25]. These techniques have been developed to efficiently encode one known special object, e.g. a human face, and require an algorithm for recognizing the face in a scene. Therefore these techniques are sometimes called knowledge-based analysis–synthesis coding techniques [12]. If the semantical meaning of the face is also considered for coding it might be called semantic coding [4, 7]. In [8] a more general strategy for analysis–synthesis coding is outlined.

The coding concept described here, is not restricted to only one special object and therefore can be applied to a more general class of scenes. It does not require a recognition algorithm. Object-oriented analysis–synthesis coding can be based on different source models for describing the objects and their motion in a scene. Depending on the source model parameter sets with different information content and different bit rates will be generated by the coder. Two source models are considered in this paper: The model of planar rigid objects with three-dimensional motion and the model of three-dimensional rigid objects with three-dimensional motion. The colour information is considered as being projected on the surface of the objects. Image analysis algorithms have been developed which estimate the shape and motion of the objects in a scene and automatically generate the three sets of parameters to be encoded by predictive or transform coding techniques. To reduce the frame-to-frame redundancy, motion compensated interframe prediction is applied and only the temporal update information is encoded.

In object-oriented analysis–synthesis coding the object-oriented information can be used to control the coding of the parameter sets. Thus by suppression of shape and colour update information of an object, geometrical distortions are introduced instead of quantization error distortions when irreversible coding techniques have to be applied in order to cut down the generated bit rate. The geometrical distortions are less annoying than quantization error distortions in situations where the modelling of an object is sufficiently exact as indicated by relatively small shape and colour update informations.

In Section 2 the new coding concept and the basic block diagram of the coder are explained. The image analysis and synthesis algorithms are described in detail in Sections 3 and 4. The coding of the parameter sets is still in a very early stage as presented in Section 5. First results obtained by a simulation of this coding concept are discussed in Section 6.

2. Concept and structure of the object-oriented analysis–synthesis coder

Object-oriented analysis–synthesis coding subdivides each image of a sequence into moving objects and describes each object i by three sets of parameters defining motion A_i, shape M_i and colour S_i information of the object. The object parameters depend on the kind of source model being applied. To explain the concept and structure of the object-oriented analysis–synthesis coder the block diagram of Fig. 1 is used and the simplified model of planar rigid objects with only translational motion is assumed.

Instead of the frame memory of block-oriented coding techniques, object-oriented coding requires a memory to store the parameters sets $A = \{A_i\}$, $M = \{M_i\}$, $S = \{S_i\}$ of the objects. The object memory of the coder and decoder contains the same parameter informations and allows the coder and decoder to reconstruct a transmitted image by image synthesis. The reconstructed image S'_k is displayed at the decoder and used for image analysis of the next input image S_{k+1} at the coder.

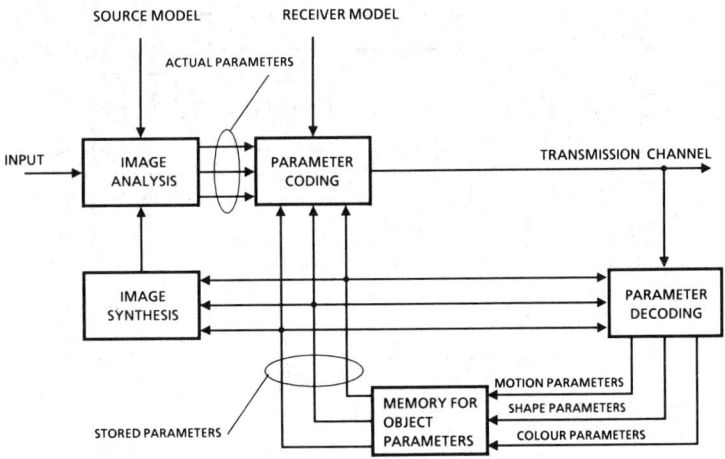

Fig. 1. Block diagram of an object-oriented analysis–synthesis coder.

In the case of the source model considered here the motion parameter set A_i of an object i contains two elements a_1, a_2 corresponding to the frame-to-frame displacement of the object in x- and y-direction. The shape parameter set M_i can be interpreted as picture elements of a bi-level image, where the white picture elements describe the shape of the object being analysed and the black picture elements represent the residual image area. The elements of the colour parameter set S_i correspond to the luminance and chrominance information of each picture element belonging to the object i. Fig. 2 illustrates the information of these parameter sets for an image with two objects.

The task of the image analysis block in Fig. 1 is to analyse the next input image S_{k+1} to be coded and to estimate the parameter sets A_i, M_i, S_i for each object i by use of the reconstructed image S'_k. A hierarchically structured procedure has been developed which starts with the estimation of A_i, M_i, S_i of the largest object in the first step of hierarchy and then analyses the smaller objects in the subsequent steps of the hierarchy. At the output of the image analysis block the parameter sets A_i, M_i, S_i are available in PCM representation as illustrated in Fig. 2.

The analysis fails in image areas which cannot be described by the source model being applied.

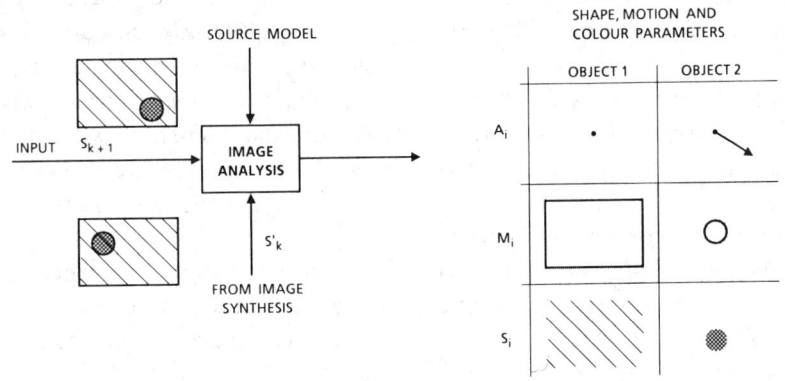

Fig. 2. Illustration of model based image analysis. (Source model of planar rigid objects with translational motion.)

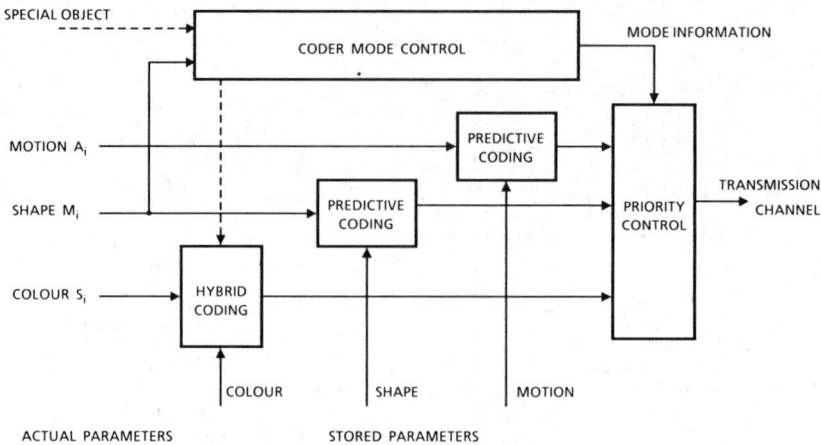

Fig. 3. Parameter coding.

Therefore the success of the image analysis is checked by a verification algorithm. Those areas which cannot be described by the model are marked in a final step of the hierarchical analysis procedure and are denoted as special objects.

The parameter sets A_i, M_i, S_i of each object i have to be encoded efficiently in order to achieve a coding gain when compared to block-oriented coding. As shown in Fig. 3 the motion parameter A_i and the shape parameter M_i are encoded by predictive coding techniques using the motion and shape information of the previous frame k. In the case of planar rigid objects the shape information describes the silhouette of an object. Therefore, contour coding techniques [5] are applied and only the temporal changes of the silhouette are encoded by predictive coding. The colour information is encoded by hybrid coding techniques, which combine motion compensating prediction with intraframe coding.

While block-oriented hybrid coding techniques [17] transmit only two parameter sets (the motion and colour information of each block), object-oriented analysis–synthesis coding transmits three parameter sets (the motion, shape and colour information of each object). Therefore, the additional bit rate R_M required for transmitting the shape information M has to be compensated by a reduction of the bit rates R_A and R_S required for motion A and colour information S in order to obtain a higher coding gain for object-oriented coding. This is achieved in two ways: First, only one motion parameter set is transmitted for a complete object covering the area of several blocks; secondly, the prediction of the colour information is improved by the use of more appropriate source models.

The efficiency of object-oriented coding depends on the size of the objects. Therefore, in the case of small objects, the coder mode control switches back to block-oriented coding. By this control the efficiency of object-oriented coding is always superior or equal to that of block-oriented coding.

The priority control in Fig. 3 allows to identify objects which can properly be synthesized without shape and colour update information, i.e. which may be encoded by motion information only in order to save bit rate. Thus geometrical distortions are introduced instead of quantization errors. Further, the priority control arranges the parameter sets of the objects in an order of decreasing priority. The transmission starts with the parameter set of the highest priority and ends with that parameter set where the bit rate available for the image is exhausted.

The encoded motion, shape and colour parameters are transmitted and decoded at the receiver as well as at the transmitter to reconstruct the PCM representations of A_i, M_i, S_i which are stored in the memory for object parameters. Using the parameters A, M, S the actual image can be synthesized.

3. Image analysis and synthesis based on moving 2D-objects

According to the explained object-oriented coding concept, the objects of a scene are described by three sets of parameters A, M, S defining the motion, shape and colour information of the objects. The entropy of each parameter set represents a part of the information which has to be transmitted to the receiver. Hence, the introduction of object-oriented coding techniques has to be justified with respect to the resulting overall bit rate. Since the parameter information and the resulting bit rate are dependent on the source model of the coding concept, it is important to develop source models and corresponding image analysis techniques that generate temporal smoothly varying parameter sets which can be encoded efficiently. Using the three parameter sets an image can be reconstructed by image synthesis. The image synthesis is determined by the source model of the image analysis part and realized by an application of the estimated parameter sets.

One of the essential problems of analysis-synthesis coding is the image analysis part, i.e. to subdivide a scene into moving objects and to describe each object by three sets of parameters defining its motion, shape and colour. From the literature [2, 18, 21, 22, 24] several approaches are known to detect moving objects and to measure their velocity. Most of them are based on the evaluation of the optical flow, i.e. of the measured displacement vector field [2, 18, 24]. The disadvantage of these approaches is that the interdependence between motion and object boundary estimation is not taken into account. For an accurate motion description, the object boundaries have to be known, while for a correct object boundary detection an accurate description of motion is

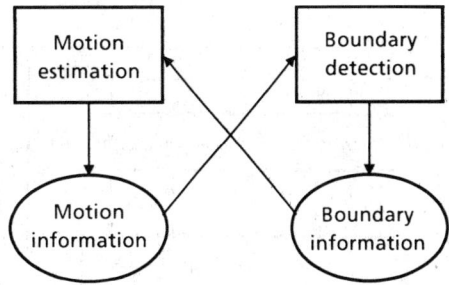

Fig. 4. Illustration of the interdependence of motion estimation and boundary detection of moving objects.

necessary. Hence, motion estimation and object boundary detection have to be treated jointly, as they influence each other: The more accurate the motion estimation, the more exact is the description of the object boundaries, and vice versa. This problem is illustrated in Fig. 4.

In this section, the source model of the image analysis is based on the assumption of rigid, planar objects moving arbitrarily in the three dimensional space. It can be shown [21, 23] that in this case the mapping of a moving object onto the camera image is defined by eight parameters—so called mapping parameters. An image analysis algorithm is presented that formulates the analysis task as a hierarchical application of object motion and boundary estimation [11]. Fig. 5 shows the structure of the algorithm which consists of three parts; the estimation of the eight mapping parameters, the internal image synthesis and the verification test.

Inputs to the image analysis scheme are the luminance signals S'_k and S_{k+1} of two successive pictures of an image sequence. The prime denotes that S'_k is the transmitted and synthesized version of S_k. In a first step, the starting hypothesis is postulated that the whole scene represents one object, which does not move. Thus, the synthesized picture $\hat{S}_0$ is identical to the picture S'_k. According to the starting hypothesis S'_k and S_{k+1} should have the same luminance values. The verification test evaluates the frame differences between S'_k and S_{k+1} and detects that area M_1 where the hypothesis is true. The area M_1 represents the object stationary

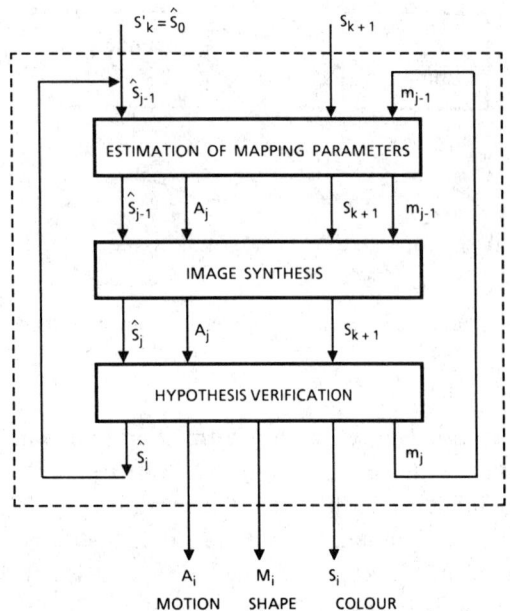

Fig. 5. Image analysis. Model: 3D-motion of planar rigid objects. (S_{k+1}, luminance signal of image $k+1$; $\hat{S}_j$, synthesized image to describe S_{k+1}; m_j, areas to be analysed; A_j, mapping parameters of analysed areas; j, index of hierarchy; i, object i.)

represent the mappings of the objects to be analysed in the third step of hierarchy and are marked in the binary mask m_2. Thus, the description of the image S_{k+1} is hierarchically refined until all objects are described in their mappings and their boundaries.

First, the blocks of the image analysis scheme are described in detail, then some important features of the whole analysis–synthesis scheme are discussed.

3.1. Estimation of eight mapping parameters

The considered source model is based on rigid, planar objects moving arbitrarily in the three dimensional space. According to the physics of the camera, each object is mapped onto the camera target by central projection (see Fig. 6). Caused by the three dimensional motion, the mapping of a point P' on a planar, rigid object is moved in the image plane from (X', Y') to (X, Y). The functional relationship between this pair of image plane coordinates can be described by a formula which depends on the location (X, Y) within the image plane and eight parameters—the so called mapping

background. Areas with non-zero frame differences indicate changed image regions where the hypothesis is not true. Each disjunct changed image region is then interpreted as the mapping of an additional object which will be analysed in its motion and boundaries in the next step of hierarchy. Therefore, these regions are marked in a binary mask m_1. In the second step of hierarchy, for each marked area of m_1, i.e. for each disjunct, changed image region, one set of eight mapping parameters is calculated by means of the synthesized image $\hat{S}_1$ and the actual image S_{k+1}. Then, for each marked area of m_1, an image synthesis is performed. If there are moving objects in front of moving objects, the assumption, that each changed region represents the mapping of only one moving object is not fulfilled and hence the mapping description is only valid in a part of the region. For that reason, the hypothesis verification yields again a detection of those image parts which have not correctly been synthesized. These image parts

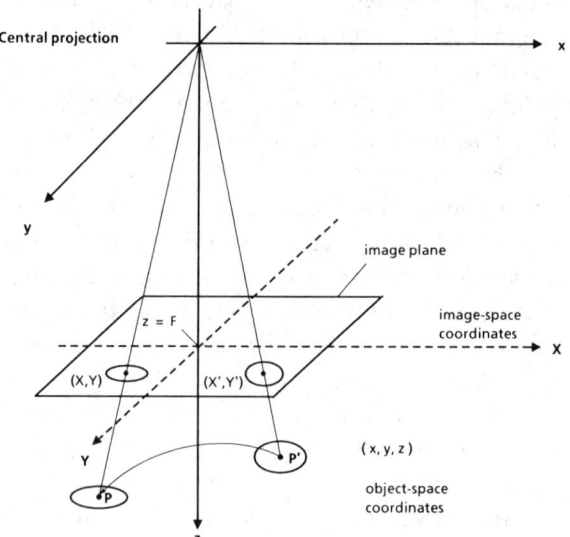

Fig. 6. Imaging of moving planar rigid objects.

parameters [23]

$$(X', Y') = F\{a_1, a_2, \ldots, a_8, X, Y\}$$
$$= \left(\frac{a_1 X + a_2 Y + a_3}{a_7 X + a_8 Y + 1}, \frac{a_4 X + a_5 Y + a_6}{a_7 X + a_8 Y + 1}\right). \quad (1)$$

These mapping parameters include both, the motion description and the position description of a planar, rigid object and can be estimated from two successive frames [11, 21]. Equation (1) is valid for the set of all mapping points (X', Y') of one moving object.

Accounting all luminance changes due to object motion, the signal description of the mapping results as

$$S_{k+1}(X, Y) = S_k(X', Y'). \quad (2)$$

Thus, the relationship between the signal and the mapping parameters can be formulated as follows

$$S_{k+1}(X, Y) - S_k(X, Y)$$
$$= S_k(X', Y') - S_k(X, Y)$$
$$= S_k\left(\frac{a_1 X + a_2 Y + a_3}{a_7 X + a_8 Y + 1}, \frac{a_4 X + a_5 Y + a_6}{a_7 X + a_8 Y + 1}\right)$$
$$- S_k(X, Y)$$
$$= FD(X, Y), \quad (3)$$

where $FD(X, Y)$ is the frame difference of two successive frames to be evaluated.

Using a Taylor series expansion to describe the image luminance in the neighborhood of (X, Y) as a function of the mapping parameters a_i, the frame difference $FD(X, Y)$ can be approximated by

$$\tilde{FD}(X, Y) = HA, \quad (4)$$

where H is a vector containing weighted local gradients and $A = (a_1, a_1, a_2, \ldots, a_8)^T$ is the mapping parameter vector.

The evaluation of (4) on the set of all mapping points (X, Y) of one moving, planar object yields the parameter vector A by linear regression [11, 21].

3.2. Image synthesis

In each step of the hierarchy of the image analysis scheme, an internal image synthesis has to be performed. For image $\hat{S}_{j-1}$, this synthesis is achieved by a motion compensating prediction of all image regions marked in the binary mask m_{j-1}. The addresses of the corresponding picture elements of a position (X, Y) in the prediction image $\hat{S}_j$ and (X', Y') in the image $\hat{S}_{j-1}$ are determined for each marked image region with the help of its mapping parameters A_i. The picture element to be predicted results as [11, 21]

$$\hat{S}_j(X, Y) = \hat{S}_{j-1}(X', Y'), \quad (5)$$

with (X', Y') according to (1) and $(a_1, a_2, \ldots, a_8)^T = A_i$ the estimated mapping parameters of the marked image region considered.

This image synthesis is repeated for each step of hierarchy within the image analysis scheme until all objects to be analysed are motion compensated.

3.3. Verification test

With help of the verification test the success of the analysis scheme is checked for each object i. The verification test controls the coincidence of the estimated and real object motion by means of the mean square displaced frame difference (DFD), because the mapping parameter estimation is based on the minimization of this signal parameter [11, 21]. For each object i of the jth step of hierarchy, the mean squared DFD(obj i) and the mean squared frame difference FD(obj i) are evaluated on all image coordinates (X, Y) belonging to the mapping of the actually considered object i

$$\overline{DFD^2}(\text{obj } i)$$
$$= \sum_{(X,Y) \in \text{obj } i} \frac{(S_{k+1}(X, Y) - \hat{S}_j(X, Y))^2}{\text{SIZE (obj } i)}$$

and

$$\overline{FD^2}(\text{obj } i)$$
$$= \sum_{(X,Y) \in \text{obj } i} \frac{(S_{k+1}(X, Y) - S'_k(X, Y))^2}{\text{SIZE (obj } i)}, \quad (6)$$

where S'_k is the transmitted and synthesized version of S_k, S_{k+1} is the luminance signal of image $k+1$, $\hat{S}_j$ is the prediction image of the jth step of hierarchy to describe S_{k+1} and SIZE (obj i) is the area of the actually considered object i in units of picture elements.

Then, the validity of the mapping description is determined by

$$\overline{\text{DFD}^2}(\text{obj } i)/\overline{\text{FD}^2}(\text{obj } i)$$
$$\begin{cases} < T_v: \text{ the mapping description of} \\ \qquad\quad \text{the object is valid} \\ \geq T_v: \text{ the mapping description is} \\ \qquad\quad \text{insufficient.} \end{cases} \quad (7)$$

If the value of the quotient in (7) exceeds a given threshold T_v, the minimization achieved by the algorithm is insufficient, i.e. a mapping description of the moving object i according to the model assumptions of the algorithm is not possible. Moving objects whose mapping description is insufficient are marked as special objects.

If the value of the quotient in (7) falls below the threshold T_v, the mapping description of the object i is accepted. By means of the accepted mapping description, uncovered image regions are separated from the mapping of the moving object i [11]. If there are moving objects in front of the actually considered object, the mapping description is only valid in a part of the object. For that reason, the verification test yields additionally a detection of those objects which are not correctly described in their mappings. These objects represent the objects to be analysed in the next step of hierarchy [11].

3.4. Improvement of image analysis by object tracking

In an analysis-synthesis coder concept, the estimated object shapes are part of the information to be transmitted. To guarantee an efficient coding of the object shapes, the shapes may vary only smoothly from image k to image $k+1$ in order to be predictable by the source model. In the case of planar, rigid objects the silhouette information of an object has to be considered. The object silhouettes of the presented image analysis algorithm can vary temporally due to the fact, that the identification of motion in uniform areas is unreliable. The image analysis algorithm is based on the hypothesis, that motion of objects generates luminance changes in the image. In uniform areas, it is difficult to distinguish between luminance changes which are caused by noise or by object motion. In order to achieve a more reliable result, the objects are tracked, i.e. the image analysis results of the actual image are used as initial guesses for the image analysis of the next picture. In this way, ambiguity is exploited to give consistent object shapes which are only changing if this is necessary because of apparent model violations.

To illustrate the function of the hierarchical image analysis algorithm, Fig. 7 shows the analysed areas of the first, second and third level of hierarchy and their superposition which have been calculated from two pictures of the test sequence "Miss America" provided by the Specialist Group for Visual Telephony in CCITT SGXV. In Fig. 7 uncovered image regions and the segmented objects are displayed with white and gray luminance values.

4. Image analysis and synthesis based on moving 3D-objects

Whereas in Section 3 considerations are restricted to moving 2-D objects, in this chapter the source model is extended to consider 3-D objects in the real world in order to improve the coding efficiency. Fig. 8 shows the relation between the three-dimensional *real world*—a view of this world called *real image*—and a three-dimensional artificial *model world* with its projection onto the image plane called *model image*. The synthesized model image approximates the real image. Goal of the modelling is to generate a model world which has a model image identical to the real image.

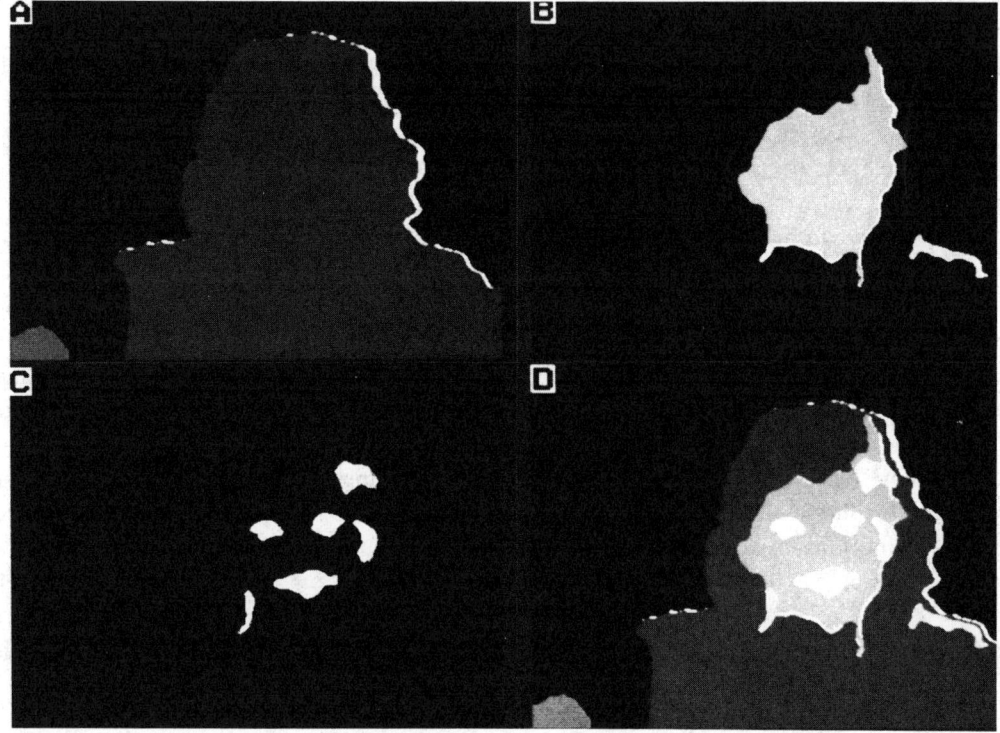

Fig. 7. Illustration of the hierarchical image analysis algorithm. (a) Analysed areas of the first level of hierarchy. (b) Analysed areas of the second level of hierarchy. (c) Analysed areas of the third level of hierarchy. (d) Superimposed, analysed areas of the first, second and third level of hierarchy.

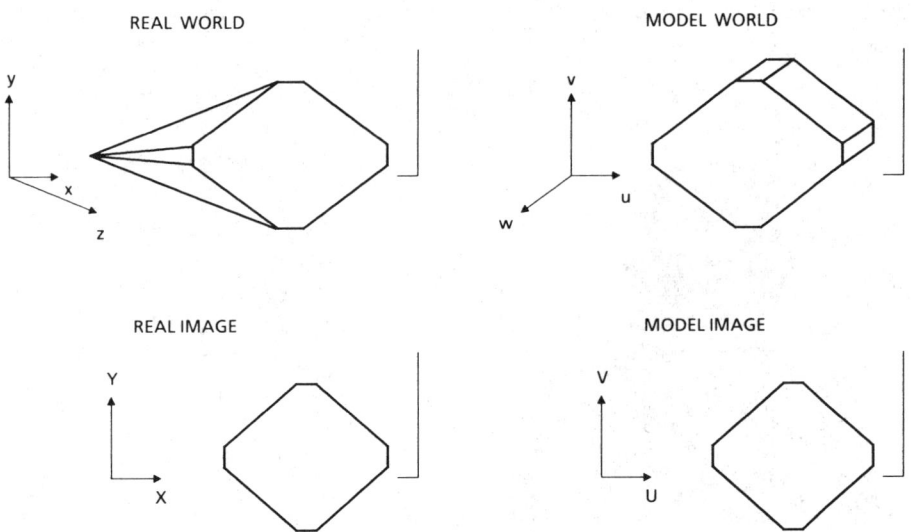

Fig. 8. Example of a real world and a model world giving the same real and model image.

A world is described by a scene, its illumination and its camera. A *scene* consists of objects and relationships between them. The applied modelling algorithm [14] requires diffuse illumination and diffuse reflecting surfaces for the model world. Furthermore, the objects have to be opaque and quasi-rigid. The real world in Fig. 8 contains one *real object*, i.e. a pyramid. The real image of the camera shows only the front face of the pyramid, i.e. an octagon. From this *reference image* the initial model world is generated without any a priori knowledge. The image analysis algorithm described in Section 3 computes *silhouettes* of moving objects. From a silhouette a *model object* is generated. It is represented by a mesh of triangles, i.e. a wire-frame. A silhouette computed from the test sequence "Claire" and a wire-frame describing the model object shape by triangles are shown in Fig. 9.

Since one image does not give any depth information, the initial three-dimensional shape of the object in the model world is estimated. Similar to the source model with 2D-objects the shape is assumed to be a planar patch. The example in Fig. 8 shows that the projections from real and model world can be identical, although their three-dimensional contents differs significantly. If the pyramid is moved, other faces than the front face will be seen in the real image. Hence, the initial guess of the model world to represent the pyramid by a planar patch will generate a difference between the new real image and the model image showing the motion compensated model object. This difference can be analysed and used for adapting the three-dimensional shape of the model object to the real world pyramid, i.e. for adapting the depth information.

In order to define the surface colours of the objects, the reference image is projected onto the initial model world. Hence the surface colours of each visible triangle of an object are defined.

If the same model world is generated at the coder and decoder, only changes of illumination and object shape, object motion, or new objects entering the scene have to be transmitted. In addition to the source model of 2D-objects, this source model based on 3D-objects allows the effective modelling of rotation of 3D-objects. Whereas the motion description of 2D-objects is implicit, i.e. the meaning of each motion parameter is not related to our imagination of real movement, the use of 3D-objects allows an explicit description of motion and shape. In coding applications this eases coder control, because every motion and shape parameter can easily be interpreted. The gain of this effective modelling of rotation and of the explicit parameter description has to be paid for. As Fig. 8 indicates, using a source model of

Fig. 9. Modelling 3D-objects. (a) Silhouette of the model object "Claire". (b) Wire-frame of the model object "Claire".

3D-objects for image analysis causes the additional problem of determining the 3D-shape of the objects. This requires two steps, in a first step the motion and in a second step the three-dimensional shape of an object has to be estimated.

Image synthesis is based on the same source model and is solved by means of central projection and the Z-buffer algorithm [19].

4.1. Image analysis

Image analysis is based on the new real image S_{k+1} of the sequence and on the current model world P'_k which is the a priori knowledge acquired from previous images. By evaluating the frame difference between the image S_{k+1} and the model image of P'_k, an update of the model world is computed. The goal of the updating is to minimize the mean square difference (MSD) between the model and the real image. According to the source model, frame differences are due to motion of objects or insufficient information about object shape, i.e. there are two causes for frame differences. Since a change of motion as well as a change of shape parameters in the model world influence the frame difference between model and real image, the cause of frame differences can not always be determined uniquely.

In order to get a stationary model world, which is very important with respect to coding, it is assumed that the frame differences are mainly caused by motion of the objects. Only frame differences which can not be compensated by motion are assumed to be due to insufficient information about the object shape.

Fig. 10 shows the structure of the image analysis algorithm for extracting the motion, shape and colour parameters of an object and for updating the model world. In contrast to Fig. 5 input of the algorithm are the model world P'_k and the new real image S_{k+1}. Output of the motion analysis are the motion parameter sets A_i of all objects i of the model world and the updated model world $\hat{P}_k$. By minimizing the MSD between the real image S_{k+1} and the model image of $\hat{P}_k$ the shape analysis

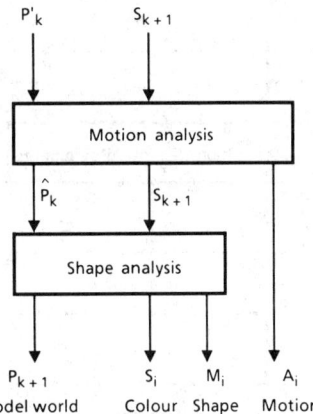

Fig. 10. Image analysis. Model: 3D-motion of 3D quasi-rigid objects. (P'_k, model world approximating real image k; S_{k+1}, colour signal of real image $k+1$; $\hat{P}_k$, model world P'_k with motion compensated objects; A_i, motion parameters of object i; P_{k+1}, model world approximating real image $k+1$; M_i, shape parameters of object i; S_i, colour parameters of object i.)

computes an update of the object shapes. Results are the shape parameter sets M_i, the colour parameter sets S_i and the model world $\hat{P}_{k+1}$ whose model image approximates S_{k+1}.

4.1.1. Motion analysis

Motion analysis will be described here using Fig. 11.

The differential estimation algorithm [13] computes the motion parameters necessary for motion compensating the objects of a model world P'_k. Input to this algorithm are the current model world $\hat{P}_{i-1}$, which equals P'_k for the first iteration, the new real image S_{k+1}, and the object area O_{i-1}, which defines the area of the image plane, in which motion parameters have to be estimated. In contrast to Fig. 5 only one object is considered for each iteration.

For each object i a motion parameter set $A_i = (T_u, T_v, T_w, R_u, R_v, R_w)$ describing the translation T and rotation R of the model object i is estimated.

Using A_i and the model world $\hat{P}_{i-1}$ a motion compensated model image $\hat{S}_i$ is computed by means of image synthesis.

The verification test looks at the actual frame difference between the current image S_{k+1} and the

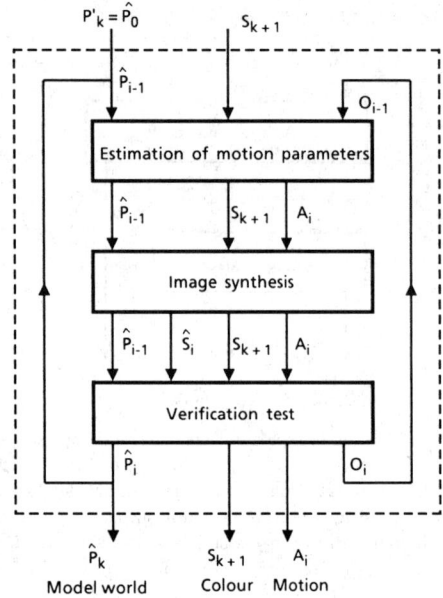

Fig. 11. Motion analysis. Model: 3D-motion of 3D quasi-rigid objects. (P'_k, model world approximating image k; S_{k+1}, colour signal of real image $k+1$; O_i, object area to be analysed; $\hat{S}_i$, model image of $\hat{P}_i$; A_i, motion parameter of object i.)

model image $\hat{S}_i$ computed from the current model world $\hat{P}_{i-1}$ and the motion parameters A_i and compares it to the frame differences between S_{k+1} and the model image of the model world $\hat{P}_{i-1}$. If the frame difference decreases in the area of O_i, the model world $\hat{P}_{i-1}$ is updated to $\hat{P}_i$, otherwise the motion parameters are rejected and if necessary object area O_i is subdivided into two areas [3].

The loop consisting of estimation of motion parameters, image synthesis and verification test inside the motion analysis block is executed until no substantial decrease of the MSD between the model and real image is achieved.

4.1.2. Shape analysis

The described motion analysis deals with objects moving as a whole. Shape analysis, on the other hand, individually moves vertices of the mesh of triangles (*control points*) of an object, in order to further decrease the MSD between the real and model image. To simplify the optimization problem, lines of perspective [13] are used (Fig. 12).

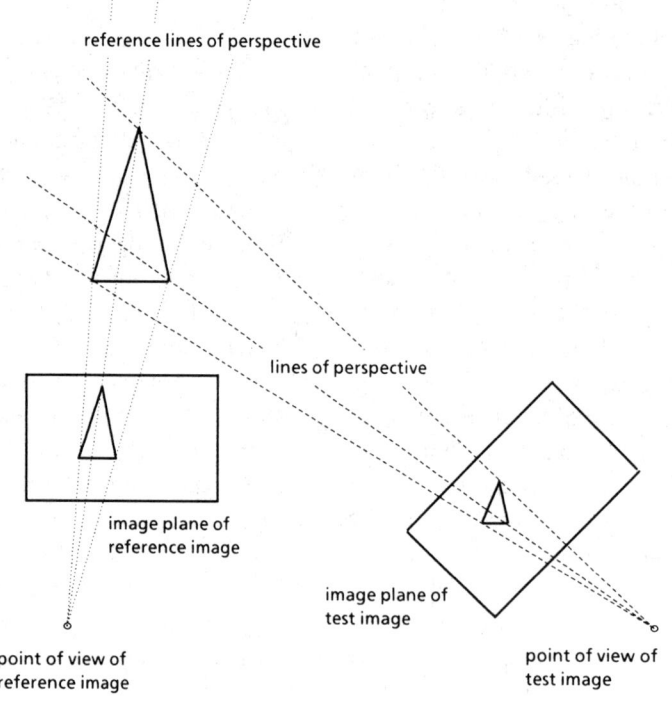

Fig. 12. Shape adaption using lines of perspective.

To each control point of a model object one *line of perspective* is assigned. A line of perspective is a ray starting at its control point in the direction of the point of focus of the camera. The line of perspective assigned to a control point when the initial model world is built up is the *reference line of perspective* of the reference image. The motion parameters determined for an object are applied to each control point and to its reference line of perspective. Hence, the motion of a triangle can also be interpreted as a view from another position. Fig. 13 shows part of an object wire-frame and how it changes when one control point is moved on its reference line of perspective. If the control point is moved on its reference line of perspective (see Fig. 12) there will be no changes in the view of the model world from the reference position but views from other positions will change. The dominant influence of the first image is justified because all luminances of the model world are extracted from the first image.

Shape analysis (Fig. 14) starts with the estimation of shape parameters. Input to this algorithm are the actual model world $\hat{P}_{i-1}$, which in the first iteration equals the output $\hat{P}_k$ of the motion analysis part, and the current image S_{k+1}. The difference signal between the image of the model world $\hat{P}_{i-1}$ and image S_{k+1} is evaluated and for the control points of object i the parameter set $M_i = (\Delta_1, \ldots, \Delta_n, \ldots, \Delta_N)$ containing one shape parameter Δ_n for each control point is estimated. A shape parameter Δ_n determines the shift of control point $P_n(u', v', w')$ on its reference line of perspective. L_n is a vector in the direction of the reference line of perspective of $P_n(u', v', w')$. Equation (8) shows how a control point $P_n(u', v', w')$ moves as a function of its reference line of perspective vector L_n and its shape parameter Δ_n to $P_n(u, v, w)$

$$P_n(u, v, w) = P_n(u', v', w') + L_n \Delta_n. \qquad (8)$$

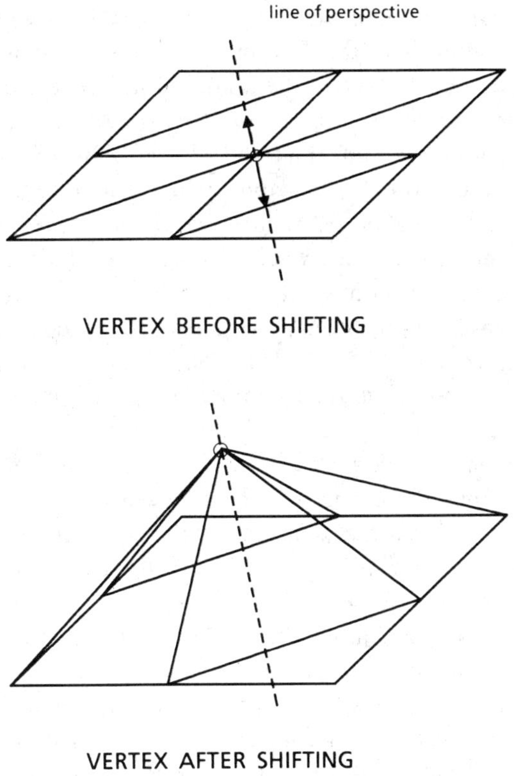

Fig. 13. Shape adaptation with triangular nets.

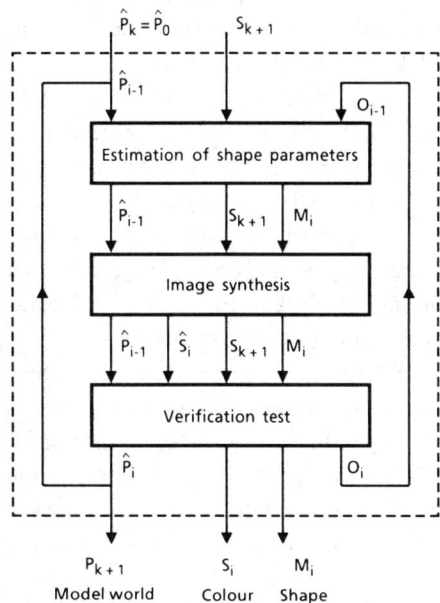

Fig. 14. Shape analysis. Model: 3D-motion of 3D quasi-rigid objects. ($\hat{P}_k$, model world with motion compensated objects; S_{k+1}, colour signal of real image $k+1$; $\hat{P}_i$, model world with partly updated shapes; M_i, shape parameters of object i; $\hat{S}_i$, model image of $\hat{P}_i$; S_i, colour parameters of object i.)

The shape parameters are computed using a simple search method [13].

The verification test simply evaluates the MSD between S_{k+1} and the synthesized model image $\hat{S}_i$ of $\hat{P}_{i-1}$ and M_i. In areas where the MSD between $\hat{S}_i$ and S_{k+1} decreased, the shape parameters Δ_n are accepted. Then the algorithm decides, whether to iterate the same object or to optimize another object. The process stops as soon as there is no substantial improvement in image quality.

4.2. Properties of image analysis based on moving 3D-objects

The chosen approach of first estimating motion and then estimating shape is essential for coding applications. First motion analysis estimates motion parameters for each object area and, if necessary, decomposes an object area into flexibly connected sub-objects. Afterwards shape analysis adapts model object shape to the shape of the real objects visible in the sequence. Hence, this image analysis yields a subdivision of a scene into objects defined by their motion, shape and colour parameters.

As an illustration of the image analysis based on arbitrarily moving three-dimensional objects Fig. 15 shows two frames of the test sequence "Claire" and results of the image analysis. The two frames (Figs. 15(a) and (b)) are used to generate a model world and to estimate the parameter sets for motion, shape, and colour. Fig. 15(c) shows the wire-frame of the model object. The object was automatically subdivided into two sub-objects indicated by different gray levels in the wire-frame. Figs. 15(d) and (f) show frame differences between the model image and the actual real image of Fig. 15(b). Fig. 15(d) shows the frame difference after motion compensation and Fig. 15(e) after motion compensation and shape adaptation. In order to demonstrate the advantage of three-dimensional object models over two dimensional object models, the frame difference using a two dimensional model object is displayed in Fig. 15(f).

5. Parameter coding

Parameter coding in an analysis–synthesis coder includes the coding of the motion, shape and colour parameters, the control of the coder modes and the priority control of the parameter transmission as shown in Fig. 3. The following explanations refer to an analysis–synthesis coder which is based on a source model with 2D-objects.

5.1. Coding of the motion, shape and colour parameters

The three parameter sets A_i, M_i, S_i defining motion, shape and colour information for each object i are generated by image analysis in PCM representation. In order to increase the coding efficiency additional individual parameter coding techniques are applied. Motion parameters are coded by known DPCM techniques using stored motion parameters from the previous image. Shape parameters of an object are coded by a contour coding algorithm [10] in combination with predictive coding. Only the temporal differences of the object boundaries are coded using stored shape parameter information of the corresponding object from the previous image. The transmission of the shape update information is suppressed by setting the temporal differences to zero if the shape of an object has not changed significantly. In this case the object shape remains unchanged. Colour information is coded with a hybrid scheme combining motion compensating prediction and intraframe coding techniques. For motion compensating prediction of the colour information a prediction image is synthezised using the previous transmitted image and the actual motion and shape information of the objects. Therefore, motion and shape information of an image have to be transmitted first. A new intraframe transform coding technique [9] is applied which is not restricted to a block structure but can be adapted to object boundaries. At present, for intraframe coding of the prediction error large objects are decomposed into internal square blocks of

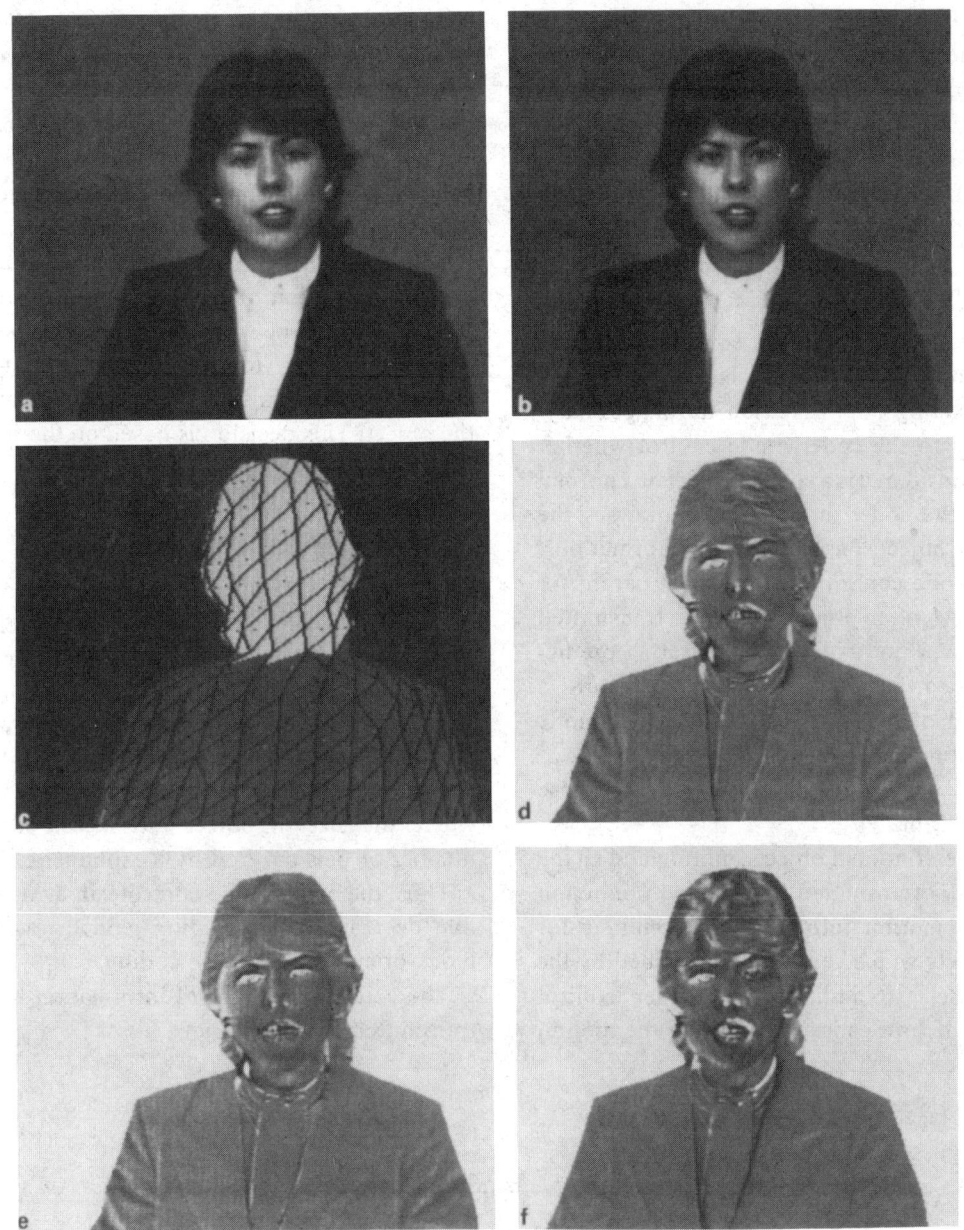

Fig. 15. Example of an image analysis based on the source model of moving 3D-objects. (a) Reference image from the test sequence "Claire". (b) Successive actual image of the sequence. (c) Wire-frame of two connected sub-objects. (d) Frame difference of model image and actual image after motion compensation. (e) Frame difference of model image and actual image after motion compensation and shape adaptation. (f) Frame difference with source model of moving 2D-objects for comparison.

picture elements and boundary blocks whereby the boundary blocks are split into segments considering the shape information. The resulting coded information R_i of each object i consists of three components R_{A_i}, R_{M_i}, R_{S_i} representing motion, shape and colour information.

5.2. Coder mode control

The object-oriented coding concept offers the possibility of an object dependent control of the parameter coding. For this reason, the image analysis indicates to the coder mode control whether the object considered is a special object or a normal object and the coder mode control analyses the size of each object. Based on these informations, the coder mode control decides which parameter sets A_i and M_i of an object have to be transmitted and whether or not motion compensating prediction is applied, i.e. whether intraframe coding is used instead of hybrid coding. The coder mode control distinguishes between four classes of objects and adapts the parameter sets to these classes (see Table 1).

In the case of normal objects, motion and shape information is transmitted by encoded prediction errors. The motion information is omitted for special objects which can not be described by the source model. In addition, the coder control informs the hybrid coder to switch off the motion compensating prediction such that only intraframe coding is applied. Also, in the case of small objects, the motion information is omitted since transmission of motion information is inefficient. Again, the coder control informs the hybrid coder to switch off the motion compensating prediction such that only intraframe coding is applied. Additionally, the coder control decides for small objects whether or not it is worthwhile transmitting the shape information. If not, the coder control generates a square shape M and thus reduces the object-oriented coding to block-oriented intraframe coding without transmitting shape information of the object. This decision is based on the following rule

$$\text{SIZE (obj } i\text{)} \begin{cases} \in [129, 256]: & \text{Block-oriented intraframe} \\ & \text{coding (small objects } B\text{),} \\ \in [1, 128]: & \text{Object-oriented intraframe} \\ & \text{coding with transmission} \\ & \text{of shape information} \\ & \text{(small objects } A\text{),} \end{cases} \quad (10)$$

where the size of object i is measured by the number of pels covered by its silhouette.

Thus, the coder mode control can avoid a possible decrease of the coding gain below that of block-oriented intraframe coding.

The coder mode control information has to be transmitted for each object.

Table 1
Coder modes

Parameter sets to be transmitted	Modes			
	Normal objects	Special objects	Small objects A	Small objects B
Motion parameters	×			
Shape parameters	×	×	×	
Colour parameters	Hybrid coding	Intraframe coding	Intraframe coding	Intraframe block-coding

5.3. Priority control

The priority control arranges the parameter sets A_i, M_i, S_i to be transmitted in an order of decreasing priority for each image. To the parameter sets A_i and M_i of each object the highest priority is assigned because these parameter sets are required for image synthesis in both cases that colour information S_i is transmitted or is omitted. This includes parameter sets M_i where the shape update information has been set to zero.

The priority $PR(S_i)$ of a parameter set S_i of an object i is determined by object features as the object size O_{si} and the quality of object synthesis O_{qi}.

By the normalization of the object features O_{si}, O_{qi}

$$O_{si} = \text{SIZE min}/\text{SIZE}(\text{obj } i) \quad (11)$$

and

$$O_{qi} = \text{MADFD}(\text{obj } i)/\text{MADFD max}, \quad (12)$$

the object features are in the range [0, 1], where high values of O_{si}, O_{qi} indicate high priority. SIZE min denotes the smallest size of the mapped objects of the scene and SIZE(obj i) the size of the actually considered, mapped object i. The parameter O_{qi} evaluates the object oriented success of the prediction of an object. MADFD max describes the maximum mean absolute displaced frame difference of all objects of an image and MADFD(obj i) describes the mean absolute displaced frame difference of the actually considered object i.

Thus, the priority $PR(\cdot)$ of the parameter sets A_i, M_i, S_i results as

$$PR(A_i) = \max_i\{PR(S_i)\},$$

$$PR(M_i) = \max_i\{PR(S_i)\},$$

$$PR(S_i) = f(O_{si}, O_{qi}), \quad (13)$$

where $f(\cdot)$ denotes the functional relationship of the priority $PR(S_i)$ and its arguments O_{si} and O_{qi}.

A simple example of the priority control is shown in Table 2. There are two objects with $O_{s1} = 0.1$, $O_{q1} = 0.1$ and $O_{s2} = 1$, $O_{q2} = 1$, i.e. object 1 is ten times the size of object 2 and has a MADFD which is one tenth of the MADFD of object 2. Object 2 is a special object. Hence, no motion information is transmitted for object 2. Each parameter set A_1, M_1, S_1, M_2, S_2 has its own priority $PR(\cdot)$. For the special priority function $PR(S_i) = O_{si} O_{qi}$ the priority queue is shown in Table 2(b). First, the parameter sets of highest priority, in this example the motion and shape information of object 1 and the shape information of object 2, are transmitted. Then, the following parameter sets are transmitted, i.e. the colour parameter set of object 2 and the colour parameter set of object 1. The transmission of the parameter sets ends if no more transmission rate is available. If, for example, the transmission rate is exhausted after the transmission of the colour parameter of object 2, geometrical distortions are introduced for object 1 instead of quantization errors.

In the case of large objects which are decomposed into internal blocks and boundary blocks the colour information is encoded separately for

Table 2

Example of the priority control. (a) Priority calculation. (b) Priority queue.

(a)

Object i	O_{si}	O_{qi}	Priority of the parameter sets
1	0.1	0.1	$PR(A_1) = 1$ (motion) $PR(M_1) = 1$ (shape) $PR(S_1) = 0.01$ (colour)
2	1	1	$PR(M_2) = 1$ $PR(S_2) = 1$

(b)

Priority function	Priority $PR(\cdot)$
$PR(A_1)$	1
$PR(M_1)$	1
$PR(M_2)$	1
$PR(S_2)$	1
$PR(S_1)$	0.01

each block. Hence, an additional parameter priority PR_p is introduced which is determined by local features of a block as the mean absolute prediction error B_p and blocks with local object boundaries B_b.

The priority PR_p results as

$$PR_p = g(B_p, B_b), \qquad (14)$$

where $g(\cdot)$ denotes the functional relationship of the priority PR_p and its arguments B_p and B_b.

By the normalization of the block features B_b, B_p

$$B_b = \begin{cases} 1, & \text{boundary block}, \\ 0, & \text{else}, \end{cases} \qquad (15)$$

$$B_p = \text{MADFD(block)}/\text{MADFD max}, \qquad (16)$$

all block features are within the range $[0, 1]$, where high values of B_b, B_p indicate high priority. The control parameter B_b denotes boundary blocks which have to be split into segments. These blocks have high priority, the segments are separately encoded. The control parameter B_p evaluates the local success of the prediction in a block. MADFD max describes the maximum mean absolute displaced frame difference of all blocks of the image and MADFD(block) describes the mean absolute displaced frame difference of the actually considered block.

Thus, the priority of a block PR_{block} based on these normalized object and block features results in

$$PR_{block} = h(PR(S_i), PR_p), \qquad (17)$$

where $h(\cdot)$ denotes the functional relationship of the priority PR_{block} and its arguments $PR(S_i)$ and PR_p.

6. Experimental results

The described analysis-synthesis coder with a simplified parameter coder has been experimentally investigated by means of computer simulations at 64 kbit/s transmission rate. The CCITT test sequence "Miss America" has been used with

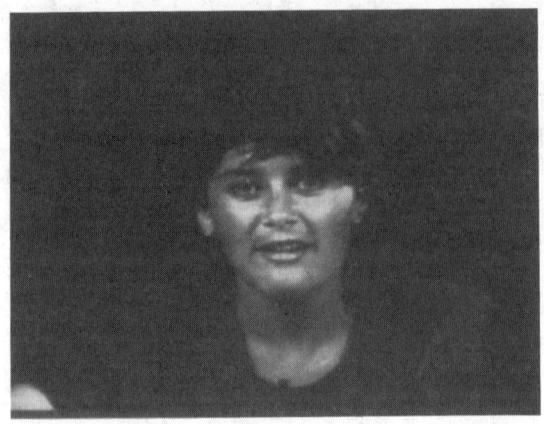

Fig. 16. Reference image from the test sequence "Miss America".

a reduced field frequency of 10 Hz and a quantization of 8 bit per sample. Each of the non-interlaced fields consists of 288 lines and 352 picture elements per line for the luminance and 144 lines and 176 picture elements for the chrominance, respectively. The test sequence "Miss America" represents a typical videophone scene showing head and shoulders in motion. Fig. 16 and Fig. 17 show two successive images of the sequence where closing eyes and an opening mouth are superimposed onto head motion.

In a first experimental implementation of the coder, the source model of 2D-objects as described in Section 3 has been applied. The shapes of the

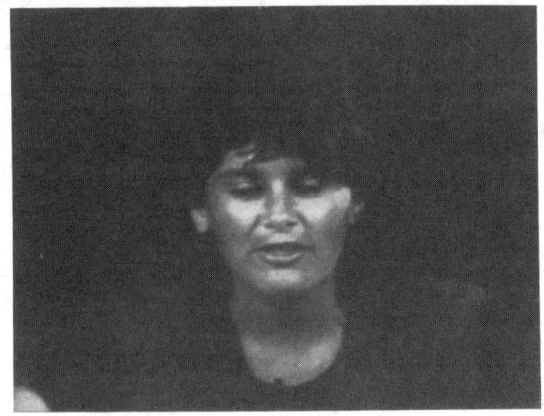

Fig. 17. Successive actual image of the test sequence "Miss America".

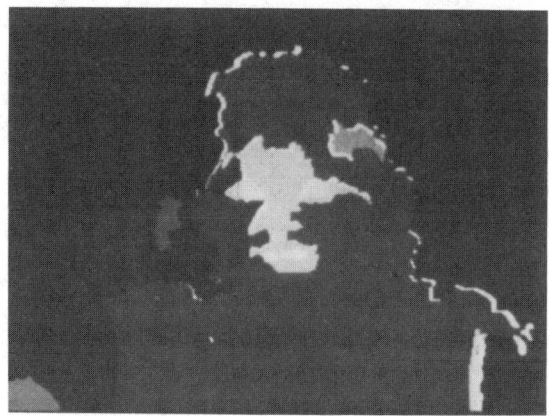

Fig. 18. Shapes of the objects found by image analysis of Figs. 16 and 17.

detected objects obtained by the image analysis are shown in Fig. 18 where uncovered image regions and the moving objects are displayed with white and different gray luminance values.

According to this source model, the motion information A_i is represented by eight mapping parameters $a_1, \ldots, a_8$ per object. With the exception of a_3 and a_6 the parameters are normalized by a factor K. This factor K is coded by 4 bits and depends on the maximum coordinates contained in the mapped object. The normalization yields an equivalent motion compensation accuracy for all objects. Each normalized parameter is coded by 6 bits. The parameters a_3 and a_6 describe the horizontal and vertical displacement of the object. They are represented with quarter pel accuracy and coded by 7 bits per parameter. Thus, $R_{A_i} = 54$ bits are needed to code the mapping parameter set of each object. No predictive coding is used in this experiment. Assuming 3 to 5 moving objects in a scene, e.g. head, shoulders and arms which are typical for videophone scenes, the total amount for the motion information results in 150 to 250 bit per image.

In order to encode the shape information, a predictive contour coding algorithm [10] has been developed which encodes the temporal differences of the object boundaries. For encoding the shape information of a large object i a bit rate R_{M_i} of about 300 bit is required. Again assuming 3 to 5 moving objects of different sizes the total amount for the shape information results in about 800 to 900 bit per image.

At present, the colour information is coded with a hybrid coding technique using object-oriented image synthesis for prediction and macro blocks for intraframe transform coding of the prediction error signal [20]. Each macro block consists of one luminance block of 16×16 pels and two chrominance blocks of 8×8 pels.

The coder mode control is reduced to use only mode 1 and mode 2 according to Table 1.

The transmission is organized via a priority control where the motion A_i and shape M_i information are transmitted with highest priority requiring about 1000 bit per image. Thus motion and shape information require a transmission bit rate which can be compared with that of the side information of a block-oriented hybrid coder. After coding of shape and motion parameters, the remaining bit rate of about 5000 bit per image is available for updating the colour information.

Fig. 19. Prediction image of an object oriented analysis-synthesis coder.

The advantage of object-oriented coding becomes obvious when prediction images are compared. Fig. 19 shows an image as generated by object-oriented coding. Fig. 20 shows the corresponding image generated by block-oriented coding. Both images can be interpreted as coder output

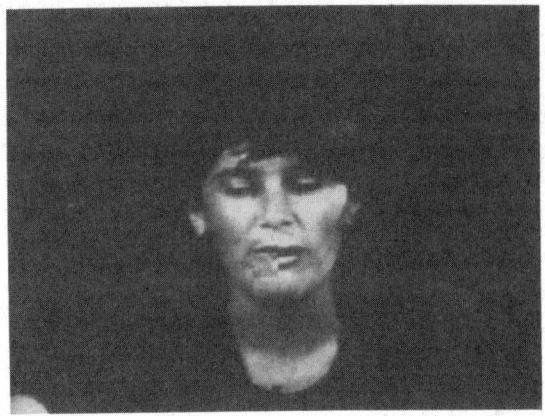

Fig. 20. Prediction image of a block-oriented hybrid coder.

when colour transmission is omitted. This example demonstrates that, with the same amount of side information, object-oriented coding generates prediction images that do not show the artefacts of block-oriented hybrid coding although there is no great difference in the mean square prediction error of both coding techniques. To take advantage of the more natural prediction image of the object-oriented coder the priority control for transmitting the colour information has to consider sophisticated criteria which are more complex than the mean square error.

In this implementation, the transmission of the colour information is organized in macro blocks by the priority control. A priority $PR(S_i)$ of a parameter set S_i according to

$$PR(S_i) = f(O_{si}, O_{qi})$$
$$= (1 + w_s O_{si})(1 + w_q O_{qi}) \quad (18)$$

and a priority PR_p according to

$$PR_p = g(B_p, B_b)$$
$$= (1 + w_p B_p)(1 + w_b B_b), \quad (19)$$

are used.

Thus, the priority of a macro block PR_{block} based on these normalized object and block features results in

$$PR_{block} = h(PR(S_i), PR_p)$$
$$= PR(S_i) PR_p$$
$$= (1 + w_s O_s)(1 + w_q O_q)$$
$$\times (1 + w_p B_p)(1 + w_b B_b). \quad (20)$$

If all weightening factors are equal to 1, a macro block achieves a high priority, if it belongs to an object of small size or to an object which can not be synthezised properly. Further, a macro block gets high priority, if the macro block contains object boundaries or if the local prediction in a macro block is inefficient.

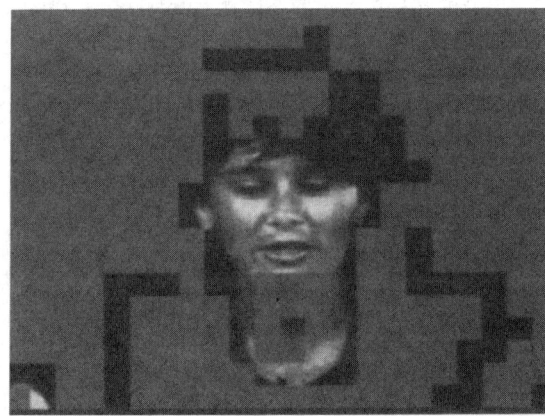

Fig. 21. Colour update information for a priority control accentuating large prediction errors and boundary blocks.

To demonstrate the influence of the priority control PR_{block}, the coding of large prediction errors and boundary blocks have jointly been accentuated by choosing $w_s = 0$, $w_q = 0$, $w_b = 20$ and $w_p = 1$ (Fig. 21). By this weightening, the so called "mosquito effects" which are typical for low bit rate hybrid coders in contour areas can be avoided since even small prediction errors of high visibility are coded. Furthermore, all blocks of high prediction error, e.g. the blocks which contain the mapping of the face are coded.

7. Conclusion

The structure of an object-oriented analysis–synthesis coder is described which segments an image into objects and encodes each object by three parameter sets.

Algorithms are presented which allow an automatic estimation of the parameter sets based on a source model of either 2D- or 3D-objects. For the case of 2D-objects the parameter coding is described. First results obtained with a simplified version of the described parameter coding are discussed.

The object-oriented analysis–synthesis coder is able to synthesize images for the prediction of colour information which look more natural than the images predicted by a block-oriented hybrid coder although the mean square prediction error may be the same or even higher. In the case of low bit rate coding where the available bit rate does not allow a perfect coding of all prediction errors, a block-oriented hybrid coder generates the known visible quantization errors while an object-oriented coder can suppress the updating of the colour information of an object to generate geometrical distortions instead of quantization errors. By transmitting the motion and shape information the object is reproduced in the right position but due to the changed projection of the object onto the camera target the non-updated colour information may lead to a loss of local resolution and locally incorrect perspective view at object boundaries. These distortions are less annoying than quantization errors. Further, the object-oriented priority control of the colour parameter transmission allows to improve the coding of important object features. It is possible e.g. to encode small objects like eyes more accurately than the other areas. In addition, the knowledge about the object boundaries can be used to improve the coding gain of the intraframe transform coder.

At present the parameter coding is still in a very early stage. Object-oriented analysis–synthesis coding provides many new possibilities for encoding the colour update information which have to be investigated in the future. There is a need for more appropriate criteria to control the colour parameter transmission since the mean square error criterion is inadequate for a quality assessment of geometrical distortions.

Furthermore, the parameter coding for the case of 3D-objects has to be developed to recognize the advantage of a source model with 3D-objects compared to a source model with 2D-objects.

Acknowledgement

This work has been supported by the Forschungsinstitut der Deutschen Bundespost beim Fernmeldetechnischen Zentralamt. We would like to express our thanks to Professor Gallenkamp for encouraging this work and to Dr. Stenger, Dr. Geuen, Dr. Billotet-Hoffmann and Mr. Heipel for many helpful discussions.

References

[1] K. Aizawa, H. Harashima and T. Siato, "Model-based synthesis image coding system", *Picture Coding Symp.* (PCS '87), Pres. No. 3.11, Stockholm, Sweden, June 9–11, 1987.

[2] G. Adiv, "Determining three-dimensional motion and structure from optical flow generated by several moving objects", *IEEE Pattern Anal. Mach. Intell.*, Vol. PAMI-7, No. 4, July 1985, pp. 384–401.

[3] H. Busch, "Subdividing non rigid 3D objects into quasi rigid parts", *IEE 3rd Int. Conf. Image Process. Applic.*, Warwick, U.K., July 1989.

[4] P. Eckman and V.W. Friesen, *Facial Coding System*, Consulting Psychologists Press Inc, 577 College Arc, Palo Alto, 1977.

[5] M. Eden and M. Kocher, "On the performance of a contour coding algorithm in the context of image coding—Part I: Contour segment coding", *Signal Process.*, Vol. 8, No. 4, July 1985, pp. 381–386.

[6] R. Forchheimer and O. Fahlander, "Low bit rate coding through animation", *Picture Coding Symp.* (PCS '83), Pres. No. 13.5, Davis, CA, March 1983.

[7] R. Forchheimer, O. Fahlander and T. Kronander, "A sematic approach to the transmission of face images", *Picture Coding Symp.* (PCS '84), Pres. No. 10.5, Cesson-Sevigne, July 3–5, 1984.

[8] W. Geuen and F. Kappei, "Principle strategy of model based source coding", *Picture Coding Symp.* (PCS '87), Pres. No. 12.2, Stockholm, Sweden, June 9–11, 1987.

[9] M. Gilge, "Coding of arbitrarily shaped image segments using moment theory", in: J.L. Lacoume et al., eds., *Signal Processing IV, Theories and Applications* (*Proc. 4th Eur. Signal Processing Conf. EUSIPCO '88*), Grenoble, France, September 1988, Elsevier, Amsterdam 1988.

[10] K.-W. Hahn, "Untersuchungen zur strukturierten Beschreibung und Codierung von Bildsegmenten für ein Konturcodiersystem", Diplomarbeit University of Hannover, Hannover, Fed. Rep. Germany, July 1989.

[11] M. Hötter and R. Thoma, "Image segmentation based on object oriented mapping parameter estimation", *Signal Process.*, Vol. 15, No. 3, October 1988, pp. 315-334.

[12] M. Kanako, A. Koike and Y. Hatori, "Codings with knowledge-based analysis of motion pictures", *Picture Coding Symp.* (PCS '87), Pres. No. 12.3, Stockholm, Sweden, June 9-11, 1987.

[13] F. Kappei, "Modellierung und Rekonstruktion bewegter dreidimensionaler Objekte aus einer Fernsehbildfolge", Ph.D. Thesis, University of Hannover, Hannover, Fed. Rep. Germany, 1988.

[14] F. Kappei and C.-E. Liedtke, "Modelling of a natural 3D scene consisting of moving objects from a sequence of monocular TV images", *Proc. SPIE*, Vol. 860, p. 126.

[15] S. Murahami, H. Ichihara and T. Miyata, "Model-based coding and facial image transformation for intelligent video communications", *Picture Coding Symp.* (PCS '88), Pres. No. 4.7, Torino, Italy, September 12-14, 1988.

[16] A.N. Netravali and B.G. Haskell, *Digital Pictures*, Plenum Press, New York, 1988.

[17] R. Plompen, Y. Hatori, W. Geuen, J. Guichard, M. Guglielmo and H. Brusewitz, "Motion video coding in CCITT SG XV—The video source coding", *Proc. IEEE GLOBECOM*, Vol. II, December 1988, pp. 31.2.1-31.2.8.

[18] J.L. Potter, "Velocity as a cue to segmentation", *IEEE Trans. Syst. Man. Cybern.*, May 1975, pp. 390-394.

[19] D.F. Rogers, *Procedural Elements for Computer Graphics*, McGraw-Hill, New York, 1985.

[20] H. Schiller and B.B. Chaudhuri, "Efficient coding of side information in a low bit rate hybrid image coder", *Signal Processing*, accepted for publication.

[21] P. Spoer, "Schätzung der 3-dimensionalen Bewegungsvorgänge starrer, ebener Objekte in digitalen Fernsehbildfolgen mit Hilfe von Bewegungsparametern", Ph.D. Thesis, University of Hannover, Hannover, Fed. Rep. Germany, 1987.

[22] R. Thoma, "A segmentation algorithm for motion compensating field interpolation", *Picture Coding Symp.* (PCS '87), Pres. No. 6.1, Stockholm, Sweden, June 9-11, 1987.

[23] R.Y. Tsai and T.S. Huang, "Estimating three-dimensional motion parameters of a rigid planar patch", *IEEE Trans. Acoust. Speech, Signal Process.*, Vol. ASSP-29, No. 6, December 1981, pp. 1147-1152.

[24] S. Ullmann, *The Interpretation of Visual Motion*, M.I.T. Press, Cambridge, MA, 1979.

[25] W.J. Welsh, "Model-based coding of moving images at very low bit rates", *Picture Coding Symp.* (PCS '87), Pres. No. 3.9, Stockholm, Sweden, June 9-11, 1987.

Tree-Structured Scene Adaptive Coder

PETER STROBACH, MEMBER, IEEE

Abstract—A new type of scene adaptive coder has been developed. The described coder involves a quadtree mean decomposition of the motion compensated frame-to-frame difference signal followed by a scalar quantization of the local means. As a fundamental property, the new coding algorithm treats the displacement estimation problem and the quadtree construction problem as a unit. The displacement vector and the related quadtree are jointly optimized in order to minimize the direct frame-to-frame update information rate (in bits) which turns up as a new and more adequate cost function in displacement estimation. This way the highest possible data compression ratio at a given quality threshold is always guaranteed. Excellent results have been obtained for coding of color image sequences at a rate of 64 kbits/s. The presented quadtree concept attracts with a much lower computational complexity when compared to the conventional motion compensated transform coder while achieving a subjective image quality that is as good or better than the traditional transform-based counterpart.

I. INTRODUCTION

DIGITAL transmission of image *sequences* at very low bit-rates has gained increasing interest recently because of its application to satellite and carrier communications of television (TV) signals (videophone, conference, industrial, and network TV). A global digital communications network, the ISDN, is branching towards reality. The new services are expected to be the starting point of a rapidly growing consumer market including a large number of video equipment for use in the new cost-effective 64 kbit/s networks. Under this perspective, major research in the field of digital image sequence transmission is focused on image sequence coding, i.e., removing *redundancy* and *irrelevancy* from image sequence data and—eventually—removing also a considerable portion of *relevance* data in order to meet or achieve a certain channel rate specification with a picture quality that should remain as natural as possible after decoding.

Traditional coding algorithms for single grey-level images exploit the characteristic property that in case of natural images, the given data is spatially high correlated. As is well known, the condition $r > 0.9$ (where r is the first-order correlation coefficient) is satisfied for almost all grey-level images and thus, transform coding [2], [4], [8], was considered to be a very appropriate coding method for single grey-level images. In transform coding, the given data are mapped into a new coordinate system where the transformed data is much less correlated.

A. Interframe Image Sequence Coding

The situation changes completely as soon as image *sequences* are considered. Although the single images, as members of a sequence, are again highly correlated in the spatial directions, the *temporal* correlation between successive images in a sequence may become *even much higher*. This observation gave rise in the development of *interframe* coding techniques for image sequences which primarily seek to remove the *temporal correlation* in a sequence [13]. It was

Paper approved by the Editor for Image Processing of the IEEE Communications Society. Manuscript received January 6, 1988; revised October 3, 1988.

The author is with Siemens AG, Zentralbereich Forschung Technik, ZT ZTI INF 121, Otto-Hahn-Ring 6, D-8000 Munchen 83, West Germany.

IEEE Log 9034843.

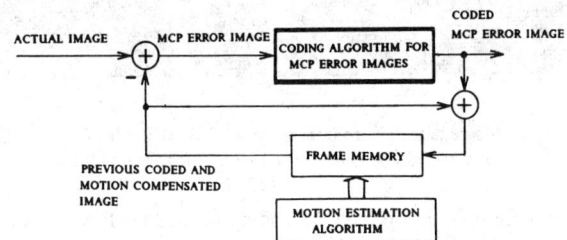

Fig. 1. Block diagram of a motion compensated interframe image sequence coder.

found, that these procedures possess the inherent ability of yielding a considerably higher data compression efficiency than achieved by simply coding the images independently [1], [5], [6]. Fig. 1 shows a general block diagram of an *interframe image sequence coder*. The coder consists of a difference pulse code modulation (DPCM) structure in the *temporal* direction which can be split in two main building blocks. This is first a *motion estimation algorithm* which determines the motion of active objects in the sequence by an appropriate and possibly *local matching* of the actual (incoming) image and the frame memory content (previous coded image). The motion of active objects is then *compensated* by reading a *shifted* version of the local frame memory content which is used to compute the *motion compensated prediction (MCP) error image*. Second, an appropriate coding algorithm is required to encode the resulting MCP error image. The coded MCP error image, along with the *motion vector* which describes the shifted local readout from the frame memory, are finally transmitted to the receiver.

B. Motion Estimation

There has been quite a lot of effort gone into the development of a wide variety of motion estimation algorithms [14], [15]. One of the important characteristics, which is common to all these algorithms is that they seek for the best "matching" between the previous (possibly coded) image and the incoming (actual) image with respect to an arbitrary matching criterion or cost function. This can either be a *correlation type* (second-order) cost function like, e.g., the well-introduced *normalized cross correlation function* (NCCF) [15], or a much simpler (first-order) cost function like the mean absolute difference (MAD) error criterion. In practice, it was found that the MAD error criterion works satisfactorily well but it must be noted that none of the cost functions, which are currently in use tries to optimize the matching with respect to, or in interaction with the coding algorithm for the resulting MCP error images. It is intuitively expected, however, that some sort of joint optimization or connected operation of the motion estimation algorithm and the coding algorithm for MCP error images could greatly improve the overall coding efficiency with respect to a more effective objective function which guarantees that both the motion estimation algorithm and the MCP error coding algorithm are operated in a joint optimum mode. This will be a central theme of this paper. But the objective of the paper is twofold. First, we present an analysis of a very popular configuration of an image sequence coder, namely, the well-introduced motion compensated transform coder [3] where motion estimation is based on block matching (BM) using the MAD error criterion. The coding algorithm for the MCP error images is simply a transform coder based on the discrete cosine transform (DCT) [7]. It is important to note that in such a system there exists no interaction between the mo-

Reprinted from *IEEE Transactions on Communications*, Volume 38, Number 4, April 1990, pages 477-486. Copyright © 1990 by The Institute of Electrical and Electronics Engineers, Inc. All rights reserved.

Fig. 2. (a) Image depicted from the sequence ALEXIS. (b) Corresponding MCP error image (four times magnified, offset = 128).

tion estimation algorithm and the coding algorithm. In other words, the motion estimation algorithm is operated independently of the prediction error coding algorithm and is based entirely on arbitrary or heuristic matching functions. This paper presents an approach where the displacement of motion compensation is optimized in the sense such that the frame-to-frame update information can be coded with a minimum number of codebits.

Therefore, the second part of this paper is devoted to a completely new type of a scene adaptive coder, where the objective is to optimize both motion estimation and coding jointly in a sense such that the number of bits which is required for encoding the frame-to-frame information in each subblock is minimized with respect to a given quality threshold. It is demonstrated that the presented coder directly determines the minimum number of bits needed for updating an actual image from its predecessor with a given MCP error coding algorithm.

C. Analysis of MCP Error Images

The idea of developing such a coder was aided by two very clear and fundamental observations. First, the procedure of motion compensation can be understood as a certain kind of inverse filtering of the image sequence. Not only the temporal correlation is removed, but also the spatial correlation decreases dramatically. For MCP error images, we have measured a typical correlation coefficient varying between $r = 0.3$ and $r = 0.5$. Additionally, it is important to realize that MCP error images exhibit the characteristics of a "line drawing," that is, the error image has significant amplitudes mainly along the boundaries and high contrast regions of moving objects, whereas homogeneous or unmoved regions correspond with an MCP error image that is totally flat and close to zero. To illustrate this, Fig. 2(a) depicts an image of the test sequence ALEXIS which is a standard sequence in the area of 64 kbit/s videophone coding. Fig. 2(b) is the related MCP error image when a conventional $16 * 16$ MAD-BM algorithm was used for motion compensation. It is seen that the MCP error energy is considerably concentrated in the "boundary lines" of the moving object. The MCP error image is clearly completely nonstationary. Subsequently, it is easy to demonstrate, that there exists no transformation that can further decorrelate such a type of signal significantly or, in other words, no transformation can yield a significant further concentration of the MCP error energy. Similar observations have been reported in [9], [11], and [12]. Thus, the consequence is that the traditional and widely applied idea of transforming image data does not work well in the case of MCP error images. On the other hand, since the MCP error energy has already been sufficiently concentrated in the boundary lines of moving objects due to the motion compensation process, there is no doubt that we can encode the MCP error images without any intermediate processing if we only find an appropriate coding method which takes advantage of the special characteristics of MCP error images.

D. Optimum Coding of MCP Error Images—The QSDPCM-Algorithm

A coding technique that is likely to succeed in coding the MCP error images should possess the following important properties. First, the coding process should be isotropic, i.e., no preassumption should be made about the signal texture since MCP error images are completely nonstationary. Second, the desired coding technique should be capable of describing line structures like those appearing in MCP error images effectively. Clearly, both demands can be satisfied by quadtree-based regular decomposition methods [16]–[25]. Recall that quadtree techniques have been applied with great success in the area of sparse line-structured binary image data compression [18] where the problem is very similar to the present MCP error image coding problem. Thus, our step was to introduce an adaptive quadtree mean decomposition for encoding of the MCP error images. A statistical description and an analysis of quadtree mean decomposition coding will be presented in [26]. In this concept, the MCP error image is adaptively segmented in blocks of variable size, wherein the error image can be approximated satisfactorily by its local sample means. When implemented in a recursive bottom-up realization, the quadtree mean decomposition of each subblock can be carried out with a total operations count of only one addition per pixel, independent of the subblock size.

This extremely low computational complexity for the quadtree mean decomposition offers the possibility of computing it eventually many times in one subblock. On the other hand it was found that the total number of bits which is required to encode the resulting means of a certain subblock decomposition can vary dramatically in dependence of motion compensation. Clearly, a motion estimation algorithm based on an arbitrary matching criterion might not find the motion vector which is optimum in the sense that the total number of bits required for encoding the quadtree means approaches an absolute minimum. The situation is especially crucial for high-contrast moving objects where an arbitrary matching criterion is oftentimes incapable of finding the motion vector which corresponds with the best, i.e., minimum update quadtree decomposition. Thus, in the presented technique a simple hierarchical BM algorithm is only used to provide an initial guess of the best motion vector. The optimum motion vector and the best quadtree decomposition are determined in a closed-loop optimization procedure as follows. Since the recursive bottom-up quadtree mean decomposition can be determined with only one addition per pixel, it can be repeatedly computed for a number of adjacent motion vectors around the initial guess. For each such decomposition, the total number of bits which would be required for coding the local means is determined via a simple table lookup in bits-per-codeword tables. Only the quadtree and the motion vector which are considered to provide the absolute minimum update information are finally coded and transmitted. The simulations have shown that a search interval of only $+/-1$ pixels in each spatial direction around the initial guess is sufficient to determine the optimum decomposition. This equals a total number of 9 decompositions per subblock or a total computational complexity of 9 additions per pixel. The method was called quadtree structured difference pulse code modulation (QSDPCM) [27]–[29]. Note finally that the QSDPCM optimization process also takes into account the nonlinear dependency between the given codewords (quadtree means) and the length of the resulting code when a variable length coding scheme (e.g., Huffman coding) is involved.

Coding results are shown for two different typical single-speaker color image sequences at a net-rate of 61 kbits/s. The results clearly confirm the excellent performance of the new QSDPCM coder. The decoded images appear to be free of disturbing block artifacts at edges of moving objects. Additionally, the presented QSDPCM algorithm attracts with a much lower computational complexity when compared with conventional transform-based hybrid coders and exhibits architectural properties which are best suited to a VLSI realization.

The paper is organized as follows. Section II provides an analysis of conventional motion compensated hybrid coders. Section III introduces the principles of regular mean decomposition and quadtrees and presents the QSDPCM algorithm. Section IV scans the architecture of QSDPCM. Some experimental results are discussed in Section V. Section VI gives the conclusion of this paper.

II. Analysis of Hybrid Motion Compensated Transform Coding

Transform coding has a long history in image data compression [7], [8]. When applied on high correlated data, an appropriately chosen energy preserving transform has the property that maximum energy (or maximum information) is packed into a minimum number of samples in the transform domain, hence facilitating efficient encoding.

When interframe image sequence coding became more attractive, transform coders were soon applied on the problem of MCP error coding [1], [13]. Configurations of this type where the transform is operated in a motion compensated DPCM structure have attracted much attention recently and are commonly referred to as "hybrid motion compensated transform coders" [5].

This section is concerned with an analysis of the effectiveness and efficiency of a transform when operated in a motion-compensated DPCM structure. In our analysis, we used real data of single speaker sequences in order to obtain realistic results. The measurements are shown for the sequence ALEXIS [Fig. 2(a)] which is a widely used characteristic test sequence in the area of videophone coding at a rate of 64 kbits/s. Similar results have been obtained for other single speaker test sequences.

We first introduce a few notations along with some fundamental principles of transform coding. Subsequently, the effect of a transform when applied on an MCP error image, like the one displayed in Fig. 2(b), is investigated. The situation is first illuminated on a one-dimensional example. The analysis is then readily extended to two dimensions. Consider the transform matrix T and an input signal x of length N samples

$$x = [x_1, x_2, \cdots, x_N]^t. \quad (1)$$

The transformed signal $\hat{x}$ is then obtained via the transformation,

$$\hat{x} = Tx \quad (2a)$$

where

$$x = T^{-1}\hat{x} \quad (2b)$$

is the corresponding reconstruction (inverse transformation). Next, we recall the following properties of the transform matrix T.

1) Overall Energy Preserving Property: The condition,

$$\hat{x}^t\hat{x} = x^t T^t Tx = x^t x \quad (3)$$

is satisfied if and only if $T^t T = I$ where I is the identity matrix.

2) Local Energy Compression Property: The transform matrix T should be determined in a sense that the signal energy is packed into a minimum number of samples in the transform domain.

For example, it is easy to find a transform matrix that exhibits the local energy compression property when the given data set x is a smooth function as the luminance function of the natural image in Fig. 2(a). The situation changes completely as soon as a nonstationary and impulsive signal such as the MCP error image of Fig. 2(b) is considered. If a signal as the one displayed in Fig. 2(b) is given, a transformation can fail in providing a further energy compression on the signal. But the situation appears to be even more dramatic. When a transformation is applied on an impulsive signal, this can result in an energy expansion, i.e., the transformed signal needs more bits for encoding than the original signal prior to transformation.

A. The Efficiency-of-Transform Test

From the introductory discussion it is clear that the energy compression efficiency of a given transform is not only a function of the transform matrix T, but also depends heavily on the characteristics of the input signal x. Clearly, we need an objective test in order to evaluate whether or not a given transform is efficient with respect to a given signal. In the sequel, such an "efficiency-of-transform test" is introduced. If the overall energy preserving property (3) is satisfied then it is clear that

$$\sum_{v=1}^{N} x^2(v) = \sum_{v=1}^{N} \hat{x}^2(v) \quad (4)$$

holds, but

$$\sum_{v=1}^{N} x^k(v) \neq \sum_{v=1}^{N} \hat{x}^k(v) \text{ for } k > 2 \; (k: \text{even}). \quad (5)$$

Obviously, the higher moments of x and $\hat{x}$ will usually be different, but, in consideration of (4), they may reflect the energy compression in the signal vectors. It is intuitively clear that the value of a higher moment of x or $\hat{x}$ will increase when the energy compression in the respective vector increases. Thus we can measure the energy compression efficiency of a given transform with respect to a given signal is we only compare the higher moments of x and $\hat{x}$. This leads to the definition of the energy compression coefficient ρ_k as follows:

$$\rho_k = \rho_k(x, T) = \frac{\sum_{v=1}^{N} \hat{x}^k(v)}{\sum_{v=1}^{N} x^k(v)} \quad k > 2 \; (k: \text{even}). \quad (6)$$

ρ_k is the energy compression coefficient to the power k. The transformation is considered to be efficient if $\rho_k > 1$ is satisfied. Else the transformation is considered to be inefficient. The definition of ρ_k can be readily extended to two dimensions.

We have measured the distribution function of the energy compression coefficient ρ_4 for the discrete cosine transform [7] since this is the most widely used transform. The blocksize was chosen to be $16 * 16$ pixels. A conventional $16 * 16$ MAD-BM algorithm was used for motion compensation and the transformation was applied on the MCP error images. Several single speaker sequences were processed. Here again we show the results obtained from ALEXIS. These results were found to be typical also for other single speaker videophone sequences. 120 MCP error images of size $288 * 288$ pixels were processed. Fig. 3(a) is the normalized distribution function of ρ_4. It is seen that the distribution function of ρ_4 in case of the MCP error images is approximately centered around $\rho_4 = 1$. In 36% of all transformed blocks the value of ρ_4 was less than one and hence, for these blocks the application of the transform causes an energy expansion. For those blocks, transform coding is clearly inappropriate. Similar results have been obtained by other authors [9], [11].

As an improved concept, one could suggest a coder where the transformation is switched on and off in dependence of ρ_k. Indeed, hybrid coders of a similar type have appeared recently in the literature [10]. Such refined configurations, however, are even more complex than conventional hybrid motion compensated transform coders. Additionally, the decision transformation YES/NO requires one more bit per block which might compensate the advantage when very low bit-rate coding is an issue.

As an interesting comparison, we have also computed the normalized distribution function of ρ_4 which is obtained by simply computing the efficiency-of-transform test for the original sequence ALEXIS rather than the sequence of MCP error images. The result is displayed in Fig. 3(b). Here, it is seen that transform coding works efficiently on the highly correlated natural images. The normalized distribution function of ρ_4 attains its maximum approximately at $\rho_4 = 250$. For this example ($16 * 16$ unitary DCT) $\rho_4 = 256$ would indicate the absolute maximum of compression.

B. Entropy Measure

In addition to the efficiency-of-transform test, we have also provided an entropy measure of MCP error images and we have compared the results with entropy measurements of the sequence of transformed MCP error images. Here again we have used the $16 * 16$ DCT

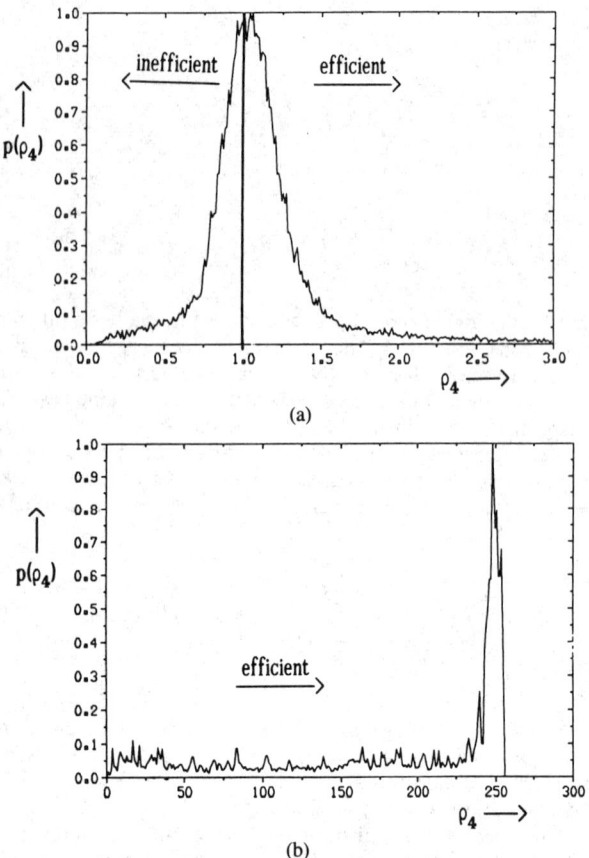

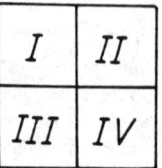

Fig. 4. Basic operation of quadtree regular decomposition: subdividing a subimage into four quadrants I, II, III, and IV.

Fig. 3. (a) Peak normalized distribution function of ρ_4 for a sequence of 120 MCP error images of ALEXIS when a $16*16$ MAD-BM motion estimation algorithm was combined with a two-dimensional $16*16$ DCT. (b) Peak normalized distribution function of ρ_4 when the sequence of natural grey-level images (ALEXIS) was transformed using the $16*16$ DCT transform.

block transform. First, the zeroth-order entropy $H(x)$ was computed,

$$H(x) = -\sum_{k=1-L}^{L} p_k \log_2 p_k \qquad (7)$$

where p_k is the probability that a quantized sample x takes a value r_k, say, from a set of $L = 2^n$, ($n = 8$ here) values. The evaluation of (7) gives the average information rate derived from one sample distribution function to which all samples in the MCP error sequence contribute. The same average information rate was computed for the sequence of transformed MCP error images. This average information rate was denoted by $H(\hat{x})$. Finally, we have computed the information rates for each coefficient in the $16*16$ DCT transform blocks independently. This measurement reflects the coding gain obtained when each coefficient is independently optimum coded in consideration of its individual statistics. The total information rate (assuming such individual encoding of the coefficients) is thus given by the relation

$$H^*(\hat{x}) = -\frac{1}{N^2} \sum_{i=0}^{N-1} \sum_{j=0}^{N-1} \sum_{k=1-M}^{M} p_k^{(i,j)} \log_2 p_k^{(i,j)} \qquad (8)$$

where $p_k^{(i,j)}$ is the probability that a quantized DCT coefficient $x_{i,j}$ takes a value r_k, say, from a set of $2M$ values (M sufficiently large).

Here again we have obtained very similar results for several single speaker sequences. In case of ALEXIS, the following information rates have been obtained:

Sequence of MCP error images: $H(x) = 2.480$ bits/pixel
Sequence of transformed MCP error images: $H(\hat{x}) = 2.504$ bits/pixel
Sequence of transformed MCP error images: $H^*(\hat{x}) = 2.498$ bits/pixel.

These results clearly demonstrate that transforming MCP error image in most cases provides no gain in compression. Sometimes, the average information rate was found to be even higher after transformation. The result that $H^*(\hat{x})$ is only slightly smaller than $H(\hat{x})$ indicates that line-structured, nonstationary MCP error images correspond with transformed images where all coefficients have approximately the same distribution which indicates the almost "white" characteristic of this type of signals.

III. QUADTREE STRUCTURED DIFFERENCE PULSE CODE MODULATION

The previous section was devoted to an analysis of the effectiveness of a transform when applied on MCP error images. The important conclusion that can be made is that a transform does obviously not provide a further reduction of the average information rate of MCP error images. Therefore, this section is focused on the direct coding of MCP error images. Clearly, a direct coding of the MCP error images possibly leads to much simpler algorithms for image sequence coding since the computationally burdensome transformation can be omitted.

A direct coding technique for MCP error images should have the following properties. First, the coding process should make no preassumption about the spatial structure of the signal and second, the coding method should be capable of describing random line-structured data effectively. Both properties are ideally represented by quadtree-based regular decomposition techniques which have been applied with great success in the area of sparse line-structured binary image data compression which is a problem very similar to MCP error coding. This important conjunction gave rise in the development of a quadtree-based mean decomposition algorithm for direct MCP error coding. In the sequel, we give a review on some fundamental principles of regular decomposition and quadtrees as far as it will be required in this context. The quadtree structured difference pulse code modulation (QSDPCM) algorithm which is a new and efficient quadtree-based algorithm for direct coding of MCP error images is then presented in the second part of this section.

A. Principles of Regular Decomposition and Quadtrees

The quadtree is a hierarchical data structure for describing two-dimensional regions. Quadtrees are often used to store binary pictures [18], [19]. A good history of the development of quadtrees is available in the papers of Klinger and Dyer [16] and Klinger [17]; however, only the basic ideas will be needed here. The quadtree has the following important properties. First, it allows a straightforward representation of size and shape and second, it facilitates the adaptive segmentation and efficient description of possibly very complex two-dimensional structures. When the quadtree is used in describing an image, the image is usually presegmented in blocks of a fixed size. Each block can be subdivided into four smaller units (subblocks). After each subdividing operation the size of the resulting subblocks is a quarter of the predecessor. Fig. 4 illustrates the basic operation of subdividing a subimage into four quadrants, labeled I, II, III, and IV.

The subdividing operation can be repeated recursively many times, until there is no further subdividing needed. The resulting segment

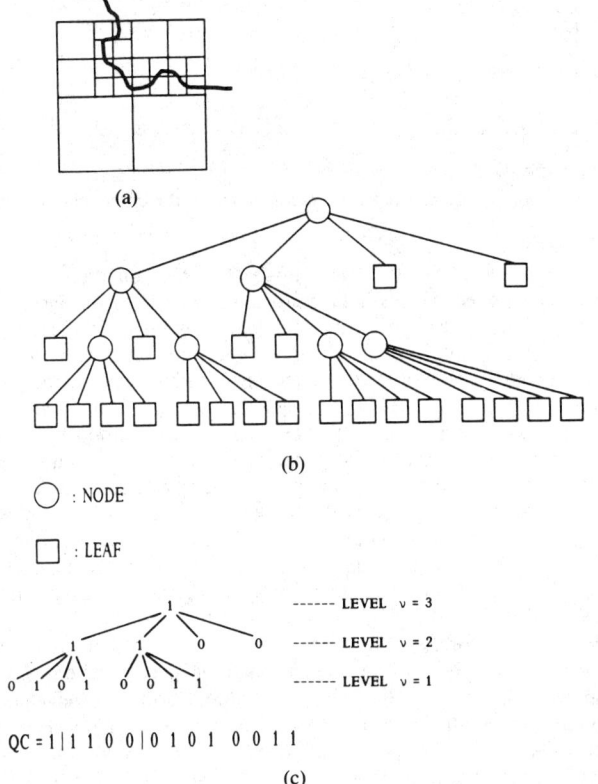

(a)

(b)

○ : NODE

□ : LEAF

------ LEVEL $v = 3$
------ LEVEL $v = 2$
------ LEVEL $v = 1$

QC = 1 | 1 1 0 0 | 0 1 0 1 0 0 1 1

(c)

Fig. 5. Quadtree-based regular decomposition and its description. (a) Segmented region. (b) Corresponding quadtree. (c) Generation of a variable wordlength quadtree code (QC).

structure is described by the quadtree. In the quadtree each node, unless it is a leaf, generates four children. Each node corresponds to a subblock that is uniquely determined, both in size and location, by its position in the tree. At each node a test is performed to see if the subblock presented by the node is homogeneous in the property of interest. If the test is positive then the node becomes a leaf, otherwise the children of the node are generated and examined in turn. The effect of this recursive and adaptive quadtree segmentation is illustrated in Fig. 5(a) where a line structure crosses a predetermined block. The block was quadtree segmented into subblocks of variable size, describing the line structure accurately. Fig. 5(b) is the corresponding quadtree. The quadtree describes the structure of segmentation. It can be encoded via a variable length code with very little redundancy. See Fig. 5(c). With structures like quadtrees, a small overhead rate is achieved by the idea of decomposing the data into subblocks whose size, shape and location are predetermined.

Until now, we have only considered the construction of a quadtree when the subdivide operation is used. Another possibility of constructing a quadtree exists when the inverse operation, namely, the merge operation is employed. In such a procedure, four adjacent subblocks are tested if they are homogeneous with respect to some criterion. If the test is positive, the four subblocks are merged to a new subblock which has four times the size of its predecessors. The procedure can be repeated recursively until the largest possible blocksize is reached. This was called a bottom-up construction of the quadtree in contrast to the subdividing method which is called a top-down construction of the quadtree. For an illustration of both procedures see Fig. 6.

Next, we consider the test which is involved in both the merge or subdivide operations. Among several possibilities, only the test which was used in this low bitrate application will be reported here. A more detailed discussion about the properties of different hypothesis tests in the merge or subdivide operations is available in [30]. The interested reader is referred to [30] for a more detailed discussion

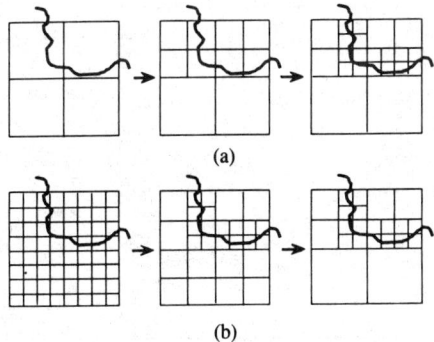

Fig. 6. (a) *Top-down* construction of a quadtree based on the *subdivide* operation. (b) *Bottom-up* construction of a quadtree based on the *merge* operation.

and analysis of hypothesis tests which can be used in the adaptive quadtree segmentation process.

In the following, the subblock and the quadrants I, II, III, and IV are represented by their sample means. This corresponds with a zero-order model of the lumiance function inside a block. Such a simple model was shown to be sufficient in case of nearly decorrelated data [26]. Higher order models may be applied in such applications where highly correlated signals are to be coded. Such approaches are slightly more involved and therefore their discussion is postponed to another paper [31].

In the case of a zero-order model, we require the sample mean of the subblock of size $\{m\}$ given by

$$M = \sum_{\{m\}}\sum x(i, j); \quad i, j \in \{m\} \tag{9}$$

where $x(i, j)$ is the pixel at location i, j.

As a second input to the test, we need the subblock sample means M_k, $k = $ I, II, III, IV (see Fig. 4) determined by

$$M_k = \sum_{\{m_k\}}\sum x(i, j); \quad i, j \in \{m_k\} \tag{10}$$

where $k = $ I, II, III, IV, respectively.

Now, the test is performed via the following decision operation:

Merge, if and only if the following condition

$$(|M/4 - M_{\text{I}}| < \sigma) \wedge (|M/4 - M_{\text{II}}| < \sigma) \wedge (|M/4 - M_{\text{III}}| < \sigma)$$
$$\wedge (|M/4 - M_{\text{IV}}| < \sigma) = \text{.true.} \tag{11}$$

is satisfied where σ is a predefined quality threshold. In the following, we only consider this bottom-up (merge) realization, since it has the distinct advantage that the sample means required in the merging test (11) can be computed recursively via the following relation:

$$M = M_{\text{I}} + M_{\text{II}} + M_{\text{III}} + M_{\text{IV}}. \tag{12}$$

Thus, it is easy to check that in the case of a bottom up construction of the quadtree mean decomposition, as described above, the total computational complexity is only one addition per pixel with an additional amount of decision operations in (11). The bottom-up regular mean decomposition thus provides us with a computationally very efficient way of encoding a two-dimensional image whose structure is random and impulsive. After decomposition, the local means (leafs) of the quadtree are independently quantized and Huffman coded. The information about the structure is mapped into the quadtree code [QC, see Fig. 5(c)]. The information about the local activity in the image is represented by a string of Huffman codewords following the QC. A theoretical consideration of this coder, however, goes beyond the scope of this paper. A detailed analysis of the described quadtree coder in terms of the rate distortion the-

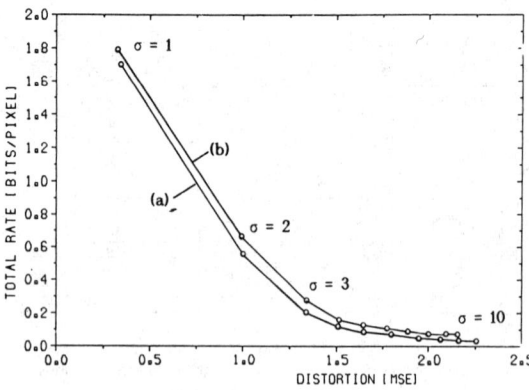

Fig. 7. Overall experimental rate distortion characteristics of the quadtree mean decomposition coder for the sequence ALEXIS. (a) Direct encoding of MCP errors. (b) DCT domain encoding.

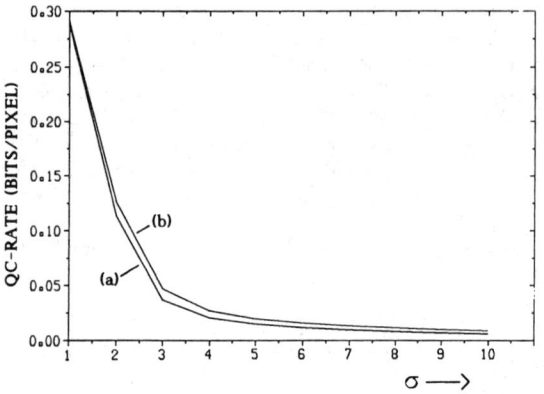

Fig. 8. Contribution of structural information (QC) to the overall rate of Fig. 7 (a) Direct encoding of MCP errors. (b) DCT domain encoding.

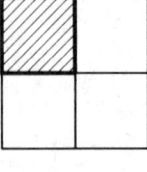
EXAMPLE 1

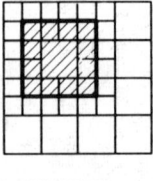
EXAMPLE 2

Fig. 9. Complexity of a quadtree as a function of the object placement.

ory will be provided in [26]. There, it was found that the regular mean decomposition coder based on quadtrees approaches the Shannon rate distortion lower bound closely as soon as the data is weakly correlated.

B. Original or Transform Domain Decomposition

Nevertheless, it is interesting to investigate, whether it is better to apply the regular decomposition coder in the transform domain, or directly on the MCP error images without any transformation. Recall that the zeroth-order entropy of the MCP error images was found to be slightly smaller (or approximately the same) as the zeroth-order entropy of the corresponding DCT coefficients. Fig. 7 shows the overall experimental rate distortion characteristics of the quadtree mean decomposition coder when applied directly, or when applied in the transform domain. This is an important test, since the random MCP error signal generally corresponds with a transformed signal which is random in its structure as well. Therefore, the application of a coding algorithm which makes no preassumption about the signal structure is also justified in the transform domain. Here again we show the results obtained from evaluating 120 images of the sequence ALEXIS. Again we used the 16 * 16 DCT. The result confirms a slightly better rate distortion characteristics in case of direct encoding of the MCP error images. This is a very nice result since it justifies the decision to drop the computationally burdensome transformation. Fig. 8 shows the contribution to the overall rate (Fig. 7) which is due to the quadtree code (QC). This confirms that the overhead of structure information is relatively small in case of the quadtree.

C. Sensitivity and Ambiguity of Displacement—The QSDPCM Algorithm

So far, we have considered the case where the MCP error images are generated independently by an arbitrary BM motion compensation algorithm. The MCP error images are then quadtree decomposed and encoded. Such a hybrid procedure where the displacement of the previous image is determined independently from the quadtree mean decomposition process, however, was found to provide not an optimum compression of the data. The effect of insufficient data compression is crucial especially for sequences containing high-contrast moving objects (e.g., ALEXIS). This can be understood by viewing the sensitivity of placement of the quadtree mean decomposition process, as reported in [19]. Suppose we are given the following problem. A shaded square with the size of a quadrant is embedded in a white subblock. Then, the complexity of the corresponding quadtree in terms of the required subdivisions is highly dependent on the placement of the shaded square. This *sensitivity* of placement problem is illustrated in Fig. 9.

Obviously, a correct placement of the quadtree can be a serious problem. Although in the presented quadtree mean decomposition coder the placement of the quadtree is predetermined and cannot be optimized, a similar problem exists in a considerable sensitivity of the quadtree with respect to the displacement between the actual image and the displaced (motion compensated) subblock of the previous image. This observation gave rise in the important question whether the displacement can be optimized in a sense such that the quadtree obtained from the corresponding regular mean decomposition process approaches a minimum complexity. For this purpose, we suggest the following system. First, an initial guess is made about the unknown displacement by simply employing a conventional two-stage MAD-BM motion estimation algorithm. Then, the quadtree mean decomposition is computed repeatedly for each displacement in a displacement interval of $+/-1$ pixels around the initial guess in order to determine the final displacement which gives the quadtree of minimum complexity. Clearly, the term minimum complexity could be defined in terms of a minimum number of subdivisions. On the other hand, there exits the attractive opportunity to measure, for each decomposition, the total number of bits which would be required for encoding the means of this specific decomposition. This can be performed by a very simple table lookup where some bits-per-codeword tables are addressed by the means, providing the number of bits required for this specific mean value taking into account the characteristic of some optimum variable length code for the means. This way, we can easily measure the total complexity of each decomposition in terms of the number of bits which would be required for encoding. Subsequently, the displacement which yields the optimum quadtree in terms of a minimum bit-rate can be determined and only the quadtree which is associated with this optimum displacement is finally coded and transmitted. Note, however, that the minimum bit-rate is oftentimes ambiguous, that is, there might exist more than one displacement yielding a minimum bit-rate. To resolve this problem, the MAD error criterion is computed in parallel for each decomposition inside the described optimization loop. Only the displacement which minimizes both the bit-rate and the MAD error criterion is finally considered as the optimum displacement. This method was named quadtree structured difference pulse code modulation (QSDPCM).

IV. THE ARCHITECTURE OF QSDPCM

In this section, the architecture of a videophone codec based on QSDPCM is described. The codec operates at a net-rate of 61 kbit/s. Fig. 10 shows the overall block diagram of the codec. After some preprocessing, the video signal is stored in the frame memory AC-

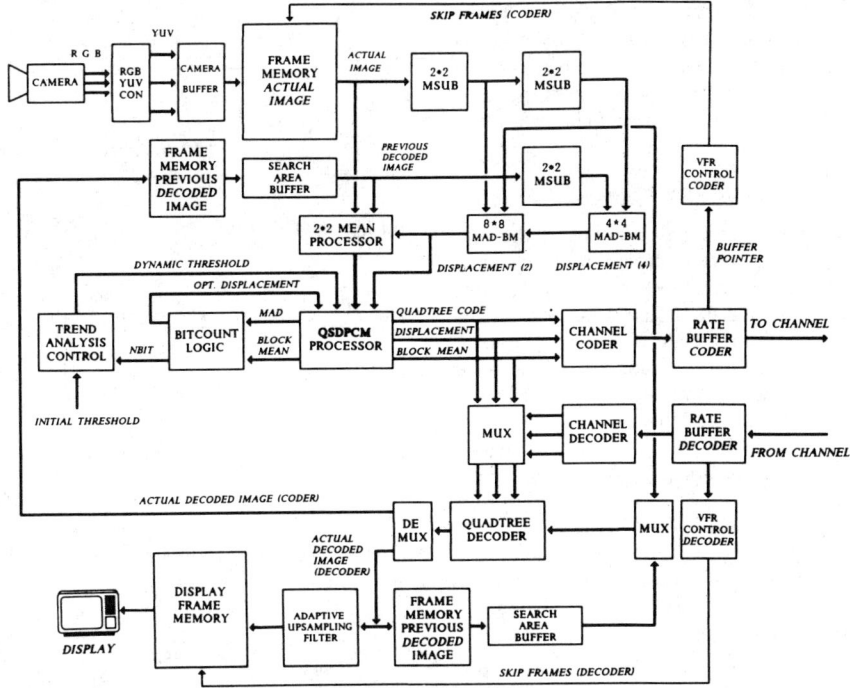

Fig. 10. Architecture of a 64 kbit/s videophone codec based on QSDPCM.

TUAL IMAGE. The organization of the frame memories is such that both the luminance and chrominance components are stored in one frame memory. The chrominance components are subsampled by a factor of two in each spatial dimension. An identical coding process is applied on both the luminance (Y) and chrominance (U; V) signals. The coder operates with the common intermediate format (CIF) with 288 lines and 352 pixels per line. As a reference, the previous decoded image is stored in the frame memory PREVIOUS DECODED IMAGE. This reference image has only half the resolution of the actual image in each spatial dimension. The actual image is presegmented in blocks of size $16 * 16$ pixels which are coded independently.

A. Initial Motion Estimation

In a first step, the actual image is subsampled by a factor of two in each spatial direction utilizing a simple $2 * 2$ mean subsampling processor (MSUB), i.e., each pixel in the resulting subsampled frame is the mean of four adjacent pixels in the corresponding original frame. The subsampling process is applied a second time in order to obtain $4 * 4$ mean subsampled images. Those are used to provide a first initial guess of the displacement (motion) vector which is obtained by a conventional blocksize $4 * 4$ MAD-BM algorithm with a search interval of $+/-4$ pixels (full search) in each spatial direction in the $4 * 4$ subsampled image. The resulting displacement vector is used as an initial guess in the second stage where a blocksize $8 * 8$ MAD-BM algorithm with a search interval of $+/-2$ pixels (full search) is applied on the $2 * 2$ subsampled image. The so-obtained refined (but not full resolution) displacement vector is then used as an initial displacement for the QSDPCM algorithm.

B. Mean and QSDPCM Processor

After the initial displacement has been computed, an actual subimage of size $16 * 16$ pixels along with the corresponding previous coded and initially displaced subimage are loaded into the mean processor. The mean processor computes a $16 * 16$ MCP error subimage for each displacement (full resolution now) in a search interval of $+/-1$ pixels around the initial displacement. Each of these $16 * 16$ MCP error subimages is then mean subsampled by a factor of two in each spatial direction and the resulting $8 * 8$ subsampled MCP error block is loaded into the QSDPCM processor which computes the quadtree mean decomposition, as described in Section III. In the presented

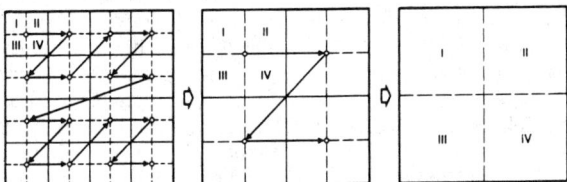

Fig. 11. Three-level merging procedure of the QSDPCM processor.

coder, the quadtree decomposition process has three steps. See Fig. 11. First, adjacent pixels in the $8 * 8$ block are tested whether they can be merged to $2 * 2$ subblocks. Second, adjacent $2 * 2$ subblocks—if available—are tested whether they can be merged to a larger $4 * 4$ subblock and finally, the test is applied on four adjacent $4 * 4$ blocks—if available—whether they can be merged to the largest $8 * 8$ block. As an important feature of this coding scheme, we note that motion estimation and compensation is carried out with pixel accuracy. The motion compensated prediction error is computed as the difference of the actual image and the zero-order interpolated and pixel accuracy displaced previous decoded image. The so-obtained motion compensated prediction error is then $2 * 2$ mean subsampled prior to quadtree coding.

C. Bitcount Logic and Trend Analysis Control

The resulting local means and the MAD value of the actual displacement are loaded into the bitcount logic where the total bit-rate is predicted which would be required for encoding the means. For this purpose, each mean value serves as an address of a bit-per-codeword table providing the accurate number of bits required for encoding the respective mean value. The bitcount logic finally determines the optimum displacement where both the predicted bit-rate and the MAD error criterion are minimized. The control signal opt. displacement is activated each time a block was detected which is optimum with respect to the already examined blocks. This signal causes the QSDPCM processor to store the decomposition result and after the search procedure (9 search positions around the initial guess are examined) is terminated, the optimum decomposition result along with the optimum displacement vector is send to the channel coder and the quadtree decoder.

At this state of encoding, the final number of bits which will be needed to encode the means of the current block is already known and used as input to the trend analysis control unit which controls the dynamic threshold of the quadtree decomposition appropriately in order to smooth the fluctuations in the primary data rate of the coder.

D. Channel Coder, Rate Buffer, and VFR Control

The channel coder provides the Huffman encoding of the optimum block updates (mean values as resulting from the quadtree decomposition). The optimum displacement vector is also Huffman coded. Finally, a codeword consisting of an active/inactive bit, the coded displacement vector, the quadtree-code (QC) and a series of mean codes is assembled and written into the rate buffer. The buffer fullness counter is incremented and the variable frame rate control (VFR-control) determines the number of input frames which must be skipped in dependence of the actual buffer fullness. Note that the active/inactive bit which carries the information whether a $16*16$ block has been updated, appears 594 times in a coded image when the described CIF image format is used. This "overhead" information can be interpreted as a binary image of size $33*18$ which can be quadtree coded. Tests have shown that this procedure saves roughly 150 bits per coded image compared to the uncoded case where 594 active/inactive bits must be transmitted.

E. Quadtree Decoder

The optimum displaced previous coded $16*16$ subimage is loaded into the quadtree decoder and is added to a $2*2$ zeroth-order interpolated version of the quadtree segmented block update. At this point it is very important to realize that the resulting updated $16*16$ subimage contains higher frequency components since the underlying displacement of the previous coded image has pixel accuracy. For a stable operation of the DPCM-loop it is therefore essential to compute a $2*2$ mean subsampled version of the updated subimage. The so-obtained $8*8$ block of the coded actual image is then used to overwrite the corresponding $8*8$ block in the frame memory PREVIOUS DECODED IMAGE in both the coder and decoder DPCM loops.

F. Decoder

The decoder (included in Fig. 10) exhibits an extremely simple structure. After the input rate buffer and the channel decoder, the update information is decomposed into the quadtree code (QC), the displacement vector and the block updates (decoded means). A quadtree decoder which is exactly the same building block as described above in case of the coder provides the update of the previous coded image to obtain the actual coded image. The signal skip frames is reconstructed from the buffer fullness in the receiver and is used to select between the mode "output repeated frame" or "output updated frame."

G. Optimum Upsampling Filter

As described in part E of this section, the reconstructed image after decoding is only available in a $2*2$ subsampled version. The *a priori* knowledge that the reconstructed image has the characteristics of a $2*2$ mean subsampled image allows the design of an optimum upsampling filter to convert the decoder output to the full CIF format. In the following, we describe a two-dimensional upsampling filter with 6 taps which resulted in high-quality reconstructed images.

The filter consists of the following two-dimensional coefficient mask

$$F^{(I)} = \begin{matrix} A1 & A2 & A4 \\ A2 & A3 & A5 \\ A4 & A5 & A6 \end{matrix} = [F^{(I)}_{i,j}]; \quad i = -1, 0, 1; \quad j = -1, 0, 1 \quad (13)$$

TABLE I
SET OF COEFFICIENTS FOR OPTIMUM UPSAMPLING

A1 = 0.0285	A4 = -0.0285
A2 = 0.1519	A5 = -0.1357
A3 = 0.9787	A6 = 0.0159

and the rotated coefficient masks

$$F^{(II)} = \begin{matrix} A4 & A2 & A1 \\ A5 & A3 & A2 \\ A6 & A5 & A4 \end{matrix}; \quad F^{(III)} = \begin{matrix} A4 & A5 & A6 \\ A2 & A3 & A5 \\ A1 & A2 & A4 \end{matrix};$$

$$F^{(IV)} = \begin{matrix} A6 & A5 & A4 \\ A5 & A3 & A2 \\ A4 & A2 & A1 \end{matrix} \quad (14)$$

which are used to reconstruct the pixels $s^{(I)}_{k,l}, s^{(II)}_{k,l}, s^{(III)}_{k,l}, s^{(IV)}_{k,l}$ according to the rule

$$s_{k,l} \rightarrow \begin{matrix} s^{(I)}_{k,l} & s^{(II)}_{k,l} \\ s^{(III)}_{k,l} & s^{(IV)}_{k,l} \end{matrix} \quad (15)$$

where $s^{(I)}_{k,l}$ is obtained via the following filter operation:

$$s^{(I)}_{k,l} = 0 \quad (16)$$

FOR $i = -1, 0, 1$
$\begin{bmatrix} \text{FOR } j = -1, 0, 1 \\ [s^{(I)}_{k,l} = s^{(I)}_{k,l} + s_{k+i,l+j} * F^{(I)}_{i,j}. \end{bmatrix}$

The pixels $s^{(II)}_{k,l}, s^{(III)}_{k,l}$, and $s^{(IV)}_{k,l}$ are reconstructed by the same procedure, employing the rotated coefficient masks (14). The design of the filter coefficients $A1-A6$ requires some care. These coefficients have been designed by a least-squares optimization procedure in a sense such that the mean squared error (MSE) of a typical reconstructed image is minimized. The simulation results in Section V demonstrate the ability of this filter to reduce the reconstruction error significantly when the following coefficients (Table I) are used:

V. SIMULATION RESULTS

Simulation results are presented in this section in order to demonstrate the behavior of the new QSDPCM videophone codec. We show the results obtained from the sequences ALEXIS and MISS AMERICA which are widely used in the development of videophone coders. The Figs. 12(a) and 13(a) show typical coded images of the sequences MISS AMERICA and ALEXIS, respectively. The Figs. 12(b) and 13(b) are the corresponding error images (four times magnified, offset = 128) when the coded image is compared to the original. There is one important difference between the coding results of the new QSDPCM coder and conventional motion compensated transform coders, namely, there are absolutely no "ringing effects," noise in the background near moving objects or other typical effects of large block transforms visible in the new QSDPCM coder. For worst case sequences where the motion compensation does not work perfectly, we have observed an almost similar breakdown behavior than the motion compensated transform coder. Interestingly, there is not a sharp breakdown of the QSDPCM algorithm even in case of heavily moving objects. This observation clearly contradicts the widely held believe that a transform helps very much in worst case sequences with heavy motion. The next images illustrate the operation of the new QSDPCM coder. The Figs. 12(c) and 13(c) show the frame-to-frame update information, i.e., the segmented and quantized MCP error images. The Figs. 12(d) and 13(d) are the corre-

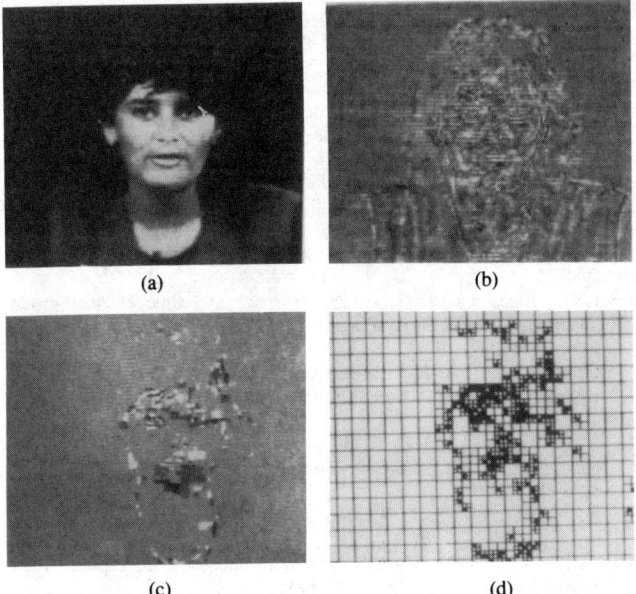

Fig. 12. Illustration of QSDPCM coder behavior for test sequence MISS AMERICA. (a) Coded image MISS AMERICA. (b) Coding error four times magnified, offset = 128. (c) Frame-to-frame update information four times magnified, offset = 128. (d) Associated quadtree segmentation structure.

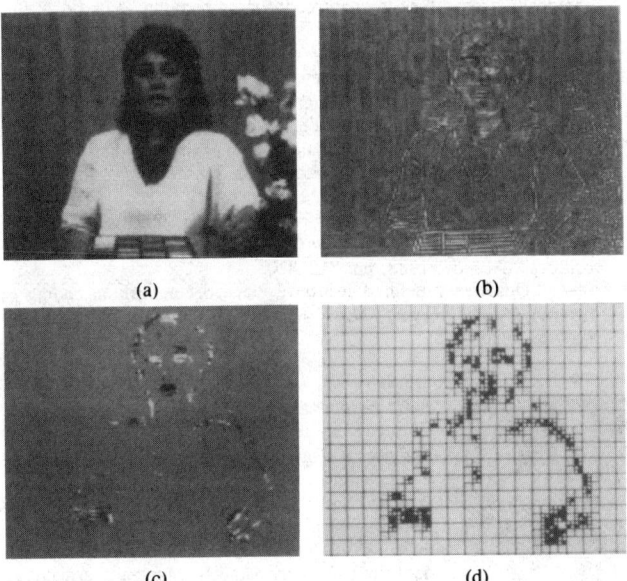

Fig. 13. Illustration of QSDPCM coder behavior for test sequence ALEXIS. (a) Coded image ALEXIS. (b) Coding error four times magnified, offset = 128. (c) Frame-to-frame update information four times magnified, offset = 128. (d) Associated quadtree segmentation structure.

sponding optimum quadtree segmentation structures as obtained by the QSDPCM algorithm. Fig. 14 shows the MSE curves obtained for both sequences. Here we have compared the results of a simple zeroth-order interpolation with the results obtained by the optimum 6-tap upsampling filter. Fig. 15 displays the number of skipped frames versus the transmitted frames for both sequences which illustrates the behavior of the trend analysis control and the variable frame rate control. More precisely, this last diagram shows how many times the previous frame has been repeated (frame repetition in the decoder) until the new coded image was displayed. The input frame rate in this experiment was 25 Hz.

VI. Conclusions

The method of quadtree structured difference pulse code modulation (QSDPCM) has been introduced as a new technique in inter-

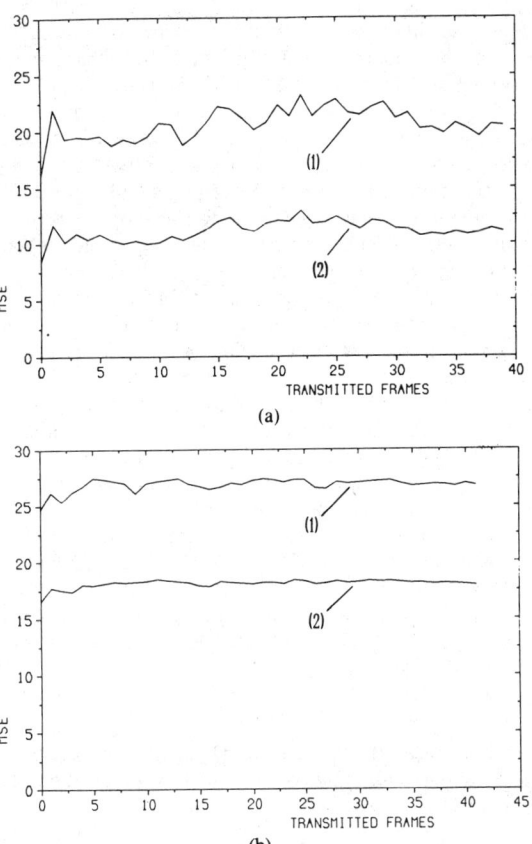

Fig. 14. Mean squared error curves. (a) Miss America. (b) Alexis. (1) Zeroth-order interpolation. (2) Optimum 6-tap interpolation.

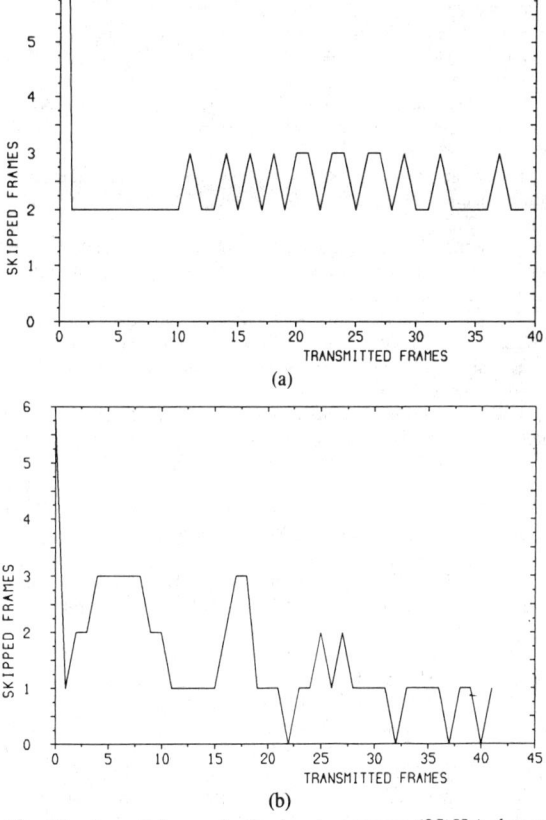

Fig. 15. Number of frames in the input sequence (25 Hz) that must be skipped while an actual frame is coded and transmitted. For each skipped frame in the coder, the decoder displays the previous transmitted frame by frame repetition. (a) Miss America. (b) Alexis.

frame image sequence coding. It has been demonstrated, that the QSDPCM method approaches a high coding efficiency and a regular algorithm structure. The QSDPCM algorithm resulted from a number of theoretical considerations and a consequent analysis of existing coding concepts and their typical behavior. The QSDPCM method combines two fundamental properties. First, there is no more transformation required and second, the QSDPCM algorithm facilitates a direct minimization of the frame-to-frame update bit-rate. The simulation results have shown very encouraging results when compared to the widely discussed motion compensated transform coder. Besides the low-bitrate application, the QSDPCM coding technique can be a very useful technique in the area of high definition television (HDTV) broadcast video coding in future HDTV broadcast video networks. This aspect arises due to the fact that QSDPCM is a typical "asymmetric" coding technique where the computational complexity is mainly concentrated in the coder. The QSDPCM decoder requires only a single addition per pixel for reconstruction of the image sequence. This allows the construction of a decoder that is expected of having a computational complexity that is roughly two orders of magnitude smaller than typical transform based concepts. Another justification of QSDPCM for HDTV coding is given by the increased frame rate in HDTV systems. Such high frame rates result in an even higher interframe correlation of the data which is best exploited by QSDPCM. For a more detailed discussion of QSDPCM in HDTV applications see [29], [30].

ACKNOWLEDGMENT

The author wishes to thank Prof. D. Schütt for several fruitful discussions about multidimensional signal decomposition and tree data structures.

REFERENCES

[1] F. A. Kamangar and K. R. Rao, "Interfield hybrid coding of component color television signals," *IEEE Trans. Commun.*, vol. COM-29, pp. 1740–1753, Dec. 1981.
[2] W. H. Chen and W. K. Pratt, "Scene adaptive coder," *IEEE Trans. Commun.*, vol. COM-32, pp. 225–232, Mar. 1984.
[3] G. Kummerfeldt, F. May, and W. Wolf, "Coding television signals at 320 and 64 kbit/s," in *Proc. SPIE Int. Conf. Image Coding*, 1985, pp. 119–128.
[4] P. M. Farrelle and A. K. Jain, "Recursive block coding—A new approach to transform coding," *IEEE Trans. Commun.*, vol. COM-34, pp. 161–179, Feb. 1986.
[5] R. Srinivasan and K. R. Rao, "Motion compensated coder for videoconferencing," *IEEE Trans. Commun.*, vol. COM-35, pp. 297–304, Mar. 1987.
[6] S. C. Kwatra, C. M. Lin, and W. A. Whyte, "An adaptive algorithm for motion compensated color image coding," *IEEE Trans. Commun.*, vol. COM-35, July 1987.
[7] N. Ahmed, T. Natarjan, and K. R. Rao, "Discrete cosine transform," *IEEE Trans. Comput.*, vol. C-23, pp. 90–93, 1974.
[8] A. K. Jain, "Image data compression: A review," *Proc. IEEE*, vol. 69, pp. 349–389, 1981.
[9] A. Furukawa, T. Koga, and K. Niwa, "Coding efficiency analysis for motion compensated interframe DPCM with transform coding," in *Proc. IEEE GLOBECOM*, New Orleans, LA, 1985, pp. 689–693.
[10] M. Kaneko, Y. Hatori, and A. Koike, "Improvements of transform coding algorithm for motion compensated interframe prediction errors—DCT/SQ coding," *IEEE J. Select. Areas Commun.*, vol. SAC-5, pp. 1068–1078, Sept. 1987.
[11] B. Girod, "The efficiency of motion-compensated prediction for hybrid coding of video sequences," *IEEE J. Select. Areas Commun.*, vol. SAC-5, pp. 1140–1154, Sept. 1987.
[12] W. A. Pearlman and P. Jakatdar, "The effectiveness and efficiency of hybrid transform/DPCM interframe image coding," *IEEE Trans. Commun.*, vol. COM-32, pp. 832–838, July 1984.
[13] T. Koga, K. Iinuma, A. Hirano, Y. Iijima, and T. Ishiguro, "Motion compensated interframe coding for videoconferencing," in *Proc. NTC'81*, New Orleans, LA, 1981, pp. G.5.3.1–G.5.3.5.
[14] J. R. Jain and A. K. Jain, "Displacement measurement and its application in interframe image coding," *IEEE Trans. Commun.*, vol. COM-29, pp. 1799–1806, 1981.
[15] H. G. Musman, P. Pirsch, and H. J. Grallert, "Advances in picture coding," *Proc. IEEE*, vol. 73, pp. 523–548, 1985.
[16] A. Klinger and C. R. Dyer, "Experiments on picture representation using regular decomposition," *Comput. Graph. Image Processing*, vol. 5, pp. 68–105, 1976.
[17] A. Klinger, "Picture decomposition, tree data structures, and identifying directional symmetries as node combinations," *Comput. Graph., Image Processing*, vol. 8, pp. 43–77, 1978.
[18] Y. Cohen, M. S. Landy, and M. M. Pavel, "Hierarchical coding of binary images," *IEEE Trans. Pattern Anal. Machine Intell.*, vol. PAMI-7, pp. 284–298, 1985.
[19] D. S. Scott and S. S. Iyengar, "A new data structure for efficient storing of images," *Pattern Recognition Lett.*, vol. 3, pp. 211–214, 1985.
[20] L. L. Jones and S. S. Iyengar, "Space and time efficient virtual quadtrees," *IEEE Trans. Pattern Anal. Machine Intell.*, vol. PAMI-6, pp. 244–247, 1984.
[21] C. H. Shaffer and H. Samet, "Optimal quadtree construction algorithms," *Comput. Vision, Graph., Image Processing*, vol. 37, pp. 402–419, 1987.
[22] S. L. Tanimoto and T. Pavlidis, "A hierarchical data structure for picture processing," *Comput. Graph., Image Processing*, vol. 4, pp. 104–119, 1975.
[23] K. R. Sloan and S. L. Tanimoto, "Progressive refinement of raster images," *IEEE Trans. Comput.*, vol. C-28, pp. 871–874, Nov. 1979.
[24] K. S. Fu and J. K. Mui, "A survey on image segmentation," *Patt. Recognition*, vol. 13, pp. 3–16, 1981.
[25] D. J. Vaisey and A. Gersho, "Variable block-size image coding," in *Proc. Int. Conf. Acoust., Speech, Signal Processing*, Dallas, TX, 1987, pp. 1051–1054.
[26] P. Strobach, "A computation of quadtree rate distortion functions," *IEEE Trans. Inform. Theory*, Feb. 1988, to be published.
[27] P. Strobach, D. Schütt, and W. Tengler, "Space-variant regular decomposition quadtrees in adaptive interframe coding," in *Proc. Int. Conf. Acoust., Speech, Signal Processing*, paper M7.8, New York, Apr. 1988, pp. 1096–1099.
[28] P. Strobach, "QSDPCM—A new technique in scene adaptive coding," in *Proc. 4th European Signal Processing Conf.*, (EUSIPCO-88), Grenoble, France, Sept. 1988, pp. 1141–1144.
[29] —, "Motion compensated regular decomposition coding of HDTV signals," in *Proc. Second Int. Workshop Signal Processing HDTV*, L'Aquila, Italy, Feb. 1988, pp. 223–230.
[30] —, "Quadtree-structured interframe coding of HDTV sequences," in *Proc. SPIE Int. Conf. Visual Commun. Image Processing*, Cambridge, MA, Nov. 1988, pp. 812–820.
[31] —, "Quadtree-structured recursive plane decomposition coding of two-dimensional images," *IEEE Trans. Acoust., Speech, Signal Processing*, June 1988.

Peter Strobach (M'86) was born in Passau, West Germany, on February 6, 1955. He received the Engineer's degree in electrical engineering from Fachhochschule Regensburg in 1978, the DiplomIngenieur degree in statistics and computer science from Technical University Munich, Munich, Germany, in 1983, and the Ph.D. degree from Bundeswehr University Munich, Munich, Germany, in 1985.

From October 1976 to February 1977, and during the summer of 1977, he was a visiting scholar at CERN Nuclear Research Laboratory, Geneva, Switzerland. From 1978 to 1981, he was temporarily with Messerschmitt-Boelkow-Blohm Research Center, Munich, Germany, where he worked on aircraft radar systems. Since 1981, he held a Friedrich-Ebert-Scholarship. From 1983 to 1985, he was a Research Assistant at the Mathematics and Computer Science Institute, Bundeswehr University, Munich, Germany, where he worked on architectures for adaptive signal processing and the development of numerically robust estimation algorithms for finite arithmetic applications. Since May 1986, he has been with SIEMENS AG, Zentrale Forschung und Entwicklung (Information Systems Laboratory) in Munich.

Dr. Strobach has written more than 30 technical papers in the areas of parameter estimation, detection, image processing and coding and is the author of the book *Linear Prediction Theory: A Mathematical Basis for Adaptive Systems*, SPRINGER Series in Information Sciences, vol. 21, 1990. Dr. Strobach is a member of the German "Informationstechnische Gesellschaft" (ITG), the European Association for Signal Processing (EURASIP), and the IEEE Acoustics, Speech and Signal Processing Society. He is a corecipient of the 1988 ITG paper price award for the best paper of a German author under 40 years old.

Combined Source-Channel Coding of Images Using the Block Cosine Transform

JAMES W. MODESTINO, SENIOR MEMBER, IEEE, DAVID G. DAUT, MEMBER, IEEE, AND ACIE L. VICKERS, STUDENT MEMBER, IEEE

Abstract—An approach is described for exploiting the tradeoffs between source and channel coding in the context of image transmission. The source encoder employs two-dimensional (2-D) block transform coding using the discrete cosine transform (DCT). This technique has proven to be an efficient and readily implementable source coding technique in the absence of channel errors. In the presence of channel errors, however, the performance degrades rapidly, requiring some form of error-control protection if high quality image reconstruction is to be achieved. This channel coding can be extremely wasteful of channel bandwidth if not applied judiciously. The approach described here provides a rationale for combined source–channel coding which provides improved quality image reconstruction without sacrificing transmission bandwidth. This approach is shown to result in a relatively robust design which is reasonably insensitive to channel errors and yet provides performance approaching theoretical performance limits. Analytical results are provided for assumed 2-D autoregressive image models, while simulation results are provided for real-world images.

I. INTRODUCTION

A COMBINED source–channel coding approach is described for the efficient encoding, transmission, and reconstruction, of image data. The approach is an extension of previous work [1], employing two-dimensional (2-D) DPCM source encoding to block transform image coding. In particular, as in [1], we demonstrate that joint design of the source and channel encoders can lead to rather dramatic improvements in reconstructed image quality in the presence of channel errors while maintaining a fixed transmission bandwidth. This improvement is achieved by exploiting the tradeoffs between image reconstruction accuracy and channel-error effects.

Previous work on block transform image coding (cf. [2]-[4]) has, for the most part, concentrated almost exclusively upon the problem of image representation accuracy, with little consideration given to the effects of channel errors. In some cases, simulation results are provided, indicating, if only qualitatively, the sensitivity of block transform coding schemes to channel errors. Here we describe the effects of channel errors both qualitatively, through simulation, and quantitatively, through the development of explicit expressions for overall image reconstruction accuracy under various system constraints and specific stochastic image modeling assumptions.

Block transform image coding, like other source coding schemes, is very sensitive to channel errors. As a result, some form of error-control protection must be applied if high quality image reconstruction is to be achieved. Since channel coding generally entails a bandwidth expansion, this operation can be extremely wasteful of channel bandwidth unless applied judiciously. By trading quantization accuracy for error-control protection through channel coding, we demonstrate that it is possible to significantly improve the reconstructed image quality without sacrificing transmission bandwidth and yet provide performance approaching an achievable rate-distortion bound. While explicit results are provided only for the 2-D discrete cosine transform (DCT), the approach is applicable to arbitrary unitary transforms.

The overall block transform coding system employing the 2-D DCT is described in Section II and includes typical performance without channel coding. An analysis of the reconstructed output signal-to-noise ratio performance is provided in Section III. System performance dependence on transform block size is described in Section IV. In Section V we develop a methodology for combined source–channel coding employing the DCT. Simulation results demonstrating the efficacy of this approach are provided for typical real-world images in Section VI. Finally, in Section VII, a summary and suggestions for future research are provided.

II. PRELIMINARIES

We assume that an image can be modeled as a 2-D autoregressive random field described according to

$$S(i,j) = \sum_{k=0}^{K} \sum_{l=0}^{L}{}' a(k,l) S(i-k, j-l) + W(i,j); i,j \geq 0 \quad (1)$$

where the prime is intended to indicate that the point $k = l = 0$ is excluded from the double summation, and $\{W(i,j)\}$ is a 2-D zero-mean sequence of independent and identically distributed (i.i.d.) random variables possessing common variance σ_w^2. We assume that the initial values $S(-k, -l)$ for $k = 0, 1, \cdots, K-1$, and $l = 0, 1, \cdots, L-1$ have been specified.

As a concrete example of a 2-D autoregressive process, we note the 2-D separable and stationary Gauss-Markov random field. Here

$$S(i,j) = \rho_R S(i-1,j) + \rho_C S(i,j-1)$$
$$- \rho_R \rho_C S(i-1,j-1) + W(i,j) \quad (2)$$

with ρ_R and ρ_C the correlation coefficients in the vertical (row) and horizontal (column) directions, respectively, and $\{W(i,j)\}$ a 2-D i.i.d. zero-mean Gaussian sequence possessing common variance $\sigma_W^2 = \sigma_S^2(1 - \rho_R^2)(1 - \rho_C^2)$. The quantity σ_S^2 represents the common variance of the resulting stationary sequence $\{S(i,j)\}$.

The underlying principle of monochrome image transform coding is that the 2-D transform of an image possesses an energy distribution in the spatial transform domain which is more suitable for coding than the original representation in the spatial domain. For a 2-D *separable* unitary transform, the transform coefficients associated with a square image array $\{S(i,j)\}$ of size $N \times N$ are given by

$$S(u,v) = \sum_{i=0}^{N-1} \sum_{j=0}^{N-1} S(i,j) A_C(i,u) A_R(j,v);$$

$$u, v = 0, 1, \cdots, N-1 \quad (3)$$

where $A_R(j,v)$ and $A_C(i,u)$ represent the row and column transform kernels, respectively. For unitary transforms we require

$$\sum_{u=0}^{N-1} A_C(k,u) A_C^*(i,u) = \delta(k-i) \quad (4a)$$

and

$$\sum_{v=0}^{N-1} A_R(l,v) A_R^*(j,v) = \delta(l-j). \quad (4b)$$

An alternative representation is to express the $N \times N$ matrix or array S of transform coefficients in the form $S = A_C^\dagger S A_R$ where[1] $A_C A_C^\dagger = I$ and $A_R A_R^\dagger = I$. Here A_R and A_C are $N \times N$ matrices with (i,j) elements $A_R(i,j)$ and $A_C(i,j)$, respectively, S represents the original input image array, and I is the $N \times N$ identity matrix.

In a typical application, the image array is segmented into blocks of size $M \times M$ and 2-D transforms taken separately and independently in each block to produce corresponding blocks of transform coefficients. Elements of the transform blocks are selectively chosen for subsequent quantization and transmission while the remaining elements are set equal to zero. The received data are then inverse transformed block-by-block to reconstruct the original image. An overall diagram of the block transform coding system is provided in Fig. 1.

The efficiency of the various unitary 2-D transforms depends upon their energy compaction characteristics. That is, the degree to which significant energy is concentrated in a few (generally low sequency) components. The 2-D DCT

[1] Here $A^\dagger$ represents the complex conjugate transpose of the square matrix A.

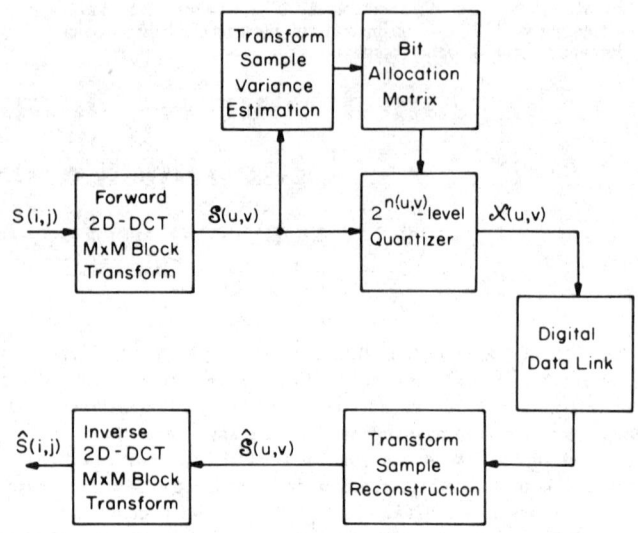

Fig. 1. Block diagram of two-dimensional transform image encoding/decoding system.

[5]–[7] has been shown to provide relatively efficient and robust performance in a variety of image coding applications and will be used exclusively in what follows. The 2-D DCT is defined by

$$S(u,v) = \frac{2}{M} C(u) C(v) \sum_{i=0}^{M-1} \sum_{j=0}^{M-1} S(i,j) \cos\left[\frac{(2i+1)u\pi}{2M}\right]$$
$$\cdot \cos\left[\frac{(2j+1)v\pi}{2M}\right]; \quad u,v = 0,1,\cdots,M-1 \quad (5)$$

where $C(0) = 1/\sqrt{2}$ and $C(u) = 1$, $u = 1, 2, \cdots, M-1$. Similarly, the 2-D inverse discrete cosine transform (IDCT) is given by

$$S(i,j) = \frac{2}{M} \sum_{u=0}^{M-1} \sum_{v=0}^{M-1} C(u) C(v) S(u,v) \cos\left[\frac{(2i+1)u\pi}{2M}\right]$$
$$\cdot \cos\left[\frac{(2j+1)v\pi}{2M}\right]; \quad i,j = 0,1,\cdots,M-1. \quad (6)$$

The 2-D DCT is image independent and possesses a fast computational implementation.

In Fig. 1, the sequence $\{X(u,v)\}$ represents the transmitted 2-D sequence whose values assume one of $L(u,v) = 2^{n(u,v)}$ possible output levels of the $n(u,v)$-bit quantizer. A number of bit assignment algorithms are available to determine the number of levels $n(u,v)$ to be allocated to quantization of the spectral element $S(u,v)$, $u, v = 0, 1, \cdots, M-1$, subject to a constraint on the average number of bits $\bar{n}$ available for each block of M^2 samples. These algorithms generally assign $n(u,v)$ proportional to the variance $\sigma^2(u,v)$ of the corresponding spectral elements. Elements for which $n(u,v) = 0$ are simply discarded, resulting in significant data compressions. The bit assignment algorithm employed here is a modification of one originally proposed by Habibi and Wintz [8] and later refined by Wintz and Kurtenbach [9]. Additional details can be found in [10].

Given the bit allocation matrix, the transmitted samples are quantized using a uniform $n(u, v)$-bit quantizer. The uniform quantizer is designed to minimize the mean-square reconstruction error under the assumption of Gaussian statistics.[2] With $L(u, v) = 2^{n(u,v)}$ the quantizer output levels can be represented as[3] $X_l = [l - (L - 1)/2] \cdot \Delta_L \sigma(u, v)$, $l = 0, 1, \cdots, L - 1$. Here Δ_L represents the uniform step size normalized to the standard deviation $\sigma(u, v)$ of the transform coefficient $S(u, v)$. In what follows, we assume that the output level X_l is coded into the natural binary representation of the integer l. It will be assumed that individual bit streams are available for subsequent modulation/coding and transmission. In particular, the modulation/coding is allowed to be different for each of the $n(u, v)$ serial bit streams associated with the output of the quantizer.

Typical block transform coding results using the 2-D DCT of selected 256 × 256 real-world images partitioned into 16 × 16 blocks and in the absence of channel errors are illustrated in Figs. 2 and 3 for an outdoor scene and antenna image, respectively. Clearly, transmission at an average rate of $\bar{n} = 1$ bit/pixel is possible with acceptable quality image reconstruction. Image clarity begins to show signs of degradation at $\bar{n} = 0.5$ bit/pixel, primarily due to a lack of edge definiteness. The effects of channel errors on the outdoor scene can be observed in Fig. 4. Here the channel is modeled as a binary symmetric channel (BSC) with bit error probability $P_b = 10^{-3}$. Subjective tests have indicated that a sharp threshold exists at this point with performance degrading rapidly as P_b increases above this value. That is, reconstructed image quality deteriorates as entire subimages are incorrectly decoded. Clearly, for channels operating close to this threshold, some form of error-control coding must be provided if acceptable quality image reconstruction is to be achieved. In the next section we provide an analysis of the output signal-to-noise ratio using block transform coding, which allows quantitative assessment of the effects of channel errors and provides the basis for a combined source-channel coding approach.

III. ANALYSIS OF OUTPUT SIGNAL-TO-NOISE RATIO:

The output signal-to-noise ratio (SNR_0) associated with the block transform encoding of an $M \times M$ image block S is given by

$$SNR_0 = \frac{\sigma_S^2}{e_T^2} \quad (7)$$

where σ_S^2 is the variance of the assumed zero-mean stationary 2-D sequence $\{S(i,j)\}$ and

$$e_T^2 = \frac{1}{M^2} E\{\|S - \hat{S}'\|^2\} \quad (8)$$

[2] The Gaussian assumption is generally justified on the basis of central limit theorem considerations (cf. [5, ch. 10]).
[3] For notational convenience we will often write n and L for $n(u, v)$ and $L(u, v)$, respectively, with the implicit understanding that these quantities depend upon the spatial frequency variables (u, v).

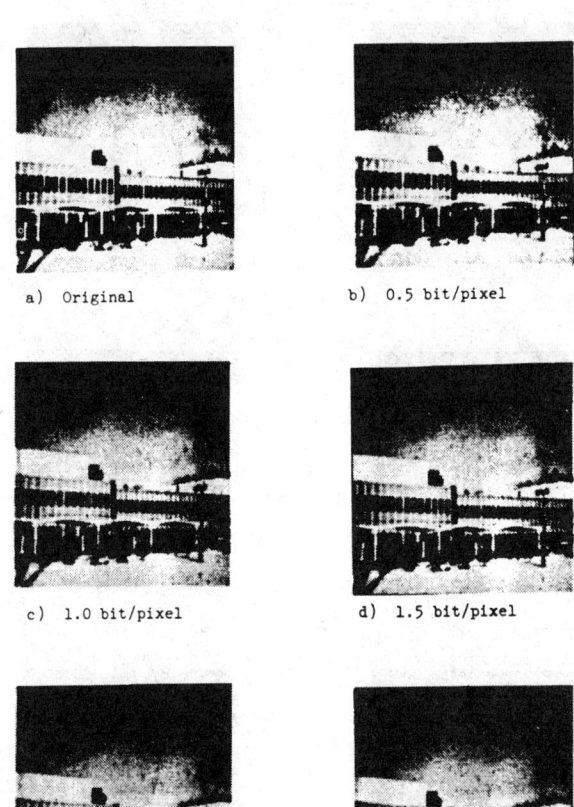

a) Original   b) 0.5 bit/pixel

c) 1.0 bit/pixel   d) 1.5 bit/pixel

e) 2.0 bit/pixel   f) 2.5 bit/pixel

Fig. 2. Block transform coding results for outdoor scene; 16 × 16 2-D cosine transform; Gaussian uniform quantizer; noiseless channel.

is the resulting mean-square reconstruction error. Here we make use of the norm $\|\cdot\|$ defined on the space of $M \times M$ matrices [11] according to

$$\|B\|^2 = tr\, BB^\dagger = \sum_{i=0}^{M-1} \sum_{j=0}^{M-1} |b(i,j)|^2. \quad (9)$$

Due to the unitary nature of the 2-D DCT, the expression for e_T^2 can be alternately stated in the spatial transform domain according to

$$e_T^2 = \frac{1}{M^2} E\{\|S - S'\|^2\} \quad (10)$$

where S is the $M \times M$ array of transform coefficients associated with the original image array S, and $\hat{S}'$ is the reconstructed estimate of S at the receiver. The array $\hat{S}'$ differs from S due to block quantization effects and the effects of channel noise. We model these effects as additive so that the received estimate of the spectral component $S(u, v)$ is given by

$$\hat{S}'(u, v) = S(u, v) + Q(u, v) + N(u, v). \quad (11)$$

Here, $Q(u, v)$ represents the additive quantization noise associated with the (u, v) spatial transform component and

Fig. 3. Block transform coding results for antenna image; 16 × 16 2-D cosine transform; Gaussian uniform quantizer; noiseless channel.

Fig. 4. Channel-error effects on block transform coding of antenna image; 16 × 16 2-D cosine transform; Gaussian uniform quantizer; $P_b = 10^{-3}$.

$N(u, v)$ represents the effects of channel errors. The corresponding arrays of quantization and channel noise elements are expressed as Q and N, respectively.

Substitution of this last expression into (10) shows that e_T^2 can be expressed as the sum of three separate components, according to

$$e_T^2 = \epsilon_q + 2\epsilon_m + \epsilon_c. \tag{12}$$

Here,

$$\epsilon_q \triangleq \frac{1}{M^2} E\{\|Q\|^2\} = \frac{1}{M^2} \sum_{u=0}^{M-1} \sum_{v=0}^{M-1} E\{Q^2(u,v)\} \tag{13}$$

represents the mean-square quantization noise normalized on a per pixel basis. Similarly,

$$\epsilon_c \triangleq \frac{1}{M^2} E\{\|N\|^2\} = \frac{1}{M^2} \sum_{u=0}^{M-1} \sum_{v=0}^{M-1} E\{N^2(u,v)\} \tag{14}$$

represents the normalized mean-square error contribution due solely to channel errors. Finally,

$$\epsilon_m = \frac{1}{M^2} tr E\{QN^\dagger\} = \frac{1}{M^2} \sum_{u=0}^{M-1} \sum_{v=0}^{M-1} E\{Q(u,v)N(u,v)\}$$

(15)

represents a mutual error term due to the interaction of quantization and channel errors. There is a tendency to assume the quantization and channel errors are independent and zero-mean and hence $\epsilon_m = 0$. However, this is not the case in general. This point has been emphasized by Totty and Clark [12], among others.

Consider first the evaluation of the normalized mean-square block quantization error ϵ_q given by (13). Recall that the uniform quantizer characteristics are chosen to minimize the mean-square quantization error. That is, the single parameter Δ_L is chosen to minimize the quantity

$$E\{Q^2(u,v)\} = \sum_{l=0}^{L(u,v)-1} \int_{E_l}^{E_{l+1}} [\xi - X_l]^2 p(\xi; u,v) d\xi$$

(16)

where $p(\xi, u, v)$ is the probability density function (pdf) associated with the transform coefficient $S(u, v)$, $u, v = 0, 1, \cdots, M - 1$ and E_l, $l = 0, 1, \cdots, L(u, v) - 1$ represents the input bin boundaries associated with the uniform quantizer.[4] Since the 2-D DCT is computed as a weighted sum over elements of the original block, it is generally assumed that

---

[4] Note that $E_0 = -\infty$, $E_L = \infty$ while $E_l - E_{l-1} = X_l - X_{l-1} = \Delta_L \sigma(u,v)$ for intermediate values of l.

$S(u, v)$ is zero-mean Gaussian.[5] That is,

$$p(\xi; u,v) = \frac{1}{\sqrt{2\pi}\,\sigma(u,v)} \cdot \exp\left\{-\frac{1}{2}\frac{\xi^2}{\sigma^2(u,v)}\right\};$$
$$-\infty < \xi < \infty \quad (17)$$

where $\sigma^2(u, v)$ is the variance associated with the transform coefficient $S(u, v)$. Tabulations of the optimum Δ_L for various numbers of quantization levels up to $L = 32$ have been provided by Max [13]. The values of Δ_L for $L > 32$ have been obtained by extending the Max results, as described in [10].

After an appropriate renormalization, (16) can be evaluated according to[6]

$$E\{Q^2(u,v)\}$$
$$= 2\sigma^2(u,v) \sum_{l=1}^{L/2-1} \int_{(l-1)\Delta_L}^{l\Delta_L} [y - (l-1/2)\Delta_L]^2 \hat{p}(y)\,dy$$
$$+ 2\sigma^2(u,v) \int_{(L/2-1)\Delta_L}^{\infty} [y - (L-1)\Delta_L/2]^2 \hat{p}(y)\,dy$$
$$\quad (18)$$

where $\hat{p}(y) \triangleq \sigma(u,v) p(\sigma(u,v)y; u, v)$ is a normalized Gaussian pdf possessing zero-mean and unit variance. This expression is readily evaluated for specified values of L, Δ_L and $\sigma^2(u, v)$. In the particular case of the separable 2-D Gauss–Markov process, it is readily shown that $\sigma^2(u, v) = \sigma_C^2(u)\sigma_R^2(v)$ with

$$\sigma_C^2(u) = \frac{2\sigma_S}{M} C^2(u) \sum_{i=0}^{M-1}\sum_{j=0}^{M-1} \rho_C^{|i-j|}$$
$$\cdot \cos\left[\frac{(2i+1)u\pi}{2M}\right] \cos\left[\frac{(2j+1)u\pi}{2M}\right] \quad (19a)$$

and

$$\sigma_R^2(v) = \frac{2\sigma_S}{M} C^2(v) \sum_{i=0}^{M-1}\sum_{j=0}^{M-1} \rho_R^{|i-j|}$$
$$\cdot \cos\left[\frac{(2i+1)v\pi}{2M}\right] \cos\left[\frac{(2j+1)v\pi}{2M}\right] \quad (19b)$$

where $u, v = 0, 1, \cdots, M - 1$. Substitution into (13) yields the normalized mean-square block quantization error ϵ_q.

Similarly, in evaluating the normalized mean-square component ϵ_c due to channel-error effects from (14), observe that

$$E\{N^2(u,v)\} = \sum_{k=0}^{L-1}\sum_{l=0}^{L-1} (X_k - X_l)^2 P_{k|l} P_l, \quad (20)$$

which is merely the mean-square error incurred if X_l were transmitted and decoded as the level X_k averaged over the probability of all such error events. The quantity $P_{k|l}$ is the conditional probability that level X_l was transmitted and decoded as level X_k while P_l is the a priori probability of transmitting level X_l. This last expression can be written as

$$E\{N^2(u,v)\} = \Delta_L^2 \sigma^2(u,v) \sum_{k=0}^{L-1}\sum_{l=0}^{L-1} (k-l)^2 P_{k|l} P_l. \quad (21)$$

Following the approach in [1], it can be established that[7]

$$E\{N^2(u,v)\}$$
$$= \Delta_L^2 \sigma^2(u,v) \left\{\sum_{i=0}^{n-1} P_{b_i}(1-P_{b_i})2^{2i} \right.$$
$$\left. + \sum_{l=0}^{L-1}\left[\sum_{i=0}^{n-1} P_{b_i}(1-2l_i)2^i\right]^2 P_l\right\} \quad (22)$$

where P_{b_i}, $i = 0, 1, \cdots, n(u, v) - 1$ is the bit error probability associated with each of the successive bit positions in the $n(u, v)$-bit quantizer output word. Here l_i, $i = 0, 1, \cdots, n(u, v) - 1$ represents coefficients of the binary expansion of the integer l according to

$$l = \sum_{i=0}^{n-1} l_i 2^i; \quad l_i = 0, 1. \quad (23)$$

For the particular case of equal bit error probability $P_{b_i} = P_b$, $i = 0, 1, \cdots, n(u, v) - 1$, then (22) reduces to

$$E\{N^2(u,v)\}$$
$$= \Delta_L^2 \sigma^2(u,v) P_b \left\{(1-P_b)\left(\frac{L^2(u,v)-1}{3}\right)\right.$$
$$\left. + P_b \sum_{l=0}^{L-1} [L(u,v)-1-2l]^2 P_l\right\} \quad (24)$$

where we recall $L(u, v) = 2^{n(u,v)}$. In either case, the quantity $E\{N^2(u, v)\}$ is readily evaluated for various values of $L(u, v)$ and corresponding optimum Δ_L. The quantity $\sigma^2(u, v)$ is easily calculated, as described earlier. Substitution for $E\{N^2(u, v)\}$, $u, v = 0, 1, \cdots, M - 1$, into (14) allows explicit evaluation of the error contribution ϵ_c due to channel-error effects.

Finally, consider the mutual error term ϵ_m given by (15). Again, following the approach described in [1], it is a relatively simple matter to demonstrate that

$$E\{Q(u,v)N(u,v)\}$$
$$= 2\Delta_L \sigma^2(u,v)\left[\sum_{l=L/2}^{L-1}\left\{\sum_{i=0}^{n-1}(1-2l_i)P_{b_i}2^i\right\}\epsilon_l'(u,v)\right]$$
$$\quad (25)$$

---

[5] Here it is implicitly assumed that the mean value of the transform coefficients has been removed.
[6] For notational simplicity we have used the notation $L = L(u, v)$ in limits of summation.
[7] Again for notational convenience we have written $L = L(u, v)$ and $n = n(u, v)$ in upper limits of summation.

where again P_{b_i} is the bit error probability associated with the transmission of the ith bit, $i = 0, 1, \cdots, n(u, v) - 1$ and the quantity

$$\epsilon_l'(u,v) = \int_{E_l/\sigma(u,v)}^{E_{l+1}/\sigma(u,v)} \{y - [l - (L(u,v) - 1)/2]\Delta_L\} \cdot \hat{p}(y)\,dy \quad (26)$$

is the average normalized quantization error given that the lth level was transmitted. For the particular case where the bit error probability is constant for each bit position we have

$$E\{Q(u,v)N(u,v)\} = -4\Delta_L \sigma^2(u,v) P_b$$
$$\cdot \left[\sum_{l=L/2}^{L-1} \{l - (L(u,v) - 1) - 1/2\} \cdot \epsilon_l'(u,v) \right]. \quad (27)$$

In either case, the quantity $E\{Q(u,v)N(u,v)\}$ is readily computed as a function of $\sigma^2(u,v)$ and $L(u,v)$ together with the channel error probability. Substitution into (15) allows evaluation of the normalized mutual error term ϵ_m. Numerical evaluation has indicated that this component is generally negligible compared to the other error components ϵ_q and ϵ_c.

With the evaluation of the three error contributions ϵ_q, ϵ_c, and ϵ_m, the total mean-square reconstruction error e_T^2 can be evaluated according to (12). This allows explicit evaluation of SNR_0 from (7) for various assumed stochastic image models.

In Fig. 5 we illustrate the behavior of SNR_0 for an assumed separable 2-D Gauss–Markov model of the outdoor scene. That is, least squares estimates of the image row and column correlation coefficients ρ_R and ρ_C are used in the 2-D Gauss–Markov model given by (2). The least square estimates of ρ_R and ρ_C for the antenna image and outdoor scene are provided in Table I. Individual quantizer bits associated with each block transform coefficient $S(u, v)$ were serially transmitted using coherent binary phase-shift keyed (BPSK) modulation over an additive white Gaussian noise (AWGN) channel. The bit error probability in this case is given by

$$P_{b_i} = Q\left(\sqrt{\frac{2E_{si}}{N_0}}\right); \quad i = 0, 1, \cdots, n(u,v) - 1 \quad (28)$$

where

$$Q(x) \triangleq \frac{1}{\sqrt{2\pi}} \int_x^\infty \exp\{-y^2/2\}\,dy \quad (29)$$

and E_{si} is the signal energy per transmitted binary channel symbol while $N_0/2$ is the double-sided noise spectral density in W/Hz. The curves are parameterized by the quantity

$$\bar{n} = \frac{1}{M^2} \sum_{u=0}^{M-1} \sum_{v=0}^{M-1} n(u,v) \quad (30)$$

representing the average number of bits transmitted per pixel.

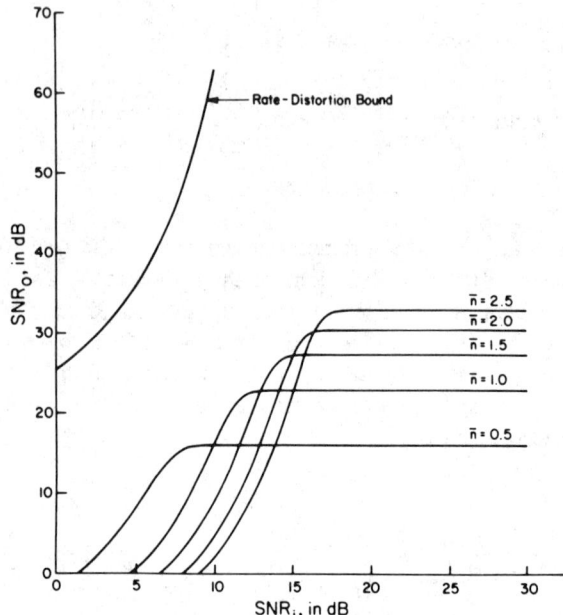

Fig. 5. Uncoded block transform encoder performance for outdoor scene; 16 × 16 2-D cosine transform; Gaussian uniform quantizer.

TABLE I
ESTIMATED ROW AND COLUMN CORRELATION COEFFICIENTS FOR TEST IMAGES

Image	Row Correlation ρ_R	Column Correlation ρ_C
Outdoor Scene	0.957	0.967
Antenna	0.974	0.942

In Fig. 5, the quantity SNR_0 is plotted as a function of the channel signal-to-noise ratio on a normalized per pixel basis. That is, if $N_C(u, v)$ uses of the channel are employed to transmit the $n(u, v)$-bit quantizer output word corresponding to the transform coefficient $S(u, v)$, then the channel signal-to-noise ratio associated with the transmission of this element is defined according to[8]

$$SNR_i(u,v) = \sum_{i=0}^{N_C - 1} \{2E_{si}(u,v)/N_0\} \quad (31)$$

where $E_{si}(u, v)$, $i = 0, 1, \cdots, N_C(u, v) - 1$, is the signal energy associated with the ith use of the channel in transmitting the $n(u, v)$-bit representation of $S(u, v)$. Actually, in Fig. 5 $N_C(u, v) = n(u, v)$, while we assume constant signal energy so that $E_{si}(u, v) = E_s$, $i = 0, 1, \cdots, n(u, v) - 1$. It will prove convenient when employing channel coding to allow the generality afforded by (31). The bandwidth expansion factor associated with the transmission of a quantized version of $S(u, v)$ is then $N_C(u, v)/n(u, v)$. Finally, the average channel signal-to-noise ratio per pixel is given by

$$SNR_i = \frac{1}{M^2} \sum_{u=0}^{M-1} \sum_{v=0}^{M-1} SNR_i(u,v), \quad (32)$$

[8] Again in upper limits of summation, N_C is written for $N_C(u,v)$.

while the average number of channel uses per pixel in transmitting a block of quantized transform samples is given by

$$\bar{N}_C = \frac{1}{M^2} \sum_{u=0}^{M-1} \sum_{v=0}^{M-1} N_C(u,v). \tag{33}$$

Note that in the particular case of constant signal energy and no bandwidth expansion, we have $\text{SNR}_i = \bar{n}(2E_s/N_0)$ where $\bar{n}$ is the average number of bits per pixel given by (30)

Also included in Fig. 5 is the rate-distortion bound on SNR_0 for operation over an AWGN channel. This is obtained by equating the rate-distortion function $R(D)$ computed under a mean-square fidelity criterion, to the channel capacity and solving for SNR_0 as a function of SNR_i. The evaluation of $R(D)$ for 2-D Gaussian autoregressive sources has been described previously in [1], while the capacity of the AWGN channel with signal energy E_{si} is given by the well-known expression [14]

$$C = \tfrac{1}{2} \log_2 \left[1 + \frac{2E_{si}}{N_0} \right] \text{(bits/channel use)}. \tag{34}$$

Under the assumption of equal energy use of the channel, the maximum output SNR for $\bar{N}_C$ channel uses satisfies

$$R(\sigma_S^2 \, \text{SNR}_0^{-1}) = \frac{\bar{N}_C}{2} \log_2 \left[1 + \frac{\text{SNR}_i}{\bar{N}_C} \right], \tag{35}$$

allowing solution of SNR_0 in terms of SNR_i. Actually, the curve labeled rate-distortion bound in Fig. 5 represents the limiting performance as $\bar{N}_C \to \infty$, thereby avoiding presentation of a series of curves parameterized by $\bar{N}_C$. The resulting bound then represents performance obtainable for large $\bar{N}_C$, or, equivalently, large bandwidth expansion.

Several things should be observed from Fig. 5. In the first place, note the sharp threshold effect which becomes more pronounced as the average number of bits per pixel $\bar{n}$ increases. For SNR_i in excess of approximately 20 dB, channel errors are rare and the performance is limited solely by the block quantization noise. An increase in the average number of bits per pixel results in a commensurate increase in SNR_0. For smaller SNR_i we see a complete reversal of this behavior. For example, at $\text{SNR}_i = 12$ dB, relative performance measured in terms of SNR_0 actually improves by decreasing the quantization accuracy. This is an illustration of the behavior observed previously[9] in Fig. 4. It should be noted that this threshold behavior occurs at error probabilities typical of that provided on many space and military data links.

The second observation to be made from Fig. 5 is that the 16 × 16 block transform coding scheme using the DCT is relatively inefficient compared to the rate-distortion bound. In Section V, following the development in [1], we describe ultimate performance bounds to be achieved through channel coding. These bounds are based upon information theoretic considerations and apply to all classes of codes. Results indicate relative performance arbitrarily close to the ultimate performance bounds over a useful range of SNR_i. Later we demonstrate that these performance bounds are realistic in the sense that they can be closely approximated with an easily implemented class of convolutional codes.

IV. CHOICE OF TRANSFORM BLOCK SIZE

Previous work on block transform image coding has considered the overall system performance as a function of transform block size only in the absence of channel errors (cf. [7]). In any realistic image transmission system, however, the channel is imperfect and, subsequently, errors are introduced into the received data sequence. It becomes necessary then to consider the effects of channel errors on choice of block size. Exclusive use of the 2-D DCT will be made, while a symmetric uniform Gaussian quantizer will be employed. The 2-D separable Gauss–Markov image model is assumed.

The performance of the block transform encoder as a function of block size M and in the absence of channel errors is illustrated in Fig. 6, where the image model parameters were chosen according to Table I to match the outdoor scene. Here, and in the sequel, system performance is determined by computing the output signal-to-noise ratio as described in Section III for a specified average number of bits/pixel $\bar{n}$ and block size M. In the case of error-free transmission, reconstructed image quality increases as the transform block size increases. Furthermore, for any fixed block size M the performance is monotonically increasing in $\bar{n}$ as to be expected.

Corresponding performance for various values of SNR_i, again employing BPSK modulation of the AWGN channel, is illustrated in Figs. 7-9. The channel signal-to-noise ratio SNR_i is given by (32) and the corresponding bit error probability can be determined from (28). Observe from Fig. 7 that for $\text{SNR}_i = 16$ dB, representing a reasonably high quality image, system performance for $\bar{n} = 2.5$ actually degrades as the block size M increases. In particular, when block transform image transmission is utilized under these channel conditions with $M \geq 8$, it is best to encode with $\bar{n} = 2.0$ bits/pixel. Again, in Fig. 8 system performance for $\text{SNR}_i = 10$ dB is seen to degrade as the block size increases whenever $\bar{n} \geq 1.0$. In fact, when the channel is very noisy there is a complete reversal in behavior compared to that of the noiseless channel. This is illustrated in Fig. 9 for $\text{SNR}_i = 4$ dB where performance degrades uniformly with increasing block size for $\bar{n} = 0.5$ up to $\bar{n} = 2.5$ bits/pixel, with the former yielding relatively superior overall performance. This phenomenon is related to the total number of bits being transmitted in each system realization. When channel noise is significant, more bits transmitted per block results in a larger number of quantizer levels being decoded incorrectly, thereby lowering the system output SNR.

The optimum block size is that which gives the highest SNR_0 for a particular $\bar{n}$ bits/pixel and specified channel SNR. It is seen that for a large SNR_i the larger block sizes yield the best performance. However, for low SNR_i the

---

[9] The correspondence between the threshold behavior illustrated in Fig. 5 and the reconstructed images in Fig. 4 are only qualitative in the sense that it is P_b and not SNR_i held constant in the latter.

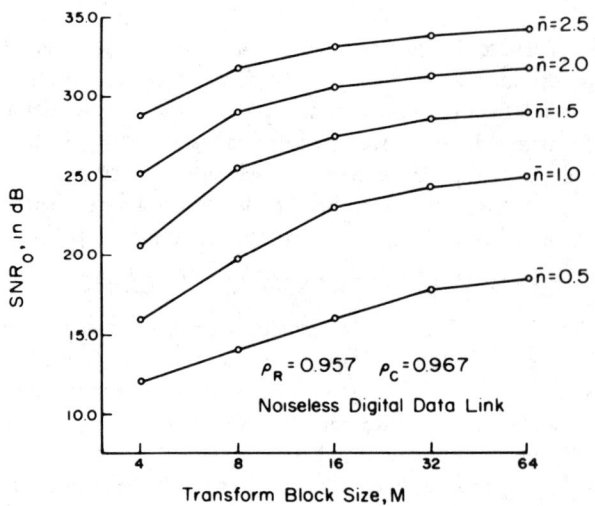

Fig. 6. Uncoded block transform encoder performance as a function of block size; noiseless channel; 2-D cosine transform; Gaussian uniform quantizer.

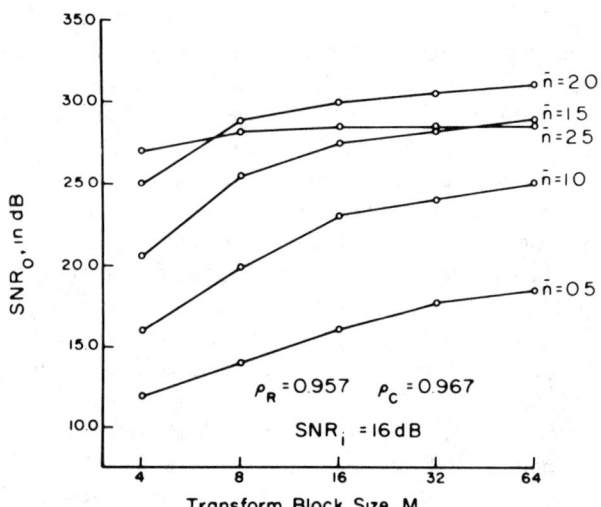

Fig. 7. Uncoded block transform encoder performance as a function of block size for $SNR_i = 16$ dB; 2-D cosine transform; Gaussian uniform quantizer.

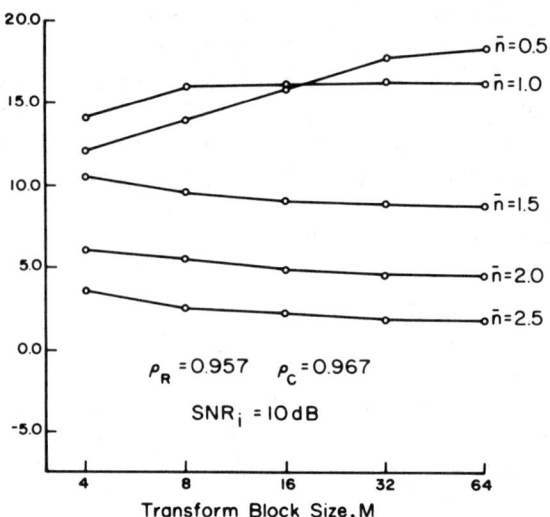

Fig. 8. Uncoded block transform encoder performance as a function of block size for $SNR_i = 10$ dB; 2-D cosine transform; Gaussian uniform quantizer.

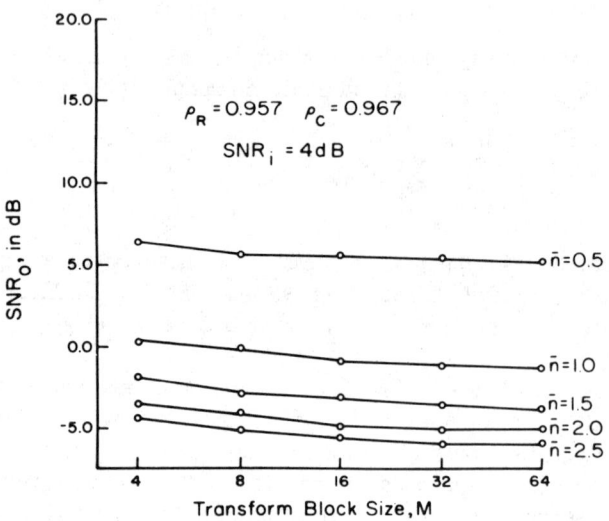

Fig. 9. Uncoded block transform encoder performance as a function of block size for $SNR_i = 4$ dB; 2-D cosine transform; Gaussian uniform quantizer.

smaller block sizes are preferred in order to achieve the best reconstructed image quality. A compromise choice, which will be employed in some of the experimental results, is $M = 16$. This choice leads to performance which is never more than a few decibels from the optimum value.

V. A METHODOLOGY FOR COMBINED SOURCE-CHANNEL CODING

In this section we extend the methodology described in [1] for assessing the source-channel coding tradeoffs to block transform image coding with mean-square error as the performance criterion. This analytically based approach will proceed on two levels: in the first, "potential" performance can be assessed through use of information theoretic bounds valid for all classes of codes, while in the second level, "practically achievable" system performance can be assessed through the use of exponentially tight bounds on bit error probability for specific and readily implemented classes of codes. The advantage of such an analytically based approach is that it provides clear and unequivocal guidance in assessing the performance gains to be achieved through combined source-channel coding approaches.

A. Modulation/Coding Options:

The generality of the output signal-to-noise ratio analysis presented in Section III allows evaluation of various combined source-channel coding strategies. Recall that it is assumed that individual bit streams are available for subsequent modulation/coding and transmission. The modulation/coding is allowed to be different for each of the $n(u, v)$ serial bit streams associated with the output of the $n(u, v)$-bit quantizer. In this study a hierarchy of system configurations is investigated. Each system assumption varies in the degree to which the modulation/coding can be tailored to the individual transform coefficients $S(u, v), u, v = 0, 1, \cdots, M - 1$. The system options considered include:

System Option 1 – Modulation/coding is the same for each bit of each quantized transform coefficient $S(u, v)$.

System Option 2 — Modulation/coding is the same for each bit of a specified quantized transform coefficient $S(u, v)$, but is allowed to vary for different coefficients.

System Option 3 — Modulation/coding is allowed to be different for each bit of each quantized transform coefficient.

Option 1 is the simplest situation from an implementation standpoint. Variations of Options 2 and 3 consist of situations where the coding but not the modulation is allowed to vary. In this case, the separate channel encoder outputs are multiplexed through a single modulator. These options are illustrated schematically in Fig. 10. First we will develop ultimate performance bounds on SNR_0, as well as performance bounds for practical coding schemes, which can be achieved through combined source–channel coding.

B. Theoretical Performance Bounds

A useful *upper* bound on SNR_0 can be obtained by *lower* bounding the bit error probability $P_{b_i}, i = 0, 1, \cdots, n(u, v) - 1$ associated with each of the bits in the $n(u, v)$-bit quantizer output word representing the transform coefficient $S(u, v)$. For simplicity, consider the case where the modulation/coding system treats each bit of each transform coefficient independently and identically. That is, the quantizer output words associated with a transform block are concatenated and individual bits fed serially to a fixed channel encoder/modulator cascade. Assuming a memoryless channel, each bit is received with bit error probability P_b independent of all other bits. Recall that an average $\overline{N}_C$ uses of the channel are required to transmit each pixel that is quantized to an average of $\overline{n}$ bits/pixel. The normalized code rate in bits per channel use is then $R = \overline{n}/\overline{N}_C$. Under the AWGN assumption, channel capacity is given by (34) with $E_{si} = E_s$, the constant energy per channel use. The converse to the coding theorem (cf. [14], [15]) then provides the desired lower bound on the common bit error probability P_b. Specifically, at rates above the capacity C of the AWGN channel, the bit error probability achievable by any rate R code is bounded away from zero by

$$P_b \geq H^{-1}(1 - C/R) \tag{36}$$

where $H^{-1}(\cdot)$ represents the inverse of the *binary entropy function*

$$H(x) = -x \log_2 x - (1-x) \log_2(1-x); \quad 0 < x < 1. \tag{37}$$

At rates below capacity P_b can be made negligibly small. For purposes of numerical evaluation, P_b will be computed according to the right-hand side of (36) for $R > C$, and we set $P_b = 0$ for $R \leq C$. While the resulting performance is achievable only in the limit of infinitely long codes, these results are nevertheless useful in providing a perspective in assessing the efficacy of combined source–channel coding.

C. Practical Channel Code Performance Bounds

It is important to demonstrate the degree to which the ultimate performance bounds, obtained as described above, can be approached by practical coding schemes. In particular,

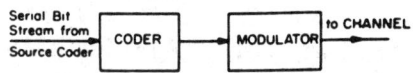
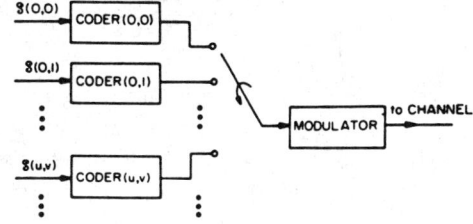
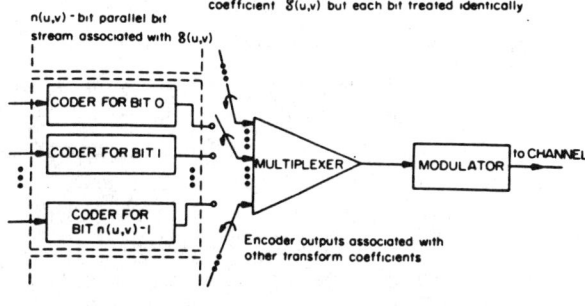

Fig. 10. Illustration of three system options in channel coding for block transform encoded imagery.

we restrict attention to short constraint length convolutional codes of rates $R = 1/2, 1/3$, and $1/4$, decoded using the Viterbi algorithm, an excellent description of which can be found in [16]. Use of the optimum binary codes tabulated by Odenwalder [17] and Larsen [18] is assumed in what follows.

A useful exponentially tight bound on bit error probability obtained with Viterbi decoding on memoryless channels can be expressed in the general form

$$P_b \leq K_0 \left. \frac{dT(N, D)}{dN} \right|_{N=1, D=D_0} \tag{38}$$

where $T(D, N)$ is the code generating function (cf. [16] for details), while the constants K_0 and D_0 depend upon the particular code employed, the modulation strategy in use, and the channel parameters. For example, for BPSK modulation on the AWGN channel, we have

$$K_0 = Q\left(\sqrt{\frac{2d_f RE_b}{N_0}}\right) \exp\left\{\frac{d_f RE_b}{N_0}\right\}, \tag{39}$$

while $D_0 \triangleq \exp\{-RE_b/N_0\}$ where d_f is the free distance of the code, R is the normalized code rate in information bits transmitted per channel use, and, finally, E_b/N_0 is the energy per information bit normalized to the single-sided noise spectral density N_0 W/Hz. The quantity E_b is related to the energy per channel symbol E_s according to $E_s = RE_b$.

Similar bounds can be obtained for soft-decision decoding of linear (N, K) block codes (cf. [19]). In the particular case of binary antipodal signaling on the AWGN channel, the bit error probability can be bounded by

$$P_b \leq \frac{d_{\min}}{N} \sum_{w=d_{\min}}^{N} N_w Q\left(\sqrt{\frac{2wRE_b}{N_0}}\right) \quad (40)$$

where $R = K/N$ is the code rate in bits per channel use, $d_{\min}$ is the minimum distance of the code, and N_w is the weight spectrum of the code. That is, N_w is the number of code words of Hamming weight w. Two block codes considered in the sequel are the Hamming (8, 4) and the Golay (24, 12) code, whose performance is easily bounded according to (40).

D. Combined Source-Channel Coding Results:

In Fig. 11 we illustrate typical performance results for the outdoor scene employing the modulation/coding approach of System Option 1. Here the modulation is assumed to be BPSK and held fixed for all bits, with an average of $\overline{N}_C = 1.0$ bits transmitted per pixel. Options include an uncoded system with $\bar{n} = 1.0$, or use of fixed-rate $R = 1/2$ codes in conjunction with $\bar{n} = 0.5$. The coded performance curves in Fig. 11 illustrate clearly the significant gains to be realized at low-to-moderate SNR_i by trading quantization accuracy for error-control protection. For large SNR_i, however, a penalty is paid in the reduction of saturation level SNR_0. In addition to the upper bound on system performance employing $R = 1/2$ codes, we have indicated the performance achievable using a number of practical $R = 1/2$ codes. The convolutional code with constraint length $K = 9$ performs better than all other codes, while the Hamming (8, 4) block code offers the least error protection of the codes considered. Due to the superior performance and simplicity in the implementation associated with the convolutional codes, attention will be restricted exclusively to these codes in the sequel.

Also included in Fig. 11 is a dotted curve labeled R_0^* bound which is displaced some 2-3 dB from the rate-distortion bound. The quantity R_0^* represents the upper bound on the critical or union bound rate R_0 for operation over an AWGN channel. This quantity represents an upper bound on the range of rates R for which reliable communication is possible for reasonable decoder complexity. In Fig. 11 the curve labeled R_0^* bound is then obtained by equating R_0^* to the rate-distortion function $R(D)$ and solving for SNR_0 as a function of SNR_i. For reasons described previously in [1], we feel that this curve represents a more realistic bound on the "practically achievable" performance to be realized with coding. From Fig. 11, performance using $K = 9$ convolutional code is roughly 5-6 dB from the R_0^* bound, indicating relatively efficient performance with only a modest increase in system complexity.

Typical performance results using combined source-channel coding under System Option 2 are illustrated in Fig. 12 for the outdoor scene, again modeled as a 2-D separable Gauss-Markov process. Here we have the option of providing selective error-control protection to the most significant spectral coefficients (MSC's), and all other coefficients are unprotected. The coding, however, is identical for each bit of

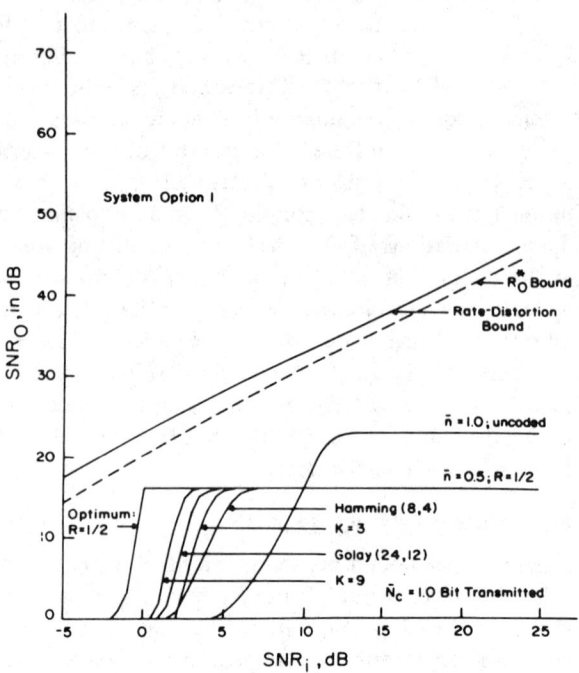

Fig. 11. Block transform encoder performance for outdoor scene under System Option 1; 16 × 16 2-D DCT; Gaussian uniform quantizer; practical convolutional and block code performance; $\overline{N}_C = 1.0$ bits/pixel transmitted.

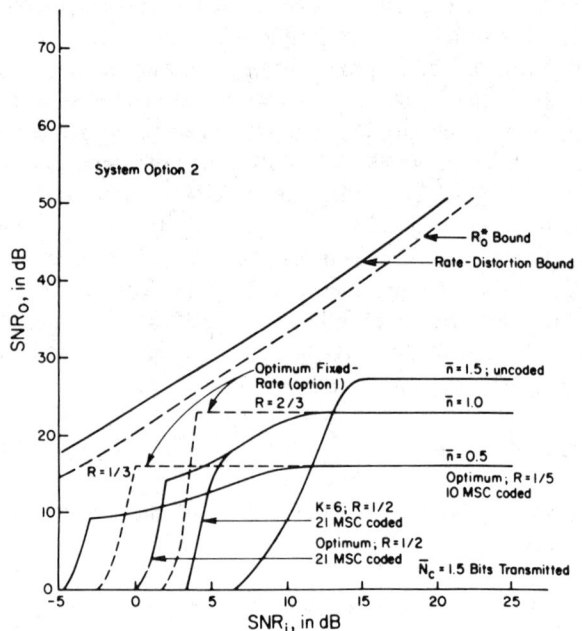

Fig. 12. Block transform encoder performance for outdoor scene under System Option 2; 16 × 16 2-D DCT; Gaussian uniform quantizer; selected optimum and practical convolutional code performance bounds; $\overline{N}_C = 1.5$ bits/pixel transmitted.

the MSC's selected for error protection. The argument underlying this strategy is that it is more important to provide error-control protection to the transform coefficients possessing larger variance $\sigma^2(u, v)$, since they contribute most heavily to reconstructed image quality. In Fig. 12, an average of $\overline{N}_C = 1.5$ bits are transmitted per pixel and some selected System 2 design options are illustrated. It is clear that Option 2 provides a substantial improvement over the uncoded case in the threshold region, even when only a fraction of the transform coefficients are protected. Other options, for which optimum performance is illustrated in Fig. 12, include $\bar{n} = 0.5$ with an $R = 1/3$ code applied to each bit or $\bar{n} = 1.0$ with $R = 2/3$ coding. These fixed-rate coding schemes are included, of course, in System Option 1.[10] The fixed-rate coding schemes of Option 1 generally outperform Option 2 stategies for moderate-to-large SNR_i, but result in sharper threshold characteristics and typically require relatively unusual rational code rates such as $R = 2/3, 3/4$, etc., for which good code constructions are not readily available.

Clearly, the real advantage of System Option 2 vis-à-vis Option 1 is that it allows performance not "practically" achievable using the fixed-rate coding approach of System Option 1. As an example, note from Fig. 12 that the System Option 2 result with $\bar{n} = 1.0$ bits/pixel can achieve SNR_0 in excess of 20 dB at $SNR_i = 10$ dB using practical $R = 1/2$ coding of the 21 MSC's with the remaining coefficients unprotected. Observe that the optimum fixed-rate (Option 1) result with $\bar{n} = 1.0$ bits/pixel offers similar performance but requires less familiar $R = 2/3$ codes.[11] In this sense System Option 2 allows filling performance gaps resulting from the nonavailability of arbitrary rational rate code constructions required with System Option 1. Furthermore, as illustrated in Fig. 12, System Option 2 results in a more gradual threshold characteristic. Both of these considerations taken together allow practically achievable performance closer to the R_0^* bound.

In Fig. 13 we illustrate typical performance results for the outdoor scene under System Option 3 operating with an average of $\bar{N}_C = 2.0$ bits transmitted per pixel. In this case, we have chosen to allocate additional error-control protection to the most significant bits (MSB's) of the quantizer word representing $S(u, v)$ and commensurately less protection to the least significant bits (LSB's). Again, the argument here is that errors in the MSB's contribute most critically to reconstructed image quality. Generally, under System Option 3 different transform coefficients have a varying degree of error-control protection in that there is a combination of coded and uncoded bits in the $n(u, v)$-bit quantizer output codeword for $S(u, v)$.

While the selected System Option 3 results illustrated in Fig. 13 are by no means exhaustive, they do illustrate the potential relative performance gains over the uncoded system. For comparison purposes we have illustrated some optimum performance bounds for several selected System Option 1 configurations. Again, System Option 3 allows filling performance gaps associated with System Option 1 constraints. For example, the optimum performance indicated in Fig. 13 for $\bar{n} = 1.5$ under System Option 1 requires codes with $R =$

---

[10] The fixed-rate System Option 1 approach requires codes of rate $R = \bar{n}/\bar{N}_C$, whereas, as indicated previously, good convolutional code constructions are generally available only for rates $R = 1/2, 1/3$, and 1/4.

[11] It should be noted that recent work by Paaske [20] has described some $R = 2/3$ short-constraint length convolutional codes requiring some qualification of this comment, although the argument is true more generally.

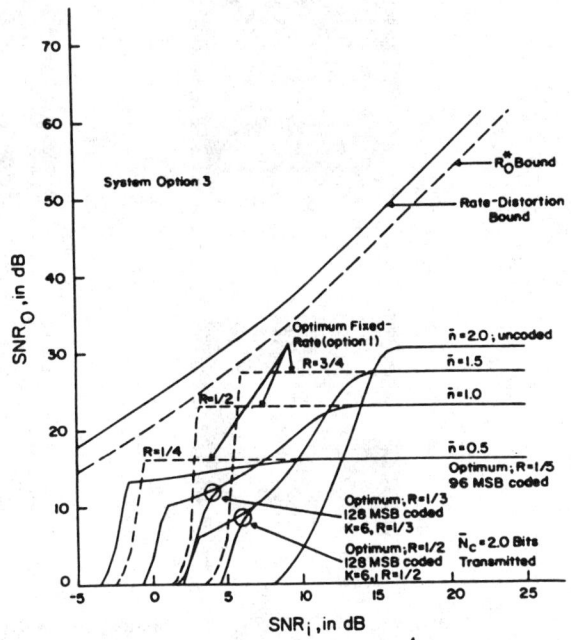

Fig. 13. Block transform encoder performance for outdoor scene under System Option 3; 16 × 16 2-D DCT; Gaussian uniform quantizer; selected optimum and practical convolutional code performance bounds; $\bar{N}_C = 2.0$ bits/pixel transmitted.

3/4, and hence not readily implementable. Nevertheless, this performance is approximated under System Option 3 with $\bar{n} = 1.5$ and employing practical $R = 1/2$ coding of the 128 MSB's with the remaining bits unprotected. A meaningful comparison with System Option 2 performance, on the other hand, is more difficult to quantify. Nevertheless, as demonstrated in [10], because of practical implementation considerations, there are situations where System Option 3 allows filling in performance gaps which are not practically achievable using either of the other two system options. In summary then, System Option 3 affords the greatest flexibility in tailoring error-control protection to various transform coefficients and, when exploited appropriately, can yield significant improvements in block transform system performance.

VI. SIMULATION RESULTS

The effectiveness of the combined source–channel coding scheme for the 2-D DCT employing selected constraint length $K = 6$ convolutional codes is illustrated in the case of the outdoor scene by the simulation results provided in Figs. 14 and 15 for $\bar{N}_C = 1.0$ and 1.5, respectively. Corresponding analytical performance evaluation is illustrated by the respective curves in Figs. 11 and 12 for System Options 1 and 2. Similar results are provided in [10] for System Option 3. In these figures, SNR_i is constant across a row while the average number of quantization bits $\bar{n}$ is held constant for each column. The transmission bandwidth requirements, as indicated by the average number $\bar{N}_C$ of channel uses per pixel, is constant for all reconstructed images on a figure. Representative choices for SNR_i in each case were made just below and above pronounced thresholds in the SNR_0 curves described in the preceding section. The actual coding assign-

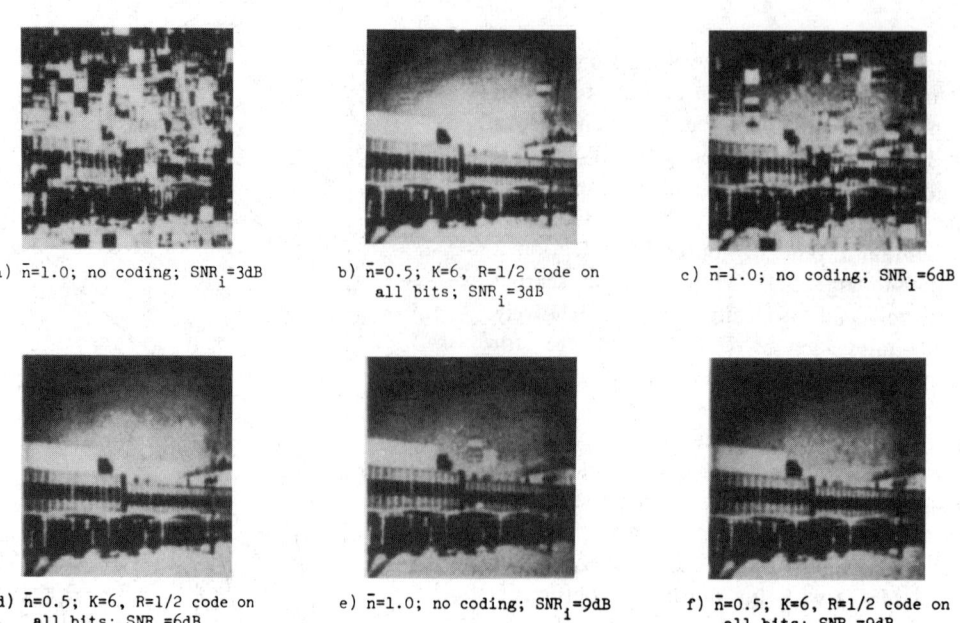

Fig. 14. Simulation results for outdoor scene; $\bar{N}_C = 1.0$ bits/pixel transmitted.

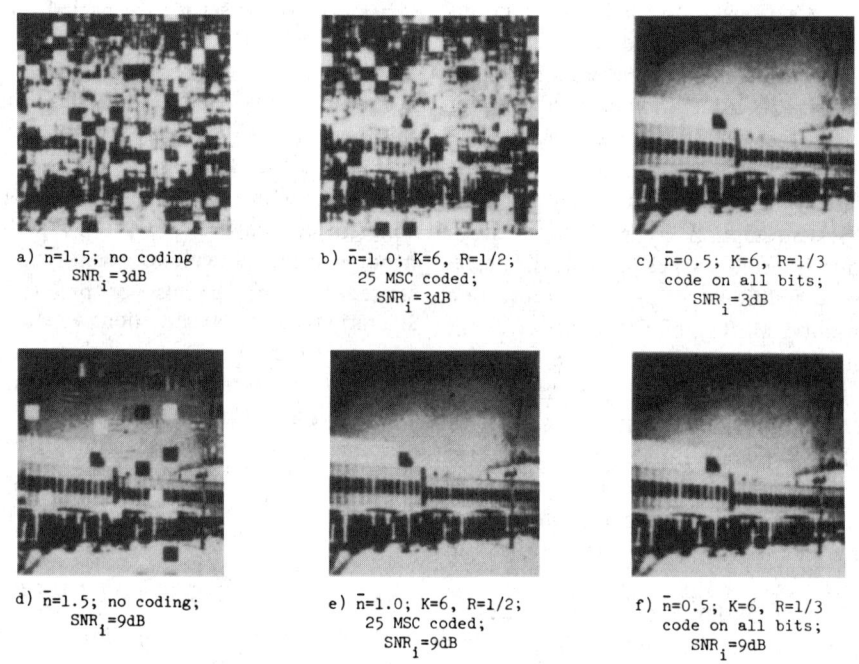

Fig. 15. Simulation results for outdoor scene; $\bar{N}_C = 1.5$ bits/pixel transmitted.

ments differ slightly from that illustrated in Figs. 11 and 12, since the bit allocation matrix resulting from coding of the real-world image differs somewhat from that computed for the 2-D separable Gauss–Markov image model. Additional simulation results for selected System 2 options with $\bar{N}_C = 2.0$ are illustrated in Fig. 16. The corresponding measured values of SNR_0 are provided in Table II.

These figures illustrate the dramatic improvements in subjective reconstructed image quality resulting from a judicious tradeoff between block transform quantization accuracy and error-control protection in a fixed transmission bandwidth. For example, in Fig. 16 we see clearly the advantages in allocating excess transmission bandwidth to channel error control rather than in attempting to improve the block transform quantization accuracy by increasing the average number of bits/pixel used exclusively for source coding. In this example, block quantization with an average of 1.0 bit/pixel employing a $K = 6$, $R = 1/2$ convolutional code on all quantizer bits provides far superior reconstructed image quality than the 2.0 bit/pixel uncoded system.

VII. SUMMARY AND CONCLUSIONS:

We have described an approach to the combined source-channel coding of a particular class of image sources using

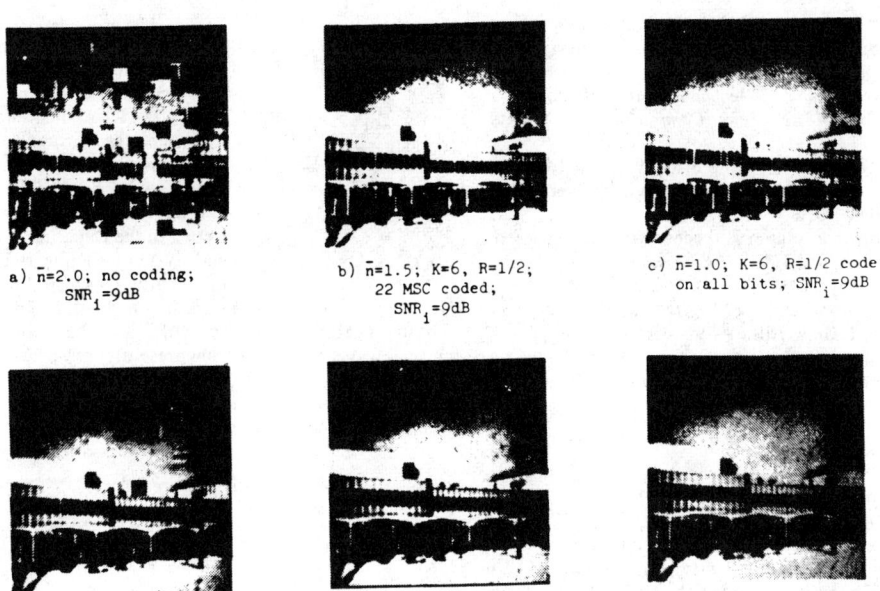

a) $\bar{n}=2.0$; no coding; $SNR_i=9$dB

b) $\bar{n}=1.5$; K=6, R=1/2; 22 MSC coded; $SNR_i=9$dB

c) $\bar{n}=1.0$; K=6, R=1/2 code on all bits; $SNR_i=9$dB

d) $\bar{n}=2.0$; no coding; $SNR_i=12$dB

e) $\bar{n}=1.5$; K=6, R=1/2; 22 MSC coded; $SNR_i=12$dB

f) $\bar{n}=1.0$; K=6, R=1/2 code on all bits; $SNR_i=12$dB

Fig. 16. Simulation results for outdoor scene; $\bar{N}_C = 2.0$ bits/pixel transmitted.

TABLE II
MEASURED SNR_O VALUES FOR COMBINED SOURCE-CHANNEL CODING SIMULATIONS OF OUTDOOR SCENE UNDER SYSTEM OPTIONS 1 AND 2; 2-D DCT BLOCK TRANSFORM; M-16

N_C	SNR_i	Quantization Accuracy $\bar{n}$, Bits/Pixel			
		0.5	1.0	1.5	2.0
1.0	3.0dB	11.56dB	-1.53dB	-	-
	6.0	12.10	2.95	-	-
	9.0	12.10	13.93	-	-
1.5	3.0	11.73	-2.24	-3.29dB	-
	9.0	12.10	14.87	4.25	-
2.0	9.0	-	15.36	15.02	2.39
	12.0	-	15.36	16.87	11.71

the 2-D DCT. This approach offers theoretical performance approximating a practically achievable rate-distortion bound. We have shown how this theoretical performance can, in turn, be approximated by a class of practical short constraint length convolutional codes and demonstrated the performance gains through selected simulations on real-world images. The major deficiency lies in the lack of good rational-rate code constructions required to achieve the near optimum behavior indicated by the fixed-rate code performance results, in particular, the results shown for System Option 1. More specifically, we have been forced to utilize previously tabulated optimum codes for rates $R = 1/2, 1/3$, and $1/4$. This severely compromises the flexibility of the approach in those situations where extremely high quality image reconstruction is required, i.e., high saturation level SNR_O at low SNR_i. Work is in progress to determine and tabulate the properties of good short constraint length codes operating at rational rates $R = (n-k)/n$, $k = 1, 2, \cdots, n-1$ and for $n = 2, 3, \cdots, 8$. This should extend the flexibility of the approach considerably.

ACKNOWLEDGMENT

The authors would like to acknowledge the constructive comments of two anonymous reviewers which helped to improve an earlier version of this paper.

REFERENCES

[1] J. W. Modestino and D. G. Daut, "Combined source-channel coding of images," IEEE Trans. Commun., vol. COM-27, pp. 1644-1659, Nov. 1979.

[2] H. C. Andrews and W. K. Pratt, "Fourier transform coding of images," in Proc. Hawaii Int. Conf. Syst. Sci., pp. 677-679, Jan. 1968.

[3] ——, "Television bandwidth reduction by encoding spatial frequencies," J. Soc. Motion Picture Television Engineers, vol. 77, pp. 1277-1281, Dec. 1968.

[4] W. K. Pratt, J. Kane, and H. C. Andrews, "Hadamard transform image coding," Proc. IEEE, vol. 57, pp. 58-68, Jan. 1969.

[5] W. K. Pratt, Digital Image Processing. New York: Wiley-Interscience, 1978, ch. 6 and 10.

[6] A. K. Jain, "A fast Karhunen-Loeve transform for finite discrete images," in Proc. NEC, Chicago, IL, Oct. 1978, pp. 223-328.

[7] N. Ahmed, T. Natarajan, and K. R. Rao, "Discrete cosine transform," IEEE Trans. Comput., vol. C-23, pp. 90-93, Jan. 1974.

[8] A. Habibi and P. A. Wintz, "Optimum linear transformations for encoding two-dimensional data," in Picture Bandwidth Compression, T. S. Huang and O. J. Tretiak, Eds. New York: Gordon and Breach, 1972, pp. 575-619.

[9] P. A. Wintz and A. J. Kurtenbach, "Waveform error control in PCM telemetry," IEEE Trans. Inform. Theory, vol. IT-14, pp. 650-661, Sept. 1968.

[10] D. G. Daut, "A combined source-channel coding approach to image transmission," Ph.D. dissertation, Rensselaer Polytechnic Institute, Electrical, Computer and Systems Engineering Department, May 1981.

[11] E. Kreyszig, Introductory Functional Analysis with Applications. New York: Wiley, 1978.

[12] R. E. Totty and G. C. Clark, "Reconstruction error in waveform transmission," IEEE Trans. Inform. Theory, vol. IT-13, pp. 336-338, Apr. 1967.

[13] J. Max, "Quantizing for minimum distortion," IEEE Trans. Inform. Theory, vol. IT-6, pp. 7-12, Mar. 1960.

[14] R. C. Gallager, Information Theory and Reliable Communication. New York: Wiley, 1968.

[15] F. Jelinek, *Probabilistic Information Theory*. New York: McGraw-Hill, 1968.
[16] A. J. Viterbi, "Convolutional codes and their performance in communication systems," *IEEE Trans. Commun.*, vol. COM-19, pp. 751–772, Oct. 1971.
[17] J. P. Odenwalder, "Optimum decoding of convolutional codes," Ph.D. dissertation, Systems Science Dept., University of California, Los Angeles, 1970.
[18] K. J. Larsen, "Short convolutional codes with maximal free distance for rate 1/2, 1/3, and 1/4," *IEEE Trans. Inform. Theory*, vol. IT-19, 371–373, May 1973.
[19] A. Viterbi and J. Omura, *Principles of Digital Communication and Coding*. New York: McGraw-Hill, 1979.
[20] E. Paaske, "Short binary convolutional codes with maximal free distance for rates 2/3 and 3/4," *IEEE Trans. Inform. Theory*, vol. IT-20, pp. 683–689, Sept. 1974.

James W. Modestino (S'60–M'68–SM'81) was born in Boston, MA, on April 27, 1940. He received the B.S. degree in electrical engineering from Northeastern University, Boston, MA, in 1962, the M.S. degree in electrical engineering from the University of Pennsylvania, Philadelphia, in 1964, and the M.A. and Ph.D. degrees from Princeton University, Princeton, NJ, in 1968 and 1969, respectively.

He has held a number of industrial positions including positions with RCA Communication Systems Division, Camden, NJ, AVCO Systems Division, Wilmington, MA, GTE Laboratories, Inc., Waltham, MA, and MIT Lincoln Laboratory, Lexington, MA. From 1970 to 1972 he was an Assistant Professor in the Department of Electrical Engineering, Northeastern University. In 1972 he joined Rensselaer Polytechnic Institute, Troy, NY, where he is presently a Professor in the Department of Electrical, Computer, and Systems Engineering. There he has been responsible for teaching and research in the communication and information processing systems area. His specific interests include communication in fading dispersive channels, detection, estimation, and filtering in impulsive noise environments, and digital signal and image processing.

David G. Daut (S'76–S'78–M'79–S'79–M'80) was born in Paterson, NJ, on October 11, 1954. He received the B.S. degree in electrical engineering from New Jersey Institute of Technology, NJ, in 1976, and the M.S. and Ph.D. degrees in electrical engineering from Rensselaer Polytechnic Institute, Troy, NY, in 1977 and 1981, respectively.

From 1976 to 1980 he was a Research Assistant in the Department of Electrical, Computer and Systems Engineering, Rensselaer Polytechnic Institute, where his doctoral research had focused on image transmission techniques in the presence of noisy communications channels. In 1980 he joined Rutgers University, Piscataway, NJ, where he presently is an Assistant Professor in the Department of Electrical Engineering. His current research interests include image data/bandwidth compression techniques, digital communications, and information theory and coding.

Acie L. Vickers (S'77–M'80–S'80) was born in Jacksonville, FL, on February 24, 1955. He received the B.S. and the M.Eng. degrees in electrical engineering from Rensselaer Polytechnic Institute, Troy, NY, in 1976 and 1980, respectively.

Since 1976 he has been a Research and Teaching Assistant in the Department of Electrical, Computer, and Systems Engineering, Rensselaer Polytechnic Institute, where he is currently studying for the Ph.D. degree. His doctoral research is focused on image modeling and system identification in the context of texture discrimination and classification.

Optimal Block Cosine Transform Image Coding for Noisy Channels

VINAY A. VAISHAMPAYAN AND NARIMAN FARVARDIN

Abstract—The two-dimensional block transform coding scheme based on the discrete cosine transform has been studied extensively for image coding applications. While this scheme has proven to be efficient in the absence of channel errors, its performance degrades rapidly over noisy channels. In this paper, we present a method for the joint source-channel coding optimization of a scheme based on the 2-D block cosine transform when the output of the encoder is to be transmitted via a memoryless binary symmetric channel. Our approach involves an iterative algorithm for the design of the quantizers (in the presence of channel errors) used for encoding the transform coefficients. This algorithm produces a set of locally optimum (in the mean-squared error sense) *quantizers* and the corresponding *binary codeword assignment* for the assumed transform coefficient statistics. To determine the *optimum bit assignment* among the transform coefficients, we have used an algorithm based on the steepest descent method, which under certain convexity conditions on the performance of the channel-optimized quantizers, yields the *optimal* bit allocation. Simulation results for the performance of this locally optimum system over noisy channels have been obtained and appropriate comparisons against a reference system designed for no channel errors have been rendered. It is shown that substantial performance improvements can be obtained by using this scheme. Furthermore, theoretically predicted results and rate distortion-theoretic bounds for an assumed 2-D image model are provided.

I. INTRODUCTION

THE two-dimensional (2-D) block cosine transform coding scheme has been well studied in image coding situations from a rate distortion-theoretic perspective. Apart from providing good performance it is image independent and can be efficiently implemented using fast algorithms [6], [11], [12], [13].

It is known that the performance of the above system degrades rapidly in the presence of channel errors. In particular, work done in [1] has shown that a careful selection of the parameters of the block cosine transform coder, as well as channel coding and modulation schemes, are essential for maintaining a good performance when data are to be transmitted over a noisy channel. Specifically, the approach taken in [1] has been that of assessing various modulation/coding options for providing channel error protection to the various transform coefficients, while maintaining a constant transmission rate (in bits/pixel transmitted).

Our approach differs from that taken in [1] in that we do not use explicit channel coders for error protection. Instead, we formulate the problem as an optimization problem in which the mean-squared error of the transform coding scheme over a noisy channel is minimized, subject to a constraint on the average transmission rate when the transform coefficients are encoded using zero-memory encoders. We show that the optimization problem can be reduced to the following.

1) The optimal allocation of bits for encoding the transform coefficients in such a way that both the source and the channel characteristics are taken into consideration.

2) The design of optimal zero-memory encoder/decoder pairs for the transmission of each of the transform coefficients over a noisy channel.

It has been shown [2] that even when a noisy channel is present, the optimal structure of a zero-memory encoder for a stationary random process, under the mean-squared error criterion, consists of a quantizer followed by a codeword assignment to each of the quantization intervals. For a given bit allocation vector, we apply the results of a new algorithm [5], [10] for the design of an optimal quantizer, its associated codeword assignment and decoder (referred to as the encoder/decoder pair) so as to minimize the total average reconstruction error across a noisy channel. We then optimize the allocation of bits among the transform coefficients by formulating it as an integer programming problem and applying an incremental bit allocation procedure based on the method of steepest descent [3]. Under certain convexity conditions, it is possible to show that this algorithm yields the optimal bit allocation, in a number of steps equal to the total number of bits to be allocated per block.

We compare the performance of the optimal system, as applied to images, against a reference system where each of the transform coefficients are encoded using Lloyd-Max quantizers followed by the natural binary code assignment. We then compare the theoretically predicted performance of the optimal system against the above reference system and against the optimum performance theoretically attainable (OPTA), based on a 2-D separable Gauss–Markov model for the image source. The performance gains of the optimal system over the reference system are extremely encouraging. Simulation studies have revealed improvements in the signal-to-noise ratio (SNR) of up to 8 dB, at a transmission rate of 1 bit/pixel, a block size of 32×32, and for a binary symmetric channel with a crossover probability of 0.05. The results are just as encouraging from a subjective viewpoint. The quality of the reconstructed image for the optimal system is seen to be far superior to the reference system, especially as the channel gets noisier. An important point is that these performance improvements are not obtained at the expense of transmission bandwidth.

The rest of this paper is organized as follows. In Section II, we develop notation and describe the system under consideration. In Section III, we present an analysis of the system and describe the algorithm used to design the optimal encoder/decoder pairs and the algorithm that does the optimal bit allocation. Section IV contains a description of the system as implemented, theoretically predicted performance results and the OPTA for a 2-D image model and simulation results based on two test images. Finally, in Section V, the paper is summarized and conclusions are drawn.

II. PRELIMINARIES

In what follows we assume that the source is an L-dimensional vector source represented by a zero mean, stationary, discrete-parameter stochastic process $\{X_n\}$ whose autocovariance matrix is denoted by Φ_{XX}. In a typical block transform coding scheme the source output vector[1] $X = (X_0, X_1, \cdots, X_{L-1})^T$ is transformed to a vector

---

Paper approved by the Editor for Image Processing of the IEEE Communications Society. Manuscript received September 21, 1987; revised August 3, 1988. This paper was presented at the 20th Conference on Information Sciences and Systems, Princeton, NJ, March 1986.

V. A. Vaishampayan is with the Department of Electrical Engineering, Texas A&M University, College Station, TX 77843-3128.

N. Farvardin is with the Department of Electrical Engineering, Institute for Advanced Computer Studies and Systems Research Center, University of Maryland, College Park, MD 20742.

IEEE Log Number 8933660.

[1] The parameter index has been dropped since the source is stationary.

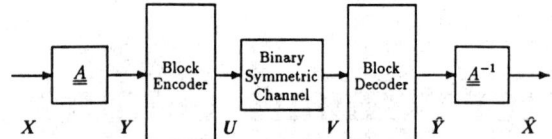

Fig. 1. Block diagram of a generic block transform coding scheme.

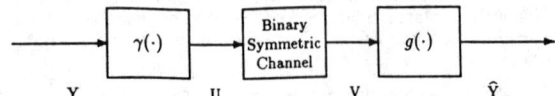

Fig. 2. A typical zero-memory encoder/decoder pair.

$Y = (Y_0, Y_1, \cdots, Y_{L-1})^t$ by a nonsingular $(L \times L)$ transformation matrix $\underline{A}$ according to

$$Y = \underline{A}X. \tag{1}$$

Each of the L components of Y (also referred to as the *transform coefficients*) is separately quantized and encoded using fixed-length binary codewords. The resulting vector of binary codewords $U = (U_0, U_1, \cdots, U_{L-1})^T$ is transmitted across the communication channel. We call the set of L encoders the "*block encoder*." Here we assume that the communication channel is modeled as a memoryless binary symmetric channel (BSC) with crossover probability ϵ. However, this assumption is not necessary; the method described here is general enough to handle any stationary, memoryless, discrete alphabet channel for which the transition probability matrix can be computed.

The received vector $V = (V_0, V_1, \cdots, V_{L-1})^T$, each component of which is a binary sequence, is decoded component-wise by a decoder, and the resulting vector $\hat{Y}$ is then transformed by $\underline{A}^{-1}$ to yield a representation vector $\hat{X}$, of the source vector X, in the receiver, i.e.,

$$\hat{X} = \underline{A}^{-1}\hat{Y}. \tag{2}$$

The block diagram of this coding scheme is illustrated in Fig. 1. The ith component U_i of U is an r_i-bit codeword and the vector $r = (r_0, r_1, \cdots, r_{L-1})^T$ is called the *bit allocation* vector. For a given bit allocation vector r, the average number of bits used to represent a source symbol r_{av} is described by

$$r_{av} \triangleq \frac{1}{L}\sum_{i=0}^{L-1}r_i. \tag{3}$$

Here, r_{av} is used as a measure of the channel bandwidth required for transmission.

III. PROBLEM STATEMENT AND ANALYSIS

For the system described in the previous section, we wish to minimize the mean-squared error

$$D = \frac{1}{L}E\{tr[(X - \hat{X})(X - \hat{X})^T]\}, \tag{4}$$

subject to a constraint on the average number of bits per-symbol required to transmit the source output, i.e.,

$$r_{av} = \frac{1}{L}\sum_{i=0}^{L-1}r_i \leq \tilde{r}, \tag{5}$$

and subject to a constraint on the minimum and the maximum number of bits that can be allocated to a single coefficient, i.e.,

$$0 \leq r_i \leq r_{max}, \quad i = 0, 1, \cdots, L-1 \tag{6}$$

where the r_i's and $L\tilde{r}$ are assumed to be integer-valued and r_{max} is a prescribed integer. If $\underline{A}$ is chosen to be an orthonormal matrix, the distortion may be simplified to

$$D = \frac{1}{L}E\{tr[(Y - \hat{Y})(Y - \hat{Y})^T]\}, \tag{7}$$

which can then be expressed as a sum of the component distortions by

$$D = \frac{1}{L}\sum_{i=0}^{L-1}E(Y_i - \hat{Y}_i)^2. \tag{8}$$

The ith component distortion, $E(Y_i - \hat{Y}_i)^2$, is a function of the number of bits r_i, allocated for transmitting the ith component and will be denoted hereafter by $d_i(r_i)$. For a *given* bit allocation vector $r = (r_0, r_1, \cdots, r_{L-1})^T$, in order to minimize D, it suffices to minimize each of the component distortions. Let $d_i^*(r_i)$ denote the minimum value of the ith component distortion when r_i bits are used to transmit the ith transform coefficient. Then the minimum average distortion for a given bit allocation vector r, denoted by $D^*(r)$ is given by

$$D^*(r) = \frac{1}{L}\sum_{i=0}^{L-1}d_i^*(r_i). \tag{9}$$

Let us assume that the values of $d_i^*(r)$, $i = 0, 1, \cdots, L-1$, and $r = 0, 1, \cdots, r_{max}$, are known. In order to solve the optimization problem, it remains to determine the optimal bit allocation, say r^*, that satisfies the constraints in (5) and (6) and such that $D^*(r^*) \leq D^*(r)$ for all r which satisfy the same constraints.

In the rest of this section we will first briefly describe an algorithm that optimizes the performance of the zero-memory encoder/decoder pair across a noisy channel, thus providing us with the (locally) optimal distortion figures for the component distortions. We will then describe an optimal bit allocation algorithm, that, under some mild conditions, yields the optimal r^* in $L\tilde{r}$ steps. Together, these algorithms are then used to solve the constrained optimization problem as formulated at the beginning of this section.

A. Optimal Zero-Memory Encoder/Decoder Design

In this section we describe an algorithm to minimize the component distortions $d_i(r_i)$ for a given r_i. Since the optimization procedure is the same for each of the L transform coefficients, we shall consider a generic term and denote it by $d(r)$.

We refer to an earlier paper [5] in which we describe an iterative algorithm that converges to a locally optimal encoder/decoder design for the system shown in Fig. 2. This procedure results in the optimal value of the component distortion $d(r)$ for a given value of r.

A zero-memory encoder/decoder pair is illustrated in Fig. 2. The encoder, represented by the mapping γ, essentially consists of an N-level scalar quantizer followed by a codeword assignment map. The decoder, represented by the map g, maps the output of the channel to a set of reconstruction levels. As shown in [5], the average squared-error distortion is a function of the following parameters:

1) the set of quantization threshold levels $T = (T_0, T_1, \cdots, T_N)^T$;
2) the value of N, the number of quantization intervals;
3) the codeword assignment, i.e., the codewords to which the quantizer intervals should be mapped, and,
4) the set of reconstruction levels in the decoder.

The distortion[2] $d(r)$ can be expressed as

$$d(r) = \int_{-\infty}^{\infty} p_Y(y)E\{(y - \hat{Y})^2|Y = y\}\,dy, \tag{10}$$

in which $p_Y(\cdot)$ denotes the probability density function (pdf) of the source to be encoded (in our application, a generic transform coeffi-

---

[2] The distortion also depends on γ and g but, for the sake of brevity, this is not explicitly reflected in our notation.

cient), and $E\{\cdot\}$ is the expectation operator. Our goal is to determine the optimum encoder and decoder maps so as to minimize (10) subject to a constraint on the rate (measured in bits/source symbol). The necessary conditions for optimality are developed by deriving the following.

a) The necessary and sufficient conditions for optimizing the decoder mapping g for a fixed encoder mapping γ.

b) The necessary and sufficient conditions for optimizing the encoder mapping γ for a fixed decoder mapping g.

The system that satisfies the above two conditions simultaneously is a locally optimal system. The optimal decoder mapping for a fixed encoder mapping follows directly from a well-known result in estimation theory and is given by

$$R_i = E\{Y|V = v_i\}, i = 1, 2, \cdots, M. \tag{11}$$

On the other hand, for a fixed decoder mapping, it is straightforward to show that the optimal encoder mapping is such that it maps a value of $Y = y$ to a codeword u_i, if and only if,

$$E\{(y - \hat{Y})^2|U = u_i\} \leq E\{(y - \hat{Y})^2|U = u_j\}, \forall j \neq i. \tag{12}$$

It is important to note that when the channel is noisy we do encounter codewords to which no source samples are mapped. This occurs when there exists a codeword u_i, for which (12) is not satisfied for any $y \in R$. Equation (12) thus provides us with a method of *identifying* a subset of codewords which should be used to encode the output of the source. If the number of codewords in this subset is N, $N \leq 2^r$ then (12), in effect, tells us that an N-level quantizer is optimum for minimizing the mean-squared error. In [5], [10] we describe a method for obtaining the endpoints of the quantization intervals in the encoder, even in situations where some of the codewords are not to be transmitted. By successive application of this method and (11), an iterative design algorithm is developed that converges to a locally optimal encoder/decoder pair. In order to be brief we shall not describe this algorithm here but shall refer the interested reader to [5], [10]. We do mention, however, that the algorithm presented in these references is general enough to handle stationary memoryless channels for which the channel transition probability matrix can be computed.

It is interesting to mention, however, that for a Gaussian source and a BSC with a crossover probability of 0.01 and a rate of 8 bits/sample, our results indicate a (locally) optimal quantizer that possesses only 29 of the possible 256 intervals.

We used this algorithm to generate the (locally) optimal, distortion versus rate performance $d^*(r)$ needed for the bit allocation algorithm described next. We mention at this point that the distortion versus rate performance of the optimal encoder/decoder pair, was observed to be convex for rates up to 8 bits/sample, and for a Gaussian source density. This observation is important since convexity is required in the development of the optimal bit allocation algorithm.

B. Optimal Bit Allocation Algorithm

In the absence of an analytical expression for the distortion versus rate performance of the optimal encoder/decoder pairs described above, we resort to an integer programming algorithm to determine the optimal bit allocation vector r^*. The algorithm described in the previous section yields the following distortion values:

$$d_i^*(r_i), i = 0, 1, \cdots, L-1; r_i = 0, 1, \cdots, L\tilde{r}. \tag{13}$$

We shall assume that the functions $d_i^*(\cdot)$ are convex and decreasing for all $i = 0, 1, \cdots, L-1$. Here, by convexity, we mean that $d_i(r-1) - d_i(r) \geq d_i(r) - d_i(r+1)$, for all integers $r \geq 1$. Let us consider the problem of minimizing

$$D^*(r) = \frac{1}{L} \sum_{i=0}^{L-1} d_i^*(r_i), \tag{14}$$

subject to[3]

$$\frac{1}{L} \sum_{i=0}^{L-1} r_i = \tilde{r}, \tag{15}$$

and

$$r_i \geq 0, \quad i = 0, 1, \cdots, L-1. \tag{16}$$

After describing a steepest descent algorithm that yields the optimal bit allocation r^* for the above problem, we will show how the same algorithm may be used to determine the optimal bit allocation, when an additional constraint is placed on the *maximum* number of bits that can be allocated to each component, i.e., when

$$r_i \leq r_{\max}, \quad i = 0, 1, \cdots, L-1. \tag{17}$$

The algorithm proceeds as follows [3].

1) Set $k = 0$; Set $r_i = 0$, $i = 0, 1, \cdots, L-1$.

2) Set $k = k + 1$; compute the index i_k which satisfies

$$d_{i_k}^*(r_{i_k}) - d_{i_k}^*(r_{i_k} + 1) = \max_{0 \leq i \leq L-1} \{d_i^*(r_i) - d_i^*(r_i + 1)\}. \tag{18}$$

3) Set $r_{i_k} = r_{i_k} + 1$. If $k < L\tilde{r}$, go to step 2; else stop.

We state the following theorem without proof, details of which may be found in [3].

Theorem 1: If the distortion functions in (13) are convex and nonincreasing, then the steepest descent algorithm as described above, yields the bit allocation vector r^* that minimizes (14) subject to the constraints in (15) and (16).

In order to use the steepest descent algorithm to solve the problem under the additional constraint on individual bit allocations, as stated in (17), we define a new set of distortion functions $\tilde{d}_i(r)$ by[4]

$$\tilde{d}_i(r) \triangleq \begin{cases} d_i^*(r), & \text{if } 0 \leq r \leq r_{\max}, \\ d_i^*(r_{\max}), & \text{if } r > r_{\max}, \end{cases} \quad i = 0, 1, \cdots, L-1. \tag{19}$$

The corresponding average distortion $\tilde{D}(r)$ is given by

$$\tilde{D}(r) = \frac{1}{L} \sum_{i=0}^{L-1} \tilde{d}_i(r_i). \tag{20}$$

The following theorem establishes that the minimization of $\tilde{D}(r)$ subject to (15) and (16) is equivalent to the minimization of $D^*(r)$ subject to (15)–(17).

Theorem 2: If the functions described in (13) are convex and strictly decreasing, then the bit allocation vector r^*, that minimizes $\tilde{D}(r)$ subject to (15) and (16), minimizes $D^*(r)$ subject to (15), (16), and (17).

Proof: Clearly, the set of bit allocation vectors that satisfy constraints (15), (16), and (17) is contained in the set of bit allocation vectors that satisfy constraints (15) and (16). The functions $\tilde{r}_i(t)$, $i = 0, 1, \cdots, L-1$, are convex and nonincreasing. Hence, by Theorem 1, the bit allocation vector r^* that minimizes $\tilde{D}(r)$ subject to (15) and (16), is obtained by the steepest descent algorithm, as described in steps 1–3 in the above algorithm. Further, the steepest descent algorithm will never allocate more than $r_{\max}$ bits to any of the L components. To see this, assume, without loss of generality, that at the kth step of the bit allocation process, $r = (r_{\max}, r_1, \cdots, r_{L-1})^T$ where $r_i < r_{\max}$, $i = 1, 2, \cdots, L-1$. At the $(k+1)$st step of the steepest descent algorithm, an index i_{k+1} is selected for which (18)

---

[3] An equality constraint, rather than the more general inequality constraint (5) is considered, since for $L\tilde{r}$ an integer and for $d_i^*(r)$ a decreasing function of r, $i = 0, 1, \cdots, L-1$, the average distortion is minimized when the inequality constraint is achieved with equality.

[4] It is assumed implicitly that $r_{\max} \leq L\tilde{r}$.

is true. Since $(\tilde{d}_0(r_{\max}) - \tilde{d}_0(r_{\max}+1)) = 0$, it follows that $i_{k+1} \neq 0$. Also from (17), $\tilde{r} \leq r_{\max}$, hence the algorithm must stop at, or prior to, the step at which $r_i = r_{\max}$, $i = 0, 1, \cdots, L-1$, hence proving the theorem.

The main difference between the bit allocation problem solved here and those solved in [3], [4], is that, here, the optimum bit allocation vector also depends on the channel crossover probability. By using the overall distortion (i.e., the distortion measured across the channel.) versus rate performance of the encoder/decoder pair rather than just the source encoder distortion versus rate performance, we were able to incorporate the effects of the noisy channel on the optimum bit allocation vector.

IV. Performance Results

We have implemented an image coding system using the method outlined in the previous sections. The 2-D discrete cosine transform (2-D DCT) has been chosen as the source transformation and we have assumed that the image can be modeled by a stationary 2-D Gaussian random field. In order to compute the theoretically predicted performance, we have made the additional assumption, that the model has a 2-D separable, first-order, Gauss–Markov structure. These results serve as a useful benchmark of system performance. The 2-D Gauss–Markov random field is described according to

$$X(i, j) = \rho_r X(i-1, j) + \rho_c X(i, j-1) - \rho_r \rho_c X(i-1, j-1) + W(i, j), i, j = 0, 1, \cdots, L-1 \quad (21)$$

where ρ_r and ρ_c are the vertical (row) and horizontal (column) correlation coefficients, respectively, and $W(i, j)$ is a 2-D sequence of independent and identically distributed Gaussian random variables with zero-mean and variance σ_W^2. It is assumed that the values of $X(-1, j)$ are known for $j = -1, 0, 1, \cdots, L-1$ and the values of $X(i, -1)$ are known for $i = 0, 1, \cdots, L-1$. For a stationary process the source variance σ_X^2 and σ_W^2 must be related by [1]

$$\sigma_W^2 = \sigma_X^2 (1 - \rho_r^2)(1 - \rho_c^2). \quad (22)$$

The image frame is divided into blocks of size $L \times L$. These blocks are then operated upon by the 2-D DCT defined by [1]

$$Y(m, n) = \frac{2}{L} C(m) C(n) \sum_{i=0}^{L-1} \sum_{j=0}^{L-1} X(i, j)$$
$$\cdot \cos \frac{(2i+1)m\pi}{2L} \cos \frac{(2j+1)n\pi}{2L}$$
$$m, n = 0, 1, \cdots, L-1 \quad (23)$$

where $C(0) = 1/\sqrt{2}$ and $C(m) = 1$ for $m = 1, 2, \cdots, L-1$. The inverse transform (2-D IDCT) is defined by

$$X(i, j) = \frac{2}{L} \sum_{m=0}^{L-1} \sum_{n=0}^{L-1} C(m) C(n) Y(m, n)$$
$$\cdot \cos \frac{(2i+1)m\pi}{2L} \cos \frac{(2j+1)n\pi}{2L},$$
$$i, j = 0, 1, \cdots, L-1. \quad (24)$$

The 2-D DCT is a separable orthonormal transformation and the analysis of Section II extends to two dimensions along exactly the same lines. In particular, the source output is now represented by a matrix $\underline{\underline{X}}$ and by using the orthonormality of the transformation, we can express the average squared-error distortion as

$$D^*(\underline{r}) = \frac{1}{L^2} \sum_{m=0}^{L-1} \sum_{n=0}^{L-1} d_{mn}^*(r_{mn}) \quad (25)$$

where $\underline{r}$ is now the bit allocation *matrix*, and $d_{mn}^*(r_{mn})$ is the optimal

 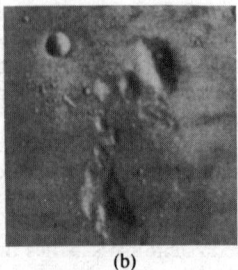

Fig. 3. Original images. (a) "GIRL." (b) "MOON."

distortion incurred in transmitting the (m, n)th transform coefficient across the channel using r_{mn} bits. The optimal bit allocation algorithm now requires $L^2 \tilde{r}$ steps to complete the allocation where $L^2 \tilde{r}$ is the total number of bits that are to be allocated to the image block of size $L \times L$.

Since the source is assumed to be Gaussian, each of the transform coefficients is also Gaussian, which implies that the component distortions may all be expressed in terms of a set of (at most) $r_{\max}$ variance-normalized distortion functions as

$$d_{mn}^*(r_{mn}) = \sigma_{mn}^2 d_{\text{nor}}^*(r_{mn}), m, n = 0, 1, \cdots, L-1. \quad (26)$$

Here, $d_{\text{nor}}^*(r)$ is the minimum distortion achievable by a zero-memory encoder/decoder pair designed for a *unit-variance Gaussian* source as a function of the transmission rate, r bits/sample. Also σ_{mn}^2 is the variance of the (m, n)th transform coefficient.

For the 2-D DCT and the 2-D Gauss–Markov model as described by (21), the variance σ_{mn}^2 may be expressed [1] as the product of $\sigma_c^2(m)$ and $\sigma_r^2(n)$ which are defined by

$$\sigma_c^2(m) \triangleq \frac{2\sigma_X}{L} C^2(m) \sum_{i=0}^{L-1} \sum_{j=0}^{L-1} \rho_c^{|i-j|}$$
$$\cdot \cos \frac{(2i+1)m\pi}{2L} \cos \frac{(2j+1)m\pi}{2L},$$
$$m = 0, 1, \cdots, L-1, \quad (27)$$

and

$$\sigma_r^2(n) \triangleq \frac{2\sigma_X}{L} C^2(n) \sum_{i=0}^{L-1} \sum_{j=0}^{L-1} \rho_r^{|i-j|}$$
$$\cdot \cos \frac{(2i+1)n\pi}{2L} \cos \frac{(2j+1)n\pi}{2L},$$
$$n = 0, 1, \cdots, L-1, \quad (28)$$

respectively.

A. Numerical Results

In order to compute the theoretically predicted performance for the assumed 2-D Gauss–Markov image model, we have estimated the values of ρ_r, ρ_c, and σ_X^2 from the "GIRL" and the "MOON" images, each of size 256×256 pixels. We will hereafter, refer to the set of parameters obtained from the "GIRL" image as PARSET1, and to those obtained from the "MOON" image as PARSET2. The original "GIRL" and "MOON" images are provided in Fig. 3. The values of ρ_r, ρ_c, and σ_X^2 are summarized in Table I. The variances of the transform coefficients (for an $L \times L$ transformation) have then been computed using (27) and (28), following which, the optimal bit allocation matrix and the corresponding performance results have been obtained using the steepest descent algorithm, described in Section III, with $r_{\max}$ set to 8 bits. Results based on the 2-D Gauss–Markov model have also been computed for a *reference* system in which the transform coefficients are quantized by Lloyd–Max quantizers

TABLE I
IMAGE STATISTICS

	IMAGE	MEAN	VARIANCE	ρ_r	ρ_c
PARSET1	GIRL	73.57	1816.56	0.9790	0.9746
PARSET2	MOON	127.23	823.78	0.9017	0.9090

TABLE II
NUMERICAL RESULTS (SNR IN dB); 1 BIT/PIXEL; PARSET1

BLOCK SIZE	$\epsilon = 0.0$		$\epsilon = 0.005$		$\epsilon = 0.01$		$\epsilon = 0.05$	
	REF.	OPT.	REF.	OPT.	REF.	OPT.	REF.	OPT.
8 × 8	25.78	25.78	12.12	20.18	9.21	18.64	2.39	12.59
16 × 16	28.16	28.16	12.21	21.06	9.26	19.37	2.41	12.89
32 × 32	29.29	29.29	12.18	21.42	9.22	19.67	2.36	13.00
OPTA	32.09		31.72		31.42		29.48	

TABLE III
NUMERICAL RESULTS (SNR IN dB); 0.5 BIT/PIXEL; PARSET1

BLOCK SIZE	$\epsilon = 0.0$		$\epsilon = 0.005$		$\epsilon = 0.01$		$\epsilon = 0.05$	
	REF.	OPT.	REF.	OPT.	REF.	OPT.	REF.	OPT.
8 × 8	19.25	19.25	12.11	16.85	9.55	15.88	3.03	11.56
16 × 16	22.54	22.54	11.99	18.86	9.19	17.61	2.45	12.25
32 × 32	24.04	24.04	12.16	19.67	9.31	18.28	2.52	12.53
OPTA	26.95		26.62		26.37		24.69	

TABLE IV
NUMERICAL RESULTS (SNR IN dB); 1 BIT/PIXEL; PARSET2

BLOCK SIZE	$\epsilon = 0.0$		$\epsilon = 0.005$		$\epsilon = 0.01$		$\epsilon = 0.05$	
	REF.	OPT.	REF.	OPT.	REF.	OPT.	REF.	OPT.
8 × 8	16.42	16.42	11.57	14.48	9.34	13.68	3.17	10.22
16 × 16	17.58	17.58	11.85	15.36	9.47	14.49	3.13	10.73
32 × 32	18.14	18.14	11.96	15.85	9.51	14.94	3.105	10.98
OPTA	20.46		20.11		19.84		18.07	

TABLE V
NUMERICAL RESULTS (SNR IN dB); 0.5 BIT/PIXEL; PARSET2

BLOCK SIZE	$\epsilon = 0.0$		$\epsilon = 0.005$		$\epsilon = 0.01$		$\epsilon = 0.05$	
	REF.	OPT.	REF.	OPT.	REF.	OPT.	REF.	OPT.
8 × 8	11.94	11.94	9.87	10.83	8.48	10.32	3.49	8.17
16 × 16	13.11	13.11	10.36	11.92	8.70	11.38	3.27	8.91
32 × 32	13.74	13.74	8.59	12.48	8.88	11.91	3.29	9.26
OPTA	15.85		15.58		15.37		13.98	

designed for a Gaussian source and encoded using the *natural binary code*. The bit allocation matrix used here is the one that is optimal for the case where no channel errors are present ($r_{max} = 8$ bits/sample). These results, referred to as the *numerical results* are presented in Tables II and III for PARSET1, at rates of 1 bit/pixel and 0.5 bit/pixel, respectively, and in Tables IV and V for PARSET2, at rates of 1 bit/pixel and 0.5 bit/pixel, respectively.[5] We also present in the last row of these tables, the optimum performance theoretically attainable (OPTA), obtained by evaluating the distortion-rate function of the 2-D Gauss-Markov image model [14] at the channel capacity (measured in bits/pixel.). Each of these tables contains results for block sizes of 8 × 8, 16 × 16, and 32 × 32, at values of $\epsilon = 0.0, 0.005, 0.01$, and 0.05.

It is obvious from the numerical results that the optimal system results in improvements in signal-to-noise ratio over the reference system. These improvements are particularly significant for very noisy channels. To be specific, the numerical results for PARSET1 indicate performance improvements of approximately 8 dB at a rate of 1 bit/pixel, for a block size of 8 × 8 and a channel crossover probability of 0.005. The performance improvements are seen to increase as the block size increases and as the channel crossover probability increases. By comparing corresponding values for PARSET1 and PARSET2, it can also be seen that the improvements are larger for PARSET1, which possesses the higher correlation coefficients of the two image models considered. In comparing the results of the optimized system to the OPTA, it is interesting to note that for the image model with the lower correlation coefficients the results are closer to the theoretically optimum values, than for the image model with the higher correlation coefficients. Also, for both the image models, the results are closer to OPTA at 0.5 bit/pixel than at 1.0 bit/pixel. Finally, we note that the performance of the reference system does not always improve as the block size is increased or as the bit rate is increased for a *fixed* channel crossover probability. It does, however, for the optimal system, a result that is to be expected. We caution the reader against comparing results for different values of the encoding rate, if the BSC is being used as a model for a binary modulation system over a waveform channel. For a real binary modulation system and for a fixed information rate (in pixels/s), the signaling interval must decrease as the encoding rate increases, which in turn leads to a larger channel crossover probability for the BSC model. Hence, for each encoding rate, the reader must compute the correct crossover probability in order to make meaningful comparisons.

To illustrate the effect of the noisy channel on the bit allocation matrix we have also presented in Figs. 6-8 sample bit allocation matrices at 1 bit/pixel for the optimal system designed for values of $\epsilon = 0.0, 0.01$, and 0.05. The size of these bit allocation matrices is 32 × 32 and they have been obtained for the 2-D Gauss-Markov image model with PARSET1. The sample bit allocations for the optimal system indicate that as the channel crossover probability increases, there is a tendency to allocate more bits to the high energy coefficients (those in the top left corner of the matrix) and thus provide greater channel protection to these coefficients at the expense of more distortion for the lower energy coefficients.

B. Simulation Results

Monte-Carlo simulation results for real-world images have also been obtained, without any modeling assumptions. Here, each image of size 256 × 256 pixels has been divided into blocks of size $L \times L$ for $L = 8, 16$, and 32. Each block has then been transformed using the 2-D DCT, and the variances of the transform coefficients have been estimated from the transformed image data. We assume that the mean and variance data of the transform coefficients is available at the receiver, and that when zero bits are allocated to any transform coefficient, it is decoded to its mean value in the receiver. Simulations have also been run for the reference system which was described earlier. Examples of reconstructed image quality obtained through simulations are illustrated in Figs. 4 and 5. These figures illustrate the performance of the optimal system, as well as the reference system, for values of $\epsilon = 0.005, \epsilon = 0.01$, and $\epsilon = 0.05$, for a block size of 32 × 32, at an average rate of 1 bit/pixel. The performance results obtained through simulations are summarized in Tables VI and VII for the "GIRL" image and in Tables VIII and IX for the "MOON" image. These results are presented for block sizes of 8 × 8, 16 × 16, and 32 × 32, at values of $\epsilon = 0.0, 0.005, 0.01$, and 0.05.

The trends in the simulation results are seen to be similar to those in the numerical results, though the performance improvements are not quite as large. For example, an improvement of 2.3 dB is observed by simulating the system for the "GIRL" image, at a rate of 1 bit/pixel, a block size of 8 × 8 and for a channel crossover probability of 0.005. The corresponding figure predicted by the numerical results is approximately 8 dB. We believe that the difference between the numerical results and the simulation results, is, in part, a result of inappropriate modeling of the source. The Gaussian assumption is not always a good one as shown in [7]. But what is perhaps more important is the fact that nonstationary image models are inherently superior to stationary image models [8], [9]. It would be useful to note here that the system optimization method is general enough to handle situations where the transform coefficients are non-Gaussian, with (possibly) distinct pdf's.

The examples of reconstructed image quality at 1 bit/pixel, confirm the trends indicated by the numerical and simulation results.

---
[5] Our results in Tables II–XII are in terms of signal-to-noise ratio (SNR) in dB, described by $10 \log_{10} \sigma_X^2 / D$.

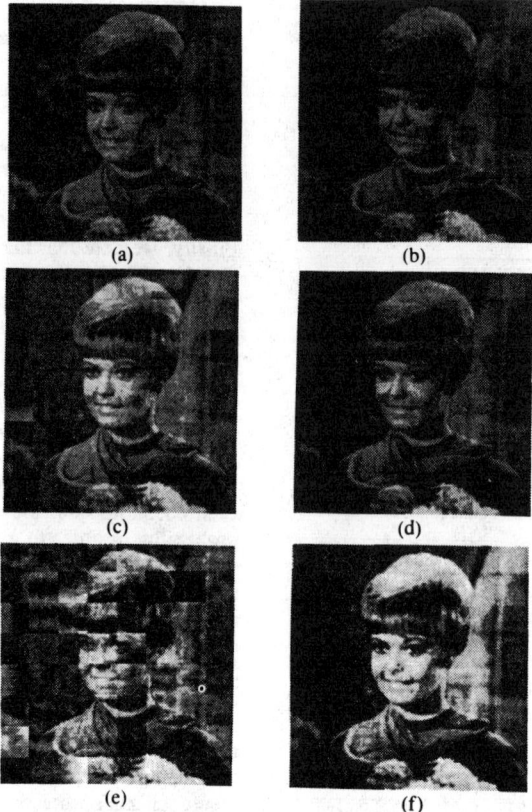

Fig. 4. Simulation results for the "GIRL" image at 1 bit/pixel; block size 32 × 32. (a) Reference system, $\epsilon = 0.005$. (b) Optimum system, $\epsilon = 0.005$. (c) Reference system, $\epsilon = 0.01$. (d) Optimum system, $\epsilon = 0.01$. (e) Reference system, $\epsilon = 0.05$. (f) Optimum system, $\epsilon = 0.05$.

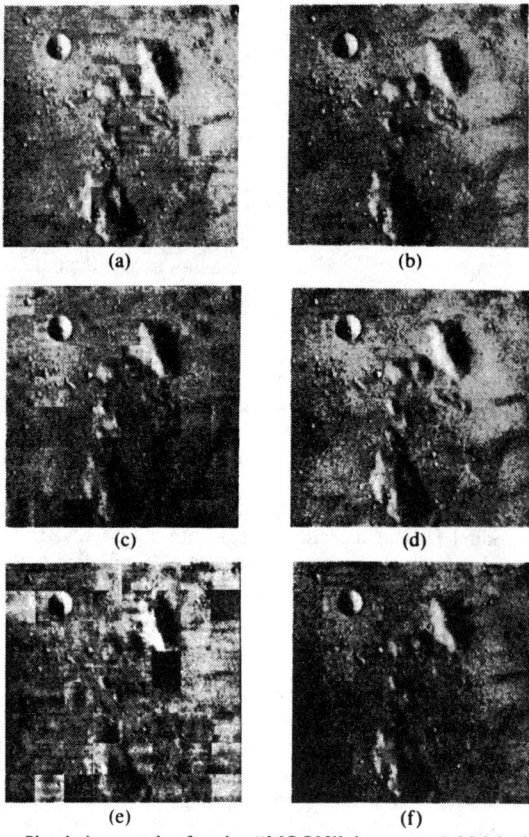

Fig. 5. Simulation results for the "MOON" image at 1 bit/pixel; block size 32 × 32. (a) Reference system, $\epsilon = 0.005$. (b) Optimum system, $\epsilon = 0.005$. (c) Reference system, $\epsilon = 0.01$. (d) Optimum system, $\epsilon = 0.01$. (e) Reference system, $\epsilon = 0.05$. (f) Optimum system, $\epsilon = 0.05$.

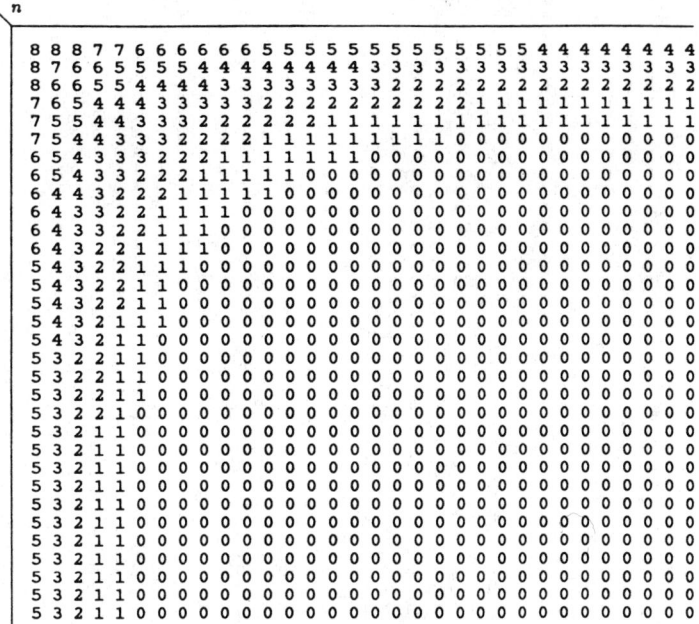

Fig. 6. Bit allocation matrix for the optimal system; 1 bit/pixel; block size 32 × 32; channel crossover probability, $\epsilon = 0.0$.

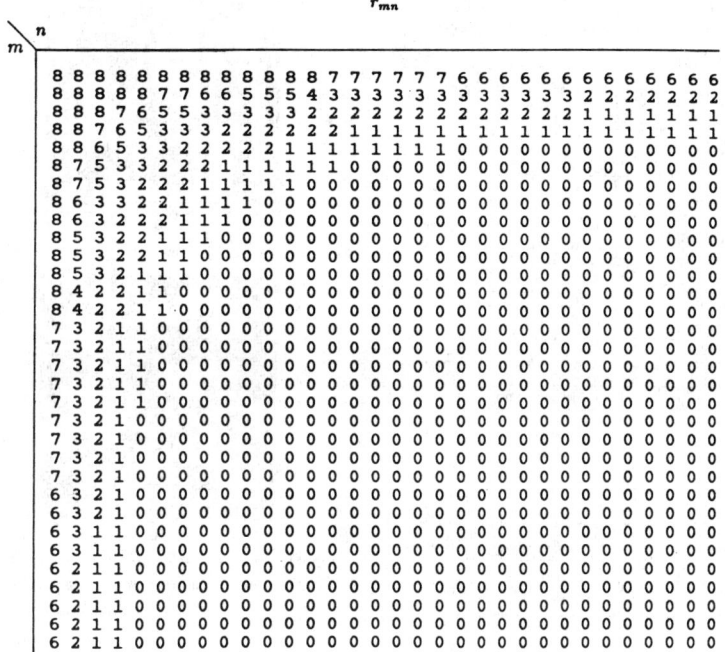

Fig. 7. Bit allocation matrix for the optimal system; 1 bit/pixel; block size 32 × 32; channel crossover probability $\epsilon = 0.01$.

The image quality for the optimal system is definitely superior to that of the reference system, and the improvements in quality are more noticeable for the highly correlated "GIRL" image than for the "MOON" image.

C. Channel Mismatch

As a final point, we have considered the sensitivity of this scheme to mismatch in the channel statistics. It is interesting to know the extent of the performance degradation that results, when the actual channel crossover probability ϵ_a, is different from the design value ϵ_d, for which the system was designed. We present theoretically predicted mismatch SNR's, for a 2-D Gauss-Markov image model, having the same correlation coefficients as the "GIRL" and "MOON" images in Tables X and XI, respectively. These results were computed for a block size of 32 × 32 and a rate of 1 bit/pixel. Mismatch results for the "GIRL" and "MOON" image have also been obtained through simulation and are presented in Figs. 9 and 10, respectively. These figures demonstrate the reconstructed image quality when a system designed for a channel crossover probability of $\epsilon_d = 0.0, 0.005, 0.01$, and 0.05 is applied in a noiseless channel situation ($\epsilon_a = 0.0$). The associated SNR's are tabulated in Table XII.

As can be expected, there is a loss in performance when a system designed for a noisy channel is applied to a noiseless channel. This

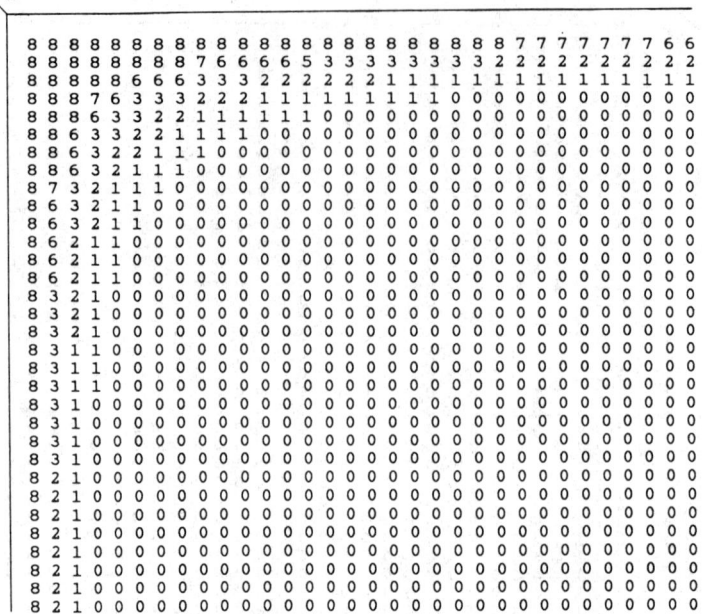

Fig. 8. Bit allocation matrix for the optimal system; 1 bit/pixel; block size 32×32; channel crossover probability $\epsilon = 0.05$.

TABLE VI
SIMULATION RESULTS (SNR IN dB); 1 BIT/PIXEL; "GIRL" IMAGE

BLOCK SIZE	$\epsilon = 0.0$		$\epsilon = 0.005$		$\epsilon = 0.01$		$\epsilon = 0.05$	
	REF.	OPT.	REF.	OPT.	REF.	OPT.	REF.	OPT.
8×8	15.87	15.87	11.83	14.13	9.34	13.34	3.34	9.79
16×16	17.05	17.05	12.06	14.80	8.66	13.70	3.07	9.94
32×32	18.66	18.66	12.38	15.62	8.22	14.30	2.67	10.89

TABLE VII
SIMULATION RESULTS (SNR IN dB); 0.5 BIT/PIXEL; "GIRL" IMAGE

BLOCK SIZE	$\epsilon = 0.0$		$\epsilon = 0.005$		$\epsilon = 0.01$		$\epsilon = 0.05$	
	REF.	OPT.	REF.	OPT.	REF.	OPT.	REF.	OPT.
8×8	13.55	13.55	10.77	12.19	8.56	11.64	3.42	8.95
16×16	14.45	14.45	11.55	13.00	8.67	12.19	3.36	9.22
32×32	15.72	15.72	11.34	13.80	7.63	12.82	2.66	10.14

TABLE VIII
SIMULATION RESULTS (SNR IN dB); 1 BIT/PIXEL; "MOON" IMAGE

BLOCK SIZE	$\epsilon = 0.0$		$\epsilon = 0.005$		$\epsilon = 0.01$		$\epsilon = 0.05$	
	REF.	OPT.	REF.	OPT.	REF.	OPT.	REF.	OPT.
8×8	11.22	11.22	9.05	10.14	7.46	9.70	2.69	7.58
16×16	12.53	12.53	10.11	10.71	7.59	10.37	2.65	8.20
32×32	14.11	14.11	10.36	12.73	7.99	12.14	2.33	9.14

TABLE IX
SIMULATION RESULTS (SNR IN dB); 0.5 BIT/PIXEL; "MOON" IMAGE

BLOCK SIZE	$\epsilon = 0.0$		$\epsilon = 0.005$		$\epsilon = 0.01$		$\epsilon = 0.05$	
	REF.	OPT.	REF.	OPT.	REF.	OPT.	REF.	OPT.
8×8	9.19	9.19	7.68	8.52	6.76	8.22	2.75	6.71
16×16	10.35	10.35	8.44	9.11	7.20	8.90	2.70	7.27
32×32	11.65	11.65	9.33	10.79	7.82	10.38	2.25	8.20

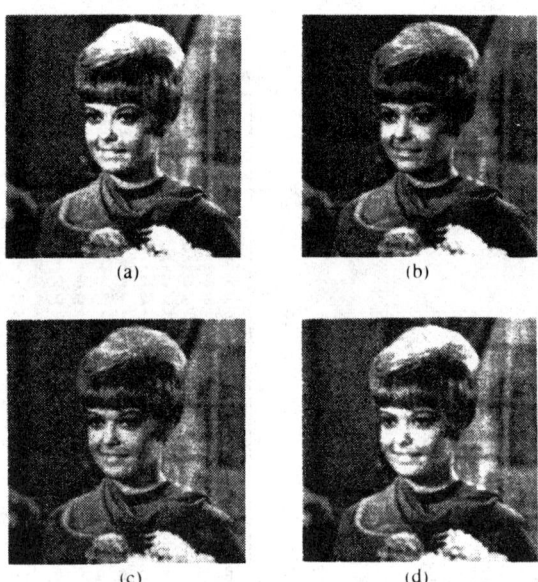

Fig. 9. Mismatch results using a system designed for a noisy channel with crossover probability ϵ and applied to a noiseless channel for the "GIRL" image at 1 bit/pixel; block size 32×32. (a) $\epsilon = 0.00$. (b) $\epsilon = 0.005$. (c) $\epsilon = 0.01$. (d) $\epsilon = 0.05$.

loss in performance can, in fact, be quite large. For example, in Table X, a system designed for $\epsilon_d = 0.05$ performs 10 dB lower than the system designed for $\epsilon_d = 0.0$. But, the significant point is that the system designed for the higher value of channel crossover probability is *less* sensitive to variations in the channel crossover probability. For example, in Table X, when the design value for the crossover probability is $\epsilon_d = 0.0$, the SNR varies by approximately 27 dB as the actual crossover probability varies from 0.0 to 0.05. The corresponding variation in SNR for a system designed with $\epsilon_d = 0.05$ is only 6 dB. Another observation, based on these numerical results, is that the mismatch sensitivity is much greater for the image model with the higher correlation coefficients. This result can be explained as follows. For a given channel crossover probability, as the source becomes more correlated, there is a tendency to allocate higher rate quantizers to the more significant transform coefficients. Our results indicate that for a given ϵ_d, the high rate quantizers are far more sensitive to variations in channel crossover probability, than the low rate quantizers, from which the above observation follows.

The mismatch results obtained through simulation follow the same trends as those obtained for the image model. However, the mismatch sensitivities are observed to be much smaller. Perceptually, no dramatic performance loss can be observed, though we do ob-

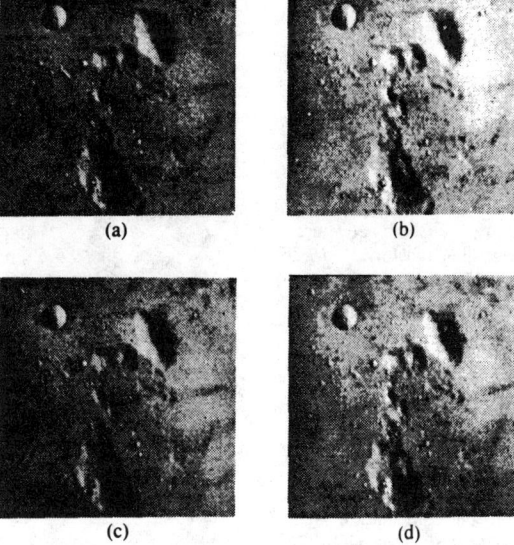

Fig. 10. Mismatch results using a system designed for a noisy channel with crossover probability ϵ and applied to a noiseless channel for the "MOON" image at 1 bit/pixel; block size 32×32. (a) $\epsilon = 0.00$. (b) $\epsilon = 0.005$. (c) $\epsilon = 0.01$. (d) $\epsilon = 0.05$.

TABLE X
MISMATCH SNR FOR THE GAUSS-MARKOV IMAGE MODEL; PARSET1; 1 BIT/PIXEL, BLOCK SIZE 32×32

	$\epsilon_d = 0.0$	$\epsilon_d = 0.005$	$\epsilon_d = 0.01$	$\epsilon_d = 0.05$
$\epsilon_a = 0.0$	29.29	24.17	22.92	19.01
$\epsilon_a = 0.005$	12.18	21.42	21.41	18.40
$\epsilon_a = 0.01$	9.22	19.03	19.67	17.77
$\epsilon_a = 0.05$	2.36	9.48	10.71	13.00

TABLE XI
MISMATCH SNR FOR THE GAUSS-MARKOV IMAGE MODEL; PARSET2; 1 BIT/PIXEL, BLOCK SIZE 32×32

	$\epsilon_d = 0.0$	$\epsilon_d = 0.005$	$\epsilon_d = 0.01$	$\epsilon_d = 0.05$
$\epsilon_a = 0.0$	18.14	17.07	16.57	14.63
$\epsilon_a = 0.005$	11.96	15.85	15.78	14.29
$\epsilon_a = 0.01$	9.51	14.69	14.94	13.94
$\epsilon_a = 0.05$	3.11	8.38	9.29	10.98

TABLE XII
MISMATCH SNR FOR FIGS. 9 AND 10; $\epsilon_a = 0.0$

	$\epsilon_d = 0.0$	$\epsilon_d = 0.005$	$\epsilon_d = 0.01$	$\epsilon_d = 0.05$
GIRL	18.66	16.75	15.88	13.51
MOON	14.11	13.25	13.00	11.56

serve an increase in graininess and a loss in detail as ϵ_d is increased. Also some of the block boundaries become faintly visible.

As a final remark on the system complexity, we note that as the channel for which the system is designed becomes noisier, the complexity of the zero-memory encoder decreases because the number of quantization intervals in the encoder decreases. However the complexity of the decoder remains fixed and is the same as the complexity of a decoder for a Lloyd-Max quantizer.

V. SUMMARY AND CONCLUSIONS

We have optimized the performance of the 2-D discrete cosine transform image coding scheme over a noisy channel by 1) optimizing the bit allocation among the transform coefficients and 2) designing optimal encoder/decoder pairs for transmission of the transform coefficients over a noisy channel.

We have obtained theoretically predicted performance results based on an assumed 2-D Gauss-Markov model, as well as simulation results for real-world images. In both cases it is shown that the optimal system offers noticeable performance improvements over the conventional system based on Lloyd-Max quantization of the transform coefficients. The performance improvements are more noticeable at higher bit rates and for noisier channels. Furthermore, it is shown that the channel-optimized scheme offers some robustness with respect to variations in the assumed channel error probability.

An important feature of the optimal system proposed in this paper is that for a fixed transmission rate, the complexity of the system actually *decreases* with increasing channel crossover probability. This is due to the fact that the number of quantization intervals in the scalar quantizers used in the optimal system actually decreases with increasing channel crossover probability, thus leading to a decrease in encoding complexity, [5], [10]. Furthermore, the proposed encoding scheme does not introduce any additional encoding delay. This is in contrast with those encoding schemes where some type of error control coding is utilized to combat the channel error effects [1].

An interesting open problem which deserves further study, is that of nonstationary and non-Gaussian image models, as there is some evidence that such models are better representatives of real-world imagery.

ACKNOWLEDGMENT

We wish to thank the anonymous reviewers for their suggestions which have resulted in an improved and complete presentation.

REFERENCES

[1] J. W. Modestino, D. G. Daut, and A. L. Vickers, "Combined source-channel coding of images using the block cosine transform," *IEEE Trans. Commun.*, vol. COM-29, pp. 1261-1274, Sept. 1981.

[2] T. Fine, "Properties of an optimum digital system and applications," *IEEE Trans. Inform. Theory*, vol. IT-10, pp. 287-296, Oct. 1964.

[3] A. V. Trushkin, "Optimal bit allocation algorithm for quantizing a random vector," *Prob. Inform. Transmission*, pp. 156-161, Jan. 1982.

[4] A. Segall, "Bit allocation and encoding for vector sources," *IEEE Trans. Inform. Theory*, vol. IT-22, pp. 162-169, Mar. 1976.

[5] N. Farvardin and V. Vaishampayan, "Optimal quantizer design for noisy channels: An approach to combined source-channel coding," *IEEE Trans. Inform. Theory*, vol. IT-33, pp. 827-838, Nov. 1987.

[6] M. J. Narasimha and A. M. Peterson, "On the computation of the discrete cosine transform," *IEEE Trans. Commun.*, vol. COM-26, pp. 934-936, June 1978.

[7] R. C. Reininger and J. D. Gibson, "Distribution of the two-dimensional DCT coefficients for images," *IEEE Trans. Commun.*, vol. COM-31, pp. 835-839, June 1983.

[8] B. R. Hunt and T. M. Cannon, "Nonstationary assumptions for Gaussian models of images," *IEEE Trans. Syst., Man, Cybern.*, pp. 876-882, Dec. 1976.

[9] . A. Habibi, "Survey of adaptive image coding techniques," *IEEE Trans. Commun.*, vol. COM-25, pp. 1275-1284, Nov. 1977.

[10] V. Vaishampayan, "Optimal quantizer design for noisy channels," M.S. thesis, Dep. Elec. Eng., Univ. Mayland, College Park, MD, May 1986.

[11] B. G. Lee, "A new algorithm for the discrete cosine transform," *IEEE Trans. Acoust., Speech, Signal Processing*, vol. ASSP-32, pp. 1243-1245, 1984.

[12] Z. Wang, "On computing the discrete Fourier and cosine transforms," *IEEE Trans. Acoust., Speech, Signal Processing*, vol. ASSP-33, pp. 1341-1344, Oct. 1985.

[13] H. Malvar, "Fast computation of the discrete cosine transform through the fast Hartley transform," *Electron. Lett.*, vol. 22, pp. 352-353, Mar. 1986.

[14] D. G. Daut, "Rate distortion function for 2-D image model," unpublished RPI Tech. Rep., Apr. 1978.

Vinay A. Vaishampayan was born in Bombay, India, on November 7, 1959. He received the B.Tech degree in electrical engineering from the Indian Institute of Technology, Delhi, in 1981, and the M.S. degree in electrical engineering from the University of Maryland, College Park, in 1986, where he is currently working towards the Ph.D. degree in electrical engineering.

He worked as a Geophysical Engineer for Schlumberger Technical Services from 1981 to 1983. His research interests are in the areas of data compression, statistical communication theory, and information theory.

Nariman Farvardin was born in Tehran, Iran, on July 15, 1956. He received the B.S., M.S., and Ph.D. degrees in electrical engineering from Rensselaer Polytechnic Institute, Troy, NY, in 1979, 1980, and 1983, respectively.

During 1980-1981 and 1982-1983 he was a Research Assistant in the Electrical, Computer, and Systems Engineering Department at Rensselaer Polytechnic Institute. He received an IBM fellowship during 1981-1982 academic year. Since January 1984 he has been with the Electrical Engineering Department at the University of Maryland, College Park, MD, where he is currently an Associate Professor and holds a joint appointment with the Institute for Advanced Computer Studies. His research interests include information theory, digital communications and signal processing with application to speech/image coding and transmission.

Dr. Farvardin is the Associate Editor for Quantization, Speech/Image Coding of the IEEE TRANSACTIONS ON COMMUNICATIONS. In 1987, he received the Presidential Young Investigator Award from the National Science Foundation.

Chapter 5: Emerging Topics

This chapter comprises six reprinted papers on some of the most recent topics that have applications in image processing. The first paper, by Mallat, is a survey paper on multifrequency channel decomposition of images and wavelet models. Specifically, models developed in psychophysiology, vision processing, and image processing are reviewed. The second reprinted paper, by Maragos and Schafer, is a general overview of morphological systems for multidimensional signal processing. This paper reviews applications of mathematical morphology to several problems drawn from nonlinear filtering and image analysis. Realizations of several nonlinear and linear operators as a combination of simple morphological operations are illustrated in detail.

The next reprinted paper, by Zhou, Chellappa, Vaid, and Jenkins, illustrates how a simple Hopfield model can be used for a standard image-restoration problem. The particular approach taken in this paper is an example of a large body of work[1-5] in which a Hopfield network or its variation is used for minimization of energy functions arising in specific image-related problems.

The following reprinted paper, by Daugman, describes a three-layered neural network for computing two-dimensional Gabor transforms for the purposes of image compression and analysis. The computation of two-dimensional Gabor transforms is complicated, owing to the nonorthogonality of the basis functions. This paper presents an elegant approach for obtaining the coefficients required for the computation of two-dimensional Gabor transforms. A biological motivation for representation using Gabor transforms is also provided.

Most image-restoration algorithms assume an additive Gaussian noise model. Very often, the real images are corrupted by a contaminated Gaussian noise, defined as

$$\omega(i,j) = \eta(i,j), \text{ with probability } 1 - \beta$$

and

$$\omega(i,j) = \upsilon(i,j), \text{ with probability } \beta$$

where $\eta(i,j)$ is a white Gaussian noise, $\upsilon(i,j)$ is an outlier process, and β is the percentage of outliers present. The classical LS or Gaussian ML methods do not perform very well, even if only a small number of outliers is present. In the next reprinted paper, by Kashyap and Eom, the authors develop two robust parameter-estimation algorithms for the case in which the original image is represented by a two-dimensional, nonsymmetric half-plane (NSHP) model and the corrupting noise is contaminated as modeled above. One of the specific parameter-estimation methods developed is a generalization of the popular M-estimator.[6] A proof for the convergence of the estimate is given. The second method represents the original image as a two-dimensional Gaussian NSHP model and estimates the model parameters and the original image using a two-dimensional generalization of the "filter-cleaner" method proposed by Kleiner, Martin, and Thomson.[7] Comparisons of restoration using the robust approach, α-trimmed mean filter, and median filter are given for a number of real images. Related work on two-dimensional robust spectral estimation is reported by Sharma and Chellappa[8] and Hansen and Chellappa[9,10] for the case of two-dimensional NSHP and noncausal models corrupted by contaminated noise. Recent workshops on robust methods for image processing and analysis[11,12] reflect the increasing importance of this area.

The final reprinted paper in this chapter, by Tonge, discusses some image-processing issues related to higher-definition television (HDTV). HDTV is expected to be one of the most popular consumer electronics products well into the 21st century; hence, it has attracted a lot of attention from both academia and industry. After defining picture-quality targets, Tonge reviews techniques for achieving a wider picture format, improving resolution in both vertical and horizontal components, and improving color reproduction.

Chapter 5 References

1. J.J. Hopfield and D.W. Tank, "Neural Computation of Decisions in Optimization Problems," *Biological Cybernetics*, Vol. 52, 1985, pp. 141-152.
2. M. Takeda and J.W. Goodman, "Neural Networks for Computation: Number Representations and Programming Complexity," *Applied Optics*, Vol. 25, Sept. 1986, pp. 3033-3046.
3. C. Koch, "Analog Neuronal Networks for Real-Time Vision Systems," *Proc. Workshop Neural Network Devices and Applications*, Feb. 1987.
4. J. Hutchinson et al., "Computing Motion Using Analog and Binary Resistive Networks," *Computer*, Mar. 1988, pp. 52-63.
5. Y.T. Zhou and R. Chellappa, "Computation of Optical Flow Using A Neural Network," *Proc. IEEE Int'l Conf. on Neural Networks*, Vol. 2, 1988, pp. 71-78.
6. P.J. Huber, *Robust Statistics*, John Wiley & Sons, Inc., New York, N.Y., 1981.
7. B. Kleiner, R.D. Martin, and D.J. Thomson, "Robust Estimation of Power Spectra," *J. Royal Statistical Soc.*, Series B, Vol. 41, 1979, pp. 313-351.
8. G. Sharma and R. Chellappa, "An Iterative Algorithm for 2-D Robust Spectral Estimation," *Proc. Int'l Conf. Acoustics, Speech, and Signal Processing*, Mar. 1984.
9. R.R. Hansen, Jr., and R. Chellappa, "Two-Dimensional Robust Spectral Estimation," *IEEE Trans. Acoustics, Speech, and Signal Processing*, Vol. ASSP-36, July 1988, pp. 1051-1066.
10. R.R. Hansen, Jr., and R. Chellappa, "Empirical Robust Estimators for 2-D Noncausal Autoregressive Models," *Proc. Int'l Conf. Acoustics, Speech, and Signal Processing*, May 1990.
11. *Workshop on Robust Computer Vision*, organized by A. Rosenfeld, Univ. of Maryland, College Park, Md., July 1989.
12. *International Workshop on Robust Computer Vision*, organized by R.M. Haralick and W. Forstner, Univ. of Washington, Seattle, Wash., Oct. 1990.

Multifrequency Channel Decompositions of Images and Wavelet Models

STEPHANE G. MALLAT

Abstract—In this paper we review recent multichannel models developed in psychophysiology, computer vision, and image processing. In psychophysiology, multichannel models have been particularly successful in explaining some low-level processing in the visual cortex. The expansion of a function into several frequency channels provides a representation which is intermediate between a spatial and a Fourier representation. We describe the mathematical properties of such decompositions and introduce the wavelet transform. We review the classical multiresolution pyramidal transforms developed in computer vision and show how they relate to the decomposition of an image into a wavelet orthonormal basis. In the last section we discuss the properties of the zero crossings of multifrequency channels. Zero-crossings representations are particularly well adapted for pattern recognition in computer vision.

I. Introduction

WITHIN the last 10 years, multifrequency channel decompositions have found many applications in image processing. In the psychophysiology of human vision, multichannel models have also been particularly successful in explaining some low-level biological processes. The expansion of a function into several frequency channels provides a representation which is intermediate between a spatial and a Fourier representation. In harmonic analysis, this kind of transform appeared in the work of Littlewood and Payley in the 1930's. More research has recently been focused on this domain with the modeling of a new decomposition called the wavelet transform. In this paper we review the recent multichannel models developed in psychophysiology, computer vision, and image processing. We describe the motivations of the models within each of these disciplines and show how they relate to the wavelet transform.

In psychophysics and the physiology of human vision, evidence has been gathered showing that the retinal image is decomposed into several spatially oriented frequency channels. In the first section of this paper, we describe the experimental motivations for this model. Biological studies of human vision have always been a source of ideas for computer vision and image processing research. Indeed, the human visual system is generally considered to be an optimal image processor. The goal is not to imitate the processings implemented in the human brain, but rather to understand the motivations of such processings

Manuscript received March 17, 1989. This work was supported by NSF Grant IRI-8903331.
The author is with the Computer Science Department, Courant Institute of Mathematical Sciences, New York University, New York, NY 10012.
IEEE Log Number 8931327.

and analyze their application to computer vision problems. From this point of view, the recent experimental findings in psychophysics and physiology open challenging questions. In order to get a better understanding of multichannel decompositions, we review the main mathematical results in this domain. The best-known decomposition which is intermediate between a spatial and a frequency representation is the window Fourier transform. The window Fourier transform is used in signal processing for coding and pattern detection [47]. We describe its properties but also show why it is not a convenient decomposition for image analysis. The wavelet transform was introduced by Morlet to overcome the shortcomings of the window Fourier transform. It is computed by expanding the signal into a family of functions which are the dilations and translations of a unique function $\psi(x)$. Grossmann and Morlet [20] have shown that any function in $L^2(R)$ can be characterized from its decomposition on the wavelet family $(\sqrt{s}\, \psi(s(x-u)))_{(s,u) \in R^2}$. A wavelet transform can be interpreted as a decomposition into a set of frequency channels having the same bandwidth on a logarithmic scale. We review the most important properties of a wavelet transform and describe its discretization as studied by Daubechies [11]. A very important particular case of discrete wavelet transform was found by Meyer [45] and Stromberg [55]. They proved that there exist some wavelets $\psi(x)$ such that $(\sqrt{2^j}\psi(2^j(x - 2^{-j}n)))_{(j,n) \in Z^2}$ is an orthonormal basis of $L^2(R)$. Wavelet orthonormal bases provide an important new tool in functional analysis. Indeed, it was believed that we could not build simple orthonormal bases of $L^2(R)$ whose elements have a good localization both in the spatial and Fourier domains. These bases have already found many applications in pure and applied mathematics [27], [33], [57], in quantum mechanics [15], [48], and in signal processing [30].

In computer vision, multifrequency channel decompositions are interpreted through the concept of multiresolution. Generally, the structures that we want to recognize have very different sizes. Hence, it is not possible to define *a priori* an optimal resolution for analyzing images. Several researchers [22], [42], [52] have developed pattern matching algorithms which process the image at different resolutions. Some pyramidal implementations have been developed for computing these decompositions [4], [10], [50]. A multiresolution transform also decomposes the signal into a set of frequency channels of constant bandwidth on a logarithmic scale. It can be interpreted as a discrete wavelet transform. We review the wavelet multiresolution model [38] which provides a mathematical interpretation of the concept of resolution. We see in particular that a large class of wavelet orthonormal bases can be computed from quadrature mirror filters [39].

Multifrequency channel decompositions are well adapted for data compression in image coding. We show that this efficiency is due to the intrinsic statistical properties of images and to the ability of such representations to match the sensitivity of human vision. For pattern recognition applications, it is also necessary to build a signal representation which translates when the signal translates. Indeed, the representation of a pattern should not depend upon its position. When a pattern is translated, its representation should be translated without being modified. The pyramidal multiresolution representations as well as discrete wavelet transforms do not have this translation property. In the last section, we study the properties of representations based on zero crossings of multifrequency channels. These representations do translate, and for a particular class of band-pass filters, the zero crossings provide the location of the signal edges. It remains to show that a zero-crossing representation can provide a complete and stable signal decomposition. We review previous results on zero-crossings properties and explain how the problem can be expressed through the wavelet model.

II. Multichannel Models in Psychophysics and Physiology of Vision

In this section, we summarize some experimental results showing that a multifrequency channel decomposition seems to be taking place in the human visual cortex. For further details, we refer to tutorials by Georgeson [18] and Levine [34]. Over the past 20 years, a large effort has been devoted in psychophysics and physiology to analyze the response of the human visual system to stimuli having particular orientation and frequency tunings. Linear models have been partly successful in explaining some experimental data. The simplest, which was first developed in psychophysiology, approximates the human visual system with a linear filter. Fig. 1 illustrates the anatomical pathway in the human visual system. Photoreceptors in the eyes measure the light input intensity. This information is processed by bipolar and ganglion cells in the retina and is transmitted through the optic nerve. The optic nerve ends in a relay station (the lateral geniculate nucleus) whose axons extend to the visual cortex.

Replacing these different stages by a global linear filter is clearly an extremely simplified model, but it gives some insights about the visual system sensitivity. Given this hypothesis, Campbell and Green [6] tried to measure the global transfer function of the visual system. In their experiments, the visual stimuli shown to the observer were vertical sinusoidal gratings of different spatial frequencies (see Fig. 2).

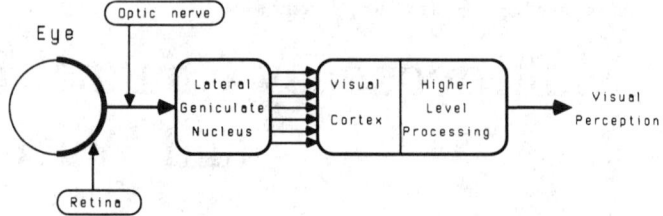

Fig. 1. Illustration of the anatomical visual pathway. The higher level processes are the least understood and are difficult to evaluate in psychophysical experiments.

Fig. 2. This image is a typical visual stimulus used in psychological experiments for computing the transfer function of the visual system. It consists of a sinusoidal grating whose frequency varies during the experiment. In order to evaluate the sensitivity to orientation, these gratings are rotated.

In psychophysics, frequencies are measured in cycles per degree of visual angle subtended on the eye. The transfer function $H(\omega)$ of the visual system is defined as the ratio of the contrast perceived by the observer to the real contrast of the stimulus for sinusoidal gratings of frequency ω. The contrast is given by

$$C = \frac{L_{\max} - L_{\min}}{L_{\max} + L_{\min}},$$

where $L_{\max}$ and $L_{\min}$ are the maximum and minimum luminance of the stimuli. In order to estimate this transfer function, a solution which is widely adopted is to measure the *Contrast Sensitivity Function*. At each frequency ω, we measure the minimum contrast $C_t(\omega)$ necessary to distinguish the sinusoidal gratings from a uniform background. This contrast is called the contrast threshold. The contrast sensitivity function is then defined by

$$CSF(\omega) = \frac{1}{C_t(\omega)}, \quad \text{and} \quad H(\omega) = CSF(\omega).$$

Many experiments [5], [6], [31] have been performed to measure the function $CSF(\omega)$ and they agree approximately with the function shown in Fig. 3. Although this linear model is clearly oversimplified, it shows qualitatively the sensitivity of the human system to stimuli of different frequencies.

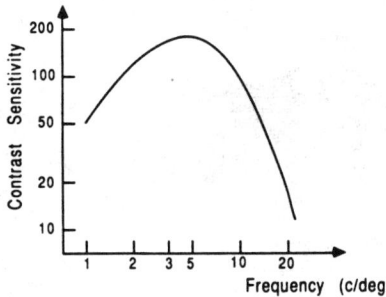

Fig. 3. Contrast Sensitivity Function (redrawn from Kulikowski and King-Smith [31]). The visual system has the maximum sensitivity to contrast when the frequency of the stimulus is around 5 cycles/deg.

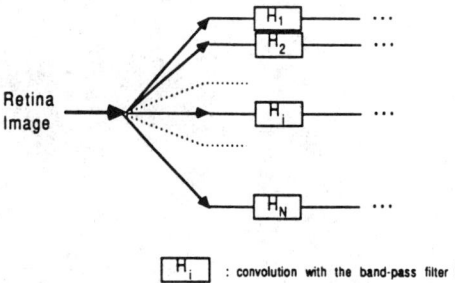

Fig. 4. Multichannel model. The retinal image is supposed to be filtered by independent band-pass filters. These filters have approximately the same bandwidth on a logarithmic scale and have a spatial orientation selectivity.

With further experiments, Campbell and Robson [8] have shown that the retinal image is likely to be processed in separate frequency channels. These experiments were based on adaptation techniques. If a stimulus is shown to an observer for a long time, the visual sensitivity for the same kind of stimuli decreases. This behavior is called an adaptation process. Campbell and Robson [8] have shown that if the visual system adapts to a sinusoidal grating of a given frequency ω_0, the sensitivity decreases for any stimuli whose frequency is in a frequency band around ω_0. However, outside this frequency band, the sensitivity is not affected. These experiments indicate that at some stage, the visual information in different frequency bands is processed separately. Researchers in psychophysics have tried to measure the width of these bands. In order to simplify the analysis of the problem, Campbell and Robson supposed that the retinal image is decomposed through independent band-pass linear filters as shown in Fig. 4. Their first estimate of the frequency bandwidth of these filters was very narrow. However, other experiments by Georgeson [17] and Nachmias [46] have since contradicted their results. They showed that the frequency bandwidth of these filters is more likely to be around one octave. In other words, the retina image seems to be decomposed in several frequency bands having approximately the same width on a logarithmic scale.

Other psychophysical experiments have shown that the visual sensitivity to a sinusoidal grating also depends upon its spatial orientation. The results of Campbell and Kulikowski [7] show that the human visual system has a maximum sensitivity when the signal has an orientation of 0° or 90°. In between, the sensitivity decreases monotonically reaching a minimum at 45°. The filters of the model shown in Fig. 4 must therefore have a spatial orientation selectivity.

This filter bank model only provides a qualitative description of some low-level processing of the visual system. In particular, it does not take into account the nonlinearities of the biological processes. However, recent physiological experiments support such approaches. Cell recordings are generally performed on cats and monkeys which have a visual cortex similar to the human one. In the cat's visual cortex, Hubel and Wiesel [23] discovered a class of cells whose response depends upon the frequency and orientation of the visual stimuli. These cells are called simple cells. Maffei and Fiorentini [35] have shown that their response is reasonably linear and that they can be modeled with linear filters. Several groups of researchers have recorded the impulse responses of simple cells [2], [36], [59]. These studies showed that the bandwidths of simple cells range from 0.6 to 2.0 octaves with an average value of 1.3 octaves. The response of simple cells also depends upon the spatial orientation of the stimuli. Fig. 5 shows the two-dimensional impulse response of simple cells measured by Webster and De Valois [61]. These impulse responses have been modeled by Daugmann [12], [13] with Gaussians modulated by sinusoidal waves. As explained in the next section, these functions generate a particular window Fourier transform called the Gabor transform. Fig. 5 shows the comparison between the impulse response of a simple cell and the corresponding Gabor function model. These graphs clearly show that a simple cell behaves like a band-pass filter with a spatial orientation tuning. The support of the impulse response of a cell is called the receptive field. It corresponds to the domain of the retina where the input light influences the cell firings. Simple cells have a receptive field of varying size depending on their frequency tuning [49].

Much evidence has now been gathered about this multifrequency channel modeling of the low-level visual cortex processing. However, we do not know what type of information is extracted from this decomposition and how it relates to further processing by complex and hypercomplex cells [49]. Since the human visual cortex is an excellent image processor, this low-level biological model raises important questions from an image processing point of view. What is the advantage of decomposing a signal into several frequency channels? Is it related to the intrinsic statistical properties of images? Does it lead to a better reorganization of the image information? If we do accept that such a decomposition offers a useful representation of images, it remains to find out how to process these different frequency channels. What type of information do we want to extract? Should we process each channel independently or compare the values of the signal from band to band? In the following sections, we show that some

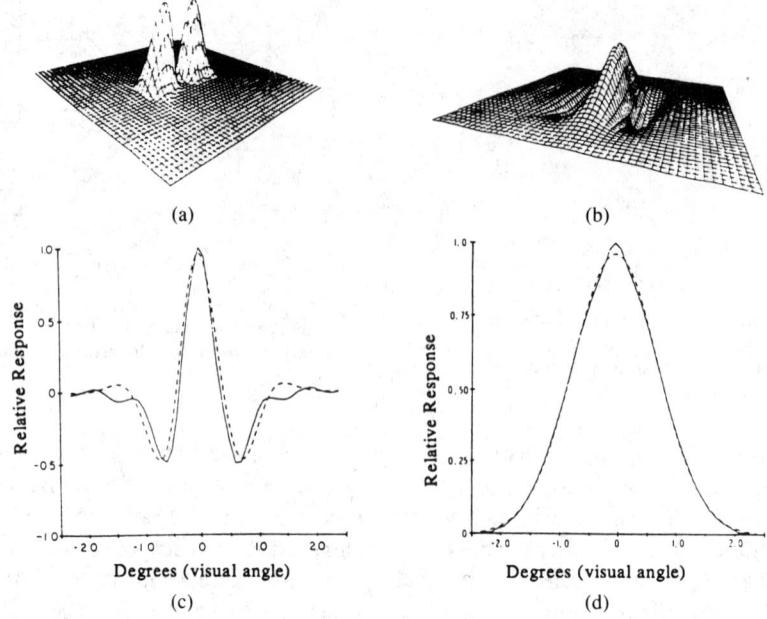

Fig. 5. (Reprint from Webster and De Valois [61].) (a) This surface is the two-dimensional transfer function of a simple cell. It is a band-pass oriented filter. Its bandwidth is 0.94 octaves. (b) Impulse response computed by taking the inverse Fourier transform of (a). (c) and (d) Cross sections of the impulse response respectively along the x and y axes. The dashed lines give the best fitting Gabor functions.

results in mathematics, computer vision, and image coding give elements of answers to these questions. Our primary goal is not to build a model of the human visual cortex but rather to justify the use of such decompositions in image processing.

III. MATHEMATICAL ANALYSIS OF MULTICHANNEL MODELS

In this section we review the mathematical properties of multifrequency channel decompositions. We do believe that a good mathematical understanding of these decompositions is necessary in order to evaluate their range of applications in image processing. We summarize the most relevant mathematical results in this domain. No proof is written, but references to original works are given. Most results are first introduced for one-dimensional functions and then generalized to two dimensions if needed. We review the properties of the window Fourier transform which is the most well-known intermediate decomposition between spatial and Fourier representations. This decomposition has already found many applications in signal coding and pattern detection [47]. We describe the drawbacks of the window Fourier transform for analyzing signals like images. The wavelet transform is then introduced and compared to the window Fourier transform. More details can be found in a complete article by Daubechies [11] and an advanced functional analysis book by Meyer [44].

Notation: Z, R, and R^+ denote, respectively, the sets of integers, real numbers, and positive real numbers. $L^2(R)$ denotes the Hilbert space of measurable, square-integrable one-dimensional functions $f(x)$. We suppose that our signals are finite energy functions $f(x) \in L^2(R)$. For a pair of functions $f(x) \in L^2(R)$, $g(x) \in L^2(R)$, the inner product of $f(x)$ with $g(x)$ is written

$$\langle g(x), f(x) \rangle = \int_{-\infty}^{+\infty} g(x)\overline{f(x)}\, dx, \quad (1)$$

where $\overline{f(x)}$ is the complete conjugate of $f(x)$. The norm of $f(x)$ in $L^2(R)$ is given by

$$\|f\|^2 = \int_{-\infty}^{+\infty} |f(x)|^2\, dx. \quad (2)$$

We denote the convolution of two functions $f(x) \in L^2(R)$ and $g(x) \in L^2(R)$ by

$$f * g(u) = \int_{-\infty}^{+\infty} f(x)g(u-x)\, dx. \quad (3)$$

The dilation of a function $f(x) \in L^2(R)$ by a scaling factor s is written

$$f_s(x) = \sqrt{s}\, f(sx). \quad (4)$$

The reflection of $f(x)$ about 0 is written

$$\tilde{f}(x) = f(-x). \quad (5)$$

The Fourier transform of $f(x) \in L^2(R)$ is written $\hat{f}(\omega)$ and is defined by

$$\hat{f}(\omega) = \int_{-\infty}^{+\infty} f(x)e^{-i\omega x}\, dx. \quad (6)$$

A. Definition of a Window Fourier Transform

From the Fourier transform of a function $f(x)$, we get a measure of the irregularities (high frequencies) but this information is not spatially localized. Indeed, the Fourier transform $\hat{f}(\omega)$ is defined through an integral which covers the whole spatial domain. It is therefore difficult to find the position of the irregularities. In order to localize the information provided by the Fourier transform, Gabor [16] defined a new decomposition using a spatial window $g(x)$ in the Fourier integral. This window is translated along the spatial axis in order to cover the whole signal. At a position u and for a frequency ω, the window Fourier transform of a function $f(x) \in L^2(R)$ is defined by

$$Gf(\omega, u) = \int_{-\infty}^{+\infty} e^{-i\omega x} g(x - u) f(x) \, dx. \quad (7)$$

It measures locally, around the point u, the amplitude of the sinusoidal wave component of frequency ω. In the original Gabor transform, the window function $g(x)$ is a Gaussian. It has since been generalized for any type of window function and is called a window Fourier transform [28]. The window function is generally a real even function and the energy of its Fourier transform is concentrated in the low frequencies (see Fig. 6). It can be viewed as the impulse response of a low-pass filter. For normalization purposes, we suppose that the energy of $g(x)$ is equal to 1:

$$\|g\|^2 = \int_{-\infty}^{+\infty} |g(x)|^2 \, dx = 1.$$

Let us denote

$$g_{\omega_0, u_0}(x) = e^{i\omega_0 x} g(x - u_0).$$

A window Fourier transform can also be interpreted as the inner products of the function $f(x)$ with the family of functions $(g_{\omega, u}(x))_{(\omega, u) \in R^2}$:

$$Gf(\omega, u) = \langle f(x), g_{\omega, u}(x) \rangle. \quad (8)$$

In quantum physics, such a family of functions is called a family of coherent states. The Fourier transform $g_{\omega, u_0}(x)$ is given by

$$\hat{g}_{\omega_0, u_0}(\omega) = e^{-iu_0\omega} \hat{g}(\omega - \omega_0), \quad (9)$$

where $\hat{g}(\omega)$ is the Fourier transform of $g(x)$. A family of coherent states thus corresponds to a translation in the spatial domain (parameter u) and in the frequency domain (parameter ω) of the function $g(x)$ (see Fig. 6). This double translation is represented in a phase-space where one axis corresponds to the spatial parameter u and the other to the frequency parameter ω (see Fig. 7). Families of coherent states have found many applications in quantum physics because they make it possible to analyze simultaneously a physical phenomena in both the spatial and frequency domains.

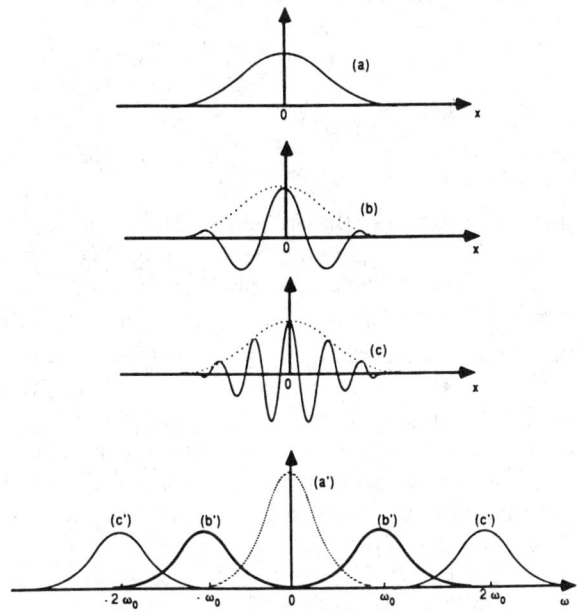

Fig. 6. (a) Window function $g(x)$. (b) Graph of $g(x) \cos(\omega_0 x)$. (c) Graph of $g(x) \cos(2\omega_0 x)$. All these curves have the same support but the number of cycles varies with the frequency of the sinusoidal modulation. The curves (a'), (b'), (c') are, respectively, the Fourier transform of $g(x)$, $g(x) \cos(\omega_0 x)$, and $g(x) \cos(2\omega_0 x)$. They have the same bandwidth but different positions on the frequency axis.

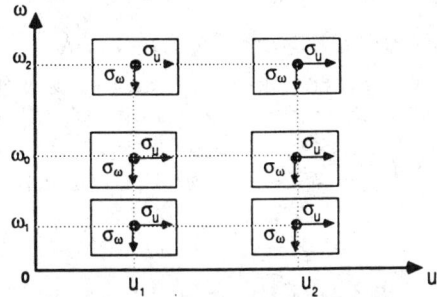

Fig. 7. Phase-space representation. The vertical axis gives the frequency ω whereas the horizontal axis gives the spatial position u. A window Fourier coefficient $Gf(\omega_0, u_0)$ provides a description of $f(x)$ within the resolution cell of $[u_0 - \sigma_u, u_0 + \sigma_u] \times [\omega_0 - \sigma_\omega, \omega_0 + \sigma_\omega]$.

Let us now describe how a window Fourier transform relates to a spatial or a frequency representation. Let σ_u be the standard deviation of $g(x)$

$$\sigma_u^2 = \int_{-\infty}^{+\infty} x^2 |g(x)|^2 \, dx. \quad (10)$$

Let σ_ω be the standard deviation of the Fourier transform of $g(x)$

$$\sigma_\omega^2 = \int_{-\infty}^{+\infty} \omega^2 |\hat{g}(\omega)|^2 \, d\omega. \quad (11)$$

The function $g_{\omega_0, u_0}(x)$ is centered in u_0 and has a standard deviation σ_u in the spatial domain. Its Fourier transform given by (9) is centered in ω_0 and has a standard deviation

σ_ω. By applying the Parseval theorem on (8), we get

$$Gf(\omega_0, u_0) = \int_{-\infty}^{+\infty} f(x)\overline{g_{\omega_0, u_0}(x)}\, dx$$

$$= \int_{-\infty}^{+\infty} \hat{f}(\omega)\overline{\hat{g}_{\omega_0, u_0}(\omega)}\, d\omega. \quad (12)$$

The first integral shows that in the spatial domain, $Gf(\omega_0, u_0)$ essentially depends upon the values of $f(x)$ for $x \in [u_0 - \sigma_u, u_0 + \sigma_u]$. The second integral proves that in the frequency domain, $Gf(\omega_0, u_0)$ depends upon the values of $\hat{f}(\omega)$ for $\omega \in [\omega_0 - \sigma_\omega, \omega_0 + \sigma_\omega]$. The spatio-frequency domain which is covered by $Gf(\omega_0, u_0)$ can thus be represented in the phase-space by the resolution cell $[u_0 - \sigma_u, u_0 + \sigma_u] \times [\omega_0 - \sigma_\omega, \omega_0 + \sigma_\omega]$ as shown in Fig. 7. The surface and shape of the resolution cell is independent from u_0 and ω_0. The uncertainty principle applied to the function $g(x)$ implies that

$$\sigma_u^2 \sigma_\omega^2 \geq \frac{\pi}{2}. \quad (13)$$

The resolution cell can therefore not be smaller than $2\sqrt{2\pi}$. The uncertainty inequality reaches its upper limit if and only if $g(x)$ is a Gaussian. Hence, the resolution in the phase-space is maximized when the window function is a Gaussian as in the Gabor transform.

B. Properties of a Window Fourier Transform

A window Fourier transform is an isometry (to a proportionality coefficient) from $L^2(R)$ into $L^2(R^2)$

$$\int_{-\infty}^{+\infty} |f(x)|^2\, dx = \frac{1}{2\pi} \int_{-\infty}^{+\infty} \int_{-\infty}^{+\infty} |Gf(\omega, u)|^2\, d\omega\, du. \quad (14)$$

The function $f(x)$ is reconstructed from $Gf(\omega, u)$ with the formula

$$f(x) = \frac{1}{2\pi} \int_{-\infty}^{+\infty} \int_{-\infty}^{+\infty} Gf(\omega, u) g(u - x) e^{i\omega x}\, d\omega\, du. \quad (15)$$

Equations (14) and (15) are proved by applying the Parseval theorem and using the definition of $Gf(\omega, x)$ given in (7).

A window Fourier transform is a redundant representation. If instead of computing $Gf(\omega, u)$ for all values $(\omega, u) \in R^2$ we sample uniformly both ω and u, the representation can still be complete and stable. Let u_0 and ω_0 be the sampling intervals in both domains. A discrete Fourier transform is defined by

$$\forall n \in Z, \quad \forall m \in Z \quad G_d f(m, n) = Gf(m\omega_0, nu_0)$$

$$= \int_{-\infty}^{+\infty} e^{-im\omega_0 x} g(x - nu_0) f(x)\, dx. \quad (16)$$

This discretization corresponds to a uniform sampling of the phase-space as shown in Fig. 8. A discrete window

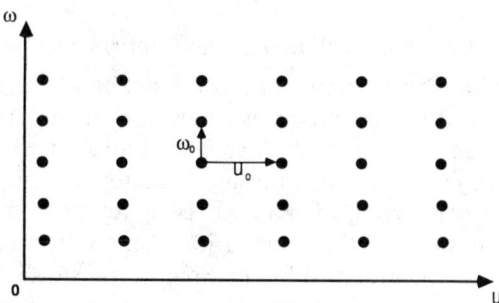

Fig. 8. Sampling pattern of a discrete window Fourier transform in the phase-space. Since the resolution cells are identical everywhere in the phase-space, the sampling is uniform.

Fourier transform is equivalent to a division of the frequency axis into intervals separated by ω_0 (see Fig. 6). In each of these intervals, the signal is sampled at a rate $1/u_0$. Daubechies [11] made a thorough study of the completeness and stability of a discrete window Fourier transform. Intuitively, the sampling intervals u_0 and ω_0 must be chosen in order to cover the whole phase-space with the resolution cells shown in Fig. 7. Formally, to reconstruct any function $f(x) \in L^2(R)$ from the set of sample $(G_d f(n, m))_{(n,m) \in Z^2}$, the operator

$$L^2(R) \xrightarrow{G_d} l^2(Z^2)$$

must be invertible on its range and have a bounded inverse. Each sample $G_d f(n, m)$ can also be expressed as an inner product in $L^2(R)$

$$G_d f(m, n) = \langle f(x), e^{im\omega_0 x} g(x - nu_0) \rangle$$

$$= \langle f(x), g_{m\omega_0, nu_0}(x) \rangle. \quad (17)$$

The properties of a discrete Fourier transform thus depend upon the family of functions $(g_{m\omega_0, nu_0}(x))_{(n,m) \in Z^2}$. In order to invert G_d, Daubechies [11] has shown that ω_0 and u_0 must verify

$$\omega_0 u_0 < 2\pi.$$

When $\omega_0 u_0 = 2\pi$, we reach the Nyquist frequency limit and G_d does not have a bounded inverse. When $\omega_0 u_0 < 2\pi$, the range of Gd has a complicated structure.

Although several researchers have tried to model the impulse response of simple cells with Gabor functions, it is unlikely that the human visual cortex implements some type of window Fourier transform. Indeed, we saw that a window Fourier transform decomposes a function into a set of frequency intervals having the same size. On the other hand, experimental data indicate that the retinal image is decomposed into a set of frequency channels having approximately a constant bandwidth on a logarithmic scale (octave). The measured impulse responses of simple cells do not have an increasing number of cycles for a constant envelope as in a window Fourier transform (see Fig. 6). Rather, they have a support (receptive field) of varying size.

Although some researchers [58] have been using the Gabor transform in computer vision, this decomposition has several drawbacks when applied to image analysis.

We saw that the spatial and frequency resolution of a window Fourier transform is constant. In the spatial domain, the information provided by this decomposition is therefore unlocalized within intervals of size σ_u. The standard deviation σ_u of $g(x)$ defines a resolution of reference. If the signal has a discontinuity such as an edge, with a window Fourier transform, it is difficult to locate this edge with a precision better than σ_u (see Fig. 9). This localization limit is generally not acceptable. If the signal has important features of very different sizes, we cannot define an optimal resolution for analyzing the signal. This is typically the case with images. For example, in the image of a house, the pattern we want to analyze might range from the overall structure of the house to the details on one of the window curtains. With a given window size, it is difficult to analyze both the fine and the large structures. This fixed resolution also introduces misleading high frequencies when decomposing local features. Let $e(x)$ be an edge as shown in Fig. 9, and suppose that

$$e(x) = \begin{cases} 0 & \text{if } x \leq x_0 - \dfrac{\Delta x}{2} \\ \dfrac{1}{2} + \dfrac{1}{2}\sin\left(\dfrac{\pi}{\Delta x}(x - x_0)\right) \\ & \text{if } x_0 - \dfrac{\Delta x}{2} < x < x_0 + \dfrac{\Delta x}{2} \\ 1 & \text{if } x \geq x_0 + \dfrac{\Delta x}{2}. \end{cases}$$

Let us denote $\omega_0 = \pi/\Delta x$. One would expect that at the point x_0, the decomposition coefficients $Ge(\omega, x_0) = \langle e(x), e^{i\omega x} g(x - x_0) \rangle$ decrease very quickly when ω gets larger than ω_0. Indeed, in the neighborhood of x_0, the edge $e(x)$ is a sinusoidal wave of frequency ω_0. In reality, this property does not hold because the edge is very localized and has only half of the sinusoidal wave period. As a consequence, when the frequency ω is large with respect to ω_0, the modulus of the coefficients $Ge(x_0, \omega)$ decreases slowly. Although the signal $e(x)$ is locally a pure sinusoidal wave of frequency ω_0, at a frequency $2\omega_0$, the window Fourier coefficient $|Ge(x_0, 2\omega_0)|$ is still about half the value of $|Ge(x_0, \omega_0)|$. This numerical property makes it hard to interpret the window Fourier coefficients when the features are very localized with respect to the size of the support of $g(x)$. More details about this property can be found in the article of Daubechies [11]. A window Fourier transform is better suited for analyzing signals where all the patterns appear approximately at the same scale.

In order to avoid the inconvenience of a transform having a fixed resolution in the spatial and frequency domains, Morlet defined a decomposition based on dilations. In the next section, we describe the properties of this decomposition which is called the wavelet transform.

C. Definition of a Wavelet Transform

Morlet [20] defined the wavelet transform by decomposing the signal into a family of functions which are the translation and dilation of a unique function $\psi(x)$. The

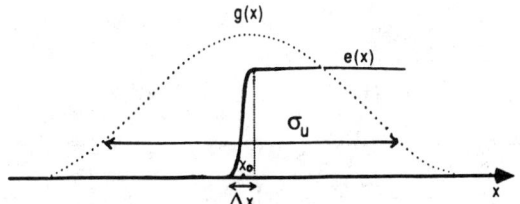

Fig. 9. With a window Fourier transform, a local feature such as an edge $e(x)$ cannot be located with a precision better than the variance σ_u of the window function $g(x)$. Since the variation step Δx of the edge $e(x)$ is small with respect to σ_u, in the neighborhood of x_0, the window Fourier transform of $e(x)$ decreases slowly when the frequency ω gets larger than $\omega_0 = \pi/\Delta x$.

function $\psi(x)$ is called a wavelet and the corresponding wavelet family is given by $(\sqrt{s}\,\psi(s(x - u)))_{(s,u) \in R^2}$. The wavelet transform of a function $f(x) \in L^2(R)$ is defined by

$$Wf(s, u) = \int_{-\infty}^{+\infty} f(x)\sqrt{s}\,\psi(s(x - u))\,dx. \quad (19)$$

The idea behind the wavelet decomposition is not new. It is very much related to some other types of spatial-frequency decompositions such as the Wigner–Ville transform. Some versions of the wavelet transform have been studied independently under other names such as the scale-space decomposition of Witkin [62], and in mathematics its origin can be traced back to be beginning of the century. However, the formalization effort of Morlet and Grossmann [20] opened a broader field of applications and has led to important new mathematical results. Let us denote the dilation of $\psi(x)$ with a factor s by

$$\psi_s(x) = \sqrt{s}\,\psi(sx). \quad (20)$$

A wavelet transform can be rewritten as inner products in $L^2(R)$

$$Wf(s, u) = \langle f(x), \psi_s(x - u) \rangle.$$

It thus corresponds to a decomposition of $f(x)$ on the family of functions $(\psi_s(x - u))_{(s,u) \in R^2}$. As shown in Fig. 10, the functions $\psi_s(x)$ have the same type as $\psi(x)$, but have a support s times smaller. In the following, we suppose that the wavelet $\psi(x)$ and the signal $f(x)$ have real values. As explained later, in order to reconstruct $f(x)$ from its wavelet transform, the Fourier transform $\hat{\psi}(\omega)$ of $\psi(x)$ must satisfy

$$C_\psi = \int_0^{+\infty} \frac{|\hat{\psi}(\omega)|^2}{\omega}\,d\omega < +\infty. \quad (21)$$

This condition implies that $\hat{\psi}(0) = 0$, and that $\hat{\psi}(\omega)$ is small enough in the neighborhood of $\omega = 0$. The function $\psi(x)$ can be interpreted as the impulse response of a bandpass filter. For normalization purposes, we suppose that the energy of $\psi(x)$ is equal to 1. Let us denote $\tilde{\psi}_s(x) = \psi_s(-x)$. We can rewrite the wavelet transform at a point u and a scale s as a convolution product with $\tilde{\psi}_s(x)$

$$Wf(s, u) = f * \tilde{\psi}_s(u). \quad (22)$$

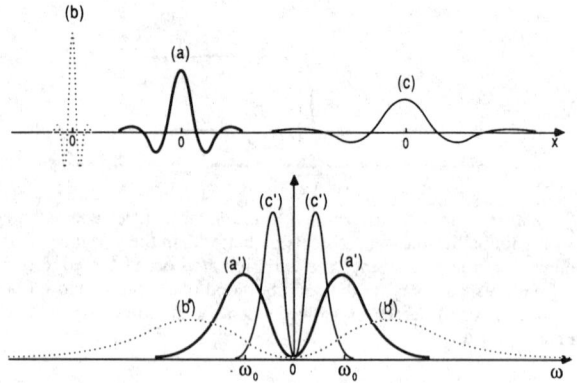

Fig. 10. (a) Graph of a wavelet $\psi(x)$. (b) Graph of $\psi_{s_1}(x)$ for $s_1 > 1$. (c) Graph of $\psi_{s_2}(x)$ for $s_2 < 1$. The curves (a'), (b'), and (c') are, respectively, the Fourier transform of the function shown in (a), (b), and (c). They have the same rms bandwidth on a logarithmic scale.

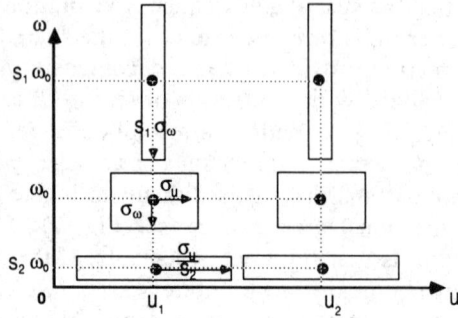

Fig. 11. In the phase-space, the shape of a wavelet resolution cell depends upon the scale. When the scale increases, the resolution increases in the spatial domain and decreases in the frequency domain. The surface of all the resolution cells is the same.

A wavelet transform can therefore be viewed as a filtering of $f(x)$ with a band-pass filter whose impulse response is $\tilde{\psi}_s(x)$. From (20), we derive that the Fourier transform of $\psi_s(x)$ is given by

$$\hat{\psi}_s(\omega) = \frac{1}{\sqrt{s}} \hat{\psi}\left(\frac{\omega}{s}\right).$$

In opposition to a window Fourier transform which has a fixed resolution in the spatial and frequency domain, the resolution of a wavelet transform varies with the scale parameter s. Since $\psi(x)$ is real, $|\hat{\psi}(\omega)| = |\hat{\psi}(-\omega)|$. Let ω_0 be the center of the passing band of $\hat{\psi}(\omega)$

$$\int_0^{+\infty} (\omega - \omega_0)|\hat{\psi}(\omega)|^2 \, d\omega = 0.$$

Let σ_ω be the rms bandwidth around ω_0

$$\sigma_\omega^2 = \int_0^{+\infty} (\omega - \omega_0)^2 |\hat{\psi}(\omega)|^2 \, d\omega.$$

It is clear that the center of the passing band of $\hat{\psi}_s(\omega)$ is $s\omega_0$ and that its rms bandwidth is $s\sigma_\omega$. On a logarithmic scale, the rms bandwidth of $\hat{\psi}_s(\omega)$ is the same for all $s \in \mathbf{R}^+$. Hence, a wavelet transform decomposes the signal into a set of frequency bands having a constant size on a logarithmic scale (see Fig. 10).

Let σ_u be the standard deviation of $|\psi(x)|^2$ around zero. One can also show easily that the wavelet $\psi_s(x - u_0)$ has an energy concentrated around u_0 within a standard deviation σ_u/s. In the frequency domain, we saw that its energy is concentrated around $s\omega_0$ within a standard deviation $s\sigma_\omega$. In the phase-space, the resolution cell of this wavelet is therefore equal to $[u_0 - (\sigma_u/s), u_0 + (\sigma_u/s)] \times [s\omega_0 - s\sigma_\omega, s\omega_0 + s\sigma_\omega]$. As opposed to a window Fourier transform, the shape of the resolution cell varies with the scale s. This is illustrated in Fig. 11. When the scale s is small, the resolution is coarse in the spatial domain and fine in the frequency domain. If the scale s increases, the resolution increases in the spatial domain and decreases in the frequency domain (see Fig. 11). In the next section, we show that this variation of resolution enables the wavelet transform to zoom into the irregularities of the signal and characterize them locally.

For some applications, it can be useful to use a complex wavelet $\psi(s)$ in order to separate a phase and modulus component from the wavelet transform. For this purpose, Morlet and Grossmann are using wavelets whose Fourier transform $\hat{\psi}(\omega)$ is equal to zero for $\omega < 0$ [20]. Such functions are called Hardy functions. The wavelet transform $Wf(s, u)$ is then a complex number. When the scale s is fixed and u varies, the function $Wf(s, u)$ is also a Hardy function. The phase and the modulus of the wavelet transform can easily be separated for any given scale s and position u. Separating the phase and energy component of the wavelet transform signal has found some applications in speech processing [30].

Remark: There is a common misunderstanding in the psychophysiological and computer vision literature around Gabor and wavelet transforms. A Gabor function is a Gaussian modulated by a sinusoidal wave. A Gabor function satisfies the condition (21) and is therefore an admissible wavelet. If we build a transform based on a dilation of this function, it will be a wavelet transform and not a Gabor transform (window Fourier transform). Indeed, in order to define a Gabor transform, we must modify the frequency of the sinusoidal modulation without changing the size of the window function. This is much more than a terminology problem since the properties of a wavelet transform and a Gabor transform are very different.

D. *Properties of a Wavelet Transform*

Morlet and Grossmann [20] have shown that the wavelet transform is an isometry (to a proportionality coefficient) from $L^2(\mathbf{R})$ into $L^2(\mathbf{R}^+ \times \mathbf{R})$

$$\int_{-\infty}^{+\infty} \int_0^{+\infty} |Wf(s, u)|^2 \, ds \, du = C_\psi \int_{-\infty}^{+\infty} |f(x)|^2 \, dx. \tag{23}$$

The constant C_ψ is defined by

$$C_\psi = \int_0^{+\infty} \frac{|\hat{\psi}(s\omega)|^2}{s} \, ds = \int_0^{+\infty} \frac{|\hat{\psi}(\omega)|^2}{\omega} \, d\omega < +\infty.$$

Equation (23) is proved by applying the Parseval theorem and using the definition of $Wf(s, u)$ given in (19). Similarly, we can derive that the reconstruction of $f(x)$ from $Wf(s, u)$ is given by

$$f(x) = \frac{1}{C_\psi} \int_{-\infty}^{+\infty} \int_0^{+\infty} Wf(s, u)\psi_s(x - u) \, ds \, du. \quad (24)$$

Like a window Fourier transform, a wavelet transform is redundant. In other words, the value of $Wf(s', u')$ depends upon the values of $Wf(s, u)$ for $s \neq s'$ and $u \neq u'$. By inserting (24) in the definition (19) of a wavelet transform, one can show that the function $Wf(s, u)$ satisfies the following reproducing kernel equation [21]:

$$\forall (s', u') \in \mathbf{R}^+ \times \mathbf{R}, \quad Wf(s', u')$$
$$= \int_{-\infty}^{+\infty} \int_0^{+\infty} Wf(s, u) K(s, s', u, u') \, ds \, du, \quad (25)$$

where

$$K(s, s', u, u') = \frac{1}{C_\psi} \int_{-\infty}^{+\infty} \psi_s(x - u)\psi_{s'}(x - u') \, dx.$$

$K(s, s', u, u')$ is called a reproducing kernel. It expresses the redundancy between $Wf(s, u)$ and $Wf(s', u')$ for any two pairs of points (s, u) and (s', u'). Equation (25) shows that, a priori, any function $F(s, u) \in L^2(\mathbf{R}^+ \times \mathbf{R})$ is not the wavelet transform of some function $f(x) \in L^2(\mathbf{R})$. One can easily prove that there exists a function $f(x) \in L^2(\mathbf{R})$ such that $F(s, u) = Wf(s, u)$, if and only if

$$\forall (s', u') \in \mathbf{R}^+ \times \mathbf{R}, \quad F(s', u')$$
$$= \int_{-\infty}^{+\infty} \int_0^{+\infty} F(s, u) K(s, s', u, u') \, ds \, du. \quad (26)$$

The function $f(x)$ is then given by

$$f(x) = \frac{1}{C_\psi} \int_{-\infty}^{+\infty} \int_0^{+\infty} F(s, u)\psi_s(x - u) \, dx \, du. \quad (27)$$

The reproducing kernel equation is an important characterization of a wavelet transform that we use later.

The wavelet transform can be discretized by sampling both the scale parameter s and the translation parameter u. In order to build a complete representation, we must cover the phase-space with the resolution cells shown in Fig. 11. This can be done with an exponential sampling of the scale parameter. We first select a sequence of scales $(\alpha^j)_{j \in \mathbf{Z}}$, where α is the elementary dilation step. We saw in (22) that the wavelet transform $Wf(\alpha^j, u)$ can be rewritten

$$Wf(\alpha^j, u) = f * \tilde{\psi}_{\alpha^j}(u). \quad (28)$$

For each scale α^j, $\tilde{\psi}_{\alpha^j}(x)$ has a Fourier transform centered in $\alpha^j \omega_0$ with an rms bandwidth of $\alpha^j \sigma_\omega$. Equation (28) can therefore be interpreted as a decomposition of $f(x)$ in a set of frequency channels centered in $\alpha^j \omega_0$ and whose rms bandwidth is $\alpha^j \sigma_\omega$. In order to characterize the decom-

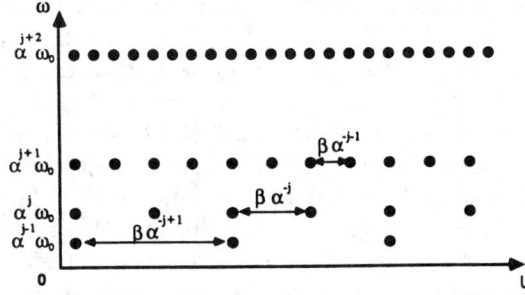

Fig. 12. Sampling of the phase-space corresponding to a discrete wavelet transform (adapted from Daubechies [11]). Each sample corresponds to an inner product with a particular wavelet. This sampling pattern is adapted to the shape of the wavelet resolution cells at the different scales (see Fig. 11).

posed signal in each channel, we must sample it uniformly at a rate proportional to α^j. Let α^j/β be the sampling rate at the scale α^j. The discrete wavelet transformed is defined by

$$W_d f(j, n) = Wf\left(\alpha^j, \frac{n\beta}{\alpha^j}\right) = \int_{-\infty}^{+\infty} f(x)\psi_{\alpha^j}\left(x - \frac{n\beta}{\alpha^j}\right) dx$$
$$= f * \tilde{\psi}_{\alpha^j}\left(\frac{n\beta}{\alpha^j}\right). \quad (29)$$

Fig. 12 illustrates this sampling pattern in the phase-space. When the scale increases, the density of samples increases.

It is not possible to understand the properties of this transform by using the Nyquist theorem since the Fourier transform of $\psi(x)$ does not have a compact support (it is not strictly band-limited). With an approach similar to her study of the discrete window Fourier transform, Daubechies [11] analyzed the main properties of a discrete wavelet transform. She made a clear comparison of these two types of multichannel decompositions from a mathematical point of view. In order to reconstruct a function $f(x)$ from the discrete wavelet transform $(W_d f(j, n))_{(n,j) \in \mathbf{Z}^2}$, the operator

$$L^2(\mathbf{R}) \xrightarrow{W_d} l^2(\mathbf{Z}^2) \quad (30)$$

must be invertible on its range and have a bounded inverse. Since

$$W_d(j, n) = \left\langle f(x), \psi_{\alpha^j}\left(x - \frac{n\beta}{\alpha^j}\right)\right\rangle, \quad (31)$$

the properties of the operator W_d depend upon the family of functions $(\psi_{\alpha^j}(x - (n\beta/\alpha^j)))_{(n,j) \in \mathbf{Z}^2}$. Daubechies [11] studied the properties of this family of functions and gave some necessary and sufficient conditions on α, β, and $\psi(x)$ so that the operator W_d admits a bounded inverse.

A very important class of discrete wavelet transform was found independently by Meyer [45] and Stromberg [55]. They showed that there exist some wavelets $\psi(x) \in L^2(\mathbf{R})$ such that $(\psi_{2^j}(x - (n/2^j)))_{(n,j) \in \mathbf{Z}^2}$ is an orthonormal basis of $L^2(\mathbf{R})$. These particular wavelets are called *orthogonal wavelets*. A wavelet orthonormal basis corresponds to a discrete wavelet transform for $\alpha = 2$ and

$\beta = 1$. Wavelet orthonormal bases can be built for sequences of scales other than $(2^j)_{j \in Z}$, but we will concentrate on dyadic scales which lead to simpler decomposition algorithms. These new orthonormal bases had a striking impact in functional analysis. It was indeed believed that one could not find simple orthonormal bases whose elements have a good localization both in the spatial and frequency domains. Any function can be reconstructed from its decomposition into a wavelet orthonormal basis with the classical expansion formula of a vector into an orthonormal basis

$$f(x) = \sum_{j \in Z} \sum_{n \in Z} \langle f(u), \psi_{2^j}(u - n2^{-j}) \rangle \psi_{2^j}(x - n2^{-j}). \tag{32}$$

The Haar basis is a well-known particular case of wavelet orthonormal basis. The orthogonal wavelet corresponding to the Haar basis is given by

$$\psi(x) = \begin{cases} 1 & \text{if } 0 \leq x < \frac{1}{2} \\ -1 & \text{if } \frac{1}{2} \leq x < 1 \\ 0 & \text{otherwise.} \end{cases} \tag{33}$$

The Haar wavelet is not continuous, which is a major inconvenience for many applications. Meyer [45] showed that we can find some orthogonal wavelets $\psi(x)$ which are infinitely continuously differentiable and whose decay at infinity are faster then any power x^{-n}, $n > 0$. In Section IV-A, we show that the Fourier transform of a large class of orthogonal wavelets can be expressed from the transfer function of a quadrature mirror filter [38]. The decomposition of a function in such a wavelet orthonormal basis can be computed with a quadrature mirror filter bank. Fig. 13 gives the graph of a particular orthogonal wavelet and its Fourier transform. This wavelet is a cubic spline studied independently by Lemarie [32] and Battle [3].

An important property of a wavelet transform is to easily characterize the local regularity of a function. This can have a particularly interesting application for discriminating image textures. In mathematics, it leads to a simple characterization of the classical functional spaces such as the $L^p(R)$ spaces, the Sobolev spaces, the Holder spaces, etc. Let us give an example. One way to measure the local regularity of a function is to measure the lipschitz exponent. A function $f(x)$ is lipschitz α in the neighborhood of a point x_0, if and only if, for any point x in a neighborhood of x_0,

$$|f(x) - f(x_0)| = O(|x - x_0|^\alpha). \tag{34}$$

A function which is differentiable in x_0 is lipschitz 1. The larger the lipschitz coefficient α, the smoother the function is in the neighborhood of x_0. Let us now suppose that the wavelet $\psi(x)$ is continuously differentiable. We also assume that our signal $f(x)$ is continuous and that there exist $\epsilon > 0$ such that $f(x)$ is lipschitz ϵ everywhere. Jaffard [26] proved that for any $\alpha > 0$, one can find whether

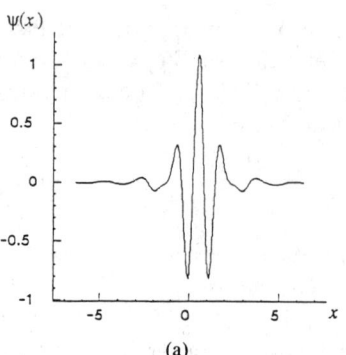

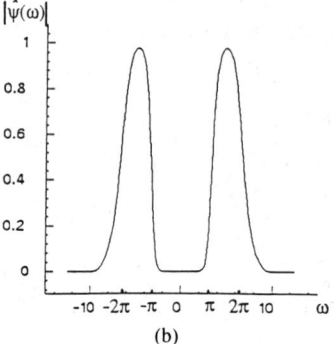

Fig. 13. (a) Example of orthogonal wavelet $\psi(x)$. (b) Modulus of its Fourier transform. The wavelet $\psi(x)$ can be interpreted as the impulse response of a band-pass filter. This particular wavelet is a cubic spline.

$f(x)$ is lipschitz α at x_0 by measuring the decay of wavelet coefficients in the neighborhood of x_0. More precisely, $f(x)$ is lipschitz α at x_0 if and only if

$$\exists C > 0, \quad \forall n \in Z, \quad |\langle f(x), \psi_{2^j}(x - n2^{-j}) \rangle|$$
$$\leq C 2^{-j(1/2 + \alpha)} (1 + |2^j x_0 - n|). \tag{35}$$

The regularity of a function at a point x_0 thus depends upon the decay rate of the wavelet coefficients in the neighborhood of x_0, when the scale increases. Other kinds of regularity, such as the derivability at any order (in the sense of Sobolev), can be derived similarly [33]. These results show that it is necessary to combine the information at different scales in order to analyze the local properties of a function. In the next section, we describe the extension of the wavelet model to two-dimensional signals. We come back to orthonormal wavelets in Section IV-A to explain their relation to the concept of multi-resolution in computer vision.

E. Wavelet Transform in Two Dimensions

The wavelet transform can be generalized in R^n, but we only consider the two-dimensional case for image processing applications. The model can first be extended without distinguishing any spatial orientation. Let $\Psi(x, y) \in L^2(R^2)$ be a function whose Fourier transform $\hat{\Psi}(\omega_x, \omega_y)$ satisfies

$$\forall (\omega_x, \omega_y) \in R^2 \int_0^{+\infty} \frac{|\hat{\Psi}(s\omega_x, s\omega_y)|^2}{s} ds = C_\Psi < +\infty. \tag{36}$$

The value of the integral (36) must be finite and constant for all $(\omega_x, \omega_y) \in R^2$. For example, this property is satisfied for a wavelet $\Psi(x, y)$ which is isotropic ($\Psi(x, y) = \rho(\sqrt{x^2 + y^2})$) and whose Fourier transform is null at the origin ($\hat{\Psi}(0, 0) = 0$). For normalization purposes, we suppose that $\|\Psi\| = 1$. The function $\Psi(x, y)$ can be interpreted as the impulse response of a band-pass filter having no preferential spatial orientation. The wavelet transform of a function $f(x, y) \in L^2(R^2)$ at the scale s and a point (u, v) is defined by

$$Wf(s, (u, v))$$
$$= \int_{-\infty}^{+\infty} \int_{-\infty}^{+\infty} f(x, y) s\Psi(s(x - u), s(y - v)) \, dx \, dy. \quad (37)$$

Let $\Psi_s(x, y) = s\Psi(sx, sy)$ and $\tilde{\Psi}_s(x, y) = \Psi_s(-x, -y)$. The wavelet transform of $f(x, y)$ at the scale s and a point (u, v) can be rewritten as a convolution product

$$Wf(s, (u, v)) = f * \tilde{\Psi}_s(u, v). \quad (38)$$

It can be interpreted as a two-dimensional band-pass filtering with no orientation selectivity. The wavelet transform in two dimensions has the same properties as a one-dimensional wavelet transform. There is an energy conservation equation

$$\int_{-\infty}^{+\infty} \int_{-\infty}^{+\infty} \int_0^{+\infty} |Wf(s, (u, v))|^2 s \, ds \, du \, dv$$
$$= C_\Psi \int_{-\infty}^{+\infty} \int_{-\infty}^{+\infty} |f(x, y)|^2 \, dx \, dy. \quad (39)$$

As in the one-dimensional case, this equation is proved with the Parseval theorem. We can also reconstruct a function $f(x, y)$ from its wavelet transform with a simple two-dimensional extension of (24):

$$f(x, y) = \frac{1}{C_\Psi} \int_{-\infty}^{+\infty} \int_{-\infty}^{+\infty} \int_0^{+\infty} Wf(s, (u, v))$$
$$\cdot \Psi_s(x - u, y - v) s \, ds \, du \, dv. \quad (40)$$

In two dimensions, a wavelet transform also satisfies a reproducing kernel equation similar to (25).

For image recognition applications, it is often necessary to have a decomposition which differentiates the local orientation of the image features. Let us define N wavelet functions $\Psi^i(x, y)$ ($1 \leq i \leq N$) whose Fourier transform $\hat{\Psi}^i(\omega_x, \omega_y)$ satisfies

$$\sum_{i=1}^{N} |\hat{\Psi}^i(\omega_s, \omega_y)|^2 = |\hat{\Psi}(\omega_s, \omega_y)|^2. \quad (41)$$

Fig. 14 shows an example of decomposition of $\hat{\Psi}(\omega_x, \omega_y)$ into the different functions $\hat{\Psi}^i(\omega_x, \omega_y)$. In the example shown in Fig. 14, the decomposition is symmetrical, but this is not a constraint of the model. Each function $\Psi^i(x, y)$ can be viewed as the impulse response of a band-pass filter having a particular orientation tuning. The wavelet

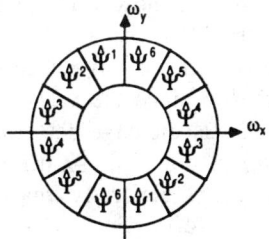

Fig. 14. Decomposition in the Fourier domain of the support of $\hat{\Psi}(\omega_x, \omega_y)$ into 6 wavelets $\hat{\Psi}^i(\omega_x, \omega_y)$ ($1 \leq i \leq 6$) having different orientation selectivities. In this example, the supports of the functions $\hat{\Psi}^i(\omega_x, \omega_y)$ are symmetrical about 0 and are rotated from one another.

transform within the orientation i is defined by

$$W^i f(s, (u, v))$$
$$= \int_{-\infty}^{+\infty} \int_{-\infty}^{+\infty} f(x, y) s\Psi^i(s(x - u), s(y - v)) \, dx \, dy. \quad (42)$$

Let $\Psi_s^i(x, y) = s\Psi^i(sx, sy)$ and $\tilde{\Psi}_s^i(x, y) = \Psi_s^i(-x, -y)$. The wavelet transform of $f(x, y)$ at the scale s and a point (u, v), within the orientation i, can be rewritten

$$W^i f(s, (u, v)) = f * \tilde{\Psi}_s^i(u, v). \quad (43)$$

It can thus be interpreted as a filtering of $f(x, y)$ with a band-pass filter having an orientation selectivity. Similar to (37), the wavelet decomposition in several orientations defines an isometry from $L^2(R^2)$ into $L^2(R^+ \times R^2)$

$$\sum_{i=1}^{N} \int_{-\infty}^{+\infty} \int_{-\infty}^{+\infty} \int_0^{+\infty} |W^i f(s, (u, v))|^2 s \, ds \, du \, dv$$
$$= C_\Psi \int_{-\infty}^{+\infty} \int_{-\infty}^{+\infty} |f(x, y)|^2 \, dx \, dy. \quad (44)$$

We can also reconstruct a function $f(x, y)$ from its wavelet transform decomposed into several directions

$$f(x, y) = \frac{1}{C_\Psi} \sum_{i=1}^{N} \int_{-\infty}^{+\infty} \int_{-\infty}^{+\infty} \int_0^{+\infty} Wf^i(s, (u, v))$$
$$\cdot \Psi_s^i(x - u, y - v) s \, ds \, du \, dv.$$

The discretization of a wavelet transform in two dimensions is similar to the discretization in one dimension. We choose a sequence of scales $(\alpha^j)_{j \in Z}$ where α is the elementary dilation step. For each scale α^j, the translation vector (u, v) is uniformly sampled on a two-dimensional grid at a rate proportional to α^j. In the next section, we study the two-dimensional extension of the orthonormal wavelet decomposition and its implementation.

IV. Computer Vision and Multiresolution Decomposition

Let us now analyze the multiresolution approach to image interpretation. A multiresolution decomposition is also an image decomposition in frequency channels of constant bandwidth on a logarithmic scale. It provides a different perspective on this kind of transform. We describe the classical pyramidal implementation of multiresolution transforms and show how it relates to a discrete wavelet decomposition.

Multiresolution transforms have been thoroughly studied in computer vision since the work of Rosenfeld and Thurston [51] on multiscale edge detection, and the Marr theory of low-level vision [40]. At different resolutions, the details of an image generally characterize different types of physical structures. For example, a coarse resolution satellite image of a coast gives a description of only the overall shape of the coast. When the resolution of the image is increased, we are able to successively distinguish the local relief of the region, and if the resolution gets even finer, we can recognize the different types of local vegetation. In order to process these different structures separately, researchers in computer vision have tried to extract the difference of information between the approximation of an image at two different resolutions. Given a sequence of increasing resolutions $(r_j)_{j \in Z}$, the details of $f(x)$ at the resolution r_j are defined as the difference of information between the approximation of $f(x)$ at the resolution r_{j+1} and the approximation at the resolution r_j.

A multiresolution representation also provides a simple hierarchical framework for interpreting the image information [29]. In some sense, the details of the image at a coarse resolution provide the "context" of the image, whereas the finer details correspond to the particular "modalities." For example, it is difficult to recognize that a small rectangle inside an image is the window of a house if we did not previously recognize the house "context." It is therefore natural to first analyze the image details at a coarse resolution and then increase the resolution. This is called a coarse-to-fine processing strategy. At a coarse resolution, the image details are characterized by very few samples. Hence, the coarse information processing can be performed quickly. The finer details are characterized by more samples, but the prior information, derived from the context, constrains and thus speeds up the computations. With a coarse-to-fine strategy, we process the minimum amount of details which are necessary to perform a recognition task. Indeed, if we can recognize an object from a coarse description, we do not need to analyze the finer details. For example, in order to distinguish a car from a house, the coarse details of the image should be enough. Such a strategy is efficient for pattern recognition algorithms. It has already been widely studied for low-level image processing tasks such as stereo matching and template matching [19], [22].

A. Pyramidal Multiresolution Decompositions

The approximation of a signal $f(x)$ at a resolution r is defined as an estimate of $f(x)$ derived from r measurements per unit length. These measurements are computed by uniformly sampling at a rate r the function $f(x)$ smoothed by a low-pass filter whose bandwidth is proportional to r. In order to be consistent when the resolution varies, these low-pass filters are derived from a unique function $\theta(x)$ which is dilated by the resolution factor $r: \theta_r = \sqrt{r}\theta(rx)$. The set of measurements $A_r f = (f * \theta_r(n/r))_{n \in Z}$ is called a discrete approximation of $f(x)$ at the resolution r. In the following, we study the approximation of a function on a dyadic sequence of resolutions $(2^j)_{j \in Z}$. The discrete approximation of a function $f(x)$ at the resolution 2^j is thus given by

$$A_{2^j} f = \left(f * \theta_{2^j}\left(\frac{n}{2^j}\right) \right)_{n \in Z}. \qquad (45)$$

Tanimoto and Pavlidis [56], Burt [4], and Crowley [10] have developed efficient algorithms to compute the approximation of a function at different resolutions. We first describe these decompositions and then explain the Burt and Crowley algorithms for computing the details at different resolutions. The details are regrouped in a pyramid data structure called a Laplacian pyramid. This simple and elegant algorithm does not define the details from the difference of information between $A_{2^{j+1}} f$ and $A_{2^j} f$. At different resolutions, the details computed with this algorithm are correlated. It is thus difficult to know whether a similarity between the image details at different resolutions is due to a property of the image itself or to the intrinsic redundancy of the representation. We review the multiresolution wavelet model which shows that the difference of information between two successive resolutions can be computed by decomposing the signal in a wavelet orthonormal basis.

In pyramidal multiresolution algorithms, the low-pass filter function $\theta(x)$ is chosen such that its Fourier transform can be written

$$\hat{\theta}(\omega) = \prod_{p=1}^{+\infty} U(e^{-i2^{-p}\omega}), \qquad (46)$$

where $U(e^{-i\omega})$ is the transfer function of a low-pass discrete filter $U = (u_n)_{n \in Z}$. Daubechies [11] studied the regularity and decay at infinity of the function $\theta(x)$ depending upon the properties of the filter $U(e^{-i\omega})$. In general, we want to have a function $\theta(x)$ which is as smooth as possible and which is well concentrated around 0 in the spatial domain.

Let us suppose that we have already computed the discrete approximation of a function $f(x) \in L^2(R)$ at the resolution $2^{j+1}: A_{2^{j+1}} f = (f * \theta_{2^{j+1}}(n/2^{j+1}))_{n \in Z}$. One can show [4], [11], [38] that the discrete approximation of $f(x)$ at a resolution 2^j is calculated by filtering $A_{2^{j+1}} f$ with the discrete low-pass filter $U = (u_n)_{n \in Z}$ and keeping every other sample of the convolution product. Let $\Lambda = (\lambda_n)_{n \in Z}$ be such that

$$\Lambda = A_{2^{j+1}} f * U, \qquad (47)$$

then

$$A_{2^j} f = (\lambda_{2n})_{n \in Z}. \qquad (48)$$

A measuring device provides the approximation of an input signal at a finite resolution. Let us suppose for normalization purposes that this resolution is equal to one. The approximation of this signal at any resolution 2^{-J}, J

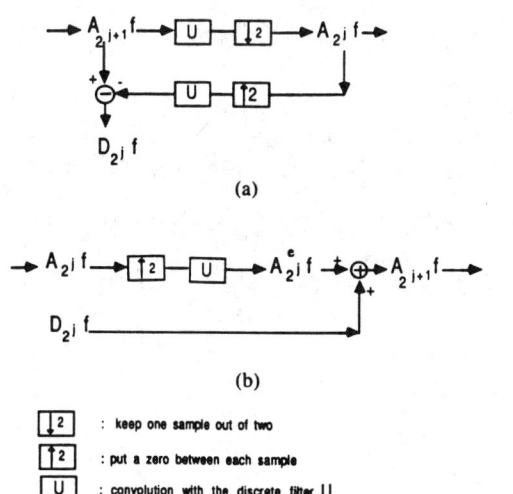

Fig. 15. (a) Decomposition of $A_{2^{j+1}}f$ into $A_{2^j}f$ and $D_{2^j}f$ when computing a Laplacian pyramid. (b) Reconstruction of $A_{2^{j+1}}f$ from $A_{2^j}f$ and $D_{2^j}f$ when reconstructing the original signal from a Laplacian pyramid.

> 0, can be computed by iterating on (47) and (48), and j varying between 0 and $J + 1$. This pyramidal algorithm is illustrated in Fig. 15(a). The set of discrete approximations $(A_{2^j}f)_{0 \geq j \geq -J}$ was called a Gaussian pyramid by Burt [4].

We now describe the algorithm of Burt [4] and Crowley [10] in order to extract the details of $f(x)$ which appear in $A_{2^{j+1}}f$ but not in $A_{2^j}f$. The discrete approximation $A_{2^{j+1}}f$ has twice as many samples as $A_{2^j}f$, so we first expand $A_{2^j}f$ by a factor of two. This is performed with a classical interpolation procedure [9]. We put a zero between each sample of $A_{2^j}f$ and filter the resulting signal with a low-pass filter. In this algorithm, the low-pass filter is the filter U defined previously. Let $A_{2^j}^e f$ be the expanded discrete signal. The details $D_{2^j}f$ at the resolution 2^j are then computed by subtracting $A_{2^j}^e f$ from $A_{2^{j+1}}f$

$$D_{2^j}f = A_{2^{j+1}}f - A_{2^j}^e f. \quad (49)$$

This algorithm decomposes a discrete approximation $A_1 f$ at a resolution of 1 into an approximation $A_{2^{-J}}f$ at a coarse resolution 2^{-J} and the successive detail signals $(D_{2^j}f)_{0 < j \leq -J}$. If the signal $A_1 f$ has N nonzero samples, each detail signal $D_{2^j}f$ has $2^{j+1}N$ samples, whereas the coarse signal $A_{2^{-J}}f$ has $2^{-J}N$ samples. Hence, the total number of samples of this representation is approximately $2N$. The signals $\{A_{2^{-J}}f, (D_{2^j}f)_{0 < j \leq -J}\}$ are regrouped in a data structure called a Laplacian pyramid [4].

The original signal can easily be reconstructed from such a decomposition. At each resolution, we compute $A_{2^{j+1}}f$ by expanding $A_{2^j}f$ by a factor two and adding the details $D_{2^j}f$. By repeating this algorithm when j is varying between $-J$ and 0, we reconstruct $A_1 f$. The reconstruction algorithm is illustrated by a block diagram in Fig. 15(b).

In two dimensions, the discrete approximation of a signal $f(x, y) \in L^2(R^2)$ at the resolution 2^j is similarly defined by

$$A_{2^j}f = (f * \Theta_{2^j}(2^{-j}n, 2^{-j}m))_{(n,m) \in Z^2}, \quad (50)$$

where $\Theta(x, y)$ is a two-dimensional low-pass filter, and $\Theta_{2^j}(x, y) = 2^j \Theta(2^j x, 2^j y)$. For image processing, the pyramidal algorithm is extended with separable convolutions along the rows and columns of the image [4]. The low-pass filter $\Theta(x, y)$ is chosen such that its Fourier transform can be written

$$\hat{\Theta}(\omega_x, \omega_y) = \prod_{p=1}^{+\infty} U(e^{-i2^{-p}\omega_x}) U(e^{-i2^{-p}\omega_y}).$$

Let us suppose that the video camera provides an image approximated at the resolution 1: $A_1 f = (f * \Theta(n, m))_{(n,m) \in Z^2}$. With a separable extension of the algorithm described in (47) and (48), we can compute the approximation of an image at any resolutions 2^j, ($j < 0$). Fig. 16 shows an image approximated at the resolution 2^j for $0 \geq j \geq -3$ (Gaussian pyramid). The detail signals $(D_{2^j}f)_{0 < j \leq -3}$ can also be computed with a straightforward extension of the one-dimensional algorithm. Fig. 17 shows the Laplacian pyramid of the image given in Fig. 16. If the original image has N^2 pixels, each detail image $D_{2^j}f$ has $2^{j+1}N^2$ pixels and $A_{2^{-j}}f$ has $2^{-J}N^2$ pixels. Hence, the total number of pixels of this representation is approximately $\frac{4}{3}N^2$.

In a Laplacian pyramid, the signals $D_{2^j}f$ do not correspond to the difference of information between $A_{2^{j+1}}f$ and $A_{2^j}f$. If they did, the total number of pixels representing the signal would be the same as in the original signal. We saw that the number of samples representing the signal is increased by a factor of 2 in one dimension and by a factor of $\frac{4}{3}$ in two dimensions. This is due to the correlation between the detail signals $D_{2^j}f$ at different resolutions. The correlation can be understood and suppressed with the multiresolution wavelet model described in [39] and [38]. It is indeed possible to extract exactly the difference of information between $A_{2^{j+1}}f$ and $A_{2^j}f$ by decomposing the signal into a wavelet orthonormal basis.

Let us first explain the multiresolution wavelet model in one dimension. We saw in (45) that the discrete approximation of a function $f(x)$ at the resolution 2^j is defined by $A_{2^j}f = (f * \theta_{2^j}(2^{-j}n))_{n \in Z}$. Let us denote $\bar{\theta}_{2^j}(x) = \theta_{2^j}(-x)$. Each convolution product in a point can be rewritten as an inner product in $L^2(R)$

$$A_{2^j}f = (\langle f(x), \bar{\theta}_{2^j}(x - 2^{-j}n) \rangle)_{n \in Z}. \quad (51)$$

Let us call the *continuous approximation* of $f(x)$ at the resolution of 2^j the best estimate of $f(x)$ given the sequence of inner products $A_{2^j}f$. By "best" we mean as close as possible to $f(x)$ with respect to the $L^2(R)$ distance (mean square distance). One can easily derive from the projection theorem that this best estimate is equal to the orthogonal projection of $f(x)$ on the vector space V_{2^j} generated by the family of functions $(\bar{\theta}_{2^j}(x - 2^{-j}n))_{n \in Z}$. The vector space V_{2^j} can be viewed as the set of all possible approximations of functions at the resolution 2^j. The sequence of vector spaces $(V_{2^j})_{j \in Z}$ is called a *multiresolution approximation* of $L^2(R)$. The proper-

Fig. 16. Gaussian pyramid. The image is approximated at the resolutions $1, \frac{1}{2}, \frac{1}{4},$ and $\frac{1}{8}$. As the resolution decreases, higher resolution details are lost and the image is characterized by fewer pixels.

Fig. 17. Laplacian pyramid. This figure shows the detail images at the resolution $\frac{1}{2}, \frac{1}{4}, \frac{1}{8}$ and the coarse image approximated at the resolution $\frac{1}{8}$. At each resolution, the pixels of the detail image have a large amplitude when the original image is not "smooth" at the corresponding location.

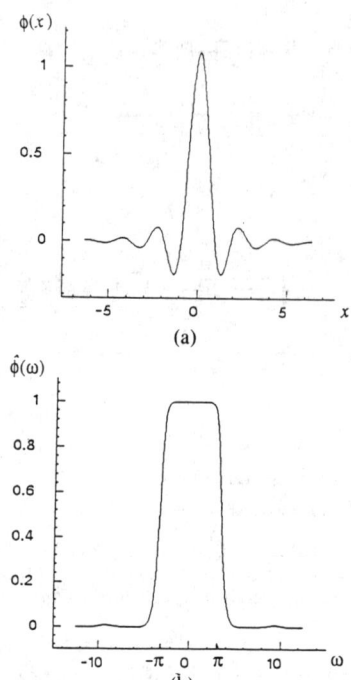

Fig. 18. (a) Example of scaling function $\phi(x)$. (b) Fourier transform $\hat{\phi}(\omega)$. A scaling function can be interpreted as the impulse response of a low-pass filter. The computation of this particular function is described in [38]. The corresponding orthogonal wavelet is shown in Fig. 13.

ties of the vector space V_{2^j} are further studied in [38] and [39]. For any function $f(x) \in L^2(R)$, the continuous approximation of $f(x)$ at the resolution 2^j is thus given by the orthogonal projection of $f(x)$ on V_{2^j}. In order to compute this approximation, we need an orthonormal basis of V_{2^j}. One can show [39] that we can build such an orthonormal basis by dilating and translating a particular function $\phi(x)$ called a *scaling function*. For any resolution 2^j, let us denote $\phi_{2^j}(x) = \sqrt{2^j}\phi(2^j x)$. The family of functions $(\phi_{2^j}(x - 2^{-j}n))_{n \in Z}$ is then an orthonormal basis of V_{2^j}. The Fourier transform of $\phi(x)$ is characterized by

$$\hat{\phi}(\omega) = \prod_{p=1}^{+\infty} H(e^{-i 2^{-p}\omega}), \qquad (52)$$

where $H(e^{-i\omega})$ is the transfer function of a discrete filter [39]. One can show that $H(e^{-i\omega})$ satisfies the condition

$$|H(e^{-i\omega})|^2 + |H(-e^{-i\omega})|^2 = 1. \qquad (53)$$

The discrete filters $H = (h_n)_{n \in Z}$ whose transfer function satisfy (53) are called *quadrature mirror* filters [14].

The orthogonal projection of a function $f(x) \in L^2(R)$ on V_{2^j} can now be computed by decomposing $f(x)$ into the orthonormal basis $(\phi_{2^j}(x - 2^{-j}n))_{n \in Z}$. Let $P_{V_{2^j}}$ be the orthogonal projection operator on V_{2^j}:

$$P_{V_{2^j}}(f)(x) = \sum_{n \in Z} \langle f(u), \phi_{2^j}(u - 2^{-j}n) \rangle \phi_{2^j}(x - 2^{-j}n). \qquad (54)$$

Let us denote $\tilde{\phi}(x) = \phi(-x)$. Since $\phi(x)$ is a low-pass filter, we can redefine the discrete approximation $A_{2^j}f$ with the function $\tilde{\phi}(x)$ instead of $\theta(x)$

$$\begin{aligned} A_{2^j}f &= (f * \tilde{\phi}_{2^j}(2^{-j}n))_{n \in Z} \\ &= (\langle f(x), \phi_{2^j}(x - 2^{-j}n) \rangle)_{n \in Z}. \end{aligned} \qquad (55)$$

The best estimate of $f(x)$ can easily be derived from this discrete approximation by using (54). Let $\tilde{H}$ be the discrete filter whose impulse response is $(h_{-n})_{n \in Z}$. From (52) and (55), one can show [38] that the discrete approximations, $A_{2^j}f$, are computed with the same pyramidal algorithm described in (47) and (48), by using the discrete filter $\tilde{H}$ instead of U. Fig. 18 gives the graph of a scaling function $\phi(x)$.

Let us now explain how to extract exactly the difference of information between the approximations of a function at the resolutions 2^j and 2^{j+1}. The approximations of a function $f(x) \in L^2(R)$ at the resolutions 2^j and 2^{j+1} are given by the orthogonal projection of $f(x)$ on the vector spaces V_{2^j} and $V_{2^{j+1}}$, respectively. Intuitively, the approximation at the resolution 2^{j+1} must give a better estimate of $f(x)$ than the approximation at the resolution 2^j. Hence, the vector spaces V_{2^j} and $V_{2^{j+1}}$ should satisfy

$$V_{2^j} \subset V_{2^{j+1}}. \qquad (56)$$

The difference of information between the approximations at the resolutions 2^j and 2^{j+1} is therefore equal to the orthogonal projection of $f(x)$ on the orthogonal complement of V_{2^j} in $V_{2^{j+1}}$. Let O_{2^j} be this orthogonal complement. The vector space O_{2^j} is orthogonal to V_{2^j} and satisfies

$$O_{2^j} \oplus V_{2^j} = V_{2^{j+1}}.$$

To compute the orthogonal projection of a function $f(x)$ on O_{2^j}, we need to find an orthonormal basis of O_{2^j}. One can show [39] that such an orthonormal basis can be built by dilating and translating a particular wavelet $\psi(x)$. For any resolution 2^j, let us denote $\psi_{2^j}(x) = \sqrt{2^j}\psi(2^j x)$. The family of functions $(\psi_{2^j}(x - 2^{-j}n))_{n \in Z}$ is then an orthonormal basis of O_{2^j}. The Fourier transform of $\psi(x)$ is given by

$$\hat{\psi}(2\omega) = G(e^{-i\omega})\hat{\phi}(\omega)$$
$$\text{with } G(e^{-i\omega}) = e^{-i\omega}\overline{H(e^{-i\omega})}. \quad (57)$$

$G(e^{-i\omega})$ is the transfer function of a discrete filter $G = (g_n)_{n \in Z}$. The filters G and H make a pair of quadrature mirror filters [54].

When the resolution 2^j varies between 0 and $+\infty$, the family of functions $(\psi_{2^j}(x - 2^{-j}n))_{(n,j) \in Z^2}$ constitutes a wavelet orthonormal basis of $L^2(R)$ [39]. This shows that the multiresolution concept and quadrature mirror filters are directly related to wavelet orthonormal bases.

Let $P_{O_{2^j}}f(x)$ be the orthonormal projection of a function $f(x) \in L^2(R)$ on the vector space O_{2^j}. $P_{O_{2^j}}f(x)$ gives the difference of information between the approximations of $f(x)$ at the resolutions of 2^j and 2^{j+1}. It can be computed by expanding $f(x)$ in the orthonormal basis of O_{2^j}

$$P_{O_{2^j}}f(x) = \sum_{n \in Z} \langle f(u), \psi_{2^j}(u - 2^{-j}n) \rangle \psi_{2^j}(x - 2^{-j}n). \quad (58)$$

This difference of information is characterized by the set of inner products

$$D_{2^j}f = (\langle f(x), \psi_{2^j}(x - 2^{-j}n) \rangle)_{n \in Z}. \quad (59)$$

Let $\tilde{G}$ be the filter whose impulse response is given by $\tilde{G} = (g_{-n})_{n \in Z}$. From (55), (57), and (59), one can derive that $D_{2^j}f$ is computed by filtering $A_{2^j}f$ with $\tilde{G}$ and keeping every other sample of the convolution product [38]. This algorithm is illustrated by the block diagram shown in Fig. 19(a); it is essentially similar to a quadrature mirror filter bank decomposition [14].

Let us now describe a simple two-dimensional extension of the one-dimensional multiresolution wavelet model. We saw that a separable multiresolution representation is computed by filtering the signal with a low-pass filter $\Theta(x, y) = \theta(x)\theta(y)$ [(50)]. Let $\tilde{\Theta}(x, y) = \Theta(-x, -y)$. The discrete approximation of a function $f(x, y) \in L^2(R^2)$ at the resolution 2^j can also be rewritten

$$A_{2^j}f = (\langle f(x, y),$$
$$\tilde{\Theta}_{2^j}(x - 2^{-j}n, y - 2^{-j}m) \rangle)_{(n,m) \in Z^2}. \quad (60)$$

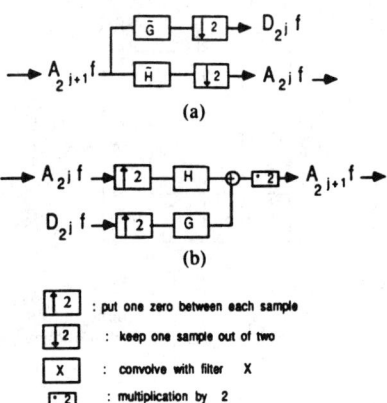

Fig. 19. (a) Decomposition of $A_{2^{j+1}}f$ into $A_{2^j}f$ and $D_{2^j}f$ when computing an orthogonal wavelet representation. The filters H and G make a pair of quadrature mirror filters. (b) Reconstruction of $A_{2^{j+1}}f$ from $A_{2^j}f$ and $D_{2^j}f$ when reconstructing the original signal from an orthogonal wavelet representation.

The extension of the one-dimensional model is straightforward. The best estimate of $f(x, y)$ given the inner products of $A_{2^j}f$ is equal to the orthogonal projection of $f(x, y)$ on the vector space V_{2^j} generated by the family of functions

$$(\tilde{\Theta}_{2^j}(x - 2^{-j}n, y - 2^{-j}m))_{(n,m) \in Z^2}. \quad (61)$$

The sequence of vector spaces $(V_{2^j})_{j \in Z}$ is called a multiresolution approximation of $L^2(R^2)$. Similarly to the one-dimensional model, the difference of information between the approximation of a signal $f(x, y)$ at the resolutions 2^j and 2^{j+1} is equal to the orthogonal projection of $f(x, y)$ on the orthogonal complement O_{2^j} of V_{2^j} in $V_{2^{j+1}}$. We can build [45] an orthonormal basis of O_{2^j} by scaling and translating three wavelets: $\Psi^1(x, y)$, $\Psi^2(x, y)$, and $\Psi^3(x, y)$. Let us denote $\Psi^i_{2^j}(x, y) = 2^j \Psi^i(2^j x, 2^j y)$ for $1 \leq i \leq 3$. The family of functions

$$\begin{Bmatrix} 2^{-j}\Psi^1_{2^j}(x - 2^{-j}n, y - 2^{-j}m) \\ 2^{-j}\Psi^2_{2^j}(x - 2^{-j}n, y - 2^{-j}m) \\ 2^{-j}\Psi^3_{2^j}(x - 2^{-j}n, y - 2^{-j}m) \end{Bmatrix}_{(n,m) \in Z^2} \quad (62)$$

is an orthonormal basis of O_{2^j}. When the resolution 2^j varies between 0 and $+\infty$, the family of functions

$$\begin{Bmatrix} 2^{-j}\Psi^1_{2^j}(x - 2^{-j}n, y - 2^{-j}m) \\ 2^{-j}\Psi^2_{2^j}(x - 2^{-j}n, y - 2^{-j}m) \\ 2^{-j}\Psi^3_{2^j}(x - 2^{-j}n, y - 2^{-j}m) \end{Bmatrix}_{(n,m,j) \in Z^3} \quad (63)$$

is a wavelet orthonormal basis of $L^2(R^2)$. Fig. 20 shows approximately the frequency support of the three wavelets $\Psi^1(x, y)$, $\Psi^2(x, y)$, $\Psi^3(x, y)$. Each wavelet $\Psi^i(x, y)$ can be interpreted as the impulse response of a band-pass filter having a specific orientation selectivity. This corresponds to a particular case of oriented two-dimensional discrete wavelet transform.

In two dimensions, the difference of information between the approximations $A_{2^{j+1}}f$ and $A_{2^j}f$ is therefore

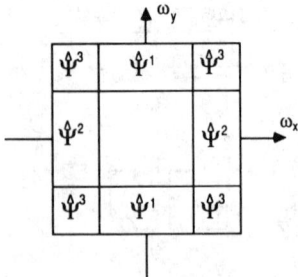

Fig. 20. Approximate repartition of the frequency support of $\hat{\Psi}^1(\omega_x, \omega_y)$, $\hat{\Psi}^2(\omega_x, \omega_y)$, and $\hat{\Psi}^3(\omega_x, \omega_y)$ in the frequency plane.

characterized by the sequences of inner products

$$D^1_{2^j}f = (\langle f(x, y), \Psi^1_{2^j}(x - 2^{-j}n, y - 2^{-j}m)\rangle)_{(n,m)\in Z^2},$$

$$D^2_{2^j}f = (\langle f(x, y), \Psi^2_{2^j}(x - 2^{-j}n, y - 2^{-j}m)\rangle)_{(n,m)\in Z^2},$$

$$D^3_{2^j}f = (\langle f(x, y), \Psi^3_{2^j}(x - 2^{-j}n, y - 2^{-j}m)\rangle)_{(n,m)\in Z^2}.$$

Each of these sequences of inner products can be considered as an image. $D^1_{2^j}f$ gives the vertical higher frequencies (horizontal edges), $D^2_{2^j}f$ gives the horizontal higher frequencies (vertical edges), and $D^3_{2^j}f$ gives the higher frequencies in both directions (corners) (see Fig. 21). Let us suppose that initially we have an image $A_1 f$ measured at the resolution 1. For any $J > 0$, this discrete image can be decomposed between the resolutions 1 and 2^{-J}, and completely represented by the $3J + 1$ discrete images

$$(A_{2^{-J}}f, (D^1_{2^j}f)_{-J\leq j\leq -1}, (D^2_{2^j}f)_{-J\leq j\leq -1},$$
$$(D^3_{2^j}f)_{-J\leq j\leq -1}).$$

This set of images is called an *orthogonal wavelet representation* in two dimensions [38]. The image $A_{2^{-J}}f$ is a coarse approximation, and the images $D^i_{2^j}f$ give the image details for different orientations and resolutions. If the original image has N^2 pixels, each image $A_{2^j}f$, $D^1_{2^j}f$, $D^2_{2^j}f$, $D^3_{2^j}f$ has $2^j \cdot N^2$ pixels ($j < 0$). The total number of pixels of an orthogonal wavelet representation is therefore equal to N^2. It does not increase the volume of data. This is due to the orthogonality of the representation.

A wavelet representation can be computed with a separable extension of the algorithm illustrated in Fig. 19(a) [38]. This extension corresponds to a separable quadrature mirror filter decomposition as described by Woods [63]. Fig. 21(b) gives the wavelet representation of the image in Fig. 16. From this representation, we can reconstruct the original image with a two-dimensional separable extension of the algorithm illustrated in Fig. 19(b) [38]. Fig. 21(c) is the reconstructed image from the wavelet representation shown in Fig. 21(b). The reconstruction is numerically stable. It enables us to use this type of rep-

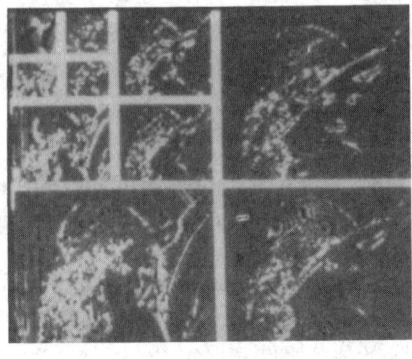

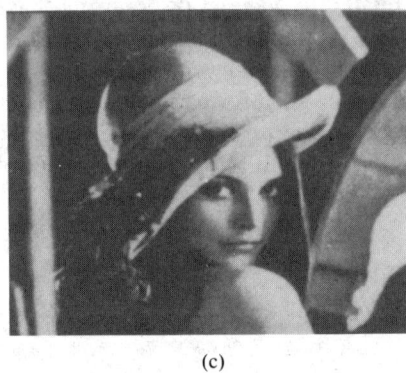

Fig. 21. (a) Labeling of the detail images shown in the wavelet representation. (b) Orthogonal wavelet representation of the lady image for $J = 3$. At a given resolution, each detail image corresponds to a particular spatial orientation tuning. (c) Reconstruction of the original image from the orthogonal wavelet representation. The reconstruction is numerically stable.

resentation for image coding. A more general nonseparable extension of the wavelet model was studied by Meyer [43]. Such extensions are, however, more difficult to implement and are computationally more expensive.

B. Applications of Multiresolution Transforms

The wavelet model gives a precise understanding of the concept of multiresolution by introducing the sequence of vector spaces $(V_{2^j})_{j\in Z}$. A noncorrelated multiresolution representation can be built by decomposing the signal into a wavelet orthonormal basis. A difficult problem when using a multiresolution representation for analyzing a scene is to relate the details appearing at different resolutions. Many ad hoc techniques have been developed for this purpose. We saw in Section III-D that the local regularity of a function is provided by the decay rate of the wavelet coefficients when the resolution increases. These theorems give a first approach for comparing the value of the decomposition at different resolutions.

Multiband image decompositions are also well adapted for coding images because it is possible to match the human visual system sensitivity and take advantage of the intrinsic statistical properties of images. The contrast sensitivity function (Fig. 3) shows that the sensitivity of human vision depends upon the frequency of the stimulus. We want to quantize each frequency band with the minimum number of bits, and at the same time try to reconstruct the best possible image for the human visual perception. For this purpose, we adapt the quantization noise to the human sensitivity along each frequency band. The more sensitive the human system, the less quantization noise is introduced. This enables us to introduce a minimum amount of perceivable distortion in the reconstructed image. Watson has done some particularly detailed psychophysical experiments to test this type of approach for image coding [60].

The statistical properties of images give another reason for using multiband decompositions in image coding. It is well known that the intensity of images is locally correlated. Predictive codings have been particularly successful to compress the number of bits used in coding an image. The wavelet coefficients give a measure of the local contrast at different scales. Since the image intensity is locally correlated, these local contrasts generally have a small amplitude [38]. We can take advantage of this property for coding the wavelet coefficients on fewer bits without introducing any noticeable distortion. As explained in the previous section, a wavelet orthogonal representation can also be imterpreted as a decomposition into a quadrature mirror filter bank. Several studies in image processing have already shown the efficiency of these filter banks for data compression [1], [63].

In order to use a multiresolution representation for pattern recognition applications, we must be able to build models of patterns within the multiresolution representation. The patterns might be located anywhere in the image. Hence, the models must be independent from the pattern location. When a pattern is translated, its model should only be translated but not modified. Let us show that a multiresolution representation does not verify this translation property. To simplify the explanation, we consider the particular case of a one-dimensional orthogonal wavelet decomposition. At the resolution 2^j, the details of a signal $f(x) \in L^2(R)$ are defined by

$$D_{2^j} f = (\langle f(x), \Psi_{2^j}(x - 2^{-j}n) \rangle)_{n \in Z}.$$

$D_{2^j} f$ can be expressed as a uniform sampling of the wavelet transform at the scale 2^j

$$D_{2^j} f = (Wf(2^j, 2^{-j}n))_{n \in Z}.$$

Let $g(x) = f(x - \tau)$ be a translation of $f(x)$ by τ. Since a wavelet transform can be written as a convolution product [(22)], it is shift invariant

$$Wg(2^j, u) = Wf(2^j, u - \tau).$$

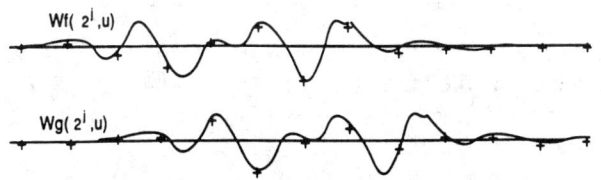

Fig. 22. This drawing shows that the sampling of a wavelet transform (given by the crosses) can be very different after translating the signal. The wavelet transform is translated but the sampling does not translate if the translation is not proportional to the sampling interval (adapted from [37]).

However, the sampling of $Wg(2^j, u)$ does not correspond to a translation of the sampling of $Wf(2^j, u)$ unless $\tau = k2^{-j}$, $k \in Z$ (see Fig. 22).

This distortion through translation implies that the wavelet coefficients of a pattern at the resolution 2^j depend upon the position of the pattern modulo 2^{-j}. This property is inherent to the notion of resolution. Indeed, at the resolution 2^j, we cannot measure anything smaller than 2^{-j} so we cannot represent a displacement smaller than 2^{-j}. One can find the same problem in all the pyramidal multiresolution representations and any uniform sampling of a wavelet transform.

A first solution to this translation problem is to sample the wavelet transform $Wf(2^j, u)$ at a rate much larger than 2^j. The samples then translate approximately when the signal translates. However, this solution considerably increases the redundancy of the representation and the translation is still not perfect. This technique is often adopted for pattern recognition algorithms based on pyramid decompositions. A second solution consists of defining a representation based on an adaptive sampling of the functions $Wf(2^j, u)$ which translates when the signal translates.

V. Zero Crossings of Multifrequency Channels

In the previous sections we studied the properties of the decomposition of a function into multifrequency channels of constant size on a logarithmic scale. We saw that such a decomposition can be interpreted as a wavelet transform. We then described the properties and applications of a discrete wavelet transform built from a uniform sampling of the continuous wavelet transform. However, we showed that such a discretization is difficult to use for pattern recognition applications because it is not invariant through translation. Here, we review the characterization of a signal from the zero crossings of a wavelet transform. Such a characterization defines a discrete representation which translates when the signal translates.

If a function $f(x)$ is translated, for each scale s, the function $Wf(s, u)$ is translated along the parameter u. Hence, the zero crossings of $Wf(s, u)$ are translated as well. Let us suppose that $\psi(x)$ is equal to the second derivative of a smoothing function $\xi(x)$

$$\psi(x) = \xi''(x).$$

A smoothing function is a function which can be interpreted as the impulse response of a low-pass filter. Any zero crossing of $Wf(s, u)$ corresponds to a point of abrupt change in the function $f(x)$ smoothed by $\xi_s(x) = \sqrt{s}\xi(sx)$. Indeed, if $\psi(x) = \xi''(x)$

$$Wf(s, u) = f * \tilde{\psi}_s(u) = s^2(f * \xi_s)''(u).$$

Hence, a zero crossing of $Wf(s, u)$ is an inflection point of the function $f(x)$ smoothed by $\xi_s(x)$. Fig. 23 illustrates this on a straight edge. This zero-crossing detection is a standard edge finding operation in computer vision [41].

Let us now study the completeness of stability of such a representation. Is it possible to reconstruct $f(x)$ from the zero crossings of $Wf(s, u)$? We know that a wavelet transform $Wf(s, u)$ defines a stable and complete representation of $f(x)$. It is therefore equivalent to study the reconstruction of $Wf(s, u)$ from its own zero crossings. If the function $Wf(s, u)$ was a priori any function of $L^2(R^+ \times R)$, it is clear that such a reconstruction would not be possible. Indeed, for a given set of zero crossings, there is an infinite number of functions in $L^2(R^+ \times R)$ whose zero crossings correspond to this set. However, we saw that a wavelet transform $Wf(s, u)$ is not any function of $L^2(R^+ \times R)$. It verifies the constraint of the reproducing kernel [(25)]. We must therefore study whether the constraint of the reproducing kernel plus the information on the zero-crossing positions is enough to have a stable characterization of $Wf(s, u)$.

An interesting particular case of wavelet transform consists of choosing a wavelet equal to the Laplacian of a Gaussian. Since a Gaussian is a smoothing function, the zero crossings of such a wavelet transform can also be interpreted as signal edges [41]. In this particular case, the intrinsic redundancy of the wavelet transform $Wf(s, u)$ can be expressed with the differential equation of heat diffusion [29]. By applying the maximum principles to the solutions of the heat differential equation, Hummel [24] proved that a function $f(x)$ is indeed characterized by the zero crossings of $Wf(s, u)$. However, Hummel also showed that this characterization is not stable. So a slight perturbation of the zero crossings may correspond a substantial perturbation of the high frequencies of the reconstructed function. Reconstruction algorithms have been developed on images by Sanz and Huang [53] as well as Zeevi and Rotem [64]. These reconstruction algorithms are iterative. They were not able to reconstruct the image perfectly in both cases. Hummel and Moniot [25] tried to stabilize the zero-crossings representation by also recording the value of the gradient of $Wf(s, u)$ along each zero crossing. By adding the gradient information, they have shown experimentally that one can then compute a stable reconstruction of $f(x)$ from the zero crossings of $Wf(s, u)$. In this algorithm, the position of the zero crossings and the value of the gradients are kept along a uniform sequence of scales: $(j\alpha)_{j \in Z}$ with $\alpha > 0$. Such a sequence is much more dense than the dyadic sequences $(2^j)_{j \in Z}$ used when we discretized the wavelet transform.

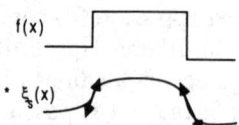

Fig. 23. The zero crossings of a wavelet transform provide the location of the inflection points (edges) of $f * \xi_s(x)$ (adapted from [37]).

Another way to stabilize a zero-crossing representation is to record the energy of $Wf(s, u)$ between two consecutive zero crossings appearing at the same scale [37]. This energy preserves an $L^2(R)$ structure to the zero-crossing representation. In particular, we can then define an $L^2(R)$ distance for pattern recognition applications. By keeping the position of the zero crossings of $Wf(s, u)$ and the local energies only along a dyadic sequence of scales $(2^j)_{j \in Z}$, we showed that the original signal can be reconstructed exactly in few iterations [37]. The reconstruction uses the reproducing kernel equation which is valid for any type of wavelet transform. We believe that the mathematical tools developed within the wavelet model give a simpler approach for analyzing the zero-crossing problem. From a practical point of view, the reconstruction algorithm developed from the reproducing kernel is simple to implement in both one and two dimensions and converges quickly (about 10 iterations).

Representations based on zero crossings of multifrequency channels are still not well understood. They are built with a nonlinear transform which is difficult to model. However, they have very good potential for pattern characterization. They characterize the position of the signal edges and are translation invariant.

VI. Conclusion

In this paper, we reviewed the application of multifrequency decompositions to image processing from several viewpoints. We covered some psychophysical and physiological data showing that such a decomposition seems to be implemented in the human visual cortex. We then described the mathematical properties of these decompositions. We first reviewed the properties of a window Fourier transform and explained why this decomposition is not convenient for analyzing signals such as images. We then introduced the wavelet transform and described its most important properties. Although the goal of this paper was not to build any psychophysiological model of the human visual system, it would be interesting to further investigate the relevance of the wavelet model to some low-level processes in the visual cortex.

In computer vision, multifrequency channel decompositions are interpreted through the concept of multiresolution. We described the classical pyramidal multiresolution algorithms and the wavelet approach to multiresolution decompositions. This model shows that the difference of information between the approximation of a function at two different resolutions is computed by decomposing the function into a wavelet orthonormal basis. We also explained the relationship between orthonormal wavelets and quadrature mirror filters. We can compute the decomposition of a function into a wavelet orthonormal basis with a quadrature mirror filter bank. A third motivation for using multiband decomposition is due to the intrinsic statistical properties of images. Images have a relatively simple decomposition into frequency subbands. These bands can be coded on fewer bits with no visible distortions.

A uniform sampling of each multifrequency channel defines a representation which is not translation invariant. It is therefore difficult to build pattern recognition algorithms from such decompositions. We reviewed the properties of zero crossing in multiband decompositions. This adaptive sampling is translation invariant but is much more difficult to analyze. We described some previous results and gave the wavelet formalization of this problem through the reproducing kernel equation.

ACKNOWLEDGMENT

I would like to thank particularly R. Bajcsy for her advice on the writing of this paper, and N. Treil for helping me draw the figures.

REFERENCES

[1] E. Adelson and E. Simoncelli, "Orthogonal pyramid transform for image coding," in *Proc. SPIE, Visual Commun. and Image Processing*, 1987.
[2] B. Andrew and D. Pollen, "Relationship between spatial frequency selectivity and receptive field profile of simple cells," *J. Physiol.*, vol. 287, pp. 163-176, 1979.
[3] G. Battle, "A block spin construction of ondelettes, Part 1: Lemarie functions," *Commun. Math. Phys.*, vol. 110, pp. 601-615, 1987.
[4] P. J. Burt and E. H. Adelson, "The Laplacian pyramid as a compact image code," *IEEE Trans. Commun.*, vol. COM-31, pp. 532-540, Apr. 1983.
[5] F. Campbell, R. Carpenter, and J. Levinson, "Visibility of aperiodic patterns compared with cortical cells compared with sinusoidal gratings," *J. Physiol.*, vol. 204, pp. 283-298, 1969.
[6] F. Campbell and D. Green, "Optical and retina factors affecting visual resolution," *J. Physiol.*, vol. 181, pp. 576-593, 1965.
[7] F. Campbell and J. Kulikowski, "Orientation selectivity of the human visual system," *J. Physiol.*, vol. 197, pp. 437-441, 1966.
[8] F. Campbell and J. Robson, "Application of Fourier analysis to the visibility of gratings," *J. Physiol.*, vol. 197, pp. 551-566, 1968.
[9] R. C. Crochiere and L. R. Rabiner, "Interpolation and decimation in signal processing," *Proc. IEEE*, vol. 69, Mar. 1981.
[10] J. Crowley, "A representation for visual information," Tech. Rep. CMU-RI-TR-82-7, Robotic Inst., Carnegie-Mellon Univ., 1987.
[11] I. Daubechies, "Orthonormal bases of compactly supported wavelets," *Commun. Pure Appl. Math.*, vol. 41, pp. 909-996, Nov. 1988.
[12] J. G. Daugmann, "Two-dimensional spectral analysis of cortical receptive field profile," *Vis. Res.*, vol. 20, pp. 847-856, 1980.
[13] —, "Six formal properties of two dimensional anisotropic visual filter. Structural principles and frequency/orientation selectivity," *IEEE Trans. Syst., Man, Cybern.*, vol. SMC-13, Sept. 1983.
[14] D. Esteban and C. Galand, "Applications of quadrature mirror filters to split band voice coding schemes," in *Proc. Int. Conf. Acoust., Speech, Signal Processing*, May 1977.
[15] P. Federbush, "Quantum field theory in ninety minutes," *Bull. Amer. Math. Soc.*, 1987.
[16] D. Gabor, "Theory of communication," *J. Inst. Elec. Eng.*, London, vol. 93, pp. 429-457, 1946.
[17] M. Georgeson, "Mechanisms of visual image processing: studies of pattern interaction and selective channels in human vision," Ph.D. dissertation, Univ. Sussex, Brighton, England, 1975.
[18] —, "Spatial Fourier analysis and human vision," in *Tutorial Essays in Psychology, A Guide to Recent Advances*. N. Sutherland, Ed. Hillsdale, NJ: Lawrence Erlbaum Associates, 1979.

[19] W. Grimson, "Computational experiments with a feature based stereo algorithm," *IEEE Trans. Pattern Anal. Machine Intell.*, vol. PAMI-7, pp. 17-34, Jan. 1985.
[20] A. Grossmann and J. Morlet, "Decomposition of Hardy functions into square integrable wavelets of constant shape," *SIAM J. Math.*, vol. 15, pp. 723-736, 1984.
[21] A. Grossman, J. Morlet, and T. Paul, "Transforms associated to square integrable group representations," *Int. J. Math. Phys.*, vol. 26, pp. 2473-2479, 1986.
[22] E. Hall, J. Rouge, and R. Wong, "Hierarchical search for image matching," in *Proc. Conf. Decision Contr.*, 1976, pp. 791-796.
[23] D. Hubel and T. Wiesel, "Receptive fields, binocular interaction and functional architecture in the cat's visual cortex," *J. Physiol.*, vol. 160, 1962.
[24] R. Hummel, "Representations based on zero-crossings in scale-space," Tech. Rep. 225, Courant Inst. Dep. Comput. Sci., June 1986.
[25] R. Hummel and R. Moniot, "A network approach to reconstruction from zero-crossings," in *Proc. IEEE Workshop Comput. Vis.*, Dec. 1987.
[26] S. Jaffard, "Estimations Holderiennes ponctuelles des fonctions au moyen des coefficients d'ondelettes," *Notes au Compte-Rendu de l'Academie Des Sciences*, France, 1989.
[27] S. Jaffard and Y. Meyer, "Bases d'ondelettes dans des ouverts de Rn," *J. Mathematiques Pures et Appliquees*, 1987.
[28] J. Klauder and B. Skagerstam, in *Coherent States*. Singapore: World Scientific, 1985.
[29] J. Koenderink, "The structure of images," in *Biological Cybernetics*. New York: Springer-Verlag, 1984.
[30] R. Kronland-Martinet, J. Morlet, and A. Grossmann, "Analysis of sound patterns through wavelet transform," *Int. J. Pattern Recogn. Artificial Intell.*, 1988.
[31] J. Kulikowski and P. King-Smith, "Orientation selectivity of grating and line detectors in human vision," *Vis. Res.*, vol. 13, pp. 1455-1478, 1973.
[32] P. G. Lemarie, "Ondelettes a localisation exponentielles," *J. Math. Pures et Appliquees*, 1988.
[33] P. G. Lemarie and Y. Meyer, "Ondelettes et bases Hilbertiennes," *Revista Matematica Ibero Americana*, vol. 2, 1986.
[34] M. D. Levine, *Vision in Man and Machine*. New York: McGraw-Hill, 1985.
[35] L. Maffei and A. Fiorentini, "The unresponsive regions of visula cortical receptive fields," *Vis. Res.*, vol. 16, pp. 1131-1139, 1976.
[36] L. Maffei, C. Morrone, M. Pirchio, and G. Sandini, *J. Physiol.*, vol. 296, pp. 24-47, 1979.
[37] S. Mallat, "Dyadic wavelets energy zero-crossings," Tech. Rep. MS-CIS-88-30, U. Penn., 1988.
[38] —, "A theory for multiresolution signal decomposition: The wavelet representation," *IEEE Trans. Pattern Anal. Machine Intell.*, vol. 11, pp. 674-693, July 1989.
[39] —, "Multiresolution approximation and wavelet orthonormal bases of L2," *Trans. Amer. Math. Soc.*, pp. 3-15, pp. 69-87, Sept. 1989.
[40] D. Marr, in *Vision*. San Francisco, CA: Freeman, 1982.
[41] D. Marr and E. Hildreth, "Theory of edge detection," *Proc. Roy. Soc. London*, vol. 207, pp. 187-217, 1980.
[42] D. Marr and T. Poggio, "A theory of human stereo vision," *Proc. Roy. Soc. London*, vol. B 204, pp. 301-328, 1979.
[43] Y. Meyer, "Ondelettes et fonctions splines," presented at the Seminaire Equations aux Derivees Partielles, Ecole Polytechnique, Paris, France, Dec. 1986.
[44] —, in *Ondelettes et Operateurs*. Paris, France: Hermann, 1988.
[45] —, "Principe d'incertitude, bases hilbertiennes et algebres d'operateurs," presented at the Bourbaki seminar, 1985-1986, Paper 662.
[46] J. Nachmais and A. Weber, "Discrimination of simple and complex gratings," *Vis. Res.*, vol. 15, pp. 217-223, 1975.
[47] J. Oppenheim and J. Lim, in *Advanced Topics in Signal Processing*, Signal Processings Series. Englewood Cliffs, NJ: Prentice-Hall, 1988, pp. 289-336.
[48] T. Paul, "Affine coherent states and the radial Schrodinger equation. Radial harmonic oscillator and hydrogen atom," preprint.
[49] D. A. Pollen and S. F. Ronner, "Visual corical neurons as localized spatial frequency filter," *IEEE Trans. Syst., Man, Cybern.*, vol. SMC-13, Sept. 1983.
[50] A. Rosenfeld, *Multiresolution Image Processing and Analysis*. New York: Springer-Verlag, 1982.
[51] A. Rosenfeld and M. Thurston, "Edge and curve detection for visual scene analysis," *IEEE Trans. Comput.*, vol. C-20, 1971.

[52] A. Rosenfeld and G. J. Vanderburg, "Coarse-fine template matching," *IEEE Trans. Syst., Man, Cybern.*, vol. SMC-7, pp. 104–107, 1977.
[53] J. Sanz and T. Huang, "Theorem and experiments on image reconstruction from zero-crossings," IBM, Res. Rep. RJ5460.
[54] M. J. Smith and T. P. Barnwell, "Exact reconstruction techniques for tree-structured subband coders," *IEEE Trans. Acoust., Speech, Signal Processing*, vol. ASSP-34, June 1986.
[55] J. Stromberg, "A modified Franklin system and higher-order systems of Rn as unconditional bases for Hardy spaces," in *Proc. Conf. Harmonic Anal. Honor of a. Zygmund*, vol. 2, Wadsworth Math Series, pp. 475–493.
[56] S. Tanimoto and T. Pavlidis, "A hierarchical data structure for image processing," *Comput. Graphics Image Processing*, vol. 4, pp. 104–119, 1975.
[57] P. Tchamitchian, "Biorthogonalite et theorie des operateurs," *Revista Matematica Ibero Americana*, vol. 2, 1986.
[58] M. Turner, "Texture discrimination by Gabor functions," *Biological Cybern.*, vol. 55, pp. 71–82, 1986.
[59] K. De Valois, R. De Valois, and E. Yund, *J. Physiol.*, vol. 291, pp. 483–505, 1979.
[60] A. Watson, "Efficiency of a model human image code," *J. Opt. Soc. Amer.*, vol. 4, pp. 2401–2417, Dec. 1987.
[61] M. Webster and R. De Valois, "Relationship between spatial-frequency and orientation tuning of striate-cortex cells," *J. Opt. Soc. Amer.*, July 1985.
[62] A. Witkin, "Scale space filtering," in *Proc. Int. Joint Conf. Artificial Intell.*, 1983.
[63] J. W. Woods and S. D. O'Neil, "Subband coding of images," *IEEE Trans. Acoust., Speech, Signal Processing*, vol. ASSP-34, Oct. 1986.
[64] Y. Zeevi and D. Rotem, "Image reconstruction from zero crossings," *IEEE Trans. Acoust., Speech, Signal Processing*, vol. ASSP-34, pp. 1269–1277, Oct. 1986.

Stephane G. Mallat was born in Paris, France. He graduated from Ecole Polytechnique, Paris, in 1984, and from Ecole Nationale Superieure des Telecommunications, Paris, in 1985. He received the Ph.D. degree in electrical engineering from the University of Pennsylvania, Philadelphia, in 1988.

Since September 1988 he has been an Assistant Professor in the Computer Science Department of the Courant Institute of Mathematical Sciences, New York University, New York. His research interests include computer vision, signal processing, and applied mathematics.

Morphological Systems for Multidimensional Signal Processing

PETROS MARAGOS, MEMBER, IEEE, AND RONALD W. SCHAFER, FELLOW, IEEE

This paper reviews the basic theory and applications of a set theoretic approach to image analysis called mathematical morphology. *The goals of the paper are: (1) to show how the concepts of mathematical morphology can quantify geometrical structure in signals and (2) to illuminate the ways that morphological systems can enrich the theory and applications of multidimensional signal processing. The topics covered include: applications to non-linear filtering (morphological and rank-order filters, multiscale smoothing, morphological sampling, morphological correlation); applications to image analysis (feature extraction, shape representation and description, size distributions, and fractals); and representation theorems, which show how a large class of nonlinear and linear signal operators can be realized as a combination of simple morphological operations.*

I. INTRODUCTION

Multidimensional signal processing has been based traditionally on the concepts and theory of linear systems and Fourier analysis (or other related transforms) [10], [11], [27], [136]. Although these classical approaches have been very fruitful in many applications, they are often of limited use for image-like signals because they do not address directly the fundamental issues of how to quantify *shape* or *geometrical structure* in signals. In contrast, mathematical morphology, which is a set-theoretical methodology for image analysis, can rigorously quantify many aspects of the geometrical structure of signals in a way that agrees with human intuition and perception. This method, which has its mathematical origins in set theory, integral geometry, convex analysis, stereology, and geometrical probabilities, was developed mainly by Matheron [80], [81] and Serra [115] in the 1960s.

The techniques of mathematical morphology are based on set-theoretic concepts, on nonlinear superpositions of signals, and on a class of nonlinear systems that we call *morphological systems*. We consider the term mathematical morphology to be a more general designation, referring to the entire body of fundamental theory of morphological systems and to the heuristics and algorithms associated with application of the theory to specific areas. Mathematical morphology has been widely used for biomedical and electron microscopy image analysis, and it has been a valuable tool in many computer vision applications, especially in the area of automated visual inspection. Industrial applications of these techniques have been spurred by the continuous development and improvement of novel computer architectures for implementing morphological signal transformations. However, in spite of its many successful applications and its deep and elegant mathematical structure, mathematical morphology has only recently become a topic of interest for academic research, and the breadth and generality of the approach are not yet widely appreciated.

A comprehensive survey of the entire field of mathematical morphology would necessarily be very superficial even if much more space were available. Instead, we focus on morphological systems, with the goals of showing how these systems can enrich the mathematical tools of multidimensional signal processing and illustrating how they can be applied to fields of growing interest such as computer vision, nonlinear filtering, and structural signal analysis. Thus, we provide a review of the fundamentals of morphological system theory and we give an introduction to some of the elegant theorems that are available for representation and analysis of morphological systems. We also attempt to illustrate ways that morphological systems can be applied by showing a limited number of examples drawn primarily from our own past and current research [64]–[74]. While limited space precludes a detailed review of all previous work in the field of mathematical morphology, we have provided an extensive bibliography and have cited relevant contributions from other researchers wherever possible.

The paper is organized as follows. Section II reviews the basic concepts behind morphological systems. Section III contains applications to nonlinear filtering: relationships between morphological and rank-order/median filters, multiscale morphological smoothing, morphological sampling, and morphological correlation. Section IV covers some applications to image analysis: edge/blob feature extraction, shape representation via skeleton transforms, shape description via shape-size distributions, and descrip-

---

Manuscript received February 21, 1989; revised July 12, 1989. This work was supported in part by the National Science Foundation under Grant MIPS-86-58150, with matching funds from Bellcore, Xerox, and Sun, and by ARO under Grant DAAL03-86-K-0171, and by the Joint Services Electronics Program under Contract DAA03-87-K0059.

P. Maragos is with the Division of Applied Sciences, Harvard University, Cambridge, MA 02138, USA.

R. W. Schafer is with the School of Electrical Engineering, Georgia Institute of Technology, Atlanta, GA 30332, USA.

IEEE Log Number 9034605.

tion/modeling of fractal images. Section V shows that simple morphological operations are the representational prototypes of a large class of nonlinear and linear signal operators.

II. General Concepts

The basis for this approach to multidimensional signal processing is the representation of signals and systems in terms of sets and set transformations. This is the key to representing and manipulating geometric structure in images and other signals.

A. Signal Representations

Let **R** and **Z** denote, respectively, the set of real and integer numbers, and let **E** be the d-dimensional (henceforth denoted d-dim) continuous space $\mathbf{R}^d$ ($d = 1, 2, \cdots$) or the discrete space $\mathbf{Z}^d$. Then a d-dim signal can be represented as a function whose domain is either $\mathbf{R}^d$ (continuous) or $\mathbf{Z}^d$ (discrete), and whose range is either **R** (continuous amplitude) or **Z** (quantized amplitude).

Binary signals can be represented by sets. For example, the image at the top left of Fig. 1 is a binary signal, where the white background region could be represented by 0 and the shaded foreground could be represented by 1. Clearly the signal may also be represented by the set X of points corresponding to the shaded region. Binary images are often obtained by thresholding a gray-level image. Thresholding can also be used to represent gray-level images by binary signals and therefore, by sets. Serra [114], [115] uses the representation of a real-valued d-dim function $f(x)$ (x is a d-dim vector) by the ensemble of its d-dim *threshold sets* defined by

$$T_a(f) = \{x: f(x) \geq a\}, \quad -\infty < a < \infty, \quad (1)$$

where the amplitude a spans all of **R** or **Z** depending on whether the signal f has a continuous or quantized range. The threshold sets have two important properties: They are

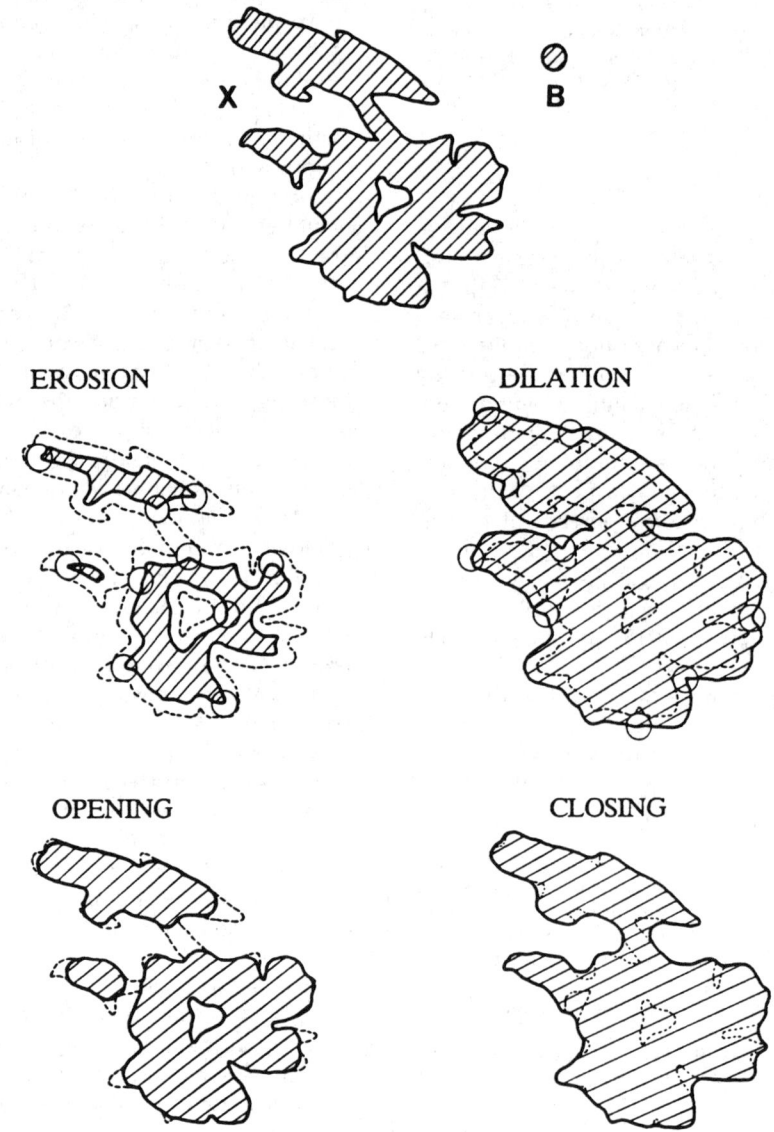

Fig. 1. Erosion, dilation, opening, and closing of X (binary image of an island) by a disk B centered at the origin. The shaded areas correspond to the interior of the sets, the dark solid curve to the boundary of the transformed sets, and the dashed curve to the boundary of the original set X. (From [73])

linearly ordered since $a < b \Rightarrow T_a(f) \supseteq T_b(f)$, and they can reconstruct the signal f uniquely since

$$f(x) = \max \{a: x \in T_a(f)\}, \quad \forall x. \quad (2)$$

This representation is illustrated for a 1-dim signal by the example of Table 1. The signal $f(x)$, shown in the second row of the table, has only four amplitude levels, and thus can be represented by the four threshold sets, each of which includes only the points indicated by dots in the next four rows of the table. (A continuous-amplitude signal would require an infinite number of threshold sets.) The final four rows show the *threshold binary signals* corresponding to the threshold sets where $f_a(x) = 1$ if $f(x) \geq a$ [i.e., $x \in T_a(f)$] and $f_a(x) = 0$ if $f(x) < a$ [i.e., $x \notin T_a(f)$], where a spans the range of $f(x)$. Obviously, the signals $f_a(x)$ convey the same information as the threshold sets $T_a(f)$. Hence, f can be reconstructed from the f_a's since

$$f(x) = \max \{a: f_a(x) = 1\}, \quad \forall x. \quad (3)$$

The validity of (2) and (3) is easily seen for the example of Table 1.

Table 1 Threshold Representation of a Discrete, Quantized Signal

x	0	1	2	3	4	5	6	7	8	9	10
$f(x)$	1	1	2	1	3	0	0	1	0	2	3
$T_3(f)$					•						•
$T_2(f)$			•		•					•	•
$T_1(f)$	•	•	•	•	•			•		•	•
$T_0(f)$	•	•	•	•	•	•	•	•	•	•	•
$f_3(x)$	0	0	0	0	1	0	0	0	0	0	1
$f_2(x)$	0	0	1	0	1	0	0	0	0	1	1
$f_1(x)$	1	1	1	1	1	0	0	1	0	1	1
$f_0(x)$	1	1	1	1	1	1	1	1	1	1	1

B. Signal Transformations

The signal transformations of mathematical morphology, which we call *morphological filters*,[1] are nonlinear signal operators that locally modify the geometrical features of multidimensional signals. We consider first the case of binary signals. Let $X \subseteq \mathbf{E}$ be the set representation of a binary input signal, and let $B \subseteq \mathbf{E}$ be a compact set of small size and simple shape (e.g. a d-dim ball). The set B is called a *structuring element*. Let $X \pm b = \{x \pm b: x \in X\}$ denote the vector *translate* of X by $\pm b \in \mathbf{E}$. The fundamental morphological operators for sets are *dilation* $\oplus$ and *erosion* $\ominus$ of X by B, which are defined as follows:

$$X \oplus B = \bigcup_{b \in B} X + b = \{x + b: x \in X \text{ and } b \in B\}, \quad (4)$$

$$X \ominus B = \bigcap_{b \in B} X - b = \{z: (B + z) \subseteq X\}. \quad (5)$$

From these definitions, it can be shown that the output of the dilation operator is the set of translation points such that the translate of the *reflected* structuring element $\check{B} = \{-b: b \in B\}$ has a nonempty intersection with the input set; i.e., $X \oplus B = \{z: (\check{B} + z) \cap X \neq \emptyset\}$. Similarly, the output

---

[1] In [56], [116] the term "morphological filters" refers only to a special class of morphological transformations (algebraic generalizations of openings), whereas we use it interchangeably with the broader term *morphological systems*.

of the erosion operator is the set of translation points such that the translated structuring element is contained in the input set.

Other operators can be defined as combinations of erosions and dilations. For example, two additional fundamental operators are *opening* $\circ$ and *closing* $\bullet$ of X by B defined as follows:

$$X \circ B = (X \ominus B) \oplus B, \quad (6)$$

$$X \bullet B = (X \oplus B) \ominus B. \quad (7)$$

To visualize the geometrical behavior of these operators it is helpful to consider 2-dim sets such as the set X and the structuring element B shown at the top of Fig. 1. Figure 1 shows that erosion shrinks the set X, whereas dilation expands X. The opening suppresses the sharp capes and cuts the narrow isthmuses of X, whereas the closing fills in the thin gulfs and small holes, in a way such that $X \circ B \subseteq X \subseteq X \bullet B$. Thus, if the structuring element B has a regular shape, both opening and closing can be thought of as nonlinear filters which smooth the contours of the input signal. Clearly, the shape and size of the structuring element will determine the nature and the degree of smoothing.

The above set operators can be extended to multilevel (i.e., non-binary) signals, represented by real-valued functions, in various ways [114], [115], [82], [89], [121], [122], [100]. Serra used the representation of a d-dim function $f(x)$ by the collection of its threshold sets in (1). Then, dilating all threshold sets of f by the same compact set B yields the sets $T_a(f) \oplus B$, which are the threshold sets of a new function $f \oplus B$, called the *dilation* of f by B. This new function can be computed either from (2) as $(f \oplus B)(x) = \max \{a: x \in T_a(f) \oplus B\}$ or, from the equivalent direct formula:

$$(f \oplus B)(x) = \max_{y \in B} \{f(x - y)\}. \quad (8)$$

Similarly, eroding all threshold sets of f by the same set B and superimposing all output sets via (2) yields a new function, the *erosion* of f by B, which can also be computed by the equivalent formula

$$(f \ominus B)(x) = \min_{y \in B} \{f(x + y)\}. \quad (9)$$

The *opening* $\circ$ and *closing* $\bullet$ of f by B are defined as $f \circ B = (f \ominus B) \oplus B$ and $f \bullet B = (f \oplus B) \ominus B$. The results of applying the erosion, dilation, opening and closing operations to the discrete quantized signal in Table 1 are given in Table 2 for the structuring set $B = \{-1, 0, 1\}$. Note that the endpoints of the outputs are undetermined because the shifts by the points of the symmetric structuring element require points outside the given domain [0, 10]. An alternative would be to assume some value for the signal outside the given interval. It is instructive to verify the results of Table 2 by using (8) and (9) and by applying the set-theoretic definitions to the threshold set representation of $f(x)$ in Table 1.

Table 2 Dilation, Erosion, Opening, and Closing of a Discrete, Quantized Signal

x	0	1	2	3	4	5	6	7	8	9	10
$f(x)$	1	1	2	1	3	0	0	1	0	2	3
$f(x) \oplus B$	–	2	2	3	3	3	1	1	2	3	–
$f(x) \ominus B$	–	1	1	1	0	0	0	0	0	0	–
$f(x) \circ B$	–	–	1	1	1	0	0	0	0	–	–
$f(x) \bullet B$	–	–	2	2	3	1	1	1	1	–	–

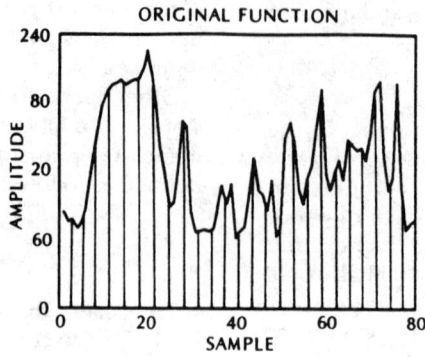

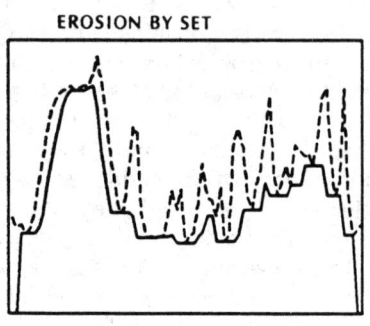
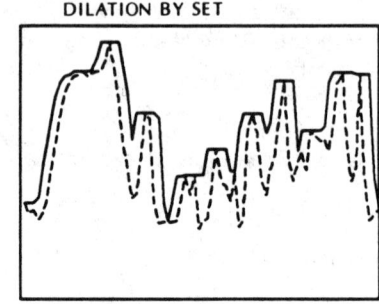
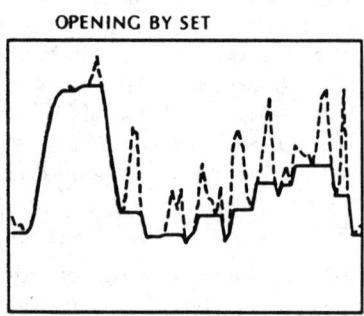
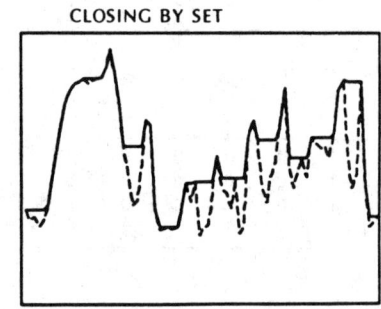

Fig. 2. Erosion, dilation, opening, and closing of a 1-dim discrete signal of 80 samples by a 1-dim set $B = \{-2, -1, 0, 1, 2\}$. The shaded region is the umbra of the input signal, and the dashed curves in the lower four plots are the input signal. (From [73])

Figure 2 shows another set of results of applying the basic morphological operators to a 1-dim signal. In Fig. 2 we see that erosion of a function f by a small convex set B reduces the peaks and enlarges the minima of the function. The dilation of f by B increases the valleys and enlarges the maxima of the function. The opening by B smoothes the graph of f from below by cutting down its peaks, and the closing smoothes the graph of f from above by filling up its valleys. Clearly, a larger 1-dim structuring set would have a greater smoothing effect.

Another extension of morphological operators to functions is due to Sternberg [121], [122], who uses the representation of a d-dim function $f(x)$ by a $(d + 1)$-dim set, its *umbra*

$$U(f) = \{(x, a): a \leq f(x)\}; \quad (10)$$

i.e., the umbra is the set of points *below* the surface represented by $f(x)$. In Fig. 2, the umbra of $f(x)$ is the shaded region. Likewise, the umbrae of the outputs of the erosion, dilation, opening, and closing would be the regions below the solid curves in respective plots in Fig. 2. In general, the umbra set extends to $a = -\infty$. The function can be reconstructed from its umbra since

$$f(x) = \max_{} \{a: (x, a) \in U(f)\}, \quad \forall x. \quad (11)$$

Dilating or eroding the umbra of f by the umbra of g yields the umbrae of new functions, i.e., the dilation or erosion of f by g. These two new functions can be computed from the direct formulae:

$$(f \oplus g)(x) = \max_{y} \{f(y) + g(x - y)\} \quad (12)$$

$$(f \ominus g)(x) = \min_{y} \{f(y) - g(y - x)\} \quad (13)$$

where for each x, y ranges over the intersection of the "support" of f and the (shifted by x) support of g. By *support* of f here we mean the set of x at which $f(x) \neq -\infty$.[2] The function g is assumed to possess a compact support and plays the role of a structuring element. The opening and closing

---

[2]For max/min operations, $-\infty$ plays a similar role to that played by 0 for additions/multiplications. Thus, to define morphological operators on functions it helps to set their values outside their supports as equal to $-\infty$.

of f by g are, respectively, the functions $f \circ g = (f \ominus g) \oplus g$ and $f \bullet g = (f \oplus g) \ominus g$.

In this paper we have presented the various theoretical concepts in a way that emphasizes intelligibility at the expense of absolute mathematical correctness. Thus, the mathematically inclined reader may find fault with some of the above definitions. For example, some of the above max/min operations may have to be replaced by sup/inf, and the assumption about real-valued signals may have to be supplemented by also allowing the signals to assume $\pm \infty$ values. Note that, for signals that assume the extreme values $\pm \infty$, the maximum in (2), (3) and (11) must be replaced with supremum. A more rigorous treatment of the morphological operators and their properties can be found in [28], [43], [47], [68], [73], [110], [115].

In [116, ch. 1, 2] Serra has extended the morphological operators to more abstract spaces such as *lattices*. Serra's lattice framework has been further investigated by Heijmans and Ronse [47], [110]. Whereas all the morphological operators discussed in this paper are translation-invariant, in [109] dilations and erosions on the Euclidean plane are considered that are invariant under rotation and scalar multiplication.

C. Historical Notes

Considerable confusion has arisen regarding the definitions of the basic operations of mathematical morphology. This confusion is primarily due to usage of the symbols $\oplus$ and $\ominus$ by different authors to mean different things. The Appendix gives a discussion of the different definitions and shows how they are related.

Parallel to the evolution of the morphological operations that we have discussed, many other researchers studied image processing techniques based on cellular array computers and similar operations of the shrink/expand type. Early papers include [40], [53], [86], [99], [113], [133]. Recent surveys of such approaches can be found in [101], [112]. Most of these efforts dealt with binary images. The extension to gray-level images was done by using concepts from fuzzy set theory [52], [142]. Nakagawa and Rosenfeld [89] introduced the local min/max operators on digital gray-level images as an extension of the shrink/expand operators on binary images. Goetcherian [39] extended many binary image processing algorithms to gray-level images. Preston [100] used an umbra-like approach to extend the morphological operators to gray-level signals by operating on binary representations of the signals' umbrae with threshold logic operators. All these related contributions can be formalized under the rich theoretical framework of mathematical morphology, as we outline in this paper.

D. Nonlinear Superpositions

Linear operators commute with additive superposition (i.e., pointwise addition) of signals. Morphological operators commute with some nonlinear signal superpositions, which are induced by set operations (unions/intersections) among the threshold sets or umbrae of two signals f and g. Specifically, for all a, it is easily shown that $T_a(f \wedge g) = T_a(f) \cap T_a(g)$ and $T_a(f \vee g) = T_a(f) \cup T_a(g)$, where the operations $\wedge$ and $\vee$ are defined by $(f \wedge g)(x) = \min \{ f(x), g(x) \}$ and $(f \vee g)(x) = \max \{ f(x), g(x) \}$. Likewise, the umbrae of $f \wedge g$ and $f \vee g$ are, respectively, the intersection and union of $U(f)$ and $U(g)$. Therefore dilation commutes with $\vee$ and erosion commutes with $\wedge$:

$$(f \vee g) \oplus h = (f \oplus h) \vee (g \oplus h)$$
$$(f \wedge g) \ominus h = (f \ominus h) \wedge (g \ominus h) \qquad (14)$$

These results can be generalized for an infinite number of signals by using $\wedge$ and $\vee$ to generally denote pointwise infimum and supremum.

Parallel superposition of morphological operators is possible by using the nonlinear signal combinations of pointwise max/min. Specifically, let $\Psi_1(f)$ and $\Psi_2(f)$ be the output signals from two morphological operators when the input is f. Then, the operator $\Psi_{max}(f) = \Psi_1(f) \vee \Psi_2(f)$ is the max-superposition of the operators Ψ_1 and Ψ_2. We can also define the min-superposition operator $\Psi_{min}(f) = \Psi_1(f) \wedge \Psi_2(f)$. For morphological set operators these parallel superpositions still apply if we replace pointwise max/min of signals with union/intersection of sets. Finally, two morphological operators can be *cascaded* by applying one of the operators to the output of the other; e.g., the opening is the cascade of an erosion and a dilation.

A helpful *classification* of morphological operators results by focusing on a specific characteristic of the input/output signals: whether they are binary (sets) or multilevel (functions). We call the operators of (12) and (13) and their cascade or parallel (using $\wedge$, $\vee$) combinations *function-processing (FP)* operators, because they accept as inputs d-dim functions and produce as outputs d-dim functions. Likewise, the morphological set operators (4)-(7) and their cascade or parallel (using $\cap$, $\cup$) combinations are *set-processing (SP)* operators. A subclass of FP operators are called *function- and set-processing (FSP)* because they can process d-dim binary signals without changing this (binary) signal characteristic; thus FSP operators can switch between two modes of operations, FP or SP. Examples of FSP operators are the FSP dilation and erosion of f by B in (8) and (9); these are special cases of the FP dilation and erosion of f by g in (12), (13) if B is equal to the support of g, and g is equal to 0 inside B and $-\infty$ outside B.

E. Implementations

The evolution of the theory of mathematical morphology has closely followed the evolution of many generations of novel (pipelined or parallel) computer architectures designed to implement morphological operations. Most of these architectures were developed as cellular automata machines to extract pictorial information. Early examples include [31], [54], [61], [120]. For relative comparisons see [23]. More recent architectures can be found in [49], [50], [77], [144], [145] and in the long list of papers on morphological systems presented in [102].

The scope of this paper does not permit explaining any of these architectures in any length. Instead we briefly discuss a *parallel* implementation of binary erosions and dilations [120] to illustrate some major issues. As (4) and (5) imply, a *global* approach to obtaining the dilation or erosion, respectively, of a binary image X by a structuring element B is to take the union or intersection of translates of X by vector points in B. Figure 3 shows an implementation of this idea, where two bit planes are needed to hold X and B and a third accumulator bit plane for the resulting transformed image. The image plane is shifted in parallel to the

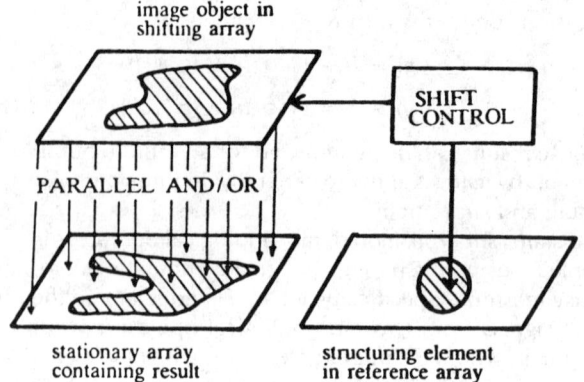

Fig. 3. Parallel implementation of binary erosion and dilation. (Adapted from [120])

accumulator plane, and the amount of shifting is controlled by the points belonging to the structuring element. The accumulator holds the parallel Boolean OR or AND of all the shifted versions of the image plane, and after all the points of B have been spanned, it will contain the dilation or erosion, respectively, of X. Alternatively, a *local* approach to compute the erosion and dilation is to shift the window B everywhere in the image plane and simultaneously perform local neighborhood operations of the Boolean type. The efficiency and scope of these simple implementations can be greatly enriched by using the rich set of algebraic properties of morphological operators. They can also be extended to gray-level images by using either max/min operations or threshold superposition (see Section II-B).

III. Applications to Nonlinear Filtering

Morphological systems, composed (at their lowest level) of erosions and dilations, can be used to modify multidimensional signals in ways that are analogous to linear filtering. The definitions of erosion and dilation indicate that these operations are similar in complexity to convolution with a finite[3] duration impulse response in the sense that the output at a given point is dependent on input values in a neighborhood of that point. However, morphological filters are nonlinear and have distinctly different properties and capabilities from linear filters. In this section we consider several types of morphological and related nonlinear filters.

A. Rank-Order and FSP Morphological Operators

Median filters and, their generalization, *rank-order filters* are nonlinear discrete[4] operators that have become popular for smoothing and enhancement of image and other signals. (See [2], [12], [17], [38], [51], [58], [91], [127], [129], for various properties and applications.) In this section, we review from [74] some interesting interrelationships among rank-order and FSP morphological operators.

The similarity between morphological filters and rank-order filters is illustrated by Fig. 4. Median filters are attrac-

---

[3]The computational structure of all the morphological and rank-order filters examined in this paper is similar to that of *non-recursive* linear filters. *Recursive* erosions and dilations have been used in [9], [112], [113] for fast computations of distance transforms. Recursive rank-order filters are defined in [91].

[4]For *analog* rank-order filters see [37], [60].

tive for removing impulsive (or salt-and-pepper) noise in images since they can remove the noise without blurring edges as would be the case for linear filtering. Figure 4 shows that in this application, the median behaves like a combined opening and closing, i.e., an open-closing $(f \circ B) \bullet B$, by a set B of size about half the size of the median window. In addition, the open-closing, while requiring less computation than the median, decomposes the noise suppression task into two steps; i.e., the opening suppresses the positive noise impulses, and the closing suppresses the negative noise impulses. The median filter does not discriminate between positive and negative impulses.

Let $W \subseteq \mathbf{Z}^d$ be a finite set called the *window* of the rank-order filter. Assume that $|W| = n$ points, where $|\cdot|$ denotes set cardinality. For $r = 1, 2, \cdots, n$, the output $RO_r(f; W)(x)$ of the rth rank-order filter with window W is obtained at any location $x \in \mathbf{Z}^d$ by *sorting* into descending order the n values of the input function f inside the shifted window $W + x$ and picking the rth number from the sorted list. If n is odd and $r = (n + 1)/2$ we have the special case of the median filter $med(f; W)$ of f with window W. Rank-order filters are FSP operators. To define their corresponding SP operators consider discrete input sets $X \subseteq \mathbf{Z}^d$. The rth SP rank-order filter is the set operator whose output is

$$RO_r(X; W) = \{p: |X \cap (W + p)| \geq r\}. \quad (15)$$

Note that computing the output from an SP rank-order filter involves only *counting* of points and no sorting. Thus, an equivalent way to implement the binary rank-order filters is to linearly convolve the binary input signal with a binary impulse response whose domain is W and then threshold the result at a level corresponding to the rank r.

The theoretical analysis of these useful filters is difficult because they are nonlinear and have nonzero memory. However, by using mathematical morphology, the framework presented in [74] facilitates the theoretical analysis of these filters, relates them to morphological filters, and provides some new realizations for them. Specifically, from the definition it is clear that the last rank-order filter $(r = n)$ is identical to the erosion by W. Likewise, the first rank-order filter $(r = 1)$ with window W is identical to the FSP or SP dilation by $\check{W}$. Further, all rank-order filters commute with thresholding [36], [51], [74], [89], [115], [130]; i.e.,

$$T_a[RO_r(f; W)] = RO_r[T_a(f); W], \quad \forall a. \quad (16)$$

This property is also shared by many FSP morphological operators. Further, if we combine it with (2), it implies that, if Ψ is any FSP operator commuting with thresholding, then

$$[\Psi(f)](x) = \max \{a: x \in \Psi[T_a(f)]\} \quad \forall x. \quad (17)$$

Therefore, as developed in [115] and [74], to transform a multilevel signal f by Ψ is equivalent to decomposing f into all its threshold sets, transforming each set by the binary counterpart of Ψ, and reconstructing the output signal $\Psi(f)$ via the threshold-max superposition of (17). This allows us to study all rank-order filters (which include erosion and dilation) and their cascade (e.g., opening and closing) or parallel (using $\vee, \wedge$) combinations by focusing on their corresponding binary filters. Such representations are much simpler to analyze and they suggest alternative implementations that do not involve numeric comparisons or sorting.

Using this approach, many interesting and useful relationships between rank-order filters and morphological fil-

Fig. 4. (a) A 256 × 256-pixel (8-bit/pixel) gray-level image f corrupted with salt-and-pepper noise; SNR = 15.1 dB. (Probability of occurrence of noisy samples is 0.1.) (b) Opening $f \circ B$ of f by a 2 × 2-pixel square set B; SNR = 19.5 dB. (c) Open-closing $(f \circ B) \bullet B$; SNR = 25.8 dB. (d) Median of f by a 3 × 3-pixel window; SNR = 29.1 dB. The SNRs were computed by $20 \log_{10}(255/e_{rms})$, where e_{rms} was the rms-value of the difference between the original and the noisy or restored images. (From [74])

ters were obtained in [74]. For example, it was shown that any rank-order filter can be represented as either a max-superposition of erosions or a min-superposition of dilations. Such implementations avoid sorting and require a fixed computation to compute each output sample. Reference [74] also presents a number of properties of median root signals and relations between median roots and close-openings and open-closings.

B. Threshold Superposition and Stack Filters

In Section II-A we showed that a function $f(x)$ can be represented exactly by the set of its threshold binary signals $f_a(x)$. If f is *nonnegative* and, say for simplicity, has integer uniformly spaced amplitudes $a = 0, 1, 2 \cdots$, then f can also be reconstructed as the pointwise sum of the f_a's; i.e.,

$$f(x) = \sum_{a \geq 1} f_a(x) \quad (18)$$

Fitch et al. [36] showed that for nonnegative digital signals f, rank-order operators Ψ obey a *threshold-sum superposition* of the form:

$$\Psi(f) = \sum_a \Psi(f_a). \quad (19)$$

This weak form of linear superposition holds because the f_a's are binary and linearly ordered; i.e., $a < b \Rightarrow f_a \geq f_b$. Note that (19) is a special case of (17) since the former applies only to nonnegative signals. Both types of threshold superposition for rank-order filters have proved to be important for VLSI [46] and optical-electronic implementations [49], [92].

Serra's general approach [114], [115, ch. XII] of creating a multilevel signal operator $f \mapsto \Psi(f)$ from a binary operator $X \mapsto \Psi(X)$ requires that Ψ has two properties: it must be *increasing* $[X \subseteq Y \Rightarrow \Psi(X) \subseteq \Psi(Y)]$ and it must be *upper semicontinuous* [for any decreasing set sequence (X_n) with $X_{n+1} \subseteq X_n$, $\Psi(\cap_n X_n) = \cap_n \Psi(X_n)$.] If these conditions hold for an arbitrary SP operator Ψ, then the $\Psi[T_a(f)]$ are legitimate threshold sets of an output function $\Psi(f)$ synthesized via (17); hence, an FSP operator is created. In [74] we applied (17) to rank-order and FSP morphological operators.

Wendt et al. [134] defined *stack* filters by using similar concepts as in [115] and [74], but from a different viewpoint, and their result was applicable only to discrete filters. In their work, the role of the set operator Ψ was played by a *positive Boolean function* β, which, due to its monotonicity, is increasing [88]. The "increasing" property is called "stacking" in [134]. Further, by filtering all threshold binary signals f_a with β and using the threshold-sum superposition (19), they defined a stack filter ST_β as

$$ST_\beta(f) = \sum_a \beta(f_a). \quad (20)$$

In [74] we showed that all stack filters are finite pointwise maxima or minima of moving local min/max operators, and vice-versa.

All the previous discussion about threshold superposition referred to FSP operators. Serra [115, p. 444] obtained analogous results for FP dilations and erosions. Similar decompositions of gray-level dilations into multiple binary dilations have been developed in [117] for VLSI architectures.

C. Multiscale Nonlinear Smoothing

In computer vision research [78] it has become apparent that various image analysis tasks have to be performed not at a single image scale but at multiple scales, because image features occur on a variety of scales. One approach to quantifying scale [16], [79], [111], [137], [140] involves varying the average "width" σ of the impulse response (e.g., a Gaussian) of a linear low-pass filter that smoothes the image. Despite the mathematical tractability of this linear filtering approach, linear filters shift and blur important image features such as edges. Alternatively, there is a large class of *nonlinear* filters including median and opening/closing filters that avoid this problem, because they can provide signal smoothing by eliminating impulses or narrow peaks/valleys while preserving its edges. In [65], [66], [69] Maragos investigated an approach for multiscale nonlinear image smoothing based on openings and closings. Some of the reasons for focusing on openings/closings are the following:

1. As developed in Matheron [81], openings and closings of sets in Euclidean spaces by convex sets of varying size (scale) can formalize the concept of size.
2. A new definition of scale is possible based on openings. Specifically, let $B \subseteq \mathbf{Z}^2$ be a finite connected set. If B is of size (by convention) one, the sets

$$nB = \underbrace{B \oplus B \oplus \cdots \oplus B}_{n \text{ times}} \quad (21)$$

define binary structuring elements of discrete size $n = 0, 1, 2, \cdots$. If B is convex, then nB is shaped like B but has size n. The *multiscale opening* of a binary image X by B at scale $n = 0, 1, 2, \cdots$ is defined [69] by

$$X \circ nB = [(X \ominus B) \ominus B \cdots \ominus B]\underbrace{}_{n \text{ times}}$$
$$\underbrace{\oplus B \oplus B \cdots \oplus B}_{n \text{ times}}. \quad (22)$$

A *dual* multiscale filter is the closing $X \bullet nB = (X \oplus nB) \ominus nB$. If $n = 0$, then $nB = \{0\}$, the origin point, and $X \circ nB = X \bullet nB = X$. The opening $X \circ nB$ eliminates from X all objects of size $< n$ (with respect to B), that is, objects inside which nB cannot fit, because, as can be shown,

$$X \circ nB = \bigcup_{(nB + z) \subseteq X} (nB + z). \quad (23)$$

That is why, the size n of nB can be considered to be synonymous to the scale at which the filter $X \circ nB$ operates. Equation (23) implies that scale could be defined as the smallest size n of a prototype pattern B that can fit inside the image X. This definition of scale is more rigorous than the approximate definition in linear smoothing.

3. An important property of the multiscale Gaussian filters for edge detection is that they do not introduce additional zero-crossings as the scale (σ) increases. Chen and Yan [18] have proved something similar for the multiscale openings; specifically, they showed that openings of 1-D boundary curvature functions of continuous binary images by disks do not introduce additional zero-crossings at coarser scales (larger disk radii).
4. Finally, Brockett [14] found a nonlinear partial differential equation that models the continuous multiscale FSP openings as a dynamical system.

The multiscale openings can be extended [69] to gray-level images $f(x)$, $x \in \mathbf{Z}^2$, as follows. Let $g(x)$ be a gray-level structuring function-element, with a finite connected support of size one. Then

$$ng = \underbrace{g \oplus g \oplus \cdots \oplus g}_{n \text{ times}} \quad (24)$$

defines structuring functions of size $n = 0, 1, 2, \cdots$. The *multiscale opening* of f by g at scale $n = 0, 1, 2, \cdots$ is defined as

$$f \circ ng = [(f \ominus g) \ominus g \cdots \ominus g]\underbrace{}_{n \text{ times}} \underbrace{\oplus g \oplus g \cdots \oplus g}_{n \text{ times}} \quad (25)$$

Likewise, $f \bullet ng = (f \oplus ng) \ominus ng$ is the *multiscale closing* of f by g. See Fig. 5 for examples.

If the image contains 1-dim line structures to be preserved, then the opening by ng will eliminate them if g has a 2-dim support. This can be avoided by using a max-superposition of openings or closings by 1-dim structuring elements oriented at various angles. Thus, for preserving edge/line features that have a predominant 1-dim structure the following multiscale morphological smoothing operators can be used:

$$[O_n(f)](x) = \max_{\theta} \{f \circ ng_{\theta}(x)\} \quad (26)$$

$$[C_n(f)](x) = \min_{\theta} \{f \bullet g_{\theta}(x)\}, \quad (27)$$

where g_{θ} is a 1-dim structuring element (binary or gray-level) rotated at angle θ. For digital implementations θ spans only a finite set of different orientations, e.g., 0°, 45°, 90°, 135°.) Applications of these parallel superpositions of oriented openings can be found in [69], [104], [115], [116], [124].

D. Morphological Sampling

Digitalization of continuous binary images by sampling them on periodic grids causes some loss of information. The issue of which morphological operators are "digitalizable," i.e., satisfy a continuity condition in the transition from the continuous to discrete domain was analyzed in [115]. The errors of derived measurements were examined in [29].

Another aspect of sampling involves multiresolution techniques [16], [111], [128], which have proven to be very useful in computer vision. Creating a multiresolution pyramid requires multiple steps of smoothing the image and sub-sampling it. Such concepts are very similar to the ones encountered in classical signal decimation/interpolation [93]. Most research in image pyramids has been based on linear smoothers. However, since morphological filters preserve essential shape features, they may be superior in many applications. Further research is required to dem-

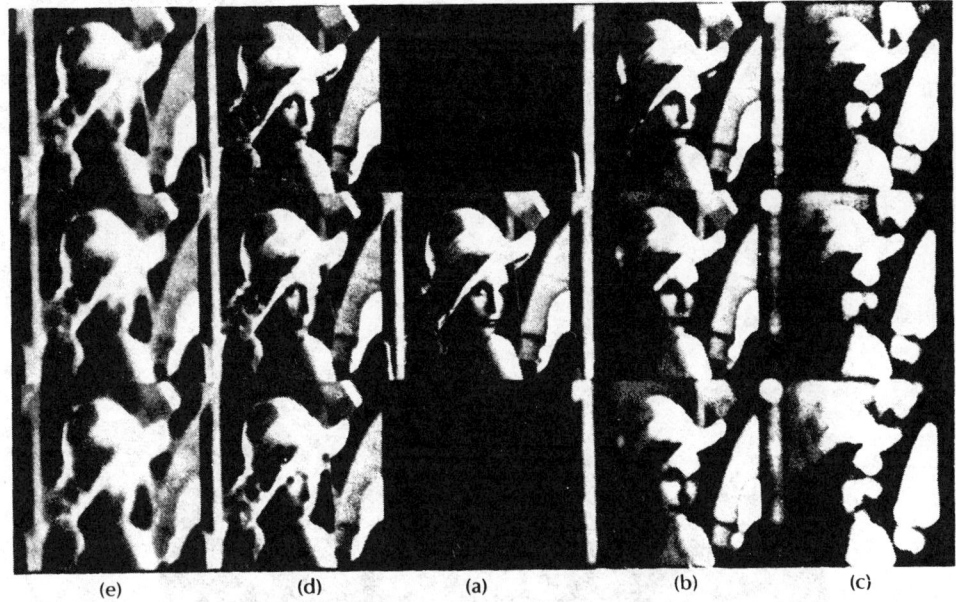

Fig. 5. Multiscale openings and closings. (a) Graytone image f (256 × 256 pixels). (b) $f \circ ng$, $n = 1, 2, 3$ (top to bottom). The pattern g is defined on $\mathbf{Z}$ as $g(x, y) = 5\sqrt{5 - x^2 - y^2}$, $0 \le x^2 + y^2 \le 5$, and $g(x, y) = -\infty$ if $x^2 + y^2 > 5$. (c) $f \circ ng$, $n = 4, 5, 6$ (top to bottom). (d) $f \bullet ng$, $n = 1, 2, 3$ (top to bottom). (e) $f \bullet ng$, $n = 4, 5, 6$ (top to bottom). (From [69])

onstrate the utility of morphological filters in forming multiresolution imagery.

Haralick, Lin, Lee and Zhuang [44], [45] have addressed some of these issues and developed a theory of morphological sampling. Their work provides a number of interesting results on reconstructing a signal after morphological smoothing and decimation. For example, they showed that if a binary signal represented by a set F has been smoothed first to $X = F \circ K$ by opening it with a structuring element K and then down-sampled to $X \cap S$ by intersecting it with a periodic sampling set S [S and K must satisfy certain conditions], then the Hausdorff distance between the smoothed signal X and its reconstruction $(X \cap S) \oplus K$ via dilation does not exceed the radius of K. By representing functions by umbrae, they have also extended these results to multilevel signals.

E. Morphological Correlation

Consider two real-valued d-dim discrete signals $f(n)$ and $g(n)$. Assume that g is a signal pattern to be found in f. To find which shifted version of g "best" matches f a standard approach has been to search for the shift lag k that minimizes the *mean squared error* $E_2(k) = \Sigma_{n \in W}[f(n + k) - g(n)]^2$ over some subset W of $\mathbf{Z}^d$. Under certain assumptions, this matching criterion is equivalent to maximizing the *linear cross-correlation* $\gamma(k) = \Sigma_{n \in W} f(n + k)g(n)$ between f and g. Such ideas have provided the foundations for many decades of research in matched filtering and signal detection. Although less mathematical tractable than the mean squared error criterion, a statistically more robust criterion is to minimize the *mean absolute error*

$$E_1(k) = \sum_{n \in W} |f(n + k) - g(n)|.$$

Mean absolute error criteria have been applied to template matching problems in image/signal processing and recently [20] to solving optimization problems in rank-order filtering.

In [67] Maragos linked the mean absolute error criterion with a nonlinear signal correlation used for signal matching. Specifically, since $|a - b| = a + b - 2 \min(a, b)$, under certain assumptions (e.g., if the error norm and the correlation is normalized by dividing it with the average area under the signals f and g), minimizing $E_1(k)$ is equivalent to maximizing the *nonlinear* cross-correlation

$$\mu(k) = \sum_{n \in W} \min[f(n + k), g(n)].$$

It was shown experimentally and theoretically that the detection of g in f is indicated by a sharper matching peak in $\mu(k)$ than in $\gamma(k)$. This is illustrated in Fig. 6. In addition, the nonlinear correlation μ (a sum of minima) is often faster than the linear (sum of products) correlation γ. These two advantages of the nonlinear correlation coupled with the relative robustness of the mean absolute error criterion make μ promising for general signal matching.

IV. Applications to Image Analysis

The applications of morphological filters in image processing and analysis are numerous. Next we shall review some of these applications to specific problems in feature extraction, shape representation and description. Additional areas of applications (not further elaborated in this paper) include biomedical image processing [1], [19], [83], [108], [115], [118], [121]; geological image processing [34]; automated industrial inspection [24], [63], [123], [138]; shape recognition [21]; shape smoothing [69], [115], [126]; enhancement and noise suppression [39], [115], [112]; texture analysis [115], [135]; radar object detection [125]; and range imagery [33].

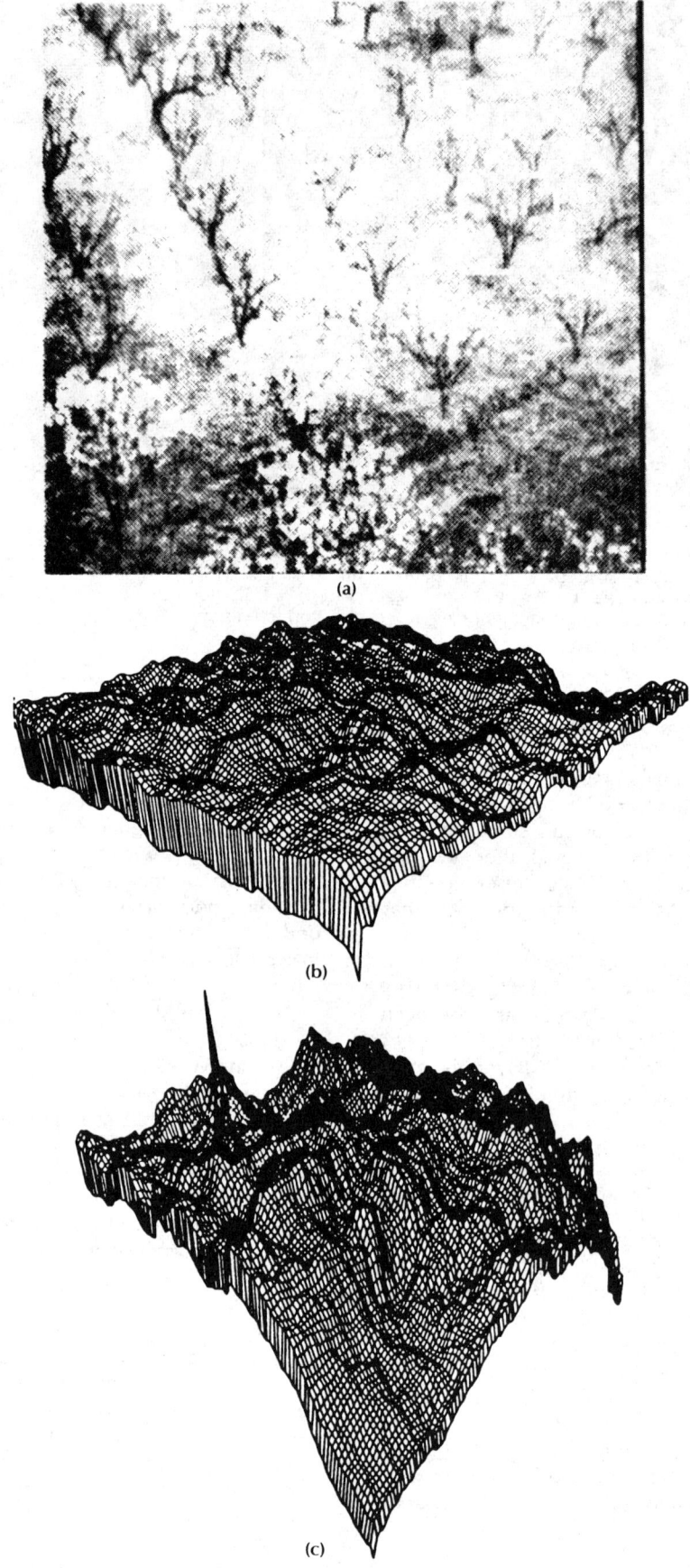

Fig. 6. (a) An image signal *f* (digitized from A. Adams' "Orchard") and a template *g* inside the window. (b) Linear correlation γ normalized by dividing it by the product of the rms value of *g* and the local rms value of *f*. (c) Morphological correlation μ normalized by dividing it by the average of the area under *g* and the local area under *f*. (From [67])

A. Feature Extraction

1) Edge/Line Enhancement and Detection: If W is a small 2-dim symmetric binary structuring element, then the set difference $X \setminus (X \ominus W)$ gives the boundary of a binary image X, and the algebraic difference

$$EG(f) = f - (f \ominus W), \qquad (28)$$

which we may call an *erosion gradient*, enhances the edges of a gray-level image f [39], [71], [82], [115]. A similar edge-enhancing operator is the *dilation gradient*

$$DG(f) = (f \oplus W) - f. \qquad (29)$$

By combining the two operators, new edge operators can be obtained that treat more symmetrically the image and its background. Examples include: 1) Beucher's morphological gradient $EG(f) + DG(f)$ in [115, p. 441] (see Fig. 7 for an example); 2) the morphological edge-strength operators $\min[EG(f), DG(f)]$ and $\max[EG(f), DG(f)]$ by Lee et al. [57]; and 3) the nonlinear Laplace operator $DG(f) - EG(f)$ in [131].

These morphological edge operators can be made more robust for edge detection by first smoothing the input image signal f either with a linear blur [57] or with an alpha-trimmed filter [35]. Another approach [131] involves combining the nonlinear Laplace filter for zero-crossing with the morphological edge-strength operators. As thoroughly investigated in [57], [131], these hybrid edge detection schemes, largely based on morphological gradients, perform comparably and in some cases better than several conventional schemes based only on linear gradients/filters; further, the morphological gradients are computationally more efficient.

In [76] it was shown that the edge operators $EG(f)$ and $DG(f)$ obey a threshold-sum superposition:

$$EG(f) = \sum_a EG(f_a). \qquad (30)$$

Thus the gray-level edge operator $EG(f)$ can be analyzed and implemented by focusing on the much simpler binary edge operator $EG(f_a) = f_a - (f_a \ominus W)$ applied to the threshold binary images f_a.

2) Peak, Valley, and Blob Detection: Opening and closings offer an intuitively simple and mathematically formal way for peak or valley detection. As suggested by the example of Fig. 2 subtracting the opening of a signal f by a set B from the input signal yields an output consisting of the

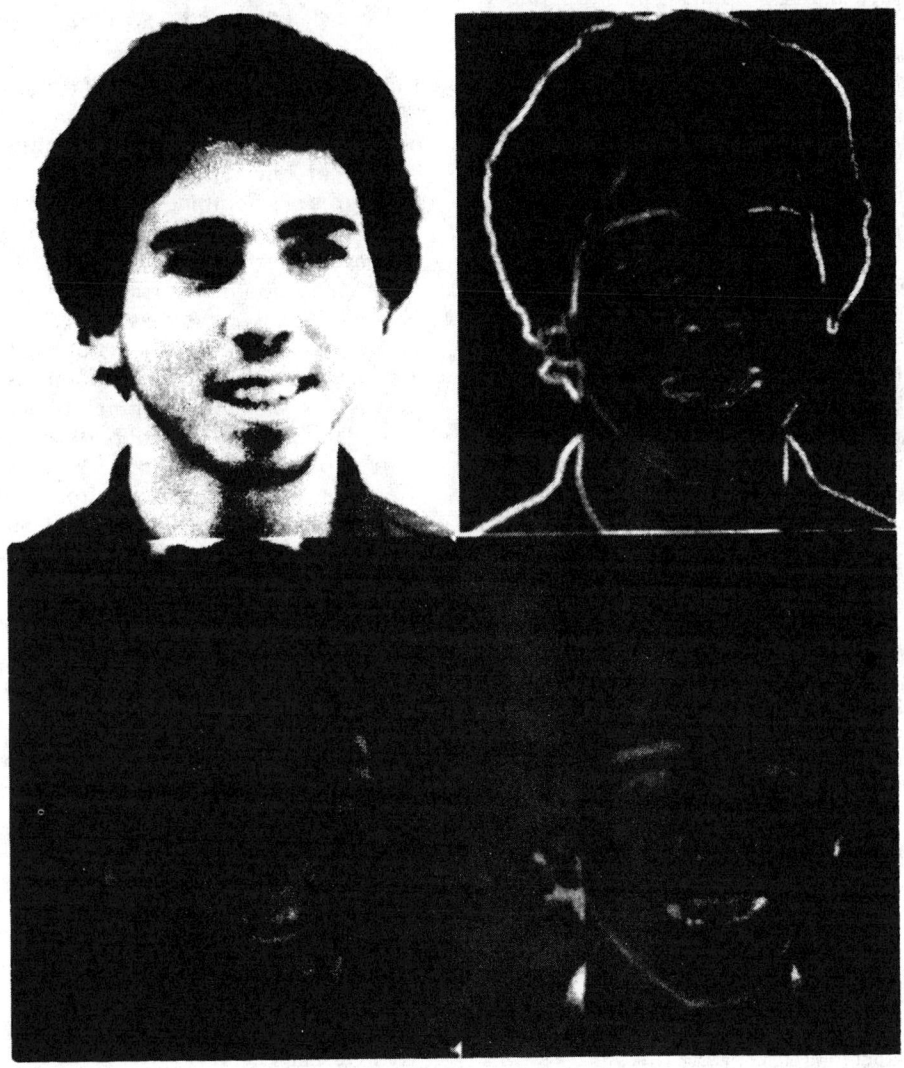

Fig. 7. Facial feature enhancement via morphological filtering. Top left: original 300 × 260-pixel image f. Top right: Edges $(f \oplus B) - (f \ominus B)$, where B is a 21-pixel discrete octagon. Bottom left: Peaks $f - (f \circ 3B)$. Bottom right: Valleys $(f \bullet 3B) - f$.

signal peaks whose support cannot contain B. This is Meyer's *top-hat transformation* [82], [83], [115],

$$P(f) = f - (f \circ B). \quad (31)$$

Since $f \circ B \leq f$, $P(f)$ is always a nonnegative signal, which guarantees that it contains only peaks. If the objective is to detect a *blob*, defined as a region with significantly brighter intensities relative to the surroundings, then we can identify the blob as a binary shape, a set B, which is the support of a corresponding peak in the intensity image function. The shape of the peak's support obtained by (31) is controlled by the shape of B, whereas the scale of the peak is controlled by the size of B. An example of application of the top-hat transformation is given in [104].

Similarly, if the blob to be detected occurs as an intensity valley, then we can approach the problem of blob detection by detecting a valley in f with a spatial support shaped like B. Thus, the operator

$$V(f) = (f \bullet B) - f \quad (32)$$

works as a general *valley* generating process. The ability of the morphological gradients to enhance edges and of the opening or closing residues to extract peaks or valleys is illustrated in Fig. 7. An example of applying these operators can be found in [141] as a pre-processing stage for extracting features such as eyes and mouth from images of human faces. Noble [90] has analyzed similar morphological feature detectors from the viewpoint of differential geometry.

In the computer vision literature there are also curvature-based approaches to extract peaks and valleys. The morphological peak/valley extractors, in addition to their being simple and efficient, have the following advantages [139] over the curvature-based approaches: 1) Curvature is an intrinsic property of 3-dim objects, which should remain invariant after 3-dim rotations. However, image functions cannot be arbitrarily rotated. Hence, the curvature estimates derived on functions are biased. 2) Using the curvature extrema to find the peak/valley boundaries may give results that do not agree with the visual perception of these boundaries. 3) Curvature requires 2nd-order derivatives, which amplify noise and are not well defined on discrete signals.

B. Shape Representation

Since the *medial axis transform* (also known as symmetric axis or skeleton transform) was first introduced by Blum [7], [8], it has been studied extensively for shape representation and description, which are very important issues in computer vision. A survey on skeletonization can be found in [112]. Next we explain how such transformations can be represented in terms of morphological systems.

Binary Images: Among the many approaches (i.e., via distance transforms [113]) to obtain the medial axis transform, it can also be obtained via erosions and openings [55], [72], [87], [115]. Let $X \subseteq \mathbf{Z}^2$ represent a finite discrete binary image and let $B \subseteq \mathbf{Z}^2$ be a binary structuring element containing the origin. The nth *skeleton component* of X with respect to B is the set

$$S_n = (X \ominus nB) \setminus [(X \ominus nB) \circ B], \quad n = 0, 1, \ldots, N, \quad (33)$$

where $N = \max\{n: X \ominus nB \neq \varnothing\}$ and $\setminus$ denotes set difference. The S_n are disjoint subsets of X, whose union is the *morphological skeleton* of X. We define the *morphological skeleton transform* of X to be the finite sequence $(S_0, S_1, \cdots, S_N)$. From this sequence we can reconstruct openings of X; i.e.,

$$X \circ kB = \bigcup_{k \leq n \leq N} S_n \oplus nB, \quad 0 \leq k \leq N. \quad (34)$$

Thus, if $k = 0$ (i.e., if we use all the skeleton subsets), $X \circ kB = X$ and we have *exact reconstruction*. If $1 \leq k \leq N$, we obtain a *partial reconstruction*, i.e., the opening (smoothed version) of X by kB. The larger the size index k, the larger the degree of smoothing. Figure 8 shows a detailed description of the skeletal decomposition and reconstruction of an image. Note that by varying k in the reconstruction phase, multiscale smoothed versions of X (its openings) can be obtained. Thus, we can view the S_n as "shape components." That is, skeleton components of small size indices n are associated with the lack of smoothness of the boundary of X, whereas skeleton components of large indices n are related to the bulky interior parts of X that are shaped similarly to nB.

A variety of skeletons results from varying the structuring element, consistent with the ability of morphological sys-

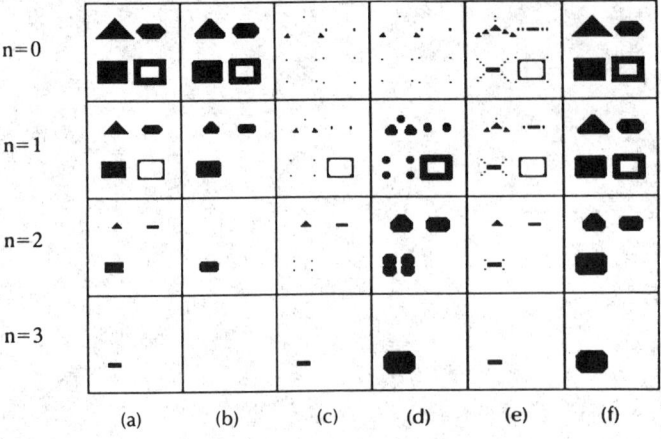

Fig. 8. Morphological skeletonization of a binary image X (top left image) with respect to a 21-pixel octagon structuring element B. (a) Erosions $X \ominus nB$, $n = 0, 1, 2, 3$. (b) Openings of erosions $(X \ominus nB) \circ B$. (c) Skeleton subsets S_n. (d) Dilated skeleton subsets $S_n \oplus nB$. (e) Partial unions of skeleton subsets $\bigcup_{N \geq k \geq n} S_k$. (f) Partial unions of dilated skeleton subsets $\bigcup_{N \geq k \geq n} S_k \oplus kB$. (From [72])

tems to extract different structural information by using different structuring elements. One application for producing multiple skeletons each with respect to a different structuring element was described in [72], where searching for the element that gives the skeleton with fewest points yielded the lowest information rate required to encode the image from its skeleton.

The morphological skeleton may be redundant. Thus, at the expense of producing a skeleton that may not look like a skeletal axis, we define the *minimal skeleton* to be a proper subset of the original skeleton whose points are sufficient for exact reconstruction, but removal of just one point would result in partial reconstruction; see Fig. 9 for an example. In [72] an algorithm was provided that finds a minimal skeleton, if it exists. Subsequent encoding of the minimal skeleton transform using Elias codes resulted in higher compression than either optimum block-Huffman or optimum runlength-Huffman coding of the original image.

A generalization of the morphological skeleton transform uses different structuring elements A_n for each skeletonization step [64, p. 191]. In this case, nB in (33) and (34) is replaced with $A_0 \oplus A_1 \oplus \cdots \oplus A_n$. A general approach for morphological skeleton-like image representations with varying structuring elements was developed in [41]. Some recent research related to morphological skeletonization includes: shape decomposition based on iterative differences between image parts and maximal openings [97]; shape matching based on features extracted from the S_n [143]; symbolic image modeling [66]; vectorized skeleton coding [13]; and extension of binary skeleton coding ideas to coding gray-level images by first decomposing them into a collection of threshold binary images [103]. Finally, note that the morphological skeleton defined above is not necessarily connected; for *connected* skeletons see [3].

Gray-level Images: In [96] the skeleton transform has been extended to gray-level images. We describe this algorithm using terminology analogous to that for binary morphological skeletons. Namely, the *n*th skeleton component of *f* with respect to a binary structuring element *B* is the nonnegative function

$$s_n(f) = (f \ominus nB) - [(f \ominus nB) \circ B], \quad 0 \leq n \leq N, \quad (35)$$

where $N = \max\{n: f \ominus nB \neq 0\}$. A skeleton of *f* can be defined as the pointwise sum

$$SK(f) = \sum_{n=0}^{N} s_n(f). \quad (36)$$

As for binary images, *f* can be reconstructed from its components s_n either exactly or partially (its openings) [64], [69]. In [76] it was shown that the above skeleton obeys a threshold sum-superposition

$$SK(f) = \sum_a SK(f_a), \quad (37)$$

As in (30), this result reduces the analysis and implementation of gray-level skeletons to the much simpler binary skeletons $SK(f_a)$ of threshold binary images f_a.

For more general gray-level skeletons see [64], [66], [69] and for thinning gray-level images see [32], [39].

C. Shaped-Size Distributions

Matheron [80], [81] considered families of openings and closings of compact sets $X \subseteq \mathbf{R}^2$ by convex compact struc-

(a)

(b)

(c)

Fig. 9. (a) Original binary image (256 × 256 pixels). (b) Morphological skeleton with respect to a 3 × 3-pixel square structuring element. (c) Minimal skeleton. (From [72])

turing elements, e.g., disks rD of radius r, for unifying all sizing (sieving) operations in Euclidean spaces. He called these parametric openings *granulometries* and their areas *size distributions*. The decreasing function $A(X \circ rD)/A(X)$, $r \geq 0$, where $A(\cdot)$ denotes area, was related in [80], [81] to probabilistic measures of the size distribution in X. Serra and his co-workers [115, ch. 10] have used extensively these size distributions in image analysis applications to petrography and biology. In [64], [65], [69] Maragos related these size distributions to a concept of a pattern spectrum. Next we discuss these ideas only for discrete binary images.

The *pattern spectrum* of a discrete binary finite image $X \subseteq \mathbf{Z}^2$ relative to a structuring element $B \subseteq \mathbf{Z}^2$ is defined [69] as the differential size distribution function

$$PS_X(n, B) = A[X \circ nB \setminus X \circ (n + 1)B]$$
$$= A(X \circ nB) - A[X \circ (n + 1)B] \quad (38)$$

The rationale behind the symbolic term "pattern spectrum" is the fact that the opening $X \circ nB$ is the union of all $(nB + z)$ with $(nB + z) \subseteq X$, that is, of all shifted patterns B of size n that can fit inside X. Thus $A(X \circ nB)$ is a measure of the pattern content of X relative to the pattern nB, and (38) measures the change of such pattern content with respect to n. In actuality, the pattern spectrum, which is a nonnegative function for all B and n, is a *shape-size histogram*. It also has some conceptual similarities with the Fourier spectrum. The pattern spectrum conveys several types of information useful for shape description and multiscale image analysis. For example, the *boundary roughness* of X relative to B manifests itself as contributions in the lower-size part of the pattern spectrum. Long capes or bulky protruding parts in X that consist of patterns sB show up as isolated impulses in the pattern spectrum around positive $n = s$. Finally, the pattern spectrum can be defined for "negative" sizes by using closings instead of openings; in this case impulses at negative sizes indicate the existence of prominent intruding *gulfs* or *holes* in X.

Observe from (34) that $S_n = \emptyset$ implies that $X \circ nB = X \circ (n + 1)B$; further, for $1 \leq k \leq N$,

$$X = X \circ kB \Leftrightarrow PS_X(n, B) = 0 \quad 0 \leq n < k. \quad (39)$$

Thus X is smooth to a degree k relative to B (i.e., $X = X \circ kB$) if and only if its first k pattern spectrum samples are zero, or if its first k skeleton components are empty.

In the theory [81], [115] of random stationary sets $X \subseteq \mathbf{Z}^2$, the size function $\lambda_x(z) = \max\{n: z \in X \circ nB\}$, $z \in X$, can be viewed as a random variable. Its probability function $p_k = \text{Prob}\{\lambda(z) = k\}$ is equal to $PS_x(k, B)/A(X)$. As explained in [69],

$$H(X/B) = -\sum_{n=0}^{N} p_n \log p_n \quad (40)$$

is the average uncertainty (entropy) of λ. It can be viewed as the *average roughness* of X relative to B, because it quantifies the shape-size complexity of X by measuring its boundary roughness averaged over all depths that B reaches. Thus $H(X/B)$ is maximum ($\log (N + 1)$) iff X contains maximal patterns nB at equal area portions in all sizes n, and minimum (0) iff X is the union of maximal patterns of only one size.

All the above ideas can be extended to gray-level images [65], [69]. In [15] the normalized pattern spectrum (called "pecstrum") was used for binary and gray-level shape recognition by computing Euclidean distances between pattern spectra of test images and reference images. Some work related to morphological size distributions can also be found in [132], [135].

C. Fractals

1) Estimating Fractal Dimension: A large variety of natural image objects (e.g., clouds, coastlines, mountains, islands, trees, leaves, etc.) can be modeled very well with *fractals* [62]. Fractals are mathematical sets with very high level of geometrical complexity; formally, their Hausdorff dimension is larger than their topological dimension. An important characteristic of fractals to measure for purposes of shape description or classification is their fractal dimension. Among the various methods [62] to estimate the *fractal dimension D* of the fractal surface of a 3-dim set F, the *covering method* is based conceptually on Minkowski's idea of finding the area of irregular sets: dilate them with spheres of radius r, find the volume $V(r)$ of the dilated set, and set its area equal to $\lim_{r \to 0} A(r)$, where $A(r) = V(r)/2r$. If the surface of F is a pure fractal, then its area $A(r)$ at different scales r behaves as

$$\log A(r) = (2 - D) \log (r) + \text{constant}. \quad (41)$$

Thus, the fractal dimension D can be estimated by fitting a straight line to a log-log plot of $A(r)$. Digital implementations and variations of the above method can be found in [25], [26], [75], [95], [119] where morphological dilations and erosions are used to create a volume-blanket as a layer either covering or being peeled off from the intensity image surface at various scales.

Similarly, if F is a 2-dim set, e.g., the graph of a 1-dim signal, we can dilate it with disks of radius r, find the area $A(r)$ of the dilated set, and compute a multiscale length $L(r) = A(r)/2r$; then, for pure fractals,

$$\log L(r) = (1 - D) \log (r) + \text{constant}. \quad (42)$$

Figure 10(a) shows an intensity image profile (the solid line) and two layers of dilations (2 dotted lines) and erosions (2 dashed lines), both at scales $r = 10$ and 20. For "real world" signals with some fractal structure, the assumption of exact self-similarity at all scales is not true. Hence, to estimate a fractal dimension for the 1-dim signal of Fig. 10(a) we fit *locally* line segments on the log-log plot of $L(r)$. Figure 10b shows the local fractal dimension, which for each r is equal to one minus the slope of a line segment fitted (using linear regression) to the log-log plot of $L(r)$ over a moving window $[r, r + 9]$ of 10 scales. The relative variation of these local estimates indicate that, for real world signals relation (42) is only approximately true; hence, it is more meaningful to estimate their fractal dimension over a small finite range of scales.

2) Modeling Fractals: Currently, there are many computer algorithms to *generate* fractals. However, the *inverse problem*, i.e., given a fractal image find a signal model and an algorithm to generate it, is much more important and very difficult. Toward solving this inverse problem, Barnsley [5] and his co-workers developed the theory of *iterated function systems*. A key idea is their *collage theorem*, which states that if we can "closely" cover a binary fractal image F with a collage of m small patches that are reduced distorted copies of F, then we can reconstruct F (within arbi-

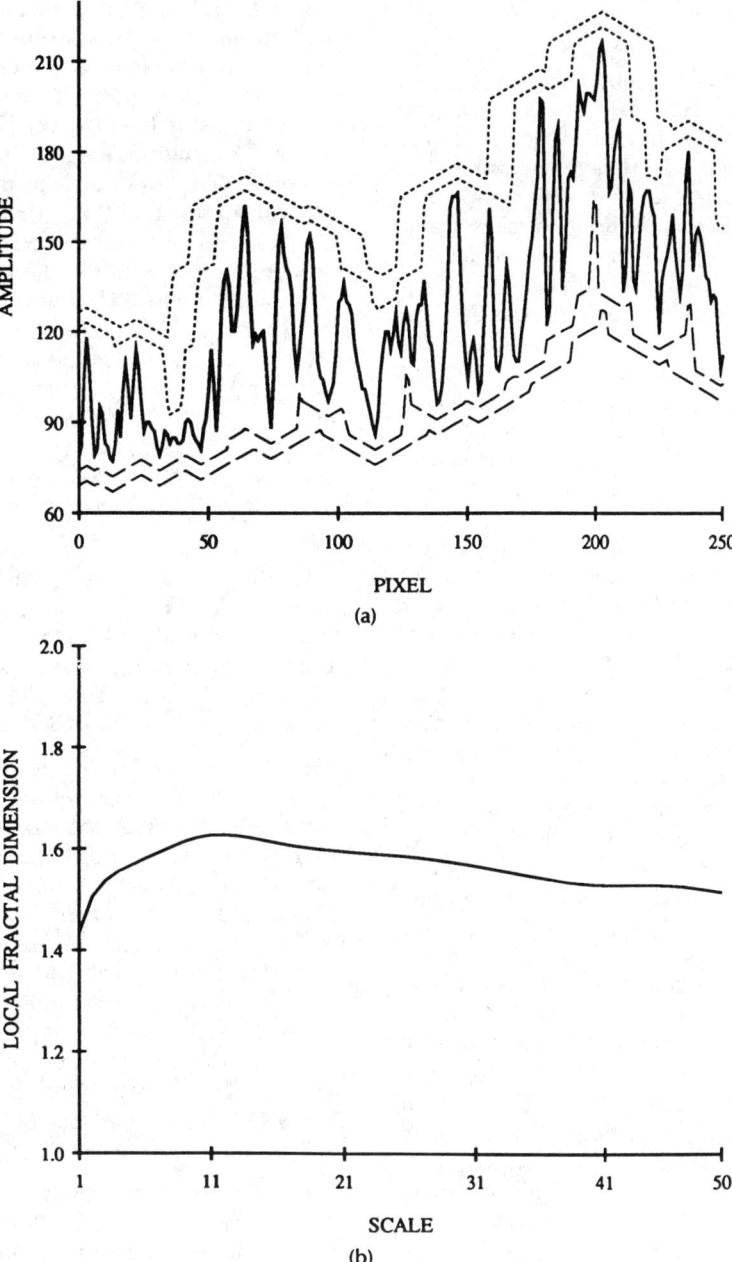

Fig. 10. (a) Discrete intensity image profile f (in solid line) with its erosions $f \ominus rg$ (dashed lines) and dilations $f \oplus rg$ (dotted lines) at scales $r = 10, 20$. The structuring function g was equal to $g(0) = 0.5$, $g(-1) = g(1) = 0$, and $g(n) = -\infty$ for $n \neq -1, 0, 1$. (b) Local fractal dimensions over a moving window of 10 scales.

trary accuracy) as the attractor of a set of m contractive affine maps (each map is responsible for one patch). Simple choices for these maps w_i, $1 \leq i \leq m$, are

$$w_i \begin{pmatrix} x \\ y \end{pmatrix} = r_i \cdot \begin{bmatrix} \cos \theta_i & -\sin \theta_i \\ \sin \theta_i & \cos \theta_i \end{bmatrix} \begin{bmatrix} x \\ y \end{bmatrix} + \begin{bmatrix} t_{xi} \\ t_{yi} \end{bmatrix}.$$

Each w_i, operating on all points (x, y) of F, gives a version of F that is rotated by angle θ_i, shrunk by a scale factor r_i, and translated by the vector (t_{xi}, t_{yi}). This theorem and a related synthesis algorithm have been very successful for fractal image modeling [5]. However, they require considerable human intervention. The difficulty lies in finding appropriate maps w_i, which (by variation of their scaling,

rotation, and translation parameters) can collage F well. An approximate solution to this problem has been provided by Libeskind-Hadas and Maragos [59] who used the morphological skeleton transform to efficiently extract the parameters of these affine maps. In their work, a major skeleton branch was associated with each map w_i. The rotation angle θ_i was found as the angle that the skeleton branch forms with the horizontal. The translation vector (t_{xi}, t_{yi}) was taken as the vector of pixel coordinates of the skeleton branch point b. Finally, the scaling factor was set equal to $r = n/N$, where n is the index of the skeleton subset containing b. This algorithm can model images F that exhibit some degree of self-similarity; i.e., when local details of F closely resemble F as a whole.

V. Representation Theorems

Several mathematical structures, known as *image algebras*, have been developed in [21], [30], [50], [84], and [105]–[107]. Their purpose is to represent many image processing operators as a finite composition of a few basic operations including erosions and dilations. The image algebras in [30], [105], [107] encompass all linear (e.g., matrix operations) and many nonlinear image operators. Although erosions and dilations are insufficient by themselves to represent all possible image operations [107], it is abundantly clear from Sections III and IV that morphological operations can be combined in many ways to solve problems in a wide variety of applications. Hence, it is interesting to know which signal processing systems can be represented morphologically. Toward this goal, a theory was introduced in [64], [68], [70] that unifies many concepts encountered in signal processing or image analysis and represents a broad class of nonlinear and linear operators as a minimal combination of morphological erosions or dilations. Here we summarize the main results of this theory, in a simplified way, restricting our discussion only to signals with *discrete* domain $\mathbf{E} = \mathbf{Z}^d$. (The corresponding part of the theory for continuous-domain signals is contained in [64], [68]).

Consider an SP operator Ψ defined on the class $\mathcal{S}$ of all subsets of $\mathbf{E}$. Ψ is called *translation-invariant* iff $\Psi(X + p) = \Psi(X) + p$, for all $X \in \mathcal{S}$ and $p \in \mathbf{E}$. Any such Ψ is uniquely characterized by its *kernel* that is defined in [81] as the subclass $\mathcal{K}(\Psi) = \{X \in \mathcal{S} : 0 \in \Psi(X)\}$ of input sets. That is, the kernel is a collection of *input* sets such that their corresponding outputs contain the origin. Ψ is called *increasing* iff $A \subseteq B \Rightarrow \Psi(A) \subseteq \Psi(B)$. The *dual* SP operator of Ψ is defined as $\Psi^d(X) = [\Psi(X^c)]^c$, $X \in \mathcal{S}$, where $(\cdot)^c$ denotes set complementation. In [64], [68], [70], the kernel representation was extended to FP operators. A d-dim FP operator ψ is called *translation-invariant* iff $\psi[f(x - y) + c] = [\psi(f)](x - y) + c$, for all $(y, c) \in \mathbf{E} \times \mathbf{R}$ and $f(x) \in \mathcal{F}$, where $\mathcal{F}$ is the class of all functions with domain $\mathbf{E}$ and range $\mathbf{R} \cup \{\pm \infty\}$. That is, ψ is translation-invariant iff it commutes with a shift of both the argument and the amplitude of its input functions. Such a ψ is uniquely characterized by its *kernel*, which is defined as the subclass $\mathcal{K}(\psi) = \{f \in \mathcal{F} : \psi(f)(0) \geq 0\}$ of input functions. Further, ψ is *increasing* iff $f \leq g \Rightarrow \psi(f) \leq \psi(g)$. The dual operator of ψ is defined as $\psi^d(f) = -\psi(-f)$, where $(-f)(x) = -f(x)$. The class of translation-invariant increasing SP or FP operators are useful because of the following two representation theorems.

THEOREM 1 (Matheron [81]). *Any translation-invariant increasing SP operator $\Psi : \mathcal{S} \to \mathcal{S}$ can be represented exactly as the union of erosions by its kernel sets and as the intersection of dilations by the reflected kernel sets of its dual operator Ψ^d.*

THEOREM 2 (Maragos [64], [68]). *Any translation-invariant increasing FP operator $\psi : \mathcal{F} \to \mathcal{F}$ can be represented exactly as the pointwise supremum of erosions by its kernel functions, and as the pointwise infimum of dilations by the reflected kernel functions of its dual operator ψ^d.*

The two theorems above require an infinite number of erosions to represent a given system. However, we can find more efficient (requiring fewer erosions) theorems by using only a substructure of the kernel. The pair $(\mathcal{K}(\Psi), \subseteq)$ is a partially ordered set with respect to set inclusion. A *minimal element* of $(\mathcal{K}(\Psi), \subseteq)$ is any set in $\mathcal{K}(\Psi)$ that is not preceded (with respect to $\subseteq$) by any other kernel set. The *basis* $\mathcal{B}(\Psi)$ of the translation-invariant operator Ψ is defined as the set of all its minimal kernel elements. It was shown in [64], [68] that $\mathcal{B}(\Psi)$ exists (i.e., is nonempty) if Ψ is increasing and upper semicontinuous. [An increasing SP operator Ψ is upper semicontinuous iff, for any decreasing set sequence (X_n) with $X_{n+1} \subseteq X_n$, $\Psi(\cap_n X_n) = \cap_n \Psi(X_n)$.] Similarly, the pair $(\mathcal{K}(\psi), \leq)$ is a partially ordered set with respect to the function ordering $\leq$. A minimal function-element of $(\mathcal{K}(\psi), \leq)$ is any function in $\mathcal{K}(\psi)$ that is not preceded (with respect to function $\leq$) by any other kernel function. Then, the *basis* $\mathcal{B}(\psi)$ of ψ is defined as the set of its minimal kernel functions, and it *exists* if ψ is increasing and upper semicontinuous [64], [68]. [An increasing FP operator ψ is upper semicontinuous iff, for any decreasing function sequence (f_n) with $f_{n+1} \leq f_n$, $\psi(\wedge_n f_n) = \wedge_n \psi(f_n)$.] The importance of the basis for SP of FP operators is revealed by the following two representation theorems.

THEOREM 3 (Maragos [64], [68]). *Any translation-invariant, increasing and upper semicontinuous SP operator $\Psi : \mathcal{S} \to \mathcal{S}$ can be represented exactly as the union of erosions by its basis sets. If the dual Ψ^d is upper semicontinuous, then Ψ can also be represented as the intersection of dilations by the reflected basis sets of Ψ^d.*

THEOREM 4 (Maragos [64], [68]). *(a)-(FP systems): Any translation-invariant, increasing and upper semicontinuous FP operator $\psi : \mathcal{F} \to \mathcal{F}$ can be represented exactly as the pointwise supremum of erosions by its basis functions. If the dual ψ^d is upper semicontinuous, then ψ can also be represented as the pointwise infimum of dilations by the reflected basis functions of ψ^d.*

(b)-(FSP systems). Let $\phi : \mathcal{F} \to \mathcal{F}$ be an FSP translation-invariant operator that commutes with thresholding, and let Φ be its respective SP operator. Then ϕ is exactly represented as the supremum of erosions by the basis sets of Φ. If the dual SP operator Φ^d is upper semicontinuous, then ϕ can also be represented as the infimum of dilations by the reflected basis sets of Φ^d.

In [73], [74] these very general theorems have been applied to various filters such as linear shift-invariant, morphological, median, rank-order, linear combinations of rank-order, and stack filters. Below we give some simple examples.

Example 1 (Linear Filters). A linear filter is translation-invariant and increasing iff its impulse response is everywhere nonnegative and has area equal to one. Consider the 2-point FIR filter $[\psi(f)](n) = af(n) + (1 - a) f(n - 1)$, where $0 < a < 1$. Then the basis of ψ consists of all functions $g(n)$ with $g(0) = r \in \mathbf{R}$, $g(-1) = -ar/(1 - a)$, and $g(n) = -\infty$ for $n \neq 0, -1$. Then Theorem 4(a) yields

$$af(n) + (1 - a) f(n - 1)$$
$$= \sup_{r \in \mathbf{R}} \left[\min \left\{ f(n) - r, f(n - 1) + \frac{ar}{1 - a} \right\} \right], \quad (43)$$

which expresses a linear convolution as a supremum of erosions. FIR linear filters have an infinite basis, which forms a finite-dimensional vector space.

Example 2 (Median filters). Many discrete FSP increasing morphological filters and all rank-order filters have a finite number of minimal elements; hence, they can be expressed as a finite max-of-erosions or min-of-dilations. Further, they commute with thresholding, which allows us to focus only on the SP versions of such filters. For example, the FSP median by the window $W = \{-1, 0, 1\}$ has an SP version of $\Phi(X) = \{p \in \mathbf{Z}: |(X \cap W + p| \geq 2\}, X \subseteq \mathbf{Z}$. Φ has 3 basis sets: $\{-1, 0\}$, $\{-1, 1\}$, and $\{0, 1\}$. Hence, Theorem 4(b) yields

$$\text{med}\,[f(x-1), f(x), f(x+1)]$$
$$= \max \begin{Bmatrix} \min\,[f(x-1), f(x)], \\ \min\,[f(x-1), f(x+1)], \\ \min\,[f(x), f(x+1)] \end{Bmatrix}. \quad (44)$$

Example 3 (Stack Filters). The definition of stack filters in (20) requires a *positive Boolean function* $\beta(x_1, \cdots, x_n)$. Such a function has an irreducible sum-of-products expression as Boolean sum of its prime implicants and an irreducible product-of-sums expression as Boolean product of its prime implicates [88]. In [134] all the 20 different stack filters with a β of $n = 3$ variables were examined in detail. For $n > 3$ there was not a direct way to find a functional definition of arbitrary stack filters. However, by using morphological concepts in [74] a general functional definition was obtained as follows. The positive Boolean function β corresponds uniquely to a translation-invariant increasing and upper semicontinuous SP operator Φ, which in turn defines uniquely an FSP operator ϕ that commutes with thresholding. That is, stack filters are the class of all discrete translation-invariant FSP finite-window filters that commute with thresholding. Given β, Φ is found by replacing Boolean AND/OR with set $\cap/\cup$; then, ϕ is obtained by replacing set $\cap/\cup$ in Φ with min/max. Further, as shown in [74], stack filters have a finite number of basis sets that are in one-to-one correspondence with the prime implicants of β. Thus the basis can be used to find the irreducible forms of β, and vice-versa. For example, the FSP opening $\phi(f) = f \circ A$, $A = \{-1, 0, 1\}$, can be viewed as a stack filter, whose functional definition is associated with the window $W = \{-2, -1, 0, 1, 2\}$. Its dual filter is the FSP closing $f \bullet A$. Let $\Phi(X) = X \circ A$ and $\Phi^d(X) = X \bullet A$ be its respective SP operator and dual SP operator. The basis sets of Φ are [64], [68] the 3 subsets $G_1 = A - 1$, $G_2 = A$, $G_3 = A + 1$ of W; the basis sets of Φ^d are the 4 subsets $H_1 = \{0\}$, $H_2 = \{-2, 1\}$, $H_3 = \{-1, 2\}$, $H_4 = \{-1, 1\}$ of W. Thus, from Theorem 4(b), ϕ can be realized as

$$f \circ A(x) = \max_{i=1}^{3} \left\{ \min_{y \in G_i} f(x+y) \right\} = \min_{k=1}^{4} \left\{ \max_{y \in H_k} f(x+y) \right\}.$$
$$(45)$$

The β corresponding to Φ and ϕ is $\beta(x_1, \cdots, x_5) = x_1 x_2 x_3 + x_2 x_3 x_4 + x_3 x_4 x_5 = x_3(x_1 + x_4)(x_2 + x_4)(x_2 + x_5)$. Thus there is one-to-one correspondence between the 3 prime implicants of β and the erosions (local min) by the basis sets of Φ, as well as between the 4 prime implicates of β and the dilations (local max) by the basis sets of Φ^d. Thus stack filters can be expressed as minimal forms of max-min operations based either on irreducible forms of their Boolean function or on their minimal kernel elements. In [74] both approaches were compared, and their theoretical equivalence was established.

Example 4 (Hybrid Linear/Nonlinear filters). There are many nonlinear filters that have both a linear and nonlinear (i.e., rank-order) component, e.g., [4], [6], [12], [22], [48], [94], [127]. They are useful because they combine desirable characteristics of both linear and nonlinear filters. The representation theory in this section applies to these filters too, if their linear parts contain positive coefficients which sum to one. A simple such filter is the *Wilcoxon* filter [22]

$$[\psi(f)](n) = \text{median}\,\{[f(n-2) + f(n+2)]/2,$$
$$[f(n-1) + f(n+1)]/2, f(n)\}, \quad (46)$$

whose basis is obtained by combining results (43) and (44); see also [64, p. 157].

The above examples show the power of the general representation theorems. An interesting area of current research is concerned with using these results as a basis for a design methodology for morphological systems.

Conclusions

In this paper we have attempted to show how a wide range of multidimensional signal processing problems can be addressed using morphological systems. We have shown that simple nonlinear operators such as erosion and dilation can be combined to create many different types of signal processing and analysis operators. A major advantage of morphological systems is their built-in ability to represent and extract shape in multidimensional signals. Another advantage is that they are well suited for simple and efficient implementations using parallel or sequential computation.

So far, many of the signal processing algorithms and analysis techniques based on morphological systems have been derived heuristically or experimentally. However, the existence of powerful representation theorems for morphological systems suggests that much more can be done to develop methodologies for designing systems of this class. The results of research in this area will impact many areas of application of multidimensional signal processing.

Appendix

Historical Notes on Definitions and Notation

Considerable confusion has arisen regarding the definitions of the basic operations of mathematical morphology. This confusion is primarily due to usage of the symbols $\oplus$ and $\ominus$ by different authors to mean different things. In [42] Hadwiger's definition of Minkowski set addition [85] was identical to our definition (4) of set dilation. Our definition of set erosion (5) is identical to an operation introduced by Hadwiger [42] and called Minkowski set subtraction. Thus, in this paper, set dilation and erosion are identical to the classical Minkowski set addition and Minkowski set subtraction. These definitions were used by Sternberg [120]–[122] in his contributions to the field.

Matheron [81] and Serra [115] used the *reflection* $\check{B} = \{-b : b \in B\}$ of B to define the set of basic operations of mathematical morphology in a somewhat different way. Minkowski addition was defined identically to Hadwiger's definition, and the symbol $\oplus$ was used for this operation. Minkowski subtraction was redefined as $X \ominus B = \cap_{b \in B}(X + b) = \{z : (\check{B} + z) \subseteq X\}$, which is the same as Hadwiger's definition except the structuring set is reflected. Matheron and Serra defined the dilation of X by B as $X \oplus \check{B} = \{z : (B + z) \cap X \neq 0\}$ where $\oplus$ means Minkowski set addition.

They defined erosion of X by B as $X \ominus \check{B} = \{z : (B + z) \subseteq X\}$, where $\ominus$ means their redefined Minkowski set subtraction (i.e., with the reflected set), thereby creating part of the confusion. Thus the two reflections cancel and the Matheron/Serra definition of erosion turns out to be identical to the classical Minkowski set subtraction, and thus, identical to the definition of this paper. Serra introduced also the *hit-or-miss* transform, which is a generalization of erosion as a Boolean matched filter. The Matheron/Serra definitions of opening and closing of X by B are $X_B = (X \ominus \check{B}) \oplus B$ and $X^B = (X \oplus \check{B}) \ominus B$. Their opening involves the same operations and gives identical result to the definition that we have presented; i.e., $X_B = X \circ B$. However, their closing by B is equivalent to our closing by the reflected B; i.e., $X^B = X \bullet \check{B}$.

In [70]–[74] we used Matheron and Serra's definitions. However, in this paper we have adopted Sternberg's definitions and his terminology (i.e., defining dilation and erosion identically to Minkowski addition and subtraction), because they are somewhat simpler. (The Matheron and Serra definitions have certain advantages in terms of duality properties). Note that Matheron and Serra's definitions become identical to Sternberg's if $B = \check{B}$, i.e., if the structuring element is symmetric. In addition we use the notation $\circ$ and $\bullet$ for opening and closing as in [43], and the group-theoretic notation $X + b$ for set translation as in [28].

References

[1] R. S. Acharya and R. Laurette, "Mathematical morphology for 3-D image analysis," in *Proc. ICASSP-88*, New York, April 1988.

[2] G. R. Arce, N. C. Gallagher, and T. A. Nodes, "Median filters: Theory for one- and two-dimensional filters," in *Advances in Computer Vision and Image Processing*, Vol. 2, T. S. Huang, Ed. CT: JAI Press, 1986.

[3] C. Arcelli, L. Cordella, and S. Levialdi, "From local maxima to connected skeletons," *IEEE Trans. Pattern Anal. Mach. Intellig.*, PAMI-3, pp. 134–143, Mar. 1981.

[4] J. Astola and O. Yli-Harja, "Gradient median filter," in *Proc. IEEE ISCAS-87*, Philadelphia, PA, May 1987.

[5] M. Barnsley, *Fractals Everywhere*. NY: Acad. Press, 1988.

[6] J. B. Bednar and T. L. Watt, "Alpha-trimmed means and their relationship to median filters," *IEEE Trans. Acoust. Speech, Signal Process.*, ASSP-32, pp. 145–153, Feb. 1984.

[7] H. Blum, "A Transformation for extracting new descriptions of shape," in *Models for the Perception of Speech and Visual Forms*, W. Wathen-Dunn, Ed. Cambridge, MA: MIT Press, 1967.

[8] ——, "Biological shape and visual senses (Part I)," *J. Theor. Biol.*, vol. 38, pp. 205–287, 1973.

[9] G. Borgefors, "Distance transformations in arbitrary dimensions," *Comp. Vision Graph. Image Process.*, 27, pp. 321–345, 1984.

[10] N. K. Bose, *Applied Multidimensional Systems Theory*. NY: Reinhold, 1982.

[11] ——, *Digital Filters: Theory and Applications*. Elsevier, 1985.

[12] A. C. Bovik, T. S. Huang, and D. C. Munson, Jr., "A generalization of median filtering using linear combinations of order statistics," *IEEE Trans. Acoust. Speech, Signal Process.*, ASSP-31, pp. 1342–1349, Dec. 1983.

[13] J. W. Brandt and A. K. Jain, "A medial axis transform algorithm for compression and vectorization of document images," in *Proc. IEEE ICASSP-89*, Glasgow, Scotland, May 1989.

[14] R. W. Brockett, Lectures in Nonlinear Science, UC Berkeley Summer School, 1987.

[15] J. F. Bronskill and A. N. Venetsanopoulos, "Multidimensional shape description and recognition using mathematical morphology," *J. Intellig. Rob. Syst.*, 1, pp. 117–143, 1988.

[16] P. J. Burt and E. H. Adelson, "The Laplacian pyramid as a compact image code," *IEEE Trans. Commun.*, COM-31, pp. 532–540, Apr. 1983.

[17] A. R. Butz, "A class of rank order smoothers," *IEEE Trans. Acoust. Speech, Signal Process.*, ASSP-34, pp. 157–165, Feb. 1986.

[18] M. Chen and P. Yan, "A multiscaling approach based on morphological filtering," *IEEE Trans. Pattern Anal. Mach. Intell.*, PAMI-11, pp. 694–700, July 1989.

[19] C. H. Chu and E. J. Delp, "Impulsive noise suppression and background normalization of electrocardiogram signals using morphological operators," *IEEE Trans. Biomed. Enginr.*, BME-36, pp. 262–273, Feb. 1989.

[20] E. J. Coyle, "Rank order operators and the mean absolute error criterion," *IEEE Trans. Acoust. Speech Signal Process.*, vol. ASSP-36, pp. 63–76, Jan. 1988.

[21] T. R. Crimmins and W. R. Brown, "Image algebra and automatic shape recognition," *IEEE Trans. Aerosp. and Electron. Syst.*, vol. AES-21, pp. 60–69, Jan. 1985.

[22] R. J. Crinon, "The Wilcoxon filter: A robust filtering scheme," in *Proc. IEEE ICASSP-85*, Tampa, FL, Mar. 1985.

[23] P.-E. Danielsson and S. Levialdi, "Computer architectures for pictorial information systems," *IEEE Computer Mag.*, Nov. 1981, pp. 53–67.

[24] A. M. Darwish and A. K. Jain, "A rule based approach for visual pattern inspection," *IEEE Trans. Pattern Anal. Mach. Intellig.*, PAMI-10, pp. 56–68, Jan. 1988.

[25] B. Dubuc, C. Roques-Carmes, C. Tricot, and S. W. Zucker, "The variation method: a technique to estimate the fractal dimension of surfaces," in *Proc. SPIE 845: Visual Communications and Image Processing II*, 1987.

[26] B. Dubuc, J. F. Quiniou, C. Roques-Carmes, C. Tricot, and S. W. Zucker, "Evaluating the fractal dimension of profiles," *Phys. Rev. A*, vol. 39, pp. 1500–1512, Feb. 1989.

[27] D. E. Dudgeon and R. M. Mersereau, *Multidimensional Digital Signal Processing*. Englewood Cliffs, NJ: Prentice-Hall, 1984.

[28] E. R. Dougherty and C. R. Giardina, *Image Processing-Continuous to Discrete*. Englewood Cliffs, NJ: Prentice-Hall, 1987.

[29] ——, "Error bounds for morphologically derived measurements," *SIAM J. Appl. Math.*, 47, pp. 425–440, Apr. 1987.

[30] ——, "Image Algebra-induced operators and induced subalgebras," in *Proc. SPIE 845: Visual Communications and Image Processing II*, 1987.

[31] M. J. B. Duff, D. M. Watson, T. J. Fountain, and G. K. Shaw, "A cellular logic array for image processing," *Pattern Recogn.*, vol. 5, pp. 229–247, 1973.

[32] C. R. Dyer and A. Rosenfeld, "Thinning algorithms for gray-scale pictures," *IEEE Trans. Pattern Anal. Mach. Intellig.*, PAMI-1, pp. 88–89, Jan. 1979.

[33] T. Esselman and J. G. Verly, "Applications of mathematical morphology to range imagery," MIT Lincoln Lab Tech. Rep. 797, Dec. 1987.

[34] A. G. Fabbri, *Image Processing of Geological Data*. NY: Reinhold, 1984.

[35] R. J. Feehs and G. R. Arce, "Multidimensional morphological edge detection," in *Proc. SPIE 845: Visual Communications and Image Processing II*, 1987.

[36] J. P. Fitch, E. J. Coyle, and N. C. Gallagher, Jr., "Median filtering by threshold decomposition," *IEEE Trans. Acoust., Speech, Signal Processing*, ASSP-32, pp. 1183–1188, Dec. 1984.

[37] ——, "The analog median filter," *IEEE Trans. Circ. Syst.*, CAS-33, pp. 94–102, Jan. 1986.

[38] N. C. Gallagher, Jr. and G. L. Wise, "A theoretical analysis of the properties of median filters," *IEEE Trans. Acoust. Speech, Signal Process.*, ASSP-29, pp. 1136–1141, Dec. 1981.

[39] V. Goetcherian, "From binary to grey tone image processing using fuzzy logic concepts," *Pattern Recognition*, vol. 12, pp. 7–15, 1980.

[40] M. J. E. Golay, "Hexagonal parallel pattern transformations," *IEEE Trans. Comput.*, C-18, pp. 733–740, Aug. 1969.

[41] J. Goutsias and D. Schonfeld, "Image coding via morphological transformations: A general theory," in *Proc. IEEE Conf. CVPR-89*, San Diego, CA, June 1989.

[42] H. Hadwiger, *Vorlesungen über Inhalt, Oberfläche, und Isoperimetrie*. Berlin: Springer Verlag, 1957.

[43] R. M. Haralick, S. R. Sternberg, and X. Zhuang, "Image analysis using mathematical morphology," *IEEE Trans. Pattern Anal. Mach. Intell.*, PAMI-9, pp. 532-550, July 1987.

[44] R. M. Haralick, C. Lin, J. S. J. Lee, and X. Zhuang, "Multiresolution morphology," in *Proc. 1st ICCV*, London, 1987.

[45] R. M. Haralick, X. Zhuang, C. Lin, and J. S. J. Lee, "The digital morphological sampling theorem," *IEEE Trans. Acoust., Speech, Signal Process.*, vol. ASSP-37, pp. 2067-2090, Dec. 1989.

[46] R. G. Harber, S. C. Bass, and G. W. Neudeck, "VLSI implementation of a fast rank order filtering algorithm," in *Proc. IEEE ICASSP-85*, Tampa, FL, Mar. 1985.

[47] H. J. A. M. Heijmans and C. Ronse, "The algebraic basis of mathematical morphology Part I: Dilations and erosions," Rep. AM-R8807, CWI, Amsterdam, June 1988.

[48] P. Heinonen and Y. Neuvo, "FIR-median hybrid filters," *IEEE Trans. Acoust. Speech, Signal Processing*, ASSP-35, pp. 832-838, June 1987.

[49] J. M. Hereford and W. T. Rhodes, "Nonlinear Optical Image Filtering by Time-Sequential Threshold Decomposition," *Optical Enginr.*, Apr. 1988.

[50] K. S. Huang, B. K. Jenkins, and A. A. Sawchuk, "Binary image algebra and optical cellular logic processor design," *Comp. Vision Graph. Image Process.*, 45, pp. 295-345, 1989.

[51] B. I. Justusson, "Median filtering: statistical properties," in *Two-Dimensional Digital Signal Processing II: Transforms and Median Filters*, T. S. Huang, Ed. NY: Springer Verlag, 1981.

[52] A. Kaufmann, *Introduction to the Theory of Fuzzy Subsets*. NY: Acad. Press, 1975.

[53] R. A. Kirsch, L. Cahn, C. Ray, and G. H. Urban, "Experiments in processing pictorial information with a digital computer," in *Proc. Eastern Joint Comput. Conf.*, 1957.

[54] J. C. Klein and J. Serra, "The texture analyzer," *J. Microscopy*, vol. 95, pt. 2, pp. 349-356, Apr. 1972.

[55] C. Lantuejoul, "Skeletonization in quantitative metallography," in *Issues of Digital Image Processing*, R. M. Haralick and J. C. Simon, Eds. Groningen, The Netherlands: Sijthoff and Noordhoff, 1980.

[56] C. Lantuejoul and J. Serra, "M-Filters," in *Proc. IEEE ICASSP-82*, Paris, May 1982.

[57] J. S. J. Lee, R. M. Haralick, and L. G. Shapiro, "Morphologic edge detection," *IEEE Trans. Rob. Autom.*, vol. RA-3, pp. 142-156, Apr. 1987.

[58] Y. H. Lee and S. A. Kassam, "Generalized median filtering and related nonlinear filtering techniques," *IEEE Trans. Acoust. Speech, Signal Process.*, ASSP-33, pp. 672-683, June 1985.

[59] R. Libeskind-Hadas and P. Maragos, "Application of iterated function systems and skeletonization to synthesis of fractal images," in *Proc. SPIE 845: Visual Communications and Image Processing II*, 1987.

[60] H. G. Longbotham and A. C. Bovik, "Relating analog and digital order statistic filters," in *Proc. IEEE ICASSP-88*, New York, Apr. 1988.

[61] R. M. Lougheed, D. L. McCubbrey, and S. R. Sternberg, "Cytocomputers: Architectures for parallel image processing," in *Proc. Workshop Picture Data Descr. Manag.*, Pacific Grove, CA, 1980.

[62] B. B. Mandelbrot, *The Fractal Geometry of Nature*. San Francisco, Freeman, 1982.

[63] J. R. Mandeville, "Novel Method for Analysis of Printed Circuit Images," *IBM J. Res. Develop.*, vol. 29, pp. 73-86, Jan. 1985.

[64] P. Maragos, "A unified theory of translation-invariant systems with applications to morphological analysis and coding of images," Ph.D. dissertation, School Electr. Enginr., Georgia Inst. Technology, Atlanta, GA, July 1985.

[65] —, "Morphology-based multidimensional signal processing," in *Proc. 21st Annual Conf. Inform. Sci. Syst.*, Johns Hopkins Univ., Baltimore, MD, Mar. 1987.

[66] —, "Morphology-based symbolic image modeling, multiscale nonlinear smoothing, and pattern spectrum," in *Proc. IEEE Conf. CVPR-88*, Ann Arbor, MI, June 1988.

[67] —, "Morphological correlation and mean absolute error criteria," in *Proc. IEEE ICASSP-89*, Glasgow, Scotland, May 1989.

[68] —, "A representation theory for morphological image and signal processing," *IEEE Trans. Pattern Anal. Mach. Intellig.*, PAMI-11, pp. 586-599, June 1989.

[69] —, "Pattern spectrum and multiscale shape representation," *IEEE Trans. Pattern Anal. Mach. Intellig.*, PAMI-11, pp. 701-716, July 1989.

[70] P. Maragos and R. W. Schafer, "A Unification of Linear, Median, Order-Statistics, and Morphological Filters under Mathematical Morphology," in *Proc. IEEE ICASSP-85*, Tampa, FL, March 1985.

[71] —, "Applications of morphological filtering to image processing and analysis," in *Proc. IEEE ICASSP-86*, Tokyo, April 1986.

[72] —, "Morphological skeleton representation and coding of binary images," *IEEE Trans. Acoust., Speech, Signal Process.*, ASSP-34, Oct. 1986, pp. 1228-1244.

[73] —, "Morphological filters—Part I: Their set-theoretic analysis and relations to linear shift-invariant filters," *IEEE Trans. Acoust. Speech, Signal Processing*, ASSP-35, pp. 1153-1169, Aug. 1987.

[74] —, "Morphological filters—Part II: Their relations to median, order-statistic, and stack filters," *IEEE Trans. Acoust. Speech, Signal Process.*, ASSP-35, pp. 1170-1184, Aug. 1987. Also "Corrections," *ibid*, ASSP-37, p. 597, Apr. 1989.

[75] P. Maragos and F. K. Sun, "Measuring fractal dimension: Morphological estimates and iterative optimization," in *Proc. SPIE 1199: Visual Communications and Image Processing*, Nov. 1989.

[76] P. Maragos and R. D. Ziff, "Threshold parallelism im morphological feature extraction, skeletonization, and pattern spectrum," in *Proc. SPIE 1001: Visual Communications and Image Processing*, 1988.

[77] M. Maresca and H. Li, "Morphological operations on mesh connected architecture: A generalized convolution algorithm," in *Proc. IEEE Conf. CVPR-86*, Miami, FL, June 1986.

[78] D. Marr, *Vision*. San Francisco, Freeman, 1982.

[79] D. Marr and E. Hildreth, "Theory of edge detection," *Proc. R. Soc. Lond. B 207*, pp. 187-217, 1980.

[80] G. Matheron, *Élements pour une Théorie des Milieux Poreux*. Paris: Masson, 1967.

[81] —, *Random Sets and Integral Geometry*. NY: J. Wiley, 1975.

[82] F. Meyer, "Contrast feature extraction," in *Special Issues of Practical Metallography*. Stuttgart: Riederer Verlag GmbH, 1978. (Proc. 2nd European Symp. on Quant. Anal. of Microstruct. in Materials Science, Biology and Medicine, France, Oct. 1977.)

[83] —, "Iterative image transformations for an automatic screening of cervical smears," *J. Histochem. and Cytochem.*, vol. 27, 1979, pp. 128-135.

[84] P. E. Miller, "Development of a mathemtical structure for image processing," Perkin-Elmer Optic. Div. Tech. Rep., 1983.

[85] H. Minkowski, "Volumen und Oberflache," *Math. Annalen*, vol. 57, pp. 447-495, 1903.

[86] G. A. Moore, "Automatic scanning and computer processes for the quantitative analysis of micrographs and equivalent subjects," in *Pictorial Pattern Recognition*, G. C. Cheng et al., Eds. Washington, DC: Thompson, 1968.

[87] J. C. Mott-Smith, "Medial axis transformations," in *Picture Processing and Psychopictorics*, B. S. Lipkin and A. Rosenfeld, Eds. NY: Acad. Press, 1970.

[88] S. Muroga, *Threshold Logic and Its Applications*. NY: Wiley, 1971.

[89] Y. Nakagawa and A. Rosenfeld, "A note on the use of local min and max operations in digital picture processing," *IEEE Trans. Syst., Man, and Cybern.*, SMC-8, 1978.

[90] J. A. Noble, "Morphological feature detectors," in *Proc. 2nd ICCV*, Trapon Springs, FL, Dec. 1988.

[91] T. A. Nodes and N. C. Gallagher, Jr., "Median filters: Some modifications and their properties," *IEEE Trans. Acoust. Speech Signal Process.*, ASSP-30, pp. 739-746, Oct. 1982.

[92] E. Ochoa, J. P. Allebach, and D. W. Sweeney, "Optical median filtering by threshold decomposition," *Appl. Opt.*, 26, pp. 252-260, Jan. 1987.

[93] A. V. Oppenheim and R. W. Schafer, *Discrete-time Signal Processing*. Englewood Cliffs, NJ: Prentice-Hall, 1989.

[94] F. Palmieri and C. G. Boncelet, Jr., "Ll filters—a new class of

[94] —, "order statistic filters," *IEEE Trans. Acoust. Speech Signal Process.*, ASSP-37, pp. 691–701, May 1989.
[95] S. Peleg, J. Naor, R. Hartley, and D. Avnir, "Multiple resolution texture analysis and classification," *IEEE Trans. Pattern. Anal. Mach. Intell.*, PAMI-6, pp. 518–523, July 1984.
[96] S. Peleg and A. Rosenfeld, "A min-max medial axis transformation," *IEEE Trans. Pattern. Anal. Mach. Intell.*, vol. PAMI-3, pp. 208–210, Mar. 1981.
[97] I. Pitas and A. N. Venetsanopoulos, "Shape decomposition by mathematical morphology," in *Proc. 1st ICCV*, London, 1987.
[98] W. K. Pratt, *Digital Image Processing*. NY: Wiley, 1978.
[99] K. Preston, Jr., "Feature extraction by Golay hexagonal pattern transforms," *IEEE Trans. Comput.*, C-20, pp. 1007–1014, Sep. 1971.
[100] —, "Ξ-Filters," *IEEE Trans. Acoust., Speech, and Signal Process.*, ASSP-31, pp. 861–876, Aug. 1983.
[101] K. Preston, Jr., M. J. B. Duff, S. Levialdi, P. E. Norgren, and J.-I. Toriwaki, "Basics of cellular logic with some applications in medical image processing," *Proc. IEEE*, vol. 67, pp. 826–856, May 1979.
[102] *Proc. IEEE Workshop CAPAIDM*, Miami FL, Nov. 1985.
[103] S. A. Rajala, H. A. Peterson, and E. J. Delp, "Binary morphological coding of grayscale images," in *Proc. IEEE ISCAS-88*, Espoo, Finland, June 1988.
[104] C. H. Richardson and R. W. Schafer, "Application of mathematical morphology to FLIR images," in *Proc. SPIE 845: Visual Communications and Image Processing II*, 1987.
[105] G. X. Ritter, and P. D. Gader, "Image algebra techniques for parallel image processing," *J. Paral. Distr. Comput.*, 4, 7–44, 1987.
[106] G. X. Ritter and J. N. Wilson, "Image algebra in a nutshell," in *Proc. 1st ICCV*, London, June 1987, pp. 641–645.
[107] G. X. Ritter, J. L. Davidson, and J. N. Wilson, "Beyond mathematical morphology," in *Proc. SPIE 845: Visual Communications and Image Processing II*, 1987.
[108] K. Rodenacker, P. Gais, U. Jutting, and G. Burger, "Mathematical morphology in grey images," in *Proc. 1983 European Signal Processing Conference*.
[109] J. B. T. M. Roerdink and H. J. A. M. Heijmans, "Mathematical morphology for structures without translation symmetry," *Signal Processing*, vol. 15, pp. 271–277, 1988.
[110] C. Ronse and H. J. A. M. Heijmans, "The algebraic basis of mathematical morphology. Part II: Openings and Closings," Manuscript M291, Philips Res. Lab, Brussels, Feb. 1989.
[111] A. Rosenfeld, Ed., *Multiresolution Image Processing and Analysis*. NY: Springer-Verlag, 1984.
[112] A. Rosenfeld and A. C. Kak, *Digital Picture Processing*. vols. 1 & 2. NY: Acad. Press, 1982.
[113] A. Rosenfeld and J. L. Pfaltz, "Sequential operations in digital picture processing," *J. ACM*, 13, pp. 471–494, Oct. 1966.
[114] J. Serra, "Morphologie Pour Les Fonctions: a peu pres en tout ou rien," Tech. Rep. 406-61, Centre de Morphologie Mathematique, Fontainebleau, 1975.
[115] —, *Image Analysis and Mathematical Morphology*. NY: Acad. Press, 1982.
[116] —, Ed., *Image Analysis and Mathematical Morphology*, Vol. 2: Theoretical Advances. NY: Acad. Press, 1988.
[117] F. Y.-C. Shih and O. R. Mitchell, "Threshold decomposition of gray-scale morphology into binary morphology," *IEEE Trans. Pattern Anal. Mach. Intell.*, PAMI-11, pp. 31–42, Jan. 1989.
[118] M. M. Skolnick, "Application of morphological transformations to the analysis of two-dimensional electrophoretic gels of biological materials," *Comput. Vision, Graph., Image Process.*, 35, pp. 306–332, 1986.
[119] M. C. Stein, "Fractal image models and object detection," in *Proc. SPIE 845: Visual Communications and Image Processing II*, 1987.
[120] S. R. Sternberg, "Parallel architectures for image processing," in *Proc. IEEE Conf. Comput. Softw. Applic.*, Chicago, 1979.
[121] —, "Cellular computers and biomedical image processing," in *Biomedical Images and Computers*, J. Sklansky and J. C. Bisconte, Eds. Berlin: Springer Verlag, 1982. (Presented at US–France Seminar on Biomedical Image Processing, St. Pierre de Chartreuse, France, 1980.)
[122] —, "Grayscale morphology," *Comput. Vision, Graph., Image Proc.* 35, pp. 333–355, 1986.
[123] S. R. Sternberg and E. S. Sternberg, "Industrial inspection by morphological virtual gauging," in *Proc. IEEE Workshop Comput. Archit. Pattern Anal. Image Datab. Manag.*, Pasadena, CA, Oct. 1983.
[124] R. L. Stevenson and G. R. Arce, "Morphological filters: Statistics and further syntactic properties," *IEEE Trans. Circ. and Syst.*, CAS-34, pp. 1292–1305, Nov. 1987.
[125] F.-K. Sun and S. L. Rubin, "Algorithm development for autonomous image analysis based on mathematical morphology," in *Proc. SPIE 845: Visual Communications and Image Processing II*, 1987.
[126] S. Suzuki and K. Abe, "New fusion operations for digitized binary images and their applications," *IEEE Trans. Pattern Anal. Mach. Intell.*, PAMI-7, Nov. 1985, pp. 638–651.
[127] H. D. Tagare and R. J. P. de Figueiredo, "Order filters," *Proc. IEEE*, 73, pp. 163–165, Jan. 1985.
[128] S. L. Tanimoto, "A hierarchical cellular logic for pyramid computers," *J. Parallel Distrib. Comput.*, 1, 105–132, 1984.
[129] J. W. Tukey, *Exploratory Data Analysis*. Reading, MA: Addison-Wesley, 1977.
[130] S. G. Tyan, "Median filtering: Deterministic properties," in *Two-Dimensional Digital Signal Processing II: Transforms and Median Filters*, T. S. Huang, Ed. New York: Springer-Verlag, 1981.
[131] L. J. van Vliet, I. T. Young, and G. L. Beckers, "A nonlinear Laplace operator as edge operator in noisy images," *Comp. Vision Graph. Image Process.*, 45, pp. 167–195, 1989.
[132] R. C. Vogt, "Morphological operator distributions based on monotonicity and the problem posed by digital disk-shaped structuring elements," in *Proc. SPIE 938*, 1988.
[133] S. H. Unger, "A computer oriented to spatial problems," *Proc. IRE*, vol. 46, pp. 1744–1750, 1958.
[134] P. D. Wendt, E. J. Coyle, and N. C. Gallagher, "Stack filters," *IEEE Trans. Acoust., Speech, Signal Process.*, ASSP-34, pp. 898–911, Aug. 1986.
[135] M. Werman and S. Peleg, "Min-max operators in texture analysis," *IEEE Trans. Pattern Anal. Mach. Intell.*, PAMI-7, Nov. 1985, pp. 730–733.
[136] A. S. Willsky, *Digital Signal Processing and Control and Estimation Theory: Points of Tangency, Areas of Intersection and Parallel Directions*. Cambridge, MA: MIT Press, 1979.
[137] A. Witkin, "Scale-space filtering," in *Proc. IJCAI*, Carlsrue, W. Germany, 1983.
[138] I. T. Young, "Modern digital image analysis," in *Proc. IEEE ICASSP-89*, Glasgow, Scotland, May 1989.
[139] A. Yuille, personal communication, 1989.
[140] A. Yuille and T. Poggio, "Scaling theorems for zero crossings," *IEEE Trans. Pattern. Anal. Mach. Intellig.*, PAMI-8, pp. 15–25, Jan. 1986.
[141] A. Yuille, D. Cohen, and P. Hallinan, "Face recognition by deformation templates," in *Proc. IEEE Conf. CVPR-89*, San Diego, CA, June 1989.
[142] L. A. Zadeh, "Fuzzy sets," *Inform. Control*, 8, 338–353, 1965.
[143] Z. Zhou and A. N. Venetsanopoulos, "Morphological skeleton representation and shape recognition," in *Proc. IEEE ICASSP-88*, New York, Apr. 1988.
[144] D. Casasent and E. Botha, "Optical symbolic substitution for morphological transformations," *Appl. Optics*, vol. 27, pp. 3806–3810, Sept. 1988.
[145] S. S. Wilson, "Morphological networks," in *Proc. SPIE*, vol. 1199: Visual Communications and Image Processing IV, Nov. 1989.

Petros Maragos (Member, IEEE) was born in Kalymnos, Greece, in 1957. He received the Diploma degree in electrical engineering from the National Technical University of Athens, Greece, in 1980, and the M.S.E.E. and Ph.D. degrees from the Georgia Institute of Technology, Atlanta, in 1982 and 1985, respectively.

From 1980 to 1985 he was a Research Assistant at the Digital Signal Processing Lab of the Electrical Engineering School at

Georgia Tech. In 1985 he joined the Faculty of the Division of Applied Sciences at Harvard University, Cambridge, where he is currently an Associate Professor of Electrical Engineering. He teaches and conducts research in the general areas of signal processing, image processing and computer vision, speech processing and recognition, and neural networks.

Dr. Maragos received a National Science Foundation Presidential Young Investigator Award in 1987. In 1989 he received the IEEE Acoustics, Speech, and Signal Processing Society's Paper Award for a publication in the Transactions of the Society. He is currently serving as an Associate Editor for the *IEEE Transactions on Acoustics, Speech, and Signal Processing*.

Ronald W. Schafer (Fellow, IEEE) received the B.S.E.E. and M.S.E.E. degrees from the University of Nebraska, Lincoln, in 1961 and 1962 respectively, and the Ph.D. degree from the Massachusetts Institute of Technology, Cambridge, in 1968.

From 1968 to 1974 he was a member of the Acoustics Research Department, Bell Laboratories, Murray Hill, New Jersey, where he was engaged in research on speech analysis and synthesis, digital signal processing techniques, and digital waveform coding. Since 1974 he has been on the faculty of the Georgia Institute of Technology as John O. McCarty Professor and Regents' Professor of Electrical Engineering. He is coauthor of the widely used textbooks, *Digital Signal Processing*, *Digital Processing of Speech Signals*, and the new text *Discrete-Time Signal Processing*. He has been active in the affairs of the IEEE Acoustics, Speech, and Signal Processing Society, having served as Associate Editor of the Transactions, member of several committees, Vice-President and President of the Society, and Chairman of the 1981 ICASSP.

Dr. Schafer is a Fellow of the IEEE and the Acoustical Society of America and he is a member of Sigma Xi, Eta Kappa Nu, and Phi Kappa Phi. He was awarded the Achievement Award and the Society Award of the IEEE ASSP Society in 1979 and 1983 respectively; the 1983 IEEE Region III Outstanding Engineer Award; and he shared the 1980 Emanuel R. Piore Award with L. R. Rabiner. In 1985 he received the Class of 1934 Distinguished Professor Award at Georgia Tech.

Image Restoration Using a Neural Network

YI-TONG ZHOU, STUDENT MEMBER, IEEE, RAMA CHELLAPPA, SENIOR MEMBER, IEEE, ASEEM VAID, AND B. KEITH JENKINS, MEMBER, IEEE

Abstract—A new approach for restoration of gray level images degraded by a known shift-invariant blur function and additive noise is presented using a neural computational network. A neural network model is employed to represent a possibly nonstationary image whose gray level function is the simple sum of the neuron state variables. The restoration procedure consists of two stages: estimation of the parameters of the neural network model and reconstruction of images. During the first stage, the parameters are estimated by comparing the energy function of the network to a constrained error function. The nonlinear restoration method is then carried out iteratively in the second stage by using a dynamic algorithm to minimize the energy function of the network. Owing to the model's fault-tolerant nature and computation capability, a high-quality image is obtained using this approach. A practical algorithm with reduced computational complexity is also presented. Several computer simulation examples involving synthetic and real images are given to illustrate the usefulness of our method. The choice of the boundary values to reduce the ringing effect is discussed, and comparisons to other restoration methods such as the SVD pseudoinverse filter, minimum mean-square error (MMSE) filter, and modified MMSE filter using the Gaussian Markov random field model are given. Finally, a procedure for learning the blur parameters from prototypes of original and degraded images is outlined.

I. Introduction

RESTORATION of a high-quality image from a degraded recording is an important problem in early vision processing. Restoration techniques are applied to remove 1) system degradations such as blur due to optical system aberrations, atmospheric turbulence, motion, and diffraction; and 2) statistical degradations due to noise. Over the last 20 years, various methods such as the inverse filter [1], Wiener filter [1], Kalman filter [2], SVD pseudoinverse [1], [3], and many other model-based approaches have been proposed for image restorations. One of the major drawbacks of most of the image restoration algorithms is the computational complexity, so much so that many simplifying assumptions such as wide sense stationarity (WSS), availability of second-order image statistics have been made to obtain computationally feasible algorithms. The inverse filter method works only for extremely high signal-to-noise ratio images. The Wiener filter is usually implemented only after the wide sense stationary assumption has been made for images. Furthermore, knowledge of the power spectrum or correlation matrix of the undegraded image is required. Often times, additional assumptions regarding boundary conditions are made so that fast orthogonal transforms can be used. The Kalman filter approach can be applied to nonstationary image, but is computationally very intensive. Similar statements can be made for the SVD pseudoinverse filter method. Approaches based on noncausal models such as the noncausal autoregressive or Gauss Markov random field models [4], [5] also make assumptions such as WSS and periodic boundary conditions. It is desirable to develop a restoration algorithm that does not make WSS assumptions and can be implemented in a reasonable time. An artificial neural network system that can perform extremely rapid computations seems to be very attractive for image restoration in particular and image processing and pattern recognition [6] in general.

In this paper, we use a neural network model containing redundant neurons to restore gray level images degraded by a known shift-invariant blur function and noise. It is based on the method described in [7]–[9] using a simple sum number representation [10]. The image gray levels are represented by the simple sum of the neuron state variables which take binary values of 1 or 0. The observed image is degraded by a shift-invariant function and noise. The restoration procedure consists of two stages: estimation of the parameters of the neural network model and reconstruction of images. During the first stage, the parameters are estimated by comparing the energy function of the neural network to the constrained error function. The nonlinear restoration algorithm is then implemented using a dynamic iterative algorithm to minimize the energy function of the neural network. Owing to the model's fault-tolerant nature and computation capability, a high-quality image is obtained using this approach. In order to reduce computational complexity, a practical algorithm, which has equivalent results to the original one suggested above, is developed under the assumption that the neurons are sequentially visited. We illustrate the usefulness of this approach by using both synthetic and real images degraded by a known shift-invariant blur function with or without noise. We also discuss the problem of choosing boundary values and introduce two methods to reduce the ringing effect. Comparisons to other restoration methods such as the SVD pseudoinverse filter, the minimum mean-square error (MMSE) filter, and the modified MMSE filter using a Gaussian Markov random field model are given using real images. The advantages of the method developed in this paper are: 1) WSS assumption is not required

---

Manuscript received February 22, 1988. This work was supported in part by AFOSR Contract F-49620-87-C-0007 and AFOSR Grant 86-0196.

The authors are with the Signal and Image Processing Institute, Department of Electrical Engineering—Systems, University of Southern California, Los Angeles, CA 90089.

IEEE Log Number 8821366.

for the images, 2) it can be implemented rapidly, and 3) it is fault tolerant.

In the above, the interconnection strengths (also called weights) of the neural network for image restoration are known from the parameters of the image degradation model and the smoothing constraints. We also consider learning of the parameters for the image degradation model and formulate it as a problem of computing the parameters from samples of the original and degraded images. This is implemented as a secondary neural network. A different scheme is used to represent multilevel activities for the parameters; some of its properties are complementary to those of the simple sum scheme. The learning procedure is accomplished by running a greedy algorithm. Some results of learning the blur parameters are presented using synthetic and real image examples.

The organization of this paper is as follows. A network model containing redundant neurons for image representation and the image degradation model is given in Section II. A technique for parameter estimation is presented in Section III. Image generation using a dynamic algorithm is described in Section IV. A practical algorithm with reduced computational complexity is presented in Section V. Computer simulation results using synthetic and real degraded images are given in Section VI. Choice of the boundary values is discussed in Section VII. Comparisons to other methods are given in Section VIII. A procedure for learning the blur parameters from prototypes of original and degraded images is outlined in Section IX, and conclusions and remarks are included in Section X.

II. A Neural Network for Image Representation

We use a neural network containing redundant neurons for representing the image gray levels. The model consists of $L^2 \times M$ mutually interconnected neurons where L is the size of image and M is the maximum value of the gray level function. Let $V = \{v_{i,k}$ where $1 \leq i \leq L^2, 1 \leq k \leq M\}$ be a binary state set of the neural network with $v_{i,k}$ (1 for firing and 0 for resting) denoting the state of the (i, k)th neuron. Let $T_{i,k;j,l}$ denote the strength (possibly negative) of the interconnection between neuron (i, k) and neuron (j, l). We require symmetry:

$$T_{i,k;j,l} = T_{j,l;i,k} \quad \text{for } 1 \leq i, j \leq L^2 \text{ and}$$
$$1 \leq l, k \leq M.$$

We also allow for neurons to have self-feedback, i.e., $T_{i,k;i,k} \neq 0$. In this model, each neuron (i, k) randomly and asynchronously receives inputs $\Sigma T_{i,k;j,l} v_{j,l}$ from all neurons and a bias input $I_{i,k}$:

$$u_{i,k} = \sum_j^{L^2} \sum_l^M T_{i,k;j,l} v_{j,l} + I_{i,k}. \quad (1)$$

Each $u_{i,k}$ is fed back to corresponding neurons after thresholding:

$$v_{i,k} = g(u_{i,k}) \quad (2)$$

where $g(x)$ is a nonlinear function whose form can be taken as

$$g(x) = \begin{cases} 1 & \text{if } x \geq 0 \\ 0 & \text{if } x < 0. \end{cases} \quad (3)$$

In this model, the state of each neuron is updated by using the latest information about other neurons.

The image is described by a finite set of gray level functions $\{x(i, j)$ where $1 \leq i, j \leq L\}$ with $x(i, j)$ (positive integer number) denoting the gray level of the pixel (i, j). The image gray level function can be represented by a simple sum of the neuron state variables as

$$x(i, j) = \sum_{k=1}^M v_{m,k} \quad (4)$$

where $m = (i - 1) \times L + j$. Here the gray level functions have degenerate representations. Use of this redundant number representation scheme yields advantages such as fault tolerance and faster convergence to the solution [10].

By using the lexicographic notation, the image degradation model can be written as

$$Y = HX + N \quad (5)$$

where H is the "blur matrix" corresponding to a blur function, N is the signal independent white noise, and X and Y are the original and degraded images, respectively. Furthermore, H and N can be represented as

$$H = \begin{bmatrix} h_{1,1} & h_{1,2} & \cdots & h_{1,L^2} \\ h_{2,1} & h_{2,2} & \cdots & h_{2,L^2} \\ \vdots & \vdots & \cdots & \vdots \\ h_{L^2,1} & h_{L^2,2} & \cdots & h_{L^2,L^2} \end{bmatrix} \quad (6)$$

and

$$N = \begin{bmatrix} N_1 \\ N_2 \\ \vdots \\ N_L \end{bmatrix} = \begin{bmatrix} n_1 \\ n_2 \\ \vdots \\ n_{L^2} \end{bmatrix},$$

$$N_i = \begin{bmatrix} n(i, 1) \\ n(i, 2) \\ \vdots \\ n(i, L) \end{bmatrix} = \begin{bmatrix} n_{(i-1) \times L + 1} \\ n_{(i-1) \times L + 2} \\ \vdots \\ n_{i \times L} \end{bmatrix} \quad (7)$$

respectively. Vectors X and Y have similar representations. Equation (5) is similar to the simultaneous equations solution of [10], but differs in that it includes a noise term.

The shift-invariant blur function can be written as a convolution over a small window, for instance, it takes the form

$$h(k, l) = \begin{cases} \frac{1}{2} & \text{if } k = 0, l = 0 \\ \frac{1}{16} & \text{if } |k|, |l| \leq 1, (k, l) \neq (0, 0); \end{cases} \quad (8)$$

accordingly, the "blur matrix" H will be a block Toeplitz or block circulant matrix (if the image has periodic boundaries). The block circulant matrix corresponding to (8) can be written as

$$H = \begin{bmatrix} H_0 & H_1 & 0 & \cdots & 0 & H_1 \\ H_1 & H_0 & H_1 & \cdots & 0 & 0 \\ \vdots & \vdots & \vdots & \cdots & \vdots & \vdots \\ H_1 & 0 & 0 & \cdots & H_1 & H_0 \end{bmatrix} \quad (9)$$

where

$$H_0 = \begin{bmatrix} \frac{1}{2} & \frac{1}{16} & 0 & \cdots & 0 & \frac{1}{16} \\ \frac{1}{16} & \frac{1}{2} & \frac{1}{16} & \cdots & 0 & 0 \\ \vdots & \vdots & \vdots & \cdots & \vdots & \vdots \\ \frac{1}{16} & 0 & 0 & \cdots & \frac{1}{16} & \frac{1}{2} \end{bmatrix},$$

$$H_1 = \begin{bmatrix} \frac{1}{16} & \frac{1}{16} & 0 & \cdots & 0 & \frac{1}{16} \\ \frac{1}{16} & \frac{1}{16} & \frac{1}{16} & \cdots & 0 & 0 \\ \vdots & \vdots & \vdots & \cdots & \vdots & \vdots \\ \frac{1}{16} & 0 & 0 & \cdots & \frac{1}{16} & \frac{1}{16} \end{bmatrix} \quad (10)$$

and $\mathbf{0}$ is null matrix whose elements are all zeros.

III. Estimation of Model Parameters

The neural model parameters, the interconnection strengths, and bias inputs can be determined in terms of the energy function of the neural network. As defined in [7], the energy function of the neural network can be written as

$$E = -\frac{1}{2} \sum_{i=1}^{L^2} \sum_{j=1}^{L^2} \sum_{k=1}^{M} \sum_{l=1}^{M} T_{i,k;j,l} v_{i,k} v_{j,l} - \sum_{i=1}^{L^2} \sum_{k=1}^{M} I_{i,k} v_{i,k}. \quad (11)$$

In order to use the spontaneous energy-minimization process of the neural network, we reformulate the restoration problem as one of minimizing an error function with constraints defined as

$$E = \frac{1}{2} \| Y - H\hat{X} \|^2 + \frac{1}{2} \lambda \| D\hat{X} \|^2 \quad (12)$$

where $\|Z\|$ is the L_2 norm of Z and λ is a constant. Such a constrained error function is widely used in the image restoration problems [1] and is also similar to the regularization techniques used in early vision problems [11]. The first term in (12) is to seek an $\hat{X}$ such that $H\hat{X}$ approximates Y in a least squares sense. Meanwhile, the second term is a smoothness constraint on the solution $\hat{X}$. The constant λ determines their relative importance to achieve both noise suppression and ringing reduction.

In general, if H is a low-pass distortion, then D is a high-pass filter. A common choice of D is a second-order differential operator which can be approximated as a local window operator in the 2-D discrete case. For instance, if D is a Laplacian operator

$$\nabla = \frac{\partial^2}{\partial i^2} + \frac{\partial^2}{\partial j^2} \quad (13)$$

it can be approximated as a window operator

$$\frac{1}{6} \begin{bmatrix} 1 & 4 & 1 \\ 4 & -20 & 4 \\ 1 & 4 & 1 \end{bmatrix}. \quad (14)$$

Then D will be a block Toeplitz matrix similar to (9).

Expanding (12) and then replacing x_i by (4), we have

$$\begin{aligned} E &= \frac{1}{2} \sum_{p=1}^{L^2} \left(y_p - \sum_{i=1}^{L^2} h_{p,i} x_i \right)^2 + \frac{1}{2} \lambda \sum_{p=1}^{L^2} \left(\sum_{i=1}^{L^2} d_{p,i} x_i \right)^2 \\ &= \frac{1}{2} \sum_{i=1}^{L^2} \sum_{j=1}^{L^2} \sum_{k=1}^{M} \sum_{l=1}^{M} \sum_{p=1}^{L^2} h_{p,i} h_{p,j} v_{i,k} v_{j,l} \\ &+ \frac{1}{2} \lambda \sum_{i=1}^{L^2} \sum_{j=1}^{L^2} \sum_{k=1}^{M} \sum_{l=1}^{M} \sum_{p=1}^{L^2} d_{p,i} d_{p,j} v_{i,k} v_{j,l} \\ &- \sum_{i=1}^{L^2} \sum_{k=1}^{M} \sum_{p=1}^{L^2} y_p h_{p,i} v_{i,k} + \frac{1}{2} \sum_{p=1}^{L^2} y_p^2. \end{aligned} \quad (15)$$

By comparing the terms in (15) to the corresponding terms in (11) and ignoring the constant term $\frac{1}{2} \Sigma_{p=1}^{L^2} y_p^2$, we can determine the interconnection strengths and bias inputs as

$$T_{i,k;j,l} = -\sum_{p=1}^{L^2} h_{p,i} h_{p,j} - \lambda \sum_{p=1}^{L^2} d_{p,i} d_{p,j} \quad (16)$$

and

$$I_{i,k} = \sum_{p=1}^{L^2} y_p h_{p,i} \quad (17)$$

where $h_{i,j}$ and $d_{i,j}$ are the elements of the matrices H and D, respectively. Two interesting aspects of (16) and (17) should be pointed out: 1) the interconnection strengths are independent of subscripts k and l and the bias inputs are independent of subscript k, and 2) the self-connection $T_{i,k;i,k}$ is not equal to zero which requires self-feedback for neurons.

From (16), one can see that the interconnection strengths are determined by the shift-invariant blur function, differential operator, and constant λ. Hence, $T_{i,k;j,l}$ can be computed without error provided the blur function is known. However, the bias inputs are functions of the observed degraded image. If the image is degraded by a shift-invariant blur function only, then $I_{i,k}$ can be estimated perfectly. Otherwise, $I_{i,k}$ is affected by noise. The reasoning behind this statement is as follows. By replacing y_p by $\sum_{i=1}^{L^2} h_{p,i} x_i + n_p$, we have

$$I_{i,k} = \sum_{p=1}^{L^2} \left(\sum_{i=1}^{L^2} h_{p,i} x_i + n_p \right) h_{p,i}$$

$$= \sum_{p=1}^{L^2} \sum_{i=1}^{L^2} h_{p,i} x_i h_p + \sum_{p=1}^{L^2} n_p h_{p,i}. \quad (18)$$

The second term in (18) represents the effects of noise. If the signal-to-noise ratio (SNR), defined by

$$\text{SNR} = 10 \log_{10} \frac{\sigma_s^2}{\sigma_n^2} \quad (19)$$

where σ_s^2 and σ_n^2 are variances of signal and noise, respectively, is low, then we have to choose a large λ to suppress effects due to noise. It seems that in the absence of noise, the parameters can be estimated perfectly, ensuring exact recovery of the image as error function E tends to zero. However, the problem is not so simple because the restoration performance depends on both the parameters and the blur function when a mean-square error or least square error such as (12) is used. A discussion about the effect of blur function is given in Section X.

IV. RESTORATION

Restoration is carried out by neuron evaluation and an image construction procedure. Once the parameters $T_{i,k;j,l}$ and $I_{i,k}$ are obtained using (16) and (17), each neuron can randomly and asynchronously evaluate its state and readjust accordingly using (1) and (2). When one quasi-minimum energy point is reached, the image can be constructed using (4).

However, this neural network has self-feedback, i.e., $T_{i,k;i,k} \neq 0$. As a result, the energy function E does not always decrease monotonically with a transition. This is explained below. Define the state change $\Delta v_{i,k}$ of neuron (i, k) and energy change ΔE as

$$\Delta v_{i,k} = v_{i,k}^{\text{new}} - v_{i,k}^{\text{old}} \quad \text{and} \quad \Delta E = E^{\text{new}} - E^{\text{old}}.$$

Consider the energy function

$$E = -\frac{1}{2} \sum_{i=1}^{L^2} \sum_{j=1}^{L^2} \sum_{k=1}^{M} \sum_{l=1}^{M} T_{i,k;j,l} v_{i,k} v_{j,l} - \sum_{i=1}^{L^2} \sum_{k=1}^{M} I_{i,k} v_{i,k}. \quad (20)$$

Then the change ΔE due to a change $\Delta v_{i,k}$ is given by

$$\Delta E = -\left(\sum_{j=1}^{L^2} \sum_{l=1}^{M} T_{i,k;j,l} v_{j,l} + I_{i,k} \right) \Delta v_{i,k}$$

$$- \frac{1}{2} T_{i,k;i,k} (\Delta v_{i,k})^2 \quad (21)$$

which is not always negative. For instance, if

$$v_{i,k}^{\text{old}} = 0, \quad u_{i,k} = \sum_{j=1}^{L^2} \sum_{l=1}^{M} T_{i,k;j,l} v_{j,l} + I_{i,k} > 0$$

and the threshold function is as in (3), then $v_{i,k}^{\text{new}} = 1$ and $\Delta v_{i,k} > 0$. Thus, the first term in (21) is negative. But

$$T_{i,k;i,k} = -\sum_{p=1}^{L^2} h_{p,i}^2 - \lambda \sum_{p=1}^{L^2} d_{p,i}^2 < 0$$

with $\lambda > 0$, leading to

$$-\frac{1}{2} T_{i,k;i,k} (\Delta v_{i,k})^2 > 0.$$

When the first term is less than the second term in (21), then $\Delta E > 0$ (we have observed this in our experiment), which means E is not a Lyapunov function. Consequently, the convergence of the network is not guaranteed [12].

Thus, depending on whether convergence to a local minimum or a global minimum is desired, we can design a deterministic or stochastic decision rule. The deterministic rule is to take a new state $v_{i,k}^{\text{new}}$ of neuron (i, k) if the energy change ΔE due to state change $\Delta v_{i,k}$ is less than zero. If ΔE due to state change is > 0, no state change is affected. One can also design a stochastic rule similar to the one used in stimulated annealing techniques [13], [14]. The details of this stochastic scheme are given as follows.

Define a Boltzmann distribution by

$$\frac{p_{\text{new}}}{p_{\text{old}}} = e^{-\Delta E/T}$$

where p_{new} and p_{old} are the probabilities of the new and old global state, respectively, ΔE is the energy change, and T is the parameter which acts like temperature. A new state $v_{i,k}^{\text{new}}$ is taken if

$$\frac{p_{\text{new}}}{p_{\text{old}}} > 1 \text{ or if } \frac{p_{\text{new}}}{p_{\text{old}}} \leq 1 \text{ but } \frac{p_{\text{new}}}{p_{\text{old}}} > \xi$$

where ξ is a random number uniformly distributed in the interval [0, 1].

The restoration algorithm is summarized as below.
Algorithm 1:
1) Set the initial state of the neurons.
2) Update the state of all neurons randomly and asynchronously according to the decision rule.
3) Check the energy function; if energy does not change, go to step 4); otherwise, go back to step 2).
4) Construct an image using (4).

V. A PRACTICAL ALGORITHM

The algorithm described above is difficult to simulate on a conventional computer owing to high computational complexity, even for images of reasonable size. For instance, if we have an $L \times L$ image with M gray levels, then $L^2 M$ neurons and $\frac{1}{2} L^4 M^2$ interconnections are required and $L^4 M^2$ additions and multiplications are needed at each iteration. Therefore, the space and time complexities are $O(L^4M^2)$ and $O(L^4M^2K)$, respectively, where K, typically 10–100, is the number of iterations. Usually, L and M are 256–1024 and 256, respectively. However, simplification is possible if the neurons are sequentially updated.

In order to simplify the algorithm, we begin by reconsidering (1) and (2) of the neural network. As noted earlier, the interconnection strengths given in (16) are independent of subscripts k and l and the bias inputs given in (17) are independent of subscript k; the M neurons used to represent the same image gray level function have the same interconnection strengths and bias inputs. Hence, one set of interconnection strengths and one bias input are sufficient for every gray level function, i.e., the dimensions of the interconnection matrix T and bias input matrix I can be reduced by a factor of M^2. From (1), all inputs received by a neuron, say the (i, k)th neuron, can be written as

$$u_{i,k} = \sum_{j}^{L^2} T_{i,\cdot;j,\cdot} \left(\sum_{l}^{M} v_{j,l} \right) + I_{i,\cdot}$$

$$= \sum_{j}^{L^2} T_{i,\cdot;j,\cdot} \cdot x_j + I_{i,\cdot} \quad (22)$$

where we have used (4) and x_j is the gray level function of the jth image pixel. The symbol "·" in the subscripts means that the $T_{i,\cdot;j,\cdot}$ and $I_{i,\cdot}$ are independent of k. Equation (22) suggests that we can use a multivalue number to replace the simple sum number. Since the interconnection strengths are determined by the blur function, the differential operator, and the constant λ as shown in (16), it is easy to see that if the blur function is local, then most interconnection strengths are zeros and the neurons are locally connected. Therefore, most elements of the interconnection matrix T are zeros. If the blur function is shift invariant taking the form in (8), then the interconnection matrix is block Toeplitz so that only a few elements need to be stored. Based on the value of inputs $u_{i,k}$, the state of the (i, k)th neuron is updated by applying a decision rule. The state change of the (i, k)th neuron in turn causes the gray level function x_i to change:

$$x_i^{\text{new}} = \begin{cases} x_i^{\text{old}} & \text{if } \Delta v_{i,k} = 0 \\ x_i^{\text{old}} + 1 & \text{if } \Delta v_{i,k} = 1 \\ x_i^{\text{old}} - 1 & \text{if } \Delta v_{i,k} = -1 \end{cases} \quad (23)$$

where $\Delta v_{i,k} = v_{i,k}^{\text{new}} - v_{i,k}^{\text{old}}$ is the state change of the (i, k)th neuron. The superscripts "new" and "old" are for after and before updating, respectively. We use x_i to represent the gray level value as well as the output of M neurons representing x_i. Assuming that the neurons of the network are sequentially visited, it is straightforward to show that the updating procedure can be reformulated as

$$u_{i,k} = \sum_{j}^{L^2} T_{i,\cdot;j,\cdot} \cdot x_j + I_{i,\cdot} \quad (24)$$

$$\Delta v_{i,k} = g(u_{i,k}) = \begin{cases} \Delta v_{i,k} = 0 & \text{if } u_{i,k} = 0 \\ \Delta v_{i,k} = 1 & \text{if } u_{i,k} > 0 \\ \Delta v_{i,k} = -1 & \text{if } u_{i,k} < 0 \end{cases} \quad (25)$$

$$x_i^{\text{new}} = \begin{cases} x_i^{\text{old}} + \Delta v_{i,k} & \text{if } \Delta E < 0 \\ x_i^{\text{old}} & \text{if } \Delta E \geq 0. \end{cases} \quad (26)$$

Note that the stochastic decision rule can also be used in (26). In order to limit the gray level function to the range 0–255 after each updating step, we have to check the value of the gray level function x_i^{new}. Equations (24), (25), and (26) give a much simpler algorithm. This algorithm is summarized below.

Algorithm 2:
1) Take the degraded image as the initial value.
2) Sequentially visit all numbers (image pixels). For each number, use (24), (25), and (26) to update it repeatedly until there is no further change, i.e., if $\Delta v_{i,k} = 0$ or energy change $\Delta E \geq 0$; then move to the next one.
3) Check the energy function; if energy does not change anymore, a restored image is obtained; otherwise, go back to step 2) for another iteration.

The calculations of the inputs $u_{i,k}$ of the (i, k)th neuron and the energy change ΔE can be simplified furthermore. When we update the same image gray level function repeatedly, the input received by the current neuron (i, k) can be computed by making use of the previous result

$$u_{i,k} = u_{i,k-1} + \Delta v_{i,k} T_{i,\cdot;i,\cdot} \quad (27)$$

where $u_{i,k-1}$ is the inputs received by the $(i, k-1)$th neuron. The energy change ΔE due to the state change of the (i, k)th neuron can be calculated as

$$\Delta E = -u_{i,k} \Delta v_{i,k} - \tfrac{1}{2} T_{i,\cdot;i,\cdot} (\Delta v_{i,k})^2. \quad (28)$$

If the blur function is shift invariant, all these simplifications reduce the space and time complexities significantly from $O(L^4M^2)$ and $O(L^4M^2K)$ to $O(L^2)$ and $O(ML^2K)$, respectively. Since every gray level function needs only a few updating steps after the first iteration, the computation at each iteration is $O(L^2)$. The resulting algorithm can be easily simulated on minicomputers for images as large as 512×512.

VI. Computer Simulations

The practical algorithm described in the previous section was applied to synthetic and real images on a Sun-3/160 Workstation. In all cases, only the deterministic decision rule was used. The results are summarized in Figs. 1 and 2.

Fig. 1 shows the results for a synthetic image. The original image shown in Fig. 1(a) is of size 32×32 with three gray levels. The image was degraded by convolving with a 3×3 blur function as in (8) using circulant boundary conditions; 22 dB white Gaussian noise was added after convolution. A perfect image was obtained after six

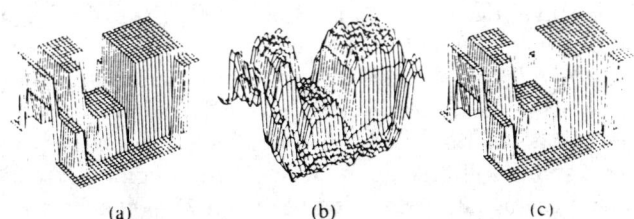

Fig. 1. Restoration of noisy blurred synthetic image. (a) Original image. (b) Degraded image. (c) Result after six iterations.

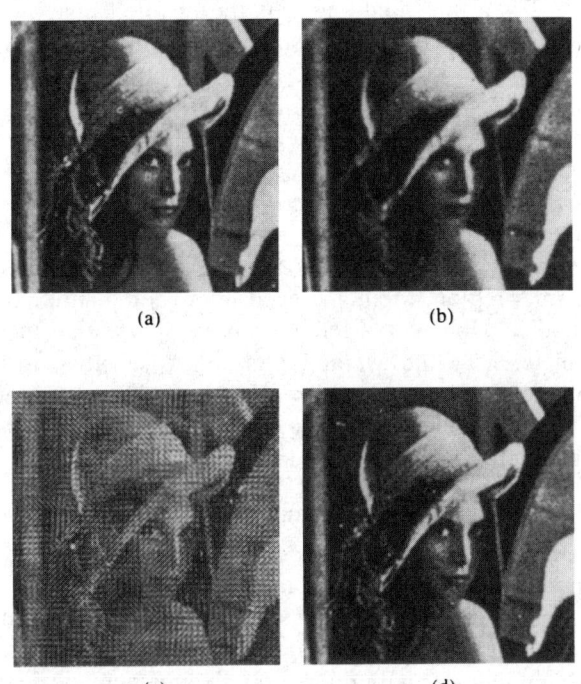

Fig. 2. Restoration of noisy blurred real image. (a) Original girl image. (b) Image degraded by 5×5 uniform blur and quantization noise. (c) The restored image using inverse filter. (d) The restored image using our approach.

iterations without preprocessing. We set the initial state of all neurons to equal 1, i.e., firing, and chose $\lambda = 0$ due to the well conditioning of the blur function.

Fig. 2(a) shows the original girl image. The original image is of size 256×256 with 256 gray levels. The variance of the original image is 2797.141. It was degraded by a 5×5 uniform blur function. A small amount of quantization noise was introduced by quantizing the convolution results to 8 bits. The noisy blurred image is shown in Fig. 2(b). For comparison purpose, Fig. 2(c) shows the output of an inverse filter [15], completely overridden by the amplified noise and the ringing effects due to the ill-conditioned blur matrix H. Since the blur matrix H corresponding to the 5×5 uniform blur function is not singular, the pseudoinverse filter [15] and the inverse filter have the same output. The restored image by using our approach is shown in Fig. 2(d). In order to avoid the ringing effects due to the boundary conditions, we took 4 pixel wide boundaries, i.e., the first and last four rows and columns, from the original image and updated the interior region (248×248) of the image only. The noisy blurred image was used as an initial condition for accelerating the convergence. The constant λ was set to zero because of small noise and good boundary values. The restored image in Fig. 2(d) was obtained after 213 iterations. The square error (i.e., energy function) defined in (12) is 0.02543 and the square error between the original and the restored image is 66.5027.

VII. CHOOSING BOUNDARY VALUES

As mentioned in [16], choosing boundary values is a common problem for techniques ranging from deterministic inverse filter algorithms to stochastic Kalman filters. In these algorithms, boundary values determine the entire solution when the blur is uniform [17]. The same problem occurs in the neural network approach. Since the 5×5 uniform blur function is ill conditioned, improper boundary values may cause ringing which may affect the restored image completely. For example, appending zeros to the image as boundary values introduces a sharp edge at the image border and triggers ringing in the restored image even if the image has zero mean. Another procedure is to assume a periodic boundary. When the left (top) and right (bottom) borders of the image are different, a sharp edge is formed and ringing results even though the degraded image has been formed by blurring with periodic boundary conditions. The drawbacks of these two assumptions for boundary values were reported in [16], [2], [18] for the 2-D Kalman filtering technique. We also tested our algorithm using these two assumptions for boundary values; the results indicate the restored images were seriously affected by ringing.

In the last section, to avoid the ringing effect, we took 4 pixel wide borders from the original image as boundary values for restoration. Since the original image is not available in practice always, an alternative to eliminate the ringing effect caused by sharp false edges is to use the blurred noisy boundaries from the degraded image. Fig. 3(a) shows the restored image using the first and last four rows and columns of the blurred noisy image in Fig. 2(b) as boundary values. In the restored image, there still exists some ringing due to the naturally occurring sharp edges in the region near the borders in the original image, but not due to boundary values. A typical cut of the restored image to illustrate ringing near the borders is shown in Fig. 4. To remove the ringing near the borders caused by naturally occurring sharp edges in the original image, we suggest the following techniques.

First, divide the image into three regions: border, subborder, and interior region as shown in Fig. 5. For the 5×5 uniform blur case, the border region will be 4 pixels wide due to the boundary effect of the bias input $I_{i,k}$ in (17), and the subborder region will be 4 or 8 pixels wide. In fact, the width of the subborder region will be image dependent. If the regions near the border are smooth, then the width of the subborder region will be small or even zero. If the border contains many sharp edges, the width will be large. For the real girl image, we chose the width

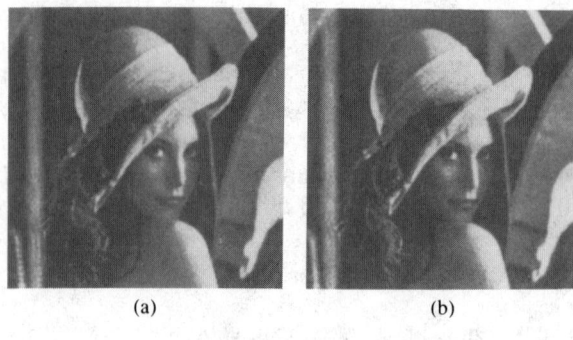

Fig. 3. Results using blurred noisy boundaries. (a) Blurred noisy boundaries. (b) Method 1. (c) Method 2.

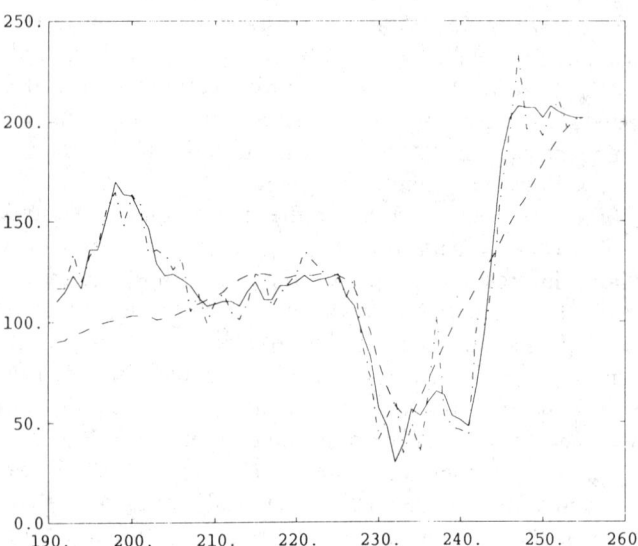

Fig. 4. One typical cut of the restored image using the blurred noisy boundaries. Solid line for original image, dashed line for blurred noisy image, and dashed and dotted line for restored image.

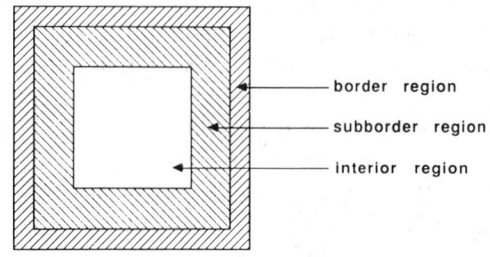

Fig. 5. Border, subborder, and interior regions of the image.

of the subborder region to be 8 pixels. We suggest using one of the following two methods.

Method 1: In the case of small noise, such as quantization error noise, the blurred image is usually smooth. Therefore, we restricted the difference between the restored and blurred image in the subborder region to a certain range to reduce the ringing effect. Mathematically, this constraint can be written as

$$\|\hat{x}_i - y_i\| \leq T \quad \text{for } i \in \text{subborder region} \quad (29)$$

where T is a threshold and $\hat{x}_i$ is the restored image gray value. Fig. 3(b) shows the result of using this method with $T = 10$.

Method 2: This method simply sets λ in (12) to zero in the interior region and nonzero in the subborder region, respectively. Fig. 3(c) shows the result of using this method with $\lambda = 0.09$. In this case, D was a Laplacian operator.

Owing to checking all restored image gray values in the subborder region, Method 1 needs more computation than Method 2. However, Method 2 is very sensitive to the parameter λ, while Method 1 is not so sensitive to the parameter λ. Experimental results show that both Methods 1 and 2 reduce the ringing effect significantly by using the suboptimal blurred boundary values.

VIII. COMPARISONS TO OTHER RESTORATION METHODS

Comparing the performance of different restoration methods needs some quality measures which are difficult to define owing to the lack of knowledge about the human visual system. The word "optimal" used in the restoration techniques usually refers only to a mathematical concept, and is not related to response of the human visual system. For instance, when the blur function is ill conditioned and the SNR is low, the MMSE method improves the SNR, but the resulting image is not visually good. We believe that human objective evaluation is the best ultimate judgment. Meanwhile, the mean-square error or least square error can be used as a reference.

For comparison purposes, we give the outputs of the inverse filter, SVD pseudoinverse filter, MMSE filter, and modified MMSE filter using the Gaussian Markov random field (GMRF) model [19], [5].

A. Inverse Filter and SVD Pseudoinverse Filter

An inverse filter can be used to restore an image degraded by a space-invariant blur function with high signal-to-noise ratio. When the blur function has some singular points, an SVD pseudoinverse filter is needed; however, both filters are very sensitive to noise. This is because the noise is amplified in the same way as the signal components to be restored. The inverse filter and SVD pseudoinverse filter were applied to an image degraded by the 5×5 uniform blur function and quantization noise (about 40 dB SNR). The blurred and restored images are shown in Fig. 2(b) and (c), respectively. As we mentioned before, the outputs of these filters are completely overridden by the amplified noise and ringing effects.

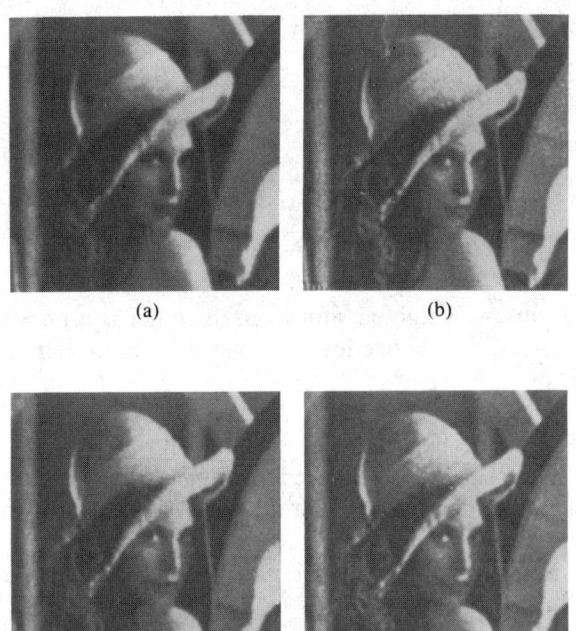

Fig. 6. Comparison to other restoration methods. (a) Image degraded by 5 × 5 uniform blur and 20 dB SNR additive white Gaussian noise. (b) The restored image using the MMSE filter. (c) The restored image using the modified MMSE filter. (d) The restored image using our approach.

B. MMSE and Modified MMSE Filters

The MMSE filter is also known as the Wiener filter (in the frequency domain). Under the assumption that the original image obeys a GMRF model, the MMSE filter (or Wiener filter) can be represented in terms of the GMRF model parameters and the blur function. In our implementation of the MMSE filter, we used a known blur function, unknown noise variance, and the GMRF model parameters estimated from the blurred noisy image by a maximum likelihood (ML) method [19]. The image shown in Fig. 6(a) was degraded by 5 × 5 uniform blur function and 20 dB SNR additive white Gaussian noise. The restored image is shown in Fig. 6(b).

The modified MMSE filter in terms of the GMRF model parameters is a linear weighted combination of a Wiener filter with a smoothing operator (such as a median filter) and a pseudoinverse filter to smooth the noise and preserve the edge of the restored image simultaneously. Details of this filter can be found in [5]. We applied the modified MMSE filter to the same image used in the MMSE filter above with the same model parameters. The smoothing operator is a 9 × 9 cross shape median filter. The resulting image is shown in Fig. 6(c).

The result of our method is also shown in Fig. 6(d). The D we used in (12) was a Laplacian operator as in (13). We chose $\lambda = 0.0625$ and used 4 pixel wide blurred noisy boundaries for restoration. The total number of iterations was 20. The improvement of mean-square error between the restored image and the original image for each method is shown in Table I. In the table, the "MMSE (o)" denotes that the parameters were estimated from the

TABLE I
MEAN-SQUARE ERROR IMPROVEMENT

Method	MMSE	MMSE (o)	Modified MMSE	Neural Network
Mean-square error	1.384 dB	2.139 dB	1.893 dB	1.682 dB

original image. The restored image using "MMSE (o)" is very similar to Fig. 6(a). As we mentioned before, the comparison of the outputs of the different restoration methods is a difficult problem. The MMSE filter visually gives the worst output which has the smallest mean-square error for the MMSE (o) case. The result of our method is smoother than that of the MMSE filter. Although the output of the modified MMSE filter is smooth in flat regions, it contains some artifacts and snake effects at the edges due to using a large sized median filter.

IX. PARAMETER LEARNING FOR LINEAR IMAGE BLUR MODEL

Apart from fine-grain parallelism, fast (and preferably automatic) adaptation of a problem-solving network to different instances of a problem is a primary motivation for using a network solution. For pattern recognition and associative memory applications, this weight training is done by distributed algorithms that optimize a distance measure between sample patterns and network responses. However, in feedback networks, general problems that involve learning higher order correlations (like the exclusive OR) or combinatorial training sets (like the Traveling Salesperson problem) are difficult to solve and may have exponential complexity. In particular, techniques for finding a compact training set do not exist.

A. Learning Model

For model-based approaches to "neural" problem solving, the weights of the main network are computed from the parameters of the model. The learning problem can then be solved by a parallel, distributed algorithm for estimating the model parameters from samples of the inputs and desired outputs. This algorithm can be implemented on a secondary network. An error function for this "learning" network must be constructed, which will now be problem-dependent.

For the linear shift-invariant blur model (5), the problem is that of estimating the parameters corresponding to the blur function in a $K \times K$ small window centered at each pixel. Rewrite (5) as

$$y(i,j) = z(i,j)^t h + n(i,j) \quad i,j = 1, 2, \cdots, L \quad (30)$$

where t denotes the transpose operator and $z(i,j)$ and h are $K^2 \times 1$ vectors corresponding to original image samples in a $K \times K$ window centered at (i,j) and blur function, respectively.

For instance, for $K = 3$, we have

$$h = \begin{bmatrix} h_1 \\ h_2 \\ h_3 \\ \vdots \\ h_9 \end{bmatrix} = \begin{bmatrix} h(-1, -1) \\ h(-1, 0) \\ h(-1, 1) \\ \vdots \\ h(1, 1) \end{bmatrix} \quad (31)$$

and

$$z(i,j) = \begin{bmatrix} z(i,j)_1 \\ z(i,j)_2 \\ z(i,j)_3 \\ \vdots \\ z(i,j)_9 \end{bmatrix} = \begin{bmatrix} x(i-1, j-1) \\ x(i-1, j) \\ x(i-1, j+1) \\ \vdots \\ x(i+1, j+1) \end{bmatrix}. \quad (32)$$

We can use an error function for estimation of h, as in the restoration process, because the roles of data $\{x(i, j)\}$ and parameter h are simply interchanged in the learning process. Therefore, an error function is defined as

$$E = \sum_{(i,j) \in S} [y(i,j) - h^t z(i,j)]^2 \quad (33)$$

where S is a subset of $\{(i, j), i, j = 1, 2, \cdots, L\}$ and $y(i, j)$ and $z(i, j)$ are training samples taken from the degraded and original images, respectively. The network energy functions is given by

$$E = -\sum_{k=1}^{K^2} \sum_{l=1}^{K^2} w_{kl} h_k h_l - \sum_{k=1}^{K^2} \theta_k h_k \quad (34)$$

where h_k are the multilevel parameter activities and w_{kl} and θ_k are the symmetric weights and bias inputs, respectively. From (33) and (34), we get the weights and bias inputs in the familiar outer-product forms:

$$w_{kl} = -\sum_{(i,j) \in S} z(i,j)_k z(i,j)_l \quad (35)$$

$$\theta_k = 2 \sum_{(i,j) \in S} z(i,j)_k y(i,j). \quad (36)$$

A greedy, distributed neural algorithm is used for the energy minimization. This leads to a localized multilevel number representation scheme for a general network.

B. Multilevel Greedy Distributed Algorithm

For a K^2 neuron second-order network, we choose Γ discrete activities $\{f_i, i = 0, 1, \cdots, \Gamma - 1\}$ in any arbitrary range of activities (e.g., $[0, 1]$) where we shall assume without loss of generality that $f_i > f_{i-1}$ for all i. Then, between any two activities f_m and f_n for the kth neuron, we can locally and asynchronously choose the one which results in the lowest energy given the current state of the other neurons because

$$E_{h_k = f_m} - E_{h_k = f_n} = [\theta_k - \zeta_k - (f_m + f_n) w_{k,k}] \cdot [f_m - f_n] \quad (37)$$

where

$$\zeta_k = \sum_{i, i \neq k}^{K^2} w_{i,k} h_i$$

is the current weighted sum from the other neuron activities. Thus, we choose level m over n for $m > n$ if

$$\zeta_k > \theta_k - (f_m + f_n) w_{k,k}. \quad (38)$$

Some properties of this algorithm follow.
1) Convergence is assured as long as the number of levels is not decreasing with time (i.e., assured if coarse to fine).
2) Self-feedback terms are included as level-dependent bias input terms.
3) The method can be easily extended to higher order networks (e.g., based on cubic energies). Appropriate lower order level-dependent networks (like the extra bias input term above) must then be implemented.

The multilevel lowest energy decision can be implemented by using variations of feedforward min-finding networks (such as those summarized in [20]). The space and time complexity of these networks are, in general, $O(\Gamma)$ and $O(\log \Gamma)$, respectively. However, in the quadratic case, it is easy to verify from (38) that we need only implement the decision between all *neighboring* levels in the set $\{f_i\}$; this requires exactly Γ neurons with level-dependent inputs. The best activity in the set is then proportional to the sum of the Γ neuron outputs so that the time complexity for the multilevel decision can be made $O(1)$. This means that this algorithm is similar in implementation complexity (e.g., the number of problem-dependent global interconnects required) to the simple sum energy representation used in [10] and in this paper. Also, in the simple sum case, visiting the neurons for each pixel in sequence will result in conditional energy minimization. Otherwise, from the implementation point of view, the two methods have some properties that are complementary. For example, we have the following.
1) The simple sum method requires asynchronism in the update steps for each pixel, while the greedy method does not.
2) The level-dependent terms arise as *inputs* in the greedy method as compared to *weights* in the simple sum method.

C. Simulation Results

The greedy algorithm was used with the weights from (35) and (36) to estimate the parameters from original and blurred sample points. A 5×5 window was used with two types of blurs: uniform and Gaussian. Both real and synthetic images were used, with and without additive Gaussian noise.

TABLE II
RESULTS FOR PARAMETER LEARNING. THE NUMBER Γ OF DISCRETE ACTIVITIES IS 256 FOR ALL TESTS. A: ARBITRARY CHOICE OF PIXELS FROM IMAGE. L: PIXELS CHOSEN FROM THRESHOLDED LAPLACIAN

Image	Noise	Blur	Samples	Methods	Iterations	MSE
Synthetic		Gaussian	68	A	49	0.000023
Synthetic		Uniform	100	A	114	0.000011
Real		Uniform	50	A	94	0.00353
Real		Uniform	100	L	85	0.00014
Real	20 dB	Uniform	100	A	72	0.00232
Real	20 dB	Uniform	100	L	83	0.00054

The estimated parameters for all types of blur matrices were numerically very close to the actual values when synthetic patterns were used. The network took longest to converge with a uniform blur function. The levels chosen for the discrete activity set $\{f_i\}$ were 128-256 equally spaced points in [0, 1] with 50-100 sample points from the image. Results for various cases are summarized in Table II.

When the sample pixels were randomly chosen, the errors increased by two orders of magnitude for a real image [Fig. 2(b)] as compared to synthetic ones. This is due to the smooth nature of real images. To solve this problem, sample points were chosen so as to lie close to *edges* in the image. This was done by thresholding the Laplacian of the image. Using sample points above a certain threshold for estimation improved the errors by an order of magnitude. The results were not appreciably degraded with 20 dB noise in the samples.

X. CONCLUSION

This paper has introduced a new approach for the restoration of gray level images degraded by a shift-invariant blur function and additive noise. The restoration procedure consists of two steps: parameter estimation and image reconstruction. In order to reduce computational complexity, a practical algorithm (Algorithm 2), which has equivalent results to the original one (Algorithm 1), is developed under the assumption that the neurons are sequentially visited. The image is generated iteratively by updating the neurons representing the image gray levels via a simple sum scheme. As no matrices are inverted, the serious problem of ringing due to the ill-conditioned blur matrix H and noise overriding caused by inverse filter or pseudoinverse inverse filter are avoided by using suboptimal boundary conditions. For the case of a 2-D uniform blur plus small noise, the neural network-based approach gives high-quality images compared to some of the existing methods. We see from the experimental results that the error defined by (12) is small, while the error between the original image and the restored image is relatively large. This is because the neural network decreases energy according to (12) only. Another reason is that when the blur matrix is singular or ill conditioned, the mapping from X to Y is not one to one; therefore, the error measure (12) is not reliable anymore. In our experiments, when the window size of a uniform blur function is 3 × 3, the ringing effect was eliminated by using blurred noisy boundary values without any smoothing constraint. When the window size is 5 × 5, the ringing effect was reduced with the help of the smoothing constraint and suboptimal boundary conditions. We have also shown that a smaller secondary network can effectively be used for estimating the blur parameters; this provides a more efficient learning technique than Boltzman machine learning on the primary network.

REFERENCES

[1] H. C. Andrews and B. R. Hunt, *Digital Image Restoration*. Englewood Cliffs, NJ: Prentice-Hall, 1977.
[2] J. W. Woods and V. K. Ingle, "Kalman filtering in two dimensions: Further results," *IEEE Trans. Acoust., Speech, Signal Processing*, vol. ASSP-29, pp. 188-197, Apr. 1981.
[3] W. K. Pratt, *Digital Image Processing*. New York: Wiley, 1978.
[4] R. Chellappa and R. L. Kashyap, "Digital image restoration using spatial interaction models," *IEEE Trans. Acoust., Speech, Signal Processing*, vol. ASSP-30, pp. 461-472, June 1982.
[5] H. Jinchi and R. Chellappa, "Restoration of blurred and noisy image using Gaussian Markov random field models," in *Proc. Conf. Inform. Sci. Syst.*, Princeton Univ., Princeton, NJ, 1986, pp. 34-39.
[6] N. H. Farhat, D. Psaltis, A. Prata, and E. Paek, "Optical implementation of the Hopfield model," *Appl. Opt.*, vol. 24, pp. 1469-1475, May 15, 1985.
[7] J. J. Hopfield and D. W. Tank, "Neural computation of decisions in optimization problems," *Biol. Cybern.*, vol. 52, pp. 141-152, 1985.
[8] J. J. Hopfield, "Neural networks and physical systems with emergent collective computational abilities," *Proc. Nat. Acad. Sci. USA*, vol. 79, pp. 2554-2558, Apr. 1982.
[9] S.-I. Amari, "Learning patterns and pattern sequences by self-organizing nets of threshold elements," *IEEE Trans. Comput.*, vol. C-21, pp. 1197-1206, Nov. 1972.
[10] M. Takeda and J. W. Goodman, "Neural networks for computation: Number representations and programming complexity," *Appl. Opt.*, vol. 25, pp. 3033-3046, Sept. 1986.
[11] T. Poggio, V. Torre, and C. Koch, "Computational vision and regularization theory," *Nature*, vol. 317, pp. 314-319, Sept. 1985.
[12] J. P. LaSalle, *The Stability and Control of Discrete Processes*. New York: Springer-Verlag, 1986.
[13] N. Metropolis *et al.*, "Equations of state calculations by fast computing machines," *J. Chem. Phys.*, vol. 21, pp. 1087-1091, 1953.
[14] S. Kirkpatrick *et al.*, "Optimization by stimulated annealing," *Science*, vol. 220, pp. 671-680, 1983.
[15] W. K. Pratt *et al.*, "Visual discrimination of stochastic texture fields," *IEEE Trans. Syst., Man, Cybern.*, vol. SMC-8, pp. 796-814, Nov. 1978.
[16] J. W. Woods, J. Biemond, and A. M. Tekalp, "Boundary value problem in image restoration," in *Proc. Int. Conf. Acoust., Speech, Signal Processing*, Tampa, FL, Mar. 1985, pp. 692-695.
[17] M. M. Sondhi, "The removal of spatially invariant degradations," *Proc. IEEE*, vol. 60, pp. 842-853, July 1972.
[18] J. Biemond, J. Rieske, and J. Gerbrand, "A fast Kalman filter for images degraded by both blur and noise," *IEEE Trans. Acoust., Speech, Signal Processing*, vol. ASSP-31, pp. 1248-1256, Oct. 1983.
[19] R. Chellappa and H. Jinchi, "A nonrecursive filter for edge preserv-

ing image restoration," in *Proc. Int. Conf. Acoust., Speech, Signal Processing*, Tampa, FL, Mar. 1985, pp. 652-655.

[20] R. P. Lippmann, "An introduction to computing with neural nets," *IEEE ASSP Mag.*, pp. 4-22, Apr. 1987.

Aseem Vaid was born in Jammu, India, on January 8, 1963. He received the B.Tech. degree in electrical engineering in May 1985 from the Indian Institute of Technology, New Delhi.

Currently he is working on the Ph.D. degree at the University of Southern California, Los Angeles. His research interests are in neural networks and optical computing.

Yi-Tong Zhou (S'84) received the B.S. degree in physics from the East China Normal University, Shanghai, China, and the M.S. degree in electrical engineering from the University of Southern California, Los Angeles, in 1982 and 1983, respectively.

He is currently a Research Assistant at the Signal and Image Processing Institute, University of Southern California, Los Angeles, and is working toward the Ph.D. degree in electrical engineering.

His research interests include image processing, computer vision, neural network algorithms, optical computing, and biomedical signal processing. He has published about a dozen technical papers in these areas.

B. Keith Jenkins (M'85) received the B.S. degree in applied physics from the California Institute of Technology, Pasadena, in 1977, and the M.S. and Ph.D. degrees in electrical engineering from the University of Southern California, Los Angeles, in 1979 and 1984, respectively.

He was employed at Hughes Aircraft Company, El Segundo, CA, from 1977 to 1979 where he worked on holography for use in head-up displays. From 1984 to 1987 he was a Research Assistant Professor in the Department of Electrical Engineering, University of Southern California, where he presently is Assistant Professor of Electrical Engineering. He has also participated in advisory panels to government and industry, and has been a consultant to JPL, TRW, and Odetics. His research has included work in the areas of optical digital computing, neural networks and their optical implementation, learning algorithms, optical interconnection networks, parallel computation models and complexity, computer-generated holography, and optical 3-D position sensing systems.

Dr. Jenkins is a member of the Optical Society of America and the Association for Computing Machinery. He was awarded The Northrop Assistant Professor of Engineering at USC in 1987, and is a recipient of the 1988 NSF Presidential Young Investigator Award.

Rama Chellappa (S'78-M'79-SM'83), for a photograph and biography, see this issue, p. 1066.

Complete Discrete 2-D Gabor Transforms by Neural Networks for Image Analysis and Compression

JOHN G. DAUGMAN

(*Invited Paper*)

Abstract—A three-layered neural network is described for transforming two-dimensional discrete signals into generalized nonorthogonal 2-D "Gabor" representations for image analysis, segmentation, and compression. These transforms are conjoint spatial/spectral representations [10], [15], which provide a complete image description in terms of locally windowed 2-D spectral coordinates embedded within global 2-D spatial coordinates. Because intrinsic redundancies within images are extracted, the resulting image codes can be very compact. However, these conjoint transforms are inherently difficult to compute because the elementary expansion functions are not orthogonal. One orthogonalizing approach developed for 1-D signals by Bastiaans [8], based on biorthonormal expansions, is restricted by constraints on the conjoint sampling rates and invariance of the windowing function, as well as by the fact that the auxiliary orthogonalizing functions are nonlocal infinite series. In the present "neural network" approach, based upon interlaminar interactions involving two layers with fixed weights and one layer with adjustable weights, the network finds coefficients for complete conjoint 2-D Gabor transforms without these restrictive conditions. For arbitrary noncomplete transforms, in which the coefficients might be interpreted simply as signifying the presence of certain features in the image, the network finds *optimal* coefficients in the sense of minimal mean-squared-error in representing the image. In one algebraically complete scheme permitting exact reconstruction, the network finds expansion coefficients that reduce entropy from 7.57 in the pixel representation to 2.55 in the complete 2-D Gabor transform. In "wavelet" expansions based on a biologically inspired log-polar ensemble of dilations, rotations, and translations of a single underlying 2-D Gabor wavelet template, image compression is illustrated with ratios up to 20:1. Also demonstrated is image segmentation based on the clustering of coefficients in the complete 2-D Gabor transform. This coefficient-finding network for implementing useful nonorthogonal image transforms may also have neuroscientific relevance, because the network layers with fixed weights use empirical 2-D receptive field profiles obtained from orientation-selective neurons in cat visual cortex as the weighting functions, and the resulting transform mimics the biological visual strategy of embedding angular and spectral analysis within global spatial coordinates.

I. INTRODUCTION

SEVERAL broad classes of problems for which neural networks appear to show promise involve the extraction or exploitation of redundancy. Examples include content addressable memory [1], pattern classification and learning [2], signal reconstruction from partial information [3], separation of signals from noise [4], cooperative and fault-tolerant processing [5], estimation and prediction [6], and data compression. The last of these is perhaps both the simplest and the most generic example because it most directly depends upon the exploitation of redundancy. In principle, data compression is possible for a nonrandom signal by virtue of the fact that its value at some points can be predicted from its values at other, possibly remote, points or sequences. Correlation structure in a signal can take many forms and can involve different statistical orders, but in information-theoretic terms [7], its existence implies that the entropy or statistical complexity of the source is less than the entropy of the channel, as determined by its resolution (e.g., 8 bits/pixel). Whenever this situation exists, compression of the signal to a lower bound specified by the elimination of redundancy is in principle possible, without loss of information (cf. Theorems 4.5.1 and 4.5.2 of [7]).

Ordinary images are examples of signals having high degrees of self-correlation. Fundamentally, mutual information arises within an image because of the fact that physical objects and scenes tend to have internal morphological consistency, including first-order correlations (locally similar luminance values), second-order or dipole correlations (e.g., oriented edge continuation), as well as higher-order correlations (e.g., homogeneity of textural signature). These correlations are attributes which distinguish real images from random noise, a distinction that is not exploited in the standard pixel-by-pixel image representation. The analysis, communication, and storage of image information would benefit from an efficient means to encode image structure in ways that extracted and exploited these correlations.

A second typical goal in signal processing is to find a representation in which certain attributes of the signal are made explicit. Often this involves transformations into representations in which the attributes or features sought for in the signal are used as the expansion functions. But it is only for certain transforms that the coefficients for projecting the signal onto that chosen set of functions can be easily obtained. If the desired elementary functions are not orthogonal, for example, then simply computing their inner products with the signal will not produce the correct coefficients. A further problem may be that the primitive functions of interest for extracting certain kinds of signal

---

Manuscript received December 17, 1987. This work was supported by an NSF Presidential Young Investigator Award and by AFOSR U.R.I. Contract F49620-87-C-0018.

The author is with the Departments of Psychology and Electrical, Computer, and Systems Engineering, 950 William James Hall, Harvard University, Cambridge, MA 02138.

IEEE Log Number 8821369.

structure may not constitute a complete basis, or it may be difficult to establish whether or not they do except under strong constraints.

One conjoint transform which illustrates the desirability of obtaining the expansion coefficients on a set of overlapping *non*orthogonal, yet complete, elementary functions is portrayed by Figs. 1 and 2. Displayed in Fig. 1 is a pixel histogram of the 8-bit "Lena" picture commonly used in image processing research. This gray-scale distribution of 65 536 pixels has an entropy of $S = 7.57$, where entropy is defined as average self-information of the pixel ensemble

$$S = -\sum_{i=1}^{n} P_i \log_2 P_i \qquad (1)$$

given that

$$\sum_{i=1}^{n} P_i = 1 \qquad (2)$$

where the P_i are the relative rates of occurrence of each of the n (in this case 256) gray levels in the picture. Characteristically, the pixel histogram is broad and multimodal, with large entropy. (Uncorrelated 8-bit white noise would have only slightly more entropy, namely, $S = 8$.) But when the Lena picture is transformed into a *complete, discrete, 2-D Gabor* representation (to be defined later), the coefficient values in the transform have the far more compact distribution shown in Fig. 2. Quantized again to 8-bit resolution, the set of 65 536 complete 2-D Gabor coefficients has an entropy of only 2.55, while capturing all of the image structure in the original picture and permitting its exact reconstruction. (The reconstruction may be seen in Fig. 8.) For data compression purposes, one consequence of this observation is that the information cost per pixel for transmitting or storing this 8-bit image could be reduced dramatically without any loss of information. By constructing a code whose word length varies inversely with the frequency distribution shown in Fig. 2, such images could in principle be encoded with a compression factor amounting to 5 fewer bits per pixel. This conjoint 2-D Gabor transform is also useful for image analysis and segmentation, since it extracts locally windowed 2-D spectral information concerning form and texture without sacrificing information about 2-D location or more global spatial relationships, as does a Fourier transform.

The problem is that the overlapping elementary functions which form the projection vectors for this transform are not orthogonal, and so finding their coefficients is difficult. In research to date, it has only been possible to find these coefficients under limiting restrictions on the relationships between the conjoint sampling rate parameters of the elementary functions, and through the use of auxiliary biorthogonal functions [8] expressed as nonlocal infinite series. The main purpose of this paper is to describe a simple neural network architecture for finding optimal coefficient values in arbitrary two-dimensional signal

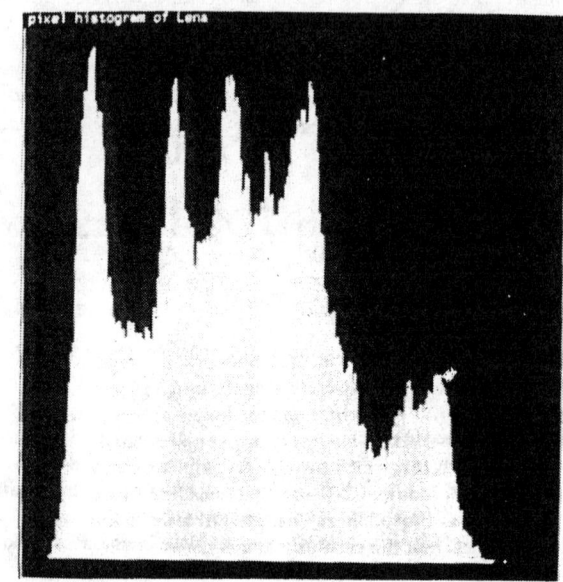

Fig. 1. Pixel histogram of the Lena image, comprising 65 536 8-bit pixels. The entropy of this pixel ensemble is 7.57, only slightly smaller than the entropy of random 8-bit noise with uniform density (namely, 8). Representing images by ensembles of independent pixels does not exploit their intrinsic correlation structure.

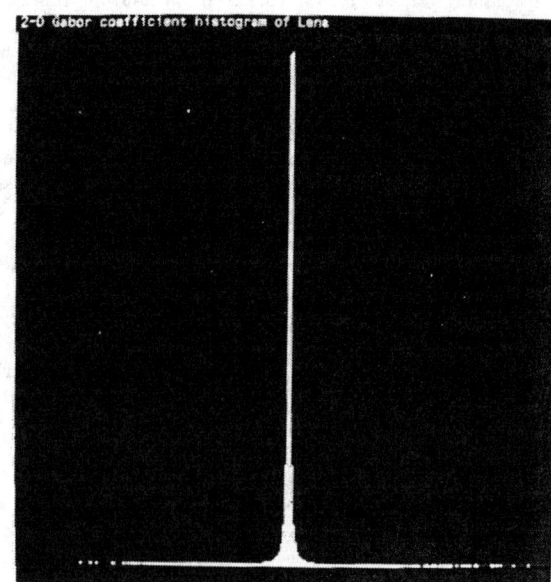

Fig. 2. Histogram of 65 536 coefficients in a complete discrete 2-D Gabor transform, quantized to 8 bits each as was the pixel histogram of Fig. 1 but obviously far more compactly distributed. The entropy of this ensemble of 2-D Gabor coefficients is only 2.55 bits, yet they completely capture the Lena image and allow its exact reconstruction (as shown in Fig. 8). The 2-D Gabor transform itself is shown in Fig. 7.

transforms which in general might be neither complete nor orthogonal. The application of this coefficient-finding scheme to generalized two-dimensional signal transforms is useful for purposes such as image analysis, feature extraction, and data compression. It also leads to an interpretation of the biologically measured two-dimensional anisotropic visual neural receptive field profiles, which have to a large extent motivated the development of the 2-D Gabor transform [10], [15].

II. Neural Network for Finding Projection Coefficients

The general neural network architecture for finding the coefficients in (possibly nonorthogonal and noncomplete) signal transforms is shown in Fig. 3. We shall deal with some discrete two-dimensional signal $I[x, y]$, say, an image supported on $[256 \times 256]$ pixels in $[x, y]$, which we wish to analyze or compress by representing it as a set of expansion coefficients $\{a_i\}$ on some set of two-dimensional elementary functions $\{G_i[x, y]\}$. We may regard a given image $I[x, y]$ as a vector in a 65 536-dimensional vector space, and different representations of the image based on complete orthonormal expansions constitute different bases of this vector space. For example, the conventional pixel representation projects the image onto a set of unit basis vectors, one for each pixel, with coefficients representing lightness values. At the other extreme from the unit basis, each of the linearly independent orthonormal basis vectors might be a 2-D Fourier component, with the associated coefficient being the inner product projection of the image onto this basis vector. More generally, for certain purposes such as feature extraction, we might also wish to represent $I[x, y]$ on a set of linearly *dependent* vectors, which may or may not completely span the vector space; even if they are neither orthogonal nor complete, we can still find *optimal* projections of the image onto each one by satisfying global optimization criteria.

Thus, we wish to represent $I[x, y]$ either exactly or in some optimal sense by projecting it onto a chosen set of vectors $G_i[x, y]$. This requires finding projection coefficients $\{a_i\}$ such that the resultant vector $H[x, y]$

$$H[x, y] = \sum_{i=1}^{n} a_i G_i[x, y] \quad (3)$$

is either identical to $I[x, y]$ (the complete case) or generates a difference-vector $I[x, y] - H[x, y]$ of minimal length (the optimization case). If the elementary functions $\{G_i[x, y]\}$ form a complete orthogonal set, then the representation in $H[x, y]$ is exact (the difference-vector is zero) and the solution for $\{a_i\}$ is simple:

$$a_i = \frac{\sum_{x,y} (G_i[x, y] I[x, y])}{\sum_{x,y} G_i^2[x, y]}. \quad (4)$$

If they do not, however, then in general the representation $H[x, y]$ will be inexact and the desired set of coefficients $\{a_i\}$ must be determined by an optimization criterion, such as minimizing the squared norm of the difference-vector:

$$E = \| I[x, y] - H[x, y] \|^2$$
$$= \sum_{x,y} (I[x, y] - H[x, y])^2. \quad (5)$$

The norm E will be minimized only when its partial derivatives with respect to all of the n coefficients $\{a_i\}$ equal zero:

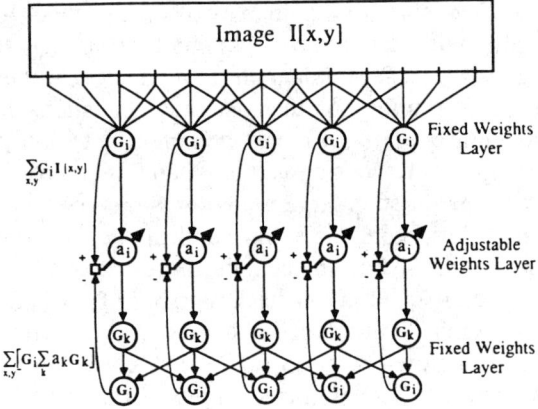

Fig. 3. A three-layered neural network for finding the optimal coefficients in arbitrary image transforms which in general may be neither orthogonal nor complete, nor limited by constraints on sampling uniformity. The first and third layers have fixed weights (in the present work taken to be 2-D Gabor elementary functions as seen in Fig. 4), while the middle layer has weights which are adjusted by interlaminar interactions. In the stable state when equilibrium is reached [see (6) and (9)], the cost function E is minimized and the weight values of the middle layer correspond to the desired transform coefficients.

$$\forall_i, \quad \frac{\partial E}{\partial a_i} = -2 \sum_{x,y} (I[x, y] G_i[x, y])$$
$$+ \sum_{x,y} \left[2 \left(\sum_{k=1}^{n} a_k G_k[x, y] \right) G_i[x, y] \right] = 0. \quad (6)$$

Satisfying this condition for each of the a_i then generates a system of n simultaneous equations in n unknowns:

$$\left| \sum_{x,y} (I[x, y] G_i[x, y]) \right.$$
$$\left. = \sum_{x,y} \left[\left(\sum_{k=1}^{n} a_k G_k[x, y] \right) G_i[x, y] \right] \right|. \quad (7)$$

Thus, the solution which minimizes the squared norm of the difference-vector [(5)] amounts to finding the set of coefficients $\{a_i\}$ such that the inner product of each vector $G_i[x, y]$ with the entire linear combination of vectors $\Sigma\, a_k G_k[x, y]$ is the same as its inner product with the original image $I[x, y]$. It should be noted that in the case when the $\{G_i[x, y]\}$ form a set of orthogonal vectors, then the inner products in the right-hand side of (7) are nonzero only for $k = i$, and so each of the n equations then has only a single unknown, and it is immediately apparent that the minimal-difference-vector solution for each a_i is identical to that given earlier in (4) as the familiar orthogonal case.

Even in the nonorthogonal case, the system of n equations [(7)] could still be exactly solved in principle by algebraic means to find the set of optimal coefficients $\{a_i\}$. But unless the enormous (65 536 × 65 536) matrix generated by (7) is very sparse (requiring strictly compact support for the members of $\{G_i[x, y]\}$), it would be completely impractical to solve this huge system of simultaneous equations by algebraic methods such as matrix manipulation, since the complexity of such methods grows factorially with the number of simultaneous equations. (Using Stirling's approximation for the factorial, the general matrix solution for the system of equations in (7) would require $2.5 \times 10^{287\,157}$ floating-point multiplications to find.) Methods based upon iterative improvement are far faster for such large n, although they converge on an exact solution only as a limit, and can become trapped in local minima. Fortunately, the difference-vector cost function (5) is quadratic in each member of $\{a_i\}$, and so a unique global minimum for E exists. The neural network architecture shown in Fig. 3 converges through iteration upon the desired image representation $\{a_i\}$ by implementing gradient descent along the $E(a_i)$ surface, which expresses the quadratic cost function's dependency on all of the $\{a_i\}$ coefficients.

A common feature of neural network architectures is the combination of layers of neurons having adjustable (or adaptive) synaptic weights, and layers with fixed weights. The present scheme begins with a layer of fixed connection strengths which are specified by an arbitrary set of (generally nonorthogonal) elementary functions $\{G_i[x, y]\}$; by summing the different image pixels through these weights, the output of the ith neuron in this layer is simply the inner product of the ith elementary function, $G_i[x, y]$, with the input image $I[x, y]$ in that region. This is precisely the neurophysiological concept of a (linear) neuron's "receptive field profile," which refers to the spatial weighting function by which a local region of the retinal image is multiplied and integrated to generate that neuron's response strength. The second layer contains adjustable weights for multiplying each of these outputs, according to a control signal which arises from interlaminar interactions. The third layer is identical to the first layer and stores the same fixed set of elementary functions. The adjustable weights of the middle layer constitute the transformed image representation as the set of coefficients $\{a_i\}$. The adaptive control signal adjusts each of the weights by an amount Δ_i, given by the difference between a feedforward signal and a feedback signal. The feedforward signal is the level of activity of the neuron from the first layer, and the feedback signal is the inner product of the weighting function of the corresponding neuron in the third layer with the weighted sum of all the other neighboring neurons in that layer with which it is connected. Thus, the weight adjustment is

$$\Delta_i = \sum_{x,y} \left(G_i[x, y] \, I[x, y] \right)$$
$$- \sum_{x,y} \left[G_i[x, y] \left(\sum_{k=1}^{n} a_k G_k[x, y] \right) \right] \quad (8)$$

and the iterative rule for adjusting the value of each coefficient is $a_i \Rightarrow a_i + \Delta_i$. It should be noted that the network does not require a "teacher" that generates the weight adjustment signal by comparing the current representation with a separate copy of the desired pattern. Rather, the adaptive control signal Δ_i arises only from interlaminar network interactions.

It can be seen by inspecting [6] and [8] that the weight adjustment rule is equivalent to

$$\Delta_i = -\frac{1}{2} \frac{\partial E}{\partial a_i}.$$

It should be noted that the minus sign implies that the weight adjustment is always in the downhill direction of the cost surface $E(a_i)$, and that the adjustment is proportional to the slope of the cost surface at this point. A fuller discussion of gradient descent methods may be found in [4, ch. 4]. The equilibrium state of the network that is reached when all $\Delta_i = 0$ is the state in which the cost function E representing the difference-vector squared norm $\|I[x, y] - H[x, y]\|^2$ has reached its minimum; this is the point at which the partial derivative of E with respect to all of the adjustable weights is nil:

$$\forall_i, \quad \Delta_i = 0 \Leftrightarrow \frac{\partial E}{\partial a_i} = 0. \quad (9)$$

Thus, in the stable state, the middle layer of the network has weights which represent the optimal coefficients $\{a_i\}$ for the projection of the signal $I[x, y]$ onto any set of elementary functions $\{G_i[x, y]\}$ which, as noted earlier, need be neither orthogonal nor complete.

III. 2-D GABOR ELEMENTARY FUNCTIONS AND BIOLOGICAL VISION

The particular choice of nonorthogonal elementary functions which will be used in the remainder of this paper for the fixed-weight layers of the network are taken from actual neurophysiological measurements of the two-dimensional anisotropic receptive field profiles describing single neurons in mammalian visual cortex [9], [10], [15]. A scientific topic of great interest to neural network researchers is the investigation of the properties and functioning of "real" (biological) neural networks. In the case of the mammalian visual nervous system, a great deal is now known about neural signal processing strategies for the extraction and representation of image structure, at least in the earlier levels of visual processing (retina, lateral geniculate, and primary visual cortex). Among the many questions which can fruitfully be studied regarding signal processing strategies in biological visual systems are the following: how image structure is encoded at various levels; the efficiency of these codes in terms such as dynamic range compression, entropy, noise characteristics, and invariances; the interweaving of multiple coding dimensions within single channel firing rates and across separate channels; the roles of spatiotemporal filtering and of nonlinear operations; and the transformations of image information which support higher level visual cognition. For all of these questions, a potential dialogue between neural network theory, signal processing theory, and experimental neurobiology is an exciting prospect, and the potential mutual benefits for all three disciplines could be high.

The several cortical visual areas of mammals contain

many populations of neurons, some linear and many nonlinear, with selectivities for a variety of stimulus attributes. These include location in 2-D visual space, orientation, motion, color, stereoscopic depth, size or spatial frequency, symmetry, and others [11]. In the primary visual cortex (Area 17), perhaps the most striking of these is orientation selectivity [12], which imparts to individual neurons a pronounced dependency between their firing rate and the planar orientation of a stimulus such as an edge or bar. Moreover, assemblies of neurons are organized into "columns" which share the same orientation preference, and on a larger scale, these columns reveal a functional "sequence regularity" of systematic shifts in their preferred orientation [13]. The sequence regularity of columnar orientation preference is one of the most crystalline features of visual cortical architecture now known, and it clearly plays a crucial role, although an as yet unspecified role from a signal processing viewpoint, in the logic of the brain's representation of the visual world. A second striking feature, although true only of the linear class of neurons (so-called "simple cells"), is their pairing by symmetry into quadrature phase pairs: adjacent simple cells have spatial receptive field profiles which share the same location in space and the same orientation preference but differ by 90° in their phase [14]. This quadrature phase relation in neural receptive field pairs is suggestive of a kind of local harmonic expansion of image structure.

One suitable model of the two-dimensional receptive field profiles encountered experimentally in cortical simple cells, which captures their salient tuning properties of spatial localization, orientation selectivity, spatial frequency selectivity, and quadrature phase relationship, is the parameterized family of "2-D Gabor filters," as seen in Fig. 4. This neural model was originally proposed in 1980 simultaneously by Daugman [15] in two-dimensional form and by Marcelja [16] in one-dimensional form. The 2-D form has the virtue of capturing explicitly the critical neurobiological variables of a given neuron's orientation and spatial frequency preference, the tuning bandwidths for these variables, the receptive field dimensions, and the relationships among all of these parameters as captured by generalized uncertainty relationships [10] which the 2-D filter family (in complex form) optimizes.

The general functional form of the 2-D Gabor filter family is specified in (10) and (11), in terms of the space-domain impulse response function $G(x, y)$ and its associated 2-D Fourier transform $F(u, v)$:

$$G(x, y) = \exp\left(-\pi[(x - x_o)^2\alpha^2 + (y - y_o)^2\beta^2]\right)$$
$$\cdot \exp\left(-2\pi i[u_o(x - x_o) + v_o(y - y_o)]\right) \quad (10)$$

$$F(u, v) = \exp\left(-\pi\left[\frac{(u - u_o)^2}{\alpha^2} + \frac{(v - v_o)^2}{\beta^2}\right]\right)$$
$$\cdot \exp\left(-2\pi i[x_o(u - u_o) + y_o(v - v_o)]\right). \quad (11)$$

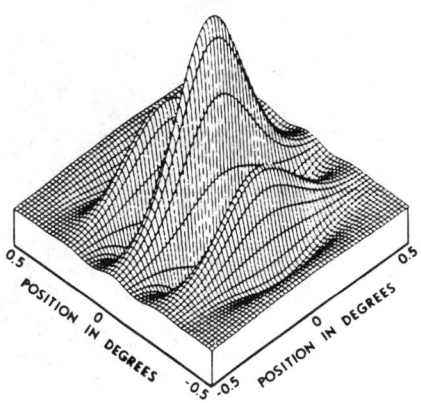

SPATIAL FILTER PROFILE

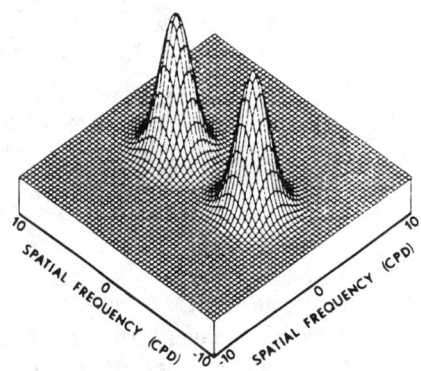

FREQUENCY RESPONSE

Fig. 4. Example of a 2-D Gabor elementary function (real part) and its 2-D Fourier transform, as originally proposed by Daugman in 1980 [15]. These functions have optimally compact support in conjoint 2-D spatial 2-D spectral representation, and they achieve the lower bound in the general uncertainty relation (12). In the present network (Fig. 3), they provide the weighting functions $\{G_i[x, y]\}$ for the first and third layers.

This family of 2-D elementary functions constitutes a generalization of the 1-D elementary functions proposed in 1946 by Gabor [17] in his famous monograph, "Theory of communication." It should be noted that the 2-D Gabor filter impulse response function $G(x, y)$ and its 2-D Fourier transform $F(u, v)$ have identical functional form; the 2-D Fourier transform theorems for shift, similarity, and modulation are reflected in the position parameters (x_o, y_o), the modulation parameters (u_o, v_o), and the two scale parameters (α, β). If $\alpha \neq \beta$, then a further degree of freedom [for simplicity not included in (10) and (11)] is coordinate rotation of (x, y) out of the principal axes corresponding to (α, β), which in the Fourier domain results in the same coordinate rotation of (u, v). These "noncanonical" members of the 2-D Gabor family simply have additional cross terms in xy in (10) and in uv in (11).

An important property of the family of 2-D Gabor filters is their achievement of the theoretical lower bound of joint uncertainty in the two conjoint domains of (x, y) visual space and (u, v) spatial frequency variables. Defining uncertainty in each of the four variables by the nor-

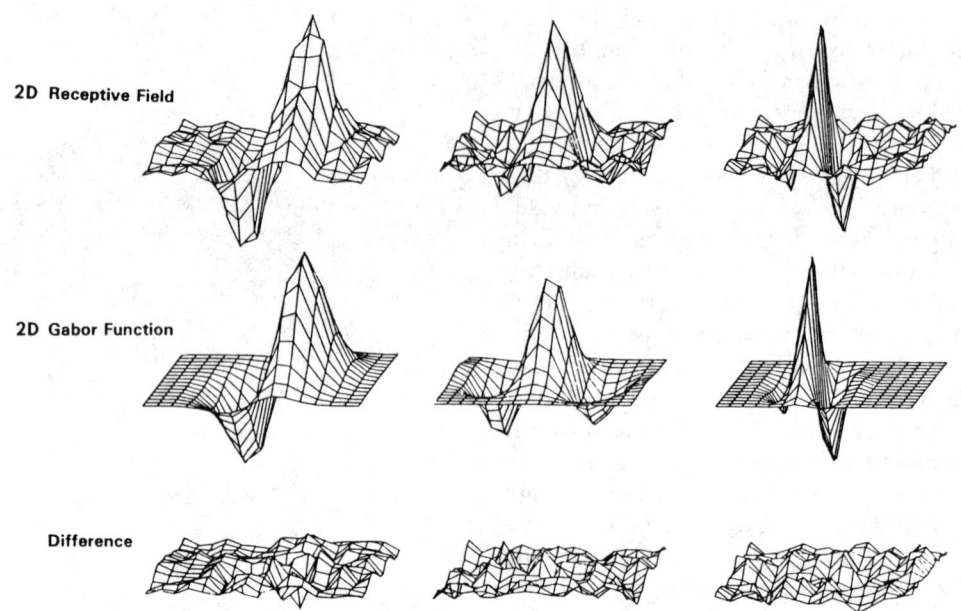

Fig. 5. Top row: illustrations of empirical 2-D receptive field profiles measured by J. P. Jones and L. A. Palmer (personal communication) in simple cells of the cat visual cortex. Middle row: best-fitting 2-D Gabor elementary function for each neuron, described by (10). Bottom row: residual error of the fit, indistinguishable from random error in the Chi-squared sense for 97 percent of the cells studied.

malized second moments (Δx), (Δy), (Δu), (Δv) about the principle axes (see Daugman [10] for details), it may be shown that a fundamental uncertainty principle exists:

$$(\Delta x)(\Delta y)(\Delta u)(\Delta v) \geq 1/16\pi^2 \quad (12)$$

and that the lower bound of the inequality is achieved by the family of 2-D Gabor filters [(10) and (11)]. In this sense, these filters achieve the maximal possible joint resolution in the conjoint 2-D visual space and 2-D Fourier domains. These elementary functions also can be regarded as forming a continuum between the opposite extremes of either Kronecker delta functions in the space domain (inherent in the pixel representation of an image) or Kronecker delta functions in the frequency domain (inherent in the 2-D Fourier representation of an image). These limiting cases arise when the parameters (α, β) in (10) and (11) become either very large or very small; in the mixed case when one is very large and the other very small, the representation corresponds to taking 1-D Fourier transforms on each raster line in a rastered image. In general, we will work with intermediate values of (α, β) in self-similar conjoint representations, because this situation appears to have great neurobiological significance.

It is interesting that the great majority of mammalian cortical simple cells (97 percent in the studies described in [9] and [10]) have 2-D receptive field profiles which can be well fit, in the sense of satisfying statistical chi-squared tests, by members of the family of 2-D Gabor elementary functions. Three examples of such empirical studies by J. Jones and L. Palmer (personal communication) are presented in Fig. 5. The top row shows the empirical 2-D receptive field profiles measured with small spots of light spanning a (16×16) position grid, plotted as the excitatory or inhibitory effect of the stimulus on the neuron's firing rate. The middle row shows the best-fitting 2-D Gabor elementary function for each cell; and the bottom row shows the residual error of the fit. Extensive discussions of the experimental and analytic methods are provided in [9].

Clearly, the parameters in the 2-D Gabor family of elementary functions directly capture the chief neurophysiological properties of localization in visual space (x_o, y_o), spatial dimensions (α, β), preferred orientation and spatial frequency (captured by converting the Cartesian (u_o, v_o) parameters into polar coordinates), and the tuning bandwidths for orientation and spatial frequency (determined jointly by u_o, v_o, α, and β). To this extent, because the neural receptive field profiles $G(x, y)$ are localized *both* in (x, y) visual space *and* in (u, v) 2-D spectral coordinates, we can describe the biological early visual cortical analysis of image structure as forming a conjoint spatial/spatial frequency signal representation with optimized joint resolution, subject to the 4-D uncertainty principle of (12). Roughly speaking, such a representation facilitates the extraction of local 2-D spectral information (texture, scale, axes of modulation) without sacrificing concurrent extraction of information about 2-D location and metrical relationships. For example, the textural structure of a given image region can be separated into its identifying 2-D spectral constituents, while in the same representation, the global spatial structure of the image can be separated into the distinct regions in which a given 2-D spectral structure appears. This scheme of image representation might be considered analogous to a speech spectrogram, generalized to four dimensions; separate signal components having conjoint support in one domain can be given disjoint support in the other domain, a strategy of proven utility in statistical pattern recognition [19]. Further discussion about conjoint 2-D/2-D anisotropic filter representations and neurobiological mechanisms may be found in [10], [15], and [18].

IV. Complete Discrete 2-D Gabor Transforms

For machine vision, the utility of representing image structure in terms of 2-D Gabor elementary functions is complicated by the fact that they do not constitute an orthogonal basis. The inner product of two members of the set specified by (10), in the same location (x_o, y_o) but parameterized differently by i and j, is nonzero:

$$\langle G_i(x, y); G_j(x, y) \rangle$$
$$= \exp\left(-\pi \left[\frac{(u_i - u_j)^2}{(\alpha_i^2 + \alpha_j^2)} + \frac{(v_i - v_j)^2}{(\beta_i^2 + \beta_j^2)}\right]\right). \quad (13)$$

One solution to this problem, developed by Bastiaans [8], is to introduce an auxiliary biorthogonal function $\gamma[x, y]$ which allows one to find the correct coefficients by the usual inner product rule for projecting the signal onto the elementary functions. Thus, in the discrete case, if the elementary functions $\{G_i[x, y]\}$ form a complete but nonorthogonal set on which the image $I[x, y]$ can be exactly represented as

$$I[x, y] = \sum_{i=1}^{n} a_i G_i[x, y], \quad (14)$$

then it may be possible under specific restrictions on $\{G_i[x, y]\}$ to find an auxiliary function $\gamma[x, y]$ such that the desired coefficients $\{a_i\}$ can be found directly by the rule

$$a_i = \sum_{x, y} \gamma[x - x_i, y - y_i]$$
$$\cdot \exp\left[-2\pi i(u_i x + v_i y)\right] I[x, y]. \quad (15)$$

Thus, Bastiaans' auxiliary function $\gamma[x, y]$ is biorthogonal to the (invariant) Gaussian window of the chosen elementary functions $\{G_i[x, y]\}$, and it is derived by demanding that the Kronecker delta inner product rule for orthogonal basis functions be satisfied. Although Bastiaans' 1-D solution can be readily generalized to the 2-D case as a Cartesian product, it is expressed only as an infinite series [8], and so in practice an approximation must be found. More importantly, its derivation depends upon certain severe restrictions on the elementary functions $\{G_i[x, y]\}$; in particular, they must all share the same windowing function. This entails that the spatial frequency bandwidths (in octave terms) and orientation bandwidths of the elementary functions will both be inversely proportional to their center frequencies. We would prefer to relax this requirement, in part because the biological 2-D receptive field profiles tend to have a roughly invariant template shape across scales as illustrated by the

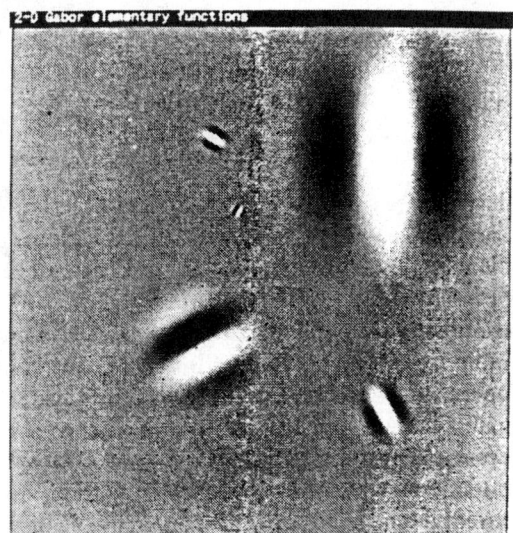

Fig. 6. Five examples of 2-D Gabor elementary functions displayed as luminance primitives. These biologically modeled "wavelets" can all be generated from a single complex member by dilations, rotations, and translations, as specified by (22).

luminance profiles in Fig. 6, lending them constant log-polar bandwidths, rather than having a window of constant size which would entail constant linear bandwidths. A further motivation for averting the requirements of the Bastiaans' biorthogonal approach is that we would also like to be able to find optimal conjoint coefficients $\{a_i\}$ even when the elementary functions do *not* form a complete set, as arises from irregular sampling rules. In these cases, the auxiliary $\gamma[x, y]$ biorthogonal function approach to obtaining the coefficients is not helpful, but the approach based on the neural network architecture illustrated in Fig. 3 is.

Before applying the network to the general (nonorthogonal *and* noncomplete) case, we first demonstrate its ability to accomplish the same goal as the Bastiaans method for regular sampling with invariant window function (the nonorthogonal yet complete case). Here the 2-D Gabor elementary functions are parameterized for an invariant Gaussian window which is positioned on (fully overlapping) Cartesian lattice locations

$$\{x_m, y_n\} = \{mM, nN\} \quad (16)$$

for integers (m, n) and corresponding lattice cell dimensions M, N. The complex exponentials which modulate these overlapping Gaussians are accordingly parameterized for a Cartesian lattice of 2-D spatial frequencies $\{u_r, v_s\}$ appropriate to the M, N spatial lattice:

$$\{u_r, v_s\} = \left\{\frac{r}{M}, \frac{s}{N}\right\} \quad (17)$$

for integer increments of (r, s) spanning $\{-(M - 1/2), (M - 1/2)\}$ and $\{-(N - 1/2), (N - 1/2)\}$, respectively. Thus, for the neural network shown in Fig. 3, we use for the fixed weighting functions of the first and third layers the 2-D Gabor elementary functions

$$G_{mnrs}[x, y] = \exp\left(-\pi\alpha^2[(x - mM)^2 + (y - nN)^2]\right)$$
$$\cdot \exp\left(-2\pi i \left[r\frac{x}{M} + s\frac{y}{N}\right]\right) \quad (18)$$

and allow the network to converge to its stable state, when (9) is satisfied, at which point we may read out the desired coefficients a_{mnrs} from the adjustable weights of the middle layer.

These obtained coefficients a_{mnrs} constitute a complete 2-D Gabor transform of the input image. Each coefficient is complex, but because the input image is real, there is conjugate symmetry among the coefficients: over both parameters r and s, the real part of a_{mnrs} has even symmetry and its imaginary part has odd symmetry. Fig. 7 displays the nonredundant halves of the complete set of real and imaginary coefficients a_{mnrs} as a (256×256) image, giving a complete 2-D Gabor transform of the Lena picture. It is noteworthy that the fundamental uncertainty principle expressed in (12) is implicit in the space/spectral sampling rules expressed in (16) and (17). The larger the size of each spatial lattice cell M or N, which means the fewer the number of spatial sampling positions, the larger is the number of spatial frequency components required in each patch in the corresponding dimension, as expressed above by the ranges of the indexes r and s. Thus, the product of the ranges of the four indexes m, n, r, s is a constant, and in the complete case, is equal to the number of pixels in the image.

The (m, n) lattice that was used in constructing the complete 2-D Gabor transform shown in Fig. 7 is apparent by the periodic clusters of points, which correspond to the centers of the overlapping Gaussian envelopes. Although the size of each $(M \times N)$ lattice cell here was (16×16) pixels, each of the overlapping elementary functions in this transform is fully supported on (32×32) pixels, with Gaussian space constant $(1/\alpha\sqrt{\pi})$ equal to ± 9 pixels at the $1/e$ points; thus, the value at which the overlapping Gaussians are finally truncated and equated to zero is 0.05. Although the value of the Gaussian scale constant α in (18) is arbitrary from the standpoint of completeness and only affects the amount of effective overlap of the 2-D elementary functions across neighboring m, n lattice locations, it does determine the required support size (number of pixels) of each elementary function so that the truncation of the Gaussian tails is negligible. Since the degree of effective overlap of the Gaussians is a free parameter, as was the particular tradeoff between the m, n spatial sampling density and the number of r, s spatial frequency components per patch, these can be manipulated in a signal-dependent fashion without affecting the completeness of the representation. These are signal-dependent flexibilities of the present neural network approach, which are not possible in the biorthogonalizing approach that requires uniform sampling rules and an invariant Gaussian window throughout the image.

Within each of the (m, n) lattice cells apparent in Fig.

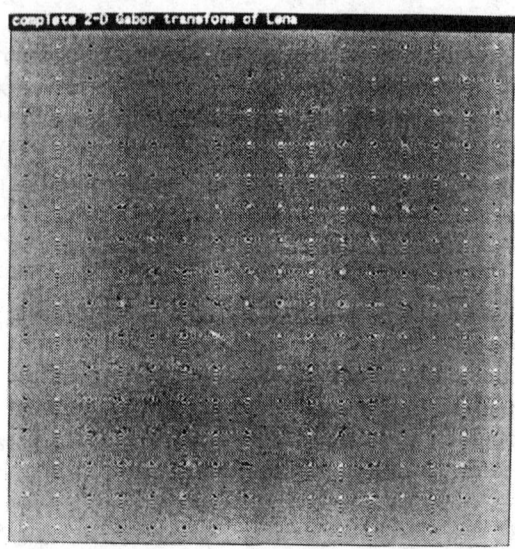

Fig. 7. Complete 2-D Gabor transform of Lena computed by the network of Fig. 3. The amplitude coefficients $\{a_{m,n,r,s}\}$ are quantized to 8-bits and plotted as pixel values (gray being zero), with the spatial center positions m, n of the overlapping elementary functions constituting the global (16×16) lattice centers, and with their 2-D spectral parameters r, s mapped out within each of these local lattice regions. Coefficient histogram shown in Fig. 2; complete reconstruction of Lena from this transform shown in Fig. 8.

7 are embedded the coefficient values a_{mnrs} as (r, s) span their ranges. Thus, the conjoint character of the 2-D Gabor transform is made clear by the way in which local *spectral* variables (r, s) are embedded within the global *spatial* image variables (m, n), for representing the image as the set of coefficients a_{mnrs} on the overlapping, nonorthogonal, elementary functions $G_{mnrs}[x, y]$.

Finally, the completeness of the representation found by the neural network is demonstrated in Fig. 8, which shows the exact reconstruction of the Lena picture from the 2-D Gabor transform of Fig. 7. Each of the transform coefficients was quantized to 8 bits (as in the original pixel image), and the reconstructed picture in Fig. 8 was simply created by the sum of all of the 2-D Gabor elementary functions weighted by their coefficients:

$$H[x, y] = \sum_{m,n,r,s} a_{mnrs} G_{mnrs}[x, y]. \quad (19)$$

The dark points specify the (m, n) lattice locations, and the mean-squared-error of the recovered image is close to zero. Recalling the original entropy comparisons of Figs. 1 and 2, it is striking that all of the image structure seen in Fig. 8 was recovered from the seemingly very impoverished image in Fig. 7, whose histogram has an entropy of only 2.55 bits. Indeed, with the complete 2-D Gabor transform of Fig. 7 quantized to 8 bits, so that each coefficient becomes an integer between -127 and $+128$, about 75 percent of all the coefficients fall within 3 bins of zero. (See Fig. 2.) This means that nearly all the image structure that was recovered in Fig. 8 was contained in just a small subset of the complete 2-D Gabor transform coefficients. For this reason, dramatic factors of data compression are possible by representing images in terms

Fig. 8. Reconstruction of the Lena picture from the complete 2-D Gabor transform displayed in Fig. 7, at only 2.55 bits/pixel. Dark points represent lattice centers for the overlapping 2-D Gabor elementary functions.

of these nonorthogonal elementary functions, whose coefficients can be found by the neural network.

V. Image Representation in Self-Similar 2-D Gabor "Wavelet" Sets

By eliminating degrees of freedom in the family of 2-D Gabor elementary functions so that they all are dilations, rotations, and translations of each other, with the spectral parameters of the set distributed in a 2-D log-polar lattice, it is possible to represent images on a sparse self-similar family of primitives with advantageous reductions in complexity. In this more biologically inspired scheme as was illustrated in Fig. 6, the different 2-D Gabor elementary functions $G_{mnrs}[x, y]$ have sizes distributed in octave steps (and hence, preferred frequencies also changing in octave steps). In (10), this corresponds to setting α and β proportional to u_o and v_o, thus eliminating two degrees of freedom which correspond to orientation bandwidth and spatial frequency bandwidth. (See [10, Fig. 2] for clarification.) The orientations of the elementary functions, given by

$$\theta_o = \tan^{-1}\left(\frac{v_o}{u_o}\right), \quad (20)$$

are chosen from a fixed set of angles (e.g., six distinct orientations differing in 30° steps). The spectral characteristics of one such set of *log-polar* parameterized 2-D Gabor elementary functions are illustrated in Fig. 9. All the elementary functions in this example have spectral envelopes with a 2:1 aspect ratio (a reflection of their 30° orientation bandwidth and 1.5-octave spatial frequency bandwidth), with center frequencies distributed on a log-polar radial octave grid (the defining 2-D spectra sampling rule), and with self-similarity across all scales, reflecting the invariant shape of the image-domain templates.

Fig. 9. 2-D Fourier transforms of the Gabor elementary functions employed in one log-polar radial octave "wavelet" scheme. Following physiological data [9], [10], these primitives have logarithmically dispersed center frequencies, ±15° orientation bandwidths, 1.5 octave spatial frequency bandwidths, and hence a constant template shape and a 2:1 bandwidth aspect ratio.

In certain of these respects, this set of elementary functions resembles the "wavelet" expansions developed recently by Meyer, Daubechies, Grossmann, Morlet, and Mallat (see [20]–[25]) for analyzing 1-D signals into a self-similar family of wavelets, all of which can be generated by dilations and shifts of a single basic wavelet. Families of wavelets have been recently developed which have strictly compact support and which constitute complete orthonormal bases for $L^2(R)$ functions ([20]). All wavelet schemes, including the present nonorthogonal one, are parameterized by a geometric scale parameter m and position parameter n which relate members of the family to each other:

$$\Psi_{mn}(x) = 2^{-m/2}\Psi(2^{-m}x - n). \quad (21)$$

Generalizing to two dimensions and incorporating discrete rotations θ into the generating function (21) together with shifts p, q and dilations m, the present 2-D Gabor "wavelet" set can be generated from any given member by

$$\Psi_{mpq\theta}(x, y) = 2^{-m}\Psi(x', y') \quad (22)$$

where

$$x' = 2^{-m}[x \cos(\theta) + y \sin(\theta)] - p \quad (23)$$

$$y' = 2^{-m}[-x \sin(\theta) + y \cos(\theta)] - q. \quad (24)$$

By using the network of Fig. 3 to find optimal coefficients on this self-similar multiresolution wavelet scheme in which 2-D Gabor elementary functions serve as the $\Psi_{mpq\theta}(x, y)$, significant further factors of code compression may be achieved as illustrated in Fig. 10. Each column of Fig. 10 corresponds to a different choice for the number of distinct orientations in the wavelet set, and the

Fig. 10. Image compression achieved by the 2-D Gabor "wavelet" transform. Columns: different numbers of distinct wavelet orientations, ranging from six to two. Rows: different quantization depths for each Gabor coefficient, ranging from 8 bits to 5 bits. Overall bit/pixel rates as indicated.

different rows reflect different degrees of quantization of the computed coefficients ranging from 8 bits to 5 bits per coefficient, with the coarsest level always having 2 bits higher quantization accuracy than the finest level. There are 6 distinct values of the scale parameter m of (22)–(24) employed in each decomposition scheme, producing a five-octave range of resolution scales in one-octave steps. Thus, for example, the image in Fig. 10, marked "3 orientations, 1.03 bit/pixel" was reconstructed from 2-D Gabor wavelets present in 3 orientations (changing in 60° steps), 2 quadrature phases, and a total of 2610 positions spanning 5 levels of resolution with variable quantization depth. It is remarkable that rather high image quality is achieved here at only 1 bit/pixel using the coefficients found by the network, even though as few as 3 distinct orientations are represented by the elementary function wavelets.

VI. Image Segmentation

Finally, by examining the distributions of the 2-D Gabor coefficients found by the network in different image regions, it is possible to achieve image segmentation on the basis of spectral signature [26] as demonstrated in Fig. 11. Here the input image to the network (top left panel) is texture consisting of a collage of anisotropically filtered white noise fields, with the noise in different regions of the image having different 2-D bandpass principal orien-

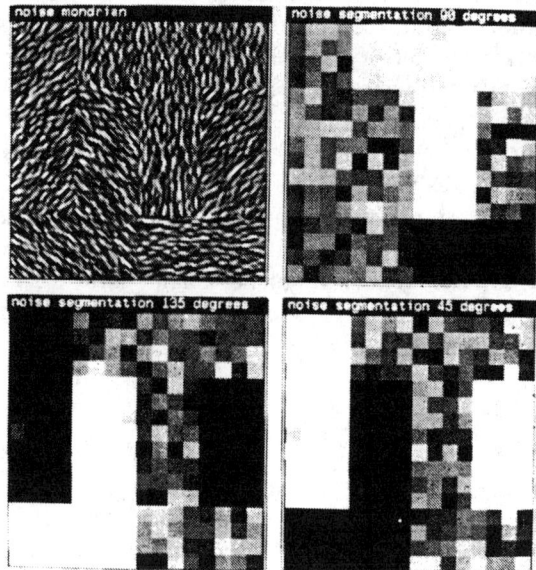

Fig. 11. Image segmentation of anisotropic white noise texture collage (upper left), by the dipole clustering of coefficients in the complete 2-D Gabor transform displayed in Fig. 12.

tations. The complete 2-D Gabor transform of this texture image is displayed in Fig. 12. Close inspection of the transform reveals that associated with each local image region, the 2-D Gabor coefficients a_{mnrs} have significant amplitudes that tend to form dipoles of distinct orienta-

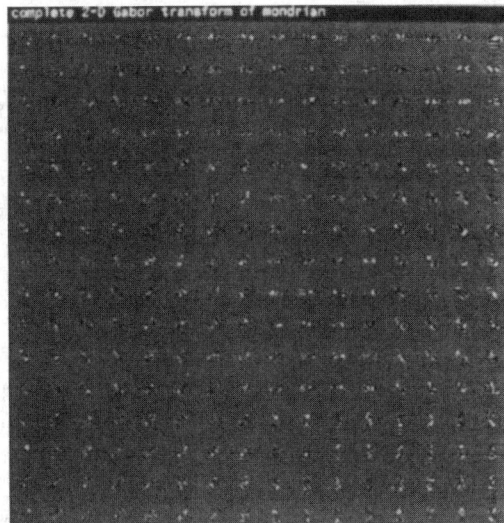

Fig. 12. Complete 2-D Gabor transform of the anisotropic white noise mondrian displayed in Fig. 11. Different local spectral dipoles are apparent in regions of the transform corresponding to regions of the image described by different anisotropic texture moments.

tions. These orientations correspond to the predominant anisotropic texture moment in that region of the image. On this basis, the original textured image was segmented into distinct regions characterized by a certain spectral signature, as demonstrated in the other three panels. Since the 2-D Gabor coefficients which the network generated as shown in Fig. 12 constitute a conjoint space-spectral representation, spectral information remains localized in the image; hence, it can be associated with particular regions of the image having a given textural signature. Many studies [26]–[33] have confirmed the utility of deriving such regional spectral measures for various signal processing applications. We have seen that the neural network of Fig. 3 for computing the transform coefficients on nonorthogonal 2-D Gabor elementary functions can also be used for texture-based image segmentations.

References

[1] T. Kohonen, *Associative Memory—A System-Theoretical Approach.* New York: Springer-Verlag, 1977.
[2] K. Fukushima, S. Miyake, and T. Ito, "Neocognitron: A neural network model for a mechanism of visual pattern recognition," *IEEE Trans. Syst., Man, Cybern.*, vol. SMC-13, pp. 826–834, 1983.
[3] D. Psaltis and N. Farhat, "Optical information processing based on an associative-memory model of neural nets with thresholding and feedback," *Opt. Lett.*, vol. 10, pp. 98–100, 1985.
[4] B. Widrow and S. Stearns, *Adaptive Signal Processing.* Englewood Cliffs, NJ: Prentice-Hall, 1985.
[5] J. Hopfield, "Neural networks and physical systems with emergent collective computational abilities," in *Proc. Nat. Acad. Sci. USA*, vol. 79, pp. 2554–2558, 1982.
[6] A. Lapedes and R. Farber, "Nonlinear signal processing using neural networks: Prediction and system modelling," Los Alamos Nat. Lab., preprint LA-UR-87-2662, 1987. (Submitted to *Proc. IEEE*.)
[7] R. Gallager, *Information Theory and Reliable Communication.* New York: Wiley, 1968.
[8] M. Bastiaans, "Gabor's expansion of a signal into Gaussian elementary signals," *Proc. IEEE*, vol. 68, pp. 538–539, 1980.
[9] J. Jones and L. Palmer, "An evaluation of the two-dimensional Gabor filter model of simple receptive fields in cat striate cortex," *J. Neurophysiol.*, vol. 58, pp. 1233–1258, 1987.
[10] J. Daugman, "Uncertainty relation for resolution in space, spatial frequency, and orientation optimized by two-dimensional visual cortical filters," *J. Opt. Soc. Amer.*, vol. 2, no. 7, pp. 1160–1169, 1985.
[11] D. Van Essen, "Hierarchical organization and functional streams in the visual cortex," *Annu. Rev. Neurosci.*, vol. 2, pp. 227–263, 1979.
[12] D. Hubel and T. Wiesel, "Receptive fields, binocular interaction, and functional architecture in the cat's visual cortex," *J. Physiol. (London)*, vol. 160, pp. 106–154, 1962.
[13] —, "Sequence regularity and geometry of orientation columns in the monkey striate cortex," *J. Comput. Neurol.*, vol. 158, pp. 267–293, 1974.
[14] D. Pollen and S. Ronner, "Phase relationships between adjacent simple cells in the visual cortex," *Science*, vol. 212, pp. 1409–1411, 1981.
[15] J. Daugman, "Two-dimensional spectral analysis of cortical receptive field profiles," *Vis. Res.*, vol. 20, pp. 847–856, 1980.
[16] S. Marcelja, "Mathematical description of the responses of simple cortical cells," *J. Opt. Soc. Amer.*, vol. 70, pp. 1297–1300, 1980.
[17] D. Gabor, "Theory of communication," *J. Inst. Elec. Eng.*, vol. 93, pp. 429–457, 1946.
[18] J. Daugman, "Six formal properties of two-dimensional anisotropic visual filters: Structural principles and frequency/orientation selectivity," *IEEE Trans. Syst., Man, Cybern.*, vol. 13, pp. 882–887, 1983.
[19] R. Duda and P. Hart, *Pattern Classification and Scene Analysis.* New York: Wiley, 1973.
[20] Y. Meyer, "Principe d'incertitude, bases hilbertiennes, et algebres d'operateurs," Seminaire Bourbaki, 1985–1986, no. 662.
[21] J. Morlet, G. Arens, I. Fourgeau, and D. Giard, "Wave propagation and sampling theory," *Geophysics*, vol. 47, pp. 203–236, 1982.
[22] A. Grossman and J. Morlet, "Decomposition of Hardy functions into square integrable wavelets of constant shape," *SIAM J. Math. Anal.*, vol. 15, pp. 723–736, 1984.
[23] A. Grossman, J. Morlet, and T. Paul, "Transforms associated to square integrable group representations. I. General results," *J. Math. Phys.*, vol. 26, pp. 2473–2479, 1985.
[24] I. Daubechies, A. Grossmann, and Y. Meyer, "Painless nonorthogonal expansions," *J. Math. Phys.*, vol. 27, pp. 1271–1283, 1986.
[25] S. Mallat, "A theory for multiresolution signal decomposition: The wavelet representation," *IEEE Trans. Pattern Anal. Machine Intell.*, vol. 10, 1988, in press. (Univ. Pennsylvania GRASP LAB 103. MS-CIS-87-22.)
[26] J. Daugman, "Image analysis by local 2-D spectral signatures," *J. Opt. Soc. Amer. (A)*, vol. 2, p. P74, 1985.
[27] Y. Zeevi and M. Porat, "Combined frequency-position scheme of image representation in vision," *J. Opt. Soc. Amer. (A)*, vol. 1, p. 1248, 1984.
[28] M. Turner, "Texture discrimination by Gabor functions," *Biol. Cybern.*, vol. 55, pp. 71–82, 1986.
[29] M. Clark, A. Bovik, and W. Geisler, "Texture segmentation using a class of narrowband filters," in *Proc. Int. Conf. Acoust., Speech, Signal Processing 87*, 1987, pp. 571–574.
[30] R. Hecht-Nielsen, "Nearest matched filter classification of spatiotemporal patterns," *Appl. Opt.*, vol. 26, pp. 1892–1899, 1987.
[31] R. Haralick, K. Shanmugam, and I. Dinstein, "Textural features for image classification," *IEEE Trans. Syst., Man, Cybern.*, vol. SMC-3, pp. 610–621, 1973.
[32] H. Szu, "Two-dimensional optical processing of one-dimensional acoustic data," *Opt. Eng.*, vol. 21, no. 5, pp. 804–813, 1982.
[33] H. Szu and H. Caulfield, "The mutual time-frequency content of two signals," *Proc. IEEE*, vol. 72, pp. 902–908, 1984.

John G. Daugman was born in 1954. He received the B.A. degree in physics in 1976 and the Ph.D. degree in psychology in 1983, both from Harvard University, Cambridge, MA.

His main research interests include neural networks, multidimensional signal processing, and neurophysiological and psychophysical studies of biological visual systems. He serves as a consultant to Lincoln Laboratories and as Scientific Advisor for the Hecht-Nielsen Neurocomputer Corporation. He belongs to the Editorial Board of *Neural Networks*. Since 1985–1986 he has been an Assistant Professor of Psychology and of Electrical, Computer, and Systems Engineering at Harvard University.

Dr. Daugman is the recipient of a 1988 NSF Presidential Young Investigator Award.

Robust Image Modeling Techniques with an Image Restoration Application

RANGASAMI L. KASHYAP, FELLOW, IEEE, AND KIE-BUM EOM, MEMBER, IEEE

Abstract—We develop a robust parameter estimation algorithm for a nonsymmetric half-plane (NSHP) autoregressive model, where the driving noise is a mixture of a Gaussian and an outlier process. The convergence of the estimation algorithm is proved.

We also develop an algorithm to estimate parameters and original image intensity simultaneously from the impulse noise corrupted image, where the model governing the image is not available. The robustness of the parameter estimates is demonstrated by simulation.

We develop an algorithm to restore realistic images. The entire image generally does not obey a simple image model, but a small portion (e.g., 8 × 8) of the image is assumed to obey an NSHP model. We divide the original image into windows and apply the robust estimation algorithm for each window. The proposed restoration algorithm is tested by comparing it to traditional methods on several different images.

I. Introduction

THE importance of model based techniques for image processing tasks such as edge detection, image synthesis, image coding, image restoration, etc., has been well documented. However, in all of these models, the image intensity array is assumed to be a multivariate Gaussian distribution. The Gaussian assumption is used primarily in estimating parameters of the image model fitted to the image. The corresponding estimation procedure is relatively easy; for example, for the nonsymmetric half-plane (NSHP) autoregressive model, the maximum likelihood method is the same as the least squares method. However, when the image contains impulse noise, the parameter estimates obtained from the Gaussian model do not appear to be appropriate.

A more realistic assumption for the noise sequence in the image is a contaminated Gaussian noise

$$\xi(i,j) = \begin{cases} w(i,j), & \text{with probability } 1 - \beta \\ v(i,j), & \text{with probability } \beta \end{cases} \quad (1.1)$$

where $w(i,j)$ is a regular white Gaussian noise and $v(i,j)$ is an outlier process and the ratio of outlier β is assumed small (less than 5 percent).

Unfortunately, least squares estimators or maximum likelihood estimators under the Gaussian assumption are very sensitive to minor deviations from the Gaussian noise assumption. Even a single bad data (outlier) among 1000 observations can cause large error in the estimator. Because of this excessive sensitivity of least squares estimators, robust estimators are needed in image models. A robust estimator should possess the following property.

1) It should have a reasonably good (optimal or nearly optimal) efficiency at the assumed noise distribution.

2) It should be robust in the sense that the degradation in performance caused by a small number of outliers is relatively small.

3) Somewhat larger deviations from the assumed distribution should not cause a catastrophe.

Many different robust estimation algorithms have been developed in the last 20 years. These robust estimation algorithms can be classified into three large types of estimators: M-estimator, L-estimator, and R-estimator. An M-estimator is a maximum likelihood-type estimator, and it is obtained by solving a minimization problem. An L-estimator is a linear combination of ordered statistics. An R-estimator is derived from the rank tests. We are mostly interested in M-estimators for the application to the image models. It is easy to extend M-estimators to the problem of image models, but other types of estimators are difficult to be used in problems other than location parameter estimation.

Even though a robust procedure is necessary in most of the image processing applications, very little research has been done on the use of robust procedures in image processing. In this paper, we develop estimation algorithms for the nonsymmetric half-plane autoregressive image model and apply this robust method to the image restoration problem.

Restoration of an image in the presence of noise is a fundamental problem in image processing. There are many image restoration methods based on the Gaussian noise assumption. Chellappa and Kashyap [18] used a spatial interaction model to represent image intensity array and restored images with minimum mean square error criterion. Geman and Geman [10] restored images by a stochastic relaxation method with *maximum a posteriori* criterion. Bovick *et al.* [19] used an order constrained least squares method. Wu [20] used a multidimensional Kalman filtering approach and nonsymmetric half-plane autoregressive model. Chan and Lim [21] used a cascade of four 1-D adaptive filters in four different directions.

Manuscript received July 3, 1986; revised February 8, 1988. This work was supported in part by the Office of Naval Research under Grant N00014-85-K-0611 and by the National Science Foundation under Grant IST 8405052.

R. L. Kashyap is with the School of Electrical Engineering, Purdue University, West Lafayette, IN 47907-0501.

K.-B. Eom is with the Department of Electrical and Computer Engineering, Syracuse University, Syracuse, NY 13244-1240.

IEEE Log Number 8821857.

Unfortunately, most image restoration methods based on the Gaussian noise assumption are not effective in the presence of impulse noise [1]. The impulsive component of the noise, which is also called salt and pepper noise, is only a small portion (usually less than 5 percent) of the total image, but it is difficult to be removed by the methods based on the Gaussian noise assumption because its amplitude is much higher than signal amplitude.

The importance of this problem has been recognized for a long period of time. Traditionally, nonlinear filtering methods such as median filter [1] or α-trimmed mean filter [8] are used to remove impulse noise from the image. However, the edges are often smeared, and the output image is often blurred in these traditional nonlinear filtering approaches. Of course, there have been some approaches to reduce these blurring effects of the traditional impulse noise removing methods. For instance, Yasuoka and Haralick [17] used a facet model based approach, and Kundu et al. [22] used a generalized mean filter.

We develop a restoration method based on the robust image model in this research. In our method, the image intensity array is represented by an NSHP autoregressive model, and a robust parameter estimation algorithm and data cleaning algorithm are applied to restore images from impulse noise contamination. The method presented in this paper can effectively remove impulse noise from the image, and does not smear edges and does not blur image after restoration. The restoration algorithm based on the robust image modeling approach is tested with several images. The experiment shows that the new approach based on the robust modeling gives better results than traditional methods such as median filter or α-trimmed mean filter in the presence of impulse noise.

Our contributions are threefold. We first develop an algorithm for the robust estimation of parameters of a nonsymmetric half-plane image model in which the driving white noise process is a mixture of a Gaussian and an outlier process. It is an M-estimator. We prove the convergence.

Next we consider the robust estimation of the parameters of a model where the image obeying the model is not available, but a noise corrupted version of the image is available, the corrupting noise being a mixture of a Gaussian process and an outlier process. We develop an algorithm to recover the parameters of the model from the noisy image. The procedure involves alternate application of parameter estimation and data cleaning. We provide intuitive reasons for the convergence of the procedure and confirm our intuition by several simulations. Finally, we use the above results to restore an image corrupted by a mixture-type noise. The original image is divided into windows, and each window is assumed to obey a nonsymmetric half-plane autoregressive model. Again, we give extensive examples for restoring noise corrupted images.

II. ROBUST PARAMETER ESTIMATION IN NONSYMMETRIC HALF-PLANE AUTOREGRESSIVE MODEL

A. The Nonsymmetric Half-Plane Autoregressive Model

We will introduce here the nonsymmetric half-plane model which behaves very much like one-dimensional time series models. Assume that the image intensity of an image follows the nonsymmetric half-plane model. Let (i, j) be an index for the coordinate location, and $y(i, j)$ be the intensity at the coordinate (i, j).

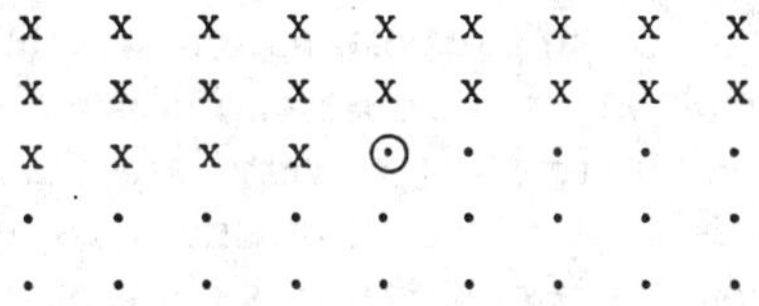

```
x  x  x  x  x  x  x  x  x
x  x  x  x  x  x  x  x  x
x  x  x  x  ⊙  ·  ·  ·  ·
·  ·  ·  ·  ·  ·  ·  ·  ·
·  ·  ·  ·  ·  ·  ·  ·  ·
```
Fig. 1.

Let us define a nonsymmetric half-plane Ω_- as follows:

$$\Omega_- = \{(i, j): (i = 0 \quad \text{and } j < 0)$$
$$\text{or } (i < 0 \quad \text{and } j \text{ is arbitrary})\}. \quad (2.1)$$

The Ω_- is illustrated in Fig. 1. The nonsymmetric half-plane members are indicated by x; $\odot$ is the origin.

Let s and r be indexes for two-dimensional coordinate locations. One important property of Ω_- is: if $r \in \Omega_-$ and $s \in \Omega_-$ then $(s + r) \in \Omega_-$.

An NSHP autoregressive model can be written as

$$y(s) = \sum_{r \in N_1} \theta_r y(s + r) + \alpha + \sigma \zeta(s) \quad (2.2)$$

where i) the noise $\zeta(\cdot)$ is zero mean, unit variance, and uncorrelated, and ii) the neighbor set N_1 is a subset of the nonsymmetric half-plane Ω_-. Equation (2.2) can be rewritten in the linear vector equation form

$$y(s) = \theta^T z(s) + \sigma \zeta(s), \quad (2.3)$$

where θ is a parameter vector and $z(s)$ is a vector which consists of intensities of pixels in the neighbor set N_1 and unity. The last element of the vector $z(s)$ is required to represent a constant gray level in the image

$$z(s) = \text{col.} \left[\{ y(s + r), r \in N_1 \}, 1 \right]. \quad (2.4)$$

For example, if

$$N_1 = \{(0, -1), (-1, 0), (-1, -1)\},$$

then the model in (2.2) can be rewritten as follows:

$$y(i, j) = \theta^T z(i, j) + \sigma \zeta(i, j)$$

$$z(i, j) = \begin{bmatrix} y(i, j-1) \\ y(i-1, j) \\ y(i-1, j-1) \\ 1 \end{bmatrix}. \quad (2.5)$$

The model given in (2.5) is called a three neighbor causal autoregressive model, and this model is used in our experiment, even though the theory is applicable to any NSHP model.

B. The Criterion Function

Consider the parameter estimation in the NSHP model. In the least squares estimation, we need to minimize the following function, with respect to θ:

$$\sum_{i,j} \left(y(i, j) - \theta^T z(i, j) \right)^2. \quad (2.6)$$

The idea of a least squares estimation is to minimize the residuals. However, if one observation is an outlier, then the corresponding residual is very large, and the least squares estimator is greatly influenced by this outlier. Thus, the least squares estimator is not robust. To ensure robustness of the estimator, we first scale the residuals by a scale factor σ, which is noise intensity in the NSHP model (2.3). Next, instead of using a quadratic function, we use a nonquadratic function ρ, which is a differentiable function possessing a bounded derivative, and it is symmetric about origin with $\rho(0) = 0$.

Robust M-estimators are defined by the minimization of a nonquadratic function of normalized residuals. Let

$$Q(\theta, \sigma) = \frac{1}{mn} \sum_{i,j} \left[\rho\left(\frac{y(i,j) - \theta^T z(i,j)}{\sigma}\right) + \frac{1}{2} \right] \sigma. \quad (2.7)$$

The residual should be normalized by the scale factor σ in the above criterion function because the M-estimator is not scale invariant. M-estimators are robust because the bounded function ρ limits the influence of outliers to a final estimator. Thus, the M-estimators of NSHP autoregressive model are defined by the following minimization problem:

$$\text{Minimize } Q(\theta, \sigma). \quad (2.8)$$

The M-estimator can also be obtained by solving the following two equations simultaneously:

$$\nabla_\theta Q(\theta, \sigma) = \frac{-1}{mn} \sum \psi\left(\frac{y(i,j) - \theta^T z(i,j)}{\sigma}\right) \cdot z^T(i,j) = 0 \quad (2.9)$$

$$\frac{\partial Q(\theta, \sigma)}{\partial \sigma} = \frac{1}{2} - \frac{1}{mn} \sum \chi\left(\frac{y(i,j) - \theta^T z(i,j)}{\sigma}\right) = 0 \quad (2.10)$$

where $\psi(x) = \partial \rho(x)/\partial x$ and $\chi(x) = x\psi(x) - \rho(x)$, and the function ψ is continuous and bounded.

A good choice of the ψ function is important not only for the robustness of estimator, but also for the fast convergence of the iterative procedure. We will introduce two popular choices of ψ functions in this section. The function ψ_{HL} in (2.11) is a hard limiter-type ψ function. Because of the monotonicity of the function ψ_{HL}, the solution of (2.9) and (2.10) is the global minimum of (2.7).

$$\psi_{HL}(x) = \begin{cases} c, & x > c \\ x, & -c \leq x \leq c \\ -c, & x < -c. \end{cases} \quad (2.11)$$

Typical values for c are between 1.5 and 2 in the above ψ function.

Another interesting ψ function—the redescending ψ function—is also continuous but returning to zero outside of some interval. It is known that the redescending ψ function yields higher efficiencies than the monotone ψ function for extremely heavy tailed distributions [2], [3]. The above advantage of the redescending ψ function is also confirmed in our experiment: the procedure converges much faster with the redescending ψ function (2.12) than with the monotone ψ function (2.11). This function performed best with parameters $a = 2$, $b = 2.5$, $c = 4.5$ in our experiment.

$$\psi_{HA}(x) = \begin{cases} x, & |x| \leq a \\ a \, \text{sgn}(x), & a < |x| \leq b \\ \frac{(c - |x|)}{(c - b)} a \, \text{sgn}(x), & b < |x| \leq c \\ 0, & |x| > c. \end{cases} \quad (2.12)$$

These two different ψ functions are compared in the experiment, and the best performing function is chosen in our algorithm. The redescending ψ function in (2.12) performed better than the hard-limiter-type ψ function in our experiment.

However, we should be careful using the redescending ψ function because it may converge to a local minimum of (2.7). Consequently, we need to iterate only a few times when using the redescending ψ function. However, the experiment shows that both robust estimation algorithms with the redescending ψ function (2.12) are stable for more than ten iterations in all images tested. More details of the experiment will be discussed in Section IV.

C. The Minimization Algorithm and Its Theoretical Convergence

The robust estimator of the NSHP autoregressive model parameters defined in (2.8) has many desirable properties. The robust M-estimator in (2.8) is asymptotically Gaussian and consistent with a monotonic ψ function. The asymptotic property is shown by Nasburg and Kashyap [16].

However, the computation of the M-estimator is generally difficult, since it involves the minimization of a nonquadratic function of multiple parameters. In this section, we will introduce an efficient algorithm to minimize the criterion function (2.7). Also, we will show that the estimator obtained by the iterative algorithm converges to the robust M-estimator with the monotonic ψ function. The algorithm explained in this section can be implemented by a small modification of a standard least squares algorithm. The iteration begins from a least squares estimator. Because the algorithm begins with the solution which minimizes a convex function (quadratic function), the risk of converging to a local minimum after a few iterations is small even with a nonmonotonic ψ function.

To compute the robust M-estimator of the NSHP model, we need to minimize the criterion function $Q(\theta, \sigma)$ in (2.8). The minimization is done in the following way. First, fix the parameter σ and change the parameter θ to obtain a guaranteed decrease of the criterion function $Q(\theta, \sigma)$. Second, fix the parameter θ and change the parameter σ to obtain a guaranteed decrease of the criterion function $Q(\theta, \sigma)$. We repeat the above two steps alternately until the difference in the estimates of successive iterations is small. The iterative robust estimation algorithm explained above is summarized in the following.

Algorithm 1 (Estimation with Perfect Observation):

1) Let $\theta^{(0)}$ and $\sigma^{(0)}$ be initial estimates (conventional least square estimator can be used).

2) At the kth iteration, we have $\theta^{(k)}$ and $\sigma^{(k)}$. Compute the residual $r^{(k)}$

$$r^{(k)}(i,j) = y(i,j) - \theta^{(k)T}z(i,j), \quad (2.13)$$

where $z(i,j)$ is defined in (2.4). Compute the censored residual $\hat{r}^{(k)}$.

$$\hat{r}^{(k)}(i,j) = \psi\left(\frac{r^{(k)}(i,j)}{\sigma^{(k)}}\right)\sigma^{(k)}. \quad (2.14)$$

3) Compute $\theta^{(k+1)}$ and $\sigma^{(k+1)}$ as follows:

$$\theta^{(k+1)} = \theta^{(k)} + \tau^{(k)}, \quad (2.15)$$

where

$$\tau^{(k)} = \left[\sum_{i,j} z(i,j)z^T(i,j)\right]^{-1}\left[\sum_{i,j} z(i,j)\hat{r}^{(k)}(i,j)\right] \quad (2.16)$$

$$\sigma^{(k+1)2} = \frac{1}{mn}\sum_{i,j}[\hat{r}^{(k)}(i,j)]^2. \quad (2.17)$$

4) Repeat steps 2)–3) until the differences $\|\theta^{(k+1)} - \theta^{(k)}\|$ and $|\sigma^{(k+1)} - \sigma^{(k)}|$ become negligible.

The following Lemma 1, Lemma 2, and Theorem 3 summarize the theoretical properties of the iterative method (Algorithm 1) to compute a robust M-estimator. Proofs are given in the Appendix. Lemma 1 and Lemma 2 show the decrease of Q in (2.7) with the update of parameters θ and σ at each iteration. Let $Q(\theta^{(k)}, \sigma^{(k)})$ be the cost involved with the estimates $\theta^{(k)}$ and $\sigma^{(k)}$ at the kth iteration of Algorithm 1. That is,

$$Q(\theta^{(k)}, \sigma^{(k)})$$
$$= \frac{1}{mn}\sum_{i,j}\left[\rho\left(\frac{y(i,j) - \theta^{(k)T}z(i,j)}{\sigma^{(k)}}\right) + \frac{1}{2}\right]\sigma^{(k)}. \quad (2.18)$$

Lemma 1: At every iteration step, $\theta^{(k+1)}$ in (2.15) with the ψ function as in (2.11) reduces the Q function for fixed $\sigma^{(k)}$, i.e.,

$$Q(\theta^{(k)}, \sigma^{(k)}) - Q(\theta^{(k+1)}, \sigma^{(k)})$$
$$\geq \frac{1}{2\sigma^{(k)}mn}\tau^{(k)T}\left[\sum_{i,j} z(i,j)z^T(i,j)\right]\tau^{(k)}. \quad (2.19)$$

Lemma 2: At every iteration step, $\sigma^{(k+1)}$ in (2.15) with the ψ function as in (2.11) reduces the Q function for fixed $\theta^{(k)}$, i.e.,

$$Q(\theta^{(k)}, \sigma^{(k)}) - Q(\theta^{(k)}, \sigma^{(k+1)}) \geq \frac{(\sigma^{(k+1)} - \sigma^{(k)})^2}{2\sigma^{(k)}}. \quad (2.20)$$

The iterative estimation algorithm (Algorithm 1) decreases the value of the function Q in (2.7) as the number of iteration increases, and it converges to the minimum value of function Q. The estimated parameters also converge to the parameters which minimize the function Q in (2.7). The above property of the algorithm is summarized in the following Theorem 3.

Theorem 3: The sequence $\{(\theta^{(k)}, \sigma^{(k)})\}$ converges to $(\hat{\theta}, \hat{\sigma})$, a unique solution of (2.9) and (2.10), and an estimator which minimizes (2.7). ∎

A proof of Theorem 3 is in the Appendix.

III. PARAMETER ESTIMATION WITH NOISY IMAGE AND IMAGE RESTORATION

In this section, we consider the parameter estimation from an image corrupted by impulse noise. We assume that the original process $y(i,j)$ follows the NSHP model and is not directly observable.

$$y(i,j) = \theta^T z(i,j) + \sigma\zeta(i,j), \quad (3.1)$$

where $\zeta(i,j)$ is a standard Gaussian process, θ is a parameter vector, and $z(i,j)$ is defined in (3.2).

$$z(i,j) = \text{col.}\left[\{y((i,j)+r), r \in N_1\}, 1\right]. \quad (3.2)$$

We assume that the observation $x(i,j)$ is corrupted by a noise process containing outliers. The observation $x(i,j)$ can be represented by the following equation:

$$x(i,j) = y(i,j) + \xi(i,j). \quad (3.3)$$

The white noise process $\xi(i,j)$ contains a small fraction of outliers.

To estimate the parameters in the above model, we cannot directly use the function given in (2.7), since the original image $y(i,j)$ is not available. However, we find that we cannot separate the problem of parameter estimation from the problem of recovery of the original image. One possible solution to the recovery problem is to minimize a modified version of the Q function in (2.7) to account for the fact that the ideal image $y(i,j)$ is not available. Kleiner, Martin, and Thomson [4] consider this approach for the corresponding one-dimensional problem: specifically, original process $y(i)$ obeys a one-dimensional autoregressive process and is not available, and $x(i)$ is the observation corrupted by a noise process containing outliers.

$$y(i) = \theta^T z(i) + \sigma\zeta(i,j), \quad (3.4)$$

where

$$z(i) = \text{col.}[y(i-r), r = 1, \cdots, m], \quad (3.5)$$

m is the order of process

$$x(i) = y(i) + \xi(i), \quad (3.6)$$

where $\xi(i)$ is a white noise process containing outliers. Define $\hat{y}(i)$ as an estimate of $y(i)$, and $\hat{z}(i)$ as the corresponding estimate of $z(i)$ computed from (3.5) by replacing $y(i)$ by $\hat{y}(i)$. They give an iterative procedure which claims to minimize the following function, with respect to $\hat{y}(i)$ and $\hat{\theta}$, simultaneously:

$$\sum_i \rho\left(\frac{x(i) - \theta^T \hat{z}(i)}{\sigma}\right). \quad (3.7)$$

If we are dealing with an $M \times M$ image and (θ, σ) is of dimension m, then the above function will involve $M^2 + m$ variables. Even if $M = 10$, $m = 2$, we are dealing with 102 variables, such a function will have many local minima, and it is not clear how one can guarantee the achievement of the global minimum by any algorithm. In addition, they have not demonstrated the effectiveness of these estimates when the additive noise $\xi(i)$ in (3.6) is impulsive.

Here we approach the problem in a different way. We apply robust parameter estimation and data cleaning alternately. Suppose that at the kth iteration, the estimate of the ideal image y is $y^{(k)}$. Then, we can minimize the Q function defined in (2.7) with y replaced by $y^{(k)}$, and get the estimates $\theta^{(k)}$ of θ. Then, we need a method of getting an improved estimate of y, the so-called data cleaning. This is achieved by a method appropriately called the data cleaning algorithm. The idea of data cleaning is the following: if the observation is contaminated by an outlier, the residual will be large. If the normalized residual is large, we modify the observation to reduce the effect of outlier using the ψ function. The estimation procedure is given in Fig. 2(a) and Algorithm 2.

Algorithm 2 (Estimation with Noisy Observation):

1) Initially, set $y^{(0)}(i, j) = x(i, j)$. Compute the initial estimate $\theta^{(0)}$ and $\sigma^{(0)}$ from the noisy observation $\{x(i, j)\}$ by the least squares algorithm.

2) Consider kth iteration, $y^{(k)}$ and $\theta^{(k)}$ are available. Get the updated estimate of $y(\cdot)$ from $y^{(k)}(\cdot)$ to $y^{(k+1)}(\cdot)$ by the following formula:

$$y^{(k+1)}(i, j) = \theta^{(k)T} z^{(k)}(i, j)$$
$$+ \psi\left(\frac{y^{(k)}(i, j) - \theta^{(k)T} z^{(k)}(i, j)}{\sigma^{(k)}}\right) \sigma^{(k)}$$
$$(3.8)$$

where

$$z^{(k)}(i, j) = \text{col.}\left[\left\{y^{(k)}((i, j) + r), r \in N_1\right\}, 1\right]. \quad (3.9)$$

3) Obtain estimators $\theta^{(k+1)}$ and $\sigma^{(k+1)}$ from the cleaned data $y^{(k+1)}$ by minimizing the following function:

$$\frac{1}{mn}\sum_{i,j}\left[\rho\left(\frac{y^{(k+1)}(i, j) - \theta^T z^{(k+1)}(i, j)}{\sigma}\right) + \frac{1}{2}\right]\sigma. \quad (3.10)$$

This can be computed by the Algorithm 1.

4) Repeat Steps 2) and 3) until the differences of estimates between iteration become small.

The above robust estimation algorithm is different from the algorithm in [4]. Specifically, the algorithm in [4] contains the data cleaning step (3.8), but instead of minimizing the function in (3.10), a quadratic function of the same argument ($y^{(k)}(i, j) - \theta^T z^{(k)}(i, j)$) is minimized.

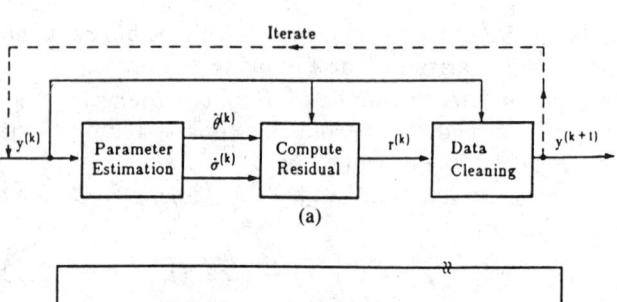

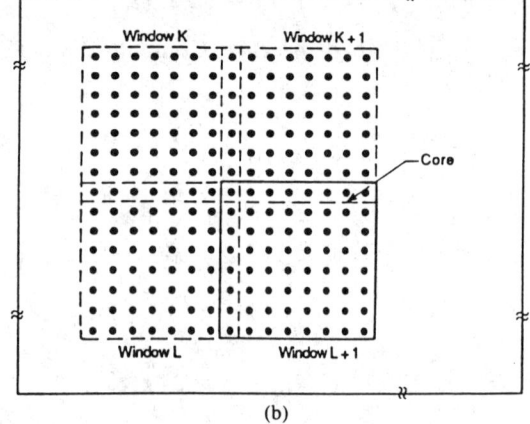

Fig. 2. (a) Block diagram of the estimation algorithm from noisy observation. $y^{(k)}$ and $y^{(k+1)}$ are cleaned data at kth and $(k+1)$th iterations, respectively, $\hat{\theta}^{(k)}$ and $\sigma^{(k)}$ are parameter estimates obtained by Algorithm 1, and $r^{(k)}$ is the residual. (b) Division of the image into small windows: the windows are applied in raster scanning direction. One column or one row is overlapped between two adjacent windows.

We have not been able to show the theoretical robustness of the algorithms, but the simulation results show the robustness of the algorithm.

A. Justification by Simulation

One-hundred images of size 25×25 are generated by the following equations (3.11) and (3.12) for the percentage of outliers from 0 to 10.

$$x(i, j) = y(i, j) + \xi(i, j) \quad (3.11)$$

where $y(i, j)$ is two-dimensional data that follow the NSHP model in (3.12), and $\xi(i, j)$ is the outliers sequence which occupies β percent of image.

$$y(i, j) = \theta^{0T}[y(i, j-1), y(i-1, j),$$
$$y(i-1, j-1)]^T + \sigma\zeta(i, j) \quad (3.12)$$

$\theta^0 = \text{col.}[0.3, 0.3, 0.3]$, $\sigma = 5$, and $\{\zeta(i, j)\}$ is a white Gaussian $(0, 1)$ noise sequence. The three parameters corresponding to the three neighbors are estimated by both a least squares method and the robust estimation algorithm. The robust estimators are obtained after three iterations with the redescending ψ function given in (2.12). The experiments are repeated 100 times with different values of β, the percentage of outliers, ranging from 0 to 9. The results are given in Table I.

For all three parameters, the mean square error of the robust parameter estimator is smaller than the mean square error of the least squares estimator except when $\beta = 0$ (no outlier). The least squares estimator is very sensitive to outliers, but the robust method is much less sensitive to outliers. For 9 percent of outliers, the mean square errors of the least squares method and robust method on the pa-

TABLE I
Comparison of Robust Estimator and Least Square Estimator for Causal Autoregressive Model with Noisy Observation; β is the Percentage of Outlier, Number of Runs $N = 100$, $\theta_1^0 = \theta_2^0 = \theta_3^0 = 0.3$.

	$\frac{1}{N}\sum_i(\hat{\theta}_{1,i}-\theta_1^0)^2$		$\frac{1}{N}\sum_i(\hat{\theta}_{2,i}-\theta_2^0)^2$		$\frac{1}{N}\sum_i(\hat{\theta}_{3,i}-\theta_3^0)^2$	
β	LS	robust	LS	robust	LS	robust
0	0.001	0.001	0.001	0.001	0.002	0.003
1	0.007	0.001	0.007	0.002	0.004	0.002
2	0.012	0.002	0.012	0.002	0.010	0.002
3	0.018	0.002	0.020	0.003	0.015	0.002
4	0.029	0.002	0.026	0.004	0.019	0.003
5	0.032	0.002	0.032	0.005	0.024	0.003
6	0.036	0.002	0.036	0.006	0.031	0.003
7	0.042	0.003	0.039	0.006	0.035	0.004
8	0.048	0.004	0.045	0.007	0.041	0.004
9	0.048	0.004	0.048	0.007	0.043	0.006

rameter θ_1 are 0.048 and 0.004, respectively. The difference between these two methods is significant. The advantage of the robust method can also be observed for a small percentage of outliers. For 1 percent of outliers, the mean square errors of the least squares method and robust method on the parameter θ_1 are 0.007 and 0.001, respectively. The advantage of the robust method can also be observed for the parameters θ_2 and θ_3. Thus, the experiment demonstrates the robustness of the estimator obtained by Algorithm 2.

B. Image Restoration of Realistic Images

The purpose of image restoration is to remove noise, including impulse noise, from the image. The image degradation process can be represented by the following equation:

$$x(i, j) = y(i, j) + \xi(i, j)$$

where x is the observation, y is the original image intensity, and ξ is the noise process with outlier. Image restoration is an estimation of original intensity y from the observation x.

In the previous section, we considered the problem of recovering an image when it is contaminated by outlier noise. The only assumption is that the entire image obeys an NSHP model. In practice, a realistic image, say 256 × 256, will not obey a simple model. However, we can divide the entire image into individual windows, and we can model the image in each window, say 8 × 8, by an NSHP model.

These windows are applied from the upper left corner to lower right corner in the raster scanning direction, but two adjacent windows overlap only for one column or one row [Fig. 2(b)]. By overlapping one column or one row with previously processed window, we can ensure continuity of the image at the boundary pixels and eliminate so-called boundary effects. For each window, we apply Algorithm 2, and the pixels inside of the window, namely, the 7 × 7 core of the window, are replaced by the cleaned data $\hat{y}$ given by the Algorithm 2.

The window size is not critical to the performance of the algorithm. The window size is determined so that the image intensity array in the window can be modeled by an NSHP model. We choose an 8 × 8 window for the convenience, and it performed well in the experiment.

The restoration method based on the robust image model has an advantage over conventional methods such as median filter or α-trimmed mean filter. The robust image model based method does not blur images after restoration. Conventional methods, such as median filter or α-trimmed mean filter, replace every pixel by its location estimates. Because these methods are based on the constant intensity assumption, the details of the original image are significantly blurred.

IV. Experimental Results

The restoration algorithm based on the robust modeling approach is applied to the five different pictures as shown in Fig. 3. Fig. 3(a) is a 256 × 256 picture of a bridge; Fig. 3(b) is a 256 × 256 picture of a monkey; Fig. 3(c) is a 256 × 256 picture of a girl; Fig. 3(d) is a 256 × 256 picture of an outdoor scene; and Fig. 3(e) is a 512 × 512 aerial picture of the Purdue University campus. All of these pictures are digitized into 256 gray levels. To measure the performance of different algorithms on noisy pictures, contaminated images are constructed by adding both Gaussian (0, 100) noise and 5 percent of impulse noise to the originals given in Fig. 3. The impulse noise is generated to have equal probabilities of having gray levels 0 (black) and 255 (white). In the robust model based algorithm, redescending ψ-function in (2.12) is used in all experiments. Experiments are performed in three different aspects with contaminated pictures. First, the convergence of the restoration algorithm is shown with these noisy pictures and the rate of convergence is measured experimentally. Second, the mean square error of three different restoration algorithms—model based algorithm, median filter, and α-trimmed mean filter—are compared to different window sizes and different images. Third, the overall performances of three different restoration algorithms are compared qualitatively for different noisy images. In Experiments 1 and 2, the mean square error criterion is used. The mean square error criterion is already used in the previous studies on the image restoration from impulse noise [8]. Other types of criteria can be used for the performance measurement of the restoration algorithm, but performance with other criteria such as absolute error will be similar to the results given in this paper.

A. Convergence of the Image Restoration Algorithm

The robust model based restoration algorithm is applied to the contaminated images. Mean square error of the cleaned image is computed at each iteration. The change of mean square error by the progress of iteration is plotted with the number of iterations.

Fig. 4(a), (b), and (c) shows plots of mean square error with respect to number of iterations from zero to ten for the outdoor scene [Fig. 3(d)], the girl's image [Fig. 3(c)], and the bridge scene [Fig. 3(a)], respectively. Contami-

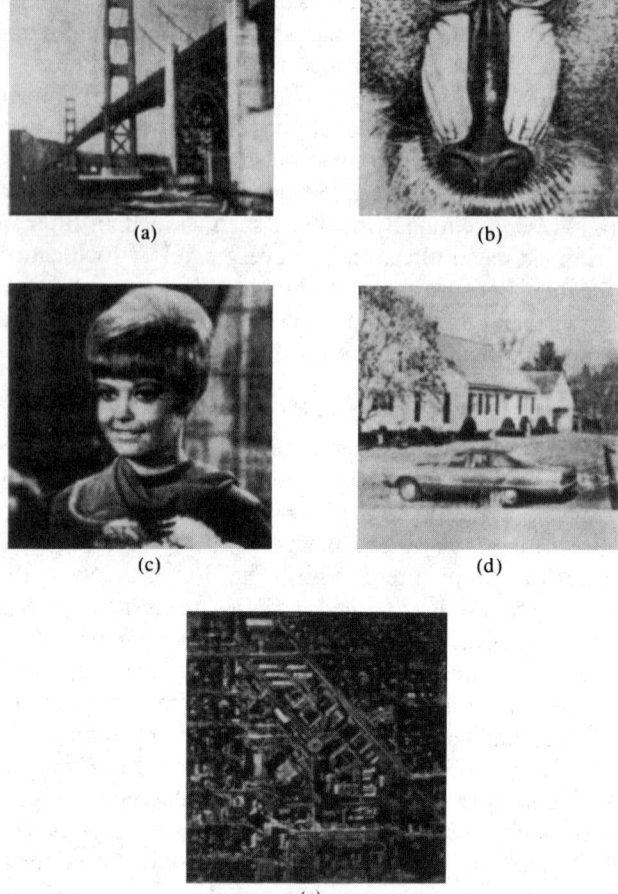

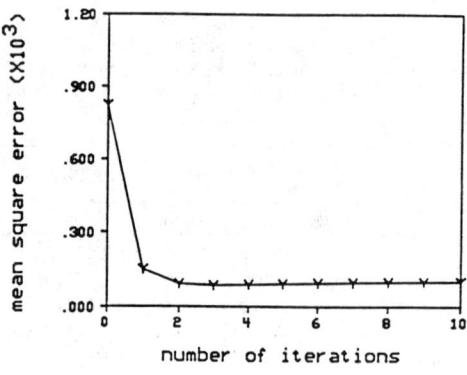

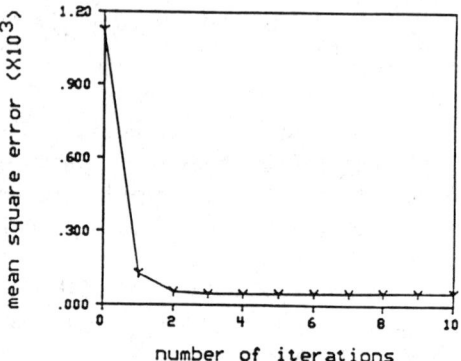

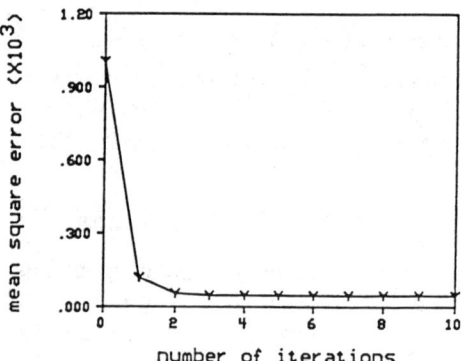

Fig. 3. Originals. (a) Bridge. (b) Monkey. (c) Girl. (d) Outdoor scene. (e) Purdue campus.

Fig. 4. Convergence of mean square errors for the outdoor scene, the image of a girl, and the bridge scene—from top to bottom.

nated pictures are made by adding Gaussian (0, 100) noise and 5 percent of impulse noise to the images in Fig. 3. Initial mean square errors of all cases are large because of the additive noise, but they decrease considerably fast in the first two iterations. The mean square error stabilizes in less than three iterations. The convergence of the data cleaning method is also fast (less than three iterations).

B. Mean Square Error Comparison of Image Restoration Methods

Four different types of image restoration methods with different sizes of windows of 3×3, 5×5, and 7×7 are used in this experiment. These are mean filter, median filter, α-trimmed mean filter with the trimming ratio $\alpha = 0.15$, and the robust model based method with window size 8×8. Note that the popular choice of α is in the range from 0.1 to 0.15, and the method performed best with choice $\alpha = 0.15$ in our experiment. For the robust model based method, the fixed window size of 8×8 is used. The choice of 8×8 is from the convenience, and the small change of window size would not affect the performance, because the fitted image model will not change significantly.

Four contaminated images are obtained from the originals in Fig. 3 by the same procedure explained in the above section. Different restoration methods which we discussed in the above are applied to those contaminated images and mean square error of restored images are computed. For the median filter, mean filter, and α-trimmed mean filter, the mean square error is computed with different window sizes, but for the robust model based method, the fixed window size 8×8 is used. The computed mean square error is plotted with respect to window size.

Fig. 5(a), (b), (c), and (d) shows plots of mean square error computed by different methods for the originals of the outdoor scene [Fig. 3(d)], girl's image [Fig. 3(c)], bridge scene [Fig. 3(a)], and aerial picture of the Purdue University campus [Fig. 3(e)], respectively. The results

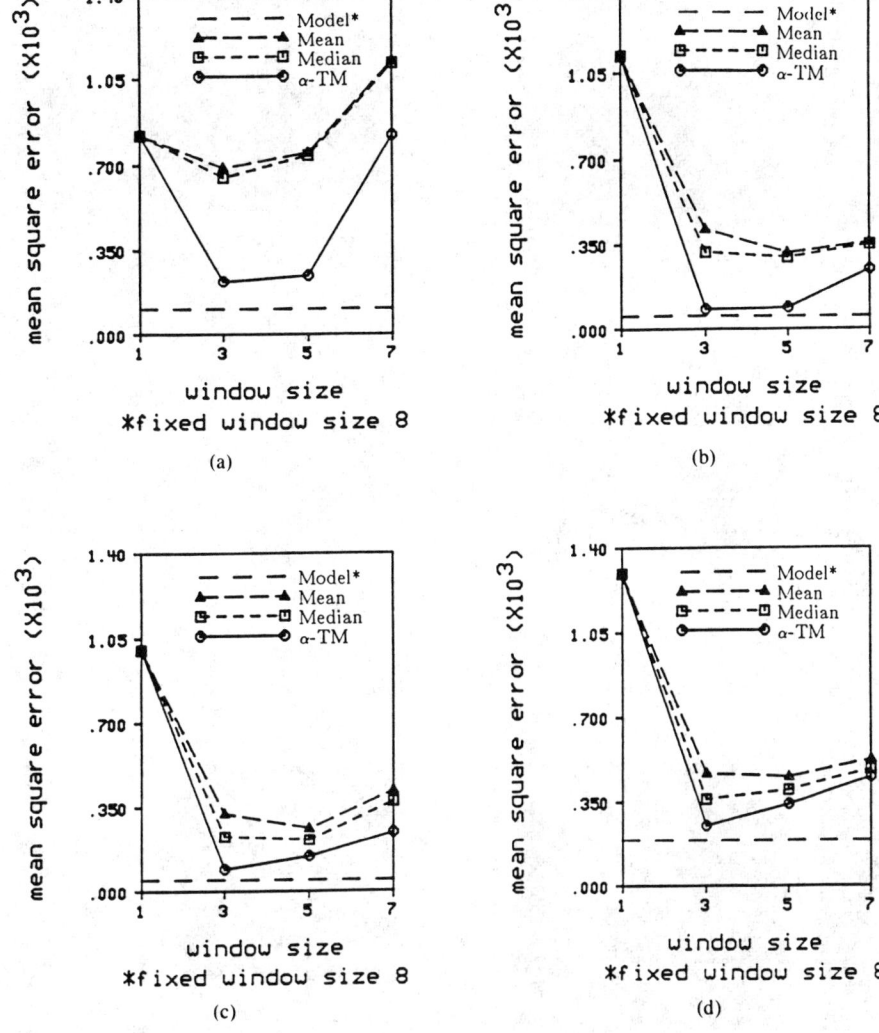

Fig. 5. Mean square error comparisons of different methods. (a) Comparison for outdoor scene. (b) Comparison for girl image. (c) Comparison for bridge picture. (d) Comparison for Purdue campus.

TABLE II
MEAN SQUARE ERROR COMPARISON OF DIFFERENT RESTORATION METHODS ON FOUR DIFFERENT TYPES OF IMAGES

Image	MSE* of mean filter	MSE* of median filter	MSE* of α-TM filter	MSE* of robust method
Outdoor	690.1441	651.1638	220.222	103.9669
Girl	318.9122	300.3172	80.6720	52.5648
Bridge	264.6290	216.3370	92.1115	47.3367
Campus	453.9291	401.6255	253.7658	189.1433

*MSE $= (1/MN) \Sigma_{i,j} (\hat{y}(i,j) - x(i,j))^2$; MN = number of pixels in the image.

are consistent for all different types of images. All traditional methods result in large mean square error on most of the images, especially on the images having many edges (see Table II). For example, in the outdoor scene, the minimum values of mean square errors of mean filter, median filter, and α-trimmed mean filter are 690.1441, 651.1638, and 220.2222, respectively. In contrast, the mean square error of the robust approach is 103.9669. The difference, which is significant, corresponds to the fact that the intensity in a window cannot be approximated by a constant because of edges and corners. Traditional methods have small mean square error at the window sizes 3 × 3 or 5 × 5, depending on the types of images. The mean filter performs worst on all images tested as expected, and the median filter has slightly lower mean square error than those of the mean filter. The α-trimmed mean filter performed better than the median filter or mean filter, but its mean square error is always larger than that of the robust model based method. The mean square error comparison shows that the robust model based method performs better than any other conventional methods on tested images. The minimum values of mean square error in conventional methods are 220.2222 for the outdoor scene, 80.6720 for the girl, 92.1115 for the bridge, and 253.7658 for the Purdue campus, respectively. Mean square errors of our approach are 103.9669 for the outdoor scene, 52.5648 for the girl, 47.3367 for the bridge, and 189.1443 for the Purdue campus. The levels of mean square error of conventional methods are always higher than that of the robust model based method.

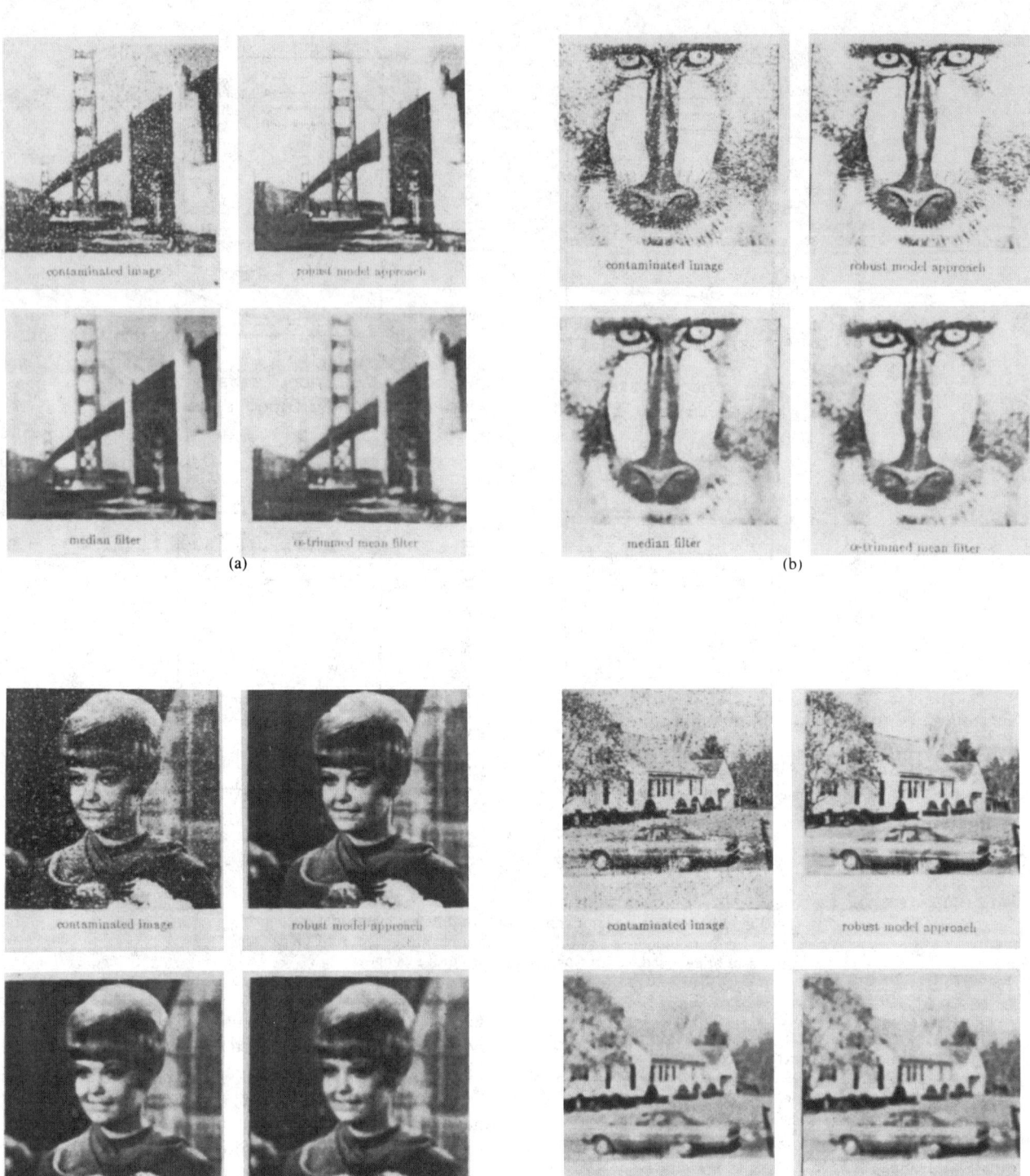

Fig. 6. (a) Qualitative comparison for bridge [Fig. 3(a)]. Most of the details, such as guy wire, are clearly shown in the result of the model based approach, but are not clear in others. (b) Qualitative comparison for monkey [Fig. 3(b)]. Most of the details, such as hair, eyes, etc., are clearly shown in the result of the model based approach, but are not clear in others. (c) Qualitative comparison for girl [Fig. 3(c)]. Most of the details, such as flowers, eyes, etc., are clearly shown in the result of the model based approach, but are blurred in others. (d) Qualitative comparison for outdoor scene [Fig. 3(d)]. Most of the details, such as leaves, windows, etc., are clearly shown in the result of the model based approach, but are blurred in others. (e) Qualitative comparison for Purdue campus [Fig. 3(e)]. Most of the details, such as roads, buildings, etc., are clearly shown in the result of the model based approach, but are blurred in others.

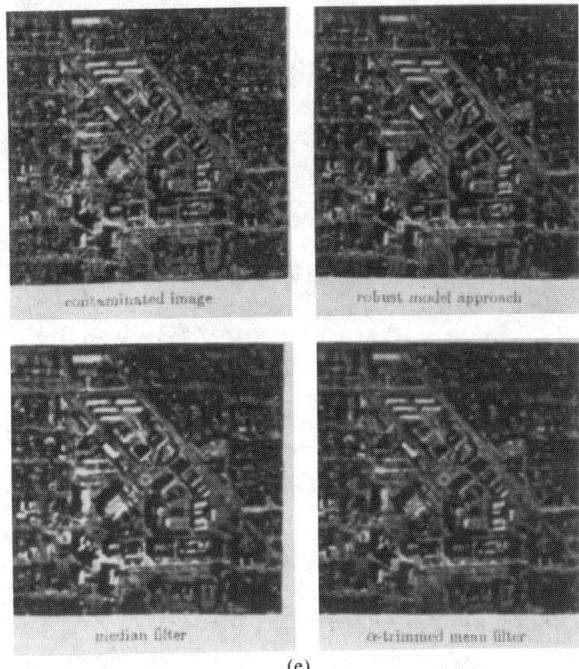

(e)

Fig. 6. (*Continued*)

C. Qualitative Comparison of Image Restoration Methods

The noisy images and images restored by different restoration algorithms are shown in Fig. 6(a)-(e). Fig. 6(a)-(e) shows results on Fig. 3(a)-(e) in the same order. The upper-left corner of each picture of Fig. 6(a)-(e) is the noisy picture contaminated by noise and is generated by adding white Gaussian (0, 100) noise and 5 percent of impulse noise to the original. This image shows typical salt and pepper noise pattern as well as Gaussian noise degradation. This noisy picture is used to obtain restored images by different methods.

The upper-right corner of each picture in Fig. 6(a)-(e) is the restored image by the robust model based method. This image is obtained after three iterations of the data cleaning process. The impulsive noise is almost completely absent, and residual Gaussian noise is hardly noticeable. The fine details of the original in Fig. 3 are well shown in this picture. For example, the guy wire of the bridge [Fig. 6(a)], hair of the monkey's face [Fig. 6(b)], eyes of a girl's face [Fig. 6(c)], leaves of trees [Fig. 6(d)], etc., have sharp edges.

The lower-left corner of each picture of Fig. 6(a)-(e) is the image restored by the median filter with a 5 × 5 window. Note that a 5 × 5 window gives the lowest mean square error as well as a 3 × 3 window in the experiment of the former section. Most of the impulse noise is removed in this picture, but it is much more blurred than the result of the robust model based method. This blurring effect can be easily observed in the images with many edges and corners. Guy wire and details of the bridge frame [Fig. 6(a)], hairs and eyes of monkey's face [Fig. 6(b)], eyes and mouth of girl's image [Fig. 6(c)], leaves of the tree and details of the car and windows of the house in the outdoor scene [Fig. 6(d)], and most details in the aerial picture [Fig. 6(e)] are blurred. The regions with small intensity variations are replaced by constant gray level, and the transitions between different regions are rather abrupt. This effect is typical in the median filter, and it is because the median filter fails in smoothing images. These effects can be observed in the tower region of the bridge [Fig. 6(a)], windows and wheels of the car [Fig. 6(d)], etc.

The lower-right corner of each picture of Fig. 6(a)-(e) is the image restored by the α-trimmed mean filter with a 5 × 5 window and $\alpha = 0.15$. Note that the choice of $\alpha = 0.15$ is considered a good choice in previous studies [3], [13]. Even though the α-trimmed mean filter has smaller mean square error than the median filter, the restored image given by this method is more blurred than by the median filter. Edges and corners of the image convey more information, and the image restored by the α-trimmed mean filter is worse than the median filter in the qualitative comparison. For example, the tower and guy wire in the bridge [Fig. 6(a)], hairs and eyes of monkey's face [Fig. 6(b)], eyes and flowers in girl's image [Fig. 6(c)], most of the tree, car, and shrubs in the outdoor scene [Fig. 6(d)], and most details of the aerial picture [Fig. 6(e)] are blurred. It is also not successful in removing impulse noise and has a lot of residual noise caused by impulse noise. These residual noises can be observed in almost all images [Fig. 6(a)-(e)].

V. Discussion and Conclusions

Robust estimation in a nonsymmetric half-plane autoregressive model is considered in this paper. First, we consider the robust parameter estimation in a nonsymmetric half-plane autoregressive model in which the driving white noise is a mixture of a Gaussian and outliers. An iterative algorithm is presented in this paper. The convergence of the proposed algorithm is proved.

Next, we consider the case where the original image is not available and a noisy version of the image is available. The corrupting noise is mixed with impulse noise. We consider the simultaneous estimation of parameters and the original image intensity. We develop a procedure assuming that the entire image obeys an NSHP model. The robustness of the proposed procedure is demonstrated by simulations.

The robust estimation procedure is applied to restore several realistic images corrupted by a mixture-type noise. The restored images compare favorably both quantitatively and qualitatively to the restored images from other methods.

Appendix
Proofs of Lemmas 1 and 2 and Theorem 3

These proofs are valid only for the ψ function as given in (2.11). The proofs have been adapted from those given in [2] for the regression problem.

Lemma 1: At every iteration step, $\theta^{(k+1)}$ in (2.15) reduces the Q function for fixed $\sigma^{(k)}$; i.e.,

$$Q(\theta^{(k)}, \sigma^{(k)}) - Q(\theta^{(k+1)}, \sigma^{(k)})$$
$$\geq \frac{1}{2\sigma^{(k)}mn} \tau^{(k)T} \left[\sum_{i,j} z(i,j) z^T(i,j) \right] \tau^{(k)}.$$

Proof of Lemma 1: Rewrite $Q(\theta^{(k)} + \tau, \sigma^{(k)})$ in (2.18) by using (2.13) and (2.15).

$$Q(\theta^{(k)} + \tau, \sigma^{(k)})$$
$$= \frac{1}{mn} \sum_{i,j} \left[\rho\left(\frac{r^{(k)}(i,j) - \tau^T z(i,j)}{\sigma^{(k)}} \right) + \frac{1}{2} \right] \sigma^{(k)}. \quad (A.1)$$

Construct a comparison function $W(\theta^{(k)}, \tau, \sigma^{(k)})$ which agrees with Q at $\tau = 0$, and lies above Q.

$$W(\theta^{(k)}, \tau, \sigma^{(k)}) = Q(\theta^{(k)}, \sigma^{(k)}) + \frac{1}{2\sigma^{(k)}mn}$$
$$\cdot \sum_{i,j} \left[(\hat{r}^{(k)}(i,j) - \tau^T z(i,j))^2 - (\hat{r}^{(k)}(i,j))^2 \right] \quad (A.2)$$

where

$$\hat{r}^{(k)}(i,j) = \psi\left(\frac{r^{(k)}(i,j)}{\sigma^{(k)}} \right) \sigma^{(k)}.$$

The gradients of $Q(\theta^{(k)} + \tau, \sigma^{(k)})$ and $W(\theta^{(k)}, \tau, \sigma^{(k)})$ with respect to τ are given by the following:

$$\nabla_\tau Q(\theta, \sigma^{(k)})$$
$$= \frac{-1}{mn} \sum_{i,j} \psi\left(\frac{r^{(k)}(i,j) - \tau^T z(i,j)}{\sigma^{(k)}} \right) z^T(i,j) \quad (A.3)$$

$$\nabla_\tau W(\theta^{(k)}, \tau, \sigma^{(k)})$$
$$= \frac{-1}{\sigma^{(k)}mn} \sum_{i,j} (\hat{r}^{(k)}(i,j) - \tau^T z(i,j)) z^T(i,j). \quad (A.4)$$

By (A.1) and (A.2),

$$\left[W(\theta^{(k)}, \tau, \sigma^{(k)}) - Q(\theta^{(k)} + \tau, \sigma^{(k)}) \right]_{\tau=0} = 0. \quad (A.5)$$

By (A.3) and (A.4),

$$\nabla_\tau \left[W(\theta^{(k)}, \tau, \sigma^{(k)}) - Q(\theta^{(k)} + \tau, \sigma^{(k)}) \right]_{\tau=0} = 0. \quad (A.6)$$

Also, because $1 - \psi'(x) \geq 0$ for all x, where $\psi'(x) = \partial \psi(x)/\partial x$,

$$\nabla_{\tau\tau} \left[W(\theta^{(k)}, \tau, \sigma^{(k)}) - Q(\theta^{(k)} + \tau, \sigma^{(k)}) \right]$$
$$= \frac{1}{\sigma^{(k)}mn} \sum_{i,j} \left[1 - \psi'\left(\frac{r^{(k)}(i,j) - \tau^T z(i,j)}{\sigma^{(k)}} \right) \right]$$
$$\cdot z(i,j) z^T(i,j) \geq 0. \quad (A.7)$$

Thus, by (A.5), (A.6), and (A.7),

$$W(\theta^{(k)}, \tau, \sigma^{(k)}) \geq Q(\theta^{(k)} + \tau, \sigma^{(k)}) \quad \text{for all } \tau. \quad (A.8)$$

However, from (A.2),

$$W(\theta^{(k)}, \tau^{(k)}, \sigma^{(k)}) = Q(\theta^{(k)}, \sigma^{(k)}) - \frac{1}{2\sigma^{(k)}mn}$$
$$\cdot \sum_{i,j} \left[2\tau^{(k)T} z(i,j) \hat{r}^{(k)}(i,j) - \tau^{(k)T} z(i,j) z^T(i,j) \tau^{(k)} \right].$$

By substituting $\sum_{i,j} [z(i,j) \hat{r}^{(k)}(i,j)] = \sum_{i,j} [z(i,j) z^T(i,j)] \tau^{(k)}$ into the above equation, we have the following equation:

$$W(\theta^{(k)}, \tau^{(k)}, \sigma^{(k)}) = Q(\theta^{(k)}, \sigma^{(k)}) - \frac{1}{2\sigma^{(k)}mn} \tau^{(k)T}$$
$$\cdot \left[\sum_{i,j} z(i,j) z^T(i,j) \right] \tau^{(k)} \quad (A.9)$$

where

$$\tau^{(k)} = \left[\sum_{i,j} z(i,j) z^T(i,j) \right]^{-1} \left[\sum_{i,j} z(i,j) \hat{r}^{(k)}(i,j) \right].$$

Therefore, by (A.8) and (A.9),

$$Q(\theta^{(k)}, \sigma^{(k)}) - Q(\theta^{(k+1)}, \sigma^{(k)})$$
$$\geq \frac{1}{2\sigma^{(k)}mn} \tau^{(k)T} \left[\sum_{i,j} z(i,j) z^T(i,j) \right] \tau^{(k)}. \quad (A.10)$$
∎

Lemma 2: At every iteration step, $\sigma^{(k+1)}$ in (2.15) reduces the Q function for fixed $\theta^{(k)}$; i.e.,

$$Q(\theta^{(k)}, \sigma^{(k)}) - Q(\theta^{(k)}, \sigma^{(k+1)}) \geq \frac{(\sigma^{(k+1)} - \sigma^{(k)})}{2\sigma^{(k)}}.$$

Proof of Lemma 2: Rewrite $Q(\theta^{(k)}, \sigma)$ in the following:

$$Q(\theta^{(k)}, \sigma) = \frac{1}{mn} \sum_{i,j} \left[\rho\left(\frac{r^{(k)}(i,j)}{\sigma} \right) + \frac{1}{2} \right] \sigma. \quad (A.11)$$

Define $\chi(x) = x\psi(x) - \rho(x)$. $\chi(x) = \frac{1}{2}[\psi(x)]^2$, since ψ obeys (2.11). Then the derivative of $Q(\theta^{(k)}, \sigma)$ with respect to σ is given by the following:

$$\frac{\partial Q(\theta^{(k)}, \sigma)}{\partial \sigma} = \frac{1}{2} - \frac{1}{mn} \sum_{i,j} \chi\left(\frac{r^{(k)}(i,j)}{\sigma} \right). \quad (A.12)$$

Construct a comparison function $U(\sigma, \theta^{(k)}, \sigma^{(k)})$

$$U(\sigma, \theta^{(k)}, \sigma^{(k)}) = Q(\theta^{(k)}, \sigma^{(k)}) + \frac{1}{2}(\sigma - \sigma^{(k)})$$
$$+ \frac{1}{mn} \sum_{i,j} \chi\left(\frac{r^{(k)}(i,j)}{\sigma^{(k)}}\right)$$
$$\cdot \left[\frac{\sigma^{(k)2}}{\sigma} - \sigma^{(k)}\right]. \quad (A.13)$$

Then the derivative of $U(\sigma, \theta^{(k)}, \sigma^{(k)})$ with respect to σ is given by the following:

$$\frac{\partial U(\sigma, \theta^{(k)}, \sigma^{(k)})}{\partial \sigma} = \frac{1}{2} - \frac{1}{mn}\sum_{i,j}\chi\left(\frac{r^{(k)}(i,j)}{\sigma^{(k)}}\right)\left(\frac{\sigma^{(k)}}{\sigma}\right)^2. \quad (A.14)$$

By (A.11) and (A.13),

$$U(\sigma^{(k)}, \theta^{(k)}, \sigma^{(k)}) - Q(\theta^{(k)}, \sigma^{(k)}) = 0, \quad (A.15)$$

and by (A.12) and (A.14),

$$\frac{\partial}{\partial \sigma}\left[U(\sigma, \theta^{(k)}, \sigma^{(k)}) - Q(\theta^{(k)}, \sigma)\right]_{\sigma = \sigma^{(k)}} = 0. \quad (A.16)$$

Define $f(v) = U(1/v, \theta^{(k)}, \sigma^{(k)}) - Q(\theta^{(k)}, 1/v)$, $v > 0$. Then $f(v)$ is convex since $\rho(x)/x$ is convex for $x < 0$, and it can be written

$$f(v) = -\frac{1}{mn}\sum_{i,j}\frac{1}{v}\rho[vr^{(k)}(i,j)] + a + bv \quad (A.17)$$

where a and b are appropriate constants. By (A.15), (A.16), and the convexity of $f(v)$, $f(v)$ has a horizontal tangent at $v = 1/\sigma^{(k)}$ and it is zero at there. Thus, $f(v) \geq 0$ for all $v > 0$. It follows that

$$U(\sigma, \theta^{(k)}, \sigma^{(k)}) \geq Q(\theta^{(k)}, \sigma) \quad \text{for all } \sigma > 0. \quad (A.18)$$

After some algebraic manipulations with (2.14) and (2.17), and using the relation $\psi^2(x) = 2\chi(x)$, we can have the following expression for $\sigma^{(k+1)2}$:

$$\sigma^{(k+1)2} = \frac{2}{mn}\sum_{i,j}\chi\left(\frac{r^{(k)}(i,j)}{\sigma^{(k)}}\right)\sigma^{(k)2}.$$

Therefore,

$$U(\sigma^{(k+1)}, \theta^{(k)}, \sigma^{(k)})$$
$$= Q(\theta^{(k)}, \sigma^{(k)}) + \frac{1}{2}(\sigma^{(k+1)} - \sigma^{(k)})$$
$$+ \frac{1}{2}\left(\frac{\sigma^{(k+1)}}{\sigma^{(k)}}\right)^2\left[\frac{\sigma^{(k)2}}{\sigma^{(kH)}} - \sigma^{(k)}\right]$$
$$= Q(\theta^{(k)}, \sigma^{(k)}) - \frac{(\sigma^{(k+1)} - \sigma^{(k)})^2}{2\sigma^{(k)}}. \quad (A.19)$$

Therefore, by (A.18) and (A.19)

$$Q(\theta^{(k)}, \sigma^{(k)}) - Q(\theta^{(k)}, \sigma^{(k+1)}) \geq \frac{(\sigma^{(k+1)} - \sigma^{(k)})^2}{2\sigma^{(k)}}. \quad (A.20)$$

■

Theorem 3: The sequence $\{(\theta^{(k)}, \sigma^{(k)})\}$ converges to $(\hat{\theta}, \hat{\sigma})$, a unique solution of (2.9) and (2.10), and an estimator which minimize (2.7).

Proof of Theorem 3: Let $\Phi = \{(\theta, \sigma) | \sigma \geq 0, Q(\theta, \sigma) \leq b\}$. Φ is closed by the global continuity theorem because Q is continuous and $Q(\Phi)$ is bounded. Also, the boundedness of Q implies the boundedness of Φ. Thus, the sequence $\{(\theta^{(k)}, \sigma^{(k)})\}$ has at least one cluster point $(\hat{\theta}, \hat{\sigma})$.

Let $\{(\theta^{(k_p)}, \sigma^{(k_p)})\}$ be a subsequence converging toward $(\hat{\theta}, \hat{\sigma})$. Then, by Lemma 1,

$$Q(\theta^{(k)}, \sigma^{(k_p)}) - Q(\theta^{(k_p+1)}, \sigma^{(k_p)})$$
$$\geq \frac{1}{2\sigma^{(k_p)}mn}\tau^{(k_p)T}\left[\sum_{i,j}z(i,j)z^T(i,j)\right]\tau^{(k_p)} \to 0. \quad (A.21)$$

It follows that

$$\sum_{i,j}\hat{r}^{(k_p)}(i,j)z(i,j)$$
$$= \sigma^{(k_p)}\sum_{i,j}\psi\left(\frac{y(i,j) - \theta^{(k_p)T}z(i,j)}{\sigma^{(k_p)}}\right)$$
$$\cdot z^T(i,j) \to 0. \quad (A.22)$$

Therefore, in the limit,

$$\sum_{i,j}\psi\left(\frac{y(i,j) - \hat{\theta}^T z(i,j)}{\hat{\sigma}}\right)z^T(i,j) = 0. \quad (A.23)$$

The above equation corresponds to (2.9).

By the convergence of subsequence and Lemma 2,

$$Q(\theta^{(k_p)}, \sigma^{(k_p)}) - Q(\theta^{(k_p)}, \sigma^{(k_p+1)})$$
$$\geq \frac{(\sigma^{(k_p+1)} - \sigma^{(k_p)})^2}{2\sigma^{(k_p)}} \to 0. \quad (A.24)$$

It follows that

$$\left(\frac{\sigma^{(k_p+1)}}{\sigma^{(k_p)}}\right)^2 = \frac{2}{mn}\sum_{i,j}\chi\left(\frac{y(i,j) - \theta^{(k_p)T}z(i,j)}{\sigma^{(k_p)}}\right) \to 1. \quad (A.25)$$

Therefore, in the limit,

$$\frac{1}{mn}\sum_{i,j}\chi\left(\frac{y(i,j) - \hat{\theta}^T z(i,j)}{\hat{\sigma}}\right) = \frac{1}{2}. \quad (A.26)$$

This corresponds to (2.10). By the convexity of Q, the solutions of (2.9) and (2.10) also minimize (2.7). ■

References

[1] W. K. Pratt, *Digital Image Processing*. New York: Wiley, 1978.
[2] P. J. Huber, *Robust Statistics*. New York: Wiley, 1981.
[3] W. J. J. Rey, *Introduction to Robust and Quasi-Robust Statistical Methods*. New York: Springer-Verlag, 1983.
[4] B. Kleiner, R. D. Martin, and D. J. Thomson, "Robust estimation of power spectra," *J. Roy. Soc.*, Series B, vol. 41, no. 3, pp. 313-351, 1979.
[5] R. D. Martin and D. J. Thomson, "Robust-resistant spectrum estimation," *Proc. IEEE*, vol. 70, pp. 1097-1114, 1982.
[6] S. A. Kassam and H. V. Poor, "Robust techniques for signal processing," *Proc. IEEE*, vol. 73, pp. 433-481, Mar. 1985.
[7] Y. H. Lee and S. A. Kassam, "Generalized median filtering and related nonlinear filtering techniques," *IEEE Trans. Acoust., Speech, Signal Processing*, vol. ASSP-33, pp. 672-683, June 1985.
[8] A. C. Bovick, T. S. Huang, and D. C. Munson, Jr, "A generalization of median filtering using linear combinations of order statistics," *IEEE Trans. Acoust., Speech, Signal Processing*, vol. ASSP-31, pp. 1342-1350, Dec. 1983.
[10] S. Geman and D. Geman, "Stochastic relaxation, Gibbs distributions, and Bayesian restoration of images," *IEEE Trans. Pattern Anal. Machine Intell.*, vol. PAMI-6, pp. 721-741, Nov. 1984.
[11] E. J. Delp, R. L. Kashyap, and O. R. Mitchell, "Image data compression using autoregressive time series models," *Pattern Recognition*, vol. 11, pp. 313-323, Dec. 1979.
[12] R. L. Kashyap, "Analysis and synthesis of image patterns by spatial interaction models," in *Progress in Pattern Recognition*, vol. 1, L. N. Kanal and A. Rosenfeld, Eds. Amsterdam, The Netherlands: North-Holland, 1981, pp. 149-186.
[13] P. J. Bickel and K. A. Doksum, *Mathematical Statistics*. Oakland, CA: Holden-Day, 1977.
[14] J. W. Tukey, *Exploratory Data Analysis*. Reading, MA: Addison-Wesley, 1971.
[15] R. L. Kashyap and K.-B. Eom, "Texture boundary detection using long correlation model," in *Proc. Int. Geosci. Remote Sensing Symp.*, Amherst, MA, Oct. 1985.
[15] R. E. Nasburg and R. L. Kashyap, "Robust parameter estimation in dynamic systems," in *Proc. 1975 Conf. Inform. Sci. Syst.*, Baltimore, MD, 1975.
[17] Y. Yasuoka and R. M. Haralick, "Peak noise removal by a facet model," *Pattern Recognition*, vol. 16, no. 1, pp. 23-29, 1983.
[18] R. Chellappa and R. L. Kashyap, "Digital image restoration using spatial interaction models," *IEEE Trans. Acoust., Speech, Signal Processing*, vol. ASSP-30, pp. 461-472, June 1982.
[19] A.C. Bovick, T. S. Huang, and D. C. Munson, Jr., "Edge sensitive image restoration using order-constrained least squares methods," *IEEE Trans. Acoust., Speech, Signal Processing*, vol. ASSP-33, pp. 1253-1263, Oct. 1985.
[20] Z. Wu, "Multidimensional state-space model Kalman filtering with application to image restoration," *IEEE Trans. Acoust., Speech, Signal Processing*, vol. ASSP-33, pp. 1576-1592, Dec. 1985.
[21] P. Chan and J. S. Lim, "One-dimensional processing for adaptive image restoration," *IEEE Trans. Acoust., Speech, Signal Processing*, vol. ASSP-33, pp. 117-126, Feb. 1985.
[22] A. Kundu, S. K. Mitra, and P. P. Vaidyanathan, "Application of two-dimensional generalized mean filtering for removal of impulse noises from images," *IEEE Trans. Acoust., Speech, Signal Processing*, vol. ASSP-32, pp. 600-609, June 1984.

Rangasami L. Kashyap (M'70-SM'77-F'79) received the D.I.I.Sc. and M.E. degrees from the Indian Institute of Science, Bangalore, India, in 1960 and 1962, respectively, and the Ph.D. degree in engineering from Harvard University, Cambridge, MA, in 1965.

He is currently a Professor of Electrical Engineering and Associate Director of the National Science Foundation supported Engineering Research Center on Intelligent Manufacturing at Purdue University, West Lafayette, IN. He was a Postdoctoral Research Fellow in Applied Mathematics at Harvard University during 1965-1966. During the Fall semester of 1974, he was a Visiting Professor at Harvard University. During the Spring semester of 1974, he was a Visiting Research Associate at the University of California, Berkeley. His current research interests are pattern recognition, the role of random fields in image processing, system identification, applications of artificial intelligence methods in manufacturing, and robotics.

Dr. Kashyap won the 1967 National Electronic Conference Annual Best Research Paper Award for his paper "Optimization of stochastic finite-state machines." He was an Associate Editor of the IEEE TRANSACTIONS ON AUTOMATIC CONTROL. He has been the Program Chairperson for several meetings of the IEEE Computer Society in the area of pattern recognition and image processing. He is a member of the Association for Computing Machinery and Sigma Xi.

Kie-Bum Eom (S'82-M'85) was born in Seoul, Korea, on June 15, 1954. He received the B.S. degree in electronics engineering from Sogang University, Seoul, Korea, in 1976, the M.S. degree in electrical science from the Korea Advanced Institute of Science, Seoul, Korea, in 1978, and the Ph.D. degree in electrical engineering from Purdue University, West Lafayette, IN, in 1986.

From 1977 to 1981 he was with Taihan Electric Company, Seoul, Korea, as an Engineer. From 1983 to 1986 he was a Graduate Instructor of Research in the School of Electrical Engineering of Purdue University. In 1986 he joined Syracuse University, Syracuse, NY, where he is currently an Assistant Professor in Electrical and Computer Engineering. His research interests include image processing, signal processing, pattern recognition, and artificial intelligence.

Dr. Eom is a member of Tau Beta Pi and Eta Kappa Nu.

Image Processing for Higher Definition Television

GARY J. TONGE

(*Invited Paper*)

Abstract — The paper discusses the application of digital image-processing techniques to broadcast television with the goal of picture quality improvement. After defining picture quality targets and levels of system compatibility, a review of techniques is presented. These fall into the categories of achieving a wider picture format, improving vertical and horizontal resolution, and improving accurate color reproduction. Specific algorithms for vertical resolution improvement by display scan conversion and horizontal resolution improvement by three-dimensional signal processing are described. Many other approaches are also summarized and referenced, with a particular emphasis on European work.

I. Introduction

OF THE MANY developments in digital image processing, one which will have an impact on most of the population, is in the area of consumer television. Digital storage and processing are already finding their way into consumer television equipment (teletext memories, picture-in-picture facilities, etc.), and the future promises much more. This paper addresses the increasing amount of research and development with the goal of higher definition television ("Hi-fi TV"). Some of the image processing being considered is of a complexity which is currently hard to imagine in the consumer environment. Nevertheless, the prospect of VLSI volume production makes it possible to consider some of the relatively complex approaches, provided that the improvement is worthwhile.

II. Picture Quality Targets

In a very general sense, the target is to produce a picture presentation in the home which is a sufficient improvement over the current norm to justify the extra expense. Typically, the improved quality will not be exploited to give a better picture definition as seen by the eye (at a typical viewing distance) but rather to enable a larger screen presentation.

Subjective tests in Japan [1] and in Europe [2] have shown that a larger viewing angle can increase the sense of involvement in a televised scene. Given that domestic television viewing disances are typically set more by practical constraints (room size, furniture, etc.) than by technical, this implies an increased screen size. The Japanese work also highlighted the importance of having a wider aspect ratio for large-screen television.

More specifically, targets for "high-definition television" (HDTV) have been set as an improvement in comparison with conventional television systems[1] in both vertical and horizontal resolution of about 2:1 in conjunction with a wider aspect ratio of around 5:3 [3]. This implies, for the same picture definition as seen by the eye at a fixed viewing distance, an increase in screen height by a factor of about 2 and screen width by a factor of around $2\frac{1}{2}$, as shown in Fig. 1.

The image-processing techniques described here can be used to achieve a broad range in the degree of improvement over conventional systems. The specific targets discussed above represent a tangible benchmark of quality which has been called "HDTV." It is not clear, however, what reduction in picture quality is necessary before an image ceases to be HDTV. With conventional television standards, for example, a domestic VCR provides a degraded picture. Nevertheless, from a users' point of view, this does not imply a destruction of the service. For this reason, it can be argued that the distinctive feature of "HDTV" is the wider aspect ratio format while the picture quality criteria are vague. Nevertheless, any improvements which can be provided by image-processing techniques in a cost-effective way are likely to find definite application, and an increasing future trend toward higher quality consumer television can be predicted.

III. Compatibility

Image-processing techniques for picture quality improvement can be applied in a number of different ways. At one extreme, they can be applied retrospectively to current TV services by processing in the receiver alone. At the other extreme, they can be particular to a proposed new completely different TV service. In the technical description which follows, the techniques are subdivided into four categories of "compatibility" with current systems.

Manuscript received February 14, 1987; revised June 11, 1987.
The author is with the Independent Broadcasting Authority, Crawley Court, Winchester, Hants, England.
IEEE Log Number 8716563.

[1] Recent standardization efforts for HDTV studio production have been based on these targets with respect to the currently agreed digital *studio* television standard. This implies a higher standard than that considered here, where the relevant comparison is with current *broadcast* standards (NTSC/PAL/SECAM).

Fig. 1. A simple comparison between conventional television (small border) and high-definition television (large border) on the basis of picture size.

A. Compatible-Level 1

These are techniques which can be applied to current NTSC/PAL/SECAM broadcasts by receiver processing alone.

B. Compatible-Level 2

These are techniques which can be applied to the current NTSC/PAL/SECAM broadcast formats but which require processing both at the receiver and at the source.

C. Compatible-Level 3

These are techniques which can be applied to 625 or 525 line systems only in channels using MAC[2] color coding.

D. Noncompatible Systems

These are techniques which assume a different scanning format from those used in conventional television transmission. It is assumed that a noncompatible system is completely separate from existing systems. In the home, it would use different equipment with a different display. The only constraints considered here are those of transmission or storage bandwidth.

These subdivisions are important since they concern broadcasting system concepts which affect significantly the receiver cost and also have political standardization implications. From a purely technical point of view, they represent constraints on the extent to which the wide range of possible image processing techniques can be applied.

Of particular importance in Europe at this time are techniques in the third category, that is, compatible with MAC. A large collaborative work program under the EUREKA framework (project EU95: Compatible High Definition Television System) is underway on this topic with participation from major industries, broadcasters, and institutions. The goal is the introduction of very high quality TV pictures in the home by a method which is operationally very similar to the introduction of color television. The broadcasting medium is by direct broadcast satellite, although of course home recording is also considered. Many of the image-processing techniques in this paper are the subject of intensive coordinated studies in this program.

IV. Aspect Ratio

In this section, we consider methods of achieving a transition from the current aspect ratio of 4:3 to a wider aspect ratio format. Although a wider aspect ratio is normally considered in conjunction with improved definition, it is in its own right a valid target. Indeed, as far as the general public is concerned, a wider picture format is likely to be a major distinctive feature of any new "hifi" service. It remains a property of the system, however poor the signal strength or however poor the viewing conditions! The precise picture aspect ratio considered in most cases here is 16:9 (5.33:3). This format (33 percent wider than the current 4:3) is the one now generally agreed on for HDTV production in preference to the earlier assumed figure of 5:3.

Despite their importance, the image-processing content of methods for achieving a wide aspect ratio is not great, and so techniques are described here only very briefly. The descriptions are subdivided according to the compatibility headings introduced in Section III.

A. Compatible-Level 1: Receiver Processing Alone

If the broadcast picture aspect ratio is 4:3, the only way in which a wide aspect ratio receiver can process the picture so as to fill the display area while maintaining correct picture geometry is to discard the top and/or bottom of the picture content. This is unlikely to be satisfactory from the point of view of picture composition. It is more likely, therefore, that a wide aspect ratio TV set of the future will process received 4:3 aspect ratio images so as to fill only part of the screen width. It has been suggested [4] that the spare display area could be put to good use in these circumstances by providing a "preview" facility of three other services in a small format (Fig. 2).

B. Compatible-Level 2: Source and Receiver Processing

In principle, it is possible to consider changing at source the aspect ratio of current NTSC/PAL/SECAM broadcasts to a wider format such as 16:9. The effect of this on a conventional 4:3 receiver without adjustment would be to give a geometric distortion of 33 percent. This is hardly "compatible." European receiver manufacturers are considering incorporating a scan height switch into new receivers which would enable future 16:9 broadcasts to be displayed with the correct geometry but reduced picture height. In this way, it is foreseen that a compatible change to wide aspect ratio could take place provided that it were sufficiently far into the future that all receivers in the market were equipped with this scan height control.

---

[2] Multiplexed Analog Components—a time division multiplex format for color TV coding using time compression which is standardized in Europe for direct broadcast satellite transmissions. In North America, such formats are under discussion in the ATSC (Advanced Television Systems Committee).

Fig. 2. A suggestion for the use of a wide aspect ratio display format when available services are in the current 4:3 aspect ratio.

C. Compatible-Level 3: MAC Systems

On services which use the MAC standard, it may be possible to consider a compatible change to wide aspect ratio at a much earlier stage than that considered above for NTSC/PAL/SECAM. The flexibility of the MAC coding structure can be used to provide a dual aspect ratio specification.

There are broadly two approaches to achieve this [5]. One involves coding the picture "side" information (that part of the wide aspect ratio picture width beyond the boundaries of 4:3 aspect ratio) into the field-blanking interval and into a portion of the "line-blanking" interval. The other involves having the same transmitted format for both 4:3 and 16:9 aspect ratios but having two different sets of time expansion ratios in the MAC decoder. At least one domestic receiver chip-set in an advanced state of development [6] incorporates the necessary facilities for either of these approaches to give correct pictures for the conventional 4:3 display for either transmitted aspect ratio. In this way, direct broadcast satellite services can change to a wider aspect ratio in a compatible evolutionary way.

D. Non-Compatible Systems

Providing a wider aspect ratio is a trivial matter with a noncompatible system; the new system is simply defined to use the new aspect ratio.

V. Vertical Resolution Improvement

We turn now to the core topic of this paper: methods for improving television picture definition by digital

(c)

(d)

Fig. 2. *Continued*

image-processing techniques. We start by considering improvements in the vertical direction.

A. Compatible-Level 1: Increasing Vertical Resolution by Receiver Processing

How is it possible to increase the vertical resolution provided on television transmissions by processing in the receiver alone? It is worthwhile first considering what the vertical resolution provided by conventional television actually is.

1) Current Resolution Limits: Clearly, the limits to vertical resolution are set by the number of lines in the system. If we assume a perfect sampling process, then the 485 active lines (vertical samples) in the 525-line system should be able to carry vertical frequencies up to the Nyquist limit of 242 cycles per picture height. This corresponds to an "equivalent" horizontal frequency of 323 cycles per picture width, or 6.1 MHz. The comparable calculation for 625-line systems yields a figure of 7.4 MHz.

It has been evident from the early days of television that these ideal figures are not provided in practice and that a reduction factor (the "kell factor") applies. The scanning imperfections which give rise to the kell factor are discussed in [7] and [8]. It emerges that a significant contribution to the perceived loss of resolution with current television standards is due to the use of interlace, especially in the display. This is because any high vertical frequencies in the source tend to be dominated on display by "interline flicker" effects. In the extreme case of a "Nyquist" frequency of 242 cycles per picture height, the display will show alternate lines as "black" and "white," which, due to interlace, will appear as alternate plain black and white fields. In this way, a purely vertical frequency of (242 c/ph, 0 Hz) is aliased to appear as a purely temporal frequency of (0 c/ph, 30 Hz). In a similar way, a frequency of (200 c/ph, 0 Hz), for example, is aliased to appear as lower vertical frequency flickering at 30 Hz (i.e., 42 c/ph, 30 Hz). These aliasing defects tend to mask the high

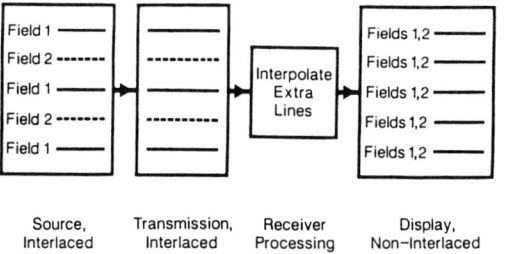

Fig. 3. Increasing vertical resolution by interlaced to noninterlaced display scan conversion.

vertical frequencies and, hence, limit vertical resolution in interlaced systems. If an electronic vertical frequency sweep (gamma-corrected to provide an optical sine wave sweep on display) is used as a test, then the "kell factor" for the 525- or 625-line system can be put at something just below 0.5.

2) Receiver Processing for Display Scan Conversion: Receiver processing can be applied to increase the line-scanning standard for display only so as to overcome some of these limitations. The potential for picture improvement in this way has been widely recognized and this area is one of active research worldwide [9]–[14]. In particular, scan conversion for noninterlaced (progressive or sequential) display has received attention. If interpolation is used to provide additional display lines for 525/60 or 625/50 noninterlaced display, as illustrated in Fig. 3, then significant picture quality improvement can result on static pictures. The improvement applies for static pictures since, in this case, all of the information in the two interlaced fields can be combined into each single noninterlaced field ("temporal interpolation"). With pictures containing significant movement, this would produce multiple-image or blurring defects, and so an alternative strategy is applied for moving images.

Subjective tests in Japan [9] have shown improvements in the range +2.6 to +1.4 on a seven-grade comparison scale for scenes with little or no movement. In our laboratories, many have commented on the high-definition appearance resulting from such scan conversion using component-coded television signals. Not only is interline flicker removed for static pictures, but also a noticeable absence of "busyness" occurs in the line structure of the noninterlaced display. If the electronic vertical frequency sweep referred to above is used as a test, then the improvement in vertical resolution offered by this technique is almost the full factor of 2:1. This would imply, however, that a 525-line 60-Hz system with 2:1 interlace offers no greater vertical resolution than a noninterlaced system with 262 lines. With real picture material, this is not the case and an improvement factor more in the region of 1.5:1 results. This is primarily because the modulation depth of the high vertical frequency detail in conventional scenes is much less than the extreme case (100 percent) of the electronic sweep.

Improvement in perceived resolution is not achieved, however, in parts of scenes which have significant motion. The use of interlace in transmission does imply inevitably

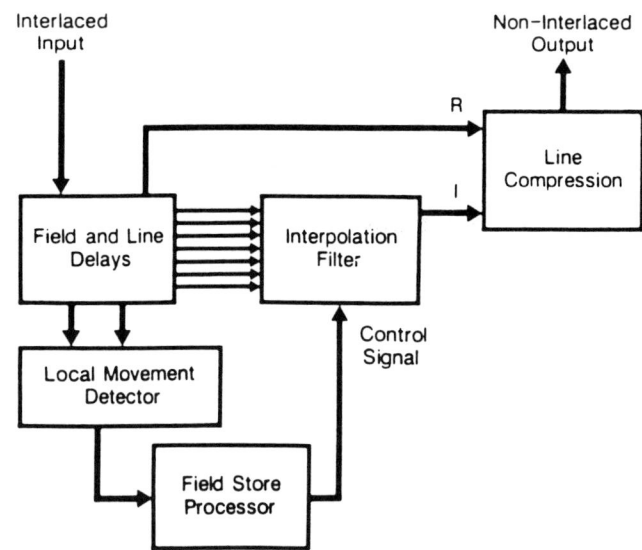

Fig. 4. The interlaced to noninterlaced scan conversion technique developed at the IBA. Processing for the digital luminance signal.

a reduced vertical resolution with motion. If the algorithm which is used to interpolate the extra lines for display is fixed, then any improvement in static picture quality is offset by a motion degradation. For this reason, most of the research has pursued the option of a motion-adaptive interpolation procedure to achieve the improvement for static pictures described above, while maintaining the conventional motion portrayal capabilities of interlace.

B. Compatible-Level 1: A Specific Algorithm for Noninterlaced Display Scan Conversion

We shall now describe briefly the specific approach for noninterlaced scan conversion developed at the IBA [11], [15], [16]. The system was developed as part of a chain to prove the feasibility of improved quality systems using MAC transmission. The processing operates on digitized decoded luminance and color difference signals and so can be applied also to decoded PAL or SECAM signals. Although the system operates with 625-line signals, the principles are equally applicable to 525 lines.

The processing for the color difference components is simple and nonadaptive. It was found that the presence of "interline flicker" on color is not a particularly annoying artifact, and so fixed vertical interpolation (within a single field) is used. Furthermore, it was found that a simple line-averaging algorithm gave better subjective results than a higher order interpolation, especially on color signals which have already been through the alternate-line coding of MAC.

A block diagram of the adaptive processing for the digital luminance component is shown in Fig. 4. The block entitled "Field and Line Delays" contains two fields delays and several line delays to make available to the interpolation filter the line positions indicated in Fig. 5. Appropriate weighted sums of the signal values from these positions are used in the interpolation filter to provide the signal value for the interpolated line whose position is

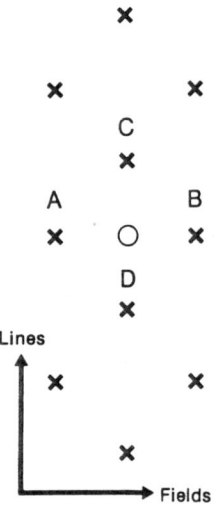

Fig. 5. Line positions (marked by ×) available for the interpolation of the "missing line" marked by O.

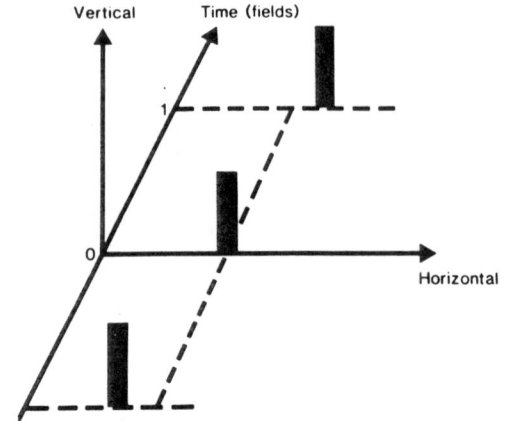

Fig. 6. A horizontally moving bar over three television fields.

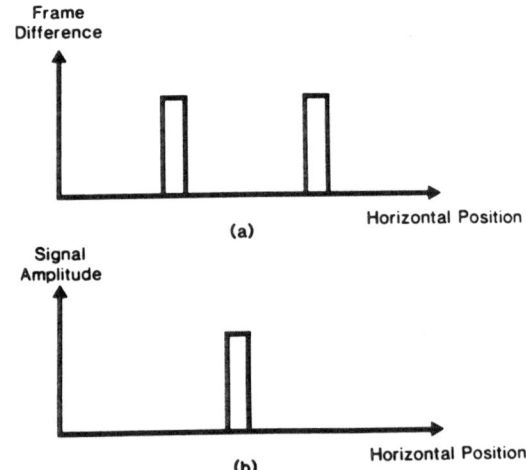

Fig. 7. The frame difference signal (a) compared with the picture signal itself (b) for the moving bar of Fig. 6 in Field O.

marked by a circle. The field and line delay block also provides the "real" (unfiltered) lines (R), suitably delayed to be combined with the interpolated lines (I), and outputs to the movement control loop (consisting of a local movement detector and a field store processor).

1) The Interpolation Filter: Although filters which use the whole range of points available were examined, it was found that it was sufficient to use only points A, B, C, and D in Fig. 5. One of the disadvantages of using more points is the visibility of filter "ringing" on sharp transitions due to the step response of the vertical interpolation. When the control signal indicates no motion, then temporal interpolation is used (averaging A and B), and when the control signal indicates full motion, then vertical interpolation is used (averaging C and D). Intermediate states involving a weighted sum of A, B, C, and D are used for intermediate levels of the control signal, but, in practice, these are in operation for only a small proportion of the time.

For program material originated on film and played at 25 Hz, a better solution is to use a nonadaptive interpolation process where the interpolated line uses signal values A or B on alternate fields. In this way, each film frame is simply repeated twice on the 50-Hz noninterlaced output. This can be implemented by incorporating a simple "film motion detector" into the signal processing.

2) The Local Movement Detector (LMD): The local movement detector is the first part of the control loop which indicates to the interpolation filter the most suitable interpolation to apply for a given picture point.

The basis of the local movement detector is an absolute frame difference signal. For a particular line to be interpolated, this is given as the absolute value of the difference between the signal amplitude on the line of the same vertical position in the previous field, and a similar line in the subsequent field, or $A - B$ from Fig. 5.

Although other starting points involving the comparison between $A - B$ and $C - D$ have been investigated, we have found none more suitable than this simple case. In the local movement detector, the frame difference signal is followed by a "coring threshold" which minimizes the effect of low-value difference signals occurring due to noise in the picture. This threshold can be adapted according to measures of scene brightness and accumulated noise statistics.

3) The Nonlocal Field Store Processor: There are certain types of motion which would bypass the local detection technique if this were used alone to provide the control signal. A simple example, which occurs, in practice, within electronically generated moving captions, is a moving narrow bar. Consider a horizontally moving vertical bar as illustrated in Fig. 6. The task is to interpolate the "missing lines" within this bar in field O. By comparing the frame difference signal which results (Fig. 7(a)) with the signal amplitude of the bar itself (Fig. 7(b)), it can be seen that during the bar itself the frame difference value is zero (indicating no change) even though the bar is moving. Thus, if the frame difference signal were used to control directly the interpolation to be used, then a wrong result would emerge. The absence of a motion indication within the bar would imply the use of temporal interpolation, and the background signal level would be inserted. It has been shown [15] that this effect is a fundamental feature of the

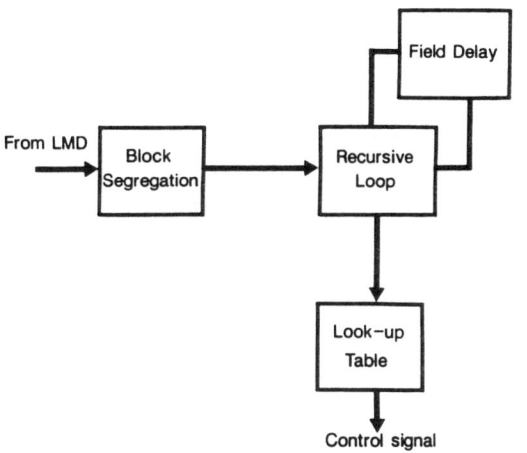

Fig. 8. The field-store processor in the motion control loop of the IBA display scan converter.

processing being attempted and that it cannot be suitably overcome on a purely local basis. The purpose of the field-store processor is to suitably "spread" the local detection signal so that the "gaps" left by such types of movement are filled, and, hence, the correct (vertical) interpolation method is used within the bar.

A block diagram of the processor is shown in Fig. 8. The local movement detection signal is separated into blocks since very fine spatial resolution is not required for this part of the processing. The signal values within a block are accumulated and coded with few quantization levels. The block signals are then modified according to previous field values by use of a recursive loop containing a field delay element. This results in a "spreading" of the signal in areas of motion. It emerges that the field storage requirements are very modest because of the block nature of the signal and the few quantization levels employed. The advantage of using field storage in this way is that the spreading which results is equally applicable for all speeds and directions of motion. Other options (using horizontal processing, for example) tend to be restrictive in this regard.

A recursive loop is used, rather than a simple single field delay, since particularly awkward motion (for example, a letter M moving horizontally with critical speed) can lead to the absence of a frame difference signal for more than one field. Finally, the output of the recursive loop is fed into a look-up table which performs a second "coring threshold" function.

By suitable choice of block size (e.g., 6 samples × 4 lines), and the use of horizontally and vertically overlapping blocks, it is found that the same control signal value can be applied to the interpolation process for all positions within a block without detrimental effects on the picture quality.

This technique has been found to be effective with all electronically generated moving captions tested so far and also with less critical motion. Furthermore, the immunity of the motion detection process to noise is remarkably good and very effective down to luminance signal-to-noise ratios of around 30 dB.

For higher noise levels than this, the system is configured to be able to adapt its coring thresholds according to an accumulated measure of noise statistics. The immunity to noise means also that the approach is suitable for decoded composite (NTSC, PAC, SECAM) systems when the luminance signal is contaminated by cross-color.

4) Line Compression: The final stage in the conversion process (Fig. 4) is to combine the "real" and "interpolated" lines to give the noninterlaced output. This implies time compression by a factor of 2 and a doubling of bandwidths. In our implementation, the luminance input bandwidth is 10 MHz (sampling frequency is 22.5 MHz) while the output bandwidth is 20 MHz ($f_s = 45$ MHz).

5) Discussion: Despite the complexity of the motion detection in the above description, techniques such as these could soon be implemented in domestic TV receivers since the techniques lend themselves to large-scale integration. The major limitation is probably the field storage, although already field-stored integrated circuits are beginning to be used by receiver manufacturers [17]. The use of double scan-rate displays in the home is not seen as a stumbling block. Indeed, such displays (using very simple interpolation techniques in scan conversion) are already coming onto the market.

The scan conversion described here is of course only one example. Another which is of particular interest in Europe is the conversion to 100-Hz field rate. The purpose of this is to reduce large-area flicker on bright displays. The motion-adaptive processing requirements for this task are even more stringent than those discussed here. Since completely new time samples are required, the only way to maintain accurate motion portrayal is to use *motion-compensated* interpolation.

This necessitates the derivation of a control signal which not only indicates the presence or absence of motion but the *velocity* of motion. The derivation of such information in television signal processing is a research topic of increasing importance which is dealt with later in this paper.

C. Compatible-Level-2: Vertical Resolution Improvement by Pre- and Post-Processing

The noninterlaced display scan conversion procedure described above still exhibits any of the vertical resolution limitations inherent in the source. For example, the vertical resolution obtained with interlaced television cameras is typically rather limited due to the effective line-scanning profile. To a first approximation, the scanning beam in a camera tube "wipes the slate clean" of charge with every field scan. This implies a vertical averaging over the width of one field line, i.e., 1/242 picture heights for 525-line systems and 1/288 picture heights for 625-line systems. This in turn implies a slow roll-off vertical frequency response with a null at 242 or 288 c/ph, respectively. The use of a higher line-scan rate at source, with suitable down-conversion for transmission, could improve on this.

A second incentive to consider pre-processing as well as post-processing for compatible vertical resolution improvement is that more controlled pre-filtering can be applied to

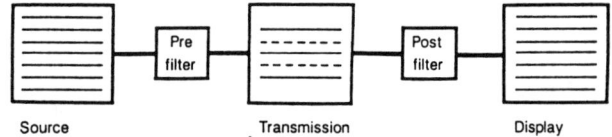

Fig. 9. Pre- and post-processing for vertical resolution improvement.

the signal, especially with motion. The need for this is apparent when observing moving picture material using display conversion only. The major remaining picture defect is the aliasing evident with fine detail and vertical motion. The use of a higher line-rate source with pre-filtering could replace this aliasing defect by a reduction in vertical resolution for motion.

A generalized diagram of the chain including pre- and post-processing for vertical resolution improvement is shown in Fig. 9. Following the previous example, the source and display formats could be 525/60 or 625/50 noninterlaced. Alternatively, the source and display formats could be 1050/60 or 1250/50 interlaced. This latter example has received more attention and has been the subject of much study in Europe [18], [19]. Motion-adaptive pre- and post-filtering is used.

Despite the promise of further improvements beyond the use of display scan conversion alone, subjective tests on simulations by Wendland [20] showed very little difference between the results of this approach and that of the previous section.

Taken to its limit with even higher line-scan rates for source and display, this approach offers the promise of reducing to an absolute minimum kell factor limitations from the 525- or 625-line transmission [7]. Under such circumstances, a kell factor in the region of 0.9 would apply, indicating the ratio of optimum filter bandwidth to half-sampling-frequency for a vertical sampled TV signal.

D. Compatible-Level 3: Opportunities with a MAC Signal

For the luminance component, the MAC system offers no difference with respect to composite systems in terms of vertical resolution. One feature of the system which could be used in this context, however, is the presence of a digital channel to carry digital audio and data services. This digital channel could be used to convey motion detection control information from the source to the receiver [15], [21]. This would be of particular use for the case of pre- and post-processing since it wold be desirable to have source and receiver motion detectors locked together.

For the color difference components, the MAC system in fact has inferior vertical resolution. Pre- and post-processing techniques can be used, however, to effectively change the transmitted color line structure to a better format [15], [19].

E. Noncompatible Systems

The range of techniques discussed here could equally be applied in conjunction with a noncompatible transmitted scanning structure. One example of this approach, which is reported in [22], has been called the FCFE Frame Conversion Fineness Enhance (FCFE) system. In this example, an 1125/60 interlaced source signal is first converted to an interlaced transmission format with 35 percent fewer lines (i.e., approx. 735/60). A frame store scan converter is then used to provide a noninterlaced scan display with this reduced number of lines. This is claimed to provide an equivalent quality to the original 1125-line picture while providing a 35-percent reduction in transmission bandwidth.

VI. Horizontal Resolution Improvement

We turn now to picture quality improvements in the horizontal direction.

A. Compatible-Level 1: Receiver Processing for Composite Systems

Composite systems are impeded in picture quality by cross-color (the misinterpretation by the receiver of high-frequency luminance detail as color) and cross-luminance (the misinterpretation by the receiver of color information as high-frequency luminance detail). These impose effective limitations to luminance and color difference horizontal resolution which can be reduced by improved decoding techniques. Improved decoding incorporating line-delay "comb-filters" has been known for some time [23], [24], while, more recently, processing (fixed or motion adaptive) incorporating field stores has been studied [10], [25]–[27]. The improvements potentially offered by these more complex NTSC and PAL decoding techniques are measurable, but not of very high significance in terms of the targets set in Section II. This work has been targeted at decoding both for studio applications as well as in the domestic receiver.

B. Compatible-Level 2: Pre- and Post-Processing with Composite Systems

It is fundamentally impossible to completely remove the cross-effects described above by receiver processing alone, although the use of motion-adaptive decoding can be effective in most practical cases. It is possible, however, to eliminate cross-effects altogether by a combination of improved NTSC or PAL coding and decoding. The nature of the precise subcarrier frequencies in NTSC and PAL imply a frequency offset in horizontal, vertical, and temporal frequency for the color information with reference to the luminance [28], [29]. This means that, by using digital two- or three-dimensional pre- and post-filtering for the luminance and color difference signals, it is possible to convey "clean" NTSC or PAL signals while maintaining the full horizontal resolution specification.

Furthermore improvements in horizontal resolution which are beyond those of the normal specifications for NTSC (4.2 MHz) and PAL (5–6 MHz) are possible within existing transmission bandwidths by introducing extra high frequency luminance information on a second subcarrier within the band (32). The subcarrier frequency is chosen to be essentially the same as the color subcarrier frequency, but with a shifted phase. An improvement for the luminance resolution in NTSC (certainly to 6 MHz and even up to 10 MHz) is claimed.

C. Compatible-Level 3: Approaches Based on MAC Transmission

While efforts towards compatible high-definition television in North America are tending to concentrate on NTSC-based approaches [32]–[34], in Europe the emphasis is clearly on a MAC-based approach, which offers a significantly greater flexibility in signal-processing terms.

Firstly, the absence of subcarriers for color or sound with MAC make it easier to simply widen the bandwidth of the video signal. The "basic" specification for the European MAC/packet family of systems gives a transmission video bandwidth of 8.4 MHz. This gives a decoded luminance bandwidth of 5.6 MHz (time compression factor is 1.5) and a color difference bandwidth of 2.8 MHz (time compression factor is 3). These figures in themselves represent a significant improvement over composite systems as typically received in the home. By suitable attention to the RF characteristics of a direct broadcast satellite channel, it is possible to widen the transmission video bandwidth to something in the region 10–11 MHz, which corresponds to around 7 MHz for the luminance.

Secondly, the absence of a color subcarrier with MAC enables a much greater flexibility in the use of "spectrum folding" techniques in which high-frequency luminance detail is carried on a suppressed "subcarrier" at the top of the band.

1) Spectrum-Folding Techniques: The horizontal sampling along each television line in digital processing introduces the opportunity to convey a reduced rate nonorthogonal sampling structure in a transmission channel, in order to enable transmission bandwidth efficiency. This approach can be used to convey an improved horizontal resolution in a MAC transmission channel. The same basic technique has been referred to as sub-Nyquist sampling [35], [36], offset sampling [18], 3-D filtering [37], frequency interleaved coding [38], or colloquially as "spectrum folding."

The basic concept is illustrated in one-dimensional frequency terms in Fig. 10. A television signal with bandwidth B is sampled with frequency f_s where $B = 0.4\ f_s$, say. As shown in Fig. 10(a), this represents "super-Nyquist" sampling with no spectral overlap between the baseband spectrum and those generated by the sampling process.

Assume then that half the samples are omitted to give a sampling rate of $f_s/2$. There then appears to be spectral overlap which leads to confusion (aliasing) in the signal (Fig. 10(b)). However, it is possible to apply filtering to the signal prior to subsampling which has a fine "comb" structure based on the harmonics of line and/or field or frame frequency. If the subsampling is then based on a nonorthogonal (offset) structure, it is possible to arrange that the "teeth of the comb" in the filtered spectra of the baseband and the adjacent repeats do not overlap but instead interleave, as illustrated in the expanded il-

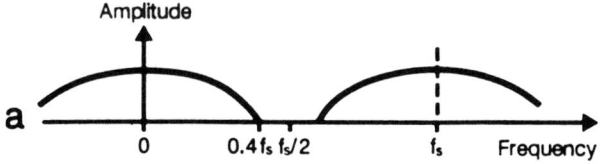
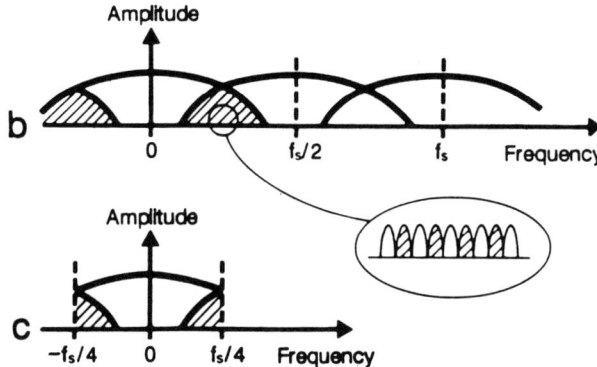

Fig. 10. A one-dimensional frequency view of spectrum folding. See text for explanation.

lustration of Fig. 10(b). In reconstruction, it is then possible to use another comb filter to restore the original comb-filtered spectrum. In this way, signal frequencies of up to $0.4\ f_s$ are conveyed by a sampling frequency of $0.5\ f_s$, appearing to violate the Nyquist limit of $0.25\ f_s$. All of the signal information can now be carried in a bandwidth of $0.25\ f_s$ (Fig. 10(c)), which represents a bandwidth saving of nearly 40 percent compared with the original $0.4\ f_s$. An infinitely sharp transmission filter with cutoff at $0.25\ f_s$ cannot be realized, but any filter which has an amplitude response of 0.5 at $0.25\ f_s$ with skew-symmetry around this point will enable accurate transmission of the samples.

The case most relevant to luminance coding for the European MAC/packet family of systems is where $f_s = 27$ MHz. The transmission "cutoff" frequency of $0.25\ f_s$ is then 6.75 MHz (-6 dB) in luminance terms, which corresponds to 10.125 MHz in MAC transmission terms. The luminance video bandwidth offered in this example is $0.4\ f_s$, which corresponds to 10.8 MHz. This approximately achieves the target for HDTV set in Section II. This improvement is merely an example. The extent to which the horizontal resolution is improved depends solely on the extent to which the spectrum is "folded back."

The limits on this are likely to be set by the visibility of this added information (the hatched region of the transmitted spectrum in Fig. 10(c)) on the simple "compatible" receiver which has no reconstruction comb filters.

Another way of viewing the process illustrated in Fig. 10 is to look at the television signal spectrum in three-dimensional terms (horizontal, vertical, and temporal frequency). This will be done by reference to an example system which was implemented in our laboratories in 1982 [39], [40].

2) An Example Using Three-Dimensional Filters and Field-Quincunx Sampling: Consider the example of Fig. 10 but viewed on axes of horizontal, vertical, and temporal frequency. The original sampled signal of Fig. 10(a) is

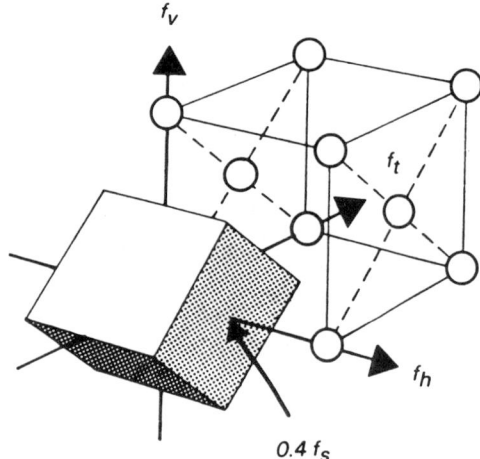

Fig. 11. The sampled television signal spectrum of Fig. 10(a) shown in three-dimensional frequency terms. The axes are horizontal frequency (f_h), vertical frequency (f_v), and temporal frequency) (f_t).

shown in Fig. 11. The block shape represents the extent of the baseband spectrum in three dimensions. The horizontal limits are set by the filtering applied with cutoff at 0.4 f_s, while the vertical/temporal boundaries are purely notional ones representing the capabilities of interlace. If the initial scanning standard had been higher, then it would have been possible to define such vertical/temporal boundaries by prefiltering. In such a case, the "diamond" shown in Fig. 11 would be merely an example of the many possible choices. The circles represent the centers of the repeat spectra generated by the image sampling.

Those displaced horizontally are due to the horizontal sampling frequency f_s, while those displayed vertically and temporally are due to the interlaced scanning. Consider now the effect of a three-dimensional "comb" filter.

A finite impulse response digital filter with 35 taps spread over a grid of 11 samples horizontally, 5 lines vertically, and 3 fields temporally was implemented with a frequency response as indicated in Fig. 12. Fig. 12(a) shows the horizontal–vertical frequency amplitude response, while Fig. 12(b) shows the horizontal–temporal frequency amplitude response. There is no filtering applied in the vertical–temporal frequency sense. The response of Fig. 12(a) indicates a loss in diagonal resolution while maintaining full horizontal resolution. The response of Fig. 12(b) indicates a loss of "temporal resolution" with high horizontal frequencies. This is difficult to interpret, and so Fig. 12(c) illustrates the horizontal frequency response of the filter as a function of motion velocity, measured in picture widths per second (pw/s).[3] The horizontal frequency axis is scaled for $f_{hs} = 6.75$ MHz (the horizontal sampling frequency after downsampling). It is seen that the horizontal bandlimiting effect of the filter is more severe as the motion velocity increases. In practice, the most significant loss noticeable (especially with TV camera pictures which are significantly temporally filtered in any

---

[3] The response is shown here within the constraints of a temporal frequency of less than 25 Hz. Beyond this frequency, the response repeats. This is not shown in the diagram for clarity.

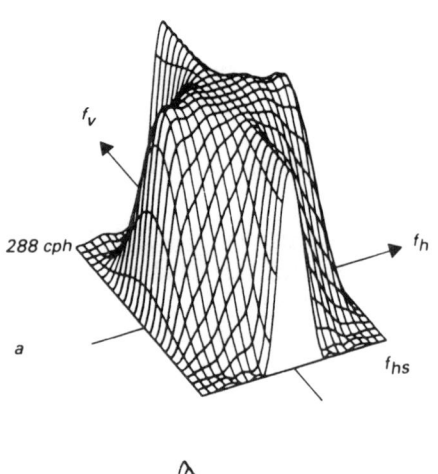
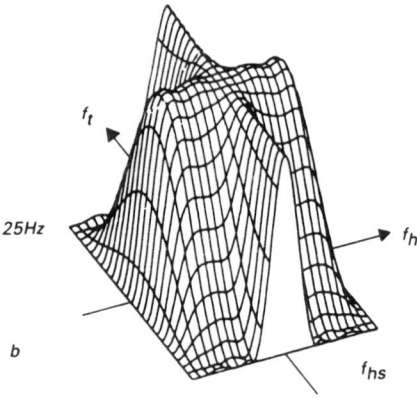
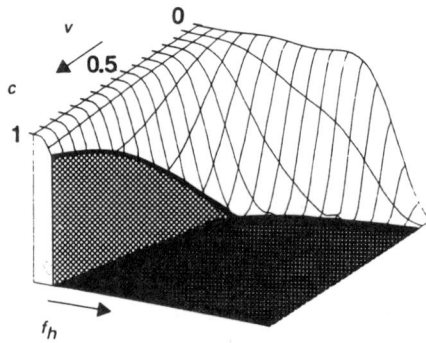

Fig. 12. Amplitude versus frequency response for a three-dimensional comb filter applied in the spectrum folding example. (a) Horizontal and vertical frequency. (b) Horizontal and temporal frequency. (c) Horizontal frequency and motion velocity.

case due to the light integration effect) is with fairly slow motion of a finely detailed image.

The effect of this filtering on the 3-D view of the baseband spectrum is indicated in Fig. 13; the "corners" are removed. If the signal is now "downsampled" by a factor of two in a particular nonorthogonal manner, then this filtered baseband spectrum is repeated on a different pattern of repeat spectra as illustrated in Fig. 14 (this is now analogous to Fig. 10(b)). The filtering is such that this shape tesselates on this pattern of repeat spectra. The "field-quincunx" nonorthogonal sampling pattern required for this is illustrated in Fig. 15.

The black squares indicate the retained samples while the white squares indicate the omitted samples from the original sampled image. The sampling frequency is now $f_s/2$ and it is possible to transmit the signal in an analog

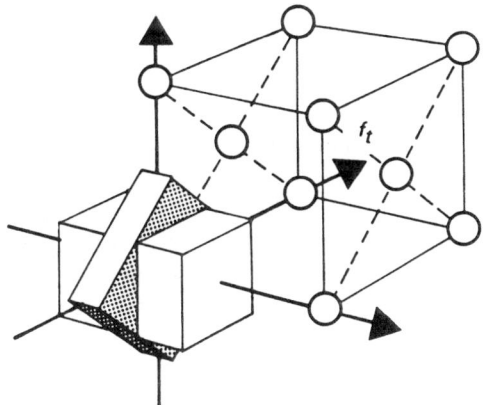

Fig. 13. The effect of the 3-D filter of Fig. 12 on the sampled television signal spectrum of Fig. 11.

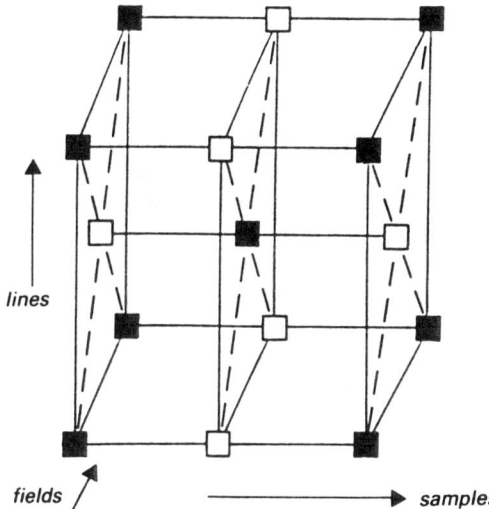

Fig. 15. A representation of the field-quincunx sampling pattern.

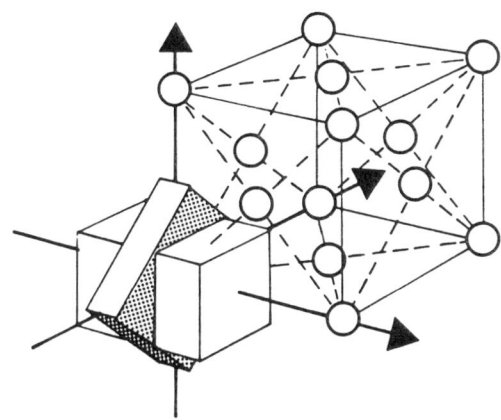

Fig. 14. Downsampling the signal of Fig. 13 (in a field-quincunx pattern) introduces extra spectral repeats. The filtered spectrum shape illustrated does not overlap its neighbors when repeated on this pattern.

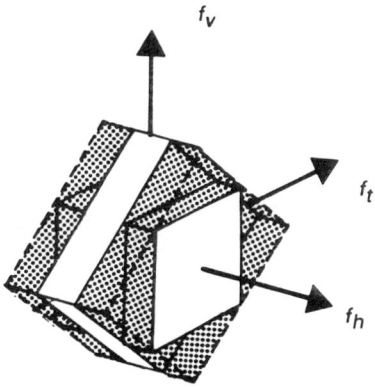

Fig. 16. The transmitted signal spectrum, analogous to Fig. 10(c).

channel of bandwidth $f_s/4$ (-6 dB). The 3-D transmitted signal spectrum is as illustrated in Fig. 16 (analgous to Fig. 10(c)). The shaded corners are now the extra horizontal resolution "folded" within the band.

At the receiver, a simple decoder will merely display the information as transmitted; the shaded corners will be spurious information. However, an improved decoder will sample the signal in a field-quincunx pattern and use a 3-D filter similar to the one at source to reconstruct the spectrum of Fig. 13, with the improved horizontal resolution.

3) Discussion: Despite the elegance of the above technique using nonadaptive 3-D filters, efforts more recently have tended to concentrate on the use of motion-adaptive filtering (19). These promise slightly improved performance but at the expense of the need for motion detection. Adaptive techniques promise to show a significant improvement in the area of motion compensation. By determining local motion velocity information, it is possible in principle to adapt the pre- and post-filtering and the downsampling pattern according to *velocity* and thus maintain more horizontal resolution with motion.

One difficulty here is in the accurate determination of motion velocity information (also known as the "optical flow" of an image). This is an area of very active research worldwide [41], both in the field of broadcast television research and also in the field of artificial intelligence (robot vision).

The opportunity offered by the digital channel in the MAC system is perhaps particularly important here. Motion velocity information can be derived at source (perhaps at great expense) and conveyed to the receiver using part of the MAC data signal (21). A second difficulty lies in determining the best use of the motion velocity information in a practical coding scheme. Typically, a scene will be divided into blocks to which a particular velocity determination is applied. It is clearly important that block boundaries are not evident in the final image.

As mentioned earlier, the major limitation of any spectrum-folding technique from a compatibility point of view is the visibility of the "spurious information" of Fig. 10(c) or Fig. 16 in the simple receiver. It can be argued that this is typically less than the dot-crawl visibility of a color subcarrier when a composite color picture is received on a monochrome TV set, but the extent to which this is tolerable for future MAC services is a matter of debate.

Because of these questions, the IBA in 1982, laid aside work on spectrum folding to concentrate on developing a "simple" system with an optimally wide-band channel [42]. Nevertheless, some form of spectrum folding is the only way in which the HDTV target of Section II of approx. 2.5× (conventional horizontal resolution) will be achieved within the appropriate channel bandwidth limitations.

D. Noncompatible Systems

Spectrum-folding techniques have also been proposed as a means of bandwidth compression for noncompatible HDTV systems. For example, the MUSE system [36] compresses an 1125/60 integrated signal with 5:3 aspect ratio into around 8 MHz by these methods. In this system, a "double downsampling" is used to reduce the sample rate of the initially sampled digital signal by 4:1. The resulting nonorthogonal sampling pattern is a line-quincunx downsampled version of a field-quincunx downsampled pattern.

Motion adaptive filtering is used with motion compensation for the special case of translatory motion for the whole scene (simple camera pans and tilts). Although there are no limits on the extent of "folding" due to compatibility constraints, it is found that it is necessary to keep the bottom 2 MHz of the transmitted spectrum "clean" to enable the receiver motion detector to function satisfactorily.

VII. Combined Horizontal–Vertical Resolution Improvement

Although the foregoing discussions on compatible systems have assumed separable improvements to vertical and to horizontal resolution, it is possible to consider an approach where both methods are combined into one. For example, the sample pattern for MUSE described above could be applied in a very similar way for a 1250-line 50-Hz system as opposed to the 1125/60 system. By "shuffling" alternate samples into a 625-line grid, it would then be possible to transmit a MUSE-type signal in a manner which is semicompatible with MAC [43]. A similar argument could apply to a 1050-line "MUSE" system transmitted on 525 lines. One variant of this concept has been proposed with NTSC compatibility [44]. Instead of the four-field MUSE sampling pattern, a six-field "Triscan" pattern is used. The benefit of these approaches is that a "true" 1250- or 1050-line signal can be transmitted on a 625- or 525-line grid. However, the price paid for the improved resolution promised is that the visibility of artifacts on a simple receiver is likely, in this case, to be greater than with most other examples of spectrum folding so far discussed.

Other methods are conceivable in which a "difference" signal is generated between a wide-band 1250-line source and a 625-line MAC signal. Such a difference signal could be coded coarsely in a digital form and sent through the MAC data channel as a horizontal–vertical resolution enhancement signal.

VIII. Nonlinear Correction and Constant Luminance

The picture quality of current composite and MAC color television systems is restricted not only by simple limitations in luminance and color horizontal and vertical resolution but also by effects resulting from the "failure of constant luminance." This means that when the transmitted luminance signal is displayed it is not a true representation of luminance perceived by the eye. Some of the "true" luminance information is in fact conveyed in the color-difference signals, which are more severely band-limited. This implies that some defects due to color band-limitation (especially with highly saturated colors) affect the perceived luminance, and are, hence, more visible. A second drawback relates to the visibility of transmission noise introduced in the color signals. For both composite and MAC signals in an FM channel (such as is used in satellite transmission or video tape recording), color noise can be more severe than luminance noise.

Since the transmitted color signals contain some true luminance content, the transmission color noise becomes visible as perceived luminance errors. This significantly affects the noise visibility.

The reason for the failure of constant luminance is twofold. The first relates to gamma-correction. The light output versus signal input characteristic of a CRT display follows an approximately exponential ("gamma") law. The approximately linear RGB signals generated by a TV camera are "gamma-corrected" at source rather than at the display for practical reasons. The color matrix which calculates the transmitted luminance and color-difference signals operates on these nonlinearly corrected signals rather than on linear versions, and, hence, the outputs do not represent true luminance and color difference in the linear domain.

The second reason relates to the use of the wrong color matrix at source, at least in Europe. The matrix values used are based on NTSC display phosphors, while the more typical PAL display phosphors give rise to a completely different matrix. Despite this, errors due to this mismatch tend to be less significant than those due to gamma-correction.

During the early days of the definition of color TV standards, there was much fundamental work on these aspects [45], [46]. More recently, work towards future improved television systems is addressing this topic again in an attempt to restore, at least partially, the constant luminance principle [47]. Noncompatible systems clearly have the advantage here, although there is still an opportunity for improvements by signal processing in a compatible manner. Most work in this area is still at an early stage. However, one technique which is established is the addition of a compensation signal to the transmitted luminance [47]. This signal is derived by modeling in the coder the receiver-eye combination and, hence, calculating the perceived luminance at the home display.

The "true" luminance is also calculated and a difference signal is generated in the gamma-corrected domain which is then added to the transmitted luminance signal. The result of this process is to effectively leave the transmitted luminance signal unaffected for frequencies within the color-difference channel passband but to send a gamma-corrected "true luminance" for frequencies outside this band. This technique can, in principle, overcome the color band-limiting deficiencies of the failure of constant luminance, but it does not affect at all the perception of transmission noise, and it does not address the errors due to incorrect matrix values. Techniques which might go some way towards offsetting these errors in a compatible way are starting to be studied, but it remains unclear whether cost-effective improvements will prove possible.

IX. Conclusions

A survey has been given covering some of the digital image-processing techniques being studied for television picture quality enhancement. The end goal for much of this work is a television picture capable of large-screen display with wide aspect ratio to give a completely different viewing experience.

The targets set at the beginning were a vertical resolution improvement of around 2:1, a horizontal resolution improvement of around 2.5:1, and a wider aspect ratio of around 5:3 (the preferred figure is now 16:9, or 5.33:3). Can these be achieved?

With composite color television signals (NTSC, PAL, SECAM) on conventional channels, improvements can certainly be made, but it is most unlikely that these targets can be reached. A particular difficulty is in the area of achieving a change to wide aspect ratio.

With MAC color television signals for satellite broadcasting, the likelihood of being able to achieve these goals in a "compatible" manner is much greater. The flexible format includes an option for dual aspect ratio. The transmission channel bandwidth is wider than for conventional terrestrial channels. The absence of a color subcarrier enables much more flexibility in possibilities with "spectrum-folding" techniques. Finally, the digital data channel enables the transmission of control information as part of the processing task.

With a noncompatible transmission standard, the limits are set only by the transmission bandwidth and it is perhaps even more likely that the targets can be met.

In the transition towards an improved television picture quality in the home, it is unclear how many stages will be passed through. One school of thought says that a "clean" 525 or 625 signal in its own right is an impressive improvement over what is currently achieved and is a sufficient target for the next few years. Another says that the next step should be a big one: immediately to large-screen wide aspect ratio with "high-definition" quality.

What is clear, however, is that digital image processing is central to either philosophy and will play an ever-increasing role in the consumer television field.

References

[1] I. Yuyama, "Large-Screen Effects," *NHK Tech. Mon.*, vol. 32, pp. 14-20, June 1982.
[2] E. van der Zee, M. H. W. A. Boesten, and A. L. Duwaer, "The influence of size constancy on the subjective evaluation of image quality," *IPO Ann. Prog. Rep.*, vol. 18, 61-66 (1983).
[3] "The present state of high definition television," CCIR (1982-1986) Interim Meet. Rep. 11/239, Draft Rep. 801-1 (MOD I).
[4] J. S. Nadan, "A glimpse into future television," *Byte*, pp. 135-150, Jan. 1985.
[5] G. J. Tonge, "Wide aspect ratio MAC," in *Proc. Third Int. Conf. on New Systems and Services in Telecoms* (Liege), Nov. 12-14, 1986, pp. 5.1-5.8.
[6] L. A. Ronningen, "The Nordic-VSLI chip set for the C/D/D2-MAC/packet receivers," in *Proc. Third Int. Conf. on New Systems and Services in Telecoms*, Nov. 12-14, 1986 pp. 5.14-5.19.
[7] G. J. Tonge, "The television scanning process," *SMPTE J.*, vol. 93(7), pp. 657-666, 1984.
[8] S. C. Hsu, "The kell factor: Past and present," *SMPTE J.*, vol. 95(2), pp. 206-214, 1986.
[9] T. Nishizawa and Y. Tanaka, "New approach to research and development of high definition television," *NHK Tech. Mon.*, vol. 32, pp. 98-101, June 1982.
[10] M. Achiha, K. Ishikura, and T. Fukinuki, "A motion adaptive high definition converter for NTSC color TV signals," in *Proc. 13th Int. TV Symp.* (Montreux), 1983.
[11] T. J. Long and G. J. Tonge, "Scan conversion for higher definition television," in *Proc. 10th Int. Broadcasting Conv.* (Brighton), Sept. 1984, pp. 116-119.
[12] D. Uhlenkamp and E. Guttner, "Improved reproduction by standard television signals," *NTZ Archiv*, vol. 4, pp. 313-321, 1982 (in German).
[13] D. W. Parker and L. G. van der Polder, "Display standards for extended definition component television signals," in *Proc. 10th Int. Broadcasting Conv.* (Brighton), Sept. 1984, pp. 120-124.
[14] A. Roberts, "The improved display of 625 line television pictures," BBC Research Dept. Rep. 1983/8.
[15] G. J. Tonge, "Signal processing for higher definition television," *IBA Tech. Rev.*, vol. 21, pp. 13-26, 1983.
[16] B. Flannaghan, "A motion detector for television applications," in *Proc. Int. Conf. on Digital Processing of Signals in Communications* (Loughborough), Apr. 1985, pp. 199-203.
[17] M. J. M. Pelgrom et al., "A digital field memory for television receivers," *IEEE Trans. Consumer Electronics*, vol. CE-29(3), Aug. 1983.
[18] B. Wendland, "High definition television studies on compatible basis with present standards," in Television Technology in the 80's, *SMPTE*, pp. 151-165, 1981.
[19] M. J. J. C. Annegarn et al., "HD-MAC: A step forward in the evolution of television technology," *Philips Tech. Rev.*, vol. 43(8), 1987.
[20] B. Wendland and H. Schroder, "Signal processing for new HQTV systems," in Television Image Quality, *SMPTE*, pp. 336-353, 1984.
[21] R. Storey, "HDTV motion adaptive bandwidth reduction using DATV," in *Proc. Eleventh Int. Broadcasting Conv.* (Brighton), Sept. 1986, pp. 167-172.
[22] "High definition television by satellite," CCIR Report 1075, XVIth Plenary Assembly, Dubrovnik, 1986.
[23] J. P. Rossi, "Colour decoding a PCM NTSC television signal," *SMPTE J.*, vol. 83(6), pp. 489-495, 1974.
[24] S. J. Auty, D. C. Read, and G. D. Roe, "Colour picture improvement using simple analogue comb filters," *BBC Engineering*, pp. 28-33, Dec. 1977.
[25] C. K. P. Clarke, "High quality decoding for PAL inputs to digital YUV studios," in *Proc. Ninth Int. Broadcasting Conv.* (Brighton), Sept. 1982, pp. 363-366.
[26] C. J. Dalton and P. A. Dixon, "The conversion of PAL signals for use in the component environment," in *Proc. Tenth Int. Broadcasting Conv.* (Brighton), Sept. 1984, pp. 64-67.
[27] D. M. Creed, "Hardware investigations into high quality digital PAL decoding and encoding for the component video environment," in *Proc. Tenth Int. Broadcasting Conv.* pp. 58-63.
[28] J. O. Drewery, "The filtering of luminance and chrominance signals to avoid cross-colour in a PAL colour system," *BBC Engineering*, pp. 8-39, Sept. 1976.
[29] E. Dubois, M. S. Sabri, and J. Y. Ouellet, "Three-dimensional spectrum and processing of digital NTSC color signals," *SMPTE J.*, vol. 91(4), pp. 372-378, 1982.
[30] Y. Faroudja and J. Roizen, "Optimizing NTSC to RGB performance," Faroudja Labs Inc., Sunnyvale, CA.
[31] E. Dubois and P. Faubert, "Two-dimensional filters for NTSC colour encoding and decoding," in *Proc. Eleventh Int. Broadcasting Conv.* (Brighton), Sept. 1986, pp. 252-255.
[32] T. Fukinuki, Y. Hirano, and H. Yoshigi, "Extended definition TV fully compatible with existing standards—Proposal and experimental results," in Television Image Quality, *SMPTE*, pp. 354-368, 1984.
[33] J. L. LoCicero, M. Pazarci, and S. Rzeszewski, "A compatible high-definition television system (SLSC) with chrominance and aspect ratio improvements," *SMPTE J.*, vol. 94(5), pp. 546-558, 1985.
[34] W. E. Glenn, "Compatible terrestrial HDTV transmission," in *1986*

NAB Engineering Conf. Proc., pp. 271–274.
[35] K. H. Barratt and K. Lucas, "An introduction to sub-nyquist sampling," *IBA Tech Rev.*, vol. 12, pp. 3–15, 1979.
[36] Y. Ninomiya, Y. Ohtusuka, and Y. Izumi, "A single channel HDTV broadcast system—The MUSE," NHK Lab. Note 304, Sept. 1984.
[37] M. D. Windram, G. J. Tonge, and R. Morcom, "MAC—A television system for high-quality satellite broadcasting," IBA Experimental and Development Report 118/82, Aug. 1982. (See Appendix E: Resolution Enhancement Techniques.)
[38] J. P. Rossi, "Reduction of bandwidth for high definition television," presented at Int. Broadcasting Symp., Tokyo, Session 2(2), Nov. 1982.
[39] G. J. Tonge, "The sampling of television images," IBA Experimental and Development Report 112/81, May 1981.
[40] G. J. Tonge, "Three dimensional filters for television sampling," IBA Experimental and Development Report 117/82, June 1982.
[41] T. S. Huang, Ed., *Image Sequence Processing and Dynamic Scene Analysis*. Berlin: Springer-Verlag, 1983.
[42] M. D. Windram, R. Morcom, and T. Hurley, "Extended definition MAC," *IBA Tech. Rev.*, vol. 21, pp. 27–41, 1983.
[43] G. De Haan and W. Crooijmans, "Subsampling techniques for high definition MAC," in *Proc. Eleventh Int. Broadcasting Conv.* (Brighton), Sept. 1986, pp. 158–162.
[44] R. J. Iredale, "A proposal for a new high definition NTSC broadcast protocol," *IEEE Trans. Consumer Electronics*, vol. CE-33, pp. 14–27, Feb. 1987.
[45] D. C. Livingston, "Colorimetric analysis of the NTSC color television system," *Proc. IRE*, vol. 42, pp. 138–150, 1954.
[46] I. J. P. James and W. A. Karwowski, "A constant luminance colour television system," *J. Brit-IRE*, vol. 23(4), pp. 297–306, 1962.
[47] R. Schafer, "High definition television production standard—An opportunity for optimal color processing," *SMPTE J.*, vol. 94(7), pp. 749–758, 1985.

Gary J. Tonge graduated from the University of Southampton with the B.Sc. degree in physical electronics in 1977 and the Ph.D. degree in applied mathematics in 1980. Since then he has worked on digital image processing for bandwidth compression and for enhanced quality television in the Independent Broadcasting Authority in Winchester, UK, where he is currently Head of Engineering Secretariat.

Chapter 6: Bibliography of Selected Additional Literature

Books

Aleksander, I., ed., *Neural Computing Architectures*, MIT Press, Cambridge, Mass., 1989.
Andrews, H.C., and B.R. Hunt, *Digital Image Restoration*, Prentice-Hall, Englewood Cliffs, N.J., 1977.
Anderson, D.Z., *Neural Information Processing Systems*, American Institute of Physics, Denver, Colo., 1988.
Anderson, J.A., and E. Rosenfeld, eds., *Neurocomputing: Foundations of Research*, MIT Press, Cambridge, Mass., 1988.
Arbib, M.A., and A.R. Hanson, *Vision, Brain, and Cooperative Computation*, MIT Press, Cambridge, Mass., 1987.
Ballard, D.H., and C. Brown, *Computer Vision*, Prentice-Hall, Englewood Cliffs, N.J., 1982.
Bates, R.H.T., and M.J. McDonnell, *Image Restoration and Reconstruction*, Oxford University Press (Clarendon), London/New York, 1986.
Baxes, G.A., *Digital Image Processing: A Practical Primer*, Prentice-Hall, Englewood Cliffs, N.J., 1985.
Beauchamp, K.G., *Applications of Walsh and Related Functions with an Introduction to Sequency Theory*, Academic Press, Inc., New York, N.Y., 1985.
Burrus, C.S., and T.W. Parks, *DFT/FFT and Convolution Algorithms*, Wiley, New York, N.Y., 1985.
Beck, J., B. Hope, and A. Rosenfeld, eds., *Human and Machine Vision*, Academic Press, Inc., New York, N.Y., 1983.
Castleman, K.R., *Digital Image Processing*, Prentice-Hall, Englewood Cliffs, N.J., 1979.
Chariglione, L., ed., *Signal Processing: Image Communication " Theory, Techniques, and Applications*, Elsevier, The Netherlands, 1989.
Chellappa, R., and A.A. Sawchuk, eds., *Digital Image Processing and Analysis " Volume 1: Digital Image Processing; Volume 2: Digital Image Analysis*, IEEE CS Press, Los Alamitos, Calif. 1985
Clarke, R.J., *Transform Coding of Images*, Academic Press, Inc., New York, N.Y., 1985.
Combes, J.M., A. Grossmann, and P.H. Tchamitchian, eds., *Wavelets*, Second Edition, Springer-Verlag, Germany, 1990.
Davies, E.R., *Machine Vision*, Academic Press, London, UK, 1990.
Denker, J.S., *Neural Networks for Computing*, American Institute of Physics, New York, N.Y., 1986.
Duda, R.O., and P.E. Hart, *Pattern Classification and Scene Analysis*, John Wiley-Interscience, New York, N.Y., 1973.
Durbeck, R.C., and S. Sherr, *Output Hardcopy Devices*, Academic Press, Boston, Mass., 1988.
Eckmiller, R., and C.V.D. Malsburg, eds., *Neural Computers*, Springer, Berlin, 1988.
Elliott, D.F., and K.R. Rao, *Fast Transforms Algorithms, Analysis, and Applications*, Academic Press, Inc., New York, N.Y., 1982.
Fu, K.S., *Digital Pattern Recognition*, Springer-Verlag, New York, N.Y., 1980.
Gonzalez, R.C., and P. Wintz, *Digital Image Processing*, Second Edition, Addison-Wesley, Reading, Mass., 1987.
Grossberg, S., *The Adaptive Brain*, Vol. 1: *Cognition, Learning, Reinforcement, and Rhythm;* Vol. 2: *Vision, Speech, Language, and Motor Control*, North-Holland, Amsterdam, 1987.
Hall, E.L., *Computer Image Processing and Recognition*, Academic Press, Inc., New York, N.Y., 1979.
Horn, B.K.P., *Robot Vision*, McGraw-Hill, New York, N.Y., 1986.
Hanson, A.R., and E.M. Riseman, eds., *Computer Vision Systems*, Academic Press, Inc., New York, N.Y., 1978.
Huang, T.S., ed., *Picture Processing and Digital Filtering*, Second Edition, Vol. 6, *Topics in Appl. Phys.*, Springer-Verlag, New York, N.Y., 1979.
Huang, T.S., ed., *Two-Dimensional Digital Signal Processing, I: Linear Filters*, Vol. 42, *Topics in Appl. Phys.*, Springer-Verlag, New York, N.Y., 1981.
Huang, T.S., ed., *Two-Dimensional Digital Signal Processing, II:Transforms and Median Filters*, Vol. 43, *Topics in Appl. Phys.*, Springer-Verlag, New York, N.Y., 1981.
Huang, T.S., ed., *Image Sequence Analysis*, Vol. 6, *Information Science*, Springer-Verlag, New York, N.Y., 1981.
Huang, T.S., *Image Reconstruction from Incomplete Observations*, JAI Press, Greenwich, Conn., 1984.
Huang, T.S., ed., *Image Enhancement and Restoration*, JAI Press, Greenwich, Conn., 1986.
Jain, A.K., *Fundamentals of Digital Image Processing*, Prentice-Hall, Englewood Cliffs, N.J., 1989.
Jayant, N.S., and P. Noll, *Digital Coding of Waveforms: Principles and Applications to Speech and Video*, Prentice-Hall, Englewood Cliffs, N.J., 1984.
Kak, A.C., and M. Slaney, eds., *Principles of Computerized Tomographic Imaging*, IEEE Press, New York, N.Y., 1988.
Kanal, L.N., and A. Rosenfeld, eds., *Progress in Pattern Recognition*, Vol. 1, North-Holland, Amsterdam, The Netherlands, 1981.
Kanal, L.N., and A. Rosenfeld, eds., *Progress in Pattern Recognition*, Vol. 2, North-Holland, Amsterdam, The Netherlands, 1981.
Koch, C., and I. Segev, eds., *Methods in Neuronal Modeling " From Synapses to Networks*, MIT Press, Cambridge, Mass., 1988.
Klimasauskas, C.C., *A Bibliography of Neurocomputing*, MIT Press, Cambridge, Mass., 1988.
Lynch, T.J., *Data Compression: Techniques and Applications*, Lifetime Learning Publications, Belmont, Calif., 1985.
Marion, A., *An Introduction to Image Processing*, Chapman and Hall, New York, N.Y., 1991.
McClelland, J.L., et al., *Parallel Distributed Processing: Explorations in the Microstructure of Cognition*, Vol. 1: *Foundations;* Vol 2: *Psychological and Biological Models*, MIT Press, Cambridge, Mass., 1986.
McClelland, J.L., and D.E. Rumelhart, *Explorations in Parallel Distributed Processing*, MIT Press, Cambridge, Mass., 1987.

Netravali, A.N., and B.G. Haskell, *Digital Pictures: Representation and Compression*, Plenum, New York, N.Y., 1988.
Niblack, W., *An Introduction to Digital Image Processing*, Strandberg, Denmark, 1985.
Nielsen, R.H., *Neurocomputing*, Addison-Wesley, Mass., 1990.
Pavlidis, T., *Structural Pattern Recognition*, Vol. 1, *Springer Series on Electrophyics*, Springer-Verlag, New York, N.Y., 1977.
Pavlidis, T., *Algorithms for Graphics and Image Processing*, Computer Science Press, Md., 1982.
Pentland, A.P., ed., *From Pixels to Predicates: Recent Advances in Computational and Robot Vision*, Ablex, Norwood, N.J., 1986.
Pratt, W.K., *Digital Image Processing*, Second Edition, John Wiley and Sons, New York, N.Y., 1991.
Pratt, W.K., ed., *Image Transmission Techniques*, Academic Press, New York, N.Y., 1979.
Rao, K.R., *Discrete Transforms and Their Applications*, Van Nostrand, New York, N.Y., 1985.
Rosenfeld, A., and A.C. Kak, *Digital Image Processing*, Vols. 1 and 2, Academic Press, New York, N.Y., 1982.
Rosenfeld, A., ed., *Digital Picture Analysis*, Vol. 2, *Topics in Applied Phyisics*, Springer-Verlag, New York, N.Y., 1976.
Rosenfeld, A., ed., *Human and Machine Vision II*, Academic Press, New York, N.Y., 1986.
Rosenfeld, A., *Picture Languages*, Academic Press, New York, N.Y., 1979.
Schalkoff, R.J., *Digital Image Processing and Computer Vision*, Wiley, New York, N.Y., 1989.
Schowengerdt, R.A., *Techniques for Image Processing and Classification in Remote Sensing*, Academic Press, New York, N.Y., 1983.
Selected Papers in Multidimensional Signal Processing, IEEE Press, New York, N.Y., 1986.
Serra, J., *Image Analysis and Mathematical Morphology*, Academic Press, New York, N.Y., 1982.
Sherr, S., *Input Devices*, Academic Press, Boston, Mass., 1988.
Stark, H., ed., *Image Recovery: Theory and Application*, Academic Press, Orlando, Fla., 1987
Touretzky, D., ed., *Advances in Neural Information Processing Systems*, Morgan Kaufmann, San Mateo, Calif., 1989.
Yaroslavsky, L.P., *Digital Picture Processing: An Introduction*, Springer, Berlin, 1985.
Young, T.Y., and K.S. Fu, eds., *Handbook of Pattern Recognition and Image Processing*, Academic Press, Orlando, Fla., 1986.
Vemuri, V., ed., *Artificial Neural Networks: Theoretical Concepts*, Computer Science Press, Rockville, Md., 1988.
Wahl, F.M., *Digital Image Signal Processing*, Artech House, Norwood, Mass., 1987.
Wasserman, P., *Neural Computing: Theory and Applications*, Van Nostrand, N.Y., 1989.
Wechsler, H., *Computational Vision*, Academic Press, New York, N.Y., 1990.

Special Periodical Issues and Sections

Artificial Neural Systems, *Computer*, Vol. 21, Mar. 1988, pp. 8-117.
Computer Analysis and Processing, *Signal Processing*, Vol. 3, July 1981, pp. 215-284.
Computer Analysis of Time-Varying Images, *Computer*, Vol. 14, Aug. 1981, pp. 1-136.
Computer Architecture for Pattern Analysis and Image Database Management, *IEEE Trans. Computers*, Vol. C-31, Oct. 1982, pp. 921-1031.
Computer Architectures, *IEEE Trans. Pattern Analysis and Machine Intelligence*, Vol. PAMI-11, Mar. 1989, pp. 225-265.
Computer Vision, *Artificial Intelligence*, Vol. 17, Aug. 1981, pp. 1-508.
Computer Vision, *Computer Vision, Graphics, and Image Processing*, Vol. 22, Apr. 1983, pp. 1-205.
Computerized Tomography, *Proc. IEEE*, Vol. 71, Mar. 1983, pp. 291-448.
Current Issues and Trends in Computer Vision (papers presented at the Third IEEE Computer Society Workshop on Computer Vision: Representation and Control), *Computer Vision, Graphics, and Image Processing*, Vol. 36, Nov.-Dec. 1986, pp. 137-391.
Digital Encoding of Graphics, *Proc. IEEE*, Vol. 68, July 1980, pp. 755-929.
Digital Image Processing and Applications, *IEEE Trans. on Circuits and Systems*, Vol. CAS-34, Nov. 1987, pp. 1261-1439.
Image Bandwidth Compression, *IEEE Trans. Communications*, Vol. COM-25, Nov. 1977, pp. 1249-1440.
Image Processing, *IEEE Trans. Automatic Control*, Vol. AC-23, Oct. 1978, pp. 800-855.
Image Processing, *Proc. IEEE*, Vol. 69, May 1981, pp. 499-657.
Industrial Machine Vision and Computer Vision Technology " Part I, *IEEE Trans. Pattern Analysis and Machine Intelligence*, Vol. PAMI-10, Jan. 1988, pp. 1-125.
Industrial Machine Vision and Computer Vision Technology " Part II, *IEEE Trans. Pattern Analysis and Machine Intelligence*, Vol. PAMI-10, May 1988, pp. 289-416.
Knowledge Based Image Analysis, *Pattern Recognition*, Vol. 17, 1984, pp. 1-176.
Multidimensional Signal Processing (Fifth MDSP Workshop, Noordwijkerjout, The Netherlands, Sept. 14-16, 1987), *Signal Processing*, Vol. SP-15(3), Oct. 1988, pp. 223-350.
Multidimensional Signal Processing " Part II, *Signal Processing*, Vol. SP-16, Jan. 1989, pp. 1-82.
Multidimensional Signal Processing in Image Analysis, *IEEE Trans. Acoustics, Speech, and Signal Processing*, Vol. ASSP-37, Dec. 1989, pp. 2006-2174.

Multiresolution Representation, *IEEE Trans. Pattern Analysis and Machine Intelligence*, Vol. PAMI-11, July 1989, pp. 673-748.
Neural Computation, *J. Complexity*, Vol. 4, Sept. 1988, pp. 175-255.
Neural Computing, *J. of Parallel and Distributed Computing*, Vol. 6, Apr. 1989, pp. 183-449.
Neural Networks, *IEEE Trans. Acoustics, Speech, and Signal Processing*, Vol. ASSP-36, July 1988, pp. 1107-1190.
Papers for the Third International Conference on Pattern Recognition, *Pattern Recognition Letters*, Vol. 4, pp. 221-314 and Sept. and Oct. 1986, pp. 317-411.
Papers from the 1978 Princeton Workshop on Pattern Recognition and Artificial Intelligence, *IEEE Trans. Pattern Analysis and Machine Intelligence*, Vol. PAMI-1, Apr. 1979, pp. 125-235.
Papers from the 1985 Alvey Computer Vision and Image Interpretation Meeting, *Image and Vision Computing*, Vol. IVC-3, Nov. 1985, pp. 145-222.
Pattern Recognition and Image Processing, *Pattern Recognition*, Vol. 12, 1980, pp. 279-347.
Pattern Recognition and Image Processing, *Proc. IEEE*, Vol. 67, May 1979, pp. 707-859.
Shape Analysis in Image Processing, *Pattern Recognition*, Vol. 13, 1981, pp. 97-187.
Special Memorial Issue for Professor King-Sun Fu, *IEEE Trans. Pattern Analysis and Machine Intelligence*, Vol. PAMI-8, May 1986, pp. 290-404.
Time-Varying Imagery, *Computer Vision, Graphics, and Image Processing*, Vol. 21, Jan.-Feb. 1983, pp. 1-304.
Visual Communication Systems, *Proc. IEEE*, Vol. 73, Apr. 1985, pp. 499-836.
Visual Motion, *IEEE Trans. Pattern Analysis and Machine Intelligence*, Vol. PAMI-11, May 1989, pp. 449-541.

Review Papers

Ahuja, N., and B. Schachter, "Image Models," *Comput. Surv.*, Vol. 13, Dec. 1981, pp. 373-397.
Andrews, H.C., "Digital Image Restoration: A Survey," *Computer*, Vol. 7, May 1974, pp. 36-45.
Andrews, H.C., "Digital Image Processing," *IEEE Spectrum*, Vol. 16, Apr. 1979, pp. 38-49.
Cannon T.M., and B.R. Hunt, "Image Processing by Computer," *Sci. Am.*, Vol. 245, Oct. 1981, pp. 214-225.
Fu, K.-S., and A. Rosenfeld, "Pattern Recognition and Image Processing," *IEEE Trans. Computers*, Vol. C-25, Dec. 1976, pp. 1336-1345.
Halel, J.A.G., and P. Satga, "Digital Image Processing," in *Pattern Recognition: Ideas in Practice*, B.G. Batchelor ed., pp. 177-202, Plenum, New York, N.Y., 1978.
Huang, T.S., "Trends in Digital Image Processing Research," in *Advances in Digital Image Processing: Theory, Application, and Implementation*, pp. 21-30, Plenum, New York, N.Y., 1979.
Huang, T.S., "Recent Advances in Picture Processing and Digital Filtering," in *Picture Processing and Digital Filtering*, T.S. Huang ed., pp. 283-292, Springer-Verlag, New York, N.Y., 1979.
Hunt, B.R., "Digital Image Processing," *Proc. IEEE*, Vol. 63, Apr. 1975, pp. 693-708.
Martin, W.N., and J.K. Aggarwal, "Survey: Dynamic Scene Analysis," *Computer Vision, Graphics, and Image Processing*, Vol. 7, June 1978, pp. 356-374.
Mersereau, R.M., and D.E. Dudgeon, "Two-Dimensional Digital Filtering," *Proc. IEEE*, Vol. 63, Apr. 1975, pp. 610-623.
Nagel, H.H., "Analysis Techniques for Image Sequences," in *Proc. Fourth Int'l Joint Conf. Pattern Recognition*, 1978, pp. 186-211.
Nagel, H.H., "Recent Advances in Motion Interpretation Based on Image Sequences," *Proc. Int'l Conf. Acoustics, Speech, and Signal Processing*, 1982, pp. 1179-1188.
Pavlidis, T., "A Review of Algorithms for Shape Analysis," *Computer Vision, Graphics, and Image Processing*, Vol. 7, Apr. 1978, pp. 243-258.
Reeves, A.R., "Parallel Computer Architectures for Image Processing," *Computer Vision, Graphics, and Image Processing*, Vol. 25, Jan. 1984, pp. 68-88.
Rosenfeld, A., "Picture Processing: 1976," *Computer Vision, Graphics, and Image Processing*, Vol. 6, Apr. 1977, pp. 157-183.
Rosenfeld, A., "Picture Processing: 1977," *Computer Vision, Graphics, and Image Processing*, Vol. 7, Apr. 1978, pp. 211-242.
Rosenfeld, A., "Recent Developments in Image and Scene Analysis," in *Machine-Aided Image Analysis*, W.E. Gardner, ed., pp. 24-69, 1978.
Rosenfeld, A., "Picture Processing: 1978," *Computer Vision, Graphics, and Image Processing*, Vol. 9, Apr. 1979, pp. 354-393.
Rosenfeld, A., "Picture Processing," in *Encyclopedia of Computer Science and Technology*, J. Belzer, A.G. Holzman, and A. Kent, eds., Vol. 12, pp. 90-110, Dekker, New York, N.Y., 1979.
Rosenfeld, A., "Image Processing and Recognition," in *Advances in Computers*, M.C. Yovitg, ed., Vol. 18, pp. 1-57, Academic Press, Inc., New York, N.Y., 1979.
Rosenfeld, A., "Picture Processing: 1979," *Computer Vision, Graphics, and Image Processing*, Vol. 13, May 1980, pp. 46-79.
Rosenfeld, A., "Picture Processing: 1980," *Computer Vision, Graphics, and Image Processing*, Vol. 16, May 1981, pp. 52-89.

Rosenfeld, A., "Picture Processing: 1981," *Computer Vision, Graphics, and Image Processing*, Vol. 19, May 1982, pp. 35-75.

Rosenfeld, A., "Picture Processing: 1982," *Computer Vision, Graphics, and Image Processing*, Vol. 22, June 1983, pp. 339-387.

Rosenfeld, A., "Picture Processing: 1983," *Computer Vision, Graphics, and Image Processing*, June 1984, pp. 347-393.

Rosenfeld, A., "Picture Processing: 1984," *Computer Vision, Graphics, and Image Processing*, Vol. 30, May 1985, pp. 189-242.

Rosenfeld, A., "Picture Processing: 1985," *Computer Vision, Graphics, and Image Processing*, Vol. 34, May 1986, pp. 204-251.

Rosenfeld, A., "Picture Processing: 1986," *Computer Vision, Graphics, and Image Processing*, Vol. 38, May 1987, pp. 147-225.

Rosenfeld, A., "Image Analysis and Computer Vision: 1987," *Computer Vision, Graphics, and Image Processing*, Vol. 42, May 1988, pp. 234-293.

Rosenfeld, A., "Image Analysis and Computer Vision: 1988," *Computer Vision, Graphics, and Image Processing*, Vol. 46, May 1989, pp. 196-264.

Rosenfeld, A., "Image Analysis and Computer Vision: 1989," *Computer Vision, Graphics, and Image Processing*, Vol. 50, May 1990, pp. 188-240.

Rosenfeld, A., "Image Analysis and Computer Vision: 1990," *Computer Vision, Graphics, and Image Processing: Image Understanding*, Vol. 53, May 1991, pp. 332-365.

Shapiro, L.G., "Data Structures for Picture Processing: A Survey," *Computer Vision, Graphics, and Image Processing*, Vol. 11, Oct. 1979, pp. 162-184.

Image Models

Chellappa, R., "Two-Dimensional Discrete Gaussian Markov Random Field Models for Image Processing," *Progress in Pattern Recognition*, Vol. 2, L.N. Kanal and A. Rosenfeld, eds., North-Holland, Amsterdam, 1985, pp. 79-112.

Conners, R.W., and C.A. Harlos, "Toward A Structural Textural Analyzer Based on Statistical Methods," *Computer Vision, Graphics, and Image Processing*, Vol. 12, Mar. 1980, pp. 224-256.

Frieden, B.R., "Statistical Models for the Image Restoration Problem," *Computer Vision, Graphics, and Image Processing*, Vol. 12, Jan. 1980, pp. 40-59.

Gagalowicz, A., and S.D. Mass, "Model Driven Synthesis of Natural Textures for 3-D Scenes," *Computers and Graphics*, Vol. 10, 1986, pp. 161-170.

Hassner, M., and J. Sklansky, "The Use of Markov Random Fields as Models of Texture," *Computer Vision, Graphics, and Image Processing*, Vol. 12, Apr. 1980, pp. 357-370.

Huang, T.S., "Mathematical Models of Graphics," *Computer Vision, Graphics, and Image Processing*, Vol. 12, Feb. 1980, pp. 127-135.

Kanal, L.N., "Markov Mesh Models," *Computer Vision, Graphics, and Image Processing*, Vol. 12, Apr. 1980, pp. 371-375.

Kashyap, R.L., R. Chellappa, and N. Ahuja, "Decision Rules for Choice of Neighbors in Random Fields Models of Images," *Computer Vision, Graphics, and Image Processing*, Vol. 15, Apr. 1981, pp. 301-318.

Kashyap, R.L., and K.B. Eom, "Robust Image Models and Their Applications," in *Advances in Electronics and Electron Physics 70*, P.W. Hawkes, ed., pp. 79-157, Academic Press, New York, N.Y., 1988.

Kube, P., and A. Pentland, "On the Imaging of Fractal Surfaces," *IEEE Trans. Pattern Analysis and Machine Intelligence*, Vol. PAMI-10, Sept. 1988, pp. 704-707.

Jain, A.K., "Partial Differential Equations and Finite-Difference Methods in Image Processing, Part 1: Image Representation," *J. Optim. Theory and Appl.*, Vol. 23, 1977, pp. 65-91.

Jain, A.K., and Angel, E., "Image Restoration, Modeling, and Reduction of Dimensionality," *IEEE Trans. Computers*, Vol. C-23, May 1974, pp. 470-476.

McClure, D.E., "Image Models in Pattern Theory," *Computer Vision, Graphics, and Image Processing*, Vol. 12, Apr. 1980, pp. 309-325.

McCormick, B.H., and S.N. Jayaramamorthy, "Time Series Model for Texture Synthesis," *Int'l. J. Inform. Sci.*, Vol. 3, Dec. 1974, pp. 329-343.

Miles, R.E., "A Survey of Geometrical Probability in the Plane with Emphasis on Stochastic Image Modeling," *Computer Vision, Graphics, and Image Processing*, Vol. 12, Jan. 1980, pp. 1-24.

Modestino, J.W., R.W. Fries, and D.G. Daut, "Generalization of the Two-Dimensional Random Checkboard Processes," *J. Opt. Soc. Am.*, Vol. 69, June 1979, pp. 897-906.

Powell, S.R., and L.M. Silverman, "Modeling of Two-Dimensional Covariance Functions with Application to Image Restoration," *IEEE Trans. Automatic Control*, Vol. AC-19, Feb. 1974, pp. 8-13.

Ranganath, S., and A.K. Jain, "Two-Dimensional Linear Prediction Models " Part I: Spectral Factorization and Realization," *IEEE Trans. Acoustics, Speech, and Signal Processing*, Vol. ASSP-33, 1985, pp. 280-299.

Schachter, B.J., "Long Crested Wave Models," *Computer Vision, Graphics, and Image Processing*, Vol. 12, Feb. 1980, pp. 187-201.

Tekalp, A.M., H. Kaufman, and J.W. Woods, "Fast Recursive Estimation of the Parameters of a Space-Varying Autoregressive Image Model," *IEEE Trans. Acoustics, Speech, and Signal Processing*, Vol. ASSP-33, Apr. 1985, pp. 469-472.

Tou, J.T., "Pictorial Feature Extraction and Recognition via Image Modeling," *Computer Vision, Graphics, and Image Processing*, Vol. 12, Apr. 1980, pp. 376-406.

Zucker, S., "Toward a Model of Texture," *Computer Vision, Graphics, and Image Processing*, Vol. 5, 1976, pp. 190-202.

Image Enhancement

Abdelmalek, N.N., "Noise Filtering in Digital Images and Approximation Theory," *Pattern Recognition*, Vol. 19, 1986, pp. 417-424.

Abramatic, J.-F., and O.D. Faugeras, "Sequential Convolution Techniques for Image Filtering," *IEEE Trans. Acoustics, Speech, and Signal Processing*, Vol. ASSP-30, Feb. 1982, pp. 1-10.

Ahmad, M.O., and D. Sundararajan, "A Fast Algorithm for Two-Dimensional Median Filtering," *IEEE Trans. Circuits and Systems*, Vol. CAS-34, Nov. 1987, pp. 1364-1374.

Arce, G.R., "Statistical Threshold Decomposition for Recursive and Nonrecursive Median Filters," *IEEE Trans. Information Theory*, Vol. IT-32, Mar. 1986, pp. 243-253.

Arce, G.R., and M.P. McLoughlin, "Theoretical Analysis of the Max/Median Filter," *IEEE Trans. Acoustics, Speech, and Signal Processing*, Vol. ASSP-35, Jan. 1987, pp. 60-69.

Arce, G.R., and N.C. Gallagher, Jr., "Stochastic Analysis for the Recursive Median Filter Process," *IEEE Trans. Information Theory*, Vol. IT-34, July 1988, pp. 669-679.

Arce, G.R., "Multistage Order Statistic Filters for Image Sequence Processing," *IEEE Trans. Signal Processing*, Vol. SP-39, May 1991, pp. 1146-1163.

Astola, J., P. Heinonen, and Y. Neuvo, "On Root Structures of Median and Median-Type Filters," *IEEE Trans. Acoustics, Speech, and Signal Processing*, Vol. ASSP-35, Aug. 1987, pp. 1199-1201.

Astola, J., and Y. Neuvo, "Optimal Median Type Filters for Exponential Noise Distributions," *Signal Processing*, Vol. 17, 1989, pp. 95-104.

Basu, A., and C.M. Brown, "Algorithms and Hardware for Efficient Image Smoothing," *Computer Vision, Graphics, and Image Processing*, Vol. 40, Nov. 1987, pp. 131-146.

Bovik, A.C., "Streaking in Median Filtered Images," *IEEE Trans. Acoustics, Speech, and Signal Processing*, Vol. ASSP-35, Apr. 1987, pp. 493-503.

Butz, A.R., "Some Properties of A Class of Rank Order Smoothers," *IEEE Trans. Acoustics, Speech, and Signal Processing*, Vol. ASSP-34, June 1986, pp. 614-615.

Cole, R., and C.K. Yap, "A Parallel Median Algorithm," *Information Processing Letters*, Vol. 20, 1985, pp. 137-139.

Coyle, E.J., "Rank Order Operators and the Mean Absolute Error Criterion," *IEEE Trans. Acoustics, Speech, and Signal Processing*, Vol. ASSP-36, Jan. 1988, pp. 63-76.

Coyle, E.J., and J.-H. Lin, "Stack Filters and the Mean Absolute Error Criterion," *IEEE Trans. Acoustics, Speech, and Signal Processing*, Vol. ASSP-36, Aug. 1988, pp. 1244-1254.

Davies, E.R., "On the Noise Suppression and Image Enhancement Characteristics of the Median, Truncated Median and Mode Filters," *Pattern Recognition Letters*, Vol. 857, 1988, pp. 87-97.

Davies, E.R., "Edge Location Shifts Produced by Median Filters: Theoretical Bounds and Experimental Results," *Signal Processing*, Vol. 16, 1989, pp. 83-96.

Fitch, J.P., E.J. Coyle, and N.C. Gallagher, Jr., "Root Properties and Convergence Rates of Median Filters," *IEEE Trans. Acoustics, Speech, and Signal Processing*, Vol. ASSP-33, Feb. 1985, pp. 230-240.

Gandhi, P.P., I. Song, and S.A. Kassam, "Nonlinear Smoothing Filters Based on Rank Estimates of Location," *IEEE Trans. Acoustics, Speech, and Signal Processing*, Vol. ASSP-37, Sept. 1989, pp. 1359-1379.

Hall, C.F., and E.L. Hall, "A Nonlinear Model for the Spatial Characteristics of the Human Visual System," *IEEE Trans. Systems, Man, and Cybernetics*, Vol. SMC-7, Mar. 1977, pp. 161-170.

Harwood, D., et al., "A New Class of Edge-Preserving Smoothing Filters," *Pattern Recognition Letters*, Vol. 6, 1987, pp. 155-162.

Heinonen, P., and Y. Neuvo, "FIR " Median Hybrid Filters," *IEEE Trans. Acoustics, Speech, and Signal Processing*, Vol. ASSP-35, June 1987, pp. 832-838.

Hodgson, R.M., et al., "Properties, Implementations and Applications of Rank Filters," *Image and Vision Computing*, Vol. 3, 1985, pp. 3-14.

Huang, T.S., "Noise Filtering in Moving Images," *Proc. IEEE Conf. Pattern Recognition and Image Processing*, IEEE CS Press, Los Alamitos, Calif., 1981, pp. 1161-1164.

Jaggernauth, J., A.C.P. Loui, and A.N. Venetsanopoulos, "Real-Time Image Processing by Disturbed Arithmetic Implementation of Two-Dimensional Digital Filters," *IEEE Trans. Acoustics, Speech, and Signal Processing*, Vol. ASSP-33, Dec. 1985, pp. 1546-1555.

Kasparis, T., and G. Eichmann, "Vector Median Filters," *Signal Processing*, Vol. 13, 1987, pp. 287-299.

Kundu, A., S.K. Mitra, and P.P. Vaidyanathan, "Application of Two-Dimensional Generalized Mean Filtering for Removal of Impulse Noises from Images," *IEEE Trans. Acoustics, Speech, and Signal Processing*, Vol. ASSP-32, June 1984, pp. 600-609.

Kundu, A., and W.-R. Wu, "Double-Window Hodges-Lehman (D) Filter and Hybrid *D*-Median Filter for Robust Image Smoothing," *IEEE Trans. Acoustics, Speech, and Signal Processing*, Vol. ASSP-37, Aug. 1989, pp. 1293-1298.

Kutka, R., "A Variable Median Filter for Image Restoration Adaptable to Different Types of Spike Noise," *Signal Processing*, Vol. 18, 1989, pp. 217-224.

Lee, Y.H., and A.T. Fam, "An Edge Gradient Enhancing Adaptive Order Statistic Filter," *IEEE Trans. Acoustics, Speech, and Signal Processing*, Vol. ASSP-35, May 1987, pp. 680-695.

Lee, Y.H., and S.A. Kassam, "Generalized Median Filtering and Related Nonlinear Filtering Techniques," *IEEE Trans. Acoustics, Speech, and Signal Processing*, Vol. ASSP-33, June 1985, pp. 672-683.

Leszczynski, K.W., and S. Shalev, "A Robust Algorithm for Contrast Enhancement by Local Histogram Modification," *Image and Vision Computing*, Vol. 7, 1989, pp. 205-209.

Li, H., and H.S. Yang, "Fast and Reliable Image Enhancement Using Fuzzy Relaxation Technique," *IEEE Trans. Systems, Man, and Cybernetics*, Vol. SMC-19, 1989, pp. 1276-1281.

Liao, G.Y., T.A. Nodes, and N.C. Gallagher, Jr., "Output Distributions of Two-Dimensional Median Filters," *IEEE Trans. Acoustics, Speech, and Signal Processing*, Vol. ASSP-33, Oct. 1985, pp. 1280-1295.

Lynch, D.K., "Range Image Enhancement via One-Dimensional Spatial Filtering," *Computer Vision, Graphics, and Image Processing*, Vol. 15, Feb. 1981, pp. 194-200.

Mastin, G.A., "Adaptive Filters for Digital Image Noise Smoothing: An Evaluation," *Computer Vision, Graphics, and Image Processing*, Vol. 31, July 1985, pp. 103-121.

McLoughlin, M.P., and G.R. Arce, "Deterministic Properties of the Recursive Separable Median Filter," *IEEE Trans. Acoustics, Speech, and Signal Processing*, Vol. ASSP-35, Jan. 1987, pp. 98-106.

Mitra, S.K., and T.-H. Yu, "Transform Amplitude Sharpening: A New Method of Image Enhancement," *Computer Vision, Graphics, and Image Processing*, Vol. 40, Nov. 1987, pp. 205-218.

Mueller, P.F., and G.O. Reynolds, "Image Restoration by Removal of Random-Media Degradations," *J. Opt. Soc. Am.*, Vol. 57, Nov. 1967, pp. 1338-1344.

Naaman, L., and A.C. Bovik, "Least-Squares Order Statistic Filters with Coefficient Censoring," *Signal Processing*, Vol. 16, 1989, pp. 139-153.

Nagao, M., and T. Matsuyama, "Edge Preserving Smoothing," *Computer Vision, Graphics, and Image Processing*, Vol. 9, Apr. 1979, pp. 394-407.

Nahi, N.E., "Role of Recursive Estimation in Statistical Image Enhancement," *Proc. IEEE*, Vol. 60, July 1972, pp. 872-877.

Nahi, N.E., and A. Habibi, "Decision-Directed Recursive Image Enhancement," *IEEE Trans. Circuits and Systems*, Vol. CAS-22, Mar. 1975, pp. 286-293.

Narendra, P.M., and R.C. Fitch, "Real-Time Adaptive Contrast Enhancement," *IEEE Trans. Pattern Analysis and Machine Intelligence*, Vol. PAMI-3, Nov. 1981, pp. 655-661.

Nieminen, A., P. Heinonen, and Y. Neuvo, "A New Class of Detail-Preserving Filters for Image Processing," *IEEE Trans. Pattern Analysis and Machine Intelligence*, Vol. PAMI-9, 1987, pp. 74-90.

Oflazer, K., "Design and Implementation of a Single-Chip 1-D Median Filter," *IEEE Trans. Acoustics, Speech, and Signal Processing*, Vol. ASSP-31, Oct. 1983, pp. 1164-1168.

Palmieri, F., and C.G. Boncelet, Jr., "*L1* Filters: A New Class of Order Statistic Filters," *IEEE Trans. Acoustics, Speech, and Signal Processing*, Vol. ASSP-37, May 1989, pp. 691-701.

Peleg, S., "Iterative Histogram Modification, 2," *IEEE Trans. Systems, Man, and Cybernetics*, Vol. SMC-8, July 1978, pp. 555-556.

Perlman, S.S., et al., "Adaptive Median Filtering for Impulse Noise Elimination in Real-Time TV Signals," *IEEE Trans. Communications*, Vol. COM-35, June 1987, pp. 646-652.

Peterson, S.R., Y.H. Lee, and S.A. Kassam, "Some Statistical Properties of Alpha-Trimmed Mean and Standard Type *M* Filters," *IEEE Trans. Acoustics, Speech, and Signal Processing*, Vol. ASSP-36, May 1988, pp. 707-713.

Pitas, I., "Study of the Computational Complexity of Algorithms in Multidimensional Digital Signal Processing," *Signal Processing*, Vol. 9, 1985, pp. 142-143.

Pitas, I., and A.N. Venetsanopoulos, "Nonlinear Order Statistic Filters for Image Filtering and Edge Detection," *Signal Processing*, Vol. 10, 1986, pp. 395-413.

Rabbani, M., "Bayesian Filtering of Poisson Noise Using Local Statistics," *IEEE Trans. Acoustics, Speech, and Signal Processing*, Vol. ASSP-35, Aug. 1988, pp. 1326-1337.

Ranade, S., and M. Shneier, "Using Quadtrees to Smooth Imáges," *Proc. IEEE Conf. Pattern Recognition and Image Processing*, IEEE CS Press, Los Alamitos, Calif., 1981, pp. 812-816.

Rao, V.V.B., and K.S. Rao, "A New Algorithm for Real-Time Median Filtering," *IEEE Trans. Acoustics, Speech, and Signal Processing*, Vol. ASSP-34, Dec. 1986, pp. 1674-1675.

Rosenfeld, A., and L.S. Davis, "Iterative Histogram Modification," *IEEE Trans. Systems, Man, and Cybernetics*, Vol. SMC-8, Apr. 1978, pp. 300-302.

Scher, A., F.R.D. Velasco, and A. Rosenfeld, "Some New Image Smoothing Techniques," *IEEE Trans. Systems, Man, and Cybernetics*, Vol. SMC-10, Mar. 1980, pp. 153-158.

Schreiber, W.F., "Image Processing for Quality Improvement," *Proc. IEEE*, Vol. 66, Dec. 1978, pp. 1640-1651.

Tagare, H.D., and R.J.P. De Figueuiredo, "Order Filters," *Proc. IEEE*, Vol. 73, Jan. 1985, pp. 163-165.

Vainio, O., Y. Neuvo, and S.E. Butner, "A Signal Processor for Median-Based Algorithms," *IEEE Trans. Acoustics, Speech, and Signal Processing*, Vol. ASSP-37, Sept. 1989, pp. 1406-1414.

Wampler, J.E., "Enhancing Real-Time Perception of Quantum Limited Images from a Doubly Intensified SIT Camera System," *Computer Vision, Graphics, and Image Processing*, Vol. 32, Nov. 1985, pp. 208-220.

Image Restoration

Aboutalib, A.O., and L.M. Silverman, "Restoration of Motion Degraded Images," *IEEE Trans. Circuits and Systems*, Vol. CAS-22, Mar. 1975, pp. 278-286.

Aboutalib, A.O., M.S. Murphy, and L.M. Silverman, "Digital Restoration of Images Degraded by General Motion Blurs," *IEEE Trans. Automatic Control*, Vol. AC-22, June 1977, pp. 294-302.

Anderson, B.D.O., and E.I. Jury, "Stability Test for Two-Dimensional Recursive Filters," *IEEE Trans. Audio Electroacoust.*, Vol. AU-21, Aug. 1973, pp. 366-372.

Anderson, G.L., and A.N. Netravali, "Image Restoration Based on a Subjective Criterion," *IEEE Trans. Systems, Man, and Cybernetics*, Vol. SMC-6, Dec. 1976, pp. 845-853.

Arce, G.R., and M.P. McLoughlin, "Theoretical Analysis of the Max/Median Filter," *IEEE Trans. Acoustics, Speech, and Signal Processing*, Vol. ASSP-35, Jan. 1987, pp. 60-69.

Astola, J., and Y. Neuvo, "Optimal Median Type Filters for Exponential Noise Distributions," *Signal Processing*, Vol. 17, 1989, pp. 95-104.

Basu, A., and C.M. Brown, "Algorithms and Hardware for Efficient Image Smoothing," *Computer Vision, Graphics, and Image Processing*, Vol. 40, Nov. 1987, pp. 131-146.

Biemond, J., J. Rieske, and J.J. Gerbrands, "A Fast Kalman Filter for Images Degraded by Both Blur and Noise," *IEEE Trans. Acoustics, Speech, and Signal Processing*, Vol. ASSP-31, Oct. 1983, pp. 1248-1256.

Boutalis, Y.S., D.S. Kollias, and G. Carayannis, "A Fast Multichannel Approach to Adaptive Image Estimation," *IEEE Trans. Acoustics, Speech, and Signal Processing*, Vol. ASSP-37, July 1989, pp. 1090-1098.

Bovik, A.C., "Streaking in Median Filtered Images," *IEEE Trans. Acoustics, Speech, and Signal Processing*, Vol. ASSP-35, Apr. 1987, pp. 493-503.

Bovik, A.C., T.S. Huang, and D.C. Munson, Jr., "Edge-Sensitive Image Restoration Using Order-Constrained Least Squares Methods," *IEEE Trans. Acoustics, Speech, and Signal Processing*, Vol. ASSP-33, Oct. 1985, pp. 1253-1263.

Bracewell, R.N., "An Imaging Problem: Restoration of Blurred Digital Characters," *Computer Vision, Graphics, and Image Processing*, Vol. 29, Mar. 1985, pp. 329-335.

Chan, P., and J.S. Lim, "One-Dimesional Processing for Adaptive Image Restoration," *IEEE Trans. Acoustics, Speech, and Signal Processing*, Vol. ASSP-33, Feb. 1985, pp. 117-126.

Chang, L.-W., and K.-L. Leu, "A Fast Algorithm for the Restoration of Images Based on Chain Codes Description and Its Applications," *Computer Vision, Graphics, and Image Processing*, Vol. 50, June 1990, pp. 296-307.

Combettes, P.L., and H.J. Trussell, "Methods for Digital Restoration of Signals Degraded by a Stochastic Impulse Response," *IEEE Trans. Acoustics, Speech, and Signal Processing*, Vol. ASSP-37, Mar. 1989, pp. 393-401.

Davies, E.R., "Edge Location Shifts Produced by Median Filters: Theoretical Bounds and Experimental Results," *Signal Processing*, Vol. 16, 1989, pp. 83-96.

Deekshatulu, B.L., "Quantitative Evaluation of Enhancement Techniques," *Signal Processing*, Vol. 8, 1985, pp. 369-375.

Dudgeon, D.E., "Two-Dimensional Recursive Filter Design Using Differential Correction," *IEEE Trans. Acoustics, Speech, and Signal Processing*, Vol. ASSP-23, June 1975, pp. 264-267.

Frieden, B.R., "Restoring with Maximum Likelihood and Maximum Entropy," *J. Opt. Soc. Am.*, Vol. 62, Apr. 1972, pp. 511-518.

Galatsanos, N.P., and R.T. Chin, "Digital Restoration of Multichannel Images," *IEEE Trans. Acoustics, Speech, and Signal Processing*, Vol. ASSP-37, Mar. 1989, pp. 415-421.

Habibi, A., "Fast Suboptimal Wiener Filtering of Markov Sequences," *IEEE Trans. Computers*, Vol. C-26, May 1977, pp. 443-449.

Harris, J.L., Sr., "Image Evaluation and Restoration," *J. Opt. Soc. Am.*, Vol. 56, May 1966, pp. 569-574.

Harwood, D., et al., "A New Class of Edge-Preserving Smoothing Filters," *Pattern Recognition Letters*, Vol. 6, 1987, pp. 155-162.

Helstrom, C.W., "Image Restoration by the Method of Least Squares," *J. Opt. Soc. Am.*, Vol. 57, Mar. 1967, pp. 297-303.

Hentea, T., and B.E.A. Saleh, "Image Restoration Utilizing Spatial Masking of the Visual System," *IEEE Trans. Systems, Man, and Cybernetics*, Vol. SMC-8, Dec. 1978, pp. 883-888.

Hou, H.S., and H.C. Andrews, "Least Squares Image Restoration Using Spline Basis Functions," *IEEE Trans. Computers*, Vol. C-26, Sept. 1977, pp. 856-873.

Huang, T.S., and P.M. Narendra, "Image Restoration by Singular Value Decomposition," *Appl. Opt.*, Vol. 14, Sept. 1975, pp. 2213-2216.

Huang, T.S., D.S. Barker, and S.P. Berger, "Iterative Image Restoration," *Appl. Opt.*, Vol. 14, May 1975, pp. 1165-1168.

Hummel, R.A., B. Kimia, and S.W. Zucker, "Deblurring Gaussian Blur," *Computer Vision, Graphics, and Image Processing*, Vol. 38, Apr. 1987, pp. 66-80.

Hunt, B.R., "The Application of Constrained Least Squares Estimation to Image Restoration by Digital Computer," *IEEE Trans. Computers*, Vol. C-22, Sept. 1973, pp. 805-812.

Hunt, B.R., and O. Kubler, "Karhunen-Loeve Multispectral Image Restoration, Part 1: Theory," *IEEE Trans. Acoustics, Speech, and Signal Processing*, Vol. ASSP-32, June 1984, pp. 592-600.

Jain, A.K., "A Semicausal Model for Recursive Filtering of Two-Dimensional Images," *IEEE Trans. Computers*, Vol. C-26, Apr. 1977, pp. 343-350.

Jeng, F.-C. and J.W. Woods, "Inhomogeneous Gaussian Image Models for Estimation and Restoration," *IEEE Trans. Acoustics, Speech, and Signal Processing*, Vol. ASSP-36, Aug 1988, pp. 1305–1312.

Karayiannis, N.B., and A.N. Venetsanopoulos, "Regularization Theory in Image Restoration: The Stabilizing Functional Approach," *IEEE Trans. Acoustics, Speech, and Signal Processing*, Vol. ASSP-38, July 1990, pp. 1155-1179.

Kasturi, R., J.F. Walkup, and T.F. Krile, "Adaptive Point Estimation in Signal-Dependent Noise," *IEEE Trans. Systems, Man, and Cybernetics*, Vol. SMC-15, May/June 1985, pp. 352-359.

Katsaggelos, A.K., et al., "A Regularized Iterative Image Restoration Algorithm," *IEEE Trans. Signal Processing*, Vol. SP-39, Apr. 1991, pp. 914-929.

Kaufman, H., et al., "Estimation and Identification of Two-Dimensional Images," *IEEE Trans. Automatic Control*, Vol. AC-28, July 1983, pp. 745-756.

Kim, H.M., and N.K. Bose, "Approaches Toward Restoration of Bilinearly Degraded Images," *IEEE Trans. Acoustics, Speech, and Signal Processing*, Vol. ASSP-35, Feb. 1987, pp. 181-197.

Ku, F.-N., and J.-M. Hu, "A New Approach to the Restoration of an Image Blurred by a Linear Uniform Motion," *Computer Vision, Graphics, and Image Processing*, Vol. 34, Apr. 1986, pp. 20-34.

Kutka, R., "A Variable Median Filter for Image Restoration Adaptable to Different Types of Spike Noise," *Signal Processing*, Vol. 18, 1989, pp. 217-224.

Lagendijk, R.L., J. Biemond, and D.E. Boekee, "Regularized Iterative Image Restoration with Ringing Reduction," *IEEE Trans. Acoustics, Speech, and Signal Processing*, Vol. ASSP-38, July 1990, pp. 1180-1191.

Lagendijk, R.L., J. Biemond, and D.E. Boekee, "Identification and Restoration of Noisy Blurred Images Using the Expectation-Maximization Algorithm," *IEEE Trans. Acoustics, Speech, and Signal Processing*, Vol. ASSP-36, Aug. 1988, pp. 1313-1325.

Leahy, R.M., and C.E. Goutis, "An Optimal Technique for Constraint-Based Image Restoration and Reconstruction," *IEEE Trans. Acoustics, Speech, and Signal Processing*, Vol. ASSP-34, Dec. 1986, pp. 1629-1642.

Lim, J.S., "Image Restoration by Short Space Spectral Subtraction," *IEEE Trans. Acoustics, Speech, and Signal Processing*, Vol. ASSP-28, Apr. 1980, pp. 191-197.

Liu, Z.-Q., and T. Caelli, "A Sequential Adaptive Recursive Filter for Image Restoration," *Computer Vision, Graphics, and Image Processing*, Vol. 44, Dec. 1988, pp. 332-349.

MacAdam, D.P., "Digital Image Restoration by Constrained Deconvolution," *J. Opt. Soc. Am.*, Vol. 60, Dec. 1970, pp. 1617-1627.

Mahalanabis, A.K., and K. Xue, "An Efficient Two-Dimensional Chandrasekhar Filter for Restoration of Images Degraded by Spatial Blur and Noise," *IEEE Trans. Acoustics, Speech, and Signal Processing*, Vol. ASSP-35, Nov. 1987, pp. 1603-1610.

Naaman, L., and A.C. Bovik, "Least-Squares Order Statistic Filters with Coefficient Censoring," *Signal Processing*, Vol. 18, 1989, pp. 139-152.

O'Connor, B.T., and T.S. Huang, "Application of Phase Unwrapping to Image Restoration," *Computer Vision, Graphics, and Image Processing*, Vol. 32, June 1984, pp. 592-600.

Oja, E., and H. Ogawa, "Parametric Projection Filter for Image and Signal Restoration," *IEEE Trans. Acoustics, Speech, and Signal Processing*, Vol. ASSP-34, Dec. 1986, pp. 1643-1653.

Oppenheim, A.V., R.W. Schafer, and T.G. Stockham, Jr., "Nonlinear Filtering of Multiplied and Convolved Signals," *Proc. IEEE*, Vol. 56, Aug. 1968, pp. 1264-1291.

Ostrem, J.S., "Homomorphic Filtering of Specular Scenes," *IEEE Trans. Systems, Man, and Cybernetics*, Vol. SMC-11, May 1981, pp. 385-387.

Papoulis, A., "Approximations of Point Spreads for Deconvolution," *J. Opt. Soc. Am.*, Vol. 62, Jan. 1972, pp. 77-80.

Perlman, S.S., et al., "Adaptive Median Filtering for Impulse Noise Elimination in Real-Time TV Signals," *IEEE Trans. Communications*, Vol. COM-35, June 1987, pp. 646-652.

Peyrovian, M.J., and A.A. Sawchuk, "Image Restoration by Spline Functions," *Appl. Opt.*, Vol. 17, Feb. 1978, pp. 660-666.

Pratt, W.K., "Generalized Weiner Filtering Computation Techniques," *IEEE Trans. Computers*, Vol. C-21, July 1972, pp. 636-641.

Rajala, S.A., and R.J.P. De Figueiredo, "Adaptive Nonlinear Image Restoration by Modified Kalman Filtering Approach," *IEEE Trans. Acoustics, Speech, and Signal Processing*, Vol. ASSP-29, Oct. 1981, pp. 1033-1042.

Restrepo, A., and A.C. Bovik, "Adaptive Trimmed Mean Filters for Image Restoration," *IEEE Trans. Acoustics, Speech, and Signal Processing*, Vol. ASSP-36, Aug. 1988, pp. 1326-1337.

Robbins, G.M., and T.S. Huang, "Inverse Filtering for Linear Shift-Variant Imaging Systems," *Proc. IEEE*, Vol. 60, July 1972, pp. 862-872.

Sanz, J.L.C., and T.S. Huang, "A Unified Approach to Noniterative Linear Signal Restoration," *IEEE Trans. Acoustics, Speech, and Signal Processing*, Vol. ASSP-32, Apr. 1984, pp. 403-409.

Schafer, R.W., R.M. Mersereau, and M.A. Richards, "Constrained Iterative Restoration Algorithms," *Proc. IEEE*, Vol. 69, Apr. 1981, pp. 432-450.

Singh, S., S.N. Tandon, and H.M. Gupta, "An Iterative Restoration Technique," *Signal Processing*, Vol. 11, 1986, pp. 1-11.

Stockham, T.G., Jr., T.M. Cannon, and R.B. Ingebretsen, "Blind Deconvolution Through Digital Signal Processing," *Proc. IEEE*, Vol. 63, Apr. 1975, pp. 678-692.

Tekalp, A.M., H. Kaufman, and J.W. Woods, "Identification of Image and Blur Parameters for the Restoration of Noncausal Blur," *IEEE Trans. Acoustics, Speech, and Signal Processing*, Vol. ASSP-34, Aug. 1986, pp. 963-972.

Tekalp, A.M., and H. Kaufman, "On Statistical Identification of a Class of Linear Space-Invariant Image Blurs Using Non-Minimum-Phase ARMA Models," *IEEE Trans. Acoustics, Speech, and Signal Processing*, Vol. ASSP-36, Aug. 1988, pp. 1360-1363.

Trussell, H.J., and B.R. Hunt, "Sectioned Methods for Image Restoration," *IEEE Trans. Acoustics, Speech, and Signal Processing*, Vol. ASSP-26, Apr. 1978, pp. 157-164.

Trussell, H.J., and B.R. Hunt, "Improved Methods of Maximum *A Posteriori* Restoration," *IEEE Trans. Computers*, Vol. C-28, Jan. 1979, pp. 57-62.

Trussell, H.J., "The Relationship Between Image Restoration by the Maximum *A Posteriori* Method and a Maximum Entropy Method," *IEEE Trans. Acoustics, Speech, and Signal Processing*, Vol. ASSP-28, Feb. 1980, pp. 114-117.

Trussell, H.J., "Convergence Criteria for Iterative Restoration Methods," *IEEE Trans. Acoustics, Speech, and Signal Processing*, Vol. ASSP-31, Feb. 1983, pp. 129-136.

Trussell, H.J., and M.R. Civanlar, "The Feasible Solution in Signal Restoration," *IEEE Trans. Acoustics, Speech, and Signal Processing*, Vol. ASSP-31, Apr. 1984, pp. 201-212.

Tugnait, J.K., "Constrained Signal Restoration via Iterated Extended Kalman Filtering," *IEEE Trans. Acoustics, Speech, and Signal Processing*, Vol. ASSP-33, Apr. 1985, pp. 472-475.

Wolberg, G., and Pavlidis, T., "Restoration of Binary Images Using Stochastic Relaxation with Annealing," *Pattern Recognition Letters*, Vol. 3, 1985, pp. 375-388.

Woods, J.W., S. Dravida, and R. Mediavilla, "Image Estimation Using Doubly Stochastic Gaussian Random Field Models," *IEEE Trans. Pattern Analysis and Machine Intelligence*, Vol. PAMI-9, Mar. 1987, pp. 245-253.

Wu, Z., "Multidimensional State-Space Model Kalman Filtering with Application to Image Restoration," *IEEE Trans. Acoustics, Speech, and Signal Processing*, Vol. ASSP-33, Dec. 1985, pp. 1576-1592.

Image Data Compression

Algazi, V.R., and J.T. DeWitte, Jr., "Theoretical Performance of Entropy-Encoded DPCM," *IEEE Trans. Communications*, Vol. COM-30, May 1982, pp. 1088-1095.

Anastassiou, D., W.B. Pennebaker, and J.L. Mitchell, "Gray-Scale Image Coding for Freeze-Frame Videoconferencing," *IEEE Trans. Communications*, Vol. COM-34, Apr. 1986, pp. 382-394.

Arce, G.R., and N.C. Gallagher, Jr., "BTC Image Coding Using Median Filter Roots," *IEEE Trans. Communications*, Vol. COM-31, June 1983, pp. 784-793.

Bowling, C.D., and R.A. Jones, "Motion Compensated Image Coding with a Combined Maximum *A Posteriori* and Regression Algorithm," *IEEE Trans. Communications*, Vol. COM-33, Aug. 1985, pp. 844-857.

Bourbakis, N.G., and A. Klinger, "A Hierarchical Picture Coding Scheme," *Pattern Recognition*, Vol. 22, 1989, pp. 317-329.

Brainard, R.C., and A. Puri, "Compact Coder for Component Color Television," *IEEE Trans. Communications*, Vol. COM-38, Feb. 1990, pp. 223-232.

Cafforio, C., F. Rocca, and S. Tubaro, "Motion Compensated Image Interpolation," *IEEE Trans. Communications*, Vol. COM-38, Feb. 1990, pp. 215-222.

Chang, P.-C., and R.M. Gray, "Gradient Algorithms for Designing Predictive Vector Quantizers," *IEEE Trans. Acoustics, Speech, and Signal Processing*, Vol. ASSP-34, Aug. 1986, pp. 679-690.

Chen, T.-C., "A Lattice Vector Quantization Using A Geometric Decomposition," *IEEE Trans. Communications*, Vol. COM-38, May 1990, pp. 704-714.

Davisson, L.D., "Rate-Distortion Theory and Applications" *Proc. IEEE*, Vol. 60, July 1972, pp. 800-808.

Dubois, E., and J.L. Moncet, "Encoding and Progressive Transmission of Still Pictures in NTSC Composite Format Using Transform Domain Methods," *IEEE Trans. Communications*, Vol. COM-34, Mar. 1986, pp. 310-319.

Eggerton, J.D., and M.D. Srinath, "A Visually Weighted Quantization Scheme for Image Bandwidth Compression at Low Data Rates," *IEEE Trans. Communications*, Vol. COM-34, Aug. 1986, pp. 840-847.

Ericsson, S., "Fixed and Adaptive Predictors for Hybrid Predictive/Transform Coding," *IEEE Trans. Communications*, Vol. COM-33, Dec. 1985, pp. 1291-1302.

Ersoy, P.K., and C.H. Chen, "Transform-Coding of Images with Reduced Complexity," *Computer Vision, Graphics, and Image Processing*, Vol. 42, Apr. 1988, pp. 19-31.

Farrelle, P.M., and A.K. Jain, "Recursive Block Coding: A New Approach to Transform Coding," *IEEE Trans. Communications*, Vol. COM-34, Feb. 1986, pp. 161-179.

Farvardin, N., and J.W. Modestino, "Rate-Distortion Performance of DPCM Schemes for Autoregressive Sources," *IEEE Trans. Information Theory*, IT-31, May 1985, pp. 402-418.

Farvardin, N., and J.W. Modestino, "Adaptive Buffer-Instrumented Entropy-Coded Quantizer Performance for Memoryless Sources," *IEEE Trans. Information Theory*, Vol. IT-32, Jan. 1986, pp. 9-22.

Fischer, T.R., "A Pyramid Vector Quantizer," *IEEE Trans. Information Theory*, Vol. IT-32, July 1986, pp. 568-583.

Freeman, H., "On the Encoding of Arbitrary Geometric Configurations," *IRE Trans. Electron. Comput.*, Vol. EC-10, June 1961, pp. 260-268.

Gonzales-Smith, M.E., and J.A. Storer, "Parallel Algorithms for Data Compression," *J. ACM*, Vol. 32, 1985, pp. 344-373.

Goldberg, M., and H. Sun, "Image Sequence Coding Using Vector Quantization," *IEEE Trans. Communications*, Vol. COM-34, July 1986, pp. 703-710.

Goldberg, M., P.R. Boucher, and S. Shlien, "Image Compression Using Adaptive Vector Quantization," *IEEE Trans. Communications*, Vol. COM-34, Feb. 1986, pp. 180-187.

Goldberg, M., and L. Wang, "Comparative Performance of Pyramid Data Structures for Progressive Image Transmission," *IEEE Trans. Communications*, Vol. C-39, Apr. 1991, pp. 540-548.

Grenez, F., "Chebyshev Design of Filters for Subband Coders," *IEEE Trans. Acoustics, Speech, and Signal Processing*, Vol. ASSP-35, Feb. 1988, pp. 182-185.

Habibi, A., "Comparison of the nth-Order DPCM Encoder with Linear Transformations and Block Quantization Techniques," *IEEE Trans. Communications Tech.*, Vol. COM-19, Dec. 1971, pp. 948-956.

Habibi, A., "Hybrid Coding of Pictorial Data," *IEEE Trans. Communications*, Vol. COM-22, May 1974, pp. 614-624.

Habibi, A., "An Adaptive Strategy for Hybrid Image Coding," *IEEE Trans. Communications*, Vol. COM-29, Dec. 1981, pp. 1736-1740.

Hang, H.-M., and J.W. Woods, "Predictive Vector Quantization of Images," *IEEE Trans. Communications*, Vol. COM-33, Nov. 1985, pp. 1208-1219.

Haskell, B.G., "Semicompatible High Definition Television Using Field Differential Signals," *IEEE Trans. Communications*, Vol. COM-34, Oct. 1986, pp. 1031-1037.

Hofmann, W.D., and D.E. Troxel, "Making Progressive Transmission Adaptive," *IEEE Trans. Communications*, Vol. COM-34, Aug. 1986, pp. 806-813.

Huang, J.J.Y., and P.M. Schultheiss, "Block Quantization of Correlated Gaussian Random Variables," *IEEE Trans. Communications Syst.*, Vol. CS-11, Sept. 1963, pp. 289-296.

Hwang, C.J., and K.R. Rao, "Channel Error Propagation in Adaptive TV Coders," *Signal Processing*, Vol. SP-10, 1986, pp. 171-183.

Ikonomopoulos, A., and M. Kunt, "High Compression Image Coding via Directional Filtering," *Signal Processing*, Vol. 8, 1985, pp. 179-203.

Johnsen, O., and A.N. Netravali, "Progressive Transmission of Two-Tone Images," *IEEE Trans. Communications*, Vol. COM-29, Dec. 1981, pp. 1934-1941.

Judell, N., and L. Scharf, "A Simple Derivation of Lloyd's Classical Result for the Optimum Scalar Quantizer," *IEEE Trans. Information Theory*, Vol. IT-32, Mar. 1986, pp. 326-328.

Kanefsky, M., and C.-B. Fong, "Predictive Source Coding Techniques Using Maximum Likelihood Prediction for Compression of Digitized Images," *IEEE Trans. Information Theory*, Vol. IT-30, Sept. 1984, pp. 722-727.

Kaneko, T., and M. Okudaira, "Encoding of Arbitrary Curves Based on the Chain Code Representation," *IEEE Trans. Communications*, Vol. COM-33, July 1985, pp. 697-707.

Kappagantula, S., and K.R. Rao, "Motion Compensated Interframe Image Prediction," *IEEE Trans. Communications*, Vol. COM-33, Sept. 1985, pp. 1011-1015.

Kim, D.S., and S.U. Lee, "Image Vector Quantizer Based on a Classification in the DCT Domain," *IEEE Trans. Communications*, Vol. C-39, Apr. 1991, pp. 549-556.

Kronander, T., "A New Approach to Recursive Mirror Filters with A Special Application in Subband Coding of Images," *IEEE Trans. Acoustics, Speech, and Signal Processing*, Vol. ASSP-35, Sept. 1988, pp. 1496-1500.

Kumar, C.S., Comments on "Subband Coding of Images" by J.W. Woods, and S. O'Neil, *IEEE Trans. Acoustics, Speech, and Signal Processing*, Vol. ASSP-36, July 1988, pp. 1089-1090.

Kundu, M.K., B.B. Chaudhuri, and D.D. Majumder, "A Generalized Digital Contour Coding Scheme," *Computer Vision, Graphics, and Image Processing*, Vol. 30, June 1985, pp. 269-278.

Kundu, A., and W.-R. Wu, "Wilcox-Mann-Whitney Rank Test-Based Filter for Removing Streak Noise in Transmitted DPCM Images," *IEEE Trans. Communications*, Vol. COM-38, Feb. 1990, pp. 150-155.

Landy, M.S., and Y. Cohen, "Vectorgraph Coding: Efficient Coding of Line Drawings," *Computer Vision, Graphics, and Image Processing*, Vol. 30, 1985, pp. 331-344.

Langdon, G.G., Jr., and J. Rissanen, "Compression of Black-White Images with Arithmetic Coding," *IEEE Trans. Communications*, Vol. COM-29, June 1981, pp. 858-867.

Lempel, A., and J. Ziv, "Compression of Two-Dimensional Data," *IEEE Trans. Information Theory*, Vol. IT-32, Jan. 1986, pp. 2-8.

Lelewer, D.A., and D.S. Hirschberg, "Data Compression," *Comput. Surveys*, Vol. 19, 1987, pp. 261-296.

Li, C.E., and K.R. Rao, "Component Coding of the NTSC Color TV Signal," *Signal Processing*, Vol. 10, 1986, pp. 265-277.

Lu, F.-S., and G.L. Wise, "A Further Investigation of Max's Algorithms for Optimum Quantization," *IEEE Trans. Communications*, Vol. COM-33, July 1985, pp. 746-750.

Malvar, H.S., and D.H. Staelin, "The LOT: Transform Coding Without Blocking Effect," *IEEE Trans. Acoustics, Speech, and Signal Processing*, Vol. ASSP-37, Apr. 1989, pp. 553-559.

Modestino, J.W., D.G. Daut, and A.L. Vickers, "Combined Source-Channel Coding of Images Using the Block Cosine Transform," *IEEE Trans. Communications*, Vol. COM-29, Sept. 1981, pp. 1261-1274.

Modestino, J.W., N. Farvardin, and M.A. Ogrinc, "Performance of Block Cosine Image Coding with Adaptive Quantization," *IEEE Trans. Communications*, Vol. COM-33, Mar. 1985, pp. 210-217.

Netravali, A.N., "On Quantizers for PCM Coding of Picture Signals," *IEEE Trans. Information Theory*, Vol. IT-23, May 1977, pp. 360-370.

Netravali, A.N., and C.B. Rubinstein, "Luminance Adaptive Coding of Chrominance Signals", *IEEE Trans. Communications*, Vol. COM-27, Apr. 1979, pp. 703-710.

Ngan, K.N., K.S. Leong, and H. Singh, "Adaptive Cosine Transform Coding of Images in Perceptual Domain," *IEEE Trans. Acoustics, Speech, and Signal Processing*, Vol. ASSP-37, Nov. 1989, pp. 1743-1750.

Nill, N.B., "A Visual Model Weighted Cosine Transform for Image Compression and Quality Assessment," *IEEE Trans. Communications*, Vol. COM-33, June 1985, pp. 551-557.

O'Gorman, L., and A.C. Sanderson, "A Comparison of Methods and Computation for Multi-Resolution Low-and Band-Pass Transforms for Image Processing," *Computer Vision, Graphics, and Image Processing*, Vol. 37, Mar. 1987, pp. 386-401.

O'Neal, J.B., Jr., "Differential Pulse-Code Modulation (PCM) with Entropy Coding," *IEEE Trans. Information Theory*, Vol. IT-22, Mar. 1976, pp. 169-174.

Pearlman, W.A., "Adaptive Cosine Transform Image Coding with Constant Block Distortion," *IEEE Trans. Communications*, Vol. COM-38, May 1990, pp. 698-703.

Pechura, M., "File Archival Techniques Using Data Compression," *Communications of the ACM*, Vol. 25, 1982, pp. 605-609.

Prabhu, K.A., and A.N. Netravali, "Motion Compensated Component Color Coding," *IEEE Trans. Communications*, Vol. COM-30, Dec. 1982, pp. 2519-2527.

Prabhu, K.A., "A Predictor Switching Scheme for DPCM Coding of Video Signals," *IEEE Trans. Communications*, Vol. COM-33, Aug. 1985, pp. 373-379.

Pratt, W.K., "Spatial Transform Coding of Color Images," *IEEE Trans. Communications Tech.*, Vol. COM-19, Dec. 1971, pp. 980-992.

Ramamurthi, B., and A. Gersho, "Classified Vector Quantization of Images," *IEEE Trans. Communications*, Vol. COM-34, Nov. 1986, pp. 1105-1115.

Ramamurthi, B., and A. Gersho, "Nonlinear Space-Variant Postprocessing of Block Coded Images," *IEEE Trans. Acoustics, Speech, and Signal Processing*, Vol. ASSP-34, Oct. 1986, pp. 1258-1268.

Ramponi, G., and G. Sicuranza, "Quadratic Digital Filters for Image Processing," *IEEE Trans. Acoustics, Speech, and Signal Processing*, Vol. ASSP-36, June 1988, pp. 937-939.

Rao, K.R., M.A. Narasimhan, and K. Revuluri, "Image Data Processing by Hadamard-Haar Transform," *IEEE Trans. Computers*, Vol. C-24, Sept. 1975, pp. 888-896.

Reddy, B.R.K., and A.L. Pai, "Reed-Muller Transform Image Coding," *Computer Vision, Graphics, and Image Processing*, Vol. 42, Apr. 1988, pp. 48-61.

Rissanen, J., "A Universal Data Compression System," *IEEE Trans. Information Theory*, Vol. IT-29, Sept. 1983, pp. 656-664.

Roe, G.M., "Quantizing for Minimum Distortion," *IEEE Trans. Information Theory*, Vol. IT-10, Oct. 1964, pp. 384-385.

Saghri, J.A., and A.G. Tescher, "Adaptive Transform Coding Based on Chain Coding Concepts," *IEEE Trans. Communications*, Vol. COM-34, Feb. 1986, pp. 112-117.

Sakrison, D.J., and V.R. Algazi, "Comparison of the Line-by-Line and Two-Dimensional Encoding of Random Images," *IEEE Trans. Information Theory*, Vol. IT-17, July 1971, pp. 386-398.

Sayood, K., S.M. Schekall, "Use of ARMA Predictors in the Differential Encoding of Images," *IEEE Trans. Acoustics, Speech, and Signal Processing*, Vol. ASSP-36, Nov. 1988, pp. 1791-1795.

Sheinwald, D., A. Lempel, and J. Ziv, "Two-Dimensional Encoding by Finite-State Encoders," *IEEE Trans. Communications*, Vol. COM-38, Mar. 1990, pp. 341-347.

Smith, M.J.T., and S.L. Eddins, "Analysis/Synthesis Techniques for Subband Image Coding," *IEEE Trans. Acoustics, Speech, and Signal Processing*, Vol. ASSP-38, Aug. 1990, pp. 1446-1456.

Song, I., and S.A. Kassam, "A New Noiseless Coding Technique for Binary Images," *IEEE Trans. Acoustics, Speech, and Signal Processing*, Vol. ASSP-34, Aug. 1986, pp. 944-951.

Srinivasan, R., and K.R. Rao, "Predictive Coding Based on Efficient Motion Estimation," *IEEE Trans. Communications*, Vol. COM-33, Aug. 1985, pp. 888-896.

Srinivasan, R., and K.R. Rao, "Motion-Compensated Coder for Videoconferencing," *IEEE Trans. Communications*, Vol. COM-35, Mar. 1987, pp. 297-304.

Storer, J.A., and T.G. Szymanski, "Data Compression via Textual Substitution," *J. ACM*, Vol. 29, Oct. 1982, pp. 928-951.

Todd, S., G.G. Langdon, Jr., and J. Rissanen, "Parameter Reduction and Context Selection for Compression of Gray-Scale Images," *IBM J. R&D*, Vol. 29, 1985, pp. 188-193.

Tseng, H.-C., and T.R. Fischer, "Transform and Hybrid Transform/DPCM Coding of Images Using Pyramid Vector Quantization," *IEEE Trans. Communications*, Vol. COM-35, Jan. 1987, pp. 79-86.

Vembar, M., and S. Mohan, "Tree Encoding of Line Drawings," *IEEE Trans. Acoustics, Speech, and Signal Processing*, Vol. ASSP-36, Sept. 1988, pp. 1542-1549.

Walker, D.R., and K.R. Rao, "Motion-Compensated Coder," *IEEE Trans. Communications*, Vol. COM-35, Nov. 1987, pp. 1171-1178.

Werness, S.A., "Statistical Evaluation of Predictive Data Compression Systems," *IEEE Trans. Acoustics, Speech, and Signal Processing*, Vol. ASSP-35, Aug. 1987, pp. 1190-1198.

Woods, J.W., "Stability of DPCM Coders for Television," *IEEE Trans. Communications*, Vol. COM-23, Aug. 1975, pp. 845-846.

Yan, J.K., and D.J. Sakrison, "Encoding of Images Based on Two-Component Source Model," *IEEE Trans. Communications*, Vol. COM-25, Nov. 1977, pp. 1315-1322.

Yamaguchi, H., T. Sugi, and K. Kinuhata, "Movement-Compensated Frame-Frequency Conversion of the Television Signals," *IEEE Trans. Communications*, Vol. COM-35, Oct. 1987, pp. 1069-1082.

Yuan, S., and K.-B. Yu, "Zonal Sampling and Bit Allocation of HT Coefficients in Image Data Compression," *IEEE Trans. Communications*, Vol. COM-34, Dec. 1986, pp. 1246-1251.

Zabele, G.S., and J. Koplowitz, "Fourier Encoding of Closed Planar Boundaries," *IEEE Trans. Pattern Analysis and Machine Intelligence*, Vol. PAMI-7, Jan. 1985, pp. 98-102.

Emerging Topics

Aleksander, I., "Adaptive Pattern Recognition Systems and Boltzmann Machines: A Rapprochement," *Pattern Recognition Letters*, Vol. 6, 1987, pp. 113-120.

Bischof, W.F., and T. Caelli, "Parsing Scale-Space and Spatial Stability Analysis," *Computer Vision, Graphics, and Image Processing*, Vol. 42, May 1988, pp. 192-205.

Carpenter, G.A., and S. Grossberg, "A Massively Parallel Architecture for a Self-Organizing Neural Pattern Recognition Machine," *Computer Vision, Graphics, and Image Processing*, Vol. 37, Jan. 1987, pp. 54-115.

Curtis, S.R., S. Shitz, and A.V. Oppenheim, "Reconstruction of Nonperiodic Two-Dimensional Signals from Zero-Crossings," *IEEE Trans. Acoustics, Speech, and Signal Processing*, Vol. ASSP-35, 1987, pp. 890-893.

Gidas, B., "A Renormalization Group Approach to Image Processing Problems," *IEEE Trans. Pattern Analysis and Machine Intelligence*, Vol. PAMI-11, Feb. 1989, pp. 164-180.

Hartmann, G., "Recognition of Hierarchically Encoded Images by Technical and Biological Systems," *Biological Cybernetics*, Vol. 57, 1987, pp. 73-84.

Hinton, G.E., "Connectionist Learning Procedures," *Artificial Intelligence*, Vol. 40, Sept. 1989, pp. 185-234.

Huberman, B.A., and T. Hogg, "Phase Transitions in Artificial Intelligence Systems," *Artificial Intelligence*, Vol. 33, 1987, pp. 155-171.

Khotanazad, A., and J.-H. Lu, "Classification of Invariant Image Representations Using a Neural Network," *IEEE Trans. Acoustics, Speech, and Signal Processing*, Vol. ASSP-38, June 1990, pp. 1028-1038.

Koenderink, J.J., "Scale-time," *Biological Cybernetics*, Vol. 8, 1988, pp. 159-162.

Kunii, T.L., I. Fujishiro, and X. Mao, "G-Quadtree: A Hierarchical Representation of Gray-Scale Digital Images," *The Visual Computer*, Vol. 2, 1986, pp. 219-226.

Li, Z.-N., and L. Uhr, "Pyramid Vision Using Key Features to Integrate Image-Driven Bottom-Up and Model-Driven Top-Down Processes," *IEEE Trans. Systems, Man, and Cybernetics*, Vol. 17, 1987, pp. 250-263.

Mallat, S.G., "A Theory for Multiresolution Signal Decomposition: The Wavelet Representation," *IEEE Trans. Pattern Analysis and Machine Intelligence*, Vol. PAMI-11, July 1989, pp. 674-693.

Manjunath, B.S., T. Simchony, and R. Chellappa, "Stochastic and Deterministic Networks for Texture Segmentation," *IEEE Trans. Acoustics, Speech, and Signal Processing*, Vol. ASSP-38, June 1990, pp. 1039-1049.

Maragos, P.A., "A Representation Theory for Morphological Image and Signal Processing," *IEEE Trans. Pattern Analysis and Machine Intelligence*, Vol. PAMI-11, June 1989, pp. 586-599.

Maragos, P.A., "Pattern Spectrum and Multiscale Shape Representation," *IEEE Trans. Pattern Analysis and Machine Intelligence*, Vol. PAMI-11, 1989, pp. 701-716.

Maragos, P.A., and R.W. Schafer, "Morphological Skeleton Representation and Coding of Binary Images," *IEEE Trans. Acoustics, Speech, and Signal Processing*, Vol. ASSP-34, Oct. 1986, pp. 1228-1244.

Maragos, P., and R.W. Schafer, "Morphological Filters " II: Their Relations to Median, Order-Statistic, and Stack Filters," *IEEE Trans. Acoustics, Speech, and Signal Processing*, Vol. ASSP-35, Aug. 1987, pp. 1170-1184.

Martens, J.B.O.S., and G.M.M. Majoor, "The Perceptual Relevance of Scale-Space Image Coding," *Signal Processing*, Vol. 17, 1989, pp. 353-364.

Meer, P., et al., "Robustness of Image Pyramids Under Structural Perturbations," *Computer Vision, Graphics, and Image Processing*, Vol. 44, Dec. 1988, pp. 307-331.

Meer, P., "Stochastic Image Pyramids," *Computer Vision, Graphics, and Image Processing*, Vol. 45, Mar. 1989, pp. 269-294.

O'Gorman, L., and A.C. Sanderson, "A Comparison of Methods and Computation for Multi-Resolution Low-and Band-Pass Transforms for Image Processing," *Computer Vision, Graphics, and Image Processing*, Vol. 37, 1987, pp. 386-401.

Peleg, S., M. Werman, and H. Rom, "A Unified Approach to the Change of Resolution: Space and Gray-Level," *IEEE Trans. Pattern Analysis and Machine Intelligence*, Vol. PAMI-11, 1989, pp. 739-742.

Porat, M., and Y.Y. Zeevi, "The Generalized Gabor Scheme of Image Representation in Biological and Machine Vision," *IEEE Trans. Pattern Analysis and Machine Intelligence*, Vol. PAMI-10, July 1988, pp. 452-468.

Ranganathan, N., and M. Shah, "A VLSI Architecture for Computing Scale Space," *Computer Vision, Graphics, and Image Processing*, Vol. 43, Aug. 1988, pp. 178-204.

Roth, M.W., "Survey of Neural Network Technology for Automatic Target Recognition," *IEEE Trans. on Neural Networks*, Vol. 1, Mar. 1990, pp. 28-43.

Sandbank, C.P., and I. Childs, "The Evolution Towards High-Definition Television," *Proc. IEEE*, Vol. 73, Apr. 1985, pp. 638-645.

Sayegh, S.I., Y.L. Kok, and J.H. Hong, "An Algorithm to Find Two-Dimensional Signals with Specified Zero-Crossings," *IEEE Trans. Acoustics, Speech, and Signal Processing*, Vol. ASSP-35, Jan. 1987, pp. 107-111.

Tan, C.L., and W.N. Martin, "An Analysis of A Distributed Multiresolution Vision System," *Pattern Recognition*, Vol. 22, 1989, pp. 257-265.

Toet, A., "Image Fusion by a Ratio of Low-Pass Pyramid," *Pattern Recognition Letters*, Vol. 9, 1989, pp. 245-253.

Toet, A., "A Morphological Pyramidal Image Decomposition," *Pattern Recognition Letters*, Vol. 9, 1989, pp. 255-261.

Unser, M., and M. Eden, "Multiresolution Feature Extraction and Selection for Texture Segmentation," *IEEE Trans. Pattern Analysis and Machine Intelligence*, Vol. PAMI-11, July 1989, pp. 717-728.

About the Author

Rama Chellappa was born in Tanjore, Madras, India, in 1953. He received his BS (with honors) in electronics and communication engineering from the University of Madras in 1975 and his MS (with distinction) in electrical communication engineering from the Indian Institute of Science, Bangalore, in 1977. He received his MS and PhD degrees in electrical engineering from Purdue University in 1978 and 1981, respectively.

From 1979 to 1981, Chellappa was a faculty research assistant at the Computer Vision Laboratory, University of Maryland. From 1981 to 1991, he was a faculty member in the Department of Electrical Engineering-Systems, University of Southern California. From 1988 to 1990, he was also the Director of the Signal and Image Processing Institute at USC. Effective August 1, 1991, he became a professor in the Department of Electrical Engineering at the University of Maryland, where he is also affiliated with the Center for Automation Research, Computer Science Department, and the Institute for Advanced Computer Studies.

Chellappa is coeditor of two volumes of selected papers on digital image processing and analysis published in 1985. He was an associate editor for *IEEE Transactions on Acoustics, Speech, and Signal Processing* from 1987 to 1989. Currently, he is a coeditor-in-chief of *Computer Vision, Graphics, and Image Processing: Graphic Models and Image Processing* and is an associate editor for *IEEE Transactions on Neural Networks* and *IEEE Transactions on Image Processing*.

During the period from 1969 to 1975, Chellappa received a national scholarship from the Government of India, and he received the 1975 Jawaharlal Nehru Memorial Award from the Department of Education, Government of India. In addition, he received the 1985 National Science Foundation (NSF) Presidential Young Investigator Award and the 1985 IBM Faculty Development Award. In 1990, he received the Excellence in Teaching Award from the School of Engineering at USC.

Chellappa was the general chairman of the IEEE Computer Society Conference on Computer Vision and Pattern Recognition and of the IEEE Computer Society Workshop on Artificial Intelligence for Computer Vision, both held in San Diego in June 1989. He was a program cochairman for the NSF-sponsored Workshop on Markov Random Fields, also held in San Diego in June 1989.

Chellappa's current research interests are in signal and image processing, computer vision, and pattern recognition. He is a Fellow of the IEEE.

IEEE Computer Society Press

Press Activities Board

Vice President: Yale N. Patt, University of Michigan
James H. Aylor, University of Virginia
James Farrell, III, VLSI Technology Inc.
Michael Mulder, IBM Research Division
Guylaine Pollock, Sandia National Laboratories
Murali Varanasi, University of South Florida
Rao Vemuri, University of California, Davis
Ben Wah, University of Illinois
Staff Representative: True Seaborn, Publisher

Editorial Board

Editor-in-Chief: Rao Vemuri, University of California, Davis
Oscar N. Garcia, The George Washington University
Joydeep Ghosh, University of Texas, Austin
Uma G. Gupta, University of Central Florida
A.R. Hurson, Pennsylvania State University
Krishna Kavi, University of Texas, Arlington
Ez Nahouraii, IBM
Frederick E. Petry, Tulane University
Dhiraj K. Pradhan, University of Massachusetts
Charles Richter, MCC
David Rine, George Mason University
A.R.K. Sastry, Rockwell International Science Center
Ajit Singh, Siemens Corporate Research
Pradip K. Srimani, Colorado State University
Murali R. Varanasi, University of South Florida
Staff Representative: Henry Ayling, Editorial Director

Press Staff

T. Michael Elliott, Executive Director
True Seaborn, Publisher

Henry Ayling, Editorial Director
Catherine Harris, Production Editor
Anne Copeland, Production Editor
Lisa O'Conner, Production Editor
Robert Werner, Production Editor
Penny Storms, Editorial Production Assistant
Edna Straub, Editorial Production Assistant

Douglas Combs, Assistant Publisher
Thomas Fink, Advertising/Promotions Manager
Frieda Koester, Marketing/Customer Service Manager
Becky Straub, Marketing/Customer Service Admin. Asst.
Beverly Anthony, Order Processor

Offices of the IEEE Computer Society

Headquarters Office
1730 Massachusetts Avenue, N.W.
Washington, DC 20036-1903
Phone: (202) 371-0101 — Fax: (202) 728-9614

Publications Office
P.O. Box 3014
10662 Los Vaqueros Circle
Los Alamitos, CA 90720-1264
Membership and General Information: (714) 821-8380
Publication Orders: (800) 272-6657 — Fax: (714) 821-4010

European Office
13, avenue de l'Aquilon
B-1200 Brussels, BELGIUM
Phone: 32-2-770-21-98 — Fax: 32-3-770-85-05

Asian Office
Ooshima Building
2-19-1 Minami-Aoyama, Minato-ku
Tokyo 107, JAPAN
Phone: 81-3-408-3118 — Fax: 81-3-408-3553

IEEE Computer Society

IEEE Computer Society Press Publications

Monographs: A monograph is an authored book consisting of 100-percent original material.

Tutorials: A tutorial is a collection of original materials prepared by the editors, and reprints of the best articles published in a subject area. Tutorials must contain at least five percent of original material (although we recommend 15 to 20 percent of original material).

Reprint collections: A reprint collection contains reprints (divided into sections) with a preface, table of contents, and section introductions discussing the reprints and why they were selected. Collections contain less than five percent of original material.

Technology series: Each technology series is a brief reprint collection — approximately 126-136 pages and containing 12 to 13 papers, each paper focusing on a subset of a specific discipline, such as networks, architecture, software, or robotics.

Submission of proposals: For guidelines on preparing CS Press books, write the Editorial Director, IEEE Computer Society Press, PO Box 3014, 10662 Los Vaqueros Circle, Los Alamitos, CA 90720-1264, or telephone (714) 821-8380.

Purpose

The IEEE Computer Society advances the theory and practice of computer science and engineering, promotes the exchange of technical information among 100,000 members worldwide, and provides a wide range of services to members and nonmembers.

Membership

All members receive the acclaimed monthly magazine *Computer*, discounts, and opportunities to serve (all activities are led by volunteer members). Membership is open to all IEEE members, affiliate society members, and others seriously interested in the computer field.

Publications and Activities

Computer **magazine:** An authoritative, easy-to-read magazine containing tutorials and in-depth articles on topics across the computer field, plus news, conference reports, book reviews, calendars, calls for papers, interviews, and new products.

Periodicals: The society publishes six magazines and five research transactions. For more details, refer to our membership application or request information as noted above.

Conference proceedings, tutorial texts, and standards documents: The IEEE Computer Society Press publishes more than 100 titles every year.

Standards working groups: Over 100 of these groups produce IEEE standards used throughout the industrial world.

Technical committees: Over 30 TCs publish newsletters, provide interaction with peers in specialty areas, and directly influence standards, conferences, and education.

Conferences/Education: The society holds about 100 conferences each year and sponsors many educational activities, including computing science accreditation.

Chapters: Regular and student chapters worldwide provide the opportunity to interact with colleagues, hear technical experts, and serve the local professional community.

IEEE Computer Society Press Titles

MONOGRAPHS

Analyzing Computer Architectures
Written by Jerome C. Huck and Michael J. Flynn
(ISBN 0-8186-8857-2); 206 pages

Branch Strategy Taxonomy and Performance Models
Written by Harvey G. Cragon
(ISBN 0-8186-9111-5); 150 pages

**Desktop Publishing for the Writer:
Designing, Writing, and Developing**
Written by Richard Ziegfeld and John Tarp
(ISBN 0-8186-8840-8); 380 pages

Digital Image Warping
Written by George Wolberg
(ISBN 0-8186-8944-7); 340 pages

**Integrating Design and Test —
CAE Tools for ATE Programming**
Written by Kenneth P. Parker
(ISBN 0-8186-8788-6); 160 pages

**JSP and JSD —
The Jackson Approach to Software Development
(Second Edition)**
Written by John R. Cameron
(ISBN 0-8186-8858-0); 560 pages

National Computer Policies
Written by Ben G. Matley and Thomas A. McDannold
(ISBN 0-8186-8784-3); 192 pages

**Optic Flow Computation:
A Unified Perspective**
Written by Ajit Singh
(ISBN 0-8186-2602-X); 256 pages

Physical Level Interfaces and Protocols
Written by Uyless Black
(ISBN 0-8186-8824-2); 240 pages

**Protecting Your Proprietary Rights in Computer
and High-Technology Industries**
Written by Tobey B. Marzouk, Esq.
(ISBN 0-8186-8754-1); 224 pages

X.25 and Related Protocols
Written by Uyless Black
(ISBN 0-8186-8976-5); 304 pages

TUTORIALS

Advanced Computer Architecture
Edited by Dharma P. Agrawal
(ISBN 0-8186-0667-3); 400 pages

Advances in Distributed System Reliability
Edited by Suresh Rai and Dharma P. Agrawal
(ISBN 0-8186-8907-2); 352 pages

Architectural Alternatives for Exploiting Parallelism
Edited by David J. Lilja
(ISBN 0-8186-2642-9); 464 pages

**Autonomous Mobile Robots:
Perception, Mapping and Navigation — Volume 1**
Edited by S. S. Iyengar and A. Elfes
(ISBN 0-8186-9018-6); 425 pages

**Autonomous Mobile Robots:
Control, Planning, and Architecture — Volume 2**
Edited by S. S. Iyengar and A. Elfes
(ISBN 0-8186-9116-6); 425 pages

**Broadband Switching:
Architectures, Protocols, Design, and Analysis**
Edited by C. Dhas, V. K. Konangi, and M. Sreetharan
(ISBN 0-8186-8926-9); 528 pages

Computer and Network Security
Edited by M. D. Abrams and H. J. Podell
(ISBN 0-8186-0756-4); 448 pages

Computer Architecture
Edited by D. D. Gajski, V. M. Milutinovic, H. J. Siegel, and B. P. Furht
(ISBN 0-8186-0704-1); 602 pages

Computer Arithmetic I
Edited by Earl E. Swartzlander, Jr.
(ISBN 0-8186-8931-5); 398 pages

Computer Arithmetic II
Edited by Earl E. Swartzlander, Jr.
(ISBN 0-8186-8945-5); 412 pages

**Computer Communications:
Architectures, Protocols, and Standards (Third Edition)**
Edited by William Stallings
(ISBN 0-8186-2710-7); 368 pages

Computer Graphics Hardware: Image Generation and Display
Edited by H. K. Reghbati and A. Y. C. Lee
(ISBN 0-8186-0753-X); 384 pages

Computer Graphics: Image Synthesis
Edited by Kenneth Joy, Nelson Max, Charles Grant,
and Lansing Hatfield
(ISBN 0-8186-8854-8); 380 pages

Computer Vision: Principles
Edited by Rangachar Kasturi and Ramesh Jain
(ISBN 0-8186-9102-6); 700 pages

Computer Vision: Advances and Applications
Edited by Rangachar Kasturi and Ramesh Jain
(ISBN 0-8186-9103-4); 720 pages

Digital Image Processing (Second Edition)
Edited by Rama Chellappa
(ISBN 0-8186-2362-4); 400 pages

Digital Private Branch Exchanges (PBXs)
Edited by Edwin Coover
(ISBN 0-8186-0829-3); 394 pages

Distributed Computing Network Reliability
Edited by Suresh Rai and Dharma P. Agrawal
(ISBN 0-8186-8908-0); 357 pages

Distributed–Software Engineering
Edited by Sol Shatz and Jia-Ping Wang
(ISBN 0-8186-8856-4); 294 pages

Domain Analysis and Software Systems Modeling
Edited by Ruben-Prieto Diaz and Guillermo Arango
(ISBN 0-8186-8996-X); 312 pages

Formal Verification of Hardware Design
Edited by Michael Yoeli
(ISBN 0-8186-9017-8); 340 pages

**Groupware:
Software for Computer-Supported Cooperative Work**
Edited by David Marca and Geoffrey Bock
(ISBN 0-8186-2637-2); 500 pages

Hard Real-Time Systems
Edited by J. A. Stankovic and K. Ramamritham
(ISBN 0-8186-0819-6); 624 pages

For further information call toll-free 1-800-CS-BOOKS or write:

IEEE Computer Society Press, 10662 Los Vaqueros Circle, PO Box 3014,
Los Alamitos, California 90720-1264, USA

IEEE Computer Society, 13, avenue de l'Aquilon,
B-1200 Brussels, BELGIUM

IEEE Computer Society, Ooshima Building, 2-19-1 Minami-Aoyama,
Minato-ku, Tokyo 107, JAPAN

Integrated Services Digital Networks (ISDN) (Second Edition)
Edited by William Stallings
(ISBN 0-8186-0823-4); 406 pages

Knowledge-Based Systems: Fundamentals and Tools
Edited by Oscar N. Garcia and Yi-Tzuu Chien
(ISBN 0-8186-1924-4); 512 pages

Local Network Technology (Third Edition)
Edited by William Stallings
(ISBN 0-8186-0825-0); 512 pages

Microprogramming and Firmware Engineering
Edited by V. M. Milutinovic
(ISBN 0-8186-0839-0); 416 pages

Modeling and Control of Automated Manufacturing Systems
Edited by Alan A. Desrochers
(ISBN 0-8186-8916-1); 384 pages

Nearest Neighbor Pattern Classification Techniques
Edited by Belur V. Dasarathy
(ISBN 0-8186-8930-7); 464 pages

New Paradigms for Software Development
Edited by William Agresti
(ISBN 0-8186-0707-6); 304 pages

Object-Oriented Computing, Volume 1: Concepts
Edited by Gerald E. Petersen
(ISBN 0-8186-0821-8); 214 pages

Object-Oriented Computing, Volume 2: Implementations
Edited by Gerald E. Petersen
(ISBN 0-8186-0822-6); 324 pages

Parallel Architectures for Database Systems
Edited by A. R. Hurson, L. L. Miller, and S. H. Pakzad
(ISBN 0-8186-8838-6); 478 pages

Reduced Instruction Set Computers (RISC) (Second Edition)
Edited by William Stallings
(ISBN 0-8186-8943-9); 448 pages

Software Engineering Project Management
Edited by Richard H. Thayer
(ISBN 0-8186-0751-3); 512 pages

Software Maintenance and Computers
Edited by David H. Longstreet
(ISBN 0-8186-8898-X); 304 pages

Software Design Techniques (Fourth Edition)
Edited by Peter Freeman and Anthony I. Wasserman
(ISBN 0-8186-0514-6); 730 pages

Software Reuse — Emerging Technology
Edited by Will Tracz
(ISBN 0-8186-0846-3); 400 pages

Software Risk Management
Edited by Barry W. Boehm
(ISBN 0-8186-8906-4); 508 pages

Standards, Guidelines and Examples on System and Software Requirements Engineering
Edited by Merlin Dorfman and Richard H. Thayer
(ISBN 0-8186-8922-6); 626 pages

System and Software Requirements Engineering
Edited by Richard H. Thayer and Merlin Dorfman
(ISBN 0-8186-8921-8); 740 pages

Test Access Port and Boundary-Scan Architecture
Edited by Colin M. Maunder and Rodham E. Tulloss
(ISBN 0-8186-9070-4); 400 pages

Visual Programming Environments: Paradigms and Systems
Edited by Ephraim Glinert
(ISBN 0-8186-8973-0); 680 pages

Visual Programming Environments: Applications and Issues
Edited by Ephraim Glinert
(ISBN 0-8186-8974-9); 704 pages

Visualization in Scientific Computing
Edited by G. M. Nielson, B. Shriver, and L. Rosenblum
(ISBN 0-8186-8979-X); 304 pages

Volume Visualization
Edited by Arie Kaufman
(ISBN 0-8186-9020-8); 494 pages

REPRINT COLLECTIONS

Distributed Computing Systems: Concepts and Structures
Edited by A. L. Ananda and B. Srinivasan
(ISBN 0-8186-8975-0); 416 pages

Expert Systems: A Software Methodology for Modern Applications
Edited by Peter G. Raeth
(ISBN 0-8186-8904-8); 476 pages

Milestones in Software Evolution
Edited by Paul W. Oman and Ted G. Lewis
(ISBN 0-8186-9033-X); 332 pages

Object-Oriented Databases
Edited by Ez Nahouraii and Fred Petry
(ISBN 0-8186-8929-3); 256 pages

Validating and Verifying Knowledge-Based Systems
Edited by Uma G. Gupta
(ISBN 0-8186-8995-1); 400 pages

ARTIFICIAL NEURAL NETWORKS TECHNOLOGY SERIES

Artificial Neural Networks — Concept Learning
Edited by Joachim Diederich
(ISBN 0-8186-2015-3); 160 pages

Artificial Neural Networks — Electronic Implementation
Edited by Nelson Morgan
(ISBN 0-8186-2029-3); 144 pages

Artificial Neural Networks — Theoretical Concepts
Edited by V. Vemuri
(ISBN 0-8186-0855-2); 160 pages

SOFTWARE TECHNOLOGY SERIES

Computer-Aided Software Engineering (CASE)
Edited by E. J. Chikofsky
(ISBN 0-8186-1917-1); 110 pages

Software Reliability Models: Theoretical Development, Evaluation, and Applications
Edited by Yashwant K. Malaiya and Pradip K. Srimani
(ISBN 0-8186-2110-9); 136 pages

MATHEMATICS TECHNOLOGY SERIES

Computer Algorithms
Edited by Jun-ichi Aoe
(ISBN 0-8186-2123-0); 154 pages

Multiple-Valued Logic in VLSI Design
Edited by Jon T. Butler
(ISBN 0-8186-2127-3); 128 pages

COMMUNICATIONS TECHNOLOGY SERIES

Multicast Communication in Distributed Systems
Edited by Mustaque Ahamad
(ISBN 0-8186-1970-8); 110 pages

ROBOTICS TECHNOLOGY SERIES

Multirobot Systems
Edited by Rajiv Mehrotra and Murali R. Varanasi
(ISBN 0-8186-1977-5); 122 pages

NEW RELEASES

AUTONOMOUS MOBILE ROBOTS: Perception, Mapping, and Navigation — Volume 1
edited by S. S. Iyengar and Alberto Elfes

Building intelligent robotic systems that can reason while functioning in unstructured environments is a challenging task. This book provides a basic foundation in autonomous mobile robotics — a crucial topic in artificial intelligence. It explores the successful deployment of industrial tele-operated and reprogrammable robots as well as more exacting scientific applications in remote, unstructured, and hazardous environments.

The tutorial provides a perspective on mobile robotics as a whole. This volume discusses topics in research areas such as sensor-based knowledge acquisition, problem solving under uncertainty, multi-sensor interpretation and integration, path planning and navigation, advanced parallel computing, and machine learning.

552 pages. December 1991. ISBN 0-8186-9018-6.
Catalog # 2018 $80.00 / $55.00 Member

AUTONOMOUS MOBILE ROBOTS: Control, Planning, and Architecture — Volume 2
edited by S. S. Iyengar and Alberto Elfes

This companion text describes the navigational capabilities required to enable autonomous machines to operate within unstructured environments and presents many challenging problems. Volume 2 discusses potential applications that have motivated advances in robotic component technologies, particularly in the areas of sensing, planning and control.

Autonomous Mobile Robots: Control, Planning, and Architecture covers, robot design and control, task-level planning, reactive planning, dynamic planning, prior planning for precompiled plans, real-world modeling, sensor control and global monitoring, and control of robotic systems. This tutorial also investigates wheeled mobile robots modeling and control, kinematic and dynamic modeling, control issues, system-level decision making and control, and AI approaches.

536 pages. December 1991. ISBN 0-8186-9116-6.
Catalog # 2116 $80.00 / $55.00 Member

COMPUTER VISION: Advances and Applications
edited by Rangachar Kasturi and Ramesh Jain

This tutorial describes recent research results and technological advancements in this maturing field. The tutorial is comprised of more than 45 papers on topics such as modeling light reflection, active perception, object recognition and localization, shape schemes from interreflections, depth recovery, CAD-based vision, 3-D object features, motion field and optical flow, estimation of object motion, and perceptual organization and representation.

The text follows the same chapter organization as its companion volume and details the latest research advances for each topic. As a conclusion, the last chapter, Applications, presents a representative set of papers that describe five machine vision application areas: aerial image analysis, document image interpretation, medical image analysis, industrial inspection and robotics, and autonomous navigation.

720 pages. September 1991. ISBN 0-8186-9103-4.
Catalog # 2103 $85.00 / $65.00 Member

COMPUTER VISION: Principles
edited by Rangachar Kasturi and Ramesh Jain

Computer Vision: Principles, introduces fundamental topics in computer vision and describes principles, concepts, and commonly used algorithms for vision systems that generate scene interpretations from image data. It includes over 30 articles covering subjects such as intensity and range images, edge detection, region-based and model-based image analysis, optical flow techniques, and knowledge analysis and representation. This volume also discusses image capture and enhancement, image segmentation, feature extraction, dynamic-scene analysis systems, and the techniques of image understanding and knowledge engineering and their impact on computer vision.

The tutorial includes descriptions of practical applications of machine vision technology for the practicing engineer and investigates recent research advances for the active researcher in the field.

728 pages. October 1991. ISBN 0-8186-9102-6.
Catalog # 2102 $85.00 / $65.00 Member

from IEEE COMPUTER SOCIETY PRESS

To order any of these titles or for information on other books,
call 1-800-CS-BOOKS or order by *FAX* at (714) 821-4010

(in California call 714-821-8380)